VOLUME 18

M to Mexico City

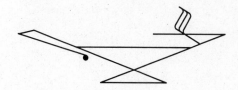

THE ENCYCLOPEDIA
AMERICANA
INTERNATIONAL EDITION

COMPLETE IN THIRTY VOLUMES   FIRST PUBLISHED IN 1829

AMERICANA CORPORATION   International Headquarters: 575 Lexington Avenue, New York, New York 10022

Eastfoto

MANCHURIA: Workers silhouetted against the glare of open-hearth furnaces in Anshan.

M. In the Sinaitic script, now believed to be a link between ancient Egyptian writing and Semitic alphabets, there is a symbol, apparently intended to represent the crests of waves on the surface of open water, viz. ∿∿ (not yet observed in Cretan). This appears to be identical with the hieroglyphic ∿∿∿, interpreted to mean "water," as well as the Semitic symbols ᛘ (Moabite), ᛘ (Phoenician), the five-stroke *m* (ᛙ or ᛙ) of some Greek alphabets (for example, the Corinthian and the Chalcidian) and of the ancient abecedaria found in Italy; and, finally, of the oldest Latin alphabet (ᛙ, right to left, on the Praenestine fibula). The Latin symbol early became a four-stroke straddling **M** (in Republican times, later **M** and **M**), though the five-stroke form survived as the abbreviation of the personal name Manius, and is represented in modern printed texts as M'. In hieroglyphic, however, the value of the wavy line symbol is *n*, whereas in the Semitic and derivative alphabets it is *m*. The most probable explanation of this discrepancy is that the Semitic *m* and *n* (compare the article N) are differentiated forms of a common original *n*-symbol, the hieroglyphic *m* being totally different (an owl). Such differentiation is not uncommon (Latin c and G, Greek O and Ω Greek P and ꝶ). It would be facilitated by the character of the two sounds themselves, both being nasals, and necessarily differentiated by accompanying consonants even in cognate words (German *Ankunft* beside *kommen,* English *count* beside *compute*). This account of *m* is not inconsistent with the Semitic name (*mēm*) of the letter, or of its apparent meaning, "water." The Greek name (*mū*) points in the same direction, for evidently it is modelled on *nū,* the name of *n* (Semitic *nūn*). Moreover, the syllable *mu* naturally was felt as indicating the closed lips (as in the pronunciation of *m*), and Greek actually has a verb μύειν meaning "to close the lips (or eyes, or both)." A similar idea, though not connected directly, or indirectly, with the Greek letter-name, is reflected in such words as Latin *mutus* "dumb," Sanskrit *múkham* "mouth," both derived from an Indo-European root *mu-* that must have been onomatopoetic.

The *m*-symbol is 13th in order in the Phoenician and Greek alphabets, 14th in the Cyrillic (13th again in modern Russian, and in modern western European alphabets), 12th in Latin; in Arabic, it is 24th; in Ethiopian (South Semitic) 4th. It has to be distinguished from **M** of early Greek alphabets (representing the Semitic *ṣādē*) which has the value of *sigma* (Ƨ); and also from another sibilant sign, the *shin* (ᛤ) of the Semitic alphabets, from which the Greek *sigma,* in the shape Ƨ , is actually de-

rived. That there was, however, some confusion, at least of the sibilant signs, in ancient Greek alphabets is evident, and the precise details of their history and substitution for one another have not been determined.

The sound *m* is produced in the same way as *b,* save that for *m* the nasal passage is open, so that the current of voice escapes through the nose. Hence it is described as a bilabial nasal. Usually it is voiced, as just indicated; but Welsh has a breathed *m,* and so had some ancient Greek dialects—written *mh* and μh respectively. Moreover, it is a feature of the Keltic languages that the nasals undergo "mutation" (along with certain other consonants); for example, in the local name *Llanfair-fechan* "The Church of St. Mary the Less," *-fair* stands for *Mair* (Mary). Conversely "in Bangor" is *ym Mangor* (for *yn +* *Bangor*). Such changes are normal in spoken language, though they are not often carried through consistently and are more usually unrepresented in writing than not. A final *m,* for example, may nasalize a preceding vowel so completely as to be absorbed into it; this accounts for the "loss" of the Latin *m* that is a marked feature of the Romance languages as compared with Classical Latin. Like *n, l,* and *r,* in a weakly accented syllable, *m* itself may become syllabic, as in English *film,* though the tendency asserts itself to insert a supporting vowel (as in the vulgar pronunciation *filum*); compare *baptism, chasm, bottom.* Archaic writings appear in *phlegm, psalm, hymn, drachm,* so that the final *m* is in those words consonantal, not syllabic. In *Pontefract* (Yorkshire) the pronunciation is the same as in *Pomfret* (Conn.); *Banff* has a Gaelic *m.* Normally *mm* is no other than *m* in sound (for example *hammer*), but a lengthened *m* is heard in *immure.* Initial *sm* is sometimes heard with *m* breathed (that is, voiceless), as a result of assimilation, as in *smile;* Latin disposed of the difficulty by getting rid of the *s* (compare the cognate *mirus*). Otherwise, voiceless *m* is abnormal in English (*mmm* "yes," *ahem, humph* all show it, and all are exclamatory rather than strictly linguistic in character). The combinations *mr, ml* commonly insert a glide *b* (compare *number:* Latin *numerus; bramble:* Old English *brēmel,* gen. *brēmles*). Before a dental, *m* becomes *n,* hence *ant* (Old English *æmete,* modern dialect *emmet*). The phoneme *m* occurs in English initially (*mat*), finally *-m* (*dim*), and medially (*glimmer*); before *u* it is followed by consonantal *i* (as in *muse*).

M as an abbreviation for "1000" (Latin *mille*) stems from the superfluous Greek Φ , half of which (namely, D) was used for "500."

For bibliography see the article A; see also
ALPHABET.

JOSHUA WHATMOUGH,
Professor of Comparative Philology, Harvard University.

MA'AN, mă-ăn', an ancient town, Jordan, capital of a district of the same name, 180 miles east of Suez. Important since Biblical times, it is on the early caravan route between Syria and the Gulf of 'Aqaba and on the later road taken by pilgrims en route to Mecca. The Hejaz Railway, from Syria to Arabia, passed through Ma'an; when the southern section fell into disuse after World War I the town became the southern terminus of the line. During that conflict the Turkish garrison at Ma'an was attacked in September 1917 by Arabs led by "Lawrence of Arabia" (see LAWRENCE, THOMAS EDWARD) in one of his most spectacular feats; early in 1918 the Arabs occupied the town temporarily, and in September they secured final possession. Subsequently Ma'an became one of the largest towns of the kingdom of Transjordan (now Hashemite Kingdom of the Jordan) having a considerable trade in agricultural products. Pop. (1961 census) 6,643.

MAARTENS, màr'těns, **Maarten** (pen name of JOOST MARIUS WILLEM VAN DER POORTEN-SCHWARTZ), Dutch novelist: b. Amsterdam, Netherlands, Aug. 15, 1858; d. Zeist, Aug. 4, 1915. He attended school in England, and at Bonn, Germany, and studied law at the University of Utrecht. Although admitted to the bar and later teaching law he soon adopted a literary career. His first published work was *The Morning of a Love and Other Poems* (1885), written, as were all his subsequent volumes, in the English language. *The Black Box Murder* (1889), a detective story, was the first to appear under his pen name ("that English readers might possibly be able to pronounce"), and success came to him with publication of *The Sin of Joost Avelingh,* 2 vols. (1889), which gave a graphic and realistic picture of peasant and bourgeois life in the Netherlands of his time. Between 1889 and 1912 he wrote a total of 14 novels and four volumes of short stories, including *An Old Maid's Love,* 3 vols. (1891); *A Question of Taste* (1891); *God's Fool: A Koopstad Story,* 3 vols. (1892); *The Greater Glory,* 3 vols. (1894); *My Lady Nobody* (1895); *Some Women I Have Known* (1901); *The New Religion* (1907); *The Price of Lis Doris* (1909).

MAAS, mäs, name for the lower course, in the Netherlands, of the river Meuse (q.v.).

MAASIN, mä-ä'sēn, name of two towns, in the Philippines: (1) In Iloilo province, south central Panay Island, a rice growing center; municipal pop. (1960) 21,510. (2) In southwestern Leyte, on Cánigao Channel, an agricultural center producing coconuts, rice, and hemp; municipal pop. (1960) 39,185.

MAASTRICHT or MAESTRICHT, mästriĸt', commune, Netherlands, capital of the Province of Limburg, on the left bank of the Maas, at the confluence of the Geer. It lies close to the Belgian frontier, 19 miles northeast of Liége, Belgium, and 56 miles east of Brussels. Among fine buildings of architectural interest are the Church of St. Servatius, oldest in the Netherlands, partly Romanesque and partly Gothic, founded in the 6th century; the Romanesque Church of Onze Lieve Vrouw dating from the 11th century; a 15th century Gothic building once the town hall and now a museum; and a town hall completed in the 17th century. The fortifications of Maastricht were dismantled between 1871 and 1878. The town carries on an active transit trade with Belgium, and has manufactures of glass and earthenware, tobacco and cigars, and metalware; the breweries of Maastricht produce a noted type of beer. About three miles from the town is the Pietersberg (Peter's Hill) on which stands the fort of St. Pierre and under which are extensive sandstone quarries of extraordinary interest; excavation is supposed to have been begun by the Romans, and it continued until the close of the 19th century, by which time the labyrinths covered an area of 125 square miles. Maastricht, known to the Romans as Trajectum Superius (Upper Ford), was part of the domains of the Franks in the 4th century. The town was besieged and taken in 1579 by the Spaniards under the duke of Parma, 8,000 of its inhabitants being massacred; it was taken by Louis XIV in 1673, and again by the French in 1748 and 1794. A vital part of the Low Countries' defense system in World War II, Maastricht soon fell before the German onslaught in May 1940. Pop. (1965) 94,939.

MAAT, mà-ät', or **MA'T,** in ancient Egypt, the goddess linked with Ra and Thoth (qq.v.) as personifying physical and moral law; as the goddess of truth she was identified with the Greek Themis (q.v.).

MAB, the fairy queen of Connaught and a familiar name in Celtic folklore. Mab has been celebrated by Shakespeare and other English poets. The name is of uncertain origin, being variously derived from the Midgard of the Eddas, the Habundia or Dame Abonde of Norman fairy lore, and from the Cymric *mab,* a child. According to some authorities, Mab was not the fairy queen, the same as Titania, this dignity having been ascribed to her only by mistaking the use of the old English word *queen* or *quean,* which originally meant only a woman. In Shakespeare's *Romeo and Juliet* Queen Mab is the "fairies' midwife" who brings to birth men's secret hopes in the form of dreams by driving "athwart their noses" in her chariot as they lie asleep. In the *Nymphidia* of Michael Drayton (q.v.) she is the wife of Oberon and queen of the fairies. Queen Mab is also mentioned in *Amyntas,* the pastoral comedy of Thomas Randolph; Ben Jonson's *Satyr;* Milton's *L'Allegro;* and Herrick's *Hesperides.* Shelley wrote the poem *Queen Mab* (q.v.).

MABERY, mā'bèr-ĭ, **Charles Frederic,** American chemist: b. New Gloucester, Maine, Jan. 13, 1850; d. Portland, June 26, 1927. He was graduated from Harvard in 1876, and until 1883 he continued at the university as an assistant instructor in chemistry at the Lawrence Scientific School. Thereafter he was professor of chemistry at the Case School of Applied Science, Cleveland, Ohio, until his retirement in 1911. His investigations into petroleum brought him into national prominence, and he also did valuable work in connection with electric smelting. A pioneer experimenter in the electrical production of aluminum, he invented a process for the preparation of anhydrous aluminum chloride.

MABIE, mā′bĭ, **Hamilton Wright,** American editor, critic, and essayist: b. Cold Spring, N. Y., Dec. 13, 1845; d. Summit, N. J., Dec. 31, 1916. He was graduated from Williams College in 1867 and from the Columbia University Law School in 1869. In 1879, after some years of practicing law, he joined the editorial staff of the *Christian Union,* at that time under the direction of Henry Ward Beecher and Lyman Abbott (qq.v.); the latter, who became editor in chief in 1881, made him associate editor in 1884. Mabie continued in this post after the paper was renamed the *Outlook* in 1893, and his connection with it lasted until his death. Through his writing and lecturing he did much to promote American culture. As an exchange professor in Japan he also helped to establish closer cultural ties between the two countries. Well known as a critic and interpreter of literature and ethics, he wrote and compiled many excellent books for both young and old. Among his works are: *William Shakespeare—Poet, Dramatist, and Man* (1900); *Backgrounds of Literature* (1903); *Myths Every Child Should Know* (1905); *Fairy Tales Every Child Should Know* (1905); *Legends Every Child Should Know* (1906); *American Ideals, Character, and Life* (1913); *Japan Today and Tomorrow* (1914).

MABILLON, mȧ-bē-yôn′, **Jean,** French Benedictine monk and scholar: b. St. Pierremont Champagne, Nov. 23, 1632; d. Paris, Dec. 27, 1707. He became a monk at Reims in 1653, and in 1664 he was sent to the abbey of St.-Germain-des-Prés, Paris, famous for its great output of literary works. Between 1668 and 1702 he edited and published the 9-volume *Acta sanctorum ordinis Sancti Benedicti,* and in 1681 completed *De re diplomatica;* this latter, his greatest accomplishment, virtually established the science of Latin paleography. He was sent to Germany in 1683, and to Italy two years later, to acquire documents and books for the library of Louis XIV, and in 1690 he edited the works of St. Bernard. Selected to refute Armand J. Le B. de Rancé (q.v.), abbot of La Trappe, who had condemned the custom of permitting monks to study, he produced the soundly argued *Traité sur les études monastiques* in 1691. Among much other work, he prepared the first four volumes of the *Annales ordinis Sancti Benedicti* (1703–1739). A collection of his *Oeuvres posthumes* appeared in 1724.

MABINOGION, măb-ĭ-nō′gĭ-ŏn, a collection of 12 ancient Welsh tales, first published in an English translation by Lady Charlotte Guest (1812–1895) in 1838–1849. Mabinogion is derived from the Welsh word *mabinog,* meaning an aspirant to bardic honor. The tales comprise 11 prose pieces from the *Red Book of Hergest,* compiled in the 14th and 15th centuries and dealing with old Celtic legends and mythology, and *Taliesin,* which is largely in verse.

Consult Ellis, T. P., and Lloyd, J., *The Mabinogion* (New York 1929).

MABLY, mȧ-blē′, **Gabriel Bonnot de,** French philosopher and historian: b. Grenoble, France, March 14, 1709; d. Paris, April 23, 1785. His family name was Bonnot, his younger brother being Étienne Bonnot de Condillac (q.v.), the philosopher. His *Droit publique de l'Europe* (1748), which achieved a remarkable success, was followed by *Observations sur les Grecs* (1749); *Observations sur les Romains* (1751); *Entretiens de Phocion* (1753); *Observations sur l'histoire de France* (1755); *Principes des négociations* (1757); *De la manière d'écrire l'histoire* (1773); *De la législation* (1776); and *De l'idée de l'histoire* (1778). He visited Poland in 1771 at the request of the government in order to prepare a code of laws, and in 1781 published *Du gouvernement de la Pologne.* He was also consulted by the United States Congress in 1783 on the preparation of the Constitution, and embodied his views in his *Observations sur le gouvernement et les lois des États-Unis d'Amérique* (1784). In this work he foretold the speedy downfall of the United States. He was an idealizer of ancient Rome, and was enamored of the socialistic state and a community of property. From his pessimistic views on modern social organization he was known as the "prophet of woe."

MABUCHI, mä-bōō-chê, Japanese writer and religious teacher: b. 1697?; d. 1769. He was distinguished as a scholar, and utilized his great learning in the endeavor to purify the native religion, Shintō, from the accretions of Chinese and Buddhist philosophy, whereby he regarded it as having been corrupted. His love and knowledge of antiquity enabled him to present the native faith in its original simplicity, and his teachings were exemplified in his own life. To him modern students are largely indebted for direct access to ancient Japanese poetry. He added greatly to the knowledge of the past. He was the first of the three great scholars (Norinaga Motoöri and Atsutane Hirata being the others) who dedicated themselves to this work of simplifying the ancient faith of the country.

MABUSE, mȧ-büz′, or **MALBODIUS,** măl-bō′dĭ-ŭs, **Jan** (real name JAN GOSSAERT or JENNI GOSSART), Flemish historical and portrait painter: b. Maubeuge, France, 1478?; d. Antwerp, Belgium, ?1533. In 1508 he went to Italy with Philip of Burgundy, illegitimate son of Philip the Good, visiting Verona and Florence and residing for a year in Rome. He seems to have been the first of the Flemish painters to go to Italy, and from his time to that of Rubens and Van Dyck it was considered the proper thing for all Netherland painters to go to that country. After Philip's death in 1524, he entered the service of Adolphus of Burgundy. When Christian II of Denmark visited the Low Countries he asked Mabuse to paint his dwarfs, and in 1528 he requested the artist to design the tomb for his queen, Isabella, in the abbey of St. Pierre, near Ghent. Mabuse also painted portraits of the children of Christian II—John, Dorothy, and Christine—which came into the collection of Henry VIII of England. Mabuse designed and erected the tomb of Philip of Burgundy in the church of Wyck. Karel van Mander's biography accuses him of habitual drunkenness, but the great works produced by him, as well as their number, prove that he was a hard-working and painstaking artist, perfectly in command of his powers.

Mabuse was a transitional artist, working in the period between the great primitive masters of Flemish painting and the Renaissance art of Peter Paul Rubens. He was trained in the traditional Flemish school, but after his trip to Italy, his work gradually acquired various characteristics of Italian painting. He was thus among the first to introduce the art of the Italian Renaissance into Flemish painting, which in time merged with the new form and completely lost its original character. In Mabuse, however, this Italianization was largely superficial and was restricted to the use of classical architecture in his backgrounds, the realistic presentation of the nude, and the choice of subject. He remained essentially in the Flemish tradition, and his monumental paintings retain a Gothic quality, observable in the careful attention given to minute architectural detail, whether Gothic or Renaissance in design, in his manner of rendering the nude figure, and in his brilliant coloring, later somewhat subdued. He was an expert craftsman, and his work conveys a strongly plastic sense. Artistically he was most successful in his portraits in the Italian manner, and his sensitive portrayal of the subject's hands is notable. Among his major works are the *Adoration of the Kings* (National Gallery, London), *St. Luke Painting the Virgin* (cathedral, Prague), *Epiphany* (London), *Agony in the Garden* (Berlin), and many fine portraits in galleries throughout the world.

MAC (frequently contracted to Mc or M'), a Gaelic word signifying son. The term was prefixed to personal names to form Irish and Scottish surnames, such as McGregor, MacDonald, and MacCarthy, McCarthy, and M'Carthy. Mac corresponds to Ap in Welsh names (Ap Jones) and to O' in Irish names (O'Neill).

MACABEBE, mä-kä-bā'bå, municipality, Philippines, Pampanga Province, Luzon, located near the Pampanga River delta, eight miles south of San Fernando. It lies in an agricultural region growing rice and sugar cane. Macabebe was long a recruiting center for the Spanish civil guard and later for the Philippine scouts attached to the United States Army. Pop. (1948) 17,647.

McADAM, John Loudon, British engineer: b. Ayr, Scotland, Sept. 23, 1756; d. Moffat, Dumfriesshire, Nov. 26, 1836. On the death of his father in 1770, young McAdam was placed in the charge of a merchant uncle in New York City, where he lived until the close of the American Revolution. As a partner in John McAdam and Co. from 1777 to 1780, and from 1781 to 1783 in McAdam, Watson and Co., he conducted a flourishing business at his auction room. In New York newspapers, he advertised the sale of captured "rebel" vessels (at least 452) and their cargoes. In 1783 he returned to Ayrshire, a displaced Loyalist. There he engaged in coal tar manufacture until 1798, when he moved to Falmouth and resumed his American wartime occupation of prizemaster, but now of captured French ships. The Peace of Amiens (1802) ended this employment and he removed to Bristol.

Paving commissioner in Bristol as early as 1806, McAdam first attracted note by a memorial to Sir John Sinclair's Select Committee of the House of Commons on Highways and Turnpike Roads (1811). In 1816 he accepted appointment as general surveyor of the Bristol Turnpike Trust, of which he was a leading member. Although the largest (149 miles) and one of the wealthiest in Britain, this trust was almost bankrupt and its roads in a ruinous state. Success in Bristol brought him immediate national attention, and his "system" spread rapidly through the kingdom. A promoter, administrator, and publicist, rather than a creative thinker and inventor, McAdam wrote four little books delineating his methods and defending himself against his detractors. The best known, *Remarks on the Present System of Roadmaking . . . ,* went through nine English editions (1816–1827), was printed in the United States (1821), and was published in German translation (1825). He created a dynasty of turnpike trust engineers and administrators, including sons and grandsons, nephews and cousins. By June 1823 he and his three sons (William, James, and John Loudon, Jr.) were employed by 71 trusts controlling about 1,800 miles of turnpike roads, representing perhaps 10 per cent of the total mileage in England and Wales. During the 1820's large areas of Europe, North America, and British India were utilizing his principles.

Although varying in detail from year to year, the basic features of the "McAdam system" may be summarized briefly:
(1) accommodate the road to the traffic;
(2) standardize road engineering procedures;
(3) form the road surface of uniformly small, artificially broken metal (stone) of the best quality available, unmixed with sand or earth;
(4) construct the road perfectly flat (he later recommended a three-inch camber), uniformly 10 inches thick, and build it on the natural subsoil without special foundation;
(5) prepare carefully phrased and specific instructions for all contractors and subordinates;
(6) engage only competent surveyors, who are scrupulously honest;
(7) submit turnpike trust administration to a mild yet effective measure of parliamentary control.

He insisted on proper drainage procedures and gradually became convinced that turnpike trust administration should be centralized in London, a reform he helped to initiate. McAdam surfaced a few city streets with the much used stone setts, but he did not employ asphalt, tar, or concrete.

Claiming constant study of roads since 1785 and asserting great financial sacrifice in extensive travels, McAdam in 1819 sought compensation from the nation. In 1820, on warrants issued by the Post Office, he was paid two grants of £2,000, and Parliament in 1825 voted him a final grant of £2,000 for significant public service. His son James was named first general surveyor of the Metropolis Turnpike Trust and was created a baronet in 1834. The man and his methods were widely heralded in poetry and prose. Thomas Hood directed a long *Ode to Mr. M'Adam.* His public career, from 1816 to 1836, coincided almost exactly with the coaching days, which ended abruptly with the introduction of the railroad.

Robert H. Spiro, Jr.

MACADAM, a system of roadmaking developed by John L. McAdam (q.v.). See Roads and Highways—*Roads in the Middle Ages and Early Modern Period.*

McADOO, măk'å-dōō, **William Gibbs,** American lawyer: b. near Marietta, Ga., Oct. 31, 1863; d. Washington, D.C., Feb. 1, 1941. McAdoo was descended from a distinguished family which lost its wealth in the general devastation in the South following the Civil War; his father, William Gibbs McAdoo, was a state attorney general in Tennessee and a state judge in Georgia. Young McAdoo entered the University of Tennessee, but in his junior year was obliged to leave school and to earn his living as a deputy clerk of the United States Sixth Circuit Court of Appeals. Nevertheless, he was admitted to the bar in 1885 and practiced law in Chattanooga, Tenn., until 1892, when he opened a law office in New York.

A project to connect New York City with New Jersey by tunneling under the Hudson River had been begun (1878) and was abandoned as impracticable. McAdoo, who had gained some experience in public transportation by operating a street railway in Knoxville, organized the Hudson and Manhattan Railroad Company (1902) and raised $4 million to complete the project. His company finished the first tunnel on March 8, 1904, and by 1909 three more had been constructed.

Becoming active in Democratic Party politics, McAdoo supported Woodrow Wilson in the New Jersey gubernatorial campaign of 1910 and in 1912 was vice chairman of the Democratic National Committee. During most of the subsequent campaign he was acting chairman. Following Wilson's election to the presidency, McAdoo became secretary of the treasury, March 6, 1913. He was soon absorbed in the enormous financial transactions in which the government was involved during World War I; his achievements included successfully floating four Liberty Loans (1917–1918), which collected over $18 billion, financing the Allied belligerents, and establishing the war risk insurance law, which later was extended to include life insurance for the armed forces. In addition he was chairman of the Federal Reserve Board, (which he helped to institute in 1913), the Federal Farm Loan Board, the War Finance Corporation, and the United States section of the International High Commission. When the railroads and coastwise and intercoastal shipping were temporarily nationalized on Jan 1, 1918, McAdoo was appointed their director general, but resigned on Jan. 10, 1919, after he had resigned from the Treasury on Dec. 16, 1918.

He was twice a prominent candidate for the Democratic presidential nomination: in 1920 he led on the first ballot, but lost to James M. Cox; and again in 1924 he led on the first ballot, but after a long deadlock with Alfred E. Smith, a compromise candidate was found in John W. Davis. McAdoo moved to Los Angeles, Calif., where he continued his law practice. As chairman of the California delegation to the Democratic Convention in 1932, he cast California's vote for Franklin D. Roosevelt on the fourth ballot, resulting in Roosevelt's nomination for president. McAdoo was elected United States senator from California in 1932. In Washington he supported Roosevelt's New Deal policies and specialized in legislation concerning banking and finance. He retired from political life at the end of his term (1939). Then until his death he served as chairman of the board of directors of the American President Lines.

In 1914, McAdoo married as his second wife Eleanor Randolph Wilson, the president's daughter. They were divorced in 1934. McAdoo supported the League of Nations, woman suffrage, and prohibition. He wrote *The Challenge— Liquor and Lawlessness Versus Constitutional Government* (1928) and *Crowded Years* (1931), an account of his career until 1919.

McADOO, borough, Pennsylvania, located in Schuylkill County, 18 miles northeast of Pottsville; altitude 1,800 feet; served by the Lehigh Valley and the Pennsylvania railroads. There are rich deposits of anthracite in the area (east central part of the state) and coal mining is the principal industry. Other industries in McAdoo are the manufacture of paper boxes and textiles. There are waterfalls nearby and the surrounding scenery is picturesque. The borough was founded in 1880 and was incorporated in 1896. Pop. 3,560.

McAFEE, măk′á-fē, **Mildred Helen** (married name HORTON), American educator: b. Parkville, Mo., May 12, 1900. She was educated at Vassar College (B.A. 1920) and the University of Chicago (M.A. 1928). From 1923 to 1925 she was acting professor of economics and sociology in Tusculum College, Greenville, Tenn.; from 1927 to 1932 was dean of women and professor of sociology at Centre College, Danville, Ky.; from 1932 to 1934 was executive secretary of the Alumnae Association of Vassar College; was dean of women at Oberlin College from 1934 to 1936; and was president of Wellesley College from 1936 to 1949. Miss McAfee was appointed first director of the Women's Reserve of the United States Naval Reserve (WAVES, 1942–1946), with the rank of lieutenant commander, and in 1943 she was promoted to captain. In 1945 she married the Reverend Douglas Horton.

MACAIRE, má-kâr′, a French CHANSON DE GESTE (see CHANSONS DE GESTE) of the 12th century, based on two favorite medieval themes: the wife unjustly accused of infidelity and the dog who brings the murderer of his master to justice. Blanchefleur, queen of Charlemagne, is slandered by the royal favorite, Macaire, after she has repulsed his advances. She is banished from France, accompanied only by the faithful knight Aubri. Macaire kills Aubri, whose dog, Dragon, shows such hatred toward Macaire that suspicion is aroused. Man and dog are summoned to single combat; Macaire is overcome, confesses his treason against the queen and the murder, and is executed. Written in a mixed Franco-Venetian dialect, the poem was edited and translated by François Guessard in *Macaire* (1886).

The episode of the dog was so popular that it was retold in many languages and finally was given a definite date: Jean de la Taille, in *Discours notable des duels* (1607), says that the encounter with the dog occurred under Charles V in 1371. The story found its way into prints and paintings, and from its depiction in the great hall in the castle of Montargis, Dragon came to be known as the *chien de* (dog of) *Montargis*. A melodrama on the subject, *Le chien de Montargis* (1814) by Guilbert de Pixérécourt was enormously successful. Another melodrama, *L'auberge des Adrets* (1823) by Benjamin Antier, used the name Robert Macaire for the villain, a murderer and bandit, and the celebrated actor Frédéric Lemaître made his reputation in this role. Lemaître and Antier collaborated on a sequel, *Robert Macaire* (1834), in which the hero is now a reformed murderer and an active swindler. In this work, which followed the Revolution of

July 1830 in Paris, Théophile Gautier saw "the great triumph of revolutionary art." "Frédérick Lemaître," says Gautier, "created in the character of Robert Macaire a kind of humor that is almost Shakespearean. In it we find terrible gaiety, sinister laughter, bitter derision, pitiless raillery and a biting sarcasm, mingled with elegance, suppleness and astonishing grace. Robert Macaire and Bertrand [his accomplice] are Don Quixote and Sancho Panza in crime." Such was its popularity that Honoré Daumier executed a series of about 100 drawings depicting Robert Macaire as banker, lawyer, journalist, and so forth.

McALESTER, măk-ăl'ĕs-tẽr, city, Oklahoma; seat of Pittsburg County; altitude 750 feet. It is situated 83 miles south-southeast of Tulsa and is served by the Chicago, Rock Island and Pacific and the Missouri-Kansas-Texas railroads. There is a municipal airport. The surrounding area includes much fertile farmland, producing cotton, corn, livestock, dairy products, and peanuts. There is also timber-producing forest land. Coal is mined, and oil and natural gas wells are important. The city processes cotton, cottonseed, soybeans, peanuts, and petroleum, and there are meat-packing establishments, and manufactures of aluminum products and concrete. J. J. McAlester, pioneer settler for whom the city is named, founded a store at a crossroads in what is now North McAlester in 1870, and with the aid of Chickasaw and Choctaw Indians developed the coal deposits. North McAlester was incorporated in 1899. South McAlester was organized civically in 1900, and they were consolidated, as McAlester, under a city charter in 1906. Government is by mayor, commissioners, and city manager. Pop. 17,419.

MACALESTER COLLEGE, a liberal arts, coeducational institution in St. Paul, Minn., founded in 1885 under the auspices of the Presbyterian Church. It grants the degree of A.B. in liberal arts and business administration. The average enrollment of students is about 1,800.

MACALISTER, măk-ăl'ĭs-tẽr, SIR **Donald,** Scottish physician and anatomist: b. Perth, May 17, 1854; d. Cambridge, Eng., Jan. 15, 1934. He was educated at Liverpool Institute and St. John's College, Cambridge, and was a fellow of St. John's from 1877 until his death. Macalister studied medicine at Cambridge, at St. Bartholomew's Hospital, London, and in Leipzig. He practiced and lectured at Cambridge, and in 1907 was appointed principal of Glasgow University. He held this office until 1929, when he resigned, becoming chancellor of the institution. He was created a baronet in 1924.

Macalister was chairman of the committee which prepared the *British Pharmacopoeia* (1898) and its revision (1914). He was the author of the medical works, *Nature of Fever* (1887) and *Antipyretics* (1888). Macalister was also an accomplished linguist and published *Echoes* (1907), a volume of verse translations. His interest in gypsy lore resulted in *Romani Versions* (1928).

MACALISTER, Robert Alexander Stewart, Irish archaeologist and historian: b. Dublin, July 8, 1870; d. Cambridge, Eng., April 26, 1950. He was educated in Dublin, in Germany, and at Cambridge University. He was

director of excavations of the Palestine Exploration Fund, 1900–1909 and 1923–1924, and professor of Celtic archaeology at University College, Dublin, 1909–1943. From 1926 to 1931 he was president of the Royal Irish Academy.

Among Macalister's publications are *Studies in Irish Epigraphy* (3 vols., 1897–1907); *A History of Civilization in Palestine* (1912; 2d ed., 1921); *Muiredach, Abbot of Monasterboice, His Life and Surroundings* (1914); *The Life of Ciaran of Clonmacnois* (1921); *A Text-Book of European Archaeology* (1921); *Ireland in Pre-Celtic Times* (1921); *The Secret Languages of Ireland* (1936); *The Book of the Taking of Ireland* (4 vols., 1938–1941); and *Monasterboice, Its History and Monuments* (1946).

McALLEN, măk-ăl'ĕn, city, Texas; in Hidalgo County; altitude 122 feet. It is situated in the lower Rio Grande Valley, 50 miles westnorthwest of Brownsville, and is served by the Missouri Pacific and the Southern Pacific railroads. McAllen is a port of entry from Mexico; being connected by road—by way of Hidalgo, Texas, and Reynosa, Tamaulipas—with Monterrey, Mexico. Citrus fruits, cotton, and truck garden crops are grown on irrigated land around the city, and there are oilfields. McAllen's chief industry is the canning, freezing, and dehydrating of foodstuffs; petroleum is refined, and chemicals and canvas products are manufactured. The city was settled in 1904, incorporated as a town in 1910; as a city in 1927. Government is by mayor and council. Pop. 32,728.

McALLISTER, măk-ăl'ĭs-tẽr, **Addams Stratton,** American electrical engineer: b. Covington, Va., Feb. 24, 1875; d. Clifton Forge, Va., Nov. 26, 1946. He was educated at Pennsylvania State College and Cornell University. After serving with private concerns, he taught electrical engineering at Cornell, 1901–1904, and in 1905 became associate editor of the *Electrical World.* He was editor of that publication, 1912–1915. During this period he was also lecturer on engineering at Pennsylvania State College, 1909–1914. In 1917 he became an adviser to the Council of National Defense, and after World War I became connected with the Bureau of Standards as electrical engineer, 1921–1923; engineer-physicist after 1923; assistant director of the bureau, 1930–1945.

McAllister was the inventor of alternating-current electrical machinery, and formulated the law of conservation as applied to illumination engineering calculations. He contributed many papers to technical journals and was the author of *Alternating Current Motors* (1906) and *Standard Handbook for Electrical Engineers* (1907).

McALLISTER, Samuel Ward (called WARD), American social leader: b. Savannah, Ga., December 1827; d. New York, N. Y., Jan. 31, 1895. He came of a family several of whose members were prominent at the bar. With his father, in 1850, he went to California to establish a law firm, remaining until 1852, when he had made a comfortable fortune. Moving to New York, he married Sarah Gibbons, the daughter of a wealthy Georgian. He lived in Europe for several years, and when he returned lived most of the time at Newport, R. I. He entered social life in New York with the advantages of personal qualifications and family prestige. As a raconteur as well as an epicure he had already attained prominence within a select circle, when, in shortening a list for a ball in 1892, he boasted that there were "only about 400 people in New York society." As "the Four Hundred" the phrase aroused a storm of controversy and ridicule throughout the country, quickly gaining a place as an American idiom. About 20 years earlier McAllister, presumably to offset the excessive power of a small wealthy group, organized "the Patriarchs," comprising heads of old New York families, whose invitations thenceforth would confer social recognition. He contributed articles to newspapers and magazines and wrote *Society As I Have Found It* (1890).

MACALLUM, mà-kăl′ŭm, **Archibald Byron,** Canadian educator and biochemist: b. Belmont, southern Ontario, Canada, April 7, 1858; d. London, Ontario, April 5, 1934. He was educated at the University of Toronto and Johns Hopkins University, receiving his Ph.D. from the latter in 1888. He joined the faculty of Toronto University in 1887 as lecturer in physiology, was professor of physiology and physiological chemistry from 1890 to 1908 and professor of biochemistry from 1908 to 1918. He joined the faculty of McGill University, Montreal, in 1920 and taught biochemistry there until 1929. He was recognized as a pioneer in medical research in Canada, and received honorary degrees from universities in Great Britain and the United States. His scientific articles were published in the *Journal of Physiology; Proceedings of the Royal Society; Quarterly Journal of Microscopical Science; American Journal of Morphology;* and *Journal of Anatomy and Physiology.*

McALPINE, măk-ăl′pĭn, **William Jarvis,** American civil engineer: b. New York, N. Y., April 30, 1812; d. Staten Island, N. Y., Feb. 16, 1890. In a career of over half a century, McAlpine became one of the pioneers in providing publicly owned water supplies for cities, and had a directing hand in some of the greatest improvements of docks, bridges, and rail and highway transportation.

After attending elementary schools in Newburgh and Rome, N. Y., McAlpine was apprenticed at 15 to John B. Jervis, civil engineer, and eight years later succeeded him as chief engineer of the eastern division of the Erie Canal. From 1846 to 1849 he was engineer in charge of construction of the vast stone dock of the Brooklyn Navy Yard. Then began a series of projects which over the next 30 or 40 years were to improve or enlarge the water-works serving Albany (1850), Brooklyn and Chicago (1851), Montreal, Canada (1869), Philadelphia (1875), and New York (1882 and later). As chief engineer of the Third Avenue drawbridge over the Harlem River, New York (1860–1861), McAlpine pioneered in the design and sinking of the caissons for the piers. He later acted as chief or consulting engineer in the building of a number of the nation's largest bridges, among them the Eads Bridge over the Mississippi at St. Louis (1865); the Niagara-Clifton bridge at Niagara (1868), and the Washington Bridge spanning the Harlem in New York City (1885–1888). He also directed the construction of the New York State Capitol at Albany in 1873, and later, as engineer of parks for New York City, built the famous Riverside Drive.

Just before his death he was planning an "arcade railway" which was to provide an underground transit system for New York, as well as second-level streets beneath the more congested thoroughfares. Although remarkable in conception and in many respects practicable, McAlpine's plan met with much opposition from property owners and was later abandoned.

For many years he was the only American who could claim membership in the British Institution of Civil Engineers; for his paper on "The Supporting Power of Piles," presented before that body, he received the Telford Gold Medal (1868). McAlpine was a frequent contributor to technical publications, and in addition to reports and original papers wrote a textbook, *Modern Engineering* (1874).

McANENY, George, American civic administrator and city planner: b. Greenville, N. J., Dec. 24, 1869; d. Princeton, N. J., July 29, 1953. He graduated from the Jersey City High School in 1885 and entered journalism, serving on several New York newspapers until 1892. He then began his long civic career, starting with his efforts in behalf of civil service reform through the National Civil Service Reform League (since 1945 the National Civil Service League) and its local affiliate, the New York Civil Service Reform Association. He served as an officer of both organizations from 1927 until his death. In 1902, as a member of the New York Civil Service Commission, he helped draft the civil service rules adopted by New York City. As borough president of Manhattan (1910–1913), he fought for zoning regulations and paved the way for adoption of the first zoning ordinance regulating the height of buildings in the city. After serving as executive manager of the New York *Times* from 1916 to 1921 he became the first chairman of the State Transit Commission appointed by Gov. Nathan D. Miller to regulate the city's muddled rapid-transit system and unify the lines. He served on state and city boards and was president of the Regional Plan Association for 10 years from its inception in 1930, and thereafter its chairman. He was president and then chairman of the corporation that organized and operated the New York World's Fair, held in 1939–1940. Lectures he had given at Yale were published under the title *Municipal Citizenship* (1915).

MACAO, mà-kou′ or mà-kä′ô (Port. MACAU), seaport and Portuguese colony, Kwangtung Province, southeast China, on the South China Sea. It is at the southwest entrance of the Pearl (or Canton) River, 40 miles west of Hong Kong and 65 miles south of Canton. The colony, six square miles in area, consists of the peninsula of Macao and the small islands of Taipa and Colôane. The city of Macao, formerly an island but now united by a 700-foot wide, three-mile long isthmus with the deltaic island of Heungshan, commands magnificent views particularly along its quay or Praia Grande, which affords a drive or promenade along the sea wall. The city has a cathedral, 120 schools, a college, and a seminary. There are statues to Vasco da Gama, Portuguese navigator who in 1497 and 1502 visited India and the Far East, and to his compatriot the poet Luiz Vaz de Camoëns, who while in exile here about 1558–1559 wrote part of his *Lusiad,* celebrating da Gama's first voyage.

The oldest foreign settlement in the Far East it is noted as a pleasure and gambling resort. It is an important transit port for fresh and salted fish, tea, rice, tobacco, cement, preserves, oranges, anise, wine, lacquer, cassia and cassia oil, and opium. Fishing is the most important local industry.

History.—Established in 1557 as the first center of trade between Europe and China, Macao became a haven for European traders and missionaries in times of uprisings. Starting in 1563, and for nearly 300 years, Portugal paid the Chinese government a yearly rental or tribute for the colony, until in 1849 the Portuguese declared Macao a free port. Disputes continued, however, until 1887, when China signed a treaty formally recognizing Portugal's sovereignty. Macao enjoyed its most flourishing period during the 18th and part of the 19th centuries, when it and Canton were the only ports in China open to European commerce. But the silting up of its harbor, together with the growth of Hong Kong (ceded by China to Great Britain in 1842) as a rival port, gradually robbed it of its pre-eminent position. While continuing to ship fish, rice, oil, and other products, it gained a nefarious reputation for its coolie traffic and opium smuggling. The trade in narcotics extended until long after World War I and required strenuous efforts of the League of Nations before it was reduced. In the 1920's Macao spent over $10,000,000 in harbor improvements, including the dredging of a 4-mile channel to deep water. During World War II the Japanese threatened the military occupation of Macao, in 1943 firing upon and seizing the British steamer *Sian.*

The colony's population, highly intermixed, declined from 187,772 in 1950 to 169,299 in 1960.

MACARONI, măk-à-rō′nĭ (It. *maccheroni*), a dough or paste prepared from a special variety of wheat flour and made into tubes, ribbons, sticks, strands, and other shapes. Supposedly originating in Italy, macaroni is used extensively in many countries. The hard or durum wheat, rich in gluten and protein, which makes the distinctive macaroni paste and formerly was obtainable only in the warm countries of southern Europe and northern Africa, has for years been successfully grown in North Dakota and other western states of the United States. Numerous macaroni factories have been established in certain sections of Canada. Virtually all the macaroni consumed in the United States—about one billion pounds a year since 1945—is produced there; only a fraction of the total is imported, and exports far exceed imports.

Among the most commonly used macaroni products are spaghetti, noodles, ravioli, lasagne, rigatoni (especially for stuffing), and macaroni itself in various forms, such as elbow macaroni. Their size varies from the largest tubes or pipes such as grooved macaroni or rigatoni to the medium-sized ones like spaghetti and spaghettini, and the smallest, vermicelli and fedelini. They are made in over 100 shapes—stars, discs, triangles, circles, bowknots, shells, quills, twists, wagon wheels, and letters of the alphabet. Several companies offer complete meals in dry form as well as precooked dishes, canned or frozen, generally in combination with mushroom or marinara sauce, meat balls, or grated cheese.

The process of manufacturing macaroni has become highly mechanized. The ground durum wheat, called semolina or middlings, is sifted into various degrees of fineness, then often blended and enriched with gluten or wheat germ and thoroughly mixed in a dry state. From the blender the mixture passes to a hopper, where hot water is added to make a dough of the right consistency. This dough is pressed or extruded through forms or dies that give it the desired shape. The macaroni is finally dried on racks that travel slowly through constantly circulating warm air.

MACARONIC VERSE, măk-à-rŏn′ĭk (It. *maccheronico,* relating to macaroni, hence mixed or jumbled), a type of humorous poetry in which modern words, given Latin endings, are introduced into Latin verse. The name is also given to poetry that is merely a mixture of Latin (in some cases Greek) and the vernacular of the author. Macaronic verse is said to have originated with Teofilo Folengo (1491–1544), a learned Benedictine monk, who left his monastery and lived a worldly life, supporting himself by writing ridiculous poetry under the pseudonym of Merlin Coccai. His *Liber Macaronicus* appeared in 1517 and was highly successful. It greatly influenced Rabelais' *Voyage of Pantagruel* (1532), and was imitated by a number of minor Italian poets. Molière made use of macaronic verse in *Le malade imaginaire* (1673).

MACAROON, măk-à-rōōn′, a small, rich, glazed cookie. Formerly a French delicacy, macaroons now are baked in many countries from simple recipes. They are made by combining almond paste or extract, coconut, flaked cereal, flour, egg whites, sugar, and salt.

MacARTHUR, măk-är′thĕr, **Arthur,** American general: b. Springfield, Mass., June 2, 1845; d. Milwaukee, Wis., Sept. 5, 1912. He entered the service during the Civil War as a first lieutenant in the 24th Wisconsin Infantry, in August 1862. Thereafter he saw action in the battles of Perryville, Stone River, Dandridge, Franklin, and in the Atlanta campaign. He was mentioned in dispatches for gallant and meritorious service, and in 1890, was awarded the Congressional Medal of Honor for bravery in the battle of Missionary Ridge (1863). By the end of the war, he had been brevetted a colonel.

In February 1866, he entered the regular army. From then until 1886, he was stationed in the West and Southwest, where he took part in several Indian campaigns. In May 1898, shortly after the beginning of the Spanish-American War, he was appointed brigadier general of volunteers, and was assigned to the Philippines. In August of that year, he was commissioned major general of volunteers. In 1899, under Gen. Elwell Otis, he led a division against Aguinaldo. In 1900, he was appointed commander of the Division of the Philippines, and succeeded General Otis as military governor of the islands. He was promoted to brigadier general in the regular army in January 1900, and in 1906 was made assistant chief of staff of the United States Army, with the rank of lieutenant general. During the Russo-Japanese War, he was detailed as a special observer with the Japanese Army (1905). He was retired from active service in June 1909.

Lieutenant General MacArthur was the father of General Douglas MacArthur.

MacARTHUR, Douglas

One of the great war heroes of the United States, General Douglas MacArthur was also one of the nation's most controversial military leaders. As commander of Allied forces in the Southwest Pacific during World War II, he led his armies to victory over Japan. After the war, he administered the Allied occupation of Japan, restoring that shattered nation to prosperity.

When the Korean War broke out in 1950, MacArthur was named United Nations commander in Korea. Through a series of daring maneuvers, he drove the invading North Koreans out of South Korea. But after Communist China entered the war, MacArthur wanted to extend the fighting to the Chinese mainland, and openly criticized President Harry S Truman's orders to limit the war to Korea. This controversy led to MacArthur's dismissal from command. After 52 years of military service, the 71-year-old general returned home to live a quiet, private life.

In an age when war had become increasingly complex, MacArthur showed complete mastery over all aspects of his profession. He combined supreme self-confidence with unflinching courage. His unusual strategic sense and his intuitive understanding of the enemy led him to make insightful, often brilliant, wartime decisions. Impressive in appearance and dramatic in action, he demanded and received unquestioning obedience.

But the qualities that made MacArthur great were also the sources of his weaknesses. He was extremely egotistical and would tolerate no criticism. Remote and authoritarian, he seemed to lose touch with the common man. Although he insisted on complete loyalty from his subordinates, he often disagreed bitterly with his superiors. During World War II, he strongly opposed Allied strategy in the Pacific, taking his case to President Franklin D. Roosevelt. And when he was dismissed from command in the Korean War, he was convinced that he was the victim of a communist plot. He believed that highly placed officials in Washington, aided by British officials, were active members of the conspiracy.

MacArthur's complex personality inspired both love and fear. His admirers gave him their wholehearted devotion. His critics seemed to find fault with almost everything he did. Few persons could be indifferent to this proud and colorful warrior. And no one could deny that he had served his country well during the difficult period when it moved away from a policy of isolation to assume leadership of the free world.

Boyhood and Education

Early Years. Douglas MacArthur was born on Jan. 26, 1880, at the U.S. Army arsenal barracks in Little Rock, Ark. He was the son of Arthur MacArthur, a professional army officer, and Mary Pinkney Hardy MacArthur, the daughter of an old Virginia family. He had two older brothers —Malcolm, who died at the age of five, and Arthur III, who graduated from the U.S. Naval Academy and served in the Spanish-American War and in World War I.

Young Douglas inherited his striking good looks from his mother. From her, he also received his determination and profound belief in his own destiny. In his father the boy found a model for his future career. The elder MacArthur had achieved fame as the "boy colonel" of the Civil War. Joining the Union army as a first lieutenant

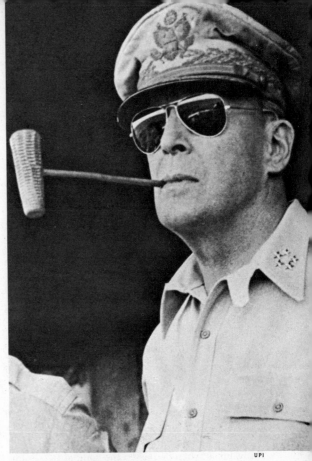

UPI

WORLD WAR II HERO Gen. Douglas MacArthur became almost as well known for his gold-braided hat, corncob pipe, and sunglasses as for defeating the Japanese.

when he was 17, he won the Congressional Medal of Honor for his conduct at the Battle of Missionary Ridge. In 1865, at the age of 19, he received the temporary rank of lieutenant colonel. After the war, he served at frontier outposts, and in 1900 became commander of army forces and military governor in the Philippines. When he retired in 1909 as a lieutenant general, he was the highest-ranking officer in the U.S. Army.

Douglas had an irregular education during his early years. His father's assignments forced the MacArthurs to move from one army post to an-

MacArthur in Profile

Born at Little Rock, Ark.—Jan. 26, 1880.
Graduated from West Point—June 11, 1903.
Served in France during World War I—1917–1919.
Named Superintendent of West Point—June 12, 1919.
Appointed Chief of Staff, U.S. Army—Nov. 21, 1930.
Drove Out the "Bonus Army" of dissatisfied veterans from Washington—July 28, 1932.
Appointed Military Adviser to the Philippine Commonwealth —Oct. 2, 1935.
Retired from the U.S. Army—Dec. 31, 1937.
Served as Field Marshal in the Philippine army—1938–1941.
Recalled to Active Duty to command U.S. Army Forces in the Far East—July 26, 1941.
Left the Philippines after Japanese forced American troops to retreat to Bataan—March 11, 1942.
Appointed Commander of Allied forces in the Southwest Pacific—April 18, 1942.
Returned to the Philippines with the Allied invasion—Oct. 20, 1944.
Received Surrender of Japan—Sept. 2, 1945.
Commanded Occupation of Japan—1945–1951.
Named U.N. Commander in Korea—July 8, 1950.
Dismissed from Command by President Truman over disagreement on Korean policy—April 11, 1951.
Died at Washington, D.C.—April 5, 1964.

FATHER AND SON. Douglas followed in the footsteps of his father, Arthur MacArthur, a U.S. Army officer who won a Medal of Honor in the Civil War.

WEST POINT CADET MacArthur graduated first in the Academy's Class of 1903.

other, frequently interrupting the boy's schooling. But Douglas worked hard at his studies, because he had set his heart on attending the U.S. Military Academy at West Point. His family was living in Milwaukee when he passed the competitive examination for West Point in 1898 and received an appointment as a cadet.

At the Academy. MacArthur entered West Point in 1899. Mrs. MacArthur moved nearby to be with her son while her husband was in the Philippines, and Douglas visited her every day.

MacArthur's achievements at West Point gave rich promise of an outstanding career. First in his class, he made a scholastic record that had not been equaled in many years. He won the coveted appointment of first captain, the highest military honor at the academy. He also played varsity football and managed the baseball team. Graduating in 1903, he was commissioned a second lieutenant in the corps of engineers.

Young Officer

First Assignments. MacArthur's first assignment was in the Philippines as an engineer. After a year there, he was sent to work in the Army Engineer Office in San Francisco. In 1905 he went to the Far East as an aide to his father, who had been appointed official U.S. observer of the Russo-Japanese War. Although the war had ended by the time the MacArthurs reached Manchuria, they had an opportunity to learn much about the Japanese army. Before returning to the United States in 1906, they made a nine-month tour of the Orient, visiting China, India, and many countries of Southeast Asia.

MacArthur's career in the years before World War I followed the usual pattern for most young officers. He attended a number of army schools and held a wide variety of posts, including service with the general staff. His promotions came rapidly during this period, and by the time the United States entered World War I in 1917, he had reached the rank of major.

World War I brought MacArthur into national prominence for the first time. The young major helped organize the famed 42d Infantry (Rainbow) Division, made up of National Guard units from various states. As the division's first chief of staff, with the rank of colonel, MacArthur quickly prepared the men for overseas service. He sailed with them to France in October, 1917. In August, 1918, after being promoted to brigadier general, he became commander of the division's 84th Infantry Brigade.

During the war, MacArthur led his brigade with an enthusiasm and dash that earned him the loyalty and affection of his men. Wounded twice, he received many decorations for his bravery in battle. He also won recognition for his skill in strategical and tactical matters. In his dress, he affected a distinctive uniform that set him apart from other officers. He carried no weapons, only a riding crop, and refused to wear a helmet or gas mask. Because of his elegant appearance, reporters nicknamed him the "Beau Brummel of the A.E.F." (American Expeditionary Force).

Between the Wars

Postwar Years. After the war, MacArthur was named superintendent of West Point, beginning his duties in 1919. At the time, the academy had an outdated curriculum. MacArthur set about with much success to modernize the institution and raise its academic level. He placed great emphasis on athletics, and wrote the motto that still appears on the wall of the West Point gymnasium: "Upon the fields of friendly strife are sown the seeds that, upon other fields, on other days, will bear the fruits of victory."

MacArthur left West Point in 1922. From then until 1930 he held various posts in the United States and in the Philippines, which he came to regard as a second home. In 1925 he was promoted to major general, and in 1928 he attended the Olympic Games in Amsterdam as president of the U.S. Olympic Committee.

AS CHIEF OF STAFF of the U.S. Army during the 1930's, MacArthur appointed Dwight D. Eisenhower as his aide.

LANDING AT LEYTE, MacArthur waded ashore with American troops that invaded the Philippines in 1944. MacArthur had promised the people that he would return when he was forced to leave in 1942 after the Japanese invasion.

One of the most important events of these years for MacArthur was his membership on the court-martial of Brig. Gen. William (Billy) Mitchell in 1925. Mitchell, an aviator-hero of World War I, was charged with insubordination for his outspoken criticism of the U.S. War and Navy departments. During the trial, attention was focused on his claim that military leaders failed to recognize the importance of air power. The court convicted Mitchell by secret ballot, and many persons believed that MacArthur had voted for conviction. MacArthur later wrote, however, that he had voted for acquittal.

Chief of Staff. In November, 1930, President Herbert C. Hoover named MacArthur chief of staff of the U.S. Army, with the temporary rank of full general. At the age of 50, MacArthur was the youngest man to have been appointed to this post. He took office in the worst days of the Great Depression, when the American people were bitterly disillusioned with war.

Opinions About MacArthur

Gen. Enoch Crowder: "I thought that Arthur MacArthur was the most flamboyantly egotistic man I had ever seen—until I met his son." (As quoted in *The Riddle of MacArthur* by John Gunther.)

President Lyndon B. Johnson: ". . . General MacArthur dedicated his entire life to selfless service in the defense of freedom." (From the proclamation issued at the time of MacArthur's death, April 5, 1964.)

Marine Corps poem:
And while possibly a rumor now,
    Some day it will be fact
That the Lord will hear a deep voice say,
    Move over God, it's Mac.

(As quoted in *The General and the President* by Richard H. Rovere and Arthur M. Schlesinger, Jr.)

Paul V. McNutt, U.S. high commissioner of the Philippines: "I wouldn't hesitate to call President Quezon [of the Philippines] 'Manuel,' but I never called the General 'Doug.'" (As quoted in *The General and the President*.)

Field Marshal Viscount Montgomery: "He was the best soldier the United States produced during World War II." (From a tribute at the time of MacArthur's death.)

Shigeru Yoshida, prime minister of Japan: " . . . It [was] your firm and kindly hand that led us . . . on the road of recovery and reconstruction. . . . In the name of the Japanese Government and people, I send you our nation's heartfelt thanks." (From a tribute after the signing of the Japanese Peace Treaty, Sept. 8, 1951.)

MacArthur had to spend much time and energy convincing Congress to appropriate adequate funds for his plans to reorganize the army and make it more efficient. He achieved much of his program, but was generally unsuccessful in his efforts to strengthen air and armored units and to integrate them with the ground force.

MacArthur's most controversial action during his five-year service as chief of staff was his rout of the Bonus Army on July 28, 1932. About 15,000 men, most of whom were unemployed veterans of World War I, had streamed into Washington to demand payment of federal war bonuses. The police were unable to handle such a large crowd, and President Hoover ordered the army to clear them out of the capital. In full uniform, polished boots, and beribboned blouse, with his aide Maj. Dwight D. Eisenhower at his side, MacArthur personally carried out the order. Using tanks and mounted cavalry, he easily routed the veterans and drove them from their camp. For many persons, the use of such force created an image of MacArthur as a potential military dictator.

Military Adviser in the Philippines. MacArthur completed his duty as chief of staff in October, 1935. He then was appointed military adviser to the newly created Philippine Commonwealth. He received the appointment at the request of Manuel Quezon, who had been elected first president of the Philippines. MacArthur's program for Philippine defense called for a small regular army, a militia, and air and naval units. Such a force, MacArthur believed, would discourage any enemy from attacking the islands.

MacArthur retired from the U.S. Army on Dec. 31, 1937, but continued as Philippine military adviser with the rank of field marshal. During this period he adopted the gold-braided hat, sunglasses, and pipe that became his hallmark.

MacArthur's Family. MacArthur was married twice, first in 1922 to Henrietta Louise Cromwell Brooks. This marriage ended in divorce by mutual consent in 1929. He married his second wife, Jean Marie Faircloth, in 1937. They had one son, Arthur, born on Feb. 21, 1938.

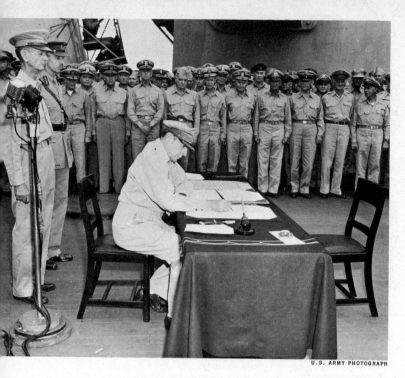

JAPANESE SURRENDER was signed by MacArthur aboard the U.S.S. "Missouri" on Sept. 2, 1945, in the presence of important Allied officers who fought in the Pacific. After the war, MacArthur led the Allied occupation of Japan and rebuilt that war-torn nation into a major industrial power.

Hero of the Pacific

"**I Shall Return.**" On July 26, 1941, as war with Japan threatened in the Pacific, the 61-year-old MacArthur was recalled to active duty as commander of the newly formed U.S. Army Forces in the Far East. Officials hoped that MacArthur's assignment would serve notice of American determination to halt Japanese aggression.

On Dec. 7, 1941, Japan began the Pacific war by attacking Pearl Harbor in Hawaii. About eight hours later, the Japanese bombed Clark Field, north of Manila in the Philippines, destroying half the bombers of MacArthur's Far East Air Force. For reasons that never have been entirely explained, the bombers were lined up unprotected on the field.

The Japanese landed large forces north and south of Manila on December 22. Three days later, MacArthur declared Manila an open city and moved to Corregidor, an island fortress off Bataan Peninsula at the entrance to Manila Bay. During the next two weeks, under heavy Japanese pressure, American troops withdrew to Bataan, where they continued to resist the Japanese heroically for three months. Although the gradual withdrawal to Bataan had been executed with great skill, some observers felt that MacArthur should have followed another plan of retreat prepared before the war. Under that plan, the defenders would have fallen back on Bataan immediately after the war began, thus saving supplies and food.

In March, 1942, President Franklin D. Roosevelt ordered MacArthur and his family to go to Australia. Strategists felt that MacArthur was too valuable to be lost in the hopeless defense of the Philippines, which finally fell to the Japanese in early May. On the trip to Melbourne, MacArthur made his famous statement of determination. "I came through," he declared, "and I shall return." He received the Medal of Honor on March 25, and on April 18 was formally named Supreme Commander of the Southwest Pacific Area.

MacArthur's first task was to protect Australia. Planning to cut Australia's sea-lanes to the United States, the Japanese sought to capture Port Moresby on the south coast of New Guinea. After the Japanese failed to take this objective by sea, they were stopped on land in September, 1942, by Australian troops under MacArthur's command. The Allies then took the offensive and began a long and difficult campaign to drive the enemy out of strongholds in New Guinea. By February, 1943, the Allies had won control of the Papuan Peninsula on southeast New Guinea and eliminated the Japanese threat to the sea-lanes.

Road to Victory. MacArthur's victory in New Guinea was one of the first steps in a campaign that took his Southwest Pacific forces westward toward the Philippines. During this campaign, South Pacific units led by Adm. William Halsey were placed under MacArthur's strategic command. As more troops, planes, and supplies arrived from the United States, the tempo of the Allied offensive increased. After advancing up the chain of the Solomon Islands, MacArthur's troops seized the Admiralty Islands and neutralized the Japanese base at Rabaul in early 1944. They then moved by giant steps along the northern New Guinea coast, bypassing large Japanese forces along the way. By September 15, the Allies had reached Morotai in the Moluccas, about 300 miles south of the Philippines.

While MacArthur was pursuing his offensive toward the Philippines, Adm. Chester Nimitz, commander of the Pacific Fleet, was advancing toward the inner defenses of Japan by way of the Gilbert, Marshall, and Mariana islands in the Central Pacific. MacArthur opposed this second offensive, which was largely naval in character, because he considered it an unnecessary diversion of effort. However, Nimitz's route was a shorter, perhaps more decisive one to Japan and had strong support from strategists in Washington. As a compromise, military leaders decided to pursue both the MacArthur and Nimitz offensives, but, if necessary, to give priority to the Central Pacific drive under Nimitz.

Considerable disagreement also arose about the objective of the Pacific advance. MacArthur insisted that the Philippines should be the major objective before the Japanese mainland. Other military leaders, notably Adm. Ernest King, chief of naval operations, argued for Formosa (Taiwan) or the China coast. In July, 1944, at a conference at Pearl Harbor, MacArthur presented his case to President Roosevelt and was permitted to attack the Philippines.

On Oct. 20, 1944, MacArthur's forces invaded Leyte in the central Philippines. The general waded ashore with his troops, fulfilling his promise to return made more than two years earlier. On December 18, three days after his troops landed on Mindoro, he was promoted to the rank of five-star general of the army. In early January, 1945, MacArthur's army invaded Luzon, the main island of the Philippines, and by the end of February had recaptured Corregidor and Manila.

Occupation of Japan. On Aug. 14, 1945, after the atomic bombing of Hiroshima and Nagasaki, the Japanese accepted Allied terms of surrender. The next day, MacArthur was named Supreme Commander in Japan for the Allied powers. On September 2, at ceremonies aboard the battleship *Missouri* in Tokyo Bay, he received the formal surrender of the Japanese.

At an age when most men retire, the 65-year-old general now began a new career as commander of the occupation of Japan. Remote and unapproachable, surrounded by a devoted staff, and regarded with awe by the Japanese people, he seemed almost superhuman to those who knew him during the occupation. Under his guidance, Japan emerged from defeat to prosperity. He disarmed the military, established a liberal government, instituted land reform, and restored the country's shattered industry. He also abolished the nobility and brought about other social changes that had an important effect on Japanese society by making it more democratic. Referring to his role in transforming Japan from a militaristic nation into a peaceful one, MacArthur later wrote: "Could I have but a line a century hence crediting a contribution to the advance of peace, I would gladly yield every honor which has been accorded me in war."

Korean War

MacArthur was still in Japan when communist North Korea attacked South Korea on June 25, 1950. Although the general had no responsibility for South Korea, President Harry S Truman ordered him to take command of a small American military mission stationed there and to provide United States air and sea support for the South Korean army. MacArthur flew to Korea on June 28 to study the situation, and on his recommendation the President authorized the use of American ground forces to help the South Koreans. The United States then succeeded in having the United Nations assume nominal responsibility for the defense of South Korea. On July 8, MacArthur was named commander of a unified international force established to repel the communist attack.

Advance to the Yalu. The 70-year-old general faced a formidable task in Korea. By the time the first American troops arrived on July 1, the North Koreans had overwhelmed South Korean defenses, captured the capital city of Seoul, and were pushing rapidly southward with little opposition. By early September they had forced the defenders into a small beachhead, called the Pusan perimeter, at the southeast tip of the Korean peninsula.

U.S. ARMY PHOTOGRAPH

IN THE KOREAN WAR, MacArthur commanded the United Nations troops against the communist invaders.

WIDE WORLD

WITH PRESIDENT TRUMAN, MacArthur conferred on Korean strategy in October 1950. Six months later, Truman dismissed MacArthur over policy disagreements.

On September 15, MacArthur executed a daring outflanking maneuver by landing troops at Inchon, west of Seoul. At the same time, the American Eighth Army launched a massive counteroffensive from within the Pusan perimeter. The North Koreans, pursued from the south and in danger of being trapped in the north, fled toward the 38th parallel, the boundary between North and South Korea. By the end of the month, United Nations forces had recaptured most of South Korea.

With total victory so close, MacArthur received permission, with some qualifications, to send his army into North Korea to destroy its military forces. On October 8, United Nations troops crossed the 38th parallel and moved northward toward the Yalu River—the boundary between North Korea and Communist China. U.N. advance units reached the Yalu on October 26.

Dismissal from Command. MacArthur's attempt to subdue North Korea ended in failure because of Communist China's entry into the war. MacArthur had known that the Chinese were massing large forces north of the Yalu, but when he met President Truman on Wake Island on October 15, he assured the President they would not attack. On the basis of this assurance, the President had permitted MacArthur to drive on to the Yalu. Toward the end of October, United Nations units reported contact with Chinese troops, but MacArthur ordered the offensive to continue.

The Chinese attacked in force on November 24 and sent MacArthur's army reeling back over the 38th parallel. MacArthur began a counterattack in February, 1951. But it proved indecisive, and the Korean War settled into a stalemate.

After China intervened, MacArthur contended that the Korean struggle had become a "new war." He proposed various measures to achieve victory, including bombing supply centers in Manchuria and "unleashing" the Chinese Nationalists on Formosa against the communist-held mainland. Presi-

UPI

"Old Soldiers Never Die"

General MacArthur made a famous farewell address to a joint session of Congress on April 19, 1951, after President Harry S Truman had dismissed him from command in Korea. The general is shown in the picture with Vice-President Alben Barkley and House Speaker Sam Rayburn. MacArthur's speech, a stirring defense of his views on Korea, ended with these words, as quoted in the *Congressional Record*:

"I have just left your fighting sons in Korea. They have met all tests there and I can report to you without reservation they are splendid in every way. It was my constant effort to preserve them and end this savage conflict honorably and with the least loss of time and a minimum sacrifice of life. Its growing bloodshed has caused me the deepest anguish and anxiety. Those gallant men will remain often in my thoughts and in my prayers always.

"I am closing my 52 years of military service. When I joined the army even before the turn of the century, it was the fulfillment of all my boyish hopes and dreams. The world has turned over many times since I took the oath on the plain at West Point, and the hopes and dreams have long since vanished. But I still remember the refrain of one of the most popular barrack ballads of that day which proclaimed most proudly that—

"'Old soldiers never die; they just fade away.'

"And like the old soldier of that ballad, I now close my military career and just fade away—an old soldier who tried to do his duty as God gave him the light to see that duty.

"Good-by."

dent Truman feared that such actions might cause a larger war and rejected MacArthur's proposals. The general then made public his disagreement with the President. In a letter read to Congress by Representative Joseph W. Martin, Jr., on April 5, MacArthur defended his recommendations, saying "there is no substitute for victory." Six days later, President Truman dismissed him from command. In a speech to the nation that evening, the President said he had taken this step "to prevent a third world war." "General MacArthur is one of our greatest military commanders," he continued, "but the cause of world peace is more important than any individual."

MacArthur returned to the United States for the first time in 15 years. Everywhere he went, as he crossed the country from San Francisco to New York, he received a hero's welcome. On April 19, he addressed a joint session of Congress. His speech, a stirring defense of his policy, closed with a line from an old army ballad: "Old soldiers never die; they just fade away."

Later Years

But the old general did not fade away. In 1952 he became board chairman of the manufacturing firm of Remington Rand. That year he also played an important role at the Republican National Convention. MacArthur had become a leading figure in Republican politics in 1948, when he was one of the candidates for the party's presidential nomination. At the 1952 convention, he delivered the keynote address, and again was mentioned as a possible candidate. The nomination went to his former aide, Dwight D. Eisenhower, whose command in Europe during World War II paralleled MacArthur's in the Pacific.

During his later years, MacArthur lived in a suite in the Waldorf-Astoria Hotel in New York City. There he assumed the same remoteness he had shown during the occupation of Japan. He seldom appeared in public and entertained little. Each year a delegation of West Point cadets called on him, and on his birthday old comrades honored him with a dinner.

In 1961, MacArthur and his wife made a sentimental trip to the Philippines, where he was treated as a national hero. In 1962, Congress authorized a gold medal struck for him, and passed a resolution citing "his outstanding devotion to the American people." That year he also received West Point's Sylvanus Thayer Award for service to his country. In accepting the award, MacArthur delivered a memorable address on the ideals of the American soldier and the meaning of the West Point motto—*Duty, Honor, Country.* He ended his speech with these words: "Today marks my final roll call with you, but I want you to know that when I cross the river my last conscious thought will be The Corps . . . . I bid you farewell."

MacArthur entered Walter Reed Hospital in Washington on March 2, 1964. During the next month he underwent three operations for an abdominal illness. Throughout this ordeal, he hung on grimly, but on April 5 he lost the battle and died at the age of 84. President Lyndon B. Johnson declared a period of national mourning, and the general's body lay in state in the rotunda of the national Capitol. On April 11, MacArthur was buried with full military honors in a memorial built for him by the city of Norfolk, Va., his mother's hometown.

LOUIS MORTON
Professor of History, Dartmouth College

MacArthur Bibliography

Gunther, John, *The Riddle of MacArthur: Japan, Korea, and the Far East* (New York: Harper & Brothers, 1951).

Hunt, Frazier, *The Untold Story of Douglas MacArthur* (New York: Devin-Adair, 1955).

MacArthur, Douglas, *Reminiscences* (New York: McGraw-Hill, 1964).

Morton, Louis, *United States Army in World War II: War in the Pacific: Fall of the Philippines* (Washington: U.S. Government Printing Office, 1953).

Rovere, Richard H., and Schlesinger, Arthur M., Jr., *The General and the President* (New York: Farrar, Straus, 1951).

Whitney, Courtney, *MacArthur* (New York: Knopf, 1956).

Willoughby, Charles A., and Chamberlain, John R., *MacArthur, 1941–1951* (New York: McGraw-Hill, 1954).

MacARTHUR, Duncan, American soldier and political figure: b. Dutchess County, N.Y., Jan. 14, 1772; d. near Chillicothe, Ohio, 1839. His family removed in 1780 to the western frontier of Pennsylvania, and at 18 years of age he went to seek his fortune in the wilderness, and participated as a ranger or scout in the warfare with the Indians in Kentucky and Ohio, until the victory of General Anthony Wayne in 1794 gave peace to the Western country. In 1796 he was married, and settled near Chillicothe, Ohio, as a surveyor and land speculator. In 1805 he became a member of the Ohio legislature, and in 1808 was appointed major general of the state militia. In the War of 1812 he received the commission of brigadier general in the army, and in 1814 succeeded General William Henry Harrison in command of the army of the West. After the war, as a joint commissioner with General Lewis Cass, he negotiated the treaty with the Indians of Ohio for the sale of their lands in that state, which was ratified in 1818. He served intermittently in the Ohio legislature (1815–30), and in 1823–25 was a representative in Congress from that state. In 1830 he was elected governor of Ohio.

McARTHUR, William Pope, American naval officer and hydrographer: b. Ste. Genevieve, Mo., April 2, 1814; d. aboard ship Dec. 23, 1850. In February 1832 he was appointed midshipman in the United States Navy, spent several years in the South Pacific station, and later attended the naval school at Norfolk, Va. During the second Seminole War (1837–1838) he commanded one of the vessels in the expedition to the Everglades. He was assigned to duty with the United States Coast Survey in 1840, and in the following year, took part in the survey of the Gulf coast. Promoted lieutenant in 1841, in 1848 he commanded the hydrographic party that made the first preliminary survey and reconnaissance of the Pacific coastline from Monterey to the Columbia River. He died of acute dysentery as his ship entered Panama Harbor on the return voyage.

McARTHUR, town of southern Ohio, the seat of Vinton County, 75 miles southeast of Columbus, on the Chesapeake and Ohio Railway. Local clays provide raw materials for brick-making, the town's chief industry. Fruit and vegetables are grown and stocks raised in the surrounding area; there also are a coal mine and oil and gas wells in the vicinity. McArthur was platted in 1815 and incorporated in 1851. Pop. 1,529.

MacARTHUR, P.I. See Ormoc.

MACASSAR or **MAKASSAR,** mà-kăs'ĕr, is a major seaport of Indonesia, and the capital of the province of South Sulawesi. It is situated near the southwest tip of Celebes (Sulawesi) island, at the southeast end of Macassar Strait, which separates Celebes from the island of Borneo. Macassar has an airport and is served by the state-owned Garuda Indonesian Airways. Its natural harbor is a port of call for big cargo ships from Europe and other parts of Asia; here imported goods are transshipped to smaller boats serving the other ports of Celebes, New Guinea, and the Molucca Islands. Teakwood, vegetable oils, coffee, spices, gums and resins, and rattan are exported. There are few Europeans, but a large Chinese group. The climate is very hot and humid and the vegetation of the surrounding area is of the tropical rain forest type.

Before Indonesian independence, Macassar was divided into two parts—a Dutch section called Vlaardingen, and a Malay section. Vlaardingen, the port area, was founded in the era of the East India Company. It now has broad avenues with modern buildings. The port is dominated by old Fort Rotterdam, originally built by the Portuguese; in front of it is a wide square surrounded by government buildings.

The new museum contains a valuable collection of objects illustrative of the native arts and industries, arms, costumes, and jewelry. The native Macassarese and Bugi are branches of the Malay people, and the Makassar language is one of the most important of the Malay group. The Portuguese claim to have visited Macassar as early as 1512, but their first permanent settlement is probably of much later date. During the 17th century the Dutch came often in conflict with the sultan of Macassar and with the Portuguese; in 1667 the sultan submitted, then the Portuguese were driven out and the Dutch East India Company won complete control. All attempts by the British to supplant the Dutch were unsuccessful, and the Dutch remained masters until the end of the second World War.

Hasanuddin University in Macassar was founded as a school of economics in 1949 and became a state university in 1956. Pop. (1961) 384,159.

MACASSAR OIL, the trade name for an unguent that made its appearance in England early in the 19th century. It took its name from the district of Macassar, where it was first produced, being pressed from the fruit, or seed, of the *Schleichera trijuga,* the East Indian kusum tree. This fixed vegetable oil is used by the natives for cooking, illuminating and for medicinal purposes. The name "macassar oil" is also used for a pomade made of almond, olive, or peanut oil, to which other substances were added to give color and perfume.

MACASSAR STRAIT is an arm of the Pacific Ocean between the islands of Celebes and Borneo, in Indonesia. The strait, connecting the Celebes Sea with Java and Flores seas, is the shortest route from Java to the Philippines. It reaches a width of almost 250 miles in the south, while in the north it is only 80 miles wide; the depth is mostly 3,000 feet, except an area in the north where it reaches almost 10,000 feet. Macassar is the most important harbor. Here on Jan. 23, 1942, took place the naval engagement in which American and Dutch warships and planes opposed a Japanese armada of some 100 ships in the Strait of Macassar between Borneo and Celebes. In the battle, which raged for five days and nights, the Japanese lost over 30 ships sunk or damaged, including one battleship and an aircraft carrier, and between 25,000 and 30,000 men drowned. Although Japanese losses were high, the battle proved to be principally an Allied delaying action, and in February of that year Japanese forces again advanced on Java, established bases on both sides of Celebes, and occupied Amboina Island, second most important naval base in the Dutch East Indies, and Timor, north of Australia.

MACAULAY, Sɪʀ **James Buchanan,** Canadian jurist: b. Niagara, Canada, Dec. 3, 1793; d. Toronto, Nov. 26, 1859. After serving as a lieutenant with a Canadian unit of the British Army in the War of 1812, he was admitted to the bar in 1822. In 1829, he was appointed a judge of the King's Bench in Upper Canada, as Ontario was then known. He served as first chief justice of the provincial Court of Common Pleas (1849–1856), and briefly thereafter as judge of the Court of Error and Appeal. Macaulay was responsible for the consolidation of the statutes of Upper and Lower Canada into a compact code, completed in 1859—a necessary prerequisite to dominion federation. He was knighted shortly before his death.

MACAULAY, Rose, English novelist: d. London, England, Oct. 30, 1958. Daughter of a lecturer in literature at Cambridge University, she spent much of her youth in Italy and published her first novel, *The Valley Captives,* in 1911. Her first major success came with *Potterism* (1920), a bitingly satirical novel of English middle class life, comparable to the slightly later work of Sinclair Lewis in the United States. *Told by an Idiot* (1923) and *Staying with Relations* (1930) are in the same vein. After World War II, Miss Macaulay published several notable travel books, including *The Fabled Shore* (1949) and *The Pleasure of Ruins* (1953). *The World My Wilderness* (1950) is a novel of the difficulties of an adolescent girl, brought up in the chaos of occupied France, who is transplanted to the orderly society of England after the war. *The Towers of Trebizond* (1956) is a seriocomic adventure story of a young Englishwoman in the Middle East.

MACAULAY, Thomas Babington, English essayist, poet, historian, and statesman: b. Rothley Temple, Leicestershire, England, Oct. 25, 1800; d. Holly Lodge, Kensington, London, Dec. 28, 1859.

Thomas Macaulay

The Bettmann Archive

His parents were Selina Mills Macaulay, a Quaker's daughter, and Zachary, a vigorous opponent of the slave trade who had for a time been governor of the free colony of Sierra Leone on the west coast of Africa. The elder Macaulay returned to England on a slave ship that deposited its human cargo in the West Indies. What he saw on this trip of the brutal mistreatment of Negro slaves filled him with a lifelong hatred of the institution and an unshakable resolve to see it abolished.

Macaulay's boyhood and early youth were spent in Clapham, then a suburb of London, where the family lived with a group of abolitionists who came to be known as the Clapham Sect. He proved amazingly precocious, writing a *Compendium of Universal History* at the age of eight and memorizing Sir Walter Scott's *Lay of the Last Minstrel* in its entirety. At 13, he was sent to a private school kept by a Reverend Mr. Preston near Cambridge. There young Macaulay studied Greek, wrote verses in Latin, read widely in history and literature, and took a lively interest in current political issues. These interests continued and increased when the school was moved the next year to Hertfordshire. He entered Trinity College, Cambridge, in the fall of 1818.

At the university, Macaulay distinguished himself in several ways: as a debater and talker, as a brilliant student of every subject except mathematics, and as something of a poet. Two times, in 1819 and 1821, he won the Chancellor's Medal for English verse. After twice failing in his application, he was elected a fellow of Cambridge in 1824. With the honor went £300 a year, "two pats of butter for breakfast and a yearly grant of the school's best audit ale." Macaulay studied law and began writing poems and essays for *Knight's Quarterly Magazine.* In 1826 he was called to the bar and joined the Northern Division of the Circuit Court at Leeds. His brilliant essay, *Milton,* had appeared in the famous Whig *Edinburgh Review* the year before and won him a reputation throughout the British Isles. He was to continue to publish frequently in this quarterly for 19 years and to do much to bolster its popularity.

Early Parliamentary Career.—In 1828, Macaulay was named a commissioner of bankruptcy. His continued writings for the *Review,* however, were mainly responsible for his election to Parliament in 1830 from the "pocket borough" of Calne, the political gift of Lord Lansdowne (Henry Petty-Fitzmaurice, 3d marquess of Lansdowne), a wealthy Whig who controlled several seats in the House and knew how to seize upon a brilliant young man when one was available. Macaulay was to be left "entirely free to act, according to his conscience."

The year 1830 was a propitious time for a rising young liberal to enter politics. Reforms in the social structure of the empire had been needed since Napoleon's defeat 15 years before, but a succession of Tory measures had thwarted practically all of them. Jewish emancipation, Catholic emancipation, the abolition of rotten boroughs, the extension of the franchise, the recognition of the rights of the expanding industrial cities to a just share in the privilege of determining the nation's laws—all these issues were clamoring for determination.

Macaulay sided with the reformers, as was natural. Having already achieved entree into the leading Whig social circles, notably into the mansion of Lord and Lady Holland (Henry Richard Fox, 3d Baron Holland), Macaulay was present when important political strategy was formulated, and he aided in translating it into law. Enactment of the so-called Reform Bills of 1832 owed much to his eloquent advocacy. "Whenever he rose to speak," William Ewart Gladstone remarked, "it was a summons like a trumpet-call to fill the benches." In 1832 he was elected to represent Leeds, after making it plain to the voters that he would not bind himself "to support any particular motion" no matter how urgent it might appear to them. This principle of the right of independent judgment was one he never surrendered.

India and Return to Parliament.—Subsequent political activities were devoted to the removal of civil disabilities against the Jews and to East Indian affairs, regarding which he soon became an authority. This latter interest led to his appointment as a member of the Supreme Council of India at a salary of £10,000 a year. He accepted, although it meant leaving all but one member of his family, to which he was devoted; his sister Hannah went with him (1834). Several years of service in India, Macaulay reasoned, would make him financially independent for life. It did just that, although the competence was well earned. His most notable accomplishment there was in drawing up a penal code for the entire country, published in 1837 and enacted into law (after some revision) in 1860; further revision was not seriously called for until well into the present century.

Macaulay returned to England in 1838, accompanied by his sister (now married to Charles Edward Trevelyan), Charles himself, and Margaret, their first born. A hard choice faced him: should he become involved in politics again or devote his restless energies to literature? He toured the Continent, mainly Italy, in the fall, trying to settle himself, and began, incidentally, the first of the 11 volumes of "journals" which he never published. He had continued to write for the *Edinburgh Review* while in the Orient, and had contemplated a detailed history of England from 1685 to the death of George III in 1820.

Politics won out. Macaulay was elected to Parliament from Edinburgh in 1839 despite attacks from the Tory press to the effect that the only thing he had accomplished in India was to amass a fortune of £30,000 at the expense of the public purse. He served briefly (1839–1841) in the cabinet as secretary of state for war. In 1842 he published a volume of poems, *Lays of Ancient Rome* (q.v.), a few of which, notably *Horatius at the Bridge,* are still enjoyed by young people. The following year he published his *Essays* (see MACAULAY'S ESSAYS) out of popular demand for an edition which he himself had supervised. Pirated and garbled versions had already appeared both in England and America.

Macaulay remained in Parliament for eight years, serving briefly in the cabinet again as paymaster general (1846–1847). He gave his support to the Maynooth grant to maintain a Catholic university in Ireland, and this fact roundly offended his constituents. He also crossed certain of the more important of them in other ways, such as treating them brusquely when they came to London to present grievances they wanted redressed. Notably, he alienated the whiskey traders of Edinburgh, who wished the tax on their commodity reduced. Macaulay assured them that he would do all in his power to have it raised. He was defeated at the polls (1847), but took comfort in the fact that he could now devote himself without interruption to his long deferred *History of England from the Accession of James the Second.*

"History of England."—Macaulay traveled extensively in the British Isles, Holland, and France in search of material for the *History.* The opening sentence of the work announced his bold but never accomplished design: "I purpose to write the history of England from the accession of King James the Second down to a time which is within the memory of men still living." Volumes 1 and 2 appeared in 1849 and proved immensely popular. Even in the United States, an agent wrote, 60,000 copies were disposed of in a few months. He added that "no book has ever sold like this with the American public, unless it was the Bible." Macaulay was named rector of the University of Glasgow and a fellow of the Royal Society. In 1852, with no effort on his part, he was returned to Parliament by the penitent voters of Edinburgh.

His health, however, began unaccountably to fail him that year. In the few speeches he made in Parliament, "the old voice, the old manner, and the old style"—all were there, but when he sat down he was visibly trembling and scarcely able to acknowledge the congratulations of friends. He was further vexed in 1853 by being driven into publishing his *Speeches,* a "wretched" bookseller, Henry Vizetelly, having announced a collected edition of them "by special license." Volumes 3 and 4 of the *History* appeared in December 1855. "Thank God," he wrote, that part of it was over at last.

Honors came thick upon him, once the *History* began to be read. He was made a member of the academies of Utrecht, Munich and Turin, and a knight of the Order of Merit by special decree of the king of Prussia (Frederick William IV). Soon afterward he was elected to the Institut de France and was named a trustee of the British Museum. This was followed by the degree of doctor of civil law from Oxford. Meanwhile the *History* was selling to an astounding extent. In 1856 his publishers, Thomas and William Longman, sent him a single check for £20,000, remarking that "in all the chronicles of the book trade no single sum equal to that amount had ever been paid to an English author."

What made the *History* such a successful performance has interested students down to the present. Its limitations were apparent even in his own day, notably his tendency to describe characters in vivid but black-and-white terms—his heroes being invariably Whigs and his villains Tories. The judgment of Sir Charles Firth in his detailed *Commentary on Macaulay's History of England* (1938) is perhaps the most reliable we shall have. The author failed to discuss England's American and colonial trade. He neglected to comment on the army. As for the relations of his country with those on the Continent, they, too, are left largely unexplored; there is an insularity about the work, in short, that reflects the insularity of its author.

Yet the virtues of the study survive all efforts that have been made to discredit them. Entirely apart from its triumphant readability, Macaulay rendered one invaluable service to history by enlarging inquiry into the past far beyond the scope of his predecessors. He was the first to examine journals and diaries for his purposes; indeed no human document was foreign to him. His style, however, is what chiefly absorbs the reader no matter what his degree of literacy. It is always clear and usually dramatic with the sense of present or impending events of major significance.

Last Years.—Continuing bad health led Macaulay to resign from the House in 1856, after confessing to friends his inability to perform "even in an imperfect manner, those duties which the public has a right to expect from every member." He traveled on the Continent, as he had done often before, avoiding the famous people there as much as possible. Back home, on Aug. 28, 1857, while he was dining out, as he did so often in these last years, a letter was delivered from the prime minister, Lord Palmerston (Henry John Temple, 3d Viscount Palmerston), with an offer of a peerage. Macaulay wrote in his journal, "the Queen's pleasure already taken. . . . It was necessary that I choose a title off hand. I determined to be Baron Macaulay of Rothley."

He attended the meetings of the House of Lords, but parliamentary matters, as compared with his *History,* had largely lost their interest for him. Although he persevered, volume 5 of the *History* did not appear until after his death. So rich and detailed was his knowledge of his subject that he proved able to complete only 17 years of his bravely projected span. It concludes with the death of King William III in 1702.

So far as the records reveal such matters, Macaulay was never in the conventional sense "in love." He directed his affections toward his family, for whom he was for many years the main support. Assuming such a responsibility meant sacrifices to an uncommon degree. In the last month that was left, he epitomized the story of his life in his journal: "Twenty-five years ago I was worth exactly and literally nothing." Now he was rich. "Indeed I cannot reckon my whole property at less than eighty thousand pounds. . . . And yet I am unhappy—more unhappy than I have been these many years. I am sick of life. I could wish to lie down and sleep, never to wake." His wish was soon granted. He died in his sleep, in his library—as was proper—and was buried in Westminster Abbey, with highest honors.

Bibliography.—The best edition of the *History of England* is that by Charles Harding Firth, 6 vols. (London 1913–15). Firth's *A Commentary on Macaulay's History of England* (London 1938) is a valuable analysis of its virtues and defects. The standard biography is by Macaulay's nephew, George Otto Trevelyan, *The Life and Letters of Lord Macaulay,* 2 vols. (London 1876). *The Public Life of Lord Macaulay* by Frederick Arnold (London 1862) contains a number of his hustings speeches that are not available elsewhere. Arthur Bryant published a brief but readable study, *Macaulay* (London 1932). The full-length critical biography by Richmond C. Beatty, *Lord Macaulay, Victorian Liberal* (Norman, Okla., 1938), is based on access to the "Journals" granted by Macaulay's great nephew, George Macaulay Trevelyan. C. D. Dharker edited *Lord Macaulay's Legislative Minutes* (London 1946).

RICHMOND CROOM BEATTY,
Professor of English, Vanderbilt University.

MACAULAY'S ESSAYS. The achievement of Thomas Babington Macaulay (q.v.) as an essayist consists of 9 contributions to *Knight's Quarterly Magazine* while he was a fellow at Trinity College, Cambridge; 36 to the *Edinburgh Review* between the years 1825 and 1844; and 5 biographical sketches for the *Encyclopaedia Britannica.* Most of them he collected and published in 1843 in three volumes, being driven to this necessity because of the fact that garbled and pirated versions were being circulated both in America and England.

Style.—Macaulay's subjects may be broadly classified as historical and literary, and with the first one of importance, *Milton,* he became immediately popular. Francis Jeffrey, editor of the *Edinburgh Review,* wondered where he could "possibly have picked up that style." What impressed him chiefly was a device Macaulay was to use over and over, the device of paradox coupled with an antithesis. In broad and sweeping lines he drew his contrast between the Cavalier and Puritan of John Milton's day. The latter

"prostrated himself in the dust before his maker; but he set his foot on the neck of his King." As for the Cavaliers, or Royalists, who supported Charles I, "they thought that they were doing battle for an injured beauty, while they defended a false and loathsome sorceress." Again, "though nothing could be more erroneous than their political opinions, they possessed in a far greater degree than their adversaries, those qualities which are the grace of private life." Other sweeping generalizations follow: No person can be a poet without a certain unsoundness of mind. As civilization advances, the art of poetry necessarily declines. In his first important work Macaulay had defined his style and manner.

The major essays on literary men indicate, primarily, Macaulay's fondness for Elizabethan and 18th century figures. Francis Bacon was his favorite. He was corrupt as a man but praiseworthy beyond measure as a practical philosopher. The ambition of Bacon was to see human society produce "fruit," which meant the multiplying of human enjoyments and the mitigating of suffering. The inductive or experimental method was the agency through which this objective could be attained. "Two simple words form the key to the Baconian doctrine," Macaulay wrote. They are "Utility and Progress." To make men perfect was no part of his plan. "His humble aim was to make imperfect men comfortable." Macaulay dismissed the idealisms of mankind, chiefly those of Plato, by saying that "they filled the world with long words and long beards and they left it as wicked and as ignorant as they found it."

Bias.—The Bacon essay has been mentioned in some detail because it is typical. In his review of John Wilson Croker's edition (1831) of James Boswell's *Life of Samuel Johnson, L.L.D.,* Macaulay wrote the following of the man who is the author of the most famous biography in the English language: "Boswell was one of the smallest men that ever lived. . . . He was always laying himself at the feet of some eminent man and begging to be spit upon. Servile and impertinent, shallow and pedantic, a bigot and a sot . . . such was this man and such was he proud to be."

Further glittering if biased statements illuminate the essays, which are generally praised more for their brilliance than for their accuracy. Macaulay had no use for Edmund Spenser's *Faerie Queene:* its pervading fault was that of "tediousness." As for the drama of the Restoration (1660–1685), he declared, "this part of our literature is a disgrace to our language and our national character."

Macaulay delighted in quarreling, either with people long dead or with his contemporaries. He was a Whig in politics—that is to say a liberal by his standards—and he gave rough treatment to those who were not of his persuasion. Their names seem almost as decisively unimportant now, as they once appeared illustrious—Henry Neele, James Mill, Robert Montgomery, and a host of others. Guiding Macaulay in his opinions about them was his considered judgment: "We are wiser than our ancestors."

Range.—Listing these brilliant essays would be an act of supererogation; they are still available for the world to read. *William Pitt, The Civil Disabilities of the Jews, Lord Clive* are titles suggestive of their ranging contents.

Yet they were not as ranging as an innocent reader might suspect. They indicate, moreover, a limitation of interest. Macaulay never seems to have noticed the Middle Ages. They were for him the "Dark Ages." Moreover, he cared little for the major figures of the romantic movement, with the possible exception of Lord Byron. William Wordsworth, Samuel Taylor Coleridge, Percy Bysshe Shelley, and John Keats were "poor creatures" to him and writers of "gibberish." What made Macaulay popular with his contemporaries, and continues to find readers for him today, is his always lucid style and his dramatic way of presenting a subject.

Bibliography.—A lengthy chapter on the essays appears in Richmond C. Beatty, *Lord Macaulay, Victorian Liberal* (Norman, Okla., 1938). George Malcolm Young edited *Prose and Poetry* (Cambridge 1953).

RICHMOND CROOM BEATTY.

McAULEY, măk-ô'lĭ, **Catherine (Elizabeth),** Irish Catholic religious leader: b. Stormanstown House, County Dublin, Ireland, Sept. 29, 1787; d. Dublin, Nov. 11, 1841. Of Catholic parentage, she was orphaned at an early age and brought up by Protestant relatives. The last of these—a well-to-do family named Callahan—allowed her to practice the Catholic religion unhampered, adopted it themselves eventually, and left her a large fortune, which she decided to use for the benefit of the poor.

On Sept. 24, 1827, in Dublin, she opened a commodious dwelling, the House of Our Blessed Lady of Mercy, staffed by herself and two female companions as a secular institution where poor children were taught and homeless young women received board and lodging. This developed into a religious order which was, however, not formally established until Catherine and her two associates had passed through their novitiates and taken their vows as nuns (Dec. 12, 1831) in a convent of the Order of the Presentation of the Blessed Virgin Mary. They then reconstituted the home as the mother house of the New Order of the Sisters of Mercy.

The new order was formally approved by Pope Gregory XVI in 1835, its rule being a modified version of that of the Presentation Order. Its foundress, now known as Mother Mary Catherine, served as mother superior until her death. The order spread rapidly to England, the United States, and other English-speaking countries, and is now worldwide.

See also MERCY, SISTERS OF.

Consult Degnan, Sister Mary Bertrand, *Mercy unto Thousands; Life of Mother Mary Catherine McAuley* . . . (Westminster, Md., 1957).

McAULEY, Jeremiah (known as JERRY McAULEY), Irish-American mission worker: b. Ireland, ?1839; d. New York, N.Y., Sept. 18, 1884. Abandoned by his parents in infancy, he was sent to live with a sister in New York City in 1852. He soon became a professional thief, serving a term (1857–1864) in Sing Sing Prison on a false charge of highway robbery. Some time later he permanently reformed and threw himself with great success into rescue work among the outcasts of the New York City slums. He founded the McAuley Water Street Mission (1872) in the Bowery, and the Cremorne Mission (1882) in the midtown area, both still in existence. Largely illiterate, he dictated his autobiography, *Transformed, or the History of a River Thief,* in 1876. His early death was due to consumption.

Consult Offord, Reverend Robert M., ed., *Jerry McAuley, an Apostle to the Lost* (New York 1907).

MACAW, mȧ-kô', a name used for about 23 kinds of birds belonging to the order of parrots (Psittaciformes). All have long, pointed tails and in most the face is bare of feathers. While many are noted for gaudiness of plumage, others are chiefly dull green. The macaws range in the American tropics from Mexico to Uruguay and Argentina, with a concentration of at least 12 kinds in Brazil alone. They are at home in the great rain forests, where they usually stay high in the trees, feeding on fruits and nuts which they are able to crack with their immensely powerful

Dode Thornton from National Audubon Society

Macaws.

beaks. They are monogamous, and when seen in flight along the great rivers of South America, or high above the trees, they are invariably in pairs or small family parties of three or four. Two or three white eggs are laid in a cavity in a tree.

Macaws are familiar to many as inhabitants of zoological gardens but are also frequently kept as household pets. Most of the specimens seen in captivity have been taken from the nest in their native lands and reared by hand so that, if well treated, they remain tame and gentle. On the other hand, those that may have been mistreated, as well as those captured as adults, may be savage and even dangerous to persons who approach them too closely, since they are able to inflict serious wounds with their great beaks. Gentle specimens make charming pets and often learn to speak a few words in deep, guttural voices. They seldom, however, can be taught to refrain from emitting occasional raucous screams. Macaws are best kept on stands, rather than in cages, since they often damage their long tails by climbing on the wire. The practice of keeping a macaw chained to a perch by one leg has some suggestion of cruelty, but pets can often be taught to remain upon a perch unrestrained and prevented from sliding down the support by placing a broad tray below it. Clipping a few feathers in one wing will generally suffice to discourage those inclined to fly.

Species.—The most brightly colored of the macaws is the red and blue (*Ara macao*). It is scarlet in general, with a band of yellow across the wings; the lower back and tips of the tapering tail feathers are light blue. The long feathers of the wing are dark blue above and reddish gold on the reverse. In overall length, this is the largest of the macaws, measuring 36 inches from tip of bill to tip of tail. It inhabits tropical lowland forests from southern Mexico, through Central America to South America, east of the Andes, as far south as Peru and east to Brazil. A commonly imported species, it is popular with pet lovers and zoological gardens the world over.

The blue and yellow macaw (*A. ararauna*), while less gaudy than the preceding, is perhaps even more beautiful. Excepting only a small area of greenish color on the crown, the entire upper parts are a fine scintillating blue, while the under parts from the black chin to the tail are deep yellow. The under surfaces of the long feathers of the tail and wing are greenish yellow. This species is a little shorter than the red and blue in length, measuring 34 inches from tip to tip. The blue and yellow macaw is found from Panama over the lowlands of South America as far south as northern Paraguay. Like the red and blue macaw, this species is frequently seen in zoological collections and in private homes.

Of similar length, but heavier in beak and body, is the green-winged macaw (*A. chloroptera*). The general coloration of this bird is deep maroon, with the lower back pale blue and a bluish green zone across the wings. The long tail feathers are red and blue above and reddish yellow below, while the flight feathers of the wings are dark blue externally and reddish yellow on their inner surfaces. The range of this handsome species extends from eastern Panama southward across South America to Paraguay and northern Argentina. For some reason it is less common in captivity than the two preceding species.

Two birds almost identical in coloration and differing principally in size are the great green macaw (*A. ambigua*) and the military macaw (*A. militaris*). Both are light green, with a red band across the forehead, the lower back light blue and the tail reddish brown interspersed with blue. The great green, however, is a large and powerful bird, measuring 34 inches. It ranges from Nicaragua to Ecuador. The military macaw is much slighter in build and measures only 27 inches. Its home extends from Mexico to the northern borders of Argentina.

Still smaller but certainly more beautiful is the Spix macaw (*A. spixii*) from eastern Brazil. It is pale blue in color and 22 inches in length. There are also a number of small macaws, chiefly dull green in color, ranging down to the noble macaw (*A. nobilis*), which is found in northern South America and is 13 inches long. The great

hyacinthine macaw (*Anodorhynchus hyacinthinus*) is entirely deep blue, with bare skin at the base of the lower bill and bright yellow around the eyes. It has a particularly powerful bill and heavy body, with a length of 34 inches. Related species are Lear's macaw (*Anodorhynchus leari*), in which the head is grayish, and the glaucous macaw (*Anodorhynchus glaucus*), which is paler blue throughout. All come from the Brazilian area, but exact distributions are uncertain. See also PARROT.

Consult Hastings, William S. R., *Parrots and Parrotlike Birds in Aviculture* (London 1929); Plath, Karl, and others, *Parrots Exclusively* (Fond du Lac, Wis., 1953); Eastman, William R., and Hunt, Alexander C., *The Parrots of Australia* (Sydney 1966).

LEE S. CRANDALL,
General Curator Emeritus, New York Zoological Park.

MACAW TREE (*Acrocomia sclerocarpa*), a palm (family Palmae) native to eastern Latin America south to Rio de Janeiro, Brazil, and north to Cuba. The trunk atttains a diameter of 1 foot and a height of 50 feet, and possesses many black 1- to 4-inch spines. The 12-foot long pinnate leaves have leaflets 1 to 3 feet long. The yellowish fruit resembles a small apricot and produces an oil which is a butterlike, sweetish, yellow substance with a fragrance resembling violets. It is used extensively in toilet soaps. Propagation is by seeds and suckers. This palm is called the grugru in the West Indies, and corozo, macaoba, or mucuja in other areas. Some confusion exists concerning the precise identity of closely related species which often go by these names. It is cultivated in southern Florida and occasionally along the Gulf coast and in California.

HUGH N. MOZINGO.

MAÇAYÓ, the former name of Maceió, the capital of Alagoas state in northeastern Brazil. The city is on the Atlantic coast, 130 miles south of Recife. See MACEIÓ.

MACBETH, măk-běth′, king of Scotland: d. Lumphanan, Aberdeenshire, Scotland, Aug. 15, 1057. Marmoar (chief) of the district of Moray, he married Gruoch, granddaughter of King Kenneth III, and thus had a remote claim to the crown of Scotland. Turning against his sovereign, Duncan I, he purportedly slew him near Elgin, Morayshire, on Aug. 14, 1040, and seized the throne, yielding the northeast part of the country to his ally, Thorfinn, Norse earl of Orkney, the late Duncan's enemy. In 1050, Macbeth made a pilgrimage to Rome, distributing alms to the poor, perhaps to atone for his regicide. His reign in Scotland is recorded in the chronicles as a time of prosperity. In 1054, however, Siward, earl of Northumbria, invaded the country on behalf of Duncan's son Malcolm, who defeated and killed Macbeth at Lumphanan three years later, succeeding to the throne as Malcolm III Canmore. William Shakespeare's play *Macbeth* (q.v.) is based on the legends which grew up around the king.

MACBETH, a tragedy by William Shakespeare, written and produced in 1606, but not printed until the Folio of 1623, which provides the only substantive text. Compliments in the play to King James I, a descendant of Banquo (the supposed progenitor of the Stuart line) and the visit of James' brother-in-law, King Christian IV of Denmark, make it probable that the composition was at least partly motivated by royal occasion, and modern evidence argues for a performance at Hampton Court on Aug. 7, 1606. The playhouse copy given to the publishers was an acting version with prompt directions, and provided one of the shortest texts of all of Shakespeare's plays. If abridged and rehandled, it also includes interpolations: the role of Hecate; Act III, scene 5; and parts of Act IV, scene 1 are probably the work of Thomas Middleton. The songs which appear in *Macbeth* by title only are printed in full in Middleton's play, *The Witch* (c. 1615), which has other Shakespearean echoes.

Shakespeare freely adapted the story of Macbeth (q.v.), 11th century king of Scotland, which he found in Raphael Holinshed's *Chronicles of England, Scotland, and Ireland* (1577). Under the circumstances Banquo could not remain an accomplice and a regicide; Duncan, in the original an incapable ruler who fell in battle, in Shakespeare meets his death under conditions applicable to another king in Holinshed. The opening matter is compressed, and the time of action telescoped. Perhaps most important, the supernatural agencies were altered to become the witches of contemporary superstition. The consequence of association with those who sold themselves to the devil was a subject of particular interest to James, who had written a book on demonology. Consequently the first scene of the play, the caldron scene, the appearance of Banquo's ghost, and Lady Macbeth's sleepwalking are of Shakespeare's invention; indeed Lady Macbeth is only briefly referred to in the *Chronicles*.

The dramatist's freedom of treatment clearly shows something of his intention. Macbeth is unlike Shakespeare's other tragic heroes. Though he shares with them the qualities of a man of position, stature, and character, he differs in that he knowingly does evil, suffers without repentance, and justly dies for his crimes. Macbeth has free will; his actions are not determined by the unnatural solicitings of the witches, nor by the forceful persuasions of his wife—in Holinshed's original she is ambitious for herself, but not here. Macbeth's actions represent externally what is already in his thought and desire, and the choice of evil is his.

Macbeth is the tragedy of a noble man who goes wrong and pays for it terribly. Consequently, Macbeth is less sympathetic than most of Shakespeare's tragic heroes, or at least the sympathy aroused is of a different kind. We cannot excuse or condone as we do for a man who is deceived by another or placed in a situation beyond his control, or who makes an error of judgment subsequently regretted. The sympathy arises here from recognitions: of the consequences, the fruitlessness, and the disillusion. The pity is that such a man, in a wider sense man himself, can fall so low; there but for the grace of God go I! There are subsidiary warnings, too: Lady Macbeth cracks under the strain; Banquo strongly suspects Macbeth's guilt but fails to communicate his suspicions—he, too, pays the penalty. Reprisal is inevitable. The moral lessons are more direct than is usual in Shakespeare's tragedies.

Macbeth is also perhaps the most atmospheric of the tragedies. Despite the many short scenes, the lack of pace after the swift first three acts, the difficult alternation in the fourth, and the absence of the great closing scene, all of which might make for loss of interest or disintegration, the play is compulsively unified by the evil which broods over it. The imaginative effects are shown in the reactions of minor characters, otherwise

Culver Service

Maurice Evans as Macbeth.

undercharacterized; in the wild scenes of the witches' incantations; in the unnatural violences; in the agonies of Macbeth and his lady; and in the terse and often horrible concentration. The poetic imagery is designed to create or to deepen these effects. Daylight is beneficent, and darkness is hidden evil: Macbeth succumbs to the power of darkness; much of the action takes place at night, a night of sleeplessness, without rest. Blood is everywhere, on the wounded, on weapons, on the besmeared grooms, on Banquo, on Lady Macbeth's hands; at the end Macbeth is decapitated. The chaos is created by abnormality, and the results are pervasive and overwhelming. No wonder that *Macbeth* generally makes such a distinctive impression on audiences when it is performed in the theater.

The impression has not always, however, been deep upon audiences, and there is a theatrical tradition that *Macbeth* is bad luck. There is only one actual record of a performance before the closing of the theaters in 1642. A mangled and spectacularized version by William Davenant (1606–1668), in which Thomas Betterton played, held the stage from the Restoration to the time of David Garrick (1717–1779), who restored some parts but modified others. The true text was not acted until the production by Samuel Phelps in 1847, though Macbeth had already become one of the great roles of William Charles Macready (1793–1873). Notable later Macbeths and Lady Macbeths have included Henry Irving (1838–1905), John Gielgud (1904–), Godfrey Tearle (1884–1953), Maurice Evans (1901–); and Ellen Terry (1847–1928), Helena Modjeska (1840–1909), Sybil Thorndike (1882–), and Judith Anderson (1898–). The play is now frequently performed.

Bibliography.—There is full early commentary in the *New Variorum*, ed. by Horace Howard Furness, Jr. (Philadelphia 1903), but the most useful modern edition is by John Dover Wilson (Cambridge, Eng., 1947); good, inexpensive texts are provided by Matthias Adam Shaaber (New York 1949) and Alfred Bennett Harbage (Baltimore 1956). For further discussion, consult Walker, Roy, *The Time Is Free* (London 1949); Paul, Henry Neill, *The Royal Play of Macbeth* (New York 1950); Stoll, Elmer Edgar, *Art and Artifice in Shakespeare*, reprint (New York 1951); and Bradley, Andrew Cecil, *Shakespearean Tragedy*, reprint (New York 1955).

ROBERT HAMILTON BALL, *Professor of English, Queens College of the City of New York.*

McBRIDE, măk-brīd', **Mary Margaret,** American radio commentator and author: b. Paris, Mo., Nov. 16, 1899. Brought up in farm country, she developed an early ambition to be a writer and had worked her way through the University of Missouri to a bachelor of journalism degree by 1919. Upon her graduation, she was an immediate success as a reporter with the Cleveland *Press*. In 1920 she came to New York as assistant to the publicity director of the Interchurch World Movement, and from the end of that year to 1924 was a reporter for the New York *Evening Mail*. Having already contributed material to the national magazines she soon became a freelance writer and a collaborator on several successful books of non-fiction.

In 1934, when the depression had reduced the market for her writings, she entered radio and began to be heard regularly, as "Martha Deane," on a constantly increasing number of stations of the Mutual Broadcasting System. In later years she worked under her own name for each of the other networks.

Her weekday radio program, originally designed to consist only of motherly hints to the housewife, soon developed into something more closely resembling a regular visit from a friend. Her frank, extemporaneous comments, homey midwestern accent, winning personality, and absorbing accounts of her daily activities among famous and active people made her one of the most popular figures in radio and perhaps the most effective saleswoman of all time. By 1948 her estimated audience had risen to about 6 million and her annual mail to over a quarter of a million letters. Among her published books were *Paris is a Woman's Town* (With Helen Josephy, 1929); *Story of Dwight Morrow* (1930); *Here's Martha Deane* (1936); and *How Dear to My Heart* (1940).

McBRIDE, SIR **Richard,** Canadian statesman: b. New Westminster, British Columbia, Canada, Dec. 15, 1870; d. London, England, Aug. 6, 1917. Of Irish parentage, he was educated in the schools of New Westminster and in Dalhousie University in Halifax and became a lawyer in Victoria in 1892. In 1895 he was elected to the provincial legislature, became minister of mines (1900–1901), leader of the Conservative opposition (1902–1903), and premier of British Columbia in 1903. Taking the leadership at a time of fiscal crisis he succeeded in giving the province several years of financial surpluses and was instrumental in securing better terms of support from the Dominion. His administration was marked by considerable road and railway building, great increases in commercial activity and population, and the planning and endowment of the provincial university. He resigned in 1915, was knighted (K.C.M.G.), and was appointed agent general for British Columbia in London.

McBURNEY, măk-bûr'nĭ, **Charles,** American surgeon and teacher: b. Roxbury, Mass., Feb. 17, 1845; d. Brookline, Mass., Nov. 7, 1913. He graduated from Harvard in 1866 and from the College of Physicians and Surgeons of Columbia University in 1870, joining that school three years later as assistant demonstrator of surgery. He was made professor in 1889 and was visiting and consulting surgeon at Saint Luke's, Roosevelt, New York Orthopedic and other hospitals.

Achieving his success at a time when advances in the techniques of antiseptic surgery were for the first time making abdominal operations practicable, McBurney's greatest contribution was in the treatment of appendicitis. He discovered "McBurney's point," a pressure point the knowledge of which made the disease easier to diagnose, and instituted an operative method in appendectomy, called "McBurney's incision," which avoided the necessity of cutting across the abdominal muscle fibers.

McBURNEY, **Robert Ross,** American Y.M.C.A. leader: b. Castleblayney, Ireland, March 31, 1837; d. Clifton Springs, N. Y., Dec. 27, 1898. Two years before his arrival in the United States in 1854, an organization patterned after the Young Men's Christian Association of England had been established in New York City. McBurney became its first paid secretary in 1862. After the International Convention of American and European Y.M.C.A. leaders in 1865, he began a series of improvements and elaborations in his New York organization which made it the pilot branch and model for the growing chapters elsewhere in the country. The first true Y.M.C.A. building in America was built through his agency for a little less than $500,000 and incorporated most of the activities at present associated with the organization. His personal influence in the formative stages of the development of the association was tremendous and his occupation of the general secretaryship around which that development took place was largely responsible for the effective centralized system of leadership at present in effect in the Y.M.C.A.

McCABE, mȧ-kāb', **Charles Caldwell,** American Methodist bishop: b. Athens, Ohio, Oct. 11, 1836; d. New York City, Dec. 19, 1906. He was educated at Ohio Wesleyan University. In 1860 he entered the Methodist Episcopal ministry and in 1862 was appointed chaplain of the 122nd Ohio Infantry. He was captured at the Battle of Winchester and held in Libby Prison for four months. After the war he became a remarkably successful fund raiser on behalf of the United States Christian Commission, then as financial agent for Wesleyan University, and, from

1884, as secretary of the Methodist Missionary Society. He was made a bishop in 1896 and chancellor of the American University in Washington, D.C., in 1902.

McCABE, Joseph, British rationalist philosopher, writer, and lecturer: b. England, Nov. 11, 1867; d. London, Jan. 10, 1955. Of Irish ancestry, he was educated at St. Francis' College, Manchester; St. Antony's, Forest Gate; and Louvain University. When 16 he entered the Franciscan Order, and was ordained a priest in 1890, becoming also professor of scholastic philosophy and, in 1895, rector of Buckingham College. The following year he renounced his faith, giving his reasons in *Twelve Years in a Monastery* (1897); thereafter he embarked on a career of lecturing and prolific writing in which he became an ardent exponent of rationalist philosophy and evolution, and directed much criticism at revealed religion in general and the Roman Catholic Church in particular. Besides such books as *The Decay of the Church of Rome* (1909), *The Evolution of Mind* (1910), and *A Candid History of the Jesuits* (1913), he wrote several biographies, notably of Peter Abélard (1901), St. Augustine (1902), Goethe (1912), and George Bernard Shaw (1914); historical works such as *The Hundred Men who Moved the World* (1931) and *The Golden Ages of History* (1940); and was author of a one-volume *Rationalist Encyclopaedia* (1948).

MACCABEES, măk'à-bēz, or **MACHABEES, The,** the name given to a Jewish family whose members led the fight for religious and political independence against the Seleucid Empire in the 2d century B.C. Originally a nickname bestowed on Judas (Judas Maccabaeus), third son of the priest Mattathias (or Mattathiah), "Maccabee" was later applied to his brothers and then extended to his supporters and to all who took part in the struggle; for example, the seven brothers of II Maccabees 7 are traditionally called "Maccabees." The meaning of the name is uncertain, but it may be derived from *maqqaba,* hammer.

The occasion of the Maccabean uprising was the attempted Hellenization of the Jewish people under Antiochus IV Epiphanes (r. 175–164 B.C.). An ardent promoter of Greek culture, manners, and religion, the king gave his support to the influential minority of priests and aristocrats in Jerusalem who wished to modernize the Jewish way of life and to assimilate it to the manners of the Gentile world. From the introduction of Greek athletics, dress, political institutions, and other aspects of Greek culture, he proceeded to forbid, under pain of death, such observances as circumcision and dietary laws and to force the Jews to take part in pagan worship. Finally he introduced into the Temple itself the worship of Greek deities, with the sacrifice of swine. The majority of the people were bitterly opposed to these measures, and many fled from Jerusalem to the Judaean hill country to evade the persecution. At the little village of Modin, 20 miles northwest of Jerusalem, Mattathias and his sons organized an armed revolt (167 B.C.), of which Judas became the leader.

His rapid success is vividly narrated in I Maccabees 3 and following chapters. At first winning skirmishes with the local police and increasing his numbers and resources with each success, he became powerful enough to defeat the larger forces sent against him by the central government. After a victory over the Syrian general Lysias, he was able to occupy Jerusalem and to blockade the king's garrison in the citadel. Just three years after its profanation, he solemnly purified the Temple (December 164 B.C.) and reestablished there the cult of the Lord.

In 163 B.C., Lysias defeated Judas at Bethzacharias and besieged Jerusalem. But a sudden crisis in Syrian politics forced him to make terms and to withdraw, granting to the Jews freedom to practice their religion. Thus the primary object of the uprising was achieved. But Judas and his brothers saw the possibility of further gains: the elimination of the Hellenizing party among the people and the eventual attainment of political independence. Nicanor, general of Demetrius I Soter, attempted to support the Hellenizers, but was defeated and killed by Judas. However, his successor, Bacchides, returned with a larger force, and the Maccabee, supported by only 800 men, died in the Battle of Bereth (160 B.C.).

Judas was followed by his youngest brother, Jonathan, in the leadership of the nationalist party, but at first Jonathan's forces were too weak to face the Syrians in battle, and he reverted to the status of a guerrilla leader. If the Seleucid Empire had been under the firm control of a single ruler, the Jewish nationalists would have been speedily crushed. But the constant dynastic rivalries in Antioch prevented any consistent policy, and by skillfully playing off one party against another Jonathan gradually increased his power. In 152 B.C. he accepted, from one of the claimants to the Seleucid throne, the title of high priest and, in 150 B.C., the titles of civil and military ruler of Judaea. He had gained control of most of central Palestine and the coast, when, in 142 B.C., he was captured and put to death by Tryphon, a rebellious Syrian general.

The last of the Maccabee brothers, Simon, succeeded to Jonathan's position. His independence was acknowledged by successive Seleucid kings, and in gratitude for his and his family's services the Jews voted that he should be their high priest, general, and governor (I Maccabees 14). Equivalently, though not in name, he became king and is reckoned the founder of the Hasmonaean (also called Asmonaean) dynasty, a name supposedly derived from that of one of his ancestors. Thus the last of the Maccabees' objectives was achieved, and Simon's reign was a time of peace and prosperity for the Jews. He died, assassinated by his son-in-law Ptolemy, in 134 B.C.

Simon's third son, John Hyrcanus (r. 134–104 B.C.), succeeded his father. After an initial setback at the hands of the Seleucid Antiochus VII Evergetes (or Sidetes), Hyrcanus successfully resumed Simon's expansionist policy, subjugating the Idumaeans, whom he forcibly converted to Judaism, and the Samaritans, whose temple on Mount Gerizim he destroyed. His long reign was prosperous, but was marked by internal strife between Pharisees and Sadducees. The king had transferred his support to the latter, who in spirit at least had much in common with the Hellenizers, whom his uncles had fought so strenuously. The Pharisees, feeling themselves heirs of the *Hasidim* (the Pious), who had been Judas' allies, bitterly resented the "secularization" of the Jewish state, where now the high priest was also a king and warrior. Hyrcanus, more interested in territorial expansion than in religion, despised the Pharisees. His son, Aristobulus I, reigned only a year

(104–103 B.C.) and was succeeded by another son, Alexander Jannaeus (r. 103–76 B.C.), a violent man and a skillful military leader. He brought all Palestine under his rule, recovering almost the full area of David's ancient kingdom. His army was largely composed of pagan mercenary troops, and many devout Jews so detested him that at one time they actually supported the Seleucid king against this grandson of the Maccabees. Jannaeus crushed this revolt with extreme cruelty, crucifying 800 of the Pharisaic party whom he had captured. Yet on his deathbed, he is said to have recommended to his wife, Salome Alexandra, that she make peace with the Pharisees. Certainly her reign (76–67 B.C.) was their "golden age." After her death, her two sons, Hyrcanus II (d. 30 B.C.) and Aristobulus II (d. 48 B.C.), were rivals for power. The dispute at first was peaceably settled, to the advantage of the latter, but was revived by the intrigues of the Idumaean Antipater, who aimed at being the power behind Hyrcanus' throne. Both parties appealed to the Romans for support; and Pompey the Great (Gnaeus Pompeius Magnus), who was then in Syria, came to Jerusalem with an army, besieged and captured it (63 B.C.), and subjected all Palestine to Roman control. Thus the political achievements of the Maccabees were short-lived, but they are remembered for the religious heroism which characterized their beginnings. See also MACCABEES (MACHABEES), BOOKS OF THE.

Bibliography.—Bevan, Edwyn R., *Jerusalem Under the High Priests* (London 1904); Bickerman, Elias, *The Maccabees*, tr. by Moses Hadas (New York 1947).

R. A. F. MACKENZIE, S.J.,
Jesuit Seminary, Toronto, Canada.

MACCABEES (MACHABEES), Books of the, four books dealing with Jewish history and theology. The first two are of much greater importance than the third and fourth, both historically and because they are Biblical books. They are two nearly contemporary accounts of the successful Jewish revolt against alien domination in the 2d century B.C. They are not (like the books of Samuel, for instance) successive histories, but independent and partly parallel treatments of the same events. See also MACCABEES or MACHABEES, THE.

I Maccabees was written about the end of the 2d century B.C. It is extant in a good early Greek translation, the original Hebrew having been lost. Its author, a Palestinian Jew, had access to excellent sources of information on the events narrated. The history begins with the accession of Antiochus IV Epiphanes in 175 B.C. and describes the fortunes of the Jews in Judaea down to the death of Simon Maccabee (Simon Maccabaeus) in 134 B.C. The introduction (I Maccabees 1 and 2) presents the situation and the two opposing parties: Hellenism, the prevailing pagan culture of the time, promoted by some of the priests and leading men and supported by the impious and persecuting Antiochus; and Judaism (the word occurs for the first time in II Maccabees), the way of life codified in the Mosaic law as then interpreted. To this the majority of Jews were obstinately faithful, and their representative was the aged Mattathias, father of the Maccabees. Thereafter, the book is divided into three main sections, following the successive leadership of three of Mattathias' sons: 3:1–9:22, Judas (Judas Maccabaeus); 9:23–12:53, Jonathan (Jonathan Maccabaeus); 13:1–16:24, Simon. With Simon's

death and the succession of his son John Hyrcanus the story ends, having thus covered a crucial period of 40 years.

The author is an enthusiast for the achievements of the Maccabees and the glory of the Hasmonaean dynasty (namely, Simon and his descendants, who took the title of king). He imitates the style of the books of Samuel and Kings, implicitly comparing the exploits of his heroes with the earlier "wars of the Lord." His religious faith is deep, but restrained in expression (he uses reverent circumlocutions for the name of God). By skillfully balancing and contrasting his characters and his narratives, he opposes the faith and the devotion on the orthodox Jewish side to what he considers impiety and arrogance in the Hellenizers. His own doctrine is conservative; he shows no belief in a life after death, but has a strong sense of the witness that must be borne to the Lord by His people. Above all, the Mosaic law is for him an absolute obligation, from which all other laws, such as those of morality and worship, derive.

II Maccabees was written about the same time as I Maccabees, but in Greek. The work is prefixed by two letters (1:1–9; 1:10–2:18) addressed to Jews in Egypt and concerned with the festival of the rededication of the Temple (*Hanukkah*). The first is dated 124 B.C.; the second, if genuine, would come from 164 B.C. The book then proceeds with an introduction (2:20–33), in which the author explains that his book is a summary of a work in five books by one Jason of Cyrene. Following this, five sections can be distinguished, presumably corresponding to Jason's five books: the inviolability of the Temple (3); the wrath of God upon Israel and the expiation of the martyrs (4–7); God's mercy, leading to Judas' success and the purification of the Temple (8:1–10:9); the purification of the land (10:10–13:26); the inviolability of the Temple and the destruction of another would-be profaner, Nicanor (14–15). The period covered is about 175–160 B.C.

In both style and ideas, II Maccabees contrasts strongly with I Maccabees. It is not primarily a work of history, but a piece of religious rhetoric, an oratorical presentation of an already well-known story, intended to edify and to inspire its readers. The opening letters indicate the theme and the tone: the author wishes to stimulate, by this highly colored account of divine protection, reverence for the Temple and devotion to the law among non-Palestinian Jews. Thus the style is that found in other works of Hellenistic rhetoric, which to modern taste may seem bombastic and unconvincing, but which was then both acceptable and effective. II Maccabees is also more explicitly religious. It stresses God's love for Israel, outlines a theology of martyrdom, promises a glorious resurrection for the just, and affirms the intercession of the dead for the living and the living for the dead. Finally, allowance being made for stylistic exaggeration and embellishment, II Maccabees is an important historical source, often supplementing or correcting the first book. In particular, the many contemporary documents quoted in it (not always in the right context) are now considered by most critics to be substantially authentic.

These two books have been preserved to us by Christian interest and were, until modern times, little valued in Jewish tradition (hence the loss of the Hebrew text of I Maccabees). This fact was due to the violent enmity between the Hasmonaeans, descendants of the Maccabees, and the

Pharisees, who founded the tradition of normative Judaism. A contributing cause may have been the value set by the Maccabees upon their alliance with Rome, and the consequent praise of the Romans in I Maccabees 8. This soon became very distasteful to the Jews in Palestine, who from the 1st century A.D. onward, considered the Romans as their archenemies. The books therefore survived in Greek Bibles and in the Latin Vulgate. They are regarded as canonical by Roman Catholics, but the Protestant churches place them among the Apocrypha.

III Maccabees has in reality nothing to do with the Maccabees as such; it gained this title because it is constantly associated in the manuscript tradition with the first two books. It is a legendary account, written in Greek by a Hellenistic Jew, of how the Jews in Egypt were threatened with total destruction, and were miraculously rescued by the power of God. Their enemy is Ptolemy IV Philopator (r. 221–203 B.C.), who, being miraculously prevented from entering the Temple in Jerusalem, conceives an intense hatred for his Jewish subjects and plans to have them all trampled to death by savage elephants in the hippodrome of Alexandria. But God first confuses the king's wits, so that he cannot give the right orders; then, when the massacre is about to take place, a vision of angels changes the king's mind completely. Convinced that the Jews are divinely protected, he decrees their liberation, and they celebrate a feast in memory of their deliverance. In theme, though not in details, the story has a certain parallelism with the Book of Esther. It is narrated in a bombastic and extravagant style, without much regard for plausibility. In outlook and treatment, it has much in common with II Maccabees and the Letter of Aristeas, and is a typical example of the propaganda literature put out by the Alexandrian Jews in the 2d and 1st centuries B.C. It may be dated toward the end of this period.

IV Maccabees is, in outward form, a philosophical treatise with historical examples; its original title appears to have been "The Sovereignty of Reason." It is written in excellent Hellenistic Greek, and with full command of the vocabulary and concepts of Stoic philosophy. Even the theme is borrowed from Stoic sources, which taught that in the true philosopher all passions must be under the entire control of right reason. But the Jewish author has adapted this theorem to his own religious purpose, and the content of the book is as Jewish as the form is Greek. Reason is here understood as obedience to the will of God expressed in the Mosaic law, which ensures the practice of all other virtues and makes possible a perfect control of the passions. The author cites examples of this obedience and consequent virtue from his people's history, and dwells at length on the stories of the heroic martyrdoms of Eleazar, the scribe, and of the seven brethren and their mother. These are taken from II Maccabees 6 and 7, with the gruesome details of the tortures still further elaborated, the better to convey the martyrs' heroism. The book can be dated only approximately, between 100 B.C. and 100 A.D., or even slightly later. Its place of origin may be Alexandria, or Antioch in Syria.

The title of "V Maccabees" is given in one ancient manuscript to a Syriac translation of book VI of Flavius Josephus' *The Antiquities of the Jews*. It has also been applied, in modern times, to a medieval Arabic summary of part of this work of Flavius Josephus.

Bibliography.—Abel, Félix-Marie, *Les Livres des Maccabées* (Paris 1949); Tedesche, Sidney S., and Zeitlin, Solomon, *The First Book of Maccabees* (New York 1950); id., *The Second Book of Maccabees* (New York 1954); Hadas, Moses, *The Third and Fourth Books of the Maccabees* (New York 1953); Dancy, John C., *A Commentary on I Maccabees* (Oxford 1954).

R. A. F. MacKENZIE, S.J.,
Jesuit Seminary, Toronto, Canada.

MACCABEES, The, a fraternal benefit society. Founded in 1878 in London, Ontario, Canada, as the Knights of the Maccabees of the World, its name was changed to its present one in 1915, when it merged with the society then known as the Knights of the Modern Maccabees. Since that time many other fraternal benefit societies have merged with it. The organization is named after Judas Maccabaeus (2d century B.C.). Its headquarters are in Detroit, Mich. It has over 1,000 lodges in the United States and Canada with a membership of about 300,000.

McCALL, mà-kôl', George Archibald, American army officer: b. Philadelphia, Pa., March 16, 1802; d. West Chester, Pa., Feb. 25, 1868. He was graduated from the United States Military Academy in 1822 and saw service in Florida against the Seminoles and in the Mexican War. He resigned in 1853, having reached the rank of inspector general. In 1861, at the start of the Civil War, he was given command of the Pennsylvania Reserves, with the rank of brigadier general of volunteers, and participated in some of the battles of the Army of the Potomac, particularly in the Peninsula Campaign of 1862 (q.v.), in which his division was engaged at the battles of Mechanicsville, Gaines' Mill, and Frayser's Farm (qq.v.). On June 30, 1862, he was taken prisoner during the Battle of Frayser's Farm and was confined for several weeks in Libby Prison. In August he was released during an exchange of prisoners, but impaired health prevented his return to service.

MacCALLUM, William George, American pathologist: b. Dunnville, Ontario, Canada, April 18, 1874; d. Baltimore, Md., Feb. 3, 1944. He was graduated from the University of Toronto in 1894 and from the medical school of Johns Hopkins University in 1897. In 1900 he became associate professor of pathology at the latter school and, in 1908, professor of pathological physiology. In 1909 he went to Columbia University as professor of pathology. In the same year he and Carl Voegtlin (1879–) showed that calcium metabolism is controlled by the parathyroid gland. In 1917 he returned to Johns Hopkins University as professor of pathology and bacteriology. In 1919 he discovered the stain known as MacCallum's stain, which is used to render visible under a microscope influenza bacilli and Gram-positive organisms (Hans Christian Joachim Gram, 1853–1938). His stain is a combination of Goodpasture's stain (Ernest William Goodpasture, 1886–) with gentian violet. His *A Text-book of Pathology* (1st ed., 1916; 7th ed., 1940) was for a long time the standard work in its subject. He also wrote *Inflammation* (1922) and the biography *William Stewart Halstead, Surgeon* (1930).

MacCAMERON, mà-kăm'ẽr-ŭn, Robert Lee, American genre and portrait painter: b.

The Metropolitan Museum of Art

Robert Lee MacCameron's *The Daughter's Return,* an example of his compelling treatment of human emotion.

Chicago, Ill., Jan. 14, 1866; d. New York, N.Y., Dec. 29, 1912. Brought up in the small town of Necedah, Wis., he had little schooling, worked while a boy as a lumberjack, but was able to develop his artistic bent by study in Chicago and by illustrating jobs there, in New York, and in London, England, where he went at the age of 22. Soon afterward he settled in Paris, France, studying at the École des Beaux Arts under Jean Léon Gérôme, and getting some instruction also from Raphael Collin and James Abbott McNeill Whistler. MacCameron's reputation rests chiefly on his interpretations of theatrical and café life, and on his profound and moving studies of human degradation. His most notable pictures include *Groupe d'Amis,* popularly known as "The Absinthe Drinkers" (Corcoran Gallery, Washington, D.C.), *The Daughter's Return* (The Metropolitan Museum of Art, New York City), *Les Habitués* (*The Old Customers;* Memorial Hall, Philadelphia), and *The People of the Abyss* (Luxembourg Gallery, Paris), the last-named a study of five outcasts seated on a bench on the Thames embankment, London. He painted many portraits of prominent people, including Auguste Rodin (Metropolitan Museum), Presidents William Howard Taft and William McKinley, and Justices John Marshall Harlan and David Josiah Brewer.

McCARRAN, mȧ-kăr'ăn, **Patrick Anthony,** American politician: b. Reno, Nev., Aug. 8, 1876; d. Hawthorne, Nev., Sept. 28, 1954. After graduating from the University of Nevada in 1901, he became a farmer and stock raiser in Nevada and, in 1903, was elected to the Nevada legislature. He was admitted to the bar in 1905 and practiced law for two years in Tonopah and Goldfield, Nev. From 1907 to 1909 he was district attorney of Nye County, Nev., and then practiced law in Reno until 1912, when he was elected an associate justice of the Supreme Court of Nevada, later serving as chief justice (1917–1918). In 1919 he returned to private practice and in 1926 made an unsuccessful campaign for the United States Senate. In 1932 he was elected to the Senate, and was thrice reelected, serving until his death, and occupying posts as chairman of the Judiciary Committee (1943–1946, 1949–1953) and of the special subcommittee on foreign economic cooperation (1950–1952). A Democrat who was in constant disagreement with the Democratic administrations of his time, Senator McCarran was chiefly known

for his sponsorship of two highly controversial measures—the McCarran-Wood Act of 1950 and the McCarran-Walter Act of 1952—which Congress passed over President Harry S. Truman's vetoes. The former, also known as the Internal Security Act, required the registration of all Communists with the attorney general and made it unlawful for those with Communist affiliations to participate in defense or government work. The latter, also known as the Immigration and Nationality Act, codified existing immigration legislation; tightened the laws governing the admission, exclusion, and deportation of dangerous aliens; limited immigration from eastern and southeastern Europe; and provided for selective immigration on the basis of skills. At other times in his career, Senator McCarran opposed President Franklin Delano Roosevelt's "court-packing" proposals; voted against the British loan of 1941 and the reciprocal trade agreements; favored closer cooperation with Spain, increased aid to Nationalist China, and a curb on the president's treaty-making powers; and strongly supported Senator Joseph R. McCarthy (q.v.). He was active in legislation establishing the Civil Aeronautics Administration in 1938, and, as leader of the silver bloc, introduced many bills favoring silver.

McCARTAN, mȧ-kär't'n, **Edward,** American sculptor: b. Albany, N.Y., Aug. 16, 1879; d. New Rochelle, N.Y., Sept. 20, 1947. He studied in Brooklyn, New York, at Pratt Institute, under Herbert Adams, and at the Art Students' League under George Grey Barnard and Hermon Atkins MacNeil; and in Paris (1907–1910) at the École

Diana, by Edward McCartan. His sculpture is distinguished by the exceptional finish of his bronze pieces.

The Metropolitan Museum of Art

des Beaux Arts under Jean Antoine Injalbert. His many groups and figures are characterized by beauty of line and design, by skillful blending with environment, especially in garden statuary, and by the exquisite finishes of his bronzes. Typical are his *Diana* (the Metropolitan Museum of Art, New York City) ; *The Kiss,* a mother and child (Albright Art Gallery, Buffalo, N.Y.) ; the Eugene Field Memorial in Lincoln Park, Chicago, Ill., a fairy hovering over two sleeping children; *Spirit of the Woods,* a dancing nymph holding a baby in her outstretched hands; *Nymph and Satyr; Girl with Goat;* and *Isoult.* Also notable are his two heroic limestone figures, representing Transportation and Industry, supporting the gigantic clock on the façade of the Grand Central Building, New York City, as it faces north over Park Avenue; and his pediment for the Department of Labor and Interstate Commerce Building, Washington, D.C. His bust of Washington Irving is in the Hall of Fame, New York City, and his work is also represented in the City Art Museum, St. Louis, Mo., Brookgreen Gardens, Brookgreen, S.C., and the Fogg Museum, Cambridge, Mass.

McCARTHY, Eugene Joseph, American political leader: b. Watkins, Minn., March 29, 1916. He graduated from St. John's University in Collegeville, Minn., and received an M.A. degree from the University of Minnesota in 1939. He was a high school teacher and then professor of economics and education at St. John's University. After World War II service as a civilian technical assistant in the War Department's military intelligence division, he taught sociology and economics at the College of St. Thomas.

In Congress. As a Democratic-Farmer-Labor party candidate in 1948, McCarthy was elected to the House of Representatives and served 10 years. In 1958 and 1964, he was elected to the Senate, where he served on the finance and foreign relations committees, established a liberal voting record, and gained respect for his scholarly mind, acerbic wit, and independent views.

Presidential Candidacy. McCarthy opposed President Lyndon Johnson on several issues, notably the U.S. involvement in Vietnam. He attacked the Vietnam policy on military, diplomatic, economic, and moral grounds, claiming that it distracted the nation from the task of solving serious domestic problems.

On Nov. 30, 1967, McCarthy said he would challenge the President in state presidential primary elections in 1968. He called for disengagement and a negotiated peace in Vietnam. Though at first not taken seriously as a candidate, he soon attracted wide support, especially among students, young voters in general, and better educated voters in both parties. Supporters admired his intellect and his sincere and soft-spoken manner. McCarthy captured most of the delegates in New Hampshire. Johnson then decided not to seek reelection. McCarthy swept three primaries against little opposition, but then lost four of five contests to Senator Robert Kennedy. After Kennedy's death, party professionals supported Vice President Hubert Humphrey, who defeated McCarthy at the Democratic convention, which also rejected a platform plank reflecting McCarthy's opposition to the war.

Despite his defeat, McCarthy had helped effect the retirement of the President, helped force the opening of peace talks, and attracted to his campaign thousands of persons new to politics.

McCARTHY, Joseph Raymond, American politician: b. Grand Chute, Wis., Nov. 14, 1909; d. Bethesda, Md., May 2, 1957. Leaving high school at the age of 16 to work on his father's farm, he later attended night school while clerking in a grocery store; beginning in 1929, he worked his way through Marquette University, graduating with the degree of LL.B. in 1935. Four years later, after practicing law at Waupaca and Shawano, Wis., he was elected a circuit judge. During World War II he served in the United States Marine Corps, rising from private to captain and winning the Distinguished Flying Cross and the Air Medal in combat duty as a tail-gunner. Returning to Wisconsin after the war, he was re-elected circuit judge, and in 1946 was elected as a Republican to the United States Senate.

McCarthy first achieved national prominence when he charged in a speech at Wheeling, W. Va., on Feb. 9, 1950, that he had a list of "card-carrying Communists" in the State Department (on various occasions at this period he alleged that there were 57, 205, and 81 Communists, pro-Communists, or "security risks" in the State Department). When he was unable to prove these charges to an investigating committee headed by Sen. Millard E. Tydings (Democrat, Maryland), the group, in a majority report (representing Democrats and liberal Republicans), dismissed his charges as "a fraud and a hoax" (a minority report, representing right-wing Republicans, termed the investigation "superficial and inconclusive"). McCarthy's role in the defeat of Senator Tydings in the November 1950 elections was investigated by one Senate committee, while another questioned some of his financial dealings.

Dismissing those who criticized his methods as disloyal Americans or stupid, McCarthy continued to denounce those he claimed were Communists or Communist sympathizers, and made blistering attacks on such public figures as Secretary of State Dean Acheson and General of the Army George C. Marshall. With the reluctant support of Gen. Dwight D. Eisenhower, he was re-elected to the Senate in 1952. Soon, however, he began to oppose President Eisenhower on various issues. Long accustomed to referring to the administrations of Presidents Franklin D. Roosevelt and Harry S. Truman as "20 years of treason," in May 1953 he altered this to "21 years of treason" to include the Eisenhower administration. In 1953, as chairman of the Permanent Subcommittee on Investigations, Senator McCarthy launched 157 inquiries, notably into the Voice of America and the Army Signal Corps installation at Fort Monmouth, N.J. His search failed to unearth any cases of provable subversive activity or disloyalty, and the manner in which he conducted his investigations brought him into open conflict with the army. From April 22 to June 17, 1954, this dispute was aired in acrimonious, nationally televised hearings. Although the results of the hearings were inconclusive, allegations about McCarthy led to Senate action. A committee headed by Sen. Arthur V. Watkins (Republican, Utah) considered 46 charges brought against him by his colleagues, and on Dec. 2, 1954, the Senate censured him with a 67–22 vote of condemnation. Thereafter his political influence declined, and, with his health failing, he was almost inactive until his death.

Senator McCarthy's defenders maintained that he made a real contribution to the fight against communism by causing security precautions to be increased and by driving subversives to cover. His critics insisted that these ends did not justify his violation of democratic procedures, that he hampered the fight against communism by creating an atmosphere of fear and suspicion among government employees, and that by his undemocratic methods he damaged American prestige abroad.

McCARTHY, Justin, Irish politician, historian, and novelist: b. Cork, Ireland, Nov. 22, 1830; d. Folkestone, England, April 24, 1912. A Nationalist from youth, he divided his career between promoting Irish freedom and prolific writing. He worked for the Liverpool *Northern Daily Times* from 1853 to 1859, and for the London *Morning Star* from 1859 to 1868, the last four years as editor. In 1868–1871 he toured the United States, being associated for a time with the weekly New York *Independent*. Returning to England, he became an editorial writer for the London *Daily News*. He was already an established novelist when, in 1879, he was elected a member of the British Parliament for County Longford, Ireland—the start of a continuous parliamentary career during which he represented various Irish constituencies until 1900. After the fall of Charles Stewart Parnell in 1890, McCarthy was for six years chairman of the Irish Home Rule Party (anti-Parnellites). His most important literary work was *A History of Our Own Times,* 5 vols. (1–4, 1879–1880; 5, 1897), beginning with Queen Victoria's accession. He also wrote *Lady Judith* (1871), *Dear Lady Disdain* (1875), *Miss Misanthrope* (1878), and other novels; biographies of Pope Leo XIII (1896) and William Ewart Gladstone (1897); an autobiography, *The Story of an Irishman* (1904); and *The Four Georges and William IV* (1884–1901), the latter half of which was written by his son, Justin Huntly McCarthy (q.v.).

McCARTHY, Justin Huntly, English novelist, playwright, and historian: b. England, Sept. 30, 1860; d. London, March 20, 1936. The eldest son of Justin McCarthy (q.v.), he was educated at University College School and University College, London. He began writing at the age of 21 and was a Nationalist member of Parliament from 1884 to 1892. In 1894 he married Marie Cecilia ("Cissie") Loftus, music hall star and once leading lady for Sir Henry Irving. They were divorced in the United States in 1899. McCarthy wrote *If I Were King* (1901), a bestselling novel about François Villon, which he quickly adapted for the stage (1901) and on which later was based (Charles) Rudolf Friml's popular operetta *The Vagabond King* (1925). He wrote more than 20 novels and over 15 plays. Among his historical works *The French Revolution* (4 vols., 1890–1897) won wide acclaim.

McCAULEY, Mary Ludwig. See PITCHER, MOLLY.

McCAUSLAND'S RAID, mà-kôz'lăndz rād, a raid on the town of Chambersburg, Pa., made on July 30, 1864, by Confederate forces under Brig. Gen. John McCausland. The foray was ordered by Lieut. Gen. Jubal Anderson Early in retaliation for the burning of crops, homes, and villages in the Shenandoah Valley by the Union commander, Maj. Gen. David Hunter. McCaus-

land's orders were to occupy Chambersburg, demand a ransom of $100,000 in gold or $500,000 in currency, and, should the ransom not be paid, to burn the town. Crossing the Potomac on July 29 with about 2,500 men, McCausland took Chambersburg next morning with little opposition. As the residents could not pay the ransom, he burned the town and quickly withdrew westward to McConnellsburg, Pa., and later across the Potomac. About 3,000 people were left homeless.

MACCHIAVELLI, Niccolò. See MACHIAVELLI, NICCOLÒ.

McCLELLAN, mà-klĕl'ăn, **George Brinton,** American army officer: b. Philadelphia, Pa., Dec. 3, 1826; d. Orange, N.J., Oct. 29, 1885. Known to his soldiers and the public as "Little Mac," McClellan was short, stocky, handsome, and magnetic. He was an important and in some ways a unique military figure. Elevated to high command in 1861 at the age of 34, he commanded one of the largest Northern field armies and for a time was general in chief of all armies. In 1864, while still holding a commission in the Army, he was the Democratic presidential candidate against Abraham Lincoln. He was a controversial figure during the war and he has been a center of historical altercation ever since. Some writers contend that he was the greatest of the Northern generals, denied victory by political interference. Others argue that he was temperamentally unfit for high command.

After attending preparatory schools and the University of Pennsylvania, McClellan entered West Point in 1842, graduating second in his class in 1846. As a second lieutenant in the Engineer Corps, he immediately saw service in the Mexican War. He was with Gen. Winfield Scott in the victorious campaign against Mexico City and was twice cited for brevets. After the war he served as an assistant instructor at West Point and in the Southwest. In 1855, then a captain, he was appointed to a board of officers to study European military systems. The board visited the principal European countries and observed the siege of Sevastopol in the Crimean War. In his report McClellan proposed, among other recommendations, a new type of saddle for the United States Army; known as the McClellan saddle, it became standard equipment in the Army. In 1857, McClellan, seeking more lucrative employment, resigned his commission. He became chief engineer and later (1858) vice president of the Illinois Central Railroad and president of the eastern division of the Ohio and Mississippi Railroad (1860).

At the outbreak of the Civil War, McClellan accepted a commission as major general of the Ohio volunteers and commander of Ohio's forces. Then the national government appointed him major general in the Regular Army, in command of the Department of the Ohio. Troops under his direction cleared western Virginia of Confederates; and, in July 1861, after the Federal reverse at the First Battle of Bull Run or Manassas, President Lincoln called him to Washington to command the forces being concentrated around the capital. McClellan forged these troops into the dogged fighting force known as the Army of the Potomac. Even his severest critics concede that he was a fine trainer of men. In November 1861, while retaining command of his field army, he also became general in chief of all Federal armies.

During the winter of 1861–1862, McClellan began to demonstrate traits that aroused impatience in Lincoln and anger in other leaders. Insisting that he could not advance until he had organized a large army, he refused to attack the Confederates at Manassas. He magnified the dangers in his front and the size of the enemy forces. He consorted with Democratic politicians and let it be known that he opposed emancipation of the slaves, thereby stirring the ire of the powerful Radical Republicans. To Lincoln he seemed timid and hesitant and to some of the Radicals he appeared a Southern sympathizer.

McClellan had a plan for the spring campaign of 1862. It was to move against Richmond on one of the waterways from the east, either the Rappahannock or the York-James rivers line. Although Lincoln feared that the operation might uncover Washington, he permitted McClellan to execute it, at the same time relieving McClellan as general in chief. McClellan decided on the York River line and in March he began to move his army to Fortress Monroe, between the York and the James. Lincoln, believing that McClellan had violated instructions to leave Washington safe, detained a corps of the Army south of the capital. McClellan still had some 100,000 men in his command. Taking Yorktown by siege, he advanced along the York line and, by June 1, he was within a few miles of Richmond.

About this time Gen. Robert Edward Lee (q.v.) became commander of the Confederate Army. With his army reinforced to 85,000, he attacked McClellan's right flank north of the York on June 26, beginning the offensive known as the Seven Days. Although McClellan was confused and convinced that he faced a superior enemy, he skillfully retired his army to the James, repulsing Lee at Malvern Hill (July 1) and reaching Harrison's Landing. The high command in Washington now decided to withdraw the Army to northern Virginia, where it would be joined to a force under Maj. Gen. John Pope (q.v.), the whole to be commanded by McClellan.

Early in August the movement began by water. But Lee hurried north with the intention of destroying Pope before McClellan could join him. This forced the government to send McClellan's troops to Pope as they arrived. When Pope faced Lee at Second Manassas, most of McClellan's army was with him or en route. After Pope's defeat, McClellan was placed in command of the disorganized troops and rapidly reorganized them. He then moved to meet Lee's invasion of Maryland. Believing that a part of Lee's army was occupied at Harper's Ferry, he attacked the enemy at the Battle of Antietam (Sept. 17, 1862). But the absent Confederate forces had returned or were returning, and Lee managed to hold his lines. He was forced, however, to retire to Virginia. Lincoln, convinced that McClellan had not followed up his success, replaced him with Maj. Gen. Ambrose Everett Burnside (q.v.) on Nov. 7.

McClellan's military career was now ended. But in 1864, the Democrats made him their presidential candidate. An advocate of continuing the war, he was embarrassed by the platform's call for a cessation of hostilities. He resigned his commission on election day. Lincoln won 212 electoral votes to McClellan's 21, but McClellan's popular vote was only 400,000 less than Lincoln's.

Culver Service

George Brinton McClellan (1826–1885). The Civil War commander remains a subject of historical controversy.

After his defeat he spent three years abroad. Returning to the United States, he became chief engineer of the New York City Department of Docks from 1870 to 1872 and served as governor of New Jersey from 1878 to 1881. See also ANTIETAM, THE BATTLE OF; BULL RUN, FIRST BATTLE OF; CIVIL WAR IN AMERICA; PENINSULA CAMPAIGN OF 1862, THE; POTOMAC, ARMY OF; SEVEN DAYS' BATTLES; YORKTOWN, SIEGE OF.

Bibliography.—McClellan wrote his own account of his war experiences, *McClellan's Own Story* (New York 1887), which is naturally biased, but contains valuable letters. Two early treatments of his campaigns are remarkably balanced: William Swinton, *Campaigns of the Army of the Potomac* (New York 1866) and Alexander S. Webb, *The Peninsula* (New York 1881). Biographies of McClellan concentrate on his military career and are strongly pro or anti. Peter S. Michie views him critically in *General McClellan* (New York 1901). Favorable to McClellan, but nonetheless scholarly and of value to the general reader and beginning student, are William S. Myers, *A Study in Personality: General George Brinton McClellan* (New York 1934); Hamilton J. Eckenrode and Bryan Conrad, *George B. McClellan* (Chapel Hill 1941); Warren W. Hassler, Jr., *General George B. McClellan, Shield of the Union* (Baton Rouge 1957). For McClellan's role in the command system see T. Harry Williams' *Lincoln and His Generals* (New York 1952); id., *McClellan, Sherman and Grant* (New Brunswick, N.J., 1962).

THOMAS HARRY WILLIAMS,
Louisiana State University.

McCLELLAN, George Brinton, American politician and educator: b. Dresden, Germany, Nov. 23, 1865; d. Washington, D.C., Nov. 30, 1940. The son of George Brinton McClellan (q.v.), American army officer, he was born in Germany while his parents were on a tour. Graduating from Princeton University, he worked as a newspaper reporter, attended New York

Law School, was admitted to the bar in 1892, and in that year joined Tammany Hall. From 1895 to 1903 he served as a Democrat in the United States House of Representatives. In 1903 he was elected mayor of New York City; re-elected in 1905, he broke with the Tammany Hall leader, Charles Francis Murphy (q.v.) over patronage, and in the next four years gave the city an honest, able government, during which he initiated the projects for the Queensboro and Manhattan bridges over the East River, and for the Catskill water supply, while also establishing municipal ferries and improving docks, parks, and subways. A strong neutralist, he nevertheless volunteered when the United States entered World War I, serving overseas and rising to lieutenant colonel. In 1911 he became a lecturer on public affairs at Princeton, and the following year was appointed professor of economic history—a post he held until 1931. He wrote *The Oligarchy of Venice* (1904), *The Heel of War* (1916), *Venice and Bonaparte* (1931), and *Modern Italy* (1933).

McCLELLAN, John Little, American legislator and lawyer: b. Sheridan, Ark., Feb. 25, 1896. His father was a sharecropper and schoolteacher who read law with borrowed books and was admitted to the bar; the son studied law in his father's office, and at the age of 17, although four years under the minimum age, was admitted to the bar by a special act of the Arkansas legislature. He served in World War I as a Signal Corps 1st lieutenant (1917–1919), became prosecuting attorney for the Arkansas Seventh Judicial District (1927–1930), and served two successive terms as a Democrat in the United States House of Representatives (1935–1939). In 1938 he made an unsuccessful bid for the Democratic nomination for United States senator from his state; four years later he won the nomination and was elected to the Senate, and he was re-elected in 1948 and 1954. As a member of the House of Representatives during the depression of the 1930's, McClellan supported many New Deal measures, but as a senator he embarked on a middle course as a southern Democrat of conservative but independent mind; he supported such measures as the Taft-Hartley labor-management relations act (1947), favored United States participation in the United Nations and the North Atlantic Treaty, and was an advocate of government economy. In the early 1950's, as the ranking Democrat on the Senate's Government Operations Committee and its Permanent Subcommittee on Investigations, he became an outspoken critic of Sen. Joseph R. McCarthy, of Wisconsin, and his handling of the subcommittee's activities; later he was on the committee that investigated the conflict between McCarthy and the army, and was among those who voted in 1954 to condemn the Wisconsin senator for his conduct.

Succeeding to the subcommittee's chairmanship in 1955, McClellan conducted further investigations that led to the establishment in January 1957 of the Senate Select Committee on Improper Activities in the Labor or Management Field, of which he became chairman. The committee's investigation of the giant International Brotherhood of Teamsters, Chauffeurs, Warehousemen and Helpers of America that immediately followed revealed shocking corruption in the union's management, and McClellan denounced two of its officials, Dave Beck and James R. Hoffa, as leaders of a "racket-ridden, gangster-infested, and

scandal-packed" union. Its inquiry into this and other unions—and into antiunion practices of some managements—brought recommendations from the committee in 1958 for legislation to regulate and control union funds, ensure union democracy, and curb the activity of middlemen in labor disputes. In these investigations, and in inquiries into the coin-machine industry and other fields in 1959, McClellan, with his stern demeanor, deep-pitched voice, and carefully articulated words, established himself as a relentless inquisitor but a strong defender of proper judicial procedures and of the rights of witnesses.

A Baptist of quiet habits, McClellan has suffered much tragedy in his private life. His first wife died after they were divorced; his second wife also died, and he lost all three of his sons by illness or accident. He married his third wife, Mrs. Norma Myers Cheatham, in 1937.

ROLAND GASK,
Staff Editor, "The Encyclopedia Americana."

McCLERNAND, mȧ-klûr'nănd, **John Alexander,** American army officer and politician: b. near Hardinsburg, Ky., May 30, 1812; d. Springfield, Ill., Sept. 20, 1900. He was admitted to the bar at Shawneetown, Ill., in 1832, served in the Black Hawk War, became a newspaper editor and an Illinois assemblyman (1836–1843), and a member of the United States House of Representatives (1843–1851, 1859–1861). During the Civil War he was a brigadier general of volunteers, commanded the Union right flank at Fort Donelson, was promoted to major general, and led a division at Shiloh. In January 1863, after superseding Maj. Gen. William Tecumseh Sherman in command of the river expedition against Vicksburg, he captured the Confederate redoubt at Arkansas Post, Ark., with the aid of Rear Admiral David Dixon Porter's gunboat flotilla; afterward, as 13th Corps commander under Maj. Gen. Ulysses S. Grant, he was prominent in the Vicksburg campaign. During the various campaigns, McClernand was in frequent conflict with his colleagues; he angered Grant by crediting the victory at Fort Donelson largely to his own division, wrote to President Lincoln after Shiloh criticizing Grant's strategy, was accused by Grant of ignoring his orders at Champion's Hill, and was relieved of his corps command in June 1863 after issuing a congratulatory order, without authorization, extravagantly extolling his own troops in the Vicksburg campaign. Subsequently (February 1864) his command was restored but illness soon forced his resignation. After the war he served as circuit judge for the Sangamon, Ill., district (1870–1873), was active in Democratic politics, and was appointed to the Utah Commission in 1893 by President Grover Cleveland.

MACCLESFIELD, măk''lz-fēld, municipal borough, England, in Cheshire, on the river Bollin, about 15 miles south of Manchester. It is built on a hill, from the crest of which the ancient Church of St. Michael, founded in 1278 by Queen Eleanor, dominates the lower town, which is reached by descending a long flight of stone steps. Immediately east of the city lies Macclesfield Forest, an immense stretch of moorland rising to 1,600 feet and commanding excellent views of the mountains of the Peak District. Macclesfield is the center of England's silk-milling industry and also manufactures cotton and mixed textiles. Other industries are leather tanning and the manufacture of silk-milling machinery, paper, plastics, light metal products, and electrical equipment. In the Domesday Book it was recorded as part of the estate of the earl of Chester. Its first charter was granted in 1261. It has a grammar school founded in 1502, an interesting town hall, a small museum, and ancient iron stocks. The first silk mill was established in 1756 and the manufacture of cotton textiles was begun in 1785. Pop. (1961) 37,578.

McCLINTIC, mà-klĭn′tĭk, **Guthrie,** American theatrical producer and director: b. Seattle, Wash., Aug. 6, 1893; d. Sneden's Landing, near Palisades, Rockland County, N.Y., Oct. 29, 1961. He was educated at the University of Washington and the American Academy of Dramatic Arts in New York City. For several years he was an actor, appearing first in 1913, and played with Grace George in New York and with the stock company of Jessie Bonstelle before becoming associated with Winthrop Ames, the producer, for whom he became casting director. His first venture as producer and director was with A. A. Milne's *The Dover Road* in New York in 1921. On September 8 of that year he married Katharine Cornell, (q.v.), an actress whom he had "discovered" while scouting talent for Mr. Ames. Working together as director and leading lady, they enriched the American theater with a series of notable plays. The first of these was *The Green Hat* (1925). It was followed by *The Barretts of Wimpole Street* (1931); George Bernard Shaw's *Saint Joan* (1936); *Candida* (1937), and *The Doctor's Dilemma* (1941); Anton Pavlovich Chekhov's *The Three Sisters* (1942), and Christopher Fry's *The Dark Is Light Enough* (1955). Among other plays which he produced or directed were Maxwell Anderson's *Saturday's Children* (1927); *Winterset* (1935); *The Wingless Victory* and *High Tor* (1936), and *Key Largo* (1939); S. N. Behrman's *Brief Moment* (1932); Sidney Howard's *Yellow Jack* (1934), and Du-Bose and Dorothy Heyward's *Mamba's Daughters* (1939). He wrote of his life and work with Miss Cornell in *Me and Kit,* published in 1955.

McCLINTOCK, Sir **Francis Leopold,** British naval officer and explorer: b. Dundalk, Ireland, July 8, 1819; d. London, England, Nov. 17, 1907. He entered the British Navy in 1831 and was commissioned lieutenant in 1845. He was a member of the 1848, 1850, and 1852 expeditions which searched for Sir John Franklin (q.v.) and his party, and by his long-distance sledge journeys, and by improvements he devised in this form of travel, greatly advanced Arctic sledge exploration. In 1857–1859 McClintock commanded an expedition aboard the yacht *Fox* dispatched by Franklin's second wife, Lady Jane Franklin, to follow up clues concerning the explorer's fate discovered by John Rae (q.v.), and from this voyage he returned with documentary and other evidence of Franklin's death and the loss of his crew. His book, *The Voyage of the Fox in the Arctic Seas* (1859) tells the story of this expedition. McClintock afterward held various naval posts, including commander in chief of the North America and West Indies station (1879–1882). He was knighted in 1860, and became vice admiral in 1877 and admiral in 1884.

Consult Markham, Sir Clements Robert, *Life of Admiral Sir Leopold McClintock* (London 1909).

McCLINTOCK, John, American Methodist Episcopal clergyman and educator: b. Philadelphia, Pa., Oct. 27, 1814; d. Madison, N.J., March 4, 1870. Educated at the University of Pennsylvania, he taught mathematics and classical languages at Dickinson College, Carlisle, Pa. (1836–1848), being meanwhile ordained an elder of the Methodist Episcopal Church (1840), and then edited the *Methodist Quarterly Review* (1848–1856). He was pastor of St. Paul's Church, New York City, in 1857–1860 (and again for a short time beginning in 1864), and was pastor of the American Chapel, Paris, France, in 1860–1864—a period during which he was an eloquent exponent of the Union cause in the Civil War. From 1867 until his death he was the first president of Drew Theological Seminary at Madison, N.J. In 1853, with James Strong, he began work on the *Cyclopaedia of Biblical, Theological and Classical Literature,* 10 vols. (1867–1881; supplement, 1885–1887), three volumes of which appeared before his death. Among other works, he published, with Charles E. Blumenthal, a translation of Johann August Wilhelm Neander's *Das Leben Jesu Christi,* under the title, *The Life of Jesus Christ in Its Historical Connexion and Development* (1848); and *Sketches of Eminent Methodist Ministers* (1854).

McCLINTOCK CHANNEL, a passage, Northwest Territories, Canada, in Franklin District, between Victoria Island on the west, and Prince of Wales Island on the east. About 170 miles long and from 65 to 130 miles wide, it connects in the north with Viscount Melville Sound, and in the south with Franklin, James Ross, and Victoria straits.

McCLOSKEY, mà-klŏs′kĭ, **John,** American Roman Catholic prelate: b. Brooklyn, N.Y., March 10, 1810; d. New York, N.Y., Oct. 10, 1885. The son of Irish parents who came to the United States in 1808, he received his early education at Thomas Brady's classical school in New York and in 1828 was graduated from Mount St. Mary's College, Emmitsburg, Md. At the age of 24 he was ordained priest, the first native of New York State to enter the secular priesthood. From 1835 to 1837, he studied in Rome, Italy. Upon his return to the United States he was assigned to St. Joseph's Church, New York. When St. John's College, now Fordham University, was opened in 1841, he became its first president. He returned to parish work a year later. At the petition of Bishop John Joseph Hughes, of the New York diocese, for an assistant in his latter years, Pope Gregory XVI appointed Father McCloskey, who in 1844 was consecrated titular bishop of Axiere and coadjutor of New York with the right of succession. In 1847, however, Bishop McCloskey was transferred to the newly formed see of Albany, N.Y. He headed this diocese for 17 years, during which he built the Cathedral of the Immaculate Conception at Albany, and established many other churches and educational and charitable institutions. In 1864 he became archbishop of the New York diocese, succeeding Archbishop Hughes, and in 1875 was preconized cardinal, the first American cardinal. He was chiefly responsible for the completion of St. Patrick's Cathedral, on Fifth Avenue, New York City—begun in 1858 but suspended because of the Civil War—and dedicated it at the opening ceremonies in 1879.

McCLOY, mȧ-kloi′, **John Jay,** American lawyer and administrator : b. Philadelphia, Pa., March 31, 1895. After graduating from Amherst College in 1916, he went to Harvard Law School, interrupted his studies there to serve overseas (as a field artillery captain) in World War I, but returned to take his law degree in 1921. From then until 1940 he practiced law in New York. In 1940 he was appointed special consultant by Secretary of War Henry Lewis Stimson—a fellow Republican serving in the Democratic administration of President Franklin D. Roosevelt —and, in the following April, became assistant secretary of war, serving throughout World War II and on until November 1945. In this capacity he attended the San Francisco Conference on International Organization and helped to formulate plans for the war crimes trials. Later, in Washington, he assisted in framing policies for the administration of liberated and occupied enemy territories. On Feb. 28, 1947, after a brief return to private law practice, he assumed the presidency of the International Bank for Reconstruction and Development. From 1949 to 1952 he served in western Germany as the first civilian United States high commissioner, as chief Economic Cooperation Administration representative, and as the United States member of the three-power council exercising Allied authority. During this period he played an important role in establishing the German Federal Republic. Returning to the United States, he became chairman of the board of the Chase Manhattan Bank in 1953. He is a director of many other large industrial organizations; a trustee of the Ford Foundation, Rockefeller Foundation, and various educational and cultural institutions; and chairman of the board of the Council of Foreign Relations, Incorporated. He is the author of *The Challenge to American Foreign Policy* (1953).

McCLURE, mȧ-kloōr′, **Alexander Kelly,** American editor, politician, and lawyer : b. Sherman's Valley, Perry County, Pa., Jan. 9, 1828; d. Philadelphia, June 6, 1909. He supported Whig political principles as editor and publisher (1846– (1850) of the *Juniata Sentinel* at Mifflintown, Pa., and Whig-Republican aims as editor and owner of the *Franklin Repository* (1850–1856, 1862–1864) at Chambersburg, Pa. At various times he was a state representative and senator, and he was admitted to the bar in 1856. He helped organize the Republican Party, and at the national convention in 1860 succeeded, with Andrew G. Curtin, in swinging the pivotal Pennsylvania delegation to Abraham Lincoln; afterward, as state Republican committee chairman, he directed the campaign that won Pennsylvania's electoral votes for Lincoln and the governorship for Curtin. During the Civil War he became an assistant adjutant general in the army, and placed 17 regiments in the field. McClure supported the nomination of Ulysses S. Grant in 1868, but in 1872 was a leader of the Liberal Republican Party that nominated Horace Greeley. He opened a law office in Philadelphia in 1868, was defeated for mayor of that city in 1874, and in 1875, with Frank McLaughin, founded (and edited until 1901) the Philadelphia *Times*. His writings included *Abraham Lincoln and Men of War Times* (1892), *Our Presidents and How We Make Them* (1900), a book of personal recollections (1902), and *Old Time Notes of Pennsylvania,* 2 vols. (1905).

McCLURE, Sir **Robert John Le Mesurier,** British naval officer and Arctic explorer : b. Wexford, Ireland, Jan. 28, 1807; d. London, England, Oct. 17, 1873. He entered the British Navy in 1824 and in 1836 made his first Arctic voyage. In 1848 he joined the Arctic expedition of Sir James Clark Ross, which was sent to search for Sir John Franklin (q.v.) and his party. Two years later McClure was given command of the *Investigator* in an expedition to search for Franklin via the Bering Strait, and in October 1850, looking across the ice from the northeastern tip of Banks Island to Melville Island, he became the first to discover the existence of the Northwest Passage (see POLAR EXPLORATION, NORTH). In September 1851 the *Investigator* was caught in the ice off Banks Island, and two years later was abandoned, McClure and his crew sledging eastward across the ice to Dealey Island and a rendezvous with Sir Edward Belcher's expedition. On his return to England in 1854, McClure was knighted, and he and his crew shared a £10,000 prize for discovery of the Northwest Passage.

McCLURE, **Samuel Sidney,** American editor and publisher : b. Frocess, County Antrim, Ireland, Feb. 17, 1857; d. New York, N.Y., March 21, 1949. Brought to the United States at the age of nine by his widowed mother, he lived a poverty-stricken youth in Indiana. He worked his way through Knox College, Galesburg, Ill., graduating in 1882, and then went to New York City with $6 in his pockets. For two years he held various minor editorial positions. In 1884 he started the McClure Syndicate, the first newspaper syndicate in the United States, supplying written material for simultaneous release by all member newspapers. In 1893 he founded and thereafter edited *McClure's Magazine,* a leader among low-priced news and literary periodicals. Among writers he presented to the American readers were Rudyard Kipling, Sir Arthur Conan Doyle, Robert Louis Stevenson, William Dean Howells, and Mark Twain. Being a popular outlet for social critics, the magazine promoted many reform movements. It published Ida Minerva Tarbell's "The History of the Standard Oil Company," (Joseph) Lincoln Steffens' "The Shame of Minneapolis," and Ray Stannard Baker's "The Right to Work." Some other contributors were O. Henry, Finley Peter Dunne, Jack London, and William Allen White. The magazine ceased publication in 1929. McClure was the author of *Obstacles to Peace* (1917); *The Achievements of Liberty* (1935); *What Freedom Means to Man* (1938).

McCLURE STRAIT, channel, Northwest Territories, Canada, in Franklin District, between Banks Island, on the south, and Melville Island, on the north. About 170 miles long and 60 miles wide, it leads into the Beaufort Sea of the Arctic Ocean in the west, and into Viscount Melville Sound in the east.

MacCOLL, mȧ-kŏl′, **Evan,** Scottish-Canadian poet : b. Kenmore, Argyllshire, Scotland, Sept. 21, 1808; d. Toronto, Ontario, Canada, July 25, 1898. He emigrated to Canada during his 42d year and became known as the bard of the St. Andrew's Society at Kingston, Ontario, where he served as a customs officer. His *Clàrsach nam beann (Poems and Songs in Gaelic)* published in Glasgow in 1838, created much enthusiasm among his compatriots. He is also author of many English poems, such as *My Rowan Tree; The Mountain Minstrel* (1887).

McCOLLUM, mȧ-kŏl'ŭm, **Elmer Verner,** American physiological chemist: b. near Fort Scott, Kansas, March 3, 1879. Graduating from the University of Kansas and Yale University, he taught at the University of Wisconsin from 1907 to 1917, afterwards accepting a professorship in biochemistry at the School of Hygiene and Public Health, Johns Hopkins University, a position he held until 1944 when he was made professor emeritus.

McCollum has specialized in the study of vitamins and the relation of diet to growth. Among his important discoveries were the "fat-soluble" vitamin A in 1913, later, vitamin B in milk sugar, and in 1922 the importance of vitamin D in the treatment of rickets. He was a member of the International Committee on Vitamin Standards, League of Nations, 1931; after 1939 the chairman of the Nutrition section, Pan-American Sanitary Bureau; and after 1942 a member of the Food and Nutrition Board, National Research Council. In 1943 the United States Army called him as a consultant to its Industrial Hygiene Division. McCollum has written extensively in the fields of chemistry and nutrition.

McCOMB, mȧ-kōm', **John,** American engineer and architect: b. New York, Oct. 17, 1763; d. there, May 25, 1853. He became prominent for his designs for both public and private buildings in New York, Philadelphia and the Eastern States. He designed the front of the old government house in New York in 1790, Saint John's Church, and was supervising architect of the city of New York at the time of the erection of the city hall. The Montauk (1795), Eaton's Neck (1798), and Cape Henry (1791) lighthouses were also his designs.

McCOMB, city, Mississippi, in Pike County, 60 miles east-southeast of Natchez on U.S. Highway 51 and the Illinois Central Railroad. Located in a timber and agricultural region producing cotton, vegetables, and dairy products, McComb is a trading and shipping center, with lumber mills and railroad shops. Manufactures include cotton textiles, clothing, and cottonseed products. It was founded about 1857 by Col. H. S. McComb, the president of the New Orleans, Jackson, and Northern Railroad, which was built in that year. After the establishment of railroad shops here, McComb grew rapidly and soon became important for its textile industries. The city has a mayor-council form of government. Pop. 12,020.

MacCONMIDHE, mȧ-kŏn'mĭ-dē, **Giolla-Brighde** or **Gillabrighde,** Irish historian and poet: b. about 1180; d. around 1260. He was descended from the hereditary poets of the O'Neills, and it is recorded that Brian O'Neill, chief of the Cinel Eoghain, on one occasion paid him 20 horned cows for a poem and on another, 20 cows besides gold and clothing. He traveled in many parts of the country, and at the Battle of Down in 1260, he was with O'Neill when that chief was killed by the Lord Justice Stephen Longespée. His 280-word lament on the defeat and death of Brian is his greatest work. He

also wrote religious verse and a poem on King Cathal Croibhdhearg O'Conor (d. 1224). See also GAELIC LITERATURE—*Bardic Poetry.*

McCONNELL, mȧ-kŏn"l, **Francis John,** American Methodist Episcopal bishop: b. Trinway, Ohio, Aug. 18, 1871, d. Lucasville, Ohio, Aug. 18, 1953. He was educated at the Ohio Wesleyan University and entered the ministry in 1894. He held pastorates in Massachusetts and in 1909 became president of De Pauw University, a post in which he served until 1912 when he was elected bishop.

McCONNELLSVILLE, mȧ-kŏn"lz-vĭl, town, Ohio, seat of Morgan County, 27 miles southeast of Zanesville on the navigable Muskingum River. Altitude 710 feet. It is served ·by state highways and the Baltimore and Ohio Railroad at Malta, across the river. Located in a farming region, it has a few industries, including the manufacture of meat products, lumber, and cigars. There are also gas and oil wells in the vicinity. It was laid out in 1817 by Gen. Robert McConnell. After 1827 keel boats traded between McConnellsville, Zanesville, and Pittsburgh and by 1850 there was a flourishing river trade connecting with Mississippi ports. With the development of overland travel, however, river traffic declined. Pop. 2,257.

McCOOK, mȧ-kŏok', **Alexander McDowell,** American soldier: b. Columbiana County, Ohio, April 22, 1831; d. Dayton, Ohio, June 12, 1903. He was graduated at West Point in 1853, and with the commission of second lieutenant of the 3d Infantry was ordered to New Mexico. In 1861 he gained his captaincy and saw much service during the Civil War. He commanded the Ohio volunteers at Bull Run and rapidly gained promotion, being appointed major general of volunteers in 1862.

McCook's brilliant military reputation was made at the battles of Shiloh, Murfreesboro, Chickamauga, and others, and in 1865 he was brevetted brigadier general in the regular army. He was subsequently placed in command of the military school at Fort Leavenworth, was commissioned major general in 1894 and retired the following year. He represented the United States at the coronation of the czar in 1896 and in 1898–1899 was a member of a commission appointed by President McKinley to investigate the work of the War Department during the War with Spain.

General McCook came of a fighting family. He was the son of Daniel McCook who was killed by Morgan's guerillas in 1863. Seven of the general's brothers took part in the War for the Union, three of whom, like their father, were killed. Four of the eight McCook brothers attained the rank of general.

McCOOK, Anson George, American soldier and politician: b. Steubenville, Ohio, Oct. 10, 1835; d. New York, Dec. 30, 1917. At the outbreak of the Civil War he entered the Federal army as captain of an Ohio company recruited by himself, became colonel of 194th Ohio Infantry and at end of the war was brevetted brigadier general. He was United States assessor of internal revenue at Steubenville, Ohio, and removed to New York in 1873. In 1876 he was elected as a Republican to the

House of Representatives from the 8th Congressional District, New York, and was re-elected in 1878 and 1880. From 1884 to 1893 he served as secretary of the United States Senate, and from 1895 to 1897 as chamberlain of New York City. He was a first cousin of Alexander McDowell McCook and brother of Edward Moody McCook (qq.v.).

McCOOK, Edward Moody, United States army officer: b. Steubenville, Ohio, June 15, 1833; d. Chicago, Ill., Sept. 9, 1909. A brother of Anson George McCook (q.v.), he went to Colorado in 1849, practiced law, and in 1859 served as a member of the legislature of Kansas Territory. At the outbreak of the Civil War he joined the Kansas Legion in Washington, D.C., and then became a cavalry officer. He fought with distinction in the campaigns of 1862 and 1863 and rose to the rank of lieutenant colonel. In 1864 he was appointed brigadier general of volunteers and commanded the cavalry of the Army of the Cumberland, performing signal service at the siege of Atlanta, Ga., where he cut off the city's communications to the south. At the end of the war he was promoted major general of volunteers, and served briefly as military governor of Florida. He resigned his commission in 1866 to accept an appointment as United States minister to Hawaii, where he remained until 1869, when he became governor of the Territory of Colorado, serving except for a short period (1873–1874) until 1875.

McCOOK, city, Nebraska, seat of Red Willow County, situated at an altitude of 2,510 feet, on the Republican River, 65 miles south of North Platte. It is served by the Chicago, Burlington & Quincy Railroad, and by Western Air Lines. The city is the trading center of a rich agricultural region, and serves as a railroad division point. Railroad repair shops and food-packing and shipping plants are important. McCook Junior College is located here. Founded as Fairview in 1881, the city was renamed in 1882 for Gen. Alexander McDowell McCook. It was incorporated as a town in 1883 and as a city in 1933. It has a city manager type government. Population: 8,301.

McCORMACK, mǝ-kôr′mǝk, **John,** Irish-American tenor: b. Athlone, Ireland, June 14, 1884; d. Boosterstown, County Dublin, Sept. 16, 1945. He was educated at Summer Hill College, County Sligo, and in 1902 won the gold medal for singing at the National Irish Festival. In the following year he became a member of the choir of Dublin Cathedral and studied with its organist, Vincent O'Brien, and later in Milan. He made his operatic debut at Covent Garden, London, in 1907, and in New York City with the Manhattan Opera Company in 1909. Subsequently he sang with the Metropolitan, Chicago, and Monte Carlo opera companies. In 1913 he turned to the concert stage, where he achieved great popularity as a singer of Irish folk songs and ballads. He became a United States citizen in 1919, and was made a papal count in 1928. His retirement was marked by a farewell tour in 1938.

McCORMACK, John William, American legislator: b. Boston, Mass., Dec. 21, 1891. He was elected speaker of the U.S. House of Representatives in January 1962, succeeding the late Sam Rayburn. When Lyndon B. Johnson became

president after the assassination of John F. Kennedy in November 1963, McCormack, as speaker, stood next in line of succession to the presidency for the rest of the term. A Democrat, he had been a member of the House since 1929.

After studying law in a private office, McCormack was admitted to the Massachusetts bar in 1913 and began to practice in Boston. From 1920 to 1926 he was a member of the Massachusetts legislature. He was elected to the U.S. House of Representatives in 1928. From 1940 to 1961 he was majority floor leader, except for two intervals (1947–1949 and 1953–1955) when the Republicans controlled the House. During those periods he was minority whip. McCormack won a reputation as a tax expert. A moderate liberal, he became known for his sharp wit in floor debate and for his influence with members of both the liberal and conservative wings of the Democratic party.

McCORMICK, mǝ-kôr′mĭk, **Anne O'Hare,** American journalist: b. Wakefield, Yorkshire, England, May 16, 1881; d. New York, N.Y., May 29, 1954. She was educated in Columbus, Ohio, and traveled extensively in Europe after her marriage to Francis J. McCormick, an importer.

In 1921 she started to write for the New York *Times,* and her accurate forecast of the rise of Benito Mussolini in Italy won her a place as a regular correspondent the next year. By 1936 her European reporting had earned her a position as the first woman on the editorial board of the *Times.* Her column "Abroad" appeared three times weekly on the editorial page of the paper. In 1937 she was awarded the Pulitzer Prize for foreign correspondence. She wrote *The Hammer and the Scythe: Communist Russia Enters the Second Decade* (1928). A selection of her writings, *World at Home,* appeared in 1956.

MacCORMICK, mǝ-kôr′mĭk, **Austin Harbutt,** American penologist: b. Georgetown, Ontario, Canada, April 20, 1893. He grew up in Boothbay Harbor, Me., and graduated (1915) from Bowdoin College, where he became interested in prison reform. In 1917 he became executive officer at the U.S. Naval Prison in Portsmouth, N.H. While here, he initiated many reforms in the treatment of inmates. His studies of penal institutions in the United States led to his writing (with Paul W. Garrett) the *Handbook of American Prisons* (1926) and the *Handbook of American Prisons and Reformatories* (1929). *The Education of Adult Prisoners* appeared in 1931. MacCormick was assistant director of the U.S. Bureau of Prisons (1929–1933) and commissioner of correction in New York City (1934–1940). In 1940 he became executive director of the Osborne Association, a leading penological research and welfare organization. He was appointed professor of criminology at the University of California (Berkeley) in 1951.

McCORMICK, mǝ-kôr′mĭk, **Cyrus Hall,** American inventor: b. Rockbridge County, Va., Feb. 15, 1809; d. Chicago, Ill., May 13, 1884. His father, Robert McCormick (1780–1846), a Virginia landowner, had patented several farming implements, but had worked without success for many years to perfect a mechanical reaper. In July 1831, Cyrus succeeded in producing a model reaper with all the essential components of later commercial machines. Patenting his invention in 1934, after Obed Hussey had announced (1833) the construction of a reaper of his own, Mc-Cormick started to manufacture the machine on the family estate in 1837 and six years later began to license its manufacture in other parts of the country. In 1847 he set up a factory in Chicago, Ill., founding what eventually became one of the greatest industrial establishments in the United States. After his original patent expired (1848), he was faced with growing competition from Hussey and others, and was engaged in a long series of legal actions involving such figures as Abraham Lincoln, Edwin M. Stanton, and William H. Seward as lawyers for one side or the other. McCormick managed to outdistance all his rivals, initiating new methods of advertising, consumer financing, and rationalization of production to promote his product. Amassing a large fortune, he invested widely in later years in railroad and mining enterprises. He was a liberal benefactor of the Presbyterian Church (see McCORMICK THEOLOGICAL SEMINARY).

LEANDER JAMES McCORMICK (1819–1900), his brother, was associated with him as superintendent of manufacturing operations in Chicago from 1849 and became a partner 10 years later, retiring in 1881. He endowed the Leander McCormick Observatory (q.v.) at the University of Virginia.

CYRUS HALL McCORMICK (1859–1936), Cyrus' son, succeeded him as president of McCormick Harvesting Machine Company in 1884. In 1902 he organized a combination of the McCormick and rival firms as the International Harvester Company, of which he was president until 1919, when he became chairman of the board.

Consult Hutchinson, William Thomas, *Cyrus Hall McCormick*, 2 vols. (New York 1930–35).

McCORMICK, Lynde Dupuy, United States naval officer: b. Annapolis, Md., Aug. 12, 1895; d. Newport, R.I., Aug. 16, 1956. Graduated from the United States Naval Academy in 1915, he served on the U.S.S. *Wyoming* in World War I, and during the 1920's was a submarine commander. When the Japanese attacked Pearl Harbor in December 1941, he was assistant war plans officer of the Pacific Fleet. Promoted war plans officer the following April and rear admiral in July, he took part in the battles of the Coral Sea, Midway, and Guadalcanal, and from October 1943 to March 1945 was in Washington, D.C., as assistant chief of naval operations for logistics plans. As chairman of the logistics committee of the Joint Chiefs of Staff, he accompanied Admiral Ernest Joseph King to the second Quebec (1944) and Yalta (1945) conferences. In March 1945, McCormick assumed command of a battleship division which participated in the Okinawa operations, and the following December he was named deputy commander of the Pacific Fleet. In April 1950 he became vice chief of naval operations, and in August 1951 commander of the Atlantic Fleet, with the rank of admiral. Early the next year he was named supreme Allied commander of the Atlantic under the North Atlantic Treaty Organization (NATO). He resigned on April 12, 1954 to become president of the Naval War College, where he remained until his death.

McCORMICK, Robert Rutherford, American newspaper editor and publisher: b. Chicago, Ill., July 30, 1880; d. Wheaton, April 1, 1955. His father, Robert Sanderson McCormick (1849–1919), nephew of Cyrus Hall McCormick (q.v.), was United States envoy to Austria, Russia, and France successively from 1901 to 1907. His mother was the daughter of Joseph Medill (q.v.), editor and publisher of the Chicago *Tribune*. Robert graduated from Yale University in 1903 and was admitted to the Illinois bar in 1907. In 1910 he and his cousin Joseph Medill Patterson (q.v.) gained control of the *Tribune* after the death of Joseph's father, Robert W. Patterson (q.v.). McCormick served as a major of cavalry on the Mexican border in 1916–1917, and during World War I fought in France as a colonel of artillery. After the war he and Patterson founded (1919) the New York *Daily News,* with Patterson in active charge, while McCormick ran the *Tribune;* the management of the two papers was formally separated in 1925, though they continued to be jointly owned. Under McCormick's direction, the *Tribune* gained the largest circulation of any newspaper in the Midwest and was an outspoken champion of the extreme right wing in American politics, strongly isolationist in editorial policy. McCormick condemned internationalism, the welfare state, and labor unions, and opposed the foreign policy of the United States after World War II, especially the Marshall Plan and the United Nations. In 1949, after the death of Eleanor Medill Patterson, Joseph's sister, McCormick purchased the Washington *Times-Herald,* which she had owned; but the venture did not pay, and he sold it again in 1954. A close student of American history, he published *Ulysses S. Grant, the Great Soldier of America* (1934), *The American Revolution and Its Influence on World Civilization* (1945), and *The War Without Grant* (1950).

(JOSEPH) MEDILL McCORMICK (1877–1925), his brother, served on the Chicago *Tribune* as a reporter and then briefly as publisher until 1910. A leading supporter of Theodore Roosevelt's unsuccessful bid for re-election as president in 1912, he was United States congressman from Illinois in 1917–1919 and senator thereafter until his death.

RUTH HANNA McCORMICK (1880–1944), Medill's wife and daughter of the Republican leader Marcus A. Hanna (q.v.), was prominent in Republican Party affairs for many years and United States congresswoman from Illinois in 1929–1931. She married Albert G. Simms, New Mexico lawyer and banker, in 1932.

McCORMICK, Samuel Black, American clergyman and educator: b. Westmoreland County, Pa., May 6, 1858; d. Coraopolis Heights, April 18, 1928. Graduated from Washington and Jefferson College in 1880, he studied law, was admitted to the bar in 1882, and practiced in Denver, Colo. (1883–1887). In the latter year he entered Western Theological Seminary in Allegheny (now part of Pittsburgh), Pa., and in 1890 was ordained a Presbyterian minister, serving churches in Allegheny and Omaha, Nebr., until 1897, when he was named president of Coe College in Cedar Rapids, Iowa. In 1904 he became chancellor of the Western University of Pennsylvania, renamed the University of Pittsburgh (1908, q.v.), which he built up into a major institution of higher education. During his first decade in office, schools of education and business administration, a graduate school, and the Mellon Institute of Industrial Research were added, as well as the Summer Session, Evening Division, and

Extension Division. He retired in 1920.

McCORMICK, Stephen, American inventor: b. Auburn, Va., Aug. 26, 1784; d. there, Aug. 28, 1875. In 1816 he invented a cast-iron plow with detachable parts, a great advance over the earlier invention (1797) of Charles Newbold. Patenting his invention in 1819, he began to manufacture it at Auburn and later established two more factories in Virginia, besides licensing other manufacturers to produce the device, which appeared in 12 models for various purposes. It is estimated that by 1840, more than 10,000 McCormick plows were in use in Virginia and other Southern states. The contemporary Northern market was supplied with plows based on the invention of Jethro Wood of Cayuga County, N.Y., who patented his cast-iron plow a few months after McCormick.

McCORMICK, Vance Criswell, American newspaper publisher and political leader: b. Harrisburg, Pa., June 19, 1872; d. Cedarcliff Farms, Cumberland County, June 16, 1946. Graduated from Yale University in 1893, he entered politics in Harrisburg as a Democrat and was mayor of the city in 1902–1905. To further his program of political reform, he purchased the Harrisburg *Patriot,* a morning daily paper, and founded the *Evening News,* both of which he continued to publish until his death. With A. Mitchell Palmer, who later became attorney general of the United States, McCormick led the Pennsylvania delegation at the Democratic National Convention of 1912 in support of Woodrow Wilson's candidacy for the presidential nomination. After running unsuccessfully for governor of Pennsylvania in 1914, he managed Wilson's victorious campaign for re-election against Republican candidate Charles Evans Hughes in 1916. When the United States entered World War I, McCormick was named head of the War Trade Board, serving until 1919. He was also one of President Wilson's leading advisers at the Paris Peace Conference, where he served on the Allied Blockade Commission as chairman.

McCORMICK OBSERVATORY. See LEANDER McCORMICK OBSERVATORY.

McCORMICK THEOLOGICAL SEMINARY, a Presbyterian institution in Chicago, Ill., founded in 1829 under the auspices of the Synod of Indiana as a department of Hanover Academy, Hanover, Ind. In 1840 it removed to New Albany, Ind., and another move in 1859 brought the seminary to Chicago as a result of the benefaction of Cyrus H. McCormick (q.v.). It was called McCormick Theological Seminary in 1886, and so legally designated in 1943. Lane Seminary of Cincinnati, Ohio, in combination with Lebanon, united with the seminary in 1931, and the Presbyterian College of Christian Education was merged with it in 1949. Located on the northwest side of Chicago near Lincoln Park, the seminary occupies 20 acres. The curriculum includes courses in the Biblical, historical, theological, and practical fields. Admission requirements are a bachelor of arts degree or its equivalent from an accredited college or university; the seminary grants the bachelor of divinity degree after three years of prescribed and elective courses. An additional year of graduate study leads to the master of theology degree. A master's degree in Christian education or church social work is also granted.

THOM HUGH HUNTER.

McCOSH, má-kŏsh', **James,** Scottish-American philosopher and educator: b. Ayrshire, Scotland, April 1, 1811; d. Princeton, N.J., Nov. 16, 1894. Educated at the universities of Glasgow and Edinburgh (M.A., 1833), he became a preacher of the Established Church of Scotland, with pastorates in Ayrshire, and in 1843 followed his former teacher at Edinburgh, Thomas Chalmers, into the Free Church of Scotland. In 1850 he published *The Method of the Divine Government, Physical and Moral,* an indirect response to the naturalistic tendency of John Stuart Mill's *System of Logic* (1843). As a result of this work, McCosh was named professor of logic and metaphysics at Queen's College, Belfast, Ireland, where he remained from 1852 to 1868, when he went to the United States to accept the presidency of the College of New Jersey (now Princeton University). During his 20 years at Princeton he proved an able and liberal administrator. He organized schools of science, philosophy, and art, instituted a balanced system of elective studies and graduate work, and erected new buildings on the campus. In his classes on the history of philosophy and psychology, he was a stimulating teacher, and as a theologian he was one of the first to defend the theory of evolution. He resigned as president of Princeton in 1888 because of age, but continued to teach until his death. His writings on theology, philosophy, and psychology include *The Intuitions of the Mind Inductively Investigated* (1860); *An Examination of Mr. J. S. Mill's Philosophy; Being a Defence of Fundamental Truth* (1866); and *The Laws of Discursive Thought, Being a Textbook of Formal Logic* (1870). His *Christianity and Positivism,* published in 1871, was an attempt to reconcile science with religion, and *The Scottish Philosophy, Biographical, Expository, Critical, from Hutcheson to Hamilton,* which appeared in 1875, provides the background of the so-called "Princeton school" of philosophy. A two-volume work, *Psychology,* appeared in 1886–1887, and his *Realistic Philosophy Defended in a Philosophic Series,* also two volumes, was published in 1887.

Consult Sloane, William Milligan, *The Life of James McCosh* (New York 1896), containing autobiographical material and complete bibliography; Howe, M. A. DeWolfe, *Classic Shades* (Boston 1928); Egbert, Donald D., and Lee, Diane M., *Princeton Portraits* (Princeton 1947).

McCOY, má-koi', **Frank Ross,** United States army officer: b. Lewiston, Pa., Oct. 29, 1874; d. Washington, D.C., June 4, 1954. Graduated from the United States Military Academy in 1897, he fought in Cuba during the Spanish-American War (1898), winning two Silver Stars for gallantry at Las Guásimas and San Juan Hill. From 1901 to 1906 he was aide to Gen. Leonard Wood in Cuba and the Philippines. In World War I he served as secretary of the general staff of the American Expeditionary Forces and later as commander of the 165th Infantry Regiment (the "Fighting 69th" of the famous Rainbow Division). After the war, McCoy acquired valuable political experience as aide to Governor General Wood in the Philippines (1921–1925), and from this time on he was given increasingly important diplomatic assignments in addition to his military duties. In 1928 he was

United States representative at the Pan American Conference in Washington, D.C., and in November of that year he supervised the presidential elections in Nicaragua. In 1929 he was head of a commission to arbitrate the dispute over the Gran Chaco boundary between Bolivia and Paraguay, and in 1932 he was a member of the League of Nations' Lytton Commission to investigate the Japanese invasion of Manchuria. McCoy was successively in command of the 7th, 6th, and 2d Corps areas from 1933 to 1938, when he retired from the army with the rank of major general. He was a member of the commission, headed by Supreme Court Justice Owen J. Roberts, to investigate the Pearl Harbor disaster of December 1941, and of the military court which tried the eight Nazi spies who landed on Long Island, N.Y., in 1942. From 1945 to 1949 he was chairman of the 11-nation Far Eastern Commission (FEC) which controlled the occupation of Japan following World War II. He published *Principles of Military Training* (1918).

McCOY, Isaac, American missionary and Indian agent: b. near Uniontown, Pa., June 13, 1784; d. Louisville, Ky., June 21, 1846. Reared in Kentucky, he moved to southern Indiana in 1804 and shortly thereafter was ordained a minister of the Maria Creek Baptist Church. In 1817 he was appointed missionary to the Miami and Kickapoo Indians in the valley of the Wabash River, and later to the Pottawatomie and Ottawa tribes in Michigan. His work convinced him that the welfare of the Indians necessitated their removal from the influence of the encroaching white settlements, and he agitated for the establishment of an Indian territory west of the Mississippi River. In 1828 he was appointed a member of a commission to conduct a survey and aid the Indians in selecting new reservations in the proposed territory. During the following 10 years he was constantly in the wilderness area of the present states of Kansas, Nebraska, and Oklahoma, selecting and surveying locations for transplanted Indian tribes. In 1842 he became secretary and general agent of the American Indian Mission Association at Louisville, Ky., serving until his death. His published works include *Remarks on the Practicability of Indian Reform* (1827), and *A History of Baptist Indian Missions* (1840).

McCOY, Joseph Geating, American pioneer cattleman: b. Sangamon County, Ill., Dec. 21, 1837; d. Kansas City, Mo., Oct. 19, 1915. Beginning as a cattle farmer in Illinois, he purchased (1867) the township of Abilene, Kans., on the newly built Kansas Pacific Railway, as a shipping point for cattle from Texas. Here he constructed his own stockyards and shipping pens, and surveyed a trail from Corpus Christi, Texas, to Abilene, with pasturage and watering facilities. His plan to drive herds of cattle in the grazing season across the plains of the Indian Territory (now Oklahoma) to the railhead was at first ridiculed; but from September 1867 to the end of that year 35,000 head of beef cattle reached the railroad and were shipped east, and all in all it is estimated that 10 million cattle reached the market over this trail. McCoy's contract with the railroad was repudiated, and at the end of the second year of operation he had to bring suit to obtain some $200,000 due him in royalties. He collected the amount several years later, but in the interim the railroad had refused to renew the contract. He later established cattle drives to Cottonwood Falls and Wichita, Kans., and helped open the famous Chisholm Trail. He was the author of the important source book *Historic Sketches of the Cattle Trade of the West and Southwest* (1874, reprinted 1951).

McCOY, Samuel Duff, American journalist and author: b. Burlington, Iowa, April 17, 1882; d. Uniondale, N.Y., April 7, 1964. He attended Princeton University from 1901 to 1903 and went into newspaper work in Washington, D.C. In February 1923 he was employed by the New York *World* to investigate the conditions of convict labor in the lumber and road camps of Florida. In a long series of articles which received nationwide publicity, McCoy exposed the abuses of the state's penal system. This resulted in a recodification of the state's laws regarding the corporal punishment of prisoners, and other important reforms. The following year, the New York *World* was awarded the Pulitzer Prize for its "disinterested and meritorious public service" in publishing the articles. McCoy was appointed assistant director of the Federal Writers' Project in New York State to compile the first official guide of New York City in 1935. He is the author of several mystery stories, a novel, and a book of poetry. His other works include *This Man Adams, the Man Who Never Died* (1928); with Hall Roosevelt, *Odyssey of an American Family, an Account of the Roosevelts . . ., from 1613 to 1938* (1939); and *Nor Death Dismay: a Record of Merchant Ships and Merchant Mariners in Time of War* (1944).

MacCRACKEN, mȧ-krăk′ĕn, **Henry Mitchell,** American Presbyterian clergyman and educator: b. Oxford, Ohio, Sept. 28, 1840; d. Orlando, Fla., Dec. 24, 1918. He was graduated from Miami University, Oxford, Ohio, in 1857, and studied at the United Presbyterian Theological Seminary in Xenia, Ohio, and at Princeton Theological Seminary in New Jersey. Ordained in 1863, he became minister of Westminster Church, Columbus, Ohio, and then of the First Presbyterian Church at Toledo (1868–1881). In 1881 he was named chancellor of the Western University of Pennsylvania (now the University of Pittsburgh), and three years later professor of philosophy at the University of the City of New York (now New York University), where he became vice chancellor in 1885 and chancellor in 1891. Under his administration the university grew and prospered, and became one of the leaders in the field of American education. Before he resigned in 1910, a graduate school had been established, schools of commerce and pedagogy were founded, and the medical school had been united with the Bellevue Hospital Medical College. At University Heights, the Hall of Fame (q.v.), a memorial to famous Americans, was erected in 1900. Besides numerous articles on education, religion, and philosophy, his works include *The Lives of the Leaders of Our Church Universal*, 3 vols. (1879); *Cities and Universities* (1882); *The Metropolitan University* (1892); *Educational Progress in the United States* (1893); *The Three Essentials* (1901); *The Hall of Fame* (1901); and *Urgent Eastern Questions* (1913). His sons, Henry Noble MacCracken (q.v.) and John Henry MacCracken, both became presidents of American colleges.

Consult MacCracken, John Henry, and others, *Henry Mitchell MacCracken: in Memoriam* (New York 1923).

MacCRACKEN, Henry Noble, American educator: b. Toledo, Ohio, Nov. 19, 1880. Son of Henry Mitchell MacCracken (q.v.), he graduated from New York University in 1900 and taught English at the Syrian Protestant College in Beirut, Lebanon, until 1903. He then served as instructor and assistant professor of English at the Sheffield Scientific School, Yale University (1908–1913), and professor of English at Smith College (1913–1915). In the latter year he was named president of Vassar College, Poughkeepsie, N.Y., where he was active until his retirement in 1946. MacCracken published editions of the works of Geoffrey Chaucer (1913) and John Lydgate (2 vols., 1912, 1934), and various collections of the plays of William Shakespeare. His other works include the autobiographical *Family on Gramercy Park* (1949); *Hickory Limb* (1950); and *Old Dutchess Forever! the Story of an American County* (1957).

JOHN HENRY MacCRACKEN (1875–1948), his brother, was president of Westminster College, Fulton, Mo. (1899–1903), professor of politics at New York University (1903–1915), and president of Lafayette College, Easton, Pa. (1915–1926). He was the author of *College and Commonwealth* (1920).

McCRADY, má-krā'dĭ, **Edward,** American Confederate officer and historian: b. Charleston, S.C., April 8, 1833; d. there, Nov. 1, 1903. Admitted to the bar in 1855, he joined the Confederate Army as a captain at the beginning of the Civil War, rose to the rank of lieutenant colonel, and was badly wounded at the Second Battle of Bull Run (Manassas) on Aug. 30, 1862. After the war he returned to the practice of law in Charleston. As a member of the state legislature (1880–1890) he drafted the South Carolina Election and Registration Law (1882), known as the "Eight Ballot Box Law," designed to disfranchise the Negroes. In 1883 he published an essay on education in colonial South Carolina, and from this time on devoted much of his energy to research on the early history of the state. The result was a monumental study, *The History of South Carolina . . .*, in four parts, covering the years 1670–1783. Despite its rather narrow state-loyalty bias, it remains a reputable source book in the field.

McCRAE, má-krā', **John,** Canadian physician and poet: b. Guelph, Ontario, Canada, Nov. 30, 1872; d. Boulogne, France, Jan. 28, 1918. Educated at the University of Toronto, he received his medical degree in 1898, and in 1899–1900 served as a junior officer in the South African War. On his return to Canada, he was connected as a pathologist with McGill University and various hospitals in Montreal. When World War I began, he volunteered to serve as a medical officer with the first Canadian troops to go to France, and from 1915 was in charge of the medical department at the general hospital in Boulogne, attaining the rank of lieutenant colonel. He died there of pneumonia. McCrae is best remembered for the poem, *In Flanders Fields*, written in a dressing station at Ypres and published anonymously in *Punch* on Dec. 8, 1915. His verses were collected and published after the war under the title *In Flanders Fields, and Other Poems* (1919).

THOMAS McCRAE (1870–1935), his brother, was associate professor of medicine (1906–1912) at Johns Hopkins University, and from 1912 until his death professor of medicine at Jefferson Medical College in Philadelphia, Pa. A close associate of Sir William Osler, he collaborated with him on *Cancer of the Stomach* (1900) and brought out posthumous revised editions of Osler's *Modern Medicine* and *Principles and Practice of Medicine*.

McCRARY, má-krâr'ĭ, **George Washington,** American jurist and legislator: b. Evansville, Ind., Aug. 29, 1835; d. St. Joseph, Mo., June 23, 1890. Brought up in the present area of Van Buren County, Iowa, he studied law at Keokuk and was admitted to the bar in 1856. In 1861–1865 he served in the state Senate, and from 1869 to 1877 was a member of Congress, where as chairman of the committee on canals and railroads he sponsored legislation foreshadowing the later creation (1887) of the Interstate Commerce Commission. He also played a leading part in the formation of the Electoral Commission which settled the disputed Hayes-Tilden election of 1876; and when Rutherford B. Hayes was confirmed as president, he appointed McCrary secretary of war. In this post (1877–1879), he supported Hayes' civil service reform measures, effected the withdrawal of federal troops from the South, and sent the army into action in the railroad strike of 1877. After his retirement from the cabinet, he served as justice of the United States Circuit Court, 8th Circuit, until 1884, when he took up residence in Kansas City, Mo., as general counsel for the Atchison, Topeka & Santa Fe Railroad. He was the author of *A Treatise on the American Law of Elections* (1875) and *McCrary's Reports*, 5 vols. (1881–84), a summary of the cases tried in his court.

McCREA, má-krā', **Jane,** American Revolutionary heroine: b. Bedminster (now Lamington), N.J., c. 1753; d. near Fort Edward, N.Y., July 27, 1777. She resided with her brother near Fort Edward, north of Troy, N.Y., at the beginning of the Revolutionary War. While she was visiting friends, news arrived of Gen. John Burgoyne's advance in the Saratoga campaign, alarming the populace. Her brother sent for her, but a band of Indians, allies of Burgoyne, descended upon the household and captured the inmates. Jane McCrea's scalped body was later found by a roadside. The Indians claimed that she was accidentally killed by a random shot from a pursuing American detachment. Some authorities credit the story that her suitor, David Jones, a lieutenant in Burgoyne's army, had hired the Indian Duluth to escort her to his camp, where they were to be married, and that she was killed in a controversy with another Indian party under Wyandot Panther. Her exact manner of death remains a mystery. Burgoyne, shocked by the incident, called a council of his Indian chiefs to reprove them, and many of them deserted shortly thereafter. The massacre roused the countryside and stimulated recruiting, hundreds volunteering for service against the British, who were subsequently defeated at Saratoga in October.

Consult Wilson, David, *The Life of Jane McCrea, with an Account of Burgoyne's Expedition in 1777* (New

York 1853); Hill, William H., *Old Fort Edward Before 1800* (Rutland, Vt., 1929); *New York State Guide* (New York 1935).

McCREIGHT, mà-krāt', **John Foster,** first prime minister of British Columbia: b. Caledon, County Tyrone, Ireland, 1827; d. Hastings, Sussex, England, Nov. 18, 1913. He was educated at Trinity College and King's Inns, Dublin, and called to the Irish bar in 1852. After a period at Melbourne, Australia, he settled in Victoria, British Columbia, in 1860 and engaged in the practice of law. When the province entered the Dominion of Canada on July 20, 1871, he was appointed its first prime minister and attorney general. He served until the end of 1872, and in 1880 was appointed a justice of the Supreme Court of British Columbia, retiring in 1897.

McCULLERS, mà-kŭl'ērz, **Carson** (nee SMITH), American novelist and playwright: b. Columbus, Ga., Feb. 19, 1917; d. Nyack, N.Y., Sept. 29, 1967. She attended writing classes at Columbia and New York Universities, New York City (1935–1936), and in 1940 published her first novel, *The Heart Is a Lonely Hunter,* which was an immediate critical and popular success. Set in a Southern mill town, it tells the life stories of a group of "lower depths" characters in their own words, as they talk to a deaf-mute. *Reflections in a Golden Eye* (1941) was less effective, but *The Member of the Wedding* (1946) surpassed the success even of her first book. A sensitive story of a summer in the life of a motherless adolescent girl, it was dramatized in 1950 by Mrs. McCullers and won the Critics Award as the year's best play. *The Ballad of the Sad Café* (1951), a novelette, was dramatized by Edward Albee and produced in 1963. Other works by Mrs. McCullers included a play, *The Square Root of Wonderful,* produced in 1957, and a novel, *Clock Without Hands* (1961).

McCULLOCH, mà-kŭl'ŭk, **Ben,** American scout and Indian fighter: b. Rutherford County, Tenn., Nov. 11, 1811; d. Pea Ridge, Ark., March 7, 1862. Having followed his Tennessee neighbor Davy Crockett to Texas in 1836, he took part in the Battle of San Jacinto (April 21) in the Texan War of Independence, and settled in Gonzales as a surveyor. In the Mexican War (1846–1848) he commanded a company of Texas Rangers, did important work as a scout, and fought in the battles of Monterey and Buena Vista, and in the siege of Mexico City. He went to California in the gold rush of 1849, but returned to Texas three years later and served as United States marshal for the coastal district from 1853 to 1859. During the Civil War he joined the Confederate Army as brigadier general in command of the troops in Arkansas, and under Gen. Sterling Price defeated Gen. Nathaniel Lyon at Wilson's Creek, Mo., on Aug. 10, 1861. He later commanded a brigade at the Battle of Pea Ridge (Elkhorn Tavern), Ark., where he was killed by a sharpshooter.

McCULLOCH, Hugh, American banker and public official: b. Kennebunk, Me., Dec. 7, 1808; d. Prince George's County, Md., May 24, 1895. He attended Bowdoin College, studied law in Boston, and in 1833 moved to Fort Wayne, Ind., where two years later he became cashier and manager of the Fort Wayne branch of the State Bank of Indiana. He held this post until 1856, when he was named president of the bank. Although he had opposed the National Bank Act of 1863, establishing federal control over the issue of currency by the state banks, McCulloch was invited by Secretary of the Treasury Salmon P. Chase to assume the new office of federal comptroller of the currency, which the act had created, to carry out its provisions. McCulloch served until 1865, when Abraham Lincoln, at the beginning of his second term as president, named him secretary of the treasury. As secretary, he labored to reduce the Civil War debt and advocated the retirement of legal tender (greenback) notes and a return to specie payments—a program which Congress adopted on a limited scale in 1866 and abandoned again in 1868. Retiring from office at the end of Andrew Johnson's administration (1869), he became a partner in Jay Cooke's banking house and ran the branch in London, England, during the 1870's. He served as secretary of the treasury again in the last six months of President Chester A. Arthur's administration (1884–1885).

McCULLOCH, mà-kŭl'ŭk, **John Ramsay,** Scottish economist and statistician: b. Withorn, Wigtownshire, Scotland, March 1, 1789; d. London, England, Nov. 11, 1864. Educated at Edinburgh University, he edited the *Scotsman* (1818–1820) and began to write on economic subjects for the *Edinburgh Review,* to which he contributed regularly until 1837. In 1820 he went to London, where for some years he conducted lecture courses and discussion groups on economic theory. He was professor of political economy at University College, London, from its foundation in 1828 until 1832, and comptroller of the stationery office from 1838 until his death.

A friend and disciple of David Ricardo (q.v.), McCulloch published *The Principles of Political Economy* . . . (1825), a popularized exposition of Ricardo's ideas, which went through five editions in his lifetime and was reprinted for many years after. His *Essay on the Circumstances Which Determine the Rate of Wages* . . . (1826) was an influential presentation of the wages-fund theory, that the total amount of wages available to labor is fixed in relation to the amount of capital invested; but he also favored labor unions as a force guaranteeing labor its maximum share. In the *Treatise on the Principles, Practice, and History of Commerce* (1831) he appeared as an outspoken advocate of free trade. Of most lasting importance was his pioneering work in the fields of statistics and economic history, represented by such publications as *A Dictionary* . . . *of Commerce and Commercial Navigation* (1832), *A Descriptive and Statistical Account of the British Empire* (1837), and *The Literature of Political Economy* (1845).

McCUMBER, mà-kŭm'bēr, **Porter James,** American legislator: b. Crete, Will County, Ill., Feb. 3, 1858; d. Washington, D.C., May 18, 1933. Brought up near Rochester, Minn., he took a law degree at the University of Michigan in 1880 and began to practice at Wahpeton in the Dakota Territory. In 1899 he was chosen United States senator (Republican) from North Dakota, and served until 1923. McCumber was a leading advocate of pure food and drug legislation, adopted in 1906 (see PURE FOOD ACTS). In 1922, as chairman of the Senate Finance Committee, he sponsored the Fordney-McCumber Tariff with Representative Joseph W. Fordney, restoring the high protective rates of the Dingley (1897) and Payne-Aldrich (1909) acts on manufactured goods and extending protection to many farm products. In his last years, McCumber practiced law in Washington, D.C.

MacCUNN, mȧ-kŭn', **Hamish,** Scottish composer: b. Greenock, Scotland, March 22, 1868; d. London, Aug. 2, 1916. Was educated in Greenock and at the Royal College of Music, London, made his début in the musical world in 1887, and in 1888 became a junior professor of harmony in the Royal Academy of Music, which position he resigned in 1894. As a composer he attained high rank; his productions are rich in melody, and his command of the orchestra is remarkable. His work is typically Scottish in character and in choice of subject. Among the more important of his numerous works are overtures, etc., *The Land of the Mountain and the Flood; Chior Mhor; The Dowie Dens o' Yarrow; The Ship o' the Fiend;* dramatic cantatas, *Lord Ullin's Daughter; Bonny Kilmeny; Lay of the Last Minstrel,* and the operas, *Jeannie Deans* and *Diarmid.*

MacCURDY, mȧ-kûr'dĭ, **George Grant,** American anthropologist: b. Warrensburg, Mo., April 17, 1863; d. Greenwood Township, N.J., Nov. 15, 1947. He graduated from Harvard College in 1893 and took his Ph.D. at Yale in 1905. MacCurdy taught anthropology at Yale from 1898, and was curator of the university's anthropological collections from 1902 until his retirement in 1931. In the field of physical anthropology, he did studies of the cranial characteristics of the inhabitants of New Britain in the Bismarck Archipelago and of skeletal remains from Peru. His publications included *Antiquity of Man in Europe* (1910); *Human Origins* (2 vols., 1924); and *The Coming of Man* (1932).

McCURDY, **James Frederick,** Canadian Orientalist: b. Chatham, New Brunswick, Canada, Feb. 18, 1847; d. Toronto, March 31, 1935. He was educated at the University of New Brunswick and at Princeton Theological Seminary. He was assistant professor in Oriental languages at Princeton, 1873–1882; and Stone lecturer there in 1885–1886. In 1886 he was appointed lecturer in University College of Toronto, and from 1888–1914 was professor of Oriental languages in that college. Among his works are *Aryo-Semitic Speech* (1881); *History, Prophecy and the Monuments* (3 vols., 1894–1901); *Life and Work of D. J. Macdonnell* (1897); an original commentary on Haggai, and various translations for the American edition of *Lange's Commentary.*

McCURDY, **Richard Aldrich,** American capitalist: b. New York City, Jan. 29, 1835; d. Morristown, N. J., March 6, 1916. He was graduated at Harvard University in 1856, and engaged in the practice of law in New York. He became attorney for the Mutual Life Insurance Company in 1860, vice president in 1865 and was president in 1885–1906. The investigation of his company in 1905 revealed mismanagement and gross extravagance, particularly in the matter of salaries for the officials. He resigned and retired in 1906.

McCUTCHEON, mȧ-kŭch'ŭn, **George Barr,** American novelist: b. near Lafayette, Ind., July 26, 1866; d. New York, N.Y., Oct. 23, 1928. He attended Purdue University in Lafayette but left, before graduating, to become a reporter on the Lafayette *Morning Journal,* at a salary of $6 a week. Prior to that time he had written a series of dialect letters for the *Sunday Leader,* of Lafayette, under the caption *Waddleton Mail,* published in that paper in 1890. After three years on the *Journal,* he became city editor of the Lafayette *Daily Courier,* serving in that capacity until June 1902, when newspaper work was abandoned for novel writing alone. While with the *Courier,* he contributed to that newspaper a serial story entitled *The Wired End,* which has never been published in book form; and also contributed short stories to various magazines during these years. He went to Chicago to reside in 1902, and in July 1910 removed to New York City.

His novels include *Graustark* (1901), dramatised; *Castle Craneycrow* (1902); *Brewster's Millions* (1903), dramatised; *The Sherrods* (1903); *The Day of the Dog* (1904), novelette; *Beverly of Graustark* (1904), dramatised; *The Purple Parasol* (1905), novelette; *Nedra* (1905); *Cowardice Court* (1906), novelette; *Jane Cable* (1906); *The Flyers* (1906), dramatised, novelette; *The Daughter of Anderson Crow* (1907); *The Husbands of Edith* (1908), novelette, dramatized; *The Man from Brodney's* (1908); *Truxton King* (1909), dramatized; *A Fool and His Money* (1913); *Black is White* (1914); *The Prince of Graustark* (1914); *Mr. Bingle* (1915); *The Light That Lies* (1917); *Shot with Crimson* (1918); *Sherry* (1918); *Anderson Crow, Detective* (1920); *Yollopp* (1922); *Oliver October* (1923); *East of the Setting Sun* (1924); *Romeo in Moon Village* (1925).

McCUTCHEON, **John Tinney,** American cartoonist: b. near South Raub, Ind., May 6, 1870; d. Lake Forest, Ill., June 10, 1949. He was graduated from Purdue University in 1889 and was connected with the leading newspapers of Chicago from 1889, his work as a cartoonist becoming famous in the campaign of 1896. He started around the world on dispatch boat *McCulloch* in January 1898; was on board that vessel, during the war with Spain, in the Battle of Manila Bay 1898. In 1899 he made a tour of special service in India, Burma, Siam, and Cochinchina and later in northern China, Korea, and Japan, returning to the Philippines during the fall campaign there. He followed the various campaigns on the islands until April 1899 when he was sent to the Transvaal. He joined the Boers in the interest of his paper and furnished political cartoons for the Chicago *Record* during the campaign of 1900. In 1909–1910 he visited Africa, the while contributing articles and cartoons for the Chicago *Sunday Tribune.* He went to Mexico as special correspondent in 1914; was with the Belgian and German armies in the autumn of the same year, and in France, Salonika and the Balkans in 1915–1916. He has published *Stories of Filipino Warfare* (1900); *Cartoons by McCutcheon* (1903); *Bird Centre Cartoons* (1904); *The Mysterious Stranger and Other Cartoons* (1905); *Congressman Pumphrey the People's Friend* (1907); *In Africa* (1910); *T. R. in Cartoons* (1910); *Dawson '11—Fortune Hunter* (1912); *An Heir at Large.* In 1931 he was awarded a Pulitzer Prize for the excellence of his cartoons.

McDANNALD, măk-dăn"ld, **Alexander H.,** American editor and author: b. Warm Springs, Va., Sept. 20, 1877; d. Delray Beach, Fla., Dec. 18, 1957. Educated at the Virginia Polytechnic Institute and the University of Virginia (B.L., 1898), he began his career as a journalist. He became a reporter for the Baltimore *News* in 1906 and transferred to the Baltimore *Evening Sun* in 1910. On the latter paper he served as political editor from 1912 until 1919, when he joined the staff of THE ENCYCLOPEDIA AMERICANA as managing editor. The following year he was made editor in chief, a position he held for nearly 30 years. He supervised the complete revision of the encyclopedia in the early 1920's, when it was expanded from 20 to 30 volumes. The first distinctively American reference work (originally published 1829–33), THE ENCYCLOPEDIA AMERICANA, under McDannald's guidance, grew in scope, prestige, and circulation to become one of the world's foremost reference sets. In 1923 he established THE AMERICANA ANNUAL, which he also edited until he retired in 1948. He was the author of *Across Germany* (1914); *Costs of the World War* (1920); and *The Storied Hudson* (1927). Other reference works which he edited were *Hayward's Key to Knowledge* (9 vols., 1929–30); and *The Concise Encyclopedia* (8 vols., 1937).

McDIARMID, măk-dĭr'mĭd, **Hugh** (pseudonym of CHRISTOPHER MURRAY GRIEVE), Scottish poet: b. Langholm, Scotland, Aug. 11, 1892. Educated at the University of Edinburgh, he was a founder of the Scottish Nationalist Party and a leading advocate of independence for Scotland. He became a prominent figure in the Scottish literary revival of the 1920's, writing on the culture and politics of Scotland in poetry and prose. Written in a language which is his own rich blend of native Scots and English, his poetry reveals his great gifts as a satirist and lyrist. He is credited with re-creating a native Scottish literature and is considered the greatest poet his country has produced since Robert Burns (1759–1796). Among his collections of verse are *Sangschaw* (1925); *A Drunk Man Looks at the Thistle* (1926); *Scots Unbound* (1932); *Kist of Whistles* (1947); and *Selected Poems* (1954). A few of his prose works are *At the Sign of the Thistle* (1934), a collection of essays; *What Lenin Has Meant to Scotland* (1935), which shows his strong leftist sympathies; and *Scottish Eccentrics* (1936). The argumentativeness which is a defect of much of his prose and some of his poetry is not found in his excellent travel books, such as *The Islands of Scotland* (1939). Published in 1943, his *Lucky Poet* was announced as the first volume of an autobiographical trilogy.

MACDONALD, măk-dŏn"ld, **Angus Lewis,** Canadian political leader: b. Dunvegan, Nova Scotia, Aug. 10, 1890; d. Halifax, April 13, 1954. Educated at the universities of St. Francis Xavier (B.A., 1914) and Dalhousie (LL.B., 1921), he was admitted to the bar in 1921. He then taught law at Dalhousie from 1922 to 1929. Entering politics, he became leader of the provincial Liberal Party in 1930. In the 1933 elections he led the party to victory, won a seat in the provincial legislature, and became premier of Nova Scotia. Re-elected in 1937, he was active in initiating old-age pensions and improving highways and schools. In 1940, Macdonald resigned as premier to become Canada's first minister of national defense for naval services and to enter the federal House of Commons. Supervising the expansion of the Canadian Navy from a few ships and about 2,000 men to a powerful wartime fighting force, he was called "the father of the Royal Canadian Navy." He resigned from the cabinet in 1945 and returned to Nova Scotia, where he again served as premier until his death in 1954.

MacDONALD, Betty (nee ANNE ELIZABETH CAMPBELL BARD), American author: b. Boulder, Colo., March 26, 1908; d. Seattle, Wash., Feb. 7, 1958. Educated in public schools and the University of Washington, she worked for federal government agencies from 1931 until her marriage to Donald C. MacDonald in 1942. She then began to write and became famous with the publication of her first book, *The Egg and I* (1945). It was a very amusing account of her difficulties in managing an isolated chicken ranch with Robert E. Heskett, her first husband, whom she married in 1927 and divorced in 1931. Her crisp style, optimism, and good humor had wide appeal, and over a million copies of the book were quickly sold. In a similar humorous vein were *The Plague and I* (1948), describing her convalescence in a tuberculosis sanitarium; *Anybody Can Do Anything* (1950), about job hunting during the depression; and *Onions in the Stew* (1955). She also wrote children's books, such as *Nancy and Plum* (1952) and the Mrs. Piggle-Wiggle series (1947–1957).

McDONALD, Eugene Francis, Jr., American businessman and explorer: b. Syracuse, N.Y., March 11, 1890; d. Chicago, Ill., May 15, 1958. In 1923 he formed the Zenith Radio Corporation, of which he became president and board chairman, and organized the National Association of Broadcasters. His major contribution in the field of communications was the development of new uses for radio. He provided Donald B. MacMillan with short-wave equipment for his Arctic expedition of 1923 and accompanied him to the Arctic in 1925, when they made radio contact with a United States Navy unit 12,000 miles away. This feat caused short-wave radio to become an integral part of naval communications. He led archaeological expeditions to Isle Royale, Lake Superior (1928); the Galápagos Islands (1929); and Georgian Bay, Lake Huron (1930). Under his supervision Zenith made many electronic advances and developed air-driven generators, automatic tuners, and low-priced hearing aids and radio sets.

MACDONALD, Flora, Scottish Jacobite heroine: b. Milton, South Uist, Scotland, 1722; d. Kingsburgh, March 5, 1790. When she was quite young, her father died, and her mother was abducted. Later she was given a home by Lady Margaret and Sir Alexander Macdonald, who provided her with more education than was usual for girls at that time. She was visiting at Benbecula, when Prince Charles Edward Stuart (q.v.) was forced to flee after the defeat of the Jacobites at Culloden Moor in 1746. Returning to her stepfather's house at Skye, she agreed to include the prince in her party disguised as one of her maidservants. When it was discovered that Flora had helped him to escape, she was imprisoned in the Tower of London, but she was soon afterward permitted to live outside the prison, although under charge of a jailer. The Indemnity Act of 1747 secured her complete liberty. She was married to Allan Macdonald in 1750. In 1774 they emigrated to North America and settled in Fayetteville, N.C. Her husband served in the British Army in the Revolutionary War and was taken prisoner. Flora returned alone to Scotland in 1779 and was later rejoined by her husband. Dr. Samuel Johnson, whose account of Flora's adventures was recorded by James Boswell, found her "a woman of soft features, gentle manners, and elegant presence."

Consult MacGregor, Alexander, *Life of Flora Macdonald*, 5th ed. (Stirling 1932).

MACDONALD, George, Scottish novelist and poet: b. Huntly, Aberdeenshire, Scotland, Dec. 10, 1824; d. Ashtead, Surrey, England, Sept. 18, 1905. He was educated at King's College, Aberdeen University, graduating in 1845, and prepared for the Congregational ministry at Highbury College, London. He was ordained in 1850 and preached at Arundel, Sussex, for three years, resigning owing to ill health. He moved to Manchester and later to London, devoting himself to lecturing, preaching, and, above all, writing. His first book, a dramatic poem *Within and Without,* was published in 1855. Macdonald's numerous works include poetry, religious writings, fairy tales, and novels which portray the life of the Scottish countryside with sympathy, understanding, and realism. The best known of his novels are *David Elginbrod* (1863); *Robert Falconer* (1868); and *Castle Warlock* (1882). Among his religious works *The Miracles of Our Lord* (1886) was well received. His stories for children are considered classics and have been reprinted many times. They include *At the Back of the North Wind* (1871); *The Princess and the Goblin* (1872); and the *Light Princess* (1905). His *Poetical Works* appeared in two volumes in 1893 (new ed. 1911).

Consult Macdonald, Greville, *George Macdonald and His Wife* (New York 1924).

MACDONALD, Sir Hector Archibald, British soldier: b. near Dingwall, Ross and Cromarty County, Scotland, April 13, 1853; d. Paris, France, March 25, 1903. The youngest son of a crofter mason, he enlisted as a private in the 92d Gordon Highlanders in 1870 and rose rapidly to high military position. He first saw active service in the Second Afghan War of 1879 and won the popular sobriquet of "Fighting Mac" for his prowess and bravery in the field. In 1880 he was with Lord Roberts (see ROBERTS OF KANDAHAR, PRETORIA, AND WATERFORD, 1st Earl) on his march from Kabul to the relief of Kandahar. Returning home from India, he disembarked at Natal and took part in subduing the revolt of the Transvaal Boers, 1880–1881. In 1883, posted to Egypt, he participated in the Upper Nile expedition of 1885 in command of a garrison at Asyut. Commissioned a captain, he served with distinction in the indecisive Sudan campaign of 1888–1891 and in the latter year was promoted to the rank of major. During the reconquest of the Sudan by Gen. Lord Kitchener (see KITCHENER, HORATIO HERBERT), 1896–1898, he commanded a brigade of Egyptian troops in the capture of Dongola in 1896; and at the annihilation of Khalifa Abdullah's army at Omdurman in 1898 his brilliant tactics and maneuvers outwitted a strong flank attack. Macdonald returned to England a popular hero and, brevetted a colonel, he was appointed an aide-de-camp to Queen Victoria. In 1899 he was stationed in India and in December of the same year he was called to South Africa to command the Highland Brigade with the rank of major general. Under Lord Roberts he distinguished himself in the South African War, preparing the way for the relief of Kimberley by capturing Koodoesberg in 1900. He engaged in other campaigns and was present at the surrender of Gen. Piet Arnoldus Cronje at Paardeberg. Macdonald was created a knight in 1900; received command of the Belgaum district, southern India, in 1901; and in 1902 accepted command of the troops in Ceylon. Early in 1903 he returned to London to answer charges of improper conduct and committed suicide in a Paris hotel. A memorial tower, overlooking his birthplace, was erected at Dingwall in 1907.

MACDONALD, mȧk-dô-nȧl', **Jacques Étienne Joseph Alexandre,** DUKE OF TARANTO, marshal and peer of France: b. Sancerre, near Sedan, France, Nov. 17, 1765; d. Courcelles, near Guise, Sept. 24, 1840. The son of a Scottish Jacobite, who had followed James II to France, and a near relative of Flora Macdonald, he entered the army about 1784. He distinguished himself in the French Revolutionary and Napoleonic wars. In 1797 he was made a general of a division in the army which captured Rome and overran the Kingdom of Naples. He became governor of the Roman Republic in 1798 and aided in the founding of the short-lived Parthenopean Republic (q.v.) in 1799. In 1805 his lost favor with Napoleon for his support of Jean Victor Moreau, but, restored in 1809, was given command of the army in Italy. He immediately marched north, joined forces with Napoleon, and crushed the Austrian center at the Battle of Wagram, July 5–6, 1809. Napoleon made him a marshal of France on the battlefield and later created him duke of Taranto. He served in the Peninsular War in Spain in 1810, commanded the left wing of the Grand Army in the invasion of Russia in 1812, and was defeated by the Prussians at Katzbach (Kocaba) in 1813. He was one of two marshals selected by Napoleon to deliver his abdication to the Allies in 1814 and he also signed the Treaty of Fontainebleau, April 11, 1814. At the Restoration (q.v.) of Louis XVIII, May 3, 1814, he was created a peer of France, remaining loyal to the throne during the Hundred Days. He became grand chancellor of the Legion of Honor in 1815 and a major general of the royal bodyguard in 1816. He retired from active service in 1830.

MacDONALD, mȧk-dŏn″ld, **James Ramsay,** British prime minister and statesman: b. Lossiemouth, Morayshire, Scotland, Oct. 12, 1866; d. aboard the *Reina del Pacifico* in mid-Atlantic, Nov. 9, 1937. Reared in a two-roomed "but and ben" by his grandmother and his unwed mother, he attended the parish school at Drainie until 15 years of age. He moved to Bristol in 1885, and later to London, where after a period of unemployment he obtained a secretaryship to Thomas Lough, a politician.

His early interest in social reform led him to join the Social Democratic Federation in 1885 and the Fabian Society (q.v.) in the following year. In 1894 he applied for membership in the newly organized Independent Labour Party, founded the year before by James Keir Hardie (q.v.). He soon became one of its leaders and served as secretary and subsequently treasurer of the Labour Representation Committee from 1900 to 1924. This committee, formed to obtain greater labor participation in politics, evolved in 1906 into the British Labour Party, which chose MacDonald as the chairman of its parliamentary group in 1911.

From 1901 to 1904, MacDonald was a member of the London County Council. In the general elections of 1906 and 1910 he was elected to Parliament from Leicester. As the leader of the party, he opposed Great Britain's entry into World War I and resigned his chairmanship on Aug. 5, 1914. However, he loyally supported the war effort and the wartime coalition government of David Lloyd George.

MacDonald was defeated by a small majority in the by-elections of 1918 and 1921. In 1922, with the rising reaction against Lloyd George's policies, he was returned to Parliament by a comfortable margin. Invited to form a government after the general election of 1923, he became prime minister and secretary of state for foreign affairs in the first Labour government of Great Britain, Jan. 23, 1924. In the following October the Conservatives were returned to power, largely owing to the publication, a few days before the election, of the alleged Zinoviev letter.

In 1929 the Labour Party was once more in power, for the first time with a preponderant majority, and MacDonald again assumed the premiership. Faced with a growing deficit, he pressed for economies sufficient to balance the budget, including a reduction in unemployment insurance. The cabinet resigned in protest on Aug. 24, 1931, and on the next day MacDonald was again invited to form a new government.

The National Coalition Cabinet was formed on Aug. 25, 1931, containing the leaders of the Conservative and Liberal parties, with MacDonald as prime minister. He was immediately denounced by his followers and was asked to resign. Vindicated in the general election of October 1931, he remained at the head of the coalition government for four years, during which Britain made an impressive recovery from the depression.

On June 7, 1935, MacDonald resigned his premiership because of failing health, but accepted the post of lord president of the council in Stanley Baldwin's cabinet. He died suddenly on a holiday voyage to South America.

An author of note, his publications include *What I Saw in South Africa* (1903); *Socialism and Government* (1909); *The Government of India* (1919); *Parliament and Democracy* (1919); *Socialism: Critical and Constructive* (1924); and *American Speeches* (1930). The expanded tribute to his deceased wife *Margaret Ethel MacDonald: A Memoir* (1912) is somewhat autobiographical.

Consult Elton, Godfrey E., *Life of James Ramsay MacDonald (1866–1919)* (New York 1939); and Sacks, Benjamin, *J. Ramsay MacDonald in Thought and Action; An Architect for a Better World* (Albuquerque 1953).

MacDONALD, James Wilson Alexander, American sculptor: b. Steubenville, Ohio, Aug. 25, 1824; d. Yonkers, N.Y., Aug. 14, 1908. He studied under the painter Alfred Waugh in St. Louis, moving to New York City after the Civil War. Among his numerous works are statues of *General George Armstrong Custer* at West Point, N.Y., and of the poet *Fitz-Greene Halleck* in Central Park, New York City.

MACDONALD, Sir John Alexander, Canadian statesman: b. Glasgow, Scotland, Jan. 11, 1815; d. Ottawa, Ontario, Canada, June 6, 1891. At five years of age he emigrated with his parents to Kingston, Ontario, Canada. He was educated at country schools, and at the Royal Grammar School in Kingston. In 1830 he was articled to a Kingston lawyer and six years later he was admitted to the bar.

Macdonald's professional abilities were quickly recognized, and in 1844 he was elected from Kingston to the Legislative Assembly of the Province of Canada, a united province formed in 1841 by the union of Upper Canada and Lower Canada, and thenceforward, almost continuously until his death, represented Kingston in the Canadian Parliament. In 1847, with only three years of political experience, Macdonald accepted the portfolio of receiver general and became a minister of the crown. In 1854 he became attorney general for Upper Canada; in 1857 he was prime minister; from 1858 to 1862 he served successively as postmaster general and as attorney general for Upper Canada.

Macdonald proposed a general federation, which, among other things, would provide more effectively for British North American defense and would settle the question of the future government of the Hudson's Bay Company's territories. In 1864 were held two conferences, one at Prince Edward Island and the other at Quebec, and a plan for a federal union of all British North America was elaborated. At both of these conferences Macdonald played a most influential part.

In 1867 the British North America Act, based on the Quebec resolutions and passed by the British Parliament, created the Dominion of Canada; and Macdonald became its first prime minister. The acquisition of the Hudson's Bay Company's territories, the creation of the Province of Manitoba in 1870, the entrance of British Columbia into confederation in 1871 and of Prince Edward Island in 1873—all of which were accomplished by Macdonald's government—enlarged the original union to continental dimensions. The first attempt at a Pacific railway ended in his discredit by the so-called Pacific Scandal in 1873; but in 1878 he regained the prime ministership, which he held until his death, and aided in the completion of the Canadian Pacific Railway in 1885.

Macdonald believed firmly in Canadian autonomy and in the plural conception of the Empire-Commonwealth which has prevailed in modern times. He was convinced, however, that for Canada the task of surviving as a separate nation in a continent dominated by the United States was more important and more difficult than that of winning complete and formal sovereignty inside the empire. He tried repeatedly to negotiate a broad reciprocal trade agreement with the United States and in the election of 1891 he successfully defeated the Liberal proposal of unrestricted reciprocity or commercial union with the neighbor to the south. He was made a knight commander of the Order of the Bath in 1867 and in 1884 he was awarded the Grand Cross of the Bath.

D. G. CREIGHTON,
Author of "John A. Macdonald, The Young Politician" and "John A. Macdonald, The Old Chieftain."

MACDONALD, John Sandfield, Canadian statesman: b. St. Raphael, Quebec, Canada, Dec. 12,

1812; d. Cornwall, Ontario, June 1, 1872. He was self-educated and admitted to the bar in 1840, practicing successfully in Cornwall. In 1841 he was elected to the Canadian Parliament as member from Cornwall. He was solicitor general in 1849–1851; and was speaker of Parliament in 1852–1854. During the brief Brown-Dorion administration in 1858 he served as attorney general, and was premier from 1862–1864. He was the first premier of the Province of Ontario, 1867–1871.

MACDONALD, Lucy Maud Montgomery, Canadian novelist: b. Clifton, Prince Edward Island, Canada, 1874; d. Toronto, Ontario, April 24, 1942. She was authoress of *Anne of Green Gables* (1908), which was described by Mark Twain as "the sweetest creation of child life ever written"; *Anne of Avonlea* (1909); *Anne of the Island* (1915); *The Watchman* (1916); *The Blue Castle* (1926); and *Jane of Lantern Hill* (1937).

MacDONALD, Malcolm, British statesman: b. Lossiemouth, Scotland, Aug. 17, 1901. He attended Bedales School, Petersfield, England, and afterward was graduated from Queen's College, Oxford. A Laborite, he entered the British House of Commons in 1928 representing the Bassetlaw Division of Nottingham. Two years later he entered the British ministry as parliamentary under secretary of state for Dominion affairs, and in 1935 he became a member of the Cabinet as secretary of state for the colonies—a post which he again held in 1938–1940. Meanwhile, in 1935–1938 he served as secretary of state for Dominion affairs, and again held the post in 1938–1939. He was made a privy councilor in 1935. In 1941 he was chosen to succeed Sir Gerald Campbell as British high commissioner to Canada, a position he held until 1946, when he was appointed governor general of Malaya and British Borneo. He has been commissioner general for the United Kingdom in southeast Asia since 1948.

MacDONALD, William, American journalist and historian: b. Providence, R. I., July 31, 1863; d. New York, New York, Dec. 15, 1938. He was graduated at Harvard in 1892, and was professor of history and economics at Worcester Polytechnic Institute, 1892–1893. He was professor of history and political science at Bowdoin, 1893–1901; was professor of history at Brown University, 1901–1917; on the editorial staff of *The Nation*, 1918–1931; and lectured on American history at Yale, 1924–1926.

He edited *Select Documents Illustrative of the History of the United States* (1898); *Johnston's High School History of the United States* (1901); *Documentary Source Book of American History* (1908); *Parkman's Oregon Trail* (1911). He was author of *Jacksonian Democracy* (1905); *A New Constitution for America* (1923); *The Intellectual Worker and his Work* (1923); *Three Centuries of American Democracy* (1923); and *The Menace of Recovery* (1934).

MACDONALD, Sir William Christopher, Canadian capitalist and philanthropist: b. Glenaladale, Prince Edward Island, Canada, 1831; d. Montreal, June 9, 1917. He early engaged in business in Montreal and achieved a large financial success as importer, merchant, and tobacco manufacturer. He was a director of the Bank of Montreal, chancellor of McGill University to which he contributed large gifts, and governor of Montreal General Hospital. He also served as president of the Legislative Council of Prince Edward Island. He founded the Macdonald Agricultural College, and made large gifts to the normal school at Ste. Anne de Bellevue, Quebec, and to the Ontario Agricultural College. He was knighted in 1898.

McDONALD, borough, Pennsylvania, in Allegheny and Washington counties; on the Mountour and Pennsylvania railroads; 18 miles southwest of Pittsburgh. McDonald is a coal mining and oil field community; a large coal washing plant is located near by. Pop. 3,141.

MacDONALD, Lake, lake, Australia, in the western part, 540 miles south of Wyndham. It is 12 miles wide and 20 miles long. During most seasons it is dry, but is surrounded with swamps.

MacDONELL, măk-dŏn'ĕl, **Alexander,** Canadian Roman Catholic prelate: b. Inverness, Scotland, July 7, 1762; d. Dumfries, Jan. 14, 1840. He was educated at the Scots College, Spain, entered the priesthood in 1787, and was for several years a missionary. He assisted in the organization of the Glengarry Fencibles and was their chaplain and in 1803 established for its disbanded members a colony in Glengarry County, Ontario, Canada. He also assisted in raising the Canadian regiment of Glengarry Fencibles, which was actively engaged in repelling the American invaders in the War of 1812–1814. In 1819 he was made vicar apostolic of Upper Canada and through his influence 48 parishes were established in Upper Canada. He was the first Roman Catholic bishop in Upper Canada, being consecrated bishop of Kingston, Feb. 14, 1826. He was called to the Legislative Council in 1831. He died in Scotland while on a mission to obtain funds for the founding of Regiopolis College, Kingston, and is buried in his episcopal city. His *Reminiscences* were published in 1888.

MacDONELL, măk-dŏn"l, **Arthur Anthony,** English Sanskrit scholar: b. Lochgarry, India, May 1, 1854; d. Dec. 28, 1930. He was educated at Göttingen and at Corpus Christi College, Oxford. He was teacher of German at Oxford, 1880–1899; and professor of Sanskrit in 1888–1899, after which he was Boden professor of Sanskrit there. He made a tour of study and research in India in 1907–1908, and in 1914 received the Campbell Memorial Gold Medal for Oriental Research from the Royal Asiatic Society of Bombay. He was keeper of the Indian Institute; and a fellow of Balliol College and of the Royal Danish Academy.

He was author of *Sanskrit-English Dictionary* (1892); *Vedic Mythology* (1897); *A History of Sanskrit Literature* (1900); *The Brhaddevatā,* translated and critically edited, 2 vols. (1904); *Vedic Grammar* (1910); *A Vedic Grammar for Students* (1916); and *India's Past . . .* (1927).

MacDONNELL, Antony Patrick, BARON MACDONNELL OF SWINFORD, British government administrator: b. March 7, 1844; d. London, England, June 9, 1925. He was educated at Queen's College, Galway, and entered the Indian Civil Service in 1865. He was appointed acting chief commissioner of Burma in 1889, chief commissioner of the Central Provinces in 1890, and acting lieutenant governor of Bengal in 1893. As lieutenant governor of the Northwestern Provinces and Oudh (1895–1901), he initiated legislation to benefit the agricultural workers and headed a commission which prepared an important report on famine relief. Recalled to England in 1902 to become undersecretary of state in Ireland, he served in that capacity until his resignation in 1908, in which year he was raised to the peerage.

MacDONNELL, Scot. măk-dŏ-nĕl', Ir. măk-dŏn'l, **Sorley Boy,** Scoto-Irish chieftain: b. probably in Dunanynie Castle, near Ballycastle, County Antrim, Ireland, c. 1505; d. there, 1590. The son of a Scottish laird, who had inherited a claim to the region known as the Glynns in Ireland, he was active in his clan's warfare against the MacQuillins, over whose territory, called the Route, he established his lordship. His powerful position made him the target of Queen Elizabeth I's diplomacy, which then aimed to create a rivalry between Sorley Boy and Shane O'Neill. He was defeated by the latter near Coleraine in 1564 and in the next year was captured and was held by the O'Neills until Shane was murdered by the MacDonnells in 1567. His subsequent activities provoked further English attempts to subdue him, and in 1575 most of his family and retainers were murdered on Rathlin Island at the instigation of Walter Devereux, the earl of Essex. After this, Sorley Boy captured Carrickfergus and strengthened his position by an alliance with Turlough Luineach O'Neill. In 1586, however, he submitted to the English, relinquished his claims to Ulster, and received both the rights of denization in the region where he was born and the constableship of Dunluce Castle.

MACDONOUGH, măk-dŏn'ŭ, **Thomas,** American naval officer: b. The Trap (now Macdonough), New Castle County, Del., Dec. 31, 1783; d. at sea, Nov. 10, 1825. After entering the navy in 1800, he served as a midshipman during the Barbary Wars on the *Constellation* and then on the *Philadelphia*. Before the capture of the latter frigate by the Moors (1803), he had been transferred to a captured Moorish vessel as second officer. Subsequently transferred to the *Enterprise,* commanded by Capt. Stephen Decatur, he participated in the latter's burning of the captured *Philadelphia* and the attack on Tripolitan gunboats (1804). In 1806 he returned to the United States to assist Capt. Isaac Hull in new naval construction and, as a lieutenant, later was assigned to further duties at sea.

Soon after the outbreak of the War of 1812, Macdonough was ordered to take command of the squadron on Lake Champlain. There he developed an effective fighting force in the face of many difficulties of logistics and personnel. In 1814 a powerful British fleet, in conjunction with the British Army, advanced toward Plattsburg where Macdonough's vessels were anchored. By skillful maneuvering, Macdonough finally forced the British to surrender, after having lost 57 men against British losses of over 100. This victory (Sept. 11, 1814), which was one of the most decisive of the war, forced the British retreat into Canada and earned for Macdonough many honors and a captaincy (1814). He subsequently served as commandant of the Portsmouth Navy Yard (1815–1818), as captain of the frigate *Guerrière* (1818–1820), and then the *Ohio* (1820–1824), and finally as commander of the Mediterranean squadron (1824).

MacDOUGAL, măk-dōō'găl, **Daniel Trembly,** American botanist: b. Liberty, Ind., March 16, 1865. Educated at De Pauw and Purdue universities and at Leipzig and Tübingen in Germany, he taught botany at the University of Minnesota (1893–1899) before moving to New York, where he was associated with the New York Botanical Garden (1899–1905). From 1905 to 1933 he was connected with the Carnegie Institution in Washington, D.C. He made important contributions to the physiology, heredity, and mutation of plants, studied cambial activity and growth in trees, and designed a dendrograph. His writings include *Botanical Features of North American Deserts* (1908); *Water-Balance of Succulent Plants* (1910); *Conditions of Parasitism in Plants* (1910); *Alterations in Heredity Induced by Ovarial Treatment* (1911); *Hydrostatic System of Trees* (1926); *Pneumatic System of Plants, Especially Trees* (1933); *Studies in Tree Growth by the Dendrographic Method* (1935); and *Tree Growth* (1938).

McDOUGALL, măk-dōō'găl, **Alexander,** American patriot and general: b. Islay, Inner Hebrides, Scotland, July or August 1732; d. New York, N.Y., June 9, 1786. When he was six years old, his parents brought him to North America and settled in New York City. McDougall, who had shown an early interest in seafaring, by 1756 had become the master of a British privateer, but in 1763 abandoned the sea for a business career in New York. One of the founders of the secret organization, Sons of Liberty, in New York, he gave voice (1769) to the growing resentment against British trade restrictions in a broadside addressed "to the Betrayed Inhabitants of the City and Colony of New York," which contained a bitter attack on the General Assembly and led to his imprisonment. His confinement lasted until 1771 and aroused considerable public opinion in his favor.

McDougall became one of the radical leaders in the New York Committee of Fifty-One and in the first and second Provincial congresses. During the American Revolution he took part in the battles of White Plains and Germantown and subsequently played, as major general, an important role in the defense of the Highlands of the Hudson, where he replaced Maj. Gen. Benedict Arnold as commander at West Point in 1780. In 1781 he declined an appointment as minister of marine but he continued his political activities as a member of the Continental Congress (1781–1782; 1784–1785) and as New York state senator (1783–1786).

McDOUGALL, Alexander, American inventor and shipbuilder: b. Port Ellen, Island of Islay, Inner Hebrides, Scotland, March 16, 1845; d. Duluth, Minn., May 23, 1923. When still a child, he immigrated with his parents to Nottawa, Ontario, Canada, where he worked as a farm hand and then as a blacksmith's apprentice before shipping as a deck hand on a vessel bound for Chicago, Ill., in 1861. By 1870 he was commanding a large lake ship and in the next year participated in the construction of three passenger ships for the Anchor Line. During the next 10 years he developed a radically new design (patented 1881) for Great Lakes freighters, the so-called whalebacks, many of which he constructed at the American Steel Barge Company in Duluth, Minn., and in Superior, Wis. Moving to the Pacific Northwest, he built the first steel-ship yard there (Everett, Wash.) in 1892 and later acquired shipbuilding enterprises in Collingwood, Ontario, and St. Louis, Mo. He also patented many inventions pertaining to ship construction, grain loading, and dredging; perfected a method of processing sand iron ores of the western Mesabi Range; and with his son designed a seagoing canal boat in 1914.

McDOUGALL, George Millward, Canadian missionary: b. Kingston, Upper Canada, 1820; d. in a snowstorm near Calgary, Alberta, Jan. 23, 1876. Educated at Victoria College, Cobourg, he became a Methodist missionary, settling at Garden River, near Sault Ste. Marie (1851–1860), and then at Rossville in the Hudson's Bay Company's territories. As a youth, he had learned the ways and the language of the Indians, and his subsequent missionary activities, together with those of his son, contributed much to the establishment of civilized communities in the Canadian West.

McDOUGALL, John, Canadian missionary: b. Owen Sound, Ontario, Canada, Dec. 27, 1842; d. Calgary, Alberta, Jan. 15, 1917. Son of the Reverend George Millward McDougall (q.v.), he was educated at Victoria University and was also a Methodist missionary (ordained 1874) among the Indians on the Canadian frontier. He assisted the government in negotiating treaties after its purchase of the Hudson Bay territories in 1869. His understanding of the Indians was particularly valuable during Riel's Risings (q.v.) of 1869–1870 and 1885. Among his writings on frontier life is the biography of his father *George Millward McDougall, the Pioneer, Patriot and Missionary* (1888). Other works include *Forest, Lake and Prairie* (1895), *In the Days of the Red River Rebellion* (1911), and *On Western Trails in the Early Seventies* (1911).

MacDOUGALL, Sir Patrick Leonard, British general: b. Boulogne, France, Aug. 10, 1819; d. Kingston Hill, Surrey, England, Nov. 28, 1894. Educated at the Military Academy in Edinburgh and the Royal Military College at Sandhurst, he served as regimental officer in Canada (1844–1854); as superintendent of the Royal Military College at Sandhurst (1854–1855, 1856–1858), and as adjutant general of the Canadian militia (1865–1869), which he organized with great effectiveness during the Fenian raid of 1866. From 1873 to 1878 he headed the Intelligence Branch of the British War Office and in the latter year was appointed commander of the Dominion forces in Canada. He returned to England in 1883 and retired two years later. Among his several writings in the field of military affairs and history was *The Theory of War: Illustrated by Numerous Examples from Military History* (1856); 2d ed., 1858), a widely used textbook.

McDOUGALL, William, English psychologist: b. Chadderton, Lancashire, England, June 22, 1871; d. Durham, N.C., Nov. 28, 1938. After graduation from Owens College, Manchester, in 1890 and from Cambridge University in 1894, he studied medicine in London for a few years. In 1898 he accompanied a group of anthropologists to the Torres Strait Islands, Australia, where he became deeply interested in psychological studies. After his return to Europe he studied at Göttingen, Germany, under Georg Elias Müller, who stimulated his interests in a career in psychology. After a brief experience (1902–1904) in London, where he founded a laboratory for experimental psychology, he was appointed Wilde reader in mental philosophy at Oxford University, a position which he held from 1904 to 1920. There, too, he established some laboratory work in experimental psychology.

In 1908, McDougall constructed one of the most important and influential sets of principles on social behavior that had appeared up to that date. His *Introduction to Social Psychology* (1908), brought him into attention as a major theorist in the field of psychology. He expounded in this book the views which he maintained throughout the rest of his life. He emphasized the irrational, instinctual drives which control human actions. Through the processes of evolution they comprise the unlearned determinants of behavior. Situations are perceived in certain ways because of these innate propensities, appropriate behavior is initiated, and a purposeful adjustment is effected. By reason of the evolutionary processes, the propensities in man and animals are purposive or teleological in nature. The strivings, therefore, are central in all behavior. Hence, he coined the phrase hormic psychology (Gr. *horme,* "purposeful striving") for his system of psychology.

McDougall went to Harvard University as professor of psychology in 1920. Like his eminent predecessor, William James, he was greatly interested in occult phenomena. He took the initiative in trying to combat prevalent mechanistic theories of psychology which were then popular in the United States. For his students he prepared textbooks which emphasized his purposeful, or teleological, views and which, he hoped, would disprove the validity of stimulus-response theories. His insistence upon instincts, or propensities, won few disciples in the United States. His enthusiasms for serious inquiries into occult phenomena were shared by few. Therefore, in 1927 he accepted a position at Duke University, where his zeal to develop his theories about the purposeful nature of behavior and to apply the methods of scientific research to what has become known as parapsychology received more encouragement than at Harvard.

McDougall's contributions to the basic theory of psychology were often misrepresented by his critics. In particular, his views about the primacy of instincts were expounded at a time when the concept was being derided. Professor Knight Dunlap, in an address to the American Psychological Association, in 1919, delivered what many thought to be the death blow to instincts. The controversies between McDougall and John Broadus Watson, the radical behaviorist, aroused much popular interest, with the prevalent opinion being that Watson had won the arguments. Later, however, a more dispassionate consideration of McDougall's theories established him as one of the eminent theoreticians in the history of modern psychology.

His writings include *Body and Mind* (1911); *Psychology: The Study of Behaviour* (1912); *An Outline of Psychology* (1923); *An Outline of Abnormal Psychology* (1926).

PHILIP L. HARRIMAN,
Bucknell University.

MacDOWELL, măk-dou′ĕl, **Edward Alexander,** American composer; b. New York, N.Y., Dec. 18, 1861; d. there, Jan. 23, 1908. He was the third son of Thomas MacDowell and his wife Frances Knapp. His father was of Scottish ancestry and his mother was of Irish descent. The boy's extraordinary talent for music was greatly encouraged by his father, a businessman, who himself had wanted to be a painter. Edward had his first lesson with the South American-born Juan Buitrago, a friend of the Brazilian pianist, Teresa Carreño. At 15, accompanied by his mother, he went to Paris, where, after a year with Antoine François Marmontel, he won a scholarship at the Conservatoire. He enrolled in 1877, becoming a fellow student of Claude Achille Debussy. In the summer of 1878 he left Paris for Germany and, following a short term at the Stuttgart Conservatory, entered Karl Heymann's class at the Frankfurt am Main Conservatory. Until this time MacDowell had intended to become a pianist, but, after studying composition with Joseph Joachim Raff, director of the Frankfurt Conservatory, he decided to become a composer. He wrote his *First Modern Suite* for piano and his First Piano Concerto and at Raff's suggestion played them for Franz Liszt. Liszt arranged that MacDowell play the *First Modern Suite* for the General Society of German Musicians and recommended both the suite and the concerto to the firm of Breitkopf and Härtel, which published them in 1883 and 1885, respectively.

By this time MacDowell had established himself in Germany as a piano teacher as well as a composer and in 1884 he married one of his pupils, Marian Nevins, an American. The couple lived first in Frankfurt and then in Wiesbaden. MacDowell continued to teach, to concertize, and to compose, and in Europe won recognition with his early orchestral works, *Hamlet and Ophelia* (1885), *Lancelot and Elaine* (1888), *The Saracens and The Lovely Alda* (1891), and the Second Piano Concerto (1890) for solo instrument and orchestra, as well as with several piano pieces that his friend Teresa Carreño was introducing in the United States. After Liszt had died in 1886 (four years after Raff's death), MacDowell decided to return to the United States. Settling in Boston in 1888, he continued his career of composing and teaching, and made extended concert tours. In 1896 he accepted an invitation from Seth Low, president of Columbia University, to take charge of its new department of music. At first he hoped that he might create a department at the university that would combine the fine arts in an integrated educational plan. During his absence on sabbatical leave in 1902–1903, however, the new president, Nicholas Murray Butler, reorganized the department. MacDowell did not agree with Butler's ideas; he felt that the president was concerned more with showy results than with quality in teaching. After a controversy that brought wide publicity and recriminations, MacDowell resigned early in 1904. For a year he engaged in private teaching, but in 1905 he was incapacitated by a mental disorder, to which he later succumbed.

For many years after his death MacDowell's place in American music was unique. He had been the first American to achieve in Europe recognition as a composer of individuality and to be accepted in his own country on his own merits. He had no sympathy with the movement to achieve nationalism self-consciously through using Indian or Negro folk themes. His music was essentially in the postromantic tradition, but the idiom which he developed was so much his own that his American temperament and environment inevitably became apparent in his works, particularly in those written after his return to the United States: the Second "Indian" Suite for orchestra (1897), and for piano the *Woodland Sketches* (1896), *Sea Pieces* (1898), and *New England Idyls* (1902).

By mid-20th century his Second Piano Concerto and his "Indian" Suite were still popular and several of the shorter piano pieces and songs were included in the standard repertoire of recitalists, but the place which MacDowell once held as the foremost American composer was being seriously challenged by several composers who came into prominence after his death. MacDowell lived in the United States when there were relatively few composers who had the necessary equipment and training to compete with the best foreign composers. In the 1950's there were dozens who could do so, with the result that MacDowell's pre-eminence waned—partially, no doubt, because of the popular 20th century reaction to the postromanticism that characterized his music.

MARIAN NEVINS MacDOWELL (1857–1956) survived her husband by 48 years. During that almost half century she devoted herself to the establishment and support of the MacDowell Colony at Peterboro, N.H., where she and her husband had their summer home. Together they had envisaged a colony where composers, writers, and artists could work undisturbed and enjoy each other's companionship. By the time of Mrs. MacDowell's death the colony had been used by 489 writers, 207 composers, and 170 artists and had produced 22 Pulitzer Prize-winning works.

Consult Gilman, Lawrence, *Edward MacDowell* (New York 1908); Currier, T. P., "MacDowell As I Knew Him,". *Musical Quarterly*, January 1915 (New York); Erskine, John, "MacDowell at Columbia," *Musical Quarterly*, October 1942 (New York); Howard, John Tasker, *Our American Music*, 3d ed. (New York, 1954).

JOHN TASKER HOWARD.

McDOWELL, măk-dou′ĕl, **Ephraim,** American surgeon: b. in Rockbridge County, Va., Nov. 11, 1771; d. Danville, Ky., June 25, 1830. The son of Samuel McDowell, who played an important role in the convention which drew up the Kentucky constitution, he was educated in medicine under Dr. Alexander Humphreys in Staunton, Va., and Dr. John Bell in Edinburgh, Scotland. From 1795 he lived in Danville, Ky., where he gained a considerable reputation as a surgeon and a teacher. A pioneer in abdominal surgery, he performed in 1809 an ovariotomy by abdominal section on Mrs. Jane Todd Crawford, who consented to the operation in spite of his warning that it had never before been performed without fatal results. This operation (the first ovariotomy in medical history) was successful, and the patient, who was 47 at the time, lived to be 78 years old. McDowell wrote little and the few published notices of his work were ignored at first; but by 1829 he had performed 12 ovariotomies as well as numerous other abdominal operations. Among his patients was James Knox Polk, later president of the United States. McDowell was one of the founders (1819) of Centre College in Danville.

Consult Schachner, August, *Ephraim McDowell, Father of Ovariotomy and Founder of Abdominal Surgery* (Philadelphia 1921).

McDOWELL, Irvin, American army officer: b. Columbus, Ohio, Oct. 15, 1818; d. San Francisco, Calif., May 4, 1885. After graduating from the United States Military Academy in 1838, he served successively with the 1st Artillery on the Canadian frontier, as a tactical officer at the Military Academy, and as aide-de-camp to Gen. John Ellis Wool during the Mexican War and in the Army of Occupation. He then filled various staff positions until the early days of the Civil War, when he was made brigadier general and was assigned command of the Army of the Potomac, which was just then being formed. Pressed by circumstances beyond his control to move against the Confederate Army at Manassas Junction, he suffered defeat at the First Battle of Bull Run (July 21, 1861) and his command was given to Gen. George Brinton McClellan (see BULL RUN, FIRST BATTLE OF). In 1862, McDowell was promoted to be major general of volunteers and was placed in command of the 1st Corps of the Army of the Potomac, from which his forces were separated later to become the Army of the Rappahannock and then, after the Peninsular campaign, the 3d Corps of Gen. John Pope's Army of Virginia. After the second Union disaster at Bull Run (Aug. 27-30, 1862), McDowell was again relieved of his command, but a subsequent inquiry cleared his name of any blame. Thereafter he held various territorial commands and in 1872 was promoted to be major general in the Regular Army. He retired in 1882 and then served as commissioner of parks in San Francisco until his death.

MacDOWELL, măk-dou'ĕl, **Katherine Sherwood** (nee BONNER, bŏn'ẽr; pen name SHERWOOD BONNER), American short-story writer and novelist: b. Holly Springs, Miss., Feb. 26, 1849; d. there, July 22, 1883. Her early years in the Old South and certain episodes of the Civil War left deep imprints in her memory and provided much of the material for her stories, the first of which was published in Nahum Capen's *Massachusetts Ploughman,* when she was only 15 years old. After her marriage to Edward MacDowell of Holly Springs (1871) had ended in a separation, she arranged for the care of their only child, a daughter, with relatives and moved to Boston, where she became a secretary to Nahum Capen and amanuensis to Henry Wadsworth Longfellow. Both men encouraged her literary efforts, and her stories began to appear in periodicals from 1875 onward. Her novel, *Like Unto Like,* dedicated to Longfellow, was published in 1878, and her earlier tales were subsequently collected into the volumes *Dialect Tales* (1883) and *Suwanee River Tales* (1884). Her later stories increased in realism, and the gloomy intensity of "The Volcanic Interlude," published in *Lippincott's Magazine* (April 1880), is reported to have caused a sharp decline in that journal's subscription.

MACDOWELL, Patrick, Irish sculptor: b. Belfast, Northern Ireland, Aug. 12, 1799; d. London, England, Dec. 9, 1870. After attending a boarding school in Belfast, he went to England and in 1813 was apprenticed to a London coachbuilder. On the subsequent bankruptcy of his master, he entered the house of the French sculptor Pierre François Chenu, where he gained his first experience in sketching and modeling. His designs and busts began to attract attention; he exhibited in the Royal Academy in 1822 and from 1826 to 1829, and was subsequently elected an associate (1841), and then a full, member (1846) of that institution. His best-known works are the marble statues of William Pitt and the earl of Chatham in St. Stephen's Hall in the Royal Palace of Westminster, London, and *Europa,* a large group symbolical of the nations of Europe, in the Albert Memorial in Hyde Park, London.

MACDUFF, măk-dŭf', THANE or EARL OF FIFE, a half or wholly mythical Scottish knight: fl. 1057. The chief sources for his life are the chronicles of John of Fordun (d. ?1384) and Andrew of Wyntoun (1350?–?1420), and the unreliable emendations of Hector Boece (1465?–1536) in his *Historia Scotorum* (*History of the Scots,* 1527). According to John of Fordun, he assisted Malcolm III MacDuncan, surnamed Canmore, to overthrow the usurper Macbeth, who had forced Macduff by threats to sail to England. From England he and Malcolm returned to defeat Macbeth at Lumphanan in Aberdeenshire on Aug. 15, 1057. In William Shakespeare's tragedy, *Macbeth* (1606; published 1623), which was based on the account in Raphael Holinshed's *Chronicles* (1578), Macduff was the slayer of Macbeth, but according to Wyntoun, Macbeth was killed by one of Macduff's knights. The Cross of Macduff, the traditional family sanctuary, stood near Newburgh in the pass leading to Strathearn, but was destroyed in 1559 by the Protestant reformers, who left only its pedestal.

McDUFFIE, măk-dŭf'ĭ, **George,** American public official and orator: b. probably in Columbia County, Ga., Aug. 10, 1790[1]; d. in Sumter District, S.C., March 11, 1851. Educated at South Carolina College, he was admitted to the South Carolina bar in 1814, a year after his graduation, and served two terms in the South Carolina legislature beginning in 1818. In 1821 he succeeded Eldred Simkins, his law partner, in the federal House of Representatives and began his legislative career as a nationalist, publishing a newspaper article in the same year directed against state sovereignty. But he soon began to support the interests of the states against the federal government. Aiming his attack against the protective tariff, he advocated a prohibitory tax on Northern goods in 1828 and in 1830 expounded his "forty-bale" theory by which he attempted to show that, because of the tariff, Southern planters were giving away 40 out of every 100 bales of cotton that they produced.

McDuffie soon became noted for his oratorical eloquence, which was often marred by excessive passion and extravagant phrases. His interests having led naturally to his ardent support of nullification, he served as a delegate to the South Carolina Nullification Convention in 1832. Two years later he resigned from Congress to become governor of South Carolina, in which office he served two terms before returning to private law practice. From 1842 to 1846 he filled the unexpired term of William Campbell Preston in the United States Senate, during which time, however, his influence in South Carolina politics waned as that of his colleague John Caldwell Calhoun increased. His later years were plagued by ill-health, due in some degree to an injury he suffered in a duel.

[1] The date of his birth is given by some authorities as 1788.

MACE, mās, a spice derived from the fruit of the nutmeg tree, *Myristica fragrans.* Structurally, mace is the fleshy, much-branched, scarlet aril which forms a covering over the hard, seed or nutmeg. The aril is removed from the fruit, flattened, and dried to form the yellowish-brown spice. Mace is delicately flavored and is chiefly used in making sauces, in baking, and in condiments.

The nutmeg tree is a native of the Moluccas or Spice Islands, but is now grown in the tropics of both hemispheres. The principal areas of supply are the East Indies and the British West Indies.

Mace and nutmeg were introduced into Europe during the 12th century. The Spice Islands were discovered in 1512 by the Portuguese, who subsequently held a monopoly over the distribution of these spices until the Dutch captured the islands early in the 17th century. The Dutch monopoly was broken when the French and the British smuggled trees into their own tropical possessions.

FRANK G. LIER.

MACE, in medieval times, a weapon of war. It was a heavy club surmounted by a spiked metal knob, which was effective against the strongest armor, and was used chiefly by knights. Maces were often borne by a royal bodyguard to protect the king in processions, but in the course of time (by the 14th century) they assumed more ceremonial functions and lost their warlike appearance, as they began to be decorated with jewels and precious metals.

The ceremonial mace, usually about four feet in length, survives today as a symbol of authority. Notable instances of its use are found in the sessions of the British House of Commons, where it is placed on the treasury table, and in the sessions of the United States House of Representatives, where it is placed to the right of the speaker. A mace is carried also in academic and ecclesiastical processions, particularly in English-speaking countries, and often before higher magistrates in Great Britain.

MACEDO, mà-sā'thōo, Joaquim Manoel de, Brazilian littérateur: b. Itaboraí, Brazil, June 24, 1820; d. Rio de Janeiro, April 11, 1882. Although trained in medicine, he taught history in the College of Dom Pedro in Rio de Janeiro and gained considerable renown for his sentimental novels of bourgeois family life, which were among the first novels by a native Brazilian. Among his fictional works are *A moreninha* (1844); *O moço louro* (1845); *Os dois amorces* (1848); *Vincentina* (1853); and many others. He also wrote plays and librettos for operettas and vaudevilles, and several poems, the best of which is *A nebulosa* (1857).

MACEDO, José Agostinho de, Portuguese poet and pamphleteer: b. Beja, Portugal, Sept. 11, 1761; d. Pedrouços, Oct. 2, 1831. Ousted from the Augustinian Order in 1792 for irregular behavior, he was subsequently reinstated in the church as a secular priest and commenced a career of preaching and writing. He had little talent for poetry, and his effort to outshine the great Luiz Vaz de Camões by writing an epic *O gama* (1811), later rewritten as *O oriente* (1814), was a failure. He nevertheless had a trenchant, biting wit, by which he served the cause of a reactionary governmental absolutism and regaled his gener-

ation with virulent criticisms of people living and dead. His poetry, which was mostly didactic and often revealed his interests in philosophy and science, enjoyed an ephemeral success. The chief value of his works lies in the useful picture which they present of the literary and political life of his times.

MACEDONIA, măs-ĕ-dō'nĭ-à, region in the south-central part of the Balkan Peninsula, bounded approximately by the Albanian Highlands to the west, the Shar Mountains to the north, the Rhodope Mountains to the east, and the Aegean Sea to the south. No precise limits can be set, since in modern times there has never been a Macedonian state uniting all the territories commonly called Macedonian. Since 1913, Macedonia has been divided between Greece, Yugoslavia (Serbia before 1918), and Bulgaria.

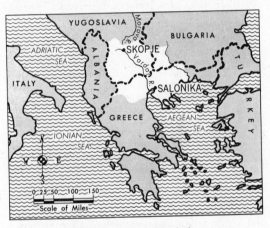

Location map of Macedonia.

Geography.—The country is mountainous, and good agricultural land is broken into a series of relatively small basins, linked by rivers that cut their path to the Aegean through a series of gorges. This broken topography is articulated into three major river systems: the Aliakmon in the west, the Vardar in the center, and the Strymon in the west.

Of the three, the Vardar is the largest and by far the most important. Its valley may be regarded as the spinal cord of Macedonia, for it offers a fairly easy route northward from the Aegean and links up, over a low watershed, with the valley of the northward-flowing Morava River. The two valleys thus constitute a north-south route connecting the Danube and central Europe with the Aegean. Migrant peoples, merchants, and imperial armies have followed this route from time immemorial.

A second and almost as important route traverses Macedonia from east to west. This is the ancient Roman *Via Egnatia,* connecting Durazzo on the Albanian coast with Constantinople (Istanbul) on the Bosporus. It crosses Macedonia by descending from Lake Ochrid in the northwest over a series of passes to Salonika and thence follows the coastal plain along the north Aegean.

The city of Salonika lies at the junction of these two routes, at the point where the Aegean Sea makes its most northerly encroachment upon the Balkan Peninsula. It is thus the natural capital of Macedonia, but in recent times its importance has suffered from the proximity of international boundaries that artificially restrict the city's hinterland.

Population.—The population of Macedonia is very mixed, in spite of drastic population exchanges that followed World War I. Under the Ottoman regime, prior to 1912, the Slav peasant majority was mingled with Turks, Greeks, Vlachs, Albanians, Jews, Gypsies, and half a dozen lesser groups. There was a tendency for linguistic and religious differences to coincide with occupational differentiation: the Turks, Greeks, and Jews followed mainly urban occupations, while the Slavs farmed and the Vlachs specialized in herding. There were, however, some districts where Greek or Turkish peasants tilled the soil.

After World War I this ethnic tangle was simplified by large-scale transfers of population. In the Greek portion of Macedonia, nearly all the Turks and Slavs were expelled between 1912 and 1927 and were replaced by Greeks coming from Asia Minor and Bulgaria. The German occupation in World War II led to the destruction of the Jewish communities in Salonika and other towns. The result was to make Greek Macedonia almost wholly Greek in population, but in Yugoslav Macedonia no such drastic reshuffle occurred, so that considerable communities of Turks and other minorities still survive there.

According to the Yugoslav census of 1961, the population of Yugoslavia Macedonia was 1,406,003 persons, while the 1961 Greek census enumerated 1,896,112 inhabitants for Greek Macedonia.

Natural Resources and Industry.—The land is primarily agricultural. Its isolated basins are often very fertile, especially when irrigated to supplement the scant summer rainfall. A large variety of crops are grown, including tobacco, cotton, sunflowers, vetch, alfalfa, grapes, melons, and other fruits and vegetables. Cereals, however, occupy by far the largest area—wheat, rye, and corn. The mountain sides offer rough pasture for sheep and goats, and in the plains a few cattle and water buffalo are kept.

The natural resources of Macedonia have not been much developed in times past, largely because of disturbed political conditions. Deposits of a large number of minerals are known to exist, including chrome, asbestos, lead, silver, antimony, sulphur, and lignite. A few mines are in operation, but mostly on a rather small scale.

Factories are unimportant, although there are some textile mills in Salonika and elsewhere. Handicrafts, often following very ancient methods, and small shops are more characteristic of Macedonian towns than larger scale enterprises.

Until World War II, village life was largely self-sufficient, and age-old peasant customs, folk songs, and costumes vigorously survived. After World War II, however, agricultural programs conducted by both the Greek and Yugoslav governments brought far-reaching changes, and it is doubtful whether the old peasant ways of life will long continue.

Culture.—In the 14th century, Macedonia was the seat of a notable art style, intermediate between Byzantine and Italian Renaissance painting. It is preserved today in the form of frescoes on the walls of a few monasteries. After the establishment of Turkish rule in the 15th century, however, only peasant arts and crafts flourished.

Under the Turks, Macedonia was as much divided religiously as it was linguistically. The majority was Orthodox Christian, but quarrels between followers of the Greek patriarchate in Constantinople and adherents of the Bulgarian exarchate (established 1870) were bitter and often violent. Since the division of Macedonia between Greece, Serbia, and Bulgaria (1913), the respective national churches have extended their jurisdiction over the orthodox within the territory that fell to each nation.

The educational systems in each part of Macedonia are supported and controlled by the state and generally follow European models. Schools rivaled the churches as means of inculcating national sentiments in the days when the Turks still ruled the country, and schools continue today to teach a very emphatic brand of patriotism, together with Communist doctrines in Yugoslav and Bulgarian Macedonia.

In Yugoslav Macedonia, since the establishment of Marshal Tito's Communist regime in 1945, there has been an effort to develop a distinct Macedonian literary language and culture, building upon local peasant tradition. In Greek Macedonia, on the other hand, the inhabitants have been assimilated into the larger body of Greek society and cannot be said to have any separate cultural existence. Thus, the University of Salonika is a provincial copy of the University of Athens, whereas the new University of Skoplje, established in 1946, at least attempts to use the Macedonian Slav dialect for its instruction.

Cultivation of Macedonian cultural autonomy in this fashion is the Yugoslav Communist answer to the "Macedonian question" which disturbed the peace of the Balkans from 1870 until 1949. During these years Macedonian Slavs attempted to win national independence through the Internal Macedonian Revolutionary Organization (IMRO), established in 1893, while agents of the Bulgarian, Greek, and Serbian nations attempted at the same time to win the loyalty of the population to their respective governments. Efforts by Ottoman authorities to keep control over the area, together with diplomatic and military intervention by the major powers of the world, added still further complications to the problem. Chronic guerrilla war began about 1895 and flickered fitfully thereafter until 1949. Whether the new cultural policy of the Yugoslav government will solve the Macedonian question permanently or international intrigue playing upon the discontents of the population will lead to further disorder cannot be foreseen. (For the cultural aspects of the ancient Macedonian Empire, see the appropriate sections in Greece and Middle East.)

History.—Macedonia was one of the earliest parts of Europe to be settled by farming populations, which came, perhaps, from Asia Minor. Sometime before 2000 B.C. a new stream of migration, coming from the north via the Morava-Vardar route, brought the Macedonians of classical times into the country. These people spoke a language related to Greek, and built a loosely consolidated kingdom on the periphery of the classical Greek world. Under King Philip II (r. 359–336 B.C.) and his son Alexander III the Great (r. 336–323 B.C.) the Macedonian Army overran first Greece itself and then the entire Persian Empire.

In the centuries that followed, the kingdom of Macedon remained one of the great powers of the ancient world, until the Romans defeated and at length annexed the country (146 B.C.). For an account of the forming of the Macedonian Empire and a map showing its greatest extent, see ALEXANDER THE GREAT. For its impact on the Mediterranean world see GREECE—*2. Ancient History and Culture: to 330 A.D.* (Greece under Macedonian Domination).

Thereafter Macedonia played a subordinate role in the Roman world. Flourishing Graeco-Roman cities rose along the major routes, and the Book of Acts in the New Testament records how St. Paul found converts in these cities. Three of St. Paul's Epistles were addressed to the new Christian communities of Macedonia, which thus ranks with Rome itself as the earliest seedbed of Christianity in Europe.

After the collapse of the Western Roman Empire (476 A.D.), Macedonia remained an important province of the Eastern Roman or Byzantine empire, but control of the area was frequently disputed between the Byzantine rulers and a long series of invaders, including Goths, Huns, Avars, Bulgars, and others. A decisive change came with the arrival of Slavic tribesmen, who infiltrated from the north between the 5th and 7th centuries. These invaders absorbed or expelled the earlier inhabitants and made most of Macedonia a Slavic land. When they began to build large states of their own, Macedonia played a critical role by virtue of its strategic lines of communication. Thus both the Second Bulgarian Empire of the 13th century and the Serb Empire of the 14th century found their major centers in Macedonia.

The Ottoman conquest of the Balkan-Peninsula also turned upon the ability of the Turks to seize Macedonia as a base from which to isolate and eventually to conquer Constantinople. Their decisive success came in 1389, when Sultan Murad I defeated the Serb armies at Kosovo, just to the north of Macedonia. Thereafter the Serb principalities became tributary to the Ottoman Turks and Macedonia came under direct Turkish administration. Considerable numbers of Muslims settled in the area. Some of these immigrated from Asia Minor, while others were local converts from Christianity. Most of these Muslims were assimilated to the ruling nation and came to be counted as Turks. The great majority of the inhabitants, however, remained faithful to their Christian faith and kept their Slavic, Greek, or Vlach speech. The Jewish community of Macedonia arrived after 1492, when the Turks offered a refuge to Jews evicted from Spain by Ferdinand and Isabella. This community soon became dominant in large-scale trade and maintained its Spanish dialect.

When, in the 19th century, ideas of nationalism began to penetrate the Balkan area from Europe, this tangle of languages and religions in Macedonia became an explosive mixture. The strategic and commercial importance of the routes that traverse Macedonia made this region a vital target for the rival national ambitions of Bulgars, Greeks, and Serbs. It was equally vital to the Turks, if they were to maintain themselves in Europe. In 1912 the Bulgar, Serb, and Greek armies combined to drive the Turks from Macedonia, but in the wake of their victory the allies quarreled over the division of the spoils; in a second Balkan war in 1913 the Serbs and the Greeks (together with the Rumanians and the Turks) defeated the Bulgars and excluded them from all but a small northeastern corner of Macedonia.

Since the Bulgars had been the most successful of the Balkan nationalities in their propaganda among the Macedonian Slavs, this result was a bitter disappointment to them. In both World Wars I and II, consequently, the Bulgars joined with Germany, on the strength of promises that Macedonia would revert to them. In fact, the Bulgars occupied most of Macedonia in 1915–1918 and again in 1941–1944, but each time the peace settlements forced them to surrender what they had won.

After World War II, Balkan Communists planned to unite Macedonia and to make it an autonomous republic in a Balkan federation. The guerrilla war in Greece, 1946–1949, was supported by the Communist governments of Bulgaria, Yugoslavia, and Albania at least partially with this end in view; but after the quarrel between Tito and the Russians (1948), the Yugoslavs ceased to help the Greek Communist insurgents, and by degrees Tito veered round to an alliance with the Greek government (1954). This alignment confirmed the partition of Macedonia between Yugoslavia and Greece—a partition first made in 1913.

Bibliography.—Books on Macedonia are nearly all violently partisan and often unreliable. For geography and resources see Jovan Cvijic, *La peninsule balkanique* (Paris 1918) and Werner Markert, *Osteuropa Handbuch: Jugoslawien* (Köln-Gräz 1954). For ancient times see Stanley Casson, *Macedonia, Thrace and Illyria* (London 1926). For more recent times see Henry N. Brailsford, *Macedonia* (London 1906) and Elizabeth Barker, *Macedonia, Its Place in Balkan Politics* (London 1950).

WILLIAM H. McNEILL,
Professor of History, University of Chicago.

MACEDONIAN, The. See UNITED STATES AND MACEDONIAN, BATTLE OF.

MACEDONIAN DYNASTY, a dynasty of the Byzantine Empire. See BYZANTINE EMPIRE; BASIL I; BASIL II; GREECE—*3. History of Byzantine Period: 330–1453.*

MACEDONIANS. See MACEDONIUS.

MACEDONIUS, măs-ê-dō'nĭ-ŭs, Eastern Church prelate: d. about 362. One of the rival claimants to the see of Constantinople after the death of Eusebius of Nicomedia (c. 341), he seems to have held this office from about 342 until 360, when he was deposed by the Arian Council of Constantinople. He is the traditional founder of the Macedonians, also called Pneumatomachi, a Christian heretical sect, whose tenets, however, modern scholarship has not been able to trace to Macedonius himself.

MACEIO, mà-sā-ô' (formerly MAÇAYÓ), city, Brazil, capital of Alagoas State, located 130 miles south of Recife on a strip of land between the Atlantic Ocean and Lagoa do Norte, a shallow lagoon which serves as a port for seaplanes. Maceió has two airports and is connected by railroads with Recife to the north and Palmeira dos Índios in the interior. Its chief industries are textile milling, furniture making, food processing, sugar refining, distilling, and manufacture of soap and cigarettes. Sugar and cotton are exported. Pop. (1960) 153,305.

MACEO, mä-sā'ō, **Antonio,** Cuban patriot, b. Santiago de Cuba, July 14, 1848; d. near Mariel, Dec. 2, 1896. A distinguished general in the Ten Years' War (1868–1878) against Spain, Maceo refused to sign the Peace of El Zanjón and went abroad to seek support for the Cuban cause. In 1895 he returned to Cuba in another effort to win Cuba's independence, but was surrounded by a Spanish force and killed.

José Raphael Maceo (1846–1896), his brother, also played a conspicuous role in the Ten Years' War and the rebellion of 1895, but, like his brother, lost his life in the latter struggle.

MACERATA, mä-chä-rä′tä, city and commune, Italy, capital of the Province of Macertata, which extends east and southward from the Adriatic coast over an area of 1,071 square miles in the territory known as the Marches. Located on a hill between the Potenza and the Chienti rivers, the city of Macerata is a trading center and a bishopric for an agricultural region. Its chief manufactures are agricultural equipment, cotton textiles, cutlery, and macaroni.

The charter of Macerata dates from the 12th century and its medieval walls still stand. Other evidences of its flourishing past are the university, founded in 1290, and several palaces dating from the 16th and 17th centuries. Its cathedral was built in the 18th century. The city suffered much damage from air attacks during World War II. Pop. (1951) city 21,875; commune 31,514.

MacEWEN, măk-ū′ĕn, **Walter,** American artist: b. Chicago, Feb. 13, 1860; d. New York, March 20, 1943. He studied under Cormon and Tony Robert-Fleury in Paris, and lived much abroad. His work includes landscapes, portraits, decorative panels, and figure subjects, and is marked by excellent sense of line and strong feeling for color. He executed panels for the Liberal Arts Building at the Columbian Exposition, Chicago, and for the Congressional Library, Washington, and many of his paintings have been acquired by public galleries. Among them are *Sunday in Holland* (in the Luxembourg Museum, Paris), *An Ancestor* (Corcoran Gallery, Washington), and *Judgment of Paris* (Art Institute, Chicago).

MACEWEN, Sir **William,** Scottish surgeon: b. Rothesay, Scotland, June 22, 1848; d. Glasgow, March 22, 1924. He was educated at Glasgow University, and became regius professor of surgery there in 1892; president of the British Medical Association in 1922; knighted, 1902. He was noted as a pioneer in the surgery of the brain and spinal cord and in the field of bone grafting. Among his works are *Osteotomy* (1880); *Atlas of Head Sections* (1893); *Pyogenic Diseases of the Brain and Spinal Cord* (1893); and *The Growth of Bone* (1912).

MACFARREN, măk-făr′ĕn, Sir **George Alexander,** English composer: b. London, England, March 2, 1813; d. there, Oct. 31, 1887. Educated at the Royal Academy of Music, London, he became a professor of composition there in 1834 and in 1876 principal. In 1875 he had also been elected professor of music in Cambridge University. Among his compositions are the operas *The Devil's Opera* (1838), *Robin Hood* (1860), and the oratorios *St. John the Baptist* (1873) and *King David* (1883). He also wrote several books, notably *Rudiments of Harmony* (1860), which had 14 editions. He was knighted in 1883.

Walter Cecil Macfarren (1826–1905), his brother, was a distinguished pianist and taught that instrument at the Royal Academy of Music from 1846 to 1903.

MAC FLECKNOE, or A SATYR UPON THE TRUE-BLEW-PROTESTANT POET, T. S., a satire by John Dryden (q.v.), published in 1682 to ridicule Thomas Shadwell, who later replaced him as poet laureate (1689). Dryden here introduced the name of Richard Flecknoe (1600–?1678), who by the author is represented as an Irish priest famed for his dull verse, but who is described by Andrew Marvell as "an English priest at Rome." Flecknoe was disliked by Dryden because of the former's abuse of actors and his attacks on their morality or rather absence of it. The name served also as a stalking-horse from behind which Shadwell might be pilloried as the "adopted" son (Gaelic *Mac*) and heir of Flecknoe. The satire served Pope as model for his *Dunciad.* The authorship of *Mac Flecknoe,* long disputed and attributed to Dryden, was called in question in 1918 when there appeared a possibility that it might have been written by John Oldham, Dryden's friend. A manuscript of the latter's poems in the Bodleian Library contains *Mac Flecknoe,* but Dryden claimed authorship of the piece and his friend Oldham never did.

MacGAHAN, mà-găn′, **Januarius Aloysius,** American journalist: b. near New Lexington, Ohio, June 12, 1844; d. Istanbul, Turkey, June 9, 1878. He followed different callings in Western states, then went to Europe and studied law in Brussels. Upon the outbreak of the Franco-Prussian War in 1870 he went to the field as correspondent of the New York *Herald,* and was with Bourbaki's army. He visited Bordeaux and Lyon and his interviews with clerical, monarchical, and republican leaders attracted wide attention. He was the only newspaper correspondent in Paris during the whole period of the Commune and narrowly escaped death. In 1873, after heroic exertions, with extreme hardships, he reached the Russian army before Khiva, and sent to the *Herald* reports of the campaign which won for him high admiration both at home and in Europe, his account of the capitulation of the city being regarded as a masterpiece of military journalism. Returning to America, he went to Cuba to report on the *Virginius* affair, then to Spain, upon the Carlist uprising, where he spent 10 months with the army of Don Carlos, was captured by the Republicans, mistaken for a Carlist, condemned to death and saved by the intervention of the United States minister. He then went to England, and in 1875 accompanied the Arctic expedition on the *Pandora.* In 1876 he joined the Turkish Army, in the service of the London *Daily News,* and did memorable work in his description of the Bulgarian atrocities, his accounts standing approved before the world in face of all attempts to discredit them. On behalf of Bulgaria he appealed to Russia, was at the front in the Russo-Turkish War that followed, and was hailed as a chief instrument of Bulgaria's resulting independence. While nursing his friend Lieut. Francis V. Greene he contracted typhus which in a few days caused his death. In 1884 the Ohio legislature secured the removal of his body from its foreign grave to its final resting place at New Lexington. He wrote *Campaigning on the Oxus, and the Fall of Khiva* (1874); *Under the Northern Lights*

(1876), and *Turkish Atrocities in Bulgaria* (1876).

McGEE, mà-gē', **Thomas D'Arcy**, Irish-Canadian journalist and statesman: b. Carlingford, Ireland, April 13, 1825; d. Ottawa, Ontario, April 7, 1868. In 1842 he emigrated to the United States, but having attracted the notice of Daniel O'Connell, he went to London as a correspondent of the *Freeman's Journal* and, later, the *Nation,* an organ of the Young Ireland party. The failure of the revolt of his party caused him to seek refuge in the United States in 1848. McGee then founded and edited the New York *Nation* and, soon after, the *American Celt* at Boston. In 1857, however, having become converted to constitutional methods for the redress of Irish grievances, he went to Montreal where he edited *The New Era,* advocating the creation of a Canadian nation. He entered Parliament in 1857; was president of the council, 1862–1863; and minister of agriculture, 1864–1868; living to see the confederation which his eloquence and persuasiveness had done much to popularize. His opposition to the extremists of the Fenian Brotherhood is believed to have been the cause of his assassination. Among his works are *A History of the Irish Settlers in North America* (1851); *Speeches and Addresses, Chiefly on the Subject of the British American Union* (1865); and *A Popular History of Ireland,* 3 vols. (1862–1869).

McGEE, William John, American scientist: b. near Farley, Iowa, April 17, 1853; d. Washington, D.C., Sept. 4, 1912. He was self-educated, and from 1873 to 1875 surveyed land and practised in the courts He also improved several agricultural implements, some of which he patented. In 1877–1881 he made geologic and topographic surveys of northeastern Iowa, and for the United States Geological Survey he surveyed and mapped 300,000 square miles in the southeastern part of the country, and performed many other important services in the departments of geology, ethnology and anthropology. From 1893 to 1903 he was ethnologist in charge of the Bureau of American Ethnology. He was president of the American Anthropological Association, chief of the Department of Anthropology and Ethnology of the Louisiana Purchase Exposition and associate editor of the *National Geographic Magazine.* He wrote *Geology of Chesapeake Bay* (1888); *Pleistocene History of Northeastern Iowa* (1891); *The Lafayette Formation* (1891); *Potable Waters of the Eastern United States* (1894); *The Siouan Indians* (1897); *Primitive Trephining in Peru* (1897); *The Seri Indians* (1898); *Primitive Numbers* (1900); *Soil Erosion* (1911); *Wells and Subsoil Water* (1913), and many scientific memoirs.

McGIFFERT, mà-gĭf'ẽrt, **Arthur Cushman,** American theologian: b. Sauquoit, N. Y., March 4, 1861; d. Dobbs Ferry, N. Y., Feb. 25, 1933. He was graduated at the Western Reserve College in 1882, and at Union Theological Seminary in 1885, and continued his studies at the universities of Berlin and Marburg, Germany, and in France and Italy. In 1888–1890 he was instructor in church history at Lane Theological Seminary, Cincinnati, and professor there 1890–1893, in 1893–1927 he was professor of church history and in 1917–1926 president of Union Theological Seminary, New York. In 1897 he published *A History of Christianity in the Apostolic Age,* and because of criticism and threatened denominational disturbance, involving his possible trial for heresy, to which this book gave rise, he withdrew from the Presbyterian ministry, and later, while still retaining his professorship, joined the Congregational Church. His other publications include *Dialogue Between a Christian and a Jew* (doctor's thesis, 1888), and a translation of Eusebius' *Church History,* with prolegomena and notes (1890); *The Apostles' Creed* (1902); *Protestant Thought Before Kant* (1911); *Martin Luther, the Man and his Work* (1911); *The Rise of Modern Religious Ideas* (1915); *The God of the Early Christians* (1924); *A History of Christian Thought,* 2 vols. (1931–1932).

McGIFFIN, mà-gĭf'ĭn, **Philo Norton,** American naval officer: b. Washington County, Pa., Dec. 13, 1860; d. New York, Feb. 11, 1897. He was graduated in 1882 at the United States Naval Academy and was stationed in China, and at the outbreak of the war between China and France was permitted to resign from the United States Navy to enter the service of China. He established a naval academy at Weihaiwei, of which he had charge. When the Sino-Japanese War broke out he was placed in command of the *Chen Yuen,* and was the first American or European to command a modern warship in action. He was in command at the Battle of Yalu River, Sept. 17, 1894, in which action he was so severely injured that he afterward shot himself at a hospital in New York.

McGILL, mà-gĭl', **James,** Canadian philanthropist: b. Glasgow, Scotland, Oct. 6, 1744; d. Montreal, Dec. 12, 1813. He was educated in Glasgow and in 1770 moved to Canada, where he engaged in the northwest fur trade, afterward becoming a merchant in Montreal. McGill was a member of the Parliament of Lower Canada and held the rank of brigadier general in the War of 1812. He used much of his wealth in philanthropic work and at his death founded McGill University (q.v.) in Montreal.

McGILL UNIVERSITY, Montreal, Canada, founded through a bequest of the Honorable James McGill, a leading merchant and prominent citizen of Montreal who died in 1813 and in his will left money for a university "for the purpose of education and advancement of learning." In 1821 the university was established, by a royal charter granted by the crown of the United Kingdom, and to this day the governor general of Canada is ex officio the visitor of the university.

The McGill campus is situated in the heart of the great Canadian metropolis, with a compact group of buildings housing the various faculties and schools, the stadium, gymnasium-armory-swimming pool, libraries, laboratories and research institutes, and the adjacent Royal Victoria Hospital, one of the teaching hospitals of the university. Its first building was erected on the land given by James McGill which was a farm on the outskirts of the city, but in the intervening century and a half the city grew up around the university property, so that in 1950 the value of the buildings and grounds was close to $50,000,000. However, Macdonald College, on a separate campus twenty miles from Montreal, houses the faculty of agriculture, the school of household science and the school for teachers, and was provided and generously endowed in 1907 by another leading merchant and philanthropist of Montreal, Sir William Macdonald. This part of the university is a residential college which houses more than 800 students.

The campus in Montreal comprises Douglas Hall and Wilson Hall, men's residences, and the Royal Victoria College for women students. Actually, however, only a small proportion of the students of the university live in residence, the majority finding homes in the city.

Many generous benefactors have made possible the great development of this Canadian university, one of the few privately endowed institutions. Situated in the French Canadian Province of Quebec, it has not received any large measure of financial support from the provincial government.

In recent times, principals of McGill University have included Gen. Sir Arthur Currie, G.C.M.G., K.C.B., who had been the commander of the Canadian Army Corps in Europe in World War I, and who served as principal from 1920 to 1933; Mr. Lewis Williams Douglas, later American Ambassador at London, England, who served from 1937 to 1939, and Dr. F. Cyril James, a native of London, England, who was a professor in the Wharton School of Finance and Commerce at the University of Pennsylvania. Dr. James became principal of McGill University in 1940.

On the battlefields in the two world wars students and staff of the university made a notable contribution. There were 6,500 on active service, 272 were killed or died, 618 received military decorations, and 359 served with the United States Army and 151 in the United States Navy.

The faculties embrace arts and science, law, music, divinity, agriculture, medicine, dentistry, engineering; there are schools of commerce, architecture, physical education, social work, graduate nursing, physiotherapy and the library school. Between 1930 and 1950 the faculty of graduate studies and research saw its enrollment of students increase from 100 to over 700, many coming to this center of higher studies from the United States and other parts of the world. The faculty of medicine is known all over the world and receives over 2,000 applications each year from students who wish to pursue their medical studies at McGill, but the annual admissions are restricted to 100, owing to the shortage of the facilities for clinical teaching. Sir William Osler was for some years a professor at McGill, and the magnificent Osler Library in the Medical Building is presided over by his nephew, Dr. W. W. Francis. The three teaching hospitals of the university comprise the Royal Victoria Hospital, the Montreal General Hospital and the Children's Memorial Hospital.

The Neurological Institute which houses the university department of neurology and neurosurgery was founded in 1933 with financial assistance from the Rockefeller Foundation and has become a recognized world center for the study of brain and diseases of the nervous system. The Allan Memorial Institute of Psychiatry was similarly founded through a generous grant from the Rockefeller Foundation and provides for the study, treatment, and cure of psychiatric ailments. The Pathological Institute houses the departments of pathology and bacteriology. The faculty of engineering, which has sent its graduates into all corners of the earth, has about 1,500 students in the courses leading to degrees in various branches of engineering and in architecture. The Institute for Pulp and Paper Research, which is also on the McGill campus, is a joint undertaking of the federal government, the pulp and paper industry of Canada, and the university.

In many of its scientific departments McGill University is prominent. The laboratories of the departments of chemistry and physics occupy a high place, and played a significant role in wartime problems. Among the discoveries was the production of RDX, an explosive more powerful than TNT. The only cyclotron and radiation laboratory in Canada is at McGill, and a large corps of research workers engage on problems of nuclear physics. The Eaton Electronics Laboratory was opened in October 1950.

Important studies of the medical and biological departments during World War II included blood storage, the treatment of shock, the cure of motion sickness in aviation and, in the agricultural departments, many problems of nutrition, human and animal, are being solved.

The athletics facilities include the Percival Molson Stadium which has been enlarged to accommodate 23,000, and the Sir Arthur Currie Memorial Gymnasium-Armoury and War Memorial Hall and Swimming Pool.

The adult education program of the university embraces accountancy diploma courses, summer schools in French and geography and, for teachers, extension lectures, and a comprehensive program for rural adult education which began with the support of the Carnegie Corporation about 1930 and has become self-supporting.

To accommodate the record enrollment of students after the close of World War II, the university took over two former air force stations, one at Lachine, Que. and one at St. Johns, Que. Dawson College, as it became known, at St. Johns, at the height of its activity housed over 1,800 students and provided there complete courses of instruction and laboratories in the subjects of the first and second years of science, commerce and engineering, the regular university staff making the daily journey from nearby Montreal to give lectures there as well as on the Montreal campus. Owing to the graduations of veterans and the prospect of a return to normal numbers these two residences were closed by the university at the end of the 1949–1950 session.

Before the outbreak of World War II in 1939 McGill University enrolled approximately 3,000 students in the full-time courses leading to degrees and diplomas, but during the postwar era its registration increased to 8,500, half of whom were veterans who had returned from active service to academic studies under the government plan of subsidizing their education. In 1950 the enrollment was approximately 7,500 and there were only about 1,000 veterans left.

MACGILLICUDDY'S REEKS, mà-gĭl'ĭ-kŭd-ĭz rēks, mountain range, Ireland, located in County Kerry, extending for 13½ miles from the Lakes of Killarney on the east to Lough Carra on the west, and covering an area of 28 square miles. It is the loftiest mountain range in Ireland, culminating in Carrantuohill, 3,414 feet high.

McGILLIVRAY, mà-gĭl'ĭ-vrā, **Alexander,** chief of the Creek Indians: b. in Alabama about 1759; d. Pensacola, Fla., Feb. 17, 1793. His father was a Scottish merchant of good family and his mother a half-breed. He received a good education at Charleston, S.C.; was placed in a mercantile establishment in Savannah; but soon returned to the Creek country, where he became partner in a large trading house and rose to a high position among the Indians. After the death of his mother, a member of the ruling stock, he became chief of the Creeks, having received a call from a formal council, and styled himself Emperor of the Creek Nation. During the Revolution the McGillivrays, father and son, were zealous adherents of the royal cause, the former holding the rank of a colonel in the British service. After the war Alexander McGillivray, in behalf of the Creek confederacy, entered into an alliance with Spain, of which government he was made a commissary, with the rank and pay of colonel. In 1790 he was induced by President Washington to visit New York, where he eventually signed a treaty yielding certain disputed lands lying on the Oconee. He was also persuaded to withdraw from Spanish service and was rewarded with an appointment as agent for the United States, with the rank and pay of brigadier general.

McGILVARY, mà-gĭl'và-rē, **Evander Bradley,** American educator: b. Bangkok, Siam (Thailand), July 19, 1864; d. Madison, Wis., Sept. 11, 1953. Born of American missionary parents, he graduated from Davidson College in 1884 and received his Ph.D. in 1897 from the University of California. From 1891 to 1894 he was a translator for the Presbyterian Board of Foreign Missions in Siam, and he and his mother translated several New Testament books into the Lao dialect. In 1894 he joined the University of California faculty, leaving in 1899 to become Sage professor of ethics at Cornell. In 1905 he went to the University of Wisconsin where, until he retired in 1934, he was chairman of the Philosophy Department.

McGLYNN, mà-glĭn', **Edward,** American Roman Catholic clergyman: b. New York, N.Y., Sept. 27, 1837; d. Newburgh, Jan. 7, 1900. He was educated at the College of the Propaganda in Rome, and in 1866 was appointed pastor of St. Stephen's Church in New York City. He favored the education of children by the state rather than in parochial schools and in 1886 warmly supported the candidacy of Henry George for the mayoralty, thereby bringing upon himself the censure of the church for his political activities. He was summoned to Rome to exculpate himself, but refused to go, pleading his ill-health. Persisting in his refusal, he was excommunicated in 1887.

McGlynn was one of the founders of the Anti-Poverty Society and was its president. In 1892, after a hearing before the papal delegate, Msgr. Francesco Satolli, the ban of excommunication was removed, after the signing of a document drawn up by the apostolic delegate to the effect that McGlynn's economic views were not in conflict with the Catholic faith. He was in charge of St. Mary's parish in Newburgh, N.Y., at his death.

McGOVERN, mà-gŏv'ern, **John,** American author: b. Troy, N.Y., Feb. 18, 1850; d. Chicago, Ill., Dec. 17, 1917. He was connected for 16 years with the Chicago *Tribune,* and after 1880 was engaged in literary work and lecturing. His expert testimony won the suit brought against Edmond Rostand by Samuel E. Gross, who claimed priority of authorship in connection with *Cyrano de Bergerac,* and obtained a restraint against its presentation in the United States. Among his books are *The Empire of Information* (1880), *American Statesmen* (1898), *Famous Women of the World* (1898), and several novels.

McGRANERY, mà-grăn'ēr-ē, **James Patrick,** American public official: b. Philadelphia, Pa., July 8, 1895; d. Palm Beach, Fla., Dec. 23, 1962. After service in World War I, he graduated from Temple University Law School in 1928. He entered politics, was a member of the United States House of Representatives (1937–1943); assistant to the attorney general (1943–1946); federal district judge in Philadelphia (1946–1952); and United States attorney general succeeding James Howard McGrath (q.v.) in 1952. He dropped the special crime investigating juries called by McGrath and announced that the Department of Justice would take its own action against corruption in government departments. Numerous resignations, removals, and prosecutions followed. He resigned in January 1953, and resumed law practice in Philadelphia.

MacGRATH, mà-grăth', **Harold,** American novelist and journalist: b. Syracuse, N.Y., Sept. 4, 1871; d. there, Oct. 29, 1932. He was educated in Syracuse and began his career as a reporter on the Syracuse *Herald.* His first novel, *Arms and the Woman,* appeared in 1899 and was quickly followed by many other popular successes. He also contributed the early silent cinema serials *The Perils of Pauline* and *The Million Dollar Mystery.*

McGRATH, James Howard, American public official: b. Woonsocket, R.I., Nov. 28, 1903. He graduated from Boston University in 1929, and after serving as United States district attorney from 1934 to 1940, was governor of Rhode Island from 1940 to 1945. In 1946 he was elected to the United States Senate, and in 1949 was named United States attorney general by President Harry S. Truman. His term of office was a stormy one; charges of corruption in government departments were made, and in 1952 the president requested that McGrath carry out a cleanup. As a result of disagreements with Newbold Morris, a special investigator appointed by the president, McGrath resigned in April 1952.

McGRATH, Sir Patrick Thomas, Canadian journalist and statesman: b. St. John's Newfoundland, Dec. 16, 1868; d. there, June 14, 1929. He was educated locally in the Christian Brothers' School, and in 1889 turned to journalism. In 1894 he became Newfoundland correspondent for the London *Times,* a post he held for 35 years. He was twice president of the Legislative Council of Newfoundland, from 1915 to 1919 and from 1925 to 1929. He also assisted in the preparation of the colony's case concerning the French and American fisheries. He was honorary secretary of the Newfoundland Patriotic Fund and of the Newfoundland War Pensions

Board after 1914, and chairman of the Cost-of-Living Commission from 1917. Knighted in 1918, he was author of *From Ocean to Ocean . . .* (1911) and *Newfoundland in 1911* (1911), a history and guidebook.

McGRAW, må-grô', **John Joseph,** American baseball player and manager: b. Truxton, N.Y., April 7, 1873; d. New Rochelle, Feb. 25, 1934. He joined the Baltimore Orioles in 1891 as a third baseman, and was manager of the New York Giants (National League) from 1902 to 1932. His teams won 10 league pennants, a record which, 25 years after his retirement, was still unmatched by any other major league manager; he also won three World Series. McGraw, a strict disciplinarian and autocratic leader, was considered by many the game's keenest strategist. He was chosen one of the original members of the Baseball Hall of Fame at Cooperstown, N.Y.

Consult Graham, Frank, *McGraw of the Giants* (New York 1944); McGraw, Blanche, *The Real McGraw* (New York 1953).

McGREADY, må-grä'dĭ, **James,** American Presbyterian clergyman and revivalist: b. western Pennsylvania, c. 1758; d. Henderson County, Ky., February 1817. Educated for the ministry at Upper Buffalo and Canonsburg, Pa., he was licensed to preach in 1788 and became pastor of a church in Orange County, N.C., about 1790, removing to Logan County, Ky., in 1796. Here in 1797–1799 he began a revivalist movement which spread throughout the Western and Southern states, resulting in the Great Revival of 1800–1805. He is considered the originator of the outdoor camp meeting, lasting several days, which became a prominent feature of the American frontier. Another result of McGready's preaching was the formation of the schismatic Cumberland Presbyterian Church (1810), with which he refused, however, to associate himself. In 1811, he was sent as a preacher to establish churches in southern Indiana, where he remained until 1816. After his death his sermons were published as *The Posthumous Works of the Reverend and Pious M'Gready,* edited by James Smith, 2 vols. (1831–33).

Consult Cleveland, Catherine C., *The Great Revival in the West, 1797–1805* (Chicago 1916).

MacGREGOR, må-grĕg'ẽr, or **CAMP-BELL,** kăm'bĕl, **Robert** (known as ROB ROY), Scottish outlaw: bap. Buchanan parish, Stirlingshire, Scotland, March 7, 1671; d. Balquhidder, Perthshire, Dec. 28, 1734. Second son of Lt. Col. Donald MacGregor of Glengyle, he assumed the maternal name of Campbell to escape the proscription of the MacGregors by the Scottish Parliament. He received the nickname Rob Roy (Gaelic for Red Rob) because of his ruddy complexion and shock of dark red hair. Early in life he engaged in raising black cattle for the English market. To protect his herds from cattle raiders, he maintained a band of armed kinsmen, and for a tax levied on his neighbors, offered protection to them as well. James Graham, 1st duke of Montrose, advanced money to extend Rob Roy's business, but by 1711 he was in financial difficulties. He was declared a fraudulent bankrupt and outlaw, and his estates were seized by the duke. Rob Roy fled to his familiar Highlands and collected a band of followers to make open war on the duke. In 1722, through the intervention of John Campbell, 2d duke of Argyll, Rob Roy submitted to the authorities and was confined in Newgate. In 1727 he was sentenced to transportation to Barbados, but was pardoned. He spent his last years in Balquhidder, where he is buried. As a brave and romantic outlaw in the Robin Hood tradition, he is the chief figure in Sir Walter Scott's novel *Rob Roy* (q.v.).

Consult Frewin, Leslie R., *Legends of Rob Roy* (London 1954).

McGUFFEY, må-gŭf'ĭ, **William Holmes,** American educator: b. Washington County, Pa., Sept. 23, 1800; d. Charlottesville, Va., May 4, 1873. Graduated from Washington (now Washington and Jefferson) College, Washington, Pa., in 1826, he was professor of languages at Miami University, Oxford, Ohio, until 1836, when he was named president of Cincinnati College and then (1839) of Ohio University at Athens. From 1845 until his death he was professor of moral philosophy at the University of Virginia. McGuffey is famous for his series of six *Eclectic Readers* (1836–1857) for elementary schools, of which an estimated 122 million copies were sold.

Consult Minnich, Harvey C., *William Holmes McGuffey and His Readers* (New York 1936).

McGUIGAN, må-gwĭ'găn, **James Charles,** Canadian Roman Catholic prelate: b. Hunter River, Prince Edward Island, Canada, Nov. 26, 1894. Educated at St. Dunstan's University (A.B., 1914) in Charlottetown and at the Grand Seminary and Laval University (D.D., 1918) in Quebec, he was ordained a priest in 1918 and two years later went to Edmonton, Alberta, where he held various diocesan offices. In 1930 he was consecrated archbishop of Regina, Saskatchewan, and in December 1934 became fifth archbishop of Toronto. Invested cardinal in 1946, he was the first native English-speaking Canadian to be so honored. He has been a leader in promoting the expansion of Catholic education and social welfare measures in his diocese.

MACH, mäк, **Ernst,** Austrian physicist, psychologist, and philosopher: b. Turas, Moravia, Austria, Feb. 18, 1838; d. near Munich, Germany, Feb. 19, 1916. He took his doctor's degree in physics at the University of Vienna (1860) and in 1864 was appointed professor of mathematics at Graz. Three years later he became professor of physics at Prague, where he published his highly influential *Die Mechanik in ihrer Entwicklung, historisch-kritisch dargestellt* (1883; Eng. tr., *The Science of Mechanics,* 1893). In *Beiträge zur Analyse der Empfindungen* (1886; Eng. tr., *The Analysis of Sensations,* 1897), Mach considered the nature of sensations as ingredients in individual minds and, on the other hand, the starting point for physical science. In 1895 a chair in the philosophy of the inductive sciences was created for him at the University of Vienna, where he published in 1896 his *Principien der Wärmelehre* and his *Populärwissenschaftliche Vorlesungen* (Eng. tr., *Popular Scientific Lectures,* had already appeared in 1894). In 1898 he was crippled by a paralytic stroke, but managed to complete his most systematic philosophical work *Erkenntnis und Irrtum* (1905), which incorporated a set of essays he originally wrote for *The Monist* (1901–03). These were separately published in 1906 as *Space and Geometry.* His last important work, *Die Prinzipien der physikalischen Optik*, was published posthumously in 1921 (Eng. tr., *The Principles of Physical Optics*, 1925).

As a technical physicist, Mach's name is commemorated in the Mach numbers (see MACH NUMBER) used to measure air flow. He is best known, however, as a philosopher of science. Scientific statements, he argued, are no more than an economical way of summarizing our experiences, useful to us because they enable us rapidly to recall our past experience when we are confronted by unfamiliar situations. Any physical theory which refers to objects not reducible to sensory experiences must be rejected as metaphysical. Thus, for example, science must abandon such conceptions as absolute space and absolute time. The physicist can compare the duration of a process with the revolution of hands on a clock face but never with the progress of absolute time. This side of Mach's teaching had a considerable influence on Albert Einstein and, within philosophy, on American pragmatism and European logical positivism, which originated in Mach's old department at Vienna. Equally influential was his doctrine that both the human mind and physical objects are constructed out of what he called "elements," which from the point of view of psychology are sensations and from the point of view of physics the constituents of things. Thus there is no sharp gap between mind and matter; both have exactly the same ingredients. Similarly, all science is unified; physics and psychology consider precisely the same material although from different points of view. American "new realism," Bertrand Russell's "neutral monism," and Rudolf Carnap's "physicalism," all reveal the influence of Mach's teachings on this point.

Consult Henning, Hans, *Ernst Mach als Philosoph Physiker und Psycholog* (Leipzig 1915); Bouvier, Robert, *La pensée d'Ernst Mach* (Paris 1923); Weinberg, Carlton B., *Mach's Empirio-Pragmatism in Physical Science* (New York 1937); Frank, Philipp G., *Modern Science and Its Philosophy* (Cambridge, Mass., 1951); Passmore, John A., *A Hundred Years of Philosophy* (London 1957).

JOHN A. PASSMORE,
Professor of Philosophy in the Australian National University, Canberra.

MACH NUMBER, named after Ernst Mach (q.v.), a numerical value establishing the ratio between the speed of an object through a gas and the speed of sound through the gas. Indicated by a *machmeter* in modern high-speed aircraft, this value determines whether the speed of the aircraft is subsonic ($<$ Mach 1), transonic (approximately equal to Mach 1), or supersonic ($>$ Mach 1). The reciprocal of the Mach number, or the ratio of the speed of sound to the speed of the aircraft, also yields the sine of the angle between the axis of the aircraft (or missile) and the envelope of the *Mach shock wave* produced by its supersonic flight. This angle is a critical function in aerodynamics. See also AERODYNAMICS—*5. Compressibility.*

FERGUS J. WOOD.

MACHADO Y MORALES, mä-chä'thō ê mô-rä'läs, **Gerardo,** Cuban statesman: b. Santa Clara, Cuba, Sept. 29, 1871; d. Miami Beach, Fla., March 29, 1939. He fought in the Cuban Revolution against Spain (1895–1898), serving also as mayor of Santa Clara, and in 1906 supported the revolt of the Liberal Party, led by José Miguel Gómez, who became president in 1909. In 1916, Machado took part in the Liberals' uprising against President Mario García Menocal, and in 1924 he was elected president of Cuba on the Liberal Party ticket. His first term of office was marked by progressive administrative reforms, public works, and an effort to promote native Cuban industry, ending its dependence on the United States. In 1928, however, he secured a constitutional amendment increasing the presidential term to six years, and after his re-election, set up a dictatorial regime. This led to open rebellion, and Machado had to flee (1933). See also CUBA—*10. History* (Republic of Cuba).

MACHAERODONTINAE, mȧ-kē-rô-dŏn-tī'nē, an extinct subfamily of cats (Felidae), referred to as the "sabertooths," of which *Smilodon* from the American Pleistocene is the best known. Fine skeletons have been found in the Rancho LaBrea tar pits of southern California. Machaerodonts evolved from the typical cats (Felinae) during the Oligocene, some 40 million years ago. In contrast to the active, fast-moving Felinae, they were heavy and slow with a jaw that could be opened to about a right angle. Their principal characteristic was the development of the canine teeth into stabbing and slicing structures well adapted for penetrating thick-skinned animals and reaching vital organs, causing copious bleeding. Powerful neck muscles coupled with the weight of the body gave power to the thrust. With the decline of the large, slow mastodons, mammoths, and giant ground sloths upon which they preyed, sabertooths could not compete in the quest for food with the agile typical cats, and vanished about 10,000 years ago.

DONALD W. FISHER.

McHENRY, măk-hĕn'rĭ, **James,** American patriot and signer of the Constitution: b. Ballymena, County Antrim, Ireland, Nov. 16, 1753; d. Baltimore, Md., May 3, 1816. He emigrated to Philadelphia in 1771, and after attending the academy at Newark, Del., studied medicine under Benjamin Rush. In 1775 he joined the Continental Army as a surgeon and was captured by the British at Fort Washington on Harlem Heights, N.Y. (November 1776). Exchanged in March 1778, he was private secretary to George Washington until 1780, when he was transferred to the marquis de Lafayette's staff. He served in the Maryland Senate (1781–1786, 1791–1796) and the Continental Congress (1783–1786), and was a delegate to the Constitutional Convention (1787) and the Maryland ratifying convention. In January 1796 he was appointed secretary of war by President Washington, holding office until May 1800, when President John Adams demanded McHenry's resignation because he favored Alexander Hamilton's policy on the threatening trouble with France. Thereafter McHenry lived in retirement at Fayetteville, Md. Fort McHenry, at Baltimore, was named for him.

McHENRY, Fort. See FORT McHENRY.

MACHIAS, mȧ-chī'ȧs, town, Maine, Washington County seat, situated near the mouth of the Machias River, 65 miles southeast of Bangor, on the Maine Central Railroad. There are truck and poultry farms nearby, and some granite quarrying; lumbering and shipbuilding are also local industries. A state normal school is in Machias, and at East Machias are Washington Academy and the summer surveying school of the Massachusetts Institute of Technology. A trading post was established here in 1633 by Englishmen, but they were soon driven out by the French. The first permanent English settlement was made in 1763 and in 1784 the town was incorporated.

In the Revolutionary War Machias participated prominently in the harassing of the British along the coast; in 1775 Machias seamen captured the British armed schooner *Margaretta* and, in reprisal, the town was partly burned by forces from the ship *Ranger*. In 1863, in observance of the town's centennial, an anniversary memorial was published. Pop. 2,614.

MACHIAVELLI, mä-kyä-věl′lê, **Niccolò,** Italian political thinker: b. Florence, Italy, May 3, 1469; d. there, June 22, 1527. Those who want to point out differences between the Middle Ages and the modern world often refer to Niccolò Machiavelli as symbolizing such a break and as indicating an approach to politics characteristic of modern times but unknown to previous centuries. The idea of the autonomy of politics and of a special reason of state, the concept of a political morality different from and not bound by the usual ethical norms, the insistence on power as the decisive factor in political life—all these fundamental problems which puzzle and disturb the mind of modern man were first raised in the writings of the great Florentine political thinker.

The period in which Machiavelli lived and the city in which his activities unfolded were conducive to a re-examination of the validity of traditional political thought. He was 25 years of age when, in 1494, Charles VIII of France invaded Italy and thereby opened an era of wars between France, Spain and the Austrian Habsburgs for the possession of the Italian peninsula. When he died, in 1527, all Western and Central Europe had been sucked into this conflict and an interconnected state system revolving around the struggle between the Habsburg ruler of Austria and Spain and the French king had emerged. Florence, an important factor in Italian politics at the beginning of this era, had become a pawn in the rivalry between pope, emperor, and French king and was reduced to a purely nominal independence. This decline of Florentine power was sharply felt by the inhabitants of a city who were proud of its long tradition of republican freedom; on the basis of an intense economic activity and of great wealth Florence had developed a rich cultural life, so that it could claim to be the intellectual center of Europe. A passion for speculation, a search for rational explanations was natural in this atmosphere.

Thus Machiavelli belonged to an entire school of Florentine writers concerned with an examination of political and historical problems. If his works alone have been of general and lasting importance, this is chiefly due to the inexplicable individual factor which might be called the unique brilliance of his intellect. However, the external circumstances of his life and career had their part in fitting him to the role which he plays in the development of political thought. Machiavelli's life divides into two parts; all his important writings were composed after 1512, when, after the return of the Medici from exile, he had been relieved of his official functions. This removal from political activity, which he regarded as the great tragedy of his life, was actually a good fortune because it forced him to enter upon the career of a political writer on which his claim to lasting fame is based. However, the realism which distinguishes Machiavelli's political thought owes much to the experience which he had acquired while serving as an official of the Florentine republic.

Machiavelli in Public Life.—From 1498 until the return of the Medici in 1512 Machiavelli served in the chancellery of the Florentine republic. We have no information about his earlier life, about his training and education, but it seems certain—and it is confirmed by his writings—that he was educated in the classics as this was the prerequisite for employment in the chancellery. The head of the chancellery was a well-known humanist; Machiavelli was the second in command and in addition was secretary of the Ten of Balìa, an important government committee, in charge of diplomatic negotiations and, in case of war, entrusted with the supervision of military operations. His work as secretary of this committee involved him in administrative tasks and diplomatic missions. Throughout this period the prime object of Florentine policy was the reconquest of Pisa. Machiavelli was frequently sent to the army camp which the Florentine government maintained before Pisa and gained first-hand knowledge of the manner in which military affairs were handled. His diplomatic missions brought him in contact with many of the Italian rulers of the Renaissance period. He spent long weeks with Cesare Borgia and became an eyewitness of the unscrupulous manner in which Cesare got rid of the small rulers of the Romagna who stood in his way. Diplomatic missions led him also to other parts of Europe; he was sent to France (1500, 1504, 1510, 1511), and to Germany (1507/1508). Machiavelli's reports about Germany and France have been preserved and show keen understanding for the relation between political institutions and political strength.

Machiavelli's most discussed political activity developed from the initiative he took to introduce a new military organization in Florence. The disadvantages of the system of mercenary armies, which prevailed in Renaissance Italy, were obvious. The armies represented a continuous drain on the treasury; their leaders, the Condottieri, were unreliable, willing to serve whoever paid them most. Machiavelli suggested that Florence should introduce conscription, and this suggestion was accepted. He was instrumental in organizing this new military force; when, in 1512, the troops of the emperor approached Florence to reinstall the Medici, part of the Florentine army was formed by this indigenous force.

The role which Machiavelli had played in the time of the republic was his undoing when the republic was overthrown and the Medici returned to Florence in 1512. Machiavelli was dismissed. Suspected of participation in a conspiracy against the new rulers, he was tortured and, for a year he was ordered not to enter into the city of Florence.

Machiavelli in Retirement.—Barred from practical politics, Machiavelli settled in San Casciano on a small estate a few miles outside Florence and embarked on a literary career.

Machiavelli's important literary productions in this period were of a political and historical nature: *The Prince* (q.v.), written in 1513; *The Discourses,* completed by 1519; *The Art of War,* written between 1519 and 1520; and *The Florentine History,* completed 1525. Of these four, *The*

Art of War and *The Florentine History* are less significant. *The Art of War* advocates his favorite idea of a national army based on conscription, but he accepts the military organization of the ancient Romans so completely as the ideal pattern to be imitated in all details that the book has a somewhat unreal and romantic flavor. His *Florentine History* is in the pattern of the humanist historical writings of the period; in presenting the history of Florence from its foundation to the death of Lorenzo the Magnificent in 1492, he follows rather uncritically the well-known narrative sources. He embellishes his account, in typically humanist fashion, by elaborate battle scenes and long speeches. However, the book has its interest because of the attention given to domestic affairs and because of some specifically Machiavellian ideas inserted in the speeches.

Machiavelli's Political Thought.—The gist of Machiavelli's political thought will be found in *The Prince* and *The Discourses*. In form, these two writings are widely different. *The Prince* gives advice to a new ruler on how to found a state and how to maintain himself in power; *The Discourses* are commentaries on the first 10 books of Livy's *History of Rome;* but the purpose of the two books is identical: an endeavor to discover the laws of political behavior which lead to success in political action. Such laws, Machiavelli believes, cannot be found outside the realm of politics, as, for instance, in ethics; they must be abstracted from political practice, that is, from the political practice of his own time as well as from the experiences of history. What he has seen in his own time—whether the successful ruthlessness of a Cesare Borgia or the undecided flounderings of his own government—enters into his presentation. But in Machiavelli's view the most perfect example of successful political action is to be found in the history of Rome, and this approach leads him to an idealization of everything the Romans did. Contemporary politics and Roman history, then, form the material out of which he forms those generalizations which by their very neglect of customary morality have shocked the world, such as "it is much more secure to be feared, than to be loved," and "a prudent ruler can not and should not observe faith when such observance is to his disadvantage."

Although these amoral aspects of his doctrines have attracted the greatest attention, they do not exhaust the content of his political thought. He was aware that success in politics needed more than precise rational calculations; he knew that all clever planning could come to naught if it lacked an irrational element, the strength of will power. In Machiavelli's own language, politics is a struggle between fortune and virtue (virtue in the sense of strength and not of Christian ethics), and a chief concern of his was the problem of how to produce political virtue. It could be possessed by an individual—thus Machiavelli admired Cesare Borgia because he believed that in him he had seen political virtue in action—but he was mainly interested in the conditions which produced political virtue in an entire state. He believed the institutions of Rome had been ideally designed to produce virtue in the Roman people and hoped to introduce a constitution in Florence which might achieve the same end. Although, with *The Prince,* he was the author of a handbook for tyrants, his true love was a free republic.

Few writers have been as passionately discussed as Niccolò Machiavelli. In the 16th and 17th centuries not many would have openly acknowledged themselves his followers, but the importance of his influence can be deduced from the vehemence with which he was attacked; there was a whole anti-Machiavellian school of political writers. With the rise of absolutism in the 17th and 18th centuries, the importance and validity of his doctrines were frankly recognized. A new interest developed in the 19th century, particularly in Germany and Italy. Machiavelli was interpreted not so much as saying that politics has no morality but that it has a morality of its own, and such a doctrine seemed justified and almost prophetic in a period in which the achievement of national unity and of a national state was regarded as the highest aim, to which everything else must be subordinated. Although contemporary scholarship may have its reservations about this 19th century transformation of Machiavelli into a prophet of the modern national state, the interest in his writings has continued and increased because, with the rise of totalitarianism, the problems which he raised have received a new vitality.

Bibliography.—A good modern critical edition of Machiavelli's works is by Guido Mazzoni and Mario Casella (Florence 1929). For Machiavelli's official reports, the older edition by L. Passerini and G. Milanesi (Florence and Rome 1873–77) is still useful. Machiavelli's correspondence, his *Lettere Familiari*, was edited by Eduardo Alvisi (Florence 1883). *The Prince* and *The Discourses* are available in many English translations. A critical edition of *The Prince*, with extensive comments, was published by Lawrence Arthur Burd (Oxford 1891), and of *The Discourses* by L. Walker (New Haven 1950).

The standard biographies are Oreste Tommasini's *La vita e gli scritti di Niccolò Machiavelli* (Turin 1883), and Pasquale Villari's *Niccolò Machiavelli e i suoi tempi* (Florence 1877–82; Eng. tr., London 1929). Consult also Whitfield, John H., *Machiavelli* (Oxford 1947); Chabod, Federico, *Machiavelli and the Renaissance*, tr. by D. Moore (Cambridge 1959); Ridolfi, Roberto, *Life of Niccolò Machiavelli*, tr. by C. Grayson (Chicago 1963); Prezzplini, Giuseppe, *Machiavelli*, tr. by G. Savine (New York 1967).

FELIX GILBERT,
Professor of History, Bryn Mawr College.

MACHINE GUN, mà-shēn′ gŭn, an automatic small arm capable of rapid fire over sustained periods of time, so long as pressure is maintained on the trigger and ammunition is supplied. The gun is recoil or gas operated, and air or water cooled. Ammunition is commonly fed from fabric or metal-link belts, or from magazines. The gun fires the same ammunition as the shoulder weapon (rifle) of the country by which it is used. It is generally fired from a stable mount, which is designed to permit accurate fire on targets not within the gunner's field of vision, for instance in night firing or indirect fire over land masks.

There is no distinct dividing line between the machine gun and other weapons having the same general characteristics. The automatic rifle or machine rifle is capable of fully automatic fire, but not for sustained periods, because of its lighter construction; being primarily a shoulder weapon, it also lacks the stable mount. The submachine gun or machine pistol is made for fully automatic firing of shorter-range pistol ammunition. Weapons of larger caliber which perform all or part of the firing cycle automatically are classified as artillery; projectiles of 37-mm. diameter (about 1.5 inches) are the largest that can be fired with machine gun rapidity. The so-called automatic pistol is misnamed; it is merely autoloading, since the trigger must be pulled each time a shot is fired.

Historical Development.—As soon as gun-

Above: The 1892 Maxim, first true machine gun, used the recoil principle.

West Point Museum

MACHINE GUN

Left: 1917 version of the Browning, standard American machine gun for 40 years.

Below: German-influenced U.S. Army M-60 replaced the Browning in 1957.

U.S. Army Photographs

Above: The 1911 Lewis gun, first lightweight machine gun, conceived for aircraft, was used by the infantry in World War I.

Below: The German MG-42, produced in 1942, strongly influenced machine gun design and production after World War II.

West Point Museum

powder began to be used in warfare (early in the 14th century), a variety of multibarreled volley guns appeared. Known as organ guns because of their appearance, they consisted of several musket or cannon barrels mounted parallel on carts. Leonardo da Vinci (1452–1519) designed some of these guns. Used in large numbers as late as the 16th century, they were eventually discarded because they were too cumbersome and took too long to reload.

Although various forms of multifiring weapons continued to be devised, a fully automatic gun was not possible until the 19th century, when an adequate metallic cartridge was developed that could be mass produced. An important milestone in the development of rapid-fire guns was the Gatling gun, first patented in 1862 by Richard Jordan Gatling, which evolved in the 1890's into a weapon that could fire 3,000 rounds per minute from its 10 barrels when driven by a built-in electric motor. However, this was not a true machine gun, since continuous fire was accomplished originally by means of a manually operated handle or lever, and later by the electric motor.

The first true machine gun was the Maxim gun, using the recoil principle; it was patented in 1885 by Hiram Stevens Maxim. In 1892 the first successful gas-operated machine gun was patented by John Moses Browning. Another early machine gun was the Hotchkiss gun, patented in 1896 by Laurence V. Benét and Henri A. Mercié and named in honor of their company's deceased founder, Benjamin Berkeley Hotchkiss. The Lewis gun (1911), patented by Isaac Newton Lewis, was the first lightweight automatic machine gun; although developed primarily to be fired from aircraft, it saw extensive infantry use in World War I. Gatling and Browning were Americans, as were Maxim, Hotchkiss, Benét, and Lewis; but the United States showed so little interest in the inventions of the last four that they went abroad to develop, market, and produce their weapons. Maxim became a British subject, knighted by Queen Victoria in 1901.

The Browning machine gun and Browning automatic rifle (BAR), although perfected by 1900, were not produced in sufficient quantity to see extensive use in World War I. The Lewis gun was not adopted by the United States Army in that war, even though the other Allies accepted and produced it in large numbers for their own use. United States troops were equipped with automatic weapons of European manufacture, including the inferior and highly unpopular French Chauchat automatic rifle. An estimated 92 per cent of all World War I casualties were inflicted by machine guns.

Browning machine guns and automatic rifles were the most effective automatic weapons in the hands of Allied troops during World War II and the Korean conflict. The Germans produced the MG-34 and MG-42 light machine guns. With a high rate of fire of up to 1,500 rounds per minute, these were remarkable not only for their combat effectiveness but also for their simplicity and suitability to mass production.

Tank and Airplane Machine Guns.—Space restrictions inside a tank present special design criteria; for example, the machine gun's receiver (generally, that portion rearward of the barrel) should be as short as possible. Standard machine guns, however, are used satisfactorily.

Conventional aircraft use .50-caliber machine guns, usually in groups of six or eight, for aerial combat and strafing. Jet aircraft, however, introduce special problems of speed, altitude, and temperature that make standard machine guns obsolete. In their place, various types of 20-mm. and 30-mm. automatic guns are used. Some of these are of the revolver type and have a single barrel; others resemble the old Gatling gun in that they have multiple barrels which are revolved by an electric motor. Since these weapons depend on a source of electric power, they are classified as automatic guns rather than machine guns.

Trends.—Just as invention of the first true machine gun had to await development of the proper type of ammunition, the next revolutionary step in the progress of automatic weapons depends on invention of a new type of cartridge. Mechanically the machine gun has approached the maximum rate it can fire while using a metallic cartridge, which must be extracted and ejected before a new round can be loaded and fired. A desirable development would be the production of a self-consuming cartridge. This might be made of a solid propellant that would also serve as the cartridge. Another possibility would be to produce a cartridge case made of a material that would be completely consumed when firing took place. This type of cartridge would leave the chamber entirely clear for the next round. See also ARTILLERY—*Types of Artillery.* For a description of submachine guns, see SMALL ARMS—*Modern Small Arms.*

MARK M. BOATNER, 3D,
Lieutenant Colonel, United States Army.

MACHINES, mà-shēnz'. Machines in one sense are as old as the human organism; for man, when deprived of his specifically human traits, can be reduced to a machine, as René Descartes pointed out in the 17th century, and man's organs served as the original models for the simple tools and utensils out of which more complicated machines were constructed. In turn, the more complex automatic machines and utilities of our own day, governed by cybernetic controls—above all, the electronic computers themselves—have uncanny resemblances to human beings, in function if not in physical appearance, including the capacity to exercise a particular kind of intelligence, to record experience (that is, to remember), and even to detect and correct their own errors. In general, one may say that the machine is an instrument for isolating and greatly enlarging in durable external form special capacities that were once confined to animal organisms and subject to their limitations.

Viewed from the standpoint of technics, the machine represents the last stage of a long development, which began with the invention of simple tools—the stone to supplement the fist, the stick to extend the reach of the arm. These early adaptations may be as old at least as the discovery and preservation of fire; but the dawn period of technics probably lasted tens of thousands of years before the deliberate chipping of flint tools with sharp edges began, and possibly man's earliest lessons in standardization and repetition came through the development of language. While we lack evidence of Paleolithic language, it is plain from remains in the Aurignacian caves (see PALEOLITHIC ART—*Aurignacian and Perigordian Periods*) that man's symbolic skill in painting far exceeded his skill in shaping stone tools.

The first development of machines specially constructed to shape, move, or control the material environment came apparently in the Neolithic period; this was associated with the development of agriculture and the building of settled village communities. At this time the simple machines of classic mechanics were developed: the inclined plane, the lever, and the wheel, all of them notably of use in building. The earliest form of the wheel, the potter's wheel, and the cart wheel appeared between 3500 and 3000 B.C. in Mesopotamia.

Machines As Distinguished from Tools, Utensils, and Utilities.—Machines may be distinguished from tools in that the latter are relatively undifferentiated and may be used for more than one kind of operation, always under the control of the worker, whereas machines are designed to perform one particular function, with an accuracy, speed, or regularity not readily attained by the individual worker. Machines must also be distinguished from utensils and utilities, which occupy a whole realm of technology, that of the containers and transformers. The machine represents the dynamic processes, derived ultimately from such organic tools as the teeth, the hands, and the limbs, while utensils and utilities stand for the more passive, static, chemical and physiological processes, such as those of the stomach, the womb, the circulatory system, and the skin. If the machine long had a subordinate place, it was because man's first great step in controlling the environment—the development of organized agriculture and cities—was largely dependent on utilities, such as planted fields, buildings, vats, dams, reservoirs, irrigation ditches, and canals, rather than on machines.

Roman catapult, an early machine of war.

Antiquity: Collective Human Machines.— The slow development of the machine in early civilizations contrasts with the swift and powerful development of utilities on the largest scale, such as the irrigation system in Mesopotamia and the Great Pyramid in Egypt. But it is a mistake to think that works of this character could have been constructed without the aid of machines. The fact is that in premechanical civilizations the machine took a form that has left no visible artifacts behind except the works that it produced, because the parts of the machine were composed of human bodies, of varied capabilities and functions, organized into great work armies, each part restricted in function and wrought into a highly complex mechanism of interdependent parts directed to a single end. The division of labor, specialization of function, and automatic response to remote control gave a work army of 100,000 men, such as employed by Cheops (Khufu) of ancient Egypt, all the attributes of a great machine; but it took many thousands of years before such a machine or group of machines could be translated into nonhuman forms. The Sumerian phalanx, which dates back to about 2000 B.C., was likewise a machine, achieving, by discipline and drill, a capacity to perform military work far beyond that of its dispersed parts.

The collective human machine thus antedates wood and iron mechanisms worked by extraorganic forms of energy; but the psychological conditioning needed to create such machines—the restriction, regimentation, repetition, and automatism—has its basis in the human organism, not merely in the system of reflexes, but also in the prevalence of acquired habits. Psychologists have remarked the sense of security that seems to accompany many repetitive activities, with the elimination of the capricious and the unexpected along with spontaneous creativity. These human properties, first embodied in languages, taboos, and moral codes, slowly took command over the working life. Without this basic need of collective order, the machine itself could hardly have taken form. These regularities are already established in the physiology of the human organism, in the relatively uniform temperature of the human body, the relatively standardized normal heartbeat, to say nothing of the periodicities of menstruation and gestation. One must not therefore regard the mechanical aspect of life as altogether alien to human nature or to human needs; rather, it is part of the groundwork out of which invention, creativity, and spontaneity manifest themselves.

Influence of Warfare and Religion.—Once the wheeled cart, the potter's wheel, the spindle, the loom, and the plow were invented (all before 3000 B.C.), religion and warfare were the chief beneficiaries of the machine almost up to the Christian era. The huge catapults which threw stones into besieged cities and the battering rams which breached their walls were the mechanical forerunners of the cannon and tank of the present century; while Heron (Hero) of Alexandria's invention of the hot-air engine (aeropile) was dedicated to the impressive mystery of opening the temple doors without use of the human hand. Though the Greeks did not follow through their own initiatives, their invention of the screw and the wood turner's lathe by the 5th century B.C. and of the water mill by the 3d century B.C. set the scene for the large-scale mechanization which took place after the 13th century A.D. in western Europe. The water mill is important as the first extrahuman prime mover, the prototype of all the other engines that utilize the energies available in nature (sunlight, wind, running water, coal, petroleum, uranium).

If the army, with its drill and regimentation, was the earliest human pattern for the machine, the next great influence was the Benedictine monastery. The whole routine of the monastery was based on a fixed and inflexible order, with the day divided into even canonical hours and every human impulse repressed except that which served the collective life directly. For the first

The Bettmann Archive

A 16th century drawing of a smelting furnace regulated by bellows and driven by a water wheel.

time, work itself became regarded as an honorable activity, not just as servile, brutalizing toil; and this elevation of work led to the concentration of human intelligence upon its adequate and economic performance. Machines themselves were welcome in the monastery as a means of releasing the soul from worldly preoccupations and enabling it to dwell more fully on matters more important to salvation. The monastery's concern with timekeeping fostered habits of mind favorable to the invention of a more reliable kind of clock than the sundial, the hourglass, or the water clock. The mechanical clock, invented in the 13th century, spread timekeeping to the rest of the community, synchronizing its activities, and became the pattern of regularity and order, making the movements of the planets a pattern for men.

Monastic discipline led even more directly to the other key invention of the machine age, the printing press. In the copying of manuscripts, the monastic scribes had achieved a form of lettering so free from personal embellishments, so uniformly perfect, that it had only to be copied to serve as a model for the type fonts that came in with the invention of printing from movable type, a process devised in Korea and perfected in both type punches and press, in western Europe in the middle of the 15th century. Though mass production had been achieved in pottery making and perhaps even in textiles in the ancient world, printing serves as the first

modern example of standardized mass production by a machine operating with interchangeable and removable parts (that is, the type itself).

Development of Materials and Power.— For the perfection of the machine, two more improvements were needed: an abundance of metals, particularly of iron, and a cheap source of power not subject to the climatic irregularities of wind and water. The technical development of iron mining, through the use of pumping machinery, elevator machinery, and railroads, also brought the utilization of coal for operating the steam engine. With these facilities at hand by the middle of the 18th century, it at last became possible to build large, complex machines of a kind that had hitherto been almost unimaginable, and to house them in a complex organization of supply, productive power, and human labor called a factory. The skill that was once directly applied by the worker in the manipulation of tools was now built into the process itself, putting the heaviest burden on the machine and utilizing only a fragment of the attendant worker's capacities.

At this point we may cease to talk about machines as individual inventions, more or less supplementing human effort in a mainly handicraft operation; the machine becomes a collective product. By its command of power, by its facility for mass production, it tends to drive out more individualistic methods of production, and the order it achieves not only prevails in the factory but spreads into the office, the market, and even the home. The final step in this process, already reached in certain industries, is complete automation.

Role of Fantasy.—The enlargement of the role of machines took place in fantasy long before it was realized in fact; and it was made possible and acceptable by a radically new approach to human experience introduced in a large way by the scientists and mathematicians of the 17th century. Up to the 13th century, the machine had been viewed with indifference, if not apprehension. The introduction of one machine or another, at intervals of centuries, did not tear the whole tissue of life; even the disruptive force of gunpowder when used in cannon has been greatly exaggerated by technically innocent historians. As for apprehension over the machine, this was chiefly manifested in fables about malicious gnomes and dwarfs who worked in the mountains and forged swords and armor and cunning mechanical contraptions; the typical fairy-tale gnome's costume is in fact simply that of the medieval miner.

Beginning with Roger Bacon, a 13th century Franciscan monk, fantasies of future mechanical triumphs are recorded. Bacon predicted the motor car, the airplane, the submarine, and the telegraph; and from this time on, writers of a new kind of literature, the utopia, devote a large part of their description of future felicities to mechanical improvements, from the mechanical incubator, described by Thomas More in his *Utopia* (1516), to the telephonic diffusion of music, described by Edward Bellamy (*Looking Backward: 2000-1887*, 1888). In the fragments of a utopia called *The New Atlantis* (1627), and even more in his *Advancement of Learning* (1605), Francis Bacon tied up the progress of mechanical invention with the advancement of experimental science, pursued systematically. Though the advance of hydrostatics did in fact have an immediate effect upon the development of the pump, Bacon's predictions were not realized on a large scale until the 19th century, when the researches on electromagnetism by Joseph Henry, Michael Faraday, Karl Friedrich Gauss, and Georg Simon Ohm led directly to the invention of the dynamo, the electric motor, and the electric telegraph.

In the 19th century Edward Bulwer-Lytton, in *The Coming Race* (1871), described a new source of energy, "vril," which anticipated nuclear energy; while Jules Verne's fantasies of submarine exploration and a rocket trip to the moon set the stage for many other fictional anticipations of the present mechanical world. Similar fantasies now form a voluminous literature, familiar to 20th century readers as science fiction.

Role of Science.—The advance of physical science, on the assumptions laid down by Galileo in the 17th century, established a new confidence in the principles of mechanical order. By discarding all the distinctive attributes of life associated with the so-called secondary qualities such as form, color, odor, taste, sensitivity, and feeling, Galileo found himself left with an abstract physical world of mass and motion capable of being observed by the eye, manipulated by the hand, and reduced to changes of quantity and position that could be described by mathematics. By bestowing an extra certificate of reality upon this kind of world, science gave the machine priority over other departments of human culture. As a result, the doctrine of mechanical progress became the watchword of the 19th century, though the advances that were so palpably manifested in the world of machines were accompanied by a degradation of the industrial worker himself, whose housing, food, and medical care remained at or below the level of mass labor in nonmechanical civilizations. The Victorian assumption that mechanical improvements must automatically register themselves in human gains, and that this sort of gain is in fact the only kind that matters, cannot be explained except as an ideological aberration so general that it resulted in a defective interpretation of actual conditions and events. Detached observers, like the economist, John Stuart Mill, were powerless to counteract this collective prejudice. Even the severest revolutionary critics of the capitalist regime, such as Karl Marx, treated the machine as if it had an existence independent of other human interests and values, yet necessarily dominating them.

Advance of the Machine.—Within its own department, the machine took over and transformed the whole business of handicraft production. It succeeded first, as in printing, spinning, and weaving, in those processes that had already under handicraft become highly standardized and mechanized. In exchange for the variations and adaptations introduced by the individual worker, the machine process prided itself on its own undeviating perfection, once the original pattern was set; the thousandth example was as good as the first. In this changeover the worker became an incidental part of the machine, performing an operation that demanded a rudimentary intelligence not yet built into the machine; or he served as a kind of "machine-herd," correcting minor breakdowns in the process, such as a broken thread in spinning. Because of the small demand on either physical power or intelligence, children and women were introduced into the factory system, since they were cheap and equally efficacious. At the same time, the pattern of the machine was applied to the large-scale organization of the working force in factory and office, progressively dispensing with the need for human labor. Today, business machines (for typewriting, manifolding, record keeping, and accounting) play a part comparable to those in industrial production.

The Bettmann Archive

Primitive steam engine designed in 1629. A steam jet impinging on the blades of a paddle wheel produced rotary motion to operate a stamping mill.

If the first step in mechanization is an increase in power and productivity, the next step is the advance toward complete automation, which releases all manpower other than the original designers of the process and machinery and the supervisors and controllers of the plant in operation. This is the ideal goal of the whole machine system, long ago foreseen—only to be dismissed —by Aristotle in the 4th century B.C., when he predicted that slavery would end only when the lyre could play and the shuttle weave by itself.

Benefits and Drawbacks.—While the beneficence of these changes is usually taken for granted, a few observers have begun to appraise the negative results of modern man's wholesale commitment to the machine. One of these has been called by the economist Stuart Chase "technological tenuousness"; that is, the delicate interdependence of all the parts of this mechanized environment, so that a break in power lines, perhaps by a thunderstorm, can not only bring production to a halt, but can stop the cooking of food and ruin vast quantities of provisions in deep-freeze lockers. So, too, a break in the channels of worldwide transport, disrupting the supplies of manganese, tungsten, chromium, and nickel, can undermine high-grade metallurgy and machine building. While this interdependence should, ideally, foster cooperation and unity on a scale never achieved before, it has also promoted efforts at monopoly or domination, increasing the frictions and anxieties that exist between countries.

Even more dubious is the tendency of machine production to repeat the fable of the sorcerer's apprentice, that is, to overwhelm the consumer with unconsumable quantities of goods automatically produced while leaving him with an insufficiency, perhaps, of less mechanized and less standardized products. The "compulsion to consume" is one of the questionable byproducts of automation, in a system that so far lacks built-in controls or regulators. A secondary effect is mass production in taste. To use a trivial example, when bread was sold unsliced, the consumer could cut it thick or thin according to taste; now in the United States it is difficult to buy an uncut loaf, and the consumer must accept the machine-regulated slice, chemically treated to counteract premature drying and standardized to fit the requirements of another machine, the automatic toaster.

A further consequence of standardization and mass production, with its need for a continued outlet, is that products are now built for early obsolescence and replacement, either by being deliberately made shoddy or by being restyled from year to year, with the implied demand to be in fashion.

On the credit side, the machine has been able to supplant a large part of human labor in agriculture, industry, transportation, and commerce; it has thus removed the ancient curse of slavery and freed human energy for other activities, giving to mankind at large—at least potentially—the leisure and opportunity once monopolized by a restricted minority. The narrow monopoly of knowledge and power imposed by limited productivity has been eliminated. With the aid of the machine, the limitations on long-distance transportation and communication have been lifted to such an extent that for certain purposes the whole planet has become as close as a village. Though the first advances of the machine were in control of the physical world, it now is an important accessory in every biological and social process, and in turn benefits by scientific advances in these departments. Studies of the human ear aided Alexander Graham Bell in inventing the telephone, while the study of locomotion in animals, particularly birds, actively led to the invention of the airplane. In turn, the electronic devices used in cybernetics have thrown fresh light on the mechanism of the human nervous system. The machine has established a pervasive sense of order, transferring the regularities and predictabilities first associated with the heavenly bodies to human institutions, training people in habits of punctuality, objectivity, and impersonality, and giving them confidence in man's power to understand the forces around him and to devise means of controlling and adapting them to his own ends. This groundwork of order seems a fundamental contribution to human creativity, more important than any particular labor-saving or power-enlarging device.

The weaknesses of the machine come largely through exaggeration of its successes. In order to run the system more effectively, a mechanized personality, conditioned to accept the machine and its products without question, is brought into

Ford Motor Company

A factory worker guides automobile engine blocks into a giant drilling machine. The machine consists of 19 drilling stations and puts 100 tools into operation.

existence—the being described by William H. Whyte in his book, *The Organization Man* (1956). Apart from this, there is little doubt that the general mechanization of life has suppressed activities and interests that do not fit into the mechanical pattern. Many activities, once spontaneous and under the direct control of the actor, have been turned over to mechanized collectives, as storytelling by parents has largely yielded to television performances or recorded readings. By the same token, the general use of the motor has undermined the habit of walking, at least in the United States, even for short distances. Even more important, the practice of standardization and mass production has, in many departments, reduced the area of choice: while increasing quantity and raising the lowest level of consumption, it has sanctioned mediocrity and curtailed variety. This has happened even in agriculture, where a few varieties of apples, pears, corn, and potatoes have supplanted the vast wealth of choices open even half a century ago.

Since creativity in all its forms presents a departure from the habitual and the expected, the general success of the machine may result in a curtailment of creativity in every department. The practice of a great corporation (Bell Telephone Company) in sending its junior executives back to college for nontechnical courses in order to release the imagination is perhaps an early acknowledgment of the dangers of tailoring men too successfully to fit limited mechanical tasks. But the deeper weaknesses of the machine, it would appear, come from another sector and are more threatening: the sense of compulsion and automatism that machine technology has introduced, which makes it expand over wider and wider areas at a faster and faster rate, even when its premature applications—as with nuclear energy—lack elementary safeguards and controls. A machine whose pace cannot be altered, whose advancement cannot be halted, whose destination cannot be plotted and directed, is a dangerous instrument, and without a farsighted system of human control the whole system of mechanization may finally wreck itself just for lack of brakes, reverse gears, and steering wheel. Hence the problem posed by the success of the machine is how to restore those human goals that have been abandoned in the pursuit of extra-human powers, without forfeiting the gains that the machine has brought into existence.

See also AUTOMATION; INDUSTRIAL REVOLUTION; INVENTIONS; MASS PRODUCTION.

Bibliography.—Singer, Charles Joseph, and others, eds., *A History of Technology,* 5 vols. (London 1954–58); Forbes, Robert James, *Man the Maker,* rev. ed. (New York 1958); Mumford, Lewis, *Technics and Civilization* (New York 1963); Chapanis, Alphonse, *Man-Machine Engineering* (Belmont, Calif., 1965).

LEWIS MUMFORD,
Visiting Bemis Professor, School of Architecture and Planning, Massachusetts Institute of Technology.

MACHPELAH. See HEBRON.

MACHU PICCHU, mä'chōō pēk'chōō (also known as MACHUPICCHU or MACCHU PICCHU), templed citadel of the Incas, situated about 50 miles northwest of Cuzco, Peru. A natural fortress, it is perched at an altitude of about 6,750 feet on a narrow ridge between the mountain heights Machu Picchu (old peak) and Huayna Picchu (young peak); 2,000 feet below is the Urubamba River. The age of Machu Picchu is unknown, but it appears to have been the residence and last stronghold of the Incas after the Spanish conquest. When the last ruler was slain in the 16th century, it was abandoned and lost. Hiram Bingham of Yale University rediscovered the city in 1911, calling it Machu Picchu although the Inca name was probably Vilcapampa. Its mortarless stonework of white granite survives today in fair condition. A railway now links the city with Cuzco, and the five-mile-long Hiram Bingham Highway climbs the approach to the ancient citadel.

Consult Bingham, Hiram, *Lost City of the Incas; the Story of Machu Picchu and Its Builders* (New York 1948).

MACIA Y LLUSA, mä-thē-ä' ê lōō-sä', **Francisco,** Catalan nationalist leader: b. Villanueva y Geltrú, Spain, Oct. 21, 1859; d. Barcelona, Dec. 25, 1933. His early career was in the army, where he rose to the rank of colonel of engineers. Joining the Catalonian separatist movement, he was elected to the Spanish Cortes in 1907 and was active in various extremist groups before and after 1920. In 1924, during the dictatorship of Miguel Primo de Rivera, Maciá y Llusá went to France, and two years later attempted unsuccessfully to organize a Catalan revolution. First imprisoned, then exiled, he returned to Spain after the fall of the monarchy in 1931 and was named president of an independent Catalan republic. Under his leadership Catalonia became an autonomous region of the Spanish Republic on Sept. 25, 1932.

McINTIRE, măk'ĭn-tīr, **Samuel,** American architect and woodcarver: b. Salem, Mass., bap. Jan. 16, 1757; d. there, Feb. 6, 1811. Having learned the housewright's trade from his father, he established a reputation in his early 20's for his part in designing the Jerathmeel Peirce (or Peirce-Nichols) house in Salem. Most of his life thereafter was devoted to the design and construction of the great mansions of Salem shipping merchants, and he has been called "the architect of Salem."

The scheme of the McIntire houses was similar to some previously built in Massachusetts—cubical, three stories high, with a hipped roof and level cornice all about. The focal point of each room was the fireplace with its decorated mantel. McIntire, however, possessed a higher degree of skill than his predecessors in the handling of proportions and decorative detail. The Peirce house and other early structures were massive and heavy in effect, but from 1793 on, due to the influence of the Boston architect, Charles Bulfinch, his work took on a more graceful, refined elegance with a use of Adam decoration. The Lyman house in Waltham, Mass. (begun 1793), and the Elias Hasket Derby mansion on Essex Street, Salem (1795–1799, destroyed 1815), are examples of this style. The interior woodwork of the Derby "mansion," so called to distinguish it from other Derby houses, was lavishly decorated with capitals, medallions, roses, and festooned draperies carved by the architect. Another fine mansion, still preserved, is the John Gardner house (also called the Pingree house, 1805) in Salem. From 1805 on, his work showed a growing tendency toward classic austerity. He also built a number of Salem's churches and public buildings, notably the South Church (begun 1804), which was destroyed in 1903; the Assembly House (begun c. 1782, remodeled 1796), now a private home; and Hamilton Hall (c. 1805–1807), still standing. In 1792 he submitted a design for the national Capitol at Washington.

McIntire lavished his skill in decorative woodcarving, not only on interior woodwork but on furniture, with such motifs as eagles, baskets of fruit, urns, sprays of grape and laurel, and others already mentioned; in this field he was unsurpassed. He also executed portrait sculpture in wood in his later years. Some of his carvings are preserved in the Essex Institute, Salem, the Boston Museum of Fine Arts, and the Pennsylvania Museum of Art.

Consult Kimball, Fiske, *Mr. Samuel McIntire, Carver, the Architect of Salem* (Portland, Me., 1940).

MACINTOSH, măk'ĭn-tŏsh, **Charles,** Scottish chemist and inventor of waterproof fabrics: b. Glasgow, Scotland, Dec. 29, 1766; d. near there, July 25, 1843. While working as a clerk in early youth, he devoted his spare time to the study of science, especially chemistry, attending lectures at Glasgow and Edinburgh universities. At 20 he began to manufacture sal ammoniac (ammonium chloride) and other chemicals in his own plant at Glasgow, and in 1797 he established the first alum manufactory in Scotland. Macintosh is best known as the inventor of the waterproof material called mackintosh (patented in 1823), made by cementing two fabric thicknesses together with rubber dissolved in naphtha. He also patented a method for converting malleable iron into steel in 1825, but this proved commercially impracticable. Three years later he assisted James Beaumont Neilson in putting his hot-blast process of iron manufacture into operation.

McINTOSH, măk'ĭn-tŏsh, **(Margaret) Millicent Carey,** American educator: b. Baltimore, Md., Nov. 30, 1898. She graduated from Bryn Mawr College (1920) and received the Ph.D. from Johns Hopkins University in 1926. After teaching English at Bryn Mawr (1926–1930) and serving also during this period as dean of freshmen and acting dean of the college, she became headmistress of the Brearley School, New York City (1930–1947). In 1932 she was married to Rustin McIntosh, M.D. Mrs. McIntosh was chosen dean of Barnard College, Columbia University, succeeding Virginia Gildersleeve in 1947, and in 1952 she was named the first president of Barnard. She retired in 1962. One of her major interests in education was to improve the status of teachers by raising salaries and giving teachers a more important place in the community. She also advocated greater emphasis on humanistic studies in school and college.

MacIVER, mȧ-kē′vŭr, **Robert Morrison,** Scottish-American sociologist: b. Stornoway, Outer Hebrides, Scotland, April 17, 1882. Educated at Edinburgh and Oxford universities, he taught at Aberdeen and Toronto, before coming in 1927 to Columbia University, where he was Lieber professor of political philosophy and sociology, 1929–1950. He is the author of several textbooks and works on social philosophy, among them *The Web of Government* (1947) and *Pursuit of Happiness* (1955).

MACK, Connie (real name CORNELIUS ALEXANDER McGILLICUDDY), American baseball player and executive: b. East Brookfield, Mass., Dec. 23, 1862; d. Philadelphia, Pa., Feb. 8, 1956. He began as a catcher on a team in his native town, turned professional in 1884, and entered the major leagues in 1886, by joining the Washington club of the National League. Four years later, he joined the Buffalo (N.Y.) team of the Players' League and the following season went to the Pittsburgh club in the National League, becoming club manager in 1894. He became manager of the Western League's Milwaukee organization in 1897. From 1901 to 1950, while he was manager of the Philadelphia Athletics, his team won nine American League championships and five World Series.

MACK VON LEIBERICH, mäk′ fôn lī′bĕ-rĭk, BARON **Karl,** Austrian military officer: b. Nennslingen, Franconia, Germany, Aug. 24, 1752; d. Sankt Pölten, Austria, Oct. 22, 1828. He entered the Austrian Army in 1770, and rose to the rank of field marshal in 1797. After the Peace of Campoformio, he was appointed by the king of Naples to command his troops, and occupied Rome in 1797; but popular protests against his conclusion of an armistice with the French forced him to take refuge in the French camp (1798). He was taken to Paris as a prisoner, but escaped in 1800. In 1805 he was sent by the Austrians to check the French advance along the line of the Iller, but he was encircled at Ulm, and had to capitulate with his army to Napoleon. He was sentenced to death by an Austrian court-martial; the emperor commuted the penalty to expulsion from the army and 20 years' imprisonment, and in 1808 he was set free.

MACKAY, mȧ-kī′, **Charles,** British poet and journalist: b. Perth, Scotland, March 27, 1814; d. London, England, Dec. 24, 1889. An editor of the *Glasgow Argus* and the *Illustrated London News,* he lectured in the United States, 1857–1858, and was a special correspondent of the London *Times* in New York during the Civil War (1862–1865). Mackay was famous for his songs, some of which he set to music of his own.

MACKAY, măk′ĭ, **Clarence Hungerford,** American financier: b. San Francisco, Calif., April 17, 1874; d. New York, N. Y., Nov. 12, 1938. The son of John William Mackay (q.v.), he succeeded on the death of his father to the latter's vast business interests. Much of his boyhood was spent in France and in England. He was chairman of several leading American cable companies, and a director of the Metropolitan Opera Company. He was made a Knight of Malta by Pope Pius XI in 1931.

McKAY, mȧ-kā′, **Claude,** American Negro writer: b. Sunny Ville, Jamaica, BWI, Sept. 15, 1890; d. Chicago, Ill., May 22, 1948. He settled in the United States in 1912, and studied at Tuskegee, Ala., and at the Kansas State College. Previously he had published two volumes of poetry, *Songs of Jamaica* (1911) and *Constabulary Ballads* (1912). After World War I he traveled widely, visited Russia, and lived in France and Germany. A new collection of poems, *Spring in New Hampshire* (1920), was brought out in London. For a while McKay joined other radical writers as a contributor to the *Liberator;* but he eventually turned away from communism and became affiliated with the Catholic Youth Organization. His other writings include the novels, *Home to Harlem* (1927), *Banjo* (1929), and *Banana Bottom* (1933); the autobiography *A Long Way from Home* (1937); and *Harlem: Negro Metropolis* (1940).

McKAY, Donald, American shipbuilder: b. Shelburne County, Nova Scotia, Sept. 4, 1810; d. Hamilton, Mass., Sept. 20, 1880. After learning the shipbuilding trade in New York, he began to work in the trade at Newburyport, Mass. In 1845 he established a shipyard at East Boston where he built many large trading ships of the clipper type. The *Great Republic,* which he constructed in 1853, a ship of 4,500 tons, was one of the largest vessels of its day.

McKAY, Douglas, American public official: b. Portland, Oreg., June 24, 1893; d. Salem, Oreg., July 22, 1959. A graduate of Oregon State College in 1917, he was a lieutenant of infantry in World War I. Subsequently he became an insurance and automobile salesman. In 1927 he established his own car agency in Salem, Oreg. He was mayor of Salem, 1933–1934, and thereafter sat for a number of terms in the Oregon State Senate. He served again in the armed forces in World War II, and in 1948 was elected governor of his state to complete the unexpired term of Governor Carl Snell, who had been killed in a plane crash. From 1953 to 1956, he served as secretary of the interior in President Dwight D. Eisenhower's administration. That fall he lost the contest for Oregon's Senate seat to Sen. Wayne Morse who accused him of sponsoring in his cabinet post a "giveaway" program of government resources.

McKAY, Gordon, American inventor and manufacturer: b. Pittsfield, Mass., May 4, 1821; d. Newport, R.I., Oct. 19, 1903. A cotton manufacturer's son, he invented shoe-making machines, including the heeler, and lasting-nailing-machines that revolutionized the industry. At the outbreak of the Civil War he offered to make shoes for the Union Army, and within three years had leased his

machines to more than 60 other shoe-manufactur-
ing firms, receiving handsome royalties for the
rental of these machines. With Lyman Reed
Blake he obtained a patent in 1865 for manufacturing shoes with turned soles. After years of
bitter competition with the welt-shoe process of
Charles Goodyear (q.v.), the two businesses
merged in 1880; and in 1895, having realized
about $40,000,000 from his inventions, McKay re-
tired from the business. He founded the McKay
Institute in Kingston, R.I., for Negro students
and bequeathed a trust fund to Harvard University to establish a department of applied science.

MACKAY, măk'ĭ, **John William,** American miner and financier: b. Dublin, Ireland, Nov.
28, 1831; d. London, England, July 20, 1902.
Brought to the United States at the age of nine,
he became apprenticed to a shipbuilder in New
York City soon afterward. In 1851 he joined
the mining rush to the West, working for several
years in California and Nevada mines and eventually striking out for himself. In 1865, in partnership with others, he acquired the Hale and
Norcross mine near Virginia City, Nev., and
in 1873 the nearby bonanza mine, Virginia Consolidated, which yielded more than $100 million
in gold and silver. Now a millionaire, Mackay
acquired wide holdings and in 1876 moved to New
York City, but thereafter spent much of his time
in Europe. He started to break the wireless
monopoly of Jay Gould (q.v.) and Western
Union in 1883, when he organized the Commercial Cable Company in partnership with James
Gordon Bennett (q.v.). In the next year he laid
two cables to Europe and won the ensuing struggle with Gould. In 1886 he established the Postal
Telegraph Cable Company for land operations
and began to lay a Pacific Ocean cable in 1902.

MACKAY, mȧ-kī', seaport, Australia, situated on the east coast of Queensland, on the
Pioneer River. A tropical city, warm and humid
in climate, it is 598 miles by rail (751 miles by
road) northwest of Brisbane. The lowlands of
the coastal plain and hinterland, with abundant
rainfall, comprise one of Queensland's largest
cane sugar-growing areas, for which Mackay,
with seven sugar mills, serves as a processing and
export center. Vegetables and tropical fruits are
also grown, while dairying and cattle raising are
important. Gold and copper, the chief minerals
in the area, have been mined since the 1870's.
There are several nearby seaside resorts. A
deepwater harbor, enclosed by two stone breakwaters, was opened in 1939, an ocean oil terminal
was added in 1955, and a bulk sugar export terminal—the first in Queensland—was completed
in 1957. Mackay is named after Capt. John Mackay, discoverer of the Pioneer River in 1860.
Pop. (1954) 14,764.

MacKAYE, mȧ-kī', **Percy,** American dramatist and poet: b. New York, N.Y., March 16,
1875; d. Cornish, N.H., Aug. 31, 1956. Son of
the actor and producer, Steele MacKaye (q.v.),
he graduated at Harvard University in 1897 and
studied at the University of Leipzig in 1899 and
1900. He then taught in a private school (1900–
1904) and later lectured on the theater at Harvard, Columbia, Yale, and other universities.

MacKaye wrote several plays, including *The
Canterbury Pilgrims,* a comedy, published in
1903; *Jeanne d'Arc* (1906), a drama; *Sappho and

Phaon (1907), a tragedy; and the tetralogy,
*The Mystery of Hamlet, King of Denmark; or
What We Will* (1950). His artistic aim was to
create a native American poetic drama. *The
Canterbury Pilgrims* was produced also as an
opera, in 1917, with music by Reginald De
Koven; and MacKaye and De Koven collaborated
on a folk opera, *Rip Van Winkle,* produced in
1920. Among MacKaye's many volumes of
poetry are *Dogtown Common* (1921) and *My
Lady Dear, Arise!* (1940). He is also the author
of various prose works, including *Tall Tales of
the Kentucky Mountains* (1926) and works on
the theater.

MacKAYE, (James Morrison) Steele,
American actor, dramatist, and producer: b. Buffalo, N.Y., June 6, 1842; d. Timpas, Colo., Feb.
25, 1894. When 16 years old, he studied painting
in Paris and a few years afterward served in the
American Civil War. After trying various occupations, he returned to Paris in 1869 to study
dramatic expression with François A. N. C. Del-
sarte (q.v.), whose method he later tried to promote in the United States. In 1872 he made his
acting debut in New York City. He began to
write plays and, in order to produce them,
opened the Madison Square Theatre (1879), one
of the first "intimate" theaters, for which he
devised a double or elevator stage and overhead
and indirect lighting. Here his greatest success,
the melodrama *Hazel Kirke,* was presented in
1880, enjoying a spectacular run of over a year.
Later he built the Lyceum Theatre, in connection
with which he founded the first dramatic school
in the United States, now the American Academy
of Dramatic Arts. The vast cycloramic spectacle
on Christopher Columbus, called *The World
Finder,* which MacKaye projected for the
World's Columbian Exposition at Chicago
(1893) never became a reality, except in the
form of a working model. He was the author of
over 20 plays, which have largely been forgotten.
His son, Percy MacKaye (q.v.), wrote his biography, *Epoch . . .* (2 vols., 1927).

McKEAN, mȧ-kēn', **Thomas,** American political leader and jurist: b. New London, Chester
County, Pa., March 19, 1734; d. Philadelphia,
Pa., June 24, 1817. After studying in a law
office in New Castle, Del., he was admitted to
the bar at the age of 20 and soon established a
large practice. In 1762 he became a member of
the Delaware Assembly, serving there for 17
years. Vehemently opposed to the Stamp Act
measure, he was a delegate to the Stamp Act
Congress in 1765. In 1772 and 1773 he was
speaker of the Delaware Assembly. In the next
year he established a home in Philadelphia, where
he became active in Pennsylvania politics, but
also continued to hold office in Delaware. He was
a leader in the fight for American independence,
representing Delaware in the Continental Congress during the years 1774 to 1776 and 1778 to
1783, serving as president of the Congress in
1781. On July 1, 1776, he voted in Congress for
independence, but because of a tying "no" by his
colleague, McKean sent for the third Delaware
delegate, whose affirmative vote on July 2 procured Delaware's support of the independence resolution. McKean helped to frame the Delaware
constitution in 1776 and again was elected speaker
of the Assembly in 1777. He signed the Declaration of Independence after Jan. 18, 1777, and the

Articles of Confederation were also signed by him. From September to November 1777, he served as acting president of Delaware, and from 1777 to 1799 as chief justice of Pennsylvania. As a member of the state convention in 1787, he played an active part in securing Pennsylvania's ratification of the Constitution. McKean became a strong supporter of Thomas Jefferson and a leader of the Republican Party of that day. From 1799 to 1808 he served as governor of Pennsylvania. With James Wilson he wrote *Commentaries on the Constitution of the United States of America* (1792).

McKEES ROCKS, borough, Pennsylvania, situated in Allegheny County, on the Ohio River at the mouth of Chartiers Creek, 4 miles northwest of the center of Pittsburgh, of which it is an industrial suburb. It is served by the Pittsburgh & Lake Erie, the Pittsburgh, Chartiers & Youghiogheny, and the Pittsburgh, Allegheny McKees Rocks railroads. There are bituminous coal mines nearby. The borough has railroad shops and industrial establishments producing iron and steel, locomotive parts, chemicals, paint, and enamelware.

McKees Rocks is on the site of a trading post established in 1743, and of a fort built by Christopher Gist (q.v.) in 1753. It was named for Alexander McKee, who acquired the land and settled here about 1764. It was incorporated as a borough in 1892. Government is by mayor and council. Pop. 13,185.

McKEESPORT, city, Pennsylvania, situated in Allegheny County, at an altitude of 750 feet, at the confluence of the Monongahela and Youghiogheny rivers and on their east banks, 10 miles southeast of Pittsburgh. It is served by the Pennsylvania, the Baltimore & Ohio, the Pittsburgh & Lake Erie, and the McKeesport Connecting railroads. The city is laid out on ground rising fairly steeply from the riverbanks, with the newer residential section on heights overlooking the business and industrial districts. McKeesport is the retail center of a thickly settled area, its neighboring towns including Clairton, East McKeesport, Glassport, Duquesne, Elizabeth, Wilmerding, Port Vue, and East Pittsburgh. The city's industrial history is closely associated with the development of the surrounding bituminous coal and natural gas region. McKeesport is one of the world's largest producers of steel pipe and tubing, and is sometimes called the Tube City. It also has important sheet steel and tin plate industries, and is the home of the first United States producers of stainless steel. Among the other products of the city's industrial establishments are shell and tool steel, steel castings, fabricated steel, structural steel products, chromium sheets, automobile wheels and bodies, tools and dies, cans, candy, meat products, and lumber. The city's public school system includes two high schools, and there is a Carnegie free library.

McKeesport was settled in 1755 by David McKee, a native of Ireland, who purchased a tract of 844 acres and from 1769 operated a ferry for which official authority was granted in 1775. The area was the center of the Whiskey Rebellion (q.v.) in 1794. The town was laid out in 1795 by John McKee, son of the original settler, 200 city lots being platted and sold. Growth was slow until about 1830, when the rich coalfields nearby were opened. Until the 1850's barge

building was a thriving industry. The first ironworks was established in 1851, and industrial expansion was steady thereafter. McKeesport was incorporated as a borough in 1842, and chartered as a city in 1890. Government is of the commission type. Pop. 45,489.

McKEEVER, William Arch, American educator and author: b. Jackson County, Kans., April 12, 1868; d. July 8, 1940. He was graduated from the University of Kansas in 1898, and later studied at the University of Chicago and Harvard University. From 1900 to 1913 he taught philosophy at Kansas State Agricultural College, and from 1913 to 1920 was head of the department of child welfare at the University of Kansas. He then became director of the School of Psychology, Oklahoma City. He was the author of *Psychology and the Higher Life* (1908); *Psychologic Method in Teaching* (1909); *Farm Boys and Girls* (1912); *Training the Boy* (1913); *Training the Girl* (1914); *Outlines of Child Study* (1915); *The Child and the Home* (1923); *The Creative Mind* (1925); *You and Your Life* (1930); and *Living a Century* (1935).

McKELL, SIR **William John,** Australian statesman: b. Pambula, New South Wales, Sept. 26, 1891. From 1917 to 1947 he was a Labour member of the Legislative Assembly of New South Wales. He served as minister of justice of the state from 1920 to 1922 and again from 1925 to 1927, minister for local government from 1930 to 1931, minister of justice from 1931 to 1932, and prime minister from 1941 to 1947, when he was appointed governor general of Australia. He was knighted in 1951. Field Marshal Sir William Slim succeeded him in the governor generalship early in 1953.

MacKELLAR, Thomas, American printer, type founder, and poet: b. New York City, Aug. 12, 1812; d. Dec. 29, 1899. He went to work as a compositor at the age of 14, and in the following year was employed by the publishing house of John and James Harper, where he learned the printer's trade. Shortly before he was 21, he went to Philadelphia and became a proofreader in the type foundry of Lawrence Johnson and George F. Smith. In 1845 he became a partner in the firm, and in 1860 the head of its successor, MacKellar, Smiths & Jordan, which he developed into the leading type foundry in the United States. From 1855 to 1884 he edited the *Typographic Advertiser.* He was the author of a popular work on typography, *The American Printer* (1866), as well as of a number of volumes of poetry. Among the latter are *Droppings from the Heart* (1844); *Tam's Fortnight Ramble* (1847); *Rhymes Atween-Times* (1873).

McKELWAY, Saint Clair, American journalist: b. Columbia, Mo., March 15, 1845; d. July 16, 1915. In 1853 his family moved to New Jersey, where he was privately educated. He studied law and was admitted to the New York bar in 1866, but never practiced. In that year he joined the staff of the New York *World,* and from 1868 to 1870 was Washington correspondent of that paper and the Brooklyn *Daily Eagle.* He was a member of the editorial staff of the *Eagle* until 1878, when he became editor of the Albany *Argus.* In 1884 he became editor in chief of the *Eagle,* which achieved a national reputation during his editorship, due in large part to his independent, courageous editorials. He was a regent of the University of the State of New York from 1883, becoming vice chancellor in 1900, acting chancellor in 1905, and chancellor in 1913.

McKENDREE COLLEGE, mà-kĕn′drē, a coeducational institution at Lebanon, Ill., founded in 1828 as Lebanon Seminary. It is the oldest United States College continuously under the operation of the Methodist Church. The name was changed in 1830 to honor William McKendree, the first American-born Methodist bishop, and the school's present charter was secured with the assistance of Abraham Lincoln. Baccalaureate degrees in arts and science are awarded. Many ministers, political leaders, and distinguished educators are numbered among the alumni.

WEBB B. HARRISON.

McKENNA, Reginald, British financier and politician: b. London, England, July 6, 1863; d. there, Sept. 6, 1943. Educated at King's College, University of London, and Trinity Hall, Cambridge, he was called to the bar in 1887. In 1895 he was elected to Parliament as a Liberal, serving until 1918. After a term as president of the Board of Education (1907–1908), he became first lord of the Admiralty (1908–1911) and while in this office won approval for the construction of eight battleships. He was home secretary (1911–1915) and, in 1915, during World War I, became chancellor of the exchequer. To finance the war effort he sharply raised income taxes and duties on such foodstuffs as sugar, tea, and coffee, and imposed taxes on many items, including amusements, railway tickets, and excess profits. Taxes on such profits reached 60 per cent. Leaving the exchequer in December 1916, he held the chairmanship of the Midland Bank, Limited, from 1919 until his death.

MACKENNAL, mà-kĕn″l, SIR **(Edgar) Bertram,** British sculptor: b. Melbourne, Australia, June 12, 1863; d. Torquay, England, Oct. 10, 1931. He studied sculpture in Melbourne, London, and Paris, and began to exhibit about 1886. In 1889 he won the competition to decorate Government House in Melbourne. After his *Circe* figure had received honorable mention at the Paris Salon of 1893, numerous commissions were offered him, including memorials to Queen Victoria in India and Australia. He executed the Edward VII memorial tomb at Windsor, unveiled in 1921, and that monarch's equestrian statue in Waterloo Place, London; the male figure, *Here Am I,* for Eton College playing fields; and the Parliament war memorial in St. Stephen's Hall, Houses of Parliament, London. Mackennal was knighted in 1921.

MACKENSEN, mäk′ĕn-zĕn, **August von,** German military leader: b. Haus Leipnitz, Saxony, Germany, Dec. 6, 1849; d. near Celle, Nov. 8, 1945. He entered the army in 1869, serving shortly after in the Franco-Prussian War. In 1908 he was made commanding general of the 17th Army Corps, which he led on the eastern front at the beginning of World War I. Under him German troops defeated Russians at the Battle of Masurian Lakes (September 1914). Later he commanded the 9th Army and the 11th Army, distinguishing himself in the 1915 campaign by expelling the Russians from Galicia. He was made a field marshal in 1915 and in the same year led the offensives in Poland and Serbia, overrunning the latter country. A German-Bulgarian army under him entered Rumania in 1916 and completed its subjugation by January 1917. At the Armistice von Mackensen became an Allied prisoner until December 1919. He retired from the army in 1920 and became leader of the Stahlheim, a monarchist veterans' organization. In 1933 he supported Adolf Hitler.

MACKENZIE, mà-kĕn′zĭ, SIR **Alexander,** Scottish explorer in North America: b. Stornoway, Scotland, c. 1764; d. Moulinearn, near Pitlochry, March 12, 1820. Brought to New York as a youth, he was employed by a Canadian fur-trading firm in 1779 and remained active in that business most of his life. Before or about 1788 he was given supervision of the Northwest Company's fur-trading affairs near Lake Athabasca (now in Alberta). His predecessor was Peter Pond, who had visited Great Slave Lake in northern Canada and suspected the existence of an outlet from that lake to the Pacific—the long-sought Northwest Passage. Mackenzie, with a party in three canoes, left Fort Chipewyan on Lake Athabasca on June 3, 1789, to explore this possibility. Paddling down the Slave River to Great Slave Lake, he located the western river outlet and drifted down this stream, which now bears his name, to Beaufort Sea of the Arctic Ocean, where further progress was barred by ice. Thus failing to find the Western Sea, he called his river the River of Disappointment. The round trip between Fort Chipewyan and the Arctic lasted 102 days.

In 1793 Mackenzie tried again to reach the Pacific, setting out by canoe on May 7 from a post on the Peace River. He ascended the Peace and its tributary, the Parsnip, discovered the turbulent Fraser River and followed it for a short distance, then struck out overland. Traveling on various rivers and by land, he crossed the Rocky Mountain coast ranges to the tiny Bella Coola River, which he descended to its mouth in a Pacific tidal inlet. Thus he made the first journey overland to the Pacific coast north of Mexico. Remaining in the fur trade during the following years, he is said to have amassed some wealth. In 1801 he published the narrative of his explorations (see *Bibliography*), and this work brought him recognition and a knighthood in 1802. Elected to the Legislative Assembly of Lower Canada in 1805, he served several years, but returned to Scotland in 1808, remaining there the rest of his life. See also AMERICA, DISCOVERY AND EXPLORATION OF—*Search for the Western Sea.*

Bibliography.—Mackenzie, Sir Alexander, *Voyages from Montreal . . . Through the Continent of North America to the Frozen and Pacific Oceans in . . . 1789 and 1793* (London 1801; reprinted in 2 vols., New York 1922); Wade, Mark S., *Mackenzie of Canada* (Edinburgh 1927); Woollacott, Arthur P., *Mackenzie and His Voyageurs* (London 1927); Mirsky, Jeannette, *The Westward Crossings; Balboa, Mackenzie, Lewis and Clark* (New York 1946).

MACKENZIE, Alexander, Canadian statesman: b. Logierait, Perthshire, Scotland, Jan. 28, 1822; d. Toronto, Ontario, Canada, April 17, 1892. Apprenticed to a stonemason at 14, he migrated to Canada in 1842 and worked in the building trade at Kingston and at Sarnia, Ontario (then Upper Canada). Keenly interested in politics, he became editor of the Lambton *Shield,* a Liberal paper, in 1852. He entered the Legislative Assembly of the Province of United Canada (comprising Upper and Lower Canada, now Ontario and Quebec), in 1861 and here he supported the Canadian confederation movement. In 1867 he was elected to the first House of Commons of the newly created Dominion of Canada. During the following years he led the Liberal opposition to the Conservative government under Sir John Alexander Macdonald (q.v.) and, when that government fell on the issue of the transcontinental railway scandal, Mackenzie became prime minister in 1873, taking for himself the ministry of public works. Under his government acts were passed for the construction of the Pacific railway and the completion of the railway to Nova Scotia and New Brunswick, and a supreme court was established for the Dominion. Mackenzie declined the honor of knighthood in 1875. In 1878, a time of economic depression, the Conservatives were victorious at the polls and Mackenzie resigned. Again he led the Liberal opposition in Parliament until his health failed in 1880, but he retained his seat therein until his death. Although he was not especially notable as prime minister, his integrity and his industry were beyond question.

MACKENZIE, Sir **Alexander Campbell,** British composer, conductor, and teacher: b. Edinburgh, Scotland, Aug. 22, 1847; d. London, England, April 28, 1935. He received his musical education at Sondershausen, Germany, and at the Royal Academy of Music, London, where he won the King's Scholarship in 1862. While at the Royal Academy, he also played violin in theater orchestras. Returning to Edinburgh about 1866, he established himself as a violinist, teacher, and choral conductor, and produced several compositions, including chamber music and the overture *Cervantes* (1877). For nearly a decade until 1888, he spent most of his time in Florence, Italy, composing choral and orchestral works. His opera *Colomba* (1883) and the oratorio *The Rose of Sharon* (1884) won him a high rank among British composers and led to his appointment as principal of the Royal Academy. He served in this post from 1888 to 1924, teaching classes and administering the school, to the welfare of which he devoted most of his energy. He was knighted in 1895. Occasionally he undertook a series of choral or orchestral concerts—thus he conducted the London Philharmonic Society from 1892 to 1899—and he continued to compose in his spare time, but his reputation rests principally on his earlier works.

As a violinist and as one much exposed to the music of the Continent, Mackenzie remained relatively free from the repressive influence sometimes exercised by the British musical climate, based principally on music for the church. His output was extensive, although he wrote no symphonies or sonatas. His musical conceptions were basically in the Italian or German idiom, but he imparted the flavor of his native Scotland to some works, especially the *Pibroch Suite* for violin and orchestra (1889) and the three Scottish Rhapsodies for orchestra (*Rapsodie écossaise,* 1880; *Burns,* 1881; and *Tam o'Shanter,* 1911).

MACKENZIE, Alexander Slidell, American naval officer and author: b. New York, N.Y., April 6, 1803; d. Tarrytown, N.Y., Sept. 13, 1848. Originally Alexander Slidell (brother to John Slidell, the Confederate agent), he legally added his uncle's name, Mackenzie, in 1838. Entering the United States Navy in 1815, he spent much of his life on naval vessels and also in traveling at his own expense. On these experiences were based his several popular travel books, including *A Year in Spain* (2 vols., 1829) and *The American in England* (2 vols., 1835). These were followed by *The Life of Commodore Oliver Hazard Perry* (2 vols., 1840) and *The Life of Paul Jones* (2 vols., 1841). In 1841 he became a naval commander and was assigned in 1842 to the training ship *Somers.* Discovering, while on a return voyage from the coast of Africa, that a mutiny was planned, he hanged three ringleaders from the brig's yardarm. This incident aroused a storm of controversy in the United States, but he was exonerated by a court of inquiry and a court-martial. He published *The Life of Stephen Decatur* in 1846 and saw service in the Mexican War.

Consult Van de Water, Frederic F., *The Captain Called It Mutiny* (New York 1954).

MACKENZIE, Sir **(Edward Montague) Compton,** English author: b. West Hartlepool, England, Jan. 17, 1883. He was educated at Magdalen College, Oxford, and served with distinction during World War I in the Greek area. In 1928 he became one of the founders of the Scottish National Party. He was rector of Glasgow University from 1931 to 1934 and from 1931 to 1935 was literary critic of the London *Daily Mail.* He was knighted in 1952.

Known primarily as a novelist, Mackenzie published his first novel, *The Passionate Elopement,* in 1911. His second was *Carnival* (1912), and his third, the quasi-autobiographical *Sinister Street* (2 vols., 1913–14), achieved marked success. Regarded as his best, this novel has been called brilliant in style and original in conception, especially manifesting its author's unusual skill in developing the atmosphere of a locale (Edwardian Oxford). Mackenzie followed these novels with many more, of varied types and subject matter. Among them are *Guy and Pauline* (1915); *The Altar Steps* (1922); *The Monarch of the Glen* (1941); and the six books of the series *Four Winds of Love* (1937–45). *Whisky Galore* (1947) was made into a successful comedy film called *Tight Little Island* (1949) and was published in the United States under that title in 1950. Mackenzie has been called the "one particular genius of British humor," but critics disagree on the value of his work and many feel that the later novels generally have not lived up to the promise revealed in *Sinister Street.*

Mackenzie has entered various other fields of literary activity. Among these are four plays, one of which is his own dramatization (1912) of his novel *Carnival.* An enthusiast of recorded music, he founded the magazine *Gramophone* in 1923 and has served as its editor since that date. He wrote several books of war reminiscence, of which one, *Greek Memories* (1932), was suppressed by the government because official secrets were revealed, but later (1940) was reissued. Other works are his spirited defense of the former Edward VIII in *The Windsor Tapestry* (1938) and his biographical studies, *Mr. Roosevelt* (1943) and *Dr. Beneš* (1946).

MACKENZIE, Sir **George,** Scottish lawyer and writer: b. Dundee, Scotland, 1636; d. Westminster, London, England, May 8, 1691. After study at St. Andrews and Aberdeen universities, he was called to the bar at Edinburgh in 1659. He quickly distinguished himself by his eloquence and legal ability and in 1677 became king's advocate. As such, he ruthlessly prosecuted the Covenanters (q.v.), earning the epithet "Bloody Mackenzie." Out of office from 1686, he was reinstated in 1688. After the revolution of 1688–1689 had deposed James II and seated William III (q.v.) on the English throne, Mackenzie was one of a minority dissenting to the dethronement of James in Scotland. Thus out of favor with the new government, he retired to study and to write at Oxford University. He was the author of *Aretina, or the Serious Romance* (1661) with an account of the English Civil Wars, and various philosophical and legal works.

MACKENZIE, Henry, Scottish novelist and essayist: b. Edinburgh, Scotland, July 26, 1745; d. there, Jan. 14, 1831. Educated at the University of Edinburgh, he entered the legal profession, became attorney for the crown in exchequer matters and eventually, in 1799, comptroller of taxes for Scotland. His first and best-known novel, *The Man of Feeling,* was published anonymously in 1771. A loosely connected story of a well-meaning, but incompetent, hero, *The Man of Feeling* was instantly popular. Upon claim of authorship by one John or Charles Eccles, Mackenzie was forced to announce the novel as his. Mackenzie's next novel was *The Man of the World* (1773), the tale of a seducer, and this was followed by *Julia de Roubigné* (1777), a teary affair in the manner of Samuel Richardson. As a novelist, Mackenzie was perhaps closest to Laurence Sterne (q.v.), but decidedly inferior to him in characterization and dialogue. He wrote also several plays, of which only *The Prince of Tunis* (1773) was moderately successful.

As member of an Edinburgh literary society, Mackenzie was active in publishing a weekly periodical entitled *The Mirror* (1779–1780), modeled after Joseph Addison's *Spectator.* Nearly half of the essays for *The Mirror* were written by Mackenzie, and an even larger proportion for its successor, *The Lounger* (1785–1787), including a glowing tribute to Robert Burns. A member of the Highland Society of Scotland, he was chairman of its committee to determine the authenticity of the alleged translation of Ossian (q.v.) made by James Macpherson (q.v.). The committee report of 1805 concluded that Macpherson had altered and added to the poetic fragments traditionally attributed to the Celtic bard.

Consult Thompson, Harold W., *A Scottish Man of Feeling; Some Account of Henry Mackenzie . . . and of the Golden Age of Burns and Scott* (New York 1931).

MACKENZIE, Ian Alistair, Canadian statesman: b. Assynt, Sutherland County, Scotland, July 27, 1890; d. Banff, Alberta, Canada, Sept. 2, 1949. Graduated from Edinburgh University in 1911, he continued with research in Celtic languages, and received also a law degree from his alma mater in 1914. Migrating to Vancouver, British Columbia, in 1914, he served with the Canadian forces overseas in World War I. On his return to Canada, he was called to the bar and sat in the British Columbia legislature (1920–1928), serving for a short time as provincial secretary. An authority on parliamentary law, Mackenzie was a member of the federal House of Commons from 1930 to 1948 and held various cabinet posts under Prime Minister William Lyon Mackenzie King. Minister of immigration in 1930, he returned to the cabinet as minister of national defense (1935–1939), directing the initial stages of Canada's military planning in World War II. As minister of pensions and national health (1939–1944), Mackenzie proposed a national social insurance plan in 1943 which led the way toward the adoption of more comprehensive federal health and welfare plans beginning in 1944. He was minister of veterans' affairs from 1944 to 1948 and in the latter year was appointed to the Senate. His papers are in the Public Archives of Canada.

ROBERT ENGLAND.

MACKENZIE, SIR Morell, English physician and laryngologist: b. Leytonstone, England, July 7, 1837; d. London, Feb. 3, 1892. He studied medicine in London and on the Continent and took his medical doctorate at London University in 1862. A specialist in diseases of the throat, he became highly skilled in laryngeal surgery, with the result that he was called in May 1887 to attend the crown prince of Germany (later Emperor Frederick III). The royal patient's illness had been diagnosed as cancer of the larynx by German physicians, but Mackenzie took the view that the growth might be noncancerous and therefore curable by means other than removal of the larynx, as planned by the Germans. By November the cancerous nature of the disease was beyond question, and the prince, after becoming emperor in March 1888, died in June. The case induced a violent professional quarrel, with political overtones, between Mackenzie and the German doctors. The latter published a medical account of the case, while Mackenzie replied with a popular one, *The Fatal Illness of Frederick the Noble* (1888). Mackenzie previously had been knighted by Queen Victoria (1887) and decorated by the German emperor before his death. Despite this one notorious failure, Mackenzie did valuable pioneer work in his field and wrote several books on laryngoscopy and diseases of the nose and throat.

Consult Stevenson, Robert S., *Morell Mackenzie; the Story of a Victorian Tragedy* (London 1946).

McKENZIE, (Robert) Tait, Canadian-American sculptor and director of physical education: b. near Almonte, Ontario, Canada, May 26, 1867; d. Philadelphia, Pa., April 28, 1938. Graduated from McGill University in 1889, he took his medical doctorate there in 1892 and then taught anatomy and physical training there from 1895 to 1904. He served as director of physical education at the University of Pennsylvania from 1904 to 1931. During World War I he did valuable rehabilitation work as a member of the Royal Army Medical Corps. Among his medical publications is *Exercise in Education and Medicine* (1909; 3d ed., 1923).

While at McGill, McKenzie discovered his sculptural ability while making a statuette of a crouching athlete for classes in anatomy. About 1902 he began to exhibit chiefly athletic figures. Among his larger and more recent works are *The Youthful Benjamin Franklin* (1914, University of Pennsylvania); the war memorial at Cambridge, England (1922); the Scottish-American war memorial at Edinburgh (1927); and the statue, *Gen. James Wolfe* (1930, London).

Consult Hussey, Christopher, *Tait McKenzie: A Sculptor of Youth* (London 1929).

MACKENZIE, Sɪʀ **William,** Canadian financier and railway builder : b. Kirkfield, Ontario, Canada, Oct. 30, 1849; d. Toronto, Ontario, Canada, Dec. 5, 1923. Becoming a railroad contractor in 1871, he constructed portions of the Canadian Pacific Railway and the Victoria Railway (now part of the Canadian National system). About 1886 he formed a partnership with Donald Mann. They built several transportation lines and in 1899 organized the Canadian Northern Railway, buying or building connecting lines to form a system. Mackenzie was the financier of this venture, which possessed some 9,500 miles of track about 1915. During World War I the Canadian Northern was acquired by the government and eventually was merged in Canadian National Railways. Both Mackenzie and Mann were knighted in 1911.

MACKENZIE, William Lyon, Canadian journalist and political agitator : b. Dundee, Scotland, March 12, 1795; d. Toronto, Ontario, Canada, Aug. 28, 1861. Migrating to Upper Canada (now Ontario) in 1820, he established at Queenston the newspaper *Colonial Advocate* in 1824, and moved to York (now Toronto) later in that year. In the *Colonial Advocate* he supported the cause of popular government against the ruling oligarchy called the Family Compact (q.v.). His printing office at York was damaged in 1826 by a mob of government sympathizers, but he was awarded damages and continued publication to 1834. Rapidly gaining prominence during these years, he was elected to the Legislative Assembly for Upper Canada in 1828, subsequently expelled for abusive language, and alternately re-elected and expelled several times. In 1832, presenting a Reform Party petition for redress to the government in England, he obtained the dismissal of several colonial officials. Mackenzie became first mayor of the new city of Toronto in 1835. In the same year he was re-elected to the Assembly, along with a Reform majority, and therefore allowed to take his seat. A grievance committee headed by Mackenzie accomplished the recall of the governor, Sir John Colborne (q.v.), but the more autocratic rule of his successor, Sir Francis Bond Head (q.v.), produced even greater resentment in the province.

Mackenzie failed to retain his Assembly seat in 1836. Embittered, he established a new newspaper, the *Constitution,* in which he advocated a republican form of government. Discouraged with the ineffectiveness of constitutional agitation, he plotted open revolt, consulting with Louis Joseph Papineau (q.v.), reform agitator in Lower Canada. On Dec. 4, 1837, appearing near Toronto at the head of 800 men, he demanded from the governor a convention to settle grievances. Refusing the demand, the governor sent troops, who decisively defeated the rebels on December 7. Mackenzie fled to the United States. Establishing headquarters on fortified Navy Island, on the Canadian side of the Niagara River, he tried to continue the rebellion with the aid of United States sympathizers. These activities, leading to the Caroline Affair (q.v.), were to result in a period of strained relations between the two countries. Abandoning Navy Island in 1838, Mackenzie was imprisoned by the United States for breaking the neutrality laws. After his release he engaged in writing and newspaper work in the United States, returning to Canada on the proclamation of amnesty in 1849. Although his revolt had been a complete failure, he succeeded in attracting the home government's attention to colonial abuses, and his agitation led ultimately to responsible popular government in Canada. He served in the Legislative Assembly of United (Upper and Lower) Canada from 1851 to 1858, but he no longer wielded his former influence. Mackenzie was the grandfather of William Lyon Mackenzie King (q.v.). See also CANADA—40. *Under British Rule to Confederation: 1760–1867.*

Consult Lindsey, Charles, *William Lyon Mackenzie,* rev. ed., vol. 11 in Makers of Canada series (Toronto 1909); Guillet, Edwin C., *The Lives and Times of the Patriots; an Account of the Rebellion in Upper Canada, 1837–1838* . . . (Toronto 1938).

MACKENZIE, district, Northwest Territories, Canada, bounded on the west by Yukon Territory, on the south by the provinces of British Columbia, Alberta, and Saskatchewan, on the east by the District of Keewatin, and on the north by the Arctic Ocean. It is one of three provisional districts (Mackenzie, Keewatin, and Franklin) into which Canada's vast Northwest Territories is divided for administrative purposes. More than 500,000 square miles in area, the district was created in 1895 and its present boundaries were defined in 1918. It is the most important of the three districts in terms of population and economic development, a largely untapped treasure house of mineral riches. The district contains Canada's greatest river, the Mackenzie (q.v.), from which it takes its name, and also the two largest lakes wholly within Canadian territory—Great Bear and Great Slave, each of which is larger than either Lake Ontario or Lake Erie.

At Great Bear Lake, just south of the Arctic Circle, are Canada's first uranium mines, opened early in the 1930's and still productive. Yellowknife, on the northern arm of Great Slave Lake, has become one of North America's great gold mining camps. The richness of its ore easily offsets the high cost of operation and transportation several hundred miles to the nearest railroad. Created during the gold rush of the early 1930's, Yellowknife has become the district's largest population center (pop. 1956, 3,126) and is now a settled community of homes, churches, and schools. At Norman Wells on the Mackenzie River are rich oilfields, now used primarily to serve the mining and transportation interests of the region, but during World War II constituting the base of the Canol Project for piping crude petroleum across the mountains to Whitehorse in the Yukon Territory. This project was later abandoned. Aklavik, in the Mackenzie Delta, is near the site of a novel industry, the Canadian government's reindeer station for breeding and preservation of the species. In earlier times trapping for fur was the region's basic industry.

Administration of this vast, but sparsely populated, empire is centered in the national capital, Ottawa, and is in the hands of the commissioner of the Northwest Territories, who heads a nine-man council. Four members of the council are elected by citizens of the District of Mackenzie. The other five are appointed by the Canadian government, which therefore holds majority control. The commissioner by custom is the deputy minister of northern affairs and national resources and has powers of taxation to maintain municipal institutions, administration of justice, public health, education, property and civil rights, and various types of licensing. The recently created constituency of Mackenzie River now elects one member to the Canadian House of Commons.

The district administrator and his staff are at Fort Smith, on the Slave River at the southern border of the district. Fort Smith is headquarters and report center for the Royal Canadian Mounted Police, who serve the area, mining recorders scattered at various points adjacent to known mineral deposits, government medical officers stationed at nine settlements throughout the region, and other officials required in an organized community. It is well served by main-line scheduled air routes as well as nonscheduled feeder lines operating into the more isolated areas. Pop. 14,895.

Leslie Roberts.

MACKENZIE, river, Northwest Territories, Canada, issuing from the western end of Great Slave Lake in the Mackenzie District and flowing generally northwest over 1,000 miles to empty into the Arctic Ocean through a huge 15-pronged delta. It is Canada's greatest river. The Mackenzie is the main stream of a complex river system extending into British Columbia, Alberta, and Saskatchewan, comprising the Hay, Slave, Peace, Athabaska, and other headstreams, whose waters flow north into Great Slave Lake and thus feed the Mackenzie. The longest part of the system—the Mackenzie, Slave, Peace, and Finlay rivers—is in excess of 2,500 miles, thus, among the rivers of North America, second only to the Mississippi-Missouri combination.

The Mackenzie - Slave - Athabaska shipping route, including Great Slave Lake, is of major importance economically. Canadian National Railways travels north from Edmonton, Alberta, 300 miles to where the Athabaska becomes navigable, at Waterways (near Fort McMurray). Thence goods are shipped north by freight steamer on the Athabaska for approximately 300 miles to the western corner of Lake Athabaska, thence to the point where the Peace and Athabaska rivers merge to form the Slave, and thence on the Slave 250 miles to Great Slave Lake. The lake is then traversed westward to the point where it drains into the Mackenzie proper, which flows on for a further 1,000 miles to the Arctic Ocean. With the exception of a nine-mile portage on the Slave near Fort Smith, covered by truck roads, the entire route of more than 1,700 miles is navigable from the end of the steel rail to the northern ocean. It is heavily used for freighting from mid-June to mid-October, but passenger steamers have given way to the airplane. Economically the Athabasca, Slave, and Mackenzie rivers comprise one continuous river system.

The Mackenzie was named for Sir Alexander Mackenzie (q.v.), who discovered and explored the river in 1789. At this time Indian tribes lived and fought in the country north from Great Slave Lake to the Arctic Circle. North of this, to the coast, were Eskimos. The fur trade followed Mackenzie and was the region's economic base until well into the 20th century, when the mining and oil men arrived. Old fur-trading posts, however, remain the commercial centers along the river. They were built for defense as well as for trade, as their names imply—Forts Providence, Simpson, Wrigley, Norman, and Good Hope on the Mackenzie proper; others on tributaries and on the southern reaches of the waterway. (In some cases the word *Fort* has tended to disappear in modern usage.) Arctic Red River, slightly north of the Arctic Circle and dividing line between Indian and Eskimo country, is the only settlement of importance not designated a fort, except for Aklavik, in the heart of the delta and thus in Eskimo country.

Aklavik is a busy fur trade center, the cathedral town of a Church of England diocese constituting the largest mission area in the world, the seat of a Roman Catholic mission and school, and a large hospital. The population comprises 350 whites, a like number of Eskimos, and some Indians.

The economic future of the Mackenzie Valley is not easily assessed. Each trade settlement here and in the tributary area is a one-product community. When fur prices collapse, the trapper starves—or moves on. Base metal areas, as on the south bank of Great Slave Lake adjacent to the Mackenzie outlet, depend on world markets and are faced by the high cost of long lines of communication. The region's oil has no outside market as yet. Thus there are population shifts as economic changes occur, and even the white man tends to be a nomad in this vast, slowly tamed wilderness.

Consult Lane, Ferdinand C., *Earth's Grandest Rivers* (New York 1949); Roberts, Leslie, *The Mackenzie,* (New York 1949).

Leslie Roberts.

McKENZIE, city, Tennessee, located in Carroll and Weakley counties, 10 miles north-northwest of Huntingdon. Its altitude is 515 feet. Served by the Nashville, Chattanooga, and St. Louis Railway and the Louisville and Nashville system, McKenzie is a processing and shipping center for agricultural products, timber, and clay, and it manufactures flour and cheese. It is also the home of Bethel College. The community was incorporated in 1869 and became a city in 1923. It is governed by a mayor and aldermen. Pop. 3,780.

MACKEREL, măk′ẽr-ĕl, a designation applied as a group name to the fishes of order Scombroidei and to the mackerel family, Scombridae, but chiefly to the common mackerel, *Scomber scombrus* Linnaeus, a valuable food fish found in the Atlantic Ocean from Labrador to North Carolina and from Norway to Spain; a very close relative, *S. japonicus,* runs in the Pacific Ocean. There are large commercial fisheries for mackerel in waters of the United States, Japan, Scandinavia, the Netherlands, Spain, Portugal, and the British Isles. Found in huge schools in the open ocean, the mackerel is usually caught in nets and is not fished by anglers. In colder weather it migrates southward, offshore and into deeper water, while at the beginning of warm weather it approaches the coasts.

The common mackerel is a fusiform, streamlined fish, black along the dorsal ridge and vivid greenish blue on the upper sides, with dark wavy lines from the dorsal ridge to slightly below the lateral line; below this, the body is silvery. There are small, cycloid scales, but no band or corselet of enlarged scales, such as is found in some of the other members of the group (for example, the chub mackerel and the tuna). The fish is also distinguished by the lack of an air bladder. It averages about a foot long and a pound in weight, but may run as high as six or seven pounds. The mackerel's 2 dorsal fins are separated from each other, and there are 11 or 12 spines in the first dorsal. The ventral and pectoral fins are short. In the adult, both dorsal and anal fins are followed by small finlets. In the very young mackerel of less than an inch, these finlets are not separated from the main fins, but, at a length of about two inches, the young fish looks like the adult. The snout is long and the mouth is large, with small teeth in the jaws and on vomer and palatines. Mackerel food consists of smaller fishes and crustaceans. The female mackerel is reported to produce as many as 546,000 eggs, which, according to Robert Morgan, take five days to hatch at about 56° F. These eggs are buoyant, nonadhesive, and about 1.25 millimeters in diameter.

A number of other well-known food and game fishes belong to the mackerel tribe. They all have the characteristic small finlets and one to three keels on the caudal peduncle. The fish most often confused with the common mackerel is the chub mackerel, which not infrequently runs in mackerel schools, but the wavy black lines on the upper sides of this fish are much finer and more numerous than in the common mackerel and there is a translucent spot near the snout. Another profitable commercial and sports fish in the group is the tuna or tunny (q.v.). Still other edible and sports fishes are the albacore, bonito, and Spanish mackerel, and the wahoo is also a member of the family. In the order Scombroidei, but in different families and without finlets and some of the other characteristics of the common mackerel, are the speared fishes: sailfish, swordfish, spearfish, and marlins. All the fishes in the order are very widely distributed.

For current information on mackerel fisheries consult the fishery departments for the localities concerned.

CHRISTOPHER W. COATES.

MACKEREL SHARK, a name used for the family Isuridae, especially for the porbeagle, Atlantic species, *Lamna nasus* (Bonnaterre); Pacific form, *L. ditropis* (Hubbs and Follett); the sharp-nosed mackerel shark or mako (Atlantic form, *Isurus oxyrhynchus* Rafinesque; Pacific form, *I. glaucus* Müller and Henle); and, finally the white or man-eater shark, *Carcharodon carcharias* (Linnaeus).

The porbeagle and the mako may be told apart by their teeth: in the porbeagle there are small lateral cusps on either side of most of the narrowly triangular, smooth-edged central cusps, but these lateral cusps are not present in the mako. There is also a secondary caudal keel on either side of *Lamna*'s caudal fin, not present in *Isurus*. The man-eater shark has broadly triangular teeth with serrated edges.

There are authenticated reports of attacks on man by two of these sharks: the man-eater, which seems to attack, when, in the pursuit of food, it gets into water unsuitably shallow for it; and the mako, which seems to be harmless in United States waters, but is considered a menace to bathers off Australia.

All three fishes are caught by anglers, but the mako is a famous game fish, staging a spectacular fight when hooked and often leaping higher than a mast or over a small boat.

CHRISTOPHER W. COATES.

McKIM, mà-kĭm', **Charles Follen,** American architect: b. Isabella Furnace, Chester Coun-

ty, Pa., Aug. 24, 1847; d. St. James, Long Island, N.Y., Sept. 14, 1909. Son of the abolitionist James Miller McKim (q.v.), he studied at the Paris École des Beaux Arts from 1867 to 1870. After a period of employment with an architectural firm, and some commissions of his own, in 1878 he formed a partnership with William Rutherford Mead and William B. Bigelow, who was succeeded in 1879 by Stanford White. The partners' early style was based on classic precedents, but due to the enthusiasm of Joseph M. Wells, who joined the firm's staff in 1879, they adopted Italian Renaissance as their most usual style. A long series of important commissions came to them, with the result that many famous buildings bear the stamp of their design.

A commission in 1882 for the Villard group of homes in New York City (now used by the Roman Catholic archdiocese) led to that for the Boston Public Library (1887), which was primarily the work of McKim. The style was Italian Renaissance, with a façade resembling the Library of Ste. Geneviève, Paris. McKim took great care with the decoration, on a scale hitherto unknown in the United States, procuring rare marbles and bronzes, and the famous murals by Edwin Austin Abbey, Pierre Puvis de Chavannes, and John Singer Sargent. In 1891 the old Madison Square Garden in New York City was designed; in 1892, the Rhode Island State Capitol (built 1896–1903); and in the same year (1892) he was active in planning several buildings for the Chicago World's Columbian Exposition. From 1897 to 1901, McKim worked on the plan for the Columbia University campus at Morningside Heights, New York City, including the design of Low Library and several other buildings. Meanwhile he designed the University Club in New York City (1900), considered by some his masterpiece.

Along with Augustus Saint-Gaudens and others, McKim was chosen to prepare a plan for the development of Washington, D.C., in 1901; his portion of the work consisted of the central design from the Capitol to the Potomac River, including the Arlington Memorial Bridge and preliminary sketches for the Lincoln Memorial. In 1902 and 1903 he undertook additions and alterations to the White House for President Theodore Roosevelt and at about this time designed the Pierpont Morgan Library, New York City. The Pennsylvania Railroad terminal in New York City, in classical Roman style, was begun in 1904 and finished in 1910.

To give art students from the United States the advantage of first-hand acquaintance with the treasures of Europe, McKim founded in 1894 the American Academy in Rome for promising students of architecture, music, painting, and sculpture. The academy was supported in its early years by his own efforts, and he was its first president.

Consult Reilly, Charles H., *McKim, Mead, & White* (London 1924); Moore, Charles, *The Life and Times of Charles Follen McKim* (Boston 1929).

McKIM, James Miller, American abolitionist: b. Carlisle, Pa., Nov. 14, 1810; d. Orange, N.J., June 13, 1874. He graduated at Dickinson College in 1828, studied at Princeton Theological Seminary, and became a Presbyterian pastor at Womelsdorf, Pa., in 1835. An original member of the American Anti-Slavery Society (1833), McKim became the organization's lecturing agent in October 1836, and spoke throughout Pennsylvania, often at great personal danger. In 1840 he removed to Philadelphia, where he was publishing agent of the Pennsylvania Anti-Slavery Society and later corresponding secretary until 1862. In November 1862 he called a public meeting in Philadelphia to provide for 10,000 slaves suddenly liberated by the capture of Port Royal, S. C. As a result, the Philadelphia Port Royal Relief Committee was formed. This committee was expanded in November 1863 into the Pennsylvania Freedman's Relief Association, of which McKim became the corresponding secretary, in which capacity he was active in the establishment of Negro schools in the South. In 1865 he assisted in founding and became a proprietor of the New York weekly *Nation*. During the Civil War he was an advocate of the enlistment of Negro troops, and as a member of the Union League of Philadelphia assisted in the recruiting of 11 colored regiments.

MACKINAC ISLAND, măk'ĭ-nô, island, Michigan, in Mackinac County, at an altitude of 596 feet, at the entrance to the Straits of Mackinac in Lake Huron. It lies 255 miles northwest of Detroit. The island is 3 miles long and 2 miles wide. It is coextensive with Mackinac Island city and has been a state park since 1895. It came into prominence when the early missionaries and explorers realized its strategic value. It has steamboat connections with lake ports. It has a Daughters of the American Revolution library, a historical museum and an emergency hospital. Among local points of interest are the John Jacob Astor house, old forts, and a "most historical spot of Michigan" monument. The name is a shortened form of the Indian *Michilimackinac* meaning "great turtle." Pop. 942.

MACKINDER, mă-kĭn'dĕr, RIGHT HONORABLE SIR **Halford John,** English author and educator: b. Gainsborough, England, Feb. 15, 1861; d. England, March 6, 1947. He was educated at Christ Church, Oxford; in 1883 was president of the Oxford Union; barrister, Inner Temple, 1886; 1903–1908 director of the London School of Economics and Political Science. He was leader of the Mount Kenya expedition, 1899; member (Unionist) for the Camlachie division of Glasgow, 1910–1922. He was made privy councillor, 1926; vice president of the Royal Geographic Society, 1933–1936; Gold Medallist, American Geographical Society, 1943. He was author of *The Rhine* (1908); *Elementary Studies in Geography* (18th edition, 1930); *Democratic Ideals and Reality* (1919). See also GEOPOLITICS.

McKINLEY, mă-kĭn'lĭ, **William,** American statesman, 25th president of the United States: b. Niles, Trumbull County, Ohio, Jan. 29, 1843; d. Buffalo, N. Y., Sept. 14, 1901. He was educated at Union Seminary, Poland, Ohio, and Allegheny College, Meadville, Pa., 1860–1861. Forced by illness to discontinue his college course, he taught in the public schools, was a clerk in the Poland post office, and on June 11 enlisted for the Civil War as a private in Company E of the 23d Ohio Volunteer Infantry. His first battle was that of Carnifex Ferry, Sept. 10, 1861, and on April 15, 1862, while in camp at Fayetteville, western Virginia, he was promoted commissary sergeant. For conspicuous service at Antietam, Sept. 17, 1862, he was made second

lieutenant of Company D. His subsequent appointments were, first lieutenant, Company E (Feb. 7, 1863); captain, Company G (July 25, 1864); and brevet major (March 14, 1865). When mustered out on July 26, 1865, he was acting assistant adjutant general on the staff of Gen. S. C. Carroll, commanding the veteran reserve corps stationed at Washington. Among other actions in which he participated were those of South Mountain, Sept. 14, 1862, Lexington, June 10, 1864, Kernstown, July 24, 1864, Opequan Creek (Winchester, Sept. 19, 1864), Fisher's Hill (Sept. 22, 1864), and Cedar Creek (Oct. 19, 1864). During his subsequent political career he was generally known, especially in Ohio, as Major McKinley. At the close of the war he began the study of law at Youngstown, Ohio (1865–1866), continued it at the Albany (N. Y.) Law School (1866–1867), in March 1867 was admitted to the bar at Warren, Trumbull County, Ohio, and at once entered practice at Canton. In 1870–1871 he was prosecuting attorney of Stark County, and during the campaign between R. B. Hayes and William Allen for the governorship of the state, spoke effectively against the "greenback" craze. He was elected to Congress as Republican representative from the 17th Ohio district in 1877, and served continually in the 45th, 46th and 47th Congresses (1877–1883). It was asserted by the Republicans that he was elected in 1882 to the 48th Congress by a majority of eight ballots; but, although he had received the certificate of election, his seat was successfully contested by J. H. Wallace, who was not, however, seated until June 1884. He represented the 20th district in the 49th Congress (1885–1887), and the 18th in the 50th and 51st Congresses; but in 1890 was defeated in the 16th for the 52d Congress by 300 ballots by J. G. Warwick, Democrat, lieutenant governor of the state a short time previously. His defeat was attributed to the gerrymandering of the district by a Democratic legislature. His service in Congress was notable. In 1877 he was appointed a member of the Judiciary Committee, and in December 1880 of the Ways and Means Committee to succeed James A. Garfield; and in 1881 was chairman of the committee in charge of the Garfield memorial exercises in the House. In 1889–1890 he was chairman of the Ways and Means Committee. He was a candidate for speaker of the 51st Congress, but was defeated by T. B. Reed on the third ballot in the Republican caucus. He was known among the foremost orators of the House; and his speeches on arbitration as a solution of labor troubles (April 2, 1886) and in support of the civil service laws (April 24, 1890) were most favorably received. But his principal efforts were made in connection with the tariff, which, from his first appearance in the House, was the chief object of his study. On April 6, 1882, he spoke in advocacy of protection; on April 30, 1884, in opposition to the Morrison tariff bill, making what was esteemed the ablest argument against that measure; and on May 7, 1890, in support of the general tariff bill, now known by his name, which, as chairman of the Ways and Means Committee, he had introduced before the House on April 16. The bill was passed by the House on May 21, by the Senate on September 11, and on October 6 became a law. His bill obtained for him an international reputation, and eventually the Presidency. In 1884 he was delegate at large from Ohio to the Republican National Convention at Chicago, where he supported James Blaine's candidacy, and where, as chairman of the committee on resolutions, he helped to determine the platform of his party, which he read before the convention. In the Republican National Convention at Chicago in 1888, he was again a delegate and chairman of the committee on resolutions. He supported the candidacy of John Sherman, although, when it was finally learned that Blaine would decline the nomination, he was himself the choice of many delegates and was strongly urged to permit the use of his name. At the Minneapolis convention of 1892 he was once more a delegate and was elected permanent chairman of the assembly. He supported the renomination of President Harrison, and though refusing the use of his own name, received the ballots of 182 delegates. He then left the chair and moved to make Harrison's nomination unanimous, which was accordingly done. In the ensuing campaign he took a very active part, traveling, it was estimated, more than 16,000 miles and speaking to more than 2,000,000 voters.

In 1892–1896 McKinley was governor of Ohio, having been elected in 1891 by 21,500 plurality, and in 1893 by the unusual plurality of 80,995. Labor riots occurred during his administration, necessitating the placing of 3,000 militia troops in active service, but the difficulties were successfully adjusted. He also personally directed the relief work for the starving miners of the Hocking Valley district.

McKinley was nominated for the presidency by the Republican National Convention which met at Saint Louis, June 16, 1896, and was elected by a plurality of 601,854 over W. J. Bryan, receiving a popular vote of 7,104,779, and in the electoral college a vote of 271 to 176 for Bryan. Throughout the campaign he remained in Canton, where he made over 300 speeches to more than 750,000 visitors. Under his administration decided increase in business prosperity followed the passage of the Dingley tariff measure. The most important event of his term was the Spanish-American War, which he had believed might be prevented and had done all in his power to avert. When an independence movement developed among the inhabitants of the Philippine Islands, the President appointed a commission to study the situation and report on the most suitable mode of government for the new territory. On July 7, 1898 he approved the joint resolution of Congress for the annexation of the Hawaiian Islands, and in 1898 he also selected a delegation to represent the United States in The Hague Peace Conference which convened in May 1899. The original Philippine Commission having rendered a report (Jan. 31, 1900), the President appointed a new commission, known from its head, Judge W. H. Taft, as the Taft Commission, under whose direction civil government was instituted in the islands on Sept. 1, 1900. (See PHILIPPINES—*History.*)

In 1900 the President stood conspicuously for justice in the settlement of the difficulties in China which marked that summer. He was renominated for the Presidency by the Republican National Convention which met at Philadelphia on June 25, 1900, receiving the entire vote of the 930 delegates. He was elected by a popular vote of 7,206,677 to the 6,374,397 for W. J. Bryan, receiving the largest popular majority ever given a candidate for the Presidency up to that time. He obtained 292 electoral votes and carried 28 States. On Sept. 5, 1901 he delivered at the Pan-American Exposition, Buffalo, N. Y., an important address, summarizing the problems then before the nation and his policy for their solution.

On September 6, while holding a reception in the Music Hall of the Exposition, McKinley was twice shot by Leon Czolgosz, an anarchist. He died on September 14, and four days afterward a day of mourning and prayer was called throughout the country by his successor, President Theodore Roosevelt. Unprecedented honors were paid to McKinley's memory in foreign capitals, notably in London, where memorial services were held in Westminster Abbey and Saint Paul's Cathedral. A statue was erected in his honor at Columbus, Ohio. See also UNITED STATES—*18. The Age of Industrial Growth.*

Bibliography.—The official biography of McKinley is by Charles S. Olcott, *Life of William McKinley* (Boston 1916). Other useful sources are Robert P. Porter's *Life of William McKinley, Soldier, Lawyer, Statesman* (Cleveland 1896); Herman H. Kohlsaat's *From McKinley to Harding* (New York 1923); Margaret Leach's *In the Days of McKinley* (New York 1959); and H. W. Morgan's *William McKinley and His America* (Syracuse 1963).

McKINLEY, Mount (Russian BOLSHAYA, bŭl-y'-skȧ'yȧ), a peak of the Rocky Mountains, the highest in North America (20,320 feet above sea level) south of the central part of Alaska, about 155 miles north of Cook Inlet. The Indian name for this peak is Traleyka. The fact that this is the highest land on the continent was not known till 1896 when W. A. Dickey explored the Sushitna River and the land near its source, naming the peak in honor of president William McKinley. In 1903 it was visited by members of the United States Geological Survey and in 1917 the Mt. McKinley National Park was created.

Attempts to climb the peak began in 1903 but no expedition was successful until the Hudson Stuck expedition reached the top on June 7, 1913. It has been climbed several times since then and the mountain was used to test U.S. Army Air Force equipment in 1942.

McKINLEY ACT, a name popularly given to a tariff bill reported to Congress, May 21, 1890, by the Ways and Means Committee of the House of Representatives, of which William McKinley was chairman. It became a law in October 1890 and was repealed in 1894. It increased the duties on wool, woolen manufactures, on tin-plate, barley and some other agricultural products and remitted the duty on raw sugar. The reciprocity feature was an important part of the bill, providing for the remission of duty on certain products from those countries which should remove duties on American imported products. See TARIFF.

McKINNEY, Mrs. Glen Ford. See WEBSTER, JEAN.

McKINNEY, mȧ-kǐn'ĭ, city, Texas, seat of Collin County, 30 miles north of Dallas on the Southern Pacific Railroad and state and federal highways. Altitude 612 feet. In a rich agricultural area, McKinney has dairy and stock farms, poultry dressing and pecan shelling plants, and manufactures dairy products, textile products, clothing, feeds, beverages, confectionery, and mattresses. Among the public services of the community are a city library, a city-county hospital as well as a 1,000-bed veterans hospital, and a municipal pool and playground. About 10 miles to the south-southeast the Lavon Reservoir (capacity 423,300 acre-feet) on the East Fork of the Trinity River is surrounded by game preserves and a recreational area.

The city was named for, and has a monument to, Collin McKinney, a signer of the Texas declaration of independence. The Collin McKinney home was built in 1836 and is now located in the city park. McKinney was founded in 1842 and has a commission form of government. Pop. 13,763.

MACKINTOSH, Charles Rennie, Scottish architect and painter: b. Dennistoun, Glasgow, Jan. 7, 1868; d. London, Dec. 10, 1928. A student at the Glasgow School of Art and a member of the firm of Honeyman and Keppie, he traveled abroad on the Alexander Thomson scholarship in 1890, and in 1894 submitted the prize-winning designs for the new building of the Glasgow School of Art. This building, completed in 1909, was representative of the originality and freedom from tradition characteristic of all his work. In 1897 he undertook, in collaboration with George Walton, the decoration and furnishing of Miss Cranston's Tea-Rooms in Glasgow, which embodied the features of what was later termed in Germany the "Glasgow School style."

Gaining considerably more renown on the Continent than in his own country, Mackintosh had commissions and exhibitions in many European cities, and, although he had no followers in Great Britain, he founded the so-called *Jugendstil* in Germany. After World War I he devoted his time to water colors and became one of the first British masters of abstract design.

MACKINTOSH, măk'ĭn-tŏsh, **Sir James,** Scottish historian and philosophical writer: b. Aldourie, Inverness-shire, Oct. 24, 1765; d. London, May 30, 1832. He was educated at Aberdeen and Edinburgh; studied medicine and took the M.D. degree in 1787; published his *Vindiciae Gallicae* in answer to Burke's *Reflections on the French Revolution;* quitted the medical profession and was called to the English bar in 1795. By reason of his brilliant lectures on the *Laws of Nature and Nations,* and his defense of Jean Gabriel Peltier, who was prosecuted for a libel on Napoleon Bonaparte, he acquired fame at the bar, and in 1804 was appointed recorder of Bombay and received the honor of knighthood.

After an honorable career in India, Mackintosh returned to England, entered Parliament for Nairn and afterward for Knaresborough, was professor of law at Haileybury College (1818–1824), a member of Privy Council, and in 1830 commissioner of the Board of Control. Among his writings may be mentioned his *History of England,* a fragment extending only to the reign of Elizabeth; *Dissertation on the Progress of Ethical Philosophy* in the *Encyclopaedia Britannica;* a *Life of Sir Thomas More* in Lardner's *Cabinet Cyclopaedia,* and nine chapters of an unfinished work on the revolution of 1688.

MACKINTOSH, a water-proof overcoat, or outer garment, one of the products of modern rubber manufacture. It derives its name from the inventor, Charles Macintosh of Manchester (1766–1843). See RUBBER.

MACKLIN, măk'lĭn, **Charles,** Irish actor and dramatist: b. Ireland, May 1, 1697; d. London, July 11, 1797. He was the son of an Irish gentleman named McLaughlin and in 1733 appeared in minor parts at Drury Lane, London. He steadily rose in public favor, until in 1741 he appeared in his greatest role, Shylock. He was accounted from this period among the best actors of the time. His last performance was at Covent Garden in May 1789, at past the age of 90. In 1735 he accidentally killed a brother actor in a quarrel and was tried for murder, and was frequently afterward engaged in disputes and actions at law. Of his own plays only *The Trueborn Irishman; Love a-la-Mode* (1759), and *The Man of the World* (1781) have been printed.

MACKUBIN, mà-kŭb'ĭn, **Florence,** American artist: b. Florence, Italy, May 19, 1861; d. Baltimore, Md., Feb. 2, 1918. She was of American parentage, and studied under Louis Deschamps and Julius Rolshoven in Paris and Herterrich in Munich, also miniature painting under Mlle J. Devina in Paris. She specialized in portrait and miniature painting, and was officially commissioned to execute various portraits for the Executive Mansion and State House, Maryland, among them a copy of Van Dyck's portrait of Queen Henrietta Maria, and portraits of Governors Calvert and Eden of Maryland. Other portraits are those of Sir Charles Drury at the Admiralty House, Chatham, England, and Sir William Van Horne, Canada. Her miniatures won a medal at the Tennessee Exposition.

McLACHLAN, măk-làk'làn, **Alexander,** Scottish Canadian poet: b. Johnstone, Renfrewshire, Scotland, Aug. 12, 1818; d. Orangeville, Ontario, March 30, 1896. He went to Canada in 1841, was Canadian immigration agent to Scotland in 1862, and in 1874 delivered in Scotland a series of lectures on Canadian life. He lectured also in Canada and the United States.

McLachlan was a man of broad and democratic sympathies and was deeply interested in the betterment of conditions among the working classes. Among his publications were *Poems, Chiefly in the Scottish Dialect* (1855); *Lyrics* (1858); *The Emigrant and Other Poems* (1861); *Poems and Songs* (1874).

McLANE, măk-lān', **Allan,** American soldier and jurist: b. Philadelphia, Aug. 8, 1746; d. Wilmington, Del., May 22, 1829. In 1774 he settled in Kent County, Del., and in the revolution he took a prominent part. He became a lieutenant in Thomas Rodney's regiment of Delaware militia, where he rendered important service at Long Island and White Plains and also in the New Jersey campaign. In 1777 he was made captain and was in command of the American guard about Philadelphia, taking active part in the battle of Monmouth. With the rank of major under Gen. Henry Lee he participated in the capture of Stony Point and Paulus Hook and attained colonel's rank.

At the close of the war McLane was appointed judge of the Delaware Court of Appeals. From 1790 to 1798 he was United States marshal of Delaware under Washington's appointment, and from 1808 until his death collector of Wilmington (Del.) port. He also served in the Delaware legislature, being for a time speaker of the lower house.

McLANE, Louis, American statesman: b. Smyrna, Kent County, Del., May 28, 1786; d. Baltimore, Md., Oct. 7, 1857. The son of Allan McLane, he entered the navy at an early age and served as a midshipman under the elder Stephen Decatur. At 16 he began to study law and was admitted to the bar in 1807. He represented Delaware in the House of Representatives from 1817 to 1827, when he became a United States senator. President Andrew Jackson appointed him minister to England in 1829, and two years later secretary of the treasury. He differed with Jackson, however, in the Bank of the United States controversy, and after serving as secretary of state in 1833–1834, resigned from the cabinet.

From 1834 to 1837 McLane was president of the Morris Canal and Banking Company of New York, and in 1837 he became president of the Baltimore and Ohio Railroad, which office he held for 10 years. In 1845 President James Knox Polk appointed him minister to England where he negotiated the compromise between the two countries in regard to the Oregon boundary line. In 1850 he became a member of the convention called to reform the constitution of Maryland.

McLANE, Robert Milligan, American statesman and diplomat: b. Wilmington, Del., June 23, 1815; d. Paris, France, April 16, 1898. The son of Louis McLane, he attended St. Mary's Academy in Baltimore, Md., and the Collège Bourbon in Paris, and was graduated from the United States Military Academy at West Point in 1837. After seeing active service in the Seminole War in Florida and against the Cherokee Indians in Georgia, he resigned from the army in 1843 and began to practice law in Baltimore, Md. He was a member of the House of Representatives from 1847 to 1851, and in 1853 was appointed commissioner to China, but resigned the following year because of ill health. In 1859 President James Buchanan appointed him minister to Mexico, where he remained until the eve of the Civil War.

In 1861 he was a member of a special committee appointed by the Maryland legislature to confer with President Abraham Lincoln regarding allegedly unconstitutional acts of the federal government in that state. In 1878 he was again elected to Congress, where he worked for the reduction of tariffs and for a pure food bill. He became governor of Maryland in 1883, and during his brief term attempted to better labor conditions, especially for working women and children. He resigned the governorship in 1885 to become minister to France, where he negotiated concerning the rights of French-born citizens of the United States, whom France attempted to press into military service. After the election of President Benjamin Harrison, he resigned, but continued to live in Paris until his death.

MACLAREN, măk-lăr′ĕn, Ian. See WATSON, JOHN.

MacLAREN, Murray, Canadian physician and government official: b. Richibucto, New Brunswick, Canada, April 30, 1861; d. St. John, New Brunswick, Dec. 24, 1942. He was graduated from New Brunswick University in 1880 and received his medical degrees from Edinburgh University in 1884 and 1888. He practiced

medicine in St. John for many years, and during World War I commanded a Canadian general hospital overseas. He sat in the Canadian House of Commons from 1921 to 1934, and was minister of pensions and national health for Canada from 1930 to 1934. He resigned to become lieutenant governor of New Brunswick and served until 1940.

McLAREN, William Edward, American churchman: b. Geneva, N. Y., Dec. 3, 1831; d. New York, N. Y., Feb. 19, 1905. He was graduated from Jefferson (now Washington and Jefferson) College, Washington, Pa., in 1851, was ordained a Presbyterian minister in 1860, and entered the ministry of the Protestant Episcopal Church in 1872. Three years later he was appointed bishop of Illinois and subsequently became bishop of Chicago when the Illinois diocese was divided. He founded the Western Theological Seminary at Chicago in 1881 and Waterman Hall, a school for girls at Sycamore, Ill., in 1885. He also summoned the first diocesan retreat held by the Episcopal Church in this country. Among his writings are *Catholic Dogma: The Antidote of Doubt* (1883); *Analysis of Pantheism* (1885); *The Holy Priest* (1889); and *The Essence of Prayer* (1901).

McLAUGHLIN, măk-lăf′lĭn, Andrew Cunningham, American historian: b. Beardstown, Ill., Feb. 14, 1861; d. Chicago, Ill., Sept. 24, 1947. He was graduated from the University of Michigan in 1882 and from its law school in 1885, and was professor of history at the university from 1888 to 1906, when he became head of the history department at the University of Chicago. He was director of the Bureau of Historical Research of the Carnegie Institution, Washington, D.C., from 1903 to 1905, and managing editor of the *American Historical Review* from 1901 to 1905. He retired from the University of Chicago faculty in 1929. Among his writings are: *Lewis Cass,* in *American Statesmen* series (1891); *History of Higher Education in Michigan* (1891); *The Confederation and the Constitution* (1905); *The Courts, the Constitution and Parties* (1912); *History of the American Nation* (rev. ed. 1913); *Steps in the Development of American Democracy* (1920); ed., with Albert Bushnell Hart, *The Cyclopedia of American Government,* 3 vols. (1914); *Foundations of American Constitutionalism* (1932); *A Constitutional History of the United States* (1935).

McLAUGHLIN, Mary Louise, American painter, noted for manufacture and decoration of porcelain: b. Cincinnati, Ohio, Sept. 29, 1847; d. there, Jan. 17, 1939. She began to make a porcelain called Losanti in 1898, and in 1899 won an award for decorative metalwork at the Paris Exposition. She also won awards for her painted china and porcelain at expositions in Chicago and Buffalo. Examples of her work are in the Cincinnati Museum, the Philadelphia Museum, and the Boston Museum of Fine Arts.

MACLAURIN, măk-lô′rĭn, Colin, Scottish mathematician and physicist: b. Kilmodan, Argyllshire, Scotland, Feb. 1698; d. Edinburgh, June 14, 1746. He was educated at the University of Glasgow and began to teach mathematics in Aberdeen in 1717. In 1719 he was elected to the Royal Society and the following year published his *Geometria organica,* a work on curves. He received a prize from the French Academy of Sciences in 1724 for a dissertation on the impact of bodies, and in 1725 he was made professor of mathematics at the University of Edinburgh. A controversy with Bishop George Berkeley led him to write his most important work, *A Treatise of Fluxions* (1742), which contains his essay on tides. His *Account of Sir Isaac Newton's Philosophy* and *A Treatise of Algebra* were published posthumously in 1748.

MACLAURIN, Richard Cockburn, kŏ′bĕrn, American educator and physicist: b. Lindean, Scotland, June 5, 1870; d. Boston, Mass., Jan. 15, 1920. After graduating from Auckland University College in New Zealand and Cambridge University, he was professor of mathematics at the University of New Zealand from 1898 to 1905 and dean of the law faculty there, 1905–1907. In the latter year he was invited to Columbia University as professor of mathematical physics. Two years later he was appointed president of the Massachusetts Institute of Technology, and he remained in that office until his death. Under his presidency the institute underwent considerable expansion and moved to its new site in Cambridge, Mass. He wrote *Title to Realty* (1900); *Theory of Light* (1909); and *Lectures on Light* (1909).

McLAWS, măk-lôz′, **Lafayette,** United States army officer: b. Augusta, Ga., Jan. 15, 1821; d. Savannah, Ga., July 24, 1897. He was graduated from the United States Military Academy in 1842, served in the Mexican War, and held various other posts in the United States Army until the outbreak of the Civil War. He then joined the Confederate forces, was commissioned brigadier general in 1861 and major general in 1862. He saw action in a number of major battles including Antietam, Fredericksburg, Gettysburg, and Chicamauga. During Sherman's march to the sea he commanded the defenses of Savannah and had charge of the military district of Georgia. In 1875 he was appointed collector of internal revenue and in 1876 postmaster of Savannah.

MACLAY, mă-klā′, **Edgar Stanton,** American author: b. Foochow, China, April 18, 1863; d. Washington, D.C., Nov. 2, 1919. The son of the missionary Robert Samuel Maclay, he lived in China and Japan until 1881, when he entered Syracuse University. After graduating, he worked on the Brooklyn *Daily Times,* the New York *Tribune,* and briefly on the New York *Sun* until 1895, when he was appointed lighthouse keeper at Old Field Point, Long Island. Five years later he received an appointment at the New York Navy Yard. Meanwhile he had published the *Journal of William Maclay* (1890) and *A History of the United States Navy,* 2 vols. (1894), which was used as a textbook at the United States Naval Academy. In the third volume of the *History,* published in 1901, Maclay charged Rear Admiral Winfield Scott Schley (q.v.) with cowardice in the naval fight off Santiago, Cuba, July 3, 1898, and as a result was dismissed from the navy yard by President Theodore Roosevelt. He subsequently found employment on the Brooklyn *Standard Union* and then was engaged in research in Washington, D.C.

Maclay also wrote *Reminiscences of the Old Navy* (1898), *A History of American Privateers* (1899), and several naval biographies.

MACLAY, Robert Samuel, American Methodist Episcopal minister: b. Concord, Pa., Feb. 7, 1824; d. San Fernando, Calif., Aug. 18, 1907. He was graduated from Dickinson College, Carlisle, Pa., in 1845, entered the Methodist ministry in 1846, and the next year went to Foochow, China, as a missionary. He soon became the leading figure in the Methodist mission in China. He helped to translate the New Testament into the Foochow dialect, and in 1870, together with C. C. Baldwin, published *An Alphabetic Dictionary of the Chinese Language in the Foochow Dialect.* In 1872 he was transferred to Japan to establish the first Methodist mission there. He founded the Anglo-Chinese College at Foochow in 1881, the Anglo-Japanese College at Tokyo in 1883, and the Philander Smith Biblical Institute in Tokyo in 1884. In the latter year he also established the first Christian mission in Korea. He returned to the United States in 1888 to become dean of the Maclay College of Theology at San Fernando, Calif., which was later transferred to Los Angeles as the University of Southern California College of Religion. His writings include *Life Among the Chinese* (1861).

MACLAY, William, American army officer and political leader: b. New Garden, Chester County, Pa., July 27, 1734; d. Harrisburg, April 16, 1804. He was educated in Chester County and served as a lieutenant in the French and Indian Wars under Gen. John Forbes at Fort Duquesne and later under Col. Henry Bouquet. He was admitted to the bar in York County in 1760 and subsequently took up residence in Northumberland County, which he represented in the state legislature from 1781 to 1785. During the American Revolution he served in the Pennsylvania militia, and in 1789 he became a senator from Pennsylvania in the First Congress of the United States. During his two years in that office he vigorously opposed the financial program of Alexander Hamilton and consequently was defeated for re-election by a Federalist in 1791. His journal, which was first published in part in 1880, is an invaluable historical record of the unreported senatorial debates of those years.

Maclay was elected again to the state legislature in Pennsylvania in 1795 and 1803, and was a county judge from 1801 to 1803.

Consult *The Journal of William Maclay,* ed. E. S. Maclay (new ed., 1927).

MACLE, măk′l, in mineralogy, a variety of andalusite, also called chiastolite, whose crystals appear tessellated in cross section, because of the arrangement of impurities. The term is also used in the diamond industry for twin crystals.

MacLEAN, măk-lēn′, **George Edwin,** American educator: b. Rockville, Conn., Aug. 31, 1850; d. Washington, D.C., May 5, 1938. He was graduated from Williams College in 1871 and from Yale Divinity School in 1874, and for seven years served as a minister in New Lebanon and Troy, N. Y. He then went to study at the University of Leipzig in Germany, and in 1883 became professor of English language and literature at the University of Minnesota.

From 1895 to 1899 he was chancellor of the University of Nebraska, and from 1899 to 1911 president of the State University of Iowa. In 1914–1916 he made a study of higher education in Great Britain for the United States Office of Education. Among his writings are: *A Chart of English Literature* (1892); *A Decade of Development in American State Universities* (1898); *Studies in Higher Education in England and Scotland, with Suggestions for Universities and Colleges in the United States* (1916); *The New International Era* (1923).

McLEAN, George Payne, American lawyer and political leader: b. Simsbury, Conn., Oct. 7, 1857; d. there, June 6, 1932. He was admitted to the bar in 1881 and practiced in Hartford. After serving in the Connecticut House of Representatives and Senate, he was elected governor of the state in 1901 and gained recognition for his advocacy of representation in the legislature according to population instead of by towns. He was in the United States Senate from 1911 until 1926, and was the author of the Federal Migratory Bird Bill which became law in 1913.

MacLEAN, măk-lān', James Alexander, Canadian educator: b. Mayfair, Ontario, Canada, Aug. 2, 1868; d. London, Ontario, Jan. 18, 1945. He was educated at the University of Toronto and Columbia University, and in 1894 became professor of political science at the University of Colorado. In 1900 he was appointed president of the University of Idaho, and in 1913 president of the University of Manitoba, Canada. He retired in 1934.

MACLEAN, John, American chemist and educator: b. Glasgow, Scotland, March 1, 1771; d. Princeton, N. J., Feb. 17, 1814. He was graduated from Glasgow University in 1786 and continued his studies in Edinburgh, London, and Paris, with the intention of becoming a surgeon. He returned to Glasgow in 1790 and the next year became a member of the faculty of physicians and surgeons at the university there. In 1795 he went to the United States and, at the suggestion of Dr. Benjamin Rush, took up residence at Princeton, N. J., where he was soon appointed professor of chemistry and natural history at the College of New Jersey (now Princeton University). He thus became the first professor of chemistry in any American college except for medical schools. In 1805 he was elected a member of the American Philosophical Society, and two years later became a naturalized citizen of the United States. In 1812 he joined the faculty of William and Mary College, Williamsburg, Va., but resigned the following year because of ill health. He published *Two Lectures on Combustion* (1797) in support of the antiphlogistic theory of Antoine Laurent Lavoisier.

MACLEAN, John, American educator: b. Princeton, N. J., March 3, 1800; d. there, Aug. 10, 1886. He was graduated from the College of New Jersey (now Princeton University) in 1816, and from 1818 taught mathematics and later classical languages there. In 1829 he became vice president of the college, and in 1854 president. Under his leadership the physical plant of the institution was expanded and eminent scholars were brought into the faculty. His *History of the College of New Jersey,* 2 vols., was published

in 1877. His other writings include *Lecture on a School System for New Jersey* (1829), and *Letters on the True Relations of the Church and the State to Schools and Colleges* (1853).

McLEAN, John, American jurist and statesman: b. Morris County, N. J., March 11, 1785; d. Cincinnati, Ohio, April 4, 1861. He moved with his parents to Warren County, Ohio, in 1799, and later went to Cincinnati, where he studied law. He was admitted to the bar in 1807, and commenced practice at Lebanon, Warren County, Ohio. He was a member of Congress from 1812 to 1816 and from 1816 to 1822 judge of the Supreme Court of Ohio. In July 1823 he was appointed postmaster general of the United States by President James Monroe. The Post Office Department was then in a very disordered and inefficient condition. Under his administration this branch of the public service was restored to order, and managed with a vigor, method, and economy that soon secured an almost unexampled degree of applause and public confidence.

In 1829 McLean became associate justice of the Supreme Court of the United States. In the Dred Scott case he dissented from the decision of the court as given by Chief Justice Roger Brooke Taney, and expressed the opinion that slavery had its origin merely in power, was against right, and was sustained only by local law.

MACLEAN, John, Canadian churchman: b. Portsoy, Banffshire, Scotland, Nov. 17, 1828; d. Saskatchewan Province, Canada, Nov. 7, 1886. He was graduated from King's College, Aberdeen, in 1851, and in 1858 was ordained a minister of the Church of England. In the same year he went to Canada and became assistant to the bishop of Huron at London, Ontario. In 1866 he became rector of St. John's Cathedral at Winnipeg, Manitoba, and warden of St. John's College there. He was consecrated first bishop of Saskatchewan in 1874 and had charge of this diocese until his death.

MACLEAN, John, Canadian clergyman and author: b. Kilmarnock, Scotland, Oct. 30, 1851; d. Winnipeg, Manitoba, Canada, March 7, 1928. He was educated at Victoria University, Cobourg, Ontario, and at Wesleyan University, Bloomington, Ill., and was ordained a minister in the Methodist Church in 1880. He then spent nine years as a missionary among the Blood Indians near Macleod, Alberta, and subsequently was pastor at several places in Saskatchewan and Manitoba. In 1888 he was appointed a member of the Northwestern Board of Education, and from 1902 to 1906 he edited *The Wesleyan.* His writings include: *The Indians, Their Manners and Customs* (1889); *The Hero of the Saskatchewan* (1891); *The Warden of the Plains, and Other Stories* (1896); *The Great Northwest* (1902); and several biographies.

MACLEAN, John Bayne, Canadian publisher: b. Crieff, Ontario, Canada, Sept. 26, 1862; d. Toronto, Ontario, Sept. 25, 1950. He was educated in the public schools and at the Royal School of Artillery in Kingston, Ontario, and began his journalistic career as a reporter on the Toronto *World.* Subsequently he was commercial editor of the *Mail* and financial editor of the *Empire* in Toronto. He gained prominence in

1887 when he founded the *Canadian Grocer,* the first Canadian trade paper. Numerous other trade publications followed, in the most diversified fields, from men's wear to engineering. Among his most important publications were *Maclean's Magazine* and the *Financial Post.* Maclean served for over 40 years in the Canadian militia, in which he attained the rank of lieutenant colonel.

McLEAN, Sarah Pratt. See Green, Sarah Pratt McLean.

MACLEAN, William Findlay, Canadian journalist: b. Ancaster, Ontario, Canada, Aug. 10, 1854; d. near Toronto, Dec. 7, 1929. He was graduated from the University of Toronto in 1880, and in the same year founded the Toronto *World,* of which he remained editor and proprietor until 1921, when it ceased publication. He sat in the Canadian House of Commons from 1892 to 1926, and at the time of his retirement was "dean" of that body. He advocated public ownership of hydroelectric power and railways, and complete home rule for Canada.

McLEAN, măk-lēn', William Lippard, American newspaper publisher: b. Mount Pleasant, Pa., May 4, 1852; d. Germantown, Pa., July 30, 1931. He was educated in the public schools, and began his career in the circulation department of the Pittsburgh *Leader* in 1872. While there, he assisted in the compilation of the first newspaper almanac published in Pittsburgh, which gave him the idea for the *Bulletin Almanac and Yearbook,* which he established later. When he was only 26, he was asked to become business manager of the Philadelphia *Press* and did much to improve its position. Seven years later in 1895, he purchased the Philadelphia *Evening Bulletin,* the oldest afternoon paper in Pennsylvania. Within a year its circulation increased fivefold, and eventually under his management exceeded 500,000, almost 100 times what it had been when he bought the paper.

From 1896 until 1924 McLean was a director of the Associated Press and in 1900 assisted in its reorganization; he was also on the board of the American Newspaper Publishers' Association. Among his public gifts were the Tudor Room in the Pennsylvania Art Museum, $100,000 toward a statue of Benjamin Franklin for the Franklin Memorial Museum, and a scholarship at Princeton in memory of his eldest son.

MACLEHOSE, măk'lĕ-hōz, Agnes (Craig), Scottish poet: b. Glasgow, Scotland, April, 1759; d. Edinburgh, Oct. 22, 1841. She was married in 1776 to James Maclehose, a Glasgow lawyer, but after four years they were separated. In 1787 she met the poet Robert Burns in Edinburgh, and for a number of years they carried on a romantic correspondence under the names of Clarinda and Sylvander. In her letters were included a number of poems of her own composition, some of which Burns praised. Their last personal meeting in 1791 was immortalized by Burns in the poem *Ac Fond Kiss.* Mrs. Maclehose later attempted to rejoin her husband in Jamaica, where he had gone after their separation, but was rejected, and she spent the remaining years of her life in Edinburgh. Her correspondence with Burns was first pub-

lished without her consent in 1802 and has since been included in standard editions of the poet's works.

MacLEISH, măk-lēsh', Archibald, American poet: b. Glencoe, Ill., May 7, 1892. He was graduated from Yale University in 1915, and in 1917 enlisted as a private in the United States Army, attaining the rank of captain by the end of World War I. In 1919 he was graduated from Harvard Law School, but he abandoned the law in 1923 to devote his time to poetry. He became one of America's outstanding poets.

During the ensuing decade MacLeish published *The Happy Marriage* (1924); *The Pot of Earth* (1925); *Nobodaddy,* a verse play (1925); *Streets in the Moon* (1926); *The Hamlet of A. MacLeish* (1928); and *New Found Land* (1930). *Conquistador* (1932) won him the Pulitzer Prize for poetry in 1933. This was followed by *Frescoes for Mr. Rockefeller's City* (1933); *Union Pacific—A Ballet* (1934); and *Panic,* a verse play (1935). He also pioneered in verse drama for radio with *The Fall of the City* (1937) and *Air Raid* (1938).

In recognition of his contribution to American literature, MacLeish was appointed to a number of government offices, beginning in 1939. He was librarian of Congress from 1939 to 1944, and during part of the same period was assistant director of the Office of War Information, 1942–1943. In 1944–1945 he was assistant secretary of state for public and cultural relations. He was United States delegate to the conference of Allied ministers of education in London in 1944, and chairman of the United States delegation to the conference in London which drew up the final constitution of the United Nations Educational, Scientific, and Cultural Organization (UNESCO) in 1945.

MacLeish became a director of the American Academy of Arts and Letters in 1948, secretary in 1949, and chancellor in 1951. In 1949 he was appointed Boylston professor of rhetoric and oratory at Harvard University. His *Collected Poems, 1917–1952* won him a second Pulitzer Prize and the Bollingen and National Book awards for poetry in 1953.

McLEMORE'S COVE, Ga., Military Operations at. The cove is located in the extreme northwest of the state, between Lookout Mountain and Pigeon Mountain, a few miles from Chattanooga, Tenn. During the Civil War, in September 1863, it was the scene of a series of maneuvers between a Union army under Gen. William Starke Rosecrans and a Confederate force under Gen. Braxton Bragg, who was trying to prevent Rosecrans from reaching Chattanooga. Bragg failed to interpose his army between the Union forces and the city as he hoped to do, and although he inflicted a costly defeat on Rosecrans in the Battle of Chickamauga (q.v.), the Union general was able to occupy Chattanooga immediately thereafter.

McLENNAN, măk-lĕn'ăn, John Cunningham, Canadian physicist: b. Ingersoll, Ontario, Canada, April 14, 1867; d. on a Paris to Boulogne train, Oct. 9, 1935. He was educated at the universities of Toronto and Cambridge, and in 1899 began to teach physics at Toronto. He became director of the physics laboratory there in 1904, and professor of physics in 1907. He conducted important researches in radioactivity, spectroscopy, and the treatment of cancer by radium, and in 1923 succeeded in liquefying helium. During World War I he collaborated with Ernest (later Lord) Rutherford in developing magnetic devices for the detection of submarines. He was elected a fellow of the Royal Society, London, in 1915 and president of the Royal Society of Canada in 1924.

McLENNAN, John Ferguson, Scottish sociologist: b. Inverness, Scotland, Oct. 14, 1827; d. Hayes Common, Kent, England, June 16, 1881. He was educated at King's College, Aberdeen, and Trinity College, Cambridge. After two years as a journalist in London, he returned to Edinburgh and was called to the bar in 1857. His first important publication was the article "Law" in the eighth edition of the *Encyclopedia Britannica* (1857). This was followed in 1865 by his most famous work, *Primitive Marriage: An Inquiry into the Origin of the Form of Capture in Marriage Ceremonies,* in which he expounded his theory of the evolution of modern marriage customs out of the more promiscuous primitive practices. The next year he published two articles entitled "Kinship in Ancient Greece" in the *Fortnightly Review,* and in 1876 this and the preceding work were reprinted along with various new materials under the title of *Studies in Ancient History.* An unfinished work, directed against Sir Henry James Sumner Maine's patriarchal theory, was completed and published in 1885 by McLennan's brother Donald under the title of *The Patriarchal Theory.* In 1896 a second series of *Studies in Ancient History,* treating of the evolution of the idea of kinship, was brought out by McLennan's widow and Arthur Platt. Although McLennan's ideas are no longer regarded as sound, the study of primitive society received a powerful impetus from his important investigations.

McLEOD, măk-loud', **Alexander,** American clergyman: b. Mull, Inner Hebrides, Scotland, June 12, 1774; d. New York, N. Y., Feb. 17, 1833. He came to the United States in 1792 and was graduated in 1798 from Union College, Schenectady, N. Y. The following year he was licensed to preach, and in 1800 became minister of the First Reformed Presbyterian Church in New York. He remained its pastor for the rest of his life. He was a vigorous opponent of slavery, and helped to organize the American Colonization Society. His writings include *Negro Slavery Unjustifiable* (1802); *Ecclesiastical Catechism* (1806); *Scriptural View of the Character, Causes, and Ends of the Present War* (1815); *The Life and Power of True Godliness* (1816).

MACLEOD, Donald, Scottish clergyman: b. Campsie, Stirlingshire, Scotland, March 18, 1831; d. Feb. 11, 1916. He was educated at the University of Glasgow, and after some years of travel abroad, became minister at Lauder and later at Linlithgow. In 1869 he was called to the ministry of Park Church in Glasgow, where he remained for forty years. In 1872 he took over the editorship of the periodical *Good Words,* which had been founded by his brother Norman Macleod 12 years before, and continued to conduct it until 1905. He was chaplain successively to Queen Victoria, Edward VII, and George V.

He wrote *Sunday Home Service* (1885) and *Christ and Modern Society* (1893).

MACLEOD, Fiona, pseudonym of William Sharp (q.v.).

MACLEOD, Henry Dunning, Scottish economist: b. Edinburgh, Scotland, March 31, 1821; d. Southall Norwood (now Southall), Middlesex, England, July 16, 1902. He was educated at Trinity College, Cambridge, studied law in London, and was called to the bar in 1849. He became interested in the theory of banking in 1854 when, as a director of the Royal British Bank, he represented that institution in a law suit. Two years later he published his most important book, *The Theory and Practice of Banking,* 2 vols. (1856), which contained a valuable historical account of the policies of the Bank of England and an original discussion of the nature of credit and its creation by the banks. Although he lectured on banking at several British universities, he was never able to secure a professorship. He was, however, employed by the British government from 1868 to 1870 in making a digest of laws relating to bills of exchange. Among his many writings were: *Elements of Banking* (1876); *A History of Banking in All the Leading Nations,* 2 vols. (1896); *The Theory of Credit,* 2 vols. (1889–1891).

McLEOD, Hugh, American army officer: b. New York, N. Y., Aug. 1, 1814; d. Dumfries, Va., Jan. 2, 1862. He was graduated from the United States Military Academy in 1835 and served on frontier duty at Fort Jessup, La., until June 1836, when he resigned. He then joined the Texans in their struggle against Mexico. In 1841, as brigadier general of the Texas militia, he was appointed by President Mirabeau B. Lamar of Texas to command an expedition to Santa Fe to extend the jurisdiction of Texas to the Rio Grande, but was taken prisoner by the Mexicans and not released until the following year, when the United States government intervened in his behalf. He settled in Galveston, served in the Texas Congress, and was a member of the state legislature after Texas was annexed to the United States. He joined the Confederate Army in 1861 and served on the Rio Grande and in Virginia, where he died in camp.

McLEOD, John, Canadian pioneer: b. Stornoway, Island of Lewis with Harris, Scotland, 1788; d. Montreal, Canada, July 24, 1849. He entered the service of the Hudson's Bay Company in 1811, and three years later was put in charge of its post at the forks of the Red River of the North. He distinguished himself in the defense of the post against raids by the rival North West Company. In 1821 he was given the rank of chief trader, and from 1822 to 1826 served in the Columbia district on the Pacific Coast. He continued in the service of the Hudson's Bay Company until 1848. His diary has been published in the *Collections of the State Historical Society of North Dakota,* vol. 2 (Bismarck, N. D., 1908).

MACLEOD, John James Rickard, Scottish physiologist: b. New Clunie, Perthshire, Scotland, Sept. 6, 1876; d. Aberdeen, March 16, 1935. He was educated at the universities of Aberdeen, Leipzig, and Cambridge, and in 1903 went to the

United States as professor of physiology at Western Reserve University, Cleveland, Ohio. While there he began the study of diabetes and the metabolism of carbohydrates, for which he was later to become famous. In 1918 he was appointed professor of physiology at Toronto, and there collaborated with Sir Frederick Grant Banting in discovering insulin, for which he and Banting received a Nobel Prize in 1923. In 1928 he accepted an appointment as professor of physiology at the University of Aberdeen, where he remained until his death. His works include: *Diabetes, Its Physiological Pathology* (1913); *Fundamentals of Human Physiology,* with R. G. Pearce (1916); *Physiology and Biochemistry in Modern Medicine* (1918; 9th ed., 1941); *Insulin and Its Use in the Treatment of Diabetes,* with W. R. Campbell (1925); *Carbohydrate Metabolism and Insulin* (1926); *The Fuel of Life* (1928).

MACLEOD, Norman, Scottish clergyman and author: b. Campbeltown, Argyllshire, Scotland, June 3, 1812; d. Glasgow, June 16, 1872. He attended Glasgow University and in 1831 went to Edinburgh to study for the ministry under Dr. Thomas Chalmers. He was ordained as parish minister for Loudoun, Ayrshire, in 1838. In the controversy which split the Scottish church five years later, Macleod took a middle course and remained in the established church. He became pastor at Dalkeith, near Edinburgh, in 1843, and from 1849 edited the *Christian Instructor* there. In 1851 he became pastor of the Barony Church in Glasgow where he did outstanding work among the poor. He was appointed chaplain to Queen Victoria in 1857, and three years later assumed the editorship of the periodical *Good Words,* published in London, to which he was also a prolific contributor. After his death, Queen Victoria gave two windows in his memory to the Crathie Church. His books include *Eastward* (1866), an account of his journey to Egypt and Palestine in 1864; and *Reminiscences of a Highland Parish* (1867).

MACLISE, măk-lēs' Daniel, Irish painter: bap. Cork, Ireland, Feb. 2, 1806; d. London, England, April 25, 1870. He went to school in Cork and studied art at the Cork Academy. He first attracted notice with a drawing of Sir Walter Scott, made when the novelist visited Cork in 1825. Two years later Maclise went to London, where he enrolled in the school of the Royal Academy. Under the pseudonym, Alfred Croquis, he drew a series of highly successful portraits of literary celebrities for *Fraser's Magazine* (1830–1838), which were republished as the *Maclise Portrait Gallery* (1871). At the same time his paintings in oil were being exhibited regularly at the Royal Academy, of which he was elected a full member in 1840. His favorite subjects were historical and literary scenes, especially scenes from Shakespeare. About 1838 he became acquainted with Charles Dickens, and soon was a member of the novelist's intimate circle. His portrait of Dickens (1839) is one of his most celebrated works.

In 1857 Maclise was commissioned to decorate the royal gallery in the House of Lords. The two large frescoes which he did there, *Wellington and Blücher* and *The Death of Nelson,* completed in 1864, were the crowning achievement of his career.

McLOUGHLIN, măk-lŏk'lĭn, John, Canadian pioneer and fur trader: b. Rivière du Loup, Canada, Oct. 19, 1784; d. Oregon City, Oreg., Sept. 3, 1857. He studied medicine in Quebec, became a licensed physician, and entered the service of the North West Company in which he became a partner in 1814. For some years he was in charge of the Rainy Lake district in Ontario. When the North West merged with the Hudson's Bay Company in 1821, he was made a chief factor and sent to the Columbia department. In 1825 he built Fort Vancouver (now Vancouver, Washington) in the Oregon country, and this remained his headquarters for the next 20 years. He resigned from the Hudson's Bay Company in 1846, and retired to Oregon City, where he spent the last years of his life. He is known as the "Father of Oregon." McLoughlin Institute in Oregon City was established in his memory in 1907.

McLOUGHLIN, măk-lŏf'lĭn, Maurice Evans, American tennis player: b. Carson City, Nev., Jan. 7, 1890; d. Hermosa Beach, Calif., Dec. 10, 1957. A Pacific coast tennis star, he was selected as a member of the United States Davis Cup team in 1909 and went to Australia with Melville Long in an unsuccessful effort to win the cup. In 1911 he went to New Zealand with William Augustus Larned and Beals Wright, but again the team failed to win. McLoughlin won the United States national singles championship in 1912 and 1913 and in the latter year was a member of the team which won the Davis Cup from England. Australia recaptured the trophy in 1914, but McLoughlin won both his singles matches against the great Australian players, Norman E. Brookes and Anthony F. Wilding. Known as the California Comet because of his furious energy and dazzling spectacular style, McLoughlin is credited with having changed the whole temper of the game, and in large measure he may be said to have started tennis on the way to becoming a national sport. He wrote *Tennis as I Play It* (1915).

McLUHAN, mək-lōō'ən, Herbert Marshall, Canadian educator and writer on mass media: b. Edmonton, Canada, July 21, 1911. Marshall McLuhan's observations on the human consequences of technological change in communications attracted the attention of major mass media and made him one of the most celebrated and controversial commentators on popular culture. His contributions include aphorisms, mixed-media and typographic innovations, and "happenings" inspired by his views on the effects of electricity in permitting total sensory participation without either a story line or a fixed point of view. His fame rode the crest of a wave of social and cultural turmoil marking the coming of age of the first generation born in the television era.

Life.—After studying engineering for a time, McLuhan shifted to English literature and received a B.A and an M.A. from the University of Manitoba. Then, at Trinity Hall, Cambridge University, he read for the honors examination in English literature, earning another B.A., M.A., and, in 1943, a Ph.D.; his doctoral dissertation was on the history of ancient, medieval, and Renaissance communication procedures.

McLuhan began his teaching career at the University of Wisconsin in 1936. He subsequently taught at St. Louis University (1937–1944); Assumption University of Windsor (now University of Windsor), Ontario (1944–1946); and, from 1946, St. Michael's College of the University of Toronto. At Toronto he was the founder and director of the Centre for Culture and Technology. In 1967–1968, McLuhan was Schweitzer Professor of the Humanities at the Center for Communications, Fordham University.

Theories.—McLuhan set forth his ideas about communications media in a series of widely discussed books, including *The Mechanical Bride: Folklore of Industrial Man* (1951), *The Gutenberg Galaxy: The Making of Typographic Man* (1962), *Understanding Media: The Extensions of Man* (1964), *The Medium is the Massage: An Inventory of Effects* (with Quentin Fiore, 1967), and *War and Peace in the Global Village* (with Quentin Fiore, 1968).

For McLuhan, a communications medium determines ways of sensing and organizing experience through the particular mixture of the senses it activates. His major theme is that electric technology is the extension of man's central nervous system, restoring the human family to a state he refers to as the "global village." Phonetic writing transformed the oral into the visual; later, printing imposed, especially on Western man, a visual and private, individualized logic and consciousness. Later still came television, which, in McLuhan's terms, is a "cool" medium because its relatively "low definition" engages the viewer actively (print is a "hot" medium, whose "high definition" encourages detachment in the reader and relative isolation). Because each medium encourages some styles of communication and rejects other styles, regardless of what it "talks about," the "medium is the message."

McLuhan's critics asserted that, at the very least, this is technological overdeterminism. They found little evidence to support his psychological suggestions and objected that his fixating on the differences between the media could impoverish analysis of the various types of messages in the same medium, or of similar messages across media.

GEORGE GERBNER
*Annenberg School of Communications
University of Pennsylvania*

Consult Rosenthal, Raymond, ed., *McLuhan: Pro and Con* (New York 1968).

MACLURE, măk-lōōr′, **William,** American geologist: b. Ayr, Scotland, Oct. 27, 1763; d. San Ángel, Mexico, March 23, 1840. Having acquired a considerable fortune as a member of a mercantile firm in London, he went to the United States in 1796 and became a naturalized citizen. In 1803 he was sent to France as a member of a commission to settle the claims of United States citizens for damages to property during the French Revolution. While in Europe, he became interested in geology, and on his return to America he undertook to make a geologic survey of the United States east of the Mississippi River, at his own expense. His *Observations on the Geology of the United States,* together with a geological map, was published by the American Philosophical Society in 1809, and a revised edition of the work appeared in 1817. The original volume antedated William Smith's parallel work for England and Wales by six years; and Maclure may rightfully be called the "father" of American, as Smith has been of English, geology.

Maclure took up residence in Philadelphia, and in 1817 was elected president of the Academy of Natural Sciences there, a position to which he was re-elected annually for the remainder of his life. He gave the greater part of his library and specimen collections to the academy. From 1819 to 1824 he lived in Spain, where he attempted to found an agricultural school for poor farmers, but the 10,000 acres which he had purchased for that purpose was confiscated in the revolution of 1824. On his return to the United States he attempted to carry out a similar project at Robert Owen's New Harmony community in Indiana, but this also failed. In 1828 he took up residence in Mexico for his health. His letters from Mexico to the New Harmony *Disseminator* on political and economic subjects were published as *Opinions on Various Subjects, Dedicated to the Industrious Producers,* 2 vols. (1831–1837).

McMAHON, Bernard, American horticulturist: b. Ireland, c. 1775; d. Philadelphia, Pa., Sept. 18, 1816. He came to the United States in 1796, settling in Philadelphia, where he started a seed and nursery business. At the same time he set up an experimental garden outside the city for the cultivation of rare flowers and plants. His work attracted the attention of botanists like William Darlington and Thomas Nuttall, and the latter named the evergreen *Mahonia* in his honor. Thomas Jefferson mentioned in his correspondence that McMahon had undertaken to cultivate in his greenhouses all the new varieties of plants brought back to the East by Meriwether Lewis from his famous expedition with William Clark in 1804–1806.

In 1806 McMahon published the *American Gardener's Calendar,* the first important horticultural work to be produced in the United States. It remained a standard reference book for more than half a century, with an 11th edition in 1857.

MacMAHON, màk-mȧ-ôn′, COMTE **Marie Edme Patrice Maurice de,** French marshal and statesman: b. Sully, Saône-et-Loire, France, June 13, 1808; d. Paris, Oct. 17, 1893. He was a descendant of an Irish family that fled to France with the Stuarts after 1688; his father was a peer of France. After graduating from the military school at St. Cyr, he was assigned to duty in Algeria, where he remained almost continuously until 1854. He served in the Crimean War as a divisional commander, and led the assault on the Malakhov fortress (Sept. 8, 1855) which resulted in the capture of Sevastopol. In 1856 he was made a senator. During the Italian War against Austria (1859) he commanded an army corps and won an important victory at Magenta, for which he was created a marshal of France and duke of Magenta. From 1864 to 1870 he was governor general of Algeria.

At the outbreak of the Franco-Prussian War (1870–1871), MacMahon was given command of the First Army Corps. He suffered a series of defeats, culminating in the decisive Battle of Sedan, which broke the back of French resistance. When the Third Republic was formed, MacMahon became its second president in 1873. He was aligned politically with the monarchists, and after repeated electoral victories by the republican parties, he resigned the presidency in January 1879.

Consult Daudet, Ernest L. M., *Souvenirs de la présidence du maréchal de MacMahon* (Paris 1880);

LaFarge, L., *Histoire complète de MacMahon, maréchal de France, duc de Magenta,* 3 vols. (Paris 1898).

McMANUS, măk-măn'ŭs, **George,** American cartoonist: b. St. Louis, Mo., Jan. 23, 1884; d. Santa Monica, Calif., Oct. 22, 1954. He began his newspaper career in 1899 as cartoonist on the St. Louis *Republic* and joined the New York *World* in 1905 and then the New York *American* in 1912. He created several comic strips, the most famous being *Bringing Up Father* (Jiggs and Maggie), published in newspapers throughout the world, ultimately appearing in 750 newspapers and 27 languages. Other series originated by him include *Snookums; Rosie's Beau; The Newly Weds and Their Baby; Panhandle Pete;* and *Let George Do It.*

MacMANUS, măk-măn'ŭs, **Seumas,** Irish writer: b. Mount Charles, County Donegal, Ulster, Ireland, Dec. 31, 1869; d. New York, N.Y., Oct. 23, 1960. At 18 he became a teacher and began contributing to newspapers and magazines in Dublin and London. He published his first book of poems, *Shuilers from Healthy Hills,* in 1893. His subsequent works include poems, plays, short stories, Donegal folk tales, and his autobiography, *The Rocky Road to Dublin* (1938). He was widely known in the United States as a lecturer at many colleges and a contributor to leading American periodicals. Some of the best known of his works are *Through the Turf Smoke* (1899); *Donegal Fairy Stories* (1900); *Ballads of a Country Boy* (1905); *Yourself and the Neighbors* (1914); *The Donegal Wonder Book* (1926); *Bold Blades of Donegal* (1935); *Heavy Hangs the Golden Grain* (1950).

McMASTER, măk-màs'tẽr, **John Bach,** American historian: b. Brooklyn, N.Y., June 29, 1852; d. Darien, Conn., May 24, 1932. After graduating from the College of the City of New York in 1872, he remained there for a year as instructor in English, then studied and practiced engineering and map making, and in 1875 received the degree of civil engineer from the same college. He published *Bridge and Tunnel Centres* (1875) and *High Masonry Dams* (1876). From 1877 to 1883 he was instructor in civil engineering at the College of New Jersey (Princeton University) and during the summer of 1878 was in charge of the Princeton scientific expedition to Wyoming in search of fossils.

In 1883, McMaster published the first volume of his *History of the People of the United States* and also was appointed professor of American history at the University of Pennsylvania, becoming professor emeritus in 1920. The first eight volumes of his major work, completed in 1913, traced the development of the United States from the close of the Revolution in 1783 to the outbreak of the Civil War. A ninth volume, published in 1927, carried the history through the administration of Abraham Lincoln.

As a historian, McMaster was a pioneer in showing the influence of social and economic forces in national evolution and in using contemporary sources of information, such as newspapers, magazines, and memoirs. Among his other important historical works are *Benjamin Franklin as a Man of Letters* (1887); *Origin, Meaning and Application of the Monroe Doctrine* (1896); *Daniel Webster* (1902); *Struggle for the Social, Political and Industrial Rights of Man in America* (1903); *Life and Times of Stephen Girard* (1918).

McMASTER, William, Canadian senator and philanthropist: b. County Tyrone, Ireland, Dec. 24, 1811; d. Toronto, Ontario, Canada, Sept. 22, 1887. He emigrated to Canada in 1833 and after several years' experience in a large wholesale dry goods firm in Toronto went into business for himself. In 1867 he founded the Canadian Bank of Commerce and was its president until 1886. He was elected a member of the Legislative Council for the Midland division of Canada in 1862 and held the seat until he was called to the Canadian Senate by royal proclamation in 1867. A prominent Baptist, he took a leading part in founding McMaster University (q.v.) and left the bulk of his estate to endow it.

McMASTER UNIVERSITY, a coeducational institution of higher learning, Hamilton, Ontario, Canada. Named for William McMaster (q.v.) who provided its original endowment, the university was located in Toronto until 1930, when it was transferred to Hamilton, where it has a campus of more than 100 acres bordered by the varied land and water park areas of the Royal Botanical Gardens. The gardens have been affiliated with the university since 1946 and provide it with an extensive experimental and conservation area. The university operates under an Act of Incorporation granted by the Legislative Assembly of Ontario in 1887 (revised in 1949) and confers degrees in all branches of university work. It maintains a broad program of university extension and summer school studies and an extensive research program on nuclear fission.

The corporation of the university consists of a board of governors elected from and by the Baptist Convention of Ontario and Quebec, which also contributes to the university budget. The academic work is directed by a senate, which consists of the members of the board of governors and representatives of the university faculty and the graduates. The university includes three colleges: the Divinity School, a college of theology, mainly postgraduate; University College (arts); and Hamilton College (sciences) with departments of physics, chemistry, mathematics, geography, geology, botany, zoology, and nursing education, and special provision for scientific research. Hamilton College, incorporated January 1948, is administered by its own board of governors under the academic supervision of the university senate.

MacMECHAN, măk-mĕk'ăn, **Archibald M'Kellar,** Canadian educator and author: b. Berlin (now Kitchener) Ontario, Canada, June 21, 1862; d. Halifax, Nova Scotia, Aug. 7, 1933. A brief period of high school teaching followed his graduation from the University of Toronto in 1884, but he was only 27 when in 1889 he received his doctorate of philosophy from the Johns Hopkins University and was appointed professor of English language and literature at Dalhousie University, Halifax, a post which he retained for 42 years. His most important book was *Headwaters of Canadian Literature* (1924), a critical survey of Canadian writing; and his books about Nova Scotia, such as *Sagas of the Sea* (1923) and *Old Province Tales* (1924), are well known. He also edited works by Thomas Carlyle and Alfred Tennyson. The best known of his works include

The Porter of Bagdad (1901); *The Life of a Little College* (1914); *The Winning of Responsible Government* (1915); *Sagas of the Sea* (1923); *Headwaters of Canadian Literature* (1924); *The Book of Ultima Thule* (1927); *There Go the Ships* (1928); *Red Snow on Grand Pré* (1931); *Late Harvest*, poems (1934).

McMECHEN, măk-měk′ĕn, city, West Virginia; in Marshall County; altitude 710 feet. It is situated on the Ohio River, six miles south of Wheeling, and is served by the Baltimore and Ohio Railroad. McMechen is a residential community, with local industries. Nearby, at Moundsville, is the Grave Creek Mound, one of the best known Indian mounds in the country. McMechen was settled in 1823, incorporated as a city in 1895, and has a mayor and council. Pop. 2,999.

MACMILLAN, măk-mĭl′ăn, **Daniel**, Scottish bookseller and publisher, founder of Macmillan & Co.; b. Upper Corrie, Isle of Arran, Sept. 13, 1813; d. Cambridge, Eng., June 27, 1857. He took service with a Cambridge bookseller in 1833, and with Messrs. Seeley, Fleet Street, London in 1837. He set up in business for himself in London in 1843, but soon moved to Cambridge, where in 1844 he became a publisher, quickly establishing a prosperous business. He published Charles Kingsley's *Westward Ho!* in 1855, and Thomas Hughes' *Tom Brown's School Days* in 1857, but he was established chiefly by educational publications and the works of Isaac Todhunter and F. D. Maurice.

ALEXANDER MACMILLAN (b. Irvine, Ayrshire, Oct. 3, 1818; d. London, Jan. 25, 1896) became associated with his brother in 1843, and after the latter's death, opened a branch in London, which in 1863 became the headquarters of the firm. He was joined in the enterprise by his son GEORGE MACMILLAN (1855–1936), and two sons of Daniel, SIR FREDERICK ORRIDGE MACMILLAN (1851–1936; knighted in 1909) and MAURICE CRAWFORD MACMILLAN (1853–1936); and through the establishment of numerous branches overseas the firm became one of the leading publishers of the English-speaking world. *Macmillan's Magazine,* the first of the shilling monthlies, made its appearance in 1859 and continued publication until 1907.

In 1893 Macmillan & Co. became a limited-liability company under the chairmanship of Sir Frederick. The branch opened in New York in 1869 became a separate concern, The Macmillan Company, in 1896, although the directors of the parent company retained control through stock ownership until Jan. 22, 1951, when it became wholly independent.

Consult Hughes, T., *Memoir of Daniel Macmillan* (London 1882); Graves, C. L., *Life and Letters of Alexander Macmillan* (London 1910); *The House of Macmillan (1843–1943)* (London and New York, 1944).

McMILLAN, SIR **Daniel Hunter**, Canadian administrator: b. Whitby, Ontario, January 1846; d. Winnipeg, April 14, 1933. He was educated in Canada and in 1864 served with the Canadian Volunteers on the Niagara frontier. He afterward took part in the military operations during the Fenian Raid in 1866; the Red River expedition of 1870; and in the Northwestern rebellion of 1885 he was awarded a medal. He represented Centre Winnipeg in the Manitoba Legislative Assembly, 1880–1900, and became a member of the Manitoba government in 1889. In 1900–1911 he was lieutenant governor of Manitoba. He was knighted in 1902.

MacMILLAN, **Donald Baxter**, American Arctic explorer: b. Provincetown, Mass., Nov. 10, 1874. He was graduated from Bowdoin College in 1898, and took postgraduate courses in anthropology at Harvard. In 1908 he joined the Peary Arctic Expedition, which culminated in 1909 in the discovery of the North Pole. He was a member of the Cabot Labrador Expedition in 1910, and in 1911–1912 did ethnological work in that region.

MacMillan organized his first independent expedition in 1913. This had for one of its purposes the solution of the problem of Crocker Land, which Peary believed he had seen on one of his earlier expeditions. MacMillan remained in the Arctic regions until 1917, proving the nonexistence of Crocker Land, and exploring a large part of the hitherto unvisited Grant Land on Ellesmere Island. MacMillan was appointed professor of anthropology at Bowdoin College in 1918. In 1920 he explored in the Hudson Bay region. In the next year he organized and commanded an expedition to Baffin Land (now called Baffin Island); followed in 1923–1924 by researches on the glaciers of Kane Basin, and in 1925 by an expedition whose chief purpose was to reach the North Pole by airplane. Commander Richard E. Byrd was in charge of the aeronautical part of the expedition. MacMillan visited Labrador, Baffin Island and Greenland in 1926 and 1927–1928; in 1944 commanded an expedition which made aerial surveys of Greenland, Baffin Island, and Labrador; and led expeditions to Ellesmere and Baffin islands in 1948 and 1949.

McMILLAN, **Edwin Mattison**, American physicist: b. Redondo Beach, Calif., Sept. 18, 1907. He was educated at the California Institute of Technology (B.S., 1928; M.Sc., 1929) and received his Ph.D. at Princeton University in 1932. He became a national research fellow at the University of California, 1932–1934; staff member of the Radiation Laboratory there from 1934; research associate, 1934–1935; instructor in physics, 1935–1936; and was assistant professor from 1936 until 1941, when he was called by the government to work on radar and, later in the same year, on sonar for the navy. McMillan also assisted in the development of the atomic bombs of the Hiroshima and Nagasaki types.

In 1940 McMillan was codiscoverer, with Philip Hauge Abelson, of element 93, which was named neptunium, obtained by bombarding the uranium isotope 238 with neutrons. His work on element 94, plutonium, was interrupted by World War II, but his experiments were continued by Glenn Theodore Seaborg, with whom he shared the Nobel Prize for chemistry in 1951.

Returning to the University of California as a full professor in 1946, McMillan developed the particle accelerator known as the synchrotron, a major advance over the cyclotron.

MacMILLAN, SIR **Ernest Campbell**, Canadian musician and composer: b. Mimico, near Toronto, Aug. 18, 1893. He was educated at the universities of Toronto and Oxford, and studied in Edinburgh and Paris. He was in Germany at the outbreak of World War I and was interned at the Ruhleben prison camp until November 1918. At performances there he gained his first experience as a conductor and wrote his doctoral dissertation, a setting for chorus and orchestra of Algernon Charles Swinburne's ode *England*. The degree was granted in absentia by Oxford in 1918. From 1926 to 1942 he was principal of the Toronto Conservatory of Music and from 1927 to 1952 dean of the faculty of music at the University of Toronto. He was conductor of the Toronto Symphony Orchestra from 1931 to 1956 and developed it into one of the major orchestras in the Western Hemisphere. He was knighted in 1935.

MACMILLAN, (Maurice) Harold, British statesman: b. London, England, Feb. 10, 1894. Educated at Balliol College, Oxford, he served as an officer in World War I, and was aide-de-camp to the governor general of Canada in 1919–1920. From 1920 to 1940 he was a director of Macmillan and Company, Ltd., the publishing house founded by his grandfather. Except for the years 1929 to 1931, Macmillan sat continuously in Parliament after 1924 as a Conservative. During the 1930's he was a critic of Conservative policy and with Winston Churchill was considered a party rebel. In Churchill's World War II government he was parliamentary undersecretary of state for the colonies (1942), and from 1942 to 1945, British resident minister at Allied Headquarters in North Africa. When the Conservatives returned to office in 1951, he rose rapidly in government ranks as minister of housing and local government (to October 1954); minister of defense (to April 1955); secretary of state for foreign affairs (to December 1955); and chancellor of the exchequer. He held this post, endeavoring to strengthen Britain's financial position, until January 1957, when he was chosen to succeed Sir Anthony Eden as prime minister of Britain and leader of the Conservative Party. In the general election of October 1959 the party won a majority of 100 in Parliament and Macmillan was reelected by the largest plurality of his career.

As prime minister, he traveled widely in the interests of international amity, conferring often with Presidents Dwight D. Eisenhower and John F. Kennedy and other Western leaders, and in February 1959 in Moscow with Soviet Premier Nikita S. Khrushchev. While standing firm against threats by Russia, he worked to find a basis for negotiations. He believed in talks among heads of states, and tried to save the Paris summit meeting of May 1960 from collapse. His attempt to get Britain into the European Common Market failed in January 1963 because of French opposition, and his government was shaken later that year by a scandal concerning the private life of War Secretary John Profumo. He resigned because of failing health on Oct. 18, 1963, after undergoing surgery. His books, advocating a liberal economy, include *Planning for Employment* (1935), *The Middle Way* (1938), and *Economic Aspects of Defence* (1939).

McMINNVILLE, măk-mĭn'vĭl, city, Oregon, seat of Yamhill County, in the Willamette Valley, 40 miles southwest of Portland. It is a residential college center in an agricultural region notable for berries and vegetables, grains, walnuts and filberts, turkeys, and dairying. Lumbering, important in the past, has waned and the community is known for the McMinnville plan to attract business and industry, which has brought factories producing cookies, house trailers, and woolen fabrics. Linfield College, a four-year liberal arts college under American Baptist auspices, founded in 1849, is situated here. The college has maintained the Linfield Research Institute, specializing in the sciences and in economics. One result of its work has been an electronics industry specializing in portable X-ray equipment. The settlement was named by William T. Newby in 1855 for his home town in Tennessee. It was incorporated as a town in 1876 and as a city in 1882. It is governed by mayor and council. Pop. 7,656.

KENNETH L. HOLMES.

McMINNVILLE, town, Tennessee, seat of Warren County, about 70 miles southeast of Nashville by highway. It is an agricultural and dairy products center, and is noteworthy for many shrub and tree nurseries. There is a municipal airport. The town lies in the foothills of the Cumberland Mountains, near recreation areas, notably Center Hill Reservoir. It was established in 1809 on land acquired by treaty from the Cherokee Indians, and named for Joseph McMinn, speaker of the State Senate, later governor of Tennessee. A nationally known school of photography was conducted here from 1904 to 1929 by W.S. Lively, who built the world's largest camera, 11 by 6 by 5 feet. Government is by mayor and council. Pop. 9,013.

FRAN W. PATTER.

MacMONNIES, măk-mŏn'ĭz, **Frederick William,** American sculptor: b. Brooklyn, N.Y., Sept. 28, 1863; d. New York, March 22, 1937. He studied in New York with Augustus Saint-Gaudens (1880–1884) and in Paris with Alexandre Falguière at the École des Beaux Arts, where he twice (1886, 1887) won the Prix d'Atelier, the highest award open to foreigners. At the 1891 Paris Salon his statues of Nathan Hale (now in City Hall Park, New York) and James S.T. Stranahan (Prospect Park, Brooklyn) won the Second Medal, the first ever awarded to an American. MacMonnies won fame by his *Columbian Fountain* for the World's Columbian Exposition, Chicago, 1893. Succeeding works included the controversial *Bacchante with Infant Faun* (1894; rejected by the Boston Public Library, now in The Metropolitan Museum of Art, New York; duplicate in the Luxembourg Gallery, Paris); *Victory* (1895), for the battle monument, West Point, N.Y.; the central bronze doors and statue of William Shakespeare (1898), Library of Congress; and the Army and Navy groups in the Soldiers' and Sailors' Arch (1900), Prospect Park, Brooklyn.

An imaginative artist and a careful craftsman, MacMonnies specialized in vigorously animated pieces and group scenes, achieved by combining bold conceptions with brilliant plastic realism. However, he was frequently accused of replacing idealism and significance in art with purely technical virtuosity, and this complaint culminated in the removal of the group *Civic Virtue* (1919) from New York City Hall Park. Major works of his later period include equestrian statues of Theodore Roosevelt (1905) and Gen. George B. McClellan (1906) and the massive granite Marne Battle Monument (1926) on the battlefield near Meaux, France.

MacMURRAY COLLEGE, a coordinate, Methodist-related institution in Jacksonville, Ill. The College for Women was founded in 1846 as Illinois Conference Female Academy, later renamed Illinois Woman's College, and again renamed in 1930 for Senator James E. MacMurray, a major benefactor. The College for Men was founded in 1955. The curriculum, leading to the bachelor of arts degree, is liberal arts oriented. The library contains about 75,000 volumes. More than 900 full-time and 250 evening and summer students are enrolled. The women's college is centered in the north of the 60-acre campus and the men's college in the south. Students share educational facilities, and operate under the same faculty, administration, and board of trustees. Student governments and most extracurricular activities are separate. The colors of the women's college are yellow and blue; those of the men's college, blue, green, and red. Athletic teams are nicknamed the Highlanders.

WENDELL S. DYSINGER.

MacMURROUGH, măk-mûr′ŏ, **Dermot** (Irish DIARMAID MAC MURCHADHA), king of Leinster: b. about 1110; d. Ferns, Leinster, 1171. Succeeding his father as king in 1126, he was notorious for his cruelty and aggressiveness. When Roderic O'Connor, his former ally, became high king of Ireland in 1166, he expelled Mac-Murrough from the country. Seeking help from Henry II of England, MacMurrough received his permission to enlist English adventurers in his cause, and was joined by Richard de Clare (called Strongbow), 2d earl of Pembroke, to whom he promised his daughter Eva in marriage and right to the succession in Leinster. In 1169 the first English forces landed and captured the town of Wexford. With the arrival of Strongbow in 1170, Waterford and Dublin were taken, and Henry arrived the next year to establish English rule over Ireland. See also IRELAND—*History to 1601 A. D.* (Anglo-Norman Penetration).

McMURRY, măk-mûr′ĭ, **Frank Morton,** American educator: b. near Crawfordsville, Ind., July 2, 1862; d. Pawling, N.Y., Aug. 1, 1936. Educated at the University of Michigan and abroad, he was professor of pedagogics and dean of Teachers College, University of Buffalo, from 1895 to 1898, and professor of elementary education at Teachers College, Columbia University, from 1898 to 1926. He was the author of *Tarr and McMurry Common School Geographies* (1900), with Ralph S. Tarr; *Method of the Recitation* (1903), with his brother, Charles Alexander McMurry; *How to Study and Teaching How to Study* (1909); and *Social Arithmetic* (1926), with Charles B. Benson.

McMURRY COLLEGE, a senior coeducational liberal arts college in Abilene, Texas, owned and operated by the Northwest Texas Conference of the Methodist Church. Virtually all denominations of the Christian faith are represented in its student body of 1,400. Strong emphasis is given to preprofessional training on the undergraduate level, especially in science. Four degrees are granted: the bachelor of arts, bachelor of business administration, bachelor of science, and master of education. Named after William Fletcher McMurry, then a bishop of the Methodist Episcopal Church South, the college

was opened in September 1923 with 191 students. Throughout the year colorful ceremonies on the campus depict the college's nickname, the Indians. The president of the college is known as "chief of the reservation." Football, basketball, and track are the principal sports. School colors are maroon and white.

GORDON R. BENNETT.

McMURTRIE, măk-mûr′trē, **Douglas Crawford,** American typographer, printing historian, and bibliographer: b. Belmar, N.J., July 20, 1888; d. Evanston, Ill., Sept. 29, 1944. He studied electrical engineering at the Massachusetts Institute of Technology but left the institution to begin a printing career in New York City. He was director of the Columbia University Printing Office (1917–1919) and then founded the Arbor Press, for which he built a plant in Greenwich, Conn., that became the Condé Nast Press, of which he was general manager from 1921 to 1923. He was director of typography for the Cuneo Press in Chicago (1925–1926) and from 1927 until his death for the Ludlow Typograph Company of Chicago. He designed several type faces: McMurtrie Title, Vanity Fair Capitals, and Ultra-Modern.

As chairman of the educational commission of the International Association of Printing House Craftsmen from 1940 until he died, he edited *The Gutenberg Documents* (1941) and was responsible for the publication of *The Invention of Printing: a Bibliography* (1942). In 1937 he was named editor of the American Imprints Inventory, a Works Progress Administration project for publishing a bibliography of American imprints before 1877, and his contribution in this post may be regarded as his most important. He projected a *History of Printing in the United States,* but only volume 2 was published (1936). His best-known book, a general history of printing published in 1927 as *The Golden Book,* revised as *The Book* in 1937 and 1943, was not a scholarly work. He was an authority on work with crippled children and was director of the Red Cross Institute for Crippled and Disabled Men (1917–1918).

FREDRIC J. MOSHER,
Associate Professor, School of Librarianship, University of California.

McNAGHTEN RULES. See INSANITY; LEGAL PSYCHOLOGY; MENTAL HEALTH—*Applications of Mental Health Principles* (Law Enforcement Problems).

McNAIR, măk-nâr, **Lesley James,** American army officer: b. Verndale, Minn., May 25, 1883; d. near St. Lo, France, July 25, 1944. He graduated from the United States Military Academy in 1904 and was commissioned a 2d lieutenant of artillery. He served with Gen. John J. Pershing's punitive expedition into Mexico in 1916 and with the American Army in France in 1917–1918 (World War I), being promoted to brigadier general and receiving the Distinguished Service Medal. He fulfilled various assignments, and in July 1940, before World War II, he was charged with the combat training of American troops as chief of staff, General Headquarters, and after the Army reorganization in 1942 as commanding general, Army Ground Forces, with the rank of lieutenant general. His program was rigorous, including obstacle courses, tactical exercises with live ammunition, and maneuvers involving armies under simulated combat conditions. He produced a trained army of about 8 million men. In July 1944 he asked for field duty and was sent to France. While on an observation mission, he was killed in an accidental bombing.

McNAMARA, mak-nə-mar'ə, **Robert Strange,** American business executive and secretary of defense: b. San Francisco, Calif., June 9, 1916. McNamara was a frail child (although his hobbies in later years included skiing and mountain climbing), but he was quick to learn and was favored with a sponge-like memory. The University of California at Berkeley, from which he graduated in 1937, elected him to Phi Beta Kappa as a sophomore. After graduating in 1939 from Harvard University's graduate school of business administration, he joined its faculty and was known as an exacting teacher.

Barred by weak eyes from active duty in World War II, McNamara developed and conducted a course at Harvard for the Air Force on statistical systems to control the flow of matériel, men, and money. He installed these systems in Air Force units around the world.

Ford Motor Company. After the war, McNamara and nine other Air Force control experts were hired by the Ford Motor Company. Most of the "Whiz Kids," as they were called, rose to high position. As controller, McNamara reputedly knew of every expenditure, and he induced the company to compete in the middle and higher income auto market. Later as vice president he developed the compact car and promoted seat belts and the long-term warranty. Chosen president of Ford in 1960, McNamara served only a month, until President-elect John F. Kennedy invited him to become secretary of defense. McNamara accepted at enormous financial sacrifice.

Secretary of Defense. Serving seven years in the post, McNamara, with his keen intellect, industrial experience, and abundant confidence, brought off feats that eluded his predecessors. He wrested control of the Pentagon from professional military men. In the cause of efficiency and economy he consolidated and centralized his department's structures and processes, applied systems analysis techniques to decision making, established elaborate controls over the use of departmental resources, and (angering many congressmen) closed down uneconomical military bases and left unspent money appropriated for weapons systems of which he did not approve.

The secretary overcame deficiencies in conventional weaponry and established an invulnerable second-strike nuclear capability. To avoid the spread of nuclear capability among European nations, he sought to integrate their nuclear efforts into the NATO structure.

His probing intelligence and broad background made McNamara a favorite, wide-ranging adviser to presidents Kennedy and Lyndon B. Johnson. His influence extended into domestic questions. For example, he reduced racial discrimination in the armed forces.

Vietnam commanded much of McNamara's attention. He was the President's chief deputy in overseeing the war. In 1964 the conflict was spoken of as "McNamara's War," but by 1967 he had become increasingly aware of domestic opinion opposed to the war and was known to doubt the efficacy of continued bombing of North Viet-

nam. Expressions of hope for an early peace gave way to a restlessness that by 1967 had led him to view the economic development of nations as more promising for peace and security than armies. This conviction led to his resignation as secretary and his assumption in 1968 of the presidency of the International Bank for Reconstruction and Development (the World Bank).

In 1968, McNamara published *The Essence of Security: Reflections in Office.*

Louis W. Koenig, *New York University*

McNARNEY, mək-när'nē, **Joseph Taggart,** American general: b. Emporium, Pa., Aug. 28, 1893. He graduated from West Point in 1915 and completed his flying training in 1917. In World War I he commanded air observation groups with the U.S. Army in France. After transferring to the Air Service in 1920, he served in flight training, command, and staff assignments. In 1940 he became a member of the Permanent Joint Defense Board for Canada and the United States. Following the Japanese attack on Pearl Harbor in 1941, he was made chairman of the reorganization committee of the War Department.

When the reorganization plan was made effective in March 1942, emphasizing the role of the Air Forces, McNarney was appointed deputy chief of the general staff of the United States Army, with the duty of establishing policy and supervising budgetary and legislative affairs, and speaking for the War Department before the public and Congress. In October of that year he was named deputy supreme commander in the Mediterranean area and commander of the United States forces there. He was named a temporary general in March 1945 and was commander of the American forces in Europe and military governor of Germany from November 1945 to March 1947, when he became commanding general of the matériel command in charge of procurement, research, and air power development and for technical training. He retired in 1952 as a major general to join the General Dynamics Corporation.

McNARY, mək-nâr'ē, **Charles Linza,** American lawyer and legislator: b. near Salem, Oreg., June 12, 1874; d. Fort Lauderdale, Fla., Feb. 25, 1944. He was educated at Leland Stanford University and by private tutors and was admitted to the Oregon bar in 1898. He practiced law in his brother's office until 1913, when he was named to complete an unexpired term on the Oregon Supreme Court. Defeated for election to the bench in 1915, he was chairman of the Republican state central committee for a year and on June 1, 1917, was appointed to the United States Senate for two years of an unexpired term.

He was elected five times successively to the Senate, where he was known for his efforts to aid the farmer. Between 1926 and 1928, bills which he sponsored with Representative Gilbert H. Haugen of Wisconsin, designed to meet the problem of surplus crops, were vetoed by President Calvin Coolidge. After 1933, McNary was minority leader of the Senate. A skillful negotiator with a pleasing manner, he was regarded as a liberal and was generally moderate in his opposition to President Franklin D. Roosevelt's New Deal measures, although he directed the vigorous strategy that defeated the plan to enlarge the Supreme Court of the United States. In 1940, when Wendell Willkie was defeated as

Republican candidate for president, McNary ran with him for vice president. He served in the Senate until his death.

McNAUGHTON, măk-nô't'n, **Andrew George Latta,** Canadian army officer: b. Moosomin, Sask., Feb. 25, 1887; d. Montebello, Que., July 11, 1966. Educated at McGill University, he served with the Canadian artillery in World War I, was wounded twice, and was promoted to brigadier general in 1918. He remained in the army, attending the Royal Staff College, Camberley, and the Imperial Defense College, London, England, and in 1929 was named major general and chief of the Canadian General Staff. From 1935 to 1939, he was president of the National Research Council, and at the beginning of World War II he went overseas as commander of the 1st Canadian Division. He commanded the 1st Canadian Army in 1942–1943, was promoted to general in September 1944, and retired from the army in November, serving as minister of national defense until August 1945. A distinguished scientist, he was a joint inventor of the cathode ray direction finder (1926).

He was chairman of the Canadian section of the Canada–United States Permanent Joint Board on Defense (1945–1959), and Canadian section chairman of the International Joint Commission, dealing with administrative affairs involving Canada and the United States (1950–1962). He was Canadian representative on the United Nations Atomic Energy Commission (1946), president of the Atomic Energy Board of Canada (1946–1948), and permanent delegate to the United Nations and Canada's representative on the Security Council (1948–1949).

MacNEICE, măk-nēs', **Louis,** Irish poet: b. Belfast, Ireland, Sept. 12, 1907; d. London, England, Sept. 3, 1963. He was educated in England at Marlborough School and at Oxford, then appointed lecturer in classics at the University of Birmingham (1930–1936) and lecturer in Greek at Bedford College, London (1936–1940). In 1941 he became a staff writer and producer of the British Broadcasting Corporation and continued to live mainly in London.

His first volumes of verse, *Blind Fireworks* (1929) and *Poems* (1935), and the long topical poem *Autumn Journal* (1939) established him as a member of the W.H. Auden group of young British poets of social protest, and *Letters from Iceland* (1937) was written with Auden. Representative poems are his *Turf Stacks* and *An Eclogue for Christmas,* contrasts of town and country; *Sunday Morning,* suburban life; *Birmingham* and *Morning Sun,* the city; and satirical pieces such as *Bagpipe Music* and *The British Museum Reading Room.* His later volumes include *Springboard* (1944), war poems; *Ten Burnt Offerings* (1952), inspired by a sojourn in Greece as director of the British Institute in Athens (1950–1951); and an assortment of short verses in *Visitations* (1957) and *Solstices* (1961). In *Eighty-five Poems* (1959) he included a selection from three decades of work. MacNeice uses colloquial idiom, effective wit and satire, and striking imagery to depict and evaluate contemporary life. For radio he had done verse plays and an abridged translation of Goethe's *Faust.* His critical writing includes *Modern Poetry* (1938) and *The Poetry of W.B. Yeats* (1941).

WILLIAM BRACY.

MacNEIL, măk-nēl', **Hermon Atkins,** American sculptor: b. Chelsea, Mass., 1866; d. New York, N.Y., Oct. 2, 1947. He studied in Paris under Henri M.A. Chapu and Jean A.J. Falguière, and did decorative work for the expositions in Chicago, Paris, Buffalo, and St. Louis. Among his other works, which included many on Indian themes, were *The Coming of the White Man* (City Park, Portland, Oreg.); McKinley Memorial (Columbus, Ohio); *General Washington* (Washington Arch, New York City); and samples at the Art Institute, Chicago; Peabody Institute, Baltimore; and The Metropolitan Museum, New York City. In 1916 he designed the United States 25-cent piece, showing a standing figure of Liberty, which was circulated for 16 years.

McNEILE, măk-nēl', **(Herman) Cyril** (pseudonym SAPPER), English novelist: b. Bodmin, Cornwall, England, Sept. 28, 1888; d. West Chiltington, Aug. 14, 1937. Educated at Cheltenham and the Royal Military Academy, Woolwich, he entered the Royal Engineers in 1907. He received the Military Cross in World War I. Retiring from the army in 1919 with the rank of lieutenant colonel, he quickly developed a talent for writing crime and adventure fiction. His best-known novel, *Bull-Dog Drummond,* an exciting tale of fast-paced action, published in 1920, has as its hero a demobilized army officer who is bored with retirement and seeks adventure as a private investigator. It was immediately popular, and a dramatized version, with Gerald du Maurier in the title role, had a successful run in London (1921–1922). A film version was produced in 1929, the first of a series based on subsequent Bull-Dog Drummond stories that poured from his prolific pen.

ALLAN M. FRASER.

McNUTT, măk-nŭt', **Paul Vories,** American lawyer and politician: b. Franklin, Ind., July 19, 1891; d. New York, N.Y., March 24, 1955. He was educated at Indiana University and Harvard Law School and taught at the Indiana University School of Law (1917–1925) and was its dean (1925–1933). He was governor of Indiana from 1933 to 1937 and high commissioner to the Philippines from 1937 to 1939. He next held several administrative posts in Washington, D.C.: federal security administrator (1939–1945); director of Defense, Health and Welfare Services (1941–1943), and chairman of the War Manpower Commission (1942–1945). He then returned to the Philippines as high commissioner and in 1946 was appointed ambassador to the new Republic of the Philippines, resigning in 1947 to practice law in Washington and New York City. He served in World War I as an artillery officer and was national commander of the American Legion (1928–1929).

MACOMB, mà-kōm', **Alexander,** American general: b. Detroit, Mich., April 3, 1782; d. Washington, D.C., June 25, 1841. He entered the United States Army in 1799 as a cornet of cavalry, later serving in the engineers. When war began in 1812 he was transferred at his own request to the artillery and commissioned colonel. In January 1814 he was promoted brigadier general and placed in command of that part of the northern frontier bordering on Lake Champlain. At Plattsburgh, on Sept. 11, 1814, he sustained the attack of a greatly superior British force under Sir George Prevost, which, after the defeat of the British squadron on Lake Champlain on the same day, retreated to Canada. For his firmness and courage on this occasion he was commissioned a brevet major general, and received the thanks of Congress and a gold medal. In 1828, he succeeded to the office of commander in chief of the Army, which he held until his death.

MACOMB, city, Illinois, seat of McDonough County, 37 miles in an air line south-southwest of Galesburg. It is a trade and industrial center in an agricultural and coal-mining region. Clay and steel products, poultry incubators, and beverage dispensers are manufactured. Western Illinois University is situated here. Settled largely by emigrants from New England, it was laid out in 1831 and originally was called Washington. The name was changed in honor of Gen. Alexander Macomb (q.v.). It was incorporated as a village in 1841 and as a city in 1856. Government is by mayor and council. Pop. 12,135.

MARY LOUISE HALL.

MACON, mā′kŭn, **Nathaniel,** American legislator: b. Macon Manor, Edgecombe (later Bute, now Warren) County, N.C., Dec. 17, 1758; d. Buck Springs, June 29, 1837. He studied at the College of New Jersey (now Princeton University) from 1774 to 1776, served briefly in the New Jersey militia, and studied law in North Carolina for three years. From 1780 to 1782 he was a private in the Continental Army, refusing a commission, and then was elected to the North Carolina State Senate for three terms. He opposed the Constitution of the United States, believing that it concentrated too much power in the central government. Elected to the federal House of Representatives in 1791, he remained until 1815, and was speaker from 1801 to 1807. He was a leader among the Republicans in the House, a friend of Thomas Jefferson, and a foe of Alexander Hamilton and the Federalists. His point of view was parochial, and his vote on many issues was often negative. He served in the United States Senate from 1815 to 1828, as president pro tempore in the last two years. In 1835 he was president of a convention called to revise the North Carolina state constitution.

MÂCON, mä-kôn′, city, France, capital of the Department of Saône-et-Loire, on the Saône River, 275 miles southeast of Paris and 38 miles north of Lyon. It developed as a way station and river port between Dijon and Lyon, and lies on the route from Paris to the Riviera and the Alps. Founded in Gallo-Roman times (ancient name Matisco), it became the seat of a feudal county between Burgundy and the bishopric of Lyon, passed to the control of Burgundy in 1435, and was brought into the royal French domain in 1477.

Its historical monuments reflect its comparatively quiet history. The oldest surviving structure, St. Mayeul Church, dates from the 11th century. The medieval (12th–13th century) Cathedral of St. Vincent was destroyed during the French Revolution, except for a chapel, still used; the façade, and the towers. The seat of the prefecture dates from the 17th century and the city hall from the 18th. The poet-statesman Alphonse Marie Louis de Prat de Lamartine (q.v.) was born here. The city's chief industrial and commercial activities are associated with the bottling and distribution of the region's famous Burgundy wines. Recently the growth of pleasant riverside suburbs has been fostered by the development of mechanical, metallurgical, and chemical industries. Pop. (1962) city, 25,012; commune 27,669.

JEAN CANU.

MACON, mā′kŭn, city, Georgia, seat of Bibb County, situated on both sides of the Ocmulgee River, 86 miles by highway south-southeast of Atlanta. Near the geographic center of the state, it is sometimes called "the Heart of Georgia." It is a manufacturing and processing center, whose economy is closely allied with agriculture. Chartered in 1823, it was named for Nathaniel Macon, a United States Senator from North Carolina, from where the first settlers came.

Products from farms, forests, and mines in the vicinity are processed. These include peaches, peanuts, pecans, watermelons, and other crops; cotton textiles, farm machinery, fertilizer, kaolin, brick clays, and pulpwood products. One of the world's largest deposits of kaolin, a fine clay used in ceramics, is nearby. The municipal airport is Cochran Field.

Mercer University (Baptist), founded in Penfield, Ga., in 1833 and moved to Macon in 1871, has one of the oldest theological schools in the South. Also in the city are Wesleyan College (Methodist), founded in 1836, said to be the first chartered college to grant degrees to women, and Georgia Academy for the Blind. The Washington Memorial Library, headquarters for a six-county regional library system, contains a bust of the poet Sidney Lanier, born in Macon, by Gutzon Borglum. The municipal auditorium, covered by a copper dome, was built in 1925, and the Macon hospital, one of the finest in the South, in 1956. The city has 22 parks and playgrounds, with swimming pools and golf courses. Central City Park is the site for winter training of harness race horses and of Georgia's oldest state agricultural fair (1846). At the Ocmulgee National Monument near the city are prehistoric mounds and remains of several ancient Indian civilizations. Robbins Air Force Base is about 20 miles south of Macon. A mayor-council form of government was adopted in 1832.

The original settlement, Fort Hawkins, authorized in 1806 by President Thomas Jefferson and named for Benjamin Hawkins, an Indian agent, was a rendezvous for troops in the War of 1812. When the fort was abandoned in 1821, the settlement was named Newtown, and became part of the city of Macon in 1829. Macon was a market and trade center for 16 counties, linked by transport on the Ocmulgee with the seaport of Darien, and later it became a railroad center. Military camps were located here in the Spanish-American War and in both World Wars. Pop. 122,876.

KATHERINE McCAMY POWERS.

MacPHAIL, măk-fāl′, **Agnes Campbell,** Canadian politician: b. Proton Township, Grey County, Ontario, Canada, March 24, 1890; d. Toronto, Feb. 13, 1954. Educated at Stratford Normal School, she taught in Ontario and Alberta. She was the first woman to be elected to the Canadian House of Commons. An agrarian reformer and a supporter of the cooperative movement, she sat as a member of the United

Farmers of Ontario Party from 1921 to 1940. An ardent advocate of social justice, she campaigned for pensions for the aged, the blind, and the disabled; for improved health services and prison reform. Defeated in the federal election of 1940, she was elected to the Ontario legislature as an Independent (1943–1945) and as a member of the Co-operative Commonwealth Federation (CCF) Party (1948–1951). In 1929, she was a member of the Canadian delegation to the League of Nations.

ALLAN M. FRASER.

MACPHEE, John Joseph, American neurologist: b. Prince Edward Island, Canada, July 8, 1860; d. New York, N. Y., Feb. 18, 1941. He was educated at Prince of Wales College, Charlottetown, and at the University of Vermont, receiving his M.D. degree in 1890. From 1891 to 1894 he was pathologist at the Post-Graduate Medical School in New York City, and then became professor of nervous and mental diseases at the New York Polyclinic Medical School and Hospital. He also served as consulting neurologist at St. John's Hospital, Brooklyn; Beth Israel Hospital, New York; and St. Francis Hospital, New York. He contributed numerous articles to medical periodicals.

MACPHERSON, SIR David Lewis, Canadian statesman: b. Castle Leathers, near Inverness, Scotland, Sept. 12, 1818; d. at sea, Aug. 16, 1896. He was educated at the Royal Academy in his native city, and moved to Canada in 1835. In 1842 he became a partner in a forwarding firm in Montreal, and in 1851 secured with others a charter for a railway from Montreal to Kingston, the beginning of the Grand Trunk Railway. In 1872 he became president of the Interoceanic Railway Company, the rival of the Canadian Pacific in competition for the transcontinental railway charter. He sat in the Legislative Council of Canada from 1864 to 1867, when he entered the Dominion Senate, becoming its speaker in 1880. From 1883 to 1885 he served as minister of the interior. He was knighted in 1884. He was the author of several pamphlets on finance.

McPHERSON, Edward, American journalist: b. Gettysburg, Pa., July 31, 1830; d. there, Dec. 14, 1895. After his graduation from Pennsylvania (now Gettysburg) College in 1848, he studied law but soon entered journalism, becoming editor of the Harrisburg *American* in 1851. For the next 44 years he was connected with various Pennsylvania newspapers, including the Philadelphia *Press* (1877–1880) and the Gettysburg *Star and Sentinel* (1880–1895). He served as a member of Congress for two terms and as clerk of the House for 16 years. He was also active in the Republican Party and was the author of several valuable political source books including *The Political History of the United States of America During the Great Rebellion* (1864); and *The Political History of the United States of America During the Period of Reconstruction* (1871). He published the *Political Manual* annually from 1866 to 1869, and the *Handbook of Politics* biennially from 1868 to 1894.

MACPHERSON, James, Scottish author and translator: b. Ruthven, Inverness, Oct. 27, 1736; d. Belville in Badenoch, Inverness, Feb. 17, 1796. He studied at King's College and Marischal College in Aberdeen, and at Edinburgh University. After he published *Fragments of Ancient Poetry, collected in the Highlands of Scotland, and translated from the Gaelic or Erse Language* (1760), a subscription was raised to enable him to collect additional specimens of national poetry. As the fruit of his research, he produced *Fingal, an Ancient Epic in Six Books* (1762), followed by *Temora* (1763), and a collected edition entitled *The Works of Ossian* (1765), all alleged translations from Gaelic originals ascribed to the 3d century bard Ossian (q.v.).

The question of the authenticity of the works provoked a violent controversy, Dr. Samuel Johnson being one of Macpherson's greatest opponents. It may be concluded that Macpherson's prose epics were founded on traditional narratives current in the Highlands; but the date of the oldest of the lays is comparatively modern, and it is now impossible to ascertain the precise extent of his obligations to Gaelic bards. Macpherson never made any serious attempt to vindicate himself against the charge of forgery. He had a life allowance from the government, was agent to Mohammed Ali, nabob of Arcot, and held a seat in the House of Commons from 1780 until his death. He was the author of several historical works and of an inadequate translation of Homer's *Iliad*. He was buried in Westminster Abbey.

McPHERSON, James Birdseye, United States army officer: b. Clyde, Ohio, Nov. 14, 1828; d. Atlanta, Ga., July 22, 1864. He was graduated from the United States Military Academy in 1853. Appointed brevet 2d lieutenant of engineers, he became assistant instructor of practical engineering at West Point (1853–1854). After working on the construction of defenses for New York Harbor and the improvement of the Hudson River, he was given charge of the construction of Fort Delaware and of the defenses of Alcatraz Island in San Francisco Bay.

At the opening of the Civil War, he applied for active employment in the field. In May 1862, he was appointed brigadier general of volunteers and was with Gen. Henry W. Halleck at the siege of Corinth. For his services on this occasion he was made major general of volunteers in the following October. He took an important part in the siege and capture of Vicksburg and in consequence was promoted to the rank of brigadier general in the regular army, Aug. 1, 1863. In March 1864, he was made commander of the Army of the Tennessee and performed distinguished services in the campaign of Georgia. The following July he commanded in the engagement around Atlanta and was killed during a reconnaissance.

McPHERSON, city, Kansas, seat of McPherson County; altitude 1,495 feet; 27 miles northeast of Hutchinson; served by the Chicago, Rock Island and Pacific; the Union Pacific; the Missouri Pacific; and the Atchison, Topeka and Santa Fe railroads. The surrounding area raises wheat and corn. The city is the central Kansas trade center for rich oil and gas fields, discovered in the region in 1929. Important industries include oil refinery plants, oilfield supply houses, flour and feed mills, and cement mills. Mc-

Pherson College (q.v.) and Central College are located in the city. Government is by commission. The city was incorporated in 1874. Pop. 9,996.

McPHERSON COLLEGE, an accredited, coeducational institution, located in McPherson, Kans. It was chartered in 1887 and opened in 1888. The college is the property of the Church of the Brethren, sometimes known as the Dunkers. It offers courses leading to the bachelor of arts and bachelor of science degrees. The campus covers about 13 acres.

McQUAID, mà-kwād', **Bernard John**, American Roman Catholic prelate: b. New York City, Dec. 15, 1823; d. Rochester, N. Y., Jan. 18, 1909. After studying in Canada, he completed his course at St. John's College, Fordham, N. Y., where he was graduated in 1843, and for the next three years held the position of tutor. He studied theology first with the Lazarists of New York City and later at St. John's College, Fordham, being ordained priest January 1848. Having built churches at Morristown and Springfield, N. J., he was engaged upon one at Mendham when summoned to the newly created diocese of Newark, N. J., 1853. In 1856, Father McQuaid founded Seton Hall College at Madison, N. J. (now Seton Hall University, located in South Orange, N. J.), and was its first president, retaining the office for 10 years. He was consecrated first bishop of the diocese of Rochester, N. Y., by Archbishop John McCloskey in New York City, July 12, 1868. With characteristic energy he discharged his episcopal duties, the cause of Catholic education ever appealing to him as one of paramount importance. With a view to advancing it, he invited the Sisters of St. Joseph to conduct new parochial schools in his diocese and likewise founded St. Andrew's Preparatory Seminary.

MACQUARIE ISLANDS, mà-kwôr'ĭ, a group of small islands in the South Pacific Ocean, about 850 miles southeast of Tasmania, Australia, by which it is administered. The largest island, also called Macquarie, has an area of about 89 square miles. The crest of a submarine mountain, it rises to a height of about 1,400 feet. It is rocky and has some small glacial lakes. Formerly it was good seal-hunting ground, but the seals have been practically exterminated. Penguins and other sea fowl abound, and there are large herds of sea elephants.

The islands were discovered in 1810 and until the destruction of the seals were visited by the sealers. Its only inhabitants at the time it was made a base of the Mawson Australasian Antarctic Expedition (1911–1914) were a few men stationed there for the purpose of rendering sea elephant and penguin blubber. There is now a permanent weather and relief station on the island and there are also radio stations.

Consult Mawson, Sir Douglas, *The Home of the Blizzard*, 2 vols. (1914).

MacQUEARY, mà-kwē'rĭ, **Thomas Howard**, American educator: b. Charlottesville, Va., May 27, 1861; d. St. Louis, Mo., July 1930. He was graduated from the Episcopal Theological Seminary at Alexandria, Va., in 1886, took orders in the Protestant Episcopal Church, and in 1887 became rector at Canton, Ohio. His religious views having undergone a radical change, he was tried by an ecclesiastical council for denial of miracles and suspended from the ministry for six months. He accordingly resigned from it in September 1891, and was for some time in the Universalist ministry. He returned to college for special work and in 1898 took his M.A. degree at the University of Minnesota, later (1901) finishing the work for the Ph.D. degree in history and economics at the University of Chicago, although he did not publish his thesis and take the degree. He founded Unity House Social Settlement in Minneapolis; from 1900–1906 was superintendent of the Parental School in Chicago; and from 1906 was head of the department of history and head assistant in Soldan High School, St. Louis, Mo. He also lectured frequently for Chautauquas and other societies. He was the author of *The Evolution of Man and Christianity* (1889), and *Topics of the Times* (1891).

McQUILLEN, **John Hugh**, American dentist: b. Philadelphia, Pa., Feb. 12, 1826; d. there, March 3, 1879. He began the study of medicine and dentistry in 1847, engaged in the practice of dentistry in 1849, took his M.D. at Jefferson Medical College in 1852, and his D.D.S. at the Philadelphia College of Dental Surgery in 1853. He became professor of operative dentistry and dental pathology at the Pennsylvania College of Dental Surgery in 1857. In 1863 he was instrumental in securing a charter for the Philadelphia Dental College and he was from that time until his death its dean and professor of anatomy, physiology, and hygiene. He was president of the American Dental Association, the Pennsylvania Association of Dental Surgeons, and the Odontographic Society of Philadelphia. From 1865 to 1872 he was editor in chief of the publication *Dental Cosmos*.

MACRAUCHENIA, măk-rô-kē'nĭ-à, a genius of three-toed, long-necked fossil ungulates, from the Pleistocene of South America. They form a connecting link between the palaeotherium and the camel family. In form they resemble the llama, but are as large as a hippopotamus. Their remains have been gathered from the pampas of Argentina and Bolivia.

MACREADY, măk-rē'dĭ, **William Charles**, English tragedian: b. London, March 3, 1793; d. Cheltenham, April 27, 1873. His father was the manager of several small theaters. William Charles received his education at Rugby, and originally had the intention of adopting one of the learned professions; but his father's failure in management changed his plans for a career, whereupon he joined his father's troupe then acting in Birmingham. He appeared there for the first time in 1810 in the character of Romeo, in which he was successful. On Sept. 16, 1816, he made his first appearance on the London stage at Covent Garden Theatre, acting the role of Orestes in *The Distressed Mother*. He did not achieve an immediate triumph in London, but gradually rose in popular favor. In 1819 his portrayal of Richard III established him as a leading tragedian, and the following year his Virginius gained him tremendous praise. In 1826 he made his first tour in the United States, making his debut in New York City on October 2 of that year as Virginius. From 1837 to 1839 he was manager of Covent Garden.

In 1841 he became manager of the Drury Lane, but met with little success and resigned in 1843. On his third visit to America in 1848–1849, he became involved in an unfortunate quarrel with the American actor Edwin Forrest (q.v.) which culminated in a riot on May 10, 1849, at the Astor Place Opera House, New York City, where Macready was playing Macbeth (see ASTOR PLACE RIOT). The disturbance forced the actor to leave the United States, and he returned to London for several farewell performances before retiring from the stage in 1851. Despite his mercurial temperament, Macready was recognized as perhaps the greatest English character actor of his day.

McREYNOLDS, măk-rĕn″ldz, **James Clark,** American public official: b. Elktown, Ky., Feb. 3, 1862; d. Washington, D.C., Aug. 24, 1946. Graduated from Vanderbilt University in 1882 and from the law department of the University of Virginia in 1884, he engaged in successful law practice at Nashville, Tenn., and was professor of law (1900–1903) at Vanderbilt University. As assistant attorney general of the United States (1903–1907), he was active in prosecuting violators of the Sherman Antitrust Act. Appointed attorney general (1913) in President Woodrow Wilson's cabinet, he initiated the government's cases against the Union Pacific-Southern Pacific railroad merger and the alleged monopoly practices of the American Telephone and Telegraph Company and other giant corporations. In 1914 he was named an associate justice of the Supreme Court, retiring in 1941. During the administration of President Franklin D. Roosevelt, McReynolds was a stanch defender of states' rights and a literal interpretation of the Constitution, voting against more New Deal measures than any other justice.

MACRINUS, mà-krī′nŭs, **Marcus Opellius,** Roman emperor: b. Caesarea, Mauretania (now Cherchel, Algeria), 164 A.D.; d. in Bithynia (now in Asiatic Turkey), 218. As praetorian prefect commanding the imperial bodyguard, he arranged the assassination of Emperor Caracalla and succeeded him in 217—the first Roman sovereign who was not a senator. His defeat near Nisibis (Nusaybin, Asiatic Turkey) by Artabanus IV, king of Parthia, from whom he then purchased peace; his severe military discipline; and his policy of retaining European-enlisted legions in Asia caused the army there to proclaim as emperor Heliogabalus (Elagabalus), who falsely claimed to be Caracalla's son. Macrinus, fleeing from battle near Antioch, Syria, escaped into Asia Minor, where he was captured and killed.

P. R. COLEMAN-NORTON.

MACROBIUS, mà-krō′bĭ-ŭs, **Ambrosius Theodosius,** Latin author: fl. 400 A.D. The country of his birth is uncertain, but he speaks of Latin as a foreign tongue, and was possibly of African origin. Macrobius was the author of the symposium *Saturnalia,* in seven books, a miscellany of philology, history, and mythology, containing important quotations from various classical writers, and valuable for its record of ancient customs and manners. He also wrote *Commentarii in Somnium Scipionis,* a Neo-Platonic commentary in two books on Cicero's *Somnium Scipionis;* this was much read by scholars during the Middle Ages. A grammatical treatise, *De differentiis et societatibus Graeci Latinique verbi,* is preserved only in fragments.

Consult Whitaker, Thomas, *Macrobius* (Cambridge, Eng., 1923).

MACROCOSM. See MICROCOSM AND MACROCOSM.

MacSWINEY, măk-swē′nĭ, **Terence,** Irish patriot: b. Cork, Ireland, March 27, 1879; d. London, England, Oct. 25, 1920. He was educated at the Royal University, Dublin, and worked as an accountant for 16 years. A member of the Sinn Fein movement for Irish independence from its founding in 1905, he edited revolutionary journals and helped to organize the Easter Rebellion of 1916. He was elected a member of Parliament from County Cork in 1918, and was chosen lord mayor of Cork two years later. Arrested and tried on charges of sedition, MacSwiney was sentenced to two years' imprisonment. On the day of his arrest (Aug. 12, 1920), he began a hunger strike that ended in his death after 74 days. His martyrdom resulted in an upsurge of Irish revolutionary fervor and in the subsequent disavowal by Sinn Fein leaders of the hunger strike as a political weapon.

MACTAN, măk-tän′, island, Philippines, in Bohol Strait, one mile off the east coast of Cebu Island. Its area of 24 square miles consists chiefly of coral lowland. The natives grow coconuts and engage in fishing. Opon is the principal town. The Portuguese navigator Ferdinand Magellan was killed here by natives in 1521. Mactan was liberated from Japan by United States forces in March 1945, and became the site of a United States military base in 1947. Pop. (1948) 44,396.

MACU, mä-kōō′. This name and closely similar variants of it are applied to four entirely different South American native peoples, none of them well known: (1) Macú, a numerous people occupying a considerable territory between the Rio Negro and Japurá River in the northwestern corner of Brazil. Their language has been classified in the Puinave family. (2) Mácu, a small tribe on the middle Auarí River in the extreme north of the Rio Branco Territory in Brazil. They speak an isolated language. (3) Maco, a division of the Piaroa tribe on the Ventuari River in southern Venezuela. (4) Maco, a division of the Cofán tribe in eastern Ecuador. The spelling "Macu" is also used for the last two names, and accents may or may not be consistently written.

Consult *Handbook of South American Indians,* Bureau of American Ethnology, Bulletin No. 143, vol. 3, pp. 813, 864–867 (Washington 1948).

JOHN HOWLAND ROWE.

MacVEAGH, măk-vā′, **Franklin,** American businessman, civic leader, and cabinet officer: b. near Phoenixville, Pa., Nov. 22, 1837; d. Chicago, Ill., July 6, 1934. He graduated from Yale College (1862) and Columbia Law School (1864), and in 1866 went to Chicago, where he entered the wholesale grocery business. After the fire of 1871, he organized Franklin MacVeagh and Company, which for 60 years was one of the major wholesale grocery firms in the United States. MacVeagh was the first president (1874) of the Citizens' Association of Chicago, and was active in many other civic groups. As secretary of the treasury (1909–1913) in President William How-

ard Taft's cabinet, he effected a reorganization of
the department in the interest of efficiency and
economy. He was the brother of (Isaac) Wayne
MacVeagh (q.v.).

MacVEAGH, (Isaac) Wayne, American
public official: b. near Phoenixville, Pa., April
19, 1833; d. Washington, D.C., Jan. 11, 1917.
He was graduated from Yale College in 1853,
was district attorney of Chester County, Pa.,
from 1859 to 1864, and served as an officer of the
Pennsylvania militia during the Civil War. He
soon became prominent as a Republican leader in
the state, and after serving as minister to Turkey
(1870–1871), led the opposition to party boss
Simon Cameron, who was his father-in-law. In
1877 the so-called MacVeagh Commission, which
he headed, settled party differences in Louisiana,
ending the reconstruction there. MacVeagh was
the friend and trusted adviser of many presidents
of the United States, a consistent opponent of
machine politics, and a vigorous champion of
government reform. He served briefly as attorney
general (1881) in the cabinet of James A. Garfield, but in 1892 switched this allegiance to the
Democratic Party, and was appointed ambassador to Italy (1893–1897) by Grover Cleveland.
Later he was chief counsel for the United States
in the Venezuela arbitration before the Hague
Tribunal (1903).

MACY, mā′sĭ, **Anne Mansfield Sullivan,**
American teacher and companion of Helen Adams
Keller: b. Feeding Hills, Mass., April 14, 1866; d.
Forest Hills, N.Y., Oct. 20, 1936. Her eyesight
was seriously weakened by an infection during
childhood, and she entered the state infirmary at
Tewksbury, Mass., at the age of 10. In 1880 she
went to the Perkins Institute for the Blind, near
Boston, where she learned the manual alphabet
and graduated with a brilliant scholastic record
in 1886. In the meantime, her eyesight had been
restored through a series of operations, and the
following year she became the teacher of the
blind and deaf Helen Keller, then seven years old.
Miss Sullivan taught her the sign langauge and
Braille system, and assisted her education at the
Perkins Institute (1889–1893), the Cambridge
School for Young Ladies (1896–1900), and Radcliffe College (1900–1904), communicating the
content of class lectures to her pupil by means of
the touch alphabet. She later accompanied Miss
Keller on numerous travels and lecture tours. In
1905 she married John Albert Macy (q.v.), but
continued her remarkable relationship with Miss
Keller, even though her eyesight deteriorated
slowly to nearly total blindness by 1935.
Consult Braddy, Nella, *Anne Sullivan Macy: the
Story Behind Helen Keller* (New York 1933); Keller,
Helen Adams, *Teacher: Anne Sullivan Macy; a Tribute
by the Foster-Child of Her Mind* (New York 1955).

MACY, John Albert, American literary
critic: b. Detroit, Mich., April 10, 1877; d.
Stroudsburg, Pa., Aug. 26, 1932. He graduated
from Harvard College in 1899, and from 1901 to
1909 was associate editor of *Youth's Companion.*
His first major work, *Edgar Allan Poe* (1907),
established his reputation as a perceptive critic.
In 1909, Macy became a Socialist, and his interest
in social problems was reflected in his next important book, *The Spirit of American Literature*
(1913), a pioneering work in its field, which
championed literary realism and recognized the
merits of such writers as Edith Wharton and

Theodore Dreiser. Macy was literary editor of
the Boston *Herald* (1913–1914) and of the *Nation*
(1922–1923), and literary adviser to William
Morrow & Company, publishers, from 1926. His
marriage (1905) to Anne Mansfield Sullivan was
unhappy and resulted in separation. Macy's other
books include *Socialism in America* (1916), *The
Critical Game* (1922), *The Story of the World's
Literature* (1925), *The Romance of America As
Told in Our Literature* (1930), and *About
Women* (1930). He also edited Helen Keller's
The Story of My Life (1903).

MACY, Rowland Hussey, American merchant: b. Nantucket Island, Mass., Aug. 30, 1822;
d. Paris, France, March 29, 1877. After serving
as a cabin boy on a whaler, he operated small
stores in Boston and California without success,
and in 1851 opened the "Haverhill Cheap Store"
in Haverhill, Mass., where he first tried out many
of the ideas that he later used successfully in New
York City, notably standardized prices, undersell-
ing competitors, and the use of effective advertising. When this business also failed, Macy spent
a year as a real estate speculator in Superior,
Wis., and in 1858 opened the R. H. Macy fancy
dry-goods store (chiefly ladies' accessories) on
Sixth Avenue just south of 14th Street in New
York City. Aided by the business boom of the
Civil War years, success came almost immediately. Macy soon transformed his business into a
genuine department store, putting in many individual sections, including a glassware and china
department operated on concession by Lazarus
Straus and his two sons, Isidor and Nathan
Straus. He also employed as a trusted aide the
first woman department store executive, Margaret Getchell, a distant relative. Some years
after his death, the major ownership of the store
passed into the hands of the Straus family.

Consult Hower, Ralph M., *History of Macy's of New
York, 1858–1919,* Harvard Studies in Business History,
No. 7 (Cambridge, Mass., 1943).

MAD ANTHONY, a nickname given to Gen.
Anthony Wayne (q.v.), on account of the great
daring of his military feats in the American
Revolutionary War.

MADÁCH, Imre, mŏ′däch, Hungarian poet
and dramatist: b. Alsó-Sztregova, Hungary, Jan.
21, 1823; d. Alsó-Sztregova, Oct. 5, 1864. His
work belongs to the romantic movement that affected Hungarian literature in the 1800's. His
best known work is the dramatic poem, *Az ember
Tragédiája,* published in 1861 and translated in
1908 as *The Tragedy of Man.* It traces the corruption of human society in 15 scenes spanning
history from the Garden of Eden to a future Ice
Age. The play challenged the contemporary belief
in inevitable progress, although the principal
characters, Adam and Eve, ultimately refuse to
abandon hope.

Madách, the son of landed gentry, was educated for the law at Budapest. He took part in
the unsuccessful revolution of 1848–1849 and was
briefly imprisoned. The failure of the revolution
and an unhappy marriage drove Madách into
retirement on his country estate, where he devoted his time to writing. A comedy, *The Civi-
lizer,* was published in 1859, and the religious
drama, *Mózes* in 1860. *The Tragedy of Man*
brought Madách wide renown. He was elected to
parliament in 1861 and served until his death.

MADAGASCAR, măd-á-găs'kĕr, is an island in the Indian Ocean off the southeast coast of Africa. It extends from northeast to southwest, opposite Mozambique on the continent, from which it is separated by the Mozambique Channel, 250 miles across at its narrowest point. The island is the home of the Malagasy Republic.

With an area of 228,000 square miles, about the size of Nevada and New Mexico together, Madagascar is the fourth-largest island in the world. Only Greenland, New Guinea, and Borneo are larger. Madagascar's length, from north to south, is 980 miles; its greatest width is 360 miles. The island's coastline is about 3,000 miles long.

A central mountain chain runs down the length of Madagascar. Called the High Plateaus, the chain has an average altitude of between 3,000 and 5,000 feet. Three of its ranges have peaks rising above 6,000 feet. The 9,450-foot Tsaratanana is the highest peak.

Vales and ravines crisscross the High Plateaus in all directions. Here and there great bowl-shaped alluvial depressions form swampy plains.

The east coast, about 30 miles wide, stands between the High Plateaus and the Indian Ocean. A low-lying region of old rock strata, it is marked by eroded hills and swamps. It rises to the south, forming cliffs and high dunes.

The west coast is 120 miles wide in some places. It is made up of a series of tiers of sedimentary formations from all geologic ages. In the west and northwest are vast plains, whose rich soils produce abundant tropical vegetation.

Most of Madagascar's many rivers have their sources in the High Plateaus. One watershed faces east on the Indian Ocean. The other faces west on the Mozambique Channel. The east coast rivers, short and torrential, are navigable only for short distances. The most important is the Mangoro, 130 miles long. The west coast rivers are navigable for longer stretches. The main ones are the Betsiboka, 272 miles, and the Mangoky, 310 miles.

Along the coasts the weather is generally hot and humid. Inland it is more temperate. The hot or rainy season lasts from November to April on the High Plateaus. It is longer on the east coast and shorter on the west coast. The cool or dry season lasts the remainder of the year.

The east coast gets an average of 118 inches of rain a year. The north gets 52 inches, and the southwest coast only 12 inches. The High Plateaus are cool and pleasant, no hotter than 85°F, no colder than 35°F.

Thick forests once covered Madagascar, but these have been mainly burned off or chopped down in order to clear the land for farming. Dense forests still grow along parts of the High Plateaus and along the coasts. On the plateaus are such trees as the palisander, rosewood, and ironwood. Along the coasts are mangrove, raffia palms, and fruit trees.

On the plateaus also grow wide stretches of grassland. Here are many rice paddies and plantings of European fruits and vegetables. The south is a land of thick, spiny underbrush and giant grasses mingling with stunted trees and varieties of cactus.

Most of the animals that inhabit continental Africa have never appeared on Madagascar. The island is the home of many kinds of lemurs. Hedgehogs, bats, wild boars, fossas (a big cat-like, meat-eating animal), and tiny, insect-eating geogales, one of the smallest mammals in the world, live on Madagascar.

Partridges, pigeons, teals, waders, and owls inhabit the woods and swamps. Crocodiles are in all the lakes and rivers, except in the coldest parts of the plateaus. Among other reptiles are great sea turtles, land turtles, chameleons, lizards, and nonvenomous snakes.

Madagascar insects include grasshoppers, termites, cockroaches, and many kinds of butterflies. Malaria-carrying mosquitoes are found in the low, wet places.

See also MALAGASY REPUBLIC.

MADAMA BUTTERFLY, mä-dä'mä bŭt'-ĕr-flī, an opera in three acts by Giacomo Puccini, with libretto by Giuseppe Giacosa and Luigi Illica, after David Belasco's play based on a story by John Luther Long. It was first performed in a two-act version in Milan, Italy, on Feb. 17, 1904, and in its present version at Brescia on May 28, 1904. The cast consists of the following characters: Cio-Cio-San, or Madama Butterfly (soprano); Suzuki, a servant (mezzo-soprano); Kate Pinkerton (mezzo-soprano); Lieutenant B. F. Pinkerton, United States Navy (tenor); Goro, a marriage broker (tenor); Sharpless, United States consul (baritone); Prince Yamadori (baritone); the Bonze, Cio-Cio-San's uncle (bass); Trouble, Cio-Cio-San's child (silent role); an Imperial Commissioner (bass); an Official Registrar (baritone); and other relatives, officials, and servants. The locale is Nagasaki, Japan, in the late 19th century.

Act I.—A Japanese house, terrace, and garden. Pinkerton is about to contract a Japanese marriage with Butterfly, who mistakenly believes that it will be binding. Having renounced her ancestral faith, Butterfly signs the marriage contract. During the ensuing festivities, the Bonze denounces her and persuades her other relatives to leave. Pinkerton and his bride enter their house.

Act II.—Inside Butterfly's house, two years later. Pinkerton is in America, but has promised to return. Suzuki suspects that he has deceived her mistress, who meanwhile has given birth to a fair-haired child. Pinkerton has written Sharpless to tell Butterfly of his "real" marriage to an American girl. Seeing the letter in the consul's hand, but not understanding it, the happy Butterfly rejects a wealthy Japanese suitor brought to her by the marriage broker. Pinkerton's ship arrives. Butterfly and Suzuki deck the house with flowers and themselves in holiday clothes. As night creeps on, Suzuki and the child sleep, but Butterfly remains awake, waiting.

Act III.—In the house, the next morning. Pinkerton and Sharpless tell Suzuki the truth. The unhappy Pinkerton leaves, but Sharpless remains to convince Suzuki that the new Mrs. Pinkerton will adopt Butterfly's child. Butterfly enters, looking for Pinkerton, but instead encounters his wife. Shatteringly convinced of the actual situation, she wishes Kate Pinkerton well and asks her to send Pinkerton for the child in half an hour. Left alone, Butterfly bids the child farewell and then stabs herself. Pinkerton and Sharpless return to find her dead.

Puccini's score is notable for its delicacy, for its use of both genuine and invented Japanese themes, and for its pervasive sentimentality. Particularly effective numbers include Butterfly's first entrance (*Ancora un passo*), the Butterfly-Pinkerton love duet beginning *Viene la sera,* Butterfly's passionate statement of belief in Pinkerton's return (*Un bel dì vedremo*), the "humming chorus" heard during Butterfly's nocturnal vigil (*Nello shosi*), the Pinkerton-Sharpless duet (*Addio, fiorito asil*), and Butterfly's farewell to her child (*Tu, tu, piccolo iddio*).

HERBERT WEINSTOCK,
Author of "Music as an Art."

MADAME BOVARY, mä-däm′ bô-vä-rê′, the first and most celebrated novel of Gustave Flaubert. Its original publication serially (1856–1857) in the *Revue de Paris* shocked many readers because of the sordidness of its story of a provincial wanton, narrated in realistic detail. Like Charles Baudelaire's *Les fleurs du mal,* which also appeared in 1857, the book led to the prosecution of the author on a charge of immorality. The case against Flaubert ended in a qualified acquittal, and he insisted on printing the court pleadings and judgment when the novel was published in book form later in 1857.

The theme of *Madame Bovary* is the banality of provincial life and the futility of revolt against it by such essentially vulgar souls as his protagonist. The convent-bred daughter of a farmer, Emma Rouault is an avid reader of romantic poetry and novels. She marries a widower, Charles Bovary, a medical practitioner (though not an M.D.), who is a good citizen but in no way corresponds to her ideal man. Seeking escape from boredom, she has a platonic affair with Léon Dupuis, a law student, and then, after failing to find consolation in religion, gives herself to Rodolphe Boulanger. This liaison ends disastrously, and Emma turns again to religion briefly. Meeting an older and more sophisticated Léon, she becomes his mistress and ruins her husband financially; but Léon, tiring of her, abandons her. When Rodolphe, too, finally rejects her, Emma kills herself with poison, retaining to the last the love of her infatuated husband, who dies of grief after discovering her infidelity.

The work, a masterpiece of style, called by Paul Bourget "the very ideal of the literary artist," is one of the great novels of the 19th century and has had considerable influence on the development of the art of fiction. A minor character, M. Homais, a druggist-demagogue, has become for the French the prototype of the narrow provincial philistine. As Pierre Mille observes: "Emma is the eternal, the universal type of the amorous, romantic woman, who mingles the vulgar and the humdrum with a touching need of love." Another French critic, Louis Bertrand, coined the word "bovaryism" to signify a kind of sentimentally distorted view of life found in many women and some men.

DRAKE DE KAY,
Senior Editor, "The Encyclopedia Americana."

MADARIAGA, mä-thä-ryä′gä, **Salvador de,** Spanish author and diplomat: b. La Coruña, Spain, July 23, 1886. Educated at technical schools in Madrid and Paris, he moved to London in 1916 to engage in journalism, and later (1928–1931) held the chair of Spanish literature at Oxford University. He was director of the disarmament section of the League of Nations Secretariat in Geneva (1922–1927), Spanish ambassador to the United States (1931) and France (1932–1934), and permanent delegate to the League of Nations (1931–1936). Madariaga is the author of several volumes of poetry, novels, and plays, including the novel *War in the Blood* (1957), but is most distinguished as a social and political philosopher and interpreter of Spanish culture. He has written much in English, and translates his own works. Among his books are The *Genius of Spain . . .* (1923), *Englishmen, Frenchmen, Spaniards* (1928), and *Spain* (rev. ed., 1958); biographies of Christopher Columbus (1939), Hernán Cortés (1941), and Simón Bolívar (1952); books on international problems, such as *The World's Design* (1938) and *Portrait of Europe* (1952); and a two-volume history of the Spanish colonial empire in America (1947).

MADAWASKA, măd-à-wŏs′kà, town, Maine, comprising the villages of Madawaska and St. David in Aroostook County. It is situated at an altitude of 595 feet on the St. John River, opposite Edmundston, New Brunswick, Canada, and constitutes a port of entry into the United States. The town is served by the Bangor and Aroostook Railroad. The establishment of paper mills in 1926 brought industrial activity to the community, which is otherwise chiefly agricultural. Originally settled in 1785 by Acadians immigrating from Nova Scotia, it was incorporated as a town in 1869. Pop. 5,507.

MADDALONI, mäd-dä-lō′nê, town and commune, Italy, in Caserta Province, Campania, 15 miles north-northeast of Naples. It is in an agricultural region where grapes and citrus fruits are cultivated on the slopes of the surrounding hills. There are a medieval castle and an aqueduct erected in 1753–1764 by the architect Luigi Vanvitelli to supply water for the royal gardens of King Charles III of Spain, conqueror of Naples, at Caserta. Maddaloni was the site of a battle between Giuseppe Garibaldi's revolutionary forces and royal troops in 1860. Pop. (1951) town 24,242; commune 28,089.

MADDER, măd′ẽr, plants in the genus *Rubia,* but especially *R. tinctorum;* also the root of *R. tinctorum,* an extract from the root used as a dye, or the color resulting from it. *Rubia* includes some 40 species, native of the Mediterranean region, South Africa, South America, and Asia. *R. tinctorum,* of southern Europe and Asia Minor, is a perennial herb, ascending or climbing to several feet, with narrow, rough, prickly leaves (four to six in a whorl); minute, clustered, yellow flowers; and dark red, smooth, fleshy fruits. Fasciated plants with as many as 40 leaves to a whorl occur.

The root of madder long served as a valuable source of dye for cloth, the decorticated main root of a two- to three-year-old plant yielding the best product. The dye is red or Turkey red, or shades of pink, purple, orange, and black—depending upon the preparation and treatment. There are various constituents, of which alizarin (q.v.) is the most important. Since this was made synthetically in 1868, it has largely replaced the natural product. Indian or Bengal madder, *R. cordifolia,* furnishes dye in India. *R. peregrina* has also been used.

Field madder is the related genus *Sherardia arvensis,* native of the Old World, which also grows in waste places in eastern North America. It is a small procumbent annual with whorled leaves and tiny pink-to-blue flowers in heads.

EDWIN B. MATZKE.

MADEIRA, village, Ohio, Hamilton County, is located 15 miles northeast of Cincinnati (3 miles from the corporate limits), of which it is a residential suburb, on the Baltimore and Ohio Railroad. It is incorporated and has a mayor-council government. Pop. 6,744.

MADEIRA, mà-dẹr'ä (Port. mà-tħā'ê-rà, mà-tħǎ'ê-rà), a group of islands in the eastern Atlantic Ocean belonging to Portugal and forming the Portuguese administrative district of Funchal. They lie opposite to and about 360 miles distant from Morocco, off the west coast of Africa, about 535 miles southwest of Lisbon, north of the Canary Islands and southwest of the Azores. They include Madeira and Porto Santo islands and two groups of uninhabited islets, the Desertas and Salvages (or Selvagens), with a combined area of 315 square miles.

The main island, Madeira, is 35 miles long and up to 13 miles wide. It is made up of mountains of volcanic origin the highest of which is Pico Ruivo, 6,056 feet high. The east portion of the island is elevated, but less so than the west. From the central mass steep ridges extend to the coast where they form precipices from 1,000 to 2,000 feet high. These cliffs are indented by a few small bays where richly cultivated valleys approach the water between abrupt precipices or backed by rugged hills, and here are located the villages of Madeira. The most striking features of the mountain scenery are the jagged ridges and the deep gorges which cut through the highest mountains almost to their base.

Wine and sugar are the staple products; sugar cane, sweet potatoes, onions, some cereals, fruit, and cattle for dairying are raised. The chief industries are embroidery, wine making, sugar milling, the manufacture of wicker furniture and baskets, and fishing. The principal exports are Madeira wines and embroideries, wickerwork, bananas, pineapples, dairy products, and fish.

The mean annual temperature of Madeira is 65°F., and the climate from its constant and temperate warmth makes the island a favorite resort of invalids. Funchal, the capital, is a submarine cable station and port-of-call. It has been an Episcopal see since 1514, and has a late 15th century cathedral. Pop. (1960) 43,301.

The Madeiras were known to the Romans under the name of *Purpurariae Insulae.* They were rediscovered in 1418 by the Portuguese navigator, Joãs Gonçalves Zarco, who in 1421 founded Funchal. The name Madeira was given to the principal island because of the magnificent forests of building timber (in Portuguese *madeira*) which covered it. From 1580 to 1640 the islands, with Portugal itself, were under Spanish rule, and twice have been occupied by the British, in 1801 and again in 1807–1814. The British developed the wine industry, and are still the most numerous among foreign visitors to the islands. Pop. (1960) *268,937* total; Madeira Island, 267,957.

MADEIRA, river, Brazil, the most important affluent of the Amazon, formed by the united streams Beni and Mamoré on the frontiers of Brazil and Bolivia. The length from the source of the Mamoré is 2,100 miles.

MADELEINE, Marie Angélique de Sainte, French abbess, prioress of the convent of Port Royal, Paris. See under baptismal name, Jacqueline Arnauld, in ARNAULD—*Port Royal.*

MADELEINE, mà-dlĕn', **La,** France, a type station, or rock shelter, of late paleolithic culture in the valley of the Vézère, midway between Moustier and Les Eyzies. The Madelenian, or Magdalenian, epoch in archaeology was named from this cave.

MADELEINE, La, a church in Paris, in a square of the same name, begun in 1764. It was remodeled and changed after the Revolution, and was completed and consecrated in 1842. The church is built in the form of a Greek temple and is 100 feet high, 354 feet long and 141 feet wide. The bronze doors by Henri de Triqueti are 35 feet high and 16 feet in width. The building, which has no windows, is lighted from above.

MADEMOISELLE DE MAUPIN, mō-păN', a novel written by the French author, Théophile Gautier, when he was only 24 years of age (1835). It expresses the most salient features of romanticism. In the somewhat long preface is found the key to the interpretation of this highly imaginative work. Gautier cries out against the shammed respectability of that period and condemns the prudish stand of literary critics who according to him are merely hypocrites actuated by envy. Violently opposed to classical traditions and ideas, Gautier, who had been trained as a painter, keeps in this work the painter's vision, and emphasizes primarily form and color, while defending art for art's sake. Digressions on the supreme value of beauty are found frequently throughout the pages, and the vivid imagination of the author is fruitful to the point of exaggeration. The heroine, brought up according to tradition, rebels against it, and, disguised as a man, like the Amazons of old, resolves to study life at first hand. After many unusual adventures she becomes for one day the long-sought ideal of a romantic poet who had searched in vain until then for the "woman" of his dreams and who found her only to lose her immediately. As a novel the work is crude both in subject matter and in development, showing that it comes from a young man whose passions were not yet calm. It is, however, essentially artistic; the style is full of color and abounds in beautiful descriptions and lyric passages. While the novel did succeed in amazing placid citizens and is still classed as dangerous reading, it must not be considered as a study of any type of French character, but as a flight of imagination, a descriptive fantasy artistically worked out by a talented writer of the Romantic school.

LOUIS A. LOISEAUX.

MADERA, mà-dâr'à, city, California, Madera County seat, is located 22 miles northwest of Fresno, on the Santa Fe, and Southern Pacific railroads. It is in a lumber and vineyard area. Pop. 14,430.

MADERO, mä-tħā'rō, **Francisco Indalecio,** president of Mexico: b. San Pedro, Coahuila, Oct. 4, 1873; d. Mexico City, Feb. 22, 1913. He came of a wealthy family and was a grandson of a former governor of Coahuila. He was educated at a Jesuit college in Mexico and at the University of California and spent the years

A modern Buddhist temple at Sanchi in Madhya Pradesh.

Fine examples of ancient Buddhist architecture at Sanchi.

1889 to 1895 studying in France. After devoting some time to managing his extensive estates in northern Mexico and instituting certain social reforms among the peons, he moved to Mexico City where he worked to spread his ideas on political reform. By 1905 he was the acknowledged leader of the opposition to the government of Porfirio Díaz, on whom he made an open attack in his book, *La sucesión presidencial en 1910,* published in 1908. Two years later he ran against Díaz for the presidency on the platform of more effective suffrage and single presidential terms. Díaz had him imprisoned until after his re-election, but Madero escaped to Texas where he was able to contact rebellious groups and returned to head a revolution. An independent government was set up at Ciudad Juárez in May 1911 and Díaz was soon forced to resign; six months later Madero was elected president.

Madero's regime was marred by continued revolts and obstructionism, and he was accused of indecision and peculation. His commander in chief, Gen. Victoriano Huerta, joined the revolutionists and overthrew him in February 1913. He was arrested and shot while allegedly trying to escape. See also MEXICO—*27. Modern Mexico* (Outbreak of the Revolution).

MADHYA PRADESH, mäd′yà prä′dĕsh, state, India, located in central India and bordered by the states of Uttar Pradesh on the north, Bihar on the northeast, Orissa on the east, Andhra Pradesh on the southeast, Bombay on the south and southwest, and Rajasthan on the west and northwest. The second largest of the Indian states after its reorganization of Nov. 1, 1956, it has an area of 171,201 square miles and includes the former states of Madhya Bharat, Vindhya Pradesh, and Bhopal, the Sironj subdivision of Rajasthan, and the Hindi-speaking districts of former Madhya Pradesh. The population (1951 census, adjusted to 1956 reorganization) is 26,071,637. The city of Bhopal (pop., 1951, 102,333) became the capital after the merger.

The country is composed of mountains and plateaus, and is irrigated mainly by the Son, Mahanadi, Narbada, and Wardha rivers. The rainfall, affected by the monsoons, is heavy. Forests cover a large area, and are the source of the best quality of teakwood to be found in India. The state is rich in mineral deposits, such as coal, iron, bauxite, manganese, and copper, as well as marble, limestone, and sandstone.

Madhya Pradesh has a predominantly agricultural economy, in which 78 per cent of the population is engaged. Major crops include wheat, rice, jowar (Indian millet), pulse, oilseeds (such as flax, peanuts, and sesame), cotton, tobacco, and sugarcane. In addition to cottage industries of spinning, weaving, and leatherworking, there are a number of factories: a newsprint plant, the first in India, was built in 1949, and there is a steel mill with a productive capacity of one million tons. A network of railways and airlines connects with other parts of the country; important rail and air centers are Nagpur, Jubbulpore, and Bhopal.

The people, who live mostly in villages, are divisible into two distinct groups: the aborigines and the descendants of later settlers. The rate of literacy, 13.5 per cent, is one of the lowest in India. The University of Nagpur, established in 1923, has three constituent and 21 affiliated colleges, and the University of Saugor, established in 1946, has 20 affiliates.

The state government consists of a governor, council of ministers, and Legislative Assembly, with 288 members. There are seven administrative divisions, each headed by a commissioner.

History.—Madhya Pradesh has an outstanding cultural heritage. Buddhist stupas at Sanchi and Bharhut, cave temples near Bhilsa and Bagh, monolithic pillars near Mandasor, and the medieval fort at Gwalior, are part of its rich past. Early in the 17th century it came under the sway of the Moguls and in the 18th century it was conquered by the Marathas; the British acquired it by separate treaties and organized it as a single province in 1861. With the addition of Berar in 1903 it was known as Central Provinces and Berar. In 1950 it became a constituent state of the new Republic of India and its name was changed to Madhya Pradesh.

ASHA PRASAD.

MADISON, măd'ĭ-s'n, **Dolley** (nee PAYNE), wife of James Madison, 4th president of the United States: b. Guilford County, N.C., May 20, 1768; d. Washington, D.C., July 12, 1849. Dolley (her spelling of her name with an *e* has been substantiated by scholars) was the third child of Quaker parents, John and Mary Payne, who gave her scrupulous care but little education. At the age of 15 she moved with her family to Philadelphia, Pa., and in 1790 she was married to the Quaker, John Todd, Jr. The couple had two sons: John Payne Todd (1792–1852), and a younger child who, like his father, died in the yellow fever epidemic of 1793. Senator Aaron Burr introduced the young widow to James Madison (q.v.), then a congressman, and 17 years her senior; they were married Sept. 15, 1794. Their marriage, although childless, was very happy.

When James Madison, the new secretary of state, moved to Washington in 1801, Dolley's charm and informal friendliness resulted in her becoming the official hostess for the widowed President Thomas Jefferson. Eight years later, when her husband assumed the presidency, she blossomed into a more elegant figure. Still generally admired, she was adept in creating a harmonious atmosphere while refraining from active political participation. From 1817 to 1836 she lived quietly with her husband at Montpelier in Orange County, Va., but after his death in 1836 she returned to Washington where, in spite of financial difficulties, she once again resumed a role in Washington society.

Consult Dean, Elizabeth Lippincott, *Dolly Madison, The Nation's Hostess* (Boston 1928).

MADISON, James, 4th president of the United States: b. Port Conway, Va., March 16, 1751 (March 5, 1750, Old Style); d. Montpellier (now Montpelier), near Orange, Va., June 28, 1836. A descendant of John Madison, ship carpenter, who emigrated from England in 1653, he was the eldest child of James Madison and Nelly Conway of Orange County, Va., and was born during a visit of his mother to her maternal home.

Education.—Madison's primary education at home was followed by five years at the school of Donald Robertson in King and Queen County, Va. Two years' tutelage under an Anglican rector prepared him in 1769 for the College of New Jersey (now Princeton University), where he remained an additional six months after graduation in 1771. His studies, in addition to literature, emphasized philosophy, theology, and principles of government. Intense application, however, temporarily undermined his health.

At home Madison continued studies of public law and theology, but with no indication of an intention to become a lawyer or a clergyman. Never a church member, he spoke later of a Unitarian preference.

Early Experience in Public Affairs.—Madison shared the growing revolutionary spirit of the British colonies and fumed against the persecution of Baptists. On Dec. 22, 1774, he was elected to the Orange County revolutionary committee, of which his father was named chairman. He also enlisted in a military company, but could not stand the physical strain. He became a delegate to the Virginia Convention, which on May 15, 1776, requested the Continental Congress to declare the colonies independent. During the drafting of the Virginia Declaration of Rights, he reworded the article on religious liberty to eliminate the idea of mere toleration of dissenters and secured a declaration of equal right to the free exercise of religion. Refusal to treat voters to liquor led to his defeat for re-election, but he helped to direct war work by serving two years on the Council of State.

Continental Congress.—At the end of 1779 the legislature appointed him to the Continental Congress. Although the youngest member of that body, he took leadership in committee work. He drafted instructions to Minister John Jay, who was seeking an alliance with Spain, upholding the American claim to British crown lands east of the Mississippi River, and asserting a right to navigation of the lower river through Spanish territory. He was a strong supporter of the Franco-American alliance and defended Benjamin Franklin against anti-Gallic attacks. He initiated and guided the legislation that made vacant Western lands a national domain. Recognizing the weakness of the Articles of Confederation, he asserted, without pressing the point, that Congress had implied power to coerce the states, then worked for amendments to create a federal revenue power. The chevalier de la Luzerne, the French minister, termed him "the man of the soundest judgment in Congress." After compulsory retirement under the three-year limit, he entered the Virginia legislature, where he defeated support of religion by taxation, opposed paper money, promoted waterway improvements, sponsored the Potomac River compact between Virginia and Maryland, and asserted the supremacy of national treaties over state laws. His efforts to initiate the use of federal power to raise revenue and regulate commerce led to the calling of the Annapolis Convention of 1786 and the Philadelphia Convention which drafted the federal Constitution of 1787.

Contributions to the Framing and Adoption of the Constitution.—In preliminary letters to George Washington and Governor Edmund Jennings Randolph of Virginia, Madison advocated a constitution that would "at once support a due supremacy of the national authority, and leave in force the local authorities as far as they can be subordinately useful." He amplified his ideas in the Virginia (or Randolph) Plan, accepted by the convention as the basis of a constitution. It called for a supreme national government divided into an executive, a judiciary, and a two-house legislature, with Congress empowered to legislate in all cases where the individual states were incompetent or wherein separate action might injure harmony. An article giving Congress power to negate state laws was supplanted by judicial review. In the debates Madison contended that rule by the people was safer in a large federal republic than in a small republic, because enlargement of the sphere would divide the people into too many interests to permit the rise of an oppressive majority. This argument helped to produce liberal suffrage provisions and to exempt Congress from the property safeguards imposed on the state. In addition to his leading role as a delegate, which won him the appellation of "father of the Constitution," he took daily notes of debates. Purchased by Congress after his death, these became the principal record of the convention's work.

Besides .leading the fight for ratification by Virginia, with victory over Patrick Henry, George Mason, and other formidable opponents, Madison joined Alexander Hamilton and John Jay in writing the *Federalist Papers* (see FEDERALIST, THE) expounding the Constitution. Hamilton wrote 51 of the papers, Madison 29, and Jay 5. Here Madison gave final form to his theory of conflicting property interests as the most important source of political faction. Through detailed analysis and by comparison with ancient and modern confederacies, he sought to show that the Constitution established a proper balance between power and liberty.

Member of the United States Congress.— Madison defeated the anti-Federalist James Monroe for the new House of Representatives. In 1789 he began eight years' service by sponsoring the Bill of Rights, offering the first revenue bill, and advocating counterdiscrimination against foreign regulations injurious to United States commerce. He broke with Secretary of the Treasury Hamilton over the manner of funding of the public debt, seeking unsuccessfully to protect the original holders (chiefly war veterans) of defaulted and depreciated securities. The danger of total defeat of the funding bill brought Hamilton and Madison together in a reluctant compromise on federal assumption of state war debts, Madison dropping his opposition in exchange for acceptance of his previously defeated amendments and permanent location of the national capital on the Potomac River. Thomas Jefferson, who returned from France during the funding controversy, joined Madison in opposition to Hamiltonian policies and speedily rose to national leadership of the developing Republican (later Democratic-Republican) Party, which Madison headed in Congress. They both denied the constitutionality of national banks, but Madison as president revised his attitude sufficiently to sign a bank bill. He opposed appropriations to give effect to Jay's 1794 treaty with England, regarding it as a surrender of national rights.

Secretary of State.—In 1794 Madison had married Mrs. Dolley Payne Todd (see MADISON, DOLLEY) whose attractive qualities contributed to a happy partnership and the maintenance of friendly social contacts without regard to politics. During three years of retirement from federal office, he wrote the Virginia Resolutions of 1798 against the Alien and Sedition Acts and the legislative report of 1800 on those resolutions. In combination they affirmed the right of the states to interpose collectively against unconstitutional laws but not to nullify them.

Becoming President Jefferson's secretary of state in 1801, Madison skillfully promoted the purchase of the Louisiana Territory. He worked unsuccessfully against the impressment of United States seamen into the British Navy and in support of the right of neutrals to trade with the colonies of belligerents. He approved Jefferson's shipping embargo as a measure midway between war and submission.

First Term as President.—Jefferson's strong support helped Madison win the presidency in 1809 over the combined candidacies of Federalist Charles C. Pinckney and two dissident Republicans, James Monroe and George Clinton. He inherited a rebellious Congress, nominally controlled by his own party.

For two years, until he dismissed a secretary of state (Robert Smith), appointed to placate hostile senators, Madison wrote all important diplomatic letters. Monroe then became secretary of state. In his first month as president, Madison secretly informed Great Britain that he would ask Congress to declare war on France if Great Britain agreed to stop molesting United States commerce and France failed to do likewise. A similar offer in reverse was made to France. A settlement reached with the British minister in Washington violated the latter's instructions and was repudiated in London. The next British minister was expelled by Madison for using offensive language. In 1810 the president encouraged a revolt in the portion of West Florida claimed as a part of Louisiana and sent troops to occupy it. Notification by France (Aug. 5, 1810) of revocation of her Berlin and Milan decrees, under which United States ships were being confiscated, led to a proclamation (Nov. 2, 1810) banning trade with England. This step, Madison informed the French minister, would inevitably lead to war with England unless she repealed her orders in council banning United States trade with France.

During the next 18 months Madison pressed continuously for British repeal, but his warnings of war were weakened by Federalist support of Great Britain and continuance of French spoliations under new guises. He sought larger military and naval appropriations than Congress would grant, and endeavored to restrain the congressional War Hawks while working to stimulate the reluctant. Great Britain's apparently final refusal to revoke the orders in council brought a presidential request for a declaration of war which Congress passed on June 18, 1812. The orders in council were then being repealed. Informal cease-fire proposals by British commanders in Canada were rejected as inadequate but Jonathan Russell, the United States chargé d'affaires in London, was empowered to make an armistice. Madison notified France that peace with England would mean immediate war with her unless French depredations ceased. England's refusal to give up impressment blocked an armistice, but her offer to negotiate a treaty extended peace discussions throughout the conflict.

Second Term as President.—Antiwar feelings narrowed Madison's 1812 re-election margin over DeWitt Clinton, a rival Republican supported by the Federalists. The war was marked on land by successive reverses for the United States, and at sea by brilliant victories, until the emergence of capable young commanders brought vigor and discipline to the army in 1814, by which time British naval power shut United States warships in port. Madison showed determination and strategic understanding. He foresaw the effect of inadequate preparation and New England's refusal to furnish troops. He failed to foresee the incompetence of cabinet ministers and generals who directed early operations and later left the national capital open to attack. Gen. Andrew Jackson's triumph at New Orleans, in January 1815, brought exultation as the conflict ended. The orders in council having been repealed and impressment having vanished with Napoleon's overthrow, the Treaty of Ghent (signed Dec. 24, 1814) brought only peace, with no settlement of the causes of the war. The war enlarged United States industry, exalted national spirit,

Right: A present day view of Montpelier, the home of James Madison, in Orange County, Va.

JAMES MADISON

Right: An old print showing Montpelier as it was during the time of Madison's residence.

Below: A famous portrait of Madison, painted by Gilbert Stuart for James Bowdoin.

Below: Dolley Madison, the president's wife, was much admired for her charm and elegance.

and destroyed the political party that opposed it.

During the final two years of his presidency Madison ended Algerian hostilities by naval action, fostered protection of new industries, and began a national program of internal improvements.

Years of Retirement.—After his retirement from public office (March 4, 1817), Madison seldom left his estate, Montpellier. His scientific farming practices won national attention. A slaveholder opposed to slavery, he was active in the American Colonization Society (q.v.). He gave advance approval to the Monroe Doctrine, became rector of the University of Virginia, and was co-chairman of the state constitutional convention of 1829–1830. Though critical of nationalistic court decisions, he strongly defended federal judicial supremacy (which he had enforced in 1809 over the armed opposition of Pennsylvania), and furnished powerful constitutional arguments against the South Carolina doctrine of nullification.

Character and Historical Stature.—Madison was known for delightful conversation and humorous anecdotes. His small figure (5 feet 6 inches) and mild demeanor gave plausibility to the Federalist assertion that he was timid and irresolute, but British Minister Francis James Jackson called him "obstinate as a mule." "Curt, spiteful, passionate," was French Minister Louis Marie Turreau's appraisal. He strengthened executive authority both by argument and by action. Henry Clay rated him as the greatest of American statesmen after George Washington. The popular belief that he was swayed by Jefferson is disproved by their correspondence. Madison's writings, inspired by current events, were lifted by intellect and scholarship into enduring works of political philosophy. See also UNITED STATES— *16. The Founding of the Nation, 1763–1815* (Decline of the Federalists, 1796–1801; Jeffersonians in Power; The War of 1812, 1812–1815).

Bibliography.—Hamilton, Alexander, Madison, James, and Jay, John, *The Federalist* (any edition); Rives, William C., *History of the Life and Times of James Madison,* 3 vols. (Boston 1859–68); Gay, Sydney H., *James Madison* (New York and Boston 1884); Adams, Henry, *History of the United States of America,* 9 vols. (New York 1889–91); Hunt, Gaillard, *The Life of James Madison* (New York 1902); Smith, Abbot E., *James Madison, Builder* (Elmira, N.Y., 1937); Burns, Edward McN., *James Madison, Philosopher of the Constitution* (New Brunswick, N.J., 1938); Koch, Adrienne, *Jefferson and Madison* (New York 1950); Padover, Saul K., ed., *The Complete Madison* (New York 1953); Brant, Irving, *James Madison,* 6 vols. (Indianapolis 1941–1961); Hutchinson, William T., and Rachel, William M. E., eds., *The Papers of James Madison,* vols. 1–4 (Chicago 1962–65).

IRVING BRANT,
Author of "James Madison."

MADISON, town, Connecticut, in New Haven County, 17 miles east of New Haven, on the Hammonasset River and Long Island Sound, at an altitude of 30 feet. It is served by the New York, New Haven, and Hartford Railroad. It is a popular summer resort and has some beautiful old 17th and 18th century houses. Originally part of Guilford township, it was incorporated as the town of Madison in 1826. Pop. 4,567.

MADISON, town, Florida, the seat of Madison County, about 50 miles east of Tallahassee, at an altitude of 135 feet. The Seaboard Airline Railroad serves the city, which is the trading center of a farming region. It was settled in 1838 by cotton planters from South Carolina. Government is administered by a council and manager. Pop. 3,239.

MADISON, village, Illinois, in Madison County, on the Mississippi River, 5 miles north of East St. Louis, at an altitude of 425 feet. It is an industrial and transportation suburb of St. Louis, producing steel, wood, meat and asphalt products, and railroad equipment and is served by 15 railroad lines. It was incorporated in 1890 and is administered by a mayor and council. Pop. 6,861.

MADISON, city, Indiana, the seat of Jefferson County, on the Ohio River opposite Milton, Ky. with which it is connected by bridge, and 40 miles northeast of New Albany, at an altitude of 497 feet. It is on the Pennsylvania Railroad and is a distributing center for a tobacco-raising region. Manufactures include containers, shoes, and work clothes; meat packing is the major industry. Two miles west of the city is the recreational area of Clifty Falls State Park. The city was settled about 1809, and is governed by a mayor and council. Pop. 10,488.

MADISON, town, Maine, in Somerset County, on the Kennebec River, 20 miles northwest of Waterville, at an altitude of 260 feet. The Maine Central Railroad serves the town, which has woolen, lumber, and paper mills. There were settlers here before the American Revolution; the town was incorporated in 1804. It has the council-manager type of government. Pop. 3,935.

MADISON, borough, New Jersey, in Morris County, at an altitude of 250 feet, four miles southeast of Morristown, of which it is a residential suburb. Truck farming and dairying are carried on in the surrounding area; rose growing is an important activity of the borough, which also produces flavoring extract and cement blocks. The Delaware, Lackawanna, and Western Railroad provides transportation.

The borough was called Bottle Hill when it was settled in 1685. Sayre House, built in 1745, was used as a headquarters by Anthony Wayne during the American Revolution. In 1834 Madison became the official name of the community. Drew University, founded in 1867 as Drew Theological Seminary, is located here. Incorporated in 1889, Madison is governed by a mayor and council. Pop. 15,122.

MADISON, city, South Dakota, seat of Lake County, 38 miles northwest of Sioux Falls, near lakes Madison and Herman, at an altitude of 1,670 feet. It is an agricultural trading center on the Chicago, Milwaukee, St. Paul, and Pacific Railroad and has grain elevators, flour mills, and packing plants. General Beadle State Teachers College was founded here in 1881. The city was laid out in 1873 and has a city manager type of government. Pop. 5,420.

MADISON, city, Wisconsin, state capital and seat of Dane County, situated about 83 miles west of Milwaukee in an agricultural and dairy region in the southern part of the state, at an altitude varying from 850 to 955 feet. The city fills and overflows a gently curving isthmus between Lake Mendota on the north and Lake

Monona on the south, connected by the Yahara River. These bodies of water, along with Lake Waubesa and Lake Kegonsa to the south, are known as the Four Lakes. In the southwestern part of the city is Lake Wingra. Madison is served by the Chicago, Milwaukee, St. Paul, and Pacific, the Chicago and North Western, and the Illinois Central railroads, and by North Central and Northwest airlines. In addition to the city airport there is a seaplane base on each of the isthmus lakes. U.S. and state highways provide for truck and motorbus transportation in many directions.

Economic Life.—Government service—municipal, county, state, and federal—provides employment for thousands of Madison's residents. Many residents work in the offices and stores of the wholesale and retail trades, in the railroad shops, or in the city's factories. Madison's most important manufactures are meat and dairy products, dry-cell batteries, machine tools, die castings, farm machinery, chemical fertilizers, paper boxes, bottle caps, hospital equipment, tin containers, balances, and automobile parts.

Education and Cultural Institutions.—In addition to the state university and public and parochial schools, educational institutions include Edgewood College of the Sacred Heart (Roman Catholic, for women) and Madison College (business). Among Madison's library facilities are the Free (public) Library, the Wisconsin Legislative Reference Library (in the Capitol), the extensive libraries of the university, the State Historical Society, and the Wisconsin Academy of Sciences, Arts, and Letters (all located on the university campus), and the important collection of the United States Forest Products Laboratory. See also WISCONSIN, UNIVERSITY OF.

Buildings.—Madison, with its extensive lake frontage, its many parks, and its fine public and private buildings, is an attractive residential and industrial center. One of its most imposing buildings in the State Capitol, which occupies a commanding site near the heart of the city on grounds which cover 14 acres. Designed in Italian Renaissance style and constructed between 1906 and 1917, its exterior, including even the dome, is of white granite. Within the building are works of art by such noted American painters and sculptors as Edwin H. Blashfield, Kenyon Cox, and Daniel Chester French.

Two of the city's churches are more than a century old. St. Raphael's (Roman Catholic) was built in 1854; Grace Episcopal Church is younger by a few years (1858), although its parish dates from 1839 and was the first religious organization in Wisconsin. Wisconsin's first synagogue, also erected in 1858, still stands. Among the buildings originally constructed as private dwellings is the mansion (built in 1854), which was used for a number of years by Wisconsin's governors and is now the university's graduate student center. Near Lake Monona is the B. O. Webster Home, once the residence of Robert M. La Follette (1855–1925), United States senator from Wisconsin and three times governor of the state.

History.—Almost as soon as the Territory of Wisconsin was organized in 1836, its legislators chose the site for its capital, named it Madison after the fourth president of the United States who had died a few months before, and made it the seat of Dane County. In 1837 the townsite was laid out and in 1846, with a population of

Monkmeyer

An aerial view of Madison, Wis., capital of the state.

about 625, Madison was incorporated as a village. Ten years later, a thriving community of several thousand residents, it was incorporated as a city. By that time Wisconsin had outgrown its first statehouse and the erection of a new one was begun in 1857, which served for the next half century. The city government is administered by 20 councilmen, elected at large, and a mayor.

The regular population, a large part of which is of German or Scandinavian extraction, is augmented by a considerable number of university students, and by visitors who, like its residents, enjoy the water sports on its lakes. Pop. 126,706.

Campus scene at the University of Wisconsin, in Madison.

Ewing Galloway

MADISON COLLEGE, Harrisonburg, Va., a general, multipurpose, state-operated, senior college founded in 1908 by act of the General Assembly of Virginia. First called the Normal and Industrial School for Women, the name was changed to the State Normal School for Women at Harrisonburg in 1914, the State Teachers College at Harrisonburg in 1924, and Madison College in 1938, in honor of the fourth president of the United States.

Strong liberal arts, preprofessional, and vocational curricula were added to the original teacher-training courses; more recently a program of general education was instituted, with instruction organized in four divisions: the humanities, the natural sciences, mathematics, the social sciences, and teacher education. In 1954–1955 a graduate program was inaugurated, offering the master's degree in a number of fields.

Since World War II men have also matriculated, constituting about 10 per cent of the student body.

The college is situated on a 62-acre campus with an adjoining farm of 240 acres. Madison is fully accredited by the Southern Association of Colleges and Secondary Schools and the National Council on Accreditation of Teacher Education.

LOUIS GLENN LOCKE,
Head of the English Department and Director of the Division of Humanities.

The Madonna and Child in the Church of Santa Maria Maggiore, Rome, is attributed to Saint Luke the Evangelist.

Anderson

MADISON RIVER, river, Montana and Wyoming, 183 miles in length, one of the three smaller rivers which unite just northeast of Three Forks, Montana, to form the Missouri. Beginning at the confluence of the Gibbon and Firehole rivers in the northwest corner of Yellowstone National Park, it flows westward into Montana and then northward to meet the Jefferson and Gallatin rivers. Hebgen Dam near the Montana state line forms Hebgen Reservoir, 15 miles long; another dam at Ennis Lake also provides hydroelectric power.

MADISONVILLE, măd'ĭ-s'n-vĭl, city, Kentucky, seat of Hopkins County, 33 miles north of Hopkinsville, with an altitude of 515 feet. It is on the Illinois Central and the Louisville and Nashville railroads and has an airport. In addition to being the center of an oil, coal, and lumber area, the city is an important loose-leaf tobacco market for the western part of the state. Manufactures include stationery, tiles, shirts, and food products. Interesting Indian artifacts have been found along nearby streams. Madisonville was settled in the year 1807; the city government is administered by a mayor and council. Pop. 13,110.

MADOG (in full MADOC AB OWAIN GWYNEDD), mà'dŏg ăb ŏ'wăn gŏŏ'ĭ-nĕth, legendary Welsh prince. A 15th century Welsh poem tells of his discovery of America about 1170, and of his second voyage to this unknown land. An account of his journeys is contained in Richard Hakluyt's geographical works (see HAKLUYT'S VOYAGES), and his feat is celebrated by Robert Southey's epic poem, *Madoc* (1805). The authenticity of the legend was rejected by certain later scholars, such as Thomas Stephens (*Madoc, an Essay on the Discovery of America . . . ;* published posthumously in 1893).

MADONNA IN ART, The, mà-dŏn'à. A painted or sculptured representation of the Blessed Virgin Mary, the mother of Christ, is commonly called a Madonna. This word, of Italian origin, is the equivalent of "My Lady" and originally was a title of honor given to ladies of distinction. In the late Middle Ages it was applied to sacred persons, such as St. Elisabeth and the Virgin Mary. As early as the 16th century the word was used in Italy to designate the image of the Virgin, and by 1644 this usage had been introduced into English.

Representations of the Virgin Mary are innumerable in Christian art and show the greatest variety. They exist as individual figures or in scenes from the Virgin's life. In most cases, naturally, they are combined with presentations of Christ or occur in scenes from his life. Their relative frequency and their varying forms and emphasis are a good indication of changes in religious beliefs and attitudes.

Portraits from Life.—St. Augustine (354–430) complained that no portrait of the Virgin Mary was known. Nevertheless, some images of her were, and indeed some still are, venerated as authentic portraits. The best known are those which legend avers were painted by St. Luke the Evangelist, such as the painting in Santa Maria Maggiore in Rome. Most of these portraits are Byzantine works or later imitations of them. An interesting byproduct of the legend of portraits made from life are represen*ations, particularly popular in the 15th and 16th centuries, in which St. Luke is depicted painting the Madonna. These representations, such as Giorgio Vasari's altarpiece (c. 1570) in the Painters' Chapel of Santissima Annunziata, Florence, sometimes owed their existence to painters' guilds, of which St. Luke was the patron saint.

Early Representations.—Images of the Virgin are found as far back as the 2d century. They appear first in the catacombs in Rome, in scenes such as the Annunciation, the Birth of Christ, and the Adoration of the Magi. Even at an early date a special worship of the Virgin led to representations, as for example in the 3d century version in the Catacombs of Priscilla, Rome, in which she is shown alone, in classic garments, seated with the nude Child on her lap. After the Council of Ephesus (431) had proclaimed her Theotokos (Mother of God), such worship became more universal and artists developed a great variety of representations of her. See also CATACOMBS—*Frescoes.*

Among the early types of Madonnas is the *orans,* one of the rare representations of Mary without the Child, in which her arms are raised in prayer. An 8th century example in mosaic can be seen in San Marco, Florence, or an earlier 4th century example—in which the Child does appear—in the Coemeterium Majus, Rome. The enthroned Virgin, which had already appeared in the Adoration of the Magi and in the Annunciation, was to become one of the most popular versions. In Byzantine art it took several forms, among them the *nicopoeia,* in which the Virgin solemnly holds the Child frontally on her lap, as in the 6th century mosaic in Poreč, Yugoslavia. The *orans* in Byzantine art was called the *blacherniotissa,* after the monastery Blachernae in Constantinople, which owned a famous image of this type. From the *blacherniotissa* developed the *platytera,* an *orans* with the Child in a medallion before the Virgin's breast, as in the marble relief of St. Mark's Basilica, Venice. A famous full-length, standing Madonna, with the Child on her arm, was the *hodegetria,* so called after another monastery in Constantinople. An example of this type is the 12th century mosaic in the Cathedral of Torcello, Italy. While these types show the Madonna in severe hieratic fashion, others such as the *glykophilusa* or the *galaktotrophysa* stress the human element; in the former, the Child nestles closely to the Mother, as in the marble relief in St. Mark's, Venice, and in the *galaktotrophysa,* she nurses him, as in the 12th century mosaic on the façade of Santa Maria in Trastevere, at Rome.

Most of these representations show the full figure; however, some of the more intimate ones show the half figure. All are characterized by a formal stiffness. The Virgin is usually soberly dressed in a red tunic, with a blue cloak drawn over her head, and a white veil framing the serious face. The Child is dressed and often is giving a blessing. Both figures have halos. At times Mary is shown as the Queen of Heaven clothed in ornate garments and with the crown of a Byzantine empress; seated on a richly decorated throne. Much gold is employed for a star on her veil, as borders on the garments, as highlights on the folds.

These Madonnas, and many other similar ones that developed during the first millennium, are found in mosaic and in fresco in the apses and vaults and on the walls and triumphal arches of churches, where they often overpower through their size. They exist in marble, metal, and ivory reliefs; in coins, cut stones, small pictures, and miniatures. The small objects particularly were carried everywhere and became the prototypes for nearly all later representations.

From the names of the Madonnas it is obvious that, after modest beginnings in the West, it was the Greek East which was mainly responsible for the formulation of this ideal of the Madonna. In the East such types lasted into the early part of the 20th century, but became more and more stereotyped. Often they became known under new names taken from images in the famous pilgrimage churches, as for example, the Madonna of Vladimir, at Smolensk in the Soviet Union, or at Częstochowa, Poland. In the West, their main features persisted, but Western artists so varied the original themes, that they eventually became almost unrecognizable.

Growth of Literature About the Virgin.— The development of representations of the Virgin in the West in the late Middle Ages and in more recent times cannot be understood without a knowledge of the vast literature on the Virgin which these times produced. The Gospels, particularly St. Luke's and St. Matthew's contained rather scanty information about the Virgin, but these accounts were soon supplemented with stories about the childhood of Mary in the Protevangelium of James and other Apocryphal texts, which in the 13th century were popularized in the West by writers such as Vincent of Beauvais, and through the *Golden Legend* (q.v.). The stories of the death and the Assumption of the Virgin also came from the East, where the day of the death of the Virgin was commemorated earlier than in the West. From such sources, in the late Middle Ages, numerous accounts of the life of the Virgin were written in verse and prose, in Latin and the vernacular languages, and sometimes in the form of plays; in these forms the various episodes were told in great detail, so that artists found all the information they needed.

At the same time, a didactic type of literature illustrated the virtues and glories of the Virgin, for example, her humility, and above all her purity and virginity. Its arguments were mainly symbolical, and artists found no difficulty in using its imagery, parallels, and allusions. Among the parallels quoted from the Old Testament were the burning bush of Moses, represented in a picture (1476) by Nicolas Froment d'Uzès, in the Cathedral of Aix, France; and the *porta clausa* (closed door; Ezekiel 44: 1–3), found in many pictures of the Annunciation. Mary is contrasted with Eve and called the New Eve, because she participated in the redemption of man; examples of this contrast are pictures of the Annunciation with the Fall of Man by Giovanni da Fiesole (Fra Angelico, 1387–1455) and Lorenzo di Credi (1459–1537). Mary was identified with the bride in the *Canticle of Canticles* (q.v. *Canticum canticorum*), and many symbols of her were drawn from its poetic language: the rose, the lily, the cedar, and the enclosed garden. The latter subject was the most popular in the 15th century, as can be seen from pictures by the German painters Stephan Lochner (d. 1451) and Martin Schongauer (d. 1491). A wood-block book of the 15th century also shows in detail this use of the *Canticum canticorum.* The "woman clothed with the sun, and the moon under her feet" (Revelation of John 12:1) is

Above left: The Visitation, Mary with Elisabeth, by Ghirlandaio.
Above right: The Virgin and Child, painted by Giovanni Cimabue.

(Above left and right) Fratelli Alinari

MADONNA IN ART

Left: A detail from Raphael's *Disputa del Sacramento* in the Vatican, Rome.

Below: The Coronation of the Virgin by Fra Angelico.

(Left) Anderson; (below) Fratelli Alinari

Titian's *Pesaro Madonna* shows the family which commissioned it, kneeling before Mary and Jesus.

Anderson

The Mother and Child have frequently been shown seated in the lap of St. Anne, as in this well-known painting by Leonardo da Vinci.

Fratelli Alinari

Michelangelo's *Pietà* at St. Peter's in Rome is the most famous representation of this subject.

Fratelli Alinari

The death of the Virgin is depicted in a 12th century Byzantine mosaic in the Church of the Martorana at Palermo, Sicily.

Fratelli Alinari

A Madonna on a crescent moon, engraved by Albrecht Dürer.

identified with the Virgin and is the source of the many Madonnas on a crescent and surrounded by rays of light, as in engravings by Albrecht Dürer (1471–1528).

Ancient lore regarding animals, as contained in *Physiologus* (2d century A.D.; *The Naturalist*) and similar natural history books popular in the Middle Ages (see BESTIARIES), was used as a source and furnished, for instance, the unicorn as a symbol for Mary's virginity, which was used in the French tapestries entitled *The Hunt of the Unicorn* (c. 1500; now in The Cloisters, New York City). Most of this symbolism and other types that developed later were eventually gathered in the Litany of Loreto (16th century and following). In such didactic fashion, using parallels from the Old Testament and other sources, comments were made on episodes in the Virgin's life. Comprehensive surveys of such symbolic treatment of the sacred stories, most of them extensively illustrated, were: *Biblia pauperum*, q.v. (*Bible of the Poor*), which was very popular in the 14th and 15th centuries, but whose origins go further back; *Speculum humanae salvationis* (*Mirror of Human Salvation*) of the 14th century; and *Defensorium inviolatae virginitatis Beatae Mariae*, also of the 14th century, which set out to "defend the immaculate Virginity of Mary." Mention should also be made of the vast devotional literature, often illustrated, on the mysteries of the Rosary, which has flourished since the 15th century and is responsible for representations of Mary as Queen of the Rosary, as for example in Dürer's picture (1506) in Prague; and of Mary surrounded by scenes of the Seven Joys or Sorrows. Many of these ideas have persisted up to the present and have had a constant bearing on art. See also ROSE IN ART AND SYMBOLISM.

Representations from the 14th to 18th Centuries.—In Romanesque art the Byzantine types still lingered, while in the Gothic period they became less schematic and more humanized, and a variety developed from the 14th to the 18th centuries which defies classification. So long as monumental sculpture still determined the character of art, as it did in the Gothic cathedrals, only the relation of the Mother and Child was varied in seated and standing Madonnas by the introduction of playful features; in these works the Child acted like a real child, though the Virgin still maintained the dignity of a queen, often wearing a crown. Some of the great painted Madonnas, such as those by Giovanni Cimabue (c. 1240–c. 1302), Duccio di Buoninsegna (c. 1255–1319), Giotto (1266?–1337), and Raphael (1483–1520), portrayed her still in the old fashion, in majesty, surrounded by angels; but in smaller devotional images a kind of religious genre developed, employing the new means of painting—that is, the study of nature and of perspective. The more intimate half figure also became frequent.

The former gold background gave way to architectural settings which developed from the Virgin's throne. The Madonna was shown by Jan van Eyck (d. 1441), for example, in realistically portrayed interiors. She was seated in a garden or landscape. As in the work of Gerard David (d. 1523), she might be feeding the Child; she might nurse it, as in many examples since the 14th century. She might read or hold a book, as in Raphael's *Alba Madonna* (c. 1508/1510), in the National Gallery of Art, Washington, D.C., or she might play with the Child. Often others were present: Joseph, as part of the Holy Family, or the child St. John the Baptist, either with or without his mother Elisabeth, as shown in the work of Raphael. From the 13th century the Madonna and Child were represented seated in the lap of St. Anne; the best known example of this is the painting by Leonardo da Vinci (1452–1519) in the Louvre at Paris. Sometimes all the relatives of the Holy Family were present, as in Lucas Cranach the Elder's *Heilige Sippe* (1509; *Holy Kinship*) in the Städel Art Institute, Frankfurt am Main, Germany. In another type of scene, the *sacra conversazione* (*holy conversation*), the Madonna was surrounded by saints, among them patron saints of churches, religious orders, and individuals. This is exemplified in the altar (1505) by Giovanni Bellini in San Zaccaria, Venice. Often the donor or his whole family knelt before her, as in Titian's *Pesaro Madonna* (1519–1526) in Santa Maria Gloriosa dei Frari, Venice, or in Hans Holbein the Younger's *Meyer Madonna* (1525–1526) in Darmstadt, Germany. The whole range of possibilities, from an almost secular to a sublime religious conception, can best be seen in the numerous Madonnas of a painter such as Bartolomé Esteban Murillo (1616/1618–1682).

Many of the Madonnas of this period were known by special names which were associated with historical events: for example, Andrea Mantegna's *Madonna della vittoria* (1495–1496; *Madonna of Victory*), a votive offering made after the Battle of Fornovo di Taro (1495) and now in the Louvre. Often they referred to a miraculous image, such as the 16th century Madonna of Loreto, who was seated on the Casa Santa (Holy House) of Loreto, Italy; or to a special symbolism, as the *Madonna della sapienza (Madonna of Wisdom)* in Jan and Hubert van Eyck's altarpiece in the Cathedral of St. Bavon at Ghent, Belgium. In a 14th century example and in Raphael's *Alba Madonna,* the *Madonna of Humility* is seated on the ground. The *Madonna della misericordia (Madonna of Mercy)* spreads her robe over the kneeling faithful in a picture by Fra Filippo Lippi (1406?–1469) in Berlin. Assisted by saints, such as St. Sebastian, she might act as protector against the plague. In Murillo's paintings of Immaculatas, the Madonna praying alone in clouds of angels illustrates the dogma of the Immaculate Conception.

The thousands of Madonna pictures and sculptures served public and private devotion. They were created for altars dedicated to the Virgin, for façades of churches, for private homes, and for tabernacles on street corners. On tombs they indicated the role of the Virgin in the Last Judgment. There was scarcely an aspect of life in which the Virgin Mary did not play her role, and for each event there was a representation of the Madonna close at hand.

Scenes of the Life and Apotheosis of the Virgin.—Scenes from the Virgin's life are found either individually (the Annunciation) or in cycles. Among the latter are cycles by Giotto (c. 1305) in the Scrovegni (Arena) Chapel, Padua, Italy, and by Orcagna on the tabernacle enshrining the miraculous image of the Virgin in Orsanmichele, Florence (1352–1360); also Dürer's woodcut series of her life.

Scenes describing events in the lives of St. Anne and Joachim, which culminate in the birth of the Virgin, occurred as early as the 5th century in the columns of the altar tabernacle of St. Mark's in Venice. Giotto's series depicts the following: Joachim rejected from the Temple; Joachim returning to his shepherds; an angel announcing to Anne the birth of her daughter; Joachim's sacrifice; an angel appearing to Joachim; the meeting of Anne and Joachim at the Golden Gate; and the Birth of the Virgin Mary. It continues with the presentation of the child Mary in the Temple, where she was educated. Then follow episodes from the marriage of the Virgin: the suitors presenting their wands to the high priest; the suitors praying before the altar, on which the wands are deposited; the marriage scene, in which Joseph holds the wand that flowered; and finally the marriage procession. Some of these scenes became popular and occur by themselves, as in Andrea del Sarto's *Birth of the Virgin* (1514; Santissima Annunziata, Florence); Titian's *Presentation of the Virgin in the Temple* (1534–1538; Galleria dell'Accademia, Venice); and Raphael's *Sposalizio* (1504; *Marriage of the Virgin,* Pinacoteca di Brera, Milan).

The Annunciation and the Visitation.— The most popular scene from the life of the Virgin, the Annunciation, has been rendered in many variations, ranging from the solemn, formal mosaic (4th century) in Santa Maria Maggiore in Rome to the intimate works of the early Flemish masters, such as Jan van Eyck's painting in the National Gallery of Art, Washington, D.C. Known throughout Italy is a composition which originated in the 14th century and reproduces the still-famous miraculous image in Santissima Annunziata in Florence.

Good examples of the Visitation (the meeting of Mary and Elisabeth, the mother of St. John the Baptist) are two statues of the 13th century on the Cathedral of Reims, France, and a picture (1491) by Ghirlandaio, in the Louvre.

The Nativity.—The Birth of Christ is preceded by various episodes: Joseph's doubts of Mary's virtue; the voyage to Bethlehem; and the payment of the taxes. The scene of the Nativity itself, often combined with the Adoration of the shepherds, places Mary as much in the center of interest as the Child. It may include legendary traits and symbols which allude to the purity of the Virgin; the story of the two midwives, for example, is treated in Gentile da Fabriano's altar (1423), now in the Galleria degli Uffizi, Florence. Some artists, among them Fra Filippo Lippi and Lorenzo di Credi, made a special subject of the Adoration of the newborn Child by the Virgin.

The Childhood of Jesus.—After the Nativity, Mary appears in scenes from the life of Christ: in the Circumcision; in the Adoration of the Magi, where she holds the child in her lap as in the ordinary Madonna picture; in the Presentation in the Temple (the Purification of the Virgin); and in the Flight into Egypt. An episode of the latter, not easily distinguished from the portrayal of the Holy Family in a landscape, is the Rest on the Flight. Such a picture is Correggio's *Madonna della scodella* (1530; *Madonna of the Bowl,* Galleria Nazionale, Parma, Italy). Dürer shows us the Holy Family earning its livelihood in Egypt. It was there that the Virgin was said to have begun work on the garment of Christ for which the soldiers threw dice on Golgotha. The Return from Egypt has been painted by Domenico Feti (1589–1624), in a picture now in Vienna. Among various childhood scenes of Christ, as for example, the Holy Family traveling, or an encounter between the families of Christ and St. John, only the scene of Christ disputing in the Temple is frequently found, because the episode is treated in the canonical Gospels (Luke 2:42–52). Based on apocryphal tradition is the scene of the death of Joseph, attended by Christ and Mary, which was a favorite in the 18th century.

The Passion and Crucifixion of Christ.— In the public life of Christ until the Passion, Mary appears only in the Marriage at Cana (John 2:1–11), as depicted by Giotto, and in the picture by Paolo Veronese (1528–1588) in the Louvre. The Passion cycle is preceded by a scene of Christ taking farewell of his mother, in a woodcut by Dürer. Mary accompanies her son on the way to Calvary in Raphael's *Lo spasimo (The Spasm),* in the Prado, Madrid. With St. John she is present under the Cross in nearly all representations of the Crucifixion (John 19:25–27), either standing in quiet grief, as she was shown in all medieval formulations until about 1300, or swooning in the arms of St. John or her women companions, as in pictures by Giotto or in the work of Rogier van der Weyden (1399?–1464) in the Philadelphia Museum of Art, Philadelphia, Pa. The same occurs in the *Descent from the Cross* (c. 1541) by Daniele da Volterra in the Church of Trinità dei Monti, Rome, and in Peter Paul Rubens' painting (1611–1614) in the Cathedral of Antwerp, Belgium, as well as in Raphael's *Entombment* (1507) in the Galleria Borghese, Rome. In the Deposition, or Lamentation for Christ, Mary is one of the central figures. Her last farewell has often been depicted in the most touching way, as for example in the work of Sandro Botticelli (1444?–1510) in Munich, Germany, and the painting by Fra Bartolommeo (1475–1517) in the Palazzo Pitti, Florence. Often the group of Mary with the body of Christ on her lap has been isolated and used as a special devotional image, the *Pietà* (q.v.). This was first done in the 14th century, and the most famous example is Michelangelo's group (1498) in St. Peter's in Rome. Other reductions of these last scenes are: the Body of Christ between the Virgin and St. John, which may be seen in the work (1457) in Munich attributed to Hans Multscher, and the *Mater dolorosa* (*Sorrowful Mother*), usually the head alone, as in the work of Guido Reni (1575–1642), or sometimes a half figure with the heart pierced by seven swords (the Seven Sorrows). A rare scene, which Dürer treated in a small woodcut of the Passion, is the apparition of Christ to his mother.

Christ's Ascension.—Since the early Middle Ages, the Virgin has been shown as present at the Ascension of the Lord and at the Descent of the Holy Ghost (Pentecost), usually in the most prominent position in the center of the assembled Apostles. Such scenes may be seen in the 14th century frescoes in the Cappellone degli Spagnoli of the Cloisters of Santa Maria Novella, Florence.

The Death and Assumption of the Virgin.—The last scenes from the life of the Virgin center around her death, which found its classical formulation in Byzantine art, as in the 12th century mosaic in Martorana, a church in Palermo, Italy, where Christ is shown taking the soul of Mary to heaven, while the Apostles surround the bed. This subject remained popular and was later treated in an etching (1639) by Rembrandt and in a painting by Michelangelo da Caravaggio (1573?–1610) in the Louvre. The Apocryphal writings suggested other scenes to accompany it. An angel announcing the hour of death to the Virgin was treated by Orcagna (Orsanmichele, Florence). Additional scenes are: the Apostles traveling to arrive before Mary's death; the farewell of Mary and the Apostles, as painted by Taddeo di Bartolo in fresco (1407; Palazzo Pubblico, Siena, Italy); the burial procession, with some miraculous incidents, as depicted in a 14th century relief in the Cathedral of Notre Dame, Paris; and the deposition of the body in the tomb, as portrayed by Taddeo di Bartolo. In the early version of the Assumption of the Virgin, she is carried to heaven by angels. This can be seen in a 9th century ivory by Tuotilo in St. Gallen, Switzerland. She ascends to heaven in later versions, such as the work (1516–1518) by Titian in Santa Maria Gloriosa dei Frari, Venice. Orcagna, in Orsanmichele, Florence, combined with the Assumption of the Virgin the scene of St. Thomas receiving the Virgin's belt, and Dürer combined with it the Coronation, although the latter is usually a separate scene. The earliest example of the Coronation is the mosaic (c. 1140) in the apse of Santa Maria in Trastevere, Rome, and this scene is the center of the great Mariological cycles of the French Gothic cathedrals (Notre Dame in Paris, and the Cathedral of Chartres), and there are innumerable later examples in the works of artists such as Fra Angelico and Fra Filippo Lippi.

The Last Judgment.—The Virgin is often included at the Last Judgment (q.v.), occasionally enthroned with Christ, as in Orcagna's fresco in Santa Maria Novella, Florence, or on one side of Christ while St. John the Baptist is on the other, interceding for humanity. Examples of the latter are the 12th century mosaic in the Cathedral at Torcello, Italy, and a work by Jan van Eyck in the Metropolitan Museum of Art, New York City. Her role in Michelangelo's fresco in the Sistine Chapel, Vatican City, combines these two possibilities. A mosaic on the façade of San Miniato al Monte, Florence, and Raphael's *Disputa* show a related scene, the *deësis* (invocation), where Christ is enthroned between the Virgin and St. John.

Legends and Miracles.—Many legends were told of miracles worked by the Virgin after her death, which were reflected in art. Already in the 6th century St. Gregory of Tours reported a number; they multiplied greatly and were gathered in large collections from the 13th to the 15th centuries. Richly illustrated is a manuscript, *La vie et miracles de Notre Dame* (1456; *The Life and Miracles of Our Lady*) by Jehan Miélot in the Bibliothèque Nationale in Paris. One of the best-known legends is that of Theophilus, shown in sculptures on Notre Dame in Paris and 13th century stained glass windows in Laon and Le Mans, France. Purely symbolic is the Marriage of St. Catherine, as seen in the picture by Hans Memling (c. 1430–1494) in the Louvre, in which the Madonna is shown with the saint pledging herself to Christ.

The Virgin and the Religious Orders.—Three great saints and their religious orders greatly propagated the worship of the Virgin and, consequently, are often represented with her: the Cistercian, St. Bernard of Clairvaux, as in Filippino Lippi's *Virgin Appearing to St. Bernard* (1486–1488), in the Badia, a church in Florence; St. Dominic, whose order first spread the prayer of the Rosary and who is depicted in such work as Giovanni Battista Tiepolo's *Institution of the Rosary* (1737), on the ceiling of the Church of the Gesuati, Venice; and St. Francis of Assisi, who is represented by various artists, among them Pietro Lorenzetti (c. 1280–?1348), in San Francesco, at Assisi. Other orders with the Virgin as their patron contributed their own version of the Madonna theme: the Carmelites, the Hermits of St. Augustine, the Servites, or Servants of Mary, some of the equestrian orders, and many, mostly local, lay confraternities.

Protestantism and the Virgin.—Since the attitude of the Reformation toward the worship of the Virgin was almost completely negative, no Protestant ideal of a Madonna ever evolved. Martin Luther (1483–1546) himself had on the wall a Madonna made by his friend Lucas Cranach and did not seem to have objected to a proper devotional use of such pictures. In general, however, the Reformation on the Continent, as well as in England, was responsible for the destruction of many images of the Virgin, particularly some of the most famous ones—those, for example, at the well-known pilgrimage church of Walsingham, Norfolk, England. Today, however, many Anglican churches have a Lady chapel with an image of the Virgin. Protestantism also had some share in certain attempts at the end of the 19th century to translate the sacred stories into contemporary, everyday garb, often with a flavor of social consciousness. Fritz von Uhde (1848–1911) and others, for example, portrayed the Virgin as a peasant or as a woman of the working class.

Representations Since the 18th Century.—With the end of the unity of art and religion in the 18th century, the Madonna as a theme in art began to suffer. Although the Catholic Church was still in need of images of the Virgin, and even wanted new ones, such as the Madonna of Lourdes, few of the better artists were interested in treating the theme. Most religious art became mediocre, and no worthy artistic formulation was ever found for the Madonna of Lourdes. When renowned artists occasionally attempted to create Madonnas or scenes from her life, the results were superficial, as in the bravura performances of the French salon artists like Adolphe William Bouguereau (1825–1905) or Pascal Adolphe Jean Dagnan-Bouveret (1852–1929). Even a work that has great artistic merit, such as Jean Auguste Dominique Ingres' *Madonna and Louis XIII* (1824; Cathedral, Montauban, France), rather chills through its formal perfection, and is no match for the Madonnas by Raphael by whom it was inspired. The attempts to revive religious art by returning to primitive styles were sincere enough but artificial, and failed to create a new religious art.

The German Nazarenes (q.v.), and similar painters elsewhere, such as Ary Scheffer (1795–1858) in France, painted Madonnas distinguished by their true feeling; the Pre-Raphaelites (q.v.) also tried to bring about reforms, but found no wide response. These beginnings were all swept away by the naturalism of the second half of the 19th century, which at its best turned religious subjects into sociological, psychological, or archaeological studies. The reform of the Benedictine School of Beuron, a monastery in Germany, and of painters such as Pater Willibrord Verkade (1868–1946) and Maurice Denis (1870–1943), took place in a more favorable climate, toward the end of the century. Beginning to develop at that time, 20th century art overcame the striving for external technical perfection and for the greatest effect of reality, and is much more capable of expressing the real meaning of such artistic themes as that of the Madonna. Its ultimate success in the expression of this and other religious themes will depend on the relation which may develop between the churches and the modern artists.

See also Ivory Carving; Manuscripts, Illuminated; Painting—*Medieval Painting* and *Modern Painting;* Paintings of the Great Masters; Renaissance Painting; Sculpture—*History* (Gothic) (The Renaissance), and (The 20th Century) ; and articles on art under various countries; also biographies of individual artists.

Ulrich Middeldorf,
Kunsthistorisches Institut, Florence, Italy.

Bibliography.—Anna Brownell Jameson's *Legends of the Madonna,* 5th ed. (London 1872), is still by far the most useful book. Consult also Gumppenberg, Gulielmus, *Atlas Marianus* (Ingolstadt, Germany, 1657–59); Rohault de Fleury, Charles, *La Sainte-Vierge,* 2 vols. (Paris 1878); Venturi, Adolfo, *La Madonna* (Milan 1900; French tr., Paris 1902); Muñoz, Antonio, *Iconografia della Madonna* (Florence 1905); Beissel, Stephan, *Geschichte der Verehrung Marias in Deutschland während des Mittelalters* (Freiburg im Breisgau, Germany, 1909); Rothes, Walter, *Die Madonna in ihrer Verherrlichung durch die bildende Kunst aller Jahrhunderte,* 2d ed. (Cologne 1909); Beissel, Stephan, *Geschichte der Verehrung Marias im 16. und 17. Jahrhundert* (Freiburg im Breisgau 1910); Jenner, Katherine Lee, *Our Lady in Art* (Chicago 1910); Van Dycke, John Charles, *The Madonna in Art* (New York 1917); Vloberg, Maurice, *La Vierge et l'Enfant dans l'art français,* 2 vols. (Grenoble, France, 1933); Vavala, Evelyn (Sandberg), *L'iconografia della Madonna col Bambino nella pittura italiana del dugento* (Siena, Italy, 1934); Palais des Beaux-Arts (Paris), *La vierge dans l'art français* (Paris 1950); Guitton, Jean, *The Madonna* (New York 1963).

Kulwant Roy

The High Court, opened in 1892, in the city of Madras.

MADRAS, má-drăs', state, India, situated at the extreme southeastern point of the subcontinent, with an area of 50,110 square miles. The total population at the 1961 census was 33,686,-953, an 11.85 per cent increase over the 1951 total of 29,974,936. Madras is triangular in shape, and bordered by the states of Mysore and Andhra Pradesh on the north, the Bay of Bengal on the east and southeast, and the state of Kerala on the west. Prior the 1953, when the Telugu-speaking state of Andhra was carved out of its territory, and to 1956, when its Kannada- and Malayalam-speaking areas were transferred to the states of Mysore and Kerala respectively, Madras was two and one-half times its present size. What it lost in size, however, it gained in cultural homogeneity, because Tamil, adopted in 1958 as the state language, is native to 67.4 per cent of the present inhabitants. Other languages spoken are Malayalam (14.6 per cent), Telugu (9.3 per cent), and Kannada (Kanarese; 3.4 per cent). Although only 10th in area, Madras is 5th in population among the Indian states. In 1961 Hinduism was the predominant religion, and only 5.23 per cent of the population was Christian and 4.6 per cent Muslim. The principal cities of the state, with their 1961 populations, are Madras, the capital (1,729,141), Madurai (424,810), Tiruchirapalli (249,862), and Salem (249,145). Madras State has two universities, Madras University (q.v.), founded in 1857, and Annamalai University, which was founded in 1929.

Government.—The government, with its administrative center located in the city of Madras is organized on the pattern generally prevalent in India: a centrally appointed governor advised by a council of ministers—in this case 8—headed by a chief minister. The bicameral legislature of 256 members is elected on the basis of adult franchise, except for 9 nominated by the governor.

Industrial Development.—Agriculture is the main occupation of the people; the chief crops are rice, millet, peanuts, coffee, tea, and cotton. In the past, some sections have suffered from the lack of irrigation, in spite of the utilization of the one large river, the Kaveri (Cauvery), and the other smaller rivers. Lack of coal or other sources of power prevented the full exploitation of the basic mineral deposits, such as iron ore, bauxite, gypsum, and magnesite. With the achievement of Indian independence in 1947, and particularly through the implementation of the First and Second Five-Year Plans (1951–1961), efforts were made to augment the agricultural and industrial output. Although attention was directed chiefly to irrigation and power projects which would make possible the development of new industries based on the agricultural and mineral resources of the state, expansion of the hand-loom weaving industry was also given major encouragement. By 1960 there were about 5,000 factories in operation; important among these were the government quinine factories.

History.—The region within the present boundaries of Madras has a long history extending back to very ancient times. Geologically, it may be said to be the oldest land mass of the Indian subcontinent. From the 7th to the 3d centuries B.C. it was the reputed seat of the Dravidian civilization, and during the early and medieval periods of the present era it saw the flourishing of the Hindu empires of the Pandyas, Cheras, Cholas, and Pallavas. The highly developed Tamil language and literature, the lofty spires and exquisite rock sculptures in Madurai, Tanjore, Mamallapuram (Mahabalipuram), and Kanchipuram, the fine craftsmanship of Tanjore, and the delicate movements of the dancers of the traditional Bharata Natyam school still bear evidence of the remarkable culture which arose in the past. This culture was not confined to the land of its birth, but, in addition to influencing the general cultural growth of India, it also spread to various parts of Southeast Asia as a result of the expeditions of Tamil traders and colonists.

Although the beginnings of Muslim conquest were felt early in the 14th century, it was not until the defeat of the great Hindu kingdom of Vijayanagar in 1565 that Muslim rule subjugated the entire area. With the advent of Portuguese colonists and Dutch, French, and British trading companies in the 16th and 17th centuries, the modern history of Madras began. The East India Company established its first trading post at Peddapali (now Nazampatam, Andhra Pradesh) in 1611, and in 1639 acquired the site for a fort and settlement that is now occupied by the city of Madras. In 1653 the locality was designated a presidency. During the 18th century the British expanded their rule through conflicts with the French and native rulers, and by the beginning of the 19th century the modern boundaries had been approximately established.

ASHA PRASAD.

MADRAS, city, India, capital of the State of Madras, about 640 miles southeast of Bombay, on the Coromandel Coast. It is intersected by the Cooum River and bounded on the south by the Adyar River. The third largest city in India, it is a railway and commercial center, as well as a seaport, and covers an area of about 50 square miles.

Industry and Commerce.—For a city of its size, Madras has relatively few large industries. Prominent among these are cotton mills, engineering works, tanneries, cement factories, dye works, and iron foundries.

The harbor is the third largest in India. Entirely artificial, it was begun in 1875, and was considerably enlarged and improved after World War II. Major imports include iron and steel products, coal, timber, cereals, sugar, and machinery. Among the principal exports are raw cotton, peanut and sandalwood oil, tea, coffee, tobacco, cigars, leather, and hides.

The city has two canals which carry inland traffic, and in addition to excellent rail and road facilities there is an airport at nearby Minambakkam.

Religious and Cultural Centers.—Madras has many important connections with both Hinduism and Christianity. The Mylapore residential district was the legendary home of the great Tamil poet Tiruvalluvar, author of the *Kural,* while the district of Tiruvottiyur was the scene of a religious reformation brought about by Shankara (Śaṅkara, fl. 800), the founder of Advaita. The city is equally famous for its associations with St. Thomas the Apostle, who is believed to have lived from time to time on Little Mount just south of the city and to have been martyred on Big Mount (now St. Thomas' Mount). His relics are said to be contained in the Cathedral of St. Thomé (São Tomé).

Central Museum, established in 1854, contains masterpieces from all periods of South Indian art, as well as parts of a stupa from Amaravati. In addition to Madras University (q.v.), with its many affiliated institutions, the city has several scientific and industrial research centers. Among the important libraries is the Madras Government Oriental Manuscript Library, containing rare manuscripts in Sanskrit and South Indian languages.

A devotee in a temple in Madras.

Kulwant Roy

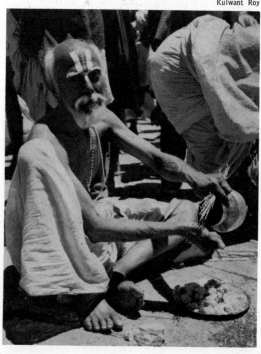

Madras is said to have one of the finest marinas, or esplanades, in the world, stretching from St. Thomé Cathedral in the south past Madras University and the Senate House to Napier Bridge over the Cooum River, then continuing north past Fort St. George to the harbor.

History.—Madras was founded in 1639, when the village of Madraspatam was granted to Francis Day, chief agent of the East India Company at Armagon, by the rajah of Chandragiri. A small fortification, Fort St. George, was erected in 1640, and to the north grew the settlement of Black Town, renamed George Town in 1906, which later developed into the densely populated business center of the city. Many smaller towns were drawn into the orbit of the fort, and Madras soon became the most important settlement of the first East India Company. The municipal corporation, constituted in 1688 under the charter of James II, is the oldest in India.

The city was blockaded in 1702 by Daud Khan and was unsuccessfully attacked by the Marathas in 1741. It was occupied for two years by the French (1746–1748) and suffered incursions from Haidar Ali, the sultan of Mysore, in 1769 and 1780. Pop. (1966) 1,896,000.

Consult Srinavasacarya, C. S., *History of the City of Madras* (Madras 1939); Visvanathan, S., *Madras, The Emerald City by the Sea*, 2d (Madras 1954).

RODERICK MARSHALL,
Fulbright Lecturer in India 1957–1959.

Kulwant Roy

A building at the University of Madras, founded in 1857.

MADRAS, University of, Madras, India, an institution of higher learning founded by an act of the Legislative Council of India dated Sept. 5, 1857. It was organized on the model of the University of London (see LONDON, UNIVERSITY OF) as an affiliating, examining, and degree-conferring body. The high school of the collegiate institution, which had been started 14 years earlier, became known as Presidency College and housed the new university until 1873. In 1881 the number of colleges affiliated with the university reached 27, and by 1904 there were 68. In that year the scope and function of the university were widened by the governor general so as to include teaching and research.

The three earliest departments under this new system—Indian history and archaeology, Indian economics, and comparative philology—were established in 1914–1915. Doctoral degrees were introduced for the first time in January 1923, and a research degree in Oriental languages was offered at about the same time. The Institute of Advanced Oriental Study and Research was opened in 1925 and research departments in zoology, botany, and biochemistry were established soon afterward, although laboratory buildings were not completed until 1936. By 1947 seven more departments of teaching and research had been created: statistics, Indian music, geography, anthropology, politics and public administration, technology, and psychology. In 1951 the departments of applied physics, geology, geophysics, Hindi, and legal studies were established; in 1953, analytical chemistry; in 1955, business management; and in 1957, archaeology. In addition to 26 departments there were (1960) 22 constituent and 92 affiliated colleges located in Madras or its environs.

RODERICK MARSHALL.

MADRAZO, mä-thrä'thō, the name of a family of celebrated Spanish painters.

JOSÉ DE MADRAZO Y AGUDO: b. Santander, Spain, 1781; d. Madrid, 1859. He worked with Jacques Louis David in Paris and spent some time in Rome before returning to Spain, where Charles IV appointed him court painter and director of the Royal Academy of Fine Arts of San Fernando. A lithographer as well as a painter of historical subjects and portraits, his work, as shown in the *Death of Viriatus* (Prado, Madrid), was characterized by the academicism of the neoclassicists.

FEDERICO DE MADRAZO Y KUNTZ: b. Rome, Italy, Feb. 9, 1815; d. Madrid, June 10, 1894. The son of José de Madrazo, he studied in Madrid and with Jean Auguste Dominique Ingres in Paris, where he was soon acclaimed for his work, particularly his *Godfrey of Bouillon Proclaimed King of Jerusalem* (1837). In 1842 he returned to Madrid and was appointed to the posts held by his father, as well as heading the National Museum of Paintings and Sculpture (Prado). In addition to the neoclassicism of his master, his historical and religious works showed the influence of the Nazarene school at Rome. He also painted over 400 portraits of the Spanish nobility, and edited *Historia de la pintura del siglo XVIII* (*History of 18th Century Painting*).

LUIS DE MADRAZO (1825–1897), brother of Federico de Madrazo, is best remembered for his *Burial of St. Cecilia* (1855).

RAIMUNDO DE MADRAZO Y GARRETA: b. Rome, July 24, 1841; d. Paris, Sept. 15, 1920. The son of Federico de Madrazo, he was taught mostly by his father, although he also worked under Léon Cogniet at the Beaux Arts in Paris. His genre works, such as *Girls at a Window* (Metropolitan Museum, New York City), received wide acclaim, as did his graceful portraits of Spanish aristocrats and prominent members of French and American families. Among the latter are *Maria Christina, Queen Regent of Spain* and *Samuel P. Avery* (1876; Metropolitan Museum).

MADRE DE DIOS RIVER, mä'thrä thâ thyōs', river, Peru and Bolivia, rising on the eastern slopes of the Cordillera de Carabaya, Cuzco Department, Peru, uniting with a branch rising in Madre de Dios Department, and flowing about 700 miles east and northeast to join the Beni River at Riberalta in northern Bolivia. Navigable for small boats as far as Puerto Heath on the Peru-Bolivia border, it was formerly used for the transportation of rubber collected from forests along its course.

MADREPORE, a name applied to certain types of true or stony corals. See CORAL AND CORAL REEFS.

MADRID, mà-drĭd', Span. mä-thre[th]', province, Spain, located in the center of the country, with an area of 3,089 square miles. Triangular in shape, it is bounded on the east by Guadalajara and Cuenca provinces, on the south by Toledo Province, and on the west by Ávila and Segovia provinces. Most of the country is a plateau 2,000 feet or more above sea level; the Sierra de Guadarrama, part of the Cordillera Carpeto-Vetónica, runs along the western border and reaches a height of 7,890 feet in the Pico de Peñalara. The tributaries of the Tagus (Tajo) River drain the province, whose soil is mostly clay and sand except in the more fertile southern and southeastern portions. Winds from the sierra in winter and the south in summer make a rigorous climate with extremes of heat and cold and shifts of as much as 50 degrees in one day. The northwest is wooded and contains mineral deposits of iron, copper, and lead; granite, lime, and gypsum are quarried. The main occupation is agriculture, consisting largely of growing grapes, oranges, olives, wheat, rye, barley, vegetables, and esparto grass. Sheep, goats, and bulls for the bull ring are raised widely.

Madrid (q.v.), the capital of the country as well as of the province, is its industrial and commercial center. National railways and state and provincial highways converge on the city, six miles northeast of which is the international and transoceanic airport of Barajas. The only other sizable communities are Aranjuez (pop., 1960, 27,251), the site of a royal palace built by Philip II (r. 1556–1598), and Alcalá de Henares (pop., 1960, 25,123), the birthplace of Miguel de Cervantes Saavedra (1547–1616). Of special interest is El Escorial (see ESCORIAL, THE), where the world-famed monastery and museum is located. Twenty-five miles northwest of Madrid is the Valley of the Dead, a shrine dedicated to the Spanish Civil War dead. It is carved out of mountain rock.

The province, which was formed in 1833, was part of the historical region of New Castile (see CASTILE). It is administered by a civil governor, who also acts as delegate to the central government, and a provincial council made up of one delegate from each legislative division. Population: (1960) 2,606,254.

MADRID, city, Spain, capital of both the country and Madrid Province, located in approximately the geographical center of the Iberian Peninsula. It lies at an elevation of 2,150 feet on a series of sandy hills that slope toward the Manzanares River, a tributary of the Jarama. The Sierra de Guadarrama 30 miles northwest of the city influences the climate, which is extremely hot in summer and cold in winter, and provides an abundance of pure water, conveyed to the city by means of the Lozoya River and the Isabella II Canal.

Plan of the City.—The nucleus of the present city is the old quarter, which was surrounded by walls, the remains of ancient fortifications, until the end of the 19th century. Two of their gates remain: Puerta de Alcalá, built by Charles III (r. 1759–1788), and Puerta de Toledo, built by Ferdinand VII (r. 1808 and 1814–1833). The center of the old quarter is a square, Puerta del Sol (Gate of the Sun), where the city's eastern gate once stood. The chief commercial streets of the city radiate from here.

By 1860 the city had begun to expand to the north, east, and south, with the streets laid out in a gridiron fashion; the deep gorge of the Manzanares has prevented much westward growth. To the east lies the wealthy residential district of Salamanca. Between it and the old quarter runs a broad parkway, El Prado, the northern continuation of which is called La Castellana; one of the most attractive avenues of Madrid, it holds many of the notable public buildings. To the northwest is Ciudad Universitaria (University City), housing most of the University of Madrid (see MADRID, UNIVERSITY OF), an architecturally outstanding group of buildings which has been largely rebuilt since the Spanish Civil War (1936–1939). To the north is the Prolongación de la Castellana, a governmental center.

Transportation.—Madrid has considerably improved its means of transportation in order to keep up with its increasing population. In addition to streetcars and buses there are subway lines. The Toledo and Segovia bridges are outstanding among several crossing the Manzanares. Three principal railway stations and the airport at Barajas serve the city.

Industry and Commerce.—Madrid's industries, while numerous, are mostly keyed to the needs of its residents. Among the important products are machinery, optical instruments, electric appliances, radio and telephone equipment, agricultural implements, jewelry, leather goods, textiles, furniture, pharmaceuticals, chemicals, plastics, glassware and chinaware, and paper. Wine, beer, and flour are processed; printing, publishing, and motion picture production are flourishing pursuits. Commercial activities are for the most part confined to residents of the city and the surrounding region.

Government.—The municipality has a town council headed by a mayor who is appointed by the central government. The other councilors are elected; the number varies according to the size of the population.

Buildings and Cultural Institutions.—Unlike other Spanish cities, Madrid has no important medieval buildings. Its churches are small; the most interesting are those of the baroque period. The most imposing structure in the city is the Royal Palace, now a museum. It was built in 1737–1764 on the site of an ancient Arab fortress which Habsburg kings improved and embellished for use as a castle. The architect was Giovan Battista Sacchetti, who employed a modification of the style of Giovanni Lorenzo Bernini, and Giovanni Battista Tiepolo decorated some of the ceilings with frescoes. Other important buildings, erected in the reign of Charles III (r. 1759–1788), are the Ministerio de Hacienda (Ministry of the Treasury), Observatorio Astronómico, and the

Above: The Puerta del Sol, a public plaza in the old quarter of Madrid, is traditionally considered the hub of the city.

Waagenaar-PIX

MADRID

Above: The Royal Palace, on the Plaza de Oriente, is a museum, housing one of the richest libraries in Europe.

Left: The Avenida de José Antonio, also called the Gran Vía, is the site of Madrid's best shops and hotels.

Below: University City, containing the University of Madrid, was rebuilt after the Civil War of 1936–1939.

(Above) Black Star; (left) Screen Traveler, from Gendreau; (below) Ewing Galloway

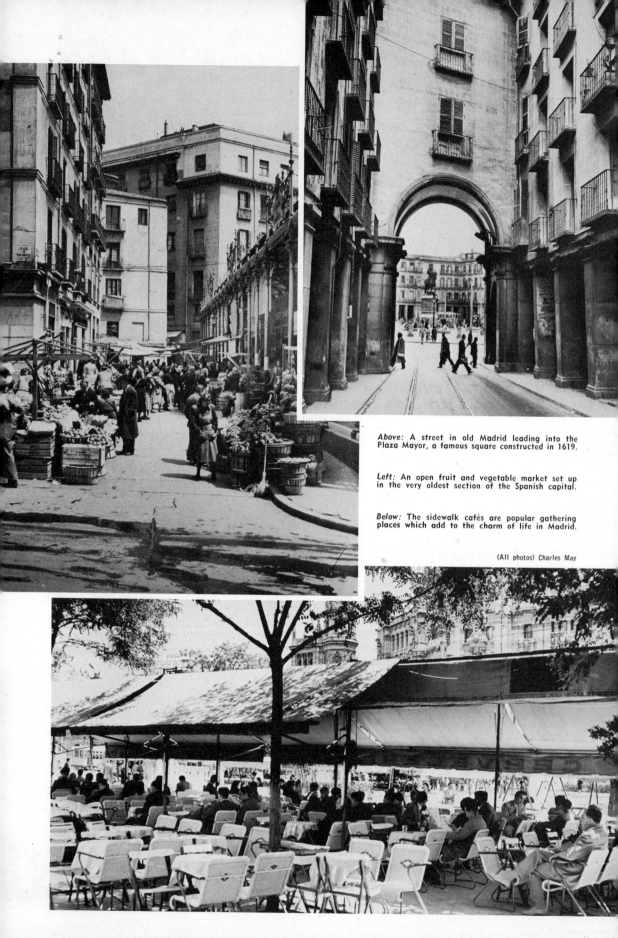

Above: A street in old Madrid leading into the Plaza Mayor, a famous square constructed in 1619.

Left: An open fruit and vegetable market set up in the very oldest section of the Spanish capital.

Below: The sidewalk cafés are popular gathering places which add to the charm of life in Madrid.

(All photos) Charles May

Museo del Prado. This last houses one of the finest collections of paintings in the world, with more than 2,500 pictures of Flemish, Italian, and other schools, and is particularly rich in its Spanish selections. Other museums include the Museo Arqueológico Nacional and the Colección Lázaro Galdiano. The most important library in Spain is the Biblioteca Nacional. Among other national cultural institutions are the Academia Española and the Academia de Bellas Artes de San Fernando.

In addition to the University of Madrid there are many official and private primary schools, as well as specialized schools and colleges.

Plazas and Parks.—In old Madrid there are numerous squares or plazas, such as Plaza Mayor and Plaza de Oriente, the latter having an equestrian statue of Philip IV designed by Diego Rodríguez de Silva y Velázquez (1599–1660). Modern plazas are those of Neptuno, Cibeles, and Independencia, each adorned with 18th century monuments. Among the many parks are the Jardín Botánico (Botanical Gardens), Parque del Oeste, and the beautiful Retiro, formerly the site of a royal palace, covering almost 300 acres.

History.—The Arab village of Magerit was an outpost of Toledo when it was conquered by Ramiro II of León in 932, but it was not until its capture by Alfonso VI (Alfonso I of Castile) about 1083 that it remained in Spanish hands. After 1329 some of the rulers of Castile and León spent long periods in Madrid, to which they were attracted by the hunting available in the surrounding forests, but Philip II was the first to make it his official residence and only court in 1561. He chose this humble town for his capital so that he could govern without pressure from the aristocracy or clergy. Philip III moved his court to Valladolid from 1601 to 1606, but on his return to Madrid its position as an artistic and political center was strengthened.

The city was beautified in the 18th century under the Bourbon rulers. The French occupied it during most of the Peninsular War (1808–1814), although they were driven out briefly by the popular uprising of May 2, 1808, an event strikingly depicted in the works of Francisco de Goya. The reign of Isabella II (r. 1833–1868), although marked by political clashes, was one of the most constructive the city had known. During the Spanish Civil War, Madrid remained loyal to the Republican government until the entrance of Gen. Francisco Franco's forces on March 28, 1939.

Population.—The largest metropolitan area in Spain, Madrid has increased in population more than four times between 1900 and 1960. Its growth has been due partly to internal development and migration, but more largely to the annexation of adjacent districts. The municipality includes the satellite towns of Aravaca, Barajas, Carabanchel Alto, Carabanchel Bajo, Canillas, Canillejas, Charmartín de la Rosa, El Pardo, Fuencarral, Horteleza, Vallecas, Villaverde, and Vicalvaro. Population: (1960) 2,259,931.

FERNANDO CHUECA GOITIA
Director
Museo de Arte Contemporáneo, Madrid

Bibliography.—Erskine, Beatrice, *Madrid, Past and Present* (New York 1923); García Cortés, Mariano, *Madrid y su fisonomía urbana* (Madrid 1950); Chueca, Fernando, *El semblante de Madrid* (Madrid 1951); Martineau, Gilbert R., ed., *Spain* (Paris 1954); Chueca, Fernando, *Madrid y sitios reales* (Barcelona 1958); Ruano, Guonzalez, *Madrid* (Barcelona 1963).

MADRID, University of, Madrid, Spain, one of 12 state universities. It was founded in 1508 at Alcalá de Henares by Francisco, Cardinal Jiménez de Cisneros, and moved to Madrid in 1836–1837 where it merged with the College of Dŏna Maria de Aragon, established in 1590, the College of San Carlos, instituted in 1783, and other faculties. Until 1928 it was the only university in Spain granting a doctorate degree. It is composed of the faculties of philosophy and letters, science, law, medicine, pharmacy, political science and economics, and veterinary medicine. The library is the second largest in Spain. See also SPAIN—*7. Education* (University Education).

MADRIGAL, măd'rĭ-găl, a variety of pastoral poem or the musical genres related to it. The word derived ultimately from the Latin *mater,* with possible influence of the Greek *mandra* (flock).

Italian madrigal texts of the 14th century often consisted of two or more strophes (stanzas) of three lines each, two lines in each strophe rhyming, and a final rhyming couplet called a ritornello, the lines being of 7 or 11 syllables. The earliest known madrigals inclined toward amorous subjects, but their connection with the *pastourelles* of the troubadours of the Middle Ages persists in pastoral sentiments. Fourteenth century Italian madrigals were customarily composed for two or three voices, each voice intended to be sung by several singers. No accompaniment was indicated, but instruments almost certainly were employed. The melody was usually identical for all the strophes and different in the ritornello. Such 14th century composers as Jacopo da Bologna, Giovanni da Cascia (fl. 1340), and Francesco Landino (1325–1397) developed the madrigal toward a sensuousness and charm that marked the end of Gothic and the beginning of Renaissance music.

The second, more familiar, form of Italian madrigal flowered in the 16th century. It was composed first by Netherlandic musicians in Italy, later by their Italian successors. This was a vocal piece for three to six singers, an intimate genre suggesting chamber music, and dealing with nature, love, and death. It did not follow a set poetic pattern and was not in itself a definable form so much as an atmosphere and a style. At first these 16th century madrigals tended to consist of a primary melodic line with accompanying lines in secondary voices; for example, Jakob Arcadelt, Philippe Verdelot, Girolamo Carlo, Costanzo Festa. Later the texture became an interweaving of several equally important voices; for example, Adrian Willaert, Ciprien de Rore, Philippe de Monte, Andrea Gabrieli, Orlando di Lasso, Giovanni da Palestrina, Claudio Monteverdi, Luca Marenzio, Carlo Gesualdo. Particularly "modern" harmonic usages appeared in the madrigals of Gesualdo. Some late madrigals were secular counterparts of the sacred motets.

Madrigals were composed widely outside Italy, but only England developed an important native school. After the middle of the 16th century, wonderfully original examples (sometimes called ayres or balletts) were written by William Byrd and Thomas Morley. Thereafter, as a result of the direct influence of the Italians, notably Marenzio and Gesualdo, many English madrigals became more Italianate in style. The chief later composers in England (late 16th and early 17th centuries) were Thomas Bateson, Orlando Gibbons, Giles Farnaby, Thomas Weelkes, and John Willbye. Thereafter the madrigal all but died out, though examples still are composed occasionally. See also ITALY—7. *Music*.

Consult Fellowes, Edmund Horace, *English Madrigal Composers,* 2d ed. (New York 1948); Einstein, Alfred, *The Italian Madrigal,* tr. by Alexander H. Krappe and others, 3 vols. (Princeton, N.J., and London 1949).

HERBERT WEINSTOCK,
Author of "Music as an Art."

MADRILENA. See BOLERO.

MADRONA, mà-drō'nyà, **MADRONE,** or **MADRONO,** a tree of the genus *Arbutus* (q.v.), chiefly *A. menziesii,* with a straight reddish brown trunk 50 to 120 feet high and 2 to 5 feet in diameter. The crown is columnar in young trees, broad and rounded in old. The dark, shiny, evergreen leaves are borne on red branches. Small white flowers in erect panicles appear in May and June, followed in the autumn by abundant brilliant orange-red berries. Madronas are found in high well-drained slopes from British Columbia to California.

FRANK G. LIER.

MADURA, mà-dōōr'à, island, Indonesia, in the Java Sea, separated from the northeast coast of Java by Madura Strait, 2 to 40 miles wide. The island, which has a total area of 1,762 square miles, is over 100 miles long and from 25 to 30 miles in width. Generally level, it rises to hills of 1,545 feet in the central portion. Although some parts are too arid for agriculture, in other sections rice, corn, cassava, coconuts, kapok, peanuts, and tobacco are grown. Other pursuits are cattle raising, fishing, and salt panning, a government monopoly. Teakwood is obtained from forests in the northwest, and oil deposits are found near the southwestern coast. Part of East Java Province, the administrative center is Pamekasan; other towns are Sumenep, Bangkalan, and Sampang. The inhabitants are of the Madurese race, and mostly Muslim in religion.

Madura was dominated by the rulers of Java when the Dutch landed there in 1747. After a period of division into three regencies, they attached it to Java as a residency in 1885. It fell to the Japanese in 1942, and in 1948 became one of the United States of Indonesia; in 1950 it was made an integral part of the new republic. Pop. (1952) 1,811,764.

MADURAI, mà-dōōr'ī, city, India, in Madras State, capital of Madurai District, on the Vaigai River, 265 miles southwest of the city of Madras. A railway junction with an airport, it is one of the largest trade and industrial centers of southern India. The weaving and dyeing of silk and muslin cloth is its best known industry; other products are agricultural implements, brasswork, and woodcarvings. Exports include rice, tobacco, and cardamom, which are grown in the surrounding district. The extensive hydroelectric systems of Pykara and Papanasam meet here, providing needed irrigation as well as power for the area.

The city has two colleges affiliated with Madras University, Madurai and American colleges, and in addition a women's college and industrial schools. The Great Temple of Madurai is composed of twin temples forming a huge parallelogram and surrounded by nine gopuras, the tallest of which is 152 feet high. Dating from the 16th century, it was beautifully rebuilt and decorated by Tirumala Nayak (1623–1659), whose palace nearby is used for public offices.

Madurai was the capital of the Pandya Empire from the 5th century B.C. through the 11th century A.D., and of the Nayak kings from the middle of the 16th century until about 1736. At that time it came under the rule of the Carnatic nawabs, who ceded it to Great Britain in 1801. It was formerly known as Madura. Pop. (1961) 424,975.

MADVIG, màth'vĕg, **Johan Nicolai,** Danish classical scholar: b. Svaneke, Denmark, Aug. 7, 1804; d. Copenhagen, Dec. 12, 1886. After graduating from the University of Copenhagen, he was appointed professor of Latin language and literature, a post which he held for many years (1829–1879). He was an outstanding philologist, and his edition of Marcus Tullius Cicero's *De finibus bonorum et malorum* (1839; amended ed. 1876), as well as his Latin grammar (1841) and Greek syntax (1846), were very highly regarded.

Madvig served as minister of education from 1848 to 1851, devoting himself to improving classical training in the schools. From 1856 to 1863 he was president of the council and leader of the National Liberal Party. His autobiography, *Livserindringer,* was published in 1887; a supplement, edited by his son, appeared in 1917.

MAEBASHI, mä-yĕ-bä-shē, city, Japan, capital of Gumma Prefecture, central Honshu. It is 60 miles northwest of Tokyo, on the left bank of the Tone River, and on the Ryomo line of the national railway. An important center of the silk industry, it produces raw silk as well as silk yarn and textiles. From Maebashi Park there is a fine view of the Mt. Akagi Range. The town formerly belonged to the castle of a lord of the Matsudaira family. Pop. (1960) 181,937.

MAECENAS, mē-sē'nàs, **Gaius,** Roman statesman and literary patron: d. 8 B.C. The member of an Etruscan family of Arretium, he was a close friend and counselor of Octavian (later Augustus), helping to arrange the latter's marriage with Scribonia (40 B.C.), bringing about a reconciliation between Octavian and Antony (38 B.C.), and acting as one of the chief negotiators of the treaties of Brundisium and Tarentum. Although without an official title, he held absolute administrative power over Rome and all of Italy while Octavian was absent in Sicily (36 B.C.) and during his later absences in the provinces. The attentions which Augustus paid to Maecenas' wife, Terentia, somewhat cooled their friendship, however.

Maecenas is perhaps best remembered as a wealthy and generous patron of the literary men of his time, particularly Horace and Virgil; in return he persuaded them to write in praise of the age of Augustus. Some fragments of his own writings which have survived have not been too highly regarded. When he died he left his immense wealth and his palatial residence on the Esquiline to Augustus.

MAELSTROM, māl'strŏm (Nor. MALSTRØM or MOSKENSTRØM), strait, Norway, in the North Sea between two of the Lofoten Islands, Moskenesøy and Mosken. The current in the strait runs with the tides, alternating six hours from south to north, and thus produces a whirlpool with immense whirls. The depth of the water around does not exceed 20 fathoms, though immediately to the west the soundings are from 100 to 200 fathoms. When the wind is northwest and opposed to the reflux of the waves it attains its greatest fury, but in ordinary circumstances it may be traversed without difficulty. An imaginative description was given by Edgar Allan Poe in *A Descent into the Maelstrom.*

MAENAD, mē'năd, (Greek, mad woman), in Greek mythology, one of the alternative names for the Bacchaes, the frenzied female companions of Bacchus (q.v.) or Dionysus.

MAERLANT, màr'länt, **Jacob van,** Flemish poet: b. near Bruges, 1235? d. Damme, Belgium, ?1300. Besides writing original poems, he made free translations of French romances into rhymed verse. He rendered the *Biblia Scolastica* of Petrus Comestor into a rhymed Biblical history, but his most ambitious work was *The Mirror of History,* inspired principally by the *Speculum Historiale,* of Vincent of Beauvais. Maerlant, who founded the didactic school in the Netherlands, was one of the most learned men of his time.

MAES or **MAAS,** màs, **Nicolaes,** Dutch genre and portrait painter: b. Dordrecht, 1632; d. Amsterdam, Nov. 24, 1693. He entered the studio of Rembrandt at Amsterdam about 1650 and studied there about four years, attaining a style of execution and coloring so similar to that of his master that many of his paintings were for a long time believed to be Rembrandt's work. He returned to Dordrecht in 1654, and in the succeeding 10 years he did his best work, which retained the influence of Rembrandt, particularly in coloring. From the time of his going to Antwerp in 1665 his style changed and he abandoned the domestic genre type of work for that of portraiture, and his subsequent pictures show the influence of Van Dyck. So different were the characteristics of the two periods that at one time it was believed that there were two artists of the same name. Of his earlier and better period notable examples are *The Reverie; Card Players; The Eavesdropper; Young Girl Peeling an Apple; Hagar's Departure,* long believed to be a Rembrandt and *The Listening Girl.* Numerous other examples exist in the galleries of Berlin, Brussels, Munich, The Hague, Frankfort, and Hanover.

MAESTRICHT. See MAASTRICHT.

MAETERLINCK, mà'tēr-lǐngk, COUNT **Maurice,** Belgian poet, dramatist, and essayist: b. Ghent, Aug. 29, 1862; d. at his villa on the French Riviera, near Nice, May 6, 1949. He was educated in a Jesuit school in Ghent, and at the university, and in 1886 he was admitted to the bar. On a visit to Paris the next year he came under the influence of Philippe Villiers de l'Isle Adam (1838–1889) and other writers of the symbolist school, and soon thereafter gave up the law to devote himself to literature. He settled in Paris in 1896 but retained his citizenship as a Belgian. In 1911, he was awarded the Nobel Prize for literature, and during World War I he engaged in relief work in France and Belgium; on his 70th birthday the king of the Belgians raised him to the rank of count. He had visited the United States on a lecture tour in 1919, and in 1940, following the surrender of France in World War II, he visited New York City, returning to France several years later to pass the rest of his life writing his memoirs. His works, comprising lyric verse, dramas, and philosophical essays, were written in French, and many of them achieved an international reputation; a large number are available in English translation. While his verse is imaginative, it lacks in any strong degree the melodic quality. Superlatively praised and extravagantly censured, Maeterlinck has described his plays as written for marionettes, and his prose as verse in solution. As a rule his plays depend on mood rather than movement, suggestion of the event rather than its presentation; they are attempts to clothe mystical conceptions in concrete form. His chief absorption is with the mystery of life. The marks of his method have been described as parallelism, symbolism, suggestion, and the use of realistic means for romantic effects. To many, the essays are his ultimate test as a force in literature, the most interesting things that Maeterlinck did. Plays translated into English comprise: *The Princess Maleine* (1892); *Pelleas and Melisande* (1892); *Alladene and Palomedes* (1898); *Aglavaine and Selysette* (1899); *The Death of Tintageles* (1899); *The Blue Bird* (1909); *Betrothal* (1912); *The Wrack of the Storm* (1916); *The Burgomaster of Stilemonde* (1918). English translations of his essays and philosophical works are: *The Treasure of the Humble* (1897); *Wisdom and Destiny* (1898); *The Buried Temple* (1902); *The Double Garden* (1904); *The Life of Space* (1922); *The Magic of the Stars* (1930); *The Hour Glass* (1936). Works on natural history in English translation comprise: *The Life of the Bee* (1901); *The Life of the White Ant* (1926); *The Life of the Ant* (1931); *Pigeons and Spiders* (1936); *The Great Beyond* (1947); and an autobiographical book of memoirs entitled *Blue Bubbles* (1949).

MAEVIAD AND BAVIAD. See BAVIAD.

MAFEKING, măf'ü-kǐng, Union of South Africa, town of the Cape of Good Hope province, approximately 750 miles northeast of Capetown. Standing at an elevation of 4,194 feet above sea level, it is close to the border of the Bechuanaland Protectorate; it contains the administrative headquarters of that protectorate, and thus is in the unique position of serving as the capital of a country beyond its frontiers. Mafeking is also the headquarters of South Africa's railway system between Kimberley and Bulawayo, and it is the chief business center for the western Transvaal and Bechuanaland Protectorate. The surrounding district is pastoral, and the town contains creameries and malt and cement works. A mile distant from the town proper, on either side of the Milopo river, is the native *stad,* or town, which serves as headquarters of the Barolong tribe; the chiefs retain administrative and judicial powers there. Mafeking was founded in 1885, after a force under Sir Charles Warren had suppressed the republics of Stellaland and Goshen and effected the annexation of British Bechuanaland (that part of the Cape province in which Mafeking lies). The town was the starting place of the Jameson Raid (see JAMESON, SIR LEAN-

DER STARR), and was the base of subsequent operations against the Matabele. During the South African War a British force under Col. Robert S. S. (later Baron) Baden-Powell (q.v.) was besieged in Mafeking from Oct. 12, 1899, until May 17, 1900. Pop. (1966) 6,346.

MAFFEI, mäf-fe′ē, MARCHESE **Francesco Scipione di,** Italian dramatist and archaeologist: b. Verona, June 1, 1675; d. there, Feb. 11, 1755. He studied at the Jesuit College, Parma, for five years, and from 1698 at Rome. During 1703–1704 he served as a volunteer in the war of the Spanish succession, being present at the Battle of Höchstadt on the Bavarian side. His literary career began in 1710 with the publication of *Della scienza cavalleresca,* a censure of dueling. He was one of the founders of the *Giornale dei Letterati,* and he edited, with introductions, some of the best plays of the Cinquecento (16th century).

In 1713 appeared his own play *Merope* (since frequently reprinted), one of the most brilliant successes achieved in the history of dramatic literature. While *Merope* lacks a love motif, it is considered a masterpiece of Italian tragedy. Voltaire adapted it for the French stage, declaring it to be "worthy of the most glorious days of Athens."

Maffei's versatility and scientific attainments are shown in subsequent works, which include *Teatro italiano* (1723–1725); *Storia diplomatica* (1727); *Le cerimonie* (1728), a comedy; and *Verona illustrata* (1732). From 1732 he spent four years in travel in France and England, returning by way of Holland and Germany, and wrote *Galliae antiquitates* (1733); *Storia teologica* (1742); *Dell'impiego del denaro* (1746), justifying loans on interest; and *Arte magica* (1749–1754). He was also associated with Muratori in the great collection of the *Rerum italicarum scriptores,* which occupied 15 years and was published in 25 folio volumes (1723–1738).

See also MEROPE.

MAFIA, mä′fē′ä, an island off the East African coast, 11 miles from the mouth of the Rufiji River. It was within that portion of the domains of the sultanate of Zanzibar transferred in 1888 to German East Africa and now a part of Tanzania. The island, 170 square miles in area, is fertile, supporting large numbers of coconut palms. At Tirene Bay, on the southwest of the island, are the principal harbor and Chobe, the largest village. Traces of early settlement by Arabs have been found at Kua, on the neighboring small island of Dshuani. Pop. (1958) 12,199.

MAFIA, mäf′ē-ə, collectively denotes the organized outlaw groups that operate chiefly in the rural areas of central and western Sicily. Originating in the local management of feudal estates, the Mafias emerged in the 1800's as regional, independent associations of political criminals. Mafia membership, often based on family ties, is kept secret and disciplined by strict enforcement of an unwritten code of honor (*omerta*) forbidding cooperation with established authority. Like the Irish Sinn Fein (q.v.), the Stern Gang of Israel, and the Mau Mau of Kenya, the Mafia (or "Honored Society"), has served as a resistance movement during times of foreign domination. In spite of repeated efforts by the Italian government to crush this underground movement,

it was strong enough in 1943 to facilitate the capture of Sicily by the Allied forces.

Due to certain similarities in organization and methods used in acquiring power (such as smuggling, bribery, and extortion for "protection"), organized crime in the United States is sometimes called "the Mafia." There is no concrete evidence of any direct connection between the two types of criminal society. See COSA NOSTRA.

R. A. LAUD HUMPHREYS
Southern Illinois University

MAFRA, mä′frä, Portugal, a town in Estremadura province, 20 miles northwest of Lisbon. Its principal architectural feature is a huge monastery which, with cloister and church, was built by John V between 1717 and 1732 to replace a small Franciscan friary. The monastery, modeled after the Escorial, in Spain, contains more than 800 rooms. The church, richly built and lavishly decorated, has twin towers, each containing a chime of 57 bells.

MAGADHA, mu′gə-də, an ancient kingdom of India, in what is now southern Bihar state. See INDIA—*20. Ancient and Medieval History.*

MAGADI, mä-gä′dē, a "lake" in Kenya, East Africa, the surface of which is solid, being entirely composed of carbonate of soda. It lies at an elevation of 1,978 feet above sea level, southwest of Nairobi and immediately north of the border of Tanzania. Bore holes, which have been put down to a depth of 10 feet over a 30 square mile area, have proved some 40 million surface tons of carbonate of soda, and the total deposit is estimated at 200 million tons.

MAGALHÃES, mə-gə-lyĭns′, **Domingo José Gonçalves de,** VISCOUNT OF ARAGUAYA, Brazilian poet and diplomat: b. Rio de Janeiro, Aug. 13, 1811; d. Rome, Italy, July 10, 1882. He was educated in medicine, but entered upon a diplomatic career in 1836, when he became an attaché at the Brazilian embassy in Paris. From 1859 till 1867 he was minister at Vienna, and for the next four years he was ambassador at Washington, D.C. At the time of his death he was ambassador at Rome.

He began the writing of verse at an early age and attained a considerable reputation, being regarded as the leader of the romantic school of Brazilian poetry. His more important works were *Suspiros poéticas* (1836); *A Confederação dos Tamóios* (1857); *Mistérios* (1858); and *Urânia* (1862). In 1834 he published a literary history of Brazil. His *Obras completas* were published in Paris in 1864.

MAGALHÃES, Fernando de. See MAGELLAN, FERDINAND.

MAGALLANES, mä-gä-yä′näs, Chile, a province lying in the southern extremity of the republic, south of latitude 49° S. It comprises all mainland between the Pacific and the frontier of Argentina, together with all islands off that coast; the latter include most of the Fuegian archipelago and the western portion of Tierra del Fuego. The total area is 52,271 square miles. The islands are barren, but there are extensive forests on the mountainous mainland. Beautiful bays and fjords are characteristic of the coasts. The climate is cold, foggy, and stormy. Animal life is not abundant, but there are seals and sea otters along the coast. The Alacaluf Indians who inhabit the area formerly subsisted on shellfish and sea mammals. They now engage in sheepherding and lumbering, the chief industries of Magallanes. The province was formed in 1929, with its capital at Punta Arenas. Pop. (1960) 73,358.

MAGDA, măg′dà, the English title of the four-act German drama *Heimat* (1893; Eng. tr., *Magda,* 1896) by Hermann Sudermann (q.v.). It is a variation upon the theme of the returned prodigal. Ten years before the action opens, Magda Schwartze, rebelling against the stuffiness of official society in a small city, had gone to Berlin to study music. Her martinet father had disowned her. Now, as a famous singer under her stage name of Maddalene dall' Orto, she returns as the star of a music festival. Grudgingly received by her father and stepmother, she appears as a benefactress, providing the dowry without which her younger sister cannot marry. But the nagging questions of her father and her aunt reveal that she was once the mistress of von Keller, now a rising local councillor. Her father insists that she marry von Keller, who imposes humiliating conditions. As the arrangements are concluded, her father dies of a stroke, leaving Magda apparently hopelessly caught in the domestic web she loathes. The play is not a tragedy, however. Given the resolute character displayed by Magda throughout the antecedent action and most of the play itself, it is impossible to imagine her remaining long in the trap where the final curtain leaves her. The play is an outstanding example of the influence of Henrik Ibsen on the generation of dramatists that followed him, and, like Ibsen's plays, it is superbly good theater.

DeLancey Ferguson.

MAGDALA, mäg′dà-là, or **MAKDALA,** village, Ethiopia, in Wallo Province, about 180 miles north of Addis Ababa. It is situated on a narrow plateau, 9,110 feet above sea level. It was a capital of Ethiopia under Emperor Theodore II, who in 1863 imprisoned a British diplomatic mission there. He committed suicide in 1868 when an expedition under Sir Robert Cornelis Napier (q.v.) stormed and destroyed the fortifications and rescued the prisoners. Pop. 1,000.

MAGDALA (also Magadan), town, ancient Galilee, Palestine, the home of Mary Magdalene. Its exact location is uncertain, but it was on the west shore of the Sea of Galilee and had a harbor (Matthew 15:39), and lay on the Nazareth-Damascus caravan route. It has been variously identified with the ancient Tarichaea, a fishing and shipbuilding center, and with the modern village of Migdal (Arabic, El Majdal), about 3 miles northwest of Tiberias.

MAGDALEN. See Mary Magdalene.

MAGDALEN COLLEGE, môd′lĭn, Oxford, England, one of the constituent colleges of Oxford University. It was founded in 1458 by William of Waynflete (q.v.), bishop of Winchester and lord high chancellor of England. The College of St. Mary Magdalen (the foundation's full title) had its origins in Magdalen Hall, established some ten years earlier, and was built on the site of the old Hospital of St. John. Under the existing stat-

utes there are five types of fellows, as well as honorary fellows. There are fellowships attached to the Waynflete professorships of chemistry, metaphysical philosophy, physiology, and pure mathematics in the university, and others to the

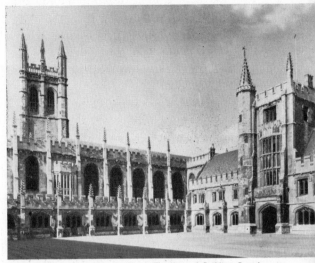

The National Buildings Record

The Great Quad at Magdalen College.

Sherardian professorship of botany, the Serena professorship of Italian studies, the Nuffield professorship of clinical medicine, and the professorship of psychology. Up to 40 junior demyships, stemming from the original foundation, and a number of other scholarships and exhibitions are available to undergraduates. There are normally from 300 to 350 students in residence. The college buildings, erected in the late 15th century on a quadrangular plan including a cloister, are among the most beautiful in Oxford, and stand in extensive grounds. Former students have included such notables as Joseph Addison, William Camden, John Foxe, Edward Gibbon, John Hampden, John Lyly, Henry Sacheverell, William Tyndale, and Thomas Cardinal Wolsey.

Consult Wilson, Henry A., *History of Magdalen College* (London 1899); Glasgow, Edwin, *Sketches of Magdalen College* (London 1901); *Handbook to the University of Oxford* (annual); *Oxford University Calendar* (annual).

Richard E. Webb.

MAGDALEN ISLANDS, măg′dà-lĕn (Fr. Îles de la Madeleine), a group of islands in the south central part of the Gulf of St. Lawrence, eastern Quebec, Canada. About 100 miles southwest of Newfoundland, they cover an area of 102 square miles. The chief islands in the group are Amherst, Grindstone, Alright, and Coffin; the chief villages are Étang du Nord on Grindstone, and Havre Aubert (Amherst) on Amherst. Fishing (cod, herring, lobster, mackerel) and sealing are the chief industries. In the 19th century gypsum was quarried. The islands were discovered by Jacques Cartier in 1534, became the property of Sir Isaac Coffin in 1787, and in 1903 were purchased by the Magdalen Island Company. The population is mainly of French origin, and the islands are administered as part of Gaspé County. Pop. 13,213.

MAGDALENA, măg-dȧ-lē′nȧ, department, Colombia, bordering on the Caribbean Sea, between the Magdalena River on the east and Venezuela on the west. It has an area of 19,162 square miles. The capital is Santa Marta (pop. 1951, 37,005). From marshy lowlands on the coast the land rises abruptly to the 18,950-foot Pico Cristóbal Colón in the Sierra Nevada de Santa Marta range. Magdalena has a dry, tropical climate, with a rainy season from May to September. Bananas are the chief export crop; cotton, corn, beans, rice, henequen, yucca, and coffee (in the highlands) are also raised. Coastal forests produce mahogany, cedar, rubber, and kapok. The chief mineral resources are petroleum, copper, gold, iron, coal, and marble. There is pearl fishing at Ríohacha; Santa Marta and Ciénaga are centers for deep-sea fishing and canning. The inhabitants are mostly of mixed Spanish-Indian and Spanish-Negro ancestry. Pop. (1951) 457,393.

MAGDALENA, river, Colombia. It rises in the southwestern part of the country, in the Cordillera Central, and flows northward for about 1,060 miles into the Caribbean Sea near Barranquilla. Its main tributary is the Cauca (q.v.). The Magdalena is navigable from its mouth to the rapids at Honda, and above Honda to Neiva, 150 miles from its source. There is a railroad around the rapids from Honda to Ambalema. The river is a main trade artery for Colombia, and its fertile valley produces cacao, cotton, sugarcane, and tobacco. The chief oil-producing area of Colombia is around the river port of Barrancabermeja, which is connected by pipeline with Cartagena. The river was discovered in 1501 by Rodrigo de Bastidas, and was explored in 1536 by Jiménez de Quesada.

MAGDALENA, municipality and city, Mexico, in Sonora State, about 50 miles south of Nogales. It is situated at an altitude of 2,464 feet, in a region producing silver and copper, and is the center of a farming area raising wheat, cotton, fruit, chick peas, and vegetables. Its placer gold mines were known to the Aztecs. It is a pilgrimage center for annual Indian festivals in October honoring St. Francis Xavier. Pop. (1950) municipality 9,034; city 6,116.

MAGDALENA BAY, an inlet of the Pacific Ocean on the southwest coast of Lower California, Mexico, about 17 miles long and 12 miles wide, providing one of the best harbors on the Pacific Coast. Santa Margarita and several other islands shelter its entrance.

MAGDALENE COLLEGE, môd′lĭn, Cambridge, England, a constituent college of Cambridge University. It was founded in 1542 by Thomas, Baron Audley of Walden, whose coat of arms it now bears, to replace Buckingham College established in 1519 by Edward Stafford, duke of Buckingham, in connection with an already existing hostel for Benedictine student monks. The mastership is in the gift of the holder of the barony of Braybrooke as representing the founder. The college houses 259 undergraduates in buildings surrounding two courts, restored and altered in 1880, and has a 15th century chapel and hall and the Pepysian library, built in 1688. An amendment to the governing statutes in 1942 provides for nine fellowships, four of them founders' fellowships. Up to 21 entrance scholarships

and exhibitions are awarded annually, and there are other awards and prizes of various types available to undergraduates, including the Pepysian Benefaction usually awarded by the master to poor and deserving students. Among its distinguished undergraduates have been Samuel Pepys, Charles Kingsley, and Charles Stewart Parnell.

Consult *The Students' Handbook to the University and Colleges of Cambridge,* annual; *The Annual Register of the University of Cambridge.*

RICHARD E. WEBB.

MAGDALENIAN, măg-dȧ-lē′nĭ-ăn, a late paleolithic culture named from La Madeleine, a cave site in Dordogne Department, France. Magdalenian man lived in caves and hunted reindeer and other large animals of the last ice age. He had well-made tools of bone and antler, and a highly developed art in bone engraving and cave painting. Centered in France and northern Spain, Magdalenian culture extended into northern Switzerland and southern Germany. See also STONE AGE—*Upper Paleolithic.*

MAGDALENO, mȧg-dȧ-lā′nō, **Mauricio,** Mexican novelist, playwright, and short story writer: b. Villa del Refugio, Zacatecas State, Mexico, May 13, 1906. His childhood was spent during the bitterest years of the Mexican revolution, to which he often refers in his work. As a young man he moved to Mexico City, where in 1927 his first novel, *Mapimí 37,* was published. In the 1930's he lived in Madrid, Spain, and contributed two short stories, *El compadre Mendoza* (*Godfather Mendoza*) and *El baile de los Pintos* (*Dance of the Pintos*), to the newspaper *El Sol,* then edited by the Mexican writer Martín Luis Guzmán.

On his return to Mexico, Magdaleno founded with Juan Bustillo Oro the group Teatro de Ahora (Theater of Today) for producing socially conscious and political plays. For this group he wrote *Pánuco 137,* a dramatization of his first novel, which was an exposé of the oil companies; *Emiliano Zapata,* about the revolutionary leader; and *Trópico* in which he inveighed against the exploitation of Mexican land by foreign capital. Collected in one volume, these plays were published in Spain in 1933. Three psychological novels followed: *Campo Celis* (1935), *Concha Bretón* (1936), and *El resplandor* (1937; Eng. tr., *Sunburst,* 1946), the latter representing the culmination of his art, fusing his maturest stylistic resources with his political ideas about the revolution.

If his more recent novels, *Sonata* (1941) and *La tierra grande* (1949; *The Great Earth*), have not added to his stature as the author of *El resplandor,* his short stories, such as *El héroe de Peñuelas* (1948; *The Hero of Peñuelas*), place him among the masters of that genre. A collection of short stories, *El ardiente verano,* was published in Mexico in 1954; also a volume of essays, *Arte, sciencia y libertad.*

MAGDEBURG, măg′dĕ-bûrg, city, Germany, in Magdeburg District. It was the capital of the former Saxony Province of Prussia. Situated on the Elbe River at the eastern terminal of the Weser-Elbe Canal, 80 miles southwest of Berlin, it is a railway and industrial center in an important sugar beet region; potash and lignite mines are nearby. Industries include sugar refining, metalworking, and zinc smelting; and the manufacture of paper, textiles, and synthetic oils, and steel products, machinery, automobiles, cranes, elevators, sewing machines, chemicals, and glass.

Founded by Charlemagne in 805, Magdeburg became an archibishopric in 968; it was a leader in the Hanseatic League; and in 1524 it accepted the Reformation. During the Thirty Years' War it was destroyed after its capture by the forces of the count of Tilly in 1631, and thousands of its citizens lost their lives. The French took the city in 1806, but it was restored to Prussia in 1814. Again destroyed during World War II, it was occupied by U.S. troops in 1945. After the war, it was included in East Germany and was rebuilt. Pop. (1965) 265,968.

MAGELANG, mä-gȧ-läng', town, Indonesia, in central Java, about 25 miles northwest of Djokjakarta. It is situated at an altitude of 1,312 feet, in the highlands between Mount Sumbing and Mount Merapi. It has textile mills and is a trading center for a rich agricultural area. The ancient temple of Borobudur (q.v.) is 8 miles to the south. Pop. (1960) 96,454.

MAGELLAN, mȧ-jĕl'ȧn, **Ferdinand** (Port. FERNÃO DE MAGALHÃES; Span. FERNANDO DE MAGALLANES), Portuguese navigator: b. Sabrosa, Vila Real District, Trás-os-Montes Province, Portugal, about 1480; d. Philippine Islands, April 27, 1521. Of noble family, he served as a page at the court of King John II, and of John's successor King Emanuel (Manuel I). From 1505 to 1512, he served with distinction with the Portuguese forces in India and the East Indies, was at the taking of Malacca, and accompanied an expedition to the Moluccas (Spice Islands). He fought in Morocco (1513–1514), where he was wounded and lamed for life. Accused of trading with the Moors, Magellan lost the king's favor and was

tween Spain and Portugal as to the limits of the spheres of influence allotted to each country by the bull of 1493 of Pope Alexander VI. Magellan argued that he would be able to prove that the Moluccas lay within the Spanish sphere. His proposal was accepted, and on Sept. 20, 1519, he set sail from Sanlúcar de Barrameda with five ships under his command on his remarkable voyage of discovery. Besides his flagship the *Trinidad,* there were the *San Antonio,* the *Santiago,* the *Concepción,* and the *Victoria.* After crossing the Atlantic, the fleet put in briefly at Guanabara Bay, on Dec. 13, 1519. On Jan. 10, 1520 they entered the Río de la Plata, which they explored, thinking it might be the sought-for western passage, then coasted southward, and in March established winter quarters in San Julián Bay, Patagonia. A mutiny began among some of the Spanish captains, but was firmly put down by Magellan. The *Santiago* was wrecked on a scouting expedition, but her crew was saved.

In August the fleet set sail again, and on Oct. 21, 1520, they sighted the eastern entrance to the strait which now bears Magellan's name, but which he called the Strait of All Saints. The passage through the strait took about five and one-half weeks. As the *San Antonio* had deserted for Spain, there were now three vessels which for 98 days sailed across the unknown waters of the ocean which Magellan called the Pacific. They ran low on food and water, were beset by sickness and starvation, and in order to stay alive were forced to eat rats and the leather from the ships' rigging. They reached Guam in the Marianas on March 6, 1521, and the Philippines on March 16, 1521. Magellan persuaded the king of Cebu to swear allegiance to Spain, but on April 27 was killed by the natives of neighboring Mactan Island in his attempt to capture it. One of the remaining ships, the *Victoria,* under Juan Sebastian del Cano,

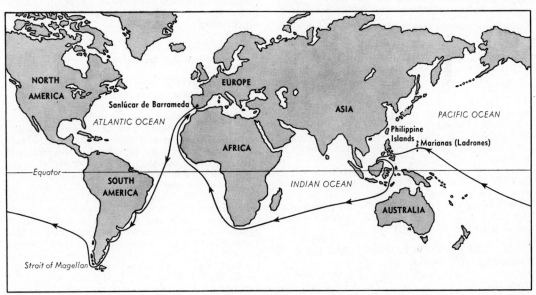

Route of Magellan's voyage.

dismissed from his service. Thereupon, in 1517, he entered the Spanish service under Charles I (later Emperor Charles V).

In Spain Magellan proposed that King Charles support an expedition to seek a westward route to the Moluccas and thus settle the controversy be-

returned to Spain via the Cape of Good Hope, reaching Sanlúcar on Sept. 6, 1522 with a crew of 18 and a cargo of spices that more than paid the cost of the expedition.

The chief sources for the history of the voyage are the accounts written by Antonio Pigafetta, an Italian who accompanied Magellan and returned on the *Victoria*. One account, written for

Bettmann Archive

Ferdinand Magellan, a portrait taken from an old print.

Charles V, was soon published in several languages. A second, longer manuscript was discovered in a Milan library and published in 1800.

Consult Stanley, Henry Edward John, Baron Stanley of Alderley, *The First Voyage Round the World by Magellan*, tr. from Pigafetta for the Hakluyt Society (London 1874); Guillemard, Francis H. H., *Life of Ferdinand Magellan* (London 1890); Pigafetta, Antonio, *Magellan's Voyage Around the World*, original text of the Ambrosian manuscript with Eng. tr. by James A. Robertson, 2 vols. and index (Cleveland 1906); Stefansson, Vilhjalmur, and Wilcox, Olive R., eds., *Great Adventures and Explorations*, chap. 9 (New York 1947); Parr, Charles McKew, *Ferdinand Magellan* (New York 1964).

MAGELLAN, Strait of, a strait at the southern tip of South America, separating the mainland from the archipelago of Tierra del Fuego, and linking the Atlantic and Pacific oceans. It is about 370 miles long, from 2 to 20 miles wide, follows a winding course, and is difficult to navigate because of fog and wind. Except for its eastern extremity, which borders Argentina, it is in Chile. The city of Punta Arenas is the chief port. The strait was discovered in 1520 by Ferdinand Magellan (q.v.). The eastern entrance to the strait is flanked by Capes Vírgenes (north) and Espíritu Santo (south).

MAGELLANIC CLOUDS, măj-ĕ-lăn'ĭk, in astronomy, two nebulae whose diffuse aggregations of glowing gas illuminated by stars are individually known as the Large Cloud and the Small Cloud. They are located in Southern Hemisphere skies in right ascensions $5^h 26^m$ and $0^h 50^m$, and declinations $-69°$ and $-73°$, respectively, and form an equilateral triangle with the south celestial pole. Both are visible to the unaided eye from positions south of the equator, and were named in honor of Ferdinand Magellan (1480?-1521), the Portuguese navigator. In terms of rela-

tive brightness, the Small Cloud only is obliterated by the light of the full moon. The Large Cloud lies mainly in the constellation of Dorado (the goldfish), while the Small Cloud is almost wholly in Tucana (the toucan).

The two clouds resemble dislocated portions of the Milky Way, but are physically independent of this system. They are the nearest extragalactic objects (objects beyond the Milky Way), and form adjacent satellite members in a system sometimes known as the Metagalaxy. Possessing ragged outer edges and lacking any well-defined, uniform cores of high luminosity or any evidence of rotational symmetry, both of the Magellanic clouds are typical examples of a class of celestial objects termed irregular nebulae. The Large Cloud is approximately 75,000 light years, and the Small Cloud about 85,000 light years distant from the earth, when corrections are included for the effects of light-absorbing material in the galaxy. The Large Cloud appears as an object about 7° in angular diameter and the Small Cloud measures about 4°. They are separated by an angular distance of approximately 23° in the sky; however, radio-astronomical observations reveal nonvisible outer portions in both clouds, as well as hydrogen extensions between them, and indicate that the clouds apparently form a physically related pair revolving in an orbit around each other.

Typical Cepheid variable stars (see STARS—*Variable Stars*) were initially discovered within the Small Cloud, and variable stars abound in both objects. Many supergiant stars (see GIANT STAR) and over 30 globular clusters are found in the Large Cloud. The individual stellar components of the two clouds differ between the clouds themselves, but the various star types found are similar to those of the galaxy. Within the Large Cloud, gas and dust are known to exist, while the Small Cloud contains gas only, an indication of differing cycles of star formation within the two clouds. See also NEBULA—*Extragalactic Nebulae*.

FERGUS J. WOOD,
Program Director, Foreign Science Program, National Science Foundation.

MAGENDIE, mȧ-zhăN-dē', **François,** French experimental physiologist: b. Bordeaux, France, Oct. 6, 1783; d. Sannois, near Paris, Oct. 7, 1855. He studied anatomy with the celebrated surgeon Alexis Boyer, and at 20 was appointed assistant anatomist and demonstrator in the faculty of medicine; later, he turned to medicine and physiology. He was elected a member of the Academy of Science in 1821, and 1831 became professor of physiology and pathology at the College of France. A pioneer in experimental physiology, he made important studies of the functions of the cerebellum, heart, and the nervous and vascular systems, and demonstrated what is known as Magendie's law—that the anterior spinal roots are motor and the posterior roots are sensory. He was the first to give a clear description of the cerebrospinal fluid (1825), and to describe the medial foramen in the membranous roof of the fourth ventricle of the brain, called after him the foramen of Magendie. He studied the localized action of various drugs on the human system, and introduced the use of new drugs as remedies in medical practice. His *Précis élémentaire de physiologie* (1816) went through many editions and was translated into several languages. From 1821 to 1831 he published the *Journal de physiologie expérimentale*.

MAGENTA, mȧ-jĕn′tȧ, commune and town, Italy, in Milano Province, Lombardy, 15 miles west of Milan, in a rice-growing area. There is a silk mill and alcohol distillery in the town, as well as foundries and furniture and match factories. Magenta is famous for the battle fought here on June 4, 1859 in which French and Sardinian forces defeated the Austrians. For this victory Comte Patrice de MacMahon, leader of the French troops, was made a marshal of France and duke of Magenta. Pop. (1951) commune, 15,513; town, 14,227.

MAGENTA or **ANILINE RED,** a dye which consists of a mixture of the hydrochlorides of rosaniline and pararosaniline, and produces a brilliant bluish-red color known as magenta or fuchsia. It may be prepared from aniline oil by digesting the aniline with arsenic acid or with nitrobenzene and ferrous chloride. When oxidation is complete, common salt is added; the rosaniline hydrochloride is precipitated because it is sparingly soluble in salt solutions. Magenta dyes wool, silk, and leather directly; for cotton a mordant is needed. The dye is also known as fuchsin or fuchsine.

MAGGIORE, mäd-jō′râ, **Lake** (also called LAGO VERBANO; Lat. VERBANUS LACUS), between Piedmont and Lombardy in Italy, with the northern end of the lake in the Swiss Canton of Ticino. Forty miles long, it is second in size only to Lake Garda among the Italian lakes. Small steamers ply between Locarno, at the Swiss end of the lake, and the several resort towns along the shores. Off the west shore are the Borromean Islands (q.v.).

MAGGOT. See FLIES—*Larvae.*

MAGI, mā′jī (Lat. plural of *magus,* from Gr. *magos,* from Old Persian *magu*), the priestly caste of the ancient Persian Zoroastrian or Mazdian religion. Their form of worship is described by Strabo (book 15, chap. 3, sects. 13–15), who said they were also called Pyraethi, fire-lighters; it may also be seen in a relief published by Franz Cumont (*Religions orientales,* fig. 10). Some Greek writers gave them the name Magousaeans. The ritual consisted in part in pouring libations of milk, oil, and honey on the ground while hymns and prayers were chanted. The priests' mouths were covered by turbans to prevent their breath from defiling the sacred flame. Their doctrines were those of the Zoroastrian religion: the sovereignty of Ahura-Mazda, the heaven-god, surrounded by his court of archangels, which were deified abstractions like Good Thought and Immortality; his eventual victory over Ahriman, the personified principle of evil in the universe; the existence of nature spirits such as Anahita or Anaitis, the spirit of fertilizing waters; Atar, fire; and Mithras, the spirit of pure light, also identified with the sun. (See also ZOROASTRIANISM.) These basic ideas were taken over by Mithraism, which spread widely over the Roman empire between the 1st and 3d centuries.

But in its westward advance the old Persian religion had come in contact with Babylonian beliefs and practices, from which it derived a strong interest in astrology, demonology, and magic. By the time it reached the Graeco-Roman world (via Mesopotamia, Armenia, Cappadocia, and Asia Minor), it was practically identical, in the popular view, with astrology and magic. Hence the use of the term "wise men" in Matthew 2:1 (the "wise men from the east" were astrologers, not kings); and the term "sorcery" (magic) in Acts 8:9–11, and "sorcerer" (magician) in Acts 13:6 Neither ancient Judaism nor early Christianity countenanced these practices.

Consult Cumont, Franz V.-M., *Les religions orientales dans le paganisme romain* (Paris 1906); 4th ed. (Paris 1929); tr. from the French by Grant Showerman as *Oriental Religions in Roman Paganism* (Chicago 1911); Nock, A. D., "St. Paul and the Magus," in *Beginnings of Christianity,* ed. by Frederick J. Foakes Jackson and Kirsopp Lake, vol. 5, pp. 164–188 (London 1933); Bidez, Joseph and Cumont, Franz V.-M., *Les mages hellénisés,* 2 vols. (Paris 1938); vol. 2 containing a full collection of the relevant texts.

FREDERICK C. GRANT,
Union Theological Seminary, New York City.

MAGIC, măj′ĭk, the prescientific art in which, according to primitive belief, a result may be achieved by means of a formula which would not otherwise be within the personal power of the practitioner to attain. Magic differs from science in that the magician assumes that there is a causal relationship between performance of the formula and the end phenomenon, whereas the scientist makes no assumptions and investigates each step of the process. Magic operates impersonally. Its efficiency is based on strict adherence to the formula—repeating the incantation word for word, or preparing the charm, taboo, or hex correctly. If magic fails to work, this is attributed to some deviation from the formula.

An early 16th century German woodcut showing witches brewing a magic potion.

Sir James Frazer, in a classic analysis of the principles of magic, distinguished two main types of magical practice. *Imitative magic* is based on the principle that "like produces like." When a voodoo practitioner in Haiti makes a wax figure of the intended victim and then pierces it with pins or melts it over a fire, he is practicing imitative magic. A pin through the head should produce head pains or madness; a pin in the stomach, internal disorders; destruction of the figure, death. When a Hottentot priest in South Africa causes a

Left: In Haiti, voodoo dancers perform a ritual about a pole set amidst magic symbols and burning candles.

Upper right: Because he is believed to have strong magical powers, this East African medicine man commands fear and respect in his community.

MAGIC

Center left: Eggs strung on wires and posts before a house in Puerto Rico are said to induce fertility and insure a large family.

Center right: Wearing grotesque costumes and masks, the magicians of a New Guinea village hope to frighten off evil spirits.

Left: A young Zulu of South Africa hopes to enchant the girl of his choice by placing a charm—an animal horn—in the thatch of her hut.

Right: A West African fetish figure kept by a surviving twin to appease the spirit of his dead twin.

(Top left) Eve Arnold from Magnum; (center right) H. Armstrong Roberts; (bottom right) The American Museum of Natural History; (others) Ewing Galloway

fire to send up great billows of cloudlike smoke to produce rain, he is likewise working imitative magic. *Contagious magic* is based on the belief that things which have been in contact continue to act on each other at a distance after the physical contact has ended. A magician can take nail parings, hair clippings, castoff clothing, even the spittle of an intended victim and, it is believed, injure the former owner by performing the prescribed formula over these objects. For this reason people in societies where contagious magic is practiced secretly bury everything of the kind to prevent magic being worked against them.

Ewing Galloway

In some rural areas, hex signs painted on the side of a barn are believed to ward off evil.

Magic can be worked for good as well as evil. The village chief in the Trobriand Islands near New Guinea has special magical incantations to insure the fertility of the village gardens. In this case magic supplements careful cultivation, as a kind of insurance. In Polynesia tribal chiefs planning a feast place a magical taboo on certain trees and gardens so that the fruit and vegetables will not be picked until time for the feast. There is also much countermagic practiced against evil magic. In Islamic countries quotations from the Koran are worn in necklaces as amulets against possible evil, and in the Mediterranean area blue beads are hung on donkeys as a charm against evil eye. Magic has not completely disappeared from modern scientific societies, as is attested by the pinch of salt thrown over the shoulder to ward off the evils consequent on spilling salt, knocking on wood to counteract the possible adverse effects of an optimistic statement, and other familiar gestures of European-American culture. See also WITCHCRAFT.

ELIZABETH E. BACON.

Bibliography.—Frazer, Sir James G., *The Golden Bough*, 3d ed., vols. 1 and 2 (London 1911); Evans-Pritchard, Edward E., *Witchcraft, Oracles, and Magic Among the Azande* (London 1937); Howells, William W., *The Heathens*, chap. 4 (New York 1950); Thorndike, Lynn, *A History of Magic and Experimental Science*, 8 vols. (New York 1923–1958); Vetter, George, *Magic and Religion* (London 1959).

MAGIC FLUTE, The (German title DIE ZAUBERFLÖTE), opera in two acts by Wolfgang Amadeus Mozart; libretto by Emanuel Schikan-

eder. It was first produced in Vienna on Sept. 30, 1791. The cast of characters is as follows: Queen of the Night (soprano); Pamina, her daughter (soprano): Papagena, a bird-girl (soprano); Tamino, an Egyptian prince (tenor); Monostatos, a temple slave (tenor); Papageno, a bird-man (baritone); Sarastro, high priest of Isis and Osiris (bass); priests, ladies, genii, guards, slaves, a speaker.

The story of *The Magic Flute* mixes farce, tragedy, serious philosophy, political commentary, pageantry, and the supernatural. Sarastro, who has imprisoned Pamina to save her from the Queen of the Night's evil influence, agrees to let Tamino win her if he can pass the tests set for him by Sarastro and his priests. The high-minded Tamino is accompanied by the charming, earthy Papageno, who desires not wisdom and the truth, but only food, wine, comfort, and "a little Papagena"—a little wife. Tamino is protected by the power of a magic flute, Papageno by a chime of magic bells. Papageno at last finds his Papagena. Tamino and Pamina, passing unharmed through ordeals by fire and water, are hailed by the wise Sarastro, who unites them.

The exalted music has kept this singular opera in the active operatic repertoire for more than 165 years. Its appeal as a stage work is unquestionable; it has something meaningful for everyone, from the unsophisticated child to the most serious and intellectual student.

Johann Wolfgang von Goethe was so impressed by the symbolic significance in *The Magic Flute* libretto that he wrote a sequel to it, and it has been studied for its Masonic symbolism, its philosophic and religious significance, and its references to the Austrian politics of Mozart's time. Ludwig van Beethoven held it to be Mozart's greatest work.

HERBERT WEINSTOCK.

MAGIC LANTERN, an optical instrument equipped with a light and lenses, and used for projecting magnified images upon a screen or other adapted surface.

MAGIC MOUNTAIN, The (German title, *Der Zauberberg*), a novel by Thomas Mann (q.v.), which was published in Berlin in 1924. An English translation by H. T. Lowe-Porter was issued in New York in 1927.

The scene of the story is a tuberculosis sanatorium at Davos Platz in the Swiss Alps; the action occurs in the years 1907–1914. Hans Castorp, a young engineer from Hamburg, is about to enter his apprenticeship as a shipbuilder. Feeling slightly fagged, he decides to spend his three-week holiday with his cousin, Joachim Ziemssen, a patient in the sanatorium. During the visit, medical examination discloses that Castorp, too, is infected. His three-week stay lengthens into seven years, and even then is terminated only by the outbreak of war.

The major theme of the book is the psychological effect of isolation and regimented idleness upon the inmates of the sanatorium. They gradually become detached from life; some who are discharged as cured find it impossible to re-enter the active world. In this artificial atmosphere normal emotions atrophy. Thus Castorp admires at a distance the exotic beauty of Clavdia Cauchat, half French and half Russian, yet never seeks a real meeting with her. It takes the momentary release of carnival night to fling them into each other's arms in a gust of passion which has no sequel and no repetition.

Castorp is purposely depicted as a somewhat naive and simple soul, without strong convictions, but given, in his isolation and enforced idleness, to wondering about the meaning of life. At first he studies books on physical and biological science, which only intensify his sense of loneliness in the universe. He listens attentively to the arguments of his two most literate and vocal fellow patients, who expound opposing views. One of these is Ludovico Settembrini, an Italian humanist who preaches romantic individualism; the other is Elie Naphta, a Jesuit-trained scholar who preaches ascetic denial of the world and the flesh. Castorp listens, but, like Omar Khayyám, evermore comes out by the same door wherein he went. Later on, he finds greater stimulus in Pieter Peeperkorn, an almost inarticulate Hollander who dominates people not by ideas but by sheer weight of personality. Music, too, and the suprarational experiences of trance, hallucination, and psychic experiment, seem at times to bring him closer to comprehension.

By contrast, Joachim Ziemssen is a man whose single purpose is to return to the realm of action—to the Flatlands, as most of the inmates call their lost working-day world—and take his appointed place as an officer in the German Army. He returns to duty before the doctors can certify him as cured. Exposure brings on a relapse which kills him. Old Peeperkorn, rather than face lingering invalidism, commits suicide.

The story has been described as an allegory of middle-class German life before World War I, but the theme is larger than that. It is rather that life without action ceases to be life; that we learn its meaning not by thinking about it, but by living. See also JOSEPH AND HIS BROTHERS.
DeLANCEY FERGUSON.

MAGIC SQUARES, arrangements of positive numbers placed in cell subdivisions of squares which possess the following property: the sums taken along the horizontal, or vertical, or the main diagonal cells are always equal. The square itself

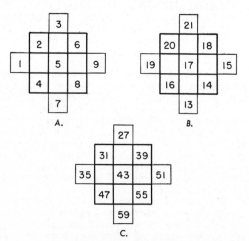

Fig. 1. Odd order magic squares: formation of diagonals.

is so subdivided that there is the same number of cells on each side of the square. There are two kinds of magic squares, depending on the number of the cells on the side of the square. There are

even (with 4, 6, 8, . . . cells on each side) and odd (with 3, 5, 7, . . . cells on each side) magic squares. The number of the cells on the side of a magic square denotes the order of the magic square.

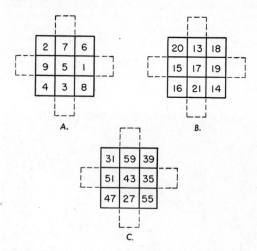

Fig. 2. Transposition of cells into Fig. 1 magic squares.

Magic squares are constructed according to definite schemes. One of these methods is presented here. There are many other methods and the reader is referred to the literature on this subject at the conclusion of this article.

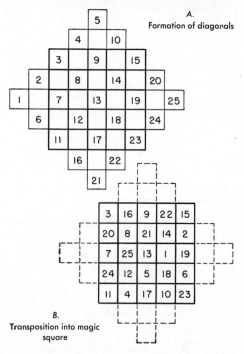

Fig. 3. Odd order magic square with 25 cells.

Odd-Order Magic Squares.—Of these, the magic square with 9 cells (3 cells on each side) is the simplest. The method presented here is applicable to all odd-order magic squares. They are constructed as follows (see Fig. 1): Write the first 9 positive numbers (1, 2, 3, 4, 5, 6, 7,

8, 9), or any other 9 consecutive positive numbers (13, 14, 15, 16, 17, 18, 19, 20, 21), or any other series of positive numbers, any two of them differing by a constant positive interval (27, 31, 35, 39, 43, 47, 51, 55, 59) as shown in Fig. 1, *A, B,* and *C*.

Transpose the numbers outside the cells of the squares so that each outside number is placed in the vacant cells farthest from it (see Fig. 2, *A, B,* and *C*).

A magic square of the 5th order, with 5 cells on each side, is constructed as follows (see Fig. 3): Write the first 25 positive numbers (1 to 25), as shown in Fig. 3*A,* or any other consecutive 25 positive numbers, or any other series of positive numbers, any two of them differing by a constant interval (such as 42, 48, 54).

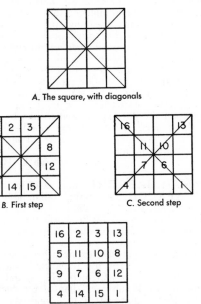

A. The square, with diagonals

B. First step

C. Second step

D. Completed magic square

Fig. 4. Construction of simple even order magic square.

Transpose the numbers which are in the cells outside the square into the vacant cells within the square so that each number outside the square occupies a vacant cell farthest from it (Fig. 3*B*).

Even-Order Magic Squares.—These squares, of which the magic square with 16 cells (4 cells on each side) is the simplest, are con-

structed as follows (see Fig. 4): Construct a square with 16 cells and draw the two major diagonals (Fig. 4*A*). Start with the upper left-hand corner, writing the first 16 positive numbers, or any other 16 consecutive numbers, or any other series of 16 positive numbers, any two of them differing by a constant interval; but do not write in the cells containing portions of the major diagonals. Thus, the numbers 1, 4, 6, 7, 10, 11, 13, and 16 are not written (Fig. 4*B*). Write these numbers in another square (Fig. 4*C*), starting with the largest number (16) by placing it in the upper left-hand corner cell and filling up those cells which contain portions of the two major diagonals. Finally superimpose the squares 4*B* and 4*C*. The resulting square 4*D* is a magic square.

A magic square with 64 cells (8 cells on each side) is subdivided into four 16-cell squares (see Fig. 5), and the major diagonals are drawn in each of the four 16-cell squares (Fig. 5*A*). The first 64 positive numbers may be employed, or any 64 consecutive positive numbers, or any series of 64 positive numbers in which any two consecutive numbers differ by some constant interval. The procedure is the same as in the case of the 16-cell square. Write the numbers in their ascending order of magnitude starting with the upper left-hand cell, but omit those cells which contain portions of the major diagonals. Using another square (Fig. 5*B*), fill in those cells through which the major diagonals pass, but write the numbers in the descending order of magnitude. Superimpose the squares 5*A* and 5*B*. The square 5*C* is a magic square.

The construction of magic squares presented above represents one of numerous known methods. The method presented here is the simplest of them.

For the construction of those even-order magic squares which, when subdivided into four smaller squares, result in odd-order squares (as, for example, a square with 36 cells subdivided into four 9-cell squares), the reader is referred to R. V. Heath's *Mathemagic,* p. 93. His method for a 36-cell square may be extended to any other magic square of this type.

Properties of Magic Squares.—Magic squares containing the series of natural numbers starting with the number 1 are considered primitive. All other magic squares are derived.

The sum of the numbers in a row, column, or along the main diagonal of a primitive magic square with *n* cells is given by the formula $S_n = \frac{1}{2}n(n^2 + 1)$. Thus, for the first few primi-

Fig. 5. Construction of an even order magic square with 64 cells.

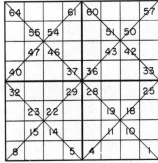

A. First step

B. Second step

C. Completed magic square

tive magic squares the sums are as follows: for 3 cells the sum is 15; for 4, 34; 5, 65; 6, 111; 7, 175; 8, 260; 9, 369; 10, 505; and 11, 671.

Magic squares were known to men from the early days of civilization. Originally, magic squares were considered to have been endowed with supernatural properties and powers. Magic squares were used as amulets and talismans to ward off illness and evil spirits, and to provide all sorts of protection from disease and misfortune.

Magic squares possess many interesting purely mathematical properties, as, for example, the indestructibility of a magic square if some of its columns or rows are transposed. Many other geometric configurations, such as triangles, pentagons, hexagons, circles, and cubes, are amenable to the construction of numerical configurations possessing properties similar to those of magic squares.

Bibliography.—Kraitchik, Maurice, *Mathematical Recreations* (New York 1942); Bakst, Aaron, *Mathematics, Its Magic and Mastery,* 2d ed. (New York 1952); Heath, Royal V., *Mathemagic* (New York 1953); Bakst, Aaron, *Mathematical Puzzles and Pastimes* (New York 1954); Bakst, Aaron, *Amusements mathématiques* (Paris 1956); Andrews, W. S., *Magic Squares and Cubes* (New York 1960); Ball, W. W. Rouse, *Mathematical Recreations and Essays* (New York 1960).

AARON BAKST,
Associate Professor, School of Commerce, New York University.

MAGINN, mȧ-gĭn', **William,** Irish journalist and humorist: b. Cork, Ireland, July 10, 1793; d. Walton-on-Thames, England, Aug. 21, 1842. After graduating from Trinity College, Dublin, in 1811, he taught school. In 1819 he began to write, contributing under various pseudonyms to *Blackwood's Magazine* and the *Literary Gazette,* and in 1823 he went to London. With Hugh Fraser he founded *Fraser's Magazine* (1830), which his contributions helped make famous. Maginn was a brilliant writer, and his short story *Bob Burke's Duel with Ensign Brady* (1834) has been described as the funniest Irish story extant, but he was an alcoholic, and his gifts were already failing when he died shortly after being discharged from debtors' prison. He was the original of Captain Shandon in William Makepeace Thackeray's *Pendennis.*

MAGINOT, mȧ-zhē-nō', **André,** French politician: b. Revigny-sur-Ornain, France, Feb. 17, 1877; d. Paris, Jan. 7, 1932. Elected deputy representing Bar-le-Duc in 1910, he became undersecretary of state for war in 1913. He joined his regiment at the outbreak of World War I, and was severely wounded in November 1914. Although permanently crippled, between 1917 and 1931 he served variously as minister of colonies, of pensions, and of war. He was largely responsible for the Maginot Line, named in his honor, which was constructed to protect the eastern border of France from Switzerland to Luxembourg with a series of underground forts connected by casements and pillboxes. For financial and political reasons the line was not extended along the Belgian frontier, and the Germans were able to bypass it at this point when they invaded France in World War II.

MAGINOT LINE. See FORTIFICATIONS— *Modern Fortifications* (World War II): MAGINOT, ANDRÉ; WORLD WAR II—*Fall of the Low Countries and France.*

MAGISTRATE, măj'ĭs-trāt, in law, a generic term having no single or universal meaning. In a general sense, a magistrate is a public official exercising a public authority. In a more limited sense, and in accord with popular usage, a magistrate is an inferior judicial officer, such as a justice of the peace (q.v.). Thus used, the term describes a judge who has summary jurisdiction in matters of a criminal nature and who has the power to issue a warrant for the arrest of a person charged with the commission of a crime or public offense. A United States commissioner is a kind of magistrate. A committing magistrate is one who conducts the preliminary hearing of persons charged with crime, and has the authority either to discharge them, commit them to jail to await trial, or release them on bail. A police magistrate is a state or municipal officer having the authority to administer local police laws.

In its broader meaning, magistrate refers to a legislative or executive officer, as well as a judge, and thus may include an alderman, burgess, county commissioner, consul, or notary public. The president of the United States is the chief magistrate of the nation, and a governor is the chief magistrate of his state. Also, the mayor of a city may be considered a magistrate. Depending upon the powers granted to him by statute, a clerk of a court may or may not be included in the term. A district attorney would not ordinarily be considered a magistrate.

RICHARD L. HIRSHBERG.

MAGLIABECHI, mä-lyä-bā'kĕ, or **MAGLIABECCHI, Antonio,** Italian bibliographer: b. Florence, Italy, Oct. 28, 1633; d. there, June 27, 1714. Until he was 40 he worked as a goldsmith, an occupation he relinquished in order to devote himself to literary pursuits. Through constant reading and study he acquired great learning and became famous for his remarkable memory and his eccentricities. Cosimo III, grand duke of Tuscany, made him custodian of the ducal library (Biblioteca Palatina) in 1673, and gave him free access to the Laurentian Library and the Oriental manuscripts, of which he published a catalog. Magliabechi left his fortune to be distributed to the poor and his personal library (Magliabechiana) to the grand duke to be set up as a public library. It is now a part of the Biblioteca Nazionale of Florence.

MAGLIONE, mä-lyō'nä, **Luigi,** Italian cardinal and Vatican diplomat: b. Casoria, Italy, March 2, 1877; d. there, Aug. 22, 1944. He was educated in Rome at the Gregorian University and the University of St. Apollinaris, was ordained priest in 1901, and in 1905 began a two-year course at the Academy of Noble Ecclesiastics in preparation for the Vatican diplomatic service. He taught at the academy from 1908 to 1918, and in the latter year was sent as representative of the Holy See to Switzerland. Created titular archbishop of Caesarea in Palestine in 1920, he was made nuncio to Switzerland, and in October 1926 became nuncio to Paris, France, where he remained nine years. In appreciation of his work there the French government awarded him the Grand Cross of the Legion of Honor. On Dec. 16, 1935, Pius XI created him cardinal, sending his red hat for presentation to him by President Albert Lebrun, in accordance with accepted custom when affairs of the nunciature prevent return to the Vatican to receive it.

Pope Pius recalled him to Rome and appointed him prefect of the Congregation of the Council. On March 11, 1939, Pope Pius XII appointed Cardinal Maglione his secretary of state, the office that he himself had occupied under Pius XI.

MAGMA, măg′mà, rock which is in a fluid condition due to heat, and commonly said to be molten. For a discussion of the modern conception of a magma see the article on ROCKS.

MAGMATIC STOPING, the process by which a fluid rock mass (magma) heats the overlying rock till it fractures and portions break off and settle into the magma, there to be assimilated or to remain as solid blocks or xenoliths. The process is believed to be important in the mechanics of igneous intrusion.

MAGNA CARTA, măg′nà kär′tà, or **MAGNA CHARTA** (GREAT CHARTER). In its earliest form this was a grant of liberties extorted from King John of England (1199–1216) in 1215 by a group of rebellious barons. It was reissued with modifications and omissions in 1216 by the regency headed by William Marshall, earl of Pembroke, ruling for the infant Henry III (1216–1272). In 1217 the regency reissued the charter as two separate documents: the charter of liberties and the charter of the forest. In 1225, after Henry III had been declared of age, these charters again were issued in essentially the same form as in 1217. The charters of 1225 became the accepted version and were placed at the beginning of all medieval collections of English statutes. The original text of John's charter was not known to scholars until the 17th century.

Background.—Ever since the Norman conquest of England in 1066 the English kings had striven to develop their power at the expense of that of the feudal class: the barons, their vassals, and their rear-vassals. The barons had opposed this process and had risen occasionally in open revolt. When Henry I (1100–1135) ascended the throne, he issued a charter of liberties in which he promised to stop certain practices of his father and elder brother. Stephen (1135–1154) and Henry II (1154–1189) each issued similar charters. But these promises had little effect on the actual policies of the royal government. All these monarchs with the exception of Stephen steadily increased the royal power.

Henry II's sons, Richard I (1189–1199) and John, followed the example of their predecessors with great enthusiasm. This was particularly true of John. The late 12th and early 13th centuries was a period of rising prices, in which the costs of government also increased rapidly and the incomes of those who drew their revenues directly from the land also increased. The feudal class as a whole was steadily growing richer, but, as most royal revenues were fixed by custom, it was difficult for the king to tap the new wealth. John tried every means which an ingenious and not too scrupulous mind could devise. He abused his feudal rights by demanding exorbitant reliefs when heirs inherited their fathers' fiefs. He sold heiresses in his custody, both maidens and widows, to the highest bidder. John also levied scutages (payments to avoid feudal military service) far more frequently than former kings and on several occasions without actually conducting a campaign. In addition he used novel forms of taxation. He twice collected income and property

levies. He experimented with customs duties. Finally he attempted to increase the annual rents on farms owed by the sheriffs for the counties which they administered. John also continually expanded the jurisdiction and hence the revenues of the royal courts at the expense of the baronial courts. In short, while in general John followed the policies set by his predecessors, he did so with extraordinary vigor and with little regard for protests.

At the same time John aroused the personal enmity of many of his barons. He was both cruel and licentious. He either murdered or procured the murder of his nephew, Arthur, duke of Brittany. When the wife of a baron made an indiscreet reference to this crime, John crushed her family's power, drove her husband and one son into exile, and starved the baroness and her eldest son to death in a dungeon. He seduced the sister of at least one great lord, and there probably were similar cases. But perhaps John's chief fault was that he trusted no one and hence no one trusted him.

Baronial Revolt.—In the autumn of 1214, King John returned from an expedition against King Philip Augustus of France. John and his allies had been crushingly defeated. This blow to the king's military prestige greatly encouraged the discontented barons. A group of these lords met at Bury St. Edmunds to discuss their grievances. These nobles not only hated John personally, but also they felt that he had deprived them of specific things to which they were entitled, such as lands, castles, privileges, and hereditary offices.

With the barons was Stephen Langton, archbishop of Canterbury, who had suffered from King John's enmity. Since he had been elected archbishop in the papal court without the king's assent, John had refused to admit him to England. For seven years Langton had waited in France until peace between John and Pope Innocent III allowed him to assume his office. During that time his relatives and friends were driven from England by John. Langton was one of the most able theologians and canon lawyers of his day. Having devoted a large part of his time to applying canon law throughout Christendom, he believed that, just as there was a canon law to govern the internal polity of the church and its relations to the lay world, there should be a recognized system of law to rule the affairs of secular states. Langton persuaded the barons to suppress for the moment their personal hatreds and ambitions and to sponsor a general program which would appeal to the entire feudal class. The assembled barons swore in the abbey church of Bury St. Edmunds that if John refused to grant their demands, they would wage war against the king. While it is impossible to discover which lords attended this meeting at Bury St. Edmunds, it seems probable that they numbered about a fifth of the English baronage.

In January 1215 the rebellious barons conferred in London with their king, who listened to their grievances and promised to give them an answer by Easter. Between January and June 1215, John's policy was extremely complicated. He had no intention of surrendering any of the royal authority and he was certain that eventually he could crush his foes. But only a small part of the four fifths of the English baronage not in the rebel ranks was willing to support the king actively, since most of the barons disliked both parties and remained neutral. Hence John sent agents to Flanders and Aquitaine to hire mercenary troops. He also sent men throughout England to place the royal castles in a state of defense. Then he dispatched messengers to Pope Innocent III, whose vassal he was, to complain of the behavior of the barons. At the same time the king engaged in more or less continuous negotiations with the rebels.

The barons committed their first overt act of rebellion in April, when they gathered in arms at Stamford. Thence they marched to lay siege to the great royal castle of Northampton. Finding this castle too strong for them, they moved against Bedford, which was held by one of their number. The barons knew that John was mustering troops and would soon have an army which they could not meet in the field. Since they needed a secure refuge, they opened negotiations with the citizens of London and on May 17 they occupied the city without meeting any resistance. The capture of London was the victory which won Magna Carta. Since John could hardly hope to collect a force large enough to expel the rebels from the city, his only course was to make peace.

Issuance.—On June 15, 1215, King John and his supporters met the rebel leaders on a meadow called Runnymede lying in the valley of the river Thames between Windsor and Staines. The barons presented to the king a document embodying their demands—the Articles of the Barons. John agreed to accept the demands and ordered his clerks to attach his seal to the document. Then the royal clerks set to work to incorporate the clauses of the articles in a formal charter. This was no simple task. The clauses of the articles were not very well arranged and many were loosely drawn and hence vague. The expert royal clerks rearranged the clauses and tightened the wording. Some changes were made in the text—presumably by mutual consent. On June 19, King John notified his officials that peace had been made and directed them to execute the provisions of the charter, which was to be read publicly in every shire. Thus it seems likely that a complete draft had been made by June 19. But the work of the royal clerks continued. There was to be a copy for every sheriff and for every cathedral chapter—a total of some 47 copies. It seems likely that this task took several weeks. Moreover, since the clerks improved the drafts to some extent as they proceeded, all the copies are not exactly alike. Four of these copies are still extant: one in Lincoln cathedral, one in Salisbury cathedral, two in the British Museum in London. That at Lincoln is generally believed to be the nearest perfect.

Content.—The provisions of Magna Carta fall naturally into three groups. Fifteen chapters treat the feudal relations between the king and his vassals. Thirty-two are concerned primarily with the procedures and policies of the royal administration. These 47 chapters seek to redress general grievances—mostly long-standing ones. They could have been aimed at Henry II or Richard I as appropriately as at John. The last 12 chapters canvass the immediate situation—the king's quarrel with his barons and the resulting revolt. They express practical terms of peace rather than basic principles of law.

The chapters on feudal relations discuss such questions as the relief to be paid by the heir of a tenant-in-chief of the crown, the marriage of ladies in the king's wardship, and the custody of fiefs during minorities. Only one of these clauses is of modern interest. The 12th chapter provides that no scutage or aid could be levied without the "common counsel of our realm" except for three occasions on which aids were sanctioned by feudal custom: the ransoming of the king if he were captured, the knighting of his eldest son, and the marrying of his eldest daughter. The 14th chapter defines the body competent to give this "common counsel of the realm" as an assembly of all tenants-in-chief of the crown. As the king had many petty tenants-in-chief and hence this assembly would have been large and unwieldy, it is rather doubtful that it ever was summoned. This chapter, in fact, was dropped when the charter was reissued in 1216. But the principle embodied in it was observed. John's successors did not levy such scutages or aids without the consent of some assembly. For a while it was usually simply the great council of barons and prelates which was called, but later this became a prime function of Parliament. Hence the principle that the government could not ask for a special levy without the approval of some competent assembly was clearly expressed in Magna Carta.

Most of the chapters dealing with the policies and procedures of the government are also of temporary importance. The problems which they solved were of that day and are now forgotten. Some of them severely hampered the financial administration and were omitted when the charter was reissued. Chapter 21, providing that earls and barons could be amerced only by their peers, is probably the remote origin of the privileges of the peerage. But the most significant clause is chapter 39, which states that no free man can be arrested, imprisoned, deprived of his property, outlawed, exiled, or "in any way destroyed" except by "legal judgment of his peers or by the law of the land." Scholars have argued and will continue to argue about what this meant to the men of the time, but all admit that it forbade arbitrary action by the government. It was a guarantee of "due process of law"—we simply cannot be sure what sort of process is described. In all probability it meant trial in a feudal court by one's peers, when that was the proper procedure for the case, and otherwise by the established customary law.

The last group of chapters discussing John's relations with the rebel barons and their allies are no longer of any interest except to the historian. The last chapter attempted to create machinery by which John could be compelled to observe the charter. Twenty-five barons were to be elected to serve as a committee to hear complaints. If the king refused to correct the grievances which this committee presented to him, they were to wage war on him. The problem was a real one—how to oblige the king to obey the law which he recognized—but the establishment of a partisan commission was not an adequate solution.

Significance.—The conception of government limited by law was implicit in the feudal system. The feudal custom in each fief, be it petty barony or kingdom, was molded by the vassals of the lord in his court. Every feudal lord was subject to the law made in his court. Magna Carta makes this explicit for the kingdom of England. John admitted that he was bound by law. Then chapter 39 (cited above) safeguards the individual from arbitrary action by the government. It is true that Magna Carta did not apply to all the people of England. Its first chapter clearly defines the beneficiaries: "all the freemen of our realm." This included the whole feudal class, agricultural tenants by such free tenures as socage, and probably the townsmen. The mass of the agricultural population was excluded. But as that agricultural population, the villeins, obtained freedom, they fell heir to the rights granted by the charter. Thus the principles of limited monarchy and individual liberties are embedded in Magna Carta.

Later History.—The Englishmen of the later Middle Ages fully realized the importance of Magna Carta as an admission of the king's submission to the law. Whenever the barons or later the Parliament felt that the king was being too high-handed, they were inclined to insist that he confirm Magna Carta. It was confirmed 44 times before the death of Henry V (1413–1422). For the men of this period it was still a living document. Its next great era began in the reign of Elizabeth (1558–1603). Lawyers and scholars used it to confound contemporary monarchs. This was especially true during the reigns of the first two Stuarts (1603–1649), who were inclined to base their procedure on the practices of the Tudor monarchs (1485–1603) and whose opponents sought medieval precedents to oppose them. Magna Carta was used extensively by the great Sir Edward Coke (1552–1634). And it was Coke and his contemporaries and their immediate successors who wrote the legal treatises which shaped the thought of men like Thomas Jefferson. Thus Magna Carta forms part at least of the background of the political ideas which shaped the United States.

SIDNEY PAINTER,
The Johns Hopkins University.

Bibliography.—The standard scholarly work on Magna Carta itself is W. S. McKechnie's *Magna Carta* (Glasgow 1914). The most recent account of the political and constitutional background is given in J. E. A. Jolliffe, *The Constitutional History of Medieval England* (London 1937). Sir Maurice Powicke's *Stephen Langton* (Oxford 1928) is extremely important for an understanding of the charter's relation to the political ideas of the time. Sidney Painter's *The Reign of King John* (Baltimore 1949) discusses the background of the charter and the document itself. For discussion of important details *Magna Carta Commemoration Essays* (London 1917) is very useful. The later history of Magna Carta is thoroughly and ably covered by two books by Faith Thompson, *The First Century of Magna Carta* (Minneapolis 1925) and *Magna Carta, Its Role in the Making of the English Constitution* (Minneapolis 1948). A more recent study is J. C. Holt's *Magna Carta* (London 1965).

MAGNA GRAECIA, măg′nà grē′shà, "Great Greece," the name commonly given in ancient times to that part of southern Italy which was inhabited by Greek colonists. Apparently the name was in use as early as the time of Pythagoras (586–506 B.C.). Strabo includes the Greek cities of Sicily under the appellation, but the name refers generally only to the Greek cities in the south of Italy, including those on the shores of the Tarentine Gulf and the Bruttian Peninsula, with Velia, Posidonia and Laüs, on the west coast of Lucania. The name was not at first territorial or coextensive with any region, but applied merely to the Greek cities on the coasts. Cumae was the most ancient of all the Greek settlements in Italy, but from its remote position it was in a great measure isolated from the later Greek settlements. The Achaeans were the real colonizers of southern Italy, their first

settlement being Sybaris (720 B.C.). A few years later (708 B.C.) Spartan colonists founded Tarentum (modern Taranto), and to counteract their encroachments the Achaeans founded Metapontum, on the frontier of the territory of the Tarentines, between 700 and 680 B.C. The Locrians founded further south the city known as Locri Epizephyrii, nearly contemporary with Crotona (710 B.C.). The Chalcidic colony of Rhegium, on the Strait of Messina, claims to have been more ancient even than Sybaris. The Greek cities on the shores of Bruttium and Lucania were, Velia excepted (540 B.C.), offshoots from the earlier settlements, and not founded by colonists direct from Greece. The arrival of Pythagoras at Crotona (530 B.C.) produced a marked change in the cities of Magna Graecia, and led to the introduction of great political changes. He and his followers were ultimately expelled from Crotona. Very little of the early history is known. The coast cities were essentially mercantile. Trade was well developed, and in the 6th century there was an extensive commerce, especially with Greece. The colonists who pushed to the interior subdued the opposing natives and developed the fertile plains into agricultural settlements. There was a high development of intellectual life. At various times there were temporary alliances among the cities. Warfare was common, and to this fact is largely due the decline of the territory. Magna Graecia comprised the provinces of Campania, Apulia, Iapygia, Lucania, and Bruttium.

MAGNALIA CHRISTI AMERICANA, măg-nā′lĭ-à krĭs′tī à-mĕr-ĭ-kā′nà, an ecclesiastical church history of New England, from 1620 to 1628, published by Cotton Mather in 1702. It treats more extensively of the early history of the country than its title seems to indicate, and is divided into seven books: the first treating of the early discoveries of America and the voyage to New England; the second is *Lives of the Governors;* the third, *Lives of many Reverend, Learned and Holy Divines;* the fourth, *Of Harvard University;* the fifth, *The Faith and the Order in the Church of New England;* the sixth, *Discoveries and Demonstrations of the Divine Providence in Remarkable Mercies and Judgments on Many Particular Persons;* the seventh, *Disturbances Given to the Churches of New England.* In the sixth book the author gives accounts of the wonders of the invisible world, of worthy people succored when in dire distress, of the sad ending of many wicked ones, and of the cases of witchcraft at Salem and other places.

MAGNENTIUS, măg-nĕn′shĭ-ŭs, **Flavius Popilius,** Roman emperor of the West: d. Aug. 11, 353. Having been entrusted by Constans with a high military command he availed himself of his office to plot the emperor's overthrow. On Jan. 18, 350, presenting himself in imperial purple at a great banquet given by one of the conspirators at Autun, he was saluted with the title of Augustus; and assassins sent for the purpose having dispatched Constans, Magnentius was acknowledged as emperor by all the western provinces except Illyria. Constantius II, on hearing of his brother's murder, hastened from the confines of Persia and defeated Magnentius (351). These disasters led to the defection of all the countries that had recognized the usurper. Constantius then became master of the entire empire, and Magnentius fled to Gaul, where he committed suicide.

MAGNESIA, măg-nē′shà, the oxide of magnesium, MgO. See MAGNESIUM.

MAGNESITE, măg′nê-sīt, an industrial mineral, magnesium carbonate, $MgCO_3$, in which silica magnesium compounds, calcium carbonate, and iron oxide are always present. It has a hardness of 3.5 to 4.5 (Mohs scale) and a specific gravity of 3.0 to 3.1, and is colored white, grey, brown, or yellow, ranging from transparent to opaque. Magnesite occurs in three forms:

(1) As crystals, commonly a resultant of hydrothermal activity by magnesium solutions associated with granitic intrusives, it is found in Manchuria, Russia, Austria, Czechoslovakia, Brazil, British Columbia, Quebec, Washington, and Nevada.

(2) As sedimentary beds, it is cryptocrystalline, dense, and exceedingly fine. Usually shallow, the beds may be of great lateral extent, typical of desert conditions, as in San Bernardino and Kern counties, Calif., and Clark County, Nev.

(3) As veins and replacements in other rocks, it occurs in the Coast and Sierra Nevada ranges, Calif., and in deposits in Lower California of Mexico and in Venezuela.

Magnesite also is made synthetically by processing dolomite and sea water.

Magnesite is used chiefly in the production of refractory bricks and in the manufacture of chemicals, cement, fertilizers, and artificial stone flooring.

See also MINERAL WEALTH OF THE WORLD.

MAGNESIUM, măg-nē′shĭ-ŭm, a silvery white, very light, metallic metal, which, although it does not occur free in nature, is the eighth most abundant element in the earth's crust. Its mineral compounds are very widely distributed in most countries of the world, and sea water, which contains about 0.13 per cent magnesium, is virtually an inexhaustible source.

History.—Magnesium, in an impure state, was first obtained by Sir Humphry Davy in 1808. He electrolyzed a mixture of magnesia and mercuric oxide and distilled the mercury from the magnesium amalgam. In 1829, Antoine Bussy obtained the metal in larger quantity and in a purer form by heating anhydrous magnesium chloride to redness with potassium. On dissolving out the residual chlorides, the metal appeared as a powder which could be fused readily into globules of relatively pure metal. In 1833, Michael Faraday became the first to produce metallic magnesium by electrolysis of a fused magnesium salt, and his method is the forerunner of the modern electrolytic process. Robert Wilhelm Eberhard von Bunsen was the first to recognize the importance of an anhydrous cell feed. In 1852 he electrolyzed fused anhydrous magnesium chloride, and Augustus Matthiessen, in 1856, improved this electrolyte by substituting mixed potassium, magnesium, and ammonium chloride, which was more easily prepared in the anhydrous form.

The first commercial production of magnesium occurred in 1866 in Germany by using a modified Bunsen electrolytic cell. Germany led the way as a producer of magnesium until 1915, when, because of the 1914–1918 wartime need for pyrotechnics, it became essential to produce magnesium elsewhere, and the United States, the United Kingdom, France, and Canada all entered the field. During 1916–1917 eight companies produced magnesium in the United States. However, with the war's end, only the Dow Chemical Company and the American Magnesium Corporation continued production. In 1927 the latter company discontinued this activity and only Dow remained.

Peacetime requirements for magnesium were sufficient to cause small increases in production and some advances were made in the technology. It was the immense stimulus of World War II which advanced magnesium to the forefront as a structural metal. Confronted by huge military requirements for pyrotechnics and for a light-weight structural metal for use in building aircraft and airborne equipment, the United States government undertook construction of magnesium production facilities on an unprecedented scale. Between 1939 and 1943, 15 plants were built in the United States, 13 by the government and 2 by private companies.

Production of primary magnesium in the United States reached its peak in 1943 at 183,584 tons, and the peak of consumption was reached in 1944 at 132,698 tons—all for war purposes. In 1944 military needs decreased drastically and the government began to close its plants. By the end of 1945 the defense plants had been shut out and only Dow's plant at Freeport, Texas, remained active. Six of the government-owned plants were reactivated in 1951 and produced at varying capacities during the Korean War.

The history of magnesium production and consumption in the United Kingdom, Canada, and Germany has followed a somewhat similar pattern to that in the United States, in that production has flourished in wartime and fallen in peacetime. Various other countries, including Norway, France, Japan, Switzerland, Italy, Australia, and Russia have produced magnesium. Only Norway and Canada, with large quantities of raw material and power available at low cost, are able to produce at prices competitive with those of the producers in the United States. Information on production in Russia is unreliable. The table shows a summary of world production in recent years by countries.

Occurrence.—The principal magnesium-rich minerals are magnesite, dolomite, hydromagnesite, brucite, carnallite, kieserite, kainite, serpentine, and olivine. Those which are abundant and widespread in the United States are magnesite, $MgCO_3$, which occurs in crystalline form in many parts of the nation and in cryptocrystalline form in California; brucite, $Mg(OH)_2$, which occurs in commercial quantity only in Nevada, where it adjoins very large magnesite deposits; and dolomite, $CaCO_3$. $MgCO_3$, which is widespread throughout the United States. Olivine, Mg_2Fe SiO_4, and serpentine, $H_4Mg_3Si_2O_9$, the magnesium silicates, occur in huge deposits in the United States, but have not as yet been used commercially as a source of magnesium. In many of the above-mentioned mineral sources magnesium is readily available by calcining the mineral to produce magnesia, which then can be used for thermal reduction to the metal, or the oxide may be transformed to magnesium chloride for electrolytic reduction. Sea water, waste liquors from the potash industry, and well brines from salt wells are the other sources of magnesium chloride readily made suitable for use as cell feed in the electrolytic production of magnesium metal.

Methods of Production.—Two main types of production processes for the extraction of metallic magnesium have emerged. The first of these, the electrolytic decomposition of fused magnesium chloride, has become the cheapest and is used extensively in the United States. Its only disadvantage is that a cell feed of high purity is required. The second type, thermal reduction of

WORLD PRODUCTION OF MAGNESIUM METAL BY COUNTRIES
(metric tons)[1]

	1948	1961	1962	1963	1964	1965
Canada	...	6,927	7,997	8,080	8,485	10,100
China (mainland)[2]	...	1,000	1,000	1,000	1,000	1,000
France	546	2,075	2,174	1,797	989	2,832
Germany, West:						
Secondary	...	2,912	3,288	3,187	3,141	2,187
Hungary	0	40	29	27	9	0
Italy	0	5,617	5,704	5,810	6,028	6,313
Japan:						
Primary	0	2,247	2,087	2,439	2,937	3,785
Secondary	...	2,776	1,933	1,412	2,248	4,164
Norway	0	14,531	14,582	18,081	20,935	26,432
Poland[3]	...	231	266	266	247	258
USSR[2]	...	30,000	32,000	32,000	32,000	33,000
United Kingdom[3]	2,540	5,286	5,043	4,736	4,784	5,400
United States:						
Primary	9,075	36,963	62,555	68,805	72,110	73,809
Secondary	6,852	7,371	8,718	8,369	10,696	12,353
World Total[4]	*10,000*	*72,000*	*99,000*	*108,000*	*115,000*	*127,000*

Source: United Nations Statistical Yearbook, 1963. Unless otherwise noted, the figures relate to the total production of primary magnesium from domestic and imported ores and concentrates. Secondary magnesium is derived from scrap.
[1] One metric ton = 1.1 short tons.
[2] Figures from U.S. Bureau of Mines.
[3] Includes secondary magnesium.
[4] Primary magnesium only; excluding mainland China and USSR.

magnesium oxide by ferrosilicon or carbon, while applicable with ease to the main mineral compounds of magnesium, is subject to the economic drawbacks associated with batch processes, such as high labor costs and lost production time during cleanouts of furnaces at the end of each run.

In the electrolytic process the most desirable cell feed is anhydrous magnesium chloride. The source of this magnesium chloride varies with the particular installation and may be sea water, waste liquors from the potash industry, salt well brines, magnesite, dolomite, or brucite. Although it is important that water should be eliminated carefully, complete dehydration is not considered essential.

Where the starting material is sea water, the intake from the sea is treated with lime to precipitate magnesium hydroxide, which is neutralized with hydrochloric acid to form dilute magnesium chloride solution. This is then evaporated and substantially dehydrated to give magnesium chloride containing two molecules of water, which is reasonably efficient as cell feed. Alternatively, the magnesium hydrate precipitate may be calcined and the resulting magnesium oxide treated with chlorine gas, usually recycled from the reduction step, to give anhydrous magnesium chloride.

Where the source material is magnesite, dolomite, or brucite, the first step is calcination to give magnesium oxide, which is treated in turn with chlorine gas, thus producing anhydrous magnesium chloride, which is suitable for cell feed without any need for dehydration.

The electrolytic processes, regardless of the source of raw material, are basically the same as used by Faraday; they are based on the decomposition, by a direct electric current, of substantially anhydrous magnesium chloride into metallic magnesium and chlorine gas.

The modern cell is a fabricated steel structure or casting insulated to conserve heat. The size, design, and number of cells in series vary with the installation. The anodes are carbon and the cathodes, on which the liberated magnesium collects, are iron or steel. When the amount of liberated magnesium is sufficient, it rises to the surface of the electrolyte, because it is lighter than the bath and is dipped or pumped off for casting. Magnesium produced by this method has a purity of 99.9 per cent.

In the thermal reduction process, using ferrosilicon, magnesite and dolomite are the common starting materials. Dolomite has the advantage that its lime content acts as the slagging agent for any silica which is present. The starting material is ground, mixed with pulverized fer-

A light-weight magnesium delivery platform of the United States Air Force is dropped from a cargo plane and lowered to earth by parachutes.

Brooks & Perkins, Inc.

rosilicon, briquetted, and charged into steel retorts. The charge is heated under vacuum to such temperature (approximately 2200° F.) that the magnesium evolves in vapor form and condenses in the cool end of the retort. It is then remelted and cast into magnesium ingots (99.5 per cent purity, or better).

When carbon is used as a reducing agent, magnesium oxide, from a magnesite or dolomite source, is mixed with a carbon in suitable form and heated to approximately 3600° F. in a closed electric arc furnace. Magnesium is evolved as vapor together with carbon monoxide, and this is swept from the furnace into a cooling chamber. The reaction has a very strong tendency to reverse, unless the gases are cooled very rapidly by "shock" methods; such cooling is accomplished by using natural gas, hydrogen, or other suitable agents. The magnesium is deposited on suitably cooled surfaces in the form of magnesium dust with a magnesia covering. Magnesium metal of 99.5 per cent purity or better is then distilled from this mixture as a final step.

Physical Properties.—The principal physical properties of pure magnesium (99.9 per cent) are given below:

Symbol		Mg
Atomic number		12
Atomic weight		24.32
Crystal structure		close-packed, hexagonal
Mass numbers of the isotopes		24, 25, 26
Relative frequency of the isotopes	per cent	77, 11.5, 11.1
Density at 20° C.	gram/cu. cm.	1.74
(68° F.)	lb./cu. ft.	108.6
Electrical resistivity at 20° C.	microhms/cm.	4.46
(68° F.)	ohms/circular Mil-foot	26.83
Mean coefficient of expansion, in./in./deg.	(20°–500° C.) (68°–932° F.)	0.0000299 0.0000166
Mean specific heat	(0° – 100° C.)	0.249
Latent heat of fusion	calories/gram Btu./lb.	88.8 159.8
Latent heat of evaporation	calories/gram Btu./lb.	1,300–1,500 2,340–2,700
Thermal conductivity, 0°–100° C. (32°–212° F.)	cal/cm/cm²/° C./sec. Btu./in./ft.²/° F./hr.	0.376 1,090
Modulus of elasticity	kg/mm² lb./sq. in.	4,570 6.5×10^6
Modulus of rigidity	kg/mm² lb./sq. in.	1,700 2.42×10^6

Chemical Properties.—Chemically, magnesium is a dyad. It is a very reactive element, as is indicated by the fact that it exists in many combined forms in nature. The metal exhibits good resistance to the atmosphere, although the surface becomes dull grey in color owing to the formation of a protective film of oxide. Magnesium resists attack by pure water and most alkaline solutions, but is not resistant to most acid solutions or to those containing chlorides. It is resistant to many common organic chemicals. Protection of the surface may be desirable in many applications; this protection may consist of chemical surface treatment, application of paint systems, or a combination of these measures.

Alloys.—Pure magnesium has only moderate strength; but since its light weight is particularly advantageous from the point of view of many structural applications, it has been alloyed extensively with aluminum, zinc, manganese, or combinations of these, and, to lesser extent, with zirconium, thorium, and some of the rare earths. Aluminum and zinc improve the strength, manganese enhances corrosion resistance, zirconium produces a finer grain structure and improved mechanical properties, rare earths and thorium improve the properties at elevated temperatures.

The magnesium alloys exhibit properties similar to those of pure magnesium, but possess, in varying degrees, greatly increased strength. They are among the lightest of structural metals, being about two thirds the weight of aluminum and one fourth that of steel. They have excellent machining properties; a good surface finish and high dimensional accuracy may be obtained with heavy cuts and at high speeds with low requirements of power.

Magnesium alloys are fabricated in the form of sand, permanent mold and die castings, forgings, sheet and plate, extruded shapes, tubing, and wire. Recent advances in magnesium technology have overcome forming problems associated with its hexagonal crystal structure. Forming of wrought products is accomplished by the commonly used processes. Also magnesium and its alloys may be joined by riveting, bolting, screwing, and by the use of adhesives. Welding is commonly done by modern arc-welding techniques and by resistance methods.

Uses.—The uses of magnesium alloys can be divided into two types: nonstructural and structural. Among the important nonstructural applications of magnesium is its use as an important alloying constituent of other metals, the most common application of which is in the production of certain aluminum alloys, where it enhances the strength, corrosion resistance, and weldability. It is also used in large quantities as a reducing agent in some metallurgical production processes; for example, titanium, uranium, hafnium, and others. Pure magnesium is also employed as a deoxidizer and desulphurizer in the metallurgical industry. It is used as a scavenger in the production of brass, bronze, and nickel, and in combination with calcium to remove bismuth from lead. In the production of iron it nodularizes the structure and hence increases the ductility of the metal. Miscellaneous applications include the use of pure magnesium in the form of powder as an ingredient of pyrotechnics. Marine and railroad signals, miscellaneous fireworks, and photographic applications are similar, but limited to peacetime uses. Shavings and coarse powder are also used in the well-known Grignard reaction for synthesizing certain organic chemicals.

One of the largest and most important nonstructural uses of magnesium is in sacrificial or cathodic protection of other metals. Magnesium, because of its high position in the electromotive series of metals, acts as an anode when connected to a structure called the cathode, which requires protection from its external or internal environment. It has been used to protect such metal structures as underground oil and gas lines, oil well casings, buried tanks of all types, telephone and telegraph cables, marine structures, such as steel piers and ships hulls, and such equipment as industrial and domestic hot-water heaters. A magnesium anode, when connected to such an installation by a suitable conductor, will dissolve gradually over a period of years. During this time the structure remains intact with this protection.

The structural uses of magnesium in its alloyed forms have grown to rank about equally with the nonstructural uses from the viewpoint of tonnage consumed. Modern developments in production, and particularly in fabricating, techniques have been responsible for extending the structural uses so widely. The best-known applications of magnesium structural alloys have been, and still are, in the aircraft industry, where, in the form of sand, permanent mold and die castings, extrusions and forgings, they form such aircraft parts as landing gear, engine parts, many parts of the fuselage and airborne equipment. In recent years magnesium alloys are also finding very substantial use in highway and railroad transport. Magnesium, with its excellent combination of light weight, high strength, and stiffness, is a logical material for structural members of trucks, trailers, buses, and railroad rolling stock. Similarly, equipment which moves or has to be moved by exertion of energy may be improved by lightweight magnesium alloys. Also, where it is desirable to reduce inertia or reciprocating and moving parts of machines, magnesium alloys are a logical choice as the material of construction. Somewhat similarly, the portable tool industry uses magnesium alloys for a wide variety of manually handled equipment.

Compounds.—The most important compounds of magnesium are those from which the metal is derived (see under *Occurrence*). Some of these same materials are used for the production of caustic-calcined and refractory magnesia, the important applications for which are magnesia bricks and refractories for high-temperature uses.

Other important magnesium compounds are magnesium chloride, used as a dressing and filler for cotton and woolen fabrics and as a filler for papers and building products, in cement, refrigerating brines, and ceramics; magnesium carbonate, magnesium bicarbonate and magnesium hydroxide of various grades, used as filler for insulating materials and for chemical and medicinal purposes; and magnesium sulphate (Epsom salts), used chiefly for medicinal purposes.

See also MINERAL WEALTH OF THE WORLD.

I. H. JENKS,
Head, Publications Division, Aluminium Laboratories Limited, Kingston, Ontario, Canada.

MAGNET, măg'nĕt, a physical device characterized by the property of magnetic polarity and capable of attracting certain other objects to it by the force of its magnetism. It consists usually of a suitably formed piece of metal whose opposite ends possess centers of magnetic attraction or repulsion called the *poles* of the magnet.

Magnets are of three general types: (1) those in which the magnetic properties are inherent within the substance, known as *natural magnets;* (2) those in which the property of magnetism is induced by artificial means either permanently or semipermanently, and known as *artificial magnets;* and (3) those in which the property of magnetism is acquired only temporarily by the action of an electrical current flowing through a coil of wire (solenoid) surrounding a soft iron core, and known as an *electromagnet*.

Theories of the Magnet.—According to an earlier and still partially usable concept known as the *molecular theory of magnetism,* an unmagnetized, but potentially magnetizable, substance may be thought of as consisting of a host of minute molecular particles possessing opposite magnetic "charges" (positive and negative) at their individual diametrical extremes. These particles are, as a group, disorganized and lacking in any common orientation. When the property of magnetism is acquired, the particles become aligned in parallel arrays, with the individual positively charged ends (north poles) pointing collectively in one direction and the negative (south) poles together pointing in the opposite direction. Thus a unified magnetic field is formed, and a full-scale magnetic polarity is achieved. Modern electron theory follows a somewhat related reasoning, but abandons the charge concept and ascribes magnetic polarity to the acquired orientation of small magnetic *domains* or grains of many-atom proportions within the substance. The actual process involves an alignment of the magnetic moments associated with spinning electrons in the atoms of the substance to bring these moments into parallelism with an applied external field. (See MAGNETISM—*Ferromagnetism.*)

Magnetostatics.—Lines of force (called *flux*) emanate from and flow from north pole to south pole between the poles of a single magnet or between two adjacently placed magnets as shown in Figs. A and B, respectively. A basic law of magnetism states that the ends of magnets having the same magnetic polarity repel and those having opposite polarity attract each other.

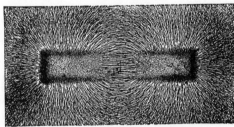

Fig. A

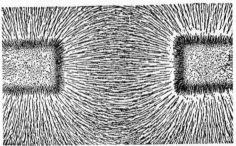

Fig. B

The force of magnetic attraction between two magnets varies in a fashion very similar to that expressed in Sir Isaac Newton's law of universal gravitation (see GRAVITATION); magnetic attraction (or repulsion) varies directly as the product of the pole strengths of the two magnets and inversely as the square of the distance between their poles, considered as points. This law was discovered by Charles Augustin de Coulomb in 1785.

Symbolically represented, it is: $F = C\, m_1 m_2 / r^2$, where m_1 and m_2 represent the strengths of the respective magnetic poles, r is the distance between them, and C is a constant involving the magnetic *permeability* of the medium through which the force is acting. $C = 1/\mu$, where μ represents the magnetic permeability. (μ has the value 1 in a vacuum and is approximately equal to 1 in air and in all nonmagnetic bodies.) F represents the resulting force between the two poles expressed in dynes, if r is in centimeters. The dyne is the unit of force required to give to a mass of one gram an acceleration of one centimeter per second per second.

If two thin, light bar magnets are supported close to each other in a horizontal position by means of pivots through their centers, they will swing toward each other in such a fashion that the north or positive pole of one points toward the south or negative pole of the other. If the magnets are forcibly arranged with like poles pointing toward each other, these like poles will repel each other and the magnets will spin around their centers in such a way as to resist this alignment and will assume a stable orientation with unlike poles adjacent.

It is a fact of common observance that some substances, such as iron and steel, are attracted strongly by any form of magnet, whereas other substances, such as aluminum, copper, brass, and zinc, are not. The difference lies in the aforementioned property of magnetic permeability. This quantity, μ, is a measure of the ease with which a given magnetic flux may be established in any substance compared with air. Substances which are strongly attracted by a magnetic field and which are readily magnetized are known as *ferromagnetic* substances; examples include iron and steel, cobalt, nickel, magnetite, and a few alloys of manganese. Substances having a comparatively weak aptitude for being magnetized or for being attracted by a magnetic field, but which experience this attraction in greater degree than that for a vacuum (that is, which have a permeability greater than, but not far in excess of, unity) are classified as *paramagnetic* substances; examples include air, oxygen, cast iron, ferrous sulphate, ferric sulphate, and palladium. Those substances whose capacity for acquiring magnetism is less than that of a vacuum and which under certain conditions are even slightly repelled by proximity to either pole of a magnet are termed *diamagnetic*. Diamagnetic substances usually tend to align themselves across, rather than parallel to, magnetic lines of force. Examples are bismuth, antimony, zinc, and glass.

Natural Magnets.—Magnetic rock material is found in nature in a form of iron ore known scientifically as magnetite (q.v.). The historical English name for this mineralized rock possessing magnetic properties is *loadstone* (alternate form, *lodestone*). The word "magnet" derives from the Latin word *magnes*, translatable as "(stone) of Magnesia" (undoubtedly a loadstone), which stems in turn from early discoveries of the native iron ore magnetite in large quantities near Magnesia in Asia Minor. In the 4th century B.C., Plato regarded "magnetic virtue" as divine. The mystical Samothracian rings, cast of magnetic iron ore, were objects of superstitious worship among ancient peoples. These mystical ideas persisted well into the 15th century. The first practical use of the mariner's compass began in the late 12th century, when it was discovered that a loadstone suspended on a piece of wood and floated in water assumed an orientation along a (magnetic) north-south line.

Permanent Magnets.—Permanent magnets may be created only from substances which possess a strong capacity for acquiring and maintaining a magnetic polarity. Substances of relatively high permeability, such as hard steel, cobalt, nickel, and numerous alloys thereof, possess this ability. Permanent magnetism may be acquired by one of several different processes by which the magnetic moments of the spinning electrons composing the substance become preferentially orientated to produce magnetic polarity: (1) striking a sharp, hard blow to a magnetically permeable substance while it is aligned parallel to the direction of the earth's magnetic field (along a magnetic meridian); (2) bringing such a substance in contact with another magnet or stroking it with a pole of this magnet; (3) placing a ferromagnetic substance in the electromagnetic field associated with a powerful electric current—usually by inserting it in a current-carrying solenoid; or (4) heating a highly permeable substance and allowing it to cool while its principal axis is maintained in the direction of the earth's magnetic field.

Permanent magnets may possess several distinct structural shapes. A *bar magnet* consists of a single, straight piece of metal, either cylindrical or rectangular in its cross section, with its positive and negative poles located at opposite ends. A *horseshoe magnet* is curved in this characteristic shape so that the positive and negative poles form separate, but more closely adjacent, ends. This type of magnet has frequent application in devices where mechanical rotation and generation of electricity are functions, such as in magnetogenerators, speedometers, and d'Arsonval galvanometers. In the first two cases rotation of a coil between the poles of a horseshoe magnet continuously cuts lines of force joining the magnetic poles and produces an electric current; in the third case, passage of current through a coil rotates the coil in the field of the permanent magnet. (See also GALVANOMETER; GENERATORS, ELECTRIC.) A *compound magnet* or *magnetic battery* is composed of a group of laminated magnets bound together with like poles adjacent to give increased pole strength.

Electromagnets.—These magnets usually consist of a coil of specially fine insulated wire surrounding a core of soft iron (the solecore). The property of magnetism may be induced temporarily in this core and will disappear almost immediately upon cutoff of the current flow by a suitable switch or by a make-and-break circuit. Because of the purpose for which such electromagnets are most commonly employed, in lifting and depositing scrap metal, actuating electrical relays, telegraphic devices, doorbells, annunciators, and a host of similar contrivances, it is desirable that no residual magnetism be displayed by the core and that its property of attraction for other substances be nullified almost instantaneously upon release of the current flow. Accordingly, substances, such as soft iron, which are weak in their ability for retention of an induced magnetic field are chosen for this usage. See also ELECTROMAGNETISM.

The Compass as a Magnet.—As expressed in the classic work *De magnete, magneticisque corporibus* (1600) by the British experimental scientist William Gilbert (q.v.), the earth itself may be considered a huge magnet in spheroidal form. Its total magnetic field is equivalent to that which would be produced by 800 quintillion (billion billion) parallel one-pound bar magnets, if it were possible to locate these at the earth's center. Because of this magnetic field of the earth, direction finding by magnetic means is made possible. A simple bar magnet suspended in a horizontal plane by a thread passing vertically through its center or caused to float on a block of wood or a cork in a horizontal position in a pan of undisturbed water will assume an orientation directed toward the north and south magnetic poles of the earth. A lightweight magnetized needle, supported by a pivot pin at its center, similarly aligns itself along a magnetic meridian. Each is an example of a rudimentary magnetic compass (see COMPASS, MAGNETIC). The end of the magnetized object which points toward the north magnetic pole is termed the north-seeking end or simply the *north pole* of the magnet; that end directed toward the earth's south magnetic pole is termed the south-seeking or *south pole*. Through convention, these poles are also sometimes known in physics as the positive and negative poles, respectively. The suspended bar or needle will assume, everywhere on or above the earth's surface, a position in a vertical plane passing through the north and south magnetic poles and known as a magnetic meridian. This direction of compass pointing is indicated on a magnetic map of the earth's surface by an *isogonic line* (q.v.), a line passing through all points of equal compass variation (declination) from the direction of the true or geographic poles. If a thin, magnetized needle is mounted in a similar fashion in a vertical plane so that it is free to rotate around a horizontal axis, it becomes a *dipping needle* (q.v.) or *magnetic inclinometer,* which measures the vertical component of the earth's magnetic field. Since the earth's magnetic lines of force extend outward from one magnetic pole, level off over the geomagnetic equator, and bend downward to converge on the opposite magnetic pole, the needle of this instrument will point vertically at the earth's magnetic poles and horizontally at the magnetic equator.

A magnetic compass needle is subject to any of the deflective influences peculiar to a magnet as well as to any forces which tend to alter its magnetic properties, such as (1) the proximity of other magnetized substances; (2) the receipt of any sudden, hard blow; (3) regular or random fluctuations in the earth's magnetic field, caused by sunspots and terrestrial magnetic effects; and (4) changing electrical currents produced in the earth or in its atmosphere.

See also TERRESTRIAL MAGNETISM.

FERGUS J. WOOD,
United States Coast and Geodetic Survey.

MAGNETIC POLE, măg-nĕt'ĭk, a point on the earth's surface to which the needle of a compass is directed. There are two such points, the North Magnetic Pole and the South Magnetic Pole. New research in 1965 established the former at 75.5° north latitude and 100.5° west longitude, at about the southern part of Bathurst Island, Canada, in the Arctic Ocean. At the same time the South Magnetic Pole was fixed at 66.5° south latitude and 139.9° east longitude, off the Adélie Coast in Antarctica. The magnetic poles vary in position over the years, occupying successive locations that may be 100 miles or more apart.

MAGNETISM, măg'nĕ-tĭz'm, in physics, is concerned with the magnetic forces which moving electrical charges exert on each other. Examples of such forces are (1) a beam of electrons in a vacuum—for instance, in a television tube—deflected by a nearby magnet; (2) the moving charges constituting the current in a conductor experiencing, in the presence of a magnetic field, a force which they transmit to the conductor—as in an electric motor; (3) the electrons moving around an atomic nucleus or spinning about their own axes—for example, in an atom in a magnet—exerting forces which can easily be felt as an attraction or repulsion between magnets held in one's hands. Moving charges produce magnetic fields, and magnetic fields exert forces on moving charges.

Magnetic Fields.—Magnetic fields may be demonstrated by means of powders of strongly magnetic materials, such as iron. If we prepare a powder of magnetized particles and scatter it in the vicinity of a magnet, each particle will tend to orient itself parallel to the local magnetic field. These magnetized particles will form chains which show the geometry of the field. Typical magnetic fields surrounding magnetized objects are shown in Figs. A and B of the preceding article on MAGNET. Fig. A shows the field around a bar magnet, while Fig. B shows the field between poles of opposite sign in two bar magnets. Of course, what we see in the figure is not the field itself, merely the manifestation of the field, actually the effect of the field on small magnetic particles which it has oriented.

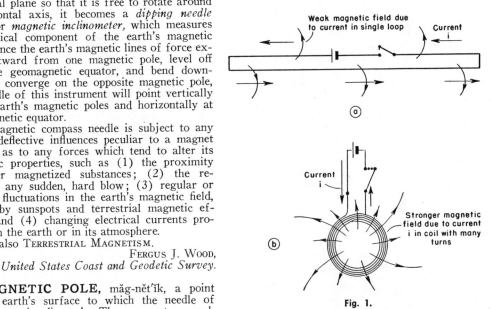

Weak magnetic field due to current in single loop

Current i

Current i

Stronger magnetic field due to current i in coil with many turns

Fig. 1.

To show the significance of a magnetic field surrounding charges in motion let us consider the simple experiment shown in Figs. 1 (a) and 1 (b) of the present article. An electric current in a wire is due to the flow of electrons along the wire. With the switch in the circuit closed and a current flowing around the circuit, the electrons have a certain momentum. That is, they tend to keep moving in the direction of motion, and forces are required to stop them. If we open the switch, thus breaking the circuit, we should expect the electrons to tend to keep on moving, like a fast-moving car after first applying the brakes. This behavior is observed, and if we notice very carefully in a darkened room, we may see a small spark jump across the terminals of the switch when it is opened. As the circuit is opened, electrons press against the bare surface of the switch at the point where the circuit is broken and tend to jump across the gap as a result of their inertia. We should expect that when the wire of the conductor, as in 1 (b), is wound into a coil, the nature of the spark at the switch when it is opened would be unchanged. With the same current, the electrons should have the same momentum and should have the same tendency to jump across the open switch. This experiment, however, reveals a marked difference. The spark in case 1 (b) is many times as great, revealing a much greater momentum, a much greater tendency to continue in motion than in case 1 (a). A detailed examination shows that this is due to the fact that the electrons are not just little individual particles each having a given mass, but the magnetic fields with which they are surrounded when in motion are a part of them and contribute to their mass. We can specify the amount of mass per unit volume associated with a magnetic field of given intensity. The greater spark in case 1 (b) can be accounted for in terms of the greater field surrounding the current in the coiled conductor and the consequently greater electromagnetic mass of the electrons.

The important part that magnetic fields play in our thinking about nature is further revealed by the manner in which a radio antenna broadcasts energy to a distant receiver. The energy supplied by an oscillator to an antenna does not move through the conducting wire, but through the space around the wire. The wire is merely a guide for the energy. This energy flow may be described in terms of the electric and magnetic fields surrounding the wire. Electric fields are necessary to maintain the current. When the current is flowing, there are additional magnetic fields. Whenever we have this combination of electric and magnetic fields in space, energy moves. The energy is guided by the wire to the antenna, where it pulsates in and out, some of it being shaken loose at every pulsation. We can pick up a part of this energy flow in a receiver and show that our electromagnetic theory of the motion of energy in space is correct.

Atoms and Molecules.—Atoms are made of a central core or nucleus, which is exceedingly small compared to the atom itself and which contains almost all the mass as well as a positive charge equal to the negative charge of its surrounding cloud of electrons.

An important point in the classification of atomic electron clouds for the purposes of magnetic analysis relates to the spinning or whirling motion of the electrons in the atoms. All atoms may be classified according to their rotational motion. Either there is no angular motion and the atom behaves mechanically like a little rigid sphere at rest or it is spinning violently and has the properties of a gyroscope to a very marked extent. It is a very striking fact that there is, in the absence of a magnetic field, no in-between region here in which we have slowly rotating atoms. The atoms are either completely at rest or rotating very fast indeed. The speed of the outer electrons is of the order of magnitude of approximately one hundredth of the velocity of light, or the surface of the atom is rotating at the rate of some millions of billions of times per second. The significance of this difference between atoms is illustrated in Fig. 2. Fig. 2 (a) shows an atom with no resultant

angular momentum or no resultant rotational motion. This is not to say that the electrons are at rest. On the contrary, there is every reason to suppose that they are in very violent motion. We merely indicate here that there is no resultant motion around an axis and, consequently, no angular momentum. If we choose an axis arbitrarily, we shall find as many electrons circulating in one sense as in the opposite. This sort of atom is analogous to an inert macroscopic object. It would behave in collisions like a marble or a baseball with no spin.

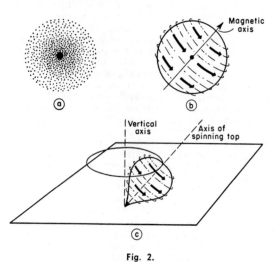

Fig. 2.

An atom of the second type, illustrated in Fig. 2 (b), is one in which there is a resultant rotary motion around an axis, labeled the "Magnetic Axis" in the illustration. This atom with its rapidly circulating electric charge has marked magnetic properties. An experimental fact about these atoms and one which has no direct analogy in the case of familiar macroscopic objects is that the rotational motion of an atom of the type shown in Fig. 2 (b) cannot be slowed down. This motion is fixed and inherent in the particle itself. An atom with angular momentum will behave like a little gyroscope, particularly if a torque or twist is applied. When an attempt is made to reorient its magnetic axis it will precess, just as a mechanical top whose point of support is so disposed that the gravitational forces tend to reorient its axis of spin will precess as illustrated in Fig. 2 (c).

Since atoms can be magnetic, we should expect atoms to form closely bound magnetically neutral pairs. Thus, for example, although individual hydrogen atoms have angular momentum and are similar to little permanently magnetized spheres, a pair of hydrogen atoms, forming an H_2 molecule, has no resultant angular momentum and is not itself a little permanently magnetized object. It resembles in some ways the pair of canceling magnets in Fig. 3 (a). Although this tendency for atoms to cancel their magnetic properties in pairs is quite common, it is not universal; they may come together to form a larger resultant, as in Fig. 3 (b). An example of this rarer sort of combination is the O_2 molecule, oxygen, which retains a resultant magnetic axis.

Similar principles govern the magnetic properties of individual atoms. Atoms with an even number of electrons tend not to have any resultant angular momentum. They behave as though the electronic angular momenta canceled in pairs, leaving a nonmagnetic atom. If an odd number of electrons is present, such a combination is impossible, and it is the atoms with odd numbers of electrons that are predominantly magnetic. Here, again, this is not a universal rule.

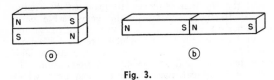

Fig. 3.

Laboratory experiments may be made to determine the magnetic strength of an atom and how it is oriented with respect to a magnetic field. These data will determine the force acting on it, if the field is not homogeneous. If the atomic magnet is pointing in the direction of the field, it will be attracted toward regions of greater field strength. If it is pointing against the field, it will be forced from regions of great field strength to regions of low field strength.

In the atomic beam experiment illustrated in Fig. 4, atoms are vaporized in a furnace, and by means of a system of slits a beam of atoms is selected and is allowed to pass through a highly evacuated region to a detector, for example, a photographic plate. If the magnet M is not turned on, the undeflected beam arrives at O. The field of the magnet M is inhomogeneous, being stronger near the sharp pole. As the magnet is turned on, atoms whose magnetization is parallel to the field

an angle $180° - \theta$ will also be a possible orientation.

A second kind of measurement to be made is the determination of the precession frequency of the atomic magnet. Since rotating atoms have a magnetic axis, there will be a torque in the presence of a magnetic field tending to make this axis parallel to the applied field. But when a magnetized particle having marked angular momentum is subjected to a twist of this kind, it will precess around the direction of the applied field, just as the top in Fig. 2 (c) precesses around the vertical gravitational axis. In electromagnetic experiments, if a macroscopic magnet is rotated in the vicinity of a small coil, there will be induced across the terminals of the coil a voltage having the frequency of rotation of the magnet. This is an "induced" electromotive force, which can likewise be detected when atomic or nuclear magnets precess in a magnetic field. Atomic or nuclear magnetic induction experiments give important information not only concerning the precessing particles, but also concerning local fluctuations and variations of fields in solids and liquids.

A third type of investigation relates to atomic diamagnetism. This diamagnetic magnetization gives rise to forces which tend to drive atoms out of a magnetic field. If we have a cloud of electrons, for example, in a spherically symmetrical atom with no angular momentum, we may think of this cloud as a gas composed of electrons, whose motion is subject to forces in the same way that the motion of free electrons in a wire is determined by electromagnetic forces. If a magnetic field is established in the vicinity of such an atom, the cloud of electrons will be acted on

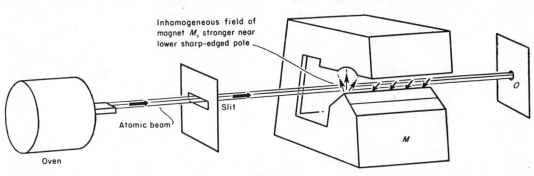

Inhomogeneous field of magnet M, stronger near lower sharp-edged pole

Atomic beam

Slit

Oven

O

M

Fig. 4.

will be drawn downward toward the greater fields near the sharp pole, while atoms magnetized in a direction opposite to the field will be drawn upward toward the weaker field near the broader pole. In this way the strength and orientation of atomic magnets may be measured by noting the upward or downward deflection of the beam when the magnetic field of M is turned on. It has also been shown by atomic beam experiments that atoms do not take up all possible orientations in the field. Some kinds of atoms, like hydrogen for example, when undisturbed, point either parallel or antiparallel to the field. Other kinds of atoms may take on one or more intermediate orientations. However, these possible orientations are always symmetrical about the field direction, with corresponding angles parallel or antiparallel to the field. Thus, if an atomic magnet is found capable of taking on an orientation making an angle θ with the field, then

by induced electromotive forces in exactly the same way as are the charges in a coil of wire. It results further that the direction of the magnetization induced in an atom by an increasing field is opposite to the direction of the applied field. If the change in the field is stopped, the forces producing this induced motion stop. In the case of the electrons in a wire, the resistance of the wire gradually brings the electrons to rest and the induced currents disappear. In the case of the atom, however, there is no resistance—the induced motion persists and the atom retains the magnetization in the direction opposite to the applied field. Thus diamagnetism is a universal property of matter resulting from its electrical structure and is observable only in otherwise nonmagnetic substances because of the very small magnitude of diamagnetic effects.

Diamagnetism and Paramagnetism.—Excluding ferromagnetic materials, such as iron, that can be permanently magnetized, matter can be classified into two classes of magnetic materials. One class is called *diamagnetic* and is characterized by the fact that, when samples are brought near an electromagnet, they are repelled. The second class is called *paramagnetic* and is characterized by the fact that, when samples are brought near an electromagnet, they are attracted. In both these classes, the degree of magnetization is proportional to the strength of the applied field. In diamagnetic materials, the magnetization is antiparallel to the field, while in paramagnetic materials it is parallel to the field.

Most substances are diamagnetic because of the very marked tendency for atomic magnetic moments to cancel in pairs. Thus water, living tissue, glass, wood, plastic substances, many rocks, and many metals are diamagnetic.

Typical paramagnetic materials are composed of atoms or molecules which possess angular momentum and which are therefore small magnets. In the absence of a magnetic field the magnetic axes of the atoms present in a sample will, in general, point randomly in all directions, particularly if the atoms are far enough apart so that there is no interaction between them and no tendency for one atom to orient its neighbors. In a gas of oxygen molecules, for example, we find that this condition is satisfied. In the absence of any magnetic field, the magnetic axes of the oxygen molecules are oriented at random in space. We have seen also that the application of a magnetic field will merely make each atom precess around the direction of the magnetic field. We should expect, therefore, that there is no magnetization produced in a collection of randomly oriented atoms of this kind, even when a field is applied. This is contrary to fact. We can perform further experiments to show that oxygen in the air is magnetized, that the magnetic axes are partially aligned parallel to the applied field, that the oxygen molecules are attracted into the region between the poles of a magnet, and that in this region of high magnet field there is consequently a slightly higher pressure than at remote points away from the magnet. To understand this we must take into account the fact that the oxygen atoms make collisions with each other; also that during these collisions the forces acting on the atomic or molecular magnetic axes are not simply the torques supplied by the external field, but include other forces as well. After the collision there will, in general, be a reorientation of the oxygen atoms and a tendency for more axes to be pointed parallel to the applied field than antiparallel to it. It is as a result of these phenomena that magnetization actually occurs. As we might expect, the degrees of magnetization of any substance not only is dependent on the strength of its atomic and molecular magnetization and the strength of the applied field, but also involves certain considerations about collisions, or about conditions relating to the thermal motion of the constituent particles. Magnetic substances composed of atomic or molecular particles having individual atomic magnetic moments will become magnetized to an extent determined by both the applied field strength and the temperature. In assemblages of atoms or molecules which are far apart and do not interact magnetically with each other very strongly, the degree of magnetization will be directly proportional to the strength of the applied field and inversely proportional to the absolute temperature. This law

was discovered by Pierre Curie, the husband of Marie Curie, famous for her work on radioactivity. At very low temperatures, substances of this kind are more easily magnetizable than at high temperatures.

Many substances are very feebly paramagnetic —much more feebly so than might be expected on the basis of their atomic magnetic properties and the thermal tendency to produce disorientation. In these substances the very feeble paramagnetism is due to the interaction of atomic and molecular magnets which are so locked together that it is difficult to produce appreciable reorientation and observable magnetization. To discover typical paramagnetic substances which obey Curie's law and which have a magnetizability that is inversely proportional to the temperature, we must look for substances in which the atomic magnets are far apart. An example of such a substance is an aqueous solution, consisting of a salt—whose ions are magnetic— dissolved in water. If the concentration is sufficiently low, so that the individual magnetic ions are far apart, they will interact with each other only very slightly. Such substances are the typical paramagnetic ones discussed above. Another example of such paramagnetic substances is instanced by certain kinds of crystals in which magnetic ions are present, but in which there are a great many waters of crystallization, so that, as in the solution, the magnetic ions are kept far apart. These crystals have a magnetic susceptibility (degree of magnetization) inversely proportional to the temperature, at least until very low temperatures are reached. When the temperature is sufficiently low, so that the energy involved in thermal collision processes becomes small compared with the energy of interaction of neighboring atomic magnets, we must expect a new interlocking tendency to arise. This is actually found in paramagnetic salts and may have the tendency to increase or to decrease their magnetizability.

Conditions of paramagnetism or diamagnetism in a substance are most readily distinguished through the force of attraction or repulsion exerted on a sample thereof by a magnet. A simple way of observing the very small forces involved is to suspend a small rod of the material to be examined so that it can rotate about its mid-point, and to place the sample so that it makes an angle of 45° with the magnetic axis at the mid-point of a magnet as in Fig. 5. When the field is

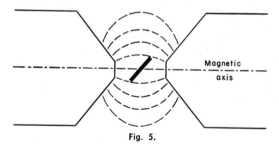

Magnetic axis

Fig. 5.

turned on, the sample will be found to rotate. If the sample is paramagnetic, it will tend to set itself parallel to the axis of the magnet; if it is diamagnetic, it will move perpendicular to the axis of the magnet. This is because the field of a magnet like that shown is inhomogeneous, being stronger near the poles and weaker in the median plane. The ends of a paramagnetic rod will be attracted toward the strong fields near the poles, but in a diamagnetic rod will be repelled by the poles. This effect has nothing to do with the direction of the field and would be absent if the field were perfectly uniform.

Ferromagnetism.—We now come to that outstanding class of magnetic materials which can exert much stronger forces than the above-mentioned paramagnetic and diamagnetic substances. The most common representatives of this class are iron and the related steels. Ferromagnetic materials are distinguished not only by the fact that they are very strongly magnetic, but also by the fact that they can retain this magnetism in the absence of an externally applied field. See also MAGNET—*Permanent Magnets.* However, there is a critical temperature at which even ferromagnetic materials lose their strong magnetic properties. Above a magnetic transformation temperature, called the Curie temperature, they behave like ordinary paramagnetic substances. Iron, nickel, and cobalt have Curie temperatures hundreds of degrees above room temperature. That is, only at these elevated temperatures is the disorienting tendency due to thermal motions sufficient to overcome the aligning forces of neighboring magnets in their atomic structure. But we know the strength of atomic magnets and the strength of the magnetic forces acting between them, and it can be shown that the magnetic forces tending to produce ferromagnetic alignment would be overcome by thermal agitation at a temperature of about one degree absolute, or $-272°$ C., and that much stronger forces must be present to produce the observed ferromagnetic effects up to several hundred degrees Celsius. The nature of these forces was unraveled by Werner Heisenberg during the early days (after 1925) of the development of the quantum theory of atomic structure; the forces that give rise to ferromagnetism are the same forces which produce other chemical and optical effects in atoms.

A model of ferromagnetic substance proposed by Sir Alfred Ewing, and illustrated in Fig. 6, proves enormously helpful in explaining, at least qualitatively, how magnetic properties may be interpreted. In Fig. 6 (a) a magnetized Ewing model is illustrated. All the elementary magnets are pointing in the same direction and the model is magnetized to "saturation," or to the maximum degree of which it is capable. However, if a demagnetizing process is simulated—for example, if we set each individual magnet spinning rapidly, as it might at high temperatures, and then allow it to settle down in the absence of any orienting magnetic field—we shall find a situation like that shown in Fig. 6 (b). A tendency is still apparent for neighboring atoms to point in a parallel direction, but there exist separate regions, or "magnetic domains," as they are often called. In each domain the magnetization points in some one direction, but the direction of magnetization of neighboring domains is different. Domains of this kind have actually been observed on a variety of magnetic materials by means of very finely divided magnetic powders. Much about their size and shape and about the magnetization process is known. Qualitatively, this magnetizing process is very much the same as that which can be observed on the Ewing model exposed to a slowly increasing uniform field. If, for instance, a magnetic field is applied along a cube edge in Fig. 6 (b), we find that those domains whose magnetization is parallel to the applied magnetic field

tend to grow at the expense of those regions in which the direction of magnetization makes some angle, 45° or 90°, to the applied field. In the absence of a field, we may think of a layer of atoms adjacent to a domain boundary as belonging with comparable probability to either of the domains separated by the boundary in question. This situation persists, however, only as long as

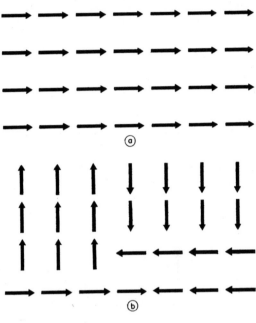

Fig. 6.

no magnetic field is applied. When a sufficiently strong field is applied parallel to the magnetization of one domain, it becomes magnetically preferable for atoms in the boundary to join this domain. Magnetization may proceed by this process of growth of one domain at the expense of its neighbor. The movement of a boundary, or a "domain wall," as it is also called, will in general not be perfectly free and reversible for a variety of reasons. There may be, for example, in a ferromagnetic crystal inclusions or impurities which make it difficult for the boundary to move past. This occasions irreversible effects known as *hysteresis.* Or again, we may find that a group of domains readjust their orientations at some particular applied field strength and do not return to their original orientations when the field is again reduced. This also causes irreversible effects. The magnetization of a typical ferromagnetic material is shown in Fig. 7.

The magnetization of a demagnetized sample starts at the origin and follows along a curve like the dark curve shown in the figure. The slope of this curve determines the *permeability* (see MAGNET—*Magnetostatics*) of the sample being described. If the sample is magnetized from the initially demagnetized state at the origin to some point such as 1, by the application of a magnetizing field H_1 and if the field is then reduced to zero, it will be found that the magnetization does not return to zero. The intensity of magnetization after the removal of the applied field measures the *remanence* (remaining magnetism) of the material being described and is shown by point 2. If now the field is reversed and increased, we find that there is a further point, 3, at which the magnetization is reduced to zero. The strength of the reversed field required to demagnetize the sample is called the *coercive force* H_c. In general, permanent magnets with strong coercive forces and high remanence are desired, the former so that they will retain their magnetization even under adverse

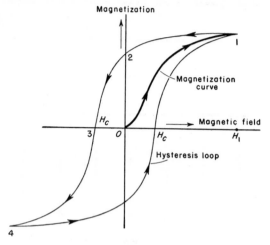

Fig. 7.

conditions and the latter so that they may be strongly magnetic. This process may now be continued. As the reversed field is increased, the magnetization will eventually reach point 4. Points 1 and 4 in Fig. 7 are near the limits of magnetization termed magnetic saturation. If the magnetization is again reversed to take the specimen back to point 1, it will follow along a symmetrically placed path.

The entire loop which has been plotted is called the *hysteresis loop* of the material. For some applications, materials having very small hysteresis loops are wanted, for example, in magnetic materials in which very small currents are expected to produce large effects. Materials having a high permeability and very little hysteresis are called soft magnetic materials and are used, for example, in communication lines.

The magnetic properties of materials are called "structure sensitive" in that small imperfections, inclusions of foreign substances, small flaws, or mechanical deformations all have a marked effect on their magnetic properties.

The effect of extremely low (cryogenic) temperatures on magnetic materials is particularly unusual. Such temperatures have caused the virtual disappearance of resistance to the flow of electric current in a conductor. Extremely powerful magnets have been devised that will operate in extreme cold.

See also ELECTROMAGNETISM; TERRESTIAL MAGNETISM; ZEEMAN EFFECT.

Bibliography.—Bozorth, R. N., *Ferromagnetism* (New York 1951); Bitter, F., *Currents, Fields, and Particles* (New York 1956); Parasinis, D. S., *Magnetism: from Lodestone to Polar Wandering* (New York 1961); Lee, E. W., *Magnetism* (Baltimore 1963).

FRANCIS BITTER,

*Massachusetts Institute of Technology.
Revised by the Editors*

MAGNETISM, Animal. See HYPNOSIS.

MAGNETITE, măg'nĕ-tīt, or **MAGNETIC IRON ORE,** măg-nĕt'ĭk ī'ẽrn ōr, an oxide of iron, Fe_3O_4, often found with small parts of titanium or magnesium. A common, strongly magnetic mineral of the igneous rocks, it contains, when pure, 72.4 per cent iron, has a hardness of from 5.5 to 6.5 and a specific gravity of 5.18, and is black in color with metallic or submetallic luster. It crystalizes in the isometric system, commonly in octahedra, but also in dodecahedra, and is often found in massive and granular forms. Magnetite with permanent magnetic polarity is known as loadstone. It occurs in large deposits in various parts of Europe, Australia, and North and South America. See also IRON—*8. Iron Ore Districts of the United States* and *9. World Supplies.*

MAGNETO, măg-nē'tō, a device employed to generate electric current for ignition in an internal-combustion engine. See INTERNAL-COMBUSTION ENGINE—*Ignition;* GENERATORS—*Special Types of Generators.*

MAGNETOMETER. See GEOPHYSICAL EXPLORATION.

MAGNETRON. See ELECTRONICS; RADAR.

MAGNIFICAT, măg-nĭf'ĭ-kăt, in the Latin version of the Bible, the name given to the song of the Virgin Mary in Luke 1:46–55, which begins *Magnificat anima mea dominum* (My soul doth magnify the Lord). As a canticle, it is chanted at vespers in the Roman Catholic Church and at evensong is sung or said in Anglican churches.

MAGNIFICENT AMBERSONS, The, by Booth Tarkington, a novel which traces the fortunes of two families in an Indiana town. Published in 1918, it was awarded the Pulitzer Prize in 1919. Realism in *The Magnificent Ambersons* is less diluted with sentimentalism than is usual in Tarkington's works. The Ambersons, who have risen on the fortune made by old Major Amberson, dominate the town. Due to a misunderstanding with her sweetheart, Eugene Morgan, the major's daughter, Isabel, has made a loveless marriage. When her spoiled son, George, is grown, Eugene, now a widower with a daughter, returns to the town to start an automobile factory. George and Eugene's daughter, Lucy, fall in love in spite of her awareness of his egotism, and their parents find their old affection returning. After his father's death, however, George prevents his mother's remarriage, and having quarreled with Lucy, takes his mother away, finally bringing her home to die. The Amberson fortune is now exhausted, and the family's former position in the social scale is occupied by the Morgans. In the end, Eugene and Lucy are reconciled with George.

MAGNITNAYA, mŭg-nyĕt'nà-yà, mountain, USSR, in the Russian SFSR, in the Ural Mountains, west of the Ural River. It is 2,020 feet high and is remarkable for its large magnetite deposits. Magnitogorsk (q.v.) is at its base.

MAGNITOGORSK, măg-nē'tô-gôrsk, Russ. màg-nyĭ-tû-gôrsk', city, USSR, located in the

Chelyabinsk Region of the RSFSR, on the Ural
River and the South Siberian Railroad, 135 miles
southwest of Chelyabinsk. Originally a small village, it underwent a tremendous development after
the Soviet government began in 1929 the exploitation of the rich magnetic iron ore deposits of
nearby mountains and built huge plants for the
production of iron and steel. Magnitogorsk soon
became one of the chief Soviet metallurgical
centers. Chemicals, rubber, and machinery are
also manufactured. Pop. (1966) 352,000.

MAGNITUDE, in astronomy. See STARS.

MAGNOLIA, city, Arkansas, seat of Columbia County, situated 35 miles west of El Dorado
and served by the Louisiana and North West
Railroad and Trans-Texas Airways. There are
rich oil and gas deposits nearby. Cotton ginning,
gasoline refining, lumbering, and the production
of cotton textiles, cottonseed oil, foundry products,
and beverages are the main industries. Southern
State College is located here. Settled in 1852
and incorporated in 1855, the city is governed by
a mayor and council. Pop. 10,651.

MAGNOLIA, a genus of ornamental, widely
cultivated evergreen or deciduous trees and shrubs
of the family Magnoliaceae. The 35 to 40 species
are mostly native to the United States, India,
China, and Japan. They are characterized by
large, alternate, entire leaves; large, solitary,
terminal flowers, often highly fragrant and white,
purple, pink, or yellowish in color; and cone-
shaped, often red, decorative fruits. Most of the
deciduous species can be grown as far north as
Massachusetts, but the evergreen kinds are not
hardy in cold weather. As a rule, magnolias thrive
best in fairly rich, open, moist, peaty or sandy
loams, but they generally prove satisfactory in any
garden soil. They may be propagated by layers
or grafts or by seeds planted when ripe and stratified in sand and kept outdoors where they cannot
become dry. The plants should be transplanted
when new growth begins.

Among the most popular cultivated American
species are the bull bay or big laurel (*Magnolia
grandiflora*), an evergreen tree which often attains a height of 75 feet and has very large, fragrant, white flowers; the sweet bay or swamp bay
(*M. virginiana*), which reaches a height of 20
feet and bears fragrant cream-colored flowers; the
cucumber tree (*M. acuminata*); and the large-
leaved cucumber tree (*M. macrophylla*). Asian
species include the yulan (*M. denudata*), a native
of China, where it has been cultivated for more
than 1,000 years; and *M. stellata, M. liliflora,* and
M. obovata, handsome Japanese kinds. By crossing, hybridizing, and selection many choice horticultural varieties have been produced.

MAGNUS, king of Denmark. See MAGNUS,
kings of Norway—*Magnus I.*

MAGNUS, măg′nŭs; Nor. mäng′nŏŏs, the
name of seven kings of Norway.

MAGNUS I (called MAGNUS THE GOOD): d.
Skibby, Denmark, Oct. 25, 1047. The son of Olaf
II (St. Olaf), he succeeded Canute II as king of
Norway in 1035. Three years later he concluded
a treaty with Hardecanute of Denmark whereby,
in the event of the death of either monarch, the
other would succeed to his throne. Accordingly,
on Hardecanute's death in 1042, Magnus also

became king of Denmark, but he met with much
opposition from his Danish subjects.

MAGNUS II HARALDSSON: b. 1035; d. 1069. A
son of Harold III, he ruled Norway jointly with
his brother, Olaf III, from 1066 to 1069.

MAGNUS III (called MAGNUS BAREFOOT): b.
1073; d. near Dublin, Ireland, Aug. 24, 1103. The
son of Olaf III, he came to the throne in 1093
(until Haakon Magnusson's death in 1095 he
ruled over only southern Norway) and spent most
of his short reign in warfare. In 1098–1099 he
raided the Orkneys and Hebrides, for the next
two years fought Sweden; and died while attacking Ireland.

MAGNUS IV (called MAGNUS THE BLIND): b.
about 1115; d. at sea, Nov. 12, 1139. The son of
Sigurd I, he became king in 1130. Defeated in a
civil war (1134–1135) with the pretender Harold
Gille, he was blinded and imprisoned. He died
in a naval battle with Harold's sons.

MAGNUS V ERLINGSSON: b. 1156; d. at sea,
June 15, 1184. The son of Erling Skakke, he
became king of Norway in 1162 and ruled under
a regency until 1164, when he was crowned at
Bergen. Defeated in a civil war with Sverre
Sigurdsson, he fled to Denmark in 1179. He died
in a naval battle while endeavoring to regain his
throne.

MAGNUS VI (called MAGNUS LAGABØTER): b.
1238; d. Bergen, Norway, May 9, 1280. The son
and successor of Haakon IV, he inherited a war
with Scotland when he became king in 1263.
Three years later he made peace by ceding the
Hebrides and the Isle of Man. Magnus is best
known for the code (1276) by which he thoroughly revised the laws of the kingdom.

MAGNUS VII ERIKSSON. See MAGNUS, kings
of Sweden—*Magnus II.*

MAGNUS, măg′nŭs; Swed. màng′nŭs, the
name of two kings of Sweden.

MAGNUS I (called MAGNUS LADULÅS): b.
1240; d. Dec. 18, 1290. The second son of Birger
of Bjälbo, he came to the throne in 1275 by
deposing his brother Waldemar. His reign was
marked by the revision of the feudal system.

MAGNUS II (known as MAGNUS ERIKSSON):
b. 1316; d. at sea, Dec. 1, 1374. The grandson of
Haakon V of Norway, he became king of Sweden
and, as MAGNUS VII, king of Norway in 1319.
Until 1332 he ruled through the regency of his
mother. He devoted most of his attention to
Sweden, and in 1343 yielded the Norwegian throne
to his young son Haakon VI, for whom he served
as regent until 1355. Another son, Eric XII, deposed his father in 1356 and ruled as king of
Sweden for three years. Restored in 1359, Magnus was again deposed, by the Royal Council, in
1363. He was succeeded by his nephew Albert,
with whom he fought for two years. Defeated
and imprisoned by Albert, he escaped to Norway
in 1371.

MAGNUS, măg′nŏŏs, **Heinrich Gustav,** German chemist and physicist: b. Berlin, Germany,
May 2, 1802; d. there, April 4, 1870. After studying in Berlin, under Jöns Jakob Berzelius in
Stockholm, and in Paris, he taught at the University of Berlin, becoming a lecturer in 1831,
extraordinary professor in 1834, and ordinary
professor in 1845. His researches covered a wide
field, including studies of selenium, platinum, and
tellurium; the absorption of gases in the blood;
thermoelectricity; and what is now known as the

Magnus effect of a rotating cylinder in an air current.

MAGOFFIN, mà-gŏf'ĭn, **Beriah**, American political leader: b. Harrodsburg, Ky., April 18, 1815; d. there, Feb. 28, 1885. After graduating from Centre College of Kentucky, he completed the law course at Transylvania College in 1838 and practiced in Harrodsburg. An active Democrat, he was elected state senator in 1850 and governor in 1859. As the Civil War approached, he favored calling a state convention on the question of secession, but met opposition in the legislature. Refusing President Abraham Lincoln's call for troops in April 1861, he proclaimed Kentucky neutral, but troops of both sides violated the state's neutrality. The legislature became increasingly favorable to the Union, and a resolution ordering the Confederates to evacuate Kentucky was passed over Magoffin's veto. Finding his position untenable, he resigned in August 1862.

MAGOG. See GOG AND MAGOG.

MAGOG, mā'gŏg, city, Quebec, Canada, situated in Stanstead County, at the northern end of Lake Memphremagog, on the Canadian Pacific Railway, 17 miles southwest of Sherbrooke. It is a resort center for the surrounding lake country, and has steamer connections with other points on Memphremagog. The city is also known for its textile manufactures and has woodworking and butter and cheese factories. Founded by Loyalists from the United States in 1776, Magog was incorporated in 1890. Pop. 13,797.

MAGONIGLE, mà-gŏn'ĭ-g'l, **Harold Van Buren**, American architect: b. Bergen Heights, N.J., Oct. 17, 1867; d. Bain Harbor, Vt., Aug. 29, 1935. He learned his profession in the offices of prominent New York and Boston architects, and after traveling in Europe on a fellowship from 1894 to 1896, went into practice in New York, first in a partnership and after 1904 by himself. He is known chiefly for his monuments, which include the McKinley National Memorial in Canton, Ohio (1904); the National Maine Monument, New York City (1911); and the Liberty Memorial, Kansas City, Mo. (1923). He also designed the United States embassy and consulate in Tokyo, Japan. He published *Architectural Rendering in Wash* (1921) and *The Nature, Practice and History of Art* (1924).

MAGOON, mà-gōōn', **Charles Edward**, American lawyer and administrator: b. Steele County, Minn., Dec. 5, 1861; d. Washington, D.C., Jan. 14, 1920. After attending the University of Nebraska, he studied law and was admitted to the bar in 1882, practicing in Lincoln, Nebr., until 1899. In the latter year he became law officer of the Bureau of Insular Affairs in the War Department, specializing in questions arising from the acquisition of Puerto Rico, the Philippines, and Cuba after the Spanish-American War. In 1904–1905, as general counsel for the Isthmian Canal Commission, he prepared laws for the Panama Canal Zone, and in 1905–1906 served as governor of the zone and minister to Panama. From 1906 to 1909 he was provisional governor of Cuba. He published *The Law of Civil Government in Territory Subject to Military Occupation* (1902).

MAGPIE, măg'pī, the common name of any of several birds of the genus *Pica* of the family Corvidae, distinguished by an extremely long, wedge-shaped tail. The European magpie (*P. pica*) is represented in North America by the variety *P. pica hudsonia,* lustrous black in color with a varied iridescence and sharply contrasting white under parts and patches on the shoulders and wings. This variety is confined to the West, its range reaching from Alaska to Arizona, and is especially common in the Rocky Mountains. The yellow-billed magpie (*P. nuttali*) of California is similar, except that it is a little smaller (about 17 inches), and the bill and a naked area at its base are yellow instead of black. Magpies are known for their thieving habits, often robbing the nests of other birds. Their own nests are ingeniously constructed, consisting of a large, domed structure protected by a thick layer of thorns and twigs, through which a narrow passage leads to a deep cup plastered with mud and lined with fibers. Six to nine greenish drab eggs, spotted with brown, are laid. The young are hatched in a rather undeveloped state and remain in the nest for some time after hatching.

MAGRUDER, mà-grōō'dēr, **John Bankhead**, American Confederate general: b. Winchester, Va., Aug. 15, 1810; d. Houston, Texas, Feb. 18, 1871. He was graduated from the United States Military Academy in 1830, saw service in the Seminole and Mexican wars, and by 1847 had risen to the rank of lieutenant colonel. Following the outbreak of the Civil War in 1861, he resigned from the United States Army and accepted a Confederate colonelcy. After his victory at Big Bethel (q.v.) in June 1861, he was made a brigadier general and, in October, a major general. Assigned to the Yorktown district, he fortified the Peninsula and, with a force of 12,000, held it against the Union forces in April 1862, but failed to press his advantage in the Seven Days' Battles. (See also PENINSULAR CAMPAIGN OF 1862, THE.) In October 1862, he was appointed commander of the district of Texas, and on Jan. 1, 1863, he recaptured Galveston. After the war, in 1866–1867, he served as a major general in the army of Emperor Maximilian of Mexico.

MAGSAYSAY, măg-sī-sī, **Ramón**, Philippine statesman: b. Iba, Luzon, Philippines, Aug. 31, 1907; d. Cebu Island, March 17, 1957. Educated at the University of the Philippines (1927–1931) and José Rizal College in Manila (1932–1933), he worked for a transportation company until the outbreak of war in 1941, when he joined the United States Army. Commissioned a captain in April 1942, he led guerrilla forces, which he had helped to organize in western Luzon, all through the Japanese occupation. In February 1945 he was appointed military governor of Zambales by Gen. Douglas MacArthur, and when the Philippines were granted independence in 1946, he was elected to the new Congress. Re-elected in 1949, he began a vigorous attack on the Communist-led Hukbalahap guerrillas ("Huks") and on the conditions which had produced them. As secretary of national defense (1950–1953), he reorganized the army and eradicated Huk terrorism. He was awarded the United States Legion of Merit in 1952.

Magsaysay was elected president of the Philippines in 1953, and worked tirelessly to improve the social and economic conditions of the poor. His administration was noted for programs of public works, social welfare, and land reform. A firm supporter of the West, he was a sponsor of the Southeast Asia Treaty Organization (SEATO), established in Manila in 1954. He met his death in an airplane crash.

MAGUEY. See AGAVE.

MAGYARS. See HUNGARY.

MAH-JONGG, mä′jong′, is a four-handed game of Chinese origin. The name is also spelled *Mah Jong.* The game is a form of rummy played with tiles or blocks. The object is to obtain a hand containing valuable combinations of tiles.

Mah-Jongg tiles. The game is played with 144 pieces.

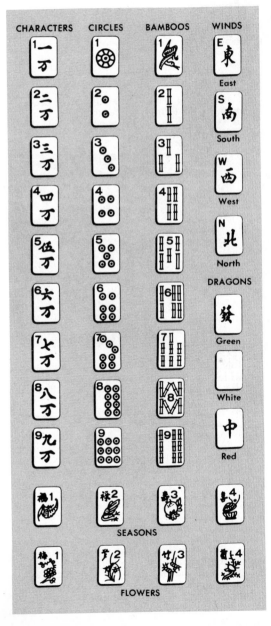

The United States began to import sets from China about 1920, and, shortly after, American sets were made. Mah-Jongg, under various names, became a "fad." But it lacked generally accepted laws, and attempts at standardization from 1922 to 1925 and again in 1937 were not successful. The trend was away from the scientific Chinese viewpoint and toward big scores. The popularity of the game faded late in 1926, and while sets have continued to be sold, efforts at a large-scale revival have failed.

A Mah-Jongg set contains 144 tiles, usually wood blocks with bone facing. There are 3 suits —bamboos, circles, and characters—each with 4 tiles numbered 1–9, making 36 tiles per suit. There are 28 honors, 4 each marked Red Dragon, White Dragon, Green Dragon, East Wind, North Wind, West Wind, and South Wind. The set is completed with 4 Seasons and 4 Flowers. Each set also contains tile racks, dice, "sticks" or markers for scoring, and a set of rules.

A game is started by shuffling the tiles and building them into a hollow square, each side 2 tiles high and 18 long. The "wall" is broken according to the roll of the dice, and each player draws 13 tiles, with East (who plays first) getting 14 and discarding one. The turn to play rotates and consists of the draw of one tile and then a discard.

Players strive for combinations or "sets." A "chow" is 3 tiles of the same unit in numerical sequence. A "pung" is 3 tiles of the same suit and denomination, or 3 similar honors. A "complete hand" consists of four sets of 3 plus a pair. Such a hand is tabled without discarding and wins the game. Flowers and Seasons are bonus tiles and are immediately "grounded" by placing in front of the owner. A "kong" is a pung plus the fourth corresponding tile. The last tile of a kong is grounded. Grounded tiles are replaced by drawing loose tiles. Kongs, pungs, and bonus tiles count in scoring, but chows are useful only in filling a complete hand.

Any player, irrespective of turn, may claim a discarded tile, but he must use it immediately to complete a set. When a player wins, or "woos," he collects from each adversary. The others settle among themselves according to their scores. Routine of play varies slightly, but scoring varies widely. It is best to use the scoring shown in the rules with the set or accepted by the group playing.

Consult Foster, Robert F., *Foster on Mah Jong* (New York 1924); Irwin, Florence, *The Complete Mah Jong Player* (New York 1924).

FRANK K. PERKINS
Authority on Games

MAHĀBHĀRATA, mà-hä′bä′rà-tà (GREAT [TALE OF THE] DESCENDANTS OF BHARATA), the title of one of the two great classical Sanskrit epics of ancient India. It is attributed to the sage Vyāsa, but its authorship is multiple, and the composition of the text covers a period of roughly eight centuries, the earliest portion dating from perhaps the 4th century B.C. This is the longest work in literary history. It consists of approximately 100,000 metrical couplets (*śloka*) and is about four times longer than India's court epic poem, the *Rāmāyana* (q.v.), or about eight times the length of the *Iliad* and *Odyssey* combined. It is arranged into 18 books (*parvan*) and is supplemented by the *Harivaṁśa,* more than 16,000 stanzas on the lineage of the god Hari.

The content of this folk epic includes numerous myths, martial legends, anecdotal fables, long religious poems, and didactic sections, bearing on a central core narrative involving the inter-clan war between the 100 sons of Kuru, called the Kauravas, and the 5 sons of Pāṇḍu, called the Pāṇḍavas. The intercalculations on theology, morality, and statecraft make the *Mahābhārata* an encyclopedia of information on classical Indian civilization, and the most important single source for Hindu ideals as differentiated from earlier Vedic or Brahmanic culture.

Although the Kauravas may represent an older aristocracy, the real heroes of the epic are the Pāṇḍavas. In the main narrative, the Kauravas employ a skilled dice player to defeat the eldest brother and leader of the Pāṇḍavas, Yudhiṣṭhira. His total loss results in 12 years' exile, after which the Pāṇḍavas regain their rightful kingdom through an 18-day battle, traditionally dated 3102 B.C., at Kurukshetra (*Kurukṣetra*), a plain near Delhi. The epic concludes with their successful rule, performance of elaborate coronation ceremonies, and eventual journey to heaven in the company of their wife, Draupadī.

During the course of their peregrinations, the Pāṇḍavas visit many hermitages and are consoled in their misery by various edifying tales. Two of the most literary of these interpolations are the stories of Nala and Damayantī—a kind of Hindu Romeo and Juliet—and Sāvitrī, an ideal Hindu wife whose faith and devotion rescue her husband from Death (Yama).

Perhaps the most significant sections of the epic deal with theology and philosophy. These later portions are best represented by the *Mokṣa-dharma,* but other tracts are better known. The most important of these treatises is the *Bhagavad Gītā,* which concerns the refusal of the Pāṇḍava hero Arjuna to participate in the battle against his Kaurava kinsmen. He is persuaded to do so on sociological, philosophical, and theological grounds by Krishna (*Kṛṣṇa*), an incarnation of the god Vishnu (*Viṣṇu;* see BHAGAVAD GITA). The immense popularity of this work may be partially accounted for by its democratic social viewpoint, its philosophical synthesis, and its moderation and simplicity of doctrine. Other significant philosophical works are the *Sanatsujātīya,* which undertakes an investigation of death, and the *Anugītā,* which further develops themes set by the *Bhagavad Gītā.*

The appeal of the *Mahābhārata* is localized in place, but not in time. Through easily identified symbols, it provides a living mythology with men and gods as part of an ordered scheme of life. The ethics of the work are bound up with chivalry, asceticism, and social obligation (*dharma*). The theology incorporates notions of a god incarnate (Krishna), polytheism, monotheism (favoring Vishnu, also called Hari), and abstract monism from the earlier Upanishadic tradition. Its philosophy seeks to relate the individual with the divine either through sacrificial action, metaphysical knowledge, meditative discipline, or simple pious devotion. Over all, however, the *Mahābhārata* displays the epic qualities of exaggeration of person, place, and circumstances, and represents the familiar Indian themes of transmigration, the force of destiny, and *Weltschmerz.*

See also INDIA—II. Literature.

ROYAL W. WEILER,
Professor, Department of Near and Middle East Languages, Columbia University.

MAHALLA EL KUBRA, EL, mȧ-hăl′ȧ ĕl kōo′brȧ (Ar. AL MAHALLAH AL KUBRA), city, Egypt (UAR), in Gharbiya Province, Lower Egypt, in the center of the Nile Delta, about halfway between Alexandria and Cairo. It is the headquarters of the Misr Spinning and Weaving Company, established in 1927, with completely integrated plants for spinning, weaving, and finishing cotton and wool fabrics. Its machinery and processes are among the most modern in the world, and its cotton exports are a major earner of needed hard currency. Pop. (1960) 178,000.

SAADAT HASAN.

MAHAN, mȧ-hăn′, **Alfred Thayer,** American naval officer and historian: b. West Point, N.Y., Sept. 27, 1840; d. Washington, D.C., Dec. 1, 1914. He was the son of Dennis Hart Mahan, professor of military art and engineering at the United States Military Academy. He attended Columbia College in New York for two years and graduated from the United States Naval Academy in 1859. During the Civil War he served on the South Atlantic and Gulf coasts and for a year was instructor at the Naval Academy, where a lifelong friendship began with another naval scholar, Stephen B. Luce. His first professional article was published in 1879 and his first book, *The Gulf and Inland Waters,* a volume on the naval history of the Civil War, in 1883. The next year he accepted an invitation to lecture at the new United States Naval War College, tended by its founder, Luce, whom he succeeded in 1886.

Alfred Thayer Mahan

Culver Service

Mahan's lectures evolved into the two works for which he is most famous, *The Influence of Sea Power upon History, 1660–1783* (1890) and *The Influence of Sea Power upon the French Revolution and Empire, 1793–1812* (2 vols., 1892). In the introduction and opening chapter of the first he outlined his seapower theory. These works, coinciding with the beginning of modern navies, and with their pro-British flavor, became especially popular in Great Britain. While in command of the cruiser *Chicago* (1893–1895) in European waters, Mahan received many honors, including degrees from Oxford and Cambridge universities. Acclaim in the United States came more slowly, but he had powerful admirers, among whom was Theodore Roosevelt.

In 1890, Mahan had begun publishing articles on the importance of seapower for the United States, specifying the need for a strong Navy, a Panama Canal, and bases in Hawaii. Retiring in 1896, he was recalled to serve on the Naval War Board directing operations in the Spanish-American War, and was a delegate in 1899 at the first Hague Disarmament Conference, where he strongly differed with the pacifism of the other American delegates. Promoted to rear admiral on the retired list in 1906, he also served on a board for reorganization of the Navy Department, but he devoted himself primarily to writing. He published an autobiography, *From Sail to Steam* (1907) and also *The Harvest Within, Thoughts on the Life of a Christian* (1909), for he was a devout Episcopalian.

Mahan's literary reputation rests mainly on his *Sea Power* works, but his later efforts, especially his essays, had an influence on the policy of the United States greater perhaps than the work of any other historian. Following World War I, his work fell into disrepute because he was blamed for having helped to bring on that conflict. The triumph of Allied seapower in World War II vindicated him.

Consult William D. Puleston, *Mahan* . . . (New Haven 1939), which contains a list of Mahan's 21 books, his unreprinted essays, and some important letters to the press.

JOHN D. HAYES,
Rear Admiral, United States Navy (Retired).

MAHANADI RIVER, mà-hä′nà-dĭ, river, India, rising in the highlands of Bastar in southernmost Madhya Pradesh and flowing 512 miles to the Bay of Bengal. In its upper course, the Mahanadi ("great river") flows northward, then eastward, traversing the basin of Chhattisgarh, where it is augmented by the Seonath. Thence the flow is southeastward into Orissa, passing through the Sambalpur Basin and being joined by the Tel River before penetrating the gorge (Sonpur to Naraj) and reaching the great delta, 125 miles across. Rainfall of 60 to 80 inches (June to October) in the drainage area of some 60,000 square miles causes extreme seasonal fluctuation of its discharge, the maximum near its mouth being as large as that of the Ganges.

The Mahanadi is little used for transportation except timber floated down from the Orissa hills and navigation of small boats in the delta, but it has increasing value for irrigation and power. After Indian independence, plans were drawn by Indian engineers for a 16-mile dam of masonry and earth at Hirakud, 9 miles above Sambalpur, with 123,000-kilowatt hydroelectric installations and over 500 miles of irrigation canals located in interior and coastal Orissa. The completion of the Hirakud project entirely under Indian direction and finance was a major achievement of the First and Second Five-Year Plans (1951–1961). Availability of cheap power has promoted the development of the alumina smelter at Sambalpur and the Austrian-built steelworks at Rourkela in the Brahmani Valley. Industrial centers developing in Madhya Pradesh are the Korba coalfield (mining and thermoelectricity) near Bilaspur and the Russian-built steelworks at Bhilai near Raipur.

JOHN E. BRUSH,
Professor of Geography, Rutgers—The State University of New Jersey.

MAHANOY CITY, mä′[h]à-noi, borough, Pennsylvania, in Schuylkill County, on Mahanoy Creek, 36 miles by road southwest of Wilkes-Barre. The name refers to a salt lick here, once used by deer (Delaware Indian *mahoni,* "lick"). The mining of anthracite coal was once the main industry. Now, however, clothing plants, a brewery, and a cigar factory are part of the economy.

Founded in 1859 and incorporated as a borough in 1863, Mahanoy City is governed by a burgess and council. Pop. 8,536.

THELMA FAUST.

MAHARAJA or **MAHARAJAH,** mà-hä′rä′jà (Sanskrit *mahārāja,* great king), a title given to ruling chiefs of the former great native states of India and indicating a rank above that of raja (rajah), or simple king. It was often applied in courtesy to all rajas and sometimes to persons of high rank or even to holy men. The corresponding feminine form is maharani (maharanee), applied in a woman's own right or by virtue of marriage to a "maharaja."

MAHARASHTRA, ma-hä′räsh′tra, state, India, in the west-central part of the country, with a western coastline stretching 330 miles along the Arabian Sea from the former Portuguese colonies of Goa on the south to Daman on the north (both now parts of the Union Territory of Goa, Daman, and Diu). It is also bounded by the states of Gujarat on the northwest, Madhya Pradesh on the north and east, Andhra Pradesh on the southeast, and Mysore on the southwest. The third largest state of India, both in area (118,717 square miles) and population (39,553,718 in 1961), Maharashtra was formed in 1960 by separating the Marathi and Gujarati linguistic areas of former Bombay State. The city of Bombay became the capital.

The People.—To other Indians, all Marathi speakers are Marathas, whereas to a Marathi speaker himself, Maratha refers to the majority group of non-Brahman castes. The people of Maharashtra are noted for their characteristically vigorous and often violent approach to social and political problem solving. Their frugality, thriftiness, and a certain bluntness in social relations are sometimes mistaken by other Indians for a lack of sophistication and taste.

Over 75 percent of the population speaks Marathi; other languages are Gujarati, Urdu, Kannada, and tribal tongues. Almost 90 percent of the people are Hindu, but Muslims, Parsis, Christians, and Jews are represented. At the top of Maharashtra's Hindu social structure are several Brahman and other "advanced" castes (6 percent of the total); in the middle, a large number of "intermediate" non-Brahman castes (77 percent, the Marathas being the most important); and at the bottom, a dozen or so former "untouchable" castes (17 percent, of which the Mahars are the most important).

Subregions.—While Maharashtra as a cultural region is easily distinguished from the other regions of India on such bases as language, literary and historical traditions, diet, and dress, the state itself comprises five subregions with distinctive physiographic, historical, economic, and cultural characteristics.

Konkan.—This coastal area between the crest of the Western Ghats and the Arabian Sea has a high annual rainfall (75-100 inches), which permits rice to be the dominant crop. Cashews, mangoes, and vegetables are also important. Significant deposits of bauxite, manganese, iron, and other minerals are found in Ratnagiri District. The Konkan is dominated by Bombay (1961 pop. 4,152,056), though land communications between the city and the southern districts is difficult because of rugged terrain; a string of small ports provides fair-weather contact by coastal steamer.

Associated Press Photos of India

The Pārvatī Temple (18th century) at Poona.

Bombay draws from the Konkan districts a large proportion of its industrial labor force, domestic servants, and policemen. A large percentage of the Konkan's population are Brahmans. Of particular significance to all of Maharashtra is the continuous migration of Konkanastha (Chitpavan) Brahmans into other subregions since 1700; by 1900 Chitpavans were in the forefront of all political and sociocultural activities throughout the Marathi-speaking region.

Desh (Deccan).—Maharashtra's central and most representative subregion, the Desh, comprises seven districts on the Deccan lava (basaltic) plateau at an average height of 1,750 feet above sea level. The principal rivers are the Godavari, Bhima, and Krishna, which rise in the Western Ghats and flow southeastward to the Bay of Bengal. The Godavari Valley is the historic cradle of Maharashtrian culture. Here the modern Marathi language emerged, the "poet-saints" lived and taught (see MARATHA SAINTS), and the all-Maharashtra cult of Vithoba developed. The modern focus of political and cultural life has shifted westward to Poona (1961 pop. 737,426), Maharashtra's second largest city.

Much of the Desh lies in the rain shadow of the Western Ghats (average annual precipitation is 25 inches), and for centuries it suffered periodic famines. Millets, particularly jowar and bajra, are the favored grains, while cotton, oilseeds, and sugarcane are the cash crops.

Khandesh.—This subregion comprises the two districts of the Tapti (Tapi) River valley, where the alluvial bottomlands produce cotton, oilseeds, and tobacco. Khandesh is of historical importance as an often fought-over transitional zone between northern and southern India.

Marathwada.—This name is given to the five Marathi-speaking districts that were part of the former princely state of Hyderabad. Dependence on agriculture as a source of livelihood is greater in this subregion than in any other. The most important features of Marathwada are architectural: the rock-cut temples of Ajanta and Ellora (qq.v.). The state government in 1958 opened Marathwada

University in Aurangabad, and is proceeding with plans for large-scale educational advances. The 1961 census showed that Marathwada had the lowest literacy rates in the state.

Vidarbha.—These eight easternmost districts focus on Nagpur, the third largest city in Maharashtra (1961 pop. 690,302). The basaltic Deccan lavas reach their eastern limit in the vicinity of Nagpur, so that Vidarbha has the cotton, oilseeds, and millets of the black-soil valleys in its western sector and the rice and tropical forests of the higher rainfall eastern section. In the eastern, nonbasaltic area, very large deposits of iron, coal, and manganese are exploited.

Industry.—While agriculture is central to the state's economy, Maharashtra is second only to West Bengal as India's most industrialized area. The cotton textile industry, centered on Bombay, has since World War II been joined by a number of greatly diversified industries, including general and electrical engineering, chemicals, soaps, pharmaceuticals, and sugar. New industrial areas have been established in Nasik, Poona, Kolhapur, and Nagpur.

Power.—The Western Ghats were the site of pioneering hydroelectric schemes established before 1915 by the Tata family of industrialists; by 1947 the Tata plants accounted for 47 percent of India's total capacity, most of it used for Bombay's industrial development. New schemes, in particular the Koyna Valley project in southern Maharashtra's Satara District, are rapidly bringing electric power to the countryside and permitting more efficient exploitation of the substantial local mineral resources.

Education.—Maharashtra's general literacy rate (1961 census) was 29.8 percent (42 percent for males and 16.8 percent for females). However, this rate covered a range of 58.6 percent in Bombay to 15.1 percent in two Marathwada districts. The state ranked eighth in India.

Maharashtra has a well-developed educational system, which embraced over 45,000 higher, secondary, and primary institutions in 1960; however, they are unevenly distributed, with a dearth of schools in Marathwada, for instance. There are six universities: Bombay (see BOMBAY, UNIVERSITY OF); Poona; Nagpur; Marathwada, at Aurangabad; Shreemati Nathibai Damodar Thackersey Women's University, at Bombay; and Chhatrapati Shivaji, at Kolhapur, founded 1962.

See also BOMBAY (city and former state); MARATHAS or MAHRATTAS; MARATHI LANGUAGE AND LITERATURE.

MAUREEN PATTERSON,
South Asia Bibliographic Specialist and Instructor in Indian Civilization, University of Chicago.

MAHATMA, mȧ-hät′ma, (Skr. *mahātman,* great-souled one), a title given by Hindus to an individual, such as Mohandas K. Gandhi, who has come to be regarded as more than usually wise and spiritually developed. In theosophy (q.v.) the word is applied to saints said to live in Tibet but who can transmit their spirit of all-inclusive love to sensitized minds.

MAHĀYĀNA, mȧ-hä′yä′nȧ (GREAT VEHICLE), that form of Buddhism dominant in India from the 1st to 11th centuries and now prevalent in Tibet, China, Japan, and Mongolia, as distinguished from the Theravāda (Doctrine of the Elders) or Hīnayāna (Little Vehicle) practiced chiefly in Ceylon, Burma, and Thailand. From Mahāyāna sources it appears that the major point of difference was that the Hīnayāna sought salvation through individual self-effort, whereas Mahāyāna advocated salvation for all creatures through the worship and grace of the Buddha or buddhas ("enlightened ones") and bodhisattvas (Buddhist saviors, whose "essence is enlightenment"). The Mahāyāna emphasis on light and saviors suggests Iranian influences. Pali, probably a mercantile language, was used for the Theravāda canon, whereas the Mahāyāna canon is partially preserved in Sanskrit, and fully in the Tibetan *Tanjur* and *Kanjur* as well as in Chinese renditions of these texts.

Doctrine.—The cult of the Buddha developed after his death (?483 B.C). with the distribution of his relics, which were enshrined in semispherical mounds called stūpas. The veneration of these memorial shrines and the influences of Hindu ritualism and theism promoted deification of the Buddha. The Buddha, called Tathāgata ("one who has gone thus") or Bhagavat ("blessed one"), is the central figure of Mahāyāna. However, several buddhas are worshiped besides the historical Siddhārtha Gautama (called Śākyamuni, "sage of the Śākyas," the two most important being Vairocana ("descendant of the sun, Virocana") and Amitābha ("of infinite light"). The Tibetan Panchen Lama is regarded as an incarnation of Amitābha. These buddhas rule various world systems (*loka-dhātu*) or buddha-fields (*buddha-kṣetra*), of which this world is one and heaven, the pure land (*sukhāvati*), is another. A later development postulates the celestial Buddha as a trinity, having three bodies: of the doctrine (*dharma-kāya*), of enjoyment (*sambhoga-kāya*), and of magic transformation (*nirmāṇa-kāya*), which accounts for the appearance of the historical Buddha.

The major scriptures of Mahāyāna are the *Saddharma-puṇḍarīka* (Lotus of the True Doctrine), the *Sukhāvatī* texts, and the lengthy philosophical treatises dealing with the perfection of wisdom (*Prajñāpāramitā*, q.v.), to which class the popular *Vajracchedikā* (Diamond-Cutter) belongs.

The deified Buddha in Mahāyāna is in many respects superseded by attention given to the ideal man, the bodhisattva, who is characterized by his formulation of a vow (*praṇidhāna*) to forgo final enlightenment until all creatures are saved, and his perfection of virtues, especially wisdom (*prajñā*). To fulfill this vow, he frequently performs acts of compassion (*karuṇā*), in which he is prepared to sacrifice life or limb at the slightest request of a supplicant, in recognition or insight (*prajñā*) into the true meaning of the Buddha's doctrine (*dharma*). Other virtues are charity (*dāna*), patience (*kṣānti*), heroism (*vīrya*), meditation (*dhyāna*), and morality (*śila*). These qualities are best described by Śāntideva (c. 650 A.D.), in his *Bodhicaryāvatāra* (Introduction to the Path of Enlightenment). Through the perfection of these virtues the bodhisattva advances through various stages (*bhūmi*) on his way to enlightenment, stopping just short of the final goal. The bodhisattva is further able to transfer merit to others, by virtue of his being grounded in welfare (*kuśala-mūla*). The principal bodhisattvas are Avalokiteśvara ("lord of that which is to be looked down upon [in compassion]"), whose Chinese counterpart is the female Kwan Yin and whose incarnation on earth is the Dalai Lama; Mañjuśrī, lord of speech and wisdom; and Maitreya, the

bodhisattva of compassion, who is to be the next Buddha on earth.

Devotion.—The worship of buddhas and bodhisattvas may involve simply copying one of the scriptures, or the repetition of the Buddha's name, especially by the Amida (Amitābha) sect in Japan. Repetition of magical formulas (*dhāraṇī*), especially the *Oṁ maṇipadmā Hūṁ* in Tibet (see Oṁ), is highly regarded. Confession of sins (*pāpadeśanā*), burning of incense, reverence to icons, the use of rosaries (*japamālā*), and similar devotions are essentials of the ritual.

Philosophical Concepts.—The major philosophical concepts of the Theravāda, such as the four Aryan Truths, the impermanence of all phenomena, dependent causation (*pratītya-samutpāda*), and the denial of an essential self are accepted by the Mahāyāna. The numerous *Prajñāpāramitā* texts suggests that all phenomena are emptiness (*śūnyatā*). Nāgārjuna (fl. 2d century A.D.) built a significant philosophical system, sometimes referred to as nihilism, on this premise. A kind of absolute reality, called "suchness" (*tathatā* or *bhūtatathatā*) was postulated by Aśvaghoṣa (1st century A.D.), which in some respects is analogous to the Brahma (*brahman*) of the Hindu Upanishads. A further argument equated nirvana (*nirvāṇa*) with the phenomenal world of bondage (*saṁsāra*). This identity was realizable through a doctrine of relative and absolute truths and meditation (*dhyāna*), which set the theme for the Chinese Ch'an school and Japanese Zen. The purpose of Mahāyāna logic was to undermine the categories of rational thought. Another significant point of view was developed from the idealism of the *Laṅkāvatāra* text by the brothers Asaṅga and Vasubandhu (4th century A.D.). In this school (the Chinese Wei-Shih and Japanese Hosso), everything was held to be merely thought (*citta*) or consciousness-only (*vijñāna; vijñapti*). A later development of the Mahāyāna in India was the Vajrayāna (Diamond Vehicle), which argued that to the pure everything is pure, and in its stress on the worship of female saviors (*tārā*) it set the stage for degeneration in Buddhist ethics.

See also BUDDHA AND BUDDHISM; INDIA—13. *Religion and Philosophy;* TIBET—*Religion.*

ROYAL W. WEILER,
Professor, Department of Near and Middle East Languages, Columbia University.

MAHDI, Al-, mä'dĕ (Ar., literally "the guided one," technically "the divinely guided one"), a term that has had different usages in the history of Islam. Some used it as a proper noun. To orthodox Muslims (Sunnites) it generally meant renewer of the faith and restorer of Islam to its original purity. The bulk of Shī'ites, however, use it more in its eschatological sense: the descendant of the Prophet who before the "end of time" shall appear to usher in a short millennium of equity and prosperity, restore the unity of believers, and conquer the whole world for Islam. A suppressed, frustrated minority, the Shī'ites personified their hopes in a Messiahlike leader, whom they identified with their 12th imam, Muhammad, who mysteriously disappeared in 878 at a mosque in Samarra, Iraq. The most renowned of historic al-Mahdis was 'Ubaydullah (r. 909–934), founder of the dynasty of the Fatimids (q.v.) in North Africa. One of the latest was the Sudanese Madhi who fought the British from 1883 to 1885 (see MOHAMMED AHMED).

PHILIP K. HITTI.

MAHÉ, island, Indian Ocean. See SEY-CHELLES.

MAHÉ, mà-[h]ā', former French enclave, India, part of the Union Territory of Pondicherry. It comprises the port town of Mahé, originally called Mayyazhi, and Nalutherara, a separate rural area—3¼ square miles in all. Kerala State surrounds the enclave except at the port, which is on high ground overlooking the small Mahé River and the Arabian Sea. Access is limited to small sailing craft and river boats. Rice and coconuts are produced. Acquired by France in 1725 and held intermittently by Great Britain between 1761 and 1817, Mahé passed under Indian administration in 1954 with Pondicherry, Karikal, and Yanam (Yanaon) on the east coast. A treaty between France and India confirming the transfer of sovereignty was signed in 1956 and was formally completed in 1962 after ratification by the French National Assembly. Pop. (1959) 18,300.

JOHN E. BRUSH.

MAHICAN INDIANS, mà-hē'kăn (meaning "wolf"), an Algonquian tribe of American Indians formerly occupying the Hudson River valley. They were closely related to the Delaware and the Mohegan, the collective tribe being known as the Loup or Wolf Indians. At one time there was a settlement of 40 villages near the site of Albany, N.Y. The Iroquois and white settlers diminished the tribe until its remnants became merged with the Delaware. In 1736 those who remained in Massachusetts, to which they had moved some years before, came together at Stockbridge and assumed the name Stockbridge Indians; some 500 live on the Stockbridge-Munsee Reservation in Wisconsin. They are also known as the Housatonic Indians, and are the tribe about whom James Fenimore Cooper wrote *The Last of the Mohicans.*

Consult Wissler, Clark, "The Indians of Greater New York and the Lower Hudson," American Museum of Natural History, *Anthropological Papers,* vol. 3 (New York 1909); Skinner, Alanson, *The Indians of Greater New York* (Cedar Rapids, Iowa, 1915); Smith, Chard Powers, *The Housatonic, Puritan River* (New York 1946).

FREDERICK J. DOCKSTADER.

MAHJONG. See MAH-JONGG.

MAHLER, mä'lĕr, **Gustav,** Austrian composer and conductor: b. Kalischt, Bohemia, Austria-Hungary (now Kaliště, Czechoslovakia), July 7, 1860; d. Vienna, Austria, May 18, 1911. Mahler, who was born into a large German-speaking family, experienced an unhappy homelife with his incompatible parents. After attending grammar school in Iglau (now Jihlava), he left for Vienna to be enrolled, at the age of 15, in the conservatory. There he received grounding in piano, harmony, and composition, shared a room for a while with Hugo Wolf (1860–1903), and fell under the influence of Anton Bruckner (1824–1896). He graduated with honors in 1878, attended lectures at the university until 1879, and embarked in 1880 on his eminently successful career as a conductor of opera.

The Conductor.—After gathering experience in provincial towns, Mahler was called to Kassel (1883–1885), Prague (1885–1886), and Leipzig (1886–1888). With his reputation steadily rising, he became director of opera in Budapest (1888–1891), chief *Kapellmeister* in Hamburg (1891–1897), and in 1897 director of the Imperial Opera

in Vienna. During the 10 years he spent in Vienna, the peak of his career, he won for himself an international reputation. He enlarged the repertory of operas, presenting uncut performances of those by Wagner, and wiped out the debts of the court opera. Unfortunately, his fiery temperament won him powerful enemies. Disputes and too much work overtaxed his health. He resigned his position in 1907, only to accept another one, in the same year, as conductor of the New York Metropolitan Opera and, in 1909, as conductor also of the New York Philharmonic Symphony Orchestra. His American successes were interrupted by February 1911 by a physical collapse from which he never recovered.

Gustav Mahler

Culver Service

The Composer.—Mahler created nine symphonies and left a tenth unfinished. Restless in mood, and changing from the naive to the complex, from the sensuously lyrical to the fiercely dramatic, these symphonies, influenced by Beethoven, Bruckner, and particularly Wagner, constitute his major output along with 44 lieder, the early cantata *Das klagende Lied,* and the symphonic cycle *Das Lied von der Erde (The Song of the Earth).*

With a predilection for the grandiose, Mahler lengthened the individual movements of the symphony, increased their number, and greatly enlarged the performing forces, including vocal soloists and chorus. Aided by his experience as a conductor, Mahler became a master of orchestration. He exploited instruments plastically, both in their characteristic tone colors and in unusual registers and combinations; he employed them in delicately scored groups, as well as in massive sonorities. Striking effects are produced by his instructing certain players to perform backstage and by his calling for instruments not found in the conventional orchestra: mandolin, guitar, cowbells, piano, organ, and even a hammer. His harmonic language is rich in modulation, in chromaticism, in the juxtaposition of major and minor triads (a heritage of Schubert), and, in his later works, in sharp dissonances that suggest polytonality and atonality. An innovation is Mahler's scheme of beginning a symphony in one key and concluding it in another. Unconventional is his aim to contrast, for irony, ideas lofty in inspiration with others that are commonplace.

Early Period.—The folklike was a prime source of inspiration for Mahler in his early lieder and first four symphonies. Although these songs are personal essays, their folklike quality has a ring of authenticity. Some are saturated with the spirit of the *Ländler,* an Austrian peasant dance.

Others are imbued with the energy of *Soldaten-lieder* (soldiers' songs). Their texts, aside from those of his earliest five songs and from the four of the *Lieder eines fahrenden Gesellen* (*Songs of a Wayfarer*), were drawn from *Des Knaben Wunderhorn* (The Youth's Marvelous Horn), a rich repository of German folk poetry. The early symphonies absorb the atmosphere of these lieder. Mahler introduces long folklike vocal solos into three of these symphonies, several of the solos being actual quotations from his songs. However, he aims to create not merely the folklike in these symphonies, but an entire world in each. In the awe-inspiring finale of the Second in C minor, the best known of the four symphonies, he paints doomsday and the world beyond through a giant orchestra and chorus that ring forth with Klopstock's *Ode to Immortality*.

Middle Period.—The works of this period, which include the Fifth, Sixth, and Seventh symphonies, are manifestly polyphonic. Besides writing fugal and canonic passages, Mahler combines contrasting melodies and, at climaxes, presents themes simultaneously that were heard individually earlier in the movement. In these purely instrumental symphonies, Mahler's expressionistic tendencies became overt. The works are markedly metaphysical and symbolic. Spiritually, they are closely related to his ten introspective Rückert songs, written during the same period. But actual quotations from the songs in these symphonies are few, indeed.

Late Period.—The most striking of Mahler's late works is the titanic Eighth Symphony, dubbed the Symphony of a Thousand by an enterprising manager. It requires the largest mass of performers Mahler ever assembled. Its two huge movements, in which the chorus is prominent throughout, are settings of the Gregorian hymn *Veni Creator spiritus* and the conclusion of Goethe's *Faust*. *Das Lied von der Erde*, which Mahler, with justification, subtitled a symphony, comprises six songs for tenor, contralto (or baritone), and orchestra which are based on Chinese poetry in German adaptations by Hans Bethge. The composer captures the subtle fragrance of the text through his use of the pentatonic scale, ostinato figures, and his lucid orchestral coloring. Passages of romantic nostalgia alternate with others of sublime exaltation and delicate pathos. This creation, the most readily acceptable of Mahler's longer works, together with his Ninth Symphony is imbued with a mood of resignation.

Although Mahler's lieder are accepted as masterpieces, the historic position of his symphonies has been much debated. Their loose and yet complex construction and their length are factors involved in endless controversy. Nevertheless, most critics agree that his influence upon contemporary composers—Shostakovich and Prokofiev as well as Schoenberg, Berg, and Webern—and his position as heir to the entire romantic tradition are above question.

EDWARD F. KRAVITT,
Department of Music, Hunter College.

Consult Engel, Gabriel, *Gustav Mahler, Song-Symphonist* (New York 1933); Mahler, Gustav, *Gustav Mahler Briefe, 1879–1911* (Vienna 1936); Mahler, Alma Maria, *Gustav Mahler: Memories and Letters*, tr. from the German by Basil Creighton (London 1946); Newlin, Dika, *Bruckner-Mahler-Schoenberg* (New York 1947); Redlich, Hans Ferdinand, *Bruckner and Mahler* (London and New York 1955); Mitchell, Donald, *Gustav Mahler: The Early Years* (London 1958); Mahler, Alma Maria, *And the Bridge is Love* (New York 1958); Walter, Bruno, *Gustav Mahler* (New York 1958); Cardus, Neville, *Gustav Mahler* (New York 1965).

MAHMUD, mä-mōōd′, Turk. mäк′mōōt, the name of two sultans of Turkey:

MAHMUD I, 24th Ottoman sultan: b. Edirne (Adrianople), Turkey, Aug. 2, 1696; d. Istanbul, Dec. 13, 1754. The eldest son of Sultan Mustafa II, he acceded to the throne on Oct. 1, 1730, during the social revolt led by Patrona Khalil and the Janissaries, which forced his uncle Ahmed III's abdication. Mahmud's reign was marked by a gradual but little-noticed decline in Ottoman power. Except for a brief period of peace in 1732, there was war against Persia until 1736, when the frontiers reverted to those under Murad IV (r. 1623–1640). Another war with Persia under Nadir Shah, from 1743 to 1746, was concluded on the basis of the 1736 frontiers. Hostilities with Russia and Austria, begun in 1736, ended with the Treaty of Belgrade (1739), restoring that city to Turkey and providing for Russian demolition of the Azov fortifications. The long peace with Europe that followed probably helped sap Ottoman power, which depended largely on almost continuous war against the infidel. Serious internal revolts in the provinces, notably those under the puritanical unitarian Wahhabis of Arabia, and under Sari Beyoghlu of Aydin in 1739, were suppressed. The sultan's personal interest in affairs of state and his employment of fairly responsible ministers helped maintain reasonable solvency. He was served by 16 grand viziers and by such able officials as the governor and diplomat Raghib Pasha, the French renegade general Comte Claude Alexandre de Bonneval (q.v.), and the powerful chief eunuch Beshir Agha, dominant until his death at 96 in 1746. The younger Beshir Agha then succeeded in establishing his authority until assassinated in 1752.

Mahmud was a good archer and swimmer, a fair musician, fond of literature, and a keen patron of architecture. Greek residents of the Phanar district of Istanbul were first appointed princes of Moldavia and Walachia under Mahmud I. The first 17 Islamic books printed on the state press authorized in 1727 and run by the Hungarian renegade Ibrahim Muteferrika (1674–1744) appeared between 1729 and 1742. By granting France the notorious capitulation of 1740, Mahmud reconfirmed on a broader base the extraterritorial rights of foreigners in Turkey. This treaty later involved the empire in awkward, protracted negotiations with European states. Mahmud died on horseback entering Tophapu Palace as he returned from Friday noon prayers, and was succeeded by his younger brother Osman III.

MAHMUD II, 30th Ottoman sultan: b. Istanbul, Turkey, July 20, 1785; d. there, July 1, 1839. He succeeded his deposed elder brother Mustafa IV in 1808 on the assassination of their cousin, the enlightened reformer Selim III, who was to have been restored to the throne. Mahmud sought to avoid foreign wars in order to consolidate his power against rebellious or virtually independent subjects, notably: Ali (q.v.), pasha of Janina (Ioannina) in Epirus; Husayn, pasha of Bosnia; the Greeks and Serbs; the Chapanoghlu and other *derebeys* ("lords of the valley") in Anatolia; Kurdish chieftains; Sulayman, pasha of Baghdad; the unitarian Wahhabis in Arabia (see WAHHABISM); and Muhammad 'Ali (see MOHAMMED ALI), pasha of Egypt. He subdued all save the Greeks and his Egyptian viceroy.

Mahmud properly considered this restoration of central authority a prerequisite to effective military, administrative, and social reforms which he initiated during the last 13 years of his reign after the destruction of the reactionary Janissaries on June 15, 1826. The Russian war that had broken out in 1806 had ended with the peace of Bucharest (1812), whereby Turkey ceded Bessarabia to Russia. The insurrection of the Greeks had begun in 1821 and was to culminate in their complete independence, secured with European help, in 1830. Mahmud's greatest triumph, his destruction of the Janissary standing army when it resisted reform, abolished what had been for almost 500 years the core of the Ottoman forces but had deteriorated into an unruly mob (see JANIZARIES). The sultan then undermined the traditional economic and judicial power of the conservative hierarchy of Muslim jurists, and proscribed the Bektashi dervish order, both of which had usually sided with the Janissaries against modernization. New troops, recruited from the Turkish population, were hastily organized and trained in European fashion. By effectively destroying the main forces blocking reform, Mahmud succeeded where his exemplar Selim III and earlier sultans had failed. He thus paved the way for his own reforms, necessarily preliminary, and for the later, more basic period of reorganization known as the *Tanzimat*.

Mahmud introduced modern methods of drill and new equipment and clothing into the reorganized army; he created a joint supreme commander and minister of war; he began the practice of training cadets in Europe and invited European military instructors to Turkey. The sultan needed competent officers and bureaucrats with ability in European languages. Hence he revived the military and naval schools, opened a medical school in 1827, and in 1838 planned new civilian schools. He created ministries to further centralize state authority, and provided more security for public officials by renouncing in 1826 his right to confiscate their property on their death. He abolished feudalism, undertook a census and land survey in 1831, and consolidated the administration of *vakf* (religious trust property) in the state. Turkey's first official gazette appeared in 1831, and a postal system in 1834. Civilian clothing regulations issued in 1829 replaced the traditional turban with the North African fez. However, the Holy Law of Islam was not tampered with.

The last nine years of Mahmud's reign were complicated by the contest with Muhammad 'Ali of Egypt. In 1828, Russia had declared war, and Turkey had been forced to sign the Treaty of Adrianople (1829) granting Greek autonomy and payment of a large indemnity to Russia. When Muhammad 'Ali's army under his son Ibrahim Pasha crossed Syria in 1831, defeated the sultan's forces at Konya the next year, and occupied central Anatolia, Mahmud had little choice but to accept Russian aid and troops. The Russians did not leave until Turkey had concluded the defensive alliance of Unkiar Skelessi (Hunkâr Iskelessi; see UNKIAR SKELESSI, TREATY OF) in 1833, with a secret clause forbidding access to the Straits to non-Russian warships. Mahmud renewed the war against Muhammad 'Ali in 1839, but on June 24 the troops of Ibrahim Pasha routed the Turkish Army at Nizip, north of Aleppo. The sultan died before he could hear this news, or word that the Ottoman admiral Ahmed Pasha had treacherously surrendered the fleet to Muhammad 'Ali at Alexandria. The European powers intervened to curb Muhammad 'Ali's ambitions for the sultanate but confirmed his hereditary governorship of Egypt.

Mahmud was a strong personality who accomplished much against fantastic odds, virtually singlehanded. He was an expert calligrapher, a competent musician, a patron of music and architecture, and a kindly father. He was well versed in Oriental statecraft but ignorant of European languages and affairs. He labored indefatigably to enlighten and modernize his empire. Often compared to Peter the Great, he faced far more profound problems than the Russian, but managed to initiate more changes with far fewer able officials.

See also TURKEY—*4. History* (The Ottoman Empire) : Westernization and Collapse of the Empire (The Reforms of Selim III and Mahmud II).

Consult Creasy, Sir Edward S., *History of the Ottoman Turks,* pp. 350–377, 492–530 (London 1877); Kramers, J.H. "Mahmud I" and "Mahmud II," *Encyclopaedia of Islam,* 1st ed., vol. 3, pp. 124–128 (Leiden 1936); Lewis, Bernard, *The Emergence of Modern Turkey,* pp. 74–104 (London 1961).

HOWARD A. REED,
Associate Director, The Danforth Foundation.

MAHMUD OF GHAZNI, sultan of Ghazni: b. Nov. 1/2, 971; d. Ghazni, Afghanistan, April 30, 1030. The eldest son of Subuktigin, founder of the Ghaznavid (Ghaznawid) dynasty of Afghanistan, he was one of the most renowned Muslim conquerors. Young Mahmud helped his father, a Turkish slave of the governor of Khurasan, to carve for himself a kingdom at the expense of the Samanids, an Iranian dynasty in Bukhara, which owed nominal allegiance to the 'Abbasid caliph at Baghdad. Mahmud inherited Khurasan and in 998 wrested Ghazni from his brother. Baghdad recognized him in 999 as the undisputed ruler of the new realm and conferred on him the title of *Yamin al-Dawlah* (the Right Arm of the State). He thus heralded the new era of Turkish dominance in Islamic affairs.

In the next 30 years, Mahmud, a zealous Sunnite, conducted no less than 17 campaigns against idolatrous and wealthy India. From one campaign he returned with a fortune of 3 million dirhams, a large number of elephants, and captives so numerous as to reduce the price of a slave to a couple of dirhams. He penetrated India as far as the Ganges on the east and Sind on the west. With the plundered money he adorned Ghazni and patronized poets such as al-Firdausi and scholars such as al-Biruni. His last campaign, against the Shi'ite Buwayhids, netted him the Persian Iraq, including al-Rayy and Isfahan. History and legend never tire of singing his exploits.

PHILIP K. HITTI.

MAHOE, mà-hō', a shrub or small tree, *Hibiscus tiliaceus,* of the mallow family (Malvaceae), occurring in the tropics of both hemispheres. It is found along seashores and tidal streams and in mangrove swamps. In the United States, mahoe grows only in southern Florida. The plant becomes 15 to 30 feet tall and has leathery leaves that are downy beneath, four to eight inches long, and reminiscent of linden leaves. The flowers, one and one half to three inches long, have five petals that are yellow at first but turn red with age. The seedpods are egg shaped, and hairy and contain many kidney-shaped dark seeds one quarter inch long. Mahoe wood is durable in seawater. It is whitish, soft, and light, and is used in making floats, planking, tool handles, and light boxes. The plant is especially valued for the fiber obtained from its bark and employed for cordage and mats. Mahoe is also called wild or coast cotton tree, yellow mallow tree, and sea hibiscus.

JOHN W. THIERET,
University of Southwestern Louisiana.

MAHOGANY, mà-hŏg'a-nĭ, large trees of the genus *Swietenia* (true mahogany), found in southern Florida, the West Indies, Mexico, Central America, Colombia, Venezuela, and the upper Amazon region. A widely used cabinet wood, mahogany is considered to be the most valuable timber tree in tropical America. It is hard enough to resist abrasion, does not warp readily, is easy to work and to finish, and possesses a beautiful grain and rich reddish brown or golden brown color. Ideal for making veneers, it can take a natural finish or lend itself to a reddish brown stain. Glued joints hold well and the shrinkage factor is low.

Mahogany leaves are compound, with the leaflets arranged in a featherlike (pinnate) fashion on both sides of the stem; the small whitish or greenish flowers appear in a loose, irregularly branched (panicled) cluster; the fruit is egg shaped (ovoid), consisting of five-valved chambers two to six inches long, seeds and valves finally falling away to leave a five-winged receptacle; the bark of the tree resembles that of the elm in having surfaced ridges.

European colonists of the 16th century built elaborate structures of mahogany. The Cathedral of Santo Domingo, completed in 1540, has some of the finest carved mahogany in the world. The American wood was originally classified by dealers into Spanish and Honduras mahogany, the former originating in the Spanish American possessions. The genus was first described by Nikolaus von Jacquin in 1760 as *S. mahogani*, found in the Bahamas. This species also grows in southern Florida and the West Indies. The second species, *S. humilis*, originating in southwestern Mexico, was described by Joseph Zuccarini in 1836. It flourishes in dry areas along the Pacific coast down to Costa Rica. The third species, *S. macrophylla*, was located at Calcutta, India, about 1886. It had originated in Central America and thrives in regions of great rainfall from the Yucatan Peninsula to Colombia and Venezuela. A considerable amount also grows in eastern Peru and western Brazil.

True-Mahogany Substitutes.—African mahogany refers to the genus *Khaya*. These trees are native to tropical Africa, where they grow in the largest quantities in the rain forest of the west coast. In general appearance and in many characteristics African mahogany is the nearest substitute for true mahogany. The larger pores of *Khaya* give the wood a coarser appearance. The texture is somewhat softer, and the wood is lighter in weight

The lauans, trees producing lumber commonly called Philippine mahogany, include a number of moderately light-to-heavy and soft-to-hard woods of the dipterocarp family. These woods resemble mahogany in general appearance and compare favorably in strength, color, and weight. Red lauan (*Shorea negrosensis*) has an interlocking grain that often produces a quartered surface resembling a ribbon figure of alternate light and dark stripes. The pores are larger than those of true mahogany. The lauans are said to produce about 95 percent of all export shipments of wood. They are often marketed in the United States as dark red Philippine mahogany. This wood is used in the construction of boats and sailing craft. Because of its large size, it is in demand for outsized planking and for decks.

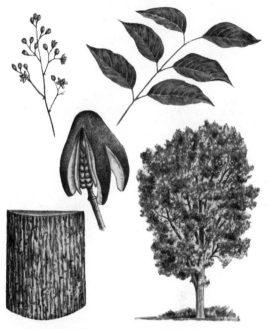

Swietenia mahogani, one of the mahogany species, showing flowers, leaves, fruit, bark, and tree silhouette.

Spanish cedar (*Cedrela odorata*) is a broadleafed wood which is closely related to true mahogany. It is also called cigar-box cedar. One authority divides Cedrelacae into two suborders: Swieteniae and Cedrelae.

Primavera (*Cybistax donnellsmithii*), sometimes termed white mahogany, belongs to the Bignoniaceae family, which also includes the catalpas. It grows in Central America and in Mexico, and is often associated with true mahogany, which it resembles even to the conspicuous pores of *Swietenia*. It differs only in color—the finished wood is a golden yellow.

East Indian or Ceylon satinwood is from *Chloroxylon swietenia*, a relative of mahogany. It is hard, heavy, durable, close grained, brittle and smooth like boxwood. The cream-colored heartwood has a fine satinlike appearance when highly polished. This costly wood is used only in very fine cabinetwork.

CHRIS H. GRONEMAN,
Head, Department of Industrial Education, Texas A & M University.

MAHOMET. See MOHAMMED.

MAHONE, mà-hōn', **William,** American Confederate officer and United States senator: b. Southhampton County, Va., Dec. 1, 1826; d. Washington, D.C., Oct. 8, 1895. After graduating from the Virginia Military Institute in 1847, he became a civil engineer and served in the Confederate Army during the Civil War, rising to brigadier general in 1864. When the war ended, he became president of the Atlantic, Mississippi and Ohio Railroad (Norfolk and Western Railway) and was a principal organizer (about

1878) and leader of the Readjusters, chiefly a faction of the Democratic Party in Virginia who favored the forcible readjustment of the state debt on terms involving conditional or partial repudiation. Mainly by the supporters of this movement, he was elected in 1880 to the United States Senate, where, however, he acted with the Republicans, making the vote of the Senate a tie and disappointing the Democrats of their expected majority. By this and other acts of his senatorial career he lost favor with his constituents and was not re-elected.

MAHONY, mä′ŏ-nǐ, **Francis Sylvester** (pseudonym FATHER PROUT), Irish humorist: b. Cork, Ireland, about 1804; d. Paris, France, May 18, 1866. Admitted to the Order of Jesuits, and in 1830 given the post of master of rhetoric at the Jesuit college at Clongoweswood, Ireland, Mahony fell into difficulties with his superiors and left the order. His wit and facility in composing Greek and Latin verse, as well as French, made him widely known among the literati of his day. As Father Prout he contributed to *Fraser's Magazine* (1834–1836) a series of papers afterwards published as *Reliques of Father Prout.* He had a trick of translating works of his contemporaries into Latin and Greek, and then playfully accusing them of plagiarism. He traveled widely; from Rome he was correspondent for the London *Daily News,* and from Paris for the *Globe.* In 1881 a collected edition of his works was published. *The Bells of Shandon,* one of his original poems, has always been greatly admired.

MAHRATTAS. See MARATHAS.

MAI, mä′ê, **Angelo,** Italian classical scholar and cardinal: b. Schilpario, Province of Bergamo, Italy, March 7, 1782; d. Castel Gandolfo, near Rome, Sept. 9, 1854. Having entered the Jesuit Order, Mai became professor of Latin and Greek in the Jesuit college at Naples (1804). Transferred to Milan, his scholarship soon procured him the post of curator of the Ambrosian Library. Here his examination of ancient manuscripts and palimpsests (q.v.) led to the discovery of fragments of Cicero and other Latin writers, never before published. The pope called him to the Vatican Library at Rome in 1819, where his findings included further writings of Cicero, works of many ancient historians, and a Greek MS. of the Bible. In 1838 he was created a cardinal. Collections of his classical discoveries were published in 10 volumes (1828–1838), and a final series, *Nova Patrum Bibliotheca,* between 1845 and 1853.

MAIA, mä′yà, in Greek mythology, the eldest daughter of Atlas and Pleione, and mother of Hercules by Zeus. With her six sisters, who were pursued by Orion, the Hunter, she was placed in the stars, where they are known as the Pleiades. The Romans also worshiped a Maia, who was also called Majesta, and was later identified with the daughter of Atlas. See also MAY (fifth month).

MAIANA (formerly HALL ISLAND), island, Gilbert Islands, in the west central Pacific Ocean, forming a part of the British colony of Gilbert and Ellice Islands (q.v.). It is nine miles long, with an area of 10.3 square miles. The principal product of the island is copra. Pop. (1947) 1,425.

MAIANO, Benedetto Da. See BENEDETTO DA MAIANO.

MAID MARIAN, a name given to the fictitious character of Matilda, daughter of Fitz-Walter, baron of Bayard and Dunmow, who eloped with Robert Fitzooth, earl of Huntingdon (known as Robin Hood, the outlaw), and lived with him in Sherwood Forest. Originally the May Queen in old May games and morris dances, and the partner of Friar Tuck, Maid Marian was transferred to the old ballads of Robin Hood, and has figured in numerous romances and poems ever since. Alfred Noyes made her the heroine of his poetic drama *Sherwood* (1911), and she appeared in films in 1937 and later. See also ROBIN HOOD.

MAID OF ATHENS, a poem by Lord Byron, whose original is said to be Theresa Macri, the beautiful 15-year-old daughter of a Greek woman in whose household Byron lived while in Athens in 1809–1810. In later years she suffered poverty, and a public appeal was issued in England by the friends of the poet, for her relief.

MAID OF ORLEANS. See JOAN OF ARC.

MAID OF ORLEANS, The (*Jungfrau von Orleans*), a romantic tragedy by Johann C. F. von Schiller (q.v., 1801).

MAID OF THE MIST, the name of a small steamboat formerly used on the Niagara River below the Falls, to carry passengers close to the cataract. It was badly damaged by fire, April 1955.

MAIDEN, The, or **THE WIDOW,** an instrument of capital punishment introduced into Scotland from Halifax. It was used during the 16th century, and was the prototype of the French guillotine. Its first victim is said to have been one of the lesser agents in the assassination of David Rizzio in 1566. In 1581 it was used on James Douglas, earl of Morton, who had brought it into Scotland.

MAIDEN QUEEN, a popular title bestowed upon Queen Elizabeth I of England.

MAIDENHAIR FERN. See FERNS AND FERN ALLIES.

MAIDENHEAD, town, England, in Berkshire on the Thames River, 27 miles west of London. For generations it has been a popular resort in summer for visitors who pole the punts up and down the river, which here has many fine abbeys, churches, and estates, many of the latter, like Cliveden, now belonging to the National Trust and open to the public. A fine 18th century bridge carries the Bath road into Buckinghamshire, and a railway bridge serves the Great Western Railway. Maidenhead is a market town, has breweries and grain mills, and handles timber. Pop. (1961) 35,374.

MAIDSTONE, mād′stŏn, municipal borough, England, county town of Kent, on the Medway River, 30 miles southeast of London. It is a crossroads for routes in all directions, older than the Roman occupation, when it was a station on a Roman road. It was well-known in the Middle

Ages as a way station for Canterbury pilgrims, and is a flourishing market town in the 20th century. Hops and fruit are extensively grown, paper is manufactured, beer is brewed, and some machinery made. There are several ancient churches, a 16th-century grammar school, a hospital founded in 1260 and an Elizabethan manor house now a museum. In World War II it was a center of Royal Air Force activity during the Battle of Britain and the buzz bomb attacks. Pop. (1961) 59,761.

MAIDU, mī′dōō (meaning man or people), an aboriginal Indian tribe dwelling in northern California, chiefly in the Sacramento valley. They belong to the Pujunan linguistic family, and had three divisions. Their houses were built of poles, bark, brush, and grass, covered with earth, and were circular, with conical roofs and a smokehole at the top. They lived mainly on acorns, seeds, and a little fish or game. They wore little clothing, and knew nothing of weaving. Their only art was basketry, in which they excelled. Coiled, or sewn, baskets were even used for cooking by dropping hot stones inside. They had shamans, or witch doctors, rites for puberty of both boys and girls, ritual dances, special huts for sweat baths and for the men alone, and a religious belief in a Great Man who created the earth and revealed himself in the lightning.

First mentioned by explorers in 1838–1842, they suffered ill treatment, were cleared out of their area in the search for gold, and now survive in small numbers in foothills and in the Round Valley Indian reservation, where the Indians farm, but still live in their bush huts.

Consult "Maidu", *Handbook of North American Indians* (Washington, D.C. 1907).

MAIL, flexible armor of interlinked rings. The term "mail," as used by extension to cover body armor in general, is a literary affectation of comparatively recent times. The popular and generally acceptable phrase "chain mail" is, nevertheless, a pleonasm, since the word mail is derived from the Latin *macula* (the mesh of a net) through the Italian *maglia* and the French *maille*. Mail was the normal body defense in Europe from before the time of the Norman Conquest until it was largely superseded by plate armor in the 14th century. See ARMS AND ARMOR; CHAIN MAIL.

MAIL ORDER, a method of selling which results in orders received by mail. The sales message may reach the customer through coupon advertising in newspapers and magazines; catalogues, circulars, letters, and similar printed material mailed to prospects (direct mail); radio and television advertising; coupon advertising on matchbook covers, and through similar methods. The seller's purpose, in all cases, is to secure orders by mail.

Modern mail order selling dates back to some time before 1900. Richard Sears, then a telegraph clerk in a Minnesota railroad station, conceived the idea of selling a consignment of watches which had been refused by a local jeweler, to other telegraph operators. He received the orders by mail, and when the original watches were exhausted, arranged for the watch supplier to ship the watches and collect the amount due. The success of this simple idea led him to leave his job to start a mail order business. This was the beginning of Sears, Roebuck & Co.

The first mail order catalogues were small and advertised only a few, carefully selected items. As ordering from catalogues became more popular more and more items were added to supply the needs of customers.

Reasons for Growth.—(1) *Price advantage.* Because of their great volume of sales, the mail order houses can usually offer lower prices.

(2) *Variety of selection.* Few stores in rural communities can match the wide selection of merchandise available through catalogues.

(3) *Ease of ordering.* Since the catalogue is always on hand, ordering by mail is fast and easy. The catalogues also describe items in such minute detail that the customer is well-informed in making his purchasing decisions.

(4) *Return privilege.* Mail order houses build confidence by readily accepting any merchandise returned as unsatisfactory. Many offer, in addition, to extend credit on purchases.

Selling of Specialties.—Many mail order firms, unlike the huge catalogue houses, sell only a single product or a group of closely related products. Cigars, books, colonial furniture, fish, lumber, men's ties, and vitamin pills are some of the specialties sold successfully through mail order. However, the product being sold must be chosen with great care since not all products can be sold profitably by mail. The item must offer advantages over competing items available locally. It must be in strong demand and must fill a consumer need.

Media of Sales.—*Publication Advertising.*— The mail order seller buys space in a newspaper, magazine, or newspaper supplement. He may or may not include a coupon but readers are asked to send orders by mail. In some cases, the advertiser offers to send a booklet further describing the product. Some newspapers and magazines devote several pages or sections to mail order advertisements. These pages are meant to serve as a directory of hard-to-find goods and services.

There is a minimum of detail and bother connected with running mail order advertisements. In most cases an advertising agency prepares and places the ads, making no charge for its services. The agency receives a commission from the periodical on the space used.

One disadvantage of mail order advertising in magazines is that ads must usually be scheduled months in advance. This sometimes makes it impossible for the mail order advertiser to follow up successful ads quickly. If selling seasonal items, this delay can be serious.

Advertising rates vary greatly depending on circulation. A page ad may cost from $30 in a low-circulation journal to $15,000 in a mass-circulation magazine. However, by using small space, the advertiser can test the sales appeal of his product at little cost.

Direct Mail.—This method entails mailing letters, circulars, booklets, catalogues, brochures, post cards, self-mailers, and similar printed material to lists of customers and selected prospects. These lists of prospect names may be procured from many sources. They may be compiled by the mailer or bought or rented from a list compiler. List brokers offer a wide selection of lists which are available for a one-time rental. Directories, telephone books, public records, club membership lists, magazine subscription lists, are a few additional sources of names. The mailer may also arrange to exchange mailing lists with a non-competitive mailer.

The mailing list is the most important single factor in a successful mailing. The most compelling offer fails if it doesn't reach a prospect who needs and can pay for the product. For this reason, great care is taken in selecting lists. For most purposes, the five-part mailing piece is most productive. It consists of a letter, circular, reply card or order form, business reply envelope, and outside envelope. The letter presents the sales story in logical sequence and describes the benefits of the product in personal terms. The circular pictures the product, supplies necessary descriptive details, and dramatizes major sales appeals through illustrations and layout techniques. The order form and reply envelope simplify ordering and fix the terms of the sale. All of these are inserted in the outside envelope which bears the stamp, address, and other mailing information.

This complete mailing piece has proved its value over the years. However, post cards, self-mailers, booklets, and other simple mailing pieces also play an important part in mail order selling. The type of mailing selected for a specific sales effort depends on a number of factors, among them the amount of money appropriated, the length and complexity of the sales story, the impression to be created, and the familiarity of prospects with the product.

One reason for direct mail's wide use is its personal character. A letter, circular, or catalogue addressed to the prospect and delivered to his home promotes a personal relationship between buyer and seller. Direct mail also offers the benefit of great flexibility. Letters, catalogues, and so on, can be as long or short as necessary, mailings can be released at the precise moment selected by the mailer, lists used can vary from a few names to millions of names, mailings can be elaborate or simple, every element going into the mailing can be controlled by the mailer. On the other hand, direct mail involves a sea of details. Arrangements must be made with printers, envelopes must be addressed, lists rented, the various elements gathered together and mailed. However, service organizations, including letter-shops (see section on *Service Organizations*) stand ready to relieve mailers of many of these details.

Radio and Television.—Household goods and similar items lend themselves to these media. Time spots, as well as programs, can be purchased. In radio and television the mail order advertiser faces a problem absent in direct mail and coupon advertising. Spoken words and television images are fleeting and can't be recaptured. While the prospect may examine letters, catalogues, and ads at his leisure, he must react to radio and television advertising as it is being presented. The mail order advertiser therefore adapts his presentation to this condition. He does so by repeating and rephrasing salient points, by emphasizing and repeating his address and by concentrating on the effort to gain attention.

Mail Order Techniques.—*Copy.*—Mail order efforts, whether printed or spoken, must complete the sale without outside help. The words used to describe the product and to convince the buyer (copy), are therefore vitally important. Mail order copy must be complete, persuasive, and action-getting. The mail order copywriter must think in terms of his prospect's needs and desires. He must dramatize the benefits to be derived from his product, and he must convince the prospect of his sincerity and of the truth of his statements.

Testimonials from satisfied users are often used to strengthen confidence.

The copy should answer in advance any objections or questions the prospect might have. To secure the maximum return, ordering should be made as simple as possible. To overcome human inertia some incentive such as a free premium is often offered for quick action.

Layout.—In periodical advertising and direct mail the arrangement of the copy and illustrations on the page also take on great importance. Since every inch of space is expected to pay its own way in orders, there is little room for empty decoration and meaningless art work. The function of the layout is to supplement and complement the copy so that the two, working together, form an effective selling unit.

Testing and Keying.—So that they may trace their orders, mail order sellers key their mailings, advertisements, and commercials. This is done by assigning distinguishable codes to the specific sales efforts being made. These codes usually appear somewhere on the coupon or order form. By keeping a record of orders received bearing such code, the mailer can test the comparative worth of various copy approaches, the order-pulling power of different magazines, or lists, and the demand for his product in various sections of the country. The information thus gained is extremely valuable in planning and expanding his mail order campaigns.

Timing.—Some items, such as Christmas cards, ski equipment, and tulip bulbs, have a seasonal appeal which determines the best time for mailings and advertisements. Sales results for the majority of products sold by mail, however, tend to follow a general pattern. January, February, March, September, and October are normally the most productive months. May and June are normally the poorest. Mail order firms usually schedule their mailings and advertisements to conform with this pattern.

Analyzing Results.—By intelligent testing, the mail order man is able to expand those efforts which succeed and eliminate those that fail. One widely used basis for evaluating the success of an effort is the cost per order. This is arrived at by dividing the total cost of the mailing or ad by the number of orders received. This is compared to a "break-even" figure representing the maximum cost per order possible for a successful operation.

Another factor important in analyzing results is the volume of repeat business. Satisfactory profits rarely come from the original sale. The basis for a sound mail order business is almost always a mailing list of satisfied customers who can be reached easily. Repeat orders and orders for additional products from these customers represent profitable business obtained at low cost. Some mailers are prepared to show little or no profit on first orders, because they expect subsequent orders to provide profits.

Postal Service.—Post office regulations provide certain aids to mailers. Advertising literature may be mailed in bulk at reduced rates (3d class mail). Business reply cards and envelopes included in mailings enable the customer to send orders to the advertiser without postage. The advertiser pays the postage due on receipt.

The post office offers other services which are valuable in keeping mailing lists up to date. When "Return Postage Guaranteed" is printed on the outside of the envelope, any undeliverable mailing pieces are returned. This enables the mailer to delete these names from his mailing list. By another method the post office notifies the sender of changes of address on form 3547. The post office will also undertake to correct mailing lists for a nominal charge, when the names and addresses are submitted for checking. Because of the great waste involved in sending out undeliverable mail, these services are widely used.

Service Organizations.—With the growth of the mail order business, numerous organizations have been set up to meet the needs of mail order concerns. Among these are:

(1) *List brokers.* Finding appropriate names in adequate quantity is a problem that continually faces mailers. By devoting the time, energy, and knowledge of his organization to the task, the broker acts as a clearing house for lists, specializing in lists of people who have bought services or products by mail.

(2) *List compilers.* Often a mailer may have need for a list of specialized people or organizations. A list compiler will arrange to compile the list if he does not already have it available. As opposed to the list broker, the compiler usually handles only lists which he himself owns or controls.

(3) *Lettershops.* The various processes involved in assemblying the parts of a mailing, sorting, tying, folding, and delivery to the post office, are time consuming and trying. Small errors can prove very costly. The lettershop, with its inserting machines, automatic addressing equipment, stamping machines and other labor and time-saving equipment provides a valuable service. Most lettershops are prepared to handle all the details of mailing. All the mailer has to do is have his envelopes, circulars, letters, and any other material delivered to the lettershop. When the mailing has been delivered to the post office, the lettershop presents a post office receipt showing quantity mailed as proof that the job has been completed.

Future.—In spite of the automobile and the spread of department stores to the suburbs, mail order continues to grow and to expand. The ease of ordering, the convenience of having goods delivered to the home, the price advantage often enjoyed, these factors help to explain mail order's continued popularity. Basically, mail order succeeds because it fills a need. Consumers want to be told about new products, they want to be sure they get their money's worth, they want to buy things to make life easier, richer, and more pleasant. Mail order gives them the opportunity to do so easily and economically.

JOSEPH R. VERGARA.

Bibliography.—Graham, I., *How to Sell Through Mail Order* (New York 1950); Mayer, E., *How to Make More Money With Your Direct Mail* (New York 1953); Cassels, J. W., *How to Sell Successfully by Direct Mail* (London 1954); Stone, R. F., *Successful Direct Mail Advertising and Selling* (New York 1955).

MAILER, Norman, American novelist: b. Long Branch, N. J., Jan. 31, 1923. He was educated in Brooklyn (N. Y.) schools and in 1939 entered Harvard where his ambition to become an aeronautical engineer was abandoned in favor of authorship. He graduated in 1943 and, while waiting to be drafted, wrote his first novel *A Transit to Venus* (unpublished). Drafted into the army in the spring of 1944, his foreign service included tours in the Philippines and Japan. Discharged in May 1946, he wrote *The Naked and the Dead* (1948), which painted obscene and repulsive aspects of a soldier's life and harrowing scenes of battle. Though plainly motivated by personal disgust with army life, critics acclaimed it a major war novel. His *Barbary Shore* (1951) and *Deer Park* (1955) received a poor press.

MAILLOL, mà-yôl', **Aristide,** French painter: b. Banyuls-sur-Mer, France, Dec. 25,

1861; d. there, Oct. 5, 1944. Although Maillol studied painting at the École des Beaux-Arts, Paris, and was interested in engraving and in tapestries, he found his real talent at the age of 40, sculpturing in wood, wax, metal, stone, and marble. He specialized in the nude female figure, and was influenced by the classical Greek tradition of the 5th century, even more after visiting Greece in 1909. Auguste Rodin, whom he does not in the least resemble, greatly praised his work, and many consider him the greatest sculptor of his time.

He executed figures for war memorials, *Fame* for a monument to Paul Cézanne, terra cotta figures, and *Seated Woman* (1901) in the Tuileries, Paris, which is the most photographed of all his figures. His *River* is in the Museum of Modern Art, New York. He was killed in an automobile accident near his home.

MAIMON, mī'mŏn, **Salomon,** German philosopher: b. Minsk, Polish Lithuania 1754; d. Siegersdorf, Lower Silesia, Germany Nov. 22, 1800. Of Jewish descent, Maimon gave up orthodoxy after reading Maimonides His discovery of Immanuel Kant in 1788 led to the publication of *Versuch über die Transcendental-philosophie* (1790), in which he limits philosophy to the realm of pure thought Taking up a position between Kant and David Hume, he influenced later criticism.

MAIMONIDES, mī-mŏn'ĭ-dēz (MOSES BEN MAIMON, also known as RAMBAM), Jewish philosopher: b. Córdoba, Spain, March 30, 1135; d. Cairo, Egypt, Dec. 13, 1204. Called IBN-MAYMŪN by the Arabs, Maimonides led the life of a respected Hebrew scholar in Córdoba until a Mohammedan invasion from Africa, and the persecution which followed, sent the family on its travels. Settling eventually in Cairo, Maimonides became the recognized head of the Jewish community in Egypt, as well as physician to the sultan and the royal family. There he wrote the most important of his works: a commentary in Arabic, *Siray* (*The Illumination*), on the Mishnah, or law book of the Jews; *Mishneh Torah,* his chief work in Hebrew; and *Dalālat al-Hā 'irin* (*Guide of the Perplexed*). In these three works he introduced a new period in Jewish theology and life. In *The Illumination,* on which he spent seven years, he interpreted the collection of laws in the light of philosophy. His method was to explain each entry by a paraphrase. He introduced the Thirteen Principles or beliefs, which became incorporated in the Daily Prayer Book, but not universally accepted as a creed or dogma.

In the *Mishnch Torah* (*Second Law*), Maimonides undertook to bring order out of the chaos of the Talmud, which had been derived from the Mishnah and was even more difficult to follow. Ten years' work produced a clear exposition of the Jewish laws of life and their religious observances. Many Jews objected to this codifying of their beliefs, but it was the *Guide to the Perplexed* that divided them into two parties, and even led to a public burning of the work by his opponents.

In this philosophical work, written in Arabic, Maimonides attempted to combine the philosophy of Aristotle, whom he knew in translation, with Biblical texts that were part of the Hebrew theology. When he could not reconcile Aristotle with the Jewish belief in the creation of the material world, he made creation an article of faith. God must remain in control of the physical world or the possibility of miracles could not exist, but Maimonides interpreted the Biblical miracles allegorically. Since the Deity was conceived of as incorporeal, Maimonides posited a world of nine spheres ruled by "angels" through which the immaterial acted on the material world.

The philosopher followed Aristotle in his belief in the Absolute, or universal intelligence, and taught that man, although material, may attain a knowledge of this pure intelligence, thus giving immortality to the soul. This confers on man freedom of will to work out his salvation by following the laws of God. Matter, he taught, was the source of evil and imperfection. He believed that the soul lives on after death, but he did not follow the orthodox Jewish belief in resurrection. The soul was punished after death by awareness of its failures. He also deviated from Aristotle in his views on prophecy, which he considered a divine illumination translated by the soul into figurative form. Moses alone he conceived to have been directly inspired.

His teaching influenced both Jewish and Christian philosophers and teachers of Biblical law for many generations. Such men as Thomas Aquinas, Albertus Magnus, Duns Scotus, Leibniz, and Herbert Spencer knew and discussed his works.

As a physician he was almost equally famous. After a morning spent in Cairo tending the royal family and officers, he returned to his home to tend hundreds of private patients. Only the Sabbath could be given to religious activities. Combating superstition and astrology, he was a forerunner of psychological therapy, and his success has left a tradition exemplified to this day in pilgrimages of the sick to his synagogue in Cairo as well as to his tomb in Tiberias.

The Code of Maimonides, tr. from the Hebrew, is in the Yale University Judaica series (1949–1952) ; and the *Mishneh Torah,* Hebrew text with English translation by Moses Hyamson, is available (1952).

Consult Yellin, D., and Abrahams, I., *Maimonides* (Philadelphia 1903); Singer, C., *The Legacy of Israel* (Oxford 1927); Roth, Leon, *The Guide for the Perplexed* (New York 1948); Bokser, Ben Zion, *The Legacy of Maimonides* (Toronto 1950).

MAIN, mān, a river of Germany, which has its source in the northeastern part of Bavaria, about 13 miles northwest of Bayreuth. It flows northwest to the border of Bavaria and then makes a succession of remarkable zigzags, continuing, however, in a westerly direction, till it reaches the border of Hesse, which it enters. It then flows circuitously west and joins the Rhine a little above the town of Mainz, after a course of over 300 miles. The principal cities which it passes are Wurzburg, Aschaffenburg, and Frankfurt. It is navigable for about 200 miles. By means of Ludwigs Canal (Ludwigs-Donau-Main-Kanal) navigation to the Danube is possible.

MAIN CURRENTS IN AMERICAN THOUGHT, An Interpretation of American Literature from the Beginnings to 1920, by Vernon Louis Parrington, in 3 volumes, the first two of which were published in 1927 and the following year won the Pulitzer Prize for history; the last volume, in fragment form, completed only to 1900, was edited by Professor E. H. Eby and published posthumously in 1930.

Volume 1, *1620–1800, The Colonial Mind,* examines those ideas which have become traditionally recognized as American, how and from

where they came, and what influence they exerted in determining our characteristic ideals and institutions. The author describes the pressure of American environment on the 17th and 18th century European ideals from which resulted the overthrow of aristocracy and monarchy and the development of the principle of democracy. Volume 2, *1800–1860, The Romantic Revolution in America,* is concerned with the influence of French romantic theories, the rise of capitalism, and the transition to an industrial from an agricultural state. Social progress in terms of the emergent middle class was the predominant philosophy. Volume 3, *1860–1920, The Beginnings of Critical Realism in America,* is the author's analysis of the decay of the romantic optimism and the source of that decay is laid to three causes: the stratifying of economics under the system of centralization; the evolvement of a mechanistic science; and the development of a philosophy of skepticism which is resulting in the questioning of the ideal democratic spirit.

The author's main purpose, as a liberal thinker, was first to examine and understand in a true scholarly spirit the various points of view expressed in American literature, being guided by historical significance rather than aesthetic judgment, before offering his personal critique. Three phases of his method become apparent: he treats the literature of America as the outgrowth of racial strains, environment, and period; to this treatment he applies the theory of economic determinism as a means for a true understanding; and, he considers American literature as American thought, that is, the literature of a country is the reflection of its thought which in turn has been the result of economic forces acting on political, social, and religious institutions. Parrington, famous for his ability to reduce his thesis to a single phrase, sentence, or expressive figure, has summarized our intellectual history in three phases: "Calvinistic pessimism, romantic optimism, and mechanistic pessimism."

MAIN CURRENTS IN NINETEENTH CENTURY LITERATURE (*Hovedstrømninger i det 19. Aarhundredes europæiske Litteratur*). This great work of Georg Brandes (1842–1927, q.v.) established its Danish-Jewish author's reputation as one of the greatest champions of freedom of inquiry and freedom of thought in the last quarter of the 19th century. Its six volumes consist of the following separate studies: *The Literature of the French Emigrés* (1872) ; *The Romantic School in Germany* (1873) ; *Reaction in France* (1874) ; *Naturalism in England* (1875) ; *The Romantic School in France* (1882) ; *Young Germany* (1890).

An English translation of the *Main Currents* was published 1901–1905. A partisan of French revolutionary ideals, an ardent admirer of his friends Taine, Renan, and John Stuart Mill, he sought in these volumes, based on lectures, to liberate Scandinavia from its provincial prejudices. He was an inveterate foe of romanticism.

MAIN STREET, a novel by Sinclair Lewis (q.v.), published in 1920. The following year it was dramatized by Harvey O'Higgins and Harriet Ford.

The central figure of the story is Carol Milford, an attractive, quick-minded, college educated librarian from the Twin Cities. Of a mercurial temperament and possessed by somewhat vaporous cultural enthusiasms, she allows herself to marry Will Kennicott, a phlegmatic small-town physician, and as his wife she attempts to reform both the unsightly material fabric and the provincial spirit of the raw Minnesota community in which Kennicott has established his not unlucrative practice. In the course of her crusade, Carol acquires a handful of sympathetic allies: Vilda Sherwin, an erotic, sharp-tongued schoolteacher; the ineffectual yet perceptive lawyer, Guy Pollock, who has tarried too long in Gopher Prairie and become permanently infected by what Lewis calls the "village virus"; and Miles Bjornstam, odd-jobman extraordinary, who is a combination of resident agnostic, "radical," and gadfly.

Balked by Main Street's hostility, intolerance, smugness, and ignorance and by its worship of dullness made God, Carol lives out the years before World War I in a state of uncertainty, satisfied neither by marriage nor by parenthood. Somewhat in despair, she drifts into an abortive love affair. Flight to wartime Washington with her child and the two years spent there give her an opportunity to review her life and her relations with her community. In the end her patient husband takes her back to Gopher Prairie, which she ultimately comes to accept as a place where, as she says of herself, she may not have won a single victory nor even have fought the good fight, but where, in spite of everything, she has steadfastly kept faith.

Originally conceived as a novel on the theme of the village virus, with Guy Pollock as the fatally infected protagonist, *Main Street* underwent a long period of incubation in its author's mind. His sixth serious novel, it was written to please himself rather than either his publisher or his hitherto modest public, and there is reason to believe that few, if any, expected it to be the very great popular success that it was, much less one of the foremost novels of the 1920's in the United States and other countries. As was the case with certain of its successors, notably *Babbitt* and *Arrowsmith* (qq.v.), *Main Street* caught a wave of inarticulate discontent and rode it in swelling triumph up the beach. That particular wave of national self-criticism has since subsided; yet detailed, acidulous, and authentic literary embodiment lives on in the mimic-history of Carol Kennicott. The argument of the book has elevated the concept of the universal Main Street into a social symbol, and its considerable artistry can still leave with the responsive reader the wistful, lingering essence of a life which is seen as permanently settled, its onetime elixir evaporated, the motionless, cloudy sediment of day-to-day existence alone remaining.

MARKHAM HARRIS,
Department of English, University of Washington.

MAINE, mān, SIR **Henry James Sumner,** English jurist: b. near Leighton, England, Aug. 15, 1822; d. Cannes, France, Feb. 3, 1888. He was educated at Christ's Hospital and at Pembroke College, Cambridge, where he served as regius professor of civil law from 1847 to 1854. Meanwhile, in 1850, he was called to the bar, and two years later became reader on Roman law and jurisprudence at the Inns of Court. As legal member of the council of the viceroy of India (1863–1869), he assisted in the codification of Indian law. On his return to England he was appointed to the chair of jurisprudence at Oxford, which he held until 1878. From 1877 until his death he was master of Trinity Hall, Cambridge, where he also served (1887–1888) as Whewell professor of international law. Maine was a pioneer in the study of the history of law, whose development he traced from early customs. Among his best-known works are *Ancient Law* (1861); *Village-Communities in the East and West* (1871); *Lectures on the Early History of Institutions* (1875); *Dissertations on Early Law and Custom* (1883); and *International Law* (1888).

MAINE, mān, Fr. mân, old province, France, bounded on the north by Normandy, on the east by Île-de-France and Orléanais, on the south by Touraine and Anjou, and on the west by Brittany. The capital was Le Mans. A countship in the 10th century, Maine was joined to Anjou in 1126 and so came under the control of the Angevin kings of England. In 1204 it was united to the French crown by Philip Augustus, but in 1246 Louis IX gave it to his brother, Charles of Anjou. Reunited to the crown with the accession of Philip VI in 1328, it subsequently became an appanage of other members of the royal family and was not finally rejoined to the crown until 1584. In 1790 the territory of Maine was divided into the present departments, most of it passing to Mayenne and Sarthe, but parts also to Orne, Eure-et-Loir, and Loir-et-Cher.

MAINE, mān, New England state, United States, bounded on the north by the Canadian provinces of Quebec and New Brunswick, on the east by New Brunswick, on the southeast and south by the Atlantic Ocean, and on the west by New Hampshire and Quebec. Its greatest length, measured from north-northeast to south-southwest, is about 322 miles; its greatest width, from east to west, about 207 miles.

The name "Maine" was used as early as 1622 to distinguish the mainland from the islands. In the charter of 1606 to the Plymouth Company the area was called the "Province of Main," and in the Mason and Gorges patent of 1629, "the Mayn Land of New England." From 1677 until its admission to the Union as a state in 1820, Maine was part of Massachusetts.

The most easterly state in the Union, Maine is almost as large as all the rest of New England. Lumbering, shipbuilding, and fishing, the chief occupations of the early settlers, are still of primary importance in its economy, but they have been supplemented by a variety of manufactures and a growing vacation industry.

State flag
(Adopted March 9, 1904)

Total area	33,215 square miles
Land area	31,040 square miles
Water area	2,175 square miles
Latitude	43°4'—47°28'N.

Longitude	66°57′—71°7′W.
Altitude (average)	600 feet
High point, Mount Katahdin	5,268 feet
Low point, Atlantic Ocean	Sea level
Population (1960)	969,265
Capital city—Augusta; population	21,680
Admitted as the 23d state	March 15, 1820
State bird (adopted in 1927)	Chickadee
State flower (adopted in 1895) White pine cone and tassel
State tree (adopted in 1945)	White pine
State song (adopted in 1937)	*State of Maine Song*
State motto (adopted in 1820)	*Dirigo* (I direct)
State nickname	Pine Tree State

State seal
(Adopted June 9, 1820)

A discussion of Maine's geography, government, social and economic life, and history is presented under the following headings:

1. Physical Features
2. Population and Political Divisions
3. Government
4. Education, Health, and Welfare
5. Economic Activities
6. Transportation and Communications
7. Cultural Life
8. Places of Interest
9. History
10. Bibliography

1. PHYSICAL FEATURES

Topography.—While the northeastern and a portion of the southwestern boundary lines of Maine are straight, the others are irregular. This is especially true of the coastline, which from Portland northeastward is deeply indented by numerous inlets and bays, giving it a shore length of over 2,300 miles, although a direct line drawn between its two extremities would be only about a tenth as long. Offshore are hundreds of islands; the largest is Mount Desert Island, on which is located the well-known summer resort of Bar Harbor. Southwest of Portland the rugged, rock-bound coast gives way to wide, sandy beaches. Maine has more good harbors than any other state on the Atlantic seaboard. Portland, on Casco Bay, is the principal port; among others are Bath, Rockland, Belfast, Searsport, Bangor, and Eastport.

There are two general mountain slopes, one of which extends from north of the source of the Magalloway River in Oxford County northeastward across the state to Mars Hill. South of the main divide are Mount Katahdin (5,268 feet high), in Piscataquis County, and Saddleback Mountain (4,116 feet), Mount Abraham (4,049 feet), and Blue Mountain (3,187 feet), in Franklin County. There is no long mountain range in Maine.

That portion of the state north of the main divide is drained almost wholly by the St. John River and its tributaries, through which the waters of a large number of the lakes of Maine find their outlet. The principal Maine tributaries of the St. John are the Aroostook and the Allagash. The area south of the main divide is drained chiefly by the Androscoggin, Kennebec,

Penobscot, and St. Croix rivers, which flow generally south to the Atlantic Ocean.

Maine is justly famed for its beautiful lakes and ponds, which are said to number about 2,500. Among the best known are the Rangeley Lakes, near the New Hampshire line; Sebago Lake, near Portland; and the largest, Moosehead Lake, which is about 35 miles long and covers 117 square miles in the central portion of the state. Many Maine lakes bear Indian names, among them Nicatous, Pocumcus, Cobbosseecontee, Mattawamkeag, and Mattamiscontis.

The nature of the geological formation of Maine shows that it belongs to one of the oldest parts of the United States. The marks of the glacial period may be plainly traced in several areas, the changes in the extent and form of the river beds and lakes being shown by nearby rock formations and by the nature of the deposits brought from the mountains to the valleys. The northern portion of the state belongs to the Devonian period, and the region about Penobscot Bay to the Silurian. In the south fossiliferous clays are found. There are a number of low ridges that evidently were once portions of mountain ridges, but which usually formed angles with the two great ranges that at one time extended across the state.

Climate.—The climate of Maine differs widely from the north to the much milder coastal zone. In Aroostook County the temperature may go as low as −54° F. in winter, and the annual snowfall approximates 100 inches; in the southern tip of the state the snowfall is not much more than 50 inches. The growing season (free of killing frosts) lasts about three months in the north and five in the south, while precipitation averages 36 inches annually in the north and 42 inches in the south. The normal average temperature for the state as a whole is about 41° F.; in January it is 20°, and in July 65°.

Plant Life.—Trees and plants common to the northeastern United States flourish in Maine. Among the trees are the alder, American elm, white, yellow, and gray birch, white and red (Norway) pine, white, black, and red oak, beech, hemlock, cedar, maple, ash, spruce, fir, tamarack, and poplar. Wild shrubs and grasses abound, as do the royal, ostrich, Christmas, evergreen wood, marsh, lady, spinulose, shield, cinnamon, and New York ferns. From the trailing arbutus and flowering dogwood of early spring to the goldenrod and asters of late summer and fall wild flowers are numerous. Wild roses are common, and in the ponds grow yellow pond lilies, white water lilies, and pickerelweed, and in the moist places, pitcher plants, marsh marigolds, cardinal flowers, rose pogonias (snakemouth), grass pinks, and the graceful meadow lilies and meadow rue. In the woods one finds the dainty, fragrant twinflower, as well as the bloodroot, anemone, purple, yellow, and white violets, lady's-slipper, goldthread, groundnut, bunchberry, checkerberry, Indian pipe, and partridgeberry, to name only a few. The commoner field flowers include white and oxeye daisies, yellow and orange hawkweed, buttercups, and Queen Anne's lace. Among the edible wild berries are the blackberry, raspberry, huckleberry, lowbush and highbush blueberry, cranberry, and strawberry.

Forests have always been Maine's major natural resource. It was because of the large extent of the pine forests that once existed within its limits that Maine became known as the Pine

MAINE

1960 Final Census 969,265; 1967 Est. 973,000

COUNTIES

Androscoggin (C7) 86,312
Aroostook (F2) 106,064
Cumberland (C8) 182,751
Franklin (B5) 20,069
Hancock (G6) 32,293
Kennebec (D7) 89,150
Knox (E7) 28,575
Lincoln (D7) 18,497
Oxford (B7) 44,345
Penobscot (F5) 126,346
Piscataquis (E4) 17,379
Sagadahoc (D7) 22,793
Somerset (C4) 39,749
Waldo (E6) 22,632
Washington (H6) 32,908
York (B9) 99,402

CITIES and TOWNS

Abbot Village (D5) Δ404
Acton (B8) Δ501
Addison (H6) Δ744
Albion (E6) Δ974
Alexander (H5) Δ220
Alfred◉ (B9) Δ1,201
Allagash (F1) Δ557
Allens Mills (C6) 320
Alna (D7) Δ347
Alton (F5) Δ303
Amherst (G6) Δ168
Andover (B6) Δ762
Anson (D6) Δ2,252
Appleton (E7) Δ672
Argyle (F5) 95
Ashdale (D8) 60
Ashland (G2) Δ1,980
Ashville (G7) 100
Athens (D6) Δ602
Atkinson (E5) Δ280
Atlantic (G7) 98
Auburn◉ (C7) 24,449
Auburn-Lewiston (urban area) 65,253
Augusta (cap.)◉ (D7) 21,680
Aurora (G6) Δ75
Ayers (J6) 50
Bailey Island (D8) 220
Bancroft (H4) Δ94
Bangor◉ (F6) 38,912
Bar Harbor (G7) Δ3,807
Bar Harbor (G7) 2,444
Baring (J5) 175
Bar Mills (C8) 600
Bass Harbor (G7) 450
Bath◉ (D8) 10,717
Bay Point (D8) 30
Bayside (F7) 100
Beals (H7) Δ640
Beddington (H6) Δ14
Belfast◉ (F7) 6,140
Belgrade (D7) Δ1,102
Belgrade Lakes (D6) 600
Belmont (E7) Δ295
Benedicta (G4) Δ200
Benton (D6) Δ1,521
Berry Mills (C6) 150
Berwick (B9) Δ2,738
Berwick (B9) 1,557
Bethel (B7) Δ2,408
Bethel (B7) 1,117
Biddeford (B9) 19,255
Biddeford Pool (C9) 400
Bingham (D5) Δ1,308
Bingham (D5) 1,180
Birch Harbor (H7) 170
Blaine (H2) Δ945
Blanchard (D5) Δ57
Blue Hill (F7) Δ1,270
Bolsters Mills (B7) 125
Boothbay (D8) Δ1,617
Boothbay Harbor (D8) 2,252
Bowdoinham (D7) Δ1,131
Bowerbank (E5) Δ17
Boyd Lake (F5) 50
Bradford (F5) Δ690
Bradford Center (F5) 109
Bradley (F6) Δ951
Bremen ‡(E8) Δ438
Brewer (F6) 9,009
Bridgewater (H3) Δ999
Bridgton (B7) Δ2,707
Bridgton (B7) 1,715
Brighton (D5) Δ62
Bristol (D8) Δ1,441
Brooklin (F7) Δ525
Brooks (E6) Δ758
Brooksville (F7) Δ603
Brookton (H4) 225
Brownfield (B8) Δ538
Brownville (E5) Δ1,641
Brownville Junction (E5) 850
Brunswick (C8) Δ15,797
Brunswick (C8) 9,444
Bryant Pond (B7) 65
Buckfield (C7) Δ982
Bucks Harbor (J6) 169
Bucksport (F6) Δ3,466
Bucksport (F6) 2,327
Burkettville (E7) 160
Burlington (G5) Δ353
Burnham (E6) Δ755
Buxton ‡(C8) Δ2,339
Buxton Center (B8) 93
Byron (B6) Δ108
Calais (J5) 4,223
Cambridge (E5) Δ354
Camden (F7) Δ3,988
Camden (F7) 3,523
Canaan (D6) Δ800
Canton (C7) Δ728
Cape Porpoise (C9) 450
Caratunk (C5) Δ90
Cardville (F5) 160
Caribou (G2) Δ12,464
Caribou (G2) 8,305
Carmel (E6) Δ1,206
Carrabassett (C5) 25
Carroll (G5) Δ147
Carthage (C6) Δ370
Cary (H4) Δ208
Casco (B7) Δ947
Castine (F7) Δ824
Center Lovell (B7) 250
Center Montville (E7) 40
Centerville (H6) Δ47
Chapman (G2) Δ376
Charleston (F5) Δ750
Charlotte (J5) Δ260
Chebeague Island (C8) 247
Chelsea (D7) 1,893
Cherryfield (H6) Δ780
Chester (F5) Δ261
Chesterville (C6) Δ505
Chesuncook (D3) 20
China (E7) Δ1,561
Chisholm (C7) 1,193
Citypoint (E7) 75
Clark Island (E8) 100
Clarks Mill (B8) 75
Clayton Lake (E2) 39
Cliff Island (C8) 100
Clifton (G6) Δ227
Clinton (D6) Δ1,729
Columbia (H6) Δ219
Columbia Falls (H6) Δ442
Cooper (H6) Δ106
Coopers Mills (E7) 150
Corea (H7) 300
Corinna (E6) Δ1,895
Cornish (B8) Δ816
Cornville (D6) Δ585
Costigan (F5) 140
Cranberry Isles (G7) Δ181
Crawford (H5) Δ83
Crescent Lake (C7) 150
Criehaven (F8) 25
Crouseville (G2) 250
Crystal (G4) Δ285
Cumberland Ctr. (C8) Δ2,765
Cundys Harbor (D8) 80
Cushing (E7) Δ479
Cutler (J6) Δ654
Damariscotta (E7) Δ1,093
Danforth (H4) Δ821
Danville (C7) 700
Darkharbor (F7) 132
Dayton ‡(B8) Δ451
Deblois (H6) Δ26
Dedham (F6) Δ438
Deer Isle (F7) Δ1,129
Denmark (B8) Δ376
Dennysville (J6) Δ303
Derby (E5) 500
Detroit (E6) Δ564
Dexter (E5) Δ3,951
Dexter (E5) 2,720
Dixfield (C6) Δ2,323
Dixfield (C6) 1,334
Dixmont (E6) Δ551
Dover-Foxcroft (E5) Δ4,173
Dover-Foxcroft◉ (E5) 2,481
Dover South Mills (E5) 25
Dresden (D7) Δ766
Dryden (C6) 650
Dry Mills (C8) 220
Dyer Brook (G3) Δ180
Eagle Lake (F1) Δ1,138
East Andover (B6) 165
East Baldwin (B8) 188
East Blue Hill (G7) 200
East Boothbay (D8) 510
East Brownfield (B8) 70
East Corinth (F5) 200
East Dixfield (C6) 225
East Dixmont (E6) 100
East Eddington (F6) 200
East Franklin (G6) 75
East Hiram (B8) 400
East Holden (F6) 350
East Jackson (E6) 125
East Knox (E7) 200
East Lebanon (B9) 1,100
East Limington (B8) 150
East Livermore (C7) 350
East Machias (J6) Δ1,198
East Madison (D6) 300
East Millinocket (F4) Δ2,392
East Millinocket (F4) 2,295
East New Portland (D6) 43
Easton (H2) Δ1,389
East Orland (F6) 190
East Otisfield (B7) 50
East Parsonfield (B8) 125
East Peru (C7) 130
East Poland (C7) 500
Eastport (K6) 2,537
East Stoneham (B7) 316
East Sullivan (G6) 350
East Sumner (C7) 114
East Union (E7) 100
East Vassalboro (D7) 270
East Waterboro (B8) 179
East Wilton (C6) 550
East Winn (G5) 70
Eaton (H4) 85
Eddington (F6) Δ958
Edgecomb (D8) Δ453
Edmunds (J6) 290
Eliot (B9) Δ3,133
Ellsworth◉ (F6) 4,444
Ellsworth Falls (G6) 550
Emery Mills (B8) 95
Enfield (F5) Δ1,098
Etna (E6) Δ486
Eustis (B5) Δ666
Exeter (E6) Δ707
Fairbanks (C6) 197
Fairfield (D6) Δ5,829
Fairfield (D6) 3,766
Fairfield Center (D6) 500
Falmouth ‡(C8) Δ5,976
Falmouth Foreside (C8) 1,062
Farmington (C6) Δ5,001
Farmington◉ (C6) 2,749
Farmington Falls (C6) 450
Fayette (C7) Δ328
Five Islands (D8) 154
Forest City (H4) 24
Forest Station (H4) 16
Fort Fairfield (H2) Δ5,876
Fort Fairfield (H2) 3,082
Fort Kent (F1) Δ4,761
Fort Kent (F1) 2,787
Fort Kent Mills (F1) 422
Frankfort (F6) Δ692
Franklin (G6) Δ627
Freedom (E7) Δ406
Freeport (C8) Δ4,055
Freeport (C8) 1,801
Frenchboro (G7) 70
Frenchville (G1) Δ1,421
Friendship (E7) Δ806
Frye (B6) 131
Fryeburg (A7) Δ1,874
Gardiner (D7) 6,897
Garland (E5) Δ568
Georgetown (D8) Δ790
Gilead (B7) Δ136
Glenburn (F6) Δ965
Glen Cove (E7) 285
Goodrich (H2) 400
Goodwins Mills (B8) 125
Goose Rocks Beach (C9) 275
Gorham (C8) Δ5,767
Gorham (C8) 2,322
Gouldsboro (H7) Δ1,100
Grand Isle (G1) Δ978
Grand Lake Stream (H5) Δ219
Gray (C8) Δ2,184
Great Pond (G6) 50
Great Works (F6) 450
Greene (C7) Δ1,226
Green Lake (F6) 50
Greenville (D5) Δ2,025
Greenville (D5) 1,893
Greenville Jct. (D5) 400
Grindstone (F4) 60
Grove (J5) 125
Guilford (E5) Δ1,880
Guilford (E5) 1,372
Haines Landing (B6) 9
Hallowell (D7) 3,169
Hamlin (H1) Δ374
Hampden (F6) Δ4,583
Hampden Highlands (F6) 800
Hancock (G6) Δ806
Hanover (B7) Δ240
Harmony (D6) Δ712
Harpswell Center (D8) 100
Harrington (H6) Δ717
Harrison (B7) Δ1,014
Hartford (C7) Δ325
Hartland (D6) Δ1,447
Hartland (D6) 1,016
Haynesville (G4) Δ187
Hebron (C7) Δ465
Hermon (F6) Δ2,087
Highland Lake (C8) 600
Highpine (B9) 125
Hinckley (D6) 500
Hiram (B8) Δ699
Hodgdon (H3) Δ926
Hollis Center (B8) Δ1,195
Hope (E7) Δ525
Houghton (B6) 15
Houlton (H3) Δ8,289
Houlton◉ (H3) 5,976
Howland (F5) Δ1,362
Howland (F5) 1,313
Hudson (F5) Δ542
Hulls Cove (G7) 250
Indian River (H6) 74
Intervale (C8) 45
Island Falls (G3) Δ1,018
Isle au Haut (F7) Δ68
Isleboro (F7) Δ444
Islesford (G7) 95
Jackman (C4) Δ984
Jackman Station (C4) 350
Jacksonville (J6) 200
Jay (C7) Δ3,247
Jefferson (D7) Δ1,048
Jemtland (G1) 30
Jimpond (B5) 8
Jonesboro (J6) Δ428
Jonesport (H6) Δ1,563
Jonesport (H6) 914
Keegan (G1) 900
Kenduskeag (E6) Δ584
Kennebago Lake (B5) 4
Kennebunk (B9) Δ4,551
Kennebunk (B9) 2,804
Kennebunk Beach (C9) 125
Kennebunkport (C9) Δ1,851
Kents Hill (D7) 180
Kezar Falls (B8) 850
Kingfield (C6) Δ864
Kingman (G4) 336
Kingsbury (D5) Δ8
Kittery (B9) Δ10,689
Kittery (B9) 8,051
Kittery Point (B9) 1,259
Knox (E6) 439
Kokadjo (E4) 25
La Grange (F5) Δ424
Lake Moxie (D5) 36
Lake View (F5) Δ18
Lambert Lake (H4) 178
Lamoine (G7) Δ484
Lebanon (B9) Δ1,534
Lee (G5) Δ555
Leeds (C7) Δ807
Leeds Junction (C7) 81
Levant (F6) Δ765
Lewiston (C7) 40,804
Lewiston-Auburn (urban area) 65,253
Liberty (E7) Δ458
Lille (G1) 200
Limerick (B8) Δ907
Limestone (H2) Δ13,102
Limestone (H2) 1,772
Limington (B8) Δ839
Lincoln (G5) Δ4,541
Lincoln (G5) 3,616
Lincoln Center (G5) 300
Lincolnville (E7) Δ867
Lincolnville Center (E7) 300
Linneus (H3) Δ607
Lisbon (C7) Δ5,042
Lisbon (C7) 1,542
Lisbon Center (C7) 200
Lisbon Falls (D7) 2,640
Litchfield (D7) Δ1,011
Little Deer Isle (F7) 215
Littleton (H3) Δ982
Livermore (C7) Δ1,363
Livermore Falls (C7) Δ3,343
Livermore Falls (C7) 2,882
Locke Mills (B7) 380
Long Cove (E8) 79
Long Island (C8) Δ57
Long Pond (C4) 30
Lovell (B7) Δ588
Lowell (F5) Δ132
Lubec (K6) Δ2,684
Lubec (K6) 1,289
Ludlow (G3) Δ274
Machias (J6) Δ2,614
Machias◉ (J6) 1,523
Machiasport (H6) Δ980
Macwahoc (G4) Δ165
Madawaska (G1) Δ5,507
Madawaska (G1) 4,035
Madison (D6) Δ3,935
Madison (D6) 2,761
Madrid (B6) Δ108
Mainstream (D6) 200
Manchester (D7) Δ1,068
Mapleton (G2) Δ1,514
Mars Hill (H2) Δ2,062
Mars Hill (H2) 1,458
Masardis (G3) Δ408
Matinicus (F8) Δ100
Mattawamkeag (G5) Δ945
Mechanic Falls (C7) Δ2,195
Mechanic Falls (C7) 1,992
Meddybemps (J5) 86
Medford (F5) 18
Medford Center (F5) 77
Medway (G4) Δ1,266
Mercer (D6) Δ272
Mexico (B6) Δ5,043
Mexico (B6) 3,951
Milbridge (H6) Δ1,101
Milford (F6) Δ1,572
Millinocket (F4) Δ7,453
Millinocket (F4) 7,318
Milo (F5) Δ2,756
Milo (F5) 1,802
Minot (C7) Δ780
Minturn (G7) 55
Monarda (G4) 143
Monhegan (E8) Δ65
Monmouth (D7) Δ1,884
Monroe (E6) Δ497
Monson (E5) Δ852
Monticello (H3) Δ1,109
Montville (E7) Δ366
Moody (B9) 100
Moosehead (D4) 4
Moose River (C4) Δ205
Morrill (E7) Δ355
Mount Desert (G7) Δ1,663
Mount Vernon (D7) Δ596
Naples (B8) Δ735
Newagen (D8) 75
Newburgh (F6) Δ636
Newcastle (D7) Δ1,101
Newfield (B8) Δ319
New Gloucester (C8) Δ3,047
New Harbor (E8) 525
New Limerick (G3) Δ394
Newport (E6) Δ2,322
Newport (E6) 1,589
New Portland (C6) Δ620
New Sharon (C6) Δ712
New Sweden (G2) Δ713
New Vineyard (C6) Δ357
Nobleboro (D7) Δ679
Norcross (F4) 60
Norridgewock (D6) Δ1,634
North Amity (H4) 325
North Anson (D6) 750
North Belgrade (D7) 300
North Berwick (B9) Δ1,884
North Berwick (B9) 1,295
North Bradford (F5) 70
North Bridgton (B7) 600
North Brooksville (F7) 200
North Chesterville (C6) 150
North Cutler (J6) 100
North Dexter (E5) 100
North Dixmont (E6) 100
North East Carry (D4) 5
Northport (E7) Δ648
North Fryeburg (B7) 185
North Gorham (B8) 80
North Haven (F7) Δ384
North Jay (C6) 600
North Leeds (C7) 47
North Limington (B8) 350
North Livermore (C7) 165
North Lovell (B7) 72
North Lubec (J6) 380
North New Portland (C6) 250
North Newry (B6) 79
North Parsonfield (A8) 60
North Penobscot (F7) 150
North Perry (J5) 100
Northeast Hbr. (G7) 700
Northfield (H6) Δ79
North Raymond (C8) 90
North Searsmont (E7) 100
North Shapleigh (B8) 90
North Sullivan (G6) 200
North Turner (C7) 350
North Vassalboro (D7) 700
North Waldoboro (E7) 160
North Waterboro (B8) 150
North Waterford (B7) 550
North Wayne (C7) 91
North Whitefield (D7) 200
North Windham (C8) 500
North Woodstock (B7) 75
North Yarmouth (C8) Δ1,140
Norway (B7) Δ3,733
Norway (B7) 2,654
Norway Lake (B7) 350

◉County seat. ΔPopulation of township. ‡Name not on map.

All figures available from 1960 final census are supplemented by local official estimates.

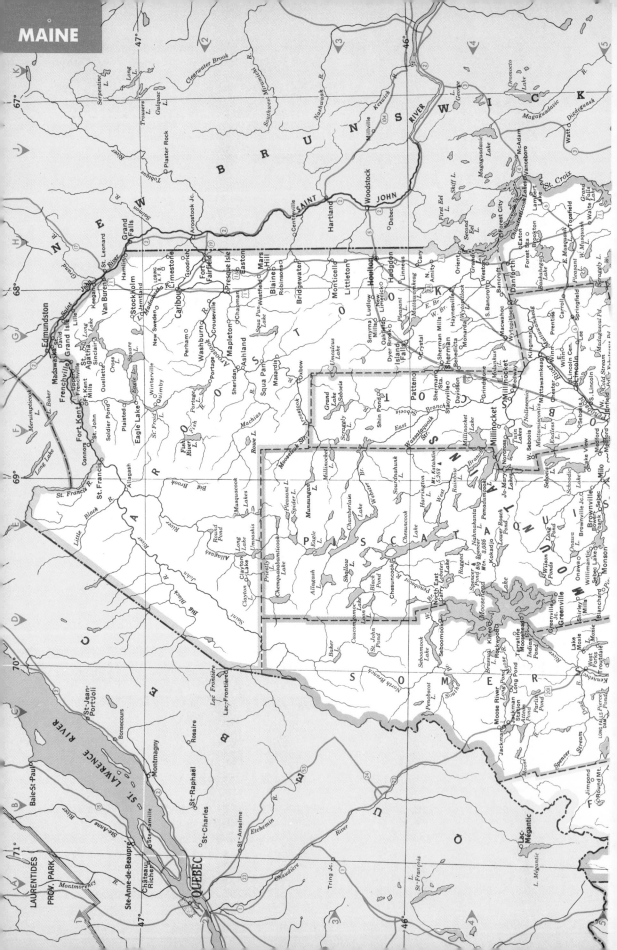

MAINE

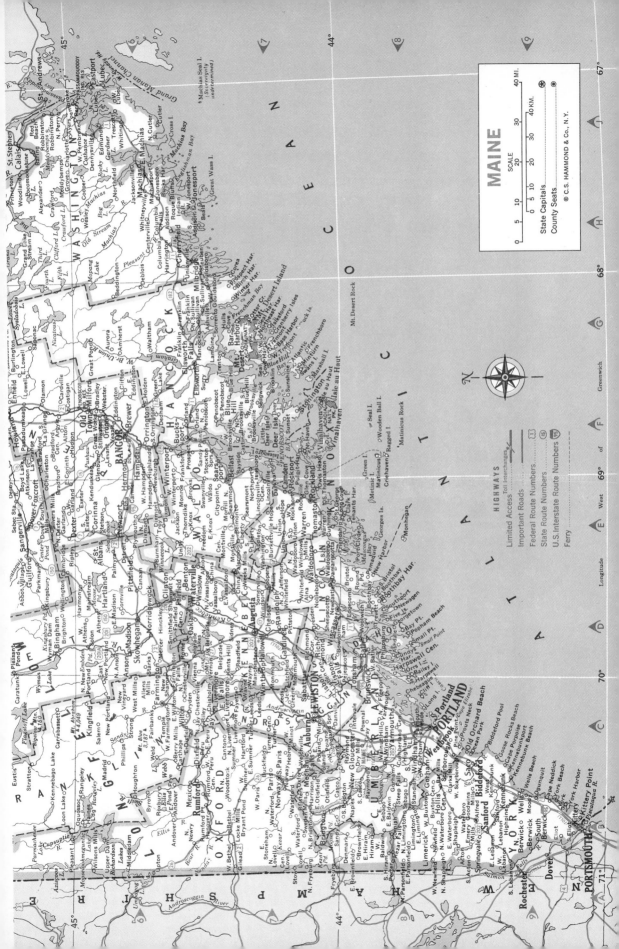

MAINE

SCALE

State Capitals ⊛

County Seats ⊙

© C.S. HAMMOND & Co., N.Y.

HIGHWAYS

Limited Access Toll Interchanges

Important Roads

Federal Route Numbers

State Route Numbers

U.S. Interstate Route Numbers

Ferry

MAINE (Continued)

1960 Final Census 969,265; 1967 Est. 973,000

Oakfield (G3) ▲848
Oakland (D6) ▲3,075
Oakland (D6) 1,880
Ocean Park (C9) 165
Ogunquit (B9) 550
Olamon (F5) 600
Old Orchard Beach (C9) ▲4,580
Old Orchard Beach (C9) 4,431
Old Town (F6) 8,626
Onawa (E5) 23
Oquossoc (B6) 150
Orient (H4) ▲124
Orland (F6) ▲1,195
Orono (F6) ▲8,341
Orono (F6) 3,234
Orrington (F6) ▲2,539
Orrs Island (D8) 350
Otisfield (B7) ▲549
Otter Creek (G7) 250
Ouellette (G1) 100
Owls Head (F7) ▲994
Oxbow (G3) ▲137
Oxford (B7) ▲1,658
Palermo (E7) ▲528
Palmyra (E6) ▲1,009
Paris (B7) ▲3,601
Parkman (D5) ▲530
Passadumkeag (F5) ▲355
Patten (F4) ▲1,312
Patten (F4) 1,099
Pejepscot (D8)
Pemaquid (E8) 210
Pembroke (J6) ▲871
Penobscot (F7) ▲706
Perham (G2) ▲512
Perry (J6) ▲564
Peru (C6) ▲1,229
Phillips (C6) ▲1,021
Phippsburg (D8) ▲1,121
Pine Point (C8) 650
Pittsfield (E6) ▲4,010
Pittsfield (E6) 3,232
Pittston (D7) ▲1,311
Plaisted (F1) 112
Pleasant Pond (D5) 11
Plymouth (E6) ▲494
Poland (C7) ▲1,537
Poland Spring (C7) 500
Popham Beach (D8) 100
Portage (G2) ▲458
Port Clyde (E8) 400
Porter (B8) ▲975
Portland◉ (C8) 72,566
Portland (urban area) 111,701
Pownal (C8) ▲778
Prentiss (G5) ▲227
Presque Isle (H2) 12,886
Princeton (H5) ▲829
Prospect (F6) ▲412
Prospect Harbor (H7) 400
Prouts Neck (C8) 12
Pulpit Harbor (F7) 25
Quimby (F2) 357

Randolph (D7) ▲1,724
Randolph (D7) 1,585
Rangeley (B6) ▲1,087
Raymond (B8) ▲732
Readfield (D7) ▲1,029
Red Beach (J5) 200
Richmond (D7) ▲2,185
Richmond (D7) 1,412
Richmond Corner (D7) 125
Riley (C6) 175
Ripley (E5) ▲317
Robbinston (J5) ▲476
Robinsons (H3) 543
Rockland◉ (E7) 8,769
Rockport (F7) ▲1,893
Rockville (E7) 196
Rockwood (D4) 300
Rome (D6) ▲367
Roque Bluffs (H6) ▲152
Round Mountain (B5) 15
Round Pond (E8) 500
Roxbury (B6) ▲344
Rumford (B6) ▲10,005
Rumford (B6) 7,233
Rumford Center (B7) 325
Rumford Point (B6) 125
Sabattus (C7) 1,620
Saco (C8) 10,515
Saint Agatha (G1) ▲1,137
Saint Albans (E6) ▲927
Saint David (G1) 1,000
Saint Francis (E1) ▲1,058
Saint George (E7) ▲1,588
Saint John (F1) ▲407
Salem (C6) 75
Sandy Creek (B7) 150
Sandy Point (F7) 300
Sanford (B9) ▲14,962
Sanford (B9) 10,936
Sangerville (E5) ▲1,157
Scarborough (C8) ▲6,418
Seal Cove (G7) 190
Seal Harbor (G7) 325
Searsmont (E7) ▲628
Searsport (F7) ▲1,838
Sebago Lake (B8) 383
Sebec (E5) ▲384
Sebec Lake (E5) 108
Sebec Station (E5)
Seboeis (F5) ▲77
Seboomook (D4) 18
Sedgwick (F7) ▲574
Shapleigh (B8) ▲515
Shawmut (D6) 225
Sheepscott (D7) 100
Sheridan (F2) 385
Sherman (G4) ▲1,034
Sherman Mills (G4) 600
Sherman Station (F4) 250
Shin Pond (F3) 28
Shirley Mills (D5)
Sidney (D7) ▲988
Silvers Mills (E5) 52
Sinclair (G1) 320
Skowhegan (D6) ▲7,661

Skowhegan◉ (D6) 6,667
Small Point (D8) 34
Smithfield (D6) ▲382
Smyrna Mills (G3) ▲331
Smyrna Mills (G3) 212
Soldier Pond (F1) 816
Solon (D6) ▲669
Somerville (D7) ▲254
Sorrento (G7) ▲196
South Acton (B8) 200
South Addison (H6) 170
South Bancroft (G4) 9
South Berwick (B9) ▲3,112
South Berwick (B9) 1,773
South Blue Hill (F7) 113
South Bridgton (B8) 125
South Bristol (D8) ▲610
South Brooksville (F7) 99
South Casco (B8) 100
South China (D7) 205
South Eliot (B9) 1,730
South Exeter (E6) 40
South Harpswell (C8) 300
South Hiram (B8) 150
South Hope (E7) 100
South La Grange (F5) 71
South Lebanon (B9) 190
South Liberty (E7) 47
South Lincoln (F5) 141
South Orrington (F6) 300
South Paris◉ (C7) 2,063
South Penobscot (F7) 171
Southport (D8) ▲416
South Portland (C8) 22,788
South Robbinston (J5) 150
South Sanford (B9) 600
South Thomaston (E7) ▲732
South Union (E7) 100
South Waldoboro (E7) 400
South Warren (E7) 150
South Waterford (B7) 110
Southwest Harbor (G7) ▲1,480
South Windham (C8) 1,142
Springfield (G5) ▲426
Springvale (B9) 2,379
Squa Pan (G2) 75
Stacyville (F4) ▲673
Standish (B8) ▲2,095
Starks (D6) ▲306
Steep Falls (B8) 400
Stetson (E6) ▲420
Steuben (H6) ▲673
Stillwater (F6) 800
Stockholm (G1) ▲649
Stockton Springs (F7) ▲980
Stonington (F7) ▲1,408
Stow (A7) ▲108
Stratton (B5) 650
Strong (C6) ▲976
Sullivan (G6) ▲709
Sumner (C7) ▲481
Sunset (F7) 450
Sunshine (G7) 70
Surry (F7) ▲547

Swans Island (G7) ▲402
Swanville (E6) ▲514
Sweden (B7) ▲119
Tarratine (D4) 2
Temple (C6) ▲314
Tenants Harbor (E8) 800
Thomaston (E7) ▲2,780
Thomaston (E7) 2,342
Thorndike (E6) ▲457
Topsfield (H5) 210
Topsham (D8) ▲3,818
Topsham (D8) 2,240
Tremont (G7) ▲1,044
Trenton (G7) ▲375
Trescott (J6) 125
Trevett (D8) 245
Troutdale (D5) 19
Troy (E6) ▲469
Turner (C7) ▲1,890
Turner Center (C7) 300
Union (E7) ▲1,196
Unionville (H6) 78
Unity (E6) ▲983
Upper Dam (B6) 2
Upper Frenchville (G1) 500
Upton (B6) ▲35
Van Buren (G1) ▲4,679
Van Buren (G1) 3,589
Vanceboro (J4) ▲389
Vassalboro (D7) ▲2,446
Veazie (F6) ▲1,354
Vienna (D6) ▲160
Vinalhaven (F7) ▲1,273
Waite (H5) ▲73
Waldo (E7) ▲395
Waldoboro (E7) ▲2,882
Walnut Hill (C8) 350
Waltham (G6) ▲153
Warren (E7) ▲1,678
Washburn (G2) ▲2,083
Washburn (G2) 1,055
Washington (E7) ▲636
Waterboro (B8) ▲1,059
Waterford (B7) ▲834
Waterville (D6) 18,695
Wayne (D7) ▲498
Webster (F6) 4,747
Weeks Mills (E7) 100
Welchville (C7) 400
Weld (C6) ▲348
Wellington (D5) ▲231
Wells (B9) ▲3,528
Wells Beach (B9) 550
Wesley (H6) ▲145
West Athens (D6) 200
West Bath (D8) ▲766
West Bethel (B7) 300
Westbrook (C8) 13,820
West Brooksville (F7) 145
West Buxton (B8) 254
West Enfield (F5) 546
West Farmington (C6) 500
Westfield (G2) ▲569
West Forks (D5) ▲53
West Franklin (G6) 135

West Gardiner (D7) ▲1,144
West Garland (E5) 50
West Gouldsboro (G7) 105
West Hampden (E6)
West Jonesport (H6) 425
West Kennebunk (B9) 375
West Lebanon (B9) 150
West Lubec (J6) 320
West Mills (C6) 342
West Minot (C7) 300
West Newfield (B8) 175
Weston (H4) ▲202
West Paris (B7) ▲1,050
West Pembroke (J6) 485
West Peru (C7) 300
West Poland (C7) 275
West Rockport (E7) 300
West Scarborough (C8) 875
West Sumner (B7) 161
West Tremont (G7) 250
West Winterport (E6) 30
Whitefield (D7) ▲1,068
Whiting (J6) ▲339
Whitneyville (H6) ▲229
Willimantic (E5) ▲137
Wilsons Mills (B6) 95
Wilton (C6) ▲3,274
Wilton (C6) 1,761
Windsor (D7) ▲878
Winn (G5) ▲526
Winslow (D6) ▲5,891
Winslow (D6) 3,640
Winslows Mills (E7) 200
Winter Harbor (G7) ▲756
Winterport (F6) ▲2,088
Winterville (F2) ▲215
Winthrop (C7) ▲3,537
Winthrop (C7) 2,260
Wiscasset◉ (D7) ▲1,800
Woodland (H5) 1,393
Woolwich (D8) ▲1,417
Wyman Dam (D5) 451
Wytopitlock (G4) 260
Yarmouth (C8) ▲3,517
Yarmouth (C8) 2,913
York (B9) ▲4,663
York Beach (B9) 500
York Harbor (B9) 950

OTHER FEATURES

Abraham (mt.) C 5
Acadia National Park G 7
Allagash (lake) D 3
Allagash (river) E 2
Androscoggin (river) C 7
Aroostook (river) G 2
Attean (pond) C 4
Aziscoos (lake) A 5
Baker (lake) D 3
Baskahegan (lake) H 4
Bear (river) B 6
Bigelow (mt.) C 5

Big (brook) E 2
Big (lake) H 5
Big Black (river) D 2
Big Spencer (mt.) D 4
Black (pond) D 3
Blue (mt.) C 6
Blue Hill (bay) G 7
Bog (lake) H 6
Brassua (lake) D 4
Casco (bay) C 8
Cathance (lake) J 6
Caucomgomoc (lake) D 3
Center (pond) E 5
Chamberlain (lake) E 3
Chemquasabamticook (lake) D 3
Chesuncook (lake) E 3
Chiputneticook (lakes) H 4
Clayton (lake) D 2
Clifford (lake) H 5
Cold Stream (pond) G 5
Crawford (lake) H 5
Cross (isl.) J 6
Cross (lake) G 1
Cupsuptic (river) B 5
Dead (river) C 5
Deer (isl.) F 7
Dow A.F.B. F 6
Duck (isls.) G 7
Eagle (lake) E 3
Eagle (lake) F 1
East Machias (river) H 6
East Musquash (lake) H 5
Elizabeth (cape) C 8
Ellis (pond) B 6
Ellis (river) B 6
Embden (pond) D 6
Endless (lake) F 5
Englishman (bay) J 6
Eskutassis (pond) G 5
Fifth (lake) H 5
Fish (river) F 2
Fish River (lake) F 2
Flagstaff (lake) C 5
Fourth (lake) H 5
Frenchman (bay) G 7
Gardner (lake) J 6
Georges (isls.) E 8
Graham (lake) G 6
Grand (lake) H 4
Grand Falls (lake) H 5
Grand Lake Seboeis (lake) F 3
Grand Manan (channel) K 6
Great Wass (isl.) J 7
Green (isl.) F 8
Harrington (lake) E 4
Haut (isl.) G 7
Indian Pond (lake) D 4
Islesboro (isl.) F 7
Jo Mary (lakes) E 4
Katahdin (mt.) F 4
Kennebec (river) D 7
Kezar (lake) B 7

Kezar (pond) B 7
Kingsbury (pond) D 5
Little Black (river) E 1
Little Madawaska (river) G 2
Lobster (lake) D 4
Long (lake) B 7
Long (lake) E 2
Long (lake) G 1
Long (pond) C 4
Long (pond) D 6
Long (pond) E 5
Long Falls (dam) C 5
Longfellow (mts.) B 6
Loon (lake) D 3
Loring A.F.B. H 2
Lower Roach (pond) E 4
Lower Sysladobsis (lake) G 5
Machias (bay) J 6
Machias (river) F 2
Machias (river) H 6
Machias Seal (isl.) J 7
Madagascal (pond) G 5
Marshall (isl.) G 7
Matinicus Rock (isl.) F 8
Mattamiscontis (lake) F 4
Mattawamkeag (lake) G 4
Mattawamkeag (river) G 4
Meddybemps (lake) J 5
Metinic (isl.) E 8
Millinocket (lake) F 4
Millinocket (lake) F 3
Molunkus (lake) G 4
Monhegan (isl.), 65 E 8
Moose (pond) B 7
Moose (pond) D 6
Moose (river) D 4
Moosehead (lake) D 4
Mooseleuk (stream) F 2
Mooselookmeguntic (lake) B 6
Mopang (lake) H 6
Mount Desert (isl.) G 7
Mount Desert Rock (isl.) G 8
Moxie (lake) D 5
Munsungan (lake) E 3
Muscongus (bay) E 8
Musquacook (lakes) E 2
Nahmakanta (lake) E 4
Nicatous (lake) G 5
Nollesemic (lake) F 4
Old (stream) H 6
Onawa (lake) E 5
Parlin (pond) C 4
Parmachenee (lake) B 5
Passamaquoddy (bay) J 5
Passamaquoddy Ind. Res. J 5
Pemadumcook (lake) E 4
Penobscot (bay) F 7
Penobscot (lake) C 4
Penobscot (river) F 5

Penobscot Ind. Res. F 6
Pierce (pond) C 5
Piscataqua (river) B 9
Piscataquis (river) E 5
Pleasant (lake) E 3
Pleasant (lake) G 3
Pleasant (lake) H 5
Pleasant (river) H 6
Pocomoonshine (lake) H 5
Portage (lake) F 2
Priestly (lake) E 2
Pushaw (lake) F 6
Ragged (isl.) F 8
Ragged (lake) E 4
Rainbow (lake) E 4
Rangeley (lake) B 6
Richardson (lakes) B 6
Rocky (lake) J 6
Round (pond) E 2
Rowe (lake) F 2
Saco (river) B 8
Saint Croix (river) J 5
Saint Francis (river) E 1
Saint Froid (lake) F 2
Saint John (pond) D 3
Saint John (river) G 1
Salmon Falls (river) B 9
Sandy (river) C 6
Schoodic (lake) F 5
Scraggly (lake) F 3
Scraggly (lake) H 5
Seal (isl.) F 8
Sebago (lake) B 8
Sebasticook (lake) E 6
Seboeis (lake) E 4
Seboeis (river) F 3
Seboomook (lake) D 4
Shallow (lake) E 3
Small (point) D 8
Sourdnahunk (lake) F 3
Spencer (pond) D 4
Spencer (stream) C 5
Spider (lake) E 3
Squa Pan (lake) G 2
Square (lake) G 1
Sunday (river) B 6
Swift (river) B 6
Third (lake) H 5
Twin (lakes) F 4
Umbagog (lake) A 6
Umcalcus (lake) G 3
Umsaskis (lake) E 2
Union, West Branch (river) G 6
Vinalhaven (isl.) F 7
Wassataquoik (stream) F 4
Webb (lake) B 6
Webster (brook) E 3
West Grand (lake) H 5
West Musquash (lake) H 5
West Quoddy (head) K 6
Wilson (ponds) E 5
Winnecook (lake) E 6
Wooden Ball (isl.) F 8
Wyman (lake) C 5
Wytopitlock (lake) G 4

Tree State. Although the majestic mast pine, furnished for many British and American ships, is a thing of the past, pine trees still grow in large numbers. The greater part of the state is wooded, most of the northern and central areas being not only wooded but lacking in permanent settlements. Of the 17,425,000 acres of forest land in Maine in the 1960's, commercial forest land covers 17,169,000 acres, divided as follows: privately owned, 16,964,000 acres; owned by the . state, counties, or municipalities, 139,000; federally owned or managed, 66,000.

Animal Life.—Among the wild animals of Maine are the white-tailed or Virginia deer, black bear, beaver, red fox, otter, mink, weasel, flying, red, and gray squirrels, snowshoe rabbit, porcupine, muskrat, woodchuck, and wildcat. Approximately 40,000 white-tailed deer are killed each year by Maine and out-of-state hunters. The caribou, once common, has become extinct, and small numbers of moose are protected by law.

Canada geese, black duck, wood duck, woodcock, ruffed grouse, pheasant, and many other game birds are found in the state. The American eagle is native to Maine, as are several varieties of gulls, hawks, and owls. Crows, starlings, and grackles migrate to the state in large numbers, and many kinds of songbirds spend part or all of the year there. Robins, bluebirds, orioles, catbirds, bobolinks, blue jays, kingbirds, kingfishers, sandpipers, flycatchers, and swallows are among the commoner varieties. Loons abound on Maine lakes, where their eerie calls can often be heard in the night.

Lakes and streams teem with black bass, pickerel, salmon, and trout, and the Department of Game and Inland Fish rears millions of trout and salmon for restocking purposes. Saltwater fishing along the coast offers sea bass, Atlantic salmon, tuna, cod, and flounder. See also section 5. *Economic Activities*—Fisheries.

Conservation.—The soil of Maine shows the effects of the glacial period, for the greater part consists of till, glacial debris, or heavy clay. The old lake beds, now dry land, and river margins, however, are largely alluvial, and in these limited areas the soil is very fertile, as in the Aroostook potato district. Some 16,485,000 acres, or 83 per cent of the area of the state, are included in 15 soil conservation districts.

With the growing scarcity of accessible old-growth trees in Maine's forests, both private owners and the state government have emphasized conservation and reforestation. State and federal agencies carry on disease and insect research and control, and white pine blister rust has been brought under control since it was first discovered in the state in 1916. By education and other means the Maine Forest Service tries to prevent or limit fire damage. Fire lookout towers and weather stations are located at strategic points, and forest wardens use telephone, walkie-talkie, mobile radio, trucks, and airplanes as part of their equipment in fighting fires. As a result of the disastrous fires which destroyed many acres of timberland and hundreds of houses in Bar Harbor, Brownfield, and other places in 1947, the service was given greater powers and additional men and equipment.

2. POPULATION AND POLITICAL DIVISIONS

Population Characteristics.—The population of Maine is chiefly of English, Scotch Irish, French, and German stock. The first settlers were the English at Kittery, who were soon joined by some Scotch Irish. Farther north, around Waldoboro, German families from Brunswick and Saxony settled in the 1740's. Irish gave Limerick its name, and French Protestants settled along the coast. In 1870, Swedes took up farms in the northeast, forming the colony of New Sweden. The nonwhite population is small: at the 1960 census there were 1,879 Indians, 3,318 Negroes, and 777 members of other races. Only two tribes of Indians are now represented in Maine, the Penobscots and Passamaquoddies, most of whom live on reservations. There are three reservations in the state, one for Penobscot Indians at Indian Island, Old Town, and two for Passamaquoddy Indians in Washington County. (See also PASSAMAQUODDY INDIANS; PENOBSCOT INDIANS.)

The first census of Maine, taken in 1790, returned a population of 96,540. The population increased at each census thereafter, except that of 1870, passing 200,000 between 1800 and 1810, 500,000 between 1830 and 1840, 700,000 between 1900 and 1910, and 800,000 between 1930 and 1940. Between 1940 and 1950 it rose from 847,226 to 913,774, or 7.9 percent, and by 1960 to 969,265, or 6.1 percent more than 1950. At the 1960 census, residents of rural areas numbered 472,151, or 48.7 percent of the total. Women outnumbered men by 490,211 to 479,054.

Political Divisions.—Maine is subdivided into 16 counties, 21 cities, 415 incorporated towns, 56 plantations, and 416 unorganized (unincorporated) townships.

Principal Cities.—Portland, the largest city (pop., 72,566), is the center of the largest standard metropolitan area (120,655) in the state. It is a trading and shipping center for southern Maine, with some industry and tourist trade. Bangor (38,912) fills a similar function for the Penobscot Valley. The twin cities of Lewiston (40,804) and Auburn (24,449) have been leading textile and shoe centers, although the textile mills of Lewiston have lost ground. Biddeford (19,255) and its twin city of Saco (10,515), long identified with textiles and textile machinery, have been forced to new endeavors with the gradual curtailment of the Maine textile industry. Augusta (21,680), the capital, is also a paper, textile, and shoe manufacturing city.

Counties.—The largest county, covering 6,805 square miles, is Aroostook, and the smallest is Sagadahoc, with 257 square miles. The most heavily populated county is Cumberland, with 182,751 inhabitants, and the least populous is Piscataquis, with 17,379. A list of counties and county seats follows.

County	County Seat	County	County Seat
Androscoggin	Auburn	Oxford	South Paris
Aroostook	Houlton	Penobscot	Bangor
Cumberland	Portland	Piscataquis	Dover-Foxcroft
Franklin	Farmington	Sagadahoc	Bath
Hancock	Ellsworth	Somerset	Skowhegan
Kennebec	Augusta	Waldo	Belfast
Knox	Rockland	Washington	Machias
Lincoln	Wiscasset	York	Alfred

3. GOVERNMENT

The state constitution was adopted by the people on Dec. 6, 1819, and went into effect in the following year, when Maine was admitted to the Union. Amendments require approval by a state convention or a two-thirds vote of both houses of the legislature, followed in either case by the approval of the voters. Since there is no constitutional initiative provision, changes cannot be made directly by the voters. The 99 amendments adopted by 1965, all of which were made by legislative proposal, did not basically alter the original constitution.

Executive.—The governor is the only state official elected by the voters; there is no lieutenant governor, and department heads are appointed by the governor and council or elected by the legislature. The legislature elects the secretary of state, treasurer, attorney general, auditor, and commissioner of agriculture. The term of the governor and legislators was one year until biennial election was adopted in 1879. In 1957 the governor's term was increased from two to four years, effective in 1959. In case of a vacancy in the office of governor the president of the Senate and the speaker of the House of Representatives are in the line of succession.

The governor has veto power but no pocket or item veto. He is further limited by the constitutional and legislative powers of the executive council of seven members, who are elected biennially by the houses of the legislature in joint session, one from each of seven council districts. The council meets at the governor's call and advises him on many matters. It has the power to confirm or reject nominations for appointive office, including those for heads of departments and judges. In addition, it has fiscal and electoral powers and sits with the governor as a board of pardons.

GOVERNORS OF MAINE

William King	Democrat	1820–1821
William D. Williamson (acting)	"	1821
Benjamin Ames (acting)	"	1821
Albion K. Parris	"	1822–1827
Enoch Lincoln	"	1827–1829
Nathan Cutler (acting)	"	1829–1830
Joshua Hall (acting)	"	1830
Jonathan G. Hunton	"	1830–1831
Samuel E. Smith	"	1831–1834
Robert P. Dunlap	"	1834–1838
Edward Kent	Whig	1838–1839
John Fairfield	Democrat	1839–1840
Edward Kent	Whig	1840–1841
John Fairfield	Democrat	1841–1843
Edward Kavanagh (acting)	"	1843–1844
Hugh J. Anderson	"	1844–1847
John W. Dana	"	1847–1850
John Hubbard	"	1850–1853
William G. Crosby	Whig and Free Soil	1853–1855
Anson P. Morrill	Republican	1855–1856
Samuel Wells	Democrat	1856–1857
Hannibal Hamlin	Republican	1857
Joseph H. Williams (acting)	"	1857–1858
Lot M. Morrill	"	1858–1861
Israel Washburn	"	1861–1863
Abner Coburn	"	1863–1864
Samuel Cony	War Democrat	1864–1867
Joshua L. Chamberlain	Republican	1867–1871
Sidney Perham	"	1871–1874
Nelson Dingley	"	1874–1876
Selden Connor	"	1876–1879
Alonzo Garcelon	Democrat and Greenback	1879–1880
Daniel F. Davis	Republican	1880–1881
Harris M. Plaisted	Democrat and Greenback	1881–1883
Frederick Robie	Republican	1883–1887
Joseph R. Bodwell	"	1887
Sebastian S. Marble (acting)	"	1887–1889
Edwin C. Burleigh	"	1889–1893
Henry B. Cleaves	"	1893–1897
Llewellyn Powers	"	1897–1901
John F. Hill	"	1901–1905
William T. Cobb	"	1905–1909
Bert M. Fernald	"	1909–1911
Frederick W. Plaisted	Democrat	1911–1913
William T. Haines	Republican	1913–1915
Oakley C. Curtis	Democrat	1915–1917
Carl E. Milliken	Republican	1917–1921
Frederic H. Parkhurst	"	1921
Percival P. Baxter	"	1921–1925
Owen Brewster	"	1925–1929
William T. Gardiner	"	1929–1933
Louis J. Brann	Democrat	1933–1937
Lewis O. Barrows	Republican	1937–1941
Sumner Sewall	"	1941–1945
Horace A. Hildreth	"	1945–1949
Frederick G. Payne	"	1949–1952
Burton M. Cross	"	1952–1955
Edmund S. Muskie	Democrat	1955–1959
Clinton A. Clauson	Democrat	1959
John H. Reed	Republican	1959–1967
Kenneth M. Curtis	Democrat	1967–

Legislature.—The legislature is composed of a Senate of 34 members and a House of Representatives of 151 members, all of whom are elected biennially in even-numbered years. It meets in regular session the first Wednesday of January in odd-numbered years. Special sessions may be called by the governor, who may deliver messages and suggest programs but cannot limit the time or subject matter of any session. Senators are chosen by counties on the basis of population, and representatives are elected from districts consisting of a city or of one or more towns. A system of determining representative districts that favored the smaller towns was eliminated by an amendment which was adopted in 1949 and became effective with the 1957 legislature. In response to a federal court order, the legislature reapportioned the Senate in 1961. A constitutional amendment to reapportion the House was passed in 1963, approved by the voters, and implemented in a 1964 special session.

Revenue bills originate in the House of Representatives. Impeachments also originate there, but the cases are judged by the Senate. The governor's veto may be overruled by a two-thirds vote of each house.

Judiciary.—There are three levels of courts: (1) probate and district courts; (2) the superior court; and (3) the Supreme Judicial Court. The only judges who are elected are the probate judges, one to each county, who are chosen for four-year terms. All others are appointed by the governor with the consent of the council for seven-year terms.

The district courts, established by the legislature in 1961 to replace municipal and trial justice courts, hear a variety of petty criminal cases and a smaller number of civil cases. They also serve as juvenile courts. The state has 13 districts and a total of 17 district judges. Appeals from a district court go to the superior court of the county.

The lower courts hold preliminary hearings in important criminal cases to determine whether the suspect shall be held for the grand jury. If the grand jury finds an indictment, the accused is brought before a superior court judge and a jury for trial. Civil actions of consequence start in the superior court.

The superior court contains 10 judges who are assigned by the chief justice of the Supreme Judicial Court to court terms in the various counties, one judge to a term. The 6-member Supreme Judicial Court has the usual function of deciding appeals on legal questions and the less common duty of rendering advisory opinions when requested to do so by the legislature or the governor.

Independent Bodies.—Special independent bodies include the Maine Turnpike Authority, established in 1941, which built toll roads from Kittery to Portland (1947) and from Portland to Augusta (1955); and the Maine Port Authority, which operates a public pier in Portland. A bridge connecting Maine and New Hampshire is under the Maine-New Hampshire Interstate Bridge Authority. Among other quasi-independent agencies are the Maine State Retirement System, the Maine Maritime Academy, and the University of Maine, each of which is administered by its board of trustees.

Taxation and Revenue.—Automobile registration and license fees are collected by the Motor Vehicle Division of the secretary of state's office, but the principal revenue-collecting agency is the Bureau of Taxation in the Department of Finance and Administration, which collects sales, gasoline, cigarette, inheritance, estate, and other taxes. Maine has no state property taxes or state or local personal income taxes; a 2 per cent sales tax was adopted in 1951, and the rate was increased to 4 per cent in 1963. Principal sources of state revenue are the gasoline tax, federal subsidies, the sales tax, motor vehicle and driver's license fees, liquor revenues, the cigarette tax, inheritance and estate taxes, and the public utility tax.

Suffrage and Elections.—Qualifications for voting include citizenship in the United States, attainment of the age of 21, residence in the state for six months and in the voting area for three months, and ability to pass a literacy test. Paupers and persons under guardianship are excluded from the franchise. Prior to 1955, Indians living on state reservations also were not allowed to vote. Although the use of voting machines was authorized in 1935, the printed ballot is commonly employed in state, city, county, and national elections. Towns use the officially printed Australian ballot if the citizens vote to do so; otherwise they retain the older method of voting, using unofficial ballots.

Party primary elections for state, county, and national offices are held in June. Maine was the only state which elected United States senators and representatives in September, along with state and county officials. The early election was watched eagerly for trends, and Maine clung to it because of the advertising received nationally through the slogan, "As goes Maine, so goes the Union." Finally, in 1957, an amendment to the state constitution, effective in 1960, changed the date of state and county elections to November, thus ending a picturesque custom which had come to be considered of dubious political advantage. Local election dates vary; city elections generally occur in the fall or winter, while towns hold their town meetings in March. Maine sends two senators and two representatives to the United States Congress.

Local Government.—Despite the lack of home rule provisions in its constitution, Maine allows local units much self-government. Cities must appeal to the legislature for their charters, but a new or revised charter is seldom denied and, having passed the legislature, is then customarily submitted to the voters in a local referendum election. In the fields of education, highways, health, and welfare there is a considerable amount of state control and assistance, but local taxation and civil service are largely free from supervision.

The basic feature of town government is the annual town meeting, at which officers are elected and taxes and appropriations are voted. Between meetings administration is handled by a board of selectmen, consisting of three, five, or seven persons, and such officers as the tax collector, treasurer, assessors, overseers of the poor, and

road commissioner. Cities are governed by either the mayor and council or the manager and council form of government, and many towns have also adopted the manager plan. At the end of 1965, Maine had 149 manager communities; over half of the population, a larger percentage than in any other state, were living under the manager type of government. Incorporated villages are not common, but there are a few, such as Ogunquit and Farmington village, which have governmental functions. More than half of the area of the state, largely in the northern and eastern sections, is surveyed into unorganized townships, which have no local government and little population. In addition, there are a number of lightly settled local units called plantations, which possess a rudimentary form of government somewhat like that of the towns. The counties serve chiefly as court and law enforcement units. In each of them the voters elect a three-member board of county commissioners, a sheriff, clerk of courts, register of deeds, county attorney, probate judge, and treasurer. Maine counties have little authority over roads and bridges and none over education, welfare, or property assessment. The governor appoints the county medical examiner, and he also has power to remove the sheriff or the county attorney for cause. See also TOWN AND TOWN MEETINGS.

Ewing Galloway

The state capitol building, Augusta.

4. EDUCATION, HEALTH, AND WELFARE

Education.—Parcels of state land were set aside in 1828 to create a public school fund, and money or timber from these lands formed the basis for a permanent fund. A law providing for free high schools was passed in 1873, and two years later education was made compulsory. Between 1900 and the school year 1965–66 enrollment in public elementary and secondary schools rose from 130,918 to an estimated 235,000. Although the trend away from one-room schools was rapid after 1940, towns did not readily accept the idea of further consolidation in school districts embracing several towns. In 1957, therefore, the legislature enacted the Sinclair bill, designed to encourage establishment of consolidated schools operated by districts covering two or more towns. The program is administered by a five-member School District Commission.

Public elementary and secondary education is free to all residents of the state between the ages of 5 and 21, and education is compulsory for all between the ages of 7 and 18. The state administers its teacher certification law, curriculum supervision, and school building standards through a Department of Education, which is headed by a commissioner chosen by the 10-member Board of Education. The department operates the state's four vocational-technical institutes, at South Portland, Auburn, Presque Isle, and Bangor. Subject to state standards, each town and city has broad powers over its school system and bears the bulk of the cost through local property taxes. Each community has a school board that supervises the school system with the aid of a school superintendent, who usually works for several towns.

More than 50 academies and institutes survive from the 19th century era of private secondary schools, and many of them are operated as town high schools or with town aid. Among them are Fryeburg Academy (1791); Hebron Academy (1804); Coburn Classical Institute, Waterville (1829); Gould Academy, Bethel (1836); Oak Grove School, Vassalboro (1849); and Maine Central Institute, Pittsfield (1869). There are a number of elementary and secondary schools operated by the Roman Catholic Church.

The state administers five teachers colleges: Gorham State College; Farmington State College; Washington State College, Machias; Aroostook State College, Presque Isle; and Fort Kent State College. All of these schools train elementary teachers. Farmington offers secondary school training in home economics, and Gorham prepares secondary school teachers in industrial arts. Specialization is also possible in physical education at Aroostook, in business education at Washington, in art and music education at Gorham, and in librarianship at Farmington.

Training of elementary and secondary school teachers is also offered by the College of Education at the University of Maine at Orono. In addition, the university has colleges of arts and sciences, agriculture, technology, and business administration. It has a branch and a law school at Portland. The Marine Maritime Academy is at Castine.

Private colleges include Bates College and Bliss College, Lewiston; Bowdoin College (for men), Brunswick; Colby College, Waterville; Nassau College, Springvale; Ricker College, Houlton; Thomas College, Waterville; and Westbrook Junior College (for women), Portland. In Bangor are the Northern Conservatory of Music, Bangor Theological Seminary (Congregational), and Husson College, a business school. There are three Roman Catholic colleges: Oblate College and Seminary (for men), Bar Harbor; St. Joseph's College (for women), North Windham; and St. Francis College (for men), Biddeford. Between 1900 and 1965 enrollment in the state's institutions of higher education rose from 1,520 to 22,999.

Libraries.—Maine's first library was founded by Sir William Pepperell in the York-Kittery area in 1751. In 1765 a library was established at Falmouth (now Portland), which ultimately became the Portland Public Library, second largest in the state. Maine passed a free public library law in 1854, and in the following year Castine opened the first library under the act.

There are about 300 libraries in the state, including the manuscript material of the Maine Historical Society in Portland and the Longfellow collection of the Bowdoin College Library. Bangor has the largest public library in the state. Colby College and the University of Maine also have notable libraries, and the state maintains a free library for the legislature and the citizens of the state in the State House at Augusta.

Public Health and Welfare.—Health and welfare agencies are combined in the Department of Health and Welfare, which administers a variety of programs, including old-age assistance, aid to dependent children, aid to the blind, mothers' aid, and the work of district health officers and nurses. Many of the programs are financed partially with federal funds. The commissioner of health and welfare, who is appointed by the governor and council, administers the state's three tuberculosis sanatoriums: Northern Maine Sanatorium, Presque Isle; Central Maine Sanatorium, Fairfield; and Western Maine Sanatorium, Hebron. There are 10 state institutions, each of which is headed by a superintendent under the direction of the commissioner of institutional service, as follows: Augusta State Hospital, for the mentally ill; Pineland Hospital, for the mentally retarded, Pownal; Maine State Prison, Thomaston; State Reformatory for Men, South Windham; State Reformatory for Women, Skowhegan; State School for Boys, South Portland; State School for Girls, Hallowell; Maine School for the Deaf, Portland; and the Military and Naval Children's Home, Bath.

Unemployment compensation is in the charge of the three-member Employment Security Commission, which also administers employment service offices throughout the state. In 1957 the maximum duration of unemployment benefits was increased from 23 to 26 weeks. The state workmen's compensation law, which was broadened in 1945 to include occupational diseases, is administered by the five-member Industrial Accident Commission. In 1942 a law was passed granting state employees retirement and disability privileges, and in 1947 the schoolteachers of the state were brought into the general state retirement system.

5. ECONOMIC ACTIVITIES

In 20th century Maine industry far outranks agriculture in value of product and in number of employees. Yet the leading industrial group depends on a type of agriculture—silviculture, or the growing and harvesting of the trees which cover three fourths of the land area of the state. Paper, lumber, and wood products mills employ almost one third of the industrial work force and produce over one third of the value of goods manufactured. Maine is one of the leading producers of paper and paper products in the United States, is the largest manufacturer of toothpicks, and is said to have the world's largest snowshoe factory and the largest dowel mill.

Next in value of product comes food-processing, principally the canning and freezing of vegetables, berries, and fish. This is followed by leather tanning and leather goods manufacturing, the textile industry, and the production of transportation equipment, chiefly ships and boats. Altogether, 36.7 per cent of the nonagricultural workers were employed in manufacturing as of 1965.

The second largest employment group, accounting for 18.9 per cent of the nonagricultural

Employment in the service trades rises sharply in July and August with the influx of summer tourists. So many farmers do their own work or

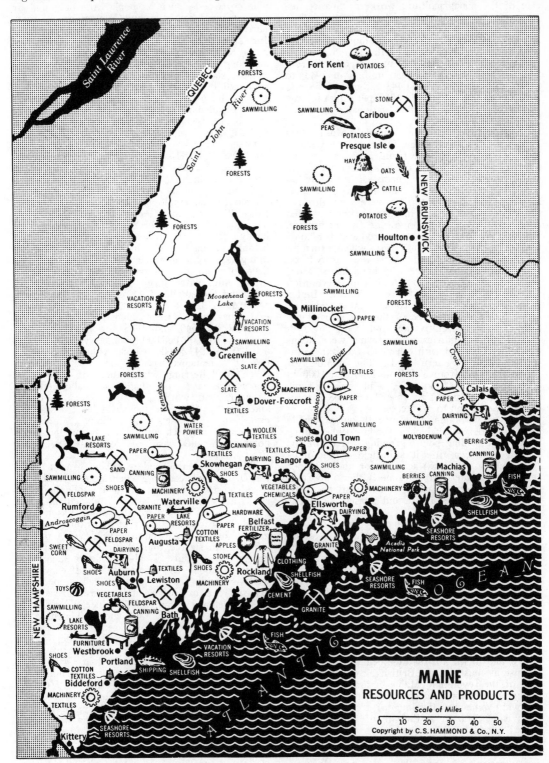

MAINE
RESOURCES AND PRODUCTS
Scale of Miles
0 10   20   30   40   50
Copyright by C.S. HAMMOND & Co., N.Y.

workers, is wholesale and retail trade. Federal, state, and local government (including teachers) is third (18.5 per cent); and the service and miscellaneous group (11.7 per cent) is fourth.

employ only seasonal labor that it is hard to judge where agricultural employment should be ranked, but it may be fifth or sixth, with transportation and public utilities (5.7 per cent of nonagricultural employment) occupying the remaining place among the first six employing groups. Contract construction employs 5.1 per cent of the nonagricultural workers; finance, insurance, and real estate, 3.4 per cent. While membership in labor unions has risen steadily since the 1930's, it has grown more slowly in Maine than in other states of the Union.

Personal income in the state increased from $444 million in 1940 to $856 million in 1945, to $1,087 million in 1950, to $1,443 million in 1955, and to $2,245 million in 1965. In 1965, per capita income was $2,277 compared with a national average of $2,894.

Agriculture.—Life in colonial Maine was hard and dangerous. The frontiersmen wrested much of their livelihood from ocean and forest, but they also practiced a crude agriculture. Oxen, cattle, hogs, and sheep furnished meat, hides, wool, and tallow. The animals ran wild in summer and fall, and those that were kept through the winter were penned in rude shelters and fed hay until they could again forage for themselves. Butter, milk, and cheese were produced for home use, and corn, pumpkins, rye, wheat, turnips, potatoes, and other vegetables were grown on small plots cleared of trees by hand labor. More peaceful times after the American Revolution allowed settlements to spread inland. Better farming methods and the commercial growing of crops followed, but much of the land proved too hilly or rocky for cultivation, and in the late 19th and the 20th centuries many farms were abandoned or combined with others to facilitate competition with Western lands. The number of farms declined from 39,000 in 1940 to 30,000 in 1950 and to 17,000 in 1959, while in the same period the average size rose from 108.3 acres to 137.7 acres and to 178 acres.

The only Maine county with large fertile areas is Aroostook, which in the late 19th century became the leading potato-growing district of the United States, a title it still held in the mid-20th century. Potatoes account for about 30 per cent of the state's crop income. Other important crops, in order of value, are forest products, apples, berries, greenhouse and nursery products, hay, oats, and peas.

Since 1900 the raising of dairy cattle has expanded considerably, but mechanization has forced many small dairymen to sell out to the larger owners. The most spectacular growth has taken place in the growing of poultry, especially broilers, and since World War II Maine has become one of the leading broiler states. Between 1946 and 1959 income from poultry rose from $6.5 million to over $61 million, or more than that from potatoes.

Lumbering.—The earliest settlers used wood for home building and fuel, boatbuilding and furniture, and in the 1650's trade began in tall pines for use as masts in the British Navy. About the time of the revolution, Maine became a leader in lumber production, and until after the Civil War the white pine was the king of trees. The sawmills which started at the site of York in 1623 moved inland as the coastal areas were stripped of the huge pine trees, which often grew over 100 feet in height. In the 19th century the greatest concentration of sawmills was near Bangor, which from 1830 to 1880 was one of the world's great lumber ports.

The character and utilization of the forest stand changed considerably from the 19th to the 20th century. Pine and spruce were the trees most commonly exported as long lumber. As the old growth was cut, use was made of less valuable softwoods, such as poplar for pulp and fir and hemlock for pulp and lumber. In addition, hardwoods were used more extensively, especially for spools, dowels, furniture, skis, snowshoes, sleds, toys, and novelties. At the same time, pulp and long lumber continued to figure prominently in the state's economy, large quantities being produced during the emergency of World War II and the paper and building material shortage that prevailed after the war. Of the 31,282 million board feet of live saw timber in Maine (1963), 20,657 million are softwood. See also LUMBER INDUSTRY—*Lumber Industry in the United States* (Historical Background).

Fisheries.—As early as 1765, Maine was a leader in codfishing, and by 1820 it had about a fifth of the ships engaged in fishing in the United States, employing about 2,600 fishermen. Since 1900 the character of the fishing industry has changed. While the catching of lobsters by hardy men in small boats has continued, codfishing sailing vessels have been replaced by draggers, large engine-driven ships which scoop fish up from the bottom of the ocean. Small motor ships catch large numbers of herring in nets, and the smaller herring are packed in tins as sardines. Lubec, Eastport, Rockland, and several other coastal towns have sardine canneries.

Between 1940 and 1965 the total catch increased from 88,088,000 pounds, valued at $2,606,400, to 204,846,000 pounds, valued at $21,922,000. The principal species are rosefish (ocean perch) and herring, while others of commercial importance are cod, haddock, hake, pollack, flounder, shad, whiting, mackerel, tuna, alewives, and smelts. Shellfish include lobsters, scallops, crabs, clams, mussels, and shrimps. Maine carries on a research and propagation program, notably in the case of lobsters. See also FISHERIES.

Mining.—Maine had extensive granite quarries in the 19th century, when stone was shipped to other states for use in such public buildings as Grant's Tomb and the Philadelphia mint. Limestone and slate were also mined extensively, but their production, like that of granite, declined greatly in the 20th century. Feldspar and mica deposits are sizable, and Maine is a leading producer of sheet mica. It also produces such semiprecious stones as tourmalines and beryls, as well as sand, gravel, and crushed stone. Peat deposits are extensive, and several areas have been developed commercially since World War II. Deposits of silver, gold, and molybdenum are under exploration in north central and eastern Maine. There are large undeveloped deposits of low-grade manganese in Aroostook County. Copper mines opened near Blue Hill in 1966.

Manufacturing.—Since the construction of the *Virginia* in 1607 (see section 9. *History*) shipbuilding and ship fitting have been Maine traditions. In the mid-19th century, Maine was the leading United States producer of wooden ships, and until 1900 nearly half the nation's ocean vessels were built in the state. As the day of wooden ships passed, however, the shipyards closed, one by one. World War I revived the shipbuilding industry in Maine, and World War II brought an even greater boom. Although the boom collapsed when the war ended, the navy yard at Kittery has continued to build submarines, a privately owned shipyard at Bath constructs naval craft, and small yards build wooden pleasure boats. (See also SHIPBUILDING INDUSTRY AND CONSTRUCTION—*United States*.)

The manufacture of cotton and woolen goods began in the latter part of the 18th century and reached its peak about 1914; since then textiles have declined in importance, with many mills closing or curtailing their operations. These losses have been more than offset, however, by the expansion of the paper industry and the development of new industries in electronics and other fields.

Samuel Waldo and Thomas Westbrook built a paper mill at Presumpscot Falls, Falmouth, in 1731, and a second mill at Stroudwater two years later. At that time, there were only three other paper mills in the United States. The Maine paper industry received a great impetus from the introduction of wood pulp, which was first produced in the state in 1868–1869. Sulphite pulp was first produced in Maine in 1889, and other sulphite, soda pulp, and ground wood mills followed in rapid succession. Until about 1950 it was thought that spruce and other softwoods were needed for paper, but with the development of newer methods such hardwoods as birch and maple have been used increasingly. Paper products constitute Maine's largest industry, and there are big paper mills in Bucksport, Woodland, Millinocket, Lincoln, Brewer, Madison, Westbrook, Madawaska, Winslow, and Rumford. Almost every mill has its specialty, such as magazine paper, book paper, or newsprint.

Many small tanneries developed in the 19th century, but most of them disappeared when the supply of hemlock bark diminished. Modern processes no longer depend on hemlock, and since World War II several new tanneries have been built. The shoe industry has grown steadily from manufacture in small home shops to the operation of large factories. The first factory, set up in New Gloucester in 1844, had 17 employees. By 1914 there were 50 plants, employing 9,371 workers, and Auburn was the leading shoe center. By the 1950's there were shoe and moccasin factories in a number of Maine towns and cities.

Power.—Hydroelectric power from Maine's many lakes and swift-flowing streams is a major resource. It was long believed that this power would prove ample and dependable, but tremendously increased use of electricity and frequent water shortages after 1945 changed the picture. To meet the demand for power several small diesel plants were built, and larger oil-fired steam plants were constructed. By the end of 1964 developed water power capacity totaled 493,000 kilowatts, and capacity for power produced by steam and internal combustion engines amounted to 648,000 kilowatts. It was estimated that an additional 1,660,000 kilowatts of water power capacity could be developed.

Electricity is produced and distributed in Maine almost wholly by private corporations. The three largest are Central Maine Power, serving southwestern and central Maine; Bangor Hydro-Electric, serving the north central and eastern sections; and Maine Public Service, serving the north. The largest power dam is Wyman Dam, at Bingham, and the biggest steam plant is the Cousins Island (Yarmouth) plant of the Central Maine Power Company.

An interesting idea was the plan of Duncan C. Cooper to utilize the power generated by the tides of the Bay of Fundy, whose flow is so great that it was estimated that power could be generated 16 hours in every 24 hours. Originally proposed as an international project, the Passamaquoddy Tidal Power Development Project, it was later modified to be built without Canadian participation. The Franklin D. Roosevelt administration constructed Quoddy Village and began work on the dams, but in 1936 Congress refused to appropriate funds and work was abandoned after some millions of dollars had been spent. With greater demands for power interest was revived in the project, and in 1950 the Canadian and United States governments made studies of the engineering and economic feasibility of developing tidal power.

Banking and Insurance.—Maine banks are regulated by the state bank commissioner. In the mid-1960's, there were 32 savings banks, 21 trust companies, and 26 savings and loan associations. There were also 22 national banks, supervised by the United States comptroller of the currency. Most insurance in the state is sold by agents representing outside companies. Maine's oldest (1848) and largest native company is the Union Mutual Life Insurance Company of Portland. There are also a stock life insurance company and a number of mutual fire insurance companies. All insurance companies are under the jurisdiction of the state insurance commissioner and must be licensed by him in order to do business in Maine.

Trade.—Major retail and wholesale centers are located at Portland and Bangor, both of which are strategically located with relation to rail, air, water, and highway transportation. Portland, on Casco Bay, supplements trade, service, and transportation with canneries, a rolling mill, and light industries. Bangor is the trading center of Penobscot County and portions of several other counties. Although it has some industry, principally shoe factories, it relies most heavily on trade and service activities. Houlton, Presque Isle, and Caribou are trading centers for the Aroostook pulp and potato industries. Exports from Maine include poultry products, milk, apples, and blueberries; fresh, frozen, and canned fish and lobsters; a wide variety of paper and pulp products, wooden ware and novelties, lumber, boats, and canoes; and canned foods, machinery, shoes, textiles, and steel ships.

For additional production statistics, see THE AMERICANA ANNUAL.

6. TRANSPORTATION AND COMMUNICATIONS

Roads.—Colonial Maine relied almost entirely on water routes. A few roads developed from Indian trails in the 17th and 18th centuries, and wagon roads eventually evolved into stagecoach routes. In 1788 mail service was begun from Boston to Portland, and by 1825 there were many stagecoach lines in Maine. Roads were slow in reaching the interior and northern areas of the state, however, and in the mid-20th century much of north central and northwestern Maine was still inaccessible by automobile, depending on the airplane or on woods roads and foot trails. As of 1964, Maine had 20,998 miles of public roads, of which 10,846 miles were state highways. U.S. Highway No. 1 runs from Madawaska in northern Maine to Calais and then along the coast all the way to Florida. The Maine Turnpike Authority operates a 106-mile toll road from Kittery to Augusta. There are many modern bridges, such as the Waldo-Hancock Bridge over the Penobscot River and the Augusta, Bath, and Portland structures, although a few wooden covered bridges are still in use. Motor vehicle registrations increased from slightly over 220,000 in 1942 to more than 400,000 in the mid-1960's. Several bus and truck lines, some of which are affiliated with the railroads, operate in the state.

Railroads.—The first Maine railroad, completed in 1836, hauled lumber from the Old Town sawmills to Bangor for shipment by boat. The first important line, built from Portland to Portsmouth, N.H., in 1841, gave rail service to Boston. In 1853 the Atlantic and St. Lawrence Railway was completed from Portland to Montreal, giving Canada its first Atlantic port connection. The railroads were eventually continued along the coast to Bangor and beyond and, in the late 1890's, into Aroostook County. Mileage increased from 1,915 miles in 1900 to 2,295 miles in 1920. By the mid-1960's it had risen to more than 2,500 miles.

Of the eight railroads operating in the state, the Maine Central and the Bangor and Aroostook are the leading lines. Their service is limited to freight hauling. The Boston and Maine, last of the passenger-carrying lines, discontinued regular service in 1965. The only remaining passenger service is on Canadian lines.

Air Service.—Maine had 170 public and commercial airports in the mid-1960's. It is served by one commercial airline, Northeast Airlines, which links the state with Boston and New York City.

Water Transport.—Waterways brought the early explorers and settlers to Maine, and they remained the chief means of communication until after the Civil War. Large quantities of lumber products and dried cod were shipped by sea before the revolution, and for much of the 19th century Bangor was the leading United States lumber port. Portland was a center of coastwise and transatlantic shipping. Canadian wheat, Maine lumber, paper, and manufactured goods were shipped out, and a wide variety of cargo was brought in. During World War II, Portland was a center of naval operations. Except for oil tankers and freighters handling paper, lumber, and potatoes, most of the oceanborne commerce to and from Maine ports has ended. Portland and Searsport are chief shipping points. The Canadian National Railways operates a ferry between Yarmouth, Nova Scotia, and Bar Harbor, Me.

Postal and Telephone Services.—Maine had 561 first, second, third, and fourth class post offices in 1965. The New England Telephone and Telegraph Company and its subsidiaries, together with several small local companies, provide telephone service in most of the settled areas, and the Maine Forest Service reaches many of the forested areas as part of its fire-control and rescue service. The number of telephones in the state increased from 186,000 in 1947 to more than 380,000 in the mid-1960's.

Radio and Television.—The first radio station in Maine was WABI, established in Bangor in 1922. Television was also introduced to the state through this station in 1953. By the mid-1960's there were more than 30 commercial radio stations and 9 television stations in Maine.

Newspapers.—Maine's earliest newspaper was the Falmouth *Gazette* (1785), printed in what is now Portland. The first daily was the *Courier,* begun in Portland in 1826. Leading papers of the 19th century were the *Eastern Argus* of Portland and the Bangor *Whig and Courier.* In the mid-1960's there were 9 daily newspapers and about 40 others, mostly weeklies. The largest in circulation is the Bangor *News.* Second is the Portland *Press-Herald,* which is put out by the Guy Gannett Publishing Co., which also prints the Portland *Evening Express.*

7. CULTURAL LIFE

Architecture.—Maine developed two general types of houses, of which the more prevalent is the simple story or story-and-one-half cottage type. In contrast are the elaborate two- and three-story mansions built by the wealthy merchants, shipowners, and timber barons. One of the earliest of these is the William Pepperell House (1682) at Kittery. Also at Kittery is the Lady Pepperell Mansion (1765), considered an outstanding example of Georgian architecture. In South Berwick is the home of Sarah Orne Jewett, built about 1780, which is notable particularly for its Doric portico and its central hall and stairway. Wiscasset is a charming small town with many fine homes built by sea captains and shipping merchants, an elegant example being the Nickels-Sortwell House (1807–1808). The Wedding Cake House in Kennebunk, too ornate to be considered of architectural merit, represents the scroll-saw era. The Ruggles House at Columbia Falls (1818) has a beautiful doorway, a flying staircase, and fine carvings. The Tate House (1755), the oldest in Portland, has noteworthy wainscoting and interesting slave quarters. Also in Portland is the Wadsworth-Longfellow House (1785–1786), which was Longfellow's boyhood home. An example of the Classic Revival is the Blaine House in Augusta, now the Executive Mansion.

Picturesque white churches are numerous in Maine, and many are architectural gems. Although most of the interesting old taverns have disappeared, the Burnham Tavern in Machias (1770) survives. To it was brought the mortally wounded captain of the British ship *Margaretta* after the first naval battle of the American Revolution.

Art, Music, and the Theater.—Artists and art colonies flourish in Maine, especially along the coast. Summer colonies center around Ogunquit, Kennebunkport, Boothbay Harbor, and Monhegan Island. Among the artists born in Maine are Benjamin Paul Akers (Saccarappa [now part of Westbrook], 1825–1861), sculptor, whose *Dead Pearl Diver* is described in *The Marble Faun;* Franklin Simmons (Lisbon [now Webster], 1839–1913), sculptor, whose bronze statue of Longfellow is in Portland; Frederic Porter Vinton (Bangor, 1846–1911), portrait painter; Marsden Hartley (Lewiston, 1877–1943), best known for his paintings of Mount Katahdin; and Waldo Peirce (Bangor, 1884–), painter. Well-known painters who have lived and worked in Maine include Winslow Homer (1836–1910), John Marin (1872–1953), Carl Sprinchorn (1887–), Stephen Etnier (1903–), and Vincent Hartgen (1914–).

The most important musical movement in Maine since the Maine Musical Festival of the first quarter of the 20th century has been the growth of school music, which has resulted in the development of hundreds of local musical groups performing creditably on dozens of local occasions and giving exchange concerts, appearing in regional contests, and attending summer music camps. In addition, there are college groups and local orchestras, such as the Bangor Symphony Orchestra. Summer theater colonies are found at Ogunquit, Kennebunkport, and Camden, but the best known is Lakewood, which was founded in 1901 near Skowhegan. Famous actors often appear at the summer playhouses, whose productions range from experimental plays to Broadway hits. To the musical and theatrical worlds Maine has contributed John Knowles Paine (Portland, 1839–1906), music teacher and composer; Annie Louise Cary (Wayne, 1842–1921), operatic and concert contralto; Lillian Nordica (pseudonym of Lillian Norton; Farmington, 1859–1914), operatic soprano; and Maxine Elliott (stage name of Jessie Dermot; Rockland, 1871–1940), actress.

Men of Letters.—Notable writers born in Maine include Sally Sayward Barrell Wood (York, 1759–1855), one of the first novelists to use American scenes and characters; Jacob Abbott (Hallowell, 1803–1879), who wrote chiefly juveniles; the celebrated poet Henry Wadsworth Longfellow (Portland, 1807–1882); Elijah Kellogg (Portland, 1813–1901), author of books for boys; Rebecca Sophia Clarke (pseudonym Sophie May; Norridgewock, 1833–1906), who wrote books for girls; Charles Farrar Browne (near Waterford, 1834–1867), humorist who wrote under the pseudonym Artemus Ward; Charles A. Stephens (Norway, 1847–1931), who wrote many stories for the *Youth's Companion;* Sarah Orne Jewett (South Berwick, 1849–1909), author of *The Country of the Pointed Firs,* perhaps the first important book about Maine by a native of the state; Edwin Arlington Robinson (Head Tide, 1869–1935), poet, who won the Pulitzer Prize three times; Kenneth Roberts (Kennebunk, 1885–1957), historical novelist; Mary Ellen Chase (Blue Hill, 1887–), educator and author; Robert P. Tristram Coffin (Brunswick, 1892–1955), poet, essayist, and novelist; Edna St. Vincent Millay (Rockland, 1892–1950), poet; and Dorothy Clarke Wilson (Gardiner, 1904–), author of religious novels. Adopted sons and daughters include Kate Douglas Wiggin (1856–1923), author of *Rebecca of Sunnybrook Farm;* Margaret Deland (1857–1945), novelist; Ben Ames Williams (1889–1953), novelist, who spent his summers in Maine; and Gladys Hasty Carroll (1904–), who wrote *As the Earth Turns.*

Other Famous Persons.—Among Maine men who became celebrated in public life are Rufus King (Scarboro, 1755–1827), member of the Continental Congress and the Constitutional Convention and twice minister to Great Britain; Hannibal Hamlin (Paris Hill, 1809–1891), vice president of the United States during the Civil War; Joshua L. Chamberlain (Brewer, 1828–1914), a Civil War general who was delegated to receive the surrender of Robert E. Lee's army, and from 1871 to 1883 served as president of Bowdoin College; William Pierce Frye (Lewiston, 1831–1911), United States senator from 1881 to 1911; Nelson Dingley (Durham, 1832–1899), member of Congress and chief author of the Dingley Act of 1897; Melville Weston Fuller (Augusta, 1833–1910), chief justice of the United States from 1888 until his death; and Thomas Brackett Reed (Portland, 1839–1902), twice

Maine Development Commission

An elm-shaded street in the city of Bath.

speaker of the United States House of Representatives. William Pitt Fessenden (1806–1869), secretary of the treasury, and James G. Blaine (1830–1893), secretary of state and presidential candidate, were residents of the state.

Persons of note in other fields include Dorothea Lynde Dix (Hampden, 1802–1887), humanitarian; Neal Dow (Portland, 1804–1897), temperance advocate; Henry Varnum Poor (Andover, 1812–1905), economist and founder of Poor's *Manual of the Railroads of the United States;* and the inventors Sir Hiram Stevens Maxim (Sangerville, 1840–1916) and Hudson Maxim (Orneville, 1853–1927). Among natives of Maine in publishing were George Palmer Putnam (Brunswick, 1814–1872), founder of the firm now known as G. P. Putnam's Sons, Inc.; Cyrus H. K. Curtis (Portland, 1850–1933), publisher of the *Ladies' Home Journal* and *Saturday Evening Post;* Frank Andrew Munsey (Mercer, 1854–1925), publisher of the New York *Evening Sun* and *Evening Telegram* and *Munsey's Magazine;* and Clara S. Littledale (Belfast, 1891–1956), first editor of *Parents' Magazine.*

Organizations and Publications.—Portland is the seat of the Maine Historical Society and the Portland Society of Natural History, both of which maintain museums. The *New England Quarterly* is published in Brunswick, and *Maine Farm Research,* also a quarterly, is issued by the Maine Agricultural Experiment Station at Orono. Near Bar Harbor on Mount Desert Island are the Roscoe B. Jackson Memorial Laboratory (cancer research) and the Mount Desert Biological Laboratory (marine biology).

Religion.—Christian religious activity in Maine can be traced back to 1604, when the French brought missionaries with them to St. Croix Island. Later the Jesuits began to convert the Indians. Father Sébastien Râle (Rasle), one of the most famous of the early missionaries, was successful with the Norridgewock Indians on the Kennebec River, but he was killed when the English made a surprise attack on the Indians in 1724. The Indians of Maine have been predominantly Roman Catholic since colonial times.

The first English settlers, early in the 17th century, were members of the Church of England, and Robert Jordan of Cape Elizabeth was the leading churchman prior to the American Revolution. When Massachusetts obtained control over Maine, the Congregational Church became paramount, and it remained so until well into the 19th century. It was at the Williston

Congregational Church in Portland that the International Society of Christian Endeavor (q.v.) was founded in 1881. The Baptists and Methodists gained a foothold in the late 18th century and gradually became stronger in the 19th century. At one time the Shakers had three settlements in Maine, at Alfred, Gorham, and New Gloucester, but by 1958 only the New Gloucester settlement survived, and with only a handful of members. Leading Protestant churches of the 20th century are the Baptist, Congregational Christian, Episcopal, Methodist, and Universalist. By far the largest Christian church is the Roman Catholic, with over 230,000 adherents in the state as of 1957.

8. PLACES OF INTEREST

Maine attracts many tourists and vacationists, especially in summer, and sportsmen continue to come well into the fall for the hunting season. Camping, canoeing, swimming, boating, and golf are among the popular sports available. Drawn by cool nights and clear air, visitors return summer after summer, to build or rent cottages along the splendid beaches of southern Maine, or at Bar Harbor or in the many other picturesque towns in the bays and inlets of the rugged coast from Portland to Eastport. Since 1900 the forest-rimmed lakes of the interior have also become increasingly popular and have helped to give Maine its name of Vacationland.

Frank E. Gunnell, from Frederic Lewis

Coastal scene in Acadia National Park.

Though small, Acadia National Park provides a unique combination of lake, mountain, forest, and rugged shoreline. Established by act of Congress in 1916 as Sieur de Monts National Monument and enlarged by gift and purchase to cover 30,651 acres, it is situated chiefly on Mount Desert Island. One section occupies Schoodic Peninsula on the mainland, and another a part of Isle au Haut. The road leading to the summit of Mount Cadillac (1,532 feet) is famous for its extensive views of land, sea, and islands.

Baxter (193,254 acres), largest of Maine's 10 state parks, was created in 1931 through the gift of ex-Governor Percival Baxter. It is maintained as a wildlife sanctuary and as a resort for campers and hikers. The park contains Mount Katahdin, marking the start of the Appalachian Trail

extending into Georgia. Camden Hills (4,962 acres), established near Camden in 1948, contains beautiful wooded hills and lakes, trails, and camping areas. Lake St. George (5,311 acres), near Liberty, has a beautiful lake. Mount Blue (4,921 acres), created in 1937 near Weld, is noted for its 3,187-foot peak, accessible by a well-marked trail, and for Webbs Pond. In Sebago Lake (1,296 acres), established in 1939, is the lake from which the landlocked salmon originated and derived its name, *Salmo sebago.* The park features camping sites and fine beaches. Reid (792 acres), in Georgetown, has fine saltwater beaches and a sheltered lagoon for swimming. Fort Knox (124 acres) is in Prospect, on Penobscot Bay. Begun in 1846, the impressive granite fort was used as a training center in the Civil War and was garrisoned in World War I. All its tunnels and galleries can be explored, and there is a fine view of the Penobscot River from above the fort. Other state parks are maintained at Bradbury Mountain in Pownal (242 acres), Lamoine (55 acres), and Aroostook at Presque Isle (520 acres).

Three art museums are worthy of note: the L.D.M. Sweat Memorial Museum in Portland, which contains a variety of 19th century paintings, as well as examples of the works of many Maine artists; the Walker Art Gallery at Bowdoin College, Brunswick, with paintings by Winslow Homer, John Singleton Copley, Gilbert Stuart, John La Farge, and other notable artists; and the Farnsworth Museum, Rockland, which has paintings and objects of historical interest. The Abbe Museum on Mount Desert Island has the state's best collection of Indian relics, and the Penobscot Museum at Searsport contains ship models, charts, logs, and other mementos of Maine's memorable role in the building and sailing of ships. The State House in Augusta, built originally in 1829–1832 and enlarged in 1911, houses the State Museum. York Gaol, York, built as a jail in 1653, is now a museum of colonial and Indian relics. The Black Mansion in Ellsworth is filled with fine furniture, silver, and other treasures of the early 19th century. Other places of particular architectural interest are described in section 7. *Cultural Life.*

9. HISTORY

Maine is supposed to have been visited by the earliest explorers, including John and Sebastian Cabot, who explored the coast in 1498–1499. Bartholomew Gosnold, later one of the founders of Jamestown, Va., visited Maine in 1602, as did Martin Pring in 1603, Pierre du Guast, sieur de Monts, in 1604, and George Weymouth in 1605. The first attempt to settle the territory was made by the French under de Monts, who, having received a patent from Henry IV, planted a small colony on St. Croix Island in the St. Croix River in 1604. The first settlement attempted by the English was made at the mouth of the Sagadahoc (now Kennebec) River by George Popham and Raleigh Gilbert in 1607. A fort and a number of other buildings were erected, and here the *Virginia,* the first vessel built in the country, was launched. The colony at Sagadahoc was broken up by the death of Popham and the great hardships endured by the colonists, who returned to England in the autumn of 1608. In 1613, French Jesuits established a mission on Mount Desert Island, but they were expelled by the English under Sir Samuel Argall. The coast was visited from

England in 1614 by John Smith, who found a few scattered settlers around Pemaquid Bay and on Monhegan Island.

In 1616, Sir Ferdinando Gorges, who had previously dispatched Pring and Popham to Maine, sent his agent, Richard Vines, to Saco to remain during the winter to explore the country and test the climate. In 1622, Gorges and John Mason received a patent of territory between the Merrimac and Kennebec rivers, and the next year Gorges sent his son Robert as governor and lieutenant general of the country. The territory was divided in 1629, Gorges receiving the land between the Piscataqua and Kennebec rivers, to which he gave the name New Somersetshire, and Mason obtaining the remainder. In 1639, Charles I granted to Gorges a charter under which, in 1641, he established the borough of Accomenticus (Agamenticus). A year later the settlement, under the name Gorgeana (q.v.), became the capital of the province and the first incorporated city in the present United States. A fort was built there, and efforts were made to protect the settlers against the Indians. Between 1630 and 1632 settlements were begun in Saco, Biddeford, Scarboro, Cape Elizabeth, and Portland, all of which continued to prosper until King Philip's War.

In 1677, Massachusetts purchased from the heirs of Gorges all their interest in the province of Maine. A new charter, issued by William and Mary in 1691, combined the provinces of Massachusetts, Plymouth, Acadia, Maine, and Sagadahoc into the Royal Province of Massachusetts Bay. Meanwhile, King Philip's War (1675–1676) began a series of six wars between the Indians and the British, in four of which the French combined with the Indians. The settlement of the eastern and interior areas of Maine was long delayed by these struggles, which were finally ended by the Treaty of Paris (1763).

Almost immediately disputes began with the mother country, and Maine joined Massachusetts in resisting the Stamp Act. The people formed nonimportation societies and staged their own tea party at York. Among the first soldiers in active service in the Revolutionary War were men from Maine, who fought as Massachusetts troops, and a regiment from Maine was present at Bunker Hill. In 1775 the British fleet attacked and destroyed Falmouth (now Portland), and off Machiasport was fought a battle in which the British ship *Margaretta* was captured. Castine was occupied by the British in 1779. At the close of the war, Massachusetts retained possession of the country, which was called the District of Maine. The people of the district were divided in their allegiance to Massachusetts, and during the War of 1812 the separatist movement gained ground. On March 15, 1820, Maine was admitted to the Union as a state. Meanwhile, there were several seasons of bad weather, especially the winter of 1816, and many persons left Maine for Ohio.

The northeastern boundary remained a source of dissension between the people of Maine and New Brunswick until after 1842, when the Webster-Ashburton Treaty (q.v.) practically settled the eastern boundary between the United States and Canada. (See also MAINE BOUNDARY TREATY; UNITED STATES—1. *Area and Boundaries:* Boundaries.)

Maine took the lead in the movement to regulate intoxicating liquors. In 1821 a license law was passed, and in 1846 a second law limited the sale of spirits to medicinal and industrial purposes.

This law was not well enforced, and, under the leadership of Neal Dow, the Maine Law, prohibiting the manufacture and sale of intoxicating liquors, was enacted in 1851. The Maine Law became part of the state constitution in 1884, but

Gramlich, from Frederic Lewis

View of Boothbay Harbor on the Maine coast.

enforcement was always difficult, and the constitutional amendment was finally repealed in 1934. (See also PROHIBITION.)

From the time Maine had been admitted to the Union as part of the Missouri Compromise, feeling ran strong against slavery, and when the Civil War broke out in 1861, Maine men responded quickly. More than 6,000 Maine men took part in the Battle of Gettysburg, and about 73,000 served during the war, 10 per cent being killed.

Between 1865 and 1900, Maine citizens were absorbed in such political issues as enfranchisement of the Southern Negro, Greenbackism, and prohibition. Through such leaders as William Pitt Fessenden, Nelson Dingley, James G. Blaine, and Thomas B. Reed (see section on *Cultural Life*), the state exerted great influence on national affairs. State politics was marked by the gradual decline of the Democratic Party and the dominance of the Republican Party from 1882 onward. In the late 1870's the Greenback Party found many adherents in Maine, and for a few years it surpassed the Democratic Party, with which it was usually allied. In the election of 1878 a three-way contest for the governorship was thrown into the Senate, which selected the minority candidate, Dr. Alonzo Garcelon, a Democrat. Although a Democratic governor, Harris M. Plaisted, was elected in 1880, the Republicans swept the field in 1882 and since then have lost control of the legislature only rarely.

In the 1954 state elections the Democratic Party came into power during a period of economic recession. Democrat Edmund Muskie was elected governor, and the Democrats gained 15 seats in the state legislature. In 1956, Muskie was reelected, and Frank Coffin was elected to the U.S. House of Representatives to become the first Maine Democrat sent to Washington in 22 years. In 1958, Muskie ended his second term as governor and was elected to the U.S. Senate. Democrat Clinton Clauson succeeded him as governor.

Clauson's death in 1959, after one year of a four-year term, led to a Republican restoration. Clauson was succeeded by John Reed, Republican president of the state Senate. After serving three years of Clauson's term as governor, Reed won election by a margin of a few hundred votes in 1962. He was defeated in 1966 by Kenneth M. Curtis, a Democrat.

In the meantime, Maine's economy had changed slowly from an agricultural toward a manufacturing base. Industrial growth in the 19th century had been most marked in textile and paper mills and shoe factories. In the 20th century, two world wars contributed to further diversification of Maine's economy, tourism became a growing industry, and the state came out of its geographical isolation.

10. BIBLIOGRAPHY

Bibliographical Aids: Williamson, Joseph A., *A Bibliography of the State of Maine from the Earliest Period to 1891,* 2 vols. (Portland 1896); Ring, Elizabeth, ed., *A Reference List of Manuscripts Relating to the History of Maine,* 3 vols. (Orono 1938–41).

DESCRIPTION: Hubbard, Lucius L., *Woods and Lakes of Maine* (Boston 1884); Emerson, Walter C., *The Latchstring to Maine Woods and Waters* (Boston 1916); id., *When North Winds Blow* (Lewiston 1922); Dole, Nathan H., and Gordon, Irwin L., *Maine of the Sea and Pines* (Boston 1928); Coffin, Robert P. T., *Kennebec, Cradle of Americans* (New York 1937); Federal Writers' Project, *Maine: A Guide 'Down East'* (Boston 1937); Munson, Gorham, *Penobscot: Down East Paradise* (Philadelphia 1959); Lund, Morten, *Cruising the Maine Coast* (New York 1967).

GOVERNMENT AND ADMINISTRATION: Hormell, Orren C., *Maine Towns* (Brunswick 1932); Starkey, Glenn W., *Maine: Its History, Resources, and Government,* 4th ed. (New York 1947); Dow, Edward F., *County Government in Maine* (Augusta 1952); *Revised Statutes of the State of Maine, 1954,* 5 vols. (Charlottesville, Va., 1954); *Maine Register* (Portland, annually).

HISTORY: Williamson, William D., *The History of the State of Maine; from Its First Discovery, A.D. 1602, to the Separation, A.D. 1820, Inclusive,* 2 vols. (Hallowell 1832); Chamberlain, Joshua L., *Maine: Her Place in History* (Augusta 1877); Baxter, James P., ed., *Sir Ferdinando Gorges and His Province of Maine,* 3 vols. (Boston 1890); Sylvester, Herbert M., *Maine Pioneer Settlements,* 5 vols. (Boston 1909); Burrage, Henry S., *The Beginnings of Colonial Maine, 1602–1658* (Portland 1914); Maine Historical Society, *Documentary History of the State of Maine,* 24 vols. (Portland 1896–1916); Hatch, Louis C., ed., *Maine, a History,* 5 vols. (New York 1919); Burrage, Henry S., *Gorges and the Grant of the Province of Maine, 1622* (Portland 1923); Coe, Harrie B., ed., *Maine: Resources, Attractions, and Its People,* 5 vols. (New York 1928–31); Rowe, William H., *The Maritime History of Maine* (New York 1948); Hebert, Richard A., *Modern Maine,* 4 vols. (New York 1951); Day, Clarence A., *A History of Maine Agriculture, 1604–1860* (Orono 1954); Smith, Marion J., *A History of Maine from Wilderness to Statehood,* rev. ed. (Manchester, Me., 1961); Rich, Louise D., *State o' Maine* (New York 1964).

EDWARD F. DOW, *University of Maine*
Revised by the Editors of "The Encyclopedia Americana"

MAINE, a battleship of the United States Navy whose destruction by explosion in Havana Harbor, Cuba, at 9:40 P.M. on Feb. 15, 1898, is considered the direct cause of the Spanish-American War. The 6,682-ton ship, commissioned in 1895, had been ordered from Key West, Fla., to Havana on January 24 to protect American lives and property. When the explosion occurred, all but 4 of the crew of 26 officers and 328 men were on board; 2 officers and 250 men were killed at once, and 8 men were fatally injured. After a month's investigation a United States court of inquiry reported (March 21) that the ship had been destroyed by the explosion of a submarine mine, but responsibility could not be fixed on any person or persons. A Spanish court of inquiry (March 28) attributed the disaster to an accidental internal explosion. Part of the wreck was raised in 1911 and was sunk at sea, with appropriate ceremonies, in 1912. A United States board made a further investigation at that time and confirmed the verdict of its predecessor, but the mystery of the explosion has never been solved. See also SPANISH-AMERICAN WAR—*Background and Causes.*

MAINE, University of, a coeducational institution of higher education situated at Orono, Me., about eight miles northeast of Bangor. Its campus of more than 200 acres borders a branch of the Penobscot River. A part of the public educational system of the state, the university is a land-grant institution established in 1865 as the State College of Agriculture and the Mechanic Arts under the provisions of the Morrill Act of 1862, and opened for instruction in 1868. The original name was changed to the University of Maine in 1897.

The university includes colleges of Arts and Sciences, Agriculture, Education, and Technology. The Maine Agricultural Experiment Station was established as a division of the institution in 1887. A college of law was opened in 1898 but was discontinued in 1920. Since 1923 graduate work has been a separate division. In 1957, Portland Junior College was merged with the university; the University of Maine at Portland offers a two-year program in liberal arts and a two-year terminal course in business education to young men in the Portland area.

The summer session offers a wide variety of academic and educational courses, and extension work in agriculture, forestry, and home economics is carried on throughout the state in cooperation with the United States Department of Agriculture. In addition, a limited amount of work in other fields is offered through extension courses given by various departments.

The degree of B.A., with specification of the major subject, is conferred on students completing a curriculum in the College of Arts and Sciences, and the degree of B.S. is conferred on those completing, in accordance with requirements, four years' work in the colleges of Agriculture and Technology. The degree of B.S. in education is awarded in the College of Education. For one year's graduate work completed with distinction the degrees of M.A., M.S., and M.Ed. are awarded. A Ph.D. degree is conferred for three years' graduate work completed with distinction in chemistry.

Men may live in fraternity houses, in private homes, or in dormitories. Women live only in dormitories, one of which is run cooperatively.

LLOYD H. ELLIOTT,
President.

MAINE BOUNDARY TREATY, a treaty signed in Washington, D.C., in 1910 by Secretary of State Philander Chase Knox for the

United States and Ambassador James Bryce for Great Britain. It finally determined the boundary line between New Brunswick and Maine south of the source of the St. Croix, which had not been definitely established by the treaty of 1842 (see WEBSTER-ASHBURTON TREATY, THE).

MAINE DE BIRAN, mân'dĕ bē-rän' (real name MARIE FRANÇOIS PIERRE GONTHIER DE BIRAN), French philosopher: b. Bergerac, France, Nov. 29, 1766; d. Paris, July 16, 1824. He entered the Life Guards of Louis XVI in 1785 and was present at Versailles on Oct. 5–6, 1789, but was not concerned in the revolution. In 1797 he became a member of the Council of Five Hundred. He opposed Napoleon in the latter part of his reign and became a legitimist at the Restoration. In 1816 he was made a councilor of state. His chief philosophical essays are *Influence de l'habitude sur la faculté de penser* (1802; Eng. tr., *The Influence of Habit on the Faculty of Thinking,* 1929); *La décomposition de la pensée* (*The Decomposition of Thought,* 1805); *L'aperception immédiate* (*Immediate Apperception,* 1807); and *Rapports du physique et du moral* (*Physical and Spiritual Interrelations,* 1814). Little of his writing appeared in his lifetime, but in 1834 some of his essays were published by Victor Cousin, who in 1841 brought out a more nearly complete edition. The publication of his major writings by Ernest Naville (3 vols., 1859) made possible the first connected study of his philosophical development. Maine de Biran's philosophy, which emphasized the activity of the will in the development of thought, influenced Cousin. A complete edition of his works was published by Pierre Tisserand (14 vols., 1920–1949).

MAINE-ET-LOIRE, mân'ā-lwàr', department, France, situated in Anjou and bounded on the north by Mayenne and Sarthe; on the east by Indre-et-Loire; on the south by Vienne, Deux-Sèvres, and Vendée; and on the west by Loire-Atlantique and Ille-et-Vilaine. It has an area of 2,787 square miles. The capital is Angers. The fertile soil of the department produces grain, wine grapes and other fruit, vegetables, hemp, flax, and potatoes. Pop. (1962) 556,272.

MAINS. See ELECTRICAL TERMS.

MAINTENANCE, mān'tĕ-năns, in law, a technical term meaning the officious intermeddling in a lawsuit of a stranger or of one having no legitimate relationship to any of the parties. Under the early English common law maintenance was a misdemeanor punishable by fine or imprisonment, but in modern times it has not been considered or punished as a crime. According to present day standards, maintenance is committed only if the act done is performed with a bad motive and tends to obstruct justice or promote unnecessary litigation. Maintenance includes champerty and embracery (qq.v.), and is similar to barratry (q.v.). The term "maintenance" may also be used in law in its ordinary meanings of the preservation or upkeep of property, or the sustenance or support of one individual by another, such as the maintenance of a child by his father or of a wife by her husband.

RICHARD L. HIRSHBERG.

MAINTENON, mănt-nôn', MARQUISE DE (FRANÇOISE D'AUBIGNÉ), mistress and second wife of Louis XIV: b. Niort, France, Nov. 27, 1635; d. St.-Cyr. April 15, 1719. The granddaughter of THEODORE Agrippa d'Aubigné (q.v.), she lived in Martinique from 1639 until her father's death in 1645, when she returned to France with her mother. She was for a time entrusted to a Protestant aunt but was later converted to Roman Catholicism. In 1652 she was married to the wit Paul Scarron, through whom she was introduced to literary society. After his death (1660) she received a royal pension. Her charm and good sense impressed Louis XIV's mistress, Madame de Montespan, and in 1669 she was entrusted with the education of the latter's children by the king. In 1674 she purchased the estate of Maintenon, which was made a marquisate in 1678. Gradually she superseded Madame de Montespan in the king's favor, and soon after Queen Marie Thérèse died she and Louis were secretly married. The ceremony probably took place in November 1683. Although her influence over the king in the field of public affairs, particularly with regard to the revocation of the Edict of Nantes, has been exaggerated, she did imprint her own moral sense and religious devotion on court life. After the king died (1715), she retired to the school she had founded at St.-Cyr. Her letters, which have considerable literary value, were published by Théophile Sébastien Lavallée (1854–1866) and others.

MAINZ, mīnts (Fr. MAYENCE), city, Germany, capital of the State of Rhineland-Palatinate, situated on the left bank of the Rhine River at its junction with the Main, 20 miles west-southwest of Frankfurt am Main. A river port, it also has establishments producing chemicals, vehicles, railroad equipment, machinery, precision instruments, furniture, hardware, leather, carpets, tobacco, soap, beer, hats, and gold and silver wares. Many of its old buildings, including the electoral palace, were destroyed in World War II. Among those surviving are the 11th century Romanesque cathedral, the 14th century Church of St. Stephen, and the 18th century grand-ducal palace. Johannes Gutenberg was born in Mainz, and there is a statue of him by Bertel Thorvaldsen. Mainz is the seat of the Johannes Gutenberg University (founded in 1447, closed in 1816, and reopened in 1946), the Max Planck Institut für Chemie, the Gutenberg Gesellschaft, and the Akademie der Wissenschaften und der Literatur. It has a large library and several museums.

Mainz owes its foundation to a Roman camp pitched nearby in 13 B.C. It became the seat of an archbishop in the 8th century and a free city in 1118. The archbishops were imperial electors, and the city flourished as a center of trade and culture. It declined after the 15th century, however, and in 1816 passed to Hesse-Darmstadt. Before World War II it was the capital of Rhenish Hesse. After the war it lost its suburbs on the right bank of the Rhine to Hesse and itself became the capital of Rhineland-Palatinate. Pop. (1956) 115,812.

MAIOLICA. See MAJOLICA.

MAIPO, mī'pô, or **MAIPU,** mī-pōō', river, Chile, rising in the Andes at the foot of the volcano Maipú, and flowing northwest and west for about 155 miles through a fertile valley to the Pacific Ocean at La Boca. Just southwest of Santiago and about 10 miles north of the river was fought on April 5, 1818, a battle in which the Spaniards were decisively defeated and Chile's independence was assured.

MAIR, mâr, **Charles,** Canadian writer: b. Lanark, Ontario, Canada, Sept. 21, 1838; d. Victoria, British Columbia, July 7, 1927. After attending Queen's University, he entered the Canadian civil service but soon left it to become a journalist. As a reporter for the Montreal *Gazette,* he covered the rebellion of Louis Riel in 1869–1870 and thereafter lived in western Canada. In 1889 he was made a fellow of the Royal Society of Canada. Mair actually wrote very little —a volume of poetry, *Dreamland and Other Poems* (1868); a closet poetic drama, *Tecumseh* (1886); and *Through the Mackenzie Basin* (1908)—but in these books and in his journalistic articles he was one of the first to illustrate the literary value of Canadian material, particularly life on the prairies.

MAISIERES, Philippe de. See MEZIERES, PHILIPPE DE.

MAISON CARREE, mā-zôn′ kȧ-rā′, a Roman temple at Nîmes, France, erected in 16 B.C., and considered the finest of its type remaining. It stands on a podium 12 feet high and measures 40 by 82 feet. Its 30 Corinthian columns, of which 6 are in front, 6 in the rear, and the rest along the sides, support an ornate entablature. The Maison Carrée now houses a museum containing sculpture, mosaics, ceramics, and coins.

MAISONNEUVE, mā-zô-nûv′ SIEUR DE (PAUL DE CHOMEDY), French colonial administrator: b. Neuville-sur-Vannes, France, February 1612; d. Paris, Sept. 9, 1676. After a military career he was selected in 1641 by the Company of Notre-Dame de Montréal to establish a new settlement in Canada. Accompanied by a band of colonists, he arrived in Quebec on Aug. 20, 1641, and on May 18, 1642, founded Ville-Marie, the future city of Montreal. As governor of the settlement, he displayed great administrative ability until 1663, when he was removed from office by the marquis de Tracy. Two years later he returned to France, where he remained until his death.

MAISONS-ALFORT, mā-zôn′ȧl-fôr′, commune and town, France, situated in the Department of the Seine, on the Seine River, 5.5 miles from the center of Paris. An industrial suburb, it has establishments producing cement, furniture, hosiery, surgical goods, soap, and chemicals. It is the seat of the École Nationale Vétérinaire d'Alfort, founded in 1766. Pop. (1962) commune, 51,689; town, 50,965.

MAISTRE, měs′tr′, COMTE **Joseph Marie de,** French philosopher: b. Chambéry, Savoy, April 1, 1753; d. Turin, Piedmont, Feb. 26, 1821. Of French descent, he studied law at Turin and entered the Savoy magistracy in 1774. In 1788 he became a senator, but went into exile when the French invaded Savoy in 1792. From 1802 to 1816 he served as Victor Emmanuel I's ambassador at St. Petersburg, and then returned to Turin. A conservative in politics, religion, and philosophy, he opposed the French Revolution and believed that the power of the pope should be absolute. He was a better writer than most of his liberal opponents, and he advanced his views ably

in such works as *Considérations sur la France* (*Reflections on France,* 1796); *Essai sur le principe générateur des constitutions politiques* (1810; Eng. tr., *Essay on the Generative Principle of Political Constitutions,* 1847); *Du pape* (*On the Pope,* 1819); *Les soirées de Saint-Pétersbourg* (*St. Petersburg Evenings,* 1821); and *De l'église gallicane* (*On the Gallican Church,* 1821). His letters were published posthumously (2 vols., 1851–1858).

His brother, COMTE XAVIER DE MAISTRE (1763–1852), was a novelist who lived for many years in Russia. His works include *Voyage autour de ma chambre* (1794; Eng. tr., *A Journey Round My Room,* 1829); *Le lépreux de la cité d'Aoste* (1811; Eng. tr., *The Leper of Aosta,* 1825); and *Expédition nocturne autour de ma chambre* (1825; Eng. tr., *A Nocturnal Expedition Around My Room,* 1886).

MAISUR. See MYSORE.

MAITLAND, māt′lănd, **Edward,** English mystical writer: b. Ipswich, England, Oct. 27, 1824; d. Tonbridge, Oct. 2, 1897. The nephew of Sir Peregrine Maitland (q.v.), he was educated at Caius College, Cambridge (B.A., 1847). He went to California in 1849, and then to Australia, where he became a commissioner of crown lands. Returning to England in 1857, he devoted himself to literature, in which he endeavored to find a spiritual basis for life. He published three romances: *The Pilgrim and the Shrine* (1867), largely autobiographical; *The Higher Law* (1869); and *By and By* (1873). It was through the last of these that he met Anna Kingsford, vegetarian and antivivisectionist, with whom he wrote *The Keys of the Creeds* (1875); and *The Perfect Way; or, the Finding of Christ* (1882). Meanwhile, he had become a mystic, and he stated that he had acquired a sense which enabled him to see the condition of people's souls and that he remembered his own previous reincarnations. With Mrs. Kingsford he founded the Hermetic Society (1884), and later he established the Esoteric Christian Union (1891). He maintained that he was in communication with Mrs. Kingsford after her death (1888), and that she inspired him in writing *Clothed with the Sun* (1889); *The New Gospel of Interpretation* (1892); and *Anna Kingsford; Her Life, Letters, Diary, and Work* (2 vols., 1896).

MAITLAND, Frederic William, English legal historian: b. London, England, May 28, 1850; d. Las Palmas, Canary Islands, Dec. 19, 1906. He was educated at Eton and at Trinity College, Cambridge (B.A., 1873; M.A., 1876). Called to the bar in 1876, he practiced law until 1884, when he was appointed reader in English law at Cambridge. Four years later he received a professorship. Maitland's particular interest was the development of early English law, and in 1887 he founded the Selden Society to further its study. Besides editing a number of volumes for the society, he wrote several authoritative works on legal history, including *The History of English Law Before the Time of Edward I* (2 vols., with Sir Frederick Pollock, 1895); *Domesday Book and Beyond* (1897); *Roman Canon Law in the Church of England* (1898); *English Law and the Renaissance* (1901); and *The Constitutional History of England* (1908). See also LAW—*Approaches to Legal Science.*

MAITLAND, James. See LAUDERDALE, 8th EARL OF.

MAITLAND, John. See LAUDERDALE, DUKE OF.

MAITLAND, John Alexander Fuller-. See FULLER-MAITLAND, JOHN ALEXANDER.

MAITLAND, SIR Peregrine, English soldier and colonial administrator: b. Long Parish, Hampshire, England, July 6, 1777; d. London, May 30, 1854. Commissioned an ensign in the 1st Foot Guards in 1792, he became a captain in 1794 and a lieutenant colonel in 1803. Meanwhile, he saw service in Flanders, Portugal, and Spain. In 1814 he was appointed a major general, and in the following year distinguished himself at Waterloo. From 1818 to 1828 he served as lieutenant governor of Upper Canada, where his reactionary policies aroused opposition. He was governor of Nova Scotia from 1828 to 1834, and from 1836 to 1838 commanded the army of Madras. He ended his career as governor and commander in chief at the Cape of Good Hope (1844–1847), and in 1846 he was raised to the rank of a full general.

MAITLAND, SIR Richard, LORD LETHINGTON, Scottish lawyer, poet, and collector of verse: b. East Lothian, Scotland, 1496; d. Edinburgh, March 20, 1586. He was educated at the universities of St. Andrews and Paris and became one of the leading lawyers of Scotland. Although he became blind in 1561, he was appointed that year to the Privy Council and made an ordinary lord of session. From 1562 to 1567 he was also keeper of the great seal. He is best known, however, as the collector of ancient Scottish poems and as the author of verse satires. His manuscript collection of Scottish poetry is preserved in the Pepysian collection at Magdalene College, Cambridge. A selection from his collection, together with his own poems, was published as *Ancient Scottish Poems* (2 vols., 1786), and his poems were reprinted in 1830 by the Maitland Club, a literary organization founded in his honor in Glasgow in 1828.

MAITLAND, William (known as SECRETARY LETHINGTON), Scottish statesman: b. about 1528; d. Leith, Scotland, June 9, 1573. The eldest son of Sir Richard Maitland, Lord Lethington (q.v.), he was educated at St. Andrews and on the Continent. In 1558 he was appointed secretary of state by the queen regent, Mary of Guise, but in the following year joined the Calvinists against her. He was one of the commissioners who concluded the Treaty of Berwick in 1560, and later that year served as speaker of the Scottish Parliament. From 1561 to 1566 he was secretary of state to Mary, Queen of Scots, and in this capacity endeavored to reconcile Scotland and England, whose crowns he hoped might one day be united. He was probably implicated in the murders of David Rizzio (1566) and Lord Darnley (1567). In 1568 he helped Mary escape from Lochleven, but he fought against her at Langside. After the assassination of the earl of Moray in 1570, he became the leader of the queen's party, and in the following year joined Sir William Kirkcaldy at Edinburgh Castle. Captured at its surrender in 1573, he died in prison soon thereafter.

MAITLAND, municipality, Australia, situated in New South Wales, on the Hunter River, 16 miles northwest of Newcastle, with which it is connected by rail. The river divides it into East Maitland and West Maitland. There are important coalfields nearby, and in the surrounding area dairy cattle and abundant crops of grain, fruit, and vegetables are raised. Bricks and tiles are manufactured in the town. Pop. (1954) 21,334.

MAIZE. See CORN AND CORN CULTURE— *Origin and Types* (Indian Corn).

MAJAPAHIT. See JAVA—*History.*

MAJESTY, măj′ĕs-tĭ (Lat. *majestas*), in ancient Rome the sovereign power and dignity of the Roman people and, by extension, of the Roman state. It was ascribed also to dictators, consuls, and, eventually, emperors. The term became an honorific title which devolved on the Holy Roman emperors as heirs to those of imperial Rome, and in the 16th century was extended also to kings. Henry VIII was the first English monarch to whom the title was generally given.

MAJOLICA, mà-jŏl′ĭ-kà (Ital. MAIOLICA), an Italian term used in the modern sense to indicate a particular type of pottery developed and brought to perfection in Italy during the 15th and 16th centuries. Its distinctive feature is its opaque, generally white glaze obtained from stannic (tin) oxide. This glaze is used to conceal the natural color of the clay and to provide a suitable ground for painted decoration. When submitted to firing the surface of tin-glazed wares becomes vitrified, while the colors laid upon it remain fixed and fused into it without any such shifting or blurring of the design as happens with lead-glazed wares. Painted decoration, swiftly carried out over the absorbent surface of the unfired glaze, accounts for the aesthetic appeal of majolica and makes it one of the most accomplished artistic expressions of the Italian Renaissance.

The shapes of majolica wares are simple and such as the clay naturally assumes on the wheel: jugs, bowls, basins, dishes, plates, and cylindrical drug pots (albarelli). The colors used in the decoration were obtained from various metallic oxides. The earliest pigments were dark manganese purple and copper green. To these were added yellow from antimony, blue from cobalt, orange from iron rust, and black from a mixture of several oxides. Besides ordinary colors, Italian potters made very effective use of luster colors, pigments containing oxides of silver and copper which produced a metallic sheen varying from a mother-of-pearl iridescence to a brassy yellow or a resplendent ruby red. Since luster colors are too volatile to resist the high temperatures necessary to melt tin glaze and ordinary pigments, their application required a third firing at a lower temperature. This technique was developed about 1500 in imitation of the famous Spanish lusterware imported from Valencia in the 15th century.

Actually, the word *maiolica* is a corruption of Majorca (Span. Mallorca), the name of the island off the Spanish coast from which lustered wares were believed to come, and at first the Italians used it exclusively to designate lustered pottery. Later the term was applied to all Italian tin-glazed pottery, as well as to wares decorated in the polychrome Italian style in countries to which Italian potters emigrated during the 16th century. A special type of pottery akin to majolica and produced in Italy at the same time consists of lead-glazed wares with incised decorations. These wares, as well as some lustered wares erroneously believed to be lead glazed, were for some time called *mezzamaiolica* (semimajolica). Modern scholars have rejected this term in favor of sgraffito or sgraffiato ware (scratched ware). Sgraffito pottery, which was made especially at Bologna and Padua, only rarely attained the artistic excellence of regular majolica.

Although majolica was made in very many places in central and northern Italy and potters often moved from one town to another, it is possible to distinguish several centers of production with marked characteristics of color and decoration. These were, in the 15th century, Orvieto, Florence, and Faenza; in the 16th century, Faenza, Siena, Deruta, Cafaggiolo, Casteldurante (now Urbania), Gubbio, Venice, and Pesaro; and, in the 17th century, Genoa, Montelupo Fiorentino, Castelli, and Sicily.

Early Majolica.—Tin glaze seems to have been used by Italian potters as early as the 14th century. The earliest pieces found around Florence, at Orvieto, and at Faenza are decorated with simple designs of birds, leaves, and heraldic motifs, or with a peculiar crosshatched ground traced in purple alone or in purple and a bright copper green.

About the middle of the 15th century, Florentine pottery became distinguished for the excellence of its simple yet monumental shapes and for its decorative feeling. Especially attractive are the handsome apothecary jars ornamented with an allover pattern of oak leaves painted in a thick, dark blue, and the large, flat-bottomed basins displaying the figure of a horseman or an animal, painted in pale blue and purple. An interesting group, slightly later in date, is represented by the Florentine jugs and drug pots decorated with Hispano-Moresque motifs—vine or parsley leaves—like those of the lusterware imported from Valencia.

Plate: "The Death of Achilles." By Niccolò or Nicola Pellipario, Casteldurante, about 1520.

About 1480, Faenza, a small town near Bologna, emerged as the leading center of pottery making. Its craftsmen are credited with inventing such original motifs as large, coiled iris leaves and arrangements of peacock feathers. A partic-

ularly vigorous use of color, consisting of a dominant deep blue accompanied by ocher, green, and purple, confers a severe and forceful grandeur on the Faenza wares of this period.

Golden Age.—After 1500 a basic change in feeling and in the forms of decoration developed under the influence of the Renaissance. Traditional formal motifs gave way to ornament of classical inspiration, while figure subjects were used increasingly as the main or the only decoration. As pictorial perfection increased, majolica pieces were designed for the sake of their aesthetic appeal, for display on sideboards and tables rather than for use. The individual character of their decoration revealed the personalities of the leading majolica painters, who often identified themselves by signatures or monograms. In other cases, a distinctive style enables one to group together several pieces by the same hand.

Dish. Deruta, about 1515.

Such technical excellence was attained between 1500 and 1530 that this period can be termed the golden age of majolica. At Faenza active workshops, like those of the Pirota, Bergantini, and Manara families, specialized in elegantly decorated wares in the new style, which were often exported to distant places. The new art attracted princely patronage, and in 1506 the factory of Cafaggiolo was founded near Florence. Here wares of great distinction and entirely Renaissance in character were made for the Medici family. A particular refinement in delicate draftsmanship and the handling of classical motifs was achieved in the drug pots, dishes, and tiles made at Siena. At Deruta, near Perugia, the secret of luster painting was discovered about 1500. Here the potters specialized in large decorative dishes with borders of foliage or imbrications framing the bust of a lady or of a warrior or a figure subject, often enhanced with lavish yellow or deep red luster. The secret of this technique was brought from Deruta to Gubbio by Giorgio Andreoli (1465?–?1553). From 1518 onward, Maestro Giorgio, as he was called, directed the main workshop in Gubbio. He became celebrated for the flaming red and splendid gold of his lustered wares, which often were signed and dated. A series of pieces made at Casteldurante between 1508 and 1520, painted with allegorical compositions, playing children, or coats of arms and remarkable for their ceramic perfection, are probably the work of one Giovanni Maria. This painter may have originated the formal symmetrical designs in blue and gray that are characteristic of Casteldurante wares.

Pictorial School.—The next phase in the development of Italian majolica was due to the influence of one of the greatest ceramic painters of the Renaissance, Niccolò or Nicola Pellipario (d. 1547), who settled in Urbino around 1528. An artist of exquisite talent, he was first active in Casteldurante, where he was possibly a pupil of Giovanni Maria. Pellipario treated his plates as small panel paintings, completely suppressing borders and formal ornament. On the large services that represent his output he depicted landscapes and buildings with swift draftsmanship and delicate water-color effects. The cool shades of his earlier work were replaced after 1530 by a warmer palette dominated by yellows and oranges. The use of these colors, together with the habit of borrowing compositions from contemporary engravings, especially those of Marcantonio Raimondi, became characteristic of the pictorial majolica produced at Urbino until the end of the 16th century.

A follower of Pellipario was Francesco Xanto Avelli of Rovigo (fl. 1530–1542), to whom we owe many signed pieces painted in warm, rich colors. Pellipario's son, Guido Durantino (called Fontana, d. 1576), became the head of a workshop run under the protection of Guidobaldo II delle Rovere, duke of Urbino, which produced imposing plates and wine coolers, splendidly painted and sometimes having details in relief. About 1560–1570, Guido's son, Orazio Fontana (d. 1571), introduced a new form of decoration, using light, grotesque ornaments against a brilliant white ground. The Patanazzi family at the close of the century were the last to produce wares, caskets, and inkstands decorated with typical Urbino motifs, though these were distinctly inferior in artistic quality.

Urbino majolica had great influence on the contemporary production of other centers, especially Faenza, Pesaro, and Venice, but a reaction soon appeared to its excessive use of color. About 1550, Virgiliotto Calamelli (d. 1570) specialized at Faenza in wares emphasizing the whiteness of the glaze, with only light designs sparingly applied in blue and pale yellow. At the same time, Venice made original majolica, strongly Oriental in flavor, which was remarkable for its blue-and-white decoration, arabesque patterns, and lavender-stained glaze.

Later Majolica.—In the 17th century, Italian majolica gradually lost its original character. At Genoa, Savona, and Albissola new factories tried to imitate the style of Chinese blue-and-white porcelain or the designs of contemporary French faience and Spanish Talavera de la Reina pottery. Much colorful peasant majolica was produced at Montelupo Fiorentino in Tuscany, while imitations of earlier Casteldurante of Faenza wares were made in several places in Sicily. Beginning in 1650 pictorial decoration was revived at Castelli in the Abruzzi by the Grue and Gentili families, who used pale, cool colors, following engravings of Annibale Carracci and Jacopo Bassano. Finally, in 1748, a short-lived majolica factory was opened in Milan by Felice Clerici, whose wares, inspired by Chinese and German porcelains, are not without a playful and original charm of their own.

The most comprehensive collections of majolica are found at the Metropolitan Museum of Art in New York, the Victoria and Albert Museum in London, and the Louvre in Paris.

See also FAIENCE; POTTERY.

Bibliography.—Bode, Wilhelm von, *Die Anfänge der Majolikakunst in Toskana* (Berlin 1911); Rackham, Bernard, *Victoria and Albert Museum: Guide to Italian Maiolica* (London 1933); Ballardini, Gaetano, *Corpus della maiolica italiana*, 2 vols. (Rome 1933–38); Rackham, Bernard, *Victoria and Albert Museum: Catalogue of Italian Maiolica*, 2 vols. (London 1940); Chompret, Joseph, *Répertoire de la majolique italienne*, 2 vols. (Paris 1949); Rackham, Bernard, *Italian Maiolica* (New York 1952).

OLGA RAGGIO,
Assistant Curator, Renaissance and Post-Renaissance Art, The Metropolitan Museum of Art.

MAJOR, mā′jẽr, **Charles** (pseudonym SIR EDWIN CASKODEN), American novelist: b. Indianapolis, Ind., July 25, 1856; d. Shelbyville, Ind., Feb. 13, 1913. After studying law in his father's office he was admitted to the Indiana bar in 1877, and established a practice in Shelbyville. His avocation was the study of history, and in 1898 he published his first historical novel, *When Knighthood Was in Flower*, which sold 200,000 copies within two years. The work was successfully dramatized, as was *Dorothy Vernon of Haddon Hall* (1902). In the same vein were *Yolanda, Maid of Burgundy* (1905), *A Gentle Knight of Old Brandenburg* (1909), and *The Little King* (1910), but Major turned to Hoosier themes for such novels as *The Bears of Blue River* (1901) and *Uncle Tom Andy Bill* (1908). Although his historical novels were deficient in characterization, they were based on sound research, and their colorful backgrounds made them very popular.

MAJOR, in military science, a field-grade officer of the air or ground forces ranking next above captain and just below lieutenant colonel. Until after World War I battalions were generally commanded by majors; since then they have been commanded by lieutenant colonels in most armies. Majors now command companies in the British service, whereas captains lead them in other armies. In the French Army a major is addressed socially as *commandant;* officially he is called *chef de bataillon* (infantry), *chef d'escadron* (artillery), or *chef d'escadrons* (calvary).

A sergeant major is generally the senior noncommissioned officer in a headquarters. A major general ranks next above brigadier general and just below lieutenant general; the latter paradox stems from the fact that the title was originally sergeant major general. The naval rank corresponding to major is lieutenant commander.

MARK M. BOATNER, III.

MAJOR, in music. See CHORD; INTERVAL; MINOR.

MAJOR BARBARA, a play by George Bernard Shaw (q.v.), first performed in 1905. The few men able to look evil in the face without illusion have been called cynics, said Shaw, and he created Andrew Undershaft, millionaire munitions manufacturer, to prove his point. Undershaft's daughter, Barbara, is a major in the Salvation Army who is determined to save the souls of the poor of the London slums. Her fiancé, Adolphus Cusins, sometime professor of Greek, has joined the Salvation Army to win Barbara for himself. When the play opens, Andrew Undershaft has been separated from his family for many years. To guarantee their children a private income, Lady Britomart, Barbara's mother, calls Undershaft to their home. When it is discovered that his money, considered tainted because it is earned by war, can buy even the services of the Salvation Army, Barbara resigns her commission. Cusins is persuaded to become heir to the munitions business, and Barbara marries him, hoping to do God's work among the munitions workers. Shaw's central theme is that poverty is the greatest moral crime and truest evil in the world. Since Andrew Undershaft has removed poverty as a threat to the lives of his employees, he is moral. Barbara and Adolphus are made to see that man's soul is beyond salvation as long as there is poverty or the threat of poverty. According to Shaw, it is impossible for man to care about ethical or political considerations on an empty stomach.

MAJOR GENERAL. See MAJOR.

MAJORCA. See MALLORCA.

MAJORIAN, mȧ-jō′rĭ-ăn (Lat. JULIUS VA-LERIUS MAJORIANUS), Roman emperor in the West: d. near Tortona, Italy, Aug. 7, 461 A.D. Commander of the Imperial Guard under Valentinian III, Petronius Maximus, and Avitus, he became friendly with Ricimer, who had him proclaimed emperor in 457. A good administrator who revised the laws of the empire, he also was able to defeat the Vandals, in 458. Two years later, however, he lost his fleet to the Vandal Genseric, and on Aug. 2, 461, was forced to abdicate. He died five days later, probably at the hand of Ricimer.

MAJORITY RULE, mȧ-jŏr′ĭ-tĭ rōol, in the United States, governance by a quantity more than half of the total. The English use of the relative majority, meaning the largest number, is similar to the American plurality. Majority rule is based on the concept of equality among voters. Marsilius of Padua (1290?–?1343), the Italian philosopher, said that "the legislator is the people, or a majority of them," and that the people may delegate authority to an individual or to a group, thus setting forth the principle of representative government responsible to the majority. American democracy is built on the foundation of popular sovereignty operating through formally adopted constitutions for the nation and the states; it acknowledges the rights and liberties of the individual and provides protection for minorities. The South African government operates through majority rule within the white minority.

In setting forth majority procedures, constitution makers must determine the basis for calculating the majority; all citizens, all adult citizens, all of those eligible to vote, all who do vote, or all who vote on a given issue. In legislative bodies, unless an absolute majority of the membership is required, a vote may be taken as a majority of those voting. A quorum in either branch of the United States Congress is a majority of the total membership, but a quorum in the British House of Commons is 40 members, or less than 7 per cent of that body. In the absence of special provisions a popular referendum is approved by a majority of votes. In the United States the Electoral College elects a president

and vice president by an absolute majority; otherwise the House of Representatives, voting by states and requiring a majority of all the states to elect, elects the president, and the Senate by majority vote elects the vice president.

SPENCER D. ALBRIGHT.

MAKAH, mä-käh′, meaning "cape people," an Amerindian tribe living around Cape Flattery, Puget Sound, Washington. Closely related to the Nootka Indians (q.v.), the Makah are the southernmost tribe of the Wakashan linguistic stock and the only such group within the United States. Originally they held a large territory between Flattery Rocks and the Hoko River, which they ceded to the United States in 1855. They were then settled on the Neah Bay Reservation, where a few hundred still live. The Makah make a characteristic form of baskets, and use roughly carved wooden masks in their religious ceremonies.

FREDERICK J. DOCKSTADER.

MAKALU, mŭ′kȧ-lōo, mountain peak, Nepal and Tibet, rising to a height of 27,790 feet in the Himalayas, 15 miles southeast of Mount Everest. It was first climbed in 1955, by a French party led by Jean Franco.

MAKARIOS III, ma-kä′rē-ōs, **Archbishop** (given name MICHAEL CHRISTODOULOS MOUSKOS), prelate of the Orthodox Church of Cyprus and first president of Cyprus: b. Panagia, Cyprus, Aug. 13, 1913. A farmer's son, he left school in Cyprus to study law and theology in Athens, where he remained through the German occupation of Greece during World War II. After the war he won a theological scholarship to Boston University. In 1948 he returned to Cyprus as bishop of Kition. Two years later, at the age of 37, he was elected archbishop of Cyprus.

During the British rule of Cyprus, Makarios worked ceaselessly for the island's union (*enosis*) with Greece and traveled extensively in Britain, the United States, and the Middle East, seeking international support for the cause. He became the first president of Cyprus when the island gained its independence on Aug. 16, 1960. A man of personal charm, wit, and humor, he showed great political and diplomatic ability on many occasions. But he was distrusted by the Turks and was criticized by many observers for his handling of the complex racial crisis that threatened the island with disaster.

NANCY CRAWSHAW
Former Special Correspondent, "Manchester Guardian," in Greece and Cyprus

MAKAROV, mŭ-kȧ′rôf, **Stepan Osipovich,** Russian naval officer: b. Kiev, Russia, Dec. 27, 1848; d. Port Arthur, Manchuria, March 31, 1904. He entered the Russian Navy in 1864, and in 1872 was attached to the Ministry of Marine. During the Russo-Turkish War of 1877–1878 he was decorated for his daring attacks on Turkish ports, and by 1890 he had risen to the rank of rear admiral. In 1897 he became a vice admiral and was placed in command of the Baltic fleet. At the outbreak of the Russo-Japanese War in 1904, he was sent to the Far East to direct naval operations. He converted the blockaded squadron at Port Arthur into an active naval force, but was lured out of the harbor by a decoy squadron. Discovering the main Japanese fleet trying to intercept him, he was about to re-enter the harbor, when his flagship, the *Petropavlovsk,* was destroyed by one of the sunken mines laid by the Japanese across the passageway, and Makarov, his guest, Vasili Verestchagin (q.v.), the famous war artist, 16 staff officers and over 800 sailors perished.

MAKART, mäk'ärt, **Hans,** Austrian painter: b. Salzburg, May 28, 1840; d. Vienna, Oct. 3, 1884. He began his art studies in the Academy of Vienna. In 1859 he went to Munich, and painted in the studio of Piloty, under whose teaching (1861–65) he developed remarkable talent as a colorist. His earliest success was a Rembrandtesque picture of *Lavoisier in Jail* (1862). His first work to gain him wide fame was his three-paneled picture, *The Seven Deadly Sins* or *The Plague in Florence,* which aroused a storm of adverse criticism, wonder and admiration in Paris and Germany. In 1869 the Emperor Francis Joseph built him a fine studio in Vienna, and he produced his series of *Abundantia* pictures, *Fruits of the Earth; Fruits of the Sea.* In 1873 followed the picture which attracted so much attention in the Exhibition of

German art to a sense of color, and broke free from the traditions of a somewhat stiff and pedantic method, gaining in life and intensity what he sacrificed of academic correctness.

MAKE-UP. The last two decades have seen make-up progress from its early category of woman's conceit to become an art and an integral part of feminine beauty and psychology. Chief credit for this about-face in the acceptance of widespread use of cosmetics should go to the motion picture industry, which set new standards of beauty and, through its motion picture studio laboratories and experimentation on the screen itself, brought new products and principles of application and use to the world's women.

Make-up as troop camouflage was an important part of World War II. Topflight make-up artists were drawn into the armed forces to put their skill to work in prosthesis. Today, make-up picks up where plastic surgery leaves off.

The war proved that make-up forms a part of feminine morale. In hard-pressed England, cosmetics were named a luxury. When, as an experiment, lipstick was again provided for

COLOR CHART

Skin	Foundation	Powder	Lipstick	Cheek rouge	Hair
Blonde light skin	Natural (very light)	Lightweight non-coloring	Light orange-red	Light orange-red	Light blonde
Blonde, medium skin	Faintly pink	Lightweight non-coloring	Pale strawberry	Pale strawberry	Medium blonde
Blonde, sallow skin	A light blue-red	Lightweight non-coloring	Light blue-red	Light blue-red	Dark blonde
Blonde, reddish skin	A peach buff	Lightweight non-coloring	True pepper red	True pepper red	Ash blonde
Blonde, dark skin	A warm copper	Lightweight non-coloring	Medium blue-red	Medium blue-red	Reddish blonde
Red head, light skin	A faintly pink or light blue-red	Lightweight non-coloring	Pale strawberry	Pale strawberry	Strawberry blonde
Red head, medium skin	A pale peach buff	Lightweight non-coloring	True pepper red	True pepper red	Copper blonde
Red head, sallow skin	A warm rose glow	Lightweight non-coloring	Medium blue-red	Medium blue-red	Medium red
Red head, reddish skin	A peach buff	Lightweight non-coloring	Medium blue-red or pale strawberry	Medium blue-red or pale strawberry	Light auburn
Red head, dark skin	A warm copper	Lightweight non-coloring	True pepper red	True pepper red	Light brown
Brunette, light skin	Faintly pink or a light blue-red	Lightweight non-coloring	Medium blue-red	Medium blue-red	Medium brown
Brunette, medium skin	A pale peach buff	Lightweight non-coloring	Medium blue-red or a pink-red	Medium blue-red or a pink-red	Dark brown
Brunette, sallow skin	A warm rose glow	Lightweight non-coloring	Medium blue-red	Medium blue-red	Henna brown
Brunette, reddish skin	A peach buff	Lightweight non-coloring	Medium blue-red or a pink-red	Medium blue-red or a pink-red	Black
Brunette, dark skin	A warm copper	Lightweight non-coloring	Deep blue-red	Deep blue-red	Dark gray
Gray, light skin	Light blue-red	Lightweight non-coloring	Light blue-red	Light blue-red	Medium gray
Gray, medium skin	Faintly pink or a warm rose glow	Lightweight non-coloring	A light blue-red	A light blue-red	Light gray
Gray, dark skin	A peach buff	Lightweight non-coloring	A pink-red	A pink-red	White

Note:—A peach buff foundation is particularly good for summer-to-winter transition on any type, and is flattering to ruddy, sallow or freckled skins.

Philadelphia (1876), his *Venice Doing Homage to Caterina Cornaro.* He traveled in the East during the winter (1875–1876), and his Egyptian sketches materialized in his *Cleopatra, Antique Hunt on the Nile,* etc. His *Entry of Charles V into Antwerp* (1875–1878) gained a medal at the Paris Exposition of 1878 and his *Diana's Hunting Party* is one of the most successful of his larger paintings, combining superb coloring and modeling of the nude with grand landscape effect. It is in the Metropolitan Museum of New York and is most characteristic of the gorgeous sensuousness of a painter who woke the intellectualists of

women defense workers, output increased and women's whole general attitude changed.

The basic principles for the application of make-up as evolved for motion pictures remain the same for street, black and white and color motion pictures, stage, black and white and color portraiture, and 16-mm. photography. Television make-up alone deviated at first, but it now follows stage principles to a degree.

Street Make-up for Women.—The principles of corrective make-up are based on the classification of women's faces into seven different types: oval, square, round, triangle, oblong, inverted triangle, and diamond. In straight make-up the attempt is always to create the illusion of the perfect, oval contour. Cheek rouge is the greatest single factor in corrective street make-up, because it absorbs light. All make-up should be used in minimum, and no street make-up should ever appear obvious or blatant. Cosmetic items should be chosen to match skin tones and to complement the color of hair, eyes, and skin.

It is well for teen-age girls to remember that women in the middle twenties and upward use make-up only to achieve the appearance of fresh, youthful skin. The author does not approve of girls from 12 to 14 using other than a light coating of lipstick. From 14 to 16 they may augment this with a little powder and a very light application of cheek rouge for evening.

It is of great importance that women past 35 remember that as the years pass, their skin is undergoing a change, gradually becoming lighter. By the same token, they should begin to turn to the lighter shades of rouge and lipstick. Women in their sixties, for instance, are most flattered by a cameo-pink shade. Dark tones against a light skin are harsh and aging.

In preparing for application of a street make-up, the skin should first be cleansed with two applications of cleansing cream removed with tissue. Skin freshener should then be patted over the face with absorbent cotton. Freshener should not be allowed to remain on the face, but in turn should be patted off with tissue or a soft towel.

The choice of base make-up depends both upon the subject's age and skin type. For normal skins, choice is optional among cream foundations, liquid-cream, or lanolin cake. Cream foundation is best for dry skins, because it acts as a daytime lubricant. For oily skins, too, either a cream or liquid-cream foundation is advisable, because such bases allow normal oil excretion and absorb it. In overactive areas around the nostrils and on the chin when shininess becomes apparent, pressing those areas with tissue to remove excess oil and then repowdering keeps make-up looking perfect throughout the day.

The subject's choice of base is then applied in minimum, and the manufacturer's direction for use should be followed closely. The base should be smoothed over the face to form a thin, equally distributed film and should be carried over and under jaw and chin lines and blended out so that no line of demarcation is apparent. In application, an upward, outward circular motion, the fundamental massage movement, should be used. This same movement should be used in all cream applications and in washing face and neck, because it tends to keep tissue firm. Downward pulling movements weaken underlying tissue and promote sagging and wrinkles.

Next and probably the most important step in street make-up is the application of cheek rouge. There are two types: cream and dry rouge. Cream rouge should never be applied over a dry base, that is, cake. Dry rouge only should be used. Cream rouge should be used directly over cream and liquid-cream foundations *before powdering*. Dry rouge is used after powdering if it is found that insufficient cream rouge has been used. Application should be with a large art brush or powder brush, dusting the color on lightly over the same area originally covered with cream rouge.

Cheek rouge on the face should seem never to end. In other words, its use should be so subtle that it appears only as a faint, natural blush and no definite area of application should be apparent. The edges of the rouge area should be blended subtly into the surrounding foundation area by patting with the fingers. The value of cheek rouge as a corrective make-up item cannot be overemphasized. Because it forms a shadow and absorbs light, its proper use can camouflage a square face, add width to a thin face. (See Face Type illustrations.) Study of the average face and comparison with the Face Type illustrations will indicate to the individual the area of proper application.

Eyeshadow is applied sparingly on the center of the eyelids, and is blended outward to the corners of the eyes and upward to the eyebrow line. It should not be used on the inside corners of the eyelids next to the nose. Preferably, eyeshadow should be one of two natural shades, to match the eyes: blue-gray or brown. Any other shades, such as green or purple, destroy the natural appearance of the make-up.

Powder is an important finishing step in any make-up. If a base is used, the best choice is a lightweight, noncoloring foundation powder. This type does not add to or distort the color of the base. Being feather-light, its use does not provide a mask-like appearance. If no foundation make-up is used, a medium-weight, tinted powder should be used.

Whether or not a base is worn, powder should always be patted onto the face. Rubbing does not provide a smooth application. This is especially true when it is employed over any type of foundation. Powder should be used generously over the face, the patting procedure continuing until the base has absorbed as much powder as is necessary to "set" it. Excess powder is then removed with a powder brush, baby brush, or piece of absorbent cotton. A small, stiff-bristle brush should be used to remove powder from the eyebrows and around the hair line.

Eyebrow pencil should be used only when eyebrows are colorless or sparse, or when additional arching is needed. The pencil should never be used in a single, hard, continuous stroke. It should be sharpened to a flat point, and application should be with quick, short hairstrokes. After application, a small, stiff-bristle brush should be used to soften the outline.

Now if it is found that insufficient cream rouge was used, dry rouge is used to retouch the cheeks and is powdered over for smoothness.

Proper application of lipstick is an art that should be practiced, because the mouth can so easily detract from or add to an illusion of beauty. Study of the face type illustrations will indicate correct mouth make-up according to type of face. In this manner, lipstick is used as a corrective cosmetic. Since the ideal mouth has perfect balance between upper and lower lips, the aim in employment of lipstick should be to camouflage too thin or too wide lips. This is done by drawing a new outline either above or below the normal lip outline. Lips should always be made up in a gradual curve. A mouth should never appear as a "cupid's bow" or as a wide splash of sulky color. Lips should be perfectly dry before application is started.

For the best results, a No. 5 art brush should be used as a dressing table brush during the initial make-up of the day. Once the correct outline of the lips is established, purse brushes

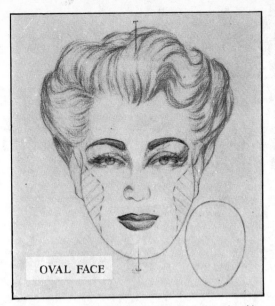

OVAL FACE

This type, with the forehead slightly wider than the chin, is considered the ideal. *Moist Rouge:* Apply in the center of the cheek, blend upward over the cheekbones toward the temple. *Lipstick:* Follow the natural lines of the mouth, retaining a full lip curve. *Eyebrows:* Retain a natural eyebrow line. Regardless of face type, the eyebrows should always start directly above the inside corners of the eyes. *Hair Style:* Retain the oval outline in coiffure; styling should be simple, with the hair drawn back from the forehead.

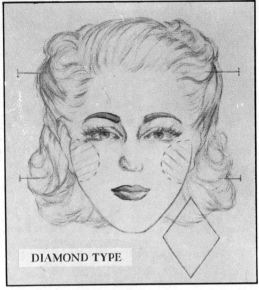

DIAMOND TYPE

This type has a narrow forehead, high and wide cheekbones, and a narrow chin. *Moist Rouge:* Apply on the highest point of the cheekbone, blend carefully in a circular field. *Lipstick:* Gently curve the lips to moderate width, thereby adding an appearance of breadth across the lower part of the face. *Eyebrows:* Arch slightly. *Hair Style:* Keep fullness of hair above and below the ears. Hair should be combed back from, and dressed closely at a point even with the cheekbones. Use a short, diagonal part to give an appearance of greater forehead width.

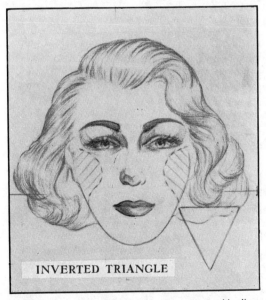

INVERTED TRIANGLE

This type has a wide forehead and a narrow chin line. *Moist Rouge:* Apply to the highest point of the cheekbone, carrying it upward toward the temple. *Lipstick:* Softly curve the upper lip; balance it with the lower lip for natural contour. *Eyebrows:* Retain the natural shape with a suggestion of an angle to disguise width of forehead. *Hair Style:* Retain simplicity on the crown. Begin fullness at a point above the ears and back of them. Greatest fullness should be even with the mouth line, making the lower part of the face appear wider.

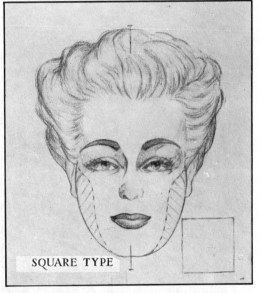

SQUARE TYPE

This type has a straight hair line and a square jaw line. *Moist Rouge:* Apply in a circle under the eye's outer corner; blend toward the ear and down the jaw line very lightly to create a shadow on the lower face. *Lipstick:* Carry to the mouth's natural corners to reduce the width of the lower face. Curve the lips, with an upward tilt at the corners. *Eyebrows:* Arch slightly. *Hair Style:* Dress softly and loosely. An upward, balanced sweep from the temples minimizes squareness of features. Height is provided to add length to them.

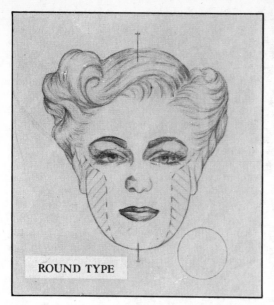

ROUND TYPE

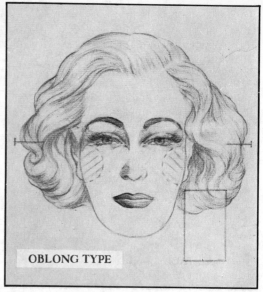

OBLONG TYPE

This type has a round hair line and a round chin. *Moist Rouge:* Use the darkest tone that blends with the complexion on the outer part of the cheek, carrying it toward the temples and down to shade the jaw faintly. *Lipstick:* Carry to the mouth's natural corners to reduce width across the lower face. Make up lips delicately with a natural curve. *Eyebrows:* Avoid a simple curve by arching subtly to a silght center angle. *Hair Style:* Avoid severity, and retain a soft outline at hair line. Create an illusion of length with a fullness above the ears.

A long, narrow face with hollow cheeks is characteristic of this type. *Moist Rouge:* Apply in a carefully blended circular area in the center of the cheek, avoiding cheek hollows. *Lipstick:* Retain a natural outline. The lower lip should remain full at the corners of the mouth. *Eyebrows:* Follow the natural, structural eyebrow line. *Hair Style:* Style hair closely to the top of the head to reduce length of features. Create fullness behind the ears on a line even with the mouth to provide an appearance of greater facial width.

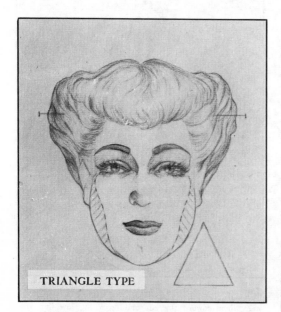

TRIANGLE TYPE

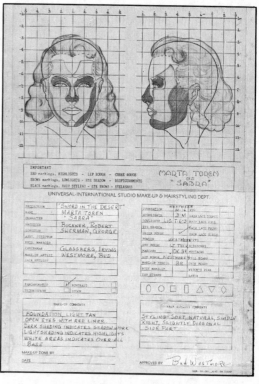

This type has a narrow forehead, a wide jaw and chin line. *Moist Rouge:* Apply in a modified triangle, shading up to the temple and blending faintly over the jaw line. Rouge should cover the outer half of the cheek. *Lipstick:* Carry to the natural corners of the mouth, and use a gently curved, perfectly balanced lip line. *Eyebrows:* Counteract squareness with a gentle curve, natural in width. *Hair Style:* A soft, fringe bang makes the forehead seem wider. Bring it into balance with an upward sweep from the temples.

A chart made by a master make-up man during make-up tests for motion pictures. Indicating the areas for make-up and listing the proper types, it provides a key for future work.

or the stick itself can be used throughout the day to renew color. The art brush should be balanced by placing the elbow of the brush-wielding hand on the dressing table and the little finger against the chin. Using the flat of the brush, application should begin at the center of the upper lip and the outline drawn in a gradual curve to end *just before the corner of the mouth is reached*. This should be a continuous, hard stroke. When the upper lip has been completed, the flat of the brush is again employed on the lower lip, starting at the extreme corners of the mouth and drawing toward the center of the lip. On both upper and lower lips, if any outline irregularity is noticeable, the tip of the brush may be employed for final correction. The purpose of ending the upper lip outline within the actual corners of the mouth is to prevent a drooping line.

Upon completion of application, tissue should be placed between the lips; then should be pressed against the lips to remove excess color. The latter process should be continued until color fails to leave a tissue impression. When lips are too wide for beauty, foundation should be carried over the normal outline and powdered over as with the remainder of the face. This disguises normal outline, and lip rouge is employed in a corrective outline.

Mascara is the last step in a street make-up. It is preferable in most instances to apply it only to the tips of the upper lashes. If the eyes are inclined to be close together, it is applied only from the center of the eyes outward to the corners on both upper and lower lids.

Motion Picture Make-up.—*Black and White Photography.*—The actual steps in make-up and cosmetics used, with exceptions of cream rouge and shades of foundation, remain identical with those outlined for street make-up. Because cheek rouge creates a dark shadow in black and white screen photography, no cream rouge is used. When a feminine star's make-up is completed, a very light dusting of dry rouge is made simply for mental "lift." The amount of make-up used is comparatively the same as used for a good evening make-up.

Corrective make-up application is based on the premise that shadow absorbs light; highlights reflect light. Thus, to minimize any structural prominence a dark foundation would be used; to bring structural weakness into relief, a light foundation, or highlight, would be used. In the examples which follow, a shadow is a color three to five shades darker than the overall base color, and is applied before the highlight. A highlight is three to five shades lighter than the overall base and is applied after the shadows and before moist rouge and powder. (For corrective street make-up, highlight is one to two shades lighter than overall base; shadow, one to two shades darker.)

If a chin has a tendency to recede, we use a foundation three shades lighter than that used on the remainder of the face. Where the two shades meet, they are blended expertly together by patting with the fingertips. Creation of such highlight on the chin brings it into a stronger relief. A sagging, double, or prominent chin is disguised with use of a dark foundation.

When a protruding forehead is a problem, we choose a foundation three shades darker than that used on the remainder of the face, follow the same blending process. The darker founda-

tion becomes a shadow, accepts light, thereby minimizing forehead prominence.

In contradiction to the foregoing use of shadow, a darker foundation is never used on a large, prominent nose. Use of shadow in such a manner would appear as discoloration. The size of the nose is minimized by using a lighter foundation on the cheeks at the sides of the nose, blending it off across the upper lip immediately under the nostrils. The nose itself and the remainder of the face are made up with a foundation cream that matches the normal skin tone, creating an illusion of fullness in the cheeks to minimize the nose. If a nose is short and flat, then a lighter foundation cream is used from the point between the eyes, straight down the bridge to end at the nose tip.

When the greater prominence lies in the cheekbones, a dark foundation is used over the cheekbones, a light foundation in the hollows of the cheeks and the recessions at the temples. The remainder of the face is made up with foundation matching normal skin tone.

These examples best explain the principles of corrective make-up and the use of highlights and shadows.

In the creation of a straight character make-up for the screen, where latex (sponge rubber) is not used to change facial structure, the subject's face is treated as an artist's canvas. An overall base, or primer (regular man's or woman's base color), is first applied to face and neck. Using artists flat sable brushes, numbers ranging from 1 to 20, highlight and shadows are applied in broad brush strokes, and are then blended with the fingertips. Wrinkles are accentuated with pencil. To promote an appearance of age on the mouth, base is carried over the lips, and pencil is used to stress normal lip wrinkles. Hair whitener is used to age eyebrows and temples. If a white head of hair is desired, a wig is used.

To create an age make-up, all hollows, crevices, and lines of expression are first covered with a dark brown foundation. When this procedure is finished, the face should somewhat resemble a skull. The subject's forehead is then forced into the deepest possible wrinkles, and all foundation is carefully wiped off the mounds of the wrinkles. As a result, the brown base is retained in the wrinkle crevices. Next, the subject squints one eye to obtain the deepest possible corner wrinkles, then the other, and the same procedure outlined above is followed. Then the lips are pursed, and the same method is followed on the wrinkled area surrounding the mouth. With completion of the mouth, all wrinkles and natural expression lines are accentuated.

Choice of shade for overall foundation would be dependent on the character to be portrayed. If a ruddy skin is characteristic, then a dark basic color (two shades lighter than wrinkle base) would be used; if pale, a lighter shade of overall base. Overall base should not be used in the shadow areas, such as temples and cheek hollows.

Shadow work now comes into play. In the wrinkling process, dark brown foundation was used in all hollows, including temples and cheeks. These same areas are now retraced with shadow. Care should be taken not to disturb the original application. Shadow placement is at the temple line, inside corners of the eyelids, down the outside planes of the nose, and from the nostrils to the outside corners of the mouth. For extreme gauntness, shadow is applied in the cheek hollows.

Highlights follow shadows. Previously applied foundation is retraced with highlight; when it crowds onto the wrinkle areas, the wrinkling process should be repeated so as not to destroy previous work. Highlight coloring should be applied to all protruding points of the head's bone structure, that is, frontal forehead bones, nose bridge, cheekbones, nostril sidewalls.

Eyeshadow should be used only in the inside corners of the eyelids. On men, red foundation is used on the lower eyelid ledge, but is not extended beyond the outer corner of the eye. On women, no lining of any kind is used.

For powdering, use plain talc and repeat the entire wrinkling process while powdering. Excess powder is removed with a powder brush.

On men, no lip rouge is used; on women, very little is used, and the lower lip is thinned and the corners droop.

Hair whitener is used on eyebrows to conform with hair. No mascara is used and powder is allowed to remain in the lashes.

To age the neck, chin and neck are stretched backwards, and shadow is applied on either side of the neck cords. After shadowing, highlight is applied to the mounds of the cords. The chin is then dropped, and revealing lines or wrinkles are traced with brown pencil, and the mounds of the wrinkles highlighted.

In straight make-ups, no hand make-up is used unless the general make-up is very dark or very light. Hands should then be made up to match the face, because dramatic action often brings hands into play close to the face. To age hands, shadows are created between the sinews and veins. Hands are hung in a drooping position until the veins are outlined, and blue shadow is then used on the veins proper and between the sinews. The hands are then closed into fists, the tops of the knuckles highlighted, and from the ends of the fingers, a highlight is carried back to the wrist, accentuating sinews and cords of each finger. No overall base is used.

Historical character portrayals or extreme old age make-ups (Agnes Moorehead in *Lost Moment*), where change of bone structure is needed for the first and sagging and loose tissue for the latter, are handled with the use of latex (sponge rubber), otherwise called appliance make-ups. Appliance make-ups are very effective, but they are prohibitive from the standpoint of cost to the layman. Not only does their employment demand a complete laboratory set-up, but the formulas themselves are secret, varying with various requirements.

Make-up as such, however, is applied in exactly the same way over rubber as described in the foregoing. It is also the same make-up, with the exception of the base. Known as rubber grease, it is an evaporated oil base, necessary because any regular oil base discolors and deteriorates rubber.

Color Photography.—Continued experimentation with color film has necessarily brought about some changes in make-up principles. Where formerly the basic tone for a screen color make-up was light gray, the basic tone now is a light gray-green which is warmed with the desired shades through the use of primary mixing colors. The mix is according to part requirements and the story setting. For instance, if it is an outdoor picture, men's make-up would have a tendency to be on the brown side. Bases for women are brought up to the desired pink tone, dependent on individual coloring, although if it is an indoor, or drawing-room type of picture, the mix has a pinker tone. Only pre-picture testing can prove or disprove a correct color make-up.

The amount of corrective work done for color motion pictures is held at a minimum. While the principles remain the same, shadows and highlights must be handled much more subtly. Very little shadowing is done, and any highlights or shadow used are mixed with the base color so that only a suggestion of their use remains after application. Great pains are taken in blending highlights and shadows, since absolutely no hint of demarcation can remain. By the same token, any latex appliances used must be extremely subtle.

All color make-up is applied in absolute minimum, a straight make-up for women, for instance, utilizing only about half the amount of that customarily used for a street make-up. For women, both moist rouge and dry rouge are used, the former directly over the base and before powder; the latter after powder. Moist cheek rouge is first mixed with base color to avoid a "hot" rouge color. Matching colors in lipstick and cheek rouge are of the greatest importance, and those used for women are on the cameo-pink side because of the intensification of red in photography.

No cheek rouge is employed on men, and any lipstick is on the brown side. Applied very lightly, it is wiped off, the very limited residue serving to provide a faint definition.

Brown eyebrow pencil is used. All desired depth is acquired with brown. The use of black pencil results in an undesirable harshness. Mascara, too, is preferably brown, although sometimes there is occasion to use a dark brown shade on a very dark brunette.

Powder must be neutral (foundation powder) so that color value of base tones, highlights or shadows is not changed.

Stage Make-up.—Basic principles of application remain the same as for black and white photography. However, because at a distance of 40 feet a performer's face loses audience perspective, stage make-up must exaggerate the essential features.

Stage lighting is extremely important in judging stage make-up. A straw-colored light will dull blue and pink; blue light changes rouge to purple and deadens pink and yellow; a light pink spotlight on an actor's face will intensify all pink and red tints in his make-up, and tend to wash out the yellows and blues. Stage make-up, therefore, is better inspected under actual stage illumination than under dressing room lights.

The liquid and paste bases used for stage make-up run from flesh color through healthy sunburn for juvenile men; for older men, flesh through the lighter sallow shades. Standard for young leading ladies is peaches-and-cream, and a light sallow for older women.

Shadows range from dark through light brown; dark through light gray; medium blue through light gray and blue-gray. Both eyebrow pencil and mascara are black.

Powder, with the exception of character make-up requirements, should match the overall base color. For character make-up, base-colored powder is mixed in the proportion of one-third base color to two-thirds plain talc. Such a mix-

Straight

Character

Elderly

FEMININE STAGE MAKE-UP. These four drawings illustrate the basic principles of feminine theatrical make-up for the professional or amateur theater. The same model was used for each sketch, demonstrating how one person can be made up for each of the four basic types: straight, character, elderly, and grotesque.

Straight

Character

Grotesque

MAKE-UP
(FOR THE STAGE)

MASCULINE STAGE MAKE-UP. These four drawings illustrate the basic principles of masculine theatrical make-up for the professional or amateur theater. Again, the same model was used for each sketch to demonstrate how one person can be made up for each of the four basic types. Detailed instructions for applying make-up, and the requirements, will be found in a subsection of the accompanying article.

Elderly

Grotesque

ture effectively reveals all highlight, shadow, or corrective work that has been done. For extreme old age, plain white talc is used. Because it is transparent, it not only reveals highlight and shadow work, but adds the white appearance of aged skin.

Adhesives in use include gutta percha, spirit gum, and resin, the last diluted with alcohol. These are used to fasten on wigs, moustaches, and beards, where hair is already on a piece. Nonflexible collodion is used over fish skin to create scars. Flexible collodion (collodion with 20 per cent castor oil mixed) can be used over cotton, before the base color, to provide a firm surface for a necessary change of facial contour. Application before foundation prevents base make-up absorption and allows retention of the modeled shade. Neither collodion nor nonflexible collodion should be applied directly to the skin. Rubber liquid adhesive can be used with cotton modelings. It is applied directly on the skin to hold the cotton, as well as on the cotton before application of the flexible collodion.

Feminine Stage Make-Up.—The basic role of stage make-up is to exaggerate the essential features of the character to be portrayed. The treatment of the hair and the selection of the costume, naturally, contribute tellingly to the final effect. The following instructions apply to the illustrations accompanying this article, on which are shown examples of the four basic types of feminine stage make-up: straight, character, elderly and grotesque.

Straight.—(1) Overall base: liquid pink (peaches-and-cream) applied sparingly to the exposed areas, the eyelids, neck and ears, inside and out.

(2) Shadow: Two shades darker than the base.

(3) Highlights: Two shades lighter than the base. If, however, the shadows and highlights are used for corrective purposes, apply them sparingly and blend them into the overall base, leaving no line of demarcation.

(4) Eye shadow: Blue-gray, green or brown. Apply over the base before powdering, but use only enough to define the color, about three times as heavy as used for the street.

(5) Eye liner: Black pencil. Use to line the eye at the upper lash line, extending the line a quarter of an inch beyond the outer corner of the eye. Line the lower lash line, starting at a point below the middle of the eye and extending a quarter of an inch beyond the corner, leaving a quarter-inch space between the upper and lower black lines. Blend with a small dry brush. Apply white foundation (clown white) with a make-up stump on the ledge of the lower eyelid, and extend it beyond the corner of the eye into the space between the upper and lower black lines. The eyes will then retain an "open" appearance.

(6) Cheek rouge: Very bright. Smile, and place moist rouge on the high point of the smiling cheek, as indicated in the illustration. Carefully blend the rouge under the outside corner of the eye up into the temple area and downward onto the lower cheek. Use three times the amount used for the street.

(7) Powder: Pat peaches-and-cream powder generously over the entire area and brush away the excess. Remove the surplus from the eyelids with absorbent cotton.

(8) Mascara and eyebrow pencil: Black, no matter what the individual's coloring. If the hair coloring is very light, apply very lightly. If the eyes are small, use mascara only on the tips of the lashes. The eyebrow should never be higher above the eye than the normal opening of the eye itself.

(9) Lip rouge: Very bright. The mouth should be sharply defined and made up with full, round and curved lines. The corners should turn upward.

Character.—Character make-up is really a matter of portrait painting; a new personality is painted over the performer's face. As in the case of the Chinese make-up which is illustrated, a photograph or other likeness is obtained and a duplicate painted on the face. The placement of rouge and the treatment of the eyes and eyebrows in the illustration should be carefully noted. Black liner is drawn from the inner corner of the eye over the upper lid to end in an upward tilt about half an inch from the outer corner. The lower lid is lined in the same fashion, with the points of the lining meeting at both inner and outer corners to achieve an olive shape. One half of the normal eyebrow is covered with overall foundation and a thin, slanting brow, drawn in with black pencil, replaces it.

Elderly.—(1) Base for wrinkles: Dark brown. First cover all hollows, crevices and lines of expression with a dark brown foundation. Then wrinkle the forehead and wipe the foundation off the mounds of the wrinkles so that the brown color is retained in the crevices. Next, squint one eye and then the other to the fullest extent, and purse the lips, following the same procedure around the mouth.

(2) Hair whitener: Use this for graying or whitening hair. (A wig is used in the illustration.)

(3) Overall base: Peaches-and-cream, or lighter, according to character. The overall base should not be used in shadow areas (see illustration), such as temples and cheek hollows.

(4) Shadow: Light brown. In applying the base for wrinkles, dark brown is used in all hollows, including the temples and cheeks. These areas should be retraced with shadow, using care not to disturb the earlier application. Shadows are placed at the temple line, on the inside corners of the eyelids, down the nose planes, and from the nostrils to the outer corners of the mouth. If an extreme gauntness is desired, shadow should be placed in the cheek hollows.

(5) Highlights: These should be practically white. Retrace over the overall base previously applied, giving highlight coloring to all protruding points of the head's bone structure, such as the frontal bones of the forehead, the cheekbones, the bridge of the nose, and the walls along the sides of the nostrils.

(6) Eye shadow: Blue-gray or gray. Apply only in the inside corners of the eyelids. The outside bulge of the upper lid is highlighted to give an appearance of heaviness.

(7) Cheek rouge: Pale, or omitted, according to character.

(8) Powder: Plain talc. The wrinkling process must be repeated when powdering.

(9) Lip rouge: A minimum is used. The lower lip is thinned more than in a younger character and the corners droop. ·

Hair whitener may be used on the eyebrows, as in the illustration, to conform with the hair.

In cases of extreme make-up, the overall foundation is applied to the eyebrows. Any powder should be allowed to remain in the lashes. No mascara or eye liner is used.

Grotesque.—Following a portrait-painting procedure, extreme use of highlight and shadow is made deliberately, applied with a brush over the basic foundation. The center area of the brush stroke must retain the full density of color. At the edges, however, shadow or highlight become a part of the overall foundation, being carefully blended with the finger tips to avoid any line of demarcation. The mouth contour is further changed by the use of lip rouge, as in the illustration. In the creation of a scar, fishskin is used as a base to prevent burning the skin, and is applied before the make-up. After determining the scar area, cut the fishskin one inch wider and longer than the scar. Tear the edges carefully to blend with the skin and affix with spirit gum. After it is placed, create the desired scar on the fishskin with nonflexible collodion.

Masculine Stage Make-Up.—The following instructions apply to the illustrations accompanying this article, on which are shown examples of the four basic types of masculine stage make-up: straight, character, elderly and grotesque. References below apply to the preceding subsection of this article, *Feminine Stage Make-Up.*

Straight.—(1) Overall base: A healthy tan. Apply sparingly to the exposed areas, the eyelids, the neck and back of neck, and the ears, inside and out.

(2) Shadow: Two shades darker than base.

(3) Highlights: Two shades lighter than base. If, however, the shadows and highlights are used for corrective purposes, apply them sparingly and blend them into the overall base, leaving no line of demarcation.

(4) Eye shadow: Dark brown on blonds and black on brunets. It is used to create contrast for the whites of the eyes. Apply sparingly, with full density at the upper lash line. It must be blended with the base color at the upper limit of the eyeball.

(5) Eye liner: Use black lining pencil. Follow procedure outlined for feminine straight make-up.

(6) Cheek rouge: Rust color. In applying, start at the high point of the cheekbone and blend carefully down over the jaw line. Avoid a harlequin look. Use three times the amount of color used for a woman's street make-up.

(7) Powder: A healthy tan. Apply generously, brushing off the excess. Remove the surplus from the eyelids with absorbent cotton.

(8) Mascara and eyebrow pencil: Black mascara may be brushed both on lashes and eyebrows, or a brown or black eyebrow pencil may be used to emphasize the eyebrows. Angular eyebrows give an impression of dramatic masculinity.

(9) Lip rouge: Very dark. Men seldom need lip rouge for the stage. When necessary, a very dark shade should be used to indicate the desired shape and then wiped off, leaving only a faint trace. Too much lip rouge on a man can defeat an entire characterization.

(10) Dry cheek rouge: A small amount of rust-colored rouge should be used over the powder to retrace the moist rouge area.

Character.—Follow the feminine character make-up procedure, noting the shadow and highlight work on the accompanying illustration.

For artificial beards and mustaches, use crepe hair, which comes in variously colored braids. The complete make-up is applied over all areas of the face, except those where the artificial hair is to be used, before the beard or mustache is applied. Paint the hair area with spirit gum and allow it to dry. Pull the prepared crepe hair together in a point, paint the hair area with a second coat of spirit gum, and affix the hair. When the spirit gum has set firmly, comb the hair together and trim with scissors to the desired contour. The same method is used for applying eyebrows or in changing the front hairline. Crepe hair may be whitened just like natural hair.

Elderly.—(1) Base for wrinkles: Dark brown. Follow the feminine elderly make-up procedure.

(2) Hair whitener: Use for graying or whitening hair. The older the character, the further over the hair should be parted.

(3) Overall base: This depends on the character to be played. If a ruddy skin is desired, a dark basic color two shades lighter than the wrinkle base should be used. For a pale skin use a lighter shade of overall base. The overall base should not be used in shadow areas, such as the temples and cheek hollows.

(4) Shadow: Two shades darker than the overall base. Follow the feminine elderly make-up procedure.

(5) Highlights: Two shades lighter than the overall base. Follow the procedure outlined for feminine elderly make-up.

(6) Eye shadow: The same color as the overall base, or darker, depending on the character. It should be used only on the inside corners of the lids.

(7) Cheek rouge: Very light, or none, depending on the character. If used, dry rouge should be applied only to the high point of the cheek, after powdering.

(8) Powder: Use a plain talc. Repeat the entire wrinkling process when powdering.

(9) Tooth enamel: Black tooth enamel may be used to black out teeth. To fill or match teeth in exact color, apply white tooth enamel and allow it to dry.

No eye liner is used. A red foundation should be used on the lower eye ledge, extending no further than the corner of the eye. No mascara or eyebrow pencil is used. Apply hair whitener to the eyebrows. Allow powder to remain on the lashes. No lip rouge is used; the overall base should be carried over the lips.

Grotesque.—Follow the feminine grotesque make-up, noting the extreme use of shadow and highlight on the accompanying illustration. The sketch there is that of a prize fighter. The change in nose shape is accomplished by the use of cotton and collodion. Before any other make-up is applied, spread a thin coat of spirit gum on the nose area. Place small pieces of cotton on the bridge of the nose and build the new shape. Brush the edges with spirit gum. After the desired shape has been obtained, cover the entire area of cotton with flexible collodion, extending the collodion a quarter of an inch beyond the edges of the cotton to make it secure. Allow the collodion to dry between the applications. The drying may be hastened with a fan or blower. Before applying the base foundation, add a quarter-ounce of base foundation to a quarter-ounce of flexible collodion, mix thoroughly, and apply over the entire area of cotton, remaining an eighth of an inch inside the margin line of the original spirit gum application. This will bind the edges of the applied spirit gum, cotton, and collodion.

The process just described is not, however, as permanent as the use of nose putty, which is manufactured in several colors to match the foundation make-up. Warmed to body temperature in the hand, it is modeled on the nose. The putty adheres to the flesh, and make-up is applied directly to it.

To achieve a cauliflower ear, bend a hairpin around the ear to hold it in the desired position and then cover it with adhesive tape. Create the necessary contours with spirit gum and cotton. Cover with a single coat of collodion and apply the foundation to all surfaces.

Television Make-up.—As continued developments in color film and photographic technique occur and as make-up is altered to meet those changes, so are the rules for television make-up elastic. Television make-up generally follows stage principles: intensification of color and exaggeration of essential features. Shadow for television is two shades darker than base color; highlight, two shades lighter.

Because red is burned out and becomes a highlight, only a light dusting of cheek rouge is permissible after powdering. Here again, as in black and white motion picture work, it is used for psychological effect only.

Lip rouge for women is a garnet shade. After initial application it is powdered, excess powder is removed, and lipstick is again applied. This is to avoid any shine or glow. Lipstick, if used for men, is on the brown side, as for stage use, and is wiped off to leave only faint definition.

The overall base for men is a dark tan; shadow, a dark brown. For masculine leads, shadow work consists usually only of under-chin work or along the sides of the nose. The overall base for women is a light tan. These bases are on the true brown side, with an avoidance of pink or definite red tones. Television lighting washes out red, thereby resulting in glaring highlight.

Powder matches the overall base. As with stage make-up, both eyebrow pencil and mascara are black for greater definition.

Photographic Make-up: Amateur and Professional.—For 16-millimeter use, the make-up procedure as outlined for black and white motion pictures is correct. For color, the best possible make-up is that designated for street, with the exception of cheek rouge and lipstick, which should be two shades lighter than that customarily worn by the subject for street.

The most important single make-up item, photographically speaking, is the base. Not only is it flattering to the subject, but also its use saves hours of retouching. The base color is that used ordinarily by the model for street. Exceptions are platinum or bleached blondes, when skin and hair tones are so often similar that definition is lacking. The same is often true of brunettes with olive skins. For blondes who present this problem, foundation liquid or cream should be at least two shades darker than that used for street; for brunettes, one shade lighter.

In black and white still photography, Hollywood photographers often omit the use of powder, if a subject's skin is unblemished and freckles are not too apparent. They use only cream or liquid foundation without powder. The result is

lustrous, highlighted skin, with normal skin texture showing through.

For color stills or home movies, eyeshadow should be used very sparingly. If brown is used, it should be mixed with a little of the base, using only enough base color to bring the eyeshadow down to a smooth tan instead of brown. After mixing, it should be two shades lighter than in its original form. Blue-gray shadow should not be mixed.

For black and white portraiture, the subject should pass the tip of the tongue lightly over both upper and lower lips before each shot. The result is the nice lip highlights seen in Hollywood portraiture. Interesting highlights on bare shoulders are achieved by smoothing on a very little cold cream or petroleum jelly, then toning it down with tissue.

If a bathing suit model has an even, overall tan, it can be effectively highlighted by covering it with an application of baby oil and by removing the excess with tissue.

Hairstyling.—The importance of feminine hairstyling cannot go unrecognized, for by following the general rules for hairstyling for the seven face types, women not only minimize faults, but also emphasize good points. Hair is the frame for the face, and correct balance is the secret of fine hairstyling. No matter how perfect the make-up, if hair is incorrectly or unbecomingly styled, beauty is destroyed.

BUD WESTMORE,
Director of Make-up and Hairstyling, Universal International Studios
AND
BERTHA JANCKE,
Publicity Director, The House of Westmore.

MAKEYEVKA, mŭ-kā'yĕf-kȧ (formerly DMITRIYEVSK), city, USSR, located north of the Sea of Azov and about 12 miles northeast of Stalino, in the Stalino Oblast, eastern Ukrainian Soviet Socialist Republic. Originally a czarist Russian workers' settlement, Makeyevka in the Soviet era has become one of the Union's centers for the production of iron, steel, steel pipe, coal, coke, nitrate fertilizer, and explosives. The output of pig iron alone exceeds 1,300,000 metric tons per annum. From 1941 to 1943, during World War II, the city was occupied by the Nazis and suffered enormous war damage. By 1957 the war-devastated factories, mines, housing, and public utilities were restored, and industrial production exceeded the prewar level. Pop. (1956) 311,000.

ELLSWORTH RAYMOND.

MAKHACHKALA, mä-ĸȧch-kä-lä' (formerly PETROVSK), city, USSR, a Caspian seaport located on the east coast of the Caucasian isthmus, north of the Caucasus Mountains. It is the capital of the Dagestan Autonomous Soviet Socialist Republic of the Russian Soviet Federated Socialist Republic. As a transshipment point for timber, oil, grain, sugar, and cotton between the Caspian Sea and the Rostov-Baku railway, it is, in volume of freight, one of the largest seaports of the Soviet Union. From the city an important oil pipeline extends to the Caucasian coast of the Black Sea and to the Donets coal basin of the Ukraine. Major industries are oil refining, metalworking, fishing, fish canning, and textile manufacture. Pop. (1956) 106,000.

ELLSWORTH RAYMOND.

MALABAR COAST, măl'à-bär, is the southwest coast of India. It stretches 550 miles from Goa to the southern tip of the Indian peninsula. On the west is the Arabian Sea; on the east are the Western Ghats mountains, 30 to 70 miles inland. The region is very humid, with a rainfall between 80 and 120 inches; on the mountain slopes, of more than 200 inches. Its mean temperature is 82° F. Forests of teak, ebony, and sandalwood grow on the mountains. Along the coast, fishing is an important industry. Coconuts, rice, pepper, spices, rubber, and cinchona bark are raised. Its chief ports include Cochin and Calicut.

It is reputed that the Apostle Thomas came here as a missionary about 52 A.D. Nestorians and Jews settled here in the 5th–7th centuries A.D. The coast was visited between 1498 and 1503 by Portuguese, who founded trading posts. The Dutch came in 1656, the French in the 1720's, and the British in the late 18th century.

MALACCA, mà-lăk'à, state, Federation of Malaysia, in the southwestern part of the Malay Peninsula. It is about 640 square miles in area. It is largely agricultural and its main crop is rubber.

In the 14th–15th centuries Malacca was an influential kingdom, which fell to the Portuguese in 1511 and was captured by the Dutch in 1641. It was held by the British from 1795 to 1802 and from 1811 to 1818 and was ceded to them in 1824. From 1826 to 1946 it formed with Penang and Singapore a single government known as the Straits Settlement. Malacca was part of the short-lived Malay Union (1946–1948). In 1948 it became a state in the Federation of Malaya, which won independence from Britain in 1957 and joined the Federation of Malaysia in 1963.

The capital of the state is Malacca, a port for coastal shipping located on the Strait of Malacca about 125 miles northwest of Singapore. Pop. (1962) of the state, 361,152.

MALACHI, Book of, măl'à-kī. This is the last book of the collection of the "Twelve [minor] Prophets" and of the Protestant Old Testament. It is actually an anonymous work, the name "Malachi," meaning "my messenger," having been taken from Malachi 3:1.

The general date of the book is practically unquestioned. It certainly dates from the Persian period, as is shown by the reference to the governor (1:8); it looks back upon a disaster which had recently befallen the Edomites (1:3 ff.), an event undoubtedly to be equated with the Nabatean conquest of Edom, which occurred at some time between 587 and 312 B.C.; more precisely, the spiritual ills with which the book is concerned are those which occupied the attention of the reforming governor Nehemiah, whose first administration began in 444 B.C. The book is probably to be dated in the decade which preceded his coming, that is, about 450 B.C.

The situation which the prophet faced was that of widespread indifference, if not actual hostility, to the traditional religion, generated by a feeling that God had shown Himself indifferent to the fate of His people. The Jews had returned from the Exile filled with hopes for a glorious future, such as had apparently been promised by the Second Isaiah. Instead, their new life on Palestine was characterized by famine, recurrent economic depression, enmity of hostile neighbors, and constant pressure of a growing population in the inadequate resources of their much-diminished country. They could conclude only that God had forsaken them or that He was not a God of justice (2:17; 3:14 ff.). The Book of Malachi consists of a series of reasoned discourses addressed to those who felt this way. Its first argument (1:2–5) is that God has shown His love and care for His people by punishing their treacherous enemies, the Edomites (Esau). This is sufficient to prove that God is not indifferent to the claims of justice. The next argument (1:6–2:9) is that whatever difficulties the nation faced were the just recompense for their scandalous neglect of God's worship. The clergy were degraded and made no effort to teach the people the kind of reverence due to the temple and the altar; they were willing to countenance the offering of blind and otherwise imperfect animals in sacrifice (1:7 ff., 13 ff.). Even the heathen, although ignorant of whom they worshiped, were more devoted than the people of Israel and offered worship more acceptable to God (1:11). In addition to profaning the principle of sacrifice, the people had incurred God's anger by failure to pay their tithes (3:6–12) and, on the ethical plane, by permitting the degradation of marriage (2:10–16). The third argument advanced by the prophet is that God's justice, which then seemed veiled, would be perfectly revealed and His honor would be vindicated in the final judgment, which was soon to come. God would purify the priests, so that they would once again offer acceptable sacrifices, and would punish the wicked who seemed, for the moment, to flourish with impunity (3:1–5). As for the righteous, who seemed to be suffering unjustly, God would not forget their fidelity and would acknowledge them as His own on that great day. Then everyone would see that God is just and that the good and the bad, the faithful and the unfaithful, are rewarded according to their deserts (3:16–4:3).

The only passage in the book that is generally regarded as being by a later hand is 4:4–6. Verse 4 attempts to summarize (in quite unprophetic language) what some editor felt to be the principal message of the Twelve Prophets. Verses 5 and 6 are an exegetical comment identifying the "messenger" of 3:1 with the prophet Elijah.

Although the prophet "Malachi" does not stand in the company of the greatest prophets of Israel, he is nevertheless a noble and appealing figure who makes his own special contribution to the history of Old Testament thought. While no mere ceremonialist, he recognized that contempt for the externals of worship may well be the symptom of a profound spiritual disease. He was deeply concerned with the ethical problem (2:10–16; 3:5) and was unique in his generous attitude toward the worship of foreigners (1:11), his conception of the relation of theology and ethics (2:10), and his condemnation of divorce (2:16).

Bibliography.—Smith, John M. P., "Malachi," *International Critical Commentary on the Holy Scriptures . . .*, vol. 24 (New York 1912); Smith, George A., *The Book of the Twelve Prophets*, rev. ed., vol. 2 (London 1929); Horst, Friedrich, "Maleachi" in *Die Zwölf Kleinen Propheten*, 2d rev. ed. (Tübingen 1954); Dentan, Robert C., "Malachi," *The Interpreter's Bible*, vol. 6 (New York 1956).

ROBERT C. DENTAN,
Professor of Old Testament Literature and Interpretation, General Theological Seminary, New York City.

MALACHITE, măl′à-kīt, a native basic copper carbonate, with the formula $Cu_2(OH)_2$ (CO_3) or $CuCO_3.Cu(OH)_2$. The monoclinic crystals are rare; the mineral usually occurs in mammillary or botryoidal forms with an internal radial fibrous structure, or as incrustations and earthy masses. It is bright green in color, with a pale green streak. The specific gravity is about 4, and the hardness 3.5 to 4. It is subtransluscent, and the luster varies from silky or velvety in the fibrous types to dull and earthy. Although more common than azurite, with which it is commonly associated, it is a minor copper ore, occurring in the upper oxidized zone of copper deposits. It is found in many of the copper mines of Arizona, Nevada, New Mexico, Utah, and Chile. It is also found in the Congo (Léopoldville), Zambia, Rhodesia, and South West Africa. The most famous source is Nizhni Tagil, in the Ural Mountains, USSR, where one large banded mass containing over 500,000 pounds was found. Cut into blocks and slabs, it was used for ornamental purposes.

LEWIS S. RAMSDELL,
University of Michigan.

MALACHY, măl′à-kĭ (Irish MAELMAEDHOIG UA MORGAIR), SAINT, Irish prelate and reformer: b. Armagh, Ireland, 1094?; d. Clairvaux, France, Nov. 2, 1148. He served as abbot of Bangor (1123–1124), bishop of Connor (1124–1132), archbishop of Armagh (1132–1136), and bishop of Down (1136–1148). He introduced Roman usages into his dioceses, restored clerical discipline, and combated paganism. In 1140, during his first journey to Rome, he began his friendship with St. Bernard of Clairvaux, who became his biographer. He returned to Ireland as papal legate and continued his work of bringing the Irish Church into conformity with that of Rome.

To St. Malachy are attributed 112 short prophecies concerning future popes. Modern scholarship has discredited completely the entire document (discovered in 1595), entitled *Prophetia de futuris pontificibus Romanis.*

St. Malachy was canonized in 1190. His feast is on November 3.

MÁLAGA, mä′lä-gä, province, Spain, in the far south, on the Mediterranean Sea. It is bounded by Cádiz province on the west, Córdoba and Seville on the north, and Granada on the east. Its area is 2,813 square miles. The climate is quite mild in winter and semitropical in summer. Málaga's scenery varies from wide beaches to stretches of rocky coast, from fishing villages to mountain towns. The province is drained by the Guadalhorce and Guadiaro rivers and by tributaries of the Guadalquivir River.

Agriculture is concentrated in the irrigated lowlands. Fruits, olives, almonds, sugarcane, and cotton are the chief agricultural products. Grapes are grown on the lower mountain sides. The province's manufacturing industries produce cottons, iron and steel, chocolate, and lumber. The mountains yield iron, lead, nickel, platinum, gold, bismuth, and coal. Its wineries produce the sweet white Malaga wines, which are as distinctive and almost as famous as sherry. Coastal villages carry on extensive fishing; many are seaside resorts.

The antiquity of the province is shown by Phoenician relics; excavations still uncover Carthaginian, Roman, and Visigothic coins; ruined Roman and Moorish walls, bridges, and aqueducts remain in many towns; ancient watchtowers stand on lonely headlands. After its capital, Málaga (q.v.), the next largest town is Ronda, with its tremendous gorge and its history of smugglers and bullfighters. The Malagueños (inhabitants of Málaga) are typical Andalusians: golden-skinned, dark-eyed, slim, graceful, indolent, pleasure-loving people, possessing the Andalusian passion for music; to this art they have contributed the malaguena, high pitched and haunting, which they sing and dance to the accompaniment of guitar and castanets. Pop. (1960) 781,690.

DOROTHY LODER,
Author of "The Land and People of Spain."

MÁLAGA, city, Spain, capital of the province of the same name, located on a narrow coastal plain along the Mediterranean Sea shore, 260 miles south of Madrid. It is an important Mediterranean port. One of the oldest cities in Europe, having been founded by the Phoenicians c. 1100 B.C., it became in turn Carthaginian, Roman, and Visigothic. It fell to the Moors in 711 A.D. and remained Moorish until captured by the army of the Spanish monarchs Ferdinand and Isabella in 1487. During the Civil War of 1936–1939, troops of Gen. Francisco Franco took the city from the Loyalists after a battle lasting from Jan. 13 to Feb. 8, 1937.

Málaga retains a strong Moorish flavor. In the old quarter, white houses huddle in a maze of narrow streets. On the Gibralfaro, a hill rising 1,000 feet above the harbor, an 8th century fortress stands intact; its garden still contains caves and dungeons where prisoners languished during the Middle Ages. A walled passage descending from the fortress of the Gibralfaro connects with the Alcazaba, a castle on a nearby hill, which in the 14th century was converted into a citadel by the Moorish rulers who built the Alhambra at Granada. Recently restored, the Alcazaba lodges an archaeological museum with the finest collection of Hispano-Moorish ceramics in Spain. From the towers of the Gibralfaro it is possible to see, on a clear day, the mountains of North Africa. Promenades, parks, and public squares, with their green of palms, pines, eucalyptus, plane, and locust trees, soften the glare of buildings; villas are set among exotic gardens; orange and lemon groves fan out to a semicircle of rose-colored hills beyond. As Málaga averages only 30 rainy days a year, the Guadalmedina River often cuts a dry gash through the town, but a heavy downpour frequently widens it into a flood.

The city exports Malaga wines and olive oil and manufactures fertilizers, shoes, cardboard, candy, flour, olive oil, and brandy. Although a commercial center, Málaga is also a pleasure resort. The luxuriant subtropical vegetation and its climate explain why the Moors called it "an earthly Paradise." Sea breezes temper summer days; the winter, said to be the mildest in Europe, attracts visitors to the fine hotels, shops, beaches, and other playgrounds. During Holy Week, members of church societies, wearing masks and bright costumes, walk through the streets beside richly decorated religious floats. These ceremonies are less publicized than those of Seville, but many who have seen both prefer Málaga's celebrations as being more impressive. Pop. (1960) 296,432.

DOROTHY LODER.

MALAGASY REPUBLIC, măl-à-găs'ē, an independent republic in the French Community, occupies the island of Madagascar (q.v.) in the Indian Ocean. Madagascar was annexed by France in 1896. It became the autonomous Malagasy Republic within the French Community in 1958 and gained full independence two years later.

The People. In physical appearance the Malagasy people resemble the people of nearby continental Africa, but their language—Malgache —is closely related to the Maanyan language of Borneo. This linguistic relationship indicates that the Malagasy people originated in what is now Indonesia, from which they may have departed about 2,000 years ago. These ancient Indonesians first settled on the East African coast, where they intermarried with Africans. Then they moved on to Madagascar. More Africans followed the first Indonesian-Africans to the island.

In the Malagasy people today, it is impossible to tell where Africa stops and Asia begins. There are several main groups. The largest is the Merina, who live in the central highlands of Madagascar. The Sakalava inhabit the western plains, and the rain forest of the east coast is occupied by the Antaisaka, Tanala, and Antaimoro. Most of the east-northeast littoral is inhabited by the Betsimisaraka. Northern Madagascar is peopled mainly by the Tsimihety. The semiarid south includes the Antandroy and the Bara.

On the island there are about 70,000 Europeans, 13,000 Indians, and 8,000 Chinese. These people are important in Malagasy's business and industry as owners and managers.

About a sixth of all the Malagasy people are Roman Catholic, and another sixth are Protestant. About 400,000 are Moslems. Most of the rural people practice ancient tribal religions.

Information Highlights

Official name: Malagasy Republic.
Form of government: Republic; member of the French Community.
President: Philibert Tsiranana.
Area: 230,035 square miles.
Population (1963): 6,016,000.
Capital: Tananarive; pop. (1962) 270,268.
Chief languages: French and Malgache.
Chief exports (1962): coffee, 61,767 tons; sugar, 64,943 tons; rice, 54,664 tons; peanuts, 37,478 tons; sisal, 24,037 tons; vanilla, 666 tons.
Value of trade (1964): imports $136,000,000; exports, $92,000,000.

The Economy. Malagasy's major economic activity is agriculture. The most productive farms are in the Lake Alaotra basin in the east, the valleys of the Betsiboka River in the northwest, and parts of the central highlands. The most important food crops are rice (per capita consumption is about 350 pounds a year), manioc (cassava), yams, corn, beans, potatoes, peanuts, and peas.

The principal exports include coffee, vanilla, rice, tapioca, cocoa, spices, sugarcane, cotton, and such oilseeds as peanuts. Vanilla, imported mainly by the United States, ranks second to coffee in earnings. The island is second only to Zanzibar in clove production. Over all, France is Malagasy's most important trading partner.

Livestock is another important source of wealth. Malagasy farmers own about 8,000,000 head of cattle and 350,000 hogs. The zebu, with its heavy hump, is bred in the great prairies of the west and south. The native goats are being replaced by Angoras. Their mohair-producing wool has created a new Malagasy industry.

Malagasy is a leading producer of graphite. Among its rare and relatively costly minerals are rhombic mica, piezoelectric quartz, uranium, and thorium. Other minerals are phosphates, columbite, industrial beryl, and various semiprecious stones. Chromite deposits at Ranomena are estimated at 400,000 tons. Nickel deposits at Valrozo contain some 70,000 tons of ore. Coal seams in the southwest Sakoa mines hold an estimated 3 billion tons, but the coal is not high grade.

The island's major industries process its agricultural products. There are rice, peanut oil, and aleurite mills; starch plants; sugar refineries; rum and perfume distilleries; canneries; sisal-processing plants; soap factories; tanneries; and cement works. About 10 percent of the nonfarm workers belong to labor unions. In 1963, 11 companies had more than 1,000 workers each, and industrialization is slowly increasing.

Malagasy earns an average $80,000,000 each year from exports. Its imports average $120,000,-000. The resulting deficit is partly made up by French economic and technical assistance. This amounted to about $500,000,000 between 1949 and 1963.

Imports of consumer goods, although still heavy, have been steadily declining. Imports of raw materials and capital goods have been rising. Fuels, mining equipment, clothing, cement, machines, and automobiles are among the chief imports. Trade with the United States more than doubled in the early 1960's. Most of Malagasy's trade, however, remains with France and the French-speaking countries of Africa.

Malagasy has 528 miles of railroad track, most of which links Tananarive, the capital, with the port of Tamatave on the Indian Ocean. It has some 500 miles of inland waterways, of which the 400-mile Pangalanes Canal is the most heavily traveled, and about 18,000 miles of roads. Arivonimano, near Tananarive, is an international airport.

Government. Malagasy's government is based on its 1959 constitution. The president of the republic is elected for a seven-year term by an electoral college. This is made up of members of both legislative houses, the six provincial councils, and special delegates from rural and municipal communes. The constitution invests the presidency with broad powers. The president appoints the members of his cabinet and determines general government policy.

The legislature is composed of a 107-member National Assembly and a 54-member Senate. Deputies to the National Assembly are elected by the people for five-year terms. They are chosen from electoral lists in each of the provinces and the city of Tananarive. The provincial councils and the rural and municipal commune delegates elect 36 of the senators. The other 18 senators are appointed by the government. All senators serve six-year terms.

The nation has several political parties. The major party is the Social Democratic Party (Parti Social Démocrate).

History. Masudi, the Arabian geographer and historian, visited Madagascar in the 900's and brought the first reliable reports of it to the outside world. An Arab town dating back to about 1100 has been uncovered near Vohemar, and small chiefdoms are known to have existed along the coast. Malgache words for seasons, months, days, and coins show Arabic influence, and Islam had made inroads before the 1600's.

Europe did not know of the island before the Portuguese came upon it by accident in 1500. The Portuguese were sailing around Africa to set up trade with Southeast Asia. During the 1600's pirates used Madagascar as a supply base and also took part in the slave trade. The French settled the Fort Dauphin area between 1643 and 1671.

The 1600's and 1700's saw the rise and fall of the great Sakalava kingdoms of Menabe and Boina and of the Betsimisaraka kingdom on the east coast. The growth of the Merina state after the 1780's was a turning point—the island became unified for the first time. Rivalry between the British and the French in the Indian Ocean furthered the process of unification. Britain granted military aid and recognized Radama I as king of Madagascar in 1817. By the 1850's, the Merina were in complete control.

The Anglo-French rivalry was settled in 1885 when France recognized certain British rights in continental Africa and Britain recognized the French protectorate in Madagascar. A decade later, Madagascar became a colony of France.

The first 50 years of French rule brought both good and bad. Under the administration of General Gallieni, from 1896 to 1905, nonethnic districts were set up; bondage was eliminated; and education was taken away from the church and expanded beyond the confines of the capital city.

The administrations that followed did not continue Gallieni's policies. Public education was again confined to Tananarive. European companies drew enormous profits from their Madagascar operations, but reinvested little. In the 1920's a moderate nationalist movement demanded full French citizenship rights for the people, but the movement was suppressed.

After World War II, political and administrative reforms introduced by France were obstructed by the colonial administrators. Despite their interference, the popular Mouvement Démocratique de la Rénovation Malgache (MDRM) won 64 out of 92 provincial assembly seats in the 1946 elections. But by using the dual electoral college, which gave the few thousand Europeans on the island a vote almost equal to that of the millions of Malagasy people, the colonial administrators saw to it that MDRM would not profit by its victory at the polls.

Early the next year, a revolt broke out. War veterans led by men from the MDRM had united to protest the denial of the MDRM election victory. After a short struggle, the revolt was crushed. Casualty estimates ranged between 60,000 and 90,000.

The revolt had one healthy effect. Within a few years the old colonial administrators were gone, and the island was governed directly from Paris. A 10-year plan of new social and economic policies was started.

In 1958 the Malagasy voters approved a new constitution making Malagasy an autonomous republic within the French Community. The next year the Malagasy National Assembly elected Social Democrat Philibert Tsiranana president. The republic attained full independence on June 26, 1960. In 1965, Tsiranana won an overwhelming victory in the nation's first popular presidential election.

Malagasy remained in the French Community and joined the United Nations, the Organization of African Unity, and the Afro-Malagasy Union. It is an associate member of the European Economic Community.

MALARIA, mȧ-lâr′ĭ-ȧ, a disease of man characterized by periodic chills and fever, splenic enlargement, and anemia; due to infection with sporozoon parasites of the genus *Plasmodium,* transmitted by *Anopheles* mosquitoes. Females of at least 60 of some 200 species of *Anopheles* transmit human malaria. When they take malarious blood into their stomachs, certain male and female parasites in the blood, called gametocytes, are not digested, as they would be in other than anopheline mosquitoes, but the gametocytes mate and produce cysts which develop on the stomach wall. When these are ripe, they burst open and their seeds, called sporozoites, move into the salivary glands. This development within the mosquito, from gametocyte to sporozoite, lasts from 7 to 25 or more days, being slower at lower temperatures. After the parasites are in its glands, the insect, whenever it feeds, injects sporozoites into its victim's blood stream. Male mosquitoes cannot penetrate the skin and so are harmless.

In man the sporozoites invade the liver, where they develop and produce broods of young parasites which enter the blood stream and penetrate the red blood cells, that is, the erythrocytes. Here the parasites grow and then most of them split into segments called merozoites. A few become gametocytes. The parasitized cells disintegrate and the merozoites attack other erythrocytes. This cycle continues until checked by immunity, or treatment, or the patient's death. Death may result from severe anemia, from choking of capillaries of the brain or another vital organ by masses of parasites, or from excessive fever.

The periodic liberation of merozoites, parasite metabolic products (such as pigment), and red blood cell debris into the blood plasma upsets the body's heat-regulating mechanism, inducing typical paroxysms of shivering, fever, and sweating. These are timed by the development period of the infecting parasite. Species attacking man are: *Plasmodium vivax,* called the tertian parasite, its cycle about 48 hours, chills and fever coming typically every other day; *P. ovale,* a less common tertian parasite; *P. malariae,* the quartan parasite with a 72-hour cycle; and *P. falciparum,* the least regular, having either a daily or a tertian periodicity. The incubation period, from infection to first fever, averages 12 days in falciparum malaria, 14 days in vivax and ovale, 20 or more days in malariae. There are many other species of *Plasmodium,* infecting chiefly bats, birds, monkeys, and reptiles. Because the symptoms and the course of malaria are often atypical, positive diagnosis of malaria depends upon observing the parasites in blood smears examined microscopically.

Man has little natural immunity to malaria and there are no protective or curative serums or vaccines. But once the body has been invaded, strong defenses are aroused, so that the chances of recovery are excellent. Often not much immunity persists even after several attacks. Strong tolerance occurs only in those who from birth are exposed to repeated infections, for example, certain tropical Africans.

Treatment of the Disease.—For over 300 years, treatment of malaria depended on cinchona bark or quinine. But during World War II, the synthetic quinacrine hydrochloride (mepacrine hydrochloride, Atabrine) was widely used. By 1957, research had developed still better antimalarials, for instance, amodiaquin (Camoquin) and chloroquine diphosphate (Aralen). A total of 8 to 10 tablets of either drug, taken over a period of three days, is highly effective. For malaria prophylaxis, 2 tablets of amodiaquin or of chloroquine, or 25 milligrams of pyrimethamine (Daraprim) once a week, or 1 tablet daily of chlorguanide hydrochloride (Paludrine) are usually effective, if taken during exposure and for one to four weeks thereafter.

Prevalence and Control.—Malaria in the 19th century extended to the St. Lawrence River in North America, the northern Dvina River in Europe, and Lake Baikal in Asia; to Chile and Argentina in South America, the Umvoti River in Africa, and to about 30° S. in Australia. But by the 1960's, owing to natural causes and to control measures, malaria has retreated notably. North America north of Mexico, Jamaica, Trinidad and Tobago, Argentina, Guyana, French Guiana, Venezuela, Chile, Europe north of 43° N., Italy, Bulgaria, Cyprus, Taiwan (Republic of China), and Australia were practically nonmalarious. Unfortunately there are a number of areas where malaria is still a problem and annually there are many cases of the disease.

Ancient authors said swamp vapors caused intermittent fevers. In medieval Italy, people blamed bad air, *mala aria,* later *malaria.* The germ theory of disease led scientists to search for malaria parasites, which were found on Nov. 6, 1880, by Charles Louis Alphonse Laveran (1845–1922) in North Africa. Next, in 1894, Patrick Manson (1844–1922) published his belief that mosquitoes transmitted malaria. The first proof came on Aug. 20–21, 1897, when Ronald Ross (1857–1932) in India found malaria parasites of man growing as cysts on the stomach wall of *Anopheles* mosquitoes. Then, on July 4, 1898, Ross observed sporozoites of bird malaria in a *Culex* mosquito's salivary glands. These two discoveries explained malaria transmission. In November 1898, Italian scientists, Giuseppe Bastianelli (1862–1959), Amico Bignami (1862–1929), and Giovanni Battista Grassi (1854–1925), demonstrated sporozoites of human malaria in the salivary glands of *Anopheles* mosquitoes.

Since early Roman times, observers had noted that drainage sometimes controlled intermittent fevers. Ross provided an explanation, stimulating more widespread antimosquito drainage. Soon it became apparent that species of malaria mosquitoes differ greatly in habitats. For example, although eggs, larvae, and pupae of all anophelines are aquatic, not all are found in marshes; some prefer millponds, rice fields, hill streams, wells, puddles, or springs. So malaria control became more carefully focused and included not only drainage, but also killing the aquatic stages of vector anophelines with insecticidal oils and Paris green, and also screens and bednets, since *Anopheles* mosquitoes generally feed at night.

In the 1930's malaria control became more often an attack on adult anophelines, through the use of pyrethrum sprays. Then, in 1939, Paul Hermann Müller (1899–) in Switzerland discovered the insecticidal properties of DDT (q.v.).

DDT and similar insecticides, for example, BHC (1, 2, 3, 4, 5, 6-hexachlorocyclohexane) and Dieldrin, had the useful property of a long-lasting killing effect after being sprayed on surfaces. One or two sprayings might be effective for a year. So these residual insecticides, as they were called, did not need to contact mosquitoes at the time of spraying; when a susceptible insect stood on a sprayed surface, small particles of the poison would cling to its feet and be transferred to its body, with lethal effect. Since most female anophelines take blood every other night, resting before and after feeding on walls and ceilings, there was a good chance that, if their resting places were sprayed with insecticide, no mosquito could live long enough to germinate the sporozoites. Obviously, if a high percentage of malaria-carrying mosquitoes died before they could infect, then malaria transmission would be prevented. The parasites in man would thereafter gradually die out and malaria would disappear. Observations have indicated that malaria cannot sustain itself in a community in which, for three consecutive years, there has been no transmission of the disease by mosquitoes. So in practice, the residual insecticides have made eradication of malaria economically feasible in many countries.

By the mid-1960's, thanks largely to an anti-malaria campaign begun in 1955 by the UN World Health Organization (WHO), over 1.2 billion people lived in regions free or almost free from malaria. Besides WHO, the groups engaged in anti-malaria activities include the Pan-American Sanitary Bureau, the UN Children's Fund, and the U. S. International Cooperation Administration.

Malaria Bibliography

Boyd, Mark F., ed., *Malariology,* 2 vols. (Philadelphia: W.B. Saunders, 1949).
Kamm, Josephine, *Malaria Ross* (London: Methuen, 1963).
Macdonald, George, *Epidemiology and Control of Malaria* (New York: Oxford University Press, 1957).
Pampana, Emilio A., *Textbook of Malaria Eradication* (New York: Oxford University Press, 1963).
Russell, Paul F., *Malaria* (Springfield, Ill.: C.C. Thomas, 1952); *Man's Mastery of Malaria* (New York: Oxford University Press, 1955); "World-Wide Malaria Distribution, Prevalence, and Control," *American Journal of Tropical Medicine and Hygiene,* vol. 5, pp. 937–965 (Baltimore: 1956).
Russell, Paul F., and others, *Practical Malariology,* 2d ed. (New York: Oxford University Press, 1963).
Sandosham, A.A., *Malariology: with Special Reference to Malaya* (New York: Oxford University Press, 1959).

PAUL F. RUSSELL, M.D.,
Medical Consultant to the Malaria Committee, World Health Organization.

MALATYA, mä-lä-tyä′, city, Turkey, is the capital of the vilayet (province) of the same name. The city is located in east central Turkey, about 10 miles west of the Euphrates River and 112 miles northeast of Gaziantep. It is a railway junction and trade center for the surrounding farming region.

Malatya, known to the ancients as Melitene, was part of the kingdom of Cappadocia. It was the headquarters for the Roman 12th (Thundering) Legion after 70 A.D. and the capital of various Roman-controlled Armenian provinces after the early 300's. The city was taken by the Persians in 577. From the 600's to the 1100's it was ruled alternately by the Arabs and the Byzantines. Many ruined mosques remain from the Arab occupation. The Byzantines held the city from 934 until 1102, when it finally fell to the Turks. Malatya was rebuilt after 1893, when it was leveled by an earthquake. In 1895 it was the scene of a massacre of Armenians.

Malatya vilayet has an area of 4,761 square miles. The land is mountainous and generally not highly productive. Pop. (1960) of the city, 64,519; of the vilayet, 342,835.

MALAWI, mä-lä′wē, is a landlocked country in southeast Africa, about as large as the state of Pennsylvania. Formerly known as Nyasaland, it was part of the British-controlled Federation of Rhodesia and Nyasaland from 1953 through 1963. It is now an independent member state of the British Commonwealth of Nations.

Most of Malawi is a long, narrow strip of land, 50 to 100 miles wide, on the west shore of Lake Nyasa. Zambia borders this portion on the west, and Tanzania on the north. The rest of Malawi, south of Lakes Nyasa, is bordered on three sides by Mozambique.

Information Highlights

Form of Government: Republic.
Head of State: President.
Head of Government: President.
Legislature: National Assembly (one chamber).
Area: 46,066 square miles.
Population: (1964) 3,900,000.
Capital: Zomba.
Largest City: Blantyre-Limbe.
Official Language: English.
Major Religions: Tribal religions; Muslim, Roman Catholic.

The People. Of Malawi's population of nearly 4 million, almost all are Africans of Bantu stock. About 25,000 are Asians, Europeans, and Coloreds. It is difficult to count the African population accurately. At all times, as many as one third of the Malawi men are out of the country, working in Rhodesia or South Africa.

Some of the major African tribes in Malawi are the Anayanja, Ngoni, Awemba, Awa-Nkonde, Wakonde, Chewa, Tonga, and Yao. Old tribal ties are breaking down as Malawi becomes more closely knit as an independent nation.

The principal African language is Chinyanja. Others are Chiyao, Chitumbuka, Chitonga, and Kyangonde. Many people speak English. Swahili, the common language of East Africa, is gaining in usage.

Malawi's population density averages about 60 people per square mile. About half of all the people live in the Southern Province, where the density figure is as high as 800 to the square mile. The largest cities are Blantyre-Limbe, the chief commercial center; Zomba, the capital; Kota Kota; and Lilongwe.

The Land. Malawi has lakes and low valleys, plateaus and high mountains. The land is cut along its length by the Great Rift Valley, which extends through East Africa from the Gulf of Aden. Within the deep trough formed by the valley lies Lake Nyasa, third-largest lake in Africa. The lake is 355 miles long and over 50 miles wide at its broadest point. It goes as deep as 2,250 feet.

Nearly all of Malawi's rivers flow from the west into Lake Nyasa. However, the country's most important river, the Shire, flows from the southern tip of Lake Nyasa to join the Zambezi River in Mozambique.

The Nyika uplands in northern Malawi rise to about 8,000 feet above sea level. South of Lake Nyasa is Mount Mlanje, which reaches an altitude of nearly 10,000 feet. Malawi's lowest area is Port Herald, on the Shire River, about 100 feet above sea level.

Malawi's year has a wet season, October to April, in which 90 percent of the rain falls. However, heavy mists and light rains are common in the highlands in June and July. Rainfall ranges from 50 to 130 inches a year in the southern highlands and from 25 to 35 inches in the Shire Valley and near the lake. Snow sometimes falls on Mount Mlanje. At the other extreme, temperatures higher than 120° F have been recorded in the lower Shire Valley.

The Economy. Malawi is almost entirely an agricultural country. It raises barely enough for itself and exports only small quantities of tea, tobacco, cotton, corn, peanuts, and tung oil. It imports cotton manufactures, vehicles and parts, industrial machinery, petroleum, cement, electrical products, iron and steel manufactures, wheat, and sugar.

Before 1950, Malawi had few factories. Since then, small plants have been set up to assemble motors and to make bricks, soap, furniture, cement, blankets, and nails. The rivers offer good sources of hydroelectric power, but only a few hydroelectric generators are now at work.

Malawi has about 7,000 square miles of woodlands. Some of the better woods are Mlanje cedar, mahogany, African ebony, and eucalyptus. There is a little coal, and asbestos, bauxite, mica, corundum, gold, gypsum, and graphite deposits have been discovered.

History and Government. Little is known about what went on in the Malawi area before the 1850's. The Portuguese were the first Europeans to explore the region, but Portugal paid more attention to its colonies in Angola on the west coast of Africa and Mozambique, Malawi's neighbor, on the east coast.

The first European to make history in the area was the British missionary-scientist, David Livingstone. He entered from the east and reached the shores of Lake Nyasa on Sept. 16, 1859. He came at a time when the tribes were at war and many slaves were being taken. The wars and slave taking were encouraged by Arab slave traders in the area.

Livingstone's descriptions of the ravages of the slave trade spotlighted this obscure corner of Africa. Other missionaries soon came. Livingstone also attempted to attract European traders. Finally, in 1891, the British government established a protectorate over the area, which was given the name Nyasaland District. British officers led Sikh troops from India to wipe out the Arab slave trade.

Between World Wars I and II, several British commissions considered the possibility of joining together Northern Rhodesia, Southern Rhodesia, and Nyasaland. The possibility became a reality when the Federation of Rhodesia and Nyasaland was created in 1953. Under its constitution, Nyasaland was given 7 seats in the 35-member Federal Legislative Assembly.

Most Africans in Nyasaland were opposed to the formation of the federation. They did not like being associated with the white-dominated Rhodesias, and they looked forward to complete independence.

Independence was hastened when Hastings K. Banda returned to Nyasaland after an absence of 40 years. Born in Nyasaland in 1906, he received medical education in the United States, set up a practice in London, but always kept close touch with his homeland. Banda led the fight that resulted in Nyasaland's secession from the federation on Dec. 31, 1963. Under his leadership, the country, renamed Malawi, gained full independence on July 6, 1964, and became a republic in 1966.

MALAYSIA, mə-lā′zhə, is an independent country in Southeast Asia, about as large as the state of New Mexico. It was originally formed in 1963 by the merger of the former Federation of Malaya, the state of Singapore, and the former British colonies of North Borneo (now called Sabah) and Sarawak. But in 1965 the state of Singapore withdrew from the federation. Malaysia is a member of the Commonwealth of Nations.

Malaysia is made up of three separate parts. Malaya itself projects like a finger pointing south from the Indochinese peninsula into the South China Sea. More than 400 miles to the east of Malaya, along the north coast of the island of Borneo, are Sabah (formerly North Borneo) and Sarawak. Except for the British-controlled sultanate of Brunei, which lies between Sarawak and Sabah on the northwestern coast of the island, the remainder of Borneo is part of the Republic of Indonesia.

Kuala Lumpur, in Malaya, is the capital of Malaysia. Other important Malaysian cities are George Town, on Penang Island, Malaya; Ipoh, also in Malaya; Kuching, in Sarawak; and Jesselton, in Sabah.

Information Highlights

Official name: Federation of Malaysia.
Form of government: Constitutional monarchy; member of the Commonwealth of Nations.
Paramount Ruler: Sultan Ismail Nasiruddin Shah.
Prime Minister: Tunku Abdul Rahman Putra Al-Haj.
Parliament: House of Representatives and Senate.
Area: 128,318 square miles.
Population (1964 est.): 9,125,000 (excluding Singapore).
Capital: Kuala Lumpur, Malaya; population (1957) 316,230.
Official language: Malay.
Chief imports: food, petroleum products, crude rubber, machinery, transport equipment, metallic ores and scrap, and textiles.
Chief exports: rubber ($407,000,000), tin ($203,000,000), petroleum products, timber and lumber, and iron ore.
Value of trade (1963): imports, $828,000,000; exports, $884,000,000.

The People. Malaysia has a population of more than 9,000,000. About 85 percent of the people live in Malaya. Over half of the Malaysian people are under 20 years of age.

More than 35 percent of the people are of Malay origin. The Malays include people originally from Sumatra and Java, in Indonesia. Almost 35 percent of the people are of Chinese origin, and about 10 percent were originally from India or Pakistan. The rest, mainly in Sarawak and Sabah, belong to such tribes as the Dyaks.

Malay is the official language, but English is widely used in government, in business, and in the schools. Chinese also is widely spoken.

The official religion of Malaysia is Islam. The ruler of each Malaysian state is also automatically the head of the Islamic faith in that state. The Chinese follow their national faiths, and Malaysians from India are mainly Hindu. The people of Sabah and Sarawak have various tribal religions.

About 50 percent of the people of Malaya can read and write. Only about 25 percent of the people in Sabah and Sarawak are literate. The nation's education problem is complicated by the large number of people under the age of 20 and by the fact that separate school systems are needed for the different ethnic groups.

In comparison with other Asians, the people of Malaysia have a high standard of living. Per capita income varies widely by regions, but is highest in Malaya, where it totals about $270 a year. It is lowest in Sarawak, where per capita income averages less than $185 a year.

The Land. In Malaya, mountain ranges run from north to south down the center line of the peninsula. The highest peaks, Gunong Tahan and Gunong Korbu, both rising to more than 7,100 feet, are in the north. Thick forests grow on the mountains and in the surrounding lowlands. Most of Malaya's developed land is along the west coast. Several good seaports, the best farmlands, and the most productive mines are in this area, although much of the west coast is covered with swamps and mud flats. Almost 80 percent of Malaya is covered by jungle and swamp.

Both Sabah and Sarawak have swampy, alluvial coastal plains. Beyond its coastal plain, Sarawak has an area of rolling country which extends into a mountainous region. Three fourths of Sarawak is covered by tropical rain forest. Much of Sabah is also jungle, but along its west coast are fertile rubber and rice lands, where most of the people live.

Malaysia's climate is generally hot, humid, and rainy. Temperatures in Malaya average 74° F to 87° F throughout the year. Rainfall varies from 80 to 120 inches a year in the lowlands and up to 200 inches in the highlands. In Sabah and Sarawak rainfall is about the same, and temperatures are even higher.

The Economy. Malaysia relies heavily on the production and export of rubber and tin for its income. Other important exports are iron ore, vegetable oils, and timber. About 45 percent of all Malaysian products are exported.

Farming is the most important industry. Malaysia is the world's largest producer of natural rubber. Rubber makes up about 18 percent of the total national product and about 35 percent of total exports. About 20 percent of all Malaysia's workers are employed in rubber growing and processing.

Most of the rubber is grown on Malaya's western side. Large estates raise about 58 percent of the rubber harvest; small farms raise the rest. More and more estates are being split up into small farms.

Faced with increasing competition from synthetic rubber, the Malaysian government is financing improved rubber production. Old, low-producing trees are being replaced with a higher-yield kind that grows about 540 pounds per acre each year, three times as much as the old trees.

Rice is the second most important crop in Malaysia, but not enough is grown to satisfy all needs. Malaya grows about 80 percent of the rice it consumes, and Sabah and Sarawak must import about half their rice supply. Most of Malaysia's rice is grown on small farms.

Another major food crop is coconuts. Most of the Malaysian coconuts, however, are pressed into coconut oil for export. Palm oil is another important agricultural product.

The Malaysian people eat large quantities of fruit—bananas, durians, papayas, rambutans, and mangosteens. Pineapples are canned or crushed into canned juice. Pepper and other spices are important exports.

Forest reserves comprise about 26 percent of Malaysia's total land area. The government sets aside these areas in programs to conserve soil, to build reservoirs, and to develop timber resources.

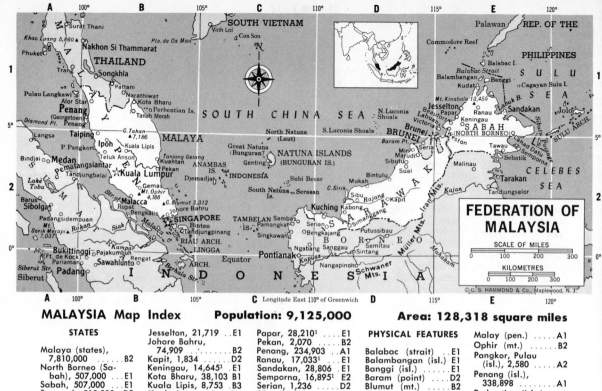

MALAYSIA Map Index Population: 9,125,000 Area: 128,318 square miles

Private companies can rent forest areas from the government for logging operations.

Cutting logs, sawing them into lumber, and making wood products make up one of Malaysia's big industries, ranking third after rubber and rice. Plywood is fabricated, and manufacturing plants turn out furniture, doors and window frames, flooring, and boxes and crates. *Meranti* and *Kuring* are leading export lumbers.

Hundreds of thousands of tons of fish are caught in Malaysian waters each year, but not enough to fill the people's needs. More fish must be imported. Small fishing craft that operated under sail are being replaced by powered boats.

Malaysia is the world's largest supplier of tin. About a third of the free world's tin comes from Malaysia. The most productive tin field in the world is the Kinta Valley in Perak, Malaya. In all, Malaya has more than 700 tin mines.

After rubber, tin is the second most important source of Malaysia's export earnings. The United States is Malaysia's best tin customer. Japan is second.

Malaysia is the largest iron ore producer in the Far East. Most of the ore is exported, but steel-making plants are being set up in Malaya. Most of the exported ore now goes to Japan. Other important Malaysian ores are bauxite (aluminum ore) and gold.

For many decades, processing rubber and tin for export was the most important manufacturing activity. Since becoming an independent nation,

Malaysia has striven to diversify its industrial output. Today consumer goods manufacturing is important—foods, vegetable oils, chemicals and drugs, building materials, wood products, tires, textiles, clothing. Other products of Malaysian industry are refined petroleum, rolled aluminum, and steel pipe. Sugar refineries and shipyards are being built.

The Malaysian government encourages new industries by offering such incentives as exemptions from taxes and import duties. It furnishes financial help in building new plants.

Transportation and Communications. Malaysia is linked to the rest of the world by a network of shipping lines and airlines. Malaya has good rail and highway services, particularly for carrying freight from inland supply sources to the seaports. In Sabah and Sarawak, most freight is carried by inland river vessels, although the road systems, particularly in Sabah, are being substantially improved. Coastal shipping moves cargo among the three parts of the federation.

Malaysia is equipped with modern communications systems. Telephones, radio telephones, and telegraph services are widely used. Radio broadcasts are made in several languages, including English, Malay, Tamil, and several Chinese dialects. Television is becoming increasingly popular.

Government. The government of Malaysia is modeled after that of Britain. It is a monarchy with a constitution and with a parliament elected by the people The constitution provides for a federal system of government.

The central government is headed by a prime minister chosen from the political party with the most seats in parliament. Parliament has two houses—a Senate and a House of Representatives. The House of Representatives, like the British House of Commons, is the more important of the two. Elections to the House of Representatives must be held at least every five years. Senators serve six-year terms. Their duties are similar to those of members of the British House of Lords. The Senate has 48 members, and the House of Representatives has 144 members.

Malaysia is made up of 13 states: the 11 states that formerly made up the Federation of Malaya (now usually called simply Malaya), and the former British colonies of North Borneo (now known as Sabah) and Sarawak. Each state has its own executive and legislature.

Of the 13 states, nine are governed by "hereditary rulers." The other four are administered by governors appointed by the central government. Elected state government officials are responsible to the state legislature. The ruler or governor appoints a chief minister, who is the leader of the party with the most seats in the state legislature.

The nine hereditary rulers elect one of their own number as paramount ruler (monarch) of all Malaysia. He acts as head of state in ceremonial functions. During his five-year term, his duties as head of his own state are carried out by a regent. When his term is up, he resumes as head of his own state. The paramount ruler, while largely a figurehead, serves as a symbol of unity among the 13 states of the federation.

Since 1957, when Malaya won its independence, the Alliance Party has been the majority party in the House of Representatives. It is a coalition of the parties representing the three most numerous groups—Malays, Chinese, and Indians. The present prime minister is Tunku (prince) Abdul Rahman Putra Al-Haj. He is a Malay.

History. Men have lived in Malaysia since very ancient times. The Niah caves in Sarawak show evidence of human life before 50,000 B.C. There were settled communities 2,000 years ago that traded with China, India, and other eastern lands.

The first Malay kingdoms may have been established north of the Malay Peninsula. These were Buddhist in religion. Another Buddhist Malay kingdom was later founded on the island of Sumatra, and by the 800's A.D. it ruled all of Malaya. Singapore was settled in the 1200's. During the same century Arab traders brought the religion of Islam to the Malay world.

For the next 300 years, three great religious and cultural forces competed in what is now Malaysia—Buddhism, Hinduism from India, and Islam. By the early 1500's a fourth rival joined in the struggle for control of the Malay world—European Christianity. In 1509 a Portuguese fleet reached Malacca, and in 1521 the Portuguese explorer Ferdinand Magellan arrived at Brunei on his globe-circling expedition for the king of Spain.

The Portuguese took control of the Malay lands, but lost out to the Dutch in 1641. In the second half of the 1700's the British East India Company entered the competition, to secure bases for its trade with China. A seesaw struggle for possession of the Malay area followed. The British gained a long-term foothold when Sir Stamford Raffles took possession of Singapore in 1819. In 1826, Penang, Malacca, and Singapore were formed into the British colony of the Straits Settlements.

The British brought much trade to the area. Immigrant Chinese workers developed the tin mines, and tax revenues increased. Yet piracy was rampant in the South China Sea, and the local rulers were constantly at war with one another. Violence was put down only when British resident governors were installed in several of the Malay states.

In 1840 an Englishman named James Brooke helped put down a revolt against the sultan of Brunei's viceroy in Sarawak. As a reward, the sultan appointed Brooke viceroy, or raja, of Sarawak. The United States recognized Sarawak as an independent country in 1850. Brooke continued to rule, and was succeeded by his nephew and then by the nephew's son. The Brooke family rule of Sarawak ended in 1946.

After the opening of the Suez Canal in 1869, Malay trade vastly increased. Rubber trees were brought to Malaya from Brazil in 1877. Tin mining expanded. Limited self-rule was gradually introduced in the area, through municipal committees and legislative councils.

Between World Wars I and II, Malaya and the Borneo territories suffered from the trade recession of the 1920's and the worldwide economic depression of the 1930's. Yet new roads and railways were built, and medical and educational services were expanded. Independence, however was little considered.

When World War II started in 1939, the rubber, tin, and oil of Malaya and Borneo helped the British. Japan entered the war in December 1941 and, by February 1942, had taken Malaya, Borneo, and Singapore. Under Japanese control, rubber and tin production stagnated, and the people suffered great hardships. At the same time, the dream of independence arose—freedom from wartime Japanese occupation and peacetime British rule.

World War II ended in 1945. When the Japanese withdrew, the jungle had taken over the rubber plantations, the tin mines were destroyed, and their mining equipment was sacked. With the war's end came a new threat—international communism. Like most of Southeast Asia, the Malay lands looked ready for communist take-over. The first step was to stir up labor unrest—strikes, arson, other types of violence and intimidation. The government declared a state of emergency.

The state of emergency did not end until 1960. During the dozen years of emergency rule the government took strong steps to put down the communist terrorists. It created a Home Guard force in each community. It gathered up the people living on the edges of the jungle and settled them in "strategic villages," adequately defended against the communist guerrillas. Despite the threats, the government kept up normal daily activities. Trains ran on time, shops stayed open, boys and girls went to school.

The progress against communism and toward economic self-sufficiency proceeded so well that the Federation of Malaya won independence in 1957. Soon Singapore, Sarawak, and North Borneo (now Sabah) were asking for their freedom and union with Malaya.

But a new threat arose. Indonesia's President Sukarno accused the British of "neo-colonialism," claiming that an independent Federation of Malaysia would be only a cover-up to maintain British influence in the area.

The new Federation of Malaysia came into being on Sept. 16, 1963. Indonesia remained hostile to the federation, and initiated a campaign to "crush Malaysia," landing guerrilla fighters within

Malaysia's boundaries. Continuing tension between the ruling Malays and the large Chinese population in Singapore resulted in Singapore's withdrawal from Malaysia in August 1965. Internal upheaval in Indonesia, beginning in late 1965, virtually eliminated the Indonesian military threat against Malaysia. On Aug. 11, 1966, Malaysia and Indonesia formally ended their difficulties by signing a peace agreement.

See also SINGAPORE.

MALCOLM, mal'kəm, is the name of four kings of Scotland. MALCOLM I MACDONALD (d. 954) succeeded to the throne in 943. He secured cession of Cumbria in 945 from Edmund I, king of the West Saxons. MALCOLM II MACKENNETH (d. 1034) came to the throne in 1005. During his reign Lothian and Strathclyde were secured to Scotland. MALCOLM III MACDUNCAN, surnamed CANMORE (d. near Alnwick, Northumberland, Nov. 13, 1093), was the son of Duncan I, who was slain in 1040 by Macbeth (Maelbaethe), mormaor of Moray. With the help of his uncle, Siward, earl of Northumberland, he defeated Macbeth in 1054 and killed him in 1057. He was crowned at Scone. His marriage in about 1067 to Margaret, sister of Edgar the Aetheling, Saxon pretender to the throne of England, provoked retaliation by William the Conqueror in 1072. From 1077 to 1080 he waged war against England, and in 1093 he invaded Northumbria. He was slain while laying siege to Alnwick. His reign had an important bearing on the consolidation of Scotland. Margaret, who died a few days later, was afterward canonized; she was largely responsible for the ecclesiastical reform effected in Scotland by her husband. MALCOLM IV, surnamed the MAIDEN (b. 1141; d. Jedburgh, Dec. 9, 1165), succeeded his grandfather, David I, in 1153. He suppressed two rebellions in Scotland, but in 1157 he was forced by Henry II of England to relinquish Northumberland and Cumberland.

MALCOLM X, American Negro leader: b. Omaha, Nebr., May 19, 1925; d. New York, N.Y., Feb. 21, 1965. Originally named Malcolm Little, he left school early and served time in prison. Early in the 1950's he joined the Black Muslims (q.v.) and in time became a chief lieutenant of Elijah Muhammad (q.v.), their leader. Dissension arose, however, and Malcolm was suspended in 1963. An eloquent and provocative speaker, he founded his own black nationalist movement, the Organization for Afro-American Unity, in 1964. Hostility between the two groups resulted in acts of violence, and Malcolm was shot to death as he addressed a rally. Three Negroes were convicted of his murder. *The Autobiography of Malcolm X* was published posthumously in 1965.

MALDEN, môl'dən, is a residential and manufacturing city in Massachusetts. It is in Middlesex County, on the Malden River, five miles north of Boston. The chief manufactures are shoes, clothing, and leather goods.

About 1640 the first settlers built homes along the Mystic River, of which the Malden is a branch, and called the place *Mystic Side*. In 1649, Malden became a separate municipality. It received a city charter in 1881. The city is governed by a mayor and a bicameral body composed of a board of aldermen and a city council. Population: 57,676.

MALDIVE ISLANDS, mal'dīv, are a chain of coral atolls in the Indian Ocean, southwest of Ceylon, that make up the independent sultanate of the Maldives. Their total area is 115 square miles. The capital is Male Island, in the northern part of Male Atoll, in the central part of the Maldives chain.

The economy is primarily agricultural. Coconuts, millet, and fruit are grown, but the islanders' basic food is rice, which is imported chiefly from Ceylon. Dried fish is exported.

The Maldives were ruled by a sultan for centuries. From 1887 to 1965 they were a British-protected state. They were a republic for a brief period in 1953, but the sultan was restored in 1954 and Britain continued to administer their foreign affairs. In 1965 the Maldives gained complete independence, but Britain retained an airbase and other facilities on Gan Island in Addu Atoll. Population: (1963 est.) 93,290.

MALEBRANCHE, mal-bräNsh', **Nicolas de,** French metaphysician: b. Paris, Aug. 6, 1638; d. there, Oct. 13, 1715. He was the youngest child of Nicolas de Malebranche, secretary to Louis XIII, and Catherine de Lauzon, sister of a viceroy of Canada. In 1660, after studying theology at the Sorbonne, he entered the Congregation of the Oratory. He ranks second only to René Descartes, greatest of French thinkers, in the history of French metaphysical speculation. The essence of his philosophy, which was founded upon that of Descartes, is a sort of mystical idealism. As set forth in Malebranche's brilliant work *Recherche de la vérité* (Search For the Truth), we have cognizance of things and objective realities as subjective thoughts and feelings, through the idea which resides in our souls. But this idea is in God, so that we perceive everything in God (*vision en Dieu*) as the primal cause of all existences and things. Hence the famous doctrine of Occasionalism or Interference, in accordance with which the objective thing and the subjective impression are made on every occasion to coincide, by the direct interposition of God, in whom alone we think and feel. In the history of philosophy, Malebranche may be regarded as the connecting link between Descartes and Spinoza. The difference between Malebranche's philosophy and that of the pantheist Spinoza is that to him the Universe was in God, and to Spinoza God was, in fact, in the Universe. See also CARTESIANISM; DESCARTES, RENÉ; FRANCE—23. *Science and Philosophy.*

MALENKOV, mäl-yen-kôf', **Georgi Maksimilianovich,** Russian political leader: b. Orenburg (now Chkalov), Russia, Jan. 8, 1902. Malenkov became premier of the USSR after the death of Joseph Stalin in 1953. He held that post until he was replaced by Nikolai Bulganin in February 1955. Malenkov was demoted to the position of minister of power stations. He held that office until 1957, when he was again demoted and made manager of the Ust-Kamenogorsk hydroelectric power station in northeast Kazakhstan.

MALESHERBES, mal-zerb', **Chrétien Guillaume de Lamoignon de,** French statesman: b. Paris, Dec. 6, 1721; d. there, April 22, 1794. He was educated in Paris and entered the legal profession. In 1745 he became counselor to the Parlement of France, and in 1750 he was made president of the Court of Aids in Paris and director of the press. His liberal policy in this last office made it possible for Denis Diderot to publish the *Encyclopédie* (1751–1772). Malesherbes opposed the dissolution of Parlement by Louis XV and was removed from office and exiled from Paris in 1771. On the accession of Louis XVI, he was recalled and made minister of the interior in 1775; but his support of Anne Robert Jacques Turgot's financial reform measures as well as his own memoranda on royal taxation forced his resignation in 1776. After this he spent some years in travel and writing. One of his essays was influential in bringing about the recognition of Protestant marriages by the civil authorities. In 1787 he returned to the ministry at the request of the king, but at the beginning of the revolution in 1789 he retired to private life. He subsequently acted as Louis XVI's counsel when the king was brought to trial before the National Convention in December 1792, was arrested himself shortly thereafter, and executed as a royalist.

MALET, mȧ-lĕ′, **Claude François de,** French army officer: b. Dôle, France, June 28, 1754; d. Paris, Oct. 29, 1812. Having entered the army at an early age, he became an ardent republican, and in 1790 was made a major in the National Guard at Dôle. Two years later he began serving in the armies of the Rhine and Italy as a battalion commander, attaining the rank of brigadier general in 1799. His hostility to Napoleon led him to take part in the unsuccessful conspiracy of 1808, as a result of which he was dismissed from the army and imprisoned. While Napoleon was away on his Russian campaign, Malet escaped from prison on Oct. 22, 1812, and released a number of his fellow conspirators. With counterfeit documents, he managed to convince military and police officials in Paris that Napoleon had been killed and that a provisional government had put him in command of the city. By this ruse he gained brief control of the government. His identity was discovered the following day, however, and he was brought to trial and executed.

MALEVICH, mŭ-lyā′vyĭch, **Kasimir (Severinovich),** Russian painter: b. Kiev, Russia, Feb. 11, 1878; d. Leningrad, 1935. In Moscow he began painting in the manner of the French postimpressionists about 1908. With the Jack of Diamonds group he exhibited cubist pictures in 1911, and the following year began to paint in the manner of Fernand Leger. He is famous for the creation of a style of geometric abstractionism which he called suprematism and which he initiated in 1913, showing a canvas with a perfect black square on a white background. In a manifesto published in 1915, he explained that the principal elements of suprematism were the circle, the square, and the triangle and that "the pure emotion" produced by the combination of geometrical shapes was for him the supreme essence of painting. He painted a number of suprematist compositions with variations of these shapes in clear colors on white backgrounds. An extreme of nonobjectivity was reached in 1919 when he painted a white square on a white background, entitled *Suprematist Composition: White on White* (Museum of Modern Art, New York City).

Malevich became an instructor at the National School of Applied Art in Moscow in 1919, but when modern art lost favor with the Soviet government, he was transferred to the Academy of Leningrad. An elaboration of his manifesto was published as *Die gegenstandlose Welt* (1927). With Piet Mondrian and Vasili Kandinski, he stands as a pioneer of abstract art.

Consult Barr, Alfred H., Jr., *Cubism and Abstract Art* (New York 1936); Haftmann, Werner, *Painting in the Twentieth Century* (New York 1960).

MALGACHE REPUBLIC. See MALAGASY REPUBLIC.

MALHERBE, mȧ-lĕrb, **François de,** French poet: b. Caen, France, 1555; d. Paris, Oct. 16, 1628. The scion of a family of magistrates of moderate means, he studied in Paris, Basel, and Heidelberg and then served as secretary to the governor of Provence, Henri, duke of Angoulême. During the earlier part of his life, he associated with the poets of the Renaissance Pléiade movement, and wrote as they did, rich, elegant, sonorous poetry. His best-known work of this period is *Les larmes de Saint Pierre* (1587). This time of his life was also a constant struggle to gain the favor of the king and achieve financial security. In 1605, he succeeded in becoming court poet to the king, then Henry IV, a post he kept until his death, under the regency of Marie de' Medici and under King Louis XIII. For about 23 years, all his ambitions seemed to have been fulfilled. He was respected and influential, many poets were his disciples, and he was a frequent guest at the literary salon of Madame de Rambouillet, where he helped to form the opinions and tastes of his time.

Gradually, Malherbe became increasingly critical of the writings of his former Pléiade friends, and he turned his efforts to purifying the French language and setting up rules to govern versification. Words of Italian origin, words lacking in "nobility," new coinings, especially when the French language already had an equivalent word, all these were to be rigorously banned. Poetry was submitted to a like discipline; rhymes were strengthened and a system of logic and clarity was imposed which left the poet much less scope.

Although Malherbe's later works, written according to these norms, have often been called stilted and lacking in true poetic inspiration, his better poems are admired for their great simplicity, purity, and precision of expression. The most famous are the *Consolation à M. Du Périer* (1599), a poem written for a friend on the death of his daughter; the *Sonnets à Caliste* (1609); and, above all, the beautiful *Paraphrase du Psaume CXLV* (*N'espérons plus, mon âme, aux promesses du monde;* 1628).

Malherbe's influence on the great writers of his generation was increasingly appreciated. The poet and critic Boileau (Nicolas Boileau-Despréaux) stated that French poetry began with Malherbe: *Enfin, Malherbe vint!* (At last, Malherbe came!). The classical literature of the years 1661–1685 owes much of its perfection of form to Malherbe.

Consult Brunot, Ferdinand, *La Doctrine de Malherbe* (Paris 1891); de Celles, J., *Malherbe* (Paris 1937); Cart, A., *La Poésie française du XVIIe Siècle* (Paris 1943); Lebègue, R., *Nouvelles études malherbiennes* (Paris 1947).

PIERRE BRODIN,
Director of Studies, Lycée Français de New-York.

MALI, mä′lē, is a landlocked country of West Africa that is about three times the size of California. Shaped like an hourglass, it extends southwest from the Sahara and links North Africa with the lands south of the Sahara. Mali is the largest of the former French West African territories. It has been an independent republic since 1960.

Mali is surrounded by seven other countries. To the north and west are Algeria and Mauritania; to the west and southwest, Senegal and Guinea; to the south and southeast, Ivory Coast and Upper Volta; and to the east, Niger.

Bamako, the capital, in the southwest, is the only sizable city. Other towns in the southwest are Kayes, Ségon, and Sikasso. Timbuktu is in central Mali, near the Niger River. Gao is farther down the river, to the east.

Information Highlights

Official name: Republic of Mali.
Area: 464,873 square miles.
Population: 4,832,000 (1968 est.).
Capital: Bamako (1965 population est., 165,000).
Major Languages: French (official) and tribal languages.
Principal Religion: Islam.
Weights and Measures: Metric system.
Flag: Green, yellow, and red vertical stripes. See also FLAG.

The People. About five sixths of Mali's total population are black tribesmen who live in the central and southern plains. Most of them are Mandingo, divided into several tribes. In the north, along the Sahara border, are the nomadic Moors and Tuareg, along with some Arab tribesmen. Living in the vast savanna country are the people called Fulah, or Fulani. Most of the Mali people are Muslims.

The population is very young. Only one person in 20 is over 60 years of age, and more than half are under 20. Mali has no common language of its own, so French is the official language of the country.

Only two or three out of every 100 people in Mali can read and write. About 10 percent of the school-age children go to school, but enrollment is increasing steadily.

The Land and Natural Resources. Most of Mali is a low plateau—the average elevation is less than 1,000 feet above sea level. The plateau is broken by sandstone heights in the south and by the Fouta Djallon mountain range near the Guinea boundary. The Niger River crosses Mali from west to east, dividing the desert region of the north from the savannas and plains of the south.

The north is hot and dry, averaging less than 10 inches of rainfall a year. Its frequent sand storms permit few animals or plants to live. South of the Niger River, the land is studded with green forests and abundant plant life. Humid monsoons blow in from the Atlantic Ocean. In the extreme southwest the annual rainfall is 40 inches. The Niger River yearly floods the surrounding plains, making this area a fertile farming region. The Mali government plans to harness the Niger River for hydroelectric power.

Mali's mineral resources, largely unexplored, may prove to be extensive. Initial surveys indicate large deposits of phosphates. Mali also has gold, bauxite, copper, zinc, tin, tungsten, and manganese. Salt is mined at Taoudeni, and small amounts of iron are mined near Kayes.

The Economy. The people living north of the Niger River depend mainly on cattle and other livestock for their livelihood. South of the river, most of the people are small farmers. They grow millet, rice, corn, manioc, yams, fonio, and other cereal crops. They eat most of what they grow themselves, and trade the rest for their few other necessities. Little cash changes hands in these transactions.

Some crops are raised for export—peanuts, almonds, cotton, and rubber. Surplus rice, cattle, and fish also are exported. They are sold in nearby countries such as Ghana and Ivory Coast. Manufacturing is limited to some small food-processing plants. The foods they process are sold in Mali.

Little more than half of Mali's 7,000 miles (12,000 km) of roads is usable throughout the year. A railroad links Bamako with Dakar (in Senegal), and Bamako has an international airport.

History and Government. The Republic of Mali is regarded as the modern re-creation of the medieval Mandingo Empire of Mali. This empire reached its height during the reign (1312–1337) of Mansa (King) Musa. After his death the empire was torn by civil wars and invasions. It began to decline as rival states were set up within its borders. The Mali Empire completely disintegrated in the 17th century. See also MALI EMPIRE.

French armies began to occupy the western Sudan in the late 1800's. In 1904 the territories of French West Africa were established, and the area roughly occupied by Mali today was called French Soudan. However, stiff resistance was put up by such warriors as El Hadj Omar and Samory Touré, and the last pockets of resistance were not wiped out until 1918.

In 1958 the country attained self-government as the Soudanese Republic within the newly formed French Community. Early in 1959 a short-lived union, called the Mali Federation, brought together the Soudanese Republic and Senegal. In June 1960 the Mali Federation withdrew from the French Community.

Only three months later, internal strife and a struggle for power brought the collapse of the Mali Federation. Finally, on Sept. 22, 1960, the Soudanese Republic proclaimed its independence, assuming the name Republic of Mali in commemoration of the old Mali Empire. A week later Mali was admitted as a member of the United Nations.

Mali's first president was Modibo Keita, who was secretary general of the governing party, the Union Soudanaise. The party's program was "African socialism and nationalism"—a combination of planned economy, financed by government and private funds, and freedom from any kind of European control. In 1962, Mali withdrew from the West African franc zone and issued its own currency, the Mali franc. However, economic conditions steadily worsened. In 1967 the government signed an agreement with France providing for Mali's progressive reentry into the West African franc zone.

The economy continued to decline, and on Nov. 19, 1968, President Keita and his government were overthrown in a bloodless coup by junior army officers. Lt. Moussa Traoré, who led the coup, became the head of a National Liberation Committee. A provisional government, responsible to the National Liberation Committee, was established with Capt. Yoro Diakhité as its head.

MALI EMPIRE, mä'lē, a rich and powerful West African state of the 13th to 15th centuries, created by the Mandingo (Mandinka), a people of the upper Niger Valley. The name Mali means "where the *mansa* (master, or king) resides," and therefore signifies a royal capital and the country ruled from it; Mandingo and Mandinka mean "people of Mali."

Early History. As the ancient kingdom of Ghana decayed after its defeat by the Almoravids of North Africa about 1076, many groups competed for its political and economic heritage. Ghana, whose territory corresponded to the western part of the present republic of Mali, had been the principal entrepôt for the profitable exchange of gold and slaves from the western Sudan in return for Saharan salt and North African products. Around 1235 victory went to the Keita, a southern Mandingo clan that had trading interests extending eastward along the Niger.

The Keita had an outstanding general, Sundiata, who established a powerful new monarchy incorporating ancient Ghana and its tributary states. This kingdom, Mali, extended its territory by conquering other Sudanic peoples, especially to the east down the Niger. The Niger provided essential communications for Mali and its trade, leading to the cities of Timbuktu and Gao, from which ran the shortest caravan routes to North Africa.

Gao, conquered by 1300, was also important as the capital of the Songhai, a river-dwelling people who controlled navigation on the Niger from Djenné to the borders of Hausaland. In the 14th century Mandingo merchants penetrated Hausaland, and Djenné became a base for the development of new trade routes southeast to the gold resources of Lobi and Ashanti.

Mali at Its Height. Mali reached its peak of prosperity and power under Mansas Musa (reigned 1312–1337) and Sulayman (reigned 1340–1360). Arabic writers depicted a well-ruled empire that extended 1,500 miles (2,400 km) from the Atlantic Ocean eastward to Hausaland, and from the edge of the forest northward into the Sahara. The ruling merchant and urban classes were Muslim. Mansa Musa's pilgrimage to Mecca in 1324–1325 was notable for its lavish display of wealth. Timbuktu and other cities were centers of Islamic scholarship and culture.

Mali commanded a wide network of trade and tribute throughout the western Sudan and dominated trade with North Africa. Its wealth was used to enforce law and order throughout the empire to the further enhancement of urban and commercial life. Mali's merchants were widely influential beyond its borders, promoting the economic growth of the Hausa cities and Islamizing their kings and merchants. Mali also influenced the political and economic development of Ashanti and the Gold Coast.

Mali's Decline. In the 15th century, competition for wealth and power among Mali's ruling factions sapped its military strength, which was needed to retain control of the subject peoples. The regaining of independence by the Songhai in the middle of the 15th century ended Mali's ascendancy. A remnant kingdom survived in the upper Niger Valley, but the eastern empire became the basis for a new and more extensive Songhai dominion.

J. D. FAGE
University of Birmingham, England

MALICIOUS MISCHIEF, ma-lish'ŭs, in law, a criminal offense: willful injury to or destruction of property with a malicious intent. Although the elements of the common-law crime of this designation are somewhat indefinite, the acts constituting it are now usually specified by statute. A wide variety of laws exist in different jurisdictions, applying to domestic animals, buildings, telephone wires, agricultural crops, and other kinds of real and personal property.

RICHARD L. HIRSHBERG

MALIK, ma'lēk, **Jacob** (Russ. JAKOV) **Aleksandrovich,** Soviet government official: b. Kharkov, Ukraine, 1906. Trained in economics at the Institute of People's Education in Kharkov, he graduated in 1937 from the Soviet Institute of Foreign Affairs at the University of Moscow and entered the Foreign Office. In 1939 he was assigned to the Soviet embassy in Tokyo, serving there as ambassador from 1942–1945. After two years in Moscow as deputy foreign minister for Far Eastern affairs, in 1948 he replaced Andrei Gromyko as permanent delegate to the United Nations, where he represented his government on the Security Council, the Atomic Energy Commission, and in the General Assembly. A somewhat less colorful figure than Gromyko, he nevertheless attracted a great deal of attention by his frequent use of the Soviet veto and bitter denunciations of the United States as the chief cause of world tension. Superseded at the United Nations in 1952, he was appointed ambassador to Great Britain, a post he held from 1953 to 1960. At the many international conferences where he represented the Soviet Union, he was regarded as a prominent Soviet spokesman, but not a policymaker.

MALLARD. See DUCK.

MALLARMÉ, ma-làr-mä', **Stéphane,** French symbolist poet: b. Paris, March 18, 1842; d. there, Sept. 9, 1898. His subtle, occasionally elusive verse is remarkable for its exquisite imagery, musical cadences, and for its evocative power.

Mallarmé became an English teacher in 1863 and continued in that profession until his retirement in 1893. He began writing poetry at an early age, although his first published poems appeared only in 1866 in the review *Parnasse contemporain.* In the 1860's also, he began work on *Hérodiade* (1871) and perhaps his most famous work, *L'Après-midi d'un faune* (1876), which inspired Debussy's tone poem (1894) of the same name. *Toast funèbre,* in memory of the author Théophile Gautier, appeared in 1873.

From the early 1880's until his death, Mallarmé was the center of a group of French writers in Paris, including Gide, Valéry, and Proust, to whom he communicated his ideas on poetry and art. Among his last major works were *Poésies* (1887) and *Vers et prose* (1893).

MALLOCK, măl'ŭk, **William Hurrell,** English author: b. near Crediton, Devonshire, England, Feb. 7, 1849; d. Wincanton, Somerset, April 2, 1923. Graduated from Balliol College, Oxford, he never entered a profession but devoted himself entirely to literary work. His philosophical and sociological writings include *Is Life Worth Living;* (1879); *Social Equality, a Study in a Missing Science* (1882); *Atheism and the*

Value of Life (1884) ; *Property and Progress* (1884) ; *Labour and the Popular Welfare* (1893) ; *Classes and Masses* (1896) ; *Aristocracy and Evolution* (1898) ; *Religion as a Credible Doctrine* (1902) ; *The Reconstruction of Belief* (1905) ; *The Nation as a Business Firm,* and *Social Reform* (1914). He also wrote several works of fiction, most of which deal with the same problems as the above works, including *The New Republic* (1877), in which he introduced many well-known contemporaries under thin disguises. Other works include his *Memoirs of Life and Literature* (1920).

MALLORCA, mä-[l]yôr′kä, or **MAJOR-CA,** mä-jôr′kä, island, Spain, largest of the Balearic Islands, in the Mediterranean Sea, about 115 miles from the Spanish coast, 1,405 square miles in area. It is irregular in shape and deeply indented, especially in the northeast. The climate is so mild that the Catalan painter and writer Santiago Rusiñol y Prats (1861–1931) called it a "lotusland where men are never in a hurry, women never grow old." The scenery is highly varied. Along the northwest coast is a mountain ridge, which reaches 4,741 feet in Puig Mayor. In the east, near Manacor, are the famous Cuevas del Drach (Caves of the Dragon) with their remarkable underground lakes. Farther to the north, near Artá, are other caves with beautiful stalactite and stalagmite formations.

Mallorca, like the rest of the Balearic Islands, was seized successively by the Phoenicians, Carthaginians, Romans, Vandals, Byzantines, and, in 797, by the Moors, from whom it was recaptured in 1229 by James I the Conqueror, king of Aragon. The island has limestone and marble quarries ; lead, iron, and coal are also mined. In the valleys, on terraced, irrigated slopes, are olive groves with trees twisted into grotesque shapes, and rich orchards of figs, oranges, lemons, and almonds. The importance of the harvest is shown by the variegated dance festivals the country people celebrate, such as the *pelades de ametles* (dance of the almond pickers), the *mateixa de figueral* (dance of the fig harvest) in August, and the *canción de la almazara* (song of the oil miller who presses the olives). Mallorca has a very ancient tradition of folk dances such as the *copeo* and the *mateixa,* which some consider of Moorish origin.

Other important industries on the island are fishing, wine and brandy making, jewelry, ceramics, embroidery, and various agricultural processing enterprises.

The capital is Palma (q.v.), one of the loveliest cities in Mediterranean Spain. Other urban centers, besides those mentioned previously, are Inca, Pollensa, Soller, and La Puebla.

Mallorca has always been the paradise of philosophers, poets, and musicians, who gather at Miramar, on the coast about 11 miles north of Palma. Here, in the last quarter of the 13th century, Raymond Lully (Ramón Lull), greatest of native Mallorcans, founded a Franciscan school of Arabic and Chaldean studies. A famous episode in the modern history of the island was the romance of Frédéric Chopin and George Sand who spent the winter of 1838–1839 at the former Carthusian monastery in Valldemosa. Pop. (1950) 375,227.

See also BALEARIC ISLANDS.

WALTER STARKIE,
Author of "The Road to Santiago."

MALLOW, măl′ō, popular name of plants of the genus *Malva,* family Malvaceae, including annuals, biennials, and perennials. There are about 30 species native to Europe, northern Africa, and Asia, several of which have been naturalized in North America. The rose or white flowers, generally large, are found solitary or clustered in the axils of the leaves, with the numerous stamens united in a hollow staminal column around the several pistils. The lobed or divided leaves possess demulcent and emollient properties, a characteristic from which the name mallow is derived.

The musk mallow (*M. moschata*), with its large, showy, white- to rose-colored flowers, and the curled mallow (*M. crispa*), with its attractively curled leaves, are frequently cultivated in gardens.

Some related genera in the mallow family are poppy mallow (*Callirhoë*), tree mallow (*Lavatera*), marsh mallow (*Althaea*), and rose mallow (*Hibiscus*). Indian mallow (*Abutilon Theophrasti*) supplies a coarse fiber with the characteristics of jute.

FRANK G. LIER.

MALMÖ, mäl′mû, city, Sweden, seat of Malmöhus County (Län), located near Sweden's southwest tip on the Öresund, 16 miles east-southeast from Copenhagen, Denmark. A large seaport and naval base, Malmö is also a center of rail and air transportation, its airport being located at the suburb of Bulltofta. It is a busy industrial city as well, with sugar refineries, textile mills, machine shops, and chemical works. Malmö possesses canals and other interesting relics of its historic past, including Malmöhus Castle (begun 1434, rebuilt 1542), now a museum. This was the stronghold where Bothwell, husband of Mary, Queen of Scots, was imprisoned from 1567 to 1573, after his escape from Scotland.

Founded in the 12th century as a Danish possession, Malmö's present charter dates from 1353. It became an important herring-fishing port, and in 1658 was annexed to Sweden as part of the region of Skåne (Scania). The development of its harbor and port facilities was begun in 1775. Pop. (1958) 245,027.

MALNUTRITION, măl-nû-trĭsh′ŭn, a condition occurring in man and animals in which there is a lack of required fats, carbohydrates, minerals, proteins, and vitamins in the diet. Such a situation is found in people in depressed socio-economic conditions ; in those adhering to dietary fads, chronic alcoholism, and drug addiction ; and in psychiatric patients, including the senile. In addition, there are many chronic disease processes which involve malnutrition, among them nephritis, colitis, diabetes mellitus, sprue, tuberculosis, and chronic liver disease. Of these, sprue is of particular interest because it appears to be a self-perpetuating dietary deficiency involving a macrocytic anemia, sore tongue, chronic intestinal disturbance, and fatty stools.

Accepted clinical standards indicate that the normal adult needs 1,400 to 1,800 calories daily, of which the protein source should be one gram per kilogram of body weight. Fat is necessary but should not exceed 25 per cent of the calorie intake to avoid the danger of arteriosclerosis. Carbohydrates provide the remaining calories.

Vitamin deficiencies occur when adequate daily intake is impaired. To avoid beriberi or polyneuritis, 1.5 mg. (milligrams) of thiamine (B_1) is recommended, and similarly 1.8 mg. of ribo-flavin (B_2) safeguards against black tongue or pellagra. Niacin (B_3) should be present, at least in the amount of 15.0 mg. daily. Scurvy, or the scorbutic state, follows the loss of ascorbic acid (vitamin C) from dietary intake to levels below 75.0 mg. daily. A deficiency of the fat-soluble vitamins A, D, and K produce, respectively, night blindness, rickets, and hemorrhagic disease. Mineral requirements of potassium, sodium, mag-nesium, calcium, phosphorus, and iron must be carefully checked to avoid depletion. All these minerals participate in the maintenance of elec-trolyte and fluid balance in the individual.

See also NUTRITION OF MAN; VITAMINS.

REAUMUR S. DONNALLY, M.D.

MALONE, mȧ-lōn', **Edmund** or **Edmond,** Irish Shakespeare scholar: b. Dublin, Ireland, Oct. 4, 1741; d. London, England, April 25, 1812. After practicing law, he settled in London (1777) as a literary scholar and critic. He was the first of the great Shakespeare textual scholars to use modern methods of research, and his *Attempt to Ascertain the Order in Which the Plays Attri-buted to Shakespeare Were Written* (1778) was the first authoritative study of the chronology of the plays. He published an 11-volume edition of Shakespeare in 1790 and left material for a 21-volume variorum edition, published in 1821. In 1782 he was the first to detect the false antiquity of Thomas Chatterton's "Rowley" poems, and in 1796 exposed William Henry Ireland's Shake-speare forgeries. The *Life of Johnson* (1791) by James Boswell owed much to Malone's editorial assistance.

MALONE, village, New York, seat of Franklin County in northern New York, on the Salmon River 30 miles east-southeast of Massena at an altitude of 755 feet. The village is served by the New York Central Railroad, Colonial Air-lines, and state and federal highways. The center of an agricultural area, it ships vegetables, grain, and dairy products; and its location at the edge of the northern Adirondack foothills makes it a pleasant summer resort. Manufactures include aluminum and bronze powder, shoes, men's cloth-ing,.concrete blocks, lumber, paper, and cheese.

Settled about 1800, the village was named for Edmund Malone, the Irish Shakespeare scholar. It was incorporated in 1833, and in 1866 and 1870 was used by the Fenians (q.v.) as a base for their unsuccessful raids on Canada. It is governed by a mayor and council. Pop. (1960) 8,737.

MALORY, măl'ô-rĭ, SIR **Thomas,** English author of the famous compendium of Arthurian legends, *Le Morte Darthur;* d. March 12, 1471.[1] Since the end of the 19th century, he has been convincingly identified with the Sir Thomas Mal-ory of Newbold Revell, an estate in Warwick-shire, and Winwick in Northamptonshire; but most of the facts of his life have been brought to light only in the last few decades. The date of his birth is unknown, but he succeeded to his father's estates in 1433 or 1434. He was, accord-ing to (Sir) William Dugdale's *Antiquities of Warwickshire* (1656), in the retinue of Richard Beauchamp, earl of Warwick, at Calais, in the time of Henry V, presumably in 1415; but since

[1] The date March 12 has been established by modern research. March 14 is given on Malory's tombstone.

Dugdale speaks of a siege of Calais and there was no siege at this time, some have supposed that the reference should be to the time of Henry VI, when (in 1436) Calais was threatened with siege. The date is of interest chiefly for the light it might throw on Malory's age.

In the Parliament of 1445, Malory represented Warwickshire, but he seems already to have had a brush with the law. In 1443, Malory and one Eustace Burneby were charged by Thomas Smythe of Northhamptonshire with assault and the carrying off of goods and chattels. What be-came of the charge is not known. While such incidents were not uncommon in this turbulent period, later events show that Malory was not the most peaceable of citizens. In an inquisition at Nuneaton he was charged with a series of of-fenses. It was claimed that in January 1450, along with 26 other armed malefactors, he lay in ambush in the woods near his Newbold estate for the purpose of murdering Humphrey, duke of Buck-ingham. Other charges included a cattle raid, extortion, and threats to the prior and convent at Axholme. While in custody at Coleshill, he had escaped from prison by swimming across the moat, and the following two days, with a large number of followers, twice broke into Coombe Abbey, threatened the abbot and monks, and carried off plunder.

How much of this melancholy tale is to be ac-cepted at face value it is impossible to say. To all of these charges Malory pleaded not guilty. In any case he spent most of the next 10 years in various prisons, and in the last of the judicial records so far found (1460), he is committed to the sheriff of Middlesex in the prison at Newgate, London. How long he remained in custody thereafter we do not know. He was twice excluded from general pardons in 1468, probably for political reasons. At the close of *Le Morte Darthur,* which Malory tells us was completed in the year ending March 3, 1470 (the 9th year of the reign of Edward IV), he begs the reader to "pray for me while I am on live [alive] that God send me good deliverance." From this and two similar references within the work, and from the fact that upon his death he was buried in a chapel at the nearby Grey Friars, we must conclude that he probably spent most of his later life in prison. There can be little doubt that *Le Morte Darthur* (published by William Caxton in 1485), a book which has delighted many generations of readers, was the product of his enforced leisure.

See also MORTE DARTHUR, LE.

Consult Kittredge, George Lyman, "Who Was Sir Thomas Malory?" in (Harvard) *Studies and Notes in Philology and Literature,* vol. 5, pp. 85–106 (Cambridge, Mass., 1896); Hicks, Edward, *Sir Thomas Malory: His Turbulent Career* (Cambridge, Mass., 1928); Vinaver, Eugène, *Malory* (Oxford, 1929); Baugh, Albert C., "Documenting Sir Thomas Malory," *Speculum,* vol. 8, pp. 3–29 (Cambridge, Mass., 1933).

ALBERT C. BAUGH,
Professor of English Language and Literature, University of Pennsylvania.

MALPIGHI, mäl-pē'gê, **Marcello,** Italian anatomist: b. Crevalcuore, Italy, March 10, 1628; d. Rome, Nov. 29, 1694. He received a medical education in Bologna and was granted a doctor's degree in 1653. In 1656 he became professor of medicine at Pisa, where he formed a friendship with the mathematician Borelli, who encouraged him to proceed with researches in anatomy. His health failing he returned to Bologna and continued his investigations, which resulted in discoveries which established facts undisputed in the modern world of science and placed the world's knowledge of physiology on a new footing; his researches in botany and entomology were highly important. In 1691 he was summoned to Rome as first physician to Innocent XII, in which office he died.

He published numerous scientific works of great value, a complete edition of which was published in Venice 1743. The principal of these are *Observationes anatomicae* (1661) and *Epistolae anatomicae* (1665).

MALPLAQUET, Battle of, măl-plà-kā′, the bloodiest engagement in the war of the Spanish Succession. It took place Sept. 11, 1709, between the allied forces under the command of the Duke of Marlborough and Prince Eugène of Austria and the French under Claude de Villars. Allied casualties were over 20,000 almost double the French and so excessive that the victory over the French was indecisive. Malplaquet is a village in northern France, the Department of the Nord, near the Belgian border. See also SUCCESSION WARS.

MALRAUX, màl-rō′, **André,** French novelist and man of action. Born Nov. 3, 1901 in Paris, he studied at the École des Langues Orientales and left in 1923 for French Indochina where he became interested in Khmer archaeology. His difficulties with the colonial administration over valuable statues illegally brought back from the jungle, as well as his later activity on behalf of the incipient Indochinese independence movement, earned him an adventurer's dubious repute. His first important work, *La tentation de l'Occident* (1926), is a rather stilted but stimulating parallel between Eastern and Western culture. His first novel, *Les conquérants* (1928; Eng. tr., *The Conquerors,* 1929), deals with a revolutionary strike and its European organizers in Canton; the second, *La voie royale* (1930; Eng. tr., *The Royal Way,* 1935), is a tale of adventure and archaeology in the Indochinese jungle. Next came Malraux's most famous novel, for which he received the Prix Goncourt, *La condition humaine* (1933; Eng. tr., *Man's Fate,* 1936), whose heroes are involved in a Communist uprising in Shanghai and in the party's later annihilation at the hands of former ally Chiang Kai-shek. Autobiographical elements are undoubtedly present but the real story of Malraux's Far Eastern experiences is not well known.

During the 1930's, the novelist backed many antifascist and leftist causes. In 1935, he published *Le temps du mépris* (Eng. tr., *Days of Wrath,* 1936) in which Nazi police brutalities are evoked. During the Spanish civil war, he played a commanding role in the Air Force of the International Brigades, then wrote *L'espoir* (1937; Eng. tr., *Man's Hope,* 1938), a vast fresco of Republican Spain in combat, which he made into a film the following year. During World War II Malraux fought on the French front in 1940. Wounded and taken prisoner, he escaped and joined the Resistance movement where once again he was wounded, taken prisoner and a second time escaped his German captors.

Malraux emerged from the underground a warm supporter of General de Gaulle, and in 1945 served briefly as minister of information. In 1958, when de Gaulle returned to power Malraux, becoming one of his closest collaborators, was entrusted with cultural affairs. During the interval between these two cabinet posts, he had published some monumental essays on the plastic arts, notably, *Les voix du silence* (1951; Eng. tr., *The Voices of Silence,* 1953), which first appeared in a less complete version between 1947 and 1949 as *La psychologie de l'art.* The central idea is that of the "imaginary museum" or confrontation of all works of art, past and present, which our historical knowledge both makes possible and demands. Relativism and nihilism must be experienced and transcended in a quasi-mystical realization of man's esthetic creativity. These essays have been attacked by professional art historians but they undoubtedly express, in their exacerbated individualism, an essential aspect of contemporary sensibility. They bring to the fore some obsessive themes which already underlie the novels and they reveal the latter as transfiguration rather than as factual accounts of experience, as was formerly believed. In all these novels, Western and bourgeois civilization appears almost as a form of prejudice, or as a "sin" from which the heroes try to purge themselves, through violence and blood, in order to reach the tragic truth of the "human condition" and a really universal vision.

Malraux is a Nietzschean for whom nihilism must be faced squarely in order to be surmounted, but the negative aspects of his work are more striking and powerful than his attempt at a positive conclusion. His passion for the exotic and the primitive, his predilection for the most intense sensations, his slightly theatrical individualism, and the increasing flamboyance of his style stamp him as the heir of Châteaubriand and Maurice Barrès; he is the creator of a latter-day romanticism suited to the spirit of our time.

Consult Picon, Gaëtan, *André Malraux* (Paris 1946); Frohock, W.M., *André Malraux and the Tragic Imagination* (Stanford, Calif., 1952).

RENÉ GIRARD,
Johns Hopkins University.

MALT AND MALTING. See BREWING AND MALTING

MALTA, môl′ta, is an island country in the Mediterranean Sea, about 60 miles south of Sicily. Formerly a British colony, it became an independent nation in the British Commonwealth in 1964. Malta consists of the islands of Malta (95 square miles) and Gozo (26 square miles), and several islets. The capital, Valletta, is on the island of Malta.

Most of the people are Roman Catholics. Their language, Maltese, belongs to the Semitic family. English is also widely spoken. Population (1963) 326,000.

Economy.—As Britain's chief Mediterranean naval base, Malta depended heavily on military spending. When independence was negotiated, Britain agreed to supply $140 million in aid for 10 years, and was to retain its military bases on the islands for the same period. For the future, Malta looked to greater tourist trade as a source of income.

Agriculture is important, but production is generally insufficient for the islanders' needs and is achieved with difficulty, due to the thin, porous layer of calcareous soil which covers Malta's limestone foundations. Terracing is practiced on a large scale. Moisture, too, constitutes a problem, as there are no rivers; but rain falls, especially in winter, and many springs and subterranean basins are found. In summer, the hot, dust-laden sirocco blows from the Libyan deserts, but otherwise the climate is mild. Products grown are wheat, potatoes, beans, onions, cotton, oranges, grapes, and cumin seeds. The islanders also raise livestock and manufacture lace, buttons, gloves, hosiery. and textiles.

History and Government.—At the time of Christ, Malta was a Roman possession. St. Paul is thought to have been shipwrecked here, in St. Paul's Bay, in 58 A.D. The Arabs seized the island in 870. From 1090 to 1530 it was attached to Sicily. Then Emperor Charles V bestowed it on the Knights Hospitalers of St. John of Jerusalem who performed great feats of arms in defending it against Moslem assaults and won for their order the title of Knights of St. John of Malta. The famous siege (1565), in which troops under Grand Master Jean de La Valette estimated at from 6,000 to 9,000 men repulsed in a four-month campaign 29,000 or more Turks, earned the order imperishable glory. Six years later the Knights participated in the victory of Lepanto. Napoleon seized Malta in 1798 and his forces were blockaded here by the British fleet. At the request of the inhabitants Malta was made a British protectorate and finally annexed by the Treaty of Paris (1814).

Malta became a vital British naval base because it commanded the trade lifeline between England and India through the Mediterranean. It was heavily bombed during World War II.

In 1947 Malta gained internal self-rule and established a 40-member legislature elected by universal suffrage. The Maltese, however, wanted independence or complete integration with the United Kingdom. After riots occurred in 1958, self-government was suspended from 1959 to 1962. The country became fully independent on Sept. 21, 1964.

The form of government is a constitutional monarchy, with Britain's monarch as head of state. The country has a 50-member elected legislature. G. Borg Olivier, a conservative, became the first prime minister.

MALTA, Knights of. See St. John of Jerusalem, Knights of the Order of the Hospital of.

MALTE-BRUN, màl-tĕ-brŭn', **Conrad** (original name Malte Conrad Brunn), Danish geographer: b. Thisted, Denmark, Aug. 12, 1775; d. Paris, France, Dec. 14, 1826. He devoted himself to literature and politics in Copenhagen, but having given offense by writing in favor of the liberty of the press and the enfranchisement of the peasants, was banished to Sweden in 1800. He went later to Paris, where he became famous as a geographer. He edited the foreign political department of the *Journal des debats,* but is best known for his *Précis de géographie universelle* (8 vols., 1810–29). The first six volumes only were completed by Malte-Brun. Another important undertaking of his was the publication of the series *Annales des voyages, de la géographie et de l'histoire* (24 vòls., 1808–14).

MALTESE CROSS. See Crosses and Crucifixes—*Heraldic Crosses.*

Combine Photos

Overlooking the waterfront of Valletta, Malta's capital.

MALTHUS, măl'thŭs, **Thomas Robert,** English political economist: b. near Guildford, Surrey, England, Feb. 14, 1766; d. Bath, Dec. 29, 1834. He studied theology at Cambridge and was ordained in the Church of England, continuing to pursue his profession as a teacher while holding a small living in Surrey. In 1805 he was appointed professor of history and political economy at Haileybury College. In his famous *Essay on the Principles of Population* he propounded (1798) what is known as the Malthusian Doctrine, namely, that the increase of population advances at a geometrical, the increase of the means of life at an arithmetical, ratio; that this condition of things renders the condition of the poor more and more hopeless; that unless famine or war interfere to diminish population the means of life will eventually prove inadequate; that discouragement of early and improvident marriages and the cultivation of self-restraint must be employed to avert the danger. These positions have been the subject of long and widespread discussion. His other writings include *An Inquiry into the Nature and Progress of Rent* (1815); *Principles of Political Economy* (1826); *Definitions in Political Economy* (1827).

See also Economics—*Classical Economics* (Thomas Robert Malthus); Social Reform Programs and Movements—*Remedies Proposed to Solve the Problems of the Industrial Revolution.*

Consult Bonar, J., *Malthus and His Work,* 2d ed. (London 1924); Keynes, J. M., "Robert Malthus" in *Essays in Biography* (New York 1933).

MALUS, mà-lŭs', **Étienne Louis,** French physicist and military engineer: b. Paris, France, June 23, 1775; d. there, Feb. 23, 1812. He was educated at the École Polytechnique, and upon leaving the school received a captain's commission in the corps of engineers, and served during the campaign of 1797 with the army of the Sambre and Meuse. Subsequently he participated in the campaign in Egypt, and in 1804 superintended the construction of fortifications at Antwerp and Strasbourg. Whatever time could be spared from his professional labors was devoted to scientific pursuits. Malus discovered the polarization of light, which finding he first published in his essay *Sur une propriété de la lumièrè réfléchie par les corps diaphanes* (*On a Property of Light Reflected from Transparent Bodies,* 1809). Malus' other scientific works include the mathematical essay *Traité d'optique analytique* (*Treatise on Analytical Optics*), published in 1810, and *Théorie de la double réfraction de la lumière dans les substances cristallines* (*Theory of the Double Refraction of Light in Crystalline Substances*), published in 1811, which won him election (1810) to the Académie des Sciences.

MALVACEAE, măl-vā'sê-ē, the mallow family of flowering plants with 40 to 50 genera and 1,000 to 1,500 species in temperate and tropical countries. Representatives of the family are economically important sources of fiber; it also includes ornamental and a few food plants.

The plants are herbs, shrubs, and trees with alternate, simple, usually palmately lobed leaves. The flowers are regular, almost always bisexual, chiefly five-parted, and white, red, yellow, or purple in color. The family is sharply characterized by the tubular column which results from the fusion of the stamens around the pistil. The two- to many-celled superior ovary forms a fruit which may be a capsule, achene, or follicle, or sometimes is berrylike. Mucilaginous sap is characteristic of many members. The pollen grains are usually large and spiny.

The mallow family includes the following well-known plants: mallow (*Malva*), hollyhock (*Althaea rosea*), flowering maple (*Abutilon*), cotton (*Gossypium*), okra (*Hibiscus esculentus*), and rose of Sharon (*H. syriacus*). See also separate articles on the above.

FRANK G. LIER.

MALVAN, town, India, in Maharashtra State, on the Arabian Sea, 200 miles south of Bombay and 50 miles north of Goa. It is a port and fish-curing center, and also produces coconuts and coconut products. It was a stronghold of the Marathas (q.v.) in the 18th century. Pop. (1951) 29,851.

MALVERN, măl'vẽrn, city, Arkansas, Hot Spring County seat, located 17 miles southeast of Hot Springs, on the Chicago, Rock Island & Pacific, and the Missouri Pacific railroads, at an altitude of 312 feet. It is in a timber, mining, and farming area producing lumber, cotton, corn, sweet potatoes, clays, barite, titanium ore, and marble. Malvern has a metal plant, two foundries, a shoe factory, and wood products mills. Incorporated as a city in 1876, it has a mayor-council form of government. Pop. 9,566.

MALVERN, môl'vẽrn, city, Australia, in the State of Victoria. It is a residential suburb, southeast of Melbourne, on Port Phillip Bay. Pop. (1954) 46,953.

MALVERN, urban district, England, in Worcestershire, 5 miles west of the Severn near the Welsh border, and 7 miles southwest of Worcester. The name covers a group of small villages in an area of 12 square miles on the east side of the Malvern Hills, a lovely scenic region. Chief of the villages is Great Malvern, which has notable mineral spas and is the site of Malvern College (public school, founded 1863), and of a 15th century priory church incorporating an 11th century Norman nave. Other villages are Malvern Link, to the north, with asbestos, asphalt, and chemical plants; Malvern Wells, southwest, also a spa; and Little (or West) and North Malvern, residential suburbs. Little Malvern contains the remains of a 12th century Benedictine priory. Since 1928, an annual Malvern dramatic festival has honored George Bernard Shaw. Great Malvern is the burial place of Jenny Lind. Pop. (1961) 24,373.

MALVERN HILL, Battle of, măl'vẽrn, in the American Civil War, an engagement fought on July 1, 1862, on the south bank of the James River in Virginia, 18 miles southeast of Richmond, during the Peninsula Campaign of 1862 (q.v.). After failing to take Richmond from the sea, Union general George B. McClellan, commanding the Army of the Potomac, fell back to the shore of the James. He was constantly harassed by the pursuing Confederates in a series of sharp engagements (see SEVEN DAYS' BATTLES), of which Malvern Hill was the last. In this battle, the Northern forces successfully stood off a series of spirited Southern assaults.

The Union Army was drawn up on top of Malvern Hill—an elevated open plateau—with both its flanks resting on the James and protected by gunboats. The approach to the Union position was over 400 to 500 yards of open uphill terrain, commanded by Northern artillery. When the pursuing Confederates, including divisions commanded by Maj. Gens. Thomas J. (Stonewall) Jackson and Daniel Harvey Hill, came in sight of Malvern Hill, they felt out the Union strength in minor skirmishes. Upon the arrival of Maj. Gen. John B. Magruder with additional troops about 2 P.M., two Southern brigades with four mounted batteries were at once ordered up the hill. The batteries were promptly knocked to pieces, as they emerged from sheltering woods, by the fire of over 60 Union guns, and the attack was quashed.

This assault had fallen on the far left of the Union line, where units commanded by Brig. Gens. Fitz-John Porter and Darius N. Couch conjoined. At 5:30 P.M., this sector was again assailed by Magruder with the reorganized elements of the first two brigades plus three fresh ones. These, too, were mowed down as they came up the hill. Three more brigades thrown in after them were similarly chewed up.

On Magruder's left, D. H. Hill, with five Confederate brigades, was having no better luck in an assault on Couch's right. His troops withered under Union fire on the uphill slope. Half an hour later, two Confederate brigades under Brig. Gens. Paul J. Semmes and Joseph B. Kershaw unsuccessfully assaulted Porter at the point where Magruder had already failed. Fighting ebbed as twilight fell, but it was 9 P.M. before the firing ceased and quiet settled on the bloody field.

Sixteen Confederate brigades had been repulsed by nine Northern brigades heavily supported by artillery. The Confederate loss was over 5,500 killed, wounded, and missing. Union casualties were less than 2,000.

MALVERNE, măl′vẽrn, village, New York, in Nassau County, Long Island. It is located 8 miles southeast of the Jamaica area of the Borough of Queens, New York City, on the Long Island Rail Road, at an altitude of· from 21 to 37 feet. Malverne is a nonindustrial home-owning suburb of New York City in the midst of·a truck farming region. Hempstead Lake State Park borders it on the south. Malverne was settled about 1790, and was originally called Norwood, but the name was changed in 1913 in honor of Malvern, England. The final *e* was added by mistake in the railroad timetable, and has been kept ever since. Malverne was incorporated as a village in 1921, and has a mayor-council form of government. Pop. 9,968.

MALVEZZI, mäl-vät′tsẽ, **Cristofano,** Italian composer and musical editor: b. Lucca, Italy, July 27, 1547; d. Florence, Dec. 25, 1597. *Maestro di cappella* (choirmaster) to the grand duke of Tuscany from 1571, he is best known for his edition (1591) of a group of dramatic intermezzi for voices and instruments (chiefly lutes and viols) by himself and others, which foreshadowed later dramatic music. The intermezzi were composed for the wedding of Malvezzi's patron, Grand Duke Ferdinand I, in 1589.

MALVOLIO, măl-vō′lĭ-ō, in William Shakespeare's comedy *Twelfth Night* (q.v.), the steward of Countess Olivia. He is represented as a ridiculously conceited, self-righteous person, roundly disliked by everyone in her household. To make a laughingstock of him, Sir Toby Belch, Sir Andrew Aguecheek, and Maria forge a love letter, purportedly from Olivia, bidding him dress and act in an outlandish fashion to show that he returns her love.

MALVY, màl-vẽ′, **Louis Jean,** French political leader: b. Figeac, France, Dec. 1, 1875; d. Paris, June 9, 1949. First elected to the Chamber of Deputies in 1906 as a Radical Socialist, Malvy held several lesser cabinet posts before becoming minister of the interior under Premier René Viviani in June 1914. He served continuously in that capacity during World War I until 1917 when, savagely attacked as a defeatist by Georges Clemenceau, he was forced to resign (August 31). The Senate, sitting as a high court, acquitted him (Aug. 6, 1918) of charges of corresponding with the enemy and treason, but found him guilty of culpable negligence and banished him for five years, which he spent in Spain. Returning to France, he was re-elected deputy (1924) and served briefly (1926) as interior minister under Premier Aristide Briand. In World War II, he voted (July 10, 1940) with rightist deputies at Vichy to abolish the republican constitution, and was expelled from the Radical Socialist Party after France's liberation.

MALWA, mäl′wä, tableland, India, northeast of Bombay, in the west central part of the country, extending north of the Vindhya Mountains and south to the Narbada River valley. Under British rule, it comprised some 25 feudatory states, which in 1950, when the Republic of India was proclaimed, were united in the State of Madhya Bharat (from 1956 included in Madhya Pradesh). The site of ancient Hindu states from at least the 6th century B.C., Malwa was annexed by the Mogul Empire in 1561, liberated by the Hindu Marathas (q.v.) in the 18th century, and conquered by the British in 1817. It is a fertile agricultural area, drained by many rivers; cereals, cotton, and poppy are grown.

MALYNES or **MALINES** or **DE MALINES,** dě mă-lēn′, **Gerard,** English merchant and writer on economics: b. Antwerp, Belgium; fl. 1586–1641. Member of an Anglo-Flemish commercial family, he became a wealthy merchant and held various government economic posts under Elizabeth I and James I. During the latter's reign he took part in several business ventures to develop English natural resources, such as lead and silver mines. These failed, as did another scheme in which Malynes had an interest, to mint farthing tokens under private auspices; the latter failure landed him in prison for debt (1619) for a short time. In 1622, he advocated a system of government-controlled pawnshops to protect the poor from usurers.

Malynes' writings are still of value to economic historians. He was an exponent of mercantilism with its state-controlled foreign trade, but his works show some intimation of the natural-law theories that later developed into laissez-faire capitalist economics. Chief among his writings is *Consuetudo vel lex mercatoria, or the Ancient Law Merchant* (1622).

MAMADYSH, mŭm-à-dĭsh′, city, USSR, in the Tatar Autonomous Republic of the Russian SFSR. It is located on the Vyatka River, about 75 miles east·of Kazan, near the European slope of the Ural Mountains. The city is noted for its distilleries, and has metal and woodworking plants. It was developed under the czars as a copper-smelting center in the 1740's, and given an imperial charter by Catherine the Great in 1781. Pop. (1936 est.) 7,200.

MAMAEA, mă-mē′à, **Julia,** mother of Roman emperor Marcus Aurelius Alexander Severus (q.v.): b. Emesa (now Homs), Syria; d. near Mainz, Germany, 235 A.D. She was the second daughter of the matriarch Julia Maesa, sister-in-law of Emperor Lucius Septimius ·Severus (r. 193–211 A.D.). Mamaea's husband was Gessius Marcianus. She was a competent, virtuous woman who largely dominated the reign (222–235) of her son. Working through Alexander, she improved the·efficiency and honesty of the imperial administration and stimulated a revival of religion, but antagonized the European legions by favoring the Asiatics. In Gaul to repel a German invasion, Mamaea and her son offered to purchase peace from the enemy. The outraged legions mutinied and murdered the emperor and his mother.

MAMARONECK, mă-măr′ô-nĕk, village, New York, in Westchester County, located on Long Island Sound, at an altitude of 50 feet, 20 miles northeast by rail from Grand Central Station in New York City. It lies between the village of Larchmont to the southwest and the city of Rye to the northeast, and is served by the New York, New Haven and Hartford Railroad. A residential suburb of New York City, it also has light industries which manufacture aircraft equipment, asbestos packing, chemicals, dental plates, food products, machinery, motorboats, perfume oils, raincoats, and wood and metal products.

The village's name is Indian, and is variously said to mean "He assembles the people" and "Where the salt water meets the fresh." Settled after 1660, the village was incorporated in 1895. J. Fenimore Cooper made his home here for some years. It has a mayor and council, and a village manager. Pop. 17,673.

MAMBA, măm′bä, a venomous African tropical snake, the *Dendraspis angusticeps,* which grows to 14 feet, also called the tree cobra. Olive green to black, it has no hood.

MAMBAJAO, măm-bä′hou, municipality, Philippine Islands, in Misamis Oriental Province, situated on the northwestern coast of Camiguin Island, which lies off the northeast coast of Mindanao Pop. (1960) 15,433.

MAMBER, măm′běr, a widely diffused colloquial name for the common wild goat (*Capra aegagrus*) of southwestern Asia.

MAMBUSAO, măm-boo′sou, municipality, Philippine Islands, in the Province of Capiz, island of Panay, on the west tributary of the Panay River, opposite Ibajay and 17 miles southwest of Capiz, the provincial capital. Pop. (1960) 19,516.

MAMELUKES, măm′ĕ-lūks (from the Arabic *mamlūk,* a slave), in Egypt, slaves from the Caucasian countries, who from menial offices were advanced to dignities of state.

In the 13th century the Seljuk Turks, whose greatest chief had been the Sultan Saladin, were masters of Egypt and western Asia. It was a Turkish custom to carry off boys from conquered territories as slaves, and to train them as military bodyguards for the sultans.

Such a bodyguard of white slaves, or Mamelukes, was formed in Egypt. The Mamelukes became an invaluable fighting force; their leaders were taken from their own ranks and in 1250 their commander Kotuz (Mozaffar Saif aldin) overturned the government, and made himself sultan of Egypt. Ten years later, another Mameluke captain, Bibars (Baybars I, 1233–1277) slew Kotuz and seized the sultanate. From this time the Mamelukes were masters of Egypt, and successive Mameluke sultans ruled until the conquest of the Ottoman Turks in 1517.

The series of Mameluke rulers is divided into two groups, the Turkish (Bahri, 1250–1390) and the Circassian (Burji, 1390–1517). The succession of each sultan was usually secured by the violent death of his predecessor. Lesser Mameluke chiefs ruled the provinces under a kind of feudal system.

The Mameluke sultans were, on the whole, able rulers, and raised Egypt to great prosperity. They were also patrons of literature, architecture, and other arts. After the Ottoman conquest, Egypt was officially placed under a Turkish pasha, but practically under Mameluke beys, who controlled the several provinces. They formed a fine body of cavalry, and attacked the French with the greatest fury when they landed in Egypt; but they were unable to withstand the European artillery, and many of them soon joined the French. The pasha of Egypt, Mehemet Ali, destroyed the Mameluke beys, March 1, 1811, by a perfidious stratagem, and immediately afterward ordered a general massacre of the Mamelukes in every province of Egypt. Some hundreds managed to escape into Lower Nubia, where they built a small town, and endeavored to keep up their force by disciplining Negroes in their peculiar tactics. They did not succeed, however, and shortly afterward dispersed. See also EGYPT—*History.*

MAMEY or **MAMMEE APPLE.** See MAMMEE APPLE.

MAMEY SAPOTA, măm′ē sà-pō′tà, a large tree (*Calocarpum mammosum*) of the family Sapotaceae, native of tropical America. The leaves are large, obovate, glabrous; the flowers small and inconspicuous; and the fruit globose or egg-shaped, rusty brown, and three to seven inches long, with a single large seed. The fruit is very popular in the tropics, especially in Cuba, and is sometimes shipped to the United States. It is eaten fresh, or used for sherbets or marmalade. The tree is grown in Florida and California, but so far not very successfully.

MAMMALIA. See MAMMALS.

MAMMALS. The mammals are warm-blooded backboned animals, nourishing their young with milk produced by the mammary glands. They possess a self-regulatory system tending to develop a relatively high and stable body temperature despite external variation. Such control has permitted the occupation of areas of extreme cold, where cold-blooded vertebrates cannot survive. Temperature regulation is, however, relatively poor in the more primitive mammals, such as monotremes and sloths. Foremost factor in the thermoregulatory system is the presence of an insulating hairy coat (suppressed in some aquatic mammals) and a richly glandular skin. Here are sebaceous (oil) glands serving to lubricate skin and hair and conserve body heat and sudoriferous (sweat) glands acting to cool the surfaces and lower the body temperature. A four-chambered heart with the circuit to the lungs efficiently separated from the systemic circulation and a muscular diaphragm providing forced air draught to the lungs are other key mammalian characters associated with efficient heat control. There are four functional limbs in all mammals except the whales and sirenians, in which mammals the rear pair are secondarily lost. Mammals, except for the egg-laying monotremes, are born alive. It is a character of the class that the period for care of the young is progressively extended. This is in part coupled with the dependence of the young on maternal nourishment, and in part owing to the need for lengthened instructional processes. In size the mammals range from minute mice and shrews, weighing less than a dime, to whales weighing 150 tons and measuring 115 feet in length.

Ancestry.—The mammals had their origin among the therapsid reptiles of the Permian and Triassic, a group having no modern representatives. These reptiles are best known from the rich deposits of their bones in the Karroo beds of South Africa. They developed representatives increasingly efficient in running which more and more abandoned the reptilian bent-leg, flaring-elbow, manner of walking, in favor of an opening-up of the angles of the elbows and knees, and an alignment of the planes of movement of the limbs with that of the direction of motion. The Cynodontia and Ictidosauria groups of therapsid reptiles represented in the South African Triassic, developed far toward the pattern of the mammals. They show a progressive regional specialization of the teeth, and the dental roots, as in the mammals, lie in sockets. The occipital condyle, which is a single process in most reptiles, is transversely spread to furnish double articulation with the broadened first vertebra, the atlas. A secondary bony palate is formed, foreshadowing the almost complete separation of air and food passages of the mammals. The single pair of temporal openings in the skull which characterize the Therapsida, in the cynodonts, migrate towards the top of the skull and their convergence produces a sagittal crest as is typical for so many mammals. The cynodont reptiles seem to have had the prerequisite characters of ancestors of the insectivorous mammals of the Jurassic.

Classification.—The living mammals may be divided into two divergent lines: the Prototheria, or egg-laying mammals, and the Theria, or live-bearing mammals. A third group, the Allotheria, is known only by a fossil order, the Multituberculata of the Jurassic, Cretaceous, Paleocene, and Eocene beds. The Theria are composed of 12 orders of extinct mammals and 17 orders represented by animals yet living. These larger groups are subdivided into families, genera, and species. Over 900 genera of living mammals and almost 3,000 living and extinct are recognized today. Approximately 4,500 species are living in our time.

The classification is built for the greater part upon the analysis of structural characters and their combinations, which, with the evidence from the fossil record and from geographic distribution, give a basis for an arrangement which indicates in part the relationship of groups of common origin. The system of classification undergoes constant refinement as knowledge expands. That which follows is abstracted from the classification set up by George G. Simpson. In it subordinal group names are given only for the living mammals and among these the superfamilies and all subfamily groups are omitted except as they may be indicated by vernacular names. Quotation marks embracing some of the vernacular names (a few of which do not follow Simpson) indicate that the name falsely implies relationship, as in the marsupial "mole." The surname following each scientific name is that of the individual who first established the name. Such designation is a necessity for clarity because subsequent writers have occasionally used the identical name for a different group of animals. (Extinct subordinal groups are omitted. A dagger (†) indicates extinct groups. The smallest units given are families.)

Class MAMMALIA Linnaeus.
  Subclass PROTOTHERIA Gill.
    Order MONOTREMATA Bonaparte. Monotremes
      Tachyglossidae Gill. Spiny-anteaters or echidnas.
      Ornithorhynchidae Burnett. Duckbill or platypus.
  †Subclass ALLOTHERIA Marsh.
    †Order MULTITUBERCULATA Cope.
  Subclass THERIA Parker and Haswell. Viviparous mammals.
    †Infraclass PANTOTHERIA Simpson.
      †Order PANTOTHERIA Marsh.
      †Order SYMMETRODONTA Simpson.
    Infraclass METATHERIA Huxley.
      Order MARSUPIALIA Illiger. Marsupials.
        Didelphidae Gray. Opossums.

Dasyuridae Waterhouse. Pouched "mice," native "cats," Tasmanian devil, Tasmanian "wolf," etc.
Notoryctidae Ogilby. Marsupial "mole."
Peramelidae Waterhouse. Bandicoots.
Caenolestidae Trouessart.
Phalangeridae Thomas. Phalangers, koala, etc.
Phascolomidae Bonaparte. Wombats.
Macropodidae Owen. Kangaroos, wallabies.
  Infraclass EUTHERIA Gill. Placental mammals.
    Cohort UNGUICULATA Linnaeus.
      Order INSECTIVORA Bowdich. Insectivores.
        Solenodontidae Dobson. Alamiqui.
        Tenrecidae Gray. Tenrecs.
        Potamogalidae Allman. African otter-shrew.
        Chrysochloridae Mivart. Cape golden-mole.
        Erinaceidae Bonaparte. Hedgehogs.
        Macroscelididae Mivart. Elephant-shrews.
        Soricidae Gray. Shrews.
        Talpidae Gray. Moles, shrew-moles, desmans, etc.
      Order DERMOPTERA Illiger.
        Cynocephalidae Simpson. Colugo or "flying lemur."
      Order CHIROPTERA Blumenbach. Bats.
        Suborder MEGACHIROPTERA Dobson. Fruit bats.
          Pteropidae Gray. Flying "foxes," etc.
        Suborder MICROCHIROPTERA Dobson.
          Rhinopomatidae Dobson. Mouse-tailed bats.
          Emballonuridae Dobson. Sheath-tailed bats, proboscis bats, etc.
          Noctilionidae Gray. Hare-lipped bat, mastiff bat.
          Nycteridae Dobson. Hispid bats, etc.
          Megadermatidae Allen. False vampires, etc.
          Rhinolophidae Bell. Horseshoe bats.
          Hipposideridae Miller. Old World leaf-nosed bats, etc.
          Phyllostomatidae Coues and Yarrow. New World leaf-nosed bats, etc.
          Desmodontidae Gill. Vampires.
          Natalidae Miller. Tall-crowned bats, etc.
          Furipteridae Miller. Furies.
          Thyropteridae Miller. Disk-winged bats, etc.
          Myzopodidae Thomas. Sucker-footed bats.
          Vespertilionidae Gray. Brown bats, etc.
          Mystacinidae Simpson. New Zealand short-tailed bats.
          Molossidae Gill. Free-tailed bats, mastiff bats, etc.
      Order PRIMATES Linnaeus.
        Suborder PROSIMII Illiger.
          Infraorder LEMURIFORMES Gregory.
            Tupaiidae Mivart. Tree-shrews.
            Lemuridae Gray. Lemurs.
            Indridae Burnett. Sifakas, indris, avahis.
            Daubentoniidae Gray. Aye-aye.
          Infraorder LORISIFORMES Gregory.
            Lorisidae Gregory. Lorises, pottos, galagos.
          Infraorder TARSIIFORMES Gregory.
            Tarsiidae Gill. Tarsier.
        Suborder ANTHROPOIDEA Mivart.
          Cebidae Swainson. Most American monkeys.
          Callithricidae Thomas. Marmosets.
          Cercopithecidae Gray. Old World monkeys.
          Pongidae Elliot. Apes.
          Hominidae Gray. Men.
      †Order TILLODONTIA Marsh.
      †Order TAENIODONTA Cope.
      Order EDENTATA Cuvier. Edentates.
        Suborder XENARTHRA Cope.
          Infraorder PILOSA Flower.
            Myrmecophagidae Bonaparte. Anteaters.
            Bradypodidae Bonaparte. Tree sloths.
          Infraorder CINGULATA Illiger.
            Dasypodidae Bonaparte. Armadillos.
      Order PHOLIDOTA Weber. Pangolins.
        Manidae Gray. Pangolins.
    Cohort GLIRES Linnaeus.
      Order LAGOMORPHA Brandt. Pikas, rabbits, hares.
        Ochotonidae Thomas. Pikas.
        Leporidae Gray. Hares and rabbits.
      Order RODENTIA Bowdich. Rodents.
        Suborder SCIUROMORPHA Brandt.
          Aplodontidae Trouessart. Sewellel.
          Sciuridae Gray. Squirrels.
          Geomyidae Gill. Pocket gophers.
          Heteromyidae Allen and Chapman. Pocket mice, kangaroo rats, spiny mice.
          Casteridae Gray. Beavers.
        ?SCIUROMORPHA *incertae sedis:*
          Anomaluridae Gill. Scaly-tailed "squirrels."
          Pedetidae Owen. Spring haas.

Suborder MYOMORPHA Brandt. Rats, mice, etc.
  Cricetidae Rochebrune.
  Spalacidae Gray. Mole-rats.
  Rhizomyidae Miller and Gidley. Bamboo
    rats.
  Muridae Gray. Rats, mice.
  Gliridae Thomas. Dormice.
  Platacanthomyidae Miller and Gidley. Spiny
    dormice.
  Seleviniidae Argyropulo and Vinogradov.
  Zapodidae Coues. Jumping mice.
  Dipodidae Waterhouse. Jerboas.
Suborder HYSTRICOMORPHA Brandt.
  Hystricidae Burnett. Old World porcupines.
  Erethizontidae Thomas. New World porcu-
    pines.
  Caviidae Waterhouse. Cavies, etc.
  Hydrochoeridae Gill. Capybara.
  Dinomyidae Alston. Long-tailed paca.
  Dasyproctidae Smith. Lowland pacas.
  Chinchillidae Bennett. Vizcacha, chinchilla,
    etc.
  Capromyidae Smith. Hutia, coypu.
  Octodontidae Waterhouse. Degu, etc.
  Ctenomyidae Tate. Tucu tucu.
  Abrocomidae Miller and Gidley. Rat-chin-
    chilla.
  Echimyidae Miller and Gidley. Spiny rats.
  Thryonomyidae Pocock. Cane rat.
  Petromyidae Tullberg. Rock rat.
?HYSTRICOMORPHA incertae sedis:
  Bathyergidae Waterhouse. Blesmol, etc.
?HYSTRICOMORPHA or ?MYOMORPHA incertae
    sedis:
  Ctenodactylidae Zittel. Gundis.
Cohort MUTICA Linnaeus.
  Order CETACEA Brisson. Whales.
    Suborder ODONTOCETI Flower. Toothed whales.
      Platanistidae Gray. River dolphins.
      Ziphiidae Gray. Beaked whales.
      Physeteridae Gray. Sperm whales.
      Monodontidae Gray. White whale, narwhal.
      Delphinidae Gray. Long-beaked dolphin,
        porpoise, killer whale, etc.
      Phocaenidae Bravard. Porpoises.
    Suborder MYSTICETI Flower. Whalebone
      whales.
      Rhachianectidae Weber. Gray whale.
      Balaenopteridae Gray. Finback, hump-
        backed whale, sulphur-bottom whale, etc.
      Balaenidae Gray. Right whales.
Cohort FERUNGULATA Simpson.
  Superorder FERAE Linnaeus.
    Order CARNIVORA Bowdich.
      Suborder FISSIPEDA Blumenbach.
        Canidae Gray. Dogs, wolves, foxes, etc.
        Ursidae Gray. Bears.
        Procyonidae Bonaparte. Raccoon, coati,
          kinkajou, panda, etc.
        Mustelidae Swainson. Weasels, wolver-
          ine, badgers, skunks, otters, etc.
        Viverridae Gray. Genet, civet, mongooses.
        Hyaenidae Gray. Hyenas.
        Felidae Gray. Cats.
      Suborder PINNIPEDIA Illiger.
        Otariidae Gill. Eared seals.
        Odobenidae Allen. Walrus.
        Phocidae Gray. True seals.
  Superorder PROTUNGULATA Weber.
    †Order CONDYLARTHRA Cope.
    †Order LITOPTERNA Ameghino.
    †Order NOTOUNGULATA Roth.
    †Order ASTRAPOTHERIA Lydekker.
    Order TUBULIDENTATA Huxley.
      Orycteropodidae Bonaparte. Aardvark.
  Superorder PAENUNGULATA Simpson.
    †Order PANTODONTA Cope.
    †Order DINOCERATA Marsh.
    †Order PYROTHERIA Ameghino.
    Order PROBOSCIDEA Illiger. Elephants.
      Suborder ELEPHANTOIDEA Osborn.
        Elephantidae Gray.
    †Order EMBRITHOPODA Andrews.
    Order HYRACOIDEA Huxley.
      Procaviidae Thomas. Hyraxes.
    Order SIRENIA Illiger.
      Suborder TRICHECHIFORMES Hay.
        Dugongidae Gray. Dugongs.
        Trichechidae Gill. Manatees.
  Superorder MESAXONIA Marsh.
    Order PERISSODACTYLA Owen.
      Suborder HIPPOMORPHA Wood. Horses,
        †brontotheres, †chalicotheres, etc.
        Equidae Gray. Horses, asses, zebras.
      Suborder CERATOMORPHA Wood.
        Tapiridae Burnett. Tapirs.
        Rhinocerotidae Owen. Rhinoceroses.
  Superorder PARAXONIA Marsh.

Order ARTIODACTYLA Owen.
  Suborder SUIFORMES Jaeckel.
    Infraorder SUINA Gray.
      Suidae Gray. Hogs.
      Tayassuidae Palmer. Peccaries.
    Infraorder ANCODONTA Matthew.
      Hippopotamidae Gray. Hippopotami.
  Suborder TYLOPODA Illiger.
    Camelidae Gray. Camels.
  Suborder RUMINANTIA Scopoli.
    Infraorder TRAGULINA Flower.
      Tragulidae Milne-Edwards. Chevrotain.
    Infraorder PECORA Linnaeus.
      Cervidae Gray. Deer.
      Giraffidae Gray. Okapi, giraffe.
      Antilocapridae Gray. Pronghorn.
      Bovidae Gray. Cattle, antelopes, sheep,
        goats.

Structure of Mammals.—The generalized
body form of primitive mammals may be roughly
exemplified by the common opossum of North
America, a species capable of terrestrial locomotion, tree climbing, and limited digging. Depar-
tures from such a generalized type may be illustrated by citing such extremes as the bat, whale,
elephant, mole, kangaroo, and sloth. With specialization to varied modes of life as exemplified
by these there are also profound changes in the
organs and organ systems of the mammals. The
range of these is partly indicated in the outline
which follows.

Skeleton.—The mammal skeleton is composed
of a skull, a vertebral column specialized into
neck, thoracic, lumbar, sacral, and tail regions,
a cage of ribs protecting the lung and heart region, pectoral and pelvic girdles, and four limbs.

The spinal column functions to protect the
spinal cord which it houses and to serve as the
basis for longitudinal rigidity. A typical vertebra
is composed of a solid body, the centrum, and
above it a bony arch forming a neural canal.
Processes serve for articulation with ribs and
other vertebrae and to provide point of origin
and insertion of the muscles. The number of
cervical (neck) vertebrae in mammals is remarkably constant and, with the exception of
the manatees and sloths, there are always seven.
The manatees have six cervicals, the sloths six,
eight, or nine. In such neckless or short-necked
forms as the whales and certain leaping and burrowing mammals, some of the cervicals may be
fused but their number is constant. In the giraffe
the number also remains seven. There are generally 17 to 24 vertebrae in the trunk region, but
even within one species the number of ribs is subject to some variation and there is no pronounced
pattern in ratio of thoracic to lumbar vertebrae.
The sacral vertebrae, to which the pelvic girdle
attaches, number one to three, and these are
usually fused as are additional vertebrae, the
pseudosacral, which do not articulate with the
girdle. The caudal vertebrae tend to be unimportant among mammals. In number they vary from
3 in man to 49 in such long-tailed forms as the
pangolins. These tail vertebrae assume greatest
importance in whales and some other aquatic
mammals, and in kangaroos where their role as
a tripod leg is important. In the African hero-
shrew, the trunk vertebrae are firmly knit with
accessory processes to form a strong arch of unknown significance. In the pocket mice (*Perog-
nathus*), the tail vertebrae have transverse planes
of weakness along which the vertebrae may
easily break if an enemy seizes the tail.

The ribs vary greatly in number between
groups. They function chiefly to protect the
heart and lungs but when moved also assist in
breathing. In the manatees the ribs become

massive and heavy in association with aquatic habits. In all mammals there is a sternum that is in part cartilaginous. The anterior ribs are attached to the sternum by costal cartilages. In the monotremes there is a presternal interclavicle, a reptilian bone lacking in other adult mammals.

The skull consists of a brain case and rostrum, together with the three movable bones of the middle ear, the hyoid or tongue bones, and the dentary bone or lower jaw. Though the cranial bones are for the greater part firmly knit, the sutures between constituent bones usually remain distinct. Basically the skull serves to protect the delicate and essential tissues of the brain and special sense organs, and to hold the teeth and support the masticatory apparatus. It may support on its roofing bones either deciduous bony outgrowths, the antlers, or bony cores for horns. The tympanic ring may be free from the skull or may be united. The tympanic bullae are in some species greatly inflated, probably as a means of increasing hearing acuity. The hyoid bones, homologous with a gill arch of fishes, serve to support tongue and larynx. The basihyal is cupped and greatly inflated in male howler monkeys to serve as a resonating chamber for their voices.

The pectoral girdle in the typical mammals is composed of the shoulder blade or scapula and the clavicle or collar bone. The latter is completely absent in the ungulates, whales, sirenians, and seals, and is best developed in climbing, flying, and digging mammals. The forelimb is always present, as are the humerus, radius, and ulna, a variable number of wrist bones, and the bones of five or fewer digits. The whales have supplementary phalanges in the hand. The extreme of reduction is attained in the horse, where only the center digit is functional.

The pelvic girdle articulates with the vertebral column at the sacrum and to this girdle the hind limbs are attached. In the placental mammals the pelvis is composed of the paired ilium, ischium, and pubis. The pubic symphysis is firmly fused in most mammals, but in some the union is loosened under hormonal control at the time of parturition, and the birth canal thus enlarged. In the monotremes and marsupials there is also a pair of prepubic bones, extending forward in the abdominal wall. The bones of the hind limbs are the femur, tibia, fibula, the ankle bones, and the phalanges. As in the forelimb, the bones of the hind limb of ungulates are reduced by loss of lateral digits and fusion of some other elements. The modern whales and sirenians completely lose the hind limbs, though internal skeletal vestiges persist in a number of cases.

A bony exoskeleton is present in the armadillos, but in no other modern mammal. For the greater part this armor remains unconnected with the endoskeleton but the ossicles over the rump of a small burrowing species, the pichiciago, are fused to the spines of the posterior vertebrae and make a strong plate used to block the earth tunnel against pursuers. A few independent bones also occur in some mammals such as the baculum or *os penis* of carnivores, rodents, bats, insectivores, and subhuman primates; the *os cordis* of the heart of deer and cattle.

Teeth.—The teeth are borne in the outer borders of the premaxillae and maxillae of the skull and the dentary bones which constitute the mandible. The nipping teeth of the premaxilla are known as incisors and these are matched by corresponding teeth in the lower jaw. A single pair of piercing teeth, the canines, grow immediately behind the suture between premaxillae and maxillae, and are matched by canines below. The premolars and molars occur in the maxilla and dentary bones. There are but two successional sets of teeth. The first, except for the molars, are replaced by a second set of permanent teeth. In elephants and sea-cows the premolars and molars are replaced from the rear as the forward teeth wear out. There are rarely more than 44 teeth, exceptions occurring in the marsupials and cetaceans. In the porpoise the number rises to 246. Teeth are completely lacking in the adult baleen or right whales, the monotremes, pangolins, and American anteaters. In the sperm whales teeth occur in the lower jaw only. Teeth in their evolution have shown extreme plasticity in adaptation to varied foods and to fighting. This, combined with their frequent preservation as fossils, have made them of particularly great use in the study of mammalian evolution.

Teeth are usually composed of dentine, a derivative of areolar tissue of the jaws, enamel, a thin dense capping material formed by the epithelium of the gums, and cement, which grows about the roots and may fill in areas between the enamel ridges of the crown of the tooth. The enamel is absent from the teeth of some species. In the greater number of mammals the teeth cease to grow after they erupt from the gums, but in teeth in which the pulp cavities remain widely open, as in elephant tusks and rodent incisors, growth continues throughout life. Teeth have evolved from the dermal scales of the fish, which were ancestral to the mammalian line of evolution.

Integument.—The integument of mammals characterizes the group more than does any other organ system, for of it are the hair, the oil, sweat, scent, and mammary glands. Because they are directly exposed to the environment, the integumental structures show great diversity in their adaptation to the numerous ways of life. Hair is modified to become heat-conserving fur, protective spines, tactile vibrissae, insect-repelling scales, or to serve other purposes. Horn, claws, and hoofs are developed from the skin. In its heat-conserving or regulating functions, the epidermis provides not only hair, but sweat glands that give a secretion which cools the body in evaporation; and blood capillaries under control of the autonomic nervous system which by regulating the flow of blood near the surface assist in the rapid dissipation of heat, or its conservation. An integumentary blanket of fat, the blubber, is developed in whales and serves much the same role as fur in conserving body heat.

Hair is developed from the epidermis, or superficial layer of the skin, though the hair root extends into the dermis and there receives nourishment from tiny blood vessels in a papilla. Around the papilla fits the hair bulb. In this are the only living cells of the hair. By their growth and division the older part of the hair shaft is pushed outward and the cells become horny. The typical shaft has a thin cuticle of transparent scales overlapping as shingles. The next layer is a mass of horny material containing pigment and air spaces. The medulla, a central area of larger air spaces, is present in larger hairs and, in the deer particularly, this gives the hair a good insulating though fragile quality. With each hair there is associated a sebaceous gland which keeps the hair and skin oily. There is also a small smooth muscle associated with the involuntary nervous system and this may cause the hair to stand erect to the end of increasing the apparent size of the animal as a means of intimidation, or of increasing the insulating quality of the coat.

Hairs are typically shed and replaced twice yearly but, as in man and in the tails and manes of ungulates, may grow persistently throughout life. The character and color of the coat may also change with the seasonal shedding, as in the assumption of white and warm pelages by some arctic mammals at the approach of winter. The range of color and shade in mammal hair is from black to white and includes grays, yellows, browns, and reds. Patterns are diverse as illustrated by the zebra, skunk, chipmunk, leopard, and other animals. The common pattern, however, is one of obliterative shading in which the upper parts are darker than the undersurface.

The sweat glands of the skin lie deep in the dermis, have a tightly coiled fundus, and a long duct to the surface. They function not only to cool the body by providing a liquid for evaporation but supplement the kidneys in excreting urea, salt, and other waste products. It is from these glands that the great variety of scent glands of mammals are modifications.

The mammary glands are believed to be modified sweat glands, and are nonfunctional in the males. In echidna and the platypus the glands secrete a sticky material into the region of the pouch and the young lick it from the body hair. In other mammals the ducts of these glands lead into nipples from which young obtain the milk. In a few mammals these are limited to a single pair. An African rat has as many as twelve pairs.

Circulatory System.—The most profound circulatory specialization of the mammalia is the division of the heart into four chambers—two muscular-walled ventricles and two thin-walled auricles. The right side pumps blood to the lungs, from which it returns aerated to the left side and is in turn circulated through the body. The red blood cells lose their nuclei and are, except in the camels, in the form of biconcave disks.

Excretory System.—Although the skin acts to a minor extent in excretion, the greater part of the liquid waste products of mammals are concentrated by the kidneys from which they flow through the ureters to a collecting organ, the bladder, to pass eventually to the outside through the urethra. Only in the monotremes do the ureters pass directly into a common reproductive and excretory passage, the cloaca.

Respiratory System.—The mammals are exclusively air breathers, even in those instances of extreme readaptation to aquatic life. The passage of air in and out of the lungs is forced by a muscular diaphragm, lying between the thorax and the abdominal cavity, plus the action of the cage of ribs, the diameter of which is increased or reduced by the partially involuntary action of the intercostal muscles. In the whales there is a special system of minute muscular valves serving to constrict the millions of small bronchioles and to control the escape of air from the lungs under the conditions of great pressure in the oceanic depths.

Nervous System.—The chief advance of the nervous system of the mammals over that of other vertebrates is the increase in relative brain size, particularly of the cerebrum. In most mammals the surface of the cerebrum is marked by fissures and convolutions increasing the surface area to provide for greater association centers. The cerebral hemispheres of monotremes, insectivores, rodents, and some bats are, however, relatively smooth surfaced. In all mammals except the monotremes and marsupials there is a band of nerve tissue (the *corpus callosum*) connecting the two halves of the cerebrum.

The organs of special sense are variously developed among the mammals. The eye tends to be as adaptive as the whole mammal and many degrees of specialization may be found. Only a few burrowing insectivores and rodents, and the river dolphin of the muddy rivers of India, have completely lost their vision.

The ear in mammals is quite different from that of other animals. There is a chain of ear bones, the malleus, incus, and stapes, which are represented in the reptiles by the articular, quadrate, and columella. Thus the reptilian bones of jaw articulation, functionally replaced in the mammals by the squamosal and dentary, have been put to new use as hearing aids and the old reptilian columella, now called the stapes, has retained its function as a transmitter of vibrations to the inner ear. An intricately coiled structure of the inner ear, the cochlea, increases auditory acuity. This pattern of hearing efficiency probably attains its greatest development in the bats. These animals are able to fly blindly by hearing the echoes of their supersonic voices reflected back from large or small objects near their course of flight.

Distribution.—Species and higher groups of mammals are limited to but part of the earth's surface by factors of physiological and anatomical specialization and by the historic factors of point of origin, the history of barriers and interspecific competition. It is apparent that arboreal species will not exist far from trees, aquatic species in the absence of water, nor cold-adapted species in the tropics. Many species are not present in suitable areas, however, by reason of their history, for if they evolve in a land separated from the unoccupied region by insuperable barriers they will not occupy the new land until conditions change. Thus there were no mammals in New Zealand before their introduction by man, because the ocean barrier was too great for any land mammal to surmount. Other islands on which nonnative mammals have been introduced have similar histories, as the rabbits in Australia, the mongooses of Jamaica, and goats on numerous other islands. The same principles, however, have held within a continent and species have changed their ranges as rivers have changed their courses, as forests have been removed, or predators decimated. The nature of the barrier may be much less apparent, however, than a body of water, a mountain range, or a dense forest. To digging animals unfavorable soil types may hinder spread, for soils too coarse or too heavy are not occupied by species adapted to a limited medium.

The greatest single controlling factor of mammalian distribution appears to be temperature, and Clinton Hart Merriam mapped "life zones" of North America on the basis of selected isothermal lines which he considered critical for many mammals. These life zones serve to emphasize the similarity of northern biotic associations and the parallel zones at higher altitudes in southern mountains, but they also tend to obscure patterns of species distribution which ignore the areas of thermal similarity.

Where a family of mammals contains several genera, the family range is greater than that of any of its constituent genera and, similarly, the range occupied by a genus is generally broader than that of any contained species. Some genera have extremely extended ranges, notably *Canis* (the dogs), which occur in every zoological region except the Antarctic. Similarly the cats (*Felis*) are almost cosmopolitan. Even single species have been successful in becoming established widely over the world. Man is the most widely distributed of all, but his commensals, the house mice and house rats, have followed him almost everywhere. The sperm whale occurs in all oceans except the polar ones. The puma is found from southern Canada to Patagonia. Conversely many species, even large ones, are quite restricted. Some small mammals, particularly island species, have ranges of but ten square miles or less.

The ranges of some groups of mammals are much less today than in the past. The rhinoceroses were common in North America in the Tertiary and in Europe even into the Quaternary, but today they are limited to Africa and the Oriental region. Lemurs (Lemuroidea) too were common in North America and Europe during the Eocene but today the true lemurs are limited to Madagascar, though related forms are found in Africa, southern Asia, and some neighboring islands. Horses once abundant in the New World, occur there now only by reintroduction.

A few instances may be cited of genera whose species are widely separated. The manatee of the west African rivers has no relatives nearer than the two species of the American coasts and rivers. The tapirs (sometimes considered as two genera) are present in Malaya and tropical America but in modern faunas are unrepresented elsewhere, the intermediate territory, once occupied, now being inhospitable to their kind.

Within the broader limits of a mammal's range there may sometimes be but small areas that are occupied in fact. Aquatic mammals do not move far from the water courses; certain small species may be found only in favorable strips of meadow, of forest border, or beach. The conditions of cover, food, and competitive species may all affect local distribution and cause seasonal change in range.

The ranges of the individuals of a species may be very restricted but some larger animals cover great distances within their times. The humpback whale of the Atlantic spends its summers off Greenland and its winters near Bermuda. The migrations of the caribou, which moves in vast herds between the summer range in the Barren Grounds and the winter range near the northern limit of trees, is a well known phenomenon. The red bat migrates great distances across open water and has come aboard ship 240 miles offshore. Some mammals, such as the mountain lion, may range an area of 100 square miles, the males being the greater wanderers. American otters may follow circuits 30 miles in diameter but other mammals, particularly herbivores, large and small, are restricted to very small tracts. The white-tailed deer, or Virginia deer, may occupy a territory but a half square mile. Extensive studies on small rodents have shown that very little range is normally covered. Rats in a city have been found to stay pretty well within areas 100 feet in diameter.

Although the ranges of two species of mammals are probably never identical because of ecological and other specializations, there are broad patterns of distribution of faunas which are linked with the geological history of the region and this fact permits one to divide the world into geographic realms the mammals of which have certain common patterns of history and present distribution. Of the several systems of division proposed, that of Philip L. Sclater is the most generally satisfactory. The regions proposed by him are as follows:

Palaearctic Region.—Including the whole of Europe, Asia north of the Himalayas, and North Africa. The sheep and goats are particularly characteristic of this area. Deer, moles, and pikas are common but are not limited to the Palaearctic.

Ethiopian Region.—Included are Africa south of the Sahara, southern Arabia, and Madagascar. The ungulate mammals show great diversity in this region. The giraffes, hippopotami, pigs, antelopes, and horses exemplify this. True cattle (*Bos*) and deer are, however, completely lacking. The hyraxes are characteristic as is also the African elephant. Among the carnivora, wolves, true foxes, bears, and raccoons are absent, but there is great diversity among the cats and civets. Primates are present in wide variety from lemurs to the great apes. The aardvark is limited to the region. The region, though now easily definable on the basis of present day distributions was not always so, for in recent geological times many peculiarly African types were shared with Europe and southern Asia.

Oriental Region.—Included are India south of the Himalayas, the Malay Peninsula, the Indonesian islands, and the Philippines. The area shares some groups with Africa, such as the elephants, rhinoceros, antelopes, scaly anteaters, lorisine lemurs, great apes, civets, lions, and leopards, but there are also striking differences such as the presence of tree shrews, colugos, and a great variety of deer, true oxen, and bears in the Oriental region. Bats are very abundant and, of bat families, only the neotropical vampires are absent.

Australasian Region.—Australia, Tasmania, New Zealand, and islands to the north including the Celebes, Lombok, and New Guinea compose this region. Here the fauna is strikingly distinct owing to long separation from the other land areas. New Zealand had no mammals whatsoever previous to introductions by man. The monotremes are found only in this region and the marsupials are now completely confined to it except for the New World opossums (Didelphidae) and opossum-rats (Caenolestidae). The only higher mammals which have invaded the Australasian region are bats, murine rodents, the dingo in Australia, the pig in New Guinea and several other species which reached the Celebes. These latter include one bovine (the anoa), a hog (the babirusa), the Celebes "ape," and the tarsier.

Nearctic Region.—Greenland and North America southward to Middle America are here included. The faunal relationships of this region with the Palaearctic are so strong that the two are sometimes grouped as one region, the Holarctic. Such common forms are the musk oxen, caribou, wapiti, moose, bison, lynxes, bears, otters, wolverines, wolves, foxes, beavers, squirrels, marmots, hares, and others. The hollow-horned ungulates are uncommon and limited to the muskox, bison, pronghorn, mountain sheep, and mountain goats. Rodents are represented by several types peculiar to the region, among them the pocket gophers (Geomyidae) and the sewellel (Aplodontidae). The cricetine mouse *Peromyscus* is charactertistic of the Nearctic and, except by introduction, there are no murine rats or mice. Muskrats and pocket mice and kangaroo rats are other groups peculiar to the region. Several species from the Neotropical occur within the southern limits of the region, such as the armadillo and the coati. No primates except man now occur in the Nearctic.

Neotropical Region.—Included are South and Middle America and the West Indies. Here some characteristic mammals are the sloths, anteaters, and armadillos, a great variety of opossums and the opossum-rats (Caenolestidae). There are also two families of primates, the Callithricidae (marmosets) and the Cebidae. The rodents have attained their maximal specialization in the neotropics, such hystricomorph types as the guinea pigs, capybara, and chinchillas being representative. Among the bats, the vampires alone are, as a family, limited to the neotropics.. There is wide variety among the dog, cat, and raccoon families. The camels are represented by the genus *Lama* and the pigs by peccaries. The Cervidae are represented by several genera of aberrant deer of the subfamily Odocoileinae of which *Mazama* is the most widely distributed. There are no antelopes, sheep, or oxen, and but one perissodactyl, the tapir.

Adaptive Radiation.—The mammals have proven very plastic in adapting themselves to diverse modes of life, on land, in the earth, the trees, the air, and the waters, and to diets ranging from strictly vegetarian to strictly carnivorous. They have occupied the polar regions and the tropics, deserts and forests. They dive to more than a mile below the ocean surface and ascend to the summit of all but the highest mountains.

Aquatic Adaptations.—Most mammals are able to swim at least short distances, and almost every degree of aquatic specialization is represented, to the extreme of the whales. Only these animals and the sirenians are completely independent of land, even producing their young in the water. Of the monotremes, the duckbill is notably aquatic, having developed webbed feet and water repellent fur. Of the marsupials, the yapok of Middle America is the only truly natatorial form. Among the insectivores there are desmans and water shrews, but the West African otter-shrew is the most completely adapted. It has a fusiform body, laterally compressed sculling tail, webbed hind feet, and an otter-like fur. No bats are aquatic, though some, at least, can swim, and some are fish catchers, scooping up surface swimmers with their interfemoral membranes. Many rodents are aquatic; one need only cite the beaver, muskrat, and coypu as examples. Of the ungulates, the hippopotami are the most specialized for aquatic life. Of the edentates none are water-adapted unless one can so consider an armadillo (*Dasypus*) which, by inflation, can float as it swims, or by deflation, can

walk on the bottom of a pond. The carnivora present many water dwellers, among them the otters, sea-lions, and seals. The latter come ashore occasionally to rest and for the birth of their young. Adult male elephant seals do not leave the rookery in the breeding season and for six to eight weeks have no food or water. Sub-human primates swim poorly or not at all.

The extreme of aquatic specialization as exemplified by the whales, entails the loss of a hairy coat and the development of a thick insulating layer of fat, the blubber. The ear pinnae are lost, the neck is shortened, the body becomes fusiform, the forelimbs are modified to paddles, the hind limbs are lost, and the tail develops heavy horizontal flukes as the principal propelling agent. Dorsal fins are developed in some species. Changes in the peripheral circulation and the breathing apparatus are profound. Among one group of whales, the Mysticeti, or whalebone whales, the teeth are lost and great fringed horny plates, the baleen, are developed to strain minute animals from the sea water for food. So fully are the sperm whales fitted to water life that they can dive to a depth of a mile. The beaked whale has been reported to stay submerged for two hours.

Digging Specializations.—Some burrowing activity occurs in each of the orders of mammals except the primates (man excepted), bats, colugos, sea-cows, whales, ungulates, and hyraxes. Specialization to almost exclusively subterranean life is found among marsupials (*Notoryctes*), insectivores (golden-moles, true moles), and rodents (pocket gophers, mole-rats). In each of these the body is cylindrical; there is almost a complete loss of visual function, reduction of the external ear, shortening or loss of the tail, and change of the hair character. In some moles there is tremendous increase in size of the hand and profound changes in the shoulder girdle. In the mole-rats the incisor teeth are angled forward and become important earth-loosening structures.

Flight.—True flight is found only among the bats, where it is attained through extreme modification of the hand to support flying membranes. To varied extent similar membranes extend to the hind legs and between these to the tail, where such exists. Mechanically, the flight of bats is basically like that of the birds. Coupled with flight and the habit of many bats of feeding in flight, there is developed a technique for guidance by echo-location. Besides the audible (to our ears) sounds of bats, there are emitted in flight a series of ultrasonic cries which, reflected from an obstacle in the bat's path, enable the bat, through perception of the echo, to avoid the obstacle or to locate the winged prey.

A gliding flight has been independently evolved several times among mammals. Such flight occurs among the marsupials (*Acrobates, Petaurus*), the colugos (Dermoptera), and rodents (Petauristinae, Anomaluridae). In each instance the animal takes off from a tree or other height, spreads the furred membranes that extend between its legs, and coasts to a lower point, usually a tree trunk, on which it lands vertically to scramble up, perhaps to take another glide. An Australian flying phalanger, *Schoinobates,* is reported to have made a measured glide of 400 feet.

Arboreal Life.—Life in the trees has developed in several manners as, for example,

MAMMALS

(1) Hippopotamus, *Hippopotamus amphibius*, Africa. (2) Pygmy elephant, *Loxodonta cyclotis*, West Africa. (3) Malay tapir, *Tapirus indicus*, Malay Peninsula, Sumatra. (4) Cheetah, *Acinonyx jubatus*, Africa, southern Asia. (5) Tiger, *Felis tigris*, southern and eastern Asia. (6) Giraffe, *Giraffa camelopardalis*, Africa. (7) Spotted cuscus, *Phalanger maculatus*, New Guinea. (8) Axis deer, *Axis axis*, India and Ceylon. (9) Mandrill, *Mandrillus sphinx*, West Africa.

Painted for "THE ENCYCLOPEDIA AMERICANA" by A. Seidel

MAMMALS

(1) Ring-tailed lemur, *Lemur catta*, Madagascar. (2) Little brown bat, *Myotis lucifugus*, North America. (3) Duck-billed platypus, *Ornithorhynchus anatinus*, eastern Australia and Tasmania. (4) Central American two-toed sloth, *Choloepus hoffmanni*, Central America, northwestern South America. (5) North American pika, *Ochotona princeps*, western United States to Alaska, at high altitudes. (6) Giant pangolin, *Manis gigantea*, West Africa. (7) Crested porcupine, *Hystrix cristata*, Italy, northern Africa. (8) European hedgehog, *Erinaceus europaeus*, Europe, Asia. (9) Manatee, *Trichechus manatus*, North Carolina to northeastern South America. (10) Bottle-nosed dolphin, *Tursiops truncatus*, the North Atlantic Ocean.

Drawn for "THE ENCYCLOPEDIA AMERICANA" by A. Seidel

brachiation (the spider monkey and the gibbon), and the upside down suspension of the sloths. Arboreal structures encountered are curved claws (as in cats), grasping hands (opossum, primates), suction pads on the feet (tarsiers, tree hyraxes), elongated limbs, prehensile tails (marsupials, pangolins, American monkeys, and other animals), and suspension hook feet (sloths). The sloths have evolved so completely to arboreal life that they walk most awkwardly on the ground. With their reversed position, they have changed the direction of hair growth. Many primates have specialized in rapid locomotion through the trees and, in some forms, long leaps between the trees. Gibbons are reported to clear as much as 40 feet in a single swing between supports. Arboreal kangaroos are comparatively short footed, and their leaps are more for vertical progression than horizontal.

Cursorial Adaptations.—Speed has become important to many mammals, but particularly to those inhabiting open country where there is little space to hide. The horses especially have evolved in this direction, and among the predatory animals the hunting leopard or cheetah is another capable of sustained high speed. Physical attributes include an elongation and straightening of the limbs which move rapidly in an antroposterior plane. In the ungulates development of speed has been accompanied by a progressive reduction of the area of contact with the ground, reaching its extreme in the horses, wherein only a single toe is in contact. Some extremes of speed reported are: man, 22 miles per hour; horse, 42; springbok, 59; cheetah, 70.

Hopping Specializations.—Speed and dodging ability have been attained in other mammals by emphasis of the hind limbs for hopping bipedal progression, as in kangaroos, jerboas, and kangaroo rats. As in the ungulates, there is a tendency for reduction of the digits, reaching its extreme in the kangaroos in which the fourth digit is the largest, and the jerboa, *Dipus,* where the toes are reduced to three. Usually the forelimbs are so reduced as to serve almost no locomotor function except when foraging. The tails of bipedal leapers are elongated or enlarged and serve the multiple function of balancing organs and the third leg of a tripod. The large kangaroos are reported capable of a speed of 30 miles per hour and a single leap of 12 feet.

Feeding Specializations.—The majority of mammals are omnivorous to a degree but specializations are occasionally extreme. The koala, for example, subsists entirely on the leaves of about twelve species of eucalyptus, while the giant panda lives largely on bamboo. The anteaters and pangolins are so specialized to feed on ants and termites, that they are toothless and their food as adults is limited to such diet. The whalebone whales subsist on the smaller animals of the sea which they strain from the water in the manner already described—with fringed horny plates (baleen) which are suspended from the roof of the mouth. Killer whales are wholly carnivorous and predatory, feeding on the larger whales and pinnipeds. Sperm whales have a diet mostly of octopus and squid. Vampire bats feed on blood alone whereas other bats are exclusively fruit eaters or insectivorous. In each food-limited mammal, characters of locomotion, of dentition and digestive tract are correlated to a pattern that robs the animal of the versatility of its generalized ancestors.

Cold Climates.—Mammals living in climates which in winter are frigid must migrate (as caribou, mountain sheep, fur seals), hibernate, or develop habits and structures fitting them to active life in a time of cold, snow, ice and scarcity of food. Meeting the challenge of cold are high and constant body temperature, thick layers of fat (walrus, etc.), rich fur hair (foxes, mink), herding (muskox), elaborate nest or shelter construction (muskrat, beaver, man). To traverse loose snow, feet may be seasonally enlarged by hair growth (snowshoe hare). Permitting removal of ice-cover from food supplies are enlarged specialized hoofs (Peary's caribou), protruding teeth (Greenland hare), and seasonally developed heavy claws (lemming). Rendering some species less conspicuous (and lessening heat radiation) the pelage may become white (ermine, arctic fox, arctic hare) or remain permanently so (polar bear). Also reducing heat radiation, arctic representatives of widespread species tend to be larger, for surface area is proportionately less in larger sized bodies; and ears are smaller and tails are reduced, or well haired.

Food storage is frequent in non-hibernating species. Pikas make and store hay; squirrels hide nuts, mushrooms, and pine cones; moles store earthworms, and beaver place winter supplies of branches below the water of their ponds.

Hibernation as a means of meeting winter conditions is employed to varied degrees. It is pronounced in many ground squirrels, marmots, jumping mice, and bats. Skunk, raccoon, badger, and opossum become torpid, but venture out in mild weather. Northern bears become inactive. In deep hibernation metabolism is lowered, and the body temperature drops to within less than one degree above surrounding temperature. The animal becomes insensible and lacks response even to strong stimuli; respiration and heart beats may become almost imperceptible. The presence of abundant fat appears a necessity. Animals of the extreme north do not hibernate because all retiring places are below freezing.

Dry, Open Lands.—Steppe and desert demand of their mammals adaptation to periodic scarcity of food and water, to lack of ground cover and, often, to extremes of temperature and wind. Smaller mammals, particularly the rodents, construct burrows in which they spend the unfavorable hours and seasons. Water requirements are minimized by avoidance of the hot sun, paucity of skin glands, concentration of urine, and metabolic manufacture of water through the breakdown of carbohydrates. Many species (aardvark, some rodents, insectivores, and lemurs, etc.) estivate, remaining torpid through the period of maximum aridity. The lack of good cover is met by close correlation between soil and pelage color. Swift movement and dodging ability are aids, and are particularly well developed in many bipedal forms (jerboa, kangaroo rats, marsupial jumping mice, etc.). In sandy areas the feet may develop hairy coverings (sand cat, gerbils, jerboas, etc.) and hairiness protects the nostrils, eyes and ears from blowing sand and dust (camels). External ears are large in many species (desert foxes, jack rabbits, jerboas, horses), in part to provide greater heat regulation, in part better to detect sounds.

In larger species swift movement is at a premium: among the predators (cheetah, hunting dog) to catch their prey without benefit of stalking cover; among the vegetarians (antelopes, kangoroos, hares) to escape and to hasten long journeys in search of water and food. Even the newborn of the larger ungulates must be ready to follow their mothers within a few hours of birth. Quick feeding is often a necessity and some small rodents have cheek pouches in which they carry food to their burrows and so lessen exposure to enemies. The rumen, a section of the stomach for temporary storage and fermentation of coarse vegetation, is of advantage to the plains-dwelling cud chewers.

Herd formation (bison, antelope, guanaco) is prevalent among the large open-country herbivores, for it promotes safety of the individual and provides warmth in winter huddling.

Early Life.—All mammals for some time after their birth are dependent on their mothers for care. The relative age at birth varies greatly. In the common opossum, for example, the newborn young are blind, naked, their hind limbs but imperfectly formed, and in other characters larval in development. They are able, however, to find their way from the vaginal orifice to the maternal pouch. Here they find a nipple and become firmly attached to it for many days. They stay in the pouch for about two months, almost five times the period in the uterus. The young of ungulates and of whales, by contrast, are capable of independent locomotion from almost the moment of birth. A newborn porpoise rises to the air immediately but a mother porpoise will push a stillborn young to the surface. A mother sea lion has been photographed leading her young into the water for a first swim, while the pup still dragged the fresh placenta. But though some mammals may early lead their young afield, nursing may be protracted. The walrus is said to nurse for two years since its tusks must develop before it is capable of securing clams, the principal adult food.

Parental instruction of the young is extensive in many mammals such as the carnivores, primates, and ungulates. The young of some rodents, however, are away from their parents in a few days. Young field mice are blind and helpless at birth but in ten days are weaned and ready to lead independent lives. The young of gregarious mammals may spend their lives in the herd and slowly learn such manners of the species as are necessary.

Reproductive Life.—Meadow mice mature in 21 days and the females bear their first litter at 45 days. The female blue whale is mature in three years, by which time she may be over 70 feet long. An elephant, however, requires about 30 years to reach sexual maturity. Those animals with a low rate of mortality bear few offspring, often but one a year or less. In the meadow mice, one female may produce as many as 17 litters in one year and an average of seven young per litter. The life expectancy is, however, correspondingly short. Promiscuity is general among small rodents, insectivores, and bats. Polygamy is most marked among the ungulates and some such pinnipeds as the fur seal. Monogamy for a season or two is reported for some canids, beavers, and a gibbon. Among some carnivores, as is true of the foxes, the male may take a responsible part in providing the young with food.

The period of gestation of mammals represents a spread of from 13 days in the opossum to 641 days in the elephant. Some representative examples (figures are mostly approximate) are: brown bat, 50 days; chimpanzee, 216-261; polar bears, 210-250; lion, 105-113; porpoise, 183; sperm whale, 365; hare, 42; white-tailed deer, 210; zebra, 365.

Longevity.—Although the potential life span of mammals is rarely attained in nature and the life span of captive mammals is scarcely representative, such data are of interest in interspecific comparisons. Again a few examples may be given, the figures all in years: fruit bat, 17; chimpanzee, 40; man, 100; bear, 34; lion, 30; seal, 19; deer mouse, 5½; porcupine, 20; elephant, 69; bison, 22.

Intercommunication.—The mammals communicate by sounds, odors, and actions. We are most aware of the acoustical signals which may be vocal or mechanical. The chimpanzee has 32 or more expressive sounds, and the howler monkeys produce as many as 20 vocalizations. A California ground squirrel, by varying the character of its single alarm chirp, indicates to others in its colony whether an enemy is a hawk, a snake, or such a mammal as coyote or man. The whales, too, produce a variety of sounds. A few mammals, such as the giraffe and rabbit, are normally silent. Rabbits thump the earth with their hind feet and white-footed mice drum with the toes of their forefeet, but the messages conveyed, if any, remain unknown to us. The skins of mammals may be rich in odor glands. These may be on the feet, on the back, the sides, the face, anal, or preputial. They serve to mark out the territory of the individuals and to keep the species together. Some glands are active only in the rut and must serve to bring the males and females together. Visual intercommunication may be illustrated by the rump-hair flashing of the pronghorn, the actions of face and tail in the dog, and the spine-raising of the porcupine. Tactile actions expressive of emotion are varied.

Defense and Protection.—The major defense of some mammals is fecundity, but concealing coloration and habits, speed, and aggressiveness are common modes of protection, and size a contributing factor of protection. Defensive structures, used in specific or interspecific competition, include the poison spurs of the monotremes, the antlers, horns and hoofs of ungulates, the spines of porcupines, hedgehogs, and others, the obnoxious odors of skunks and varied other carnivores and insectivores, the armor of pangolins and armadillos, the teeth of many more. Herd behavior may be important, as notably among the musk oxen where a ring is formed by the older individuals, all facing horns-out, protecting young animals in the center from wolf attacks, a behavior suicidal against the newer danger of men with guns. A device aiding escape in a few mammals is a weak tail structure, permitting easy separation of that member should it be caught. Some mammals by the very factor of gigantism have been largely immune from predation, except by man. Largest mammal is the blue whale which attains a length of 115 feet and a weight of 150 tons. Largest of present day land mammals is the African elephant, which may attain a shoulder height of 12 feet and a weight of 4 tons, but this was greatly exceeded by an extinct giant rhinoceros, *Baluchitherium,* which stood 18 feet at the shoulder. The other extreme of size is represented by certain pigmy shrews and pigmy mice which weigh less than one ounce and must find their protection in hiding, aggressiveness, or fecundity.

In the matter of color, the adaptive seasonal change of such arctic animals as the ermine and arctic fox wherein the summer pelage is dark, the winter pelage white, is among the most remarkable. There is a distinct tendency for many mammals to be colored much as the background against which they usually appear. This character in deer mice has been demonstrated to have strong survival value when owls are the predator.

Migrations.—The migrations among mammals, in which there is a seasonal change of area with a later return to the original range, are not so common or spectacular as among birds and fish. Among larger aquatic mammals and the ungulates, such migrations are well marked. The Alaskan fur seal, for example, migrate annually from the open ocean to the south to the breeding grounds on the Pribilof Islands. Some of the whales have pronounced shift in range, following food supply and perhaps temperature changes. Mountain-living ungulates usually move down to lower altitudes in winter, often a very short distance. Some bats make seasonal range changes and the red bat and hoary bat from the American mainland sometimes winter in Bermuda.

Economic Importance.—Mammals of greatest economic importance to us are those which we have domesticated, the ox, the horse, hog, sheep, dog, camel, and others. These may serve many uses, such as for food, or for leather, hair, wool, and labor. Others, under controlled breeding but not domestic, such as the mink and fox, are important for the single resource of fur. The wild animals too, in many instances, are of marked utility, providing furs, bristles, and fats (notably from whales). The value of a single year's production of wild furs in the United States is estimated at $50,000,000. Yet there are numerous other aspects of wild animal life which are economically significant. Examples are crop and stock destruction by a host of species from mice to elephants; the support of many large industries supplying sportsmen; the spread of disease (as tularemia, rabies, sleeping sickness, and plague); the important role of tilling of the soil and so aiding in its improvement by aeration, by increasing its water absorptive qualities, and by carrying organic material to lower levels. The insect-destroying habits of many mammals (as bats, shrews, and skunks) give them marked beneficial status. The extirpation of a single mammal species, or man's misplacement of it, has frequently had profound and unexpected results on our economy. One may illustrate with the classic case of the introduction of five rabbits in Australia, where none of the rabbit's natural enemies were present. As a result, these animals have become the worst of agricultural pests and millions of dollars have been spent in rabbit-proof fencing.

Bibliography.—Flower, W. H., and Lydekker, R., *An Introduction to the Study of Mammals, Living and Extinct* (London 1891); Beddard, F. E., *Mammalia* (London 1902); Burrell, Harry, *The Platypus* (Sydney 1927); Parker, T. J., and Haswell, W. A., *Text Book of Zoology* (New York 1928); Seton, Ernest Thompson, *Lives of Game Animals* (New York 1929); Howell, A. B., *Aquatic Mammals* (Baltimore 1930); Scott, W. B., *History of the Land Mammals of the Western Hemisphere* (New York 1937); Hamilton, W. J., Jr., *American Mammals* (New York 1939); Simpson, G. G., *The Principles of Classification and a Classification of the Mammals* (American Museum of Natural History, New York 1945); Romer, A. S., *Vertebrate Body* (Philadelphia 1949); Bourlière, François, *The Natural History of Mammals* (New York 1964);

Walker, E. P., *Mammals of the World*, 3 vols. (Baltimore 1964); Morris, D., *The Mammals* (New York 1965).

ROBERT T. HATT,
Cranbrook Institute of Science.

MAMMARY GLANDS, măm'à-rĭ, the milk glands of mammalian animals (see also BREAST). They are present in all mammals, in both sexes, but in the male are usually rudimentary, their functional activity being limited to the female, who secretes in these glands the milk for nourishing her young during a natural period after birth. In all mammals they are placed in pairs, but vary much in position and number in different groups. Zoologists give them names according to their position near the armpits (axillary), on the chest (pectoral), on the belly (ventral or abdominal), or near the groin (inguinal). They are never situated on the back. The number in an individual may be from 2 to 12 or more, and is usually even. The structure of the cow's udder is due to the uniting of the same number of mammae as there are of teats, the number of which, when more than two, usually corresponds to that of the young produced at each birth. The mammary glands of Marsupialia (q.v.) are contained in the pouch. In monotremes—duckbills and echidnas—the nipple is not present. See also PROTOTHERIA.

Diseases of the Mammary Glands.—The common inflammation of the glands (mastitis) is often attended by much swelling, with fever and painful tenderness. The formation of pus is apt to result in a slowly pointing abscess. Great care in diet and regulation of the bowels should be observed. Purgatives and fomentations may be necessary, and, in many cases, the placing of the arm on the affected side in a sling. Drawing off the milk and evacuating the pus may be practicable and will afford great relief. Pain in the breasts may result from many causes, of which sore nipples is one of the most frequent. The nipples are also subject to cracks and ulcerations which occasion much difficulty and pain to the mother when nursing the child. Lotions of an astringent character, such as tannin, have a remedial effect in these disorders, as have also collodion and lunar caustic (nitrate of silver), when applied to the sore nipple. Metallic shields are used in severe cases for protection of the affected point. Among many specific disorders to which the mammary glands are liable are cancer and galactocele and other forms of tumor. See also MILK FEVER.

MAMMEE APPLE, măm'ē, **SANTO DOMINGO APRICOT,** or **MAMEY,** mà-mā', a tropical tree of the species *Mammea americana* (family Guttiferae), which bears a large russet-colored drupaceous fruit, oblate to round in form, from four to six inches in diameter. The yellow pulp is sweet and juicy and resembles the apricot in taste. It may be eaten raw or cooked.

The tree, 40-60 feet in height, has large oblong leaves which are of a richer shade of green than those of most trees and much glossier. It has fragrant white flowers from which a liqueur, known as eau de créole or crème de créole, is distilled in the French West Indies. The tree grows well in a light sandy soil and seedlings will come into bearing after six or seven years.

MAMMON, a term popularly held to be a mere personification of riches. It is used in

Matt. vi, 24 and Luke xvi, 9. Milton makes Mammon a fallen angel of sordid character.

MAMMOTH, măm′ŭth, an elephant (*Elephas primigenius*) which inhabited the temperate parts of the northern world during the glacial period; it spread northward with the retreat of the ice, and survived until the Neolithic period of human history. Some account of the origin and probable wanderings of the species is given in the paragraph relating to fossil elephants under ELEPHANT. Mammoth remains have been found in intimate association with the handiwork of savage man; and upon a piece of bone a portrait of this animal was found scratched, the accuracy of which shows a close acquaintance by the cave dwellers of France with the animal in life, and much artistic skill. This elephant, although the word "mammoth" has become an expression for hugeness, was little if any larger, on the average, than the modern Asiatic elephant, to which it was nearly related. Its remains are abundant and enable us to reconstruct its form and features completely, especially since the remarkable discovery, first in 1799, of carcasses frozen into the icy cliffs along the Arctic coast of Siberia. One of the most important discoveries of this kind occurred in 1801. Since the earliest known times ivory from buried tusks of these animals has been obtained from northern Siberia and Alaska, and many curious stories were invented to account for its origin, especially among the Chinese, who had never seen an elephant; but the specimens above mentioned contained not only the tusks still in their sockets and every bone in its place throughout the skeleton, but a great part of the flesh was in a condition fit for sledge-dogs to eat and enjoy, and was covered with thick skin still clothed with long dark hair, beneath which was a dense woolly fur, well fitted to protect the animal against Arctic cold. The ears were much smaller than those of modern elephants. This specimen of 1801, which was preserved in the Leningrad Museum in the attitude in which it was found buried, measured 16 feet 4 inches from the forehead to the extremity of the tail; its height was 9 feet 4 inches, and the tusks, along the outer or greater curve, measured 9 feet 6 inches. Of other well-known specimens, the skeleton mounted in Chicago is one of the largest known, and its tusks measure 9 feet 8 inches. The largest tusks on record are a pair found in Alaska which measure 12¾ feet in length. All mammoth tusks show an outward and upward sweep very distinct from the growth of elephant tusks. The mammoth seems to have been extremely numerous all over northern Europe, Asia and North America, especially during post-glacial times, when northern Asia was covered with pine forests to the borders of the Arctic Sea, affording plentiful food in their leaves and twigs upon which these animals browsed. The disappearance of these forests, due to slow climatic changes, is supposed to be the principal influence which led to the extermination of the species, a fact otherwise not easily to be explained. It is probable that human hunting had much to do with the mammoth's extinction. See also MASTODON.

Bibliography.—Lucas, F. A., *Animals of the Past* (New York 1901); Beddard, F. E., *Mammalia* (New York 1902); Herz, O. F., *Frozen Mammoth of Siberia* (Washington 1904); Scott, W. B., *History of Land Mammals in the Western Hemisphere* (New York 1913); Pfizenmayer, E. W., *Siberian Man and Mammoth* (Toronto 1939); Bourlière, F., *Natural History of Mammals* (New York 1954).

MAMMOTH CAVE, a remarkable American cavern, located in Kentucky, about 85 miles southwest of Louisville. It was established as a national park in 1936, with 50,696 acres of grounds. There are over 150 miles of passageway in the cave, including avenues, chambers, pits, domes and rivers. What is termed the Main Cave is three miles long, varying in width from 40 to 175 feet and in height from 40 to 125 feet. Its greatest enlargement is known as the Chief City (or Temple), an oval room 541 feet long, 287 feet wide and 125 feet high; anciently a rendezvous of the Indians, whose torches and other relics have been found in abundance. The Star Chamber mimics the starry heavens by reason of its lofty ceiling of black oxide of manganese flecked by snowy crystals of gypsum. The cavern exists in five successive tiers, through which, at various points, shafts have been cut, which are styled pits or domes, according to the point of view. The largest are the Bottomless Pit, Gorin's Dome, the Mammoth Dome and the Maelstrom, and their average depth is about 100 feet. Oval depressions, locally known as "sink-holes," drain through the pits and chasms and form subterranean lakes and rivers; which finally find an outlet to the neighboring Green River. The largest, the Echo River, gets its name from the wonderful reverberations of sound along its course. Boats are provided for short voyages. Eyeless fish abound, of which there are three or four species; in addition blind crawfish, blind crickets, flies, beetles, spiders and other abnormal fauna are found on the walls and under the rocks. The structure and habits of these animals have been studied with great care.

Beyond River Hall long avenues extend, many adorned by marvelous gypsum rosettes and brilliant arches of crystal efflorescence in the most fantastic diversity. Cleveland's Cabinet is frequently mentioned as a treasure-house of cave flowers, but some of the smaller rooms, for instance, Charlotte's Grotto, can boast of finer displays. The great cavern was long believed to end at Croghan's Hall, where the Maelstrom is located, but subsequent exploration revealed that there were long, wide avenues beyond this point. The so-called Frozen Niagara, made up of onyx cascades, stalactites, stalagmites, and many fascinating gypsum formations, was discovered in 1923, and additional caverns were found in 1938. Everywhere, even in the deepest pits, the atmosphere is both chemically and optically pure; the temperature is uniformly about 54° F. all the year around, as has been determined by a long series of exact scientific observations, in order to discover the temperature of the crust of the earth.

The discovery of the Mammoth Cave is usually credited to a hunter named Hutchins, in 1809; but one of the managers of the estate found that the county records, in 1797, fixed the entrance to this cavern as a landmark for a piece of real estate. The locality first gained notoriety by reason of its immense deposits of saltpeter, which were used in the manufacture of gunpowder during the War of 1812. After passing through the hands of several owners, the cave was bought by Dr. John Croghan, who willed it to his nephews and nieces, with instructions that at their death it should be sold at auction. In 1926 an act of Congress authorized the establishment of Mammoth Cave National Park. The caves continued to be operated as a tourist attraction by private owners until 1930, when the property was acquired by the State of Kentucky. In 1936 it was turned over to the federal government for administration and protection as a national park. See also CAVE.

MAMMOTH HOT SPRINGS. See YELLOWSTONE NATIONAL PARK.

MAN. See ANTHROPOLOGY; ARCHAEOLOGY; ETHNOLOGY; MAN, PREHISTORIC TYPES OF; PSYCHOLOGY.

MAN, Isle of, one of the British Isles. It is situated in the Irish Sea about 30 miles (48 km) from both England and Northern Ireland and 16 miles (25 km) south of Burrow Head, Scotland. Favored with a mild climate, the Isle of Man is a popular resort for vacationers. It extends 33 miles (53 km) in a northeasterly direction and is about 12 miles (19 km) wide. The island is generally hilly, except for an area of sand dunes and gravel at its northeast end. Snaefell (2,034 feet, or 620 meters) is the highest point. Cliffs fringe the coast—Spanish Head in the south rises to 400 feet (122 meters)—and there are many bays and beaches. Off the south end of the island is the Calf of Man, a 600-acre (240-hectare) rocky islet preserved as a bird sanctuary.

The Isle of Man is a self-governing community owing allegiance to the British crown, which is represented by a lieutenant governor. Domestic legislation passed by the Manx parliament—called the Tynwald Court—may be reviewed by the British government. The Tynwald Court consists of the Legislative Council and the popularly elected House of Keys. Bills passed by the parliament are still promulgated on Tynwald Day (July 5) from Tynwald Hill, at St. John's, meeting place of the parliament for over 1,000 years.

Catering to tourists is the islanders' principal occupation. The only other large industry is agriculture. Oats, turnips, and potatoes are the chief crops. The principal towns are Douglas, the capital and chief port, Ramsey, Peel, and Castletown, the former capital. The airport is at Ronaldsway. At Castletown are King William's College (founded 1668), for boys, and Buchan College for Girls (1875). There is a good natural history collection in the Manx Museum in Douglas, and at Port Erin is a Marine Biological Research station. Typical old island houses are displayed at the Manx Open Air Museum in Cregneish. At Peel and Castletown there are 13th century castles.

History. Norsemen conquered the island in the 9th century. Orry, the first Norse ruler, established the Tynwald Court and House of Keys. He also divided the island into its present six counties, or "sheadings." Scotland acquired the island in 1266, but it came under English control in 1341. In 1406, Henry IV gave Man to Sir John Stanley, later Earl of Derby, and in 1736 it passed to the dukes of Atholl. The lordship of Man reverted to the British crown in 1765. The native Manx language, akin to Gaelic, persisted into the 1800's. Pop. (1966) 50,423.

GORDON STOKES,
Author of "English Place-Names."

MAN, Prehistoric Types of. The history of the biological sciences is replete with examples of hypotheses which have been advanced on the basis of indirect evidence, and subsequent attempts to put them to the test by seeking evidence of a more direct nature. Perhaps one of the most remarkable instances of the verification of a hypothesis of this sort is the confirmation of Charles Robert Darwin's inferences regarding man's descent from lower forms of life. Although in Darwin's time practically no fossil evidence was available to support his thesis of human evolution, today this evidence has been accumulated in quite impressive quantities as a result of subsequent discoveries of fossil remains of intermediate types such as he had postulated. Indeed, we now have an almost continuous geological record, ranged in a temporal succession covering something like a million years, which leads from apelike creatures with brains hardly larger than those of a modern gorilla to beings indistinguishable in their skeletal structure from *Homo sapiens.* Before giving a brief account of the various types represented by these fossil remains, it will be well to make reference to some general aspects of the kind of evidence available.

Dating Fossil Remains. The time factor is obviously an essential element in the interpretation of fossil remains and in the solution of evolutionary problems. Hence it is a matter of great importance that the antiquity of fossils should be determined with confidence. There are several ways in which this can be done. Relative dating can often be established by stratigraphical geology, that is, by determining the relative levels of different strata in which fossils are found to be embedded. The more recent strata are superimposed on the earlier strata so that, in a succession of stratigraphic levels, the more ancient fossils are those which occur at the lower levels.

Chemical analysis of various elements may also assist in the determination of relative antiquity; for example, when a bone becomes fossilized and lies buried for many thousands of years, it slowly takes up fluorine from the percolating waters of the soil, and this element combines with the bony substance to form a very stable compound, fluorapatite. Consequently, in any one geological deposit, the older fossils will be found to contain a higher percentage of fluorine. However, since the amount of fluorine in the soil may vary considerably from place to place, obviously the fluorine content cannot be used for comparing the antiquity of fossils derived from *different* deposits. There are also methods available by which the absolute chronological age of fossils in terms of years can be estimated; some of these methods are being actively developed and still further refined at the time of writing. The method based on the estimation of radioactive carbon, carbon-14, has proved particularly reliable if it is carried out with due care; it depends on the fact that *living* organic material contains a known proportion of carbon-14 which, after death, undergoes a very gradual disintegration at a known rate. With the techniques at present available, this method permits a fairly accurate estimation of antiquity up to a limit of about 40,000 years. (See RADIOCARBON DATING.)

It now seems clear that the latter stages in the evolution of man, culminating in the emergence of *Homo sapiens,* occurred throughout the geological period called the Pleistocene epoch (q.v.). During the earlier part of this period, perhaps indeed covering almost the first half of its extent, the prevailing climate of the northern and southern hemispheres was becoming gradually colder. The second part of the Pleistocene was marked by an oscillating climate with a succession of glaciations during which much of the northern region of Europe and North America (and of corresponding latitudes in the southern hemisphere) was covered by ice sheets and glaciers. It is now generally agreed that there were four of these glaciations. They differed in their length and severity, and were separated by warmer interglacial periods of variable duration. The total length of this Ice Age, as it is often called, is estimated to have been about 500,000 years, while the total length of the Pleistocene, including the period preceding the first glaciation, was approximately 1,000,000 years. Oscillations of climate also occurred in the tropical regions of the world, marked by pluvial periods of increased rainfall, and interpluvial periods of relative aridity. There is some reason to suppose that, broadly speaking, these pluvial and interpluvial periods corresponded to the glacial and interglacial periods of the more northern and southern latitudes.

It will be realized that this rhythmic sequence of glacial and interglacial, or pluvial and interpluvial, periods can provide additional evidence of the greatest value for establishing a relative chronology in human prehistory. For if (as is often the case) the geologist can refer a particular deposit to its proper place in the sequence, the chronological position of the indigenous fossils (human or otherwise) can be likewise determined. Moreover, since there is good evidence that the climatic changes affected distant parts of the earth more or less synchronously, they permit some degree of correlation in time of the remains of prehistoric man discovered in widely separated regions.

Defining "Man."—In his book *The Descent of Man* (1871), Darwin anticipated that, with the accession of fossil material representing "connecting links" with an apelike ancestral stock, it might become difficult to decide at what particular point in the series the application of the term "man" would be appropriate. He went on to suggest, however, that this was not a difficulty of any great importance. In a sense he was no doubt quite right, but he did not foresee the sort of confusion of thought which has sometimes arisen because writers on evolutionary problems use the term with different connotations; indeed, it has not infrequently happened that quite ridiculous and unnecessary argumentation has derived from the fact that one of the opposing parties in a controversy uses the term as though it refers only to modern *Homo sapiens*, while the other applies it to a much wider range of hominid species, including primitive types which lived many thousands of years ago and are now extinct.

It is the present convention that the term "man" is taken to refer to all those types of hominid with a mental capacity sufficiently highly developed to make possible the deliberate fabrication of implements. In other words, while some animals can be described as tool *users*, the essential characteristic of "man" is tool *making*. The terms "man" and "human" are not, of course, scientific terms, and are better avoided in strictly scientific discussions. But, in order to avoid in-

convenient pedantry, we shall use them in the following account where their meaning is in no possible doubt. However, in discussing the earlier extinct hominids, where these colloquial terms may be of dubious application, we shall use the more scientific nomenclature of zoological taxonomy. Thus the zoological family Hominidae (and its adjectival form, hominid) refers to the whole evolutionary sequence which gave rise to *Homo sapiens* as well as to other allied genera and species now extinct.

Now, it is generally supposed that the Hominidae arose in the geological period called the Miocene—about 20 or 30 million years ago—from a common ancestral stock which also gave rise to the anthropoid ape family, Pongidae. On the other hand, in spite of intensive explorations, no convincing evidence has yet been found that any stone artifacts are older than the beginning of the Pleistocene. It seems evident, therefore, that a very long period of time intervened between the initial segregation of the Hominidae as an independent line of evolution and the point in its progressive development at which the terms "man" and "human" can properly be applied. This extended period may conveniently be called the prehuman phase of hominid evolution. In this connection it is of particular importance to emphasize once again that the zoological term "hominid" is not to be equated with the colloquial term "human," for much confusion has arisen from using them as though they were synonymous.

HOMO SAPIENS

All the modern varieties of mankind are included in the single species *Homo sapiens*. The major racial divisions today are, of course, easily distinguishable by superficial differences, such as those of skin pigmentation, hair texture, nose shape, and so forth, but it is not possible so readily to distinguish them by internal anatomical characters. Contrary to popular supposition, even the racial differences in the skull are often so poorly defined as to make a racial diagnosis on cranial evidence alone very uncertain. Consequently, it is only rarely that the racial affinities of a fossilized skeleton can be identified with any degree of assurance, though there may be no doubt that it is the skeleton of a man of modern type, that is, of the species *Homo sapiens*.

Antiquity of *Homo sapiens*.—The evidence for the great antiquity of this species is now fairly substantial; let us consider this evidence in the course of a backward journey in time from the Neolithic into the Paleolithic period of human culture.

The Neolithic (or New Stone Age) phase of human culture was probably flourishing about 7000 B.C. in the Middle East, though it did not reach western Europe until 3,000 years later. The culture was characterized by the use of polished stone implements, and by the beginning of plant cultivation and the domestication of animals. The Paleolithic (or Old Stone Age) period of culture, which extended over a vastly longer stretch of time from the Early Pleistocene, was characterized by stone industries in which implements were chipped or flaked by repeated blows, but not polished by grinding. Although in the early stages of the Paleolithic such implements were excessively crude, in the later stages techniques were developed which led to the production of a great variety of tools and weapons,

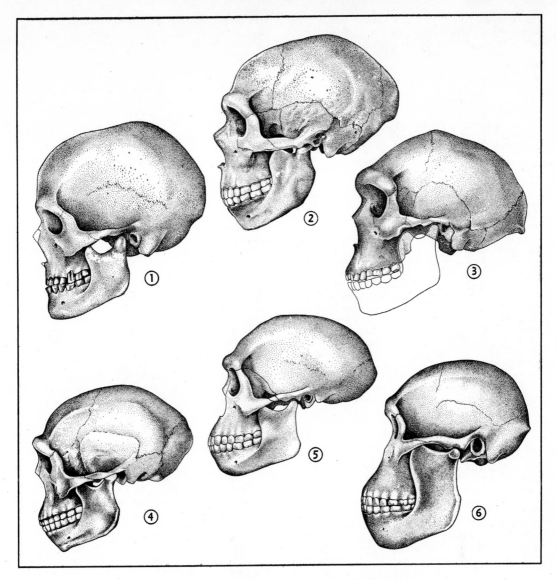

SKULLS OF SIX IMPORTANT TYPES OF PREHISTORIC MAN

(1) Cro-Magnon man (*Homo sapiens*), Menton, French-Italian Mediterranean coast. After Verneau.
(2) Neanderthal man (*Homo neanderthalensis*), Chapelle-aux-Saints, Corrèze, France. Mainly after Boule.
(3) Rhodesian man (*Homo rhodesiensis*), Broken Hill, Northern Rhodesia, Africa. Lower jaw unknown. Known part after Woodward.
(4) Peking man (*Sinanthropus pekinensis*), female skull, restored. After Weidenreich.
(5) Pithecanthropus (*P. erectus*), female skull, No. 11, Sangiran, Java. Face restored from other specimens. Cranium after von Koenigswald.
(6) *Australopithecus*, Sterkfontein, Transvaal, south Africa.

often of considerable delicacy and refinement. After the last major glaciation reached its climax, about 50,000 years ago, there followed a series of somewhat less extreme climatic oscillations. The last of these cold oscillations is termed the Magdalenian period, or sometimes (because of the presence of reindeer, together with other arctic or subarctic mammals, in Europe during this time) the Reindeer Age. It was during this period that the cave art of Paleolithic man reached its highest pitch of perfection—as shown, for example, in the caves at Lascaux in France. (See PALEOLITHIC ART.)

Still more ancient than the Magdalenian was the Aurignacian period. The Aurignacian people were also quite advanced culturally and, like the Magdalenians, left behind for posterity a fine collection of cave drawings and sculptures. By the carbon-14 method it has been possible to determine with considerable accuracy the antiquity of these Upper Paleolithic civilizations. Thus, it is now established that the Magdalenian period was already flourishing in France about 15,000 years ago, while the development of the Aurignacian culture began some 10,000 years earlier. It is of particular interest, therefore, that all the human remains dating from these periods which have been discovered (and many are excellently preserved) are precisely similar in all their anatomical characters to *Homo sapiens*. In other words, members of our own species, apparently indistinguishable from ourselves, were already in existence and (as we know from cultural re-mains) had already developed a complex social organization at least 25,000 years ago.

Racial Distinction.—There is some doubt whether the populations which inhabited Europe in the Upper Paleolithic were always identical racially with their modern successors. Certainly in some cases it is not possible to make any dis-tinction; for example, the skeletons discovered at Cro-Magnon in the Dordogne region of France conform in all details with those of modern Europeans. But there are two possible exceptions to which attention may be called. In 1888 a skeleton of Magdalenian antiquity was excavated at Chancelade in France and studied by the dis-tinguished French anatomist Jean-Léon Testut. He commented on certain resemblances which the skull shows with that of Eskimos. By some anthropologists, indeed, it has even been sug-gested that the Magdalenians *were* Eskimos, and that with the final retreat of the last glaciation they followed the reindeer north and finally settled in the Arctic regions which they now in-habit. This interpretation seemed to be reinforced by certain similarities in the design of their im-plements (for example, their barbed harpoons, bone needles, and so forth). However, more detailed comparisons have considerably lessened the strength of the anatomical evidence, for in certain important features the Chancelade skeleton actually shows quite marked differences from the modern Eskimos.

The other example of a possible racial intru-sion into Europe dates from the Aurignacian and consists of two skeletons found in Italy at Grimaldi (across the border from Menton, France) in 1901, and reported to show Negroid traits. Here again, however, the anatomical evidence for such a conclusion has been seriously questioned, and it has to be admitted that the so-called Negroid traits refer to features which in their development do not exceed the range of variation found in the skeleton of European populations.

Steinheim and Swanscombe Fossils.—We have seen that *Homo sapiens* can be traced back at least to the postclimacteric stages of the first part of the last glaciation. The question now arises whether there is any evidence that the species was in existence at a still earlier date. Here the fossil evidence is far from abundant, but what there is makes it clear that *Homo sapiens*, or at least a type of man not markedly different from *Homo sapiens,* was certainly living in Europe during the third interglacial period (that is, immediately preceding the last, or fourth gla-ciation), and probably even during the second interglacial period.

At Fontéchevade in France and Steinheim in Germany, for example, fossil human skulls simi-lar to those of our own species have been exca-vated in deposits referred to the last intergla-cial period. The Steinheim skull certainly shows an exaggerated development of the brow ridges, but it is not established that this feature is un-paralleled in some of the more primitive races of modern *Homo sapiens.* Portions of a skull found at Swanscombe, England, in 1935 are of particular importance, for all the evidence derived from various sources (geological, archaeological, flu-orine analysis, and so forth) accords with an antiquity corresponding to the second interglacial period, an antiquity which must certainly exceed 100,000 years. Unfortunately the skull itself is very incomplete, but the three cranial bones which have come to light, the occipital and the two parietals, are in a very good state of preservation. Except for their unusual thickness, they all fall within the range of variation of modern human skulls. There is one possible exception to this statement—at the front end of the basal portion of the occipital bone is the impression of one of the air sinuses of the nose. This indicates that the air sinus system must have been very extensively developed, a feature all the more unusual because (since the cranial sutures were still open) the age of the individual could hardly have been more than 20 or 25 years. The total capacity of the skull is estimated to have been rather more than 1,300 cc. (cubic centimeters), which is almost identical with the average cranial capacity in modern *Homo sapiens.* Moreover, an endocra-nial cast makes it clear that the convolutional pattern of the brain was just as complicated.

Because the Swanscombe skull is so fragmen-tary, and because it is an isolated specimen of the European population of the second interglacial period, conclusions based on it must be advanced with caution. However, it may be stated that, *on the evidence of the three bones available,* the skull suggests a type of prehistoric man not markedly different in anatomical features from *Homo sapiens;* if this conclusion is correct, our own species must be very ancient indeed.

Worldwide Distribution of Prehistoric *Homo sapiens.*—Hitherto we have been discuss-ing the antiquity of prehistoric types of *Homo sapiens* in Europe. But it is almost certain that the species did not have its evolutionary origin there. Although we do not certainly know in what part of the world it did arise, there is some reason to suppose it may have been in Africa, partly because of the wide distribution over the continent of primitive stone industries referable to all successive phases of the Paleolithic.

Africa.—Unfortunately, the skeletal evidence of the antiquity of *Homo sapiens* in Africa is too meager to permit any conclusions about its extreme limits, but in 1933 at Florisbad in the Union of South Africa a human skull was found which belongs to a period of Paleolithic culture older than the Aurignacian of Europe. Carbon-14 analysis of peat from the deposit in which the skull lay has given an estimated date of 37,000 years. There is no doubt that the Florisbad skull is that of *Homo sapiens,* even though it is more closely comparable with the primitive variants of this species which exist today. Ob-viously, then, populations of *Homo sapiens* must have been living in south Africa before the Upper Paleolithic civilizations of western Europe. Still more ancient remains of *Homo sapiens* have been reported from east Africa, but the geological evidence for their dating has proved to be too insecure for any reliance to be placed on them.

Asia and Australia.—The oldest remains of *Homo sapiens* so far discovered in eastern Asia were found in cave deposits at Choukoutien, near Peking, China. They consist of several skeletons associated with an Upper Paleolithic culture, and belong to individuals who were probably more or less contemporaneous with the European Au-rignacians. Their racial affinities are indetermi-nate, but they have been said to show some Mon-golian features. In Australia, a human skull was found at Keilor near Melbourne in 1940 which is quite similar to that of the aboriginal natives of today. Although this fossil is not nearly so old as was initially claimed by some, carbon-14 dating has given it an antiquity of at least 8,500 years. Thus the colonization of Australia by *Homo sapiens* took place quite early, and the discovery of Australoid skulls at Wadjak in Java, in deposits which probably date from the terminal part of the Pleistocene, suggests the route by which these ancient colonists reached the continent.

America.—The prehistory of *Homo sapiens* in America has only comparatively recently been elucidated. For many years it had been supposed that man only began to occupy the New World in what may be called historic times. Then, in 1930, it was established from discoveries in New Mexico that a stone industry of Paleolithic type was already in existence at a period when North America was inhabited by Pleistocene animals such as the mammoth and an extinct species of bison. Moreover, the remains of the hearths and campfires of the makers of the stone implements have been found, and carbon-14 analyses of the charcoal from these sites make it certain that they date from at least 9000 B.C. It appears, therefore, that human populations reached America during the recession of the last glaciation, probably by way of Bering Strait.

At Tepexpan, a little north of Mexico City, a human skeleton was found in 1947 embedded in a well-stratified lake deposit. The skeleton was associated with the remains of extinct Pleistocene animals, and a carbon-14 dating of organic material from a layer overlying it (and therefore more recent) gave an antiquity of over 4,000 years. In none of its characters does the Tepexpan skeleton show any appreciable difference from Mexican Indians of modern times. It has been claimed, on the basis of carbon-14 analysis of charcoal from prehistoric sites in Nevada and Texas, that Paleolithic immigrants may have reached America even so far back as 30,000 years ago, but doubts have been expressed on these particular analytical results, and they will therefore need to be checked by further studies. Meanwhile, it may be taken as fairly established that men of modern type were certainly in the New World as long as 10,000 years.

NEANDERTHAL MAN

The Aurignacian period in Europe was preceded by the Mousterian period of Paleolithic culture, a culture whose terminal phases coincided with the onset of the last glaciation. The men inhabiting western Europe at that time had remarkable, and quite distinctive, anatomical characters. They are commonly included under the general term Neanderthal man, for the reason that the first described representative consisted of skeletal remains which were found in 1856 in a valley of that name, near Düsseldorf, Germany. At the time of this discovery, attention was drawn to the simian appearance of the skull as shown, for example, in the receding forehead, the enormous development of the brow ridges, and the flatness of the cranial roof. Some authorities even supposed that it might be a pathological specimen, for example an acromegalic idiot. Thomas H. Huxley pronounced it to be the most apelike human skull that he had ever seen, but he expressed some doubt whether it transcended the variational limits of the more primitive races of modern mankind. Others regarded it as a distinct species to which they applied the name *Homo neanderthalensis*.

Today there are available for study the skull and skeletal remains of numerous specimens of Neanderthal man, and they seem to demonstrate once and for all that, far from being aberrant or pathological types, they comprise a remarkably homogeneous population. In particular, careful biometrical studies have shown that in the sum total of their cranial characters they by no means intergrade with *Homo sapiens,* and this contrast has provided the clearest justification for relegating them to a distinct species.

Physical Characteristics.—Apart from the features just mentioned, the Neanderthal skull is characterized by its unusual thickness, the large size of the orbital and nasal apertures, the massive, chinless jaws, the powerful ridges on the occipital bone for the attachment of exceptionally strong neck muscles, and a backward tilt of the *foramen magnum* on the base of the skull. The limb bones are relatively thick and robust, and they display certain features which have suggested (but not very conclusively) that Neanderthal man walked with a somewhat stooping and lumbering gait. Naturally enough, with all these primitive characters, it was at one time supposed that the Neanderthal species was the parent stock which gave rise to *Homo sapiens,* a sort of "missing link" partly bridging the gulf between modern man and apelike ancestors. But it is now evident from the archaeological and geological evidence that it was the product of a divergent line of evolution which reached the climax of its development in Mousterian times. At the end of the latter period the species rather suddenly disappeared, to be abruptly replaced by a population of quite modern type. The latter, it is presumed, invaded western Europe from more easterly regions and was probably responsible for the final extinction of the Neanderthals.

One particularly remarkable feature of Neanderthal man is the size of his brain; it was considerably larger (average cranial capacity, 1,450 cc.) than that of modern man (average cranial capacity, 1,300 cc.). Although some anthropologists have expressed themselves as puzzled to know why, living under such primitive conditions, he should have needed so large a brain, his mode of life possibly supplies the very answer to the problem. Perhaps we may put it this way. If we ourselves had to endure the severities and hazards of the Ice Age, and to contend with such creatures as mammoths, woolly rhinoceroses, and cave bears with no more elaborate weapons than crude stone axes, no doubt we should need every ounce of grey matter to survive at all! It may be, indeed, that with the invention of more efficient weapons and the development of a more elaborate social organization for the maintenance of collective defense, shelter, and food supplies, the survival value of a large brain in more advanced hominids actually became reduced.

Geographical Variants.—At about the time Neanderthal man lived in Europe, or perhaps a little later, somewhat similar types of prehistoric man inhabited regions so widely separated as Africa and eastern Asia. Several skulls from Ngandong in Java bear witness to the massive size of the brow ridges, and the huge development of the muscular crests in the occipital region for the attachment of the neck muscles. In Northern Rhodesia and in the Union of South Africa at Saldanha Bay near the cape, fossil skulls showing the same sort of construction have been found. In spite of their general similarity to the European Neanderthals, these prehistoric

Asian and African types differ in certain details, particularly of the cranial base and the facial skeleton, and this has led to doubts whether they are at all closely related. Until more evidence is forthcoming, however, it seems reasonable to regard them as geographical variants of the Neanderthal stock which, like the latter, became extinct when they were supplanted by immigrants of modern type.

PITHECANTHROPUS

Conventionally, the Pleistocene period is subdivided into three parts: Upper, Middle, and Lower. There has been much controversy on the precise delimitation of these subdivisions, and we shall adopt here the scheme on which geologists now are generally agreed, a scheme (it is important to note) which includes with the Lower Pleistocene what has for many years been regarded as the terminal phase of the preceding geological period, the Pliocene. The Middle Pleistocene extends from the first to the third glaciation of the Ice Age, and, as we have already seen, there is evidence that toward its close prehistoric types closely resembling (and perhaps identical with) *Homo sapiens* were already in existence. But the most characteristic hominid fossils of the Middle Pleistocene are those which belong to the extinct genus *Pithecanthropus*. The first remains of this genus were discovered in 1891 in Java, and consist of no more than a skull cap and a thigh bone.

The skull cap displays remarkably simian features in the low, flat cranial roof, and in the astonishingly small size of the brain case, while the thigh bone is quite similar to that of modern man. So long as only these fragmentary remains were available, they naturally gave rise to a good deal of speculation, and for a long time opinions were about equally divided whether they represented: (1) an exceedingly primitive type of man, (2) an extinct type of large ape such as a giant gibbon, or (3) a real "missing link," about halfway between ape and man. In more recent times further remains of *Pithecanthropus* have been discovered in Java and also in China. Those found in China were at first allocated to a distinct genus, *Sinanthropus,* but (although this term is still retained as a sort of historical label by some authorities) it has been well established that they are not distinguishable generically from *Pithecanthropus*. It is possible, however, that they represent a different species. All this material has made it quite clear that the first of the three opinions mentioned above is correct.

Physical Characteristics.—The distinctive characters of *Pithecanthropus* may be summarized as follows. The cranial capacity is small, averaging about 900 cc. in the Javanese fossils and about 1,000 cc. in the Chinese. On the other hand, it was evidently extremely variable, ranging from less than 800 cc. to about 1,200 cc. In other words, the cranial capacity at its lowest level approached very closely the largest capacity so far recorded for a modern gorilla (685 cc.) and at its uppermost level reached well within the limits of *Homo sapiens*. The forehead region is flat and retreating. The brow ridges project forward as a continuous shelf of bone overhanging the orbital apertures. As a result of the flatness of the cranial roof, the widest part of the brain case is in the lower temporal region (and not high up in the parietal region of the skull as in *Homo sapiens*). The area on the back of the skull for the attachment of the neck muscles is very extensive. The nasal aperture is exceptionally broad. The palate is capacious. The jaws are massive and show a marked degree of prognathism (that is to say, they project very noticeably in advance of the rest of the face). There is no chin eminence. The teeth are large, and (at least in some individuals) the upper canine teeth may project beyond the level of the adjacent teeth and even interlock to a slight degree with the lower canines.

In all these features, *Pithecanthropus* undoubtedly makes a far closer approach to the anthropoid apes than does *Homo sapiens,* or even *Homo neanderthalensis.* By contrast, the limb bones (so far as they are known) show no features by which they can be certainly distinguished from those of modern man. It thus appears that in the later stages of hominid evolution the limbs acquired their modern shape and proportions long before the skull, brain, and jaws did so, and it is a matter of some interest to note that such a sequence of events (that is, the precocious evolution of limb structure) seems to have been a common feature of mammalian evolution in general.

From the circumstances of their discovery, it is known that the Chinese representatives of *Pithecanthropus* were cave dwellers, and lived in hunting communities. Moreover, they fabricated simple stone implements, and they had already learned the use of fire for culinary purposes. When it is realized that they lived in the early part of the Middle Pleistocene, going back to perhaps as much as 300,000 years or more ago, it seems astonishing that at such an early time they should have been relatively so far advanced culturally.

Distribution.—For many years there was no evidence that the genus *Pithecanthropus* extended its domain outside eastern Asia, and it was this apparently limited distribution which was partly responsible for the thesis that the evolutionary emergence of man took place in the Far East. However, in 1954 there were discovered in sandy deposits in Algeria three lower jaws, and also a parietal bone, of a primitive type of hominid so similar in all important respects to *Pithecanthropus* that it must certainly be regarded as generically identical (in spite of the fact that it was at first assumed to be a new genus, *Atlanthropus*). These fossils were associated with animal remains which include a saber-toothed tiger and an extinct elephant (*Elephas antiquus*), and with stone implements of a very archaic Paleolithic culture called Early Acheulian. The evidence makes it clear that they date from the early part of the Middle Pleistocene. Another fossil relic which may well belong to *Pithecanthropus* is the famous Heidelberg jaw, found in 1907, 80 feet down in a sand pit at Mauer, near Heidelberg, Germany. This fossil, which also probably dates back to the beginning of the Middle Pleistocene, shows certain differences from the known jaws of *Pithecanthropus,* but it seems doubtful whether these can be taken by themselves to justify a generic distinction.

It is generally accepted that the genus *Pithecanthropus* bears an ancestral relationship to *Homo,* and the fossil evidence so far available is strongly in favor of this interpretation. In the first place, there is now a continuous and closely graded series of fossil specimens linking *Pithecanthropus* anatomically with modern man, a gradation which is marked by no perceptible structural hiatus. Second, the geological dating of *Pithecanthropus* fits in quite well with such a conclusion, for, although it is probable that some representatives of the genus persisted to a later date in some parts of the world, the earliest remains so far discovered certainly antedated the earliest known remains which can be attributed to *Homo*. Thus the temporal sequence indicative of an ancestral relationship is in good accord with the evidence of the morphological sequence.

AUSTRALOPITHECUS

Up to 1925 no fossil remains of hominids earlier, or more primitive, than *Pithecanthropus* were known. In that year was announced the first discovery in south Africa of a type of Early Pleistocene hominid which, in skull proportions and brain size, approaches the anthropoid apes so closely that at first considerable doubt was expressed regarding its real nature. Indeed, the generic name by which the type was christened, *Australopithecus* (meaning "southern ape"), has proved to be rather misleading. For, in contradiction of some early statements advanced prematurely on the basis of inadequate material and inaccurate statistical studies, it has now been firmly established that *Australopithecus* is properly to be placed in the family Hominidae and not in the anthropoid ape family (Pongidae).

Significant Physical Characteristics.—Its taxonomic status was made perfectly clear when it was shown, from detailed and critical comparative studies of great numbers of fossil specimens, that it had already developed a long way in the direction which has characterized the hominid line of evolution, and quite opposite to the direction followed by the pongid line of evolution. The so-called simian characters of *Australopithecus* are primitive characters which must certainly have persisted in the hominid line for some considerable period after its segregation from the pongid line as an independent line of evolution. They are particularly emphasized in the small size of the brain and the massive jaws. The cranial capacity actually shows considerable variation, reaching at its upper limits almost to 700 cc. (and according to some estimates, over 700 cc.). In its absolute size, therefore, the brain probably did not exceed by very much that of a big male gorilla, but there is some reason to suppose that in proportion to body size it was quite definitely larger.

It was the small size of the brain which led some anatomists at first to deny hominid status to *Australopithecus*. But this line of argument was evidently based on a confusion between the zoological term "hominid" and the colloquial term "human," for it is well recognized that, while the evolutionary sequence of the Hominidae dates back to Miocene or Early Pliocene times, there is no evidence that a large brain was acquired before the Pleistocene. In spite of their massiveness, the jaws are fitted with teeth of typically human pattern. Thus, the canine teeth are not tusklike, interlocking teeth as they are in the apes; they are small and spatulate in shape, and in the earliest stages of wear they became worn down flat from the tips just as they do in modern man. Similarly, the lower premolar teeth have the bicuspid pattern typical of the Hominidae, and quite different from the pointed cutting teeth characteristic of the apes. The milk dentition, too, is entirely hominid in all important features.

Because comparative odontology has proved so reliable a criterion for determining evolutionary relationships in the study of fossils in general, this evidence of the dentition is particularly important for assessing the taxonomic position of *Australopithecus*.

Certain features of the australopithecine skull have a particular significance in that they first suggested the probability that these ancient hominids were already erect, bipedal creatures. They include the relatively forward position on the base of the skull of the occipital condyles (whereby the skull articulates with the spinal column), and the small size of the area on the occipital bone for the neck muscles. Both these features led to the inference that the skull was balanced on the top of a more or less vertical spine as in later hominids, and not held in position at the end of a forwardly sloping spine by powerful neck muscles as in the anthropoid apes. This inference was further supported by the anatomical details of the lower end of the thigh bone and of one of the ankle bones (talus).

Finally, it was fully and dramatically confirmed by the discovery at different sites of four specimens of the hipbone, all of which are designed on the human pattern. Now, no part of the skeleton is more distinctive of the Hominidae as compared with the anthropoid apes than this bone. In the apes the blade of the hipbone (ilium) is narrow and elongated; in the hominid type it is broad and flattened in direct adaptation to the erect posture. The broad blade provides an extensive area for the attachment of the buttock muscles, which are used for balancing the trunk on the lower limbs in standing and walking; it gives a wider attachment to the abdominal muscles, which are concerned with the maintenance of abdominal tone in the standing position; and it also plays a part in directly supporting the abdominal viscera in the upright posture. Many other features of the hipbone likewise can only be interpreted on the assumption that *Australopithecus* was adapted for an erect bipedal gait (though, as of course might be expected in such a primitive type, there are also indications that this had not been developed to the degree of perfection found in modern *Homo sapiens*). It is interesting to note that the anatomical evidence of posture is quite consistent with the geological evidence of the environment in which the south African representatives of *Australopithecus* lived, for this indicates a relatively arid climate and open veldt-like country, and certainly not a tropical forest habitat of the kind for which modern anthropoid apes are adapted.

Toolmaking Capacity.—We have noted the generally accepted convention that the terms "man" and "human" should be reserved for those later stages of hominid evolution marked by the ability to fabricate implements. The question therefore arises whether the australopithecine hominids had attained such a level of intelligence. Some suggestive evidence was provided at the site of the original discovery by numbers of fossil baboon skulls, a large proportion of which appeared to have sustained depressed fractures of the cranial roof, which (it was reasonably argued) were possibly caused by well-aimed blows with an implement of some sort. Quite recently more direct evidence of a toolmaking capacity has been furnished by the discovery of crude stone implements embedded in deposits containing fossil jaws and teeth of *Australopithecus*. Since no remains of hominids of a more advanced type have (at the time of writing) been found in these particular deposits, it seems a fair inference that the implements were actually fabricated by australopithecines. On the other hand, it has been argued that such a primitive hominid with so small a brain can hardly be credited with the intelligence required for such manipulative and inventive skill. But this argument is based on quite uncertain assumptions regarding the minimal amount of brain substance which is a necessary prerequisite for this level of intelligence.

The fact is, of course, that while the fossil skulls of *Australopithecus* can provide information about the size of the brain and its external configuration, it can supply no information about the complexity of its functional organization. Nevertheless, it is prudent to await the accumulation of further evidence before coming to a decision on the possible toolmaking capacity of *Australopithecus*. If stone implements of the same primitive type should be discovered at a number of different sites containing remains of this genus (and no remains of any more advanced hominid), then the application to it of the terms "man" and "human" would obviously become appropriate.

Sir WILFRED E. LE GROS CLARK,
Professor of Anatomy, Oxford University.

ZINJANTHROPUS

Fossil evidence indicating that two, or even three, distinct hominid species may have lived in the veldt-like regions of South Africa at the time of *Australopithecus* was uncovered by Louis S. B. Leakey, the British paleontologist. At Olduvai Gorge, Tanganyika, in 1959, Leakey found the complete skull of a 500,000-year-old hominid with a brain capacity significantly larger than that of *Australopithecus*. Associated with the skull in the same layer, or horizon, were pebble tools, stone flakes, a hammerstone, and the food remains of birds, fish, lizards, and frogs. Leakey termed this individual *Zinjanthropus* and theorized that it represented a direct link between *Australopithecus* and *Homo Sapiens*. Related discoveries in Kenya, the Vaal Valley in South Africa, and Ain Hanech in Algeria offered persuasive evidence that the basic toolmaking tradition, dating back a half million years, was also widespread as it evolved on the African continent.

See also ANTHROPOLOGY; ARCHAEOLOGY; CULTURE; STONE AGE.

Bibliography.—MacCurdy, George G., *Early Man* (Philadelphia 1937); McGregor, James H., "Human Origins and Early Man," in Franz Boas and others, *General Anthropology*, Chap. 2 (Boston 1938); Romer, Alfred S., *Man and the Vertebrates*, 3d ed. (Chicago 1941); Howells, William W., *Mankind So Far* (New York 1944); Hooton, Earnest A., *Up From the Ape*, 2d ed. (New York 1946); Montagu, M. F. Ashley, *An Introduction to Physical Anthropology*, rev. 2d ed. (Springfield, Ill., 1951); Zeuner, Friedrich E., *Dating the Past* (London 1952); Leakey, Louis S. B., *Adam's Ancestors*, 4th ed. (London 1953); Clark, Sir Wilfred E. Le Gros, *The Fossil Evidence for Human Evolution* (Chicago 1955); Boule, Marcellin, *Fossil Men*, new ed. by Henri V. Vallois, Eng. tr. by Michael Bullock (New York 1957); Clark, Sir Wilfred E. Le Gros, *History of the Primates* (Chicago 1957); Oakley, Kenneth P., *Man the Toolmaker* (Chicago 1957); Piveteau, Jean, *Traité de paléontologie* (Paris 1952–   ): Vol. 7, *Primates* (1957); White, Leslie A., *The Evolution of Culture* (New York 1959); Clark, J. Grahame D., *The Prehistory of Southern Africa* (Hammondsworth, England, 1959); Braidwood, Robert J., *Prehistoric Man* (Chicago 1961); Clark, J. Grahame D., *World Prehistory: An Outline* (London 1961); Howells, W. W., *The Emergence of Man* (New York 1961); Washburn, Sherwood L., *Social Life of Early Man* (New York 1961); Cornwall, Ian W., *World of Ancient Man* (New York 1964).

MAN AND SUPERMAN (subtitled A COMEDY AND A PHILOSOPHY), a play by George Bernard Shaw (q.v.), published in 1903. Except for *Back to Methuselah* it is the longest, and perhaps the wittiest, of his plays.

As its dedicatory preface states, the work is Shaw's response to the suggestion of the English critic Arthur B. Walkley that he write a Don Juan play. Using a modern setting, Shaw centers the play on four of the traditional characters of Mozart's opera *Don Giovanni:* Don Juan Tenorio (John Tanner); Doña Ana (Ann Whitefield); the Commander (Roebuck Ramsden); and Leporello (Henry Straker, Tanner's chauffeur). He makes Tanner and Ramsden Ann's joint guardians, and adds the subplots of Octavius Robinson's hopeless love for Ann and of the secret marriage of Octavius' sister Violet to Hector Malone, a young American whose wealthy father wants him to marry a lady of title.

The Shavian twist to this standard set of characters makes Ann the pursuer and Tanner the pursued. The latter, regarded by Ramsden as a dangerous radical (Shaw prints his "Revolutionist's Handbook" as an appendix to the play), is both the hero and the *raisonneur,* who discusses Shaw's ideas. He expounds a Lamarckian philosophy of evolution in which woman, as the embodiment of the Life Force, seeks to advance the evolutionary process by finding a mate capable of fathering the Superman. This need makes the highly intelligent Tanner Ann's quarry, and she captures him.

The play is in four acts. The third, which deals with Tanner's capture by Mendoza, a philosophical Spanish bandit, includes a long dream sequence in which Tanner, Ann, and Ramsden, reverting to their operatic prototypes, discuss life and morality with the Devil. This section, usually omitted in staging, has been produced as an independent dramatic reading under the title *Don Juan in Hell.*

DeLANCEY FERGUSON.

MAN IN THE IRON MASK, The, a mysterious prisoner confined in France during the time of Louis XIV: d. Paris, Nov. 19, 1703. When a new superintendant, Bénigne de Saint-Mars, took charge of the Bastille in Paris, Sept. 18, 1698, he brought with him a prisoner whose identity was concealed by a mask of black velvet (not of iron). The prisoner died there in 1703 and was buried in the cemetery of St. Paul under the name of Marchioli (or Marchioly). This much is known for certain. In addition it is said that the same man had been in the custody of Saint-Mars earlier at Pignerol (Pinerolo, Italy) and on Ste.-Marguerite, one of the Îsles de Lérins near Cannes. Rumors were circulated about him even during his lifetime, but it was probably Voltaire who aroused most interest in the case in his *Siècle de Louis XIV* (1751), and he is usually credited with originating the legend that the mask was of iron.

Although there is still debate on the subject, probably the most widely accepted theory is that the prisoner was Conte Ercole Antonio Mattioli (q.v.), a minister of the duke of Mantua. Mattioli was arrested for revealing to foreign powers secret negotiations by which France attempted to acquire the fortress of Casale from Mantua. Critics of this theory point out that since it was widely known that Mattioli was imprisoned at Pignerol in 1679, there would be no need to hide the fact later, yet the French royal family continued to keep the identity of the masked prisoner a secret even after his death. Adherents to another popular theory maintain that the prisoner was one Eustache Dauger de Cavoye, whose offense to the king is unknown.

A more romantic explanation is the one which holds that the Man in the Iron Mask was a twin brother of Louis XIV whose existence was concealed from the public to avoid dispute over the throne. This version was first published by Jean Louis Giraud Soulavie in his *Mémoires du maréchal duc de Richelieu* (1790), and it has been used by various playwrights and novelists, including Alexandre Dumas père. *Le Vicomte de Bragelonne* (1848) by Dumas includes a section, sometimes published separately as *The Man in the Iron Mask,* which is the most popular literary treatment of the case.

Consult Mongredien, Georges, *Le masque de fer* (Paris 1952); Furneaux, Rupert, *The Man Behind the Mask* (London 1954); Ross Williamson, Hugh, "The Man in the Iron Mask," *Enigmas of History*, pp. 207–228 (New York 1957).

MAN O' WAR, American race horse, by Fair Play out of Mahubah, foaled near Lexington, Ky., in 1917. Bred by August Belmont and sold in 1918 to Samuel D. Riddle, he had a pedigree which included the three great English sires: Matchem, Herod, and Eclipse. Racing only as a two-year-old and three-year-old (1919–1920), he set five world records and won 20 out of 21 races, defeated only by Upset at Saratoga, N.Y., in 1919. He was probably the most famous stallion in the history of horse racing and became a leading sire. His offspring won about $3,250,000. When he died (1947), he was embalmed and buried at Faraway Farm near Lexington. See also HORSE RACING.—*In the United States.*

MAN-O'-WAR BIRD. See FRIGATE BIRD.

MAN-OF-WAR, a warship of a recognized navy, almost always armed for active hostilities. See WARSHIPS, MODERN.

MAN WITHOUT A COUNTRY, The, a short story by Edward Everett Hale (q.v.). A patriotic parable, it was first published in the *Atlantic Monthly* for December 1863. Its popularity, in the midst of the Civil War, was immediate.

Hale tells the story of Philip Nolan, a young lieutenant in the United States Army, who was court-martialed for participation in Aaron Burr's conspiracy to set up an independent nation in the Louisiana territory. Asked by the court if he would affirm his allegiance to the United States, he exclaimed, "Damn the United States! I wish I may never hear of the United States again!" The court pronounced sentence: He should have his wish. He was shipped aboard a naval vessel bound for a foreign station. The officers whose mess he sometimes shared were under orders never to mention the country in his presence; his reading matter was censored, and allusions to the United States deleted. When the ship completed its foreign tour, Nolan was transferred to another outward-bound cruiser. In a frigate action during the War of 1812, Nolan gallantly helped to serve a gun; the commander mentioned him favorably in dispatches and urged his pardon, but nothing came of it. His exile continued until his death at sea in the spring of 1863. On his deathbed, when he was told by one of the officers about

the growth of the United States, he revealed that he had prayed daily for the welfare of the country and had tried to guess at the significance of the new stars in the flag.

Though Hale's story continued to be immensely popular for at least two generations after the Civil War, it was primarily a tract for the times. Hale even named Southern leaders—Braxton Bragg, Matthew Maury, and others—as equal in their treason to the real Burr and the fictitious Nolan. Sectional bitterness is revealed also in sneering references to the Virginian presidents Thomas Jefferson and James Madison. The early readers of the story saw only the patriotic parable; later readers are more likely to notice both the implausibility of the narrative machinery and the actual cruelty of Nolan's punishment. In 1937, at the Metropolitan Opera House in New York, an opera entitled *The Man Without a Country* had its first performance. The music was by Walter Damrosch, and the libretto by Arthur Guiterman was based on Hale's story.

DeLancey Ferguson.

MANADO, mä-nä'dō, or **MENADO,** mä-nä'dō, town, Indonesia, the capital of North Sulawesi Province, located at the northeastern tip of the island of Celebes (Sulawesi), about 600 miles northeast of Makassar. On the Celebes Sea, it is the chief port for the northern part of the island and is the trading center for the surrounding agricultural and lumbering region. Its exports include copra, sugar cane, coffee, spices, and tropical woods. Pop. (1951 est.) 50,000.

MANAGEMENT, măn'ij-mĕnt, the art of coordinating the elements or factors of production toward the achievement of the purposes of an organization. It is the accomplishment of objectives through the use of men, materials, and machines. The traditional economic classification of the factors of production includes land, labor, capital, and coordination. The management function is a major segment of coordination.

Any enterprise or association, whether public or private, whether run for profit or not, must be controlled. The control of an enterprise is effected through *administration* and *management.* These two functions are not the same, although they are often confused. Administration consists of the determination of the goals and the policies of the enterprise. In a business organization, these goals usually include economical production, sale of production at a profit, and growth of the enterprise at least to the point at which diminishing returns are encountered. In nonbusiness enterprises, policies must also be determined. The carrying out of these policies to achieve the aims of the enterprise is management. The confusion arises because management personnel often influence policy determinations.

For administration and management to function effectively, there must be a proper structuring of the enterprise. This is *organization,* which is necessary to, but distinct from, both administration and management. Organization has been termed the keystone on which the entire structure of any enterprise is based. Management is now seen as the carrying out of the policies of administration through the framework of organization.

The form which the organization of an enterprise will take is determined by the nature of the problems encountered, the conditions under which the problems will have to be solved, and the character of the personnel that are available.

Because of the increasing specialization of management functions, the organization of management has become a major problem of administration. The main problem is coordination. The usual solution is a division of management units along such functional lines as finance, production, and personnel. This type of organization must be tempered, however, by a consideration of the most effective coordination, and possible centralization, of management activities.

Management has been called both a science and an art. The development of scientific management has demonstrated the fact that many techniques of management are susceptible to measurement and factual determination. Such techniques have in part replaced reliance on personal judgment. To this extent, management may be said to be a science. But in coordinating these techniques and in enlisting the cooperation of individual employees, management may still be considered an art.

Although the principles of management have been developed primarily in the field of business, the same basic principles can be applied to all forms of enterprise. It is this similarity of application that holds the greatest promise for a further systematization of management as a science.

WILLIAM N. KINNARD, JR.
Head, Finance Department
University of Connecticut

Bibliography

Barry, William S., *The Fundamentals of Management* (London: Allen and Unwin, 1963).
Bowman, Donald M., and Fillerup, Francis M., *Management: Organization and Planning* (New York: McGraw-Hill, 1963).
Chandler, Margaret K., *Management Rights and Union Interests* (New York: McGraw-Hill, 1964).
Enrick, Norbert L., *Management Operations Research* (New York: Holt, Rinehart, and Winston, 1965).
McLarney, William J., *Management Training, Cases and Principles*, 4th ed. (Homewood, Ill.: Irwin, 1965).

MANAGUA, mä-nä′gwä, is the capital and largest city of Nicaragua. It is also the country's communications, financial, and industrial center. The city is situated on the southwestern shore of Lake Managua, in western Nicaragua. Its sultry climate is tempered by breezes from the lake. The residential areas south of the city are higher and cooler. Population: (1960 est.) 240,000.

Managua is on the route of the Inter-American Highway and is connected by paved road with the Pacific port of Puerto Somoza. Government-owned railroads connect it with the cities of Granada and León and with the port of Corinto. Manufactures are limited to food processing and to such products as cement, soap, and textiles, chiefly for local consumption.

At the time of the Spanish conquest, there was a large Indian settlement in Managua. The city's growth was slow until 1858, when it was chosen as the national capital in a compromise solution to the rival claims of Granada and León. United States Marines were stationed in Managua almost continuously from 1912 to 1933 in an effort to maintain order in Nicaragua.

The city was almost destroyed by earthquake and fire in 1931. It was rebuilt in modern style, with evenly spaced streets and avenues. Most of its civic buildings are modern in design. The national capitol and the cathedral are situated in the Parque Central, one of the city's main plazas. Managua is also the site of Nicaragua's national museum and library. In a park on the southwest-

ern edge of the city, footprints of prehistoric men and animals are preserved in lava. There are two active volcanoes in the vicinity—Momotombo to the northwest and Momotombito on an island in Lake Managua.

The department of Managua, of which Managua city is the capital, has an area of 1,330 square miles and a population (1960) of 300,341.

MANAGUA, Lake, mä-nä′gwä, is the second-largest lake in Nicaragua. It is situated in the departments of León and Managua at an altitude of 127 feet, and drains into Lake Nicaragua, to the southeast, through the Tipitapa River. Lake Managua is 38 miles long and 16 miles wide. Fishing and the hunting of alligators, whose skins are exported, provide a livelihood for the people who live on its shores. The lake contains the only known species of freshwater shark (*Eulamia nicaraguensis*). The city of Managua, on the southwestern shore, is the lake's only large port.

MANAKIN, man′ə-kin, is any one of the small perching birds of the family Pipridae. The family has 59 species. Their habitat is the American tropics. The typical manakin is about the size of a sparrow, but is stockier and has a shorter, square tail and weaker legs. The males of many species have a striking plumage, usually deep black with bold contrasting areas of crimson, gold, or blue. The females, and the males of some species, have a dull, inconspicuous plumage.

The males, who take no part in building the nest, incubating the eggs, or raising the young, are noted for their curious method of courtship. This consists of repeated snappings and rattling of the wings. The sounds produced apparently take the place of song in attracting the females or in warning off competitors, since manakins are voiceless.

The best known species is Gould's manakin (*Manacus vitellinus*) of Central America, which is mainly green in color but adorned with a deep black cap and wings and brilliant patches of orange gold on the cheeks and throat.

CHARLES VAURIE
Department of Ornithology
American Museum of Natural History

MANAMA, ma-na′mə, is the capital, chief port, and commercial and financial center of the sheikhdom of Bahrain (Bahrein) in Southwest Asia. The sheikhdom consists of a group of islands in the Persian Gulf. Manama extends a mile and a half along the northern coast of Bahrain Island, the largest of the group. A 1.7-mile causeway connects Bahrain Island with the adjacent island of Muharraq. The residences of the sheikh and of the British political agent are in Manama.

Until the discovery of petroleum here in 1932, Manama was noted primarily for its pearl-fishing industry. The rise of the oil industry shifted the emphasis to oil refineries. Other local industries include fishing, boatbuilding (small dhows), and the manufacture of reed matting and sailcloth. Manama is also a transshipment point for goods destined for Saudi Arabia. In 1958 it was declared a free port, and in 1962 a deepwater harbor was constructed. Oil royalties have financed the construction of schools and roads and brought improvements in sanitation. There is also an American hospital in Manama. Population: (1959) 55,541.

MANASAROWAR LAKE, măn'à-sà-rō'ĕr, lake, Tibet, 12 miles long and 14 miles wide, located in the Himalayas in southwestern Tibet, at an altitude of 14,950 feet. Along with smaller lakes, sometimes grouped with it as the Manasarower Lakes, it is situated in a divide between Kailas peak to the north and Gurla Mandhata to the south. Except when it is icebound or during periods of unusual dryness, it drains via the river Ganga Chu into Rakas Lake (or Rakas Tal). It is a sacred pilgrimage center for Hindus. According to tradition it was created by Brahma's soul and is the source of the Brahmaputra, Ganges, Indus, and Sutlej rivers, all of which originate in this part of Tibet. Actually, it is thought to contribute water only to the Sutlej by way of Rakas Lake and underground channels.

MANASQUAN, măn'à-skwŏn, borough, New Jersey, in Monmouth County, seven miles south of Asbury Park, on the Atlantic coast at the mouth of the Manasquan River, an entrance to the Intracoastal Waterway. It is primarily a resort, but there is some commercial fishing. Fruit, vegetables, and poultry are agricultural products of the vicinity. It is served by the New York and Long Branch, Central of New Jersey, and Pennsylvania railroads. It was incorporated in 1887. Robert Louis Stevenson wrote part of *The Master of Ballantrae* while staying here in 1888. Pop. 4,022.

MANASSAS, First and Second Battles of. See BULL RUN, FIRST BATTLE OF; BULL RUN, SECOND BATTLE OF.

MANASSEH, mà-năs'ĕ, in the Old Testament, the first son of Joseph and Asenath, founder of a chief tribe of Israel. Born in Egypt, he was given this name (from the Hebrew *naseh* "to cause to forget") because with a son God had made Joseph forget his family's troubles (Genesis 41:51). Traditionally Manasseh, as first-born, would have inherited a double share of his father's estate, but he was subordinated to his younger brother Ephraim (q.v.) by Jacob, his grandfather, who believed that Ephraim's descendants would be greater (48:5–20). Although Manasseh's descendants were allotted a large expanse of desirable land in Canaan, they were eventually surpassed in numbers and influence by the tribe of Ephraim. Among prominent leaders of the Manasseh tribe were Gideon, Gilead, and Jephthah.

MANASSEH (or in Greek form MANASSES), king of Judah: r. about 687 to 642 B.C. A son of Hezekiah and Hepzibah, he succeeded his father when he was 12 years old. Although his reign was long and peaceful, he was regarded as one of the most wicked kings of Judah because, under the influence of Assyrians, he recognized such alien cults as Baalism and the worship of Astarte and Moloch. There is little mention of him in the Bible except for the story of his wickedness as told in II Kings 21:1–18 and II Chronicles 33:1–20. The latter version includes a happy ending in which he repented, while a captive in Babylon, and returned to cast out the false gods. A vassal of the Assyrian kings Sennacherib, Esarhaddon, and Ashurbanipal, he was succeeded by his son Amon. A penitential psalm attributed to him is included in the Apocrypha (q.v.) as the Prayer of Manasseh.

MANASSEH BEN ISRAEL, bĕn ĭz'-rà-ĕl, or **MENASSEH BEN ISRAEL,** Jewish theologian: b. c. 1604; d. Middelburg, Netherlands, Nov. 20, 1657. His birthplace is uncertain (perhaps La Rochelle, France), but he grew up in Amsterdam, where his parents had settled after fleeing from the Inquisition in Portugal. Educated there, he became chief rabbi of the Amsterdam synagogue, and in 1626 he established the first Hebrew printing press in Holland. He gained prominence with his most famous work, *El conciliador* (1632–51), an attempt, written in Spanish, to reconcile contradictory passages in the Old Testament. Seeking readmission of Jews to England, he wrote *Esperança de Israel* (1650) and went to London in 1655 to petition for the repeal of anti-Semitic legislation. He stayed in England for two years, and his *Humble Addresses to the Lord Protector on behalf of the Jewish Nation* (1655) was favorably considered by Oliver Cromwell, but Manasseh ben Israel did not live to see protection officially guaranteed to Jews in England. He published in Latin, Spanish, and Portuguese many scriptural interpretations and various works defending the Jews, including *Vindiciae Judaeorum* (1656). Rembrandt painted a portrait of him and etched illustrations for one of his works.

Consult Roth, Cecil, *Life of Menasseh ben Israel, Rabbi, Printer, and Diplomat* (Philadelphia 1934).

MANATEE, măn-à-tē', an aquatic, herbivorous mammal, genus *Trichechus* (or *Manatus*), of the order Sirenia (q.v.). Large and robust, it weighs from 450 to 2,000 pounds and averages from 7 to 12 feet in length. It has a blunt head, small eyes, thick lips, and a bristly muzzle. The adult's skin is gray and almost hairless. Its forelimbs are broad flippers, and lacking hindlimbs, it has a broad flat tail. Although it is a mammal, it is helpless on land, yet it must come to the surface of the water to breathe every 10 to 15 minutes. Sensitive to cold, it lives in the warmer rivers and estuaries of the Atlantic coasts, feeding on seaweed and other aquatic vegetation, of which it consumes up to 100 pounds a day. It lacks ways to defend itself and is preyed upon by crocodiles and sharks and is hunted by man. Its meat is tasty, and its fat makes an excellent cooking oil. Four species are known: the Florida manatee (*Trichechus latirostris*), found from the Carolinas to Florida and the Gulf of Mexico; the West Indies manatee (*T. manatus*) around Caribbean islands; the Amazon manatee or Natrerer's manatee (*T. inunguis*), which inhabits the rivers of northeastern South America; and the African manatee (*T. senegalensis*), which lives in Lake Chad as well as in the rivers of western Africa. Once far more common, the manatee has diminished in number, especially in North America. It is now protected by law in Florida. Manatees are placid, sociable animals, which become quite tame in captivity. Often affectionate and playful, they have been observed to kiss and to swim about with linked flippers. Both males and females are solicitous parents and may take turns caring for the young. It is thought that legends of mermaids were inspired by manatees because of the very human way the female holds a nursing pup to the mammary glands on her chest. One or two pups are produced at a birth, weighing about 60 pounds.

MANATEE, Florida. See BRADENTON.

MANAUS, mà-nous, or **MANAOS**, city of northwestern Brazil, the capital of Amazonas state, on a height over the left bank of the Rio Negro, about 10 miles above its junction with the Amazon River. Although it is located almost 1,000 miles inland from the Atlantic by river, ocean-going vessels can reach its busy harbor, built in 1902; because of the marked changes in the water level floating wharves were constructed. Manaus is the trade and distribution center for the whole upper Amazon region; rubber, cacao, Brazil nuts, tonka beans, horns and hides, hardwoods, and dried fish are exported. There is a regular air service with Belém and Rio de Janeiro. The city is completely surrounded by tropical forests and has a very hot and humid climate. It is well built, with broad streets, electricity, a good water supply, and several modern government buildings; a large cathedral rises in the center of the town, which has been an episcopal see since 1892. Manaus is also a cultural and educational center, with high schools, an industrial school, a chemical institute, an historic-ethnographic museum. The botanical and zoological gardens are famous. Manaus was founded in 1660 by Francisco da Motta Falcão as São José do Rio Negro; the name was changed to Manaos after 1825 and Manaus after 1939. It was the capital of Rio Negro province before it became in 1850 the capital of the newly-created state of Amazonas. At the end of the 19th century and at the beginning of the 20th Manaus had a period of incredible prosperity due to the wild rubber boom. The golden-domed opera house, now in disuse, the ornate buildings, and the harbor were then constructed. When the rubber trade practically ceased, the city suffered decline; but following World War II trade began to revive. Pop. (1966) 210,000.

MANBY, George William, English inventor: b. Denver, Norfolk, Nov. 28, 1765; d. Southtown, Great Yarmouth, Nov. 18, 1854. He was educated at the military college of Woolwich, and became in 1803 barrack master at Great Yarmouth. His attention having been drawn to calamities resulting in cases of shipwreck, from the difficulty of establishing communication with the shore, he attempted casting a rope from the shore to the wreck by the agency of gunpowder. Chains were unable to stand the shock of the discharge, but stout strips of rawhide closely platted together were found to answer, and on Feb. 12, 1808 the entire crew of the brig *Elizabeth*, wrecked within 150 yards of the beach, were rescued by the simple contrivance of Captain Manby.

In 1810 his invention was brought before a committee of the House of Commons, and having been favorably reported on, he received a grant of money, and all the dangerous stations on the British coasts were supplied with his apparatus. He also contrived shells filled with luminous matter, to enable the crew to perceive the approach of the rope, in the manufacture of which he suggested several improvements.

MANCHESTER, town, Connecticut, in Hartford County; altitude 140 feet; on the New York, New Haven and Hartford Railroad; 8 miles east of Hartford. The township (which includes South Manchester) is situated in a fertile area growing fruits, vegetables, tobacco and nursery products. The Cheney silk mills, established here in 1838, form the town's chief industry. Other manufactures include woolens (made here before 1790), soap, paper and fiber board, parachutes, electrical instruments, needles, clothing, baseballs, toys, leather novelties, machinery and tools, and chimes. Manchester has the Whiton Memorial Library, and South Manchester, the Mary Cheney Library. There is a state trade school here.

Settled in 1672, it was a part of Hartford, and then of East Hartford, until its incorporation as a town in 1823. Town government is operated under a special legislative charter. Pop. 42,102.

MANCHESTER, măn′chĕs-tēr; -chĭs-tēr; county borough and city, England, in Lancashire County, 188 miles north of London and 30 miles east of Liverpool, on the Irwell River, an affluent of the Mersey, and since 1894 connected with the sea at Eastham, on the Mersey, by the Manchester Ship Canal. It is one of the principal manufacturing cities of the world, and the cotton center of Great Britain. Railways (steam and electric) and motor omnibuses communicate with the surrounding towns and villages.

Geography.—The city lies in the southeast corner of Lancashire, bordered by the low Pennine Hills on the north and east, and entering the fertile Cheshire plain on the south. The city center is 133 feet above sea level.

Climate.—The climate is temperate; the prevailing wind is southwest. The city, with 30 inches rainfall, is damp rather than wet, with fogs and mists in winter and with sunshine reduced by the industrial smoke pall. This damp climate and ample water supply contributed to the establishment of the cotton industry.

Geology.—Thick deposits of glacial drift, sands, gravels and boulder clay overlie heavily faulted Triassic, Permian and Carboniferous rocks which often reach the surface. The "Pendleton fault" gives rise to occasional earth tremors. Wells in the Triassic rock form a source of industrial water. Coal is mined at two pits within the city and extensively throughout the surrounding area. To the south, vast salt beds feed the local chemical industries, and other mineral deposits abound.

HISTORY

Ancient.—The Romans established a fort at Mancenion in 79 A.D. to guard a military road: a small portion of the wall and Roman objects from the site are still extant. The Romans left Mancenion in 426 and though the place is occasionally mentioned in surveys, little is known until 870, when the Danes destroyed the town. In 920 it was rebuilt by Edward the Elder: in 1028 King Canute gave Manchester the right to coin money. Manchester is briefly mentioned in the Domesday survey of 1086 as poor and sparsely populated.

Medieval.—Manchester's importance dates from the 13th century. In 1229 Henry III granted an annual fair and in 1330 the first signs of industrial activity were seen in the settlement of immigrant Flemish manufacturers. About 1500, vegetable cotton, known as "cotton wool," was introduced. The antiquary John Leland, appointed by Henry VIII, described Manchester in his 1536 survey as "the fairest, best builded, quikkest and most populous towne in all Lancashire." From 1645 Manchester was represented by a member of Parliament. In 1650, Manchester manufactures were given as "woollens, frizes, fustians, sack-cloths, mingled stuffs, inkles, topes and prints" and in 1690 the art of calico printing was introduced from France.

Recent.—In 1717 Manchester's population was 8,000. In the following 200 years, the coming of the Industrial Revolution brought the greatest growth, for by 1900 the population was 543,872. The discovery and exploitation of steam power, and the opening up of road and river communications, paralleled a multitude of mechanical inventions for cotton manufacture. In 1761, the first of a network of canals was built; in 1785 the culminating invention of the power loom for weaving was made, and about the same time the first steam engine was used in cotton manufacture in Miller Street, Manchester. In 1821, the *Manchester Guardian* newspaper was established; in 1830 the Manchester and Liverpool Railway was opened: by 1850 there was a direct rail link with London.

In 1832 Manchester became a Parliamentary borough with two members. Social progress was interrupted in the 1830's and 1840's by food shortage, and despite the repeal of the Corn Laws, great distress was caused in the 1860's by restriction of cotton imports due to the American Civil War. In 1851 Owens College (later the Manchester University) was opened, and in 1894 the Manchester Ship Canal, making Manchester an inland port for ships up to 15,000 tons, was completed. In 1929 land was acquired for a 4,000 acre satellite town at Wythenshawe, and in the following year the first air service from Manchester to the European continent was inaugurated. During World War II, more than 600 Manchester citizens lost their lives in heavy air raids, many of the town's buildings were destroyed, and 30,000 houses were damaged.

Municipal.—In 1301 the lord of the manor granted a charter appointing officers, making rules for town management and defining the functions of the courts, but in practice the lord of the manor remained all-powerful until the latter half of the 18th century when Parliament set up town commissioners. Successful administration was not achieved, however, until 1838, when Manchester was granted, under an Act of 1838, a charter of incorporation giving it an elected municipal council with wide powers of local government. In 1838, the acreage was 4,293; in 1900 the acreage, by absorption of neighboring authorities, was 13,000, and in 1931 the present acreage of 27,255 was attained. Manchester became a city in 1853.

CONTEMPORARY MANCHESTER

Industry and Commerce.—Manchester is the metropolis of southeast Lancashire—one of the principal industrial areas of the world—housing within the city boundary many great industrial plants and, even more significantly, providing packing, marketing, selling, banking, insurance, stockbroking, exchange, and other services for the whole region. Two misconceptions arise from Manchester's reputation as the home of cotton manufacture—that this manufacture is carried out within the city boundary, and that it is the sole important local industry. In fact, cotton manufacture within the city is negligible. The spinning, bleaching, weaving, dyeing, printing, and finishing processes are carried on in the surrounding towns, and the research, marketing, and other commercial facilities are provided in Manchester.

Moreover, although cotton manufacture is still the principal local industry, the heavy engineering and chemical industries are now almost equally important, and the volume of production in the city is considerable. Other major products include rubber and leather, wires, ropes, aircraft, storage batteries, clothing, asbestos, belting and chains, and light industrial goods. Much research is carried on by individual firms and a degree of coordination is achieved through the Manchester Joint Research Council, comprising members of the Manchester Chamber of Commerce and Manchester University, and formed in 1944 to bring together science and industry, disseminate new knowledge, encourage research, and inquire into industrial, scientific, economic and sociological problems. Research into cotton problems is performed by the Shirley Institute at Didsbury.

Manchester is an important financial center, with a branch of the Bank of England and with a bankers' clearing house. The Stock Exchange has 120 members. The Royal Exchange is primarily a cotton exchange, but its 4,000 (in 1951) members deal in all classes of goods. Other exchanges deal in coal, food and produce, and real property.

Manchester is a newspaper publishing center comparable with London, publishing three morning, two evening, five weekly, and two Sunday newspapers. Northern editions of five national papers are also printed and published in Manchester.

Transport.—Manchester is linked with the sea by the 35 mile Manchester Ship Canal, with surrounding towns by a comprehensive network of railways and roads, and with other regions by barge-carrying canals. There are four principal railway stations, many smaller stations and extensive sidings. Municipal airports provide facilities for transcontinental aircraft at Ringway, and for private flying and air-taxi work at Barton upon Humber.

Central Government.—*Administration.*—Manchester is a center of national government, housing the regional offices of 16 ministries and local offices of 41 other government departments. Ten members represent the city in Parliament.

Local Government.—The elected Manchester City Council of 144 members (36 aldermen and 108 councillors), has 40 committees, most of whose proceedings require ratification by the City Council. The chairman of the Council and "first citizen" is styled "lord mayor." Manchester's municipal services resemble those of other county boroughs, it is not necessary to enumerate them all. Outstanding examples are the water supply, drawn by pipeline from lakes Thirlmere and Haweswater, nearly 100 miles distant, and supplied to a population of 1,140,000; the municipal gas, electricity and transport undertakings, serving the city and surrounding districts; the city markets, drawing food from and distributing it to a wide area; the municipal airports, of which Manchester had in 1929 the first in the world; the support of the Manchester Ship Canal enterprise, in which the Corporation holds £6,750,000 share capital and appoints 11 directors out of 21; and the Wythenshawe Estate, a satellite town projected in 1926 and since visited by sociologists and planners from all parts of the world. Built on "neighborhood unit" principles, with segregated industrial, residential and agricultural areas, Wythenshawe when complete will house 60,000 people in the true community of interest which towns of the past have lacked. The municipality is also responsible for the Henry Watson Music Library, the Rutherston Loan Scheme, and the Cunnington Costume Collection, more fully described hereafter.

The Courts.—Manchester has a Court of Assize and a District Registry of the High Court of Justice, and seven other courts of law sit within the city boundary. The lord mayor is ex-officio the chief magistrate; there are 136 magistrates on the roll for service on the bench at the magistrates' courts.

Religion.—The Manchester Cathedral (the Parish Church) is the local nucleus of the Established (Protestant Episcopal) Church (The Church of England), and in the city there are 106 parish and district churches. Manchester has also been a notable home of nonconformity, since the Act of Uniformity in 1662 resulted in the expulsion in Lancashire alone of over 100 ministers of the Established Church who would not subscribe to the Anglican Prayer Book. The first dissenting meetinghouse, Cross Street Chapel (now Unitarian) was built in 1693, and meetinghouses were also built by the Friends (1732), the Wesleyans (now Methodists) (1752) and the Independents (now Congregationalists) (1761). There are 19 Free Church denominations in the city, many of which are represented on an active Free Church Federal Council, and on the Manchester Council of Churches. Manchester's importance as a religious center is emphasized by the presence of seven theological colleges—Baptist, Methodist, Congregational, Talmud Torah, Moravian, Unitarian, and Roman Catholic. Connected with these are many religious societies whose work is closely interwoven with that of the local voluntary bodies, and who maintain 120 day schools in conjunction with the Municipal Education Committee. At nearby Fairfield is a Moravian settlement, more fully described hereafter.

Medicine.—Manchester, a center of medical research and treatment, has twenty-one voluntary (privately supported) and twelve municipal hospitals, served by a distinguished group of specialist doctors and surgeons. The Royal Infirmary (with the Manchester University medical school the nucleus of medicine in the city) provides 875 beds, and the Christie Cancer Hospital and Holt Radium Institute is the foremost center of cancer research and treatment in the British Commonwealth.

Education and Culture.—The Victoria University of Manchester is the hub of the Northern British universities group. The university bears a fine reputation and has led the world in research into atomic structure: in the university laboratories, professors Ernest Rutherford, James Chadwick, John Douglas Cockcroft, and (William) Lawrence Bragg first watched the atom disintegrate, discovered the neutron and first mechanically disintegrated the atom. Research continues. The university is closely connected with the municipal College of Technology, where technical degrees are taken. At the Manchester Grammar School, founded in 1515 by Hugh Oldham, Bishop of Exeter, many distinguished British statesmen and citizens began their education. The city's schools include a number of religious training colleges, a college of music, and, under the municipality, an art school, domestic economy college, schools of commerce,

adult education centers and several hundred day schools.

The Municipal Art Galleries house a fine collection of works of the English school of the last century and of the Pre-Raphaelite Brotherhood, with many specimens of the work of 18th and 19th century painters and contemporary artists, and foreign works. Special collections include statuary, furniture, silver, glass, enamels and ceramics. Under the Rutherston Loan Scheme, Manchester's art treasures are loaned to other British towns.

Platt Hall (municipal) the first museum in Britain devoted exclusively to costume, exhibits the collection of English women's costumes formed by Dr. C. Willett Cunnington. Acquired for Manchester by public subscription, the collection of dresses and dress accessories, books, periodicals, and fashion plates covers a period of two hundred years.

The Whitworth (private) Art Gallery contains an important collection of English water colors and textile fabrics from the 1st century onwards. The Manchester Museum of the University possesses one of the most comprehensive collections of Egyptian antiquities in Britain, in addition to collections of fossils, plants, animals, and arts and crafts.

The municipal libraries comprise a central library and 36 branch libraries. The Manchester Central Library houses the finest municipal reference collection in the country, a technical and patents library, a commercial library, and the Henry Watson Music Library. The last is acknowledged the finest and largest music collection for public borrowing in the world, with 73,549 volumes and 309,474 pieces of sheet music available for borrowing, and with many rare books, manuscripts and instruments. A former baronial hall, c.1425, houses the Chetham Library and Bluecoat School for poor boys, founded by Humphrey Chetham in 1653. The library, the earliest free library in Europe, is essentially a scholars' library with its 100,000 volumes of classical, historical, topographical, philosophical, theological, archaeological, and antiquarian works.

The John Rylands Library (for reference and research), a center of attraction for scholars and lovers of rare and beautiful books from all parts of the world, includes the Spencer Althorp Collection (reputed by some the finest private library ever compiled) and holds unsurpassed collections of block books, incunabula, Aldines, Caxtons, and Bibles. The manuscripts, which include the 6,000 item collection of the earls of Crawford, illustrate the history of writing and illumination in the principal world languages from the fourth millennium B.C. to the present day. There are several thousand early charters, 20,000 proclamations from the principal countries of Europe of the 15th century, and autographs, prints and historic bindings.

Manchester has a wealth of literary and artistic societies. To the Literary and Philosophical Society, the foremost British scientists have first disclosed fundamental and revolutionary discoveries—including the atomic theory of matter, first propounded there by John Dalton. Visual art is represented by several vigorous groups of modern artists, and there are more than 300 local amateur dramatic societies. Manchester's musical background is especially noteworthy. An influx of German and Austrian merchants in the last century led to the formation of the internationally famous Halle Orchestra, whose 90 musicians under their conductor John Barbirolli now play to audiences of 6,000 at the Kings Hall, Belle Vue, tour the British Isles and fulfill many engagements on the European Continent. There are numerous other orchestras and chamber concert societies, five amateur symphony orchestras, and several amateur vocal societies, whilst an important annual musical festival takes place at Alderley Edge nearby.

The city possesses six theaters, over 200 cinemas, and the celebrated Belle Vue Zoological amusement gardens of 80 acres, founded in 1836, which with their zoo, amusement park, sports stadium, dance floors and concert halls are visited annually by five million people.

Notable Buildings.—Among these are the Town Hall (Victorian Gothic revival) with historical mural paintings by Ford Madox Brown, the Central Library (Greek revival), and the Town Hall Extension (Modern), which together form a municipal block; the Cathedral, built between the 13th and 19th centuries, with its fine interior woodwork; the Rylands Library (late Gothic revival) in Deansgate, internally and externally an architectural gem; the Free Trade Hall, Assize Courts and Royal Exchange, all severely damaged by air raids; and the university, a group in varying styles. Modern functional examples include Ship Canal House, King Street; Kendal Milne's department store, Deansgate; and Midland Bank Building, King Street. Older buildings include Chethams Hospital, previously mentioned; the Wellington Inn, the last of the City's Elizabethan inns; and the more recent Moravian settlement at Fairfield. Founded by religious refugees from central Europe in 1785, this settlement (late Georgian style) includes a church, two schools, a textile factory, and nearly 100 dwelling houses. The original character remains, and descendants of the original families occupy the buildings.

Population.—The population greatly increased between 1841 and 1931 as will be seen by the following figures: (1841) 242,983; (1871) 351,-189; (1891) 505,368; (1931) 766,378. This increase may be partially accounted for by the extension of the city boundaries which began in 1885. There was no census taken during World War II but the estimated population in 1939 was 727,600 and the 1961 census records the total as 661,041.

Bibliography.—Axon, W. E. A., *Annals of Manchester* (1886); Tait, J., *Mediaeval Manchester* (1904); Mills, W. H., *The Manchester Guardian: a Century of History* (1921); Bruton, F. A., *A Short History of Manchester and Salford*, 2d ed. (1927); Clay, Henry, and Brady, K. R., *Manchester at Work: a Survey* (1929); Redford, A., *A History of Local Government in Manchester*, 3 vols. (1939–40); Nicholas, R., *City of Manchester Plan*, published by Manchester City Council (1945); *Official Handbook* (Annual).

TERENCE F. USHER,
Information Officer, Manchester Corporation.

MANCHESTER, city, Iowa, and Delaware County seat, altitude 919 feet, on the Maquoketa River and on the Illinois Central and the Manchester and Oneida railroads (the latter steam), 130 miles northeast of Des Moines; also on state and federal highways. Situated in an agricultural region, the city is a dairying center and a trading point for the farmers of the county. There is a public library here.

Settled in 1850, as the town developed it was first known as Burrington; the present name was adopted in 1856. Incorporation as a city was effected in 1886. Manchester is governed by a mayor and council, and has a city manager. Pop. 4,402.

MANCHESTER, town, Massachusetts, in Essex County; altitude 14 feet; on Massachusetts Bay; 6 miles southwest of Gloucester; on the Boston and Maine Railroad. Originally a fishing village, it began to develop into a summer resort about 1850. Settled about 1626, the place was known as Jeffrey's Creek until 1645, when the name was changed and the town was incorporated. There is a library, and the historical society has quarters in an old home. A brick building in which ammunition was stored during the War of 1812 stands on Powder House Hill. Pop. 3,932.

MANCHESTER, city, New Hampshire, one of the county seats of Hillsboro County, on the Merrimack River at the mouth of the Piscataquog, 18 miles south by east of Concord, and on the Boston and Maine Railroad. The first settlement was made in 1722 and for a number of years it was called Amoskeag and Tyngstown. In 1751 it was incorporated as Derryfield and in 1810 the name was changed to Manchester. It was chartered as a city in 1846.

The Amoskeag Falls (55 feet) in the Merrimack, above the city, provide extensive waterpower which, by means of canals, is made available for manufacturing. Cotton goods manufactures and woolen goods manufactures are the city's largest industries and for many years the mills of the Amoskeag Manufacturing Company were considered the largest cotton manufacturing plant in the world. Competitive conditions made the enterprise unprofitable after the depression of 1929 and the plant was closed. Local business men, determined to save for the city this valuable industry, bought the plant and leased parts of it to scores of small manufacturing enterprises which have since operated successfully. The mills have been operated for more than a century, having been founded in 1810. There are numerous other important industries in the city, especially the shoe industry. The city's area of about 35 square miles is well laid out and its residential districts present an attractive appearance. It has been seat of a Roman Catholic bishop since 1884. Nearby are two notable Catholic schools, Mount St. Mary, at Hooksett; and St. Anselm's College, at Goffstown. The Carpenter Memorial Library is one of the finest structures of its kind in New England, and other outstanding buildings are those of the Currier Gallery of Art; the Institute of Arts and Sciences; the Association Canado-Américaine; and the Manchester Historic Association. City Hall, built from red brick of local manufacture, dates from 1845.

Manchester was the home of Gen. John Stark (q.v.), hero of the French and Indian, and the American Revolutionary wars. Stark Park, in which the general is buried, is one of the most beautiful in the vicinity, overlooking the Merrimac River and the Uncanoonuc Mountains; the Stark home is owned by the Daughters of the Revolution; and the site of the old Stark family homestead forms a part of the grounds of the State Industrial Home. Other points of interest are Rock Rimmon, with its story of an Indian maiden's love tragedy; Mast Road, on the Piscataquog River, so named because giant pines reserved for the British Navy were transported over it; and Goffs (originally Goffe's) Falls, near which the Goffe family, the first white settlers in the area, built their homestead.

Manchester has many fine summer homes and is a popular summer resort, as is Lake Massabesic four miles to the east. The city has an altitude of 175 feet and is on a federal highway and several state highways; its airport is served by Northeast Airlines. Pop. 88,282.

MANCHESTER COLLEGE, North

Manchester, Indiana, is a coeducational church-related college of liberal arts and sciences. The college had its origin in a United Brethren Seminary which was founded in Roanoke, Ind., in 1869 and moved to North Manchester in 1889. In 1895 the campus was purchased by representatives of the Church of the Brethren, and in 1932 Mount Morris College of Mount Morris, Ill., merged with Manchester College. The college was operated primarily as a Bible school and academy in its early years, but the academy was discontinued in 1923 and the Bible school became a department of religion and philosophy in the liberal arts college.

The college offers undergraduate courses leading to the bachelor of arts and bachelor of science degrees. Strong emphasis is given in its curriculum to peace studies, teacher education, and rural life.

Manchester College has been accredited by the North Central Association of Colleges and Secondary Schools since 1932, and is a member of the Association of American Colleges and the American Council on Education.

ROBERT J. NELSON, JR.

MANCHESTER SCHOOL, a group of

members of Parliament and businessmen, mostly from the city of Manchester, England, who represented the extreme free-trade viewpoint between 1820 and 1860. The passage of the Corn Law of 1815 forbidding the import of grain until the price of domestic grain had reached virtually famine heights resulted in increasing discontent from 1820 onward. The successful protest against this protectionist move was instigated by the Manchester Chamber of Commerce. Led by Richard Cobden and John Bright (qq.v.), the group continued agitation for unlimited free trade and for a laissez-faire approach to all areas of economic activity. They believed that the establishment of worldwide free trade would represent a major step toward ultimate world peace.

Cobden's Anti-Corn-Law League was formed in 1839. The league's efforts were crowned in 1846 when the corn laws were repealed. After 1860 free trade and laissez faire declined in influence, as did the Manchester school. On the Continent, the French political economist Frédéric Bastiat was the leading exponent of the Manchester group's principles. He failed to enlist support among business leaders, however. The rise of protectionism in the latter part of the 19th century spelled the end of the Manchester school's influence.

Consult Roll, Erich, *History of Economic Thought*, 3d rev. and enl. ed. (London 1954).

WILLIAM N. KINNARD, JR.

MANCHESTER SHIP CANAL, England,

in southern Lancashire and northern Cheshire, which connects Manchester with the Mersey River estuary, thereby making this inland city accessible to ocean-going vessels. Begun in 1887 and opened in 1894, the canal allowed the economic development of Manchester's textile industry based on the import of raw materials and export of finished goods. It is 35½ miles long, from 28 to 30 feet deep, and generally 120 feet wide at the bottom. There are five sets of locks, with a total rise of 60½ feet. The western terminus is at Eastham. It communicates with the principal railway and canal systems of Great Britain.

MANCHESTER TERRIER. See DOG—

Terrier Group (Manchester Terrier).

MANCHURIA, măn-chŏŏr'ĭ-à, region, northeastern China, comprising the three provinces of Heilungkiang, Kirin, and Liaoning, and the eastern part of the Inner Mongolian Autonomous Region.[1] It is known to the Chinese as Tungpei (the Northeast), and was formerly known as the Three (or Four) Eastern Provinces; it was called Manchukuo during the period of Japanese domination. Manchuria is China's chief industrial region and one of its most important agricultural areas. It is also rich in mineral resources and in unreclaimed arable land. In political and economic organization, as well as in social and cultural patterns, Manchuria in the mid-20th century is not unlike the rest of China. The total area of Manchuria is about 600,000 square miles, or nearly one sixth of the total area of China. It is situated roughly between latitudes 38° and 53° north and longitudes 115° and 135° east—over a thousand miles in each direction—and is bounded

Location map of Manchuria.

on the northwest, north, and east by the Soviet Union, a boundary of over 2,000 miles; on the southeast by North Korea; on the west by the Mongolian Plateau; and on the south by North

[1] The author has described the natural region of Manchuria, which in the northwest extends beyond the Great Khingan Mountains to the borders of Outer Mongolia and in the southwest extends to the western boundary of Jehol. The term Manchuria is sometimes applied to the more limited region comprising the three provinces of Heilungkiang, Kirin, and Liaoning.—*Editor.*

China and the Yellow Sea, giving it 700 miles of seacoast. In 1958 the estimated population of Manchuria exceeded 50 million.

For the convenience of the reader this article is divided into the following sections:

1. The Land
2. The People
3. Economy
4. Culture and Welfare
5. History

1. THE LAND

Manchuria consists of a vast central plain enclosed on the south by the sea and on three sides by mountains: the Yin and Great Khingan mountain ranges in the west, the Little Khingan range in the north, and the Changpai range in the east. The highest point in Manchuria is the extinct volcano Paitou Shan, on the Korean border, which rises to a height of 9,003 feet; only a few other mountains exceed 5,000 feet. Five rivers define boundaries with neighboring countries: the Argun, the Amur—with 2,340 miles in Manchuria it is China's fourth longest river—and the Ussuri rivers form natural boundaries with the Soviet Union on the northwest, north, and east, while the Tumen and Yalu rivers define Manchuria's southeastern border with Korea. The Sungari, which is a tributary of the Amur and the fifth longest river in China (1,150 miles), constitutes, with its tributaries the Nonni and Mutan, the most important river system in northern Manchuria. Southern Manchuria is drained by the Liao (900 miles). Manchurian rivers have great hydroelectric potential and are to a large extent navigable, though for only half the year.

Manchuria lies in the cold temperate zone. Its climate is continental, with a very cold winter, a hot summer, and a short spring and autumn. In the north the frozen season extends from October to May and the temperature sometimes drops to − 50° F. It is considerably warmer in the south. Average annual precipitation is 21 inches, most of it falling during the summer. The soil, especially the black earth belt, is among the most fertile in the world. Despite intensive exploitation during the Japanese occupation, virgin forests cover about one fifth of the entire area of Manchuria, constituting China's largest forest reserve. Northern Manchuria abounds in wild animals and birds. Rivers are well stocked with fish.

2. THE PEOPLE

Population.—Over 90 per cent of the population of Manchuria is Chinese. The other two main ethnic groups are the Manchu-Tungusic and the Mongol. The Manchu-Tungusic group numbers over one million. It includes the settled Manchus and the Gold or Fishskin Tatar, Solon, and Orochon tribal peoples. There are also some non-Tungusic Gilyak tribesmen along the Amur River. These tribal peoples, who formerly dominated the northern woodland area, have been largely assimilated, and by the 1950's comparatively few still depended on fishing and hunting for a livelihood. The Manchus, who gave their name to Manchuria, have become almost completely assimilated with the Chinese except in the far north, where Manchu villages are still to be found. There are no Manchu autonomous territorial units. There are probably somewhat less than a million Mongols, mostly in western Manchuria, and over a million Koreans, mostly in the area adjoining Korea. In September 1952 the Chinese Communist authorities created the Yenpien Korean Autonomous District from a segment of Kirin Province along the Korean border, where about half a million Koreans constitute three quarters of the total population. Manchuria's European population does not exceed 10,000; it consists almost solely of Russians: Soviet advisers and technicians, and remnant White Russian émigrés.

The average density of population is about 35 persons per square kilometer (1 square kilometer equals 0.3861 square mile), about half the average density of China, but the distribution of population is very uneven. The mass of population is concentrated in the Manchurian plain, in southern and central Manchuria, where the density reaches 100 to 150, and in some areas even 400, whereas in the northeastern regions it is less than one person per square kilometer. While in China males constituted 51.8 per cent of the population in 1953, the percentage for Manchuria was over 55 per cent, largely because of heavy male immigration.

Although Manchuria is still predominantly rural (only about 20 per cent of its people resided in urban area in 1953), it is more urbanized than the rest of China; of the 21 largest Chinese cities, 7 are located in Manchuria. The largest are Shenyang (Mukden), the fourth largest city in China, with a 1953 population of 2,300,000; Harbin (Pinkiang), with 1,200,000; Lushun (Port Arthur), which has the best naval base in China, and Talien (Dairen), one of the three most important ports in China, with a combined population of 1,200,000; and Changchun, with 800,000. Other important cities are Fushun (coal), Anshan and Penki (iron and steel), Kirin, and Tsitsihar.

Settlement and Immigration.—No reliable population statistics are available other than those provided by the Japanese census of 1940 and the Chinese Communist census of 1953. Chinese settlement in the lower valley of the Liao River and on the Liaotung Peninsula antedates the beginning of the Christian era, but the modern large-scale colonization of Manchuria began in 1878, when the Manchu government relaxed its restrictions on Chinese settlement in Manchu territory. In 1890 the population of Manchuria was estimated to be 10 million, in 1910 from 15 to 18 million, in 1927 over 25 million, in 1932 over 30 million and in 1940 over 45 million. The tripling of population in the first half of the 20th century is in part due to large-scale immigration from famine areas of North China. From 1925 to 1940 alone, over 10 million Chinese crossed into Manchuria, and about half this number remained as permanent settlers. The Communist regime has encouraged immigration to Manchuria, urging immigrants to settle the virgin lands in the north rather than swell the cities. The urban areas nonetheless showed a remarkable increase in the first decade of Communist control.

At the height of Japanese domination there were more than 1.5 million Japanese in Manchuria, excluding the Kwantung Army, which at its peak numbered well over a million officers and men. Almost all Japanese were repatriated during the first postwar years. There had long been some Korean settlement west of the Tumen River, and after 1932 the Japanese encouraged Korean settlement throughout Manchuria. By the end of World War II Koreans numbered about 1.5 million, of whom about a quarter returned to Korea after its liberation from Japanese rule. Close to

200,000 Russians, both White Russian émigrés and Soviet citizens, lived in Manchuria during the 1920's and early 1930's. Most of the Soviet citizens returned to the USSR after the sale of the Chinese Eastern Railway in 1935. The émigrés, of whom there were still some 70,000 in 1945, were largely forced to accept Soviet citizenship during the Russian occupation of Manchuria in 1945–1946. They were encouraged to return to the Soviet Union and most of them did so, although no effort was made to dissuade those who wished to remain or emigrate elsewhere. There were never more than 5,000 other foreigners—chiefly Poles, Germans, British, Americans, and French—in Manchuria, and only a handful of them remained after 1948.

3. ECONOMY

The construction of the first railroads in Manchuria by the Russians at the turn of the century had a tremendous impact on the development of Manchurian economy. It made possible large-scale Chinese immigration and colonization and in turn the production and export of an agricultural surplus. Manchuria's development as a major industrial area came later and must be credited to the Japanese.

Agriculture.—In spite of rapid industrialization, the economy of Manchuria is still based on agriculture, which occupies about three fourths of the population. Dry farming is almost universal and some 40 different crops are raised. The principal crop is soybeans; Manchuria has accounted for over 60 per cent of the world's soybean production. Other important crops are kaoliang, millet, wheat, corn, and rice. Soybeans are raised throughout the region, but especially in the northern part of the Manchurian plain, where they occupy a third of all arable land. Kaoliang, the staple food of the population, is the next largest crop; it is likewise cultivated in all parts of the region. Rice is grown chiefly by the Koreans in the southeast. Principal industrial crops include cotton (mainly in the south), hemp, flax, tobacco, and wild silk. Vegetables and fruit are grown for local consumption.

Manchuria is the largest agricultural surplus area in China and has regularly exported grain to China proper as well as to foreign countries. Moreover it has been estimated that only about one half of the arable land of Manchuria has been brought under cultivation, and that there are still huge tracts of fertile uncultivated land. Some economists feel that Manchuria can support 100 million inhabitants.

The Chinese Communists, in practical control of the countryside since 1946 and of all Manchuria since the end of 1948, have taken a number of measures to increase agricultural production, starting with a vast land reform, which was completed well ahead of similar reforms in other parts of China. Huge state farms specializing in mechanized farming were set up in the sparsely populated north. It was reported in late 1957 that, since 1950, 120 state farms in the north had reclaimed 2.2 million hectares (1 hectare equals 2.471 acres) of virgin land. Simultaneously antiflood and antidrought precautions were taken. In 1951 protective forest belts were planted in the west. Lumbering, a prominent industry in northern Manchuria, accounts for about one fifth of the total product of the Heilungkiang Province. Cattle, horses (primarily Mongolian breeds), donkeys, mules, goats, sheep, pigs, camels, and chickens are raised, but stockbreeding is distinctly subordinate to agriculture. Fishing is carried on along the coast of the Yellow Sea and in the rivers and lakes.

Natural Resources and Industry.—In mineral resources Manchuria is one of China's richest regions. It has enormous deposits of coal, especially in the south; the Fushun open-pit mine is the world's largest. Low-grade iron ore is abundant in the Anshan-Penki area. Other minerals mined include lead, zinc, copper, manganese, magnesium, gold, silver, aluminum, molybdenum, quartz, talc, asbestos, and salt.

Prior to the Japanese occupation Manchuria was a region of light consumer industry, such as soybean-oil-extracting plants, flour mills, beet-sugar refineries, distilleries, paper mills, tobacco-processing plants, match factories, and small machine shops for repairing railroad equipment. The Japanese meticulously surveyed Manchuria's natural resources, brought in fresh capital, managerial and technical know-how, and advanced machinery, and proceeded to build a heavy industry base. In a little over a decade of Japanese rule the production of coal was tripled, electric power output was increased 700 per cent and great advances were made in heavy industry (pig iron and steel, nonferrous metals, liquid fuels, and lubricants). In 1943, at the height of the Japanese war effort, Manchuria produced over nine tenths of China's iron and steel, four fifths of China's electric power, and almost half of China's coal.

The Russians during their brief nine-month occupation (1945–1946) systematically dismantled Manchurian plants and shipped to the Soviet Union much of their most modern equipment, especially heavy manufacturing, mining and chemical machinery, power generators, electric motors, and equipment from experimental plants and laboratories. The Chinese civil war (1946–1948) further disrupted Manchurian mining and industry, so that by 1948 production had dropped 90 per cent from its 1943 peak. Four years of

This youth planted 4,000 willows in a day, in a large scale Kirin Province afforestation project.

Eastfoto

intensive reconstruction followed, and some of the wartime production figures were matched by late 1952.

Although China's long-range industrial development plan called for a more even distribution of industry throughout the country, the first five-year plan (1953–1957) emphasized the strengthening of the existing industry in Manchuria, in order to provide the means for achieving the long-range goal. It has been estimated that the Chinese have invested about half their available capital in Manchuria. Beginning in the early 1950's many projects were planned and built in cooperation with the Soviet government, utilizing Soviet technology and machinery. One such project was the first Chinese automobile plant in Changchun, which began production in October 1956. It was said to have a capacity of 30,000 trucks a year, but a year later it was operating at only one fifth of capacity. Other new factories turned out precision instruments, tractors and agricultural machinery, mining equipment, locomotives and railroad cars, machine tools, chemicals, pharmaceutical products, and rubber tires. Hydroelectric plants on the Sungari and Yalu rivers were reconstructed and newly built, and others were planned on the Amur and elsewhere. All the new industrial projects were built by the state; after a decade of Communist rule, some four fifths of all industrial enterprises in Manchuria were state owned. By the end of the first five-year plan, Manchuria's industrial production was at an all-time high. Leading manufacturing centers are Shenyang (Mukden, the heavy industry center of China), Harbin (Pinkiang), Changchun, Talien (Dairen), and Fushun. The Anshan-Fusin-Shenyang-Fushun-Penki area can be truly called the Ruhr of the Orient. In August 1957 the Anshan iron and steel works, the largest industrial enterprise in China, claimed to have tripled the maximum production rate attained by the Japanese in 1943.

Transportation.—The principal mode of transportation in Manchuria is the railroad. At the end of World War II the total railroad mileage was a little over 7,000 miles, or about half of China's total. About one third of the track was laid by the Russians at the turn of the century, and about one half by the Japanese during the 1930's. The main artery cuts across northern Manchuria, linking the Trans-Siberian Railway with Vladivostok; a branch from Harbin to Lushun (Port Arthur) passes through the heart of Manchuria. Other important railroads connect Manchuria with North China and North Korea. The Japanese built a number of lines leading toward the Soviet border, but these are of limited economic importance. Up to 1957 Communist railroad construction was restricted to light railroads, for lumbering operations in the northwest.

Manchuria has 30,000 miles of roads, most of which were either constructed or improved by the Japanese. In winter the frozen rivers also serve as roads. Some 4,000 miles of Manchurian rivers are navigable from six to nine months a year; as a Chinese inland water route, the Sungari is second in importance only to the Yangtze. Ice-free Talien is the best port in Manchuria and one of the best in China. Other Manchurian ports were left relatively undeveloped by the Japanese concentration on Talien; three of the best are Yingkow, Antung, and Hulutao. Manchuria is connected by air routes with other parts

Eastfoto

Assembly line of "Liberation-brand" lorries at the No. 1 Motor Vehicle Plant in Changchun, Manchuria.

of China as well as with North Korea and the Soviet Union.

4. CULTURE AND WELFARE

Culturally and socially Manchuria has become an integral part of China.

Religion.—The majority of the Chinese population of Manchuria are adherents to Confucianism, Buddhism, and Taoism. Some 150,000 are Muslims. The Mongols are Lamaists, while the Tungusic tribes in the north practice shamanism. Latest Japanese statistics in the early 1940's listed some 125,000 Roman Catholics, and 50,000 Protestants. Under the Communist regime all religions have been frowned upon, but persecution and suppression of individual cults varied in accordance with Peking's policy. Taoists and Christians are perhaps the most persecuted, Muslims the least.

Education.—Much has been claimed by the Communists in the fields of education, information and mass communication, and public health. Campaigns for the eradication of illiteracy have involved millions of peasants and workers in Manchuria, formerly a region of high illiteracy. The Communist goal announced in 1955 was that 70 per cent of all young people in rural villages would be literate by 1962. There was a great increase in the publication of books, newspapers, and periodicals, in radio broadcasting, and in film production. Publications appear not only in Chinese but in Mongol, Korean, and other minority languages.

Since Manchuria is the greatest industrial base of China, it is also a center of China's technical and scientific education and research. There are several full-fledged universities and specialized colleges of agriculture, forestry, engineering, geology, mining, surveying, fisheries, navigation, and medicine. The Automobile and Tractor Institute in Changchun was the first school of its kind in China. At least nine of the institutes and laboratories of the Chinese Academy of Sciences in the scientific and technical fields are located in Manchuria.

The Arts and Literature.—Harbin, Shenyang, and other Manchurian cities are among the cultural centers of China; most large cities maintain orchestras. The Tungpei (Northeast) Lu Hsun Institute of Arts and Literature and the Tungpei (Northeast) School of Music and Art, as well as one of the three Chinese state film studios, are in Manchuria.

No major Chinese writer is a Manchurian by birth, although during the Japanese occupation of Manchuria, Hsiao Hung and other writers from Manchuria vividly described the guerrilla warfare against the Japanese aggressors. Chou Li-po's novel, *The Hurricane,* winner of the Stalin Prize in 1951, deals with agrarian reform in Manchuria.

Health.—The Communists claim a sharp drop in the mortality rate. In 1955 they boasted of having vaccinated 90 per cent of the population, eradicated flies, rats, and other disease carriers, and spread elementary health information. To carry out this program thousands of young "activists of public health" were trained.

5. HISTORY

Early History.—Manchuria is one of the most ancient habitats of man in East Asia. Archaeological discoveries point to the existence of man there since Paleolithic times. Manchurian history is essentially the record of interaction between the nomadic tribes that roamed through the area and the Chinese, who began to settle in southern Manchuria around 1000 B.C. During the past 3,000 years, intermarriage between the Chinese and the native peoples, though at times proscribed by one side or the other, has been almost constant. At times southern Manchuria was incorporated into the Chinese Empire (beginning with the 3d century B.C.); at other times the tribes paid tribute to the Chinese court; at still other times warlike tribes from Manchuria invaded North China and established their rule in China proper (notably from the 10th into the 14th centuries and again between 1644 and 1911). During the latter period China's Manchu rulers treated Manchuria as their special domain and forbade the Chinese to settle there. The Russians reached Manchuria in the 17th century, but they were defeated by the Manchu Army and had to retreat (Treaty of Nerchinsk, 1689). In the mid-19th century, however, the Chinese were forced to cede to Russia large territories north of the Amur River (1858) and east of the Ussuri (1860).

Modern History (1895–1945).—Manchuria first attained world prominence in the 1890's, and for the next 60 years it remained one of East Asia's trouble spots and an object of big-power rivalries. During this time Manchuria was not under the effective control of the central Chinese government; in fact, most of the time it was occupied by Russia or Japan or both. Yet it was during this period that Manchuria became almost completely Sinicized.

Following the humiliating Sino-Japanese War (1894–1895), China was forced to cede the Liaotung Peninsula to Japan. Russia, however, coveted Manchuria as a potential colonial area, and with the support of Germany and France forced Japan to renounce her claims. In 1896 Russia and China concluded a secret treaty of alliance, directed against Japan, which gave the Russians the right to construct a railroad in northern Manchuria, linking Vladivostok with the Trans-Siberian Railway. In 1898 Russia expanded her sphere of influence in Manchuria by obtaining a 25-year lease on the Liaotung Peninsula, the very territory she had denied Japan. The Russians proceeded to build a naval base at Port Arthur (Lushun), at the tip of the Liaotung Peninsula, and to connect it with the railroad running through northern Manchuria. As a result of the Boxer Rebellion (1900) Russian troops occupied all of Manchuria. This eventually led to a war with Japan, fought largely on Manchurian soil. The Russo-Japanese War (1904–1905) ended disastrously for Russia. By the Treaty of Portsmouth (1905) Russia was forced to give up the Liaotung Peninsula, and to transfer to Japan the section of the railroad south of Changchun together with all mines and other enterprises belonging to the railroad company.

The two former enemies soon realized, however, that their best chance of exploiting Manchuria lay in cooperation against other powers and not in competition with each other. In a secret agreement (1907) they divided Manchuria into two spheres of influence, roughly the south for Japan and the north for Russia. China, though alarmed, could only look on helplessly. Russo-Japanese rapprochement was increased by unsuccessful American attempts to internationalize Manchurian railroads (Knox-Harriman plans, 1909).

China's political instability after the revolution of 1911 and the preoccupation of world powers in Europe during World War I provided Japan with a golden opportunity to expand her influence in China. Seven of the infamous Twenty-One Demands presented to China in 1915 dealt with the extension of Japanese influence in southern Manchuria for 99 years. After the Russian Revolution an Allied commission headed by an American was set up to run the Chinese Eastern Railway. Nevertheless the Japanese contrived to entrench themselves in northern Manchuria.

In 1916 the pro-Japanese warlord Chang Tsolin was appointed military governor of one of the Manchurian provinces; in 1918 he became inspector general and *de facto* ruler of all the Three Eastern Provinces. His death was engineered by the Japanese in 1928, when he began to show signs of independence. He was succeeded by his son, Chang Hsueh-liang, who tried unsuccessfully in 1929 to oust the Soviets from joint control over the Chinese Eastern railway, which they had regained by the Sino-Soviet treaty of 1924.

The Japanese, fearing the consolidation of Chinese power, decided to strike first. On Sept. 18, 1931, Japanese troops in Manchuria provoked an incident which gave Japan a pretext to occupy all of Manchuria. In March 1932 the Japanese transformed Manchuria into the puppet state of Manchukuo under Henry Pu-yi, the last Manchu emperor of China. In 1933 they annexed the Province of Jehol. When a League of Nations commission of inquiry under the earl of Lytton found Japan guilty of aggression (October 1932), Japan announced its withdrawal from the League, launched an intensive campaign to destroy a quarter of a million guerrillas in Manchuria, and consolidated her position on the continent by pushing on into Inner Mongolia and North China. Japanese occupation of Manchuria gave Japan (1) a rich territory with tremendous agricultural and industrial potential, and an enormous supply of cheap labor; (2) a huge area for large-scale

MANCHURIA

Above: Western-looking Chung-Shan Road in Dairen, industrial city and major seaport.

Right: Blast furnaces at Anshan, metallurgical center and heart of China's industrialization.

Below left: Opencut mining at Fushun, which has the world's thickest coal seam.

Below right: Peasants of a farming cooperative cheer the arrival of their newly bought tractors.

Eastfoto

immigration from the overpopulated Japanese islands; and (3) a strategic base for further expansion into China proper and Mongolia, if not into eastern Siberia. The Soviets had left Manchuria peaceably in 1935 after selling their share of the Chinese Eastern Railway but two armed clashes in 1938 and 1939 convinced the Japanese of Soviet strength in the Far East. Between 1935 and 1943, the Japanese spared no efforts in Manchuria to increase agricultural productivity, to build up the mining and manufacturing industries, and to expand transportation and communications. When the Pacific war began in December 1941, Manchuria had become the most important supply base for the Japanese Empire.

Apart from a few American bombing raids on industrial centers, Manchuria was relatively unaffected by the military operations until the very last stages of the war. The Cairo Conference (November 1943) between President Franklin D. Roosevelt, Prime Minister Winston L. S. Churchill, and Generalissimo Chiang Kai-shek resulted in a declaration that all territories stolen by Japan from the Chinese, among them Manchuria, would be restored to the Republic of China. At the Crimea (Yalta) Conference (February 1945), however, Roosevelt, Churchill, and Joseph Stalin, without the consent of China, agreed to the re-establishment of Russian influence in Manchuria. The American president was to obtain Chinese concurrence to this agreement. Following negotiations in Moscow during July and August 1945, a Sino-Soviet Treaty of Friendship and Alliance was signed on Aug. 14, 1945, almost simultaneously with the surrender of Japan. Essentially, this treaty assured Chinese compliance with the Yalta arrangements: the main railroad trunk lines formerly known as the Chinese Eastern Railway and the South Manchurian Railway were combined as the Chinese Changchun Railway, to be jointly owned and operated by China and the Union of Soviet Socialist Republics for a period of 30 years; Port Arthur (Lushun) was declared a joint Sino-Soviet naval base, to be garrisoned by Soviet forces for the same period; and Talien (Dairen) was made a free international port, under the control of a Russian harbormaster, and with some facilities leased to the Soviets.

History Since 1945.—The first postwar decade (1945–1955) in Manchuria witnessed the disappearance of the Japanese rulers, the re-establishment of Russian influence, civil war and the victory of the Chinese Communists, and, finally, the gradual retreat of the Soviet Union from its privileged position in the area. Beginning in 1955, for the first time in 60 years, Chinese sovereignty in Manchuria was not limited by special rights of foreign countries. In the same decade Manchuria was also transformed from a Communist base with a considerable measure of autonomy and a degree of independence from Peking to a position very like that of parts of China proper, that is, thoroughly subordinated to the central government. Economically speaking, the disastrous Soviet occupation and the civil war were followed by feverish reconstruction and further intensive economic development.

Soviet Occupation (August 1945–May 1946).—On Aug. 8, 1945, the Soviet Union declared war on Japan, and the following day three Soviet armies began their advance from the northwest, north and east into Manchuria on a 2,500-mile front. The Red armies met with resistance from the once-formidable Kwantung Army, which was already decimated by withdrawals of crack units to other theaters of the Pacific war. The Soviet troops captured the city of Hailar in the northwest on August 9; they did not occupy the key Manchurian cities of Tsitsihar, Changchun, Mukden, Harbin, Kirin, Dairen, and Port Arthur until August 19–23, after the surrender of Japan. By the end of the month Soviet occupation of Manchuria was complete. The Soviets were in control of Manchuria for less than a year, but they succeeded in that time in achieving their four major objectives. (1) They eliminated the Japanese from the scene by sending Japanese troops to the Soviet Union as prisoners and shipping Japanese civilians to Japan. (2) They reinforced their own position in Manchuria by confiscating as war booty all commercial and industrial concerns that had worked for the Kwantung Army, as well as buying up other Japanese firms with military currency. (3) They helped hasten the reconstruction of their war-ravaged homeland by using the slave labor of over half a million Japanese prisoners of war for several years, and by wholesale dismantling and removal of the most modern Manchurian industrial equipment, estimated by the Edwin W. Pauley Mission to be worth close to $1 billion, with a resulting damage to Chinese industry amounting to double that figure. (4) They helped the Chinese Communists gain control of Manchuria (and thus indirectly helped them win the civil war in China) by supplying them with captured Japanese munitions, and by obstructing the Nationalists who were sent to take over when the Russian armies finally withdrew.

The Civil War (1946–1948).—Units of the Chinese Communist forces in North China began crossing into Manchuria shortly after the surrender of Japan. By early 1946, aided by local guerrilla bands and reinforced by Japanese munitions made available to them by the withdrawing Soviet army, they were reorganized as the United Democratic Army under Gen. Lin Piao. Many local administrative units were set up during and immediately following Soviet occupation. Nationalist troops, long hindered from establishing government control in Manchuria, were able to enter Mukden in March of 1946, but in April other principal Manchurian cities—among them Harbin, Changchun, Kirin, and Tsitsihar—were seized by the Communists. Nationalist troops counterattacked in May and succeeded in capturing Szeping (May 20), Changchun (May 23) and Kirin (May 29), and in reaching the Sungari River 76 miles from Harbin. The Communists retained control of much of the countryside, however, and of all northern Manchuria, where they had established effective local administration as early as March 1946. In August a congress of people's representatives at Harbin elected a "people's government," the Administrative Committee of the Northeast. The principal resolutions passed at the congress called for the confiscation of land belonging to the landlords, the nationalization of businesses owned by Japanese and traitors, and the granting of autonomy to the Mongols. An unsuccessful Nationalist drive toward Harbin in September was followed by a Communist counteroffensive north of Changchun. By 1947 the Nationalists were on the defensive, and by the end of 1948 the Nationalist resistance had collapsed in Manchuria. Chang-chun fell in October and Mukden, the last bastion, in November.

The Communist Regime (1949–).—In April 1949 the Communists divided Manchuria into six provinces and several municipalities (the territory west of the Khingan range formed part of the Inner Mongolian Autonomous Region, established in May 1947). In August 1949 the Northeast People's Government was set up under Kao Kang, a top-ranking Communist. For the first few years Manchuria enjoyed a large degree of autonomy and served as a testing ground for many economic, social, and political measures and reforms. In July 1949 a Manchurian trade delegation went to Russia to conclude a Soviet-Manchurian trade agreement. Manchuria had its own central bank, its own currency and its own official gazette.

In 1951 the Peking government began to crack down on Manchurian autonomy. In May 1951 a widespread counterrevolutionary plot was reported to have been smashed and a wave of terror spread over most urban areas. The charges of germ warfare dramatized drastic sanitary drives. The People's government was reduced to the Northeast Greater Administrative Area (end of 1952) and then abolished altogether. Kao Kang was purged and reportedly committed suicide. In August 1954 Manchuria was divided into three provinces under the direct control of the central government.

During the first several years of Communist control the Soviet Union steadily retreated from its re-established sphere of influence in Manchuria. In February 1950, a new Sino-Soviet treaty was signed in Moscow. By this treaty, the Russians agreed to transfer immediately to China without compensation all the plants and properties they had confiscated or purchased from the Japanese in 1945–1946, to reduce the period of joint operation of the Chinese Changchun Railway from 30 to 3 years, and to give up the Port Arthur naval base upon the conclusion of a peace treaty with Japan. The railroad was officially turned over to China without compensation at the end of 1952, other property shared in Manchuria was returned by the end of 1954, and the naval base was relinquished in May 1955, although no peace treaty with Japan had been negotiated.

Sino-Soviet relations in Manchuria nonetheless remained close. In August 1956 an agreement was signed for the joint development of the natural resources of the Amur basin, including the planning and building of a 13-million-kilowatt system of hydroelectric power stations on the Amur, Argun, and Ussuri rivers. In June 1957 Soviet and Chinese specialists began joint work on hydroelectric, irrigation, water-supply, navigation, and flood-control facilities on the Sungari River. In the summer of 1957 a delegation from the Communist Party of the Maritime Territory, USSR, visited Harbin at the invitation of the Heilungkiang Party organization while Chinese party workers from Manchuria visited the Soviet Far East. In the middle 1950's Soviet influence was probably greater in Manchuria than in any other part of China.

Bibliography.—REFERENCE WORKS: Carnegie Endowment for International Peace, *Manchuria: Treaties and Agreements* (Washington 1921); Gibert, Lucien, *Dictionnaire historique et géographique de la Mandchourie* (Hong Kong 1934); *The Manchoukuo Year Book* (Hsinking, Manchukuo, 1942); Berton, Peter A., *Manchuria, an Annotated Bibliography* (United States Library of Congress, Washington 1951).

GEOGRAPHY: Fochler-Hauke, Gustav, *Die Mandschurei, eine geographische-geopolitische Landeskunde auf Grund eigener Reisen und des Schrifttums* (Heidelberg 1941); Shabad, Theodore, *China's Changing Map*, pp. 206–239 (New York 1956).

ECONOMY: Schumpeter, Elizabeth B., ed., *The Industrialization of Japan and Manchukuo, 1930–1940* (New York 1940); Clubb, Oliver E., *Chinese Communist Development Programs in Manchuria* (Institute of Pacific Relations, New York 1954).

HISTORY AND DEVELOPMENT: Clyde, Paul H., *International Rivalries in Manchuria, 1689–1922*, 2d rev. ed. (Columbus, Ohio, 1928); Young, Carl W., *The International Relations of Manchuria* (Chicago 1929); id., *Japan's Jurisdiction and International Legal Position in Manchuria*, 3 vols. (Baltimore 1931); Li, Chi, *Manchuria in History, a Summary* (Peiping 1932); Lattimore, Owen, *The Mongols of Manchuria* (New York 1934); id., *Manchuria, Cradle of Conflict* (New York 1935); Willoughby, Westel W., *The Sino-Japanese Controversy and the League of Nations* (Baltimore 1935); Stimson, Henry L., *The Far Eastern Crisis*, 3d ed. (New York 1938); Lattimore, Owen, *Inner Asian Frontiers of China* (New York 1940); Jones, Francis C., *Manchuria Since 1931* (London 1949); Chao, Kuo-chün, *Northeast China (Manchuria) Today* (Massachusetts Institute of Technology, Cambridge, Mass., 1953); *A Regional Handbook on Northeast China* (Human Relations Area Files, Inc., New Haven 1956).

PETER A. BERTON,
Acting Curator, North Asia Collections, The Hoover Institution on War, Revolution, and Peace, Stanford University.

MANCHUS, măn'chōoz, a people originating in the modern Province of Kirin, China, from a Tungus border tribe known as Jurchen (Ju-chên, Nü-chên), who overran north China in the first half of the 12th century and established the dynasty known as Chin (Kin, 1115–1234). When the Manchus emerge in history they were under the leadership of a minor chieftain named Nurhachu (Nurhachi, 1559–1626). The men were good horsemen and skilled as mounted archers. They depended largely on farming and the breeding of cattle for a livelihood. From the Chinese in Manchuria they learned to live in walled towns and to engage in trade. They early (1616) established an organization of eight banners, possibly after the manner of their Jurchen ancestors. This banner system started as a military institution but developed into a socio-administrative one, into which Mongols, Koreans, and a large number of Chinese in Manchuria were pressed, under the leadership of Manchu nobles.

During the first decades of the 17th century the Manchus made several raids into North China, and in 1644 they attacked Peking in force. By 1659 the last of the Ming princes was driven into Burma and the whole country came under Manchu control. They called their dynasty Ta Ch'ing and maintained it until 1912. The empire was the largest in the history of eastern Asia except for that of the Mongols; at its greatest extent, in the 18th century, it stretched from Kokand in the west to include Korea and Taiwan in the east, and from the Stanovoi Mountains of Siberia in the north to encompass Yunnan and Hainan in the south. The central government was patterned after that of the Ming, and accepted Chinese in posts of every rank. Being military conquerors the Manchus encouraged the military arts among their men, and maintained the system of eight banners to the end. But their numbers were limited, and as their fitness to rule and their military spirit waned they succumbed without a struggle to the resurgent Chinese.

Although officially the Manchus supported

Confucianism, privately they continued their national religion, a kind of shamanism. After 1912 they practically lost their identity, having been swallowed up by the Chinese; even their spoken language is virtually extinct. Their script was derived (c. 1600) from that of the Mongols. See also CHINA—8. *History* (The Ch'ing, 1644–1912).

Bibliography.—Gibert, Lucien, *Dictionnaire historique et géographique de la Mandchourie* (Hong Kong 1934); Michael, Franz, *The Origin of Manchu Rule in China* (Baltimore 1942); Hummel, Arthur W., ed., *Eminent Chinese of the Ch'ing Period, 1644–1912*, 2 vols. (Washington 1944–45).

L. CARRINGTON GOODRICH,
Professor of Chinese, Columbia University.

MANCINI, män-chē′nĕ, the name of a noble Italian family, of which the most famous members were the five daughters of Michele Lorenzo Mancini and his wife, Girolama Mazzarino, who was the sister of Jules Cardinal Mazarin. They were summoned to the French court by their uncle during the early years of the reign of Louis XIV, and won the favors of the king.

LAURE MANCINI: b. Rome, Italy, 1635; d. Paris, France, 1657. In 1651 she was married to Louis de Vendôme, duc de Mercoeur (a natural grandson of Henri IV), and became the mother of Louis Joseph, duc de Vendôme, marshal of France and one of Louis' most brilliant generals.

OLYMPE MANCINI: b. Rome, 1639?; d. Brussels, Flanders (now Belgium), 1708. In 1675 she became the wife of Prince Eugène Maurice de Savoie-Carignan (who was made comte de Soissons), and was appointed mistress of the queen's household. Accused of engaging in a plot to poison the king, she was forced to flee from France in 1680.

MARIE MANCINI: b. Rome, 1640?; d. Pisa, 1715. She was passionately loved by Louis, but because of strong opposition to her marriage to the king, Mazarin arranged a match in 1661 with Prince Lorenzo Onofrio Colonna, constable of Naples. She ran away from her husband in 1672 and, when Louis refused to receive her at court, lived in Savoy, Flanders, and at a convent in Madrid, Spain, before returning to Italy in 1705 after her husband's death.

HORTENSE MANCINI: b. Rome, 1646?; d. Chelsea, England, 1699. The most beautiful of the sisters, she married the marquis de La Meilleraye, who was given the title of duc de Mazarin. Her husband's jealousy caused her to leave him in 1666; after several adventures she went to England, where she became a favorite of Charles II.

MARIE ANNE MANCINI: b. Rome, 1649; d. Clichy, France, 1714. The spoiled darling of the French court, she married Godefroy Maurice de la Tour, duc de Bouillon, in 1662. Her salon was a center of social and intellectual life, and she was a patron of Jean de la Fontaine, Pierre Corneille, and Molière. With her sister Olympe, she was banished from the French court in 1680.

MANCINI, Pasquale Stanislao, Italian jurist and statesman: b. Castel Baronia, Avellino Province, Italy, March 17, 1817; d. Rome, Dec. 26, 1888. He practiced law and taught jurisprudence at the University of Naples, but after participating in the Revolution of 1848 he was forced to flee to Turin in Piedmont, where he occupied the chair of international law at the University there. His *La nazionalità come fonte del diritto delle genti* (1851; *Nationality as a Source of the Law of Nations*) was acclaimed as stating the juridical-political doctrine of the Italian Risorgimento.

When Italy became independent in 1860 Mancini was chosen deputy from Ariano Irpino to the first national parliament, and in 1862 he served briefly as minister of public instruction. In 1872 he joined the faculty of the University of Rome, and the next year was named president of the Institute of International Law, with headquarters at Geneva, Switzerland. From 1876 to 1878 he served as minister of justice, and from 1881 to 1885 as minister of foreign affairs; during this period he negotiated a treaty with Germany and Austria-Hungary known as the Triple Alliance (1882). He published a number of works on jurisprudence and international law, and was the promoter and first editor (1884–1888) of *Enciclopedia giuridica Italiana.*

MANCO CAPAC, mäng′kō kä′päk (MANCO INCA), Inca ruler of Peru: b. 1500?; d. 1545. He was the son of the Inca Emperor Huayna Capac, who died in 1525 without designating a successor. His eldest brother, Huáscar, was crowned king, but another brother, Atahualpa, revolted and put Huáscar to death. He himself was executed in 1533 by the Spanish conquistador, Francisco Pizarro. Shortly afterward Manco Capac announced his claim to the throne and asked the protection of Pizarro, who after the capture of Cuzco placed him on the throne.

When he was not allowed to exercise his sovereignty, Manco escaped from the Spanish and roused the Inca nation against the invaders. With a host of Indians, estimated at 180,000, he laid siege to Cuzco in April 1536. They destroyed a large part of the city by fire and killed some 800 Spaniards before scarcity of food forced them to withdraw in February 1537. Defeated in a subsequent battle by Diego de Almagro, Manco fled to the Andes, where for several years he carried on guerrilla warfare with the aid of a few loyal followers. He was killed by a party of Spaniards who took refuge in the Inca camp after the defeat by Spanish royalists of their leader, Diego de Almagro the younger.

Consult Prescott, William H., *History of the Conquest of Peru* (any edition).

MANDAEANS, măn-dē′ănz, a Gnostic sect, some 6,000 of whom still survive in towns and villages of lower Iraq and the adjoining area of Iran. They speak Arabic but still use among themselves a dialect of East Aramaic and work as craftsmen, particularly silversmiths. Locally they are called Subba (baptists, Sabians), and to Christians often represent themselves as Christians of St. John (John the Baptist), but they call themselves Nasurai (true believers, Nasoreans) and Mandai (gnostics), the people of Manda d'Hayye, the lord who gives knowledge of life.

The sect seems to have originated in Mesopotamia about the 5th century A.D. and has drawn heavily on Biblical, Syriac Christian, and Manichaean sources for its teachings, though also incorporating some more ancient Mesopotamian ideas and practices. Their technical religious vocabulary is hardly explicable apart from the Peshitta (a Syriac Bible used by Nestorian and Jacobite Christians), and their scriptures show clear evidence of having been redacted in Islamic times.

The more important texts that have been published are the *Ginza* (*Treasure*), the *Drasha d'Yahya* (*Book of John*), the *Qolasta* (*Liturgies*), the *Sfar Malwasha* (*Zodiac Book*), and the *Diwan Abathur* (*On Purgatory*).

Though called Baptists the lustrations of the sect are rather daily purification rites in running water, and concern pots and pans as well as humans. Their religious gatherings are on Sunday, but their ceremonies are usually in the open air, in courtyards or by streams. Their priestly families are strictly separated from lay families, and they have a high reputation for virtue.

Consult Pallis, Svend A.F.D., *Mandaean Studies,* 2d rev. ed., tr. from the Danish by E. H. Pallis (New York 1926); Stevens, Ethel S. (Lady Drower), *The Mandaeans of Iraq and Iran* (London 1937).

ARTHUR JEFFERY.

MANDALAY, măn'dȧ-lā', town, Burma, situated on the left bank of the Irrawaddy River 386 miles north of Rangoon. It is the second largest city in Burma, a port serving busy river traffic and a railroad junction connecting Rangoon in the south with Lashio and Myitkyina in the north. Its importance as an administrative, commercial, and cultural center has grown considerably since Burma became independent in 1948. In addition to the traditional handicrafts for which Mandalay is famed—silk weaving, gold and silver work, jade cutting, and wood carving—it has a government-operated brewery and distillery which produce ale and rum. In the great Zegyo Bazaar outside the walled city, as well as in a number of smaller bazaars, the produce of all north Burma is sold as well as imported goods. The University of Mandalay, with a pioneer agricultural school, was created in 1957 from the former Mandalay College, which had been a two-year affiliate of Rangoon University.

Mandalay was founded in 1857 by King Mindon, and was the last capital of the kingdom of Burma (1860–1885) before the British took control of the country. During World War II it was occupied by the Japanese, and about 85 per cent of the old city was destroyed in the course of its capture in 1942 and recapture by Allied armies in 1945. The old city, surrounded by walls and moat, had the royal palace in the center, and many monasteries and temples. Mandalay is the center of Burmese Buddhism. The Queen's Golden Monastery remains, built of teakwood profusely decorated with heavily gilded carving; also the Kuthodaw Pagoda at the foot of Mandalay Hill, with 729 small pagodas in the shadow of the parent shrine housing stone-inscribed Buddhist scriptures. Three miles south of the city is the Arakan Pagoda, with a 12-foot brass image of Buddha said to have been brought over the hills from Arakan in 1784. The city was immortalized in the English-speaking world by Rudyard Kipling's poem *Mandalay* (in *Barrack-Room Ballads,* 1892), set to music by Oley Speaks in *On the Road to Mandalay* (c. 1907). Pop. (1964) 322,000.

RICHARD PAW U,
Regional Office, United Nations Economic Commission for Asia and the Far East, Bangkok.

MANDAMUS, măn-dā'mŭs (Lat., we command, from *mandare,* to command), in law, a court order commanding the performance of a specific act. It may be directed to a public officer in the judicial, executive, or legislative branch of the government, to an association or corporation, or to a private individual. It is used chiefly to compel the performance of a ministerial duty, and is not available to direct the exercise of judgment or discretion in a particular way.

Since its purpose is to require affirmative action, mandamus differs from most types of injunction, the purpose of which is to prohibit the doing of harmful acts. Mandamus is an extraordinary writ which is issued only where the right involved, and the duty sought to be enforced, are clear and certain. The remedy is granted in the exercise of sound judicial discretion, rather than as a matter of right, and the court issuing the writ must be convinced that no other fully adequate remedy exists. See also INJUNCTION; WRIT.

RICHARD L. HIRSHBERG.

MANDAN, măn'dăn, the name of a North American Indian tribe of Siouan stock, which has become affiliated with the Hidatsa and Arikara on Fort Berthold Reservation in North Dakota. In 1953 they had 389 tribal members, of whom 3 were full bloods and the rest mixed with other tribes and with whites. They depend on farming and cattle raising for a livelihood. Their tribal myths and music reveal their long association with the Hidatsa.

History records the Mandan as a friendly people of above medium height, handsome, graceful, and neat in appearance, and noted for their beautiful costumes. They were agriculturists in earliest times and lived in villages of earth-covered lodges, where they also made fine pottery. They occupied an important position on the upper Missouri River when they were visited by Sieur de La Vérendrye in 1738 and by Meriwether Lewis and William Clark in 1804. Wars with Dakota and Assiniboin tribes, followed by epidemics decimated their numbers; estimated at 1,600 in 1837, they were soon reduced by small-

Ornately-carved golden roof of the Arakan Pogoda.

Camera Press—Pix

pox to between 125 and 145. They were allotted lands in severalty in 1894.

Bibliography.—Catlin, George, *Letters and Notes on the Manners, Customs, and Condition of the North American Indians,* vol. 1 (New York 1841); Hodge, Frederick W., ed., *Handbook of American Indians North of Mexico,* part 1 (Washington 1912); Densmore, Frances, *Mandan and Hidatsa Music* (Washington 1923); Report 1953 from Fort Berthold Indian Agency, North Dakota.

MURIEL H. WRIGHT.

MANDAN, city, North Dakota, seat of Morton County, altitude 1,646 feet, at the confluence of the Heart and Missouri rivers, five miles west of Bismarck. On U.S. Highway No. 10, it is served by the Northern Pacific Railroad and by two airlines, and is a railroad division point with car shops. The city lies in a wheat-growing and stock-raising area and has flour mills and creameries as well as beverage and tile industries. In the vicinity are Fort Abraham Lincoln State Park and a United States agricultural experiment station.

Mandan was founded in 1872 on the site of an early village of the Mandan Indians, and was incorporated as a city in 1881; it has had a commission form of government since 1907. Pop. (1950) 7,298; (1960) 10,525.

MANDARIN, măn′dȧ-rĭn (Port. *mandarim,* from Malay *mantri,* minister of state, from Sanskrit *mantrin,* counselor), term applied to government officials under the Chinese Empire. The nine grades were distinguished by the color of the button on the hats of office, and promotion was based on passing civil service examinations on the literary classics.

The term Mandarin language originally referred to the language spoken by officials—the dialect of Peking—and this is the national language of China. By extension Mandarin is applied to closely related dialects spoken in north and central China. See also CHINA—*10. Language* (Historical Development).

MANDARIN DUCK, an exceedingly beautiful little fresh water duck (*Aix galericulata*) native of China and Japan. The drake, in breeding plumage, is the most ornamental of all ducks with its vivid blue, green, purple, orange, and chestnut plumage set off by areas of glossy black and pure white. It is adorned by a very large ruff of glossy chestnut feathers springing from the lower cheeks and two large bright orange fan-shaped wing feathers, called "sails," which expand upward from the lower back. The mandarin duck has been domesticated by the Chinese for many centuries and introduced throughout the world in ornamental ponds in public parks and private estates. In some regions of Europe, including England, birds descended from some that had escaped are now breeding in a feral state. The mandarin duck is related to the American wood duck (*A. sponsa*) and has similar habits, such as perching in trees and nesting in a hollow stump or other natural cavity in a tree.

CHARLES VAURIE.

MANDAT, män-dȧ′, or **MANDAT TERRITORIAL,** the name given to a form of paper money issued in March 1796 by the French Directory government. The *mandats territoriaux* replaced the assignats (q.v.), first issued in 1790, differing from them in that specific pieces of confiscated property, enumerated in a table, were pledged for their redemption. Despite a forced circulation they dropped rapidly in value, and became worthless when the gold franc was introduced in February 1797.

MANDATES SYSTEM, măn′dāts sĭs′tĕm (Lat. *mandatum,* in Roman law, a contract for gratuitous service), the form of government for dependent territories ceded after World War I by Germany and Turkey to the principal Allied powers. These powers appointed the mandatories and approved the mandates subject to confirmation by the League of Nations Council, in accord with Article 22 of the Covenant. This article declared that to ceded territories "which are inhabited by peoples not yet able to stand by themselves under the strenuous conditions of the modern world, there should be applied the principle that the well-being and development of such peoples form a sacred trust of civilization" and that "the tutelage of such peoples should be entrusted to advanced nations" to be "exercised by them as Mandatories on behalf of the League."

The location of sovereignty in these areas was controversial but practice indicated that it was vested in the League which supervised the mandatory's administration and had ultimate authority to change the status of the territories. Each mandatory was required to report annually to the League on the territories committed to its charge. The League defined the degree of control to be exercised through an instrument known as the mandate, and, with the advice of the Permanent Mandates Commission, criticized any failure to observe this instrument. The mandated territories were divided into three groups.

A mandates were applied to former Turkish territories; Palestine, Transjordania, and Iraq were placed under British mandate, Syria and Lebanon under French. These communities were considered to have reached a stage of development where their independence could be provisionally recognized subject to the administrative advice and assistance of the mandatory until they were able to stand alone.

B mandates were applied to former German colonies in central Africa; the Cameroons (divided into British and French spheres), Togoland (likewise partitioned), Tanganyika (British mandate), and Ruanda-Urundi (Belgian mandate). In these territories the mandatory was responsible for administration under specified conditions designed to prevent abuses and to ensure that the welfare of the inhabitants would be the first consideration. The mandatory was obliged to secure equal opportunities for the trade and commerce of all members of the League of Nations.

C mandates were given for territories which, it was thought, might best be administered as integral portions of the mandatory's territory. The laws of the mandatory might be applied, with modifications to conform to the terms of the mandate which safeguarded the interests of the natives, as in the case of B mandates, but the open door to trade was not required. The C mandates comprised South West Africa (assigned to the Union of South Africa), eastern New Guinea (to Australia), Western Samoa (to New Zealand), Nauru (to the British Empire, to be administered by Australia), and the Caroline, Mariana, and Marshall island groups (to Japan). The mandatories were forbidden to establish defense bases in the mandated territories or to organize native military forces for use outside the territories, although the latter proviso was waived in respect to the French spheres of the Cameroons and Togoland. The United States secured by treaties with the mandatories the same rights as League members in respect to all the territories except New Guinea, Western Samoa, Nauru, and South West Africa.

The mandates were approved by the League of Nations between 1920 and 1922, with the exception of Iraq. Relations between that country and Great Britain, the mandatory, were regulated by a treaty which was approved by the League as the mandate in 1924. On advice of Great Britain the League recognized the independence of Iraq in 1932 and admitted it as a member. The remaining A mandates were terminated during or soon after World War II; the last was Palestine, which was divided by the United Nations between Israel and Jordan in 1948.

The United Nations Charter provided that the International Trusteeship System which it established should apply to "territories now held under mandate," if the mandatory agreed. All did so except the Union of South Africa, which, according to an advisory opinion of the International Court of Justice, continued to administer South West Africa as a mandate with the United Nations General Assembly substituted for the League of Nations Council as the supervising authority. The United States, which had occupied the Japanese mandated islands, agreed to administer them under the trusteeship system. By 1960 all of the former B mandates had become, or were about to become, independent states.

The mandate system marked an advance in colonial administration, begun in the Berlin treaty of 1885 on central Africa, and carried further by the United Nations. Humane treatment, education, and eventual self-determination of the inhabitants, and equal commercial opportunity in the territories, were assured by supervision of the administration by an international authority.

Consult Wright, Quincy, *Mandates Under the League of Nations* (Chicago 1930); League of Nations, *The Mandates System* (New York 1945); *Everyman's United Nations,* pp. 355 fol., 6th ed. (New York 1959).

QUINCY WRIGHT,
Professor of International Law, University of Virginia.

MANDAUE, män-dou′ä, municipality, the Philippines, on the east coast of Cebu Island opposite Mactan Island, four miles north of Cebu city. The chief crops are corn (maize) and coconuts, and salt is produced from sea water. The municipality has 27 barrios. Pop. (1948) 19,068.

MANDER, män′dẽr, **Karel van,** Dutch-Flemish painter and writer: b. Meulebeke, Flanders, May 1548; d. Amsterdam, Netherlands, Sept. 2, 1606. He studied with Lukas de Heere and Pieter Vlerick, and spent three years (1574–1577) in Rome, Italy, studying and painting. In 1583 he settled in Haarlem in Holland, where he opened an academy for painters; among his pupils was Frans Hals. His painting, mostly in the mannerist style, included portraits and religious subjects, but he is best known for his biographies of painters in *Het schilder boeck* (1604; *The Book of Painters*), prefaced by a poem in 14 chapters on the technique of painting. Part of this work was translated into English as *Dutch*

and Flemish Painters (tr. by Constant van de Wall, 1936).

MANDEVILLA, măn′dẽ-vĭl-à, a genus of woody vines of the dogbane family (Apocynaceae), native from Mexico south to Argentina. The genus is large and contains about 100 species, one of which, the Chilean jasmine (*Mandevilla laxa*), is grown as an ornamental in greenhouses or warm climates.

The petioled leaves are ovate in shape, 2 to 6 inches long, and 1 to 6 inches wide. The fragrant white or pinkish flowers are borne in axillary or terminal racemes. They are funnelform and 5-parted, have stamens with very short filaments, anthers united to the stigma, and 2 ovaries containing many ovules. The fruit consists of 2 cylindrical follicles 10 to 16 inches long.

The genus was named after Henry John Mandeville, a British minister at Buenos Aires, Argentina.

FRANK G. LIER.

MANDEVILLE, măn′dẽ-vĭl, **Bernard,** Dutch-English satirist and physician: b. Dort (Dordrecht), Netherlands, 1670?; d. Hackney, England, Jan. 21, 1733. After receiving a medical degree from the University of Leiden in 1691 he went to England and settled permanently in London. His medical practice was small; he received a pension from some Dutch merchants, and apparently did public relations work for distillers. He enjoyed a reputation as a conversationalist and wit among such distinguished men as Joseph Addison, Benjamin Franklin, and the lord chief justice, Lord Macclesfield, and he published a number of satirical works on social problems of the day.

His most famous work was a doggerel poem first published in 1705 as *The Grumbling Hive, or Knaves Turned Honest* and republished anonymously in 1714 under its better-known title, *The Fable of the Bees, or Private Vices Public Benefits,* together with *Remarks* and an *Enquiry into the Origin of Moral Virtue.* Another edition appeared in 1723 with the addition of an *Essay on Charity and Charity Schools* and *A Search into the Nature of Society.* Using a hive of bees as a symbol of human society, Mandeville described the disruption of their community when they attempted to reform by practicing self-denial and renouncing self-interest and the accumulation of wealth. He rejected the concept of a natural moral sense advocated by Anthony Ashley Cooper, 3d Earl of Shaftesbury (1671–1713), and maintained that the progress and prosperity of a society were not the result of virtue, but of such vices as egotistical ambition and the desire for gain and showy expenditure—that "private vices are public benefits." This inspired heated controversy, and the 1723 edition was presented as a public nuisance by the grand jury of Middlesex. The work was very popular, however, and impressed such scholars as Samuel Johnson. *The Fable of the Bees* developed the economic philosophy of Thomas Hobbes and paved the way for Jeremy Bentham and his doctrine of utilitarianism.

Consult Robertson, John M., *Pioneer Humanists* (London 1907); Kaye, Frederick B., "The Influence of Bernard Mandeville," *Studies in Philology,* vol. 19, Jan. 12, 1922.

MANDEVILLE, SIR **John,** the putative author of the most popular medieval travel book,

Mandeville's Travels, originally written in Norman French about 1360, and rendered into every major European tongue by 1400. The first of the four English versions, made about 1385, is the earliest monument of secular English prose; long attributed to Mandeville himself, it won him the title of father of English prose. Modern scholarship has transferred this honor to an unknown translator, has reduced the author's role to that of an armchair traveler who pilfered most of his book from the works of earlier writers, and has seriously questioned the very existence of Mandeville both as an author and as a person. Was Sir John, as stated in the *Travels,* born in the English town of St. Albans and did he "pass the sea" in 1322 to return home 34 years later in 1356 to "put these things written in this book"? Can we believe the story told by the often untrustworthy Liège chronicler, Jean d'Outremeuse (1338–1400), that a certain Jean de Bourgogne, locally called John with the Beard, revealed to him on his deathbed in 1372 that he was actually Sir John Mandeville who had fled England in 1322 for having killed a nobleman? We have well-authenticated records that a tomb in a church near Liège bore an inscription to a Sir John Mandeville, deceased in 1372; much less authentic is the inscription still shown in the abbey at St. Albans, claiming the abbey as his burial place. Amid this confusion, scholars continue to speculate variously, interpreting the meager evidence to support their contradictory judgments. Of the two most recent investigators, Malcolm H. I. Letts endorses d'Outremeuse's report, while Josephine W. Bennett rejects the entire Liège episode as an imposture. In default of further substantial evidence, the authorship of the *Travels* bids fair to remain a controversial issue. On one point there is general agreement—the author was quite certainly an Englishman.

Whoever the author, the book remains a masterpiece of literary collage, fabricated with consummate artistry from wide reading of the accounts of genuine travelers to the Holy Land and the Orient and from the reports of natural and unnatural wonders in numerous writings, conveniently summarized in Vincent of Beauvais' encyclopedic *Speculum majus* (1260?). For the first part of the simulated voyage, terminating in Egypt, the principal source was the *Itinerarius* (1336; *Itinerary*) of the German monk William of Boldensele; for the far more entertaining continuation through the Middle East and the Orient the *Itinerarium* (1330) of the Italian friar Odoric of Pordenone was quite thoroughly pillaged. The triumph of Mandeville consists in his ability to transform the raw material of his multiple sources into an artistically unified and absorbingly entertaining narrative, to cast an air of veracity around the most incredible fictions in a style designed to win from the reader that willing suspension of disbelief which characterizes the greatest imaginative writings. He knew how to stress the picturesque detail, to invent new adventures, to imagine fantastic marvels.

It was Mandeville who fired the curiosity of Western Europe about the mysterious East, with his vivid accounts of the Fountain of Youth, the Dog-faced People, the Vegetable Lamb, the Gold-digging Ants, the Valley Perilous, and the court of the Great Khan of Cathay. More than any other book, the *Travels,* ably seconded by the graphic illustrations supplied by the excited imagination of the miniaturists, stimulated the enormous and finally successful efforts of 15th century Europeans to persevere through sea and land to the fabulous people and places so plausibly described. Long after the plausibility of the *Travels* was shattered the many printed editions continued to delight mature readers with their preposterous quaintness and to stir the imagination of the young with the glamour of prodigious adventures amid strangely exotic surroundings. Few travel books have enjoyed such enduring popular favor and such a controversial history.

Bibliography.—TEXTS: *The Travels of Sir John Mandeville,* ed. by A. W. Pollard, 5th ed. (London 1923), the Cotton version (MS. Cotton Titus c. xvi, British Museum) in modern spelling, is best for the general reader. Sir John Mandeville, *Travels,* ed. by Malcolm H. I. Letts, 2 vols., Hakluyt Society, Series 2, vols. 101–102 (London 1953), the Egerton version (MS. Egerton 1982, British Museum) in modern spelling, is annotated, with the texts of the oldest French manuscript and of the Bodleian version (Bodleian Library, Oxford), and a comprehensive introduction. COMMENTARIES: Malcolm H. I. Letts, *Sir John Mandeville, the Man and His Book* (London 1949), gives a thorough analysis of the *Travels* and its sources, and assumes that Mandeville adopted the name of John of Bourgogne to conceal his identity. Josephine W. Bennett, *The Rediscovery of Sir John Mandeville* (New York 1954), examines in detail the genesis and fortunes of the *Travels,* refuting the identification of Mandeville with John of Bourgogne, and gives an extensive bibliography of manuscripts and printed editions in 10 languages.

ALBERT DOUGLAS MENUT,
Professor of Romance Languages, Syracuse University.

MANDINGO, măn-dĭng'gō, **MANDE,** măn'dĕ, or **MENDE,** mĕn'dĕ, a group of West African peoples, numbering several million, who speak related languages. They extend from Senegal, French West Africa, on the west to the upper Niger River on the east, and from western Liberia on the south into the Sahara Desert on the north. Two physical types are distinguishable. A slender type is thought to represent the ancestral Mandingo; a shorter, stockier, darker-skinned type is associated with the aboriginal population.

Among the most populous groups are the Bambara or Banmana, who dwell in the east and have long been settled agriculturists. Their religion is centered around a village ancestor cult. In the west the Mandingo proper occupy numerous small chiefdoms established by Mandingo warriors who conquered the aborigines in their quest for slaves. These latter were employed in the fields and served as a medium of exchange. Secret societies are strongly developed among the Mandingo. The Dyula, who are merchants and traders scattered throughout the area have long been Muslims.

ELIZABETH E. BACON.

MANDOLIN, măn'dô-lĭn, a stringed musical instrument belonging to the lute family, with a deep, pear-shaped back. There are two types of mandolin. The Neapolitan has four pairs of strings—the lower usually of gut spun over with silver or copper, the upper of steel only—which are set in vibration by a plectrum. The strings are tuned in fifths, and there are 17 frets across the fingerboard. The rarer Milanese type has five or six pairs of strings. The *mandolino* originated in Italy as a popular instrument, but was introduced into England in 1713 in concert. Wolfgang Amadeus Mozart composed a serenade for mandolin in Act II of *Don Giovanni,* and Ludwig van Beethoven wrote a piece for the instrument.

Related to the mandolin is the Spanish *bandurria,* which is played with a plectrum but has a flat back. The number of strings increased from three pairs in the 17th century to six pairs in the 20th. The *bandurria* is used in playing serious as well as popular music; such musicians as Manuel de Falla and Isaac Albéniz have composed pieces for the *bandurria*.

MANDRAKE, măn′drāk, historically, the common name for perennial herbs of the genus *Mandragora* in the potato family (Solanaceae), with three species native to the Mediterranean region. They are nearly stemless plants with large, sinuately toothed leaves and large taproots. The flowers are purplish to pale violet or white, with bell-shaped corollas; the berries are globular. The root is sometimes forked, giving it a fancied resemblance to the human form, a characteristic which has given rise to many legends of its magical properties; reference to it is common in the older literature, such as the Bible (Genesis 30:14–16) and the plays of William Shakespeare (*Romeo and Juliet,* Act IV, scene 3). In some places the plant is cultivated for its historical interest, but it has little horticultural merit. The plant parts contain poisonous narcotic principles similar to those of belladonna, a relative, and were used by the ancients as narcotics and aphrodisiacs.

In the United States the name is applied to the May apple, *Podophyllum peltatum,* an herbaceous member of the barberry family (Berberidaceae) that also has a perennial and sometimes divided rootstock. It has two large, peltate, deeply lobed leaves and a solitary nodding white flower 1 to 2 inches across. The 2-inch fleshy berry is yellow and edible when ripe and is sometimes used for preserves. The rhizome, foliage, seeds, and green fruits, however, are poisonous. This native of the eastern United States grows in moist open woods and pastures, from which its rhizomes are collected by herb gatherers. Preparations of the rhizome are used in cathartics, but in overdoses may prove fatal.

RICHARD M. STRAW,
Assistant Professor of Botany, Los Angeles State College.

MANDRILL, măn′drĭl, *Mandrillus sphinx,* a forest-dwelling baboon (q.v.) native to West Africa. The mandrill is large—about three feet long—with a stumpy tail. Vividly hued, the face has a nose of bright red and blue, a yellow beard, and whitish patches behind the ears, while the sitting pads are of violet surrounded by crimson; between the colorful extremities the body is black. Its inch-long canine teeth make the mandrill dangerous, but it does not attack man unless provoked. See also DRILL.

MANES, mā′nēz, in ancient Rome the spirits of the dead, who were thought of collectively as *di (dii) manes,* the good gods. (1) They were believed to return to visit the living during Parentalia or All Souls (February 13–21), when families decorated the graves and made offerings of food to placate the spirits of their dead kinsmen. On the final day there was a public ceremony, Feralia, for all the spirits of the community. During the nine days of Parentalia the temples were closed, the magistrates laid aside their official dress, and no marriages took place.

(2) When a town was founded in ancient Italy a round pit was dug and a stone (*lapis manalis*) placed at the bottom of it, representing the gateway to the underworld. On specified dates, which varied from town to town, the stone was removed to give passage to the spirits and gods of the dead and sacrifices were made at the pit.

(3) According to another belief hungry spirits prowled around dwellings on the nights of May 9, 11, and 13, a period called Lemuria, and had to be driven out by a magic formula performed by the head of the household.

MANET, mȧ-nĕ′, **Édouard,** French painter: b. Paris, France, Jan. 23, 1832; d. there, April 30, 1883. The son of a wealthy bourgeois family, he had registered as an apprentice officer in the merchant marine and made a crossing to South America before he decided to become a painter. At the age of 17 he entered the studio of the academic artist Thomas Couture in Paris. There he remained for about seven years, learning much of lasting value, though his own tastes and strong artistic personality were in little sympathy with the rigid and arid standards of his master. Early in his career he established his lifelong loyalty to the great tradition of European painting, copying in the Louvre the works of such old masters as Titian, Peter Paul Rubens, and Diego Velázquez. He also traveled extensively during his twenties, visiting museums in the Netherlands, Germany, and Italy. The pictures that he studied during these trips stimulated in him a great admiration for Spanish art. The influence of Velázquez and Francisco José de Goya led him to the use of much black and subtle tones of gray and directed him toward Spanish subject matter; this predominates in his work from 1860, when he painted the *Guitarist* (in the Metropolitan Museum, New York City), until 1865, when he made a brief voyage to Spain. The actuality disappointed him and as a result of this visit he formulated his intention to devote the broad free style that he was developing to the celebration of intrinsically French subjects drawn directly from contemporary life.

Édouard Manet's portrait sketch of George Moore.

The Metropolitan Museum of Art, Gift of Mrs. Ralph J. Hines, 1955

In 1861 he exhibited the *Guitarist* and a double portrait of his parents at the Salon in Paris, and from this time until the year before his death, when he showed the brilliant *Bar at the Folies Bergère* (National Gallery, London), Manet sent contributions to the official exhibitions of painting and often had the satisfaction of acceptance. This consistent courting of popular approval, perhaps more than anything else, separates Manet from the established impressionist group that numbered among others Claude Monet, Auguste Renoir, and Camille Pissarro, though his works, like theirs, seemed to the conventional Parisian gallery visitors and critics incredibly shocking in both choice of subject and technique. Two paintings by Manet now included among the Louvre's greatest treasures, *Olympia* and *Breakfast on the Grass,* both of 1863, were the objects of hostile attack and were regarded as scandalous affronts to decency. Actually the first, a youthful reclining nude attended by her servant and a black cat, pays tribute to Goya's *Nude Maja,* and the other takes its theme from works by the Renaissance Italians, Raphael and Giorgione. The shocking quality of these paintings was due less to what they represented than to the fresh vision and the bold brush stroke so foreign to the smooth, facile handling characteristic of the academic French painting to which people were accustomed at the time.

Manet played a significant role in the development of impressionism (q.v.), although he himself was never a dedicated member of the impressionist group nor did he contribute to their exhibitions. His courage and daring were of incalculable value to the young impressionists who in turn exerted considerable influence on him, especially in the direction of working out of doors and in the adoption during the early 1870's of a much lighter palette. This use of paler, brighter tones and a new increased preoccupation with the effects of light changed greatly the appearance of the pictures that Manet painted in the last decade of his life. Though the Salon continued to reject many of his contributions his work was much noticed and admired, and from about 1875 he was notably successful. The critics Théodore Duret and Émile Zola supported him and he was much in demand for society portraits. Some of these, executed in a technique combining oil and pastel which he perfected and used extensively at the end of his life, may be counted among his most beautiful and successful works.

Manet was one of the most important painters in France during the 19th century. He was also a personage of great distinction, possessing beside his tremendous artistic gifts a figure and bearing of marked elegance and a cultivated aristocratic mind and spirit.

Bibliography.—Duret, Théodore, *Histoire d'Édouard Manet et de son oeuvre* (Paris 1902), tr. by J. E. C. Flitch as *Manet* (New York 1937); Rey, Robert, *Manet,* tr. from the French by Eveline B. Shaw (New York 1938); Hamilton, George H., *Manet and His Critics* (New Haven 1954).

MARGARETTA M. SALINGER,
Research Associate in the Department of Paintings, The Metropolitan Museum of Art.

MANETHO, măn'ĕ-thō, Egyptian priest and historian: fl. 3d century B.C. A native of Sebennytus in Lower Egypt, he served as a priest at Heliopolis during the reigns of Ptolemy I (r. 304–283 B.C.) and Ptolemy II (r. 285–246 B.C.). From the temple archives he wrote a history of Egypt, *Aegyptiaca* (Egyptian Annals), which listed 30 dynasties of kings with their names, accession dates, and the notable events of each period. His work, which was written in Greek, survives only in the epitomes and extracts of later writers, most fully in the *Chronographia* of Georgius Syncellus, a 9th-century Byzantine monk. Early Christian and Jewish scholars attempted to correlate Old Testament events with Manetho's chronology. When, over 2,000 years after Manetho compiled his history, European scholars began to decipher the inscriptions carved on Egyptian monuments they used his king list as a guide in working out a chronology of Egyptian history. Although the surviving copies of the king list have been distorted by copyists' errors, on the whole his names check with those found on inscriptions, and his scheme of 30 dynasties arranged in three main periods—the Old, Middle, and New kingdoms—is basic to modern chronologies of Egyptian history. See also CHRONOLOGY— *Egyptian Chronology.*

MANEUVERS. See ARMY, NAVY, AND AIR FORCE MANEUVERS.

MANFRED, măn'frĕd, king of Sicily: b. about 1232; d. Benevento, Feb. 26, 1266. A natural son of Frederick II, Holy Roman emperor and king of Sicily, Manfred studied in Paris and Bologna and in his father's court at Palermo, a center of Arabic-Norman science. On his father's death in 1250 Manfred became prince of Taranto and regent of Italy in the name of his half-brother Conrad IV, who was absent in Germany. When Conrad died in 1254 Manfred made himself regent for his young nephew, Conradin, and continued the struggle with the papacy for control of Italy which had been begun by Frederick II. Supported by Saracen (Muslim) troops, Manfred was successful against Pope Innocent IV (d. 1254), and on Aug. 10, 1258, following an invented report of Conradin's death, he had himself crowned king of Sicily. Succeeding popes, Urban IV (d. 1264) and Clement IV (d. 1268) called on Charles I of Anjou, brother of Louis IX of France, to defend the Holy Church, and in 1266 Manfred was killed while fighting against the French army.

A poet and patron of the arts, Manfred was a benign ruler, but too indolent to organize a strong defense against the forceful Charles. His daughter Constance became queen of Sicily in 1282 when the Sicilian people, revolting against Charles' harsh rule, offered the throne of Sicily to her husband, Pedro III of Aragon.

MANFRED, a dramatic poem in three acts by George Gordon Byron, published in 1817. This powerful and imaginative witch drama was composed under the spell of the awe-inspiring scenery of the Alps, which Lord Byron had visited in 1816 on the tour through Germany and Switzerland recorded in the third canto of *Childe Harold.* The hero is a sort of combination of Faust and of the Byronic type portrayed in the earlier verse tales, a lofty and defiant spirit, dwelling alone in a dark castle among the higher Alps, haunted by remorse for an act the nature of which we are left to guess. Seeking to interview the spirit of the dead Astarte, the victim of his crime, and to obtain her forgiveness, he calls up the spirits over whom he has control and at length resorts to the abode of the evil principle itself. The ghost is evoked, but returns an ambiguous answer to his question. On the morrow Manfred expires, after resisting a summons to repent from the old abbot of St. Maurice and defying the demons who have come to possess his soul.

Some biographers have seen in the poem a reflection of its author's relation with his half sister, Aurora Leigh. In any case Byron has made his hero in his own image, infusing into him the characteristic Byronic spirit of proud rebellion and passionate despair. In style the poet aims at and partly succeeds in achieving an imaginative grandeur commensurate with his superhuman theme. Manfred attracted the favorable notice of Johann Wolfgang von Goethe, to whose Faust, translated in his presence by Matthew Gregory Lewis (Monk Lewis) in 1816, Byron is indebted for some of the essential elements in his drama.

Consult Ward, Adolphus William and Waller, A. R., eds., *Cambridge History of English Literature,* vol. 12, pp. 31–56 (London 1916).

JAMES H. HANFORD,
Author of "John Milton, Englishman" and "A Restoration Reader."

MANGABEY, măng′gȧ-bā, a slender, long-tailed monkey of the genus *Cercocebus,* found across tropical Africa from the Congo Basin to Kenya. It resembles the macaque, to which it is related, in its large cheek pouches where food can be stored, but differs in having fingers and toes webbed at the base and white upper eyelids. There are two distinct groups, one with a tuft of hair on the head forming a crest, the other without this tuft. Each type includes several species. Mangabeys make docile pets.

MANGALDAN, măng-gäl-dän′, municipality, Republic of the Philippines, in the province of Pangasinan, Luzon, 11 miles northeast of Lingayen, the provincial capital. It is on the coast road overlooking Lingayen Gulf and is served by a railroad running from San Fernando to Manila. An agricultural municipality comprising 30 barrios, its chief products are rice, copra, and maize (corn). Pop. (1960) 33,422.

MANGALORE, măng′gȧ-lōr, city, India, a seaport on the west coast, at the mouth of the Netravati River, 190 miles west of Bangalore. It is the capital of the district of South Kanara, Mysore State. The harbor is a tidal lagoon; larger vessels must anchor in the roadstead two miles from the city. A rail terminus, Mangalore is a major shipping center for coffee; pepper, tea, cashew nuts, and sandalwood are also exported. In addition to a cottage industry in spinning and weaving cotton, industries include the manufacture of tiles and glazed pottery, as well as coffee curing and sugar milling. It is the seat of a Roman Catholic bishopric and the headquarters of the Basel Luthern Mission of India. There is a Jesuit college and two affiliates of Mysore University.

Mangalore was active in the Persian Gulf trade in the 14th century, and the Portuguese established a trading post there in the 16th; the Dutch East India Company controlled the area from 1669, to be followed by the British in 1688. Haidar Ali, the Muslim soldier-adventurer of Mysore, held the city between

1763 and 1783, making it a boat-building center, and his son Tipu Sahib regained it from the British in 1784 and held it until 1799, when the city again became a part of British India. About one quarter of the inhabitants are Indian Christians, the remainder Muslims. Pop. (1966) 156,317.

MANGAN, măng′gȧn, **James Clarence,** Irish poet: b. Dublin, Ireland, May 1, 1803; d. there, June 20, 1849. The son of a grocer who went bankrupt, Mangan was forced to leave school at the age of 13. Employed for small wages as a copyist and clerk and tormented for his eccentricities by his fellow clerks, he became an alcoholic, so that when better positions were offered he could not hold them for any length of time. After a series of illnesses he died during a cholera epidemic, probably of starvation rather than cholera.

Mangan began to write verse for Dublin almanacs in 1822. Later he contributed extensively to the journal of the Comet Club, which he joined in 1831, and to the *Dublin University Magazine,* the *Nation,* and other Irish journals. He had studied Latin, French, Italian, and Spanish in school. He taught himself German and published a number of translations of German poetry which were collected in *German Anthology* (2 vols., 1845). His old Gaelic poems, rendered by him into English verse from prose translations made by friends, were collected in two volumes: *The Poets and Poetry of Munster* (1849) and *The Tribes of Ireland* (1852). His work was uneven, but at his best, as in *The Dark Rosaleen,* a free rendering from the Gaelic, and in his autobiographical *Nameless One,* he is regarded by many as the greatest of the Irish poets writing in English.

Consult Sheridan, John Desmond, *James Clarence Mangan* (Dublin 1937).

MANGANESE, măng′gȧ-nēs, a metallic element widely distributed in nature as an oxide, carbonate, or silicate. The most common compound, the dioxide MnO_2, was believed to be a compound of iron until 1774, when Karl Wilhelm Scheele proved it to contain a new element. The metal had no commercial importance until 1856 when Sir Henry Bessemer used it as an addition to steel. The practice of adding manganese to steel has since become almost universal and an average of 14 pounds of manganese is added to every ton of steel produced. This use of manganese dominated the commercial picture to such an extent that the important properties and uses of manganese as a nonferrous metal in its own right were not adequately recognized until the middle of the present century.

Ferromanganese.—Manganese is commonly added to steel not as the metal but as manganese iron carbide, known as ferromanganese or spiegeleisen depending on the manganese content. These alloys are made by carbon reduction of the oxide ores of manganese. To produce ferromanganese, which contains 80 per cent manganese, high grade ores are required containing 48 per cent or more manganese and not over 10 per cent iron. Such ores are not produced in quantity in the United States, but must be imported from Africa, Brazil, or India. (The Union of Soviet Socialist Republics has a large supply, producing almost 50 per cent of the world total in 1965.) For this reason manganese has been listed as a strategic mineral to be stockpiled against an emergency which would close ocean shipping. This fact has led to the erroneous assumption by some people that manganese itself is scarce in the United States. This is not true; there is an abundance of low grade ores suitable for products other than ferromanganese.

As a general practice manganese is added to steel not as an alloying metal but as a scavenger to remove sulphur and other impurities. The manganese remaining has very little effect on the steel. When it is desirable to add less carbon to the steel than standard ferromanganese (containing about 7 per cent C), the oxidic ores are reduced in part with silicon, which produces medium- and low-carbon ferromanganese. It is not possible in this way to produce pure manganese metal.

Pure Manganese Metal.—Commercial production of pure manganese metal by the electrolytic process was begun in 1941, and had expanded so that in the 1960's millions of pounds of pure metal were produced. The electrolytic manganese produced in the 1960's was made from manganese ammonium sulphate solutions using a diaphragm cell. Although other electrolytes appeared to have advantages they had not been adopted commercially. The manganese in the spent electrolyte is replenished by manganous oxide produced by reducing the usual oxidic ores. This metal has standards of purity usual to commercial nonferrous metals such as copper, lead, and zinc, and forms the basis of a new approach to the metallurgical uses of manganese.

The pure metal in the form stable at room temperature is brittle and has no engineering uses; however, it exists in three allotropic forms, alpha, stable up to 742° C., beta, stable from 742° C. to 1100° C., and gamma, stable from 1100° C. to the melting point, 1240° C. The alpha and beta forms have a complicated cubic structure and are brittle, but the gamma form is face-centered tetragonal in structure and is soft and ductile.

The gamma form is rendered stable at low temperatures by alloying with copper, nickel, iron, and a number of other elements, hence pure manganese can be used as an alloying element either as the base metal or as the secondary metal. An alloy having a manganese base of 72 per cent Mn, 18 per cent Cu, and 10 per cent Ni is widely used as the high expansion component of thermostatic metal; another alloy of 80 per cent Mn and 20 per cent Cu is used in cams and other friction drives because of its unusual elastic properties. Pure manganese is also used in new grades of stainless steel in which up to 15 per cent manganese replaces part of the nickel in the older compositions.

Valence and Compounds.—Chemically, manganese has 5 valences—2, 3, 4, 5, and 7. In the divalent state, its oxide is quite basic and can be dissolved even in weak acids to form manganous salts. The divalent oxide MnO is formed by heating the higher oxides in a moderately reducing atmosphere or by oxidizing the metal with even a small percentage of acidic flux such as SiO_2. Manganese salts with valences of 2 or 7 are much more stable in solution than compounds with the other valences. Tetravalent and tervalent manganese salts hydrolyze rapidly; pentavalent salts disproportionate in acid solution to form the stable manganous salt and permanganate.

Manganese carbonate occurs naturally as rhodochrosite (q.v.). The pure compound is produced commercially in treating low grade ores by the carbamate process in which manganese in the ore is reduced to MnO and dissolved in ammonium carbamate. This solution on heating precipitates manganese carbonate. The pure manganese carbonate so produced is an intermediate for other manganese compounds, such as battery oxide and the metal itself.

An important use of manganese is as battery oxide, the depolarizing component of dry cells. Originally a special grade of natural oxide obtained from the Gold Coast of Africa was used for this purpose, but synthetic oxides have come increasingly into use. The requirement for battery oxide goes beyond chemical purity and the products produced electrolytically and by thermal treatment of the carbonate have shown outstanding performance.

In addition to the compounds discussed, manganese sulphate is used as a fertilizer, the chloride is used to add manganese to magnesium alloys, and the naphthenate and resinate are used as paint driers.

See also ELECTROCHEMICAL INDUSTRIES—*Electrometallurgy: Electrolysis of Aqueous Solutions* (Manganese); METALS; STEEL—*4. Steel Technology.*

Bibliography.—Dean, Reginald S., *Electrolytic Manganese and Its Alloys* (New York 1952); Mathewson, Champion H., ed., *Modern Uses of Nonferrous Metals*, 2d ed. (American Institute of Mining and Metallurgical Engineers, New York 1953); Sully, Arthur H., *Manganese* (New York 1955); Varentsov, I. M., *Sedimentary Manganese Ores* (Amsterdam 1964).

REGINALD S. DEAN,
Metallurgical Engineer and Consultant.

MANGANESE BRONZE, brŏnz, a metallic element in which the copper forming the base of the alloy is mixed with a certain proportion of ferromanganese, and which has exceptional qualities in the way of strength and hardness. Various qualities of the bronze are manufactured, each suited for certain specific purposes. One quality, in which the zinc alloyed with the treated copper is considerably in excess of the tin, is made into rods and plates, and when simply cast is said to have a tensile strength of about 24 tons per square inch. Another quality has all the characteristics of forged steel without any of its defects. Still another quality is in extensive use for toothed wheels, gearing, brackets, and all kinds of machinery supports. Because of its nonliability to corrosion, manganese bronze is widely used for steamship propellers. See also ALLOYS—*Alloys for Specific Purposes.*

MANGANITE, măng′gȧ-nīt, native hydrated oxide of manganese, $MnO(OH)$, or $Mn_2O_3H_2O$. It crystallizes in the orthorhombic system, but also occurs in columnar and stalactitic forms. It is brittle and has a hardness of 4 and a specific gravity of about 4.3. In color it is steel gray to iron black, and is opaque with a submetallic luster. It occurs in the Harz region, Germany, in Norway and Sweden, and in the British Isles. In the United States it is found in the Lake Superior mining district, and in Douglas County, Colo. It also occurs in Nova Scotia and New Brunswick, Canada. Manganite is used as a source of manganese for the preparation of spiegeleisen and other alloys, and also in the manufacture of pigments and dyes. See also MANGANESE.

MANGATAREM, mäng-gä-tä'rĕm, municipality, Republic of the Philippines, in the Province of Pangasinan, Luzon, 17 miles south of Dagupan, near the Agne River. Comprised of 47 barrios, it is an agricultural center for rice, copra, and maize (corn). Pop. (1948) 20,425.

MANGE, mänj, a communicable disease affecting both humans and domestic animals, caused by parasites burrowing into the epidermal layer of the skin. Follicular mange, produced by *Demodex folliculorum,* infests the hair follicles of dogs; sarcoptic mange or scabies, produced by *Sarcoptes scabiei,* is the type most often found in humans. Various local applications are used in curing the disease. See also CATTLE—*4. Cattle Diseases* (Cattle Mites); DOG, DISEASES OF THE—*Mange;* HORSE—*Care and Diseases of the Horse* (Skin Parasites); ITCH MITE; SCAB, or SCABIES.

MANGEL-WURZEL. See BEET—*Mangel-Wurzel, or Mangel.*

MANGIN, män-zhăn', **Charles Marie Emmanuel,** French general: b. Sarrebourg, France, July 6, 1886; d. Paris, May 12, 1925. On leaving the military academy at St.-Cyr in 1888 he served in the Sudan (1890–1894), and commanded the military escort for Jean Baptiste Marchand on his historic journey from the sources of the Ubangi, a tributary of the Congo, to Fashoda on the White Nile (1896–1898). After three years in Tonkin, French Indochina (1901–1904) he was posted to West Africa (1907–1911). While serving under Marshal Lyautey in Morocco (1912–1913) he drove the insurgent El Hiba from Marrakesh, a feat which won him the award of the Legion of Honor. His book, *La force noire* (1910) expressed his belief in the vast resources of France's African empire.

Mangin proved himself a brilliant general and tactician in World War I. As brigadier general of the Fifth Army he withstood the shock of the German onset at Charleroi, Belgium. He participated as division commander in the battles of the Marne and Aisne and in 1916 recaptured the forts of Douaumont and Vaux at Verdun. Because of a setback in April 1917 he was relieved of his post, but with the accession of Georges Clemenceau he was returned to active duty. In June 1918 he led a counterattack which broke the German offensive in Champagne and had pressed on to Lorraine when the armistice was signed on Nov. 11, 1918. After the armistice he was in charge of the army of occupation on the Rhine. In 1920–1921 he was sent on a mission to South America, and on his return was named inspector general of colonial troops and a member of the supreme war council, posts held until his death.

MANGO, mäng'gō, a tropical fruit of the genus *Mangifera,* chiefly *M. indica,* belonging to the family Anacardiaceae. The fruit is a fleshy drupe, 3 to 5 inches long, with an orange, yellow, or red pulp possessing a rich aromatic flavor. The mango tree is a large evergreen plant reaching 90 feet in height with tapered, shiny, dark green leaves and large panicles of small pink flowers.

Mango trees are grown commercially in many tropical countries, especially in India where it is an important food plant. In the United States it is grown in Florida and California. Most of the fruits are eaten fresh, but some are used in preserves, salads, jams, and chutneys. The tree has been under cultivation for at least 4,000 years; it is believed to have originated in the India-Burma region.

FRANK G. LIER.

MANGOSTEEN, măng'gŏ-stēn, a fruit of the tropical plant *Garcinia mangostana,* has been considered by many as the world's best flavored fruit. The small tree, 25 to 30 feet high, is a native of the Malayan region and is common in the East Indies and Ceylon. A few plants are grown in the West Indies, but not on a commercial basis.

The fruit is a dark red-purple berry 2 to 3 inches in diameter with persistent, adhering, light green calyx lobes. The rind is thick and tough and encloses the 5 to 7 fleshy, white segments which are eaten. The texture of the pulp of these segments is so delicate that it melts in the mouth with a delicious flavor.

FRANK G. LIER.

MANGROVE, măng'grōv, a tree of worldwide tropical distribution, is found growing on mud flats of coastal tidal swamps. The red mangrove, *Rhizophora mangle* (Rhizophoraceae), is economically most important. It is a large tree which at maturity reaches a height of 100 feet. The aerial stiltlike roots which support the stem 10 feet or more above the water are characteristic. The wood is hard and heavy and is used in some tropical countries for rafters, posts, piling, railroad ties, and charcoal. Its most important use is as a source of tanning for tanning sole and other thick leathers. Mangrove bark, which contains from 20 to 30 per cent tannin, is dried and pulverized to a fine powder. It may be used in this form or, more commonly, a solid extract is prepared of 55 to 60 per cent tannin. Most of the powdered bark and extract are shipped to the United States from the East Indies, East Africa, and Central America.

FRANK G. LIER.

MANGUM, măng'gŭm, city, Oklahoma, seat of Greer County, 125 miles southwest of Oklahoma City on Salt Fork, a branch of Red River, at an altitude of 1,580 feet. It is at the junction of the Chicago, Rock Island, and Pacific, and the Missouri-Kansas-Texas railroads. A trade center for an agricultural area, its industries include cotton ginning, the processing of cottonseed products and flour, and the manufacture of brick and tile. The city was laid out in 1883 and incorporated in 1900; it has had a city manager since 1914. Pop. (1960) 3,950.

MANGYAN or **MANGUIAN,** män-gyän', a name applied to the primitive tribes inhabiting the interior of Mindoro Island in the Philippines. Sparsely scattered through the forested highlands, these tribes have retained their pagan religions, and for a livelihood they depend on hunting with bow and arrow to supplement the produce of a crude shifting agriculture. Those in the north and central mountains are among the most primitive peoples in the Philippines, while those in the south raise cotton and weave the cloth for their simple garments, make pottery, and do some work in iron. One group on the central plateau has writing, inscribing on bamboo the letters of an alphabet introduced from India in the early centuries of the Christian era.

MANHATTAN, măn-hăt"n, city, Kansas, seat of Riley County, on the Kansas River near its confluence with Big Blue 50 miles west of Topeka, at an altitude of 1,010 feet. It is on the Union Pacific and the Chicago, Rock Island, and Pacific railroads, and has an airport served by Continental Air Lines. A trading center and distribution point for a farming and cattle region, its industries include poultry packing, bottling, and paint manufacture. Kansas State College opened here in 1863. The city, which was founded in 1854 as Boston, renamed Manhattan in 1855, and incorporated in 1857, has a city manager form of government. Pop. (1960) 22,993.

MANHATTAN, borough, New York, one of the five boroughs comprising New York City, occupies the island of Manhattan, and includes also the islands of Welfare, Randall's, and Ward's in the East River and the small section of Marble Hill on the mainland across Spuyten Duyvil Creek. New York County is coextensive with the borough, as was the city of New York until 1874 when parts of Westchester County was joined to it. Manhattan was first incorporated as a borough in 1898.

In addition to its railroad and subway connections, Manhattan as of 1958 was linked with the other boroughs and New Jersey by 7 vehicular bridges, 4 underwater tunnels, and 5 ferry routes. Its waterfront along the North and East rivers, containing 39 piers which receive ocean-going vessels, is among the most active in the world. Its famous skyscrapers include the Empire State Building (1,248 feet) and the Chrysler Building (1,046 feet), as well as such feats of architecture as the group of 16 buildings (as of 1959) at Rockefeller Center, the home of the United Nations, and the Coliseum exposition center. Manhattan's reputation as the cultural center of the nation is embodied in the Metropolitan Opera House, Carnegie Hall, the American Museum of

Natural History, the Metropolitan Museum of Art, the Museum of Modern Art, the City Center of Music and Drama, and the projected Lincoln Center for the Performing Arts. Educational facilities include New York University, Columbia University, Hunter College, City College of the City of New York, Cooper Union for the Advancement of Science and Art, the Juillard School of Music, and several theological seminaries and medical schools. The New York Public Library has one of the largest research libraries in the United States. In 1960 there were 32 theaters in the Broadway area as well as a number of smaller off-Broadway playhouses.

The financial and commercial heart of New York is found in lower Manhattan, where the Wall Street district houses the New York Stock Exchange and the main offices of many of the country's greatest banks. In midtown, between Sixth and Tenth avenues, is the nation's greatest garment industry, while the name Madison Avenue has become synonymous with advertising and public relations, as has Fifth Avenue with fashion. Manhattan is the leading publishing center of the country, and four major radio networks and three television networks have their headquarters here. The hotels, restaurants, theaters, and night clubs serve a vast tourist trade. Pop. (1950) 1,960,101; (1960) 1,698,281. See also NEW YORK.

MANHATTAN, island, New York, at the southeastern corner of the state, approximately 12½ miles long by 2½ miles wide, with a total area of 22 square miles. It is bounded on the south by New York Bay, on the west by the Hudson River, on the north and northeast by Spuyten Duyvil Creek and Harlem River, and on the east by the East River. The island was discovered in 1524 by Giovanni da Verrazano, a Florentine navigator, and was visited by Henry Hudson in 1609. The island takes its name from the Manhattan Indians, who occupied the island until 1626, when they sold it to the Dutch West India Company. Fort Amsterdam, which was built by the company at the southern tip of the island, developed into the village of New Amsterdam (1637); other hamlets sprang up at New Haerlem, Stuyvesant's Bouwery, and Sapohannican. When the English took over the island in 1664 they renamed the village New York. See also NEW YORK—9. *History.*

MANHATTAN BEACH, city, California, in Los Angeles County 13 miles southwest of downtown Los Angeles, on a branch line of the Atchison, Topeka, and Santa Fe Railroad, at an altitude of 190 feet. Its beautiful beach on the Pacific Ocean makes it a popular residential and resort city. Industries consist of ceramics and fishing tackle. Incorporated in 1912, it has a city manager government. Pop. (1950) 17,330; (1960) 33,934.

MANHATTAN COLLEGE, New York, N.Y., an institution directed by the Brothers of the Christian Schools, founded in 1853 at 131st Street and Broadway, Manhattan, under the name of Academy of the Holy Infancy. It was chartered as a college in 1863, and moved to its present site in the Riverdale section of the Bronx in 1923.

The college is divided administratively into three schools: arts and sciences, engineering, and

Architectural model of Lincoln Center with its separate units for dance, music, opera, drama, and study.

Ezra Stoller

business administration. Its liberal arts program is built on the four-year historical study of western civilization as the modern equivalent of the seven liberal arts. The Engineering School offers degrees in civil, sanitary, electrical, and mechanical engineering.

The annual enrollment is about 2,700 men students. The faculty consists of religious and laymen.

MANHATTAN PROJECT, The. The genesis of the American effort in the development of the atomic bomb lay in an informal announcement made at Princeton, N.J., in January 1939 by the world famous nuclear physicist, Niels Bohr, of Copenhagen, Denmark. He told of the nuclear fission hypothesis of Lise Meitner and her nephew Otto R. Frisch, which interpreted the results of the recently completed laboratory experiments and discoveries of Otto Hahn and Fritz Strassmann in Germany as being the fission of uranium atoms when bombarded with neutrons, with the consequent release of enormous quantities of energy. This led quickly to confirmatory experiments in many laboratories, particularly in the United States, but in other nations as well.

The possibility of military applications in the explosives field, as well as of the generation of power, at once became evident to physicists throughout the world, including a number in the United States. Starting in March 1939 efforts were made by a small group of scientists, mostly at Columbia University, New York, N.Y., and many of them recent émigrés to the United States, to create governmental interest and to secure federal support. They were greatly concerned lest Germany devote a major effort to fission development and if successful secure complete mastery of the world.

Early Governmental Sponsorship of Uranium Research.—The first attempts of the Columbia group to secure support were unsuccessful, but in the fall of 1939 it was arranged that a letter from Albert Einstein be given to President Franklin D. Roosevelt. He promptly appointed an advisory committee on uranium and within a few months an initial allotment of government funds ($6,000) was made for the purchase of uranium oxide. The governmental responsibility in connection with the research was carried during the initial period by this committee, headed by Lyman J. Briggs, then head of the United States Bureau of Standards.

With the organization by President Roosevelt of the National Defense Research Committee in June 1940 under the chairmanship of Vannevar Bush, top jurisdiction in uranium research was assigned to the latter. The first research contract was let in November 1940, and by November 1941 16 projects, with an estimated total cost of about $300,000, had been approved. In December 1941, after the completion of a number of studies and an interchange of views with several British scientists who were working on the problem, Bush, with the approval of President Roosevelt, decided to enlarge and generally reorganize the program. The next months saw a considerable expansion in the overall scientific effort and a number of reorganizations of the responsible committees.

Establishment of Manhattan Engineer District.—In March 1942, in a generally optimistic report, Bush recommended to the president that the United States Army be brought into the project for the construction of full-scale plants for the production of fissionable materials. This recommendation was approved, and on June 18 this responsibility was assigned to Col. James C. Marshall, Corps of Engineers, United States Army. The Manhattan Engineer District was established on Aug. 13, 1942. From that time on the entire effort became known generally as the Manhattan Project.

On Sept. 17, 1942, Brig. Gen. Leslie R. Groves of the Corps of Engineers was placed in complete charge of all the Army's responsibilities relating to atomic bomb development. Secretary of War Henry L. Stimson appointed a Military Policy Committee, under the chairmanship of Bush, which was a great source of strength to Groves throughout the entire project, as it gave him sound, experienced scientists and military men with whom to advise and consult.

Soon after Groves' assignment, Bush and he agreed that existing laboratory research should be progressively transferred to the Manhattan Engineer District. This was done piecemeal with no interruption in the progress of the work, and it was not until May 1943 that the last research contracts were formally turned over. In July 1943, at Groves' request, James B. Conant and Richard C. Tolman became his scientific advisers. Coordination of the scientific and technical programs was maintained by constant liaison and by frequent meetings of those concerned in the particular matter involved.

By September 1942 the work was in the main being carried on by major research efforts in three government-supported laboratories at Columbia University, the University of Chicago, and the University of California. There were also a number of smaller efforts at various other academic and industrial laboratories. All of the research up to this time had been essentially basic, aimed at gaining knowledge as to the best avenues of approach to the innumerable, varied scientific problems in the relatively unknown field of atomic energy.

Development of Production Facilities.—In June 1942 Stone and Webster, Inc., was selected by the Manhattan Engineer District to handle the overall engineering and construction work. Immediately upon assuming his responsibilities Groves reviewed the project and concluded that it was too large, too complicated, and too widespread to be carried on by a single organization, no matter how able its management and its personnel or how great its experience in the engineering field. Promptly major segments of the engineering responsibilities were split off and assigned to other organizations.

Within a few months a decision was reached to develop three major processes for the production of fissionable materials, one through the transmutation of uranium into plutonium and two for separating uranium 235—one through the electromagnetic process and the other through gas diffusion.

Plutonium Process.—E. I. du Pont de Nemours and Company was selected to design, construct, and operate the plutonium production plant based on theories to be developed at the Metallurgical Laboratory at the University of Chicago under the direction of Arthur H. Compton. Because of the unknown and unpredictable but appreciable hazards involved in the completely undeveloped process, the original plan to put the plutonium plant with the rest of the plants at Oak Ridge, Tenn., was abandoned. Instead it was located on a large, well-isolated area at Hanford in southeastern Washington. A small-scale semi-works plant was built at Oak Ridge, primarily to assist in the basic research.

Electromagnetic Process.—The basic research for the electromagnetic plant was carried on in the Radiation Laboratory at the University of California, under the direction of Ernest O. Lawrence. Stone and Webster continued to be responsible for the engineering and construction of this plant as well as the general features of Oak Ridge. Tennessee Eastman, a subsidiary of Eastman Kodak Company, agreed to operate the plant, as well as to advise on its design features.

Gas-Diffusion Process.—The basic research for the gas-diffusion process of separating U-235 was carried on at a special laboratory at Columbia University under Harold C. Urey. The engineering design was carried on under the Kellex Corporation, a subsidiary of the M. W. Kellogg Company, while the construction was the responsibility of J. A. Jones, Inc. The Union Carbide and Chemicals Company agreed to operate the plant and to advise on its design.

Atomic Bomb Production.—The design of the bomb, including the basic research and the final assembly, was undertaken at a laboratory established at Los Alamos, N.Mex., near Santa Fe. This work was carried on under the auspices of the University of California, with J. Robert Oppenheimer as the director. There were many other smaller installations and laboratories operated under the general direction of the District Engineer, first Colonel Marshall and later Col. Kenneth D. Nichols.

Under Enrico Fermi's direction at the Chicago laboratory, on Dec. 2, 1942, the first self-sustaining chain reaction was initiated, using an experimental uranium and graphite atomic pile. This opened the atomic age.

Other Responsibilities of the Manhattan Project.—In 1943 it was agreed by President Roosevelt and Prime Minister Winston Churchill that the joint atomic effort would be carried on in the United States and Canada, with the major effort in the United States. A number of British scientists came to the latter country to work in certain phases of the Manhattan Project.

The Manhattan Project was also responsible for the security of the entire effort and for counterintelligence; for the gathering and appraisal of information concerning nuclear activities in enemy countries; the planning and preparation of the necessary personnel, equipment, and facilities and the preparation of the basic directives for the use of the atomic bomb; the securing of adequate supplies of uranium ore; the development of knowledge as to the location of uranium ore throughout the world; and for advice and assistance in diplomatic relations with other nations on atomic matters. (President Roosevelt kept the atomic effort secret from Secretary of State Cordell Hull. Shortly before the Crimea Conference the new secretary, Edward R. Stettinius, Jr., was acquainted with the general nature of the effort at Groves' request.) In the main, these responsibilities were not originally assigned. Some were assumed at the request of Secretary Stimson or the Chief of Staff, Gen. George C. Marshall; others were assumed as being necessary to the success of the general effort.

Dropping the First Bombs.—The work proceeded at such a pace that shortly before President Roosevelt left for Yalta it was possible to inform him that the first bombs should be ready to drop on Japan in August 1945; that the chances of the bombs being successful were at least 99 per cent; and that it was believed that two bombs would end the war.

It was deemed essential that a plutonium bomb be exploded in this country prior to its actual use in Japan. This took place on July 16, 1945, in the vicinity of Alamogordo, N.Mex. The results came up to full expectations and President Harry S. Truman was so informed at Potsdam, Germany. He then issued his ultimatum to Japan. By the date set as necessary to permit a reply (July 31) the first bomb was ready. Unfavorable weather prevented its use until Aug. 6, 1945, when it was exploded over Hiroshima, Japan. This was a previously untested U-235 bomb and not the plutonium type tested at Alamogordo. The second bomb of the latter type was exploded as soon as material could be produced, on August 9, over Nagasaki, Japan. Each of these bombs exploded with an equivalent force of some 20,000 tons of TNT. The Japanese surrendered on August 14.

Creation of Atomic Energy Commission.—With its widespread operations and with the importance which it held for the future peace of the United States and the world, it was unthinkable that the Manhattan Project should be demobilized. Most of the personnel, particularly the scientific and technical, were anxious to return to their former pursuits, but despite the pressing need for prompt action the necessary legislation was not passed until July 1946. The Atomic Energy Commission (q.v.) set up by this act was not appointed until November and did not take over its responsibilities until Jan. 1, 1947.

This interim period of over 16 months proved to be a very difficult one. The organization had to be reconstituted if it were to continue on a more permanent basis, due to the lack of legislation doubt was necessarily present as to permanency. Many of the senior personnel—scientific, technical, and management—had to be replaced. The primary effort was devoted to continuing to produce at full capacity the essential fissionable materials. This was done in order that no permanent impairment of the defensive capacities of the United States would result. Steps were also taken to bring about improvements in production methods, and great strides were made in this direction.

The Manhattan Project was concluded on Jan. 1, 1947, when its responsibilities were turned over to the new civilian Atomic Energy Commission. It had been one of the greatest combined scientific, technical, engineering, and industrial achievements in history.

LESLIE R. GROVES,
Lieutenant General, United States Army (Retired).

MANHATTAN TRANSFER, a novel by John Dos Passos, published in 1925. It is a study of the diversified life of New York City up to and during the prohibition era. Using a broken plot pattern, the author treats of the lives of many characters and their reactions to an industrial, urban environment. The characters include Ellen Thatcher, an actress who marries three times without finding happiness; two of her husbands, Jimmy Herf, an idealistic newspaperman who cannot find a satisfactory place for his ideals in society; and George Baldwin, an opportunistic lawyer; as well as the only man she loves, the alcoholic Stan Emery. The only ultimately contented individuals portrayed in the book are the nonintellectuals—small politicians, bootleggers, an occasional businessman—who mold themselves into acceptable social patterns.

Essentially a study of contemporary social history, *Manhattan Transfer,* Dos Passos' first major work, employs the camera-eye technique characteristic of his writing. The novel is like a surgical cross section in which the nerves and arteries of the subject are displayed with a modicum of protective covering. There is a wealth of naturalistic detail which gives a terrifying reality to the pains and small triumphs of the characters.

MANHATTANVILLE COLLEGE OF THE SACRED HEART, an accredited college of liberal arts for women, conducted by the Religious of the Sacred Heart, at Purchase, N.Y. The institution began its educational work in New York City as Manhattanville Academy in 1841 and changed its name to College of the Sacred Heart in 1917 when it first received a college charter, adding "Manhattanville" in 1937. In 1952 it moved to its campus of 250 acres in Westchester County.

Manhattanville offers four degrees: Bachelor of Arts, Bachelor of Music, Bachelor of Fine Arts, and Bachelor of Sacred Music. The last is conferred by the Pius X School of Liturgical Music, founded in 1918, which is affiliated with the Pontifical Institute of Sacred Music in Rome, Italy. A small number of men students are admitted to this school.

The average enrollment is 1,000 students, including resident and day.

MANHEIM, măn′hīm, borough, Pennsylvania, in Lancaster County, on the Reading Railroad 10 miles northwest of Lancaster, at an altitude of 400 feet. It produces asbestos, clothing, rubber products, and metalware, and has stone quarries in the vicinity.

First settled in 1716, the town was laid out in 1762 by Henry William Stiegel, who established here the first glass factory in America to make flint glass. (See GLASS—*Historical Background:* North America.) The town was incorporated in 1848 and is governed by a mayor and council. Pop. 4,790.

MANIC-DEPRESSIVE PSYCHOSIS. See PSYCHOSIS.

MANICALAND, mȧ-nē′kȧ-lănd, a region in southeast Africa along the border of Mozambique and Southern Rhodesia. There are rich gold deposits in the border district between Macequece in Mozambique and Umtali in Southern Rhodesia.

MANICHAEANS, măn-ĭ-kē′ănz, the followers of Mani, the Persian sage, sometimes called the last of the Gnostics, who founded in the 3d century of our era a religion which for a while seemed a serious rival to Christianity. From the 4th to the 12th centuries it spread widely, in the west as far as France and in the east to the China coast, where Marco Polo found Manichaean communities at the end of the 13th century. Nineteenth century scholars had to base their study of Manichaeism on material gleaned from Greek and Latin sources, and some few in Syriac and Arabic, usually hostile to the movement. In the 20th century there has come fresh material from these sources; in addition extraordinary finds in Central Asia, as well as a remarkable find in Egypt, have provided us with actual Manichaean documents in Pahlavi, Parthian, Sogdian, old Turkic, Chinese, and Coptic. These comprise hymnbooks, catechisms, theological tractates, homilies, epistles, liturgies, and numerous historical fragments; and though by no means all the material is as yet published, what has been published has revolutionized the study of Mani and his movement.

Mani was born of Persian parents about 216 A.D. in Babylonia and piously reared in a local baptist sect. In his 12th year he underwent a religious experience and 12 years later he experienced another, as a result of which he went forth to preach a new religion, claiming that the God who had sent prophets to various peoples had now sent him as the final prophet, indeed the Paraclete promised by Jesus. He journeyed to northwest India where Shapur I, the son of the Sassanian King Ardashir, was fighting and there preached his new religion. When Shapur was recalled to succeed Ardashir Mani also returned, met the new monarch at the capital, and on the coronation day in 243 was given recognition. This was remembered as the Manichaean Day of Pentecost. There followed missionary journeys throughout Shapur's realms and the sending of disciples as missionaries south to Egypt, east to Bactriana (Bactria), and north to the region of the little Zab. The enmity of the Mazdean priesthood was aroused, however, and when Bahram I came to the throne they succeeded in having Mani accused, imprisoned, and, about 277, put to death. Persecution thereupon drove his followers far and wide and the religion spread with extraordinary rapidity northward and eastward in Asia and southward and westward through North Africa and Europe. St. Augustine (354–430) was for nine years a Manichaean "hearer" before he became a Christian.

Mani taught a doctrine of the two "roots" and the three "moments." One root was light, a kingdom of peace and goodness, with its ruler and its spirits. The other was darkness, a kingdom of turmoil and evil, with its ruler and its spirits. The first moment was the past, when these two kingdoms existed apart. Then came an uprush when the darkness invaded the light and brought about the mixed. This is the present, and our world with all it contains belongs to the mixed, being partly good and light, partly evil and darkness. The third moment will be the future when the two kingdoms are again separate. The coming of that third moment depends on us, for when we do evil we increase the mixture, but as we eschew evil we are separating the dark and evil from the good and light, and thus are working toward the separation. Mani's community consisted of: (1) the elect, who lived ascetic lives, laboring at separation; (2) the hearers, who followed the teaching but lived less ascetically; and (3) the adherents, who were interested but undertook no obligations.

Bibliography.—Burkitt, Francis Crawford, *The Religion of the Manichees* (London 1925); Jackson, Abraham V. W., *Researches in Manichaeism* (New York 1932); Schmidt, Karl, and Polotzky, Hans Jakob, *Bin Mani-Fund in Ägypten* (Berlin 1933); Waldschmidt, Ernst, and Lentz, Wolfgang, *Manichäische Dogmatik* (Berlin 1933); Andreas, Friedrich Karl, and Henning,

Walther, *Mitteliranische Manichaeica,* parts 1–3 (Berlin 1932–34); Polotzky, Hans Jakob, *Manichäische Homilien* (Stuttgart 1934); id., *Abriss der manichäischen Systems* (Berlin 1935); Henning, Walther, *Ein manichäisches Bet- und Beichtbuch* (Berlin 1937); Allberry, Charles Robert Cecil, *A Manichaean Psalm-Book,* part 2 (Stuttgart 1938); Schmidt, Karl, and others, *Kephalaia* (Stuttgart 1940); Puech, Henri Charles, *Le manichéisme, son fondateur, sa doctrine* (Paris 1946); Widengren, Geo, *Mesopotamian Elements in Manichaeism* (Uppsala, Sweden, 1946); Boyce, Mary, *The Manichaean Hymn-Cycles in Parthian* (London 1954).

ARTHUR JEFFERY.

MANIFEST DESTINY, măn′ĭ-fĕst dĕs′-tĭ-nĭ, in United States history, a catchword implying divine sanction for the territorial expansion of the young nation. Its original journalistic use was in an anonymous article, in the July–August 1845 issue of the *United States Magazine and Democratic Review,* which proclaimed "our manifest destiny to overspread the continent allotted by Providence for the free development of our multiplying millions." The article, probably written by the editor, John L. O'Sullivan, had specific reference to the annexation of Texas effected earlier in the year. The key phrase "manifest destiny," appealing to the popular imagination, was used by advocates of other annexations, as of Mexican territory after the Mexican War (1846–1848), the Oregon country disputed with Great Britain, and the plotted seizure of Cuba from Spain in the 1850's. Though a Democratic Party tenet, Whigs and later Republicans adopted it. The Alaska Purchase of 1867 and even the extracontinental annexations at the end of the 19th century (such as Hawaii and Guam), all achieved under Republican administrations, were hailed as instances of the operation of "manifest destiny."

DRAKE DE KAY.

MANILA, mȧ-nĭl′ȧ, city, Republic of the Philippines, the chief port and the governmental center of the Philippine Islands. It is on Manila Bay at the mouth of the Pasig River, on the southwest coast of Luzon, the largest island, at an altitude of 25 feet. It lies 1,479 air miles northeast of Singapore, 693 miles southeast of Hong Kong, and 1,863 miles southwest of Tokyo.

Area and Population.—Manila proper covers only 14.78 square miles, but together with its rapidly growing suburbs it comprises a metropolitan area that extends for more than 25 miles along Manila Bay and inland for as much as 10 miles at its widest point, the Manila-Quezon City portion. This huge urban complex had a population of more than 2 million in the 1960 census, that of Manila proper being 1,138,611. In 1965, according to estimates, the city's population had grown to 1,356,000.

Government.—Although Quezon City, which adjoins Manila on the northeast, was designated the official capital in 1948, the City of Manila continued to be the seat of many departments of the national government. The city itself, which is divided into 14 districts, is governed by an elected mayor and legislative council. It was incorporated as a city in 1901.

Transportation and Communications.—Manila is connected with other world ports by both passenger and freight steamship lines, as Manila Bay has one of the best harbors of Asia. A dozen international airlines use the Manila international airport, probably the second busiest air terminal in monsoon Asia. Philippine Air Lines, Inc., discontinued its trans-Pacific routes in 1954 but maintained its service to Hong Kong.

Interisland transportation is provided by various ships and boats, most of them converted World War II naval vessels, and by Philippine Air Lines' domestic service that serves some 45 cities and towns with DC 3's and Convairs. A rural feeder service links the principal air center with some 20 lesser communities.

Intraisland traffic is principally by railroad and bus, the latter constructed of a locally built body placed on a truck chassis. The Manila Railroad extends from Manila southeast to Legaspi in Albay Province and north to San Fernando in La Union Province, a total route length of 585 miles. Within the city passenger service is principally by bus or "jeepney"—a jeep chassis with a locally constructed body that accommodates 6, 8, or 10 passengers—but is supplemented by a normal supply of taxicabs, a few *calesas* (horse-drawn carriages), and a few pedicabs.

Telephones in the city numbered 42,200 in 1957; there were 18 radio broadcasting stations and 1 television station in 1958.

Manufacturing.—The Philippines is becoming the most industrialized nation of Southeast Asia and Manila is the center of this manufacturing, although most of the recently constructed plants are located outside the corporate limits. Most industries are small; they include the manufacture of cigars and cigarettes, rubber products, paint, drugs, aluminum fabrications, rope and cordage, shoes, textiles, coconut oil, soap, and furniture, as well as various handicraft or cottage industries. There are probably a dozen truly modern industrial plants.

Description.—The architecture in the city is diverse. There are modern governmental buildings, hotels, apartment houses, and offices of reinforced concrete. A few old Spanish stone houses with barred windows, balconies overhanging the street, and tiled roofs still remain. There are many new homes of modern design, some of them surrounded with spacious grounds. Structures of nipa thatch are no longer permitted, but many people live in makeshift dwellings of scrap lumber, galvanized iron, or other salvaged materials.

The city is composed of 14 districts, 7 on either side of the river. The original Manila, a medieval walled town called the Intramuros, lies on the south (left) bank of the river. It was completely destroyed at the time of liberation from Japanese occupation (1945) and for the most part was not rebuilt, the only section of the city that in 1959 still showed the ravages of war. To the south of the Intramuros lies the Luneta, the only sizable park in Manila, and beyond the Luneta is the Ermita District with many of the principal hotels and government buildings, most of the foreign embassies and larger legations, some superior residences, and several large apartment and office buildings. Inland along the river are the Paco and Pandacan districts, the most industrialized portion of the city but with residential areas as well.

North of the river are the Santa Ana, Tondo, Binondo, Santa Cruz, Quiapo, and Sampaloc districts. Santa Ana, nearest Manila Bay, has most of the old Spanish buildings, and is largely residential and wholesale in character. Tondo is the most densely populated portion of the city. Binondo contains the principal shopping center, the Escolta, a street that parallels the river between Jones Bridge and MacArthur Bridge (formerly

Santa Cruz Bridge), and has a Chinese section. Santa Cruz also contains an important shopping street, Rizal Avenue, and most of the better motion picture theaters. In many ways the modern Rizal Avenue since World War II has displaced the Escolta as Manila's principal retail trade area. Quiapo is another very congested area and a secondary commercial district, with Quiapo Cathedral as its focal point.

Beyond Quiapo is Sampaloc, the site of the famous University of Santo Tomas, the oldest university in the Philippines and the temporary residence of several thousand civilian internees during the Japanese occupation (1942–1945).

Education and Culture.—The Republic of the Philippines is undergoing an educational revolution. School buildings and classes are overcrowded from the first grade through college level. Manila is the educational center of the country and most of the better colleges and universities are situated in the Manila area. Foremost is the University of the Philippines, the only state-supported university, which has a post-World War II campus in Quezon City, a medical campus and an extension division in the Ermita section of Manila, and an agricultural and forestry campus at Los Baños, Laguna Province. Enrollment at the University of the Philippines was 16,821 in 1956–1957.

Equally famous is the University of Santo Tomas, founded by Dominican missionaries in 1611. Before World War II its school of medicine was well known throughout the Far East. The largest universities in terms of enrollment figures are Far Eastern University (22,000 students in 1954) and the University of the East (18,500 students in 1954). The Philippine Women's University is one of the few women's universities in Asia. Philippine Normal College is the foremost teacher-training school of the country, although all universities have a college or school of education and offer a teacher-training curriculum. Other well-known schools in the Manila area include Ateneo de Manila (Jesuit), La Salle College, Mapua Institute of Technology, Adamson University, University of Manila, Araneta Institute of Agriculture, Centro Escolar University, Manila Central University, and San Juan de Letran.

The libraries and museums were destroyed at the time of the liberation and as of 1959 had been only partially replaced. The National Museum is the best known, especially for its anthropology and archaeology exhibits. The Institute of Science and Technology (formerly the Bureau of Science) has one of the better reference libraries of the Philippines. The Bureau of Mines maintains a small geological museum. The library at the University of the Philippines is noted particularly for its section of Filipiniana. A very good historical library is maintained by the United States Embassy. The Manila Observatory, founded by Jesuit Fathers in 1865, has gained worldwide recognition for its studies and observations of earthquakes and typhoons. When it was re-established after World War II it was moved to a mountain at Baguio for better observation, so that its facilities are no longer readily accessible to Manila.

Churches.—Manila's oldest churches are Catholic. The Church of San Agustin in the Intramuros is the oldest and fortunately was not severely damaged at the time of liberation. The Manila Cathedral, also in the Intramuros, was

Philip Gendreau

Manila's downtown business section seen from across the Pasig River and Jones Bridge.

completely destroyed and was not rebuilt until 1958. Other famous Catholic churches include the San Sebastian Cathedral in the San Miguel District, Quiapo Cathedral with its famous black image of Christ, and the modernistic dome-shaped cathedral on the grounds of the University of the Philippines.

There are more than 20 Protestant churches, several of them interdenominational. The Presbyterians, Methodists, Baptists, Episcopalians, Seventh-Day Adventists, Church of Christ, Scientists, and others have strong missions in the Philippines with headquarters in Manila.

Health.—Health conditions vary in different parts of the city, but in general are superior to those of other cities in the Far East. The Manila water supply is properly treated and safe. The Philippine General Hospital and the Quezon Institute (for tubercular patients) are well known. The Veterans Hospital in Quezon City is well equipped and modern in every respect. Many of the better hospitals are mission hospitals, such as St. Luke's (Protestant Episcopal), Mary Johnson (Methodist), and Manila Hospital and Sanitarium (Seventh-Day Adventist). Other good hospitals include San Juan de Dios (Catholic), Doctor's Hospital, and American Hospital.

History.—In 1571, 50 years after Ferdinand Magellan claimed the Philippines for Spain, the Spanish governor, Miguel López de Legazpe, established the seat of government in the native village of Manila. The city suffered attacks by both Dutch and British during their wars with Spain in the 18th century, and was in the hands of the British from October 1762 to February 1763. During the Spanish-American War the city surrendered to United States forces on Aug. 13, 1898, following Commodore George Dewey's defeat of the Spanish Fleet at the Battle of Manila Bay. Because of native unrest it remained under military rule until a civil government was established in 1901, and it continued to function as the official capital when commonwealth status was inaugurated in 1935. When the United States was drawn into World War II Manila was declared an open city by Gen. Douglas MacArthur and suffered little damage at the time of the Japanese invasion and capture on Jan. 2, 1942; but between October 1944 and Feb. 27, 1945, when MacArthur's forces re-entered the city, it was subject to intense offshore and aerial bombardment to force out Japanese entrenched within and behind the walls of the Intramuros. As a result probably no other city in the Pacific theater suffered such complete destruction. Reconstruction was begun almost at once, however, and except for the Intramuros the city has been largely rebuilt.

ALDEN CUTSHALL,
Professor, Department of Geography, University of Illinois.

MANILA, University of, a privately operated, coeducational university in the city of Manila, Republic of the Philippines. The forerunner of the present institution, the Instituto de Manila, was founded in 1913, offering elementary and high school courses, and in 1921 was reincorporated as a university. It is composed of a College of Liberal Arts, College of Law, College of Business Administration, College of Education and Normal College, School of Foreign Service, Department of Graduate Studies, Preparatory Department for high school and elementary students, and Department of Military Science. The buildings are located in the Sampaloc and Tondo districts of Manila, and the university also operates Dagupan Colleges at Dagupan City. Its publications include the *University of Manila Journal of East Asiatic Studies* and the *Law Gazette.* Average annual enrollment is about 8,000 students.

MANILA BAY, Republic of the Philippines, an inlet of the South China Sea on the southwest coast of Luzon. It is 35 miles wide (11 miles at the entrance), reaches 32 miles inland, and is bordered by the provinces of Bataan, Pampanga, Bulacan, Rizal, and Cavite. Most of the shoreline is level but the entrance to the bay is protected by the hills of Bataan Peninsula and the rugged promontories of Batangas and southern Cavite provinces. The fortified island of Corregidor lies at the entrance, less than two miles from the nearest point of the Bataan Peninsula. The Pampanga River (Rio Grande de la Pampanga) together with lesser streams draining into the bay, has built a large delta, much of it tidal swamp, along the shores of Pampanga and Bulacan. The shorter Pasig River connects Laguna de Bay, a freshwater lake, with Manila Bay. The city of Manila lies on the eastern shore at the mouth of the Pasig and, with its suburbs, lines the bay shore from Malabon on the north to Cavite city and naval base on the southwest, a distance of some 25 miles.

Manila Bay is the finest harbor in east Asia with good protection, huge anchorage space, and unobstructed deep water. However, the shoreline along the upper margins of the bay is shallow, largely because of silting, and the port of Manila needs constant dredging to permit large ocean vessels to tie at the piers. Because typhoon winds make the waters of the bay extremely rough on occasion large breakwaters have been constructed. It was in Manila Bay that Commodore George Dewey won a victory over the Spanish Fleet, May 1, 1898. During the liberation of the Philippines in 1944 and 1945 by Allied forces under Gen. Douglas MacArthur a large number of Japanese vessels were sunk in the bay and the Manila port area was completely demolished. The port facilities have since been rebuilt and the sunken vessels removed.

ALDEN CUTSHALL,
Professor of Geography, University of Illinois.

MANILA BAY, Battle of. See SPANISH-AMERICAN WAR—*Military and Naval Operations.*

MANILA HEMP or **ABACÁ,** ä-bä-kä′, a hard fiber derived from the leaf stalks of several species of tropical wild plantains. The chief source of the fiber is *Musa textilis.* This plant resembles the edible banana but has narrower leaves and inedible fruits. It is a treelike herb growing to a height of 20 feet with stems formed by overlapping leaf sheaths. A crown of spreading leaf blades 3 to 6 feet in length surmounts the stem. The plant is most often propagated from young sucker shoots or by divisions of the rootstock and takes 16 to 28 months to mature.

The fibers are obtained from the outer portions of the leafstalk and are removed either by hand or by machine. Each fiber strand ranges from 3 to 9 feet in length and is glossy, stiff, light in weight, cream colored, and resistant to salt water. The two chief areas of production are the southern Philippines, Malaya, and Sumatra in the East and Panama, Costa Rica, Honduras, and Guatemala in the Western Hemisphere. The chief producer of manila hemp or abacá is the Philippines, which accounts for over 95 per cent of the average annual world output of 100,000 to 125,000 metric tons.

The fiber is chiefly used in the manufacture of high grade cordage ranging in size from binder twine to marine cables. Some is used in making coarse textiles and heavy construction paper. It is the strongest of the commercial plant fibers, three times as strong as cotton, twice as strong as sisal, and a little stronger than true hemp. See also CORDAGE; FIBER, NATURAL—*Names of Fibers and Fiber Plants.*

FRANK G. LIER.

MANILIUS, mà-nĭl′ĭ-ŭs, **Gaius,** Roman statesman: fl. 1st century B.C. In his second year as tribune of the people (67–66 B.C.) he proposed that Gnaeus Pompeius Magnus (Pompey) be given command of the war with Mithradates VI Eupator and administrative power over all the provinces of Asia Minor. In this he was supported by Marcus Tullius Cicero, whose *Pro lege Manilia* was his first speech on public matters. After leaving the tribuneship Manilius was prosecuted by an enemy of Pompey on the charge of accepting a bribe, and condemned.

MANILIUS, Marcus, Roman poet: fl. late 1st century B.C. and early 1st century A.D. Nothing is known about him except that he is the author of an astrological poem entitled *Astronomicon,* of which five books have survived. Whether there were originally more books or whether the poem was left unfinished has not been definitely ascertained. The work describes the creation of the heavens, the signs of the zodiac, and their influence on the men born under them. Although technically inaccurate, the writer is eloquent and shows a mastery of hexameter verse forms. The five books have been the subject of critical editions (*M. Manilii Astronomicon*) by three well-known Latinists, Joseph Justus Scaliger (1579), Richard Bentley (1739), and Alfred Edward Housman (2d rev. ed., 1937).

MANIN, mä-nēn', **Daniele,** Italian patriot and statesman: b. Venice, Italy, May 13, 1804; d. Paris, France, Sept. 22, 1857. His father, of Jewish origin, changed the family name at the time of his conversion to Christianity from Medina to Manin, the name of the patrician who became his godfather. After receiving his doctorate in law at the University of Padua in 1825 Daniele Manin practiced in Venice, where he became known as an eminent jurist and patriot. On the election of Pope Pius IX (q.v.) in 1846 Manin joined with Niccoló Tommaseo in the so-called legal struggle to stir up dissatisfaction with Austrian rule among the Venetian people. He played a leading part in the congress of Italian scientists held in Venice in September 1847 where science was used to mask political discussion. For this he was arrested in January 1848. News of an insurrection in Vienna led to a popular uprising in Venice during which Manin was released (March 17). When the Austrian emperor offered to grant a constitution, Manin rejected this concession and organized a revolt to drive the Austrians from Venice. On March 23, after other leaders had attempted to form a provisional municipal government, Manin was acclaimed president of the republic of Venice. The dream was that Venice should join the other states of Italy in, forming a great federation. Toward this end Venice agreed to a merger with Piedmont on July 4, but when that state signed an armistice with Austria Manin set up a provisional government in Venice (Aug. 11). When Austrian forces called on Venice to submit, the people resolved (April 2, 1849) to resist under Manin's leadership. During the siege that followed they held out through bombardment, famine, and cholera, and when finally forced to capitulate on Aug. 22, remained united in their desire for independence.

Manin had accepted no salary from the state while he was in office; as he went into exile the municipality gave him 20,000 lire in recognition of his services. In Marseille his wife died of cholera. In Paris, where he settled, he supported himself by giving Italian language lessons. There he formulated the program of a united monarchical Italy headed by the house of Savoy, and his last years were devoted to winning over other Italian nationalist leaders to this program. After the liberation of Venice, 11 years after his death, his remains were brought back to Venice and interred with public ceremony in the basilica of San Marco.

Consult Pascolato, Alessandro, *Manin e Venezia nel 1848–1849* (Milan 1916); Trevelyan, George M., *Manin and the Venetian Revolution of 1848* (London 1923).

MANIOÇ. See Cassava.

MANIPLE, măn'ĭ-p'l (Lat. *manipulus,* a handful), *in ancient Rome,* one of 30 subdivisions of a legion, composed of 120 to 200 men. It had two centurions, one of whom was the commander, and its own standard or *signum.*

In ecclesiastical usage, part of the ritual vestments worn in the Roman Catholic, Armenian,

and Greek churches. See Costume, Ecclesiastical—*Christian.*

MANIPUR, mä'nĭ-pōŏr, Union territory, Republic of India, in the extreme northeast section of the country, bordered by Burma on the east and southeast and by the state of Assam on the north and west. It has an area of 8,628 square miles and a total population in 1951 of 577,635. The capital, Imphal (pop., 1951, 132,-000), lies on the main road between Assam and Burma and is the trade and commercial center of the territory.

The country consists of a high plateau, 2,600 feet above sea level, surrounded by the rugged Manipur Hills with an average elevation of 5,000 to 6,000 feet and peaks rising to 8,500 feet. These merge with the Naga Hills in the north and the Chin and Lushai hills in the south. The central valley is drained by the Manipur River, which rises in the northern hills and flows southward into Burma. In the southern valley is Loktak Lake, a large, marshy water drained by the Manipur River. The Barak River, called the Surma after it passes into Assam, rises near the headwaters of the Manipur and flows south along the western border of Manipur. The climate is warm and humid, varying from 85° F. in summer to 40° F. in winter, with an average rainfall of 65 inches.

The population is largely Mongoloid in physical type and Tibeto-Burmese in speech. The settled Manipuri (Meithei), who numbered 377,-191 in 1951, occupy the fertile valleys, while in the hills are the warlike Naga (95,528) and Kuki-Chin (80,545) tribes. Most of the Manipuri have become Hindus but the tribal peoples are pagans believing in a multiplicity of nature spirits (see Kuki-Chins). Only 5 per cent of the population is Muslim. Religious festivals are marked by community dancing, in which both men and women join; the Manipuri dance style is one of the most famous in India.

Manipur is an agricultural area, with rice grown in the plains in sufficient quantity for export. Mustard, sugarcane, and tobacco are also produced. In the hills fruit is raised and silk cultivated, and the forests are exploited for their bamboo and teak. Manipur is the home of polo, and its horses are especially prized for polo ponies.

Industry is at the cottage level. About 150,000 persons are engaged in the hand-loom weaving of cotton and silk; their fine craftsmanship and excellent designs are noted throughout India. Carpentry is a second industry.

The territory, taken over by the government of India on Oct. 15, 1949, is centrally administered by the Indian Government through a chief commissioner appointed by the president of India. It elects three members to the national parliament, and since Aug. 15, 1957, has had a territorial council of 30 elected and 2 nominated members which has autonomy over local issues.

Manipur was an independent kingdom until conquered by the Burmese in 1813. The raja appealed to the British for aid, and at the end of the first Burmese war the Burmese agreed to recognize Manipur as an independent state. In 1890 the raja was deposed by his brother; when the British chief commissioner of Assam tried to intervene and was slain a British force entered the country and set up a boy raja under a British political agent. The rajas of Manipur were assisted by political agents until the end of World War I, when a Kuki revolt led to a partition into three administration regions. During World War II, when the Japanese invaded Manipur and besieged Imphal, both Kukis and Nagas supported the British in the severe fighting. Manipur came under Indian control when it acceded to the Indian Union on Aug. 15, 1947.

MANIS, PANGOLIN, or SCALY ANT-EATER,

mā'nĭs, păng-gō'lĭn, skāl'ĭ ănt'ēt-ēr, an edentate mammal, belonging to the group Squamata, coextensive with which is the family Manidae. The body and long, thick tail are covered with horny, imbricated scales. The legs are short and very strong, and the toes are armed with powerful claws, enabling the animals to burrow rapidly. These animals can roll themselves into a ball, and are then protected by their scales, and they exhibit remarkable strength in holding their bodies in this protective attitude. The scales are regarded as formed of agglutinated hairs; in the Asiatic species true hairs grow between the scales and extend beyond them. All dwell in burrows, come abroad only at night and subsist almost altogether on ants and termites, which they capture by means of their long, ropelike, sticky tongues. They have no trace of teeth; and in general structure show a close resemblance to the American anteaters. They range in size from the African *M. Gigantea,* six feet, to two and one-half feet. They are comparatively common in some rocky districts of India and China. The latest review of the family shows that it contains seven species.

MANISTEE,

măn-ĭs-tē', city, Michigan, and Manistee County seat, altitude 581 feet, on Lake Michigan at the mouth of the Manistee River, on the Chesapeake & Ohio Railroad, and on state and federal highways; about 95 miles northwest of Grand Rapids. It has a natural harbor, which has been improved by extensive engineering works. The river flows through the city from Lake Manistee to Lake Michigan, and is navigable for vessels of moderate draft. A municipally owned and operated airport is three miles to the north, on a federal highway. The United States Coast Guard maintains a Manistee station with three power boats.

Products of the city's industries are salt, chemicals, paper, drop forgings, motorboats, furniture, clothing, highway markers, pumps, and a varied line of miscellaneous articles. Lumbering, formerly the foremost local industry, has been largely replaced by exploitation of salt and bromine deposits underlying the city. In its public and parochial schools Manistee has almost 2,000 pupils; its public library contains more than 30,000 volumes, and its parks total 50 acres. Orchard Beach State Park is two miles north of the city, on a bluff overlooking Lake Michigan. Eighteen denominations are represented in the city's churches. There is a modern hospital. Service and civic clubs, two music clubs, women's clubs and a country club contribute to the community's social and civic resources. Before the white man came, the Indians occupying the land about the site of the present city were Chippewas. White traders and missionaries of early times frequently camped hereabout. Father Jacques Marquette visited the locality. It was in 1841 that the first permanent white settlement was made. In that year one John Stronach and his son Joseph

set up a sawmill. Here they found a strategic location for the lumber industry, as the river flowed through pine forests. In Manistee Lake there was good storage space for logs, and they could easily be floated down the stream to the mills for cutting. It was in 1882 that the salt deposits were discovered. Nineteen hundred feet underground is a stratum of salt rock 32 feet thick, and brine is pumped from a still lower depth, for use in manufacturing commercial salt. Manistee County was organized in 1855, and Manistee became a city in 1869. In 1861 the population was not more than 1,000; the Civil War and a disastrous fire retarded its development, but by 1869, the year of its incorporation as a city, the population had trebled. In 1871 the city was again almost destroyed by fire. A monument at the junction of state and federal highways marks a point on the old Chippewa Indian trail. Manistee is an Indian word meaning Spirit of the Woods. Commission government has been adopted by Manistee, and there is a city manager. The commissioners, elected by districts, one from each district, choose a mayor from their own number. The water-supply system is municipally owned and operated; the water comes from wells. Pop. (1960) 8,324.

MANISTIQUE,

măn-ĭs-tēk', city, Michigan, and Schoolcraft County seat, altitude 613 feet, on the north shore at the eastern end of Lake Michigan, at the mouth of the Manistique River; on the Soo Line and the Manistique and Lake Superior railroads, and on state and national highways, 107 miles by rail southwest of Sault Sainte Marie. The Ann Arbor Railroad Company, in connection with its train service between Toledo and Manistique, operates a car ferry between Manistique and Frankfort, Michigan. U.S. Highway No. 2 crosses the Manistique River on a highway bridge that has a roadbed several feet lower than the surface of the water. Its construction and the control of the water level was considered a fine piece of engineering. The surrounding region has lumber and limestone. The city's manufactures and industries include paper, fitted lumber, wooden novelties, pulpwood, and brooms. Manistique has a public library and a hospital; parks, playgrounds, and recreational centers. The National Guard Armory is located here. The public school system includes one high school. Musical interests are conserved by a Municipal band, and a choral club, and the town has its quota of social, civic, and service organizations. Manistique was incorporated as a city in 1901. The name is of Indian origin, meaning Great Sandy Beach. Administration of local government is under the supervision of a city manager. The water supply system is under municipal ownership; the water is taken from Indian River. Manistique is a summer resort and a fishing center. As an added attraction to tourists the enormous spring, called by the Indians Kitch-iti-ki-pi (big spring) is located four miles west of the city. Pop. (1960) 4,875.

MANITOBA,

măn-ĭ-tō'bȧ, one of the three prairie provinces of Canada, is situated in the geographical center of Canada and of North America as well since a line drawn from Alaska to Florida will intersect a line from Labrador to southern California in this area. Formerly known as Red River Settlement (q.v.) or Fort Garry, the name Manitoba (Indian, *Manitou, Great*

Spirit) was adopted upon the enactment by the federal parliament of the Manitoba Act (1870) by which the province was created and provision made for its admission to the new Dominion of Canada of which it became the fifth province July 15, 1870. In its early days the area of the province was so small that it was called the "postage stamp" province. Subsequent enlargements in 1881 and 1912 have brought it to its present size of 251,000 square miles (650,091 sq km). Of this area, 39,225 square miles (101,593 sq km) are fresh water including three large lakes, Winnipeg (larger than Lake Ontario), Manitoba, Winnipegosis, and innumerable smaller ones.

Coat of arms

The province is bounded on the south by the states of Minnesota and North Dakota, on the west by the Province of Saskatchewan, on the north by the Northwest Territories, and on the east by the Province of Ontario and Hudson Bay. It extends from latitude 49° to 60° N., and from longitude 95° to 102° W., and is approximately 275 to 500 miles wide.

The shield bearing the coat of arms of Manitoba is divided laterally, the upper third being a white ground bisected by a red cross, the lower two thirds a pictured representation of a bison standing on rocky ground on a field of green. The floral emblem is the crocus, adopted 1906.

For the convenience of the reader this article is divided into the following sections:

Physical Features	National and Provincial
Climate	Parks
Population	Health and Welfare
Natural Resources	Education
Water Power	Government and Courts
Agriculture	History and Political Devel-
Industry	opment
Finance	Bibliography
Transportation and Commu-	
nication	

Physical Features.—Topographically the province is interesting and unusual. It consists of five approximately parallel areas running from northwest to southeast. In the center is the fertile valley of the Red River and the large lakes, about 100 miles wide by 350 miles long. To the east is a country of granite rock, lakes, rivers, and forests, the western edge of the Pre-Cambrian shield of Canada. Further east and north is a flat, barren land bordering on Hudson Bay. To the west of the central section lies hilly agricultural country rising to about 400 feet above the valley, which is approximately 760 feet above sea level, and, in its north-

ern part, to the Duck and Riding Mountains with a maximum height of 2,800 feet. To the west of this strip, forming the southwestern portion of the province, lies the true prairie country, the area which made *Manitoba No. 1 Hard* the standard of high quality grain. From the southeast to the northwest runs a line dividing the grove and prairie areas from the heavy forests. Thus it will be seen that, though always described as the most easterly of the three Prairie provinces, much of it is not prairie country, all the more so since 40 per cent of its area is heavily forested. Five rivers of importance traverse the province— the Red River of the North, the Saskatchewan, the Nelson, the Winnipeg, and the Assiniboine.

Climate.—The climate of Manitoba is dry, clear, and invigorating with long winters, brief springs, hot summers and a clear bracing autumn. An outstanding characteristic is the amount of sunshine which at Winnipeg in 1953 totaled 2,091 hours, and for which the normal, over a period of years, is 2,113 hours. The coldest months are January and February; the hottest, July and August. Over a period of 75 years for which accurate records have been kept the average mean temperature was 35.2°F. The coldest day on record (Dec. 24, 1879) showed —53°F.; the hottest (Aug. 7, 1949), 104.2°F. Normal winter temperatures run from —10° to —20°F. Normal summer temperatures are between 70° and 80°F. but at times they rise above 90°F. and on rare occasions to over 100°F. Normal precipitation is about 20.5 inches of which 20-25 per cent is snow. June, July, and August are the months of heaviest rainfall. The fact that the periods of longest sunshine and heaviest rainfall coincide is responsible for the remarkably rapid growth of vegetation and the production of high quality grain and vegetables. The considerable depth of frost is another factor in providing bountiful moisture during the short growing season. The longest period of continuous frost free days varies from 100 to 109 days in the agricultural area.

Average mean monthly temperature over a long period of years: January 2.3°F.; February 1.8°F.; March 16.2°F.; April 37.6°F.; May 51.9°F.; June 61.9°F.; July 67°F.; August 64.3°F.; September 54.3°F.; October 41.5F°.; November 22.1°F.; December 6.6°F.

Precipitation for 1953 was 28.28 inches. Relative humidity ranged from 0 per cent to 100 per cent.

Population.—In 1870 a census was taken by the first lieutenant governor, and it showed the population at that time to be 1,563 persons. The Dominion census taken a year later listed 25,228 persons. The 1966 census showed a population of 963,006, a gain of 41,320, or 4.5 percent, in ten years.

The periods of large growth are revealed by the ten-year census figures: 1871, 25,228; 1881, 62,260; 1891, 152,506; 1901, 255,211; 1911, 461,-394; 1921, 610,118; 1931, 700,139; 1941, 729,744; 1951, 776,541; 1961, 921,686; 1966, 963,006.

Of the many ethnic groups, the largest is that tracing its origin to the British Isles, numbering in 1961 396,445, or 43.0 percent of the population. Next in size were those of Ukrainian origin, numbering 105,372, or 11.4 percent of the population, followed by those listing their origin as German (91,846), French (83,936), Dutch (47,780), Polish (44,371), Scandinavian (37,746), and Indian and Eskimo (29,427).

The capital is Winnipeg (pop. 1966, city proper, 257,005; metropolitan area, 508,759). Over half the province's population lives in the Winnipeg metropolitan area. Other cities are St. Boniface (43,214), St. James (35,685), Brandon (29,981), St. Vital (29,528), East Kildonan (28,796), West Kildonan (22,240), and Transcona (19,761). Of the total population, 317,018, or 32.9 percent, were classified as rural.

Natural Resources.—Manitoba's natural resources, other than agriculture and water power are in her mines, forests, and lakes.

Minerals.—The principal minerals produced, all found in the Pre-Cambrian shield, which covers 57 per cent of the area of the province, are copper, gold, zinc, and silver. Selenium, tellurium and cadmium are recovered as byproducts. Of the mines the most important is that of the Hudson Bay Mining and Smelting Co., at Flin Flon, 400 miles northwest of Winnipeg. In the same area there are three other producing mines. Structural minerals are also available in abundant quantities, the chief one being Tyndall stone found about 20 miles northeast of Winnipeg and much used for public buildings. Oil has recently been discovered in the southwest corner of the province. Development is continuing but production in 1967 totaled 5.6 million barrels, valued at $14 million. The total value of all minerals produced in 1967 was estimated at $186.6 million.

Forests.—Over 40 per cent of Manitoba's land is forested. This includes 30,496 square miles of productive forest, and 62,513 square miles of unproductive forest. Species include white and black spruce, jack-pine, aspen and balsam poplar, tamarack, white birch, balsam fir, and cedar. In

1967, products included lumber (41 million board feet), pulpwood (263,000 cords), and fuel wood (10,000 cords), as well as railway ties, telephone and hydroelectric poles, and fence posts. One large pulp and paper mill has been in operation for over 30 years. The total value of forest products in 1967 was $25 million. The Department of Mines and Resources is making vigorous efforts to protect and develop the forest wealth of the province.

Fisheries.—The fishing industry, important since the early days, has been developed chiefly by people of Icelandic descent. Lake Winnipeg, and other lakes in the central part of the province, are the chief sources but in the colder northern lakes an unlimited supply is being made available by air transport. The most important varieties of fish found in all these waters are pickerel and white fish, and 90 per cent of the production is sent to eastern cities in the United States. To keep the lakes well stocked the government operates five fish hatcheries. In addition to the commercial fishing, these lakes attract large numbers of tourists and sportsmen.

Commercial fishing is carried on in about 300 rivers and lakes in the province. In 1967 production totaled 29.9 million lb, with a market value of $7.5 million.

Water Power.—Hydroelectric installations are the main power sources for Manitoba's industries. Manitoba Hydro, provincially owned, is the chief generating and distributing agency in the province and supplies most of its power. It does not distribute power within the city of Winnipeg. Manitoba Hydro was established in 1961, succeeding two former provincial government utilities.

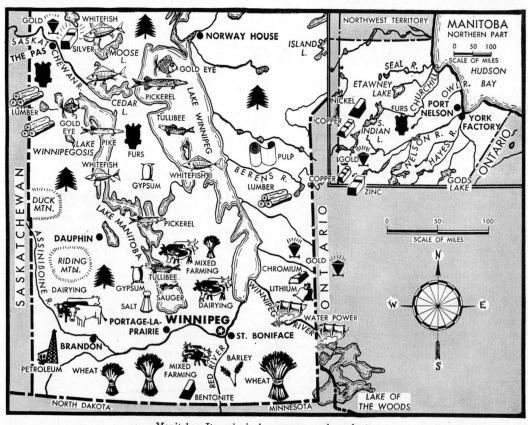

Manitoba: Its principal resources and products.

CITIES and TOWNS

Place	Pop.
Alexander (B5)	297
Allegra (F4)	66
Alonsa (C4)	169
Altamont (D5)	143
Altona (E5)	2,129
Amaranth (D4)	333
Amery (J2)	25
Angusville (A4)	208
Anola (F5)	107
Arbakka (F5)	
Arborg (E4)	891
Arden (C4)	151
Argyle (E4)	61
Arnaud (E5)	87
Arnes (E4)	10
Arrow River (B4)	150
Ashern (D3)	479
Ashville (B3)	20
Aubigny (E5)	121
Austin (D5)	404
Baden (A2)	89
Badger (G5)	110
Bagot (D5)	56
Baldur (E5)	401
Balmoral (E4)	118
Balsam Bay (F4)	100
Bannerman (C5)	118
Barrows (A2)	130
Basswood (B4)	117
Bayton (D3)	
Beaconia (F4)	62
Beauséjour (F4)	2,214
Beaver (E4)	
Bélair (F4)	
Belleview (B5)	
Bellsite (A2)	73
Belmont (C5)	341
Benito (A3)	490
Berens River (F2)	212
Beresford (B5)	55
Beresford Lake (G4)	
Berlo (E4)	
Bethany (C4)	57
Bethel (C4)	
Beulah (A4)	74
Bield (A3)	
Binscarth (A4)	490
Birch Bay (D3)	
Birch River (A2)	775
Birchview (B3)	
Bird River (G4)	
Birds Hill (F5)	220
Birdtail (B4)	
Birnie (C4)	63
Birtle (B4)	860
Bissett (G4)	584
Bluewing (A3)	
Bluff Creek (D4)	
Blumenfeld (E5)	135
Blumenort (E5)	140
Blumenort (E5)	278
Boggy Creek (A3)	350
Boissevain (C5)	1,473
Bonnie Doon (D4)	
Bowsman (A2)	558
Bradwardine (B5)	85
Brandon (C5)	29,981
Brightstone (F4)	
Broad Valley E3)	57
Brochet (H2)	612
Brokenhead (F4)	
Brookdale (C4)	104
Brooklands (E5)	4,181
Broomhill (B5)	30
Brunkild (E5)	113
Bruxelles (C5)	74
Buchan (F4)	
Bunclody (B5)	12
Butler (A5)	32
Caliento (F5)	
Camper (D3)	30
Camperville (B2)	761
Camp Morton (F4)	350
Carberry (C5)	1,265
Cardale (B4)	89
Cardinal (D5)	40
Carey (E5)	47
Carlowrie (E5)	50
Carman (D5)	1,922
Carnegie (B5)	
Carroll (B5)	88
Cartwright (C5)	409
Castle Point (C5)	16
Cayer (D3)	
Channing (H3)	509
Chater (C5)	44
Chatfield (E4)	93
Chisel Lake (H3)	
Chortitz (F5)	47
Churchill (K2)	1,689
Clandeboye (E5)	125
Clanwilliam (C4)	155
Clarkleigh (D4)	
Clearwater (D5)	104
Clematis (E4)	
Cloverleaf (F5)	
Cooks Creek (F4)	
Cordova (C4)	
Cormorant (H3)	342
Coulter (B5)	48
Cowan (B2)	120
Cracknell (A4)	10
Cranberry Portage (H3)	618
Crandall (B5)	117
Crane River (C3)	141
Crocus (B5)	
Croll (B5)	
Cromer (A5)	88
Cross Lake (J3)	168
Crystal City (C5)	600
Culross (E5)	
Cypress River (D5)	262
Dallas (E3)	480
Dand (B5)	20
Darlingford (D5)	206
Dauphin (B3)	8,655
Davis Point (D3)	
Decimal (G5)	
Decker (B4)	48
Deepdale (A3)	77
Deer Horn (E4)	
Deerwood (D5)	
Deleau (B5)	188
Deloraine (B5)	910
Delta (D4)	78
Desford (C5)	
Domain (E5)	55
Dominion City (E5)	467
Douglas (C5)	251
Drifting River (B3)	
Dropmore (A3)	47
Dry River (C5)	
Duck Bay (B2)	847
Dufresne (F5)	
Dufrost (E5)	114
Dunnottar (E4)	206
Dunrea (C5)	177
Durban (A3)	97
East Bay (D5)	
East Braintree (G5)	
East Kildonan (E5)	28,796
East Selkirk (F4)	444
Ebor (A5)	25
Eddystone (C3)	
Eden (C4)	140
Edrans (C4)	67
Edwin (D5)	
Ekhart (E4)	
Elgin (B5)	301
Elie (E5)	364
Elkhorn (A5)	575
Elk Ranch (C4)	
Elm Creek (E5)	399
Elphinstone (B4)	357
Elva (A5)	41
Emerson (E5)	834
Endcliffe (A4)	
Erickson (C4)	547
Eriksdale (D4)	303
Erinview (E4)	
Ethelbert (B3)	512
Ewart (A5)	
Fairfax (B5)	63
Fairford (D3)	56
Falcon Lake (G5)	179
Fallison (D3)	
Fannystelle (E5)	132
Faulkner (D3)	
Findlay (B5)	25
Firdale (C5)	
Fisher Bay (E3)	62
Fisher Branch (E3)	444
Fisherton (E3)	
Fishing River (C3)	
Flin Flon (H3)	9,674
Fork River (B3)	165
Forrest Station (C5)	63
Fort Alexander (F4)	
Fort Garry (E5)	‡21,177
Fortier (C5)	
Fort Whyte (E5)	800
Foxwarren (A4)	239
Franklin (C4)	62
Fraserwood (E4)	104
Gardenton (F5)	108
Garland (B3)	124
Garson (F4)	347
Geyser (E4)	
Gilbert Plains (B3)	942
Gillam (K2)	356
Gimli (F4)	2,262
Giroux (F5)	77
Gladstone (D4)	935
Glenboro (C5)	776
Glencairn (C4)	
Glenella (C4)	201
Glen Elmo (B4)	
Glenhope (C4)	
Glenlea (E5)	22
Glenora (C5)	64
Glen Souris (C5)	
Gods Lake (K3)	83
Golden Stream (D4)	
Goodlands (B5)	115
Grahamdale (D3)	51
Grande Clairière (B5)	
Grand Marais (F4)	334
Grand Rapids (C1)	454
Grandview (B3)	998
Grass River (D4)	
Graysville (D5)	115
Great Falls (F4)	255
Green Ridge (F5)	
Greenwald (F4)	
Greenway (C5)	133
Gregg (C5)	36
Gretna (E5)	561
Grifton (E3)	
Griswold (B5)	112
Grosse Isle (E4)	63
Grunthal (F5)	431
Gunton (E4)	63
Guynemer (C3)	
Gypsumville (D3)	173
Hadashville (G5)	60
Halbstadt (E5)	81
Halicz (B3)	
Hallboro (C4)	86
Hamiota (B4)	828
Hamrlik (E4)	
Harcus (D4)	20
Harding (B5)	52
Hargrave (A5)	75
Harlington (A2)	
Harmsworth (B5)	
Harperville (A4)	
Harrowby (A4)	70
Harte (C4)	
Hartney (B5)	621
Harwill (E3)	
Hayfield (B5)	87
Hayland (D3)	
Haywood (D5)	163
Hazelridge (F5)	52
Heaslip Sta. (C5)	
Helston (C4)	
Herb Lake (H3)	11
Herchmer (K2)	
High Bluff (D4)	142
Hilbre (D3)	55
Hillside Beach (F4)	
Hilltop (C4)	
Hilton (C5)	
Hnausa (E4)	71
Hochfeld (E5)	130
Hodgson (E3)	191
Holland (D5)	418
Holmfield (C5)	73
Homebrook (C3)	
Homewood (E5)	63
Horndean (E5)	139
Horod (B4)	
Horton (B5)	12
Husavick (F4)	
Ideal (E4)	
Ile des Chênes (F5)	239
Ilford (J2)	184
Indian Bay (G5)	
Indian Springs (D5)	
Ingelow (C4)	
Inglis (A4)	265
Inwood (E4)	186
Isabella (A4)	31
Janow (G5)	172
Jaroslaw (F4)	
Julius (F5)	54
Justice (C4)	45
Kaleida (D5)	
Kane (E5)	
Katrime (D4)	
Kelloe (B4)	86
Kelwood (C4)	296
Kemnay (B5)	68
Kenton (B5)	223
Kenville (A3)	115
Kergwenan (C4)	
Keyes (C4)	64
Killarney (C5)	1,836
Kinosota (D4)	
Kirkella (A4)	65
Kississing (H3)	108
Kleefeld (F5)	79
Komarno (E4)	55
Koostatak (E3)	
Kulish (B3)	
La Broquerie (F5)	305
Lac du Bonnet (G4)	886
Ladywood (E4)	25
Lake Francis (E4)	
Lakeland (D3)	
Landseer (C5)	8
Langruth (D4)	303
La Rivière (D5)	217
La Rochelle (F5)	68
La Salle (E5)	146
Lauder (B5)	56
Laurier (C4)	247
Lavenham (D5)	71
Lavinia (B4)	
Layland (D5)	
Learys (D5)	
Ledwyn (E4)	
Lena (C4)	25
Lennard (A3)	
Lenore (B5)	75
Lenswood (B2)	300
Letellier (E5)	257
Lettonia (G4)	
Lewis (F5)	
Libau (F4)	91
Lillesve (E4)	
Lily Bay (D4)	
Little Bullhead (F3)	
Lockport (E4)	293
Lonely Lake (D3)	
Long Lake (G4)	
Lorette (F5)	510
Lowe Farm (E5)	342
Lundar (D4)	649
Lydiatt (F5)	50
Lyleton (A5)	87
Lynn Lake (H2)	2,174
Macdonald (E5)	97
MacGregor (D5)	724
Macross (D5)	
Mafeking (B2)	360
Magnet (C3)	50
Makaroff (A3)	63
Makinak (C4)	66
Malonton (E4)	55
Manigotagan (F3)	186
Manitou (D5)	888
Manson (A4)	60
Marchand (F5)	114
Marco (B4)	
Margaret (C5)	64
Mariapolis (C5)	191
Marius (D4)	800
Markland (E4)	
Marquette (E4)	61
Mather (C5)	95
Matheson Island (E3)	122
Matlock (F4)	500
Mayfeld (C4)	
McAuley (A4)	181
McConnell (B4)	65
McCreary (C4)	578
McTavish (E5)	139
Meadowlands (C3)	
Meadow Portage (C3)	61
Meadows (E4)	65
Mears (B4)	
Medika (G5)	450
Medora (B5)	90
Mekiwin (C4)	
Melbourne (C5)	78
Meleb (E4)	97
Melita (A5)	1,101
Melrose (F4)	300
Menisino (F5)	
Mentmore (C4)	20
Menzie (B4)	
Merridale (A3)	
Methley (C3)	
Methven (C5)	50
Miami (D5)	372
Middlebro (G5)	151
Million (C3)	
Milner Ridge (F4)	63
Miniota (B4)	246
Minitonas (B2)	621
Mink Creek (B3)	
Minnedosa (B4)	2,305
Minnewakan (D4)	
Minto (B5)	135
Moline (B4)	
Molson (F4)	50
Monominto (F5)	
Moore Dale (C3)	
Moorepark (C4)	166
Moose Bay (C3)	
Moosehorn (D3)	250
Moose Lake (H3)	429
Morden (E5)	3,097
Morris (E5)	1,339
Mountain Road (C4)	
Mountainside (B5)	
Mowbray (D5)	75
Muir (D4)	
Mulvihill (D4)	169
Myrtle (E5)	110
Napinka (B5)	191
Narcisse (E4)	
National Mills (A2)	
Neelin (C5)	55
Neepawa (C4)	3,229
Nesbitt (C5)	77
Netley (E4)	
Neveton (E4)	
Newdale (B4)	277
Newton Siding (D5)	
Ninette (C5)	560
Ninga (C5)	108
Niverville (F5)	684
Norgate (C4)	
Norway House (J3)	676
Notre Dame de Lourdes (D5)	583
Novra (A2)	
Oakbank (C5)	292
Oak Brae (C3)	
Oakburn (A4)	347
Oak Lake (B5)	389
Oakland (D4)	10
Oakner (B4)	120
Oak Point (D4)	265
Oak River (B4)	247
Oakview (D3)	
Oakville (D5)	366
Oatfield (C5)	
Oberon (C4)	10
Ochre River (C3)	308
Ogilvie (D4)	20
Olha (B4)	
Onanole (C4)	426
Osborne (C4)	
Ostenfeld (F5)	

†Population of metropolitan area. ‡Population of municipality.

All figures available from 1966 final census are supplemented by local official estimates.

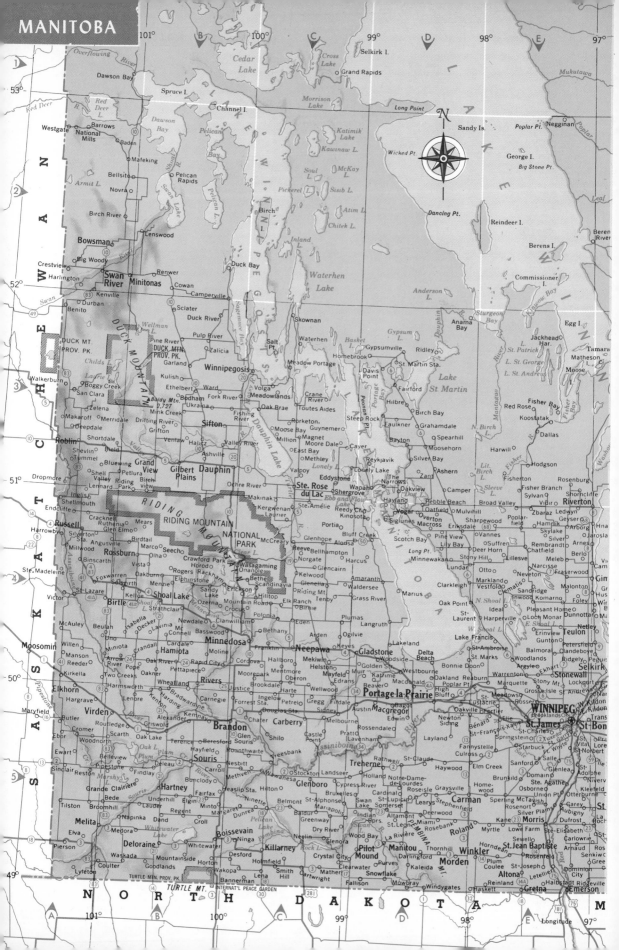

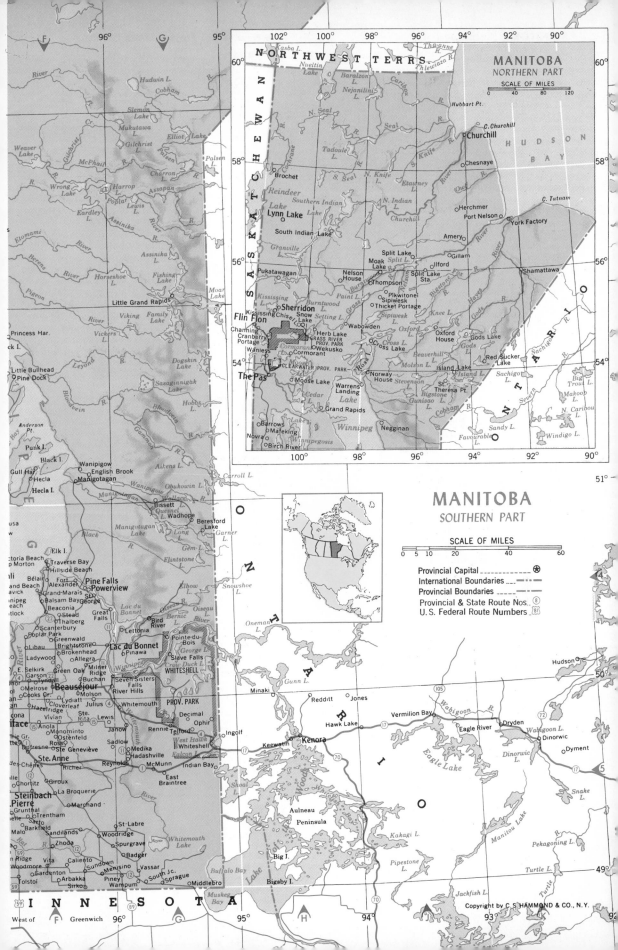

Osterwick (D5) ... 166
Otterburne (E5) ... 253
Otto (E4) ...
Overton (D4) ...
Ozerna (B4) ...
Pebble Beach (D3) ...
Peguis (F4) ...
Pelican Rapids (B2) ... 199
Petersfield (E4) ... 171
Petlura (B3) ...
Petrel (C5) ...
Pettapiece (B4) ... 30
Pierson (A5) ... 221
Pikwitonei (J3) ... 230
Pilot Mound (D5) ... 767
Pinawa (G4) ... 1,339
Pine Dock (F3) ... 112
Pine Falls (F4) ... 1,233
Pine River (B3) ... 403
Pine View (D4) ...
Piney (F5) ... 154
Pipestone (B5) ... 225
Pleasant Home (E4) ...
Plumas (D4) ... 356
Plum Coulee (E5) ... 531
Point du Bois (G4) ... 323
Polonia (C4) ...
Pope (B4) ... 50
Poplarfield (E4) ... 114
Poplar Park (F4) ... 300
Poplar Point (D4) ... 270
Portage la Prairie (D4) ... 13,012
Port Nelson (K2) ...
Powerview (F4) ... 843
Prairie Grove (F5) ... 88
Pratt (D5) ...
Pulp River (B3) ...
Purves (D5) ... 66
Rackham (B4) ... 24
Rapid City (B4) ... 449
Rathwell (D5) ... 146
Reaburn (E4) ... 10
Red Rose (E3) ... 50
Reedy Creek (C4) ...
Regent (B5) ... 50
Reinland (E5) ... 188
Rembrandt (E4) ... 25
Rennie (G5) ... 121
Renwer (B2) ...
Reston (A5) ... 556
Reykjavik (D3) ...
Rice Creek (A2) ... 42
Richer (F5) ... 333
Ridgely (E4) ...
Ridgeville (E5) ... 63
Riding Mountain (C4) ... 235
Riding Park (B3) ...
Ridley (D3) ...
River Hills (G4) ... 98
Rivers (B4) ... 1,685
Riverton (E3) ... 817
Roblin (A3) ... 1,617
Roland (D5) ... 376
Rorketon (C3) ... 277
Rosa (F5) ...
Rosebank (D5) ... 44
Roseisle (D5) ... 60
Rosenburg (E3) ...
Rosenfeld (E5) ... 266
Rosengart (E5) ... 71
Rosenort (E5) ... 197
Ross (F5) ... 89
Rossburn (B4) ... 638
Rossendale (D5) ... 137
Rosser (E5) ... 55
Rounthwaite (C5) ... 7
Routledge (B5) ...
Russell (A4) ... 1,511
Ruthenia (A4) ...
Saint Adolphe (E5) ... 320
Saint Alphonse (C5) ... 40
Saint Ambroise (E4) ... 315
Saint Andrews (E4) ... 850
Saint Boniface (F5) ... 43,214
Saint Charles (E5) ... 500
Saint Claude (D5) ... 638
Sainte Agathe (E5) ... 311
Sainte Amélie (C4) ... 44
Sainte Anne (F5) ... 923
Sainte Elizabeth (E5) ... 300
Sainte Geneviève (F5) ... 84
Sainte Madeleine (A4) ...
Sainte Rita (F5) ... 58
Sainte Rose du Lac (C3) ... 792
Saint Eustache (E5) ... 388
Saint François Xavier (E5) ... 450
Saint George (F4) ... 347
Saint James (E5) ... 35,685
Saint Jean Baptiste (E5) ... 541
Saint Joseph (E5) ... 81
Saint Labre (G5) ...
Saint Laurent (D4) ... 281
Saint Lazare (A4) ... 389
Saint Leon (D5) ... 82
Saint Lupicin (D5) ... 268
Saint Malo (F5) ... 546
Saint Marks (E4) ... 80
Saint Martin Sta. (D3) ... 54
Saint Norbert (E5) ... 1,284
Saint Pierre (F5) ... 853
Saint Vital (E5) ... 29,528
San Clara (A3) ... 176
Sandilands (F5) ... 126
Sandridge (E4) ...
Sandy Hook (E4) ... 136
Sandy Lake (B4) ... 389
Sanford (E5) ... 145
Sarto (F5) ...
Scandinavia (C4) ...
Scanterbury (F4) ... 97
Scarth (B5) ... 94
Sclater (B3) ...
Scotch Bay (D4) ...
Seech (B4) ...
Selkirk (F4) ... 9,157
Senkiw (F5) ... 150
Seven Sisters Falls (G4) ... 174
Sewell (E5) ... 50
Shamattawa (K2) ... 295
Sharpewood (E4) ...
Shellmouth (A4) ... 89
Shell Valley (A3) ...
Shergrove (C3) ... 150
Sherridon (H3) ... 117
Shevlin (A3) ...
Shoal Lake (B4) ... 836
Shorncliffe (E3) ... 173
Shortdale (A3) ...
Sidney (C5) ... 180
Sifton (B3) ... 245
Siglunes (D4) ...
Silver (E4) ...
Silver Bay (D3) ...
Silver Plains (E5) ...
Silverton Sta. (A4) ... 6
Sinclair (A5) ... 66
Sipiwesk (J3) ... 5
Sirko (F5) ... 5
Skownan (C3) ... 61
Skylake (E4) ... 140
Smith Hill (C5) ...
Snowflake (D5) ... 57
Snow Lake (H3) ... 1,349
Solsgirth (B4) ... 53
Somerset (D5) ... 649
Souris (B5) ... 1,829
South Indian L. (H2) ... 477
South Junction (G5) ... 204
Spearhill (D3) ... 69
Sperling (E5) ... 133
Split Lake (J2) ... 500
Sprague (G5) ... 403
Springstein (E5) ... 110
Spurgrave (G5) ... 140
Starbuck (E5) ... 216
Stead (F4) ... 64
Steep Rock (D3) ... 171
Steinbach (F5) ... 4,648
Stephenfield (D5) ... 10
Stockton (C5) ... 64
Stonewall (E4) ... 1,577
Stony Hill (E4) ...
Stony Mountain (E4) ... 1,451
Strathclair (B4) ... 453
Stuartburn (F5) ... 56
Suffren (E4) ...
Sundown (F5) ... 257
Swan Lake (D5) ... 312
Swan River (A2) ... 3,470
Sylvan (E3) ... 250
Tenby (C4) ... 20
Terence (B5) ... 41
Teulon (E4) ... 817
Thalberg (F4) ...
The Narrows (D3) ...
The Pas (H3) ... 5,031
Thicket Portage (J3) ... 282
Thompson (J2) ... 8,846
Thornhill (D5) ... 51
Tilston (A5) ... 93
Tolstoi (F5) ... 67
Toutes Aides (C3) ...
Transcona (F5) ... 19,761
Traverse Bay (F4) ... 14
Treesbank (C5) ...
Treherne (D5) ... 614
Trentham (F5) ... 500
Tummel (A3) ...
Tuxedo (E5) ... 2,480
Two Creeks (B4) ... 86
Tyndall (F4) ... 392
Ukraina (B3) ...
Underhill (B5) ... 4
Union Point (E5) ... 78
Uno (B4) ...
Valley River (B3) ...
Valpoy (C3) ...
Vannes (E4) ...
Vassar (G5) ... 242
Venlaw (B3) ...
Vestfold (E4) ...
Victoria Beach (F4) ... 70
Vidir (E3) ...
Virden (A5) ... 2,933
Vista (B4) ... 72
Vita (F5) ... 336
Vivian (F5) ... 47
Vogar (D4) ... 144
Volga (C3) ...
Wabowden (J3) ... 594
Wakopa (C5) ... 62
Waldersee (D4) ...
Walkerburn (A3) ...
Wampum (G5) ... 51
Wanless (H3) ... 102
Warrens Landing (J3) ... 229
Warrenton (E4) ... 237
Wasagaming (C4) ... 124
Waskada (B5) ... 282
Waterhen (C3) ...
Wawanesa (C5) ... 512
Wekusko (H3) ... 23
Wellwood (C4) ... 69
Westbourne (D4) ... 149
Westgate (A2) ... 65
West Kildonan (E5) ... 22,240
Wheatland (B4) ... 144
Whitemouth (G5) ... 387
Whitewater (B5) ... 93
Willen (A4) ...
Windygates (D5) ...
Winkler (E5) ... 2,570
Winnipeg (cap.) (E5) ... 257,005
Winnipeg (E5) ... †508,759
Winnipeg Beach (F4) ... 753
Winnipegosis (B3) ... 908
Wood Bay (D5) ... 10
Woodlands (E4) ... 126
Woodnorth (A5) ... 55
Woodridge (G5) ... 261
Woodside (D4) ...
York Factory (K2) ... 65
Zalicia (B3) ...
Zant (D3) ...
Zbaraz (E4) ...
Zelena (A3) ...
Zhoda (F5) ...

OTHER FEATURES

Aikens (lake) ... G 3
Anderson (lake) ... D 2
Armit (lake) ... A 2
Assapan (riv.) ... G 2
Assiniboine (riv.) ... C 5
Assinika (lake) ... G 2
Baralzon (lake) ... J 1
Basket (lake) ... C 3
Beaverhill (lake) ... J 3
Berens (isl.) ... E 2
Berens (riv.) ... F 2
Bigstone (point) ... E 2
Bigstone (riv.) ... J 3
Birch (isl.) ... C 2
Black (isl.) ... F 3
Bloodvein (riv.) ... F 3
Bonnet, Lac du (lake) ... G 4
Buffalo (bay) ... G 5
Burntwood (riv.) ... J 2
Carroll (lake) ... G 3
Cedar (lake) ... B 1
Channel (isl.) ... B 2
Charron (lake) ... G 2
Childs (lake) ... A 3
Chitek (lake) ... C 2
Churchill (cape) ... K 2
Churchill (riv.) ... J 2
Clear (lake) ... C 4
Clearwater Prov. Pk. ... H 3
Cochrane (riv.) ... H 2
Commissioner (isl.) ... E 3
Cormorant (lake) ... H 3
Cross (lake) ... C 1
Cross (lake) ... J 3
Crow Duck (lake) ... G 4
Dauphin (lake) ... C 3
Dawson (bay) ... B 2
Dog (lake) ... D 3
Dogskin (lake) ... G 3
Duck (mountain) ... A 3
Duck Mountain Prov. Pk. ... B 3
Eardley (lake) ... F 2
East Shoal (lake) ... E 4
Ebb and Flow (lake) ... C 3
Egg (isl.) ... E 3
Elbow (lake) ... G 4
Elk (isl.) ... F 4
Elliot (lake) ... G 2
Etawney (lake) ... J 2
Falcon (lake) ... G 5
Family (lake) ... G 3
Fisher (bay) ... E 3
Fishing (lake) ... G 2
Flintstone (lake) ... G 4
Fox (riv.) ... K 2
Gammon (riv.) ... G 3
Garner (lake) ... G 4
Gem (lake) ... G 4
George (isl.) ... E 2
George (lake) ... G 4
Gilchrist (lake) ... G 2
Gods (lake) ... K 3
Gods (riv.) ... K 3
Granville (lake) ... H 2
Grass (riv.) ... J 3
Grass River Prov. Pk. ... H 3
Gypsum (lake) ... D 3
Harrop (lake) ... G 2
Hayes (riv.) ... K 3
Hecla (isl.) ... F 3
Horseshoe (lake) ... G 2
Hubbart (point) ... K 2
Hudson (bay) ... K 2
Hudwin (lake) ... G 1
Inland (lake) ... C 2
International Peace Garden ... B 5
Island (lake) ... K 3
Katimik (lake) ... C 2
Kawinaw (lake) ... C 2
Kinwow (bay) ... E 2
Kississing (lake) ... H 2
Knee (lake) ... J 3
Laurie (lake) ... A 3
Lewis (lake) ... G 2
Lonely (lake) ... C 3
Long (lake) ... G 4
Long (point) ... D 1
Long (point) ... D 4
Manigotagan (lake) ... G 4
Manitoba (lake) ... D 4
Mantagao (lake) ... E 3
Mantagao (riv.) ... E 3
Marshy (lake) ... B 5
McKay (lake) ... C 2
McPhail (riv.) ... F 2
Minnedosa (riv.) ... B 4
Moar (lake) ... G 2
Molson (lake) ... J 3
Moose (isl.) ... E 3
Moose (lake) ... H 3
Morrison (lake) ... C 1
Mossy (riv.) ... C 3
Mukutawa (riv.) ... E 1
Nejanilini (lake) ... J 2
Nelson (riv.) ... J 2
Northern Indian (lake) ... J 2
North Shoal (lake) ... E 4
Nueltin (lake) ... H 1
Oak (lake) ... B 5
Obukowin (lake) ... G 3
Oiseau (riv.) ... G 4
Overflowing (riv.) ... A 1
Owl (riv.) ... K 2
Oxford (lake) ... J 3
Paint (lake) ... J 2
Palsen (riv.) ... G 2
Pelican (lake) ... B 2
Pelican (lake) ... C 5
Pembina (mountain) ... D 5
Pembina (riv.) ... C 5
Peonan (point) ... D 3
Pickerel (lake) ... C 2
Pigeon (riv.) ... F 2
Pipestone (creek) ... A 5
Plum (lake) ... B 5
Poplar (point) ... E 2
Portage (bay) ... D 3
Punk (isl.) ... F 3
Quesnel (lake) ... G 4
Rat (riv.) ... F 5
Red (riv.) ... E 5
Red Deer (lake) ... A 2
Reindeer (isl.) ... E 2
Reindeer (lake) ... H 2
Riding (mountain) ... B 4
Riding Mt. Nat'l Park, 210 ... B 4
Rock (lake) ... C 5
Saint Andrew (lake) ... E 3
Saint George (lake) ... E 3
Saint Martin (lake) ... D 3
Sale, Rivière (riv.) ... E 5
Sasaginnigak (lake) ... G 3
Seal (riv.) ... J 2
Setting (lake) ... H 3
Shoal (lake) ... B 4
Shoal (lake) ... G 5
Sipiwesk (lake) ... J 3
Sisib (lake) ... C 2
Sleeve (lake) ... E 3
Slemon (lake) ... G 1
Snowshoe (lake) ... G 4
Souris (riv.) ... B 5
Southern Indian (lake) ... H 2
Split (lake) ... J 2
Spruce (isl.) ... B 1
Stevenson (lake) ... J 3
Sturgeon (bay) ... E 3
Swan (lake) ... B 2
Swan (lake) ... D 5
Tamarack (isl.) ... F 3
Tatnam (cape) ... K 2
Turtle (mt.) ... B 5
Turtle (riv.) ... C 3
Turtle Mountain Prov. Pk. ... B 5
Valley (riv.) ... B 3
Vickers (lake) ... F 3
Viking (lake) ... G 3
Wallace (lake) ... G 3
Wanipigow (riv.) ... G 3
Washow (bay) ... F 3
Waterhen (lake) ... C 2
Weaver (lake) ... F 2
Wellman (lake) ... B 3
West Hawk (lake) ... G 5
West Shoal (lake) ... E 4
Whitemouth (lake) ... G 5
Whitemouth (riv.) ... G 5
Whiteshell Provincial Pk. ... G 4
Whitewater (lake) ... B 5
Wicked (point) ... D 2
Winnipeg (lake) ... E 2
Winnipeg (riv.) ... G 4
Winnipegosis (lake) ... C 2
Woods (lake) ... H 5
Wrong (lake) ... F 2

Hydroelectric power-generating stations in Manitoba, owned and operated by Manitoba Hydro, are at Pine Falls (with a total installed capacity of 82,000 kw), Great Falls (132,000 kw), McArthur Falls (56,000 kw), Seven Sisters (150,-000 kw), Grand Rapids (339,000 kw), and Kelsey (160,000 kw). The Seven Sisters, Great Falls, Pine Falls, and McArthur Falls developments are on the Winnipeg River. The Kelsey station is on the Nelson River, and the Grand Rapids station is on the Saskatchewan River. There are, in addition, two privately owned plants on the Laurie River in northern Manitoba, three thermal generating stations capable of producing 276,000 kw, and one diesel generating station capable of generating 9,720 kw.

In the mid-1960's, power stations in Manitoba had a combined generating capacity of about 1.2 million kw. Available power still undeveloped was estimated at 6.5 million kw. Hydroelectric power served approximately 50,000 farms, or over 90 per cent of the total rural establishments in the province. In 1967, more than 4 billion kw-hr of electricity were sold, for a total revenue of $46 million. The average rate for electricity used for domestic lighting, heating, cooking, and hot water heaters is 3.3 cents for the first 60 kw-hr and 1 cent per kw-hr for the balance.

Agriculture.—Farming continues to be the basic industry of Manitoba but, whereas it was once dependent on wheat, it is now much diversified. This diversification has followed three trends: first, from wheat to other cereals; second, to dairying, poultry and livestock; and third, to sugar beets, sunflowers, corn, field peas and vegetables for canning. Practically all the farms are mechanized and there is a steady development of larger farm units. The main crops are still cereals, wheat, oats, barley, rye, and flaxseed. In 1966 production of main crops was: wheat, 85 million bushels; oats, 64 million bushels; barley, 270 million bushels; rye, 3.3 million bushels; flaxseed, 11 million bushels; potatoes, 5.8 million bushels. Agricultural production had a gross value of over $500 million, with $340 million derived from field crops, $165 million from livestock, $30 million from dairy products, and $30 million from poultry products. Figures for both gross value, and value of field crops, include only initial payments for wheat, oats and barley. With the growth of livestock production has come the development at St. Boniface of the largest stockyards in Canada, capable of handling 25,000 head at one time.

Industry.—Since 1941 Manitoba's economic position has improved greatly. A major factor has been the increase in the quantity and diversity of its manufacturing. In 1941 the gross value of its manufacturing production was $211.5 million. This increased by 1966 to $984 million, involving 1,800 establishments, 47,300 employees, and a payroll of nearly $2 billion. The leading industries are meat packing, flour milling, the processing of butter, cheese, and other foodstuffs, and the manufacture of pulp and paper products, petroleum products, garments and clothing, railroad rolling stock, and beverages. Manitoba's retail sales in 1966 were about $1.1 billion, an increase of 5.8 per cent over the previous year. About 95 per cent of the province's industrial establishments are situated in the Greater Winnipeg area.

Conditions contributing to the rapid industrial development of the province are: abundant supply of cheap electrical energy, a large and stable supply of labor with varied skills, excellent transportation facilities including railroads, highways and air services spreading in every direction, ready accessibility to most primary materials, and a consumer market spreading 1,700 miles to the Pacific. This market area includes within its boundaries a population of 5,200,000 people. Time lost as a result of strikes and lockouts in Manitoba during 1967 was only 0.5 per cent of the time so lost in all of Canada, although the population of Manitoba represents 5 per cent of Canada's total population.

Finance.—For a number of years provincial finances have been handled in a sound and prudent manner. In 1939 the provincial budget was about $17 million; by 1967–1968 it had risen to $354.5 million. This is still far below the budgets of the other Western provinces with approximately the same population.

Manitoba's tax burden on its residents is the lowest of any province in Canada. Although a 5 per cent sales tax on consumer goods and services became effective in 1967, Manitoba has no per capita tax of any kind, and its gasoline taxes are among the lowest in Canada.

Provincial gross debt as of March 31, 1966, was $393.7 million, of which $183.2 million was for self-sustaining utilities, leaving a gross non-utility debt of $210.4 million. Sinking funds and other debt-retirement funds totaled $31.8 million, leaving a net dead-weight provincial debt of $178.6 million. All dead-weight debenture debt was retired by 1963.

The rural sections of the province are served by about 175 branch banks, and Greater Winnipeg alone is served by over 100 branches, representing 8 of Canada's 10 federally chartered banks. Bank clearings in Winnipeg in 1965 were $30.6 million. Seven trust and loan companies and 12 insurance companies have their head offices in the city. The Bank of Canada operates a central agency here, and there is a regional office of the Industrial Development Bank.

Transportation and Communication.—Due to Winnipeg's geographical position it has become one of Canada's great railway centers. Two great railway systems, the Canadian Pacific and the Canadian National, have their western headquarters in Winnipeg which is also served by three smaller Canadian roads and is linked with the United States by the Great Northern, Northern Pacific, and Soo lines. The Canadian Pacific has within the city the largest individually owned railway yards in the world. The area of Winnipeg is also an important air center being at the major aerial crossroads of the continent. It is peculiarly fortunate in that its commercial airport is only four miles from the downtown business center and that it is capable of indefinite expansion.

Three major airlines operate regular services from Stevenson Field: Air Canada; Canadian Pacific Air Lines; and Northwest Airlines. All three airlines have regional operation headquarters at the airport. A number of other lines offer scheduled and charter services to outlying parts of the province. Water transport is available, not only on the inland lakes, but through the port of Churchill on Hudson Bay to all parts of the world. This route from Churchill provides the shortest distance to Europe from the middle of the continent. In winter caterpillar tractors drawing strings of sleds carry heavy loads of supplies to mining developments and isolated communities in northern parts of the province where railroad service is not available.

The Manitoba Telephone System is owned by the provincial government and operated by a commission. It covers practically every inhabited section of the province through its wire lines, and serves remote mining communities by a radio-telephone connection. Its rates compare favorably with those of any part of the continent. A tremendous program of expansion has been carried on since 1946, and automatic exchange service which has operated in the cities for many years is now being extended to smaller places in the country. The present value of its plant is estimated at more than $150 million.

The Canadian Broadcasting Corporation operates Radio Station CBW, which expanded its services to include television broadcasting in 1954. In addition, 12 privately owned radio stations are operated in the province.

Daily, weekly, and monthly publications are printed in 13 languages in addition to English. Daily papers are printed in Winnipeg, Brandon, Portage la Prairie and Flin Flon. Two of these, the Winnipeg *Free Press,* and the Winnipeg *Tribune,* are recognized throughout Canada for the excellence of their coverage.

National and Provincial Parks.—Riding Mountain National Park established in 1929 lies in southwestern Manitoba just south of the Duck Mountain Provincial Park. It has an area of 1,148 square miles. Fort Prince of Wales National Historic Park covers an area of 50 acres in the extreme north near Churchill. The fort was built in 1733 by the Hudson's Bay Company to guard its rights in pioneer days. The park was established in 1941. There are seven forest reserves, having a combined area of 4,603 square miles. The best known is Whiteshell Forest Reserve (area 1,078 square miles), which is being developed as an outstanding resort area.

Health and Welfare.—The department of health is the largest department of the provincial government. In addition to widely spread and varied health services, it operates large hospitals for mental, incurable, and tubercular patients, has a far-reaching nursing service and is rapidly developing a system of health units. The Manitoba Hospital Services Plan is compulsory for all Manitoba residents. Combined individual premiums and government subsidies provide free hospital services to all. The Manitoba Medical Service limits free medical service to members. Membership is voluntary but includes over 50 per cent of the provincial population.

Winnipeg has also a well-developed department of health giving medical, dental, and nursing services to all child-caring institutions, schools, and those citizens requiring free services. There are 15 hospitals in the city, with a combined capacity of over 4,000 beds. Additions are being made to several hospitals that will greatly increase the total capacity. Outside Greater Winnipeg many hospital units have been formed, each supported by several municipalities and having nursing stations, in addition to a central hospital.

The province maintains its own system of workmen's compensation and mothers' allowances, and cooperates with the federal government in the payment of old age pensions and pensions for the blind. It also makes grants for hospital construction and for various types of disease control, research, and study. Special assistance is provided in periods of epidemic. Federal aid to this department program constitutes a substantial proportion of total expenditure in the departmental budget.

Winnipeg operates a large department of public welfare, and is the center of a wide variety of philanthropic institutions numbering 700 in all. The outstanding feature of social welfare work in Winnipeg lies in the wide use of volunteer workers under the direction of the Central Volunteer Bureau, a citizens' agency.

Education.—Elementary and high school education is free to all and compulsory for children between the ages of 7 and 16. In large centers organization usually follows a pattern of 6 years elementary, 3 years junior high, and 3 years high school training. In small districts the first 8 years are considered as elementary and the last 4 as high school. Admission to the first year at the university is awarded on completion of a grade 12 university entrance course.

The organization and content of the school curriculum and authorization of textbooks, as well as matters of general policy, are under the control of the minister of education; matters of local administration, subject to provisions of the Public Schools Act, are controlled by local school boards. The province is divided into 48 school divisions, each with a single school board responsible for all education from kindergarten to grade 12 in its division.

Education is financed under the foundation program, with the province contribution 65 per cent of the cost out of consolidated funds. The remaining 35 per cent is raised by a property tax of 9 mills on the equalized assessment for farm and residential property and 33 mills on all other property. Local costs not covered by the foundation program are made up by a special levy on property within each school division.

In 1967 there were 250,000 students and 10,-000 teachers in Manitoba's public schools. Approximately 1,000 teachers are trained annually by the faculties of education in the University of Manitoba and Brandon University.

The province owns and operates the Manitoba Institute of Technology in Winnipeg, the Northern Manitoba Vocational School at The Pas, and the Manitoba Vocational School at Brandon. These schools offer over 15 technology courses and 40 trade courses. A technical-vocational high school is operated by the Winnipeg school division under the secondary school program. Federal aid is granted for vocational school construction.

Government and Courts.—The Legislature of Manitoba consists of 57 members. It exercises supreme control over all the affairs of the province which come within the authority of the province as defined in section 92 of the British North America Act. It is elected for a term of five years but it does not always continue for the full term, it being at the option of the government to call an election at any time.

The conduct of affairs is based on the British parliamentary system. Under this system the cabinet, or executive, is chosen by the leader of the party from among the members of the party having the largest number. All cabinet members must be members of the legislature to which body the cabinet is directly responsible. Following the election in 1966 there were four parties represented in the legislature: Progressive Conservative (31 members), Liberal (14), New Democratic (former Co-operative Commonwealth Feder-

MANITOBA

The National Film Board, Canada

The Manitoba Legislative Building at Winnipeg.

Canadian National Railways

Wheat being loaded at Churchill for transshipment across Hudson Bay.

MANITOBA

Portage Avenue, the main business street of Winnipeg.

A diesel tractor near The Pas hauls a train of timber sleds.

Fields near Minnedosa dotted with shocks of wheat ready for threshing.

ation, 11); Social Credit (1). Premier Walter C. Weir headed a Progressive Conservative government. The franchise is held by all persons over 21 years of age, except the insane, criminals, Indians living on reservations, and judges. Manitoba is represented in the federal Parliament by 16 members in the House of Commons and six members in the Senate. The titular head of the government is the lieutenant governor who is the direct representative of the king and who, like the king, acts only on the advice of his ministers. He is appointed by the federal government for a term of not less than five years. Honourable Richard S. Bowles was appointed lieutenant governor in 1965.

Each department of government is directed by a minister who must be an elected member of the Legislature. The ministers, together with the premier, form the cabinet. In 1967 established departments of government were as follows: agriculture and conservation, attorney general, education, health, highways, industry and commerce, labor, mines and natural resources, urban development and municipal affairs, provincial secretary, public utilities, public works, treasury, and welfare.

Local government is highly organized, the province being divided into cities (6), towns (35), villages (37), rural municipalities (112), and some local government districts. Each has its elected council controlling local affairs with the aid and partial supervision of the province, except in the cases of the local government districts, where an appointed official carries out most of the normal duties of a council. There are no counties in the province.

The courts of Manitoba include the court of appeal, the high court of justice and the county courts. Judges of these courts are appointed and paid by the federal government. There are also police courts, juvenile courts, and a family court. Magistrates in charge of these are appointed by the provincial government. The province is divided into six judicial districts, each of which has a county court with a resident judge, the district of Winnipeg having four judges. The provincial government maintains a prison farm near Winnipeg and several jails. There are also reform schools for juveniles. The Royal Canadian Mounted Police assume the duties of provincial police.

PROVINCIAL PREMIERS SINCE CONFEDERATION

Alfred Boyd	Sept. 16, 1870
Marc Amable Girard	Dec. 14, 1871
Henry J. H. Clarke	Mar. 14, 1872
Robert A. Davis	Dec. 3, 1874
John Norquay, *Con.*	Oct. 16, 1878
David H. Harrison, *Con.*	Dec. 26, 1887
Thomas Greenway, *Lib.*	Jan. 19, 1888
Sir Hugh J. Macdonald, *Con.*	Jan. 10, 1900
Sir Rodman P. Roblin, *Con.*	Oct. 29, 1900
Tobias C. Norris, *Lib.*	May 12, 1915
John Bracken, *Lib.-Prog.*	Aug. 8, 1922
Stuart S. Garson, K.C., *Lib.-Prog.*	Jan. 14, 1943
Dufferin Roblin, *Prog. Con.*	June 30, 1958
Walter C. Weir, *Prog. Con.*	Nov. 16, 1967

History and Political Development.—Although Pierre Gaultier de Varennes, Sieur de la Vérendrye, of Quebec, was the first white man to see the site of modern Winnipeg, he was preceded by Thomas Button (q.v.), in 1612, and by Pierre Esprit Radisson and Médart Chouart, Sieur de Groseilliers (q.v.) out of whose marvelous cargo of furs came the grant from King Charles II which, in 1670, created the Hudson's

Bay Company (q.v.). Henry Kelsey was the first man to see the prairies (1691). There was no settlement until Thomas Douglas, 5th earl of Selkirk, having secured control of the company, sent out from the Scottish Highlands the first group in 1811. Those settlers suffered incredible hardships in the first years, and not until 1820 had their settlement at the junction of the Red and Assiniboine rivers a permanent basis. Thereafter it remained for 40 years an island of British folk in the great northwest, ruled by officials of the company which controlled the vast area draining into Hudson Bay. By 1860 conditions of isolation were disappearing. In another ten years Canada had bought the rights of the company for $1,500,000 and had created the Province of Manitoba which became the fifth province of the three-year-old Dominion of Canada on July 15, 1870.

Preparations for this changed status had created restlessness among the métis (French-Indian) population who were greatly in the majority, and a rebellion, led by Louis Riel (q.v.), made the early days of the new province difficult. (See RIEL'S RISINGS.) The wisdom and caution of the first lieutenant governor, Adams George Archibald (q.v.), gradually succeeded in establishing the usual institutions of representative government. Immigration came steadily from eastern Canada, followed by the first European immigrants from Europe, Mennonites from Russia in 1874, and Icelanders in 1875. In 1876 the first shipment of *Manitoba Hard* wheat was sent to eastern Canada.

Prior to 1870 there was neither steamboat nor stagecoach running regularly to Winnipeg, but with the coming of the railways the pace of development began to quicken. Winnipeg experienced a fantastic land boom which collapsed in 1882, but left more men, more money, and many substantial buildings in the city. The province, however, faced a bleak prospect. It had an area of only 14,000 square miles; its only revenue was a meager subsidy from the federal government which had kept under its control all the natural resources including the lands; the Canadian Pacific Railway had been given a railway monopoly and extensive grants of land; even larger grants had been made to the Hudson's Bay Company. At every turn the province was hampered in development, especially in settlement and in the building of local railways which made settlement possible. Under John Norquay as premier (1878–1887), and his successor, Thomas Greenway (1888–1900), a bitter struggle was waged with the federal government to secure provincial rights. A moderate extension of the province's area, and increase in the federal subsidy, which left it still inadequate, and the surrender by the Canadian Pacific of its monopoly were gradually conceded. In 1912 the area of the province was extended to its present size, but not until 1930 did the province secure control of its own resources together with a payment of $5,000,000 for those already alienated.

All through this time of struggle, the question of what schools were to be allowed kept political life at a tension. The second Riel rebellion which broke out with the return of Riel from Montana (1885), was quickly put down, but it stirred into new life the latent contest between the French-Canadian and the English-speaking populations. The Manitoba Act allowed the continuance of the church schools, the only ones then in existence. The settlement of large numbers of English-speaking Protestants from Ontario brought about a rapid decline in the numbers and importance of the French-Canadians. By 1879 their numbers in the Legislature had declined from one half to one sixth. In 1881 the Legislature ordered that the education grant, hitherto divided equally, should be distributed in proportion to the number of children of each race in each school district. In 1890 the old system was abolished. A department of education was established and given charge of all schools in which education was now to be free, all property being taxed for their support. No school which did not come under the new department was to have any grant. The validity of the law was challenged in the courts but the privy council held that the province had acted within its rights. The Manitoba School Question became a national one. In and out of Parliament this question cut across political lines. In the election of 1896 Sir Wilfrid Laurier (q.v.), himself a French-Canadian, fought for the right of Manitoba to pass her own legislation, and won. As prime minister (1896–1911) he succeeded in effecting an arrangement with the Greenway government by which bilingual instruction might be given in English and in any other language. With the coming of immigrants from many lands the bilingual privilege was grossly abused. Barely one half of the children were attending school. In 1915 a new government headed by Tobias Crawford Norris (q.v., 1915–1922), with Dr. Robert Stirton Thornton as minister of education, came into office on a policy of compulsory education, which received popular support.

Shortly after the Laurier government came to power, it embarked on an active policy of assisted immigration under the direction of Clifford Sifton (q.v.), a Manitoban, who became minister of the interior. Almost at once American farmers poured into the country followed by eastern Canadians and British, and then by large numbers from Europe. The majority of these immigrants went on farther west but thousands remained in Manitoba. Her population which had been 91,279 in 1901 increased to 461,394 in 1911 and the peak of immigration was not reached for another two years. In 1914 World War I stopped this movement. Manitoba sent large contingents to join the struggle and, in spite of a labor shortage, produced large quantities of food for the Allies. Just as her troops were returning, the most protracted general strike of labor in the history of Canada broke out in Winnipeg. For six weeks the city was without the usual services except those which could be partially continued by volunteers. In the end the strike was broken.

In 1920 the sudden fall in wheat prices brought disaster to the farmers and, in consequence, great hardship to the whole province. In their despair the western farmers turned to political organization and the progressive movement was born. It went from success to success. In Manitoba this party won the election and a farmers' government resulted under the leadership of John Bracken (q.v.). The following year the farmers of Manitoba joined those of the other prairie provinces in the decision to organize voluntary pools for the handling of wheat. Already the United Grain Growers, which had its beginning in Manitoba in 1906, had shown what could be done by voluntary association. The idea spread like wildfire and by 1924 the Manitoba

pool was in operation. In the time of high prices in the next six years the pool flourished but came to disaster when world prices again fell early in 1930. But by this time the pool was able to exercise strong pressure and the government came to its rescue. It passed successfully through the years of depression (1930–1937), repaid its loan and again became highly successful. Of the 52,000 farmers in the province somewhat more than one half were (1949) members of the pool which in the crop year of 1948–1949 handled 45 per cent of all the grain sold.

The province also suffered heavily in the depression years, but came through with its credit unimpaired—the only one of the Prairie provinces to do so. In World War II Manitoba played the same part she had in World War I in the sending of forces and food products, but her factories had by then sufficiently developed for her to share in munitions production; the basis of her present industry was laid in those years.

One of the major developments in Manitoba's history since World War II has been her cooperation with other provinces in financial arrangements with the federal government. More than a quarter of Manitoba's revenue in the 1966–1967 fiscal year was contributed by the federal government as a result of federal-provincial agreements. Total revenue from the federal government was in excess of $104 million, with $50 million derived from personal income taxes, $22 million from corporation income taxes, $3 million from succession duties, and $29 million from equalization payments. See also CANADA.

Bibliography.—Ross, Alexander, *Red River Settlement: Its Rise, Progress and Present State* (London 1856); Shortt, Adam, and Doughty, A. G., eds., *Canada and Its Provinces*, 22 vols. and Index (Toronto 1914); Buller, A. H. Reginald, *Essays on Wheat* (New York 1919); McWilliams, Margaret, *Manitoba Milestones* (Toronto 1928); Stanley, George F. G., *The Birth of Western Canada* (Toronto 1936); Morton, Arthur S., *History of Prairie Settlement* (Toronto 1936); Manitoba Historical and Scientific Society, *Transactions* (Winnipeg 1882–1949); Donnelly, Murray, *The Government of Manitoba* (Toronto 1963); Kavanaugh, Martin, *The Assiniboine Basin: A Social Study of the Discovery, Exploration, and Settlement of Manitoba* (Brandon 1966); Morton, William L., *Manitoba, a History*, 2d ed. (Toronto 1967).

MARGARET MCWILLIAMS,
Author of "Manitoba Milestones" and "This New Canada."
Revised by The Office of the Deputy Minister of Education, Manitoba, Canada.

MANITOBA, University of. Long before the formation of the Province of Manitoba in 1870, education in the Red River Settlement had been promoted by the churches. A school opened by Father Provencher in 1818 later developed into the Roman Catholic College of St. Boniface. Various schools functioned precariously under the Anglican clergy from 1820 until St. John's College was finally established in 1866 by Bishop Machray. Lord Selkirk's Scottish settlers, with the help of the Presbyterian Church, organized a school in 1847, which later, upon the arrival of Dr. George Bryce from Ontario in 1871, gave rise to Manitoba College. It was due to the vision and zeal of George Bryce and his contemporaries, and not less to the support and statesmanship of Hon. Alexander Morris, lieutenant governor from 1872 to 1877, that the University of Manitoba came into being on February 28, 1877, as an examining and degree conferring body.

The population of Manitoba in 1871 was only

25,228. New settlers from the east did not begin to arrive in any numbers until 1879. The Provincial Government, which granted the University of Manitoba charter in 1877, regarded it as premature, but yielded to the urging of its advocates who wished to secure an impartial standard in higher education and to ensure cooperation instead of sectionalism among the denominational colleges. The government of the university was vested in a council on which the original colleges were equally represented. All teaching continued to be done by the colleges according to a common curriculum, until the expense of developing scientific subjects made necessary the next major change in the university.

The first professors were appointed in 1904, five in number, to give instruction in mathematics and the natural sciences. Slowly but steadily the university expanded its teaching departments by the addition of professors of civil and electrical engineering (1907, 1909), architecture and modern languages (1913), until in 1914 for the first time it offered the full work for the bachelor's degree in arts and science. It was in 1914 that Manitoba College restricted itself to theology and its students and staff in arts transferred to the university.

Expansion inevitably brought a change in administration. The acquisition of students, staff, and building involved income and expenditure, the latter much greater than the former. The province, which since 1877 had needed to contribute little financial support, now began to be asked for increasing annual grants. An endowment of 150,000 acres of land obtained from the Dominion Government in 1898 added gradually but substantially to the university's revenue as sales were realized. The University Act of 1917 established a board of governors, appointed by the provincial government, as the plenary authority in the university. In 1934 graduates obtained the right to elect three members to this board. The university council continued to have general charge of academic work until it was replaced by the Senate set up under a new University Act of 1936. The university has had a chancellor, a vice chancellor, and a registrar since 1877.

Subsequent to the granting of the charter, other denominational colleges became affiliated with the university and now prepare candidates for the university's degrees in arts and science. The earliest of these to join was Wesley College (1888), now united with Manitoba College as United College. Later came St. Paul's College (R.C., 1931) and Brandon College (1938), which severed its connection with the Baptist Church when it sought support from public funds.

In the first half of the century, the university's rapid growth was marked by the adhesion of a number of professional schools and the establishment of others as faculties and schools of the university. These included medicine (1882), pharmacy (1902), agriculture (1907), home economics (1911), law (1914), engineering (1920), architecture (1924), education (1935), commerce (1937), interior design (1938), nursing education (1943), social work (1943), music (1944), fine and applied arts (1950). In 1949 the Committee on Graduate Studies was reconstituted as a Faculty of Graduate Studies and Research.

In 1913 the agricultural college occupied a new group of buildings five miles south of Winnipeg in the municipality of Fort Garry. To

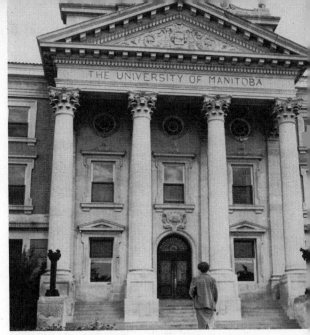

Annan Photo Features

The administration building, University of Manitoba.

this beautiful site of 1,100 acres in a bend of the Red River the university was moved gradually as other buildings were erected. In 1950 the move was complete. The law school and the faculty of medicine remained in Winnipeg. The average enrollment is over 5,900 students, and the staff numbers over 275 full time instructors.

W. M. HUGILL,
Professor of Latin and Greek.

MANITOU, măn′ĭ-tōō, a name given, among the American Indian tribes, to any spirit or supernatural being, good or evil; also applied to any object of religious awe and reverence. "The Illinois," wrote the Jesuit Father Marest, "adore a sort of genius, which they call manitou; to them it is the master of life, the spirit that rules all things. A bird, a buffalo, a bear, a feather, a skin—that is their manitou." "If the Indian word manitou," says John G. Palfrey, "appeared to denote something above or beside the common aspects and agencies of nature, it might be natural, but it would be rash and misleading to confound its import with the Christian, Mohammedan, Jewish, Egyptian, or Greek conception of Deity, or with any compound of a selection from some or all of those ideas." The word was applied to any object used as a fetish or an amulet.

MANITOULIN ISLANDS, măn-ĭ-tōō′lĭn, Canada, a group of islands in the northern part of Lake Huron, partially separating the waters of the lake from Georgian Bay and North Channel. The name is a corruption of the Indian word Manitouin, which means divinity. Except Drummond Isle, about 24 miles long and 9 miles wide, which belongs to the State of Michigan, the group is a part of the Province of Ontario. The largest island of the group is Grand Manitoulin, or Sacred Isle; about 80 miles long and 30 miles at the widest. The coast is very irregular. Cockburn, or Little Manitoulin, is nearly circular, and about eight miles in diameter. All the islands are well wooded; Grand Manitoulin and Cockburn have large pine forests. The shore waters abound in fish. About one fifth of the inhabitants are Indians of the Algonquian tribe. The cool climate in summer and the striking natural features add to the attractions of the islands and make them a favorite summer resort.

MANITOWOC, măn'ĭ-tô-wŏk, city, Wisconsin, seat of Manitowoc County and a port of entry, altitude 595 feet, is located on Lake Michigan, at the mouth of the Manitowoc River, 25 miles north of Sheboygan. It has a municipal airport. It has a good harbor, shipbuilding and repair yards, grain elevators, fisheries, and an extensive coal trade. Its manufactured products include aluminumware and castings, flour and malt products, furniture, canned vegetables, cheese, and condensed milk.

The British North West Company had a fur trading post here in 1795, and permanent settlement began with the land boom of 1835. Many Germans settled here in 1848, followed soon by Norwegians and Irish; Bohemians came in 1854, and Poles after 1865. The city was chartered in 1870. The name is an Indian word meaning "home of the Great Spirit." Pop. 32,275.

MANIWAKI, măn-ĭ-wô'kĭ, town, Canada, Quebec Province, capital of Gatineau County, is located at the confluence of the Gatineau and Desert rivers, 82 miles northwest of Ottawa, and is the terminus of a branch of the Canadian Pacific Railway. In a lumber region, it has pulp mills and sawmills. The region is also famous for winter sports, hunting, and fishing. There is a Roman Catholic college here. Maniwaki was first incorporated as a village in 1930. Pop. 6,404.

MANIZALES, măn-ĭ-zä'lĕs; -zăl'ĕs (Span. mä-nĕ-sä'läs), city, Colombia, capital of Caldas Department, is located 110 miles northwest of Bogotá, at an altitude of 7,064 feet, on a ridge of the Cordillera Central range of the Andes Mountains. An aerial tramway 45 miles long connects it with Mariquita. It is an important coffee center, and there are gold, silver, and mercury mines nearby. It has a pleasant climate, though the rainfall is heavy, and is a modern city with fine parks, schools, cathedral, library, theaters, and a stadium.

Manizales was founded in 1847 by prospectors for gold, who named it for a kind of stone they found there and called maní. It was the scene of conflict during the civil wars of the mid-19th century, was destroyed by earthquake in 1878, and by fire in 1925. Since then it has been rebuilt largely of concrete. Pop. (1964) 190,036.

MANKATO, măn-kä'tō, city, Minnesota, seat of Blue Earth County, on the Minnesota River at the mouth of the Blue Earth River, 85 miles southwest of St. Paul. It is situated in an agricultural region and in the vicinity are valuable stone quarries. Nine miles south is the Rapidan Dam, furnishing hydroelectric power for numerous southern Minnesota cities and villages. Mankato is the leading metropolis and trade center of southwestern Minnesota. Its factories produce brick, cement, clothing, leather goods, flour, foods, boxes, brooms, and numerous other items. The Mankato hog market is one of the largest in the state, and the poultry industry and the creamery

business are important factors in the city's commerce.

Mankato is the Sioux name for the blue earth found in the vicinity, specimens of which Pierre Le Sueur shipped to France in 1701 believing them to be copper bearing. The city was laid out in 1852. During its early days Indians caused much trouble. Following the uprising of 1862, over 400 Sioux Indians were tried for murdering white settlers, and 303 condemned to death were brought to Mankato and held at Camp Lincoln, now Sibley Park. President Abraham Lincoln commuted the sentences of all but 38 and these were hanged simultaneously from a single gallows on Dec. 26, 1862. Mankato was incorporated as a village in 1865, and chartered as a city in 1868. It is the seat of Mankato State College and of Bethany Lutheran College. Pop. 23,797.

MANKATO STATE COLLEGE, is a state college located in Mankato, Minnesota. Founded by legislative enactment in 1867, it offers four-year programs in liberal arts, nursing, teacher education, and preprofessional areas. An extensive graduate program is also carried out which leads to a master's degree for teaching. In addition to regular day schedules, the college carries on a varied evening and in-service program on the campus and in outlying centers.

The college, originally founded as Mankato State Normal School, became Mankato State Teachers College by legislative enactment in 1921, and Mankato State College in 1957. A second campus and a $10 million building program were under way (1961) to care for the rapidly growing enrollment and expanding college offerings. Current enrollment averages over 6,500.

MANLEY, măn'lĭ, **John,** American naval commander: b. 1734; d. Boston, Mass., Feb. 12, 1793. At the outbreak of the Revolutionary War he was given command of the armed schooner *Lee,* with which he cruised along the coast of Massachusetts Bay, making captures of great value to the American army then at Cambridge. In July 1777 his ship, the *Hancock,* was captured by a British frigate and after a rigorous confinement on a prison ship in New York harbor, he was exchanged in March 1778. In 1782 he was put in command of the *Hague* frigate, which, after lying in a perilous position off the West Indies for three days, exposed to the fire of four British ships, contrived to effect her escape, and in January 1783 captured the *Baille.* This exploit closed the regular maritime operations of the United States during the Revolutionary War.

MANLEY, Joseph Homan, American journalist and politician: b. Bangor, Me., Oct. 13, 1842; d. Augusta, Feb. 7, 1905. He was graduated in 1863 from the Albany Law School in Albany, N.Y. He was admitted to the bar in 1865. He acquired a half interest in the *Maine Farmer* in 1878, and then joined with James G. Blaine in local and national politics, dictating the editorial policy of that paper for three years. He was a delegate to the Republican National conventions of 1880, 1888, 1892, and 1900; member of the state Senate in 1903–1904; was for many years chairman of the Maine Republican State Committee; a member of the Republican National Committee, and chairman in 1896–1904; and was a notable figure in the executive committees of 1896 and 1900, which aided in the election of McKinley.

MANLEY, Mary de la Rivière, English author : b. probably on the Island of Jersey, April 7, 1663; d. London, England, July 11, 1724. She succeeded Jonathan Swift as editor of the *Examiner* in 1711. She is known for her *Secret Memoirs and Manners of Several Persons of Quality of Both Sexes: from the New Atalantis* (1709), a licentious satire reflecting on politicians of the day, that caused the arrest of both the author and the publisher though they were subsequently discharged. This work was continued in the *Memoirs of Europe* (1710).

MANLIUS, măn'lĭ-ŭs, **Marcus** (surnamed CAPITOLINUS, kăp-ĭ-tô-lī'nŭs), Roman legendary hero, of the 4th century B.C. He was called Capitolinus because of his successful defense of the Capitoline Hill. Tradition says he was aroused to action by the cackling of Juno's sacred geese just in time to prevent the surprise of the citadel by the Gauls (390 B.C.). Two years before he defeated the Aequi, and six years after (384 B.C.) he was thrown from the Tarpeian rock, having been declared guilty of plotting to become king or dictator.

MANLY, măn'lĭ, **Charles Matthews,** American inventor : b. Staunton, Va., April 24, 1876; d. Kew Gardens, N.Y., Oct. 15, 1927. After completing his education at Cornell University, where he received his mechanical engineering degree in 1898, he began work for the United States War Department as an assistant to Samuel P. Langley, who was then engaged in attempts to construct a heavier-than-air flying machine. Manly devised a 125-pound, 5-cylinder, water-cooled radial engine which was first used on an airplane in 1901. This engine was later characterized as the first modern aircraft engine. Manly took out over 50 patents on mechanical devices.

MANN, măn, SIR **Donald D.,** Canadian railroad builder : b. Acton, Ontario, March 23, 1853; d. Toronto, Nov. 11, 1934. In 1879 he began lumbering in Winnipeg and became manager for a firm of contractors who were supplying ties to the Canadian Pacific Railway; he thereafter worked continuously as a contractor until the completion of the main railway to the Pacific. In 1886, Mann formed a partnership with William Mackenzie (q.v.) and they constructed long sections of the Manitoba and Northwestern, Hudson Bay, Grand Trunk, Regina and Long Lake, and Edmonton railroads. What was later to develop into the Canadian Northern Railroad system began in 1895 when Mann and Mackenzie started securing charters for various other rail lines. By 1912 they had organized a rail system which extended from Montreal to Vancouver. The Canadian government took control over the railway in 1922 and made it part of the Canadian National Railroad Company. Mann was knighted in 1911.

MANN, män, **Heinrich,** German novelist, essayist, playwright: b. Lübeck, Germany, March 27, 1871; d. Santa Monica, Calif., March 11, 1950. The older brother of Thomas Mann (q.v.), he shared with him a deep concern for the creative artist in the modern world, but in contrast to the subtle irony of Thomas Mann, he is bitter and violent in his attacks on the upper middle class. He peoples his stories with eccentric personalities, bold adventurers, and passionate lovers, whom he often distorts to the point of grotesqueness. His style is brilliant, permeated by wit and sarcasm tinged with melancholy. He had a flair for the exotic, and in his great trilogy *Die Göttinnen* (1902–1903; Eng. tr. *The Goddess,* 1918) he was obviously under the influence of Emile Zola, Guy de Maupassant, and Gabriele d'Annunzio.

After a conventional education in his native Lübeck, he had a short apprenticeship in a publishing house, which he gave up for a literary career. His imagination was nourished by Mediterranean sensuality during a sojourn in Italy. Later, in Berlin, he experienced the impact of Prussian arrogance, and from there he moved to the more congenial Munich, where he observed the unrestrained voluptuousness of the Bohemian artistic circle. He had an opportunity to put into practice his liberal political ideas when he held an official post in the Weimar Republic. In 1933 he became a voluntary exile from Germany and in 1940 took up residence in California, where he remained until his death.

In his novel *Im Schlaraffenland* (1900; tr. into Eng. as *In the Land' of Cockaigne,* 1925), he satirizes the decadent financial and publishing circles of imperial Berlin. His best-known novel, *Professor Unrat* (1905; tr. into Eng. as *The Blue Angel,* 1932; also *Small Town Tyrant,* 1944), is a masterpiece of social satire. It depicts the pathetic entanglement of a respectable school teacher with a woman from a world without moral standards. His trilogy *Das Kaiserreich* (1917–1925; tr. into Eng. as *The Patrioteer,* 1921, *The Poor,* 1917, and *The Chief,* 1925) is a scathing satire on a conceited bourgeoisie hungry for power. His ideal of a truly enlightened democratic ruler is the hero of his historical novel *Die Jugend des Königs Henri Quatre* (1935; Eng. tr. *Young Henry of Navarre,* 1938) which together with its sequel *Die Vollendung des Königs Henri Quatré* (1938; tr. into Eng. as *Henry King of France,* 1939), was his most ambitious project.

MANN, män, **Horace,** American educator : b. Franklin, Mass., May 4, 1796; d. Yellow Springs, Ohio, Aug. 2, 1859. After his graduation from Brown University in 1819, he taught there for two years and then studied for his law degree. He was admitted to the Massachusetts bar in 1823 and thereafter had a legal practice at Dedham and Boston, Mass. From 1827 to 1833, he was a representative in the Massachusetts legislature and from 1833 to 1837 a state senator, serving from 1835 as president of the Senate. In 1837, upon the appointment by the state of a board of education to revise and reorganize the Massachusetts public school system, Mann became secretary to the board. He withdrew from politics and from a successful law practice and devoted himself entirely to the field of education. The schools throughout the state were at the time in poor condition; not only were buildings inadequate and run-down, but the quality of classroom instruction was at a low ebb. Mann launched a program of many reforms and achieved results which were to have great beneficial effect on public education in Massachusetts and throughout the rest of the country. Despite often pronounced opposition and controversy over whether taxes should be applied to help run a free school system, Mann succeeded in stimulating public interest in the problems of the schools. From this period dates the awareness of the need for training teachers, and the first system of normal schools was established for this purpose. In a series of 12 annual reports (1837–1848), Mann discussed the needs of public education and for the first time made facts and figures in the field a matter of general interest.

Mann returned to politics in 1848, being elected to Congress as an anti-slavery Whig, and he served until 1853. In 1852 he declined the nomination for the governorship of Massachusetts, at the same time accepting the presidency of the recently established Antioch College in Yellow Springs, Ohio, a position he held until a few weeks before his death. In 1900, Mann was elected to the American Hall of Fame.

MANN, James Robert, American lawyer and congressman: b. near Bloomington, Ill., Oct. 20, 1856; d. Washington, D.C., Nov. 30, 1922. He graduated from the University of Illinois in 1876 and from the Union College of Law (later Northwestern University Law School) in 1881, in the latter year being also admitted to the bar. He quickly became active in Chicago politics, holding several local public offices and becoming known for his honesty and ability. In 1896 he was elected as a Republican to the United States House of Representatives and he served continuously in that body until his death. Among important pieces of legislation associated with him are the Mann-Elkins Act of 1910 regulating railroad rates and the Mann Act (White Slave Act) which he wrote.

MANN, män, **Thomas,** German-American writer: b. Lübeck, Germany, June 6, 1875; d. Zurich, Switzerland, Aug. 12, 1955. The brother of Heinrich Mann (q.v.), he was one of the most eminent men of letters of the first half of the 20th century, winner of the Nobel prize for literature in 1929, the Goethe Prize of the city of Frankfurt-am-Main in 1939, and the recipient of numerous honorary doctorates.

With the publication of his first novel *Die Buddenbrooks* (1901; Eng. tr. 1924) his reputation was firmly established. In this massive autobiographical saga Mann uses the leitmotiv to trace the rise and decline of a prosperous family of merchants through four generations. In naturalistic style such ordinary events as festivities, meals, and daily business transactions are described in minute detail.

In *Der Zauberberg* (1924; *The Magic Mountain,* 1927), one of Mann's most significant works, the young protagonist passes through a long spiritual development guided by the exponents of three diverse cultures—northern European, Mediterranean, and Eastern. Set in a tuberculosis sanatorium in the Swiss Alps, this novel has a theme of disease and death evolved against the broad background of European culture. (See also MAGIC MOUNTAIN, THE.) The same theme of decadence is treated in solemn style and with almost Goethean perfection in the short novel *Die Betrogene* (1925; *The Betrayed*), the story of a middle-aged widow who is in love with a much younger man and who mistakes the symptoms of a fatal disease for signs of her physical rejuvenation. In other novels the heroes are victims not of physical disease but of spiritual suffering. In all Mann's writing the autobio-graphical element is discernible; the dualism of the writer's heroes is Mann's own dilemma. *Tonio Kröger* (1903; Eng. tr. 1914) is the story of a promising writer painfully aware of being an outsider, "a lost burgher," in an unresponsive world. The theme of the artist against society recurs in *Der Tod in Venedig* (1913; *Death in Venice,* 1925). In this story of an aging poet unable to master an illicit passion, death in an epidemic comes as a welcome release.

The spiritual ancestors of Mann's youth were Schopenhauer, Nietzsche, and Wagner; from them he moved gradually towards Goethe—as suggested in the preceding discussion—until his artistic work and *Weltanschauung* (world philosophy) were dominated by the impact of Goethean thought. So complete was Mann's absorption in the world of Goethe that he was able to produce an authentic image of this world in his partly documentary historical novel *Lotte in Weimar* (1939; tr. into Eng. as *The Beloved Returns,* 1940), in which the aged Goethe meets his once beloved Charlotte Buff. In *Doktor Faustus* (1947; Eng. tr. 1948), Mann turns to the 16th century Faust legend, as had Goethe, and uses it to symbolize the tragic fate of the German people in postwar Europe. This intricate story of a musical genius is saturated with erudite information, especially on musical theory.

The inspiration for another group of novels is derived from history and legend. The Joseph novels, the work of more than a decade (1933–1943), reinterpret the Old Testament story from a mythological and psychological point of view. A one-volume edition of the tetralogy was published in German in 1944 and in English in 1948 as *Joseph and His Brothers* (q.v.). *Der Erwählte* (1951; tr. into Eng. as *The Holy Sinner,* 1951) revives a 13th century verse narrative. The jesting mood and the bizarre, often archaic, language are reminiscent of James Joyce.

In his essays, Mann assumes the role of interpreter of modern European humanism, voicing succinctly his views on literature and politics. He became a respected symbol of his nation's culture in times of unrest. His political essays and speeches are collected in *Order of the Day* (1942). A representative collection of his literary essays was published in 1947—*Essays of Three Decades.*

Mann and his family left Germany in 1933. In 1938 he accepted an invitation to lecture at Princeton University, from where he moved in 1941 to southern California. He became a citizen of the United States in 1944, but returned to Europe in 1953 and took up residence in Switzerland.

BERNARD V. VALENTINI,
Department of German, New York University.

MANN, măn, **Tom,** English labor leader: b. Foleshill, Warwickshire, England, April 15, 1856; d. Grassington, Yorkshire, March 13, 1941. At the age of 11 he became a coal miner, and from 1870 to 1877 he worked as an engineering apprentice in factories in Birmingham. Going to London in 1877, he became active in programs for the betterment of working men. He joined the union movement in 1881 and became a Socialist in 1885. In 1889 he was one of the organizers and a leader of the dockworkers' strike.

MANN ACT. See MANN, JAMES ROBERT; PROSTITUTION.

MANNA, măn'å, a term used to describe (1) various plant exudates and (2) certain Biblical food plants. One of the better-known forms of manna is the exudate of the flowering or manna ash, *Fraxinus ornus,* a tree native to southern Europe and the Near East. When slits are made in the bark, a sweetish substance oozes from the wound and dries into the substance known as flake manna. One of its chemical constituents is the higher alcohol, mannitol, which is used medicinally as a mild laxative, in the treatment of certain types of high blood pressure, and as a demulcent and expectorant. Two other forms of manna are: the gummy exudate from the leaves of the camel's-thorn or prickly alhagi (*Alhagi maurorum*), from the Near East; and the honeylike secretion of the manna tamarisk (*Tamarix mannifera*) of the same region, appearing when the tender stems are punctured by a small scale insect.

Two distinct types of manna are referred to in the Bible: The manna which "rained down" from heaven (Psalms 78:24) and served as food for the Israelites is believed to have been composed of several species of the lichen genus *Lecanora.* The type of manna in the quotation, "when the sun waxed hot, it melted" (Exodus 16:21), is thought to have been a species of the blue-green alga *Nostoc,* which rapidly forms large jellylike masses on moist ground.

FRANK G. LIER.

MANNAR, må-när', **Gulf of,** an inlet of the Indian Ocean, running between the southeastern coast of India (Madras State) and the island of Ceylon. The gulf is bounded on the north by Rameswaram Island, the chain of shoals known as Adam's Bridge, and Mannar Island. The gulf is some 100 miles long and from 80 to 170 miles wide. Its waters along the coast of Ceylon are famous for their pearl fisheries.

MANNERHEIM, mån'nĕr-hām, BARON **Carl Gustaf Emil,** Finnish military leader and statesman: b. Askainen, Finland (then part of Russia), June 4, 1867; d. Lausanne, Switzerland, Jan. 27, 1951. Descended from a Swedish noble family which had settled in Finland, he attended the Nikolayev Cavalry School in St. Petersburg,

Baron Carl Gustaf Emil Mannerheim

Brown Brothers

Russia. In 1889 he became a second lieutenant in the Imperial Russian Army. He served in the Russo-Japanese War (1904–1905), receiving three decorations for his strategy in organizing the retreat from Manchuria. During World War I he was again decorated for his services.

When Finland declared her independence after the Bolshevik Revolution in October 1917 Mannerheim, then a lieutenant general, resigned from the Russian Army and returned to Finland. There he organized the White Guards, which, with German assistance, defeated the Bolshevist-supported Red Guards in Finland's brief civil war of 1918. On December 14 of that year he became regent of Finland, holding the post until his defeat in the new republic's first presidential election in July 1919. From 1919 to 1931 he lived in semi-retirement, directing the Mannerheim Child Welfare League, which he founded in 1920, and the Finnish Red Cross, of which he became president in 1921. In 1931 he was appointed head of the national defense council, and two years later was made field marshal. In the years that followed he reorganized the army and constructed a 65-mile system of defenses, later known as the Mannerheim Line, across Finland's southeastern frontier.

Mannerheim led his country's armed forces in their heroic but unsuccessful resistance to Soviet aggression in 1939–1940, and again between 1941 and 1944 when Finland, hoping to regain territory which it regarded as historically Finnish, joined the Germans in attacking the Soviet Union. Mannerheim was made marshal of Finland in 1942. In August 1944, when the Germans were falling back on the eastern front, Mannerheim was appointed president of Finland to negotiate a separate peace with the Soviet Union. Finland withdrew from the war on Sept. 4, 1944.' Mannerheim opened the new Finnish legislature in April 1945 but became seriously ill in September of that year, and on March 4, 1946, he resigned from the presidency. He spent his last years in retirement, mostly in Switzerland and Sweden.

Consult Borenius, Tancred, *Field-Marshal Mannerheim* (London 1940); *The Memoirs of Marshal Mannerheim,* tr. from the Swedish by Count Eric Lewenhaupt (London 1954).

MANNES, măn'ĕs, **David,** American violinist, conductor, and teacher: b. New York, N.Y., Feb. 16, 1866; d. there, April 24, 1959. Pupil of noted violinists, including Eugène Ysaye, he joined the New York Symphony Orchestra under Walter Johannes Damrosch (q.v.) in 1891 as a first violin and was concertmaster of the organization from 1902 to 1911. He and his wife gave sonata concerts in the United States and Europe, and until 1915 he directed the Music School Settlement and the Music School Settlement for Colored People in New York City. In 1916 he and his wife founded in New York the Mannes Music School, of which he remained codirector until 1951. During the years 1918–1948 he conducted free orchestral concerts at The Metropolitan Museum of Art. His autobiography, *Music Is My Faith,* was published in 1938.

CLARA DAMROSCH MANNES (1869–1948), a sister of Walter Damrosch, married David Mannes in 1898. A pianist, she appeared in sonata recitals with her husband from 1900, and was codirector with him of the Mannes Music School.

LEOPOLD DAMROSCH MANNES (1899–1964), their son, was a pianist, composer, and coinventor of the Kodachrome color-photography process (1936). He became president of the Mannes Music School in 1951 and reorganized it as the Mannes College of Music in 1953.

MANNHEIM, män'hīm, city, West Germany. It is situated at the confluence of the Rhine and Neckar rivers, 44 miles southwest of

Frankfurt am Main. A bridge across the Rhine connects Mannheim with Ludwigshafen. Mannheim is the major port of the upper Rhine, and a rail and highway center, as well as an important industrial city. There are modern docks along the Rhine and Neckar, and numerous canals connect the two rivers. Such products as coal, timber, grain, and the hops and wine of south Germany are transshipped here. Mannheim manufactures agricultural and industrial machinery, automobiles, electrical equipment, precision instruments, chemicals, rubber, synthetic fiber, textiles, cables, soap, pottery, paper, and wood products.

Originally a small fishing village dating back to the 8th century, Mannheim was chartered by the Elector Palatine Frederick IV as a fortified place in 1607, when it became a refuge for French and Dutch Protestant refugees. Destroyed in 1622 during the Thirty Years' War and again by the French in 1689, it was rebuilt in 1698 on the gridiron pattern, with numbered streets running at right angles to each other. From 1720 to 1778 the city was the residence of the Palatinate electors, who built an imposing baroque residence southwest of the town. In the mid-18th century, while Elector Charles Theodore held court here, Mannheim was a cultural center. The elector's court orchestra was famous throughout Europe, and the first play of Johann Christoph Friedrich Schiller (q.v.), *Die Räuber* (*The Robbers*) was given its first performance at Mannheim's National Theater in 1781.

Beginning about 1834 an expanding river trade stimulated Mannheim's rapid growth as a commercial and industrial city. Karl Benz (1844–1929), who built the first gasoline-powered automobile, established his factory in Mannheim. During World War II the city was bombed repeatedly, and most of the old city, including the magnificent baroque castle and the National Theatre was destroyed or severely damaged. Likewise the harbor and industries suffered heavily. Paintings in Mannheim's art gallery, however, were for the most part preserved, and many of the buildings have been restored. The city was taken by United States forces about March 30, 1945. It became a part of the *Land* (state) of Baden-Württemburg in the German Federal Republic (West Germany). Pop. (1965) 326,949.

MANNING, măn´ing, **Henry Edward,** English cardinal: b. Totteridge, Hertfordshire, England, July 15, 1808; d. London, Jan. 14, 1892. Youngest son of a West India merchant and member of Parliament, Manning studied at Harrow School and at Balliol College, Oxford, where he took honors in the classics in 1830. After two years in the Colonial Office he decided to enter the church and returned to Oxford, where he was elected fellow of Merton College (1832). He was ordained in December, received a curacy in Sussex, and, in the following year, a rectory. In 1833 he married the daughter of the former rector, but she died in 1837 just after his appointment as dean of Midhurst.

At the time of his ordination Manning believed in the doctrine of baptismal regeneration; his leanings led him gradually to adopt the tenets of Tractarianism (q.v.), moving ever closer to High-Church views. He had already achieved a reputation for devotion and eloquence when, in 1840, he became archdeacon of Chichester. Even in 1845, when John Henry Newman (q.v.) and other Tractarians became Roman Catholics, Manning maintained an anti-papist position, but during a trip through continental Europe in 1847–1848 he began to question seriously the Anglican doctrine and in 1848 he had an audience with Pope Pius IX. It was not until November 1850, however, when there was a popular outcry against re-establishment of the Roman Catholic hierarchy in England, that he resigned his archdeaconry. He was received into the Roman Catholic Church on April 6, 1851, and on June 14 was ordained a priest. During the next three years he spent his winters in Rome, studying at the Accademia dei Nobili Ecclesiastici; he was warmly received by the pope, who personally conferred on him the degree of doctor of divinity in 1854.

Manning made his first appearance in a Roman Catholic pulpit in a little chapel in Westminster in 1852. On his return to England in 1854 he became active in a movement for reformatories, and in 1857 Pius IX appointed him provost of the chapter of Westminster and installed him as superior of the Oblates of St. Charles, a community of secular priests in Bayswater. He also directed mission and educational work in the slums of Westminster. In 1865 Manning became archbishop of Westminster. As archbishop he greatly increased the number of Roman Catholic primary schools and the number of pupils attending them, and it was under his leadership that Westminster Cathedral was built. (It was completed in 1903.) A strong advocate of ultramontanism (the supremacy of the pope), he was regarded as the head of that movement in England. His powerful advocacy of the doctrine of papal infallibility, promulgated at the Vatican Council of 1869–1870, brought him considerable prominence, and in March 1875 he was made a cardinal. He continued his philanthropic work to the end of his life, vigorously espousing the cause of the workingman. In addition to a number of published sermons and letters, he wrote *Unity of the Church* (1842); *Temporal Mission of the Holy Ghost*, 2 vols. (1865, 1875); *England and Christendom* (1867); and *The Eternal Priesthood* (1883).

Consult Purcell, Edmund S., *Life of Cardinal Manning*, 2 vols. (London 1895); McEntee, Georgiana P., *The Social Catholic Movement in Great Britain* (New York 1927); Leslie, Shane, *Cardinal Manning, His Life and Labors* (New York 1954).

MANNING, William Thomas, American Protestant Episcopal bishop: b. Northampton, England, May 12, 1866; d. New York, N.Y., Nov. 18, 1949. He came to the United States at the age of 16 and was educated at the University of the South (B.D. 1893), in Sewanee, Tenn. Ordained a priest in 1891, he became rector of a church in Redlands, Calif., in 1892. He taught theology at his alma mater (1893–1895) and served churches in Lansdowne, Pa., and Nashville, Tenn., before going to New York City to be vicar of St. Agnes Chapel, Trinity Parish (1903–1908) and rector of Trinity Church (1908–1921). On May 11, 1921, he was consecrated bishop of New York, a post he held until his retirement in 1946.

As bishop, Manning showed himself to be an able administrator and a militant crusader in matters of faith and moral values. A tangible monument to his work is the Cathedral of St. John the Divine, one of the largest cathedrals in the world. Begun in 1892 it was still unfinished in 1960, but substantial progress was made in the building through Manning's efforts. Frequently the center of controversy because of his uncompromising views, he consistently opposed the marriage of divorced persons, denounced companionate marriage when it was advocated in the 1920's, and in 1940 was instrumental in voiding the teaching appointment in New York City of the English philosopher Bertrand Russell, branding him a "defender of adultery and disbeliever in God." He made many enemies but was loved by the large circle who admired his courage, kindliness, and nobility of character.

MANNINGTON, măn′ĭng-tŭn, city, in northern West Virginia, in Marion County, 12 miles west of Fairmont at the confluence of Pyles and Buffalo creeks. Its altitude is 975 feet. Situated on the Baltimore and Ohio Railroad, the city is a processing center for an area producing oil, gas, and bituminous coal. Manning was incorporated in 1871 Pop. 2,996.

MANNITOL. See MANNA.

MANNLICHER, män′lĭ-кĕr, **Ferdinand,** Austrian arms inventor: b. Mainz, Germany, Jan. 30, 1848; d. Vienna, Austria, Jan. 20, 1904. An engineer, he invented several small arms, of which his breech-loading repeater rifle with movable bolthead was second only to the German Mauser in its widespread use. It was adopted by the Austro-Hungarian army in 1885, and in modified form by a number of other European countries. See also SMALL ARMS.

MANNYNG, măn′ĭng, **Robert** (also ROBERT OF BRUNNE), English poet and chronicler: fl. 1288–1338. He was born in Brunne (now Bourne), Lincolnshire, England, and entered the Gilbertine monastery at Sempringham, probably as a lay brother, about 1288. His chief work is *Handlyng Synne* (1303), a free and amplified translation of William of Wadington's 13th century Anglo-Norman *Manuel des pechiez* (*Manual of Sins*). In this poem of 12,630 lines, Mannyng expounds the Ten Commandments, the seven deadly sins, the sin of sacrilege, the seven sacraments, and confession (shrift), illustrating these subjects with lively stories and anecdotes. The work is valuable for the light it throws on medieval English customs, and also because it was written in the London midland dialect, which later evolved into modern literary English (see ENGLISH LANGUAGE). Of somewhat lesser importance is Mannyng's *Story of Inglande* (1338), of which the first part is early traditional history drawn chiefly from the Norman French translation by Wace (fl. 1170), in his *Roman de Rou,* of the *Historia Regum Britanniae* (c. 1147) of Geoffrey of Monmouth; the second part is a translation of the French verse chronicle of Peter of Langtoft (d. 1307?), describing England's history up to the death of Edward I (1307). Mannyng deliberately wrote in English instead of French, in order to reach the common people, to give them the means "ffor to haf solace & gamen In felawschip when...[they] sitt samen [together]."

Consult Mannyng, Robert, of Brunne, *The Story of England,* ed. by Frederick J. Furnivall, 2 vols. (London 1887); *Robert of Brunne's "Handlyng Synne,"* ed. by Frederick J. Furnivall, with preface (London 1862); new ed., 2 vols. (London 1901–03).

MANOMETER, mȧ-nŏm′ê-têr (Greek, "thin" or "rare" + "measure"), an instrument for measuring the pressure of a gas, vapor, or vacuum. It is more accurate for recording extremely low pressures than a Bourdon tube pressure gage (q.v.). The simplest form is a U-tube containing mercury or other liquid which stands at the same height in the two legs when the pressure of the gas in each column is equal. One end of the tube is connected with the source of the gas and the other is open to the atmosphere. The difference between the levels gives the pressure of the gas being measured with the atmospheric pressure taken as 1. The reading is made on a scale between the two legs.

Instead of an open leg, some manometers are designed with that leg closed. In such a closed-tube instrument, the air above the liquid in the closed end is compressed or expanded as the liquid rises or falls in that leg. When normal pressure is known with the liquid levels the same in both columns, the pressure of the gas being measured is calculated by formula.

When gases of slight pressure are being measured, the manometer used has one leg at an incline at a great angle from the vertical. The vertical displacement of the liquid thus covers a greater distance in the inclined leg and a scale along its length gives a sensitive reading.

A Chattock gage is an example of a two-fluid manometer using liquids of nearly equal density to measure movement of their interface. It is tilted to balance accurately the pressure to be measured against that caused by the tilt and is much more sensitive than simpler manometers.

A Pirani gage, called a hot-wire manometer, measures gas pressures by determining the loss of energy by a heated wire due to conduction by the gas through which it passes.

When it is desired to obtain differences in pressure, such as friction loss between points in a pipe, a differential manometer is frequently employed. A simple form consists of an inverted U-tube with its ends connected at the two points in the pipe where the readings are to be taken. The upper portion of the U is partially filled with a nonmiscible liquid of known weight. The difference in pressure between the two points is calculated from the standing heights in the legs of the fluid flowing through the pipe.

FRANK DORR.

MANON LESCAUT, mȧ-nôn′ lĕs-kō′, novel by Antoine François Prévost d'Exiles (q.v.), known as the Abbé Prévost; first published in Amsterdam in 1731 under the title *Histoire du chevalier Des Grieux et de Manon Lescaut,* seventh and final volume of a work entitled *Mémoires . . . d'un homme de qualité . . .* (7 vols. in 3, 1730–31; *Memoirs of a Nobleman*). It is the story of a passion which wrecks two lives.

The young chevalier Des Grieux falls in love with Manon Lescaut, a courtesan, and takes her to Paris with the intention of marrying her. Manon loves him, but she loves luxury more. Manon acquires a wealthy protector and Des Grieux's father has him dragged home. Resolved to forget his mercenary mistress, Des Grieux studies for the church. But by chance he meets Manon again, and in renewed passion forgets his resolve. To maintain Manon in the luxury she craves, he resorts to gambling and cheating at cards. Both are imprisoned for robbing Manon's protector, and Manon is deported to Louisiana. Des Grieux, whose father had secured his release from jail, accompanies her and they are briefly happy in America. But Manon is sought by the governor's nephew, whom Des Grieux wounds in a duel. The lovers flee to the wilderness, where Manon dies of hardship and exposure. Des Grieux turns in repentance to religion.

In this book, says the French literary historian Gustave Lanson (1857–1934), Prévost forgot for once his habit of tearful, long-winded sermonizing and wrote swiftly, without digressions and without exaggerated scenes. The result is a classic study of an infatuation which degrades instead of elevating its victims. The novel has been widely translated into English and other languages; it has also been the direct source of hundreds of imitations, and its indirect effects are still greater. Becky Sharp, Emma Bovary, Anna Karenina, and Camille all owe something to Manon. In the field of opera, the story's most notable treatments are by Jules Massenet (1884) and Giacomo Puccini (1893).

DeLancey Ferguson.

MANOR, măn′ĕr (Old Fr. *manoir*, habitation or village), a medieval estate held by a lord who might be a king, noble, knight, bishop, or other church dignitary, and operated as a self-sufficient economic unit by the labor of serfs or tenant farmers who were more or less permanently attached to the soil.

The center of the manor estate was the residence of the lord, fortified in early times, although less strongly than a castle. Following the Norman pattern, most English manors of the 13th and 14th centuries were of masonry, rectangular in shape and often surrounded by a moat, while the entire area, including the farm buildings, was surrounded by a wall. The interior consisted principally of one great hall, which was the main living room for the lord and his family, to which were attached a kitchen and storerooms. French Norman manors generally retained the rectangular masonry structure dominated by the great hall through the 15th and 16th centuries. As Europe became more settled, the defensive features of the manor tended to disappear and more spacious living quarters were developed. In England, half-timber construction became more common. From the 16th century on, manors tended to become luxurious country houses, built of whatever material was most available or desirable, and exhibiting a wealth of decoration in the styles current in the various countries.

Near the manor house were the lord's barns, oven, and mill, and his garden, fruit trees, and beehives. At a greater distance, usually aligned along a single lane, were the huts of the peasants, each with its vegetable plot, beehive, and a few barnyard fowl. Nearby was the church. The brook furnished power for the mill, and along its banks stretched the common meadow. Surrounding the cluster of habitations were plots of cultivated land, and beyond these the woods and wastelands. Land cultivation was a prime requisite for the manor, and to this end the three-field system was used—each year one field was planted to winter crops (wheat or rye), one to summer (barley, oats, or peas), while the third lay fallow. The demesne land, reserved for the lord's own use, might stand apart in a block or be scattered among the plots parceled out to the hereditary tenants (see Serf). The tenants' holdings consisted of narrow one-acre or half-acre strips, each tenant having a number of these strips scattered through the three fields. In cultivating the strips, the tenants pooled their labor and resources, but each received only the crops from his own land.

For his beasts, each tenant was entitled to pasture and to a share of hay for winter feed.

In return for use of the plots of land, for protection, and various other benefits, the serf or villein was bound to work on the demesne land for two or three days a week, which might be stretched to five at harvesttime. In addition, he paid rent to the lord in kind or money. Although there were two general classes of serfs, the free and the unfree, actually there were many different conditions and degrees of servitude. An unfree serf could not leave the land, and sometimes his labor was completely at the lord's disposal, while a tenant of the highest class cultivated his strips in return for a fixed payment, being free to leave if he wished. All tenants had to use the lord's mill, bake oven, and wine press, giving him payment in flour, bread, and wine; and they were sometimes subject to other labor, such as repairing roads, bridges, fortifications, and the manor house. Also attached to the estate were skilled craftsmen such as the miller, the smith, the mason, the carpenter, and the herdsman. The manor was a self-sufficient, self-contained unit administered by a steward or intendant and his assistants. It was also a unit of local government, for the lord held manorial court to judge disputes and crimes within the manor. For further discussion of the manorial system see Seignorialism. See also Ninth Century—*Economic and Social Developments;* Eleventh Century—*Manorial System;* Fourteenth Century.

Bibliography.—Vinogradoff, Paul G., *The Growth of the Manor,* 3d ed. (London 1920); Gotch, John A., *The Growth of the English House . . .,* 2d ed. (London 1928); Dutton, Ralph, *The English Country House* (London 1935); Thompson, James W., and Johnson, Edgar N., *An Introduction to Medieval Europe, 300– 1500,* chap. 12 (New York 1937); *Châteaux et manoirs de France,* 14 vols. (Paris 1934–39).

MANRIQUE, män-rē′kä, **Gómez,** Spanish soldier, poet, and statesman: b. Amusco, Valencia, about 1412; d. Toledo, Castile, about 1490. Nephew of Iñigo López de Mendoza, Marqués de Santillana (q.v.), he took an active part in the turbulent Spanish politics of the times, opposing King Henry IV of Castile (r. 1454–1474) and later supporting Ferdinand and Isabella of Aragon and Castile. Manrique's verses, written in the troubadour tradition, have no great distinction. More important, as being precursors of later Spanish dramatic forms, are his religious and liturgical dramas, *Representación del nacimiento de Nuestro Señor (Representation of Our Lord's Nativity),* and *Lamentaciones fechas para la Semana Santa (Laments Performed for Holy Week).*

MANRIQUE, Jorge, Spanish poet and cavalier: b. Paredes de Nava, Castile, Spain, c. 1440; d. March 27, 1479. He was the nephew of Gómez Manrique (q.v.) and the son of Rodrigo Manrique, count of Paredes. Jorge Manrique fought in support of Isabella's claim to the throne of Castile, and again when the queen and her husband, Ferdinand II of Aragon, undertook to repress the unruly nobles in their dominions. Manrique's father was killed in 1476 while fighting the Moors, and the poet himself was mortally wounded in an assault on the castle of Garci-Muñoz in 1479. During his short life he wrote a quantity of verse, courtly *cancioneros* scarcely superior to those of other Spanish poets of the times. However, the death of his father inspired a set of elegiac verses which still rank with the greatest in Spanish poetry: *Coplas de Manrique por la muerte de su padre* (1492; *Manrique's Couplets on the Death of His Father*). See also COPLAS DE MANRIQUE.

MANSARD ROOF, măn'särd rōōf, in architecture, a roof popularized by François Mansart (q.v.), having two sets of rafters, the lower set sloping at a steep pitch and the upper at a shallow pitch. The advantage of this style of construction is that it allows greater headroom and usable floor space in an attic than was possible under the sharply pitched roofs of the French châteaux

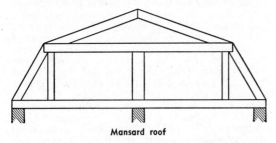

Mansard roof

built in the medieval Gothic tradition. The mansard roof was typical of French Renaissance architecture and later achieved great popularity in the Victorian period, both in Europe and the United States. Usually the lower portion is broken by dormer windows.

MANSART or **MANSARD,** män-sàr' **(Nicolas) François,** French architect: b. Paris, France, Jan. 23, 1598; d. there, Sept. 23, 1666. Of obscure origin and training, he began to receive commissions sometime after 1620, but a number of the buildings of this period, and later ones also, have since been destroyed. During 1635–1638 he constructed the Hôtel de la Vrillière in Paris (now occupied by the Banque de France), and he was employed by the duc d'Orléans to make additions to his château at Blois, which resulted in the so-called Orléans wing (1635–1640). Meanwhile King Louis XIII had made him royal architect in 1636. As the foremost architect in France, he built the beautiful Château de Maisons-Laffitte (1642–1651), near Paris, and the Hôtel Mazarin (1643–1645), which became the Bibliothèque Nationale, in Paris. He designed the Val-de-Grâce church (begun in 1645) in Paris, probably one of his best works. In 1660 he built the present façade of the Hôtel Carnavalet (now the Musée Carnavalet) in Paris.

Harmonious proportions and classic simplicity with restrained external decoration were characteristic of Mansart's work, which signaled the beginning of a new classic period in France. Although often credited with the invention of the mansard roof (q.v.), he actually only made popular a style which was already in use.

JULES HARDOUIN-MANSART or HARDOUIN-MANSARD (1646–1708), his grandnephew, was also a French architect. Born Jules Hardouin, he studied architecture under Libéral Bruant (1637–1697) and under his great-uncle, whose surname he adopted. He continued in the classic Renaissance tradition of the earlier Mansart, but with a greater degree of opulence. Chief architect for Louis XIV from 1674, he was entrusted with enlarging the royal palace at Versailles (q.v.), including the Galérie des Glaces (Hall of Mirrors,

1678–1684); the Orangerie (1684–1686); the Grand Trianon (1687–1688); and the chapel, begun in 1699. During this period he worked with tremendous speed on many other projects, among which were the Place des Victoires (c. 1684) and the octagonal plaza now called Place Vendôme (1699), both in Paris. In the latter year he was made superintendent of royal construction. Perhaps his greatest achievement was the dome of the Hôtel des Invalides (1692–1704), in which the body of Napoleon I was laid to rest in 1840. See also DOME; FRANCE—15. *Art and Architecture* (The 17th Century).

MANSFELD, mäns'fĕlt, COUNT **Peter Ernst II,** German soldier: b. Luxembourg, 1580; d. near Sarajevo, Bosnia (now in Yugoslavia), Nov. 29, 1626. He was a natural son of Count Peter Ernst Mansfeld (1517–1604), governor of Luxembourg for Charles V of the Holy Roman Empire. He fought for the Habsburgs in the Netherlands and Hungary, and was legitimized by Rudolf II (1552–1612) but when he was not given his father's property he turned against the Habsburgs. At the outbreak of the Thirty Years' War (1618), he supported the Protestant princes and was sent to aid the Bohemian revolt against Austria. He remained inactive while the newly chosen "Winter King" of Bohemia, Elector Palatine Frederick V, was driven from Prague (1620). Appointed to command Frederick's forces, he attempted to defend Frederick's original Palatine possessions with an army of mercenaries, and his troops, unpaid, survived by plundering both hostile and friendly territory. With allies, he defeated Johan Tserclaes Tilly at Weisloch in 1622, but was unable to drive out the imperial forces and Frederick dismissed him. Mansfeld became a mercenary, selling his services to various princes. In 1625 he was sent by England to recover the Palatinate, but was defeated by the imperial general Albrecht Eusebius Wenzel von Wallenstein (q.v.) at Dessau bridge (1626). Raising another army, he marched into Hungary to join Gabriel Bethlen (q.v.) but was checkmated by Wallenstein. He died soon after.

MANSFIELD, 1ST EARL OF. See MURRAY, WILLIAM.

MANSFIELD, mäns'fēld, **Katherine** (pseudonym of KATHLEEN MURRY, nee BEAUCHAMP), British short story writer and critic: b. Wellington, New Zealand, Oct. 14, 1888; d. near Fontainebleau, France, Jan. 9, 1923. She attended Queen's College in London in 1903–1906, and in 1908 returned to London, where she made her home. An accomplished violoncellist, it was only in 1908 that she decided to pursue a career in literature rather than in music. After an unhappy marriage in 1909 she spent some time in Bavaria, where she wrote the stories which were collected in *In a German Pension* (1911). In 1911 she met John Middleton Murry, with whom she became closely associated. She was coeditor and contributor to a series of journals which he edited, and in 1918, after she had obtained a divorce from her first husband, the two were married. She suffered from ill health much of her adult life, and in 1918 was found to have tuberculosis. In her last years much of her time was spent in southern France and Switzerland in search of a healthful climate.

Mansfield had been contributing to journals since 1910 and had published two collections of short stories (*Prelude,* 1918) and (*Je ne parle pas français,* 1919), but it was not until 1920, when *Bliss and Other Stories* appeared, that her reputation was established. *The Garden Party* (1922) was the last volume to be published in her lifetime. After her death her stories were collected and published in *The Doves' Nest* (1923), *Something Childish* (1924; American title *The Little Girl*), and *The Aloe* (1930), as well as her *Poems* (1923), and criticism, in *Novels and Novelists* (1930). Her self-analytical *Journal* (1927), her *Letters* (2 vols., 1928), and her *Scrapbook* (1939), were edited by her husband. Katherine Mansfield was greatly influenced by Anton Pavlovich Chekhov (q.v.). Similar to Chekhov in sensitivity and subtle choice of detail, her stories depended on atmosphere rather than plot. She, in turn, influenced writers of her own and succeeding generations, particularly in the use of the vital, arrested moment. Her work was marked by warm humanity and subtle characterization.

MANSFIELD, manz'fēld, **Michael Joseph** (1903–   ), American legislator, who became Democratic leader in the U.S. Senate in 1961. He was born in New York City of Irish immigrant parents on March 16, 1903. Reared in Montana from boyhood, he left school at 14 to join the Navy in World War I and later he served in the Army and in the Marines. After working as a copper miner, he earned two degrees from Montana State University (Missoula)—now the University of Montana—where for a decade he taught Latin American and Far Eastern history.

Mike Mansfield was elected to Congress from Montana in 1942. He served 10 years as a representative before his election to the Senate in 1952. He was elevated to assistant majority leader in 1957 on the recommendation of Lyndon B. Johnson, then the majority leader, but Mansfield so avoided the limelight that he escaped major national attention. Respected by liberals, whom he joined on most issues, and also by conservatives, he contributed to party unity in the Senate.

When Mansfield became majority leader upon Johnson's election as vice president, the contrast with the persuasive style of his former chief was startling. Mansfield encouraged legislative leadership by committee chairmen, arranged committee assignments by secret ballot in party counsels, and sought both personal accommodation and dispersal of responsibilities. He worked closely with Senator Everett Dirksen, the Republican leader, on whom he often relied for key votes to offset opposition to liberal measures from conservative Southern Democrats.

Deeply interested in foreign policy, Mansfield at times spoke only for himself rather than for the Kennedy or Johnson administrations. In 1961 he advocated that all Berlin become a free, neutralized city under international guaranties. In 1964 he suggested neutralization for both South and North Vietnam. He preferred technical assistance abroad to foreign economic aid.

FRANKLIN L. BURDETTE, *University of Maryland*

MANSFIELD, Richard, American actor: b. Berlin, Germany, May 24, 1854; d. New London, Conn., Aug. 30, 1907. Son of an English wine merchant and the singer Hermine (Erminia) Rudersdorff, he accompanied his mother on tour and in 1872 went with her to Boston, Mass., where she settled. He returned to London in 1877, where he eked out a living giving skits and playing in Gilbert and Sullivan operettas. Back in the United States in 1882, he continued to sing in operetta but struggled to break into the spoken drama.

Mansfield's first dramatic role was an instant success—a New York appearance (1882) as Baron Chevrial in *A Parisian Romance,* from the French of Octave Feuillet—but it was not until his Boston performance (1886) of the title role in *Prince Karl* by Archibald Clavering Gunter that he established himself as an actor-manager. He gradually built up a large repertoire of plays, often acting a different part every night. In 1887 he essayed the dual role of Dr. Jekyll and Mr. Hyde in the play based on Robert Louis Stevenson's story. His Shakespearean debut was made in London (1889) as Richard III, and later he added such roles as Shylock in *The Merchant of Venice* (1893), and Henry V (1900). His production of *Arms and the Man* in New York (1894), introduced George Bernard Shaw to the United States; and in 1897 he gave the premiere of Shaw's *Devil's Disciple,* in Albany, N.Y. His New York production of an English version of Edmond Rostand's *Cyrano de Bergerac* was so enthusiastically acclaimed in 1898 that he acted nothing else for a year, and Booth Tarkington's *Monsieur Beaucaire* (1901) was equally well received. In 1906 he gave the first American production of Henrik Ibsen's *Peer Gynt* in Chicago.

Richard Mansfield as Cyrano.

Brown Brothers

Mansfield was an outstanding representative of "grand style" and romantic tradition in acting, and of the era when an actor-manager could take an extensive repertoire of plays on the road; in introducing such dramatists as Shaw and Ibsen in the United States, he also helped to break ground for a new era. A versatile actor who could interpret a great variety of roles, he played with a vibrant quality which enthralled audiences.

MANSFIELD, manz'fēld, a town in eastern Connecticut, is in Tolland County, on the Willimantic River, just north of Willimantic. It comprises several villages, including Mansfield Center, Spring Hill, Merrow, Eagleville, and Storrs. Near Storrs, which is the home of the University of Connecticut, is located the Mansfield State Training School for the mentally-retarded. Mansfield is a residential center with some small farms. It was settled in 1692 and incorporated in 1703. Population: 14,638.

MANSFIELD, municipal borough, England, situated on the Maun River in Nottinghamshire, 14 miles north of Nottingham on the western edge of Sherwood Forest. Set in a coal-mining area, it is a market town and railroad center and manufactures shoes, hosiery, chemicals, machinery, and cotton.

Mansfield was the site of a Roman camp, and later the occasional abode of Mercian kings; in Norman times it often served as a base for royal parties hunting in Sherwood Forest. In 1377 it was granted a fair by Richard II. Its Church of St. Peter, built in Early Norman and Perpendicular styles, was begun in the 13th century, and it has a grammar school founded in 1561 by Queen Elizabeth I. It became a municipal borough in 1891. Pop. (1961) 53,222.

MANSFIELD, town, Louisiana, seat of De Soto Parish, located in the northwestern part of the state 33 miles south of Shreveport at an altitude of 330 feet. Situated in a fertile agricultural area where oil wells and timber are also found, it is a trading and shipping center served by the Kansas City Southern Railway. A switch line of the Texas and Pacific Railway runs through nearby South Mansfield. Its industries include cotton ginning, lumber milling, and the manufacture of trailer bodies. Mansfield was incorporated in 1847. Nearby, Mansfield Battle Park marks the site of the Battle of Sabine Crossroads (April 8, 1864), where Confederate troops defeated Union forces in the Red River campaign of the Civil War. Pop. 5,839.

MANSFIELD, town, Massachusetts, in Bristol County about 25 miles southwest of Boston at an altitude of 180 feet. Situated on the New York, New Haven, and Hartford Railroad, it is the market center for a farming area, and manufactures machine parts, metal products, and chocolate. Its commercial greenhouses specialize in gladioli. The community was settled in 1659, and made a district in 1770; the district became a town by general act in 1775. In 1921 it adopted the council-manager form of government. Pop. 7,773.

MANSFIELD, city, Ohio, the seat of Richland County in the north central part of the state, located 55 miles west of Akron on a fork of the Mohican River. Situated in a rich farming area among the western foothills of the Appalachian Mountains, its altitude is 1,155 feet. Mansfield is an industrial city, making electrical appliances, steel and rubber products, brass castings, auto bodies, machinery, and bathroom fixtures. It is served by three railroads—the Erie, the Baltimore and Ohio, and the Pennsylvania—and by Lake Central Airlines. The Ohio State Reformatory is located just outside the city.

Mansfield was founded in 1808 and named after Jared Mansfield, United States surveyor-general. During the War of 1812, Johnny Appleseed (see CHAPMAN, JOHN) saved the hamlet by speeding more than 30 miles through the night to summon troops to defend Mansfield against an Indian attack. The settlement was incorporated as a village in 1826, as a city in 1857. Its government is by mayor and council. The novelist Louis Bromfield (q.v.), who was born here in 1896, used this locale for several of his books. Pop. 47,325.

MANSFIELD PARK, novel by Jane Austen (q.v. 1775–1817), first published in 1814. Moral questions—some of them hard for modern readers to understand—are central in this book, which was said by its author to be "about ordination." Perhaps the least popular novel written by Jane Austen, it nevertheless has considerable power.

At Mansfield Park, Fanny Price is brought up by her uncle and aunt, Sir Thomas and Lady Bertram. A sensitive and conscientious girl, Fanny loves their younger son, Edmund, a candidate for holy orders. Edmund falls in love with Mary Crawford, visiting nearby with her brother Henry. Private theatricals produce a flirtation between Henry Crawford and Maria Bertram (Edmund's sister), under the nose of Maria's rich and stupid fiancé, James Rushworth. Eventually, however, Henry falls in love with Fanny, and everyone favors the match. At Sir Thomas's urging, Fanny revisits her parents' impoverished Portsmouth home, Sir Thomas nourishing the hope that the contrast with comfortable Mansfield will make her accept Henry. But Henry elopes with Maria, now married to Rushworth, and Mary condones the offense, revealing to Edmund her basic lack of principle. Finally Edmund and Fanny are united. Minor characters are excellently drawn: indolent Lady Bertram; her sister, the officious Mrs. Norris; and high-principled Sir Thomas. The American critic Lionel Trilling (1905–) has called *Mansfield Park* "a great novel, its greatness being commensurate with its power to offend."

JANE F. BLANSHARD.

MANSHIP, măn′shĭp, **Paul,** American sculptor: b. St. Paul, Minn., Dec. 24/25, 1885; d. New York City, Jan. 31, 1966. He attended evening classes in drawing at the St. Paul Institute School of Art, then took up sculpture at Philadelphia, and won a fellowship at the American Academy in Rome in 1909. During his three years in Rome he assimilated the classic spirit but developed his own manner of expression, characterized by purity and simplicity of line and a strong feeling for design. On his return from Rome, the originality of his works attracted at-

Manship's *Prometheus* fountain at Rockefeller Plaza.

Rockefeller Center, Inc.

tention. He began to accomplish a prodigious amount of work, including the following (in bronze, unless otherwise specified) : *Centaur and Dryad* (1913) ; portrait of Pauline Frances, his infant daughter (marble, 1914) ; *Infant Hercules* fountain at the American Academy in Rome (1914) ; the companion statuettes *Indian* and *Pronghorn Antelope* (both 1914) ; and marble portraits of John Barrymore and John D. Rockefeller (both 1918). In many cases several copies were made, sometimes in different years. During the early 1920's Manship's style began to change, showing more of a tendency to realism. Works of this decade include *Atalanta* and *Europa and the Bull* (1924).

Probably Manship's most famous sculpture is the *Prometheus* fountain (gilded bronze, 1934) at Rockefeller Center, New York City, while his *Moods of Time* groups (1938) and *Time and the Fates* sundial (1938), all originally in bronze, were displayed in plaster at the New York World's Fair. In 1939 he executed the *Woodrow Wilson Memorial* celestial sphere for the League of Nations in Geneva, Switzerland, and during the years 1952–1955 he completed memorials in bronze and marble for the American Military Cemetery at Anzio, Italy (*Memory and Immortality, Comrades in Arms,* and an altar triptych). His work is on display in some 35 United States cities as well as in several European countries. See also SCULPTURE—*American Sculpture*.

Consult Murtha, Edwin, *Paul Manship* (New York 1957).

MANSLAUGHTER. See HOMICIDE.

MANSON, măn's'n, SIR **Patrick,** British physician and parasitologist : b. Old Meldrum, Aberdeenshire, Scotland, Oct. 3, 1844 ; d. London, England, April 9, 1922. After taking his M.D. degree at Aberdeen University in 1866, he was appointed medical officer for Formosa to the Chinese Imperial Maritime Customs. In 1871 he became head of a mission hospital at Amoy, China, where he began research on tropical diseases. He first investigated the relationship between elephantiasis (q.v.), a disease frequently encountered among his Chinese patients, and the filaria worms (see FILARIASIS) observed in the patients' blood, as well as the possible role of the mosquito in transmitting filaria. After establishing a school of medicine in Hongkong (1883–1886) which later became the University of Hong Kong Medical School, Manson returned to Scotland. In 1892 he was appointed physician to the Seaman's Hospital Society in London, where he undertook research on malaria. On the basis of his experience with filaria he suggested that the mosquito was the host of the malarial parasite at one stage of its existence, a theory which was developed by Sir Donald Ross (q.v.). (See also MOSQUITO.) In 1897 Manson was appointed medical adviser to the British Colonial Office. In this post he was instrumental in reforming the colonial medical service and in founding the London School of Tropical Medicine (1899). Knighted in 1903, he has been called the father of tropical medicine. His *Tropical Diseases: A Manual of the Diseases of Warm Climates* (1898) became a standard work which, revised by his son-in-law Philip M. Manson-Bahr, reached its 14th edition in 1954.

Consult Manson-Bahr, Philip H., and Alcock, A. W., *Life and Work of Sir Patrick Manson* (New York 1927).

MANSUR or **MANSOUR, al-,** ăl-măn-sōōr' (also ALMANZOR or ALMANSOR), Arabic title signifying "victorious," assumed by a number of Muslim rulers. Among the more notable of these are the following.

ABU-JA'FAR 'ABDULLĀH AL-MANṢŪR, 2d Abbasid caliph : b. about 712 ; d. near Mecca, Arabia, Oct. 7, 775. His father was descended from a first cousin of the Prophet Mohammed, his mother was a Berber slave. During his reign (754–775) he firmly established the Abbasid dynasty founded by his brother, al-Saffāh. For his capital he built Baghdad, a new city on the west bank of the Tigris in Mesopotamia which was to become one of the great cities of the ancient world. He employed a Persian vizier (q.v.), a practice followed by his successors, and encouraged cultivation of the Persian science and scholarship which were to give luster to the Abbasid dynasty. He died while on a pilgrimage to Mecca. See also ABBASIDS ; ARABIC LITERATURE.

MUḤAMMAD IBN-ABI-'ĀMIR, known as AL-MANṢŪR BI-ALLAH or AL-ḤĀJIB AL-MANṢŪR, Muslim regent of Cordóba, Spain : b. 939 ; d. Medinaceli, Spain, Aug. 10, 1002. A humble professional letter writer of Yemeni Arab descent, he became a protégé of the sultana of Cordóba and eventually royal chamberlain (*hājib*) and vizier. While the immature Umayyad caliph, Hishām II (r. 976–1009, 1010–1013) was kept a prisoner in his palace, al-Manṣur ruled the state, placing his name on the coinage and the official seal of state. He reorganized the army on the regimental system, and the success of his military campaigns against the Christian kingdoms of northern Spain—León, Castile, Catalonia, and Galicia—led him to assume in 981 the title al-Manṣur bi-Allāh (victorious through the aid of Allah). He passed the viziership to a son in 991, but continued to wield the actual power until his death, which occurred as he was returning from a campaign against Castile. See also SPAIN—*15. History: 5th Century A.D. to 1492.*

ABU-YŪSUF YA'QŪB AL-MANṢŪR, Almohade caliph in northwest Africa and Spain : d. 1199. Grandson of the Berber founder of the dynasty, 'Abd-al-Mu'min, and son of a Christian slave woman, al-Manṣūr became caliph in 1184. His reign is distinguished by the glorious architectural monuments erected in Morocco and Spain, among them the Giralda tower in Seville, his capital. See also ALMOHADES.

MANSURA, El, ĕl măn-sōōr'à, city, Egypt, in the Nile River delta, 36 miles southwest of Damietta. It is the capital of Daqahliya Province. Situated on the eastern bank of the Damietta branch of the Nile, it is a rail junction and a center for cotton trade and such industries as cotton and wool processing, tanning, dairying, and metal and woodworking.

El Mansûra was founded in 1221 as a defense stronghold after Damietta had been captured (1219) in the Fifth Crusade. In 1250 the city was the scene of a Mameluke victory over crusaders led by Louis IX of France. Pop. (1947) 101,965.

MANTA. See DEVILFISH ; RAY.

MANTECA, măn-tē'kà, city, California, in San Joaquin County, in the central part of the state, 12 miles south of Stockton, at an altitude of 38 feet. In a rich agricultural region where grapes, olives, market vegetables, and sugar beets are grown, it is a shipping center for agricultural and dairy products. The Southern Pacific and Western Pacific railway lines serve the city. The first settlement was made here in 1857, in 1870 it became known as Cowell's Station, and in 1918 it was incorporated as Manteca. Pop. 8,242.

MANTEGNA, män-tĕ′nyä, **Andrea,** Italian painter and engraver: b. probably at Isola di Carturo, between Vicenza and Padua, Italy, 1431; d. Mantua, Sept. 13, 1506. The adopted son and apprentice of the Paduan painter Francesco Squarcione from about 1441, he was exposed as a youth to Florentine artistic influences also (the painters Fra Filippo Lippi, Andrea del Castagno, and Paolo Uccello, and the sculptor Donatello, qq.v.), Squarcione himself may have introduced Mantegna to the art of classic antiquity, sparking an enthusiasm which increased throughout the pupil's life. In 1448 Mantegna was painting on his own, and his contract with Squarcione was dissolved a few years later. In 1454 he married the daughter of the Venetian painter Jacopo Bellini.

An early work of great importance was Mantegna's series of frescoes on the lives of St. James and St. Christopher, in the Ovetari chapel of the Church of the Eremitani, Padua, begun about 1448 with Niccolò Pizzolo and finished by Mantegna working alone from 1454 to 1457. These frescoes survived until the World War II bombing of Padua in 1944, when all were destroyed except two which had been temporarily removed from the church. In about 1459 Mantegna finished one of his masterpieces, the altarpiece for San Zeno Maggiore in Verona, comprising the main triptych of the Madonna flanked by saints, and predella panels. The latter are now in France—the center panel of the Crucifixion at the Louvre, Paris, and the side panels at the Tours museum. On Jan. 30, 1459, Mantegna was appointed court painter to the princely family of Gonzaga at Mantua, and he lived in this city from about 1460, with occasional trips elsewhere in Italy, until his death. Of the many frescoes painted for the Gonzaga family, only one now remains, the decoration of the bridal chamber (*Camera degli Sposi*) in the Gonzaga palace (finished in 1474), which depicts scenes of the family. Nine murals entitled *Trionfo di Cesare* (*Triumph of Caesar*), painted on canvas between about 1482 and 1492, survive, although in poor condition, at Hampton Court, England. While engaged in these murals, Mantegna was called to Rome to decorate the papal Belvedere Chapel (since destroyed), and this contact with Roman antiquities during the years 1488–1490 influenced his painting greatly. No artist of his time studied classical antiquities as eagerly as Mantegna, who acquired an extensive collection of Greek and Roman fragments. He continued to paint up to his death, but in his later years was eclipsed by such artists as Michelangelo. He was buried in a mortuary chapel frescoed by his son Francesco in the Church of Sant' Andrea in Mantua.

Mantegna's art was essentially north Italian, although containing elements of Florentine, Venetian, and classic styles. He was the first great painter of the Paduan school and the foremost 15th century painter outside Venice. A perfectionist in anatomy, draftsmanship, and perspective, he endowed his figures with a singular intensity, and they have a sculptural quality which may mark the influence of Donatello. Many of his works have been destroyed or survive in poor condition. Among those now displayed in museums are his panel depicting Jesus' agony in the Garden (unknown date, National Gallery, London), and the following canvasses: *Madonna della vittoria* (1495–1496, Louvre, Paris); *Parnassus* (1497, Louvre), originally painted for Isabella d'Este, a Gonzaga by marriage; and *Cristo morto* (1506, Brera Gallery, Milan), the last-named a powerful study of the foreshortened human figure. Mantegna was also a pioneer in copperplate engraving. A number of engravings were produced at his shop, of which seven are attributed to Mantegna himself. See also PAINTING—*Modern Painting* (Early Renaissance).

Consult Kristeller, Paul, *Andrea Mantegna,* tr. from the German by S. Arthur Strong (London 1901); *Mantegna: Paintings, Drawings, Engravings,* introduction by Erika Tietze-Conrat (London 1955).

MANTELL, măn-tĕl′, **Gideon Algernon,** English geologist, paleontologist, and physician: b. Lewes, England, Feb, 3, 1790; d. London, Nov. 11, 1852. The son of a shoemaker, he studied medicine at Lewes with a surgeon who later took him into practice. He devoted his leisure time to research in geology and paleontology, making a particular study of the Wealden formations in Sussex and acquiring a large collection of fossil specimens, which he sold to the British Museum in 1839. Among other findings he discovered four of the five genera of dinosaurs known at the time of his death and demonstrated the fresh-water origin of the Wealden strata, but perhaps his chief contribution was to point the way to further research in the then infant sciences of geology and paleontology. Of the 67 books and 48 scientific papers which came from his pen, the popular *Wonders of Geology* (2 vols., 1838) ran through 6 editions in the first 10 years after publication.

Consult Spokes, Sidney, *Gideon Algernon Mantell, Surgeon and Geologist* (London 1927).

MANTEUFFEL, män′toi-fĕl, BARON **Edwin Hans Karl von,** Prussian soldier: b. Dresden, Germany, Feb. 24, 1809; d. Carlsbad, now in Czechoslovakia, June 17, 1885. Of a noble Pomeranian family, he entered the Prussian Guards in 1827, rising in rank until he became chief of the Prussian military cabinet in 1857. He served in the war with Denmark (1864), after which he became governor of Schleswig, and in the Austro-Prussian War of 1866.

During the Franco-Prussian War (1870–1871) Manteuffel commanded in turn the First Corps, the First Army, and the Army of the East South. Attacking the French Army of the East near Belfort, in the war's final stages, he drove 80,000 men across the Swiss frontier and thus out of action. He was a commander of the army of occupation in France from 1871 to 1873, and was promoted to the rank of field marshall in 1873. After serving on several diplomatic missions, he was made governor of Alsace-Lorraine (Elsass-Lothringen) in 1879, a post which he held until his death.

MANTI, măn′tī, city, Utah, situated in the central part of the state, 70 miles south of Provo, at an altitude of 5,530 feet. It is the seat of Sanpete County. Served by the Denver and Rio Grande Western Railroad, it is a processing point for the livestock, poultry, and dairy products of the surrounding irrigated region, and flour and cheese are made in the city. The city has a

National Guard armory, and a county-city jail. There is a Mormon temple here; also, three Mormon churches and a Presbyterian church. The name Manti is taken from the *Book of Mormon.* Manti has a mayor and council; the city was founded by Mormons in 1849. Pop. 1,739.

MANTINEA, măn-t'n-ē′à, or **MANTIN-EIA,** ancient city, Arcadia, Greece; on the Argolis district border of the eastern Peloponnesus, on the Ophis River. Mantinea was known for its wealth, and famous for the battles fought near it; in 418 B.C., when the Argives, Athenians, and Mantineans were defeated by the Spartans; in 385 B.C., when the city was taken and destroyed by the Spartans; and in 362 B.C., when the Thebans under Epaminondas defeated the Spartans, although the victory of the Thebans was purchased with the life of their commander. Mantinea was, in 226 B.C., surprised by Aratus of Sicyon; and in 222 B.C. taken by Antigonus III Doson; on this occasion the town was sacked, and the inhabitants were sold as slaves. Another battle was fought near Mantinea 207 B.C., between Machanidas, tyrant of Lacedaemon, and Philopoemen, general of the Achaean League. The latter was victorious, and slew the tyrant with his own hand.

The French school at Athens financed an archaeologist, G. Fougères, in uncovering a large area here in 1888. The ancient city was walled, with towers about 80 feet apart. A large mound-shaped theater was disclosed, a square market hall, and paved roads of different eras.

MANTIQUEIRA, maNn-tĕ-kā′ĕ-rà, **Serra da,** mountain range, Brazil, which is in the southeastern part of the republic and is about 75 miles from the Atlantic Ocean and extends nearly parallel with the coast for about 200 miles. The eastern end is near Rio de Janeiro. Ranges connected with the Mantiqueira are often included with this range and the name Mitiqueira applied to the whole. Mount Itatiaía, the highest peak, is 9,145 feet above the sea. Several large rivers have their sources in this range.

MANTIS, an orthopterous insect of the family Mantidae. These curious insects, allied to grasshoppers, abound in many parts of the world, and have always excited popular notice, and have been endowed with many supernatural qualities by the ignorant and superstitious of all countries. They are slender, with long, locust-like legs, oval wings, and a long necklike prothorax, terminating in an angular head with large protruding eyes. The front legs are stout, spiny, fitted for grasping their prey, and are held up in front of them in an attitude that to some suggest prayer. Hence the names praying insect, prophet, and the like often given to the more familiar species; to others they suggest other ideas, as of a horse pawing the air, whence our common species of the southern states (*Stagomantis carolina*) is known as the rearhorse, and in Europe these insects are called camel crickets. Why it should also be called mule killer is harder to explain; probably it is by confusion with a scorpion also so called.

These insects in tropical countries have come to assume various forms and hues similar to the flowers near which they lurk to catch the insects visiting the blossoms—a protective measure which comes under the head of mimicry. A large pro-

portion of the insects upon which they feed are injurious to crops, hence the mantis may be regarded as beneficial to man. Among the Japanese and Chinese they are made to minister to human amusement also, being kept in cages and made to engage in combats upon which the spectators bet money. The eggs of the mantis are laid in an oval mass upon the stem of a plant and covered with a tough case of hardened mucus which shows a curiously braided pattern of surface and is easily recognized.

MANTLE, man′təl, **Mickey,** American baseball player: b. Spavinaw, Okla., Oct. 20, 1931. He was the fourth super-star in the New York Yankee galaxy, following Babe Ruth, Lou Gehrig, and Joe DiMaggio. Primarily a home-run hitter, Mantle in 1967 became the sixth major league player to hit 500 home runs. A switch-hitter, he was named the most valuable player in the American League in 1956, 1957, and 1962. His top salary was about $100,000 a year.

Mickey Charles Mantle was named for Mickey Cochrane, a Hall of Fame catcher. The Yankees signed him for $1,000 in 1949. After two years as a shortstop in the minor leagues, he was moved to the New York outfield. He was the key man as the Yankees dominated the American League, although he was often sidelined by injuries, some of them stemming from osteomyelitis, a bone disease. In 1956 he won the Triple Crown in batting (leading in hitting, runs batted in, and home runs). He set a record for total World Series home runs with 18. In 1967, to cut down on his running and thus to prolong his career, Mantle became a first baseman.

BILL BRADDOCK, *New York "Times"*

MANTLE-ROCK (also called REGOLITH), the loose unconsolidated debris that results from rock weathering. It includes all soils except those of strictly organic origin. If they have resulted from weathering in place, without removal, the soils are called residual; if they have been carried from their place of origin by wind, glaciers, or running water, they are said to be transported. The mantle-rock varies greatly in thickness. In some places it is entirely absent, in others it is hundreds of feet deep.

MANTLING, *in heraldry,* an ornament depicted as hanging down from the helmet, and behind the escutcheon. It is considered to represent either the cointise, an ornamental scarf which passed around the body, and over the shoulder; or the military mantle, or robe of estate. When intended for the cointise, it is cut into irregular strips and curls of the most capricious forms, whose contortions are supposed to indicate that it has been torn into that ragged condition in the field of battle. When the mantling is treated as a robe of estate, the bearings of the shield are sometimes embroidered on it. A mantling adjusted so as to form a background for the shield and its accessories constitutes an "achievement of arms."

MANTRAPS, metal traps formerly used on the grounds of large estates in England to catch poachers and trespassers. The grounds were posted with the warning notice, "Man-traps and spring-guns set here." Designed with sharp teeth to clutch and hold the leg of anyone caught in them, in appearance they resembled gigantic rattraps several feet long. They may be seen in museums.

MANTUA, măn′tû-à (Ital. MANTOVA), city and commune, Italy, capital of the Province of Mantova, Lombardy, 70 miles southeast of Milan, on an almost insular site on the Mincio River, which here divides into several arms ending in a marshy lake. Communication is maintained between the islands and mainland by several bridges, the chief of which is Ponte di San Giorgio, 800 yards long. Mantua is the see of a bishop.

FOTO—ENIT

Top: The Ducal Palace. *Bottom:* The Castle of the Gonzagas. These are among the many historical buildings to be seen in Mantua.

The most remarkable edifices are the cathedral, after an elegant design by Giulio Romano; the basilica of Sant' Andrea, conspicuous from a distance by its majestic cupola and Gothic tower; the church of San Sebastiano, the Corte Reale, formerly the ducal palace of the Gonzagas; the Castello di Corte or old castle of the Gonzagas; the Torre dell' Orologio, and the Torre dello Zuccaro; the house of Giulio Romano, the Palazzo Colloredo, with enormous caryatides supporting its façade; the Palazzo Del Te, outside the walls of the town, also built by Giulio Romano, and adorned with some of that master's largest frescoes; and the Vergilian Academy of Sciences and Fine Arts.

Mantua is an agricultural and commercial center, and also a rail junction. Manufactures include macaroni, beet sugar, paper, fertilizers, pianos, furniture, bricks, pottery, and dairy machinery.

History.—Mantua was an ancient Etruscan settlement, and in the time of Virgil, a native of the region, was a Roman town. Charlemagne built its first fortifications. Soon after 1115 Mantua succeeded in making itself independent, and continued so until 1276, when it fell under the iron rule of Buonacolsi or Bonacossi. In 1328 it

found better masters in the Gonzagas, who, first as captains, then (from 1432), as marquises, and finally (from 1530) as dukes of Mantua, governed it with great ability, and distinguished themselves by the splendor of their court and their patronage of literature and art. The last of the Gonzaga family who reigned in Mantua was Ferdinando Carlo, or Carlo IV, who, having taken part with the French in the War of Succession, was declared to have incurred a forfeiture by withdrawing his allegiance from his liege lord, the emperor of Germany. The Mantuan territory was accordingly annexed to the Austrian possessions in Lombardy, and the remaining part of Montferrat was assigned to Savoy (1708). The fortifications of the town, previously formidable, were completed and put into their modern form by the Austrians and have been kept up to date by the Italian government. In 1797 Napoleon, apparently hopeless of reducing it by any other means, contented himself with keeping it under strict blockade, until famine compelled the garrison to capitulate. After the cession of the western part of Lombardy to Sardinia in 1859, Mantua, with what else of Lombardy remained to Austria, was united to Venetia, and with it was given up to Italy in 1866. The area of the department is 903 square miles. The communal population is (1951) 53,810.

MANU, măn′ōō, the reputed author of the most renowned law book of the ancient Hindus, and likewise of an ancient Kalpa work on Vedic rites. It is a matter, however, of considerable doubt whether both works belong to the same individual, and whether the name Manu, especially in the case of the author of the law book, was intended to designate a historical personage; for, in several passages of the Vedas (q.v.), as well as the Mahābhārata (q.v.), Manu is mentioned as the progenitor of the human race; and, in the first chapter of the law book ascribed to him, he declares himself to have been produced by Virâj, an offspring of the Supreme Being, and to have created all this universe. Hindu mythology knows, moreover, a succession of Manus, each of whom created, in his own period, the world anew after it had perished at the end of a mundane age.

According to theosophy, the Manu is a great Being (though once a man) who governs the earth planet; other Manus govern other planets, while the Logos (q.v.) created the universe. The word Manu is chiefly used with reference to the author of an ancient renowned Hindu law book. This work is not merely a law book in the European sense of the word, it is likewise a system of cosmogony. The chief topics of its 12 books are the following: (1) creation, (2) education and the duties of a pupil, or the first order; (3) marriage and the duties of a householder, or the second order; (4) means of subsistence and private morals; (5) diet, purification and the duties of women; (6) the duties of an anchorite and an ascetic, or the duties of the third and fourth orders; (7) government and the duties of a king and the military caste; (8) judicature and law, private and criminal; (9) continuation of the former and the duties of the commercial and servile castes; (10) mixed castes and the duties of the castes in time of distress; (11) penance and expiation; (12) transmigration and final beatitude.

MANUAL ALPHABET, alphabet for the deaf and dumb, also the letters made by the deaf and dumb with their fingers. See also DEAF, EDUCATION OF THE; EDUCATION OF THE PHYSICALLY HANDICAPPED—*History of Educational Services for Physically Handicapped Children.*

MANUAL BLOCKING. See BLOCK AND OTHER RAILWAY SIGNAL SYSTEMS.

MANUEL I, king of Portugal. See EMANUEL THE GREAT.

MANUEL II, king of Portugal: b. Lisbon, Nov. 15, 1889; d. Twickenham, England, July 2, 1932. He was the second son of Carlos I, and in boyhood, when he was known as the Duke of Beja, he was trained for a naval career. On Feb. 1, 1908, his father and his elder brother, Louis, were assassinated in the streets of Lisbon and Manuel, then 18 years of age, was called to the throne. He inherited a burden of unpopularity with which his training had not fitted him to cope, and republican victories at elections in Lisbon and Oporto were followed in October 1910 by a naval revolt which forced the young king to flee the country. By way of Gibraltar he made his way to England after a reign of only 32 months, and the remainder of his life was spent in exile. While he never officially abdicated, he took no action to regain his throne. A man of great wealth, he led the life of a cultured country gentleman, among his books, his artistic pictures, and his sporting interests. He possessed a collection of early Portuguese books said to have no rival outside of the British Museum. In 1913 he married Augusta Victoria, daughter of Prince William of Hohenzollern; there was no issue. His body was returned to Portugal in August 1932 for burial in Lisbon's Pantheon, where funeral services were attended by the president of the Portuguese republic; he bequeathed his entire Portuguese estate to the government.

MANUEL, mä-nwĕl', DON **Juan,** Spanish prince and writer: b. Escalona, Spain, May 5, 1282; d. 1349. He was a nephew of Alfonso X and cousin of Sancho IV. During the minority (1320–1325) of Alfonso XI he served as a coregent, and he also commanded a Spanish army fighting the Moors. His chief claim to remembrance, however, is as a writer of prose works notable for singular simplicity and charm. The finest of these was *Libro de Patronio,* more commonly known as *El Conde Lucanor,* a collection of tales written in a high moral tone.

MANUEL I COMNENUS, măn′ū-ĕl kŏm-nē′nŭs, Byzantine emperor: b. 1120?; d. Sept. 24, 1180; r. 1143–1180. The valor he had displayed against the Seljuk Turks induced his father John II Comnenus to bequeath the crown to him rather than to his elder brother Isaac, who Axuch, the deceased emperor's minister, imprisoned. A valiant knight and admirer of Western chivalry rather than a great general, Manuel was involved in wars both in the East and the West which lasted with brief intermissions throughout his reign. In 1145 he subjected Raymund, the rebellious prince of Antioch. During 1146–1147 he fought against Mas'ud, sultan of the Seljuk Turks, with no great measure of success, though he reached the enemy's capital, Iconium (Konya). In 1147 he allowed the armies of the Second Crusade, led by Conrad

III of Germany and Louis VII of France, to reach Constantinople and pass through Byzantine territory. The tension which resulted, together with the crusade's failure, upset the previous Byzantine policy of alliance with Germany against the growing danger of the Normans who, also in 1147, suddenly seized Corfu, devastated several Greek islands, and captured Thebes and Corinth.

In alliance with Venice, Manuel recaptured Corfu in 1149 but hostilities with the Serbians and Hungarians, instigated by Roger II, the Norman King of Sicily, prevented him from invading that island and kept him occupied with the Hungarians as late as 1152.

After Roger's death in 1154, Manuel's armies landed in southern Italy and seized Bari but Roger's successor, William I, defeated them at Brundisium (Brindisi) and took Negropont in Euboea and Halmyrus in Thessaly in 1157. The following year Manuel signed a peace pact with William and also repressed a rebellion of the Armenians in Cilicia. His Western policy of seeking to restore the unity of the empire led him to support the pope and the Italian cities against the German emperor Frederick Barbarossa and earned him Frederick's enmity.

The subsequent years of Manuel's reign were marked by a new war with the Hungarians who were defeated near present Semlin in 1168; by the complete severance of relations with Venice (1167) followed by the arrest of all Venetians on Byzantine territory and the confiscation of their property (1171); and, finally, by war against the Seljuk sultan, Kilij Arslan II, Mas'ud's successor, in the hands of whom Manuel experienced a terrible defeat at Myriocephalon, in the mountains of Phrygia, in 1176. From this battle, which historians regard as a death blow to the Comnenian era, Manuel never really recovered, even though the peace terms that followed were not dishonorable. His many military campaigns weakened the empire financially and his failure to stem the Moslems led to its ultimate collapse.

He was succeeded by Alexius II Comnenus.

MANUEL II PALAEOLOGUS, pā-lē-ŏl′ō-gŭs, Byzantine emperor: b. 1350; d. 1425. When his father John V Palaeologus died in 1391, Manuel, a hostage of the Ottoman sultan, Bajazet I, at Brusa, escaped to Constantinople and ascended the throne. But for a period of coregency with John VII Palaeologus from 1398 to 1412, he reigned as sole emperor until the year of his death. Blockaded by Bajazet in Constantinople until 1395, he enjoyed a brief respite when the Ottoman Turks were diverted from their siege by the crusade of Hungarians, Germans, and French under Sigismund, king of Hungary. However, after the crusaders' defeat at Nicopolis (Nikopol) in 1396, a second Ottoman siege of Constantinople started. Seeking help from the West and a union between the Greek and the Roman churches, Manuel made a journey to Italy, Germany, and England between 1399 and 1403, but failed in his efforts. His capital, this time, was saved by the advance into Asia Minor of the Tatars under Tamerlane (Timur) who defeated Bajazet at Angora (Ankara) in 1402. Although with Bajazet's successor, Mohammed I, Manuel remained at peace, this was not so with Murad II, Mohammed's successor, who set siege to Constantinople in 1422 and compelled the Byzantine emperor to pay tribute.

Manuel was a prolific writer, composing poetry

and writing books on rhetoric and theology. He was succeeded by John VIII Palaeologus.

MANURES AND MANURING. See FERTILIZER.

MANUS, mā'nŭs, largest of the Admiralty Islands, in the southwest Pacific, a group comprised within the Australian-administered Territory of New Guinea. It is situated 160 miles west of Lavongai, in the Bismarck Archipelago; it is 52 miles long by 13 miles broad, and has an area of 650 square miles. The island is densely wooded and mountainous, the highest elevations approximating 3,000 feet. Lorengau, at the northeastern end of the island, is the chief port and administrative headquarters. Manus contains numerous coconut plantations, and off the coasts lie valuable trochus and pearl shell fisheries. During World War II the United States constructed an extensive naval base on Manus, harnessing the Lorengau River to secure hydroelectric power and building a bridge across Loniu Passage to the neighboring island of Los Negros. Manus was discovered in 1616 by Willem Cornelis Schouten (q.v.), visited by Antoine Raymond Joseph de Bruni the chevalier d'Entrecasteaux (q.v.) in 1791, and surveyed by the *Challenger* Expedition (q.v.) in 1875. It was agreed between the governments of Australia and the United States after World War II that the naval forces of both powers would have the use of the Manus base.

MANUSCRIPTS, măn'ŭ-skrĭpts (Lat. *manu scriptus,* written by the hand), literally writing of any kind, whether on paper or any other material, in contradistinction to printed matter. Previous to the introduction of printing all literature was contained in manuscripts. All the existing ancient manuscripts are written on parchment or on paper. The paper is sometimes Egyptian (prepared from the real papyrus reed), sometimes cotton or silk paper (*charta bombycina*), which was invented in the East about the year 706 A.D., and was used until the introduction of linen paper, and in common with this until the middle of the 14th century; sometimes linen paper, the date of the invention of which, though ascribed to the first half of the 13th century, on the authority of a document of the year 1243, written on such paper, is nevertheless exceedingly doubtful.

The earliest mention of quill pens is in the 7th century. The most common ink is the black and the oldest ink generally consisted of soot, lampblack, burned ivory, pulverized charcoal. Red ink of a dazzling beauty is also found in manuscripts of ancient times. With it were written the initial letters, the first lines, and the titles, which were thence called *rubrics,* and the writer *rubricator.* More rarely, but still quite frequently, blue ink is found in ancient manuscripts; yet more rarely green and yellow. Gold and silver were also used for writing either whole manuscripts (which, from their costliness, are great rarities), or for adorning the initial letters of books. With respect to external form, manuscripts are divided into rolls (*volumina,* the most ancient way, in which the troubadours in France wrote their poems at a much later period), and into stitched books or volumes (properly *codices*).

Among the ancients the writers of manuscripts were mainly freedmen or slaves (*scribae librarii*). Some of the professional copyists in Rome were women. When Origen undertook the revision of the Old Testament (231 A.D.), St. Ambrose sent to his assistance a number of deacons and virgins skillful in calligraphy. Subsequently the monks, among them the Benedictines in particular, were bound to this employment by the rules of their order. In all the principal monasteries was a *scriptorium,* in which the *scriptor* or scribe could pursue his work in quiet, generally assisted by a *dictator,* who read aloud the text to be copied; the manuscript was then revised by a *corrector,* and afterward handed to the *miniator,* who added the ornamental capitals and artistic designs.

It is more difficult to form a correct judgment respecting the age of Greek manuscripts from the character of the writing than it is respecting that of Latin manuscripts. In general it is to be remarked that in a Greek manuscript the strokes are lighter, easier, and more flowing the older it is, and that they become stiffer in the progress of time. The absence or presence of the Greek accents is in no respect decisive. Some Greek papyri are earlier than the Christian era, but most are not earlier than about the 6th century. The characters in Latin manuscripts have been classified partly according to their size (majuscule or minuscule); partly according to the various shapes and characters which they assumed among different nations or in various periods (*romana antiqua,* Merovingian, Lombardic, Carolingian, to which has been added since the 12th century the Gothic, so called, which is an artificially pointed and angular character); and for all of those species of writing particular rules have been established, affording the means of estimating the age of a manuscript. Before the 8th century punctuation marks rarely occur; even after the introduction of punctuation, manuscripts may be met with destitute of points, but with the words separate. Manuscripts which have no capital or other divisions are always old. The catchword, as it is termed, or the repetition of the first word of the following page at the end of the preceding, belongs to the 12th or subsequent centuries. The fewer and easier the abbreviations of a manuscript are the older it is.

Finally, in the oldest manuscripts the words commonly join each other without break or separation. The division of words first became general in the 9th century. The form of the Arabic ciphers, which are seldom found in manuscripts earlier than the first half of the 13th century, also assists in deciding the age of a manuscript. Some manuscripts have at the end a statement when, and commonly also by whom, they were written (dated codices).

The most ancient manuscripts still preserved are those written on papyrus which have been found in Egyptian tombs. Next to them in point of age are the Latin manuscripts found at Herculaneum, of which there is a rich collection in the National Museum of Naples. Then there are the manuscripts of the imperial era, among which are the *Vatican Terence* and *Septuagint* and the Biblical codices in the British Museum. From the middle of the 19th century many manuscripts of Greek writings have been found in Egypt.

It was the custom in the Middle Ages to obliterate and erase writings on parchment for the purpose of writing on the materials anew, and these manuscripts, many of them of great value, are known as palimpsests. See also BOOK—*The Medieval Manuscript;* CODEX; ILLUMINATED MANUSCRIPTS; PALEOGRAPHY; PALIMPSEST; PAPYRUS; PARCHMENT; WRITING.

MANUTIUS, mȧ-nū'shĭ-ŭs (Ital. MANUZIO, MANUCCI), the Latin name of a family of Italian printers who set up and operated the Aldine press (q.v.).

ALDUS MANUTIUS (Aldo Manuzio): b. Bassiano, Velletri, Italy, 1450; d. Venice, Feb. 6, 1515. He first studied at Rome and then at Ferrara where he learned Greek under Battista Guarini. After a stay with the humanist Giovanni Pico Della Mirandola at Mirandola, he settled in Venice in 1490 and, with the support of Alberto Pio, prince of Carpi, set up a printing press there. The printer of many Greek and Latin classics as well as of works by Italian writers, he was the author of prefaces to these publications as well as of books such as *Vita di Ovidio* (1502) and *De metrorum generibus* (1509).

ALDUS MANUTIUS (Aldo Manuzio): grandson of the first Aldus: b. Venice, Feb. 13, 1547; d. Rome, Oct. 28, 1597. At the age of 14 he published *Orthographica Ratio,* a book on Latin spelling. Among his later publications was a commentary on the *Ars poetica* of Horace (1576). Although a scholar of ability, as a typographer he was less remarkable than the other members of his family. In 1590 he was entrusted by Pope Clement VIII with the direction of the papal press, a post he held until his death. None of his children continued the Aldine press.

MANX CAT. See CAT, DOMESTIC.

MANX LANGUAGE. See CELTIC LANGUAGES.

MANX LITERATURE. See CELTIC LITERATURES.

MANZANILLO, män-sä-nē'yō, city, Cuba, and port of entry in the western part of Oriente Province, on the Gulf of Guacanayabo. It has a large harbor which is protected by smaller islands and is a trading center for the area, the chief products of which are coffee, fruit, sugar, and hardwoods. Pop. (1961) 50,900.

MANZANO MOUNTAINS, a range on the east side of the Rio Grande Valley in Bernalillo, Torrance and Valencia counties southeast of Albuquerque, N. Mex. It extends from Tijeras Canyon on the north to Abo Pass on the south, a distance of 45 miles. The highest summits are Manzano Peak, 10,103 feet; Osha Peak, 10,023 feet, and Mosca Peak, 9,723 feet, which are about 5,000 feet above the Rio Grande. To the east is the Estancia Valley, long famous for its salt lakes. Near Bosque Peak is a large spring. The region is forested with yellow pine, piñon and juniper, and is included in the Manzano Forest Reserve. Deer, bear and wild turkeys and many minor wild animals remain in these mountains. Gold, lead and silver are mined on the west slope. Most of the long canyons on the eastern slope contain streams from large springs.

MANZONI, män-dzō'nĕ, **Alessandro (Francesco Tommaso Antonio),** Italian poet and novelist: b. Milan, March 7, 1785; d. there, May 22, 1873. He studied at Milan and Pavia, and published in 1806 his poem on the death of his friend Carlo Imbonati, which was followed in 1815 by his *Sacred Hymns (Inni Sacri).* In 1820 appeared his first tragedy, *Il Conte di Carmagnola,* the first drama in which an Italian defied the

unities. This play was reviewed and praised by Goethe, who took a warm interest in every subsequent production of Manzoni. The death of Napoleon inspired one of the finest odes of the century, *Il Cinque Maggio (The Fifth of May).* In 1822 his second tragedy, *Adelchi,* appeared. This, as well as its predecessor, finds more favor in personal reading than on the stage. After this Manzoni divided his time between country pursuits at his residence in the neighborhood of Milan and the composition of his romance *I Promessi Sposi (The Betrothed),* a Milanese story of the 17th century, published 1825–1827, and which has been translated into most of the European languages (see ITALY—*Literature*). Manzoni was devoted to the ideals of Italian independence and unification, participating, with his sons, in the Milanese revolt of 1848, and declining all honors from the Austrians; he became a senator of the Italian kingdom, however, in 1860. His *I Promessi Sposi* is regarded as a model of Italian prose, and its influence, when revised (1840) in the Tuscan dialect, had an important bearing on the establishment of Tuscan as the official form of the Italian language—a development which he warmly supported. Verdi's *Manzoni Requiem* (1874) is a magnificent musical tribute to his memory.

MAO TSE-TUNG, mou dzǝ-dŏong, Chinese Communist leader: b. Shaoshan, Hunan province, Dec. 26, 1893. The son of a small farmer and a peasant woman, he was born in a village 30 miles west of Hsiangtan. His ancestors, as far back as can be traced, were Hunan peasants. His father was a choleric man who liked to keep his family of three sons and one daughter in order by quoting Confucian texts and punishing them regularly; his mother was a kindly woman devoted to Buddhism.

At the age of five Mao was set to work in the fields. At seven he was spending part of the day learning to read and write, and was beginning to read the novels *Monkey, All Men are Brothers,* and *The Romance of the Three Kingdoms,* which were to influence his life and thought profoundly. These novels are essentially accounts of heroic rebellions against authority, and by the age of 11 or 12 he was beginning to conduct spasmodic revolts against his father. At 14 he was married, and in the same year he abandoned his wife and went off to the Tungshan primary school at Hsianghsiang, his mother's native town.

He was an impressive student at the primary school, where he was noted for the wide range of his reading and the elegance of his essays. He entered the Teachers' Training School at Changsha in 1913 and did equally well. Here he paid particular attention to the brilliant classical essays of the 8th century philosopher Han Yü, who was ironical and cynical, somewhat in the manner of Jonathan Swift. With the discovery of Han Yü, whose style he continued to imitate, Mao's intellectual groundwork was complete.

Changsha stands at the crossroads of China, and inevitably Mao found himself caught up in the turmoil following the revolution of 1911 and the downfall of the Manchus. Those were years of famine and civil war, which he watched at close quarters. His instincts were scholarly, and, except for leading a group of students to Peking, where they hoped to take ship for France to learn Western ways, he was indistinguishable from thousands of other quietly contemplative students with little prospect of a successful career. For a brief period in the winter of 1911 he had joined the revolutionary army, but that unhappy adventure had long since been forgotten. In the fall of 1918 he was an underpaid clerk in the library of Peking University. It was an ideal occupation, for it gave him time to read and study (at this time he was chiefly interested in anarchism). Here, too, he met Ch'en Tu-hsiu, Chang Kuo-t'ao, and Li Ta-chao, who were impressed by the Russian Revolution and discussing the prospects of a Communist revolution in China. In 1921, Mao attended the first Congress of the Chinese Communist party, which was held in Shanghai.

Thereafter his fortunes were linked with the party, in which he gradually rose to a position of prominence and prestige. His chief interest, however, lay in the peasant movement in Hunan, where he set up local Communist organizations and study circles. In 1925, when the boundaries between the Communists and the Kuomintang were not yet fixed, he became the secretary of the propaganda department of the Kuomintang in Canton and the editor of the *Political Weekly,* the secret bulletin issued to high party members. As the split between the parties widened, he abandoned his role as alternate member of the Kuomintang central executive committee and became head of the peasant department of the Chinese Communist party, with headquarters in Shanghai. In January 1927, after a brief visit to Hunan, he wrote *A Report of an Investigation into the Peasant Movement of Hunan,* a vivid and powerful plea for an immediate peasant insurrection. There is nothing essentially Marxist in the report; the traditional anarchism of the Hunan peasants was allied to a violent revolutionary temper.

In the autumn of the same year Mao led the Autumn Harvest Uprising in Hunan and Kiangsi, aimed at the capture of Changsha. With this uprising the Chinese Red Army came into existence, only to be crushed by local Kuomintang forces. Scattered remnants of the army made their way to Chingkanshan, in the mountainous area between Hunan and Kiangsi. In this impregnable fastness, hidden in the winter mists, the real story of the Chinese Communist conquest of China begins.

When Chu Teh (q.v.) joined Mao on Chingkanshan in the spring of 1928, there was forged a duumvirate that would dominate the Chinese Communist party for 20 years. Both Chu and Mao were gifted strategists with an intimate knowledge of peasant life, and both were capable of extraordinary daring. The Red armies survived four successive annihilation campaigns, growing stronger with each campaign. Their intention was to capture Changsha, which in July 1930 was held for a few hours by P'eng Teh-huei, one of Mao's comrades who rose to become secretary of defense in the 1950's, but many years passed before they were in a position to capture any large industrial town. In October 1934, fearing that a fifth annihilation campaign might prove disastrous, the Red Army broke through the Kuomintang blockade and began the Long March through Southwest China and by way of the unexplored hinterland to Shensi, where they arrived exactly 12 months later. With the success of this legendary march, during which Mao was elected chairman of the Chinese

Mao Tse-tung

Communist party, the prestige of the Chinese Communists increased, even though they were never able to establish soviets along the line of the march. From their new capital in Yenan Chu Teh and Mao continued to dominate Chinese Communist strategies, their armies growing larger and their influence spreading out of all proportion to their effective means. Though surrounded by a tight censorship and receiving little or no aid from Russia, they were already a dominant force capable, under favorable circumstances, of wresting power from the national government.

Yenan became the training ground for resourceful experiments in guerrilla warfare, first against the Japanese and then against the Kuomintang. The theoretical justification for Chinese Communist actions was provided by Mao in a series of speeches, essays, and handbooks written in a style at once hard-hitting, elegant, and authoritative. The most important of these—*Strategic Problems of China's Revolutionary Wars, On the Protracted War,* and *The New Democracy*—were directed as much against the Kuomintang as against the Japanese invaders. He also composed a collection of poems called *Wind Sand Poems,* never officially published, though a few of the poems were widely known and most of them were published many years later.

With the end of World War II, when efforts were made by the Allies to bring about a truce between the Kuomintang and the Chinese Communists, Mao paid a prolonged visit to Chungking, the capital of the Nationalist government. The conferences, outwardly friendly, proved to be abortive, although Mao and Chiang Kai-shek (q.v.) signed what appeared to be an agreement in principle in October 1945. The long-awaited civil war had already begun; it was to smolder through the two following years, and with the fall of Peking in January 1949 the Chinese Communist Army was poised for a massive onslaught on the rest of mainland China. By October most of mainland China had been conquered, and Mao became the first chairman of the People's Republic of China and the undisputed ruler of the country.

Thereafter his history becomes inseparable from the history of the Chinese mainland. While Chu Teh fell into gradual oblivion, Mao became the sole ruler, the fountain of all power, the artificer of all social changes, "the sun in the east." With all the resources of propaganda at his disposal, he was able to exert an extraordinary influence on his countrymen. He succeeded against opposition in instituting a communal system that abruptly changed the social organization of the peasantry, but his short-lived campaign for open criticism ("Let the Hundred Flowers blossom") came to an end when he realized that the criticism was largely directed against his dictatorship. In the mid-1960's he was thought to be ailing and in semiretirement, but he suddenly emerged in the spring of 1966 as the leader and instigator of the "Red Guards," who swept across China proclaiming his doctrines. The Red Guard movement, with its emphasis on youth and an elementary form of communal life, was also fostered by Mao's fourth wife, Chiang Ch'ing, a former movie actress, who by 1968 had risen to a position of high rank among Communist China's leaders. The Red Guards have injected a new excitement into a regime oppressed by the inevitable Communist bureaucracy, but it is uncertain whether the experiment can be continued indefinitely.

A brilliant strategist, profoundly nationalist and ignorant of the rest of the world, more an anarchist than a Communist, half scholar, half warrior, Mao succeeded in shaping China according to his will as no emperor had ever done. He was the greatest of the Chinese tyrants, and the most enduring.

ROBERT PAYNE, *Author of "Mao Tse-tung"*

Bibliography.—Payne, Robert, *Mao Tse-tung*, rev. ed. (New York 1969); Siao-Yu, *Mao Tse-tung and I Were Beggars* (Syracuse, N.Y., 1959); Snow, Edgar, *Red Star Over China*, rev. and enl. ed. (New York 1968).

MAORIS, mä′ȯ-rĭz, mou′rĭz, or mä′rĭz, a Polynesian people inhabiting New Zealand. Their traditional clothing is a loose garment woven from *harakeke* (New Zealand flax, *Phormium tenax*). Tattooing is a highly developed art among them. They formerly tattooed the faces of a young warrior after his first successful combat, adding fresh designs for each new exploit. Their religion combined ancestral cult with deification of natural forces; they held that the soul was distinct from the body, and survived it. *Tapu* (taboo) was a strong force. Social organization, founded on kinship through common descent, is evidently a remnant of the waves of immigration, the most important of which was the "fleet" of about 1350 A.D. The largest unit is the *waka* (canoe), a loose affiliation of *iwi* (tribes), which are subdivided into *hapu* (clans), and these into *whanau* (family groups). The villages (*kainga*) are usually built around a central meeting place (*marae*), and were usually situated near a fort (*pa*) for defense. Before the coming of Europeans, they lived mainly on agricultural products (particularly the *kumara,* sweet potato), other roots, and fish. See also NEW ZEALAND.

MAP, măp (Latinized as MAPES, mā′pēz), **Walter,** Welsh author and wit: b. probably in Herefordshire, England, about 1140; d. about 1209. He studied at the University of Paris, became a favorite at the court of Henry II, and attended the third Lateran Council in Rome in 1179. He was appointed archdeacon of Oxford in 1197. Map's fame rests chiefly on the tradition, accepted in the Middle Ages, that he was the author (or part author) of the prose romance *Lancelot du Lac,* but that belief has been largely rejected by modern scholarship. His reputed authorship of some well-known goliardic poems (see GOLIARD) is likewise questionable. Curiously, one work which definitely is credited to him es-

caped the notice of medieval scholars: the satirical collection *De nugis curialium* (Courtiers' Trifles), consisting of pieces of folklore, historical tales, and anecdotes, written between 1181 and 1193. The work was published in English in 1924.

MAP. The word derives from the Latin *mappa* meaning napkin, cloth, sheet (just as we speak now of topographic "sheets"). A map is a symbolized picture of the earth pattern drawn to scale on a horizontal projection, to which lettering usually is added for identification. Abstraction and symbolization often go far from the original conception of a picture, as for instance on a political map.

Scale.—Every map is on a definite size relationship with the part of the land it represents, which can be expressed in three different ways:

(1) Numerical scale, or representative fraction, as 1:1,000,000, meaning that one inch on a map represents 1,000,000 inches in nature, or nearly 16 miles.

(2) Inch to mile scale, as 1 inch to 8 miles (1:506,880), meaning that one inch on the map represent 8 miles in nature.

(3) Graphic scale, as $\overset{0}{\rule{0pt}{0pt}}\!\!\underset{}{\rule{1.5cm}{0.4pt}}\!\overset{}{\underset{}{\rule{1.5cm}{0.4pt}}}\!\overset{10}{\rule{0pt}{0pt}}$ miles, which has the advantage that it remains true even if the map is photographed larger or smaller.

Enlarging and Reducing Maps.—Changing the scale of maps can be accomplished by:

(a) The quadrangle method, by drawing closely set nets of parallels and meridians both on the original map and for the new drawing on larger or smaller scale. All features are filled in by hand. This method is especially good if the projection system is also changed.

(b) Photostat or photograph, which, however, often shows some distortion.

(c) Pantograph, which instrument is based on a parallelogram with free-moving angles and can enlarge or reduce drawings with great precision.

(d) By various arrangements of lenses, mirrors, or prisms an enlarged or reduced image can be projected upon the drawing paper.

Maps on a scale of 1:1,000,000 and smaller are called *small-scale* maps; *large-scale* maps are over 1:100,000; in between are *medium-scale* maps.

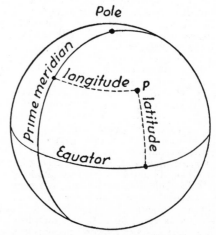

Fig. 1.—Latitude and longitude.

MAP   253

Parallels and Meridians.—The ancient Greeks established a co-ordinate system dividing the arc between the equator and the poles into 90° in parallel circles which get smaller nearer the equator. Similarly the equator is divided into 360 parts and through the division points and the two poles are 180 semicircles or meridians. Distance from the equator measured along a meridian and expressed in degrees (minutes and seconds) is called *latitude*. Distance in degrees reckoned from a chosen *prime meridian* measured along a parallel is called *longitude*. While all degrees of latitude are equally long (about 69 miles), degrees of longitude vary from 69.17 miles at the equator to 0 at the pole. For any degree

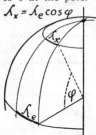

Fig. 2.—Longitude varies with the cosine of the latitude. λ_x=longitude on any parallel. λ_e=longitude on the equator. ϕ=latitude.

of longitude where ϕ is the latitude, for instance 1° of longitude at lat. 60° is one half of 1° long. at the equator, cos 60° being 0.5.

In all these considerations the Earth is regarded as a perfect sphere. As the exact form of the Earth is more nearly a rotational ellipsoid, the degrees of latitude are slightly smaller near the equator, 68.7 miles, and larger near the poles, 69.2 miles. Prime meridians changed a great deal during history from the Fortunate Islands of Ptolemy to Ferro in the Canary Islands. Even Washington, Philadelphia, Boston, and Hartford were used as prime meridians. By international agreement, at present the meridian at the Royal Observatory in Greenwich, England, is used for prime meridian.

Most maps are oriented with north on top, but this is conventional. Other orientations are often used at present to bring out hidden relationships.

Projections.—The spherical surface of a globe cannot be flattened into a map without stretching or tearing. If only a small part of the Earth's surface is shown, as on large-scale maps, distortion is negligible, but on medium-scale maps, and especially small-scale maps of the whole Earth, considerable distortion is necessary.

Several geometrical methods were tried. If the globe is enveloped into a cylinder and the surface is projected upon this surface and then the cylinder is cut open and laid out flat, we have a *cylindrical projection*. Similarly, if we cap the globe with a conical band, project upon the cone, split open the cone along one of its elements and lay it out flat, we have a *conical projection*. Also, if the surface of the globe is projected upon a tangent board from some eye point at a selected distance, we have an *azimuthal projection*.

These projections are derived from actual perspective projection from a point or points upon a surface. Except for a few azimuthal projections, however, no perspective projections are in actual use. Most of them are simply some kind of network of parallels and meridians to suit the map maker's purpose. A map projection can be defined as *any orderly network of parallels and meridians upon which a map can be drawn.*

As the problem of flattening spherical surfaces is impossible, there can be no perfect projection. We can choose from dozens of imperfect solutions the one which is most suitable for our particular purpose. Some projections have special merits. *Equal-area* or *equivalent* projections are those in which every part of the map, and the map as a whole, has the same area as the corresponding part of the Earth's surface. To achieve this, shapes and angles have to be considerably distorted. *Conformal* or *orthomorphic* projections are those in which every small portion has the same shape as the corresponding part on the globe. Not only are the parallels and meridians right angles to each other, but they have also the correct proportions. To achieve this, the scale of the map has to vary a great deal. Some projections are not equal-area nor conformal but have small scale errors.

It is obvious from the foregoing that on any map only the parallels or only the meridians or certain other lines can be true to scale; all other distances are distorted. Which lines are selected to be *true to scale,* that is the same scale as on the corresponding globe, is the fundamental consideration in projections. Several hundred projections occur but only a few selected projections are presented here.

Rectangular Even-spaced Projection.—This is the simplest of projections, consisting of even-spaced horizontal parallels and vertical even-spaced meridians. Meridians are spaced on the central parallel of the map according to

$$\lambda_x = \lambda_e \cos \phi \text{ (see Fig. 2).}$$

Mercator Projection.—The equator is divided truly for vertical meridians. Parallels are horizontal, spaced conformally; that is, their relation

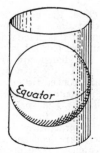
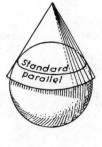
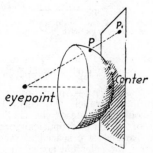

Fig. 3.—Cylindrical, conical and azimuthal projections.

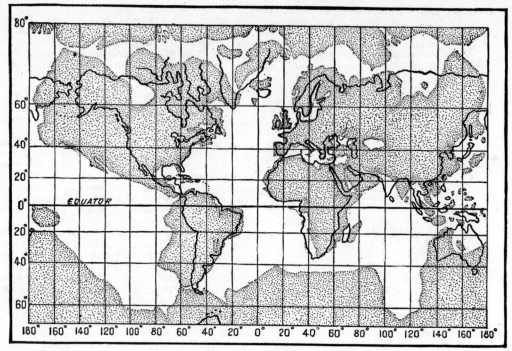

FIG. 4.—Mercator's projection from his World Map of 1569. Mercator's delineation of the land is dotted.

to the meridian is the same as on the globe. On the globe the meridians converge, but in this projection they are parallel. To get the correct proportion, the parallels are spaced at increasing distances toward the poles. The poles are at infinite distance.

The chief merit of the projection is that compass directions, or rhumb lines, appear as straight lines. (On the surface of the globe they spiral towards the poles.) For this reason the projection is ideal for navigation, in spite of the enormous variation of scale. It is less good for world maps for which it is frequently used. The pro-

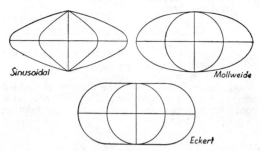

FIG. 5.—Outlines of the world and the hemisphere in various projections with horizontal parallels.

jection was delineated by Gerardus Mercator, the great Belgian cartographer, in 1569 (see Fig. 4).

Other Projections.—Among other projections with horizontal parallels and vertical meridians, mention should be made of the Gall's projection and also of Miller's cylindrical projection, in which the parallels are spaced at increasing distances nearer the poles but not so much as in the Mercator projection.

The *sinusoidal* and the *Mollweide,* or *homolographic,* projections have both horizontal parallels but the meridians converge toward the poles. Both projections are equal-area. The *Eckert* projection is similar, but the poles are represented as lines half the length of the equator. All these projections are popular for world maps and continent maps.

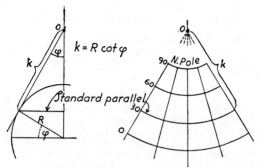

FIG. 6.—Construction of the conic projection.

In the *conic* projection, the globe is capped by a cone which touches it along a selected standard parallel. The radius of this standard parallel is $1 = R \cot \phi$. The standard parallel is obviously divided truly; the meridians are radiating straight lines, placed truly on the standard parallel, and the parallels are concentric circles. For best results usually the central parallel of the map is taken as standard. The spacing of the parallels would be uneven in the actually projected network. In the practically used conic projection, the parallels are concentric circles placed at their true distances. The projection is used for country and continent maps in the tem-

MAP   255

perate zones on account of its small scale error. The scale error is further reduced in the *conic projection with two standard parallels.* On a map of the United States the maximum scale error would not exceed 1.25 per cent.

By different spacing of the parallels, this projection can be made equal-area. The *Albers conical equal-area* projection is adopted as the best projection for the country by the United States Geological Survey. By spacing the parallels differently, the projection can be made conformal. The *Lambert conformal conic* projection has relatively straight azimuths for which it is generally used for air navigation charts.

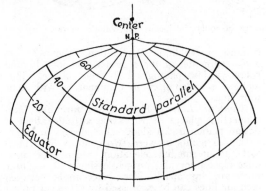

Fig. 7.—Bonne projection of the half-hemisphere centered on lat. 40° N.

The *Bonne* projection is similar to the simple conic, except that not only the standard parallel, but all parallels are divided truly, which makes the meridians curved and the projection equal-area. It is a popular all-around projection, used for all scales, from world maps to topographic sheets.

The *polyconic* projection has a truly divided vertical central meridian. The parallels are non-concentric circles, each with a radius $1 = R \cot \phi$, as if each would derive from a tangent cone. Each parallel is divided truly, the connecting lines form the meridians. The United States Geological Survey topographic sheets are on this projection.

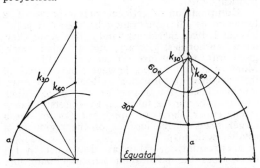

Fig. 8.—Construction of the polyconic projection.

The *azimuthal* projections derive from projecting a part of the earth's surface upon a plane surface from an eye point. The plane can be tangent at the pole, at the equator, or any other point, and all three views—polar, equatorial, and oblique—are often used.

In the *gnomonic* projection the eye point is in the center of the sphere. The projection has extreme distortions of size and shape, but it shows

all great circles as straight lines, for which it is used for laying out transoceanic sailing and flying routes. The meridians are straight lines; the parallels are hyperbolas.

Fig. 9.—Stereographic projection of the hemisphere in oblique view.

In the *stereographic* projection the eye point is at the antipodal point of the center of the map. The projection has the interesting property that not only all parallels and meridians, but also all other circular lines of the globe appear as circles on the map too. It is a conformal projection, but it is not much used on account of its considerable distortion of scale.

The eye point of the *orthographic* projection is in the infinite; the rays are parallel. The parallels and the meridians are elipses, ranging from a straight line to a circle. The great merit of this projection is its visual quality—it looks like a globe. Although the distortion on the sides of the man is enormous, we see everything in correct proportion because we perceive not a map but a picture of a three-dimensional globe. For this reason it became very popular for so-called «global» maps.

Two azimuthal projections do not derive from direct perspective methods. The *azimuthal equidistant* projection is the only one in which every point is shown, not only the correct distance, but also in correct direction (azimuth) from the center point. All other distances and directions, however, are distorted. The *Lambert azimuthal equal-area* projection is very good for hemispheres and for continent maps.

Besides these, a number of interrupted, star-formed, and other projections are used. Among these the butterfly projection of B. T. S. Cahill is particularly attractive. Another interesting group of projections derives from the oblique, or transversal development of the cylindrical and related projections. The transverse Mercator projection is particularly interesting and used for the new maps of the British Ordnance Survey.

Symbols.—As all geographic information of the map is given with the help of symbols, a good symbol is one which can be recognized without a legend, yet is simple, distinct, and does not take up more space than its importance allows. Lines, patterns, and colors can all be used. Symbols are different on small-scale maps and on large-scale maps, and it makes a great deal of difference whether colors can be used or not.

Standardization of symbols is necessary by government agencies. Private cartographers, not hampered by such regulations, are in a position

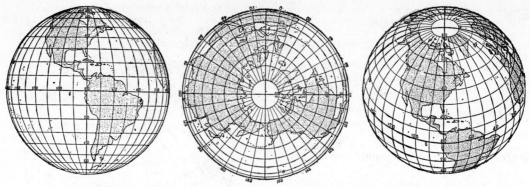

Fig. 10.—Orthographic projection of the hemisphere in equatorial, polar, and oblique views.

to design new and better symbols. Airplane photography presents a rich pattern of the earth's surface which our present symbols are not quite able to express, and a major change is expected in the appearance of maps in the future.

If colors can be used, the conventional color of *hydrography* (water features) is blue; for *hypsography* (relief features, such as hills and mountains) brown; and for *culture* or man-made features, black and red. Vegetation is usually shown with green symbols.

Relief Features.—The representation of mountains is a particularly difficult problem of cartography, essentially because we represent the mountains on maps as seen from above, while our familiar conception of mountains is as they look from below. Several methods are in use.

Hachuring.—This is the older type of representation of relief, and is usually applied to black-and-white maps. Slopes are shown by lines of variable thickness running along the «dip» of the slope, the way water would run upon that surface. The steeper the slope, the thicker the line. The method was systematized by F. G. Lehmann, a Saxonian officer in Napoleon's army.

Plastic Shading.—This method requires reproduction by half-tone method, which limits its use. Two methods are used. In «vertical illumination» the steeper the slope, the darker the tone (as in hachuring). This method is used by the topographic sheets of Norway. Much more

common is «oblique illumination,» somewhat as a plaster model of the region would look lighted sideways but photographed from above. This method is often used in combination with contour lines.

Contour Lines.—These are continuous lines connecting places of the same altitude above a datum plane, drawn along selected regular intervals. All points between two contour lines have to be at intermediate elevation. Steep slopes produce close intervals; on gentle slopes the contour lines are far apart. The exact angle between contour lines can be expressed by «feet per mile,» or graphically by «profiles.» All contour lines are horizontal and perpendicular to hachure lines. The contour interval varies with the scale of the map and the ruggedness of the land. The 1:62,000 topographic sheets of the United States have 20-foot intervals in hilly country. The datum plane is mean sea level.

Lettering.—Letters obscure by their bulk much topographic detail on maps, and they are kept as small and fine as legibility will permit. If letters are applied to an area, they are spread so as to indicate the trend or extent of the area. Letters are sometimes hand-drawn, but stamped, pasted, or templeted letters are also common. Most United States maps have «slanted» letters for hydrography, «block» or «gothic» letters for relief features, and «Roman» letters for political units.

Composition.—Sectional maps—parts of a larger map—fill a quadrangle between two parallels and two meridians, and title, scale, key, name, authorities, glossary, and all other «marginal information» are set up outside the map. Maps of a unit region, however, have often all this pertinent information collected in a «cartouche» inside the frame of the map. Much empty space can be taken up by «insets.» These insets either show an important portion on a larger scale, or the location of the region on a smaller-scale map.

Reproduction.—Maps are drawn usually 1½ to 3 times the publication size to obtain finer detail. The most common method of reproduction is by offset planography. Only if the map has to be printed together with type is it reproduced by photoengraving (q.v.). Color maps are usually printed from separate color plates drawn on separate papers. Maps reproduced in four-color process are also common. (See Lithography.)

Charts.—Marine charts for navigation differ from land maps chiefly by their emphasis on the sea. They show submarine contours, usually ob-

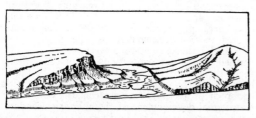

Fig. 11.—Topographical features expressed by contour lines. After the U.S. Geol. Survey.

MAP   257

tained by sounding. Almost all charts are on the Mercator projection. The datum plane is usually a low-water level for sounding, and a high-water level for land features. Charting has been greatly helped by the sonic depth finder instruments and from radar, which helps to locate exactly the point of the surveying vessel. The charts of coasts of the United States and territories are surveyed and prepared by the United States Coast and Geodetic Survey, while those of foreign waters are published by the United States Hydrographic Office (qq.v.). See also article on CHART.

Topographic Maps.—Every civilized country publishes detailed general maps of the land on 1:25,000–1:100,000 scale. In the majority of countries these maps are prepared by the army. Relief is usually shown by contours, but in reconnaissance maps plastic shading is common. The topographic sheets of the United States are prepared by the United States Geological Survey (q.v.) and also by the Corps of Engineers. The fine topographic sheets of England are prepared by the British Ordnance Survey.

Air Navigation Maps.—These are usually published on 1:500,000 to 1:1,000,000 scale, using contour lines with altitude tilts, and show all features which help airmen, especially radio beacons. The United States Army Map Service has prepared air navigation maps on 1:1,000,000 scale of the entire world.

Military Grids.—All new topographic maps have a grid system of even squares overprinted,

for easier location of spots. These grid systems are drawn upon a standard map in a specified projection and grid distances and directions are not true on any map on another projection, but as long as the area involved is small, there is not much difference. In the United States Progressive Military Grid System, the country is divided into seven grid zones, and a 1,000-yard square grid is drawn upon a polyconic projection.

Statistical Maps.—These maps show quantitatively the distribution of a certain variable, as, for instance, rainfall, acreage of wheat, reli-

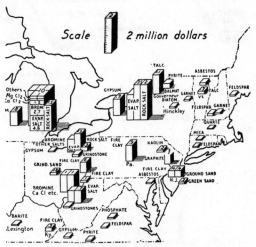

FIG. 13.—Statistical map with superimposed diagrams, showing the nonmetallic mineral production of the northeastern U.S.*

gions of people. Three methods are used: (1) isopleths, which are lines connecting equal values; (2) dot system; and (3) superimposed diagrams. The last is recommended whenever the distribution is highly variable or has to be subdivided. «Density of population» maps are the most important in this group. Usually a combination of the dot system and superimposed circular graphs are used on them.

Cartograms.—Highly abstracted diagrammatic maps are called cartograms and are used much in statistical mapping and for showing the distribution or relations of distributions of certain variables over the earth.

Land Utilization Maps.—These indicate forest, meadow, various types of cultivation, etc., and form the most important type of maps in modern cartography. Various colors, patterns, index numbers and figures are used.

Scientific Maps.—This type of map is published in increasing numbers in atlases, books, and periodicals. Not only do the Earth sciences, such as geology, meteorology, climatology, oceanography, seismology, astronomy, plant geography, and zoogeography use maps as an essential part of their presentation, but also economics, history, sociology, etc., use maps in increasing numbers.

School maps, wall maps, city maps, railway, auto-road maps, maps of art and advertising, are just a few more items each of which has its own specialized cartography. See also GLOBE.

History.—The ability of making maps is an inherent quality of mankind. Primitive people are able to draw maps of large areas in vertical projection without any difficulty. The Eskimos, the Indians, the nomads of Asia and Africa, and

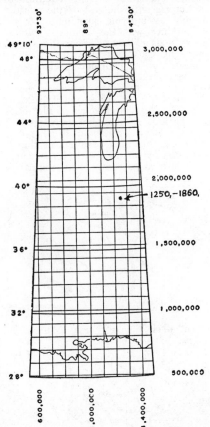

FIG. 12.—Progressive military grid of the U.S. There are seven grid zones. This is Grid Zone C.

*From Raisz, E., "Geography of the Mineral Industry," *Mining and Metallurgy 1941.*

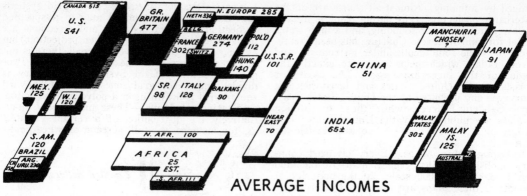

AVERAGE INCOMES

in international units per person

modified after Colin Clark, The Conditions of Economic Progress, 1940

FIG. 14.—Statistical cartogram. The base of blocks is proportionate to population. From E. Raisz: *Atlas of Global Geography.*

the South Sea Islanders are excellent map makers.

The oldest maps which survived were made by the ancient Babylonians, but records indicate that the Egyptians, Persians, and Phoenicians also made maps, few of which survived, however.

Cartography as a science was established by the ancient Greeks. The Ionian geographers of the 5th and 6th centuries B.C. drew the earth in the form of a disk floating in the oceans. In the 4th century, an oblong earth was drawn from which our expressions latitude and longitude derive. At the same time arose the idea of a spherical earth, and it was a well-established fact in the time of Aristotle. The tilt of the ecliptic was accurately measured and the equator, poles, tropics, zones were defined. The size of the earth was measured by Eratosthenes of Alexandria in the 3d century (with an error of less than 14 per cent, 28,000 miles circumference), and later by Posidonius, who, however, figured it one-third too small. This latter measurement was accepted by Ptolemy and influenced Paolo dal Pozzo Toscanelli and Columbus (qq.v.). Eratosthenes prepared a map also showing certain principal parallels and meridians in which he was attacked by Hipparchus, who advocated an even system of parallels and meridians dividing the circle into 360°, as we still use it at the present time.

The only Greek map which survived was an atlas of Claudius Ptolemy of Alexandria about 150 A.D. Much of his material is based on the Phoenician, Marinus of Tyre. His atlas, a supplement of his 8-volume *Geography,* consists of 27 detailed maps and a map of the known world. His delineation had an immense influence upon the cartography of the Renaissance, and some of his mistakes did not disappear from maps until the 18th century.

Roman cartography did not continue the scientific attitude of the Greeks. They preferred a simple map to be used for administrative and military purposes. For this they returned to the disk-like earth of the early Greeks and the Roman *Orbis Terrarum* became the standard map of the world for 13 centuries. It has east on top and we still speak of «orientation.» Most of the map is an exaggerated representation of the Roman Empire with the rest of the world represented only as outlying provinces. A peculiar Roman product was the *Tabula Peutingeriana* (see PEUTINGER'S TABLE) from the 4th century A.D., made by Castorius in which Roman roads are delineated on an enormously elongated scroll 22 feet long and only 1 foot wide. A good medieval copy of this map survived.

The early Middle Ages added little to cartography. A great number of crude maps survived in various codices, but they were mostly copies of the *Orbis Terrarum.* Further diagrammatization of this map resulted in the T-in-O maps (*Orbis Terrarum*) with Jerusalem in the center. These maps, with their regularity, ap-

FIG. 15.—Outline of Ptolemy's World Map.

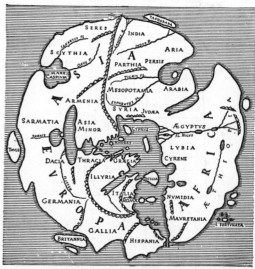

FIG. 16.—The Orbis Terrarum of the Romans. From E. Raisz: *General Cartography* (McGraw-Hill 1938).

pealed greatly to the medieval mind, not interested so much in reality but in divine harmony. A good map of England was prepared by Matthew Paris (q.v.) in St. Albans, c. 1250.

The Arabs are credited with the first school atlases dating back to the 10th century, showing highly diagrammatic maps. They measured the size of the earth with great accuracy. Their tables of latitudes and longitudes surpass anything prior. The most famous Arab map is the large world map of Idrisi (Edrisi) (1154) of rich detail. It shows, however, Christian influence as it was prepared in the court of King Roger II of Sicily.

FIG. 17.—T in ○ map from the 11th century.

Portolan Charts.—These charts appeared around 1300 and seem to be the copy of a remarkable early chart showing the Mediterranean and Black Seas with surprising accuracy. Indeed, this chart was used for actual navigation for three centuries. Over a hundred copies are known, with but few additions and improvements. The original portolan chart was based on an organized compass survey, probably under the Genoese Admiralty.

The Great Discoveries.—The introduction of the compass and improved sailing vessels made possible the voyages of Columbus, Magellan, and others. These great discoveries caused a revolution in map making, as America and its relation to Asia had to be explained to the public. The outlines of four maps below show the confusion which prevailed in the minds of cartographers in the early 16th century. Juan de la Cosa's map

FIG. 18.—Diagrammatic Arabic schoolmap from the 10th century.

ot 1500, if its date is correct (which is doubtful), is the earliest representation of the Americas. Martin Waldseemüller's (q.v.) map is the godfather of America, as it was the first to name the continent so. Diogo Ribero's map is a copy of the *padron real* or royal map of Spain. This is the first real world map showing the immensity of the Pacific Ocean, with China and India in their proper locations.

Engraving and Printing.—Hitherto all maps were manuscript and reproduced by hand. The invention of engraving and printing made maps very much cheaper and the flow of new information was facilitated. Woodcut maps were common at the end of the 15th century, but gradu-

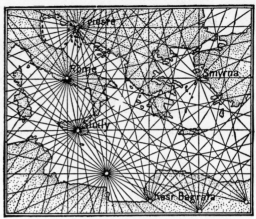

FIG. 19.—Portion of Portolan Chart, c. 1300.

ally copper engraving became the generally used method. Waldseemüller's map was engraved in copper.

Rediscovery of Ptolemy.—Ptolemy's map survived chiefly through the Arabic scholars. His work was translated into Latin around 1410 and since then it was republished perhaps a hundred times, mostly with the addition of new *Tabulae Modernae.* So great was the authority of Ptolemy that Waldseemüller replaced the good outline of the Mediterranean of the portolan charts with the far worse outline of Ptolemy.

The Dutch School.—The Low Countries, situated between England, France, and Germany, and subject to Spain, had good opportunity to obtain information from these countries. Dutch industry and talent supplied the rest, and in the 16th and 17th centuries the Low Countries were the leaders in the map making of Europe. Gerardus Mercator (q.v.) of Louvain is called the father of Dutch cartography. The projection bearing his name appeared in 1569 (see Fig. 4). Hundreds of maps embodying remarkably correct information and restrained, yet artistic rendering, bear his name. Abraham Ortelius (q.v.) published the earliest modern atlas, the *Theatrum Orbis Terrarum,* in 1570. Jodocus Hondius and Jan Janszoon followed the Mercator tradition. The House of Blaeu in Amsterdam produced perhaps the best maps of the Renaissance. Among the later Dutch map houses, the Visshers, the Donckerts, Schenck, Allard, and De Witt should be mentioned. The father of English cartography is Charles Saxton (d. 1611); his county maps are superb. The atlases of Norden, Speed, Goss, Pitt, and Seller closely followed the Dutch style.

Surveying Methods.—Hitherto almost all maps were the result of development: one person made a map, his successors improved it, and gradually a fair representation developed, supported by a few latitude measurements, otherwise unsurveyed. Yet the principles of triangulation are described by Gemma Frisius in 1526, and Willem Janszoon Blaeu actually triangulated a portion of Holland. At the end of the 17th century, the sextant, telescopic theodolite, the planetable, the barometer, and accurate pendulum clocks were available for land measurements.

The French School.—Modern cartography dates from the longitude measurements of the French Academy around 1680. About 80 longitudes were accurately measured by simultaneous

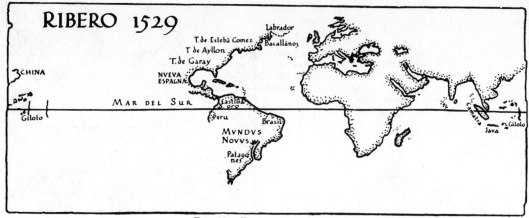

Fig. 20.—Famous map of 1529.

observations of the occulations of the satellites of Jupiter, as chronometers were not yet available. The results of these measurements were laid down on a polar map, covering the floor of the Paris Observatory, by Jean Dominique Cassini. French cartographers of the 18th century excelled in fine, accurate work, critical, scientific attitude, and less inclination for decoration. Outstanding men were Guillaume Delisle, Jean Baptiste Bourguignon d'Anville, Gilles, and Didier Robert de Vaugondy, J. N. Bellin, Philippe Buache, Rigobert Bonne and many others.

The English School.—Early British cartography was under Dutch influence. In the 18th century the fine French style prevailed, but by the end of the 18th century the British even surpassed the French in the number and excellency of their maps. The maps of John and Thomas Bowles, Thomas Jefferys, William Faden, John Rocque, John Cary, and Aaron Arrowsmith were popular even in America.

National Surveys.—The triangulation of France was organized by the Academy of Sciences under César François Cassini de Thury and accomplished in 1744. The preparation of detailed topographic sheets was the further life work of this great cartographer. This was the first great national survey, which was soon followed by Austrian Belgium, and the British Ordnance Survey 1791. In the 19th century every civilized nation produced its topographic sheets.

Diversification of Cartography.—The 19th century witnessed a great diversification of cartography. Geologic maps of William Smith, school maps of Emil Sydow, physical maps of Karl Ritter, atlases of meteorology and climates of John Bartholomew, relief models of Albert Heim, historical map reproductions of Jomard and Konrad Miller, are just a few examples of various tasks which found a cartographic answer. The International 1:1,000,000 Map of the World is the first great experiment in international cooperation in mapping.

American Cartography.—The oldest map wholly produced and published in America is John Foster's woodcut of New England from 1677. The Bonner map of Boston of 1722 is the first large city map. Lewis Evans' *Middle British Colonies* in 1755 is the most outstanding colonial map. The British naval and military maps, previous to the Revolution, by Samuel Holland (New York, New England); John Gascoigne

(South Carolina, Georgia); G. Gould (Florida); Ross (Mississippi River); Wm. Brassier (Lake Champlain); J. Montresor (New York state); John Hills (New Jersey); and many others formed a fundament for the later maps of the United States. Washington's surveyors, Thomas Hutchins, Simeon De Witt (qq.v.), and others, organized the official cartography of the new state. In the early 19th century almost every state of the Union prepared a state map on 4 to 8 miles to the inch scale. Atlases were published in great numbers since Matthew Carey's *General Atlas,* 1794. Especially famous is Henry S. Tanner's *New American Atlas,* 1823. The two Tanner brothers, John Melish, Samuel Augustus Mitchell, and later the Colton family, were especially productive.

Wax engraving was invented by Sidney Edwards Morse; his *Cerographic Atlas* appeared in 1841. This method, with its stamped-in names and mechanical appearance, imprinted its style upon American cartography for a century. More individual maps were produced by lithography, which was introduced around 1827. The county atlases of the second half of the 19th century are typical American products, and their production became a national industry.

The early explorations and mapping of the rapidly expanding country were chiefly due to the army. William Clark's map of 1810 of the Lewis-Clark transcontinental expedition; Major Stephen H. Long's map of the Platte River; Benjamin L. E. Bonneville's map of the Great Basin; Joseph N. Nicollet's map of Minnesota; John Charles Frémont's map of the West are just a few witnesses to the outstanding work of these men under constant danger from Indians.

The westward migration of people was preceded by the host of surveyors commissioned by the General Land Office to make township plots. These men did remarkable work in incredibly short time, but often characterized more by speed than accuracy.

The Coast Survey was established in 1807 under the directorship of Ferdinand Hassler of Switzerland; the first charts, however, did not appear until 1845. This office is responsible for the leveling and triangulation of the country, and since 1878 it has carried the name United States Coast and Geodetic Survey.

The many competing surveys of the West were collected in 1878 into the United States Geological Survey, which is in charge of the

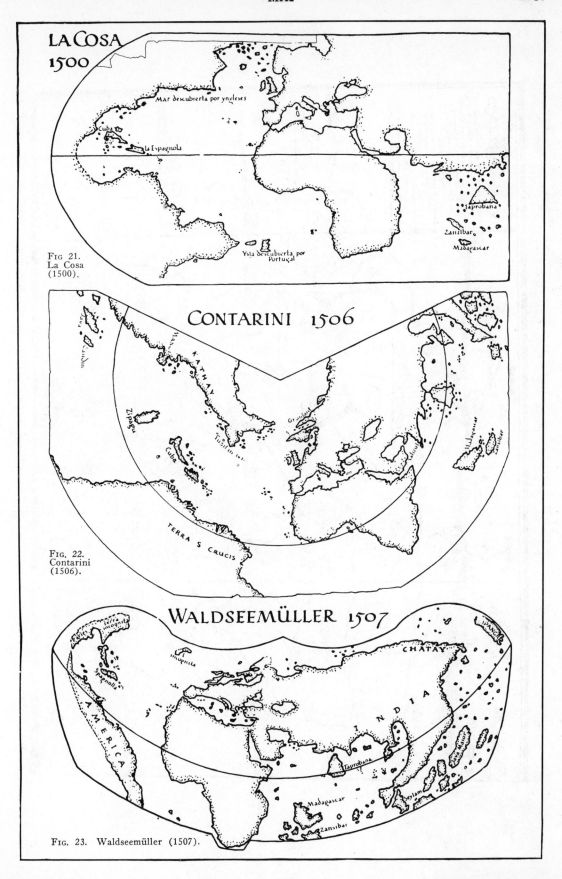

FIG. 21. La Cosa (1500).

FIG. 22. Contarini (1506).

FIG. 23. Waldseemüller (1507).

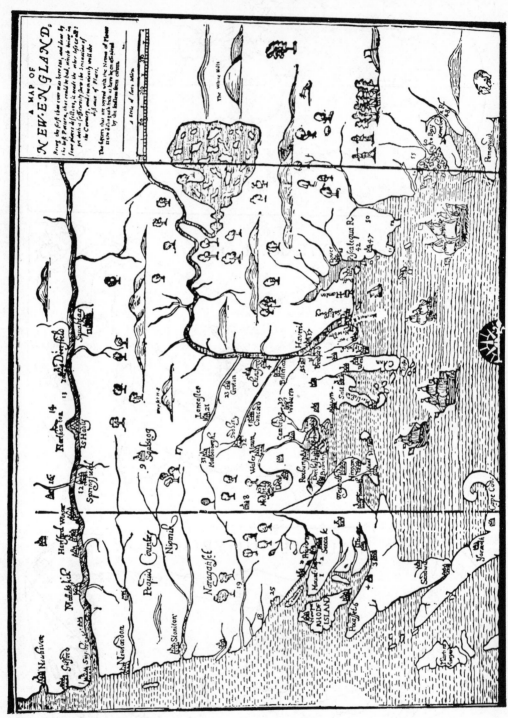

FIG. 24. The first map drawn, engraved, printed and published in the American colonies. John Foster's woodcut, Boston, 1677.

topographic mapping of the country. At the beginning of the Second World War less than half of the country was topographically surveyed. The coverage, however, was greatly expanded by the United States Corps of Engineers in recent years.

Before the war, 24 federal agencies in Washington alone produced all kinds of special maps. Add to this the maps of the various local and state agencies, the number of official maps produced yearly runs into the hundred thousands. Even this production was superceded during the war, when the Army Map Service, the Coast and Geodetic Survey, and the navy produced maps especially of foreign countries with unprecedented speed. Much of the cartographic work of these agencies was assisted materially by the utilization of aerial photography.

ERWIN RAISZ,
Lecturer on Cartography,
Institute of Geographical Exploration,
Harvard University.

Bibliography.—Deetz, Charles H., and Adams, Oscar S., *Elements of Map Projection with Applications to Map and Chart Construction,* U.S. Government Printing Office (Washington, D.C., 1928); Lloyd, Malcolm, *A Practical Treatise on Mapping and Lettering* (Philadelphia, Pa., 1930); Saunders, Howard Raymond, and Ives, Howard Chapin, *Map Drafting and Lettering* (Los Angeles, Calif., 1931); Debenham, Frank, *Exercises in Cartography* (London and Glasgow 1937); Deetz, Charles H., *Cartography,* U.S. Government Printing Office (Washington, D.C., 1936); Steers, James Alfred, *An Introduction to the Study of Map Projection,* 4th ed. revised and enlarged (London 1937); Raisz, Erwin, *General Cartography* (New York 1938); Thiele, Walter, *Official Map Publications* (Chicago 1938); United States War Department, *Topographic Drafting,* technical manual no. TM 5-230, U.S. Government Printing Office (Washington, D.C., 1940); Bagley, James W., *Aerophotography and Aerosurveying* (New York 1941); Flexner, William Welch, and Walker, Gordon L., *Military and Naval Maps and Grids* (New York 1942); Hinks, Arthur R., *Maps and Surveys,* 4th ed. (New York 1942); Tooley, Ronald V., *Maps and Map Makers* (New York 1952); Robinson, Arthur H., *Elements of Cartography* (Evanston, Ill., 1960); Bagrow, Leo, *History of Cartography,* tr. by D. L. Paisey, revised and enlarged by R. A. Skelton (Cambridge, Mass., 1964).

MAPES, māps, **Victor,** American playwright: b. New York, 10 March 1870. He was graduated from Columbia in 1891, was dramatic critic of the New York *World* 1898–99 and manager of New Theatre Chicago (1906–07). He wrote *Duse and the French* (1897); *Partners Three* (1909); *Gilded Way* (1911); and directed *The Tory's Guest* (1900); *Don Caesar's Return* (1901); *The Detective* (1908); *The Boomerang* (with Winchell Smith, 1915); *The Lassoo* (1917); *The Hottentot* (1919); and *The Amethyst* (1925). Mapes died on Sept. 27, 1943, in Cannes, France.

MAPLE, a genus (*Acer*) of trees, together with a few shrubs of the family *Aceraceae.* The species, of which there are about 100, are indigenous to the north temperate zone, being best represented in China, Japan, United States and Canada. They are characterized by opposite, palmate or lobed, exstipulate leaves; small polygamo-dioecious flowers in axillary corymbs or racemes; and compound, one- or two-seeded, long-winged nuts (samaras). The maples constitute one of the most widely useful genera of trees, being extensively employed for ornamental and street planting and for windbreaks, while the wood serves well for toolhandles, furniture, flooring and many other purposes. The flowers are rich in nectar and are sought by bees. Most of the species thrive best upon rich moist land suitable for agricultural purposes and are considered an indication of the type of soil. A few grow in wet land, and many upon mountain sides. They are readily propagated by means of seeds which, in the case of the early maturing kinds, should be sown as soon as ripe, the later ones in autumn or spring, being stratified in sand during the winter. Some choice varieties are grafted or budded and others may be increased by cuttings and layers.

In America, the best known, most widely planted and otherwise most important species is probably the rock or sugar maple (*A. saccharum*), a stately round-headed, gray-barked tree, often attaining heights of 120 feet. It is especially characteristic of rich woods from Maine to Michigan and southward in the mountains to Georgia, everywhere being noted for the rich colors of its leaves in autumn. Besides great popularity for all the purposes mentioned above, some of the trees are highly prized for their wavy-grained wood, which, being of satiny appearance and capable of high polish, is used under the name of curly maple often as veneers for choice furniture. It is further the most important of the species which yield a saccharine sap, and is a chief source of maple syrup and sugar, to obtain which the trees are «tapped,» the sap caught in buckets and evaporated. A yield of three pounds per tree annually is considered very profitable; six pounds or even more is often obtained from many specimens whose sap is either especially abundant or particularly rich in sugar. If properly done no injury results to the trees. A form of the sugar maple, the black maple (*A. saccharinum* var. *nigrum*), so called from its very dark bark, is considered a distinct species (*A. nigrum*) by some botanists. It has the same range and habitats as the preceding and in nearly every respect the same uses, including sugar production. This form is more abundant than the preceding in the Central States.

The silver maple (*A. saccharinum*) is a widely spreading tree which attains a height of 120 feet throughout the same range as the above species. Being very ornamental in form and particularly also because of its graceful leaves, which are silvery white beneath, this tree is widely planted where rapid growth and quick effects are desired. Its chief fault is its brittleness; it quickly succumbs to high winds. It will succeed upon a wide variety of soils. Its sap, though rather sweet, is less useful for sugar than the above-mentioned species.

The red, scarlet or swamp maple (*A. rubrum*) attains heights similar to the above, has about the same range, but is most frequently found in wet ground. It is named from the brilliant color of its flowers, which are borne profusely in early spring before the leaves appear and from its red fruits which appear soon after. Being of good habit it is widely planted for ornamental purposes upon all kinds of soils. Its wood is used for most of the purposes enumerated above.

The Norway maple (*A. platanoides*) is somewhat smaller than the preceding species, being more compact and umbrageous. It is widely planted in private grounds and in parks, but is less valuable for street planting than the above because of its shorter trunk. It is a native of Europe. The sycamore maple (*A.*

pseudoplatanus), another European species, is smaller still, attaining only about 70 feet. It is also widely planted in America as well as in Europe, being a vigorous, rapid grower and succeeding upon a great variety of soils. The common maple (*A. campestre*) occasionally attains 50 feet, but is usually a smaller tree or even a shrub. It is of European origin and is widely planted.

The Japanese maples (*A. japonicum, A. palmatum,* and other species) are small trees or shrubs which because of the great diversity of form of their leaves and their dainty habit have become widely popular in the parks and gardens of the United States and Europe. Their exceptionally brilliant autumnal coloring is taken advantage of in Japan where in the fall they approach the chrysanthemum in popularity.

The maples furnish food for a large number of insects, some of which live upon the green parts and others upon the wood. Several species of scale insects (q.v.) are often abundant enough to do considerable damage. The cottony maple scale (*Pulvinaria vitis*) is among the most troublesome. Several caterpillars live upon the leaves, the forest tent caterpillar (*Malacosoma disstria*), the fall webworm (*Hyphantria cunea*), and the larvae of the white-marked tussock moth (*Hemerocampa leucostigma*) being the most generally important. The maple worm (*Anisota rubicunda*), which is the larva of a moth, is frequently very destructive. Of the borers, the larvae of *Dicerca divericata* and *Glycobius speciosus,* which are beetles in the adult state, and those of *Sesia acerni,* a clear-winged moth, are among the most destructive to maples. The second beetle mentioned is known as the sugar maple borer.

Consult Bailey, Liberty H., *Standard Cyclopedia of Horticulture* (New York 1944); Carey, William, *The Book of Trees,* rev. ed. (Harrisburg, Pa., 1965); Platt, Rutherford, *The Great American Forest* (Englewood Cliffs, N.J.,1965).

MAPLE HEIGHTS, city, Ohio, is located in Cuyahoga County in the northeastern part of the state, ten miles southeast of Cleveland of which it is a residential suburb. It was incorporated as a village in 1915 and as a city in 1930, and it has a mayor-council type of government. Pop. 31,667.

MAPLE SHADE, village, New Jersey, is located in Burlington County in southwestern New Jersey seven miles east of Camden, at an altitude of 40 feet. Served by the Pennsylvania Railroad, it is principally a manufacturing and agricultural center, the chief industries being clothing, paper products, radio parts, and lumber milling. It is in a region of truck, fruit, poultry, and dairy farms. Pop. 12,947.

MAPLE SUGAR INDUSTRY, a trade term in common use, pertaining to the manufacture of sugar and sirup from the sap of the rock or sugar maple (*Acer saccharum*) or from the sap of the black maple (*Acer nigrum*). The maple trees, which are about forty years old when first tapped, are drilled with small and shallow holes a few feet from the base of the trunk during the spring when the sap is rising. The sap drips into buckets, which are hung on the tree, and the flow continues for several weeks. An average tree yields from 10 to 20 gallons of sap, although from 35 to 50 gallons of sap must

be boiled down in order to obtain one gallon of sirup.

New York and Vermont are the leading producers of maple sirup (up to about 400,000 gallons each annually in the 1960's). The next in order of importance are Pennsylvania and Ohio (each over 100,000 gallons); then Michigan and Wisconsin (60,000 gallons each); Massachusetts (44,000); New Hampshire (38,000); and finally Maryland, Maine, and Minnesota (in the tens of thousands). The total United States production of maple sirup came to over 1.2 million gallons annually in the mid-1960's. The amount of sugar contained in this sirup is slightly less than 10 million pounds. (This does not mean, of course, that the entire maple sirup output was converted into sugar.) There are no figures after 1959 for the number of maple trees in the United States that were being tapped for sirup; in that year over 4.5 million were tapped. Although in past years a greater number of trees were used for sirup production—almost 10 million in 1940 and over 8 million in 1949—the volume of sirup produced has not dropped markedly since 1949. In fact in some years it has exceeded 1949 production, although far fewer trees were being tapped, showing that these trees were being used more efficiently.

Canada is an important producer of maple sirup and maple sugar. Quebec, Ontario, New Brunswick, and Nova Scotia are its chief producers.

History.—Maple sugar and sirup were made by the early pioneers of New England and Canada. The art was a product of "necessity, the mother of invention," or an inheritance from the Indians, who were familiar with the process of making the sugar. But, in either event, the first methods employed were crude, and the article was dark in color and not attractive. Moreover, tapping trees with an axe tended to denude the forest of its maples, and the entire procedure was wasteful in the extreme. The sap was caught in troughs, hewed out of logs, thence carried in pails to the boiling place and reduced to sirup in potash kettles which were suspended by chains from a horizontal pole, supported by forked or crossed sticks at each end and surrounded by a blazing open fire. Improved methods, however, both as to tapping the maples and refining the sap, gradually followed one another, until now modern scientific methods prevail, and it is possible to reduce the sap to sugar or sirup almost immediately by using evaporators.

Adulteration.—Prior to the passage of the National Pure Food and Drugs Act, and before the federal government inaugurated its crusade against misbranding, certain sugar refineries made much more sugar and sirup, labeling it "maple," than the entire natural production. This practice, however, has been suppressed, and, though much maple sirup is sold to concerns which blend it with cane sirup, no attempt is made in marketing the product to deceive the public, the labels simply stating that the article within the container is a sirup made by blending cane and maple sirups.

MAPLEWOOD, city, Missouri, is located at an altitude of 508 feet directly to the southwest of St. Louis of which it is a residential suburb. It is served by the Missouri Pacific Railroad. Settled in about 1865 and incorporated in 1908, Maplewood has a commission type of government. Pop. 12,552.

MAPLEWOOD, township in Essex County, New Jersey, is situated six miles west of Newark on the Delaware, Lackawanna and Western Railroad. Although largely a residential suburb of Newark and New York City, celluloid, metal products, and golf clubs are manufactured here. Of historic interest in Maplewood, which was incorporated in 1922, is the Timothy Ball House often visited by Washington during the Revolutionary War. Pop. 23,977.

MAPPA, măp′pă, **Adam Gerard,** Holland-American soldier and type founder: b. Delft, Holland, Nov. 25, 1754; d. Olden Barneveld, N. Y., April 15, 1828. As a young man he entered the military service of his native country, gaining marked distinction. He later engaged in the type-founding business, but his work was interrupted by the political storms which disturbed the Netherlands in 1786–1787. Colonel Mappa again took up the sword and became a leader of volunteer militia forces which aimed at liberalizing Dutch political institutions, but in the abortive revolution of 1787 his forces were overwhelmed and he was banished forever from Delft.

Mappa then went to the court of Versailles to solicit cooperation. Louis XVI, however, had troubles enough of his own, and, as the prospects of civil liberty being established in his own country grew fainter, Colonel Mappa decided to move with his family to America.

While in Paris, Mappa became acquainted with Thomas Jefferson, then American ambassador to France, who advised him to take to America a type-founding plant. Up to this time all printers had been obliged to purchase their type in Europe since there was as yet no type foundry on the western side of the Atlantic. Accordingly, when Mappa arrived in New York in 1789, he brought with him a complete letter foundry. .

The infant industry, nevertheless, did not prosper, ad in 1794 he advertised his type foundry for sale. Later that same year he moved to Olden Barneveld, later Trenton, now Barneveld, where, as resident agent for the Holland Land Company, he played an important role for more than thirty years in helping to settle that part of New York State.

MAPU, mä′pōō, **Abraham,** Hebrew novelist: b. Slobodka, a suburb of Kovno, Lithuania, Jan. 10, 1808; d. Königsberg, Oct. 9, 1867. Noted as a Talmudist when still very young, Mapu also became well acquainted with French and Latin secular literature, both of which exerted a lasting influence on his literary endeavors. In 1848 he was appointed professor in a Jewish school at Kovno, and in 1853 his historical novel *Ahabat Ziyyon* (*The Love of Zion*) appeared. This important work, which managed effectively to symbolize the spirit of regeneration of the Jews through contact with Palestine, was a significant forerunner of the romantic movement in 19th century Hebrew literature. An English translation, *Amnon, Prince and Peasant,* written by Frank Jaffe was published in 1887. His second major historical novel, *Ashmat Shomeron* (*The Transgression of Samaria*). was published in 1865. He also wrote *Ayit Zabua* (*The Hypocrite*) (1857–1861), a Hebrew manual, and a Hebrew grammar.

MAR is the section of Scotland located between the Dee and the Don rivers. The ancient earldom of Mar, which had previously expired, was restored by being granted in 1565 to John, 6th lord of Erskine, who had been regent of Scotland. His son, the 2d earl of Mar and guardian of James VI, helped to negotiate the question of the succession of James to the English throne. The 6th earl, after helping to negotiate for the union of Scotland and England, returned to Scotland and led an unsuccessful rebellion in 1715 for the Old Pretender.

MAQUI, mä′kĕ, an evergreen shrub of the family Elaeocarpaceae, found in Chile, from the juice of whose acid berry the Chileans make a wine given to persons ill with fever. It is the best-known species of the genus *Aristotelia* (*A. maqui* or *macqui*) and is sometimes cultivated as an ornamental shrub.

MAQUIS, mä-kē′, a dense copselike growth found in the hot, dry regions of thin soil along the coasts of the Mediterranean Sea. It usually consists of a thicket of such bushes as the arbutus, cistus, holm oak, myrtle, tree heath, wild olive, or laurel. In Italy the growth is called the *macchia,* and in California it is called the chaparral, in the latter case generally consisting of dwarf evergreen oak. The name, by extension, also applied to Corsican bandits who, in evading the law, would hide in the maquis growth.

During World War II, when Pierre Laval instituted a compulsory labor draft in Vichy France in 1943, the term began to be applied to those who fled to the countryside to escape this draft and later to all who were participating in underground resistance. Such groups of men, the *maquisards,* concentrated particularly in the mountainous regions of France bordering on Italy and Switzerland. They were organized only on a local basis until 1944 when nation-wide contact was established and they became a part of the French Forces of the Interior (FFI).

MAQUOKETA, mä-kō′kĕ-tä, city, Iowa, seat of Jackson County, is located at an altitude of 685 feet on the Maquoketa River 30 miles south of Dubuque. Served by the Milwaukee Railroad, it is chiefly an agricultural trading center although the manufacturing of foundry and machine-shop products and fishing tackle is also carried on. Valuable limestone quarries are in the vicinity, and not far distant are forests which furnish excellent hardwood timber. The city owns and operates the waterworks and the electric generating plant and distribution system. Pop. 5,909.

MARA, mä′rä, in Norse legend, was a goblin that seized on men asleep in their beds and took from them all speech and motion. In Buddhist mythology Mara is the tempter, the ruling spirit of evil. Mara is also frequently identified with the incubus and with nightmares.

MARABOU, măr′a-bōō, a large African pink-white pouched stork (*Leptoptilus crumenifer*), which resembles the adjutant (q.v.) of India in appearance and habits. It gives its name to the soft and drooping feathers (coverts) which cover the root of the tail and are prized for millinery and other ornamental purposes. A large part of the "marabou feathers" sold, however, are derived from the Indian adjutant.

MARACAIBO, mǎr-à-kī′bō, Span. mä-rä-kī vỏ, city and port, Venezuela; capital of Zulia State; located in the northwest part of the country, on the west shore of a channel linking Lake Maracaibo (q.v.) and the Gulf of Venezuela, an arm of the Caribbean Sea. Second largest city in Venezuela, it is the export center of the country's petroleum industry.

Extreme humidity and a mean annual temperature of 82.4°F. hindered the city's development until 1918, but subsequent exploitation of nearby oilfields by foreign capital introduced modern sanitary and other improvements and brought an influx of inhabitants. Maracaibo was founded in 1529 but declined and was refounded by Alonzo Pacheco in 1571. Pop. (1966) 558,953.

MARACAIBO, Lake, located in northwestern Venezuela, chiefly in Zulia State. It is connected with the Gulf of Venezuela by narrows, is 75 miles wide and approximately 100 miles long, and lies in hot, unhealthful lowlands ringed by mountains. Adjacent oilfields are among the world's richest.

MARACAY, mä-rä-kī′, city, Venezuela; capital of Aragua State; located in the northern part of the country, on the northeast shore of Lake Valencia, 50 miles southwest of Caracas. It is a commercial and industrial center. Pop. (1966) 165,763.

MARAT, mà-rà′, **Jean Paul,** French revolutionist: b. Boudry, Switzerland, May 24, 1744; d. Paris, France, July 13, 1793. He studied medicine in Paris, later practicing there and in London. In 1789 at the start of the French Revolution he began journalistic activities which quickly made him known as an agitator for extreme violence. He was denounced and was compelled to go into hiding, but in 1792 was elected to the National Convention. He helped Danton and Robespierre overthrow the Girondists, June 2, 1793. He was stabbed to death in his bath by Charlotte Corday (q.v.).

MARATHA SAINTS, mà-rä′tà, heroes of a great religious revival in the Maratha country of India. It lasted almost 500 years, from the middle of the 13th to the middle of the 18th century, and produced over 50 important prophets, poets, and theologians, some of whom are worthy of a high place among the world's religious geniuses. This was a revival of Krishna (q.v.) worship with great stress on the *Bhagavad Gītā* (q.v.) socially interpreted: that is, it played down the common Krishnaite emphasis on sex and played up in a striking degree the *Bhagavad-Gītā's* emphasis on all forms of work and accomplishment as ways in which men may bind themselves to, fulfill, and make themselves one with the will and purpose of the preserver god, Vishnu incarnated as Krishna.

The most celebrated of the Maratha religious geniuses were Jñāneśvar (fl. 1290), a one-time ascetic who defied caste rules in order to assume family life and duties in accordance with what he understood to be the true meaning of the *Bhagavad Gītā*, which he paraphrased in some 10,000 Marathi verses; Nāmdēv (1270–1350), a shudra or slave-caste psalmist; Janabai, a high-caste woman who became Nāmdēv's self-made slave, courted Brahman scorn, and found union with God in the menial work of washing clothes

and grinding grain; Ēknāth (d. 1609), another Brahman who opposed caste by precept and example and left as his greatest literary work a long poetic commentary on the 11th chapter of the *Bhagavata Purana;* Tukārām (1608–1649), a grain dealer and wonderful mystic poet, who flourished in the first half of the 17th century; and Mahīpati, who commemorated in his *Bhākta Vijaya* (1762) the lives and deeds of his saintly predecessors, creating a masterpiece in his biography of Bhanudas, the grandfather of Ēknāth. It was characteristic of the Maratha Saints to find yogic bliss or mystic union with God, not in withdrawal from life or in "the great release" of moksha but in all the activities dictated by love of the divine image in all creatures.

Bibliography.—Bell, H. W., *Some Translations from the Marathi Poets* (Bombay 1913); Fraser, J. N., and Marathe, K. B., *The Poems of Tukarama,* tr., 3 vols. (London 1909–15); Kincaid, C. A., *Tales of the Saints of Pandharpur* (Bombay 1915), which is largely adapted from Mahipati; Nadkarni, M. K., *A Short History of Marathi Literature* (Baroda 1921); Fraser, J. N., *The Life and Teaching of Tukaram* (Madras 1922); Abbott, J. E., comp. and tr., *The Poet-Saints of Mahārāshtra,* Nos. 1-7, translations from original sources (Poona 1926–30).

RODERICK MARSHALL.

MARATHAS, or **MAHRATTAS,** mà-răt′tàs (from *Marāṭhās,* the people of Maratha, which is the Marathi version of the Sanskrit word *Mahārāṣṭra,* the name of a large section of western India). The Marathas are members of a racial group who lived chiefly in the western Deccan and the Bombay Presidency and are at present much scattered. They are of Scytho-Dravidian type, famous for their energy, strength, and efficiency as soldiers. They have imposed their language, Marathi, on many neighboring peoples.

Inhabitants of the hills and high tablelands of western India, the Marathas were not easily conquered by the early Aryan invaders of India and were converted to Hinduism largely by missionary work. They consider themselves a distinct nation or people and have clung to certain ancient beliefs and practices in spite of Aryan, British, and Muslim influences and rule. Their religious poetry, hymns written by the so-called Maratha Saints (q.v.), many of whom came from the lowest caste, shows a resistance to caste and a preference, mildly disguised, for goddess, as contrasted with god, worship. Like the Sikhs (q.v.), they ignored the caste rules which forbade all but the Kshatriyas (see CASTE), or born warriors, to carry arms; but they never, like the Sikhs, withdrew or were driven from the Hindu community. Also like the Sikhs, they were inveterate enemies of the Muslims, and during the decline of the Mogul Empire united under a war leader called Sivaji (1627–1680) for a career of conquest and unification which brought a large part of northern and western India under their rule.

This paramountcy of the Marathas lasted for the century from 1674, when Sivaji had himself crowned king of the Maratha Empire, to 1775, when the empire, now degenerated into a Maratha confederacy in which a number of independent princes were headed by a peshwa or prime minister, first came to blows with the British in India. After three bloody wars, the confederacy came to an end in 1818, and the rulers of most of the states became dependent monarchs under British protection. The last state to hold out against the British, Gwalior, came under their control in 1844. Had there been no Europeans in India in the 18th century, the Marathas might have established hegemony over the whole country; but it is unlikely that they would have brought India peace, since they were given to fighting among themselves and the Sikhs were ready to challenge their power.

Bibliography.—Ranade, M. G., *The Rise of the Maratha Power* (Bombay 1900); Sarkar, J., *Shivaji and His Times* (Calcutta 1919); Sen, S. N., *The Administrative System of the Marathas* (Calcutta 1923); Kincaid, C. A., and Pārasnīs, D. B., *History of the Maratha People*, 3 vols. (New York 1919–25); Sen, S. N., *Military System of the Marathas* (Calcutta 1928); Kincaid, D., *Grand Rebel: an Impression of Shivaji, Founder of the Maratha Empire* (London 1937).
RODERICK MARSHALL.

MARATHI LANGUAGE AND LITERATURE,

mà-rä'tê, is a language of the Indo-Aryan subfamily of Indo-European. It is spoken by 21 million people (census of India, 1931) in the Maratha country, which includes Bombay city and a large wedge of territory based on the coast south to Goa and extending inland eastward to Nagpur. Dialect differences are slight, except for the Konkani of the Goa coast. Historically, it is usually agreed that Marathi descends from the Māhārāṣṭrī Prakrit. It is written in the Devanagari alphabet.

Marathi literature begins in the 13th century with a series of lyric poets who drew their inspiration from worship of Vishnu (Viṣṇu). The earliest is Nāmdēv (1270–1350), some of whose verses survive in the Sikh scriptures called Adigranth. A contemporary of his was Jnāneśvar, who paraphrased the *Bhagavad Gītā* (ca. 1280). Ēknāth (d. 1609 A.D.), Muktēśwar (17th century), Rāmdās (1608–1681), Tukārām (1608–1649), Mōrōpant (Mayūra Paṇḍit, 1729–1794), all religious writers, are the greatest names from a much longer list; Tukārām is considered the greatest of all. Secular literature included love poetry, poetry in praise of the Maratha national heroes headed by Sivaji (1627–1680), and adaptations of Sanskrit folktale collections.

Modern Marathi literature vies with that of Bengal in its political and religious writings, if not so much in fiction and the drama.

See also INDIA—*Languages;* INDIA—*Literature;* PRAKRIT LANGUAGES AND LITERATURE.

Consult Grierson, G. A., *Linguistic Survey of India*, vol. 7 (Calcutta 1905); Bloch, Jules, *La formation de la langue marathe* (Paris 1919); Macnicol, Nicol, *Psalms of Marāṭhā Saints* (Calcutta 1919); Lambert, H. M., *Marathi Language Course* (New York 1943).

MURRAY B. EMENEAU,
Department of Classics, University of California.

MARATHON, măr'à-thŏn, village, Greece, located in Attica nome, near the Gulf of Petalion, 17 miles northeast of Athens. It is an agricultural community. Pop. (1940) 2,515.

MARATHON, ancient town, Greece, located in Attica, near the Gulf of Petalion, south of the modern village of Marathon, probably on a height occupied by the modern village of Vrana.

The PLAIN OF MARATHON, overlooked by the height of Vrana, extends in a broad arc south and east, between the Pentelikon massif and the Bay of Marathon, an inlet of the Gulf of Petalion. It is about six miles long; its width varies from three miles to one mile and a half. In ancient times it was bounded at the northeast and southeast by two marshes. Between the marshlands, which were drained after World War II, the plain is bisected by a brook, the Charadra, which flows through a pass at the height of Vrana and empties into the Bay of Marathon. The plain was linked to ancient Athens by a stretch of road approximately 25 miles long.

MARATHON, Battle of, the occasion of a celebrated victory of Greeks under Callimachus and Miltiades over Persians under Datis and Artaphernes, in September 490 or 491 B.C.

An Athenian force of 9,000 or 10,000 men opposed about 20,000 Persians who had established a beachhead below a marsh at the northeast edge of the Plain of Marathon, adjoining the Bay of Marathon. The Persians had been sent by Darius I (q.v.) to subdue all of Greece, beginning with Athens. Datis intended to pin down the Athenian army at Marathon while Artaphernes led a Persian naval expedition against Athens itself, where conspirators stood ready to aid the invaders.

The Athenians hoped to delay battle until promised reinforcements from Sparta should join them, but news of the impending move by Artaphernes and the arrival of 1,000 troops from Plataea, a town in alliance with Athens, nerved them to attack. The Greeks sortied from strong defensive positions in heights overlooking the plain and advanced in a phalanx of spearmen toward the Persians, drawn up along the seashore. Callimachus and Miltiades had placed most of their troops on the two wings of the Greek phalanx. As the Greeks came within range of Persian archers, they broke into a run and their wings probably outdistanced their center. The Persians pushed into the concave Greek line, their center advancing beyond their wings, which met heavier opposition. Soon the Persian center was enveloped on both flanks, with the Persian wings crushed back on it in confusion. At close quarters Persian arrows were useless, but the spears of the Greeks were deadly.

The Persians broke for their ships under close pursuit, losing 6,400 killed. The victors then marched back to Athens and prevented Artaphernes' expedition from investing the city. Athens lost 192 killed at Marathon. Their bodies were burned on a huge pyre, built on the plain, and were subsequently covered with an earthen commemorative mound 50 feet high. Excavation of this mound in 1890 revealed the remains of the Athenian dead, funeral vases, and weapons. Among the Athenians who fell were Callimachus and Cynegirus, a brother of the tragic poet Aeschylus, who also was present at the battle.

MARATHON RACE, one of the regular events of the modern Olympic Games (q.v.). It commemorates the reputed feat of Pheidippides, who is said to have run more than 20 miles to Athens with news of the Greek victory at Marathon in 490 or 491 B.C. According to tradition, Pheidippides ran into the Athenian agora, or market place, gasped out his news, and fell dead.

The Marathon Race is an outdoor road race. After 1924, its length was standardized at 26 miles, 385 yards; but otherwise Marathon courses vary, notably with respect to road grade. By analogy, any unusual feat of endurance may be called a Marathon.

MARAVEDI, măr-à-vā'dĭ, a Spanish copper coin of low denomination, in use from 1474 to 1848, varying in value from one seventh to one third of a cent. There were also, at an earlier period, maravedis of gold weighing 60 grains.

MARBLE, mär′b′l, **Alice,** American tennis player: b. Plumas County, Calif., Sept. 28, 1913. She began to play tennis at the age of 15. In 1932 she won the California women's championship, becoming No. 7 in national ranking, and by 1933 she had become No. 3. The next year she collapsed on a Paris court and was told she should never play tennis again. However, the medical diagnosis proved faulty and she resumed playing, four times winning the national singles championship (1936, 1938–1940), and, with Sarah Palfrey Cooke, the national doubles (1937–1940). She also won the British singles (1939) and doubles (1938–1939) championships at Wimbledon. In 1940 she became a professional player, also a singer, lecturer, radio announcer, and designer of tennis clothes. She wrote the autobiographical *Road to Wimbledon* (1946).

MARBLE (from Gr. *marmaros,* originally stone, boulder), a crystalline rock which, if pure, would be composed entirely of carbonate of lime (calcium carbonate, $CaCO_3$, the original material of limestone). It is a rock valued for its beauty and is widely used for making statuary and monuments, for architectural treatment in construction, and for ornamentation. Many limestones which become decorative when polished are also termed marbles.

contribute to color and color patterns in the various marbles are quartz, mica, talc, pyrites, graphite, feldspar, and iron oxides. These impurities had their origin in sands, clays, dolomites, organic material, and other substances in the original calcite (calcium carbonate). The heat in the earth's crust liberated carbon dioxide from the calcite; the remaining calcium oxide combined with silica to produce silicates, among other reactions, and a variety of minerals resulted.

Typically, commercially used marbles have a specific gravity of about 2.70 and a compressive strength of 10,000 pounds per square inch. They are capable of withstanding heat up to 1200° F. without injury and are durable in a dry atmosphere, but will deteriorate under continued damp exposure or when subjected to an acid atmosphere.

Types of Marble.—Commercial marbles are classified into three groups: high-calcium or dolomitic types (with the greatest variety of uses), onyx marbles, and serpentine marbles. Onyx marbles are crystalline, translucent rocks resulting from the deposition of lime carbonate from cold waters. Serpentine marble is an abundant, granular, hydrous silicate of magnesia widely used for making vases and for ornamental work.

Statuary-grade marbles are the purest, whitest, and most homogeneous. They must be of a single shade and free from hard or soft spots, iron inclusions, or other defects. All marbles, including limestones so classed, are distinguished on the basis of color. Uniformity in tones

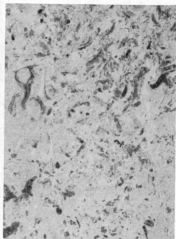

Marble Institute of America

Kinds of commercial marbles. *Left:* Vermont Pavonazzo. *Center:* Striped Brocadillo. *Right:* Trieste Buff Gray.

Composition and Physical Characteristics.—True marble is a metamorphosed, recrystallized equivalent of limestone, from which it was formed by heat, pressure, or a combination of both. A pure marble would have a chemical analysis of 56 per cent calcium oxide (lime, CaO), and 44 per cent carbon dioxide, CO_2, but even the finest grades of white marble are not completely pure. Foreign substances have been introduced, to varying degree, during the formation of all marbles used commercially. Streaks and variegated colors are caused by the action of oxides of iron and other chemicals. Among accessory minerals which

of color is important in architecture, while striking effects of varied colors determine the choice for ornamental work. Adequate crushing strength, low absorption, and uniformity of coefficient of expansion are required for building work.

Sources of Marble.—Most marbles are old geologically and date back to Paleozoic or even Precambrian times. Those used for structural purposes occur in regions of metamorphic rocks and are found associated with gneisses, schists, and other altered rocks. Deposits range from a few feet to many miles in extent, and the purest forms are generally massive, with freedom from cracks or jointing.

There are quarries of fairly pure marble in many parts of Europe, notably in France, Belgium, England, Italy, and Spain. Uruguay has a great variety of colored marbles, and there are quarries of high-grade marbles in India and Africa. The most important quarries in the United States are in the Appalachian district, and the leading producing states, by far, are Vermont, Georgia, and Tennessee. Other production comes from Alabama, Arkansas, Maryland, Missouri, Massachusetts, Maine, New York, Colorado, Utah, Arizona, California, Minnesota, and North Carolina. New sources are continually being uncovered in the Rocky Mountains and Coast Ranges. United States production includes a variety of colors, the greatest diversity being in the marbles quarried from an area 80 miles long in western Vermont, where white, black, and all manner of colored marbles are obtained. While marble has been quarried in all the provinces of Canada except Prince Edward Island, it has been mostly crushed or ground and used for marble flooring, terrazzo, stucco, poultry grit, and the manufacture of artificial stone.

Uses of Marble.—Marble has been a preferred stone for statuary and for decorative work in buildings and monuments from the very earliest ages. The ancient Greeks are famed for their genius in forming statuary and bas-reliefs from Parian marble, one of the finest and purest white marbles ever discovered. Carrara marbles from the Apuane Alps in Italy were subsequently exploited and today are still the most sought white marbles for statuary work. American sculptors prefer them to domestic marbles, although there is increasing interest in some of the pure white marble occurrences being discovered in the United States.

High-grade marble graces the exteriors of many of the world's finest buildings and, because of its high resistance to heat, it is being used increasingly in the erection of fireproof buildings, for floors, and for the overlaying of inside walls and ceilings. Among the many other uses of this so-called dimension marble, in addition to decorative work and monuments, are tiling, washbasins, interior window sills, vases, chimney pieces, veneer, ashlar, and electric power panels.

Marble Industry.—Breakage and waste in the quarries amount to 50 per cent of the stone, so there is continuing stress on the development of markets for byproducts. Marble chips are graded for making artificial stone, and dust is sold as filler material or as an abrasive for hand soap. Crushed and ground products are used for asphalt filler, cast stone, composite flooring, concrete and road stone, mineral feed, plaster, poultry grit, roofing, stucco, terrazzo, whiting, and treating the soil in agriculture.

Marble companies include those which quarry the stone and sell rough shapes and slabs for finishing by others, those which quarry and finish the marble, and those which buy rough shapes for finishing. High production costs, wastage, and high transportation charges are problems inherent to the industry. The trend is to increasing mechanization; cranes and derricks are used extensively, and other elaborate equipment has been developed. The channeling machine, consisting of a self-propelled carriage traveling on a track with one or two pistons, each powering a set of chisel-pointed drills, is most widely used for primary cuts; it cuts a channel in any direction, and wedges are driven into horizontal drill holes below to lift the channeled blocks. Line drills mounted on a stiff leg-supported bar are also used for primary cuts; deep holes are then drilled close together in a line, and a flat steel chisel, powered or hand-driven (a broaching tool), cuts out the webs between holes to form a continuous channel.

Marble Institute of America

Marble in contrasting hues and patterns decorates the main lobby of a modern office building.

Large blocks are subdivided by drilling and wedging into mill blocks. In the fabricating mills, further subdivision is done by various means, including drilling, wedging, and using gang saws and other types of saws. Lathes, pneumatic tools, surfacing machines, and much handwork are required for carving and shaping, followed by polishing to a high luster. See also QUARRYING—*Dimension Stone.*

BROR NORDBERG,
Engineering Consultant.

MARBLE CANYON or **MARBLE GORGE,** canyon of the Colorado River in Coconino County in northern Arizona. It extends about 60 miles, from the confluence of the Paria River in the north to that of the Little Colorado in the south (on the eastern end of the Grand Canyon National Park). It is sometimes considered the upper end of the Grand Canyon. Just below the Paria River, Navajo Bridge (also known as Marble Canyon or Grand Canyon Bridge), about 800 feet long, crosses the river at an elevation of about 470 feet; it is the only bridge to cross the Colorado in about 1,000 miles.

MARBLE FAUN, The (British title, TRANSFORMATION); the last completed romance of Nathaniel Hawthorne (q.v.), published in 1860.

Most of the scene is laid in Rome. The main characters are: Kenyon, a young American sculptor; his compatriot Hilda, a painter; Miriam

Schaefer, also a painter, with a hidden past; Donatello, Count of Monte Beni, a young Italian who, his friends think, resembles the marble statue of the *Faun* (or *Satyr*) by Praxiteles. The resemblance is more than physical: Donatello is gay and charming, but lacks moral responsibility.

Donatello deeply loves Miriam, who, after an encounter in the catacombs, is haunted by a mysterious man whose power over her implies some dark secret in her past. Enraged at seeing her thus tormented, Donatello one night flings the tormentor from the Tarpeian rock. Hilda, a chance witness, parts from Miriam in revulsion, but cannot bring herself to tell what she has seen. She finally, though a Protestant, unburdens herself to a confessor at St. Peter's. Shared guilt —for she had consented to his act—brings Miriam and Donatello together in an unhappy union. The greatest effect, however, is upon Donatello, in whom bloodguiltiness awakens for the first time real conscience and moral responsibility. Kenyon ultimately marries Hilda; the fate of the other two is left vague.

The book is the least satisfying of Hawthorne's romances. Too much is left unexplained; the narrative is impeded by Baedekerlike details from the author's notebooks. It poses, however, a dark problem, thus phrased by Kenyon: "Sin has educated Donatello, and elevated him. Is sin, then, ... like sorrow, merely an element in human education, through which we struggle to a higher and purer state than we could otherwise have attained?" Hilda repudiates this idea with horror; it is by no means certain that Hawthorne does.

DeLancey Ferguson.

MARBLEHEAD, mär'b'l-hĕd, town, Massachusetts, in Essex County and on Massachusetts Bay about 15 miles northeast of Boston; altitude 30 feet; on the Boston and Maine Railroad and a state highway. The southeastern projection of the double peninsula on which the town is situated is known as Marblehead Neck and creates a sheltered harbor, one reason for Marblehead being a great yachting center. Fishing, boatbuilding, and the manufacture of machine parts and shoes are the chief industries. Among the numerous places of historic interest are the King Hooper mansion (1745), headquarters of the local art association; and the Jeremiah Lee mansion (1768), housing the museum of the local historical society. Abbot Hall contains the original of the Archibald Willard painting *The Spirit of '76.*

Marblehead was settled in 1629; at first a part of Salem, it was incorporated in 1649. During the American Revolution, Marblehead privateers rendered noteworthy service to the colonial cause. During the War of 1812, the waters near Marblehead were the scene of the engagement between the American vessel *Chesapeake* and the British ship *Shannon,* and in 1814 the *Constitution* (Old Ironsides) was forced to take refuge in the harbor.

Marblehead has a town council form of government. Pop. 18,521.

MARBLES AND MARBLE PLAYING, mär'b'lz. Marbles are small balls made of painted and glazed clay, limestone, plastic, glass, or agate, used as toys and playthings for children. There are virtually numberless variations of the game played with them, many of them of local custom. What may be termed the official version in the United States is that played in the National Mar-

bles Tournament, which has been held at Wildwood-by-the-Sea, N.J., and is now held at Cleveland, Ohio.

In this competition, which is open to boys and girls 14 years old and younger, a ring 10 feet in diameter is inscribed on a smooth level surface. Two lines, at right angles, are drawn through the center of the circle to its perimeter to form a cross. Glass marbles, not more than five eighths of an inch in diameter, are placed within the circle —one at the center and three each on each of the four branches of the cross, each marble three inches away from the next one.

From a line drawn tangent to the circle a player knuckles down, that is, he places at least one knuckle on the ground and attempts to knock the marbles out of the ring with a shooter (a marble of any substance but metal and varying from one half to three quarters of an inch in diameter). The player continues to shoot so long as he knocks at least one marble outside the ring in one shot; he then gives way to the next player. There are a number of other rules for this official game, but, in essence, the game is won by the player first knocking seven marbles out of the ring. Where more than two players take part and a tie results, a new game is played to break the tie.

Of the many informal local games, some are played with holes in the ground. The winner is he who most accurately shoots his marbles into the holes—a game known in some locales as "bunny-in-the-hole." In another variation small clay ("commy") or glass marbles are shot at a larger glass ("glassie") or agate ("aggie"). The holder of the large marble keeps all the small ones that fail to hit it, and surrenders it when a hit is made, the game then resuming with roles reversed. In a "hit and span" variation a player scores a point if he comes within a hand's breadth of the large marble. Some games are on a point basis, others "for keeps"—the winning player enlarging his supply of marbles.

Parke Cummings,
Author of "The Dictionary of Sports."

MARBLING, in bookbinding. See Bookbinding—*Hand Binding* (Marbling).

MARBURG, mär'boork (also Marburg an der Lahn, än dĕr län'), city, Germany, in the State of Hesse, part of the Federal Republic of Germany (West Germany). It is on the Lahn River about 47 miles north of Frankfurt am Main. Marburg is a livestock market, and among its manufactures are precision instruments, chemicals, textiles, and pottery. Points of interest include the castle of the landgraves of Hesse and the Church of St. Elizabeth (burial place of St. Elizabeth of Hungary, Frederick the Great of Prussia, and Paul von Hindenburg), both dating from the 13th century, and the University of Marburg, founded by Philip of Hesse in 1527 as the first Protestant university in Germany. The history of Marburg goes back at least as far as the 12th century; the charter was granted in 1227. During World War II, United States troops captured the city in 1945. Pop. (1956) 39,566.

MARBURY v. MADISON, a famous case considered in 1803 by the United States Supreme Court. It is important in that it established the rule that the court can declare legislation invalid when it conflicts with the Constitution of the United States. William Marbury was appointed justice of the peace in the District of Columbia by President Adams, but the commission, though drawn up, signed and sealed, had never been delivered. Madison, when he became secretary of state, refused to deliver it. An act of Congress empowered the United States Supreme Court to issue to executive officers a writ of mandamus to force them to attend to their duties, and on the basis of this act Marbury brought suit. Now the Constitution nowhere mentions the right to issue a writ of mandamus among the cases of original jurisdiction by the Supreme Court. Chief Justice Marshall therefore decided against Marbury, and his argument, admittedly the only accurate one, established an important precedent which is found only in the courts of the United States.

MARCABRU, màr-kà-brü', a French troubadour: b. in Gascony, about 1140; d. toward the end of the 12th century. He was a special favorite at the court of Alfonso VIII of Castile, where he seems to have been the chief of the royal troubadours.

MARCASITE, mär'kà-sīt, *in mineralogy,* an iron disulphide (FeS$_2$), differing from pyrites in that it crystallizes in the orthorhombic system. It is usually a pale yellow, being thus lighter than true pyrites, but it has gray to brown-black streaks. Deposits are found in Germany, England, Missouri, Wisconsin and Illinois.

MARCEL, màr-sĕl, **Étienne**, French political leader: d. Paris, July 31, 1358. From December 1354 he was provost of the Paris merchants and actual ruler of the city. He put to death two officials of the Crown and finally persuaded the dauphin Charles (later King Charles V of France) to act as regent while King John the Good was held by the English. Not finding the Dauphin properly submissive, he obtained assistance from Charles the Bad of Navarre. He was killed during an uprising of the more wealthy and conservative citizens against his power.

MARCELINE, mär-sĕ-lēn', city, Missouri, in Linn County; altitude 858 feet; 104 miles northeast of Kansas City; on the Santa Fe Railroad. Railroading and mining have been its principal industries, but farming and food processing are advancing here. Walt Disney spent his boyhood years in Marceline. The city owns light and water supply systems. Pop. 2,872.

MARCELLINUS, mär-sĕ-lī'nŭs, Saint and pope: reigned 296–304. The Diocletian persecution raged during his reign, and he has been accused by the Donatists (q.v.) of relinquishing the sacred books and of offering incense to the gods. This is questioned by Augustine as Marcellinus died a martyr.

MARCELLUS I, mär-sĕl'ŭs, Saint and pope. reigned 308–309. After an interregnum of two years he was elected pope and found the church in great confusion after the Diocletian persecution. He restored some semblance of order by dividing Rome into 25 districts supervised by a presbyter with certain authority. He incurred the enmity of the *lapsi* for refusal to readmit them to the church without doing penance for their apostasy. The tyrant, Maxentius, seized the pope and banished him. He died in exile.

MARCELLUS II (real name MARCELLO CERVINI DEGLI SPANNOCHI), pope: reigned 1555. Of great purity of life and marked ability, Paul III appointed him prothonotary apostolic and papal secretary. He was made advisor and secretary to the pope's able nephew, Cardinal Alessandro Farnese (q.v.), and accompanied him on his various legations to the courts of Europe, participating in important negotiations. Appointed president of the Council of Trent (1545 q.v.) he incurred the enmity of the emperor, Charles V, for fearlessly upholding the interests of the church. As librarian of the Vatican (q.v.) he added priceless manuscripts to its collections. Elected pope, he set about the immediate reform within the church, but was stricken ill and died after a pontificate of 22 days. Palestrina (q.v.) dedicated his famous *Missa Papae Marcelli* to him.

MARCELLUS, Marcus Claudius, Roman general: b. 268 B.C.?; d. near Venusia, 208 B.C. In 222 being consul with Scipio he twice defeated the Insubrians in northern Italy, and with his own hand killed their king, thus winning the *spolia opima.* After the disaster of Cannae in the Second Punic War (216), Marcellus took command, gained several slight victories over the Carthaginians and hence was named "the sword of Rome," Fabius Cunctator being called "the shield of Rome." His third consulship (214) was spent in Sicily, where he attacked Syracuse, and after a two years' siege prolonged by the skill of Archimedes captured the city. In his fifth consulate after two years of varying success against Hannibal in Italy he was killed in a skirmish near Venusia.

MARCELLUS STAGE, *in geology,* a term introduced by the New York State Geological Survey for the thin rock, mostly shale, which is the lowest group of the Upper Devonian System, and which is most typically seen in New York State at the little village of Marcellus.

MARCH, märch, **Alden**, American surgeon: b. Sutton, Mass., Sept. 20, 1795; d. June 17, 1869. He was educated at Boston and at Brown University, receiving the degree of M.D. from the latter in 1820. From 1825 to 1831 he was a professor in the Vermont Academy of Medicine, from 1831 to 1833 at the Albany Medical Seminary, and in 1833–1834 at the Albany Medical School. In the latter year he founded a school of practical anatomy in Albany and in 1839 founded the Albany Medical College, in which he was professor of surgery from the foundation until his death in 1869. Dr. March also founded the Albany City Hospital, and founded the American Medical Association, of which he was president in 1863.

MARCH, Francis Andrew, American philologist: b. Millbury, Mass., Oct. 25, 1825; d. Sept. 9, 1911. He was graduated from Amherst in 1845, studied law in New York in 1849–1850, was admitted to the bar in 1850, in 1856 became adjunct professor of *belles-lettres* and English literature in Lafayette College (Easton, Pa.), and in 1857 professor there of the English language and comparative philology. He was among the earliest advocates of a historical study of the English language and of a philological study of the classic works of that language. In 1870 he published his major work, *A Comparative Grammar of the Anglo-Saxon Language . . .*, which helped clarify the position of English in the Indo-European linguistic family. He was also American editorial director for *The Oxford English Dictionary* and consulting editor for the *Standard Dictionary* (2 vols., 1893–95). Gen. Peyton Conway March (q.v.) was his son.

MARCH, Fredric (born FREDERICK MC-INTYRE BICKEL), American actor: b. Racine, Wis., Aug. 31, 1897. He graduated B.A. from the University of Wisconsin in 1920 and made his stage debut the same year under his own name, Fred Bickel, in the Sacha Guitry hit *Deburau*. In 1927 he married actress Florence Eldridge and a year later went to Hollywood, where he made many films and won an Academy Award in 1932 for his *Dr. Jekyll and Mr. Hyde*. March returned to leading roles in the theater in 1938 but continued to make motion pictures, winning a second Academy Award in 1946 for his acting in *The Best Years of Our Lives*. He appeared on Broadway with Miss Eldridge in 1956 in Eugene O'Neill's *Long Day's Journey Into Night*.

MARCH, Peyton Conway, American army officer: b. Easton, Pa.; Dec. 27, 1864; d. Washington, D.C., April 13, 1955. The son of Francis Andrew March (q.v.), he graduated B.A. (1884) from Lafayette College and B.S. (1888) from the United States Military Academy with the rank of 2d lieutenant of field artillery. March served with distinction in the Philippines during the Spanish American War (1898) and as major of volunteers in quelling the insurrection (1899–1901) which followed. Returning to the Regular Army, he was attached to the General Staff (1903–1907) and served as American observer during the Russo-Japanese War (1904). When the United States entered World War I (1917), March was sent to France as major general commanding the artillery. In 1918 he was recalled, named full general and chief of staff, and in this position worked effectively to consolidate the army, expedite the draft, and move 2,000,000 men to France. He retired in 1921. When Gen. John J. Pershing published *My Experiences in the World War* (1931), criticizing the General Staff, March replied in 1932 with *The Nation at War*.

MARCH, märch, or **MARK,** märk, a frontier or border region. The term is Germanic in origin and appears in various forms in the Germanic languages; it was also adopted at an early date into the Romance languages—hence the region in Italy called the Marche (see MARCHES, THE). The plural form is usual in English, for instance, the Welsh Marches. The word also appears in such place names as Denmark, Mark Brandenburg, and Osmark (East Mark), an ancient German (and 20th century Nazi) name for Austria. Titles of nobility in various languages (Ger. *Markgraf,* Fr. *marquis,* Ital. *marchese,* and Eng. *marquess*) are derived from this term and originally signified the lord of a frontier province.

MARCH, a military movement, usually on foot, in a steady, military manner and in a given order; more commonly, a movement of troops either by vehicle or on foot. Marches are clas-

sified as *administrative* or *tactical*. The former are employed during peace, or in war when no enemy attack is expected; the efficient use of available transportation, the comfort of the troops involved, and their speedy movement are primary considerations. Tactical marches are those in which contact with the enemy is anticipated; troops and vehicles move in combat-ready formations, and their movement is protected by reconnaissance and security detachments. When necessary, *forced marches* may be employed to expedite the arrival of troops at a desired destination; this is usually accomplished by increasing the marching hours per day rather than the rate of march.

The success of a march depends upon careful planning and effective control. The commander's order specifies when and at what point the march will begin, the route, the rate of march, the arrangement of subordinate units in the column, and (when appropriate) the point at which the march will end. Roads are reconnoitered and marked; the capacities of bridges, underpasses, and similar possible bottlenecks are determined; and measures are taken either to improve or to bypass these where necessary. Military police control traffic. Halts are made at regular intervals to rest personnel and refuel vehicles. In the absence of enemy threats, day marches are preferred since they are easier to control, permit speedier movement, and are less fatiguing. Night marches are slower and harder to control, but offer concealment from hostile observation and attack.

JOHN R. ELTING,
Lieutenant Colonel, United States Army; Department of Military Art and Engineering, United States Military Academy.

MARCH, the third month of the year, numbering 31 days and including the equinox (q.v.) on the 21st, marking the beginning of spring. March was the first month of the Roman year until 46 B.C., when Julius Caesar's calendar reform shifted New Year's Day (q.v.) to January 1. It was named after the second most important Roman deity, Mars, god of war and patron of agriculture. In Christendom, after the 4th century, when Christ's birth began to be celebrated on December 25 (see CHRISTMAS) the year was assumed to start on March 25, nine months earlier, with the Annunciation of the Virgin Mary. The Gregorian calendar, which was introduced by Pope Gregory XIII into Catholic countries in 1582 and reached England and her colonies in 1752, re-established January 1 as New Year's Day.

MARCH, a musical composition originally played as an accompaniment to military movement, its characteristic duple meter corresponding to the beat of marching feet. The value of music as a stimulus to concerted action has been known at least since Old Testament times; in the Middle Ages distinctive drumbeats were used to identify the marching armies of different European countries. As an art form, the march is found in operas by Jean Baptiste Lully (1632–1687) and George Frideric Handel (1685–1759), and subsequently in the works of such noted composers as Wolfgang Amadeus Mozart (for instance, in *The Marriage of Figaro,* 1786), Ludwig van Beethoven (*Eroica Symphony,* 1804), Franz Schubert (*Marches Militaires,* before

1826), Richard Wagner (*Tannhäuser,* 1845), and Giuseppe Verdi (*Aida,* 1871). Composers who have become noted specifically for their march music include, in England, Sir Edward Elgar (1857–1934) and, in America, John Philip Sousa (1854–1932).

MARCH TO THE SEA, an episode (November-December 1864) unique in American military history, when more than 60,000 Union troops commanded by Gen. William Tecumseh Sherman (q.v.) marched through Georgia from Atlanta to the coast at Savannah. Because of the crushing blow this exploit dealt to Southern pride and because of Sherman's "nervous-sanguine" temperament, which kept him at odds with the gentlemen of the press to the point where they once characterized him as mentally unbalanced, detractors of Sherman for years endeavored to minimize the importance of the march and to strip Sherman of any credit for initiating it. The facts do not substantiate either prejudice.

Background.—August 1864 was "the darkest month of the war" for the North. Gen. Ulysses S. Grant was stalemated in the East. In Chicago the Democrats nominated Gen. George B. McClellan for president, and the convention called for a negotiated peace. In Meadville, Pa., where John Wilkes Booth had stopped en route to a visit with his sister Asia in Philadelphia, an inscription on a windowpane announced that President Abraham Lincoln would die on the 13th of the month "by the effects of poison." In Washington the president did not believe that he stood much chance of re-election.

Against this background, late in August, Sherman unleashed the drive that swept the Confederates out of Atlanta. To the Lincoln administration—indeed to all parties in the North dedicated to prosecuting the war to the bitter end—Sherman had emerged as a hero second only to Grant. Henceforth the complete destruction of Southern armies in the field would be the North's exclusive military objective, and any means that achieved this goal would be considered justified. "We are not only fighting hostile armies," Sherman once said, "but a hostile people, and must make old and young, rich and poor, feel the hard hand of war."

Before the Battle of Atlanta, Gen. John Bell Hood replaced Gen. Joseph E. Johnston as commander of the Confederate Army opposing Sherman. Critics of Hood contend that this proud, fiery Texan was only effective as a subordinate under Robert E. Lee; yet in the weeks that followed, Hood, operating in unison with cavalry forces under the gifted Gen. Nathan B. Forrest, so harassed Sherman that he was kept constantly on the defensive to protect his lines of communication. The climactic battle came at Allatoona, Ga., a vital railroad juncture. Here were vast stores of Federal supplies and a bridge over the Etowah River; by capturing one and destroying the other, Hood could damage Sherman severely. Hood's Army of Tennessee struck first and seemed to be carrying the day; then Federal forces arrived under Gen. John M. Corse, a hard-bitten veteran of Corinth and Vicksburg, and soon from the bloody slopes at Allatoona the Signal Corps was flagging to Sherman a message from Corse, one of the most famous of the war: "I am short a cheekbone and an ear, but am able to whip all hell yet!"

At least Corse whipped Hood's troops that day, forcing the Confederates back into a defensive course that led ultimately to defeat in Tennessee. Now Sherman could divide his army, sending part to pursue Hood while the remainder marched across the state to Savannah. "I can make this march, and make all Georgia howl!" Sherman declared. Grant, in command of all Federal armies, was not so sure; and when through October the plan remained unapproved, Sherman was heard to growl that Grant's lack of support was surprising since "I stood by him when he was drunk."

Grant sent Gen. James H. Wilson to Atlanta, proposing that Sherman let Wilson and the cavalry handle the raid into Georgia; Sherman told Wilson tartly that he "had not so much faith" in horse soldiers. Sherman admitted that, if he failed, his proposed march would be called "the wild adventure of a crazy fool," but he pressed the scheme doggedly until Grant, worn down, wired Sherman in early November: "I say, then, go on as you proposed." In Washington, Lincoln confessed that he was "anxious, if not fearful" of the entire scheme.

March to Savannah.—Sherman never doubted that the march to Savannah would succeed. He divided his army into two wings—the 15th and 17th Corps under Gen. Oliver Otis Howard and the 14th and 20th Corps under Gen. Henry W. Slocum—and ordered the troops to march by four parallel roads while foraging "liberally" on the country. The power "to destroy mills, houses, cotton gins, etc." was entrusted to the corps commanders. On the night of the 14th Sherman burned Atlanta, and, an aide wrote home, "The heaven is one expanse of lurid fire"; next day, with a smoldering city behind them, Federal troops began a march not knowing where they were going, though many men called out to Sherman: "Uncle Billy, I guess Grant is waiting for us at Richmond!"

Route of Sherman's march to the sea.

In subsequent days a puzzled Grant spoke for a puzzled country when he said: "Sherman's army is now somewhat in the condition of a ground-mole when he disappears under a lawn. You can here and there trace his track, but you are not quite certain where he will come out till you see his head." The description was apt. Sherman drove fast and hard, and neither a small Confederate cavalry force under Gen. Joseph Wheeler nor the local militia could offer better than token resistance. Milledgeville, then the Georgia state capital, was reached on November 23; on the way, the home of Howell

Cobb, secretary of the treasury under James Buchanan, was burned under orders from Sherman to "spare nothing." In Milledgeville the Northerners declared themselves the "Legislature of the State of Georgia," elected a speaker, and introduced an ordinance to repeal secession. The issue, Sherman declared, was "well debated" and secession nullified "by a fair vote!"

Culver Service

View of the ruins of Atlanta after the city had been burned by Sherman's army.

Generally, however, the march produced few moments of levity. The troops pushed forward, foraging "liberally," burning anything that resembled a military installation and some dwellings that did not, and giving at least partial substance to the remark, attributed to Sherman, that he would "bring every Southern woman to the washtub." Negro women, carrying household goods and babies in their arms, joined Sherman's columns by the thousands, creating one of his gravest problems. Northern tempers flared at the sight of the prison pen in Millen, about 50 miles from Savannah, and a chaplain described the place as "hardly fit for our swine to live in."

On December 8, Sherman's troops reached Pooler's Station, about eight miles northwest of Savannah. The key to the Southern defenses was Fort McAllister; and when it was stormed and taken, the capture of Savannah, defended only by a small force under Gen. William J. Hardee, became simply a question of time. On December 22, Sherman rode into the city and wired President Lincoln that he was presenting Savannah as "a Christmas-gift" along with "about 25,000 bales of cotton" which, upon investigation, proved to be over 38,000 bales. Soon a Unionist newspaper, the *Loyal Georgian,* published the first of three issues, featuring among other items the significant news that "a Union barber shop" had been opened; and for half a century Negroes in Savannah dated events from "the time Tecumpsey was here."

Aftermath in the Carolinas.—To this point much of the infamy that was attached to the march to the sea was unjustified; houses that burned in Georgia 50 years later were blamed on Sherman. When, in late January, Sherman's army turned toward South Carolina, even the

general admitted that his men "had got the idea" that this state was the "cause of all our trouble" since in firing on Fort Sumter its people "had been in a great hurry to precipitate the country into civil war" and therefore should experience "the scourge of war in its worst form." It was an open fact, a Union chaplain said, that Gen. Hugh Judson Kilpatrick, in command of the cavalry, "fitted all the boys' saddlebags with matches before leaving Savannah," suggesting there was more than an empty threat behind Sherman's comment that the state which had bred secession should now get "a bellyful of war."

Steadily Sherman's army drove through the most highly improved and cultivated region of South Carolina, and when they conferred the name "Burnwell" on the town of Barnwell, they indicated the spirit of the march. "Fear is the beginning of wisdom," Sherman had preached; his men were trying with their trail of flame to prove the point. Charleston feared the wild harvest it seemed sure to reap, but Sherman ignored this proud old city and struck instead at Columbia, the capital of the state. Not even the people of Vicksburg, who had lived for weeks in caves while Grant and Sherman laid siege to their city, knew greater terror than Sherman's troops inflicted on Columbia during the night of Feb. 17, 1865.

William Gilmore Simms, the South's greatest novelist of the time, described how Sherman's soldiers raced through the streets with "pots and vessels containing combustible liquids" with which "they conveyed the flames with wonderful rapidity from dwelling to dwelling." Young Emma Florence LeConte, another eyewitness, spoke of

Brown Brothers

Sherman's troops destroying a railroad line during the march through Georgia.

"the drunken devils" who "roamed about setting fire to every house the flames seemed likely to spare." A night of almost indescribable horror followed; James G. Gibbes, mayor of the city, estimated that 366 acres had been destroyed, and Simms gave the number of residences and stores devastated at 1,386. Sherman's own laconic comment was: "We saved what of Columbia remains unconsumed." Confederate Gen. Wade Hampton cried: "For these deeds history will brand him as a robber and incendiary and will deservedly 'dam him to everlasting fame."

The extent of personal responsibility that Sherman must bear for the villainies his soldiers committed, especially after swinging north from Georgia, has been grossly exaggerated by his enemies. Nor do they serve history when they contend that his march was without military importance, for he was shattering forever resources on which Lee depended in his stalemate with Grant before Petersburg, Va. Mid-March found Sherman deep into North Carolina, with the remnant of the Army of Tennessee, again under the command of Johnston, contesting his progress. At Bentonville on March 19 the two armies clashed; for a time the Confederates drove the Federal forces back, then Sherman threw in fresh reserves, and thereafter, reported Col. Alexander C. McClurg, "the struggle was sharp and bloody, but it was brief . . . as the sun went down that night, it carried with it the last hopes of the Southern Confederacy."

McClurg overstated the case, and yet in less than a month the end came for Lee at Appomattox. On April 17, the day Sherman received the news that Lincoln had died (April 15) from an assassin's bullet, Sherman met Johnston at a farmhouse near Raleigh, N.C., to open negotiations for the surrender of the Army of Tennessee.

Bibliography.—Report of the Committee Appointed to Collect Testimony in Relation to the Destruction of Columbia, S.C., on the 17th of February, 1865 (n.d.); Conyngham, David Power, Sherman's March Through the South (New York 1865); Who Burnt Columbia? (Charleston, S.C., 1873); Johnston, Joseph E., Narrative of Military Operations . . . (New York 1874); Sherman, William Tecumseh, Memoirs (New York 1875); Hood, John B., Advance and Retreat (New Orleans 1890); Howe, Mark A. DeWolfe, ed., Home Letters of General Sherman (New York 1894); Thorndike, Rachel Sherman, ed., The Sherman Letters (New York 1894); Dodson, William Carey, Campaigns of Wheeler and His Cavalry (Atlanta 1899); Howard, Oliver Otis, Autobiography (New York 1907); Du Bose, John W., General Joseph Wheeler and the Army of Tennessee (New York 1912); Wilson, James H., Under the Old Flag (New York 1912); Burge, Dolly Sumner (Lunt), A Woman's Wartime Journal (New York 1918); Howe, Mark A. DeWolfe, ed., Marching with Sherman (New Haven 1927); Hay, Thomas Robson, Hood's Tennessee Campaign (New York 1929); Snowden, Yates, Marching with Sherman (Columbia, S.C., 1929); Lewis, Lloyd, Sherman, Fighting Prophet (New York 1932); LeConte, Joseph, 'Ware Sherman (Berkeley, Calif., 1937); Cate, Wirt Armistead, ed., Two Soldiers . . . (Chapel Hill, N.C., 1938); Upson, Theodore F., With Sherman to the Sea, ed. by Oscar Osburn Winther (Baton Rouge 1943); Dyer, John P., The Gallant Hood (Indianapolis 1950); Miers, Earl Schenck, The General Who Marched to Hell (New York 1951); LeConte, Emma, When the World Ended, ed. by Earl Schenck Miers (New York 1957); Connolly, James A., Three Years in the Army of the Cumberland, ed. by Paul M. Angle (Bloomington 1959).

EARL SCHENCK MIERS.

MARCHAND, màr-shäṅ', **Jean Baptiste,** French army officer and explorer: b. Thoissey, Ain Department, France, Nov. 22, 1863; d. Paris, Jan. 14, 1934. Entering the military service as an enlisted man in 1883, he won a commission in 1887 and two years later was sent to French West Africa, where he took part in expeditions up the Niger River and along the Ivory Coast. In March 1897 he set out in command of a party that went from the coast of French Equatorial Africa, up the Congo, Ubangi, and Bomu rivers about 1,700 miles to the Sudanese border. They then portaged nearly 200 miles across high ground and swamps, dragging a small steamboat, the *Faidherbe*, which they launched again in the Bahr el Ghazal, and floated down this river and

the White Nile about 375 miles to Fashoda (now Kodok), Sudan, where they encamped on July 10, 1898. To counter French claims to the area, the British sent an Anglo-Egyptian force into the Sudan under Gen. Horatio Herbert Kitchener, who confronted Marchand in Fashoda on September 19. War was narrowly averted by an agreement between the French and British governments, in Britain's favor (see also KODOK— *Fashoda Incident*). Marchand was recalled and given a hero's welcome in France for his patriotic though fruitless endeavors. After serving against the Boxers in China in 1900–1901, he retired in 1904 but returned to duty in World War I as a general of division and was severely wounded in 1915 in the Champagne offensive.

MARCHE, màrsh, region and former province, France, in the central part of the country, including the present Department of Creuse and part of Haute-Vienne. It extends from the angle of the Gartempe and Creuse rivers in the northwest across the Monts de la Marche of the Massif Central nearly to Limoges; eastward it crosses the Plateau of Millevaches (Thousand Cows) to a line 10–15 miles east of the Creuse River above the Éguzon Dam, as far south as Aubusson. Rye, potatoes, and cattle are raised in the Marche, as well as sheep whose wool has been used to make the famous Aubusson carpets and tapestries. As a border region (march) of the Duchy of Aquitaine, the province was formed in the 10th century, passed to the Lusignan family in the 13th, and was seized by King Philip IV of France in the 14th. After having been a fief of various Valois and Bourbon princes, it was repossessed by Francis I in 1527 and remained a province of France until 1790, when it was divided up into the present departments. Guéret was its capital.

MARCHES, The, màr'chĕz (Ital. *Le Marche*), region, Italy, in the east central section, stretching about 100 miles along the Adriatic Sea from the Republic of San Marino in the north to the city of Ascoli Piceno and from Umbria and the central Apennines in the west to the Adriatic. The seaport of Ancona is the capital. The region is roughly rectangular, 3,744 square miles in area, and includes from north to south the provinces of Pesaro e Urbino, Ancona, Macerata, and Ascoli Piceno. Agriculture is the chief occupation; along the narrow coastal plain, watered by a dozen rivers that flow from the Apennines, fruit, olives, vegetables, grain, and raw silk are cultivated, and domestic animals, chiefly sheep and swine, are raised. Industries of the region include the manufacture of furniture, paper, and textiles; forestry, sulphur mining; hydroelectric power production; fishing; and shipbuilding.

The area known as The Marches came under Roman rule in the 3d century B.C., and was swept by barbarian invasions early in the Christian era. The northern section was ruled by the Byzantines in the 6th century A.D. In the third quarter of the 8th century, the region was placed under the nominal rule of the popes by the Frankish kings Pepin the Short and Charlemagne. In the 10th century Holy Roman emperors began to grant fiefs in these provinces, which they called marches or border regions (hence the name); the last of these grants did not expire until 1631. Thereafter The Marches belonged wholly to the Church (or Papal) States, except during their occupation by the French in the Napoleonic Wars (1797–1815). They were finally united with the Kingdom of Italy in 1860. Pop. (1966) 1,357,588.

MARCHESI, mär-kā′zē, **Mathilde** (nee GRAUMANN), German concert singer and teacher: b. Frankfurt am Main, Germany, March 26, 1826; d. London, England, Nov. 18, 1913. Daughter of a wealthy German merchant, she turned to music at 17, when her father's business reverses forced her to take up a career. After studying with Otto Nicolai in Vienna and Manuel Garcia at the Paris Conservatory, she moved to England in 1849 and won acclaim as a concert mezzo-soprano in London and on the Continent. In 1852 she married Salvatore Marchesi, cavaliere de Castrone and marchese della Rajata (1822–1908), an Italian nobleman who had become a professional singer after taking part in the revolution of 1848 in Milan. Mme. Marchesi became famous as a teacher at the Vienna Conservatory (1854–1861, 1868–1878), where her husband also taught. In 1881 she established the École Marchesi in Paris and there trained many of the finest young singers of the day, including the French operatic soprano Emma Calvé, the American Emma Eames, and the British Nellie Melba. She published a method used in many music schools, and her memoirs (in English), *Marchesi and Music* (1897).

MARCHING THROUGH GEORGIA, the title of an American ballad, popular in the North at the end of the Civil War, written by Henry Clay Work (q.v.) in 1865 to celebrate Gen. William T. Sherman's march (see MARCH TO THE SEA) from Atlanta to Savannah, Ga.

MARCIAN, mär′shăn, Byzantine emperor: b. probably in Thrace (European Turkey), 392 A.D.; d. probably at Constantinople (Istanbul), Jan. 26, 457. An officer of the palace guards, he came to the throne (450) by agreeing to wed Pulcheria, sister of the deceased Emperor Theodosius II, on condition that she would be allowed to preserve her chastity, for which she was later canonized. Marcian's domestic policy was marked by financial economy, and he ended the enormous annual tribute (established in 424) to the Huns and reduced taxation. He is best remembered for convoking the Fourth General Council at Chalcedon (451), where 630 bishops condemned Monophysitism (the doctrine that Christ has a single composite nature) and composed the so-called Definition of Chalcedon, which has procured for itself a secure place in standard Christian doctrine. Marcian successfully defended the Eastern Roman Empire in Syria (452), in Egypt (452), and on the Armenian frontier (456). His reign was a relatively calm period —in contrast to the storms which were sinking the ship of state in the Western Roman Empire.
P. R. COLEMAN-NORTON.

MARCIANO, mär-sē-ä′nō, **Rocky,** American boxer: b. Brockton, Mass., Sept. 1, 1923. He retired as world heavyweight champion in 1956, undefeated in 49 professional bouts, 43 of which he won by knockouts. Marciano, whose real name was Rocco Francis Marchegiano, boxed while in the U.S. Army and in amateur competition in the mid-1940's. He won the heavyweight title by knocking out Jersey Joe Walcott in the 13th round in Philadelphia on Sept. 23, 1952. In his first defense he again stopped Walcott, this time in the first round. He defended his title five more times in three years and retired on April 27, 1956, having won by knockouts all but the first of two bouts with Ezzard Charles. Marciano was elected to Boxing's Hall of Fame in 1959.
BILL BRADDOCK, *New York "Times"*

MARCION, mär′shĭ-ŏn, early Christian teacher: b. probably in Pontus, Asia Minor (now in Turkey); fl. first half of 2d century A.D. He was an important and influential Christian teacher, though his views were rejected as heretical by the Roman and other leading churches. Marcionism, the movement which sprang from his teaching and organizing activities, deeply divided the church of the 2d and several later centuries. There are signs of his presence in Asia and Macedonia, but his figure emerges clearly only after he reached Rome around the year 140. Even then we see him only through the eyes of more orthodox churchmen such as Tertullian and Epiphanius, who bitterly opposed his movement. Marcion produced an apologetic work, but this has perished except for quotations appearing in later denunciations and refutations of his views. He is often described as a Gnostic but, although undoubtedly influenced by Gnosticism (q.v.), he was not typical.

Marcion held that the Creator of the world, although a real God, was to be distinguished from the otherwise unknown God revealed in Christ. The former was a God of strict justice; the latter, of love. The Jewish Scriptures were held to speak only of and for the Creator God, not the God of Christ. Christianity, therefore, was not intended to fulfill Judaism, but entirely to displace it. Christ did not actually take on sinful flesh, but only appeared to do so (see DOCETISM). The Gospel stands in absolute contradiction to the Law. The original disciples of Jesus, according to Marcion, misunderstood the radical nature of the Christian position; Paul was the only true apostle. It may be added that the Marcionites practiced a very rigid asceticism, rejecting marriage. Since the Jewish Scriptures—the later Old Testament and only Bible of the churches in the earliest period—was rejected by Marcion, he was under the necessity of setting up a new Scripture for his followers: the "Gospel and Apostle," consisting of a Gospel very similar to the Gospel of Luke and a collection of Paul's letters. This Marcionite canon was a most important factor in the origin and earliest growth of the New Testament.

Consult Harnack, Adolf von, *Marcion: das Evangelium vom fremden Gott,* 2d ed. (Leipzig 1924); Knox, John, *Marcion and the New Testament* (Chicago 1942).

JOHN KNOX,
Union Theological Seminary.

MARCIONISM. See MARCION.

MARCO BOZZARIS. See BOZZARIS, MARCO.

MARCO POLO. See POLO, MARCO.

MARCOMANNI, mär-kō-măn′ī, an ancient West German tribe, one of the Suevi, who are first reported by Julius Caesar as serving with the German Ariovistus in his invasion of Gaul about 71 B.C. Their name, which means "marchmen" (borderers), derives from the fact that they lived across the Rhine from Gaul, between the Main and Danube rivers. Attacked by the Roman consul Nero Claudius Drusus, they moved eastward (c. 8 B.C.) to the region south of the Elbe in what is now Bohemia (Czechoslovakia), across the Danube from the Roman province of Noricum. Here, under their great king Maroboduus (Marbo, dethroned 19 A.D.), they became leaders of the German tribes and, with their eastern neighbors the Quadi (q.v.), were a continual threat to the Roman Empire until they were finally defeated by Marcus Aurelius Antoninus in the Marcomannic Wars (166–180 A.D.).

During the first two centuries of the Roman Empire, the Marcomanni were the best market for Roman trade with northern Europe, and they may have begun the practice of writing Teutonic runes in characters adapted from the Latin alphabet. In the 5th century they were overwhelmed by the Huns and, after 500, migrated again, from Bohemia to Bavaria.

MARCONI, mär-kō'nĕ, Marchese **Guglielmo,** Italian inventor: b. Bologna, Italy, April 25, 1874; d. Rome, July 20, 1937. His father was Giuseppe Marconi, a successful businessman and gentleman of independent means; his mother, Annie Jameson, was the youngest daughter of Andrew Jameson of Ireland. In his early years Marconi was tutored on the parental estate; later at Leghorn he met Professor Vincenzo Rosa, under whom he studied physics. He also became acquainted with Professor Augusto Righi of the University of Bologna, a pioneer in the study of electromagnetic waves. Marconi, however, was never a student at that institution or any other university.

Guglielmo Marconi

While on vacation in the Italian Alps during the summer of 1894, Marconi picked up an electrical journal containing an article describing the electromagnetic wave experiments of Heinrich Hertz. From this he conceived the idea of using Hertzian waves for communications, and he returned to his home in Pontecchio eager to test the idea. Within several months (1895) he completed his apparatus and transmitted signals through the air from one end of the house to the other, then from the house to the garden. These experiments were in effect the dawn of practical wireless telegraphy.

Early Work in England.—Since communications at sea presented the greatest promise for development and use of the invention, Marconi decided to go to England (1896), where there

was greater shipping activity. Using the Hertz radiator at the transmitter and the coherer developed (1890) by Édouard Branly as the detector at the receiver, he conducted historic experiments on Salisbury Plain, to which British Army and Navy officials were invited. Modestly, Marconi declared that his discovery was not the result of long hours of labor and thought, but of experiments with devices invented by other men, to which he applied certain improvements. First, he increased the effectiveness of wireless by connecting both transmitter and receiver with the earth, that is, grounding them; second, he used the vertical wire, or antenna, insulated from the earth, which was the more important of the two innovations.

In 1897, Marconi rigged up a new station at The Needles on the Isle of Wight, and in 1898 the first paid Marconigrams were sent by Baron Kelvin (William Thomson) to his friend George Stokes and to Sir William Preece, engineer in chief of the British Post Office, who was deeply interested in signaling without wires. Wireless now covered a distance of 18 miles. Encouraged, Marconi built a new station at Bournemouth. Shipping interests began to evince an interest in this new form of communication, and Queen Victoria invited Marconi to establish communication between Osborne House on the Isle of Wight and the royal yacht, *Osborne.* In March 1899 he flashed the first signal across the English Channel from France to the cliffs of Dover. He was then invited to the United States by the New York *Herald,* which arranged for installation of his apparatus on the steamship *Ponce,* from which bulletins were flashed on the progress of the international yacht races off the New Jersey coast.

Transatlantic Wireless.—The dawn of the 20th century found Marconi possessed with the idea of sending messages across the Atlantic. At Poldhu, on the southwest tip of England, he built a transmitter 100 times more powerful than any previous station, and in November 1901 he went to America to install a receiving station at St. John's, Newfoundland. December 12, 1901 became a historic date in the annals of wireless when the 27-year-old Marconi received signals across the ocean from Poldhu. News of his achievement sped around the world, and he was acclaimed by outstanding scientists, including Thomas A. Edison, Michael Pupin, Charles P. Steinmetz, and Sir Oliver Lodge.

Marconi then turned his attention to the application of wireless to ships at sea, conducting historic tests from the steamer *Philadelphia.* Glace Bay, Nova Scotia, was selected as a site for a transmitter to demonstrate further the capabilities of the invention by transatlantic contacts with Poldhu. The scene then shifted to Cape Cod, Mass., and from a station built at South Wellfleet communication was established with England. An exchange of messages between President Theodore Roosevelt and King Edward VII, on Jan. 19, 1903, heralded Marconi's "wonderful triumph of scientific research and ingenuity."

Marconi next selected Clifden, Ireland, as the location for a 300-kilowatt station, and there he incorporated many new ideas and improvements which resulted from the earlier tests. So strong were the signals that Glace Bay and Clifden seemed but a short distance apart as thousands of words crossed the sea. Press and commercial service was established in the year 1907.

Wireless met its first big test in time of disaster at sea on Jan. 23, 1909, when the S.S. *Republic* was rammed by the S.S. *Florida,* 26 miles south of Nantucket Lightship. Rescue ships came from all directions, and only six lives were lost, although the *Republic* sank while the crippled *Florida* was towed to port. Three years later —on April 12, 1912—the S.S. *Titanic,* bound for New York City on her maiden voyage, crashed into an iceberg in mid-ocean, and its wireless frantically called for help as the SOS flashed from the masthead. From that day no one argued that wireless was just a dream or a toy, and honors were heaped upon Marconi as a benefactor of mankind. Previously, in 1909, his achievement had been recognized by the award of the Nobel Prize in physics, which he shared with Karl Ferdinand Braun of Germany, who pioneered in the development of the electron tube.

Later Years.—During World War I, Marconi was in Italy aiding the Italian Navy in communications. Wireless emerged from the war with new records of accomplishment, and Marconi, entranced by the possibilities of short waves, directed his experiments to that spectrum. He bought a yacht, which he named *Elettra,* equipped it as a floating laboratory, and established communication between the Mediterranean and Australia and other points around the world. From short waves he went to microwaves and, in 1922, demonstrated their possibilities, especially the directional effects and their application to radiotelephony. He predicted that a revolution in wireless was coming with the harnessing of tiny waves that would vastly improve worldwide communication. Beyond that he foresaw the possibilities of sending radiophotos and eventually pictures in motion—in other words, television.

Marconi continued his research and development activities, especially in the area of microwaves, but by 1935 his health was failing, and doctors ordered him to take a complete rest. Two years later the wireless that he developed startled the world with the news that Marconi's "race of existence" had ended with tragic suddenness in a heart attack.

On March 16, 1905, Marconi had married Beatrice O'Brien, daughter of the 14th Baron Inchiquin (Edward Donough O'Brien) of Ireland. They had three children: Degna (1908), Giulio (1910), and Gioia (1916). This marriage terminated in 1924, and in June 1927 he married Contessa Maria Cristina Bezzi-Scali, who bore him a daughter, Elettra (1930). In 1929 he was made a marchese by the Italian government and in 1930 was chosen president of the Royal Academy of Italy.

Bibliography.—Vyvyan, R. N., *Wireless Over 30 Years* (London 1933); Jacot de Boinod, Bernard L., and Collier, D. M. B., *Marconi—Master of Space* (London 1935); Marconiphone Co., Ltd., *Marconi Book of Wireless* (London 1936); Dunlap, Orrin E., Jr., *Marconi: The Man and His Wireless* (New York 1937); Di Benedetto, Giovanni, *Bibliografia Marconiana* (Rome 1950); Landini, Adlemo, *Marconi* (Turin 1955).

ORRIN E. DUNLAP, JR.

MARCOS, mär′kōs, **Ferdinand Edralin,** president of the Philippines: b. Sarrat, Philippines, Sept. 11, 1917. He was the most decorated Filipino veteran of World War II.

Marcos studied at the University of the Philippines and while a law student was convicted of the murder of assemblyman Julio Nalundasan.

He appealed his own case and was acquitted in 1940. During the Japanese occupation he distinguished himself as an intelligence officer and guerrilla leader, earning 27 decorations. After World War II, he served as a special assistant to President Manuel Roxas. Marcos was Liberal minority leader in the House of Representatives from 1949 to 1959 and a senator from 1959 to 1965. Soon after becoming senate president in 1963, he switched from the Liberal party to the Nationalist party. Marcos had married (1954) Imelda Romualdez, cousin of distinguished Leyte politicians, and with her help he campaigned successfully in 1965 against incumbent President Diosdado Macapagal.

President Marcos took office on Dec. 30, 1965. He visited the United States and Japan in 1966, and was able to reduce the leases on American bases in the Philippines from 99 to 25 years. He also won assurances of financial aid from the United States. Marcos supported a continued U.S. presence in Southeast Asia, and in 1966 sent a 2,000-man construction team to South Vietnam.

LEONARD CASPER,
Boston College.

MARCUS AURELIUS ANTONINUS, mär′kŭs ô-rē′lĭ-ŭs ăn-tô-nĭ′nŭs (original name MARCUS ANNIUS VERUS; often called simply MARCUS AURELIUS), Roman emperor: b. Rome, Italy, April 20, 121; d. Vindobona (now Vienna, Austria), March 17, 180. His descent from Roman ancestors domiciled in Spain attracted the attention of the Spanish-born Emperor Hadrian (r. 117–138), who appointed him to a priesthood (129), supervised his education, betrothed him (136) to the daughter of the heir apparent Lucius Aelius Caesar, and, as a tribute to the lad's love of truth, called him not Verus (true), but Verissimus (truest). Aurelius was taught by the ablest teachers of the time, among whom was the eminent Marcus Cornelius Fronto. The letters (discovered in 1814) exchanged between Aurelius and Fronto, even after the former entered public life, reveal Aurelius' sincere affection for and high esteem of Fronto.

Marcus Aurelius Antoninus

Bettmann Archive

Aelius died before Hadrian, in the same year (138), and Antoninus Pius (r. 138–161) succeeded to the throne. Antoninus adopted (138) as his sons Aurelius (as Marcus Aelius Aurelius Verus Caesar), who was also his wife's nephew, and Lucius Ceionius Commodus (as Lucius Verus Caesar), who was Aelius' son. Among the honors next conferred on Aurelius were the quaestorship (139), which admitted him to the Senate, and the consulship (140, 145). Most important was the tribunician power (147), which he shared with Antoninus, who thus indicated that Aurelius would succeed him. Contemporaries could have foretold Aurelius' future earlier, however, both from his adoption and from his marriage (145) to Faustina, his own cousin and the emperor's daughter, whom Antoninus had substituted (138) as Aurelius' fiancée.

From 147 to 161, Aurelius lived with Antoninus in close companionship and constant confidence; at the same time he devoted himself so deeply to the pursuit of philosophy that he became eventually one of antiquity's most distinguished Stoic philosophers. During that period he began composition of his celebrated *Meditations* (see MEDITATIONS OF MARCUS AURELIUS, THE), which record his thoughts on the meaning of life and on how life should be lived. Thus, when the time came for him to reign, Aurelius started to rule as a philosopher-king, for whom the philosopher Plato five centuries earlier had yearned as the only certain end for mankind's evils.

When Aurelius acceded to the throne in 161, his first act was to share the imperial power with his adopted brother Verus (now called Lucius Aurelius Verus Augustus), to whom he affianced his daughter Lucilla. The supreme authority, however, reposed always in Aurelius, who ruled alone after Verus' death (169), until he admitted his own son Commodus to full participation in the government (177).

Foreign Affairs.—The chief task of the new emperors was to protect the empire's frontiers. Verus and other generals repelled the Parthians from the Roman protectorate of Armenia and the Province of Syria, which they had invaded (162), and then carried the war into Parthia, until Parthia sued for peace and ceded Mesopotamia, which the Romans also made a protectorate (166). The victory was costly, however, because the returning legions brought with them a pestilence which ravaged the Mediterranean area. The Parthian War ended opportunely for the Romans to oppose the Germans, who had crossed the Danube River and were descending even into northern Italy; two years were required to repulse this threat (166–168). To prevent its recurrence, Aurelius determined (169) to subdue central and southeastern Europe beyond the Danube. The Marcomanni, the Quadi (qq.v.), and the Iazyges were conquered (170–175), and their territories received partial Romanization. Next Aurelius went to Syria and Egypt to quell a rebellion (175–176). The German tribes, again descending below the Danube, then engaged Aurelius' attention until his death (177–180).

Domestic Policy.—Aurelius continued the age of good government, commenced by Marcus Cocceius Nerva (r. 96–98) and confirmed by Trajan, Hadrian, and Antoninus Pius, with such success that Edward Gibbon's famous judgment still stands that it was "the only period of history in which the happiness of a great people was the sole object of government." Among his good works are counted: foundation of schools for poor children, endowment of orphanages and hospitals, reform of taxation, abolition of cruelty in criminal laws, suppression of informers, diminution of absolute power possessed by fathers over children and by masters over slaves, admission of mothers to equal rights to property left by their children, just government of provinces, and adoption of the principle that merit—rather than

birth, rank, or friendship—justified promotion in the public service. Against these improvements must be set: increase in the burdensome bureaucracy, decline of municipal initiative through interference by the central government, depreciation of currency to pay for wars and donations to soldiers and civilians, selection of his dissolute and disreputable son Commodus as his successor, and persecution of Christians.

Persecutions.—The only indelible blot on Aurelius' memory is the severity which he exhibited toward Christians, whom he considered superstitious, pernicious, and immoral. Perhaps he had imbibed a bitter prejudice against Christians from Fronto, who hated them, or from the Stoic Epictetus, whose writings he revered and who condemned them as fanatics; or perhaps evil counselors misrepresented the Christians' conduct to him. At any rate, his profound attachment to his ancestral religion and his fear that the ancient cult was jeopardized by Christianity's progress apparently impelled Aurelius to rigorous measures against the Roman religion's rival. The fiercest persecution occurred in Gaul, where many Christians perished, particularly at Lyon and Vienne (177), amid scenes of refined torture more to be expected of a savage chieftain than of a civilized sovereign. Certainly Aurelius' considered and contemptuous cruelty was not consistent with his character as revealed by the rest of his domestic policy and by the inspired principles of his *Meditations.*

Bibliography.—Sedgwick, Henry D., *Marcus Aurelius* (New Haven 1921); Dove, C. Clayton, *Marcus Aurelius Antoninus: His Life and Times* (London 1930); Hayward, Frank H., *Marcus Aurelius: Saviour of Men* (London 1935); Cresson, André, *Marc-Aurèle*, 2d ed. (Paris 1942); Calderini, Aristide, *Marco Aurelio Antonino: imperatore* (Milan 1950); Farquharson, Arthur S. L., *Marcus Aurelius: His life and His World* (Oxford 1951); Carrata Thomes, Franco, *Il regno di Marco Aurelio* (Turin 1953); Görlitz, Walter, *Marc Aurel: Kaiser und Philosoph* (Stuttgart 1954).

P. R. COLEMAN-NORTON,
Princeton University.

MARCY, mär'sĭ, **William Learned,** American statesman: b. Southbridge, Mass., Dec. 12, 1786; d. Ballston Spa, N.Y., July 4, 1857. Graduated from Brown University (1808), he settled in Troy, N.Y., practiced law, and after serving briefly in the War of 1812, became active in local politics as a Democrat. Attracting the attention of Martin Van Buren, he became a member of the powerful Albany Regency (q.v.) group and in 1823 was made state comptroller and later (1829–1831) associate justice of the state Supreme Court. In 1831 he was elected to the United States Senate, where he made a famous speech (January 1832) in support of Van Buren's nomination as minister to England, defending the latter's patronage methods while secretary of state by declaring "to the victor belong the spoils of the enemy," a pronouncement that gave birth to the term "spoils system."

After only a year in the Senate, Marcy was elected governor of New York, serving three terms (1833–1838). During his administration the first geological survey of the state was made, and Mount Marcy in the Adirondacks was named in his honor. When James K. Polk became president, Marcy was named secretary of war (1845–1849), conducting the affairs of the department during the war with Mexico in a generally efficient manner, despite the criticism of Gen. Winfield Scott. He was now considered a strong contender for the presidency, but he never received his party's nomination. The pinnacle of his political career came in the administration of Franklin Pierce, when Marcy was secretary of state (1853–1857), an office that he discharged with great credit to himself and the nation. Among the more notable events of his tenure were the consummation (1853–1854) of the Gadsden Purchase (see GADSDEN TREATY AND GADSDEN PURCHASE, THE); the successful handling of the Koszta case (1853) with Austria (see KOSZTA AFFAIR); negotiation of the Reciprocity Treaty (1854) providing for free trade in natural products and exchange of fishing rights with Canada; settlement of the *Black Warrior* (q.v.) incident and the subsequent Ostend Manifesto (q.v.) excitement with Spain (1854–1855); and the Townsend Harris (q.v.) mission to Japan (1855).

Consult *American Secretaries of State and Their Diplomacy,* ed. by Samuel Flagg Bemis and others, vol. 6, pp. 145–294, 420–431 (New York 1928).

MARCY, Mount, mountain, New York, about 12 miles south-southeast of the village of Lake Placid in the Adirondack Mountains in the northeastern part of the state. First surveyed (1837) during the governorship of William Learned Marcy (q.v.) and named for him, it is the highest point (5,344 feet) in the state and the point of origin of the Hudson River, which springs from tiny Lake Tear of the Clouds on its slope.

MARDI GRAS, mär′dĕ grä, French name (literally, fat Tuesday) for Shrove Tuesday (see SHROVETIDE), the last day of feasting and carnival preceding the 40 penitential days of Lent in the Christian calendar. Mardi gras, which has given its name to public merrymaking generally, is a holiday in various Catholic countries. In the United States it is observed in Alabama; in Florida, in cities where it is proclaimed; and in Louisiana, in six parishes (East Baton Rouge and five around New Orleans, where Mardi Gras has become an important annual event) and various municipalities. See also CARNIVAL.

MARDONIUS, mär-dō′nĭ-ŭs, Persian general: d. Plataea, Greece, 479 B.C. The son of Gobryas, who captured Babylon (539 B.C.) for Cyrus the Great, he was delegated by his uncle Darius I, whose daughter he had married, to command the force sent to punish Athens in 492 for her aid to the Ionian rebels in Asia Minor. Stopping first in the Ionian cities to establish the pro-Persian democratic party in power there, Mardonius proceeded with his army and navy around the northern shores of the Aegean Sea, ferried his men across the Dardanelles (Hellespont), and continued into Macedonia. During the campaign, his navy was overtaken by a great storm off Mount Athos, losing half its ships and men, and his army was defeated by the Brygi in a battle in which Mardonius was wounded; but by the end of the year, Macedonia was subdued, and he was able to return to Persia.

Mardonius did not take part in the next invasion of Greece, when the Persians were defeated at Marathon (490); but after Xerxes I succeeded his father Darius on the throne (486), Mardonius encouraged him to expand his empire. The fruit of this advice was the expedition of 480 against Greece, in which Mardonius participated, when Xerxes reached Athens and burned it. The Persian navy was defeated at Salamis in September, however, and Xerxes returned to Asia, leaving Mardonius with the army in Greece. In the spring of 479 a Greek force was raised to drive out the Persians, and Mardonius met it at Plataea, where his forces were smashed by Pausanius and Mardonius was killed.

MARDUK, mär′dŏŏk, chief god of Babylon. Originally a minor Sumerian deity, he was made supreme when the Semitic Amorites established the 1st dynasty of Babylon about 1830 B.C. Previously the chief gods of three city-states had been generally recognized as superior throughout Babylonia: Anu, of Uruk, god of heaven; Ea, of Eridu, god of the waters; and Enlil, of Nippur, god of the earth and the most powerful of the three. The triumphant kings of Babylon wanted a supreme god of their own, however, and elevated Marduk by substituting him for Enlil in the story of creation—which they wrote in Accadian as an epic poem known from its first two words as *Enuma elish* (When on high).

According to this ancient epic of creation, Marduk offered to fight the rebellious dragons of chaos, Tiamat and her timorous husband Kingu, on condition that the gods granted him supreme power; forced the winds down Tiamat's open mouth, cut her in two, and fashioned earth and sky from her body; created man from Kingu's blood; and organized the cosmos. This last work of organization was commemorated every year. During the vernal equinox, when the new year began, the king had to perform certain rites to propitiate Marduk and assure the continued stability of the world.

For the next 1,500 years, Marduk remained closely identified with the Babylonian state, and successive kings paid homage to him. At the beginning of the 17th century B.C. the great king Hammurabi made Babylon supreme in Mesopotamia; and when the famous Code of Hammurabi was engraved on a black diorite stele, it was topped with a sculpture showing the king receiving the laws from Marduk. Thereafter Marduk was acknowledged as chief god of Babylon by various occupying powers: the Kassites, Assyrians, Chaldeans (who founded the Neo-Babylonian Empire, 625–539 B.C.), Persians, and Macedonians.

In the Aramaic language of later Babylonia, Marduk was usually called Bel ("Lord"), Hebrew Baal. To the Israelite captives who were brought to Babylon by Nebuchadnezzar in 597 and 587 B.C., Bel's religion was strange and hateful. His original temple tower, or ziggurat, where Hammurabi had worshiped, is thought by some to have been the Biblical Tower of Babel, and the Hebrew prophet (Jeremiah 50:2) pronounced doom on the god as well as on the state: "Babylon is taken, Bel is confounded, Merodach is broken in pieces." According to the Apocrypha, Daniel destroyed Bel's temple and converted the Babylonian king (Daniel 14 in the Douay Bible). Cyrus, the Persian empire builder, acknowledged Marduk's influence when he captured Babylon in 539 B.C., claiming that the god had personally chosen him to rule. In 331, when Alexander the Great took the city, he gave orders to rebuild Marduk's ancient ziggurat but died (323) in Babylon before the work could be begun.

W. F. ALBRIGHT,
W. W. Spence Professor of Semitic Languages, The Johns Hopkins University.

MARE ISLAND, island, California, at the mouth of the Napa River and the head of San Pablo Bay, in Solano County, opposite Vallejo, reached by a causeway. In 1854 Mare Island was established by the United States Government as a navy yard.

MAREE, Loch, mà-rē′lŏK, Scotland, a lake in Ross and Cromarty County, forming a long and comparatively narrow expanse, stretching southeast to northwest for 12½ miles with a breadth of from one half to two miles. Its depth in most places is 60 fathoms; it has never been known to freeze. The scenery along its shores is bold and picturesque, and its surface is studded with 32 wooded islands, on one of which are found the remains of an ancient chapel, with a graveyard. One is Saint Swithin's Isle, shaped like a doughnut, enclosing a lake 750 feet long. The loch discharges itself into Loch Ewe by a small river of the same name.

MAREES, mä-rā′, **Hans von**, German historical painter: b. Elberfeld, Dec. 24, 1837; d. Rome, Italy, June 5, 1887. He painted in Munich from 1856 until 1864, when he moved to Rome, thereafter most of his life being spent in Italy. His most notable work was the execution of the frescoes in the library of the Zoological Museum in Naples, the commission for which was given to him in 1873.

MAREMMA, mà-rĕm′à, Italy, a low, swampy region in the southwestern part of Tuscany, chiefly in Grosseto Province. It extends from the mouth of the Cecina to Orbetello, having a length of 92 miles, breadth of 6 to 20 miles, and area of about 1,000 square miles. Formerly these regions were fruitful, healthful and populous; but after the 15th century the neglect of the watercourses of the district permitted the formation of marshes and they generated insects and fevers and presented an aspect of dreary desolation during the summer months, when the inhabitants fled from the pestilences. In winter, on the other hand, the Maremma were habitable and afforded a luxuriant pasturage for cattle, which grazed in summer on the Apennines. The district was gradually reclaimed and improved in the 20th century.

MARENGO, mà-rĕng′gō, city, Iowa, seat of Iowa County, located on the Iowa River 25 miles west-southwest of Cedar Rapids. It is served by the Chicago, Rock Island and Pacific Railroad. The city is the center of a fertile agricultural and stock raising region. Food processing is the principal industry. Marengo was settled in 1845 and incorporated in 1859. Government is administered by a mayor and council. Pop. 2,264.

MARENGO, village, Italy, located in southeast Piedmont 5 miles east of Alessandria. In the vicinity, on June 14, 1800, Napoleon scored one of his greatest victories, defeating the Austrians commanded by Baron Michael Friedrich Benedikt von Melas (1729–1806). The Austrians were at first successful, but with the arrival of French reinforcements a cavalry charge led by Gen. François Étienne de Kellermann (q.v.) turned what looked like certain defeat into a decisive victory. The French lost about 4,000 men, including Gen. Louis Charles Antoine Desaix de Veygoux (q.v.) ; the Austrians, 9,500. The main consequence of the victory at Marengo was the cession of northern Italy to France.

MAREOTIS, mãr-ê-ō′tĭs, or **MARYUT**, mŭr-yōōt′, Egypt, a salt lake separated from the Mediterranean on the west by the long, narrow strip of land on which stands part of the city of Alexandria. The most westerly of the lakes in the Nile Delta, it is about 28 miles long by 20 broad. At one time it was deep enough for inland navigation, and had its shores covered with beautiful gardens and vineyards. During the siege of Alexandria in 1801 the British let the sea into it, and it now yields great quantities of salt by evaporation.

MARE'S TAIL, a genus (*Hippuris*) of plants with whorled narrow leaves and small inconspicuous flowers set in their axils. They are aquatic or marsh plants. *H. vulgaris* is common in Europe and in some parts of North America.

MARESCOT, Mount, peak, highest point (3,900 feet) on Santa Isabel Island, east central Solomon Islands, in the Pacific Ocean.

MARET, mà-rĕ′, **Hugues Bernard**, DUC DE BASSANO, French statesman: b. Dijon, 1763; d. Paris, 1839. An ardent supporter of the French Revolution, he published the debates of the National Assembly in the *Bulletin de l'Assemblée*, later expanded into the *Moniteur Universel*. After the monarchy fell in 1792 he undertook a diplomatic mission to London, and the next year he was sent to Naples as ambassador of the French Republic. Seized by the Austrians, he was imprisoned at Brünn until 1796. During 1797 he conducted negotiations with Great Britain, and after Napoleon became first consul of France in 1799 Maret became the latter's confidential adviser. He was created a count in 1807 and duke of Bassano (q.v.) in 1809, and from 1811 to 1813 he was minister of foreign affairs. During the Hundred Days (q.v.) he was minister of state, but after Napoleon went into exile in 1815 he was banished from France. In 1820 he was permitted to return, and Louis Philippe created him a peer of France in 1831.

MARETZEK, mä′rĕ-tsĕk, **Max**, American musician: b. Brünn, Moravia, Jan. 28, 1821; d. Pleasant Plains, Staten Island, May 14, 1887. He was educated at the University of Vienna, but desirous of a wider field went to London and was connected for a time with its Italian Opera as chorus-master, writing in addition some music. In 1848 he came to New York, where he was appointed leader of the orchestra at the Italian Opera and subsequently at the Astor Place Theatre and the Grand Opera House. He wrote the operas of *Hamlet, Sleepy Hollow*, and an interesting book on contemporary life entitled *Crotchets and Quavers* (1858). Under his management many notable operas and artists, among the latter Adelina Patti and Pauline Lucca, were presented to American audiences.

MAREY, mà-rā′, **Étienne Jules**, French physiologist: b. Beaune, 1830; d. Paris, 1904. He became a professor of natural history on the faculty of the Collège de France in 1867, and he made investigations on the physiology of circulation and the heart, on the action of poisons, on animal heat, and motion in animals. He invented the improved form of the sphygmograph (q.v.) in 1863.

MARFA, mär′fà, city in western Texas and Presidio County seat, on the Texas and New Orleans railroad about 175 miles southeast of El Paso and about 55 miles from the Rio Grande, at the foot of the Davis Mountains; alt. 4,688 feet. It is a trading center for large livestock ranches, shipping cattle, goats, sheep and mohair. The brisk mountains in the vicinity are increasingly visited by tourists and hunters. Silver was once mined in the region. Outside Marfa is Fort D. A. Russell, an old army post set up in 1833. The city, founded in 1884, was incorporated in 1887. Pop. 2,799.

MARGARET, Saint, Christian martyr. According to legend she was martyred about 275 (other sources say 307). She is held to be identical with St. Pelagia. Known in Greek as Marina, her feast is July 17 in the Greek church. Her feast in the Western church, July 20, was dropped from the universal liturgical calendar in 1969 because her existence was questioned.

MARGARET, Saint, queen of Scotland, elder sister of Edgar Aethling, and granddaughter of Edmund Ironside: b. Hungary about 1045; d. Edinburgh, Scotland, Nov. 16/17, 1093. She and her brother Edgar went to Scotland and placed themselves under the protection of Malcolm III Canmore, the Scottish king, who, c.1067, became her husband. It was largely through her influence with the king that the Scottish Church was brought into conformity with those of England and the Continent. Margaret is said to have elevated the manners of the Scottish court and to have set a noble example to the people. In 1251 she was canonized. Her daughter Matilda married the English king, Henry I, and thus the old Anglo-Saxon line became united with that of the usurping Normans. Her feast is June 10.

MARGARET, queen of Denmark, Norway and Sweden, sometimes called "The Semiramis of the North," daughter of Waldemar IV, king of Denmark: b. Søborg, near Copenhagen, Denmark, 1353; d. Flensburg (now Germany), Oct. 28/29, 1412. Married to Haakon VI, king of Norway, in 1363, the death of her husband in 1380 placed Norway in her hands; that of her son Olaf in 1387 enabled her to secure also the throne of Denmark; and after defeating Albert of Mecklenburg, the Swedish king, she obtained possession of the throne of Sweden as well. She endeavored to place the union of the three kingdoms on a permanent basis by the celebrated Act of Union or Treaty of Kalmar (1397).

MARGARET OF ANJOU, än′jŏŏ or än-zhŏŏ′, queen consort of Henry VI of England: b. probably at Pont-à-Mousson, Lorraine, France, March 23, 1430; d. Dampièrre, near Saumur in Anjou, France, Aug. 25, 1482. The daughter of René the Good of Anjou, titular king of Naples, she was married to Henry in 1445. The imbecility of the king made her practically regent, and her power being contested by the Duke of York, a claimant of the throne by an older line, the protracted Wars of the Roses began. At first victorious, she was afterward compelled to flee to Scotland, but raising an army in the north, she secured by the battle of Wakefield (1460) and the 2d battle of Saint Albans (1461) the death of York, and the release of the king. Her army, however, was soon afterward annihilated at Towton (1461), and Edward IV, the son of the late Duke of York, was declared king. In a last attempt, Margaret, collecting her partisans, fought the battle of Tewkesbury (1471), and was totally defeated. She and her son were made prisoners, and the latter, when led into the presence of the royal victor, was killed. Henry soon after died or was murdered in the Tower, and Margaret remained in prison for almost five years. Louis XI ransomed her (1476) for 50,000 crowns. See also HENRY VI; ROSES, WARS OF THE.

MARGARET OF AUSTRIA, regent of the Netherlands, and daughter of Maximilian I of Austria: b. Brussels, now Belgium, Jan. 10, 1480; d. Mechlin, now Belgium, Dec. 1, 1530. Educated at the French court, she was betrothed to the Dauphin Charles (later Charles VIII), who, however, married Anne of Brittany. She married instead John, the Spanish crown prince, in 1497; and, after his death in the same year, married Philibert II of Savoy in 1501, only to be widowed again in 1504. Three years afterward her father made her regent of the Netherlands, where she ruled with much ability, although a bitter enemy of the Reformation. She took a prominent part in the peace of Cambrai in 1529, which is called, because negotiated by her and Louise of Savoy, the "Paix des Dames."

MARGARET OF CARINTHIA, kà-rĭn′-thĭ-à, or **MARGARET MAULTASCH,** moul′-täsh, countess of Tirol: b. 1318; d. Vienna, Austria, Oct. 3, 1369. She retained rule over the Tirol after her father's death (1335) despite the opposition of Emperor Louis IV. After divorcing her husband John Henry, son of the king of Bohemia, she married the Emperor's son, Louis, margrave of Brandenburg. In 1363 she abdicated. Also called Ugly Duchess (the title of a historical novel by Lion Feuchtwanger), she has become almost proverbial for her rancor and hideous looks.

MARGARET OF FLANDERS, countess of Flanders and Hainaut, sometimes called Margaret of Constantinople: b. Valenciennes, France, about 1200; d. Lille, France, Feb. 10, 1279. She was a daughter of Baldwin IX of Flanders and Hainaut (Baldwin I of Constantinople), who was succeeded by her older sister, Jeanne. Upon the latter's death in 1244 Margaret acceded. Her son by a first marriage, Jean d'Avesnes, took Hainaut (1246), but she retained Flanders.

MARGARET or **MARGUERITE OF NAVARRE,** nà-vär′, queen of Navarre, variously known as Margaret of Angoulême, of Orléans, and of Valois: b. Angoulême, France, April 11, 1492; d. Odos en Bigorre, Hautes-Pyrénées, France, Dec. 21, 1549. The daughter of Charles d'Orléans, Count of Angoulême, and a sister of Francis I of France, she was brought up at the court of Louis XII and married the Duke of Alençon in 1509. Widowed in 1525, she married in 1527 Henri d'Albret, titular king of Navarre. She resided at the French court or at Nérac and Pau. A protector of Protestant reformers, she was also a great patroness of men of letters. In 1533 she published a religious poem, *Le Miroir de l'Ame Pécheresse,* which incurred the censure of the Sorbonne as heretical. In 1547 a collection of her poems and other pieces was printed under the title of *Marguerites de la Marguerite des Princesses.* The *Heptaméron, ou sept Journées de la Reyne de Navarre,* a famous collection of tales long attributed to her exclusively, is probably of composite authorship. She left one child, Jeanne d'Albret; afterward mother of Henry IV of France. See HEPTAMERON, THE.

MARGARET OF PARMA, regent of the Netherlands: b. Oudenarde, 1522; d. Ortona, 1586. She was also known as Margaret of Austria. She was a natural daughter of Charles V of Spain by a Flemish woman. Brought up in Brussels, she was married to Alessandro de Medici in 1536, and in 1538 to Ottavio Farnese, duke of Parma, to whom she bore the great general, Alexander Farnese. In 1559 Philip II made her regent of the Netherlands. There she sided with Cardinal de Granvelle, introduced the Inquisition and provoked the provinces to revolt by her strong, masculine policy. She resigned in 1567 when the duke of Alva was sent to the Netherlands.

MARGARET OF VALOIS, vȧ-lwȧ', or **OF FRANCE,** known as QUEEN MARGOT: b. Saint Germain-en-Laye, France, May 14, 1553; d. Paris, March 27, 1615. She was the daughter of Henry II of France and Catherine de Médicis. She married in 1572 Henry of Navarre, afterward Henry IV of France. It was entirely a marriage of policy, and on Henry's accession to the throne their marriage was dissolved by mutual consent. She resided thereafter in Paris where her house became the rendezvous of the learning and fashion of the time. Some very agreeable poems by her are extant and her *Memoirs* (1842) are extremely interesting.

MARGARET TUDOR, queen of Scotland, wife of James IV and daughter of Henry VII of England: b. Westminster, Nov. 29, 1489; d. Methven Castle, Oct. 18, 1541. She was married to the king of Scotland when 14; bore him three children, of whom two, James, later fifth king of Scotland of that name and father of Mary Stuart, and Margaret, mother of Lord Darnley, survived her; and after the king's death (1514) married Archibald Douglas, earl of Angus, from whom she was divorced in 1527, to marry soon after Henry Stewart, lord of Methven. By descent from Margaret Tudor her great-grandson, James VI of Scotland, was Elizabeth's successor as James I of England.

MARGARETTA, The, a British armed schooner, captured by Americans near Machias, Me., June 12, 1775, in the first naval contest of the American Revolution.

MARGARIC ACID, name formerly given to an acid having the chemical formula $C_{17}H_{34}O_2$, and supposed to exist in natural fats. Later the name came to be applied only to an acid obtained by boiling cetylic cyanide with potassic hydrate solution.

MARGARINE, mär'jȧr-ĭn, a concentration of highly refined vegetable oils emulsified in fresh pasteurized skim milk. Domestic vegetable oils, primarily soybean and cottonseed, contribute practically all of the fats and oils used in American margarine. Margarine consists of 80 per cent fat content by weight which is made up of highly refined oils. Approximately 16 per cent by weight is pasteurized, cultured skim milk The remainder is made up of salt, Vitamin A, and minor ingredients. Margarines are emulsified under scientific control so that the finished product is a smooth-textured spread for bread.

Hippolyte Mège-Mouriès, a French scientist, invented the product now known as margarine as a result of a contest sponsored by Napoleon III for a palatable table fat. Mège-Mouriès won the prize and the product was patented in England in 1869. A small production in France was resumed after the Franco-Prussian War in 1870.

In 1874, margarine was introduced into the United States during a period when a surplus of farm products was being produced. Almost immediately 22 states levied discriminatory taxes on the product to give butter a frankly competitive advantage. Federal legislation, which was to last 64 years, went into effect in 1886. This legislation consisted of taxes and restrictions designed to curtail the sale of margarine. Amendments increasing the severity of the original law were passed in 1902 and 1930. Congress repealed these restrictions by the act approved March 16, 1950, effective July 1, 1950. The new law:

(1) Repealed all federal taxes on yellow and white margarine and annual license fees on retailers, wholesalers and manufacturers handling yellow and/or white margarine.

(2) Defines the product as "margarine."

(3) Stipulates labeling requirements on the package so as to leave no doubt that the consumer would be purchasing margarine.

(4) Specifies notification and serving requirements for public eating places serving yellow margarine as follows:

(a) A sign must be displayed or a notice carried on the menu stating that margarine is served and,

(b) Each separate serving must be in triangular shape or bear or be accompanied by labeling identifying it as margarine.

Margarine today bears little resemblance to the product manufactured before the turn of the century. Its ingredients and technology have radically changed. During the early part of this century, methods of refining vegetable oils were materially improved, thus leading to the gradual increase in the use of vegetable oils in margarine. Odors and flavors were eliminated, producing a blandness which would then readily absorb the flavor of the milk to be incorporated. The shortage of fats during and after World War I intensified the trend toward wider use of vegetable oils and for the first time soybean oil was used in significant quantities.

With the discovery of new processes in 1937, cottonseed oil became the major fat ingredient, supplanting coconut oil, which was temporarily a major fat contributor. Since that time American cottonseed, soybean, corn, and safflower oils have become the major fat ingredients of margarine, especially soybean oil. Margarine is second only to shortening as the major food user of soybean and cottonseed oils. Unsaturated vegetable oils are very important from the medical standpoint, because they limit the amount of cholesterol in the blood and perhaps abate the frequency of arterial hardening in humans.

In the mid-1960's over a billion pounds of soybean oil were used annually in the manufacture of margarine. The amount of cottonseed oil employed annually for the same purpose was somewhat over 100 million pounds. About 160 million pounds of corn oil were also thus used, as well as 45 million pounds of other vegetable oils (peanut, safflower, and others). Close to 100 million pounds of animal fats and oils were utilized in the manufacture of margarine in a single year. Milk products, such as skim milk, are also an important ingredient of margarine.

Margarine is manufactured and distributed under the Federal Food, Drug and Cosmetic Act and the similar laws of the various states. In 1941 the United States Food and Drug Administration established the "Definition and Standard of Identity for Oleomargarine" in order to assure consumers a product of uniformly high quality. As amended effective Aug. 18, 1952, this regulation sets forth required and optional ingredients; fixes the fat content at 80 per cent; permits coloring; and requires each pound that is fortified with Vitamin A be fortified with a minimum of 15,000 U.S.P. units. The standard, following the act of March 16, 1950, recognizes the word margarine as well as oleomargarine to describe the product.

Leading authorities have long recognized the high food value of margarine. The following nutritional experts have attested that margarine is the nutritional equal of any other table spread: The American Medical Association's Council on Food and Nutrition; The United States Department of Agriculture, which includes margarine on its "Basic 7" food list; The Food and Nutrition Board of the National Research Council; The New York Academy of Medicine's Committee on Public Health Relations; and the United States Army. One scientific test, the results of which appeared in the American Medical Association *Journal*, February 7, 1948, concluded that "Growing children experience normal growth in height and weight when their diets contain only fortified margarine as table fat, as shown by comparison with children fed on similar diets with butter as the source of table fat . . ." and "Whether the greater part of the fat of the diet is derived from vegetable or animal sources has no effect on growth and health. . . ."

The Committee of Public Health Relations of the New York Academy of Medicine has said: "From a nutritional viewpoint, when it is fortified with Vitamin A in the required amount, oleomargarine is the equal of butter, containing the same amounts of protein, fat, carbohydrates and calories per unit of weight. Moreover, since the minimum Vitamin A content of 'enriched' margarine is fixed, and the amount of this Vitamin A in butter may range from 500 to 20,000 units per pound, 'Enriched' oleomargarine is a more dependable source of Vitamin A than is butter. Since it is a cheaper product than butter, fortified oleomargarine constitutes a good vehicle for the distribution of Vitamin A and fats. . . ."

With the advent of World War II margarine consumption increased rapidly despite restrictive regulation. In 1941 the average per capita consumption of margarine was 2.7 pounds. Since then margarine consumption has risen steadily; it stands at almost 10 pounds yearly (as of the mid-1960's). Public interest in removing discriminatory restrictions on the product, manifested over many years and successful in several states, crystallized. Although a large majority—consumer, farm, labor, grocer and other groups—asked for federal and state repeal actions, butter interests almost alone sought to keep the restrictions on the grounds of protecting the price of butter. On April 28, 1948, a repeal bill was passed by the House of Representatives by a heavy majority, but adjournment prevented any action by the Senate.

Further hearings before the 81st Congress resulted in another repeal bill being passed by the House of Representatives by a large majority on April 1, 1949. On Jan. 18, 1950, the bill, with certain amendments, was easily passed by the Senate and became law as of July 1, 1950. Certain labeling requirements and other provisions were incorporated with the purpose of safeguarding the sale of margarine.

New York State and Washington State repealed bans on the sale and manufacture of yellow margarine in 1952, the latter in a popular referendum, reducing to only six the number of states still prohibiting such sale. In the six—Iowa, Minnesota, Montana, South Dakota, Vermont, and Wisconsin—consumer, dealer, and farm groups are seeking repeal.

The situation for butter is quite different. Per capita butter consumption declined from 16.9 pounds in 1940 to 6.5 pounds in 1965. The amount of milk used in buttermaking has declined since 1940, when it was 40 per cent.

Thus, though margarine consumption has nearly quadrupled since 1941, butter consumption today is less than two fifths what it was in 1940. Margarine has just about filled the consumption and nutrition gap left by the decline in the civilian use of butter in the United States. Some dietitians are satisfied with the situation.

CLARA GEBHARD SNYDER,
Food Consultant.

MARGARITA, mär-gä-rē′tä, Venezuela, an island off the northeast coast, in the Caribbean Sea, about 35 miles north of Cumana. In 1901 it was made a province and is known by the name of Nueva Esparta. Its area is 450 square miles. This island was discovered by Columbus in 1498; it was settled by the Spanish about 1525. The name Margarita, meaning "pearl," was given to it because of the pearl fisheries still existing in surrounding waters. The capital of the province in La Asunción; the chief port Pampatar. The natives are mostly civilized Indians. Pop. (1961) 85,286.

MARGATE, mär′gät, England, a seaport and popular summer watering resort of Londoners, in Kent, in the Isle of Thanet division, 64 miles by rail east of London. The restored parish church of Saint John the Baptist dates from 1050. It was originally a fishing village, but began to develop as a resort about the year 1800. Its sea walks are continuous with those of Westgate and Broadstairs.

MARGATE FISH, a handsome, pearly white, brown-striped fish (*Haemulon album*) of West Indian waters, important as a food fish.

MARGHERITA, queen dowager of Italy: b. Turin, Nov. 20, 1851; d. Jan. 4, 1926. She was the daughter of Ferdinand, Duke of Genoa. In 1868 she was married to Humbert, then crown prince of Italy, who ascended the throne of Italy in 1878. In that same year an attempt was made upon the life of the king, and the nervous shock to the queen seriously affected her health for a number of years. Her winning personality and dignified performance of her duty as queen gained her wide popularity in Italy. In 1900 her husband was assassinated and their son, Victor Emmanuel III, succeeded him as king.

MARGHERITA PUSTERLA, for many years the most popular historical novel in Italy with the exception of Manzoni's masterpiece, *I promessi sposi,* was written between 1833 and 1834 while the author, Cesare Cantù, lay in prison charged with political offenses against the Austrian authorities. Composed under great difficulties, suppressed by the foreign oppressors who felt themselves attacked through this work, the novel was not published till 1838. The theme deals with the period of the Italian despots of the 14th century—a period which had already been treated in Tommaso Grossi's *Marco Visconti* (1834), to which novel Cantù alludes in his own work. The scene is laid in Milan in 1340–1341 during the reign of Luchino Visconti. The latter attempts to seduce Margherita, the wife of the rich and noble Franciscolo Pusterla. Rebuffed by her, the tyrant seeks revenge by sending to the scaffold husband, wife and their young son, a mere child, after having had the parents condemned for treason against the state and conspiracy against his life. Vain attempts to save his master and mistress by the devoted young squire, Alpinolo, an effort to deter the vindictive Luchino from his cruel purpose on the part of the good monk Fra Buonvicino (a replica of the famous Fra Cristoforo of *I promessi sposi*), heighten the interest of this somber tale. With the exception of the impulsive and engaging Alpinolo, the sardonic court-jester Grillincervello and the saintly Fra Buonvicino, the characterization is mediocre. The book owes its success to the splendid pictures of mediaeval life and to the pathos and horror of its situations. The execution of Margherita Pusterla, a powerful but revolting scene, has been much admired. For a historian of no mean ability, Cantù, as has been justly pointed out by Mazzoni, makes curious blunders and takes singular liberties with his sources. Written when Romanticism was supreme in Italy, *Margherita Pusterla* is an imitation of *I promessi sposi* combined with an attempt to rival the vast panoramas, the highly colored realism and the violent contrasts of *Notre Dame de Paris.*

ALFRED G. PANARONI.

MARGOLIOUTH, mär-gō′lĭ-ŭth, *later* mär-gŭl-yōōth, **David Samuel,** English Arabic scholar: b. London, Oct. 17, 1858; d. Mar. 23, 1940. He was educated at Oxford, and was Laudian Professor of Arabic at Oxford in 1889–1937. His published works are associated chiefly with Arabic literature, and include *Letters of Abul Ala* (1898); *Mohammed and the Rise of Islam* (1905); *Yakut's Dictionary of Learned Men* (edited in Arabic, 1907–25); *The Homer of Aristotle* (1924).

MARGOLIS, Max Leopold, American Hebrew philologist: b. Merech, Vilna, Russia, Oct. 15, 1866; d. April 2, 1932. In 1889 he was graduated at the Leibniz Gymnasium, Berlin, and in 1890 received the degree of A.M. at Columbia University and the degree of Ph.D. the following year. In 1892 Dr. Margolis was lecturer on Jewish literature at the Glenmore School for Culture Sciences, Keene, N. Y. From 1892 to 1897 he was connected with the Hebrew Union College, Cincinnati, as assistant professor of Hebrew and Biblical exegesis. In 1897 he became professor of Semitic languages and literatures at the University of California, where he was associate professor from 1898 to 1905. In 1905–07 he held the chair of Biblical exegesis at Hebrew Union College. In 1907–1908 Dr. Margolis visited European libraries and in the following year was editor-in-chief of Bible translation for the Jewish Publication Society of American. From 1909 he was professor of Biblical philology at the Dropsie College for Hebrew and Cognate Learning, Philadelphia. He was the author of *Commentarius Isaacidis quatenus ad textum talmudicum investigandum adhiberi possit tractatu Erubhin ostenditur* (1891); *The Columbia College Manuscript of Meghilla* (1892); *An Elementary Text-Book of Hebrew Accidence* (1893); *The Theological Aspect of Reformed Judaism* (1904); *The Holy Scriptures with Commentary on Micah* (1908); *A Manual of the Aramaic Language of the Babylonian Talmud* (1910); *The Story of Bible Translations* (1917); *The Hebrew Scriptures in the Making* (1922); and contributions to philological and theological publications. In 1922 Dr. Margolis became editor of the *Journal* of the American Oriental Society.

MARGRAVE, in mediaeval times, in continental Europe, a border count or commander entrusted with the protection of a *mark,* or district on the frontier. As early as the times of Charlemagne marks and margraves appear. The margraves stood immediately under the German kings and emperors. In the 12th century margraviates became hereditary and at last the margraves acquired the rank of princes of the empire, between counts and dukes.

MARGUERITE, mär′gĕ-rēt, a popular name for several flowers of the family *Asteraceae.* The blue marguerite (*Felicia amelloides*), or blue daisy, is a native of southern Africa, and has long been popular in greenhouses and window gardens because of its simple culture and large solitary flower-heads. The Paris daisy or marguerite (*Chrysanthemum frutescens*), a native of the Canary Islands, was introduced into cultivation in Great Britain about the close of the 18th century and has continued a popular florist's flower ever since. It is the one usually obtainable throughout the year in the stores, but especially during the winter. Because of a close resemblance, the name is applied to its near relative, the ox-eye daisy (*C. leucanthemum*), which is common in mismanaged pastures and fields, especially in the New England and adjacent States. The Reine marguerite (*Callistephus hortensis*) is better known in America as China aster (see ASTER) and is one of the most popular out-of-door annuals of the garden, being easily grown from seed and readily adaptable to any garden soil. The English daisy (*Bellis perennis*) is also called marguerite, but less frequently.

MARIA II, usually known as **Maria da Gloria,** thà glô'ryà, queen of Portugal: b. Rio de Janeiro, April 4, 1819; d. Lisbon, Nov. 15, 1853. She was a daughter of Dom Pedro I of Brazil and on the death of her grandfather, John VI of Portugal in 1826, her father ceded to her the succession to the throne. Her uncle, Dom Miguel, to whom she was betrothed was appointed regent, but in 1828 upon the sailing of the young queen for Spain he usurped the throne and barred the landing of the queen. In 1832–1833 Dom Pedro instigated a civil war against his brother and, through the intervention of England and France, Maria was placed on the throne in 1834. She married Duke Ferdinand of Saxe-Coburg and though retaining her throne had a troubled and rather unsuccessful reign. Upon her death her son, Pedro V, ascended the throne.

MARIA CHAPDELAINE, a novel of French-Canadian pioneer life written by Louis Hémon while he was working on a farm, also the locale of the story, near Péribonca, Quebec. It was first published in a Paris newspaper in Jan., 1914. The lives of Samuel Chapdelaine's family revolve around the ceaseless struggle to wrest a farm from the unbroken forest of the St. Johns Lake country. Maria, his daughter, loves François Paradis, a young trapper. Before they can be married, Paradis is lost in the winter's snow and dies. In the spring, Maria refuses Lorenzo Surprenant who offers her the pleasures of civilization, and gives her promise of marriage to a neighboring farmer, choosing to live the life her parents had lived, in the open, beside the forest. This simple story of devoted resignation, unaffectedly told, gives a vivid picture of the compensations of pioneer life.

MARIA CRISTINA, queen of Spain: b. Austria, July 21, 1858; d. Madrid, Feb. 6, 1929. She was the daughter of Archduke Karl Ferdinand of Austria, and was married by proxy to Alfonso XII of Spain in 1879. At the death of Alfonso XII in 1885, she was appointed queen-regent during the minority of her daughter, Queen Mercedes, who was succeeded six months later by Alfonso XIII, a posthumous son. The queen-regent faced a difficult problem; she was a foreigner, the people were unsympathetic, and the political and financial condition of the country was in a precarious state. She formed a new cabinet with Sagasta, the Liberal leader at its head, and soon won the hearts of her people by her wise and able rule. Throughout the time of her regency she commanded the respect and admiration of the world as well as her own country for her clear, far-sighted administration of the affairs of state and her careful training of the young king whom she endeavored to inspire with her own high sense of the responsibilities of his position. Even the disastrous outcome of the Spanish-American War failed to unsettle the stability of her government which on May 17, 1902 she surrendered into the hands of her son, Alfonso XIII.

MARIA CRISTINA DE BOURBON, ma-rē'ä krĕs-tē'nä thà bôr-bôn', queen of Spain: b. Naples, April 27, 1806; d. Havre, France, Aug. 22, 1878. She was a daughter of Francis I, king of the Two Sicilies, and was married to Ferdinand VII of Spain in 1829. Upon Ferdinand's death in 1833, Maria Christina by her husband's will became regent until her daughter,

Queen Isabella, should become 18. A civil war which was waged until 1840 ensued, its purpose being to place Don Carlos on the throne, and its outcome was for a long period doubtful, but the queen-regent appeared to care only for her chamberlain, Don Fernando Muñoz, with whom she secretly contracted a morganatic marriage. Her policy as regent was entirely subject to the will of the minister of the day which naturally resulted in a reign alternately liberal and despotic. When she affixed her signature to the law concerning the Ayuntamientos the public protested so strongly that she was obliged to resign the regency to the Prime Minister, Espartero, in 1840. In 1843, after the fall of Espartero, she returned to Madrid and in 1844 publicly married Muñoz, who was made Duke of Rianzares. A revolution in 1854 compelled her to flee the country and her return to Spain in 1864 was followed by the revolution which dethroned Queen Isabella in 1868 and she was again exiled and though allowed to return to Madrid after the accession of Alfonso XII, she died in exile.

MARIA LESZCZYNSKA, lĕsh-chĭn'y-skä, queen of France: b. Breslau, June 23, 1703; d. Versailles, June 24, 1768. She was a daughter of Stanislas Leszczynska, king of Poland, and shared the obscurity which followed upon his exile. Her marriage to Louis XV in 1725 was arranged by the regent Duc de Bourbon and the minister Fleury and was regarded as an intrigue to further their interests since it antagonized Spain by sending back the young infanta with whom an alliance had been projected. The queen after a brief period in which she tried to control state matters lived very quietly and was noted for her charities.

MARIA LUISA or **MARIE LOUISE,** empress of the French and grand duchess of Parma: b. Vienna, Dec. 12, 1791; d. there, Dec. 17, 1847. The eldest daughter of Emperor Francis I of Austria, she was 18 when Napoleon, in order to have an heir and ally himself to the old royal families of Europe, divorced Josephine and, after the Battle of Wagram and capture of Vienna, demanded her hand of her father and Prince Metternich. From her first arrival in Paris (April 1810) the very cool reception accorded her by the populace which sympathized with Josephine evoked in the new empress an equal coolness toward France and the French. Napoleon, however, was deeply in love with her. While she greatly admired him and feared him a little, she seems never to have loved him. In March 1811 she gave birth to the king of Rome. During Napoleon's absences on campaign she acted as regent, but showed utter incapacity. At the close of the campaign of France, on Napoleon's instructions she quitted the menaced capital and went with her son to Blois, but refused to continue on across the Loire with his brothers. After the emperor's abdication she went to Orléans, then joined her father at Rambouillet. During the Hundred Days she was kept secluded and separated from her son whom she would not see again until at his death. In 1816 the former empress was given the sovereignty of the duchies of Parma, Piacenza and Guastalla. She lost her throne of Parma in 1831 in consequence of a popular revolt. As a ruler she was kindhearted, but her character was light and vacillating and she was devoid of political sense.

MARIA LUÍSA, Order of Queen. See DECORATIONS AND ORDERS—*Spain.*

MARIA MAGDALENA, màk-dà-lā′nà, a drama in three acts by Friedrich Hebbel. In this play, written in 1843 and published in 1844, Hebbel invigorated the middle-class tragedy in which traditional conflicts no longer represented the problems of the day. *Maria Magdalena* deals with contemporary society; the highly tragic conflict arises within the same class, indeed within the same family. This powerful and taut tragedy, which has held the stage for over a century, is the first in a long line of social dramas, leading through Henrik Ibsen, whom Hebbel anticipated by more than 30 years, to Bertolt Brecht.

As in all his tragedies, Hebbel endeavors to show that the tragic conflict arises out of the prevailing morals and customs of society. From his own standpoint each figure is right in his actions, which, though anchored in his character, are determined by the pressures of the existing social order rather than by the actions or intrigues of his opponents. Master Anton is an inflexible moral rigorist, ashamed of his tender feelings, a tyrant in his home, yet a model citizen in the eyes of the world. His son Karl, rebelling against the existing order, innocently causes the deaths of his mother and of his sister Clara, whose actions are as much determined by fear of public opinion as are those of her father. See also HEBBEL, (CHRISTIAN) FRIEDRICH.

F. E. COENEN.

MARIA PIA, Ital. mä-rē′ä pē′ä; Port. mà-rē′ä pē′à, queen of Portugal: b. Turin, Italy, Oct. 16, 1847; d. Stupinigi, July 5, 1911. The daughter of Victor Emmanuel II of Italy, she was married in 1862, at the age of 15, to Louis, king of Portugal. After the death of her husband in 1889 the queen dowager devoted herself to charitable work and took no part in public life. Following the assassination of her son, Carlos I, and his eldest son in 1908, and the overthrow of her grandson, Manuel II, in the republican revolution of 1910, Maria Pia fled to Italy, and found refuge with her sister-in-law, the queen dowager Margherita of Savoy.

MARIA THERESA, mà-rē′à tĕ-rē′sà (Ger. MARIA THERESIA) of Hapsburg, archduchess of Austria, queen of Hungary and Bohemia, empress of the Holy Roman Empire: b. Vienna, Austria, May 13, 1717; d. there, Nov. 29, 1780. The oldest daughter of Charles VI, she was made heiress to the throne by the pragmatic sanction (q.v.) of 1713. In 1736 she married Francis Stephen, duke of Lorraine, who was made grand duke of Tuscany the following year.

On the death of her father on Oct. 20, 1740, Maria Theresa assumed the government of his empire, but her right to the succession was contested by several claimants, chief among them Charles Albert, elector of Bavaria. England, Russia, and Prussia acknowledged her right to rule her father's lands, but when she also claimed the throne of the Holy Roman Empire for her husband, whom she had made coregent of Austria a month after her accession, she encountered resistance. In December 1740 Frederick II of Prussia invaded Silesia, and soon Austria was attacked by Bavaria and Spain. By the Treaty of Dresden (1745), Maria Theresa ceded Silesia to Prussia in exchange for recognition of Duke Francis as Holy Roman emperor. By the Treaty of Aix-la-Chapelle, which in 1748 brought to a close the War of the Austrian Succession, Parma, Piacenza, and Guastalla were ceded to Spain and Prussia's hold on Silesia was reaffirmed. (See also SUCCESSION WARS.) Nevertheless her conduct of the war established Maria Theresa as one of the leading rulers of Europe.

Hoping to regain Silesia, Maria Theresa formed an alliance with Russia, and also, through her able chancellor, Count Wenzel Anton von Kaunitz, with France. She was preparing to strike at Prussia when Frederick forestalled her by invading Saxony, and thus opened the Seven Years' War (q.v.). This struggle availed Austria little, and Maria Theresa was forced to recognize Prussia's right to Silesia in the Treaty of Hubertusburg, signed Feb. 15, 1763. But in 1772 Maria Theresa participated in the first partition of Poland and received Galicia as her share. In 1775 Turkey ceded Bucovina, which Austria had seized in 1774; and the Treaty of Teschen (1779), which closed the War of the Bavarian Succession, brought her the Inn district.

When Francis I died in 1765 the empress named her oldest son as Emperor Joseph II of the Holy Roman Empire and coregent of Austria, but kept her own hands on everything save military administration. Though best known for her masterful part in European politics, Maria Theresa was equally effective in internal reforms. Austrian finance was revived, agriculture encouraged, and higher education fostered; and for the first time an attempt was made to centralize the imperial administration. The empress was a strict Roman Catholic, but in the later part of her reign she was induced by her free-thinking son to enact some antiecclesiastical legislation. She was strikingly beautiful in her youth, and a devoted mother—she had 16 children altogether—as well as a strong ruler.

Consult Mahan, Jabez A., *Maria Theresa of Austria* (New York 1932); Morris, Constance L., *Maria Theresa, the Last Conservative* (New York 1937).

MARIA THERESA, Order of. See DECORATIONS AND ORDERS—*Austria.*

MARIAMNE THE HASMONAEAN, măr-ĭ-ăm′nê, hăz-mô-nē′ăn, wife of Herod the Great: b. ?57 B.C.; d. ?29 B.C. The granddaughter of the high priests Aristobulus II and Hyrcanus II, she became the second wife of Herod in 37 B.C. Flavius Josephus relates that Herod, although devoted to her, condemned Mariamne to death because of jealousy aroused by his scheming sister, Salome. Mariamne met her fate with nobility. Voltaire and Friedrich Hebbel, among other writers, based plays on her story.

MARIAN DOCTRINE. See MARY.

MARIANA, mä-ryä′nä, **Juan de,** Spanish Jesuit and historian: b. Talavera de la Reina, Spain, 1536; d. Toledo, Feb. 16, 1624. He studied at the University of Alcalá de Henares, taking holy orders at the age of 17. After teaching theology in Rome, Sicily, and Paris, he settled in Toledo in 1574. Here he wrote his noted *Historiae de rebus Hispaniae* (1592–1605; *History of Spain*) in Latin, later translating it into Spanish (1601). Although uncritical of the facts, he was the first to present Spanish history as a continuous, polished narrative. He defended, in *De Rege et Regis Institutione* (1599), killing of kings who proved tyrants.

MARIANA, mâr-ĭ-ăn'à, in American colonial history, a name given by John Mason (q.v.) to the tract granted to him between the Salem River and the Merrimac. Here he founded an agricultural settlement and formed the Laconia Company in 1629. Mason returned to England in 1633 and died there two years later. In 1691 his heirs sold all his lands and rights in New Hampshire to Gov. Samuel Allen.

MARIANA ISLANDS (commonly MARIANAS, formerly LADRONE ISLANDS) is a volcanic island group in the Pacific Ocean, north of the equator and 1,500 miles east of the Philippine Islands; from north to south, the group extends for 380 miles. The islands were discovered in 1521 by Ferdinand Magellan (q.v.), who sighted Guam and Rota, and were settled by the Spaniards, who named them Islas de los Ladrones ("Thieves Islands") because they were a rendezvous for pirates; after Jesuit missionaries were sent to the islands in 1667 by Mariana of Austria, queen of Spain, they were renamed Marianas for her. Spain ceded Guam (q.v.), southernmost of the group, to the United States in 1898, following the Spanish-American War, and in 1899 sold the remaining islands to Germany for $5,000,000; after World War I the German islands, together with the Marshalls and the Carolines, became a mandate of the League of Nations and were entrusted to Japan for administration.

The Japanese Marianas comprised 14 islands, besides islets and reefs, with an aggregate area of 246 square miles; the population in 1935 numbered 44,025, including 39,728 Japanese. Northward from Guam, the islands are Rota, Tinian, Saipan (on which was Garapan, pop. 6,000, the seat of administration), Farallon de Medinilla, Anatahan, Sarigan, Guguan, Zealandia Bank, Alamagan, Pagan, Agrihan, Asuncion, Maug, and Farallon de Pajaros—all lost to Japan in World War II. The northernmost 10 islands are volcanic and uninhabited. Sugar and cotton are grown on Saipan (15 miles long by 4 in width), Tinian (13 miles by 6), and Rota (12 miles by 4); and other crops, on most of the islands, include coconuts, rice, sugar, corn (maize), tobacco, and coffee. The breadfruit tree was first discovered on the Marianas.

Early in 1944 United States naval and air forces commenced a series of attacks to retake Guam and capture the Japanese Marianas. Troops were landed on Saipan on June 15, and on July 4 they occupied Garapan and Tanapag, a second town; the entire island fell to the Americans on July 9, the total cost being 3,426 killed and 13,099 wounded. The Japanese lost 27,586 killed and 2,161 captured, many of these being subsequently accounted for on hills and in caves to which they had retreated. The invasion of Tinian was launched on July 23, 1944, and the island was completely occupied by the end of the month, the United States suffering 1,829 casualties, of whom 314 represented men killed; 6,939 Japanese were killed, and 523 captured.

The United States governs Guam as a possession and since 1947 has administered the other Marianas for the United Nations, as part of the Trust Territory of the Pacific Islands. Population: (1961), excluding Guam, 8,414.

MARIANNA, mâr-ĭ-ăn'à, city, Arkansas, and Lee County seat, altitude 235 feet, on L'Anguille River; on the Missouri Pacific Railroad, 22 miles northwest of Helena. It is in an agricultural region, and cotton processing is the principal industry. Pop. 5,134.

MARIANNA, city, Florida, and Jackson County seat, altitude 80 to 117 feet, on the Louisville and Nashville and the Marianna and Blountstown railroads. It is the trading center for a region producing corn, cotton, pecans, peanuts and fruit. Pop. 7,152.

MARIBOR, mä'rê-bôr (Ger. MARBURG), city, Yugoslavia, capital of Maribor Oblast, Slovenia, on the Drava River, 65 miles northeast of Ljubljana. The city, the second largest in Slovenia, and a center for trade, transportation, and industry, manufactures automobiles, textiles, chemicals, and leatherware. Pop. (1961) 85,000.

MARICOPA, mär-ĭ-kō'pà (formerly Coco-MARICOPA), an Indian tribe of the Yuman linguistic family, living together with the Pima Indians on the Gila River and Salt River reservations, in Arizona. The tribe, which today has some 415 members, united with the Pima to repel the Yuma Indians in a memorable battle in 1857.

FREDERICK J. DOCKSTADER.

MARIE ANTOINETTE, mà-rē' ăn-twà-nĕt' (in full JOSÈPHE JEANNE MARIE ANTOINETTE), queen of France: b. Vienna, Austria, Nov. 2, 1755; d. Paris, Oct. 16, 1793. She was the daughter of the Emperor Francis I and Maria Theresa. In 1770 she was married to the Duc de Berri, dauphin of France, and after he ascended the throne in 1774 as Louis XVI she made enemies about the court because of youthful frivolities and extravagances. Spoken of contemptuously as *l'Autrichienne* ("the Austrian woman"), she was considered to be too much under the influence of her mother. Her name was further tarnished by the affair of the diamond necklace (q.v.), in which the Cardinal Louis de Rohan, the imposter Alessandro di Cagliostro, and the Countess de La Motte were the chief actors. Her unpopularity was increased by the enthusiastic reception given her at a banquet on Oct. 1, 1789, where the white bourbon cockades were worn and the national cockade trampled under foot. The attack on Versailles and transfer of the royal family to Paris shortly followed. The queen advised the flight of the royal family from Paris in June 1791, which ended in their capture at Varennes. From that time they were viewed as traitors. On Aug. 10, 1792, the last day of the royalty, the queen exerted all her power to induce the king to resistance. This he thought was vain, and he was led with his consort before the Legislative Assembly. She heard his deposition announced, and then accompanied him to the prison of the Temple. There, deprived of every semblance of royalty, she displayed magnanimity and patient endurance. In August 1793, she was removed to the Conciergerie, and in October was brought before the revolutionary tribunal. She was charged with having dissipated the finances, exhausted the public treasury, corresponded with foreign enemies of France, and favored its domestic foes. She replied with firmness and decision, and heard her sentence pronounced with perfect calmness. On the same day she was guillotined. Marie Antoinette's faults were due in great measure to her defective education and difficult position. Her expiation of them made her a general object of pitying interest.

MARIE BYRD LAND, mà-rē' bûrd' lănd, large section of Antarctica, situated east of Ross Sea and Ross Shelf Ice, and south of Amundsen Sea, at a latitude of approximately 73° to 85° S. and longitude 100° to 150° W. It was named for Richard E. Byrd who claimed the land for the United States in 1929.

MARIE DE FRANCE, mà-rē' dĕ frăɴs', French poetess of the 12th century, a native of Ile de France, whence her surname, who spent her life in England, where she was well known at the court of Henry II. Her *Lais,* largely based on Breton stories, and full of Celtic spirit and pathos; fables, a revision under the title *Isopet* (that is, *Aesop*) of an English collection; and a tale, *L'Espurgatoire Seint Patriz,* make up the body of her work.

MARIE DE MEDICIS, mà-rē' dĕ mā-dē-sēs (Italian Maria de' Medici), queen of France: b. Florence, April 26, 1573; d. Cologne, July 3, 1642. She was the daughter of Francesco de' Medici, grand duke of Tuscany, and was married by proxy, Oct. 5, 1600, to Henry IV of France, with whom she constantly quarreled, partly because of his inconstancy and his open favor to the Marquise de Verneuil, and partly because of her own haughty, obstinate character, which was not unmixed with ambition. For years she urged him to have her crowned queen; the ceremony took place May 13, 1610, and on the next day the king was assassinated. Marie was accused of complicity in the plot, but the charge is not proven. For seven years she acted as regent and showed a strong friendship for Spain and the Catholic Church, being advised by the nuncio and the Spanish ambassador as well as by such favorites as Concini. She quarreled with her son, later Louis XIII, was reconciled to him by Richelieu, and upon her attempt to displace the latter was forced by that great minister again to leave court in 1630. Her last years were spent in exile in Belgium, England and Cologne. The story of her poverty during these years is untrue.

MARIE GALANTE, mā-rē' gä-läɴt', island, about 16 miles southeast from Guadeloupe. The area is about 60 square miles. The chief productions are sugar, coffee, tobacco, indigo and cotton. It is a dependency of the French overseas territory of Guadeloupe. Columbus discovered it in 1493, and named it from his vessel, the *Santa Maria.* The French occupied it in 1647, and lost it several times. In 1825 it suffered severely from the hurricane which desolated Guadeloupe (q.v.). Pop. (1954) 16,037.

MARIE LOUISE, empress of France. See Maria Luisa.

MARIE THERESE or **MARIA THERESA,** queen consort of Louis XIV of France: b. Escorial, Sept. 10, 1638; d. Versailles, France, July 30, 1683. She was the daughter of Philip IV of Spain and of Elizabeth of France. By the Treaty of the Pyrenees in 1659 she renounced any claim to the Spanish throne. In the following year she married Louis XIV, but the union was unhappy. Only one of her six children, Dauphin Louis, survived her.

MARIETTA, mâr-ĭ-ĕt'à, city, Georgia, county seat of Cobb County, on the Nashville, Chattanooga and St. Louis, and Louisville and Nashville railroads, about 16 miles north by west of Atlanta. Kennesaw Mountain is west of the city. It was settled in 1834 and incorporated in 1852. A city charter was granted in 1885. It is in a fertile agricultural region in which stock-raising is one of the prominent occupations. Large marble quarries are in the vicinity. The chief manufactures are chairs, prefabricated houses, castings, hosiery, lumber, marble products, pottery, and frozen foods. There is a United States Air Force base here, and a large aircraft plant built during World War II. The Clarke Library, which contains about 5,500 volumes, is in Marietta. Marietta National Cemetery, located here, contains the graves of 10,279 soldiers.

The city government is administered by a mayor and council chosen at a popular election. Pop. 25,565.

Marietta was an intermediate objective point in Gen. William Sherman's campaign for Atlanta, and when he crossed the Etowah May 23, 1864, his columns were headed for that place by way of Dallas and New Hope Church, but Gen. J. E. Johnston threw his army in his front and checked him at New Hope Church and Dallas. After many hard-fought battles and severe skirmishing, Johnston abandoned his Dallas lines on June 4, and took position covering Marietta, his left on Lost Mountain, his right beyond the railroad and behind Noonday Creek, with a strong advanced position on Pine Mountain. Sherman repaired the railroad, established a secondary, fortified base at Allatoona Pass, and joined by Blair's Seventeenth corps advanced June 10 and confronted Johnston in his new and strong position, and by the 14th was strongly intrenched before it in a continuous line of 10 miles. Johnston abandoned Pine Mountain on the night of the 14th, and Sherman advanced his lines, bringing on the engagement at Pine Mountain (q.v.) June 15. The general movement was continued on the 16th and the right thrown forward to threaten the railroad below Marietta. On the 18th Johnston fell back to a new line, including Kennesaw Mountain, which was strongly fortified, and Sherman pressed in closely on the center and left, north of Marietta, still continuing the extension of his line to the right, south of it. Johnston, making a corresponding movement by his left, encountered Sherman's right at Kolb's Farm (q.v.) on the 22d. Sherman assaulted Kennesaw Mountain on the 27th, and was repulsed. Flanking operations were then renewed to the right to reach the railroad, and Johnston, finding it in danger and his communications with Atlanta threatened, after being 26 days under an uninterrupted cannonade and infantry fire, abandoned Marietta on the night of July 2 and fell back to a new line, previously selected and intrenched, 10 miles south of Marietta, and covering the railroad and his pontoon-bridges across the Chattahoochee, with an advanced position at Smyrna Campground. Sherman occupied Marietta on the morning of July 3. The Union loss in the operations around Marietta was 1,790 killed and missing, and 5,740 wounded, an aggregate of 7,530. Johnston reported a Confederate loss of 468 killed and 3,480 wounded.

MARIETTA, city, Ohio, seat of Washington County, on the Ohio River at the mouth of the Muskingum, 95 miles southeast of Columbus. It lies in a region of fertile valleys, with coal, iron, oil, and natural gas, and handles large quantities of fruits and vegetables, shipped to various urban markets. The city's manufactures and industries include castings of iron, brass, aluminum; drilling tools; grindstones; metal signs and markers; paints and varnishes; gas engines and ranges; chemicals; household and office furniture; harness; and a varied list of miscellaneous trade articles.

Marietta has a National Guard armory; a Civil War monument, a monument to the pioneers, and a monument commemorating French participation in the settlement of America; a public library and a state museum, the Campus Martius; and two hospitals. It is the seat of Marietta College (chartered 1835), a private, coeducational, liberal arts college with an enrollment of about 2,000 students.

The city was settled in 1788. The Ohio Company of Associates, under the leadership of Manasseh Cutler (q.v.) and Gen. Rufus Putnam, in Boston, bought lands in the southeastern part of the present State of Ohio, and Putnam led a party of settlers to Western Pennsylvania and thence down the rivers. Upon landing at the mouth of the Muskingum, they called their community by that river's name, but soon changed it to Marietta, in honor of Marie Antoinette. The city developed as the westward country opened up; in its early years it was a thriving river town. The Mound Cemetery, which was set apart for public use in 1788, has the graves of a number of officers of the Revolution; it also contains an ancient Indian mound. An interesting relic of the historic past is the old Northwest Territory land office, a small structure of hand-hewn timbers, in which the first official maps of the region were made and records of transactions in land were kept; it is one of the oldest buildings in the state. At Blennerhassett Island, in the river, Aaron Burr visited his coconspirator, Harman Blennerhassett, discussing plans for his "empire" in the Southwest.

Marietta has a mayor and council, with a service director (city manager). Pop. 16,847.

MARIETTE, mȧ-ryet', **Auguste Edouard,** French Egyptologist: b. Boulogne, France, Feb. 11, 1821; d. Cairo, Jan. 19, 1881. He was educated at the Boulogne Municipal College and in 1839 went to England as professor of French and drawing. He returned to France in 1840, took his degree at Douai in 1841 and became professor at his alma mater, the Boulogne Municipal College.

While so engaged he became interested in archaeology and in 1847 published an essay on the history of Boulogne. In 1848 he received a position in the Egyptian museum of the Louvre; and in 1850 was sent by the government to gather Coptic, Syriac, Arabic and Ethiopic manuscripts in Egypt. His excavations and discoveries in connection with his search for the true site of Memphis led to the finding of many important remains, such as the Serapeum, the first Memphian temple discovered near the three great pyramids. Beginning to excavate four miles west of the accepted site of Memphis, Mariette came first upon an avenue of sphinxes, which led directly up to the magnificent granite and alabaster temple of Serapis mentioned by Strabo, which contained the sarcophagi of the sacred bulls of Apis from the 19th dynasty to the Roman supremacy. Besides these he found no less than 2,000 sphinxes, and over 4,000 statues, bas-reliefs and inscriptions, some evidently of Greek construction; and various streets, colonnades, and other structures belonging to a great city. His excavations around the base of the sphinx near Gizeh not only disclosed the entrance to it, but proved it to be sculptured out of the solid rock.

In 1854 he returned to Paris and was made assistant conservator of the Louvre; and in 1855 was sent to Berlin to study Egyptian remains in the museums there. On his return to Egypt, in 1858, the viceroy made him conservator of the monuments and antiquities of the land, with the title of bey, later promoted to pasha, with an annual appropriation for the prosecution of his researches, and the foundation and maintenance of the museum of Boulak. His discoveries at Tanis revealed the monuments of the Hyksos dynasty, and those at Thebes explain the chronology of the various dynasties. In 1860 he made the important discovery of the mummy of Queen Aahhotep, of the 18th dynasty, with a wealth of jewels of exquisite workmanship belonging to her. In 1873 the Institute of France awarded him the biennial prize of 20,000 francs. His discoveries have been of utmost importance for the light that they have thrown upon the earliest periods of Egyptian history.

MARIGOLD, mar′ə-gōld, popular name for several unrelated plants. The pot marigold (*Calendula officinalis*) is one of the most widely popular of garden plants. It is grown for its brilliant flowers which range from white to rich orange. The genus *Tagetes* has approximately 30 species, including the African marigold (*Tagetes erecta*) and the French marigold (*Tagetes patula*) which are also widely used for ornamentation. Their flowers are usually some shade of orange or yellow. The Cape marigold (*Dimorphotheca* spp.), white, yellow, orange, or purple in color, is also grown for ornament. The marsh marigold or cowslip (*Caltha*) is a member of the crowfoot family (Ranunculaceae). It is a well-known plant in the marshes and wet meadows of North America. The name fig marigold is applied to the genus *Mesembryanthemum,* comprising several hundred species of annual or perennial herbs or low shrubs, belonging to the botanical family Aizoaceae. See also BUR-MARIGOLD; COWSLIP.

MARIHUANA, mar-ə-wä′nə, also spelled *marijuana,* is a mixture of leaves, stems, and flowering tops of the Indian hemp plant (*Cannabis sativa*). The mixture contains a drug, not currently used in medicine but used illegally for pleasurable effects. The pharmacological effects of the hemp plant have been known for a long time. A Chinese herbal dating from 2700 B.C. recommends hemp preparations for the treatment of a variety of illnesses, and hemp preparations were used as intoxicants in India before the 10th century A.D.

Drug preparations derived from the Indian hemp plant are known by a variety of names throughout the world. In the Western Hemisphere and England, the term "marihuana" is used to refer to preparations of the leaves and flowering tops of the plant. The same preparations are known as *dagga* in South Africa, *djoma* in Central Africa, *kabak* in Turkey, *liamba* in Brazil, *kif* in Morocco and Algeria, and *ganja* in India. The flowering tops can also be processed to yield a resin high in the active drug. This resin is known as *charas* in India and as *hashish* in most other parts of the world.

Source and Ingredients. Although the hemp plant is probably indigenous to Central Asia, it now grows wild throughout most of the world and can be cultivated in any area that has a hot season. Only the female plant synthesizes the chemicals responsible for the pharmacological effects of marihuana. The chemicals are found primarily in the flowering tops of the plant but may also be found to a lesser extent in the leaves, stems, and seeds.

Tetrahydrocannabinol is the chemical most active in producing the physiological effects of marihuana. The amount of tetrahydrocannabinol in a particular plant varies widely, depending on the climate, soil, and other factors. On the basis of its clinical effects, tetrahydrocannabinol is classified as a *psychotomimetic* or *hallucinogenic* drug. However, its effects on the brain appear to differ from those produced by other hallucinogens, such as LSD-25 or mescaline.

Use. The pattern of marihuana use in the United States is primarily intermittent in social situations. Solitary use or regular heavy use is much less common. Regular heavy use of marihuana or hashish leads to some tolerance. However, unlike narcotics (morphinelike drugs), barbiturates, and alcohol, the repeated use of marihuana does not cause physical dependence, and there are no withdrawal symptoms when chronic use is interrupted.

Cannabis (Indian hemp) preparations are not used in medicine, but suggestions that they may have value in the treatment of depression or as a useful alternative to the social use of alcohol have not received sufficient attention.

Physiological Effects. Marihuana acts mainly on the central nervous system. The effects it produces depend on the personality of the user, the dose, the method of administration, and the circumstances surrounding its use.

The most consistent effect of marihuana is a change in mood. Marihuana usually produces a sense of well-being (euphoria), enhanced self-esteem, and relaxation. These mood changes are frequently accompanied by changes in sensory perceptions. Distances may appear greater, and time intervals may seem longer than they really are. Sensory stimuli may also take on a more pleasant or novel quality so that ordinary sounds or objects may seem aesthetically more pleasing or interesting.

In some cases, marihuana causes a decrease in emotional control that gives rise to impulsive behavior. It is more common, however, for users to withdraw into introspective reveries. In the United States, marihuana users refer to this level of intoxication as a "high." Marihuana users generally try to avoid taking more of the drug than is necessary to reach this level.

Some users of marihuana or hashish experience illusions or visual and auditory hallucinations that are sometimes accompanied by agitation, feelings of panic, and other psychotic symptoms. It is now known that such acute intoxications are not necessarily caused by individual idiosyncrasies, as previously thought, but that in high enough doses, tetrahydrocannabinol, the active principle in marihuana, can produce such effects in most people.

Marihuana is almost always smoked. Since tetrahydrocannabinol is more potent when smoked than when taken orally, and since the onset of drug effects is rapid when the drug is smoked, it is usually possible for marihuana users to avoid overdosage by taking only as many inhalations as are required to produce a pleasant "high." However, marihuana, especially in high doses, has induced psychotic episodes in occasional users who had no previous histories of psychotic behavior.

Legal Aspect. The possession or sale of marihuana is illegal in the United States. Under federal law and under the laws of most states, the penalties for violation of the marihuana laws are as severe as the penalties for possession or sale of narcotics. The initial prohibition of the use of cannabis in the United States was based on the belief that marihuana users were subject to psychotic episodes and were likely to commit aggressive and sexual crimes. When subsequent investigations did not substantiate these assertions, a continuation of marihuana prohibition was supported on the grounds that the use of marihuana was a preliminary to experimentation with narcotics (opiates).

In spite of the legal penalties, there has been a marked increase in the use of marihuana by college students and middle-class adults. There has been no corresponding rise in the use of narcotics, or in serious aggressive crime among these groups, and there has been growing demand for the legalization of marihuana.

Many in the medical community favor the continued prohibition of marihuana, arguing that repeated self-induced intoxication is dangerous and is both a manifestation of psychiatric disturbance and a practice that retards the seeking of appropriate treatment. Other scientists distinguish between the occasional use of marihuana by stable individuals and the heavier and habitual use by individuals with personality problems. These scientists believe that the occasional use of marihuana is no more dangerous that the occasional use of alcohol, but they generally reject the comparison of marihuana and alcohol as a valid argument for making marihuana (which is a powerful intoxicant) freely available to the public. They point out that the present pattern of intermittent social use of marihuana and the low incidence of adverse effects could change if more potent preparations became generally available without appropriate controls. Authorities in other parts of the world have reported that chronic heavy use of marihuana creates health problems as serious as those caused by alcoholism in the United States.

No doubt, the penalties for possession of marihuana in the United States are far too severe for the social danger its use presents; but too little is known about marihuana to provide a rational basis for its legal distribution.

JEROME H. JAFFE, M.D., *University of Chicago.*

MARIMBA, mə-rim′bə, a musical instrument consisting of tuned bars of hardwood graduated in size and suspended over the open ends of tuned resonators. The bars, arranged like the keys of the piano, are sounded by striking with rubber-tipped mallets. The marimba is of ancient origin and is found among many primitive peoples. Its existence in the New World is due originally to the importation of Africans. At the end of the 19th century, Sebastian Hurtado of Guatemala improved the instrument, extending its compass and using as resonators wooden boxes shaped like the gourds formerly used. Near the end of each box is an opening covered with cured pig's gut which in vibrating increases the volume and imparts a stringlike tone to the instrument. Such resonators are peculiar to the Central American marimba and give it the compass and versatility of the piano. The manufactured type of marimba has a range of four octaves and uses metal tubes as resonators. In recent years the marimba has grown in popularity, attracting the attention of serious musicians. Though similar to the xylophone (q.v.), which originated in Europe, the marimba has greater range and superior tone quality.

FRANK K. MACCALLUM.

MARIN (măr'ĭn), **John Cheri,** American artist: b. Rutherford, N.J., Dec. 23, 1870; d. Addison, Me., Oct. 1, 1953. One of the few contemporary American artists whose work was almost universally admired by critics and fellow artists alike, John Marin was regarded as the greatest American water-colorist since Winslow Homer (1836–1910).

After attending Weehawken and Hoboken (N.J.) schools, Marin worked for almost a decade as a draftsman and architect, before deserting architecture for formal art training at the Pennsylvania Academy of Fine Arts (1899–1901) and at the Art Students League (1901–1903). Marin's early successes included the etchings, *L'Opéra Paris* (1908), *The Seine, Paris* (1909), and *Brooklyn Bridge* (1913). Meanwhile, with his famous *London Omnibus* (1908) sketch, Marin turned primarily to water colors, although he continued to produce etchings until the early 1930's. In March 1909 he was given his first major showing in New York City, at the "291" gallery of Alfred Stieglitz, pioneer promoter of modern art and Marin's lifelong friend. The artist's work was exhibited annually thereafter in the city, winning him wide critical acclaim as the outstanding water-colorist in American art. Although his fame and reputation were assured in the 1920's, Marin's prestige was considerably enhanced in 1936, when New York City's Museum of Modern Art held a retrospective show of more than 225 of his water colors, oils, and etchings.

Opposed to the exact representation of objects as being too static in effect, Marin subordinated line to patches or masses of color, and frequently expressed objects by employing such symbols as green triangles for pine trees, zigzags for waves, and swirling lines to suggest mountains, thereby giving his paintings a highly decorative quality. He created a variety of original effects through the use of color, and achieved cosiderable tension or movement in his works.

Representative among Marin's water colors are *Woolworth Building* (1912, 1913); *Marin Island, Small Point, Maine* (1915); *Trees and Rocks and Schooner* (1921), *From the New York Hospital* (1951), and *Sea Piece No. 1* (1951). Marin's works, which after the early 1930's came to include increasing numbers of outstanding oils, such as *Circus Forms* (1934); *Sealadies, Cape*

Split, Maine (1931–1935), and *Restaurant with Figures* (1935), are represented in the permanent collections of major American galleries, and some Marins are owned by the French government.

He received the 1948 Fine Arts Medal of the American Institute of Architects, and in 1950 his works were featured in the American pavilion of Venice's 25th biennial show of contemporary art.

Consult Benson, E. M., *John Marin, the Man and His Work* (Washington, D.C., 1935); Helm, M., *John Marin* (New York 1948); and *The Selected Writings of John Marin*, ed. by Dorothy Norman (New York 1949).

MARIN, mȧ-răn', **Louis,** French political leader: b. Faulx, Meuse Department, France, Feb. 7, 1871; d. Paris, May 23, 1960. An honor graduate of the French School of Political Sciences, he entered politics in 1905 as a deputy, and thereafter held various ministerial posts beginning in 1924. As minister of state when the Germans invaded France in 1940, he was one of a small group of French leaders who argued unsuccessfully for continuation of the war against the Nazis, and in 1944 he escaped to England in disguise. Elected to the two Constituent Assemblies after the war, he was a member of the first National Assembly (November 1946). He did not, however, seek re-election in 1951. From 1925 he headed L'Union Républicaine Démocratique, a conservative political grouping, and, as an ardent rightist, he was a leader in the opposition to Socialist Premier Léon Blum. Throughout his long political career, he was a staunch fighter for the preservation of French rights in the Rhineland, and he was regarded as a representative French scholar-statesman.

MARINATING. See COOKERY—*Supplementary Methods.*

MARINDUQUE, mä-rēn-dōō'kȧ, island and province, Republic of the Philippines, on the Sibuyan Sea southwest of Tayabas, Luzon. The area of the island is 346 square miles; the capital is Boac. Marinduque is hilly, and rich in minerals. Hemp and coconuts are exported. Until 1920 it was a subprovince of Tayabas. The inhabitants are Tagalogs. The province comprises the island of Marinduque and several offshore islands. Pop. of province (1948) 85,828; island (1939) 79,781.

MARINE BIOLOGY, that branch of biological science concerned with the nature and interrelationships of plants and animals that live in the sea. It concerns the ways in which such organisms are adapted to the complex chemical and physical properties of sea water, to the course of ocean currents and the action of waves, and to the nature of the sea floor from the intertidal shore down to the abyssal depths. From the shoreline to mid-ocean and from the surface to the bottom the sea is occupied by living things, from microscopic bacteria to the largest whales, the largest creatures that have ever lived. Being alive, all need to be studied alive and marine biology for the most part is investigated at special marine biological laboratories or institutes located on the coast of various countries throughout the world and operated in conjunction with research vessels of various kinds. The most famous are those at Naples (Italy), Plymouth (England) and Woods Hole (Massachusetts), which were started at the close of the 19th century and in that order. Now almost every country with access to the sea has established coastal research laboratories for studying sea life either for its intrinsic interest or in connection with fisheries development. The subject as a whole, however, embraces practically all of animal biology, for with the exception of amphibians and insects almost every kind of animal is to be found in the sea, and nearly half of the recognized classes of animals are exclusively marine.

In a general way marine life is classified into three groups: (1) benthos; (2) nekton, and (3) plankton. Benthic plants and animals are those that are associated with the sea floor either as attached forms or creeping or burrowing, and include the larger seaweeds and such animals as barnacles, sea squirts, snails, clams, crabs, worms, sponges, and many others. Nekton includes the more active and larger animals such as fishes, squid and whales, which are capable of swimming against currents and making migratory journeys. While plankton represents all the small or helplessly drifting plants and animals that are carried along by the currents wherever they happen to go, the phytoplankton comprising all the microscopic plants such as diatoms and certain other forms, and the zooplankton which includes not only microscopic protozoan animals such as foraminiferans, small crustaceans, and large jellyfish, but also the eggs, embryos, and larval stages of large creatures such as fish, crabs or squid which become part of the nekton or the benthos as they grow (see PLANKTON).

All animal life, whether on land or in the sea, depends directly or indirectly upon plant life for its existence. The plant life of the sea, however, is poor in variety compared with the land and consists mainly of the microscopic plant organisms of the phytoplankton, which truly constitute the pasturage of the seas, together with the large seaweeds or algae which are anchored to the sea floor in shallow water near the shore or in the intertidal zone itself. Exceptions are the sargasso or gulf weed, which not only drifts in large tangled masses at the surface of the Sargasso Sea in the middle of the North Atlantic Ocean, but perpetuates itself by vegetative propagation at the sea surface a thousand miles from any coast; and eelgrass and turtle grass which are among the very few flowering plants which have invaded the shallow coastal waters to become anchored in mud or sand flats. All plants need light, however, so that the microscopic phytoplankton is limited to a comparatively shallow layer of water at the surface of the ocean, while the seaweeds which are anchored to rocks are equally limited to the coastal regions where the sea floor is within the range of illumination. The deepest water from which growing weeds have been taken is between 300 to 400 feet, although a giant brown seaweed with fronds 200 yards long is abundant in the Strait of Magellan. Giant kelp, though not quite so large, also forms submarine forests off the Californian coast, where schools of big tuna play.

The most important plants in the sea, however, are the microscopic members of the phytoplankton, for they are the primary source of food for the animal kingdom. Individually they are minute but in aggregate they constitute a rich pasture, their concentration at any one place and time depending on the average depth to which light penetrates during the hours of daylight and upon the concentration of certain essential salts which are in shortest supply, namely, phosphates and nitrates. Requirements for abundant growth are in fact the same as for vegetation growing on land (see OCEANOGRAPHY).

The microscopic nature of the basic source of food in the sea and its limitation to the comparatively shallow depth to which light can penetrate determine to a very great extent the vast network of marine life as a whole. Thus in the open oceans throughout the world we can distinguish a vertical series of zones from the surface downwards. The uppermost layer is the most important, the relatively thin illuminated zone about 200 meters in depth (the *epipelagic* zone), for only here do the microscopic plant organisms propagate, and most of the animal life of the sea is to be found within this zone. Beneath this is the so-called twilight zone (*mesopelagic* zone) where there is still enough light for animals to make use of but insufficient for the growth of plant cells. Below the twilight zone and extending downwards for about 2,000 meters is the *bathypelagic* zone into which sunlight penetrates, while below this again is the bottom layer of water known as the *abyssal pelagic* zone. Each zone has its peculiarities, not only of light, temperature, viscosity, and oxygen, but also of the kinds of life associated with it.

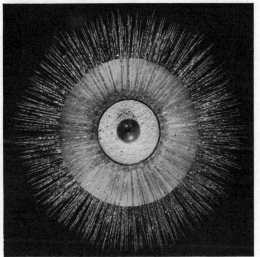

The American Museum of Natural History

Simplest of the Radiolaria, shell-less *Actissa princeps* is found in samples of plankton. Its threadlike pseudopodia extend in all directions to secure food.

The drifting life of the uppermost zone travels passively with the currents, but all of it has to contend with the force of gravity since any organism which depends upon light for carrying on photosynthesis or is feeding upon those that do must remain within the lighted region. If it sinks into the darkness below, death through starvation awaits it. Consequently both plants and animals of this zone have special devices for counteracting their tendency to sink. Single-celled organisms, whether animal or plant, have an advantage to begin with. Being minute, they have comparatively extensive surfaces relative to their size, and the viscosity of water is such that the surfaces tend to keep them from sinking in any case. All that is necessary to prevent it entirely is further extension of the organisms' surfaces, so that the diatoms, which are plants, the peridinians, which may be plantlike or

animallike in their metabolism, and the foraminiferans, which are animal, all possess numerous
slender processes extending into the surrounding
water. As long as they live they remain within
the illuminated zone, although when they die their
elaborate little skeletons of silicate or lime sink
slowly to the sea floor to add their quota to the
deep sea oozes of the abyss perhaps three or four
miles below.

The Chalk Cliffs of Dover are actually the
consolidated and elevated ooze made up of the
dead skeletons of one particular foramineran,
Globigerina, deposited many million years ago.
Except in the northern and western Pacific Ocean
and in very high altitudes, Globigerina ooze is still
the predominant kind covering the greater part
of the ocean floor and Globigerina skeletons continue to rain down from the surface waters as
their owners die. Large areas of the Pacific
Ocean are so deep, however, that the minute skeletons of lime dissolve before they reach the bottom
and the red clay of the floor itself is not covered
by ooze of any kind. In the high latitudes
in the neighborhood of the Arctic and Antarctic
circles the diatoms are the dominant form of
microscopic life and their siliceous skeletons sink
to form diatomaceous ooze instead (see Ooze).

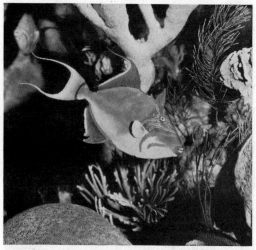

The American Museum of Natural History

A queen trigger-fish swimming amongst the corals of a
tropical reef.

Unicellular organisms such as diatoms and
the rest are too small to be eaten except by
the smallest creatures and these fall into two
categories: small copepod crustaceans, particularly those of the genus *Calanus,* and euphausid
crustaceans of a somewhat larger size, which
even as adults feed upon the primary food organisms; and the larval forms of most of the bulkier
creatures that crawl upon the sea floor or swim
in the waters above. In a general way almost
every form of life feeds upon organisms of a
somewhat smaller size and in turn is eaten by
those that are larger. Food chains thus come
into existence, with the plant producers constituting the broad but highly dispersed platform
upon which everything else is built. Chemically
the diatom crop is much like meadow hay and
in a large area of the Irish Sea, for instance,
it is reckoned to amount to roughly ten tons of
moist vegetation per acre. Numerically the individual numbers get out of hand for according to

records at the Oceanographic Institute at Woods
Hole the sea off the coast of Massachusetts contains about 400 million diatoms per cubic yard.

It takes many diatoms, however, to maintain a
single small copepod. One copepod may have as
many as 120,000 diatoms in its stomach at any
given time, while another step up the chain a
herring may have 6,000 copepods, and a humpback whale in turn a ton of herring. At any
stage, however, a step may be omitted. Newly
hatched herring are themselves too small to feed
upon copepods and feed directly on the diatoms
which they strain into their throats through a
fine grille of gill rakers, thereby getting their
green, vitamin-rich food directly. When they are
a little larger and their gill filters a little coarser,
the diatoms slip through and escape, but the young
of the copepods and other forms now enter the
mouth and are strained into the gullet. And so it
continues until the herring is pretty well full
grown, when it strains out of the stream of
water entering the mouth not merely the largest
copepods but the euphausid shrimps as well.

Food chains may be long or short. Large fish
for the most part prey on smaller fish, and so
do squid. And whales for the most part on both
fish and squid. Yet the largest animals in the sea
cut out the middlemen altogether. These are the
whalebone whales, the largest of all which have
huge filters of baleen hanging from the sides of
the mouth. They plow the seas with their mouth
open and the water straining through the great
sieves so that the euphausids are filtered out and
swallowed. A blue whale may have 300 gallons
of the shrimp in its stomach. In much the same
way the whale shark, which is a true shark and not
a mammal like the whale, browses through the
water feeding only upon the shrimp and growing
to a length of 40 feet or more.

As size increases, whether as the typical size
of adult animals or as a consequence of growth
from embryo to adult, the difficulty of remaining
within the sunlit zone increases. Compared with
its bulk the surface of any creature decreases
as the animal gets larger and accordingly the force
of gravity increases in effect. Most marine organisms large enough to be visible to the naked eye
therefore have to work to maintain position and
also have need of sense organs to direct them.
Gravity-sensitive organs of the simplest nature
are present in most inhabitants of the upper layer
of the sea, in jellyfish, squid and fish alike, which
enable the possessor to sense whether it is sinking
or rising, thus enabling it to avoid descending into
the darkness below the twilight zone. Light-sensi-
tive eyes, which are usually too simple to form
images, serve equally well during the hours of
daylight to orientate the owner towards the sea
surface and so away from the depths. Between
the two, the gravity-sensitive otolith and light-
sensitive eye or ocellus, the planktonic creatures
maintain their position within the illumination
zone where their food supply exists. Yet within
this zone their location changes regularly during
the course of the day and night in an alternating
up-and-down movement known as the diurnal
migration of the plankton.

Nearly all small creatures of the upper layers
swim towards a source of light if the intensity is
below a certain level, but away from the light
if it is too bright. Very few can tolerate the
intensity of light near the surface on a sunny
day, although each species has its own particular
maximum tolerance. Accordingly at noon the

copepod *Calanus* is to be found most abundantly between 15 and 30 meters from the surface. During the afternoon the intensity of daylight diminishes and each species of plankton animal moves slowly towards the surface, until by dusk the plankton as a whole tends to be concentrated in the uppermost layer. At night, particularly when there is no moon, light has no effect at all and the plankton organisms tend to become scattered up and down at random. But as dawn approaches and dim light reappears, they return toward the surface as they did at dusk, only to retreat to greater depths as the sun gains height and the light penetrates to greater depths. Not only do the small plankton animals migrate in regular manner according to the intensity and penetration of light during every 24 hours but so do those larger forms which feed upon them, such as fish, and so in turn the squid which feed upon the smaller fish. Such is the general pattern of life in the upper zone. Creatures in this region are usually as invisible as color or the lack of it can make them. Many forms are so watery in composition that they are completely transparent, for example the comb jellies, the smaller jelly-fishes, and the arrowhead worms, which are among the most abundant animals in the sea and the least often seen because of their virtual invisibility. Larger types are usually blue, which renders them less visible to seabirds, while most fish are blue or dark colored above and white below so that they blend with the white light descending from above or the blue reflected light below, thus camouflaging them from any angle.

In the twilight zone the basic food supply is no longer present and such animals as are present depend for the most part upon what descends to them from above. Life in the twilight zone is sparse and peculiar, and it is in this region especially that we find small fish and squid with saucerlike eyes which are large in proportion to the head, or even telescopic eyes which are elongated between front and back and are turned so that they point upwards instead of sideways or forwards. In this way the shadowy silhouettes of other creatures swimming above can be discerned against the dim background of light and can be captured as food. The twilight zone, however, quickly passes into the great depths of complete blackness and colder temperature where no light is seen except that which is produced by living animals themselves. This region comprises the great bulk of the ocean and is the least populated.

Small fish, shrimps, and squid inhabit this dismal world. Most of the fish are jet black, while the shrimp are red, which amounts to the same thing when the only light that can shine upon them is the blue-green luminescence of other creatures. In this region too the eyes of fish and squid are of extreme kind, either enlarged in order to perceive the faint gleams of light emitted by their fellow inhabitants, or imperfectly developed and blind where no use has been found for them. Light, however, is produced by the majority of the deep water forms, a luminescence produced by enzymatic action rather than combustion, and without heat. Special glands manufacture the luminescence material and usually are placed like small lanterns along the sides of the body (see LUMINESCENCE). Several purposes appear to be served by the animal light. Some shrimp and squid can eject a luminous cloud under cover of which they can escape from enemies if neces-

sary, or the cloud may serve as a lure to other creatures who may be preyed upon if they come too close. In other cases the pattern of little flashing lights probably serves for recognition, so that mating and propagation may proceed successfully. This is particularly the case with deep-sea fish, although one species of small deep-sea angler fish has solved the problem by the males becoming attached very early in life to any female they encounter and living out their lives as more or less headless parasites fastened to her skin.

Finally, in this descent from the surface, we reach the floor of the abyss where the deep sea oozes supply an insubstantial foothold. Many creatures live here, for the ooze and the water just above it are rich in decaying debris of the dead organisms sinking down from the surface layers. Crustaceans, sea snails, echinoderms and worms move with varying difficulty on or beneath the soft floor. Many anchor themselves in the ooze and grow upwards in slender form, such as the long-stalked sea lilies (echinoderms) sea pens, and the Venus sponge with its marvellously beautiful skeleton of silicon, thus raising the body clear of the engulfing ooze.

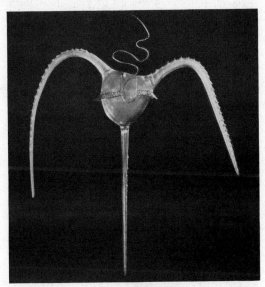

The Protozoan *ceratium* is abundant in tropic seas, where its luminescent bodies cause the sea to glow at night.

The vast majority of bottom-living animals are to be found in comparatively shallow water on the submerged shelves surrounding continents and islands. These platforms, extending from the sea's edge out to the end of the continental shelf where the sea floor suddenly dips towards the oceanic abyss, are the home of innumerable kinds of animal life—most of it in fact apart from the inhabitants of the upper illuminated layer of the open ocean. Many kinds live a stationary existence, either attached to rocks or reefs or stones, or merely embedded in the sand or gravel of the sea floor, though often within an encasing tube of their own making. For such as these there is an ever-present supply of microscopic food. The bulk of this food, however, is no longer alive and consists of detritus which is the distintegrated debris of organisms that have died. Inasmuch as some light reaches most of the platform and since currents keep the water in motion from surface to bottom, both unicellular plants such as diatoms are present in large numbers in addition to the detritus. The stationary or sessile animals that feed upon such food are filter feeders. Oysters, clams, scallops, mussels, barnacles, sea cucumbers, plume worms and sea squirts all by one means or another continually or intermittently draw water into or towards themselves and sift out the contained organic particles. Apart from closing their shells or retreating within their tubes or burrows in order to avoid being eaten by browsing fishes or other creatures, they remain rooted to the spot and move not at all. Water currents bringing the microscopic currents to the filtering system are generally created by the action of innumerable cilia, which are minute protoplasmic hairs beating against the water in a steady rhythm and covering the gills or tentacles as the case may be. Other forms, in particular certain worms such as the lugworm, burrow below the surface and swallow large quantities of mud, in the manner of an earthworm, for the sake of contained organic matter. The bivalve molluscs and worms are so generally abundant, however, that many other kinds of animals subsist by preying upon them.

The American Museum of Natural History

An octopus emerges from an undersea cavern.

Starfishes, lobsters, crabs, octopus, and many sea snails live mainly upon the various clams and mussels and their like, starfish often traveling in hordes capable of cleaning up an oyster bed overnight. Other sea snails and the sea urchins or sea eggs which are relatives of the starfish, on the other hand, feed directly upon vegetation, although upon the relative massive growths of weed in place of the microscopic kinds too small for them to handle. Many kinds of fish also feed upon the bottom-living molluscs, and sand sharks and rays have teeth arranged and shaped as crushing plates for this purpose. And some forms of course are scavengers, especially the ubiquitous hermit crabs which always drag around the empty shell of a deceased snail in which the hinder part of their body is encased.

An abundance of animal and plant life also occurs along every coast between the level of low and high tide. This region is essentially an extension of the floor of the shallow sea, though every creature and the seaweed which inhabit it must be able to withstand the twice-daily with-

drawal of the water as the tide ebbs and flows. Only animals encased in protective shells, such as molluscs and crustaceans, are usually found exposed. Others may survive partial exposure by sheltering beneath curtains of seaweed or beneath boulders. The farther up the shore from the low-tide level, the longer the exposure to the air, and only certain kinds of life are commonly found.

Whether far out on the submerged shelf or somewhere between the tides, the one common and outstanding feature of most bottom-dwelling marine animals is their comparatively large size and relatively heavy weight. Shells or skeletons of lime or bone require either a powerful swimming apparatus to keep them afloat or a platform to rest them on. The floor of the shallow seas is in fact the place above all where armor can be developed with impunity, for much greater weights can be dragged around than can be supported away from the sea floor. Lime is so readily precipitated from its solution in sea water that wherever weight is of little importance to an animal species the substance is laid down for either support or protection with little expenditure of metabolic effort. The corals precipitate it on such a scale over long periods of time that reefs are formed rising in the surface of the sea, the largest being the 1,200 mile long Great Barrier Reef of Australia (see CORAL AND CORAL REEFS).

Bibliography.—Marine biology covers a very wide field, but general accounts may be found in the following books: Russel, F. S., and Yonge, Charles M., *The Seas* (London 1949); Yonge, Charles M., *The Seashore* (New York 1950); Carson, Rachel, *The Sea Around Us* (New York 1951); Berrill, N. J., *The Living Tide* (New York 1951); Ricketts, E. F., and Calvin, J., *Between Pacific Tides* (Stanford 1952); Carson, Rachel, *The Edge of the Sea* (New York 1955).

N. J. BERRILL,
McGill University.

MARINE CITY, Michigan, is in St. Clair County, on the St. Clair River, 45 miles north of Detroit. It enjoys a considerable reputation as a summer resort, but it is also a busy manufacturing center with salt works, beet sugar factories, and shipyards. Incorporated as a village in 1865, it was named Marine City in 1867 and incorporated as a city in 1887. Pop. 4,404.

MARINE CORPS, United States, the only U.S. armed service trained for integrated land-sea-air military action anywhere at any time. The Marine Corps is a component of the Department of the Navy. The Marines have a particular competence in, and responsibility for, amphibious warfare. Although it is smaller than the other U.S. armed forces, the Marine Corps has always been noted for its pride, dedication, fighting spirit, and readiness.

Marines have performed duty both afloat and ashore since the early days of the Revolutionary War. Other major actions include the naval war with France (1798–1801), the war against Tripoli (1801–1805), the War of 1812 against England, the Seminole War (1836–1842), the Mexican War (1846–1848), the Civil War (1861–1865), the Spanish-American War (1898–1899), the Philippine Insurrection (1899–1901), the Boxer uprising in China (1900), World War I (1917–1918), World War II (1941–1945), the Korean War (1950–1953), and the Vietnam War, beginning in 1962.

Commandant. The commanding officer is a

MARINE CORPS

Above: Victorious United States Marines entering Mexico City, 1847.
Right: Painting showing marines landing near Seoul, Korea, in 1871. *Center below:* Federal marines, Civil War period. An officer stands at the left. *Bottom:* Marines at Guantanamo, Cuba, 1898, during Spanish-American War.

Official U.S. Marine Corps Photos

MARINE CORPS

Above: Marines protected the American consulate during the native war in Western Samoa, 1899. *Left:* U.S. Marines in France, World War I. *Below:* American marines were briefly pinned to the beachhead when they landed on Iwo Jima and began its conquest in the spring of 1945.

4-star general, the commandant of the Marine Corps. He answers directly to the secretary of the Navy for the total performance of the Marine Corps; however, for the Marine forces assigned to operating forces of the Navy he is responsible to the Chief of Naval Operations. When the Joint Chiefs of Staff consider a matter affecting the Marine Corps, the commandant meets with them as an equal. The commandant is appointed by the president for a term of four years.

Operating Forces. The Marine Corps is divided into three principal parts: operating forces, supporting establishment, and reserves. Fleet Marine Force Pacific and Fleet Marine Force Atlantic, containing all of the corps' combat forces, are assigned respectively to the Navy commanders in chief of the Pacific and Atlantic fleets. These FMF's consist of balanced division (ground) and wing (air) teams which are integrated with the fleets for the conduct of amphibious operations and for land fighting incident to naval campaigns. Within each FMF are Force Troops that give logistical and combat support, such as reconnaissance, engineering, and tank and artillery support. Also in the operating forces are the Marine forces afloat: guard detachments on carriers and cruisers, and battalion landing teams with Navy fleets.

Supporting Establishment. The supporting establishment includes Marine Corps Headquarters in Washington, all bases, barracks, camps, training centers and schools, aviation bases, and recruiting activities.

Major Marine installations are at Washington, D.C.; Quantico, Va.; Cherry Point and Camp Lejeune, N.C.; Beaufort and Parris Island, S.C.; Albany, Ga., Philadelphia, Pa.; Yuma, Ariz.; El Toro, Camp Pendleton, San Diego, Twentynine Palms, and Barstow, Calif.; Kaneohe, Hawaii; Iwakuni, Japan; and on Okinawa.

Much of the Marines' support comes from the Navy. Marine aviators, for example, receive basic flight training at naval air stations in Pensacola, Fla., and Corpus Christi, Texas. Navy doctors, dentists, nurses, medical corpsmen, and chaplains are provided to the Marine Corps.

Women Marines, legally limited in number to 2% of the corps, perform many important functions in the supporting establishment, in fields such as personnel administration, airfield operations, data control, supply, electronics, transportation, finance, aerology, law, and education.

Reserve. The Marine Corps Reserve exists so that the corps can expand rapidly when it is needed for war or emergency. It consists of three categories, Ready, Standby, and Retired, to be called in the order named. Within the Ready Reserve is the Organized Reserve, consisting of units that train together and can be mobilized as units. These units form the 4th Marine Aircraft Wing and 4th Marine Division, complete with combat support elements.

There are also individual Ready Reserve members. All units and individuals of the Ready Reserve may be mobilized by the president without congressional authorization. Standby and Retired categories can be called only after Congress has declared a state of war or national emergency.

Organized Reserve units are trained at regular unit drills in local training centers and through two weeks annually of active duty for training (AcDuTra) at regular military installations and often in large-scale maneuvers, integrated with regular Marines. A small staff of Marines on active duty is assigned to each Organized Reserve unit to give technical guidance and help.

Marine Corps reservists who do not belong to Organized units receive training as individuals, performing AcDuTra by attending schools or fulfilling duties in their military specialties. Many also join special Volunteer Training Units.

Specialized Warfare. With the passing of the years, the unique mission of the Marine Corps in maintaining a mobile force-in-readiness has resulted in the modern concept of land-sea-air components for a complete team capable of projecting sea power ashore.

The corps began formal training in "advance base work" in 1901, leading to the modern application of amphibious warfare techniques. In 1922 the first simulated ship-to-shore attacks were conducted during fleet exercises. In 1933 the term Fleet Marine Force, already well established in the American naval lexicon, was officially recognized as representing the heart of the Marine Corps, and formal planning got under way for the organization of two such forces, one with the Atlantic Fleet and one with the Pacific.

The Fleet Marine Forces, over half the entire corps, were to be the nation's force-in-readiness at all times, peace or war, as well as a laboratory for development of amphibious techniques in time of peace.

New tools were developed, such as the tracked landing vehicle; new techniques were applied, such as combat loading of ships; and new tactical units were created, such as the shore party battalion. Since World War II the Marine Corps has continued its role as the originator and innovator of landing force doctrine.

From the beginning, the Marine Corps considered the airplane an integral weapon, not a separate arm. Two Marine officers were among the pioneers of military aviation in 1912. Marine Corps aviation in World War I consisted of an aeronautical company in the Azores on antisubmarine patrol and the 1st Marine Aviation Force in Europe. The Germans in World War II adopted some of their techniques. Marine aviators had developed dive bombing and the airdrop of supplies during the long campaigns in Haiti and Nicaragua. Marine Corps use of close air support for ground troops also dates from these wars. Naval gunfire support was also developed as an integral part of amphibious operations, and the outbreak of World War II found the corps ready with new amphibious techniques.

The outstanding work of Marine aviators in Korea brought renewed emphasis on close air support of ground troops and special attention to the tactical use of helicopters. Marines proved the versatility of the helicopter in combat tactics as well as in reconnaissance, transport, supply, communications, and evacuation work. Tactical history was created in Korea when Marine helicopter operations moved entire battalions with their equipment into combat positions.

In the Marines' first air-amphibious assault of the Vietnam War (August 1965), three companies hit the beaches of Van Tuong Peninsula. A battalion was then landed by helicopter from a helicopter carrier, surrounding 2,000 Vietcong guerrillas who were well hidden in foxholes, tunnels, and concrete bunkers. Artillery, air strikes, and naval gunfire shattered the Vietcong regiment, and Marine casualties were light.

Marine aviation was heavily employed in Vietnam. During 1966, Marine jets flew over 70,000 sorties for day and night close air support missions; Marine helicopters flew over 529,000 sorties, and helicopter evacuation of the wounded helped reduce fatalities among the wounded to 2%.

In the first use of U.S. forces for riverine warfare, Marines in Vietnam cleared the Vietcong from areas adjacent to one of Saigon's vital river links to the sea. In 1967 the Marines published the first manual on riverine warfare.

History. The Continental Congress established the corps in a resolution on Nov. 10, 1775. It was voted that "two Battalions of Marines be raised" and that "particular care be taken that no persons be appointed to office or enlisted into said Battalions, but such are good seamen, or so acquainted with maritime affairs as to be able to serve to advantage by sea, when required."

The Marine Corps of today was established by Act of Congress on July 11, 1798, as a separate service within the naval establishment. In 1834 the president was given, and still has, authority to order Marines to duty with the Army.

In World War I a total of 78,839 officers and enlisted personnel (including 277 women reservists) served in the Marine Corps. The 4th Marine Brigade was committed to action at Belleau Wood, Soissons, Saint-Mihiel, Blanc Mont, and in the Meuse-Argonne offensive.

In World War II, when the Japanese struck on Dec. 7, 1941, Marines were stationed throughout the Pacific. Following heroic stands at Wake, Guam, Bataan, Corregidor and Midway, Marines launched the first offensive action against the Japanese of Guadalcanal on Aug. 7, 1942. Then followed occupation of the Russell Islands; the landings in New Georgia, at Bougainville, on Tarawa, and at Cape Gloucester, New Britain, in 1943. In 1944, Marines helped seize Kwajalein and captured Eniwetok in the Marshalls, landed on Saipan, Guam, and Tinian in the Marianas, and Peleliu in the Palau Islands. In 1945, Marines seized Iwo Jima and, with the Army, Okinawa. Following Japan's surrender Marines were committed to occupation duty in Japan until 1946 and in China until 1949.

The Marine Corps reached a peak strength of 475,604 officers and men and women in World War II, building from 70,425 at its outbreak. The corps was reduced to 74,279 by 1950.

The National Security Act of 1947 (PL 253—80th Congress) reaffirmed and defined the mission of the Marine Corps as an integral part of the Department of the Navy. The act provides that the corps shall be organized, trained, and equipped to provide Fleet Marine Forces of combined arms, together with supporting air components, for service with the fleet in the seizure and defense of advance naval bases and for the conduct of such land operations as may be essential to the prosecution of a naval campaign.

The law further provides that the Marine Corps shall develop, in coordination with the Army and Air Force, those phases of amphibious operations pertaining to the tactics, techniques, and equipment employed by landing forces.

The 1st Provisional Marine Brigade was activated on July 7, 1950, for duty in Korea. It was in action at Pusan a month later, supported by carrier-based Marine planes. The 1st Marine Division, later committed as a component of the Tenth Army Corps in several major actions, made an amphibious landing at Inchon that September. The division was brought up to war strength by the mobilization of reserves, drafts from the 2d Marine Division on the east coast, one battalion from the Mediterranean, and incorporation of the 1st Provisional Marine Brigade.

In 1952, the 82d Congress amended the 1947 National Security Act and assured the Marine Corps of continued division organizational structure. The amendment, known as Public Law 416, provides that "the United States Marine Corps, within the Department of the Navy, shall be so organized as to include not less than three combat divisions and three air wings, and such other land combat, aviation, and other services as may be organic therein, and except in time of war or national emergency hereafter declared by the Congress the personnel strength of the Regular Marine Corps shall be maintained at not more than four hundred thousand."

The president of Lebanon requested U.S. military aid in 1958 to stop rebellion and riot. U.S. Marines landed the next day and stayed from July through October, preserving order without incident. In the Cuban missile crisis of 1962, 30,-000 Marines were deployed, ready if needed.

Marine advisers were first sent to South Vietnam in 1962. When U.S. forces became combatants, in 1965, Marines provided the first ground elements sent into South Vietnam.

By mid-1968 the strength of the corps was 302,000, and 85,000 were in Vietnam. Marines were flying 5,000 fixed-wing and 30,000 helicopter sorties per month, and the war had changed in character. Instead of the hit-and-run guerrilla attacks of 1965 and 1966, the Vietcong and North Vietnamese were engaging in major land battles, even occasionally using entrenched fortifications.

MARINE ENGINE. See Diesel Engine; Marine Engineering.

MARINE ENGINEERING. That branch of engineering which pertains to the design and operation of the machinery required for propelling, working and handling of ships. The last two items include such details as steering, loading and unloading cargo, and in general embrace a highly complex organization of electrical and mechanical devices designed for the safety and comfort of the passengers and crew. Marine machinery must possess the highest degree of reliability without being unduly heavy or bulky.

The early history of marine engineering is a story of the development of the steam engine beginning with the rudimentary but somewhat successful pumping engines used for pumping water from mines. These early steam plants were so heavy and inefficient it was doubted if a ship equipped with an engine could ever carry enough fuel to complete a long voyage. The first steamships were simply sailing vessels with engines; the limited bunker space would permit using the engines only part of the time.

The foremost problem of the marine engineer has always been one of reducing the weight and improving the efficiency of the power plant so that the ship, by carrying less machinery and fuel, will be able to carry more cargo.

Shipboard machinery may be divided into two classes: (1) propulsion machinery, (2) ship's service machinery. All machinery directly concerned with propelling the ship through the water falls in the first category. Machinery necessary for navigation, safety, cargo handling and habitability falls in the second category.

For deep sea vessels, the fuel used is generally fuel oil with a few smaller vessels using coal. Oil fuel can be readily stored in tanks and handled by pumps and is therefore more convenient.

In modern practice, ship propulsion machinery is usually a steam plant for powers above 4,000 horsepower, and diesel engines for smaller powers. Sound economic reasons exist for these choices. Steam turbine propulsion machinery as used today is quite efficient at reasonably high powers. In addition, this type of machinery can use the lowest grade of fuel oil. In the lower powers, the efficiency of steam machinery is poor, so that the more efficient diesel must be employed. The diesel, however, must use a better grade of fuel oil so that in higher powers the cost per horsepower hour cannot compete with steam.

The Steam Plant.—Most marine propulsion steam machinery employs the highly efficient steam turbine for a prime mover. The less efficient reciprocating steam engine still finds some use,

especially where powers are low and coal must be used for fuel or for wartime emergency ship-building, since the reciprocating engine is easily built.

The cycle of steam and water in the elementary steam plant is indicated in Fig. 1. Steam, from boiling water at high pressure, is generated in the *boilers,* then superheated in the *superheaters* and passed through the main steam line to the *throttle valves.* The steam then flows through the *high pressure turbine,* the cross over pipe and the *low pressure turbine* and exhausts to the *condenser.* The steam, in passing through the turbines, is expanded and the resulting kinetic energy is given up the blades of the rotating elements. The turbine rotors are connected to a speed *reduction gear* and the useful work transmitted to the propeller shaft and propeller.

The condenser serves two purposes. First, it recovers the exhaust steam as water for return to the boilers as *feed water.* This is very im-

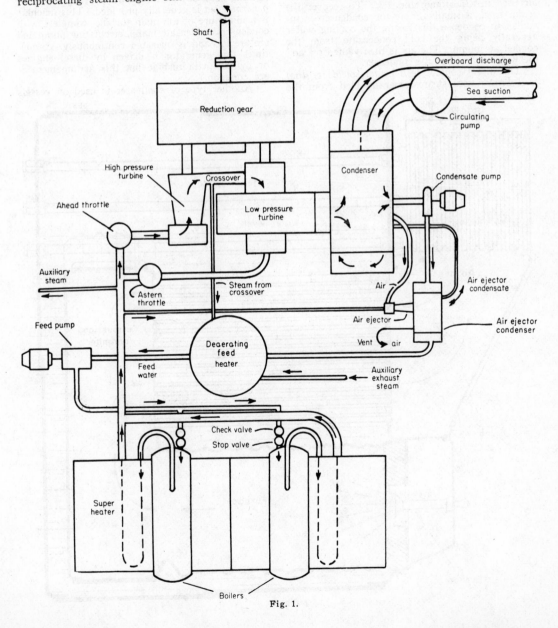

Fig. 1.

portant since fresh water must be conserved. A ship cannot possibly carry sufficient water for this purpose and salt water is unusable for generating steam. In addition, the condenser generates a high vacuum in condensing the exhaust steam to water, so that more energy is extracted per pound of steam.

The condenser consists of a bundle of tubes through which cold sea water is passed. The exhaust steam passes around the outside of the tubes, thereby being chilled, giving up the latent heat of vaporization and condensing into water.

The condensate is pumped out of the bottom of the condenser and passed to the *direct contact feed heater* by the *condensate pump*.

Since the low pressure turbine operates at below atmospheric pressure, some air leaks into the system and must be removed from the condenser by the *air ejector,* a device working on the same principle as a perfume atomizer, except that a jet of high velocity steam replaces the jet of air used in a perfume atomizer. To recover the steam used, a small air ejector condenser is installed to condense this steam, the cooling water generally being the cold condensate from the condensate pump. The air is then vented off and the water drained to the condenser.

The direct contact feed heater, or *deaerating feed heater* uses steam generally bled from the turbine crossover for feed heating. This arrangement, known as regeneration, has great thermal advantages, since it recovers the latent heat of vaporization of the bled steam after it has already done much useful work in the high pressure turbine. In some cases, exhaust steam from auxiliary machinery is also used in the feed heater. In addition to heating the feed water, the deaerating heater acts as a water storage and also drives off any entrained air.

The feed water is then pumped by the *feed pump* to the boilers and the cycle repeats.

In many plants, the feed pump is steam driven and the exhaust steam is used for the deaerating heater. It is also common for additional feed heaters to be installed, using steam extracted from various points on the turbines. The heaters are generally surface heaters, similar in principle to the condenser.

To drive the various auxiliaries and provide lighting and power for ship's service, a *turbogenerator* set is generally provided. This machine is a miniature of the main turbine, complete with condenser, condensate pump, circulating pump and air ejector and is operated continuously. Sometimes this generator is driven by diesel engines or by the main turbine but this arrangement is not common.

Another type of condenser is used on vessels

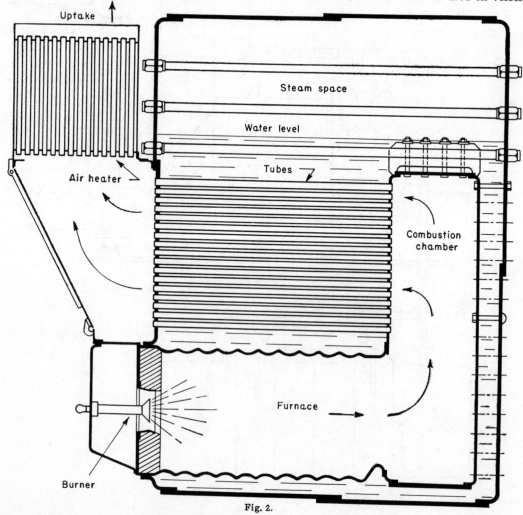

Fig. 2.

which operate in fresh water, or in harbors where their fresh water tanks can be refilled readily. This condenser is called a *jet condenser,* or *direct contact condenser.* The cooling water is sprayed directly into the chamber which receives the exhaust steam. A vacuum is produced, but the resulting mixture of condensed steam and cooling water is unfit for boiler feed unless the cooling water itself is free from impurities. Early seagoing steamships used sea water in their boilers with reasonable success according to the standards of the day. The steam plants were inefficient but the low steam pressures and types of boilers used did permit the use of sea water which was a very important consideration in the absence of a dependable surface condenser.

The demands of modern watertube steam generators in regard to boiler water can only be obtained with a tight surface condenser plus a scientific procedure of feedwater treatment to prevent corrosion and formation of scale. The deposit of scale on the heating surfaces can be prevented by chemical treatment of the boiler water, while corrosion can be prevented by maintaining the water slightly alkaline and by removing dissolved oxygen before the water enters the boiler. Oxygen can be kept out of the boiler to

a satisfactory degree by using the deaerating type of feedwater heater wherein the water and heating steam are brought into direct contact. The water enters the heater in a fine spray which exposes the highest possible surface contact with the steam jets. Under the influence of the high velocity steam the air becomes disengaged from the water particles and joins the steam flow which carries the air out of the heater. There is no waste of steam, as provision is made for condensing it after it has cleared the air from contact with the water.

The extent to which a steam engine will convert steam into mechanical power depends primarily upon its ability to permit expansion of the steam within the engine. In the multistage reciprocating engine the steam is admitted and expanded successively in two, three, or four cylinders depending upon whether it is a *compound, triple expansion,* or *quadruple expansion* engine. The extent to which the steam can be expanded is obviously limited by the size of the low-pressure cylinder. In the *steam turbine* the steam passes through the nozzles and blading at a high velocity which permits a large volume of steam to be accommodated and gives a much higher ratio of expansion than would be practicable in a piston

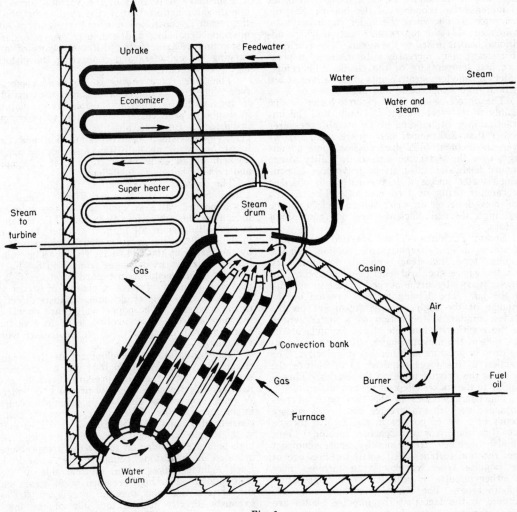

Fig. 3.

type of engine. However, this inherent efficiency of the steam turbine is not fully gained in turbines of small size. For very high powers the steam turbine has no competitor. It has been built in units as large as 60,000 horsepower per shaft.

Marine Boilers.—These are of two general types—*firetube* and *watertube*. The Scotch marine boiler, shown in Fig. 2, is the outstanding example of the firetube type. As the name implies, the hot products of combustion pass through the tubes. This type of steam generator is obsolete as far as new construction in the United States is concerned. However, many hundreds are in use in existing vessels. Contrary to this one principal type of firetube boiler, watertube boilers are manufactured in a variety of forms. In the past, each boiler manufacturer built a particular type which was referred to by its proprietary name, such as "Babcock & Wilcox." Since the various boiler companies now build all types, such designations are meaningless to one not already familiar with the boilers concerned.

Fig. 3 is a diagrammatic sketch of a watertube boiler showing the path of water and steam. It should be noted that there are three distinct sections of the boiler: (1) the *preheating section* generally referred to as an "economizer," because originally it was added to older designs in order to increase the economy of the boiler; (2) the *generator section* where the water vapor or steam is formed; (3) the *superheater* section where additional heat is added to the steam. The efficiency of a steam plant increases with increase in pressure and temperature of the steam. Therefore, boilers for modern steam plants must deliver steam at both high temperature and high pressure.

The obsolescence of the Scotch boiler is due mainly to its great weight and bulk, and the impracticability of building it for steam pressures higher than 220 pounds per square inch. However, the Scotch boiler does possess some advantages over the watertube such as its ability to use impure feedwater; also, its large volume of contained water makes it less sensitive to changes in rate of firing or feed control. The Scotch boiler is desirable in cases where weight, space and high thermal efficiency are not controlling factors.

Steam Turbines.—There are two basic types of steam turbines—*impulse* and *reaction*. In the impulse type the steam expands in stationary nozzles where the heat energy is converted to kinetic energy by virtue of the increase in velocity of the jet. The driving force is created by the impulse of the high velocity steam jet on the blades, similar to the action of a water wheel. In the reaction turbine the steam expands in the passages of the moving blades with a corresponding drop in pressure and increase in velocity. The reaction to the force required to accelerate the steam is the driving force on the blades. This is similar to the rocket effect of jet propulsion.

The characteristics of the two types of turbines are such that a greater change of energy occurs in a set of nozzles in an impulse turbine than in a blade row of a reaction turbine. Thus, impulse turbines are generally more compact than reaction turbines. All small turbines are of the impulse type, whereas large turbines may be either impulse or reaction, or a combination of both types. The combined turbine takes advantage of the fact that the impulse blades are more efficient at the high pressure, inlet end while the reaction blades are more efficient at the low-pressure end. In geared turbine drives the turbine is divided into two or sometimes three casings, which are actually separate turbines, through which the steam flows in series. This division of turbines reduces the load that any one reduction gear pinion must transmit. Also, the problems of thermal expansions and contractions are reduced by the smaller units.

Reversing turbines are required for direct or geared drives. The reversing turbine is a separate turbine mounted in the casing of the low-pressure turbine at the exhaust end. When the ship is going ahead the astern turbine runs idle opposite to its natural direction of rotation. The resulting drag on the ahead turbines is kept as small as possible by making the astern element compact without too much regard for its efficiency. When running astern the windage losses in the ahead turbines are considerable and the final power available for astern running is generally less than half the ahead power. However, this is generally sufficient. If for any reason full astern power is required from a turbine, the electric drive is advisable.

Reciprocating Steam Engine.—All modern reciprocating engines used for marine propulsion are of the multicylinder vertical inverted type. The primary difference in the various forms is one of valve action, that is, the manner in which the steam is controlled during the events of admission, expansion and exhaust. A secondary distinction relates to the different ways of arranging the cylinders and connecting the pistons to the crankshaft.

The *slide valve engine* is the most common type. The two-cylinder compound is used mainly in tugs with the triple expansion predominating in seagoing cargo vessels. The slide valve engine installed in Liberty ships has one slide valve per cylinder which controls admission and exhaust of steam at both top and bottom ends. Typical of all slide valve engines, it is simple and reliable but quite inefficient.

The *uniflow marine engine,* as built in the United States by the Skinner Engine Company, has a poppet valve at each end of the cylinder to control the admission of steam. The exhaust is controlled, as in all uniflow engines, by ports in the middle of the cylinder which are uncovered by the piston at the end of its stroke. The number of cylinders used ranges from 2 to 8. Each cylinder is independent in regard to steam flow; i.e., each cylinder receives a charge of steam at the beginning of the stroke and exhausts directly to the condenser. The poppet valves are operated by cams and can be controlled so as to give the much desired constant point of admission with variable cut-off.

Woolf Engine.—A development of the steam engine by Arthur Woolf in 1804 was a compound engine in which the high-pressure cylinder exhausted directly into the low-pressure cylinder. A recent revival of the Woolf principle occurs in the *Ajax engine.* The engine, as usually built, consists of 3 units on a 3-crank shaft. Each unit is a steeple compound arrangement with the high-pressure cylinder on top of the low-pressure cylinder, both pistons being on the same rod. Each cylinder takes steam on one side of the piston only. The high-pressure takes steam on the bottom side and then on the down stroke exhausts directly to the top side of the low-pressure cylinder. The low-pressure cylinder is

Skinner Engine Company

Three-cylinder uniflow marine engine.

MARINE ENGINEERING

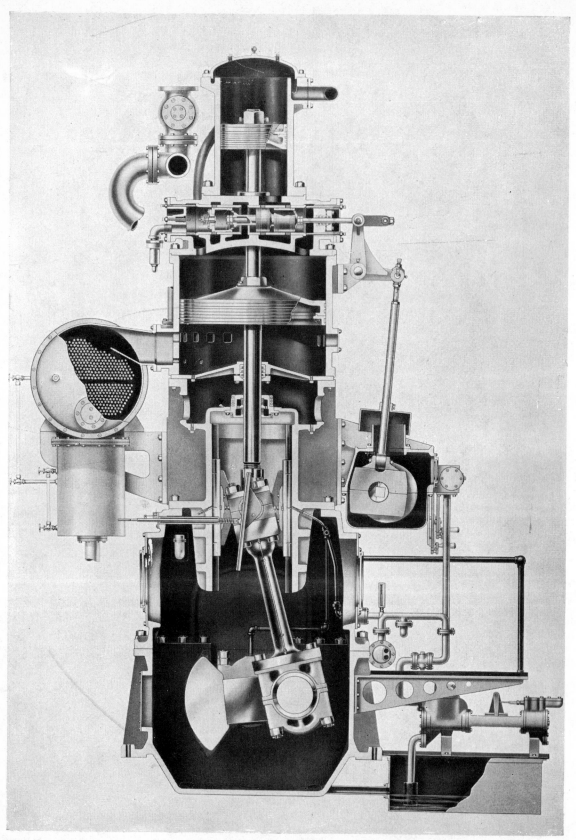

Ajax marine engine.

Ajax Iron Works

strictly single-acting uniflow and exhausts to a condenser attached to the side of the engine. One valve of the piston slide-valve type controls both admission to the high-pressure cylinder and the combined event of high-pressure exhaust and low-pressure admission.

The *Lentz engine* is a European development of the Woolf principle. It is built as a double compound engine having two high-pressure and two low-pressure cylinders. Each piston is on a separate crank with 180° crank angle between each high- and low-pressure cylinder. Thus the low-pressure cylinder of each unit is always moving opposite to its adjacent high-pressure cylinder. The steam to the double-acting pistons is controlled by poppet valves, six of which are required for each pair of cylinders. The only difference between the Lentz engine and an ordinary double-acting, poppet-valve counterflow is the manner in which the steam is exhausted directly from the high-pressure cylinder to the low-pressure instead of first being exhausted to a receiver and then being admitted to the low-pressure. This arrangement, however, gives a more efficient engine due to the elimination of the receiver and two valves between each pair of cylinders.

Reciprocating Engine Performance.—There is little difference in the relative heat efficiencies of the three engines just described; all of them are definitely superior to the standard slide valve engine. However, the attempt to increase the efficiency of any reciprocating engine by using higher-temperature steam aggravates the problem of lubricating the piston and cylinder walls. The serious aspect of the problem is not the actual providing of lubrication but the separation of the oil from the feedwater before it is returned to the boilers.

Combined Reciprocating Engines and Turbines.—Although some original designs have used reciprocating engines and turbines in combination, this arrangement is more common in conversion jobs where the power and efficiency of the propulsion plant have been increased by adding an exhaust turbine to the original reciprocating engine. The turbine must be connected through reduction gears to the propulsion shaft just aft of the main engine. In order to secure full benefit from the combination it is necessary to increase the original steam pressure and temperature and install a new condenser capable of producing a higher vacuum.

The Diesel Plant.—The modern diesel propulsion plant takes many varied forms, depending on the service and the type of drive. For long life and dependability, the diesel must be a slow turning engine. The result is a large, heavy, slow-moving engine, of either two cycle or four cycle type, directly connected to the propeller shaft and direct reversing. Such engines are very efficient and dependable and can burn comparatively poor grades of fuel.

In an effort to reduce size and weight, modern practice tends toward using higher speed engines with reduction gears and clutches or electric transmissions. For smaller powers, these efforts have been quite successful. The diesel engine is the most common form of propulsion prime mover for small craft, submarines and vessels of moderate power.

Even when employing higher speeds, however, the diesel engine cannot compete at high powers. For a more detailed discussion of this type of prime mover, see INTERNAL COMBUSTION ENGINE; DIESEL ENGINE, HISTORY AND DEVELOPMENT OF.

For large diesel engines, especially if direct connected, compressed air is generally used for starting the engine. Smaller engines are often started by electrical means.

To provide electric power for auxiliaries and lighting, a smaller *diesel generator set* is usually provided. In addition, a small boiler is installed to provide steam for ship heating and other uses. This boiler is sometimes heated by the exhaust gas from the main engines, in which case it is known as a waste heat boiler.

Propulsion.—Early steamships were propelled by *paddle wheels* not only because this method of mechanical rowing was the most obvious but because the paddle wheels were suitable for the slow-turning engines then in use. Paddle wheels proved entirely unfit for seagoing vessels. If the wheels were properly submerged when the ship was fully loaded, they would probably be entirely out of water with the vessel in light condition; also the paddles were quite likely to be damaged by waves in rough weather. Paddle-wheel propulsion is well adapted to vessels of shallow and more or less constant draft, such as river steamers.

The *screw propeller,* generally referred to simply as a *propeller* or a *screw,* is the most efficient and widely used method of propulsion. It began to replace the paddle wheel about 1837. In the first installation the engines were adaptations of the paddle-wheel engines which were fairly satisfactory at rotative speeds on the order of 30 revolutions per minute or less, but were dangerous to the wooden hulls at higher speeds on account of the vibration due to unbalanced forces. For good efficiency the propeller requires a speed of about twice that of a paddle wheel. These higher speeds were frequently obtained by the use of gearing involving wooden-toothed gears on the engine shafts driving smaller iron gears on the propeller shafts. All of these engines were a practical failure due to their great weight as well as their mechanical infirmities. The propeller came into its own with the development of better balanced multicylinder steam engines that could be run fast enough to be connected directly to the propulsion shafting. The only restriction on the use of the propeller is sufficient depth of water and draft of hull to allow it to operate completely submerged. Depending upon the size and type of ship, one to four propellers are used, and the ship is designated as single-screw, twin-screw, triple-screw, or quadruple-screw. See NAVAL ARCHITECTURE—*Model Basins;* SCREW PROPELLER.

Jet propulsion is too inefficient to be considered as a general means of moving a ship through the water. Its principle is simply one of pumping a submerged jet of water opposite to the direction in which the vessel is to be propelled. In order to obtain high efficiency the jet of water must be larger in diameter than is practicable to obtain from any type of pump. Jet propulsion can be used in the special case of a fire boat where the large pumping capacity can be used as effective if not efficient propulsion while running to or from a fire. See also JET PROPULSION.

Transmission of Power.—There are three ways of transmitting power from the main engine to the propeller: (1) By *direct drive* when the engine is connected directly to the propeller shaft. In this type of drive the rotative speeds of the engine and propeller cannot be selected independently, which may result in a very inefficient combination. The screw propeller requires a relatively low rotative speed for good efficiency whereas the steam turbine requires a high speed. The early direct-drive turbine vessels such as the *Leviathan, Majestic* and old *Mauretania* were inefficient because the shaft speed in each case was a compromise between the most efficient propeller speed and the most efficient turbine speed. The reciprocating steam engine, and the Diesel engine, can all be used successfully in direct drive.

(2) The *geared drive* was developed mainly to take advantage of the inherent efficiency of the steam turbine. Most of the turbine installations employ double reduction, double-helical gears with speed reductions running as high as 80 to 1. The single-reduction gear is used for geared Diesel jobs where the required speed reduction is not as high as for steam turbines. The purpose of the geared Diesel drive is to reduce machinery weight and provide greater reliability and ease of maintenance through the use of one or more small high-speed units instead of one large slow engine directly connected. Also, the power which can be transmitted by one shaft is considerably greater in the multiengine drive. In the geared-Diesel it is good practice to introduce a slip-type coupling between each engine and the gears so as to minimize the torque variations transmitted by the gear teeth. The two types of couplings used are the electromagnetic and the hydraulic.

(3) The *electric drive* is used primarily as a speed reducer. It permits the speed of the electric motor and propeller to be adjusted independently of the engine and generator speed. Electric energy used to drive the propulsion motor can be generated by any type of prime mover. However, steam turbines and internal combustion engines are the only engines used to any great extent in connection with electric drive. In ships of large powers alternating current is preferred to direct current on account of less weight and cost, and greater simplicity. The reduction in speed is obtained by designing a propulsion motor with more poles than the generator. Thus for alternating current the speed ratio between the generator and motor is fixed for any one pole arrangement. Although the Diesel engine has been used to some extent for alternating current electric propulsion, the turboelectric plant is the outstanding example of this drive. On the other hand, direct current propulsion finds its greatest usefulness in Diesel-electric jobs.

Aside from the matter of speed reduction the electric drive has other desirable features. In either a-c or d-c jobs it gives full power astern without changing the normal ahead operation of the main engine. In the case of direct current it also gives an exceedingly fine control of power and speed. Also, the electric drive permits pilot house control of the propulsion motors. These last two features are particularly desirable for tugs and icebreakers.

Thrust Bearing.—The interaction of the propeller and water produces a *thrust* on the propeller shaft. A special *thrust bearing* must be fitted in the shafting between the propeller and engine, or gears, so that this axial force which propels the vessel will be transmitted directly to the hull instead of to the propelling machinery. The modern type of thrust bearing consists of a collar on the shaft which bears against Babbitt-faced shoes secured to the casing of the bearing. The casing is bolted firmly to the hull. Since

the shoes are on both the forward and after sides of the collar the propeller thrust will be transmitted to the hull whether going ahead or astern.

Propeller.—Although the form of a screw propeller is similar to the helicoidal screw thread, the action of an individual propeller blade can be considered as a rotating airfoil. The thrust produced by a marine propeller is directly comparable to the lift of an airplane wing. (See AERONAUTICS.) Propeller design is based on tests of scale models made either in open water or in closed variable pressure tunnels. In comparing the behavior of a model and the full size propeller it is necessary to consider the effect of propeller size upon such quantities as thrust, power and torque. A study of dimensional analysis [1] reveals the conditions under which a model must be operated so that its performance can be used to predict full size performance. For instance, one of the conditions is that the ratio of the pressure acting on the model to the pressure acting on the full size must be the same as the ratio of their linear dimensions. That is, if the full size propeller has a diameter 20 times the diameter of the model, the pressure on the model must be one twentieth that on the full size. Since pressure acting on a ship's propeller is mainly atmospheric, it is necessary to operate the model in a partial vacuum to obtain comparable pressure conditions. Fortunately, this pressure relationship does not appreciably affect any of the propeller properties except cavitation (*cavitation* occurs when the flow of water to the propeller fails to follow the blade outline) and most testing can be conducted under atmospheric pressure.

Auxiliaries.—*Heat exchangers* include such items as condensers, evaporators, feedwater heaters, fuel oil heaters and lubricating oil coolers. Of course, the shape, proportions and details of design will vary for each type of service, but all heat exchangers are based on the principle of transferring heat from one medium to another through the walls of the tubes. In the case of heat transfer between condensing steam and water more efficient transmission will be effected if the water is confined to the tubes so that the velocity of flow along the tube walls is uniform.

The *electric plant* aboard ship is becoming more important as the shipboard uses of electricity continue to expand. The first general use of electricity aboard ship at the beginning of the 20th century was confined to lighting. On small cargo vessels the "dynamo" would be shut down during the day and oil lamps would be used in the engine and fire rooms. On modern vessels electric power is as common as on shore with additional uses such as the gyrocompass, automatic steering and other navigational aids. In some vessels all auxiliaries and hull machinery are driven by electricity. Direct and alternating current are both used, with direct current predominating, except in later naval vessels. The electric generators for auxiliary use are generally driven by geared steam turbines or Diesel engines. Small size generators, particularly those in older ships where they are referred to as dynamos, are driven by single cylinder reciprocating steam engines.

Pumps.—The *pump* is probably the oldest piece of mechanical equipment in marine use. In the development of marine engineering many new

---

[1] "Dimensional Analysis of Model Propeller Tests," by Edgar Buckingham, *Journal of the American Society of Naval Engineers*, vol. 48, no. 2, May 1936.

types have been invented. The centrifugal and other rotary types are desirable on account of compactness, uniform flow and because they can be driven directly from the shaft of an electric motor or steam turbine. However, the reciprocating piston type pump driven by direct-acting steam pistons is still common. The efficiency of the piston pump is high, but the steam end of a direct-acting pump is very inefficient. The desirable features of the piston pump are retained in the *power pump* which gives an efficient drive by using a system of gears, crankshaft and connecting rod to connect an electric motor to the reciprocating pistons.

For additional information on machinery used aboard ship see articles ENGINE; PUMPS; SHIP-BUILDING INDUSTRY AND CONSTRUCTION; SHIPPING AND SHIPBUILDING TERMS; STEAM ENGINE; TURBINE.

Bibliography.—Pounder, Cuthbert C., *Marine Diesel Engines* (New York 1959); Crouch, Holmes F., *Nuclear Marine Propulsion* (Cambridge, Md., 1960); Osbourne, Alan, ed., *Modern Marine Engineer's Manual*, 2 vols. (Cambridge, Md., 1965, 1943); Paterson, William B., *Marine Engine Room Blue Book*, 2d ed. (Cambridge, Md., 1965); Lewis, E. V., O'Brien, R., and the Editors of Life, *Ships* (New York 1965); Terry, R. D., *The Deep Submersible* (North Hollywood, 1966); Cooke, D. C., *How Atomic Submarines Are Made* (New York 1967).

JEREMY B. BLOOD,
Professor of Marine Engineering, Webb Institute of Naval Architecture.
Revised by   JENS T. HOLM,
Professor of Marine Engineering, Webb Institute of Naval Architecture.

MARINE INSURANCE. See INSURANCE —*Marine Insurance.*

MARINE SEDIMENTS, those laid down in the ocean, in contrast to terrestrial deposits laid down on land. They are usually characterized by uniformity in thickness and character over rather large areas, and commonly contain fossils of animals known to live only in the sea. The common types are conglomerates, sandstones, shales and limestones. See also OCEAN, THE: section on *Submarine Geology* in article on GEOLOGY, and section on *Sedimentary Rocks* in article on ROCKS.

MARINER'S COMPASS. See COMPASS, MAGNETIC.

MARINES IN FRANCE IN 1918—Belleau Wood, Soissons, etc.—On May 31, 1918, the Second Division of the American Expeditionary Forces was selected to go to the relief of the French Army retreating before the German drive. The Fifth and Sixth Regiments and the Sixth Machine Gun Battalion of United States Marines, forming the Fourth Brigade of the Second Division, commanded by Brigadier General James G. Harbord, were in reserve in a rest area at Montdidier, when the order to the front arrived. Reaching their destination in the early morning of June 1, they moved into line in support of the French. It was the opening of the Battle of Chateau Thierry, and found the German advance facing the Americans. Hill 165 was the enemy's objective, but the marines as expert riflemen "calmly set their sights and aimed with the same precision that they had shown upon the rifle ranges at Paris Island, Mare Island and Quantico." Their machine guns also took up the fire.. The artillery soon backed

the riflemen and, with shrapnel, added to the killing power; the Germans ran to cover raked by the American fire. This day's battle halted the German drive on Paris. But the city of Chateau Thierry remained in the enemy's hands; its liberation involved prior capture of the Bois de Belleau which was very strongly fortified, as were the flanking villages of Bouresches and Torcy. On June 6 at 5 P.M. the marines, attacking with the bayonet, captured Bouresches and penetrated Belleau Wood. The Germans resisted fanatically, but the marines with their associated infantry brigade so exhausted the three enemy divisions (197th, 237th and 10th) that the 5th Guards, and then the 28th, had to be thrown in as reinforcements. Thus, five German divisions were consumed in a three-week conflict. The last enemy nests were captured on the 28th. In the Aisne-Marne campaign launched on July 18 the brigade fought again brilliantly near Soissons, then in the St. Mihiel campaign of mid-September. Early in October they defeated the Germans once again east of Reims. The brigade's total casualties amounted to nearly 400 officers and 12,000 enlisted men. Distinguished Service crosses were awarded to 644 of its members.

MARINETTE, măr-ĭ-nĕt′, city, Wisconsin, Marinette County seat, altitude 595 feet, is located on Green Bay, at the mouth of the Menominee River, on the Chicago and North Western and the Chicago, Milwaukee and St. Paul railroads, opposite Menominee, Mich., with which it has car ferry service across Lake Michigan to Frankfort, Mich. Its manufactures include wood products, excelsior, gloves, pulp wood insulation, cardboard boxes. It has docks for small craft on the river, which flows through the center of the city, and a harbor for lake steamers. The city has a considerable lake traffic, and is a point of entry for the 37th customs district. The site of the first local sawmill is preserved as a monument to the city's early days, and there is a monument to United States Senator Isaac Stephenson (1829–1918), pioneer lumberman. Marinette was settled in 1830 on the site of an Indian village, was named for Queen Marinette (Jacobs) of the Menominee tribe, the wife of a fur trader, and received its city charter in 1887. Government is by mayor and council. Pop. 13,329.

MARINUS I or **MARTIN II,** pope: r. 882–884. Of Roman birth he was ordained a deacon and sent on three embassies to Constantinople at one of which he presided as legate over the Eighth Ecumenical Council (869). He succeeded John VIII who had made him bishop of Caere (Cerveteri) and treasurer of the Holy See. He absolved Formosus (q.v.) of all censures but condemned Photius (q.v.). Because of friendship for Alfred of England he freed the headquarters of the English in Rome from all taxes.

MARINUS II or **MARTIN III,** pope: r. 942–946. A Roman cardinal, he was elected through the power of the prince, Alberic, and instituted reforms, aided monastic development, and helped the poor. He was impotent as a temporal ruler.

MARIO, mä′ryô, **Giovanni Matteo,** MARCHESE DI CANDIA, dĕ kän′dyä, Italian tenor: b.

Cagliari, Sardinia, Oct. 17, 1810; d. Rome, Dec. 11, 1883. After serving in the Sardinian Army he went to Paris, where after two years of musical study he was appointed first tenor of the opera, changing his name at the same time from Di Candia to Mario. He made his debut Nov. 30, 1838 as Robert in *Robert the Devil,* and soon became the leading tenor of the world. Among his chief roles were Otello in Rossini's *Otello;* Almaviva in *Il Barbiere di Siviglia;* and Manrico in *Il Trovatore.* He married the famous singer, Giulia Grisi, in 1854, and together they made an operatic tour of the United States. In his later years, after his retirement from the stage in 1867, he lost his fortune through speculations, and in 1872 again made a concert tour of the United States.

MARIOLATRY. See MARY.

MARION, măr'ĭ-ŏn, **Francis,** American soldier: b. near Georgetown, S. C., in 1732; d. Pond Bluff, Feb. 26, 1795. He was the youngest in a family of six children. His grandfather, Benjamin Marion, was a Huguenot exiled from France in 1690. At 16 Francis showed his adventurous disposition by embarking on a small vessel bound for the West Indies. It was wrecked and he barely escaped death by starvation. He returned home and worked several years on a farm. In 1759–1761 he served in campaigns against the Cherokees. Thenceforth until 1775 he lived on his plantation at Pond Bluff in the parish of Saint John.

In 1775 Marion was elected member from Saint John in the South Carolina provincial congress, which adopted the bill of rights and voted money for raising troops. He was chosen captain (June 21, 1775) and took the field against the British and the Tories. He took part in the capture of Fort Johnson (Sept. 14, 1775), and because of his ability in organizing and discipline was promoted to major. He participated in the patriot victory (June 28, 1776) at Charleston, which gave the Southern States respite from active fighting for nearly three years. Appointed lieutenant-colonel, he led his regiment in the unsuccessful attack on Savannah (September 1779). In 1780 Marion, now a brigadier-general, was obliged to take refuge in forest and swamp. Beginning with a handful of men, less than 20, he gathered recruits, fearless riders and good marksmen, who formed the famed "Marion's brigade." At times they numbered several hundred. They came and went at their leader's bidding, providing their own equipment and rations. Part of the time they were at work on their farms, planting crops. These rough and ready troopers became the terror of the British regulars and the Tories, although in justice to Marion's men it should be said that they committed no acts of wanton cruelty and burned no buildings on Tory homesteads. The stories of his adventures read more like fiction than history. His scouts kept close watch of the enemy's movements, and detachments of the brigade struck blow after blow, surprising and capturing small parties of soldiers. At times they united with larger bodies of troops for important engagements. After a vain pursuit, Sir Banastre Tarleton named Marion the "Swamp Fox." Failing in his attempt against Georgetown (December 1780), he retired to Swan Island and prepared for a second attack (Jan. 13, 1781),

which was also unsuccessful. Then he joined with Col. Henry Lee in reducing Fort Watson (April 1781). After raiding 200 miles of country he commanded the first line in the battle of Eutaw Springs and took many prisoners. For his gallantry in this engagement he received the thanks of Congress. From 1782 to 1790 Marion served in the State senate and was a member of the State Constitutional Convention in 1790. He opposed harsh treatment of the Tories and condemned the Confiscation Act of 1782. In 1784 he married a wealthy cousin, Mary Videau, who survived him with no children. He was a man of attractive personality. Of slight figure, he was capable of great endurance and accustomed to abstinence. As a leader he was admired and beloved. He justly ranks among the heroes of the American Revolution.

MARION, city, Illinois, Williamson County seat, altitude 419 feet, is located 45 miles south of Mt. Vernon, on the Illinois Central; Missouri Pacific; and Chicago and Eastern Illinois railroads. It has local and county airports. To the west is Crab Orchard Lake (25,000 acres) a federal project, a large industrial area, and national wild life refuge. A United States Veterans Hospital adjoins the city. Blasting powder, mine drills, batteries, stencil machines, electric capacitors, armatures, transformers, refrigerator parts, plastics, furniture, ice cream, and ice vending machines are manufactured. Robert G. Ingersoll and John A. Logan (qq.v.) lived in Marion. Pop. 11,274.

MARION, city, Indiana, Grant County seat, altitude 811 feet, is located 28 miles northwest of Muncie, on the Pennsylvania; Chesapeake and Ohio; New York Central; and Toledo, St. Louis and Western railroads. It has an accredited airport. It is an industrial city in a farm area, with gas and oil wells nearby. Among its manufactures are insulated wires and cables, bottles, radios and equipment, automobile accessories, shoes, and paper products. The city government is administered by a mayor, a council, and a board of public works. It is the seat of Marion College (coeducational). The first land entry in Marion was made in 1825. Grant County, organized in 1831, was incorporated in 1839. The city was incorporated in 1889. It was named in honor of Gen. Francis Marion (q.v.). Pop. 37,854.

MARION, city, Iowa, Linn County, altitude 848 feet; is located on Indian Creek; 6 miles northeast of Cedar Rapids; on the Chicago, Milwaukee, St. Paul and Pacific Railroad, of which it is a division point, with shops and yards. It is in a region producing general crops, cattle, and hogs. Its fine shade trees have won for it the nickname of Grove City. Marion was once the county seat; Cedar Rapids now holds that position. A mill built in 1863 is still operating, and there are in the city chick hatcheries, an aluminum factory, and a factory making sack balers. Marion was settled in 1839, and was named in honor of Gen. Francis Marion. Pop. 10,882.

MARION, city, Ohio, and Marion County seat; altitude 986 feet; 46 miles north of Columbus; on the Erie; Cleveland, Cincinnati, Chicago, and St. Louis; and Chesapeake and Ohio railroads; with a municipal airport. In a farm region it is a railroad and manufacturing center, famous since 1874 for its steam shovels, tractors, road rollers, and farm implements. Railroad shops, foundries, and factories making steel vaults, steel bodies, locks, ornamental glass, silk goods, dresses, cigars, dairy and soybean products are here.

At the age of 19, Warren G. Harding (q.v.) became proprietor of the Marion *Star*. The house in which he campaigned for the presidency in 1920 is preserved as Harding Museum; and a mile south is the handsome Harding Memorial.

An early settler, Jacob Foos, found a fine water supply at this site. After two years as Jacob's Well, the place was named Marion in 1822 and became county seat. Marion became a city in 1890. Pop. 37,079.

MARION, town, South Carolina, and Marion County seat; altitude 68 feet; 21 miles east of Florence; on the Atlantic Coast Line Railroad. It is the business center for a cotton, tobacco, and timber region; local industries produce cotton yarn, cottonseed oil, veneer, boxes, cement blocks, clothing, lumber, and brick.

Marion was settled in 1800 as Gilesboro; in 1830 it was renamed Marion, honoring Francis Marion, the "Swamp Fox" of the American Revolution. It was incorporated as a city in 1900. Pop. 7,174.

MARION, town, Virginia, and Smyth County seat; altitude 2,124 feet; in the Walker Mountains; on Holston River; 45 miles northeast of Bristol; on the Norfolk and Western Railroad. It is in a cattle, corn, Burley tobacco, and lumber region, with limestone and manganese deposits. Marion has manufactures of furniture and tool handles, baseball bats, brick, shirts and shorts, and silk hosiery.

Here are Marion College, a junior college for girls, and the Southwestern State Hospital for the mentally ill. The novelist Sherwood Anderson edited two weekly newspapers here. After Anderson's death in 1941, his son Robert Anderson edited and later combined the two papers as *The Smyth County News.*

First settled in 1750, Marion became a town in 1832. Three miles north is Hungry Mother State Park. Pop. 8,385.

MARION ISLAND, in the Indian Ocean, is a dependency of the Republic of South Africa. It is 13 miles long and 8 miles wide.

MARIOTTE, mà-ryôt′, **Edme,** French physicist: b. probably in Dijon, ?1620; d. Paris, France, May 12, 1684. He lived for the most part at Dijon, and was made prior of Saint-Martin-sous-Beaune. He became a member of the Academy of Sciences upon its formation, and was one of the founders of experimental physics. "It is Mariotte," said Marie Jean de Caritat (Marquis de Condorcet), "who first in France introduced into physics a spirit of observation and of doubt." He discovered independently the law known by his name, also discovered by Robert Boyle (q.v.), and known as Boyle's Law.

MARIOTTE'S LAW, *in physics,* the principle that the volume of a gas, under constant, that is, unchanging, temperature and pressure, varies inversely as the pressure. It is identical with Boyle's Law (q.v.), the latter name being applied to it in the United States and England, and the former in continental Europe.

MARIPOSA GROVE, a stand of big trees in Yosemite National Park, California. It contains about 465 trees of the *Sequoia gigantea,* some of which are thousands of years old. One of the largest specimens is the Grizzly Giant, with a main limb over six feet in diameter at 200 feet above the earth and a circumference of 96 feet. The tallest tree is 272 feet high, and several are over 250 feet. A roadway 9½ feet wide has been cut through the heart of one of the giants.

MARIPOSA LILY or **BUTTERFLY LILY,** popular names for various species of *Calochortus* of the family Liliaceae. The numerous species, all of which are natives of western United States and British Columbia, are characterized by coated corms; rather leafy, generally branched stems; and showy, six-segmented flowers. Almost all the species are in cultivation for ornament, some, natives of the Colorado Desert, being suited to arid conditions, others to fairly moist soils, still others to very cold localities, as species indigenous to the Sierra Nevada. All will stand extreme cold, but not alternate freezing and thawing, hence their failure under such conditions. The bulbs should be planted in late autumn in any kind of soil. After the tops have become yellow subsequent to flowering in the following year the bulbs should be taken up, divided, and kept dry until planting time.

MARIQUINA or **MARIKINA,** town, Philippine Islands in the province of Rizal, Luzon, eight miles northeast of Manila. It is situated at the intersection of several main highways, has shoe and leather factories and medicinal iron springs. Pop. (1960) 40,642.

MARIS, mä′rĭs, **Jacob,** Dutch painter: b. The Hague, Aug. 25, 1837; d. Carlsbad, Austria, (now Czechoslovakia) Oct. 7, 1899. He began his art studies at the local academy, choosing landscape as a specialty. He studied also under Nicaise de Keyser, director of the Antwerp Academy. Going to Paris, he received instruction from Antoine Auguste Hébert; he came under the influence of the Barbizon school, and reached his full power as a painter of figures and landscape in combination. In 1871 he returned to his native town. His brush work and use of chiaroscuro are essentially French.

Among his numerous works are *View of a Town in Holland; View of Schiedam; On the Sea Shore; Mother and Children.*

MARIS, mä′rĭs, **Matthijs,** Dutch painter, brother of Jacob Maris (q.v.): b. The Hague, Holland, Aug. 17, 1839; d. London, England, Aug. 22, 1917. In his youth he traveled and worked with his elder brother; in 1855 they lived in Antwerp sharing quarters with a young student named Lawrence Alma-Tadema (q.v.); in 1860 the brothers studied and sketched in Germany and Switzerland; in 1870, in Paris, Matthijs was enrolled in the National Guard and performed military service during the siege. Shortly after he settled in London, where he remained till his death. He was a striking example of the so-called "artistic temperament"; he painted what he liked and when he liked, with the result that his works are extremely scarce. His work is characterized by fine qualities of color and imagination.

MARITAIN, mȧ-rē-tăn', **Jacques**, French philosopher: b. Paris, Nov. 18, 1882. Baptized in the Protestant faith, he first came, when a student at the Sorbonne, under the influence of the professor of biology, Félix Alexandre Le Dantec, and then was weaned away from determinism and extreme materialism by the philosopher Henri Bergson. He became a Catholic in 1906, and, after one year at Heidelberg, gave himself to the study of Thomistic philosophy. He was professor of philosophy at the Institut Catholique, Paris, visiting professor at the Institute of Medieval Studies, Toronto, and at several American universities. He was in the United States at the outbreak of World War II and was one of the first French abroad to join the de Gaulle movement, which paved the way for his appointment in 1945 as French ambassador to the Vatican. His books are a technical exposition of scholastic philosophy in its Thomistic form, and to an application of Thomistic principles to politics, art, education and religion.

His first work, *La Philosophie Bergsonnienne* (1914), was a criticism of Henri Bergson's theory of intellectual intuition; in *Reflexions sur l'intelligence et sa vie propre* (1924), he challenged Maurice Blondel's apparent distrust of abstraction and speculation; in *Three Reformers: Luther, Descartes, Rousseau* (tr. 1929), he denounced the fountainhead of modern subjectivism. *The Degrees of Knowledge* (tr. 1937), which may be considered his main work, contrasts the modern mathematical approach to the study of nature with the ancient metaphysical approach. His *Preface to Metaphysics* (tr. 1939) comprises lectures on being and its transcendental properties viewed as the basic principle of speculative thinking. What may be called his political treatises—*Things that are not Caesar's* (tr. 1930), *Freedom in the Modern World* (tr. 1936), *True Humanism* (1938), to mention but a few —are inspired by the preoccupation of safeguarding the dignity and rights of man against the encroachments of the modern totalitarian conception of the state and breathe a fervent democratic spirit, while *Art and Scholasticism* (tr. 1930), *Prayer and Intelligence* (1928), and *Religion and Culture* (1930) as well as *Education at the Cross-Roads* (1943), are typical of the manner in which the author translates into life and action the fundamental tenets of his philosophy. *Ransoming the Time* (tr. 1941), a collection of diverse essays, deals with one essential theme: the reconciliation of human conflicts through Christian wisdom.

More recent works are *Range of Reason* (1952); *Bergsonian Philosophy and Thomism* (tr. 1955); *Social and Political Philosophy* (1955).

Consult Fecher, C. A., *Philosophy of Jacques Maritain* (Westminster, Md., 1953); Michener, N. W., *Maritain On the Nature of Man in Christian Democracy* (Hull, Canada, 1955).

MARITIME LAW, măr'ĭ-tīm; -tĭm lô, a body of custom, court decision, and legislative enactment relating to the sea in general, and, more particularly, to the ownership and operation of vessels, the rights and obligations of master and crew, and the transportation of goods and passengers on the high seas and navigable waters.

The origins of this law are lost in the mists of antiquity. Because the challenge of a similar environment is likely to invoke a similar response, it is probable that some of its principles are as old as seaborne commerce itself, developing independently along analogous lines even in the absence of any direct historical connection. Thus the basic concept of a sea voyage as a joint adventure, in which the separate interests of the vessel and her cargo are bound together in a common enterprise, may be regarded as the fundamental principle underlying all systems of maritime law.

History.—What little is known of this law in the time of the Roman empire indicates that it may have been derived from customs previously developed on the island of Rhodes, a flourishing mercantile center in the pre-Christian era. This Rhodian Sea-Law was, in turn, reflected in the *Digests* of Justinian the Great compiled in 533 A.D. and subsequently incorporated in somewhat modified form in the *Basilica* of the Byzantine Emperor Leo VI (c. 888).

The barbarian invasions which overthrew the Empire of the West disrupted the avenues of maritime trade. For almost 500 years the dual menace of the Viking sea rovers in the north and of the Moslem pirates in the Mediterranean effectively discouraged seaborne commerce. When the revival of economic activity in the period of the Crusades brought merchants and ships of many lands into foreign harbors, local law and procedures were able to provide neither the rules nor the machinery for the disposition of the controversies which inevitably arose, often raising problems as alien as the tongues of the disputants. Maritime law, together with the law merchant, evolved from the application of commonly recognized customs to the resolution of such disputes.

Doubtless many of these customs were respected long before there was any need to reduce them to writing. Almost certainly they were modified in the process of oral transmission, so that it is difficult to judge how faithfully the documents which have survived reflect the original usage. Sometimes, as in the 12th century *Table of Amalfi* (*Amalfitan Tables*), and *Customs of Trani,* these customs were recorded because the amplitude and justice of their provisions warranted a more general use; sometimes, as in the *Assize of Jerusalem* (q.v.) of the same period, the Frankish ruler of a foreign land found it necessary to preserve for the guidance of his newly acquired subjects the hitherto unwritten rules governing maritime affairs.

The sea laws of northern Europe are thought to have been based on the so-called *Judgments or Laws of Oleron.* Oleron (q.v.), an island situated off the west coast of France near La Rochelle and an important center of maritime commerce in the 11th century, early obtained from its feudal overlords the privilege of adjudicating maritime claims according to the usages of the sea and the customs of merchants and mariners. The oldest known version of these *Judgments* consists of some 24 short statements setting forth the decisions in particular cases. These are assembled without any obvious order and deal with the mutual rights and obligations of masters, mariners and merchants, as well as certain aspects of collision and pilotage.

Modified and expanded to serve the needs of other localities and trade, the *Judgments of Oleron* were accorded a wide reception. Their influence is traceable in the fifth of the *Las Siete Partidas* of Alfonso X (the Wise) of Leon and Castile; they were translated into Flemish in the mid-14th century in the *Purple Book of Bruges* and are referred to in 1364 in an ordinance of Charles V of France. In 1403 a statute of Henry IV made the *Judgments of Oleron* part of the sea laws of England. When and how they were imported into that country has been the subject of considerable scholarly speculation; according to an old but somewhat unreliable tradition, they were brought back by King Richard I on his return from the Third Crusade in 1194. In any case it seems clear that the *Judgments* were accepted as evidence of established custom long before they were first (1344) mentioned in a recorded case.

The seaport town of Wisby, on the island of Gotland in the Baltic Sea, is credited with another of the most important northern maritime codes, the *Sea Laws of Wisby*. These too are a collection of early customs which, as an introductory paragraph states, "the associated shipmasters and merchants settled among themselves on shipping law." The *Sea Laws* are now thought to have been based partly on a Flemish version of the *Judgments of Oleron* and partly on an earlier code of the city of Lübeck, dating from the middle of the 13th century. The capture and virtual destruction of Wisby by the Danes in 1361 ended its importance as a commercial center, but its *Sea Laws* were reflected in the later maritime code of the Hanseatic League (1597).

Little is known about the tribunals which meted out justice in maritime disputes in the Middle Ages. It appears that on the island of Oleron this function was exercised by the mayor's court. In England the *Domesday of the Borough of Ipswich* (c. 1200) establishes that the bailiff's court was empowered to hear pleas "from tide to tide" according to the "marine law." Even before the beginning of the 15th century, the greater part of maritime disputes came under the jurisdiction of the "admiral," whose title was derived from the Arabic *amir-al-bahr* (commander of the sea). This official, in addition to commanding a fleet, was especially charged with the suppression of piracy. His appointment of ecclesiastics as deputies in the administration of his office gave rise, during the 14th century, to a Court of Admiralty with jurisdiction over other maritime cases as well. This court followed the procedures of the civil law; there was no jury, trial by battle was unknown, and its readiness to give a satisfaction *in rem* against the vessels or goods of an absent defendant soon made it a popular forum for the disposition of controversies relating to foreign trade and maritime matters. The *Black Book of the Admiralty* was compiled during the 14th and 15th centuries as a guide to the legal principles followed in the Admiral's Court; it also contains, written in Norman French, an early version of the *Judgments of Oleron.*

The extension of the jurisdiction of the Admiral's Court to include maritime contracts soon provoked the hostility of the common law judges. At the close of the 14th century statutes were enacted commanding that "the Admirals and their deputies shall not intermeddle from henceforth of any thing done within the realm, but only of a thing done upon the sea." These proved ineffectual, however, and during the succeeding two centuries the Court of Admiralty continued to provide a remedy for all types of maritime claims.

Special courts, administering a sea law different from the law of the land, are also known to have existed in the western Mediterranean area during the 13th century. In the major port cities of Spain, southern France, and Italy cases were heard and decided according to maritime usages by magistrates known as consuls of the sea who, in at least some instances, were elected by the Guild of Navigators. From references in surviving documents, these customs are believed to have been put in written form as early as 1343, but our knowledge of their provisions is largely based on the *Consolato del Mare,* written in the Catalan language and printed at Barcelona in 1494. This was a treatise for the guidance of the consuls at that port, containing, as its opening paragraph proclaims, "the good customs which regard matters of the sea which wise men who traveled all over the world communicated to our predecessors." Unlike the haphazard arrangement of the earlier sea laws, the *Consolato's* 252 chapters organize and synthesize the customs and regulations pertaining to all aspects of maritime enterprise. Translated into many languages, it represents a high-water mark in the development of a common law of the sea, founded not on the fiat of a superior authority but on a tradition of general agreement among mariners.

By the 17th century the increasing complexity of maritime trade and the growth of national states ushered in a new era of maritime codes. In France Louis XIV's great minister, Jean Baptiste Colbert, promulgated in 1681 the celebrated *Ordonnance de la Marine,* based on a thorough study of existing customs and procedures. This famous code, the authors of which are unknown, established a royal admiralty court with jurisdiction over "all actions concerning the commerce of the sea." Future resort to the consuls' courts was strictly prohibited. Charter parties, bills of lading, the rights and duties of master and crew, maritime contracts and insurance, fisheries, prizes of war and crimes committed at sea—all were included in the wide jurisdiction granted to the new court. The *Ordonnance* served as a model for the maritime codes of many other European nations and, through the Napoleonic Code of Commerce (1807), its influence may still be traced in those countries whose jurisprudence is based on the civil law.

In England, on the other hand, the 17th century saw the Court of Admiralty brought to its lowest ebb. Associated as it was with unpopular civil law principles and procedures, it was reduced after 1660 to the status of an inferior tribunal with a narrow and limited jurisdiction over "things done upon the high sea only." Not until a series of Parliamentary enactments in the period from 1840 to 1873 did the court once more regain the right to exercise its ancient powers over the conduct of maritime affairs generally.

In the United States the jurisdiction of the federal admiralty courts was never so narrowly construed. "The law, admiralty and maritime, as it has existed for ages, is applied by our Courts to the cases as they arise," Chief Justice Marshall wrote in an early decision. Procedurally, this meant that admiralty cases were tried before a judge without a jury and with a minimum of procedural technicalities; rights *in rem* were recognized and enforced, and the courts were empowered to adjudicate maritime claims no matter where the cause of action arose. The 19th century movement for codification did not leave the maritime law untouched. In the United States many of its aspects are regulated by statute. Perhaps the most important of these enactments was the law relating to limitation of liability, first passed in 1851 to encourage investment in shipping. In its present, much-amended form this statute permits a shipowner, under certain circumstances, to limit his liability for loss of property to the value of the vessel and her earnings at the termination of the voyage; his liability for personal injuries or death may be limited to an amount calculated on the basis of the vessel's tonnage.

Nevertheless, the tradition of a common law of the sea has by no means disappeared. The law in the United States relating to marine insurance and charter parties for the hire of ships is still largely unaffected by legislation. The maritime lien, which gives a proprietary interest in a vessel as security for particular types of claims, continues to retain its historical characteristics. As late as 1949 the Supreme Court of the United States quoted from the *Judgments of Oleron* in deciding a case arising out of the shipowner's ancient obligation, independent of fault on his part, to provide subsistence and medical care to a seaman injured in the service of his ship. The long-recognized principles of general average (under which a sacrifice or contribution made to avert a common peril is replaced at the expense of all interests thereby brought to safety) were clarified in 1890, and most recently in 1950, in the *York-Antwerp Rules,* adopted by private shipping interests representing many nations.

During the present century the United States has joined with other countries in accepting as part of its own law a large number of international conventions, designed to bring some degree of harmony out of the welter of discordant local shipping regulations. As a result, the contents of ocean bills of lading, international rules for preventing collisions, minimum standards for the safety of life at sea, salvage, load lines, whaling and many other subjects are now governed by agreements ratified by the major ship-owning states. The proposed creation of an Intergovernmental Maritime Consultative Organization under the aegis of the United Nations further confirms the need in the modern age for a maritime law which, as Lord Mansfield declared in 1759, "is not the law of a particular country but the general law of nations."

See also ADMIRALTY AND MARITIME JURISDICTION; CHARTER PARTY; CODE; COMMERCE—1. *History;* COMMERCIAL LAW; NAVIGATION ACTS; SHIPPING OF THE WORLD.

Bibliography.—Pardessus, Jean Marie, *Collection de Lois Maritimes* (Paris 1828–45); Twiss, Sir Travers, ed., *The Black Book of the Admiralty* (London 1871); Ashburner, Walter, *The Rhodian Sea Law* (Oxford 1909); Sanborn, Frederick R., *Origins of the Early English Maritime and Commercial Law* (New York 1930); Knoph, Ragnar, *Norsk Sjørett* (Oslo 1931); Benedict, Erastus C., (Arnold B. Knauth, ed.) *The Law of American Admiralty* (New York 1940); Dominedò, Francesco M., *Introduzione al Diritto della Navigazione* (Rome 1945); Cleveringa, Rudolph P., *Het Nieuwe Zeerecht* (Zwolle 1946); Smith, Herbert Arthur, *The Law and Custom of the Sea* (New York 1950); Ripert, Georges, *Droit Maritime* (Paris 1950); Wüstendörfer, Hans, *Neuzeitliches Seehandelsrecht* (Tübingen 1950); Higgins, A. Pearce (Colombos, ed.), *The International Law of the Sea* (London 1954); Gilmore, Grant, and Black, Charles L., Jr., *The Law of Admiralty* (Brooklyn 1957).

ELLIOTT B. NIXON.

MARITIME PROVINCES. See NEW BRUNSWICK; NOVA SCOTIA; PRINCE EDWARD ISLAND.

MARIUS, mâ′rĭ-ŭs, **Gaius,** Roman general: b. about 155 B.C., in Cereatae, in the Volscian territory; d. Rome, Jan. 13, 86 B.C. He won his first military repute at Numantia in 134, beginning his rapid rise from the ranks; was made tribune of the people in 119; increased his political power by marrying Julius Caesar's aunt; became praetor in 115; went to Spain in the next year, suppressing brigandage there; and in 109 accompanied Metallus to Africa. Two years later he was chosen consul, displaced his superior officer and made a brilliant campaign. His success was so great that he was elected consul four times in succession (104–101 B.C.)—a proceeding counter to law and entirely unparalleled—so as to meet the invasion of Italy by the Cimbri and Teutons. He defeated the latter tribe at Aix in 102, and the Cimbri near Vercellae in 101. In 100 he was again elected consul. He made the fatal mistake of plunging into party politics, allied himself with the most disreputable leaders of the popular party, and, in his envy of the rising fame of the patrician Sulla, attempted to remove him from his command in the Jugurthine War. Civil war broke out in 88. Sulla was victorious. Marius fled to Africa, whence he returned to Italy on the successful rising in Rome under Lucius Cornelius Cinna. The first great proscription followed and many of Marius' opponents were killed. Marius was elected consul for the seventh time in 86 B.C.

MARIUS THE EPICUREAN, a philosophic romance by Walter Pater (q.v.), written in 1885. It is the story of a young Roman noble of the days of Marcus Aurelius, but in the problems and experiences of young Marius in ancient Rome, Pater has given also something of the problems and experiences of a young man at the end of the 19th century. In the days of Marcus Aurelius the ancient world was changing into the medieval. Another such period was the Renaissance, in which the medieval world was changing to the modern. In our days it may be civilization may be changing to something very different from the last few hundred years. Of the first of these great changes Pater wrote in *Marius the Epicurean.* Of the second he began to give a picture in *Gaston de Latour,* a later novel of which he wrote only the first part. To the last period, his own, Pater devoted critical rather than creative thought. *Marius the Epicurean,* therefore, is deeply informed with ideas; in fact the subtitle of *Marius* is *Sensations and Ideas.*

Pater became known first as a critic; in this novel he turned to express in the form of life the ideas which he had previously presented as matter of thought. A good many of Pater's ideas will be found in *Marius:* the fundamental conception of Epicureanism is a restatement of the theory of life which had already been presented in the conclusion of the Renaissance and had since been much and sometimes severely criticized. After the novel Pater published several shorter pieces which he called *Imaginary Portraits* (1887). In each of these he presented a figure which embodies some idea or position in the philosophy of art and life. *Marius the Epicurean* is an earlier, more fully developed and imaginary portrait. Its interest is not in the story, but in the idea, or in this case in the progress of the idea. Marius grows up in the old pagan world, comes to know all the cultivation and refinement of the ancient civilization, weighs the older philosophies of life and art, and finally devotes himself to the new and growing religion of Christ. Like all of Pater's fiction the story is most sedulously careful of its surroundings and environment, and the pictures of life on the great old Roman family estate, the popular festival, the interview with the emperor, the lecture on rhetoric by Fronto are among his best known. It continues to hold a high place among the books that present adventures and experiences of the soul.

MARIVAUX, mà-rē-võ′, **Pierre Carlet de Chamblain de,** French dramatist and novelist: b. Paris, France, Feb. 4, 1688; d. there, Feb. 12, 1763. He was brought up in luxury, but as a young man became dependent on literature for his living. He edited several periodicals, the first of which, *Le spectateur français* (1722–23), showed English influence in both its name and its content. Two unfinished novels, *La vie de Marianne* (1731–41) and *Le paysan parvenu* (1735–36), are considered among his best work. Rich in background and characterization, they influenced the later development of the French novel. Marivaux is best known, however, for his plays, which include, among others, *Le jeu de l'amour et du hasard* (1730), *La mère confidente* (1735), *Le legs* (1736), *Les fausses confidences* (1737), and *L'épreuve* (1740). They are notable for the author's departure from the much-imitated comic manner of Molière and for his cultivation of his own highly personal dramatic style, called *marivaudage*—a peculiar blend of sparkling wit, bombastic self-examination, true psychological insight, and elaborate artificial plotting. He was elected to the Académie Française in 1743.

MARJORAM, mär′jô-răm, the common name for subshrubs and perennial herbs of the genus *Origanum,* comprising about 25 species in the mint family (Labiatae) native to the Old World, particularly the Mediterranean region. Especially important is the common or pot marjoram, *O. vulgare,* an erect, branching, aromatic perennial found wild on dry pastures and hedge banks from Britain through central Europe to the Himalayas. It stands about 30 inches high, has hairy, ovate, slightly toothed leaves 1½ inches long, and dense clusters of rose-purple flowers borne in terminal panicles in the summer. It is widely cultivated, its leaves being used fresh or dried as seasoning for meats, salads, sauces, and other foods. A second species in cultivation is the sweet marjoram, *O. majorana,* a one- to two-foot subshrubby plant with oblong-ovate, blunt, entire and hairy leaves, and blue, purple, or white flowers appearing in June. It is a native of northern Africa. The various species are easily grown from seed or cuttings in any warm, dry soil. They are not particularly critical of soil types, and tolerate calcium well.

RICHARD M. STRAW.

MARK, märk, SAINT, an early Christian in Jerusalem, to whom was later attributed the writing of the earliest Gospel (see MARK, GOSPEL ACCORDING TO). Very little is known about him. He appears suddenly in the Acts of the Apostles as if already known to the readers: Peter, upon

his miraculous release from prison, "went to the house of Mary, the mother of John whose other name was Mark" (Acts 12:12;[1] 1st century Jews often took additional Graeco-Roman names). When Barnabas and Saul (Paul) returned to Antioch, they took him with them (12:25), and he accompanied them on the First Missionary Journey but deserted on reaching the coast of Asia Minor and returned to Jerusalem (13:13). Later, when Paul and Barnabas were planning the Second Missionary Journey, Barnabas wished to take Mark with them, but Paul refused; Paul accordingly chose Silas to be his companion in Syria and Cilicia, while Barnabas took Mark and went off to Cyprus (15:36–40), which was Barnabas' native land (4:36). According to Colossians 4:10, Mark was Barnabas' cousin (*anepsios,* not "nephew").

The other New Testament references to Mark are indecisive. Philemon 24 and II Timothy 4:11 describe him as Paul's "fellow worker" who was "very useful" to him; it is thought that Mark had somehow recovered his lost standing with Paul and had later proved himself trustworthy. I Peter 5:13 describes him (if it is the same person) as Peter's "son," possibly meaning in the faith. But Peter was married (Mark 1:30 f.) and may have had a son. If so, and if the same Mark is meant, Peter's wife's name was Mary, a very common Jewish name (Miriam). Further, the intimate reference in I Peter, joining Mark's greetings with Peter's and those of the church in "Babylon" (Rome?), would be more natural if the relation was physical as well as spiritual. At least, it is not impossible that Mark was a relative of Peter as well as of Barnabas, though the references in Acts do not suggest it.

Later legend and imaginative interpretation have woven these few brief data into a longer story, much of it improbable. There is no evidence that Mary's house in Jerusalem was the scene of the Last Supper (Mark 14:12–16; in Luke 22:11 the owner of the house is a man), and that for this reason the disciples frequently gathered there (Acts 1:13); or that Mark was the man carrying a jar of water (Mark 14:13) or the youth who fled naked from the garden (14:51 f.). In fact Papias (c. 130 A.D.; consult Eusebius, *Church History,* book iii, chap. 39, sect. 15) said explicitly that "Mark had not heard the Lord nor been his disciple, but afterwards . . . became Peter's translator [or amanuensis]." His connection with Peter, reflected in I Peter 5:13, is presupposed in this tradition, which made him the author of the earliest Gospel and the interpreter of Peter when he taught the traditions of Jesus (according to Eusebius) "as need arose" in the Roman church. The tradition probably also presupposes that Peter was in Rome after the death of Paul (that is, after 62 or 64 A.D.), which is not improbable, but is certainly not based on historical or archaeological evidence—though the excavations under the basilica of St. Peter may eventually uncover such evidence.

The later "traditions" of Mark's connection with Alexandria, as its first bishop, and his death there as a martyr; the legend of his connection with Aquileia, and the removal of his body in 828 A.D. from Alexandria to Venice, where it was enshrined in the great basilica of San Marco; the description of him as "stub-fingered" (self-mutilated, in order to escape service as a priest

---

[1] Quotations according to Revised Standard Version throughout this article.

or Levite)—all this legendary material belongs to later church history, not to the New Testament. In fact, so little is really known about Mark that the attribution of the Gospel of Mark to him throws more light upon his character than his story contributes to the interpretation of the Gospel. See also GOSPELS, THE.

FREDERICK C. GRANT,
Professor of Biblical Theology, Union Theological Seminary, New York City.

MARK, originally, in western Europe, a weight of silver or gold, about eight ounces; also a unit of money and a silver coin. The modern German mark was established in 1873 with a par value of $0.238, re-established in 1924 as the reichsmark and in 1948 as the Deutsche mark with the same value.

MARK, Gospel According to. The earliest of the Christian Gospels, that attributed to Mark (see MARK, SAINT), was probably written at Rome about 68 A.D. Later tradition, relying upon and perhaps inspired by the connection of Mark with Peter (consult I Peter 5:13), described the work as based upon Peter's "reminiscences" or "recollections," that is, the memories or traditions of Jesus which Peter related "as need arose" (Eusebius, *Church History,* book iii, chap. 39, sect. 15) and which Mark translated into Greek or Latin. But modern literary and historical criticism has found difficulty in ascribing the Gospel to the Mark who is described elsewhere in the New Testament or in deriving its contents from Peter's preaching or teaching (presumably in Aramaic, then translated into Greek). There is much in the Gospel that can scarcely be Petrine in origin; and the author betrays no special acquaintance with Palestinian Judaism or the topography of Palestine. Marcus was one of the commonest Roman names in the 1st century A.D.; and the theory that an early Roman Christian by that name wrote down the traditions of Jesus' career, teaching, "mighty works," Passion, and Resurrection as they circulated in the Roman church in the 60's, soon after Nero's persecution and the death of the great leaders Peter and Paul, would explain the characteristic features of this Gospel far better than the ancient traditional or legendary account of its origin.

Form.—In form the work is a collection of independent narratives of episodes and incidents from Jesus' life and of separate oral accounts of his teaching. These "pericopes" were doubtless already in use in the Roman church as elsewhere for purposes of preaching, teaching (the instruction of converts and youth), and recital at the services of worship, perhaps in association with the selections from the Old Testament which the Christian church, like the Hellenistic Jewish synagogue, read in the Greek version (see SEPTUAGINT). In fact, the Gospels, and the whole New Testament, came into existence as the Christian supplement to the Greek Old Testament, as used in the church's lectionary (the "lessons" read at worship).

The purpose of the Gospel was not biographical, but didactic, that is, either apologetic, homiletical, or liturgical. Its form is a series of great "blocks" of tradition leading up to the Passion narrative, explaining why and how Jesus came to be rejected by the "chief priests, scribes, and elders," and then put to death by the Romans. Some scholars believe the arrangement of the

material to be the result of its use during the early Christian-Jewish liturgical "year," ending at the spring festival of Passover, which for them was now the celebration of Jesus' death and Resurrection (consult I Corinthians 5:7, "Christ, our paschal lamb";[1] and 15:20, "first fruits").

Contents.—The Gospel begins with an opening sentence which no doubt also (as in many ancient books) served as title: "The beginning of the gospel of [good news about] Jesus Christ, the Son of God," followed by an introduction describing "John the baptizer" and his mission (1:2–8), Jesus' Baptism and Temptation. The main narrative opens with a thematic statement of Jesus' return to Galilee with the message, "The time is fulfilled, and the kingdom of God is at hand; repent, and believe in the gospel" (1:14 f.). The rest of the chapter describes a day in Capernaum followed by the beginning of Jesus' ministry of exorcism, healing, and teaching throughout Galilee. This is the first "block" of tradition, centered in Peter's call, his home in Capernaum, and the opening of the Galilean mission.

Chapters 2:1–3:6 relate a series of controversies with the scribes and Pharisees, occasioned by Jesus' healing, forgiveness of sins, and disregard of the food and Sabbath regulations and the custom of fasting. This block concludes with the decision of the Pharisees and "Herodians" (probably the court of Herod Antipas and his partisans) to destroy Jesus (3:6). Chapter 3:7–35 describes the growing multitude of Jesus' followers, who came from all parts of Palestine and even beyond; his exorcisms; the appointment of the 12 disciples; the scribes' charge of collusion with Beelzebul and Jesus' refutation of it; and the blessing pronounced on his true followers. Then begins another group of traditions, the chapter of parables (4:1–34), which cannot be supposed to have been limited to one day, but must represent a collection of examples of his parabolic teaching. Mark's inserted explanation that the purpose of parables was to withhold the "mysteries" (or secrets) of the kingdom of God (4:11 f.) is most improbable in this connection, and is contradicted by the rest of the chapter—and indeed by the whole character of Jesus' teaching.

Then follows a series of "great miracle stories" (4:35–5:43), which are really not "miracles" (in our sense) but "mighty works" of God done through Christ, that is, manifestations of supernatural power like those described in the Old Testament, especially at the Exodus, and designed to show Jesus as the divine Son of God. In fact, the whole Gospel has been described as "the story of the mighty works of the Son of God," this title being the one best understood by converts from Graeco-Roman paganism, and the one familiar from the beginning in the gentile churches (as Paul's letters show). The failure in Nazareth (6:1–6) leads to the Mission of the Disciples (6:7–13) and the story of the death of John the Baptist (6:14–29), an interlude which fills the period of the disciples' absence. (Mark uses both titles for John: baptizer and Baptist.) Then follow more "mighty works" (6:30–10:52), interspersed with a controversy with the Jerusalem scribes who had arrived in Galilee, Peter's confession of faith in Jesus' Messiahship, the three Passion announcements, the Transfiguration, and the discourse on humility and discipleship, the

---

[1] Quotations according to Revised Standard Version throughout this article.

teaching on divorce and remarriage, and on renunciation. The great climax of the discipleship discourse is the famous saying, "For the Son of man also came not to be served but to serve, and to give his life as a ransom for many" (10:45; compare Luke 22:27).

By this time Jesus is on his way to Jerusalem, where the "triumphal entry" followed by the Cleansing of the Temple (11:1–26) immediately rouses the opposition of the priestly authorities and introduces the second series (or "block") of controversies (11:27–12:44). The following chapter (13) on the signs of the end (of the age), introduced by Jesus' prediction of the destruction of the Temple, is based on a collection of apocalyptic material commonly known as the "Little Apocalypse," ending with the sublime warning, addressed to all Christians, especially to the martyr church at Rome: "And what I say to you I say to all: Watch."

The next two chapters (14 and 15) form the Marcan Passion narrative, based on an earlier account which probably did not identify the Last Supper with the Passover, and may not have included various incidents with which it is now elaborated (for example, 14:3–9). The present narrative emphasizes the responsibility of the Jewish Sanhedrin for the death of Jesus; but the fact that he was crucified, not stoned, and upon the charge of stirring up insurrection (compare Luke 23:1–25), implies the primary responsibility of Pilate, not the Sanhedrin (see also JESUS CHRIST). The climax of the Marcan Passion narrative (and perhaps of the pre-Marcan) is the testimony of the centurion, "Truly this man was a son of God!" (15:39). It is possible that this officer, like the woman in 14:3–9 and the three men named in 15:21, was known to the Christian community in Rome. It is characteristic of tradition (as distinguished from fiction or fancy) that these persons are not further identified. The names in 15:40, 43 are added for a special purpose: they testify to the truth of the story. The finale, the discovery of the open tomb (15:47–16:8), is not an account of the Resurrection, but only of its setting. The Resurrection is presupposed by Mark, but not described.

Some have thought this Gospel incomplete, and efforts have been made since the 2d century to finish it off with materials from the other Gospels (and even from Acts). But it probably ended at 16:8, when it left its author's hands. As the earliest Gospel, Mark set the standard for all later writings of accounts of Jesus' life, teaching, death, and Resurrection. It became the basis of both Luke and Matthew, and its pattern has been followed by innumerable "lives of Christ" down to the present day.

See also BIBLE—9. *New Testament.*

Bibliography.—Weiss, Johannes, *Das älteste Evangelium* (Göttingen 1903); Bacon, Benjamin Wisner, *The Gospel of Mark* (New Haven 1925); Grant, Frederick C., *The Earliest Gospel* (New York 1943); Lightfoot, Robert H., *The Gospel Message of St. Mark* (New York 1950); Carrington, Philip, *The Primitive Christian Calendar* (London 1952); Grant, Frederick C., *The Gospels: Their Origin and Their Growth* (New York 1957). Consult also commentaries by Alfred Firmin Loisy (Paris 1912); Henry Barclay Swete (London 1898), 3d ed. (1920), reprinted Grand Rapids, Mich. (1951); Ernst Lohmeyer (Göttingen 1937); Erich Klostermann (Tübingen 1907), 4th ed. (1950); Frederick C. Grant, in *The Interpreter's Bible* (New York 1951); Vincent Taylor (London 1952).

FREDERICK C. GRANT,
Professor of Biblical Theology, Union Theological Seminary, New York City.

MARK ANTONY. See ANTONIUS, MARCUS.

MARK TWAIN. See CLEMENS, SAMUEL LANGHORNE.

MARKAGUNT PLATEAU, mär′kȧ-gŭnt, tableland, Utah, lying mostly in Iron County in the southwest part of the state, just east of Cedar City. Brian Head, on the western edge, is the highest point (11,315 feet). Cedar Breaks National Monument (established 1933) is a natural amphitheater of many-colored sandstone carved out of the Pink Cliffs of the southern escarpment, which plunge about 2,000 feet to form a series of bowls. Much of the plateau is covered with forests of fir and spruce, constituting part of Dixie National Forest.

MARKET PRICE. See MARKETING—*Price Determination and Price Policies;* INFLATION AND DEFLATION; SUPPLY AND DEMAND.

MARKET RESEARCH. See ADVERTISING —*Science of Advertising;* MARKETING—*Integration of Marketing Functions* (Marketing Research).

MARKETING, mär′kĕt-ĭng. Marketing is defined by the Committee on Definitions of the American Marketing Association as "the performance of business activities directed toward, and incident to, the flow of goods and services from producer to consumer or user." Marketing, therefore, is made up on one hand of such physical activities as transporting, storing, and selling goods, and on the other hand of a series of decisions which must be reached by any organization undertaking any part of the process of moving goods from the producer to the user.

Growth of Marketing Methods.—The importance and complexity of marketing activities have increased steadily in the years since the Industrial Revolution. In a simple village economy, the shoemaker ordinarily purchased his leather and other materials from nearby producers and took orders from his neighbors for relatively simple footwear. The quality of his work was easily recognized, and protests against poor workmanship could be made easily and directly. The shoemaker himself had no difficulty in gauging in advance what kinds of shoes would be desired by his customers or the number of shoes he should make, nor did he have to entrust any part of his relationship with those customers to others.

As specialization in production has developed and the scale of manufacturing operations has increased, producers and their customers have become widely separated in space, in time, and in knowledge. The producer of automobiles in Detroit sells throughout the United States and, indeed, throughout the world. He produces not upon the order of a particular customer for a particular automobile but rather upon the basis of anticipated future sales to unknown customers. In this anticipation of future sales, he must in turn place orders for materials and component parts well in advance of his own production period. Finally, the increasing multiplicity of goods produced has led to a lack of intimate knowledge on the part of the buyers of the inherent qualities of those goods. Millions of people buy mechanical refrigerators and other household appliances without personal understanding of how the appliances function and without the ability to judge the workmanship.

As the scope of marketing activities has broadened, the amount of effort devoted to these functions measured in employment or in dollars has naturally multiplied. Many estimates have been made as to the proportion of the consumer's dollar absorbed by production on one hand, and by marketing on the other. These estimates differ somewhat, but there is rather general agreement that marketing activities take more than half of the consumer's dollar. Figures for employment in retail trade, in wholesale trade, in transportation, in the sales departments of manufacturers and producers, in the facilitating activities of advertising agencies, publishing firms, and the like, lead to the conclusion that the steady increase in the proportion of our working population engaged in marketing activities has reached the point where they outnumber those engaged in manufacturing or production.

Although the role of marketing activities has expanded substantially since the Industrial Revolution, literature on the subject has developed only within the last 40 years. Many publications devoted to various aspects of marketing have been developed and authoritative information has become available to those interested in the subject. During this period, courses in marketing, and in the various subdivisions thereof, have become common in the colleges and universities. Latterly, marketing research has developed as a highly specialized activity, in which thousands of individuals and hundreds of specialized firms are engaged.

Principal Subdivisions of Marketing

The early literature of marketing is full of discussions as to what should be considered marketing functions. There are such physical activities as transporting and storing merchandise. There are also the functions of making decisions on such questions as how the product should be designed; how it should be packed; what retail and wholesale channels should be used; whether advertising is advisable and, if so, how much and what kinds; what prices should be set, not only to final buyers but also to whatever intermediaries may be used; and what pricing policies should be observed in regard to such matters as quantity discounts, terms of sale, and the like.

Although there is as yet little agreement on what are properly to be included as marketing functions, it is very clear, from the standpoint of the individual businessman, that these and similar questions must be answered as part of the marketing task. As one convenient way of dealing with such questions, they may be grouped under the following heads: merchandising; channels of distribution; brand or trademark policy; sales promotion (including advertising and personal salesmanship); pricing and price policies; control of marketing operations.

Merchandising.—This term has many meanings. To some it is synonymous with marketing; to others it is synonymous with retailing. In the advertising world, many men use the phrase "merchandising the advertising to the salesmen" to mean "informing and making the salesmen enthusiastic about the advertising campaign being carried on by their employer." Others say: "Merchandising is getting the goods onto the dealers' shelves; distribution is getting them off."

The meaning given to merchandising in this article is none of these, but rather "the adjustment of the merchandise produced or offered for sale to customer demand." Merchandising for the merchant means decisions and actions with regard to what goods and what quantities of them should be bought for resale. Merchandising for the manufacturer means selecting the product or products to be produced, deciding on size, appearance, form, and packaging, and determining the quantities to be produced during any given time. Thus, in manufacturing, merchandising activity can be regarded either as a part of production or as a part of marketing. It is the point at which the production department and the sales department most often come together. Effective merchandising, therefore, requires the closest coordination of those two departments.

The importance of advance knowledge as to the acceptance which will be accorded to a new product or to a redesigned version of an established product has given considerable impetus to a variety of methods of testing consumer reactions in advance of large-scale marketing efforts.

One vital factor in the merchandising task is that of coping with fashion. For some products, such as millinery and women's and misses' dresses, the merchandising task is almost entirely that of gauging fashion trends, but even automobile designers carefully study trends in the popularity of colors. Fashion is not synonymous with style. Dr. Paul H. Nystrom defines style as "a characteristic or distinctive mode or method of expression, presentation, or conception in the field of art."[1] A style is, therefore, a more or less permanent phenomenon in contrast to a fashion, which is usually temporary. A style may or may not be a fashion at any given time; it becomes a fashion when it is generally accepted by the people. Queen Anne is a style of furniture, but it does not happen to be a fashion because it is no longer in widespread use. Any fashion has its beginning when a relatively few people are influenced by it, its culmination when large numbers of people follow it, and its decline when it is gradually abandoned by more and more of its followers. Many theories as to the psychological motivation for this fashion cycle have been formulated. Fashion, like the stock market, is essentially a manifestation of group psychology. Fundamentally, these matters are still little understood, but practical businessmen have developed methods for scrutinizing the trend of sales in their own establishments and elsewhere which somewhat reduce the hazards of handling fashion merchandise.

In the merchandising of all types of goods, whether fashion is a major element or not, experience has demonstrated the importance of paying close attention to the buying motives of the potential customers. To do this it is first necessary to determine who the potential customers for the particular product or service are. They may be a handful of large corporations buying for use in their own manufacturing processes, or the general public buying to satisfy some personal need or desire.

The distinction implied in the contrast between business buyers and the general public is the basis for a classification of goods and services, of great importance in marketing, as industrial goods or consumers' goods. The latter are bought by the public for the business of living. Food and clothing are typical of relatively per-

---

[1] *Economics of Fashion*, p. 3. (New York 1928).

ishable consumers' goods, whereas washing machines, automobiles, and dwellings are typical of so-called consumers' durable goods. Industrial goods, on the other hand, are bought by business firms for use in the production and marketing of their own output. Industrial goods range from operating supplies, such as brooms and sweeping compounds, to major machinery and equipment and even the factory building itself, and from raw materials to fuel and power.

Channels of Distribution.—To the merchant, whether a wholesaler or a retailer, the decision as to what goods to buy for resale is a principal part of merchandising. To the merchant's supplier, the decision to sell to him is a part of the supplier's selection of his channels of distribution. The manufacturer of consumers' goods must decide in general what types of retail stores are the best for his product. Then he must decide whether to have his own salesmen sell direct to these retailers or to sell to wholesalers for resale to the retailers. If he elects to sell through wholesalers, he must decide which types of wholesalers, and he must also choose whether to sell to them direct through his own salesmen or through such intermediaries as brokers and manufacturers' agents.

Similarly, the manufacturer of industrial goods faces the question whether to use such intermediaries as mill supply firms and manufacturers' agents or to ultilize his own sales force, working out of the main factory office or out of sales branches strategically located throughout the country.

Policies must be formulated not only as to the types of intermediaries to be used but also as to their number. At one extreme is a policy of exclusive distribution, under which the retail or wholesale intermediary is the sole outlet for the product or service in some particular territory. Typical of this policy is the automobile industry, with each "franchised" dealer protected within a specified territory against the competition of other dealers. At the other extreme is a policy of intensive distribution, characterized by efforts to secure the maximum possible number of outlets. Typical followers of this policy are the major cigarette manufacturers, who want all the outlets they can get. Between these two extremes are many policies which may be grouped under the term "selective." Under this type of policy, certain chosen outlets are on the basis of criteria important to the manufacturer, such as prestige in the community, size, ability to provide installation or repair service, and the like.

There are three major considerations to be taken into account in arriving at a policy in regard to the number of outlets to be sought: (1) the willingness of prospective buyers of the particular product to seek out a source of purchase; (2) the ability of the intermediary to contribute to the effective promotion of the particular product; (3) the intermediary's willingness to make such promotional efforts if the benefits from those efforts accrue largely to him.

In addition to deciding what policies to follow concerning the channels of distribution to be used, the marketer must exert much effort and show much ingenuity in putting the policies selected into effect. Much of the day-to-day work of marketing consists of seeking to make particular retail stores, or wholesale establishments, of the type selected, want to carry the product.

Much of the sales promotion program must often be directed to this end. Advertising in trade and other publications, preparation of effective display and other material useful or appealing to the dealer, offering of attractive profit margins—all these are designed to supplement and reinforce the work of the salesman in inducing retailers, wholesalers, or other intermediaries to carry the product or line of products.

Brand Policy.[2]—A trademark is a distinctive word, emblem, symbol, or device, or a combination of these, used on goods actually sold in commerce to indicate or identify the manufacturer or seller of the goods.[3] In business terms a trademark is a short cut to the customers' memory. The picture of the little Dutch girl and the phrase "Old Dutch Cleanser" can be retained in the memory far more easily than could "cleanser produced by the Cudahy Packing Company." Through constant use on packages and in advertising, many trademarks have almost entirely eclipsed the name of the manufacturer. By actual test, dozens of persons know and use the trademark "Vaseline" for every one who knows Chesebrough-Pond's Inc., even in spite of the fact that every jar describes "Vaseline" as the Chesebrough-Pond's brand of petroleum jelly.

Because of their importance as a short cut to the customer's memory, well-established trademarks are considered to have substantial cash value. In transactions involving the sale of one business to another and in some court decisions, well-known trademarks have been valued at many millions of dollars. As might be expected, a body of law and precedent has developed and is continuing to develop for the protection of property of such value. The basic principle is that ownership of a trademark is acquired by prior use (that is, the first actual user in commerce is the owner), and registration of trademarks by the United States Patent Office has been provided for in a number of Congressional acts over the years, and most recently by the Lanham Act, adopted by Congress and made effective by President Truman on July 5, 1946. This act now provides the basic legislative framework for trademarks and should be studied by all interested.

Careful observance of the legal technicalities in the choice and development of a trademark is important. Of equal importance from a business standpoint is the selection of a trademark which will easily become a short cut to the customer's memory—one which lends itself readily to advertising and sales promotion and has pleasant rather than unpleasant connotations for the prospective customer. See also TRADEMARKS.

The addition of a new item to the line of a manufacturer often gives rise to the question: "Shall the new item carry the same trademark as the existing items?" The use of a so-called family brand assures the newcomer of benefits from some of the goodwill that may have de-

---

[2] A brand may include a brand name, a trademark, or both. The term "brand" is comprehensive, including practically all means of identification except perhaps the shape of the product and the package. The brand name is that part of the brand which may be vocalized. (Paraphrased from Committee on Definitions, American Marketing Association).

[3] *General Information About Protection of Trademarks*, pp. 1-4. (Government Printing Office, Washington, 1944).

veloped. On the other hand, the promotional needs of the new item may be secured more adequately by a distinctive trademark. As an extreme illustration, the well-known trademark for Ivory soap was understandably not deemed suitable for the vegetable shortening Crisco, made by the same company.

The importance of the brand which has gained public acceptance or preference as a means of controlling sales has led to the description of the widespread conflict between two opposing methods of marketing as the "Battle of the Brands."

On the one side are manufacturers of merchandise carrying brands featured in extensive magazine, newspaper, and radio advertising, often national in scope, and relying relatively little on the promotional efforts of retailers and wholesalers. With this type of brand, the retailers and wholesalers are generally little more than necessary links in the chain for making goods physically available to prospective buyers. Whatever the personal preference of the retailer, he must carry the well-known brands of cigarettes, for example, if he is to do business in tobacco products; the development of demand by the manufacturers makes this certain.

On the other side are retailers and wholesalers with their own brands of merchandise, frequently produced by manufacturers to the retailer's specifications. Such brands are often called "private" brands, although they are more accurately described as "distributor's" brands. When the corner druggist has a particular formula for cough syrup or antimosquito lotion put up under his own brand name, he is following a distributor's brand policy in a small way. But the battle is really joined when large-scale retailers, such as the great food chains, the large mail order houses, or important department stores, seek to develop wide public acceptance for a great range of products under their own brand names. Because the responsibility for maintenance of quality and the development of public acceptance rests on the owner of the brand, in this case the large-scale retailer, the manufacturer is limited to producing to specifications at as low a manufacturing cost as possible. The retailer, through his contact with the market, therefore, often becomes the dominant enterprise in the chain of service bringing goods to prospective buyers.

Sales Promotion.—The principal methods of promoting the sale of a product, aside from the inherent qualities of the product itself and its price, are personal salesmanship and advertising.

A marketing organization handling consumer goods must decide whether it will use salesmen to sell to final consumers (e.g. the retail store salesman or the house-to-house canvasser for vacuum cleaners or hosiery), to retailers, or to wholesalers, with or without the assistance of so-called missionary salesmen,[4] or whether it will rely entirely on advertising. Similarly, a marketing organization handling industrial goods must decide whether its sales should be promoted by salesmen, or whether it can rely on catalogues and other forms of advertising.

The management of sales organizations is

a field of major importance in itself. Sales management includes the selection of salesmen, their training to serve the particular needs of the firm by which they are employed, the working out of the best methods for determining their compensation, and the control of their activities. The control of salesmen's activities includes planning the number and location of customers to be solicited, possibly the laying out of the sequence in which customers are to be visited, the planning of the type of presentation to be made to prospective customers, and the appraisal of the performance of individual salesmen.

Advertising has been one of the most thoroughly studied aspects of marketing. Many types of advertising media have developed: newspapers; general circulation magazines; special circulation magazines, including so-called trade magazines, editorially devoted to the interests of particular trades or types of business executives (e.g. purchasing agents, power plant superintendents) ; radio broadcasting, both local and network; billboards along highways and city streets; car cards in public transportation systems; catalogues; direct mail advertising in many forms. The motion picture has been increasingly used as an advertising medium, often for use at large gatherings of prospective customers. Exhibits of various kinds at conventions and trade gatherings have long served the same purpose.

The marketing organization seeking an effective advertising program must give close attention to the selection of the medium or combination of media best adapted to the particular market to be sought, and the particular product to be promoted. Similarly, the construction of the advertising material to be used in these media requires careful attention to the determination of the buying motives which should be emphasized most strongly and to the most compelling ways of appealing to those buying motives. The need for specialized attention to these problems has been largely responsible for the growth of the many advertising agencies which perform these functions for their clients.

Not infrequently, the characteristics of the particular market for a particular product are such that expenditures for advertising are not likely to yield much return in sales. Sound judgment on this point by marketing organizations often has an important effect on the profit and loss statement.

Price Determination and Price Policies

The individual wheat farmer does not put a price on his crop. He is offered a price adjusted by conventional amounts from the current quotation on an organized exchange, and his decision is limited to whether he will hold or sell at that price. Only as large numbers of farmers, millers, and speculators change their decisions as to whether to hold, sell, or buy, does the price quotation change materially. Much current economic writing implies that earlier economists believed that such a condition prevailed throughout the business structure. This view may be an injustice to those earlier economists, but in any event, the plain fact is that most marketing organizations do face the problem of putting a price on their product, and not merely the question of manufacturing or not manufacturing at an established market price. The greater the degree to which the product is differentiated from other products, the more attention can be

---

[4] Missionary salesmen, known as "detail men" in some industries, call on customers to encourage the placing of orders. In the dental trade, for example, manufacturers employ "detail men" to call on dentists to encourage them to place orders for the manufacturers' products with dental supply houses.

centered on factors other than the prices of competitive products. Conversely, the more the product resembles competitive products in appearance and performance, the more competitive prices will govern price policies. Since one of the outstanding features of our industrial development has been the widespread differentiation of products, thus greatly widening the range of the consumer's choice, it follows that the problem of setting prices has tended to become more, rather than less, important to marketing managements.

In the typical situation, the pricing problem includes the establishment not only of prices to attract buyers, but also of prices to whatever successive tiers of intermediaries are included in the marketing program. It may also involve decisions as to whether special discounts are to be offered for purchases in relatively large quantities. The pricing problem often includes the decision as to whether all customers, or all customers of a particular type or class, are to be quoted the same price, or whether individual salesmen or higher officials are to be permitted to lower prices for especially vigorous bargainers, or to recognize circumstances which result in particularly low costs to the seller. Finally, the pricing problem includes decisions as to terms of sale and delivery.

The Marketing Program.—Recognition of the interrelationship of the several subdivisions of marketing described above has led experienced marketing executives to think and act in terms of a co-ordinated marketing program. Decisions on the channels to be used bear directly on the pricing problem; decisions on price are tied inseparably to the problem of the selection of channels; and both in turn directly influence decisions in regard to methods of sales promotion. Successful marketing results from the effective carrying out of a well co-ordinated marketing program, in which every element supports every other element.

MARKETING INSTITUTIONS

The principal source of quantitative statistical information concerning marketing institutions is now the census of the United States. The first such census of marketing institutions was the census of distribution of 1929. Legislation provides for a census of business every 5 years.

Basically, marketing institutions may be divided into retail institutions, wholesale institutions, and producers' marketing departments or agencies.

Retail stores may be classified in a number of different ways: as to the types of goods sold; as to whether or not they are operated as single stores, or as parts of a corporate chain, or as voluntary associations; as to whether they do principally a cash or credit business; as to their general level of prices and quality of merchandise carried, and the like.

Retail stores may also be classified according to whether they are owned and operated by chain store organizations, by individual proprietors, or whether they are members of voluntary chains or co-operative associations. The corporate retail chain has reached its greatest development in the variety and grocery fields, although it is also important in the drug, clothing, and filling station business. Chains of the type of F. W. Woolworth Company, S. S. Kresge Corporation, W. T. Grant Company, and many others do a very high proportion of the total business in the variety field. In the food trade such firms as the Great Atlantic & Pacific Tea Company, Safeway Stores Corporation, Kroger Grocery and Baking Company, and First National Stores Incorporated carry on approximately 40 per cent of the nation's retail food business.

To meet the competition of big chain enterprises, a large number of individual stores have linked themselves with wholesalers in so-called voluntary chains which use a common name, sell many items under a common trademark, and follow a number of uniform management practices. This type of enterprise has grown to considerable importance in the food field and is found occasionally among automotive supply stores. See also CHAIN STORES.

For the most part, wholesale merchants buy goods outright from manufacturers and suppliers and resell them to retailers or other outlets, usually granting credit and extending delivery service. Such firms may carry a broad line of merchandise or a relatively specialized and narrow line. In contrast to the services offered by wholesale merchants, the cash-and-carry wholesalers, as the name implies, require their customers to transport the merchandise themselves and to pay cash for it. Drop shippers never take possession of merchandise, but simply secure orders which the manufacturer or supplier fills direct to the customer.

Manufacturers' sales branches perform different parts of the wholesale function. Sales branches or offices may be established by manufacturers for the purpose of sale or resale to wholesalers, or for sale to retailers, or for sale

RETAIL STORE SALES IN THE UNITED STATES
(in billions of dollars)

Kind of business	1960	1965	1967
Food group[1]	$54.023	$66.920	$72.137
Grocery stores	48.610	61.068	66.146
Automotive group	39.579	56.266	57.556
Passenger car, other automotive dealers ...	37.038	53.217	53.695
Tire, battery, accessory dealers	2.541	3.049	3.861
General merchandise group[1]	24.085	35.840	42.174
Department stores	14.468	23.421	27.703
Mail order (department store merchandise) ...	1.874	2.581	2.767
Variety stores	3.847	5.320	6.078
Eating and drinking places	16.146	21.423	24.887
Gasoline service stations	17.588	21.765	24.011
Apparel group[1]	13.631	15.752	18.105
Men's and boys' wear ..	2.644	3.258	3.822
Women's apparel, accessory stores	5.295	6.243	6.994
Shoe stores	2.437	2.571	2.947
Furniture and appliance group	10.591	13.737	15.700
Furniture, home furnishings stores	[3]	8.538	9.384
Household appliances, TV, radio	[3]	4.223	5.245
Lumber, building, hardware, farm equipment group[1]	14.685	16.274	12.411
Lumber, building materials dealers[2]	8.567	9.302	9.350
Hardware stores	2.655	2.813	3.061
Drug and proprietary stores	7.538	9.335	10.894
Liquor stores	4.893	6.305	7.120
All retail stores ..	219.529	283.950	313.503

[1] Includes data not shown separately. [2] Also includes paint, plumbing, and electrical stores. [3] Data not available. Source: U.S. Department of Commerce.

to final buyers, either individual customers or industrial enterprises.

The general category of agents and brokers includes the following types: auction companies, merchandise brokers, commission merchants, export and import agents, manufacturers' agents, (with stocks), manufacturers' agents (without stocks), selling agents, purchasing agents, cooperative buying agents, and cooperative sales agencies.

These various categories reflect differences in the arrangements between manufacturers and agents or in the method of operation of wholesale enterprises. A common characteristic which distinguishes this group from the service and limited function wholesalers is that they do not buy and resell for their own account but serve as selling or buying representatives, usually on a commission basis.

Assemblers (mainly farm products) include: assemblers; commission buyers; co-operative marketing associations; cream stations; country grain elevators; and packers and shippers.

The census of business shows in great detail the extent to which each of these types of wholesale institutions is important for different industries and for different types of products. Every producer or manufacturer finds that one of his chief problems is to decide which of these wholesale institutions or what combination of wholesale institutions will serve him best. The great divergence in methods of operation is partly a reflection of the differences among the markets to be served and partly a reflection of individual decisions by many business managements.

In addition to the types of marketing institutions already described, there are also the marketing departments of manufacturers or producers, which are not included among the manufacturers' sales branches. Many manufacturers, notably those with limited geographical coverage or those who sell to a few large customers, have no need for sales branches and operate entirely from the factory or central office.

WHOLESALE TRADE IN THE UNITED STATES, BY TYPE OF OPERATION AND KIND OF BUSINESS
(From U. S. Census of Business, 1963)

Type of operation	Number of establishments	Sales (in billions)
Merchant wholesalers	208,997	$157.392
Manufacturers' sales branches, offices	28,884	116.443
Merchandise agents, brokers	25,313	53.245
Petroleum bulk stations, terminals	30,873	21,485
Assemblers of farm products	14,110	9.820
Kind of business		
Groceries and related products	41,890	$58.881
Motors vehicles, auto equipment	28,895	36.584
Farm products—raw materials	16,214	34.831
Machinery, equipment, supplies	48,501	33.408
Metals, minerals (except petroleum products, scrap)	8,475	26.593
Electrical goods	16,211	22.035
Petroleum bulk stations, terminals	30,873	21.485
Drugs, chemicals, allied products	11,438	20.829
Dry goods, apparel	11,756	17.468
Lumber, construction materials	14,139	13.787
Beer, wine, distilled alcoholic beverages	7,598	10.739
Paper, paper products (except wallpaper)	8,812	9.831
Hardware, plumbing, heating equipment, supplies	12,814	9.352
Furniture, home furnishings	8,119	6.565
Tobacco, tobacco products	2,824	5.374
Scrap, waste materials	8,288	3.701
Other miscellaneous products	31,330	26.923
Total wholesale trade	308,177	358.386

Source: U. S. Department of Commerce.

In addition, there are a great many marketing institutions which might be described as facilitating organizations. Advertising agencies which prepare and supervise advertising programs for their clients are prominent among these. There are also a growing number of specialized marketing research organizations which undertake to secure facts, by survey or otherwise, as to the size and character of the market for a particular product, the best type of outlets to be used, and other factors affecting marketing decisions. In a very real sense, magazines, newspapers, and radio stations are also facilitating marketing institutions because of their importance in sales promotion activities.

INTEGRATION OF MARKETING FUNCTIONS

When a single enterprise carries out all of the activities involved in moving goods to final buyers, it may be described as having integrated all of the marketing functions. An example of thoroughgoing integration, not only of marketing activities but also of production activities, is found in the petroleum industry. Many of the concerns in the petroleum industry own oil wells, pipelines and other transport facilities for moving crude oil to refineries, refineries themselves, tankers or other transportation equipment for moving the refined product to market, and wholesale and retail marketing facilities. As another example, some manufacturers of men's clothing own and operate chains of retail stores to sell their products, and the products of other manufacturers to men.

The integration of marketing functions may be complete or partial. Grocery chains, for instance, often perform what may be described as both wholesale and retail functions. They maintain large warehouses to which goods are shipped direct from manufacturers or processors in very large quantities. These large quantities are broken down at the chain warehouses into smaller quantities and shipped to the individual retail stores, usually by truck. In other words, there has been partial integration of the marketing functions but not the complete integration which would have developed if the same interests owned both the manufacturing and the chain store organization.

A different type of partial integration is found when a manufacturer or producer sets up his own sales branches with stocks of merchandise and sells from these branches to retailers. In this case, the integration has extended through the wholesale functions but has not included the retail functions. The working out of integration to the most effective degree, taking into account not only internal costs but also sales promotion factors, is an outstanding marketing problem.

New Combinations of Merchandise.—Another important problem which concerns many types of marketing institutions is the working out of new combinations of merchandise to be carried. A special aspect of merchandising activity, as described above, has featured extensive experimentation in the combinations of merchandise carried by particular kinds of wholesale or retail institutions. A notable illustration is the development of modern drugstores, many of which, starting with a relatively clear-cut line of pharmaceuticals, have expanded to include a wide range of toys, household appliances, cosmetics, tobacco products, and even some types of

Marketing for the automobile age has led to the construction of immense shopping centers, such as these two in Paramus, N.J. A shopping center clusters many chain and independent stores within a parking area larger than the congested central city can offer.

clothing. Most drugstores are much like old-fashioned general stores or modern department stores. In the grocery chains, there was much discussion during the 1920's about the addition of meats and fresh fruits and vegetables to the line; this development is now firmly established. Filling-station chains, several of which are operated by large tire manufacturers, are tending to broaden their lines markedly, almost to the point of becoming small department stores.

There have been some developments in the opposite direction—toward narrower specialization. In the shoe trade, for instance, some concerns have specialized not only in men's shoes but even in men's shoes at a single price. Perhaps the extreme in such specialization was the operation of a store devoted entirely to the sale of men's neckties.

Marketing Costs.—As already noted, marketing costs represent somewhat more than half, perhaps between 54 per cent and 59 per cent, of the total cost of producing and distributing goods. Increasing perception of this fact has caused considerable concern about the problem of high distribution costs. Two observations in regard to this problem are worth citing: (1) "Distribution costs have in part replaced production costs. Economies flowing from large-scale manufacture, and from the technical developments that it has been possible to utilize in large-scale operations, have greatly lowered the costs of producing goods; but at the same time increased marketing costs have resulted from the attempt to dispose of larger outputs in wider markets." (2) "The high cost of distribution," as Professor F. W. Taussig once remarked, "is to a considerable extent the price of consumer freedom—freedom to make choices from a great variety of goods, both in and out of season, freedom to gratify whims; freedom to return merchandise merely because of a change of mind; freedom to enjoy all kinds of collateral services, including credit, delivery, mail orders, telephone orders, demonstrations, lectures, fashion shows, and so on."

These observations do not, of course, imply that intensive efforts should not be made by business management and by public authorities to reduce marketing costs. Indeed, the large proportion of total costs devoted to marketing represents an opportunity and a challenge, since the general potential standard of living can be greatly affected by efforts in this direction. Overall estimates of aggregate marketing costs do not serve particularly well for this purpose. What is needed is detailed information as to the costs incurred by particular types of marketing institutions.

The study of marketing costs really began about World War I when the Harvard Bureau of Business Research, a division of the Harvard Graduate School of Business Administration, published its first study of the operating costs of shoe retailers. Since that time, the Harvard bureau and many other educational and trade institutions have published typical figures for operating costs of many retail and wholesale trades. The census of business has provided additional information, and there are few wholesale and retail trades for which at least some information about typical operating costs is not available. A compendium of such studies, not only for the United States but for European countries, has been published by the Harvard Graduate School of Business Administration.

Marketing Research.—There has been a notable increase in interest in marketing research. In a sense, any effort to secure facts or to correlate known facts in an orderly fashion in order to provide a rational basis for marketing decisions is marketing research. Over the years most successful enterprises have, therefore, been engaged in marketing research. Business firms, advertising agencies and publishers, and specialized marketing research organizations have also been developing a considerable body of specialized techniques which warrant particular attention.

As has been noted already, the marketing of most consumer goods is characterized by far-flung markets, with producer and consumer widely separated as to time and place. Some manufacturers of industrial goods and a few small manufacturers of highly specialized consumer goods have such a small number of potential customers that information about these potential customers may be secured by a direct, complete canvass or census. But for most sellers the number of potential customers renders it physically and financially impossible to make a complete canvass. Under these conditions, the techniques of "sampling" become important. Essentially, the use of "sampling" rests on the proposition that results obtained from studying a properly selected sample will be representative of the whole.

An important question in radio advertising is the number of listeners for particular programs. A method has been devised whereby a careful, calculated sample of people in certain cities is telephoned and asked what program is being heard. From these replies the relative popularity of different programs is calculated. Critics of this method point out that the sample is composed only of people in cities and only of those in the income group who have telephones. If this is the total group with which the marketer is concerned, the kind of sample is adequate; if, on the other hand, the marketer is interested in a cross section of the entire population, there are very important segments unrepresented in such a sample. To meet this difficulty a device has been developed which is attached to the radio and records on a tape the exact times the radio is turned on and the stations to which it is tuned. The user of this device seeks to have it attached to radios in homes

which are carefully selected to be fully representative of the entire population, taking into account geographical distributions, racial characteristics, income levels, and urban and rural differences.

The question of the popularity of particular radio broadcasts is illustrative of problems calling for continuing information. The readership of magazines (circulation is not a complete nor accurate measure of the number of actual readers) and the movement of particular brands of goods through grocery and drugstores are other illustrations of questions which receive continuing study by one means or another.

Since the end of World War II television has developed with great rapidity and has become a major method of sales promotion, particularly for large companies able to spread the very heavy cost over a large volume. The television audience has proved itself highly responsive in the case of certain products.

More often a marketer needs facts to help reach a specific nonrecurring decision. The problem may be the desirability of a particular change in a package, the use of a specific kind of advertisement or other promotional piece, or the determination of the size and character of a market, either nationally or in some smaller regional unit.

For securing information on these and a host of other questions many techniques have been developed and are used. One technique is direct observation. Observers, for instance, are stationed in liquor stores to hear and record just what happens during a transaction. How does the customer ask for merchandise? In how many instances does he ask for a specific brand of merchandise? How often does he mention price first? How often is he influenced by large special displays? The salesman, knowing of the observer's presence, may not act naturally, but the behavior of the customer is likely to be significant.

A second frequently used technique is the interview. Interviews are held in homes, on subways or other public transportation, in offices, and indeed wherever people can be induced to talk. Usually the interviewer is guided by a carefully prepared questionnaire or series of questions which is designed to bring out the information desired and to guard against false or mistaken answers.

Both the preceding methods are expensive, since they require the time of an observer or interviewer for each observation or reply. Their high cost is a major factor which has led to the very great use of mail questionnaires. Such questionnaires have become a popular butt for jokes, and in some instances they have been so poorly constructed or handled that the results have little or no validity. A great deal of experience on the construction of questionnaires has now been accumulated, however, and it should be possible to avoid the most egregious errors. Even after careful attention to the advance construction of questionnaires, experienced marketers conduct small-scale trial runs before using a particular questionnaire on a broad scale.

The careful planning of a survey in advance, including the exact definition of the information (facts or opinions) to be sought, the determination of the methods to be used in securing information, and the handling of mass data after it has been secured, is an essential to effective and low-cost marketing research. Much refinement of techniques is now in progress and those refinements will make possible more precise measurements, but the best techniques are of little value if the basic planning in terms of objectives is not carefully and skillfully done.

THE GOVERNMENT AND MARKETING

As an important part of business as a whole, marketing is, of course, affected by all federal and state legislation which deals with business activities. The present tax structure, for instance, affects marketing decisions as much as it effects decisions about production. There are, however, a number of important pieces of legislation which are primarily concerned with marketing activities. Among these may be mentioned the Pure Food and Drug Act as amended, the Federal Trade Commission Act establishing the principal federal agency which regulates marketing activities, and the statutes providing for the registration of trademarks. Important basic state legislation includes the uniform sales acts and many laws designed to prevent fraud and misrepresentation in sales transactions.

After World War II there developed a considerable legislative movement related to the regulation of prices. These legislative enactments are sometimes lumped together under the heading "Fair Trade Legislation." The Clayton Antitrust Act, passed in 1914, in conjunction with Federal Trade Commission Act, made a start toward limiting pricing freedom by forbidding discrimination among different localities designed to eliminate competition. In the middle 1930's this limitation was extended by the so-called Robinson-Patman Act, which provided, "That it shall be unlawful for any person engaged in commerce, in the course of such commerce, either directly or indirectly to discriminate in price between purchasers of commodities of like grade and quality. . . ." This act includes a series of specific exceptions to the basic rule against discrimination, the most important of which is, "That nothing herein contained shall prevent differentials which make only due allowance for differences in the cost of manufacture, sale, or delivery resulting from the differing methods or quantities in which such commodities are to such purchasers sold or delivered. . . ."

A second major piece of legislation limiting pricing freedom was the Miller-Tydings Act which permitted the states to enact legislation providing for resale price maintenance. Under such state enactments, manufacturers are permitted to require wholesalers and retailers to resell their merchandise at or above prices stipulated by the manufacturer. State legislation of this nature has been generally adopted, and resale price maintenance contracts have been widely employed, especially by manufacturers of drugs, foods, and alcoholic beverages.

A companion approach to the control of selling prices is typified by the California Unfair Practices Act, which prohibits sales below cost. A number of states have adopted this type of legislation and have defined cost variously, several setting a percentage above the price paid by the retailers or wholesalers to cover the distributors' operating costs.

STANLEY F. TEELE
Coauthor of "Problems in Retailing"
and "Distribution Costs"

Bibliography

Alderson, Wroe, and Green, P. E., *Planning and Problem Solving in Marketing* (Homewood, Ill., 1964).
Alexander, Ralph S., and others, *Industrial Marketing,* 3d ed. (Homewood, Ill., 1967).
Beckman, Theodore N., and Davidson, William R., *Marketing,* 8th ed. (New York 1967).
Britt, Steuart Henderson, and Boyd, H. W., Jr., *Marketing and Administrative Action* (New York 1963).
Bursk, Edward C., and Chapman, John F., eds. *Modern Marketing Strategy* (Cambridge, Mass., 1964).
Converse, Paul D., and others, *The Elements of Marketing,* 7th ed. (Englewood Cliffs, N.J., 1965).
Lazo, Hector, and Corbin, A., *Management in Marketing* (New York 1961).
Levitt, Theodore, *Innovation in Marketing* (New York 1962).
Lockley, Lawrence C., and Dirksen, Charles J., *Cases in Marketing,* 3d ed. (Boston 1964).
Oxenfeldt, Alfred, *Executive Action in Marketing* (Belmont, Calif., 1966).
Phillips, Charles F., and Duncan, Delbert J., *Marketing: Principles and Methods,* 5th ed. (Homewood, Ill., 1964).

MARKHAM, märk'əm, SIR **Albert Hastings,** English admiral and Arctic explorer: b. Bagnères-de-Bigorre, France, Nov. 11, 1841; d. London, England, Oct. 28, 1918. He entered the navy in 1856, saw active service in the China seas for several years, took part in the Polar expedition of George Strong Nares (1875–1876), and in that expedition attained what was then the farthest north, 83° 20′ 26″. With Sir Henry Gore-Booth he attempted to reach Franz Josef Land in 1879, but was unsuccessful; in the next year Markham explored the Galápagos Islands. Rear admiral in 1891, and second in command of the Mediterranean Fleet in 1892, he was made a vice admiral, and later an admiral. His last command was at Nore. He retired from the navy in 1906. During World War II he assisted in the minesweeping service. He was created Knight Commander of the Bath in 1903.

He wrote *The Great Frozen Sea* (1877); *A Polar Reconnaissance* (1879); *The Life of John Davis, the Navigator* (1882); *The Voyages and Works of John Davis* (1884); *The Life of Sir John Franklin* (1890); and *The Life of Sir Clements Markham* (1917), the subject of which was his cousin.

MARKHAM, SIR **Clements Robert,** English geographer and traveler: b. Stillingfleet, Yorkshire, England, July 20, 1830; d. London, Jan. 30, 1916. He was educated at Westminster School, entered the navy in 1844, accompanied the Franklin Search Expedition of 1850–1851, and then retired from the service. He traveled in Peru in 1852–1853 and 1860–1861, the second journey being undertaken to get cinchona seeds for planting in India, an experiment described in his *Peruvian Bark; Cinchona Culture in British India, 1861–1880* (1880). After spending 1865–1866 in Ceylon and India, he became assistant secretary in the India Office from 1867–1877, and curator of its geographical department in 1868. As secretary (1858–1886) and president (1889–1909) of the Hakluyt Society, and also as president (1893–1905) of the Royal Geographical Society, Markham rendered distinguished service to the history of geography and discovery by his encouragement of exploration and prolific editorial work. He published some 50 volumes of biographies, histories, geographical records, and historical romances.

MARKHAM, Edwin (real name, CHARLES EDWARD ANSON MARKHAM), American poet and reformer: b. Oregon City, Ore., April 23, 1852; d. Westerleigh, Staten Island, N.Y., March 7, 1940. The youngest child of pioneer parents who separated soon after his birth, he moved with his mother to Lagoon Valley, Calif., and was put to lonely and difficult work on her farm and ranch before he was 10 years old. He discovered books and began a long struggle with his mother for an education, at one time running away from home. With earned money, he succeeded in graduating from the State Normal School at San José, and later graduated from Christian College, Santa Rosa, and became a schoolteacher. In 1875 he married Annie Cox, whom he divorced in 1884; three years later he married Caroline E. Bailey, from whom he soon separated. In 1890 he became principal of the Tompkins School in Oakland, later the Observation School for the University of California. Here he developed a circle, including Ambrose Bierce, Joaquin Miller, and other notables in education and literature.

Markham had written verse as early as 1869 and was now publishing distinctive poems in magazines, including *Scribner's* and *Century*. His poem *The Man with the Hoe,* inspired by Jean François Millet's painting of the same name, was printed in the *San Francisco Examiner,* Jan. 15, 1899, and immediately brought him international fame. Translated into 40 languages, it was reputed to have earned $250,000 in 33 years, and was termed "the battle cry of the next thousand years." Markham moved to New York City with Anna Catherine Murphy Markham, whom he married in 1898, and their son Virgil. His poem *Lincoln; The Man of the People,* written in 1900, developed a notable fame of its own. Markham was accepted as one of the distinguished Americans of his time and was called the dean of American poets. He was for 35 years in constant demand as a lecturer. His articles on child labor, reprinted in *The Children in Bondage* (1914), are a landmark in the child labor crusade. Although much of his later verse was undistinguished, *The Ballad of the Gallows Bird* (*American Mercury,* August 1926) has unique qualities; and his 10-volume collection *The Book of Poetry* (1926) remains a valuable anthology. His *Collected Poems* were published in 1940.

Consult Downey, David G., *Modern Poets and Christian Teaching* (New York 1906); Sullivan, Mark, *Our Times, 1900–1925: Vol. 2, America Finding Herself* (New York 1927); Stidger, William Le Roy, *Edwin Markham* (New York 1933). Manuscript materials and information are preserved in the Edwin Markham Memorial Library, Wagner College.

LOUIS FILLER,
Professor of American Civilization, Antioch College.

MARKHAM, Gervase (or Jervis), English poet and writer: b. Nottinghamshire, England, about 1568; d. London (buried Feb. 3) 1637. A soldier of fortune in the Low Countries and later a captain under the earl of Essex in Ireland, he was a prolific writer on such topics as horsebreeding, agriculture, and forestry. As he compiled many separately titled works on similar subjects to supply the booksellers, he has been called the first English hack writer. His poems, historically interesting but seldom read today, include *The most Honorable Tragedie of Sir Richard Grinvile, Knight* (1595), *Poem of Poems, or Sion's Muse* . . . (1595), and *The English Arcadia* . . . (1607). He also collaborated in writing two plays, and was the author of *A Discourse on Horsemanshippe* (1593).

MARKHAM, William, English colonial governor in America: b. England, about 1635; d.

Philadelphia, Pa., June 12, 1704. It is believed that he served at one time in the English army. He was appointed deputy governor of Pennsylvania on April 10, 1681, by his cousin, William Penn. Arriving in America in July of that year, he established a council for the colony on August 3, and later helped to choose the site for Philadelphia and conferred with Lord Baltimore on the Maryland-Pennsylvania boundary. When Penn arrived in the colony on Oct. 27, 1682, Markham was elected to the council, but left immediately for England to represent Penn in the legal dispute over the territorial boundary. Returning to Pennsylvania shortly after Penn's departure in 1684, he served as secretary of the province (1685–1691), deputy governor of the lower counties, or Delaware (1691–1693), and lieutenant governor or governor of both (1693–1699). He was removed from office by the Privy Council on Aug. 31, 1699, on charges by his political enemies that he had violated the terms of his office, but was succeeded by Penn, who appointed him register general of the colony in 1703. A devoted secretary to Penn, Markham did much to advance the colony's welfare, although his services were not appreciated by the colonists.

MARKHOR, mär′kôr, a large species of wild goat. See GOAT, WILD.

MARKIEVICZ, mär-kyĕ′vĕch, COUNTESS de (nee CONSTANCE GEORGINE GORE-BOOTH), Irish revolutionist: b. Lissadel, Sligo, Ireland, 1876; d. Dublin, July 15, 1927. The elder daughter of Sir Henry Gore-Booth, she participated in aristocratic social life, being presented at court where her beauty and wit attracted many admirers. She found high society dull, however, and went alone in 1897 to study art at Paris, where she met a Polish nobleman, Count Casimir Dunin de Markievicz, whom she married in 1900. The couple settled in Dublin and became leaders of a young artistic and literary circle. Because of her interest in Irish politics as a radical advocating independence from England, the countess soon became estranged from her husband, who disapproved of her political activities.

Countess de Markievicz first came into political prominence in 1908 as the supporter of barmaids who had suffered from the effects of a new liquor-licensing law. In the strike of 1913, she supported the notorious labor leader Jim Larkin, and ran a soup kitchen for the families of strikers. A leader in the Sinn Fein movement, she commanded a detachment of 120 rebels during the Easter Rebellion of 1916 in Dublin. Besieged by British troops in the building housing the College of Surgeons, she was the last Sinn Fein leader to surrender. She was tried for treason and sentenced to death, but the sentence was commuted to life imprisonment, and she was then released in the general amnesty of 1917. Again arrested and interned in 1918, she became the first woman to win election to the British House of Commons, but refused to hold the office. Appointed minister of labor (1919) in the "shadow" cabinet of Eamon de Valera, she opposed the Anglo-Irish Treaty and was prominent in the Republican uprising of 1922. Elected to the Dail Eireann in 1922, 1923, and 1927, she refused, with other Republicans, to take her seat.

The countess was reconciled to her husband just before her death from appendicitis. Denounced by her opponents as the "Red Countess" and praised by her friends as the "Irish Joan of Arc," Countess de Markievicz was recognized by both as one of the great fighters for Irish independence.

Consult her *Prison Letters,* ed. by Eva Gore-Booth, with a biographical sketch by Esther Roper (Toronto 1934); and O'Faoláin, Seán, *Constance Markievicz; or, The Average Revolutionary: a Biography* (London 1934).

MARKING NUT, märk-ing nŭt, the common name of an evergreen tree, *Semecarpus anacardium,* of the cashew family (Anacardiaceae), native in the mountains of the East Indies. It reaches a height of 50 feet, bears oblong blunt leaves and greenish-yellow flowers in hairy terminal panicles. The one-inch fruit is a smooth black drupe whose acrid black juice is mixed with lime by the natives and used for printing and marking cotton cloth. The mark is not water-soluble. The swollen pedicel below the fruit is roasted and eaten, having the taste of an apple. The pedicels of many and the latex of all the 40 species of the genus are poisonous or irritating.
RICHARD M. STRAW.

MARKINGS OF ANIMALS. See COLORATION IN ANIMALS.

MARKLE, mär′k′l, **John,** American coal operator: b. Hazelton, Pa., Dec. 15, 1858; d. New York, N.Y., July 10, 1933. He graduated in mining engineering from Lafayette College in 1880, and became general superintendent of mines of G. B. Markle and Company, his father's firm. Upon his father's retirement, he succeeded to the presidency of the company, and was later president of the firm's successor, the Jeddo-Highland Coal Company, one of the largest of the independent anthracite coal companies. Markle represented the independent operators in the negotiations with President Theodore Roosevelt during the anthracite coal strike of 1902. He also served as president and chief engineer of the Jeddo Tunnel Company, and as a director of other industrial organizations.

MARKOVA, mär′kŏ-và, **Alicia** (real name, LILIAN ALICIA MARKS), English ballerina: b. London, England, Dec. 1, 1910. She studied ballet under Seraphine Astafieva, and at the age of 14 joined Sergei Pavlovich Diaghilev's Russian Ballet Company, with which she appeared until Diaghilev's death in 1929. From 1932 to 1935, she was with the Vic-Wells (later, Sadler's Wells) Ballet, and in May 1935 danced in *The Blue Bird* at the Drury Lane, London, before British royalty. With Anton Dolin, she formed a ballet company and toured successfully (1935–1938); she then performed as ballerina (1938–1941) of the Ballet Russe de Monte Carlo. During World War II, she appeared at the Metropolitan Opera House, New York City, with the Opera Ballet, and in April–May 1946, appeared there with the Ballet Theatre in highly successful performances of *Giselle, Firebird, Swan Lake, Romeo and Juliet,* and other notable works. Markova toured in the United States (1947) and the Far East (1948); was prima ballerina at the Festival Ballet, London, in 1950–1952 and 1954–1955; and has since made many special guest appearances. Her combined technical proficiency, refinement of gesture, and perfect balance has placed her deservingly among the world's great ballet artists.

Consult Anthony, Gordon, *Markova: a Collection of Photographic Studies* (London 1935); Beaumont, Cyril William, *Alicia Markova* (London 1935).

MARKS' MILLS, Engagement at, märks milz, a battle of the American Civil War fought on April 25, 1864, at Marks' Mills, Ark., during the Red River Campaign (q.v.) of the Union Army. A Union train of 240 wagons, escorted by 1,200 infantry, 400 cavalry, and 5 guns, under the command of Lt. Col. Francis M. Drake, 36th Iowa Infantry, left Camden, Ark., on April 23, 1864, for Pine Bluff, to get supplies for Maj. Gen. Frederick Steele's army, then cooperating with Maj. Gen. Nathaniel P. Banks' Red River expedition. At 10 A.M. on April 25, when at Marks' Mills, on the Camden and Pine Bluff road, Drake was attacked, front and rear, by Brig. Gen. James F. Fagan's Confederate force of 3,000 men—cavalry, mounted infantry, and two batteries. After a hard fight of more than three hours, during which Drake was severely wounded and had lost 250 soldiers in killed and wounded, the entire wagon train, guns, and the greater part of the cavalry and infantry were captured. About 300 men escaped and made their way to Little Rock and Pine Bluff. General Fagan's division reported losses of 41 killed, 108 wounded, and 144 missing. When General Steele heard of the disaster, he immediately abandoned the idea of joining Banks' army, evacuated Camden on April 28, fought a rear-guard action with Confederate forces commanded by Maj. Gen. Sterling Price at Jenkins' Ferry on April 30, and retreated to Little Rock.

Consult *The War of the Rebellion: a Compilation of the Official Records of the Union and Confederate Armies,* series 1, vol. 34, part 1 (Washington 1891).

MARKSVILLE, märks′vĭl, town, Louisiana, the seat of Avoyelles Parish, situated 24 miles southeast of Alexandria. It lies near the Red River, at an altitude of 90 feet, and is a station on the Texas and Pacific Railroad. The center for an agricultural area producing chiefly sugarcane, sweet potatoes, cotton, corn, and rice, Marksville processes cotton, mills lumber, and manufactures candy. Nearby are Fort de Russey, the scene of much fighting during the Civil War, and Avoyel Indian State Park, the site of a prehistoric Indian village and burial mounds. (See MOUND BUILDERS AND MOUNDS—*Burial Mounds:* North America.) The town was settled by Acadians from Nova Scotia in the latter half of the 18th century, after their expulsion from the Canadian province in 1755. Pop. 4,257.

MARL, märl, a natural mixture of calcium carbonate ($CaCO_3$) and clay in varying proportions. If the former predominates, it is called calcareous; if clay predominates, it is argillaceous marl. It consists of an earthy friable material of organic origin, secreted by animals and plants, and found chiefly in shallow lakes and marshy areas, such as those in the glaciated region of the northern United States and the coastal areas of Virginia and the Carolinas. The so-called greensand marls, such as occur in England and in New Jersey, may contain little or no calcium carbonate, and are mixtures of greensand and clay. Because of the $CaCO_3$ content, marl is used in the manufacture of portland cement, and also for agricultural purposes, to neutralize acid soil, and as a soil conditioner.
LEWIS S. RAMSDELL.

MARLATT, Charles Lester, American entomologist: b. Atchison, Kans., Sept. 26, 1863; d. Washington, D.C., March 3, 1954. Educated at Kansas State College of Agriculture and Applied Science, he received his B.S. degree in 1884, his M.S. in 1886, and taught there for two years. From 1889 to 1894 he was assistant entomologist, from 1894 to 1922 first assistant and assistant chief entomologist, from 1922 to 1927 associate chief, and from 1927 to 1933 chief, Bureau of Entomology, United States Department of Agriculture. He directed efforts to secure a federal law to prevent the importation of infested and diseased plants, which resulted in the passage of the Plant Quarantine Act of Aug. 20, 1912.

MARLBORO, märl′bûr-ô, unincorporated village, New York, situated in Ulster County, at an altitude of 180 feet, on the west bank of the Hudson River and the New York Central Railroad, 8 miles north of Newburgh. In a fruit-growing and dairying region, it has canneries, dairies, and factories producing builders' supplies. Marlboro was the home of Frederic W. Goudy (q.v.), type designer. Pop. 1,733.

MARLBOROUGH, märl′bŭ-rŭ, 1ST DUKE OF (JOHN CHURCHILL), English soldier and statesman: b. Ashe House, near Musbury, Devonshire, 1650; d. near Windsor, June 16, 1722. He attended St. Paul's School from 1663 to 1665, when he became page to the duke of York (later James II). Commissioned an ensign in 1667, he saw service at Tangier, and in 1672 was promoted to the rank of captain. In that year he accompanied the duke of Monmouth to Flanders in the expedition to assist the French against the Dutch. He distinguished himself at the siege of Maastricht in 1673, and in the following year was commissioned colonel by Louis XIV. Returning to England, he was married to Sarah Jennings, attendant of Princess (later Queen) Anne, early in 1678, and was commissioned colonel of a foot regiment. He accompanied the duke of York to the Netherlands in 1679, and later that year to Scotland. In 1682, he was created Baron Churchill of Aymouth. In the following year his wife was appointed lady in waiting to Princess Anne, with whom she became intimate. On the accession of James II in 1685, he was sent on a mission to Louis XIV and soon after his return was created Baron Churchill of Sandridge. He helped to suppress Monmouth's rebellion and was raised to the rank of major general.

He was in touch with William of Orange as early as 1687, and he joined him in the following year. Early in 1689, William appointed him a member of the Privy Council and raised him to the earldom of Marlborough. He served in Ireland in 1690, reducing Cork, Kinsale, and other towns. Suspected of intrigue with the Jacobites, he was dismissed from his positions in 1692 and committed for a short time to the Tower of London. By 1698, however, he was restored to favor at court and was appointed governor to the young duke of Gloucester and member of the Privy Council. In 1701, William appointed him commander in chief of the English forces in the Netherlands and ambassador plenipotentiary at The Hague.

On the accession of Queen Anne in 1702, Marlborough was appointed captain general of the forces in England and master general of ordnance.

He was sent to The Hague as ambassador extraordinary and arranged for English support of the Dutch in the War of the Spanish Succession. In command of a mixed force of English, Dutch, and Germans, he drove the French from Upper Gelderland and took Kaiserwerth, Venlo, and Liége. For his services he was created marquis of Blandford and duke of Marlborough. He returned to the Continent in 1703, campaigned successfully in the Rhineland, but was unable to take Antwerp because of the lack of Dutch support. In the following year he stormed the French and Bavarian lines at Donauwörth and, with Prince Eugene of Savoy, won the great victory of Blenheim (August 13). Parliament showed its gratitude by passing an act enabling the queen to award him the manor of Woodstock, and Blenheim Palace was built for him at her expense. He was victorious over the French at Ramillies in 1706, and at Oudenarde, with Prince Eugene, in 1708. In the following year he defeated the duc de Villar at Malplaquet, though at a cost ill repaid by the capture of Mons. Meanwhile, his popularity at court had declined and a new ministry, hostile to him, had taken office. He was accused of using public funds for private purposes and dismissed from his command in 1711. He went in disgust to the Netherlands in 1712, but returned to England in 1714, on the death of Queen Anne, and shortly thereafter was reappointed captain general and master of ordnance.

Consult Murray, George, ed., *Letters and Despatches of Marlborough,* 5 vols. (London 1845); Coxe, William, *Memoirs of the Duke of Marlborough,* rev. ed. (London 1847–48); Churchill, W. L. S., *Marlborough, His Life and Times,* 6 vols. (New York 1933–38); Ashley, M. P., *Marlborough* (London 1939).

MARLBOROUGH, municipal borough, England, situated in Wiltshire, in the Kennet River valley, 75 miles west of London. It serves as the trading center for the surrounding dairying and sheep-raising region. The borough is the seat of Marlborough College, a public school founded in 1843. Thomas Cardinal Wolsey is said to have been ordained at St. Peter's Church here in 1498. Pop. (1961) 4,843.

MARLBOROUGH, märl′bûr-ô, city, Massachusetts, situated in Middlesex County, at an altitude of 375 feet, on the Boston and Maine and the New York, New Haven and Hartford railroads, 15 miles east-northeast of Worcester. An industrial city, it produces shoes and slippers, paper goods, metal products, boxes, and miners' lamps. It has a public library, a museum of natural history, and a general hospital. In the building used as the headquarters of the American Legion is the John Brown Bell, taken from the engine house at Harpers Ferry in 1861 by Union soldiers from Marlborough.

Marlborough occupies the site of an Indian settlement. The first white settlers arrived in 1657, and three years later a town was incorporated and named for Marlborough, England. It was attacked by the Indians in 1676, in King Philip's War, while the townspeople were at church. Marlborough was incorporated as a city in 1890. It is governed by a mayor and council. Pop. 18,819.

MARLBOROUGH, provincial district, New Zealand, situated in the northeastern part of South Island. Its extreme length is 130 miles, breadth 60 miles; area, 4,220 square miles. The coast is deeply indented by bays and natural harbors, from which the hills rise abruptly, clothed with magnificent forests. The district is generally hilly or mountainous, with splendid scenery. The amount of arable land is restricted; in the south are the Wairau plains, one of the finest sheep tracts in New Zealand. Mining is carried on, gold, copper, and coal being found. Blenheim, the capital, is connected by rail with the seaport of Picton on Queen Charlotte Sound, an inlet off Cook Strait. Pop. (1956) 25,697.

MARLIN, mär′lĭn, city, Texas, seat of Falls County, located near the Brazos River at an altitude of 383 feet, 20 miles south-southeast of Waco, on the Southern Pacific and the Missouri Pacific railroads. It is situated in an agricultural region in which cotton is the principal product, and the ginning and compressing of cotton is the city's leading industry. Cottonseed oil is produced and shipped. Other shipments are mineral crystals, dressed poultry, and creamery products. With three hot-water artesian wells having remarkable curative properties, Marlin stands high as a health resort, and is visited by persons from all parts of the country. There are two general hospitals and a veterans hospital here. The city has good schools, a public library, and a courthouse. Government is by mayor and council. Pop. 6,918.

MARLINESPIKE, mär′lĭn-spīk, **MARLINSPIKE,** or **MARLINGSPIKE,** an iron pin tapering to a point, and principally used by sailors to separate the strands of a rope in splicing or knotting. The name is often applied to the jaeger because of the bird's long middle tail feathers.

MARLITT, E. See JOHN, EUGENIE.

MARLOW, mär′lō, city, Oklahoma, in Stephens County, on a tributary of the Washita River, 26 miles east of Lawton, served by the Chicago, Rock Island, and Pacific Railroad. Corn and watermelons are raised in the county, and there are cotton gins in the city. Pop. 4,027.

MARLOWE, Christopher, English poet and dramatist: b. Canterbury 1564; d. Deptford, June 1, 1593. In 1584 he took the A.B. degree at Corpus Christi College, Cambridge, and in 1587 the degree of M.A. Perhaps in the same year, the first part of his *Tamburlaine* was acted in London; and the rest of his life was spent in active connection with the theaters. His life seems to have been somewhat dissipated and the daring of his theological opinions gave color to an accusation of atheism. In 1593 he was killed in a tavern broil by Ingram Frisar, and was buried at St. Nicholas, Deptford.

Numerous plays have been assigned to Marlowe, including a share in the three parts of *Henry VI;* and he may very likely have had some part in others besides the following, which can with certainty be ascribed to him: *The Tragedy of Dido,* of uncertain date of acting, finished by Thomas Nash, printed 1594; *Tamburlaine the Great* (two parts), acted 1587–1588, printed 1590; *Tragedy of Dr. Faustus,* acted 1588–1589, entered at Stationer's Hall 1601; *The Jew of Malta,* acted after 1588, entered 1594, printed 1633; *Edward II,* acted 1591, printed 1593; *The Massacre of Paris,* acted 1593, printed about 1600. His *Hero and Leander* was completed after his death by George Chapman and published in 1598. Marlowe's plays attained a sudden and great popularity and his poetic reputation is testified to by numerous tributes from his contemporaries. Marlowe's dramatic activity came at a time of great emotional stir and stress. In England the ideas and ideals of the Renaissance and the Reformation had finally gained the ascendency over those of the Middle Ages. The struggle with Spain, which was just ending in the destruction of the Armada, had brought a triumphant consciousness of national greatness. From this newly-discovered England as well as from the newly-discovered America and the rediscovered world of Greece and Rome, came countless incentives for multiform activities. The drama had already become in some measure an expression of this national activity, but it still awaited the services of great literary genius. After two generations of precarious struggle, the professional companies had become firmly established in the public theaters and it was already plain that the main development of the drama was henceforth to be popular and professional rather than scholarly and amateur. In comedy, indeed, the plays of John Lyly and George Peele had already supplied refinement and a literary flavor, but in the popular drama in the main, and in tragedy in particular, there was neither refinement nor poetry.

Marlowe created English tragedy anew. He threw aside Senecan traditions and devoted himself to meeting the demands of the London theaters, but the prologue to his first play was a declaration of reform, announcing the adoption of blank verse, heroic themes and "high astounding terms." His themes were novel, and his treatment of them seems to have been dictated by a conception of tragedy formed independently of his predecessors—the heroic struggle of a great personality doomed to inevitable defeat. *Tamburlaine* is hardly a tragedy at all but rather a chronicle of the hero's greatness; but in *Dr. Faustus* and *The Jew of Malta,* heroes with ambitions as boundless and passionate as Tamburlaine's are overwhelmed in the end by the limitations that forever bound human aspiration. These plays mark the formation of the Marlowean type of tragedy, often imitated and long influential in the English drama. A protagonist distinguished by great passions and many crimes absorbs the interest of a series of scenes, brutal and sensational, full of violent action, ranting declamation, bloodshed, and villainy affording opportunity for elaborate theatrical spectacles and adorned by passages of profound intellectual suggestiveness and extraordinary beauty of diction and melody. *Edward II,* the most mature of his plays, illustrates these characteristics and also testifies to his growing power both as a playwright and as a poet. The characterization is less melodramatic, more varied and more human than in the earlier plays; the structure more coherent and organized; the style less bombastic, more even and more dramatic. Shakespeare, who clearly imitated Marlowe in *Richard III* and produced *Richard II* in rivalry of *Edward II* did not in these two plays surely surpass his master.

Marlowe's faults and deficiencies are apparent and they cannot all be credited to the immaturity and experimental nature of his art. The banalities that mar his noblest scenes and the absurdities that appear in every phase of his work, theatrical, dramatic or poetic, would doubtless have disappeared in the rapid development of dramatic art which the next 30 years witnessed. But there are no indications that, had Marlowe's life been prolonged, he would ever have excelled in humor or the individualization of character. His achievement is, nevertheless, among the most remarkable and enduring of the Elizabethan era. His poetry remains forever impressive with its fine impetuosity, its splendors of diction and melody. His tragedies, of immense influence on the theater of his day, continue to rank among the greatest of English literature in their expression of passionate ambition and aspiration. He was the first great English dramatist, and he prepared the way for Shakespeare. See also JEW OF MALTA, THE.

ASHLEY H. THORNDIKE,
Professor Emeritus of English, Columbia University.

Bibliography.—The best collected editions of his works are by Alexander Dyce (1858, 1865, and 1876), and by A. H. Bullen, 3 vols. (1885). Also consult Ward, A. W., *History of Dramatic Literature*, vol. 1 (London 1887); Ingram, J. H., *Christopher Marlowe and His Associates* (New York 1904); Bakeless, J., *Tragicall History of Christopher Marlowe*, 2 vols. (Cambridge, Mass., 1942); Kocher, P. H., *Christopher Marlowe* (Chapel Hill, N. C., 1946); Ellis, Havelock, ed., *Christopher Marlowe*, with introduction by J. A. Symonds (reissue, New York, 1948). Marlowe's life has been the theme of two modern tragedies: Richard H. Horne's *Death of Marlowe* (1837); and W. L. Courtney's *Kit Marlowe* (1890).

MARLOWE, Julia (real name SARAH FRANCES FROST), American actress: b. Caldbeck, Cumberlandshire, Eng., Aug. 17, 1866; d. New York, N. Y., Nov. 12, 1950. She came to the United States in 1871. In 1878 she joined the Juvenile Opera Company, which presented *H.M.S. Pinafore, The Chimes of Normandy* and other light operas, in which she was known as Fanny Brough. Subsequently she took a child's part in *Rip Van Winkle*. She then retired, studied in New York for three years and then made her metropolitan debut as Parthenia in *Ingomar*. Her later roles include Viola in *Twelfth Night;* Rosalind in *As You Like It;* Highland Mary in *For Bonnie Prince Charlie* (1897); Barbara Frietchie in the play of that name by Clyde Fitch (1899), and Charlotte Oliver in *The Cavalier* (1903). Other plays in which she took the title roles are *Colinet and When Knighthood Was in Flower.* On May 28, 1894 she was married to Robert Taber, who had been her leading man in her first appearance in *Romeo and Juliet* in 1888. They starred together for a season, but owing to a disagreement were later separated, and in 1900 Mrs. Taber secured a divorce. In 1904 she joined Edward Hugh Sothern, and for several years they were joint stars in Shakespearean roles. In 1911 they married, and in 1924 she retired from the stage. Their presentations of Shakespearean plays are reckoned as some of the best ever given in the United States. She received honorary degrees from George Washington University and Columbia University.

MARMADUKE, John Sappington, American Confederate soldier: b. Saline County, Mo., March 14, 1833; d. Jefferson City, Mo., Dec. 28, 1887. He studied at Yale and Harvard and graduated from West Point in 1857, and served in the United States Army in the West. At the outbreak of the Civil War he entered the service of the Confederate States and rose to the rank of major general. In 1864 he was captured and was not released until after the close of the war, when he went abroad for a time, and on his return engaged in business and also in journalism. He was editor of the St. Louis *Journal of Agriculture* (1871–1874); and he served on the Missouri Railway Commission (1880–1885). He was defeated for the governorship of Missouri in 1880, but in 1884 was elected and served until his death.

MARMALADE, a jellied or gelatinous preparation made from quinces, peaches, apricots or oranges and portions of their rinds, with a mixture of sugar and spice. It is made like the ordinary jams, poured out warm into pots or jars and sold as a confection. The marmalade tree (*Tucuma mammosa*) is of the star-apple family, producing a large egg-shaped drupe, tasting like marmalade.

MARMARA, mär'mà-rà, **Sea of** (Turkish MARMARA DENIZI; ancient PROPONTIS), an inland sea, lying between southeastern Europe and the westernmost part of Asia, communicating with the Mediterranean by the narrow strait called the Dardanelles, and with the Black Sea by the Bosporus. Length from Gallipoli to the head of the Gulf of Izmit, 172 miles; greatest breadth, which is near the center, about 45 miles; average depth over 600 feet; maximum depth, 4,000 feet. The largest of several islands is Marmara, famous for its quarries of marble and alabaster, situated near its western end; at the eastern end, on the Asiatic coast, and not far from Constantinople, is a group called the Princes Islands. A current sets from the Black Sea into the Sea of Marmara, which in turn runs into the archipelago. The tides are hardly perceptible and the navigation is easy.

MARMETTE, Joseph Etienne Eugene, Canadian author: b. St. Thomas de Montmagny, Quebec, Oct. 25, 1844; d. Ottawa, May 7, 1895. After receiving a good general education he determined to devote himself to literature. He wrote several historical novels dealing with the main events in French-Canadian history. These include *Charles et Eva* (1866); *François de Bienville* (1870); *L'Intendant Bigot* (1872); *Le Chevalier de Mornac* (1873); *Le Tomahawk et l'épée* (1877); *A Travers la vie* (1895).

MARMIER, màr-myā', **Xavier,** French author: b. Pontarlier, Doubs, June 24, 1809; d. Paris, Oct. 11, 1892. He engaged in journalism and later traveled extensively in Switzerland, Holland, Germany, Russia, Algeria, America and the East. In 1835 he accompanied the scientific voyage of the *Research* to the Arctic regions and then acquired a wide knowledge of the Scandinavian and Finnish languages and customs. In 1839 he became professor of foreign literature at Rennes and in 1841 occupied a position under the minister of public instruction. In 1846 he was appointed curator at the Bibliothèque Sainte-Geneviève in Paris, in 1870 was elected a member of the Academy; and in 1884 was made administrator. Among his publications are *Histoire de l'Islande* (1838); *Langue et Littérature Islandaises* (1838); *Histoire de la littérature en Danemark et en Suède* (1839); *Lettres sur la Rus-*

sie, la Finlande et la Pologne (1843) ; *Lettres sur l'Amérique* (1852) ; *Voyage en Suisse* (1861) ; *Voyages et Littérature* (1888), and the novels *Les fiancés du Spitzberg* (1858) ; *Gazida* (1860).

MARMION, A TALE OF FLODDEN FIELD,

a poem in six cantos by Sir Walter Scott, published in 1808, is the second of his metrical romances, and the first—after the preliminary experiment of the *Lay of the Last Minstrel*—in which he developed the full possibilities of the form. Because of the success of the earlier poem, he was offered £1,000 for this one before he had begun to write it—a circumstance which enabled Byron to barb his satire with the taunt:

> "And think'st thou, Scott! by vain conceit perchance,
> On public taste to foist thy stale romance,
> Though Murray with his Miller may combine
> To yield thy muse just half a crown per line?"

Like most of Scott's fiction, in prose or verse, the story of *Marmion* is based on the fundamental impulse to revivify the past, especially in connection with the historic associations of picturesque scenes. Hence he weaves a romance about persons, some historic and some imaginative, but always with an eye toward the climax, the account of the Battle of Flodden Field. It is significant, too, that the famous scene describing the quarrel between Marmion and Douglas (canto vi) was an afterthought, due to a suggestion from one of Scott's friends that he should plan Marmion's journey from England to Edinburgh so as to introduce the Douglas castle of Tantallon. Critical opinions have varied concerning the romantic plot of this poem, and Scott himself spoke severely of his having based it in part on the crime of forgery, characteristic "of a commercial rather than a proud and warlike age." But there can be no difference of view as to the splendid movement and glow of the more stirring scenes of the story—those of the kind in which Scott's genius was always at its best—especially the account of the Battle of Flodden, culminating in the death of Marmion. The work also contains some interesting personal poetry, in the epistles, addressed to different friends, which Scott prefixed to the several cantos, and (in canto v) one of his most popular narrative ballads, *Lochinvar*.

RAYMOND M. ALDEN.

MARMOL, mär′môl, **José,** Argentine author : b. Buenos Aires, Dec. 5, 1818 ; d. there, Aug. 12, 1871. He was a pronounced Democrat, was banished by Juan Manuel de Rosas, led the opposition against that dictator and on its successful termination became senator and librarian of Buenos Aires. A fervent orator, Marmol is better known as the author of *La Amalia* (1855), a historical novel dealing with Rosas' dictatorship, of the popular patriotic poem *El 25 de Mayo de 1843,* and of the dramas *El poeta* (1842) ; *El Peregrino* (1846) and *El Cruzado* (1851). *La Amalia* has long been familiar to European readers through French and German translations. An English translation of this work was published in New York in 1919.

MARMONT, màr-môn′, **Auguste Frédéric Louis Viesse de,** DUC DE RAGUSE, marshal of France : b. Châtillon-sur-Seine, France, July 20, 1774 ; d. Venice, March 2, 1852. He entered the army as a lieutenant of infantry in his 15th year. In 1792 he changed to the artillery, and at Toulon became acquainted with Bonaparte, who chose him for his aide-de-camp. For several years after 1805 he was military and civil governor of Dalmatia, where he initiated important public works. Being called to aid in the Austrian campaign in 1809 he assisted so efficiently that Napoleon made him a marshal and governor general of the Illyrian provinces. He was again called upon in the Spanish campaign of 1811, was severely wounded at Salamanca, and was laid up for some time. In the campaign of 1813 he held the command of an army corps in Germany, and fought in the battles of Lützen, Bautzen and Dresden. In 1814 he fought a final battle under the walls of Paris, but opposition appearing fruitless surrendered to the Allies. This proceeding was one main cause of Napoleon's immediate abdication, and brought Marmont into favor with the Bourbons. After the Restoration, Louis XVIII made him a peer of France, but he was compelled to withdraw from Paris by the revolution of 1830, and his name was struck off the army list.

MARMONTEL, màr-môn-tĕl′, **Jean François,** French writer : b. Bort, Limousin, France, July 11, 1723 ; d. Abbeville, Eure, Dec. 31, 1799. He was educated for the church, but turned to letters, and became a journalist and dramatist at Paris. In 1758–1759 he edited *Le Mercure,* and in 1763 was elected to the Academy. He wrote tragedies, including *Denys le Tyran* (1748) and *Aristomène* (1749) ; *Contes Moraux* (1761), and the works of fiction *Bélisaire* (1767) and *Les Incas* (1778). His *Poétique Française* (1763) and *Eléments de Littérature* (1787) have perhaps a more permanent worth. A collected edition of his writings appeared in 1786–1787. In 1771 he was appointed historiographer of France, and in 1783 was made secretary of the French Academy.

MARMOSET, the common name applied to a group of extremely small American monkeys constituting the family Callithricidae (Hapalidae) which differ from the related family Cebidae in the absence of the third molar tooth, leaving 32 instead of 36 teeth, and in having sharp curved claws on all the digits except the very short great toe which bears a flat nail. Their hands lack the dexterity possessed by other monkeys. The two families are united in a superfamily Ceboidea. Marmosets have soft silky fur, long nonprehensile tails, and are often described as squirrellike in appearance. The numerous species are grouped in two genera, *Callithrix* (*Hapale*), the true marmosets, and *Leontocebus* (*Midas*), the tamarins, which have longer canine teeth. Marmosets inhabit the forests of tropical South America, and one species, Geoffroy's tamarin, is found in Panama and Costa Rica. All are strictly arboreal, associate in small groups, and feed on fruits, insects, spiders and birds' eggs. The gestation period is about 150 days (S. Zuckerman), remarkably long for such small mammals. Unlike other monkeys they commonly bear two and sometimes three young at a birth. Marmosets are readily tamed and are greatly favored as pets, though in intelligence they are greatly inferior to the cebid monkeys. Some zoologists consider the marmosets the most primitive of all American monkeys, while others regard them as an adaptively specialized dwarf branch of the Ceboidea. See also MONKEYS ; PRIMATES.

MARMOT, a large ground squirrel of the genus *Marmota* (*Arctomys*), having terrestrial habits, coarse fur, no cheek-pouches, short limbs and powerful digging claws. In size it varies from about 15 to 25 inches in length, the tail adding from 3 to 12 inches. Several species inhabit the northern parts of the world, in southerly climates keeping themselves mostly upon mountain heights, but farther north inhabiting lower levels, preferring open or thinly wooded plains. All dig and dwell in burrows, some species gathering into extensive colonies, the hillocks about the mouths of the burrows forming communities similar to the "towns" of the prairie dogs; while other species dwell in families far apart from one another. They feed upon herbage and grow very fat in the autumn preparatory to hibernation during the cold months, when their dormancy is complete. Their underground sleeping-chambers are warmly furnished with dry leaves and hay. The European marmot (*M. marmota*) is found plentifully in the Alpine range, equals a rabbit in size and is light brown in color. It lives immediately below the snow line, and subsists on vegetables, insects and roots. It comes forth from its burrow during the month of April, and is said to be readily tamed. The bobac, another European species (*M. bobak*), inhabits Poland, Russia and all northern Asia. A third species is found in the Himalayan ranges; and a fourth (*M. caudatus*), the largest and handsomest of the family, dwells in the valleys of their southerly slopes. These little animals are of great value to the wandering natives of northern and central Asia, who utilize both their skins and flesh. America has two marmots, one of which is the siffleur or whistler of the tops of the northern Rocky Mountains, and the other the familiar Eastern woodchuck. The former takes its name from the loud eerie whistle with which it wakes the echoes of the crags about the lone pastures above timber line, where it makes its home; it was of great service to the mountain Indians. Other species or varieties occur in the southern mountains of the Western states. The woodchuck or ground hog (*M. monax*), is a heavy, broad-headed, grizzled animal of the woods and fields, yellowish to whitish gray in color, blackish on the back and crown and chestnut on the belly; with the feet and tail brownish black. It abounds throughout the whole country east of the dry plains, and flourishes in spite of civilization, as the farmers' meadows and gardens supply it with an increased supply of good food, and mankind thins out its worst enemies, such as wildcats, foxes, weasels, the larger serpents and birds of prey; none of these save the first is much to be feared by the full-grown woodchucks, but may kill many of the young. As a result the animals have become unpleasantly numerous in some districts of the Eastern states, where their depredations upon gardens and certain plantations, as of lettuce, carrots, and celery, are often serious.

MARNE, märn, river, France, the chief affluent of the Seine, rising in the plateau of Langres, flowing northwest past Châlons et Épernay, thence westward, joining the Seine at Charenton-le-Pont, four miles above Paris. Its length is 325 miles, 220 of which are navigable. It is connected by canals with the Rhine, the Aisne and the Seine. The Marne was the crucial fighting line of the western front during World War I. The river was reached by the American forces in August 1944, during World War II.

MARNIAN EPOCH, name given to the period known in France as the Gallic, in England the late Celtic and in Switzerland as La Tène. It extends from about 500 B.C. to the conquest of Gaul by Julius Caesar. It is named Marnian from the French department of the Marne where the richest deposits of the period have been found.

MARNIX mär′nĭks, **Philipp von,** BARON SAINT-ALDEGONDE, Flemish statesman and writer: b. Brussels, Belgium, 1538; d. Leyden, Dec. 15, 1598. He studied at the universities of Paris, Louvain, Dôle, and Pavia. While in Italy he became a strict Calvinist, and in 1566 he wrote a defense of the iconoclasts. He later was forced to flee to Bremen and East Friesland. In 1571 he took up residence in the home of William of Orange, and thereafter performed many missions for William, until he was captured by the Spanish (1573), and held prisoner for a year. In 1578 he was ambassador to the Diet of Worms. In 1585 he retired from political life after Antwerp, of which he had been burgomaster, capitulated to Alessandro Farnese. His most renowned work was *Tableau des différends de la religion* (1598). He also wrote the Flemish national song *Wilhelmuslied* and translated the Psalms of David.

MAROC. See MOROCCO.

MARONITES, mär′ŏ-nīts, a sect of Eastern Christians, whose origin was a consequence of the Monothelite controversy. In the 7th century the opinion that Christ, though He united in Himself the divine and human natures, had but one will arose among the Eastern nations. But when their last patron, the Emperor Philippicus, was deposed and exiled in 713, the Monothelites were condemned and banished by his successor, Anastasius II. The remnant of this party survived in the Maronites (so named from their founder, Maron)—a society of monks in Syria, about Mt. Lebanon, which is mentioned as early as the 6th century. Another monk, John Maro, or Maron also preached Monothelitism there in the 7th century. Regarded as rebels by the Melchites (q.v.), or Christians who adhered to the opinions of the emperor, they became, in that district of Lebanon which is now called Kisrawan, a warlike mountain people, who defended their political as well as their religious independence boldly against the Mohammedans, and who even under the Turkish government resisted the payment of a tribute, like the Druses. The political constitution of the Maronites is that of a military commonwealth. Governed by their ancient customary rights, defended from external attacks, they support themselves among the mountains by husbandry and the produce of their vineyards and mulberry trees. The revenues of all their orders of ecclesiastics are very small, but a common spirit unites them, and in simplicity of manners, temperance and hospitality they resemble the ancient Arabians. Revenge for murder is permitted among them, and as a sign of nobility they wear the green turban. Their church constitution resembles very much that of the old Greek Church. Since the 12th century they have several times accepted papal supremacy and the Roman Catholic

Church, preserving certain differences peculiar to their sect. In 1736 they accepted a new church constitution and definitely fixed their affiliation with Rome. They use the Antiochene rites of worship in Syriac or Arabic. Elected by the bishops with the approval of the pope, the head of the church is the patriarch of Antioch, who resides in Lebanon. Celibacy is not required of the clergy.

In the mid-19th century there were frequent conflicts between the Maronites and the Druses (q.v.), an extreme sect of Shī'ite Muslims, which culminated in a massacre of Christians in 1860. A French army intervened to protect the Christians, mostly Maronites, and shortly thereafter the Lebanese province of the Ottoman Empire was given a great deal of autonomy and placed under a Christian governor. Although some Maronites have settled in Cyprus, Syria, Egypt, and the United States, their largest community is still in Lebanon. They form the largest Christian sect in the country (estimated at 377,544 in 1952), and the president of Lebanon is traditionally a Maronite. See also LEBANON—5. *History.*

Consult Attwater, Donald, *The Catholic Eastern Churches* (Milwaukee 1935), rev. ed. published as vol. 1 of *Christian Churches of the East,* 2 vols. (Milwaukee 1947); Hourani, Albert H., *Minorities in the Arab World* (London 1947); Hitti, Philip K., *Lebanon in History* (New York and London 1957).

MAROT, mȧ-rō', **Clément,** French poet: b. Cahors, France, 1495?; d. Turin, Italy, September 1544. The son of Jean Marot, court poet, he became a favorite of Francis I and his sister, the future Margaret of Navarre. He went to the Field of the Cloth of Gold (1520) with the king, and on an Italian campaign he was wounded and taken prisoner with him at Pavia in 1525. When he returned to Paris, within a year, he entered the royal household, eventually succeeding his father as court poet. By temperament he was gay and lighthearted—qualities which made him popular at court but caused him difficulties with the church. He was imprisoned in 1526 for failing to observe Lent properly, but his influential patrons quickly secured his release. Because of his Protestant tendencies, he was often attacked by the faculty of the Sorbonne. Twice he fled from the capital when suspected of complicity with the Lutherans. His verse translations of the Psalms (1540?) were well received at court and by the people, which is thought to have aided the cause of the Protestants. In 1542 he had to flee from France for reasons which are obscure. He took refuge in Geneva, where he was welcomed by the Calvinists. However, he soon found the puritanical atmosphere there stultifying and went to Chambéry and then to Italy, where he died.

Marot was the last French poet of the Middle Ages and the first of the Renaissance. He began in the school of the *rhétoriqueurs* but had the taste to avoid their wordiness and emphasis on complicated forms rather than content. An important literary reformer, he made his innovations independently and did not join the Pléiade (q.v.), the leading reform group. His first major work was *Le temple de Cupido* (1515), which he presented to Francis I. *Adolescence clémentine* (1532) is a collection of his amusing verse commentaries on events at court. He described a brief imprisonment in *Enfer* (1542). For a court poet he was surprisingly unaffected. His work is characterized by charm, grace, and facile irony rather than by profundity, and he was at his best in such light forms as ballades, rondeaus, epistles,

and epigrams. He is credited with introducing the sonnet into French literature. At capturing a particular form of Gallic wit he was unexcelled until the times of La Fontaine and Voltaire. See also CHANT ROYAL.

MAROZIA, mȧ-rō'zhĭ-ȧ, Roman noblewoman: fl. 928. The daughter of Theodora and the consul Theophylact, she belonged to the noble faction which controlled Italian politics in the early 10th century. The domination of Roman government and the papacy by Theodora and her daughters has been termed "the pornocracy" (government by profligate women). Marozia was the mistress of Pope Sergius III, who may have been the father of her son John XI, and by a series of calculated marriages and intrigues she increased her power. She was successively the wife of Alberic, duke of Spoleto, Guido of Tuscany, and Hugh, king of Italy, and bore the titles of *senatrix* and *patricia.* In 928 she overthrew Pope John X, installed Leo VI (q.v.), and later elevated one of her sons to the papal throne as John XI (q.v.). By negotiating the marriage of one of her daughters to a Byzantine prince, she attempted to extend her influence to Constantinople; however, a revolution of her son Alberic II put an end to her schemes. He won all temporal power in Rome, and kept her imprisoned until she died sometime between 932 and 937.

MARPRELATE, mär'prĕ-lĭt, **Martin,** the pseudonymous name signed to a series of vituperative tracts attacking the prelacy of the Church of England, published from 1588 to 1589 by several Puritans. The controversy which arose about them is interesting because it demonstrates (1) the bitterness some Puritans felt at Queen Elizabeth's failure to rid the Church of England of what they charged were remnants of Roman Catholicism, and (2) the beginning of the development of the prose satire. A Welshman, John Penry (q.v.), who was hanged May 29, 1593 for inciting to rebellion, is generally believed to have been the chief author of the pamphlets. Others probably involved were Robert Waldegrave, a printer, who fled the country in 1589, and two Puritan preachers: John Udall, who died (1592) shortly after his release from a death sentence for libel, and Job Throckmorton, who was acquitted of complicity (1593). The Marprelate pamphlets were written in a racy, often scurrilous style, offensive even to many members of the Puritan party, and they called forth equally invective—but less inspired—rejoinders from supporters of the prelacy, including such literary lights as John Lyly and Thomas Nash.

HENRY HUMPHREY.

MARPRELATE CONTROVERSY. See MARPRELATE, MARTIN.

MARQUAND, mär-kwänd', **John Phillips,** American author: b. Wilmington, Del., Nov. 10, 1893; d. Newbury, Mass., July 16, 1960. A descendant of prominent New England families, which included the transcendentalist Margaret Fuller, he grew up in Rye, N.Y., and Newburyport, Mass. He graduated from Harvard in 1915 and then worked on the Boston *Evening Transcript.* After serving as an artillery lieutenant in World War I, he settled in New York and wrote for the *Tribune* and for an advertising agency. Marquand began his literary career in 1922 with *The Unspeakable Gentleman,* a novel first published in the *Ladies' Home Journal.* For the next 15 years he was highly successful as the author of "slick" magazine fiction—short stories, serialized novels, and a popular series about a Japanese detective, Mr. Moto. Most of his works of this period were published in the *Saturday Evening Post.* They had exciting plots and colorful settings. Despite the limitations of the "magazine formula," his characters were remarkably well drawn. With time he became more and more skillful, and in 1937 he published *The Late George Apley* (q.v.), which marked his debut as a writer of serious fiction. It was awarded the Pulitzer Prize in 1938. In this novel, in *Wickford Point* (1939), and in *H. M. Pulham, Esquire* (1941), he satirized upper-class New England social structure, depicting characters from this environment as unhappy people bound by family tradition.

In 1944 and 1945 he served as a special consultant to the war department, and World War II played an important part in several of his novels, including *So Little Time* (1943), *Repent in Haste* (1945), *B. F.'s Daughter* (1946), and *Melville Goodwin, U.S.A.* (1951). In his later novels he continued to examine New England society, showing the changing stratification and class mobility of the period following the war. *Point of No Return* (1949), about a banker unable to halt his struggle for a better position in the upper class, has been called the shrewdest picture of American life since Sinclair Lewis' *Main Street* (1920). In a similar vein he chronicled the rise of a ruthless businessman in *Sincerely, Willis Wayde* (1955). *Women and Thomas Harrow* (1958), the life of a playwright, shows the creative artist torn between his work and the ordinary world.

Successful as a commercial writer, Marquand enjoyed even greater success as a serious author. His books are quite readable and most of them have been best sellers. While some critics find an objectionable slickness in his work, most others praise his masterly craftsmanship and his gifts for characterization, dialogue, and wry humor. In his best novels he shows discriminating taste, deep understanding of human motives, and acute powers of observation. His satire is almost always gentle. Additional works are: *Thirty Years* (1954), a collection of articles and stories; *Stopover: Tokyo* (1957), another of the Mr. Moto thrillers; and *Life at Happy Knoll* (1957).

WILLIAM LIVINGSTONE,
Staff Editor, "The Encyclopedia Americana."

MARQUE, Letters of. See PRIVATEER.

MARQUESAS ISLANDS, mär-kā′sás or **MARQUEZAS ISLANDS** (Fr. ÎLES MARQUISES), French Oceania, a group of 11 small islands (aggregate area 376 square miles), in the South Pacific about halfway between Panama and Sydney, Australia. Only 7 of the islands are inhabited: Nuku Hiva, Ua Huka, and Ua Pu (North Marquesas); Hiva Oa, Tahuata, Motane, and Fatu Hiva (South Marquesas). The seats of administration are Taiohae, on Nuku Hiva, for the North Marquesas and Atuona (or Atuana), on Hiva Oa, for the South Marquesas. The South Marquesas were discovered in July 1595 by the Spanish mariner Alvaro de Mendaña de Neyra, who named them Islas Marquesas de Mendoza in honor of the wife of his patron, the viceroy of Peru. They were visited in 1774 by Capt. James Cook.

In May 1791, Capt. Joseph Ingraham, of Boston, was the first to sight the North Marquesas, naming them Washington Islands. A month later Étienne Marchand, of Marseille, planted the French flag on Ua Pu. David Porter claimed Nuku Hiva for the United States on Nov. 19, 1813, and named it Madison Island, but a rebellion wiped out the garrison he left there. Finally, in 1842, Capt. Abel Dupetit-Thouars took formal possession of both groups of islands in the name of the king of France. The islands were under military administration until 1881 when, after the annexation of Tahiti, a civilian governor was appointed for all of French Oceania.

All the islands are of volcanic origin, with mountains dropping abruptly into the sea, the rocks being fretted into fantastic shapes. A bay at the foot of a volcano's half-collapsed cone was the scene of Herman Melville's famous narrative *Typee* (1846). The climate is warm and humid, but with occasional long periods of drought. Except in the narrow fertile valleys, each of which was formerly occupied by a different tribe, the vegetation is largely thick underbrush, with giant fern on the mountain slopes, and grass on the plateaus where wild oxen and horses roam.

The Marquesans are of the purest Polynesian type, as depicted by the French painter Paul Gauguin (1848–1903), who is buried at Atuona. Once ritualistic cannibals, they are described as proud and artistic. They are skilled fishermen. Their crops include breadfruit (the basic ingredient for the traditional Marquesan dish *popoi*), yams, coconuts, mangoes, coffee, and vanilla. Copra is exported to the extent of about 3,000 tons annually. Pop. (1951) 3,259.

Consult Handy, Edward S. C., *The Native Culture of the Marquesas Islands* (Honolulu 1923); Rollin, L., *Les Iles Marquises* (Paris 1929); Robson, Robert W., *Pacific Islands Handbook* (New York 1946), rev. ed. entitled *Pacific Islands Year Book* (Sydney, Australia, 1956); Allmon, Charles, "Shores and Sails in the South Seas," *National Geographic Magazine,* pp. 73–104, January 1950.

GINETTE TUMA.

MARQUETRY, mär′kĕ-trĭ (Fr. *marqueterie*), cabinetwork in which ornamental designs of wood, metal, shell, or ivory are inlaid in furniture and smaller articles. Derived from Italian intarsia work of the 15th and 16th centuries, it was highly developed by the Dutch in the 17th century and later by the French. The best period of English marquetry was the last half of the 18th century. See also BUHL; INLAYING.

MARQUETTE, mär-kĕt′, **Jacques** (known as PÈRE MARQUETTE), French Jesuit missionary and explorer in North America: b. Laon, France, June 1, 1637; d. near present Ludington, Mich., May 18, 1675. He was the son of Nicolas Marquette (Sieur de la Tombelle), counselor-elect of Laon, and Rose de la Salle, who was the grandaunt of St. Jean Baptiste de la Salle, the founder of the Brothers of the Christian Schools (Christian Brothers). The family had a tradition of education and public service. Marquette's sister Frances founded and directed the community of School Sisters (Marquette Sisters), and at 17 he associated himself with the Society of Jesus. After completing his novitiate at Nancy, he studied at Pont-à-Mousson and taught at Reims, Charleville, and Langres.

In 1666, Marquette was summoned to report to

Quebec, New France, for missionary duty among the Indians. He arrived there the year Jean Talon, the great intendant (the king's personal representative in New France), won the war. This victory made it possible to increase both trading and missionary activities in the west. Having arrived in New France in 1625, the Jesuits were among the most active missionaries at this time, even though they had not been the first to arrive in the Canadian field. Many of them had not only learned the languages of the Indians, but had also learned how to live among them. Marquette entered training for this work on Oct. 10, 1666, being sent to the trading station at Three Rivers, 77 miles southwest of Quebec, to study Indian languages with Père Gabriel Druillettes. In 1668 he was appointed missionary to the Ottawa tribe at Sault Ste. Marie. Later he was sent to Chequamegon Bay on the southwest shore of Lake Superior, where he served the mission of La Pointe de St. Esprit. In the summer of 1671 the outbreak of war between the Sioux and the Huron tribes forced Marquette to retreat with the Hurons and Ottawas to Mackinac Island. He established the mission of St. Ignace on the north shore of the Straits of Mackinac at that time.

In December 1672, Louis Jolliet (or Joliet; q.v.), a trader, arrived at St. Ignace with news that Marquette was to join him in exploring the great river to the west. The French had learned of the Mississippi River from the Indians, but there was uncertainty as to whether it led to the Gulf of Mexico or the Gulf of California (then called the South Sea). Jolliet had been selected for the task by Governor Frontenac on the recommendation of Jean Talon. Just why Père Claude Dablon, superior general of the Jesuit missions in New France, selected Marquette to accompany Jolliet has never been determined. During the winter and spring of 1673, Marquette and Jolliet prepared for their journey, pooling their knowledge, which had been secured from Indians who traveled through the region. According to a written account of the expedition, they made a preliminary map based on what information they had. There is good evidence to indicate that the party made careful notes during the trip and constructed a very accurate map on the basis of actual experience.

Toward the middle of May 1673 (no exact date is known) Marquette and Jolliet left with five French companions. Traveling in canoes along the northern shore of Lake Michigan and the west shore of Green Bay, the party entered the Fox River and rested at the mission of St. Francis Xavier. In early June they started traveling up the Fox, guided by Mascouten Indians, who showed them a portage between the Fox and the Wisconsin rivers. After traveling 118 miles down the Wisconsin, they reached the Mississippi River on June 17. They had traveled 608 miles since leaving Sault Ste. Marie. Although Marquette christened the great river Rivière de la Conception, its Indian name (Missi Sipi) persisted.

The first white men on the upper Mississippi, the Marquette-Jolliet expedition explored it almost as far as the mouth of the Arkansas River. Near the Iowa River the party encountered the Peoria Indians, who gave Marquette a calumet (peace pipe) three feet long as a safeguard for their journey. They saw the confluence of the Missouri and the Mississippi, where the current was so swift and the disturbance so great that the waters became muddy and would not clear. Fearful of being captured by the Spanish and eager to avoid losing the information they had gained, they turned back when the Indians told them of European settlements farther downstream. Even though they had not reached its mouth, they had learned that the Mississippi led to the Gulf of Mexico.

On the voyage back, the party traveled as far north as the Illinois River, which they followed to the Chicago portage. From Chicago they pointed their canoes northward along the west shore of Lake Michigan until they reached Sturgeon Bay, where they portaged to Green Bay, and then paddled down the east shore and entered the Fox River. In this manner they returned to the mission of St. Francis Xavier. Why the party went to this mission rather than to Sault Ste. Marie or St. Ignace, where Marquette had a mission, is not known. It is possible that Marquette's health had begun to fail after the strenuous journey of more than 2,900 miles.

Marquette spent the winter of 1673–1674 at St. Francis Xavier. By May 1674 he was quite ill, but during the summer he wrote to his superior, Père Henri Nouvel, asking for an assignment for the coming winter. While awaiting a reply, he prepared whatever record he had of his journey and sent it to Père Dablon, who prepared the annual *Jesuit Relations* for publication. Dablon requested the information because the official record of the expedition was lost when Jolliet's canoe capsized in the Lachine Rapids near Montreal when the trader was returning to Quebec. The nature of Marquette's report to Dablon is a subject of controversy. Some historians contend that Marquette sent his own journal and related papers to Dablon; others assert that Marquette had kept no journal of his own, but merely a copy of Jolliet's. Most agree that Dablon's account of the expedition, as published in the *Jesuit Relations,* was not written by Marquette even though it was composed in the first person. Dablon probably rewrote what he secured from Marquette in the light of information from Jolliet.

At his own request Marquette was allowed to return to Illinois and work at Kaskaskia, an Indian village on the Illinois River which he had visited while returning from the expedition. In the company of Pierre Porteret and Jacques Largilier, two men sent by Père Nouvel, Marquette retraced the route he had pursued earlier. They arrived at the Chicago portage on Dec. 4, 1674, and spent the winter in a temporary shelter because Marquette was too ill to continue. A spring flood swept away their quarters on March 30, forcing them to move to Kaskaskia. Marquette arrived there shortly before Easter Sunday, April 14. His health deteriorated, and after only three weeks with the Illinois Indians he decided to return to Sault Ste. Marie.

With his two companions and a group of Indians, he once again made his way to the Chicago portage. This time he turned the canoes along the east shore of Lake Michigan. Marquette died near the present site of Ludington, Mich. (q.v.), May 18, 1675. He was buried there, but later a group of Indians brought to St. Ignace some remains, which they explained were those of the missionary. These were placed in the chapel at St. Ignace, which was destroyed by fire in 1706. However, in 1877 the grave was discovered, and a marker was erected in 1882.

Although he was in North America less than 10 years, Marquette achieved a great reputation because of the popular reception of his journal which contained much geographical and ethnological information on the valley of the Mississippi and its tributaries. An important result of his expedition was that it stimulated settlement of the region he explored and pushed back the frontier. Because of this and the manner of his death, he became the best known of the Jesuit missionaries in the United States and Canada. In the area where he worked, a diocese, a railroad, a university, cities, counties, and various geographical features have since been named for him, and the state of Wisconsin has placed a statue of him in the Capitol at Washington, D.C. See also AMERICA, DISCOVERY AND EXPLORATION OF—*Opening of the Mississippi Basin.*

Consult Thwaites, Reuben G., *The Jesuit Relations and Allied Documents,* vol. 59 (Cleveland, Ohio, 1900); Steck, Francis B., *The Jolliet-Marquette Expedition,* rev. ed. (Quincy, Ill., 1928); Delanglez, Jean, *The Life and Voyages of Louis Jolliet* (Chicago 1948).

ABRAHAM P. NASATIR,
Professor of History, San Diego State College.

MARQUETTE, mär-kĕt′, city, Michigan, Marquette County seat, located in the Upper Peninsula midway between Sault Ste. Marie and Ironwood, on the south shore of Lake Superior. At an altitude of 620 feet, it is on both state and federal highways. It is an important lake port for shipping iron ore and is also the rail center for a large mining, lumbering, and agricultural region. It is served by the following railroads: the Duluth, South Shore and Atlantic; Lake Superior and Ishpeming; Chicago and North Western; and the Chicago, Milwaukee, St. Paul and Pacific.

When an iron mine was opened in 1846 near Negaunee, the natural harbor at the mouth of the Carp River (at the site of the present city of Marquette) was chosen as a shipping point. Construction of a village began there in 1849, and the following year it was named for Jacques Marquette (q.v.), who contributed to the opening of the Northwest Territory. Incorporated as a village in 1859, Marquette was largely destroyed by fire in 1868. It was quickly rebuilt and incorporated as a city in 1871.

Shipping iron ore is still important to Marquette, and the ore docks are one of its most impressive sights. Other industries are the production of mining and railroad equipment, woodenware, lumber, chemicals, food products, and clothing. It is also the center of a resort area. Points of interest in the city include Presque Isle Park and Northern Michigan College. A branch of the Michigan state prison is also located there, and Marquette State Park is about five miles away. Municipal government is of the commission-manager type. Pop. 19,824.

MARQUETTE UNIVERSITY, a private, coeducational university in Milwaukee, Wis., administered by the Society of Jesus. It was chartered in 1864, and instruction began in 1881. It received university status in 1907. Located within walking distance of downtown Milwaukee, it includes 10 schools and colleges: liberal arts, business administration, journalism, nursing, speech, engineering, law, medicine, dentistry, and the graduate school. Degree programs in physical therapy and medical technology are offered through the school of medicine, and degrees and diplomas in dental hygiene are granted by the dental school. On the campus there are units of both Army and Navy Reserve Officer Training Corps.

Marquette's dental clinic is one of the largest in the United States, and speech correction services are provided for adults, children, and preschool youngsters in greater Milwaukee. Permanent centers of research include the Bureau of Business and Economic Research, the Institute of German Affairs, and the Institute of the Catholic Press (a research division of the college of journalism). The Catholic School Press Association has its headquarters at Marquette. Research projects in medicine, dentistry, and other health-related sciences have won the approval and support of such groups as the American Cancer Society, the Atomic Energy Commission, the United States Public Health Service, and the National Foundation for Infantile Paralysis.

MARQUIS, mär′kwĭs, **Don** (in full DONALD ROBERT PERRY MARQUIS), American author and humorist: b. Walnut, Ill., July 29, 1878; d. Forest Hills, N.Y., Dec. 30, 1937. After completing high school and a year of college, he tried many varied occupations before going to Atlanta, Ga., where he had his first important writing jobs, on the *Constitution* (1902–1907) and *The Uncle Remus Magazine* (1907–1909). He then went to New York, where he won fame as a newspaper columnist, writing "The Sun Dial" for the *Sun* (1912–1922) and "The Lantern" for the *Tribune* (1922–1925). To express his opinions on contemporary life he invented for these columns such humorous characters as Captain Fitzurse, a bragging adventurer; Clem Hawley, a philosophical drunkard; and Hermione and her Little Group of Serious Thinkers. The best known of his creations were "mehitabel the cat" and her friend "archy the cockroach," who supposedly wrote poetry on Marquis' typewriter at night, but lacked the strength to make capital letters. He is remembered chiefly for these characters, and his book *archy and mehitabel* (1927) is still widely read.

Marquis was quite successful as a humorist. His play *The Old Soak,* based on Clem Hawley, was favorably received when produced in New York in 1922. His collections of light verse were popular; they included *Noah an' Jonah an' Cap'n John Smith* (1921); *Sonnets to a Red-Haired Lady* . . . (1922); and *Love Sonnets of a Cave Man* (1928). The biting satire which characterized many of his newspaper columns is also present in his volumes of stories, such as *The Revolt of the Oyster* (1922); *A Variety of People* (1929); and *Chapters for the Orthodox* (1934). As a serious author, however, he was not very successful. The response was poor to the plays *The Dark Hours* (1924) and *Out of the Sea* (1927) and to his serious poetry, *Poems and Portraits* (1922) and *The Awakening* (1924). When he died, he left an uncompleted autobiographical novel, *Sons of the Puritans,* which was published posthumously in 1939.

MARQUIS, Thomas Guthrie, Canadian educator and author: b. Chatham, New Brunswick, Canada, July 4, 1864; d. Toronto, Ontario, April 1, 1936. After graduating from Queen's University, Kingston, in 1889, Marquis began a school-teaching career, rising in 1896 to the principalship of the Collegiate Institute at Brockville, Ontario. By 1901 he had tried his hand at writing, and having published five books which received some attention, he decided to devote his entire time to this field. His first major job was editing a dictionary of Canadian biography called *Builders of Canada from Cartier to Laurier* (1903), but his most notable editorial work was the production of *Canada and Its Provinces,* 22 vols. (1914–1915). His own works range through the Canadian historical field from *Marguerite de Roberval* (1899), a novel of the days of Cartier, to *Brock, the Hero of Upper Canada* (1912), a biography of Sir Isaac Brock.

MARQUIS, mär′kwĭs, or **MARQUESS** (It. MARCHESE; Fr. MARQUIS; Ger. MARKGRAF), an hereditary title of nobility, next in rank after duke and above earl. Originally officers in charge of the marches or frontier regions of a kingdom were known as marchiones. Later the title became known as marquis and was honorary. It was first used in England in the year 1385 when Richard II created his favorite, Robert de Vere, the 9th earl of Oxford, marquis of Dublin. In 1397 the same king raised John Beaufort, earl of Somerset, to the rank of marquis, a dignity which he afterwards refused to bear because of its being an innovation. The title fell into disuse until the reign of Henry VI who revived it in 1442, but it was used only rarely until 1551 when Edward VI created the marquisate of Winchester, the oldest surviving title of this rank. In present-day England the preferred form of the title is marquess (fem. marchioness).

MARR, mär, **Carl von,** German-American painter: b. Milwaukee, Wis., Feb. 14, 1858; d. Munich, Germany, July 10, 1936. After studies at the Weimar and Berlin academies he was appointed professor of painting at Munich's Academy of Fine Arts in 1893, became its director in 1919, and retired in 1925. His *Dusk* hangs in the Museum of Art, Toledo, Ohio, and *Gossip* in the Metropolitan Museum, New York City. Other works are in Continental galleries. He was decorated by Bavaria, Prussia, and Italy.

MARRAKECH, mȧ-rä′kĕsh, or **MARRA-KESH** (sometimes erroneously called MOROCCO), city, French Morocco, Africa located near the Tensift River, at an elevation of about 1,500 feet, on the western slopes of the Grand Atlas Mountains. It is connected by rail with Safi, its Atlantic port some 85 miles to the northwest; Casablanca, about 150 rail miles to the north; Rabat, and other coastal cities. Its airport dates from 1940.

The sultan's palace on the south side of the city, together with the large, central square and market place, and numerous gardens, fountains, tombs, and mosques (the best known being the 12th century Kutubyyah, or Koutoubia, also called Mosque of the Scribes, with its 220-foot tower) add color to the picturesque, medieval old city whose surrounding wall, with its numerous gateways, is now in ruins. The modern city, dating from 1913, has been constructed about one and one-half miles from the old city.

Under modern French administration, agricultural and commercial training schools are operated, and much encouragement has been given to the revival of ancient arts and the development of agriculture and industry. Manufactures include leather goods, carpets, and building materials; other industries are fruit, vegetable, and palm fiber processing; flour milling; and wool spinning. Date palm groves circle the city, and copper, lead, and graphite are mined nearby.

The site of Marrakech was chosen in 1062 by Yūsuf ibn-Tāshfin, grandson of 'Abdallāh ibn-Yāsīn, first ruler of the Almoravid dynasty. It was made the capital of Morocco in 1147 during the rule of the Almohades, who built many of its best structures. Thereafter, under the Merinides, Fez became the sultan's favorite residence, while under Sa'adi (Sherifian) rule, Marrakech again became the capital. Subsequently it served occasionally as the chief residence of the sultan. In September 1912, the city was occupied by the French under Col. Charles M. E. Mangin. It became the site of a United States airbase in World War II, following Allied landings in Morocco.

Once famed as a center of Islamic culture, the city attained its greatest importance in the 13th century when its population is believed to have reached 700,000. Thereafter, as a result of civil wars and Berber attacks, it suffered a decline, but the modern city has grown rapidly. Pop. (1936) 190,314; (1949 est.) 239,200.

MARRELLA, mȧ-rĕl′ȧ, a genus of fossil Crustacea found in the Cambrian shales of British Columbia.

MARRIAGE, History of (from Lat. *maritare,* from *maritus,* husband). In the natural history sense, marriage may be defined as a more or less durable union between one or more husbands and one or more wives, sanctioned by society and lasting until after the birth and rearing of offspring. In the legal sense, marriage is a contract between one or more males and one or more females for the establishment of a family (q.v.).

Origin and Social Function of Marriage.— Some scholars are inclined to trace the origin of marriage to pairing arrangements of animals below man. Studies reveal that a more or less permanent association between one or more males and one or more females is common among birds and higher mammals. It especially characterizes the anthropoid apes, with the association of the chimpanzee·being monogamous and durable. These more or less permanent associations between other than human animals are not marriages, for animals have no society to sanction them. Marriage involves social sanctions, and these social sanctions are in the customs and traditions of a given group. The customs and traditions of any form of marriage arise in the same way as other types of customs and traditions. Their origins, for the most part, are lost in the antiquity of the past.

The primary function of marriage is to regulate the relations between the sexes. In most societies a more or less permanent union between one or more males and one or more females is valued as a secure situation in which children can be reared.

Practically all forms of marriage are found, if one includes all societies and all historical times. While the original form of marriage is lost in the oblivion of the prehistorical period, it is safe to say that during historical times some form of marriage has been present in all societies. Whether a form of communal or group marriage has ever existed among any people has been debated by anthropologists and sociologists. The nearest approach to this is seen in the punaluan family of the Polynesians, the marriage of a group of brothers with a group of sisters. This arrangement is rare even among the Polynesians. Most scholars are unwilling to guess as to the historical origin of group marriage or any other form of marriage. Setting group marriage to one side as exceptional, the main forms of marriage are polygyny, polyandry, and monogamy.

Polygyny.—The union of one husband and two or more wives is known as polygyny. Popularly this is generally called polygamy, but this is incorrect for polygamy means multiple mates and applies to both polygyny and polyandry. In general, polygyny presupposes a considerable accumulation of wealth and is therefore very rarely practiced. It seems to have been an accompaniment of the development of a predominantly militant life and of slavery. Where polygyny is practiced, therefore, it is confined largely to the wealthy and the ruling classes, as only these can afford the luxury of having more than one wife. Polygyny is practiced today in some countries, but only by a very small per cent of the population. The remainder practices monogamy, for the number of males and females in a given population under normal conditions is relatively equal, and consequently the majority of marriages are necessarily monogamous.

Polygyny, as has been indicated, can be traced to two main factors: military and economic activities. In early warfare, such as that of the American Indians, it was a common practice to kill the men and carry off the women for secondary wives. Extra wives meant not only an outward sign of a man's wealth, but a means of increasing the wealth that a man already had. For example, among the Blackfoot Indians polygyny, which had been practiced in a limited way by chiefs and other influential persons, was greatly expanded when the fur trade changed from beaver to buffalo robes. Women almost exclusively tanned buffalo skins, and, consequently, the enlarged market for these led to a need for more female workers, and this need was met by getting more wives.

The practice of polygyny has been widespread among practically all people, even though the numbers involved have been small. Where it lacked legal sanction it frequently existed in the more or less illegal form of concubinage (q.v.), such as among the Chinese up to the beginning of the 20th century. In many cases it has received the explicit sanction of religion as in the cases of Mohammedanism and Mormonism. But among all people it has tended to die out. This has been due in large part to the diffusion of Western European culture and particularly to the spread of Christianity. The ethical views of Christianity have been against other forms of marriage than monogamy.

Polyandry.—The union of one woman with several men is a rare form of marriage found practically only in Tibet and among some of the mountain tribes of India, though within historic times it existed in Arabia. Apparently polyandry has never been a wide-spread form of marriage. There is no reason for supposing, as did John Ferguson McLennan, that in primitive times it was universal. On the contrary, it seems to exist only under certain economic and social conditions. Thus the difficulty of one man supporting a family has in the barren regions of Tibet led to the de-

velopment of polyandry. In the same region there seems to be a scarcity of women, which also favors the practice of polyandry.

The most common form of polyandry is the fraternal or Tibetan form, in which a group of brothers have a common wife, the oldest brother being the head of the household and the putative father of all the children. Among the Nairs of India, however, a non-fraternal form of polyandry exists.

Polyandry generally does not mean that one woman has the privilege of having more than one husband. It means that several men combine and share one wife. This is the case in Tibet where it is used as a way of keeping the land intact and passing it on to the next generation.

Polyandry, in contrast to polygyny, has developed among the lower social strata. This is the case of both Tibetans and Marquesans where the poor may be able to afford but one wife for two or more brothers. Thus they are able to establish a single conjugal group maintained in the interests of the wife's children.

Monogamy.—Polygny and polyandry, as we have seen, always have been exceptional forms of marriage. The prevalent form of marriage among all people today, and probably among people in all times, has been some form of monogamy, or the union of one man and one woman. This has been so by necessity, for under normal conditions the number of males and females in any given society is relatively equal. Economic conditions also have rarely made it possible to support more than one wife and her children. Besides such biological and economic reasons for the existence of monogamy, it appears to be more favorable to the care and upbringing of children. Under monogamy both the husband and wife commonly unite in the care and training of the child.

In many countries where monogamy is the socially sanctioned and legal form of marriage, there exists successive polygyny and polyandry which is permitted by the device of divorce. This is the case in the United States, where two or three husbands or wives in a lifetime is not exceptional. While this is legal, it does violate the principle of monogamy.

The Marriage Ceremony.—Among all people, both preliterate (those who have no written language) and literate, legal marriage is usually accompanied by some form of ceremony which expresses the sanction of the group upon the union. This ceremony is usually of ritualistic or religious character; in a few peoples it is apparently purely social. Betrothal (q.v.) is also frequently an occasion for some sort of religious or social ceremony.

Freedom of Choice in Marriage.—Edward A. Westermarck presents considerable evidence to show that among preliterate people marriage was originally based on the mutual attraction and consent of the parties. Almost always the male was the wooer, but the female, by having the right to accept or reject a lover, played the decisive role in mate selection. In preliterate societies the role of wife capture and wife purchase is regarded as exceptional and of minor importance. Thus it can be assumed that marriage began in free choice, and that wife capture and wife purchase were later developments.

By free choice we do not mean that it was necessarily free choice by individuals. The parental family often either chose the mate for the son or daughter or was a dominant factor in mate selection. This, of course, is the way it is today in most western European countries.

Marriage by Capture and by Purchase.— Among predatory and warlike tribes marriage by capture is often common; indeed, on account of the social and military honor attached to wife capture, it sometimes comes to be the favorite form of marriage. We know of no people, however, among whom wives are regularly captured. Manifestly such a social state would be practically impossible, even though wife capture was socially favored.

The cave man probably wrested his mate from a neighbor on the basis of brute strength and retained her by physical power. The relationship between the cave man and his mate was certainly not regulated by formal law. Little by little, as tribes and clans developed, changes in wife capture occurred. Raiding and capturing wives from other clans took the place of capturing one's neighbor's wife or daughter. The practice of "standing up" with the bride and groom evolved out of the practice of wife capture. After a mate had been seized, the friends of the bridegroom stood by to ward off the enraged kinfolk of the bride. Even in the early part of the 20th century, wedding guests in south Russia engaged in mock fights in which friends of the bride attacked those of the groom. When harmony was restored after this symbolic battle, the entire company proceeded with the service. The ring, although it has acquired a highly dignified symbolic character today, in early times was used to tie up a girl who had been captured. It was placed around her ankle or above her knee, and prevented her from escaping. In Africa the ring is placed around the neck in some tribes, and in others, through the nose. But wherever placed, the ring is supposed to make the groom sure of the bride. Incidentally, it is a growing custom in western European countries for both the husband and the wife to wear a ring. This is a reflection of the gradual emancipation of women and the general movement away from the patriarchical marriage to the companionship form.

Much more common than wife capture, but at a much later stage of cultural development, was wife purchase. This occurred particularly in preliterate societies with the development of slavery and the idea of property in persons. It was particularly instrumental in developing polygyny and the patriarchal form of the family. Many survivals of wife purchase exist among even relatively contemporary peoples.

The prospective husband paid for the privilege of carrying his bride away. Sometimes the abduction came first, the purchase price subsequently being levied to atone the "offense" and disguised as a fine. In some instances, as under very early Roman law, the woman was adopted; she then came under the "fatherly" power of the husband, and theoretically became his daughter. In all cases the wife became the property of her husband and, at the worst, she was his drudge or slave. Still the actual condition of the wife was not so hard as might be implied from her legal status, or lack of it. The injunction to obey the father was coupled with the injunction to honor the mother.

In the great Oriental monarchies of antiquity marriages were undisguisedly commercial transactions. Even then the bought wife of a citizen of Babylon was the manager of her husband's house, consulted with him in serious matters of business and even in affairs of state if he happened to be a public official.

The contractual or purchase marriage became symbolic and dramatic. The pledge given by the wooer to bind the bargain might originally have been a cow (domestic animals were real money; cattle or chattels and *pecunias* were words of identical meaning). This pledge eventually was represented by a gift to the bride—a bracelet, jewel, or other token. Sometimes a wooer made payment in personal services as in the Biblical story which relates how Jacob tended Laban's sheep for seven years in order to purchase Rachel. The bride usually received from her father a dowry or dos, which passed to the husband and remained under his control during the duration of the marriage. Among the Semites and Orientals marriage was terminated by divorce at the will of the husband. Among the early Romans marriage could be concluded at the will of the wife's father or by mutual consent. In either case the bride's dowry was returned.

Child Marriage.— Another result of wife capture and wife purchase among some peoples was the practice which we know as child marriage, that is, the uniting in formal marriage of children under 15 years of age, usually the marriage of a girl under 15 with a much older man. It developed, especially in India, under the influence of the caste system and the custom of wife purchase. More than one half of the total female population of India were married before 15 years of age, sometimes while they were mere infants. In the western provinces of India the girl remained at home with her parents until sexual maturity was reached; but in Bengal, girls commenced their married life at the age of nine years. The practice continues, as it is supported by the higher as well as by the lower Hindu castes.

Exogamy and Endogamy.— Exogamy is defined as marriage outside the group and endogamy as marriage within the group. Among practically all peoples, custom forbids the marriage of very near kin. A limited number of preliterate people do not forbid the marriage of brothers and sisters, but all view with disapproval sexual relations between parents and children. Sexual relations between brothers and sisters and parents and children are known as incest. Indeed, people not only condemn sexual relations between members of the immediate family but forbid it between other less related persons. In preliterate societies marriage between the same clan or totem group is not infrequently forbidden.

Exogamy and endogamy are almost always correlated, in that marriage outside an immediate group implies marriage within another specified group. Thus in the clan or totemic stage of social organization, which existed among most of the North American Indians at the time of their discovery, a man must take a wife outside of his clan or totem-kin group, but usually must marry within his tribe or related tribes.

The causes of such customs of exogamy and endogamy have been much debated. McLennan held that exogamy was the outgrowth of the custom of female infanticide, but there is little or no evidence in support of such a theory. Westermarck's explanation was that exogamy arose from the extension to the whole clan of the natural instinct of aversion to incest. It may be pointed out, however, that exogamy and endogamy are not customs peculiar to preliterate people. Similar rules are found regarding forbidden degrees of relationship among contemporary people. While there is no evidence to support the view that there is a natural aversion to incest, some evidence exists that there is an attraction between persons of the opposite sex who are relatively strange and unfamiliar. Among all peoples this naturally leads to marriage outside the close social group; and among preliterate people all members of a clan are regarded as practically the same as very near relatives.

Marriage Among the European Peoples.— Among the early Aryan people of Europe marriage was universally regarded, so far as we can discover, as a religious bond, since their family life was based upon ancestor worship. This early Aryan view of marriage gave way in later Rome to the view that marriage was a private contract to be made and dissolved by the parties at their pleasure. The early Christian Church combated this view of the marriage relation and sought to restore the view that marriage was a religious bond, which it finally did by making marriage one of the sacraments of the church. It was forced, however, still to recognize that consent or contract was the essential means of entering the marriage relation. "Consent marriages" continued to be recognized, therefore, though they could not be broken except through the authority of the church. The Protestant reformers put forth the idea that marriage was a civil relation, rather than a religious bond or sacrament, to be created by the state and broken by the state. In reaction to this view the Roman Catholic Council of Trent in 1563 declared that a valid marriage could only be created by the church and only annulled by the church. This still remains the Roman Catholic view of marriage. The view that marriage is a private contract, to be created and broken by individuals as any other contract, has shown a tendency to revive in modern nations among many elements of their population. The present problem of the family, therefore, centers about the question of divorce and the toleration of other forms of marriage than that of permanent marriage.

The two theories of marriage—as (1) a sacrament plus a permanent civil contract, and (2) as a civil contract as long as the contracting parties desire—are held side by side by different elements of the populations of modern nations. While one cannot be sure which form of competing theory of marriage will survive and be compatible with the standards of the future, the current trend appears to be toward the view that marriage is a contract like any other civil contract. Consequently, its permanence depends on the desires of the contracting parties.

See also Divorce; Mixed Marriage; Polyandry; Polygamy.

Bibliography.—Westermarck, Edward A., *The History of Human Marriage* (London 1891); 3d ed. (London 1901); Howard, George E., *History of Matrimonial Institutions*, 3 vols. (Chicago 1904); Thomas, William I., *Primitive Behavior* (New York 1937); Burgess, E. W., and Locke, H. J., *The Family*, 2d ed. (New York 1953).

Harvey J. Locke,
James A. Peterson,
Department of Sociology, University of Southern California.

MARRIAGE OF FIGARO, The (LE Mariage de Figaro), a play by Pierre Augustin Caron de Beaumarchais. His most popular play, and possibly the wittiest and politically the most effective, *The Marriage of Figaro* was ready for the stage in 1778 three years after the success of *The Barber of Seville* (q.v.), to which it was a sequel. But even while in manuscript, it became the center of intensely active and complicated political intrigue. Louis XVI rightly discerned in it danger to his throne, and it was not publicly presented till 1784, when it achieved a success until then unparalleled, being by strange irony most applauded by the aristocratic class whose ruin it portended. To Napoleon, after the event, it seemed "the Revolution already in action," and it certainly contributed greatly to hasten and provoke, by its leveling tendencies, the disintegration of the conventions and even the foundations of the old social regime, though this seems the result rather of Beaumarchais' delight in his own wit, of mere wantonness, than of a realization whither his work was tending or of any deliberate revolutionary purpose. Figaro in *The Marriage* is still the light-hearted, versatile, philosophic scapegrace of *The Barber;* Almaviva and Rosine are what that play would lead one to expect they would be after some matrimonial disillusion. Of the new characters Suzanne, on whom Almaviva has set his vagrant fancy and Figaro his heart, is genially conceived; and Chérubin, the page and disquietingly precocious gallant, was a really daring creation, provoking reprobation and inviting controversy. Figaro is successful in defending his beloved from the wiles of Almaviva, but it has been not unjustly said that if the object of comedy is to make vice ridiculous or odious or contemptible, *The Marriage* can hardly claim to attain it. Universal mockery, supremely vivacious, a wit whose brilliancy puts morality off its guard, ethically mar a drama whose sustained excellence in dialogue had been hardly attained even by Molière. Beaumarchais' play furnished the text for Mozart's opera *Le Nozze di Figaro* (1786; see Figaro, Le Nozze di). The best edition of *Le Mariage de Figaro* is found in *Théâtre complet de Beaumarchais,* edited by Georges d'Heylli and F. de Marescot (Paris 1869–1871).

Benjamin Wells.

MARRIAGES, Law of. The social evolution of the family from prehistoric to modern times is mirrored in specific trends in marriage laws. Marriage in early times, of course, was regulated by custom rather than by formal laws, and law today is in large part the verbal codification of accepted social practices. The following discussion includes description of (1) early marriage laws of the Hebrews, the Romans, and the Teutonic barbarians; (2) early Christian influence on marriage laws; and (3) modern marriage laws of China, the USSR, and the United States.

EARLY MARRIAGE LAWS

In historic times the articulation of legal codes in such documents as the *Code of Hammurabi,* the *Decalogue,* the *Twelve Tables,* the *Laws of the Republic,* the *Lex Romana Visigothorum,* and the *Leges Barbarorum* gives a somewhat more accurate rendition of marriage codes than we have for periods for which we have no such records. There was great diversity in these laws. Monogamy and polygamy existed side by side, but all codes seemed to have modified the severity of patriarchical controls over wife and children, particularly as the result of the impact of early Christian institutions and of the Reformation.

Hebrew Law.—In contrast to early Aryan practice, the Semites gave legal sanction to plurality of wives. Solomon need only be recalled to enforce this observation. Children born to free men of their slave women or handmaidens were considered legitimate. The strictest mandates covered sexual contacts. Adultery, intercourse during the menses, intercourse with mother, daughter-in-law, another of the same sex, mother of a wife, or beast were punishable by death. If there were prohibitions regarding marriage to relatives, there were also restrictions on endogamy in marriage. Moses commanded that girls should marry "only to the family of the tribe of their father." Virginity of brides was prized and adjudication of disputes over virginity was early rather carefully spelled out in the law. In preprophetic times all that a man had to do if his wife "found no favor in his eyes" was to write her a bill of divorcement and send her out of his house. He might not, however, remarry her. When a man had taken a new bride he was enjoined from going to war or entering into a new business for one year because "he should be free at home one year, and shall cheer up his wife which he hath taken."

Later problems faced by the Hebrews involved losing their individuality because of a growing practice of interfaith and internationality marriage. Both Ezra and Nehemiah faced this threat by vigorous and harsh statutes dissolving marriages involving women who were not Hebrew. To smite or to curse the father or the mother resulted in death. The child who would not obey could be stoned to death by the parent. Divorce came to be much restricted; grounds for divorce were carefully defined and a couple had to counsel with selected rabbis before the divorce was granted. Further restrictions on marrying outside the faith were promulgated and a man or woman were regarded as dead if they did so.

Roman Law.—Roman law recognized three kinds of formal marriage in the earlier period of Roman history. The religious form, *confarreatio* (q.v.) had to be solemnized by the *pontifex maximus* in the presence of 10 witnesses and was reserved by the old patrician families to themselves. This solemn form of marriage could be annulled only by very tremendous rites, which represented the death of the contracting parties (*diffarreatio*). Unlike the early Hebrew law, polygamy had been prohibited by praetorian edict with great severity. Among the plebeians marriages took the form of a purchase, *coemptio,* which is defined by Gaius (2d century A.D.) as a mutual mock sale of the parties whereby the wife was freed from her tutelage to her male relatives. The third form, *usus,* was prevalent only in the later period when it pervaded all social ranks. In contrast to the severe control which *confarreatio* or *coemptio* gave to the husband over the wife, *usus* held the husband's marital despotism in abeyance, for in this form of union a perfect matrimonial bond was not established until after continued cohabitation for an entire year. Thus a wife had but to absent herself from the home for one day in each year to indefinitely postpone and defeat the acquirement of tutelary and possessory rights by the husband. By contracting a *usus* marriage the women of Rome evaded the tyranny of the earlier law and enjoyed a freedom of person and property such as they have not enjoyed until very recent years. Most important of all was the establishment of the principle that marriage rested upon the consent of the parties and might, therefore, be dissolved at the pleasure of either party. To hinder a separation when a consensus had ceased to exist came to be regarded as *contra bonos mores,* or "immoral."

As to incestuous marriages, the Roman law extended the laws of Moses (which prohibited marriages between brothers and sisters, and of uncles and aunts with nephews and nieces) to connections formed by adoption or by affinity; hence a union with an adopted brother or sister was regarded as evil as in the case of blood. Cousins were allowed to marry. In fact, the Emperors Arcadius and Flavius Honorius married cousins. The Justinian Code furthermore prohibited the marriage of freeman with slave, of senators with actors or with persons of infamous occupations, such as procurers (*lenones*), tavern keepers, or daughters of tavern keepers and gladiators.

Teutonic Marriage Law.—Early Teutonic marriage law did not differ greatly in fundamentals from that of Rome. Though disguised by ceremonials, the transaction was essentially a barter. In its original form the father was given a certain amount for his daughter, depending upon the circumstances and status of the families involved. The contract was made firm, just like any other bargain, by a pledge or part payment. This pledge, the *vadium,* eventually took the form of an ornament of some value presented to the bride at the betrothal and was the predecessor of the modern practice of giving an engagement ring. Some early Teutonic laws sanctioned the "robber marriage" which was nothing more than an abduction, or, if the bride was willing, an elopement. The penalty the abductor was required to pay to the "outraged father" was usually identical in amount with the prescribed settlement or dower in the more conventional type of wedding—indicating that barter weddings and robber marriages stood on a somewhat equal footing of respectability. The Teutonic maiden when given in marriage was usually provided with equipment for housekeeping and a dowry. If it were assumed that an abducted bride would receive neither, it is understandable why some abductions were accomplished with the connivance of the bride's family.

The idea of a threefold stage in the process of acquiring a wife—the troth plighting, the wedding, and the consummation—has persisted in legal phraseology and conceptions.

The Teutonic reverence for the sanctity of marriage is reflected in the barbaric codes. Under the Burgundian and Visigothic law, adultery was punishable by death, but in Saxony the adulteress must hang herself, after which she was burned and her lover was hung over the blazing pile; as an alternative she was scourged or cut to pieces with knives by the women of her village until she was dead. Barbaric law followed the Roman in that it prohibited marriages between freeman and slave, but the penalties were more severe—in Lombardy and Burgundy such unions resulted in death. Polygamy and concubinage were forbidden. Incest was extended to the sixth degree of relationship among the Visigoths.

EARLY CHRISTIAN INFLUENCE ON MARRIAGE LAW

From the very outset Christianity opposed the looseness of the later Roman law respecting marriage and divorce. The church declared marriage to be a sacrament and, in consequence, enunciated the doctrine of the indissolubility of the matrimonial union except by death. Eventually the church used its growing power to establish a universal marriage law throughout the Christian world. The canonists accepted the principle of the Roman law that the consent of the parties is essential to the making of a legal contract of marriage. The lack of free consent, or legal incapacity of one or both of the parties (impotency, insanity, or minority), were declared insuperable impediments to the execution of the contract, and grounds for its annulment if executed. The canonists also carried over from Roman law the system of the age of consent (14 years for males and 12 for females) but they rejected the requirement for parental consent. In seeming contradiction to this principle, the father still "gave away" the bride in the marriage service.

Formidable impediments to marriage within the family, even between very distant relations, were created by the canons of consanguinity and affinity. These prohibitions, conforming to a reasonable interpretation of the older Levitical canon, were not without positive effect. The practice of intermarriage within the family had become prevalent not only among the nobility but in all social classes. Near relationship in blood or by marriage might exist among entire populations of small communes because conditions of life did not encourage travel or changes of habitation. By compelling men and women to seek mates outside their own limited circle, the church, in effect, stimulated mobility and thereby increased contact with outsiders.

The Reformation and Marriage Law.—The Reformation introduced important changes in marriage law. The Council of Trent pronounced clandestine marriages to be null and void and added the requirement of the presence of two witnesses at all weddings. The Protestant ecclesiastical law denied the indissolubility of the matrimonial bond and regarded all betrothals as *sponsalia per verba de praesenti*. Luther stated that "I will" did not express future intention but a present purpose, so that any promise to marry followed by cohabitation was to be considered a valid marriage. Indeed, cohabitation in conjugal relation was quite generally regarded as presumptive evidence of a marriage *per verba de praesenti*.

The Church of England did not accept the stand of the Reformation and continued to insist upon the indissolubility of the matrimonial bond. It also increased its control of marriage. By acts of Parliament in the second half of the 18th century and the first part of the 19th century, church weddings were required in all cases and all marriages not thus celebrated were declared void. Curiously, informal marriages not performed by the clergy in a church were still valid in Scotland and this explains how Gretna Green became a mecca for runaway lovers. While a statute of Henry the VIII permitted marriages between first cousins and abolished all disabilities growing out of affinities or relationships by marriage, the Church of England continued to oppose a marriage involving a deceased wife's sister.

MODERN MARRIAGE LAWS

Modern marriage law is, as we see by the preceding sections, the product of Hebraic, Roman, and Teutonic practices, modified first by the impact of Christianity, and more recently by industrialization, mobility, and social changes. Modern law regards marriage primarily as a civil relation. Most of the European codes make a civil marriage and its registration in the public records indispensable. A relation established by the civil authority can be dissolved by the same authority. Modern law has generally raised the age of consent and has made such consent necessary to the validity of the marriage of minors. All marriages must now be publicly contracted. In England such publicity may be obtained either through the Established Church or other religious denominations, or in accord with rules made by the public registrar or by statute. In most countries betrothal is now considered merely a promise to marry, and action to recover damages for breach of promise to marry is not permitted. The dissolubility of marriages by consent of the parties is generally disallowed, but almost everywhere divorces may be obtained by process of law. Examples of changes in modern marriage laws are cited for China, the USSR, and the United States.

CHINESE MARRIAGE LAW

For 4,000 years the extended-patriarchal-family system of China was characterized by a patriarchal organization, by filial piety, and by familism. This resulted in parental choice of mate, concubinage, the subordination of both females and children, child betrothal, and a system of gifts to the bride's parents that seemed characteristically like bride purchase. Marriage laws were incidental and simply served to reinforce the powerful group sanctions which made deviation from these practices impossible. In modern times industrialization and education have caused revolt against these norms in some places so that some organizations, such as the antimatrimonial associations which were formed in Kwangtung, indicate the revolt of Chinese women against their subordinate role in marriage and life.

In 1950 the Central People's Government Council of Communist China issued the new "Marriage Laws of the People's Republic of China." These laws strive to abolish in one code all of the above characteristics of the family. Marriage is now to be based on the mutual consent of both parties but only after the man has reached 20 years of age and the woman is at least 18. Marriages are prohibited between brother and sister, half-brother and sister, and lineal relatives by blood. Marriages are prohibited if one of the partners is impotent, has venereal disease, mental disorder, or leprosy.

Both husband and wife are guaranteed free choice of occupation, equal rights in possession and management of private property, and inheritance of each other's property. The couple is enjoined by law to enjoy equal status in the home and to live there with love and in harmony with each other.

Children must be supported and educated, and later they must support their parents. Infanticide is prohibited. Children born out of wedlock are guaranteed support by the father, if paternity is established, until they are 18 years of age. After divorce, each party must continue to assist the children. Divorce, however, is granted only after official efforts have been made to effect a reconciliation. As yet (in the mid-1950's) no appraisal has been made of this effort to change so radically a deeply rooted culture by legal edict. It is probable that these changes will be more popular in industrial areas, where young people had already rebelled against traditional methods of mate choice and familism, than in rural areas, where familistic roles are still strong.

RUSSIAN MARRIAGE LAW

The prerevolutionary family of the czarist period in Russia prior to 1861 lived under the terms of the Domestic Ordinance drawn up in the mid-16th century. This law stipulated that a wife should love her husband and should show "boundless compliance" to him. Such compliance was indicated in her inability to hold property or even to travel without her husband's consent; or in the obligation of the husband to beat his recalcitrant wife with a whip. (The whip was furnished, ironically, by the bride's father at the time of the wedding.)

Significant changes greatly liberalizing marriage and divorce laws were enacted in 1917: these required persons entering marriage to sign three statements establishing (1) intent to marry, (2) absence of impediments to marry, and (3) voluntary or mutual consent to marry. Common-law or unregistered marriages were legal but were confined in subsequent years chiefly to persons in intellectual or artistic groups. Divorce was greatly facilitated and was regarded as a private matter between the two persons involved.

In 1926 the basic law of 1917 was modified as follows: (1) the inclusion of a strong statement favoring the registration of marriage; (2) the age of marriage was raised from 16 to 18 years for females; (3) coercion of women to contract a marriage or continue cohabitation was made a punishable crime; (4) a subsequent marriage following an unregistered divorce was declared legal but divorce then had to be registered.

In 1936 and again in 1944 marriage laws were substantially altered so as to hasten the retreat from the 1917 laws which had radically departed from established custom. However, in the area of women's rights, this movement toward conservatism did not take place. The Soviet Constitution of 1936 guaranteed equal educational, medical, property, and vocational rights for women as men. The specific laws of 1936 and 1944 imposed more external obligations on the family, lightened the economic burden of parents, and tried to implement the stability of the family by the machinery of the state. Even in common-law marriages or among the unmarried, mothers had no legal ground to try to establish the fatherhood of their children. Divorce regulations were amplified, alimony was required, and nonsupport became a crime. In 1944, abortion, which previously had been generally sanctioned, was strictly regulated. It will be seen that most of the changes of the 1936 and 1944 reforms were admissions of the failure of earlier theories of Marxist freedom. Now there is a broad emphasis on the crucial importance of the family for cultural transmission and child welfare. This indicates the pivotal importance of the family unit for any cultural group.

MARRIAGE LAW IN THE UNITED STATES

The general movements of the emancipation of women, the changing status of children, and the transition of the authoritarian family into the democratic or companionship family can be seen with greatest clarity in the marriage laws of the United States. The present status of marriage law in the United States cannot be understood without some reference to the following basic social changes.

The Emancipation of Women.—About a century ago in America, the growing concept of democracy resulted in its first overt expression on behalf of women's independence. On July 19, 1848, the first convention on behalf of woman's rights convened in Seneca Falls, N. Y. Previous to this convention, women had no legal status apart from their husbands. They could not sue in court, execute a deed or a valid conveyance, claim their own wages, determine the work or custody of their children, vote, or hold property. The property they brought into marriage became that of their husbands. The children they brought into the world could be willed to the care or custody of another woman by their husbands. At the woman's rights convention in 1848 a program developed with three primary goals: (1) to free the persons and property of wives from the absolute control of their husbands; (2) to provide opportunities for higher education for women; and (3) to gain for women full political rights. Practically all of these aims have been written into the law.

This movement toward greater equality of rights had some historic antecedents which helped the cause of aspiring women. In some of the provinces of France the prerevolutionary *coutumes* gave married women below the rank of nobility nearly all the independence that later Roman jurisprudence had granted to women. These local customs together with imported aspects of the Roman law became the basis for corresponding provisions in the Code Napoléon. This code affected the law of Louisiana and other Southern states in the United States. Husband and wife by this law acquired no general interest in each other's property on marriage. The only property the wife brought into marriage was her dowry. While the husband did not become the owner of the dowry, he had the use of it during the continuance of the marriage and could sue the wife if she did not let him use it. Every species of property owned by the wife at the time of marriage or subsequent thereto could become the subject of a dotal gift.

Change in Status of the Child.—No less important has been the shift in the role of the child. Previously the child was entirely subordinate to the parent. The government kept a "hands off" policy as far as treatment of the child was concerned. The child was expected to be entirely submissive and docile. His father might put him in the factory at eight years of age and this was his inalienable right as a parent. No one raised a voice against the most arbitrary and cruel punishment. Indeed, in earlier days the father had an unquestioned right to exercise the death penalty upon his unruly offspring. Today the emphasis upon the rights of parents has given ground to a new concept of the obligations of parents. This emphasis on the welfare of the child has resulted in the state acquiring the status of *in loco parentis* to protect the child and see that the parents fulfill their obligations. The mother has increasingly been given rights regarding the disposition of her children. In most states the law now favors her cause over that of her husband in the case of contested custody. It is with this background of the evolving status of women and children that we may understand the sharp differences between modern and ancient marriage law.

Laws on Age for Marriage.—The determination to protect the child is seen in the modification of the age for marriage statutes in the United States. It will be remembered that Roman law permitted boys of 14 and girls of 12 to marry and the English common law followed this pattern. In America, however, only Idaho, Mississippi, New Jersey, and Washington allow children of this age to be married. The general minimum age of marriage without consent of parents is 21 for boys and 18 for girls. Next in frequency is the age 21 for both boys and girls. Even with the consent of parents, marriages are not permitted for those boys below 18 or those girls below 16. If, however, the fact of pregnancy is established, the law generally gives a judge the right to waive the minimum age requirement.

Civil and Common-Law Marriages.—In the United States a marriage may be either religious, civil, or common-law. Civil marriage was authorized or required in all of the New England colonies. John Milton's tracts on divorce and his denunciation of ecclesiastical "meddling" with marriage resulted in the Civil Marriage Ordinance of Oliver Cromwell in 1653. This ordinance made obligatory the celebration of the marriage before the justice of the peace, and established a system of lay notice, certification, and record. The action of the Puritans and the Independents in England found ready followers in America. For many years the celebration of a marriage before a clergyman was illegal. Later, religious marriages were sanctioned throughout New England, and long before the close of the colonial era there was established the dual civil and religious system which still prevails.

The common-law marriage, still recognized in 21 states, is nothing more than the canonical *sponsalia per verba de praesenti* under another name. In these states any agreement to marry *per verba de praesenti* which is followed by cohabitation as man and wife constitutes a legal marriage. In such marriages no license or ceremony is required. Common-law marriages were essential during frontier days because neither a justice of the peace nor a minister was near. Four states—Arizona, Illinois, Missouri, and New York—have declared such marriages null and void and eight other states have passed laws controlling them.

Formal Marriage Requirements.—In all states formalities attending marriage are prescribed by statute. Licenses to marry must be obtained, and the publication of the issuing of a license gives publicity to the action, as does the requirement of the presence of witnesses. The persons who may perform the ceremony are designated. In some states ministers must be officially licensed to marry before they may conduct weddings. The clerk issuing the license must be satisfied, by affidavit or otherwise, that there are no legal impediments to the marriage and that, in the case of minors, the consent of parents has been granted. These legal requirements vary greatly from state to state. Nevertheless, there is a general rule that a marriage which is legal in the place where it was established will be regarded as legal in all other states. This permits many parties to evade inconvenient requirements of the laws of the place of their domicile by going out of that state to make their contract and celebrate their marriage.

In an effort to prevent hasty or alcoholic marriages, many states have experimented with the imposition of a waiting period between the date of application for and deliverance of the marriage license. In 1955 there were 43 states which explicitly required a waiting period or which had a venereal disease law that serves the same purpose of interposing a period between the intention to marry and the legal right to marry. In some states the establishment of the fact of pregnancy allows the judge to waive the waiting period requirement. While a legal waiting period is novel, the posting of or reading of the banns has existed since early in the Middle Ages.

Prohibitions on Marriage.—As has been noted, consanguineous marriages have long been under the incest taboo. It is interesting that even in 8 states in America this incest taboo applies to those who are relatives only by virtue of affinity. All states, however, prohibit marriage of close blood relations. Likewise, all states with the exception of Rhode Island (which permits the marriage of Jewish uncles and nieces) prohibit marriage between uncles and nieces, grandmothers and grandsons, grandfathers and granddaughters, aunts and nephews, fathers and daughters, mothers and sons, and brothers and sisters. In 29 states the marriage of cousins, or brothers and sisters of half-blood, is prohibited.

In recent years legislation on the subject of marriage has been affected greatly by new emphasis on health considerations. North Carolina and North Dakota require a certificate stating that the man and woman are free from tuberculosis in either the infectious or advanced states; 7 states prohibit the marriage of those with transmittable disease in infectious state; 5 states require a physical examination for venereal diseases; 29 states require such an examination for syphilis; other states have similar requirements differing only in degree; and only 8 states (1955) do not require some evidence regarding freedom from venereal infection. All states regulate the marriage of those who are mentally ill or not of sound mind. In 3 states the feeble-minded are permitted to marry if they present proof of having undergone a sterilization operation; 17 states prohibit the marriage of epileptics.

In some 30 states interracial marriages are prohibited. In the statutes affecting this type of marriage the laws often define to a nicety the fractional part of African blood which vitiates the marriage. In general, whites and Mongolians may not marry in the Western states and Negroes and whites in the Southern states. Eastern and North Central states are more likely to have no regulation prohibiting miscegenetic marriages.

Impotence is defined as the inability of one of the parties to a marriage to have "ordinary and complete intercourse" with the other because of an organic or psychological infirmity. Impossibility of performance voids the marriage contract although sterility does not. Other grounds for annulment in addition to impotence are bigamy, force, fraud, insanity or lack of sound mind, and non-age. About one third of the annulments are granted because of one form or another of gross misrepresentation. One fourth result from the discovery of bigamist conditions. Duress or the use of force to obtain the promises of marriage makes that marriage null and void.

When one reviews the long history of marriage and assesses the complex antecedents of contemporary marriage law in the Roman, Teutonic, and Christian forms, it is not surprising that it is difficult to adjust this many-faceted heritage to contemporary urban marriage. Many national committees representing interdisciplinary memberships, together with the American Bar Association, are now exploring the feasibility of a thorough revision of both the divorce and marriage laws of the United States. Certainly there is a plethora of contradictions and irrational regulations that have become outmoded and today result only in confusion to the public.

See also DIVORCE; DOWER; DOWRY; HUSBAND AND WIFE; LEGITIMACY.

JAMES A. PETERSON
HARVEY J. LOCKE
Department of Sociology
University of Southern California

Bibliography.—Westermarck, Edward A., *The History of Human Marriage*, 3d ed. (London 1901); Vernier, Chester G., *American Family Laws* (Palo Alto 1931); Landis, Judson T., and Landis, Mary G., *Building a Successful Marriage*, 2d ed. (New York 1948); Pilpel, Harriet, and Zavin, Theodora, *Your Marriage and the Law* (New York 1952); Burgess, Ernest W., and Locke, Harvey J., *The Family: From Institution to Companionship* (New York 1953); Truxal, Andrew G., and Merrill, Francis E., *Marriage and the Family in American Culture* (New York 1953); Fishbein, Morris, and Kennedy, R.J.R., *Modern Marriage and Family Planning* (New York 1957); Peterson, James A., *Education for Marriage*, 2d ed. (New York 1964).

MARROW, mar'ō, is a substance of soft, vascular tissue that fills the cells and cavities in most of the bones of mammals. It contains fat, water, and both red and white corpuscles, along with traces of albumin, fibrin, and salts. Some marrows, usually of the long bones, are mostly a yellow oil. Red bone marrow, important in blood manufacture, is highly nutritious. See also BLOOD; BONE; OSTEOLOGY, HUMAN.

MARRYAT, mar'ē-ət, **Frederick,** English naval officer and novelist: b. London, England, July 10, 1792; d. Langham, Norfolk, Aug. 9, 1848. At the age of 14 he entered the navy, and from then until his retirement in 1830 he served in many exciting campaigns throughout the world. He took an active part in the First Burmese War, being given naval command of a successful expedition up the Bassein River in 1825.

Marryat wrote many popular stories of the sea, beginning in 1829 with *The Naval Officer, or Scenes and Adventures in the Life of Frank Mildmay.* The most familiar of these stories is *Mr. Midshipman Easy* (1836), in which Marryat's lifelike and circumstantial narration and his rollicking humor appear perhaps at their best. Others of the series include *The King's Own* (1830), *Newton Forster* (1832), *Peter Simple* (1834), and *Jacob Faithful* (1834). Toward the end of his career his best works were boys' books, chief among them being *Masterman Ready* (1841). From 1832 to 1835 he edited the *Metropolitan Magazine* in which most of his finest novels first appeared. After visiting Canada and the United States, he recorded his impressions in *A Diary in America* (1839).

His daughter FLORENCE MARRYAT (1838–1899) was a novelist, lecturer, operatic singer, and comedienne. Her many novels were briefly popular throughout Europe. In 1872 she published the *Life and Letters* of her father.

MARS, mȧrs, **Mlle.,** French actress: b. Paris, France, Feb. 9, 1779; d. there, March 20, 1847. Mlle. Mars was the stage name of Anne Françoise Hippolyte Boutet, daughter of the French actor Monvel. In 1799 she joined the company of the Comédie-Française where she played for 33 years. Her interpretations of ingénue and coquette parts in the comedies of Molière and Marivaux charmed her audiences, and she was a favorite of Napoleon I. She retired in 1841.

MARS, märz, is the fourth planet in order of increasing distance from the sun in our solar system and the first planet beyond the earth's orbit. Under favorable conditions Mars appears to the naked eye as a star of the first magnitude. It is called the "red planet" because of its characteristic light brick color.

For many years Mars has been a tantalizing object to man. Its surface appearance through the telescope and its apparently earthlike nature raised conjectures that an advanced form of life might conceivably exist on its surface. This possibility has been dimmed by increasing knowledge of conditions on Mars, and especially by the data returned from unmanned space probes sent past the planet on photographing missions.

The photographs taken by the U.S. Mariner space probes revealed large-scale features of the Martian surface, and the probes also collected and radioed back to earth a wealth of scientific data on heat measurements and the composition of the Martian atmosphere. Mars was shown to have a moonlike, heavily cratered surface without visible signs of water or life, including the famous "canals" that some astronomers had thought they glimpsed through earth-based telescopes.

Scientists have inferred from the space-probe data that for a very long time Mars has not had a sufficiently protective atmosphere and apparently is incapable of supporting most forms of life known on earth. However, the possibility that some simple form of life does exist on Mars, especially in the region of the polar caps, cannot be dismissed completely. The question may not be resolved until manned or unmanned spacecraft are landed on the red planet.

CHARACTERISTICS OF MARS

Mars is an earthlike planet, in contrast to Jupiter and the other gas giants of the outer solar system. It is believed to have condensed from much the same material as the earth did when the solar system was formed four to five billion years ago. However, Mars apparently contains significantly less metals, particularly iron, than does the earth.

Size and Shape. The equatorial diameter of Mars is 4,212 to 4,228 miles (6,781 to 6,807 km), about half the diameter of the earth. The mass of the planet, as indicated with increased precision by the trajectories of the Mariner space probes, is slightly greater than 0.1078 that of earth. This is equivalent to 1/3,098,500 the mass of the sun.

Mars bulges at its equator slightly more than the earth does, which indicates that Mars has a more homogeneous makeup than the earth. The

TABLE OF MARTIAN DATA

Mass	About 11% of the earth's
Volume	About 15% of the earth's
Density	About 70% of the earth's
Equatorial diameter	4,212 to 4,228 miles
Surface gravity	About 38% of the earth's
Escape velocity	3.1 miles per second
Orbital velocity	2.2 miles per second
Inclination of equator	25°
Eccentricity of orbit	0.093
Mean distance from sun	141,500,000 miles
Distance from earth:	
Opposition at perihelion	34,600,000 miles
Opposition at aphelion	62,900,000 miles
Sidereal rotation period	24 hr/37 min/22.6678 sec
Mean solar day	24 hr/39 min/35.16 sec
Sidereal revolution period	686.98 days
Synodic revolution period	779.5 days
Albedo (reflecting power)	15 percent
Surface atmospheric pressure	5 to 20 millibars
Number of satellites	2 (Deimos and Phobos)

Jet Propulsion Laboratory, California Institute of Technology, NASA

PORTRAIT OF MARS, taken by Mariner 7 in August 1969 at 281,000 miles, shows large-scale surface markings.

polar diameter of Mars is smaller than its equatorial diameter by one part in 192.

Gravitational and Magnetic Fields. The force of gravity on Mars is 38% of that on earth. The planet's volume is 15% of the earth's; and, compared to the earth's average density of 5.52, Mars has an average density of 3.96. The velocity needed to keep a surface-skimming satellite in orbit around Mars would be 2.2 miles (3.5 km) per second, compared with 5 miles (8 km) per second for a similar satellite around the earth. The escape velocities for objects leaving Mars and the earth are 3.1 and 6.95 miles (5 and 11.19 km) per second, respectively.

The Mariner space probes revealed that the magnetic field of Mars is about equivalent to that of the earth's moon, or somewhere between 1/1,000 and 1/10,000 that of the earth. The lack of a strong magnetic field explains the apparent absence of a radiation belt around Mars, and indicates that the planet probably has a solid core.

Motions. The closer a planet is to the sun, the faster must be its orbital velocity. Since Mars lies beyond the earth, it orbits the sun at a slower velocity than the earth does—15 miles (24 km) per second, compared to the earth's velocity of about 18.5 miles (29.8 km) per second. Mars completes a revolution around the sun, with respect to the fixed stars, once every 686.98 earth days.

The mean distance of Mars from the sun is 141.5 million miles (227.8 million km). However, the eccentricity of its orbit—0.093, compared with earth's 0.017—causes the distance at a given time to vary from 128 million miles at perihelion (the nearest approach to the sun) to 154 million at aphelion (the outer limit of its orbit). Because of this eccentricity, the closest distance between Mars and the earth as they pass each other in orbit varies from 34 million to 62 million miles (60.7 to 101.3 million km), with the closest approaches occurring every 15 or 17 years.

The exact rotational period of the planet—the Martian *sidereal day*—is 24 hours 37 minutes 22.67 seconds. The Martian *solar day,* which is the one that would be used by an explorer on the planet, is 24 hours 39 minutes 35.16 seconds.

Appearance from the Earth. Because Mars has a thin atmosphere, it reflects only about 15% of the solar radiation reaching it, whereas the earth reflects 35% to 40%. Not all parts of Mars reflect light equally; the brightness of the planet varies by 15% as it spins on its axis.

The magnitude of the planet's light also depends on its nearness to the earth. When Mars is on the other side of the sun from the earth, it has an average visual magnitude of +1.6, or about one and a half times the brightness of Polaris, the North Star. When Mars makes its closest possible approach to the earth, its magnitude increases to −2.9; the planet then shines more brightly than any object in the skies of earth except the sun, moon, and Venus.

CONDITIONS ON THE PLANET

That the Martian surface is subject to seasonal changes in color and surface patterns is certain. The changes have been observed, photographed, and mapped repeatedly. They have aroused intense speculation, including the possibility that they are the result of a seasonal growth and decline of some form of vegetation; the data returned by the Mariner space probes do not en-

Jet Propulsion Laboratory, California Institute of Technology, NASA

SOUTH POLAR REGION of Mars has snowdrift-like formations that are thought to consist almost entirely of carbon dioxide ice. In some areas, most notably the floors of large craters, the surface is partially bare. Photo was made by Mariner 7 from approximately 3,300 miles.

courage this theory. It is generally agreed, at any rate, that life could never have developed to a high order on Mars. The atmosphere is too thin, and the supply of oxygen and free water too scarce, to support most forms of life as they are known on earth.

Atmosphere and Surface Materials. The atmosphere of Mars, as determined by the Mariner space probes, consists mainly of carbon dioxide, with some atomic oxygen in the upper atmospheric regions. No free nitrogen was detected (although slight amounts of nitrogen may nevertheless be present), which virtually overturned earlier theories about the content of the Martian atmosphere. Although there was some evidence for the existence of a very thin haze of ice crystals in warm latitudes, the atmosphere of Mars is extremely dry.

Although the surface of Mars appears predominantly brick red through telescopes, it combines various hues ranging from white, through yellow, to dark red. The surface materials have not been positively identified, although it is generally assumed that some metals are represented there. Spectroscopic studies indicate the presence of felsite, a brown rock composed principally of aluminum and potassium silicate, while studies of the polarization of light reflected from Mars indicate the presence of limonite, a brown iron ore. These findings await further investigation.

Seasons. Because the axis of Mars is inclined to its orbital plane at an angle of about 24°, almost the same as the earth's degree of tilt, Mars has earthlike seasons. The Martian year is almost twice as long as an earth year, so it would seem that the seasons on Mars should also average twice as long as on earth; but they do not. Because of the eccentricity of Mars' orbit, seasons on the planet vary in length.

When Mars is at perihelion, it always has its south pole tipped toward the sun. Because the planet is moving more rapidly at that time, the southern summer and northern winter last 160 days of 24 hours. The southern autumn and northern spring are 199 days long. The southern winter and northern summer are 182 days long, and the southern spring and northern autumn are 146 days long. The maximum spread between seasons on Mars is therefore 53 days, as opposed to only four days on the earth.

Climate. Surface temperatures are generally lower on Mars than on the earth. In the middle of summer the noon temperature at the south pole may occasionally rise to 32°F (0°C) though the average is about 20°F (−7°C). In the south temperate zone the average noon temperature rises to about 60°F (16°C), and at the equator the temperature may reach 75°F (24°C). North of the equator at the same time of year 0°F (−18°C) is the average temperature in the temperate zone, and −40°F (−40°C) in the polar region. Night temperatures can get down to about −100°F (−73.3°C).

Whereas on earth there is little difference between temperatures on the ground and in the air immediately above it, on Mars the ground may be as much as 50°F (28°C) hotter than the atmosphere just above. In consequence, strong vertical currents are generated on Mars, and they subject the planet to severe, dust-filled windstorms.

Surface Appearance. Apart from the controversial "canals" discussed below, the surface features of Mars, as seen through earth-based telescopes, fall into three categories. There are

Jet Propulsion Laboratory, California Institute of Technology, NASA

HEAVY CRATERING OF MARTIAN SURFACE is strikingly recorded by Mariner 6 in July 1969 in this four-picture mosaic. The area covered by the pictures is 2,500 miles long. Superficially, at least, Mars resembles earth's moon more than it does the earth.

light red areas, called "deserts"; darker areas, inappropriately called "seas"; and polar caps, which wax and wane with the seasons. The nature of the difference in surface materials between the so-called deserts and seas was not determined by the Mariner space probes.

Craters. What the probes did reveal was an abundance of craters, large and small, on the surface of Mars. The planet seems to resemble the earth's moon more than it does the earth. Of all the Mariner findings, none occasioned more surprise than this.

The Mariner pictures did not reveal dynamic processes taking place on Mars such as those that created mountains and other orogenic features on earth. Because of the presence of an atmosphere, however, the craters of Mars seem to be more eroded than those of the moon; some craters, apparently quite ancient, are almost worn away. In addition, there are regions of jumbled terrain and regions that are virtually free of craters—an indication of geological processes not yet determined. Whether the surface of Mars is heavily cratered because it has not much altered in geological time, or because it lies close to the asteroid belt and hence is more subject to such collisions, is another of the many questions yet to be answered about Mars.

Deserts and Seas. The so-called deserts of Mars—the lighter-colored areas—cover from three-fourths to three-fifths of the planet's surface, while the darker-colored seas cover the remaining surface (except for the polar caps). The seas exhibit seasonal changes; they expand and grow still darker in the Martian springtime and retreat and grow lighter in the fall.

At one time it was widely believed that these dark regions, which are predominantly south of the equator, were covered with vegetation nourished by water released from the polar caps at the onset of summer. About 1900 a Swedish physicist and chemist, Svante Arrhenius, argued that an absorbent material subject to alternate periods of humidification and desiccation provided the color changes observed. The increasing evidence of the extreme scarcity of water on Mars rendered these theories untenable.

Polar Caps. The polar caps of Mars also advance and retreat with the seasons and are obviously some form of frozen material—either water ice or carbon dioxide ice—that responds to the changing temperatures on the surface. One of the Mariner probes passed over the southern cap, which in wintertime covers an area of about 4 million square miles (10.4 million sq km). Interpretations of the data vary, but it is agreed that carbon dioxide ice and small amounts of water ice are present in the cap and in clouds above it.

THE QUESTION OF CANALS

Through the telescope the surface of Mars exhibits a number of local variations of color and light intensity. Some of these smaller markings seem to be permanent features, whereas others appear to come and go with the waxing and waning of the polar caps. At least a few seem to be strictly temporary. Different observers in the past have given such markings different interpretations but many agreed that there seemed to be a discernible pattern of dark lines.

Schiaparelli's Canali. The Italian astronomer Giovanni Schiaparelli is credited with "discovering" the line pattern, though other observers had seen the markings earlier without thinking them particularly significant. In 1877, using the 8½-inch telescope at the Brera Observatory in Milan, he discerned faint, dusky streaks at the critical limit of visibility. He recorded them and called them *canali,* the Italian word for both "channels" and "canals." The second meaning, used in translation, doubtless stimulated speculation that they were of artificial origin.

Two years later, during another favorable opposition, Schiaparelli observed Mars again and discovered that some of the markings previously seen as single lines were instead now seen as double lines. Although Schiaparelli was convinced that the markings were permanent, they were not seen by others for nine years. Then, in rapid succession, other astronomers reported seeing them, and the "canals" became one of the most publicized subjects in astronomy.

Lowell's Charts. In 1894, Percival Lowell, an American astronomer, saw the "canals" and subsequently stated his conviction that they were irrigation ditches fashioned by a "higher intelligence" to carry water from the poles to the arid equatorial regions. Lowell charted the canals, drawing an incredibly fine network of intersecting straight lines that numbered at least 700 and represented channels 15 to 30 miles wide. In some cases they extended 3,000 to 4,000 miles. Lowell contended that the markings were not the canals themselves but strips of vegetation along the waterways; dark spots at the intersections of the lines were oases.

Lowell's essay was the high point of speculation on the "canals." Despite other reported sightings, numerous expert observers never saw a canal and doubted that they existed.

Probable Explanation. The Mariner space probes confirmed such doubts; thus far no sign of any really canallike features has been found in the pictures of Mars. The most likely explanation of the "canals" is found in the experience of observers who have viewed the lines on one night, and on another night have seen only fragmented markings. The lines, then, are an optical illusion, the tendency of a field of separate points or objects to seem interconnected by lines when viewed from a great distance.

SATELLITES OF MARS

Discovery of the two moons of Mars was the fulfillment of an amazing piece of speculation. In 1610, Johannes Kepler suggested that since Venus had no moon, the earth but one, and Jupiter—as known at that time—four, it was reasonable to assume that Mars (between the earth and Jupiter) had two. Others, including Jonathan Swift, later speculated on this possibility.

In 1877, Asaph Hall, director of the U.S. Naval Observatory, put the institution's new 26-inch telescope to the task of finding the moons of Mars. On August 11 he discovered the outer satellite and on August 17 the inner one. He named them Deimos and Phobos, respectively, after the Homeric attendants of Ares, the Greek god of war (the Roman Mars).

Deimos orbits Mars in 30 hours 18 minutes, at a mean distance of 14,580 miles (23,474 km) from the planet's center. Phobos completes a revolution every 7 hours 39 minutes; its mean distance is 5,826 miles (9,380 km). Phobos and Deimos are about 10 and 5 miles (16 and 8 km) wide, respectively. Deimos, the more distant one, would simply appear as a bright star in the Martian sky, varying in brightness as it passes through its phases. Both satellites are too near the planet to be visible from all Martian latitudes. Phobos does not appear at latitudes higher than 69.5° north and south; Deimos does not appear at latitudes higher than 82.5°.

PLANNED EXPLORATION OF MARS

Unmanned Probes. The success of the U.S. Mariner probes in 1965 and 1969 stimulated even greater interest in the Mars missions that have been planned for the future. Two orbital Mariners are scheduled for 1971; two years later, the first of a series of Vikings may be softlanded on the surface of the planet.

Investigations indicate that an automated biological space laboratory such as the one planned for Viking, can provide answers to questions about the possibility of life on Mars. Three such laboratories have been under research. One, called Gulliver, would employ a sensitive radioisotope technique to detect gases emitted as byproducts in metabolic processes. Samples of Martian soil, cultured in a weak acid solution in Gulliver's "broth chamber" would—if the soil contained living organism—emit carbon dioxide containing radioactive carbon-14. The radiations, in theory, would be counted by a miniature Geiger counter and the data relayed to earth by radio.

Another projected laboratory, called the Multivator, would collect dust samples from the planet's surface and test them in combination with a variety of reactive materials. The reactive materials would be selected for their ability to amplify certain steps in the metabolism of microbes. Presumably an instrument weighing 30 ounces could do the job, but, unfortunately, only relatively few organisms can be detected in this way. Fluorescent materials, subjected to light in the Multivator, might be detected electronically.

The third type of laboratory, called the "Wolf Trap," would inhale dust in the Martian atmosphere, subject it to culture experiments, and determine by photoelectric techniques whether microorganisms are present.

Manned Programs. The instrumented probes eventually will be followed by a manned landing on Mars. At present it is considered likely that this will take place in the 1980's. By 1977 the nuclear propulsion stage necessary for the trip should have become operational, and by 1975 the reusable "earth-to-orbit" space shuttle and the "tug" to navigate in earth orbit also should have come into being. With these elements it will be possible to assemble two craft, with a crew of six men in each, to leave earth for Mars. Currently, the most acute problem foreseen is the two-year interval that the flight will take; no one can fully visualize the physiological and psychological problems that will arise. The current estimate of the cost, probably quite optimistic, is $24 billion.

The Soviet Union apparently has similar plans for the exploration of Mars. Radio signals from several unpublicized Soviet space probes have been detected, and the Russians twice publicized probes directed at Mars. On Nov. 1, 1963, the Soviets launched their Mars 1 probe. On Nov. 30, 1964, two days after Mariner 4 began its journey, the Russians announced the departure of another Mars probe. However, radio contact with both probes was lost long before they reached the vicinity of the planet, and they must be considered to have failed. Subsequent Soviet Mars probes have also been unsuccessful. See also ASTRONOMY; SOLAR SYSTEM.

Bibliography.—Lowell, Percival, *Mars* (Boston and New York 1895); id., *Mars and Its Canals* (New York 1906); Antoniadi, E.M., *La Planète Mars* (Paris 1930); Hess, Seymour L., "Some Aspects of the Meteorology of Mars," *Journal of Meteorology*, Vol. 7 (1950), pp. 1–13; id., "Some Meteorology of Mars," *Sky and Telescope*, Vol. 9 (1950), pp. 155–157; Kuiper, Gerard P., *The Atmospheres of the Earth and Planets*, rev. ed. (Chicago 1952); Urey, Harold C., *The Planets, Their Origin and Development* (New Haven 1952); de Vaucouleurs, Gérard, *The Planet Mars*, tr. from the French by Patrick A. Moore, 2d ed. (New York 1953); id., *Physics of the Planet Mars* (New York 1954); Levitt, I.M., *A Space Traveler's Guide to Mars* (New York 1956); Edgeworth, Kenneth E., *The Earth, the Planets, and the Stars* (New York 1961); Moore, Patrick, *Guide to Mars* (New York 1961); Branley, Franklyn M., *Mars: Planet Number Four* (New York 1962); Gallant, Roy A., *Exploring the Planets*, rev. ed. (New York 1967).

I.M. LEVITT
Director, Fels Planetarium, Philadelphia

MARS, märz, is the god of war in Roman mythology. At an early date, he was an agricultural deity, surnamed Silvanus, and propitiatory sacrifices were offered to him as the god of fields and flocks. His transition into the Roman god of war may have occurred in one of three ways: (1) he may originally have been the supreme deity of a warlike people, and thus invested with warlike attributes; (2) he may have been a war god, pressed into service as the guardian of crops; or (3) he may have been an agricultural deity transmogrified by a warlike people. The name, contracted from the Sabine *Mavers* or *Mavors,* or the Oscan *Mamers,* was early identified by the Romans with the Greek Ares.

Mars was regarded as the father of the Roman people. According to tradition, Romulus and Remus, the founders of Rome, were his sons by Rhea Sylvia. Several temples in Rome were dedicated to him, the most important of which was that outside the Porta Capena, on the Appian Way, and that of Mars Ultor, built by Augustus in the forum. His service was celebrated not only by particular priests devoted to him, but by the College of the Salii, or priests of Mars. His festivals took place each year in the circus on August 1.

The month of March, the first month of the Roman year, was sacred to Mars and was named for him. The Campus Martius, where the Roman youth engaged in their athletic and military exercises, was also named in his honor.

MARSALA, mär-sä'lä, an Italian city, is a Mediterranean seaport in Sicily, about 55 miles southwest of Palermo. Situated in Trapani province, it is the westernmost city of Sicily. Its most important export is the strong, sweet, white Marsala wine produced in the neighborhood. Grain, soda, and salt are among the other exports. The city was known as *Lilybaeum* in the time of the Carthaginian supremacy in Sicily. The seaport obtained its present name from the Saracens, who valued it so highly that they called it *Marsa Allah* (Port of God). There is a 16th century cathedral dedicated to St. Thomas of Canterbury, and traces of the early city walls survive. In 1860, Giuseppe Garibaldi landed at Marsala with 1,000 of his famous Redshirts. His subsequent conquest of the island was an important step in the unification of Italy. Population of commune: (1961) 81,327.

MARSEILLAISE, mȧr-sā-yez', **La,** is the French national anthem. Its words and music were composed in 1792 by Claude Joseph Rouget de Lisle, a French army officer stationed at Strasbourg. Conceived as a patriotic anthem during wartime, it was entitled "Battle Song for the Army of the Rhine." Subsequently the people of Marseille took it up as a song of revolutionary France and spread it throughout the land; hence the title.

Its aristocratic author was reported to have been terrified by the tremendous effect of his composition. Suspected of Royalist activities, he was arrested during the Reign of Terror and was saved from the guillotine only by the death of Robespierre. On Jan. 8, 1795, the French government ordered the music played at all theaters. Suppressed during the Empire and Restoration, it was restored to use permanently in 1830.

The original version consisted of only six verses. The stanza beginning "Nous entrerons" was not written by Rouget de Lisle; it was composed later for a Bastille Day celebration. *La Marseillaise* was orchestrated by both Hector Berlioz and Ambroise Thomas.

LA MARSEILLAISE.

1

Allons, enfants de la patrie,
Le jour de gloire est arrivé!
Contre nous de la tyrannie
L'étendard sanglant est levé!
Entendez-vous dans ces campagnes
Mugir ces féroces soldats?
Ils viennent jusque dans nos bras
Égorger nos fils, nos compagnes!
Aux armes, citoyens, formez vos bataillons!
Marchons! marchons!
Qu'un sang impur abreuve nos sillons!

2

Que veut cette horde d'esclaves,
De traîtres, de rois conjurés?
Pour qui ces ignobles entraves,
Ces fers dès longtemps préparés?
Français, pour nous, ah! quel outrage!
Quels transports il doit exciter!
C'est nous qu'on ose méditer
De rendre à l'antique esclavage!
Aux armes, etc.

3

Quoi! ces cohortes étrangères
Feraient la loi dans nos foyers!
Quoi! ces phalanges mercenaires
Terrasseraient nos fiers guerriers!
Grand Dieu! par des mains enchaînées
Nos fronts sous le joug se ploîraient!
De vils despotes deviendraient
Les maîtres de nos destinées!
Aux armes, etc.

4

Tremblez, tyrans! et vous, perfides,
L'opprobre de tous les partis,
Tremblez! vos projets parricides
Vont enfin recevoir leur prix!
Tout est soldat pour vous combattre.
S'ils tombent, nos jeunes héros,
La terre en produit de nouveaux,
Contre vous tout prêts à se battre!
Aux armes, etc.

5

Français, en guerriers magnanimes,
Portez ou retenez vos coups!
Épargnez ces tristes victimes,
À regret s'armant contre nous.
Mais ces despotes sanguinaires,
Mais les complices de Bouillé,
Tous ces tigres qui, sans pitié,
Déchirent le sein de leur mère!
Aux armes, etc.

6

Amour sacré de la Patrie,
Conduis, soutiens nos braves vengeurs;
Liberté, Liberté, chérie,
Combats avec tes défenseurs!
Sous nos drapeaux, que la Victoire
Accoure à tes mâles accents;
Que tes ennemis expirants
Voient ton triomphe et notre gloire!
Aux armes, etc.

7

Nous entrerons dans la carrière
Quand nos aînés n'y seront plus;
Nous y trouverons leur poussière
Et la trace de leurs vertus!
Bien moins jaloux de leur survivre
Que de partager leur cercueil,
Nous aurons le sublime orgueil
De les venger ou de les suivre!
Aux armes, etc.

THE MARSEILLAISE.

1

Come, children of the fatherland,
The day of glory now is here;
By tyranny against us
The bloody banner is raised:
Do you hear in the land
Those ferocious soldiers roar?
Up to our arms they come,
Butchering our sons, our women!
To arms, citizens, form your battalions,
Let us march, let us march!
That the foul blood may drench our furrows!

2

What seeks this horde of slaves,
Of traitors and conspiring kings?
For whom these base manacles,
These irons already long prepared?
For us, Frenchmen, ah, such outrage!
What passions it must raise!
'Tis us whom they dare purpose
To restore to former slavery.

3

What! shall these foreign cohorts
Make the law in our homes?
What! shall these hireling phalanxes
Throw our proud warriors down?
Great God! with fettered hands,
Our heads bowed down beneath the yoke!
And despots vile become
The masters of our destinies.

4

Tremble, ye tyrants and traitors,
The shame of every faction,
Tremble! your parricidal projects
Shall at last gain their reward!
Each one is soldier to fight you.
And if our young heroes fall,
The land shall produce them afresh
All ready to struggle against you!

5

Frenchmen, as magnanimous warriors,
Restrain or deal your blows;
Spare those sad victims
Who reluctantly armed against us.
But those bloody despots—
Those accomplices of Bouillé—
All those tigers who pitilessly
Lacerate the bosom of their mother!

6

Sacred love of fatherland,
Guide, sustain our brave avengers;
Liberty, dear Liberty,
Fight with thy defenders!
That victory under our flags
Shall hasten to thy noble call;
And may thy dying enemies
Behold thy triumph and our glory!

7

We shall begin our career
When our elders are no more;
Yet we shall find their ashes
And the trace of their virtues!
Less eager to survive them
Than to share their tomb,
It shall be our sublime pride
To avenge or follow them!

MARSEILLE, mär-sä′, Fr. màr-sâ′y′, city, capital of the Bouches-du-Rhône Department, 26 miles east of the mouth of the Rhone River, on the northeastern shore of the Golfe du Lion, an arm of the Mediterranean Sea. Nice lies 125 miles to the east. Marseille is France's principal seaport and her largest city next to Paris, 515 miles to the northwest. Its climate is mild, dry, and sunny.

Physical Features.—At the outlet of the valley of the little Huveaune River, Marseille lies within an imposing arc of undulating hills and valleys which reach their highest point (2,340 feet) in the Étoile range. The city has grown up around its Vieux-Port (Old Harbor), running west to east, and the old section with its narrow tortuous streets resembles an amphitheater facing south on the Vieux-Port. The squalid waterfront district, legendary sailors' haven, has been entirely rebuilt since it was razed (1943) by the Germans. Across the Vieux-Port the harbor is dominated by a cliff crowned with the Basilica of Notre-Dame de la Garde and its towering golden statue of the Virgin (500 feet above sea level), a beacon for mariners and visible for many miles by land and sea.

The new city, which has developed since the end of the 17th century, is divided in two parts by the Canebière (Provençal, hemp field), a world-famous boulevard which runs east from the Vieux-Port and becomes, after the first two thirds of a mile, the postwar Boulevard de la Libération. Spreading little by little from the Canebière, the population has taken over the surrounding heights, except along the southern shore of Marseille Bay, which is cut off from the city by a line of steep hills. Here, between the sea and the gardens of fine residences which line the cliffs, has been built the Promenade de la Corniche. From the magnificent one-and-a-half-mile Corniche one has a sweeping view of the whole roadstead, one of the most beautiful spots in the Mediterranean. About a mile offshore lies the romantic islet of If, with the château made famous by the elder Dumas' *Comte de Monte Cristo.*

Economic Activities.—Marseille is tending gradually to become a great industrial center as well as a seaport. To its traditional industries (the manufacture of olive oil and soap, oil refining, and shipbuilding) have been added the processing of plastics, the manufacture of ceramics and cement, and industries based on electrometallurgical and electrochemical processes and on producing derivatives of petroleum. The commune itself is very large, covering almost 60,000 acres, and the suburbs, where a quarter of the people live, are gradually losing their agricultural character, especially in the Huveaune Valley, and are becoming industrialized.

The chamber of commerce, founded in 1599 and thus the oldest in France, continues to play a dominant role in the economic development of the city. In particular it insures the proper administration of the port and has charge of the maintenance and modernization of harbor installations. After the latter were totally destroyed in 1944 they were replaced within a few years and equipped with every modern improvement. The Vieux-Port, a natural inlet known to the Greeks as Lacydon, is now used only by pleasure craft and shipping boats. Its area was doubled in 1846 when the Joliette Basin, or dockyard, was built, and expansion continues to the north.

Just beyond L'Estaque the Rove Tunnel (1927), a sea-level canal four and a half miles long and 72 feet wide, pierces the L'Estaque range of hills northwest of Marseille and leads into the Étang de Berre (Berre Basin), a natural lagoon. From there the 29-mile canal from Port-de-Bouc to Arles connects Marseille with the Rhone. When the current of this river has been brought under control by vast works now in progress, Marseille will be linked with Central Europe by way of the Rhone and the Rhine.

Today, with its branch petroleum installations the Étang de Berre and the new Lavéra Basin, Marseille is the largest seaport of France. The harbor has nearly 1,000 acres of water surface, 17 miles of piers, and 420 acres of wharfage, served by 50 miles of railway. Possessing, besides, the most modern technical equipment, the port handles annually about 20 million tons of freight on more than 17,000 ships totaling 43 million tons burden. Since Marseille is a port of call for ships from almost every maritime country, passenger traffic is comparably heavy, and air travelers at the Marseille-Marignane Airport on the Étang de Berre, where nearly 800,000 were reported in 1956, double the total.

Cultural Life.—Marseille is the seat of an archbishopric; a district court (*tribunal de première instance*); a commercial court which is the oldest in France; two branches of the University of Aix-Marseille: the faculties of science and of medicine and pharmacy; an observatory; and schools of commerce and engineering. There are several museums, the best known being the art and natural history museums in the Longchamp Palace, and the Cantini Museum, housed in a charming 17th century residence, which has a fine collection of Provençal faïence and annually presents exhibitions of painting and sculpture.

Although Marseille is the oldest city in France, it is not rich in public monuments; only a few vestiges of antiquity remain. However, the crypts of St. Victor's Abbey Church, dating from the 13th and 14th centuries, contain one of the oldest Christian sanctuaries of ancient Gaul. The historic cathedral called La Major (Sainte-Marie-Majeure), of which only the apse and transept have been preserved, is one of the most beautiful works of the 12th century Romanesque school. The city hall and the Chapelle de la Charité, with a dome by the noted sculptor Pierre Puget, date from the 17th century. But most of the public buildings were erected during the 19th century; among them are the prefecture, exchange, Longchamp Palace, courthouse, Notre-Dame de la Garde, and the modern cathedral, which, with its eight Byzantine domes, is said to be the third largest in the world.

History.—The civilization of classical antiquity reached Western Europe through its oldest city, Marseille, settled by Ionian Greeks from Phocaea (modern Foça, western Turkey) about 600 B.C. and called Massilia. After five centuries of glory, during which it founded colonies around the Mediterranean Massilia, which had supported Pompey the Great against Julius Caesar, fell to Caesar's legions (49 B.C.) and went into eclipse. In the 4th century A.D., thanks to Cassian (Johannes Cassianus), the monk who founded the Abbey of St. Victor, Marseille helped bring Christian civilization to Gaul. At the end of the 12th century and the beginning of the 13th, the city, having become an independent commune, took part in the Crusades and brought about a revival of commerce with eastern countries, creating mercantile consulships which were the origin of French influence in the Middle East today.

Marseille passed under the rule of the counts of Provence in 1257 and of the kings of France in 1482, her port acquiring great importance as the principal commercial outlet for the kingdom. In the same period Marseille proved one of the bulwarks of France by withstanding (1524 and 1536) two sieges by Charles V's imperial armies. During the next century, Marseille was wracked by France's civil wars: the Wars of Religion (1562–1598) and the uprising of the Fronde (1648–1653); but thereafter she resumed her progress and became a free port in 1669. Traffic grew during the 18th century, thanks to the opening of a new market in the West Indies. French occupation of North Africa, beginning in 1830, and the opening of the Suez Canal (1869) crowned the work of centuries in making Marseille the queen of the Mediterranean.

Since World War II, major projects in town planning and road building, carried forward under a great modernization program initiated by the municipal authorities, have given a new look to the city. Pop. (1962) of city, 767,146; of commune 783,738.

GASTON DEFERRE,
Mayor of Marseille and Deputy representing the Bouches-du-Rhône Department.

MARSEILLES, mär-sālz, city, Illinois, in La Salle County. It lies at an altitude of 495 feet, 35 miles southwest of Joliet, on the Illinois River, the Rock Island Railroad, and a federal highway. A canal permits boats to pass the two-and-a-half-mile rapids, source of industrial power. Across the river is 400-acre Illini State Park, a bird and game refuge. In a bituminous-coal area, Marseilles has an aluminum and brass foundry and manufactures clothing, construction supplies, biscuits, and ornamental iron. Incorporated in 1861, the city has a commission form of government. Pop. (1960) 4,347.

MARSH, märsh, **Othniel Charles**, American paleontologist: b. Lockport, N.Y., Oct. 29, 1831; d. New Haven, Conn., March 18, 1899. Becoming interested in natural history, he graduated from Yale College (now University) in 1860, and continued his studies there and in Germany. In 1866 his uncle, George Peabody, endowed a natural history museum at Yale, and Marsh was named professor of paleontology there, the first in the Western Hemisphere. He soon began a series of explorations in the western United States which resulted in a large and unique collection of fossil vertebrates, which he presented to Yale and to the United States National Museum.

Marsh became a leading exponent of the natural selection theory, following publication of Charles Darwin's *Origin of Species* in 1859, and his discovery of fossil birds with reptilian characteristics and his researches on the development of the horse were acknowledged by Darwin to provide sound support for his theory of evolution. In the early 1870's Marsh made three of his most important discoveries in the Cretaceous tablelands of Kansas: the hitherto unknown birds with teeth; well-preserved mosasaurs, or marine lizards; and huge toothless pterodactyls, or flying reptiles. Forsaking his original interest, prehistoric mammals, he turned to the giant reptiles and collected or described 80 new forms of dinosaurs and 34 new genera. His most important

discoveries among the extinct mammals were tiny jawbones and teeth from the late Jurassic and late Cretaceous times, which showed the earliest genetic divergences in the class Mammalia. A leader among world scientists for nearly 40 years, Marsh served as the first vertebrate paleontologist of the United States Geological Survey from 1882 until his death.

Consult Schuchert, Charles, and LeVene, Clara M., *O. C. Marsh, Pioneer in Paleontology* (New Haven 1940).

MARSH, Reginald, American painter and illustrator: b. Paris, France, March 14, 1898; d. Bennington, Vt., July 3, 1954. The son of American parents, both painters, he studied with John Sloan and Kenneth Hayes Miller at the Art Students League in New York City, later with Jacques Maroger and in Europe, and was a teacher at the League (1934–1954). He became known as a cartoonist and illustrator through his work for the New York *Daily News, Vanity Fair, The New Yorker,* and other periodicals. His exuberant and colorful paintings of such aspects of city life as Greenwich Village, the Bowery, Coney Island, and burlesque shows were so often satirical that they won for him the title of "the Hogarth of New York." He illustrated a number of books, among them Daniel Defoe's *Moll Flanders,* Mark Twain's *Prince and the Pauper,* and Theodore Dreiser's *An American Tragedy.* He also executed historical murals for the Post Office in Washington, D.C., and the Custom House in New York City, and wrote *Anatomy of Artists* (1945).

MARSH GAS. See METHANE.

MARSH HARE. See HARE.

MARSH HAWK (more correctly HARRIER), a hawk of the genus *Circus.* The marsh hawks belong to a well-characterized group of diurnal birds of prey which are sometimes separated as a distinct subfamily, the Circinae. The group is worldwide in distribution and consists of about 14 species. Only one (*Circus cyaneus*) inhabits North America; it inhabits Eurasia as well. In the North American marsh hawk the adult female is brown and, as is the rule in hawks, larger than the male, measuring about 22 inches. The adult male is a beautiful shade of pale gray and measures about 19 inches. Both sexes have a conspicuous white rump through which they are easily identified when on the wing. The wings, and also the tail, are considerably longer than in other hawks. The marsh hawk is inoffensive and beneficial to man, as its food consists chiefly of harmful rodents. It nests on the ground and, as its name implies, frequents mainly marshes.

CHARLES VAURIE.

MARSH HEN. See GALLINULE.

MARSH MALLOW, măl'ō, the common name of a perennial herb, *Althaea officinalis,* in the mallow family (Malvaceae), native to Europe but formerly cultivated and now locally naturalized on the borders of salt- and freshwater marshes in the eastern United States. Its erect, coarse stem is two to four feet tall and bears large, ovate, toothed, and sometimes three-lobed downy leaves. The flowers are pale rose colored, with five spreading petals. The roots yield a sweet mucilaginous substance formerly the base for marshmallow confections, now made synthetically.

A well-known relative, *A. rosea,* is the garden hollyhock.

RICHARD M. STRAW.

MARSH MARIGOLD. See COWSLIP.

MARSH WREN, either of two species of North American wrens, the long-billed marsh wren (*Telmatodytes palustris*) and the short-billed marsh wren (*Cistothorus platensis*). The two birds are typical wrens—fussy, noisy little brown birds with long bills and short tails. The latter is usually cocked at a very high angle over the back. The long-billed species inhabits shallow expanses of water invaded by cattails, bulrushes, tules, or any other coarse vegetation that grows in water. The short-billed species prefers damp meadows or small shallow sedge marshes. The difference in length of bill is not very conspicuous, but the long-billed can be distinguished in the field, first of all by its wetter habitat and also by its bold white eyeline and more sharply streaked back. The males of both species are indefatigable builders, weaving a number of characteristic ball-shaped nests with a small entrance at the side; these are "dummy nests," as they are not lined or occupied for breeding. The female meanwhile builds the actual nest in which she will lay her eggs. The long-billed species is the better known, as it is less furtive in its habits than its relative and has a much louder song, rattlelike in quality, which is given forth endlessly from before dawn to late evening.

CHARLES VAURIE.

MARSHAL, mär'shăl, family name derived from the title marshal (q.v.) as it was used in the early English court. The first noteworthy bearer of the name and the title was John Marshal (d. 1164?), known also as John the Marshal or Jean le Maréchal, who married the sister of Patrick, earl of Salisbury. He was a loyal supporter of the Empress Matilda and Henry II.

John's second son, WILLIAM MARSHAL (b. 1146?; d. Caversham, England, May 14, 1219), was a great soldier-statesman, twice a regent of England. He became 1st earl of Pembroke of the Marshal line—and thus 1st earl marshal—by his marriage (1189) to Isabella, daughter and only child of Richard, 2nd earl of Pembroke of the de Clare line (see CLARE, DE).

Entering the service of Henry II (r. 1154–1189) in 1170, William was one of the principal advisers to every English sovereign for the next half century, while the monarchy took root and the nation moved out of feudal darkness. Henry II chose him as a mentor for his son Henry, and retained him in favor after the rebellious prince's death. As military commander and a regent (1190–1194) during the absence of Richard I (r. 1189–1199), William defended the crown against continuing assaults of the French and insurgent Britons; he supported John (r. 1199–1216) in the Barons' War and helped guide the king to acceptance of the Magna Carta (q.v., 1215); and as the regent for young Henry III (r. 1216–1272) as he reaffirmed the Magna Carta in 1216, defeated the land forces of Prince Louis of France at Lincoln in 1217, and helped pacify the disordered country.

William had five sons, each of whom succeeded to his titles, and five daughters. His title of earl marshal passed to the son of his oldest daughter Matilda, who had married the 3d earl of Norfolk,

and it has remained hereditary with the dukes of Norfolk. The title of earl of Pembroke passed to William de Valence, husband of the daughter of William's youngest daughter Johanna, and her descendants in the Hastings line.

MARSHAL, a title of authority derived from the Teutonic words for horse (*marah*) and servant (*scalc*) and originally given, in Frankish and medieval European courts, to deputies of the constable (q.v.), or count of the stable, who, because of the importance of cavalry in those days, was a military commander and an administrator of the royal household as well. In England the marshal, who also had jurisdiction over the court of chivalry, eventually became the military superior of the constable, beginning in the 12th century and particularly when William Marshal became 1st earl marshal in 1189 (see MARSHAL, family name—*William Marshal*). In other European countries the office of marshal developed similarly, and now the title, or its literal equivalent, indicates the highest ranking military officer: English, *field marshal;* French, *maréchal;* German, *Generalfeldmarschall;* Italian, *maresciallo.*

In the United States, in the federal government, a marshal is an officer of the executive department appointed to execute, with his deputies, the orders of the federal courts in each judicial district and to open and close court sessions. In some states, particularly in the South and West, marshals are police officers of municipal districts and boroughs, with powers generally corresponding to those of constable or sheriff. In New York City, marshals execute the orders of the municipal courts.

Marshal, as a title of superiority, appears in various compounds: for instance, provost marshal, chief of military police; fire marshal, chief of a fire department; marshal (of the day), one who is charged with arrangements for ceremonial occasions; and earl marshal, English officer of state who presides over the Heralds' College and manages state ceremonies.

MARSHALL, mär'shăl, **Alfred,** English economist: b. London, England, July 26, 1842; d. Cambridge, July 13, 1924. Graduating from Cambridge in 1865, he at first planned to devote himself to physics and then to mathematics, but instead accepted a lectureship in moral science at Cambridge (1868–1877). He turned to a study of economics to see how the "conditions of life of the British (and other) working classes" could be improved, becoming professor of political economy at Oxford (1883–1885) and Cambridge (1885–1908). His *Principles of Economics* (1890), the first of his major works, he revised in succeeding editions. *Industry and Trade* appeared in 1918, and *Money, Credit and Commerce* in 1923. He expanded the theories of the classic English economists Adam Smith, David Ricardo, and John Stuart Mill, formulated his own theories, and developed a neoclassical school of political economy. By the time of his death he was recognized as the most influential figure in contemporary English economics. His letters and miscellaneous writings were published as *Memorials of Alfred Marshall* in 1925.

MARSHALL, George Catlett, American army officer and statesman: b. Uniontown, Pa., Dec. 31, 1880; d. Washington, D.C., Oct. 16, 1959. A career soldier who rose to the rank of five-star general (general of the army) and later became secretary of state, Marshall graduated from Virginia Military Institute in 1901. After serving in the Philippines and the western United States, he graduated from the United States Infantry-Cavalry School in 1907 and the Army Staff College in 1908, teaching there for two years. He then held various posts in the United States and served again in the Philippines (1913–1916), the last year as aide-de-camp to Gen. Hunter Liggett; at this time Maj. Gen. James Franklin Bell called him "the greatest military genius since Stonewall Jackson." When the country entered World War I he was sent to France in July 1917 as a member of the general staff, and was assigned to general headquarters in July 1918; in recognition of his brilliant direction of the St. Mihiel and Meuse-Argonne offensives he was raised to the temporary rank of lieutenant colonel. From 1919 to 1924 he was aide to Gen. John J. Pershing and helped secure passage of the National Defense Act of 1920; from his permanent rank of captain he rose to that of lieutenant colonel in 1923.

After three years with the 15th Infantry in Tientsin, China (1924–1927) and a year as instructor at the Army War College in Washington, he became assistant commandant of the Infantry School at Fort Benning, Ga. (1928–1932). After other assignments, in 1938 he was made assistant chief of staff, having risen to the rank of brigadier general in 1936. In 1939 he became chief of staff and was promoted to general.

Foreseeing that the United States would be drawn into the conflict that had broken out in Europe, in 1940 Marshall insisted on peacetime conscription and calling up Reserves and National Guard, and in 1941 he helped formulate a global strategy to aid potential allies, even before American participation. After Pearl Harbor (Dec. 7, 1941), Marshall became chief military strategist for the Allied Powers and directed operations of United States forces in both the European and Pacific theaters. In December 1944 he was made general of the army. By the end of the war he had raised the army from a force of less than 200,000 to one of more than 8 million.

Within a week of resigning his wartime post, in November 1945 Marshall was sent as President Harry S. Truman's personal envoy to resolve differences between Chinese Nationalists and Communists (see CHINA—8. History: Defeat of the Nationalists); this mission effected little but a cease-fire. In January 1947 he returned to the United States to become secretary of state. On March 12 the president, with Marshall's counsel, proposed the so-called Truman Doctrine of worldwide aid to non-Communist nations (see TRUMAN, HARRY S.). Of more direct economic assistance to war-stricken Europe was the Marshall Plan, which Marshall outlined June 5, 1947, in a commencement address at Harvard University. The plan was adopted, and the Economic Cooperation Administration (q.v.) was set up to administer it in 1948; by the time it was superseded by the Mutual Security Agency on Jan. 1, 1952, the administration had extended about $12.5 billion to 16 European nations.

In 1947, Marshall attended the Inter-American Defense Conference in Brazil which drew up the Western Hemisphere Defense Pact. In the United Nations meetings in 1947–1948 he initiated a firmer stand against Russian demands. Because of ill health he resigned as secretary of state in 1949, served briefly as president of the American Red Cross, and from 1950 to 1951, during the Korean War, served as secretary of defense. In 1953 he was awarded the Nobel Peace Prize.

MARSHALL, John, fourth chief justice of the United States: b. Prince William (now Fauquier) County, Va., Sept. 24, 1755; d. Philadelphia, Pa., July 6, 1835. No jurist has left so deep an imprint on the law and government of his country as John Marshall, chief justice of the United States from 1801 to 1835. If it is true, as Justice Oliver Wendell Holmes once said, that "there fell to Marshall perhaps the greatest place that ever was filled by a judge" (Oliver Wendell Holmes, *Speeches,* p. 90, Boston 1913), it is no less true that Marshall proved able to take full advantage of the opportunity afforded him by history. To quote Felix Frankfurter ("John Marshall and the Judicial Function," *Of Law and Men: Papers and Addresses of Felix Frankfurter,* Philip Elman, ed., pp. 4–5, New York 1956): "When Marshall came to the Supreme Court, the Constitution was essentially a virgin document. By a few opinions—a mere handful—he gave institutional direction to the inert ideas of a paper scheme of government. Such an achievement demanded an undimmed vision of the union of States as a Nation and the determination of an uncompromising devotion to such insight. Equally indispensable was the power to formulate views expressing this outlook with the persuasiveness of compelling simplicity."

Even before his appointment to the Supreme Court, Marshall's services to his state and to the United States were manifold. Like so many men of action and thought who participated in the founding of the nation, Marshall was a Virginian, born in a log cabin on the frontier. He was a third cousin of Thomas Jefferson, but unlike the other Virginians Jefferson, James Madison, and James Monroe, his political commitments were early and lastingly enlisted in support of the national government. Although he was not a Republican, neither was he totally committed to the Federalists, as his vigorous condemnation of the Alien and Sedition Laws (see ALIEN AND SEDITION ACTS) adequately demonstrated. Like Civil War veteran Justice Oliver Wendell Holmes, his only rival for the accolade of greatest American judge, Marshall also served with distinction in a war in which the existence of the United States was at stake, taking an active part as a Revolutionary officer in the critical battles of Brandywine, Valley Forge, Monmouth, and Stony Point. After the war he soon became one of the leaders of the Virginia bar, a bar of an intellectual quality hardly if ever matched in the course of American history. He served in the Virginia House of Delegates intermittently from 1782 to 1790 and in 1795–1796.

In 1795 he was compelled by personal financial problems to refuse President George Washington's request that he serve as attorney general of the United States, and a year later he rejected the appointment as American ambassador to France for the same reason. In 1797, however, he went to France as one of the special envoys to negotiate the X Y Z claims (see X Y Z CORRESPONDENCE). This role earned him not only great popularity but a monetary reward from Congress large enough to ameliorate what had theretofore been a chronic economic problem, caused largely by his joint purchase of the Fairfax estate. Nevertheless, in 1798 he refused an appointment as associate justice of the Supreme Court. A year later, however, he bowed to Washington's entreaties and was elected, thanks in part to the efforts of Patrick Henry, to the House of Representatives, where he soon assumed the burdens of spokesman for the Federalist bloc. His experience in Congress was a short one, however, for in 1800, after first refusing an appointment as secretary of war, he assumed the post of secretary of state in John Adams' cabinet. One of Adams' last important acts as president, and perhaps his most important contribution to the welfare of the country, was the appointment of Marshall as chief justice on January 20, 1801. Jefferson's earlier expressed belief that the appointment of Marshall to a judicial post would remove him from the political scene and eliminate a thorn in the side of Republicanism underestimated both Marshall's capacities and the potentialities of the judiciary as a vital force in American government (consult *The Writings of Thomas Jefferson,* Federal ed., vol. 7, p. 130, New York 1905).

Marshall Court Decisions.—Of the opinions which Marshall wrote on behalf of the court in constitutional cases, *Marbury* v. *Madison* (1 Cranch 137 [1803]) must be acknowledged as the most fundamental, for here was established, once and for all so far as American history was concerned, the right of the federal courts to pass on the validity of congressional legislation. This power of judicial review was the foundation on which all the remainder of the Marshall court's constitutional doctrine rested. But once this power was established it remained to assert the principle that the federal government could exercise not only those functions specifically authorized by the Constitution but those implicitly suggested by the language of that document as well. It has seldom since been forgotten by the court that, as Marshall put it, "It is a *constitution* we are expounding" (*M'Culloch* v. *Maryland,* 4 Wheat. 316, 407 [1819]). Had the court chosen a narrow and literal reading rather than the broad construction expressed in the M'Culloch case, it is doubtful the nation would have survived Marshall's tenure of office.

That the Supreme Court could condemn state action in violation of the Constitution would seem to have followed a fortiori from the power to review national legislation (*Cohens* v. *Virginia,* 6 Wheat. 264 [1821]), but it was not a position readily acceptable to the states or the Jeffersonians. Holmes thought the doctrine of the Cohens case more vital to the continuance of the Union than the principle announced in the Marbury case (Oliver Wendell Holmes, *Collected Legal Papers,* pp. 295–96, New York 1920). The scope of the national commerce power and the implicit limitations on the rights of the states in this area were first enunciated extensively, if not finally, in *Gibbons* v. *Ogden,* (9 Wheat. 1 [1824]). Probably the fifth of the "handful" of great constitutional opinions written by Marshall was that in *Fletcher* v. *Peck* (6 Cranch 87 [1810]), in which the court assumed the right to prevent a state from arbitrarily interfering with the property rights of an individual. It will be noted that the direction of these Marshall court rulings were all in favor of the national power as opposed to that of the states, and in extension of the judicial function at the expense of the executive and legislative branches of the federal government.

While all of these and many other Marshall opinions often aroused a large part of the country to violent attacks on the chief justice and the court, probably nothing in Marshall's judicial career caused such a storm as the trial for treason of Aaron Burr (1807, q.v.) in the United States Circuit Court at Norfolk over which the chief justice presided. Marshall's rejection of the concept of constructive treason (see TREASON) and the consequent acquittal of Burr were generally unpopular, for the hatred of Burr by Jeffersonians was matched only by those who remembered him as the killer of Alexander Hamilton. The guilt of Burr is still being debated (consult, for example, Abernethy, Thomas P., *The Burr Conspiracy,* New York 1954), but there can be no doubt that the conduct of Jefferson in publicly condemning the defendant before the trial, Marshall's unfortunate attempt to subpoena Jefferson, and Marshall's presence, during the trial, at a dinner which was attended by Burr and his legal counsel, blotted the escutcheons of both these great political antagonists.

A myth grew up, due in large part to the masterly if sycophantish *Life of John Marshall* by Senator Albert J. Beveridge (new ed., 4 vols. in 2, Boston 1939), that the Marshall court was completely dominated by the chief justice; that the other justices were mere puppets. That myth is now slowly but surely being dissipated. As Justice Frankfurter has written (*The Commerce Clause . . . ,* p. 5, Chapel Hill, N.C., 1937): "Marshall himself, hardheaded as he was and free from obvious self-deception, would doubtless be greatly amused by the claim that he was the whole of his Court"; consult also William W. Crosskey, "Mr. Chief Justice Marshall," *Mr. Justice,* Allison Dunham and Philip B. Kurland, eds., p. 3 (Chicago 1956).

When Marshall died in Philadelphia on July 6, 1835, appropriately enough the Liberty Bell inexplicably cracked as it was rung in expression of mourning for the loss of the great chief justice, of whose work Donald G. Morgan appropriately said ("Marshall, the Marshall Court, and the Constitution," *Chief Justice John Marshall; A Reappraisal,* W. Melville Jones, ed., pp. 168, 185, Ithaca, N.Y., 1956): "To a great degree, the measure of Marshall's influence . . . was in his qualities of character and personal leadership. The eminence acquired by the Supreme Court during that period and the strength imparted to the Constitution are less the work of Marshall the convinced Federalist than of Marshall the man. Here was a statesman, not a zealot; an empiricist, not a dogmatist; a leader, not a tyrant."

PHILIP B. KURLAND,
Professor of Law, The Law School, The University of Chicago

Bibliography.—Dillon, John F., *John Marshall: Life, Character, and Judicial Services,* 3 vols. (Chicago 1903); Beveridge, Albert J., *Life of John Marshall,* 2 vols. (Boston 1939); Jones, W. Melville, ed., *Chief Justice John Marshall: A Reappraisal* (Ithaca, N.Y., 1956); Servies, James A., *Bibliography of John Marshall* (Washington 1956); Konefsky, Samuel J., *John Marshall and Alexander Hamilton: Architects of the American Constitution* (New York 1964); Thayer, James B., and others, *John Marshall* (Chicago 1967).

MARSHALL, Thomas Riley, 28th vice president of the United States: b. North Manchester, Ind., March 14, 1854; d. Washington, D.C., June 1, 1925. Marshall graduated from Wabash College in 1873, studied law, and was admitted to the Indiana bar in 1875, practicing his profession at Columbia City. In 1908 he was elected governor of Indiana. His administration

(1909–1913) was progressive. Several laws that he sponsored, including an employers' liability law and a child labor law, were enacted, but he failed in his endeavor to have a new state constitution adopted.

At the Democratic National Convention held in Baltimore in 1912, he was the favorite-son candidate of the Indiana delegation for the presidency, and when Woodrow Wilson was nominated for that office, Marshall was chosen for the vice presidency. Renominated and re-elected in 1916, he served with Wilson until 1921. He was a good presiding officer of the Senate and enjoyed much popularity. He became known for his humorous remarks; in 1917, during a Senate debate on the country's needs, he said, "What this country really needs is a good five cent cigar." During President Wilson's absences from Washington and during the president's illness, Marshall often received official visitors. After his term of office expired, he made his home in Indianapolis. He was a member of the United States Coal Commission in 1922.

MARSHALL, mär'shəl, **Thurgood** (1908–), American lawyer and civil rights leader, who in 1967 became the first Negro member of the U.S. Supreme Court. A moderate in the civil rights movement, he held that equal rights for Negroes must be obtained in the courts, and he frequently cautioned against civil disobedience.

Marshall was born in Baltimore, Md., on July 2, 1908. He graduated with honors from Lincoln University in Pennsylvania and was first in his law school class at Howard University. From 1933 to 1938 he had an active but unprofitable practice, devoted largely to civil rights cases, in Baltimore. Simultaneously, he was counsel for the Baltimore branch of the National Association for the Advancement of Colored People (NAACP) whose successful attack on racial barriers at the University of Maryland Law School in 1935 was Marshall's first conspicuous victory. In 1936 he became an aide to the national organization, and for 23 years beginning in 1938 he was special counsel at NAACP headquarters in New York.

Marshall argued 32 cases for the association before the U.S. Supreme Court. He won 29 of them. Many of his successful cases concerned rights of defendants in criminal cases and exclusion of Negroes from juries. Marshall also won decisions from the court outlawing exclusion of registered Negro voters from primaries in the South (1944) and invalidating restrictive covenants aimed at preventing minorities from renting and buying real estate (1948). His most important victory was in *Brown* v. *Board of Education of Topeka*, the 1954 school desegregation case that overturned the "separate but equal" doctrine on which segregated public schools had been justified for 60 years.

Marshall resigned from the NAACP in 1961 to accept an appointment as judge of the U.S. Court of Appeals in New York. From 1965 to 1967 he was U.S. solicitor general.

MARSHALL, William Louis, United States army engineer: b. Washington, Ky., June 11, 1846; d. Washington, D.C., July 2, 1920. A grandnephew of John Marshall (q.v.), he studied at Kenyon College from 1859 to 1861. He served in the Union Army in 1862–1863, and in the following year was appointed a cadet at the United States Military Academy. Graduating in 1868, he was assigned to the Corps of Engineers as a second lieutenant. He was promoted through the grades, reaching the rank of brigadier general in 1908 on his appointment as chief of engineers. In 1870–1871, Marshall was acting assistant professor of natural and experimental philosophy at West Point, and from 1872 to 1876 he was in charge of the Colorado section of the explorations west of the 100th meridian. He discovered Marshall Pass through the Rocky Mountains in 1873, and the gold placers of Marshall Basin, San Miguel River, in Colorado, in 1875. From 1876 to 1884 he was assistant engineer on river improvement projects in Alabama, Georgia, and Tennessee, and had charge of a section of the Mississippi River. From 1884 to 1899 he was in charge of harbor improvements on Lake Michigan, and he also superintended the construction of the Hennepin Canal (1890–1899). During this period he patented a breakwater and two types of dams.

Placed in charge of the fortifications and river and harbor works at New York Harbor in 1899, he completed the 40-foot Ambrose Channel and extended Governor's Island. As chief of engineers, he was in charge of river, harbor, and fortification works in the United States from 1908 to 1910, when he retired from active service.

MARSHALL, city, Michigan, seat of Calhoun County, situated on the Kalamazoo River, 12 miles southeast of Battle Creek. The surrounding area raises livestock, grain, and onions. The city's industrial establishments produce automobile parts and trailers, heating and refrigeration equipment, pharmaceuticals, medical supplies, paint, processed meat, and dairy products. First settled in 1831, Marshall was incorporated as a city in 1859. Government is of the commission type. Population: 6,736.

MARSHALL, city, Minnesota, seat of Lyon County, situated on the Redwood River, 130 miles southwest of Minneapolis. The shipping center of an agricultural area, the city processes dairy products and poultry. It was settled in 1871 and was incorporated as a city in 1901. Marshall is governed by a mayor and a council. Population: 6,681.

MARSHALL, city, Missouri, seat of Saline County, situated 88 miles southeast of Kansas City. It is the trading center of a predominantly agricultural region that raises corn, wheat, fruit, soybeans, cattle, and sheep. The city has bottling, milling, seed and fertilizer, and milk and poultry processing plants; shoes are the principal factory product. Marshall is the seat of Missouri Valley College. Settled in 1836, it was named for John Marshall (q.v.) in 1839, and incorporated in 1866. Government is of the council-manager type. Population: 9,572.

MARSHALL, city, Texas, seat of Harrison County, situated approximately 40 miles west of Shreveport, La. It is the center of a fertile agricultural region producing cotton, vegetables, and dairy products. Although the lumbering operations of earlier days have been reduced as reserves of timber have declined, second-growth pine is used in sawmilling. The presence nearby of oil and natural gas, lignite, clay, and glass sands has stimulated the city's industrial development. The principal industries are cotton compressing; flour and lumber milling; and the manufacture of iron, steel, and lignite products, brick, carbon, crates, and clothing. Educational institutions include East Texas Baptist College; St. Mary's Academy (Roman Catholic, coeducational); and two coeducational colleges for Negroes: Wiley College (Methodist, founded 1873) and Bishop College (Baptist, founded 1881). Caddo Lake and Caddo State Park are 15 miles northeast of the city. The government is of the city manager type.

Settled in 1841, incorporated as a town in 1843 and as a city in 1848, Marshall was named for Chief Justice John Marshall, who had died in 1835. During the Civil War it was the seat of the Confederate state government of Missouri, and headquarters of the Confederate ordnance, quartermaster, and commissary departments. Pop. 23,846.

MARSHALL COLLEGE, coeducational college, Huntington, W.Va. It was established in 1837 as Marshall Academy, named in honor of Chief Justice John Marshall, a long-time friend of John Laidley, traditionally accepted as the founder of the school. It was elevated to collegiate status by the Virginia Assembly in 1858, and West Virginia State Normal School was added to it in 1867, after West Virginia had achieved statehood. The educational program established in the 1837 charter was expanded in 1921 and 1923 into the four-year baccalaureate degrees offered in the Teachers College and the College of Arts and Sciences. The Graduate Division, established in 1938, became the Graduate School in 1948. Financial support for the college is supplied by the State of West Virginia, and the state Board of Education governs.

STEWART H. SMITH,
President.

MARSHALL ISLANDS, easternmost of three adjoining archipelagoes in the western Pacific which comprise the Trust Territory of the Pacific Islands, the other two being the Caroline and the Mariana Islands. Geographically the Trust Territory comprehends nearly all of Micronesia (q.v.); politically it is governed by the United States as trustee for the United Nations. The Marshall Islands consist of two parallel chains of some 34 coral atolls, the Radak Chain to the east, and the Ratik Chain to the west; they extend about 700 miles from northwest to southeast between latitudes 4° and 15° N. and longitudes 162° and 174° E., and cover an aggregate area of 160 square miles and a land area of about 66 square miles.

Marshall Islanders are broadly classed as Micronesians; closely resembling the Malaysians, they are of medium size, with brown skin, straight or wavy black hair, and Mongoloid features. Christianity is the predominant religion. The coconut palm is the backbone of island economy; copra, the dried meat of the coconut, is processed for market on almost every island of the Trust Territory, but cacao has been introduced as an additional export crop. Taro, pandanus, breadfruit, bananas, and other fruits and vegetables are grown, and poultry and pigs are raised. In 1956 a small-scale fishing industry was started in the Marshalls; before that, fishing was on an individual basis for subsistence.

Majuro Atoll, in the Ratak Chain, is the seat of the Marshall Islands District, one of the seven districts into which the Trust Territory is divided. The atolls of Bikini and Eniwetok in the north were evacuated and placed outside the jurisdiction of the administration of the Trust when atomic bomb tests were conducted there beginning in 1946, and in 1957 the United States Air Force used Eniwetok as a base for firing research rockets. The Marshall Islands Congress is a bicameral legislative body composed of an upper chamber of hereditary nobles, the House of Iroij, and a lower chamber, the House of Assembly.

Although the Spaniards discovered and explored Micronesia in the 16th century, Spain exploited only the western part. In 1885, Germany laid claim to the neglected Marshalls, and in 1899, after the Spanish-American War, Spain sold to Germany what she had left of Micronesia. When World War I broke out, Japan took over administration of the German islands, and at the end of the war was granted a League of Nations mandate over the three archipelagoes; in violation of this she proceeded to fortify them and establish sea and air bases there. After World War II the United States succeeded Japan under the United Nations trusteeship agreement which came into force July 18, 1947. Pop. Marshall Islands (1957) 13,231.

DRAKE DE KAY,
Senior Editor, "The Encyclopedia Americana."

MARSHALL PLAN. See ECONOMIC COOPERATION ADMINISTRATION, THE.

MARSHALLTOWN, mär-shăl'toun, city, Iowa, Marshall County seat. It is located about 50 miles northeast of Des Moines, on the Iowa River and on one state and two federal highways, at an altitude of 863 feet, and is served by the Chicago and North Western, Chicago Great Western, and Minneapolis and St. Louis railroads; it also has railroad shops. Meat packing and the manufacture of heating equipment, oil and gas controls, and fire apparatus are the chief industries. The principal crops of the area are corn, soybeans, hay, and oats, and large numbers of beef cattle and hogs are pastured. Settled in 1851, the city was incorporated in 1863 and has mayor-council government. Pop. 22,521.

MARSHBUNKER. See MENHADEN.

MARSHFIELD, märsh'fēld, town, Massachusetts, in Plymouth County, 15 miles east of Brockton. It is a summer resort amid cranberry bogs. Daniel Webster lived there during the latter part of his life, and his grave is in Winslow Cemetery. Settled in 1632, the town was incorporated in 1642. Pop. 6,748.

MARSHFIELD, Oregon. See COOS BAY.

MARSHFIELD, city, Wisconsin, in Wood County. Situated 185 miles northwest of Milwaukee, at an altitude of 1,288 feet, in the northern dairy belt, the city is a shipping point for butter, cheese, and other milk products, is served by the Chicago and North Western, the Omaha, and the Soo Line railroads and North Central Airlines. It is on one federal and two state highways and has a municipal airport. Besides processing of dairy and meat products, peas and beans, industries include custom foundry and tooling, and manufacture of mobile homes, store fixtures, heaters, pumps, stainless steel tanks, cement and clay products, stock feed, beekeepers' supplies, clothing, plywood products, and dairy and barn equipment. The city has a full-time recreation program and a city youth center. Central Wisconsin State Fair is held here. The town was settled about 1868, chartered as a city in 1883, and rebuilt in 1887 after a disastrous fire. Government is by mayor and council. Pop. 14,153.

MARSHMAN, märsh'măn, **Joshua,** English missionary and Orientalist: b. Westbury Leigh, Wiltshire, England, April 20, 1768; d. Serampore, India, Dec. 5, 1837. A weaver, largely self-educated, he was one of a group that the Baptist Missionary Society sent to India in 1799. Established in Serampore in West Bengal, which was then in Danish territory, the group included Marshman's eldest son, John Clark Marshman, and William Carey (q.v.). It established a number of stations and translated the Bible or parts of it into various Indian languages, and Marshman assisted Carey in preparing a Sanskrit grammar. With others he founded (1818) *Sumachar Durpun* (*Mirror of News*), the first newspaper printed in an Eastern language, and (1821) the monthly *Friend of India,* the first English magazine published there. One of the ablest Orientalists in India, Marshman also published a translation of Confucius (1809); *Elements of Chinese Grammar* . . . (1814); and the first complete edition of the Bible in Chinese, which was also the first Chinese book printed from movable metal type.

JOHN CLARK MARSHMAN (1794–1877) worked with his father on these projects, and was himself a distinguished Orientalist. He served for many years as a secular bishop at Serampore, and published a series of law books of which one, *Guide to the Civil Law . . . of the Presidency of Fort William* (2d ed., 1848) was long the Civil Code of India. He devoted all his profits to promoting education in India. In 1852 he resigned his post as official Bengali translator to the government and returned to England. His many published works include *The Life and Times of Carey, Marshman, and Ward, Embracing the History of the Serampore Mission* (1859) and *The History of India . . . to the Close of Lord Dalhousie's Administration* (3 vols., 1863–1867).

MARSIGLI, mär-sē'lyê, COUNT **Luigi Ferdinando,** Italian scientist and soldier: b. Bologna, Italy, July 10, 1658; d. there, Nov. 1, 1730. After completing his scientific studies at Bologna, he was sent to Turkey by the Republic of Venice to make a study of its natural history and military organization. In 1683, while serving under Emperor Leopold in the war against the Turks, he was wounded, captured, and sold to a pasha, accompanying him to the siege of Vienna. His release was purchased in 1684. He fought in the War of the Spanish Succession, but was cashiered by court-martial when the fortress of Alt Breisach, where he was second in command, surrendered in 1703. Thereafter he devoted himself to science, traveled widely throughout Europe to collect scientific data, and in 1712 presented his collections to Bologna, thus initiating the Bologna Institute of Science and Art. Of his more than 20 published works, the most important are *Breve*

ristretto del saggio fisico interno alla storia del mare (1711, republished as *L'histoire physique de la mer,* 1725), an account of his scientific study of the sea at Marseille; the six-volume scientific and historical study of the Danubian countries, *Danubius Pannonico-Mysicus* (1725); and *Stato militare dell' imperio ottomano* (1732), his study of Turkish military organization.

MARSILEACEAE. See FERNS AND FERN ALLIES—*Ferns.*

MARSILIUS OF PADUA, mär-sĭl'ĭ-ŭs (Ital., MARSIGLIO DEI MAINARDINI), Italian scholar and political theorist: b. Padua (Padova), Italy, c. 1270; d. Germany, c. 1343. He studied medicine and other sciences in Padua, and about 1311 went to Paris, where by 1313 he had become rector of the university. When Pope John XXII excommunicated Louis of Bavaria (later Louis IV, Holy Roman emperor) in 1324, Marsilius, with the help of John of Jandun, canon of Senlis, prepared the treatise *Defensor Pacis* (1324, first printed in Basel in 1524), directed against the temporal power of the papacy. It held that political authority should be vested in the people (adult male citizens), who would choose a council or prince to be vested with executive authority; that the church, stripped of its worldly wealth, should become a purely spiritual power, subordinate to the state; and that, in the church, all priests should share equally in the ecclesiastical power. The *Defensor Pacis* was condemned by the pope in 1327, although it was later to exert considerable influence upon such reformers as John Wycliffe (1320?–1384) and Martin Luther (1483–1546).

Marsilius accompanied Louis to Rome and was present at the latter's coronation on Jan. 17, 1328. In addition to attempting to replace John as pope by Pietro Rainalducci as Nicholas V, Louis appointed Marsilius ecclesiastical vicar of Rome, in which position Marsilius for a while persecuted the clergy who remained faithful to John. When Louis returned to Germany in 1330, Marsilius accompanied him.

MARSTON, mär'stŭn, **John,** English dramatist and satirist: b. probably at Coventry, England, c. 1575; d. London, June 25, 1634. He graduated from Brasenose College, Oxford, in 1593 or 1594. In 1598, under the pseudonym of W. Kinsayder, he published an erotic poem, *The Metamorphosis of Pigmalion's Image. And Certain Satyres,* and a volume ·of coarse poetic satires, *The Scourge of Villanie,* which was republished with additions in 1599. Both works were burned in 1599 by order of the archbishop of Canterbury.

Although Marston wrote other poems, satires, and some Latin speeches, he was especially noted for his plays, most of them written and published between 1602 and 1607 and a product of his rivalry with Ben Jonson, the two playwrights writing for competing companies of players. They include the melodramatic *History of Antonio and Mellida* and *Antonio's Revenge,* both written in 1601 and printed in 1602; the satirical comedy *The Malcontent* (1604); *The Dutch Courtezan* (1605), bitterly inveighing against women and considered his best comedy; another satirical comedy, *Parasitaster, or the Fawne* (1606); and the vigorous *The Wonder of Women, or the Tragedie of Sophonisba* (1606).

His authorship of the tragedy *The Insatiate Countess,* published under his name in 1613, is doubtful. He may have collaborated on the comedy *Histriomastix* (1610) and the farcical *Jack Drum's Entertainment* (1616), both published anonymously.

Marston, although he has been called "a screech owl among the singing birds," wrote plays that were popular in their day, whether they were comedies satirizing the follies of the court or melodramas of the type then in vogue. He was satirized by Ben Jonson in *The Poetaster* (1601) for his pompous diction and high-flown melodrama, and in turn probably collaborated with Thomas Dekker in lampooning Jonson in *Satiromastix* (1602); but he dedicated *The Malcontent* to Jonson and collaborated with him and George Chapman on *Eastward Ho!* (1605), one of the best comedies of the period, containing passages which offended the king's Scottish friends and resulted in the three authors being thrown into prison for a short time. In 1609, Marston was ordained, and in 1616 he became rector of Christchurch, Hampshire; he held this charge until 1631. His collected plays were published in 1633; his complete works, edited by James Orchard Halliwell, appeared in three volumes in 1856; and another edition in three volumes, edited by Arthur Henry Bullen, in 1887.

MARSTON, John Westland, English dramatist: b. Boston, Lincolnshire, England, Jan. 30, 1819; d. London, Jan. 5, 1890. At the age of 15 he became a clerk in his uncle's law office in London, but was more interested in literature and the theater than in law. He joined a mystical group somewhat resembling the Transcendentalists of New England, editing for it a periodical, *The Psyche.* He published a volume of verse, *Gerald, a Dramatic Poem, and Other Poems* (1842) and won recognition as a critic of poetry, his review of Algernon Charles Swinburne's *Atalanta in Calydon* being especially famous. But he is known chiefly for his dramas, many of them in blank verse, which achieved considerable success on the stage. Among them are *The Patrician's Daughter* (1841), based on the difficulties he himself encountered in his courtship and marriage; the historical drama *Strathmore* (1849), which he considered his best work; *Marie de Méranie,* another historical drama (1850); *Donna Diana* (1863), based on a play by Augustín Moreto y Cabaña (1618?–1669) and usually considered his best play; *The Favorite of Fortune* (1866); and *Broken Spells* (1873). Although the plays are not especially distinguished, they are among the few of the period that aimed at literary excellence.

His son, PHILIP BOURKE MARSTON (1850–1887), also a poet, was blind from early childhood as the result of an accident. His sensitive but somewhat monotonous poems, tending to melancholy and strongly influenced by Pre-Raphaelitism (see PRE-RAPHAELITES) were especially popular in the United States. He published *Song-tide, and Other Poems* (1871), *All in All* (1875), *Wind-Voices* (1883), and a collection of short stories, *For a Song's Sake, and Other Stories* (1887).

MARSTON MOOR, mär'stŭn mōor, plain, England, in Yorkshire, about 8 miles northwest of York. It was the scene of a great battle in the English Civil War in which on July 2, 1644 Oliver Cromwell's Parliamentary troops (about 24,000) defeated the royal forces (about 22,000) under Prince Rupert. The victory gave Parliament control of the north of England.

MARSUPIAL FROG, mär-sū'pĭ-ăl frŏg, any of several South American tree frogs (Hylidae) of the genus *Gastrotheca* which incubate the eggs in a brood pouch of skin on the back of the female. At breeding time, the female frog adopts a peculiar posture with the posterior end of the body tilted upward. The eggs are expelled from the cloaca and slide forward and downward into the pouch; on the way they are fertilized by the male frog, which holds itself clasped to the back of the female. In some species the eggs are abundantly provided with yolk, and the young live on this yolk until they emerge as fully formed little frogs. In species with less yolk in each egg, the young emerge as tadpoles and undergo subsequent development in a free-living state. Some species closely related to *Gastrotheca* carry the eggs affixed to the back, but lack the protective covering of the brood pouch.

RICHARD G. ZWEIFEL.

MARSUPIALIA, mär-sū-pĭ-ā'lĭ-à, one of three divisions of the class of vetebrate animals known as mammals. (In the Simpson classification—see MAMMALS—*Classification*—marsupials constitute an order in the infraclass Metatheria in the subclass Theria.) The name is derived from the Latin *marsupium,* meaning pouch; this pouch of skin is located on the underside of the body of the female near the hind legs. The milk glands and the teats are contained in the pouch. The newborn young are very small and undeveloped; they crawl into the pouch, where they attach themselves to the teats and continue their growth for many weeks. Not all marsupials have well-developed pouches. Marsupials at the present time are found only in the New Guinea-Australia region, and in North, Central, and South America. The best-known animals of this group are the kangaroo and the koala of Australia and the common opossums of the Americas.

Origin and Evolution.—The oldest known fossil marsupial was discovered in Montana in Upper Cretaceous strata. This "opossum," which lived about 100 million years ago, and other marsupials evolved from even more primitive mammals of a still earlier period. Evidence from other fossil remains shows that marsupials were at one time widely distributed around the world. With the rise and spread of the higher mammals (that is, members of the cat and dog families), however, marsupials could not compete, and their ranges became more and more restricted. The early marsupials that found their way to the islands of New Guinea, Australia, and Tasmania were isolated there for millions of years without competition from more advanced animals. The result was that these first marsupials gradually radiated out into the many kinds of country available and took advantage of different kinds of food. This process of slowly evolving adaptation has given us the varied marsupials listed in the classification below. Many other kinds are known from fossils; these have become extinct, it is thought, because of climatic changes or other changes in the environment with which the animals could not cope. An excellent example of the seriousness of the competition between placentals (mammals whose fetus is nourished in the uterus) and marsupials can be seen in Australia today. The European colonization of this continent, together with the introduction of dogs, cats, rabbits, foxes, Norway rats, and sheep, has resulted in the extermination of a number of species and the decimation of many more. In the United States and Canada, however, the common opossum has been remarkably successful and is rapidly extending its range.

Classification.—The living marsupials are now usually divided into five groups or super-families:

(1) *Didelphoidea*—the true opossums, small to medium-sized animals of many kinds, found chiefly in Central and South America; one species in North America.

(2) *Dasyuroidea*—the marsupial "mice" and "rats," native "cats," pouched "mole," banded "anteater," Tasmanian devil, and Tasmanian "wolf" of the Australian region.

(3) *Perameloidea*—the bandicoots, long-nosed, terrestrial animals peculiar to New Guinea and Australia.

(4) *Caenolestoidea*—small marsupial shrews found only in the Andean region of South America.

(5) *Phalangeroidea*—the brush-tailed and ring-tailed possums (in Australia "opossums" are usually called possums to distinguish them from the true opossums of the Americas), feather-tailed phalangers, honey possums, and striped phalangers; cuscuses or woolly possums; pygmy, sugar, and giant gliders or flying "squirrels"; kangaroos, wallabies (small and medium-sized kangaroos), wallaroos, rat kangaroos, koalas, and wombats of Australia, New Guinea, and many adjacent islands.

The early settlers of Australia either named the marsupials after the common English animals of their acquaintance (as will be seen from the preceding list), or adopted a form of the native aboriginal name. To the latter practice we owe some of the most delightful names in zoology; to the former, some of the most confusing.

Natural History.—To many people the red and the great gray kangaroos typify the usual concept of a marsupial. These take the place of antelopes on the Australian plains. In New Guinea and tropical North Queensland live the tree-climbing kangaroos of the mountain forests. They have relatively short hind feet and are completely at home in the trees. There are many small wallabies adapted to the most diverse habitats, from the lowland tropical rain forest to high mountain forests, grasslands, and dry rocky hills. Among the phalangers we find the most arboreal of the marsupials; some have become proficient gliders, and in the giant eucalyptus forests gliding flights up to 100 yards have been recorded. The koala, or native bear, has captured the imagination of the children of the world; the toy Teddy bear is supposed to have been developed from it. A unique arboreal animal with a diet restricted to the leaves of a few species of eucalyptus trees, the koala has been reduced by hunting and epidemic disease to a fraction of its former numbers. The wombat, with its stout, strong-clawed limbs, is an expert burrow digger; it is the Australian counterpart of the badger.

The nocturnal bandicoots, ranging in size from the black pygmy species of the New Guinea mountains to the 30-inch giant of the lowland rain forest, have an insatiable appetite for beetle grubs and other insect food. Their claws and long snouts serve them well in this search. One of the most beautiful of the marsupials, the bilby or Australian rabbit bandicoot, has long ears and silky blue-gray fur, and is able to burrow rapidly. Most peculiar of the burrowers is the marsupial "mole," which closely resembles the golden "mole" of South Africa. The pouch opens backward, the snout has a horny shield, the eyes are atrophied, and there are no external ears. Zoologists term such cases of resemblance convergent evolution.

Tasmania is the last redoubt of two large carnivorous marsupials, the Tasmanian devil and the Tasmanian "wolf." The black-haired devil is about 30 inches long, has a stocky build, and powerful crushing teeth. Its surly appearance and reputation as a killer of domestic animals contributed to its name. In captivity, however, it makes a friendly and interesting pet. The "wolf" had the misfortune to develop a taste for sheep, and as a result of bounty hunting has almost been extirpated. The combined head and body of a large male measure about 3½ feet, and the peculiar thick-based tail about 20 inches. Fifteen to 20 blackish stripes on the lower part of the back, the flanks, and the base of the tail are so striking that the name of tiger is often used. Smaller carnivores include the spotted native "cats" and the many species of *Phascogale,* or marsupial "rats" and "mice." Their diet ranges from insects and frogs to the introduced rats, mice, and rabbits. In spite of this economic service some individuals come into conflict with man as poultry killers. These marsupials are roughly the equivalent of weasels and minks of the Western Hemisphere. One of the most attractive small marsupials is the rusty-colored, brush-tailed wombat or banded "anteater." Termites, which abound in Australia, are its preferred diet. This is one of the marsupials without a pouch, but the female carries her nipple-attached young wherever she goes. The web-footed yapok or water opossum is the most handsome of the American marsupials.

Reproduction.—The majority of mammals belong to the placental subclass. These animals are nourished inside the body of the female for a relatively long period of time by means of the placenta or organ of contact of the embryo with the uterus. The young when born are relatively large and well developed. Two mammals, the platypus and the spiny "anteater," lay eggs from which the young hatch a few days later. The marsupials, in contrast to these two methods, are born in a very undeveloped state, and are nourished for weeks at the teat either in a pouch or in the mammary gland area. For many years marsupial birth was a subject of conjecture. Reliable observations now give us the following sequence of events. Normal birth from the opening of the vagina occurs; the newborn animal is very small (from one quarter of an inch to a little over one inch), but the forelimbs are well developed and the digits equipped with claws; the young, using strong and persistent reflex climbing motions of the forelimbs, progresses through the fur from the vagina to the pouch or to the mammary field where it finds a teat and attaches itself. The well-developed tongue and muscles of the mouth region combine to form a very firm attachment to the nipple, so strong in fact that the careless separation of the young from the teat may result in rupture and bleeding of the mouth tissues. For this reason, and because of the small size, many people without knowledge of anatomy once believed that the young were born from the teat. Others believed that the female aided the transfer from the vagina to pouch by picking up the newborn in her lips. Young have been seen to miss the target area and fall to the ground; the female has made no effort to rescue them. Striated muscle fibers are present among the lobes of the mammary glands; this has led some writers to suggest that in the early stages, at least, milk is forcibly expressed into the mouth of the young. In the Virginia opossum, however, sucking begins the moment contact is made with the nipple. The young may continue to use the pouch as a retreat for some time after it is able to feed and care for itself.

Bibliography.—Troughton, Ellis LeGeyt, *Furred Animals of Australia* (Sydney and London 1951); New York 1952); Hartman, Carl G., *Possums* (Austin, Texas, 1952; New York 1953); Barrett, Charles Leslie, *An Australian Animal Book*, 2d ed. (New York and London 1955); Davis, David W., and Golley, Frank B., *Principles in Mammology* (New York 1963); Bourlière, Francois, *The Natural History of Mammals*, 3d ed. (New York 1964).

HOBART M. VAN DEUSEN,
The American Museum of Natural History, New York.

MARSYAS, mär′sĭ-ăs, in Greek mythology, one of the sileni of Asia Minor, the son of Hyagnis. Athena, having invented a flute (or oboe), threw it away when she caught sight of her reflection in water while playing the instrument and saw how it distorted her features. She pronounced the severest maledictions against anyone who should take it up. Marsyas found the instrument and soon acquired such skill in playing it that he challenged Apollo to a contest. The god accepted the challenge on condition that the victor might do as he pleased with the vanquished. The Muses, or in some versions of the myth the Nysaeans, acted as judges and decided in favor of Apollo, whereupon the god bound Marsyas to a tree and flayed him alive, so fulfilling Athena's curse. A statue of Marsyas stood in the Roman Forum; others in various colonial cities were regarded as symbols of freedom.

MARTEL, Charles. See CHARLES MARTEL.

MARTEL, mär-těl′, SIR **Giffard Le Quesne**, British army officer, b. Southampton, England, Oct. 10, 1889. He was educated at Wellington College, a private school in Berkshire. In World War I he played an important part in developing the use of the tank in combat. After the war he continued his studies in this field, constructing the first one-man tank in 1925. In the years preceding World War II he was assistant director of mechanization at the British War Office (1936–1938), and deputy director (1938–1939); and in 1940 was made commander of the Royal Armoured Corps (formed by the merger of the tanks corp with the mechanized cavalry units). He was made lieutenant general in 1942, and in 1943 headed a British military mission to Moscow. His books include *In the Wake of the Tank* (1931), *Our Armoured Forces* (1945), *The Russian Outlook* (1947), *An Outspoken Soldier* (memoirs, 1949), and *East Versus West* (1952).

MARTEL DE JANVILLE, mär-těl′ dě zhän-vēl′, COMTESSE de (SIBYLLE GABRIELLE MARIE ANTOINETTE DE RIQUETI DE MIRABEAU; pseudonym GYP). French novelist: b. Château de Koëtsal, Morbihan Department, France, Aug. 15, 1850; d. Neuilly-sur-Seine, June 29, 1932. She was the great grandniece of the comte de Mirabeau. As Gyp she contributed stories to *La vie parisienne* and *La revue des deux mondes* and wrote over 100 novels presenting vivid pictures of the political life and worldly society of Paris in the late 19th and early 20th centuries. Her wit and satire are brilliant, and her dialogue is especially effective. A number of her novels she developed into successful plays. She created such well-known types of Parisian life as Loulou and Paulette as well as the Parisian man of the period, and introduced the *enfant terrible* into literature. Among her novels are *Le petit Bob* (1882); *Autour du mariage* (1883); *Autour du divorce* (1886), *Le mariage de Chiffon* (1894); and *Un ménage dernier cri* (1903). Her reminiscences of her childhood appeared as *Souvenirs d'une petite fille* (1927–1928).

MARTEN, mär′tĭn; -t′n, **Henry** or **Harry,** English statesman and regicide: b. Oxford, England, 1602; d. Chepstow, Sept. 9, 1680. In 1640 he was elected to the Long Parliament, which was to bring to a head the struggle between Charles I and Parliament. He was so vigorous in his opposition to the king that Charles attempted unsuccessfully to have him tried for treason. For saying that the royal family should be eliminated, he was expelled from Parliament and imprisoned briefly in the Tower of London in 1643. After serving as commander in chief of the Parliamentary infantry in the siege of Dennington Castle in the winter of 1644–1645, he was readmitted to Parliament in 1646, continuing his campaign against the king and becoming popular for his attacks on abuses of all kinds and for his courage, forthrightness, and "wondrous poignant, pertinent, and witty speeches."

Marten was suspicious of Oliver Cromwell's aims; it is said he planned to assassinate him at one point, and he later said: "Had I suspected that the ax which took off the king's head should have been made a stirrup for our first false general, I should sooner have consented to my own death than his"; nevertheless he joined Cromwell in the north when war again broke out in 1648 and returned to Parliament with him after Pride's Purge had eliminated the royalist members. He helped prepare for the king's trial and, as one of the judges, signed the death warrant. In 1649 he was elected a member of the council of state for the commonwealth, but disappeared temporarily from political life when Cromwell dispersed Parliament in 1653.

Outlawed for debt in 1655, Marten was imprisoned in 1656 and 1657, but was returned to Parliament in 1659 and was again a member of the council of state. When Charles II came to power and summoned the regicides to surrender, Marten obeyed the summons, pleaded not guilty at his trial on Oct. 16, 1660, and ably conducted his own defense. Although he was convicted, execution was suspended, possibly because when in power he had acted to save the lives of many endangered royalists, and he spent the rest of his life in prison.

MARTEN, mär′těn, any of several long-bodied, short-legged animals which comprise the genus *Martes* of the weasel family, Mustelidae. Martens are found in the forested regions of the Northern Hemisphere, where they feed on a variety of small mammals and are much hunted for their valuable fur. Of the eight recognized species, two are found in North America.

The pine marten (*Martes martes*) and the beech or stone marten (*M. foina*) are found in Europe and Asia. The brown fur of the pine marten is more valued than that of the lighter-colored beech marten. Both species have a yellow-white chest patch. The sable (*M. zibellina*) is the marten most valued for its fur. Although once found over a wide area of Asia, it has been so hunted that it now exists only in remote areas of Siberia. The Japanese marten (*M. melampus*), the yellow-throated marten (*M. flavigula*) of southeastern Asia, and the Indian marten (*M. gwatkinsi*) are less valued than the other species.

The American marten, known also as the American pine marten or Hudson Bay sable (*M. americana*), lives in the coniferous forests of North America. Males are about 24 inches long, of which one third is tail, and weigh about two pounds; females are 10 per cent smaller and 35 per cent lighter. The body is dark brown, the head paler, and there is a yellowish orange patch on the chest. The mating season is in July, and the young, numbering one to five, are born in March or April.

The fisher (*M. pennanti*) is the largest of the martens, males being about 37 inches long, of which 14 inches is tail, and weighing about eight pounds. The females are about 15 per cent smaller and half the weight. Fishers are dark brown, nearly black, and are often grizzled. The tail is long and bushy, giving the animal a foxlike appearance. They are found over much the same area as the American marten, and feed largely on hares, porcupines, small mammals, and carrion. They mate in April, and the young are born 50 weeks later.

The raising of martens on fur farms is difficult, and when fur prices are low few farming ventures are successful. Some sable farming is done in Russia; in Canada, in 1956, less than 1 per cent of the martens sold came from farms.

Consult de Vos, Antoon, *Ecology and Management of Fishers and Marten in Ontario,* Ontario Dept. of Lands and Forests Technical Bulletin (Toronto 1952).

RICHARD G. VAN GELDER,
Assistant Curator of Mammals, The American Museum of Natural History, New York.

MARTENS, mär′tĕns, **Frederic Frommhold de** (Russ. FYODOR FYODOROVICH MARTENS), Russian jurist and diplomat: b. Parnu, Estonia, then part of Russia, Aug. 27, 1845; d. St. Petersburg (now Leningrad), June 20, 1909. He was educated at the University of St. Petersburg, where he was later (1873–1907) professor of international law. Entering the Russian ministry of foreign affairs in 1868, he became legal adviser to the foreign office and represented the government at many international conferences, including the negotiations to end the Russo-Japanese War, which led to the Treaty of Portsmouth (1905). A recognized authority on international law and a skilled arbitrator, he was awarded the Nobel Peace Prize in 1902. His best-known published work is *The International Law of Civilized Nations* (2 vols., 1882–1883), translated into French (3 vols., 1883–1887, and into German (2 vols., 1883–1886). He also edited the important 15-volume *Recueil des traités et conventions conclus par la Russie avec les puissances étrangères* (1874–1909), a compendium of treaties between Russia and other powers, with introductions giving their diplomatic background.

MARTENSITE, mär′tĕnz-īt, a constituent of steel, being a supersaturated solid solution of carbon in iron, which is retained by sudden cooling (quenching) and confers hardness upon the steel.

LEWIS S. RAMSDELL.

MARTHA, mär′thả, the sister of Mary and Lazarus, in the gospels of Luke and John. In Luke 10:38–42 the two women appear without Lazarus; in John 11–12 they are present at the raising of Lazarus from the grave, and we are told that their home is in Bethany. In both passages Martha is an energetic, practical, positive person, while Mary is more reserved and devout. In the incident told by Luke, they entertain Jesus in their home when He is on His last journey to Jerusalem. When Martha complains that Mary is not helping her prepare the meal, but sits at Jesus' feet and listens to His teaching, Jesus replies, "Martha, Martha, you are anxious and troubled about many things; one thing is needful. Mary has chosen the good portion, which shall not be taken away from her." (The text of verse 42 is uncertain; some manuscripts read, "Few things are needful, or only one," which may mean either one dish of food or one concern in life, namely, religious devotion.) The two characters, Martha the practical and Mary the devout (although essentially they are not contradictory), have given their names in later art and literature to two types of religious devotion, as in Stephen Graham's book *The Way of Martha and the Way of Mary* (1915), a study of Eastern Christianity.

FREDERICK C. GRANT.

MARTHA, opera in four acts by Friedrich von Flotow (q.v.), with libretto by Friedrich Wilhelm Riese (W. Friedrich). It is the operatic version of a ballet-pantomime *Lady Henriette ou la servante de Greenwich,* with music by von Flotow and others, which was produced in Paris in 1844. The opera was first performed in Vienna on Nov. 25, 1847, and became widely popular. Its first performance in the United States was at Niblo's Garden, New York City, on Nov. 1, 1852. It makes use of Thomas Moore's famous song *The Last Rose of Summer* (to the tune of an Irish folksong).

The action takes place in and near Richmond, England, in the reign of Queen Anne. The cast includes Lady Harriet Durham (soprano); Nancy, her maid and confidante (mezzo-soprano); Lionel (tenor); Plunkett (bass); Sir Tristan, Lady Harriet's cousin (bass); the Judge of Richmond (bass); servants, and others.

In Act I, Lady Harriet and Nancy persuade Tristan to accompany them to the maid's market at Richmond where, disguised as the maids Martha and Julia, they pretend to seek employment and mischievously accept positions with Plunkett, a rich farmer, and his supposed foster brother Lionel. To bind the bargain they receive a small payment on account of their wages, and because money has changed hands the Judge of Richmond forces them to carry out their bargain. In Act II, Lionel falls in love with Martha, Plunkett with Julia. Sir Tristan appears, scolds the two girls, and helps them to escape during the night. In Act III, Julia rejects Plunkett's suit and Martha rejects Lionel's, revealing her identity; but through a ring he is wearing, Lionel is discovered to be the son of a wealthy man of high rank and is reinstated in his possessions. In Act IV, the happily united Julia (Nancy) and Plunkett bring Martha (Lady Harriet) and Lionel together, and all ends happily.

HERBERT WEINSTOCK,
Author of "Chopin, the Man and His Music."

MARTHA'S VINEYARD, mär'thȧz vĭn'-yẽrd, an island in southeastern Massachusetts. Vineyard Sound separates it from the Elizabeth Islands, with which it comprises Dukes County, as well as from the southernmost part of Cape Cod. It is roughly triangular in shape and of glacial formation; a ridge of boulder-strewn hills on the northerly side, the highest 311 feet, falls to a broad outwash plain broken along the ocean shore by numerous great ponds. Its greatest length is 19¼ miles, its greatest width 9⅜ miles.

The island is an important summer resort, its waters noted for yachting; fisheries and shell-fisheries are productive. Year-round air service operates to New York and Boston, steamboats to Nantucket and New Bedford, and a ferry, a 45-minute run, to Woods Hole.

The townships are: Edgartown, the county seat, a considerable whaling port in the 19th century; Tisbury, including the village of Vineyard Haven, formerly important as a port of call for coastal vessels; Oak Bluffs, a resort town evolved from a Methodist camp meeting first held in 1835; West Tisbury; Chilmark, including the seaward island of Noman's Land and the fishing village of Menemsha; and Gay Head, named for its colorful clay cliffs, an Indian reservation until 1870.

The island was discovered and named in 1602 by the English navigator Bartholomew Gosnold, and settled in 1642 by Thomas Mayhew, whose son, also named Thomas, founded a line of missionary Mayhews responsible for unbroken amity with the Indians. The sovereignty of New York, based upon a 1641 grant to Mayhew from the earl of Sterling, patentee under Charles I, continued until 1692. Pop. Dukes County 5,829, summer pop. estimated from 30,000 to 40,000 at seasonal peaks.

HENRY BEETLE HOUGH,
Editor, "Vineyard Gazette," Edgartown.

MARTI, mär-tē', **José Julian,** Cuban patriot and writer: b. Havana, Cuba, Jan. 28, 1853; d. Dos Ríos, May 19, 1895. As a youth Marti was condemned to the quarries for his political activities, and in 1871 was banished to Spain, where he studied law at Saragossa, graduating in 1876. He then taught literature and philosophy at the University of Guatemala for several years. Returning to Cuba, he was implicated in the revolutionary movement of 1879, and was again deported to Spain. In 1890 he went to New York City, serving as consul for Uruguay, Paraguay, and Argentina, and publishing *La patria,* a periodical devoted to Cuban interests. An able orator and writer, he launched a crusade for Cuban independence from Spain, founding the Cuban Revolutionary Party. In 1894 he attempted to lead a company of armed Cuban revolutionaries from the United States to Cuba,

but was intercepted in Florida. The next year he succeeded in reaching Cuba, joined Gen. Máximo Gómez y Báez, and was killed in a skirmish with Spanish forces at Dos Ríos. Not only is he credited with having done more than any other single person to secure Cuban independence, but he was also a gifted poet and regarded as one of the greatest Spanish-American prose writers, a precursor of the *modernista* movement. His writings were collected in 73 volumes as *Obras completas* (Havana 1936–1953). See also CUBA —*9. Cultural Life* (Literature), and *10. History* (Revolution of 1895).

Consult Mañach, Jorge, *Marti, Apostle of Freedom,* tr. by Coley Taylor (New York 1950); Lizaso, Félix, *Marti, Martyr of Cuban Independence,* tr. by E. E. Shuler (Albuquerque 1953).

MARTIAL, mär'shăl (Lat. MARCUS VALERIUS MARTIALIS), Roman epigrammatist: b. Bilbilis (near Calatayud), Spain, March 1, c. 40 A.D.; d. in Spain, c. 104 A.D. After his local education, Martial in 64 went to Rome, where his countrymen, the poet Lucan, the philosopher Seneca, and the orator Quintilian, helped to launch him on a literary career which rapidly resulted in his renown as antiquity's most eminent and most prolific writer of epigrammatic poetry.

Of Martial's life for 16 years after his arrival in Rome, little is known. At first he lived in an attic high in a lodging house; later he had his own house and a farm (the latter near Nomentum, 15 miles from Rome), each apparently procured through patrons whose insolence he censured, while he, as their client, flattered them by his written wit in order to win the wherewithal to live. He secured some social standing after Emperor Titus (r. 79–81) had made him an honorary military tribune. Martial was on good terms with most of his chief literary contemporaries, of whom Pliny the Younger paid his passage back to Spain when Martial, at last disgusted at his life of 35 years in the capital as a client, returned to Bilbilis in 98 to enjoy a small rural estate presented to him by a Spanish patroness, Marcella, whom he may have married.

Martial's poems fall into four parts: (1) *Liber de spectaculis (Book on Spectacles),* issued in 80 A.D., contains 33 short poems commemorating the public contests sponsored by Emperor Titus to dedicate the Flavian Amphitheater (the Colosseum) in Rome. (2–3) *Xenia (Guest Gifts)* and *Apophoreta (Gifts to Take Home),* published during 84–85, comprise, respectively, 127 and 223 poems (all but 5 in distichs), intended to be inscribed as mottoes on gifts presented at the Saturnalia (q.v.). These collections now constitute the 13th and 14th books of the *Epigrams.* (4) *Epigrammata (Epigrams),* appearing at intervals between 86 and 102, have 1,172 epigrams in 12 books and are his really characteristic work. About four fifths of Martial's total production of 1,555 poems are in elegiac couplets (a six-foot line followed by a five-foot line).

It would be difficult to name any phase of Roman life which Martial does not depict with pungent pen. He himself says, "My page smacks of human life." Here pass all classes from emperor and courtier to peddler and beggar: patron, client, physician, lawyer, philosopher, teacher, merchant, barber, auctioneer, jockey, innkeeper, fop, slave, parasite, debauchee. It is because he brings us into contact with men and women— high and low, rich and poor, virtuous and vicious —on the plane of everyday existence that Martial from his day to ours has been one of the most popular poets.

In his chosen field Martial stands without a rival, and his influence has never ceased. If the highest form of art is to conceal art, Martial is a consummate artist. The words fall into their places with fitness. The point or sting, whether dependent on pun or antithesis or unexpected twist, is usually postponed to the end of the epigram. Many of the best epigrams in modern languages are translations or adaptations of his character sketches and descriptions of social life.

While the chief characteristic of his epigrams is their wit, Martial stands accused of two faults: servility and indecency. As to the first, in antiquity literary men without independent means could not exist without wealthy patrons, who often demanded adulation as the recognized price of material support. The second charge can be confined to only a small part (about one tenth) of his poetry, but most of his objectionable poems are indescribably obscene. However, this obscenity is overshadowed by his scorn of hypocrisy, his freedom from envy, and his affection for his friends. See also EPIGRAM.

Bibliography.—The best Latin text of Martial is by Wallace M. Lindsay, *M. Val. Martialis epigrammata,* 2d ed. (Oxford 1929). The most convenient Latin text with English prose translation on opposite pages is by Walter C. A. Ker, *Martial: Epigrams,* 2 vols. (London 1919–20; Cambridge, Mass., 1947–50). Consult also Nixon, Paul, *Martial and the Modern Epigram* (New York 1927); Weinreich, Otto, *Studien zu Martial* (Stuttgart 1928); Pepe, Luigi, *Marziale* (Naples 1950).

P. R. COLEMAN-NORTON,
Princeton University.

MARTIAL LAW (from *lex martialis,* the regulations enforced by the Court of the Constable and Marshal in medieval England, charged with maintaining justice in the army in wartime or when it was on foreign service), military rule exercised by a state over its own citizens in an emergency which justifies such action, either in time of war or on any occasion when the civil authorities, because of public disorder or natural catastrophe, are unable to preserve order or enforce their laws. Martial law is the law of necessity asserting itself. Actually, martial law is not law in the ordinary sense of that word, but simply the assumption of absolute power by the executive branch of the government, backed up by military force. The will of the executive, or of the responsible military commander, is substituted for the due process of civil courts. Police power is exercised by military units; persons charged with obstructing the military in its enforcement of order may be punished by military courts.

The original meaning of the term appears to have been the same as that of present-day *military law*—those laws relating to the government of the army itself. English legal opinion during the 17th century held that martial law came into existence only on the outbreak of war or rebellion, and even then applied only to members of the armed forces. These beliefs were embodied in the Petition of Right (q.v., 1628), in which Parliament, aroused by the king's employment of the *lex martialis* to try civilians as if they were subject to military law, forbade the trial of civilians by martial law in peacetime without either definitely or impliedly legalizing its use in time of

war. Subsequent developments, including the problems of British rule in Ireland and India, led to modification of this original position. The Defense of the Realm acts (1914–1915) introduced a form of statutory martial law, while the Emergency Powers Act (1920) gave the government various powers, subject to the approval of Parliament, to deal with industrial disturbances.

On the European continent and in Latin American countries, martial law is commonly called *state of siege,* a term which has its origin in the traditional custom of transferring all civil authority in a besieged town to its military commander.

In the United States, martial law is not directly mentioned in the Constitution, but is authorized by implication in that clause (Art. 1, sect. 9, clause 2) which permits the suspension of the privileges of habeas corpus when, in cases of invasion or rebellion, such action is essential to the general safety. By decision of the Supreme Court, a state legislature may proclaim martial law whenever the public safety demands it. As in England the principal justification for the declaration of military law is the inability of the civil courts to exercise their functions; if these courts are able, with the aid of the military, to remain open and functioning, the imposition of martial law is considered unnecessary. Instances of the employment of martial law in the United States include New Orleans in 1815, in the border states during the Civil War, and during World War I. A modified form was used to restore order in San Francisco following the 1906 earthquake.

JOHN R. ELTING,
Lieutenant Colonel, Department of Military Art and Engineering, United States Military Academy.

MARTIN, mär'tĭn; -t'n, SAINT (also known as ST. MARTIN OF TOURS): b. Sabaria (now Szombathely in western Hungary, then capital of the Roman province of Pannonia); d. Tours, France, Nov. 8, ?397. Most of the facts of his life come to us through his disciple, Sulpicius Severus. The son of pagan parents who later removed to Pavia in northern Italy, he was forced unwillingly into the army at 15 and served until his discharge after the age of 20. He then went to Poitiers, France, where he became a disciple of St. Hilary, bishop of Poitiers and vigorous opponent of Arianism. Returning to Italy, Martin converted his mother to Christianity and established himself at Milan until driven out by the Arian bishop Auxentius, seeking refuge on the Isola d'Albenga in the Tyrrhenian Sea. He returned to Poitiers about 360, and having received a piece of land from Hilary, assembled about himself a group of hermits. This monastery, Ligugé, continued until 1607 and was revived by the Solesmes Benedictines in 1852. In 371 Martin, although unwilling, was chosen by the people of Tours as their bishop. He was indefatigable in preaching Christianity and combating paganism. He founded the famous abbey of Marmoutier near Tours. Many miracles are ascribed to him by early chroniclers, and he is an important figure in folklore and art. He is frequently depicted as having divided his cloak with a beggar and on the following night being rewarded by a vision of Christ making known to the angels Martin's act of charity. He vainly counseled moderation in the treatment of the Priscillianist heresy then current in Spain (see PRISCILLIAN), and opposed the execution of the Priscillianists. His name is found in the Canon of the Mass according to the Gelasian Sacramentary and the Bobbio Missal and has figured similarly in local French usage. In France he has always been one of the most popular saints; his day is November 11 in the church calendar.

Bibliography.—Severus, Sulpicius, *De vita beati Martini*, ed. by Karl Felix von Halm in the Vienna *Corpus*, vol. 1, pp. 107–216 (Vienna 1866); Babut, Charles Edouard, *St. Martin de Tours* (Paris 1912), whose destructive criticism was answered by P. H. Delahaye in *Analecta Bollandiana*, vol 38, pp. 1–136 (Brussels 1920) and by Camille Jullian in *Révue des études anciennes*, vols. 24 and 25 (Bordeaux 1922, 1923). There is an English translation of the Severus Sulpicius *Life in Niceta of Remesiania: Writings; Severus Sulpicius Writings . . .*, vol. 7 in the *Fathers of the Church* series (New York 1949), and in *The Western Fathers*, ed. by Frederick Russell Hoare, in *The Makers of Christendom* series (London and New York 1954).

ALASTAIR GUINAN,
Lecturer, Hunter College.

MARTIN I, SAINT, pope, and martyr: b. Todi, Italy; d. Chersonesus Heracleotica on the Crimean peninsula, Sept. 16, 655. Elected pope in 649 to succeed Theodore I and consecrated without the consent of the Byzantine emperor Constans II, Martin convoked a council of 105 Western bishops which discussed and condemned the Monothelite heresy (see MONOTHELETES) sponsored by the Byzantine court. Constans sent the exarch Olympius to Rome to sow dissension between the pope and the bishops, in which mission Olympius was unsuccessful. Constans then sent the exarch Theodore Calliopas (Kalliopes) to Rome in 653 to arrest Martin. After a protracted journey to Constantinople (now Istanbul) lasting from June 19, 653, to Sept. 17, 653 or 654, Martin was tried on charges of treason and, when he persistently refused to join in communion with the church of Constantinople, was condemned, degraded, and exiled. He is venerated as a martyr by the Roman Church on November 12; the Eastern churches honor him on other days.

Bibliography.—"Epistolae Martini," in *Patrologiae Latinae*, 221 vols. (Paris 1844–64): vol. 87, pp. 197–204; Jaffe, Philipp, *Regesta pontificum Romanorum*, 2 vols. (Leipzig 1885–88): vol. 1, pp. 230–243; *Liber pontificalis*, ed. by Louis Duchesne, 2 vols. (Paris 1886–92): vol. 1, pp. 336–340; Duchesne, Louis, *L'église au VI siècle* (Paris 1925); Fliche, Augustin, and Martin, Victor, *Histoire de l'église*, 6 vols. (Paris 1934–37): vol. 5, pp. 174–181.

ALASTAIR GUINAN.

MARTIN II. See MARINUS I.

MARTIN III. See MARINUS II.

MARTIN IV (SIMON DE BRION or DE BRIE), pope: b. Touraine, France, c. 1210; d. Perugia, Italy, March 28, 1285. He was actually the second pope to bear the name of Martin, but chroniclers have confused the Martins with Marinus I (r. 882–884) and Marinus II (r. 942–946). Educated at the University of Paris, Martin became canon of the Church of St. Martin in Tours, keeper of the royal seal (1260), and cardinal (1261). As papal legate in France, he concluded the treaty giving the crown of Sicily to Charles of Anjou. He was elected pope Feb. 22, 1261, succeeding Nicholas III. Because Rome was hostile to French influence, he spent most of his pontificate in Viterbo, Orvieto (where he was crowned), and Perugia. Supporting Charles' policies, he became involved in troubles with the Byzantine emperor Michael VIII Palaeologus and excommunicated him, thus breaking the union which had existed between the Greek and Latin churches; he also excommunicated Pedro III of Aragon after the Sicilians had chosen him as their king. He was a patron of the mendicant orders and opened the process of canonization of Louis IX of France.

Consult *Liber pontificalis*, ed. by Louis Duchesne, 2 vols. (Paris 1886–92): vol. 2, pp. 459–465; Gay, J.,; "Notes sur le second royaume français de Sicile . . .," in *Mélanges offerts à M. Nicolas Iorga par ses amis de France* (Paris 1933).

ALASTAIR GUINAN.

MARTIN V (OTTONE or ODDONE or OTTO COLONNA), pope: b. Genazzano, near Rome, Italy, 1368; d. Rome, Feb. 20, 1431. Noted as a canonist and made cardinal (1405) by Innocent VII, in 1409 he attended the Council of Pisa, which had been called to effect a settlement between the claims of the rival popes at Rome and at Avignon (the so-called Western Schism of the church: see ANTIPOPE; PISA, COUNCIL OF), and took part in the elections of Alexander V and John XXIII. But it was not until the Council of Constance (see CONSTANCE, COUNCIL OF) that the Western Schism was ended by Martin's accession to the papal throne on Nov. 21, 1417. Although he had previously held that the council was superior to the pope, Martin then set about restoring the primacy of the Holy See. He concluded concordats with the various European nations. Arriving in Rome in 1420, he set about restoring the sadly dilapidated city. He worked to restore order and harmony in the church, and made some, though not all, of the reforms that were needed in the Curia Romana. By conferring great powers on his Colonna relatives he foreshadowed the nepotism of the Renaissance. Among his other acts were approval (1429) of the devotion to the Holy Name of Jesus preached by Bernardino of Siena, and abolition of some of the restrictions on the Jews by forbidding (1422 and 1429) violent preaching against them and by disapproving the baptism of Jewish children under 12 without parental consent.

Consult Creighton, Mandell, *History of the Papacy During the Period of the Reformation*, 5 vols. (London 1882–94): vol. 1, pp. 397–420; vol. 2, pp. 3–32; Valois, Noël, *La crise religieuse du XVe siècle* (Paris 1909); Mollat, Guillaume, "Martin V" in *Dictionnaire de théologie catholique*, 15 vols. in 27 (Paris 1909–50).

ALASTAIR GUINAN.

MARTIN, Archer John Porter, English biochemist: b. London, England, March 1, 1910. He was educated at Cambridge University (B.A. 1932, M.A. 1935, Ph.D. 1936). From 1933 to 1938 he worked in the nutritional laboratory of the university. His researches with Richard Lawrence Millington Synge, and their experiments in chromatography provided effective starvation correctives during World War II. Together, in 1944, they devised a paper partition chromatography which made possible marked advances in bacteriological and biological research (see CHROMATOGRAPHY—*Partition Chromatography*). It furthered the discovery of new antibiotics and amino acids in bacteria and the solution of many chemical problems. For their discoveries Martin and Synge shared the Nobel Prize in chemistry in 1952. In 1953 Martin's research in gas liquid chromatographs developed a technique for fractioning mixtures and compounds in ultramicroscopic amounts. Martin was elected a fellow of the Royal Society in 1950, that year became biochemist at the National Institute for Medical

Research, London, and in 1951 was awarded the Berzelius Gold Medal of the Swedish Medical Society.

MARTIN, Everett Dean, American educator and sociologist: b. Jacksonville, Ill., July 5, 1880; d. Claremont, Calif., May 10, 1941. He was educated at Illinois College and McCormick Theological Seminary, and in 1907 was ordained as a Congregational minister. He held Unitarian pastorates in Illinois and Iowa until 1914, when he left the ministry to lecture and to write on social philosophy. He was assistant director (1917–1922) and director (1922–1938) of the People's Institute in New York City, and headed the department of social philosophy (1922–1938) at the Cooper Union Forum in New York City. In 1936 he became professor of social philosophy at Claremont Colleges. His *Behavior of Crowds* (1920), a nonfiction best seller, was one of the first popular studies of mob psychology, and his *Meaning of a Liberal Education* (1926) was an important contribution in the field of adult education. Among his other works are *Psychology and Its Use* (1926, 1933); *Liberty* (1930); and *Civilizing Ourselves* (1932).

MARTIN, mar-tăn, Félix, Roman Catholic priest and educator: b. Auray, Brittany, France, Oct. 4, 1804; d. Paris, Nov. 25, 1886. Educated at the Jesuit seminary at Auray, he became a novitiate in 1823 and was ordained in 1831. One of the missionaries sent to Canada in 1842 to re-establish the Jesuits there, in 1848 he founded St. Mary's College (Collège Ste. Marie) in Montreal and was its first rector. He did valuable Canadian historical research and, among other works, wrote *De Montcalm en Canada, ou les deniers années de la colonie française* (1867). Returning to France in 1862, he spent most of his later years at Collège Vaugirard in Paris.

MARTIN, mär'tĭn; Fr., mar-tăn', François Xavier, American jurist: b. Marseille, France, March 17, 1762; d. New Orleans, La., Dec. 10, 1846. After a good education, at the age of 17 or 18 he went to Martinique to join an uncle. From there he went to New Bern, N.C., where he taught French and developed a small publishing business. Taking up the study of law, he published a number of legal handbooks. He was admitted to the bar in 1789, and in 1792, at the request of the state legislature, made a compilation of the British statutes in force in North Carolina before the revolution; in 1794 he compiled the private acts of the assembly, and in 1803 extended Iredell's *Revisal* (see IREDELL, JAMES). He became a federal judge of Mississippi Territory in 1809, and in 1810 went to Louisiana as federal judge for the Territory of Orleans. In 1813 he became the first attorney general of the new state of Louisiana, and from 1815 until just before his death (although he became blind for the last ten years of his life) was a member of the state Supreme Court, becoming chief justice in 1836. Largely through his efforts an effective jurisprudence was established in Louisiana from the tangle of French and Spanish statutes in which the state law was enmeshed.

He wrote a *History of Louisiana* (1827) and a *History of North Carolina* (1829), but more valuable are his translation of Robert Joseph Pothier's *Treatise on Obligations* (1802); his

opinions as recorded in 51 volumes of the *Louisiana Reports;* and *A General Digest of the Acts of the Legislature of the Late Territory of Orleans and of the State of Louisiana . . .* (1816).

MARTIN, mär'tĭn; -t'n, Glenn Luther, pioneer American aviator and airplane manufacturer: b. Macksburg, Iowa, Jan. 17, 1886; d. Baltimore, Md., Dec. 4, 1955. After taking a business course at Kansas Wesleyan University, he worked as an automobile mechanic, and in 1905, when his family moved to Santa Ana, Calif., opened his own garage there and spent his spare time building and flying gliders. In 1909 he constructed and flew his first motor biplane, and that year set up a small airplane factory. By 1916 he had made several records for speed, altitude, and endurance flying, including (May 10, 1912) the first air flight over the ocean by flying a round course between Newport Beach and Santa Catalina Island, Calif. He received his first government order (for training planes) in 1913, during World War I built the first armored airplanes for the government, and ultimately became one of the largest airplane manufacturers in America. In 1917 he merged with the Wright Company, but withdrew from the merger later in the year to organize the new Glenn L. Martin Company at Cleveland, Ohio, moving it to Baltimore in 1929.

Martin developed the first plane built specifically for airmail service, the first metal monoplane, and several of the most famous military airplanes, including the army's B-26 bomber and the navy's PBM Marina flying boat. In 1933 he was awarded the Collier Trophy (the aeronautics industry's highest award) for the greatest achievement in aeronautics in America, and in 1944 received the Guggenheim Medal of the Institute of Aeronautical Sciences. In 1945 he founded the Glenn L. Martin College of Engineering and Aeronautical Sciences at the University of Maryland. In 1953 he retired from active control of the Glenn L. Martin Company.

MARTIN, Gregory, English translator of the Bible: b. Mansfield, near Winchelsea, Sussex, England, date unknown; d. Reims, France, Oct. 28, 1582. He was one of the original scholars of St. Johns College, Oxford, entering there in 1557 and remaining for 13 years. He then became tutor to the sons of Thomas Howard, 4th duke of Norfolk, and was a dominant influence in the family's adherence to Roman Catholicism. When the duke was imprisoned in the Tower of London in 1570, Martin escaped to the English College at Douai, France, where he was ordained priest in 1573. From 1577 to 1578 he helped organize the English College at Rome, Italy. He then returned to France, and at Reims, where the Douai school had moved, he spent the remainder of his life working on the translation of the Bible from the Latin Vulgate into English. The bulk of the work devolved upon Martin, although he was assisted by William Allen, Richard Bristow, and others. The New Testament was published at Reims in 1582; the Old Testament, however, was not printed until 1609–1610 at Douai. Bishop Richard Challoner's revision of this translation, first published in London in 1749–1750, known as the Douay (Douai) Bible, became officially "the Bible for English-speaking Catholics the world over."

MARTIN, Helen Reimensnyder, American author: b. Lancaster, Pa., Oct. 18, 1868; d. New Canaan, Conn., June 29, 1939. After being educated at Swarthmore and Radcliffe colleges she married Frederic C. Martin. While helping a friend to prepare a history of the Pennsylvania Dutch colonies she managed to win acceptance from the Mennonites and made a careful and sympathetic study of their manners and way of life. Probably the best-known of the novels which this study brought forth are *Tillie, a Mennonite Maid* (1904) and *Barnabetta* (1914); the latter, dramatized as *Erstwhile Susan* and played by Minnie Maddern Fiske, was highly successful on the stage, telling the story of a woman's revolt from her domineering husband. Among her other novels are *The Elusive Hildegarde* (1900); *Sabina, a Story of the Amish* (1905); *The Crossways* (1910); *Wings of Healing* (1929); and *Emmy Untamed* (1937).

MARTIN, mär-tăn', (Bon Louis) Henri, French historian: b. Saint-Quentin, France, Feb. 20, 1810; d. Paris, Dec. 14, 1883. Educated for the law, he compiled a *Histoire de France* (15 vols., 1833–1836) made up of excerpts from the works of leading historians and chroniclers. He expanded and reworked this into his own history, an extensively revised fourth edition of which appeared in 16 volumes in 1861–1865. For his work he was awarded the Gobert Prize in 1856, and the grand biennial award of the French Academy in 1869. Six additional volumes (1878–1883) brought this history up to date from 1789. He was elected a member of the National Assembly in 1871, a senator in 1876, and a member of the French Academy in 1878.

MARTIN, mär'tĭn; -t'n, Homer Dodge, American landscape painter: b. Albany, N.Y., Oct. 28, 1836; d. St. Paul, Minn., Feb. 12, 1897. Martin was largely self-taught, and from the age of 16 produced small landscapes which were excellent in composition though crude in color. His painting tours ranged from the Adirondacks and the Catskills to the Berkshires and the White Mountains. He exhibited at the National Academy in 1857, established a studio in New York in 1865, was elected to the Century Club in 1866 (where his *Lake Sanford* hangs), became an associate of the National Academy in 1868, and full member in 1875. Between 1879 and 1882 he did some illustrating, his work appearing in *Scribner's Monthly* and the *Century Magazine,* and in 1882 he and his wife, Elizabeth Gilbert Davis Martin, a journalist, went to France where they spent four years, mostly at Villerville or Honfleur. Paintings completed after his return to America are among his finest work, revealing a deeply contemplative mood and lofty melancholy. Among them, *Evening on the Seine* hangs in the National Gallery, Washington, D.C., and *Harp of the Winds* and *Sand Dunes, Lake Ontario* are in the Metropolitan Museum of Art, New York City. His last years were clouded by poverty, failing eyesight, and poor health, and his work did not receive full appreciation until after his death.

MARTIN, Joseph, Canadian statesman: b. Milton, Upper Canada (now Ontario), Canada, Sept. 24, 1852; d. Vancouver, B.C., March 2, 1923. Educated at Michigan State Normal School and the University of Toronto, he was called to the bar in 1882. A Liberal in politics, he was a member of the Manitoba Legislature from 1883 to 1892; as attorney general and minister of education of the province (1888–1891) he introduced the bill abolishing the separate school system and opposing the teaching of French, which precipitated a national crisis in politics. From 1893 to 1896 he served in the Canadian House of Commons. In 1897 he moved to British Columbia, becoming a member of the provincial legislature (1898–1903) and holding the posts of attorney general and minister of education (1898–1899) and, briefly, that of premier (1900). He was in favor of free trade, an advocate of reciprocity between the United States and Canada, and an opponent of railway monopoly. In 1899 he had been made a Queen's Counsel, and in 1908 he emigrated to England, where he was elected to the House of Commons (1910–1918). He thus served in four separate legislative bodies in the course of his career.

ROBERT ENGLAND.

MARTIN, mär'tĭn, Joseph William, Jr., American statesman: b. North Attleboro, Mass., Nov. 3, 1884; d. Fort Lauderdale, Fla., March 6, 1968. He declined a scholarship to Dartmouth College, becoming instead a newspaper reporter in his home town and in Providence, R.I. In 1908, with others, he purchased the North Attleboro *Evening Chronicle,* becoming its publisher and later its chief owner. He served in the Massachusetts House of Representatives (1912–1914) and Senate (1915–1917), took a leading role in state Republican politics, and was elected to the United States House of Representatives in 1924, and continually thereafter. As chairman of the Republican Congressional Campaign Committee in the 1938 elections, he led a campaign that resulted in almost doubling Republican membership of the House of Representatives; and with his reputation as a political strategist established, he was made minority leader in 1939 and headed the Republicans in the House in the succeeding 20 years. In the 80th and 83d Congresses (1947–1948 and 1953–1954) he was speaker. Twice chairman of the Republican National Committee (1940–1942; 1948), he was permanent chairman of Republican national conventions on five consecutive occasions between 1940 and 1956 —a record. In January 1959, at age 74, following the Republican electoral defeat in 1958, he was voted out of the minority leadership and replaced by Representative Charles A. Halleck, 58, of Indiana, amid widespread expressions of esteem and affection among his colleagues but also counterbalancing arguments by many that a change in House leadership was needed.

MARTIN, Josiah, English colonial governor in America: b. probably in Antigua, West Indies, 1737; d. London, England, 1786. He had risen to the rank of lieutenant colonel in the British Army before he was appointed royal governor of North Carolina in 1771. Although he was an able and conscientious administrator, negotiating successfully with the Regulators (q.v.), opposition to his insistence upon the royal prerogative in tax matters led to the undermining of his authority and, fearing violence, he fled from the colony in the summer of 1775, taking refuge on a British sloop. He then attempted unsuccessfully to organize the Loyalists, and took part in the British attack on Charleston in 1776 and in Cornwallis' campaign in the Carolinas in 1780–1781. His health failing, he returned to England in April 1781.

MARTIN, Lillien Jane, a pioneer American psychologist: b. Olean, N.Y., July 7, 1851; d. San Francisco, Calif., March 26, 1943. A graduate of Vassar College (1880), after having been a high school teacher of science she went to Göttingen, Germany, in 1894, to study with the psychologist Georg Elias Müller, with whom she collaborated in writing an important paper in the field of psychophysics. She was associated with the psychology department of Leland Stanford Junior University (Stanford University) from 1899 to 1943, becoming professor (1911–1916) and after that professor emeritus. In 1920, after her retirement, she founded a child guidance clinic in San Francisco, and in 1929 a psychological clinic for aged persons, thus becoming a pioneer in gerontology. She herself learned to typewrite at 65, and to drive a car at 78. Her books include *Mental Training of the Pre-School Age Child* (1923), *Salvaging Old Age* (1930), and *The Home in a Democracy* (1937).

PHILIP L. HARRIMAN.

MARTIN, mȧr-tăN′, **Louis,** French physician and bacteriologist: b. Puy, Haute-Loire Department, France, Sept. 20, 1864; d. Paris, June 13, 1946. He introduced culture media for the cultivation of typhoid bacilli (1915); the isolation of the diphtheria bacillus (1916); and the cultivation of *Leptospira icterohaemorrhagiae,* the cause of Weil's disease, infectious jaundice (1917). Codiscoverer of the antidiphtheritic serum and a pioneer in its use, in 1919 he differentiated between diphtheria and pseudodiphtheria, describing the bacillus of the latter. Elected a member of the French Academy of Medicine (1919) and of the Academy of Science (1937), he also served as honorary director of the Pasteur Institute in Paris.

MARTIN, mär′tĭn; -t′n, **Luther,** American lawyer: b. near New Brunswick, N.J., Feb. 29, ?1748; d. New York, N.Y., July 10, 1826. After graduating from the College of New Jersey (now Princeton) in 1766, he taught school and studied law in Maryland and Virginia until admitted to the Virginia bar in 1771. Settling in Somerset County, Maryland, he became attorney general of the state (1778–1805). He was a delegate to the Continental Congress (1785) and a member of the federal Constitutional Convention at Philadelphia (1787); opposing a strong central government, he refused to sign the Constitution. However, he later became a Federalist because of his dislike for Thomas Jefferson. He defended Justice Samuel Chase against impeachment (1805) and Aaron Burr (for whose daughter Theodosia he cherished a hopeless attachment) against the charge of treason (1807). He was chief judge of the court of oyer and terminer from 1813 until it was abolished in 1816. He was again attorney general of Maryland from 1818 until a stroke of paralysis forced him to retire in 1822, penniless through alcoholism and extravagance; the state legislature passed a resolution requiring every lawyer in the state to pay an annual license fee of five dollars, the proceeds to be devoted to Martin's assistance. After this was repealed in 1823 he lived with the Burrs in New York City until his death.

MARTIN, mȧr-tăN′, **Pierre Émile,** French engineer and inventor: b. Bourges, France, Aug. 18, 1824; d. Fourchambault, May 24, 1915. He attended the French School of Mines, worked with his father at the Fourchambault forges, and from 1854 to 1883 was director of the steel mills at Sireul. In 1865 he invented an open-hearth smelting method for making steel from pig iron. Known as the Martin process, this was a modification of the Siemens method, and most open-hearth steelmaking became known as the Siemens-Martin process.

MARTIN, mär′tĭn; t′n, **Riccardo** (HUGH WHITFIELD MARTIN), American operatic tenor: b. Hopkinsville, Ky., Nov. 18, 1874; d. New York, N.Y., Aug. 11, 1952. He studied composition with Edward MacDowell at Columbia University (1896–1900), intending to become a composer, but with the discovery of his voice went to Europe to study. He made his European debut at the municipal opera in Nantes, France, in 1904, and in 1906 sang Canio in *Pagliacci* at the French Opera House in New Orleans, La. On Nov. 20, 1907, the first American tenor to sing a major role there, he appeared as Faust in Arrigo Boito's *Mefistofele* at the Metropolitan Opera House in New York City. Until 1918, except for one season, 1916–1917, with the Boston Opera Company, he was one of the leading tenors at the Metropolitan, distinguishing himself in Italian operas as well as creating roles in operas by American composers. He later appeared with the Chicago Opera Company and at Covent Garden in London.

MARTIN, Thomas Commerford, Anglo-American scientific writer and editor: b. London, England, July 22, 1856; d. Pittsfield, Mass., May 17, 1924. After studying theology at the Countess of Huntingdon Theological College at Trevecca, Wales, he developed an interest in physics and scientific research. Arriving in the United States in 1877, he spent two years as an assistant in the Menlo Park laboratory of Thomas Alva Edison. After editing the *Daily Gleaner* in Kingston, Jamaica (1880–1882), he returned to the United States and became editor of *The Electrical World* (1883–1890), *The Electrical Engineer* (1890–1899), and of the two periodicals when they combined as *The Electrical World* (1899–1909). He was a founder of the American Institute of Electrical Engineers and its president from 1887–1888. He showed great ability not only as a writer on scientific subjects but also as a lecturer, traveling extensively throughout the United States, Great Britain, and France. In addition to contributing to leading encyclopedias and magazines, he was the author of such works as *The Electric Motor and Its Applications* (1887); *The Inventions, Researches and Writings of Nikola Tesla* (1894); *Edison, His Life and Inventions* (2 vols., 1910); and *The Story of Electricity* (2 vols., 1919–1922).

MARTIN, Victoria Claflin Woodhull. See CLAFLIN, VICTORIA AND TENNESSEE.

MARTIN, William Alexander Parsons, American missionary, educator, and author: b. Livonia, Ind., April 10, 1827; d. Peking, China, Dec. 17, 1916. The son of a Presbyterian minister, after his graduation from Indiana University in 1846 he studied theology at the Presbyterian seminary in New Albany, Ind., was ordained to the ministry at Salem, Ind., in 1849, and in 1850 went to China to serve at the Ninzpo mission. He was fluent in the local dialect, the literary language, and Mandarin, and served as interpreter for William B. Reed in negotiating the 1858 treaty between China and the United States. In 1863 he settled in Peking, founding a mission there and becoming in 1868 teacher of international law at T'ungwên Kuan, the government school for the special training of young Chinese in Western languages and learning. From 1869 to 1894 he was its president, and in 1898 became president of the new Imperial University. After settlement of the Boxer outbreak he became professor of international law at Wuchang University (1902–1905), and in 1911 rejoined the staff of the Presbyterian mission. Through his lectures, teaching, and writing in both English and Chinese, he made the West better acquainted with China and was a dominant influence in introducing Western culture to China. He was the author of the *Hanlin Papers* (1880, 1894); *A Cycle of Cathay* (1896); and *The Awakening of China* (1907).

MARTIN, William McChesney, Jr., American government official: b. St. Louis, Mo., Dec. 17, 1906. After graduating from Yale in 1928, he studied at Benton College of Law in St. Louis and at Columbia University, and before World War II was engaged in banking and brokerage. A governor of the New York Stock Exchange (1935–1938), at the age of 31 he was elected president of the exchange in July 1938, serving until April 1941; he was the first to hold this position with a definite term of office. In 1941 he was drafted into the army; as one of his assignments he handled much of the government's lend-lease to Russia, and rose to the rank of colonel in 1945. He was made a member of the board of directors of the Export-Import Bank in 1945, becoming chairman of the board the same year. After serving as assistant secretary of the Treasury (1949–1951) he became chairman of the board of governors of the Federal Reserve System in 1951.

MARTIN, city, Tennessee, in Weakley County. Situated 11 miles south of Fulton, Ky., at an altitude of 415 feet, it is served by the Illinois Central and the Louisville and Nashville railroads. A trade center in a timber- and truck- and dairy-farming area, it has some manufactures of clothing, shoes and chemicals. It is the seat of the University of Tennessee at Martin. Pop. 4,750.

MARTIN, a popular term usually reserved for a swallow. In England, two unrelated swallows are called martins, the house martin (*Delichon urbica*) and the sand martin (*Riparia riparia*). The house martin is restricted to the Old World, but the sand martin also inhabits North America where it is called the bank swallow. In America, the term martin is reserved for other swallows (genus *Progne*), the best-known of which is undoubtedly the purple martin (*Progne subis*). The purple martin breeds from Canada south to the West Indies and central Mexico and winters in the Amazon Valley. It is a rather stocky, heavy swallow about 8 inches in length. The old males are deep glossy blue with brown wings, and the females and young males are brownish gray below and considerably duller blue above than the adult males. Purple martins breed in colonies. Before the advent of civilized man they bred in holes or any other cavity in cliffs or trees, but now have become semidomesticated, breeding in hollow gourds, boxes, or houses set up for their benefit. They prefer open good agricultural country where flying insects are abundant, but will also nest in the midst of a small town, where they are a matter of civic pride. Another martin, the gray-breasted martin (*P. chalybea*) barely reaches the United States, breeding on the borders of southern Texas. As the name indicates, both sexes are gray below. Its habits are similar to those of the purple martin. See also SWALLOWS.

CHARLES VAURIE.

MARTIN CHUZZLEWIT, chŭz′l-wĭt, a novel by Charles Dickens (q.v.), published in 1844 after serialization in monthly parts. The complex plot turns on wealthy old Martin Chuzzlewit's distrust of all his potential heirs. Chief among these are his cousin, Seth Pecksniff, an unctuous architect, and his namesake grandson, young Martin. The latter is in love with Mary Graham, the old man's ward. By a series of contrivances young Martin, after quarreling with his grandfather, sets out for America in company with cheerful Mark Tapley. There he almost dies of fever in Eden, a fraudulent land speculation on the Ohio River. Mark nurses him back to health; he returns to England purged of his former careless selfishness, is reconciled with his grandfather, and marries Mary Graham.

A second line of plot deals with old Martin's brother Anthony, and Anthony's villainous son Jonas. As with most of Dickens' work, however, the reader remembers episode and character rather than plot. Besides Pecksniff, the immortal hypocrite, the *Chuzzlewit* gallery includes Sairey (Sarah) Gamp, the drunken nurse who is one of Dickens' most superb creations, and a collection of American caricatures. The latter were furiously resented in the United States, partly because they travestied real American types which are not yet wholly extinct.

DeLANCEY FERGUSON.

MARTIN DU GARD, mär-tăn′ dü gär, **Roger,** French novelist: b. Neuilly-sur-Seine, France, 1881; d. Bellême, Aug. 22, 1958. He studied archaeology and history at the École des Chartes, where he acquired the habit of painstaking research and careful documentation. In 1908 he published his first novel, *Devenir!*, of which he was later ashamed. From 1910 to 1913 he worked on *Jean Barois*, the novel which first brought him recognition. Written in dramatic dialogue, this vividly portrays the travail France went through largely as a result of the Dreyfus case (see FRANCE—28. History: 1815–1914: The Third Republic), when the corruption of the old order was exposed, the clash between science and religion was intensified, old loyalties broke down, and what seemed to be clean-cut moral issues became confused. He aptly described himself as "an independent writer who has escaped the fascination of partisan ideologies, and an investigator as objective as is humanly possible, as well as a novelist striving to express the tragic quality of individual lives."

During World War I Martin du Gard served in a motor transport division and began work on his cyclical novel in eight parts, *Les Thibault* (published 1922–1940; translated into English in its entirety as *The World of the Thibaults,* 1939–1941). In this he expands and enriches the same themes he dealt with in *Jean Barois,* tracing the history of the middle-class Thibault family, one of the sons a Protestant and the other a Roman Catholic, through the early years of the 20th century and World War I, discarding his method of telling the story mainly through dialogue in favor of a more conventional novelistic approach. It is a rich and moving study on a grand scale, mingling real events and people with fiction, and brought the award of the Nobel Prize for literature in 1937.

Martin du Gard also wrote essays and stories, including *Vieille France* (1933); two farces which show his understanding of French peasant life and psychology, *Le testament du père Leleu* (1914), and *La gonfle* (1928); and the drama *Un taciturne* (1931).

MARTINEAU, mär′tĭ-nō; -t′n-ō, **Harriet,** English writer and social reformer: b. Norwich, England, June 12, 1802; d. Clappersgate, Westmoreland County, June 27, 1876. An elder sister of James Martineau, she was a delicate child, hard of hearing (she later became quite deaf), and was educated mostly at home in a strict and puritanical household. By the time she was 17 she had begun to write for the Unitarian *Monthly Repository.* In 1826 her father died, leaving the family poorly provided for. Harriet helped support the family by needlework and by writing reviews for the *Repository.* In 1830 and 1831 she won three prizes totaling 45 guineas, offered by the Central Unitarian Association, for essays designed to convert Jews, Catholics, and Muslims, respectively. This money, supplemented by some small loans, enabled her to give all her time to a project she had had in mind for some time: writing stories for periodicals which would portray the sufferings of the poor and show the need for the social and economic reforms that she advocated. These stories were collected as *Illustrations of Political Economy* (9 vols., 1832–1834), *Poor Laws and Paupers Illustrated* (1834), and *Illustrations of Taxation* (1834). They had little literary merit, but they aroused public opinion and appealed to a wide audience. They made her famous and enabled her to move to London with her mother and to acquire a wide circle of influential friends, among them William and Dorothy Wordsworth, Thomas Robert Malthus, and Thomas Carlyle (whose first course of lectures she managed in 1837).

In 1834–1835 Miss Martineau visited the United States, touring the South, meeting the abolitionists in Boston, and becoming strongly abolitionist herself. Returning to England, she published *Society in America* (1837) and *A Retrospect of Western Travel* (1838), both successful in England but deeply resented in the United States for some of her criticisms and for her abolitionist views. In 1839 her novel *Deerbrook* appeared; in 1841 *The Playfellow,* a series of tales for children, and the historical romance *The Hour and the Man,* based on the exploits of Toussaint L'Ouverture; and in 1844, after she felt she had benefited from mesmerism, *Letters on Mesmerism,* which distressed many of her friends. In 1845–1846 she bought a site at Clappersgate in the English Lake country, and built her home The Knoll, writing *Forest and Game-Law Tales* (1845). A trip to Egypt and Palestine resulted in *Eastern Life, Past and Present* (1848).

Another work to attract wide attention was the *History of England During the Thirty Years' Peace* (1849) with the supplementary *Introduction to the History of the Peace* (1851), written largely from the viewpoint of philosophical radicalism. The strongly antitheological *Letters on the Laws of Man's Social Nature and Development* (1851) estranged her for a while from her brother James. In 1853 her able *Philosophy of Comte, Freely Translated and Condensed,* received the approval of Comte himself.

In 1855, threatened with a serious heart condition, Harriet Martineau began work on her autobiography. However, she continued to write on a wide variety of subjects mostly in the form of magazine articles. A journalist rather than a writer of literature—she herself said she had "earnestness and intellectual clearness within a certain range" and could "popularize, but neither discover nor invent"—courageous and honest, ardently interested in reforms of all kinds and frequently an advocate of unpopular causes, she exerted a wide influence in her time.

Consult her *Autobiography,* ed. by Maria Weston Chapman, 3 vols. (London 1877); Bosanquet, Theodora, *Harriet Martineau: An Essay in Comprehension* (London 1927); Nevill, John Cranstoun, *Harriet Martineau* (London 1943); Wheatley, Vera, *The Life and Times of Harriet Martineau* (London 1957).

MARTINEAU, James, English clergyman and theological philosopher: b. Norwich, England, April 21, 1805; d. London, Jan. 11, 1900. A younger brother of Harriet Martineau, he gave up his plans to become a civil engineer and entered Manchester College, York, as a divinity student in 1822. In 1828 he was called to a congregation in Dublin, Ireland, where he was ordained the same year. He assisted in the founding of the Irish Unitarian Christian Society in 1830, serving as its first secretary. In 1832 he became pastor of the Paradise Street Chapel in Liverpool, and then in 1840 professor of mental and moral philosophy at his old college (which had moved to Manchester, had become New Manchester College, and was to move to London in 1853). After a stay in Germany in 1848–1849, where he was much influenced by the philosophy of Friedrich Adolf Trendelenburg, he came to be recognized as a leader in the Unitarian movement (see UNITARIANISM—*England*) and one of the outstanding theological philosophers of his time. His earlier deterministic and utilitarian views gradually developed into a belief in "a divine mind and will ruling the universe," and he became a champion of free will and intuitionalism. It has been said of him that he, more than any other, sums up the history of Unitarianism and of liberal theology in general during the 19th century. His writings include *Religion as Affected by Modern Materialism* (1874); *Ideal Substitutes for God* (1879); *A Study of Spinoza* (1882), and *Essays, Reviews, and Addresses* (4 vols., 1890–91). His philosophical views are best set forth in his *Types of Ethical Theory* (2 vols., 1885), and his theology in *A Study of Religion* (2 vols., 1888) and *The Seat of Authority in Religion* (1890).

Consult Jackson, Abraham W., *James Martineau* (Boston 1900); Drummond, James, and Upton, Charles Barnes, *Life and Letters of James Martineau,* 2 vols. (London 1902); Carpenter, J. Estlin, *James Martineau* (London 1905).

MARTINELLI, mär-tĭ-nĕl'ĭ, **Giovanni,** operatic tenor: b. Montagnana, Italy, Oct. 22, 1885. He made his debut in 1910 in a Milan production of Verdi's *Ernani.* Giacomo Puccini heard him and engaged him to appear as Dick Johnson in *La Fanciulla del West* in Rome in 1911. In 1913 he joined the Metropolitan Opera Company in New York, where he was a leading tenor for over 30 years, with a repertoire of over 50 roles.

MARTINEZ, mär-tē'nĕs, city, California, seat of Contra Costa County, located in the wooded hills along Carquinez Strait, 30 miles northeast of San Francisco. A highway bridge connects Martinez with Benecia, across the strait. Products of the city's oil refineries are shipped in great quantities from Martinez in oceangoing vessels. Other industries include chemical works, fiberboard manufacturing, copper smelting, vegetable canning, and a winery. Pear raising is a diminishing industry. The city operates a small-craft harbor and a park with hiking and riding trails.

Martinez was founded by and named for Ignacio Martinez, a Mexican government land grantee, in 1849, and was incorporated in 1864. The city-manager form of government was adopted in 1946. Historic sites include the home of the naturalist John Muir. Pop. 9,604.

LAUREL ADAIR.

MARTINEZ DE CAMPOS, mär-tē'näth thä käm'pōs, **Arsenio,** Spanish soldier and statesman: b. Segovia, Spain, Dec. 14, 1831; d. Zarauz, Sept. 23, 1900. He served in Morocco in 1859, in Mexico in 1861, and in Cuba from 1869 to 1872, when he became a general. After helping to bring Alfonso XII to the Spanish throne in 1874, he inflicted a crushing defeat on the Carlists in 1876. As commander in chief in Cuba in 1877, he brought an insurrection to a close chiefly by promising concessions, which he failed to effect as premier of Spain in 1879. He was minister of war from 1881 to 1884 and president of the Senate in 1886 and 1891. In 1895 he was sent again to Cuba, but was recalled in 1896 after failing to settle the insurrection. In 1899, he was again president of the Senate.

MARTINEZ DE LA ROSA, mär-tē'näth thä lä rō'sä, **Francisco,** Spanish statesman and writer: b. Granada, Spain, March 10, 1787; d. Madrid, Feb. 7, 1862. He secured a law degree at the University of Granada, where he later taught philosophy. A deputy in the Cortes of Cádiz, he supported the Constitution of 1812 and was imprisoned when it was abolished in 1814. The insurrection of 1820 brought him liberation and appointment as premier of Spain. After alienating all parties, he resigned in 1823 and went to Paris. His early poems and plays were in the neoclassical tradition, but in Paris he became imbued with romanticism and composed historical prose dramas. Returning to Spain in 1831, he was again premier in 1834–1835, and later served as an ambassador, chairman of the council of state, and director of the Spanish Academy. His works include the first successful Spanish romantic drama, *La conjuración de Venecia* (1834), political and literary studies, and a historical novel, *Doña Isabel de Solís* (1837–1846).

MARTÍNEZ RUIZ, mär-tē'näth rōō-ēth', **José** (pseudonym AZORÍN), Spanish novelist and essayist: b. Monóvar (Alicante), Spain, June 8, 1874; d. Madrid, Mar. 2, 1967. Although trained in the law, he began to write before he was 20 and published his first work in 1893. He moved to Madrid three years later and joined a politically liberal literary circle which he was the first to term the Generation of 1898.

His first novel, *La voluntad* (1902) was based on his own life, and he adopted the surname of its protagonist, Antonio Azorín, as his nom de plume. In 1904 there followed *Las confesiones de un pequeño filósofo,* a semifictional collection of vignettes of childhood and his travels.

In much of his work he attempts to evoke the essence of Spanish tradition by isolating the timeless element present in life and customs. This is best shown in the collection of stories and impressions entitled *Castilla* (1912). This intent places him squarely within the Generation of 1898, which set about the same task in different ways. Much of his literary criticism is in the same vein, exemplified by his attempt to find the spirit of Don Quixote in the unchanged atmosphere of the places he visited. This is done in *La ruta de don Quijote* (1905). His obsession with time and the part it plays in human perception and tradition stems from his interest in the ideas of Henri Bergson, which he attempted to apply to the Spanish scene. In his later novels, this feeling has a great stylistic consequence, leading to a conscious suppression of verbs along with a return to his earlier themes dealing with the problems of will. He wrote numerous articles for newspapers and magazines. Some of his short stories have been translated into English, in *Syrens and Other Stories* (1931) and in other collections.

See also SPAIN—*11. Literature* (The 20th Century).

GREGORY RABASSA,
Associate Professor of Spanish and Portuguese, Columbia University.

MARTINEZ SIERRA, mär-tē'näth syĕr'rä, **Gregorio,** Spanish playwright and poet: b. Madrid, Spain, May 6, 1881; d. there, Oct. 1, 1947. By early training a journalist, he was soon acting in and writing for small theater groups. He married the poetess María Lejárraga, and most of the work appearing under his name was written in collaboration with her. In 1916 he founded the Teatro Eslava in Madrid and the publishing firm Renacimiento. He is generally associated with the *modernista* group of poets who were his contemporaries. His most famous play is *Canción de cuna* (1911), produced in New York as *The Cradle Song* (1926–1927). It exemplifies his delicate, rather ephemeral style, and shows his insight into feminine character. Much of his later life was spent outside of Spain. See also SPAIN—*11. Literature* (The 20th Century).

GREGORY RABASSA.

MARTINI, mär-tē'nĕ, **Simone,** Italian painter: b. Siena, Italy, c. 1284; d. Avignon, France, 1344. His surname is sometimes given as DI MARTINO and, incorrectly, as MEMMI. He was a pupil of Duccio di Buoninsegna, becoming one of the leading exponents of the Sienese school of painting. Most of his frescoes were executed in the churches of Siena, Assisi, Naples, and Orvieto, many of them in collaboration with his brother-in-law, Lippo Memmi. At the invitation of Pope Benedict XII he went to Avignon in 1339, where he executed frescoes in the cathedral and the papal palace, and where he met Petrarch and painted the portrait of Laura (now lost). Together with other painters he established a flourishing school. Very little of his late work remains, but the few pieces extant are marked by a Gothic flamboyance not shown in the lyrical delicacy of his earlier works. His color is harmonious and fresh, and his lines rhythmic. The large painting of the Madonna on the walls of the Palazzo Pubblico is his most important work at Siena (1315). In the Uffizi at Florence can be seen the famous *Annunciation,* a work which had great influence throughout central Italy.

MARTINIQUE, mär-t'n-ēk', island, in the Windward Islands, West Indies, constituting an overseas department of France. Forty miles long and 425 square miles in area, the island is one of the largest of the Lesser Antilles, lying about 370 miles southeast of Puerto Rico. The capital and chief commercial center is Fort-de-France (1954 pop., 60,648).

The island is rugged and studded with volcanic peaks, notably the 4,800-foot volcano Mont Pelée (see PELÉE, MONT) and the Pitons du Carbet (3,960 feet). There are dense, little-exploited rain forests in the mountainous north, and many narrow, fertile valleys with streams which become torrents in the rainy season. The only considerable extent of level lowland is the Plain of Lamentin, a region of sugarcane plantations adjoining the Bay of Fort-de-France. The coastline is deeply indented by numerous coves and harbors, and there are many small islets off the east coast. The generally warm, humid climate is moderated by trade winds and ocean breezes. Annual rainfall ranges from very heavy in the northern mountains and moderate in the south central Plain of Lamentin, to very light on the semiarid southwest coast.

The chief exports of Martinique are bananas, sugar, and rum; cocoa, pineapples, and coffee are also exported. Other crops, chiefly for domestic consumption, include cassava, breadfruit, sweet potatoes, mangoes, citrus fruit, tobacco, and vanilla. Martinique's industry is almost entirely confined to the production of sugar and rum, and the canning of bananas and pineapples. The bulk of the country's trade is with France.

Most of the island's population is Negro or mulatto; there is also a small group of whites of unmixed French descent. French is the official language, with a Creole patois the popular tongue.

Education through the primary level is compulsory, and secondary education is provided at separate *lycées* for boys and girls. There are two technical colleges, and the Institut Henri Vizioz offers higher education in law, politics, and economics. About 75 per cent of the adult population is literate.

The Department of Martinique is governed by a prefect, aided by an elected General Council of 36 members.

Martinique was discovered by Columbus on his fourth voyage, in 1502; but the island was subsequently ignored by the Spanish, partly because of the ferocity of the Carib inhabitants. In 1635 a group of French settlers under Pierre Belain, sieur d'Esnambuc, settled at St.-Pierre, on the northwest coast of the island. By the end of the 17th century the Caribs had been nearly wiped out, other settlements had been established, and the importation of Negro slaves had begun.

Several times occupied by the British, the island has been continuously in French possession since 1816. Slavery was abolished in 1848. During World War II, Martinique at first sided with Vichy France, but after the United States suspended food shipments to the island on March 9, 1943, an agreement was negotiated on July 8 by which the island came under the control of the Free French government. When France and its possessions were reorganized in 1946, the colony became an overseas department. Pop. (1954) 239,130. See also FRANCE—*33. The French Republic and the Community.*

Consult Roberts, Walter A., *The French in the West Indies* (Indianapolis 1942).

MARTINMAS, mär'tĭn-mås, the feast day of St. Martin of Tours (d. 397), celebrated on November 11, the day not of his death but of his burial at Tours. In England, Indian summer is sometimes called Martinmas summer or St. Martin's summer if it occurs in November.

MARTINS FERRY, mär't'nz fĕr'ĭ, city, Ohio, in Belmont County, located at an altitude of 660 feet on the west bank of the Ohio River, across from Wheeling, W.Va. It is served by the New York, Chicago, and St. Louis, the Pennsylvania, and the Baltimore and Ohio railroads which carry freight only. The city's industries center around steel and soft coal; products include galvanized steel, tinplate, pipe couplings, asphalt road materials, and wholesale baked goods.

Settled before 1785, the town was first known as Norristown. In 1835 it was settled as Martinsville and finally named Martins Ferry, after Ebenezer Martin who operated a ferry across the river. It was incorporated as a town in 1865 and as a city in 1885. Martins Ferry was the birthplace of the author William Dean Howells, and the pioneers Ebenezer and Betty Zane are buried here. A branch of Ohio University is located in the city. Government is by mayor and council. Pop. (1960) 11,919.

LAUREL KRIEG.

MARTINSBURG, mär't'nz-bûrg, city, West Virginia, seat of Berkeley County, in the eastern panhandle, 17 miles southwest of Hagerstown, Md. It is served by the Baltimore and Ohio and the Pennsylvania railroads. Situated at an altitude of 430 feet, at the head of the Shenandoah Valley, the city is in the center of a rich agricultural region. Apples, peaches, and other fruits are packed, and the city also has some light industries. There are limestone quarries in the vicinity. Named for Thomas Bryan Martin, colonel in the American Revolution, it was incorporated in 1778 as a town and became a city about 1859. Government is by mayor and council. Pop. (1960) 15,179.

MARTINSBURG, Operations at. Because of its strategic position at the top of the Shenandoah Valley, Martinsburg was an important military objective during the Civil War. Both Confederate and Union troops held it for short periods. On July 1, 1864, it was held by Union troops under Maj. Gen. Franz Sigel, but the next day he was menaced by the approach of the Confederates under Lt. Gen. Jubal Anderson Early, who had been ordered to clear out the lower valley and wreck the Baltimore and Ohio Railroad. Sigel, warned of the approaching danger, burned his stores, collected his command, and leaving

Martinsburg on the night of July 3, crossed the Potomac at Shepherdstown and occupied Maryland Heights. General Early cleared the valley and advanced on Washington. From July 11, when Martinsburg was again occupied by Union troops, the town changed hands repeatedly until September 19, on which date Maj. Gen. Philip Sheridan defeated General Early and drove him up the valley. Martinsburg was again occupied by Union troops and remained in their possession until the end of the war. See also SHENANDOAH VALLEY, MILITARY OPERATIONS IN.

MARTINSVILLE, city, Indiana, seat of Morgan County, at an altitude of 599 feet, 31 miles southwest of Indianapolis on the West Fork of the White River, served by the Pennsylvania Railroad. The surrounding area grows grain and has good timber. There is a state forest in the vicinity. Artesian mineral wells in the city make it attractive as a health resort. The industrial products include bricks, flour, canned goods, dairy products, clay goods, hickory chairs and mineral water crystals. The city was founded in 1822. Pop. 7,525.

MARTINSVILLE, city, Virginia, and Henry County seat, but politically independent of the county, situated near the Smith River, altitude 1,128 feet, in the east foothills of the Blue Ridge Mountains, 62 miles south of Roanoke. It is in a region of farms and forest, where industrialism is developing. Factories here produce furniture, garments, mirrors, fiberboard products, and nylon; and textiles are spun, knitted, and dyed. There is a large tobacco market. The city was named for Gen. Joseph Martin (born 1740). It was founded in 1793 and became a city in 1929. The government is administered by a manager and council. Pop. 18,798.

MARTINY, mär-tē′nĭ, **Philip,** American sculptor: b. Strasbourg, France, May 19, 1858; d. New York City, June 25, 1927. His boyhood was spent in France working in various studios. Early in the 1880's he came to America and made further studies under the direction of Augustus Saint-Gaudens. Martiny's efforts in decorative sculpture were conspicuously successful and his work improved this branch of art in the United States. Among his best-known works are the sculpture on the grand staircase of the Congressional Library, Washington; the Carnegie Library, Washington; the New York Hall of Records; two Chamber of Commerce groups, New York; the bronze doors of St. Bartholomew's, New York; *Soldiers' and Sailors' Monument,* Jersey City, N. J.; *McKinley Monument,* Springfield, Mass.; statue of Vice President Garrett A. Hobart at Paterson, N. J.; and the *Admiral de Gernay Monument* at Newport, R. I.

MARTYN, mär′tĭn, **Edward,** Irish dramatist: b. Masonbrook, County Galway, Jan. 31, 1859; d. Tulira Castle, Ardrahan, County Galway, Dec. 5, 1923. He was educated at Christ Church College, Oxford, and in 1899 became with William Butler Yeats and George Moore one of the founders of the Irish Literary Theatre. His was primarily the financial backing of the theater, although his play *The Heather Field* was produced with Yeats' *The Countess Cathleen* at the premier of the theatrical group in 1899. The same year Martyn founded the Palestrina Choir in Dublin, established for the reform of liturgical music, an organization that in 1903 became the Schola Cantorum for Dublin.

Martyn split with the Irish Literary Theatre in 1901 because he objected to the plays about the Irish peasants, insisting that an Irish literature must be built on higher standards. He served from 1904 to 1908 as president of Sinn Fein and in 1914 founded the Irish Theatre in Dublin, organized specifically for the production of plays in the Gaelic tongue and not about peasants, and also for productions of European masterpieces that had been translated into English. Martyn was a firm promoter of the Gaelic League, and once advocated a reform of Irish church architecture. He was a governor of Galway College and of the National University. His works include *Maeve* (1899); *The Tale of a Town* (1902), rewritten by George Moore and given in 1900 as *The Bending of the Bough; Grangecolman* (1912); and the *Dream Physician* (1918), a satire on Moore. His prose includes *Morgante the Lesser* (1890) and a pamphlet, *Ireland's Battle for Her Language.*

MARTYN, mär′tĭn, **Henry,** English missionary to India: b. Truro, Cornwall, Feb. 18, 1781; d. Tokat, Asia Minor, Oct. 16, 1812. He was graduated from St. John's College, Cambridge, in 1801; became a fellow of the same college in the next year, and, turning from the law, took orders, and landed in India in 1806. After three years at Dinapur he was transferred to Cawnpore, where he opened a church in 1810, in spite of violent opposition, and where he completed a Hindustani version of the New Testament. To perfect a translation of the New Testament into Persian and to recover his health in 1811 he traveled into Persia. In Tabriz he was taken ill with a fever, and on his hurried journey home was compelled to stop at the plague-stricken town of Tokat, where he died. In 1856 a monument to his memory was erected there. He was the great missionary hero of the Church of England up to the early part of the 19th century. Martyn's works include *Controversial Tracts on Christianity and Mohammedanism* (1824), and versions of various parts of the Bible into Hindustani, Persian and Judaeo-Persian.

MARTYN, John, English botanist: b. London, Sept. 12, 1699; d. Chelsea, Jan. 29, 1768. He was lecturer in botany at Cambridge (1732–1762), being almost wholly self-educated in the subject, and was also a practicing physician. He contributed to Nathan Bailey's *Universal Etymological English Dictionary* (1721) and wrote *Historia plantarum rariorum* (1728–1737), as well as translations of Virgil's *Georgics* (1741) and *Bucolics* (1749). He was a regular correspondent with Carolus Linnaeus.

MARTYNIA, mär-tĭn′ĭ-à, a genus of annual and perennial herb of the family Martyniaceae. The eight species have thick sub-erect stems, opposite or alternate heart-shaped leaves, showy catalpalike flowers in short terminal racemes, and horned capsules which suggest the names unicorn plant and proboscis flower (*M. lutea*). When ripe the capsules split and expose numerous black wrinkled seeds. The stems and foliage are clammy and malodorous, but the flowers of some species not unpleasantly perfumed. The species are all natives of warm parts of America. They are often planted for ornaments, as curiosities and for their capsules, which while young and tender are used as material for pickles. *M. louisiana,* to which the popular names are generally applied, is the most commonly grown.

MARTYR, Peter. See PETER MARTYR.

MARTYR (Greek for "witness"), a designation applied by the Christian Church to those persons in particular who, in the early ages of Christianity, suffered death rather than renounce their faith, and thus testified their confidence in the truth of the new doctrines. Martyrs are sometimes classified as of three classes: martyrs in will and deed, like Saint Stephen; those in will, but not in deed, like Saint John, who escaped from the death ordained for him by Domitian; and those in deed but not in will, like the Holy Innocents. An account of the life, persecutions, and death of the Christian martyrs is called a martyrology (q.v.). A tomb or oratory erected on the spot where a martyr suffered was called martyrium, martyry. Festivals in honor of the martyrs seem to have been observed as early as the 2d century. The Christians offered prayers at the martyry and thanked God for the example which they had given to the world. The rite was concluded with the sacrament of the Lord's Supper and the distribution of alms. Eulogies were also delivered, and accounts of the lives and actions of the deceased read. These festivals were called the birthdays of the martyrs, because on the day of their death they were born to eternal life. There are 14,000 martyrs commemorated in the Roman Catholic martyrology. In the early centuries of Christianity the bishop of the locality certified the names of those who were deemed worthy of the title of martyr, but after 1100 this designation became more and more reserved to the pope, especially since 1636.

MARTYRE DE SAINT SEBASTIAN, Le (THE MARTYRDOM OF SAINT SEBASTIAN), an oratorio by Achille Claude Debussy which had its first performance at Paris on May 22, 1911.

MARTYROLOGY, called also calendar of the saints, the acts of the saints, menology, anology, synaxary, a list of martyrs and other saints, in which was sometimes noted the character of their lives, and in the case of a martyr the place and date of his martyrdom and the nature of the sufferings which he underwent. Caesar Baronius, an ecclesiastical historian of the 16th century, attributes to Saint Clement of Rome, almost contemporary with the apostles, the first idea of collecting the acts of the martyrs. In the time of Gregory the Great (end of the 6th century) the Roman Catholic Church possessed a general martyrology, the author of which is said to have been Saint Jerome, who made use of materials collected by Eusebius of Caesarea. The only part of it now extant is a catalogue of the martyrs who suffered in Palestine during the last eight years of the persecution of Diocletian. There is a martyrology attributed to Bede (beginning of 8th century), but if not altogether spurious it is at least interpolated. Numerous martyrologies were produced in the next century and subsequently. In 1586, under the auspices of Sixtus V, a martyrology was printed at Rome, with notes by Baronius, with the title of *Martyrologium Universale.* Ruinart's *Acta Primorum Martyrum*

Sincera appeared at Paris in 1689, and a new edition of it was published in 1859. The *Acta Sanctorum* (q.v.) of the Bollandists comprises over 60 volumes issued at various times from 1643, but the work is still incomplete. The well-known English work of John Foxe, *The Book of Martyrs* (1563), may also be mentioned.

MARVEL, Ik. See MITCHELL, DONALD GRANT.

MARVELL, Andrew, English poet and satirist: b. Winestead, Holderness, Yorkshire, March 31, 1621; d. London, Aug. 18, 1678. He was graduated from Trinity College, Cambridge, in 1638, and after four years' continental travel he became in turn tutor at Nunappleton, Yorkshire, the scene of his lyrical poems, to Mary, daughter of Lord Fairfax and afterward duchess of Buckingham, and at Windsor to William Dutton, a nephew of Oliver Cromwell. In 1657 he was appointed John Milton's colleague in the Latin secretaryship, a post he retained until the Restoration. From 1660 he represented Hull in the House of Commons. Known in his lifetime chiefly as a Cromwellian, as a friend and colleague of Milton, as a member of Parliament, a pamphleteer, and a satirist, his fame as a poet came later. His widow published a collection of his miscellaneous poems in 1681, and an edition including the political satires was issued in 1726. The complete works did not appear until 1776. His poems, especially those on gardens and country life, display an exquisite feeling for nature and language. Those by which he is chiefly remembered are the *Horatian Ode upon Cromwell's Return from Ireland, On Appleton House, To His Coy Mistress, The Garden, The Bermudas,* and *The Nymph Regretting the Loss of Her Fawn.* In his satires he attacked the Earl of Clarendon and the court party, assailed Charles II, and, finally, condemned the house of Stuart, despaired of Parliament, and favored a republicanism after the model of Rome and Venice. In *Growth of Popery and Arbitrary Government in England* (1677) he alleged that the king sought to reestablish Roman Catholicism and make himself an absolute ruler; and in *The Last Instructions to a Painter* he satirized the conduct of the Dutch War. A copy of the 1681 edition of his poems was acquired by the British Museum in 1921. The site of the cottage at Highgate in which Marvell lived is marked by a tablet in Waterlow Park.

MARVIN, Charles Frederick, American meteorologist: b. Putnam, Ohio, Oct. 7, 1858; d. Washington, D. C., June 5, 1943. He graduated as a mechanical engineer in 1883 at Ohio State University, where he had been an instructor in mechanical drawing and laboratory practice since 1879. In 1884 he was appointed a forecaster in the United States Weather Bureau (at that time part of the Army Signal Corps), and rose to become its chief in 1913. He retired in 1934. Besides conducting experiments upon which were based the bureau's tables for computing moisture in the air, he made exhaustive investigations of anemometers and invented instruments for measuring and automatically recording rainfall, snowfall, sunshine, and atmospheric pressure. He made use of kites for determining meteorological conditions in the free air, and made studies of the registration of earthquakes and of the measurement of evaporation, solar radiation, and temperature by means of electric resistance thermometers. His work on wind velocities and standardization of the anemometer was particularly noteworthy. He invented the clinometer, an instrument to ascertain the exact height of clouds over airports. Besides publishing numerous papers on meteorology, he wrote on the simplification of the calendar. He advocated improving the Gregorian rule for leap years by omitting four leap years in 500 years; he asserted that such a change would assure accurate reckoning for more than 10,000 years.

MARVIN, Enoch Mather, American clergyman: b. Warren County, Mo., June 12, 1823; d. Nov. 25, 1877. He was self-educated, and in 1841 became a minister of the Methodist Episcopal Church as member of the Missouri Conference. Upon the division of the Methodist body in 1844 he cast his lot with the Methodist Church South. In the Civil War he was for two years a chaplain in the Confederate Army. He was chosen bishop of his church in 1866, and at the time of his death had just returned from a missionary tour which took him around the world. He published *Errors of the Papacy and Transubstantiation* (1860); *The Life of William Goff Caples* (1871); *Sermons* (1876); *The Doctrinal Integrity of Methodism* (1878); *To the East by Way of the West* (1879); and *The Methodist Episcopal Churches, North and South.*

MARVIN, Frederic Rowland, American clergyman, essayist, and poet: b. Troy, N. Y., Sept. 23, 1847; d. July 22, 1918. After attending Lafayette and Union colleges he studied at the College of Physicians and Surgeons and New Brunswick Theological Seminary. He became a professor at the New York Free Medical College for Women, and subsequently was a Congregational pastor at churches in Middletown, N. Y., Portland, Ore., and Great Barrington, Mass. In 1895 he retired in order to devote himself to study and foreign travel, and from 1900 he made his home in Albany, N. Y. His numerous books included *Literature of the Insane; Epidemic Delusions; Last Words of Distinguished Men and Women; Book of Quatrains; Excursions of a Book Lover; Poems and Translations; Companionship of Books; Christ Among the Cattle.*

MARX, märks, **Karl** (1818–1883), German political philosopher and founder of scientific socialism, whose doctrine, known as Marxism (q.v.), forms the basis of modern international communism.

Background and Education. Marx was born in the town of Trier in the Prussian Rhineland on May 5, 1818. His family was Jewish, but his father, a lawyer and public official, converted to Christianity in 1824, and all family members were baptized in the Lutheran church. Intending to pursue an academic career, Marx studied history, philosophy, and law at the universities of Bonn and Berlin, and in 1841 he received his doctorate from the University of Jena.

While in Berlin, Marx became absorbed in the study of social and political problems and joined the left-wing Young Hegelian movement. The influence of Hegel's dialectic as a method of analyzing society was to continue throughout Marx's life, although he rejected Hegelian polit-

KARL MARX is commemorated in a monument in Sverdlovsk Square, Moscow. The monument, unveiled in 1961, reads: "Workers of the world, unite!"

ical philosophy. See Hegel, Georg Wilhelm Friedrich.

Early Career and Writings. Marx's liberal political views precluded a teaching appointment in the reactionary educational circles, and he turned instead to journalism. In 1842 he became editor of a liberal Cologne newspaper, *Rheinische Zeitung.* The newspaper was suppressed in 1843, and Marx went to Paris with his bride, childhood friend Jenny von Westphalen, daughter of a Prussian aristocrat and government official. He was to spend most of the rest of his life in exile.

In Paris he edited the radical, short-lived *Deutsch-Französische Jahrbücher* and then wrote for the magazine *Vorwärts.* His political ideas developed markedly as he associated with French socialists Pierre Joseph Proudhon, Louis Blanc (qq.v.), and the Saint Simonians (see Saint-Simon, Comte de). He also met Friedrich Engels (q.v.), who remained his lifelong friend and collaborator and on whose financial assistance the Marx family depended for many years. When the staff of the radical *Vorwärts* was ordered to leave France in 1845, Marx and his family went to Brussels, and Engels followed.

The two men acquired a local German weekly, the *Brüsseler Deutsche Zeitung.* Marx published *The Holy Family* in 1845, and in 1846 he wrote two other major philosophical statements, *Theses on Feuerbach,* and, with Engels, *The German Ideology.* The last named work, directed against neo-Hegelian idealistic philosophers, was not published until 1932. In 1847, with *The Poverty of Philosophy,* Marx challenged every aspect of Proudhon's *Philosophy of Poverty.* Incorporating elements of the philosophies of Hegel, Ludwig A. Feuerbach (q.v.), Proudhon, and the Utopian socialists, and transcending them, Marx laid the foundations of his dialectical materialism.

Political Activity. In 1847, Marx and Engels joined the Communist League, an international workers' society for which they wrote the *Communist Manifesto* (1848), a definitive statement of the league's aims and beliefs. This historic document, appearing on the eve of a revolutionary period in Europe, has been called a masterpiece of political propaganda. It was the first public declaration of international socialism, attacking the state as an instrument of oppression and setting forth an economic, political, and social program to overthrow the capitalistic system. For the rest of his life Marx focused his efforts on the analysis of capitalism and its predicted downfall, attempting through writing and organizational work to accelerate the inevitable course of events toward the goals of socialism and a classless society.

Expelled from Belgium after the appearance of the *Manifesto,* Marx went briefly to Paris and then to Germany to participate in revolutionary movements there. In Cologne he revived the *Neue Rheinische Zeitung,* which was published for almost a year before being suppressed. Though acquitted of a charge of incitement to treason, he was expelled from the Rhineland. Banished also from Paris, he went to London, where he remained until his death.

Work in London. In London the Marx family lived in poverty most of the time, pawning their possessions to avoid starvation, and depending largely on Engels' generosity. Fervently dedicated and convinced that he was right, Marx was intolerant of criticism and contradiction and was often considered arrogant and conceited. Although usually in ill health, he spent day after day at the British Museum reading interminably and passionately all the literature in the field in order to develop his doctrines of political economy.

Meanwhile, to earn income he became a correspondent for the New York *Daily Tribune,* contributing, with Engels' assistance, almost 500 articles on aspects of world politics between 1852 and 1862. He also acted for a time as London correspondent for the *Oder Gazette,* a progressive Breslau paper. During these years he also published many books on political events, including *Class Struggles in France 1848–1850* (1850); *The Eighteenth Brumaire of Louis Bonaparte* (1852); *The Secret Diplomatic History of the Eighteenth Century* (1856); *Herr Vogt* (1860); *The Civil War in France* (1871); and *The Critique of the Gotha Programme* (1875).

His analysis of the economy of capitalism resulted in *A Contribution to the Critique of Political Economy* (1859) and his greatest and best-known work, *Das Kapital (Capital),* the first volume of which was published in 1867, and the second and third, posthumously, in 1885 and 1894 by Engels. *Das Kapital* was a systematic critique of capitalism with emphasis on its self-destructive tendencies, expounding Marx's theory of the inevitability of social revolution.

Turning once more to politics, he assumed leadership in 1864 of the First International of the Workingmen's Association, a group of revo-

lutionary, reformist, and labor movements. As head of the general council he formulated programs and shaped policies until the International broke into anarchist and Marxist factions in 1873, to be dissolved soon afterward.

In Marx's last years there was a slight improvement in his finances, but his health deteriorated. He died in London on March 14, 1883.

Influence. Marx's political creed exerted a long-range and powerful influence on subsequent generations, and his social philosophy and program of action for the rising proletariat inspired a great mass movement. At his death some theories were still uncoordinated and certain contradictions unreconciled; these became the source of dissension and distortion among his followers and critics.

Further Reading: Berlin, Isaiah, *Karl Marx: His Life and Environment,* 2d ed. (New York and London 1948); Mehring, Franz, *Karl Marx, The Story of His Life,* tr. by Edward Fitzgerald (London 1936, reprinted Ann Arbor, Mich., 1962); Payne, Robert, *Marx* (New York 1968); Rühle, Otto, *Karl Marx, His Life and Work* tr. by Eden and Cedar Paul (New York 1935; reprinted 1943); Marx, Karl, and Engels, Friedrich, *Selected Works* 2 vols. (Moscow 1962).

MARX, Wilhelm, German statesman: b. Cologne, Jan. 15, 1863; d. Bonn, Aug. 5, 1946. He studied jurisprudence at the University of Bonn, and subsequently served as a judge. In 1899 he was elected to the Prussian Diet, and in 1910 he entered the German Reichstag, where he became a leading member of the Catholic Centrist Party.

He was chosen president of his party in 1921, and two years later he succeeded Gustav Stresemann as chancellor of Germany, forming a minority government of Centrists, Democrats, and People's Party members. In 1924 he attended the Reparations Conference in London, and upon his return to Berlin he succeeded in securing a two thirds Reichstag vote for approval of the Dawes Plan. On the strength of this vote he tried in the fall to form a majority cabinet, and when this failed he was forced to vacate the chancellorship in favor of Hans Luther.

In January 1926, Marx was appointed minister for justice and occupied territories, and later that year, after the resignation of the Luther cabinet, he again became chancellor. He retired from political leadership when his party was weakened in the elections of May 1928.

MARXISM, märks'siz-əm, is a political and social doctrine developed by Karl Marx and Friedrich Engels (qq.v.), and officially maintained by the Communist parties (see COMMUNISM; COMMUNIST PARTIES).

Essential Features. Marxism is a comprehensive theory of the nature of history and politics, as well as a prescription for revolutionary action to bring the industrial working class to power and create a classless society of communism. The basic propositions of Marxism are that the economic forces of production determine the basic form of the class structure, the state, and the religious and intellectual superstructure of society; that society up to the present has been dominated by a ruling class of property owners who exploit the lower class; and that according to the laws of the "dialectic," each social system generates the forces that will destroy it and create a new system, with political revolution and the emergence of a new ruling class marking each transition.

According to Marxism, mankind has experienced five types of society—primitive communism, Asiatic society, ancient slave-holding society, feudalism, and capitalism. The expected breakdown of capitalism will set the stage for a proletarian revolution and the establishment of a classless communist society with the "withering-away" of the state.

Different schools of Marxism—revisionist (moderate), orthodox, and revolutionary (Bolshevik, Communist)—have differed mainly over questions of methods: democratic or violent, gradual or abrupt. Wherever Communist parties have come to power, Marxism has been made the official philosophy, but its interpretation has been controlled by each Communist government to justify its own policies. The Marxist prophecies of the classless society and the withering-away of the state have not come true; instead, the characteristic pattern of the officially Marxist societies is a bureaucratic dictatorship.

Development of Marxist Theory. The theory of Marxism was worked out by Marx and Engels over an extended period of time in the 19th century, and the different stages of their thought show different emphases and even contradictions. By 1845, when he was 27, Marx had assimilated the three main intellectual sources of his theory—German philosophy (Hegel), French utopian socialism, and British classical economic theory. In his *Economic and Philosophical Manuscripts* of 1844, Marx concluded that man was alienated from his own true nature by the class system and the exploitation of the lower class by the upper. In 1845, in *The German Ideology*, he formulated his materialist conception of history, and in 1847, in *The Poverty of Philosophy*, he produced his first systematic statement of the dialectical breakdown of capitalism and the predicted triumph of the proletarian revolution.

Beginning with the publication of their fiery summation, the *Communist Manifesto*, in January 1848, Marx and Engels devoted the next five years to revolutionary political agitation and to journalistic comments on Europe's unsuccessful revolutions of 1848–1849. From 1852 until the mid-1860's, Marx concentrated on the scholarly elaboration of his economic theory of capitalism, publishing his *Critique of Political Economy* in 1859 and the first volume of *Das Kapital* (*Capital*) in 1867. In 1864, with the organization of the International Workingmen's Association (see INTERNATIONAL), Marx renewed his interest in practical political activity. Much of his writing from that time, until illness (and possibly self-doubt) sapped his powers in the mid-1870's, was devoted to discussing programs, especially in *The Civil War in France* (1871), on the meaning of the Paris Commune, and *The Critique of the Gotha Program* (1875), on the future communist society.

After 1875 most of the development of Marxism was the work of Engels, who extended it with writings on philosophy (*Herr Eugen Dühring's Revolution in Science*, or "Anti-Dühring," in 1878, and *The Dialectics of Nature*, not published until 1925); on sociology (*The Origin of the Family, Private Property, and the State*, 1884); and on the theory of history (mainly in letters).

Marx's Social Theory. Marx's theory of society, termed by Engels "historical materialism," attributes fundamental importance to the economic aspect of life. According to Marx, the technological conditions of producing and exchanging goods (the "forces of production"), together with the system of property ownership (the "relations of production"), determine the basic division of society into two classes and the fundamental nature of government, religion, and culture in any given society. Marxism is thus a form of economic determinism, in which the economic circumstances are regarded as the "base" of the social system, and the political, legal, and religious institutions are the "superstructure," whose nature is substantially governed by the form of the base.

Together with its superstructure each society develops an "ideology," a set of official beliefs or religious doctrines justifying the power of the ruling class. Marx once defined ideology as "false consciousness," in other words a view of the world distorted by the class interests of the exploiters and upheld in order to justify those interests.

Historically, after the hypothetical epoch of primitive communism, all societies, according to Marxism, have been based on a division into two classes, the property-owning exploiters and the propertyless class of exploited workers. Social change from one system to another comes about primarily from changes in the economic base, giving rise to a new ruling class that takes political power through revolution and causes its new ideology to prevail.

The identity of each ruling class and its respective lower class depends on the state of development of the economic base. Ancient slave-holding society, based on crude agriculture, was divided into the slaves who toiled and the owners who exploited them; the superstructure was the city-state or the ancient empire, and the ideology was the pantheon of Greco-Roman religion. The concept of Asiatic society was not clearly developed by Marx and Engels, but it was intended to recognize an alternative to the slave-owning society, where the exploiters were the class of government officials who extracted taxes from the peasants. Presumably more progressive was the society of feudalism, although it is hard to find a significantly different economic base for it. In feudal society the ruling class was the nobility, which exploited the serfs; the superstructure was the monarchy; and the ideology was the Christian religion.

In elaborating his philosophy of history Marx devoted most of his attention to the transition from feudalism to capitalism (especially in England) and the rise of a new ruling class, the bourgeoisie, deriving its power from the accumulation of monetary capital and the modern technology of industrial production. He analyzed the commercial development of the 17th century and the beginnings of the Industrial Revolution in the 18th as the stage of the "primary accumulation of capital" and attributed the English Revolution of 1642 and the French Revolution of 1789 to the drive of the rising bourgeoisie to achieve political power. "Laissez-faire" liberalism, with parliamentary government that denied the vote to the workers and kept hands off business, represented to Marx the ideology and the superstructure characteristic of the capitalist society.

Following the same pattern, Marx predicted revolution by the class of industrial workers who were exploited by the capitalists. He prophesied that the workers would overthrow and expropriate the owners of capital and establish a class-less society of socialism or communism (Marx used the terms almost interchangeably).

In some of his historical writings, Marx qualified his economic determinism and conceded the role of force and political action in history. Engels in his late letters made a general acknowledgment of the possible reverse influence of the political and ideological superstructure of society on the economic base. In the "last analysis," however, economic developments were the decisive factor both in generating change and in limiting human aspirations at any stage.

Marxian Philosophy—The "Dialectic." Marx's philosophy as a whole has been termed "dialectical materialism" by his followers. It is "dialectical" because it takes Hegel's philosophy of the "dialectic" (from the Greek, meaning an argument) as its model of the process of change both in society and in the world of nature; there, a given situation (the "thesis") generates opposing forces (the "antithesis") that ultimately break up the original situation and produce a new one (the "synthesis"). The synthesis then becomes the "thesis" for the next stage of development.

The Marxian theory of society follows the dialectical model closely. Social change is prompted by the development of "contradictions" between the class system and the political superstructure on the one hand and new developments in the economic base on the other. (Where such innovation originates is never clearly explained.) Quantitative social changes are suddenly transformed into qualitative changes when the tension between "thesis" and "antithesis" erupts in revolution. In the dialectical view, social change is usually abrupt and violent, and revolution is therefore the norm.

The Marxian dialectic is "materialist" because, contrary to Hegel, it deals not with the world of ideas as the primary reality, but with the material world. Marxism is materialist in two senses: first, in rejecting any religious or metaphysically "idealist" view of the universe and, second, in asserting the primacy of material (economic) factors rather than ideas in human history. Marxism does not hold that individuals are guided only by economic self-interest, nor does it extend to the ethical materialism of extolling such motives. In fact, Marxism represents an impassioned moral protest against the rule of self-interest in human affairs. The ethical appeal of Marxism as a creed of equality and fraternity has been a major factor in its political success.

Marx had no particular scientific reason for carrying over his philosophic dialectic into his description of society; it was merely his crude way of trying to represent social problems in a dynamic developmental manner. Some Marxists, following Engels, have attempted to apply the dialectic to the physical and biological worlds. There is even less scientific merit in that.

Marx's Economic Theory. The Marxian theory of economics is primarily an analysis of capitalism, with England in Marx's own time as the model. Marx made a combined moral and economic attack on capitalism with his theory of exploitation and surplus value, and he argued, in the pattern of the dialectic, that the inherent contradictions in capitalism would ultimately destroy it.

Capitalism, according to Marx, is based on the exploitation of the working class (proletariat) by the owners of capital (factories, machinery, and working capital), whose profits come from the difference between the wages of labor and the value of the product. Marx borrowed most of his argument from the British classical economists Adam Smith, Thomas Malthus, and David Ricardo, although they wrote in defense of capitalism. He followed them on the labor theory of value, the iron law of wages, and the concept of surplus value. According to the labor theory of value (which neglects the modern attention to utility or demand), the value of a commodity is determined by the labor necessary to produce it. Wages, however, according to the iron law, are pushed down to the subsistence level by increasing population and held there by the "reserve army" of the unemployed. The difference between the wage level and the value of the product is "surplus value," which is appropriated by the capitalist as profit.

Besides his moral condemnation of surplus value of exploitation, Marx added three propositions about the development of capitalism: the law of accumulation, by which, he argued, competition forced capitalists to reinvest their profits in order to cut labor costs and increase production; the law of concentration of capital, by which big capitalist grew bigger by forcing the smaller ones out of business and into the working class; and the law of increasing misery of the proletariat, by which labor-saving machinery increased the ranks of the unemployed and thereby depressed wages.

In the later volumes of *Capital,* unpublished until his death, Marx tried to argue that the rate of profit on capital must necessarily fall as industry expands, thus contributing to the business cycle and the ultimate crisis of capitalism. Ultimately, Marx believed, capitalism would be paralyzed by the contradiction between the social nature of industry and the system of evermore concentrated private property. Capitalism would exhaust its possibilities of development and give way in the next stage of the dialectic to the proletarian revolution and socialism.

Theory of the Proletarian Revolution. Marx was convinced that his historical and economic research had created the basis for "scientific socialism," that the laws of history he believed he had discovered made the breakdown of capitalism and the rise of the proletariat just as inevitable as the overthrow of feudalism by the bourgeoisie. The proletariat would seize power as the new ruling class, abolish capitalist private ownership of the means of production, eliminate class differences, and thus usher in the classless society of communism. Since the victory of the proletariat would end the history of contradictions between the ruling class and its subjects, the whole process of the dialectic would finally come to an end. The revolution would ordinarily be violent, but where the workers had the vote, as in Britain and the United States, it might be accomplished peacefully. It would begin in the most industrially advanced countries.

While Marx hesitated to draw up a detailed blueprint for the revolution and the ensuing socialist society, he did make a number of general predictions and suggestions. The revolution must be the work of the proletariat itself, following naturally from the trend toward organization and consciousness promoted among the working class by the conditions of capitalist industry.

Capitalism would tend toward monopoly and the boom-and-bust fluctuations of the business cycle. Sooner or later there would be a crisis severe enough to bring the working class to power. The workers' first step would be to destroy the old bureaucratic government and replace it with a "dictatorship of proletariat," for which Marx took as his model the revolutionary Commune of Paris (1871). This workers' state, based on direct democracy and workers' pay for officials, would expropriate the monopoly capitalists and bring the whole working class into the administration of industry.

Following the abolition of class differences by the proletarian revolution, the state—existing primarily to enforce the exploitation of the propertyless class—could begin to wither away. Society would gradually evolve through the "first phase of communism," in which people still would be paid for their work, into the "final phase of communism," in which the state would disappear, national differences would subside, and the entire system of monetary rewards and inequalities would vanish. Then, as Marx wrote, "Society can inscribe upon its banners, from each according to his ability, to each according to his needs."

Critique of Marxism. Like any other broad theory of society Marxism is subject to many criticisms, and its significance should be weighed as a contribution to the development of modern politics and social thought rather than as a dogma that must be condemned or taken on faith.

Marxism is replete with inconsistencies and ambiguities, and has been subject to all manner of interpretations both by its detractors and by various schools among its followers. The factual weaknesses in Marxism center on the analysis of classes and the prediction of their future development. The scheme of rulers and exploited is much too simple for any period of history, and there are numerous instances of political changes that do not correspond to social and economic changes. Certain powerful historical forces—nationality, for one—cannot be explained by the class struggle, and the Marxian explanation of religious and ideological commitments is quite inadequate. Marxism has had to live with the fact that most of the movement's own leaders have been non-workers, motivated by a psychology much more complex than class interest.

Judgment of the predictive value of Marxism depends on whether one accepts the Communist revolutions as the sort of event Marx had in mind. The proletarian revolution has failed to materialize in the advanced capitalist countries, where Marx expected it, unless the gradual reform under Scandinavian and British socialism is viewed as proof of the prediction. Marx was clearly wrong on the trend toward increased misery of the working class, and he failed to foresee the rise of the salaried middle class of professional, technical, and white-collar workers.

A major weakness in the inner logic of Marxism is the question of why the dialectic should stop once capitalism has been overthrown; why not a new ruling class exploiting the masses on some new basis? Some Marxist writers have suggested that the bureaucracy of the Communist party has become a new ruling class, which exploits the masses not through private property but through its control of the state (for example, Leon Trotsky, *The Revolution Betrayed,* James Burnham, *The Managerial Revolution,* and Milovan Djilas, *The New Class*).

Certain questions were left in an unsettled or contradictory state by Marx and have been the subject of recurring controversy among his followers: the necessity of violence versus the possibility of democratic methods in the proletarian revolution; the inevitability of capitalism and the proletarian revolution for all countries versus the possibility of separate lines of development; and the efficacy of deliberate political leadership and iedological inspiration versus the rigorous determination of the future by economic circumstances. Marxism suffers from an inner duality in trying to be simultaneously a predictive science of history and a prescription for moral action. From this stem two tendencies that have repeatedly divided the Marxist movement: passivity in the face of a foreordained future and manipulation of the science to make it justify the impulses of activism.

Marxism aroused violent antagonism in most countries, as a dangerous challenge to the political, social, and religious order. As its revolutionary threat has subsided, it has gradually come to be recognized intellectually by social scientists in Europe and America as a major contribution to the method of analyzing social problems and changes, even if many of its particular predictions or prescriptions have not turned out to be valid. Marxism challenged scholars to recognize the interrelatedness of the different aspects of society —political, economic, social, and cultural—and, in particular, to give economic forces and interests their due weight in explaining the past and the present. With the concept of "ideology" as a set of beliefs that justify the purposes of a movement or a ruling class, Marx contributed to the foundations of the sociology of knowledge and the notion of relativism in the interpretation of history. These approaches, of course, are not confined to Marxists or particularly tied to Marxism. On the contrary, Communists do not look with favor on the application of such relativistic sociological analysis to their own philosophy and movement.

Influence of Marxism to 1917. In the latter part of the 19th century, Marxism was adopted by a majority of the rising labor and socialist movement in Europe (except England) and embodied as the official philosophy in the Social Democratic parties. At the same time, the political emphasis of Marxism shifted from revolution to peaceful democratic change, as encouraged by the later writings of Marx and especially of Engels. This was the position of the Labor and Socialist International (the Second International), a loose association of the Social-Democratic parties formed in 1889.

During the next two decades two opposition tendencies, based on particular interpretations of Marx, appeared within the Social Democratic movement. On the right, or moderate, side the "revisionists," led by Eduard Bernstein, wanted to bring Marx up to date and replace his idea of revolution with a democratic program of "evolutionary socialism." On the left a radical tendency, led by Rosa Luxemburg in Germany and supported by most of the Russian Marxists, emphasized the violent revolution of early Marxism. In the center the "orthodox" Marxists, led by the German socialist Karl Kautsky, stuck to the deterministic philosophy of the proletarian revolution but expected it to come by peaceful means.

One distinctly new theoretical contribution, made principally by the left-wing Marxists, was a theory of imperialism, which applied Marxism to the relations between advanced and colonial countries and suggested that monopoly capitalism in its mature stage led necessarily to the exploitation of backward nations and to war among the major capitalist powers. Supplementing this was the Austrian socialist Rudolf Hilferding's theory of "finance capitalism," which posited a final stage of monopoly dominated by big banks.

Marxism became influential in Russia in the late 1890's, just as the capitalist industrialization of the country was getting started. Georgi Plekhanov, the founder of Russian Marxism, insisted that Russia would have to pass through a stage of capitalism in order to become ready for the proletarian revolution (although Marx himself was not convinced of this). A revisionist faction of Russian Marxists (the so-called "economists") took the position that all they could do in the meantime was to work for improvements in the economic position of the workers. The others, after establishing the Russian Social Democratic Workers' party, split at their Second Congress in 1903 over the question of the means to achieve revolution—by patient democratic organization or by an accelerated revolutionary conspiracy. The more democratic position was taken by the orthodox Menshevik ("minority") faction, led by Julius Martov, while the more revolutionary, left-wing position was taken by Vladimir Lenin and Bolshevik ("majority") faction.

Lenin's Contribution to Marxism. Lenin's distinctive contribution (expounded particularly in his pamphlet "What is to be Done," 1902) was to combine with Marxism the conspiratorial organization and tactics developed by the pre-Marxist Russian revolutionary movement. His central idea, as crucial as the idea of the class was to Marx, was his concept of the party—not a party in the Western democratic sense but a disciplined organization of professional revolutionaries aiming to overthrow the government and seize power in the name of the working class. To justify an early bid for power, Lenin argued that the Social-Democratic party should take the lead in the bourgeois revolution and establish a "democratic dictatorship of the proletariat and peasantry" pending the economic development that would make a transition to socialism feasible. Later on, reiterating the Marxist theory of imperialism (in *Imperialism, the Highest Stage of Capitalism,* 1916), Lenin argued that Russia, as a backward victim of exploitation, was the "weakest link in the chain of capitalism," and hence ripe for revolution.

Lenin's fellow countryman Leon Trotsky suggested a different rationale for the early seizure of power in his "theory of permanent revolution," 1906). According to Trotsky, the outbreak of a bourgeois revolution in Russia would initiate a continuous or permanent state of revolution in which the workers could seize power temporarily in the major cities. This in turn would set up a permanent state of revolution internationally, as the Russian example triggered the mature forces of proletarian revolution in the West. The latter would come to the aid of the Russian Marxists and help clinch their victory despite Russia's backwardness. Trotsky's theory was part of the Bolshevik rationale in 1917 and helps explain their emphasis on world revolution.

Lenin's major statement of Marxist political theory was his book *State and Revolution,* written while he was in hiding in the summer of 1917. He expanded on the smashing of the old state, the establishment of the dictatorship of the proletariat, equality under the new regime, the withering away of the state, and the two phases of communism (which Lenin labeled "socialism" and "communism" respectively). The generally anarchistic ideal of *State and Revolution* was violated by Lenin himself soon after he took power, for he set up a highly centralized dictatorship and industrial administration. Shortly before his death in 1924, Lenin acknowledged that Soviet Russia lacked the economic and cultural foundation for communism and that a long period of gradual building under the tutelage of the Communist party would be necessary.

Critique of Leninism. Lenin always insisted that his actions as well as his theories were absolutely orthodox applications of Marxism, and all Communists maintain that Leninism is the only correct 20th century version of Marxism. In reality, Lenin introduced some very different implications and emphases, particularly in his doctrine of the party as the conscious, disciplined vanguard of the proletariat. Drawing on the views of the pre-Marxist Russian revolutionary movement, Lenin repeatedly warned that the proletarian revolution would not occur simply as the result of economic forces, but depended on the willful action of a revolutionary organization that seized the strategic movement. He frequently was at pains to justify the most extreme measures for seizing and holding power, and he denounced as "bourgeois" any absolute standards of democracy, morality, legality, or pacifism.

Lenin is rightly charged with having believed that the end justifies any means, and he is vulnerable to the criticism that evil means tend to become ends in themselves. In fact, in his hierarchical organization and command practices, which Lenin justified as "democratic centralism," Lenin developed such a spirit of authoritarianism that the Soviet regime quickly became a dictatorship over the workers rather than by them. Lenin's own exposition of the Marxian theory of the state became merely a piece of utopian propaganda.

Marxist Reactions to the Russian Revolution. Marxists outside Russia split deeply over the Russian Revolution and the Communist dictatorship. Those of the left wing, favorable to Soviet Russia, broke away from the Social Democratic parties and founded Communist parties that were committed to revolutionary Marxism and pledged to support Soviet Russia. Because of the imposition of Soviet control over these parties through the Third, or Communist, International (Comintern), they made relatively little independent contribution to Marxist theory. One exception is the appreciation of voluntarism to Leninism by the Italian Antonio Gramsci and the Hungarian Georg Lukacs, both of whom avowedly stressed the role of belief and force in history as against purely economic factors. The Soviet leadership, however, rejected their contribution.

Marxists who opposed the Soviet dictatorship affirmed their commitment to the democratic process and condemned the Communists for attempting socialism by means of dictatorship in a country where the industrial prerequisites were lacking. This was the argument of Kautsky, Hilferding, and Martov, and even of the "Austro-Marxists," who clung to the spirit of thorough-going socialism. In practice, all of the non-Communist Marxists became revisionists, accepting the gradual and piecemeal approach to socialism. In the 1950's the leading democratic Marxist party, the Social-Democratic party of Germany, officially dropped Marxism as its official doctrine while still according Marx a place of respect in the history of socialist thought.

Development of Stalinism. During the struggle for power in Soviet Russia just preceding and following Lenin's death the meaning and role of Marxist theory for the Communist movement was profoundly changed. Bitter disagreements had already erupted among the Russian Communists—between those ("Left Communists," "Democratic Centralists," and "Workers' Opposition") who demanded immediate steps toward the classless society and the withering away of the state and those (including Lenin) who stressed the temporary consolidation of the state and the administration of industry by centrally appointed officials.

From 1923 to 1927, Leon Trotsky led the Left opposition in calling for the democratization of the Communist party, a more revolutionary foreign policy, and systematic plans to strengthen the proletarian basis of Soviet communism by rapid industrialization. Trotsky was opposed by Nikolai Bukharin, the leading Soviet theoretician of the 1920's, who essentially continued Lenin's position of firm Communist party control and education while the industrial basis for communism grew gradually in response to market demand. Bukharin was supported until 1928 by Joseph Stalin, who as general secretary of the Communist party had built up a formidable system of personal power.

In 1924, Stalin coined the expression "Marxism-Leninism" and laid down in dogmatic form the theoretical justifications followed by the Soviet regime ever since: the necessity of violent revolution by the Communist party; the necessity of Communist party dictatorship throughout the period of the "building of socialism"; the need for "iron discipline" and unity within the party; and the "theory of socialism in one country," which maintained that Russia could overcome its backwardness and achieve socialism without the aid of international revolution ("Foundations of Leninism" and "The October Revolution and the Tactics of the Russian Communists," published in *Problems of Leninism* in 1933).

The "theory of socialism in one country" was a turning point in the role of Marxist theory, because, although it was based only on a misquotation from Lenin and was contrary to what all Communists had believed since the revolution, Stalin successfully imposed the view that it had been standard Marxism all along. He thus made the philosophical meaning of Marxism in the Soviet Union entirely subject to the authority and convenience of the leadership.

The basic premises of Stalinism took shape as a rationale for the Soviet political and economic system as Stalin reorganized it in the early 1930's, particularly in the collectivization of the peasantry and the institution of centralized economic planning. Economic equalitarianism was abandoned, with the argument that "to each according to his needs" allowed recognition of the greater needs of managerial personnel. The "withering away

of the state" was rejected in favor of recognizing the positive role of the state—even under the final phase of communism—in the promotion of economic and cultural development as well as in the defense of the country against "capitalist encirclement."

In his essay "Dialectical and Historical Materialism" (1938; reaffirmed in "Marxism and Linguistics," 1950), Stalin held that the political and ideological superstructure of society could have a decisive effect in waging class war and in promoting development of the economic base. Similarly, the individual was held responsible for his own conduct and achievements; these were not to be viewed as the product of social conditioning. All this was nearly the reverse of Marx's sociology, but Stalin's views were enforced in the name of orthodox Marxism.

Stalin's triumph over his rivals for leadership in Russia was the occasion for a series of splits in the Communist movement elsewhere, in the course of which most of the original leaders of the various Communist parties left the movement or were expelled. A small left wing sympathetic to Trotsky broke away to form the "Fourth International" (represented by the Socialist Workers party in the United States), which stressed the bureaucratic degeneration of Marxism in Russia and the need for world proletarian revolution to renew the movement. Other splinters on the right, sympathetic to Bukharin, gravitated toward the revisionism of the Social Democrats.

Critique of Stalinism. Under Stalin the official Soviet interpretation of Marxism was extensively altered, although the revised version was still asserted to be the only correct interpretation of Marxism-Leninism. Because no independent discussion of Marxism was allowed, no one was in a position to challenge interpretations by the leadership that departed from the spirit and even the letter of the original doctrine.

The real principles of Stalinism have to be inferred from the historical record: the permanent power of the dictatorial state and party; a permanently unequal social hierarchy of officials, technicians, workers, and peasants; and reliance on government coercion to accomplish the economic and cultural modernization of the country. These de facto principles have been continued by Stalin's successors, whose views are less in accord with original Marxism than they are with the elitist state socialism proposed by Saint-Simon (q.v.).

There are at least four different schools of thought among outside observers as to the function of Marxism in the Soviet regime under Stalin and his successors. One school sees Soviet Marxism still as a living faith, setting the goal of world revolution and classless society, for which the Soviet leadership must constantly work. Another school recognizes that Soviet aims are more pragmatic but suggests that Marxism is still used as a method or frame of reference for interpreting the outside world. A third approach regards the ideology as no more than propaganda, cynically manipulated by the leadership for day-to-day political effect at home and abroad. Finally, Soviet Marxism is regarded by some as a system of self-justification for the leadership, modified to fit their practical interests but nevertheless dogmatically believed and enforced. Some neo-Marxist theorists view Soviet Marxism as the "ideology" (or "false consciousness") of a new ruling class of bureaucrats in a social system of state capitalism.

Marxism in other Communist Countries.

The Soviet interpretation and use of Marxism has not changed appreciably since Stalin's time. Major developments, however, have occurred in the countries brought under Communist rule during and after World War II, wherever independence from Soviet control made it possible for other Communist governments to interpret Marxism in support of their own interests.

Yugoslavia, as the first Communist country to defy Soviet domination of the movement in 1948, made the first overt modifications of Stalinist doctrine. President Tito and Vice President Djilas asserted that Soviet Russia had deviated from the correct Marxist path into a bureaucratic state capitalism; to correct this, they revived and applied the ideal of workers' control of industry. To defend Yugoslavia's claims of independence, Tito and Djilas asserted the possibility of separate roads to socialism," on which each country might travel at its own speed rather than being obliged to copy the Soviet model. Further, they decentralized industrial administration to allow the play of market forces of supply and demand among socialized enterprises, like the Soviet practice in the 1920's. Djilas went further, extending his critique of Communist bureaucracy to Yugoslavia itself (*The New Class*, 1957), and fell from power.

At the time Poland achieved internal independence from Soviet control in 1956, there was an upsurge of genuine philosophical work by individual Marxists, notably Leszek Kolakowski. Kolakowski stressed the ethical goals in Marxism and attacked extreme determinism as an excuse for terror and dictatorship. Czech Marxism responded to a liberalization of the regime in 1968 with a "revisionist" emphasis on the democratization of all aspects of life.

The most complex development of Marxism has occurred in Communist China, reflecting the abrupt turns in Chinese internal policy and in China's relations with the rest of the Communist world. Before coming to power in 1949, the Chinese Communists subscribed to Marxism-Leninism but with Mao Tse-tung's personal emphasis on indoctrination, nationalism, and coalition tactics. Because they achieved power with intellectual leadership and a peasant rather than working-class base, the Chinese Communists reinterpreted the Marxian notion of "class" to emphasize political attitudes rather than economic origins. Mao's theory of revolution stressed cooperation of all classes—including the "national bourgeoisie"—in the "New Democracy" but required the liquidation of landlords and any elements that collaborated with foreign imperialism

When cooperation between China and Soviet Russia broke down in the late 1950's, Marxist theory became an area of political struggle rather than a tie between the two powers. With the institution of agricultural communes in 1958, China claimed to have moved ahead of Soviet Russia on the road to true communism and thereafter condemned the Soviet regime as "revisionist." A further source of discord was the question of international revolution and the inevitability of war, on which the Chinese took a bolder stand than the Soviets but one less rash than the latter accused them of.

The "cultural revolution" that began in China in 1966 bore some resemblance to the ultrarevolutionary views of the left-wing communists in Russia in the early days of the Soviet regime, particularly in attacking the influence and privileges of bureaucrats and intellectuals. In theoretical terms, however, Chinese Marxism became increasingly irrational, as a cult of the infallible wisdom of Chairman Mao.

Communism in Cuba under Fidel Castro is nominally Marxist, although Marxist theoretical influence did not appear until after Castro had come to power in 1959. Cuban Marxism, like Chinese, advocates for all of Latin America guerrilla warfare against governments that are regarded as satellites of United States imperialism.

Marxism Since Stalin.

The death of Stalin did not bring any substantial change in the structure of the Communist regimes, nor in their dogmatic use of Marxist theory. Certain reinterpretations of detail were associated with Soviet Party First Secretary Nikita Khrushchev's "destalinization" campaign of 1956 and the Communist party program of 1961—specifically that, contrary to Stalin, the class struggle would not intensify and justify terror under Communist rule and the state could indeed begin to wither away provided that its functions were taken over by the Communist party organization or "nongovernmental public organizations" such as the Young Communist League and the auxiliary police.

Khrushchev toned down considerably the international aspects of Marxism-Leninism. "Separate roads to socialism" were acknowledged; the inevitability of war was expressly rejected in favor of peaceful coexistence; and violent revolution and one-party Communist dictatorship ceased to be demanded for all countries. The major Communist parties in the West (notably in Italy and France) took this position and in practice became more or less "revisionist," while small left-wing factions in the same parties reasserted the revolutionary outlook and supported Communist China.

A major paradox of Marxism is that it has had (especially in its revolutionary form) more appeal in the less-developed countries than in the most industrialized. Marxism tends to appeal to intellectuals in backward or troubled countries as an ideology of national development and regeneration. Despite its internationalist phraseology, Marxism can be a vehicle of intense nationalism.

In the most prosperous countries of western Europe and America (Britain, Scandinavia, the United States, and Canada), Marxism has never had more than a limited and passing appeal. Rising living standards and democratic access to political power made it hard to apply the Marxian theory of proletarian revolution, however interpreted. The Labor and Socialist parties of Britain and Scandinavia are pragmatic rather than Marxist and not very different in outlook from the liberal factions in U.S. and Canadian politics. The Communist parties in these countries have always been small; they achieved their peak before and during World War II more through anti-Fascism than through Marxism.

In western Europe in the 1950's and 1960's there was a revival of non-Communist intellectual interest in the early writings of Marx, especially as a philosophy of the individual alienated from society. The German-American Marxist philosopher Herbert Marcuse became a major influence among student groups of the "New Left," with his emphasis on the psychologically alienating effect of the entire existing social order. This interpretation of Marx is not accepted in the Communist countries.

ROBERT V. DANIELS, *University of Vermont*

ROBERT V. DANIELS, *University of Vermont*

Bibliography

Cole, G. D. H., *History of Socialist Thought,* 5 vols. (London 1953–1960).
Daniels, Robert V., ed., *Marxism and Communism: Essential Readings* (New York 1965).
Daniels, Robert V., *The Nature of Communism* (New York 1962).
Feuer, Lewis S., ed., *Marx and Engels: Basic Writings in Politics and Philosophy* (New York 1959).
Hunt, R. N. C., *The Theory and Practice of Communism* (New York 1951).
Kuusinen, O. W., and others, *Fundamentals of Marxism-Leninism* (Moscow 1961).
Landauer, Karl, *European Socialism,* 2 vols. (Berkeley, Calif., 1959).
Lichtheim, George, *Marxism, an Historical and Critical Study* (New York 1961).
Marx, Karl, *Selected Works,* 2 vols. (New York, 1952).
Meyer, Alfred G., *Leninism* (Cambridge, Mass., 1957).
Meyer, Alfred G., *Marxism: The Unity of Theory and Practice* (Cambridge, Mass., 1954).
Sabine, George H., *Marxism* (Ithaca, N. Y., 1958).
Wetter, Gustav A., *Dialectical Materialism* (New York 1958).

MARY, SAINT, mâr'ĭ (BLESSED VIRGIN MARY), the mother of Jesus. Holy Scripture does not give the names of the parents of Mary. The names Joachim and Anna are known from an ancient tradition, derived ultimately, it seems, from the Apocryphal Protoevangelium of James (2d century A.D.), which contains some facts and some undoubted fantasy. Traditions vary on the place of her birth, Nazareth, Sepphoris, and Jerusalem being given. The oldest tradition favors Jerusalem, and there are references as early as the 6th century to a church built on the supposed site of the house, near the Sheep Pool. Scripture does make clear, however, that Mary was of the line of David. Her parents named her Miryam, a name which in the Old Testament belonged only to the sister of Moses but which was not rare at the time of Christ. The meaning of the name is uncertain; over 60 etymologies have been proposed. The best scientific evidence now available seems to favor the meaning "highness" or "the exalted one." It is uncertain whether Joachim and Anna had other children. John 19:25[1] does speak of "his mother's sister," but the word may easily have the broader Semitic sense of "cousin."

Life of Mary.—The Protoevangelium of James states that at an early age Mary was presented in the temple and remained there until about the age of 12. Such a presentation was not obligatory, but neither was it unlikely. Whether she remained there for several years is more questionable though not impossible. Some passages in Scripture seem to indicate a possibility of women residing there (Exodus 38:8; IV Kings 11:3; Luke 2:37); and St. Ambrose (d. 397) speaks of virgins being assigned to the temple (*De virginibus ad Marcellinam,* book 1). At an early age, probably 12, according to Jewish custom, Mary was espoused to Joseph who, though a descendant of David, was a carpenter. According to Jewish custom, the man and wife were supposed to be of the same social and economic status; hence it seems likely that Joachim was also of the artisan class. It is unlikely that Joseph was aged at this time. The opinion that he was rests on very unsatisfactory evidence. Although the espousal seems to have carried most or all of the juridical effects of marriage, it was at least contrary to custom for the partners to live together for some time afterward, commonly a year.

During this period (a few commentators think the angel came after the final marriage ceremony), Mary was visited at Nazareth by the angel Gabriel, who told her that by the power of the Holy Spirit she would conceive a son, whom she should name Jesus. He would be called the Son of the Most High, the Son of God, and would be king in the house of Jacob forever. Gabriel said that the child would be conceived because the power of the Most High would "overshadow" her. The Greek verb *episkiasei,* used by St. Luke to mean "overshadow," is the same one used in the Septuagint version of Exodus 40:35 to describe the divine presence filling the tabernacle. Mary acquiesced to the divine will, saying: "Behold the handmaid of the Lord; be it done to me according to thy word" (Luke 1:38). Since Gabriel had also told her that her relative Elizabeth was to bear a son in her old age, and was then in the sixth month, Mary went promptly to visit her, probably to Ain-Karim, about four miles west of Jerusalem. On seeing Mary, Elizabeth "was filled with the Holy Ghost" (Luke 1:41), and the child leapt in her womb. Mary replied to her greeting with the famous canticle, the Magnificat, in which she praised God for the great things He had done for her, His humble servant. After a visit of about three months, Mary returned to Nazareth.

When, some months after the Annunciation, Mary "was found with child, of the Holy Ghost" (Matthew 1:18), Joseph at first was inclined to put her away privately; but, being admonished in a dream by an angel, he concluded the final marriage ceremonies with Mary. Some months later, an edict of the Emperor Augustus required a general enrollment. The Romans commonly respected local customs; hence Joseph went to Bethlehem, the city of his ancestors, for the census. Finding no place that would afford privacy in the inn, since Mary's time was come, they took refuge in a cave outside the city. There Mary gave birth to her son, and laid him in the manger. A group of shepherds, given the good news by angels, came to visit the child. After eight days, he was circumcised, and named Jesus, as the angel had directed. Forty days later, Mary, obeying the Jewish law, went to the temple for the ceremonial purification and to present her child to God. There a holy man named Simeon met them and foretold that the child was set for the fall and the resurrection of many in Israel and that a sword would pierce Mary's own soul. Anna, a prophetess, also met the Holy Family and spoke of the child to many who looked for the redemption of Israel.

Probably some time after their return to Bethlehem, the Holy Family was visited by a group of Magi, wise men who had come from the East, probably Nabataean Arabia, or Media, following a star. They offered gifts of gold, frankincense, and myrrh, and adored Jesus. But, on the way to Bethlehem, the Magi had asked directions of King Herod. The latter, sensing a rival to his throne, cunningly asked them to report back so that he too might adore the child. The Magi, being warned in a dream not to return to King Herod, took a different road back to their own country. Herod, seeing that the Magi did not return, ordered a massacre of every male child up to two years of age in all the territory of Bethlehem. Joseph, warned in a dream, fled to Egypt with Jesus and Mary, where they remained until an angel advised Joseph that Herod

---

[1] All references and quotations in this article are according to the Douay Version of the Bible.

Metropolitan Museum of Art

Peter Paul Rubens: *The Holy Family*

Bartolomé Murillo: *Madonna*
Anderson, from Art Reference Bureau

Rijksmuseum, Amsterdam

Giovanni Cimabue: *Madonna and Child*

THE VIRGIN MARY IN ART

Pietro Lorenzetti: *Madonna and Child* (detail from panel)
Anderson, from Art Reference Bureau

had died. Joseph did not, however, settle in Bethlehem, for Herod's son, Archelaus, ruled Judaea, but returned instead to Nazareth.

When Jesus was 12 years old, he went with Mary and Joseph to Jerusalem for the Pasch (Feast of the Passover). After they had left, he stayed behind in Jerusalem. On the third day, they found him among the doctors in the temple, who were amazed at his understanding and answers. After this he went back to Nazareth, "and was subject unto them" (Luke 2:51). We next meet Mary at the wedding at Cana in Galilee, at the opening of the public life of Christ. Here, although his hour had not yet come, at her request, he performed his first miracle, changing water to wine. The Gospels next report that Mary went with his disciples to Capharnaum (John 2:12), but thereafter she is mentioned only twice before the time of his death. On one occasion, she, with his "brethren," tried to see him when a great crowd was about. Jesus, informed of their presence, replied: "Who is my mother, and who are my brethren?" And looking about, he said: "Behold my mother and my brethren. For whosoever shall do the will of my Father . . . he is my brother, and sister, and mother" (Matthew 12:47-50). This text has given rise to various interpretations. At least one point is clear. He was not giving a public rebuke to his mother. For even the most ordinary son would hardly rebuke his mother publicly even if she were guilty of some considerable fault. Mary had done nothing wrong; and he whose meat it was to do the will of the Father, would not violate the commandment: "Honor thy father and thy mother." Actually, Jesus was taking a striking means of teaching that spiritual values are above mere consanguinity. On a second occasion, when a woman in the crowd cried out: "Blessed is the womb that bore thee," Jesus answered: "Rather, blessed are they who hear the word of God, and keep it" (Luke 11:27-28). Here again he taught the same lesson.

During the Passion of Christ, Mary was present, suffering in silence with him. He commended her to the beloved apostle, John, who from that hour took her to his own. After Jesus' Ascension, we find her in the upper room with the apostles, persevering in prayer with them before the descent of the Holy Spirit. We do not have any definite information on the rest of her life in this world. One tradition holds that she died at Jerusalem. In Apocalypse (Revelation) 12:1, St. John saw a great vision of "a woman clothed with the sun, and the moon under her feet, and on her head a crown of twelve stars." Some interpreters believe the vision was of Mary. Others think it represented the church. Still others hold it is Mary as a personification of the church.

Marian Doctrine.—In general, the various Protestant denominations are disinclined to go beyond a mere recital of the Gospel narrative in regard to Mary, nor do they seek for further developments of Marian doctrine in the writings of the early fathers. The Roman Catholic Church, on the other hand, has developed an elaborate body of teaching on Mary. The Protestant attitude is founded ultimately upon the principle that the Bible, privately interpreted, is the sole rule of faith. The Catholic attitude is the result of (1) a belief that tradition is also a depository of revelation; (2) a belief that Christ gave to the church the authority to serve as a sort of supreme court to interpret revelation; and (3) a belief that in virtue of Christ's promise to send the Holy Spirit to "teach you all things, and bring all things to your mind, whatsoever I shall have said to you" (John 14:26), the church is led to an ever deepening realization of all the implications of the revelation once given through the apostles, so that truths which were known only in implicit form, or were realized only dimly in the first centuries, might later be clarified. The relation is comparable to that of a closed bud to the opened flower.

In the case of some doctrines, the clarification came very early, while others had to wait for many centuries. One of the classic examples of the longer development is the Catholic doctrine of the Immaculate Conception (q.v.), which is found in vague or implicit form in the patristic period and was not defined until 1854. In contrast, the development of the title of Theotokos (Mother of God) was very rapid. The term occurs in a papyrus which may go back even to the 2d century, and the historian Socrates Scholasticus asserts that the title was used by Origen (d. ?254); but the first incontrovertible use of it comes in a letter of St. Alexander, patriarch of Alexandria (d. 326). It was officially adopted by the general councils of Ephesus (431), Chalcedon (451), and Constantinople (553). It is easy to see that the belief in the divine motherhood was at least implicit from the very beginning. For since the Gospels teach that Christ is God and Mary is His mother, then she can be called the Mother of God—not as having produced the divine nature but as being the mother of Christ who is God. With such limitations, the term is so obviously proper that Martin Luther, Huldreich Zwingli, and the theologians of Protestant orthodoxy make frequent use of it, though many Protestants reject it.

In regard to the virginity of Mary, the virginal conception of Christ is so clearly taught in Luke 1:35 that rationalist critics have been able to deny it only by denying the authenticity of that passage, contrary to all manuscript evidence. It was believed, therefore, from the beginning. The belief in the virginity during and after the birth of Christ becomes indisputably clear and explicit in the 4th century; for example, the local Council of Milan (c. 390) teaches the virginity during birth, appealing to the Apostles' Creed, and the prophecy of Isaias (Isaiah) 7:14 ("Behold, a virgin shall conceive, and bear a son") as support; and, by about 400, the *Symbol* of Epiphanius used the word *aeiparthenos* (evervirgin). *Aeiparthenos* also occurs much earlier in a disputed text of St. Peter of Alexandria (d. 311). Clement of Alexandria (d. ?220) defends the perpetual virginity, while admitting some denied it. The most notable denial was by Tertullian (d. ?230). Earlier and less clear is the expression of St. Justin (d. ?165), who calls Mary simply "the Virgin." Several early Apocrypha (Protoevangelium of James, Odes of Solomon, and Vision of Isaias, the latter probably late 1st century) seem to reflect a contemporary belief in the perpetual virginity. In addition to Isaias 7:14, the words of Mary: "How shall this be done, because I know not man?" (Luke 1:34) are taken as scriptural foundations; for if, as the traditional view holds, the latter text expresses at least a firm resolve, if not a vow, of virginity, it is hardly conceivable that, having so strong a resolve and realizing that a special divine intervention had preserved her virginity in the conception and birth of Christ, Mary would later surrender it. The Gospels do refer to the "brothers of the Lord," but the Semitic term often means merely "cousins" in a loose sense. The perpetual virginity was officially taught by the Lateran Synod (649) under St. Martin I and the Council of Constantinople (681). Protestants take varying attitudes on the virginity of Mary. Luther, Zwingli, and others of the original Protestants believed in the perpetual virginity. The Anabaptists and some modern Protestants deny even the virginal conception of Christ.

The Catholic belief in Mary's complete freedom from personal sin rests chiefly on Genesis 3:15, where she is foretold as being at perpetual enmity with Satan, and on the conviction that the honor of Christ required her to be sinless and that God would not choose any but a sinless person to be the mother of His Son. The belief is implicit in passages in which the fathers praise her holiness and compare her with the spotless church. In the East, it becomes entirely explicit in St. Ephraem (d. ?373). In the West, St. Ambrose in 377 described her as the model of all virtues; and St. Augustine in 415 said that out of honor to Christ, he wished no question to be raised about Mary when treating of sin. The Council of Trent (1545–1563) defined Mary's complete freedom from personal sin. Protestants in general do not accept this doctrine.

The Catholic Church teaches that Mary cooperated in the Redemption: (1) by being the mother of the Redeemer, for since God willed that Christ should die to redeem man, it was necessary that He have a body in which He could die; and (2) by her association with Him on Calvary. In regard to this second phase, the popes and theologians point especially to the morally unanimous teaching of the early fathers that Mary is a New Eve. The fathers teach that just as the first Eve had a secondary but very real role in bringing down the anger of God upon mankind, so Mary shared in undoing the "knot" of sin, to use the expression of St. Irenaeus of Lyon (d. about 202). Without necessarily asserting that the early fathers realized the full implications of this New Eve teaching, Pius XII teaches that Mary's New Eve role extends even to a cooperation on Calvary; so that just as Eve in a secondary way shared in bringing down God's anger upon mankind, so Mary, through, with, and in subordination to Christ, shared in appeasing that anger and winning Redemption. Most Catholic theologians understand the popes to mean that God, in His infinite generosity, willed to accept even her immeasurably inferior, in itself hopelessly insufficient, offering as fusing, so to speak, into the one great price of our Redemption paid by Christ. Of course, her cooperation was certainly not necessary, for the Passion of Christ was superabundant, and her very ability to cooperate came entirely from and depended upon the sovereign efficacy of His death. Thus, Catholics say, while this teaching glorifies Mary, it sheds even more splendor on the limitless power of the death of Christ and on the generosity of the Father. In addition to the New Eve passages, many theologians consider this doctrine implicit in Genesis 3:15, in which a mysterious woman is promised who will be associated with the promised Redeemer in crushing the head of the serpent. There is as yet no Catholic definition of the Coredemption, although authoritative papal teaching does exist, as described. Protestant bodies reject this teaching completely.

Pius XII, in 1950, defined the Assumption, namely that Mary, after the end of her earthly life, was taken up both body and soul into heaven. Clear and explicit patristic testimonies first appear in the 6th century. Before then we have a few traces, such as the unclear statement of Epiphanius, and several Apocryphal Transitus Mariae, of uncertain value. The pope cited the patristic belief, stating it rested ultimately on Scripture, which, not in one single passage, but in an overall view, shows the close union of Mary with Jesus, "constantly sharing His lot," so that it seems impossible that she would be separated from Him, even in body. Again, since He, a most devoted son, was able to save her from the corruption of the tomb, He surely did so. Further, she was united with Him as the New Eve in the struggle and victory over sin and death foretold in Genesis 3:15. Just as His Resurrection was "an essential part and final sign of this victory," so also, since she had shared in the struggle (Coredemption), she had to share in His Resurrection by her Assumption. Again, being completely victorious over sin by the privilege of the Immaculate Conception, she was also exempt from the general law of remaining in the grave until the end of the world. Protestants in general deny the Assumption.

In establishing the feast of the Queenship of Mary, in 1954, Pius XII explained that though the feast was new, the belief was ancient. For, he said, Mary is queen because (1) she is mother of Him who is King by very nature, and (2) she is the New Eve, who shared with Him in the reconquest of the human race. Among her royal prerogatives is that of being dispensatrix of all graces, that is, in an inferior way shares with Christ in distributing all graces, for she had shared, by the Coredemption, in obtaining all. She is not thereby considered as being in any way on a par with Christ, the one Mediator. She is the New Eve, who acts only in subordination to and union with the New Adam, who alone is needed, and is sufficient without her; just as the first Adam alone could have brought original sin upon all without Eve but, in actuality, acted with her real, though inferior and secondary, cooperation.

The Catholic belief that Mary is the spiritual mother of all men is a corollary of certain doctrines already described: (1) since she is the mother of Christ, the Head of the Mystical Body, she is by that very fact also the mother of His members; and (2) she, as coredemptrix, cooperated in winning spiritual life for all, and as mediatrix, she cooperates in transmitting that life to all, and is a motherly instrument of God's Providence in caring for us.

The large place Mary holds in Catholic devotion is a consequence of the large position she holds in Catholic dogma: it is reasoned that since God Himself has honored her so much and given her so great a place, it is fitting that we imitate His ways. Mary is not, however, adored: she is given a specially high honor called hyperdulia, but not adoration, which is due to God alone. She is specially honored in the liturgy by several feasts, as well as in other lesser ways. Prominent among nonliturgical devotions are the Rosary, the Scapular, and the Litany of Loreto.

Protestants fear that honor paid to Mary detracts from Christ, the one Mediator. Thus

Luther said: "There is no harm in praying to dead saints, like Peter and Mary . . . but I would like, simply because of the abuse, that devotion to Mary be completely uprooted." Yet, in some Protestant quarters, there is seen a growing interest in Marian doctrine, and a recent survey in the United States (*Marian Studies,* vol. 6, pp. 137–163, Washington 1955) showed that a few Protestant ministers do practice Marian devotion. Some High Anglicans, who often do not wish to be called Protestant, have much Marian doctrine and devotion in common with Roman Catholics. The Orthodox Eastern churches have always held most of the same Marian doctrines as Rome, and practice a strong Marian devotion. Christian art has received much inspiration from Mary (see MADONNA IN ART, THE).

Bibliography.—Sheed, Francis J., comp., *The Mary Book* (New York 1950); Sheen, Fulton J., *The World's First Love* (New York 1952); Doheny, William J., and Kelly, J. P., eds., *Papal Documents on Mary* (Milwaukee 1954); Neubert, Emil N., *Mary in Doctrine* (Milwaukee 1954); Carol, Juniper B., ed., *Mariology,* vols. 1, 2 (Milwaukee 1955, 1957); Most, William G., *Mary in Our Life* (New York 1955); Carol, Juniper B., *Fundamentals of Mariology* (New York 1956); *Marian Studies,* Mariological Society of America (Washington, annually).

WILLIAM G. MOST,
Loras College, Dubuque, Iowa.

MARY I (MARY TUDOR), queen of England and Ireland: b. Greenwich (London), England, Feb. 18, 1516; d. London, Nov. 17, 1558. The daughter of Henry VIII and his first wife, Catherine of Aragon (qq.v.), she was brought up as heir to the throne, but was harshly treated by her father after his divorce from Catherine. Mary was forced to sign a declaration acknowledging the union of her parents to have been illegal and renouncing the authority of the pope; nevertheless, she remained faithful to the Roman Catholic religion. After her father's death she lived in retirement at her estates of Hunsdon, Newhall, and Kenninghall until the death of her half brother, Edward VI, on July 6, 1553. Despite the efforts of John Dudley, duke of Northumberland, to secure the succession for his daughter-in-law, Lady Jane Grey, Mary had popular support and was proclaimed queen in London. Her reign was inaugurated by acts of clemency toward her enemies. Parliament asserted her legitimacy and repealed the antipapal laws of Henry VIII, and the kingdom was absolved by the pope through Reginald Cardinal Pole, returning from exile as special ambassador of the Vatican.

In the face of strong popular opposition, Mary announced her intention of marrying Philip of Spain, the son of her cousin Emperor Charles V, in July 1554. Insurrections broke out, and Sir Thomas Wyatt (Wyat) marched his troops from Kent to London before he was defeated. As a result, Mary's half sister, Elizabeth, was imprisoned in the Tower of London, but was released a few months later; and Lady Jane Grey and her husband, Lord Guildford Dudley, were executed. The old laws against heresy were revived in 1555, and a stern persecution of the Protestants began. The queen, embittered perhaps by her early life, by her marital difficulties with Philip, and by recurring ill health, must bear some share of responsibility for the burning of nearly 300 persons at the stake during the last three years of her reign, which brought her the nickname of "Bloody Mary." Among those who perished were many of her political enemies, including the bishops Hugh Latimer, Thomas Cranmer, and Nicholas Ridley. Through the influence of Philip II, England was drawn into the war between Spain and France in 1557, in spite of her desperate financial condition. The loss of Calais to the French in 1558 after it had been held by the English for some 200 years proved to be the final blow in Mary's unhappy life.

Bibliography.—Mullinger, James Bass, "Philip and Mary," *Cambridge Modern History,* vol. 2, pp. 512–549 (London 1904); Hume, Martin A. S., *Two English Queens and Philip* (New York 1908); Froude, James Anthony, *The Reign of Mary Tudor* (New York 1910); Pollard, Albert Frederick, *The History of England from the Accession of Edward VI to the Death of Elizabeth* (London 1911), vol. 6 in *Political History of England;* Henderson, Daniel M., *The Crimson Queen, Mary Tudor* (New York 1933); White, Beatrice, *Mary Tudor* (New York 1935); Prescott, Hilda F. M., *A Spanish Tudor: the Life of Bloody Mary* (New York 1940).

MARY II, queen of England, Scotland, and Ireland: b. London, England, April 30, 1662; d. there, Dec. 28, 1694. She was the eldest child of James, duke of York (later James II) and Anne Hyde, his first wife. In November 1677 she was married to William, prince of Orange, the stadholder of Holland, and went to live with him near The Hague. After her father ascended the English throne in 1685 and began to show special favor to Roman Catholics, she was placed in a difficult position because her husband was a Protestant leader in Europe. She took the side of William against James, however, and supported his invasion of England with Dutch and English troops in 1688. In February of the next year she followed her husband, and the pair were proclaimed joint sovereigns, with William III (q.v.) as sole administrator, and crowned at Westminster Abbey on April 11, 1689. During the absences of William in Ireland in 1690–1691, and his campaigns on the Continent in 1692–1694, Mary acted with ability as regent, and her personal popularity was considerable.

MARY (VICTORIA MARY OF TECK), consort of King George V of Great Britain and Northern Ireland: b. London, England, May 26, 1867; d. there, March 24, 1953. Daughter of Francis, duke of Teck, and Princess Mary Adelaide of Great Britain (granddaughter of George III), she was betrothed in December 1891 to Albert Victor, duke of Clarence, eldest son of Albert Edward, prince of Wales (later Edward VII). Albert Victor died the following January, however, and, in 1893, Mary married his brother George, duke of York. In 1910 the latter succeeded to the throne as George V (q.v.), and she was crowned with him on June 22, 1911. She shared the duties of the throne with her husband, taking an active interest in the social and educational problems of their people, working tirelessly in two world wars to organize relief and visit the wounded, and assembling a notable art collection. Their eldest son became King Edward VIII in 1936, but abdicated the same year and was known thereafter as the duke of Windsor. Their second son was George VI (r. 1936–1952). They also had a daughter, Mary (1897–), the princess royal, and three other sons: Henry William, duke of Gloucester (1900–); George Edward, duke of Kent (1902–1942), and Prince John (1905–1919).

MARY, mä-rē', oblast, USSR, in the Turkmen SSR, in Soviet Central Asia, formed in 1939, with an area of 34,700 square miles. It is bordered on the south by Afghanistan and extends into the Kara Kum (desert) on the north. The Murghab (Murgab) River, which flows into the area, has created a fertile oasis of about 1,900 miles in the midst of a sandy desert through irrigation canals. The region produces cotton, grains, sugar, rice, and fruit, and is famous for its horses and karakul. In the southern part are groves of pistachio trees. Chief towns are Mary (q.v.), Bairam-Ali, and Iolatan. According to Hindu, Parsi, and Arab tradition, this region was the ancient Paradise, the cradle of the Aryans, and hence of the human race. Pop. (1947 est.) 265,000.

MARY (formerly MERV), city, USSR, capital of Mary Oblast, in the Turkmen SSR, on the Murghab (Murgab) River, 180 miles southeast of Ashkhabad, on a junction of the Trans-Caspian Railway. It trades extensively in cotton, wool, grain, and hides, and its industries include cotton ginning and milling, wool washing, metal working, flour and food processing, and the making of carpets, felt, and woolen goods. The original town is said to have been founded by Alexander the Great in the 4th century B.C., and rebuilt by Antiochus I (d. 261 B.C.) as Antiocha Margiana. In the 4th or 5th century A.D., Merv was the seat of a Christian Nestorian archbishopric, and in the 7th century the Arabs made it one of the great Islamic centers of learning. It reached its zenith under the Turks in the 11th century; but after it was overrun by Mongols in 1221, its palaces, libraries, and baths fell into decay, and in 1794 it was burned to the ground by the Bukharians. The Russians occupied the region in 1883, and early in the 19th century built a new town of Merv on the opposite side of the Murghab. The city was renamed Mary in 1937. Pop. (1939) 37,100.

MARY BEATRICE. See MARY OF MODENA.

MARY MAGDALENE, măg-dà-lē′nē, or **MAGDALEN,** măg′dà-lĕn (also MARY OF MAGDALA, măg′dà-là), in the New Testament, the name of the woman mentioned with others as being healed of evil spirits and ministering to Jesus of her substance (Luke 8:2–3). She was present at the Crucifixion, and it was to her that Jesus first appeared after the Resurrection (Mark 16:9–11). The name is generally understood as indicating that she was a native of Magdala (modern Migdal), near the northwest shore of the Sea of Galilee. Tradition identified Mary Magdalene with the unnamed penitent who anointed Jesus' feet with ointment (Luke 7:37–50).

MARY OF BURGUNDY, bûr′gŭn-dĭ (Fr. MARIE DE BOURGOGNE, mà-rē′ dĕ bōōr-gôn′y), duchess of Burgundy: b. Brussels, Brabant, Feb. 13, 1457; d. Bruges, Flanders, March 27, 1482. On the death of her father, Charles the Bold, in battle on Jan. 5, 1477, Louis XI of France seized part of her inheritance. In order to secure the aid of her remaining subjects she signed the Great Privilege (February 1477) which restored to them the rights and liberties abrogated by her father and grandfather. Rejecting the proposal of Louis XI that she marry the dauphin Charles, she married instead Archduke Maximilian of Austria (later Maximilian I, king of Germany and Holy Roman emperor), who came to her assistance with an army and defeated the French king at Guinegate, Aug. 7, 1479, although not ending the war thereby. When Mary was killed by a fall from her horse she was succeeded by her son, Philip the Handsome (later Philip I of Castile). Her daughter, Margaret of Austria, became duchess of Savoy and regent of the Netherlands.

MARY OF FRANCE (nee MARY TUDOR, tū′dẽr), consort of Louis XII of France: b. England, probably March 1496; d. Westhorpe, Suffolk, June 24, 1533. The daughter of Henry VII of England and Elizabeth of York, she was contracted in marriage to Charles, prince of Castile (later Emperor Charles V), in 1507, but in 1514 the contract was renounced in favor of marriage to Louis XII of France. Her husband, who was 52 and in poor health, died three months later, and Mary, only 18 years old, secretly wed Charles Brandon, duke of Suffolk. Her brother, Henry VIII, was persuaded to forgive the pair by the promised payment of a large sum of money for the expenses he had incurred at the previous wedding, and a public ceremony was performed at Greenwich in May 1515. Their daughter, Frances, was the wife of Henry Grey, marquis of Dorset, and the mother of Lady Jane Grey (q.v.).

MARY OF GUISE, gēz, gwēz; Fr. gü-ēz′, gēz (also known as MARY OF LORRAINE), consort of James V of Scotland: b. Bar-le-Duc, France, Nov. 22, 1515; d. Edinburgh, Scotland, June 11, 1560. The eldest child of Claude, count (later duke) of Guise and Antoinette de Bourbon, she married Louis d'Orléans, 2d duke of Longueville, in 1534. Her husband died in 1537, and the next year she married James V at St. Andrews, Scotland. Their daughter Mary, Queen of Scots (q.v.) was born December 1542, only a few days before the death of James, and James Hamilton, 2d earl of Arran, was appointed regent. Refusing to accept the betrothal of her infant daughter to Edward (later Edward VI) of England, she persuaded the Scottish parliament to agree to the child's espousal to the dauphin of France, the future Francis II, and sent her to be brought up at the French court in 1548. In her 12th year the young queen was able to transfer the regency to her mother. When John Knox and the leaders of the Protestant Reformation rebelled against Mary's suppressive policies she called on France for aid. However, English troops joined the reformers the following March, and the queen mother, in poor health, was forced to retreat to the neutrality of Edinburgh Castle, where she died still trying to effect a reconciliation between France and England.

MARY OF HUNGARY, consort of Louis of Hungary: b. Brussels, Brabant, Sept. 15, 1505; d. Cigolas, Spain, Oct. 18, 1558. The daughter of Philip I of Spain, she was espoused to Louis II, king of Hungary, in 1515, but did not join her husband until 1522. After he was killed by the Turks at the Battle of Mohács in 1526, her brother was chosen king of Hungary and Bohemia as Ferdinand I. During the latter's absence fighting his rival for the throne, John Zápolya, and the aggressive Turks, she acted as regent. In 1531 her brother, Emperor Charles V, appointed her governor of the Netherlands, which office she executed with faithfulness and devotion until 1555, when Charles relinquished the country to his son Philip (later Philip II of Spain).

MARY OF LORRAINE. See Mary of Guise.

MARY OF MAGDALA. See Mary Magdalene.

MARY OF MODENA, mô'dä-nà (Mary Beatrice), consort of King James II of England, Scotland, and Ireland: b. Modena, Italy, Oct. 5, 1658; d. Saint-Germain-en-Laye, France, May 7, 1718. She was the daughter of Alfonso IV, duke of Modena, and the Duchess Laura. In 1673 she was married by proxy to the widowed James, duke of York (later James II, q.v.), and joined him in England soon afterward. She was extremely unpopular there, both on account of her Catholicism, which she shared with her husband, and her friendship with Louis XIV of France, who had helped arrange the match. James ascended the throne in 1685, and in June 1688, Mary gave birth to her sixth and only surviving child, James Francis Edward (sometimes called the Old Pretender). Because the people disliked the queen and also knew about the bad relations between Mary and James, it was widely believed that a fraud had been perpetrated, that Mary had not in fact borne a child, and she fled to France with her son in December 1688, followed by James. She soon gave up hope of a quick restoration of the English throne, but after the death of her husband in 1701 she persuaded Louis XIV to proclaim her son the rightful king of England.

MARY, QUEEN OF SCOTS (Mary Stuart), queen of Scotland: b. Linlithgow, Scotland, Dec. 7 or 8, 1542; d. Fotheringhay, England, Feb. 8, 1587. She was the only lawful surviving child of James V and his second wife, Mary of Guise (q.v.); and through her grandmother, Margaret Tudor, the consort of James IV, she was heir to the throne of England after the children of Henry VIII. With the death of her father six days after her birth she was proclaimed queen, and on Sept. 9, 1543, was crowned at Stirling Castle. A treaty of betrothal to Henry VIII's son, Edward (later Edward VI of England), was abrogated by the Scottish parliament, and in 1548 she was betrothed to the French dauphin, Francis (later Francis II). In the same year she was sent to the French court to be brought up in the Roman Catholic faith under the supervision of her uncles, the duke of Guise and the cardinal of Lorraine, while her mother remained in Scotland to rule on her behalf. In 1558, Mary became the wife of the dauphin, and when he succeeded to the French throne the following year she was his queen consort. Both her mother and her husband died in 1560, and finding herself relegated to a secondary place by her mother-in-law, Catherine de' Medici, she decided to return to Scotland in 1561. Considered a great beauty at this time, she had a dazzling complexion, unusual charm of manner, and a fine intelligence.

Presbyterianism had been established by the Scottish Parliament the previous year, and Mary yielded to the demands of John Knox that it be maintained, while being permitted to hear Mass in her private chapel. Sought after by a number of suitors, she at first carried on negotiations with Don Carlos, son of Philip II of Spain, but when they broke down she chose her cousin, Henry Stewart (Stuart), Lord Darnley, the next lineal heir to the English throne after herself, and a representative of the English Catholic party. They were married July 29, 1565, in the chapel at Holyrood, and she bestowed on him the title of king, but refused his demand that the crown be secured to him for life and to his heirs. She soon found that Darnley was weak and incapable, and put her confidence in David Rizzio (Riccio), an Italian musician, whom she made her personal secretary, and with whom she conspired to restore Catholicism. Darnley plotted with her enemies to murder Rizzio, who was dragged from her supper table and stabbed to death on the night of March 9, 1566.

Mary never forgave her husband, although there was a formal reconciliation three months later after she had given birth to a son (later James VI of Scotland and James I of Great Britain). James Hepburn, 4th earl of Bothwell, assisted her in banishing the murderers of Rizzio, and he was suspected of superintending the subsequent murder of Darnley, whose outrageous behavior had lost him all support in Scotland. In February 1567, when Darnley was lying ill in a house in Kirk-o'-Field near Edinburgh, whither he had been conveyed by Mary, the house was blown up and he was found strangled in the yard. Bothwell was subjected to a mock trial and acquitted. A moot point in Mary's history is whether she was a party to the murder. The Scottish nobles declared they found letters from her (called the Casket Letters) in Bothwell's jewel case, but the originals have never been found and their authenticity is doubtful; irrespective of this, her guilty knowledge of the plot seems indubitable. In April, Bothwell made a show of capturing Mary while she was on her way to Edinburgh after a visit to her son at Stirling Castle and carried her off. They were married on May 15, 1567, in a Protestant ceremony, a few days after Bothwell's divorce from his wife. This act turned all the Scottish nobles against Mary, and on June 15 their forces faced hers at Carberry Hill. After a parley Mary agreed to surrender herself if Bothwell was allowed to escape, believing that she would still be treated as a sovereign. Instead, she was abused by her captors and forced to abdicate in favor of her son, with Lord James Stewart (Stuart), earl of Moray (Murray), her half brother, named as regent. On May 2, 1568, Mary escaped from Lochleven Castle where she had been imprisoned, but only a few devoted followers gathered to her standard. They were defeated at Langside by the earl of Moray on May 13, and Mary fled to England.

Elizabeth I, guided by policy rather than generosity, immediately imprisoned Mary, who for the rest of her life was moved from place to place as a captive. A commission sat at York and then at Westminster, nominally to hear the defense of the Scottish lords for their rebellion, but actually in order that their charges against Mary might be made public, and the conference was closed without giving her any opportunity to rebut their evidence. Roman Catholics and political enemies of Elizabeth subsequently formed plot after plot to liberate her and set her on the throne of England, to which, if the marriage of Anne Boleyn to Henry VIII were really invalid, she had irrefutable claim on the score of descent. Each plot was detected, but without investigation of Mary's complicity, for neither her acquittal nor her condemnation would have suited Elizabeth's plans. At length, in 1586, Sir Francis Walsingham, Elizabeth's secretary, was given a free hand, and uncovered a conspiracy with Anthony Babington (q.v.) to arrange the murder of Elizabeth. At her trial, October 14–15, Mary handled her own defense brilliantly, but letters were produced which were absolutely damning, though whether they were genuine or forged is still uncertain. Mary was found guilty, and Parliament demanded her execution. Elizabeth, after attempting to evade the issue, signed the death warrant and Mary was executed at Fotheringhay on February 8 and buried at Peterborough. She was reinterred at Westminster Abbey in 1612. (See also ELIZABETH I—*Mary, Queen of Scots.*)

The tragic figure of Mary, Queen of Scots, has appeared frequently in literature. Johann Christoph Friedrich von Schiller's dramatic tragedy, *Maria Stuart,* was produced in 1800. Sir Walter Scott used her in his romantic novel, *The Abbot* (1820). Following Bjørnstjerne Bjørnson's play, *Mary Stuart in Scotland* (1864), Algernon Charles Swinburne wrote a trilogy about her life: *Chastelard* (1865); *Bothwell* (1874); and *Mary Stuart* (1881). She was featured in Mauric Henry Hewlett's *The Queen's Quair* (1904) and in Maurice Baring's *In My End Is My Beginning* (1931). Stefan Zweig published a fictionalized biography, *Mary, Queen of Scotland and the Isles,* in 1935.

Bibliography.—Lobanov-Rostovski, Aleksandr, ed., *Lettres, instructions et mémoires de Marie Stuart, reine d'Ecosse,* 7 vols. (London 1844); Strickland, Agnes, *Lives of the Queens of Scotland, and English Princesses Connected with the Royal Succession of Great Britain,* vols. 3–7, *Mary Stuart* (Edinburgh, London, and New York 1852–59); Cust, Lionel Henry, *Notes on the Authentic Portraits of Mary, Queen of Scots* (London 1903); Henderson, Thomas Finlayson, *Mary Queen of Scots, her Environment and Tragedy,* 2 vols. (New York 1905); Rait, Robert Sangster, and Cameron, Annie T., eds., *King James's Secret* (London 1927); MacKenzie, Agnes M., *The Scotland of Queen Mary and the Religious Wars, 1513–1638* (New York 1936); Weber, Bernard C., *The Youth of Mary Stuart, Queen of Scots* Philadelphia 1941); Tannenbaum, Samuel and Dorothy, *Marie Stuart, Queen of Scots,* 2 vols. (New York 1945); Morrison, Nancy, *Mary Queen of Scots* (New York 1961); Phillips, James, *Images of a Queen* (Berkeley, Calif., 1964).

MARY TUDOR. See MARY I; MARY OF FRANCE.

MARYBOROUGH, mâr′ĭ-bŭ-rŭ, city, Australia, in southeastern Queensland, on the Mary River, 140 miles north of Brisbane. It is a rail junction and river port, trading in sugar, fruit, coal, timber, grain, and livestock. There are steel and flour mills, sugar refineries, foundries, and railway engineering works. Other industries include dairying, fishing, and shipbuilding. Pop. (1966) 19,647.

MARYBOROUGH, municipality, Australia, in west central Victoria, 85 miles northwest of Melbourne. It is the rail and commercial center of an agricultural area, and has dairy plants and flour and knitting mills. There is some gold mining in the vicinity. Pop. (1966) 7,694.

MARYBOROUGH (or PORT LAOIGHISE, pōrt lā′ĭ-shě), town, Ireland, the seat of County Laoighis or Leix, on the River Triogue; a rail junction 45 miles southeast of Dublin. The chief industries are malt making, woolen mills, and

farm implement works, and there is considerable trade in agricultural produce. Some portions of a fort built during the reign of Mary I (1553–1558) remain. The town's charter was granted in 1570. Pop. (1961) 3,133.

MARYKNOLL, popular title of the Catholic Foreign Mission Society of America and the name of the property near Ossining, N.Y., on which the society's headquarters is located. Pope Pius X, on June 29, 1911, authorized Father (later Bishop) James A. Walsh of Boston, Mass., and Father Thomas F. Price of Wilmington, N.C., to make the foundation, which opened in September 1912. In September 1918, Father Price left with three priests for Maryknoll's first mission field in Kwangtung Province, China. The growth of Maryknoll has been exceptionally rapid. In 1957 the society had houses in many dioceses of the United States, and 549 Maryknoll missioners engaged in foreign missions, including Korea, Japan, Taiwan (Formosa), and Hong Kong in Asia; Tanganyika Territory in Africa; Yucatan, Guatemala, Bolivia, Chile, and Peru in Latin America; and the Hawaiian and Philippine islands. Maryknoll's founders also prompted the foundation in 1912 of the Maryknoll Sisters, whose central house is at Ossining. The sisters work with the society in many of the same regions, as well as Yucatan, Nicaragua, and Panama, 553 being occupied in work outside of the United States in 1957.

Consult Considine, Robert, *The Maryknoll Story* (New York 1950); Lane, Raymond A., *The Early Days of Maryknoll* (New York 1951); Del Rey, Sister Maria, *In and Out the Andes* (New York 1954); Nevins, Albert J., *The Meaning of Maryknoll* (New York 1954); Del Rey, Sister Maria, *Her Name is Mercy* (New York 1957).

JOHN F. MCCONNELL, M.M., *Professor of Sacred Scripture, Maryknoll Seminary.*

MARYLAND, měr′ĭ-lănd, South or Middle Atlantic state, is one of the original 13 states of the United States. It is bounded on the north by Pennsylvania and Delaware, on the east by Delaware and the Atlantic Ocean, on the west by the District of Columbia, and on the west and south by Virginia and West Virginia. The name Maryland was bestowed in honor of Queen Henrietta Maria, wife of King Charles I of England.

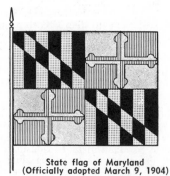

State flag of Maryland
(Officially adopted March 9, 1904)

(Colors: In first and fourth quarters, dotted areas are gold and meshed areas are black. In second and third quarters, black areas are white and shaded areas are red.)

Total area	10,577 square miles
Land area	9,881 square miles
Inland water area	696 square miles
Latitude	37°53′ to 39°43′N.
Longitude	75°04′ to 79°29′W.

Altitude	sea level to 3,360 feet
Population (1960)	3,100,689
Capital—Annapolis; population	23,385
Ratified the Constitution	April 28, 1788
State motto	*Scuto Bonae Voluntatis Tuae Coronasti Nos*

(With the Shield of Thy Goodwill Thou Hast Covered Us)

State bird (designated 1947)	Baltimore oriole
State flower (adopted April 18, 1918)	Black-eyed Susan
State tree (adopted 1941)	White oak
State song (adopted 1939)	*Maryland, My Maryland*
State nicknames	Old Line State; Free State

STATE SEAL OF MARYLAND
(Adopted March 18, 1876)

Obverse

Reverse

A discussion of Maryland's geography, government, social and economic life, and history is presented under the following sections:

1. Physical Features and Resources
2. Population Characteristics
3. Political Divisions
4. Government and Politics
5. Education and Welfare
6. Economic Activities
7. Places of Interest
8. Famous Men and Women
9. History

1. PHYSICAL FEATURES AND RESOURCES

Topography.—The state is divided by Chesapeake Bay into two major sections—the Eastern Shore and the Maryland Main or western shore. There are three principal physiographic regions: the coastal plain, the piedmont plateau, and the Appalachian region. The coastal plain encompasses the entire Eastern Shore and the western shore as far inland as the fall line, which passes from Washington, D.C., through Baltimore and Elkton. Between the fall line and the Blue Ridge to the west lies the piedmont plateau. The Appalachian region, embracing the Cumberland and other valleys and rolling plains and mountain areas, extends to beyond the western border. It includes Backbone Mountain (3,360 feet), south of Oakland in Garrett County, which is the highest point in the state. East to west, Maryland's greatest distance is 198.6 miles; north to south, 125.5 miles. At its narrowest point, located in Washington County where the Potomac River and the Mason-Dixon Line almost meet, Maryland is only 1.9 miles wide.

Both shores of Chesapeake Bay are broken by rivers, which are really tidal estuaries. The Eastern Shore rivers include the Elk, Sassafras, Chester, Choptank, Nanticoke, and Pocomoke. Among the Maryland Main rivers emptying into the bay are the Potomac, the state's major river, and the Gunpowder, Patapsco, Magothy, Severn, and Patuxent. Tributary from Maryland to the Potomac are the Monocacy River and Antietam Creek. The entire course of the Potomac, except for a portion in the District of Columbia, lies in Maryland. The large Susquehanna River enters the head of Chesapeake Bay from the north. In the western part of the state the Youghiogheny is the only Maryland river that drains away from the Atlantic Ocean.

Climate.—The mean monthly temperature for Maryland varies from 34°F. for January to 75° for July. The annual mean is 48°F. for the west, 57° for the south, and 54° for the state as a whole. Zero temperatures are rare. The state's mildest climate is found in Worcester, the only county facing upon the Atlantic Ocean, and the most rigorous winter climate occurs in Garrett, the westernmost county. Average annual rainfall varies from 25 to 55 inches, with most parts of the state receiving 38 inches or more. Average annual snowfall is 66 inches at Oakland and 16 inches in Easton. The growing season for much of the state ranges from 180 to 194 days.

Water Resources.—The state's water resources are well balanced. Irrigation is normally unnecessary, and water power potential is not notable. Principal water resource uses are shipping and recreation. Chesapeake Bay and its estuaries provide a water frontage of some 3,600 miles. Most of the state's water traffic passes through Baltimore harbor, which has a water frontage of about 40 miles. Water recreation centers principally along the Chesapeake and Atlantic shores, along the many rivers, and around Deep Creek Lake in the mountains of Garrett County.

Soils and Minerals.—Most of the coastal plain and of the piedmont plateau consists of rich farmlands. Soils on the Eastern Shore are light loam. On the western shore, sandy loam prevails. Western Maryland soils are derived principally from limestone and sandstone. The Appalachian region, particularly Allegany and Garrett counties, is rough terrain and not well adapted to agriculture.

Principal minerals available in the state are coal, sand and gravel. Others are limestone, granite, basalt, sandstone, slate, marble, kaolin and other clays, shale, and asbestos.

Plant Life.—Maryland's most common wild flowers include clematis, honeysuckle, Virginia creeper, trailing arbutus, violets, wild roses, mountain laurel, clover, black-eyed Susans, golden asters, and goldenrod.

There is very little virgin timber left in Maryland, and most of the approximately 3 million acres of forested areas comprise farm woodlands or other private holdings. Some hardwoods, principally black and white oak and beech, have survived in infrequent pure stands, but they are more often found in mixed forests. Chestnut and walnut have almost completely disappeared. Other of the 150 species which have been found in the state include poplar, locust, hickory, ash, gum, elm, hackberry, persimmon, pine, spruce, and

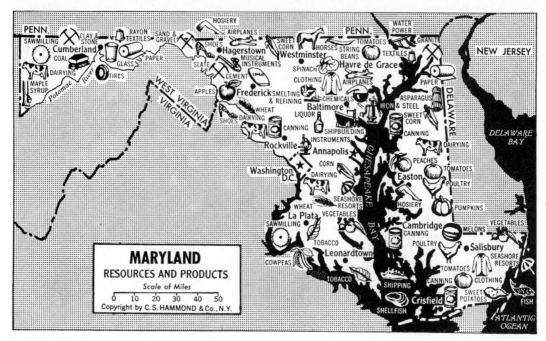

hemlock. Lumber production is very slight.

Animal Life.—Most large mammals have disappeared from the Maryland scene, although occasionally bobcats and bears appear in the mountain areas. Deer, foxes, opossums, raccoons, squirrels, and rabbits are scattered throughout the state. The seventeen-year locust and the Japanese beetle are the most destructive insects. The only poisonous snakes are the timber rattler and copperhead.

Water and shore birds are abundant in the Chesapeake Bay region, and many kinds of ducks frequent the state's waters. Inland game birds include quail, partridge, ruffed grouse, and wild turkey. The Chesapeake Bay retriever, used for hunting waterfowl, is a native Maryland breed. Bald eagles, hawks, herons, and owls are fairly common, and orioles, thrushes, finches, warblers, and whippoorwills are the principal songbirds.

In the Chesapeake and Atlantic coastal waters there are some 200 species of fish, including large quantities of oysters and crabs.

2. POPULATION CHARACTERISTICS

The population of the state has shown steady growth and promises to continue to do so. Growth is most pronounced in the metropolitan area of Baltimore (pop. 1960, 1,727,023) and in the two Maryland counties which are classified as a part of the Washington metropolitan area (698,323). Of Maryland's 23 counties, 20 gained in population between 1950 and 1960, the changes ranging from a decline of 6 per cent in Allegany County to an increase of 107.4 per cent in Montgomery County, adjacent to Washington. The following table indicates the state's population growth since 1790, the year of the first federal census.

Of the 1960 population, 1,533,000 were males and 1,567,000 were females, and 2,254,000 (73 per cent) lived in urban areas and 737,000 (27 per cent) in rural areas. Density of population was 314.0 persons per square mile. Housing units numbered 935,000, and there were 3.2 persons per household. The median age of all Marylanders

was 28.7 years. The birthrate was estimated at 18.8 per 1,000 in 1965 and the death rate was estimated at 8.7.

YEAR	POPULATION	YEAR	POPULATION
1790	319,728*	1880	934,943
1800	341,548	1890	1,042,390
1810	380,546	1900	1,188,044
1820	407,350	1910	1,295,346
1830	447,040	1920	1,449,661
1840	470,019	1930	1,631,526
1850	583,034	1940	1,821,244
1860	687,049	1950	2,343,001
1870	780,894	1960	3,100,689

*Including population of present area of District of Columbia.

Native whites numbering 2,209,000 in 1960 accounted for 82 per cent of the population; foreign-born whites (364,000), 1.1 per cent; Negroes (518,000), 16.7 per cent; and all other non-whites, including Indians, less than 1 per cent. Foreign-born whites in the state came principally from Germany, Italy, Poland, Russia, the United Kingdom, Canada, Lithuania, Latin America, and Asia.

3. POLITICAL DIVISIONS

Cities and Towns.—Baltimore City, the sixth most populous city of the United States, is the center of most of the Maryland economy. Its 1960 population of 939,024 constituted over 30 per cent of that of the entire state. Baltimore is an old city, built largely without plan and historically too much absorbed with its thriving industry to give adequate attention to its civic and physical needs. The city's cosmopolitan character is most clearly evident in its harbor, which is second in the nation in the volume of seagoing traffic. Characteristic of the city are the highly scrubbed white stone steps of the countless row houses.

The state's second city is Hagerstown (36,660). It is a growing industrial center surrounded by a fertile farming area. Cumberland (33,415), the third city in population, lies in the Allegheny Mountains where they are divided by the Potomac. Its economy is largely sustained

COUNTIES

Allegany (A2) 84,169
Anne Arundel (H4)...206,634
Baltimore (H3) 492,428
Baltimore (city) (H3) 939,024
Calvert (H6) 15,826
Caroline (L5) 19,462
Carroll (F2) 52,785
Cecil (L2) 48,408
Charles (F6) 32,572
Dorchester (K7) 29,666
Frederick (E3) 71,930
Garrett (A7) 20,420
Harford (J2) 76,722
Howard (G4) 36,152
Kent (K3) 15,481
Montgomery (E4) ...340,928
Prince Georges (G5)..357,395
Queen Annes (L4)....16,569
Saint Marys (H7)......38,915
Somerset (M8) 19,623
Talbot (K5) 21,578
Washington (C2) 91,219
Wicomico (M7) 49,050
Worcester (N8) 23,733

CITIES and TOWNS

Abell (H8) 400
Aberdeen (K2) 9,679
Abingdon (J3) 650
Accident (A7) 237
Accokeek (G6) 1,637
Adamstown (D3) 220
Aikin (K2) ....
Airey (K6) 110
Allen (M7) 250
American Corner (L5).. 40
Andrews (K7) ....
Annapolis (cap.)◉
  (H5) 23,385
Annapolis Junction
  (H4) 750
Antietam (D3) 100
Aquasco (G6) 900
Arbutus-Halethorpe-
  Relay (H4) 22,402
Ardmore (C4) 1,330
Baden (H6) 100
Baldwin (J3) 350
Baltimore◉ (H3) 939,024
Baltimore (urban
  area) 1,418,948
Barclay (L4) 142
Barnesville (E4) 145
Barstow (H6) 151
Barton (C7) 731
Bayview (L2) 150
Beaver Creek (D2) 50
Bel Air◉ (J2) 4,300
Bel Alton (G7) 700
Bellevue (K6) 289
Beltsville (C3) 4,589
Benedict (H6) 450
Bentley Springs (H2).. 150
Berlin (07) 2,046
Berwyn Heights (C4)..2,376
Bethesda (A4) 56,527
Bethlehem (L6) ....
Betterton (K3) 328
Big Pool (C2) 950
Big Spring (C2) 125
Bishop (N7) 100
Bishops Head (K7)... 300
Bishopville (07) 300
Bivalve (L7) 290
Bladensburg (C4) ...3,103
Bloomington (B8) 354
Blythedale (K2) 100
Boonsboro (D2) 1,211
Borden Shaft (C7)..... 200
Boring (G2) 197
Boulevard Heights (B5) 500
Bowens (H6) 220

Bowie (G4) 1,072
Boyds (E4) 100
Bozman (J5) 450
Bradbury Park (C5)... 200
Bradshaw (J3) 650
Brandywine (G6) 459
Brentwood (B4) 3,693
Bridgetown (L4) 39
Bristol (H5) 140
Brookeville (F4) 140
Brookview (L6) 83
Brownsville (D3) 205
Brunswick (D3) 3,555
Buckeystown (E3) ....
Burkittsville (D3) 208
Burrsville (L5) 50
Burtonsville (G4) 1,969
Bushwood (G7) 300
Butler (H2) 100
Cabin Creek (L6) 100
Cabin John (A4) 2,000
California (H7) 250
Calvert (K2) 125
Cambridge◉ (K6) ...12,239
Camp Springs (C6).... 900
Capitol Heights (C5)..3,138
Cardiff (J2) ....
Carney-Parkville (H3)..27,236
Carrollton (C4) 3,385
Carrollton (G2) 168
Castleton (J2) 343
Catoctin Furnace (E2).. 233
Catonsville (H3) 37,372
Cavetown (D2) 325
Cecilton (L3) 596
Cedar Grove (F4)..... 350
Cedar Heights (C5)...1,231
Cedartown (N8) 53
Cedarville (G6) 200
Centreville◉ (K4) ...1,863
Chance (L8) 509
Chaptico (H7) 185
Charlestown (L2) 711
Charlotte Hall (H7).... 200
Chase (J3) 900
Cheltenham (G6) 484
Cherry Hill (L2) 200
Chesapeake Beach
  (J6) 731
Chesapeake City (L2)..1,104
Chester (J5) 1,100
Chestertown◉ (K4) ...3,602
Chesterville (L3) 60
Cheverly (C4) 5,223
Chevy Chase (A4) ...2,405
Chevy Chase Section
  Four ‡(A4) 2,243
Chewsville (D2) 350
Childs (L2) 275
Chillum (B4) 6,338
Choptank (L6) ....
Church Creek (K6) 146
Church Hill (K4) 263
Churchton (J5) 1,000
Churchville (J2) 450
Claiborne (J5) 150
Clarksburg (E4) 265
Clarksville (G4) 200
Clear Springs (C2) 488
Clements (G7) 300
Clinton (C6) 1,578
Cockeysville (H3) 2,582
College Park (C4) ...18,482
Collington (G5) 150
Colmar Manor (B4) ...1,772
Colora (K2) 80
Coltons Point (H8) 300
Columbia (G3) 1,100
Compton (H7) 750
Conowingo (K2) 100
Cooksville (F3) 336
Cordova (K5) 300
Cornersville (K6) 200
Corriganville (D7) 1,200
Cottage City (B4) 1,099

Cox Station (Bel Alton)
  (G7) 700
Crapo (K7) 64
Creagerstown (E2) 325
Crellin (A8) 475
Cresaptown (C7) 1,680
Crisfield (L9) 3,540
Crocheron (K8) 165
Crownsville (H4) 80
Crumpton (L4) 281
Cumberland◉ (D7) ...33,415
Damascus (F3) 1,120
Dameron (J8) 250
Dames Quarter (L8)... 300
Daniels (G3) 460
Dargan (D3) 200
Darlington (J2) 500
Darnestown (E4) 300
Davidsonville (H5) 50
Deal Island (L8) 700
Deer Park (A8) 379
Delmar (M7) 1,291
Denton◉ (L5) 1,938
Derwood (F4) 200
Dickerson (E4) 350
District Heights (C5)..7,524
Doncaster (F7) 75
Doubs (E3) 250
Downsville (C2) 250
Drayden (J8) 360
Dublin (J2) 300
Dundalk (J3) 82,428
Eagle Harbor (H6).... 15
Earleigh Heights (H4).. 850
Earleville (L3) 60
East New Market (L6) 225
Easton◉ (K5) 6,337
Eckhart Mines (C7) ...1,800
Eden (M7) 300
Edgemere-Fort Howard-
  Sparrows Point
  (J4) 11,775
Edgewood (J3) 1,670
Edmonston (C4) 1,197
Eldersburg (G3) 500
Eldorado (L6) 80
Elk Mills (L2) 500
Elk Neck (L2) 800
Elkridge (H4) 3,000
Elkton◉ (L2) 5,989
Ellerslie (D7) 850
Ellerton (D2) 54
Ellicott City◉ (G3) ...1,500
Elliott (L7) 120
Emmitsburg (E2) 1,369
Essex (J3) 35,205
Ewell (L9) 360
Fairbank (J6) 300
Fair Hill (L2) 100
Fairland (G4) 200
Fairlee (K4) 175
Fairmont Heights
  (C5) 2,308
Fairmount (L8) 600
Fallston (J2) 600
Farmington (K2) 35
Fearer (A7) 150
Federalsburg (L6) ...2,060
Ferndale (H4) 2,500
Finksburg (G3) 500
Fishing Creek (J7) 800
Flintstone (A2) *500
Forest Glen (B4) 1,500
Forest Heights (B5)...3,524
Forest Hill (J2) 300
Forestville (C5) 5,144
Fort Foote (B6) 300
Fort Howard-Edgemere-
  Sparrows Point
  (J4) 11,775
Fort Washington (G6).. 300
Foxville (E2) 450
Frederick◉ (E3) 21,744
Freeland (H2) 200
Friendship (H6) 275

Friendship Heights (A4) 500
Friendsville (A7) 580
Frizzellburg (F2) 193
Frostburg (C7) 6,722
Fruitland (M7) 1,147
Funkstown (D2) 968
Gaithersburg (F4) ...3,847
Galena (L3) 299
Galestown (L6) 151
Galesville (H5) 600
Gamber (G3) 300
Gambrills (H4) 900
Garrett Park (A3)...... 965
Garrison (G3) 800
Germantown (E4) 200
Girdletree (N8) 400
Glenarden (C4) 1,336
Glen Arm (J3) 350
Glen Burnie (H4) 3,900
Glen Echo (A4) 310
Glen Echo Heights (A4) 900
Glenelg (G3) 40
Glenn Dale (C4) 2,094
Glyndon-Reisterstown
  (G3) 4,216
Golden Hill (K7) 98
Goldsboro (L4) 204
Golts (L3) 100
Graceham (E2) 202
Granite (G3) 600
Grantsville (B7) 446
Grasonville (K5) 1,200
Greenbelt (C4) 7,479
Green Haven (H4) ...1,302
Greenmount (G2) 225
Greensboro (L5) 1,160
Hagerstown◉ (C2) ...36,660
Halethorpe-Arbutus-
  Relay (H4) 22,402
Halfway (C2) 4,256
Hall (G5) 125
Hampstead (G2) 696
Hancock (B2) 2,004
Hanover (H4) 975
Harmans (H4) 750
Harney (F2) 450
Havre de Grace (K2)..8,510
Hebron (M7) 754
Helen (H7) 125
Henderson (L4) 129
Henryton (G3) 250
Hereford (H2) 400
Highfield (E2) 650
Highland Beach (J5).. 5
Hillcrest Heights
  (B5) 15,295
Hillsboro (L5) 201
Hillside (C5) 5,528
Hobbs (L5) 95
Hollywood (H7) 3,841
Hoopersville (K7) 300
Hopewell (L8) 300
Hudson (J6) 125
Hughesville (G6) 550
Huntingtown (H6) ... 350
Hurlock (L6) 1,035
Hutton (A8) 300
Hyattstown (E3) 157
Hyattsville (B4) 15,168
Ijamsville (E3) 150
Ilchester (G4) 200
Indian Head (F6) 780
Ingleside (L4) 154
Ironshire (07) 100
Island Creek (H7) 408
Issue (G7) 200
Jacksonville (H2) 150
Jarrettsville (H2) 300
Jefferson (E3) 267
Jennings (B7) 300
Jesterville (L7) 160
Johnsville (F2) 210
Keedysville (D3) 433
Kempton (A9) 12
Kemptown (E3) 225

Kennedyville (L3) 900
Kensington (A4) 2,175
Keymar (F2) 200
Kingston (M8) 75
Kingsville (J3) 3,230
Kitzmiller (B8) 535
Knoxville (D3) 500
Ladiesburg (E2) 71
Lakesville (K7) 37
Landover (C4) 800
Landover Hills (C4) ...1,850
Langley Park (B4) ...11,510
Lanham (C4) 2,621
Lansdowne-Baltimore
  Highlands (H3) ...13,134
Lantz (E2) 75
La Plata◉ (G6) 1,214
Largo (C5) 25
Laurel (G4) 8,503
LaVale-Narrows Park‡
  (C7) 4,031
Laytonsville (F4) 196
Leeds (L2) 175
Le Gore (E2) 500
Leitersburg (D2) 500
Leonardtown◉ (H7)...1,281
Level (K3) 325
Lewistown (E2) 500
Lexington Park (J7)...7,039
Liberty Grove (K2).... 125
Libertytown (E3) 500
Lime Kiln (E3) 176
Lineboro (G2) 250
Linkwood (L6) 176
Linthicum Heights
  (H4) 1,400
Linwood (F2) 272
Lisbon (F3) 182
Little Orleans (A2) ... 132
Loch Lynn Hts. (A8).. 476
Loch Raven (H3) 23,278
Lonaconing (C7) 2,077
Long Green (H3) 500
Lothian (H5) 70
Love Point (J4) 120
Loveville (H7) 250
Lower Marlboro (H6).. 156
Luke (B8) 587
Lusby (J7) 75
Lutherville-Timonium
  (H3) 12,265
Lynch (K3) 150
Mackall (H7) ....
Madison (K6) 400
Madonna (H2) 128
Magnolia (J3) 200
Manchester (G2) 1,108
Manokin (L8) 400
Mapleville (D2) 175
Marbury (F6) 750
Mardela Springs (L7).. 380
Marion Station (M8)... 270
Marshall Hall (F6) 365
Marydel (L4) 130
Maryland Line (H2)... 175
Maryland Park (C5)... 992
Mason Springs (F6)... 50
Massey (L3) 210
Maugansville (D2) ... 950
Mayberry (F2) 108
Mayo (H5) 583
McDaniel (J5) 190
Meadows (C5) 150
Mechanicsville (H7) ... 500
Medford (F2) 25
Melitota (K4) 100
Melrose (G2) 58
Middleburg (F2) 160
Middle River (J3) ...10,825
Middletown (E3) 1,036
Midland (C7) 737
Milestown (H7) 400
Milford (H3) ....
Millers (G2) 170
Millersville (H4) 750

◉County seat.   ‡ Name not on map.

All figures available from 1960 final census are supplemented by local official estimates.

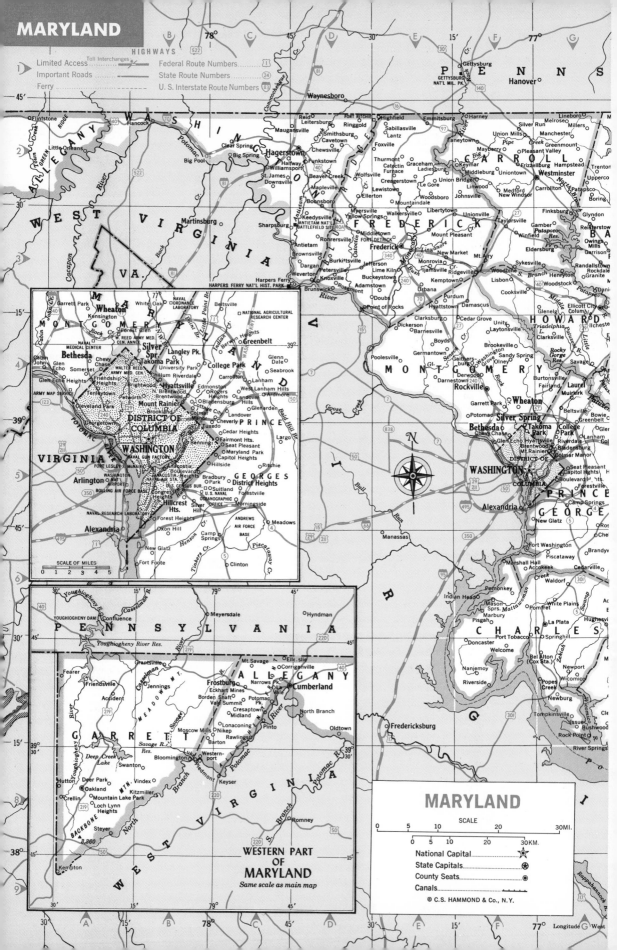

MARYLAND

WESTERN PART OF MARYLAND
Same scale as main map

MARYLAND
SCALE

0	5	10	20	30MI.
0	5	10	20	30KM.

National Capital
State Capitals
County Seats
Canals

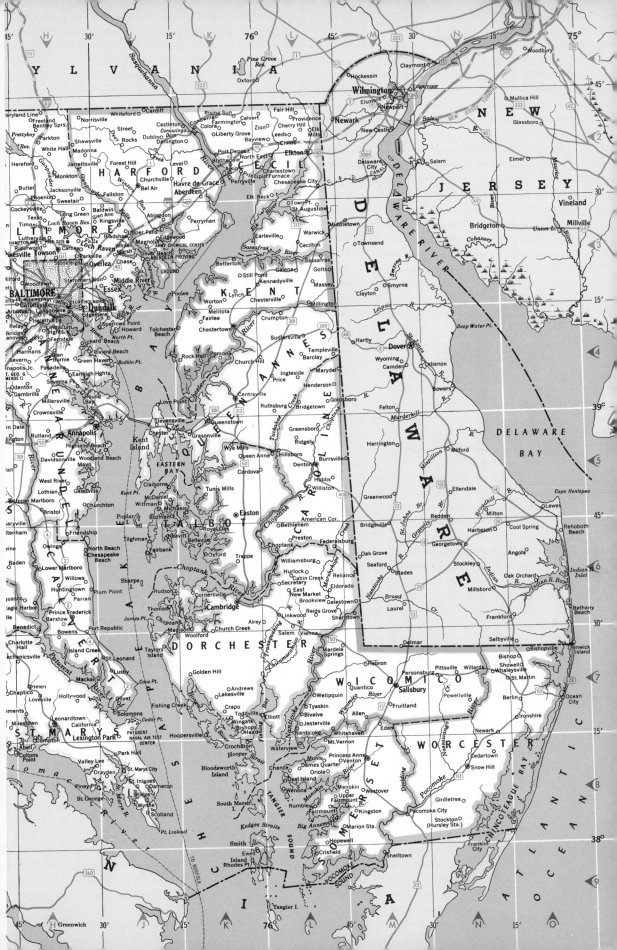

Millington (L3) 408
Monie (L8) 250
Monkton (H2) 147
Monrovia (E3) 300
Morningside (C5) 1,708
Moscow Mills (B7)...... 350
Mountain Lake Park
(A8) 975
Mountaindale (E2) 490
Mount Airy (F3) 1,352
Mount Pleasant (E3).... 260
Mount Rainier (B4)......9,855
Mount Savage (C7).......1,639
Mount Vernon (L8)....... 400
Muirkirk (G4) 500
Myersville (D3) 355
Nanjemoy (F7) 243
Nanticoke (L7) 500
Neavitt (J6) 250
Newark (N7) 265
Newburg (G7) 250
New Glatz (B6) 50
New Market (E3) 358
Newport (G7) 100
New Windsor (F2) 738
Nikep (C7) 210
Norrisville (J2) 206
North Beach (J6) 606
North Branch (D7) 70
North Brentwood (B4).. 864
North East (L2) 1,628
Oakland◉ (A8) 1,977
Ocean City (O7) 983
Odenton (H4) 1,914
Oella (G3) 500
Oldtown (D7) 450
Oliver Beach-Twin
Rivers Beach (J3).....1,426
Olivet (J7) 150
Olney (F4) 645
Orchard Beach (H4)....1,691
Oriole (L8) 268
Overlea (H3) 10,795
Owings (H6) 720
Owings Mills (G3) 3,810
Oxford (K6) 852
Oxon Hill (B6) 1,000
Park Hall (J8) 250
Parkton (H2) 500
Parkville-Carney (H3)..27,236
Parran (H6) 300
Parsonsburg (M7) 500
Pasadena (H4) 300
Patapsco (G2) 150
Perryman (K3) 560
Perryville (K2) 674
Petersville (D3) 300
Phoenix (H2) 313
Pikesville (G3) 18,737
Piney Point (H8) 990
Pinto (C7) 275
Piscataway (G6) 1,816
Pisgah (F6) 450
Pittsville (N7) 488
Pleasant Valley (G2).... 170
Plum Point (J6) ....
Pocomoke City (M8)...3,329
Point of Rocks (E3)...... 326
Pomfret (G6) 500
Pomona (K4) 25
Pomonkey (F6) 200
Poolesville (E4) 298
Popes Creek (G7) 75
Port Deposit (K2) 953
Port Republic (J6) 50
Port Tobacco (F6) 500
Potomac Park (C7) 1,016
Powellville (N7) 400
Preston (L6) 469
Price (L4) 245
Prince Frederick◉
(H6) 362
Princess Anne◉ (L8)....1,351
Principio Furnace (L2).. 300
Providence (L2) 500
Purdum (E3) 160
Quantico (M7) 200
Queen Anne (K5) 283
Queenstown (K5) 355
Randallstown (G3) 1,550
Rawlings (C7) 500
Reid (D2) 150
Reids Grove (L6) 75
Reisterstown-Glyndon
(G3) 4,216
Relay-Arbutus-
Halethorpe (H4) 22,402
Reliance (L6) 30
Rhodes Point (K9) 168
Riderwood (H3) 1,241
Ridge (J8) 400
Ridgely (L5) 886
Ridgeville (F3) 200
Ringgold (D2) 250
Rising Sun (K2) 824
Ritchie (C5) 100
Riverdale (B4) 4,389
Riverside (F7) 150
River Springs (G8) 300
Riviera Beach (J4) 4,902
Rockdale-Woodlawn-
Milford Mills (H3)..19,254
Rock Hall (K4) 1,073
Rock Point (G7) 250
Rocks (J2) 450
Rockville◉ (F4) 26,090
Rogers Heights (C4).....3,624
Rohrersville (D3) 500
Rosaryville (G5) 50
Rosemont ‡(D3) 212
Round Bay-Severna
Park (H4) 3,728
Royal Oak (K6) 575
Rumbley (L8) 125
Ruthsburg (L4) 22
Rutland (H5) 300
Ruxton (H3) ....
Sabillasville (E2) 300
Saint Augustine (L3).... 20
Saint Inigoes (J8) 400
Saint James (C2) 100
Saint Leonard (J7) ......
Saint Martin (O7) 60
Saint Mary's City (J8).. 540
Saint Michaels (J5) 1,484
Salem (L7) 40
Salisbury◉ (M7)........16,302
Sandy Spring (F4) 650
Sassafras (L3) 125
Savage (G4) 1,341
Scotland (J8) 375
Seabrook (C4) 2,347
Seat Pleasant (C5) 5,365
Secretary (L6) 351
Severn (H4) 200
Severna Park-Round
Bay (H4) 3,728
Sharpsburg (C3) 861
Sharptown (M6) 620
Shawsville (H2) 106
Shelltown (M9) 28
Shipley (H4) 200
Showell (O7) 250
Silver Hill-Suitland
(B5) 10,300
Silver Run (F2) 325
Silver Spring (B4) 66,348
Smithsburg (D2) 586
Snow Hill◉ (N8) 2,311
Solomons (J7) 183
Somerset (A4) 1,444
Sparrows Point-Fort
Howard-Edgemere
(J4) 11,775
Springhill (G7) 150
Stemmers Run (H3).....1,260
Stevensville (J5) 350
Steyer (A8) 46
Still Pond (K3) 290
Stockton (N8) 500
Stoneleigh-Rodgers
Forge (H3) 15,645
Street (J2) 250
Sudlersville (L4) 394
Suitland-Silver Hill
(C5) 10,300
Swanton (B8) 350
Sweetair (H2) 75
Sykesville (F3) 1,196
Takoma Park (B4) 16,799
Taneytown (F2) 1,519
Taylors Island (J7) 250
Taylorsville (F3) 125
Templeville (L4) 98
Texas (H3) 300
Thomas (J6) 100
Thurmont (E2) 1,998
Tilghman (J6) 900
Timonium-Lutherville
(H3) 12,265
Toddville (K7) 300
Tolchester Beach (J4).. 4
Tompkinsville (G7) 600
Town Point (L3) 50
Towson◉ (H3) 19,090
Trappe (K6) 358
Trenton (G2) 200
Tunis Mills (K5) 100
Tuxedo (C5) 500
Tyaskin (L7) 150
Union Bridge (F2) 833
Union Mills (F2) 300
Uniontown (F2) 225
Unionville (F3) 133
Unity (F4) 66
University Park (B4)....3,098
Upper Fairmount (L8).. 824
Upper Falls (J3) 800
Upper Marlboro◉ (H5).. 673
Upperco (G2) 460
Urbana (E3) 250
Vale Summit (C7) 400
Valley Lee (H8) 300
Venton (M8) 95
Vienna (L7) 420
Vindex (B8) 175
Waldorf (G6) 1,048
Walkersville (E3) 1,020
Warwick (L3) 391
Washington Grove
(F4) 576
Waterview (L8) 45
Welcome (F7) 200
Wenona (L8) 300
Westernport (C8) 3,559
West Lanham Hills
(C4) 1,090
Westminster◉ (G2) 6,123
Westover (M8) 400
West River (H5) 100
Wetipquin (L7) 75
Weverton (D3) 150
Whaleysville (N7) 800
Wheaton (A3) 54,635
Whiteford (J2) 500
White Hall (H2) 68
Whitehaven (L7) 98
White Marsh (J3) 500
White Oak (B3) 1,413
White Plains (G6) 700
Wicomico (G7) 225
Willards (N7) 531
Williamsburg (L6) 300
Williamsport (C2) 1,853
Williston (L5) 60
Willows (H6) 200
Winfield (F3) 140
Wingate (K7) 200
Wittman (J5) 403
Wolfsville (D2) 96
Woodbine (F3) 262
Woodland Beach (H5)...1,855
Woodlawn-Rockdale-
Milford Mills (H3)..19,254
Woodsboro (E2) 430
Woodstock (G3) 600
Woolford (K7) 250
Worton (K3) 300
Wye Mills (K5) 125
Wynne (J8) 300
Yellow Springs (D3).... 375
Zion (L2) 150

OTHER FEATURES

Aberdeen Proving Ground J 3
Allegheny Front (mts.) ..C 7
Anacostia (river) ....B 5
Andrews A.F.B. ....C 5
Antietam (creek) ....D 2
Antietam Nat'l Battlefield
Site ....D 3
Army Chemical Center ....K 3
Army Map Service ....A 4
Back (river) ....J 4
Backbone (mt.) ....A 8
Bald Hill Branch (river)..C 4
Big Annemessex (river) ..L 8
Big Pipe (creek) ....F 2
Bloodsworth (isl.) ....K 8
Blue Ridge (mts.) ....D 3
Bodkin (point) ....J 4
Bush (creek) ....E 3
Cabin John (creek) ......A 4
Casselman (river) ....B 7
Catoctin (creek) ....D 3
Cedar (point) ....J 7
Census Bureau, U.S. ....B 5
Chesapeake (bay) ....J 7
Chesapeake and Delaware
(canal) ....M 2
Chester (river) ....K 4
Chicamacomico (river)....L 7
Chincoteague (bay) ....N 8
Choptank (river) ....K 6
Conococheague (creek)...C 1
Conowingo (dam) ....K 2
Cove (point) ....J 7
Deep Creek (lake) ....A 8
Deer (creek) ....J 2
Detrick, Fort ....E 3
Dividing (creek) ....M 8
Eastern (bay) ....J 5
Elk (river) ....L 3
Fishing (bay) ....K 7
Fort Detrick ....E 3
Fort George G. Meade ....G 4
Fort Holabird ....H 3
Fort McHenry Nat'l
Mon. ....H 3
Fort Ritchie ....D 2
Great Seneca (creek) ...E 4
Green Ridge (mts.) ....A 2
Gunpowder (river) ....J 3
Gunpowder Falls
(creek) ....H 2
Hampton Nat'l Hist.
Site ....H 3
Henson (creek) ....B 6
Holabird, Fort ....H 3
Honga (river) ....K 7
Hooper (strait) ....K 8
Hydrographic Office,
U.S. ....C 5
Indian (creek) ....C 4
James (point) ....J 6
Kedges (straits) ....K 8
Kent (isl.) ....J 5
Kent (point) ....J 5
Linganore (creek) ....E 3
Little Choptank (river)....J 6
Little Gunpowder Falls
(creek) ....H 2
Little Paint Branch
(river) ....B 4
Little Patuxent (river)...G 4
Loch Raven (res.) ....H 3
Lookout (point) ....J 8
Manokin (river) ....L 8
Marshyhope (creek) ......L 6
Mattawoman (creek) .....F 6
Meade, Fort
George G. ....G 4
Meadow (mt.) ....B 7
Middle Patuxent
(river) ....G 3
Monocacy (river) ....E 3
Nanticoke (river) ....L 7
Nassawango (creek) .....N 8
National Agricultural
Research Center ....C 3
Naval Medical Center .....A 4
Naval Ordnance Lab. ......B 3
North (point) ....J 4
Oxon Run (river) ....B 5
Paint Branch (river)......B 4
Patapsco (res.) ....G 3
Patapsco (river) ....H 4
Patuxent (river) ....H 7
Patuxent Naval Air Test
Center ....J 7
Piscataway (creek) ....C 6
Pocomoke (river) ....N 8
Pocomoke (sound) ....L 9
Pooles (isl.) ....K 3
Poplar (isl.) ....J 5
Potomac (river) ....H 8
Prettyboy (res.) ....H 2
Ritchie, Fort ....D 2
Rock (creek) ....F 4
Rocky Gorge (res.) ....C 4
Saint George (isl.) ....H 8
Saint Marys (river) ....J 8
Sassafras (river) ....L 3
Savage (river) ....B 7
Savage River (res.) ....B 7
Severn (river) ....J 4
Sharps (isl.) ....J 6
Smith (isl.) ....K 8
South Marsh (isl.) ....K 8
Susquehanna (river) ......J 1
Tangier (sound) ....L 8
Tinkers (creek) ....B 6
Town (creek) ....A 2
Transquaking (river)......L 7
Triadelphia (lake) ....G 4
Tuckahoe (creek) ....L 5
Walter Reed Army
Medical Center Annex A 4
Wicomico (river) ....G 7
Wicomico (river) ....M 7
Winters Run (creek) ......J 2
Youghiogheny (river) .....A 8
Youghiogheny River
(res.) ....A 7
Zekiah Swamp (river)....G 7

DISTRICT OF COLUMBIA
763,956

CITIES and TOWNS

Anacostia (B5) ....
Benning (B5) ....
Brightwood (B4) ....
Brookland (B4) ....
Cleveland Park (A4)....
Congress Heights (B5)..
Georgetown (A5) ....
Petworth (B4) ....
Tenleytown (A4) ....
WASHINGTON (B5)..763,956
Washington (urban
area) (Md.-Va.)..1,808,423

OTHER FEATURES

Anacostia Naval Air
Station ....B 5
Bolling A.F.B. ....C 5
Fort Lesley J. McNair...A 5
Naval Gun Factory ....B 5
Naval Research
Laboratory ....A 5
Walter Reed Army Med.
Center ....A 4

by lumber, coal, and manufacturing, and through its functions as a trade center for surrounding areas of Maryland, West Virginia, and Pennsylvania. Next in size are Rockville (26,090), Annapolis (23,385), and Frederick (21,744).

The existence of the District of Columbia has greatly stimulated the surrounding areas in Maryland, including Prince Georges and Montgomery counties, which are considered as part of the District's metropolitan area. Many federal institutions and agencies have contributed markedly to the state's economic life. On the other hand, many Marylanders, prominent in civic and political life in the suburbs, carry on professional and economic careers in Washington. Four of Maryland's 10 most populous incorporated cities are in the Washington metropolitan area: Rockville, College Park (18,482), Takoma Park (16,799), and Hyattsville (15,168).

Southern Maryland, south from Annapolis and away from Washington, is largely unchanged from earlier years. Its people are almost exclusively English in origin, and there is a strong element of old aristocracy. Located in the region is Annapolis, the state capital, which is one of the most individual small towns of the nation.

The Eastern Shore is a place apart. Its people are vigorous, unbeholden, and keenly conscious of politics. Its economic expansion has continued steadily since the refrigerator car proved practicable for the transport of perishable produce. Salisbury (16,302) is the region's principal city and its distributing center. Ocean City, in the ocean county of Worcester, is the state's only prominent seaside resort. Cambridge (12,239), on the Choptank River and the shore's second city, has sizable packing and processing industries. Crisfield (3,540) lays its claim as the "seafood capital of the world." Smith Islanders, who inhabit a group of islands off the coast from Crisfield, are individualists par excellence. The Eastern Shore is connected to the Maryland Main by the Chesapeake Bay Bridge, a two-lane, 28-foot-wide vehicular crossing from Kent Island.

Counties.—Of the state's 23 counties, the most populous is Baltimore and the least populous is Kent. The largest county in land area is Frederick (664 square miles); the smallest is Calvert (219). A list of the counties, exclusive of Baltimore City, with their populations, areas, and county seats, follows:

County	Population (1960)	Land Area (sq. m.)	County Seat
Allegany	84,169	426	Cumberland
Anne Arundel	206,634	417	Annapolis
Baltimore	492,428	610	Towson*
Calvert	15,826	219	Prince Frederick*
Caroline	19,462	320	Denton
Carroll	52,785	456	Westminster
Cecil	48,408	352	Elkton
Charles	32,572	458	La Plata
Dorchester	29,666	580	Cambridge
Frederick	71,930	664	Frederick
Garrett	20,420	662	Oakland
Harford	76,722	448	Bel Air
Howard	36,152	251	Ellicott City*
Kent	15,481	284	Chestertown
Montgomery	340,928	494	Rockville
Prince Georges	357,395	485	Upper Marlboro
Queen Annes	16,569	373	Centreville
St. Marys	38,915	367	Leonardtown
Somerset	19,623	332	Princess Anne
Talbot	21,578	279	Easton
Washington	91,219	462	Hagerstown
Wicomico	49,050	380	Salisbury
Worcester	23,733	483	Snow Hill

*Unincorporated place.

FPG

The Maryland State House at Annapolis.

4. GOVERNMENT AND POLITICS

Maryland has been a political entity for over 300 years. Its capitol, the State House, which is still in use, was built in 1772. Although the political and executive capital is Annapolis, the administrative capital is Baltimore, where practically all the administrative establishments are.

State Constitution.—The present constitution, the state's fourth, dates from 1867. By its provisions, the question of a new constitutional convention is submitted to the voters every 20 years. Despite vigorous efforts in 1930 and again in 1950, no constitutional convention was held until 1967. The constitution drafted at the convention included major revisions in the state court structure, the legislature and the governor's office. It was rejected in a referendum in 1968.

Executive.—The principal policy-making branches of the government are the governor and the General Assembly. The governor is popularly elected for four years, but may not serve for more than two consecutive terms. There is no lieutenant governor, succession going to the president of the Senate and the speaker of the House of Delegates. The governor's veto of legislation may be overridden by a vote of three fifths of the members elected to each house. The comptroller and the attorney general are popularly elected. The treasurer is chosen by the General Assembly. Other state administrative officials are appointed. Principal departments or commissions are those of Education, State Roads, Health, Public Welfare, Corrections, and Comptroller of the Treasury.

Although there was substantial administrative reorganization under Governor Albert C. Ritchie in 1922 and extensive recommendations were made by the Sobeloff Commission in 1952, boards and commissions are still more numerous than is the case in most other states. The state service operates under a merit system which was the first in the United States on a state level to be established (1920) with a single head rather than a civil service commission. There is also an active Maryland State Planning Commission. Budgeting and central purchasing are performed by the Department of Budget and Procurement.

The following is a list of the Maryland governors:

LORDS PROPRIETARY OF MARYLAND

Cecilius Calvert, 2d Lord Baltimore	1632–1675
Charles Calvert, 3d Lord Baltimore	1675–1715
Benedict Leonard Calvert, 4th Lord Baltimore	1715
Charles Calvert, 5th Lord Baltimore	1715–1751
Frederick Calvert, 6th Lord Baltimore	1751–1771
Henry Harford	1771–1776

PROPRIETARY GOVERNORS OF MARYLAND

Leonard Calvert	1634–1647
Thomas Greene	1647–1649
William Stone	1649–1654
Commissioners (settlers appointed by Parliamentary Commissioners or Provincial Court)	1654–1658
Josias Fendall	1658–1660
Philip Calvert	1660–1661
Charles Calvert	1661–1676
Cecilius Calvert	1676
Thomas Notley	1676–1679
Charles Calvert, 3d Lord Baltimore	1679–1684
Benedict Leonard Calvert	1684–1688
William Joseph (president of council)	1688–1689

INTERVAL OF PURITAN CONTROL

Protestant Associators	1689
Convention of Freemen and John Coode, commander in chief	1689–1690
Nehemiah Blakistone	1690–1692

ROYAL GOVERNORS

Sir Lionel Copley	1692–1693
Sir Thomas Lawrence	1693
Sir Edmund Andros	1693–1694
Col. Nicholas Greenbury	1694
Sir Thomas Lawrence	1694
Francis Nicholson	1694–1699
Nathaniel Blakistone	1699–1702
Thomas Tench	1702–1704
John Seymour	1704–1709
Edward Lloyd	1709–1714
John Hart	1715–1720

PROPRIETARY GOVERNORS (RESTORED)

John Hart	1715–1720
Charles Calvert	1720–1727
Benedict Leonard Calvert	1727–1731
Samuel Ogle	1731–1732
Charles, 5th Lord Baltimore	1732–1733
Samuel Ogle	1733–1742
Thomas Bladen	1742–1747
Samuel Ogle	1747–1752
Benjamin Tasker	1752–1753
Horatio Sharpe	1753–1769
Robert Eden	1769–1776
The Convention and Council of Safety	1776–1777

GOVERNORS OF THE STATE OF MARYLAND

Thomas Johnson		1777–1779
Thomas Sim Lee		1779–1782
William Paca		1782–1785
William Smallwood		1785–1788
John Eager Howard	Federalist	1788–1791
George Plater	"	1791–1792
James Brice		1792
Thomas Sim Lee	"	1792–1794
John H. Stone	"	1794–1797
John Henry	"	1797–1798
Benjamin Ogle	"	1798–1801
John F. Mercer	Republican	1801–1803
Robert Bowie	"	1803–1806
Robert Wright	"	1806–1809
Edward Lloyd	"	1809–1811
Robert Bowie	"	1811–1812
Levin Winder	Federalist	1812–1815
Charles Ridgely of Hampton	"	1815–1818
Charles Goldsborough	"	1818–1819
Samuel Sprigg	Republican	1819–1822
Samuel Stevens, Jr.	"	1822–1825
Joseph Kent	"	1825–1828
Daniel Martin	Anti-Jackson	1828–1829
Thomas K. Carroll	Jackson-Democrat	1829–1830
Daniel Martin	Anti-Jackson	1830–1831
George Howard	Whig	1831–1833
James Thomas	"	1833–1835
Thomas W. Veazey	"	1835–1838
William Grason	Democrat	1838–1841
Francis Thomas	"	1841–1844
Thomas G. Pratt	Whig	1844–1847
Philip Francis Thomas	Democrat	1847–1850
Enoch Louis Lowe	"	1850–1853
Thomas Watkins Ligon	"	1853–1858
Thomas Holliday Hicks	American	1858–1862
Augustus W. Bradford	Unionist	1862–1865
Thomas Swann	Unionist, later Democrat	1865–1868
Oden Bowie	Democrat	1868–1872

William Pinkney Whyte	Democrat	1872–1874
James Black Groome	"	1874–1876
John Lee Carroll	"	1876–1880
William T. Hamilton	"	1880–1884
Robert M. McLane	"	1884–1885
Henry Lloyd	"	1885–1888
Elihu E. Jackson	"	1888–1892
Frank Brown	"	1892–1896
Lloyd Lowndes	Republican	1896–1900
John W. Smith	Democrat	1900–1904
Edwin Warfield	"	1904–1908
Austin L. Crothers	"	1908–1912
Phillips L. Goldsborough	Republican	1912–1916
Emerson C. Harrington	Democrat	1916–1920
Albert C. Ritchie	"	1920–1935
Harry W. Nice	Republican	1935–1939
Herbert R. O'Conor	Democrat	1939–1947
William Preston Lane	"	1947–1951
Theodore R. McKeldin	Republican	1951–1959
J. Millard Tawes	Democrat	1959–1967
Spiro T. Agnew	Republican	1967–1969
Marvin Mandel	Democrat	1969–

Legislature.—The General Assembly meets annually for a 70-day regular session on the third Wednesday in January. The governor may call a special legislative session of no more than 30 days.

The state legislature consists of a Senate and a House of Delegates. Members of both houses serve for four-year terms. A 1965 reapportionment plan raising the number of senators from 29 to 43 and reducing house membership to 123 delegates was approved by the state courts in 1966. The Senate and the House of Delegates are equal in power, and the governor of Maryland, especially when he is a Democrat, can exercise a substantial degree of leadership in legislative matters.

The General Assembly is assisted by a Department of Legislative Reference, whose director is secretary of the Legislative Council. The council comprises 6 senators, 6 delegates, and 8 other members who function between legislative sessions to study and recommend new legislation. The council's recommendations carry great weight in the assembly.

Judiciary.—The administration of justice is performed in the 23 counties by 7 circuit courts. At the same level in Baltimore City is the Supreme Bench of Baltimore. There are four appellate circuit courts, one of which serves Baltimore City alone. The state's highest court, the Court of Appeals of Maryland, has seven justices and sits at Annapolis. Appellate judges are elected for 15-year terms, usually without opposition after endorsement by the bar and by both political parties. Lower state courts include orphans', probate, and people's courts.

Local Government.—There is great variety in Maryland local government, despite the fact that two local government forms, the town and township, are not found in the state. In 1962, 351 local governmental units were counted for the state, including 23 counties, 152 municipalities, and 176 special districts.

Governmental units range from the City of Baltimore to the incorporated municipality of only a few people and the special taxing district organized in a suburban area. Some units, such as the Baltimore Metropolitan Police District and the Maryland-National Capital Park and Planning Commission, transcend county boundaries. The entire area of the state is included in the 23 counties and Baltimore City; the latter is not included in any county. In the main, the counties are regarded as instruments of state administration. Under the county home rule provision, however, counties may alter their forms of government and free themselves from specific legislative control. Montgomery County, suburban to Washington, was the first to do so. Cities in Maryland may under certain conditions amend their own charters. This privilege was extended to Baltimore in 1915 and to other cities in 1954. The General Assembly, however, still may classify cities and pass general laws concerning municipalities.

Several counties, especially Montgomery and Prince Georges near Washington, and Anne Arundel, Howard, and Baltimore, near Baltimore City, perform municipal as well as the traditional county functions. Except for Montgomery, Wico-

beverages, and horse racing. The proceeds of several of the major sources of state revenue are shared generously with counties and cities. The percentage distribution of state expenditures the early 1960's was as follows: education, 28.5; highways, 25.4; health and hospitals, 8.9; public welfare, 7.2; public safety, 2.7; and other, 27.3.

Suffrage and Elections.—The constitution of Maryland establishes qualifications for voting, as follows: citizenship in the United States, age of 21 years or over, and minimum residence of one year in the state and six months in the

Ewing Galloway

Airview of the United States Naval Academy, Annapolis.

mico, Baltimore, and Anne Arundel counties, which have county councils, all Maryland counties are governed by a board of commissioners. In general, the great bulk of county funds support highways and schools.

City governments are organized mostly as mayor-council types, although some have the commission form and even though the number of council-manager cities is growing. The Maryland Municipal League has done much to stimulate better governmental practice since its organization in 1947. Two counties, Howard and Baltimore, contain no incorporated municipalities; at the other extreme, Prince Georges County contains 28 municipalities. Many teeming communities, like Silver Spring and Bethesda in Montgomery County and Dundalk, Wheaton, Catonsville, and Essex in Baltimore County, are unincorporated and receive governmental services from the county.

Taxation and Revenue System.—The general property tax has become unimportant as a source of revenue for the state, although it continues to be the mainstay for local governments and special governmental areas. The State Tax Commission supervises the administration of this tax through the counties and Baltimore City. With the exception of some fees and licenses, most other revenues are administered by the comptroller's department. Principal taxes include the general sales tax and levies on personal and corporate income, gasoline, motor vehicles, alcoholic

county (or legislative district of Baltimore City). The state has no poll tax requirement for voting. A requirement for voter registration is established by law. The use of voting machines is required throughout the state. Popular initiation of legislation is not used, and popular referendum is employed only for constitutional amendments and, on petition, for approval or nullification of any act of the General Assembly not involving an appropriation. Elections for state offices are held in even-numbered years in which there is not a presidential election. Maryland sends eight congressmen and the usual two senators to Washington.

Political Parties.—Maryland is more likely to be Democratic than Republican. There have been only four Republican governors of Maryland since 1900. In recent years the tendency has been toward a more even balance between the major political parties in statewide elections. Both houses of the General Assembly are generally Democratic, although the Republican minority is usually large enough to make itself felt. Republican governors find it difficult to accomplish a full measure of legislative leadership. Party candidates are nominated in primaries, with run-off primaries in the absence of a majority.

5. EDUCATION AND WELFARE

Public Education.—Schools in early Maryland were predominantly religious. The movement for free public schools grew gradually until a uniform public school system was provided for the whole state in the constitution of 1864. A compulsory school attendance law was enacted in 1911, and current required attendance ages are 7 to 16, inclusive.

Public schools are administered on a county-wide basis, with state aid forthcoming to maintain a minimum program in each county. The governor appoints county school boards, which in turn select and control the county superintendents. Baltimore City board members are appointed by the mayor. The state Department of Education is headed by a state superintendent who is selected by a seven-member state Board of Education which is appointed by the governor. The Department of Education supervises the elementary and secondary schools in the 23 counties, as well as the state colleges.

Enrollment in the 1965–1966 school year in Maryland's public elementary schools (grades 1 through 6) totaled 455,647; in the public secondary schools (grades 7–12), 330,008. There were 16,342 public elementary and 14,752 secondary school teachers.

Maryland's public schools were segregated until 1954, when the U.S. Supreme Court ruled the practice unconstitutional. Almost all of Baltimore's public schools had been integrated by 1965, and racial desegregation was progressing rapidly elsewhere in the state.

On the higher educational level, the University of Maryland at College Park and Baltimore (see MARYLAND, UNIVERSITY OF), which dates from 1807, is controlled by a Board of Regents. Appointed by the governor for long terms, the board also functions as the state Board of Agriculture. The president of the university serves the board as administrative agent for its agricultural functions. These functions are carried on by the College of Agriculture and its cognate organizations, the Agricultural Extension Service and the experiment stations. Assisting the president in the conduct of the academic university is a faculty senate.

Other state-supported institutions of higher learning include Maryland State College (1886) at Princess Anne on the Eastern Shore, a division of the University of Maryland; and state colleges at Towson, Frostburg, Salisbury, and Bowie. Morgan State College and Coppin State College are at Baltimore.

Special state schools include the Maryland School for the Blind, maintained at Overlea on the outskirts of Baltimore, and the Maryland School for The Deaf at Frederick. The state school for the deaf offers an academic education similar to that of public schools. The Maryland Workshop for the Blind, a state-aided institution, is at Baltimore.

Private Education.—Primary and secondary religious schools are numerous in Maryland, especially in areas like southern Maryland, where Roman Catholics predominate. There are several well-known private secondary schools in the state, most of which are in and around Baltimore. In 1965–1966 there were over 400 private and parochial schools in the state, which were staffed by 5,650 teachers and which served 152,400 pupils.

The first Maryland institution of higher learning, Washington College at Chestertown on the Eastern Shore, was privately established as a college in 1782. St. John's College at Annapolis was chartered in 1784, and is nationally known for its "great books" program. Western Maryland College was established at Westminster in 1868. Colleges for women include Goucher, at Towson, established in 1885, and Hood, at Frederick, founded in 1893. One of the most distinguished of the private institutions in Maryland is Johns Hopkins University in Baltimore, incorporated in 1876. Its medical school, along with the University of Maryland School of Medicine, has made Baltimore one of the nation's medical meccas.

There are a number of Roman Catholic higher institutions in Maryland. In Baltimore these include Loyola College (1852), College of Notre Dame of Maryland (1873), Mount Saint Agnes College (1867), and St. Mary's Seminary and University (1791). At Emmitsburg are located Mount St. Mary's College (1808) and St. Joseph College (1809) and in Woodstock is situated Woodstock College (1867).

Other private higher or professional institutions include the University of Baltimore, the Peabody Institute of the city of Baltimore, and the Maryland Institute at Baltimore.

Libraries.—In addition to the libraries of the various educational institutions, there are extensive public libraries in Maryland. Chief among these is the Enoch Pratt Free Library in Baltimore, established in 1882 with a gift by Enoch Pratt. The city library in Baltimore has been merged with that of the Department of Legislative Reference in City Hall. Libraries in the counties have been encouraged and subsidized by the state, and in some counties branch library and bookmobile services are maintained.

Public Health.—Maryland's public health program is administered by the State Department of Health. The department is governed by a State Board of Health, most of whose members are appointed by the governor. The department serves the state through the counties, each of which has a health board and a county health officer. The department performs a variety of functions including the operation of hospitals.

Tuberculosis hospitals in the state are Victor F. Cullen in Frederick County, Henryton at Sykesville, Mount Wilson in Baltimore County, and Pine Bluff at Salisbury. Chronic disease hospitals are Deer's Head at Salisbury and Montebello at Baltimore, and western Maryland at Hagerstown.

Public Welfare.—The State Department of Public Welfare, established in 1939, is the coordinating and directing agency for all state welfare activities. It supervises, directs, and controls each of the county welfare boards, whose six members are appointed for six-year terms by the county governing body. The welfare program includes cooperation in the federal programs of assistance to dependent children, the aged, the needy blind, and the totally disabled. The department controls the state's four training schools: Boys' Village in Prince Georges County, Maryland Training School for Boys near Towson, Barrett School for Girls at Glen Burnie, and Montrose School for Girls at Reisterstown.

The administration of the Workmen's Compensation Law (1902), the first enacted by any state, is entrusted to the State Industrial Accident Commission. Unemployment insurance is administered by the Department of Employment Security. The Department of Mental Hygiene controls the state mental hospitals of Crownsville in Anne Arundel County, Eastern Shore in Dorchester County, Spring Grove in Baltimore County, and Springfield in Carroll County, the Rosewood State Training School in Baltimore County, and the Maximum Security Hospital in Howard County.

Public Safety.—The Maryland Military Department is headed by the adjutant general, who is appointed by the governor. The principal National Guard unit allotted to Maryland is a part of the 29th Infantry Division, and there are other guard units as well as several United States Air Force detachments assigned within the state. The Maryland Civil Defense Agency, assisted by a Civil Defense Advisory Council, is headed by a director appointed by the governor. It is authorized to cooperate with federal, state, and local governments on civil defense plans, and is responsible for disaster operations when necessary.

The Department of Maryland State Police, organized in 1939, is responsible for the enforcement of state criminal and motor vehicle laws. It maintains radio and teletype communications with four bodies of troops assigned to barracks located throughout the state.

Maryland correctional and penal institutions are managed by the Department of Correction. A Board of Correction appointed by the governor chooses the superintendent of prisons, who heads the administrative department. Institutions operated by the Department of Correction are the Maryland Penitentiary at Baltimore, the State Reformatory for Males in Washington County, and the House of Correction and the State Reformatory for Women, both at Jessups. At Jessups is also located the Patuxent Institution, which directs psychiatric and psychological work at all of the Department of Correction's institutions. It has custody of defective delinquents and emotional psychopaths committed by the courts or transferred to it by the Board of Correction. Court sentences under the law are indeterminate with no maximum limit. Parole in Maryland is handled by the Board of Parole and Probation.

6. ECONOMIC ACTIVITIES

Although Maryland's economic life is varied, it centers principally around manufacturing and trade, which together account for over 40 per cent of all employment. In 1967 the state's labor force totaled 1,406,500 persons, including 30,700 agricultural workers. Manufacturing provided employment for 21.4 per cent of all nonagricultural workers; trade, 20.2; public administration 16.7; service industries 15.1; and all other activities 26.6 per cent.

Total personal income of all Marylanders approximated $10,604,000,000 in 1965, or $3,001 per capita, slightly above the national level.

Agriculture.—Small in area with about 3 per cent of its labor force engaged in farming, Maryland is not an important agricultural state. Nevertheless farming is profitable because the land is fertile, huge markets are near, and both rail and water transportation are easily accessible.

In the 1950's and 1960's, the number of farm units declined while their size increased. In 1950 there were 36,107 farms with 4,055,529 acres, while in 1959 there were 25,108 farms covering 3,897,000 acres, or about 48 per cent of the total land area. In the same nine-year span the average value per farm rose from $14,048 to $39,095.

Of cash income of $334,450,000 received by farmers for crops and livestock and livestock products in 1965, the bulk was derived from broilers, dairy products, tobacco, and corn, in order of cash receipts. Maryland ranks high among the states in broiler production, in its strawberry harvest from the Chesapeake Bay region, and in its tomato yields from the Eastern Shore.

The most impressive development in Maryland's agriculture in the early 1960's was the growth of the broiler industry on the Eastern Shore. Tobacco, the staple crop in early times and still the leading cash crop, is grown almost entirely in southern Maryland. Dairying is the principal agricultural pursuit in Baltimore, Harford, and Montgomery counties. Frederick County ranks high in the state in grain and hay yields and in livestock and milk production. Income from the sale of dairy products in the county is almost triple that of any other Maryland county. Throughout the state the production of Irish potatoes, horses, and sheep and wool steadily declined in the mid-20th century, but that of milk, chickens, and eggs rose rapidly.

Among Maryland's large number of crops of commercial importance are hay, wheat, barley, oats, rye, soybeans, tobacco, corn, tomatoes, snap beans, asparagus, apples, peaches and strawberries. The state's chief canning crops include tomatoes, corn, snap beans, cucumbers for pickles, and peas. Fruit production is dominated by apples and peaches. Other fruits raised in the state are strawberries, pears, plums, cherries, watermelons, and cantaloupes. Between 1950 and 1960, vegetables declined as a percentage of total farm products sold while field crops, horticultural specialties, and fruits and nuts increased their share of total sales. In 1960, the crops with the highest sales were tobacco, corn, soybeans, wheat, and tomatoes.

Fisheries.—The seafood industry thrives in Maryland. In the mid-1960's the commercial catch from Chesapeake Bay and Atlantic Ocean waters was valued at $13,249,000, comprising 35,030,000 pounds of fin fish and 51,641,000 pounds of shellfish. The most valuable catches were those of oysters, 8,619,000 pounds ($6,447,000), of which Maryland is a leading producer, and crabs and surf clams. Leading commercial fin fish include striped bass, shad, flounder, white perch, and menhaden.

Mineral Production.—Maryland is not a leading state in primary mineral production, although it is important as a mineral processor (see below, *Manufacturing*). Primary production was reported in 22 counties in 1960, principally sand and gravel and stone in most counties. The mining of bituminous coal in Allegany and Garrett counties, which reached its peak in the early 1900's, was in decline. Production of Maryland's minerals in 1965, valued at $77,995,000, was as follows (in short tons): sand and gravel, 16,200,-000; stone, 14,553,000; coal, 1,210,000; clays, 914,000; and lime, 37,294. Small quantities of other minerals included natural gas, cement, greens and marl, potassium salts, talc, soapstone, and oyster shells.

Manufacturing.—The state's leading source of wealth is its well-developed and diversified manufacturing industry, which is largely centered in the Baltimore metropolitan area. The earliest important Maryland manufacture was the building of boats and ships, which was begun in Baltimore by 1700 and was of major stature by 1750. The Revolutionary War further stimulated ship-

The outer ramparts of Fort McHenry, Baltimore.

building and also encouraged the growth of iron manufacture. In the early 19th century, cotton textiles and brewing entered the Baltimore area, and in the period immediately before the Civil War, woollen fabrics and chemical fertilizers attained importance. Petroleum refining was started in Baltimore in 1865 and steel production, at Sparrows Point, in 1889. The most significant new industry of the 20th century was that of aircraft manufacture, which was highly stimulated by the military demands of World War II, as was the shipbuilding industry.

The continuing growth of manufacturing in 20th century Maryland is reflected in the rise of manufacturing employment from 100,911 persons in 1899 to about 265,000 in the mid-1960's; the increase in their wages from $39,260,000 to $1,-550,000,000; and the climb in value added by manufacture from $81,722,000 to $3,001,468,000.

In the 1960's, the leading manufactures in the state were, in order of value added by manufacture, primary metals, food and food products, transportation equipment, electrical machinery, chemicals and allied products, printing and publishing, apparel and related products, non-electrical machinery, fabricated metal products, rubber and plastic products, and lumber and wood products. The largest employers in manufacturing were the primary metal industries, with about 16 per cent of total manufacturing employment; food and food products, 14.4 per cent; trans-

portation equipment, 12.5 per cent; apparel and related products, 8.9 per cent; fabricated metal products, 6.9 per cent; chemicals and allied products, 6.3 per cent; and electrical machinery, 5.6 per cent. The increase in wage rates from 1950 to 1960 was higher in the durable goods industries than in the nondurable goods industries. Also, the average hourly wage rate in the 1960's was higher in durable goods.

In 1963, 2,027 of the state's 3,451 manufacturing plants were in the Baltimore metropolitan area, where the leading industries were those relating to primary metals, transportation equipment, and processed foods and beverages. Chief products of these and other industries included steel, iron, copper, fabricated metal products, boats and ships, airplanes, motor vehicles, chemicals and chemical products, petroleum products, soaps, paints, men's and boy's apparel, and glassware. The Baltimore establishments of the Bethlehem Steel Company (at Sparrows Point) and the Martin Marietta Corporation missiles and space systems plants are among the largest of their kind. Shipbuilding is still thriving. Large factories are devoted to oil refining, spice manufacture, sugar refining, meatpacking, distilling, and canning.

There is extensive poultry, fish, and vegetable processing on the Eastern Shore, particularly at Salisbury and Cambridge, where miscellaneous other light manufacturing industries are located.

Cumberland produces Celanese, rayon, and tires, and has a railroad repair center. There is an aircraft and missile plant and a sizable machine tool industry in Hagerstown, where textiles, trucks, and pipe organs are also produced.

Electric Power.—One of the important factors supporting the state's manufacturing activities is its supply of electric power. In the 1960's, the installed capacity of all generating units operating in the state was 3,312,000 kilowatts, of which 494,000 were represented by hydroelectric capacity.

Banking.—Banking services in Maryland were being provided, in the mid 1960's by 78 state banks and trust companies, 6 mutual savings institutions and 50 national banks. Also operating in the state were about 45 chartered credit unions and 345 savings and loan associations.

Insurance.—By 1965, almost 700 licensed companies were doing business in the state, the great majority of which were Maryland-licensed operators from other states or from foreign nations. A small number of native Maryland companies were doing business in life insurance and in fire and casualty insurance.

Domestic and Foreign Trade.—To support the growing economy of the state, an extensive retail and wholesale trade has been built up. By 1963, retail sales by the state's approximately 23,900 retail establishments totaled $4,237,000,000, almost half accounted for by the Baltimore metropolitan area. Wholesale trade in the state in 1963 involved slightly over 3,600 establishments with $4,474,000,000 in sales.

In 1960 and 1962 Baltimore ranked second nationally in foreign trade tonnage. Waterborne commerce through the port in 1964 totaled 48,220,-000 net tons, including 7,145,000 tons of exports and 18,062,000 tons of imports. The port of Baltimore ranks second only to New York in the handling of bulk cargo.

Transportation.—Two factors have largely shaped the development of Maryland's transportation system. First is the existence of Chesapeake Bay, which, with its entry to the excellent harbor at Baltimore, has made cheap water transportation available. The second factor is that the main line of rail traffic southward from New York and Philadelphia traverses the state. Both the pioneer Baltimore & Ohio Railroad and the Penn Central Railroad operate main lines from New York to Washington by way of Baltimore. The Baltimore & Ohio also swings westward to western Maryland, a section that is also served by the Western Maryland Railway. In all, 13 railroads operate some 2,000 track miles within the state. The main airlines serving Maryland at Washington National Airport and Baltimore's Friendship International Airport are American, Eastern, Pan American, National, Trans World, and United.

There are many bus lines, serving all parts of the state, with all lines converging in Baltimore, and there is extensive statewide truck transportation. These and the state's 1,540,000 registered motor vehicles are served by over 23,000 miles of roads and highways, including 19,000 surfaced miles.

Principal federal highways transversing the state north and south are U.S. Highway 13 on the Eastern Shore; 301 from Baltimore to southern Maryland; 1 from the northeast corner of the state through Baltimore and Washington; 15 through Frederick; and 11 through Hagerstown.

East-west highways are 40, traversing the state from Elkton through the state's four principal cities and Garrett County in the west; and 50, beginning at Ocean City, and leading out of the state at Washington. Principal limited-access highways are those out of Washington toward Annapolis, Baltimore, and Frederick. The most important toll bridges are the Chesapeake Bay Bridge near Annapolis, the Susquehanna River Bridge near Havre de Grace, and the Potomac River Bridge carrying Highway 301 from southern Maryland to Virginia. The Baltimore Harbor Tunnel, a fourth toll facility, was opened to vehicles in 1957.

Communications.—Maryland's first radio station went into operation in 1922 at Baltimore, where also in 1947 the state's first television station was established. By the mid-1960's there were 50 AM and 28 FM radio stations and 4 television stations. In addition, there were approximately 1,800,000 telephones in the state. The nation's first telegraph line was constructed in 1844 between Baltimore and Washington.

The oldest newspaper still published in Maryland is the weekly Maryland *Gazette-News,* established as the Maryland *Gazette* in 1727 and published at Annapolis. The oldest daily newspaper is the Baltimore *Sun,* founded in 1837. Besides the *Sun,* the state's leading dailies of general circulation include the Annapolis *Evening Capital,* the Baltimore *News American,* the Cambridge *Banner,* the Cumberland *News* and *Times,* the Frederick *Post* and *News,* the Hagerstown *Mail* and *Herald,* and the Salisbury *Times.* In addition, there are 69 weeklies published in Maryland. Widely read within the state are the Washington *Post, Star,* and *News.*

7. PLACES OF INTEREST

Cities.—Of special interest to tourists are Baltimore, Annapolis, and Frederick (see individual articles on these and other Maryland cities). Baltimore is the state's chief tourist center because of its diverse historical background and because it is the state's cultural, economic, and sports center. The United States Naval Academy and the state capitol attract visitors to Annapolis. The Barbara Frietchie House and the home of Chief Justice Roger Brooke Taney make Frederick a tourist attraction.

Homes.—Throughout the state there are many beautiful old houses. One of the best examples of architecture of the period of George III is the Hammond-Harwood House in Annapolis. Another famous old Annapolis house is the Chase Home, built by Samuel Chase in 1769. Doughoregan Manor, near Ellicott City in Howard County, was built by Charles Carroll of Carrollton, as was the charming Homewood (1800), located on the Johns Hopkins campus in Baltimore. Hampton, a late 18th century Georgian mansion lying adjacent to the Goucher College campus, was designated in 1948 as part of the Hampton National Historic Site. Not far from Easton is Wye House, the leading old home on the Eastern Shore. At Wye Mills in Talbot County is the Wye Oak, estimated to be 400 years old. Not far away is Wye Chapel, consecrated in 1721. Many other old houses have been preserved on the Eastern Shore and in southern Maryland.

Historic Areas.—Fort McHenry National Monument and Historic Shrine is located in Baltimore. The Francis Scott Key Monument, near the Fort Avenue entrance to the park, commemorates the birthplace of *The Star-Spangled Banner* (q.v.). The Antietam National Battlefield and National Cemetery commemorate one of the most sanguinary battles of the Civil War. The Catoctin Recreational Demonstration Area, a federal project, contains Camp David, the presidential retreat near Thurmont.

Art, Music, and Theater.—Maryland's art activities center in Baltimore, home of the Walters Art Gallery and the Baltimore Museum of Art. The center of musical interest in Maryland is Baltimore's Peabody Conservatory of Music. The city has its own civic opera company and symphony orchestra. The Ford Theater in Baltimore presents professional road shows from New York. Summer stock productions are staged by the Hilltop Theater near Towson and in theaters at Olney and Ocean City.

Scientific Centers.—Nowhere is the impact of proximity to the national capital better illustrated than in the numerous federal scientific laboratories and installations scattered throughout the state. These establishments, most of which

Carew from Monkmeyer
Naval Medical Center, Bethesda.

employ many scientists and other specialists who live in Maryland, include the Naval Ordnance Laboratory (White Oaks), Army Chemical Center (Edgewood), Aberdeen Proving Ground, David Taylor Model Basin (Carderock), Bureau of Standards (Gaithersburg), Army Prosthetic Institute (Forest Glen), Naval Powder Factory (Indian Head), Agricultural Research Center (Beltsville), and National Institute of Health (Bethesda).

Outdoor Recreation Facilities.—For outdoor recreation, tourists are attracted to Ocean City, to both shores of the Chesapeake Bay, to the mountains in Garrett County, particularly around Deep Creek Lake, to the state's many forests, parks, and preserves, and to a varied program of sports activities, notably horse and harness racing and professional baseball.

State Forests.—Four state forests are located in Garrett County—Swallow Falls, Savage River, Potomac, and Mount Nebo. Other state forests are those of Green Ridge in Allegany County, Cedarville in Prince Georges and Charles counties, Doncaster in Charles, Pocomoke in Worcester, Seth Demonstration in Talbot, Elk Neck in Cecil, and the State Forest Nursery in Anne Arundel County.

State Parks.—Washington and Frederick counties each contain three state parks. In the former are the Washington Monument, Fort Tonoloway, and Fort Frederick state parks, and in Frederick County are situated Gambrill, Gathland, and Cunningham Falls. Other state parks are Patapsco in Howard, Wye Oak in Talbot, Elk Neck in Cecil, Sandy Point in Anne Arundel, Dan's Mountain in Allegany, The Rocks in Harford, and Seneca Creek in Montgomery County.

Wildlife Preserves.—In Maryland the federal Fish and Wildlife Service has established the Patuxent Research Refuge (1936) in Anne Arundel and Prince Georges counties, for wildlife experimental purposes, and in Dorchester County the Blackwater National Wildlife Refuge (1933). The latter area, consisting of marshes along the Big and Little Blackwater rivers, serves as a haven for ducks, Canada geese, quail, and muskrats.

Maryland state-owned game farms are located at Gwynbrook in Baltimore County, at Belle Grove in Allegany County, and at Montgomery and Wicomico in the counties for which they are named. The state operates fish hatcheries at Lewiston in Frederick County, Bear Creek in Garrett County, and Beaver Creek in Washington County.

Sports Attractions.—In Maryland, horse racing is a principal sport. The state's most notable racetrack is Pimlico in Baltimore, where the renowned Preakness is run each spring for three-year-olds. Other major flat-racing tracks are at Bowie and Laurel, while lesser tracks are located at Upper Marlboro, Havre de Grace, Cumberland, and Hagerstown. Harness races are run at Ocean Downs, near Ocean City; Rosecroft, near Washington; at the Baltimore Raceway; and at Laurel.

Revived interest in major league baseball in Maryland was instrumental in bringing the St. Louis club of the American League to Maryland in 1953, under the ancient and honored baseball team name of the Baltimore Orioles.

8. FAMOUS MEN AND WOMEN

Thomas Stone (Charles County, 1743–1787), Samuel Chase (Somerset County, 1741–1811), William Paca (near Abingdon, 1740–1799), and Charles Carroll of Carrollton (Annapolis, 1737–1832) were all Maryland signers of the Declaration of Independence. Daniel of St. Thomas Jenifer (Charles County, 1723–1790) was a pre-Revolutionary leader and signer of the United States Constitution in 1787. A few of the native Marylanders who made names for themselves in the United States government are: Roger Brooke Taney (Calvert County, 1777–1864), United States secretary of the treasury and attorney general and chief justice of the United States; William Pinkney (Annapolis, 1764–1822), lawyer, statesman, and diplomat; Reverdy Johnson (Annapolis, 1796–1876), constitutional lawyer, diplomat, and United States attorney general and senator; Charles Joseph Bonaparte (Baltimore, 1851–1921), lawyer and United States attorney general and secretary of the navy; William Wirt (Bladensburg, 1772–1834), lawyer, United States attorney general, presidential candidate in 1832 on the Anti-Masonic ticket, and author of the best seller, *The Letters of the British Spy;* Arthur Pue Gorman (Woodstock, 1839–1906); United States senator; and Simon Sobeloff (Baltimore, 1893–   ), United States solicitor general and circuit judge.

Among the state's better-known authors are Henry Louis Mencken (Baltimore, 1880–1956), editor and satirist, Maryland's most important recent literary figure; Francis Scott Key (Frederick County, now Carroll County, 1779–1843), lawyer, and author of *The Star Spangled Banner,* Mason Lock Weems, often called Parson Weems (Anne Arundel County, 1759–1825), clergyman and author; John Leeds Bozman (Talbot County, 1757–1823), historian and lawyer; John Pendleton Kennedy (Baltimore, 1795–1870), novelist; Lizette Woodworth Reese (Baltimore County, 1856–1935), author of autobiographical works and volumes of poetry; Upton Beall Sinclair (Baltimore, 1878–   ), writer and politician, awarded the Pulitzer Prize in 1943 for *Dragon's Teeth;* James Mallahan Cain (University Park, 1892–   ), journalist, author of *The Postman Always Rings Twice;* Charles Fulton Oursler (Baltimore, 1893–1952), journalist, playwright, and fiction writer; Frederick Arnold Kummer (Catonsville, 1873–1943), writer of fiction and plays; Ryder Randall (Baltimore, 1839–1908), journalist and song writer, author of *Maryland, My Maryland.*

A few native Marylanders in the field of art are: Charles Willson Peale (Queen Annes County, 1741–1827), portrait painter; James Peale (Chestertown, 1749–1831), miniaturist; Raphael Peale (Annapolis, 1774–1825), miniaturist and painter of still life; Charles Yardley Turner (Baltimore, 1850–1918), outstanding muralist; Camelia Whitehurst (Baltimore, 1875–1936), known for her portraits of children; R. McGill Mackall (Baltimore, 1889–   ), muralist and portrait painter; and William Henry Rinehart (near Union Bridge, 1825–1874), sculptor.

Several of the leading figures in American Negro history were natives of Maryland. Benjamin Banneker (1736–1806), mathematician, published an almanac in

1792 and became known in Europe as an astronomer. Frederick Douglass (1817?–1895), born a slave on an Eastern Shore plantation, became an abolitionist, orator, journalist, and served as minister to Haiti. Harriet Tubman (1821?–1913) was a fugitive slave, abolitionist, and the foremost leader of the Underground Railroad. Francis E. Watkins Harper (1825–1911) was born of free parents in Baltimore. She was well known as a poet, novelist, lecturer, and abolitionist leader.

9. HISTORY

The Chesapeake Bay region of present-day Maryland was first explored in 1608 by Captain John Smith from the Virginia colony of Jamestown. The principal Indian tribes inhabiting the territory were engaged in agriculture—various Algonquin tribes in the Eastern Shore region, the Anacostans near the present site of Washington, D.C., and the Susquehannocks at the head of the bay. These tribes were generally friendly, and in subsequent years there were only occasional troubles between them and the growing number of white settlers. Gradually and peaceably the Indians withdrew from Maryland.

Early Settlement.—After the Smith expedition, Virginians began trading freely with the Indians in the bay region, principally for furs. William Claiborne, representing a London trading company, established a trading post on Kent Island in the Chesapeake off Maryland in 1631. Active in Virginia politics, for many years he contested politically and with military force the rights of the Lords Baltimore to Maryland.

The first Lord Baltimore was Sir George Calvert, a Roman Catholic, who had visited Virginia in 1629 and who besought from the king a grant of land in the same region. The territory which he was granted was much larger than the area he was ever able to reduce to possession. Its original boundaries, the Potomac River and the 40th parallel, would have encompassed the cities of Philadelphia and Wilmington and sizable other portions of Pennsylvania and Delaware.

The first Lord Baltimore died before a charter could be granted in final form, and a charter was issued on June 20, 1632, to his son Cecilius Calvert, the second Lord Baltimore. Under the leadership of Leonard Calvert, the brother of Cecilius and the first governor of Maryland, the *Ark* and the *Dove* sailed from England in late 1633. They landed at St. Clements (now Blakistone) Island in the Chesapeake on March 25, 1634, a date celebrated in Maryland as Maryland Day. The two ships carried more than 200 persons, both Catholics and Protestants. Two days later the first settlement was made at St. Marys in southern Maryland, which became the capital of Maryland until 1694. The state's first two counties were St. Marys in southern Maryland and Kent on the Eastern Shore.

Proprietary Period.—The charter granted to the proprietor the right to make laws with the consent of the freemen or their delegates. The proprietor tried originally to exercise the law-making power in town meeting fashion, but by 1638 an assembly of freemen had assumed the power to initiate laws, and by 1650 a regular bicameral legislature was in operation that exercised full legislative powers. In 1649 the assembly approved an "Act Concerning Religion," which guaranteed religious toleration but which provided penalties for non-Trinitarians.

The fur trade very soon declined in importance, and agriculture took its place. Wheat and corn were important early crops, but tobacco soon became the staple crop and remained so until well after the colonial period. At first, indentured white servants did most of the hard labor, but they were gradually supplanted by Negro slaves.

A group of Puritans from Virginia settled on the banks of the Severn River and in 1649 established the town of Providence (now Annapolis). The following year they named their new county Anne Arundel after the wife of Cecilius Calvert. Calvert County was created in 1654 and Charles County in 1658. Prior to 1675 the Eastern Shore counties of Talbot, Somerset, and Dorchester were established, and at the head of the Chesapeake, Baltimore and Cecil counties were formed in 1659 and 1674, respectively.

A rebellion in the colony in 1689 displaced the proprietor. Shortly thereafter the crown took over political authority and Maryland became a crown colony until 1715, when it was restored to the proprietor. Under the royal government, Annapolis became the capital, laws were codified, and the lower house of the General Assembly grew in prestige and power. The Anglican Church was made the established church, and a poll tax of 40 pounds of tobacco was levied for its support. During this period the proprietor sent as his property agent Charles Carroll, who founded one of Maryland's leading families. During the royal period, two new counties, Queen Annes and Prince Georges, were created and named for the queen and her husband.

Around 1700, settlers began moving toward western Maryland, although neither the institution of slavery nor the tobacco crop moved with them. Colonization spread slowly, despite sporadic Indian troubles, and by 1730 the present site of Cumberland had been settled.

In 1723 the General Assembly authorized the establishment of a free school in each county. Catholics were disfranchised and repressed for the remaining provincial years. The town of Baltimore was settled on the Patapsco in 1729, and in 1732, German settlers from Pennsylvania penetrated western Maryland, particularly the area around present-day Frederick. Worcester County on the Atlantic was organized in 1742 and Frederick County in 1748.

A long-standing boundary dispute with Pennsylvania was firmly settled in 1732. A later survey of the joint boundary by Charles Mason and Jeremiah Dixon in the years 1763 to 1767 established the historic Mason-Dixon Line (see MASON AND DIXON'S LINE).

The last proprietor, Frederick, died in 1771, bequeathing the colony to his illegitimate son, Henry Harford, for whom Harford County was named. Caroline County, likewise established before the American Revolution, was named for the wife of Governor Robert Eden.

Movement for Independence.—Agitation for independence was as prevalent in Maryland as elsewhere in the colonies. Maryland was represented at the Stamp Act Congress of 1765, and conventions were called to protest the Townshend Acts. After these laws were repealed, however, only mild disturbances occurred in the colony during the next few years. In 1774 an informal protest organization known as the Maryland Convention, which was composed of five delegates from each county, began to assume the proportions of a regular government. It chose delegates to the Continental Congresses, appointed a committee of safety vested with interim powers, and it later enlisted troops and exercised many other governmental powers.

There was, however, considerable loyalist sentiment in conservative sections of Maryland. Advocates of independence centered in Baltimore and Frederick. The Maryland Convention resolved as late as May 1776 that it was not too late to compose differences between the colonies and England. But in June the convention authorized Maryland delegates to vote for independence.

A convention met on Aug. 14, 1776, to form Maryland's first constitution. The constitution was proclaimed on Nov. 8, 1776, without submission to the voters. The new document provided a bill of rights, a Governor's Council, a bicameral legislature comprising a House of Delegates elected annually and a Senate chosen by an electoral college for five-year terms, and a governor chosen annually by the legislature. High property qualifications, which were not abolished until 1810, were established for the suffrage, and even higher ones were imposed for officeholding. The first state governor was Thomas Johnson, who took office in 1777. A year earlier, Frederick County was divided into three counties. The central county retained the old name, the southern portion became Montgomery County, and the western portion became Washington County.

The new government of Maryland gave full support to the American Revolution. Maryland troops were commanded by Gen. William Smallwood. Other famous officers included Gen. Mordecai Gist and Col. John Eager Howard. Dr. James McHenry was one of George Washington's aides, and later became secretary of war under Presidents Washington and Adams. The bravery of Maryland troops during the Revolution earned for the state its nickname, the Old Line State. Maryland refused, until 1781, to ratify the Articles of Confederation, until those states claiming western lands agreed to cede their claims to the central government. The Continental Congress met in Annapolis in 1783 and 1784. It was there that General Washington resigned his commission on Dec. 23, 1783, and that Congress ratified the treaty terminating the Revolution on Jan. 15, 1784.

Maryland actively supported the move toward a constitutional convention. Commissioners from several states met at Annapolis in 1786 (see ANNAPOLIS CONVENTION) and agreed to meet the following year in Philadelphia. Maryland delegates to the Constitutional Convention were Luther Martin, John Francis Mercer, James McHenry, Daniel Carroll, and Daniel of St. Thomas Jenifer. Martin and Mercer refused to sign the Constitution. A Maryland convention elected for the purpose approved the federal Constitution on April 28, 1788, making Maryland the seventh state to do so. In 1791, Maryland and Virginia ceded to the national government the territory known as the District of Columbia. The Virginia portion of the District was later returned to the state, leaving the entire District to consist of former Maryland territory. In 1796, Allegany County was formed out of the western part of Washington County.

Early Statehood.—In the years following the adoption of the Constitution, Maryland prospered. Commerce grew rapidly, and Baltimore emerged as a leading American city. Even the Napoleonic wars and the War of 1812 did little lasting injury to the state's prosperity. After the war with England, Baltimore businessmen concerned themselves with western trade routes, and the Baltimore and Ohio Railroad was established.

During the War of 1812, British troops made several landings in Maryland. A sizable expedition landed on the banks of the Patuxent in August 1814, and moved toward Washington. A battle was fought at Bladensburg, where American forces were routed, and the British moved on to burn government buildings in Washington. The British fleet then moved toward Baltimore and tried to reduce Fort McHenry. During this attack, Francis Scott Key, a Marylander held on board a British ship, wrote *The Star-Spangled Banner*.

Following the War of 1812 the state legislature enacted a law in 1818 requiring all banks maintaining main offices outside the state to print their bank notes on special taxed paper. This legislation was aimed directly at the United States Bank. The act was held unconstitutional by the United States Supreme Court in the famous case of *McCulloch* v. *Maryland* (1819).

A violent contest in state politics, which erupted in 1837 and 1838, resulted in constitutional amendments providing for the popular election of the governor and the Senate and abolition of the Governor's Council. Meanwhile, Carroll County, named for Charles Carroll of Carrollton, was established in 1836 out of portions of Frederick and Baltimore counties.

Maryland's second constitution was adopted in 1851. Lasting until 1864, it provided few major changes in governmental structure. At the time of its adoption, Howard County was created out of a part of Anne Arundel, and Baltimore City was separated from Baltimore County. In the decade before the Civil War there was considerable unrest in the state, particularly in Baltimore. In 1860 the Baltimore police force was placed under state control, and from that date on the state government has not been reluctant to interfere in the city's affairs when necessary.

Civil War and Reconstruction.—Considerable distress was felt in Baltimore and throughout Maryland during the Civil War. Maryland was a border state, and its sympathies were clearly divided. Most influential in keeping Maryland officially on the Union side was Reverdy Johnson, who had earlier served as President Taylor's attorney general and as a United States senator.

A riotous attack in Baltimore in 1861 on Massachusetts troops proceeding through the city resulted in several deaths and led to military control of the city throughout the war. Marylanders fought in both the Union and Confederate armies. Armies of Generals Lee and McClelland fought the Battle of Antietam (Sept. 16–17, 1862) in Washington County. The passage of Gen. Stonewall Jackson's troops through Frederick during this campaign gave rise to Whittier's poem, *Barbara Frietchie*. The Confederate armies crossed the state again in proceeding to and from the Battle of Gettysburg in 1863, and in 1864 the two armies again met on Maryland soil at the Battle of the Monocacy (July 9). Early in the war, James R. Randall wrote *Maryland, My Maryland* to encourage those of Southern sympathies.

In 1864, Maryland's third constitution was adopted. Its principal new features were abolition of slavery, provision for establishment of a system of public education, and disfranchisement of Confederate sympathizers. The fourth constitution, adopted in May 1867 and still in effect, closely resembled that of 1864 except that it did not contain repressive features. The constitution established Wicomico County out of portions of Dorchester and Somerset. In 1872 the western part of Allegany County became Garrett County, and in 1879 the Virginia-Maryland boundary was tentatively settled, although final acceptance of the state's joint boundary was not made until 1930.

Following the Civil War, industry and commerce boomed, both in Baltimore and in the state as a whole. This growth was partly due to the increase in rail and water facilities. Transportation interests for a time dominated state politics. Arthur Pue Gorman, president of the Chesapeake and Ohio Canal Company, led in Maryland politics from 1880 until 1906. One of the prime issues of the period was machine politics.

20th Century Developments.—In the 20th century the state's development continued to be paced by the growing industrial might of Baltimore. The city's disastrous fire of February 1904, causing an estimated damage of $125,000,-000, created dislocations but did not permanently impair its industrial progress.

During World Wars I and II, Maryland contributed substantially to American war efforts. Over 60,000 Marylanders were in uniform in World War I and nearly 250,000 in World War II. In both conflicts the state contributed significantly in industrial production; its contributions in the latter struggle were most notable in shipbuilding and aircraft manufacture.

Military activities became prominent in Maryland during and after the two world wars. Among the many army, air force, and navy bases established at that time were Fort George G. Meade, Bainbridge Naval Training Center, and Andrews Air Force Base (see also above, *Scientific Centers*).

In the 1950's and 1960's, transportation facilities were improved significantly. Friendship International Airport, south of Baltimore, was opened, providing the state with its largest airport. The Chesapeake Bay Bridge, connecting the Eastern Shore with the Maryland Main, was opened in 1952. The Baltimore-Washington Expressway was opened in 1954 and the Baltimore Harbor Tunnel in 1957. In the early 1960's, the Balitmore Beltway, encircling the city, and the John F. Kennedy Memorial Highway, joining Baltimore and Wilmington, Del., were opened. Washington International Airport, a jet port west of Washington, was under construction in the mid-1960's.

In the 1960's, many factors served to knit Maryland's people more closely together than in the past. One such factor was the improved facilities for transportation and communication. Another was the increasing part the University of Maryland played in the state's affairs. Its services to agriculture and its research in other matters affecting life in the state contributed much toward integrating the state and its people. A third factor was the tremendous growth in the state's population, particularly in the Baltimore and Washington metropolitan areas. In 1960, for the second time in a decade, Maryland's growing population won the state a new seat in the U.S. House of Representatives.

Bibliography.—McSherry, James, *History of Maryland* (Baltimore 1904); Gambrill, John M., *Leading Events of Maryland History* (New York 1917); Earle, Swepson, *The Chesapeake Bay Country* (Baltimore 1924; rev. ed. 1934); Andrews, Matthew P., *History of Maryland; Province and State* (New York 1929); Essary, Jesse F., *Maryland in National Politics* (Baltimore 1932); Stieff, Frederick P., *The Government of a Great American City* (Baltimore 1935); Maryland Writers' Project, *Maryland, A Guide to the Old Line State* (New York 1940); Footner, Hulbert, *Maryland Main and the Eastern Shore* (New York 1942); id., *Rivers of the Eastern Shore* (New York 1944); Hill, Norman A., ed., *Chesapeake Cruise* (Baltimore 1944); Ray, Joseph M., and Bracken, Claire, *Maryland Fiscal Scene* (College Park 1948); Burdette, Franklin L., *Election Practices in Maryland* (College Park 1950); Clark, Charles B., *The Eastern Shore of Maryland and Virginia*, 3 vols. (New York 1950); State of Maryland, *Reports of Commission on Administrative Organization of the State* (Baltimore 1951), the Soboloff Commission reports; Bard, Harry, *Maryland Today: The State, the People, the Government* (New York 1954); Bodine, A. Aubrey, *Chesapeake Bay and Tidewater* (New York 1954); id., *My Maryland* (Baltimore 1954); Bowen, Don L., and Friedman, Robert S., *Local Government in Maryland* (College Park 1955); Kaessmann, Beta, Manakee, Harold R., and Wheeler, Joseph L., *My Maryland* (Baltimore 1956); Bodine, A. Aubrey, *The Face of Maryland* (Baltimore 1961); Crowl, Philip A., *Maryland During and after the Revolution* (Baltimore 1967); Maryland Historical Society, *Archives of Maryland* (Baltimore 1883 to date); Maryland Hall of Records, *Calendar of Maryland State Papers* (Annapolis 1943 to date); *Maryland Historical Magazine* (1906 to date); Maryland Manual, a compendium of legal, historical, and official information published biennially at Annapolis.

JOSEPH M. RAY
*President, Amarillo College
Formerly Dean, College of Special and Continuation Studies, University of Maryland
Revised by the Editors of "The
Encyclopedia Americana"*

MARYLAND, University of, state-controlled, coeducational university which, as presently established, dates from 1920 when it was formed by combining Maryland Agricultural College Park with the state professional schools in Baltimore. The School of Medicine in Baltimore had been established in 1807 and other professional schools were later added. The Maryland Agricultural College at College Park had been chartered in 1856 and had become the state's land-grant college in 1862.

Most of the individual schools and colleges comprising the university had separate existence before being absorbed in 1920. The schools of Medicine (1807), Dentistry (1840), Pharmacy (1841), Nursing (1889), and Law (1890) are located at Baltimore. At College Park are situated the colleges of Arts and Sciences (1804), Agriculture (1856), Education (1918), and Home Economics (1918); the Graduate School (1918); and the colleges of Engineering, Commerce (1938), Military Science (1946), Special and Continuation Studies (1947), and Physical Education, Recreation and Health (1949). The College of Special and Continuation Studies is unique. It arranges classes for full academic credit at military installations in the environs of Washington, D.C., and in Maryland, and at United States military establishments overseas. The governing board of the university is the Board of Regents, which also serves as the Maryland State Board of Agriculture; its 11 members are appointed by the governor and confirmed by the state senate for 7-year terms. Enrollment at the university exceeds 25,000. See also MARYLAND—*Education and Welfare* (Education).

MARYSVILLE, mâr'ĭz-vĭl, city, California, seat of Yuba County, opposite Yuba City on the Feather River at the influx of the Yuba River, 42 miles north of Sacramento, at an altitude of 60 feet. It is on state and federal highways and the Southern Pacific, Sacramento Northern, and Western Pacific railroads, and is served by the Southwest Airways. It is a trade and shipping center for a fruitgrowing region, with timber tracts and mineral deposits in the area. Formerly a trading post on the California Trail, the town was founded in 1849 as a source of supply in the gold rush and was incorporated in 1851. The government is administered by a mayor and council. Pop. 9,553.

MASACCIO, mä-zät′chô (real name TOM-MASO GUIDI, gwē′dê), Italian painter: b. San Giovanni Valdarno, Italy, Dec. 21, 1401; d. Rome, 1427 or 1428. The known facts of his life are few. In 1422 he enrolled with the guild of doctors and apothecaries, to which painters also belonged, and in 1424 he joined the painters' guild of St. Luke. He knew and was influenced by the sculptor Donatello and the architect Filippo Brunelleschi. In 1426 he painted an altarpiece for the Church of the Carmine in Pisa (since dismembered; the National Gallery in London has the central panel of the *Virgin Enthroned*). In July 1427 he was working in Florence with his younger brother, Giovanni. During this period he did panels for the churches of St. Ambrose and St. Ignatius (the masterly fresco of the Trinity is now in the Church of Santa Maria Novella) and his greatest work, the frescoes for the Brancacci Chapel of the Church of Santa Maria del Carmine, all in Florence. In 1427 or 1428 he went to Rome, where he died sometime before November 1429. While there has been some controversy as to what part of the frescoes in the Brancacci chapel were painted by Masaccio and what part by his master, Masolino da Panicale, it is now generally believed that he worked alone on *The Tribute Money, St. Peter Baptizing, St. Peter and St. John Healing the Sick, Expulsion from the Garden of Eden,* and *St. Peter Distributing Alms; St. Peter Healing the Son of Theophilus* and *St. Peter Enthroned,* begun by him, were finished by Filippino Lippi about 1485. Of all these Brancacci frescoes, *The Tribute Money* and *Expulsion from the Garden of Eden* are most frequently mentioned as Masaccio's greatest achievements. The frescoes in the Church of San Clemente in Rome, formerly attributed to him, are now believed to have been the work of Masolino.

Masaccio was highly praised by Leonardo da Vinci and Giorgio Vasari, and he influenced the work of many painters including Michelangelo and Raphael, but for several centuries his reputation was neglected. Today he is considered one of the greatest painters of the Renaissance, whose innovations in tonal and linear perspective introduced the modern era of painting. He fitted his massive figures naturally into their surroundings, and illuminated his scenes consistently from a single source.

Consult Lindberg, Henrik, *To the Problem of Masolino and Masaccio,* 2 vols. (Stockholm 1931); Berenson, Bernard, *Italian Painters of the Renaissance,* rev. ed. (London 1953).

MASADA, mə-sä′də, was the stronghold where the Jewish Zealots made a last stand against the Romans in 72–73 A.D. It is an isolated rock in Israel, rising some 1,300 feet (400 meters) near the western shore of the Dead Sea.

History. The only ancient source of information about Masada is the writings of Josephus (*Jewish Wars; Antiquities*). According to him, the rock was first fortified by the Hasmonaean high priest Jonathan, who named it Masada ("the fort"). Jonathan may be identified with King Alexander Jannaeus of Judea (reigned 103–76 B.C.). However, it was actually King Herod (reigned 37–4 B.C.) who built the citadel, as a refuge against possible attack by the Egyptians or by descendants of the old Hasmonaean dynasty. Masada was held by a Roman garrison from 4 B.C. to 66 A.D., when the Jewish revolt began and the Zealots seized the fortress.

In 72, two years after the fall of Jerusalem to the Romans, the 10th Legion, led by the Roman governor Silva, encircled the stronghold with eight siege camps and built a ramp 300 feet (90 meters) high against the western side of the rock. The next year Silva breached the walls. The Zealots' leader, Eleazar Ben Yair, then persuaded the 960 men, women, and children in Masada to die free, and they killed each other.

Excavation. In 1955–1956 a joint expedition of the Israeli department of antiquities, the Israel Exploration Society, and the Hebrew University of Jerusalem surveyed Masada and made trial excavations. A second joint expedition under Yigael Yadin excavated and restored 97% of the site in 1963–1965.

The oldest objects found on the top of Masada were coins from the reign of Alexander Jannaeus. All the large structures, dispersed over the plateau of 20 acres (8 hectares), which was surrounded by a casemate wall, had been built by Herod. The largest building was the western palace, Herod's principal residence. On the northern side of the rock, administrative buildings, storehouses, and a bathhouse had been erected, and a 3-tiered palace had been skillfully built on the edge of the cliff.

The buildings were plastered white, and some were decorated with frescoes. In the western palace were found two multicolored mosaics—the earliest of their kind yet discovered in the Holy Land. Great cisterns cut out of the side of the rock received water through an aqueduct.

The Zealots adapted the rooms in the casemate wall and in parts of Herod's palaces to their living needs. They built a synagogue, two ritual baths, and a religious schoolroom, which are the oldest known. The expedition found 700 ostraca (inscribed fragments of pottery), one of which bore the name "Ben Yair." Fragments of 14 scrolls of the books of Genesis, Leviticus, Deuteronomy, Psalms, Ezekiel, Ecclesiasticus, and Jubilee and a scroll belonging to the Dead Sea Scrolls' Community were also discovered. They were important for dating the Dead Sea Scrolls.

Remains of domestic utensils were in the ashes of the Zealots' dwellings. Parts of weapons, including rolling stones and stone balls used against the Romans, bear witness to the drama of Masada. Roman coins left by the Roman garrison between 73 and 111 A.D. and a church and some rooms built during the Byzantine period (5th–6th century A.D.) complete Masada's story.

YIGAEL YADIN, *Author of "Masada"*

MASAI, mä-sī′, are a Nilo-Hamitic people living in the Masai District of southern Kenya and in the Masai Steppe of the United Republic of Tanzania. These people speak a language of Hamitic origin. They are tall and slender, with well-defined features. Formerly the greatest warriors of eastern Africa, their numbers, variously estimated between 50,000 and 150,000, have been greatly reduced, but they still retain their ancient tribal customs. They are grouped into a number of patrilineal, exoganous clans with four endogamous sections. There is no tribal chief; the *laibon,* or medicine man, is the religious head and chief adviser to the councils of military leaders. A nomadic, pastoral people, their most important possessions are cattle, sheep, and goats, and their diet consists largely of meat and milk. Their distinctive houses are low, continuous structures surrounded by thorn fences.

MASAN, mä-sän, is a city in South Korea in South Kyongsang province. It lies along Chinhae Bay off Korea Strait, 26 miles west of Pusan. A commercial and shipping center, it is on a main railway line and has a well-protected harbor. Its industries include fishing, soy making, metalworking, and textile weaving; the chief exports are cotton, fish, and salt. Hot springs and bathing nearby make it a popular resort. The imperial Japanese fleet was defeated off Masan by the Koreans in 1598. The port was opened up to foreign trade and residence in 1899. Population: (1960) 157,547.

MASARYK, má'sà-rik, **Jan Garrigue,** Czechoslovak statesman: b. Prague, Austria-Hungary, Sept. 14, 1886; d. Prague, Czechoslovakia, March 10, 1948. The son of Tomáš Garrigue Masaryk (q.v.) and Charlotte Garrigue, an American, he was educated in Prague. He was forced to serve in the Austro-Hungarian Army through World War I, but joined his father in Prague in 1918 and aided in the establishment of the new Republic of Czechoslovakia. He was sent to Washington as first secretary to the Czechoslovak legation in 1919 and in 1920 became chancellor of the legation in London. He returned to Prague in 1923 and for two years was a secretary in the Ministry of Foreign Affairs in Prague. Appointed minister to Great Britain in 1925, he resigned in September 1938 as a protest against the British and French capitulation to Adolf Hitler at Munich. He was appointed foreign minister, and later deputy prime minister, of the government-in-exile organized by Beneš in 1940, and remained as foreign minister when the government returned to Prague in 1945. He stayed in office after the Communist coup d'état of Feb. 25, 1948, but in less than two weeks his death as a result of jumping from a window of the foreign ministry building was announced by the Communist leaders. Whether his death was caused by suicide or defenestration has never been certain.

MASARYK, má'sà-rik, **Tomáš Garrigue,** Czechoslovak statesman and philosopher: b. Hodonín, Moravia, March 7, 1850; d. Prague, Czechoslovakia, Sept. 14, 1937. The son of a coachman on an Austrian imperial estate, he was taught both Czech and German as a boy. After a brief apprenticeship to a blacksmith, he determined to fulfill his ambition of becoming a teacher and supported himself by tutoring while attending the universities of Vienna and Leipzig, where he married an American student, Charlotte Garrigue, and adopted her last name as his middle name. In 1881 he published his first important sociological work, *Suicide and Modern Civilization.* In 1882 he was invited to the newly organized Czech University of Prague, where he became professor of philosophy, and achieved an outstanding reputation in his field. He founded the critical monthly review, the *Athenaeum,* and took over the political weekly, *Time.* He soon became the spokesman for Young Czechs, a liberal political faction, and was elected to the Austrian Reichsrat in 1891, but resigned two years later to devote more time to the political education of the Czech people. In 1893 he founded a monthly review, Naše doba (*Our Epoch*), and in 1898 published another penetrating study, *The Philosophical and Sociological Foundations of Marxism.* He helped to organize the Progressive Party, popularly known as the Realist Party, which advocated a democratic, federal Austria-Hungary, and was elected to Parliament as candidate of the party in 1907. The idea of an independent nation for his people had already formed in his mind. He fearlessly exposed the duplicity of Austria-Hungary in the high treason trials at Agram (Zagreb). Still a member of the Austrian Parliament, he tried to prevent the declaration of war against Serbia in 1914. Warned of orders for his arrest he left Prague in December, ostensibly for a trip to Italy.

Making London his headquarters during the years of World War I, Masaryk devoted himself to speaking and raising money for the Czech cause, and with Eduard Beneš (q.v.), Josef Durich, and Milan Štefánik organized the national council of an independent Czech government in Paris. He helped to form Czech military units within the Allied armies, and in 1917 went to Russia to recruit a Czech regiment among the prisoners of war there. He advocated nonintervention in the Russian civil war, and eventually the Czech soldiers were sent to join the French army, although not before a clash with the Bolshevik forces. Masaryk's trip to the United States in 1918 led to an official American declaration of sympathy for the Czech aims, and by the fall of 1918 the Republic of Czechoslovakia had been formally recognized by the Allied powers. The new nation was proclaimed in Prague in October, and Masaryk was made the first president; he was re-elected in 1920, 1927, and 1934. Putting into practice the principles to which he had devoted his life, he carried through extensive land reforms, mitigated the extremes of feeling among national minorities, and attempted to reconcile the conflict between church and state. In foreign affairs he backed the League of Nations and participated in the Locarno Pact. On his resignation in December 1935 because of advancing years, he was succeeded by Eduard Beneš.

Masaryk set forth his experiences in *Světová revoluce. Za války i ve valce, 1914–1918* (1925; Eng. tr., *The Making of a State,* 1927), and in *President Masaryk Tells His Story, Recounted by Karel Čapek* (1934). One of his best-known works, *The Spirit of Russia,* was published in English editions in 1919 and 1955.

Bibliography.—Beneš, Eduard, and others, *T.G. Masaryk, 1850–1925* (Prague 1925); Ludwig, Emil, *Defender of Democracy* (New York 1936); Selver, Paul, *Masaryk* (London 1940); Hunt, Richard, *Thomas Garrigue Masaryk* (Pittsburgh 1955).

MASAYA, mä-sä'yä, is a department in southwestern Nicaragua. It has an area of 230 square miles, and is situated on a plateau. Agriculture and stock raising are the chief activities. Major products include rice, coffee, tobacco, corn, sugar, vegetables, fruits, hides, rubber, and dairy products. Population: (1963) 76,580.

MASAYA, a city in Nicaragua, is the capital of Masaya department and its chief industrial and commercial center. The city is situated at a junction of two railway lines and 19 miles southeast of Managua. It is at the foot of an extinct volcano, Masaya, in whose eastern crater is Lake Masaya. Manufactures include cigars, leather, shoes, starch, soap, and handicrafts for which the large Indian population is noted. Masaya is known as the City of Flowers, and thousands attend the fiesta of San Jerónimo every September. Population: (1963) 23,402.

MASBATE, mäs-bä′tä, is an island and province in the Philippines. The island of Masbate, one of the Visayan Islands, lies south of the southeastern end of Luzon and west of Samar. It is approximately 82 miles long and 45 miles wide, with mountainous terrain (the highest peak rises to 2,285 feet) and sizable rivers. The island is deeply indented by Asid Gulf on the southern coast. Major products of the island are rice, sugarcane, kapok, hemp, coconuts, and tobacco. Stock raising is the chief industry, and there is some lumbering, fishing, and weaving. There is extensive gold mining, and there are copper, manganese, and coal deposits. A surfaced highway connects the main cities of Aroroy, Milagros, Masbate (the capital), Dimasalang, and Cataingan. An airline links Masbate and Manila.

Masbate province consists of the islands of Masbate, Ticao, and Burias, with a total area of 1,571 square miles. In 1901 the three islands were united into a subprovince. The province was created in 1939. Population: (1960) 335,971.

MASCAGNI, mäs-kä′nyē, **Pietro,** Italian composer: b. Leghorn (Livorno), Italy, Dec. 7, 1863; d. Rome, Aug. 2, 1945. He studied at the Istituto Luigi Cherubini, and after a measure of success with some early compositions, won the patronage of a wealthy nobleman who sent him to the Milan Conservatory. There the academic routine made Mascagni restless, so he abandoned formal musical studies and for some years conducted traveling opera companies.

Mascagni had settled at Cerignola as manager of the municipal school of music when his one-act opera, *Cavalleria rusticana,* won a competition held by the publisher, Eduardo Sonzogno. It was a resounding success on its first performance in Rome on May 17, 1890, and received equal acclaim wherever it was performed. In his next opera, *L'amico Fritz* (1891), Mascagni failed to achieve a suitable relationship between his music and his libretto.

He wrote 13 more operas and an operetta, *Si,* but was never able to repeat his first success. From 1895 until 1903 he was director of the conservatory at Pesaro, and he achieved a reputation as an orchestra conductor, touring the United States in 1903 and South America in 1911. He was made a member of the Royal Academy of Italy in 1929. He also composed choral and symphonic works.

MASCARA, mas′kə-rə, is a city in Algeria, in Mostaganem department, 50 miles southeast of Oran. Mascara is on the southern slopes of the Tell, at an altitude of 1,800 feet. It is a commercial and wine-making center, and manufactures cement, footwear, rugs, agricultural equipment, and flour. Trade is chiefly in wines, cereals, tobacco, olives, and sheep. Built on the site of a Roman colony, it was the seat of a Turkish beylic from the 16th to the end of the 18th century. Abd-el-Kader was born nearby, and made it his headquarters in 1832. In 1835, it was razed by the French, who lost it to Abd-el-Kader's forces in 1838 but recaptured it in 1841. Population: (1960) 44,839.

MASCOUTAH, mas-kōō′tə, is a city in southwestern Illinois, in St. Clair County, 23 miles southeast of St. Louis. Manufactures include flour, brick, feed, beverages, and hats. The city was incorporated in 1839. Population: 3,625.

MASEFIELD, mäs′fēld, **John** (1878–1967), English writer and poet laureate. He was born June 1, 1878, at Ledbury. Orphaned at an early age, he was sent to join the training ship *Conway* at Liverpool when he was 13. He sailed around Cape Horn in a merchant ship and was on his way to an officer's post on a liner docked at New York when he decided to abandon the sea as a profession. For two years he held various jobs in and near New York, returning to London in 1897.

Masefield had determined to devote himself to writing, and he contributed to various periodicals, while at the same time serving as literary editor of the *Speaker* and writing a column of miscellany for the Manchester *Guardian.* His first book of poetry was *Salt-Water Ballads* (1902); it contained what has remained his best-known short poem, *Sea Fever.* In 1905 a book of stories, *A Mainsail Haul,* appeared, followed in 1909 by the most significant of his early novels, *Multitude and Solitude.* His interest in dramatic writing was expressed in *The Tragedy of Nan, and Other Plays* (1909) and *The Tragedy of Pompey the Great* (1910). *William Shakespeare* (1911), written for the Home University Library, was the first of his critical studies. However, it was the long narrative poem, *The Everlasting Mercy,* printed in the *English Review* of October 1911, that marked the beginning of his fame. Considered violent and even shocking at the time, it was softened by the redemption of the drunken poacher who was the hero. The vein of realism was continued in the narrative poems, *The Widow in the Bye Street* (1912), *The Daffodil Fields* (1913), and *Dauber* (1913). The passion play, *Good Friday* (1915), was the beginning of a series of dramas interweaving verse and prose.

When World War I broke out, Masefield joined a Red Cross unit in France, and later a hospital ship. He recalled the latter experience in a prose narrative of the tragic heroism of battle, *Gallipoli* (1916). A book of poetry, *Lollingdon Downs,* appearing in 1917, was noteworthy for lyrical and meditative passages. His series of lectures in the United States for the Allied cause were collected in *The War and The Future* (1918; published in England as *St. George and the Dragon,* 1919). The long and vivid poem about the hunters and the hunted, *Reynard the Fox,* appeared in 1919 and was followed the next year by one about horse racing, *Right Royal.* One of the best of his novels of adventure was *Sard Harker* (1924).

In 1930, Masefield was appointed poet laureate of England by King George V. This was considered to be an expression of Masefield's widespread popularity.

Among the continued prolific output of his later years may be mentioned a novel about the sea, *The Bird of Dawning* (1933); a verse play, *End and Beginning* (1933), based on the life of Mary, Queen of Scots; and a history of his old training ship, *The "Conway," from Her Foundation to the Present Day* (1933). His subsequent writings include *Some Memories of W.B. Yeats* (1940); *The Nine Days Wonder* (1941); three autobiographical sketches, *In the Mill,* (1941), *New Chum* (1944), and *So Long to Learn* (1952); a new collection of poetry, *Poems, Complete Edition* (1953); *The Bluebells, and Other Verse* (1961); and *Grace Before Ploughing, Fragments of Autobiography* (1966). He died at his home in Berkshire on May 12, 1967.

Further Reading: Fisher, Margery, *John Masefield* (London 1963).

MASER, mā′zər, is a device that can produce electromagnetic waves or increase the amplitude of electromagnetic waves incident on it. Both functions are performed by using fundamental properties of atoms and molecules. Masers are useful in the fields of communications, radio astronomy, precision measurement, and other applications.

Definition. A maser is a basic type of amplifier or oscillator for electromagnetic waves that uses atomic or molecular resonances in the amplifying process. Maser operation depends on the fact that electromagnetic waves of appropriate frequency can stimulate the emission of additional electromagnetic energy from excited atomic and molecular systems.

Because the first maser operated in the microwave frequency range, the word was coined as an acronym for the phrase "microwave amplification by stimulated emission of radiation." Maser amplification principles have now been used for operation at frequencies ranging from the audio-frequency range (20 to 20,000 cycles per second) to the visible and ultraviolet frequency regions of the electromagnetic spectrum, and the term has been extended to include all coherently amplifying devices that utilize molecular or atomic resonances. Hence, the word maser can be interpreted more generally as "molecular amplification by stimulated emission of radiation."

General Characteristics. A maser can be used as a low-noise amplifier of almost ideal sensitivity for applications in fields such as radio astronomy and satellite communications. Since the radiation from a maser is derived from the discrete and constant characteristic frequencies of atomic and molecular systems, it is very low in fluctuations. Thus, maser oscillators are highly monochromatic and extremely stable. Maser oscillators provide pure and extraordinarily precise frequency standards.

Masers have also functioned as oscillators or amplifiers at frequencies more than 1,000 times higher than those reached by other forms of coherent amplifiers. Because ·conventional electromagnetic oscillators depend for their operation on resonant structures with dimensions comparable to the wavelength of the radiation, it has been very difficult to build oscillators that operate at wavelengths shorter than about 1 millimeter (frequencies above 300×10^9 cycles per second). Because the resonant system in a maser is a molecular or atomic one, this requirement on the dimension of a separate resonant structure is absent, and maser oscillators and amplifiers can be built to operate at much higher frequencies.

A wide variety of masers amplify wavelengths in the infrared, visible, or ultraviolet regions of the electromagnetic spectrum where the wavelength can be as short as one three-thousandth millimeter. An optical maser, or one operating at visible frequencies, has been given the name *laser,* an acronym for "*l*ight *a*mplification by *s*timulated *e*mission of *r*adiation" (see LASER).

PHYSICAL PRINCIPLES

Although the idea that a practical oscillator or amplifier could be built by using stimulated emission is relatively new, the concept of stimulated emission goes back many years. As early as 1917, Albert Einstein showed, on the basis of thermodynamic arguments and the quantum ideas of Niels Bohr, that energetically excited atoms or molecules could be stimulated to emit electromagnetic radiation.

Energy Levels. Bohr had used Max Planck's concept of discrete "quantized" energy levels to explain the striking series of emission lines observed at different frequencies in the spectrum of radiation emitted in a hydrogen discharge. To explain the series of lines, Bohr also had to assume that a hydrogen atom in an excited state of energy E_1 would fall to a lower state of energy E_2 and emit light at a definite frequency f, as shown in the equation:

$$hf = E_1 - E_2 \qquad (1)$$

where h is Planck's constant.

The frequency defined by this relation is called a characteristic or resonance frequency of the system because transitions between the two energy levels are accompanied by the absorption or emission of light at frequency f. This terminology comes by analogy from classical mechanics, where an oscillator with a resonance frequency f can absorb or give up energy when driven by a force at frequency f.

Energy Distribution. The next important consideration is the distribution in energy of a collection or ensemble of atoms or molecules at equilibrium at a temperature T. Thermodynamics shows that the probability of occupation of a given energy level anywhere in the ensemble is given by Ludwig Boltzmann's law:

$$P = Ce^{-E/kT} \qquad (2)$$

where E is the energy of the level, k is Boltzmann's constant, and C is a constant. Thus, in temperature equilibrium, there are fewer molecules or atoms in a state of higher energy than in one of lower energy.

Emission and Absorption. Einstein considered the conditions for a collection of molecules to be in equilibrium according to Boltzmann's law (2), and also to be in equilibrium with radiation

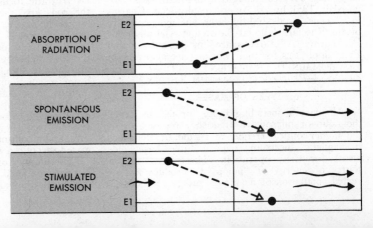

Fig. 1.
When an atom absorbs a packet of radiation energy (wavy arrow), an electron (black dot) of the atom is raised from a lower energy level E_1 to a higher energy level E_2. When an electron falls from E_2 to E_1, the atom *spontaneously* emits a packet of radiation energy (wavy arrow). Stimulated emission occurs when a packet of radiation energy interacts with an atom that has an electron in level E_2. This packet of radiation stimulates emission but is undiminished by the interaction. When the electron falls to the E_1 level, a packet of energy is emitted. Thus there are two packets of emitted radiation.

ABSORPTION OF RADIATION

SPONTANEOUS EMISSION

STIMULATED EMISSION

at the same temperature. For any pair of energy levels E_1 and E_2 of the molecules of the system, only radiation at the frequency f given by (1) will interact with the pair. He was able to show that $R(f)$, the rate of change of radiation intensity at the frequency f, was related to the radiation intensity $I(f)$ by:

$$R(f) = AN_1 + BI(f)N_1 - BI(f)N_2, \qquad (3)$$

where N_1 is the number of molecules in state E_1; N_2 is the number of molecules in state E_2; and A and B are constants.

The first term on the right side in (3) is independent of $I(f)$; that is, it does not depend on the presence of electromagnetic waves. This term represents what is called *spontaneous emission*. The second term, which is proportional to the population of the excited state and to the intensity of radiation, represents *stimulated emission*. The third term, which is proportional to the population of the ground state and to $I(f)$, represents *absorption*. (See Fig. 1.)

In thermal equilibrium, $R(f)$, the rate of change of intensity at frequency f, must be zero; and indeed, the coefficients A and B are related so that when N_1 and N_2 have their thermal equilibrium values, the right side of (3) is zero. The spontaneous emission term in (3) allows the emission from a smaller number of molecules N_1 in the higher energy state to balance the absorption due to the larger number of molecules N_2 in the lower state.

When stimulated emission takes place, the atoms and molecules of the system radiate at the frequency f in the same direction and in step (or coherently) with the electromagnetic wave already present. If there were no stimulated absorption terms, then an electromagnetic wave present initially would grow in amplitude. In a medium at thermal equilibrium, absorption will counteract stimulated emission and no such growth will occur. However, if some means is used to make the population N_1 of the upper state greater than the population N_2 of the lower state, then stimulated emission can override absorption, and a growing wave results.

The condition when N_1 is greater than N_2 is called an inverted population because Boltzmann's law (2) does not allow this condition under thermal equilibrium at any positive absolute temperature. Generally the growing wave is partially confined by reflecting surfaces so that it passes back and forth over the molecules many times in order to produce large amounts of stimulated emission. This allows the wave to build up to continuous oscillation.

The use of stimulated emission in this manner to produce an electromagnetic oscillator was proposed in 1951 by an American physicist, Charles H. Townes, and slightly later but independently by the Russians Nikolai Basov and Aleksandr M. Prokhorov. All three shared in the 1964 Nobel Prize in physics for their work. (See also ATOM; ELECTROMAGNETIC RADIATION; LIGHT—1. *Introduction, 2. Properties*; QUANTUM THEORY.)

TYPES OF MASERS

All masers, including those for use in either the radio or microwave frequency regions, or in the higher optical-frequency region of the electromagnetic spectrum, require three basic elements for their operation. These are: (1) a source of energy or "pump" to produce an inverted population of a pair of energy levels; (2)

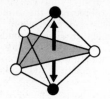

Fig. 2.
The nitrogen atom of an ammonia molecule (NH_3) moves back and forth through the plane formed by the three hydrogen atoms. The ammonia molecule can occupy either a higher energy level or a lower level.

an active region in which the population is inverted; and (3) a region in which the electromagnetic wave interacts with the molecules. Usually, the last element involves a resonant structure that stores the electromagnetic energy and promotes a strong interaction.

In the maser *amplifier,* population inversion is produced, but the losses of radiation from the resonant structure (or interaction region) to the outside are great enough to quench oscillations. However, when a signal is fed to the maser from outside, it produces a net coherent stimulated emission, and the signal emitted from the maser is amplified. The ratio of the intensity of the emitted signal to that of the incoming signal is called the gain of the amplifier.

In a maser *oscillator,* the rate of stimulated emission exceeds that of losses in the resonant structure or to the outside. The resonant structure then provides feedback to lock the emission in coherent oscillation. The signal amplitude builds up and approaches a steady state usually limited by the "pumping"—that is, the supply of energy to the molecules.

A few of the important specific types of masers that operate in the radio-frequency or microwave-frequency region are the ammonia, paramagnetic, and hydrogen masers.

Ammonia Maser. The first maser oscillator, built by Charles H. Townes, James P. Gordon, and Herbert J. Zeiger, was put in operation in 1954. This maser made use of the characteristic frequency of the ammonia molecule (NH_3). This frequency is called the ammonia inversion frequency. It corresponds to the frequency with which the nitrogen atom in the ammonia molecule moves back and forth through the triangle formed by the hydrogen atoms of the structure (see Fig. 2). The inversion frequency of ammonia is 24,000 megacycles per second (1 megacycle equals 1,000,000 cycles), which is in the microwave range.

The source of radiation in the maser is a beam of ammonia molecules traveling through an evacuated chamber (see Fig. 3). To produce population inversion, the beam passes first through a set of electrostatic focusing rods. Electric fields between the rods give the upper energy level of the ammonia inversion pair an electric dipole moment that produces a focusing component of motion for these molecules. On the other hand, they give the lower energy level an electric dipole moment of opposite sign, and hence it is defocused. The beam of ammonia molecules leaving the focuser is thus in a state of inverted population. The beam of molecules next enters a resonant microwave cavity, which is tuned to the ammonia inversion frequency. Here stimulated emission occurs, and a continuous microwave signal leaves the maser through a wave guide.

The number of molecules in an ammonia beam is relatively small, and therefore the power emitted by an ammonia maser oscillator is quite weak,

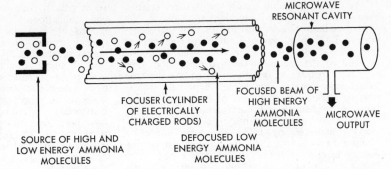

Fig. 3.
In the ammonia-beam maser, ammonia molecules in two energy levels pass into a focuser that sorts them. The lower-energy-level molecules (white) do not enter the cavity, but the upper-energy-level molecules (black) do enter. These molecules initiate an oscillating electromagnetic field in the microwave resonant cavity. The microwave-frequency radiation from the cavity is sent into a wave guide.

MICROWAVE RESONANT CAVITY

FOCUSER (CYLINDER OF ELECTRICALLY CHARGED RODS)

FOCUSED BEAM OF HIGH ENERGY AMMONIA MOLECULES

MICROWAVE OUTPUT

SOURCE OF HIGH AND LOW ENERGY AMMONIA MOLECULES

DEFOCUSED LOW ENERGY AMMONIA MOLECULES

approximately 10^{-9} watt. Furthermore, the ammonia resonance frequency is quite sharp and invariable. Hence, this maser is useful as a low-power oscillator of very constant frequency, but it cannot amplify over a wide enough range of frequencies to be generally useful as an amplifier.

Paramagnetic Maser. Paramagnetic ions in crystals can serve as the active element in a maser that has general utility as an amplifier. The energy levels of a magnetic ion in a crystal depend on the orientation of the ion magnetic moment with respect to both the crystal axes and an applied magnetic field. The frequency width of a paramagnetic ion resonance depends on interaction with other ions and with crystalline fields. By a suitable choice of a crystal and the concentration of an impurity in the crystal, the width of the resonance can be varied from a fraction of a megacycle to hundreds of megacycles. Thus, the range of frequencies (or bandwidth) over which a maser amplifier will operate can be varied widely. Furthermore, the dependence of the resonance frequency on an external magnetic field makes a paramagnetic maser quite tunable (the relationship is roughly 2.8 megacycles per gauss of applied magnetic field).

Although a wide variety of paramagnetic maser amplifiers have been proposed or put into operation, the most generally convenient type, the three-level paramagnetic maser, was suggested by Nicolaas Bloembergen in 1956 and first operated by Henry E.D. Scovil, George Feher, and Harold Seidel in 1957.

Suppose that the active medium of the maser has three energy levels, as shown in Fig. 4. A strong pump signal at the microwave frequency f_{3-1} (23,100 megacycles in this case) produces transitions between levels 1 and 3 so effectively that the system cannot return to thermal equilibrium, and the populations of these two levels become nearly equal. In this case the population of level 2, which is normally less than that of level 1 and greater than that of level 3 in thermal equilibrium, can become less than that of level 3.

The population inversion between levels 3 and 2 then permits oscillation or amplification at f_{3-2} (9,400 megacycles in the case shown). Depending on the parameters of the systems, population inversion may occur instead between levels 1 and 2, and the maser operates at f_{2-1}.

The first paramagnetic maser amplifier was a microwave resonant cavity system that used a rare-earth ion in a water-soluble crystal as the active medium. Soon afterward, paramagnetic masers with more desirable operating characteristics were designed and built by using other active media, notably ruby (chromium ions in aluminum oxide). Traveling-wave masers, which have broader bandwidth, also have replaced the cavity masers.

In order to achieve a large enough inverted population in a paramagnetic system to produce maser action, the crystal must be cooled to a low temperature. Usually this is done by using liquid helium to obtain a temperature of about $4°K$. The cooling serves mainly to make the thermal equilibrium population of levels 1 and 2 small and to reduce the rate of processes that tend to restore thermal equilibrium among the levels.

If the frequency bandwidth over which amplification occurs is indicated by Δf, then the intensity of intrinsic noise emitted by a maser amplifier is the same as what would be produced by an input signal of $\dfrac{\Delta f}{1-(N_2/N_1)}$ photons per second. (The photon is the smallest unit of electromagnetic energy, hf, that can exist.) The well-designed maser, with N_2/N_1 much less than unity, can detect a signal about as small as the intrinsic noise, Δf photons per second. This is the smallest amount of noise that a coherent amplifier is allowed by the uncertainty principle of quantum mechanics, and hence the maser represents the most sensitive amplifier that can, in principle, be constructed. Actual performance of sensitive maser amplifiers comes rather close to this ideal limit.

It is sometimes convenient to define amplifier noise in terms of effective noise temperature. The effective noise temperature of a well-designed maser approaches the value $\dfrac{hf}{k}$, or a fraction of one degree absolute in the normal microwave range. Other microwave amplifiers that were available when the maser was invented characteristically depended on the use of electron tubes, and their noise was hundreds of times stronger. Since then, another type of low-noise microwave amplifier, the parametric amplifier, has begun to compete with the maser, but it does not match the effective noise temperature of the maser.

Hydrogen Maser. In 1960, H. Mark Goldenberg, Daniel Kleppner, and Norman F. Ramsey,

Fig. 4.
The energy levels shown are for chromium ions in ruby with a particular crystalline orientation, and using a magnetic field intensity of 3,900 oersteds. The frequency of the pumping field is 23,100 megacycles per second. The oscillation frequency is 9,400 megacycles per second.

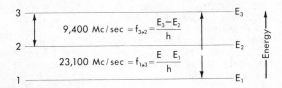

$$9{,}400 \text{ Mc/sec} = f_{3-2} = \frac{E_3-E_2}{h}$$

$$23{,}100 \text{ Mc/sec} = f_{1-3} = \frac{E\;E_1}{h}$$

Jr., reported observing maser oscillations from a beam maser that used atomic hydrogen as the active medium. The transition in this maser occurs at 1,421 megacycles. Radiation is emitted at this frequency when the nuclear-spin magnetic moment of the proton in the hydrogen atom flips over with respect to the direction of the electron magnetic moment. This same "hyperfine transition" is a source of radiation of enormous importance in the field of radio astronomy.

In the hydrogen-beam maser, population inversion is achieved by using magnetic deflecting plates that separate atoms in the upper hyperfine energy level from those in the lower one. The atoms in the upper state enter a quartz bottle inside a cavity that is resonant at 1,421 megacycles. The atoms of hydrogen bounce about in the bottle and may make as many as 10,000 collisions with the walls before falling to the lower hyperfine level. Because of the long lifetime of the excited state, the resonance frequency in this maser is extremely sharp. Thus, this maser is an exceedingly constant-frequency oscillator. (See also ELECTRONICS—*Microwave Electronics;* MAGNETISM; QUANTUM THEORY.)

APPLICATIONS

Maser-type amplification has provided the key element for a new field called *quantum electronics.* As previously in the field of electronics, there is control and use of electromagnetic waves, but the field of quantum electronics also involves utilizing ideas and devices that depend on the quantum nature of waves and of atomic or molecular systems. The new field unites the classical areas of radio and electronics with those of optics, spectroscopy, and quantum mechanics.

The general utility, flexibilty, and power of maser devices appear to be comparable to those characteristics of the vacuum tube or the transistor, although they differ in detail. While perhaps more varied in its functioning than the transistor amplifier, the maser amplifier is generally somewhat more complex and specialized, and hence is not likely to see as wide use as the transistor in everyday devices. However, masers, including lasers, have already found uses in such widely diverse applications as surgery, three-dimensional photography, diamond drilling, communications, and very high-precision scientific experiments.

Masers usually work with electromagnetic waves. However, maser ideas also have been applied to the amplification and generation of acoustic waves.

Masers display some of their most spectacular features and have their widest variety of applications in the infrared, visible, and ultraviolet regions. Man's ability to produce and control amplification at short wavelengths, and thereby obtain intense coherent beams of light, has opened up a wide variety of scientific and technological uses of optical masers, or lasers (see LASERS). Attention here will be directed toward the less extensive but important applications of masers in the microwave- and radio-frequency regions.

Communications. One of the difficulties with which the communications field must cope is the crowding of channels in the normal broadcast bands. Because a certain minimum bandwidth must be made available to a broadcaster in order to transmit messages with reasonable fidelity, stations must be assigned broadcast frequencies sufficiently separated to avoid interference. There is room for an enormous increase in the number of communications channels if broadcasting can be moved up into the microwave and higher frequency range. However, at higher frequencies, communication is limited to the distance along the line of sight. For this reason, microwave relay stations are used to extend telephone communications across the country.

Satellite relay stations can be used to provide transoceanic microwave communications. Masers have been used in a number of satellite relay systems in order to provide sensitive detection and a minimum of interference from noise. Sensitive detection greatly reduces the broadcast power that must be used.

As a test of a microwave satellite communications system, a large aluminum-coated balloon (Echo I) was launched into earth orbit in 1960. Contact was established between installations of the Bell Telephone Laboratories in Holmdel, N.J., the Jet Propulsion Laboratory at Goldstone, Calif., and the Naval Research Laboratory at Stump Neck, Md. These systems, which operated at 2,390 megacycles, used traveling-wave paramagnetic masers to provide sensitive detection of signals bounced off Echo I.

In 1962 the Telstar satellite was put in orbit and used for communication between Andover, Me., and stations at Pleumeur-Bodou in France and Goonhilly Downs in England. The Telstar system operated in two frequency bands, from 3,700 to 4,200 megacycles and from 5,925 to 6,425 megacycles. The satellite was an active relay station—it received signals, amplified them, and rebroadcasted them to the ground receivers. These receivers used traveling-wave maser amplifiers. The Early Bird satellite, which is the first one to give regular commercial service, uses the same ground-based receivers as those developed for the Telstar. A traveling-wave maser amplifier is commonly used in sensitive communications receivers.

Space-Probe Experiments. Space probes must send intelligible signals to earth from enormous distances. The power of microwave sources that can be placed aboard such probes is limited by considerations of weight. For this reason, amplifiers of great sensitivity and low noise must be used at ground stations to detect weak signals from space probes. Paramagnetic maser amplifiers have been used in a number of cases.

In 1964, the Ranger VII lunar probe broadcast TV pictures of the moon's surface back to earth —238,000 miles away. The pictures were taken at distances ranging from 1,000 miles to 1,000 feet from the lunar surface. In 1965, Mariner IV transmitted pictures of the surface of Mars to earth over a distance of 134,000,000 miles. At that time, Mariner IV was 6,118 miles from the Martian surface, after traveling 325,000,000 miles through space. In both of these projects, the transmitted signals were picked up by using a maser amplifier in the receiver system. It is likely that maser receivers will be used in most long-distance space-probe experiments of the future.

Radio Astronomy. The value of maser amplifiers to radio astronomy was very quickly apparent after their development. The first successful application of masers in this field was in 1958 when Leonard E. Alsop, Joseph A. Giordmaine, Cornell H. Mayer, and Charles H. Townes used maser amplifiers in combination with the U.S. Naval Research Laboratory radio telescope to study the effective surface temperature of Venus and Jupiter.

A very important source of discrete radiation in radio astronomy is the emission of 1,421-megacycle radiation by atomic hydrogen, the same transition as in the hydrogen maser. The intensity of the emission depends on the density of atomic hydrogen in space and its effective temperature. The frequency of the radiation may be shifted, because of the relative motion of the source and earth (see DOPPLER'S PRINCIPLE). By measuring both the intensity and frequency of the Doppler-shifted hydrogen emission line, it is possible to map the amount of hydrogen gas and its velocity distribution in our galaxy or to examine the hydrogen in other galaxies. Masers in radio telescopes have been used by Eugene Epstein at the Harvard College Observatory and others to study the hydrogen emission from galactic sources and from sources outside our galaxy.

Studies of the Doppler shift of radar signals reflected from different portions of the surface of Venus indicate that Venus is rotating in the opposite direction from other planets in the solar system. Some of these observations made use of a maser amplifier in the radio telescope.

One recent application of a microwave traveling-wave maser to radio astronomy is the detection of background sky radiation at microwave frequencies. If all the other background sources of noise are known, then any excess must be due to the sky radiation entering the antenna of the radio telescope. Since the equivalent noise temperature of a maser is low and can be determined accurately, the background sky radiation can be measured. This was done by Arno A. Penzias and Robert W. Wilson of Bell Telephone Laboratories. The presence of background radiation is not fully understood, but it may have important implications for theories of the origin of the universe.

Test of Special Theory of Relativity. The celebrated experiment by Albert A. Michelson and Edward W. Morley, first undertaken in 1881, looked for an apparent shift in the wavelength of light due to the motion of earth through a postulated medium (the ether) in which light is propagated. The absence of a shift, demonstrated by the experiment, was an essential key to the development of Einstein's special theory of relativity. A similar but far more accurate experiment making use of ammonia masers was performed by John P. Cedarholm and Charles H. Townes in 1959. In this case the motion of the beam of molecules in an ammonia maser relative to the ether should give rise to a Doppler shift in frequency, which was not observed. This experiment puts a limit on isotropy in the velocity of light, or in the velocity of the ether (if it exists), with respect to the earth, of less than one thousandth the orbital velocity of the earth.

Frequency and Time Standards. Before the advent of modern "atomic clocks," the best available frequency standards were oscillators stabilized on the frequencies of oscillation of quartz crystals. However, such standards gradually change with time, and they must be calibrated by comparison with another standard. The newer frequency standards based on atomic or molecular resonances are more truly "standard" in that their frequency is determined primarily by natural constants. At present one of the most useful and common standards of frequency is an oscillator stabilized on a characteristic radio-frequency absorption of a beam of cesium atoms. The frequency stability of the cesium atomic clock, when averaged over some time, has the impressive value

of 1 part in 10^{11} or 10^{12}, but the purity of its spectrum is not quite so high in quality.

The sharp characteristic frequencies of atomic and molecular transitions in maser oscillators suggest their use as frequency standards. The ammonia maser emits a signal that is one of the purest frequencies available. However, the oscillation frequency is in part determined by the resonance frequency of the cavity in which emission takes place, and cavity frequency drift limits the long-term stability of this maser to about 1 part in 10^{12}. In the hydrogen-beam maser, because of the extremely long lifetime of the excited state, the hydrogen resonance is so sharp that the coupling to the cavity is much less important, and a long-time frequency stability of about 1 part in 10^{13} seems to be quite practical.

The older standard of time was the solar second, which was defined in terms of the length of the solar day. It is now much more satisfactory to use a frequency standard as a time standard by defining the second as the time interval in which a fixed number of cycles of oscillation of the standard occur. The hydrogen maser is thus a candidate for being the source of our standard of time. The atomic clocks afford methods of checking the constancy of the solar second or of performing other time measurements with previously unavailable precision.

Measurement of Magnetic Fields. Another interesting application of the maser principle is in the design of magnetometers (devices for the measurement of magnetic field intensity). Measurement of resonant frequency for either nuclear or electron magnetic moments in a magnetic field offers a method of great accuracy for determining field intensity because the frequency is directly proportional to the field intensity. However, absorption of electromagnetic energy at resonance due to a collection of magnetic moments in thermal equilibrium is rather small, especially at small magnetic field intensities. To overcome this difficulty, methods of pumping have been devised that produce population inversion of the energy levels of the magnetic moments.

A. Abragam, J. Combrisson, and I. Solomon developed a magnetometer that makes use of the hydrogen nuclear magnetic moments in a sample of water. These moments are coupled to electron magnetic moments also present in the sample. When a strong signal is applied at the electron-moment resonance frequency, sufficient population inversion is produced in the nuclear moments to initiate maser oscillations. The frequency of these oscillations is directly proportional to the magnetic field around the water sample. This frequency can be measured with great precision.

Bibliography.—Gordon, James P., "The Maser," *Scientific American,* Vol. 199, No. 6, pp. 42–50 (New York 1958); Schawlow, Arthur L., "Optical Masers," *Scientific American,* Vol. 204, No. 6, pp. 52–61 (New York 1961); Townes, Charles H., "Masers," *The Age of Electronics,* ed. by Carl F.J. Overhage (New York 1962); Klein, H. Arthur, *Masers and Lasers* (New York 1963); Birnbaum, George, *Optical Masers* (New York 1964); Siegman, A.E., *Microwave Solid-State Masers* (New York 1964); Townes, Charles H., "Production of Coherent Radiation by Atoms and Molecules," *Science,* Vol. 149, No. 3686, pp. 831–841 (Washington, D.C., 1965).

CHARLES H. TOWNES
Nobel Prize Winner in Physics
Provost and Professor of Physics
Massachusetts Institute of Technology
HERBERT J. ZEIGER
Group Leader, Solid-State Theory
Lincoln Laboratory
Massachusetts Institute of Technology

MASINISSA, mas-i-nis′ə, king of Numidia: b. about 240 B.C.; d. about 149 B.C. Masinissa (also spelled *Massinissa*) at first was the ruler of only the eastern portion of Numidia. About 203 B.C., during the Second Punic War, with the help of the Romans, he defeated Syphax, the king of western Numidia. He took Syphax prisoner along with his wife, Sophonisba, who was the daughter of the Carthaginian general, Hasdrubal. She had formerly been promised to Masinissa, who now made her his wife. But Scipio the Elder, commanding the Roman forces, was fearful of her influence, and he claimed her as a prisoner of Rome. Because he was not able to resist the demands of Scipio, Masinissa sent Sophonisba a bowl that contained poison, which she voluntarily drank. Masinissa commanded the Roman cavalry on the right wing at the battle of Zama, which ended the Second Punic War (201 B.C.). As a reward the Romans gave him the territory formerly held by Syphax. In peace he proved himself an efficient administrator.

MASK, a covering for the face, often shaped so as to form a rude representation of human or animal features. The study of masks, or false faces, forms an important chapter in anthropology as well as in the history of art. Evidence of the manufacture and use of masks appears in the Old Stone Age among pictures preserved on the walls of caverns in western Europe. Perhaps the best known of these is the figure of a dancing man in the cavern of Trois Frères, Ariège, France, painted in the Magdalenian period. The head of this figure is covered by the skull of a deer, the attached skin covering his body. A visitor to Indian villages in New Mexico and Arizona may still see among other masked dancers a so-called Kachina, strikingly reminiscent of this very ancient cave dancer, his body draped in the skin of a deer, his head hidden in a grotesque mask upon which are mounted the antlers of a deer.

The best surviving cave drawings of masked dancers, however, are to be seen in the cave of Mige in France (see Keith Henderson, *Prehistoric Man.*) The heads of these dancers are covered with the skulls of chamoislike animals, the attached skins of the original living creatures falling over the dancers' bodies. So well-drawn are these figures that one can almost see the vigorous movements of the dancers.

Drawings published by George Catlin (1796–1872), Maximilian zu Wied (1782–1867) and other early explorers of the Missouri River country show us Indians of the time dancing in masks representing the heads of bears and buffalo, with their bodies draped in the skins of these animals.

The transition from the primitive realistic use of animal heads to the manufacture of imaginative demon and dragon faces seems to have been made in early Neolithic times, appearing in the art of the most ancient civilizations of 6,000 and more years ago. These evidences of antiquity in the use of masks, and the survival of their uses among all primitive peoples of the world, justify the assumption that the use of masks is as universal as speech and almost as ancient in origin. Their function as a mode of expression is so fundamental that they are still used by the most civilized peoples. That they played an indispensable role in the early evolution of the stage is obvious.

Anthropologists consider one of the most universal interests of mankind to have been the observation and study of mammals, birds, and reptiles. Primitive man was intrigued by the mysterious behavior of animals, which was everywhere interpreted in terms of human experience. Cave man art suggests that, almost from the earliest times, man chose animal characters for his fictional narratives. Surviving folk tales collected from savage peoples and those handed down to us from our pagan European ancestors indicate that the bedtime story, Uncle Remus stories, and other such tales are as old as the human race. Drawings in caves indicate that dancing began with the impersonation of real living serpents and animals with masks and costumes, leading soon to imaging grotesque demons and saints, as the case might require.

While the use of masks in the abstract is ancient and universal, masks vary in style, technique, and art to such a degree that a worldwide collection of masks throws much light on human geography, history, and archaeology. Like stone tools, metalwork, and ceramics, their classification as to place and time affords one of the most satisfactory objective records of man's career upon the earth. Hence, they play a large role in museums of anthropology, history, and art. In fact it is difficult to conceive of any study of art, graphic or theatrical, not based objectively upon collections of masks. For example, the role played by masked animal gods in the tomb and temple paintings of Egypt, in the heroic sculptures of Ur, Babylon, and other ancient Asiatic cities, is extremely illuminating, and so is the part played by the masked gods of Tibet and China, who appear in religious festival folk dances. How empty and dreary would be the mere verbal narratives of ancient and surviving primitive peoples without collections of masks to use as illustrations!

The modern geographical distribution of masks is of interest. In the New World, the Indians show special regional styles in masks. The most elaborate development appears among the coastal Indians of British Columbia and southern Alaska, where large wooden masks are in use. These objects form a large part of museum collections from that area. Both animal and human heads are depicted in these masks; some of the heads representing birds and mammals are of extraordinary size, and by means of cords the wearer can roll their eyes about, and open and snap their jaws. Other heads are double or triplicate, opened out by the dancers at will, revealing entirely different faces within. Even the Eskimos of Alaska use masks, but Eskimo masks are smaller, not so complicated.

The Indians of the Southwest, the Apache, Navajo, and Pueblo tribes, use numerous highly colored masks of wood and textile materials to impersonate gods and other supernatural creatures.

The Plains Indians formerly supported a series of ceremonies in which some animal masks were worn, but, comparatively speaking, their mask culture was weak. The same thing is true of California Indians. East of the Mississippi, the chief mask area is among the Iroquois, whose false-face ceremonies are famous. Some of the Iroquois masks are woven of cornhusks, but the most conspicuous are those of wood;

MASK

Left: This comical creature was created from a gourd by the Zuñi Indians of New Mexico.

Right: A painted wooden mask by natives of the Admiralty Islands, north of New Guinea.

Below: Fine artistic skill is shown in this creation of the Tsimshians, British Columbia.

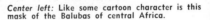

Center left: Like some cartoon character is this mask of the Balubas of central Africa.

Center right: A Tibetan devil dancer, whose visage should frighten off any evil spirit.

Lower left: Seal effigy mask, fashioned of weathered driftwood by the Alaskan Eskimos.

Lower right: A birdlike mask from Alaska. It is one of a type representing animal spirits.

Below: Wooden casque mask, worn like a helmet, is the work of Belgian Congo natives.

The American Museum of Natural History; Museum of the American Indian; Ewing Galloway; National Film Board; Musée de l'Homme

MASK

Top left: Basil Rathbone, left, and Christopher Plummer donned masks depicting God and Satan, respectively, in the drama *J.B.*

Top center: Actress Katharine Hepburn, shown in mask by the noted designer Wladyslaw T. Benda (1873–1948), for the movie *Dragon Seed.*

Top right: A pontificating judge is portrayed by a French comedian. By using masks, entertainers can satirize life with pungent effect.

Bottom left: Carved wooden mask from the Republic of Gabon, formerly French Equatorial Africa, in the Ogooué River style.

Bottom center: Kwakiutl Indian mask from Vancouver Island, off British Columbia, was used in dances to illustrate clan legends.

Bottom right: This fantastic creation, of painted bark cloth stretched over a wood frame, adorned tribal dancers in New Guinea.

Pix; Ben Washer; Watson-Guptill Publications; The American Museum of Natural History

fearful distortions of the human face used in an annual ceremony to drive away disease. In pre-Columbian Mexico, priests wore magnificent masks, decked with plumes. Warriors led their troops to battle arrayed in impressive plumed masks, as did the peoples of the Andean Highlands. The marginal peoples in both of the Americas presented far less developed mask practices, but rarely is a tribe found wholly ignorant of the art of using masks.

In the Old World, the development of masks is also uneven. Some masks were made in Africa, notably in central West Africa and in isolated parts of the Sudan, but, as a whole, the development of masks throughout the continent remained weak. India, also, has shown little interest in masks. On the other hand, the religious cults of Tibet, Siam, China, and the Malay countries reveled in the production and use of masks. New Guinea, Indonesia, and parts of Melanesia are conspicuous producers of masks and masked dancing. Polynesia, on the other hand made little use of such objects.

Australia is often thought of as devoid of crafts and arts, but often the chief actors in their elaborate ceremonies have masks built upon their bodies and faces, of almost unbelievable complexity and conceived on highly original lines. The likeness of some of these masks have been preserved by photography; usually they are destroyed in removal from the body.

Siberia and Arctic America were weak in the use of masks. Europe saw a considerable development of masks in early times, but the Romans showed less interest in them. While the old religions of ancient Mediterranean civilizations show the use of masks, these objects found their way but moderately into pre-Roman Europe. Surviving folk festivals in Europe suggest that, in early pagan times, masks were important in clownish performances rather than in serious impersonations of supernatural beings.

CLARK WISSLER.

Bibliography.—Stevenson, M. C., "The Sia," *Eleventh Report of the Bureau of Ethnology* (Washington 1893); Boas, F., "The Social Organization and Secret Societies of the Kwakiutl Indians," *Report of the United States National Museum for 1895* (Washington 1896); Hodge, G. M., *The Kachinas Are Coming* (Los Angeles 1936); Wissler, C., "Masks," *Science Guide*, American Museum of Natural History (New York 1946); Bedouin, Jean L., *Les masques* (Paris 1961)

MODERN MASKS

Masks to cover the face or head are used for playful disguising, as in masquerade and carnival; for dramatic effect or characterization, as in ballet, theater, and film; and for protection, as in sport, industry, and war.

Masquerade, carnival, and theater masks are descended from the primitive ritual falseface which identified the wearer, by mystic transference of properties and spirit, with the being represented by the mask. It is for this reason that a masker, even in this day, when a matter-of-fact attitude toward the supernatural has become common, still produces an uncanny effect.

At masquerades the domino, or halfmask, is generally worn. It covers the upper half of the face but leaves the mouth free. The halfmask, developed in the Italian masked comedy of the Renaissance, when mimes began to improvise speeches, became popular as a stock disguise in the streets at carnival time, and even fashionable as a sunshade and adjunct to coquetry. Often black, the halfmask may be colored as well; it is made of velvet, satin, or papier-mâché, shaped to fit over the forehead, cheeks, and nose, and is held on by cords or ribbons running from the sides around the head.

During carnival in Latin countries, many special masks are worn in parades and spectacles. Masks may have the form of gigantic heads, of humanized animals, or they may be fantastic. In Basel and other Swiss cities, there are masking societies which vie with each other in inventing caricatures with current application; such masks may comment upon political affairs. In the Tyrol, some carnival masks, clearly survivals of pagan times, represent demons and animistic spirits, while others are grotesques without historic models. In Mexico and Guatemala, some masks hark back to pre-Columbian times, some commemorate the coming of the conquistadores, and some are modern inventions. Carnival masks are often made of papier-mâché, and are discarded after being worn once; but some (as in the Tyrol) are of carved wood, or (as in Mexico) of tin or gesso-covered cactus pith.

Masks may be said to have an unknown tradition of use in the theater. Greek and Egyptian drama, arising from a religious ceremonial, were masked. At the height of its native development, about 100 B.C., Roman drama lost the mask, but regained it when Greek theater fashions came in at the time of Quintus Roscius. Traveling mountebanks of the Middle Ages played in masks; church drama had need of masks for the figures of God, angels, saints, and devils. In the day of Shakespeare, the court masque continued the medieval usage of players in vizors. Ballet dancers often wore masks, for ballet grew out of the court masque. The plays of the Roman playwright Terence (190?–?159 B.C.) were revived in masks when Goethe produced them at Weimar in the 18th century. English pantomimes and continental extravaganzas in the 19th century frequently used masked sprites, demons, and grotesques; a procession of "big heads," or players with oversized masks, was an expected feature of all such entertainments.

A revival of the mask in the theater at the beginning of the present century may be traced to Gordon Craig's writings in his magazine, *The Mask*, and to his mask designs. From 1910 on, V. E. Meyerhold in St. Petersburg, in his struggle against the realistic stage, used masks in his formalized productions of plays dealing with the fantastic and the subconscious. In 1914, Percy MacKaye used masks in vast open-air pageants such as his *Masque of St. Louis*. In the 1920's, there was a widespread experimentation with masks in the theatre. Edmond Dulac made masks for poetic dance-dramas by William Butler Yeats, in the manner of the classic masked Japanese drama. W. T. Benda's masks, which Benda first made for masquerades were worn by the dancer Margaret Severn. Pablo Picasso and Fernand Léger designed cubist masks for the ballet in Paris. Oscar Schlemmer made masks for mechanistic ballets at the Bauhaus in Dessau.

Eugene O'Neill, having written a scene of masked Fifth Avenue paraders for his play *The Hairy Ape* (1922), to show how the world looked through the eyes of a character in the play, devised a masked dramatization of Samuel Taylor Coleridge's *The Ancient Mariner,* then used masks for psychological effect in *Lazarus*

Laughed, and as symbols of character in *The Great God Brown.*

In 1920, Robert Edmond Jones designed a production of *Macbeth* in which the huge brooding masks of the Weird Sisters dominated the stage as part of the expressionistic scenery. Ernst Stern made masks for Max Reinhardt's productions in Germany. Norman Bel Geddes designed masks for the New York production of Reinhardt's *The Miracle.* Lee Simonson injected occasional masks into such Theater Guild productions as *The Adding Machine* by Elmer Rice, *Man and the Masses* by Ernst Toller, and *Back to Methuselah* by George Bernard Shaw. For New York revues, John Held designed caricatures of film stars, and Jo Davidson made mask portraits of drama critics. James Light fitted masks to most of the characters in the Provincetown Playhouse production of August Strindberg's *The Spook Sonata* in 1924. Remo Bufano made masks for productions of *Alice in Wonderland,* Thornton Wilder's *The Skin of Our Teeth,* and Shaw's *Androcles and the Lion.* Masks are sometimes needed to give actors the look of realistic animals or of special characters; at other times, to give them an unrealistic appearance. A masked actor may change his stature or proportions; he approaches the physical fluidity of a marionette.

Protective masks of wire, leather-covered pads, and metal mesh are worn by fencers, baseball catchers, hockey guards, and other sportsmen. Eskimos and skiers wear halfmasks with goggles to keep snow glare from the eyes. Bandits wear handkerchiefs over the lower parts of their faces. Surgeons wear protective masks to maintain antiseptic conditions, or place them over patients to administer ether. A diver's helmet is a form of head mask. Wax-lined masks are placed over the skin for beauty treatments. Dust respirators and masks for paint sprayers, welders, and workers with acids are widely used in industry. Gas masks were provided in World Wars I and II, much as metal vizors were provided for the knights of the Renaissance.

PAUL McPHARLIN,
The Puppeteers of America.

Bibliography.—Macgowan, K., and Rosse, H., *Masks and Demons* (New York 1923); Kniffin, H. R., *Masks* (Peoria 1931); Benda, W. T., *Masks* (New York 1944); Riley, Olive L., *Masks and Magic* (London 1955).

MASOCHISM, a term used in analytic psychology to denote a tendency, usual in infancy and early childhood but outgrown or sublimated in later life, to take pleasure in having pain inflicted upon oneself. The term is derived from von Sacher-Masoch, an Austrian novelist, in whose stories many of the main characters exhibited this trait in an excessive degree. A mild degree of masochism is evinced by many average men and women, particularly those who spend much of their time complaining about wrongs, injuries, pains, etc., suffered by themselves, the inference being that their unconscious masochism drives them to be occupied mentally with pain and the details of its effect upon themselves.

MASON, mā′sŏn, **Alfred Edward Woodley,** English novelist: b. May 7, 1865; d. London, England, Nov. 22, 1948. He was educated at Oxford, and among his works are *A Romance of Wastdale* (1895); *The Courtship of Morrice Buckler* (1896, dramatized 1897); *The Philanderers* (1897); *Lawrence Clavering* (1897);

Miranda of the Balcony (1899, dramatized in New York 1901); *The Watchers* (1899); *Clementina* (1901); *The Four Feathers* (1902); *The Truants* (1904); *The Broken Road* (1907); *The Turnstile* (1912); *The Four Corners of the World* (1917); *The Summons* (1920); *Running Water* (play, 1922); *The Winding Stairs* (1923); *The Three Gentlemen* (1932); *Fire Over England* (1936); and *The Life of Francis Drake* (1941).

MASON, Charles, English astronomer and surveyor: b. England, about 1730; d. Philadelphia, February 1787. He was for years assistant astronomer at the Greenwich Observatory and was sent on various expeditions in the service of science. In 1763 he was employed with Jeremiah Dixon to survey the boundary line between Maryland and Pennsylvania and they were engaged in this undertaking until 1767, the line established becoming famous in American history as the Mason and Dixon's Line. They returned to England and Mason was thereafter engaged in astronomical observations and researches until the time, the precise date of which is not known, when he returned to America. His work upon the lunar tables of Tobias Mayer which were published in London in 1787 under the title *Mayer's Lunar Tables Improved by Charles Mason,* enjoyed a high reputation for reliability. In 1860 many of his papers were accidentally discovered at Halifax, N. S.

MASON, Daniel Gregory, American composer and writer on music: b. Brookline, Mass., Nov. 20, 1873; d. Greenwich, Conn., Dec. 4, 1953. In 1895 he graduated from Harvard University; he retired from his position as chairman of the Music Department at Columbia University in 1940, but remained there as MacDowell professor of music until 1942 when he became professor emeritus. His works include *Music in My Time* (1938), and *Quartets of Beethoven* (1947).

MASON, George, American statesman: b. Stafford (now Fairfax) County, in the "Northern Neck" of Virginia, 1725; d. Oct. 7, 1792. He spent his early life on a typical plantation. The same region produced his co-workers in the cause of the American Revolution, Richard Henry Lee and George Washington (qq.v.). Mason seems to have been tutored at home, being grounded in a knowledge of the classics, both Latin and English. His younger brother, Thomson, was sent to London to study law at the Middle Temple. George Mason was married in 1750 to Ann Eilbeck, who died in 1773. Of this union there were several children. He was married again in 1780 to Sarah Brent.

As a member of the Ohio Company he was identified with his friend, George Washington, in the initial stages of the French and Indian War. In 1759 the two entered the Virginia House of Burgesses together.

Mason drafted the Non-Importation Resolutions, which the Virginia Assembly adopted in 1769, and the Resolves, which were sanctioned by the Virginia Convention and reaffirmed by the Continental Congress in 1774. In these he outlined both a nonintercourse policy with Great Britain and the scheme of a general intercolonial congress. As a member of the Virginia Constitutional Convention of 1776, he is remembered as the author of the Bill of Rights which constitutes so notable a part of the Virginia Constitution of 1776, and was probably the most complete and most advanced statement of the rights of man up to that time. Mason was a member of the Virginia Assembly from 1776 to 1780 and from 1786 to 1788. Under his leadership, acts were passed in 1776 and 1779 disestablishing the Anglican Church and leading within a few years to complete freedom of worship in Virginia. Mason declined to serve in the Continental Congress, although chosen by the legislature in 1777. In 1780 he outlined a plan, afterward adopted, for the cession of Virginia's western land claims to the federal government.

Mason was a member of the Constitutional Convention at Philadelphia in 1787, taking an active part in drafting the Constitution. He refused to sign it, however, and along with Patrick Henry, opposed its ratification by the Virginia Ratification Convention of 1788. He brought forward a number of objections, the most important stemming from the failure to include a bill of rights and from the North-South compromise on the issues of slavery (Art. 1, sect. 9, clause 1) and the tariff. In Mason's opinion, the slave trade was "disgraceful to mankind." The first ten amendments to the Constitution (1791) were the aftergrowth of his insistence on a bill of rights. Chosen one of the first United States senators from Virginia, he refused to serve.

Thomas Jefferson described Mason as "a man of the first order of wisdom among those who acted on the theater of the Revolution."

Consult Hill, Helen D., *George Mason: Constitutionalist* (Cambridge, Mass., 1938).

MASON, James Murray, United States senator and Confederate diplomat: b. Georgetown, Va. (now part of Washington, D.C.), Nov. 3, 1798; d. near Alexandria, Va., April 28, 1871. Grandson of George Mason (1725–1792), he graduated from the University of Pennsylvania in 1818 and continued with the study of law at the College of William and Mary. In 1820 he began legal practice at Winchester, Va., served in the state legislature during the years 1826–1827 and 1828–1831, and was a delegate to the Virginia Constitutional Convention in 1829.

Mason was elected to the federal House of Representatives as a Jackson Democrat in 1837, serving one term, and he was a member of the Senate from 1847 until 1861. A strong supporter of the Southern economic system, including slavery, he drafted the Fugitive Slave Act of 1850. He advocated secession after Abraham Lincoln was elected president, and on March 28, 1861, he left the Senate. In the same year he was appointed Confederate commissioner to England to secure aid for the South. While on board the British ship *Trent*, he and John Slidell, commissioner to France, were seized by federal authorities; they were held as prisoners until January 1862, when they were released at the demand of Great Britain (see also TRENT AFFAIR, THE). Although well received in England, Mason was never officially recognized, and he failed to obtain aid. He continued to represent the Confederacy until the end of the Civil War (April 1865). After residing in Canada for three years, he returned to Virginia in 1868 in response to President Andrew Johnson's second proclamation of amnesty. His biography, *The Public Life and Diplomatic Correspondence of James M. Mason* (1903), is by his daughter, Virginia Mason.

MASON, Jeremiah, United States senator and lawyer: b. Lebanon, Conn., April 27, 1768; d. Boston, Mass., Oct. 14, 1848. A direct descendant of John Mason (c. 1600–1672), Jeremiah graduated from Yale College in 1788. He then studied law and was admitted to the bar in Vermont. In 1797 he moved to Portsmouth, N.H., where he practiced law for many years, often in competition with Daniel Webster. From 1802 to 1805 he served as attorney general of New Hampshire, and was elected in 1813 to the United States Senate. He opposed the War of 1812, and, as a Federalist, resisted the rising tide of Jeffersonian democracy. Dismayed at his party's decline, he resigned in 1817 and returned to New Hampshire. He was a member of the state House of Representatives in 1820, 1821, and 1824, and was appointed president of the Portsmouth branch of the United States Bank. In 1832 he moved to Boston, where he continued to practice until 1838. His preference and perhaps his greatest ability lay in working as a trial lawyer, and he rarely lost a case.

MASON, SIR John, English diplomat: b. Abingdon, England, 1503; d. April 20 or 21, 1566. Of humble parentage, he was educated at Oxford University, graduating in 1521. Thereafter he served in diplomatic and other official positions. To gather information for Henry VIII he traveled on the Continent, and under Edward VI he served as ambassador to France (1550–1551). Under Mary I he was ambassador to the court of Holy Roman Emperor Charles V at Brussels (1553–1556). During the reign of Elizabeth I he spent most of his time in London, exerting considerable influence on foreign policy. He was chancellor of Oxford University during the periods 1552–1556 and 1559–1564. Astute and crafty as a diplomat and politician and willing to alter his religious convictions as necessary, he was able to keep on good terms with all factions during this turbulent period.

MASON, John, English colonial proprietor in America, founder of New Hampshire: b. King's Lynn, England, Dec. 11, 1586; d. London, December 1635. He was educated at Magdalen College, Oxford. Governor of Newfoundland from 1615 to 1621, he systematically explored and mapped the island. In 1620 he produced a short tract on its resources, hoping to influence Scots to settle there, and his map, completed in 1625, was the first to show the outline of the coast.

In 1622 the Council for New England granted Mason a patent for the territory called Mariana, now in Massachusetts, consisting of Cape Ann and land west and north of it to the Merrimack River. As he held various posts in England from 1624 to 1629, including that of treasurer and paymaster of the English Army in the war against France and Spain, it is doubtful whether he ever took possession of this property, which was incorporated into Massachusetts Bay Colony in 1629. The Council for New England made another grant in 1622 to Mason and Sir Ferdinando Gorges consisting of the lands between the Merrimack and Kennebec rivers and extending inland 60 miles. This was divided between the two in 1629, Mason's share being the area between the Merrimack and the Piscataqua rivers, which he named New Hampshire. With Gorges and others he formed the Laconia Company for the purpose of establishing an agricultural settlement in the region called Laconia, which included Lake Champlain, and in 1631 they also acquired the Pescataway grant on the Piscataqua River. Settlements were made under these grants. In 1632 Mason was elected vice president of the Council for New England, and in 1635 he became vice admiral of New England.

Mason's land rights were the subject of much litigation after his death, as the colonists refused to recognize the claims of his successors. The claims were sold in 1691, but subsequently were returned to his heirs. In 1746 the New Hampshire lands were sold to 12 citizens of Portsmouth, called the Masonian Proprietors, who granted 2,000,000 acres of the property to settlers. See also UNITED STATES—*15. The English Colonies in America, 1607–1763* (New England): Maine and New Hampshire.

Consult Dean, John W., ed., *Capt. John Mason, the Founder of New Hampshire* (Boston 1887). This publication includes Mason's charters and his tract of Newfoundland, as well as a memoir by Charles Wesley Tuttle.

MASON, John, English colonist and soldier in America: b. England, about 1600; d. Norwich, Conn., Jan. 30, 1672. He emigrated to Massachusetts in 1630 or soon thereafter, and in 1633 was a captain of militia in Dorchester (now part of Boston). In 1635 he migrated with other settlers to Windsor, Conn. At about this time a series of incidents provoked the hostility of the Pequot tribe of Indians. Mason was commissioned in 1637 by Connecticut authorities to proceed against the Pequots under their chief, Sassacus. He went first to the country of the Narragansetts, near Narragansett Bay, to secure aid from the sachem Miantonomo. He then marched against the Pequots with about 80 settlers and a force of several hundred Mohegans and Narragansetts, including the Mohegan sachem Uncas. Taking the Pequots by surprise near the Mystic River, he gained entrance to their fort, fired the wigwams, and surrounded the area, slaughtering about 700 men, women, and children. He pursued those who had escaped, killing them or taking them as prisoners, thus exterminating the Pequots as a tribe. Other tribes in the area kept peace for 40 years after this massacre.

Mason was then promoted to the rank of major, and in 1656 he was requested by the Connecticut General Court to write a history of the Pequot War. This was printed in 1677 as part of a work by Increase Mather; its first separate publication was in 1736, under the title *A Brief History of the Pequot War,* with a sketch of Mason's life by Thomas Prince. Mason gave many years of public service to the colony of Connecticut. He was chief military officer, handled relations with the Indians, and served in various official positions, notably as magistrate from 1642 and as deputy governor from 1660.

Consult Mason, Louis Bond, *The Life and Times of Major John Mason* ... (New York 1939).

MASON, John Mitchell, American clergyman and educator: b. New York, N.Y., March 19, 1770; d. there, Dec. 26, 1829. He graduated from Columbia College (1789) and received his theological training at the University of Edinburgh. In 1793 he succeeded his father as pastor of the Scotch Presbyterian Church on Cedar Street, New York City, and later, in 1810, founded a new congregation. Realizing the need for higher educational standards in the American ministry, he founded a theological seminary in New York (1804), becoming its first professor. This institution was the predecessor of Union Theological Seminary. Mason had been a trustee of Columbia College since 1795, and in 1811 he became its first appointee to the administrative position of provost. After five years, ill health forced him to retire from Columbia, and in 1821 from his other positions. Accepting the presidency of Dickinson College at Carlisle, Pa., in the same year, he resigned in 1824. He has been called one of the greatest among the British and American pulpit orators of the period, and his work at Columbia College considerably advanced the prestige of that institution.

MASON, John Young, American political leader and diplomat: b. Greensville County, Va., Apr. 18, 1799; d. Paris, France, Oct. 3, 1859. After graduating from the University of North Carolina in 1816, he studied at the law school of Tapping Reeve in Litchfield, Conn., and was admitted to the Virginia bar in 1819. From 1823 to 1831 he served as a member of Virginia's General Assembly, and was a delegate to the state constitutional convention of 1829–1830. A member of Congress from 1831, he generally supported the measures of President Andrew Jackson. He resigned from Congress in January 1837 to become a judge of the federal district court, and, in March 1844, was appointed secretary of the navy by President John Tyler. Retained in the cabinet of James Knox Polk, he was made attorney general, then secretary of the navy. After retiring from the cabinet in 1846, he practiced law in Richmond and was elected to the Virginia constitutional convention of 1850–1851, being chosen presiding officer of that body. From Oct. 24, 1853, until his death, he was minister to France; in 1854 he joined with Pierre Soulé and James Buchanan, ministers to Spain and Great Britain respectively, in drafting the Ostend Manifesto, which advocated that the United States take Cuba by force if Spain would not sell it, and provoked bitter discussion before it was officially disavowed.

MASON, Sir Josiah, English pen manufacturer and philanthropist: b. Kidderminster, England, Feb. 23, 1795; d. Erdington, June 16, 1881. During childhood he sold cakes, fruit, and vegetables from door to door, and from 1810 to 1824 he engaged successively in different trades. Manager in 1824 for a maker of key rings, he bought the business in 1825 and invented a method for manufacturing the rings by machinery. In 1829 he found a way to improve and cheapen the manufacture of steel pens, which had been sold in England on a small scale since 1803, thus bringing them into mass production. About 1844, he went on to make electroplated articles, such as spoons and forks. Having accumulated a fortune, he began to spend it on charity, being knighted in 1872 for his philanthropies. In 1875, Mason sold his pen business, and in 1880 he endowed a scientific college at Birmingham, now part of Birmingham University.

MASON, Lowell, American music educator and hymn writer: b. Medfield, Mass., Jan. 8, 1792; d. Orange, N.J., Aug. 11, 1872. At an early age he played several musical instruments, but at 20 he became a bank clerk in Savannah,

Ga. At Savannah he was also an organist and choirmaster, and he compiled a collection of psalm tunes, some of them adapted and others of his own composition. His collection was published in 1822 as *The Boston Handel and Haydn Society's Collection of Church Music,* a work which ran into 17 editions; Mason, however, did not wish to become known as a musician, and his name was used sparingly in the book. Returning to Boston in 1827, he became president of the Handel and

Lowell Mason

Culver Service

Haydn Society (1827–1832), and set up music classes for children. Out of these grew the Boston Academy of Music (1832), which gave instruction to children and teachers. Later Mason inaugurated music conventions, where for a two-week period he offered a variety of musical activities, especially helpful for teachers. From 1834 on, he traveled around the country, conducting conventions in various cities. His method of teaching was an application to music of the principles of Johann Heinrich Pestalozzi—teaching the student to sing before he could read music. He constantly urged the introduction of music instruction in the public schools, until the Boston public school authorities allowed him to teach without pay in 1837, giving him a regular appointment in 1838. He left the schools in 1841 to devote himself to conventions, and later to his music library of over 8,000 printed works and several hundred manuscripts, which was given to Yale College after his death. He was an able educator, and his influence on music education, particularly in the public schools, was enormous. He was a pioneer in championing music for the multitude.

Mason made numerous compilations of hymns and other church music, and composed about 1,210 hymn tunes of his own, including the well-known *Bethany* (*Nearer, My God, to Thee*), *Olivet* (*My Faith Looks Up to Thee*), and *Missionary Hymn* (*From Greenland's Icy Mountains*). He was more gifted, however, as an adapter and arranger than as a composer. His collections include *Juvenile Psalmist* (1829); *Juvenile Lyre* (1830); *The Boston Academy Collection of Church Music* (1836); *The Boston Anthem Book* (1839); and *The Song Garden* (3 parts, 1864–65).

Several of Mason's descendants made valuable contributions to music in the United States. One son, WILLIAM MASON (1829–1908), a concert pianist, teacher, and composer, studied in Europe with Franz Liszt and others, thus becoming a pioneer in bringing the European tradition of piano virtuosity to the United States. Another son, HENRY MASON (1831–1890), founded the

Mason & Hamlin Organ Company (1854) with Emmons Hamlin, branching out into piano manufacture from 1882. One of Henry's sons was Daniel Gregory Mason (1873–1953, q.v.).

Consult Rich, Arthur L., *Lowell Mason, the Father of Singing Among the Children* (Chapel Hill, N.C., 1946).

MASON, Luther Whiting, American music educator: b. Turner, Me., April 3, 1828; d. Buckfield, July 14, 1896. Self-taught, he served as superintendent of music in the schools of Louisville, Ky., from the age of 25, later at Cincinnati, Ohio, and from 1865 at Boston, Mass. While at Cincinnati he invented a system of music charts and books which achieved outstanding success. In the late 1870's, when the government of Japan began to introduce Western culture to its people, Mason was invited to organize music education in the public schools there. Accordingly he spent the years 1879–1882 in Japan, so successfully that in that country Western music in general came to be called Mason song. He was also active in giving piano lessons in the homes of the nobility. After his return to Boston, he published four "music readers," constituting *The National Music-Course* (4 vols., 1887–97). George Augustus Veazie, Jr., collaborated on the fourth reader.

MASON, Max, American educator and inventor: b. Madison, Wis., Oct. 26, 1877; d. Claremont, Calif., March 23, 1961. He graduated from the University of Wisconsin in 1898 and received a Ph.D. from the University of Göttingen in 1903. After teaching briefly at the Massachusetts Institute of Technology and the Sheffield Scientific School at Yale, he went to the University of Wisconsin in 1908 as professor of mathematical physics, holding this post until 1925. At the naval experimental station at New London, Conn., during World War I, he invented several devices for submarine detection. From 1925 to 1928 he was president of the University of Chicago, and from 1929 to 1936 president of the Rockefeller Foundation, New York City. In 1936 he became a member of the executive council of the California Institute of Technology and chairman of its council to direct construction of the Mount Palomar Observatory (completed 1948). He retired in 1950.

MASON, Otis Tufton, American ethnologist: b. Eastport, Me., April 10, 1838; d. Washington, D.C., Nov. 5, 1908. He graduated from Columbian College (now George Washington University) in 1861 and served as principal of its preparatory school from 1861 to 1884. A growing interest in ethnology led to his appointment in 1872 as collaborator in ethnology at the Smithsonian Institution. In 1884 he was appointed curator of ethnology for that organization, in connection with which he did important work in organizing the newly founded National Museum. In 1902 he became head curator of anthropology. A specialist in the field of culture and primitive technology, he was the author of *Woman's Share in Primitive Culture* (1894) and *The Origin of Inventions* (1895).

MASON, Stevens Thomson, United States senator: b. Stafford County, Va., Dec. 29, 1760; d. Philadelphia, Pa., May 10, 1803. The son of Thomson Mason, he received legal training and served as an aide to George Washington during the Yorktown campaign (1781). In 1783 he was elected to the Virginia House of Delegates, and in 1787 to the state Senate, serving there until 1790. With his uncle, George Mason (1725–1792), he opposed ratification of the United States Constitution at the Virginia Ratification Convention of 1788. Elected to the United States Senate in 1794, he opposed Jay's Treaty (q.v.), which attempted, not too successfully, to deal with postwar problems between the United States and England, and raised a storm by publishing an abstract of it before the Senate had come to a final decision. A member of the Senate until his death, he became associated with the party of Thomas Jefferson.

MASON, Stevens Thomson, American political leader, first governor of Michigan: b. Loudoun County, Va., Oct. 27, 1811; d. New York, N.Y., Jan. 4, 1843. He was a grandson of Stevens Thomson Mason (1760–1803). His parents moved to Kentucky while he was an infant, and he later attended Transylvania University (now Transylvania College) until 1828, when he had to leave college and go to work.

In 1830, Mason's father was appointed secretary of Michigan Territory, and in 1831, when his father was sent to Texas and Mexico, the younger Mason became secretary at the age of 19. In spite of opposition because of his youth, Mason performed his duties well, and in 1834 and 1835 was acting governor ex officio. He was a vigorous proponent of statehood for Michigan and a strong supporter of her claims in the boundary dispute with Ohio over the "Toledo strip." When the people of Michigan adopted a state constitution in 1835, they elected Mason as their first state governor, and he was inaugurated early in November. Michigan did not legally become a state, however, until Jan. 26, 1837, after she had assented to the loss of the Toledo strip, receiving the Upper Peninsula in return. Mason was re-elected in 1837, serving until January 1840. He aided education in the state, advocated a geological survey, and made intelligent efforts for the public good. However, his inexperience contributed to the severity of the panic of 1837 in Michigan; he was harshly criticized, and his popularity waned, so that he declined to run for a third term. In 1841 he settled in New York City, where he practiced law until his death at the age of 31. Later Mason became a romanticized figure as the "boy governor" of Michigan, and in 1905 his body was reinterred in Capitol Square Park, Detroit.

Consult Hemans, Lawton T., *Life and Times of Stevens Thomson Mason* (Lansing 1920).

MASON, Thomson, American Revolutionary leader: b. Prince William County, Va., 1733; d. Feb. 26, 1785. Brother to George Mason, he studied law at the Middle Temple in London, England, and was admitted there in 1751. After returning to Virginia to practice law, he served in the Virginia Assembly for many years, before, during, and after the Revolution (1758–1761; 1765–1774; 1777–1778; 1779; and 1783–1785). In the forefront in defense of American liberties, he wrote in 1774 nine letters signed "A British American," in which he marshaled legal arguments to uphold the rights of the colonists, counseling armed resistance if there should be no redress. One of the best legal minds in Virginia, he gave

prudent advice throughout the Revolutionary era. An outstanding contribution was the part he played in establishing the United States claim to the territory won by George Rogers Clark in 1778 by attaching it to Virginia and setting it up as the county of Illinois. He probably would have advanced further politically if it had not been for the independence of his views and his refusal to be swayed by political considerations.

MASON, William, English clergyman and writer: b. Hull, England, Feb. 12, 1725; d. Aston, near Rotherham, Yorkshire, April 7, 1797. He was educated at St. John's College, Cambridge, and through the influence of his friend, the poet Thomas Gray, he was elected a fellow at Pembroke. In 1754 he resigned the fellowship, becoming vicar at Aston on Yorkshire and retaining this post until his death. He was also appointed chaplain-in-ordinary to King George II, continuing under George III but resigning in 1773.

From about 20 years of age, Mason had been occupying himself with literary pursuits, usually submitting his efforts for Gray's approval. Among the earlier works were *Masaeus: a Monody to the Memory of Mr. Pope* (1747); the elegy *Isis* (1749); the tragedies in verse *Elfrida* (1752) and *Caractacus* (1759); and *An Heroic Epistle to Sir William Chambers* (1773), in which he satirized fashions in gardening. As Gray's literary executor, Mason spent about four years, following Gray's death in 1771, in preparing an edition of Gray's poems, with a memoir and letters. This was published in 1775 as *The Poems of Mr. Gray. To Which Are Prefixed Memoirs of His Life and Writings (Including His Correspondence).* Mason treated the letters as literary documents, editing and combining where he chose.

Mason was a cultivated clergyman of modest abilities. Talented in music and painting as well as writing, he composed church music and wrote essays on the subject. His literary work, though pretentious, was of mediocre quality, his poems generally being in imitation of Gray, whose own attitude was patronizing toward Mason.

Consult Draper, John W., *William Mason: A Study in Eighteenth Century Culture* (New York 1925).

MASON, city, Michigan, county seat of Ingham County. It is situated 12 miles south-southeast of Lansing at an altitude of 885 feet, and is served by the New York Central Railroad system. Located in a farming area, Mason produces beans, cabbage, and dairy products, and manufactures pharmaceuticals. Nearby is a state game farm.

The city was named for Stevens Thomson Mason (1811–1843). Settled in 1836, it was incorporated as a village in 1865 and as a city in 1868. It has the mayor-council form of government. Pop. 4,522.

MASON AND DIXON LINE, in United States history, originally the dividing line (drawn 1763–1767, with extension completed 1784) between Pennsylvania, on the north, and Maryland and that part of Virginia which is now West Virginia, on the south. The term later came to be applied to this line and its extensions westward which formed the boundary between the Northern and Southern states.

The original Mason and Dixon line settled a long and bitter controversy between the Calvert family, proprietors of Maryland, and the Penn family, proprietors of Pennsylvania. The Maryland charter of 1632 and the Pennsylvania charter of 1681 were so loosely drawn as to be susceptible of various interpretations with respect to adjoining borders. As a result, Pennsylvania claimed a sizable part of Maryland, and Maryland claims on her colonial neighbor included Philadelphia. After Penn's acquisition in 1682 of the so-called Lower Counties (Delaware), these counties also were involved in the dispute, and the inhabitants were subject to frequent armed attacks by the authorities of both provinces in support of their respective tax collectors. The Penn and Calvert families finally reached an agreement in 1760, under which the boundary was measured by two English astronomers and surveyors, Charles Mason and Jeremiah Dixon, between 1763 and 1767. By complex measurements and computations made in accordance with the agreement, they fixed the Maryland-Pennsylvania border at parallel 39°

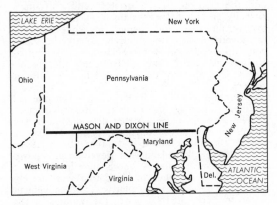

Location map of the Mason and Dixon line.

43′ 17.6″ N. beginning at Maryland's eastern boundary with Delaware, which they had previously determined. They surveyed west along parallel 39° 43′ 17.6″ N., unwittingly proceeding more than 30 miles west of Maryland's northwest corner. Here they were stopped by Indians. The survey was ratified by the crown in 1769, and a further extension of the line to mark the boundary between Pennsylvania and Virginia was completed in 1784.

During the Congressional debates over the Missouri Compromise (q.v.) in 1819 and 1820, the term Mason and Dixon line was used to include the Ohio River from Pennsylvania to its outlet in the Mississippi River. It also came to include the line set by the Missouri Compromise to separate free territory on the north and slave territory on the south. This constituted the parallel 36° 30′ west of the Mississippi, except for Missouri, which protruded north of that parallel. The original Maryland-Pennsylvania line was resurveyed between 1901 and 1903 by a joint commission of the two states.

MASON BEES, a name given to various species of wild bees of the genera *Osmia* and *Chalicodoma* which construct their nests with sand or gravel firmly glued together with saliva, placing them in crevices or fixing them to stones or walls. Like the leaf cutters and other allied forms of the family Megachilidae, they are solitary in habits and do not live in communities. Each queen bee constructs a nest of 10 to 20 or more cells, laying a single egg within each and providing it with nectar and pollen. When the nest is completed, she closes it and abandons it.

Mason bee and nest.

Among the various species of mason bees are *C. muraria* (the wall bee), found in southern Europe and northern Africa, and *O. panzer,* found in North America. The latter species is especially valuable as a plant pollenizer. See also BEE—*Leaf-cutters and Their Relatives* (*Megachilidae*).

MASON CITY, city, Iowa, county seat of Cerro Gordo County. It is located in the north central part of the state on the Winnebago River, 65 miles northwest of Waterloo, at an altitude of 1,125 feet. A railway center, it is served

Mason City Chamber of Commerce

Entrance to the Mason City Public Library.

by the Chicago Great Western; Chicago, Milwaukee, St. Paul and Pacific; Chicago, Rock Island and Pacific; Chicago and North Western; Minneapolis and St. Louis; and a local railway to Clear Lake. Braniff Airways and Ozark Air Lines furnish air transportation. Mason City is in a grain, dairy, and livestock region. Beets are grown north and west for the city's sugar mill, and nearby are clay, shale, and limestone deposits. The city's chief industrial products are processed meats, portland cement, brick and tile, beet sugar, fertilizers, dairy products, soybean products, and women's lingerie. Mason City Junior College, first public junior college in the state, is located here. Nine miles west of Mason City is Clear Lake, with two state parks and several religious and youth camps.

The first settlement in 1853 was by people largely belonging to the Masonic order, from which the community took its name. It was laid out in the following year, received its first charter in 1870, became a city in 1881, and received its present charter in 1916. A mayor and council administer the government. Pop. 30,642.

MASONIC FRATERNITY, mà-sŏn'ĭk frà-tûr'nĭ-tĭ (FREEMASONRY or ANCIENT FREE AND ACCEPTED MASONS), an oath-bound fraternal order of men, originally deriving from the medieval fraternity of operative stonemasons. Generally conceded primacy among fraternal orders, it is disseminated over the civilized world. It has no central authority, being divided into more than 100 grand jurisdictions, each autonomous, in addition to which there are a number of large and widespread concordant organizations or so-called higher degrees. The main stem, variously referred to as Craft, York, Symbolic, or Blue Masonry, consists of three degrees (Entered Apprentice, Fellow Craft, and Master Mason); it is directly descended from the fraternity and lodges of operative stonemasons and cathedral builders of the Middle Ages, which gradually over some 200 years lost their operative character and became entirely speculative. Freemasonry is cosmopolitan and, though selective in membership, somewhat democratic, bearing upon its rolls the names of noblemen, statesmen, scholars, and others of high rank, along with a much larger number of the middle class. It admits men of every nationality, religion, creed, and political persuasion; the qualifications for membership are few, such as belief in a Supreme Being, good moral character, a fair degree of intelligence, and absence of injury or defect in body which would prevent the candidate from performing his duties as a Mason. By long-continued custom, the society refrains from solicitation of candidates; all who enter must do so of their own free will and accord. The essential teachings of the craft are few and simple, illustrated by the symbolism of such working tools as the plumb, square, level, and compasses, though extensive embellishments and refinements have been adopted in higher degrees and are often emphasized in Masonic literature; as a result the doctrine has become in places highly spiritual, though the fraternity rejects all suggestion that it is a religion or rivals any religious sect.

Beginnings.—Estimates of the antiquity of Freemasonry were greatly overstated by most writers prior to the third quarter of the 19th century. The work of the British realistic school, begun about 1860, matured and was compiled in Robert Freke Gould's *History of Freemasonry* (6 vols., London 1883–87, New York 1884?–89; see also *Bibliography*—General; Condensed); its main conclusions have remained unimpaired. The consensus of modern authorities is that the society arose out of the fraternity and lodges of the English and Scottish Freemasons and cathedral builders of the Middle Ages, traces of them being found as early as the 14th century A.D.

Gothic Constitutions.—The prosperity as well as the fate of the Freemasons was strangely bound up with the Gothic style of architecture, which dominated cathedral and other ecclesiastical building for about 400 years (c. 1135–1550). The oldest Masonic documents found in England contain the legends of the craft in somewhat fabulous phrases, tracing the science of geometry or masonry from ancient times, even from Babylon, through Egypt, Palestine, and France into England by the 10th century A.D., when King Athelstan and his son, Prince Edwin, gave the Masons a charter at York and patronized them generously. The name Gothic Constitutions was attached to these documents in 1738, and by the middle of the 20th century slightly over 100 specimens of these interesting and somewhat puzzling relics have been found. In addition to the legends, they contain the charges to the masters and craftsmen. Broadly speaking, they relate to such subjects as loyalty, morality, and business principles, enjoining loyalty to king and church, honesty in workmanship, good morals, brotherly love, and mutual aid and assistance; they also include the qualifications for apprentices, followed by the oath of secrecy.

Transition.—The interruption of cathedral building caused by the Lutheran Reformation of 1517 seems to have written the doom of the lodges of operative stonemasons and architects, except for minor trade regulation. Soon afterward there followed another development known as the *transition,* that is, the change in character from operative lodges to those that were purely social, theoretical, or speculative. This movement began as early as 1600, when the minutes of the Lodge of Edinburgh, Scotland, disclose the presence of a laird, who, of course, was neither a stonemason nor a tradesman of any kind. This absorption of theoretical members was effective even earlier in England. The Masons' Company of London was a very old operative organization formed as early as 1376, having attached to it a subsidiary society called the "accepcon," where nonoperatives were "accepted." Thus the name Accepted Mason came to designate the theoretic Mason as distinguished from the Freemason or operative stonemason. Hence the name Free and Accepted Masons. The diary of Elias Ashmole, the antiquarian, states that he was admitted to membership in the lodge at Warrington in 1646, and subsequent search has shown that the lodge then contained few, if any, stonemasons.

Development of the Grand Lodge and Speculative Freemasonry.—At the opening of the 18th century, there were possibly half a dozen lodges in England. In 1716, proof can be found of six, four of which met at the Apple Tree Tavern in London to form a temporary organization, reassembling on St. John the Baptist's Day, June 24, 1717, at the Goose and Gridiron Ale House, where they elected a grand master and established a grand lodge. Although this event is commonly called the Revival of 1717, the new body was the first grand lodge of which any record can be found. It was a remarkable step for a group of so few lodges, limited to London and Westminster, and it had consequences far beyond the expectations of the participants. The founders were either so modest or so secretive that they kept no minutes for the first six years, and though *The Constitutions of the Free-Masons,* consisting of legends and charges modeled on those in the Gothic Constitutions, was published in 1723, it contained no account of prior proceedings. Nor did anything of that kind appear until 1738, when the Reverend James Anderson, author of the first edition, published a second containing purported minutes, probably largely from memory, of 14 meetings from 1716 up to June 24, 1723, on which date the minutes were taken by a newly appointed secretary.

By 1723 the English craft may be said to have become entirely speculative, though one or two lodges remained operative and unaffiliated with the London body. The organization grew rapidly in numbers and esteem, no less than 30 lodges being represented in the grand lodge in April 1723. It became the subject of much curiosity and comment, and was both imitated and opposed by other groups. In 1721 the duke of Montagu became grand master, and since that time a peer of the realm or a member of the royal family has always held that position in England.

Ireland and Scotland.—Irish records of Freemasonry are sparse, but extraneous documents indicate that nonoperative Freemasonry was familiar to Dublin in 1688 and that a grand lodge may have existed there in 1725, if not earlier, though the existence of such an institution is somewhat doubtful before 1730. Scotland had, according to preserved internal lodge records, more and older lodges than either England or Ireland. By 1700 there were about 20 lodges in Scotland. Most of them were of mixed composition, but a few kept up a purely operative routine into the 19th century. The Grand Lodge of Scotland was formed Nov. 30, 1736, by 33 of the 100 or so Scottish lodges then existing.

World Migration.—The second quarter of the 18th century witnessed the spread of Freemasonry over the world in what is believed to have been the most rapid and extensive migration of any society, philosophy, or creed in history; and that, too, entirely without any missionary zeal or proselyting. It is a striking peculiarity of Freemasonry that, although it grew up in Britain and has thrived best in Anglo-Saxon cultures, it nevertheless has had a pronounced appeal to men of every civilized country, for the most part irrespective of sect and party. Lodges were formed elsewhere as follows: Belgium and France possibly as early as 1721–1725, certainly by 1730; Spain in 1728; Bengal, India, in 1730; Philadelphia, Pa., in 1730; Boston, Mass., in 1733; Hamburg, Germany, in 1733; Savannah, Ga., in 1734; the Netherlands in 1734; Rome, Italy, in 1735; Sweden in 1735; Portugal in 1735–1736; Charleston, S.C., in 1736; Portsmouth, N.H., in 1736; Switzerland in 1736; the West Indies in 1737; Dresden, Germany, in 1738; Nova Scotia in 1738; New York in 1739; Poland in 1739; Turkey in 1738 or 1748; Berlin, Germany, in 1740; Russia in 1740; Bayreuth, Germany, in 1741; Virginia in 1741; Austria in 1742; Frankfurt am Main, Germany, in 1743; Denmark in 1743; Newfoundland in 1746; Maryland in 1749; Newport, R.I., in 1749; New Haven, Conn., in 1750; and many others in later years.

By the end of the 18th century, as countries developed a desire for autonomy, independent grand lodges had been established in most of the countries of Europe and, concurrently or later, in most other countries of the Eastern and Western hemispheres. The following list shows grand lodges now existing throughout the world (ex-clusive of those in the United States) and those which have been suppressed. The word *expired* does not indicate any inherent weakness of the Masonic body. Freemasonry is characteristically an Anglo-Saxon institution and has thrived best under republican or limited constitutional government. Totalitarian governments, sometimes aided by powerful churches, forcibly eradicate the organization, and Freemasonry is the especial object of hatred of the Fascists, Falangists, Nazis, and Communists. Persecutions beginning in the 1920's developed into complete suppression in the 1930's by every totalitarian power, though in the case of Italy, Austria, and West Germany these suppressions proved to be only temporary.

Europe: Austria (expired; revived 1945); Belgium; Denmark; England; Finland; France; Germany; Greece; Hungary (expired); Iceland; Italy; Luxembourg; the Netherlands; Norway; Poland (expired); Portugal (expired); Russia (expired); Scotland; Spain (expired); Sweden; Switzerland.

Asia and Africa: China (expired); Egypt; Israel; Japan; Philippines; Turkey.

Australia and New Zealand: New South Wales; New Zealand; Queensland; South Australia; Tasmania; Victoria; Western Australia.

Canada: Alberta; British Columbia; Manitoba; New Brunswick; Nova Scotia; Ontario; Prince Edward Island; Quebec; Saskatchewan.

Mexico: 4 national and 16 state grand lodges.

Central America and West Indies: Costa Rica; Cuba; Guatemala; Nicaragua; Puerto Rico; San Salvador; Honduras; Panama.

South America: All countries.

United States.—In proportion to population, Freemasonry has grown faster in the United States than in any other country, being represented by 49 grand lodges, 15,770 lodges, and over 4 million members. The first lodge to meet in the American colonies was one at the Tun Tavern in Philadelphia, to which Benjamin Franklin and other prominent citizens belonged. The first lodge to receive a charter of constitution from the British homeland was originally called the First Lodge (now St. John's Lodge), formed at Boston, Mass., in 1733 by Henry Price under authority of the grand lodge at London. This body also contained prominent men—among others, James Otis, who represented the citizens in the celebrated case involving writs of assistance, and Jeremy (Jeremiah) Gridley, attorney general for the king, who won this case in court but not in the hearts of his countrymen. In 1752, in the old lodge at Fredericksburg, Va., George Washington, then just under 21 years of age, was made a Freemason. By the outbreak of the Revolution, there were seven provincial grand masters in the colonies, and approximately 100 lodges, of which St. Andrew's Lodge at Boston became the most noted because of its colorful composition and patriotic activity. It had been warranted by the Grand Lodge of Scotland and included on its roll the names of John Hancock, Paul Revere, Dr. Joseph Warren, Richard Gridley, Joseph Webb, Jonathan W. Edes, Perez Morton, Col. Henry Purkett, and John Rowe the younger, some of whom, at least, took part in the Boston Tea Party. Of the 56 signers of the Declaration of Independence, 9 are clearly identified as Freemasons, and some authorities include 5 to 10 more. Of the 55 delegates to the Constitutional Convention of 1787, 15 are known to have been Freemasons and 6 delegates subsequently became members.

Before the end of the Revolution, the provincial grand lodges began falling away from British control. Grand Master Joseph Warren having lost his life at Bunker Hill, his grand lodge, on

March 8, 1777, elected his successor instead of waiting for the appointment of a grand master to be made from Britain, as was the rule. In Virginia the grand lodge became independent in 1778; in South Carolina in 1783; in Pennsylvania, Georgia, and New Jersey in 1786; in Maryland, New York, and North Carolina in 1787; in Connecticut in 1789; in New Hampshire in 1790; in Rhode Island in 1791; and in Delaware in 1806. The political and economic development of the United States, unequaled in character, rapidity, and extent, was accompanied by a like dissemination of Freemasonry. Lodges followed the covered wagons westward, and about half the grand lodges in the western states were formed before the states themselves. Exactly 100 years after the United States Constitution was declared in effect, the last of the 49 grand lodges was erected—in North Dakota in 1889. Thirteen presidents have been Freemasons. In 1959, 6 out of 11 cabinet members were Freemasons; also 5 out of 9 justices of the Supreme Court, 54 of the 96 senators, 189 of the 430 representatives, and 29 of the 49 state governors.

Concordant or Supplemental Degrees and Orders.—Freemasonry is unique in the extent to which it allows additional degrees and orders, some even non-Masonic, to be superimposed upon the first three Craft or Blue degrees. Some of these additions are open only to Master Masons, while others are open only to members of other degrees which are confined to Master Masons, thus demanding a two-step qualification. Such advanced degrees may be somewhat unrelated in substance to the required preceding degree, since the relationships have often grown up historically and the reason for them has become lost. Even a century ago this pyramiding of degrees became so extensive that there arose a new and strictly Masonic meaning of the word *rite* so as to include not merely a ceremony or formal observance but to designate a group or series of degrees or orders usually associated together and sometimes under a single administration or governing council, chapter, or other body. Thus the York or English Rite is usually deemed to include the three Craft degrees, the four degrees of the Royal Arch Chapter, the two degrees of the Royal and Select Masters, and the three orders conferred in commanderies of Knights Templar; these four divisions are also referred to, respectively, as the Craft Rite, the Capitular Rite, the Cryptic Rite, and the Chivalric Rite. The Scottish Rite (actually a Franco-Prussian rite) includes the degrees from the 1st to the 33d, though in English-speaking countries the first three degrees are conceded exclusively to the York Rite. To show how much of the elaboration and complexity must here remain unexplained, it is only necessary to add that over 1,000 degrees can be identified as having been formulated as Masonic supplemental degrees; these for the most part have been from time to time embraced in one or another of approximately 100 rites, many of them having long since fallen into disuse.

In the 20th century, the prevailing systems are fairly well limited to the York Rite of 12 degrees, chiefly though not entirely confined to English-speaking countries; the French Rite of 7 degrees worked by lodges under the Grand Orient of France; the Swedish Rite, a Christian 12- or 13-degree system worked in all Scandinavian countries; and the 30- or 33-degree system of the Scottish Rite, which is the most

prominent and widely disseminated in Latin and Latin American countries. Other orders of limited membership or special character are as follows: Royal Order of Scotland; Red Cross of Constantine; Allied Masonic Degrees; Tall Cedars of Lebanon; Veiled Prophets of the Enchanted Realm (or Grotto); and Ancient Arabic Order Nobles of the Mystic Shrine (or Shrine). The following table shows the number of bodies and members of some of the principal organizations in the United States in 1957:

Name	Units	Members
Craft or Symbolic Rite	15,770 lodges	4,085,676
Royal Arch or Capitular Rite	3,416 chapters	712,375
Royal and Select Masters or Cryptic Rite	1,411 councils	293,129
Knights Templar or Chivalric Rite	1,611 commanderies	390,541
Scottish Rite	224 consistories	907,969
Shrine	166 temples	800,332
Veiled Prophets	216 grottoes	88,101
Tall Cedars of Lebanon	112 forests	55,286

Although the confinement of membership to men is vigorously asserted and jealously guarded, more and more women's and girls' orders have attached themselves to the lodges simply by organizing and limiting their memberships to female relatives of Master Masons, or in some instances of Knights Templar or Shriners. Many of these orders use and sometimes own interests in Masonic halls. Orders confining their membership to Master Masons and female relatives are: Order of the Eastern Star, formed about the middle of the 19th century; and later, Order of the Amaranth, White Shrine, and Daughters of the Nile. The order for boys is De Molay (no requirement of Mason father) and for girls, Job's Daughters and Rainbow.

Charities.—In the United States, Canada, and the British Isles, most grand lodges as well as some supplementary orders maintain extensive homes for aged members and their widows and orphans. However, none of the Masonic bodies or affiliated organizations have any insurance features or other fixed death, disability, or annuity benefits. The use of the name or insignia of Freemasonry in connection with a commercial enterprise of any kind is not tolerated.

Anti-Masonry.—Persecutions of Freemasons which reached their culminations in several European countries during the third and fourth decades of the 20th century occasioned no surprise where Italy, Spain, and Portugal were concerned; in these countries the church-state mechanism had maintained open warfare against the fraternity for almost two centuries, beginning with the papal edict of 1738. The blows were merely more vigorously and more expertly delivered by Benito Mussolini and Francisco Franco. The Fascist Grand Council of the former expelled all Freemasons from its membership in 1923. This was followed by violence in various parts of Italy until 1926, when the state appropriated the buildings of the Grand Orient of Italy, and all Masonic lodges were dissolved; the grand master was arrested and banished to Lipari. The Grand Orient of Spain was forced to close in September 1928, and large numbers of Freemasons were imprisoned; some were executed for no other reason than that they were

Freemasons. With the arrival of Franco in Madrid, the Grand Orient went into exile in Mexico. In 1929 a special tribunal was formed to suppress Freemasonry, mere membership therein being declared a crime. Portugal remained quiet simply because the last Freemasons had been expelled about the middle of the 19th century.

Outside of the chronically anti-Masonic nations, Hungary offered examples of the first and severest persecutions, beginning under the Horthy regime as early as 1919–1920 with raids on Masonic libraries, records, and archives; there for the first time Masonic buildings were seized and used for exposing and exhibiting the contents, furnishings, paraphernalia, and regalia to crowds of sightseers. The last Grand Master of Hungary was forced to retire in 1938, when Nazi influence was dominating the country. At the close of World War II, the scourge simply passed from the hands of the Nazis to those of Communists without change of effect.

The anti-Masonic agencies in Germany were akin to those in Hungary and were as readily accepted upon an even larger scale. Beginning with the campaign of Gen. Erich F. W. von Ludendorff and his wife about 1920, the ills of Germany were blamed on alleged combined treasonous activities of Freemasons and Jews; the claim was made that they had brought about the loss of World War I by stealing secrets of the German General Staff and delivering them to Great Britain. Yet there were hardly any two elements of the German people less likely to cooperate, for the German lodges and, particularly the three most prominent and influential grand lodges, all located in Berlin, had for years been anti-Semitic so that Jews were not only rejected as candidates but also as visitors to the lodges, even though they were already Freemasons elsewhere.

The German Freemasons at first sought to placate the Nazis by converting their lodges into clubs for educational and charitable purposes, but in 1934 Hermann Göring decreed the closure of the largest grand lodge (long known as the Christian Grand Lodge). The Grand Lodge of the Three Globes, then almost 200 years old, assumed the name National Christian Order of Frederick the Great (Frederick having been an active and loyal Freemason), and the Grand Lodge of Prussia became the German Christian Order of Friendship. Only men of pure German ancestry were permitted to join these orders. In short, the leaders of German Freemasonry were compelled to become subservient to Hitler. As World War II dragged on, the Nazi temper became shorter. A grand master and his wife were seized and sent to a concentration camp; many fine lodge buildings were turned to other uses, and their contents were exposed in "Masonic Museums," with robes, costumes, symbols, and equipment arranged in ridiculous forms and combinations. Finally, in 1935, the dissolution of all lodges in Germany was decreed, accompanied by renewed charges that Freemasons had not only lost World War I but had been the cause of it by conspiring to assassinate the Austrian archduke Francis Ferdinand.

For anti-Masonry in the United States, see ANTI-MASONIC PARTY.

Bibliography.—Publications preceded by an asterisk (*) are especially valuable for the general reader.

GENERAL: Waite, Arthur Edward, A New Encyclopedia of Freemasonry . . ., 2 vols. (London and New York 1921); Ward, John S. M., Freemasonry: Its Aims and Ideals (London 1923); Waite, Arthur Edward, Emblematic Freemasonry . . . (London and New York 1925); Hunt, Charles C., Some Thoughts on Masonic Symbolism (Cedar Rapids, Iowa, 1930); Robbins, Sir Alfred Farthing, English-Speaking Freemasonry (London and New York 1930); Gould, Robert Freke, The History of Freemasonry, 6 vols. (London 1883–87; rev. by Dudley Wright, New York 1936); Begemann, Wilhelm, History of Freemasonry, tr. from the German by Douglas Knoop and Gwilym Peredur Jones (Sheffield, Eng., 1941); Crowe, Frederick J. W., What Is Freemasonry? 7th ed. (London 1943); Knoop, Douglas, and others, The Early Masonic Catechisms (Manchester, Eng., 1943); Mackey, Albert Gallatin, Encyclopedia of Freemasonry and Kindred Sciences, rev. by Robert L. Clegg, 3 vols. (Chicago 1946).

CONDENSED: Newton, Joseph F., *The Builders (Cedar Rapids, Iowa, 1915); Coil, Henry W., *Outlines of Freemasonry (Riverside, Calif., 1939); Knoop, Douglas, and Jones, Gwilym Peredur, *A Short History of Freemasonry to 1730 (Manchester, Eng., 1940); id., *Genesis of Freemasonry (Manchester, Eng., 1947); Gould, Robert Freke, *Concise History of Freemasonry, rev. by Frederick J. W. Crowe (Chicago 1920, reprinted 1951); Pick, Fred L., and Knight, Gilfred N., *The Pocket History of Freemasonry (New York 1953); Coil, Henry W., *A Comprehensive View of Freemasonry (New York 1954).

SECTIONAL AND SPECIAL: Robertson, John Ross, The History of Freemasonry in Canada (Toronto 1900); Sachse, Julius F., ed., Washington's Masonic Correspondence (Philadelphia 1915); Johnson, Melvin M., The Beginnings of Freemasonry in America (New York 1924); Pound, Roscoe, Lectures on Masonic Jurisprudence (Washington 1924); Tatsch, Jacob H., *Freemasonry in the Thirteen Colonies (New York 1929); Lobingier, Charles S., The Supreme Council 33° Mother Council of the World, A. & A. S. R., So. Juris., official ed. (Washington 1930); Jones, Bernard E., Freemasons' Guide and Compendium (New York 1950); Voorhis, Harold V., *Masonic Organizations and Allied Orders and Degrees (New York 1952).

HENRY WILSON COIL,
33°, Past Master, Riverside Lodge No. 635, F. and A.M., California.

MASONRY, mā′s′n-rĭ (Fr. maçonnerie), the art or work of building in stone. Its origins go back to antiquity. Almost all ancient temples, the Pyramids, and the massive structures of medieval times, extending down through the Renaissance, were erected in stone. In the earliest period massive foundations and walls of granite blocks, amazingly cut and proportioned, were set without mortar, which was then unknown. This is called dry masonry. Since the advancement of organized production, particularly in the present century, masonry has been subjected to striking changes. The utilization of modern machinery and up-to-date appliances points to progress commensurate to a degree with competitive industries. The more important stone works, facing higher labor and materials costs, and with emphasis placed upon speed and modern techniques, have found it necessary to subordinate or largely eliminate hand labor. The substitution to a considerable extent of steel and other materials for building stone is significant of economic and industrial pressures. Advances since the introduction of steel skeleton construction in the last quarter of the 19th century have resulted in the use of machinery to maintain masonry operations profitably. In the design of large commercial structures in the United States and Canada, high costs and requirements of industrial techniques make the matter of location, purpose of the building, and the adequacy of suitable materials a primary consideration.

Durability of building stone is essential. Classified as masonry materials are natural stones, brick, tile, and terra cotta. Also used in masonry work are (1) reinforced concrete, a conglomerate of portland cement, crushed stone, water, and sand, with steel rods or bars embedded in the concrete to supply additional strength for resisting tensile stresses; (2) concrete blocks, made of portland cement, water and crushed stone or cinders, which are durable and fire resistant; these units minimize waste in construction. Artificial stone, cast in molds, is more economical than natural stone. When rubbed to a finish this product harmonizes with other structural effects by reason of a variety of colors. The ubiquity and abundance of materials for constructing masonry units, in contrast to the limited sources of supply of other building materials, assure that masonry will continue as an important form of construction for many centuries. (See also CEMENT.)

Building stones are grouped as (1) igneous rocks, including granite—hard, durable and strong, and for centuries basically a masonry unit; also traprock, an ingredient of concrete; (2) sedimentary rocks—limestone and sandstone "in various hues," and (3) metamorphic rocks; in this group are varicolored marble and also slate. Marble takes a high polish. In the United States, building stone deposits are widely distributed (see also QUARRYING; BUILDING— Materials (Masonry, Concrete). Great Britain has an unusually wide variety of native stones, and in the Western Hemisphere, Canadian limestone (the Tyndall, the Trenton and other varieties) has been utilized during the last fifty years in the construction of buildings and also canals. Good practice calls for special care in the selection and placing of building stone. All building stones are affected by weather conditions—frost, temperature changes, and wind-driven rains, especially in cities. Sulphuric acid in the atmosphere deteriorates the stone.

Mortar (q.v.), among many cementitious materials, is selected for its particular purpose— workability. An aggregate of natural cement, sand, water, and lime is used in laying brick and setting stone. For setting solid masonry foundations a mortar of greater strength, with portland cement, lime putty, and sand as components, is used. Structural wall strength and durability are indispensable. As the stone is strong, so should the mortar be.

Masons and Tools.—Employed in masonry construction are masons, stonecutters, workers on limestone and sandstone, workers on rubble walls, layers of paving slabs, joiners, fixers who place the stone, machinists, and the masonry draftsmen, also excavators, foundation workers, bricklayers, terra cotta and fireproofing unit workers, plasterers, metalworkers, roofers and laborers. On masonry piers and bridge abutments or heavy tunnel construction, the cooperation of various other trades is sometimes required. For a time a considerable number of bombproof and gasproof underground shelters were constructed in the face of the nuclear-bomb menace, in addition to the existing shelter facilities provided by subways and also by steel-frame office and apartment buildings.

Masons' tools (see illustration) in general include: the wooden mallet, steel hammers used severally by hard-stone masons, marble masons and granite masons; and the iron hammer used as a carver's tool. The pitching tool reduces the size of rough stones. Soft-stone masons use the dummy. The punch cuts surplus hard stones. The mallet-headed point furrows the stone. Chisels include the hammer-headed for granite, mallet-headed for drafting, the boaster for draft

work, and the claw tool; also the patent claw with teeth for hard stone. Mallet-headed gouges are used for hollow moldings; the batting tool "surfaces" sandstone, the water-chisel cuts soft limestone, and the Lewising tool cuts mortises. The driver is used for soft stone, and the quirking tool cuts grooves. The steel diamond jumper is used for boring holes, and the miter tool cleans up molding intersections. The axe and the patent axe are used in dressing granite surfaces.

Machines.—The frame saw, in a swinging frame, saws stone into slabs. Cutting to size and shape is done by diamond-circular steel saw blades. Carborundum saws "joint off" marble and slate. The jointer saw is used for cutting small dimensioned stones. Planing and molding machines (two types) operate on cornices and plane surfaces; turning lathes shape columns and balusters. Hoisting appliances include nippers with hooked arms, and Lewis bolts which are fitted into dovetailed mortises in the stone to be raised.

Stone Construction.—Strength of the foundation walls is essential. Foundations now generally are composed of portland cement concrete. They should be evenly proportioned in order to prevent any unequal settling of the building. The footings are projecting courses at the wall base; they are sufficiently spread to distribute the load over as large an area as practicable. If the supporting capacity of the ground selected is not adequate, concrete piles and reinforced rafts may be used; otherwise the area of the footings is extended. In Chicago, owing to the soft soil, grillage work is necessary in the construction of many of the larger buildings. Granite is used when architectural appearance is essential. Limestone and sandstone are laminated and special care is required in placing these stones in the wall bed at right angles to the direction of the thrust.

In masonry construction, stonework comprises mainly ashlar, rubble, and trimming. Ashlar consists of carefully worked and jointed stone blocks which form the outside facing of the wall. It generally is stoneyard cut. The face of the stone may be plain, vertically tooled, truly worked, reticulated, or rusticated, finished in any of several ways. All joints are dressed to planes. The blocks vary from twelve to eighteen inches in depth, and from four to eight inches in thickness. When of uniform size and laid in continuous courses (a course is a continuous level range of masonry throughout the face of a building), the work is known as regular course ashlar. The face of the stone may be plain or have molded joints. When the blocks are laid in alternate wide and narrow courses the wall facing is called alternate course ashlar. In courses not continuous, and with stones of various sizes, the wall face is called broken ashlar or random ashlar. Rubble generally consists of irregular stones having one good face fit for an exposed wall surface. These stones are seldom cut. They are taken usually as they come from the quarry. When laid up in walls the interstices should be filled with pieces of broken stone and mortar. Coursed rubble stones are roughly quarry-squared and leveled up in twelve to eighteen inch courses.

Trimming in masonry work includes: cornices, sills, quoins, door and window facings, moldings, jambs, and copings. Ashlar facing may be backed with brick, rough stone, hollow terra cotta, or concrete blocks. The *cornice* is the

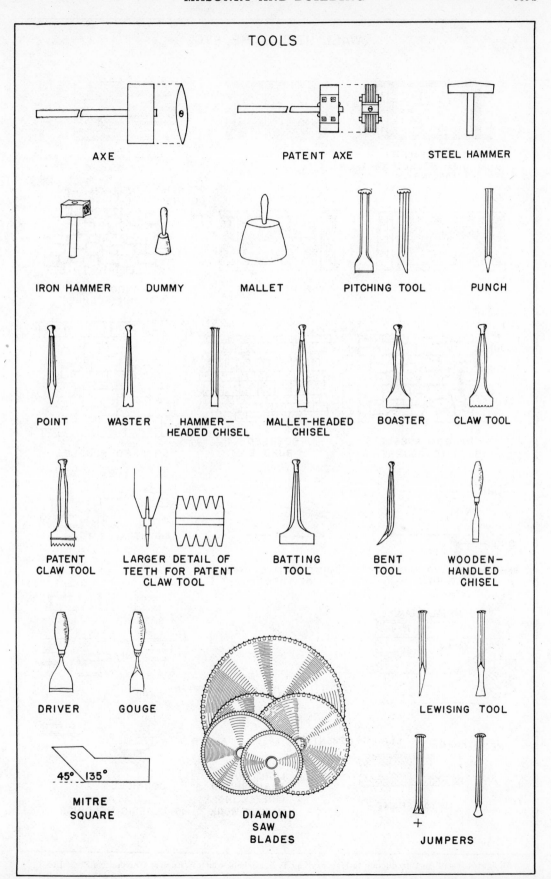

TOOLS

AXE

PATENT AXE

STEEL HAMMER

IRON HAMMER

DUMMY

MALLET

PITCHING TOOL

PUNCH

POINT

WASTER

HAMMER—HEADED CHISEL

MALLET-HEADED CHISEL

BOASTER

CLAW TOOL

PATENT CLAW TOOL

LARGER DETAIL OF TEETH FOR PATENT CLAW TOOL

BATTING TOOL

BENT TOOL

WOODEN-HANDLED CHISEL

DRIVER

GOUGE

LEWISING TOOL

45° 135°

MITRE SQUARE

DIAMOND SAW BLADES

JUMPERS

WALL STRUCTURE, ETC.

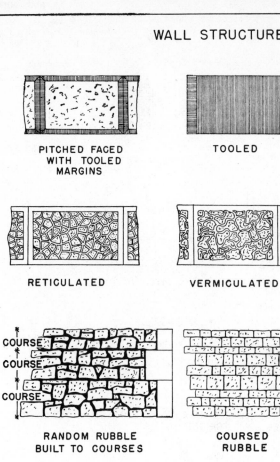

PITCHED FACED
WITH TOOLED
MARGINS

TOOLED

BOASTED

"FENCE"
COPING

RETICULATED

VERMICULATED

RANDOM OR
ROUGH RUBBLE

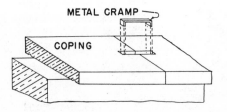

COURSE
COURSE
COURSE

RANDOM RUBBLE
BUILT TO COURSES

COURSED
RUBBLE

SNECKED RUBBLE

RAIN

DRIP

SKETCH SHOWING OBJECT
OF THROAT

ALTERNATIVE TYPE
OF THROAT

ARCHITRAVES

BASES

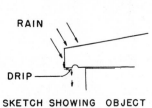

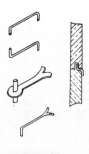

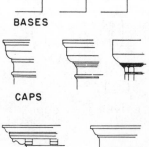

METAL CRAMP

COPING

METAL CRAMP   LEAD OR CEMENT

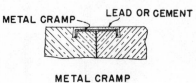

METAL CRAMP

GROUP OF
LIGHT WIRE
CRAMPS USED
CHIEFLY IN
MARBLE WORK

CAPS

CORNICES

CLASSIC MOLDINGS

All figures from "An Introduction to Masonry" by T. B. Nichols, courtesy English Universities Press Ltd.

projecting molded top course of the wall; the *gable* is the vertical wall at the end of a pitched roof. The *bed* is the lower surface upon which the stone rests; the *sill* is a broad stone at the base of a door or window; a *quoin* is a wedgelike stone at the intersection of two walls. The *coping* is the covering top course of a wall; a *molding* is a plane or curved decorative surface; a *jamb* is an upright stone at the side of an opening. The *plinth* is the lowest course of stonework projecting from the base of the main wall face. *Bond stones* in walls tie in masonry units as a whole, giving effective jointing and greater solidity. *Joints* are prepared surfaces for fitting into other stones butting against them. A *closer* is the last stone to be placed in a course. A *throat* is a groove cut under the coping or cornice to prevent rain from running down the face of the wall.

Arches generally span wall or bridge openings. In masonry they consist of wedge-shaped stones or other solid materials called voussoirs; and are usually curved. In placing such stones the layers should rest at right angles to the face of the arch. Joints between the stones radiate from the center. The weight the arch carries is, accordingly, distributed from stone to stone.

Brick Construction.—Building brick, classified as masonry units, include common brick of the kiln run; face brick, more uniform in size and shape than common brick; and glazed brick with decorative effects which are made by a special process. Common brick generally is employed to back up the masonry facing material; face brick is placed in exposed walls. Building brick, standardized in size, generally runs 2¼ x 3¾ x 8 inches. The brick is made from selected ground clay, mixed with water, molded and kiln-fired at from 1600 to 2000 degrees Fahrenheit. (See also BRICK; CLAY—*Applications:* (ceramics). During brick wall construction it is customary to tie in the bricks with metal cramps, in order to provide a unified masonry mass and thus distribute the load over the whole area. This is a form of *bonding.*

Common bond, English bond, and Flemish bond are most frequently used. Common bond consists of five stretcher courses with headers (bricks laid with their ends toward the face of the wall) and stretchers (bricks laid with their length parallel to the face of the wall) in each course. The English and Flemish bonds are more expensive to lay than the common bond. The Flemish bond is frequently used to provide an attractive wall surface. There is also an English cross-bond with alternate courses of stretchers arranged with the joints below the middle of the bricks above. Skeleton steel frame construction provides support for the outer masonry walls at each story by the use of spandrel girders. These are called "curtain" walls. Tying brick-bearing walls to the floor beams at horizontal intervals of 6 feet at each tier is a modern practice. The walls forming an angle should be carefully bonded. In brick walls, stone quoins or other solid wedgelike supports frequently are set into exterior angles like a voussoir in an arch. Window and door openings may be spanned by stone or brick horizontal lintels; the lintel supports the superstructure. It consists of one or more masonry units keyed to adjust the weight. Building brick is cheaper than stone. Engineering brick, made for heavy duty construction, and other designs meet special requirements in building.

Structural load-bearing clay tile, kiln burned, is designed to resist impact and moisture in building walls; also to support heavy and compressive loads. Non-load-bearing tile, molded and kiln treated, are made in many shapes and sizes for floor construction, fireproof interior partitions, and wall coping. Mixtures of clay and shale are employed in the manufacture of structural tile. Facing tile is made from a mixture of fire clay and water. Hollow interior spaces in the various units are designed to meet building requirements.

Historical.—Masonry's origin and development are traced through ruins of Babylonian temples, the Egyptian pyramids and tombs, and down through centuries of the Mycenaean, Greek, and Roman civilizations. Contrasted with massive masonry structures erected in Egypt, the Assyrians built temples and palaces from platforms reached by steps. Assyrian walls were of sun-dried brick, faced with kiln burned brick. "Cyclopean" and, later, Greek rectangular masonry necessitated the laying up of huge stone blocks in regular courses. The Greeks developed the Doric, Ionic, and Corinthian columns for use in monumental structures. The walls were chiefly of marble and stone blocks. The Romans adopted the columnar style of the Greeks; they also invented concrete and developed arch, vault, and concrete construction. Roman walls of rectangular stone blocks were laid up; concrete, faced and unfaced, was employed — the unfaced for foundations. Concrete vaults and cross-vaults, cast in solid mass, were extensively used. Marble and brick were employed for wall surfaces. The Romans frequently employed the circular and polygonal forms in the construction of temples and public buildings of enormous size. The key to such operations was in the arch, vault, and dome system. The arch made it possible to span wide openings. In modern times, reinforced concrete and steel-frame construction have put industrial pressure on masonry, making it imperative to use machinery in competitive operations. See also ARCHITECTURE.

ROYAL GURLEY, *Technical News Analyst.*

Bibliography.—Corkhill, T., ed., *Brickwork, Concrete and Masonry* (London 1930); Williams, C. C., *The Design of Masonry Structures and Foundations,* 2d ed. (New York 1930); Nichols, T. B., *An Introduction to Masonry* (London 1936); White, A. H., *Engineering Materials* (New York 1939); Molloy, Edward, ed., *Brickwork and Masonry* (New York 1942); Fletcher, Sir B. F., *A History of Architecture on the Comparative Method,* 12th ed., rev. and enl. (New York 1945); Bateman, J. H., *Materials of Construction* (New York 1950); Dalzell, James R., *Masonry Simplified,* 2 vols., 2d ed. (Chicago 1957); American Standards Association, *Building Code Requirements for Reinforced Masonry* (Washington, D.C., 1960).

MASONTOWN, mā′s'n-toun, borough, Pennsylvania, in Fayette County, situated on the Monongahela River about 60 miles south of Pittsburgh, at an elevation of 1,010 feet. Masontown is served by the Monongahela Railway Company and is on a state highway. Its chief industry is bituminous coal mining, and other activities are farming, oil refining, and lumber milling. First settled late in the 18th century by people of German origin, Masontown was made an incorporated borough in 1876. Pop. 4,730.

MASORAH, MASSORAH, or MASORA, mȧ-sō′rȧ (Heb. *māsōrāh,* tradition), a body of notes on the text of the Hebrew Bible, transmitted from generation to generation during the 6th to

12th centuries A.D. by the Masoretes, a group of Biblical scholars and scribes. Most of these notes were in the Aramaic language.

To aid in accurate transmission and proper understanding of the Biblical text, the Masoretes developed a tradition as to writing, paragraphing, word division, vocalization, and accentuation. To this they added a body of notes indicating peculiar forms and spellings, noting variant readings and giving statistical and other pertinent information to aid readers and assist scribes in making accurate copies of the sacred text. At first the notes were few and simple and were transmitted orally. Presently scribes began noting them down on the margins and between the lines. Gradually they grew in number and complexity. Notes between the lines or on side margins made up the Masorah parva (small Masorah), while more extensive notes on the upper and lower margins were called Masorah magna (great Masorah). Later came the practice of digesting these notes in a Masorah finalis at the end of the manuscript, while the parva and magna together were called Masorah marginalis. The term initial Masorah refers to the practice of arranging notes in elaborate patterns around the large initial letters of the various books. Much later all these notes were elaborated in special treatises, such as the famous *Oklah we Oklah* (*Ochlah wa Ochlah,* 1864).

Piety attributed the origin of the notes to Moses or to Ezra, but obviously they belong to no one time or place; they are rather a product of gradual growth. All such notes available to us assume as their basis the type of text which became canonical about 100 A.D., and are hardly older than about 500 A.D. Their presence or absence in a manuscript depended at first on the whim of the scribe, who inserted what he thought necessary. Later they were systematized at centers of Masoretic activity, and it is possible to distinguish an eastern or Babylonian tradition, and a western or Palestinian tradition, though differences within these traditions developed at such centers as Sura, Nehardea, and Pumbedita in the east, and in the schools of Aaron ben Moses ben Asher and Aaron ben Naphtali at Tiberias, Palestine. Jacob ben Ḥayyim (Chayyim) made from manuscripts then available a digest of these Masoretic notes for the Rabbinical Bible printed in Venice in 1524 and 1525. This has been the basis of most subsequent study of the Masorah, including Christian David Ginsburg's *The Massorah, Compiled from Manuscripts* (4 vols., 1880–1895). Jacob ben Ḥayyim drew, however, on relatively late manuscripts, and he failed to understand the development of the Masorah. Consequently his work has been superseded by that of Paul Kahle, who prepared the Masorah parva for the third edition of Rudolf Kittel's *Biblia Hebraica* (Hebrew Bible, 2 vols., 1929–37; 9th ed., 1954). See also BIBLE—4. *Textual Criticism of the Old Testament* (History of the Text); HEBREW LANGUAGE AND LITERATURE—*Medieval Period* (Philology).

Bibliography.—Consult the sections on the Masorah in the chief *Introductions* to the Old Testament (for example, Robert Henry Pfeiffer's *Introduction to the Old Testament,* pp. 88–97, New York 1941). Consult also Frensdorff, Solomon, ed., *Das älteste Handbuch der Massora, "Ochlah w'Ochlah"* (Hannover 1864); id., *Massoretisches Wörterbuch* (Masoretic Dictionary, Hannover 1876); Aaron ben Moses ben Asher, *Dikduke Hateamim (Diqduqe ha Te'amim, Grammatical Rules of the Accents),* ed. by S. Beyer and H. L. Strack (Leipzig 1879); Kahle, Paul, *Masoreten des Ostens* (Leipzig 1913); Ehrentreu, Ernst, *Untersuchungen über die Massora* (Hannover 1925); Kahle, Paul, *Masoreten des Westens,* 2 vols. (Stuttgart 1927–30); *Ben Asher—Ben Naphtali: Der Bibeltext der tiberinischen Masoreten,* ed. by L. Lipschütz (Stuttgart 1937); Kahle, Paul, *The Cairo Geniza* (London 1947, New York 1948); id., *Opera Minore* (Leiden 1956).

ARTHUR JEFFERY, *Columbia University.*

MASS, in physics, the quantity of matter in a body. The mass of a body is the same wherever the body may be in the universe. Two bodies have equal masses if the gravitating forces with which another body acts upon them are exactly equal at equal distances. (See GRAVITATION.) Hence two bodies have equal masses if their weights are the same at the same place on the earth; so that if the metallic "weight" used by a grocer is carried from place to place, the quantities of sugar and tea balanced by it in a good pair of scales will always be the same, for the mass of tea or sugar is in every case equal to the mass of the metallic "weight." It is to be clearly understood that as the force of gravity is different at different places on the earth, the weight of any body is different at different places. It is very important to distinguish between the mass (or quantity of matter) and the weight (or force which tends to move it downward) of a body.

MASS, in certain Christian churches, the most prominent and central act of worship, instituted by Jesus Christ at the Last Supper. The word *mass* is derived from *missa,* which in late Latin designates an act of dismissal marking the end of an audience or public gathering. In the course of the 6th century its meaning was restricted to the liturgical act. Use of the word *mass* was always limited to the Western Church; in the East the celebration of the Last Supper was called *liturgy* (public service) or *eucharist* (thanksgiving). The latter term has become widely used in the West as well.

The theological meaning of the Mass has been summed up by the Second Vatican Council fathers in the following words: "At the Last Supper, on the night He was betrayed, our Saviour instituted the Eucharistic Sacrifice of His Body and Blood. He did this in order to perpetuate the sacrifice of the cross throughout the centuries until He should come again, and so to entrust to His beloved Spouse, the Church, a memorial of His death and resurrection: a sacrament of love, a sign of unity, a bond of charity, a paschal banquet in which Christ is consumed, the mind is filled with grace, and a pledge of future glory is given to us," Abbott and Gallagher, eds., "Constitution on the Sacred Liturgy," N. 54, *The Documents of Vatican II* (New York 1966).

Christ, when he instituted the Mass as something to be *done* (Luke 22:19), and to be done in the form of a *meal,* established at the same time the character of the Mass as a ritual. To understand the true nature of this ritual, one must keep in mind that the Mass has never been taken to be a magical rite, deriving its efficacy from the exactness with which it follows a rigidly fixed formula. The fact that there is no uniformity even among the four reports of the institution of the Eucharist contained in the New Testament shows that from the very beginning a flexibility of form existed in its celebration, and excludes the idea of one original and normative "apostolic liturgy," which later became diversified.

The discussion that follows is limited to the Roman Rite, the form of liturgy that developed in the city of Rome and became the official form of celebrating the Eucharist for the great majority of Roman Catholic Christians. It is only since the Second Vatican Council that the strict uniformity of language and ceremonial has been changed, and place has been given for use of the vernacular and for adaptation to the spirit of various races and peoples.

The Last Supper. The sources of knowledge of the Last Supper are the four short accounts recorded in Matthew 26:26–29; Mark 14:22–25; Luke 22:15–20; and I Corinthians 11:23–25, all of which reflect the existing liturgical practice. The setting is a Jewish festive meal, probably the paschal meal, which Jesus celebrated with his disciples. According to Matthew and Mark the consecration of bread and wine took place together at the end of the meal; according to Luke and Paul they were separated by the meal. This latter usage is no doubt the original one, and fits well with the hypothesis that the Eucharist was instituted during the paschal meal: the consecration of the bread at the breaking of bread at the beginning of the meal, and the consecration of the wine after the meal at the third cup of blessing.

The injunction "Do this in memory of me," which Christ gave to the apostles at the end of the meal, has been interpreted by the church to mean that Christ has replaced the old *Pasch* (Passover) offered by the assembly of the children of Israel in memory of the passage from Egypt. In the new Passover he was to be the lamb offered by the church in memory of his own passing from this world to the Father. It was by the shedding of his blood that Christ redeemed man once and for all from the power of darkness and transferred him into his kingdom. It is evident that the sacrifice that the church offers in obedience to Christ's command cannot be some new sacrifice added to the one offered by Christ on the cross, but is its *memorial*. It is also evident that this memorial is more than an act of thinking of the death of Christ while one eats a piece of bread and drinks a cup of wine. The memorial sacrifice must be real, just as the meal is a real participation in the one body and the one blood of Christ. It is its *sacramental* re-presentation: which means the rendering present again, under the sacramental sign, of the one sacrifice that Christ offered, in historical reality, by the physical shedding of his blood on the cross. The fact that this sacrifice was instituted in the form of a *meal* shows that it is not only the death of Christ that is made present in this rite, but the resurrection as well. By sharing in the body of Christ and in the "blood of the new and everlasting covenant," the participants in the Eucharistic meal are filled with the life of the risen Christ, and therefore participate already in the joy of future eschatological glory.

The Early Christian Memorial. The earliest description of the celebration of the Mass, given by St. Paul (I Corinthians 11:20–26) shows that it was still celebrated in connection with a *meal*, probably the traditional Sabbath meal. The first important step in the development of the rite of the Mass was its separation from the meal, or the *agape* as it was called.

This separation and its celebration on Sunday morning resulted in the combining of the Eucharistic meal with the Reading Service. Originally, Jewish Christians had attended the Jewish synagogue service on the morning of the Sabbath. After they were expelled from the synagogues they established a new Sabbath day with their own services, which followed the order of the synagogue service but was adapted to Christian worship.

Development of Rites (4th to 6th Century). The most creative period in the development of the Mass is the time between 250 and 650. During the second half of the 3d century the church grew stronger and stronger. Assemblies for worship became public events and consequently took on an official character, with more solemn and more elaborate ceremonial. The bishops received public authority with certain judicial functions and entered, together with their assistants, priests, and deacons, into the well-defined hierarchy of state officials. A new kind of distinction between clergy and laity like that between rulers and subjects began to appear, and this distinction became part of the rite.

By the end of the 3d century the basic structure of the Mass had two parts: a Reading Service with greeting and response, lections interspersed with psalmody, sermon, dismissal of the catechumens, intercessory prayer of the faithful; followed by the Eucharist, opened by greeting and response, then the kiss of peace, offertory, Eucharistic prayer, fraction of the bread, communion, and dismissal. The first part was open to all, the second part only to the faithful.

Separation of the catechumens disappeared in the 4th century and was followed by a fusion between the two rites, of the *word* and the *sacrament*. By the end of the 5th century the same congregation attended the whole of both rites as a matter of course. One unforeseen effect of this change was that passive receptiveness, necessarily the layman's role in the first part of the liturgy, affected also his attitude during the second part. Formerly a clear distinction had been made between the listening attitude of the uninitiated and the active participation of those who through baptism had received the right to pray and to offer. Now the whole rite came to be considered a single act of worship, at which the people assisted in the attitude of recipients or beneficiaries. As a result of this fusion a desire was felt for an introduction, or entrance rite for this one act of worship. The traditional prayers of the faithful were replaced by a litany, at times moved to the entrance rite or into the Eucharistic prayer.

The adaptation of the simple pre-Nicene (325) form of worship to the public character of the post-Nicene era took on different forms according to various local needs and circumstances, and resulted in the formation of different rites. This differentiation was influenced by the different mentality of East and West. In the East the pattern of worship tended to transcend temporal life and to become immutable, hieratic, and contemplative. The West was directed toward action, seeking to pervade the temporal with the spiritual. The liturgies of the West gave more place to the change of the ecclesiastical seasons, especially in the Gallican and Visigothic rites in Gaul and Spain.

The Roman Rite stands between the Eastern and Western rites. To understand the development of the Roman Mass it is necessary to remember that Rome, properly speaking, is not a

"Western" church. It is the meeting point of East and West. The patriarchate of Rome was predominantly Greek, not Latin, and Greek long remained the liturgical language because of its cosmopolitan character. The Roman Mass reached its final shape through influences from the East as well as from the West. As late as the 7th century the Roman liturgy was influenced by the East when the Syrian prose hymn *Lamb of God* was introduced into the liturgy. On the other hand the Roman Mass shows traits characteristic of the West, especially the growing influence of the calendar of feasts on the priestly prayers, as in the preface at the beginning of the Canon. With all this openness, Rome managed to give the various borrowings from East and West a typically Roman stamp.

Codification of the Roman Mass and Its Diffusion in the West. In the latter half of the 3d century, the Roman liturgy began to change from Greek to Latin. By then, Latin had been "christened" by a long series of theological writers working in North Africa. It was probably there that Latin was first used in the celebration of the liturgy. In Rome the change was gradual and was completed only by the time of Pope Damasus (366–384).

Although the exact text of the Roman Canon at that time is not known, it is reasonable to suppose that it received its "canonical" form when it was translated into the new language. The liturgical activity of Pope Gelasius I (492–496) seems to have given to the Roman Mass its final shape, except for some minor changes made by Pope Gregory I.

Change from the Greek to the Latin language made it possible for the Roman Rite to be diffused all over the West. The Roman pontiffs' custom of celebrating the Mass in various Roman basilicas on special occasions brought with it a need of further codification, not only of texts used for the prayers and prefaces, but also of melodies and ceremonies. Prayers for the use of the bishop, arranged by outstanding popes like Leo I, Gelasius I, and Gregory I, were written down and collected in the sacramentaries. The Roman sacramentaries reflect basically the Mass as it was celebrated by the pope. None of these sacramentaries, however, were considered normative, in the present-day sense.

The desire of the Frankish kings for uniformity was ultimately responsible for the spreading of the Gelasian and the Gregorian sacramentaries into the regions north of the Alps. The most decisive step in this direction was made by Charlemagne, who obtained a copy of the *Gregorian Sacramentary* from Pope Adrian (785), which became the universal norm for the celebrating of Mass in his realm. However, it did not contain the ordinary Sunday masses after Pentecost and after Christmas. To fill this lack Charlemagne's chancellor, Alcuin, added an appendix with material from various sources, some of it of Gallican origin. With this a process began that, between the 8th and the 11th centuries, led to a considerable transformation of the original Roman (Gregorian) liturgy. The Gallo-Frankish temperament was more inclined to "drama," and to a certain exuberance foreign to Roman taciturnity. The new spirit was felt in liturgical innovations, such as the procession on Palm Sunday; the washing of the feet on Holy Thursday; the blessing of the new fire at the Easter Vigil, and the blessing of the Easter Can-

dle, with the singing of the Exsultet; and the anointing at the ordination of bishops and priests. Besides these embellishments, prayers were added that served the private devotion of the priests, as the prayers at the foot of the altar, prayers during the offertory, before and after communion, and incensations.

In this form the Mass eventually returned to Rome, in the 10th or 11th century, when the influence of the German emperors, especially Otto I and Henry II, brought about a renaissance of Rome and of the papacy. The last change was the introduction of the Creed into the Mass, at the bidding of Henry II.

From Gregory VII to the Council of Trent (1545). The transformation of the Mass under Franco-German influence was not an unmixed blessing. Under Pope Gregory VII (1073–1085) a reaction set in to restore Roman liturgy. The juridical centralization of authority in Rome began to make itself felt by the demand for conformity in matters of liturgical texts and ceremonial. The texts that had been scattered in a great variety of volumes (sacramentaries, lectionaries, antiphonals) now were collected in a single book. The Roman Missal contained everything needed for the celebration of Mass and came into use all over western Europe.

Hand in hand with this development went the custom of celebrating private Masses. These were made possible because the traditional unity between priest (bishop) and people at the celebration of the Eucharist had been weakened. Silent recitation of the Canon had become the rule in Rome by the year 1000 at the latest. The altar had been turned round and removed to the rear of the apse, so that the priest had to turn his back to the people. The altar now received a reredos, or ornamental backdrop. Candles and crucifix placed on the altar became customary in the 12th and 13th centuries. The Mass became more and more an action of the priest; the lay people were mute spectators.

At the same time Masses became more frequent. Daily celebration of the Mass became customary. With the number of clergy increasing, most of the Masses were said without a congregation, with only a "server" assisting the priest. As a result, the priest had to do all the reading himself, and soon it also was done in a whisper. Since there was nothing to be listened to anymore, the few people present turned to performing their own private devotions. All that was left of the Mass was its value as an atoning sacrifice and as a means of bringing Christ down upon the altar. The first led to an enormous increase of Requiem Masses celebrated for the souls in purgatory, and the second resulted in a desire to see the Host.

Council of Trent to Vatican II (1545–1962). The attacks on the Mass by the Reformers and the widespread dissatisfactions among Catholics with the many abuses and the liturgical chaos of the time caused the Council of Trent to start a reform of the liturgy. Confronted with doctrinal errors and with disciplinary abuses, the council Fathers first had to define again the doctrines of the church with regard to the Eucharist. Against the denials of the substantial presence of Christ under the species of bread and wine the Fathers restated the doctrine of transubstantiation. Against the rejection of the Mass as sacrifice the 22d session of the council (1562) declared that the Mass is a true sacrifice, not detracting from the bloody sacrifice of the cross, but re-presenting it in a sacramental, unbloody manner. To remedy the existing disciplinary defects the Fathers insisted on frequent reception of Communion and the preaching of sermons during the celebration of the Mass. Furthermore, a comprehensive reform of the liturgical texts was begun. This, however, proved too much for the council Fathers to accomplish. At the end of the council the matter had to be put into the hands of the Holy See.

Commissions were formed in Rome to publish authentic editions of the Breviary as well as of the Mass. The new Roman Missal appeared in 1570 under Pope Pius V. The accompanying papal decree declared this edition as normative for all bishoprics with less than a 200-year-old tradition of their own. From that time on, additions and changes could only be made by the Holy See. To implement this legislation Pope Sixtus V organized the Sacred Congregation of Rites (1588) for the task of extending this work of reform to all liturgical functions.

The publication of the Missal of 1570, together with the establishment of the Congregation of Rites, stopped any further development of the Mass in the Western Church. Only a few unimportant changes were made. Unfortunately the positive suggestions of the Council of Trent concerning regular liturgical preaching, and frequent communion by the laity, did not evoke a very enthusiastic response. With regard to the question of the use of the vernacular the council had left the door open by saying that the Fathers did not think Mass should be celebrated in the vernacular indiscriminately. The general policy of the Congregation of Rites was to restore and to keep the Roman Mass as much as possible in the form it had reached under Gregory VII. Latin was considered to be the only official liturgical language in the West and the rite of the city of Rome to be the highest norm for all liturgies.

Liturgical Movement and the Constitution on the Liturgy. The renewal of the ritual of the Mass now taking place is the result of a process that began simultaneously in various places about the middle of the 19th century and later became known as the "liturgical movement." The leading figures of its earliest stage was Abbot Gueranger (died 1875) of Solesmes, a Benedictine abbey in France. His ideal was renewal of the spiritual life of the faithful through restoration of liturgical unity through the Roman Rite, which had given way to neo-Gallican innovations in most of the dioceses of France.

The woeful lack of sound scholarship displayed in Abbot Gueranger's principal work, *Institutions Liturgiques,* led to a new phase of the liturgical movement, that of historical and critical research. To secure a sound basis for renewal, the movement needed critical editions of liturgical sources. A beginning had already been made in the latter half of the 19th century by scholars like Cardinal Pitra (died 1889) and Dom Henri Leclercq (died 1945). After the World War I the Benedictine abbey of Maria Laach in Germany became a center for liturgical research under the leadership of Abbot Ildefonse Herwegen (died 1946) with the assistance of Kunibert Mohlbert (died 1963) and Odo Casel (died 1949). Thus a firm foundation was built under the popular and pastoral phase of the movement.

At the beginning of the 20th century, Pope St. Pius X made use of the work of the monks of Solesmes for a restoration of Gregorian chant; the complete Roman Gradual for the songs of the Mass appeared in 1907. In 1905 his decree on frequent communion was published. From that time on the desire on the part of the people for active participation in the Mass became the dominant concern of the movement. It was a Belgian Benedictine, Dom Lambert Beauduin (died 1960) who initiated this phase of the liturgical movement with a famous address given in Malines, Belgium, before the National Congress of Catholic Action in 1909. For the first time the social implications of the celebration of the Mass were emphasized.

The liturgical movement in the United States had its center in St. John's Abbey, Minnesota, where Virgil Michel (died 1938) published *Orate Fratres* (now called *Worship*), a magazine devoted to liturgical renewal. In 1940 the first Liturgical Week was held in Chicago. From that time the Liturgical Conference with members from both the diocesan clergy and the religious, under the presidency of a bishop, organized annual "liturgical weeks" to spread the movement through the whole country.

In 1922 the Congregation of Rites published a decree in favor of community Masses with the responses given by the people. The feeling grew that some adaptation had to be made in the liturgy to make active participation easier. During World War II, Pope Pius XII prepared two decisive encyclicals, *Mystici Corporis* (1943), on the Church, and *Mediator Dei* (1947), on public worship. These were followed in 1951 by the restoration of the Easter Vigil, and in 1955 by the restoration of Holy Week.

The liturgical movement had succeeded in preparing the church to proclaim that the liturgy is more than a matter of rubrics, that it is the fountainhead of its spiritual life. So it was only natural that the Second Vatican Council, called by Pope John XXIII as a pastoral rather than a dogmatic council, began its work with the reform of the public worship of the church.

The *Constitution on the Sacred Liturgy* was promulgated by Pope Paul VI on Dec. 4, 1963. It is the fruit of the work that had been done during the last decade preceding the council. It indicated the changes that were to be made in the Mass to adapt the rite to modern needs and to bring about more meaningful participation. To carry out the reforms it established a postconciliar commission. The council also made provision for experimentation to evolve new liturgical forms.

Various Forms of the Mass. The original and normative celebration of the Eucharist was the pontifical Mass. The various historical documents that have come down through the centuries show clearly that this special normative position of the pontifical Mass and its essential structure have remained the same. From this pontifical, or standard, Mass there evolved the high Mass or solemn Mass, at which the chief celebrant was no longer a bishop but a priest. Originally, when the priest celebrated the Eucharist there was no notable difference in appearance from the liturgy as celebrated by his bishop. Subsequent elaboration of the pontifical rite and corresponding simplification of the rite of the presbyter's Mass made the distinction of the two rites more evident.

The rubrics of the missal published by Pope Pius V (1570) kept the high Mass, celebrated with priest, deacon, subdeacon, two acolytes, thurifer, and torchbearers as the normal form of the conventual or public Mass in the proper sense of the word, as distinguished from the private Mass, read in a low voice with the assistance of a server. In private Masses the priest absorbed the liturgies of the deacon and the subdeacon, while the server absorbed the liturgy of the faithful.

In the post-Tridentine age the private Mass became de facto the "normal" Mass, which influenced also the ritual of the high Mass and the pontifical Mass. Now, after the Second Vatican Council, pastoral considerations have become a determining factor in the evolution of the various forms of the Mass. They have led to a more elastic presentation of the forms of the Mass in the new *Ordo Missae* promulgated by Pope Paul VI on Holy Thursday 1969 through the Apostolic Constitution *Missale Romanum.* The *Ordo Missae* (or ordinary) is the basic structure of prayers and ritual of the mass. According to this document the *pontifical Mass,* presided over by the bishop surrounded by his priests, and celebrated with the full participation of God's people, keeps its place of honor as the most outstanding manifestation of the unity of the local church. Among the Masses celebrated with a congregation, the *parish Mass* and the so-called conventual Mass of religious communities are more important. At these Masses the celebrating priest should usually be assisted by a lector, a cantor, and at least one server. This form of celebration is considered as typical (*Missa typica*). A special *Ordo* is provided for a *Mass without people,* that is, a mass celebrated by a priest with only a server.

In order to manifest appropriately the unity of the priesthood the council permitted the extension of the old custom of concelebration, that is, the communal celebration and consecration of the Eucharist by several priests. In the Latin Church, concelebration in this strict sense had been limited to only a few occasions—for example, the Mass of newly ordained priests together with their bishops. The council extended the possibilities of concelebration to Holy Thursday, not only at the Mass of the Chrism, but also at the evening Mass; and to Masses during councils, bishops' conferences, and other clerical gatherings and synods.

During the protracted debate at the council on Latin as the sole language of worship in the Roman Church, it became evident that the strict uniformity of language and ritual could not be maintained in a church that had reached out into the world as a whole. As a result the bishops incorporated broad principles of evolution in the *Constitution on the Liturgy,* opening the way for a much wider variety of form. These principles guided the work begun immediately after the closing of the council by the Consilium instituted to implement the wishes of the council with regard to a reform of the liturgy. The new Ordo Missae of 1969 presents the first outlines of the new Roman Missal in various chapters on the importance, the structure, the ministers, and the various forms of the Mass, as well as on the church building, the implements needed for the celebration of the Mass, and the way to select its variable parts during the year and for special occasions.

THE RITE OF THE ROMAN MASS

Entrance Rite. According to the new Ordo the Roman Mass opens with an entrance song as the priest and the ministers approach the altar. After kissing the altar, and after all present have signed themselves with the sign of the cross, the priest turns to the people to greet them. Then follows an act of public repentance, the Kyrie, and the Gloria (on ordinary Sundays and on festive occasions), and then the entrance rite is concluded with the Collect.

The entrance song (Introit) was originally a complete Psalm with an antiphon sung by the congregation alternating with the choir. The new Ordo opens various possibilities for handling the Introit. The antiphon and the Psalm from the Roman Gradual may be sung either alternately by the choir and people or by the choir alone. A simplified form from the Simple Gradual may be used, or any other song fitting the occasion, and approved by the national conference of bishops, may be chosen. If the Introit is not sung, the antiphon from the Missal may be recited, either by all the faithful or by a group, or by the lector or also by the presiding priest, right after the greeting to the people. This salutation, which the priest addresses to the congregation immediately after kissing the altar, is the sign that the assembly is convened. It may take various forms: the traditional "The Lord be with you"; St. Paul's greeting, "The grace of the Lord Jesus Christ, and the love of God, and the communion of the Holy Spirit be with you all" (II Corinthians 13:14); or "Grace be to you and peace from God our Father, and Our Lord Jesus Christ!" (I Timothy 1:2). The people answer in the traditional way: "And with your spirit," acknowledging God's presence and blessing. The priest may at this time give a brief introduction to the Mass to be celebrated.

The penitential act, which now follows, may also take different forms. Replacing as it does the prayers at the foot of the altar, which heretofore were said privately by the priest and the ministers immediately on their arrival at the altar, the penitential act consists of a general confession of sins in an abbreviated form of the former Confiteor. It is introduced by an invitation by the presiding priest, and is closed by a general absolution. The Confiteor may also be replaced by a silent examination of conscience, followed by some verses of a penitential character; or by three invocations addressed to Christ by the priest and answered by the people:

Priest: "You who have been sent to heal the contrite of heart: Lord, have mercy."
People: "Lord, have mercy!"
Priest: You who have come to call the sinners: Christ, have mercy."
People: "Christ, have mercy!"
Priest: "You who sit at the right hand of the Father to intercede for us: Lord, have mercy."
People: "Lord, have mercy!"

Naturally whenever this form of the penitential act is used, the traditional Kyrie is dropped. Without greeting the people again, the priest invites all to pray briefly in silence, that all may become conscious of standing in the presence of God while addressing their wishes to him. The prayer that the priest then pronounces is called the Collect, because it is intended to gather together, or recapitulate, the prayers of all those present. With the confirming "Amen" of the congregation, the entrance rite is concluded.

Reading Service. The *Constitution on the Liturgy* strongly emphasizes the importance of Holy Scripture in fostering the spiritual life of the faithful and calls for a reform of the reading service to offer the faithful a more representative portion of the Holy Scriptures over a set cycle of years. To implement this demand the new Ordo provides that on Sundays and feast days the ancient custom of three lessons, one from the Prophets, one from the writings of the Apostles, and the third from the Gospels should be restored, so that the continuity of God's plan of salvation through history may have its full educational effect on the people. For weekdays special lectionaries provide two-year cycles for continuous reading of all the books of the Bible.

The people respond to the first reading with a song called the *Gradual*. The name "gradual" is derived from the old custom of the cantor's singing the verses of a Psalm from the first step (gradus) of the ambo, while the people answered repeating the responsorial verse. The present reform emphasizes the importance of this kind of response by the whole congregation as an "integral part of the liturgy of the Word." Ordinarily the responsorial Psalm should be taken from the lectionary, which provides texts that correspond to the reading. However, to facilitate their use by the people, responses and Psalms may also be chosen from special collections of a more general nature.

The *Alleluia* ("Praise ye the Lord") served in the synagogue as the response of the people during the singing of the so-called Hallel psalms. This acclamation had a special significance, because it combined into a single verbal unit the praise of the people (Hallelu) with the holy name of God (Jah).

The long, drawn-out melody of the "jubilus," on the last syllable of the Alleluia, developed on special feasts into a poem of its own, called the *Sequence*. The most famous of these are the Sequence for Easter Sunday, *Victimae paschali laudes,* and the one for Pentecost, *Veni, sancte spiritus.*

Whenever there are three readings, the Alleluia follows the second reading, except, during Lent, when in its place a Psalm (Tract) or a verse is sung. Whenever the response to the readings is not sung, however, the Alleluia or the Psalm may be omitted.

The listening to the Word of God and the singing of the congregation are followed by the *homily,* or sermon. The word "homily" means a special kind of sermon, spoken from the heart and addressed to friends. It differs from the "exhortation," which intends to lead to repentance or conversion, and also from the catechetical instruction. The Second Vatican Council that formally declared that the sermon is an official part of the liturgical service, which should draw its content mainly from scriptural and liturgical sources.

Creed. The Creed used in the Mass is known as the Creed of Nicaea-Constantinople and was originally a baptismal creed. When the Creed was taken into the Mass it was put in the second part, the Mass of the Faithful, to confront those who take part in the Eucharistic prayer with the full and orthodox faith in the true divinity and true humanity of Christ. Therefore it was always said by the entire congregation. The reform initiated by the council has restricted the recitation of the Creed to Sundays and high feasts.

Prayer of the Faithful. The intercessory Prayer of the Faithful belongs to the oldest parts of the service of the Word. The whole idea of the Prayer of the Faithful practically disappeared from the Roman Mass because of various changes introduced in the 6th century. The *Constitution on the Liturgy* restored it to its original place after the Homily (and Creed), especially on Sundays and feasts of obligation. Without determining the precise form, it generally proposed that the prayer should include, after an introductory invitation, a series of petitions "for holy Church, for the civil authorities, for those oppressed by various needs, for all mankind, and for the salvation of the entire world." A brief response like "Lord, have mercy" or "Lord, hear our prayer," is made by the congregation, the whole ending in a Collect.

Offertory. The new Ordo Missae recommends that the faithful present the gifts of bread and wine to the priest or the deacon. The bread should be of wheat and unleavened. It should have the character of real food, and there should be at least one large host that can be broken later in the course of the Mass. The faithful are also encouraged to offer other gifts for the poor or for the church, in money or goods, to be placed at a suitable place next to the altar. During this offertory procession a song or an antiphon may be sung. It is to be omitted when there is no singing. At the offering of the bread the priest says: "Be praised, Lord, God of the universe, for through your bounty we have received the bread which we offer to you, the fruit of the earth and work of man's hand. It will become to us the bread of life." Likewise, at the offering of the wine the priest says: "Be praised, Lord, God of the universe, for through your bounty we have received the wine, which we offer to you, the fruit of the vine and the work of our hands. It will become for us a spiritual drink." Both prayers may be said in a loud voice and then are answered by the people saying: "Praise be to God for evermore!" To conclude the Offertory rite the priest says the Prayer over the Offerings to prepare the way for the Eucharistic Prayer, the heart of the Mass.

Eucharistic Prayer. The term "Eucharistic Prayer" characterizes the whole act of worship beginning with the greeting "The Lord be with you!" and ending with the solemn "Amen" of the congregation. Its essential note is thanksgiving. The short dialogue between the priest and people, with which the Eucharistic Prayer opens, emphasizes its importance as well as its communal character. The exchange of greeting assures the priest and people of their mutual identity in Christ. The invitation "Lift up your hearts!" carries the priest and people from their everyday life into the new world of the Spirit. The people respond "It is right and just."

Now the priest directs, in the name of the whole congregation, the "Eucharistia"—which gives thanks to God and sanctifies the people—through Christ to the Father in the Holy Spirit. Three new Eucharistic Prayers have been added to the original Roman Canon. However, the new prayers have retained all the basic elements. The first of these elements is that of thanksgiving for the bounties of God in creation and Redemption. This is mainly expressed in the Preface. In the Eucharistic Prayers I and IV the Preface forms a part of the whole prayer. Eucharistic Prayers I and III suppose special Prefaces, differing according to the special occasion of the day, to the mystery being celebrated on a special feast, or according to the special character of the season. For this purpose the reform adds eight new prefaces to those already in use, for example, one for the Sundays of Lent to bring out better the festive, joyful character of the season—as well as its penitential nature; two for the season of Advent; and two new common Prefaces for ferial days.

The Preface is followed by an acclamation, sung or recited by the entire congregation, priest and people, the "Holy, Holy, Holy . . . ." This acclamation constitutes another element common to all four Eucharistic Prayers, expressing the communal as well as the enthusiastic character of the central part of the Mass. The reform adds to the "Holy, Holy, Holy" another acclamation, taking place right after the Consecration. To the invitation of the priest "Let us proclaim the mystery of faith" the people answer: "Christ has died, Christ is risen, Christ will come again" or a similar acclamation is the "Amen" at the end of the Eucharistic Prayer by which the people confirm all that has been said and done during this sacred action.

The third element of all Eucharistic Prayers is the "epiclesis" (invocation), one preceding the Consecration to implore the divine power to consecrate the oblation offered by man, and one following the Consecration to ask that those who participate in the holy sacrifice may become one in the Holy Spirit.

The heart of the Eucharistic Prayer is the scriptural account of the Consecration. Significantly enough, this part remains the same, with only slight variations, in all four of the Eucharistic Prayers. Its last sentence "Whenever you do this, do it in memory of me," leads to the next element of the Eucharistic Prayer, the Anamnesis, or memorial, recalling the death and the resurrection of Christ, and simultaneously offering to the Father the work of redemption that Christ has accomplished for our salvation. The invocation, which asks that the grace and peace of the Holy Spirit may fill the hearts of those who participate in the sacrifice, leads in each of the three new Eucharistic Prayers to the prayers of intercession, which manifest the spirit of communion in which the Eucharist is being celebrated, communion, that is, with the whole Church in heaven and on earth, with all its members, living and deceased.

At the end of the Eucharistic Prayer, the priest lifts the paten with the consecrated bread, and the chalice with the consecrated wine, while reciting the words of the final glorification: "Through him, with him, in him, the unity of the Holy Spirit, all glory and honor is yours, almighty Father, for ever and ever," The "Amen" of the people marks the end of the sacred action through which the sacrifice of Christ is being offered to the Father, by the Church, in the unity of the Holy Spirit.

The Lord's Prayer. Since the Eucharistic celebration culminates in the Paschal Meal, it is only natural that the Lord's Body and Blood should be received as spiritual food. In the context of the Mass the Lord's Prayer is the bridge between the Canon and the Meal. The petition for daily bread refers to the communion, and the petition that God forgive the faithful as they forgive each other cleanses their hearts before the reception of the Eucharist. As a preparation of the assembled people of God for receiving the Body and Blood of Christ, it is properly prayed aloud by all.

The Kiss of Peace. Immediately after the Lord's Prayer and its continuation prayer (embolism) for peace, the priest greets the people with the salutation "The peace of the Lord be always with you." This is an invitation to all to give one another the Kiss of Peace.

At first, to exchange the Kiss of Peace one merely turned to one's neighbor and did so. Eventually it was limited to the clergy, and its form became stylized as a distant embrace. Today it is again being given from neighbor to neighbor in the form recommended by common usage, with the words "Peace be to you," and the response "And with your spirit."

The Breaking of the Bread and the Agnus Dei. The rite of commingling by dropping a small piece of the Host into the chalice is an old custom that has always been considered a symbolic representation of the Resurrection by the reuniting of Christ's body and blood. The revised form of the Mass restores to the gesture of breaking the bread its original meaning, namely, to express that we, the faithful being many, by participating in the one Bread of Life, which is Christ, become one body. It has, therefore, been decided that the Eucharistic bread should be so made that it permits the priest who celebrates with a community to break the Host into various parts and distribute them to at least some of those who want to communicate, as an outward sign of their own union in the one Christ. To emphasize this general idea of unity, the commingling of the bread with the wine is now done as part of the breaking of the Host for Communion. The singing or reciting of the Agnus Dei naturally accompanies the breaking of the bread. In this way the revision of the rite brings clarity and simplicity into what was one of the weakest parts of the former Roman Mass.

Communion of the Faithful. As long as the nature of the Eucharist as a corporate act of worship was fully understood, it was taken for granted that the bringing of the gifts and the receiving of Holy Communion were for all the members of the laity present at the Mass. As the Mass as a whole became more and more a "devotion" of private individuals, the reception of Communion also became an act of private devotion, losing its connection with the sacrifice.

The Constitution on the Liturgy gave "hearty endorsement . . . to that closer form of participation in the Mass whereby the faithful after the priest's communion, receive the Lord's body under elements consecrated at the very sacrifice." Reintroducing the old custom of accompanying the distribution of Communion with the words "The Body of Christ," answered by the "Amen" of the faithful, helps to make the act of receiving an act of faith and a personal encounter with Christ.

The Communion Song and Prayer after Communion. It corresponds to the nature of Holy Communion that its reception should be accompanied by a song. With the decline the number of those receiving the singing was reduced to the Communion Antiphon alone. Now that the number of communicants is increasing, Psalm singing with responsories sung by the people is becoming popular again.

The Communion procession is followed by a prayer of thanksgiving for the gift of Christ's body and blood that has been received. Significantly, the Postcommunion prayers suppose that not only the priest but also all the people have received the Sacrament.

Final Blessing, the Dismissal and Recessional. The order of the Dismissal and Final Blessing has been reversed so that the Final Blessing now occurs in a more logical place before the Dismissal. Formerly there were several forms of Dismissal, but eventually these were reduced to two, the sober Roman phrase *Ite, missa est* ("Go, you are dismissed") and *Benedicamus Domino* ("Let us bless the Lord"). The latter has been dropped in the course of the post-conciliation changes. The official English version of the former, "The Mass is ended. Go in peace," is sung in a very simple tone by the deacon or said by the priest. The people answer: "Thanks be to God." Recent directives have also stressed the role of a recessional hymn sung by the people at the departure of the priest.

FULTON J. SHEEN
Titular Archbishop of Newport, England

Bibliography

Amiot, Francois, *History of the Mass* (London 1958).
Bouyer, Louis, *Liturgical Piety* (Notre Dame, Ind., 1954).
Crichton, J. D., *The Church's Worship, Consideration on the Liturgical Constitution of the Second Vatican Council* (New York 1964).
Dix, Gregory, *The Shape of the Liturgy* (Westminster, Md., 1947).
Jungmann, Josef A., *The Liturgy of the Word* (London 1966).
Jungmann, Josef A., *The Mass of the Roman Rite*, 2 vols. (New York 1951–1955).
Vagaggini, Cyprian, *Theological Dimensions of the Liturgy* (Collegeville, Minn., 1959).

MASS PRODUCTION. The material progress made by mankind during the past 100 years has exceeded that made during all previous recorded history. Inventions such as the automobile, the airplane, radio, and television have revolutionized transportation and communication, and changed the way of life of millions of people. Vacuum cleaners, automatic washing machines and clothes driers, improved canned goods, frozen and processed foods, and many other newly developed products have eliminated tiresome and often inefficient drudgery. Automatic, thermostatically controlled oil and gas furnaces and hot water heaters eliminate the need for wood chopping, coal shoveling, and ash disposal. Household repairs are facilitated by a wide variety of electrically powered tools. Mowing the lawn, once a physically tiring and unpleasant task, has been simplified by power mowers.

The invention and improvement of such devices did not in themselves insure widespread adoption and use. Their development was paralleled by the application of new techniques of manufacture and distribution which made them available at prices within the reach of the average consumer. These new techniques are generally grouped under the term mass production.

ELEMENTS OF MASS PRODUCTION

Althought the best known characteristic of mass production is the manufacture of great quantities of goods, it is more than mere quantity output. It is distinguished from all previous types of manufacture by scientific planning and management, which coordinate all available techniques for obtaining a maximum number of identical products of uniform quality at the lowest feasible unit cost.

The essential elements of mass production are: (1) simplification of product; (2) standardiza-

tion of parts; (3) use of production and machine tools; (4) careful arrangement of workers, machines, and materials in sequence, combined with the continuous motion of work; (5) high volume; (6) planning and coordination of all activities relative to production and distribution.

Product Simplification.—Probably the most publicized example of a mass produced item is the automobile. The completed vehicle, with its many hundreds of parts and assemblies, is extremely complex. For the purposes of manufacture and assembly, however, it is simplified by separation into component items, or logical units. This facilitates the study of individual parts to determine the most economical and efficient manufacturing methods. The manufacture of each part or unit is further divided into separate and successive operations which can be examined individually.

Related parts are grouped into assemblies, such as frames, transmissions, engines, and bodies, which are logical units to make up the completed automobile. This provides economical packages for shipping purposes, and simplifies operations at the location where the completed automobile is put together.

This method of dividing a complex product into component parts, and then building those parts into completed units prior to assembling the completed automobile or other product, is what is meant by the expression "product simplification" as applied to mass production. It is the foundation of the production line.

Another aspect of product simplification is the constant effort to design parts and assemblies which are particularly suited to high volume production. A relatively simple design change often leads to significant economies in production, and may even result in improved functional qualities. New materials, too, facilitate manufacture, and in many cases, improve quality. Simplified design also contributes to reduced costs.

Standardization.—The standardization of parts is another important element of mass production, making it possible to utilize high production machines, equipment, tools, dies, jigs and fixtures, and other manufacturing aids. These are especially designed or adapted for the manufacture of virtually identical parts or assemblies, with a resultant gain in efficiency, and usually represent an investment which would be prohibitive if it were not for the large quantities of items required. Uniformity of parts also greatly facilitates assembly operations, minimizing laborious and costly fitting.

From the standpoint of the consumer, standardization is equally important. Replacement parts, for those which have been damaged or have exceeded their normal useful life, are identical with original parts, and repairs can be quickly and economically effected.

The uniformity of items essential to modern manufacture extends not only to dimensions, but also to the materials from which they are made. Detailed chemical, metallurgical, and physical specifications for all raw materials are established, and laboratory analyses determine adherence to specifications. Quality control is a routine part of every stage of the production process so that quality products can be assured.

Production and Machine Tools.—Until the 19th century, the primary tools of the metal worker were the chisel, file, and hammer. These tools were slow and inefficient, and precision manufacture—and therefore standardization—was virtually impossible. The invention of the steam engine gave a source of power for metal working tools, and the coming of the machine age during the early 19th century, with its demands for increased productivity and increased precision, accelerated the development of machine tools.

Modern machine tools are power-driven and nonportable, and they include lathes, planers, drill presses, shapers, milling machines, and other tools which are designed for shaping and sizing metal parts by cutting or grinding. Early machine tools in industry were designed for general utility, and could be adjusted to accommodate parts of different sizes and shapes. The general purpose machine tool still has a wide range of application in tool and die making, and in other work where only one or a few identical parts are required.

The increasing importance of standardization and high productivity during the early 20th century led to the development of the single purpose machine tool, which is usually designed to perform a single operation or series of operations on a specific part. Once such a machine tool is correctly set up, it can produce many thousands of identical parts with a minimum of adjustment and attention, making it indispensable to mass production.

A further development, the integrated machine, has been extensively applied since World War II. Successive similar operations, hitherto performed on a series of individual machines, are combined in a multistation integrated machine tool, which incorporates mechanisms which provide automatic transfers from operation to operation.

Another significant trend has occurred in the increased use of improved materials in the tools used for cutting and forming metals. Foremost among these are the tungsten carbides, a man-made family of metals having great resistance to wear and abrasion, even at the high temperatures encountered in metal cutting operations, and having hardness approaching that of diamonds. Machines utilizing tungsten carbide tools can be run at increased speeds, can produce many more parts before the tools are worn and require changing, and can turn out parts with better and more uniform finishes than those made with conventional steel tools. Carbides are also used to make machine components where exceptional wear or abrasion is encountered. This helps to minimize repairs, and hence improves machine productivity.

Allied to machine tools are various types of presses used for shaping or forming by impact and pressure, which forces metal to conform to the shape of a die. Stamping presses are used extensively in the automotive industry for shaping sheet metal into fenders, hoods, and other body parts; for forming the various components of frames; and for making many hundreds of related small parts. Forging presses are used to shape slugs of hot metal into such items as wheel spindles and gear blanks. Cold heading machines are used to convert wire into finished bolts and other articles.

The use of dies insures reliable uniformity, and in conjunction with the enormous pressures and high speeds available in modern presses, makes it possible to manufacture parts which could not be economically produced in any other way. Where a number of successive stamping operations on a part are required, multistage dies are often used. These may be considered to correspond to integrated machines, since the parts are made in successive stages of a single die.

In the modern plant, every effort is made to utilize the full cycle time, or capacity, of stamping presses and other types of machines to the maximum practical extent. Automatic feeding of raw materials and parts, and the automatic removal of completed parts, is accomplished by magazines, loaders, extractors, and other ingenious devices. Invariably this results in semiautomatic operation, greatly improves the safety features of the work to be done, and eliminates the physical effort of manual handling.

Progress in the field of precise measurement has kept pace with the development of machine tools and dies. Modern production gages and other quality control devices, often electronic in nature, are adapted to the specific parts or dimensions they are intended to measure, and give virtually instantaneous and highly accurate readings.

It is important that precision-made parts be correctly assembled. The high volumes of mass production make it possible—and even mandatory—to utilize special jigs and fixtures to hold parts in correct alignment while they are being welded, bolted, riveted, or otherwise fastened together. These jigs and fixtures eliminate the possibility of incorrect assembly, and are designed greatly to improve the rapidity and efficiency of assembly operations.

Production Sequence.—The symbol of mass production is the continuous production line, such as the type of installation on which automobiles are assembled. Such a line, however, represents only a part of the total planning and engineering which are necessary for the manufacture of a product. Individual parts and assemblies are in themselves the products of production lines which are often located many miles away from the location where they are assembled into the completed automobile. The final assembly line can be likened to a river which, as it progresses toward the ocean, is continually augmented by a host of contributory streams.

The essential features of the modern continuous production line include: (1) production operation sequence; (2) transportation of raw materials and parts to the operation; and (3) careful synchronization of all elements to insure optimum continuity and productivity.

The first of these, production sequence, is made necessary by the complexity of many of the component parts and assemblies in an automobile. Engines, for instance, represent a complete product in themselves, and their manufacture requires highly specialized techniques. Similarly, the production of radiators, transmissions, stampings, generators, carburetors, castings, and many others is highly specialized. For this reason, many major manufacturers maintain separate plants for the production of these and similar items.

Within each such plant, a separation of activities takes place. The plants are divided into departments, each of which is responsible for a series of related processes or parts. The work on individual parts is in turn divided into opera-

MASS PRODUCTION

Upper left: First manufactured part to be built on a moving assembly line, the Ford flywheel magneto made mass production history in 1913. *Upper right:* The engine conveyor system in a modern Ford plant. *Center:* A six-station transfer machine automatically machines automobile engine blocks, two at a time. *Lower left:* Twenty-seven critical dimensions of automobile crankshafts are gauged simultaneously and automatically on an air-operated visual gauge. *Lower right:* In a stamping plant, closed-circuit television enables a man within the building to bale steel trimmings and load them, via conveyors, onto waiting freight cars.

(Center) Chevrolet Motor Division of General Motors; (others) Ford Motor Company

MASS PRODUCTION

Above: In a vacuum cleaner factory, parts are carried from one manufacturing step to another by an intricate conveyor system. *Center:* The tool-control board in an engine manufacturing plant signals a warning when a particular tool needs changing. *Lower left:* Final assembly line in the mass production of United States Air Force fighters and fighter-bombers. *Lower right:* Planning the final assembly line of an automobile manufacturing plant.

(Top) The Hoover Company; (center and lower right) Ford Motor Company; (lower left) Republic Aviation Corporation

tions, representing a series of essential steps in manufacture. Each employee in a plant is responsible for the proper performance of a certain segment of the facility. The manager of a stamping plant, for instance, becomes increasingly expert in coordinating all the activities in his plant for the efficient production of quality stampings. Foremen, specializing in the production of certain types of stampings, are similarly able to maintain and improve the effectiveness of their respective departments. The individual employees, usually performing only one or a few related operations on a single type of part or assembly, become increasingly proficient at their assigned tasks.

Parts and assemblies are transported from operation to operation with a minimum of effort and delay. The principle of the modern production line is to bring the work to the operation, eliminating waiting, excess handling, and the necessity for the employee to move from place to place. To accomplish this, many different types of conveyors are used, each adapted to the specific requirements of a series of related operations. Individual parts for assembly operations are transported by overhead monorail conveyors. The assembly conveyor itself is frequently equipped with fixtures or other devices to hold component parts in exact alignment while they are being fastened or fitted together. The conveyor is a symbol of mass production, and is used to deliver parts to a production or an assembly line, to provide a means for more effective assembly, to transport individual parts or logical units past the employee, and to store items prior to usage.

Conveyor type assembly lines afford convenience of work space, and are inherently flexible, since their output can be adjusted to seasonal fluctuations in production requirements by varying their speed and the number of employees. This flexibility also makes it possible to synchronize all subsidiary lines to the requirements of the final assembly line.

High Volume.—Mass production, with its product simplification, standardization of parts, special tools, machines, and equipment, must be supported by reliable and consistent high volume, in order to justify the significant investment needed to accomplish desired objectives.

Quantity output is both an objective and a characteristic of mass production, affording the mechanism to achieve maximum utilization of productive capacity, for maximum efficiency and economical costs.

Planning and Coordination.—Perhaps the most important element of mass production is the coordination of all the elements of the entire system.

This requires detailed and precise planning, with the overall objectives for the end product as the unifying factor. Final and subsidiary lines are all geared to meet the established objective, including raw materials, transportation, tools, and labor, to mention only a few.

The planning and coordination required for an efficient individual manufacturing or assembly line illustrates several of the considerations which are necessary in the production of an automobile.

Each operation is separately studied to determine (1) the time required for performance; and (2) the best method to be used. The output of the line can be no greater than that of its slowest operation, so every effort is made to equalize the time required for the various operations to minimize idle time and delays. This is known as "balancing" the line. The fair and equitable distribution of work among the employees on the line is also an important consideration, as is the full utilization of machine cycle time.

This type of planning and coordination, on a larger scale, must be applied to all of the major and subsidiary production lines of the modern manufacturing organization to ensure that objectives are met.

HISTORY OF MASS PRODUCTION

The elements of mass production existed, to some degree, prior to the 20th century. No one aspect, in itself, constituted mass production, which represents the successful combination of all elements, given unity by careful overall planning and coordination.

Product simplification, the division of a product into its component parts for the purpose of manufacture, is probably as old as manufacturing itself, since it is necessary whenever products are made which require different trades or skills. Early carriage makers, for instance, employed both carpenters and blacksmiths.

The first standardized interchangeable machine parts were produced by James Watt in the latter half of the 18th century. In its time, this represented a tremendous achievement, since precision tools and accurate measuring devices had not yet been developed. The earliest machine tools date from about 1780, and by 1850, as a result of developmental work by English manufacturers, machine tools capable of considerable accuracy were in general use in England and the United States. Eli Whitney is credited with the earliest quantity production of interchangeable parts, in the arms factory which he established at New Haven, Conn., in 1798.

The development of improved machine tools and jigs and fixtures received a tremendous impetus from the expansion of the bicycle industry in the United States subsequent to 1850. In general, the early automobile manufacturers adapted the methods and techniques used in the bicycle and wagon industries to automotive production.

The use of sequential steps in production and the movement of assemblies between successive operations was observed by the young Henry Ford in a Detroit railroad car factory as early as 1879.

Conveyor lines were used in meat packing houses prior to the Civil War, but were not applied to manufacturing until the 20th century. Quantity machine production is, of course, the primary characteristic of the "machine age" which started in the early 1800's.

The development of the automobile furnished an environment which was particularly favorable for the application of improved production methods. It was a product for which a widespread potential demand existed, provided the price could be low enough to place it within the reach of the average person, and provided the means to keep it in satisfactory service could be developed. Furthermore, even the early automotive market was highly competitive, which provided a strong incentive for efficient manufacture.

Many of the men associated with early automobile companies combined a broad practical engineering experience with a willingness to try new ideas. Chief among these was Henry Ford, who was the most ardent prophet, pioneer, and practitioner of mass production of his time.

The first complete application of all of the elements of modern mass production was made during the years 1912 and 1913 at the Highland Park Plant of the Ford Motor Company.

Here the most modern machine tools were used; machines and men were placed in an orderly sequence; moving conveyor lines were first used for the assembly of automobiles; and overhead conveyors and other devices for the economical and efficient movement of parts and materials were extensively employed. The entire plant was planned to provide accuracy, volume, and speed. From the Ford Motor Company, this concept rapidly spread to other companies in the automotive and allied fields.

American productive capacity was a major factor in World War II, when the demand for tremendous quantities of weapons and materiel led to the application of the methods used in automotive manufacture to a host of new and complex items. Perhaps the most notable of these applications was the manufacture and assembly of B-24 Bombers by the Ford Motor Company at Willow Run, where the continuous production of one bomber per hour was achieved.

Today, with improved techniques, improved machines and tools, improved controls, and more effective organization, it is possible to apply the principles of mass production to the economical manufacture of any item which has quantity requirements sufficient to warrant the investment in engineering, planning, tools, machines, and facilities.

FORWARD PLANNING FOR MASS PRODUCTION

Because of the complexity of modern manufacture, forward planning for a new product invariably starts several years before it is scheduled to be produced. The necessary tools, machines, and equipment must be planned and procured, and it may even be necessary to construct new plants to accommodate the manufacturing and assembly operations.

The first step in forward planning is "processing" the job, which entails planning the sequence of operations; deciding what manufacturing methods will be used; selecting the machines best suited to each operation, giving due consideration to quality and volume requirements; and designing the tools required.

Production lines are planned through plant layouts, on which machines, equipment, and other essential features are plotted to scale. These layouts are constantly reviewed to make sure that the most suitable arrangements of men and machines are being utilized, and the most effective flow of materials and parts is accomplished.

If it is necessary to build a new plant, extensive studies of various potential plant locations are made. Such factors as water supply, rail, highway, and water transportation, available utilities, labor supply, raw material supply, and location with respect to markets are examined. The facilities for the disposal of industrial wastes are another important consideration.

After the production lines for the product have been determined, the detailed design of the new plant (or any necessary redesign of an existing plant) are undertaken. The building is planned around the needs of the production lines. In other words, the space requirements are determined, the plant layouts are made, and the building is erected around and over the space required. Shipping, receiving, and storage space must be provided, with adequate aisles for the movement of materials and parts, and access to machines. The piping and wiring systems required for electricity, water, steam, compressed air, and similar items must be incorporated within the plant. Illumination and ventilation systems must be provided. Office space, parking space, employee washrooms, lunch rooms, and cafeterias are other important factors in plant design.

Concurrently with this planning, the necessary machines, tools, and equipment are designed and ordered. These are installed sufficiently in advance of the date for scheduled production to permit necessary tryout, adjustments, and refinements.

The forward planning effort involves not only the company directly responsible for the end product, but those who supply it with machines, tools, equipment, raw materials, parts, goods, and services. They, too, must plan well in advance of delivery dates their products or services.

THE MODERN ASSEMBLY PLANT

Most of the elements of mass production are amply illustrated in the modern automobile assembly plant. These elements are, of course, not confined to the automotive industry, but are to be found wherever modern methods are utilized for high volume manufacture.

The continuous, synchronized movement of parts and assemblies to points on the final line where they are incorporated into the automobile is the outstanding feature of the assembly plant. This flow starts at the receiving area, and moves to the storage area, where all components are kept ready for use. Such components as frames, axles, and front suspension systems are received and stored as subassemblies ready for final line use, while others such as the engine and transmission assemblies, and the body and front end, are built up or completed on secondary or "feeder" assembly lines. Ideally, each of these lines starts at a storage area, and all feeder lines end at the point on the final line where their products are used.

Not all of the feeder lines are within the plant itself. The modern assembly plant in the automotive industry is dependent upon thousands of suppliers for parts and subassemblies. These suppliers range in size from major manufacturing plants to small shops. They may be located adjacent to the assembly plant, or they may be hundreds of miles distant, and they may be under the same ownership as the assembly plant or they may be independently owned. Their production schedules must be coordinated with the final assembly line, irrespective of their geographical separation, since failure to deliver any component of the automobile in proper quantities on schedule will effectively disrupt production.

In addition to the raw materials and parts which become part of the end product, a steady supply of items which are consumed in the manufacture of the product is essential to the proper functioning of the production line. Modern mass production systems use immense quantities of water, electricity, petroleum products, and perishable tools of all kinds.

Modern production lines cannot function in

an economic vacuum. In the broad sense, all elements of the national economy contribute in some degree to the successful functioning of the system. Good rail, water, and highway transportation are essential to furnish raw materials to the fabricating plants; to connect feeder plants to the final assembly plant; and to distribute the end product of the company to the ultimate consumer. Many suppliers, both inside and outside the organization which maintains the production line, furnish the products and services which keep the line going.

AUTOMATION

With the development of more productive and efficient machine tools and industrial equipment, increasing emphasis has been placed on "automatic" machines and "automatic" production lines. Conventional production lines consist of a number of machines, each of which performs only one or a few operations on a part. Each machine is operated by an employee, who places the part in the machine, starts the machine, waits for the completion of the processing cycle, and unloads the part. Productivity is limited by two factors: the speed of the machine itself, and the skill of the operator in positioning the part in the machine and removing it when the operation is completed. In production lines of any length, more time is spent in feeding and unloading parts from the machines, and in transferring parts from one machine to another, than in actually performing operations on the parts in the machines themselves.

A new concept—"automation"—has contributed to an advance in mass production techniques more revolutionary than any other single development in the past century. The Ford Motor Company has pioneered in this field. As an example, its first application of automation was on a valve guide bushing—a small cylindrical cast iron part, larger in diameter at one end than at the other. Automatic handling came into play by a method of turning these parts so that the large end was always first to enter the conveyor which took the bushings through the machining operations.

These parts were simply slid down a slotted trough, which was wide enough, but too short for them, thus forcing them to tilt. Because the larger end was heavier, the small end could pass over the slot without dropping; only when the large end passed the opening did the piece drop. Thus, no matter which end passed first, each piece always fell with the large end down. Imagination of this kind soon began to be applied to the handling of other items: loading and unloading of stamping presses; operation of "iron hands" and other mechanical lifting and turnover devices for steel sheets; transfer of hot, heavy coil springs from a coiling machine to a quench tank. This latter job was called "mankilling" before automation, because the operator had to reach down, lift the hot part chest-high, then turn around and put it in a compression fixture for quenching, all in a matter of seconds. Uses of automation have since become immeasurably more complex.

In automated production lines, parts are automatically transferred to, into, and out of a series of machines which perform successive operations on a part. The only limiting factor on the productivity of the machine is the speed of the machine itself, since loading and unloading mechanisms are geared to the machine cycle. Thus the full productivity of the machine is realized, and the heavy manual effort formerly associated with many metal-working operations is reduced to a minimum.

The basic unit of automated machining lines is the transfer machine, a development of the integrated machine. Transfer machines consist of a number of individual machines, synchronized to perform dozens or even hundreds of successive operations on a part. Parts are carried through the machine by transfer mechanisms which position the part for each operation, even turning it over when necessary. Once a part is loaded in the transfer machine, the entire series of operations is performed automatically.

One further step is required for complete automation. This consists of linking transfer machines together with powered conveyors and turnover and rotation devices, all of them controlled by ingenious electrical controls which synchronize the entire operation. These controls stop automated production lines immediately in case of a malfunction; they guide parts through the various phases of the production process; and they perform many types of inspection.

Fully automated machining lines represent an approach to the realization of the "automatic factory." It is significant, however, that unlike the "automatic factory" visualized by theorists, where a single man operates a pushbutton, and electronically controlled machines produce completed parts without further attention, the modern automated factory still requires the services of hundreds of expert technicians to keep the production system functioning. The completely automatic factory, generally, is still some distance in the future.

The concepts and techniques of automation have been successfully applied to many processes in addition to machining. Among these is the production of heavy automotive body stampings. The presses in a modern plant for the manufacture of roof panels, fenders, or hoods, and other stampings, are linked together by automation equipment, which feeds a steady supply of parts into each press, and inverts or reverses parts between presses as required. All presses in the line, and the automation equipment itself, are synchronized to permit a continuous uninterrupted flow of materials and parts between operations. As a result, the maximum capacity of each press is effectively utilized and the press lines as a whole achieves optimum output.

THE MODERN MANUFACTURING PLANT

The modern manufacturing plant represents the utmost refinement of the elements of mass production possible at the beginning of the last half of the 20th century.

A typical facility—an engine plant—will be described briefly.

Design and Construction.—The modern engine plant is functionally designed to house all machining operations for the components of the engine, the completed assembly, and testing of the engine itself. Having all of these operations under one roof—and one manager—contributes importantly to the overall efficiency of the operation, since it facilitates close coordination of all aspects of engine production.

The building is typically of one-story construction, which eliminates the costly and time-consuming transfers of materials and parts from floor to floor which are necessary in older multi-story plants. Every feature of the plant, from the receiving and storage areas, through machining, testing, and shipping, is planned to facilitate the smooth and uninterrupted flow of materials, parts and assemblies. All production lines are carefully integrated and balanced to allow all operations in the plant to accomplish planned capacities. Machining lines are served by electrical substations located directly overhead, and metal cuttings are carried away from the individual machines by conveyor systems. Adequate ventilation and illumination are provided, along with conveniently located washrooms, locker rooms, and lunch rooms, all of which contribute to making such a plant a desirable place to work.

Location.—A modern plant is usually located in a suburban area of a large city, where there is sufficient room for one-story construction, employee parking lots, and possible future expansion. It is adjacent to railway lines, and also is conveniently located with respect to major traffic arteries. The suburban site is possible and increasingly desirable because of the general use of automobiles by employees as a means of getting to work, and would have been impossible prior to the development of this individual means of transportation. The suburban plant is therefore able to draw on the metropolitan area and adjoining suburbs for its labor supply. Similarly, the plant is usually located as close as possible to sources of supply for raw materials.

A number of the major components of an engine, which are machined in the engine plant, are castings produced in an adjacent modern foundry, minimizing handling and shipping costs. The rough castings are transported to the engine plant hourly, indicating the extremely close relationship between a feeder operation and a fabricating and assembly facility.

The proximity of the engine plant and the foundry leads to operating economies, since it permits common use of a central powerhouse and other facilities.

Machining.—Most of the machining operations in the modern engine plant are fully automated, utilizing transfer machines and automatic material handling systems to the fullest extent practicable. The machine tools are designed and constructed for high precision, resulting in the production of parts of uniform quality, and this quality is maintained by frequent checks at all stages of the production process. Accurate control over cutting tools is maintained, and they are replaced before they are worn to an extent which would result in deviations in quality. The machines themselves are lubricated, inspected, and maintained on a predetermined schedule to minimize the possibility of breakdowns. Working parts and lubrication points are readily accessible for inspection and maintenance, and standard electrical, hydraulic, and pneumatic components are used, simplifying the procurement of replacement parts.

Assembly.—While manufacture has capitalized extensively on the effectiveness of automation, the assembly of engines must still be left to the inscrutable coordination of the human hand and eye. However, everything possible has been done to simplify assembly work, and to reduce employee effort and fatigue. All heavy engine components are handled mechanically, and all assembly operations are performed at working heights which are most convenient for the employee. Portable power tools are extensively used in place of hand screw drivers and wrenches, and each work area is laid out to minimize employee effort.

The principle of the continuous movement of work is made possible by suspending the engines from an overhead monorail conveyor on a specially designed hanger which carries them through assembly, testing, storage, and ultimately to the shipping dock. The conveyor is powered by an endless chain, and it is possible to disengage the hanger from the chain when engines are being inspected or stored. The hanger is equipped with devices which allow the engine to be turned in any vertical or horizontal direction for convenient assembly.

Testing and Shipping.—Subsequent to assembly, the engines, still suspended from the overhead conveyor, are transported to individual test stands. Here water, oil, and fuel lines are connected, and the engine is run under its own power for the first time. Following any necessary adjustments, the engines continue to the storage area, or directly to the shipping area, where a section of the overhead monorail conveyor is lowered to allow the engine to be placed directly in a special shipping rack, and the hanger is unfastened. The hanger is carried back to the start of the assembly line to go through the system again, and the loaded engine racks are placed in railroad boxcars by a fork lift truck. The shipping racks become an integral part of the boxcar, which is especially equipped to provide maximum protection for engines in transit, and optimum utilization of space.

The "hot testing" of engines in the same plant where they are made has several advantages. It furnishes a definitive check on engine performance before the engines are shipped hundreds, or even thousands, of miles to final assembly plants; and it allows immediate corrective action to be taken when defective parts or improper assembly methods are disclosed.

This illustrates the degree of integration and preplanning which characterizes the modern engine plant. Combined with automation, efficient assembly practices, and the close coordination of all activities in the plant, this integration makes possible the production of engines of the highest quality of high volumes and economical unit costs.

MODERN MANAGEMENT

Because of the magnitude of many modern mass production enterprises and the complexity of some of their products, such as the automobile, it would be virtually impossible for any one man or small group of men to effectively supervise all aspects of an enterprise in detail. For this reason, many large companies are organized into autonomous or semiautonomous divisions, responsible for the production of a group of related products, together with a central staff for policy-making and coordination. A typical automotive company, for instance, has vehicle divisions charged with responsibility for the final assembly and marketing of the products of the company, and manufacturing divisions responsible for the production of engines, chassis parts, stampings, transmissions, and others.

The direct line of authority and responsibility for meeting production objectives extends directly from the president of the company, through division and plant managers, to department man-

Right: A tremendous range of products is mass-produced, including the 75-foot-long U.S. Air Force Atlas intercontinental ballistic missiles, here being assembled.

MASS PRODUCTION

Below: Final assembly steps in a Japanese television plant. Japanese industry quickly adopted mass production methods which made wide distribution possible.

(Right) General Dynamics Corp., Astronautics Div.; (center left) Consulate General of Japan, N.Y.; (bottom left) General Electric; (bottom right) General Motors

Below: Electric ranges have reached the stage in the assembly line where only the lower oven door and bottom storage door have to be added.

Below: The last step in the mass production of electric refrigerators is checking to make sure that all movable parts are in place.

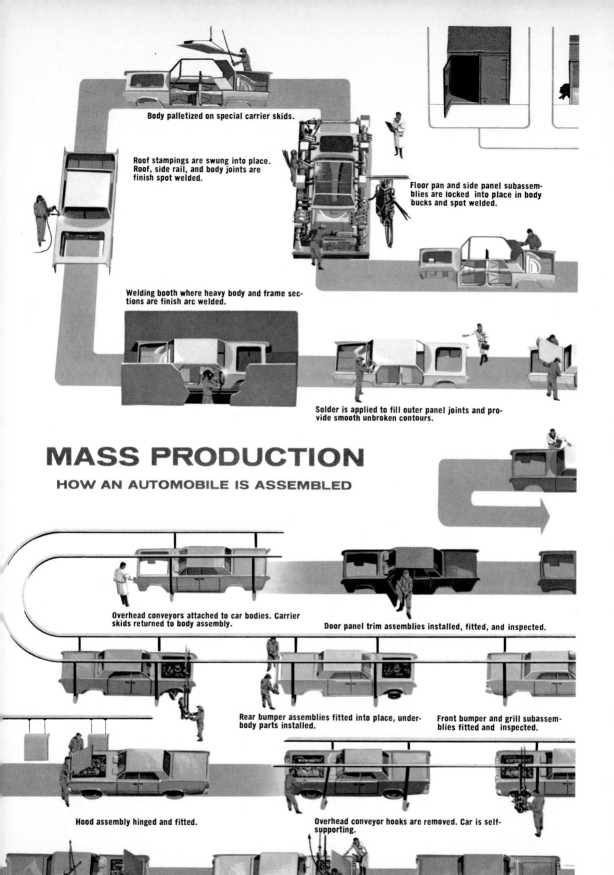

Body palletized on special carrier skids.

Roof stampings are swung into place. Roof, side rail, and body joints are finish spot welded.

Floor pan and side panel subassemblies are locked into place in body bucks and spot welded.

Welding booth where heavy body and frame sections are finish arc welded.

Solder is applied to fill outer panel joints and provide smooth unbroken contours.

MASS PRODUCTION

HOW AN AUTOMOBILE IS ASSEMBLED

Overhead conveyors attached to car bodies. Carrier skids returned to body assembly.

Door panel trim assemblies installed, fitted, and inspected.

Rear bumper assemblies fitted into place, underbody parts installed.

Front bumper and grill subassemblies fitted and inspected.

Hood assembly hinged and fitted.

Overhead conveyor hooks are removed. Car is self-supporting.

Seat subassemblies are installed.

Hydraulic fluids and gasoline installed. Engine started.

Completed car driven to inspection station. Head lamps focused.

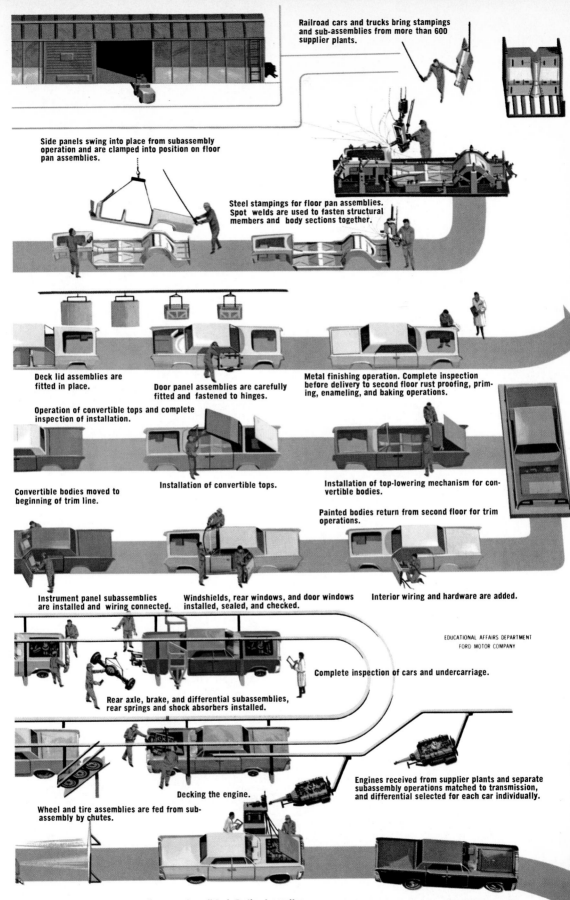

Railroad cars and trucks bring stampings and sub-assemblies from more than 600 supplier plants.

Side panels swing into place from subassembly operation and are clamped into position on floor pan assemblies.

Steel stampings for floor pan assemblies. Spot welds are used to fasten structural members and body sections together.

Deck lid assemblies are fitted in place.

Door panel assemblies are carefully fitted and fastened to hinges.

Metal finishing operation. Complete inspection before delivery to second floor rust proofing, priming, enameling, and baking operations.

Operation of convertible tops and complete inspection of installation.

Convertible bodies moved to beginning of trim line.

Installation of convertible tops.

Installation of top-lowering mechanism for convertible bodies.

Painted bodies return from second floor for trim operations.

Instrument panel subassemblies are installed and wiring connected.

Windshields, rear windows, and door windows installed, sealed, and checked.

Interior wiring and hardware are added.

EDUCATIONAL AFFAIRS DEPARTMENT
FORD MOTOR COMPANY

Complete inspection of cars and undercarriage.

Rear axle, brake, and differential subassemblies, rear springs and shock absorbers installed.

Decking the engine.

Engines received from supplier plants and separate subassembly operations matched to transmission, and differential selected for each car individually.

Wheel and tire assemblies are fed from sub-assembly by chutes.

Dynamometer roll test. Further inspection.

Completed car driven over test track before delivery to truck and rail carriers.

Above: Final body assembly point for two adding machine conveyor lines, producing two models, electric and hand-operated.

MASS PRODUCTION

Left: Calculator housings are painted, conveyed through a drying tunnel, and then are fastened to the machine bodies.

Below: Spool winding is an important step in the manufacture of tape recorders at Bayreuth, Germany.

(Top and left) Ing. C. Olivetti & C., S.p.A.; (below) German Information Center agers, supervisors, and foremen in the various plants.

The company president has overall responsibility for the proper operation of all divisions. Assisted by a staff made up of experts in all fields of management, and by committees of top executives which assist him in making policy decisions, the president sets overall objectives for the company, and, through his staff, exercises functional and financial control over the activities of the various divisions. Each division and plant manager has full responsibility for all the activities of his division, within the limits of practices and policies established by the president and the central office staffs. Normally, division and plant managers are assisted by their own staffs, which are made up of experts on each major phase of manufacturing.

Because division and plant managers are able to make decisions on most matters affecting their operations without going "through channels" to top company executives, no time is lost waiting for decisions. Furthermore, foremen and managers, accustomed to the responsibility of making their own decisions, furnish a pool of talent from which future company executives can be drawn.

INVESTMENT

The tools, machines, and equipment used in modern mass production represent a tremendous investment, as do the land, buildings, material handling systems, and other features of the modern plant. This investment would not be feasible if only a few parts were to be produced. However, where large numbers of identical products are produced, the investment cost per unit becomes progressively smaller as the number of pieces produced increases.

The continuing existence and success of any manufacturing enterprise is dependent on its receiving an adequate return on the investment in tools, machines, and facilities Business in a free economy must make a profit in order to survive.

Modern management thus has a tremendous responsibility. Production lines must be kept running, not only to secure the desired return on investment, but to keep employment at high levels. To this end, much time and effort is expended in developing products for which there is a wide actual or potential demand Advertising in newspapers and magazines is used to stimulate demand, and prices are kept in line with the income of the average consumer through efficient manufacturing methods. Competition also furnishes an important stimulus to planning a better product and developing more efficient methods of manufacturing and distribution.

EFFECTS OF MASS PRODUCTION

Mass producton has had important effects on the consumer, the employee, and the national economy itself. The wide availability of such items as automobiles, radio and television sets, household appliances, and many others has revolutionized the way of life of millions of people, adding both leisure time and a means of utilizing that leisure for pleasure, recreation, or travel.

The productivity of the American industrial worker is the highest in the world. The reason for this is the tremendous investment in modern plants, machines, tools, and equipment, all of which increase the productivity of the worker. This high productivity is reflected in high wages, a high standard of living, shorter working hours,

improved working conditions, and greater employee benefits.

Increasingly, the production worker is becoming a skilled technician. Brain, rather than brawn, is becoming the most important factor in modern industry. The increasing complexity of modern mass production machines and the adoption of automation have caused the need for great numbers of technicians to keep production lines running smoothly. Automatic machines and automated production lines have eliminated much, and in some cases all, of the fatiguing manual effort which was formerly associated with factory work. The primary function of the production employee in the modern manufacturing plant is not to feed a machine—that can now be done automatically—but to keep the machine functioning properly.

Mass production creates jobs. The automobile industry has stimulated employment in the raw materials industries, in supplier plants, and in service stations, garages, and motels, to name only a few. In addition, efficient production results in reduced prices, making products available to new markets and creating a demand for further new products, which in turn results in increased employment, both in the industry initially affected and in the related supply and service industries. Ultimately this chain reaction has a beneficial effect on the entire economy.

MANUFACTURING ENGINEERING OFFICE,
Ford Motor Company.

MASSA, mäs′sä, town, Italy, capital of Massa e Carrara Province, Tuscany, 28 miles northwest of Pisa, near the Ligurian Sea. Nearby are the famous Carrara marble quarries The 15th century Malaspina castle dominates the old town. In the new town are the Palazzo Cybo-Malaspina of that epoch, and a 16th century cathedral. Capital first of a principality, then of a duchy, it was united to Modena in 1829. For a brief time (1938–1946) the city and province were called Apuania. Pop. (1951) 50,192.

MASSACHUSET, mås-à-chōō′sĕt, a tribe of North American Indians of the Algonkian (Algonquian) stock, formerly living in the neighborhood of Massachusetts Bay, between Salem and Plymouth. Their capital, Massachusetts, was where Quincy now stands. A pestilence in 1617 greatly reduced their number and on the arrival of the white settlers the tribe numbered about 500, but a fraction of its former strength. In 1633 this number was further depleted by the ravages of smallpox. The surviving members of the tribe were placed by the whites in the missions of Natick, Nonantum, and Ponkapog in 1646 and gradually disappeared.

MASSACHUSETTS, one of the original thirteen states of the United States. The name is derived from that of an Algonkian confederacy which inhabited the region of Massachusetts Bay. It appears to be compounded from the Algonkian words, *massa* (great), *wadchu* (hill), and *set* (near), meaning "near the great hill," which probably refers to the Blue Hills near Quincy, which was the site of the confederacy's capital. It is bounded on the north by New Hampshire and Vermont, on the west by New York, on the south by Connecticut, Rhode Island, and the Atlantic Ocean, and on the east by the Atlantic Ocean. The main portion of the state is approximately 130 miles from east to west; the width from north to south is 110 miles at the widest parts and in the west is 48 miles.

State Flag of Massachusetts
(Adopted March 18, 1908; revised March 6, 1915)

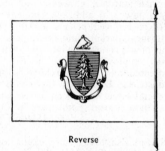

Obverse

(Colors: Commonwealth seal with blue shield on a white field)

Reverse

(Colors: Green pine tree against blue shield on a white field)

Total area	8,257 square miles
Land area	7,867 square miles
Inland water area	390 square miles
Latitude	49°10′—42°53′N.
Longitude	69°57′—73°30′W.
Altitude	sea level to 3,491 feet
Population (1960)	5,148,578
Capital—Boston; population	697,197
Ratified the Constitution	Feb. 6, 1788
State motto	*Ense Petit Placidam Sub Libertate Quietem*
	(By the Sword She Seeks Peace Under Liberty)
State bird (designated 1941)	Chickadee
State flower (adopted 1918)	Mayflower
State tree (adopted 1941)	American elm
State song (unofficial)	*Massachusetts*
State nicknames	Old Bay State; Baked Bean State; Old Colony State; Puritan State

State seal of Massachusetts
(Adopted June 4, 1885)

A discussion of the physical features, resources, government, and the social and economic life of Massachusetts is presented under the following sections:

1. PHYSICAL FEATURES AND RESOURCES

Topography.—The topography of Massachusetts may be described in four regions: western mountains, the Connecticut Valley, central plateau, and eastern lowlands. The mountains in the west, known as the Berkshire Hills, run north and south across the state and are a southern extension of the Green Mountains of Vermont, themselves a part of the Appalachian system. In the extreme west, along the border of New York State, lies the Taconic Range, which reaches an elevation of 3,491 feet in the northwest at Mount Greylock, highest point in the state, and 2,603 feet at Mount Everett in the southwest. East of the Taconic Range lies the picturesque Berkshire Valley, in which are located a number of manufacturing centers, chief of which is Pittsfield, and also residential towns which are noted as summer resorts. The Berkshire Hills to the east comprise a succession of ridges, the highest being the Hoosac Range, which reaches 2,588 feet at Spruce Hill. There is some farming, chiefly on the plateaus, but this region is noted chiefly for its scenic beauty and as a summer resort. The mountain barrier has tended to isolate Massachusetts from the region to the west, with the result that the state faces to the east and south and tends to remain, along with the rest of New England, a distinctive region. East of the Berkshire Hills the broad Connecticut Valley extends across the state from north to south. Here the deep, alluvial soil and the high summer humidity provide rich crops of tobacco, onions, and potatoes. Several manufacturing centers, such as Springfield, Holyoke, and Chicopee, are located in the valley. Dominant features of the landscape here are the traprock ridges which have resisted erosion and which rise sharply from the valley to peaks such as Mount Tom (1,202 feet), Mount Holyoke (878 feet), and Mount Toby (1,269 feet). The central plateau east of the Connecticut is a southern extension of the White Mountains of New Hampshire. It is a hilly and largely wooded region with an elevation of about 1,100 feet in the central portion, but with some higher peaks such as Wachusett Mountain (2,006 feet). East of this plateau the hills slope away to a coastal lowland which was once submerged beneath the sea. The highest point along the coast is the Great Blue Hill of Milton (635 feet). In the eastern region are located most of the population centers, constituting roughly three fourths of the state's population. The shoreline is rocky and picturesque in the north and sandy to the south, and is deeply indented by bays such as Massachusetts Bay, Cape Cod Bay, and Buzzards Bay, and by many inlets. The hook-shaped Cape Cod Peninsula in the southeast, about 65 miles in length, was formed by glacial moraine, as also were the islands of Martha's Vineyard, Nantucket, and the sixteen Elizabeth Islands, which are part of the state. This region with its mild climate, beautiful beaches, and fine harbors for sailing is one of the principal summer resort areas of New England.

Massachusetts is favored with over 4,000 miles of rivers and more than 1,100 lakes. Altogether, including the islands, Massachusetts has a coastline of 1,832 miles with a number of excellent harbors. The Connecticut, dominant river of New England, originating near the Canadian border, bisects the western half of the state from north to south, thus creating the Connecticut Valley. Tributaries from the west are the Deerfield and Westfield rivers, and from the east the Millers and Chicopee rivers. The Berkshire Valley is drained to the south by the Housatonic River, which empties into Long Island Sound, and to the north by the Hoosic River, which flows into the Hudson. The Swift River valley in the central plateau has been dammed to form the large Quabbin Reservoir. Farther east, the Merrimack River rises in New Hampshire and flows for 35 miles through the northeastern corner of Massachusetts; it is navigable by small boats for about 17 miles from Newburyport to Haverhill, but is valuable chiefly as a source of power for the industrial cities of Lowell, Lawrence, and Haverhill. The Concord River empties into the Merrimack, and the Charles River flows into Massachusetts Bay at Boston. In the southeastern part of the state the Blackstone River, valuable for waterpower, and the Taunton River drain into Narragansett Bay. Scattered throughout the state are many small lakes and ponds, mostly of glacial origin. In the Cape Cod region many glacial depressions with rich, peaty soil serve as cranberry bogs.

Along the eastern shore are the harbors of Boston, Lynn, Marblehead, Salem, Gloucester, Newburyport, Plymouth, and Provincetown. Boston and Provincetown accommodate the largest ocean-going vessels. On the south shore are the important harbors of New Bedford on Buzzards Bay, and Fall River on Narragansett Bay.

Climate.—Lying in the middle of the temperate zone, Massachusetts is in the area of recurrent conflicts between cold, dry air masses flowing from the northwest and the warmer, moisture-laden air from the south. The resultant disturbances bring storms and weather changes at fairly frequent intervals. The prevailing winds are from the northwest in winter and south to southwest in summer. Winters are long, leading to short spring seasons, with fairly warm summers, and cool, bracing fall weather. Along the eastern and southern shores the climate is tempered by the ocean, being milder in winter and less oppressive in summer than in the interior. The average January temperature at Williamstown in the northwest is nearly 23°F., while at Boston it is about 30°F., and on Nantucket 32.6°F. The average July temperature is near 70°F. throughout most of the state. The highest temperature recorded is 106°F. and the lowest −28°F. Average dates for the last killing frost in spring are two to three weeks earlier in coastal areas than in the interior and correspondingly later in the fall, so that there is considerable variation in the growing season. Precipitation in most areas exceeds 40 inches annually, with 48 inches as the highest average at any station, and it is rather evenly distributed throughout the 12 months. There is little permanent snow cover along the coast, but in mountain areas snow lies deep for much of the winter.

Water Resources.—Natural water systems and coastlines blending with the landscape constitute one of the prime resources of the state, providing power, water for industrial, agricultural, and domestic use, fish and various other seafoods, and unexcelled facilities for recreation. Combined with the state's other physical features, water resources have had a marked effect upon its development.

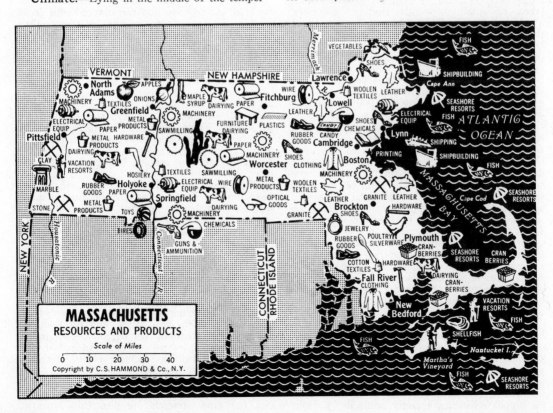

MASSACHUSETTS
RESOURCES AND PRODUCTS
Scale of Miles
0　10　20　30　40
Copyright by C. S. HAMMOND & Co., N.Y.

For example, good harbors were largely responsible for Massachusetts' early eminence in shipping. Furthermore, rivers have played an important part in the history of the state, but primarily as sources of waterpower for manufacturing and the production of electricity, rather than for navigation. The fact that no important river flowed eastward from the center of the state retarded settlement in that region, and early settlers in the Connecticut Valley ascended that river from Long Island Sound. The Connecticut River is navigable in the state only by small boats, but is a valuable source of power.

All or parts of 19 river systems, excluding the coastal streams, provide ample water supplies for domestic, recreational, and industrial purposes. The largest of the lakes, Quabbin Reservoir, 24,704 acres, and Wachusett Reservoir, 4,160 acres, are man-made and provide metropolitan Boston with an excellent supply of water.

Plentiful water resources have played an important part in the successful industrial development of the state throughout its entire history. During earlier years small factories and mills were located along the streams in order to harness the waterpower directly for driving the machines. These streams also provide an abundance of soft water for processing purposes. While much of the state's industry still tends to locate on or near streams, especially those requiring water for non-power purposes, the machines are no longer driven directly by waterpower, but by electricity, much of which is generated in turn by waterpower.

Technical developments in the use of lightweight portable overhead irrigation equipment are rapidly creating an agricultural demand for water. In 1964, over 24,000 acres of intensive crops were irrigated by pumping from streams, lakes, or small man-made storage reservoirs.

With the coming of the electrical era most of the state's waterpower facilities have been converted to generate hydroelectric power. Most of the hydroelectric plants, representing a capacity of over 400,000 horsepower, are located on the Connecticut River and its tributaries in the western half of the state. An estimate made in the mid-1960's was that about 150,000 horsepower was undeveloped.

Soils.—Massachusetts has a large variety of soils among which can be found those suitable for all crops climatically adapted to the area. Of the five million acres of land in the state 210,000, or 4.1 per cent, are suitable for intensive agriculture; 1,580,000 acres, or 31.2 per cent, are suitable for extensive agricultural purposes; while the remaining 64.7 per cent is adaptable for nonagricultural uses and is mainly covered with forest growth.

Siliceous rocks particularly granites, gneisses, schists, and quartzites, predominate in the parent rock material of Massachusetts soils, and largely account for their sandy texture. In the Berkshire region which constitutes the western end of the state, limestone formations have improved the quality of the soils.

Continental glaciation thousands of years ago rejuvenated and redistributed the pre-existent soil mantle, added freshly ground rock material, and softened a previously harsh landscape. In the period since the last invasion of an ice sheet, generous precipitation, aided by a cool climate, has caused Massachusetts soils to be leached of the soluble elements, thereby producing podsolic soils. Three hundred years of exploitative farming have further depleted the soils in some places of plant nutrients, particularly lime, potash, and nitrogen.

Thus, with the exception of those strongly influenced by limestone and those formed on recent alluvial and lacustrine deposits, Massachusetts soils have only low to moderate native fertility. However, these soils respond quickly and readily to good management. The addition of lime, organic matter, and commercial fertilizer makes it possible to maintain a high level of fertility.

Minerals.—Although important mineral resources are not associated with Massachusetts and the deposits are predominantly nonmetallic, many of the metals, including gold, silver, copper, manganese, iron, nickel, tin, and leads, have been found. The nonmetallic minerals include alum, asbestos, barite clay, kaolin, fuller's earth, anthracite, lignite, and bituminous coal, corundum, emery, cyanite, feldspar, fluorspar, garnet, graphite, lime, spondumene, mica, ocher, sienna, peat, pyrite, building and paving sand, building gravel, silica, granite, limestone, marble, sandstone, traprock, talc, soapstone and several of the less rare gem stones such as the aquamarine cheastolite, jasper, rhodonite, spinel, and tourmaline.

Flora.—A wide variety of plants may be found. There are the marsh grasses, sedges, and rushes of the seacoast; the skunk cabbage, white hellebore, marsh marigolds, white and blue violets in the low marshy parts of the uplands; the Solomon's-seal, Canada mayflower, ferns, and trilliums as well as azalea, rhodora, mountain laurel, dogwood, and viburnum on the drier slopes of the uplands. The state is the northern limit for the holly and tupelo.

Forests.—Originally almost all the land of the state except Cape Cod was covered with dense forests. The forest area now includes more than three million acres, which is over 60 per cent of the total land area of the state. The natural forests can be classified as the pine-oak region on Cape Cod, Nantucket, and Martha's Vineyard, the central hardwood region in the eastern part of the state, the white pine-transitional hardwood region in the central area, the spruce in the northwestern area, and the northern hardwood in the far western part of the state. The largest forested areas are in the western area which has a scattering of pine and hemlock in addition to the deciduous forest of maples, birches, beeches, and oaks.

Fauna.—Cape Cod deflects the Gulf Stream in such a way that the water to the south is much warmer than that to the north, and thus the state is a meeting place for many southern and northern species of fauna and flora. For example, southern fishes and other marine life are found in the water south of the cape, including the Portuguese man-of-war, while the water to the north is inhabited by entirely different ocean fauna. Whales are occasionally sighted off the coast or washed up on the beach. Fish caught in the lakes and rivers and along the coast include bass, rock bass, bluefish, butterfish, carp, catfish, cod, eel, flounder, haddock, hake, halibut, herring, mackerel, perch, pickerel, salmon, smelt, sturgeon, swordfish, and trout. The shellfish include clams, lobsters, oysters, scallops, and shrimp.

The deer population has increased in recent years and is now quite abundant. Cottontail rabbits and gray squirrels are plentiful. Muskrat,

COUNTIES

Barnstable (N6) 70,286
Berkshire (B3) 142,135
Bristol (K5) 398,488
Dukes (M7) 5,829
Essex (L2) 568,831
Franklin (D2) 54,864
Hampden (D4) 429,353
Hampshire (D3) 103,229
Middlesex (J3) 1,238,742
Nantucket (O7) 3,559
Norfolk (K4) 510,256
Plymouth (L5) 248,449
Suffolk (K3) 791,329
Worcester (G3) 583,228

CITIES and TOWNS

Abington (L4) ▲10,607
Accord (E8) 256
Acoaxet (K7) 50
Acton (J3) ▲7,238
Adams (B2) ▲12,391
Adams (B2) 11,949
Agawam (D4) ▲15,718
Allerton (E7) 500
Amesbury (L1) ▲10,787
Amesbury (L1) 9,625
Amherst (E3) ▲13,718
Amherst (E3) 10,306
Andover (K2) ▲15,878
Annisquam (M2) 260
Arlington (C6) 49,953
Ashburnham (G2) ▲2,758
Ashby (G2) ▲1,883
Ashfield (C2) ▲1,131
Ashland (J3) ▲7,779
Ashley Falls (A4) 5,000
Assinippi (E8) 500
Assonet (K5) 975
Athol (F2) ▲11,637
Athol (F2) 10,161
Attleboro (J5) 27,118
Attleboro Falls (J5) 2,100
Auburn (G4) ▲14,047
Auburndale (B7) 8,000
Avon (K4) ▲4,301
Ayer (H2) ▲14,927
Ayer (H2) 3,323
Baldwinville (F2) 1,631
Ballard Vale (K2) 1,100
Barnstable◉ (N6) ▲13,465
Barre (F3) ▲3,479
Barre (F3) 1,065
Barre Plains (F3) 532
Barrowsville (K5) 500
Becket (B3) ▲770
Bedford (B6) ▲10,969
Beechwood (F8) 200
Belchertown (E3) ▲5,186
Bellingham (J4) ▲6,774
Belmont (C6) 28,715
Berkley (K5) ▲1,609
Berlin (H3) ▲1,742
Bernardston (D2) ▲1,370
Beverly (E5) 36,108
Beverly Farms (E5) 2,000
Billerica (J2) ▲17,867
Blackinton (B2) 440
Blackstone (H4) ▲5,130
Blandford (C4) ▲636
Bolton (H3) ▲1,264
Bondsville (E4) 1,200
Boston (cap.)◉ (D7) 697,197
Boston (urban area) 2,413,216
Bourne (M6) ▲14,011
Bournedale (M5) 120
Boxborough (H3) ▲744
Boxford (L2) ▲2,010
Boylston (H3) ▲2,367
Braintree (D8) 31,069
Brant Rock (M4) 500
Brewster (O5) ▲1,236
Bridgewater (K5) ▲10,276
Bridgewater (K5) 4,296
Brimfield (F4) ▲1,414
Brockton (K4) 72,813
Brockton (urban area) 111,315
Brookfield (F4) ▲1,751
Brookline (C7) 54,044
Brookville (K4) 1,300
Bryantville (L4) 950
Buckland (C2) ▲1,664
Burlington (C5) ▲12,852
Buzzards Bay (M5) 2,170
Byfield (L1) 900
Cambridge◉ (C7) 107,716
Canton (C8) ▲12,771
Canton Junction (C8) 150
Carlisle (J2) ▲1,488
Carver (M5) ▲1,949
Caryville (J4) 150
Cataumet (M6) 500
Centerville (N6) 1,518
Central Village (K6) 800
Charlemont (C2) ▲897
Charlton (F4) ▲3,685
Charlton City (F4) 1,070
Charlton Depot (F4) 150
Chartley (K5) 800
Chatham (P6) ▲3,273
Chatham (P6) 1,479
Chatham Port (P6) 150
Chelmsford (J2) ▲15,130
Chelsea (D6) 33,749
Cherry Valley (G3) 1,300
Cheshire (B2) ▲2,472
Cheshire (B2) 1,078
Chester (C3) ▲1,155
Chesterfield (C3) ▲556
Chicopee (D4) 61,553
Chicopee-Springfield-Holyoke (urban area) 449,777
Chicopee Falls (D4) 27,000
Chilmark (M7) ▲238
Chiltonville (M5) 400
City Mills (J4) 500
Clicquot-Millis (A8) 2,588
Clifton (E6) 5,000
Clinton (H3) 12,848
Cochituate (A7) 4,500
Cohasset (F7) ▲5,840
Cohasset (F7) 2,748
Collinsville (J2) 2,500
Colrain (D2) ▲1,426
Concord (B6) ▲12,517
Concord (B6) 3,188
Conway (D2) ▲875
Cordaville (H3) 500
Cotuit (N6) 1,041
Cummaquid (N6) 300
Cummington (C3) ▲550
Cushman (D3) 250
Cuttyhunk (L7) 60
Dalton (B3) ▲6,436
Danvers (D5) 21,926
Danversport (E5) 1,500
Dartmouth (K6) ▲14,607
Dedham◉ (C7) 23,869
Deerfield (D2) ▲3,338
Dennis (O5) 3,727
Dennis Port (O6) 1,271
Dighton (K5) ▲3,769
Dodge (G4) 1,083
Dodgeville (K5) 750
Dorchester (D7) 150,000
Douglas (H4) ▲2,559
Dover (B7) ▲2,846
Dracut (J2) ▲13,674
Dudley (G4) ▲6,510
Dunstable (J2) ▲824
Duxbury (M4) ▲4,727
Duxbury (M4) 1,069
East Blackstone (H4)....
East Braintree (D8) 10,000
East Brewster (O5) 500
East Bridgewater (L4) ▲6,139
East Brookfield (G4) ▲1,533
East Brookfield (G4) 1,150
East Dedham (C8) 1,500
East Dennis (O5) 450
East Douglas (G4) 1,695
East Falmouth (M6) 1,655
East Foxboro (K4) 600
East Freetown (L5) 1,200
Eastham (O5) ▲1,200
Easthampton (D3) ▲12,326
East Harwich (O6) 650
East Lee (B3) 250
East Longmeadow (E4) ▲10,294
East Milton (D7) 7,500
East Northfield (E2) 950
East Norton (K5) 800
Easton (K4) ▲9,078
Eastondale (K4) 600
East Orleans (P5) 383
East Otis (B4) 200
East Pembroke (M4) 275
East Pepperell (H2) 2,500
East Sandwich (N6) 325
East Saugus (D6) 4,000
East Taunton (K5) 5,000
East Templeton (G2) 1,200
East Village (G4) 621
East Walpole (C8) 2,000
East Wareham (M5) 975
East Weymouth (E8) 10,000
East Whatley (D3) 425
Edgartown (M7) ▲1,474
Edgartown◉ (M7) 1,181
Egypt (F8) 600
Elmwood (L4) 350
Erving (E2) ▲1,272
Essex (L2) ▲2,238
Everett (D6) 43,544
Fairhaven (L6) ▲14,339
Fairview (D4) 2,108
Fall River (K6) 99,942
Fall River (urban area) 123,951
Falmouth (M6) ▲13,037
Falmouth (M6) 3,308
Farnams (B2) 144
Farnumsville (H4) 1,041
Fayville (H3) 975
Feeding Hills (D4) 4,000
Fiskdale (F4) 1,200
Fitchburg (G2) 43,021
Fitchburg-Leominster (urban area) 72,347
Florence (D3) 5,000
Florida (B2) ▲569
Forge Village (H2) 1,191
Foxboro (J4) ▲10,136
Foxboro (J4) 3,169
Framingham (A7) 44,526
Framingham Center (J3) 4,500
Franklin (J4) ▲10,530
Franklin (J4) 6,391
Furnace (F3) 140
Gardner (G2) 19,038
Gay Head (L7) ▲103
Georgetown (L2) ▲3,755
Georgetown (L2) 2,005
Gilbertville (F3) 1,202
Gill (D2) ▲1,203
Gleasondale (J3) 300
Glendale (A3) 300
Gloucester (M2) 25,789
Goshen (C3) ▲385
Grafton (H4) ▲10,627
Granby (E3) ▲4,221
Graniteville (J2) 975
Granville (C4) ▲874
Great Barrington (A4) ▲6,624
Great Barrington (A4) 2,943
Greenbush (F8) 650
Greenfield (D2) ▲17,690
Greenfield◉ (D2) 14,389
Green Harbor (M4) 650
Greenwood (D6) 5,000
Griswoldville (D2) 675
Groton (H2) ▲3,904
Groton (H2) 1,178
Groveland (L1) ▲3,297
Hadley (D3) ▲3,099
Halifax (L5) ▲1,599
Hamilton (L2) ▲5,488
Hampden (E4) ▲2,345
Hancock (A2) ▲455
Hanover (L4) ▲5,923
Hanson (L4) ▲4,370
Hardwick (F3) ▲2,340
Hartsville (B4) 100
Harvard (H2) ▲2,563
Harwich (O6) ▲3,747
Harwich Port (O6) 1,592
Hatfield (D3) ▲2,350
Hatfield (D3) 1,330
Haverhill (K1) 46,346
Haydenville (C3) 950
Heath (C2) ▲304
Hingham (E8) ▲15,378
Hinsdale (B3) ▲1,414
Holbrook (D8) ▲10,104
Holden (G3) ▲10,117
Holden (G3) 1,704
Holland (F4) ▲561
Holliston (A8) ▲6,222
Holliston (A8) 2,447
Holyoke (D4) 52,689
Holyoke-Springfield-Chicopee (urban area) 225,446
Hoosac Tunnel (C2) 200
Hopedale (H4) ▲3,987
Hopedale (H4) 2,904
Hopkinton (J4) ▲4,932
Hopkinton (J4) 2,754
Hortonville (K5) 150
Housatonic (A3) 1,370
Hubbardston (F3) ▲1,217
Hudson (H3) ▲9,666
Hudson (H3) 7,897
Hull (E7) ▲7,055
Humarock (M4) 200
Huntington (C4) ▲1,392
Hyannis (N6) 5,139
Hyannis Port (N6) 300
Hyde Park (C7) 34,633
Interlaken (A3) 350
Ipswich (L2) ▲8,544
Ipswich (L2) 4,617
Islington (C8) 2,300
Jamaica Plain (C7) 36,476
Jefferson (G3) 975
Kingston (M5) ▲4,302
Kingston (M5) 1,301
Lakeville (L5) ▲3,209
Lancaster (H3) ▲3,958
Lanesboro (A2) ▲2,933
Lanesville (M2) 1,046
Lawrence (K2) 70,933
Lawrence-Haverhill (urban area) 166,125
Lee (B3) ▲5,271
Lee (B3) 3,078
Leeds (D3) 1,200
Leicester (G4) ▲8,177
Leicester (G4) 1,750
Lenox (A3) ▲4,253
Lenox (A3) 1,713
Lenox Dale (B3) 500
Leominster (G2) 27,929
Leverett (E3) ▲914
Lexington (B6) 27,691
Leyden (D2) ▲343
Lincoln Center (B6) 5,613
Linwood (H4) 995
Littleton (H2) ▲5,109
Littleton Common (J2) 2,277
Longmeadow (D4) ▲10,565
Lowell (J2) 92,107
Lowell (urban area) 118,547
Ludlow (E4) ▲13,805
Ludlow Center (E4) 500
Lunenburg (H2) ▲6,334
Lynn (D6) 94,478
Lynnfield (D5) ▲8,398
Lynnfield Center (C5) 2,600
Madaket (N7) 50
Magnolia (M2) 450
Malden (D6) 57,676
Manchaug (G4) 1,800
Manchester (F5) ▲3,932
Manomet (M5) 1,800
Mansfield (J4) ▲7,773
Mansfield (J4) 4,674
Marblehead (E5) 18,521
Marion (L6) ▲2,881
Marion (L6) 1,160
Marlborough (H3) 18,819
Marshfield (M4) ▲6,748
Marshfield Hills (M4) 875
Marstons Mills (N6) 900
Mashpee (M6) ▲867
Mattapan (C7) 19,086
Mattapoisett (L6) ▲3,117
Mattapoisett (L6) 1,640
Maynard (J3) 7,695
Medfield (B8) ▲6,021
Medfield (B8) 2,424
Medford (C6) 64,971
Medway (J4) ▲5,168
Medway (J4) 1,602
Melrose (D6) 29,619
Mendon (H4) ▲2,068
Menemsha (L7) 70
Merino Village (G4) 3,099
Merrimac (L1) ▲3,261
Merrimacport (L1) 300
Methuen (K2) 28,114
Middleboro (L5) ▲11,065
Middleboro (L5) 6,003
Middlefield (B3) ▲315
Middleton (K2) ▲3,718
Milford (H4) ▲14,749
Milford (H4) 13,722
Millbrook (M4) 125
Millbury (H4) 9,623
Millers Falls (E2) 1,199
Millis-Clicquot (A8) 2,588
Mill River (A4) 350
Millville (H4) ▲1,567
Millville (H4) 1,141
Milton (D7) 26,375
Minot (F8) 375
Monroe Bridge (C2) 176
Monson (E4) ▲6,712
Monson (E4) 2,413
Montague (E2) ▲7,836
Montague City (D2) 609
Monterey (B4) ▲480
Montville (B4) ....
Monument Beach (M6) 650
Moores Corner (E2) 128
Mount Hermon (D2) 760
Mount Tom (D3) 210
Mount Washington (A4) ▲34
Myricks (K5) 500
Nabnasset (J2) 1,381
Nahant (E6) 3,960
Nantasket Beach (E7) 1,900
Nantucket (O7) ▲3,559
Nantucket◉ (O7) 2,804
Natick (A7) 28,831
Needham (B7) 25,793
Needham Heights (B7) 8,000
Neponset (D7) 5,573
New Bedford (K6) 102,477
New Bedford (urban area) 126,657
New Braintree (F3) ▲509
Newbury (L1) ▲2,519
Newburyport (L1) 14,004
New Lenox (B3) ....
New Marlboro (B4) ▲1,083
New Salem (E2) ▲397
Newton (C7) 92,384
Newton Center (C7) 18,850
Newton Highlands (C7) 7,500
Newton Lower Falls (B7) 1,215
Newton Upper Falls (C7) 3,451
Newtonville (C7) 15,000
Nonquitt (L6) 487
Noquochoke P.O. (Westport) (K6) ▲6,641
Norfolk (J4) ▲3,471
North Abington (L4) 3,906
North Acton (J2) 300
North Adams (B2) 19,905
North Amherst (E3) 1,009
Northampton◉ (D3) 30,058
North Andover (K2) ▲10,908
North Attleboro (J5) ▲14,777
North Bellingham (J4) 300
North Billerica (J2) 4,500
Northboro (H3) ▲6,687
Northboro (H3) 2,516
Northbridge (H4) ▲10,800
Northbridge (H4) 2,128
North Brookfield (F3) ▲3,616
North Brookfield (F3) 2,615
North Carver (L5) 500
North Chatham (O6) 200
North Chelmsford (J2) 4,670
North Cohasset (F7) 1,500
North Dartmouth (K6) 6,500
North Dighton (K5) 1,167
North Eastham (O5) 600
North Easton (K4) 3,800
North Egremont (A4) 265
North Falmouth (M6) 700
Northfield (E2) ▲2,320
Northfield (E2) 1,179
Northfield Farms (E2) 500
North Grafton (H4) 2,800
North Hadley (D3) 750
North Hanover (L4) 800
North Harwich (O6) 200
North Hatfield (D3) 240
North Leominster (G2) 5,700
North Marshfield (M4) 500
North Middleboro (L5) 500
North Oxford (G4) 1,466
North Pembroke (M4) 600
North Plymouth (L5) 3,467
North Reading (C5) ▲8,331
North Rutland (G3) 125
North Scituate (F8) 3,421
North Swansea (K5) 200
North Truro (O4) 500
North Uxbridge (H4) 1,882

◉County seat. ▲Population of township.

All figures available from 1960 final census are supplemented by local official estimates.

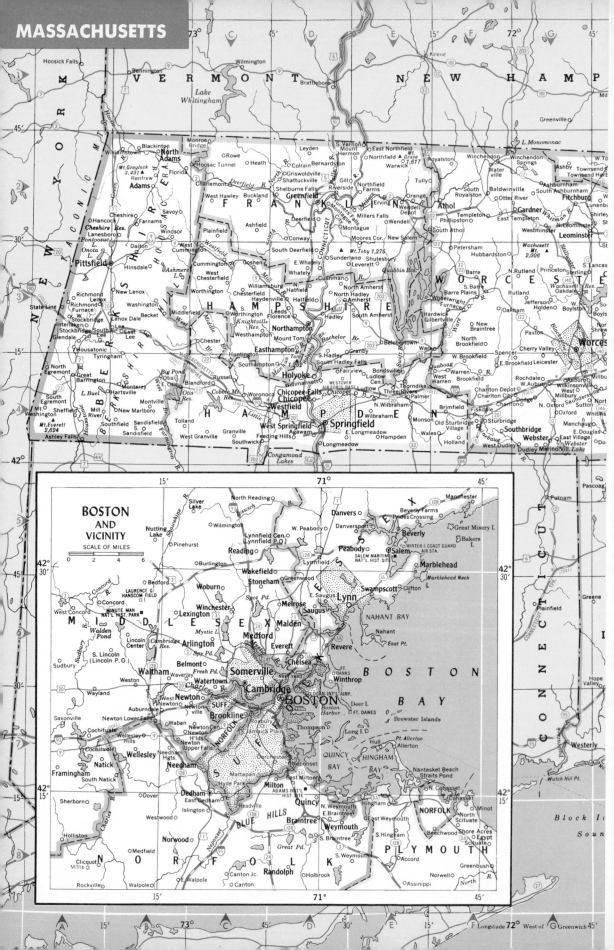

North Westport (K6)...4,000
North Weymouth (D8)... 700
North Wilbraham (E4)...3,000
Norton (H5)...▲6,818
Norton (K5)...1,501
Norwell (F8)...▲5,207
Norwood (B8)...24,898
Nutting Lake (B5)...
Oak Bluffs (M7)...▲1,419
Oak Bluffs (M7)...1,027
Oakdale (G3)... 650
Oakham (F3)... ▲524
Ocean Bluff (M4)... 300
Ocean Grove (K6)...1,500
Old Sturbridge Village (F4)...
Onset (M6)...1,714
Orange (E2)...▲6,154
Orange (E2)...3,689
Orleans (O5)...▲2,342
Osterville (N6)...1,094
Otis (B4)... ▲473
Otter River (F2)... 660
Oxford (G4)...▲9,282
Oxford (G4)...6,985
Palmer (E4)...▲10,358
Palmer (E4)...3,888
Paxton (G3)...▲2,399
Peabody (E5)...32,202
Pembroke (L4)...▲4,919
Pepperell (H2)...▲4,336
Petersham (F3)... ▲890
Phillipston (F2)... ▲695
Pigeon Cove (M2)...1,064
Pinehurst (B5)...1,991
Pittsfield◉ (A3)...57,879
Pittsfield (urban area)...62,306
Plainfield (C2)... ▲237
Plainville (J4)...▲3,810
Pleasant Lake (O6)... 200
Plymouth (M5)...▲14,445
Plymouth◉ (M5)...6,488
Plympton (L5)... ▲821
Pocasset (M6)...1,035
Pottersville (K6)...2,700
Prides Crossing (E5)... 450
Princeton (G3)...▲1,360
Provincetown (O4)...▲3,389
Provincetown (O4)...3,346
Quincy (D7)...87,409
Quissett (M6)... 300
Randolph (D8)...18,900
Reading (C5)...19,259
Readville (C8)...33,123
Rehoboth (K5)...▲4,953
Renfrew (B2)...
Revere (D6)...40,080
Richmond (A3)... ▲890
Richmond Furnace (A3) 200
Riverside (D2)... 500
Rochdale (G4)...1,058
Rochester (L6)...▲1,559
Rock (L5)... ▲487
Rockland (L4)...▲13,119
Rockport (M2)...▲4,616
Rockport (M2)...3,511
Rockville (A8)... 500
Rowe (C2)... ▲231
Rowley (L2)...▲2,783
Rowley (L2)...1,223
Roxbury (C7)...82,246
Royalston (F2)... ▲800
Russell (C4)...▲1,366
Rutland (G3)...▲3,253
Rutland (G3)...1,774
Sagamore (M5)... 900
Salem◉ (E5)...39,211
Salisbury (L1)...▲3,154
Salisbury Beach (L1)... 550
Sand Hills-Shore Acres (M4)...1,778
Sandisfield (B4)... ▲536
Sandwich (N5)...▲2,082
Sandwich (N5)...1,099
Santuit (N6)... 320
Saugus (D6)...20,666
Saundersville (G4)... 950
Savoy (B2)... ▲277
Saxonville (A7)...3,200
Scituate (F8)...▲11,214
Scituate (F8)...3,229
Scotland (L5)... 400
Seekonk (J5)...▲8,399
Segreganset (K5)... 95
Sharon (K4)...▲10,070
Sharon (K4)...5,888
Shattuckville (D2)... 150
Shawsheen Village (K2)...2,100
Sheffield (A4)...▲2,138
Shelburne Falls (D2)...2,097
Sheldonville (J4)... 300
Sherborn (A8)...▲1,806
Shirley (H2)...▲5,202
Shirley (H2)...1,762
Shirley Center (H2)...2,000
Shore Acres-Sand Hills (F8)...1,778
Shrewsbury (H3)...▲16,622
Shutesbury (E3)... ▲265
Siasconset (P7)... 200
Silver Lake (L5)... 500
Somerset (K5)...12,196
Somerville (C6)...94,697
South Acton (J3)...1,114
South Amherst (E3)... 975
Southampton (C4)...▲2,192
South Ashburnham (G2)... 975
South Athol (F2)... 131
South Attleboro (J5)...6,000
South Barre (F3)...
South Berlin (H3)... 300
Southboro (H3)...▲3,996
Southboro (H3)...1,114
South Braintree (D8)...5,600
Southbridge (G4)...▲16,523
Southbridge (G4)...15,889
South Bridgewater (L5)...2,000
South Carver (M5)... 500
South Chatham (O6)... 500
South Dartmouth (L6)...6,300
South Deerfield (D3)...1,253
South Dennis (O6)... 500
South Duxbury (M4)... 950
South Easton (K4)...3,500
South Egremont (A4)... 425
Southfield (B4)... 195
South Grafton (H4)...1,663
South Groveland (L2)... 900
South Hadley (D4)...▲14,956
South Hadley Falls (D4)...5,000
South Hanover (L4)... 800
South Harwich (O6)... 400
South Hingham (E8)... 650
South Lancaster (H3)...1,891
South Lee (A3)... 375
South Lincoln (Lincoln P.O.) (B6)... 950
South Middleboro (L5).. 486
South Natick (A7)...1,500
South Orleans (O5)... 200
South Royalston (F2)... 450
South Sandisfield (B4)..
South Sudbury (J3)...3,000
South Vernon (D2)... 125
Southville (H3)... 500
South Walpole (K4)...1,450
South Wellfleet (P5)... 450
South Westport (K6)... 250
South Weymouth (E8) 10,000
Southwick (C4)...▲5,139
Southwick (C4)...1,242
South Worthington (C3)... 42
South Yarmouth (O6)...2,029
Spencer (F3)...▲7,838
Spencer (F3)...5,593
Springfield◉ (D4)...174,463
Springfield-Chicopee-Holyoke (urban area)...449,773
State Line (A3)... 300
Sterling (G3)...▲3,193
Still River (H3)... 150
Stockbridge (A3)...▲2,161
Stoneham (C6)...17,821
Stoughton (K4)...▲16,328
Stow (H3)...▲2,573
Straits Pond (F7)... 250
Sturbridge (F4)...▲3,604
Sudbury (A6)...▲7,447
Sunderland (D3)...▲1,279
Sutton (G4)...▲3,638
Swampscott (E6)...13,294
Swansea (K5)...▲9,916
Swansea Center (K5)... 950
Taunton◉ (K5)...41,132
Teaticket (E. Falmouth P.O.) (M6)... 950
Templeton (F2)...▲5,371
Tewksbury (K2)...▲15,902
Tewksbury (K2)...1,151
Thorndike (E4)...1,552
Three Rivers (E4)...3,082
Tolland (B4)... ▲101
Topsfield (L2)...▲3,351
Townsend (H2)...▲3,650
Townsend Harbor (G2).. 197
Truro (O5)...▲1,002
Tully (E2)... 50
Turners Falls (D2)...4,917
Twin Village (J5)...
Tyngsboro (J2)...▲3,302
Tyringham (A4)... ▲197
Upton (H4)...▲3,127
Upton-West Upton (H4)...1,991
Uxbridge (H4)...▲7,789
Uxbridge (H4)...3,377
Vineyard Haven (M7)...1,701
Waban (B7)...7,300
Wakefield (C5)...24,295
Wales (F4)... ▲659
Walpole (B8)...▲14,068
Waltham (B6)...55,413
Waquoit (M6)... 400
Ware (E3)...▲7,517
Ware (E3)...6,650
Wareham (L5)...▲9,461
Wareham Center (L5)...1,739
Warren (F4)...▲3,383
Warren (F4)...1,616
Warwick (E2)... ▲426
Washington (B3)... ▲290
Watertown (C6)...▲39,092
Waterville (F2)... 296
Waverley (B6)...10,000
Wayland (A7)...▲10,444
Webster (G4)...▲13,680
Webster (G4)...12,072
Wellesley (B7)...26,071
Wellesley Hills (B7)...15,600
Wellfleet (O5)...▲1,404
Wendell (E2)... ▲292
Wendell Depot (E2)... 21
Wenham (L2)...▲2,798
West Acton (H3)...
West Auburn (G4)...
West Barnstable (N6)... 695
West Berlin (H3)... 300
Westboro (H3)...▲9,599
Westboro (H3)...4,011
West Boxford (K2)... 700
West Boylston (G3)...▲5,526
West Brewster (O5)...
West Bridgewater (K4)...▲5,061
West Brookfield (F4)...▲2,053
West Brookfield (F4)...1,250
West Chatham (O6)... 400
West Chelmsford (J2)... 300
West Chesterfield (C3).. 200
West Concord (A6)...1,556
West Cummington (B3) 96
West Dennis (O6)... 782
West Dudley (F4)... 200
West Falmouth (M6)... 700
Westfield (D4)...26,302
Westford (J2)...▲6,261
West Granville (C4)... 200
West Groton (H2)...1,100
Westhampton (C3)... ▲583
West Hanover (L4)...1,200
West Harwich (O6)... 450
West Hawley (C2)... 56
West Mansfield (K5)... 900
West Medway (J4)...1,818
West Millbury (G4)... 450
Westminster (G2)...▲4,022
Westminster (G2)...1,047
West Newbury (L1)...▲1,844
West Newton (B7)...15,000
Weston (B6)...▲8,261
West Peabody (D5)...1,100
Westport (K6)...▲6,641
Westport Point (K6)... 500
Westport P.O. (N. Westport) (K6)...4,000
West Springfield (D4)...▲24,924
West Stockbridge (A3)...▲1,244
West Tisbury (M7)... ▲360
West Townsend (H2)...1,300
West Upton-Upton (H4)...1,991
West Wareham (L5)... 800
West Warren (F4)...1,124
Westwood (B8)...▲10,354
West Yarmouth (N6)...1,365
Weymouth (D8)...48,177
Whately (D3)...▲1,037
Wheelwright (F3)... 350
Whitinsville (H4)...5,102
Whitman (L4)...10,485
Wilbraham (E4)...▲7,387
Wilkinsonville (G4)... 800
Williamsburg (C3)...▲2,186
Williamstown (B2)...▲7,322
Williamstown (B2)...5,428
Willimansett (D4)...10,181
Wilmington (C5)...▲12,475
Wilmington (C5)...2,250
Winchendon (F2)...▲6,237
Winchendon (F2)...3,839
Winchendon Sprs. (G2) 333
Winchester (C6)...19,376
Windsor (B2)... ▲384
Winthrop (D6)...20,303
Woburn (C6)...31,214
Woods Hole (M6)... 975
Woodville (H4)... 450
Worcester◉ (H3)...186,587
Worcester (urban area)...225,446
Woronoco (C4)... 425
Worthington (C3)... ▲597
Wrentham (J4)...▲6,685
Wrentham (J4)...1,790
Yarmouth (O6)...▲5,504
Yarmouth Port (N6)... 450

OTHER FEATURES

Adams Nat'l Hist. Site ..D 7
Agawam (river)...M 5
Allerton (point)...E 7
Ann (cape)...M 2
Ashmere (lake)...B 3
Assabet (river)...H 3
Assawompset (pond)...L 5
Bachelor (brook)...D 3
Bakers (isl.)...F 5
Banks, Fort...D 6
Berkshire (hills)...B 4
Big (pond)...B 4
Billingsgate (isl.)...O 5
Blackstone (river)...G 3
Blue (hills)...C 8
Boston (bay)...E 6
Boston (harbor)...D 7
Brewster (isls.)...E 7
Buel (lake)...A 4
Buzzards (bay)...L 7
Cambridge (res.)...B 6
Camp Wellfleet...P 5
Cape Cod (bay)...N 5
Cape Cod (canal)...N 5
Cape Cod Nat'l Seashore P 5
Chappaquiddick (isl.)...N 7
Charles (river)...C 7
Cheshire (res.)...A 2
Chicopee (river)...D 4
Cobble Mountain (res.) ..C 4
Cochituate (lake)...A 7
Cod (cape)...O 4
Concord (river)...J 2
Congamond (lakes)...D 4
Connecticut (river)...D 2
Cuttyhunk (isl.)...L 7
Dawes, Fort...E 7
Deer (isl.)...E 7
Deerfield (river)...C 2
Devens, Fort...H 2
East (point)...E 6
East Chop (point)...M 7
Eastern (point)...M 2
Elizabeth (isls.)...L 7
Everett (mt.)...A 4
Falls (river)...D 2
Farmington (river)...B 4
Fort Banks...D 6
Fort Dawes...E 7
Fort Devens...H 2
Fort Rodman...L 6
Fresh (pond)...C 6
Gammon (point)...N 6
Gay (head)...L 7
Grace (mt.)...E 2
Great (point)...O 7
Great (pond)...D 8
Great Misery (isl.)...F 5
Green (river)...B 2
Greylock (mt.)...B 2
Gurnet (point)...M 4
Hingham (bay)...E 7
Holyoke (range)...D 3
Hoosac (mts.)...B 2
Hoosic (river)...A 1
Housatonic (river)...A 4
Ipswich (river)...L 2
Knightville (res.)...C 3
Laurence G. Hanscom Field...B 6
Little (river)...C 4
Logan Int'l Airport...D 6
Long (isl.)...E 7
Long (point)...O 4
Long (pond)...L 5
Manhan (river)...D 4
Manomet (point)...N 5
Marblehead (neck)...F 6
Martha's Vineyard (isl.)...M 7
Massachusetts (bay)...M 4
Merrimack (river)...K 1
Mill (river)...C 3
Mill (river)...D 3
Millers (river)...E 2
Minute Man Nat'l Hist. Park...B 6
Mishaum (point)...L 6
Monomonac (lake)...G 2
Monomoy (isl.)...O 6
Monomoy (point)...O 6
Mount Hope (bay)...K 6
Muskeget (channel)...N 7
Muskeget (isl.)...N 7
Mystic (lake)...C 6
Mystic (river)...C 6
Nahant (bay)...E 6
Nantucket (isl.)...O 8
Nantucket (sound)...N 6
Nashawena (isl.)...L 7
Nashua (river)...H 3
Naushon (isl.)...L 7
Neponset (river)...C 8
Nonamesset (isl.)...M 6
North (river)...D 2
North (river)...L 4
Onota (lake)...A 3
Otis (res.)...B 4
Otis A.F.B....M 6
Pasque (isl.)...L 7
Plum (isl.)...L 2
Plymouth (bay)...M 5
Poge (cape)...N 7
Pontoosuc (lake)...A 3
Quabbin (res.)...E 3
Quaboag (river)...F 4
Quincy (bay)...D 7
Quinebaug (river)...F 4
Race (point)...N 4
Rodman, Fort...L 6
Salem Maritime Nat'l Hist. Site...E 5
Shawshine (river)...K 2
Silver (lake)...L 4
South (river)...D 2
Spot (pond)...C 6
Spy (pond)...C 6
Squibnocket (point)...M 7
Stillwater (river)...G 3
Sudbury (res.)...H 3
Sudbury (river)...A 6
Swift (river)...E 4
Taconic (mts.)...A 2
Taunton (river)...K 5
Thatcher (isl.)...M 2
Thompson (isl.)...D 7
Toby (mt.)...E 3
Tom (mt.)...D 4
Tuckernuck (isl.)...N 7
Vineyard (sound)...L 7
Wachusett (mt.)...G 3
Wachusett (res.)...G 3
Walden (pond)...A 6
Ware (river)...F 3
Watuppa (pond)...K 6
Webster (lake)...G 4
Wellfleet (harbor)...O 5
Wellfleet, Camp...P 5
West (isl.)...L 6
West (river)...H 4
West Chop (point)...M 7
Westfield (river)...C 3
Westover Air Force Base D 4
Weweantic (river)...L 5
Whitman (river)...G 2
Winter Isl. Coast Guard Air Sta....E 5

mink, skunk, raccoon, weasel, otter, bobcats, red fox, and gray fox are fur-bearing animals to be hunted.

A large variety of water, marsh, and shore birds find their homes along the seacoast and streams. The best known of the long-winged swimming birds are the gulls and terns. The ring-necked pheasant and the ruffed and Whitlow grouse are among the ground-dwelling, scratching game birds to be found. Among the birds of prey are the eagle, turkey buzzard, and many members of the hawk and owl families. The perching birds include the lark, starling, bluejay, bobolink, cowbird, blackbird, meadowlark, oriole, rusty blackbird, grackle, and twenty varieties of sparrows.

2. POPULATION AND POLITICAL DIVISIONS

Population Characteristics.—The population of Massachusetts increased from 378,787 in 1790 to 5,148,578 in 1960. During the earlier years of this period the percentage rate of growth was slightly over 10 per cent each decade. The rate of growth reached its peak during the decade 1850–1860 with an increase of 34.8 per cent. From 1880 to 1910 the growth rate was approximately 25 per cent for each decade. After that it tapered off rapidly and for the decade 1930–1940 was only 1.6 per cent. Official United States census figures indicate a resumption of the upward trend in population growth at the rate of 8.7 per cent in 1940–1950 and 9.8 per cent in 1950–1960.

During colonial days Massachusetts was typical in that its population was predominantly rural. The percentage of rural population decreased steadily from 86.5 per cent of the total in 1790 to 9.8 per cent in 1930. Thus Massachusetts has become a predominantly urban state. However, the United States censuses of 1940, 1950, and 1960 indicated a reversal of this trend, with people moving into rural areas and commuting to their urban places of employment. The rural population represented 15.6 per cent of the state total in 1950 and 16.4 per cent in 1960.

In 1960 there were 93.3 males per 100 females as compared with 97.4 for the United States as a whole. The birthrate per thousand was 18.5 (United States 18.9) and the death rate 11.3 (United States 9.5), as of 1966. The 1960 census showed 1,534,732 households with 3.23 per thousand (United States 3.38). The median age was 32.1 years.

Age groupings	Number	Per cent of total
Under 5 years	548,457	10.7
5 to 9 years	487,905	9.5
10 to 14 years	444,471	8.6
15 to 19 years	361,938	7.0
20 to 24 years	294,149	5.7
25 to 29 years	297,759	5.8
30 to 34 years	334,486	6.5
35 to 39 years	355,186	6.9
40 to 44 years	342,584	6.7
45 to 49 years	319,160	6.2
50 to 54 years	289,968	5.6
55 to 59 years	262,545	5.1
60 to 64 years	238,361	4.6
65 to 69 years	210,912	4.1
70 to 74 years	162,348	3.2
75 to 84 years	162,798	3.2
85 years and over	35,551	0.7
Total of all ages	5,148,578	100.0
21 years and over	3,245,066	

The population is approximately 89 per cent native; 97.6 per cent were white, 2.2 per cent Negro, and 0.2 per cent other races as of 1960. The foreign-born population comes from many countries, with Canada first (152,075), Italy next (86,921), and the Republic of Ireland third (51,428).

Political Divisions.—The state has 14 counties and these in turn are divided into 351 minor civil divisions, 39 of which are chartered by the General Court as cities with the city form of government and 312 are unincorporated towns with no distinction between the thickly settled urban and sparsely occupied rural areas. This creates an obvious problem of establishing arbitrary distinctions between urban and rural areas for purposes of census taking. Hence the Bureau of the Census in 1960 separately identified 39 cities, 31 "urban towns," and 122 unincorporated thickly settled "places" of 1,000 population or more.

Cities and Metropolitan Areas.—The cities ranged in size from Newburyport, with a population in 1960 of 14,004, to Boston, with 697,197. According to the 1960 census, Massachusetts had 20 cities with populations of over 50,000, a total matched only by Pennsylvania and exceeded only by California. Besides Boston, cities of more than 100,000 are: Cambridge, New Bedford, Springfield, and Worcester. Those with more than 50,000 include Brockton, Brookline, Chicopee, Fall River, Holyoke, Lawrence, Lowell, Lynn, Malden, Medford, Newton, Pittsfield, Somerville, and Waltham. (For populations of these and other cities, see individual articles and the back of the state map.)

The Census Bureau in 1960 designated 10 metropolitan areas within the state. These were Boston, Brockton, Fall River, Fitchburg-Leominster, Lawrence-Haverville, Lowell, New Bedford, Pittsfield, Springfield-Chicopee-Holyoke, and Worcester. The standard metropolitan area of Boston included the whole of Suffolk County and parts of Middlesex, Essex, Plymouth, and Norfolk counties.

The Boston metropolitan area, with a population of 2,589,301 in 1960, compared with 2,369,986 in 1950, ranked as seventh most populous in the United States. The area is also one of the nation's largest wholesale centers, a leader in per capita retail sales, one of the outstanding in-

Ewing Galloway

Monument to hardy New England whalers, New Bedford.

dustrial centers, and a leading educational center. Its activities include the usual industries associated with a large population center, with more than ordinary emphasis on confectionery, drugs, chemicals, sugar refining, soap, plastics, printing and publishing, electrical machinery, and other fine metal products.

The Lowell and Lawrence metropolitan areas, located in the Merrimack River valley, have long been centers for extensive textile manufacturing, including cottons, woolens, and worsteds. Other manufactures include such diversified products as boots and shoes, hard rubber products, soap, plastics, chemicals, paper, boxes, electronics, machinery, and a variety of metal products.

The Fall River and New Bedford metropolitan areas, located on the southern shore of the state, have climatic conditions which gave the area an early lead in the manufacture of fine cotton goods, in addition to marine equipment. In recent years, however, there has been a tendency towards diversification into other fields, such as dyeing and finishing, leather goods, rubber goods, tire fabrics, and fine metal products, including copper, brass, and silverware.

Located in the Connecticut River valley, the Springfield-Holyoke metropolitan area ranks high in the manufacture of paper and textiles of all kinds, rubber goods, chemicals, games and toys, electronics, fine metal products, and light machinery, including firearms and electrical equipment.

The Worcester area of central Massachusetts, located along the Blackstone River, is also noted for its diversity of industries, including machine tools, steel and wire products, textile machinery, grinding machines, firearms, woolens and worsteds, carpeting, and clothing.

Pittsfield, located in the Berkshires, is an attractive industrial city famed for electrical, metallurgical, chemical, and paper industries. One plant, the largest of its kind in the world, is devoted to the manufacture of transformers.

Counties.—The state is divided into fourteen counties. Nantucket with an area of 46 square miles and (1960) 3,559 persons is the smallest. Worcester County has the largest area (1,532 square miles) and Middlesex the greatest population (1,238,742). The counties and their county seats are as follows:

County	County Seat
Barnstable	Barnstable
Berkshire	Pittsfield
Bristol	Taunton, Fall River, and New Bedford
Dukes	Edgartown
Essex	Salem, Lawrence, and Newburyport
Franklin	Greenfield
Hampden	Springfield
Hampshire	Northampton
Middlesex	Cambridge and Lowell
Nantucket	Nantucket
Norfolk	Dedham
Plymouth	Plymouth
Suffolk	Boston
Worcester	Worcester and Fitchburg

3. GOVERNMENT AND POLITICS

Government.—The Massachusetts Constitution adopted in 1780 remains the basis of government and is the oldest among state constitutions still in force. Conventions for revision of the constitution were held in 1820, 1853, and 1917–1919; more than 80 articles of amendment have been adopted. Amendments may be initiated by either branch of the legislature or by initiative petition signed by a specified percentage of voters. If the proposed amendment receives the required votes in a joint session of the legislature, and likewise in the next elected legislature, it is then submitted to the voters in a state election.

Executive.—The executive branch is headed by a governor, elected annually until 1920, biennially from then until 1966, and for 4-year terms beginning in 1966. Other administrative officials, also elected for 4-year terms, are the lieutenant governor, attorney general, secretary of the commonwealth, auditor, and members of the governor's council. The latter has eight members elected by districts, plus the lieutenant governor. It acts as a check on the governor's powers, especially in judicial appointments and pardons for prisoners. The governor may exert considerable influence over legislation. He makes recommendations to the legislature and may call special sessions; he submits annually the executive budget detailing all proposed expenditures and revenues; he may veto or reduce any item in the budget as passed by the legislature. Executive vetoes may be overridden by a two thirds vote of both houses.

GOVERNORS OF MASSACHUSETTS

Governors of Plymouth Colony
Chosen annually by the people

John Carver	1620–1621	William Bradford	1639–1644
William Bradford	1621–1633	Edward Winslow	1644–1645
Edward Winslow	1633–1634	William Bradford	1645–1657
Thomas Prence	1634–1635	Thomas Prence	1657–1673
William Bradford	1635–1636	Josiah Winslow	1673–1680
Edward Winslow	1636–1637	Thomas Hinckley[1]	1680–1686
William Bradford	1637–1638	" "	1689–1692
Thomas Prence	1638–1639		

Governors of Massachusetts Bay Colony
Chosen annually under the first charter

Matthew Cradock	1629	Thomas Dudley	1645–1646
John Endecott[2]	1629	John Winthrop	1646–1649
John Winthrop	1629–1634	John Endecott	1649–1650
Thomas Dudley	1634–1635	Thomas Dudley	1650–1651
John Haynes	1635–1636	John Endecott	1651–1654
Henry Vane	1636–1637	Richard Bellingham	1654–1655
John Winthrop	1637–1640	John Endecott	1655–1665
Thomas Dudley	1640–1641	Richard Bellingham	1665–1672
Richard Bellingham	1641–1642	John Leverett	1672–1679
John Winthrop	1642–1644	Simon Bradstreet	1679–1686
John Endecott	1644–1645		

The Inter-Charter Period

Joseph Dudley became president of New England under royal commission on May 17, 1686, holding the office until December 19, the same year, when Sir Edmund Andros became governor of New England, appointed by King James II. On April 18, 1689, Governor Andros was deposed by a revolution of the people. After the dissolution of the first charter, Simon Bradstreet was governor from June 7, 1689, to May 16, 1692.

GOVERNORS OF THE PROVINCE OF MASSACHUSETTS BAY
Appointed by the king under the second charter

Sir William Phips	1692–1694	William Tailer		1730
William Stoughton[3]	1694–1699	Jonathan Belcher		1730–1741
Richard Coote	1699–1700	William Shirley		1741–1749
William Stoughton	1700–1701	*Spencer Phips*		1749–1753
The Council	1701–1702	William Shirley		1753–1756
Joseph Dudley	1702–1715	*Spencer Phips*		1756–1757
The Council	1715	The Council		1757
Joseph Dudley	1715	Thomas Pownall		1757–1760
William Tailer	1715–1716	*Thomas Hutchinson*		1760
Samuel Shute	1716–1723	Francis Bernard		1760–1769
William Dummer	1723–1728	*Thomas Hutchinson*		1769–1771
William Burnet	1728–1729	Thomas Hutchinson		1771–1774
William Dummer	1729–1730	Thomas Gage		1774–1775

UNTIL THE CONSTITUTION

A provincial congress	1774–1775	The Council	1775–1780

UNDER THE CONSTITUTION
Governors elected annually until 1920, since then biennially

John Hancock		1780–1785	Thomas Talbot	"	1879–1880
James Bowdoin		1785–1787	John D. Long	"	1880–1883
John Hancock		1787–1793	Benjamin F. Butler	Dem., Independent	1883–1884
Samuel Adams		1793–1797	George D. Robinson	Republican	1884–1887
Increase Sumner	Federalist	1797–1799	Oliver Ames	"	1887–1890
Moses Gill	"	1799–1800	John Q. A. Brackett	"	1890–1891
Caleb Strong		1800–1807	William E. Russell	Democrat	1891–1894
James Sullivan	Democrat-Republican	1807–1808	Frederic T. Greenhalge	Republican	1894–1896
Levi Lincoln	" "	1808–1809	Roger Wolcott	"	1896–1900
Christopher Gore	Federalist	1809–1810	W. Murray Crane	"	1900–1903
Elbridge Gerry	Democrat-Republican	1810–1812	John L. Bates	"	1903–1905
Caleb Strong	Federalist	1812–1816	William L. Douglas	Democrat	1905–1906
John Brooks	"	1816–1823	Curtis Guild, Jr.	Republican	1906–1909
William Eustis	Democrat-Republican	1823–1825	Eben S. Draper	"	1909–1911
Marcus Morton	" "	1825	Eugene N. Foss	Progressive-Dem.	1911–1914
Levi Lincoln, Jr.	Democrat-Federalist	1825–1834	David I. Walsh	Democrat	1914–1916
John Davis	Whig	1834–1835	Samuel W. McCall	Republican	1916–1918
Samuel T. Armstrong	"	1835–1836	Calvin Coolidge	"	1919–1920
Edward Everett	"	1836–1840	Channing H. Cox	"	1920–1925
Marcus Morton	Democrat	1840–1841	Alvan T. Fuller	"	1925–1929
John Davis	Whig	1841–1843	Frank G. Allen	"	1929–1931
Marcus Morton	Democrat	1843–1844	Joseph B. Ely	Democrat	1931–1935
George N. Briggs	Whig	1844–1851	James M. Curley	"	1935–1937
George S. Boutwell	Democrat, Free Soil	1851–1853	Charles F. Hurley	"	1937–1939
John H. Clifford	Whig	1853–1854	Leverett Saltonstall	Republican	1939–1945
Emory Washburn	"	1854–1855	Maurice J. Tobin	Democrat	1945–1947
Henry J. Gardner	American	1855–1858	Robert F. Bradford	Republican	1947–1949
Nathaniel P. Banks	Republican	1858–1861	Paul A. Dever	Democrat	1949–1953
John A. Andrew	"	1861–1866	Christian A. Herter	Republican	1953–1957
Alex H. Bullock	"	1866–1869	Foster Furcolo	Democrat	1957–1961
William Claflin	"	1869–1872	John A. Volpe	Republican	1961–1963
William B. Washburn	"	1872–1874	Endicott Peabody	Democrat	1963–1965
Thomas Talbot		1874–1875	John A. Volpe	Republican	1965–1969
William Gaston	Democrat	1875–1876	Francis W. Sargent	Republican	1969–
Alex. H. Rice	Republican	1876–1879			

[1]Mr. Hinckley was governor till the union of the colonies in 1692, except during the administration of Andros.
[2]While Cradock was governor of the Company in England, John Endecott was sent out as governor of the Plantation in Massachusetts Bay, serving under Cradock and under Winthrop until the latter arrived at Salem.
[3]Those whose names are printed in italics were acting governors.

By a constitutional amendment adopted in 1966, the governor was given extensive power to reorganize state agencies. The central administrative agency under the governor is the executive office of administration and finance. Major state departments include: agriculture, banking and insurance, civil service and registration, commerce and development, corporations and taxation, correction, education, labor and industries, mental health, metropolitan district commission, natural resources, public health, public safety, public utilities, public welfare, and public works.

Most state and many municipal positions are under civil service regulations. The division of civil service administers the examination and appointment of both state and municipal employees whose positions are classified under civil service. A division of personnel and standardization, which has considerable power, prepares detailed classification systems for all state employees and also administers the retirement and salary systems.

Legislature.—The legislature—called the General Court—consists of two houses, a Senate of 40 members and a House of Representatives of 240, both elected for a two-year term and representing in each case single member districts. A member of the House represents about 11,000 legal voters and a senator about 65,000. The powers of the two chambers are similar and each chooses its own officers. The legislature meets in annual sessions, beginning on the first Wednesday in January and often lasts nine months or longer. Massachusetts was a pioneer among state legislatures in the establishment of joint standing committees, composed of members from both houses, a system adopted to save time and prevent duplication of legislative work.

Judiciary.—The Massachusetts court system is highly regarded by students of the judiciary. At the bottom are 72 district courts, in addition to the special municipal court of Boston. These are local, non-jury courts with jurisdiction in both civil and criminal cases. There are two appellate divisions of the district courts, each consisting of five judges. There are 14 superior courts that employ judges. These courts are in session in principal centers throughout the state. Heading the judicial system is the Supreme Judicial Court of seven members, the oldest court in the United States in continuous existence. It hears cases on appeal, deciding questions of law, not of fact. Specialized jurisdiction is vested in the small claims and the juvenile sessions of district courts, the probate courts, the Land Court, and the pioneer Juvenile Court of Boston. Judges are appointed by the governor with consent of the council and hold office during good behavior. Massachusetts has adopted various devices to shorten court procedure or prevent litigation, such as the use of arbitrators and pretrial hearings at which judge and lawyers discuss the cases. Massachusetts was the first state to establish a "judicial council"; it is composed of judges and leading attorneys, and is charged with maintaining a continuing study of the judicial system and suggesting reforms.

Independent Special Bodies.—To serve the common needs of over 40 municipalities in the Boston area, the metropolitan district commission was created in 1919. It is a state commission appointed by the governor, and it controls for these municipalities the functions of sewerage, water supply (notably the Quabbin and Wachusett reservoirs in central Massachusetts), and parks and boulevards. This was the first such district to be organized and it set an example for other areas. The Massachusetts Port Authority operates the Port of Boston, with the Mystic River Bridge (toll) and Logan Airport in the Boston area. The Massachusetts Turnpike Authority constructed and operates the toll highway across the state, which was opened in 1957. Notable among agencies for interstate cooperation are the Commission on Interstate Cooperation, and the Connecticut River Valley Flood Control Commission.

Taxation and Revenue.—A large proportion of the revenue for local communities comes from property taxes. The revenue from the personal income tax is divided between the state and the localities. A sales tax, which also is divided between the state and the localities, was instituted in 1966. To promote efficiency in state finances, the executive office of administration and finance, responsible to the governor and council, prepares the annual state budget and controls the preaudit and accounting system and centralized purchasing for the state.

Suffrage and Elections.—Until 1691 the right to vote was based on church membership; the constitution of 1780 established a property qualification which was changed to tax payment in 1820, the latter being abolished in 1891. A voter must be 21 years of age, a citizen of the United States, a resident of Massachusetts for one year and of his city or town for the six months preceding an election in which he votes, and able to read and write English. The state was the first to adopt the so-called Massachusetts type of ballot, on which the names of candidates are arranged by offices rather than by party columns, an arrangement which encourages independent voting. Party candidates for state and federal offices are nominated at primaries held on the seventh Tuesday before a state election in even-numbered years. Since 1918 the state has made use of the initiative and referendum for direct participation by the voters in legislation. Since the 1960 census, Massachusetts elects 12 members to the United States House of Representatives.

Historically the Democratic Party has represented the urban population and the Republican Party the rural. If the "Yankees" have tended to vote Republican and the "Irish" Democratic, various factors are making this distinction less valid.

Local Government.—The state allows local units to draw up, approve, and revise charters for self-government. However, such powers as taxation, borrowing money, regulating elections, and disposing of parkland can be used by localities only in conformity with laws approved by the legislature. The county is a relatively unimportant unit of administration, principally for judicial purposes, and has no authority to tax. Much more important is the system of town government which developed in Massachusetts and extends throughout New England. It has made a notable contribution to the history of democratic government. The town is an area which includes one main and often minor centers of population, along with the surrounding countryside. Although unincorporated, the towns exercise wide powers within limits specified by state law. The principal agency of government is the town meeting, held annually or oftener. At the traditional "open" town meeting all citizens are free to take part in the discussion and to vote on town matters. There are many elected officials, chief of which are the selectmen, who act as agents in carrying out the decisions of the town meeting. Since 1916 towns with 6,000 population have been free to apply for the limited type of town meeting, to which representatives are elected; all voters may attend and speak, but only the representatives vote.

Under an optional charter system introduced in 1915, towns with 12,000 or more population may adopt one of five different plans of city government. Several cities have taken advantage of the optional charter plan.

4. EDUCATION AND PUBLIC WELFARE

Education.—Massachusetts was a pioneer in the development of public education in America and no state has established as many precedents which were followed elsewhere. The principle of tax-supported, state-controlled education began with the famous law of 1647 in the Bay Colony. This act stated that it was a principal aim of the "ould deluder, Satan, to keepe men from the knowledge of the Scriptures," and went on to provide that every town of 50 families should appoint someone to teach reading and writing, and that towns of 100 families should set up grammar schools to fit youth for college.

The first public high school in the country, which trained youth for business and industrial pursuits as distinct from the old Latin grammar schools, was established at Boston in 1821. Five years later a high school for girls was started there. In 1827 the General Court of Massachusetts passed the first American law requiring the establishment of high schools. The greatest figure in the history of Massachusetts education was Horace Mann. Largely due to his efforts, the first state board of education was established in 1837 and the first normal school in the country for training teachers in 1839, at Lexington. In 1852 Massachusetts enacted the first compulsory education law in the United States, requiring the attendance of children 8 to 14 years of age for 12 weeks a year.

Under present law, attendance at a public school, or other school approved by the local school committee, is compulsory for children between 14 and 16 unless they are granted employment certificates by the local school superintendent. Education is supervised by the state department of education. It is headed by a board

Above left: The beautiful pavilion covering the famous Plymouth Rock in Plymouth on which the Pilgrims are said to have landed from the "Mayflower" in 1620.

Above right: The Boston Edison Company plant on Boston Bay. Greater electrical power is needed for the state's expanding industries.

MASSACHUSETTS

Center: Dome-shaped Kresge Auditorium seen from the "moated" chapel at Massachusetts Institute of Technology. These buildings were completed in 1955.

Below left: The Minuteman statue at Lexington, in memory of the patriotic civilians who fought the first important battle of the American Revolution.

Below right: Cutting garments with an electric rotary in a factory in Boston. Apparel making has always been a leading industry in the state.

MASSACHUSETTS

Top: Woods Hole, a small summer resort at the southwest tip of Cape Cod, is known for its Oceanographic Institution, the Marine Biological Laboratory, and a fine harbor.

Center: For 300 years Eastern Point Lighthouse, on Cape Ann, near Gloucester, has warned fishermen of impending danger.

Left: A structure dating back to colonial whaling days is the old red brick Rotch Market ships' warehouse, at the foot of Main Street in cobblestoned Nantucket.

(Top) Laurence Lowry from Rapho-Guillumette; (center) Laurence Lowry from Devaney Inc.; (left) Fritz Henle from Monkmeyer Press Photo

of education appointed by the governor. The board appoints the commissioner of education, who is administrative head of the department. While the principle of local control always has been the rule exercised in the towns and cities by elected school committees the commissioner and the board have gained increased powers. The state imposes minimum standards as to buildings and health and safety in the schools, and in some cases gives substantial aid. Regionalization of schools is encouraged, especially for vocational education.

A board of higher education coordinates all public institutions of higher education. The University of Massachusetts, which was established at Amherst in 1863 with a branch organized in Boston in 1965, is growing rapidly. This institution, originally Massachusetts Agricultural College, became a university in 1947 and has a board of trustees named by the governor.

Three other types of state institutions are under the jurisdiction of the board of higher education: the state colleges, the technological institutes, and the community colleges. The trustees of state colleges oversee nine schools, located at Boston, Bridgewater, Fitchburg, Framingham, Lowell, North Adams, Salem, Westfield, and Worcester, plus the Massachusetts College of Art in Boston and the Massachusetts Maritime Academy in Buzzards Bay. The state colleges originally were teacher-preparation institutions, and they still discharge that function, but have broader curricula.

The two technological institutes, each of which has its own board of trustees, are Lowell Technological Institute and Southeastern Massachusetts Technological Institute, situated in North Dartmouth.

There are 11 two-year community colleges, with several more in the planning stage, governed by the board of regional community colleges. Massachusetts has a policy of extensive state support for vocational education and also for the education of the retarded and the physically handicapped.

Massachusetts has a large number of excellent private elementary and secondary schools and is outstanding for the number of private colleges and universities of high standing. Among the institutions of higher learning are: Harvard University (1636) at Cambridge, Williams College (1793) at Williamstown, Amherst College (1821) at Amherst, the College of the Holy Cross (1843) at Worcester, Tufts College (1852) at Medford, Boston College (1863) at Newton, Boston University (1869) at Boston, Clark University (1887) at Worcester, Springfield College (1885) and American International College (1885) at Springfield, Northeastern University (1898) at Boston, and Brandeis University (1948) at Waltham. Among the colleges for women only are Mount Holyoke College (1836) at South Hadley, Wellesley College (1870) at Wellesley, Smith College (1871) at Northampton, Radcliffe College (1879), affiliated with Harvard, Simmons College (1899) at Boston, and Wheaton College (1834) at Norton. Among institutions for specialized training are the Massachusetts Institute of Technology (1861) at Cambridge, and Worcester Polytechnic Institute (1865), the New England Conservatory of Music (1867) at Boston, and Babson Institute (1919) at Babson Park.

Libraries.—Considering the number of no-table libraries in the state, and the availability of library services to the public, probably no state is better served in this respect than Massachusetts. With the object of assisting library services, there is a bureau of library extension in the department of education. There is no town in the state without its free public library. The Boston Public Library, housed in a building noteworthy for its architecture, was the first city public library supported wholly by taxation. It is one of the great scholarly libraries in the country and has set an example in making its collections freely available to the public. The libraries at Harvard University constitute one of the principal collections in the country.

Other outstanding libraries in Massachusetts include: the Boston Athenaeum, containing the books owned by George Washington; the state library, which has a collection of the laws of foreign countries and of legislative records; the Massachusetts Historical Society Library; the New England Historic Genealogical Society Library (family records); the Essex Institute Library at Salem (marine); and the American Antiquarian Society Library at Worcester, notable for its collection of bound newspapers. The Boston Museum of Natural History and the Museum of Fine Arts (specializing in Oriental collections) are acknowledged to be outstanding in their fields.

Public Health and Welfare.—Massachusetts has a vast program of legislation and many state agencies for the promotion of public welfare and social betterment. The first state board of public health was established here in 1869 and the state has led the way in adoption of many advanced practices in public health. Activities of the department of public health include measures for control of communicable diseases, investigation and advice to communities concerning water supply and sewerage, inspection of places which process or distribute food products, laboratories for research, testing, and production of antitoxins and vaccines, a program for cancer control, and maternal and child health. State sanatoria for treatment of tuberculosis and other chronic diseases are located at Rutland, Tewksbury, Lakeville, Pondville, Westfield, the Massachusetts Hospital School at Canton, and the Lemuel Shattuck Hospital in Boston.

A department of mental health has general supervision over all public and private institutions for persons with mental disorders, epileptics, and drug addicts. State hospitals for mental disorders are the Massachusetts Mental Health Center, the Metropolitan State Hospital at Waltham, and state hospitals at Boston, Danvers, Foxborough, Framingham, Gardner, Grafton, Medfield, Monson, Northampton, Taunton, Westborough, and Worcester. State schools for mental defectives are located at Belchertown, Waltham, Taunton, and Wrentham.

A major tendency that is expanding in the field of mental health is to avoid the hospitalization of a patient if possible, and to treat minor mental disturbances through psychiatric counseling. In accord with this, the department of mental health has established clinics and treatment centers in seven regions. These are financed by the state and administered in cooperation with associations of citizens in each region who are interested in fostering mental health.

A department of public welfare has supervision over programs of public assistance and private charitable corporations. The state has centralized the administration of welfare; funds are provided almost entirely by the federal and state governments. Public assistance programs include: general relief, old age assistance, aid to dependent children, to the disabled, and to the blind. A department of industrial accidents administers the workmen's compensation law. In conformity with provisions for federal assistance, an unemployment compensation act was passed in 1937, providing for weekly benefit payments to the unemployed.

Public Safety.—The organized militia, administered by the adjutant general, constitutes chiefly the 26th Division of the National Guard, and units are trained in 58 communities. A civil defense agency created in 1950 organizes civilian activities for coping with enemy attack or natural disasters. In 1865 Massachusetts became the first state to establish a state constabulary, now the state police.

The Department of Correction has supervision over state and county penal and correctional in-

Ewing Galloway

The Massachusetts State House, Boston.

stitutions. Beginning in 1955, a reorganization has been under way, with emphasis given to the classification, diagnosis, and rehabilitation of prisoners. All establishments are now known as correctional institutions. The old state prison at Charleston was abandoned in 1956 for the modern institution at Walpole. Other institutions, more or less specialized, are located at Concord (which serves as a state classification center), at Framingham (for female prisoners), at Norfolk, and at Bridgewater.

5. ECONOMIC ACTIVITIES

Massachusetts has always been a leader in the economic development of the United States. From colonial days it has had a stable, highly skilled population. In recent years the composition of its industrial complex has been changing rapidly. Textiles and leather products were the leading industries until the early 1950's, but the state is now a major center of the electronics, nucleonics, and fabricated metals industries. Research and development firms in space-related and defense-related industries are the center of the state's economy.

This has resulted in a significant shift in the economy, especially in the labor force. Employment expanded during the 1960's in the fields of electrical and nonelectrical machinery, chemicals, printing and publishing, transportation equipment, scientific instruments, and food products. There was a slight decline, or only a moderate gain, in textile mill products, leather and leather products, pulp and paper products, rubber products, and furniture and other wood products.

In 1960 the number of persons employed in the state was 2,000,312. Of these, 709,268 were in manufacturing, 99,823 in construction, and 22,118 in agriculture. Almost all the rest were in service industries. During the 1960's the service industries expanded, with the result that by 1967 more than 60 per cent of the employment in the state was in this type of activity. Construction employment expanded slightly, due largely to the impact of urban renewal projects in major cities.

Among the expanding types of services were: government employment, education, hospitals, finance and insurance, welfare and religious employment, and retail trade. In general, service employment reflected an increasing level of education and skill, as did manufacturing employment. Thus the overall labor force showed certain trends through the late 1960's: the percentage of professional, technical, and managerial personnel increased, as did the proportion of clerical workers, while the percentage of operatives showed a decrease.

With the changes in its economy, Massachusetts remained among the ten highest states in per capita personal income during the 1950's and 1960's, with the figure in 1966 at $3,271. After 1955, about a $500 million increase in personal income for the people of the state was recorded annually; after 1964, this tended to increase to over $800 million.

Production.—*Agriculture.*—While Massachusetts is the second most densely populated state in the Union with almost 600 inhabitants per square mile, over 90 per cent of the people are crowded into thickly settled areas which constitute only 5 per cent of the space. Thus, 95 per cent of the state is open rural countryside where the remaining 10 per cent live comfortably at an average of only 50 people per square mile of land.

Approximately 80 per cent of the 100,000 families living in the rural areas reside there for residential purposes only. They depend entirely on nonagricultural income, except for small subsistence enterprises such as back-yard gardens and flocks. The remaining 20 per cent of the families (about 20,000) living in the rural areas are part-time and commercial farmers. Although there has been little change in the actual number of people living in the rural areas during the past 150 years, the proportion has decreased enormously; but recent developments, including

Right: One of the many fishnet-draped antique shops in Provincetown on Cape Cod, famed for its art colony and Portuguese fishing community.

MASSACHUSETTS

Below: Amherst College, at Amherst. Since its founding in 1821, its campus has reflected many architectural styles, as in the white-pillared portico of the gymnasium, shown here.

Right: Demonstrating a stage in early American iron manufacture, a trained guide at the Saugus Ironworks Restoration, an outdoor industrial museum north of Boston, stokes the fire in a hearth of the building where cast iron is forged into wrought iron bars. The museum, completed in 1954, is an authentic replica of the first successful ironworks in America, begun in 1646, and is an industrial landmark.

MASSACHUSETTS

Left: Leather pieces are stitched together to form uppers for men's shoes by a worker in a South Weymouth factory.

Center: Alluvial farming land in the Connecticut River valley near South Deerfield.

Lower left: A cluster of small cottages and fishing craft at the tiny village of Menemsha on Martha's Vineyard.

Lower right: Paul Revere House at 19 North Square, downtown Boston.

(Left) David F. Lawlor from Devaney Inc.; (center) Clifford G. Scofield from Frederic Lewis; (lower left) The New York, New Haven and Hartford Railroad; (lower right) David W. Corson from Devaney Inc.

the automobile and improved roads, have apparently brought about a trend toward increased numbers living in the rural areas and commuting to their work.

At the same time the number of commercial farms is growing less as the average size of each farm is increasing. This reflects the need for larger units in order to operate efficiently the expensive equipment required for mechanized farming.

Approximately 30 per cent of the land is in farms. The state ranks as one of the lowest in farm tenancy with almost 95 per cent of the farms operated by their owners.

The agricultural industry, with an output valued at almost $175 million, ranks high among the industries of the state. Slightly more than half of the annual income received by the state's farmers comes from livestock, primarily dairy and poultry products. However, only dairy products displayed a growth in cash receipts during the 1950's and 1960's. Among the important crops produced are cranberries (in which Massachusetts ranks first among the states), apples, potatoes, hay, and alfalfa.

Urbanization has brought the absorption of farmland, with industrial expansion. In the mid-1960's, it was estimated that there were about 11,000 farms in the state, but of these only 3,600 were truly commercial enterprises, with their sales of farm products averaging $10,000 annually. The other farms were operated on a part-time basis, with some farmers relying on seasonal or transient labor. A growing aspect of the agricultural sector of the economy is horticulture, especially as reflected in the greenhouse and nursery business close to major centers of population.

The major portion of land in farms is used for producing roughages for dairy cattle, such as corn silage, hay, and pasture. The improvement of land, including drainage and stone and brush removal with power machines, and modern practices, including new plant varieties, fertilization, and mechanization, have increased the production of feed nutrients in the form of roughage which in turn replaces part of the grain imports from the Western states. These modern techniques are revitalizing the livestock industry, and vegetable, fruit, and cash crop production as well.

Forest Products.—Massachusetts forests produce about 145 million board feet per year, or about 10 per cent of the total consumption. They produce approximately 150,000 cords of fuelwood annually for local consumption. Some pulpwood, cooperage, fence posts, and piling also come from the state's forests.

Forest trees most used for commercial purposes are the white pine for builders' finish, boxes, crates, toys, novelties, and patterns; hemlock for dimension stock and planks; red spruce for general lumber uses, such as planks and boards; red oak and white oak for timbers, shipping lumber, shipbuilding, and machine construction; hard maple for the manufacturing of furniture, heels, and turning; white birch for turning stock and furniture; ash for truck bodies, sporting goods, and machine construction; and red maple and other woods for fuel.

Fisheries.—Massachusetts fisheries suffered a decline from the mid-1950's to the mid-1960's, and then began to recover somewhat. Haddock, flounder, and sea scallops are the most important species caught. Both the quantity and the value of fish brought into Boston and Gloucester have declined, but New Bedford's catch has increased significantly.

Mineral Production.—Practically the entire mineral production of the state is nonmetallic and includes building stones, crushed stone, lime, sand, gravel, and clay. Granite is plentiful and is found in 11 of the 14 counties, but the most important quarrying centers are Quincy, Rockport, Westford, and Milford. Some marble is produced in Berkshire County.

Manufactures.—Although commerce, finance, education, recreation, and agriculture occupy important places in the state's economy, the manufacture of industrial products is its basic activity. There was little manufacturing in the state before the American Revolution. Although there was no local advantage due to the possession of raw materials, waterpower did encourage industrial development beginning in the early part of the 19th century. The climate of the southeastern part of the state was favorable to cotton spinning. Massachusetts has always been a leader in the textile industry. The first cotton mill was established at Beverly in 1788 and the first woolen mill at Byfield in 1794. The first power loom was set up in 1814 at Waltham. With the improvement in machinery and the development of waterpower, great centers such as Lowell, Lawrence, and Fall River arose in the 1830's. The development of these cities is in effect the story of the textile factory system. The boot and shoe industry is interwoven with the story of the growth of Lynn, Haverhill, Brockton, and many smaller municipalities. The first printing done in the American colonies was at Cambridge in 1639. From this small beginning the printing and publishing business has become an important industry in the state.

Following World War I much of the cotton textile industry was transferred to the South. For a time business pessimism prevailed. However, this was replaced with a spirit of aggressive management during the latter part of the 1930's and as a result a great diversification of industry has developed.

This diversification became more marked in the 1950's, with the growth of many small firms in defense-related and space-oriented technology. No single large employer dominates any section of the state. In the early 1950's, with the completion of a "circumferential highway" (Route 128) passing by Boston on the north, west, and south, many highly specialized firms closely related to the skilled labor supply emerged. While most of these were beyond the Boston-Cambridge area, they enjoyed close relations with the universities in this area, notably the Massachusetts Institute of Technology and Harvard.

During the late 1960's, another circumferential road, farther from Boston, was constructed from Haverhill in the north through Marlborough on the west to Foxborough on the south. This also stimulated diverse industrial development as the various sections were completed.

Between 1951 and 1964, manufacturing employment declined by about 100,000 jobs, with the loss in textile and leather industries amounting to almost 87,000. After 1965, employment was stabilized or rising gradually. Industries whose growth rate was substantial in the late 1960's included: electrical machinery, nonautomative transportation equipment, chemical, ordnance, primary and fabricated metals, and instruments.

Electric Power.—Facilities for generating electric power are expanding rapidly. From 1954 to 1965, the electric generating capacity increased from 2,749,601 kilowatts to 4,145,000 kilowatts. Of the larger figure, a capacity of 3,970,000 kilowatts was privately owned, 174,000 publicly owned, and 464,000 was in private plants.

Banking.—On Dec. 31, 1966, there were 340 banks in Massachusetts, of which 90 were national banks and 250 were state banks. Of the latter, 178 were mutual savings banks and 72 were commercial. The total assets of the banks were $18.4 billion, and the total deposits were more than $16 billion. There were more than 3.5 million savings accounts.

The banks under the supervision of the state commissioner of banks include, in addition to the state commercial, mutual savings, and private banks reported on above, trust companies, cooperative savings and loan associations, and credit unions. Massachusetts ranks high in both the amount of savings deposits per capita and the number of depositors. A state law provides for a savings bank life insurance system which operates through the savings banks.

Trade.—Mid-20th century technology is having its effect on distribution methods and channels in Massachusetts. Modern superhighways and motor hauling are causing wholesale and retail trade facilities to move from congested areas. Although the major new highways of the state have caused some industrial plants and trucking firms to move out of Boston, the city remains a central distribution and service point for all of New England. Numerous firms have their headquarters in Boston. However, there is evidence that some activity is moving toward the Worcester area, which is more centrally located.

Employment in wholesale and retail trade expanded from 323,000 jobs in 1950 to 403,300 in 1964, a gain of 14.2 per cent. This gain continued at a somewhat slower pace after 1964. Between 1958 and 1968, eight major shopping centers were opened in the Greater Boston area. These competed successfully with the retail stores in Boston and the central business districts in such cities as Cambridge, Somerville, and Quincy. However, urban renewal revitalized downtown Boston and stimulated both wholesale and retail trade in the central business district.

Other major cities—for example, Worcester, Springfield, New Bedford, Fall River, Lawrence, and Lowell—witnessed a similar dispersion of trade centers to the outlying areas, but in most cases they were able to retain substantial retail facilities in the downtown sections.

A special trade problem was posed by the difficulties of the Port of Boston, which has declined in relative importance. While imports through the port remained substantial, exports declined steadily. In 1966, imports amounted to 7,111,054 tons, and exports to only 494,649 tons. High costs for loading and discharging cargoes, compared to those of other Atlantic coast ports, seemed to be a cause of the problem.

Tourism.—As mentioned elsewhere, Massachusetts with its historical and cultural interests, natural beauty of land and waterscapes, and its interesting coastline is becoming a mecca for increasing numbers of tourists—so much so that tourism has developed into a major economic activity for the state. Several sections of Massachusetts, notably Cape Cod and the Berkshires, rely to a large extent upon tourism.

Transportation.—The state, extending midway across southern New England from east to west, occupies a strategic position in the paths of transportation and communications in the northeastern United States. Boston is the nearest large United States metropolitan center to western Europe. It is directly in the line of air traffic between the United States and Europe. Actually it is 1,200 miles nearer the Panama Canal than San Francisco and it is nearer to the ports of Argentina and Brazil than southern United States ports bordering the Gulf of Mexico. Boston has excellent shipside storage and warehousing and over 30 miles of berthing space for ocean vessels.

The metropolitan area of Boston is connected with the West by two railway systems which cross the state from east to west. These lead either directly or by branches, by way of the Buffalo gateway, to all of the industrial centers of the North Central states. One system extends from Boston to the north and east, serving Canada and all of northern New England. The other general system serving Massachusetts reaches into the South by way of New York. A network of branch lines connects the factory centers of the state with each other, with the seaboard, and with the railway systems leading north, south, and west.

The problems associated with passenger traffic on the railroads are acute in Massachusetts, as in many states. Experiments were conducted in high-speed rail transit between Boston and New York and cities to the south, in the hope that rail transportation could be revived to compete with airplane and automobile traffic. The state subsidizes railroad commuter service in the Greater Boston area.

More than 2.5 million motor vehicles are registered in Massachusetts. The figure includes 35,000 trucks. A major factor in the increasing volume of truck and automobile traffic is the complex highway network. The Massachusetts Turnpike runs from downtown Boston westward to the New York state line. Several major arteries radiate from the center of Boston, and there are two major "outer belt" or "circumferential" highways on the peripheries of the Boston area, one 10 to 15 miles from the city and the other 25 to 30 miles away.

Within the state, there are more than 100 facilities for airplanes or helicopters. The most important airport is Logan International Airport in East Boston. Built out into the harbor and connected with downtown Boston by two tunnels under the harbor, the airport has become an important center of international and domestic traffic.

Communications.—As of Jan. 1, 1966, Massachusetts had exactly 100 broadcasting stations, of which 60 were AM radio stations, 30 were FM radio stations, and 10 were television stations. These covered more than 90 per cent of the homes in the state.

Telephone coverage also was extensive, reaching 95 per cent of all homes. As of Jan. 1, 1966, there were more than 2 million residential telephones and more than 800,000 business telephones.

With consolidations, the number of post offices in the state declined from 568 to 480 from 1954 to 1966.

The state is served by 47 daily newspapers with a net paid circulation of 2,324,000 in 1966. There are eight foreign language dailies. The

MASSACHUSETTS

Cape Ann's old red sail loft, jutting into Rockport harbor, is a "natural" for artists trying their hand at local color. The street of neat wooden houses looks seaward while boulder-strewn moorlands make up the background. Rockport still quarries some granite, but lives on its fishing and tourist trades.

Reproduced by Special Permission from "National Geographic Magazine"

Kodachrome by Jack Breed © N.G.S.

MASSACHUSETTS

Top left: Harvard University campus on the Charles River at Cambridge. View is northward. Most of the university's buildings lie within a mile radius of the original 1638 site.

Top right: General store at Old Sturbridge Village, in Sturbridge, is a re-creation of a New England community of about 1790–1840. Many of its buildings are originals; others are reconstructions.

Left: Nuclear-age wiring machine in a plant at Pittsfield. It automatically wires parts for Polaris missile fire control systems.

Below: Music in the Berkshires—Boston Symphony Orchestra at Tanglewood. Its summer festival there has gained national fame.

nine Sunday newspapers have 1,603,000 circulation. The older and better-known newspapers include the *Christian Science Monitor,* the Boston *Globe,* the Boston *Herald Traveler,* and the Springfield *Sunday Republican.*

6. PLACES OF INTEREST

Art Museums and Centers.—The history of art in the United States is closely related to the early history of Massachusetts where many noted painters and sculptors were born or did much of their work. Museums throughout the state have exceptionally fine and many specialized collections. The Boston Museum of Fine Arts has the most important collection of Asiatic art in the Western World, as well as European and American paintings, an extensive textile collection, American silver, furniture, and one of the richest collections of graphic arts in the country.

Other outstanding museums include the Worcester Art Museum in Worcester and the Berkshire Museum in Pittsfield which emphasize painting and sculpture from Egyptian to modern times; the Smith College Museum of Art, Northampton, with emphasis on French painting during the last 200 years; the Fogg Art Museum, Harvard University, with a splendid display of Italian primitives; Addison Gallery of American Art, Andover, with a display of American art of the 18th, 19th, and 20th centuries; and the Sterling and Francine Clark Art Institute, Williamstown, which has an outstanding collection of paintings and fine silver. The Isabella Stewart Gardner Museum, Boston, a Venetian-style palace, contains European and American paintings of the 14th to 20th centuries, sculpture, stained glass, and furniture and is also famous for flower displays in the central court.

There are numerous art centers and schools throughout the state and several of these are museum schools. The home of the largest art colony in the country is at Provincetown. Other artist colonies are located at Cape Ann, Pigeon Cove, and on Nantucket Island.

Music Centers and Festivals.—Boston, one of the foremost musical centers of the world, is the home of the Boston Symphony Orchestra. Regular concerts are presented by the orchestra during the winter season in Symphony Hall, which is also the scene of the popular "Pops" concerts in the early summer. Tanglewood, the summer home of the Boston Symphony Orchestra, is a 200-acre estate and is the scene of the nationally famous Berkshire Music Festival each July and August. The Boston Symphony Orchestra also supports Boston's Esplanade concerts, which attract audiences that may number 20,000 or more.

The Handel and Haydn Society of Boston, organized in 1818, gives annual performances of Handel's *Messiah.* Among the numerous musical organizations presenting regular concert courses is the Springfield Symphony Orchestra and the Pioneer Valley Symphony in the Connecticut Valley, The Little Symphony of Worcester, and Pierian Sodality, the Harvard-Radcliffe Orchestra. The Boston Opera House is the scene of opera presentations of the New England Opera Company. The Boys' Choir of Malden, organized before the turn of the century, sings at regular worship services in Malden and presents programs of sacred and secular works to audiences throughout New England. The Worcester Music Festival will soon observe its centennial birthday.

Massachusetts Department of Commerce

A picnic beside the pool at Bash Bish Falls, near the town of Mt. Washington, in southwestern Massachusetts.

Literary and Theatrical Centers and Festivals.—Ted Shawn's school of the dance, Jacob's Pillow, is located near Lee. During the summer months a series of programs is presented by famous artists in addition to regular instruction in ballet.

Although Massachusetts has relatively few legitimate theaters, summer theaters are popular, especially on Cape Cod. Summer theaters include those at Williamstown and Stockbridge in the Berkshires; Holyoke in the Connecticut Valley; Sturbridge and Fitchburg in the central area; Beverly on the North Shore; Boston; and Cohasset, Dennis, Falmouth, Hyannis, Orleans, Plymouth, and Provincetown on the South Shore and Cape Cod; and Nantucket Island.

Science Museums, Centers, and Sites of Note.—The Museum of Science, Boston, was the first museum in the country to combine natural history, science, industry, public health, and a planetarium. Agassiz Museum, Harvard University, contains the Peabody Museum of Archaeology and Ethnology, the Museum of Comparative Zoology, and Botanical, Mineralogical, and Geological Museums. The famous Ware collection of Blaschka glass flowers is of particular interest in the Agassiz.

Fisher Museum, Harvard Forest, Petersham, houses the Pitman Dioramas presenting the history of land use, methods of silviculture, and soil conservation. Bourne Whaling Museum, New Bedford, contains whaling relics, replicas of a cooperage shop, sail loft, and rigging loft, and a full-rigged whale ship with equipment. Nantucket Whaling Museum on Nantucket Island has samples of gear used in the whaling industry and a full-rigged whaleboat. The John Woodman Higgins Armory Museum, Worcester, has an unusual collection of historic ancient armor and arms of all periods and masterpieces of modern pressed-steel craftsmanship. The Arnold Arboretum, Jamaica Plains, contains labeled specimens of all trees and shrubs known to grow in the climate of the area.

One of the greatest aggregations of scientific, engineering, and research talent in the world is concentrated along the Charles River in Boston and Cambridge. Here is located Harvard University, Massachusetts Institute of Technology, Boston University, hospitals with research facilities, and professional and industrial research centers. The Computation Laboratory, Harvard University, houses an automatic sequence controlled calculator and an electronic magnetic drum calculator. Harvard and Massachusetts Institute of Technology are jointly building and will operate the "atom smasher." A nuclear reactor is being built at Massachusetts Institute of Technology as a center for medical and biological research. A similar reactor has been approved for the Watertown Arsenal where the first atomic cannon was designed and built. A plant at Attleboro fabricates fuels for nuclear reactors and does precision work with uranium, zirconium, thorium, and niobium. Similar plants are located in Concord and Boston. A new electron and research center is located at Wilmington. Research at the University of Massachusetts is conducted in science, agriculture, and nutrition.

Historical Shrines and Monuments.—The state is rich in places of historical interest and merit. The Pilgrim and Puritan settlements of the 17th century, the scenes of memorable occasions of the Revolutionary period, and the literary achievements of such men as Emerson, Thoreau, and Hawthorne during the 19th century are great contributions to the history of the country. Among places of historical interest are the monument at Provincetown which marks the first landing of the Pilgrims; Plymouth Rock at Plymouth; the Myles Standish Monument at South Duxbury; Bunker Hill Monument in Charlestown; the Salem Maritime National Historic Site in Salem; the Old State House, the Old South Meeting House, the Old North Church, and Faneuil Hall in Boston; and the battlegrounds of Lexington and Concord. The historic town of Deerfield and the restored Fort Massachusetts at North Adams have significance in the history of the French and Indian Wars. The homestead of William Cullen Bryant in Cummington is now maintained by the state.

Parks and Reservations.—The oldest public park in the United States, the Boston Common, was established in 1634 for use as a "cow pasture and training field." The state's interest in public parks and recreation has never waned. Over the years it has acquired through public and semipublic agencies more than 250,000 acres of land which is devoted to outdoor recreation and forestry. Of this amount almost 80 per cent is owned by state agencies and the rest by towns, cities, and counties. The counties own less than one per cent of these lands. The state forests and parks are administered by the Division of Forests and Parks of the State Department of Natural Resources.

There are approximately 200 public recreation areas in Massachusetts. State parks and forests are located in every region of the state and provide outdoor recreation for over a million visitors annually. The 15 state parks composed of over 100,000 acres include: Clarksburg and Wahconah Falls in the Berkshires; Robinson and Joseph Allen Skinner in the Connecticut Valley; Quinsigamond in the central area; Bradley W. Palmer on the North Shore; Ashland, Cochituate, Hopkinton, and Whitehall in the suburban

area; and Cushing, Dighton Rock, Demarest Lloyd Memorial, Roland C. Nickerson, and Pilgrim Spring on the South Shore and Cape Cod.

Of approximately 172,000 acres of state forests, almost 103,000 acres are located in the 28 forests where provision has been made for outdoor recreation. These include: Bash Bish Falls, Beartown, Campbell Falls, Chester, East Mountain, Granville, Mohawk Trail, October Mountain, Pittsfield, Sandisfield, Savoy Mountain, Tolland, and Windsor in the Berkshire region; D. A. R., Erving, Federated Women's Club, and Mount Grace in the Connecticut Valley; Brimfield, Douglas, Leominster, Otter River, Spencer, and Willard Brook in central Massachusetts; Lowell-Dracut, Warren H. Manning, and Harold Parker on the North Shore; Freetown-Fall River, and Myles Standish in the South Shore area; and Martha's Vineyard on the island of Martha's Vineyard.

State owned and operated public beaches include Lynn, Nantucket, and Revere near Boston; Salisbury on the North Shore; Horseneck on the South Shore; and Scusset on Cape Cod.

The Department of Natural Resources administers 47 state forests of approximately 75 thousand acres that are devoted to scientific forest practices and wildlife management; 13 wildlife sanctuaries comprising 3,671 acres, 18 wildlife refuges (15,577 acres); four game farms of 364 acres; six fish hatcheries and two breeding pond systems of 853 acres; and the State Lobster Hatchery in Oak Bluffs on Martha's Vineyard. These areas are devoted to the scientific propagation of various types of small game and fish for stocking purposes and experimentation. The division also has leased over 75 miles of public fishing waters. These waters are stocked and offer fine fishing.

There are eight state reservations of 13,546 acres which are developed for recreational purposes. Four of these areas are administered by special unpaid commissioners appointed by the governor while the other four are under the jurisdiction of the commissioners of the county or counties in which they are located.

The Massachusetts Audubon Society has 11 wildlife sanctuaries comprising more than 4,000 acres. These wildlife sanctuaries are Pleasant Valley in the Berkshire Hills area; Arcadia in the Connecticut Valley; Cook's Canyon and Wachusett Meadows in central Massachusetts; Ipswich River, Marblehead Neck, Nahant Thicket, and Drumlin Farm in the northeast; Moose Hill, Tern Island, and Sampson's Island in the southeast and Cape Cod areas.

7. FAMOUS MEN AND WOMEN

Massachusetts, as one of the original colonies, has produced many statesmen and patriots. Among them are Benjamin Franklin (Boston, 1706–1790), statesman, printer, author, and scientist; Israel Putnam (Salem Village, now Danvers, 1718–1790), American Revolutionary soldier; Samuel Adams (Boston, 1722–1803), American Revolutionary patriot and statesman, delegate to 1st and 2d Continental Congresses, signed Declaration of Independence, and became governor of Massachusetts; James Otis (West Barnstable, 1725–1783), American Revolutionary statesman, a leader in upholding the colonial cause; Artemas Ward (Shrewsbury, 1727–1800), American Revolutionary general; John Adams (Braintree, now Quincy, 1735–1826), 2d president of the United States and signer of the Declaration of Independence; Paul Revere (Boston, 1735–1818), silversmith and patriot; John Hancock (Braintree, now Quincy, 1737–1793), merchant, statesman, first signer of the Declaration of Independence, and first governor of the State of Massachusetts; Elbridge Gerry (Marblehead, 1744–1814), statesman, member of Massachusetts Provincial Congress and Continental Congress, a signer of the Declaration of

Independence and also of the Articles of Confederation, was governor of Massachusetts and vice president of the United States under James Madison; John Quincy Adams (Braintree, now Quincy, 1767–1848), 6th president of the United States; and John Fitzgerald Kennedy (Brookline, 1917–1963), 35th president of the United States.

Among the many men and women notable in the world of literature who were born in the state are: William Cullen Bryant (near Cummington, 1794–1878), poet, editor and co-owner of the New York *Evening Post* for almost 50 years; William Hickling Prescott (Salem, 1796–1859), historian, essayist, author of the *History of the Conquest of Mexico;* George Bancroft (Worcester, 1800–1891), historian and statesman; Ralph Waldo Emerson (Boston, 1803–1882), essayist and poet; Nathaniel Hawthorne (Salem, 1804–1864), novelist; John Greenleaf Whittier (Haverhill, 1807–1892), poet, editor, and ardent abolitionist; Oliver Wendell Holmes (Cambridge, 1809–1894), teacher of anatomy, poet, and essayist; Edgar Allan Poe (Boston, 1809–1849), poet and writer of short stories; Sarah Margaret Fuller (Cambridgeport, 1810–1850), journalist and critic; John Lothrop Motley (Dorchester, 1814–1877), historian and diplomat; Richard Henry Dana (Cambridge, 1815–1882), lawyer, specializing in admiralty cases, and author of *Two Years Before the Mast;* Henry David Thoreau (Concord, 1817–1862), essayist, naturalist, and philosopher; James Russell Lowell (Cambridge, 1819–1891), poet, essayist, editor, and diplomat; Edward Everett Hale (Boston, 1822–1909), Unitarian minister and author of the well-known short story *The Man Without a Country;* Francis Parkman (Boston, 1823–1893), historian and author of *The California and Oregon Trail,* as well as other histories of early America; Charles Dudley Warner (1829–1900), essayist and novelist; Emily Elizabeth Dickinson (Amherst, 1830–1886), poet, none of whose poems (except two) were published during her lifetime; Horatio Alger (Revere, 1834–1899), author of more than 100 popular books for boys; and Henry Brooks Adams (Boston, 1838–1918), assistant professor of history at Harvard, editor of the *North American Review,* and author of many books of biography and history.

A few of those who became famous in the field of art are: John Singleton Copley (Boston, 1738–1815), portrait painter; Samuel McIntire (Salem, 1757–1811), architect and wood carver, designed many of the houses and public buildings in old Salem; Charles Bulfinch (Boston, 1763–1844), architect of Massachusetts State House on Beacon Hill and designed many public buildings in Boston, also completed the Capitol in Washington, D.C.; John Rogers (Salem, 1829–1904), sculptor, well known for his Civil War groups; James Abbott McNeill Whistler (Lowell, 1834–1903), painter and etcher; and Winslow Homer (Boston, 1836–1910), painter, known especially for his paintings of the sea.

Among Massachusetts-born inventors are Eli Whitney (Westboro, 1765–1825), inventor of the cotton gin and firearms parts; Samuel Finley Breese Morse (Charlestown, 1791–1872), artist and inventor of the telegraph; Elias Howe (Spencer, 1819–1867), inventor of the sewing machine; and Francis Blake (Needham, 1850–1913), inventor and physicist, whose telephone transmitter was purchased by the Bell Telephone Company.

Others who have become famous for various reasons are: Cotton Mather (Boston, 1663–1728), Puritan clergyman, scholar, and author; Horace Mann (Franklin, 1796–1859), educator, who revolutionized public school organization and teaching; Lucy Stone (West Brookfield, 1818–1893), reformer and pioneer in woman's rights; Clara Barton (Oxford, 1821–1912), philanthropist and Civil War worker, through whose efforts the American Red Cross was established; Charles William Eliot (Boston, 1834–1926), president of Harvard, (1869–1909), and one of the most influential leaders in educational activities in this country; Samuel Pierpont Langley (Roxbury, 1834–1906), airplane pioneer and astronomer; Lyman Abbott (Roxbury, 1835–1922), clergyman, editor, and author, who became associated with Henry Ward Beecher and succeeded him as pastor of the Plymouth Congregational Church in Brooklyn; Phillips Brooks (Boston, 1835–1893), Episcopal bishop and a great preacher, rector of Trinity Church of Boston; Dwight Lyman Moody (Northfield, 1837–1899), a layman who became one of the world's great evangelists; Oliver Wendell Holmes (Boston, 1841–1935), son of the essayist, associate justice of the United States Supreme Court for 30 years; Luther Burbank (Lancaster, 1849–1926), plant breeder and originator of many new varieties of fruit, flowers, and vegetables; Nathaniel Carll Goodwin (Boston, 1857–1919), favorite comedian of the 1880's and 1890's; and Otis Skinner (Cambridge, 1858–1942), actor.

Others of national fame who, by residence or work in Massachusetts, have brought distinction to the state are: John Eliot (1604–1690), missionary to the American Indians and founder of the Praying Towns in Massachusetts; Mary Morse Baker Eddy (1821–1910), founder of the Christian Science Church and author of *Science and Health; Louisa May Alcott* (1832–1888), author of *Little Women* and other novels; Henry James (1843–1916), novelist, who claimed Cambridge as his American home; Edwin Austin Abbey (1852–1911), mural painter, who did the *Quest of the Holy Grail* series for the Boston Public Library; John Singer Sargent (1856–1925), portrait painter and mural artist; and Calvin Coolidge (1872–1933), 29th president of the United States.

8. HISTORY

It is common knowledge that the first permanent settlement in Massachusetts was made in 1620 by the Pilgrims. But there had been for many years previous an active interest in the region due to its possibilities for fishing, trading with the Indians, and the acquisition of land. In 1602, Bartholomew Gosnold, an English navigator, skirted the coast of Massachusetts, gave Cape Cod its name, and settled briefly on Cuttyhunk Island. Captain John Smith explored the coast in 1614 and soon published his *Description of New England,* a glowing account of the region and its prospects. Active interest continued and, in 1620, the Council for New England was organized, with a royal charter granting title to all land between the 40th and 48th parallels. From this title came, directly or indirectly, the land grants of five colonies. Thus, regardless of the Pilgrims, settlement would have occurred soon.

The origin of the Pilgrim settlement goes back to a small group of folk in England, called Separatists because they worshiped in defiance of the established Anglican Church. They were molested by neighbors, and under their leaders, William Brewster, John Robinson (their pastor), and William Bradford, they left England, 1607–1609, and settled at Leyden in Holland. Here they lived peaceably for some years, working as laborers. But life there was hard, and fearful that their children would be assimilated by the Dutch, a part of the congregation decided to migrate to America. Permission was obtained from the Virginia Company of London (London Company) to settle in their territory, and capital to finance the undertaking was obtained from a group of London promoters. This small band left Holland for England and on Sept 6/16, 1620, the memorable voyage began from Plymouth on the *Mayflower.* Aside from the crew, there were 100[1] persons on the vessel, of whom 35 were from Leyden and 65 from England, many of the latter not being Separatists but persons sent over by the London promoters to work.

The plan had been to settle south of the Hudson River, but, due to stress of weather, anchor was finally dropped in Provincetown Harbor, Nov. 11/21, 1620. Since this was outside the bounds of the Virginia Company, they were without charter of government or title to land. To meet this situation, the male settlers signed the "Mayflower Compact," by which they agreed to be governed by the will of the majority until more permanent provision could be made. This first American example of pure democracy was patterned after the church covenant under which all authority was vested in the assembly of church members. During the terrible first winter about half the population died, but new settlers came, including nearly all of the Leyden congregation. By 1640 there were eight towns with 2,500 population in the Plymouth Colony. The Pilgrims were simple country folk and artisans from the middle and lower classes in England, with little

[1] On the voyage a passenger died and two were born; thus 101 landed.

or no education, and without social or political distinction. In this respect they formed a contrast to their more wealthy and aristocratic neighbors of Massachusetts Bay Colony, into which they were absorbed in 1691.

During the decade of 1620 a number of small communities were established around Massachusetts Bay. In 1622 a group of businessmen of Dorchester, England, decided to establish a permanent fishing settlement in New England, to avoid the time wasted by fishermen in annual ocean crossings. In 1623 settlement was made at the present site of Gloucester on Cape Ann. The attempt failed, but Roger Conant led a group which moved to Salem in 1626 and this became the second permanent settlement in Massachusetts. In 1628 a new company, backed by many influential Puritan gentry and merchants, obtained a grant of land from the Council for New England. Charles I in 1629 granted a royal charter incorporating this group as the Massachusetts Bay Company. From this stemmed the main settlement of Massachusetts.

This was a period of growing discontent in England. The conflict between crown and Parliament, which later led to the civil war, was growing more acute. There was a rapidly increasing number of Puritans, numerous in the towns and among the gentry, who disliked the High Church policies and repression of Archbishop William Laud. In these circumstances a group within the Massachusetts Bay Company, including John Winthrop, Thomas Dudley, and Sir Richard Saltonstall, proposed to leave England and create a Puritan refuge in America. Since the royal charter contained no clause binding the company to maintain headquarters in England—whether such a clause was omitted by accident or design is not known—it was decided to turn the charter and government of the company over to settlers who would move to New England. This move would be a protection against control of the company by groups hostile to the Puritans in England, as well as against interference by the crown. In 1630 a well-equipped fleet of vessels, carrying some 900 passengers, with Winthrop as governor, crossed the ocean and founded Boston and several towns nearby. The decade which followed witnessed a great wave of migration to America, some 15,000 going to Massachusetts and even more to the West Indies. Although the desire for religious freedom was an influential cause, this has been overstressed, and it is probable that desire for economic betterment, including land hunger, was an even more important factor.

The transfer of the company charter to America had an important bearing on the future government of the colony and its relations with England. What had been the charter of a trading corporation became the instrument for governing a colony. It was assumed in the colony that neither king nor Parliament had anything to say about the colony's affairs, and, in fact, for half a century this was almost the case. Within the colony, control was tightly vested in the hands of a narrow theocracy. Winthrop and his associates, intent on building a religious commonwealth, did not believe in democracy and felt that power must be retained in their hands. At first the General Court was composed of shareholders, called freemen, who made up less than one per cent of the inhabitants. In 1631 it was decreed that only members of an approved Puritan church

might become freemen. A representative plan was soon adopted under which the freemen of each town chose deputies to the General Court. Eventually the court split into two houses.

The clergy exerted great political influence. In its early years the colony was rent by controversies and by persecution of those who challenged the prevailing orthodoxy, such as Roger Williams and Mrs. Anne Hutchinson. The Reverend Thomas Hooker left in 1636 to found Connecticut. It was not until the 18th century that more liberal views prevailed. In the years after 1688 occurred the famous witchcraft delusion, centering in Salem where 20 persons were put to death. After the Restoration in 1660, Charles II tried to assert a greater degree of royal control, resulting in revocation of the Massachusetts charter in 1684. This was followed by the brief experiment in colonial absolutism known as the Dominion of New England. Sir Edmund Andros was sent out as governor with autocratic powers over all of New England, as well as New York and New Jersey. This aroused the most intense opposition in Massachusetts. When news reached Boston in 1689 of the "Glorious Revolution" in England, which brought William and Mary to the throne, the Bostonians had their own revolution, clapping Andros and his advisers into jail. In 1691, Massachusetts received a new charter which brought her government more into line with that of other colonies. Henceforth, there was a governor appointed by the king, with power of veto over acts of the legislature; the charter forbade religious tests for voting; and Maine and Plymouth Colony were joined to Massachusetts.

During the 17th and early 18th centuries the settlers of Massachusetts suffered severely from Indian attacks. In 1637 the Pequot War occurred, and in the years 1675–1678, the much more severe King Philip's War, in which the forces of that chieftain were crushed. The whites suffered severe losses and frontier settlement was retarded for a generation. In the subsequent wars against the French and Indians many frontier towns were ravaged. Massachusetts played a prominent role in the wars of colonial rivalry with France, 1689–1763. Under Sir William Pepperell, Massachusetts troops took the chief part in the capture of Louisburg in 1745, and they figured in various campaigns during the crucial struggle of the Seven Years' War, 1756–1763.

After the British and colonial victory over France, issues were raised which soon led to revolution in the empire. It was the British view that the colonists should pay a larger share of their cost of administration and defense. Massachusetts enjoyed prosperity from her shipbuilding industry, her trade to the West Indies, and from slave-trading expeditions to Africa. British trade regulations had been laxly enforced, and extensive smuggling had developed. British measures after 1761 to eliminate smuggling and increase colonial revenue met opposition from the mercantile classes of Massachusetts, and from leaders such as James Otis, Samuel Adams, John Adams, and John Hancock. The Massachusetts House in 1765 took the lead in calling an intercolonial Congress to resist the Stamp Act. Samuel Adams, a radical agitator of Boston who led the movement for nonimportation agreements and "committees of correspondence," did much to develop an irreconcilable revolutionary spirit. Royal troops were stationed in Boston and friction with the citizens culminated in the Boston massacre, March 5, 1770, in which soldiers, goaded by a mob, fired, killing five persons. When Parliament persisted with a tax on tea, Samuel Adams took the lead in organizing the "Boston tea party," 1773. Citizens disguised as Indians boarded the vessels in Boston Harbor and dumped the chests of tea into the water. In retaliation, Parliament passed the Boston Port Bill, closing the port to commerce. When Governor Gage dissolved the General Court in 1774, the members resolved themselves into a provincial congress and adopted plans for mustering the militia, including the minutemen. The first blood of the revolution was shed at Lexington on April 19, 1775, when General Gage sent troops to Concord to destroy military stores collected there by the colonists. At the Battle of Bunker Hill, June 17, 1775, the British suffered over 1,000 casualties in taking a hill from militia who were besieging them in Boston. For the remainder of the war, no important engagement was fought in Massachusetts.

In September 1779 a convention, authorized by the people, framed a state constitution which was ratified in June 1780.

A few years later came the episode known as Shays' Rebellion, 1786–1787. Business depression and rigorous foreclosures for debts and taxes caused an uprising of the farmers led by a former army captain, Daniel Shays. Although suppressed by the militia, it alarmed the conservative classes and played its part in the movement for a new federal Constitution. The state ratified the federal Constitution Feb. 6, 1788, after a sharp contest and after the Federalists drafted amendments which met the demand for a bill of rights.

Dominated as it was by the commercial classes, Massachusetts in the early years under the Constitution was strongly Federalist in politics, and opposed to the agrarian and democratic principles of Jefferson's party. Trade was severely restricted by the embargo under Jefferson, and almost stopped by the War of 1812. Massachusetts, in a rebellious mood, refused to allow her militia to be used outside the state and her spokesmen were active in the Hartford Convention, 1814, where there was talk of secession from the Union. Following 1815, however, a new basis for prosperity came in the rapid development of the machine textile industry, ushered in by Francis Cabot Lowell's introduction of the power loom at Waltham in 1814. The new industry was centered in Massachusetts. The state retained its pre-eminence in shipping, climaxed by the famous clipper ship era of the early 1850's. The growth of industry coincided with a decline in agriculture, brought on by competition from Western lands, which caused a migration from the farms either to Western areas or to the new industrial centers.

In the decades which followed 1830 the industrial transformation was accompanied by an intellectual and artistic awakening which constituted a kind of New England renaissance. This combined the liberalizing influence of Unitarianism in religion with the "transcendentalism" of Emerson and other literary figures, and with a mounting demand for social reform. The state produced a galaxy of literary figures: Emerson, Hawthorne, Thoreau, Holmes, Lowell, Bryant, Parkman, Prescott, and others. Horace Mann led the way in educational reform, and William Lloyd Garrison began his crusade for the abolition of slavery at Boston in 1831.

The years after 1845 were marked politically by the turbulence of the "Know-Nothing" and antislavery movements. The first great wave of emigration from Ireland came to Massachusetts in these years. A movement for native Americanism, strong in northern seaboard states, took the form of the American or "Know-Nothing" party, which in 1854 swept the polls in Massachusetts. The antislavery movement also attracted strong support. The new Republican Party with its program of halting slavery expansion carried the state in 1856 and again for Lincoln in 1860. Massachusetts responded quickly to Lincoln's call for volunteers in 1861 and gave strong support to the Union cause.

In the great industrial expansion which followed the Civil War Massachusetts retained its leading position in a number of fields, particularly in textiles and leather goods. Before 1900 about a third of the nation's woolen production came from this state, and nearly half of the boots and shoes. This period witnessed great achievements in cultural life within the state, at the same time as the swelling tide of immigration was changing the make-up of the state's population. As late as the 1930's nearly two thirds of the state's population was either foreign born or descended in part from foreign-born parentage.

Perhaps the key to understanding Massachusetts in the present generation lies in the mingling of old and new. The great cultural achievements of the nineteenth century are everywhere apparent and the state produces leaders in every field, while at the same time the more recent population strains make an increasing contribution. Although older industries have declined, the state retains its economic vitality with developments in other areas. In the field of politics the present generation has found a fairly close balance between conservatism and the tradition of liberal reform.

Bibliography.—GENERAL DESCRIPTION: Emerson, B. K., *Geology of Massachusetts and Rhode Island* (Washington, Government Printing Office 1917); Federal Writers' Project, *Massachusetts, a Guide to Its Places and People* (Boston 1937).

PHYSICAL FEATURES AND RESOURCES: Crosby, Irving B., *Report on the Mineral Resources of Massachusetts* (Boston 1932); Beaumont, A. B., *A Key to Massachusetts Soils*, Miscellaneous Publication Number 274, United States Department of Agriculture (Washington 1940).

POPULATION AND POLITICAL DIVISIONS: United States and Massachusetts State Census of Population *Reports*.

GOVERNMENT: Frothingham, L. A., *A Brief History of the Constitution and Government of Massachusetts* (Boston 1925); Sly, John F., *Town Government in Massachusetts, 1630–1930* (Cambridge 1930); Handlin, Oscar, and Mary F., *Commonwealth: A Study of the Role of Government in the American Economy: Massachusetts, 1774–1861* (New York 1947); League of Women Voters of Mass., *Massachusetts State Government, a Citizen's Handbook* (Cambridge 1956); Commonwealth of Mass., *Manual for the Use of the General Court* (Boston, biennially).

ECONOMIC ACTIVITIES: United States Department of Commerce, Census of Agriculture *Reports;* United States Department of Commerce, *Statistical Abstract* (published annually); The Council of State Governments, *The Book of States* (Chicago, published annually); United States Department of Commerce, *State Income Reports* (published annually); United States Department of Commerce, Census of Manufactures *Reports;* United States Department of Commerce, Census of Business *Reports;* United States Forest Service, *Timber Resources in Massachusetts* (1956); State Department of Natural Resources, *Annual Reports.*

PLACES OF INTEREST: Rozman, David, and Sherburne, Ruth E., *Public Land Ownership in Rural Areas of Massachusetts*, Experiment Station Bulletin No. 489, University of Massachusetts (Amherst 1955); The New England Council, *New England Museums and Historic Houses* (Boston 1957); State Department of Natural Resources, *Massachusetts State Forests and State Parks* (published annually).

HISTORY: Morison, S. E., *The Maritime History of*

Massachusetts (Boston 1921); Lockwood, J. H., ed., *Western Massachusetts: A History, 1636–1925,* 4 vols. (New York 1926); Adams, James T., *History of New England,* 3 vols. (Boston 1927); Hohman, Elmo P., *The American Whaleman* (New York 1928); Hart, A. B., ed., *Commonwealth History of Massachusetts,* 5 vols. (New York 1927–30); Morison, S. E., *Builders of the Bay Colony* (Boston 1930); Andrews, C. M., *The Colonial Period of American History,* 4 vols. (New Haven 1934–38); Wittke, Carl, *The Irish in America* (Baton Rouge 1956); Massachusetts Historical Society, *Proceedings,* and *Collections;* excellent articles in *The New England Quarterly* (Brunswick, Me.).

THEODORE C. CALDWELL,
Professor of History,
University of Massachusetts.
GEORGE W. WESTCOTT,
Economist, University of Massachusetts.
Revised by the Editors of "The Encyclopedia Americana."

MASSACHUSETTS, University of,

a co-educational institution of higher learning located near Amherst, Mass., on a campus of 700 acres. Undergraduate instruction is divided into the College of Arts and Science, College of Agriculture, schools of Engineering, Business Administration, Home Economics, Nursing, and Education, and divisions of Physical Education and Military and Air Science. The university also maintains a graduate school, and the Stockbridge School of Agriculture (a two-year vocational program), the state Agricultural Experiment Station, the Agricultural and Home Economics Extension Service, and experimental stations at Waltham and Wareham, Mass.

The state institution of the Commonwealth of Massachusetts, the university was founded in 1863 as Massachusetts Agricultural College under the provisions of the Morrill Land Grant Act of 1862, and was formally opened to students on Oct. 2, 1867. In April 1931 its name was changed by legislative enactment to Massachusetts State College, and in May 1947 the college became the University of Massachusetts.

JAMES W. BURKE.

MASSACHUSETTS BAY,

a broad inlet of the Atlantic Ocean formed by the westward curve of the Massachusetts coast, extending about 65 miles from Cape Ann on the north to Cape Cod. The northern shore is rocky and irregular, the southern low and sandy; along the shores are a number of capes, headlands, and small islands. Important arms are Gloucester and Nahant bays and Salem, Marblehead, and Lynn harbors in the north; Boston Bay in the center; and Plymouth and Cape Cod bays in the south.

MASSACHUSETTS BAY COMPANY.

On March 4, 1629 a royal charter was granted to the "Governor and Company of the Massachusetts Bay in New England," a group of English Puritans who the year before had received a grant from the Council of New England authorizing them to trade and colonize between the Merrimack and Charles rivers. Under the 1628 patent the company had been given powers of local self-government, subject to the general New England government of the council. The charter of 1629 nullified the council's authority and made the company subject only to the king. Provision was made for governing officers and a general court of stockholders, but unlike most trading company charters of the day, it did not require that the company hold its business meetings in England.

Thus when John Winthrop (q.v.) led nearly 1,000 immigrants to Massachusetts in 1630, they were able to make the charter the basic constitution for the colony's government. They landed at Salem on June 12, 1630, but soon moved on to Charlestown (founded the year before). The following autumn Winthrop and several followers founded Boston. (See BOSTON—*History.*)

Through the control which the general court exercised on admission of new members to the company, they were able to limit the suffrage to Puritans. Thus, almost at the outset the colony, though chartered as a commercial enterprise, became a Calvinist theocracy virtually independent of external control. With the outbreak of the Puritan Revolution in 1642 Massachusetts refused to accept the authority of the British Parliament, and in 1643 it invited Connecticut, Plymouth, and New Haven to join a confederation, the United Colonies of New England, for defense against Indians, Dutch, and French. Following the Restoration a commission was sent from England in 1664 to investigate the company. As a result of its report, made in 1676, that Massachusetts had committed grave errors in such matters as coining money without authority, denying freedom of worship to dissenters, and refusing to obey the Navigation Acts, the company's charter was withdrawn in 1684. The company government continued until 1686, however, when the Dominion of New England was established.

ELIZABETH BACON,
Editorial Staff, "The Encyclopedia Americana."

MASSACHUSETTS HISTORICAL SOCIETY,

the oldest historical society in the United States. It was founded by Jeremy Belknap (1744–1798) and held its first meeting in Boston, Mass., on Jan. 24, 1791. Resident membership is limited to 125 citizens of Massachusetts; 50 corresponding members are elected from other states of the Union; while 10 honorary members are elected mostly from Europe and South America. Members pay no dues, the expenses of the society and its publications being met by income from its endowment. The society meets monthly from October through May; at each meeting, a member reads a paper which is later published in the *Proceedings.* Other publications consist of the *Collections,* the *Winthrop Papers,* and the *Lives of Harvard Graduates.*

The society possesses a library of 250,000 books and pamphlets, many of which are extremely rare, and an invaluable collection of manuscripts. These include a complete collection of the private papers of Thomas Jefferson; the *Adams Papers,* which in 1957 were being edited for publication; and the Winthrop manuscripts, the greatest colonial collection in existence. Both the library and the museum, which contains many remarkable portraits and unique objects connected with American history, are open to the public free of charge.

STEWART MITCHELL.

MASSACHUSETTS INSTITUTE OF TECHNOLOGY (MIT),

an independent, co-educational, endowed institution chartered by the General Court of the Commonwealth of Massachusetts on April 10, 1861. It receives no tax support from the commonwealth.

MIT grants undergraduate degrees in aeronautical engineering, architecture, biology, chemical engineering, chemistry, civil engineering, economics, electrical engineering, food technology, geology, the humanities, industrial management, mathematics, mechanical engineering, metallurgy, naval architecture, and physics. Graduate degrees are awarded in all these fields except the humanities, and also in biochemistry, building engineering, ceramics, city and regional planning, meteorology, nuclear engineering, sanitary engineering, and textile technology. The undergraduate programs in architecture, engineering, the humanities, management, and science are so broad and fundamental as to constitute an excellent general preparation for careers in other fields as well as these. The graduate programs derive exceptional strength from MIT's extensive research activities.

MIT emphasizes fundamental research, with both undergraduate and graduate students participating in the cooperative research effort. Among the outstanding research facilities are a nuclear reactor and nuclear engineering laboratory, computation center, servomechanisms laboratory, supersonic wind tunnels, cyclotron (7 Mev., million electric volts), Van de Graaff accelerators, synchrotron (350 Mev.), spectroscopy laboratory, electronics laboratory, gas turbine laboratory, hydrodynamics laboratory, metals processing laboratory, acoustics laboratory, ship model towing tank, and insulation and high-voltage laboratories. In addition to the facilities of its own campus, MIT has field stations at the Oak Ridge National Laboratories in Alabama and at a number of eastern industrial plants. It cooperates in the Brookhaven National Laboratories and is a partner with Harvard University in the Cambridge Electron Accelerator.

The institute's first classes, delayed by the Civil War, opened in 1865 in Boston. Its first president, William Barton Rogers (1804–1882), set it on a course of intellectual leadership and public service that has given it continuing vitality and made it an institution of national and international influence. In its early years the institute pioneered in extending the laboratory method of instruction as an indispensable educational technique; later it virtually created the modern profession of chemical engineering. Its courses in electrical engineering, aeronautical engineering, and applied physics were among the first in the world, and it was the first technological institution to recognize the importance of and provide for economics in the training of engineers. During World War II, MIT trained many thousands of students for the armed forces and undertook large programs of defense research out of which grew achievements in radar, fire control, and other fields. It operates the Lincoln Laboratory in Lexington, Mass., and the Instrumentation Laboratory in Cambridge as defense research centers. In 1916 the campus was moved from Boston to Cambridge. After World War II a large building program added to the campus the Kresge Auditorium, a chapel, swimming pool, the Everett Moore Baker House (dormitory), and the Karl Taylor Compton Laboratories, all of which have won recognition as outstanding examples of contemporary university architecture.

JOHN I. MAHILL,
Assistant to the Director, Massachusetts Institute of Technology.

MASSADA. See MASADA.

MASSAGE, mà-säzh′. The word *massage* is derived from the Greek *massein,* to knead. In the healing arts, massage refers to systematic manipulation of the bodily tissues for therapeutic purposes. It represents one of the oldest forms of treatment still useful today in the alleviation of symptoms due to disease or injury. Primitive man probably used massage intuitively by rubbing or stroking an injured or painful area of the body. Ancient Hindu and Chinese writings refer to well-developed systems of massage as part of their early medical practices. In Western civilization, Hippocrates, about 400 B.C., wrote in detail about the beneficial therapeutic effects of massage and gave indications for its use. Massage has continued to be a useful form of therapy in many clinical conditions, although some claims for its effectiveness are probably highly exaggerated. Despite the ancient history of massage and its widespread use in the healing arts, knowledge concerning its effectiveness is limited by a scarcity of precise medical data.

Massage Techniques.—The techniques of massage vary widely among its practitioners. In general they can be divided into two groups: *manual* and *mechanical.* Most medical massage is performed manually, requiring the skilled hands of a trained physical therapist or nurse. The technique of manual massage is usually classified as follows: *effleurage*—long, rhythmical stroking movements of the therapist's hands applied with varying pressure over the part to be treated; *petrissage*—kneading or compression movements applied to the underlying muscle tissues; *friction*—a deep circular rolling motion of the therapist's fingers, especially around bony prominences or joints; *tapotement*—a striking or percussion movement of varying intensity over muscle and other soft tissue; *vibration*—a vibratory, or trembling movement administered through the therapist's fingers or whole hand to the part to be treated.

Mechanical massage can be administered by a wide variety of devices consisting of motor-driven vibrators, rollers, and belts. These devices, which vary much in their design and effectiveness, are more a tribute to the mechanical ingeniousness of their inventors than to their therapeutic value. It is unlikely that any mechanical apparatus will ever approach the usefulness of manual massage administered by a skilled therapist.

Effects of Massage.—The physiologic effects of massage can be described by the changes it produces in the skin and fatty tissues, the muscles, the circulation of blood and lymph, and the nervous system. Effleurage acts directly on the skin surface, removing excessive secretions and superficial deposits. The skin temperature can be elevated from 2° to 3° C. by the direct mechanical effects of massage, as well as by reflex dilatation of the underlying small blood vessels. Although it is frequently thought that massage can remove undesirable fat deposits in various regions of the body, there is no positive clinical or experimental evidence that adipose tissue can be altered by even vigorous local massage.

It is believed that massage affects muscles by both direct and reflex changes, increasing the circulation in these deeper tissues. It has been demonstrated, however, that the production of lactic acid is not increased by massage, as does occur following muscular exercise. It is generally agreed that massage does not increase muscular strength, as this can be accomplished only through exercise. Certain abnormal states of muscular activity, such as cramping, spasm, or twitching, can be significantly relieved by properly applied massage. This relief is effected by both direct action upon the muscles and reflex action mediated through the nervous and circulatory systems. Massage may also alter intramuscular connective tissue adhesions formed by disease or injury. The adhesions are stretched and proper function is restored by the mechanical effect of massage.

The circulation of blood and lymph is increased by the variable pressures exerted during massage. Rhythmic alternation of pressure, produced by the contraction of skeletal muscles and respiratory motions during normal physical activity, is called *automassage*. This type of physiologic massage is an important adjunct in aiding circulation in the veins and lymphatic channels. Swelling of the extremities may occur when muscular activity is reduced by disease, injury, or immobilization, and is due to the inefficient circulation in the veins or lymphatics. This swelling may be prevented or minimized by the proper application of massage in a centripetal direction. Aside from the direct effect of pressure on the blood and lymphatic vessels, massage can produce changes in the contraction or relaxation of the muscular walls of the blood vessels by means of nerve reflexes that are initiated by stimulation of the skin.

In addition to the reflex effects on muscle and blood vessels, massage may exert a beneficial effect on the central nervous system of the body. In the case of most individuals, massage acts as a sedative when it is applied, reducing anxiety and tension. This relief is accomplished through a variety of complicated nerve reflexes, whose nature is not too well understood at the present time. Thus, in addition to the purely physical effects, massage may have a most desirable though temporary psychotherapeutic value. Massage for this purpose has come to be quite widely employed.

CHARLES S. WISE, M.D.,
Professor of Physical Medicine and Rehabilitation, George Washington University School of Medicine, Washington, D.C.

MASSAGETAE, măs-să′gĕ-tī, a pastoral nomadic people described by the Greek historian Herodotus (I: 204–216; IV; II: 172) as living beyond the Oxus River in Central Asia. Cyrus the Great of Persia is said to have been slain in a battle with the Massagetae.

MASSASAUGA. See RATTLESNAKE.

MASSASOIT, măs′à-soit (also known as OSMEKIN or OUSAMEQUIN, Yellow Feather), American Indian chief: b. about 1580; d. in Rhode Island, 1661. He was a powerful chief of the Wampanoag tribe in the region about Bristol, R.I., whose dominion extended from Cape Cod to Narragansett Bay. His principal village was at Pokanoket (Mt. Hope), near Bristol. He had already become acquainted with white men when on March 22, 1621 he visited Plymouth with other chiefs and signed a treaty of peace and friendship with the colonists which he kept throughout his life. He visited Boston in 1638 and 1642, and in 1649 sold the site of Duxbury to the English. His son and successor, Metacomet, became known as King Philip (q.v.).

Consult Winthrop, John, *Winthrop's Journal,* James K. Hosmer, ed., vol. 1, p. 131 (New York 1908); Bradford, William, *Of Plymouth Plantation 1620–1647,* with notes and introduction by Samuel Eliot Morison (New York 1952).

MASSAWA, mà-sä′wà, city, Eritrea, Ethiopia, capital of Massawa administrative division, on the Red Sea, about 40 miles from Asmara. The chief port of Eritrea, and a road and railroad terminus, it is built on the two small islands of Taulud and Massawa and the adjacent mainland, with connecting causeways. It exports hides, coffee, dried fish, gum arabic, and oilseeds, and is the main Red Sea market for pearls and mother-of-pearl. It has shipyards, salt works, an electric power plant, water-distilling, ice-making, fish-drying, and tobacco-processing plants, and cement and brick works. Occupied by the Italians in 1885, it was the capital of Eritrea until 1897. The British made it an Allied naval base in 1941. Pop. (1963) 15,800.

MASSENA, mà-sā-nà′, **André,** French soldier: b. Levens, near Nice, France, May 6, 1758; d. Paris, April 4, 1817. Early orphaned, he served in an Italian regiment from 1775 to 1789. In 1791 he joined a volunteer battalion under the French revolutionary government, and in 1793 was made a general of brigade. He participated in the Piedmont campaign in 1794, and, as Napoleon's most trusted general in the campaign of 1796-1797, won the Battle of Rivoli. In 1799 he defeated the Russians at Zurich, and in 1800 held Genoa for four months, giving Napoleon time to strike successfully at Marengo. Made a marshal of the empire in 1804, he was given command in Italy in 1805 and occupied the Kingdom of Naples for Joseph Bonaparte. He served in Poland in 1807, and in 1808 was created duke of Rivoli. His courage at Aspern-Essling in 1809, which saved the French forces from destruction, won him the title of prince of Essling (1810). In command of the army in Portugal, 1810–1811, Masséna withstood Wellington for five months, but was compelled to withdraw to Spain, where in May 1811 he was defeated at Fuentes d'Oñoro. (See WELLINGTON, ARTHUR WELLESLEY, DUKE OF.) Recalled to France, he became commander at Marseilles. He supported the Bourbons on their return to power, and after Waterloo was named governor of Paris.

MASSENA, mă-sē′nà, village, New York, in St. Lawrence County, about 3 miles south of the St. Lawrence River and 33 miles northeast of Ogdensburg. Located on the Raquette and Grass rivers, at an altitude of 202 feet above sea level, it is served by the Grand Trunk (Canadian National), New York Central, and Massena Terminal railroads, and Eastern Airlines, and is an international airport of entry. At the focal point of the St. Lawrence Seaway and the St. Lawrence River Power Project, Massena's population grew from 13,137 in 1950 to 15,942 in 1957.

The principal seaway structures in the Massena area are the Long Sault Canal (10 miles) and the Eisenhower and Grass River locks; power structures are the Barnhart Island powerhouse, the Long Sault spillway control, the Massena intake control dam, and the Iroquois control dam.

Before the inauguration of the seaway projects the town's economy was based on dairying and industry. Three large aluminum plants employ several thousand workers. Recreational facilities include a 2,000-acre state park on Barnhart Island, an 18-hole golf course, a yacht basin, and two public beaches.

Beginning as a log cabin settlement in 1792, when Anable Fancher put up a sawmill on the

Grass River and named the place for André Masséna (q.v.), Massena was incorporated as a village in 1886, and has mayor-council government. Pop. 15,478.

MASSENET, màs-nĕ', Jules (Émile Frédéric), French composer: b. Montaud, near St. Étienne, France, May 12, 1842; d. Paris, Aug. 13, 1912. His father, an ironmaster, had served as an army engineer under Napoleon Bonaparte; his mother was a talented musician, who gave him his early training in music. At the age of 11 he entered the Paris Conservatory, and to earn living expenses, played triangle and drum in local theaters, thus gaining a practical knowledge of orchestra instrumentation. He won conservatory prizes for pianoforte and fugue, and in 1863 was awarded the Grand Prix de Rome for his cantata *David Rizzio.* Study in Rome was followed by travel in Italy and Germany before his return to Paris. His first opera to be produced, *La Grand' Tante,* was performed at the Opéra Comique in 1867. He was elected to the Académie des Beaux Arts in 1878, and from 1878 to 1896 was professor of advanced harmony at the Paris Conservatory. He became chevalier (1876) and grand officier (1899) of the Légion d'Honneur.

Massenet composed songs, oratorios, orchestral suites, and operas. His famous *Élégie* was originally written for his unpublished opera *La Coupe du roi de Thulé* and transferred to serve as incidental music for Charles Marie Leconte de Lisle's drama *Les Érinnyes.* The orchestral suite *Scènes Hongroises* (1871) and the comic opera *Don César de Bazan,* produced in 1872, placed him among the leading young composers of his day. One of his most popular operas was *Hérodiade,* first performed in Brussels in 1881 (in England called *Salomé*); but *Manon,* produced at the Opéra Comique in 1884, is usually considered his masterpiece. In it he replaced the unaccompanied recitative with dialogue over an orchestral accompaniment and adopted the use of leitmotiv in the manner of Charles François Gounod. Best known of his other operas are *Le Cid* (1885); *Werther* (1892); *Thaïs* (1894); *Sapho* (1897); *Le Jongleur de Notre-Dame* (1902); and *Don Quichotte* (1910).

Consult Bruneau, Alfred, *Massenet* (Paris 1935); Morin, A., *Jules Massenet et ses opéras* (Montreal 1944); Colson, Percy, *Massenet: "Manon"* (London 1947; also his autobiography *Mes souvenirs,* completed by Xavier Leroux (Paris 1912; Eng. tr., *My Recollections,* Boston 1919).

MASSEY, măs'ĭ, Gerald, English poet: b. Gamble Wharf, near Tring, Hertfordshire, England, May 29, 1828; d. Redcot, South Norwood, Surrey, Oct. 29, 1907. One of a large and impoverished family (his father was a canal boatman), he was put to work in a silk mill at the age of 8. At 15 he became an errand boy in London, spent what leisure time he had in reading, studying French, and writing poetry, and in 1848 published his first volume of verse, *Poems and Chansons.* He was actively interested in Chartism (q.v.), became editor of the social reform paper *The Spirit of Freedom* in 1849, and in 1850 joined the Christian Socialist movement. That year he also published his second volume of poems, *Voices of Freedom and Lyrics of Love.* His next volume, *The Ballad of Babe Christabel and other Poems* (1854), brought him immediate popularity as a poet of the people.

In later life Massey became deeply interested in spiritualism and made an intensive study of ancient Egyptian civilization as offering an explanation of psychic phenomena. His most ambitious work in this field, *Ancient Egypt: the Light of the World* (1907), is now considered of little value. George Eliot based her novel *Felix Holt, the Radical* on Massey's career.

MASSEY, Hart Almerrin, Canadian manufacturer and philanthropist: b. Haldimand Township, Northumberland County, Upper Canada (Ontario), Canada, April 29, 1823; d. Toronto, Feb. 20, 1896. He was educated at Victoria College, Cobourg, Ontario, and in 1855 became sole owner of the implement factory established by his father at Newcastle. In 1870 he became president of the Massey Manufacturing Company, and in 1891 of the Massey-Harris Company. He perfected mowing and reaping machines, the first of their kind in Canada, and introduced improvements in other farm implements. A liberal philanthropist, he founded Massey Music Hall, Toronto, and contributed generously to other cultural and philanthropic activities. The student center, Hart House, at the University of Toronto, built and endowed (1913–1919) by the Hart A. Massey Foundation, was named for him.

Consult Denison, Merrill, *Harvest Triumphant: the story of Massey-Harris* (New York 1949).

His eldest son, CHESTER DANIEL MASSEY (1850–1926) became president of the Massey-Harris Company in 1901, and, besides maintaining his father's benefactions, gave liberally to Toronto General Hospital, the Toronto Art Gallery, and many other institutions. In his later years he was chairman of the Hart A. Massey Foundation.

MASSEY, Raymond, Canadian-American actor, director, and producer: b. Toronto, Ontario, Canada, Aug. 30, 1896. The younger brother of Vincent Massey (q.v.), he was educated at the University of Toronto and at Oxford. He served with the Canadian Field Artillery in Belgium in 1916 when he was wounded, and with the Canadian Expeditionary Force in Siberia in 1918. In 1922 he made his stage debut in London as Jack in *In the Zone,* at Everyman Theatre, and in 1926 became joint manager of the theater. His first notable hit was as the Khan Aghaba in *The Transit of Venus* at the Ambassadors in 1927. Massey made his New York debut in 1931 at the Broadhurst Theatre in the title role of *Hamlet.* His most conspicuous success was as Abraham Lincoln in *Abe Lincoln in Illinois,* at the Plymouth Theatre, New York, 1938–1939. In World War II he served as major in the adjutant general's branch of the Canadian Army, and in 1944 became a United States citizen. In 1958 he played one of the leading roles, Mr. Zuss, in the prize-winning *J.B.* by Archibald MacLeish. He is author of the play *The Hanging Judge* (1952) and has appeared in a number of motion pictures and radio programs.

MASSEY, Vincent, Canadian statesman: b. Toronto, Ont., Canada, Feb. 20, 1887; d. London, Eng., Dec. 30, 1967. A grandson of Hart A. Massey (q.v.), he studied at the University of Toronto and at Oxford. Between 1921 and 1925 he was president of the Massey-Harris Company, a position he resigned to become a minister in the Liberal cabinet of Prime Minister Mackenzie King in 1925. In 1926 he was appointed first Canadian minister to the United States, where he served until 1930; from 1935 to 1946 he was high commissioner for Canada in the United Kingdom. In February 1952 he became governor general of Canada, the first Canadian appointed to the office. Among important civic offices held, Massey was chancellor (1947–1953) and member of the Board of Governors (1953–   ) of the University of Toronto; chairman of the National Gallery of Canada (1948–1952); and chairman of the Royal Commission on National Development in the Arts, Letters, and Sciences (1949–1951). He was succeeded as governor general of Canada on Sept. 15, 1959, by Gen. George Philias Vanier, a French Canadian. Massey is the author of *On Being Canadian* (1948).

MASSIF CENTRAL, mà-sēf' säN-tràl', a mountainous plateau region in south central France, centering in Puy-de-Dôme, Cantal, and Haute-Loire departments, with an area of about 33,000 square miles. Its highest point is the Puy de Sancy, 6,188 feet, in the Monts Dore Range of the Auvergne Mountains; the average elevation is about 2,600 feet. It is the chief water divide of France: the Loire River and its largest tributaries, the Allier, Cher, and Vienne, rise in the Massif Central, as do the Dordogne and tributaries of the Seine, Rhone, and Garonne. Sheep and cattle are raised and Roquefort and other cheeses made in the uplands, while grapes, olives, and mulberries are intensively cultivated in the valleys and on southeastern slopes. There are extensive deposits of coal, kaolin, and other minerals, and hydroelectric power serves metallurgical and textile industries in St.-Étienne, Roanne, and Le Creusot. Clermont-Ferrand is the center of France's rubber industry; Limoges is famous for its porcelain.

MASSILLON, mà-sē-yôN', **Jean Baptiste,** French ecclesiastic: b. Hyères, France, June 24, 1663; d. Clermont-Ferrand, Sept. 18, 1742. In 1681 he entered the Congregation of the Oratory, in 1692 was ordained priest, and in 1696 was appointed director of the Seminary of St. Magloire in Paris. Massillon became famous for the eloquence of his sermons and funeral orations; often quoted are the opening words of his oration for the funeral of Louis XIV, *"Dieu seul est grand"* (God alone is great). He was nominated bishop of Clermont in 1717; in 1718 he preached a series of sermons before the nine-year-old Louis XV which were later published as *Le petit carême* (*Sunday Lenten Sermons*). He was elected to the French Academy in 1719, and the same year retired to his diocese. His collected works (15 vols.) were published in 1745–1749.

MASSILLON, măs"l-ŭn, city, Ohio, in Stark County, about 7 miles west of Canton, on the Tuscarawas River, at an altitude of 1,030 feet. Located in a coal-mining area, it is an industrial and shipping center served by the Pennsylvania, the Baltimore and Ohio, and the Nickel Plate railroads, and is 10 miles from the Akron-Canton airport. Its manufactures include steel and aluminum products, metal bearings, machinery, furnaces, hardware, paper products, clothing, and rubber goods.

First settled by New Englanders in 1812, it was called Kendal, but in 1826 was renamed for Jean Baptiste Massillon (q.v.). With the opening of the Ohio and Erie Canal in 1832, Massillon became one of the largest wheat markets in Ohio.

A center for the manufacture of threshing machines and railroad cars, Massillon was incorporated as a village in 1853 and as a city in 1868. Its government is by mayor and council of nine. Jacob Sechler Coxey (q.v.), leader of Coxey's Army, was its mayor in 1931–1933. Pop. 31,236.

MASSINE, mŭ-syēn', **Léonide,** Russian-born dancer and choreographer: b. Moscow, Russia, Aug. 9, 1896. He studied at the Imperial Academy of Dancing, Moscow, and made his debut in 1912. Between 1914 and 1920 he was principal dancer of the Diaghilev Ballet Russe, and in 1915 succeeded Michel Fokine as choreographer of the company. From 1932 to 1941 he was choreographer, dancer, and artistic director of the Ballet Russe de Monte Carlo, and was director of the Ballet National Theatre, New York City, 1941–1944. During the period 1947–1951 he was choreographer and guest artist with Sadlers Wells Ballet, London, and leading Continental opera houses, and composed and danced in the motion pictures *The Red Shoes* (1948) and *Tales of Hoffman* (1951). His symphonic ballets were a fresh contribution to choreography. The numerous ballets conceived by Massine include *Le Tricorne* (1919), *Le Sacre du Printemps* (1920), *Symphonie Fantastique* (1936), *Seventh Symphony* (1938), and *Rouge et Noir* (1939).

MASSINGER, măs'ĭn-jẽr, **Philip,** English dramatist: b. 1583, baptized at Salisbury, England, Nov. 24, 1583; d. Southwark, London, March 1639 or 1640 (buried March 18). His father, Arthur Massinger, a confidential employee of Henry and William Herbert, 2d and 3d earls of Pembroke, had been a fellow at Merton College, Oxford, and late in life became a member of Parliament. Philip entered St. Alban Hall, Oxford, in 1602, but left after four years without taking a degree. Settling in London, he became the friend and collaborator of several playwrights, notably John Fletcher. The literary association with Fletcher began in 1613; in 1616 both men became playwrights for the acting company known as the King's Men. (See also BEAUMONT AND FLETCHER.) In 1623 Massinger transferred to the Cockpit company (the Queen's Men), and wrote three plays for them under his own name: *The Bondman* (licensed Dec. 3, 1623, printed 1624), of which Samuel Pepys saw a revival in March 1661; *The Renegado* (licensed April 17, 1624, printed 1630); *The Parliament of Love* (licensed Nov. 3, 1624). This last was ascribed to W. Rowley on the Stationers' Registers of June 29, 1660, and was first printed from an imperfect manuscript in 1805. After Fletcher's death in 1625 Massinger returned to the King's Men and wrote for them exclusively except for his play *The Great Duke of Florence* (1627, printed 1635), which he wrote for a company called the Queen's Servants.

Massinger made little money from his plays, but he had friends and patrons among the nobility. He dedicated *The Bondman* to Philip Herbert, 4th earl of Pembroke, who gave him an annual pension of 30 or 40 pounds; a number of his other plays are dedicated to various benefactors. Massinger died suddenly at his home near the Globe Theatre in Southwark, and was buried in St. Saviour's churchyard, possibly in the same grave as Fletcher. He is known to have married, for the earl of Pembroke transferred his pension to Massinger's widow. A theory has been advanced that Massinger was a convert to Roman Catholicism. This is based on certain passages in some of his plays: *The Virgin Martyr* (c. 1622), written with Dekker; *The Renegado*, in which the Jesuit Francisco is the dominant good character; and *The Maid of Honour* (1632), in which the heroine becomes a nun.

Massinger drew heavily on Italian and Spanish sources for his material. His plays show a sure knowledge of dramatic construction, plot development, and stage technique, but very little grasp of human motivation. His characters seem devised mostly to meet the demands of his plots, their virtues or villany too exaggerated and their speech too rhetorical to be convincing. His blank verse has the pace of prose rather than the lift of poetry. His own favorite among his plays was *The Roman Actor* (1626, printed 1629), in which he showed the brutalizing effects of despotism; but the most popular was the comedy *A New Way to Pay Old Debts,* probably written about 1625 or 1626, and licensed Nov. 10, 1632. The frenzy of its money-mad villain, Sir Giles Overreach, when his avaricious schemes are finally thwarted, offered such acting opportunities that the play was retained in repertoires for more than 200 years.

Massinger's political views as reflected in his plays were those of the Herbert family. He satirized George Villiers, duke of Buckingham, as Giseo in *The Bondman* and as Fulgentio in *The Maid of Honour*. One play, probably a draft of *Believe as You List,* was refused a license in January 1631 because its reference to the deposing of Sebastian of Portugal by Philip II of Spain was considered dangerous to the existing treaty friendship between England and Spain. His social views were largely those of his time. In *The City Madam* (1632) he satirizes the unsuccessful efforts of the wife and daughter of a wealthy city merchant to climb the social ladder by aping the speech and manners of court ladies. In *The Roman Actor* he extols the stage as a strong moral influence promoting practice of "the active virtues," though this is hardly borne out by the coarseness of his own plays.

Twelve of Massinger's plays may have been lost, but it is possible that some of the lost manuscripts were duplicates of existing plays. Some scholars advance the theory that he collaborated with Shakespeare on the disputed *Henry VIII,* others assign this play and *Two Noble Kinsmen* to the joint authorship of Massinger and Fletcher. Massinger is the acknowledged author of 15 extant plays—tragedies, comedies, and tragicomedies. In addition to those mentioned above, they include *The Duke of Milan* (c. 1618, printed 1623 and revived in 1816); *The Unnatural Combat* (c. 1619, printed 1639); *The Picture* (1629, printed 1630); *The Emperor of the East* (1631); *The Guardian* (1633, printed 1655); and *The Bashful Lover* (1636, printed 1655).

Bibliography.—The standard edition of Massinger's works is *The Plays of Philip Massinger,* William Gifford, ed., 4 vols. (London 1805); id., re-edited by Francis Cunningham, with the addition of *Believe as You List* (London 1868); *Selections from Philip Massinger,* Arthur Symons, ed., 2 vols., in the Mermaid Series (London 1887–1889).

For biography and criticism consult Stephen, Sir Leslie, *Hours in a Library,* 3d series, vol. 2 (London 1899); Cruickshank, Alfred H., *Philip Massinger* (Oxford 1920); Eliot, T. S., *The Sacred Wood* (London 1920); Ball, Robert H., *The Amazing Career of Sir Giles Overreach* (Princeton, N.J., 1939); Maxwell, Baldwin, *Studies in Beaumont, Fletcher, and Massinger* (Chapel Hill, N.C., 1939); Boas, Frederick S., *Introduction to Stuart Drama,* chap. 13 (New York 1946); Dunn, Thomas A., *Philip Massinger: The Man and the Playwright* (London 1957).

MASSIVE, Mount, măs'ĭv, mountain, Colorado, in the Sawatch Range of the Rocky Mountains, 10 miles southwest of Leadville, in Lake County. Mount Massive (14,418 feet) is the second highest peak in the American Rockies, after Mount Elbert, which is five miles to the southeast.

MASSON, măs''n, **David,** Scottish editor and scholar: b. Aberdeen, Scotland, Dec. 2, 1822; d. Edinburgh, Oct. 6, 1907. Educated at Marischal College, Aberdeen, he studied theology at Edinburgh University, and in 1842–1844 edited the *Banner,* a Free Church weekly. In 1847 Masson settled in London, where he contributed to leading periodicals of the day, and in 1853 was appointed professor of English literature at University College. He helped found *Macmillan's Magazine* in 1859 and edited it until 1867. In 1865 he became professor of rhetoric and English literature at Edinburgh University, where until his retirement in 1895 he worked for the admission of women into the universities. In 1893 he was appointed historiographer royal for Scotland. Most important of his many works is his *Life of Milton,* 6 vols. (1859–1880).

MASSON, mȧ-sôn', **Frédéric,** French historian: b. Paris, France, March 8, 1847; d. there, Feb. 19, 1923. Librarian in the archives of the French Foreign Office (1868–1880), he was employed by Prince Louis Napoleon to arrange the latter's collection of papers. Masson himself assembled a private collection of original documents on Napoleon I—later bequeathed to the French Institute—and devoted his career to research and writing on the French hero. The most important of his works is *Napoléon et sa famille,* 13 vols. (1897–1919). He was elected to the French Academy in 1903 and became its permanent secretary in 1919.

MASSON, măs''n, **Tom** (in full THOMAS LANSING MASSON), American humorist and editor: b. Essex, Conn., July 21, 1866; d. Glen Ridge, N.J., June 18, 1934. After graduating from high school in New Haven, he began work as an office boy. Later, while working as a traveling salesman, he began contributing to the new humorous weekly *Life.* From 1893 to 1922, the most flourishing period of that magazine, he was its managing editor. In 1922 he joined the staff of the *Saturday Evening Post.* Masson also published several books of humor, including the anthologies *Our American Humorists* (1922) and *Tom Masson's Compendium of Wit and Humor* (1927).

MASSYS, măs'ĭs, or **MATSYS,** măt'sĭs, **Quentin** or **Quinten** (also MESSYS; METSYS), Flemish painter: b. Louvain, Belgium, about 1466; d. Antwerp, between July 13 and Sept. 16, 1530. Legend says that Massys was a blacksmith who became a painter in order to win the hand of an artist's daughter. His teachers are not known. Massys painted religious scenes, portraits, and genre pictures. His most important religious works, characterized by deep spiritual feeling, are the *Legend of Ste. Anne* (1509; now in the Brussels Museum of Antique Painting); and his masterpiece, a triptych painted for the joiners' company, in the Antwerp Cathedral (1511; now in the Antwerp Museum of Fine Arts) : the principal panel portrays the *Burial of Christ;* on the wings are the *Martyrdom of St. John the Baptist,* and *St. John the Evangelist.* His best-known portrait is of Erasmus. In his genre scenes, such as the *Man with a Pair of Eyeglasses* (Städel Art Institute, Frankfurt, Germany), and *The Money Changer and His Wife* (Louvre, Paris), the artist has presented a study of human personality which sparkles with vitality and intense individualization. Massys combined the strong, lifelike forms of Italian Renaissance painting with the refinement and meticulous workmanship of Flemish tradition, to which he added his own glowing colors and vigorous concepts.

Consult Conway, Sir Martin, *The Van Eycks and Their Followers* (New York 1921); Friedländer, Max J., "Das Leben Meister Quentin. . . ," *Die altniederländische Malerei,* vol. 7, pp. 1–165 (Berlin 1929); Boon, K. G., *Quinten Massys* (Amsterdam 1950).

MASTECTOMY, mas-tek′tə-mē, a surgical operation to remove the breast. There are two basic types of mastectomies : simple and radical. In a simple mastectomy only the breast tissue is removed, while in a radical mastectomy some surrounding tissues, including chest muscle and lymph nodes, are also removed.

A simple mastectomy is usually performed when a noncancerous disease is present, although it is sometimes performed to removed a cancer. Generally, however, a radical mastectomy is performed when breast cancer is present. In the majority of cases where the cancer is detected early enough, a complete cure can be achieved.

MASTER BUILDER, The (BYGMESTER SOLNESS), a drama by Henrik Ibsen (q.v.), published in 1892 and first performed at the Lessing Theatre, Berlin, Germany, Jan. 19, 1893. It is the first of a series of four symbolic plays (the others are *Little Eyolf, John Gabriel Borkman,* and *When We Dead Awaken*) with which Ibsen ended his dramatic career.

It is the story of Halvard Solness, an aging architect, who has climbed ruthlessly, crushing rivals and sacrificing his wife's happiness in the process. Now he feels the pressure of the rising generation, represented by Ragnar Brovik, a young draftsman in his employ whom he will not allow to undertake original designs. Into this strained atmosphere comes Hilda Wangel, a young woman who has idealized Solness ever since, as a little girl, she had watched him climb the tower of the great church he had built in her town. He is now building himself a house, with a high tower which he feels too old and dizzy to climb. But urged on by Hilda he makes the attempt, reaches the summit, and then falls to his death.

The symbolism is obscure, especially in the character of Hilda, whose role seems to alternate between woman the inspirer and woman the temptress. But in the opinion of William Archer, the drama critic who popularized Ibsen's work in England, it is a mistake to regard the play as wholly a piece of symbolism. "Essentially," he says, "it is the history of a sickly conscience, worked out in terms of pure psychology."

DELANCEY FERGUSON.

MASTER OF ARTS. See DEGREE.

MASTER OF BALLANTRAE, bȧl-ăn-trā′, **The,** a romance by Robert Louis Stevenson

(q.v.), published in 1889 after serialization in *Scribner's Magazine.*

In 1745 Lord Durrie of Durrisdeer in Scotland had two sons, James, called the Master of Ballantrae, and Henry. When Prince Charles, the Stuart pretender, claimed the throne of England, the timid father decided to play safe by sending one son to the prince while the other stayed home and declared for King George. Henry claimed the honor of going, but the reckless and unscrupulous James, by the toss of a coin, won the right from his younger brother. The rebellion failed and James, attainted for treason, fled overseas. Alison Graeme, his betrothed, then married Henry, for duty, not love. James, in the intervals of adventures that included piracy, contrived to haunt Henry and Alison, endangering their safety by clandestine returns to Scotland, fostering dissension between husband and wife, and finally driving Henry to madness. The ultimate flight and pursuit brought both to their deaths in an Adirondack wilderness.

James Durrie is a study of evil free will. His destructive power over Henry derives from the basic error of the decision, responsibly made, to protect property by dividing allegiance—a decision which Henry described at the time as "cheating at cards." The evil character destroys the good ones because they had consciously put themselves in a false position.

DELANCEY FERGUSON.

MASTER OF THE ROLLS, a member of the Supreme Court of Judicature in England, who presides with the lords justices in the Court of Appeal, and ranks next to the lord chief justice. He is the keeper of all records of the Court of Chancery and of the rolls of all grants and patents that pass under the Great Seal.

MASTERS, màs′tẽrz, **Edgar Lee,** American poet and author : b. Garnett, Kans., Aug. 23, 1869; d. Melrose Park, Pa., March 5, 1950. In 1880 his family settled at Lewistown, Ill., near the Spoon River. Masters attended school here, and studied (1889) at Knox College, but was mainly self-educated through wide reading, acquiring a lifelong love of poetry. He was admitted to the bar in 1891, and the next year moved to Chicago, where he maintained a successful law practice until 1920. Meanwhile, an unnoticed part of the literary ferment of the period in Chicago, he had published poems and stories, chiefly in various newspapers.

In 1913 William Marion Reedy, editor of *Reedy's Mirror* of St. Louis, Mo., gave him a copy of *Epigrams from the Greek Anthology.* This inspired Masters' most famous work, *The Spoon River Anthology,* epitaphs spoken by about 250 persons buried in the graveyard of a village in the Middle West, revealing their inner lives in terms which are imaginative but essentially pessimistic. The first installment of *Spoon River* appeared anonymously in *Reedy's Mirror,* May 29, 1914, and was published in book form, also anonymously, in 1915. A sequel, *The New Spoon River,* appeared in 1924.

Masters published a number of volumes of verse and several novels, but these were uneven in quality and often dull. None of his later works achieved the high artistry of *Spoon River.* Masters also wrote biographies—limited by his lack of scholarship—of *Lincoln, the Man,* a bitter "debunking" of the so-called Lincoln myth

(1931) ; *Vachel Lindsay,* valuable for personal knowledge (1935) ; *Whitman* (1937) ; and *Mark Twain,* viewed as a frustrated genius (1938).

Consult Masters' autobiography, *Across Spoon River* (New York 1936).

MASTERWORT, màs'tẽr-wûrt', the rustic name of several umbelliferous plants, as those of the genus *Anethum* (see DILL), formerly much cultivated as pot-herbs, and held in great repute as a stomachic, sudorific, and diuretic.

MASTICATION, màs-tĭ-kā'shŭn, or **CHEWING,** the thorough subdivision of food in the mouth so that it can be readily acted upon by the gastric juice and other digestive secretions. The tongue, cheeks, and lips push the food material between the teeth, and by the lateral and up-and-down motions of the lower jaw it is cut and torn by the incisor, canine, and bicuspid teeth and bruised by the molar or grinding teeth. During these actions the food is softened by the saliva (insalivation), which exudes abundantly from the salivary glands by the act of mastication. Typical mastication is seen only in the higher vertebrata. "The amphibian bolts its fly, the bird its grain, and the fish its brother without the ceremony of chewing," but in man and the higher animals mastication is necessary for complete and comfortable digestion. Thorough comminution of food by mastication is analogous to the pulverizing process employed by the chemist, but associated with mastication is insalivation, as it is almost impossible to swallow substances which are very dry. Imperfect mastication of food, either by reason of rapid swallowing (bolting), or because of the absence of sound and serviceable teeth, is very frequently the cause of the numerous ailments classified under the term indigestion. Exaggerated mastication, which has been so highly recommended by certain persons as almost to constitute a panacea or complete prophylaxis, is known to lessen the secretion of gastric juices which is started by sensations of taste, to protract beyond desirable limits the time required for proper gastric digestion, and to develop the salivary deposit in a proportion relatively too great when compared with the secretion of the pancreas. It is moreover known that the teeth are likely to wear out too soon, if mastication is carried beyond a reasonable time

Exaggerated mastication and the fancied advantages accruing from it are an illustration of an indulgence in a form of securing the gratification of an unconscious desire. In infancy a great pleasure is derived merely from mouthing different objects, a pleasure originating in the mode of absorbing the early meals at the mother's breast. It has been discovered by studying the unconscious wishes of mankind that the sexual desire in the adult is a synthesis of different partial desires which in the infant are satisfied in different parts of the body, now here, now there, but which in the adult are assembled in the genital organs or are at least unified under the supremacy of the genitals. But it has been definitely proven that in some individuals this synthesis has never been successfully accomplished. Either the mouth pleasure zones or the anal or the skin or some other zone, which gave in infancy a quite absorbing sense of gratification, has failed of appropriate subordination, and has persisted into adult life, with some individuals, as a source of extraordinary pleasure.

MASTIFF, màs'tĭf, a breed of dogs of great size, recognized by the large head, short muzzle, the dependent lips, the broad, hanging ears, and by the general muscularity of the form. The mastiff in general disposition is affectionate and gentle, extremely faithful and vigilant. In Rome and in classical ages these dogs were held in high estimation for their strength and courage. The most valued breeds were obtained from Great Britain, where these dogs originated, and were used to guard flocks and herds; and watching has become instinctive with them. Roman officers were appointed to breed them and to transmit them periodically to Rome, where they fought lions and bears in the arenas of the Roman amphitheaters and were otherwise favorites. The dog now is highly valued, both as a watch-dog, and as a domestic companion. Fawn is the prevalent color, and the weight should be about 165 pounds.

MASTIGOPHORA, màs-tĭ-gŏf'ŏ-rà, a class of Protozoa "in which the flagellate form is prominent although the amoeboid and encysted conditions frequently occur." The class is synonymous with that of Flagellata (q.v.).

MASTODON, màs'tŏ-dŏn, a genus of fossil proboscideans that lived during the Pleistocene period of earth history. By extension the word *mastodon* is very generally used as a common noun and applied to many proboscideans of middle and late Cenozoic age. For such usage the word *mastodont* is also frequently employed.

The mastodonts first appeared in the Miocene period and continued from then through the Pliocene and most of the Pleistocene period. The early mastodonts were of fair size, some of them being about as large as modern oxen, and from such a beginning they evolved into giants, comparable to modern elephants, during the latter phases of the Cenozoic era.

The mastodonts were characterized by elongated noses or prosbosces, as were all but the most primitive of the proboscideans, and by tusks. In many of the mastodonts there were four tusks, two in the skull and two in the lower jaw. These tusks showed a great variety of development; they were straight, upcurved, or downcurved, long or short. In some of the mastodonts the lower tusks were even broadened and flattened to form a sort of scoop or shovel. The lower tusks of some of the later mastodonts were suppressed and in certain genera they disappeared completely. The tusks were invariably enlarged upper and lower second incisor teeth. The grinding teeth in the mastodonts were somewhat elongated and multicuspidate, and in some genera adjacent cusps of each tooth were joined by a process of transverse growth through time to form strong cross-ridges.

Perhaps the commonest use of the word *mastodon* is its application to remains of the American mastodon, *Mastodon americanus.* (Strict application of the International Rules of Zoological Nomenclature requires that the designation be *Mammut americanum,* but this usage is not commonly followed.) The American mastodon lived throughout much of North America during the Pleistocene period—the last great ice age of geologic history. Remains are found as far south as the southern tip of Florida, and as far north as Alaska. There is some evidence to indicate that this mastodon was present also in parts of

Asia. Fossils of the American mastodon are commonly found in bog deposits and swamps, in river and lake beds, and even on the floor of the Atlantic Ocean along the continental shelf. Some of the remains are remarkably fresh, and it is evident that this proboscidean persisted until a very late stage of the Pleistocene period.

by The American Museum of Natural History, New York City, through the munificence of Mr. J. P. Morgan, and it is now exhibited in that institution.

Careful archaeological and paleontological investigations of the past few decades have afforded increasing evidence that the American

Upper: Skeleton of the Warren Mastodon, male, estimated shoulder height 9 feet 2 inches in the flesh. The skeleton was found in the Hudson Highlands near Newburgh, New York. *Lower:* restoration of male *Mastodon americanus,* estimated shoulder height 10 feet 2 inches in the flesh. Illustrations after Osborn's *Proboscidea,* Vol. 1, The American Museum of Natural History.

Mastodon americanus was a large, bulky proboscidean. Large skeletons are as much as nine or ten feet in height at the shoulder. A mastodon of this size would have been much heavier than a modern elephant of similar height. The skull is rather low for a proboscidean, and it is armed with a pair of large tusks curving upward and outward. The teeth are strongly ridged by transverse cross-crests, there being three such crests in the milk molars and the first two molars, and four or five crests in the third molars. Specimens that have been frozen in the muck of Alaska show that the mastodon was covered by a heavy coat of coarse, reddish-brown hair.

Probably the most complete and famous mastodon skeleton to be discovered is the so-called Warren mastodon, unearthed a century ago from a swamp near Newburgh, New York. This skeleton was first exhibited in many towns and cities of eastern North America, but in time it came to rest in the private museum of Dr. John C. Warren of Boston. In 1909 it was purchased

mastodon was contemporaneous with early man in North America. There is good reason to think that the mastodon persisted until a very late geologic time; it was almost certainly living on the continent ten thousand years ago, and it may have lingered on until as late as four or five thousand years ago. The bones of this huge animal have been found in undoubted association with various types of artifacts. In fact, among objects of early Indian art there are some that may well represent crude attempts to depict the mastodon. The existence among the Indians of legends concerning the animal would constitute valuable evidence, of course; but no unequivocal legends of this sort have been found up to the present time.

EDWIN H. COLBERT.

MASUDI, al-, ăl măs-ōō'dē (Ar. ABU-AL-ḤASAN 'ALI IBN-ḤUSAYN AL-MAS'ŪDI), Arab traveler, geographer, and historian: b. Baghdad; d. al-Fusṭāṭ (El Fustat), Egypt, about 956. Not much more is known about his life than what is gleaned from his own writings. Urged by thirst for adventure and hunger for learning, young Masudi made journeys that took him beyond Ceylon into the sea of China, northward to the southern shores of the Caspian Sea, and southward as far as Madagascar. Being a rationalist Mu'tazilite, he had no hesitation in seeking information from Jews, Christians, Hindus, and other non-Muslims. He accepted, as might be expected, legends and tales without criticism, but contributed new information, particularly about the periphery of the Muslim world, that can be found nowhere else. The first Arab historian to make extensive use of the historical anecdote, Masudi has been styled the Herodotus of the Arabs. To his catholicity of interest and sense of curiosity no aspect of life or intellectual activity was entirely alien—religion, philosophy, ethics, politics, economics, science, and art. His presentation of the material differed from that of his predecessors who followed the annalistic method, grouping historical events around years. Masudi inaugurated the topical method, grouping events around subjects such as dynasties, kings, peoples. In this he was followed by ibn-Khaldun among other great historians.

Most of Masudi's works have been lost. The largest and most important of those which survive is *Marūj al-Dhahab wa-Ma'ādin al-Jawhar* (*Meadows of Gold and Mines of Gems*), edited and translated into French by Casimir-Adrien Barbier de Meynard and Abel Jean Baptiste Pavet de Courteille, 9 vols. (Paris 1861–77). Several Arabic editions have since been issued in Egypt. The first volume was translated into English by Aloys Sprenger (London 1841). Shortly before his death, Masudi attempted a survey and summation of his whole literary output supplemented with new data which he entitled *Kitāb al-Tanbīh w-al-Ishrāf* (*Book of Indication and Revision*). This was edited by Michael Jan de Goeje (Leiden 1893–94) and translated into French by B. Carra de Vaux (Paris 1896).

Consult Sarton, George, *Introduction to the History of Science,* vol. 1, pp. 637–39 (Baltimore 1927); Nicholson, Reynold A., *Literary History of the Arabs,* 2d ed., pp. 352–54; "al-Mas'ūdi," in *Encyclopedia of Islam,* 4 vols. (London 1911–38).

PHILIP K. HITTI.

MASULIPATAM, mŭ-sŭ-lĭ-pŭt′ăm, or **MASULIPATNAM** mŭ-sŭ-lĭ-pŭt′năm, (also BANDAR) city, India, headquarters of Krishna (Kistna) District in the State of Andhra Pradesh. Located 145 miles east-southeast of Hyderabad, Masulipatam, of all ports on the Coromandel Coast, had, in the prerailroad era, easiest access to the Deccan interior via a broad gap in the Eastern Ghats. Hence, the establishment there in 1611 of England's first major trading station on the east coast of India. Firmans, formal grants of trading privileges, were obtained from the sultan of Golconda about 1630 and from the Mughul emperor in 1690; but, despite these, there were short-lived, forceful occupations by the Dutch and French. The latter terminated in 1759 when the territory including Masulipatam was ceded to the British by treaty. In 1864 a cyclone and tidal wave destroyed the town, killing an estimated 30,000 people. The diversion of trade from the interior to larger ports with better rail links and the fact that modern ocean vessels must anchor five miles

offshore have greatly inhibited Masulipatam's economic recovery. Imports are negligible; exports consist almost entirely of agricultural produce. Though the city has a variety of handicraft industries, its once famous carpet and chintz industries are moribund. Pop. (1951) 77,953.

JOSEPH E. SCHWARTZBERG.

MA'T. See MAAT.

MATA HARI, mä′tä hä′rē (real name MARGARETHA GEERTRUIDA ZELLE), Dutch dancer, courtesan, and spy: b. Leeuwarden, Netherlands, Aug. 7, 1876; d. Vincennes, France, Oct. 15, 1917. The convent-bred daughter of a Dutch businessman, she was married at the age of 18 to Campbell MacLeod, a commissioned officer in the Dutch Army, who was then over 40 years old. Soon after the marriage a son, Norman, was born in Amsterdam, where the couple lived in a fashionable quarter. MacLeod's gambling debts threatened ruin, and his wife initiated her career as an adventuress by blackmailing a rich admirer. Another child, a daughter named Jeanne Louise, was born before the MacLeods went (1897) to Java, where MacLeod commanded a battalion in the Dutch Army.

From the outset the marriage was a miserable failure and on returning to Holland in 1902, Mrs. MacLeod instituted divorce proceedings. The courts denied the application but later granted her husband a decree. In 1903 she went to Paris, ambitious to become a dancer. While training for this profession, she earned money as an artists' model, and in other ways. During the decade preceding World War I, she gained notoriety on the vaudeville stages of Paris, Berlin, Vienna, Rome, and London. But she preferred to give private performances of her erotic dances, supposedly of symbolic religious significance, before select gatherings of persons in the upper political and social circles. Thus she came to know men who were prominent in the government and established intimate relations with them. Her middle-class Dutch origin lacking glamour, she represented herself as having been born on the Malabar coast of southern India, the daughter of a dancing girl who died in giving her birth. Taking the name Mata Hari, meaning Eye of the Dawn, she said that she had been brought up in a Brahman temple dedicated to Siva, the god of evil, and become one of his votaries. Tall, slim, and beautifully formed, with somber eyes, black hair, and amber skin, she easily convinced admirers of her Hindu pedigree.

Several years before World War I she attended the German espionage school at Lörrach. In 1914, on the day war was declared, she rode through the streets of the German capital with Berlin's chief of police. A citizen of a neutral country with property in France, she was able to return to France in 1915 despite the war. On this occasion she changed her role of an Oriental dancer to that of a rich woman of fashion. Before her arrival the French secret service had full reports on her both from its own agents and from the Italian secret service. They knew her relations with the Berlin police chief, the German crown prince, and other Reich officials. But lacking direct evidence, they were unable to prove her criminality. Furthermore, among her protectors were men high in both the French and Dutch governments. For months she skillfully avoided the numerous traps laid for her by the French Deuxième Bureau. Finally she was arrested in a Paris hotel on Feb. 13, 1917, the day after her return from Madrid where she had been observed in frequent conferences with the heads of the German military and naval intelligence services.

The evidence proving her a spy which had been accumulated over many years was at last incontrovertible. One of the most damning documents was an intercepted telegram from German Army headquarters to the embassy in Madrid instructing H21 (her code number in the German secret service) to return to Paris where 15,000 pesetas would be delivered to her. The check was found on her after her arrest. Another proof was her acceptance of 30,000 marks from the German secret service before her return to France in 1915. Her relations with French, British, and Russian officers, particularly of the flying services, had enabled her to obtain much valuable military information which she was able to forward to the Germans through seemingly innocent letters to her daughter conveyed by the Dutch diplomatic pouch from Paris. At her trial it was estimated that her espionage activities had been responsible for the death of at least 50,000 Allied soldiers. She faced a firing squad at Vincennes with surprising fortitude for a woman whose life had been a long career of debauchery.

Consult Coulson, Thomas, *Mata Hari: Courtesan and Spy* (New York 1930); Morain, Alfred, "The Case of a Spy—Mata Hari" in *Underworld of Paris* (New York 1931); Newman, Bernard, *Inquest on Mata Hari* (London 1956).

MATACO, măt′à-kō, a South American Indian stock, including several tribes, whose habitat is in the Bermejo River valley in the Chaco, in northern Argentina. They are of medium size with wavy hair and subsist by hunting, fishing, and cattle raising. Their dress is made of skins and they dwell in huts of brush.

Consult Steward, Julian H., ed., *Handbook of South American Indians*, 7 vols. (Washington 1946–59).

MATADOR, măt′à-dōr, in Spanish bull fights the man appointed to administer the fatal stroke to the bull. See BULLFIGHTING.

MATAGALPA, măt-à-găl′pà, department and city, Nicaragua. The department, covering 2,623 square miles, lies in the central highlands. Its economy is primarily agricultural, including tobacco, corn, sugar, fruits, and potatoes. Some cattle and swine are raised, and about one fifth of all Nicaraguan coffee is produced here. There is also some small-scale gold and silver mining.

The city of Matagalpa, capital of the department, is about 60 miles north-northeast of Managua, the national capital, with which it is connected by a 20-mile feeder road to the Inter-American Highway. It is an agricultural and commercial center; an old and picturesque city, it has only recently lost some of its colonial aspect because of the modern construction that has taken place. Pop. (1963) department 171,465; city 15,030.

RUSSELL H. FITZGIBBON.

MATAGORDA, măt-à-gôr′dà, name of a bay, peninsula, island, and village in Texas, on the Gulf of Mexico. The bay, an inlet of the gulf, is about 50 miles long and from 3 to 12 miles wide. It is sheltered by Matagorda Peninsula, a 50-mile-long sandspit. Pass Cavallo is the entrance to the bay, which receives the Colorado of Texas and Lavaca rivers. The waters abound in shellfish, shrimp, and oysters. La Salle's last expedition sailed into the bay in 1685. Matagorda Island is a low sandspit 36 miles long and from 1 to 4 miles wide. It lies between San Antonio Bay and the Gulf of Mexico and it has a United States Air Force bombing and gunnery range. Matagorda village, on the bay at the mouth of the Colorado River, was settled in 1825 and served as a prosperous port for Austin's colony. Today it is a commercial fishing center, has a shell market, and about 750 inhabitants.

MATAMOROS, măt-à-mōr′ōs, city, Mexico, in the State of Tamaulipas, on the right bank of the Rio Grande, about 30 miles above its mouth on the Gulf of Mexico. A frontier town and a river port opposite Brownsville, Texas, the city is a busy gateway between the United States and Mexico, and in 1963 a handsome complex of modern buildings to house immigration, customs, and other tourist facilities was opened. The city is the commercial center for the lower Rio Grande Valley and its population has increased sixfold since 1940. The Mexican government plans to modernize the port and make it one of the best on the gulf for the export of hides, wool, cotton, cottonseeds, and glass from Monterrey, 175 miles to the west, with which Matamoros is connected by a good road. The city was founded in 1824. During the Mexican War the town was occupied by American troops under Gen. Zachary Taylor on May 18, 1846. Pop. (1960) 92,327.

IRENE NICHOLSON.

MATANE, mà-tàn′, town, Quebec, Canada, in Matane County, on the southern shore of the St. Lawrence estuary at the mouth of the Matane River, about 60 miles east-northeast of Rimouski. Named for the Micmac word meaning "beaver pond," Matane was established as a fishing settlement in 1686 but had no growth until the mid-19th century, when French-Canadian colonists from overcrowded upstream parishes migrated to the area and cleared much of the fertile littoral plain for farming. Surrounding rich timber resources were soon tapped, and Matane's chief industry today is the export of pulpwood. There is also processing of agricultural products, fish freezing and storage, and the manufacture of construction materials. The town, incorporated in 1938, has long been a fashionable summer resort, especially among Montrealers. Pop. 11,109.

PETER B. CLIBBON.

MATANUSKA RIVER, măt-à-nōōs′kà, river, south central Alaska, rising in the Chugach Mountains, and flowing through Matanuska Valley to Knik Arm of Cook Inlet, near Anchorage. The valley covers about 1,000 square miles; its fertile soil and mild climate make it a rich farming and dairying region. Here in 1935 the federal government settled 208 families from the Middle West drought area. There are coal deposits at Jonesville, and Palmer is the trading center. The village of Matanuska, 30 miles northwest of Anchorage, has coal mines nearby and a population of less than 25.

MATANZAS, mă-tăn′zàs Sp. mä-tän′thäs, city, Cuba, capital of Matanzas Province, a leading seaport on the north coast, 52 miles east of

Havana. It is situated on Matanzas Bay, one of the largest, safest, and most convenient harbors of the Western Hemisphere. The city is well built with wide, regular and paved streets, handsome plazas and public buildings, and good railway communications. The caves of Bellamar and Yumuri Valley, in the neighborhood, are two popular natural resorts. Matanzas ranks in importance next to Havana in the export of sugar, molasses, rum, and coffee. It has several mills, distilleries, oil refineries, tanneries, shoe factories, and machine shops. It was founded in 1693. The city was bombarded by the United States warships during the Spanish-American War in 1898. The only casualty was an injury to a "Matanzas mule," news of which was telegraphed abroad and made the animal famous. Pop. (1953) 82,619.

MATAPAN, măt′à-păn, **Cape** (modern Greek Taínaron; ancient Taenarum), a promontory of Greece, forming the southern extremity of the Peloponnesus, in latitude 36° 23′ N. and longitude 22° 29′ E. It was sacred to Neptune, whose temple stood nearby. The British sank two Italian destroyers, three cruisers, and damaged a battleship near here in a naval battle in March 1941.

MATAS, măt′ăs, **Rudolph,** American surgeon: b. Bonnet Carre, near New Orleans, La., Sept. 12, 1860; d. New Orleans, Sept. 23, 1957. An innovator in surgical techniques, Matas graduated in medicine from Tulane University in 1880 and taught surgery there from 1895 to 1927. He was also senior surgeon (1894–1928) at Charity Hospital and chief surgeon (1905–1935) at Touro Infirmary, both in New Orleans. Matas pioneered in vascular surgery, developing an operating technique to relieve enlarged veins and arteries, and devised a preventive against lung collapse during operations. In addition, he perfected methods of intravenous feeding and for the removal of bowel contents in cancer cases, and extended the use of cocaine anesthesia. He edited the New Orleans *Medical and Surgical Journal* (1883–1895) and was president of the International Society of Surgery (1936–1938).

MATCH INDUSTRY. It was in 1669 that the Hamburg alchemist, Hennig Brand (Brandt) discovered phosphorus while experimenting with an olio he hoped he could reduce to gold. But while phosphorus was soon used in several briefly popular fire-producing forms, it was not adapted to the manufacture of matches for about 160 years.

In 1680 both Godfrey Haukwitz and Robert Boyle sold coarse sheets of paper coated with phosphorus in combination with splinters of wood tipped with sulphur. When the splinters were drawn through a fold of the paper they burst into flame. Since the price of an ounce of phosphorus in those days was the equivalent of $250 today, the clientele for these early matches was limited to the extremely wealthy, and when their interest in the novelty ebbed, both sales and experiments ceased.

Disinterest in phosphorus continued for a century, during which the world continued to rely chiefly upon flint and steel for sparks to be nursed into the fires it needed for warmth, cooking, and manufacture. Then, in 1781, began a cycle of inventiveness which was to produce modern matches.

The first of these inventions was the *Phosphoric Candle* or *Ethereal Match* which appeared in France in that year. It consisted of paper tipped with phosphorus, sealed in a glass tube. Admission of air when the glass was broken set the paper to flaming. The *Pocket Luminary* (Italy, 1786) was a small bottle lined with oxide of phosphorus. Sulphur-tipped wood splints ignited when rubbed on this coating and withdrawn. The *Instantaneous Light Box,* invented in 1805, was highly popular with American gentlemen up to the time of the Mexican War, despite obvious dangers. Like the luminary, it involved a small bottle, this one filled with sulphuric acid. The splints, treated with a composition of potassium chlorate, sugar, and gum arabic, were called *Empyrion* or *Oxymuriated Matches* in the United States and retailed for $2 for 50 together with the "box."

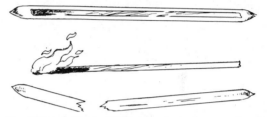

The Ethereal Match (1781) comprised of paper, tipped with phosphorus and sealed in a glass tube.

The last of these elaborate early matches was the *Electropneumatic Fire Producer,* involving the principle of the ignition of a fine jet of hydrogen gas by a spark from charged rosin. The German chemist, Johann W. Döbereiner, produced several types. He created gas by the action of sulphuric acid on zinc and directed it in a thin stream upon a platinum sponge in contact with the air. Several of Döbereiner's models still survive in museums.

Even after the birth of the match in its original modern form in 1827, inventors continued to contrive unusual means of producing fire. Self-lighting cigars of two types were introduced in Austria in 1839. In some of these a short splint of wood with a matchhead decorated with rosettes of linen was inserted in the tips. When the cigar was struck, the smoker inhaled a combination of the fumes of match composition, burning wood and linen, but he had a light. Another type wore a frilly cap of treated paper much like the lacy "socks" placed on lamb chops in some restaurants. Pellet matches (1850) made of sawdust, flour, and match composition were exploded by a plunger machine carried by users. Another pellet match came in strips like caps for a Fourth of July pistol and when detonated set fire to the paper holding them. *Wire Fixed Stars, Chinese Lights, Prussian War Fusees,* and *Latchford's Bone Stem Cigar Lights Which Will Never Fall Off, Break Or Burn The Fingers In Using* are the names of some of the novel lights appearing in the 1860's.

As late as 1882, the Diamond Match Company bought the patent for the *Drunkard's Match,* the splint of which was treated chemically so that it would not burn beyond midpoint. This match was highly popular with American *bons vivants* for twenty years. Much later the match inventors produced the *repeatedly ignitible* or *everlasting* match. In 1932, Rudolf Koenig and Zoltan Foldi, Austrian chemists, patented a *repeatedly ignitible rod* resembling a styptic pencil wrapped in Cellophane. Actually it was an elongated match head, loaded with fire retardents to make it burn more slowly. Each of these matches was good for 40 lights if carefully nursed, and packets of three were sold in Europe for approximately 5 cents. Tried out in Holland, these repeatedly ignitible rods proved unsuccessful commercially.

The Friction Match.—While Döbereiner was still manufacturing his elaborate Fire Producers, the first friction match had already been made and sold in England (1827). The records of an apothecary, John Walker of Stockton-on-Tees, show that he sold to a Mr. Hixon "100 Sulphurata Hyperoxygeneta Frict." Later analysis indicated that Walker's friction matches were tipped with antimony sulphide, potassium chlorate, gum, and starch. They were three inches long and were ignited by drawing them through a pleat of "glass paper." Two years later when Walker exhibited his matches to amazed Londoners, one of the spectators, Samuel Jones, was not too excited to note there was no protecting patent and he promptly set himself up in the match business. Jones named his

A box of Samuel Jones' *Lucifers* as they appeared in London in 1829. Users were warned to avoid the fumes.

matches *Lucifers*. Their ignition was accompanied by a series of small showers of sparks and odors so offensive that this warning was printed on their boxes: "If possible, avoid inhaling gas that escapes from the combustion of the black composition. Persons whose lungs are delicate should by no means use Lucifers."

In 1830, about 160 years after its discovery, phosphorus was adapted by Dr. Charles Sauria of France as an ingredient for match heads. Sauria substituted it for antimony sulphide in the Walker formula and in so doing improved the efficiency of matches but set off a wave of necrosis which was to exact a fearful toll of life among matchmakers and users for 80 years. Necrosis, called "phossy jaw" by workers, attacked the bones, particularly of the jaws, and resulted in maiming or death. In addition, innocent persons, babies especially, were poisoned by ingesting match heads containing phosphorus, and they furnished a widespread and easily available source of poison for suicide and even murder.

This dreadful occupational hazard plagued American factories until 1911 when William A. Fairburn of the Diamond Match Company adapted harmless sesquisulphide of phosphorus to United States climatic conditions. The new nonpoisonous formula was presented to the government for the use of all rival companies, a humanitarian gesture which won public commendation from President William Howard Taft and for which Mr. Fairburn and his company were given the Louis Livingston Seaman

Medal "for the elimination of occupational disease."

Substitution of sesquisulphide of phosphorus in the formula accomplished other things. It raised the point of ignition more than 100 degrees, a considerable safety factor, and it ended fires caused by rodents. Experiments conducted by Mr. Fairburn proved conclusively that while rats and mice would gnaw on phosphorus matches, thus igniting them sometimes, they would not touch the new match heads even when starving.

Manufacture of the dangerous phosphorus matches began in the United States in 1836 when Alonzo Dwight Phillips, a Springfield, Mass., powder maker, secured a patent for "new and useful improvements in modes of manufacturing friction matches for instantaneous light." Phillips made his phosphorus matches by hand and when he had a wagon load, sold them himself from door to door thus founding an industry which produces about 500 billion matches each year in the United States.

At that time, only one type of match existed, the wooden strike-anywhere that is sometimes called the "kitchen" match today. The discovery of red or amorphous phosphorus by Professor Anton von Schrotter in 1845 led to the development of another type of match, the safety, by J. E. Lundstrom 10 years later. The safety match differs from the strike-anywhere only in one regard: part of the ingredients necessary to create fire are in the head of the safety match, part in the striking surface on the box.

The third basic form of modern match, the paper book variety, was the invention in 1892 of an attorney, Joshua Pussey. His books contained 50 matches, had the striking surface on the inside where sparks frequently ignited the remaining matches, a danger quickly corrected by the Diamond Match Company which bought the patent in 1895. Unpopular at first and made by hand, book matches became big business in 1896 when a brewing company ordered 10,-000,000 books to advertise their brews, forcing creation of machinery for swift production in volume. Today the industry produces 300 billion book matches annually in the United States with more than 90 per cent being handed out free to customers of cigar stores, hotels, restaurants, railroads, and other businesses, a custom not practiced in any other country.

At the time of the Phillips patent, matches all over the world were made by hand on a piecework basis in the homes of the poor, a condition which led to the infection by necrosis of a considerable segment of the populations in industrial areas. The boxes also were made by hand in homes. The first American patent for a machine to cut round splints was granted to Chauncey E. Warner in 1841.

The trend toward mechanization of the industry and the centralization of efforts in factories instead of homes began in 1842 with the invention of a machine by Reuben Partridge, which cut the wooden splints in bulk, ending tedious hand methods for this important process. Other inventors contributed to match machines, each performing a function, but real mechanical impetus came in 1883 when Ebenezer Beecher of Connecticut designed three "continuous" automatic matchmaking machines by combining all functions in one device. The machines made by

Beecher for Ohio Columbus Barber, of the newly formed Diamond Match Company, became the models for all future equipment in the industry.

Modern Methods of Manufacture.—The methods used to manufacture all types of matches are basically the same. The wood or paper for the splints must be cut into proper size, dipped to create the heads, dried and assembled in books or boxes for retail sale. Hence, the making of the strike-anywhere match on the modified Beecher machine gives a good overall picture of the processes involved.

The machines, 60 feet long and two stories high, convert blocks of straight-grained pine into packaged matches in 60 minutes at a rate as high as 1,125,000 an hour. The pine blocks, cured from 12 to 18 months, are fed into the head of the machine where a row of from 42 to 57 dies cuts the splints and fixes them into perforations in an endless chain of metal plates, each with 12 rows of perforations. It is this operation which creates the visible indented collars at the holding tips of all round wooden matches.

Match splints are cut from pine blocks by sharp dies which then lodge them in perforations in steel plates.

The dies cut 350 rows of from 42 to 57 splints each minute, setting them into the plates on which they ride through a series of five dips and baths which treat the wood against afterglow, provide a collar of paraffin to speed combustion, put on the main bulb and its "eye," and finally dip the heads with a solution which protects them from weather changes. Punched out of their plates after the final drying, the matches pour down a trough to drop into endless chains of boxes waiting for them. On the larger-size boxes an ingenious device turns

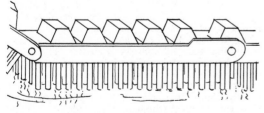

Splints are carried on steel plates in an endless chair-belt until processing of matches is completed.

the matches so that approximately half the heads are to the right, and the balance to the left, assuring a flat pack. The boxes, covers, and wrappers for the matches are made in the same factories as the matches and the output is synchronized so that matches and containers reach the packaging machinery simultaneously.

Some United States factories have as many

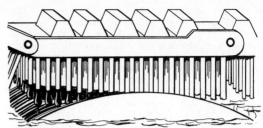

Riding on plates, splints pass through grooves on a roller rotating in a solution which creates the main bulb.

as 20 continuous automatic match machines, each capable of producing 10,000,000 matches in an eight-hour shift, a factory total of 200,000,-000 each one-shift day. Shipment of a day's output would require five freight cars.

Book matches are not made on a single continuous machine but in two separate operations under the same roof. The first machine, called "cut, set, and dip," slices rolls of pretreated cardboard into combs of 60 matches each, then carries them through paraffin and head-forming dips. The combs are then inserted in a booking machine which assembles covers and combs and stitches them together for packing in caddies of 50 books each.

Modern machinery, plus increased revenue from the advertising carried on book matches, has kept United States production costs at a minimum. As a result match prices, unlike those of most other household necessities, have remained the same for a half century despite increased labor and material charges. Five cents for a box of strike-anywhere matches and a penny for safety matches has been standard for more than two generations.

Since the turn of the century, match machinery has been constantly improved, and there have been three outstanding advances in American matches. The first of these, the nonpoisonous match, has already been discussed. The second was an improvement in the safety factor. It had been known, long before 1912, that match splints treated with an aqueous solution of ammonium phosphate retained no ember or afterglow when the match was blown out. Matches made under the veneer method (cut separately and dipped in composition in bundles) had been impregnated against afterglow simply by tossing them into vats of solution, but American matches were cut and made on a single machine which barred this method. In 1912, fresh from his triumph with the nonpoisonous match, William A. Fairburn developed a spray attachment for the continuous match machine which would impregnate matches in course of manufacture. As with his previous development, Fairburn gave blueprints to the rivals of Diamond Match Company in the interests of fire prevention.

World War II produced another advance, the waterproof match, dream of matchmakers since the birth of the industry. The United States War Department needed a match that would function in the long rainy seasons of the South Pacific and called on the industry for help. Raymond Davis Cady, chief chemist for Diamond Match, produced a formula, approved by the army, which resulted in matches which can remain under water eight hours yet still function. The match went into production Dec. 7, 1943, and was supplied at the rate of more than

10,000,000 daily to the armed forces. The Quartermaster Board, United States Army, was offered the formula for lending to other manufacturers in the war effort. Universal and Ohio Match companies were also large producers of water resistant matches for the services.

The United States makes 300 billion each of book and strike-anywhere matches and 100 billion safety matches annually, the largest national output in the world. Other large manufacturers are Great Britain, Russia, and Sweden. Before World War II, Japan ranked high in match volume and for a period flooded the United States and other countries with cheap matches, packaged in containers so nearly like those of leading manufacturers that only close scrutiny revealed their real origin.

During recent years there has been a gradual diminution in the production and use of wooden matches. Rural electrification wiped out a major market; the increase in cigarette consumption brought an added demand for book matches. Thus, out of an annual production of 500 billion matches, only two out of each five today are wooden matches of the safety and kitchen types. Pilot lights on gas stoves, broadened use of electricity for cooking purposes, and increased acceptance of cigarette lighters have contributed to hold United States match production static at 500 billion per year. Only about 5 billion matches are imported each year from Sweden, Italy, Finland, and Japan.

STUART LITTLE,
Writer and Publicist.

MATE, a deck officer in the merchant marine ranking below the captain. If there is more than one mate, they are designated first mate, second mate, and so on.

MATE, YERBA MATE, or **PARAGUAY TEA,** mä′tä, an infusion of the dried and powdered leaves of *Ilex paraguayensis,* sweetened with sugar. It is aromatic and somewhat bitter, with refreshing and restorative effects, and is sucked up through a tube which strains off the leaf particles. *Ilex paraguayensis,* a holly related to the *Ilex aquifolium* widely used for Christmas decorations, grows wild in the forests of the Paraná Plateau in Brazil, Argentina, and Paraguay, and is cultivated in Argentina. Curitiba is the center for final processing and packing of maté in Brazil, which produces about half of the world supply. Maté is widely used in southern Brazil, Paraguay, Uruguay, Chile, and Argentina (Argentina accounts for half the world consumption); attempts have been made to develop a market in Europe and the United States for the beverage.

MATEHUALA, mä-tä-wä′lä, city and municipality, Mexico, in the state of San Luis Potosí, 105 miles north-northeast of the city of San Luis Potosí. Located on a plateau at an altitude of 5,955 feet, it is the center of a mining district producing copper, silver, gold, and lead. The chief industries are copper smelting, tanning, and the manufacture of textile fibers and liquor from the maguey plant. Matehuala is served by railroad and airfield. Pop. (1950) city 14,177; municipality 34,966.

MATERA, mä-tä′rä, province, Italy, formed in 1927 from a part of Potenza Province, facing on the Gulf of Taranto in Basilicata Region. It has an area of 1,329 square miles. The region is traversed by the Apennines in the interior, and slopes gradually toward a broad coastal plain. It is watered by the Cavone and the lower courses of the Agri, Basento, Bradano, and Sinni rivers. The province is largely agricultural, with cereals, grapes, olives, fruit, and cotton the chief crops; sheep and goats are raised in the interior. Pop. (1950) 182,398.

MATERIA MEDICA, mà-tē′rĭ-à mĕd′ĭ-kà, the division of medical science which deals with drugs and drug treatment, namely pharmacology. Pharmacology has five principal branches. The first is *pharmacognosy* or the descriptive study of the physical characteristics of crude drugs. The 20th century has rendered this branch almost obsolete because of continued effort to produce drugs in their chemically pure form. *Pharmacy* is the second division of materia medica, the actual compounding and dispensing of medicines. *Pharmacodynamics* is the third subdivision of materia medica and concerns the study of the absorption, fate or distribution, and finally the excretion of drugs in man and animals. Animals (frogs or guinea pigs) are generally employed for the experimental assaying of a drug before its use in man. *Pharmacotherapeutics,* the fourth part of pharmacology, is the effort to discover the ideal and specific drug for a specific complaint. The fifth and last branch of materia medica is *toxicology* which is devoted to the study of harmful effects a given drug may have upon a patient. For example, chloromycetin is an excellent drug for pneumonia but may have the toxic effect of bone marrow destruction.

Drugs are administered in a variety of ways: locally to skin or mucous membrane, by mouth, and by injection under the skin, in the vein, muscle, peritoneum, and even on the spinal canal. Each route involves a different rate of absorption and distribution to the various organs. Materia medica catalogues this information for the physician and tells him where the drug is detoxified and how it is excreted. See also PHARMACOPEIA; PHARMACY; TOXICOLOGY.

REAUMUR S. DONNALLY, M.D.

MATERIALISM, mà-tēr′ĭ-ăl-ĭz′m, in philosophy, the theory that everything is material or results from matter. Different varieties of it may be distinguished according to how "results from" and "matter" are understood. That everything results from matter may mean no more than that matter is the sole cause, the only source of being and change; but also it may mean that everything actually consists of matter. The latter, more extreme, materialism is of most interest to metaphysicians, but for the practical man it is not significantly different from the former, or merely causal, materialism, since they affect his prospects in much the same way. Ideas of "matter," derived as they are from the natural things and processes of daily experience, have changed as the sciences have understood these better, but also as philosophers have developed contrasting ideas of immaterial principles, such, for example, as Plato's categories of conscious souls and abstract ideals or essences. Many students would refuse the title "materialists" to men who only vaguely assume that everything is an aggregate or interaction of physical objects, without any definite conception of a difference between physical and non-physical. Such has probably been the condition of the ordinary worldly citizen everywhere, as it was in some degree of the Confucian and Buddhist philosophies in the East, and, in the West, of those early Ionian philosophers (c. 550 B.C.) who would explain everything by the circulation of substances like water, air, or fire. Developed conceptions of "matter" are compiled from two rather antithetical ideas: the stuff or content of things, in contrast with their form; and the specifically physical kind of form or structure, composed of shape, size, position, motion, and the like. The latter characters, variously called "modes of extension," "primary qualities," or "quantities," lend themselves best to measurement and calculation, and hence to exact systematic description and understanding. A materialism of stuffs seeks, like the Ionian philosophy, to explain the world by their mixing, blending, and separating, their thinning or thickening, on the analogy of chemistry or cookery. It rapidly lost ground, however, before the materialism of structure, which looks for the secret in form or arrangement, on the analogy of physics and mechanics, and which soon became indifferent to, or even denied, any stuff in which the structure might be embodied.

The first pure type of materialism was presumably the ancient atomism of Leucippus and Democritus, who lived respectively in the 5th and early 4th centuries B.C. Their philosophical enemies effaced their works and lost their dates, but their doctrine was preserved by their critics and by their great popularizers, Epicurus (342?–270 B.C.) and Lucretius (96?–55 B.C.): that the world consists of indivisible particles, having no intrinsic quality except sheer being or solidity, but different sizes and shapes, distributing themselves fortuitously, that is, purposelessly, forever in the infinite void (non-being, or empty space). These not only cause but constitute all the variety of things and events, including the evolution of planets, animals, and men, and the processes of perception, thought, and the moral and political life.

Plato, though detesting materialism, gave a classic account of the physical world as mathematically structured, so that at the Renaissance Plato and Democritus were revived together. The founders of the modern scientific world view, agreeing that the geometry of matter in motion is at any rate the ultimate truth about nature as it exists outside the mind, vacillated between the Platonic dualism which coupled this with a strictly incorporeal realm of spirit (Descartes, and less decidedly, Bacon and Locke), and a view essentially that of Democritus, with only some reservations in behalf of theology, that the mathematically structured world machine embraces everything (Galileo, 1564–1642, generally; Hobbes, 1588–1679 and Gassendi, 1592–1655, vigorously; and, in his own grand fashion, Spinoza, 1632–1677).

The constant and successful scientific pressure to assimilate more and more to the physical pattern was philosophically stemmed, not by dualism, but by the idealisms which opposed the metaphysical claims of science from without and the positivisms which weakened them from within. Idealism, beginning with Leibniz and Berkeley, cut off materialism at the root with the metaphysical doctrine that matter itself is a manifestation of spirit, human or divine. Positivism, beginning with Hume, sapped it by the thesis that propositions about physical objects are just compendious ways of describing, predicting, and controlling sense experience, yet it has generally favored the materialistic attitude by teaching that only statements which ostensibly are about physical objects are significantly descriptive or explanatory, for sense experience is *as if* materialism were true (David Hume, 1711–1776; generally, Immanuel Kant, 1724–1804; Auguste Comte, 1798–1857; John Stuart Mill, 1806–1873; Herbert Spencer, 1820–1903; Thomas Henry Huxley, 1825–1895; Ernst Mach, 1838–1916). With technological philosophy dominated by idealism and positivism, downright metaphysical materialism tended to be amateurish and strident: for example, in England, Joseph Priestley (1733–1804); in France, J. O. de La Mettrie (1709–1751), Baron d'Holbach (1723–1789), Pierre Simon de Laplace (1749–1827), and Pierre Cabanis (1757–1808); in Germany, Ludwig Feuerbach (1804–1872), Karl Marx (1818–1883), Friedrich Büchner (1824–1899), and Ernst Haeckel (1834–1919).

Philosophers of the 20th century are chary of the word "materialism," generally preferring the softer terms "monism" and, later, "naturalism." The quasi materialism of positivism, however, has continued prominently, in the "physicalism" of the logical positivists, in American behaviorism, and in pragmatism (q.v.) or instrumentalism, and in some British linguistic analyses, as that of Gilbert Ryle, for example. (See Positivism; Behavior and Behaviorism.) The atheists among the French existentialists (see Existentialism) are informally or implicitly materialistic, while Marxian dialectical materialism (q.v.) goes its own conspicuous way, rather more dialectical than materialistic. George Santayana (1863–1952), who called himself "the only living materialist," was in fact only a causal materialist, believing in the Platonic realms of spirit and essence as well as matter, but denying their efficacy. Many other "new realists" of Britain and America, expressly renouncing both idealism and dualism, stand closer than he to metaphysical materialism; for example, Samuel Alexander (1859–1938), Bertrand Russell (1872–   ), William Pepperell Montague (1873–1953), Ralph Barton Perry (1876–1957), and Roy Wood Sellars (1880–   ). If most of these, though not Sellars, would disown the epithet "materialism," this is because of certain philosophic and scientific innovations widely thought to have antiquated the traditional distinction between the material and the mental. One of these is the displacement of the older scientific atomism with less lumpish principles: "neutral entities," events, waves, patterns of action, electric charges, energy fields, space strains, perspectives, frames of reference, and even probabilities. Another is the concept of "emergence," natural novelty, and levels of organization (Alexander, Perry, and Sellars, for example), which provides that, though mind ensues upon life and life on matter, as perhaps matter did on something else (primitive space-time, Alexander said) and something else will on mind, each higher level of complexity and integration has a new quality of its own, not predictable from nor reducible to the entities of any lower level. It seems as appropriate, however, to say that these views refine materialism as that they abolish it. Conceptions of energy fields and the like do cancel the antique idea that matter is intrinsically inert and impenetrable, but they perfect the cardinal materialistic principle of spatiotemporal structure. And it is far from clear how the natural emergence of novelty differs from the sweeping changes of physical configuration that materialism has always affirmed. Democritus denied novelty to the extent of believing that everything happens by inexorable natural necessity, and perhaps that any state of affairs will be repeated after a sufficiently long interval. His principle of mechanistic determinism and predictability, however, is by no means essential to materialism, and was promptly rejected, in fact, by Epicurus.

Thomas Hobbes argued for materialism *a priori,* that "incorporeal substance" is a contradiction in terms; Leibniz returned the compliment by asserting that "corporeal substance" is absurd. Few philosophers, however, think the issue so easily resolved, and materialists generally advocate their doctrine as the hypothesis best in accord with science and best confirmed by its evidence and methods. The evidence against it must consist accordingly of the phenomena it finds hardest to explain, or explain away: not especially, as is popularly supposed, religious, moral, and intellectual affairs, but rather the sheer fact of awareness and the simple qualities of sensation—colors, smells, and the like—which seem so disparate from the geometry of matter and motion that Democritus, Galileo, Hobbes, and the behaviorists roundly denied their existence in objects.

Materialism has been exalted (by Lucretius and Karl Marx) and condemned (by Christian philosophers) as the great enemy of transcendent religion. Epicurus believed in gods of a physical sort, frail, far, and powerless, but more serious materialistic religions have revered the fecundity of nature, the evolutionary impulse, or our own moral ideals, usually in the hope of human perfectibility. Materialists thus tend to convert religion into ethics, which they espouse with a seriousness that may make them revolutionaries, but which rebuts the vulgar charge that they are amoral. Their favorite ethic is hedonism, that the good is happiness or the satisfaction of interest, typically the happiness or interest of all (utilitarianism, q.v.); but they have found congenial also the ideals of rational self-possession and of self-realization.

Bibliography.—Lucretius, *On the Nature of Things* (many translations and editions); Lange, Friedrich A., *The History of Materialism,* tr. from the German by Ernest C. Thomas, 3 vols. (London 1877–1880); Haeckel, Ernst H., *The Riddle of the Universe,* tr. from the German by Joseph McCabe (London 1900); Hobbes, Thomas, *The Metaphysical System of Hobbes,* selected by Mary Whiton Calkins (Chicago 1905); Perry, Ralph Barton, *Present Philosophical Tendencies,* rev. ed. (New York 1916); Alexander, Samuel, *Space, Time, and Deity* (London 1920); Sellars, Roy W., McGill, Vivian J., and Farber, Marvin, eds., *Philosophy for the Future; the Quest of Modern Materialism* (New York 1949).

DONALD C. WILLIAMS,
Professor of Philosophy, Harvard University.

MATERIALISM, Dialectical. See DIALECTICAL MATERIALISM.

MATERNITY. See OBSTETRICS.

MATHEMATICAL COMPUTERS. See COMPUTERS.

MATHEMATICAL INDUCTION. See INDUCTION, MATHEMATICAL.

MATHEMATICAL SIGNS AND SYMBOLS. The operations of mathematics are greatly simplified by the use of a wide variety of special signs, symbols, and abbreviations. Some of the symbols are required to indicate the operations to be performed, others are very short abbreviations for a complete phrase or idea, as, for instance, when a single letter x, is substituted for "the amount of money that was invested by a broker at 6 per cent" in a more or less complicated problem. The set of symbols currently used in the more elementary branches of mathematics has been developed through many years, in many countries and languages, at the hands of many eminent mathematicians, until these symbols are almost international in their application. For readers who are interested in following the course of this development, the work of the master historian Florian Cajori in *A History of Mathematical Notations,* 2 vols. (La Salle, Ill., 1928–29) will be rewarding.

It is important that every symbol should be concise, so as to be visible at a glance, capable of rapid writing, and not too taxing on the ingenuity of the printer when a discussion is to be published. The stock of such symbols among our everyday characters is fortunately very large. First are the numbers of our decimal system, including common and decimal fractions. Then there are all the ordinary letters of our Latin alphabet, both upper and lower case; the letters of the Greek alphabet; and, for some special uses, script letters and some letters from the German, Hebrew, and Old English alphabets. Add to these the use of subscripts like x_1, x_2, x_3, primes at the upper right hand of the letters as in x', x''; and the overscore or bar, like $\bar{x}$; and the number of forms for a single character is much increased. Mathematically, the use of the upper right hand position for a superscript, called an exponent, has greatly expedited work with powers of numbers and with logarithms.

The choice of a symbol to stand for some quantity in a given branch of mathematics or in a particular problem does not mean that we cannot use the same symbol with another meaning in another phase of our work or in another problem. While we customarily try to confine our use of the letters of the first half of the alphabet to *known* quantities and the other half to *unknowns,* we must be careful to be sure from the context whether, for example, the r in a problem stands for a constant or a variable.

Based upon a study of conventional and current usage, a selection of the signs and symbols most frequently met in the various fields of elementary mathematics is given below. For a more comprehensive table, readers are referred to Glenn James and R. C. James, eds., *Mathematics Dictionary,* 2d ed., p. 467 ff. (New York 1959).

GLOSSARY OF MATHEMATICAL SIGNS AND SYMBOLS

ARITHMETIC AND ALGEBRA

a, b, c, ... The letters of the first half of the alphabet, used for *known* quantities.

p, q, r, ... The letters of the second half of the alphabet, used for *unknown* quantities; outstanding exceptions are *e* and *i.*

e or *ε* The base of the natural logarithm system (see LOGARITHMS):
$$e = \lim_{x \to \infty} (1 + 1/x)^x = 2.71828...$$

i The imaginary square root of -1; $i^2 = -1$.

∞ Infinity, both absolute infinity, and in the sense of a variable increasing without limit.

$+$ Plus, a symbol for addition and positive direction, as in $a + b$, and $+32°$ F.

$-$ Minus, a symbol for subtraction and negative direction, as in $a - b$, and $-6°$ F.

$\pm$, $\mp$ Plus or minus, and minus or plus; used when an operation requires an even root of a positive number $\sqrt{9} = \pm 3$, $-\sqrt{9} = \mp 3$.

$\times$, $\cdot$ Alternative symbols for the process of multiplication; $a \times b$, $a \cdot b$, and ab, all represent the product of a times b.

$\div$, $/$, $-$, $:$ Alternative symbols for the process of division; $a \div b$, a/b, $\frac{a}{b}$, and $a : b$ all represent the quotient of a divided by b.

$\approx$ Is approximately equal to, as $\pi \approx 3\frac{1}{7}$.

$=$, $::$ Is equal to. The equation $x^2 - 3x + 2 = 0$ asks "For what values of x, if any, is this relation true?"

The equation $a : b :: c : d$ may be rendered $\frac{a}{b} = \frac{c}{d}$

$\equiv$ Is identical with. The equation $a^2 - b^2 \equiv (a + b)(a - b)$ is true for any values of a and b. The sign $=$ is frequently used in an identity when it leads to no confusion.

$a/b = c/d$, $a : b :: c : d$ Symbols denoting proportion; a is to b as c is to d.

$>$ Greater than; in $a > b$, a is greater than b.

$<$ Less than; in $a < b$, a is less than b.

$\geqslant$, $\geqq$ Greater than or equal to; in $a \geqslant b$, a is greater than or equal to b.

$\leqslant$, $\leqq$ Less than or equal to; in $a \leqslant b$, a is less than or equal to b.

a^2, a^n The symbols for a squared, a to the nth power; $a^2 = a \cdot a$, $a^n = a \cdot a \cdot a \cdot \ldots n$ factors. See Exponents and Exponentials.

$\sqrt{}$ Root, indicating square root when no figure is placed above it.

$\sqrt{a}$, $a^{\frac{1}{2}}$ The positive square root of a, for positive a.

$\sqrt[n]{a}$, $a^{1/n}$ The nth root of a, usually the *principal* nth root.

$(\ )$, $[\ ]$, $\{\ \}$, $-$ Parentheses, brackets, braces, and vinculum are symbols setting apart an operation which is to act as a single term: $a(b + c)$, $a[b + c]$, $a\{b + c\}$, and $a\ \overline{b + c}$, all indicate the product of a and the binomial $b + c$.

$|y|$ The absolute value of y; that is its exact value without regard to the algebraic sign of y.

$\bar{y}$ The modulus of the complex number y; the mean or average value of y.

$\neq$, $\ngtr$, $\nless$ not equal to, not greater than, not less than.

$\begin{vmatrix} a_1 & a_2 & \ldots \\ b_1 & b_2 & \ldots \\ \cdots \end{vmatrix}$ The determinant

See Determinants.

$\|abc \ldots\|$ or $(abc \ldots)$ The matrix $\begin{Vmatrix} a_1 & a_2 & \ldots \\ b_1 & b_2 & \ldots \\ \cdots \end{Vmatrix}$ or $\begin{pmatrix} a_1 & a_2 & \ldots \\ b_1 & b_2 & \ldots \\ \cdots \end{pmatrix}$

$n!$, $\lfloor n$ Factorial n; the product of all the natural numbers from 1 to n inclusive.

$_nP_r$, $P(n,r)$ The number of permutations of n things taken r at a time. It is equal to $n!/(n - r)!$ See Combinations and Permutations.

$_nC_r$, $\frac{n}{r}$, $C(n,r)$ The number of combinations of n things taken r at a time: $\frac{n!}{r!\ (n - r)!}$. The $(r + 1)$th binomial coefficient.

G.C.D. or *g.c.d.* The greatest common divisor.

L.C.D. or *l.c.d.* The lowest common denominator.

L.C.M. or *l.c.m.* The lowest common multiple.

log a, $\log_{10} a$ The common logarithm of a to base 10 in the Common or Briggs logarithm system. See Logarithms.

ln a, $\log_e a$ The logarithm of a to base e ($e = 2.718...$) in the Natural or Napierian logarithm system.

antilog x, $\log^{-1} x$ The antilogarithm of x; the number whose logarithm is x.

colog x The cologarithm of a; $-\log x = \log \frac{1}{x}$.

exp x Exponential x: e^x where e is the base of the natural logarithm system ($e = 2.718...$).

$\ldots$ Sign of continuation, as, for example, 2, 4, 8, $\ldots$

$\propto$ Varies as. The volume of a sphere varies as the cube of its radius: $V \propto R^3$, that is, $V = kR^3$.

a_n The nth term of a progression.

S_n The sum of n terms of a progression. See Series.

a', a'', $\ldots$, $a^{(n)}$ used to denote quantities of the same sort as a.

ω_1, ω_2, ω_3; 1, ω, ω^2 The three imaginary cube roots of 1.

$f(x)$, $F(x)$, $\phi(x)$ Function of x. See Function.

Elementary and Analytic Geometry

A, B, C, $\ldots$ Capital (upper case) letters used to denote points.

$\angle$, $\measuredangle$ Angle, angles.

$\angle A$, $\angle BAC$ Angle A (only one angle at A); in the angle BAC, the vertex is A, the sides BA and CA.

$\llcorner$ Right Angle.

$\perp$, $\underline{\perp}$ Perpendicular, perpendiculars. In $AB \perp CD$, AB is perpendicular to CD.

$/\!/$, $/\!/$s Parallel, parallels. $AB /\!/ CD$ means that AB is parallel to CD.

$\triangle$, $\triangle$ Triangle, triangles.

$\odot$, $\circledS$ Circle, circles. A specific circle is denoted by three points on its circumference, for example, $\odot CDE$.

$\square$, $\square$, $\bigtriangledown$, $\ldots$ Squares, rectangles, trapezoids, and other geometric figures are frequently represented by rough sketches of their shapes.

$\overset{\frown}{BC}$ An arc having the ends B and C.

$\cong$, $\equiv$ Congruent; having identical shape and size.

$\sim$ Similar to; having the same shape but differing in size.

π The ratio of the circumference of a circle to its diameter; π has a numerical value of 3.14159. $\ldots$

$\therefore$, $\because$ Symbols denoting therefore and since, respectively.

Q.E.D., *Q.E.F.* Abbreviations of the Latin *quod erat demonstrandum*, which was to be proved, and *quod erat faciendum*, which was to be constructed.

(x, y), (x, y, z) Rectangular coordinates of a point in a plane, and in space. See Geometry. 4. *Analytic Geometry.*

P(x, y) The point P whose coordinates are x and y.

(r, θ) The polar coordinates of a point.

(r, θ, z) Cylindrical coordinates.

(r, θ, ϕ) Spherical coordinates.

cos α, cos β, cos γ Direction cosines of a line which makes angles α, β, and γ respectively with the x-, y-, and z-axes.

l, m, n Direction numbers, which are proportional to the direction cosines.

Trigonometry

$°$ Degrees of angle or of arc; $1° = 60'$.

$'$ Minutes of angle or of arc; $1' = 60''$.

$''$ Seconds of angle or of arc.

h, m, s Hours, minutes, seconds of time; example: $4^h 27^m 53^s$; $24^h = 360°$; $1^h = 15°$; $1^m = 15'$; $1^s = 15''$.

sin θ Sine of angle θ.

cos θ Cosine of angle θ; $\sin^2 \theta + \cos^2 \theta = 1$.

tan θ Tangent of θ; $\tan \theta = \sin \theta / \cos \theta$.

cot θ Cotangent of θ; $\cot \theta = \cos \theta / \sin \theta = 1/\tan \theta$.

sec θ Secant of θ; $\sec \theta = 1/\cos \theta$.

csc θ Cosecant of θ; $\csc \theta = 1/\sin \theta$.

vers θ Versine of θ; $\text{vers } \theta = 1 - \cos \theta$.

covers θ Coversine of θ; $\text{covers } \theta = 1 - \sin \theta$.

hav θ Haversine of θ; $\text{hav } \theta = \frac{1}{2} \text{ vers } \theta = \sin^2 \frac{\theta}{2}$.

sin^{-1}a Inverse sine of a; the angle whose sine is a.

cos^{-1}a, tan^{-1}a Other inverse functions.

sinh x Hyperbolic sine of x: $\frac{1}{2}(e^x - e^{-x})$.

cosh x   Hyperbolic cosine of x: $\frac{1}{2}(e^x + e^{-x})$.

tanh x   Hyperbolic tangent of x; $\frac{\sinh x}{\cosh x}$.

sech x, coth x, csch x   Hyperbolic functions.

sinh⁻¹y   Inverse hyperbolic sine of y. If $x = \sinh^{-1}y$, then $y = \sinh x$.

cosh⁻¹y, tanh⁻¹y   Other inverse hyperbolic functions.

s   One-half the sum of the lengths of the sides of any triangle, plane or spherical.

S, σ   One-half the sum of the angles of any spherical triangle.

E   The spherical excess; $2S - 180°$.

DIFFERENTIAL AND INTEGRAL CALCULUS

△x   An increment of x; when x changes from x_1 to x_2, $\triangle x = x_2 - x_1$.

△y   The amount by which $y = f(x)$ changes when x changes from x to $x + \triangle x$; that is, $y = f(x + \triangle x) - f(x)$.

→   Approaches. In $x \to a$, x approaches a. When $x \to \infty$, x increases without limit.

lim f(x)   The limit, as x approaches a, of $f(x)$. It is
$x \to a$ $f(a)$ if this function exists.

$\frac{dy}{dx}, \frac{df(x)}{dx}$, y', $f'(x)$, $D_x y$ The derivative of $y = f(x)$ with respect to x. $\lim\limits_{\triangle x \to 0} \frac{\triangle y}{\triangle x}$ if such a limit exists.

$\frac{d^2y}{dx^2}, \frac{d^2f(x)}{dx^2}$, y'', $\int D_x^2 y$ The second derivative of $y = f(x)$ with respect to x.

$\frac{d^ny}{dx^n}$, $D_x^n y$ The nth derivative of y with respect to x.

$\dot{x}$ The derivative of x with respect to t (time).

$\ddot{x}$ The second derivative of x with respect to t (time). If $s =$ distance, $\dot{s} = v =$ velocity; $\ddot{s} = \dot{v} =$ acceleration, a.

dx   Identical with $\triangle x$ by definition.

δy   The variation of y.

dy, df(x)   The differential of $y = f(x)$. It is the product of $\frac{dy}{dx}$ by dx. For relatively small values of dx, dy becomes a good approximation for $\triangle y$.

∫ f(x) dx   The integral of $f(x)\ dx$; that is, the function (or functions) having $f(x)dx$ as a differential. As this result involves an arbitrary additive constant, it is called an *indefinite* integral.

$\int_a^b f(x)dx$ and $x = b$ The definite integral of $f(x)dx$ between $x = a$. If $\int f(x)\ dx = Q(x) + C$, then $f(x)dx = Q(b) - Q(a)$.

$Q(x)]_a^b$ Another method of writing $Q(b) - Q(a)$.

$\oint_C, \oint_S$ An integral around a closed path C or a closed surface S which is often written without the circle: $\int_C$ and $\int_S$.

$\frac{\delta u}{\delta x}, u_x, f_x(x,y,z)$ The partial derivative of $u = f(x,y,z)$ with respect to x. It is the same as the ordinary derivative of u with respect to x when only u and x are considered as variables.

$\frac{\delta^2 u}{\delta y\, \delta x}, u_{xy}, f_{x,y}(x,y)$ The second partial derivative of $u = f(x,y)$, taken first with respect to x, then with respect to y.

∫∫   A double integral; $\iint x^2 y^3 dx\, dy$.

Σ   A sum; an algebraic sum.

$\overset{n}{\underset{1}{\Sigma}}$ or $\overset{n}{\underset{i=1}{\Sigma}}$ The sum of n terms, one for each integer from 1 to n. $\overset{3}{\underset{1}{\Sigma}} x_i^2 = x_1^2 + x_2^2 + x_3^2$.

$\overset{n}{\underset{1}{\Pi}}, \overset{n}{\underset{i=1}{\Pi}}$ The product of n factors of the sort indicated;

$\overset{3}{\underset{i=1}{\Pi}} x_i y_i = x_1 y_1 x_2 y_2 x_3 y_3$.

I   Moment of inertia.

k   Radius of gyration.

$(\bar{x}, \bar{y}, \bar{z})$ Coordinates of the center of mass.

s or σ   Length of arc.

ρ   Radius of curvature.

κ   Curvature of a curve.

τ   Torsion of a curve.

WALTER F. SHENTON,
Professor Emeritus of Mathematics, American University, Washington, D.C.

MATHEMATICAL SOCIETIES AND PUBLICATIONS. Mathematics, one of the oldest sciences, is one of the most vital and active today; probably more mathematical discoveries have been made since 1875 than in all the years before then. If these discoveries are to become known and available to others as a basis for further progress, they must be adequately reported and the reports must be adequately disseminated. Investigations, the results of which are not reported and disseminated, are quickly forgotten and, as far as the advancement of mathematical science is concerned, might well never have been undertaken at all.

Mathematical societies exist chiefly to facilitate communication between mathematicians. The older societies were for the most part local, confined to a particular university or city. However, the tendency toward national societies has been growing, and most of the stronger societies today are national in character, though possibly not in name. A number of international organizations have been formed, but these have not developed as fully as the national organizations.

Probably the oldest mathematical society still active is the Mathematische Gesellschaft in Hamburg. This society was founded in 1690 and commenced publication of its *Mitteilungen* (*Communications*) in 1881. The Wiskundig Genootschap te Amsterdam was founded in 1778 and has published a number of journals, of which the *Nieuw Archief voor Wiskunde,* founded in 1875, is still being published. The London Mathematical Society was founded in 1865, the Moscow Mathematical Society in 1866. In the years following 1866 many new mathematical organizations were established, including the Société Mathématique de France in 1873, the Edinburgh Mathematical Society in 1883, the American Mathematical Society in 1888, and the Mathematical Association of America in 1915.

The usual methods by which mathematicians, in common with other scientists, communicate their discoveries are (1) by personal correspondence with other mathematicians, (2) by presentation of results at mathematical meetings, (3) by publication of results in mathematical journals. Little need be said about private correspondence between mathematicians as a method of communication, except that it is customary for mathematicians to write one another about their common scientific interests even though they are not acquainted personally. This is an important but limited form of communication, which is assisted by the lists of members' addresses published by mathematical societies.

A primary function of mathematical societies is the organization of meetings at which the results of new mathematical investigations may be presented. Unlike private correspondence, where one may discuss conjectures and promising lines for further investigation without committing oneself, it is not customary to present results at meetings until they are firmly established. Priority of discovery can usually be established through presentation at a meeting.

Except possibly for a published abstract in the report of the meeting, presentation at a meeting does not provide a permanent record of a discovery nor does it disseminate it beyond those able to attend. A permanent record and wide dissemination of new results are obtained through publication in a mathematical journal. The sale of mathematical journals that report new discoveries is usually limited to professional mathematicians and research libraries. The circulation is necessarily small and the publication of such journals usually is not commercially profitable. They are, therefore, in most cases sponsored by mathematical societies or universities which are able to provide the necessary financial backing.

Languages of Publication.—Italian, French, German, and English are the traditional languages for scientific publication. Most scientists, no matter what their native tongue, publish in one of these languages, and it is assumed that every scientist can read scientific papers in his own field in any of the four. More recently, Russian scientists have been required to publish in Russian. Since few American mathematicians are familiar with this language, the American Mathematical Society has inaugurated a series which translates current Russian mathematical research papers into English and has prepared a Russian-English vocabulary to assist English-speaking mathematicians in reading mathematical texts in Russian.

Journals of Primary Publication.—Journals that publish the results of original research are known as journals of primary publication. Articles in such journals are usually advanced in character and devote themselves directly to the new results obtained without giving much antecedent material. The articles are intended for other specialists in the same field of mathematics and do not have much general interest even for the great majority of mathematicians. Papers published in such journals are contributed by the author, and it is not customary for the journal to pay royalties. Each journal has a board of editors which establishes editorial standards and decides whether the papers submitted meet these standards. Editorial criteria usually include appropriateness of the subject matter for the particular journal, originality, and the quality of the results presented. Membership in the organization supporting the journal is not generally a requirement for publication. When a paper has been accepted and published, the author usually receives a number of copies, perhaps 100 or so, separately bound in pamphlet form. The author may distribute these reprints to individuals he feels will be particularly interested but who may not be subscribers to the journal in which the article was published.

The principal mathematical journals of primary publication in North America are the following: *Proceedings of the American Mathematical Society; Transactions of the American Mathematical Society; Memoirs of the American Mathematical Society; American Journal of Mathematics* (Johns Hopkins Press); *Canadian Journal of Mathematics* (University of Toronto Press); *Pacific Journal of Mathematics* (University of California Press); *Annals of Mathe-*

matics (Princeton University Press); *Duke Mathematical Journal* (Duke University Press); *Communications on Pure and Applied Mathematics* (Interscience Publishing Company); and *Quarterly of Applied Mathematics* (Brown University).

The following journals are largely, though not exclusively, devoted to mathematics or closely related subjects: *Journal of Mathematics and Physics* (Massachusetts Institute of Technology); *Journal of Rational Mechanics and Analysis* (University of Indiana); *The Journal of Symbolic Logic* (Association for Symbolic Logic); *Biometrics* (Biometric Society); *Econometrica* (Econometric Society); *The Annals of Mathematical Statistics* (Institute of Mathematical Statistics); and *Mathematical Tables and Other Aids to Computation* (National Research Council). Most of these journals are issued from four to six times a year and publish from 500 to 1,000 pages annually.

Mathematical journals of primary publication are published throughout the world. A partial listing by country and sponsoring society, when there is one, follows:

Argentina.—Unión Matemática Argentina: *Revista.*
Austria.—Österreichische Mathematische Gesellschaft: *Monatshefte für Mathematik.*
Belgium.—Société Mathématique de Belgique: *Bulletin.*
Brazil.—*Summa Brasiliensis Mathematicae* (Rio de Janeiro). Sociedade de Matemática de São Paulo: *Boletim.*
China.—Chinese Mathematical Society: *Journal.*
Czechoslovakia.—Jednota Československých Matematiků a Fysiků v Praze: *Časopis pro Pěstování Matematiky.*
Denmark.—Matematisk Forening i København: *Matematisk Tidsskrift.* Societates Mathematicae Daniae Fenniae Islandiae Nouvegiae Sveciae: *Mathematica Scandinavica.*
Finland.—Societas Scientiarum Fennica: *Commentationes Physico-Mathematicae; Annales, Series A. I., Mathematica-Physica.*
France.—Société Mathématique de France: *Bulletin.* École des Hautes Études: *Bulletin des Sciences Mathématiques.* Centre National de la Recherche Scientifique: *Journal de Mathématiques Pures et Appliquées.* Institut Henri Poincaré: *Annales.* École Normale Supérieure: *Annales.*
Germany.—Deutsche Mathematiker Vereinigung: *Jahresbericht.* Mathematische Gesellschaft in Hamburg: *Mitteilungen. Journal für die reine und angewandte Mathematik* (W. de Gruyter). Forschungsinstitut für Mathematik of the Deutsche Akademie der Wissenschaften zu Berlin: *Mathematische Nachrichten. Mathematische Annalen* (Springer). *Mathematische Zeitschrift* (Springer). Mathematisches Forschungsinstitut in Oberwolfach: *Archiv der Mathematik. Zeitschrift für angewandte Mathematik und Mechanik* (Akademieverlag, Berlin).
Great Britain.—London Mathematical Society: *Journal; Proceedings. The Quarterly Journal of Mathematics* (Oxford). *The Quarterly Journal of Mechanics and Applied Mathematics* (Oxford). Edinburgh Mathematical Society: *Proceedings. Mathematika* (London).
Greece.—Société Mathématique de Grèce: *Bulletin.*
Hungary.—University of Szeged: *Acta Scientiarum Mathematicarum.* Academia Scientiarum Hungarica: *Acta Mathematica.* Institutum Mathematicum of the University of Debrecen: *Publicationes Mathematicae.*
India.—Bhârata Gaṇita Pariṣad (Lucknow): *Gaṇita* (formerly, Benares Mathematical Society: *Proceedings*). Calcutta Mathematical Society: *Bulletin.* Indian Mathematical Society: *Journal.*
Israel.—*Journal d'Analyse Mathématique* (Jerusalem).
Italy.—*Annali di Matematica* (C. Zuffi). *Giornale di Matematiche di Battaglini* (Pellerano). Unione Matematica Italiana: *Bollettino.* Circolo Matematico di Palermo: *Rendiconti.* University of Padua: *Rendiconti del Seminario Matematico.* University of Parma: *Revista di Matematica.* Scuola Normale Superiore di Pisa: *Annali.*
Japan.—Mathematical Society of Japan: *Journal.* National Research Council of Japan: *Japanese Journal of Mathematics.* Tôhoku University: *Tôhoku Mathematical Journal.* Tokyo Institute of Technology: *Kôdai Mathematical Seminar Reports.* Nagoya University: *Nagoya Mathematical Journal.* The Tensor

Society: *Tensor. Mathematica Japonicae. Osaka Mathematical Journal.*

Mexico.—Sociedad Matemática Mexicana: *Boletín.*

Netherlands.—Koninklijke Nederlandse Akademie van Wetenschappen: *Indagationes Mathematicae.* Wiskundig Genootschap te Amsterdam: *Nieuw Archief voor Wiskunde. Compositio Mathematica* (Noordhoff, Groningen).

Norway.—Norsk Matematisk Forening: *Nordisk Matematisk Tidsskrift.*

Poland.—*Fundamenta Mathematicae* (Warsaw). *Studia Mathematica* (Wrocław). *Colloquium Mathematicum* (Wrocław). Société Polonaise de Mathématique: *Annales.*

Portugal.—Sociedade Portuguesa de Matemática: *Portugaliae Mathematica; Boletim.*

Rumania.—Academia Republicii Populare Romine, Institutul de Matematică: *Studii și Cercetări Matematice.*

Spain.—University of Barcelona: *Collectanea Mathematica.* Sociedad Matemática Española: *Revista Matemática Hispano-Americana.*

Sweden.—*Acta Mathematica* (Uppsala). Kungliga Svenska Vetenskapsakademien: *Arkiv för Matematik.* University of Lund: *Communications du Séminaire Mathématique.*

Switzerland.—Schweizerische Mathematische Gesellschaft: *Commentarii Mathematici Helvetici.*

USSR.—Academy of Sciences of the USSR: *Izvestiya, Seriya Matematicheskaya; Prikladnaya Matematika i Mekhanika; Matematicheskij Sbornik; Trudy Matematicheskogo Instituta imeni V. A. Steklova.* Academy of Sciences of the Ukrainian SSR: *Ukrainskij Matematicheskij Zhurnal.* Moscow Mathematical Society: *Uspekhi Matematicheskikh Nauk.*

Yugoslavia.—Académie Serbe des Sciences: *Publications de l'Institut Mathématique.*

In addition to these, there are many journals of primary publication with a broader scientific coverage which carry some material of mathematical interest. These include the *Proceedings* of the National Academy of Sciences in Washington; the *Proceedings* of the Royal Society of London; the *Proceedings* of the Royal Society of Edinburgh; the *Comptes Rendus Hebdomadaires* of the Académie des Sciences in Paris; the *Doklady (Comtes Rendus)* of the Academy of Sciences of the USSR; the *Rendiconti* of the Accademia dei Lincei in Rome, Italy; the *Proceedings* of the Japanese Academy; and the *Proceedings* of other national academies. Altogether, throughout the world, there are more than 1,200 periodicals devoted in whole or part to mathematics.

Reviewing and Abstracting Journals.—The fact that there are over 1,200 journals which carry a substantial amount of mathematical material gives rise to another problem: How in such a multitude of journals does one locate the papers one is interested in? This need is met by the reviewing and abstracting journals, which scan the journals of primary publication on a current basis and publish reviews or abstracts of all articles of mathematical interest. The first publication of this type, *Revue Semestrielle des Publications Mathématiques,* was published from 1892 to 1935. Later this function was performed by the *Zentralblatt für Mathematik und ihre Grenzgebiete,* established in 1931 by Springer, publishers in Berlin. Due to political interference with the *Zentralblatt* by the regime of Adolf Hitler, a new reviewing and abstracting journal, *Mathematical Reviews,* was founded by the American Mathematical Society and commenced publication in 1940. The *Zentralblatt* discontinued publication for a few years during World War II, but has since started again. The *Bulletin Analytique,* founded in 1940 and published by the Centre National de la Recherche Scientifique in France, covers a wider range of subject matter but with somewhat briefer notices.

Mathematical Reviews is sponsored by the following 13 mathematical organizations: American Mathematical Society; Mathematical Association of America; Institute of Mathematical Statistics; Edinburgh Mathematical Society; Matematisk Forening i København; Wiskundig Genootschap te Amsterdam; London Mathematical Society; Société Polonaise de Mathématique; Unione Matematica Italiana; Unión Matemática Argentina; Indian Mathematical Society; Société Mathématique de France; Society for Industrial and Applied Mathematics.

To ensure the authoritativeness of its reviews, *Mathematical Reviews* has a staff of 750 professional mathematicians, including specialists in every branch of mathematics, who are qualified to review articles written in almost any language. They serve without remuneration. The reviewers are widely distributed and many nationalities are represented. Reviews are published in Italian, German, French, or English. Approximately 7,000 current mathematical articles are reviewed each year. Subject and author indices are published annually. A list of the more than 1,200 journals regularly received for reviewing in the office of *Mathematical Reviews* is published annually in the December issue and is a good source of information concerning mathematical journals.

Although reviewing and abstracting journals serve very well to locate the current literature on some topic, they lack the perspective necessary to orient the reader with respect to earlier publications on the topic. This gap is filled by the *Encyklopädie der Mathematischen Wissenschaften mit Einschluss ihrer Anwendungen,* which publishes survey articles on the various branches of mathematics. These articles, though never completely up-to-date, are rewritten from time to time to keep them from becoming obsolete. They give references to the necessary antecedent material, enabling the research worker to become well grounded in his chosen topic.

Teachers' Journals.—In addition to the journals of primary publication and the abstracting journals, there are journals which publish expository articles and articles dealing with the problems of mathematics teachers. *The American Mathematical Monthly,* published by the Mathematical Association of America, and the *Mathematical Gazette,* published by the British Mathematical Association, serve college and university teachers of mathematics, while the *Mathematics Teacher,* published by the National Council of Teachers of Mathematics, Washington, D.C., serves school teachers. *The Mathematics Student,* published by the Indian Mathematical Society, *Elemente der Mathematik,* published in Basel, Switzerland, *Mathematics Magazine,* published in Pacoima, Calif., and *L'Enseignment Mathématique,* mentioned later, all serve this same general purpose. *Scripta Mathematica,* published by Yeshiva University, is devoted primarily to the history of mathematics.

Monograph Series.—To enable a trained mathematician to obtain insight into fields of mathematics in which he has not specialized, a number of monograph series of varying degrees of difficulty are published. The American Mathematical Society publishes two such series, the *Colloquium Publications,* which deal with advanced mathematical subjects and embody new contributions to mathematical knowledge, and

Mathematical Surveys, which are careful expositions of fields of current interest in research. The Princeton University Press also publishes two series, the *Princeton Mathematical Series* and the *Annals of Mathematics Studies.* The *Carus Monographs,* published by the Mathematical Association of America, are of the same general type, but somewhat more elementary in their treatment. The *Cambridge Tracts in Mathematics and Mathematical Physics* are published by the Cambridge University Press. Other series of a similar nature are published in France, Switzerland, Germany, and Poland.

SOCIETIES

In general, mathematical societies are organized to facilitate the dissemination of mathematical information by holding meetings and by sponsoring mathematical publications, particularly journals. The principal distinction between mathematical societies is in the area they serve. Thus, we have societies which originally were of a purely local character, such as the Mathematische Gesellschaft in Hamburg, Wiskundig Genootschap te Amsterdam, London Mathematical Society, Edinburgh Mathematical Society, Circolo Matematico di Palermo, the Calcutta Mathematical Society, and the Matematisk Forening i København. Although originally local in character, some of these societies are now in point of fact national. There are also national mathematical societies, such as the Indian Mathematical Society, the Société Mathématique de France, the Unione Matematica Italiana, the Unión Matemática Argentina, the Société Polonaise de Mathématique, and the Schweizerische Mathematische Gesellschaft, and there are a few regional organizations, like the American Mathematical Society and the Mathematical Association of America which serve North America.

Libraries.—Originally one of the important functions of a mathematical society was to maintain a mathematical library. Such a library would contain, among other things, the society's own publications and those of sister organizations. To obtain accessions for its library, it became customary for a society to exchange its publications with sister organizations. Due to the improvement of university libraries, it is now less necessary for societies to maintain libraries, but the tradition of exchanging publications is still recognized, and in times when the exchange of currencies is restricted this plays an important role in securing the prompt dissemination of scientific information across national boundaries.

American Mathematical Society.—This body has enjoyed continued growth since its founding in 1888 and numbers approximately 5,000 individuals and 130 colleges, universities, and other institutions among its members. The society publishes three journals of primary publication, the *Proceedings,* the *Memoirs,* and the *Transactions;* a reviewing and abstracting journal, *Mathematical Reviews;* two monograph series, the *Colloquium Publications* and *Mathematical Surveys;* and the *Bulletin.* This last is the official organ of the society and contains reports of meetings, abstracts of scientific papers and the texts of invited addresses presented before meetings, reviews of advanced mathematical books, and personal notes. A history of the society was published to mark its semicentennial celebration in 1938, as well as a collection of papers reviewing progress in American mathematics since its founding. In 1950, the *Collected Mathematical Papers of George David Birkhoff,* one of America's most distinguished mathematicians and a past president of the society, were published in three volumes.

In 1950, the society was host to the International Congress of Mathematicians which met at Cambridge, Mass., and it published the *Proceedings* of the congress.

The society holds its annual meeting late in December, a summer meeting early in September, and nine sectional meetings. The scientific programs consist of short contributed papers presenting the results of original research and a few invited addresses. At the summer meeting, there is ordinarily a colloquium at which recent advances in some specific field of mathematics are summarized and presented by an outstanding investigator in the field. The Josiah Willard Gibbs Lecture is usually presented at the annual meeting, by a scientist prominent in mathematics or some allied field.

Early each summer, the society holds a symposium in applied mathematics. Unlike the regular meetings of the society, where any member may contribute a short paper on any branch of mathematics, each symposium has a central theme and the program is planned to present a well-rounded picture of the selected topic. Nonlinear problems in mechanics of continua, electromagnetic theory, elasticity, and fluid dynamics have been topics. The *Proceedings* of each symposium are published by the society or a commercial publisher.

The American Mathematical Society, with the support of the National Science Foundation and the cooperation of the Association for Computing Machinery, the Association for Symbolic Logic, the Biometric Society, the Econometric Society, the Industrial Mathematics Society, the Institute of Mathematical Statistics, the Operations Research Society of America, the Society for Industrial and Applied Mathematics, the Society of Actuaries, and the Mathematical Association of America maintains the Mathematical Sciences Section of the National Register of Scientific and Technical Personnel. The register is a permanent record of the fields of interest and the qualifications of persons professionally qualified in at least one of the mathematical sciences. Other sections of the register serve other fields of science and are maintained by societies serving those fields.

To help its members join the mathematical organizations of other areas, and so provide links between organizations through the members they have in common, the American Mathematical Society has entered into a number of reciprocity agreements with sister organizations. A member of two organizations united by a reciprocity agreement is entitled to reduced dues in one of them.

Mathematical Association of America.—While the American Mathematical Society is devoted to the interests of mathematical scholarship and research, the Mathematical Association of America, which was founded in 1915 and has a slightly larger membership than the society, devotes itself mainly to the problems of instruction in mathematics at the college level. There is close cooperation between them. Like the society, the association holds two national meetings each year, the summer meeting and the annual meeting, and the two organizations usually arrange to meet together at these times.

The Mathematical Association of America is divided geographically into 27 sections, each of which enjoys considerable autonomy in arranging sectional meetings. Two publications of the association, *The American Mathematical Monthly* and the *Carus Monographs,* have already been mentioned. The association also publishes a series of expository monographs under the title, *Slaught Memorial Papers.*

Society for Industrial and Applied Mathematics.—Since World War II there has been a rapid increase in the number of mathematicians employed by government and industry. This has led to a renaissance of interest in applied mathematics. In 1952 the Society for Industrial and Applied Mathematics was founded to further the application of mathematics to industry and science. In the mid-1960's the membership of this society had reached almost 4,000. The *Journal* of the society publishes research, expository, and survey papers, and papers directing attention to areas suitable for mathematical development. The society holds national meetings, frequently in conjunction with the American Mathematical Society and Mathematical Association of America, and also sectional meetings.

Canadian Mathematical Congress.—This congress meets during the summer every fourth year. Between congresses, a seminar devoted to a designated field of mathematics is held, at which a number of distinguished investigators in the field give short series of lectures. The *Canadian Journal of Mathematics* was founded by the Canadian Mathematical Congress.

Societies in Special Fields.—Societies are also formed which specialize in prescribed fields of mathematics or in the application of mathematics to allied sciences. American societies of this character include the American Statistical Association, the Institute of Mathematical Statistics, the Association for Symbolic Logic, the Association for Computing Machinery, the Industrial Mathematics Society, the Society of Actuaries, Operations Research Society of America, and the Duodecimal Society of America.

Problems arising from the logical structure within which mathematics functions are in the province of symbolic logic. These problems are of interest alike to mathematicians and philosophers. The Association for Symbolic Logic fosters interest in this area.

World War II gave a great impetus to the development of automatic high speed computers. Since then the design of computers has been greatly improved and simplified and the field of their application greatly expanded. The Association for Computing Machinery was formed to foster this development.

During World War II the scientific analysis of various phases of military operations was placed in the hands of groups variously known as operational or operations research groups. Many of the methods employed by these groups were mathematical. Since the war vigorous efforts have been made, and with considerable success, to apply these methods to industrial and governmental as well as military operational problems. The Operations Research Society of America was formed to stimulate these developments.

International Organizations and Congresses.—Among the international organizations with restricted fields of interest should be mentioned the Biometric Society, the Econometric Society, and the Tensor Society. The International Commission on the Teaching of Mathematics has published extensive reports dealing with various aspects of mathematical instruction in Germany, Italy, Austria, Spain, Switzerland, France, Belgium, the Netherlands, Hungary, Rumania, Denmark, Sweden, the United Kingdom, the United States, Australia, and Japan. *L'Enseignment Mathématique,* the official organ of the commission, has been published since 1899. The teaching, history, and philosophy of mathematics are included in its scope.

An International Mathematical Union has been formed with the assistance of the United Nations Educational Scientific and Cultural Organization. The members of the union are national groups, rather than individuals. In general, the union interests itself in problems common to its members.

Congresses.—There was an important international gathering of mathematicians in connection with the World's Columbian Exposition at Chicago, Ill., in 1893, and the first International Congress of Mathematicians was held four years later in Zürich, Switzerland. The second congress was held in Paris, France, in 1900, and since then, except for interruptions due to wars, there has been an international congress every four years. The members of a congress are individual mathematicians, not national groups. There is no permanent organization. Each congress determines where the next will be held.

Due to strong feelings after World War I, mathematicians representing the Central Powers were not invited to attend the congresses in 1920 and 1924. At other congresses every effort has been made to enable mathematicians from all parts of the world to attend. The official languages for each congress are specified in advance. For the 1954 congress, they were Russian, Italian, German, French, and English. Papers could be presented and subsequently published in any of the official languages.

In general, the purposes of the congresses are the same as those of national or local meetings. The congresses are broader in scope and there are certain topics, such as matters of terminology and notation, on which worldwide agreement is desired, which are particularly suitable for discussion at a congress. The dates and places of the congresses that have been held are listed below:

Date	Site of Congress	Attendance
1897	Zurich, Switzerland	204
1900	Paris, France	232
1904	Heidelberg, Germany	336
1908	Rome, Italy	535
1912	Cambridge, England	574
1920	Strasbourg, France	200
1924	Toronto, Canada	526
1928	Bologna, Italy	836
1932	Zurich, Switzerland	667
1936	Oslo, Norway	487
1950	Cambridge, Mass., U.S.A.	1,917
1954	Amsterdam, Netherlands	2,120
1958	Edinburgh, Scotland	2,000
1962	Stockholm, Sweden	2,400
1966	Moscow, USSR	5,000

Only mathematicians enrolled as members are counted, not the persons accompanying them.

Each congress makes provision for the publication of its *Proceedings,* so that there is a permanent record of the papers presented before it.

HOLBROOK M. MACNEILLE,
Chairman of the Department of Mathematics Washington University.

MATHEMATICS, măth-ê-măt′ĭks. The nature of a growing and changing intellectual discipline varies with time, and is thus inextricably bound up with the history of that subject. This is particularly true of mathematics, and in tracing its history from ancient to modern times we shall note how its essential character has on occasion been transformed. In the following discussion the author assumes that the reader has at least that awareness of mathematics which results from an ordinary acquaintance with the elementary portions of arithmetic, algebra, and geometry.

Empirical Nature of Pre-Hellenistic Mathematics.—There is little doubt that mathematics arose from necessity. The annual flooding of the Nile Valley, for example, forced the ancient Egyptians to develop some system of re-establishing land boundaries; in fact, the word geometry means "measurement of the earth." The need for mensuration formulas was especially imperative since, as Herodotus (5th century B.C.) remarked, taxes in Egypt were paid upon the basis of land area. The ancient Babylonians likewise encountered an urgent need for mathematics. Marsh drainage, irrigation, and flood control converted the land along the Tigris and Euphrates rivers into a rich agricultural region. Similar projects undoubtedly were undertaken in early times in south-central Asia along the Indus and Ganges rivers and in eastern Asia along the Hwang Ho and Yangtze. The engineering, financing, and administration of such projects required the development of considerable technical knowledge and its attendant mathematics. Also, the need in agriculture for a usable calendar and the demand for some system of uniformity in barter furnished pronounced stimuli to mathematical development.

Thus there is a basis for saying that mathematics beyond primitive counting originated with the evolution of more advanced forms of society in certain areas of the ancient Orient during the 5th, 4th, and 3d millenniums B.C., and that the subject was developed as a practical science to assist in engineering, agricultural, and business pursuits. Although the initial emphasis was on mensuration and practical arithmetic, it was natural that a special craft should come into being for the application, instruction, and development of the science, and that, in turn, tendencies toward abstraction should assert themselves and the subject be studied, to some extent, for its own sake.

In a study of pre-Hellenistic mathematics we are restricted essentially to that of Egypt and Babylonia. The ancient Egyptians recorded their mathematical work on stone and papyrus, the latter fortunately enduring because of Egypt's unusually dry climate; the Babylonians inscribed their work on clay tablets that afterwards were baked to a time-resisting hardness. In contrast to the use of these media, the early Indians and Chinese used perishable writing materials, like bark and bamboo. Thus it happens that we have a fair amount of definite information, obtained from primary sources, about the science and the mathematics of ancient Egypt and Babylonia, while we known very little indeed, with any degree of certainty, about these fields of study in ancient India and China.

Now it is the nature, rather than the content, of this early pre-Hellenistic mathematics that concerns us here. In this regard, it is important to note that, outside of very simple considerations, the mathematical relations employed by the Egyp-tians and the Babylonians resulted essentially from "trial and error" methods. In other words, the earliest mathematics was little more than a collection of rule-of-thumb procedures that gave numerical results of sufficient acceptability for the needs of these early civilizations. Nowhere in pre-Hellenistic mathematics do we find a single instance of what we today call a logical demonstration. In place of an argument we find a process illustrated by a large number of specific numerical cases. In short, we are instructed to "do thus and so," the apparent purpose of the instructions being to teach, by repetition and gradual introduction of complexities, certain empirically discovered procedures.

Greek Mathematics and the Introduction of Deductive Procedures.—The next important contribution to the development of mathematics came from the Greeks. The origin of early Greek mathematics is obscured by the greatness of Euclid's *Elements,* written about 300 B.C., for this work so superseded all preceding Greek writings on mathematics that the earlier works were thenceforth discarded. The debt of Greek mathematics to ancient Oriental mathematics is difficult to evaluate; that it is considerably greater than was formerly believed became evident with the 20th century researches on Babylonian and Egyptian records. But, whatever the strength of the historical connection between Greek and ancient Oriental mathematics may be, the Greeks transformed the subject into something vastly different from the set of empirical conclusions worked out by their predecessors. For the Greeks insisted that mathematical facts must be established not by empirical procedures but by deductive reasoning. It is difficult to account for this completely new viewpoint on mathematical method, and explanations based on psychological, economic, racial, and other grounds have been offered.

It is disappointing that, unlike the case of ancient Egyptian and Babylonian mathematics, there exist virtually no primary sources for the study of early Greek mathematics. We are forced to rely upon manuscripts and accounts that are dated several hundred years after the original treatments had been written. In spite of this, scholars of classicism have been able to build up a rather consistent, though somewhat hypothetical, account of the history of early Greek mathematics, and even have reasonably restored many of the original Greek texts.

According to Proclus' *Eudemian Summary,* written in the 5th century A.D., Greek mathematics essentially started with the work of Thales of Miletus in the first half of the 6th century B.C., and was then further purified by the later work of Pythagoras (fl. 530 B.C.) and his followers. At any rate, somewhere between the time of Thales in 600 B.C. and Euclid in 300 B.C. there was developed the notion of a logical discourse as a sequence of statements, obtained by deductive reasoning from a given set of initial statements assumed at the start of the discourse. The method, which neatly systematizes any body of knowledge to which it is applied, may be roughly described in its Greek form as follows: First, explanations of certain primitive technical terms of the discourse are given, the intention being to suggest to the reader what is to be meant by these primitive terms. Next, certain primitive propositions that concern the primitive terms, and that are felt to be acceptable as immediately true on the basis of the properties suggested by the initial explanations, are taken as *axioms* or *postulates* of the discourse. All the other technical terms of the discourse are defined by means of the primitive ones, and all the other propositions of the discourse are deduced by logic from the axioms or postulates. This method of developing a subject has become known as the method of *material axiomatics,* and certainly the most outstanding contribution of the early Greeks to mathematics was the formulation of and insistence upon axiomatic procedure.

By the middle of the 4th century B.C., the method had been fairly well developed, for in the *Analytica posteriora* by Aristotle (384–322 B.C.) we find much light thrown upon some of its features. By the turn of the century, the stage was set for Euclid's magnificent and epoch-making application of the method. Although Greek mathematics is largely geometrical in content, there is also in it a good deal of number theory, geometrical algebra, and trigonometry.

Transition from Ancient to Modern Times.—The glorious era of Greek mathematics, after reaching its peak with Euclid, Archimedes, and Apollonius of Perga, in the 3d century B.C., suffered a slow decline, and finally, about 400 A.D., faded away with the general breakup of ancient society. The long and sterile period known as the Dark Ages settled over Europe. During these centuries of low ebb in Western civilization, the major custodians of mathematics became first the Hindus and then the Arabs. However, the Greek concept of rigorous thinking, in fact, the very idea of proof, seemed distasteful to the Hindus. Although they excelled in computation, contributed to the devices of algebra, and played an important role in developing our present positional numeral system, they produced nothing of importance so far as basic methodology is concerned. Hindu mathematics of this period is largely empirical.

It was during Europe's Dark Ages that the Muslim culture traveled its spectacular orbit. Within a century of Mohammed's flight from Mecca to Medina, in 622 A.D., religious fervor, augmented by force of arms, had extended Moslem rule and influence over a territory reaching from India to Spain. Of considerable importance for the preservation of much of world learning was the manner in which the Arabs seized upon Greek and Hindu erudition. Numerous Hindu and Greek works in astronomy, medicine, and mathematics were industriously translated into Arabic and thus saved for later European scholars to retranslate into Latin and other languages.

It was not until the latter part of the 11th century that Greek classics in science and mathematics began to filter into Europe. The 12th century, from the point of view of mathematics, was largely a century of translators. The 13th century saw the introduction into Europe of the Hindu-Arabic number system and the rise of the early universities. The 14th century, the century of the Black Death and the start of the Hundred Years' War, was a mathematically barren one. The 15th century witnessed the beginning of the European Renaissance in art and learning. About the middle of the century, printing was invented and revolutionized the book trade, enabling knowledge to be disseminated at an unprecedented rate. During this century and the next, arithmetic, algebra, and trigonometry made forward strides under the practical influence of trade, navigation, astronomy, and surveying.

By the advent of the 17th century, the content of mathematics had increased considerably, and during that century a surprising number of new fields in the subject were opened up for investigation. It was during the 17th century that John Napier revealed his invention of logarithms; Galileo Galilei founded the science of dynamics; Johannes Kepler induced his laws of planetary motion; Gérard Desargues and Blaise Pascal formulated projective geometry; René Descartes launched modern analytic geometry; Pierre de Fermat laid the foundations of modern number theory; Pascal, Fermat, and Christiaan Huygens made distinguished contributions to the theory of probability; and, most important of all, toward the end of the century, Isaac Newton and Gottfried Wilhelm von Leibniz created the calculus.

The calculus, aided by analytic geometry, proved to be astonishingly powerful and capable of attacking hosts of problems that had been baffling and quite unassailable in earlier days. So attractive for research was this new field that it may be said, with a fair element of truth, that mathematically the 18th century was largely spent in exploiting the new tool. The era of modern mathematics had begun.

Here the path of our story must divide. After considering an important advance in the development of the nature of mathematics that occurred in the early part of the 19th century, and which was brought about by two significant events, one in geometry and one in algebra, we shall return to the story of the calculus and the part it played in molding the basic character of mathematics.

Liberation of Geometry.—Euclid had developed his *Elements* from initial postulates, one of which, the so-called *parallel postulate,* lacking the terseness, clarity, and seeming self-evidence of the others, was early called into question. Even in Greek times, unsuccessful efforts had been made to remove the objectionable postulate by deducing it from the other postulates. After the European revival of geometry following the Dark Ages, researchers returned to the elusive problem, but with no more success than had been achieved in earlier times.

Then, in a tract published in 1733, the Italian, Girolamo Saccheri, hit upon the brilliant idea of trying to establish the parallel postulate from the other postulates by an application of the method of *reductio ad absurdum.* In gist, Saccheri's idea was to deny the parallel postulate (actually an equivalent of it) and then, from this denial and the remaining postulates, to try to deduce a pair of contradictory statements. The success of such a venture would prove that the denial of the parallel postulate is untenable, and that therefore the parallel postulate must hold. In his eagerness to achieve his goal, Saccheri finally forced the desired result by some lame arguments, and thus missed the honor of becoming the first discoverer of a non-Euclidean geometry.

The bestowal of this honor awaited about a hundred years, when the Russian Nikolai Ivanovich Lobachevsky in 1829 and the Hungarian Johann Bolyai in 1832, unknown to one another, each independently discovered a non-Euclidean geometry. These men followed lines similar to those inaugurated by Saccheri, but, unlike Saccheri, they boldly asserted that they had reached no contradiction and believed that none could be reached. It took unusual imagination to entertain the possibility of a geometry different from Euclid's, for the human mind had for two millenniums been bound by the prejudice of tradition to the firm belief that Euclid's geometry was most certainly the only conceivable one.

Liberation of Algebra.—At approximately the same time that non-Euclidean geometry was discovered, a similar event occurred in the realm of algebra. In the early 19th century, algebra was considered as simply symbolized arithmetic, and it seemed inconceivable that there could exist an algebra different from this algebra of ordinary arithmetic. To attempt, for example, the construction of a consistent algebra in which the commutative law of multiplication $(a \times b = b \times a)$ fails to hold, not only probably did not occur to anyone of the time, but had it occurred it would surely have been dismissed as a purely ridiculous idea.

Such was the feeling about algebra when, in 1843, after years of cogitation, the Irish mathematician William Rowan Hamilton was led, by physical considerations, to invent his quaternion algebra in which the commutative law of multiplication does not hold. In the following year, 1844, the German mathematician Hermann Günther Grassmann published the first edition of his remarkable *Ausdehnungslehre,* in which he developed classes of algebras of much greater generality than Hamilton's quaternion algebra. By weakening or deleting various of the laws of common algebra, or by replacing some of the laws by others that also are consistent with the remaining ones, an enormous variety of algebraic structures can be created. It was by developing algebras satisfying different laws than those obeyed by common algebra that Hamilton and Grassmann opened the floodgates of modern abstract algebra.

Rise of Formal Axiomatics.—The discovery of a non-Euclidean geometry and a noncommutative algebra led ultimately to a tremendous increase in the content of mathematics. Freed from the bonds of tradition, mathematicians commenced to create and explore scores of new geometries and algebras.

But perhaps more important than this increase in the content of mathematics was the metamorphosis that took place in the nature of the subject. It became apparent that, so far as the mathematician is concerned, the postulates of a branch of mathematics can be regarded as mere hypotheses whose physical truth or falsity need not concern him; the mathematician may take his postulates to suit his pleasure, so long as they are consistent with one another. Whereas it had been customary to think of the objects that interpret the primitive terms of an axiomatic discourse as being known prior to the postulates, now the postulates came to be regarded as prior to any assignment of meaning to the primitive terms. This new viewpoint of the axiomatic method has become known as *formal axiomatics,* in contrast to the *material axiomatics* of earlier times. In a formal axiomatic treatment, the primitive terms have no meaning whatever except that implied by the postulates, and the postulates have nothing to do with "self-evidence" or "truth."

Many mathematicians have come to regard any discourse conducted by formal axiomatics as a *branch of pure mathematics.* If, for the primitive terms in such a postulational discourse, we substitute terms of definite meaning that convert the postulates into true statements about these terms, then we have an *interpretation* of the postulate system. Such an interpretation will also, if the reasoning has been valid, convert the derived statements into true statements. Such an evaluation of a branch of pure mathematics has been called a *branch of applied mathematics.* Clearly, a given branch of pure mathematics may possess many interpretations, and may thus lead to many branches of applied mathematics.

The notion of pure mathematics as an assemblage of formal axiomatic developments gives considerable sense to the famous facetious statement of Bertrand Russell (1872–) that "mathematics may be defined as the subject in which we never know what we are talking about, nor whether what we are saying is true." It also accords with the remark of (Jules) Henri Poincaré (1854–1912) that "mathematics is the giving of the same name to different things," and with the definition offered by Benjamin Peirce (1809–1880) that "mathematics is the science which draws necessary conclusions," and with the aphorism of Georg Cantor (1845–1918) that "the essence of mathematics lies in its freedom."

Formal axiomatics was first developed systematically by David Hilbert (1862–1943) in his famous *Grundlagen der Geometrie* (1899). This work did much to clarify the essentially hypothetico-deductive character of mathematics.

Calculus and the Arithmetization of Analysis.—Mathematicians have divided the great bulk of present-day mathematics into three large categories: geometry, algebra, and analysis. It is not always easy to place a given branch of mathematics unfalteringly into one of these categories, for the categories lack clearcut definitions. Nevertheless, most branches of mathematics seem to have ultimate parenthood in either Euclidean geometry, symbolized arithmetic, or the limit processes of the calculus, and can, from this point of view, be classified as above. We have noted the contributions to the development of the nature of mathematics made by the two categories of geometry and algebra. We now consider the effect of the category of analysis on this development.

Of the many remarkable mathematical discoveries made in the 17th century, unquestionably the most outstanding was the invention of the calculus. But when the theory of a mathematical operation is only poorly understood, there is the danger that the operation will be applied in a naively formal and perhaps illogical manner. This is essentially what happened to analysis during the century following the invention of the calculus. Attracted by the powerful applicability of the subject, and lacking a real understanding of the basic principles upon which the subject rests, mathematicians, even of the caliber of the great Swiss mathematician Leonhard Euler (1707–1783), manipulated analytical processes in an almost blind manner, often being guided only by a native intuition of what was felt to be valid. A gradual accumulation of absurdities resulted, until, as a natural reaction to the uncritical employment of intuition and formal manipulation, some conscientious mathematicians felt bound to attempt the difficult task of establishing a rigid foundation under the subject.

The earliest mathematician of the first rank actually to attempt a rigorous treatment of analysis was the Italian-born mathematician Joseph Louis Lagrange, whose effort, published in 1797, was far from successful. A great forward stride was made in 1821, when the French mathematician Augustin Louis Cauchy developed an acceptable theory of limits, and then defined continuity, differentiability, and the definite integral in terms of the limit concept. But the demand for an even deeper understanding of the foundation of analysis was startlingly brought to light in 1874, when the German mathematician Karl Theodor Weierstrass (1815–1897) exhibited an example of a continuous function having no derivative, or, what is the same thing, a continuous curve possessing no tangent at any of its points. This example dealt a severe blow to the employment of geometric intuition in analytical studies. Further examples revealed that beneath everything there still lay properties of the real number system that required clearer understanding. Accordingly, Weierstrass advocated a program wherein the real number system itself should first be made rigorous, and then all the basic concepts of analysis should be derived from this number system. This remarkable program, known as the *arithmetization of analysis,* proved to be intricate and difficult to carry out, but by the advent of the 20th century it had been essentially realized by Weierstrass and his followers.

The establishment of the real number system as a foundation for analysis turned out to be a far-reaching accomplishment. Euclidean geometry, through its Cartesian interpretation, can also be made to rest upon the real number system, and mathematicians have shown that most other branches of geometry are consistent if Euclidean geometry is consistent. Again, since the real number system or some part of it, can serve for interpreting so many branches of algebra, it appears that the consistency of much of algebra can also be made to depend upon that of the real number system. In short, the success of Weierstrass's program established the real number system as a foundation for the bulk of existing mathematics, and most of mathematics can be deduced from a set of postulates for the real number system.

Philosophies of Mathematics.—The arithmetization of analysis, along with the axiomatic method, led, in the 20th century, to the formulation of a number of philosophies of mathematics that endeavor to throw light on the fundamental nature of the subject. Thus there is the so-called *logistic thesis,* which claims that mathematics is a branch of logic, and which arises naturally from the effort to base the foundation of mathematics on as deep a level as possible. We have noted that the arithmetization of analysis established this foundation in the real number system. From here mathematicians pushed it back to the natural number system, and thence to set theory. Since set theory is an essential part of logic, the idea of reducing mathematics to logic suggests itself. The monumental *Principia Mathematica* (1910–1913) of Alfred North Whitehead (1861–1947) and Bertrand Russell is the definitive expression of the logistic school.

In contrast to the logistic thesis is the so-called *intuitionist thesis,* which holds that at the very base of mathematics lies a primitive intuition, allied, no doubt, to our temporal sense of before and after, which allows us to conceive a single object, then one more, and so on endlessly. In this way we obtain unending sequences, the best known of which is the sequence of natural numbers. From this initial basic sequence of natural numbers, other mathematical objects are built in a purely constructive manner and in a finite number of steps or operations. The intuitionist school (as a school) originated about 1908 with the Dutch mathematician Luitzen Egbertus Jan Brouwer (1881–   ) of the University of Amsterdam.

Again, there is the so-called *formalist thesis,* which regards mathematics as a collection of formal axiomatic systems, in which the terms are mere symbols and the statements are formulas involving these symbols. Thus, according to this thesis, the ultimate base of mathematics does not lie in logic or in the sequence of natural numbers, but in a collection of prelogical marks and a set of operations with these marks. The formalist school was founded by Hilbert and was developed by him and his co-workers shortly after 1920.

As a concluding point of interest, we recall that a mathematical theory results from the interplay of two factors: a set of postulates and a logic. The set of postulates constitutes the basis from which the theory starts, and the logic constitutes the rules by which such a basis may be expanded into a body of theorems. For some time, mathematicians had been aware of the variability of the first factor, namely the postulates, but up to 1921 the second factor, namely the logic, was universally thought to be absolute and immutable. The construction of a three-valued logic by Jan Lukasiewicz in 1921, and the subsequent construction of other non-Aristotelian logics, opened up the intriguing possibility of also varying the logical factor of a mathematical theory. Mathematics emerges as a highly arbitrary creation of the human mind, and certainly not as something dictated to us of necessity by the world in which we live. See also ALGEBRA; ARITHMETIC; GEOMETRY; NEW MATHEMATICS; TRIGONOMETRY; and articles on other branches of mathematics.

Bibliography.—Heath, Thomas L., *History of Greek Mathematics* (New York 1921); Russell, Bertrand, *Principles of Mathematics,* 2d ed. (New York 1938); Black, Max, *The Nature of Mathematics, a Critical Survey* (New York 1950); Bell, Eric Temple, *Mathematics, Queen and Servant of Science* (New York 1951); Neugebauer, Otto, *The Exact Sciences in Antiquity* (Princeton, N.J., 1957); Newman, James R., *The World of Mathematics,* 4 vols. (New York 1960); Hogben, Lancelot, *Mathematics in the Making* (New York 1960); Kline, Morris, *Mathematics and the Physical World* (New York 1963); Marks, Robert W., ed., *The Growth of Mathematics* (New York 1964); Eves, Howard W., and Newsom, Carroll V., *An Introduction to the Foundations and Fundamental Concepts of Mathematics,* rev. ed. New York 1965).

HOWARD W. EVES,
Professor of Mathematics, University of Maine.

MATHEMATICS, New. See NEW MATHEMATICS.

MATHER, măth′ẽr, **Cotton,** American colonial divine, son of Increase Mather (q.v.): b. Boston Mass., Feb. 12, 1663; d. there, Feb. 13, 1728. He graduated from Harvard in 1678, took his M.A. in 1681, and in 1685 became his father's colleague at the Second Church in Boston, where he served until his death. He was active in the rebellion in 1689 against Sir Edmund Andros, royal governor of Massachusetts, and wrote the manifesto of the insurgents. He vigorously defended the new Massachusetts charter of 1691 and supported Sir William Phips, who had been appointed governor by King William III at the request of Increase Mather. During the witchcraft excitement of 1692, Cotton Mather wrote the ministers' statement exhorting the judges to be cautious in their use of "spectral evidence" against the accused and he believed that "witches" might better be treated by prayer and fasting than by punitive legal action. In spite of this, Mather's popular reputation is that of a fomenter of the witchcraft hysteria who rejoiced in the trials and the executions. He was ardently interested in what he believed to be witchcraft and his writing and preaching may have stimulated the hysterical fear of "witches" revealed at Salem in 1692. In writing about the trials he defended the judges and their procedure more than seems consistent with his earlier warnings against "spectral evidence." He may have been too deferential to the judges in order to win their favor and he was no doubt unwise in helping to keep the witchcraft excitement alive, but the idea that he was a ruthless tormenter of the innocent is not justified by the evidence, whereas it is clear that if the court had paid more attention to his advice some lives might have been saved. The witchcraft trials ended before he was 30; most of the achievements which made him the most famous of American Puritans came later.

Renowned as a preacher, man of letters, scientist, and scholar in many fields, he read widely and wrote more than 450 books. The most celebrated is the *Magnalia Christi Americana* (1702), an "ecclesiastical" history of New England and the most important literary and scholarly work produced in the American colonies during their first century. It shows an amazing range of erudition and considerable stylistic skill. Mather's interest in science is revealed principally in other books, notably *The Christian Philosopher* (1721). He admired Sir Isaac Newton, advocated inoculation for smallpox when it was generally regarded as a dangerous and godless practice, and wrote one of the earliest known descriptions of plant hybridization. He was one of the few American colonists elected to the Royal Society of London, corresponded with foreign scholars, and was probably better known internationally than any of his countrymen before Jonathan Edwards and Benjamin Franklin. He was vain, ambitious, and hot tempered, and sometimes a pedant, but had genuine piety and worked tirelessly for moral reform. His tolerance increased with age and his later thinking moved somewhat away from the strict Puritan orthodoxy of the 17th century toward the rationalistic and deistic ideas of the 18th.

Bibliography.—There is no complete biography of Cotton Mather. The best brief life is Wendell, Barrett, *Cotton Mather* (Cambridge, Mass., 1926). Holmes, Thomas J. *Cotton Mather: A Bibliography* (Cambridge, Mass., 1940) describes each of his works. His diaries were edited by Worthington Chauncey Ford (Boston 1921–22). Beall, Otho T., and Shryock, Richard Harrison, *Cotton Mather: First Significant Figure in American Medicine* (Baltimore 1954) contains valuable information on his scientific activities and references to other works dealing with them.

KENNETH B. MURDOCK,
Professor of English Literature, Harvard University.

MATHER, Increase, American colonial divine, son of Richard Mather and father of Cotton Mather (qq.v.): b. Dorchester, Mass., June 21, 1639; d. Boston, Aug. 23, 1723. He graduated from Harvard in 1656 and took his M.A. at Trinity College, Dublin, in 1658. He preached in Guernsey and in England but in 1661, after the restoration of King Charles II, returned to Boston. He became teacher of the Second Church in 1664. He was chosen a fellow of Harvard in 1674 and in 1685 took the presidency, with the title of Rector. He held that office until 1701. In 1688 he went to England to appeal to James II on behalf of some of the New England churches for the restoration of the Massachusetts charter revoked by Charles II. Supported by some prominent nonconformists and others with political influence he pleaded his case before both James II and William III. In 1690 he was officially appointed one of Massachusetts' four diplomatic agents in London. Their attempt to win back the charter failed. William offered a new one which deprived the colonists of their right to elect their own governor and abolished the restriction of the franchise to church members, but preserved most of the powers of the elected Massachusetts Assembly. Two of the agents opposed the new charter but Mather accepted it and was given by the king the privilege of naming the royal governor and the other officers to be appointed for the first year of the new government. He chose Sir William Phips as governor and, in May 1692, returned with him to Boston.

At the time of the witchcraft hysteria at Salem, Mather joined with other ministers in urging the judges who were trying the suspected witches to be cautious in giving weight to "spectral evidence" which, he believed, might jeopardize the innocent. He also wrote, at the request of the Cambridge association of ministers, and read before that group in October 1692, a more elaborate argument against relying on "spectral evidence" as proof of guilt. In this he declared that it was better to let 10 suspected witches escape than to condemn 1 innocent person. The document was published with the approval of the association as *Cases of Conscience Concerning Evil Spirits* (1693). Phips was impressed by it and it helped to bring about the ending of the witch trials. After 1692 Mather's political influence waned but he continued to be powerful in the churches and was recognized as one of the foremost colonial Puritans of his time. He was a diligent scholar and printed more than 100 books and pamphlets. He started a scientific society in Boston in 1683, encouraged scientific study at Harvard, and advocated inoculation for smallpox in the face of opposition from doctors and laymen.

The only detailed biography is Murdock, Kenneth B., *Increase Mather* (Cambridge, Mass., 1925). Holmes, Thomas J., *Increase Mather: A Bibliography* (Cleveland 1931) gives full descriptions of Mather's writings.

KENNETH B. MURDOCK,
Professor of English Literature, Harvard University.

MATHER, Richard, American colonial divine: b. Lowton, Lancashire, England, 1596; d. Dorchester, Mass., April 22, 1669. After studying at Brasenose College, Oxford, he was ordained as minister at Toxteth Park, Lancashire, was suspended in 1633 because of his Puritanism, and in 1635 emigrated to Massachusetts where, from 1636 until his death, he was "teacher" of the Dorchester church. He was one of the authors of the famous *Bay Psalm Book* (1640, q.v.) and wrote the original draft of the *Cambridge Platform,* which, somewhat revised, was published as *A Platform of Church Discipline* (1649) and was for years the standard statement of Congregational doctrine and polity in New England. This and his other writing and his preaching made him a leader among the Puritan founders of Massachusetts. His son, Increase Mather (q.v.), wrote a brief life of him, first printed in 1670 and reprinted in Dorchester in 1850.

KENNETH B. MURDOCK.

MATHEW, măth'ū, **Theobald** (called FATHER MATHEW), Irish temperance reformer:

b. near Cashel, Tipperary, Ireland, Oct. 10, 1790; d. Queenstown, Cork, Dec. 8, 1856. He was educated at St. Canica's Academy, Kilkenny, and at Maynooth College, joined the Friars Minor Capuchins in 1808 and was ordained priest six years later. He did parochial work in Cork for almost 25 years, becoming provincial of the Irish Capuchins in 1828 and Commissary Apostolic in 1841.

The temperance campaign which made him internationally famous began in 1838 in Ireland. After great success in Ireland he made extensive and prolonged tours of England, Scotland, and, from 1849 to 1851, the United States, where he is said to have given the pledge to more than 600,000 people. The organizations known as the Catholic Total Abstinence Union of America and the Pioneers of Eire resulted largely from the momentum generated by his campaign. In all he pledged some seven million persons to abstinence and saw the consumption of alcohol in his native land, as reflected by the duties on imports of liquor, substantially reduced. He was less successful in financing his work and spent some time in prison for debt in 1847 before being granted a small pension by Queen Victoria.

MATHEWS, măth′ūz, **Shailer,** American educator and editor: b. Portland, Me., May 26, 1863; d. Chicago, Ill., Oct. 23, 1941. A graduate of Colby College and the Newton Theological Seminary, he taught rhetoric and history at Colby from 1889 until 1894, when he joined the staff of the University of Chicago. From 1906 until retirement in 1933 he was professor of history and theology at Chicago, and was dean of the Divinity School from 1908. He headed the Federal Council of the Churches of Christ (1912–1916) and the Chicago Church Federation (1929–1932), lectured extensively in the United States and Asia, edited *The World Today* (1903–1911) and *The Biblical World* (1913–1920), and wrote a score of books, including *The Social Teachings of Jesus* (1897), *The Faith of Modernism* (1924), and *The New Faith for Old: an Autobiography* (1936). He was a leading exponent of the "social gospel" and the thesis that religious and scientific truths are essentially noncontradictory.

MATHEWSON, măth′ūs-s′n, **Christopher** (known as CHRISTY MATHEWSON), American baseball player: b. Factoryville, Pa., Aug. 12, 1880; d. Saranac Lake, N.Y., Oct. 7, 1925. After playing baseball and football at Bucknell University, he joined the New York Giants in 1900 and became one of the most successful pitchers in the history of the game. A right-hander, he threw a deceptive "fadeaway," an early version of the modern "screwball." Nicknamed "Big Six" after a then famous New York City fire engine, Mathewson pitched no-hit, no-run games in 1901 and 1905, and posted such spectacular season's won-and-lost records as 30-13 (1903), 33-12 (1904), 31-9 (1905), and 37-11 (1908). During a 17-year active career he won 372 games while losing 188 and established the National League strikeout record of 2,499. In his first World Series in 1905, against Connie Mack's Philadelphia Athletics, he pitched three complete games without allowing a run, a feat never duplicated in Series play. He left the Giants in mid-1916 to manage the Cincinnati Reds. While serving in World War I, he was gassed. From 1919 to 1921 he coached the Giants. In 1923 he became president of the Boston Braves, but died of tuberculosis two years later. Mathewson was among the first five players of the modern era selected in 1936 for Baseball's Hall of Fame.

MATILDA, mà-tĭl′dà (also called MAUD), empress of the Holy Roman Empire and queen of England: b. London, England, 1102; d. near Rouen, France, Sept. 10, 1167. Her marriage in 1114 to Emperor Henry V of Germany and the Holy Roman Empire was arranged by her father, King Henry I of England. She was widowed in 1125 and German leadership passed by election to Lothair II, but she was recognized as heiress to the English crown in 1126. Two years later she married Geoffrey Plantagenet of Anjou. Upon her father's death in 1135, her claim to the English succession was contested by Stephen of Blois, who was enthroned by the barons and the Londoners and ruled England until his capture by Matilda's forces in February 1141. Matilda then took the throne, but her harsh rule caused her to be driven out of London in August. In November she was forced to release Stephen, who was crowned again on Christmas Day and fought off all subsequent attempts to dethrone him. In 1148 Matilda left England for Normandy. The eldest of her three sons by Geoffrey became king of England as Henry II in 1154.

MATINS, măt′ĭnz, in churches of the Anglican Communion, the daily office of morning prayer, composed in part of the pre-Reformation offices of Matins and Lauds. In the Roman Catholic Church it is the first part of the Divine Office, with which Lauds are usually associated. See also CANONICAL HOURS.

MATISSE, mà-tēs′, **Henri Émile Benoît,** French artist: b. Le Cateau, near St. Quentin, Picardy, France, Dec. 31, 1869; d. Nice, Nov. 3, 1954. With Pablo Picasso, Henri Matisse has been the leader of 20th century Western art.

Matisse was intended by his parents for the law, but after an illness he turned to painting. He studied in Paris at the Académie Julian and the École des Beaux-Arts, and copied old masters in the Louvre. In 1894 and 1896, Matisse exhibited in the academic Salon Nationale, but afterward he became interested in impressionism and postimpressionism. His interest in the work of Cézanne and in Japanese prints and Near Eastern art led him toward Fauvism. Meanwhile, travels in Corsica and later in North Africa inspired his pure bright palette. From 1904 to 1931 he signed his work "Henri-Matisse" to distinguish it from that of Auguste Matisse, an academic painter.

Matisse had his first one-man show in 1904 at Ambroise Vollard's, and in 1905 he exhibited the controversial *Woman with the Hat* at the Salon d'Automne (1905). In 1905 or 1906 Matisse and his group were called Les Fauves (wild beasts), from which was derived the term Fauvism. Among the most important early Fauvist works of Matisse are *Luxe, Calme, et Volupté* (1904), and *Bonheur de Vivre* (1905–1906). Matisse also made bronzes similar to those of Auguste Rodin.

In 1910, Matisse visited Moscow, where a collector, Sergei Shchukin, had commissioned two large panels, *La Danse* and *La Musique*, now in the Soviet Union. He had a retrospective show in Paris in 1910. He held New York exhibitions in 1908, 1910, and 1912 at Alfred Stieglitz's Photo-Secession Gallery. He also exhibited at the Armory Show, held in New York City in 1913, and in 1915 at the Montross Gallery there.

From 1913 until he moved to Nice, France, in 1917, Matisse painted semiabstract forms in subdued colors. Travels in North Africa introduced Oriental motifs into his work, as in *The Painter's Studio* (1911). His Nice period is noted for intimate and decorative paintings, such as the *French Window at Nice* (1919) and *White Plumes* (1919). This period ended about 1926.

In 1927, Matisse won first prize at Pittsburgh's Carnegie International for *Fruits and Flowers* (1924). Four years later New York's Museum of Modern Art exhibited his work. Matisse produced prolifically—paintings, sculptures, etchings for the poems of Stéphane Mallarmé, cartoons for tapestries, overmantel decorations, designs for glassware, ballet *décors,* and the like. His style became broad and simplified, with calligraphic emphasis; a handsome example of this period is *The Ochre Head* (1937). He became seriously ill in 1940 and was nursed by Franciscan sisters in Lyon. After recovery, he worked in bed, making drawings for books and designs for tapestries. In 1949 he returned to Nice to design murals and stained glass for the Dominican Chapel of the Rosary in Vence.

Matisse was honored by retrospectives held in 1948–1949 in Paris, Philadelphia, Lucerne, and Nice, and in 1951 at the Museum of Modern Art, and in Japan and Germany. By the time of his death,· Matisse had lived long enough to see the revolution in art he helped to launch become the status quo.

Consult Barr, Alfred H., Jr., *Matisse, His Art and His Public* (New York 1951).

ELIZABETH MCCAUSLAND,
Art Historian and Critic.

MATO GROSSO, mȧ'tŏŏ grō'sŏŏ (formerly MATTO GROSSO), state, Brazil, bordering on the countries of Bolivia and Paraguay and covering an area of 484,486 square miles. It is the second largest of the Brazilian states, but one of the least densely populated. A large part of Mato Grosso lies on the central plateau of Brazil, with tropical rain forests in the north and a marshy flood plain in the southwest. The capital is Cuiabá (pop., 1960, 43,112); other major cities are Campo Grande and Corumbá. Mineral resources in the· state are considerable but largely unexploited. Stock raising continues to be the major occupation; rice, beans, tobacco, and sugar are cultivated near the population centers; and maté is gathered in the extreme south of the state. Navigable rivers are the São Lourenço, Cuiabá, Paraná, and Paraguay. The São Paulo-Corumbá Railroad crosses Mato Grosso from east to west. Pop. (1960) 910,262 (including an estimated 400,000 Indians).

MATRIARCHY, mā'trĭ-är-kĭ, or **MATRI-ARCHATE,** mā'trĭ-är-kât, traditionally, any society, state, family, or group of individuals ruled by a woman. Sociologists often distinguish between the two terms, identifying matriarchy as a tribe, clan, or society in which descent is traced matrilineally, that is, through the female line. The Swiss anthropologist Johann Jakob Bachofen (1815–1887) suggested that matriarchal organization was the rule for all societies at a certain primitive stage in their social evolution, but most of his successors have rejected this theory. Though modified matriarchal forms have been found among primitive peoples of the modern era, notably among the Menangkabaus of Sumatra and the Pueblo Indians of North America, and matrilineal descent has been observed in several societies, no full-fledged, "mother-ruled" matriarchy has been discovered.

MATRIX, mā'trĭks. The mathematical theory of matrices has its origin in the theory of determinants (q.v.). Matrices play an important role in many branches of mathematics and in physics, engineering, statistics, and economics.

An $r \times s$ matrix is an array of rs elements arranged in r rows and s columns, as in

$$\mathbf{A} = \begin{pmatrix} a_{11} & a_{12} & . & . & . & a_{1s} \\ a_{21} & a_{22} & . & . & . & a_{2s} \\ . & . & . & . & . & . \\ a_{r1} & a_{r2} & . & . & . & a_{rs} \end{pmatrix}$$

Arthur Cayley (1821–1895) was the first to study matrices systematically. He introduced the name matrix and showed that their behavior is similar to that of single natural numbers. The matrices $\mathbf{A}$ and $\mathbf{B}$ are called equal if they have the same number of rows and the same number of columns, and if the corresponding elements a_{ik} and b_{ik} are equal for each i and k.

Assume that $\mathbf{A}$ and $\mathbf{B}$ are both $r \times s$ matrices. The sum, $\mathbf{S} = \mathbf{A} + \mathbf{B}$, is defined as the matrix with the elements $s_{ik} = a_{ik} + b_{ik}$. The addition of matrices has the same properties as the addition of ordinary numbers. If c is a number, then the product of the matrix $\mathbf{A}$ by the number c is defined as the matrix whose elements are ca_{ik}. This multiplication is called a multiplication of the matrix $\mathbf{A}$ by a scalar. It follows that $\mathbf{A} + \mathbf{A} = 2\mathbf{A}$.

We define the product of two matrices only under the assumption that the number of columns of the first factor equals the number of rows of the second factor. For instance, let $\mathbf{A}$ be an $r \times s$ matrix and $\mathbf{B}$ an $s \times t$ matrix. Then we define the product $\mathbf{P} = \mathbf{AB}$ as the matrix whose elements p_{ik} are the inner product of the ith row of $\mathbf{A}$ and kth column of $\mathbf{B}$, hence

$$p_{ik} = a_{i1}b_{1k} + a_{i2}b_{2k} + \ldots + a_{is}b_{sk}$$
$$(1 \leqq i \leqq r; 1 \leqq k \leqq t).$$

It follows from this definition that the product $\mathbf{BA}$ is defined only if $r = t$. If $\mathbf{A}$ and $\mathbf{B}$ are square matrices of the same order, then $\mathbf{AB}$ and $\mathbf{BA}$ are defined. It is easy to see that the multiplication of matrices is associative and distributive; that is, that $\mathbf{A(BC)} = \mathbf{(AB)C}$ and $\mathbf{A(B + C)} = \mathbf{AB} + \mathbf{AC}$. But it is not always commutative, even if both $\mathbf{AB}$ and $\mathbf{BA}$ are defined. For instance,

$$\begin{pmatrix} 2 & 3 \\ 8 & 4 \end{pmatrix}\begin{pmatrix} 6 & 7 \\ 1 & 5 \end{pmatrix} = \begin{pmatrix} 15 & 29 \\ 52 & 76 \end{pmatrix};$$
$$\begin{pmatrix} 6 & 7 \\ 1 & 5 \end{pmatrix}\begin{pmatrix} 2 & 3 \\ 8 & 4 \end{pmatrix} = \begin{pmatrix} 68 & 46 \\ 42 & 23 \end{pmatrix}.$$

A matrix whose elements are all zero is called a zero or null matrix. While the product of two numbers can vanish only if at least one of the factors vanishes, the product of two matrices $\mathbf{A}$ and $\mathbf{B}$ may be a zero matrix even though neither of the factors is a zero matrix.

A square matrix is called triangular if either all the elements above the main diagonal or all the elements below it are zero. If, moreover, all the off-diagonal elements are zero, then the matrix is called a diagonal matrix. The diagonal matrix of order n whose main diagonal elements equal 1 is called the unit matrix $\mathbf{I}_n$ of order n. If $\mathbf{A}$ is an arbitrary square matrix of order n, then $\mathbf{A}\mathbf{I}_n = \mathbf{I}_n\mathbf{A} = \mathbf{A}$.

If a square matrix $\mathbf{A}$ is multiplied by itself, the product is denoted by $\mathbf{A}^2$. The product of m factors $\mathbf{A}$ is called $\mathbf{A}^m$ or the mth power of $\mathbf{A}$. We call a square matrix singular if its determinant vanishes, otherwise nonsingular. For nonsingular matrices we define also negative powers. The inverse $\mathbf{A}^{-1}$ of the nonsingular matrix $\mathbf{A} = (a_{ik})$, whose determinant is D, is the matrix whose element in the ith row and kth column is $\mathbf{A}_{ki}$ divided by the determinant D, where $\mathbf{A}_{ki}$ is the cofactor of a_{ki} in $\mathbf{A}$; hence

$$\mathbf{A}^{-1} = \begin{pmatrix} \mathbf{A}_{11}/D & \mathbf{A}_{21}/D & \ldots & \mathbf{A}_{n1}/D \\ \mathbf{A}_{12}/D & \mathbf{A}_{22}/D & \ldots & \mathbf{A}_{n2}/D \\ \vdots & & & \vdots \\ \mathbf{A}_{1n}/D & \mathbf{A}_{2n}/D & \ldots & \mathbf{A}_{nn}/D \end{pmatrix}.$$

Moreover, we set $(\mathbf{A}^{-1})^m = \mathbf{A}^{-m}$. Then all the laws of exponents hold for positive and negative powers of matrices, with the exception that $(\mathbf{AB})^m = \mathbf{A}^m\mathbf{B}^m$ only if $\mathbf{A}$ and $\mathbf{B}$ are commutative.

Let us multiply $\mathbf{A}$ and $\mathbf{A}^{-1}$. We have to form the inner product of the ith row of $\mathbf{A}$ and the kth column of $\mathbf{A}^{-1}$ for each i and k. The element p_{ik} of the product becomes

$$p_{ik} = a_{i1}\mathbf{A}_{k1}/D + a_{i2}\mathbf{A}_{k2}/D + \ldots + a_{in}\mathbf{A}_{kn}/D.$$

It follows from equation 17 of the article on determinants that $p_{ik} = 1$ for $i = k$ and $p_{ik} = 0$ for $i \neq k$. Hence $\mathbf{A}\mathbf{A}^{-1} = \mathbf{I}_n = \mathbf{A}^{-1}\mathbf{A}$.

As an application, let us consider the system of n linear equations in n unknowns whose coefficient matrix is the nonsingular matrix A:

$$\begin{aligned} a_{11}x_1 + a_{12}x_2 + & \ldots & + a_{1n}x_n = k_1 \\ a_{21}x_1 + a_{22}x_2 + & \ldots & + a_{2n}x_n = k_2 \\ \vdots & & \vdots \\ a_{n1}x_1 + a_{n2}x_2 + & \ldots & + a_{nn}x_n = k_n \end{aligned}$$

Now let X and K be matrices of n rows and 1 column:

$$X = \begin{pmatrix} x_1 \\ x_2 \\ \vdots \\ \vdots \\ x_n \end{pmatrix}, \qquad K = \begin{pmatrix} k_1 \\ k_2 \\ \vdots \\ \vdots \\ k_n \end{pmatrix}.$$

Then the system of linear equations can be written in short form as AX = K, since the product AX is defined. Equating the corresponding elements of AX and K gives the system of linear equations. If we multiply both sides of the matrix equation AX = K by $\mathbf{A}^{-1}$ on the left-hand side, then we obtain $\mathbf{A}^{-1}$ AX = $\mathbf{I}_n$X = X = $\mathbf{A}^{-1}$K. Equating the elements of the ith row of X and $\mathbf{A}^{-1}$K for each i, we obtain

$$x_i = \mathbf{A}_{1i}k_1/D + \mathbf{A}_{2i}k_2/D + \ldots + \mathbf{A}_{ni}k_i/D.$$

This is the rule of Gabriel Cramer (1704–1752), in which the determinant in the numerator is expanded by the ith column. This short proof shows how useful matrices are.

Let $x_1, x_2, \ldots, x_n$ be n variables. We introduce new variables $y_1, y_2, \ldots, y_n$ and $z_1, z_2, \ldots, z_n$ such that

$$\begin{aligned} y_1 &= b_{11}x_1 + b_{12}x_2 + & \ldots & + b_{1n}x_n \\ y_2 &= b_{21}x_1 + b_{22}x_2 + & \ldots & + b_{2n}x_n \\ & \vdots & & \vdots \\ y_n &= b_{n1}x_1 + b_{n2}x_2 + & \ldots & + b_{nn}x_n \end{aligned}$$

and

$$\begin{aligned} z_1 &= a_{11}y_1 + a_{12}y_2 + & \ldots & + a_{1n}y_n \\ z_2 &= a_{21}y_1 + a_{22}y_2 + & \ldots & + a_{2n}y_n \\ & \vdots & & \vdots \\ z_n &= a_{n1}y_1 + a_{n2}y_2 + & \ldots & + a_{nn}y_n. \end{aligned}$$

If we substitute into the last n equations the values of $y_1, y_2, \ldots, y_n$ from the first system of equations, we see that $z_1, z_2, \ldots, z_n$ are linear functions of $x_1, x_2, \ldots, x_n$. We want to find the coefficients of these linear functions without computation. Since the transformations can be written in matrix form $\mathbf{Y} = \mathbf{BX}$, $\mathbf{Z} = \mathbf{AY}$, we at once obtain $\mathbf{Z} = \mathbf{ABX}$ by substituting the value for $\mathbf{Y}$. Hence the coefficient matrix is the matrix $\mathbf{AB}$.

If in a matrix $\mathbf{A}$ the rows and columns are interchanged, a new matrix is obtained which is called the transpose $\mathbf{A}'$ of $\mathbf{A}$. If $\mathbf{A}' = \mathbf{A}$, then $a_{ik} = a_{ki}$ for every i and k. Such a matrix $\mathbf{A}$ is called symmetric. Similarly, matrices are called skew-symmetric, Hermitian, orthogonal, and stochastic if their determinants are respectively skew-symmetric, Hermitian, orthogonal, and stochastic. A matrix is called positive (nonnegative) if all its elements are positive (nonnegative) numbers.

ALFRED BRAUER,
Professor of Mathematics, University of North Carolina.

Bibliography.—MacDuffee, Cyrus Colton, *The Theory of Matrices*, 2d ed. (New York 1947); Ferrar, William Leonard, *Finite Matrices* (New York 1951); Perlis, Sam, *Theory of Matrices* (Cambridge, Mass., 1951); Wade, Thomas Leonard, *The Algebra of Vectors and Matrices* (Cambridge, Mass., 1951); Aitken, Alexander Craig, *Determinants and Matrices*, 8th ed. (New York 1954); Beaumont, Ross Allen, and Ball, Richard William, *Introduction to Modern Algebra and Matrix Theory* (New York 1954); Zurmühl, Rudolf, *Matrizen*, 2d ed. (Berlin 1958); Browne, Edward Tankard, *Introduction to the Theory of Determinants and Matrices* (Chapel Hill, N.C., 1959); Albert, A. A., *Fundamental Concepts of Higher Algebra* (Chicago 1961); Wedderburn, J. H. M., *Lectures on Matrices* (New York 1964); Eves, Howard, *Elementary Matrix Theory* (Boston 1966).

MATRONALIA, măt-rô-nā'lĭ-à, the 1st of March, the New Year's day of the Roman religious calendar, sacred to Juno.

MATSUDAIRA, mä-tsŏo-dī-rä, the generic name of 52 families of territorial nobles in feudal Japan, mostly, although not all, descended from an ancestor Minamoto Chikauji of the 14th century, 11th in generation from Yoshiie who, in the village of Matsudaira, in Mikawa, espoused the daughter of Matsudaira Nobushige and took his wife's name. When, in Yedo in 1603, the Tokugawa line of shoguns was established, permission was given to the heads of allied or loyal clans to bear his name. Among the hundreds of feudal barons and others thus favored were many of the most illustrious in the period 1603–1867. After the latter date, the name, with the privilege of bearing the ancestral coat of arms, was restricted to 27 families. Their heraldic crest consists of three mallow leaves within a circle.

MATSUDAIRA, Tsuneo, Japanese diplomat and statesman: b. Tokyo, Japan, April 17,

1877; d. there, Nov. 14, 1949. After graduating from the Imperial University (1902), Matsudaira entered his country's diplomatic service, where he held important posts, which included vice minister for foreign affairs (1923); ambassador to the United States (1925–1928) and to Great Britain (1928–1936); and minister of the imperial household (1936–1945). As Japan's delegate to the London Naval Conference (1930), he succeeded in obtaining a higher ratio of naval power for his country. After World War II he was cleared of the charge of war responsibility and in 1947 became president of the House of Councillors. He was noted for his moderate views during the period of Japanese military aggression.

MATSUE, mä-tsŏŏ-ĕ, city, Japan, capital of Shimane Prefecture, 80 miles northeast of Hiroshima. An ancient castle town and inland port in western Honshu near the Sea of Japan, it is the cultural and commercial center of a broad, marshy, yet rich agricultural region. The city has modern facilities, including pleasant resort hotels with gardens lining the shore of Lake Shinji and blending with the traditional atmosphere featured by the small classical castle (c. 1601). Some machinery and food are produced. A Lafcadio Hearn museum commemorates the author's residence in Matsue. Pop. (1965) 110,-534.

MATSUKATA, mä-tsŏŏ-kä-tä, PRINCE **Masayoshi,** Japanese statesman: b. Kagoshima, Japan, 1835; d. Tokyo, July 2, 1924. The son of a samurai, he joined the revolution that overthrew the shogunate in 1867 and after 1874 was concerned with the financial administration of the central government. As minister of finance (1881–1891) he averted economic ruin in Japan after the inflation of 1878–1880 by introducing a currency reform that included the redemption of inconvertible paper money and establishment of the Bank of Japan. (See JAPAN—10. *Financial Development.*) He was twice premier (1891–1892, 1896–1898), holding the portfolio of finance during both terms and from 1898 to 1900. Matsukata was responsible for placing Japanese coinage on the gold standard (1897). He was keeper of the privy seal from 1917 to 1922, and in 1922 was created prince. Japan's economic stabilization in the late 19th century was largely due to his work.

MATSUMOTO, mä-tsŏŏ-mô-tô, city, Japan, in Nagano Prefecture, central Honshu, 110 miles northwest of Tokyo. Lying in a broad agricultural basin surrounded by high mountains, Matsumoto is somewhat isolated; nevertheless it has important silk, textile, machinery, and food industries. Its colorful history is preserved in the unusually old castle (1504) and in many stately feudal dwellings. Pop. (1965) 154,131.

MATSUOKA, mä-tsŏŏ-ô-kä, **Yosuke,** Japanese statesman and businessman: b. Yamaguchi Prefecture, Japan, March 3, 1880; d. Tokyo, June 27, 1946. An intense nationalist, Matsuoka received most of his education in the United States. Director (1920–1926), vice president (1927), and president (1935–1939) of the South Manchurian Railway, he advocated that Japan's business interests were coincidental with an aggressive foreign policy. As delegate to the League of Nations in Geneva (1932), he vigorously defended Japan's Manchurian policy. Upon the League's refusal to recognize Japan's actions, Matsuoka led his delegation out of the League, returning home a hero. Named foreign minister (1940) in Prince Fumimaro Konoye's cabinet, he activated Japan's alliance with the Axis powers, signing the Tripartite Pact with Germany and Italy on Sept. 27, 1940, and the nonaggression pact with the USSR. When Germany attacked Russia (1941), Matsuoka left the cabinet. He was indicted as a war criminal after World War II, but died before being brought to trial.

MATSUSAKA or **MATSUZAKA,** mä-tsŏŏ-zä-kä, city, Japan, in Mie Prefecture, on the Ise Peninsula of south-central Honshu, 59 miles southwest of Nagoya by rail. In the Tokugawa period (1603–1867), Matsusaka grew prosperous as a highway service town for pilgrims. The great financial house of Mitsui originated here. The city contains stockyards and is famous for the quality of its beef. Pop. (1965) 99,814.

MATSUSHIMA, mä-tsŏŏ-shê-mä (Eng. "Pine Island"), scenic area, Japan, in Miyagi Prefecture, on the Pacific coast of northeastern Honshu, about 15 miles northeast of Sendai in Matsushima Bay. One of Japan's "three beauty spots" (*Nihon-sankei*), it is an archipelago of over 800 pine-studded islets whose volcanic foundations have been eroded into an infinite variety of delicate forms. Tourist hotels and other services are provided in the bay-side town of Matsushima (1965 pop. 15,115) and in the important port of Shiogama (58,363) at the bay head. The area produces seed oysters for export and edible seaweed for domestic use. Zuiganji, a Buddhist temple and ideal example of 16th century architecture, has been designated a national treasure.

MATSUYAMA, mä-tsŏŏ-yä-mä, city and port, Japan, capital of Ehime Prefecture, northwestern Shikoku, 43 miles southeast of Hiroshima across the Inland Sea. A former castle town commanding the broad Dogo agricultural plain, it is the chief city of western Shikoku and a conspicuous example of post-World War II reconstruction, with wide streets and a modern commercial core. The imposing castle (1603) has become the center of a spacious public park that houses many handsome buildings and grounds designed by the nation's leading architects. Matsuyama now includes the ports of Takahama and Mitsuhama, as well as Dogoyuno-machi, a famous old spa. It is a vigorous industrial center, specializing in shipbuilding, machinery, textiles, steel, food processing, and most recently petroleum and petrochemicals. Pop. (1965) 282,651.

MATTAWA, măt′à-wô, town, Ontario, Canada, in Nipissing District, on the Ottawa River, 42 miles by road east of North Bay. A fur-trading post in the 18th century, by 1855 it was a center of the lumber industry. Nearby are two large installations of the Ontario Hydro-Electric Commission: the Otto Holden Station a few miles up the Ottawa, and the Des Joachims Station about 50 miles downstream. Veneer and plywood are the chief manufactures. Pop. 3,143.

MATTEOTTI, mät-tä-ôt′tê, **Giacomo,** Italian Socialist leader: b. Fratta Polesine, Italy,

May 22, 1885; d. near Rome, June 10, 1924. An implacable enemy of fascism, Matteotti was abducted and murdered after denouncing the terroristic methods used by the Fascisti, in a speech in the Chamber of Deputies. Evidence involving Prime Minister Benito Mussolini in the crime was suppressed, and national indignation over the affair forced a parliamentary crisis, during which Mussolini was able to consolidate his personal rule. After World War II a new trial was initiated against those involved in the murder. Mussolini, however, was dead, and three of the accomplices, having disappeared, were tried *in absentia*. Sentences of 30 years' imprisonment were pronounced against three defendants, and the remaining four were acquitted.

MATTER, the term used by the physical scientists to designate the things in the world about us. It is sometimes convenient to say that the realm of the physical scientists is matter and radiation. Radiation includes all forms of electromagnetic waves, from the longest radio waves to the shortest gamma rays from radio-active nuclei. We shall note later that this dichotomy may not always be justified—matter has some of the aspects of radiation and radiation has some of the attributes of matter.

Matter is ordinarily said to exist in one of three states, solid, liquid, or gaseous. There is not always a clear distinction between the various states. Water is a liquid and tends to fill the lower part of a container, whatever its shape. A substance such as asphalt, which is often called a solid, in time will flow under the action of gravity and take the shape of its container just as water does. Asphalt or even glass may be called a liquid, since they will, in time, flow or deform under forces. The time required depends on the temperature; at high temperatures the characteristics are those of an ordinary liquid. Substances such as glass or asphalt are said to be amorphous. Another group of solids, for example ice, iron, or diamonds, are crystalline. In crystalline materials the individual atoms are arranged in a definite pattern which is often evident by the regular external form of crystals, such as snowflakes. Solids in the crystalline form generally have sharply defined temperatures at which they melt and become liquids. Amorphous substances change gradually from solid to liquid as the temperature is raised or lowered. There is no definite melting point.

The effects of high pressure on the solid phase are sometimes surprising. Solids that have been stretched beyond a certain limit or distorted severely in shape often do not return to the original length or shape when the distorting applied force is removed; but under a uniformly applied pressure their behavior is different. Almost without exception solids, as well as liquids, return to their initial volume after being compressed. However, some rather startling changes do occur under high pressure. For example, at −22°C. and under a pressure of 2,200 atmospheres, ice abruptly decreases in volume until its density is greater than that of the initial water. As the pressure is again increased, other forms of ice—in fact a total of seven forms—have been observed. The last of these may be heated to the temperature of melting solder without melting, provided the pressure is kept at 45,000 atmospheres.

The properties of matter can in general be described or "explained" in terms of the atomic theory. The behavior and properties of gases are explained more satisfactorily than those of liquids and solids, but an eventual understanding of the behavior of these forms of matter based on the atomic theory appears likely. The evidence for atoms as the basic units of matter is accepted by all. In fact the theories of the structure of the atoms themselves are fairly well established. The number of atoms in any visible speck of matter is beyond our ordinary concepts. For example, if we were able to count the number of atoms in a drop of water at the rate of one million atoms per second, it would require more than 200 million years—probably longer than the time of man on the earth—to complete the task. Atoms are very small, but the nucleus occupies only a tiny fraction of the atomic volume. If the atom in a crystal is enlarged until its volume is that of an ordinary house, the nucleus becomes as large as a pin head. Therefore, it should not be surprising to discover that our ordinary concepts of space, matter, or mass, and perhaps others, no longer are valid in atomic realms.

Classical physics (previous to 1900 A.D.) taught that matter, or more precisely mass, was conserved. Whatever may have happened to a body —as long as no mass was added or subtracted from the body—its mass was unchanged. This principle is called the conservation of mass. Matter was said to be indestructible. In a similar manner, the energy of a system is said to be unchanged unless energy were added to or subtracted from the system by transfer from or to another system. Nothing one could do inside a system would change its total mass or energy.

These statements of conservation apply to relatively few things. For example, the number of people in a country will not remain the same, even though none cross its boundaries. Some die and some are born. The concepts of conservation of energy, as ordinarily interpreted, and of mass since Einstein's contribution are no longer acceptable. The question, "What is matter?" is no longer satisfactorily answered by saying it is the stuff of which atoms are made or that it is measured by the mass of a body. Energy and mass now appear basically to be identical. In fact we state that the total energy of an atom is mc^2 where m is the mass and c is the velocity of light. The term m, however, is not the classical mass, except for bodies at rest with respect to the observer. For a particle having a velocity and hence kinetic energy, we may write $mc^2 = m_o c^2 +$ kinetic energy. Here m_o is called the rest mass, the classical mass of the body. It is the quantity mc^2 which remains constant under all conditions; thus, if by some process (for example, nuclear fission), the rest mass, m_o, of an atomic system is reduced, the kinetic energy of the system will be increased. In the sense that m_o represents the "quantity of matter" in the atom, one can say that matter has been converted into energy. Energy so obtained is now called atomic or nuclear energy. On the other hand, one may also say that energy has mass, and that for the entire system, the mass (m) has not changed. It appears to us as kinetic energy.

In the descriptions given above, the particle or corpuscular nature of atoms has been assumed. One may naïvely say only such particles exhibit the property called mass. But radiation has energy, and if energy (E) and mass are related through the equation $E = mc^2$, should not radiation also have mass ascribed to it? To be consistent, the physicist must assign mass to the photons or corpuscles which describe radiation. Such photons do exert pressure on a surface just as bombarding atoms of a gas exert pressure on the container. Their mass can then be measured, and experiment and theory are in agreement. The rest mass (m_0) of the photons is zero, but the total mass (m) is such that $mc^2 = $ Energy.

The wave theory of light is adequate to locate the energy of radiation, but is not adequate for the description of the transfer of energy to matter. For this the photon or corpuscular theory is required. In a complementary manner, the location of streams of electrons or atoms is best determined by assigning a wave character and a wavelength to the moving particles. The electron microscope is an application of the theory. In designing this instrument the electrons are treated as waves whose wavelength decreases as the velocity of the electrons increases. Thus on the macroscopic scale matter may be treated as distinct from radiation. The properties of solids, liquids, and gases are described without reference to radiation. But on the microscopic scale the properties of matter and radiation merge, and their unity is becoming apparent.

See also ATOM; CRITICAL POINT; ELASTICITY; KINETIC THEORY OF GASES; LIQUEFIED AND COMPRESSED GASES; PARTICLE ACCELERATORS; RELATIVITY; SOLIDIFICATION.

J. W. BUCHTA,
Department of Physics, University of Minnesota.

MATTERHORN, măt′ĕr-hôrn, or **MONT CERVIN,** môn sĕr-văn′, mountain, Switzerland, in the Pennine Alps on the Swiss-Italian border near Zermatt. The fame of this 14,700-foot peak is due less to its height than to its forbidding appearance and to the problems its sheer cliffs have posed for climbers. The best-known expedition was the first successful one, led by Edward Whymper (q.v., July 1865), in which four members of the seven-man party died during the descent, touching off a long controversy as to the cause of the accident. All of the approaches have since been conquered, and some have been made easier by the addition of wire ropes and other aides.

MATTESON, măt′ĕ-s′n, **Tompkins Harrison,** American painter: b. Peterboro, N.Y., May 9, 1813; d. Sherburne, Feb. 2, 1884. Matteson was mostly self-taught, and had little success until the appearance of *The Spirit of '76.* From 1841 to 1850 his studio was in New York City; many of his best pieces were done during this period. After moving to Sherburne (1850), he devoted himself to local politics, and served for a time in the New York legislature. His paintings, which depict American historical and genre scenes, are still widely reproduced. Their historical inaccuracy is compensated by the artist's enthusiastic portrayal of his subject. Included are *Washington Crossing the Delaware; The First Sabbath of the Pilgrims; Eliot Preaching to the Indians; Examination of a Witch;* and *Washington's Inaugural.*

MATTEUCCI, mät-tä-ōōt′chĕ, **Carlo,** Italian physicist: b. Forlì, Italy, June 20, 1811; d. Ardenza, June 25, 1868. Known chiefly for his studies in electrophysiology, Matteucci did notable work in such diverse fields as chemistry, optics, telegraphy, geology, and politics. He was professor of physics at the universities of Bologna (1832), Ravenna (1838), and Pisa (1841); senator in the Tuscan Assembly (1848); member of the Italian Senate and director of telegraph lines (1860); and minister of public instruction (1862). His most significant work was concerned with induction, magnetism, and the effects of electric rays on animal organs. His publications include: *Traité des phénomènes électro-physiologiques des animaux* (1844); *Lezioni sui fenomeni fisico-chimici dei corpi viventi,* 2d ed. (1846).

MATTHESON, mät′ĕ-zôn, **Johann,** German musician, composer, and theorist: b. Hamburg, Germany, Sept. 28, 1681; d. there, April 17, 1764. Music director of the Hamburg Cathedral (1715–1728), Mattheson took an active part in the development of the church cantata, using his talents as composer and writer to effect a more dramatic quality in the sacred music as then performed. He was responsible for the innovation of women singers in church. After 1728 he devoted himself to writing, covering many subjects unrelated to music. His important works, such as *Das neueröffnete Orchester* (1713) and *Der vollkommene Kapellmeister* (1739), are standard sources for the history of music in Hamburg in his day. Mattheson composed 8 operas, 24 oratorios and cantatas, and much sacred and instrumental music.

Consult Cannon, Beekman, C., *Johann Mattheson: Spectator in Music* (New Haven 1947).

MATTHEW, măth′ū, SAINT, apostle of Jesus Christ and traditionally author of the first Gospel. His name stands seventh in the lists of disciples in the Gospels of Mark and Luke, eighth in Matthew and the Book of Acts. Matthew 10:3 calls him the "publican" or tax collector, and according to 9:9 he was at the tax office when Jesus called him. Presumably he was an employee of the tetrarchy of Galilee under Herod Antipas and worked near Capernaum at a border station on the highway that ran from Egypt through Palestine to Damascus. Tax collectors, whether directly in Roman employ or not, were despised by the public.

Mark 2:14, however, gives the name of Levi the son of Alphaeus to the man called at the tax office, and some manuscripts of Mark call him James the son of Alphaeus. Since Matthew and James the son of Alphaeus stand together in Matthew's list, it has been conjectured that the phrase "the publican" has been attached to the wrong name. Matthew and Levi are often thought to be the same person; but while Jews often had two names—a Jewish and a Greek name such as Saul and Paul, or a designation such as Simon the Tanner—it would be unusual for a man to have two Semitic given names. He might, of course, have been not "Matthew Levi" but "Matthew the Levite."

Certainly Matthew's name has always been attached to the first Gospel, and the heading "according to Matthew" at least affirms that it is based on tradition going back to this disciple. The earliest ecclesiastical tradition, that of Papias of Hierapolis (about 135 A.D.), says that "Matthew wrote up the oracles of the Lord in the Hebrew language, and everyone interpreted them as he was able," but it is not agreed whether Papias referred to the Gospel itself or to one of its sources. (See MATTHEW, GOSPEL ACCORDING TO.) Varying accounts of the apostolic labors of Matthew in

Macedonia, Egypt, Ethiopia, and Parthia were current in the early church, and he has been regarded by the western church as a martyr, but such traditions are late and cannot be verified.

SHERMAN E. JOHNSON,
Dean, Church Divinity School of the Pacific.

MATTHEW, Gospel According to. This Gospel, which bears the name of one of Jesus' twelve disciples, stands first in the modern canon of the New Testament and has almost always had that position. From the time of its first publication it has been the most popular of the Gospels, being quoted more frequently by the church fathers and used in worship more extensively than the others. This pre-eminence is no doubt due to the fact that it includes nearly all of Mark's narrative, adds to it stories of the birth and resurrection appearances, and gives a much fuller account of Jesus' teaching. It is, furthermore, conveniently arranged and was particularly useful to the early church because of its appeal to Old Testament prophecy.

Contents.—Matthew follows in the main the chronological outline of Mark, the earliest Gospel, but rearranges the incidents somewhat to make them fit his topical scheme, so that the groups of sayings and narratives illustrate and reinforce one another. The Gospel can be regarded as composed of five (possibly six) "books" or major sections, plus a prologue and an epilogue, thus: Prologue, The Birth and Infancy (1:1—2:23); Book I, Discipleship, narrative (3:1—4:25), discourse (5:1—7:29); Book II, The Training of an Apostle, narrative (8:1—10:4), discourse (10:5—11:1); Book III, The Secret Revelation, narrative (11:2—12:50), discourse (13:1–53); Book IV, Founding of the Church, narrative (13:54—17:27), discourse (18:1—19:2); Book V, The Judgment, narrative (19:3—22:46), discourse in two parts, (a) Against the Pharisees (23:1–39) and (b) The Last Judgment (24:1—26:2); Epilogue, The Passion and Resurrection (26:3—28:10).

It will be noted that each of the five books concludes with some such formula as "It came to pass that when Jesus had finished these words . . . ." There may be some connection between this fivefold scheme and the fact that Papias of Hierapolis (early 2d century), the first ecclesiastical writer to mention Matthew, wrote an *Interpretation of the Oracles of the Lord* in five books. There are indications that Matthew was fond of numerical schemes, perhaps as an aid to memory. As in Mark, material is often arranged in triplets. The genealogy is organized in three groups of 14 generations each (in contrast to Luke's genealogy). In chapters 8 and 9 there are three miracles of power followed by three of restoration. The expression "Woe to you" occurs seven times in chapter 23.

Purpose.—The general purpose of all the Gospels was to proclaim the good news of salvation through Jesus Christ and to awaken faith in him and in the new revelation. In order to serve this purpose they were apparently designed as manuals for teachers and new converts. Certain subsidiary motives can also be discerned in Matthew: .

(1) The evangelist thinks of Christianity as a new Law fulfilling that of the Old Testament—thus he is more conservatively Jewish in his approach than the Apostle Paul—and he collects various sayings of Jesus into the Sermon on the Mount (chapters 5 through 7) as a summary of this new Law.

(2) He writes at a time when the church is becoming more organized and must take practical decisions on moral questions facing its members. Therefore he includes sayings that exalt the authority of the apostles and of the church itself, and pictures Peter as the ideal rabbi whose decisions can be depended upon. Chapter 18 is largely devoted to church discipline.

(3) More than any other evangelist he emphasizes the authority of the Old Testament and its direct applicability to Christianity, often quoting it with such a phrase as "This came to pass that it might be fulfilled which was spoken." Jesus is claimed to be the Messiah son of David promised to the Jewish people.

(4) Passages in Mark which might cause theological difficulty or minimize respect to the apostles are often carefully edited to remove the difficulty.

(5) Many early Christians believed that the end of the present age would come in their own generation. As time passed there was danger that "the love of many will grow cold" (24:12) and that people would desert the new faith. Matthew carefully emphasized the hope of the new age. The final words of Jesus (28:18–20) sum up the specific message of this Gospel.

Sources.—It is still occasionally argued that Matthew is the earliest Gospel and the source of for Mark and Luke—in this case Matthew's sources would be mainly oral, or the Gospel the direct account of an eyewitness—or that there was an earlier Gospel which Matthew expanded and Mark abbreviated. But the prevailing opinion is that the two principal sources of Matthew were Mark and a sayings document called the Logia (or, more commonly, Q), which was also used by Luke. Matthew used practically all of Mark, and knew that Gospel in a form nearly identical with that which we now possess. Q seems to have been a document with a definite order, though Matthew and Luke may have had different forms of it. In addition, Matthew contains numerous sayings not found elsewhere which are much more conservatively Jewish than other sayings ascribed to Jesus. Since this material includes interesting parallels to the Dead Sea or Qumran scrolls (see SCROLLS, THE DEAD SEA), it may have been collected in Jerusalem or elsewhere in Palestine.

Certain other materials, such as chapters 1 and 2, are so completely in the evangelist's own style that he must have composed them from oral tradition. Further than this it is difficult to go, since the evangelists exercised the prerogatives of individual authors and did not simply copy their materials. (See also GOSPELS.)

Authorship.—If the foregoing judgments are correct, it is difficult to think of our present Gospel as the composition of an original apostle. It seems better to regard the title "According to Matthew" as referring to a special tradition embedded in the Gospel. Some students have thought of Matthew as the original collector of Q, but since Luke also used Q, Matthew may be the ultimate authority for the special materials which are so Jewish in their tendency. Such a man may have been one of the Twelve. (See MATTHEW, SAINT.)

Papias, the first Christian writer to mention the Gospel, may have thought of Matthew as the author of the complete Gospel. In any case he believed that Matthew had written in Hebrew (possibly meaning Aramaic, the vernacular of

Palestine). It is hard to accept Papias' tradition if it refers to the entire Gospel, since Matthew and Luke show clear signs of having used the Greek Mark, and those who affirm the tradition are driven to suppose that the man who translated Matthew into Greek used the Greek Mark as an aid. The author of Matthew may have been of Jewish origin, but he was thoroughly in favor of the mission to the Gentiles and contemplated a worldwide church. One of the stories which he included in his Gospel (17:24–27) teaches a doctrine of Christian freedom quite similar to that of Paul.

Date and Place of Composition.—Matthew is often thought to have been written after the fall of Jerusalem because, when compared with Mark, it seems so clearly to reflect that event. The parable of the Great Supper, for example, contains an allegorical reference to the king who sent his armies and destroyed the city of the men who rejected his invitation (22:7). Matthew may be a little later than Luke, for it bears witness to a higher development of church organization, and it is interesting that the mosaics of the Mausoleum of Galla Placidia in Ravenna picture the evangelists in the order Mark, Luke, Matthew, John. On the other hand, the differences may be due to the personalities of the evangelists and the local churches for which they wrote. Syria is often thought to be the place of writing, for there two didrachmas equaled a stater (17:27); it is, however, not impossible that the Gospel is Palestinian.

Authenticity and Value.—All three of the synoptic Gospels—Matthew, Mark, and Luke—contain ancient traditions, and many of the stories in Mark have come directly from Peter. The Q material is obviously very old and a fairly reliable report of what Jesus said. The evangelists were to some extent influenced by their presuppositions, and they had neither the interests of scientific historians nor training in their methods. Yet we can be sure that they never deliberately falsified, and by comparing Matthew with Mark we can see that he is very faithful to his sources.

Text.—The four Gospels in ancient times formed a single codex or leaf-book and were usually copied together; thus the history of the text of all four is the same. The text of the King James, or Authorized Version of 1611 is based fundamentally on the late ecclesiastical text of the Greek Orthodox Church. That of the Revised Standard Version (1946) is based mainly on the earliest manuscripts known to exist, dating in some cases from the 3d, 4th, and 5th centuries.

See also BIBLE—9. *New Testament, Introduction* through 17. *History of the English Bible.*

Bibliography.—Zahn, Theodor, *Introduction to the New Testament,* vol. 3, tr. by John M. Trout (Edinburgh 1909); McNeile, Alan Hugh, *Gospel According to St. Matthew* (London 1915); Streeter, Burnett H., *The Four Gospels* (New York 1924); Kilpatrick, George Dunbar, *Origins of the Gospel According to St. Matthew* (London 1946); Johnson, Sherman E., in *The Interpreter's Bible,* vol. 7 (New York 1951); Grant, Frederick C., *The Gospels: Their Origin and Growth* (New York 1957).

SHERMAN E. JOHNSON,
Dean, Church Divinity School of the Pacific.

MATTHEW OF PARIS. See PARIS, MATTHEW.

MATTHEW OF WESTMINSTER, an imaginary 14th-century English monk to whom was long ascribed the authorship of the *Flores historiarum,* a history of England from the Creation to 1326, written in Latin. Sir Francis Palgrave (1788–1861) and Henry Richards Luard (1825–1891) are credited with discovery and proof of the fact that the work was a composite produced by several monks at Westminster and St. Albans. It was in large part adapted from the 13th century *Chronica majorum* of Matthew of Paris. Most important to historians is the material describing events in the time of Edward I (r. 1272–1307).

MATTHEWS, măth'ūz, **(James) Brander,** American critic and teacher: b. New Orleans, La., Feb. 21, 1852; d. New York, N.Y., March 31, 1929. New York was Matthews' home during most of his life, though he was a frequent visitor to London and Paris. After his graduation from Columbia College in 1871, he attended the Columbia Law School and was admitted to the bar (1873), but turned instead to literature, contributing to periodicals and trying to establish himself as a playwright. During the 1880's Matthews became a prominent figure in New York literary and theatrical life and an active member (and founder) of writers' clubs. After lecturing at Columbia in 1891–1892, he became professor of literature there (1892–1900) and was professor of dramatic literature from 1900 until his retirement in 1924. An exponent of the "well-made play," Matthews' influence on playwrights and the public was at its height between 1890 and 1915. The Brander Matthews Dramatic Museum at Columbia contains his collection of model stage sets and costumes.

Matthews wrote several comedies, some fairly successful, and stories of New York life, including a novel, *His Father's Son* (1895); but he is best known for his books on the theater—*The Theatres of Paris* (1880), *French Dramatists of the 19th Century* (1881), *Studies of the Stage* (1894), *The Development of the Drama* (1903), *A Study of the Drama* (1910), *Molière: His Life and His Works* (1910), *Shakspere as a Playwright* (1913), *A Book About the Theater* (1916), and the essays collected in *The Principles of Playmaking* (1919), *Playwrights on Playmaking* (1923), and *Rip Van Winkle Goes to the Play* (1926), a defense of new trends. *These Many Years* (1917) is autobiographical.

MATTHEWS, Francis Patrick, American public official: b. Albion, Nebr., March 15, 1887; d. Omaha, Oct. 18, 1952. He studied law at Creighton University and was admitted to the Nebraska bar in 1913, practicing in Omaha and becoming well known as a lawyer, business official, and a prominent Catholic layman who devoted much of his time to charities. After serving as an attorney for the Reconstruction Finance Corporation (1933–1949), Matthews was appointed secretary of the navy on May 13, 1949. He took office during a period of especially intense interservice bickering attendant on the first attempt at unification of the armed forces. He drew violent criticism from military and political conservatives after firing his Chief of Naval Operations, Admiral Louis E. Denfeld, for insubordination (October 1949). Denfeld had opposed diminution of naval air authority. In 1951, Matthews resigned and was appointed ambassador to Ireland.

MATTHEWS, Stanley, American lawyer and judge: b. Cincinnati, Ohio, July 21, 1824; d. Washington, D.C., March 22, 1889. He studied law in Cincinnati and was admitted to the bar in

Tennessee in 1842, returning to Cincinnati to practice in 1844. Matthews held several state and minor federal offices in Ohio, served as a colonel of Ohio volunteers (1861–1863) during the Civil War, and was a judge on the superior court of Cincinnati (1863–1865). During the following decade he became widely known as an attorney for railroads and other large business enterprises, attracting national attention in 1877, when, after campaigning vigorously for the election of his friend Rutherford B. Hayes to the presidency, he served as an attorney before the electoral commission that reviewed the disputed returns in the Hayes-Tilden election and gave the victory to Hayes. Matthews was a United States senator from Ohio in 1877–1879. In 1881 President Hayes nominated Matthews to succeed Associate Justice Noah H. Swayne, who had resigned from the Supreme Court. His nomination was opposed on grounds that it was a political reward and that Matthews would favor large business interests. Thus it was not until James Garfield, Hayes' successor, had again submitted Matthews' name to the Senate that he was confirmed, taking office on May 12, 1881, and serving until his death. He proved an impartial, capable jurist.

MATTHEWS, măth'ūz, **Washington,** American ethnologist and physician: b. Killiney, County Dublin, Ireland, July 17, 1843; d. Washington, D.C., April 29, 1905. The son of an Irish physician who emigrated to the United States, Matthews graduated M.D. at the University of Iowa in 1864 and spent most of his active career as a surgeon at army posts in the West and Southwest. He was on duty at the Army Medical Museum from 1884 to 1890, and retired in 1895.

Matthews is known for his studies, based on careful research, of the Hidatsas (Gros Ventres of the Missouri) and Navajos, including *Grammar and Dictionary of the Hidatsa* (1873), *Ethnography and Philology of the Hidatsa Indians* (1877), *Navajo Legends* (1897), and two important papers on Navajo myth and ceremonial: "The Mountain Chant" (1887) and "The Night Chant" (1902).

MATTHIAS, mă-thī'ăs, a disciple of Jesus, probably one of the 70, who was chosen by lot to take Judas Iscariot's place among the 12 (Acts of the Apostles 1:23-26). Little is known of him. The traditions are vague and contradictory, and sometimes confuse him with Matthew. An apocryphal Gospel of Matthias, mentioned by Origen, was attributed to him. The Roman Catholic Church celebrates his feast on February 24; the Orthodox Eastern Church on August 9.

MATTHIAS, mă-thī'ăs, Ger. mä-tē'äs, Holy Roman emperor: b. Vienna, Feb. 24, 1557; d. there, March 20, 1619. He was a younger son of the Emperor Maximilian II and a brother of Rudolf II, who appointed Matthias governor of Austria in 1593. Rudolf was unbalanced, and the fortunes of the ambitious Matthias, guided from 1599 by his chancellor, Melchior Khlesl, bishop of Vienna, rose as his brother's incompetence became more and more evident. When the Protestants of Transylvania revolted under István Boeskay, Rudolf was compelled to let Matthias negotiate the Treaty of Vienna (1606) with the rebels, granting Protestantism equal status with Catholicism. Later in 1606, Matthias, supported by the other Habsburg archdukes, was declared head of the house of Habsburg and Rudolf's heir.

In 1608, allying himself with the estates of Austria, Hungary, and Moravia, he compelled Rudolf to cede to him by treaty the government of these countries, and in 1611, following a revolt of the Bohemian estates, Matthias secured Rudolf's recognition as king of Bohemia as well.

Matthias succeeded Rudolf in 1612, but as ruler of the moribund empire he proved equally ineffectual. His policy—or Khlesl's—well-intentioned but wavering, was fundamentally an attempt to reconcile two irreconcilables, the Protestant Union and the Catholic League, which had been formed toward the end of Rudolf's reign. Having secured the succession for Ferdinand of Styria (Emperor Ferdinand II), an ardent Catholic, Matthias died in 1619, the year after a Protestant uprising in Prague plunged the empire into the Thirty Years' War.

MATTHIAS CORVINUS, mă-thī'ăs kôr-vī'nŭs (also MATTHIAS I HUNYADI, Hung. MÁTYÁS HOLLÓS), king of Hungary: b. Cluj, Transylvania, probably on Feb. 23, 1440; d. Vienna, April 4, 1490. Matthias, the second son of the famous János Hunyadi, was elected king of Hungary in 1458. His rival, the Emperor Frederick III, though supported by a faction of Hungarian magnates, relinquished his claim by treaty in 1462, retaining some counties in western Hungary. To some extent Matthias was able to dominate the powerful feudal magnates in Hungary, but the foundations of his power were his family's vast possessions and numerous followers, the support the lesser Hungarian nobility and burghers gave the crown, and his standing army, whose creation freed him from complete dependence on feudal levies.

After campaigning against the Turks in the 1460's—thereafter contenting himself with a passive defense of that frontier—Matthias intervened in Bohemia against the "Hussite king" George of Poděbrad, who had been excommunicated by the pope. The Catholic party elected Matthias king of Bohemia in 1469, but the Poles also intervened and a long struggle ended in the Treaty of Olomouc (1478), by which Matthias obtained Moravia, Silesia, and Lusatia for life, while Ladislas of the Polish Jagellon dynasty became king of Bohemia (Ladislas II). Matthias now turned against his old enemy, Frederick III, whom he finally deprived of his territories. He captured Vienna in 1485, making it his capital, and added most of Austria, Styria, Carinthia, and Carniola to his dominions, emerging as head of the most powerful kingdom in Central Europe, one that dominated the upper Danube Valley. He died suddenly, at the height of his power. During much of his life his aim had been to secure the crown of the Holy Roman Empire, apparently as a first step in leading Central Europe against the Turks.

One of the greatest Renaissance princes and founder of the famous Bibliotheca Corvina at Buda, Matthias was a patron of learning and the arts and maintained a brilliant Italianate court, whose guiding spirit was his young, ambitious queen, Beatrice of Naples (1457–1508), whom he married in 1476.

Matthias' kingdom was entirely the creation of his ambition and skill as soldier and statesman. It did not survive his death. Lacking legitimate children, Matthias tried to secure the succession for his natural son JOHANNES CORVINUS, or János Hollós (1473–1504), but died before the matter was settled. Beatrice, who hoped for a share in the succeeding government, was opposed, as were the Hungarian magnates, who elected the docile Ladislas II of Bohemia. Johannes became ban of Croatia and Dalmatia.

MATTHIESSEN, măth'ĭ-sĕn, **Francis Otto,** American critic: b. Pasadena, Calif., Feb. 19, 1902; d. Boston, Mass., April 1, 1950. He was educated at Yale (B.A. 1923), went to Oxford as a Rhodes scholar (1923–1925), and received his Ph.D at Harvard in 1927. Matthiessen taught at Yale (1927–1929) and then at Harvard, where he was professor of history and literature from 1942 until his death. His early critiques, *Sarah Orne Jewett* (1929), *Translation: an Elizabethan Art* (1931), and *The Achievement of T. S. Eliot* (1935, enlarged ed. 1947), were followed by his illuminating study of a great period in American letters, *The American Renaissance: Art and Expression in the Age of Emerson and Whitman* (1941). Next came *Henry James: the Major Phase* (1944), the first of several related works— *The James Family* (1947) and editions of Henry James' stories of writers and artists (1944), his American novels and stories (1947), and his notebooks (1947, with Kenneth B. Murdock). Matthiessen also wrote *Russell Cheney* (1947), a biography of his close friend, the painter, and *From the Heart of Europe* (1948), a travel journal that reveals the basis of his convictions as a socialist. His biography *Theodore Dreiser* was published in 1951, after his suicide cut short a brilliant career in letters. *The Responsibilities of the Critic* (1952) is a selection by John Rackliffe of Matthiessen's essays and reviews.

Consult Sweezy, Paul M., and Huberman, Leo, eds., *F. O. Matthiessen (1902–1950)* (New York 1951).

MATTING, a coarse, woven or plaited fabric, made of fibrous grasses, reeds, sedges, coconut husk fibers, palm leaves, or similar materials. They are used for floor and wall coverings, table mats, furniture, screens, and many decorative purposes. Most mattings in the United States and Canada are imported from the Orient. Most are woven or plaited by hand—a notable exception is the matting made of coir fiber—and low labor costs in harvesting, curing, and manufacturing are largely responsible for their success in competitive markets.

The straw of many cereal grasses, especially rice straw (*Oryza sativa*) in the Orient and rye straw (*Secale cereale*) in Europe, is used extensively in making matting, both for floor covering and decoration. Matting made from the split stems of the giant reed (*Arundo donax*) comes from the Mediterranean region. In these mattings the straw or reed forms the woof and cotton threads the warp. Manufacture may be by hand or machines.

Japanese mattings made from the Bingo-i mat rush (*Juncus effusus*) are available in limited quantities. Others, of coarser texture and inferior quality, are made from a sedge (*Cyperus unitans*) and imported from Japan under the name Hanamushiro. So-called Chinese, or Calcutta, mat grass (*Cyperus corymbosus,* formerly called *C. tegetiformis*), which is a sedge and not a grass, once accounted for a substantial tonnage of imported mattings, but these are now primarily collector's items. The fragrant roots of the khuskhus (*Andropogon squarrosus*), a perennial grass of India, are woven into screens and exported in limited quantities.

Coir matting, machine-woven fibers from the husks of immature coconuts (*Cocos nucifera*), makes a tough, coarse, rot-resisting floor covering. Coir is also made into the common fiber door mats well known in the United States and Canada.

New Zealand flax (*Phormium tenax*) is the source of a very satisfactory floor matting, whose manufacture has become an important industry in that country. But the production is inadequate to meet domestic demands and little of the matting is exported.

Mattings hand plaited from the leaves of the screw pine (*Pandanus utilis, P. odoratissimus,* and *P. tectorius*) are used extensively in the Philippine and Hawaiian islands. In the United States these mattings are used primarily by decorators as wall coverings, screens, and table mats. In the Hawaiian homes of many Occidentals, they are used also as floor coverings. Niihau mats (*Cyperus laevigatus*) were formerly produced in Hawaii in limited quantities, especially as novelties. Abacá mats (*Musa textilis*) from the Philippines are much finer in texture, more flexible, and highly durable. They are used for floor and wall coverings.

Rattan, made from split stems of the very spiny clambering rattan palm (*Calamus* species), is used in wall coverings and screens. Malaya is a primary source. Bamboo splits from the same region, hand woven into matting and furniture, are exported to a lesser extent.

Throughout most tropical regions, mattings made by hand plaiting the leaves of the coconut palm (*Cocos nucifera*) provide durable wall materials, and many dwellings are walled with this alone. In the more arid areas, leaves of the date palm (*Phoenix dactylifera*) are equally serviceable.

Western Hemisphere.—The American bulrush (*Typha latifolia* and *T. angustifolia*) is harvested in quantity for making chair seatings, especially those of reproductions of early American furniture. Mats made of these rushes are also used in some areas as insulating coverings for the sashes of hotbeds during the winter.

The American Indian in what is now the United States made extensive use of mattings prepared from grasses and rushes—notably the giant tule (*Scirpus validus*) and the alkali tule (*S. paludosus*), both employed by California tribes. Little use is made of these materials in modern mattings. Throughout tropical America, especially north of Panama, mattings are used abundantly by indigenous peoples for wall materials, screens, rain capes (*suyucales*), furniture, and decorative articles. These are made primarily from the young leaves of native palms like *Sabal mexicana* and *Brahea dulcis*. In the highlands of Latin American countries, mattings of reeds may take the place of plaited palm leaves, although the latter are often transported and sold in highland village markets.

Efforts have been made to produce commercial mattings in Florida from leaves of the abundant native cabbage palm (*Sabal palmetto*). These were intended as a domestic substitute for imported coir fiber mattings, but sabal matting is not so flexible nor so durable as that from coir fiber and has not been produced at costs competitive with the imported product.

GEORGE H. M. LAWRENCE,
Bailey Hortorium, New York State College of Agriculture, Cornell University.

MATTIOLI, mät-tĕ-ô′lĕ, CONTE **Ercole Antonio,** Italian statesman and diplomat: b. 1640; d. Paris, Nov. 19, 1703. Nothing is known of his early life but as a young man he settled at Mantua and became the confidential secretary to Charles III and Charles IV, dukes of Mantua. His name has been passed down to posterity only because it is generally believed that he was the famed secret prisoner of Louis XIV, first referred to by Voltaire as "The Man in the Iron Mask."

From the private papers of Louis XIV it became evident that it was this man who was seized by the king for revealing to others the secret negotiations of France with Mantua for the sale of the Mantuan fortress of Casale. Mattioli was first confined at Pignerol, then at the island of St. Marguerite, and in 1698 he entered the Bastille, where he died five years later.

Much speculation was caused at the time (and later) as to the identity of the unknown prisoner. Some regarded him as the natural son of Louis XIV and others as the twin brother of the French king. Dumas père established him as the latter in his book *Vicomte de Bragelonne* (1848) in a section often published separately as *The Man in the Iron Mask.*

MATTIPI (South American name) or **FROG SNAKE,** a serpent (*Xenodon severus*) of northeastern South America. While a poisonous variety, it is slow to bite. Its posterior teeth serve as fangs, but it has no venom sacs. The bite causes temporary swelling and soreness, but is seldom fatal.

MATTO GROSSO. See MATO GROSSO.

MATTOON, mă-tōōn′, city, Illinois, in Coles County, at an altitude of 725 feet, 40 miles southeast of Decatur, and served by the Illinois Central and the Cleveland, Cincinnati, Chicago and St. Louis railroads and state and federal highways. Situated in an agricultural region, Mattoon is an industrial city, making furniture, shoes, utility equipment, roofing, Diesel engines, and brooms. Broom corn and soybeans are the major crops in the surrounding district. The two railroads serving the city have machine shops and repair shops there. The city has a public library, and nearby are a fish hatchery and Paradise Lake, formed by a dam on the Little Wabash River.

Mattoon was settled and incorporated in 1855, in connection with construction of the Illinois Central through this region, and was named for William Mattoon of that railroad, who played an important part in organization of the town. It was here, in 1861, that Ulysses S. Grant mustered the Twenty-first Illinois Volunteers into service, with himself as colonel, appointed by Gov. Richard Yates. The city has commission government, and the water supply is municipally owned. Pop. (1960) 19,088.

MATTSON, mät′s′n, **Henry Elis,** American painter: b. Gothenburg, Sweden, Aug. 7, 1887. He came to the United States in 1906 and was naturalized as a citizen in 1913. He studied briefly (1912–1913) at the School of Worcester Art Museum, Worcester, Mass., although most of his training in art is self-taught. His marines and landscapes are represented in many of the nation's finest collections, among them the Metropolitan Museum of Art, the Whitney Museum of American Art, New York; the Carnegie Institute, Pittsburgh; the Corcoran Gallery of Art and the White House, Washington, D.C. He painted under the sponsorship of the Works Progress Administration and has murals at the post office in Portland, Me. His prizes include those of the Art Institute of Chicago (1931), Corcoran Gallery of Art (1935 and 1943), and Carnegie Institute (1935).

MATURIN, măt̬′rĭn, **Charles Robert,** Irish dramatist and novelist: b. Dublin, 1782; d. there, Oct. 30, 1824. He received his education at Trinity College, Dublin, entered the ministry of the Church of Ireland, and served successively as curate at Loughrea, County Galway, and at St. Peter's, Dublin. He wrote the novels *The Fatal Revenge, or the Family of Montorio* (1807); *The Wild Irish Boy* (1808); and *The Milesian Chief* (1812), under the pseudonym of DENNIS JASPER MURPHY. The novels, written as Gothic romances, were ridiculed by the critics, but attracted the favorable attention of Sir Walter Scott, who introduced Maturin to Lord Byron. These powerful friends secured the production of Maturin's tragedy *Bertram, or the Castle of St. Aldobrand* at Drury Lane in 1816, with Edmund Kean in the leading role. It ran for 22 nights, and a French version was produced soon afterward at the Théâtre Favart, Paris. His other tragedies *Manuel* (1817) and *Fredolfo* (1819) failed totally. Among his other works were the novels *Women* (1818); *Melmoth the Wanderer* (1820); and *The Albigenses* (1824). *Melmoth* is his greatest work and was most successful in its day.

MATURIN, mä-tōō-rēn′, town, Venezuela, capital of the state of Monagas, formerly the capital of the state of Maturin. It is on the Guarapiche River, north of the Orinoco, 25 miles by rail above its port, Colorado, and 40 miles from the sea. A considerable trade with the West Indies, principally in cattle and hides, is carried on. In the neighborhood are extensive plantations of cacao, sugar cane, fruits, and cereals. Its industrial establishments turn out cigars, starch, hammocks, boots, shoes, and soaps. There are petroleum fields nearby. Maturin is the birthplace of two presidents of Venezuela, José Tadeo Monagas and José Gregorio Monagas. Pop. (1941) 10,705; (1950) 25,350.

MATZOON, mät-sōōn′, a milk food used in Armenia; prepared by exposing milk in open vessels to a heat of 90° F., and when coagulation takes place the curd is broken up by a churning process and salt is added.

MATZOTH, mät′sōth, the Hebrew name for a kind of unleavened bread or biscuit eaten by the Jews during the feast of the Passover.

MAUBEUGE, mō-bûzh′, fortress and manufacturing town, France, in the Department of Nord, occupying both banks of the Sambre, 49 miles southeast of Lille, within two miles of the Belgian frontier. The origin of Maubeuge was in a double monastery for monks and nuns founded in the 7th century. Destroyed successively by the Normans, by Louis XI, by Francis I, and by Henry II, it finally fell to France by the Treaty of Nimeguen in 1678, and was fortified by the marquis de Vauban. Previous to outbreak of World War I in 1914 it was defended by nine forts. The principal industry is the manufacture of iron and steel products. The town was occupied by the Germans in 1914 and again in 1940. Pop. (1962) city 27,208; commune 27,287.

MAUCH CHUNK, môk chŭngk (called JIM THORPE since 1954), former borough, Pennsylvania, and Carbon County seat; located 23 miles northwest of Allentown and lying at an altitude of 545 feet on the banks of the Lehigh River. It is served by the Central Railroad of New Jersey and the Lehigh Valley Railroad. Anthracite coal is mined in the surrounding areas and the town has textile and clothing factories. Mauch Chunk was first settled about 1815. On May 9, 1954, voters of Mauch Chunk and East Mauch Chunk, on the opposite side of the Lehigh River, approved the merger of the two boroughs. The new borough is called Jim Thorpe, honoring the great Indian athlete who excelled in sports while at school in Carlisle, Pa., and at the 1912 Olympic games in Stockholm, Sweden. Pop. of borough 5,945.

MAUD, môd, a poem by Alfred Tennyson (q.v.), published in 1855, which was badly received by his generation but is regarded with much interest today. Psychologically related to the work of 20th century poets like T. S. Eliot, *Maud,* according to Tennyson, is a "monodrama" in which "different phases of passion in one person take the place of different characters." It depicts, in monologue form and with great sensitivity, the character of an impoverished young man made unstable and morbid by the suicide of his father, following an unwise financial speculation encouraged by the father of Maud, a wellborn young lady whom he comes gradually, and somewhat reluctantly, to love. His ambivalence toward her and her family flares into murderous rage when he is struck by her brother, whom he then kills in a duel. Fleeing his guilty deed, he returns to the introverted life from which Maud had withdrawn him and psychotically broods on death and burial. Tennyson, whose knowledge of psychoses was drawn from the disturbed lives of two of his brothers and from the practice of a neighboring psychiatrist, Dr. Matthew Allen, was perhaps unequal to the task of depicting his young man's return to sanity, but in a sort of epilogue he has his unstable hero change his wish for self-destruction to a wish for self-sacrifice in the Crimean War, which was just beginning when the poem was written. It was this militant strain in *Maud* that shocked Tennyson's admirers.

Maud was Tennyson's favorite poem, the one he loved best to read to friends and admirers; it contains some of his most beautiful lyrics, including "Come into the garden, Maud," "I have led her home," and "O that 'twere possible," the lyric written in 1837 out of which *Maud* itself grew. Unfortunately the violent public reaction to it probably hindered his development as a writer who might foreshadow the intellectual trends of the 20th century. According to T. S. Eliot, Tennyson was "the most instinctive rebel against the society in which he was the most perfect conformist." The hero of *Maud* refers bitterly to: "The whole weak race of venomous worms, that sting each other here in the dust"; "Pickpockets, each hand lusting for all that is not its own"; "Cheat and be cheated, and die,"

he cries, "only the ledger lives." This type of social invective was badly received in Queen Victoria's golden era and Tennyson, amazed and hurt by the angry public response to *Maud,* never again attempted such a forthright sociological document.

MAUD MULLER, mŭl'ẽr, a poem by John Greenleaf Whittier, first published in the *National Era,* December 1854. It is a ballad reciting a romantic passage in the lives of a susceptible judge and a country girl.

MAUDE, SIR **Frederick Stanley,** British army officer: b. Gibralter, June 24, 1864; d. Baghdad, Turkey (now Iraq), Nov. 18, 1917. Entering the army at the age of 20, he saw his first active service in the Egyptian campaign of 1885; during the years 1900 and 1901 he saw action as a staff officer of a brigade in engagements of the Boer War. With the outbreak of World War I in 1914 he went to France as a staff officer and saw action on the Marne, the Aisne, and at Armentières. In October 1914 he was made brigadier general; in the following month he was returned wounded to England. Promoted to major general in July 1915, he was sent to the Dardanelles to take command of the 13th Division. During the Gallipoli campaign he shared in the withdrawal from Anzac Cove and Suvla Bay.

From Egypt, whither he had gone with his division, he was transferred to Mesopotamia, and there, after failure of the attempt to relieve Kut-al-Imara (now in Iraq), he became British commander in chief in August 1916. Reorganizing his forces, he began an advance in December which drove the Turks from Kut-al-Imara and carried him on to Baghdad, where he concluded his successful campaign in March 1917. After a pause for preparation came another forward move, marked by the last victory of his lifetime at Tikrit on November 6. Back in Baghdad, Maude was stricken with a fatal attack of cholera.

MAUGHAM, môm, **William Somerset,** English author: b. Paris, Jan. 25, 1874; d. Nice, Dec. 16, 1965. The sixth and youngest son of the solicitor to the British embassy in Paris, he learned French as his native tongue. His mother dying of tuberculosis when he was eight, he was orphaned at 10 and was sent to England to liv with an uncle, the vicar of Whitstable. His loneliness in this austere, religious atmosphere was made more acute because he scarcely knew English and was afflicted with a bad stammer. Sent to King's School, Canterbury, at 13, he was shy, underdeveloped and incipiently tubercular. He knew he wanted to be a writer and in 1891 attended lectures at Heidelberg University in Germany, although he did not matriculate. Urged by his uncle to choose a profession, he studied medicine for six years but never practiced, except as an intern, and his health failing, he went to the south of France. Then for the next 10 years he lived in Paris as a struggling young author. Much of his best work has been autobiographical: his early life was told in *Of Human Bondage* (the hero's crippled foot was, symbolically, Maugham's speech impediment) and his first book, *Liza of Lambeth* (1897), recounted his experiences as an intern in Lambeth, one of the poorer districts of London. *A Man of Honour,* his first play, was produced in 1903, although *Lady Frederick* in 1907 brought his earliest success; by 1908, four of his plays were running simultaneously: *Lady Frederick, Jack Straw, Mrs. Dot,* and *The Explorer.* After the publication of *Of Human Bondage* (q.v.) in 1915, which is usually considered his outstanding achievement, he wrote a steady stream of plays, short stories, and novels. His plays, most of them drawing room comedies, were performed in Europe and the United States. Among them, *The Circle* (1921), *Our Betters* (1923), and *The Constant Wife* (1927) were outstanding. His last play, *Sheppey,* written and produced in London in 1933, was not especially successful.

Several of his novels and shorter pieces are reprinted almost annually. *The Moon and Sixpence* (1919), the story of an artist, was based on the life of Paul Gauguin. *Miss Thompson,* included in a collection of short stories, *The Trembling of a Leaf* (1921), was made into a a play by John Colton and Clemence Randolph under the title *Rain* in 1922. *Ashenden, or The British Agent* (1928) was drawn from the author's experiences as an intelligence agent in Switzerland during World War I. *Cakes and Ale, or The Skeleton in the Cupboard* (1930) is a satirical story of two men of letters, who are often said to be Thomas Hardy and Hugh Walpole. In 1938 Maugham published an account of his literary experiences, *The Summing Up,* which has become a useful guidebook for persons interested in writing. *The Razor's Edge* (1944), the story of a young American's spiritual quest, brought his most immediate success, and was made into a motion picture in 1946. Among his more recent books are *The Mixture as Before* (1940), *Up at the Villa* (1941), *Then and Now* (1946), *Creatures of Circumstance* (1947), and *Catalina* (1948).

MAUI, mä'ōō-ĕ, one of the Hawaiian Islands, situated 26 miles northwest of Hawaii; it comprises two mountainous passes joined by an isthmus. The east peninsula contains Haleakala crater, 10,025 feet high, last active about 1750. There are large sugarcane and pineapple plantations. Wailuku, near the northwest coast, is the largest town and the seat of Maui County; it has supplanted Lahaina, on the southwest coast, where white men first established themselves in the island. The county of Maui comprises Maui, Lanai, and Kahoolawe. Population of the county is 42,576.

MAULE, mou'lå, Chile, a maritime province bounded north by the province of Talcá, and south by the province of Nuble. The area is 2,172 square miles. Most of the surface is occupied by the forested coast range, averaging nearly 3,000 feet in height. Agriculture, stockraising, and lumbering are the principal industries. The province takes its name from the river Maule (q.v.). Linares (q.v.) the provincial capital, is on the main line of the state railroad; branch lines connect it with Cauquenes (pop. 11,198), the former capital, and with Constitución (pop. 7,049), the chief port. Pop. (1952) 72,181.

MAULE, a river of Chile, rising in the Andes and after a westerly course of 150 miles (52 miles navigable for small vessels) entering the Pacific Ocean immediately north of Constitución; it gives its name to the province of Maule (q.v.). The Maule River is believed to have been the southern boundary of the empire of the Incas.

MAUMEE, Ohio, village in Lucas County; altitude 648 feet; on the Maumee River; 8 miles southwest of Toledo; on Nickel Plate and Wabash railroads. It makes desks, cabinets, and butter coloring. It has the mayor-council form of government. Pop. 12,063.

MAUMEE, mô-mē', a river formed by the junction of Saint Marys and Saint Joseph rivers at Fort Wayne, Ind. It flows northeast across the northwest corner of the state of Ohio, and enters Lake Erie through Maumee Bay. Its affluents are the Auglaize and the Tiffin. Its basin is 6,700 square miles in extent. The river is 150 miles long and navigable 12 miles from its mouth to the Maumee Rapids.

MAUNA KEA, mou'nä kä'ä, Hawaii, a semiactive volcano, highest peak in the Hawaiian Islands, 13,784 feet in altitude. Snow covers its upper slopes for the greater part of the year; and its sides are wooded. Coffee is cultivated on the lower slopes.

MAUNA LOA, lō'ä, Hawaii, active volcano in the central southern portion of the island, 13,680 feet in altitude; the crater is nearly five miles in circumference, and on the inner side vertical precipices tower 500-600 feet. On the eastern slope of Mauna Loa is the still larger crater of Kilauea (q.v.), about nine miles in circumference but apparently having no communication with the former since their periods of activity are independent of each other. Mauna Loa's greatest activity was in 1881; it erupted on April 26, 1942, and again on Jan. 6, 1949. A sharp earthquake, accompanying its last eruption, rocked nearby Hawaii National Park Volcano House, but no damage was reported.

MAUNDY THURSDAY, môn'dĭ, the Thursday in Holy Week, the annual memorial of the Last Supper at which Christ washed the feet of his disciples. The ceremony of washing the feet of the poor on that day was originally kept by noblemen and prelates, as well as by the pope and Roman Catholic sovereigns. In Britain the ceremony was performed by the sovereign until the reign of William III, when it was transferred to the lord high almoner; it was discontinued in 1754. The maundy usage is now confined in Britain to gifts of money at Westminster Abbey to as many old men and women as there are years in the sovereign's age, one penny for each year, together with money in lieu of the clothes formerly given; the maundy pennies, first coined under Charles II, are silver and unmilled, and are legal tender. The yeomen of the guard carry the doles, which are distributed by the lord high almoner. Maundy Thursday is sometimes called Sheer or Chare Thursday.

MAUNOURY, mō-nōō-rē', **Michel Joseph,** French military officer: b. Maintenon, Eure-et-Loire, Dec. 11, 1847; d. en route from Paris to Orleans, March 28, 1923. He became an artillery officer in 1869, and in the Franco-Prussian War of 1870–1871 he was wounded at Champigny. In 1905 he attained the rank of general of division and had charge of the artillery of the Paris forts. General Maunoury was commandant of the École Supérieure de Guerre in 1907; the following year of the 15th Army Corps with headquarters at Marseilles, and in 1909 of the 20th corps at Nancy.

He was made military governor of Paris in 1910. In World War I Maunoury was placed in charge (Aug. 19, 1914) of the army of maneuver and was rushed north in an effort to turn the flank of Alexander von Kluck's army then driving toward Paris. When Von Kluck discovered Maunoury on his right the drive was stopped and in the Battle of the Marne the invader was driven back. He was severely wounded in March 1915 and in the same year received from the president of the Republic the *médaille militaire,* the highest military honor in the gift of France. From November 1915 until March 1916 he was again military governor of Paris. He was an officer of the Legion of Honor and was posthumously created marshal of France.

MAUPASSANT, mō-pà-sän, **(Henri René Albert) Guy de,** French novelist and short-story writer: b. Château de Miromesnil, Tourville-sur-Arques, Seine-Inférieure, France, Aug. 5, 1850; d. Paris, July 6, 1893. The nobility of Guy de Maupassant's paternal ancestors was genuine but recent (18th century). His maternal grandfather, Paul Le Poittevin, was Gustave Flaubert's godfather; his mother, Laure, and his uncle, Alfred Le Poittevin, had been childhood playmates of Flaubert and his sister. Flaubert's avuncular interest in Maupassant had no more suspicious a source than this.

Maupassant grew up in his native Normandy, a rebellious student whose athletic constitution demanded open air and strenuous exercise. Those were afforded in abundance through vacations at Étretat on the seashore. The gift of a photographic memory enabled him to gather a storehouse of information about the country and its inhabitants, so that, with him, the Norman inspiration was to become basic in every sense, both as an unending supply of subject matter and as a pattern, so to speak, for the subsequent study of other *milieux,* such as the army in which he served during the Franco-Prussian War, the little world of government clerical workers which he joined for a period of eight years (1872–1880), and the salons which he frequented in later life. Between Maupassant and his province, however, there remained an unbroken affinity. Never a believer in the goodness of human nature, he brought to the depiction of Norman foibles a gusto which was akin to complicity and love, whereas the "pity" that he developed toward Parisians, for instance, actually set him apart from the crowd and implied no small measure of contempt. Maupassant's pessimism had grown more bitter with experience, part of which is ascribable to the loss of his health. Incessant headaches, alleviated by the use of ether, led to hallucinations and an ultimate mental breakdown. He died an inmate of the celebrated private asylum of Dr. Esprit Blanche at Passy, Paris.

As Maupassant's natural literary mentor, Gustave Flaubert attempted to mold him in his own image. Painstaking labor and respect for style went into the making of *Boule de suif,* the disciple's first important publication and first acknowledged masterpiece. This short story, however, appeared in *Les Soirées de Médan* (1880), an aggregate of six war stories told by Émile Zola and his younger followers. It brought Maupassant into the naturalists' camp and averred more of a taste for the naked truth than was compatible with Flaubert's lofty artistic realism. One must also remember that, in twice the time

that it took the master to write *Madame Bovary,* Maupassant issued 17 volumes of short stories (*La Maison Tellier,* 1881; *Mademoiselle Fifi,* 1882; *Contes de la bécasse,* 1883; *Clair de lune, Les Soeurs Rondoli, Yvette, Miss Harriet,* all 1884; *Toine, Contes du jour et de la nuit, Contes et nouvelles,* all 1885; *La Petite Roque* and *Monsieur Parent,* both 1886; *Le Horla,* 1887; *Le rosier de Madame Husson,* 1888; *La main gauche,* 1889; *L'inutile beauté,* 1890; *Le Père Milon,* posthumous), not to count novels, plays, and travelogues. Unlike Flaubert, therefore, Maupassant was content to control his facility; he did not damn or banish it altogether. Theirs was the difference between the dedicated artist and the craftsman.

Maupassant's predestined vehicle was the short story. For swift character and background delineation, brief but poignant drama, and "electric" finishes, he had no peer except Prosper Mérimée. The larger frame of the novel, on the other hand, proved less well suited to his talents. Of the six novels which he wrote (*Une vie,* 1883; *Bel-ami,* 1885; *Mont-Oriol,* 1887; *Pierre et Jean,* 1888; *Fort comme la mort,* 1889; *Notre coeur,* 1890), only *Pierre et Jean* achieves real concentration and unity. Its preface, an important document, shows Maupassant shifting away from naturalism, toward the so-called psychological novel in the manner of Paul Bourget (1852–1935).

There is little foundation for the widespread belief that Maupassant's treatment of obsession, in late stories such as *Le Horla,* reflects the approach of insanity. All of his themes, including that one (in *Sur l'eau*), are present in his first collection, *La Maison Tellier,* published at the height of his health and power; all are evenly distributed through his works. The topic of *Le Horla* was suggested to him by a fellow writer. The conclusion seems inescapable that Maupassant's symptoms, until they condemned him to living death, precipitated no major change of inspiration nor faltering of the writer's hand.

Bibliography.—Consult Maupassant's *Oeuvres complètes,* 15 vols., unfinished (Paris 1934–38), and, for the missing items, *Oeuvres complètes,* 29 vols. (Paris 1907–10); his short stories, translated, were published in one volume, *Complete Short Stories* (Garden City, N.Y., 1941). See also Maynial, Edouard, *La vie et l'oeuvre de Guy de Maupassant* (Paris 1906); Dumesnil, René, *Guy de Maupassant* (Paris 1933); Hoffmann, Gérard, *Le cas de Maupassant: étude médico-littéraire* (Paris 1940); Artinian, Artine, *Maupassant Criticism in France, 1880–1940* (New York 1941); Steegmüller, Francis, *Maupassant: a Lion in the Path* (New York 1949); Thoraval, Jean, *L'art de Maupassant d'après ses variantes* (Paris 1950); Sullivan, Edward D., *Maupassant the Novelist* (Princeton 1954); Vial, André, *Guy de Maupassant et l'art du roman* (Paris 1954).

JEAN-ALBERT BÉDÉ,
Professor of French, Columbia University.

MAUPERTUIS, mō-pĕr'tü-ē', **Pierre Louis Moreau de,** French mathematician and astronomer: b. St. Malo, France, July 17, 1698; d. Basel, Switzerland, July 27, 1759. He entered the army in 1718 and after five years' service resigned in order to become instructor of mathematics in the Academy of Sciences. In 1728 he went to England where he was made a member of the Royal Society and became a pupil of Isaac Newton. In 1736 he headed a scientific expedition to Lapland for the purpose of measuring the length of a degree of longitude, the result of which was confirmation of Newton's theory of the flattening of the globe at the poles. In 1744 he was summoned to Prussia by Frederick II, and in 1746 was declared president of the Academy of Sciences at Berlin. A dispute with the philosopher, König, regarding the infinitesimal calculus shortened his days.

Among his works are *Sur la figure de la terre* (1738); *Discours sur la figure des astres* (1742); *Lettre sur la comète de 1742* (1742); *Astronomie nautique* (1745); *Essai de cosmologie* (1753).

MAUREPAS, môr-pà, COMTE **Jean Frederic Phelippeaux,** French statesman: b. Versailles, France, July 9, 1701; d. there, Nov. 21, 1781. In 1725 he became administrator of the navy, in which post he used the best knowledge then available to bring the navy to a high standard of perfection. He became minister of state under Louis XV in 1738, and became his principal adviser. In 1749 he was banished from the court for an attack on Mme. de Pompadour. He lived in exile until his appointment as prime minister by Louis XVI in 1774. The chief event of his administration was the restoration of the Parliament of Paris (Nov. 12, 1774). He intrigued against Anne Robert Jackes and replaced him as minister of finance with Jacques Necker in 1776.

MAURETANIA, mô-rĕ-tā'nĭ-à, or **MAURITANIA,** ancient name for northwestern Africa, west of Numidia, varying in size at different periods but roughly corresponding to modern Morocco and western Algeria. No part of ancient Mauretania coincided with today's Mauritania. The area came under Roman influence in the first century B.C. In 42 A.D. it was divided into two provinces and brought under Roman rule. In the 400's the Vandals overran the country.

MAURIAC, mô-ryàk', **François,** French writer: b. Bordeaux, France, Oct. 11, 1885. In 1906 he went to Paris and began his career as a poet and critic, publishing volumes of poetry in 1909 and 1911. He turned to fiction in 1912, and achieved his first real success with the publication of *Le Baiser au Lépreux* (1922) and *Genitrix* (1923), translated together as *The Family* (1930), which won the Grand Prix du Roman in 1925. He was elected to the French Academy in 1933. Other English translations of his works are *Suspicion* (1932); *The Vipers' Tangle* (1933); *Woman of the Pharisees* (1946); *Thérèse* (1947); *Proust's Way* (1950); and *The Loved and the Unloved* (1952). He also achieved distinction in drama, biography, and criticism. During World War II he wrote articles for the resistance movement under the signature Forez. In 1952 he was awarded the Nobel Prize for Literature, for the "penetrating psychology and artistic intensity with which he, in the form of the novel, has interpreted the drama of human life."

MAURICE, mô'rĭs, duke and elector of Saxony: b. Freiberg, March 21, 1521; d. near Sievershausen, July 11, 1553. In 1541 he succeeded his father, Henry the Pious, as duke, and, although a Protestant, refused to join the Schmalkaldic League. He fought for Charles V, and with the latter's aid became elector in the Albertine line in 1547. Subsequently opposed to Charles, in 1552 he forced the emperor to accept the Treaty of Passau. He was mortally wounded in a battle with Albert Alcibiades.

MAURITANIA, mô-rĭ-tā'nĭ-à, is an independent, French-speaking republic on the western bulge of Africa. A desert covers about two thirds of its area. Mauritania's capital, Nouakchott, built in the 1960's, stands four miles inland from the Atlantic Ocean.

Information Highlights

Official name: Islamic Republic of Mauritania.
Form of government: Republic.
President: Mokhtar Ould Daddah.
Area: 406,400 square miles.
Population (1964): 1,000,000.
Languages: French (official): Arabic (national).
Capital: Nouakchott, pop. (1964) 6,000.
Chief products: iron ore, sheep and goats, cattle, camels, millet, dates.
Value of trade (1962): exports, $2,783,000; imports, $35,689,300.
Unit of currency: CFA (African Financial Community) franc; 246.85 CFA = $1.00.

Although nearly twice as big as Texas, the country has a population of only one million persons, most of them nomadic herdsmen. Other Mauritanians farm along the Senegal Valley and in mountainous regions. Pastoral and agricultural for centuries, Mauritania turned its economy toward industry in the 1960's with large-scale mining of its rich deposits of iron ore. The government planned further industrial expansion with income from its mining royalties.

Formerly a territory in French West Africa, Mauritania achieved independence in 1960. Although outside the framework of the French Community, the republic maintains financial and political ties with France. A 400-mile stretch of Atlantic coast forms Mauritania's western boundary. The country is bordered on the northwest and north by Río de Oro (southern zone of Spanish Sahara), on the northeast by Algeria, on the east and southeast by Mali, and on the south by Senegal.

The People.—About 80 percent of the people are Moors. They are of Arab-Berber origin and related to the Touaregs. These people are mostly herdsmen who camp in tents and lead their livestock across the sands in search of new grass springing up after rains. They live in the central region and, in lesser numbers, in the north.

About 20 percent of the people are Negro villagers who live by subsistence farming in the south. The largest tribes are the Toucouleur, Sarakolle, and Ouolof.

Most of the people of Mauritania are Moslems, and Islam is the state religion. However, the constitution guarantees freedom of worship.

Relatively few people in the country have any formal education, although Mauritania operates two systems of education—Arab and French. Nomadic living conditions limit enrollment to a small percentage of the school-age population. To overcome this handicap, some schools travel with tribes. In the 1960's there were 15,000 students in 228 primary schools and 884 students in seven secondary schools. But even this small number of students represented a 100 percent increase over the 1950's.

The Land.—Only the southern part of the country, called the sub-Sahara region, receives regular rainfall. As a consequence, most crop-farming takes place in the south. Along the Senegal River, on the southern boundary, rich alluvial soil is watered by flooding of the river and by rains that fall from July to October. The nearby Sahelian plain provides pasture for cattle and sheep despite a sparse 4-inch annual rainfall.

The Sahara region covers about two thirds of Mauritania. It extends north of a line curving from Nema on the east to Nouakchott on the west. In the mountainous Adrar, Tagant, Assaba, and Affole regions, intermittent rainfall stored by dams is sufficient for cultivation of large palm groves. From the 20th parallel of latitude northward to the Algerian border, shifting sand dunes and rocky expanses provide sparse grazing for camels and sheep.

The Economy.—Until the 1960's, Mauritania based its economy almost entirely on raising livestock and crops for subsistence. The nomad's camel and the date palm symbolized the country's resources. In 1963, however, iron-ore mining began, and became a significant new element in the economy. The venture provided Mauritania with its first major heavy industry, its first railroad, and its first improved harbor.

The ore lies in the Kedia d'Idjill mountain range, which rises 2,000 feet above the desert plain and covers an 85-square-mile triangular area near Fort Gourard. Geologists calculate that the area has at least 115 million tons of high-grade hematite ore, with an average iron content of 65 percent. Production began at 4 million tons annually, and at capacity will reach 6 million tons. Miferma, the corporation operating the mines, was formed by French, British, German, and Italian interests. The Mauritanian government receives 50 percent of the profits of the company. A railroad stretches 419 miles across the desert from the mines to Port Étienne.

Mauritania also hopes to exploit copper deposits in the desert. Two pilot copper-treatment plants have been built near Akjoujt, 100 miles south of the railroad.

Livestock continues to be a major resource. Herds number 300,000 camels and 5,500,000 sheep and goats in the central and northern regions, and 1,000,000 head of cattle in the south. Livestock furnishes the nomads with essentials for their way of life: abundant meat and milk, and hides and skins to make tents, carpets, cushions, and saddles. Some livestock is driven on the hoof for sale in Senegal and Mali.

In the mountains, some 800,000 palm trees yield 15,000 tons of dates annually. Only about 500 tons are exported.

Farmers in the Senegal Valley annually produce 60,000 tons of millet, nearly all for local use. Rice, corn, sweet potatoes, and peanuts also are grown in the valley.

Two airlines serve eight airports. Highways total 1,660 miles.

History.—European trade with the people of the region began in the late 1400's, after Portuguese navigators discovered Arguin, an island off the coast. The Portuguese bought gum arabic, as did Dutch and French traders in later centuries. By the early 1800's, Mauritania was recognized as within 'the French sphere of influence. It became a French protectorate in 1903, a colony in 1920, and a territory in 1946.

Mauritania won self-government on Nov. 28, 1958, as a republic within the French Community. It proclaimed complete independence on Nov. 28, 1960. The republic's first president, 37-year-old Mokhtar Ould Daddah, was elected in 1961 and reelected in 1966. Educated in France as a lawyer, he had previously served as prime minister.

The president and 40-member unicameral National Assembly are elected by universal suffrage for five-year terms.

MAURITIUS, mô-rish′ē-əs, a densely populated island in the Indian Ocean about 550 miles east of Madagascar, is an independent nation within the Commonwealth of Nations. Its capital, Port Louis, also administers smaller island dependencies: Rodrigues, 350 miles east, and scattered coral groups, 250 to 580 miles away.

Information Highlights

Form of Government: Constitutional monarchy.
Head of State: Queen (represented by governor general).
Head of Government: Prime Minister.
Legislature: Legislative Assembly (70 seats).
Area: 809 sq. mi. (Mauritius island, 720 sq. mi.; Rodrigues, 40 sq. mi.; Agalega Islands, about 27 sq. mi.; Cargados Carajos archipelago).
Population: 773,573 (June 1967 estimate).
Capital: Port Louis (population Dec. 1966 est., 134,000).
Major Languages: English (official); French; Creole (patois); and Hindi (spoken).
Monetary Unit: Mauritian rupee.
Main Crops: Sugar, tea, tobacco, fiber, foodstuffs.

Mauritius has a population nearly as large as Rhode Island, but the island has an area only about half the size of that state. The density of population has risen to more than 1,000 persons per square mile, largely because public health measures have brought about the control of malaria and other diseases.

The prosperity of Mauritius depends on sugar, which accounts for 97 percent of export income. Sugarcane plantations cover almost half the island. Because of its single-crop economy, Mauritius imports most of its food. Per capita income averages $226 annually, only about 10 percent of U.S. average per capita income.

The People.—About two thirds of the people are Indo-Mauritians, descendants of immigrants from India. The rest are Europeans, Negroes, Chinese, and persons of mixed origin.

Most members of the Indian community are Hindus, but more than 120,000 are Muslims. The population also includes about 200,000 Roman Catholics and a number of Chinese Buddhists.

From the 1950's to the 1960's, the island's population soared 66 percent. With births exceeding deaths by 4 to 1, the population continues to rise rapidly. The Mauritian birthrate of 30.4 per thousand is nearly twice as high as that of the U.S. Moreover, the Mauritian death rate has dropped to a record low of 8.5 per thousand, 1.2 below the U.S. rate. Most Mauritian families have at least 6 children and many have 10.

Half of the Mauritians over 15 years of age can read and write. Primary education is free but not compulsory. Enrollment in the 773 schools exceeds 181,000. The government operates a technical institute, an agricultural college, and a teacher-training college.

The Land.—The island of Mauritius is 39 miles long and 29 miles wide. Formed by volcanoes, the land slopes gradually from the coasts to a fertile plateau from 1,000 to 1,800 feet high. There are several short chains of mountains, but the three tallest peaks reach only about 2,700 feet.

Abundant rains water the eastern slopes of the central tableland with from 125 to 175 inches annually. Elsewhere rainfall ranges from 40 to 100 inches. Humidity generally runs high. Mauritius sometimes suffers from hurricanes. One of the worst recorded hurricanes struck in 1960, killing 42 persons, making 70,000 homeless, and ruining 60 percent of the sugar crop.

The Economy.—The sugar industry employs 60,000 workers to cultivate 215,000 acres of cane on plantations and operate 23 cane-crushing factories. The Sugar Syndicate, made up of more than 300 cooperative societies, exports most of the crop to Great Britain and Canada. Molasses and alcohol are by-products.

The second-largest agricultural industry, tea, employs 2,200 workers. Formerly imported, tea has risen sufficiently in production to permit small exports. Other main crops include tobacco and aloe fiber, used for making sugar sacks. Farmers raise vegetables and livestock for local use.

Only about 6,500 Mauritians work in manufacturing. They make soap, rum, tobacco products, and matches.

Chief imports are food—especially rice, flour, and meat—as well as clothing, building materials, and machinery.

Port Louis, the island's only harbor, handles up to 10 oceangoing vessels at a time. Five foreign airlines serve an airport at Plaisance. There are 77 miles of railroad and more than 800 miles of roads.

History.—Portuguese navigators discovered the island between 1507 and 1512. They called it Swan Island. The Portuguese found no human inhabitants and no signs that anyone ever lived there. They did see the dodo, an unusual flightless bird that later became extinct (see DODO).

Dutch seamen under Admiral Wybrandt van Warwyk landed in 1598 and renamed the island *Mauritius* for Prince Maurice of Nassau. The Dutch colonized the island from 1638, but they did not prosper and abandoned Mauritius in 1710.

The French took possession in 1715, sent colonists in 1721, and gave the island a new name, *Île de France*. Sugar cane cultivation was introduced by Mahé de La Bourdonnais, governor from 1733 to 1746.

British rule began in 1810 when troops commanded by Gen. Sir Robert Abercromby captured the island during the Napoleonic wars. British possession was confirmed in 1814 by the Treaty of Paris. Under the British, slavery was abolished in 1835. Indian immigrants streamed in from 1842 to 1910 to work on the sugar plantations.

Mauritius began moving toward internal self-government in 1947 with adoption of a constitution setting up an advisory council and legislative body. Continued reviews of the constitution and the granting of fuller self-government after succeeding general elections finally led to the appointment of Sir S. Ramgoolam as first prime minister of the colony in 1967. That same year the date of March 12, 1968, was set for the country's independence. Rioting in January 1968 seemed to jeopardize that goal. Factors contributing to the strife were opposition to independence, new taxes, unemployment, and ethnic rivalries; however, independence was achieved on schedule, and shortly thereafter Mauritius became a member of the United Nations.

Consult Benedict, Burton, Mauritius: *Problems of a Plural Society* (New York 1965).

MAUROIS, mô-rwà´, **André** (pseudonym of ÉMILE SALAMON WILHELM HERZOG), French writer: b. Elbeuf, Seine-Inférieure, July 26, 1885; d. Neuilly-sur-Seine, Oct. 9, 1967. His service as a liaison officer with the British Army in World War I formed the basis for his first book, *Les Silences du Colonel Bramble* (1918). He won acclaim for fictionalized biographies, notably Shelley (1924), Disraeli (1927), Byron (1930), Lyautey (1931), Tourgeniev (1931), Voltaire (1932), Dickens (1934), and Chateaubriand (1938). Among his works of fiction in English translation are *The Conversation of Dr. O'Grady* (1921), *The Weigher of Souls* (1931), and *A Time for Silence* (1942). In 1938 he was elected member of the French Academy and created knight of the Order of the British Empire. During World War II, while France was occupied by the Germans, he resided in the United States, where he wrote *Tragedy in France* (1940) and *Why France Fell* (1941). In 1942 he published the autobiographical *I Remember, I Remember.* Another personal record appeared in *Journal, Etats-Unis* (1946). Also published that year were *La Terre Promise* and a volume of short stories, *Inattendu Toujours Arrive.* His *History of the United States* and *Woman Without Love* appeared in 1948; and in 1950, *Proust: Portrait of a Genius.* Two major works appeared in translation in 1965 and 1966, respectively: *Promethus: The Life of Balzac* and *Victor Hugo and His World.*

MAURRAS, mô-rà´, **Charles,** French writer: b. Martigues, Bouches-du-Rhône, France, April 20, 1868; d. Tours, November 16, 1952. A graduate of the Catholic college of Aix, he went to Paris where he became a contributor to various periodicals including *l'Evènement* and *Revue bleue.* With Moréas and other writers he founded the *École romain* (1891) and drew up its program. A royalist by conviction, he engaged in bitter campaigns against democratic ideas in such periodicals as *le Soleil, la Gazette de France* and *le Figaro,* becoming the leading spokesman of the neomonarchist group. When *l'Action française* was converted from a semimonthly to a daily in 1908, he was associated with Léon Daudet in its editorial direction. A traditionalist, he was convinced that France could only achieve political stability by a return to the monarchy. His support of the church was not motivated by religious principles but by belief in its social values. He was twice imprisoned in 1936 for violent attacks against the Blum government, and his election to the Académie Française two years later caused considerable controversy. After the fall of France in 1940 he became a staunch supporter of the Vichy government. On Jan. 27, 1945 after a four-day trial at Lyon, having been charged with treason and intelligence with the enemy, he was sentenced to imprisonment for life. He was released on Feb. 9, 1952, to undergo hospital treatment.

Among his outstanding political works are *l'Idée de la décentralisation* (1898); *Trois idées politiques* (1899); *Kiel et Tanger* (1910); and the 4-volume *Conditions de la victoire* (1916-1918). His collected poems are in *la Musique intérieure* (1925). His *Les Amants de Venise* (1902) is a psychological study of George Sand and de Musset.

MAURY, mô´rĭ, **Matthew Fontaine,** American naval officer and hydrographer: b. Spotsylvania County, Va., Jan. 14, 1806; d. Lexington, Va., Feb. 1, 1873. He was appointed midshipman in the Navy in 1825, and during 1826-1830 he circumnavigated the globe in the *Vincennes.* A stagecoach accident in 1839 lamed him for life, and in 1842 he was appointed superintendent of the Depot of Charts and Instruments (later the

United States Naval Observatory and Hydrographic Office). He conducted researches on ocean winds and currents, and made wind and current charts of the Atlantic, Pacific, and Indian oceans; his *Physical Geography of the Sea* (1855) was the first textbook of modern oceanography. With outbreak of the American Civil War in 1861 he resigned his post to join the Confederate forces. From 1862 to 1865 he was agent of the Confederacy in Britain; and during 1865–1866 he sought to arrange with Emperor Maximilian for the settlement of Confederate veterans in Mexico. He then settled in Britain, but returned to the United States in 1868 to become professor of meteorology at the Virginia Military Institute. Maury Hall, at the United States Naval Academy, is named for him; his birthday is a school holiday in Virginia.

MAUSER, mou'zĕr, **Peter Paul,** German inventor: b. 1838; d. May 29, 1914. He was employed in the royal armory at Oberndorf, and there, with his brother, Wilhelm Mauser (1834–1882), invented a needle gun in 1863. Moving to Liége, Belgium, in 1867, the brothers invented a breech-loading gun which was adopted by the Prussian government in 1871. They purchased the arsenal at Oberndorf to manufacture their weapons, which included a pistol, a revolver, and a repeating rifle. The Mauser magazine rifle was invented by Peter Paul Mauser in the year 1897.

MAUSOLEUM (Greek, *mausoleion*), a tomb or burial place, the name of which is derived from Mausolus, a ruler of Caria, to whom a sumptuous sepulcher was raised by his wife, Artemisia, at Halicarnassus. Mausolus died 353 B.C.; and his wife was so disconsolate that she perpetuated his memory by the erection of this magnificent monument which became so famous as to be esteemed the seventh wonder of the world, and to give a generic name to all superb sepulchers. Its entire height was 140 feet, and the entire circuit 411 feet. It was overthrown, probably by an earthquake, between the 12th and 15th centuries; and when the Knights of Rhodes took possession of Halicarnassus in 1404 they availed themselves of the materials of the mausoleum to erect the fortress of San Pietro. Parts of the frieze were transported to the British Museum in 1846. Other famous mausoleums are that erected at Babylon by Alexander the Great in honor of Hephaestion, equally magnificent with that of Mausolus, though less refined; and the mausoleum of Augustus, built by him in the sixth consulate on the Campus Martius, between the Via Flaminia and the Tiber, the ruins of which are still seen near the church of Saint Roque. One of the obelisks which stood before this superb building was found in the reign of Pope Sixtus V. This mausoleum contained the ashes of Augustus, Marcellus, Agrippa, Germanicus, and of some later emperors. The mausoleum of Hadrian, at Rome, has been known since the addition of a medieval superstructure as the Castel Sant' Angelo. The most beautiful of all mausoleums is the Taj Mahal, at Agra, India, erected by Shah Jahan between 1631 and 1653 to the memory of his favorite wife, Mumtaz Mahall. Notable mausoleums of modern times include that of Napoleon under the dome of the Invalides, Paris; of President Lincoln, in Washington; of Gen. U. S. Grant, Riverside Drive, New York City; and of Nikolai Lenin, in Moscow.

MAUSOLUS, mô-sō'lŭs, ruler of Caria (ancient division of southwest Asia Minor): d. about 353 B.C. With other satraps, he revolted against Artaxerxes II (Mnemon) and made himself virtually independent, capturing much of Lycia, Ionia, and several of the islands of Greece. He removed the capital of Caria from Mylasa (now Milas, Turkey) to Halicarnassus (the modern Bodrum). The latter is the site of his celebrated tomb, erected by his wife, Artemisia. See also MAUSOLEUM.

MAUSTON, môs'tŭn, city, Wisconsin, seat of Juneau County, located in the valley of the Wisconsin River 35 miles west-northwest of Portage; it is served by the Chicago, Milwaukee, St. Paul and Pacific Railroad. The city handles the products of a fertile dairy and farming area, and engages in lumbering and the production of ladies' clothing. Mauston's original name was Maughstown. Pop. 3,531.

MAUTHNER, mout'nĕr, **Fritz,** German novelist and philologist: b. Horzitz, Bohemia, Nov. 29, 1849; d. Jan. 29, 1923. He came of a Jewish family. Moving to Prague at an early age, he studied law and in 1876 became a contributor to the *Berliner Tageblatt*. He continued writing for this newspaper in various departments, particularly as dramatic critic, until 1905. While he wrote novels and satiric romances, his greatest work was in the field of philosophical criticism of language as a means of expression. His style was smooth and brilliant.

MAUVAISES TERRES. See BAD LANDS.

MAUVE, mōv, an aniline purple coloring matter, first obtained by W. H. Perkin in 1856.

MAVERICK, măv'ĕr-ĭk, **Peter,** American engraver: b. New York City, Oct. 22, 1780; d. there, June 7, 1831. He learned the art of engraving under his father, and was engaged principally on designs for bank notes. Among his more famous engravings was that of Charles King's portrait of Henry Clay; of Samuel Lovett Waldo's portrait of Andrew Jackson; and of William Dunlap's portrait of Benjamin Moore. He was one of the founders of the American Academy of Design in 1826. His most celebrated pupil was Asher Brown Durand.

MAVERICK, an unbranded animal found straying, especially one appropriated by a chance finder. This term, in common use in the cattle country of the United States, is derived from the name of Samuel Augustus Maverick (1803–1870), a pioneer in Texas from 1835, who owned a cattle ranch of 385,000 acres. Having accepted in 1845 a herd of 400 cattle in payment of a debt, he left them in charge of one of his men. They were neglected and allowed to run wild, and when the calves were born they were of course appropriated by other ranchers and branded with their marks, and so passed to their undisputable ownership. As the ownership of the cattle was determined by the brand, the name mavericks came to be given to all calves caught when straying from the herd. From this use of the word grew a wider application to anything dishonestly come by.

MAVOR, mā'vẽr, **James,** Scottish-Canadian economist: b. Stranraer, Scotland, Dec. 8, 1854; d. Glasgow, Oct. 31, 1925. He was educated at the University of Glasgow, and was for a time editor of the *Scottish Art Review.* In 1888 he became professor of political economy at St. Mungo's College, Glasgow, and from 1892 to 1923 was professor of political economy at the University of Toronto, Canada. He was elected a fellow of the Royal Society of Canada in 1914. He published a number of works on economics, including *Economic Survey of Canada* (1914); *Applied Economics* (1914); and *A Short Economic History of Canada* (1915).

MAVROKORDATOS, mä-vrô-kôr-thä'tôs (also spelled MAVROCORDATO, MAVROCORDATOS, or MAUROCORDATOS), **Alexandros,** Greek statesman: b. Constantinople (Istanbul), Turkey, Feb. 11, 1791; d. Aegina (Aigina), Greece, Aug. 18, 1865. Member of a Phanariot family of Greek princes, he was a skilled linguist and diplomat. At the outbreak of the war for Greek independence (1821), he devoted his fortune to the equipment of a ship and the arming of volunteers. He organized the insurrection in Aetolia and Acarnania, and distinguished himself in the first defense of Missolonghi (1822–1823). As president of the first national assembly, he drew up the provisional constitution and signed the proclamation of independence. Between 1833 and 1856 he held various ministerial posts in the Cabinet, and became the first prime minister under the new constitutional monarchy proclaimed late in 1843. A Liberal in politics, he was leader of the so-called English Party. See also GREECE—*7. Modern History.*

MAVROMICHALIS, mä-vrô-mē-ка'lyês, **Petros** (also called PETRO BEY), Greek patriot: b. 1775; d. Jan. 29, 1848. Bey of Maina in 1816, he was a leader of the revolt in the Peloponnesus (1821) in the Greek Revolution; but after the liberation was imprisoned for his opposition to the pro-Russian policies of Count Johannes Antonius. He supported Otto I from 1832 and was appointed (1836) vice president of the council of state.
See also GREECE—*7. Modern History.*

MAWLAWI. See MOSLEM SECTS—*Sufism.*

MAWSON, mô's'n, SIR **Douglas,** British geographer and explorer: b. Bradford, Yorkshire, England, May 5, 1882; d. Adelaide, Australia, Oct. 14, 1958. His parents emigrated to Australia in his childhood. He was educated in mining engineering at Sydney University, taught chemistry there, and from 1920 to 1954 was professor of geology and mineralogy at the University of Adelaide. In 1903 he made a geological exploration of the New Hebrides, and as a member of Sir Ernest Shackleton's Antarctic expedition in 1907, took part in the ascent of Mount Erebus (q.v.) and helped determine the position of the south magnetic pole in Victoria Land. As leader of the Australasian Antarctic expedition, 1911–1914, he made some of the most important discoveries of the early 20th century, for which he was knighted (1914) and awarded the Founder's Medal of the Royal Geographical Society (1915). He also led the British, Australian, and New Zealand Antarctic ex-pedition of 1929–1931. He was the author of *Home of the Blizzard* (1915) and of numerous scientific papers. See also ANTARCTIC REGIONS; POLAR EXPLORATION, SOUTH.

MAX, mäks, **Adolphe,** Belgian public official: b. Brussels, Belgium, Dec. 31, 1869; d. there, Nov. 6, 1939. He was educated at Brussels University, where he received his law degree at the age of 20. Thereafter he entered the political field, serving as provincial councilor for Brabant until 1903, when he became a member of the Brussels City Council. Politically a Liberal, he soon won prestige as a stirring orator and shrewd public official. After 1903 he took up journalism for a time, acting as managing chief of *Le Soir* (Brussels) and honorary chief of the Belgian Press Association. In 1909, however, he returned to politics as burgomaster of Brussels and soon became known as the first civilian citizen of the capital city. His fame as a World War hero rests chiefly upon his defiance of the German army as it occupied Brussels and upon his leadership of the people of the city during the first part of the occupation. He was arrested in September 1914 and, despite repeated attempts to have him released, was held prisoner by the Germans until the Armistice in 1918. Returning to Brussels, he received a great welcome. He won a seat in the Chamber of Representatives (1919), was appointed minister of state, and was elected a member of the Belgian Academy.

MAX, mäks, **Gabriel von,** German painter and illustrator: b. Prague, Bohemia (then under Austrian rule), Aug. 23, 1840; d. Munich, Germany, Nov. 24, 1915. He studied with his father, the sculptor Joseph Max, and later with Karl von Piloty in Munich, where he settled, and taught at the Munich Academy from 1879 to 1883. He was known especially for his mystical figure paintings and for his book illustrations. His *The Last Token* (1874) is in The Metropolitan Museum of Art, New York City.

MAX MULLER, Friedrich. See MÜLLER, FRIEDRICH MAX.

MAXENTIUS, măk-sĕn'shĭ-ŭs, **Marcus Aurelius Valerius,** Roman emperor: r. 306–312; d. near Rome, Italy, Oct. 28, 312. The son of Maximian, Roman emperor in the West, he was not chosen to succeed his father, when the latter and Diocletian abdicated (305). But after Constantius I, Maximian's successor, died (306) and his son Constantine I had been proclaimed emperor in Britain, the Praetorian Guard in Rome raised Maxentius to the throne. On Maxentius' invitation, Maximian left his retirement to resume the purple (306) and to aid his son by reaching an agreement with Constantine, who had crossed into Gaul. Maximian and Maxentius forced Severus, rightful Roman emperor in the West, to surrender near Ravenna, Italy, and Maxentius ordered his execution (307). Then Galerius, Roman emperor in the East, invaded Italy, but was compelled to retreat (307). When Maximian tried to depose Maxentius, he failed and fled to Gaul (308). Next Maxentius recovered the Province of Africa, which had revolted (309–310). Encouraged by his successes, Maxentius challenged Constantine for control of the Western Empire. Constantine invaded Italy, and, after defeating Maxentius' forces at Turin and Verona, destroyed them in the decisive Battle of the Milvian (Mulvian) Bridge (312), four miles north of Rome. Maxentius perished in the Tiber River while trying to escape over the bridge.

P. R. COLEMAN-NORTON.

MAXEY, măk′sē, **Samuel Bell,** American soldier: b. Tomkinsville, Ky., March 30, 1825; d. Eureka Springs, Ark., Aug. 16, 1895. Upon his graduation from West Point in 1846, he was assigned to the infantry, fought in the Mexican War, and was breveted first lieutenant for bravery at Contreras. When the war ended; he resigned from the army to enter the practice of law with his father, first in Kentucky and later at Paris, Texas. At the outbreak of the Civil War he entered the Confederate service as colonel of the 9th Texas Infantry, which he organized, and fought in the campaigns east of the Mississippi. He was made brigadier general in 1862, and in 1863 was placed in command of Indian Territory, where he raised and equipped three Indian brigades and kept the Indians friendly to the Confederacy. In 1864 he was promoted major general for his defeat of Union troops attempting to effect a junction with federal forces in the Red River Valley. After the war, he returned to his law practice. He declined a federal judgeship in Texas, but from 1875 to 1887 was United States senator from Texas. As senator, he ably represented the interests of his state, advocated individual farms as the best solution of the Indian question, and opposed the system of protective tariffs.

MAXIM, măk′sĭm, SIR **Hiram Stevens,** Anglo-American inventor: b. Brockway's Mills, near Sangerville, Me., Feb. 5, 1840; d. Streatham, England, Nov. 24, 1916. He had a country school education, worked on his father's farm, and spent his spare time studying science. At the age of 14 he was apprenticed to a carriage builder in East Corinth, Me., later worked in the engineering works of his uncle, Levi Stevens, at Fitchburg, Mass., and still later was employed by Oliver P. Drake, scientific instrument maker, in Boston. He received his first patent in 1866 for an improved curling iron; and about two years later, while employed as draftsman in a shipbuilding firm in New York City, he invented a locomotive headlight which came into general use. In 1878 he became chief engineer of the United States Electric Lighting Company—the first such company in the country—and soon devised a successful method of building up carbons in the incandescent lamp by heating the filaments electrically in a hydrocarbon atmosphere.

In 1881 Maxim exhibited his electric pressure regulator at the Paris Exposition and received the Légion d'Honneur decoration, then went to England where in 1884 he organized the Maxim Gun Company to produce his most important invention (1883), an automatic, single-barrel rifle firing 10 shots a second, in which the recoil from the explosion of one cartridge was used to eject the empty shell and at the same time reload the weapon. The British Army adopted the rifle in 1889, the Royal Navy in 1892, and it was soon in use in armies throughout the world. He also invented a smokeless powder, an aerial torpedo gun, and the delayed-action fuse; his other inventions included an automatic sprinkler for fire extinguishing, automatic gas-generating plants, steam and vacuum pumps, engine governors, even an improved mousetrap. In all he received 122 United States patents and 149 British patents.

Maxim had experimented with aeronautics for many years, and in 1894 built a steam-propelled airship that left the ground but did not fly, chiefly because when it was loaded for flight its weight was too much for the engines. The Maxim Com-

Sir Hiram Stevens Maxim

Culver Service

pany merged with the Nordenfeldt Company in 1888 and with Vickers' Sons in 1896. Maxim became a British subject in 1900 and was knighted by Queen Victoria in 1901. He was a member of the American Society of Civil Engineers, the Royal Society of Arts, the British Association for the Advancement of Science, and other important societies.

His son, HIRAM PERCY MAXIM (1869–1936), also an inventor, was educated at Massachusetts Institute of Technology and Colgate University, and is best known for his invention of the Maxim silencer for firearms and the muffler for automobile motors. He was the author of *Life's Place in the Cosmos* (1933) and the autobiography *Horseless Carriage Days* (published posthumously 1937).

MAXIM, Hudson (original first name ISAAC), American inventor: b. Orneville, Me., Feb. 3, 1853; d. Landing Post Office, N.J., May 6, 1927. He was the brother of Sir Hiram Stevens Maxim (q.v.), studied chemistry and natural science at Maine Wesleyan Seminary, Kent's Hill, Me., and was for about 10 years a partner in a book business, publishing and selling a book on

Hudson Maxim

Culver Service

penmanship, first in Columbus, Ohio, and later (1883–1888) in Pittsfield, Mass. In 1888 he joined his brother in England and began experiments with smokeless powder. Upon his return to the United States late that year he continued his study of explosives and in 1889 patented a process for producing high explosives. In 1891, as chief engineer of the Columbia Powder Manufacturing Company at Squankum, N.J., he worked on producing safer dynamite, and in 1893 organized the Maxim Powder Company for the production of smokeless powder.

Maxim sold his patents to the E. I. du Pont de Nemours & Company of Wilmington, Del., in 1897, and thereafter was consulting engineer for that company. Between 1895 and 1900 he developed and perfected the shockproof high explosive, maximite, the formula of which he sold to the United States government in 1901. Among other products, he invented stabillite (q.v.) and the torpedo propellant motorite; in 1901 he patented a process for making calcium carbide. In World War I he was chairman of the committee on ordnance and explosives on the Naval Consulting Board in Washington, D.C. He was a member of the Chemists Club, the Aeronautical Society, and other scientific societies, and in 1913 Heidelberg University (now Heidelberg College), Ohio, awarded him the Doctor of Science degree. He published *The Science of Poetry and the Philosophy of Language* (1910); *Defenseless America* (1915); and *Dynamite Stories* (1916).

MAXIMA AND MINIMA, măk′sĭ-mȧ, mĭn′ĭ-mȧ, in mathematics, are the points where a curve ceases to ascend and or to descend.

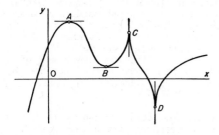

For Functions of One Variable.—A function $f(x)$ is said to have a maximum (or minimum) value when the corresponding curve $y = f(x)$ has an ordinate which is greater (or less) than its immediate neighbors. Not all functions have such values, but when they do occur the value of the function increases until the maximum is reached and then decreases as x increases from left to right; for a minimum the value of the function first decreases, then increases. In the figure, A and C are maximum points and B and D are minimum points. Since these extremes (maxima and minima) are not of necessity the greatest or least values of the entire function, they are frequently called *relative* maxima and minima. In the calculus it is shown that when a function $f(x)$ is increasing, the value of its first derivative $f'(x)$ is positive, and when the function $f(x)$ is decreasing the value of $f'(x)$ is negative. When $f'(x)$ is zero the function is neither increasing nor decreasing, hence any value of x which makes $f'(x)$ equal to zero tends to locate a maximum or minimum of the types A and B in the figure. For types C and D in the figure $f'(x) = \infty$ locates the extremes. In either case, if $f'(a) = 0$ or $f'(a) = \infty$, $x = a$ is a *critical value* for an extreme. If, as x increases from the left to the right through the value a, $f'(x)$ varies from plus through zero to minus, $x = a$ locates a maximum; while the variation of $f'(x)$ from

minus through zero to plus indicates a minimum. If no change of sign occurs, the critical value does not determine a maximum or a minimum.

For Functions of Two or More Variables. —$F(x,y)$ is usually represented in space by the surface $z = F(x,y)$. If, for such a surface, $F(x,y) \geqq F(a,b)$ for all points sufficiently near to (a,b), the function is said to have a relative minimum value at (a,b). If the inequality holds for all values of F, an *absolute* minimum is indicated. If the inequality is reversed, $F(x,y)$ has a relative maximum at (a,b). All critical values for locating maxima and minima are determined by the values of x and y which make

$$\frac{\partial z}{\partial x} = 0 \text{ and } \frac{\partial z}{\partial y} = 0.$$

Various tests, which have been recorded in calculus textbooks, exist for the identification of this type of extreme.

In a similar manner functions of many variables $w = F(x,y,z,...)$ have extreme values when

$$\frac{\partial w}{\partial x} = 0, \frac{\partial w}{\partial y} = 0, \frac{\partial w}{\partial z} = 0, ... \text{ at } (a, b, e, ...).$$

These conditions give rise to a set of simultaneous equations whose solution may determine a maximum, a minimum, or neither. If the reader would like to have details, he is referred to textbooks on advanced calculus.

The idea of maximum occurs in some of the theorems of plane geometry, such as "A circle has a greater area than any other figure with the same perimeter."

WALTER F. SHENTON,
Professor Emeritus of Mathematics, The American University, Washington, D.C.

MAXIMIAN, măk-sĭm′ĭ-ăn (Lat. MARCUS AURELIUS VALERIUS MAXIMIANUS, surnamed HERCULIUS), Roman emperor: r. 286–305, 306–308; d. February 310. Born of humble parents in Pannonia (now Yugoslavia), Maximian had had a distinguished military career before Emperor Diocletian (r. 284–305) chose him as his colleague, when he decided to divide the Roman Empire. Made Caesar (285), Maximian campaigned so successfully in Gaul that Diocletian promoted him to be Augustus (286) and then (or by 293) entrusted to him the European provinces west of the Adriatic Sea and the African provinces west of Egypt, while Diocletian retained the rest of the empire for his own rule. Maximian's successes against barbarian invaders continued until his agreed abdication with Diocletian (305). Recalled from retirement (306) by his usurping son Maxentius (q.v.), Maximian reassumed the imperial title (306) and aided Maxentius against Severus and Galerius, the rightful rulers (307). Then Maxentius, impatient of Maximian's dictation and catching him in a conspiracy to dethrone him, deposed his father (308), who fled to Gaul. There Maximian proclaimed himself emperor for the third time (308), but soon was compelled to surrender at Marseille to Constantine I, who permitted him to live. Two years later, detected in a plot against Constantine, he committed suicide.

P. R. COLEMAN-NORTON.

MAXIMILIAN, măk-sĭ-mĭl′yăn (FERDINAND MAXIMILIAN JOSEPH), emperor of Mexico and archduke of Austria: b. Vienna, Austria, July 6,

1832; d. Querétaro, Mexico, June 19, 1867. He was the younger brother of Francis Joseph I, emperor of Austria. He entered the Austrian Navy in 1846, obtained the rank of rear admiral in 1854 and was placed in command of the navy. From

Maximilian

Brown Brothers

1857 to 1859 he was viceroy of the Lombardo-Venetian possessions of Austria. In 1857 he married Princess Charlotte (Carlota) of Belgium, daughter of King Leopold I. After 1859 Maximilian traveled in Brazil. On his return to Austria he made his home at Miramar, near Trieste.

In 1863 Maximilian became the choice of a group of Mexican exiles and Napoleon III of France to become emperor of Mexico, a venture in monarchy made possible by the French intervention against the Republic of Mexico and its president, Benito Juárez. Maximilian insisted that the people of Mexico approve the offer, whereupon Achille Bazaine, French commander in chief, secured pro-imperial plebiscites in those portions of Mexico controlled by French troops. After a treaty with Napoleon III was arranged, Maximilian accepted the Mexican throne on April 10, 1864. The French army was to remain in Mexico for six years, during which the country was to be regenerated through the development of natural resources and the attraction of immigration.

Maximilian and Carlota reached Mexico City on June 12, 1864. Ignorant of the land he was to rule and temperamentally unfit for the problems facing him, Maximilian was in difficulties

Carlota

The Bettmann Archive

from the start. He refused to restore confiscated lands to the clergy, nor did he pacify the liberals. When he promoted colonization, he antagonized the landowners by initiating an inquiry into land titles. His choice of ex-Confederates from the

United States as colonists to be encouraged and subsidized offended the Mexicans and the United States government. It was impossible to support French forces and maintain an extravagant court from a bankrupt treasury. Friction between Maximilian and the French increased; Mexico was never entirely conquered.

By the spring of 1865, Napoleon realized that the Mexican venture was a failure and that he could not continue its cost in view of growing opposition in France and disturbing events transpiring in Europe. The United States refused to recognize the Mexican Empire and, once the Civil War ended in 1865, urged the withdrawal of French troops. Unofficial aid from the United States strengthened the resistance of Juárez and the republican forces. Efforts of Maximilian to arouse support in the financial centers of the United States through opportunities of investment came to nothing. In the hope of ending the resistance, the French pressed Maximilian to issue the decree of Oct. 2, 1865, ordering all Juáristas shot as bandits. Bitter indignation resulted. By July 1866, the French agreed to retire within 18

Radio Times Hulton Picture Library

Maximilian's brief reign comes to a tragic end as troops of Juárez enter Mexico City in 1867.

months. Empress Carlota went to Europe to protest the desertion of her husband before Napoleon III and the pope. The futility of her mission unsettled her reason.

As the French prepared to depart, they urged Maximilian to go with them. In October 1866 he actually drafted an abdication proclamation and sent his baggage to Vera Cruz whence it was shipped to Austria; but he allowed himself to be persuaded to remain. His forces then consisted of 15,000 to 20,000 Mexican troops and a few European volunteers. He established himself at Querétaro where he was surrounded by the Juáristas and captured through the treachery of one of his officers, Miguel López, on the night of May 14, 1867. Foreign governments petitioned Juárez to send Maximilian back to Europe; the Austrian minister to Mexico received an unlimited expense account to bribe the Mexicans, but Juárez determined to give foreign interventionists a lesson. Maximilian was court-martialed and on June 19, 1867, he and two of his officers were shot. His body was returned to Austria. The Empress Carlota lived in Belgium until 1927 without regaining her reason. See also MEXICO—*26. Mexico from 1810 to 1910* (Decisive Decade 1857–1867).

KATHRYN ABBEY HANNA, *Rollins College.*

Bibliography.—Rivera Cambas, Manuel, *Historia de la intervencion Europea y Norte Americano en Mexico y del Imperio de Maximiliano de Hapsburgo,* 3 vols. (Mexico City 1888); Gaulot, Paul, *La verité sur l'expédition du Mexique d'après les documents inédits de Ernest Louet, payeur en chef du corps expéditionaire,* 3 vols. (Paris 1890); Musser, John, *The Establishment of Maximilian's Empire in Mexico* (Menasha, Wis., 1918); Corti, Egon Conte, *Maximilian and Charlotte of Mexico,* 2 vols. (New York 1929); Dawson, Daniel, *The Mexican Adventure* (London 1935); Blasio, José Luis, *Maximilian, Emperor of Mexico* (New Haven, Conn., 1934); Hyde, Harford M., *Mexican Empire* (New York 1946).

Even better sources are the Mexican newspaper files of the period and the *Papeles del Imperio,* located in the Archives of the Nation, Mexico City.

MAXIMILIAN, known as PRINCE MAX OF BADEN (full name, MAXIMILIAN ALEXANDER FRIEDRICH WILHELM), German statesman: b. Baden-Baden, Germany, July 10, 1867; d. Constance (Konstanz), Nov. 6, 1929. He was heir presumptive to the grand ducal throne of Baden. From 1907 to 1918 he was president of the First Chamber of the Baden Diet, and during World War I did much to alleviate the sufferings of British prisoners of war in Germany and of German prisoners in Russia. On Oct. 3, 1918, he became chancellor of Germany, holding the post for five weeks. He signed the request for the armistice, announced the abdication of William II as emperor on Nov. 9, 1918, and the same day turned over the government to the Socialist leader Friedrich Ebert. In his *Erinnerungen und Dokumente* (1927; Eng. tr., *Reminiscences and Documents,* 1928) he answered some of the political charges made against him by Erich Ludendorff and other monarchists.

MAXIMILIAN, the name of two Holy Roman emperors:

MAXIMILIAN I: b. Wiener Neustadt, near Vienna, Austria, March 22, 1459; d. Wels, Austria, Jan. 12, 1519. Called "the Last of the Knights," he was the son of Frederick III, and in 1477 married Mary of Burgundy (1457–1482), daughter of Charles the Bold. The marriage made him an independent prince, but involved him in a war with Louis XI of France, in which Maximilian was successful. At Frankfort, in 1486, he was chosen king of the Romans (king of Germany), secured the Tyrol in 1490, and in 1493, on the death of his father, became Holy Roman emperor. In 1494 he married as his second wife, Bianca Sforza, daughter of the duke of Milan, and was soon at war with France for control of Milan and Naples. His defeat by the Swiss Confederacy in 1499 practically assured their independence. In 1508 he joined the League of Cambrai against Venice, and in 1513 the so-called Holy League against Louis XII of France, and the same year helped Henry VIII of England defeat the French at Guinegate (Battle of the Spurs); but in 1516 he was forced by Francis I to cede Milan to France. His son Philip married Juana, daughter of Ferdinand and Isabella of Castile, and Maximilian was succeeded by his grandson Charles V. See also GERMANY —*3. History* (Confessional Age).

MAXIMILIAN II, Holy Roman emperor: b. Vienna, Austria, July 31, 1527; d. Regensburg, Bavaria, Oct. 12, 1576. He was the son of Ferdinand I, and on the death of his father in July 1564, succeeded him as Holy Roman emperor. In 1548 he married Maria, daughter of Emperor Charles V, served as the emperor's representative in Spain (1548–1550), and from 1552 directed the defense of the Austrian territories against the Turks. He became king of Bohemia and king of the Romans (that is, king of the Germans) in 1562, and king of Hungary in 1563. In 1568 he concluded an unsatisfactory truce with the Turkish sultan Selim II, under which, while retaining his Austrian possessions, he continued to pay tribute to Turkey for the kingdom of Hungary. In 1573 a group of Polish factions offered him the throne of Poland, but the proposal collapsed in the face of strong opposition from other Polish circles. As emperor he was tolerant in his treatment of the German Protestants, though he was nominally a Catholic. He was succeeded as emperor by Rudolph, the eldest of the sons who survived him. His daughter Anne was the fourth wife of Philip of Spain, and his daughter Elizabeth was the wife of Charles IX of France.

MAXIMILIAN, the name of two kings of Bavaria:

MAXIMILIAN I (in full, MAXIMILIAN I JOSEPH): b. Schwetzingan, Baden, May 27, 1756; d. Castle Nymphenburg, near Munich, Bavaria, Oct. 13, 1825. He served as an officer in the French Army from 1777 to 1789, when he entered the Austrian service. He succeeded to the title of duke of Zweibrücken in 1795, and in 1799 became elector of Bavaria. By the Treaty of Pressburg (1805), Bavaria was given the status of a kingdom and on Jan. 1, 1806, Maximilian was recognized as its king. (See BAVARIA—*History.*) Until 1813 he supported Napoleon Bonaparte, but in that year joined the league against him and thus retained his own throne after Napoleon's fall. He opposed the consolidation of Germany at the Congress of Vienna (1814–1815), and in 1818 granted Bavaria a new constitution. He was succeeded by his son Louis I.

MAXIMILIAN II (in full MAXIMILIAN II JOSEPH): b. Munich, Bavaria, Nov. 28, 1811; d. there, March 10, 1864. The son of King Louis I, he was educated at Göttingen and Berlin universities, traveled in Italy and Greece, and came to the throne of Bavaria upon his father's abdication in 1848. A patron of art and science, he began his reign as a liberal monarch but became increasingly conservative. He was opposed to the union of Germany under the hegemony of Prussia, supported Austria in opposition to Prussia (1850), and advocated the creation of a confederation of the smaller German states, the so-called Trias, as a counterweight to Austrian-Prussian rivalry. After 1859 he instituted a moderate constitutional government.

MAXIMILIAN I (called THE GREAT), duke and elector of Bavaria: b. Munich, Bavaria, April 17, 1573; d. Ingolstadt, Sept. 27, 1651. He became duke of Bavaria upon the abdication of his father in 1597. Educated by the Jesuits, he actively opposed the Reformation. Following the formation of the Protestant Union of German princes in 1608, he organized the rival Catholic League of German states in 1609. In 1618, with the outbreak of the Thirty Years' War (q.v.), and having first ensured the neutrality of the Union by means of a treaty, he threw the support of the League to his cousin, the Emperor Ferdinand II. In November 1620 his forces, commanded by the Count of Tilly, defeated the troops of Frederick V, elector Palatinate and king of Bohemia, at White Mountain, near Prague, and occupied and devastated the Palatinate. In 1623 he became elector Palatinate (see also BAVARIA—*History*). He acquired the Upper Palatinate, restored Upper Austria to Ferdinand, and in 1630, at the Diet of Regensburg, succeeded in having Albrecht von Wallenstein removed as commander of the imperial armies. Two years later, Wallenstein was recalled to command and Maximilian was obliged to seek his help against the Swedes when, with French assistance, they occupied Munich. After several years of intermittent war with Sweden and France, Maximilian concluded a truce with them at Ulm in 1647; but the following year Bavaria was again invaded and his forces were defeated. By the Treaty of Westphalia (see WESTPHALIA, PEACE OF) signed at Munich in October 1648, Maximilian was confirmed as elector and the electorate was made hereditary in his family.

MAXIMILIAN FRANZ, măk-sĭ-mĭl′yăn fränts, archbishop and elector of Cologne: b. Vienna, Austria, Dec. 8, 1756; d. Hetzendorf, near Vienna, July 27, 1801. He became archbishop of Cologne in 1780, and the last elector of Cologne in 1784; he was also bishop of Münster. In 1786 he raised the status of Bonn Academy to that of university. He was the youngest son of Francis I and Maria Theresa, emperor and empress of Austria, and as the French Army approached to invest Cologne in 1794, he retired to Austria.

MAXIMILIAN HENRY, măk-sĭ-mĭl′yăn hĕn′rĭ, archbishop and elector of Cologne: b. Bavaria, Oct. 8, 1621; d. Bonn, June 3, 1688. The son of Duke Albert VI of Bavaria, in 1650 he became archbishop and elector of Cologne. He formed an alliance with Louis XIV of France in 1671, and took part in Louis' wars against the Netherlands, Spain, and the emperor. When Bonn was besieged by the imperial forces in 1673, he fled to Cologne, and, following the fall of the city, made peace with the enemy in 1674.

MAXIMILIAN JOSEPH, măk-sĭ-mĭl′yăn yō′zĕf (pseudonym PHANTASUS), German writer: b. Bamberg, Bavaria, Dec. 4, 1808; d. Munich, Nov. 15, 1888. A Bavarian nobleman, he followed a literary career and was the author of a number of novels and plays, and of the travel book *Wanderung nach dem Orient* . . . (1839).

MAXIMIN I, măk′sĭ-mĭn (Lat. GAIUS JULIUS VERUS MAXIMINUS, surnamed THRAX), Roman emperor (r. 235–238): b. in Thrace, 173; d. Aquileia, Italy, May 238. A shepherd turned soldier, Maximin won renown for his size, strength, endurance, courage, and military ability, which resulted first in his rapid advancement and then in his election as the first Roman emperor who ›rose from the ranks. After Emperor Alexander Severus had been assassinated in Gaul (235), Maximin, who was conducting an invasion of Germany, was acclaimed emperor by his soldiers and then was accepted by the Roman Senate. Maximin continued his campaign beyond the Rhine and the Danube rivers for almost two years (235-237), until an African insurrection brought Gordian I and II (father and son) to the throne. Proscribed by the Senate as a public enemy because of his cruelty, oppression, rapacity, and confiscation of public property and state funds, Maximin invaded Italy, where he halted to besiege Aquileia. But the Aquileians' determined defense

so prolonged the siege that his discouraged soldiers decided to terminate the civil war and murdered Maximin.

MAXIMIN II (Lat. GAIUS GALERIUS VALERIUS MAXIMINUS, surnamed DAIA or DAZA, which perhaps was his original name), Roman emperor (r. 308–314): d. Tarsus, Asia Minor, 314. Of Illyrian birth, he had been a shepherd until he decided to be a soldier. Advancement in the army was rapid and based more on his connections than on merit, for his uncle was Galerius, Roman emperor in the East, who eventually named him governor of Egypt, Syria, and southern Asia Minor (305). But when Galerius had created Licinius Roman emperor in the West after Emperor Severus' death (307), Maximin persuaded his soldiers to proclaim him emperor (308). After Galerius had died (310 or 311), Maximin maneuvered Licinius into relinquishing the rest of Asia Minor to his governance. Then a quarrel between Maximin and Licinius caused the former to invade Europe, where the latter defeated him near Heraclea Pontica in Thrace (313). Maximin escaped into Asia Minor and soon died by poison, either taken by himself or administered by his rival's agents. Maximin was notorious for his persecution of Christians in the eastern provinces.

P. R. COLEMAN-NORTON.

MAXIMS OF LA ROCHEFOUCAULD, măk′sĭmz, là rôsh-fōō-kō′. The original publication in Paris in 1665 of *Réflexions, ou Sentences et Maximes morales* (*Reflections, or Sentences and Moral Maxims*) caused a stir in the literary salons, as much because of its authorship—the anonymous book was known to be the work of François, duc de La Rochefoucauld (q.v.)—as by reason of its searching and devastating analysis of human motives. A classic of modern literature, the book was described by Voltaire a century after its publication as one of those "which have contributed most to form the taste of the French nation, and to give it the spirit of accuracy and precision." Probing into motives of conduct, La Rochefoucauld finds little to admire; in fact, he discovers *amour-propre*, self-love, at the root of all our actions. Significantly, at the head of the numbered maxims (there are 636 in his last revised edition) he places for epigraph, "Our virtues are most frequently but vices disguised." Here is a sampling of the maxims:

(2) Self-love is the greatest of flatterers.
(19) We all have strength enough to support the misfortunes of others.
(25) We need greater virtues to sustain good than evil fortune.
(39) Interest speaks all sorts of tongues and plays all sorts of characters; even that of disinterestedness.
(218) Hypocrisy is the homage vice pays to virtue.
(220) Vanity, shame, and above all, disposition, often make men brave and women chaste.
(298) The gratitude of most men is but a secret desire of receiving greater benefits.
(304) We may forgive those who bore us, we cannot forgive those whom we bore.
(409) We should often be ashamed of our very best actions if the world only saw the motives that caused them.

Five editions of the *Maxims* were published in the author's lifetime (1665, 1666, 1671, 1675, 1678), each successor containing revisions and additions. Indefatigable in revising and polishing his epigrammatic sentences, La Rochefoucauld undoubtedly owed much to the counsel of his devoted friend and fellow author, Comtesse de

La Fayette (1634–1693), in whose house he lived from 1666 until his death. The *Maxims* have been translated into all modern languages.

DRAKE DE KAY.

MAXIMUS, măk'sĭ-mŭs, SAINT (called THE CONFESSOR), Byzantine theologian: b. Constantinople, 580?; d. in exile, Aug. 13, 662. The son of a noble Byzantine family, Maximus was secretary to the emperor Heraclius from 610 to 630, when he entered the monastery of Chrysopolis (Scutari) and was made abbot. Maximus was very active in the Monothelite controversy, during which he upheld orthodoxy and the supremacy of Rome. (See MONOTHELETES.) He induced Pope Martin I to call the first Lateran council (649), at which Monothelitism was officially condemned. The doctrines advocated by Maximus running counter to imperial policy, he was imprisoned (653) and banished to Thrace in 655. Maximus was brought to Constantinople to stand trial in 662; there he was tortured, mutilated, and exiled. He was one of the major theological writers of the Greek Church; his works cover ascetism, ethics, liturgy, mysticism, and polemics. Of particular importance were his commentaries on Pseudo-Dionysius, which greatly influenced medieval mysticism and theology. His feast day is August 13.

MAXIMUS, the name of four Roman emperors.

MAGNUS CLEMENS MAXIMUS: b. in Spain; d. Aquileia, Italy, 388. Maximus proclaimed himself emperor while commanding Roman troops in Britain, defeated Emperor Gratian in Gaul (383), and was recognized by Theodosius, emperor of the East. Invading Italy, his troops were defeated, and he himself besieged by Theodosius and beheaded.

MARCUS CLODIUS PUPIENUS MAXIMUS: d. Rome, 238. Pupienus Maximus was named joint emperor with Decimus Caelius Balbinus (238) by the senate, in order to resist the barbarian emperor Maximinus Thrax, slain by his own troops. The two emperors, ruling only a few months, were killed by the discontented praetorians to avenge the loss of Maximinus.

PETRONIUS MAXIMUS: d. 455. A friend of Emperor Valentinian III, Maximus conspired in his murder (455) for personal reasons, and was proclaimed emperor. He ruled about three months, and was slain while fleeing the Vandal troops of Genseric, who sacked Rome in 455.

MAXIMUS TYRANNUS: d. Ravenna, Italy, 422. Proclaimed emperor (409) in Spain by the Roman general Gerontius, Maximus was deposed in 411 by the usurper Constantine (Flavius Claudius Constantinus). Maximus rebelled unsuccessfully (418), and was carried off to Italy and slain.

MAXWELL, măks'wĕl, the name of a Scottish family that migrated from England about 1100. Members have held the titles of earl of Morton, earl of Nithsdale, Lord Maxwell, and Lord Herries, and include the following notables:

SIR HERBERT MAXWELL won renown defending his castle Caerlaverock against Edward I in 1300.

ROBERT MAXWELL, 5TH BARON MAXWELL: d. July 9, 1546. Maxwell served as lord provost of Edinburgh, extraordinary lord of session (1533), and high admiral (1540). Taken prisoner by the English at the defeat of Solway Moss (1542), he was forced to make terms with Henry VIII.

JOHN MAXWELL, 7TH or 8TH BARON MAXWELL and EARL OF MORTON: b. April 24, 1553; d. Dryfe Sands, Scotland, Dec. 7, 1593. In constant disfavor with King James VI and his favorite, James Stewart, earl of Arran, Maxwell lost the earldom of Morton (1585), and joined with the banished lords of Scotland in driving Arran from power. He also intrigued to bring about a Spanish invasion of the British Isles in 1588. His son, JOHN MAXWELL (8th or 9th BARON MAXWELL: b. about 1586; d. Edinburgh, May 21, 1612), feuded with the Douglases over the earldom of Morton, killed the laird of Johnstone (1608) to avenge his father's death, and was beheaded for treason.

SIR JOHN MAXWELL OF TERREGLES, MASTER OF MAXWELL and 4TH BARON HERRIES (1512?–1583). A loyal supporter of Mary, Queen of Scots, Maxwell helped her escape from Lochleven, fought for her at Langside (1568), and was one of her commissioners at the conferences in England.

MAXWELL, James Clerk, Scottish physicist: b. Edinburgh, Scotland, Nov. 13, 1831; d. Cambridge, England, Nov. 5, 1879. The greatest theoretical physicist of the 19th century, Maxwell made his first scientific contribution to the Royal Society of Edinburgh at 15. He was educated at the universities of Edinburgh and Cambridge, and was appointed professor of natural philosophy at Marischal College, Aberdeen, Scotland (1856), and at King's College, London (1860), retiring to private life in 1865. In 1871 Maxwell was unanimously elected to the newly founded chair of experimental physics at Cambridge. There he directed the organization of the Cavendish laboratory, opened in 1874. In 1856 he wrote his brilliant essay *On the Stability of Motion of Saturn's Rings,* which won the Adams prize at Cambridge, and which was the forerunner to his studies on the kinetic and dynamical theories of gases. Between 1855 and 1872 he published his investigations on perception of color and color blindness; his textbook *Theory of Heat* appeared in 1871.

Maxwell's fame rests principally on his studies in electricity and magnetism, which were based on a mathematical extension and development of theories first presented by Michael Faraday. Rejecting the theory of electrical action at a distance, he sought to explain all electrical and magnetic phenomena as the results of local strains and motions in a material medium, as a corollary to which he originated the electromagnetic theory of light. Maxwell incorporated his findings in the great work *Treatise on Electricity and Magnetism* (1873), from which have stemmed many of the most significant discoveries of the 20th century. Several scientific laws have been named in his honor.

MAXWELL, SIR John Grenfell, British general: b. Liverpool, England, July 11, 1859; d. Cape Town, Union of South Africa, Feb. 20, 1929. He was sent to Egypt as a young officer in 1882, and in the winter of 1884–1885 took part in the unsuccessful effort to rescue Gen. Charles George Gordon at Khartoum. In 1892 he became a member of Sir Herbert Kitchener's staff, playing a leading role in the British conquest of the Sudan (1896–1898). He then served as a brigade commander and military governor of Pretoria during the South African War, being knighted in

1900. Promoted major general in 1906, he was placed in command of British forces in Egypt two years later, occupying this position until 1912 and again in 1914–1916, during World War I. After the Easter Rebellion in Ireland in 1916, Maxwell was sent there as British commander in chief, and succeeded in crushing the uprising. He retired from active service in 1922.

MAY, Phil(ip William), English illustrator and cartoonist: b. New Wortley, England, April 23, 1864; d. St. John's Wood, Aug. 5, 1903. The greatest black and white artist of his age, May had little formal training, and suffered years of poverty before he was employed as artist for *St. Stephen's Review* (1883). In 1885 he went to Australia to work on the Sydney *Bulletin*, completing some of his best drawings there. From 1888 to 1892 he studied art in Paris, and had his first real success with the illustrations for *The Parson and the Painter* (1891). May began his association with the *Daily Graphic* after his return to London, and joined the staff of *Punch* in 1896. The political portraits which he drew for *Punch*, however, were artistically inferior to his studies of London street life, which he portrayed with such wit and understanding that he may be called the people's illustrator of the late Victorian age. The characteristic feature of May's work was economy of line; as a drawing progressed, he eliminated stroke after stroke, until only the skeleton remained, through which he could express a sense of vitality and life equalled by no other English draftsman. Publication of his drawings include *Phil May's Winter Annual* (1892–1903); *Phil May's Sketch Book: Fifty Cartoons* (1895); and *Guttersnipes: Fifty Original Sketches* (1896).

MAY, Thomas, English poet and historian: b. 1595; d. London, England, Nov. 13, 1650. Unable to practice law because of a speech impediment, May turned to literature. He wrote the comedies *The Heir* (1622) and *The Old Couple* (published in 1658), and three unsuccessful classical tragedies, but was best known as a translator of the classics: Lucan's *Pharsalia* (1627); Virgil's *Georgics* (1628); and *Selected Epigrams of Martial* (1629). King Charles I became his patron and commissioned him to write two historical poems on the reigns of Henry II (1633) and Edward III (1635). May adopted the parliamentary cause in the civil wars, and was made secretary to Parliament (1646). In 1647 appeared his famous *History of the Parliament of England Which Began 3 Nov. 1640*, the official apology of the Parliament and its moderate leaders, while *The Breviary of the History of the Parliament of England* (1650) was a panegyric of the radical Independents. May's histories are biased, and have been accused of dishonesty and venality. After the Restoration, his body was exhumed from Westminster Abbey, and thrown into a neighboring pit.

MAY, Sir Thomas Erskine, 1st Baron Farnborough, English constitutional jurist: b. London, England, Feb. 8, 1815; d. Westminster, May 17, 1886. May was assistant librarian to the House of Commons (1831), and was called to the bar in 1838. In 1844 he published *A Practical Treatise on the Law, Privileges, Proceedings, and Usage of Parliament*, a work recognized as authoritative by Parliament, and translated

into many languages. From 1847 to 1856, May was examiner of petitions for private bills to both houses of Parliament, and from 1871 until his retirement in 1886, he was clerk of the House of Commons. May was president of the Statute Law Revision Committee (1866–1884), and in 1885 was sworn to the Privy Council. He collected and reduced to writing the *Rules, Orders and Forms of Procedure of the House of Commons* (1854); between 1861 and 1863 published the *Constitutional History of England since the Accession of George III, 1760–1860*, which is a standard authority on the subject, and in 1877 wrote *Democracy in Europe*. May was knighted in 1866, and was raised to the peerage in 1886.

MAY, the fifth month of the modern year, and the third in Roman times, has 31 days, and is commonly considered the last month of spring. The etymology of the word is uncertain, but is thought to have come from the Greek goddess Maia, mother of Hermes, or Maia Majesta, a local Italian goddess of spring, to whom sacrifices were made to insure crop growth. The many ceremonies celebrated during May stem largely from its position in the agricultural year, and May Day (q.v.) was once a very important holiday. In the United States the most notable days of the month are Mother's Day and Memorial Day (qq.v.). The Catholic Church dedicates the entire month to the Virgin Mary.

MAY, Isle of, island, Scotland, situated in Fifeshire County, in the mouth of the Firth of Forth, southeast of Crail. The island, about one mile long, has a lighthouse. There are ruins of a 13th century chapel, dedicated to St. Adrian, who was martyred by the Danes in the 9th century, as well as traces of several holy wells, which were formerly favorite places of pilgrimage.

MAY APPLE. See Mandrake.

MAY BEETLE, or JUNE BUG, a clumsy, brown beetle of the Melolonthidae family, is common throughout the United States. The adults fly at night during late spring, feeding upon the young foliage of trees and shrubs. They are less destructive than the larvae, large, soft, white grubs, with big, brown heads. The beetle has a life cycle of about three years; the first two years the grub stays in the ground where it is very harmful, feeding upon roots of grass and plants. For this reason, strawberries, corn, and other vegetables should not be planted upon newly plowed sod land. Early fall plowing is often practiced to destroy the grub.

MAY DAY, the first day of May, has been celebrated through the ages as the arrival of the season of new vegetation. May Day ceremonies are the remnants of ancient agricultural and fertility rituals, which were celebrated universally during seasonal changes. Homage was rendered to trees and leaf-covered branches, and the spirit of vegetation was symbolized in a living person or doll. Elaborate festivities, meant to insure good crops and happiness, were closely linked to numerous omens and taboos of the day. Among the old Celtic peoples, a festival called Beltane was held on May Day. Bonfires were lit and great celebrations held in rites which continue to this day in remote areas of the British Isles. In Ireland the Church

Christianized this celebration by transferring it to June 24, the feast of St. John, which is still celebrated with bonfires.

In England, as we learn from Chaucer and other writers, it was customary during the Middle Ages for all, both high and low—even the court itself—to go out on the first May morning at an early hour "to fetch the flowers fresh." Hawthorn branches also were gathered and were brought home about sunrise, with accompaniments of horn and tabor. The people then proceeded to decorate the doors and windows of their houses with the spoils. By a natural transition of ideas, they gave the hawthorn bloom the name "the May"; they called the ceremony "the bringing home the May"; they spoke of the expedition to the woods as "going a-Maying." The fairest maid of the village was crowned with flowers as the "Queen of the May" and placed in a little bower or arbor, where she sat in state, receiving the homage and admiration of the youthful revellers, who danced and sang around her. This custom of having a May queen seems a relic of the old Roman celebration of the day when the goddess of blooming vegetation, Flora, was specially worshiped.

But perhaps the most conspicuous feature of these festive proceedings was the erection in every town and village of a fixed pole—the Maypole—as high as the mast of a vessel of 100 tons, on which, on May morning, they suspended wreaths of flowers, and round which the people danced in rings nearly the whole day. A severe blow was given to these merry and often wild revels, by the Puritans, who, in their campaign of taking the joy out of life, caused Maypoles to be uprooted and a stop put to all the festivities. They were, however, revived after the Restoration.

Since the 1890's May Day has been adopted in much of the Western World as the international labor day.

MAY FLY, SHAD FLY, or DAYFLY,

members of the order Ephemerida. The species, of which about 300 have been described, nearly one third of which are North American, are fragile insects with large fore wings, small or lacking hind wings, short antennae, atrophied mouth parts and two or three thread-like abdominal filaments. Being greatly attracted to lights, the adults are often a source of annoyance in lakeside and riverside towns, and are sometimes troublesome in obscuring lights from lighthouses.

The eggs are laid in fresh water, either on the surface or the bottom. The larvae, which feed mainly on vegetable matter, are active creatures with strong legs, abdominal tracheal gills, and anal appendages. They live on the bottom, under stones, covered with mud, or in burrows. After molting about 10 times wing pads appear, and these increase with each molt until the last, which may be the twentieth. This occurs in the open air. The one previous to it occurs at the surface of the water, the insect escaping from its subimago skin rather suddenly. One striking difference the adults exhibit is the development of paired sexual organs, which do not appear in other orders of insects. The larvae may take three years to develop; the adults live only a few days, lay their eggs and die. Both adults and larvae are important food for fishes, and consequently they form a favorite bait with anglers, and are imitated in making artificial flies.

MAYA, mä′yà or mī′à, an American Indian people of Middle America. In the strict meaning of the word, the term Maya refers to the indigenous inhabitants of the Yucatán Peninsula and to their native language. The term takes on different and wider connotations when used to refer to the ancient Maya civilization, to the Maya cultural area, or to the Maya (or Maya-Quiché) linguistic stock.

Modern Maya of Yucatán.—Ethnically, the Maya still form the largest part of the population of the peninsula. Physically, they are small in stature (average height: men, five feet one inch; women, four feet eight inches), sturdily built, very round-headed, have warm copper-colored skin, and straight, coarse, black to dark brown hair. The epicanthic eye fold occurs frequently.

Culturally, the Indian way of life has been modified profoundly; first by Spanish influence, the result of conquest and colonization, and later by the impact of Western industrial civilization. These factors making for cultural change have been much less effective in the eastern part of the peninsula (Quintana Roo). The sparse Indian population of this area was in rebellion against the Spaniards throughout the colonial period, and stubbornly maintained its traditions. In 1847, after Mexican independence, the Indians living in the part of Yucatán which had been colonized by the Spaniards for three centuries, rose against their white masters. This war is called the War of the Castes. When the rebellion was suppressed, by 1850, those among the vanquished who did not want to submit again to white domination fled into the Quintana Roo jungles, where they kept up armed resistance until 1901. Even after this date, the Indian communities of interior Quintana Roo maintained their isolation and marked hostility against any interference by the federal government. Politically, they reverted to tribal patterns of organization. Only since 1935 have these Maya groups shown a tendency to become part of the Mexican nation.

Maya Languages.—Maya proper is spoken by about 350,000 individuals, two fifths of whom speak Maya only. The other three fifths speak Maya and Spanish. Roughly six sevenths of the Maya-speaking population inhabits the State of Yucatán. The remainder occupy the northern part of Campeche; Quintana Roo; the Corozal, Orange Walk, and El Cayo districts of British Honduras; and a small northeastern section of the Department of Petén, Guatemala.

The Maya (or Maya-Quiché) linguistic stock includes, besides Maya proper, a number of languages closely related among themselves and also closely related to Maya. Linguists differ on how the Maya-Quiché languages should be classified with relation to each other. Abraham Meyer Halpern classified them, in 1942, as follows:

Guatemalan-Yucatecan Family. It comprises: (1) Maya (spoken in the areas listed above), and Lacandon (the language of a group of perhaps 200 Indians in the Chiapas jungle); (2) Quiché, Cakchiquel, Tzutuhil, Kekchí, Pokoman, Pokomchí, Uspantec (all spoken in highland Guatemala); (3) Mam (southeastern Chiapas and southwestern Guatemala), Aguacatec, Jacaltec, Ixil (all three in highland Guatemala).

Chiapas-Honduras Family. It comprises: (4) Tzental, or Tzeltal, and Tzotzil (both in Chiapas); (5) Chontal (in Tabasco; formerly also southern Campeche), Chol, or Choltí, and Tojolabal, or Chañabal (both in Chiapas), Chuj (highland Guatemala), Chortí (eastern Guatemala and western Honduras).

Huaxtec (or Huastec) Family.—Composed of one group only: (6) Huaxtec (northern Veracruz, eastern San Luis Potosí). Most authors also include the Chicomucteltec language (Chiapas) in this group.

Other authors (Alfred L. Kroeber and John Alden Mason) on the one hand group together the subdivisions 1, 4, and 5 (Kroeber's Lowland Maya Speech Division), and, on the other, the subdivisions 2 and 3 (Highland Division) to form the two major divisions of the Maya linguistic stock. The separate position of Huaxtec is recognized by all authorities, but Kroeber has pointed out its relationships with groups 4 and 5, and places it as a separate branch of the lowland Maya languages.

PRE-COLUMBIAN DISTRIBUTION OF THE MAYA LANGUAGES

In addition to the 350,000 people speaking Yucatecan Maya, more than 1,000,000 speak languages belonging to group 2 above; more than 300,000 speak languages of group 3; more than 100,000 speak languages of the Tzental-Tzotzil group; some 135,000 speak languages of group 5; and about 50,000 speak Huaxtec. About 2,000,000 thus speak languages belonging to the Maya-Quiché linguistic stock.

ANCIENT MAYA

Area.—The area of interest in dealing with the pre-Hispanic Maya civilization comprises the following regions: the whole territory of present-day Guatemala and British Honduras, western Honduras, El Salvador, and, in Mexico, the eastern parts of Chiapas and Tabasco, the states of Campeche and Yucatán, and the Territory of Quintana Roo. This geographical area coincides generally with the area of Maya speech at the time of discovery by Europeans.

Two exceptions are nevertheless of importance. Although the Huaxtec (Huastec) speak a language which belongs to the Maya linguistic stock, they remain outside the pre-Hispanic Maya area. Archaeologists have proved that the Huaxtec separated from their linguistic relatives at an early date (perhaps 1000 B.C., or even before), and that Huaxtec culture differs markedly from the other Maya cultures. In contrast, we must include in the Maya area the Pipil, who at the time of the conquest occupied the Pacific coast of Guatemala and El Salvador southeast to the

Lempa River. The Pipil spoke Nahuat, a variety of the Nahuatl language of central Mexico. Nevertheless, archaeologists have proved that the history of the area inhabited by the Pipil is intimately related to the history of the Guatemalan highlands and western Honduras.

Both from a geographic and a historical point of view, the Maya area may be divided into three parts: (1) a northern Maya area, which comprises the Yucatán Peninsula roughly north of parallel 18° 30' N.; (2) a central Maya area, including the lowlands and foothills south of this line and north of the Chiapas-Guatemalan highlands; (3) a southern Maya area, comprising the Chiapas-Guatemalan highlands, the Pacific coast of Guatemala, and El Salvador west of the Lempa River.

Culturally, the Maya area formed the southern part of the larger cultural area which ethnologists call Meso-America, comprising central and southern Mexico, British Honduras, Guatemala, western Honduras, and El Salvador. Despite regional differences, the civilizations which flourished in this area in pre-Hispanic times shared a basically common culture, with roots in a formative stage of sedentary cultivation, the origins of which date back to before 1000 B.C.

Origins.—Botanists consider the Chiapas-Guatemala highland region an important center of the domestication of cultivated plants. The so-called common, or kidney, bean (*Phaseolus vulgaris*) and secondary varieties of corn (maize) may have been developed in this area. It is believed that corn originated in South America, and that in highland Guatemala, through hybridization with a wild plant of the genus *Tripsacum*, it acquired traits which enabled it to be cultivated not only in temperate zones, but also in humid tropical lowlands. This would give the southern Maya area priority in the development of the proto-Maya culture. Archaeological finds made in the late 1940's also uncovered evidence of an early cultural flowering in this region, which seems to antedate similar developments in other parts of the Maya area.

The earliest period of sedentary cultures in the Maya zone for which we have archaeological evidence is called Formative, Archaic, or Pre-Classic. This period came to an end about 200 A.D. The available data do not permit us to date its beginnings. Nevertheless, by making comparisons with other parts of Meso-America, it is possible to say tentatively that the oldest cultural remains found go back to 1000 B.C., or before.

The oldest evidence of human occupation of the southern Maya area consists of pits filled with household debris found on the outskirts of Guatemala City. The culture which corresponds to these middens belonged to a sedentary people which cultivated corn and probably other plants as well. They ground the corn on grinding stones (*metates*), and baked it in bowl-shaped dishes, ancestors of the flat *comal* of later times. They lived in settled communities and had houses of pole and thatch, with mud-daubed walls. They used obsidian blades and scrapers, and greenstone celts, and made baskets, mats, and textiles. They produced excellent pottery, baked-clay fetishes in human or monkey form, and stamps and seals. This culture is comparable to the Archaic cultures of central Mexico.

The last centuries before Christ represent a period of cultural flowering in the southern Maya area, which lasted until the beginnings of our era. The majority of the 200-odd mounds at Kaminaljuyú, a large archaeological site on the southwestern outskirts of Guatemala City, were constructed during this period. The largest of these mounds is a pyramidal platform over 65 feet high, containing two interior burial chambers. The body of the lord for whom the tomb was constructed lay on a wooden platform in the center of one of the' chambers, surrounded by human bodies, apparently sacrificed to accompany him on his trip to the other world, and by rich funerary offerings, including ornaments of jade, bone, shell, and pyrite, and fine pottery in heaps. All this is evidence of the high social position of the individuals given such an elaborate burial. Great archaeological sites are also known on the Pacific Coast.

The oldest remains of occupation known in the central Maya area are pottery, stone and bone tools, and shell ornaments found in a midden covered by buildings of a later period in the ruins of Uaxactún, Department of Petén, Guatemala. The lack of grinding stones in this midden perhaps indicates that corn was not cultivated in the central Maya area at this time. If this be true, it is possible that the staple food plants cultivated by these proto-Maya were roots, as in many tropical lowland regions of America. The oldest building found at Uaxactún, or at any other site in the central Maya area, belongs to a later period than this midden. It is a base for a temple, in the shape of a stepped and truncated pyramid, with fronts decorated with grotesque stucco faces. It was probably built between the beginning of the Christian era and 250 A.D.

Surveys made in the northern Maya area after 1940 indicate that settlement by sedentary populations in this area is as old as in the other Maya areas. The beginnings of monumental architecture are similarly as old in Yucatán as in Petén Department. A high artificial mound at Yaxuná, Yucatán, appears to belong to the same period as the above-mentioned Uaxactún temple.

Classic Period.—From about 300 A.D. to about 900, a civilization flourished in the central area which was at one and the same time the most brilliant civilization of the Maya and one of the most outstanding of pre-Hispanic America. Sylvanus Griswold Morley called it the "Old Maya Empire." This flowering is characterized by the following traits: great architectural development, and stone buildings roofed with corbeled vaults; temples on top of high pyramids (the highest is Temple IV at Tikal, height 229 feet); artistic climax in sculpture, painting, and decorated pottery; hieroglyphic writing; advanced arithmetic, including the concept of completion or zero, and a positional notation of numbers; highly developed astronomy; complex calendrical calculations (Long Count); the stele cult; and deities not directly related to the powers of nature.

These traits form what J. Eric S. Thompson has called "the hierarchic culture." They are traits of an urban culture, superimposed on the elements of a peasant culture, that is, on the complex of farming and supplementary food-producing activities, home industries, and a simpler religion directly concerned with the elemental forces of nature (Thompson's "lay culture"). The complex calendrical calculations, the Long Count system of reckoning time, and the associated stele cult were some of the most original traits of the classic Maya civilization.

Calendar.—The Long Count was the indispensable basis for complicated astronomical counts. It served as a fixed system of reference for the other two calendars, the civil year of 365 days and the magic cycle (*tzolkin*) of 260 days. It is a count of days (or multiples of days) with an initial date going back to 3114 B.C., according to the most accepted correlation between this count and our own calendar. This initial date is without a doubt much earlier than the invention of the system. We are dealing here with a retroactive count. Scholars set the real beginning of the Long Count at between about 350 B.C. and 140 A.D. The oldest known inscription of the Long Count corresponds to 320 A.D. The complexity of the astronomical calculations of the Maya is evident, if one considers that some of these calculations covered millions of years.

Steles.—The steles are memorials erected to mark time intervals. Thompson maintains that they were not erected to commemorate individual deeds, but that they constitute impersonal markers of calendrical or astronomical events related to religious ideas. There are archaeological indications that these monuments were the objects of a real cult, and traits of this cult survive among the present-day Maya.

Cultural Centers.—The main cultural centers of the classic Maya civilization seem to have been: Tikal (Department of Petén, Guatemala); Palenque (Chiapas, Mexico); and Copán (Honduras). Other sites are: Bonampak, Yaxchilán, and Piedras Negras, in the Usumacinta River drainage (Mexico-Guatemala); Uaxactún and Holmul (Petén Department, Guatemala); Calakmul (southern Campeche, Mexico); San José (British Honduras); and Quiriguá in the lower Motagua Valley (Guatemala).

Some archaeologists deny that these centers constituted real cities. They believe that their function was primarily religious, and that they were enormous sanctuaries with a small resident population formed by priests and their servants. For this reason they prefer to call them ceremonial centers. If this were true, however, one would be led to ask where the main political and commercial centers of this civilization were located. Moreover, these so-called sanctuaries were very large; the ceremonial nucleus of the Tikal ruins covers an area of at least 220 acres. Along with other archaeologists, the author believes that insufficient attention has been paid to the possible role of these centers as political and commercial capitals, to their urban extension, and to the size of their resident populations.

Southern Area.—During the Classic period, close relations existed between the southern Maya area and central Mexico. Between 300 A.D. and 600, Kaminaljuyú served as a center of diffusion of central Mexican influences in the Guatemalan highlands down to Copán. The finds made by Alfred Vincent Kidder and his collaborators in the late 1930's in the big tombs at Kaminaljuyú clarified the nature of these relations between the Maya zone and Teotihuacán, the great metropolis of the Valley of Mexico. Thompson found archaeological evidence along the Pacific Coast which seems to indicate that the Pipil may have arrived in the area between 700 and 850 A.D.

Yucatán.—In the Yucatán Peninsula, the ruins of Oxkintok (Yucatán State) and Cobá (Quintana Roo) belong to the classic period. A lintel found at Oxkintok showed a Long Count date corresponding to 475 A.D. Cobá, the center of a system of causeways radiating to outlying sites, flowered especially from about 600 A.D. to about 750. One of its causeways is 62 miles long. Many of the famous archaeological sites of Yucatán, Campeche, and Quintana Roo, such as Uxmal, Kabah, Sayil, Labná, Edzna, Santa Rosa, Xlabpak, Río Bec, Xpuhil, and the oldest buildings at Chichén Itzá are dated from 600 A.D. to 1000.

Collapse.—This civilization collapsed suddenly, apparently at the peak of its flowering, without going through a well-defined period of decadence. Between 800 A.D. and 900 or 950, one after another of the cities, or ceremonial centers, were abandoned. The cultural superstructure (Thompson's "hierarchical culture") disappeared, and only the peasant culture remained. It is probable that the population decreased markedly at this time, even in the rural areas.

The causes of this crisis are unknown. Many different hypotheses have been advanced to explain it. Some of these are wholly fantastic. Those which seem most valid attribute the phenomenon to impoverishment of the soil, or to a rebellion of the peasants against the exploitation of the ruling group. Moreover, there is archaeological evidence of warfare along the western and northern periphery of the central Maya area from 630 A.D. on. All these factors may have contributed, though it is important to note that whatever their nature, they were felt over a much wider territory than the central Maya area. Meso-America went through a general crisis during the 9th and 10th centuries.

Maya After 900 A.D.—*Yucatán.*—The centers of civilization which had flourished in Yucatán during the preceding period were similarly abandoned in the 10th century. This was nevertheless followed by a period of cultural resurgence under Toltec influence. Morley called this period in the history of Yucatán until the Spanish conquest the "New Empire." It begins with the invasion by the Itzá, who were probably Chontal from Tabasco and southern Campeche, strongly influenced by Toltec culture and perhaps led by Toltec chiefs. They established local dynasties in Yucatán, which associated in a kind of confederacy. Chichén Itzá, settled by the Itzá about 987, dominated the confederacy until about 1204. A rebellion of the lords of Mayapán and Izamal then put an end to the supremacy of Chichén Itzá. This was followed by a period in which the city of Mayapán was dominant, until a new rebellion brought this hegemony to an end about 1460. After the fall of Mayapán, Yucatán remained politically divided into some 18 independent warring lordships. Culturally, there is evidence of decadence from the fall of Chichén Itzá on.

In 1511, a dozen shipwrecked Spaniards reached the shores of Yucatán. Most of them were sacrificed by the Maya. In 1517, the expedition of Francisco Hernández de Córdoba first explored the Yucatecan coast. After Francisco de Montejo had made two unsuccessful attempts to conquer Yucatán in 1527–1528 and 1531–1535, his son Francisco de Montejo the Younger finally made Yucatán a part of the Spanish realm in 1540–1546.

Southern Area.—After the collapse of the Classic civilizations, Toltec invaders also reached the highlands of Guatemala in the southern Maya area. The invaders conquered the local population, and established dynasties which lasted until the Spanish conquest. The last centuries preceding the arrival of the Spaniards was characterized by continuous warfare. The Quiché and Cakchiquel were able to conquer a part of the rich cocoa-producing lands held by the Mam, the Tzutuhil, and the Pipil on the Pacific slopes of the highlands. Around 1500, the great Aztec conqueror Ahuitzotl waged a campaign in Chiapas, which resulted in the conquest of the Pacific coast and in the establishment of some garrisons in the highlands. However, the Aztecs did not push beyond the present-day boundary between Mexico and Guatemala. In 1524, the Spanish captain Pedro de Alvarado conquered the southern Maya area.

Central Area.—Little historical and archaeological information on this period is available for the central Maya area. From the accounts of the first Spanish expeditions it would seem that the region was sparsely populated and politically fragmented. Towns were elaborately fortified with palisades and moats. The Maya of Petén maintained their independence and their cultural traditions until 1697, when Martín de Ursúa completed the conquest of the last Maya redoubts of Lake Petén.

PEDRO ARMILLAS,
Instituto Nacional de Antropología e Historia, Mexico City.

Bibliography.—Spinden, H. J., *A Study of Maya Art* (Cambridge, Mass., 1913); *The Maya and Their Neighbors* (New York 1940); Landa, Diego de, *Relación de las cosas de Yucatán*, tr. by C. P. Bowditch, ed. by A. M. Tozzer (Cambridge, Mass., 1941); Redfield, Robert, *The Folk Culture of Yucatán* (Chicago 1941); Roys, Ralph L., *The Indian Background of Colonial Yucatán* (Washington 1943); Villa Rojas, Alfonso, *The Maya of East Central Quintana Roo* (Washington 1945); Morley, Sylvanus G., *The Ancient Maya* (Stanford, Calif., 1946); Kidder, A. V., Jennings, J. D., and Shook, E. M., *Excavations at Kaminaljuyú* (Washington 1946); Thompson, J. E. S., *Maya Hieroglyphic Writing: Introduction* (Washington 1950); Von Hagen, V. W., *The Ancient Sun Kingdoms of the Americas* (Cleveland 1960); Reed, Nelson, *The Caste War of Yucatan* (Stanford, Calif., 1964); Stierlin, Henri, *Living Architecture: Mayan* (New York 1965).

MAYAGÜEZ, mä′yä-gwäs′, a seaport city in Puerto Rico, located on the west coast, 72 miles southwest of San Juan. It exports sugar, needlework, and fruit. A federal agricultural experiment station is located here, as is the College of Agriculture and Mechanic Arts of the University of Puerto Rico.

An important manufacturing and food-processing center, the city of Mayagüez produces refined sugar, cotton clothing, furniture, tiles, cigars, beer and rum, and food products. Founded in 1760, Mayagüez suffered great damage from an earthquake and tidal wave in 1918. Pop. (1960) 50,147.

MAYAKOVSKI, mŭ-yŭ-kôf′skĭ, **Vladimir Vladimirovich,** Russian Communist poet and dramatist: b. Bagdadi (now Mayakovski), Georgia, Russia, July 19, 1893; d. (suicide) Moscow, April 14, 1930. He joined the Bolshevik Party at the age of 14 and in 1911 began to write futurist poems, of which the best known is *The Cloud in Trousers* (1915). Following the Russian Revolution of 1917 he became the official poet of the Communist government, writing iconoclastic verse for declamation that at its worst is blatantly propagandistic, but at its best—as in the long narrative poem *150,000,000* (1920)—has vitality and vivid imagery. His plays include the satire *The Bedbug* (1929). Mayakovski had a marked influence on Soviet literature.

MAYAPÁN, mī-yä-pän', is an archaeological site in Mexico, about 25 miles south-southeast of Mérida, Yucatán. The ruins belong to the pre-Columbian Maya civilization of southern Mexico, British Honduras, Guatemala, northern Honduras, and western El Salvador. According to Indian legend, Mayapán, "the banner of the Maya," was the capital of the northern provinces of the Yucatán Peninsula from the 1200's to the 1400's A.D. The city was reputedly founded by Kukulcán, the Maya equivalent of the Toltec god or culture hero Quetzalcoatl, who instituted a joint government whereby the rulers of the various provinces resided in Mayapán. Indian legend further recounts that, because of internal dissension, the government was overthrown and the city was destroyed about 1450. The older sites of Chichén Itzá and Uxmal figure prominently in these accounts of strife and dissension.

Recent archaeological researches at the ruins of Mayapán have tended to confirm the legendary date and account of the city's violent destruction. The city is surrounded by a massive, though not very high, stone wall that is pierced by a dozen ancient entrances. The wall encloses a roughly oval area that has a diameter of some two miles east-west and slightly more than one mile north-south. Within this enclosure are the remains of approximately 4,000 buildings, the vast majority of which were dwellings. A conservative estimate of the ancient population of the city is 10,000.

The main ceremonial center of the city, approximately one-quarter mile square, is a congested area of temples, shrines, colonnaded halls, and other civic and religious structures. The art and architecture are a blend of Maya and Toltec styles plus a number of new elements. Compared with the earlier Maya and Toltec remains, those of Mayapán are of inferior quality and clearly reflect the degeneration of Maya civilization. See also CHICHÉN ITZÁ; MAYA.

Bibliography.—Gann, Thomas W.H., *In an Unknown Land* (New York 1924); Noyes, Ernest, *Fray Alonso Ponce in Yucatán, 1588* (New Orleans 1932); Landa, Diego de, *Relación de las cosas de Yucatán,* tr. by Charles P. Bowditch, ed. by Alfred M. Tozzer (Cambridge, Mass., 1941); Roys, Ralph L., *The Indian Background of Colonial Yucatán* (Washington 1943); Carnegie Institution of Washington, *Year Book,* nos. 17, 37, 41, 50–57 (Washington 1918, 1938, 1942, 1951–58).

H.E.D. POLLOCK
Curator of Maya Archaeology
Harvard University

MAYBACH, mī'bäкн, **Wilhelm,** German automobile engineer and builder: b. Heilbronn, Germany, Feb. 9, 1846; d. Stuttgart, Dec. 29, 1929. He was a pioneer in the engineering and construction of automobiles. In 1883 he and Gottlieb Daimler established a workshop at Bad Cannstatt, where they constructed one of the earliest gasoline engines. As technical director from 1895 for the Daimler Motor Company, Maybach was instrumental in building the first Mercedes automobile in 1900–1901. He invented the float-feed carburetor, a shifting-gear mechanism, and the honeycomb radiator. In 1909, with Count Ferdinand von Zeppelin, he established a plant at Friedrichshafen to build airship motors and motorcars.

MAYENNE, ma̔-yen', is a department in northwestern France, formed from part of the old province of Maine. It comprises the basin of the Mayenne River. The area is 1,986 square miles. It is a generally flat agricultural region growing wheat, barley, flax, sugar beets, potatoes, and apples. It is especially noted for dairying and livestock raising. Chief manufactures are cotton cloth, linen, and rope. The capital is Laval. Population of the department: (1962) 250,030.

MAYER, mī'ər, **Julius Robert von,** German physicist: b. Heilbronn, Germany, Nov. 25, 1814; d. there, March 20, 1878. He studied medicine at Tübingen, and finished his university studies at Munich and Paris. In 1840 he went to Java as a ship's surgeon. While there, he turned his attention to studies of the blood and also made exhaustive investigations of animal heat, to which he applied the mechanical theory. He returned in 1841 to Heilbronn, where for some years he practiced medicine. In 1842 he published in Liebig's *Annalen der Chemie und Pharmacie* a preliminary statement of his revolutionary theory of heat, together with his views on the conservation and correlation of energy. Three years later he restated his results in *Die organische Bewegung in ihrem Zusammenhang mit dem Stoffwechsel,* at the same time giving a forecast of his theory of the meteoric origin of the sun's heat. The mechanical theory of heat was worked out independently at the same time by James Prescott Joule in England, and a controversy arose regarding the priority of discovery.

MAYER, mä'ər, **Louis Burt,** American motion picture producer: b. Minsk, Russia, July 4, 1885; d. Los Angeles, Calif., Oct. 29, 1957. He was taken to Canada as a child and educated in the public schools of St. John, New Brunswick. At first he worked in his father's ship-salvaging business. In 1907 he bought a theater at Haverhill, Mass., and began a career in the motion picture industry. In 1912 he became a citizen of the United States, and two years later acquired exclusive distribution rights in New England for David W. Griffith's *Birth of a Nation.* After operating a film-booking agency covering New England, in 1918 he founded the Louis B. Mayer Pictures Corporation and the Metro Pictures Corporation, a booking agency, which in 1924, through a merger, became the Metro-Goldwyn-Mayer Corporation, with Mayer as first vice president in charge of production. Hollywood's Academy of Motion Picture Arts and Sciences presented him with a special "Oscar" award in 1951.

MAYER, mī'ər, **Maria Goeppert,** German-American physicist: b. Kattowitz, Germany (now Katowice, Poland), June 28, 1906. One of the outstanding theoretical physicists of her time, she made significant contributions to solid-state theory and statistical mechanics and, most particularly, to the borderline between these disciplines—theory of phase transitions. She won her world fame and a share of the 1963 Nobel Prize in physics, however, by her recognition of a structure in the properties of the nuclei and her explanation of that structure. She explained it in terms of a picture in which the constituents of the nuclei, protons and neutrons, move independently of each other, each following its own orbit.

Contributions to Science. Maria Goeppert Mayer's contributions to science can be separated into two periods. Before 1948 she was under the influence of Max Born, Karl F. Herzfeld, and her husband, Joseph E. Mayer. Her interests lay primarily in molecular structure, the theories of solids and phase transitions, and statistical mechanics in general. The book *Statistical Mechanics,* written in collaboration with her husband, was published in 1940. Her classic paper on the theory of fusion, written with Karl F. Herzfeld, also originated in this period.

In 1948, Mrs. Mayer's attention turned to nuclear physics. She rediscovered signs of closed shells in nuclei, supporting earlier indications that they existed. Nuclei with closed shells show exceptional stability, their first excited states lie unusually high, and they exhibit properties resembling those of noble gases, which have "closed" electron shells. From these characteristics, Mrs. Mayer concluded that protons and neutrons, the constituents of the nucleus of the atom, move much more independently of each other than had been believed. She discovered that, unlike what happens in electron shells, the directions in which the constituents spin play a major role in determining the energy of the nuclear orbits.

The theory of the nuclear shell model with its spin-orbit coupling was advanced almost simultaneously by a German physicist, J. Hans D. Jensen, in collaboration with Otto Haxel and Hans E. Seuss. Jensen and Mrs. Mayer eventually collaborated on a book, *Elementary Theory of Nuclear Shell Structure,* published in 1955. In 1963, half of the Nobel Prize in physics was won by Eugene P. Wigner. The other half was shared by Drs. Mayer and Jensen for their work on nuclear shell theory. Mrs. Mayer was the second woman to win the Nobel Prize in physics; the first was Marie Curie, who received the award in 1903.

Life. Maria Goeppert was born in Upper Silesia, in an area transferred from Germany to Poland after World War I. In 1924 she entered the University of Göttingen, where she was known as "the beauty of Göttingen." Her interests at first were in the field of mathematics, but she soon decided that theoretical physics offered a greater challenge. She received her Ph.D. in physics in 1930.

She met Joseph E. Mayer, a distinguished American physical chemist, when he was a research fellow at the University of Göttingen. In 1930, soon after she received her doctorate, they were married and moved to Baltimore, Md., where they both had positions at Johns Hopkins University. She became an American citizen in 1933.

During World War II, Mrs. Mayer worked at Columbia University on the separation of the isotopes of uranium. At the same time, she taught (1941–1945) at Sarah Lawrence College. Both she and her husband became professors at the University of Chicago after the war, and Mrs. Mayer also worked for the U.S. Atomic Energy Commission at Argonne National Laboratory. In 1960 the Mayers moved to the University of California, where she became a professor of physics.

The Mayers had two children, Marianne (Mrs. Donat G. Wentzel) and Peter Conrad.

EUGENE P. WIGNER
Professor of Physics, Princeton University

MAYFIELD, mā′fēld, is a city in western Kentucky, 23 miles south of Paducah. The city is the seat of Graves County, in an agricultural area that produces tobacco, cotton, and milk. Mayfield manufactures men's and boys' clothing and condensed milk. It is an important national market for dark, fire-cured tobacco. Mayfield was founded about 1823 and incorporated in 1850. Population: 10,762.

Plimoth Plantation

Mayflower II, a replica of the original, was built in England in 1957. It is now exhibited in Plymouth, Mass.

MAYFLOWER, mā′flou-ər, was the ship in which the Pilgrim Fathers sailed to America in 1620. The Mayflower, used as a wine ship when it was hired by the Pilgrims, was a three-masted vessel of 180 tons. It set sail from Southampton, England, on Aug. 5/15, 1620 (Old Style and New Style dates) in company with the smaller *Speedwell.* The *Speedwell's* leaky condition forced the ships to put back into Dartmouth harbor. About August 23/September 2, they again set sail, but the *Speedwell* proved quite unseaworthy. The ships made port at Plymouth, England, and the *Speedwell* was abandoned. Here some passengers, disheartened, gave up the venture. On a third attempt, the *Mayflower* alone sailed from Plymouth on September 6/16 with 102 passengers and crew. On the transatlantic voyage, one passenger died, and two were born; thus 103 persons landed.

The Pilgrims aboard the *Mayflower* sighted Cape Cod on November 9/19, and their ship dropped anchor in what is now Provincetown harbor at the cape's point on November 11/21. They took on wood and water, mended their shallop, and used it to explore the coast. On December 11/21 the future Plymouth harbor was explored and judged suitable for a settlement. Five days later the *Mayflower* dropped anchor there. The ship began a return voyage to England on April 5/15, 1621, and arrived safely in London. The *Mayflower's* history after 1624, when it was again in London, is unknown.

The male passengers aboard the *Mayflower* were as follows:

THE MAYFLOWER PASSENGERS

Alden, John	Hopkins, Stephen
Allerton, Isaac	Howland, John
Allerton, John	Leister, Edward
Billington, John	Margeson, Edward
Bradford, William	Martin, Christopher
Brewster, William	Mullins, William
Britterage, Richard	Priest, Degory
Brown, Peter	Rigdale, John
Carver, John	Rogers, Thomas
Chilton, James	Soule, George
Clarke, Richard	Standish, Miles
Cook, Francis	Tilly, Edward
Crackston, John	Tilly, John
Dotey, Edward	Tinker, Thomas
Eaton, Francis	Turner, John
English, Thomas	Warren, Richard
Fletcher, Moses	White, William
Fuller, Edward	Williams, Thomas
Fuller, Samuel	Winslow, Edward
Gardiner, Richard	Winslow, Gilbert
Goodman, John	

With these 41 male passengers and heads of families came 15 male servants, whose names were as follows:

SERVANTS ON THE MAYFLOWER

Carter	Langemore	Sampson
Coper	Latham	Story
Ely	Minter	Thompson
Holbeek	Moore	Trevore
Hooke	Prower	Wilder

These first Massachusetts settlers, before debarking at Cape Cod, signed a compact on Nov. 11, 1620, providing for a "civil body politic" to make all their laws. It remained Plymouth Colony's basic governmental chapter until 1691, when that colony was absorbed by Massachusetts. The Mayflower Compact reads as follows:

In the name of God Amen! We whose names are underwritten, the loyal subjects of our dread sovereign Lord, King James, by the grace of God, of Great Britain, France and Ireland, King, Defender of the Faith, etc., have undertaken for the glory of God and the advancement of the Christian faith, and honor of our King and Country, a voyage to plant the first colony in the northern parts of Virginia; do by these presents, solemnly and mutually, in the presence of God and of one another covenant and combine ourselves together into a civil body politic for our better ordering and preservation, and furthermore of the ends aforesaid; and by virtue hereof to enact, constitute and frame just and equal laws, ordinances, acts, constitutions, and offices from time to time, as shall be thought most mete and convenient for the general good of the colony; unto which we promise all due submission and obedience. In witness whereof we have hereunto subscribed our names, at Cape Cod, the 11th of November, in the year of the reign of our sovereign Lord, King James of England, France and Ireland, the Eighteenth, and of Scotland the Fifty-fourth, Anno Domini, 1620.

Whittier, Lowell, Holmes and other poets have immortalized the *Mayflower* in well-known poems.

Consult Stoddard, Francis R., *The Truth About the Pilgrims* (New York 1952).

Mayflower II.—A gift of the English to the American people, the *Mayflower II,* designed by the naval architect William Baker and built at Brixham, Devon, by Stuart Upham, sailed from Plymouth, England, on April 20, 1957; after an uneventful 53-day voyage she dropped anchor at Plymouth, Mass. Commander Alan Villiers, Australian sailor-author, was master of a ship's company of 33 men and boys, mostly Britons. In size and rig this contemporary version of the immortal Pilgrim ship is a near replica, weighing 180 tons, having a 90-foot length, 25-foot beam and 100-foot mainmast. Anachronistic fittings include wheel in place of a tiller, a generator, electricity, and two-way radio; also a cooking galley in lieu of a sandbox hearth. After exhibition in New York from July 1 to November 15 she was given to a New England corporation for preservation as a memorial at Plymouth, Mass.

Consult the official account by Warwick Charlton, *The Second Mayflower Adventure* (Boston 1957).

MAYFLOWER. See TRAILING ARBUTUS.

MAYHEM, *in law,* the maiming of one person by another, the destroying or disabling of an arm, leg, hand or foot, putting out an eye, etc. Mayhem renders the perpetrator liable to a civil action for damages, and also to a criminal prosecution.

MAYHEW, mā'hū, **Experience,** American missionary: b. Martha's Vineyard, Mass., Jan. 27, 1673; d. there, Nov. 29, 1758. He took charge of a half-dozen congregations of Indians, and in 1709 executed for the Society for the Propagation of the Gospel in New England a translation of the Psalms and of the Gospel according to St. John into the Indian tongue. His principal writing is *Indian Converts* (1727).

MAYHEW, Henry, English journalist and author: b. London, England, Nov. 25, 1812; d. July 25, 1887. In 1831 he started, with Gilbert à Beckett, a periodical called *Figaro in London;* in 1841 produced, with à Beckett, the farce of the *Wandering Minstrel;* and not long after formed a literary partnership with his brother Augustus, the Brothers Mayhew, as they came to be familiarly known, turning out a number of most successful works of amusing fiction.

Among these may be mentioned *The Greatest Plague of Life, or the Adventures of a Lady in Search of a Good Servant* (1847); *The Image of His Father, or One Boy is More Trouble than a Dozen Girls* (1850); *Living for Appearances* (1855). In 1851 appeared the first volume of his most important work, *London Labor and the London Poor.* He was one of the founders of *Punch* (1841) and its first editor. His brothers Horace, Thomas and Edward also assisted Henry and Augustus in their enterprises, besides publishing independently.

MAYHEW, Jonathan, American clergyman: b. Martha's Vineyard, Mass., Oct. 8, 1720; d. Boston, July 9, 1766. He was graduated from Harvard in 1744, and from 1747 until his death was minister of the West Church in Boston. In a day of theological controversy he was prominent for his tracts. His views were so liberal as to exclude him from the Boston Association of Congregational Ministers. He opposed the measures of the British Society for the Propagation of the Gospel in Foreign Parts, and got into dispute about it with Thomas Secker (1693–1768), archbishop of Canterbury. In both pulpit and press he was an earnest patriot, being of much assistance to Otis and other early leaders. By the Tories he was considered to have brought about the Stamp Act riots because of a sermon in which he pleaded for the repeal of the act. From him came the suggestion of uniting the colonies in opposition to England. Among his writings are *Seven Sermons* (1749); *Discourse Concerning Unlimited Submission and Non-resistance to the Higher Powers* (1750), and *Sermons* (1756).

MAYHEW, Thomas, American colonial governor: b. England, 1592; d. Martha's Vineyard, Mass., March 25, 1682. Prior to his emigration to New England in 1631 he had been a merchant in Southampton. He settled first at Watertown, Mass., and in 1641 secured from the agent of Lord Stirling a grant of the larger part of the island of Martha's Vineyard and the title of governor. With his son Thomas he labored to convert the Indians of the island so successfully that during King Philip's War the island Indians protected the white settlers. He founded Edgartown in 1647, and after the death of his son and grandson continued their ministry and organized an Indian church.

MAYNARD, Edward, American inventor: b. Madison, N.J., April 26, 1831; d. Washington, D.C., May 4, 1891. He entered West Point in 1831; resigned because of ill-health in 1832; studied dentistry and practiced in Washington from 1836 to 1890. He invented new dental tools, discovered in 1846 the diversity of the maxillary antra, introduced the method of filling cavities with gold foil, taught dentistry in the Baltimore College of Dental Surgery and in the National University at Washington, and practiced successfully in Europe.

He is best known for his invention of small arms and new priming methods which superseded percussion caps. He patented a breech-loading rifle in 1851; a method of converting muzzle-loaders to breechloaders in 1860; a plan to join two barrels so that contraction and expansion in either would be independent of the other, in 1868, and in 1886 a registering device showing the number of cartridges in a magazine rifle. His rifle was adopted by the United States, and brought him decorations from the governments of Belgium, Prussia, and Sweden.

MAYNARD, Horace, American politician: b. Westboro, Mass., Aug. 30, 1815; d. Knoxville, Tenn., May 3, 1882. He was graduated from Amherst College in 1838; and became instructor, and later professor, in East Tennessee College, Knoxville, Tenn. He studied law, was admitted to the bar in 1844, and built up a successful practice. In 1857 he was nominated for member of Congress by the Know-Nothing Party, and elected. On the outbreak of the American Civil War he declared his loyalty to the Union and took an active part in the unsuccessful attempt to keep Tennessee from seceding; on this account he suffered persecution and heavy loss of property during the war. When the Union forces occupied his state in 1864 he was made attorney general. In 1866–1875 he was again member of Congress, being representative at large for his state in the last two years. In 1875–1880 he was appointed minister to Turkey, and in 1880 postmaster general in President Hayes' Cabinet, holding the office until March 4, 1881.

MAYNARD, town, Massachusetts, in Middlesex County, altitude 176 feet, 21 miles west-northwest of Boston. It is served by the Boston and Maine Railroad. Its principal manufactures are woolens, chemicals, and beverages. Settled in 1638; incorporated in 1871. Pop. 7,695.

MAYNOOTH, mā-nōōth′, town, Ireland, in County Kildare, 15 miles west-by-north of Dublin. Located here is famous St. Patrick's College. This college is the chief center for the training of Roman Catholic diocesan clergy in Ireland. It was established in 1795 on the site of a college founded by the earl of Kildare in the 16th century, which was suppressed by Henry VIII.

Maynooth is of historic interest as the seat of the powerful Geraldines, and has ruins of their castle, built 1176 and enlarged in 1426. Several battles with the English occurred here, notably in the rebellion of Silken Thomas in the reign of Henry VIII, and the War of the Confederates (1641–1650). Pop. (1956) 1,722.

MAYO, mā′ō, a family of distinguished American surgeons, including:

WILLIAM WORRALL MAYO: b. Manchester, England, May 31, 1819; d. Rochester, Minn., March 6, 1911. He emigrated to the United States in 1845, took a degree in medicine at the University of Missouri (1854), and began to practice as a country doctor in frontier Minnesota, from 1863 in the town of Rochester. When a destructive cyclone hit the town in 1883, Mayo cared for the injured with the help of the Sisters of St. Francis, who offered to finance a hospital for the region if Mayo agreed to head it. The result was St. Mary's Hospital, opened in 1889 with 40 beds, which became the nucleus of the Mayo Clinic, developed later by his sons.

WILLIAM JAMES MAYO: b. Le Sueur, Minn., June 29, 1861; d. Rochester, July 28, 1939. Son of the preceding, he received his medical degree at the University of Michigan (1883) and in 1889 became associate chief of staff and chief surgeon, with his brother Charles, of St. Mary's Hospital in Rochester. Here the brothers developed the world-famous Mayo Clinic, a unique private cooperative medical center with a staff eventually of over 300 specialists available to the individual patient. To bring back to Rochester the latest surgical techniques, the Mayos traveled widely each year, and in time the clinic attracted surgeons and patients from all over the world to study and benefit from their methods. In 1915 they set up out of their earnings the Mayo Foundation for Medical Education and Research, administered since 1917 by the University of Minnesota, to promote advanced medical training.

William Mayo's specialty was abdominal surgery, and he became known especially for his operations for cancer and gallstones. During World War I he alternated with his brother as chief surgical consultant to the Office of the Surgeon General, United States Army, with the rank of colonel, and was awarded the Distinguished Service Medal.

CHARLES HORACE MAYO: b. Rochester, Minn., July 19, 1865; d. Chicago, Ill., May 26, 1939. Younger brother of the preceding, he took his medical degree in 1888 from the Chicago Medical College (Northwestern University) and with William was cofounder of the Mayo Clinic at St. Mary's Hospital in Rochester. Charles made a special study of goiters and goiter operations, did much work in ophthalmology, and interested himself also in preventive medicine. For his services as consultant to the Office of the Surgeon General during World War I he was made a colonel and won the Distinguished Service Medal. He also was professor of surgery at the University of Minnesota Medical School (1919–1936).

See also MAYO CLINIC.

Consult Clapesattle, Helen, *The Doctors Mayo* (Minneapolis 1941; 2d ed., condensed, 1954).

MAYO, Henry Thomas, American naval officer: b. Burlington, Vt., Dec. 8, 1856; d. Portsmouth, N.H., Feb. 23, 1937. Graduated from the United States Naval Academy in 1876, Mayo's early service was largely in hydrographic survey work, with intervals of sea duty. As rear admiral (1913), he was put in command of the 4th Division of the Atlantic Fleet, and in this capacity was a central figure in the Tampico incident in Mexico (April 1914), when the unwarranted arrest of some of his men led him to make vehement demands for an apology from the Mexican government. The resulting situation contributed to the temporary breaking off of diplomatic relations between the two countries and the occupation by United States naval forces of the port of Veracruz. During World War I, as full admiral, Mayo was the senior United States naval officer at sea, with the title of commander in chief, Atlantic

Fleet (1916–1919), and commander in chief, United States Fleet (1919). He retired in 1920.

MAYO, county, Ireland, in the Province of Connacht (Connaught), bounded on the north and west by the Atlantic Ocean, on the east by Sligo and Roscommon, and on the south by Galway. Its greatest length, north to south, is 66 miles; greatest breadth, 54 miles; and total area, 2,084 square miles. The name means "the plain of the yew trees." The county is barren and mountainous, and several peaks rise above 2,000 feet. The most notable is Croagh Patrick (2,510 feet), where St. Patrick, according to tradition, drove the snakes out of Ireland; there is a yearly pilgrimage to this peak. Mayo has many harbors and inlets, including Killala Bay, Blacksod Bay, and Clew Bay. The Moy is the most important river, and the lakes are practically countless, but the soil is extremely poor. Fishing is a big industry, and cattle, sheep, pigs, and poultry are raised. In the extreme west, Gaelic is spoken. The chief towns are Ballina, Castlebar (the county seat), and Westport. Pop. (1961) 123,330.

MAYO CLINIC, a private medical center in Rochester, Minn., known by this name since about 1903. It originated in 1889, when St. Mary's Hospital was opened in Rochester by the Sisters of St. Francis in collaboration with Dr. William Worrall Mayo. The latter's sons, Drs. William James Mayo and Charles Horace Mayo, founders of the clinic, finding it necessary to expand their facilities for carrying on the practice that had succeeded to them from their father, gradually added more and more physicians and surgeons to their staff, and St. Mary's underwent repeated enlargements to accommodate the rapidly increasing practice of the Mayo brothers and their associates.

Originally a surgical clinic only, the Mayo Clinic about 1915 became a medical center in which medical and surgical treatment are balanced. Patient No. 1,000,000 was registered in 1938, Patient No. 2,000,000 in 1954. In the 1960's over 150,000 patients consulted the clinic annually, counting those who reregistered.

The Mayo Clinic is a private association of over 300 physicians and surgeons, administered by a Board of Governors elected from the staff. A separate entity is the Mayo Foundation for Medical Education and Research, established in 1915 by the Mayo brothers with an original endowment of $1,500,000 (increased by 1934 to $2,500,000), and since 1917 a part of the Graduate School of the University of Minnesota. It provides three-year fellowships for young people who already have their medical degrees and have completed their internships but seek graduate training in special fields of medicine and surgery and the sciences related to medicine. These fellows have the benefit of the facilities of the Mayo Clinic under the direction of its physicians and surgeons, who hold academic appointments in the Graduate School of the University of Minnesota under the Mayo Foundation. See also MAYO, family.

Consult Wilder, Lucy, *The Mayo Clinic,* rev. ed. (Springfield, Ill., 1955); Nagel, Gunther W., *The Mayo Legacy* (Springfield, Ill., 1966).

JAMES ECKMAN,
Mayo Clinic.

MAYO INDIANS, mä'yō, a tribe of Mexican Indians whose earlier homeland was located along the Mayo River in southern Sonora. They are now also found along the Fuerte River in northern Sinaloa, and in smaller numbers as far south as central Sinaloa. In 1950 they numbered about 31,000. With the Yaqui, their northern neighbors, the Mayo speak Cáhita, a language of the widespread Uto-Aztecan stock. The Mayo are agriculturists who grow irrigated crops of maize, beans, squash, wheat, melons, and chickpeas, and keep cattle, sheep, goats, pigs, fowl, and turkeys. There is still some wild-plant gathering (especially cactus fruits and maguey) and hunting of deer. Fish are taken from both the rivers and the ocean. The Mayo weave blankets, sashes, baskets, and hats, and make several types of pottery. Although the Mayo are Roman Catholics and have absorbed many Spanish and Mexican patterns of culture, they have not been completely assimilated. Each village has a headman called a *kobanáro,* who has both political and religious functions. The ceremonial life is still vigorous, with both deer dancers and pascola dancers (masked men who serve as ceremonial hosts and as clowns) performing at appropriate fiestas.

Consult Beals, Ralph L., *The Aboriginal Culture of the Cáhita Indians* (Berkeley, Calif., 1943); id., *The Contemporary Culture of the Cáhita Indians* (Washington 1945).

EVON Z. VOGT.

MAYO-SMITH, mā'ō-smĭth, **Richmond,** American political economist: b. Troy, Ohio, Feb. 9, 1854; d. New York, N.Y., Nov. 11, 1901. After graduating from Amherst College (1875) and studying for two more years in Germany, he joined the faculty of Columbia University, where the whole of his teaching career was spent. He was on the original faculty of the graduate School of Political Science, established in 1880, and pioneered the teaching of statistics and the application of statistics to social and economic problems, a field in which he was an internationally recognized authority. In 1890 he published *Emigration and Immigration,* and his later studies and recommendations led to the improvement and regular publication of United States census figures. His major work was the two-volume *Science of Statistics,* consisting of *Statistics and Sociology* (1895) and *Statistics and Economics* (1899).

MAYON, mä-yôn', an active volcano in the Philippine Islands, in the Province of Albay, on the southeastern tip of Luzon, rising to 7,946 feet. It is known as one of the world's most perfect volcanic cones, with a halo of vapor which gives off a fiery glow at night. Located near Albay Gulf, its base is 80 miles in circumference. It has had many destructive eruptions, one of considerable force occurring in 1947.

MAYOR, mā'ĕr, the chief executive in municipal government. The term is derived from the Latin *major* (greater). The medieval *major-domus* (*major-domo*) was chief of a household; from royal stewardship the term was adapted to municipal usage. In the United States, the mayor's office carries political weight in sharing with the city council the determination of policies, particularly budgetary matters, and also much administrative authority in the appointment, removal, direction, and supervision of subordinate officers and employees. This applies to the "strong mayor" type, as distinguished from the "weak mayor," who has relatively few such powers. In many

English cities the administrative duties fall to several officials who are in turn accountable to committees of the city council. In this situation the mayor serves as president of the council, with few responsibilities of an executive nature. French mayors often are closely identified with national politics, and some have served in Parlement and in the cabinet while retaining the role of mayor. In the United States and Canada the growth of the city manager form of government has resulted in the assignment of many administrative duties to the manager, who in turn is responsible to the popularly elected council. A member of the council becomes mayor, serving as chairman of the council and as ceremonial head of the city government.

See also CITY COUNCILS, AMERICAN; CITY MANAGER PLAN OF GOVERNMENT; MUNICIPAL GOVERNMENT—*Classes of Municipal Organization;* UNITED STATES—*33. State and Local Government* (Local Government).

SPENCER D. ALBRIGHT,
Professor of History and Political Science, University of Richmond.

MAYOR OF CASTERBRIDGE, The,

kăs' tẽr-brĭj, a novel by Thomas Hardy, published in 1886. It is a tragedy of character. The protagonist, Michael Henchard, as a young farm laborer had in drunken anger sold his wife Susan and child to Richard Newson, a sailor, both parties accepting the act as binding. In belated remorse Henchard vowed abstinence, and he eventually so prospered that he became mayor of Casterbridge (Hardy's native Dorchester). At this summit of his success, four people come to Casterbridge: Donald Farfrae, a young Scot who becomes Henchard's assistant; Susan and her daughter, Elizabeth Jane (Newson being supposed lost at sea); and Lucetta LeSueur, an heiress with whom Henchard had had a liaison. Each in turn contributes to Henchard's downfall, but each downward step results from a flaw in his character. Thus jealousy makes him quarrel with Farfrae and then ruin his own business in a mad effort to ruin the Scot's; possessiveness estranges him from Elizabeth Jane when he learns that she is really Newson's child, his own baby having died. The estrangement becomes complete when Newson returns and claims the girl.

The complex plot is artificial; the three women are mere shadows; coincidence, always tragic, is overworked. The book owes its continuing vitality chiefly to the character of Henchard, with the occasional racy comments of local rustics serving as a kind of Greek chorus.

DeLANCEY FERGUSON.

MAYOR OF ZALAMEA, The,

thä-lä-mä'ä (EL ALCALDE DE ZALAMEA), the title of two Spanish plays, the first by Lope Félix de Vega Carpio (1562–1635) and the second by Pedro Calderón de la Barca (1600–1681). In Lope de Vega's play are the following characters: Pedro Crespo, the mayor of the small town of Zalamea de la Serena in Extremadura; his two daughters (Isabel and Leonor); two captains (Don Diego and Don Juan); Don Lope de Figueroa; King Philip II; a sergeant, two soldiers, and a few supernumeraries. The two captains violate the daughters of Pedro Crespo who, relying on his status as mayor of the town, obliges them to marry the girls. After the ceremony, however, he condemns them to be hanged, and the sentences are carried out. On the arrival of the king, the mayor shows him the bodies of the two guilty captains. The king approves the mayor's sentences and appoints him mayor in perpetuity.

The plot of *El Alcalde de Zalamea* is based upon an incident which took place in the campaign of Philip II, leading to the annexation of Portugal in 1581. Throughout the play Lope refers to excesses committed by the troops billeted in the town and makes Pedro Crespo the mouthpiece of the victimized inhabitants. Don Lope de Figueroa, the embodiment of the noble and human qualities of the Spanish officer, was drawn from real life; he was one of the ablest brigadiers of the veteran duke of Alba and at the time of the Portuguese campaign had reached the age of 60. Lope de Vega, a man of the people and a democrat, in this as in many other plays such as *Fuenteovejuna* and *Peribáñez*, sides with the townspeople against the tyranny of the army and upholds Pedro Crespo in his defense of justice and family honor.

Calderón's play, which belongs to the first period of his production, was adapted from Lope de Vega's work. In the golden age of Spanish drama, plagiarism was not frowned upon, and playwrights frequently adapted the works of their contemporaries. Plagiarism, however, as the modern critic Marcelino Menéndez Pelayo wittily remarked, is justified only when followed by assassination, and Lope's play was forgotten when Calderón's work was acclaimed as a masterpiece. Today in Spain the latter is the most popular of all the classical plays.

Calderón simplifies the action of the original, using one heroine and one captain instead of the two victims and two seducers in Lope. He also stylizes the figure of Pedro Crespo and increases his significance so that he becomes the prototype of the Spanish father and judge. Furthermore, he creates fresh characters, such as Juan Crespo, the valiant son of the mayor; Don Mendo and Nuño, picaroons who challenge comparison with Lazarillo de Tormes; and Chispa and Rebolledo, the witty *graciosos* or clowns. Don Lope de Figueroa, too, grows in stature in Calderón as the prototype of the veteran commander whose aching wounds have made him choleric. At the end of the play Calderón adds a touch of pathos, for Crespo the mayor, who has been tied to a tree by the captain seducer, is released by his daughter instead of by a servant as in Lope.

No play is a better illustration of the antithesis existing between the spontaneous improvized drama of Lope de Vega, "the Portent of Nature" as he was called, and the close-knit, calculated art of Calderón, the ruler of the stage in the later baroque age.

WALTER STARKIE,
Director, British Institute, Madrid.

MAYORUNA INDIANS,

mä-yô-rōō'nà, a name traditionally applied to independent and hostile South American Indians living on the border between Peru and Brazil south of the Amazon and east of the Ucayali, especially on the upper Tapiche and Yavarí rivers. The name is Inca and means merely "river people." Virtually no reliable information is available regarding the language and customs of the people so designated, though at least some of them are said to speak a language of the Pano family. Secondhand reports collected by travelers and missionaries emphasize the poverty of their culture. There may be some truth in these stories, since the Mayoruna have been persecuted incessantly by aggressive Indian and white neighbors for several centuries and have learned to keep moving to avoid their tormentors.

JOHN HOWLAND ROWE.

MAYOTTE ISLAND. See COMORO ISLANDS.

MAYOW, mā'ō, **John,** English physiologist and chemist: b. London, England, May 24, 1640; d. there, October 1679. Enrolling at Wadham College, Oxford University, in 1658, he became a fellow of All Soul's College in 1660; in 1665 he was awarded the bachelor's degree and in 1670 the doctorate in civil law. He engaged initially in the study of medicine and, while practicing during the summer at Bath, made a special chemical analysis of its salt springs. His interest early turned to the similarity between combustion as a chemical process and breathing as a physiological function, and he is best known for his studies in this area. The first treatise in his *Tractatus duo, de Respiratione et de Rachitide* (1668) explained the function of the heart as a muscular pump which circulates the blood and carries air throughout the body, and the role of breathing as a means of replenishing the blood stream with oxygen. In 1674 his enlarged *Tractatus quinque Medico-Physici* was published. Mayow based his results upon a close attention to observational detail in the manner of his contemporaries Robert Boyle and Robert Hooke. He was chosen a fellow of the Royal Society in 1678. See also PHYSIOLOGY—*History;* RESPIRATION—*Historical Summary.*

FERGUS J. WOOD.

MAYS, māz, **Willie** (1931–   ), American baseball player, who was the best right-handed slugger in National League history. In 1966 he hit his 535th home run, surpassing Jimmy Foxx' career total of 534 and taking second place behind Babe Ruth, a left-handed batter, who hit 714. Mays was also rated as one of the greatest center fielders. His all-around ability and his effervescence made him not only a great favorite with the fans, but at one point the highest-paid active player—at over $100,000 a year for the San Francisco Giants.

Willie Howard Mays, Jr., was born in Fairfield, Ala., on May 6, 1931. He grew up in Alabama and was playing with the Birmingham Barons of the Negro National League when he was discovered by Giant scouts. Mays was signed for the Giants' Class B Trenton (N.J.) farm club in 1950; the Barons received $10,000 for him, and Mays received a bonus of $5,000. He started the next season with the Class AAA Minneapolis club, but in May 1951 the Giants (then in New York) brought him up from Minneapolis. He helped the Giants win a pennant that season and was voted rookie of the year.

Mays' hitting, fielding, throwing, and daring base running (with his cap flying off) made him a showpiece. He performed difficult feats with apparent ease, and he added interest to routine plays—for example, making "basket" catches of easy flies by gathering them in against his stomach with both hands.

Early in 1952 he was called into the Army. He returned to the Giants in 1954 and led them to another pennant, winning the batting championship with a .345 average. The next year he hit 51 homers, and on April 30, 1961, he became the ninth player ever to hit four home runs in one game. In August 1965 he broke a major league record by hitting 17 in one month.

Voted the National League's most valuable player in 1954 and again in 1965, he led the league in stolen bases as well as home runs several times, and he held many records for batting and scoring in All-Star games. He was made captain of the Giants in 1964.

BILL BRADDOCK, *New York "Times"*

MAYSVILLE, māz'vil, is a city in Kentucky, 62 miles by road southeast of Cincinnati, Ohio. It is the seat of Mason County. Situated on the Ohio River, Maysville is a river port, a tobacco market, and a trade and industrial center whose manufactures include power transmission equipment, canned goods, and textile and distillery products. Settled by Simon Kenton and others about 1782, it was originally known as Limestone. In 1787, when it was officially established as a town, it was renamed for John May, on whose land it was laid out. Daniel Boone and his wife owned a tavern here in the late 1780's. The city, incorporated in 1833, now has the commission form of government. The Mason County Courthouse (1838) is an impressive landmark. Pop. 8,484.

MAYWOOD, mā'wŏod, city, California, in Los Angeles County, six miles southeast of downtown Los Angeles, of which it is a residential and industrial suburb. Its plants produce automobile accessories, steel, and processed foods. The United States Air Force has a base here, which is also the site of a heliport providing service to Los Angeles. Founded in 1920, the city was incorporated in 1924 and is governed by a mayor and council. Pop. 14,588.

MAYWOOD, village, Illinois, in Cook County, a western suburb of Chicago, on the Des Plaines River, at an altitude of 630 feet. It is served by the Chicago Great Western, the Chicago and North Western, the Chicago, Aurora and Elgin, and the Indiana Harbor Belt railroads. Maywood is the site of Chicago Lutheran Theological Seminary. Its manufactures include tin cans, tubing, surgical equipment, and bottled beverages. Incorporated in 1881, it has a mayor-council government. Pop. 27,330.

MAYWOOD, borough, New Jersey, in Bergen County, at an altitude of 65 feet. A residential community 12 miles west of New York City and just northwest of Hackensack, it is served by the New York, Susquehanna and Western Railroad. Its plants manufacture chemical and pharmaceutical products. Incorporated in 1894, it is governed by a mayor and council. Pop. 11,460.

MAZAGAN, māz-à-găn' (Arab. EL JEDIDA), city, Morocco, on the Atlantic coast, about 55 miles southwest of Casablanca. Though surpassed as a port by Casablanca, its harbor is the outlet for agricultural produce from the inland Doukkala region and serves as a port for fishing and coastal ships. The city is also known as a bathing resort. The Portuguese first established a settlement here in 1502 and held it until 1769. It was their last foothold on the Moroccan coast. Pop. (1960) 34,781.

MAZAR-I-SHARIF, mà-zär'ĕ-shà-rĕf', city, Afghanistan, capital of the northern province of the same name, about 190 miles northwest of Kabul. The name means "place of pilgrimage" and refers to the mausoleum of Ali, the fourth caliph, cousin and son-in-law of Mohammed, which is located here. The city is near the site of the historic city of Balkh (q.v.).

The modern city of Mazar-i-Sharif is the center of the carpet and rug industry and the karakul fur trade in northern Afghanistan. It is also the center of export and import trade with the Soviet republic of Uzbekistan, just across the Amu Darya (Oxus) River.

The city is situated in the low-lying northern plains and is hot during the summer and rather mild in winter, except for occasional extremely cold winds from the steppes which sometimes cause damage and loss to the herds of sheep and cattle. The climate in spring is very pleasant, and the fields are covered with green and red flowers. Pilgrims from all over the country visit the shrine of Ali and participate in horse racing and "goat carrying," which are favorite sports, as well as the "red flower" festivals.

The surrounding country is irrigated by the "eighteen canals," but much of the cereal and food grain is grown by dry farming. Karakul lambs and magnificent horses are raised in the province. The city is joined by motor roads to Maimana (southwest), to Pata Kesar on the Amu Darya River (west), and to Kabul. Pop. (1956 est.) 50,000.

MAZARA DEL VALLO, mà-tsä'rä däl väl'lō, town and commune, Italy, on the western tip of Sicily, in the Province of Trapani. Marsala wines are among the principal products and exports, which include olive oil, vegetables, and wheat. The town, at the mouth of the Mazara River, also serves as a fishing port. A colony of the Sicilian Greek city of Selinus, it was destroyed with the latter in 409 B.C. by the Carthaginians, and later was the first Sicilian stronghold occupied by the Saracens (827 A.D.). There are still remains of old fortifications, the ruins of a castle, and Norman churches. Pop. (1951) town, 31,744; commune, 33,184.

MAZARIN, mà-zà-răn', **Jules** (Ital. GIULIO MAZARINI), French cardinal and statesman: b. Pescina, Italy, July 14, 1602; d. Vincennes, France, March 9, 1661. A protégé of the Colonna family, he was given a solid education under the Jesuits, distinguished himself on diplomatic missions for Pope Urban VIII, and became papal nuncio to Paris (1634–1636). Having gained the favor of Cardinal Richelieu, he acquired French citizenship and entered the service of France. Though he never took more than minor orders, his abilities were such that he was made a cardinal (1641) upon presentation by Louis XIII as a preliminary step to succeeding the ailing Richelieu.

The passing of Richelieu (1642) and then of Louis XIII (1643) threatened the entire structure of absolute monarchy in France. Mazarin's position as minister to Anne of Austria, queen regent on behalf of five-year-old Louis XIV, was essentially weak. All those whose ambitions Richelieu had mercilessly crushed—the nobility, the higher courts (Parlements)—came back to haunt his appointed heir. The bourgeoisie itself, normally the crown's stanchest ally, smarted under the burden of taxation. Final success in the war

with the houses of Austria and Spain hung in the balance.

Any appraisal of Mazarin's statesmanship must take these considerations into account. His authority derived, not from personal prestige, but from his shadowy status as confidant, lover, perhaps even (since he was not bound by priestly vows) morganatic husband to Queen Anne. Intrigue and deceit were his favorite tools, but he used them from necessity as much as from character. He lacked the stamina of his predecessor; yet he constituted himself the faithful executor of Richelieu's political testament.

The first phase of Mazarin's regime saw the triumphant conclusion of the Austrian war. The victories of the young prince de Condé (Louis II) and the vicomte de Turenne paved the way for the Treaties of Westphalia (1648), which recognized French sovereignty over most of Alsace. Other concessions to France's allies—Sweden and the German princes—foreshadowed the formation (1658) of a League of the Rhine as a bulwark against the Austrian emperor's ambitions.

Meanwhile the threatened Fronde (q.v.) or revolt of the malcontents broke out and hampered the prosecution of the war with Spain. Mazarin forthwith removed himself and the court to St.-Germain-en-Laye, the better to exploit divisions among the rebels. Further political expediency drove him to exile near Cologne (1651). From afar he urged the queen to rally around her son, by then of legal age, all partisans of order and unity. His plan was immeasurably advanced by the collusion of Condé, protagonist of the Fronde of the Princes, with the Spanish enemy. This treasonable act allowed Louis XIV to re-enter Paris to the acclaim of his subjects. Mazarin returned in his wake (1653); Condé was eventually subdued and forgiven, and the "royal party" envisioned by Mazarin emerged unchallenged from ruin and misery.

Turning his attention back to the Spanish war, Mazarin more than compensated for the loss of Holland as an ally by gaining an alliance with Oliver Cromwell. Threats of invasion both at home and in their northern possessions compelled the Spaniards to sue for peace. At the Treaty of the Pyrenees (1659), France acquired Roussillon and Artois as well as parts of Flanders, Hainaut, and Luxembourg. Not content with this splendid result, Mazarin complicated the succession to the throne of Spain by bringing about the marriage of Louis XIV with the Infanta Maria Theresa.

The cardinal at his death bequeathed to his sovereign the most powerful kingdom on the Continent. He had saved and strengthened the state by thwarting all enemies from within and without, and had trained a phalanx of public servants (Jean Baptiste Colbert among them), subsidized the arts, and preserved or created the instrumentalities of absolute monarchy. Through the Palais Mazarin and the Bibliothèque Mazarine, even his huge fortune and collections, amassed by devious means, in part at least reverted to the nation. Indeed, Louis XIV's decision to be his own prime minister thereafter was no repudiation of the past but a reaping of what Richelieu and Mazarin had sown.

Bibliography.—Moreau, Célestin, *Bibliographie des mazarinades,* containing an account of over 4,000 *mazarinades* or lampoons against Mazarin, 3 vols. (Paris 1850–51); Chéruel, Adolphe, *Histoire de France pendant la minorité de Louis XIV,* 4 vols. (Paris 1879–80); id., *Histoire de France sous le ministère de Cardinal Mazarin,*

3 vols. (Paris 1882); Hassal, Arthur, *Mazarin* (London 1903); *Lettres du Cardinal Mazarin pendant son ministère,* 9 vols. (Paris 1872–1906) in *Collection de documents inédits sur l'histoire de France;* Boulenger, Marcel, *Mazarin, soutien de l'État* (Paris 1929); Bailly, Auguste, *Mazarin* (Paris 1935).

JEAN-ALBERT BÉDÉ,
Department of Romance Languages, Columbia University.

MAZATLAN, mä-sä-tlän', city, Mexico, the country's largest Pacific coast seaport, in the State of Sinaloa, opposite the southern tip of Lower California. It has been a shipping center since Spanish colonial days. Precious metals from nearby mines, hides, tobacco, and agricultural products are among its main exports, and the fishing industry is important. In 1951 its harbor was deepened to accommodate ships drawing 24 feet of water. Beautifully situated on a peninsula overlooking Olas Altas Bay, it is also a popular resort, offering swimming, game fishing, and hunting. Its pre-Lent festival is one of Mexico's best known. Airlines and railroads connect Mazatlán with the rest of the country and the United States, and the West Coast Highway, from Nogales, Ariz., runs through to Mexico City. Pop. (1950) 41,459.

MAZDAK, măz'dăk, Persian religious leader: d. ?528 A.D. An ardent reformer, he led a socialistic movement against the established Zoroastrian religion, preaching community of property and families and the simple ascetic life. The peak of his influence was reached when the Sassanid ruler Kavadh I (Kobad; r. 488–498, 501–531 A.D.), who also opposed the orthodox Zoroastrian priesthood and the nobility, turned to Mazdak's philosophy. In the struggle over the future succession in the last years of Kavadh's reign, however, Mazdak and thousands of his followers were massacred. Kavadh's son, Khosraw I Anushirvan, completed the liquidation of the sect.

MAZEPA or **MAZEPPA,** mŭ-zyä'pŭ, Eng. mà-zĕp'à, **Ivan Stepanovich,** Ukrainian hetman: b. Podolia Province, Poland, ?1644; d. Bendery, Bessarabia, Aug. 22, 1709. His parents were Ukrainian nobles, and as a youth he was educated at the Polish court. It is said that after Mazepa made advances to a Polish noblewoman, her irate husband tied him naked to a wild horse, which carried him to the Cossacks of the Ukrainian steppes (an incident which Lord Byron immortalized in his poem, *Mazeppa,* 1819). Mazepa joined the Cossacks, became secretary to the Ukrainian hetman (ruler), and in 1687 himself became the hetman. A long-time friend of Czar Peter the Great, he aided the czar's campaigns against Turkey and Sweden, but fear of Russia's increasing power induced him (1708) to join the Swedish troops fighting Russia and invading the Ukraine. He tried to arouse the Cossacks to join the Swedish side in the Battle of Poltava (1709), but only a few thousand horsemen responded. After the great Russian victory in this battle, Mazepa fled with Charles XII of Sweden to Turkish Bessarabia. Peter subsequently crushed Ukrainian autonomy, and no hetman thereafter was permitted to wield any real power.

ELLSWORTH RAYMOND.

MAZURKA, mà-zûr'kà, a proud, lively dance and musical form. Originally a Polish folk dance, its name derives from its source in the Province of Masovia (Mazovia). The music is in $\frac{3}{8}$ or more usually $\frac{3}{4}$ time, accented on the second beat, and it is danced in a round by four or eight couples, with stamping of feet, clicking of heels, and great freedom of figures and steps. First known in Poland in the 16th century, the mazurka made its way into the social centers of Europe during the 17th and 18th centuries and thence, by the 19th century, to America. Frédéric Chopin composed more than 50 mazurkas for the piano.

MAZZINI, mät-tsē'nĕ, **Giuseppe,** Italian patriot: b. Genoa, Italy, June 22, 1805; d. Pisa, March 10, 1872. Son of Giacomo Mazzini, a well-known physician, he received his law degree from the University of Genoa in 1827 but never actively practiced his profession, preferring to devote himself to literature and art. His first publications were literary articles and reviews. In 1827, however, he had also joined the secret society of the Carbonari, of which he became a stanch supporter. Betrayed by a deceitful pledgee, he was imprisoned at Savona from Nov. 13, 1830, to Feb. 2, 1831, and although acquitted, was banished from Italy.

First Exile.—At Marseille, Mazzini launched his powerful association Giovane Italia (Young Italy, q.v.), which advocated the independence and unity of Italy under a republican form of government. The new society, with the aid of a review by the same name, rapidly spread Mazzini's revolutionary ideas throughout Italy. Meanwhile, in 1833, he addressed a celebrated letter to Charles Albert, in which he urged the young king of Piedmont to lead the patriotic movement to unite Italy and to wage war against Austria. The letter having failed of its purpose, Mazzini took part in an unsuccessful revolutionary uprising in Genoa and Lombardy and was sentenced to death in absentia. An attempt in 1834 to invade Savoy from Switzerland also failed. Undismayed by still another death sentence, he founded Giovane Europa (Young Europe) at Berne (1834), seeking to unite all Europe into a brotherhood of free peoples. He maintained that in this mission, Italy—not France—was destined to play a leading role.

Threats from France and his precarious position in Switzerland forced Mazzini to change his place of exile to London, where he arrived on Jan. 12, 1837. Here he eked out a living by teaching and writing; at the same time, with the aid of Thomas Carlyle and his wife, he enlisted the sympathy of English friends in the cause of Italian independence. In London he founded the newspaper *L'Apostolato Popolare,* addressed to the working classes, and in 1839 he reorganized the Giovane Italia to open its membership to them. Meanwhile, he helped his less fortunate countrymen in exile by establishing a free Italian school.

Revolution of 1848–1849.—In September 1847, encouraged by the liberal reforms of the newly elected Pope Pius IX, Mazzini appealed to the pontiff to carry out the greatest task of the century—the unification of Italy. In 1848, from Paris and then Milan, where he had returned after the expulsion of the Austrians in the uprising of March 1848, he continued his campaign, again urging Charles Albert to become the champion of Italian unity. His appeals were ignored, and when the Austrians reoccupied Milan in July, Mazzini again escaped to Switzerland. In February 1849 a republic was proclaimed in Rome, after Pope Pius had withdrawn, and the next month Mazzini was named one of its governing triumvirate. The republic fell in July 1849 when the French intervened on behalf of the pope, and Mazzini once more fled, first to Switzerland and then to London. Except for brief visits to Italy, especially during the wars of 1859 and 1860, and again in 1870, 1871, and 1872, Mazzini lived the remaining years of his life in exile.

Later Years.—Mazzini helped to plan the ill-fated Milanese revolutionary uprising of Feb. 6, 1853. Other scattered revolts followed, and for his part in one of them, in Genoa, he was condemned to death a third time. These seemingly useless sacrifices lessened his prestige among Italian patriots, especially when he began to attack the policies of the more moderate Conte Camillo Benso di Cavour in the review *Pensiero ed Azione* in London. However, in the renewed war with Austria in 1859, he appealed to Victor Emmanuel II, Charles Albert's son and successor, to lead the national movement for independence and unity, and he cooperated with Giuseppe Garibaldi in the Sicilian campaign against the Bourbons in 1860. Although opposed to the monarchy, Mazzini on several occasions was ready to sacrifice his republican ideal for the sake of unity and independence. After Italy was finally unified (except for Venice and Rome) in 1861, Mazzini was repeatedly elected by Messina to the Chamber of Deputies but refused to take his seat as a protest against the death sentence that still hung over him; the sentence was finally rescinded in 1866. He opposed the September Convention of 1864, pledging Italy never to attack or allow attacks on the Papal States, because he felt it a renunciation of Rome as the capital of the country. He also deemed the Treaty of Vienna (1866) to be shameful and humiliating to Italy. He continued to plot other uprisings against Victor Emmanuel, for which he was imprisoned in the fort at Gaeta from August to October 1870, at the very moment when Rome, having voted overwhelmingly in favor of union with Italy, was occupied by royal Italian troops and made the capital of the country. Tired and in ill health, he finally retired to Pisa where he died. The Italian government accorded him a public funeral.

Ideas and Philosophy.—An ardent admirer of the romantic poet and critic Ugo Foscolo, Mazzini upheld romantic doctrines in literature not only because he felt that romanticism came closest to the spirit of the people and therefore could better express and interpret their aspiration and needs, but also because it meant liberalism, a principle in full harmony with his religious faith. A basic concept in his philosophy was faith in God—not, however, as a religious confession, but rather as a means of achieving personal liberty. The attainment of freedom and the complete emancipation of mankind are goals, he believed, toward which all efforts must tend. Man's mission is constant progress, which moves forward under the moral law; and Italy, he thought, was in an ideal position to initiate this mission in Europe. Italy's first duty was to attain national independence so that she might promote the formation of an association of free nations, which would come about, not by one usurping the rights of another, but by progressive stages in the fulfillment of the moral law, or the attainment of the knowledge of God. This religious phase of Mazzini's philosophy constitutes the cornerstone of his moral and political beliefs. According to his view, life has value only insofar as it is based on "duty," and "duty" governs all action in order to achieve the victory of good over evil.

Although Mazzini was an idealist and therefore much of his work seemed wasted, his love of mankind was so consuming that he dedicated his life to its service. He exerted a powerful influence over his contemporaries, and his philosophy influenced political thought long after his death.

Bibliography.—The national edition of Mazzini's *Scritti editi ed inediti,* begun in 1905, includes 100 volumes (Imola, Italy). Of special interest are the *Scritti di letteratura e d'arte di Giuseppe Mazzini* (Florence 1931) and the *Ricordi autobiografici* (Imola 1939). Consult also Marriott, Sir John, *The Makers of Modern Italy: Mazzini—Cavour—Garibaldi* (London 1889); King, Bolton, *Mazzini* (London 1902); Salvemini, Gaetano, *Mazzini* (Rome 1920; Eng. tr., London 1956); Gentile, Giovanni, *I profeti del risorgimento italiano* (Florence 1923); Mazzini, Giuseppe, *Mazzini's Letters,* tr. by Alice de Rosen Jervis (London 1930); Griffith, Gwilym Oswald, *Mazzini: Prophet of Modern Europe* (London 1932); Barr, Stringfellow, *Mazzini: Portrait of an Exile* (New York 1935); Mazzini, Giuseppe, *The Duties of Man and Other Essays* (London 1936); id., *Selected Writings,* ed. with introduction by Nagendranath Gangulee (London 1945); Rossi, Joseph, *The Image of America in Mazzini's Writings* (Madison, Wis., 1954); Hales, Edward Elton Young, *Mazzini and the Secret Societies: the Making of a Myth* (New York 1956).

HOWARD R. MARRARO,
Professor of Italian, Columbia University.

MAZZOLA or **MAZZUOLI,** Girolamo Francesco Maria. See PARMIGIANINO, IL.

MAZZONI, mät-tsō'nê, **Guido** (called IL MODANINO), Italian sculptor: b. Modena, Italy, c. 1450; d. there, Sept. 12/13, 1518. Best known for his work in painted terra cotta, he did startlingly lifelike groups of figures such as the *Pietà* in the Church of San Giovanni in Modena. He worked for a time in Naples at the court of Ferdinand I, and after the latter's death (1494) went to France at the behest of King Charles VIII. Mazzoni remained at the French court through the reign of Louis XII, returning to Modena two years before his death.

MEAD, mēd, **George Herbert,** American philosopher and social psychologist: b. Hadley, Mass., Feb. 27, 1863; d. Chicago, Ill., April 26, 1931. He graduated from Oberlin College in 1883, and after four years spent mainly in teaching school and tutoring, went to Harvard to study philosophy. There he received another A.B. degree, based largely on his work with William James and Josiah Royce during 1887–1888. While at the universities of Leipzig and Berlin in 1889–1891, he was influenced by Hegelian philosophy, but like John Dewey, who was to become his colleague and co-worker, Mead moved on from Hegelianism to pragmatism (q.v.). He taught at the University of Michigan from 1891 to 1893 and at the University of Chicago until his death. Although Mead published only essays and reviews during his lifetime, his influence was considerable through personal conversation and through his teaching. After his death, former colleagues and students prepared four volumes drawn mainly from notes—some of them stenographic—taken from his lectures.

Mead set himself the task of formulating a scientific and empirical social psychology. Starting from the facts of evolutionary biology, he attempted to explain how the human mind, the "self," and self-consciousness come into existence. Two fundamental assumptions of his thought are: (1) that mental phenomena can be explained in behavioristic terms without dependence on anything not open to scientific observation; and (2) that radically new kinds of phenomena emerge during the evolutionary process which cannot be explained away by reducing them to their causes in the past. Mead always considered human behavior in its social context, and this led him to find in language and the entire area of communication the key to the emergence of the self and the development of the power of reflective thinking.

Although lower animals communicate with each other, Mead thought that none has the capacity to evoke in itself the response which its gestures have evoked in others. No lower animal can indicate to itself or to other animals the nature of the stimulus that will evoke a particular response. Yet men can do so because they can use words (vocal gestures) in a language. Words, then, are symbols, and through their use men are able to elicit in themselves the responses which these same words evoke in others. The user of a word can *intend* to call out in another organism the response which he has already—by his intention—called out in himself. In so doing, he has acted out in his mind the role of the other; that is, he has responded covertly to his own gesture just as the other has responded to it overtly. Thus role-taking, in Mead's terms, is the reproduction in imagination of observable behavior, while thinking is the symbolic process by which an individual carries out in imagination the possible alternative responses of others to his gestures.

This is the genesis of the self. An organism does not have a self at birth because the self emerges out of the social activities of communication and role-taking; an organism can be said to have a self only when it is able to control its own responses. According to Mead, this ability to bring about a desired result by selecting from alternative stimuli is what is meant by human freedom and choice. The chief end of knowledge itself is cooperative behavior directed to achieving predictable goals.

In later years Mead developed a metaphysics, based on his social psychology, in which the evolution of new forms continues to be of fundamental importance. In *The Philosophy of the Present,* he describes his doctrine of "sociality" as "the capacity of being several things at once." He formulated a complex theory of time and relativity to account for the fact that everything operates in more than one context. This theory has been called a pragmatic version of Alfred North Whitehead's philosophy of organism.

Bibliography.—WORKS: *The Philosophy of the Present,* ed. by Arthur E. Murphy (Chicago 1932); *Mind, Self, and Society,* ed. by Charles W. Morris (Chicago 1934); *Movements of Thought in the Nineteenth Century,* ed. by Merritt H. Moore (Chicago 1936); and *The Philosophy of the Act,* ed. by Charles W. Morris, John M. Brewster, Albert M. Dunham, and David L. Miller (Chicago 1938). *The Social Philosophy of George Herbert Mead,* ed. by Anselm Strauss (Chicago 1956), is a selection from Mead's writings. All of the above works have informative introductions.
COMMENTARY: Clayton, Alfred Stafford, *Emergent Mind and Education* (New York 1943); Lee, Grace Chin, *George Herbert Mead, Philosopher of the Social Individual* (New York 1945); Natanson, Maurice, *The Social Dynamics of George H. Mead* (Chicago 1956).

DAVID L. MILLER,
Professor of Philosophy, University of Texas.

MEAD, Larkin Goldsmith, American sculptor: b. Chesterfield, N.H., Jan. 3, 1835; d. Florence, Italy, Oct. 15, 1910. Brother of the architect William Rutherford Mead (q.v.), his first works of note were a heroic figure, *Vermont* (1857), for the dome of the state capitol at Montpelier, and a statue of Ethan Allen (1861) for the interior of the building. In 1862 he went to Italy, where he made his lifetime home, mainly in Florence. Intermittent trips to the United States brought him various commissions, notably that for the huge Lincoln monument at Springfield, Ill., a $200,000 project completed in 1883. A second statue of Ethan Allen (presented by the state of Vermont) is in Statuary Hall in the Capitol in Washington.

MEAD, Margaret, American anthropologist: b. Philadelphia, Pa., Dec. 16, 1901. Educated at Barnard College (B.A., 1923) and Columbia University (Ph.D., 1929), she was assistant curator (1926–1942) and thereafter associate curator of ethnology at the American Museum of Natural History, and in 1954 was named adjunct professor of anthropology at Columbia University. Miss Mead's first anthropological field work, in Samoa (1925–1926), resulted in the publication of *Coming of Age in Samoa* (1928), in which she demonstrated that Samoan young people pass through adolescence without the emotional crises regarded as characteristic of these years in Western society. There followed expeditions to Manus in the Admiralty Islands (1928–1929, 1953), New Guinea (1931–1933, 1938), and Bali (1936–1938, 1939), the findings of which were described in a number of works, including *Growing Up in New Guinea* (1930), *Sex and Temperament in Three Primitive Societies* (1935), *The Mountain Arapesh* (Anthropological Papers, American Museum of Natural History, vols. 36–37, 40–41, 1938–49), and *Balinese Character* (1942) with Gregory Bateson. Interested in the interrelationship between personality and culture, she made a particular study of infant and child care and adolescent and sexual behavior. In addition to her professional works, she published the popular *Male and Female* (1949).

Her interest in the psychology of culture led Miss Mead to a study of national character, reflected in such works as *And Keep Your Powder Dry* (1942), a popular analysis of American culture, and *Soviet Attitudes Toward Authority* (1951). She was also director of research programs in contemporary cultures at Columbia University (1948–1950) and the American Museum of Natural History (1951–1953). During World War II she served as executive secretary of the committee on food habits of the National Research Council, and in 1956–1957 was president of the World Federation for Mental Health. She was awarded the Viking Fund Medal for General Anthropology (1957) and was president of the American Anthropological Association for 1959–1960.

MEAD, William Rutherford, American architect: b. Brattleboro, Vt., Aug. 20, 1846; d. Paris, France, June 20, 1928. Brother of the sculptor Larkin Goldsmith Mead (q.v.), he graduated from Amherst College in 1867 and studied architecture in New York City and Florence, Italy. In 1872 he opened an office in New York City with Charles Follen McKim, and in 1879 they were joined by Stanford White, forming the famous firm of McKim, Mead & White, which produced many important buildings in the United States. Among them are the Boston Public Library, the Washington War College, and, in New York City, the General Post Office, the Municipal Building, and buildings for Columbia University. With McKim, Mead played an important part in the formation of the American Academy in Rome (founded as the American School of Architecture in Rome, 1894), and on McKim's death in 1909 he went to Rome as president of the academy, whose administration he guided until his death.

MEAD (also METHEGLIN), a drink of fermented honey and water, with fruits or spices added for flavor. Known in history and legend from classical Greek and Roman times, it is especially associated with the early Teutonic peoples as the "heavenly drink" of their gods. Beowulf's victory over the monster Grendel was celebrated with mead drunk in jeweled cups in the huge "mead-hall." Its use was common throughout Europe in the Middle Ages.

MEAD, Lake, a reservoir in northwest Arizona and southeast Nevada, at the western end of the Grand Canyon, formed from the waters of the Colorado River by Hoover Dam (completed 1936). The lake is 115 miles long, with a shoreline of 550 miles, including the 25-mile-long north arm fed by the Virgin River. With an area of 247 square miles and a capacity of 9,719,000,000,000 gallons, it is the largest artificial lake by volume in the United States and one of the largest in the world. Around its shores is the Lake Mead National Recreational Area, the largest in the country. Lake Mead's water supply serves for irrigation, power development, and flood control.

MEADE, mēd, **George Gordon,** American general: b. Cádiz, Spain, Dec. 31, 1815; d. Philadelphia, Pa., Nov. 6, 1872. Graduated from the United States Military Academy in 1835, he served as a second lieutenant in Florida during the Second Seminole War, but after a year resigned from the Army and worked as a civil engineer, mainly in survey work. Rejoining the Army in 1842, he was put into the topographical engineers and assigned to a survey of the northeastern boundaries. This was followed by service in the Mexican War (1846–1848), during which he was cited for gallant conduct at Monterey. After the war he returned to military engineering and survey work, receiving his captaincy in 1856.

In 1861, when the Civil War began, Meade was commissioned a brigadier general of volunteers and put in charge of a unit assigned to help build the defenses of Washington, D.C. Under Gen. George B. McClellan, in the Peninsula Campaign in late June 1862, he led his brigade in the Seven Days' Battles at Mechanicsville, Gaines' Mill, and Frayser's Farm (Glendale), where he was badly wounded. Barely recovered, he rejoined his brigade in late August, just in time to take part in the Second Battle of Bull Run (Manassas). He distinguished himself in temporary command of a division at South Mountain, and when Gen. Joseph Hooker was wounded a few days later at Antietam, Meade led the 1st Corps for the rest of the battle. In November he was made major general of volunteers, and after the Battle of Fredericksburg (December), he was given command of the 5th Corps, which he led effectively at Chancellorsville (May 1863). When Hooker resigned his command of the Army of the Potomac, Meade was named to succeed him (June 28, 1863) and retained this command for the rest of the war.

Meade's greatest military achievement was his victory over Gen. Robert E. Lee in the crucial Battle of Gettysburg (July 1–3, 1863). Though he later was criticized for allowing Lee to escape, he had won a major battle in a command new to him with hastily gathered forces on an unplanned site. Somewhat overshadowed thereafter by Gen. Ulysses S. Grant, who led the pursuit of Lee through Virginia as commander in chief of all Union forces, Meade served him with skill. He and the Army of the Potomac fought under Grant through the Battle of the Wilderness (May 1864), the 10-month siege of Petersburg, and on to Appomattox and the end of the war. On Grant's recommendation, he was made a major general in the Regular Army in August 1864. After the war, except for a year in Atlanta, Ga., he commanded the Military Division of the Atlantic, with headquarters in Philadelphia.

See also CIVIL WAR, AMERICAN; GETTYSBURG, BATTLE OF.

Consult Bache, R. M., *Life of General Meade* (Philadelphia 1897); Pennypacker, Isaac R., *General Meade* (New York 1901); Meade, George G., *The Life and Letters of George Gordon Meade,* 2 vols. (New York 1913).

MEADOW BEAUTY, mĕd'ō bū'tĭ, a common name for plants of the genus *Rhexia* in the Melastoma family (Melastomaceae), comprising about 15 species of erect, often bristly perennial herbs of the eastern United States and Cuba. Sometimes also called deer grass, they are the only temperate representatives of an otherwise tropical family. The leaves are opposite and linear to ovate. The flowers appear in the summer in showy terminal cymose clusters, having four crimson, roseate, or white petals that fall early in the day. There are eight stamens and a single four-loculed ovary with many seeds. The species grow commonly in moist, sandy, or marshy places, under trees or in the open.

RICHARD M. STRAW.

MEADOW LAKE, town, Saskatchewan, Canada, at the northwest end of Meadow Lake, 148 miles north of North Battleford. It is served by the Canadian Pacific Railway and has an airport. Lumbering and fishing are the chief industries. Population: 3,375.

MEADOW MOUSE. See VOLE.

MEADOW PINK, or **MEADOW CAMPION,** the common cuckooflower (q.v.), or ragged robin (*Lychnis floscuculi*). See LYCHNIS.

MEADOW RUE, a plant of the crowfoot family and of the genus *Thalictrum*. These rues are erect perennial herbs, with much-divided leaves and small flowers, usually in loose panicles. The genus contains about 75 species, scattered about the north temperate zone, of which the United States and Canada possess about 15 species. The early meadow rue (*T. dioicum*) is a slender, leafy species, of rocky woods, a foot or two in height, whose flowers, purplish and greenish with yellowish anthers, appear in April or May. The purple meadow rue (*T. dasycarpum*), common in New England woods, is distinguishable by its size (two to four feet tall), its large, bright green, waxy leaves, and its purplish stem; the flowers form a greenish fleecy bloom. A third large species is the thickleaved (*T. coriaceum*) of the Southern states, whose flowers are of different hues, the staminate flowers being white and showy, while the pistillate flowers, borne on separate plants, are purplish. The tall meadow rue (*T. polygamum*) towers to a height of 10 feet in favorable situations. All are fertilized mainly by the wind.

MEADOW SNIPE. See JACKSNIPE.

MEADOWLARK, mĕd'ō-lärk, an American songbird of the genus *Sturnella.* Despite their name, meadowlarks are not larks, family Alaudidae, but members of the American blackbird family, the Icteridae, which is restricted to the New World. North America is inhabited by two meadowlarks, the eastern (*S. magna*) and the western (*S. neglecta*). The breeding ranges of the two birds are largely geographically representative, but they overlap from Oklahoma to southern Ontario. The two meadowlarks are extremely similar in appearance: from 8 to 11 inches long, brown and streaked above, with bright yellow under parts interrupted by a bold crescent of black across the upper breast, and white outer tail feathers. They nest on the ground in grassy fields or meadows and feed largely on insects. Although it is virtually impossible to distinguish them in the field by appearance, they can readily be identified by their songs, the song of the western meadowlark being much more melodious. It consists of a deep rich melody with a bubbling quality, in contrast to the series of high-pitched. drawn-out whistles emitted by the eastern meadowlark.

CHARLES VAURIE.

MEADOWSWEET, a well-known handsome European plant (*Filipendula ulmaria*) of the rose family. It grows by the sides of streams and in damp places, has pinnate leaves and stems two feet high bearing corymbs of white fragrant flowers. It is also called queen of the meadow.

MEADVILLE, mĕd'vĭl, city, Pennsylvania, seat of Crawford County, is located on French Creek, 33 miles south of Erie, on the Erie and the Bessemer and Lake Erie railroads. It has a radio station and two airports, one municipal and one private, and is the industrial center for a diversified farming and oil producing area. Its manufactured products include castings and bearings, industrial heating equipment, rayon yarns, slide fasteners, stereoscopes, lanterns and lantern slides. The Erie Railroad has repair shops here. Allegheny College is here. The Meadville Historical Society maintains a museum, and the community supports its own symphony orchestra. The old courthouse is said to have been the scene of the first direct primary election.

Meadville was first settled about 1788 as a fortified outpost by Major David Mead, a Revolutionary soldier, for whom it was named and ·whose home built in 1797 is a point of interest. It was incorporated as a borough in 1823, as a city in 1866, and has a modified form of commission government. Pop. 16,671.

MEAFORD, town, Canada, in Ontario Province, on Nottawasaga Bay, 20 miles west of Collingwood, on the Canadian National Railway, in a fine farming section of Grey County. It has a good harbor from which fishing is carried on, and there are beaches which attract summer residents. The town does a considerable trade as outfitter to Great Lakes shipping. Local industries include furniture factories, hardwood flooring mills, and several smaller industries. The town has churches, public and high schools, a public library, two weekly newspapers, two banks,

and a board of trade. It takes its name from the birthplace in England of Admiral the Earl of St. Vincent (John Jervis), victor over Spain in the ·crucial naval battle of Cape St. Vincent (1797); several of its streets are also named after British naval officers. Pop. 3,866.

MEAGHER, mä'ĕr; -hĕr; -кĕr, **Thomas Francis,** Irish-American soldier: b. Waterford, Ireland, Aug. 23, 1823; d. near Fort Benton, Mont., July 1, 1867. He was educated at the Jesuit College, Clongowes Wood, Kildare, and at Stonyhurst College, near Preston, England. In 1845 he joined the Young Ireland party, which aimed at independence through armed revolution, and became one of its most inflammatory speakers. He was sent on a mission by the Irish Confederation to the French provisional government in 1848, and soon after his return to Ireland was arrested on a charge of sedition. He was bailed, but on passage of the Treason Felony Act was rearrested and sentenced to death for treason. The sentence was commuted to life banishment, and he was sent to Tasmania in July 1849. In 1852 he escaped to the United States, where he became a naturalized citizen, studied law, was admitted to the bar, and practiced in New York City in 1856–1861. For some time also after 1856 he was editor of the *Irish News* of New York.

At the outbreak of the Civil War in 1861, Meagher organized a company of Zouaves which as part of the 69th New York Volunteers under command of Col. Michael Corcoran took part in the first battle of Bull Run. After three months' service he recruited the Irish Brigade in New York City and was made its commander. He fought bravely at Richmond, the second battle of Bull Run, Fredericksburg and Antietam, but after Chancellorsville found his command so reduced in numbers that he resigned. Early in 1864 he was reappointed brigadier general of volunteers and was assigned to the command of the military district of Etowah. The following January he joined the forces of Gen. William Tecumseh Sherman at Savannah, and was mustered out there at the close of the war. He was appointed secretary of Montana Territory in 1865, and for about a year acted as temporary governor. At Fort Benton, Mont., on July 1, 1867 he boarded a steamer for an inspection trip down the Missouri and thereafter was never seen It is supposed that he fell overboard unperceived during the night. He published *Speeches on the Legislative Independence of Ireland* (1853); *The Last Days of the 69th in Virginia* (1861).

Consult Lyons, W. F., *Brigadier-General Thos. F. Meagher* (1870); Cavanagh, Michael, *Memoirs of Gen. Thos. Francis Meagher* (1892); O'Meagher, J. C., *Some Historical Notes of the O'Meaghers of Ikerrin* (1893); Bowers, C. G., *The Irish Orators* (1916).

MEAKIN, mē'kĭn, **James Edward Budgett,** English author and social reformer: b. London, Aug. 8, 1866; d. there, June 26, 1906. He was ·educated at Reigate grammar school. He was editor 1884–1893 of the *Times of Morocco,* a newspaper established by his father, and is best known for his books on the Moors. He was also interested in social reform and slum removal in England and organized the Shaftesbury Lectures. Among his works are *The Moorish Empire* (1899); *The Land of the Moors* (1901); *The Moors* (1902).

MEALY BUG, the name applied to any member of the family Pseudococcidae of the order Homoptera. Mealy bugs are found in practically all parts of the world and are very destructive to plant life. Small insects of an elongate oval shape, they generally are covered with a mealy or cottony wax secretion and usually possess a pair of moderately long anal filaments. The females and some of the males are wingless. Mealy bugs have sucking mouth parts and, since they frequently occur in large colonies, weaken and sometimes kill the host plant.

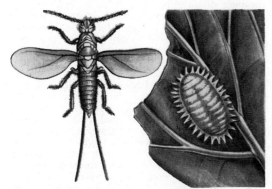

A male mealy bug, left, and a wingless female on leaf.

The citrus mealy bug, *Pseudococcus citri,* and the citrophilus mealy bug, *P. fragilis* (*P. gahani*), are cosmopolitan in distribution and feed upon a large variety of plants. The ground mealy bug, *Rhizoecus terrestris,* infests the roots of grasses and many kinds of agricultural and ornamental plants, and the pineapple mealy bug, *P. brevipes,* feeds upon pineapples and numerous other plants.
CHARLES H. CURRAN.

MEALY WING. See WHITE FLY.

MEAN VALUE. Given a finite number n of commensurable quantities, the sum of these quantities divided by their number n is called the arithmetical average or the mean value of the n quantities. For example, if the quantities are 5, 7, 9, and 11, their mean value is $\frac{1}{4}$ (5+7+9+11), or 8; and, in general, if the numbers of units in n quantities are denoted by x_1, x_2, x_3, . . . , x_n, respectively, their mean value M is given by the formula

$$M = \frac{1}{n}(x_1 + x_2 + x_3 + \ldots + x_n).$$

Quite frequently it is desirable to find the mean value of a set of quantities like those cited, where each x has a weight w, and we obtain a weighted mean M_w:

$$M_w = \frac{w_1 x_1 + w_2 x_2 + w_3 x_3 + \ldots + w_n x_n}{w_1 + w_2 + w_3 + \ldots + w_n}$$

As an illustration, suppose that a student had five percentage grades, 68, 76, 65, 82, and 76, and the instructor considered the last two grades each three times as important as each of the others. The weighted mean would be

$$M_w = \frac{68+76+66+3(82)+3(76)}{1+1+1+3+3} = 76 \text{ per cent.}$$

Should a quantity vary continuously according to some law, thereby assuming every possible value between two extremes, the number of different quantities becomes infinite, and a new definition of mean value is required. For example, suppose that it is desired to find the mean value of the ordinates of the curve $y = f(x)$ from $x = a$ to $x = b$, $b>a$. If the interval from $x = a$ to $x = b$ is divided into n equal parts and the ordinates are calculated for each of these divisions, the sum of the ordinates divided by n would be an approximation of the mean value desired. If by the calculus (q.v.) the number of divisions n be indefinitely increased, the limit of the approximation would define the mean value M as

$$M = \frac{1}{b-a}\int_a^b f(x)\,dx,$$

which is the area bounded by the curve, the x-axis, and the ordinates $x = a$ and $x = b$, divided by the length of the base b-a. Geometrically, as shown in the accompanying diagram, M is the altitude of a rectangle $ABEF$ of base b-a which has the same area as $ABCD$, bounded by the curve $y = f(x)$ between $x = a$ and $x = b$. As a simple example, the mean ordinate of a semicircle whose radius is r is given by

$$M = \frac{\frac{1}{2}\pi r^2}{2r} = \frac{\pi r}{4}.$$

Mean Value Theorem for a Function of Two Variables.—Given the function $f(x,y)$, where x lies between a and b and y lies between a' and b', the theorem is as follows: If $f(x,y)$ is continuous and has continuous first partial derivatives, there exist numbers x' and y' such that

$$f(b,b') - f(a,a') = (b-a)\,f_x(x',y') + (b'-a')\,f_y(x',y'),$$

where $f_x(x',y')$ and $f_y(x',y')$ denote the values of the first partial derivatives of f with respect to x and y, respectively, and $a<x'<b$ and $a'<y'<b'$. This theorem may be extended to any number of variables.

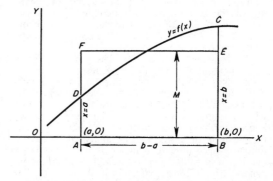

Diagram of the mean value of a continuous quantity.

Law of the Mean of the Differential Calculus.—Geometrically, this theorem states that an arc of a smooth single-valued curve has at least one tangent parallel to its secant. If the secant lies along the x-axis, the theorem is known as Rolle's theorem (from the French mathematician Michel Rolle).

Extension of the theorems cited above lead to many interesting developments in the theory of the differential and integral calculus.

WALTER F. SHENTON,
Professor Emeritus of Mathematics, The American University.

MEANDER, mē-ăn′dēr, in Greek art, an ornamental design, also known as a fret, in which lines interlock at right or oblique angles. It was often used in decorating vases and, as an architectural motif, in ornamenting cornices and the tops and bottoms of columns. The design derives its name from the Maeander (Menderes) River of Asia Minor, known for its many windings.

MEANING, a characteristic attributed to signs in a very wide sense of the word, including not only linguistic expressions, such as written or spoken words and sentences, but also markings on a map, road signs, smoke signals, the various signals produced by semaphores and traffic lights, and the sounds of a policeman's whistle or a ship's siren. Broadly speaking, the meaning of a sign is whatever the sign signifies or expresses. A certain bell signal received at a fire station, for example, may be said to have twofold meaning in this sense: (1) it conveys the information—which may be true or false—that there is a fire in a specified area, and (2) it conveys the order that appropriate action be taken.

Similarly, a sentence may possess different kinds of meaning. It may have *cognitive, or descriptive, meaning,* giving true or false information, as do, among others, the statements of mathematics and of empirical science; it may have *directive meaning,* conveying a directive, an order, a request, or a recommendation, as does, for example, the golden rule (which, making no assertion, is neither true nor false and thus lacks descriptive meaning); and it may have *affective meaning,* expressing and perhaps conveying (rather than describing) a mood, an attitude, or the like, as do, for example, certain kinds of poetry. A sentence or a group of sentences may combine any of these, and possibly other, kinds of meaning; this will usually be the case in an advertisement, a newspaper editorial, a political address, or a sermon. (On the concept of meaning in the wide sense just indicated, see works by Charles W. Morris, Charles L. Stevenson, and C. K. Ogden and I. A. Richards in the *Bibliography.*)

To indicate what a given sign means for a given person, we will have to describe the circumstances and the manner in which that person will employ the sign, and the way in which he will respond to it in specified situations: we know what a sign means for a given person if we know how he is disposed to use it. The idea that the meaning of a sign can be indicated by giving the rules according to which it is used is a basic maxim of a subtle and often highly illuminating method of meaning analysis which has been developed in contemporary analytic philosophy, especially the so-called Oxford school. (Works by Stevenson, Gilbert Ryle, and Ludwig Wittgenstein cited in the *Bibliography* illustrate the significance of this kind of meaning analysis for the clarification of philosophical issues).

Construed in the broadest sense, the meaning of a sign will obviously depend on and often vary with its user, but there are many signs which may be considered as having nearly the same descriptive meaning for different users. Indeed, such objectivity of descriptive meaning is an essential requirement for scientific terms. Thus it is reasonable and often useful to treat such signs as having definite meanings without making any explicit reference to users. This is done, for example, by the writers of dictionaries, and often also by analytic philosophers when they formulate rules governing the use of a given expression.

In the same way, logical theory deals with meanings in abstraction from the users of the signs concerned. Logic distinguishes the sense or meaning of an expression from its reference or denotation. The expressions "the author of *Waverley*" and "the author of *Ivanhoe*" are said to have different senses and yet the same reference, since both are true of or apply to the same individual, Sir Walter Scott. Similarly, the expressions "vertebrate endowed with speech" and "biped without feathers or tail," though differing in sense, have the same reference—namely, all humans. Expressions having the same sense, such as "even number" and "integral multiple of 2" are said to be synonymous. Synonymous expressions evidently have the same reference, but the converse is not generally true. This is shown by the first two examples cited for the distinction between sense and reference; another illustration is provided by such expressions as "unicorn" and "American who traveled to the moon in 1950," which have different meanings but, by reason of being true of nothing, have the same reference.

One way of specifying the meaning of a linguistic expression is to give a definition which provides a synonym for it and thus exhibits its sense; thus the meaning of the word *sibling* can be specified by stating that it is the same as that of the expression "brother or sister." Dictionaries often indicate the meaning or meanings of a term by giving approximate synonyms for the principal linguistic contexts in which it can occur.

Meanings or senses, as here considered, are abstract logical entities. The meanings of the words *irascible* and *unicorn,* for example, are said to be the properties of irascibility and of unicornhood, respectively. The meaning of a statement—that is, a declarative sentence which is either true or false—is called a proposition; it may be thought of as the objective informational content expressed by the statement. For example, the statement "Snow is white" and its French translation, *"La neige est blanche,"* have the same meaning: the proposition that snow is white. That proposition is not a linguistic entity and thus belongs to no language, but it can be expressed by statements in different languages. For the purposes of logical theory, it is of course necessary to give a more rigorous characterization of the abstract entities thus assumed and to develop a precise theoretical apparatus to deal with them. Much effort has been devoted to this task in contemporary logic, and several ingenious solutions to the problem have been proposed. (For a statement of one of these and an excellent survey of the major alternatives, see the work by Rudolf Carnap cited in the *Bibliography.*) None of these, however, has been quite generally accepted, and some influential logicians and philosophers find so much difficulty with the idea of abstract meanings that they have been concerned rather to develop methods of attaining various objectives of logical theory without reliance on that notion. (See works by Leonard Linsky and Willard V. O. Quine in the *Bibliography*.)

Bibliography.—Ogden, Charles K., and Richards, Ivor A., *The Meaning of Meaning*, 6th ed. (London and New York 1944); Stevenson, Charles L., *Ethics and Language* (New Haven 1944); Morris, Charles W., *Signs, Language and Behavior* (New York 1946); Carnap, Rudolf, *Meaning and Necessity* (Chicago 1947); Ryle, Gilbert, *The Concept of Mind* (London 1949); Linsky, Leonard, ed., *Semantics and the Philosophy of Language* (Urbana, Ill., 1952); Quine, Willard V. O., *From a Logical Point of View* (Cambridge, Mass., 1953); Wittgenstein, Ludwig, *Philosophical Investigations* (Oxford 1953).

CARL G. HEMPEL,
Department of Philosophy, Princeton University.

MEANY, George, American labor leader: b. New York, N.Y., Aug. 16, 1894. Beginning as a plumber's apprentice in 1910, he attained journeyman's status in 1915, and by 1922 had become business representative of Plumbers Local Union No. 463, New York. His forceful manner, colorful personality, and firsthand acquaintance with the problems of labor won him the presidency of the New York State Federation of Labor in 1934. In 1940, following six successful years as a state leader, he became secretary-treasurer of the American Federation of Labor (AFL), in which capacity he was active in public relations. During World War II he served on the National Defense Mediation Board (1941–1942) and the War Labor Board (1942–1945). Meany led the postwar fight against participation by United States labor in the Soviet-dominated World Federation of Trade Unions, advocating in its stead affiliation with the anti-Communist International Confederation of Free Trade Unions (ICFTU), founded in 1949.

Elected president of the AFL in 1952 to succeed the deceased William Green, he was reelected in the following year. From the outset one of his primary objectives was the reunification of the United States labor movement, which had been split since 1935, when the Committee for Industrial Organization (CIO; in 1938 renamed Congress of Industrial Organizations) was formed. On Feb. 9, 1955, Meany signed a merger agreement with Walter Reuther, president of the CIO, and on December 5, after AFL and CIO conventions had ratified the agreement, the new American Federation of Labor and Congress of Industrial Organizations (AFL-CIO), q.v., was officially established. On the same day, Meany was unanimously elected its president. In his address to the founding convention, he denied charges that labor was in the process of either founding or taking over a political party, but he insisted on workers' rights as citizens to participate "in shaping the policies of our government."

After the merger Meany directed his attention to the problem of labor corruption, which came under investigation by the U.S. Senate. Measures taken by the AFL-CIO under his leadership resulted in the expulsion of three affiliated unions in 1957, including the powerful Teamsters. Meany became a vice president of the ICFTU that year and was a delegate to the United Nations General Assembly in 1957–1958 and 1959–1960. He received the Presidential Medal of Freedom award in 1964.

MEARES, mērz, John, English navigator: b. about 1756; d. London, England, 1809. Entering the British Navy in 1771, he became a lieutenant in 1778 and served in the war with the French until peace was declared in 1783. He then transferred to the merchant service and went to India, where he established a company to engage in the fur trade on the northwest coast of North America. After exploring the coast of Alaska in 1786–1787, he brought a cargo of furs to Canton. He took two ships to Nootka Sound in 1788, and sent three to the same area in the following year. The latter, together with a locally built tender, were seized by the Spanish. Returning to England in 1790, Meares induced the British government to demand reparation from Spain. A fleet was assembled to back up the British demands, and the Spanish government agreed to make restitution. Through his expeditions, Meares did much to strengthen British claims to the Pacific Northwest. His *Voyages Made in the Years 1788 and 1789 from China to the North-West Coast of America* was published in 1790.

MEARNS, mûrnz, Hughes, American educator and writer: b. Philadelphia, Pa., Sept. 28, 1875; d. Kingston, N.Y., March 13, 1965. He received his education at the School of Pedagogy in Philadelphia and at Harvard College (B.A., 1902), and from 1902 to 1918 taught at the School of Pedagogy. After serving in the army for two years, he was appointed to the staff of the Lincoln School, Teachers College, where he remained until 1925. In that year he became associate professor of education at New York University. Appointed to a full professorship in 1926, he served as chairman of the Department of Creative Education until his retirement as professor emeritus in 1946. An inspiring teacher, he reached beyond the classroom to the general public with such works as *Creative Youth* (1925), *Creative Power* (1929), and *The Creative Adult* (1940), and he did much to further the cause of adult education. In addition, he published several novels: *Richard, Richard* (1916); *The Vinegar Saint* (1919); *I Ride in My Coach* (1923); and *Lions in the Way* (1927).

MEARS, mērz, Helen Farnsworth, American sculptor: b. Oshkosh, Wis., Dec. 21, 1876; d. New York, N.Y., Feb. 17, 1916. She began modeling in clay as a young child, and at the age of 16 became a pupil of Lorado Taft in Chicago. A few weeks later she was commissioned to create a statue, called *The Genius of Wisconsin,* for the World's Columbian Exposition of 1893. For this she received a prize of $500, which enabled her to go to New York to study at the Art Students League. There she attracted the attention of Augustus Saint-Gaudens, whose assistant she became. She then went to Paris, where she continued her studies and exhibited at the Salon. Returning to the United States, she received a number of official commissions, including one for a statue of Frances E. Willard, placed in the Capitol in Washington in 1905. *The Fountain of Life* won her a silver medal at the Louisiana Purchase Exposition in St. Louis in 1904. Three years later she was elected to membership in the National Sculpture Society. Among her other works are bas-relief portraits of Saint-Gaudens (Peabody Institute, Baltimore) and Edward MacDowell (Metropolitan Museum of Art, New York), and busts of George Rogers Clark (Milwaukee Public Library) and Dr. William T. G. Morton (Smithsonian Institution).

MEASLES, mē′z′lz (Lat. RUBEOLA), the commonest childhood disease except for the common cold. It occurs universally. In large cities about 95 per cent of the adults will have had measles before the age of 21, but the percentage is smaller in rural communities. Measles occurs in infancy and early childhood in crowded sections of large cities. Where hygiene is better, it is a disease of the early school years, but measles may occur from infancy to old age. Infants born of mothers who have had measles are variably immune from three to six months. One attack of measles generally gives immunity for life. Measles occurs in periodically recurring epidemics, commencing in the fall, becoming prevalent in winter and spring, and ending in early summer, although there are occasional cases throughout the summer.

Infection.—Measles is caused by a virus and is spread from person to person by the droplets of moisture expelled from the nose and throat of an infected person. It is highly contagious. Symptoms of the disease begin 7 to 14 days after infection, most commonly after 10 or 11 days, the interval from exposure to the onset of illness being known as the incubation period. The prodromal period extends from the beginning of symptoms to the appearance of the rash, or 3 to 7 days (most often, 3½ to 4 days). Measles is infectious from the time when symptoms start until the rash is fully developed, or about 7 or 8 days. It is not infectious during the incubation period. Nevertheless, an exposed child may be quarantined and prevented from attending school during this time.

Prevention and Modification.—Very promising measle vaccines are now available. One, consisting of a weakened live measles virus, gives complete and long-lasting immunity in 95% of cases. However, it does cause some reactions, including fever in about 50% of patients and a rash in about 20%. Gamma globulin given concomitantly with this vaccine reduces the incidence and severity of the reactions but may interfere with the immunity induced. Live virus vaccine should not be given to patients with leukemia, malignant diseases, or active tuberculosis, or during pregnancy or a serious illness.

Another vaccine, consisting of alum-adsorbed killed measles virus, gives temporary immunity when administered in 2 or 3 doses at an interval of 4 weeks. Reactions to this vaccine are infrequent, mild, and of short duration.

The manifestations of measles may be prevented or modified by the injection of gamma globulin within 8 days after the person becomes infected.

Symptoms.—The child infected by measles feels tired, uncomfortable, feverish, and at times chilly. Tearing, light sensitivity of the eyes, sneezing, and coughing follow. Tiny red spots called Koplik's spots, which appear in the mouth, are diagnostic of measles. The rash starts around the hairline of the face late in the third or early in the fourth day and then descends, becoming generalized in 36 hours. The rash, which is pink at first, becomes red, elevated, blotchy, and itching. The child is sickest, the fever highest, and the cough most annoying during the early rash stage. The rash fades quickly, leaving a staining which lasts about two weeks. The skin peels in fine branny scales. Measles is most often confused with German measles, scarlet fever, and some drug eruptions.

Treatment.—A child with measles remains in bed for about a week, although bathroom privileges may be permitted. He may not accept solid food but will and should take fluids. Medication to reduce coughing and fever and to combat complicating infections may be prescribed as indicated. Dark glasses are helpful to eliminate the annoyance of bright light.

Fever ordinarily subsides a day or two after the rash is completed, and continued fever indicates a complication, commonly pneumonia or ear infection. During convalescence the child is more susceptible to other infections.

SAMUEL KARELITZ, M.D.,
Chief of Pediatrics, Long Island Jewish Hospital.

MEASLES, German. See GERMAN MEASLES.

MEASURE, in music, the group of beats or metrical time units set off by bars in a composition. The first beat in each measure is accented. If there are two beats to the measure, the composition is said to be in duple meter or time; if there are three beats, in triple meter; and if there are four beats, in quadruple meter. Quadruple meter is also known as common meter or time. Compound meters are obtained by multiplying the simple meters by three. See also BAR.

MEASURE FOR MEASURE, a play by William Shakespeare (q.v.), usually grouped with *All's Well That Ends Well* and *Troilus and Cressida* as one of the "realistic" or "dark" or "bitter" or "problem" comedies or as tragicomedy, though all these designations are open to question. It was not published until the folio of 1623 in a quite unsatisfactory text full of contradictions and corruptions, evidence of alteration, and careless transcription from the author's foul papers, but it is generally agreed that the play in this form stems from 1604. At any rate, it was acted at court on Dec. 26, 1604, and includes references which might be thought flattering to James I.

The basic story is an old one in fact and fiction. Shakespeare's immediate source was a tedious two-part play by George Whetstone, *Promos and Cassandra* (1578), which in turn derived from a tale in *Ecatommiti* by Giambattista Giraldi (known as Cintio), used by Shakespeare at about the same time for *Othello*. It seems probable from certain correspondences that he also knew the version of the story in Giraldi's tragicomedy *Epitia,* first published in 1583, and Whetstone's prose redaction of his own play in *An Heptameron of Civil Discourses* (1582). Despite the complicated derivations, the characterization is almost wholly by Shakespeare; it is he who makes the heroine a novice, provides the substitution of another woman in an assignation as in *All's Well,* and keeps the duke ever present to supervise the action and marshal it to its conclusion.

The scene is Vienna. Its duke, Vincentio, pretends a journey and leaves the administration in the hands of a deputy, Angelo, who is instructed to enforce laws against corruption. Angelo, a rigid moralist, condemns to death Claudio for premarital intercourse with his betrothed. Claudio's sister, Isabella, comes from a nunnery to plead with Angelo for mercy. Angelo, overcome with temptation, agrees to reprieve Claudio if Isabella will yield to him. At the duke's instance, Mariana, formerly contracted to Angelo, takes Isabella's place at the rendezvous in the dark, and though Angelo retracts his promise, Claudio is saved. At the end of the complex plot, villainy is unmasked, but all the characters are pardoned and paired off in an elaborately contrived resolution. Minor personages include a fantastic debauchee, Lucio, and a clutch of low-life and largely comic reprobates from the jail and the stews.

The play has been a puzzle to critics, and there is no general agreement about its quality or its interpretation. To some the characterization has seemed inconsistent, the moods contradictory, the values of the first half different from those of the second. The difficulties have been accounted for by haste or by a change in intention on Shakespeare's part, by textual corruption, and by failure to understand that Shakespeare was writing a new type of play, either a satire or a play of ideas. Certainly the play contains some fine rhetorical poetry and three or four magnificent scenes, and some of the problems are minimized with an appreciation of contemporary practices and ideals. Later critics have stressed the presentation in the play of early 17th century attitudes toward justice and mercy, governmental ethics, and Christian humanism. The play certainly falls into clearer focus if the duke is taken to be not only the *deus ex machina* but the principal character, though it is a question whether, even so, the execution is such that it can be counted among Shakespeare's major successes.

Except for the court performance there is no record of a production of *Measure for Measure* before the closing of the theaters in 1642, and performances thereafter into the early 18th century were of mangled adaptations. From 1738 on the play provided a vehicle for actresses who wanted to interpret Isabella: Susannah Maria Cibber, Hannah Pritchard, Mary Ann Yates, Sarah Siddons, and, in the 19th century, Lilian Adelaide Neilson and Helena Modjeska. In 1906 it was revived in London by Oscar Asche, who played Angelo to Lily Brayton's Isabella, and in 1933 by Tyrone Guthrie at the Old Vic with Charles Laughton and Flora Robson. After World War II revivals were frequent in Germany, the Netherlands, Belgium, and Switzerland as well as in Great Britain, Canada, and the United States. The most notable were those at Stratford-upon-Avon, England, in 1950 with John Gielgud as Angelo; at the Stratford Shakespearean Festival in Ontario, Canada, in 1954 with James Mason; and at the American Shakespeare Festival Theatre, Stratford, Conn., in 1956 (revived at the Phoenix Theatre, New York, 1957).

Bibliography.—The best text with commentary is provided by John Dover Wilson and Sir Arthur Quiller-Couch (Cambridge, England, 1922) with a stage history by Harold H. Child. An inexpensive one is edited by Robert C. Bald (Baltimore 1956). Varying critical interpretations are provided in works by William W. Lawrence, *Shakespeare's Problem Comedies* (London 1931); Raymond W. Chambers, *Man's Unconquerable Mind* (London 1939); Oscar J. Campbell, *Shakespeare's Satire* (London 1943); George Wilson Knight, *The Wheel of Fire*, 4th ed., rev. and enl. (New York 1949); Eustace M. W. Tillyard, *Shakespeare's Problem Plays* (London 1950); and Mary Lascelles, *Shakespeare's "Measure for Measure"* (London 1953).

ROBERT HAMILTON BALL,
Professor of English, Queens College of the City of New York.

MEASUREMENTS include not only those units defining length, area, volume, capacity, and weight, but also those defining velocity, pressure, energy, electricity, temperature, illumination, force, and the like. They are determined by special instruments suitable for recording the unit involved together with its subdivisions and multiples. These instruments vary both in markings and in form for almost every occupation. The schoolboy has his desk ruler, the merchant his yardstick, the tailor his tape, the carpenter his folding rule and square, the surveyor his chain and level, the machinist his gages, calipers, and micrometer, the scientist his microscope and spectrometer. Some of the instruments are relatively crude but sufficiently accurate for their purpose, while others are remarkably delicate, precise to the millionth part of an inch and even better.

It is evident that standards have had to be authorized to avoid confusion. A yard of 36 inches has been adopted in the United States and other English-speaking countries as the standard for measuring length and the pound for weight. Most non-English-speaking countries use the metric system, which is based on the meter for length and the gram for weight. As a result of the Convention of the Meter, adopted in 1875 at a conference held in Paris in which the government of the United States participated, a platinum-iridium meter bar and kilogram (1,000 grams) were adopted and stored in a vault at the International Bureau of Weights and Measures at Sèvres, France. Prototypes were supplied to the United States and are kept at the National Bureau of Standards at Washington, D.C. The British standard of length is the imperial standard yard, a bronze bar established by act of Parliament in 1878. The British also have a copy of the international meter, and occasional comparisons between the two indicate a slight shrinkage of the bronze standard.

In 1866, Congress took its first formal step to legalize a system of weights and measures, making it "lawful throughout the United States of America to employ the weights and measures of the metric system" and setting the meter at 39.37 inches. It failed to make the metric system obligatory, thus presenting the anomalous situation of a legalized system not in common use and a customary system which has never been formally legalized. A bill was introduced in Congress in 1902 to make the metric system mandatory but was later withdrawn. The system, however, has been universally adopted by scientists both because of the ready comparison of results and because of the decimal character of the units.

By an agreement made in 1958, the inch in the United States (2.540005 centimeters) and that in Great Britain (2.5399956 centimeters) were revised to conform with the Canadian and Australian standards of 2.54 centimeters for machine-tool makers, bringing machines of the inch countries into line and providing a simple conversion factor to metric measures. Since advances in modern industrial technology require tolerances as close as a ten millionth of an inch, agreement was also reached in 1959 on an atomic wavelength standard for length measurements.

See also METRIC SYSTEM; WEIGHTS AND MEASURES.

FRANK DORR,
Associate Editor, "Popular Science Monthly."

MEASURING INSTRUMENTS, Electric. See ELECTRICAL MEASUREMENTS.

MEASURING WORM, the common name applied to the caterpillar of any moth of the family Geometridae (q.v.). These caterpillars are known also as inchworms, loopers, and spanworms—names derived from the fact that there are only two or three pairs of legs at each end of the body, and when the caterpillar travels, it draws its tail end forward until the front and hind legs almost meet and the middle of its body forms a high loop. Colors vary from yellow green to dark green, frequently striped on the upper half with brown or brown and yellow, and from pale brown to dark brown. When at rest, many of the larvae grip a branch firmly with the posterior legs and extend the body rigidly at an angle, thus resembling stubby twigs. Mature larvae may pupate in a cell in the ground or build a thin cocoon on the host plant or in ground litter.

The adults are small to medium in size and almost always are quite fragile. The wings are fairly broad and sometimes are scalloped, the front pair in some cases being angulated toward the apex. Many of the moths are of almost uniform color, but in the majority of species the wings are colored in varied patterns. Most of them are attracted to light and, when abundant, may swarm around lights in enormous numbers. The larvae of one group of small yellowish green to fairly dark green species have a peculiar habit. They cover themselves with fragments of their food plants by fastening them with silk to small projections of their bodies and replace the fragments when they turn brown. As a result, the larvae are extremely difficult for their enemies to discover.

Practically all of the species feed on the foliage of woody plants, and many of them are pests to forest and cultivated trees. The most serious of these pests in North America are the spring cankerworm (*Paleacrita vernata*) and the fall cankerworm (*Alsophila pometaria*). Both species lay their eggs in flat clusters on bark of the host plant, those of *A. pometaria* being laid in the fall and hatching the following spring. *P. vernata* overwinters as a pupa in the ground and lays its eggs in the spring. Outbreaks of these two pests occur at irregular intervals and are most severe when both species reach a peak in the same year. The herbarium moth (*Eois pteliaria*) feeds on dry herbarium plants, and the larvae spin lacelike cocoons.

CHARLES H. CURRAN,
Curator, Department of Insects and Spiders, The American Museum of Natural History, New York City.

MEAT is defined in *Regulations Governing the Meat Inspection of the United States Department of Agriculture* (Washington 1957) as "the edible part of the muscle of cattle, sheep, swine, or goats which is skeletal or which is found in the tongue, in the diaphragm, in the heart, or in the esophagus, with or without the accompanying and overlying fat, and the portions of bone, skin, sinew, nerve, and blood vessels which normally accompany the muscle tissue and which are not separated from it in the process of dressing."

Consumption of Meat.—Per capita consumption of meat in the United States varies with yearly changes in the supplies of meat animals available. In a 10-year span ending in 1967, for example, per capita consumption fluctuated from a low of 151.6 pounds a year to a high of 174.3 pounds. In 1967, Americans consumed an average of 105.5 pounds of beef per person, 61.2 pounds

of pork, 3.9 pounds of veal, and 3.7 pounds of lamb and mutton.

MEAT PRODUCTION IN THE UNITED STATES
(millions of pounds)

	1950	1955	1960	1965
Beef	9,534	13,569	14,753	18,724
Pork	10,714	10,990	11,606	11,140
Veal	1,230	1,578	1,109	1,020
Lamb, mutton	597	758	768	651

Source: U. S. Department of Agriculture, *Livestock and Meat Situation.*

Nutritive Value of Meat and the Stefansson Experiment.—As a result of increased research, the scientific standing of meat as a food has undergone a marked change in the 20th century. In the early 1920's meat was somewhat suspect as an article of diet: it was commonly believed that excessive meat eating—and some defined excessive as eating it more than two or three times a week—caused such conditions as rheumatism, hardening of the arteries, high blood pressure, and kidney trouble. In an article published in the *American Mercury* in May 1929, Dr. Logan Clendening, professor of clinical medicine at the University of Kansas and a member of the Board of Governors of the American College of Physicians, wrote that while he was "convinced that 'health' warnings against the eating of meat are not only absurd but positively harmful," nevertheless "advice about diet has become so impassioned and so involved in the United States of late that in some quarters it even acquires a plot and takes on the aspects of a ritual drama. In this drama meat is cast for the role of villain."

About this time, however, signs of a turn in the tide began to appear as scientific workers published results that cast doubt on some of the adverse thinking about the nutritive value of meat. The definite turning point came after Vilhjalmur Stefansson (q.v.), the Arctic explorer, and an associate, Karsten Andersen, followed an all-meat diet at Bellevue Hospital, New York, in 1928 and 1929 under the observation of a committee of scientists. The chairman of the committee was Dr. Raymond Pearl of Johns Hopkins University, who was assisted by Dr. Eugene F. DuBois, medical director of the Russell Sage Institute of Pathology, and others.

This unique experiment developed in this way: Stefansson had lived for years in the Arctic on an all-meat diet or its equivalent and was convinced that meat was not harmful in any way. An anthropologist of standing, a man of conviction, and a keen observer with an unusual clarity and facility of expression, he returned to the United States after his Arctic experiences to lecture. At one of his lectures, given in 1920 at the Mayo Clinic in Rochester, Minn., one of the Mayo brothers suggested that Stefansson have a checkup to see whether his all-meat diet had affected him. He was unable to do so at the time but later discussed the matter with a gastroenterologist in New York, who volunteered to gather a committee of specialists to examine him. This was done, and the physician, Dr. Clarence W. Lieb, reported in the *Journal of the American Medical Association* of July 3, 1926, that the committee had failed to discover any harmful effects of Stefansson's all-meat diet.

Some scientists contended, however, that while an exclusive meat diet might be satisfactory in a cold climate under the strenuous conditions experienced there, it was doubtful whether a human being could exist in a temperate climate

Table 1—MEAT AS A SOURCE OF PROTEINS, B VITAMINS, AND FOOD IRON
(All ratings based on cooked values)

Kind of meat	Complete protein	B vitamins			Food iron
		Thiamine (B_1)	Riboflavin (B_2)	Niacin	
Pork	excellent	excellent	fair	excellent	excellent
Beef	excellent	fair	excellent	excellent	excellent
Lamb	excellent	fair	good	excellent	excellent
Veal	excellent	good	good	excellent	excellent
Variety meats (liver, heart, kidney)	excellent	excellent	excellent	excellent	excellent
Sausage (frankfurters, bologna)	excellent	good	good	good	excellent

for long on such a diet. Stefansson was determined to dispel such doubts and proposed to the meat industry that it finance an experiment. For various reasons, the industry was somewhat reluctant to do so, but Stefansson's arguments were persuasive and, after much discussion and negotiating, agreement was reached and the experiment undertaken. This was done not with the idea of trying to promote an all-meat diet, for all the meat produced is consumed, but to establish scientifically the healthfulness and nutritive value of meat.

Publication of a number of scientific papers followed the experiment. They were summarized in effect in this comment which Dr. Lieb made later:

During the year on exclusive meat diet, 1928–9, both men said they felt better than average for them. Both looked it and were, insofar as I could tell through the clinical and laboratory studies which I made of them before, during and after. The like, I believe, was the verdict of the rest of those intimately connected with the experiment.

Stefansson and Andersen are in health today at or above the average for their years. Neither, so far as I can tell, has to date suffered any ill effect either from the Russell Sage experiment or from the numerous previous years during which they had lived exclusively or mainly on meat.

Composition of Meat.—As shown in Table 1, meat is rich in complete, high-quality proteins and in certain vitamins and minerals and also is a good source of energy. Its value as a protein lies in the fact that it provides adequate amounts of all the essential amino acids: tryptophan, phenylalanine, methionine, and lysine, among others. Scientific research has established the fact that the lysine, methionine, and tryptophan contained in meat are all well utilized. This fact is of significance, for these three acids are thought to be most limiting in the human diet. In addition, meat furnishes important amounts of the vitamin B complex, which includes thiamine (vitamin B_1) riboflavin (vitamin B_2), niacin

(nicotinic acid), pyridoxine (vitamin B_6), pantothenic acid, folic acid, and cobalamin (vitamin B_{12}).

As customarily consumed, meat makes an important contribution to the mineral needs of the diet except for calcium and iodine. Among its minerals are those required in substantial quantities as well as those required only in trace amounts. Table 2 gives the approximate amounts of essential minerals provided by muscle meat when 200 grams (7.0548 ounces) per day (the average per capita) are consumed. The minerals include those known to be essential components of the human organism—the skeletal framework and the teeth,

Laboratory researchers seek to learn more about the nutritive values of meat and its important food elements.

Armour and Company

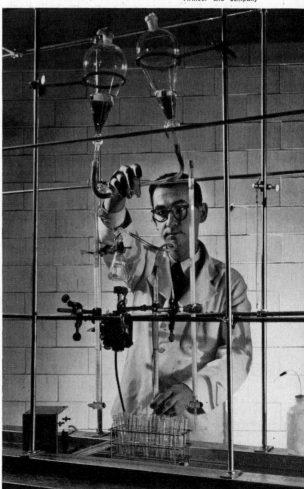

Table 2—APPROXIMATE MINERAL CONTENT OF
VARIOUS MEATS
(200-gram edible portion, uncooked)

	Beef round		Lamb leg		Pork loin		Veal shoulder	
Total minerals	2.0	gm.	1.8	gm.	1.8	gm.	2.0	gm.
Calcium	22	mg.	20	mg.	20	mg.	22	mg.
Chlorine	147	mg.	136	mg.	125	mg.	147	mg.
Copper	0.2	mg.	0.2	mg.	0.2	mg.	0.2	mg.
Iodine[1]	0.02	mg.	0.03	mg.	...[2]		0.01	mg.
Iron	5.8	mg.	5.4	mg.	5.0	mg.	5.8	mg.
Magnesium	46	mg.	42	mg.	39	mg.	46	mg.
Phosphorus	360	mg.	426	mg.	372	mg.	398	mg.
Potassium	661	mg.	610	mg.	559	mg.	661	mg.
Sodium	164	mg.	152	mg.	139	mg.	164	mg.
Cobalt[3]	0.0002	mg.	...		...[2]			
Manganese[3]	0.03	mg.	0.03	mg.	0.02	mg.	0.03	mg.
Zinc[3]	9.4	mg.	...		...[2]		...	

[1] Ohio animals; iodine content of meat varies with the iodine content of the feed of the animals. [2] Data not yet available. [3] Needed in trace amounts only.

soft tissue structures including blood, and substances concerned in regulatory functions.

The average values for iron, phosphorus, and copper of the four kinds of meat shown in Table 2 constitute about 46, 25, and 100 per cent, respectively, of the National Research Council's recommended daily allowances for adults, and the average values for chlorine, potassium, and sodium constitute about 14, 63, and 16 per cent, respectively, of estimated daily adult needs, as based on mineral balance studies. Although no specific information is available on the quantitative needs for cobalt, magnesium, manganese, and zinc, nutritional information suggests that the amounts reported in the table have nutritional significance.

Studies made by Dr. Ruth M. Leverton at Oklahoma State University of Agriculture and Applied Science have shown that the protein content of cooked meats is substantially higher and the calorie content substantially lower than previous data had indicated. Table 3 shows certain of the nutrients and total calories provided by the approximate average daily per capita consumption of meat and the percentages they represent of recommended daily dietary allowances. In the case of both protein and calories, the figures are based on earlier data than that developed by the Leverton studies.

Table 3—NUTRIENTS AND CALORIES PROVIDED BY MEAT

	Amounts per 6 ounces of average cooked meat[1]		Percentages of recommended daily dietary allowances[2]
Protein (biologically complete)	44	grams	63
Iron	5.6	milligrams	47
Phosphorus	342	milligrams	28
Niacin	9.5	milligrams	79
Riboflavin	0.44	milligrams	24
Thiamine	0.50	milligrams	42
Calories	454		19

[1] Average number of calories and average amounts of the chief nutrients furnished by 6-ounce servings of cooked meat (averages of amounts furnished by 6 ounces each of cooked beef, lamb, pork, and veal). [2] National Research Council's recommended daily allowances for a sedentary 154-pound man.

MEAT-PACKING INDUSTRY

The production of meat and of the livestock from which it is derived constitutes one of the world's greatest industries. In the United States alone, more than 4,000,000 farmers and ranchers produce the livestock processed at 4,500 plants devoted to meat packing and meat processing. Meat is sold in the United States at more than 230,000 retail outlets, supplied by about 5,000 wholesale distributors. The sale of livestock accounts for about one third of the total income of U.S. farmers and ranchers.

The meat-packing business is unusual in that its basic operating principle is not one of assembling but of disassembling: the meat animal is split up into many separate cuts and such varied byproducts as hides, hair, bones, and glandular derivatives. The industry is also somewhat seasonal, since more livestock is marketed at certain periods of the year than at others. About two fifths of the hogs, for example, are marketed during four months of the year, and greater numbers of cattle normally come to market during the late summer and fall months than at other seasons. The time of marketing is affected by many factors, including weather, availability of feed, and prices.

Meat animals are produced on large numbers of individual farms throughout the United States, and meat packers therefore have no practical way of controlling the flow of livestock. Moreover, meat is a highly perishable product, most of which must be used within a few days after it has been dressed. It is true that some meat is cured, some canned, some made into sausage, and some frozen, and that these processes lessen its perishability. In general, however, meat may be considered a perishable in uncontrolled supply. As is the case with other commodities in this classification, prices are determined by the interplay of supply and demand, adjusting to the level which will move existing supplies into consumption.

In meat packing there is some specialization. Some packers handle beef only and others pork only; some confine their operations to sausage making; still others can meat and perform no other operation. Many packers combine two or more of these operations, and a score or more throughout the United States produce a full line of meat. Some packers conduct slaughtering operations; others buy their meat from packers who do.

After meat animals have been slaughtered, they are chilled preparatory to their sales as fresh meat or to such further operations as curing or canning. Beef is sold chiefly in the side, although substantial quantities are boned for sausage making or canning. Pork usually is divided into cuts before sale; such parts as the loin, spareribs, and, at times, the shoulder are sold fresh, while the ham and the side usually are sold cured and smoked.

Animals are not all meat, and not all meat is steak and chops. A good steer weighing 1,000 pounds live yields about 590 pounds of beef in the sides, which, when made into retail cuts, yield approximately 465 pounds of eating meat, or less than half the live weight of the animal. There are 35 pounds of porterhouse, T-bone, and club steak, 40 pounds of sirloin steak, 65 pounds of round steak, 45 pounds of rib roast, 25 pounds of boneless rump roast, 100 pounds of chuck roast, 45 pounds of hamburger, and 110 pounds of stew meat and miscellaneous cuts.

Although only 75 pounds of choice steak and 45 pounds of rib roast are produced from a 1,000-pound steer, the demand for these cuts is sufficiently great that the money paid for them at retail sometimes equals the total paid for all the other cuts.

The beef from a steer generally sells at wholesale for less than the live animal cost the packer. The wholesale price is made possible by low-cost operation and by the return received from byproducts, which represent about one fourth of the live weight of the animals purchased. While some of the byproducts are produced by the packers themselves, a large part is produced by specialized trades that buy their materials from packers.

WESLEY HARDENBERGH
American Meat Institute

Bibliography

American Meat Institute, *Science of Meat and Meat Products* (San Francisco 1960).
Drury, John, *Rare and Well Done: Historical Notes on Meat and Meatmen* (Chicago 1966).
Stefannsson, Vilhjalmur, *The Fat of the Land* (New York 1956).
U.S. Department of Agriculture, *The Livestock and Meat Situation* (Washington, bimonthly).
Ziegler, Percival T., *The Meat We Eat* (Danville, Ill., 1962).

MEATH, mēth, Eire, county in the province of Leinster, with an area of 577,824 acres. It is bounded by the counties of Louth, Monaghan, Cavan, Westmeath, Offaly, Kildare, and Dublin and by the Irish Sea. The county town is Trim, and the main rivers are the Blackwater and the Boyne. The Royal Canal passes near the southern border. Most of the land is very fertile, being favorable for the principal crops which are potatoes, turnips, and oats. The chief occupations, in addition to farming, are textile-making and stock raising. There is no good harbor despite the seacoast, although the rivers provide both trout and salmon. Meath was made a county during the time of Edward I, but its boundaries were not fixed until much later. Two of the noted landmarks are the ancient round towers at Kells and Donaghmore. The royal palace at Tara, the monasteries of Duneek and Clonard, and the fort at Trim are other distinguished relics of the section's long history. Pop. (1956) 66,762.

Consult Healy, John, *History of the Diocese of Meath* (Dublin 1908).

MEAUX, mō, France, a town in the department of Seine et Marne, located 28 miles northeast of Paris, on the right bank of the Marne River. It is famous for its beautiful setting and many notable church buildings and castles. Meaux has been the seat of a bishopric since 375 A.D. The Cathedral of St. Etienne, built from the 12th to the 16th centuries, contains the tomb of Jacques Bossuet (q.v.), bishop of Meaux and a renowned orator. The ancient episcopal palace dates from the 13th to the 16th centuries. The town has been in existence since Roman days when it was the capital of the Gallic tribe of Meldi. It was besieged in the 15th century by Henry V of England and became the first Protestant town in France. During World War I it suffered from the German drive toward Paris, although the enemy was stopped here and turned back to the Aisne. Again in World War II it became the scene of fighting and was occupied by Germany until the liberation of France in 1944. Pop. (1962) 21,960.

MEBANE, North Carolina, a village located in both Alamance and Orange counties, altitude 678 feet, situated 23 miles northwest of Durham, and served by the Southern Railway. Founded in 1854 by Frank Mebane, it became an industrial and tobacco market town and the trade center for a large farm area. In addition to having the oldest furniture factory in North Carolina, its other manufactured goods include mattresses, bedsprings, and cotton yarns. The annual Six-County Fair is held each fall at Mebane. Pop. 2,364.

MECCA, mĕk'à (Arab. *Makkah*), Saudi Arabia, the holiest city of Islam, capital of the territory of Hejaz, located about 45 miles east of its Red Sea port Jidda with which it is connected by road. The Mohammedans called the city Umm-al-kora, meaning "Mother of Cities," deriving its sanctity from having been the birthplace of Mohammed. Mecca is situated in a narrow, sandy valley, enclosed by barren hills from 200 to 500 feet high. Jabal Khandama, with a height of about 3,000 feet, is located nearby. After heavy rains the water flows down from the hills into the city, often filling the streets with water.

Ancient walls barred the valley at only three points where gates led into the city. Its early importance came about because caravans crossing the desert used Mecca as a stopping place on the well-traveled incense routes. In addition, even before the time of Mohammed, it was also a holy shrine of pilgrimages, where religious festivals were held at various places in and around the city. After the people of Medina refused to recognize Mohammed as the new Prophet, he made his followers turn toward Mecca as the holy place instead of Jerusalem. In every mosque, the house of worship for Mohammedans, there is a niche in the direction in which Mecca lies, toward which the faithful look as they engage in their daily prayers.

The great mosque of Mecca, with its courtyard and colonnades, occupies a central square which divides the city into the northern upper and the southern lower towns. Lively bazaars almost surround the mosque and also occupy smaller streets. Between pilgrimages, the university hall in the mosque is used for lectures on law and science. Streets are wide and unpaved, and the stone houses are often three stories high. The city is large enough for more than three times its normal population in order to provide room for the pilgrims, as apartments in almost every house are rented to strangers. During three or four months of the year Mecca is the greatest market in the East. Since idolatrous ages, visitors have been the source of wealth for local inhabitants, who are largely settlers or children of settlers, attracted by the opportunities for prosperity. The sheriffs of Mecca, who are the descendants of Mohammed, became a numerous and wide-spread group. They wear the same costume, priding themselves on the green robe which is the identification of their heritage.

The colleges of Mecca have fallen into decay, and vast libraries which once existed have disappeared. With the exception of the mosque, there are no outstanding buildings in the city. The waterworks were constructed in 1571 by Sultan Selim II. With a strange combination of color and shabbiness, Mecca is one of the famous places of the world.

History.—The markets around Mecca attracted travelers of several tribes from many countries. Ideas were traded as well as articles, and a religious center developed in which beliefs could be exchanged. After Mohammed returned as master in 629 A.D., Mecca became primarily a religious center, with the Kaaba as the holiest site. Merchants with their caravans across the desert were secondary to the great hordes of worshippers who came to pay tribute at their holy city.

Fairs were held at varying distances from Mecca, toward which the travelers advanced until they reached the religious center. The calendar for religious ceremonies was arranged so that they coincided with a time when food products and merchandise could be sold. The people of Mecca and surrounding places flourished as a result of these annual trades. Despite the fact that the geographical location was largely desert, there was very great prosperity. Under the name of religion, commerce and business expanded. The merchants of Mecca, with the impetus of Islam, built a real empire, for all the smaller markets and fairs became secondary to those which flourished in the city of the Kaaba. The period of 930 was one of great luxury; gems, silks, precious drugs, and rare commodities from every part of the Moslem (Muslim) world, were to be had. In 930 the city was sacked by the Carmathians, the greatest loss being the theft of the sacred black stone of the Kaaba, which was returned only in 951 upon the payment of a heavy ransom. By the 13th century Mecca was controlled by the Egyptian Mamelukes, who greatly beautified the city, adding magnificent temples and sanctuaries. After 1517 Mecca was ruled by the Ottoman Turks, whose authority remained unbroken until 1916, except for a brief period (1803–1813) when the city was in the hands of the Wahhabis, a puritan sect that believed Islam was corrupt and needed reform. In 1916 the grand sherif, Husein ibn-Ali, secured Arabian independence from Turkey, and became first king of the Hejaz, with Mecca as his capital. He was ousted in 1924 by Abdul Aziz ibn-Saud (q.v.), Wahhabi leader, who later established the kingdom of Saudi Arabia. During centuries of strife and political unrest, the sacred character of Mecca has never diminished, while its political control has always had great value to Moslem rulers.

The Kaaba (Caaba, Kaabeh).—Long before Mohammed, the Kaaba was a center of worship, a repository for the idols brought by traders from many lands. With the advent of Islam, it became a shrine, and the black stone in its southeast corner, also a relic of idol-worship, became the holiest object of the faith. Pilgrims, arriving in Mecca, kiss the stone as their first obligation. The Kaaba, a small, cube-shaped, stone building within the confines of the great mosque, has been repeatedly rebuilt; according to tradition, the present structure was built by Abraham and Ishmael. The door is seven feet from the ground; there are no windows, although the 12th century writer, ibn-Jubair, speaks of five windows within the Kaaba, made of stained glass. The interior is richly decorated. There are many sacred corners in the shrine for worship and meditation, one of these being the legendary spot where Abraham stood when he built the temple. Outside is the sacred well, Zamzam, associated with Hagar and Ishmael. The peculiar importance of the Kaaba, the black stone and Zamzam, toward which all devout Moslems are oriented, has been perhaps the single greatest factor in forging a sense of oneness among the widely scattered adherents of Islam.

Pilgrimages to Mecca.—The last of the five pillars of Moslem faith is the obligation to make a pilgrimage to the holy cities. Every person, man or woman, faithful to his religion, must perform this duty once during his life, unless hindered by poverty, ill health, or other reasonable cause. The holy pilgrimage (*hajj*) takes place annually at a specified time; it is another force in developing a bond of unity among those of the faith. Here people of all races and of varying degrees of poverty and wealth meet on a basis of common devotion, for Islam does not recognize any barriers of race, nationality, or color. Pilgrims come from all parts of the Moslem world, from North and Central Africa, from Asia Minor, India, Indochina, Java and Sumatra; the four principal caravans, however, come from Egypt, Syria, Yemen, and Iraq. Those who die on the way are martyrs.

. Before entering the precincts of the holy city, the pilgrim dons a seamless garment, assuming a sanctified state (*muhrim*) during which he may not shave, cut his hair or nails; he may not hunt, shed blood, or uproot any plants. Arriving at Mecca, he makes the seven-fold circuit of the Kaaba, and the seven-fold course between the sacred hills of Safa and Marwah, commemorating Hagar's search for water for her son. At Mina, which lies between Mecca and Arafah, his goal, the pilgrim casts seven stones at each of three buttresses, known as Devil's Pillars, where the Devil appeared to Abraham and was driven away with stones. Returning to Mina, a sheep, goat, or other horned domestic animal is sacrificed. This sacrifice falls on the tenth of the month, and is celebrated throughout the Islamic world as the feast of sacrifice. After the ceremony the pilgrim returns to the secular state, by removing the seamless garment and shaving his head. He is then permitted to place the coveted title *hajj* (pilgrim) before his name.

Between the two world wars, the average number of pilgrims was about 172,000 annually. More than 1,200,000 pilgrims traveled to Mecca during the April, 1965, *hajj*. Mecca's commercial activity largely depends on the annual pilgrimages, although some income comes from oil. Population: (1963) 158,908.

Bibliography
Gaury, Gerald de, *Rulers of Mecca* (Harrap, Clarke, Irwin: London, 1951).
Hitti, Philip K., *History of the Arabs*, 5th ed. rev. (Macmillan: New York, 1951).
Kirk, George E., *A Short History of the Middle East: From the Rise of Islam to Modern Times*, rev. ed. (Frederick A. Praeger: New York, 1955).
Lipsky, George A., *Saudi Arabia* (Hraf Press: New Haven, 1959).
Philby, H., *A Pilgrim in Arabia* (Robert Hale: London, 1943).

MECHAIN, mā-shăn', **Pierre François André**, French astronomer: b. Laon, France, Aug. 16, 1744; d. Castellon de la Plana, Spain, Sept. 28, 1804. With the help of Joseph Lalande, Méchain received a government post as hydrographer in the Dépôt des cartes de la marine. The resulting financial security permitted him to distinguish himself as an astronomical observer, and he became a member of the Académie des sciences (1782), and editor of the *Connaissance des temps* (1784–1794), where he published many valuable scientific papers. Méchain collaborated in verifying the difference in longitude between the observatories of Paris and Greenwich, England (1787), and with Jean B. J. Delambre (q.v.), was appointed to measure the meridian arc between Dunkerque, France, and Barcelona, Spain, as a basis for establishing the metric system (1791). His work nearly completed, Méchain rejected the findings because of a slight discrepancy. Named director of the Bureau des longitudes (1798), dissatisfaction with his previous mission made him persuade the board to extend the arc to the Balearic Islands. He died of yellow fever while carrying out his work. Méchain is remembered as a precise observer and calculator, and the discoverer of 11 comets.

MECHANIC FALLS, town, Maine, located in Androscoggin County, altitude 300 feet, on the Little Androscoggin River. Papermaking, which was begun in 1850, is the principal industry. Population: 1,992.

MECHANICAL DRAWING. See DRAWING, ENGINEERING.

MECHANICAL ENGINEERING, mē- кăn′ĭ-kăl ĕn-jĭ nē̠r′ing. The function of the profession of mechanical engineering is the design and manufacture of machines used by industry for the transmission and transformation of energy. The mechanical engineer is a "maker," creating the tools and devices of production. His is the broadest and most varied of all of the fields of engineering, serving all industries and supplying the basic working apparatus for each.

Until late in the 18th century, mechanical engineering was only a branch of civil engineering. It emerged as a separate profession simultaneously with the Industrial Revolution, which it promoted and served importantly. Many of the pioneers of that time were only millwrights or mechanics by title, but mechanical engineers in accomplishment. The Industrial Revolution was born in England in the 1700's with the development of the steam engine by James Watt and others, and swung into full momentum with the installation by Richard Arkwright in 1771 of the cotton mill which has often been called the "first true factory." To England also goes credit for the first practical boiler and the railroad. But engineers and mechanics from all of Europe and America participated in the new development. French scientists and inventors did basic work in hydraulics and the perfection of the turbine, in the mechanics of heat, and in the manufacture of cement. Germans developed the internal combustion engine and later the diesel engine, and built the first working automobile. From Sweden came the steam turbine, helical gears, and ball bearings. British, German, and American engineers all took part in the development of steelmaking and treatment. The Americans were responsible for important contributions such as the Corliss engine and the air brake. Their principal genius, however, has been in the practical application of mechanical inventions, production engineering, and the organization of mass production. The amazing technological progress of Russia indicates corresponding advances in mechanical engineering in that country, but little is known in the West of details and methods there.

Products.—Among the classes of machines which the mechanical engineer designs and produces are the "prime movers" (engines using water, oil, gas, and steam as motive power); pumps and other hydraulic apparatus; boilers; refrigerating, ventilating, and air-conditioning equipment; the engines and apparatus of automotive transportation; railways, ships, and aviation; devices for the mechanical transmission of power; and special machines for all industries. Basic to all is the mechanical engineer's role as producer of the machine tool, that is, the machine that makes other machines. The essential features of modern mechanization—mass production, precision fitting, interchangeability of parts, and the like—have been made practicable only by this product. Closely allied to the machine tool are the machines for wood forming and those used in metals engineering, another branch of the mechanical field.

Design and Production.—As designer, the mechanical engineer is responsible for the planning of machines that will function efficiently, smoothly, and safely. His products must operate with a minimum of lost time and motion. Fundamental is his evaluation of the materials to be used. These, whether iron, steel, aluminum, or other metals or alloys, must be appraised for their strength, stiffness, elasticity, incidence of "fatigue," sensibility to temperature changes, tendency to corrosion, "processability," and many other properties.

In designing apparatus and media using fuels, gas, and steam, the engineer utilizes the laws of thermodynamics, the rules of heat transfer, and the principles of convection, conduction, and radiation. Similar considerations are involved in the design of ventilating, air-conditioning, and refrigerating machinery, as is also a knowledge of the action of the liquids, chemicals, and gases involved. In his work on pumps and water power plants, the mechanical engineer must have at his command all the details of hydrodynamics. The designer of machines deals constantly with the characteristics of matter and forces in motion. He is occupied continually with the qualities of moving parts and with application of the laws of kinetics and kinematics. Problems of tension, critical speeds, rotational momentum, concentrations of stress, and vibration are of constant concern. Devices for the transmission of power—chains, pulleys, levers, cranks, gears—must be fabricated and coordinated. Questions of friction and lubrication must be worked out.

The mechanical engineer frequently functions as plant designer, planning a whole installation. In this capacity he will determine the source of power for the enterprise, select all the main units of the installation, and plan their arrangement. He attends to proper working space, sequence of operations, supply of materials and fuel, heating and cooling necessities. He will provide for necessary services, including heat, light, water, and whatever else may be needed. He makes provision for the disposal of waste, the recovery of valuable byproducts, and the establishment of necessary stand-by and auxiliary equipment.

Management.—The mechanical engineer traditionally has been esteemed as exceptionally qualified for the task of overall management of industrial plants. The nature of his training and experience, the breadth of his interests, and his necessary awareness of the requirements of other branches of engineering, all combine to fit him for such general supervision and control. The very name and idea of a now generally accepted concept of management arose from the researches of an American mechanical engineer, Frederick W. Taylor (1856–1915, q.v.). Taylor's investigations, which began at a humble level with such studies as the determination of the proper load for the shovel of a coal heaver, grew by steady degrees into a method for evaluating the operations of a whole plant. His system of scientific management, visualizing "the efficient, functionalized organization" of an enterprise, has become a recognized guide in industrial planning and operation.

Including Taylor's concept, but broader still, is the function of industrial engineering, a profession often considered a branch of mechanical engineering but alternately regarded as a separate province of engineering in its own right (see INDUSTRIAL ENGINEERING). In any case the ties between the two are exceedingly close, and the training and experience of the mechanical engineer continue to make him a preferred candidate for positions in the broader field of management.

Research.—Research is the preoccupation of a large number of mechanical engineers and is carried on under the auspices of a great many different organizations. All industrial concerns of any size have their own research divisions and laboratories. In the United States, the American Society of Mechanical Engineers (q.v.) has conducted much basic research in such fields as machine design, the properties and processing of metals, and the mathematical data useful in mechanical engineering. Many studies are carried on by private and public organizations under grants made by other bodies, such as the United Engineering Trustees, the Carnegie Corporation, and the Rockefeller, Ford, and Sloan foundations. A marked development has been the increasing interest of the national government in engineering research and the provision of very substantial facilities for its pursuit. Agencies such as the Bureau of Standards, the Atomic Energy Commission, the National Science Foundation, and the departments of Commerce and Defense are all engaged in research in the physical sciences, including mechanics, or in the financing of such studies by outside organizations or students. In Canada, the National Research Council promotes research in these sciences. Governmental subsidizing of engineering research, now practically worldwide, has received fresh impetus in the present era of international tension, and may be expected to develop even more in the near future.

Associations.—The oldest association in this field is the British Institution of Mechanical Engineers, founded in 1847. In the United States, the American Society of Mechanical Engineers (ASME) was formed in 1880. The ASME furnishes extensive services to its members, including the carrying on of research; the publication of bulletins, periodicals, and reports; participation in regional, national, and international conferences of engineers; and an effective placement service. Its professional divisions number over 30, with corresponding committees for each division of industry and subject of interest. The activities of the ASME are paralleled in Canada by the Engineering Institute of that country, which is a participant with United States societies in the Engineers' Council for Professional Development. In Europe, the leading associations representing mechanical (as well as other) engineers are the Verein Deutscher Ingenieure of Germany and the Société des Ingénieurs Civils in France.

Education and Training.—In the United States, requirements for entrance into a college or university for training as a mechanical engineer generally include the completion of a four-year high school program that embraces courses in algebra, English, French or German, history, physics, plane and solid geometry, and plane trigonometry, as well as the passing of certain aptitude and achievement tests. As for the college curriculum in institutions particularly devoted to technical training, that of the Massachusetts Institute of Technology may be taken as illustrative. Here the mechanical engineering student in his first year takes courses in chemistry, physics, calculus, "Foundations of Western Civilization," and military or air science, combined with an elective in a related field. In the second and third years he continues his work in calculus, physics, applied mechanics, military or air science, and the humanities, and also studies machine drawing and design, machine tools, heat engineering, physical metallurgy, and fluid mechanics. The fourth and last year covers economic principles, work in mechanical engineering problems, elective courses in his field, and the preparation of a thesis. These are frequently combined with a period of practical experience in a selected industrial plant. Graduate work, looking to a master's or doctor's degree, is provided at the institute and also at an Engineering Practice School affiliated with the activities of the Atomic Energy Commission. In England and Continental Europe degrees in mechanical engineering are offered by many of the larger universities, but mechanical training is more characteristically acquired through apprenticeship or in technical schools of lower grade. Engineering training in Soviet Russia seems to differ from that in Western countries in its greater intensity within a narrower field, the subsidizing of scholars, longer hours of study, and autocratic state control. See also ENGINEERING EDUCATION.

Opportunities of the Profession.—In recent years mechanical engineering accounted for a sizable proportion of all undergraduate college enrollments in engineering in the United States. The supply of graduates does not, however, appear to come close to meeting the demands for mechanical engineering talent. Predictions indicate an accelerating automation of industry that will steadily require more engineers per thousand of a rapidly increasing world population. See also ENGINEERING.

Bibliography.—Marks, Lionel S., *Mechanical Engineer's Handbook* (New York, regularly revised); Kirby, Richard Shelton, and others, *Engineering in History* (New York 1956); Mischke, Charles R., *Elements of Mechanical Analysis* (Reading, Mass., 1963); Naparstek, Marvin I., *Mechanical Engineering* (New York 1964); Oberg, Erik V., and Jones, Franklin D., *Machinery's Handbook for Machine Shop and Drafting-Room*, 17th ed., (New York 1964); Eder, W. E., and Gosling, W., *Mechanical System Design* (New York 1965); Souders, Mott, *The Engineer's Companion: A Concise Handbook of Engineering Fundamentals* (New York 1966); Pollack, Philip, *Careers and Opportunities in Engineering*, rev. by John D. Alden (New York 1967).

WILLIAM H. DILLINGHAM.

MECHANICAL TERMS. See AERODYNAMICS—*Aerodynamics Glossary;* AIRPLANE—*Glossary of Airplane Terms;* AUTOMOBILE—6. *Automobile Glossary;* ELECTRICAL TERMS; ENGINE; ENGINEERING TERMS; LOCOMOTIVE; SHIPPING AND SHIPBUILDING TERMS; TOOLS; VALVE TERMS; WORKSHOP TERMS; and separate articles on many individual terms.

MECHANICS, mê-kăn'ĭks. "Mechanics is the science of motion; we define its task; to describe completely in the simplest manner the motions that take place in nature." Such was Gustav Robert Kirchhoff's famous definition; it would be hard to write a better one. The immediate importance of mechanics to most people is that it is the foundation of all machine and construction design. The science goes far beyond this, however, being the key to some of the deepest mysteries of the universe. With our widening exploration of the infinitely great and the infinitesimally small—the secrets of outer space on the one hand and of the atom and its constituents on the other—the basic role of mechanics in physics and astronomy is of ever-increasing significance.

It is customary to divide mechanics into *statics* and *dynamics;* statics deals with bodies at rest, and dynamics with the motions of particles and bodies. Dynamics is further subdivided into *kinematics,* or the study of motions without reference to their causes, and *kinetics,* which analyzes the relationships of bodies moving with changing velocities. The divisions are blurred, however: statics is only a special case of dynamics; conversely, by the method of inertia forces, most cases in dynamics can be reduced to those of statics; and kinetics can be described only in kinematical terms. The present article deals with the factors of motion and matter that apply in greater or lesser degree to all divisions of mechanics.

History.—The ancients were acquainted with many practical applications of mechanics, but knew very little of its rationale. The Egyptians and the Babylonians understood the mechanical advantages of the lever, the inclined plane, the wheel, the roller, and, as it now appears, perhaps the pulley also. The Greeks were the first to theorize on the laws of motion, but were stultified by their besetting aversion to testing theory by observation. Archimedes (287?–212 B.C.) was an exception, a practical man as well as a thinker, drawing deductions and putting them to use in such diverse fields as ballistics and hydrostatics, and having knowledge of the center of gravity and other basic mechanical concepts. No comparable genius in the field of mechanics appeared in the Western World until the late 16th century A.D., when a brilliant group of minds arose in Europe, seeming to catch fire from each other, and all occupied with the problems of matter, motion, and time. Galileo Galilei (1564–1642), Tycho Brahe (1546–1601), and Johannes Kepler (1571–1630) developed the basic ideas of celestial mechanics, most of which still endure. Galileo was the pioneer of controlled experiment, establishing the laws of falling bodies and of the pendulum. Simon Stevin (or Stevinus, 1548–1620) developed the principle of the composition of forces. All alike prepared the way for the great synthetizer, Sir Isaac Newton (1642–1727). Newton, putting together all that his predecessors had developed and much original thought of his own, formulated three laws of motion and an auxiliary gravitational theory, embracing in one grand sweep all the fundamentals of motion and force. Nearly all subsequent mechanics has been based upon his conclusions, and it is really astonishing to note how often the most recondite analyses in this field turn out to be only reaffirmations of his principles.

The line of succession after Newton ran first through another school of contemporaries: Johann (or Jean) Bernoulli (1667–1748); Daniel Bernoulli (1700–1782), the blind Leonhard Euler (1707–1783), and Pierre L. M. de Maupertuis (1689–1759); then, by way of Jean Le Rond d'Alembert (1717–1783), Joseph Louis Lagrange (1736–1813), Pierre Simon de Laplace (1749–1827), and others, to Siméon Denis Poisson (1781–1840), Sir William Rowan Hamilton (1805–1865), and Josiah Willard Gibbs (1839–1903, qq.v.). All these were engaged more or less on a common line of thought that had two continuing aspects. The first was perfection of methods of analysis that would facilitate solution of mechanical problems; as d'Alembert with his principle of effective forces, Poisson with that of moving axes, Lagrange with generalized coordinates and the method of virtual work, and Gibbs with vector analysis. The other aspect, which mingled with the first, was the search for a formula that would compress the laws of motion into one unified equation. In this all participated, tending toward a common conclusion, which was a concept of matter in motion taking the "minimal path." All worked within the Newtonian framework.

Definitions.—For the understanding of mechanics, definitions of certain fundamentals of matter and motion are necessary. A *body*, in mechanics, is a material object, as a rock, rod, or beam, having *mass*. Mass is a relative quantity, not the same as *weight*, with which it is frequently confused. The mass of a body is the measure of its *inertia* (q.v.), that is, its resistance to moving or to having its direction of motion changed, as compared with that of a body of standard mass. The mass of a rigid body never varies, whereas its weight may change, since weight represents the pull of gravity on the body, and gravity changes with the distance of the body from the center of the earth. Bodies are seen as composed of systems of *particles*, defined as material points whose dimensions are negligible.

Methods.—Problems in mechanics are solved by one or both of two methods: the analytical and the graphical. Analysis uses mathematical formulas and symbols in place of the diagrams of the graphical method. It is at once the more exact and the more penetrating of the two methods; it is also the more difficult to understand. In graphical solution, the objects under consideration are reduced to skeletonized or symbolic outlines; the phenomena affecting them, such as heat or pressure, are likewise shown in simplified form. These phenomena are generally *vector quantities*, that is, they possess direction and magnitude. As such, they obey all the laws of vector manipulation, including, most importantly for mechanics, the law of the resolution of a vector into its components along specified axes, as x, y, and z in Fig. 1. "A vector is portrayed graphically by a line seg-

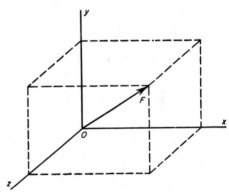

Fig. 1.

ment (such as F in Fig. 1), whose length shows to scale the size or magnitude of the acting force or quantity, with an arrow at its head to indicate the direction of its exertion and the point of its application."

Velocity, Acceleration, and Force.—The two fundamental aspects of motion are *velocity* and *acceleration*, both vector quantities. Velocity is the rate of speed of a body or particles, or the time rate of change of displacement. It is measured in centimeters (or feet) per second. *Momentum*, an important quantity, is the product of mass and velocity. Acceleration is defined as the time rate of change of velocity and is measured in centimeters (or feet) per second per second, that is, the gain (or loss) in velocity of so many centimeters (or feet) per second in a second.

Letting S be a frame of reference (as the surface of the earth), O a point fixed on it, and A a moving particle with position vector r relative to O; t being the time of motion from O; then the velocity v of A relative to S is the vector v, which is the rate of change of position vector r with respect to time t. This is frequently written, in differential calculus terminology, as:

$$v = \frac{dr}{dt}, \text{ or } v = \dot{r}$$

The dot indicates that r is to be "differentiated" with respect to time.

If r is resolved into its components along the x, y, and z axes (as discussed a little earlier), the components of velocity become $\dot{x}$, $\dot{y}$, $\dot{z}$. Then this equation can also be written:

$$v = \dot{r} = \dot{x}i + \dot{y}j + \dot{z}k$$

i, j, and k are constants.

Similarly, the acceleration a of the particle A can be defined as follows:

$$a = \frac{dv}{dt} \text{ or } a = \dot{v}$$

a can also be written in terms of the components x, y, and z. In calculus terminology, this means taking the "second differential," which is represented by two dots. Thus, the equation becomes:

$$a = \ddot{x}i + \ddot{y}j + \ddot{z}k$$

Mechanics deals not only with matter but also with *force*. What a force actually is remains even today somewhat controversial. The popular notion associates it always with a push or a pull and would call it the cause of motion. Mechanics, however, defines a force as the mutual influence between bodies, and also as the product of the mass m of a body times its acceleration a. Thus in mechanics the fundamental law for force (F) is $F = Kma$, k being a universal positive constant that depends on the units in which force, mass, and acceleration are expressed. It is obviously inconvenient to have to remember various values of k to take care of all possible combinations of units, so the choice has been made to make k equal to "1." Systems of mechanics are all set up with this end in view. Then the equation reduces to $F = ma$. See also ACCELERATION; FORCE.

Newton's Laws of Motion.—Practically the whole basis of ordinary modern mechanics was established by Sir Isaac Newton in his three laws of motion and his auxiliary theory of gravitational attraction. The first three laws, written in Latin, have been variously translated; they are most simply stated as follows:

(1) Every body continues at rest or in a state of uniform motion unless a disturbing force acts upon it.

(2) A body, acted upon by a force, experiences an acceleration in the direction of the force and proportional in amount to it, and inversely proportional to the mass of the body.

(3) To every action of a force there is an equal and opposite reaction.

The fourth law, that of gravitational attraction, was developed by Newton in his attempt to explain the motions of the heavenly bodies and the fact that all earthly bodies tend to fall downward. This law states that all particles and bodies in the universe attract each other with a force (F) proportional to the product of their masses

(M_1 and M_2) and inversely proportional to the square of their distance apart (D); or $F = G\dfrac{M_1 \times M_2}{D^2}$, G being the *gravitational constant*, a factor that must be used to make the equation numerically correct. The value of G has been established at $6.670 \times 10^{-8}\dfrac{\text{dyne cm.}^2}{\text{gm.}^2}$. See also GRAVITATION; GRAVITY.

Equilibrium.—Statics is occupied essentially with the problems of *equilibrium*, that is, the characteristics of bodies at rest. Such problems are solved by two different methods: that of *stable equilibrium* and that of *virtual work*. The first utilizes the general principle that all forces and moments acting on a body remaining at rest must be in perfect balance in all directions and about any and all axes drawn with reference to the body. The second method is discussed separately in the section *Method of Virtual Work*.

For a particle to be in equilibrium, the resultant (vector sum) of all forces acting on it must be zero. This is the *first condition of equilibrium*, the only one necessary for particles. Convenient ways of testing this condition are afforded by the facts that if a particle continues at rest, the forces acting on it, if there be three of them, will form a closed triangle when drawn in order as vectors (see Fig. 2); and that if there are more than three forces, they will form a closed

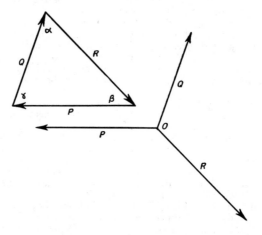

Fig. 2.

polygon. Bernard Lamy (1640–1715) expressed in his theorem this condition for three forces (P, Q, R) by the requirement that each force must be proportional to the angle between the other two; or $\dfrac{P}{\sin \alpha} = \dfrac{Q}{\sin \beta} = \dfrac{R}{\sin \gamma}$. See also EQUILIBRIUM.

Moment or Torque.—A rigid body, in addition to the motion of *translation* from one location to another, may have another type of motion, namely *rotation*, the movement of the body and all its particles in circular fashion about some axis. This rotation will be produced by some unbalanced force acting upon the body. The distance between the axis of rotation and the point of application of the force is the *lever arm;* the longer the lever arm, the greater the rotational effect. That effect, or resultant of force and lever arm, is called the *moment* about the axis, or the *torque.* This gives us the *second condition of equilibrium* —necessary in the case of bodies, not necessary for particles—which is, that the resultant of all moments about any axis drawn with reference to a body must be zero. Obviously this condition can be secured by many different combinations of force and lever arm. For instance, a force of two pounds applied two feet away from the axis will be perfectly balanced by an opposing force of four pounds applied one foot away from the axis on its opposite side. The lever arm (L_1, L_2, L_3, L_4 in Fig. 3) is always drawn perpendicularly

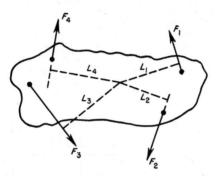

Fig. 3.

to the direction of the force (F_1, F_2, F_3, F_4). Counterclockwise torques and consequent rotation in that direction are called, by mathematical convention, positive; those involving clockwise motion, negative. Torques, having direction and magnitude, are vector quantities and are so represented and combined.

The following propositions, pertinent here, are more or less self-evident, although each is susceptible of rigorous proof. A force applied to a body may be conceived as acting at any point in that body along the line of direction of the force. This is the principle of the *transmissibility of force,* of much value in facilitating solutions of mechanical problems by vector diagrams. For a body to be in equilibrium with three nonparallel forces acting on it, these forces must lie in the same plane and meet at a point. Two parallel forces acting on a body in the same direction will be balanced by an opposing force equal to their sum and applied in the opposite direction at a point lying between their points of application. This point for the balancing force must be so located as to divide the line connecting the points of application of the two original forces into segments proportional to their respective moments. Two parallel and equal forces acting upon a body in opposite directions form a *couple.* They cannot be balanced by a single opposing force; unless they are opposed by another couple, the result will be rotation of the body. Practically all members of any structure are subject to forces that, if not balanced by other forces, would cause translation or rotation. From this arises the extreme importance of the foregoing principles in construction and the design of building members. See also MOMENT.

Center of Mass and of Gravity.—Calculation of the *center of mass* of a body is highly important in problems of stability. That center is the point with respect to which the moments of all

points in the body cancel out or add to zero. For all balancing purposes, the body may be treated as if its whole mass were concentrated at this point. Since the gravity force on a particle is proportional to the mass of the particle, the *center of gravity* of a body corresponds to the center of mass in all cases in ordinary mechanics, that is, those in which the gravity lines of force pulling on the various particles can be regarded as parallel. With symmetrical objects or systems having uniform density, the center of mass and gravity is easily determined by mere inspection: with a solid globe, it will be the geometric center; with a rectangular block of metal, it will be the intersection of its interior diagonals.

Circular Motion.—The first noteworthy characteristic of circular motion is that it is continuously accelerated. Objects in circular motion have constant change of direction; this implies acceleration even though there may be no change in speed. This acceleration (a_n) is always directed toward the center of revolution; it is given by the

formula $a_n = r\omega^2 = \dfrac{v^2}{r}$, where r is the radius, ω

is the angular velocity, and v is the linear velocity (Fig. 4). When the circular motion is uniform, there is no other acceleration acting. When the velocity of the moving particle or body is increasing in magnitude, however, there is also a tangential acceleration, given by the expression $a_t = r\alpha$, α being the angular acceleration. The acceleration directed toward the center of revolution tends to

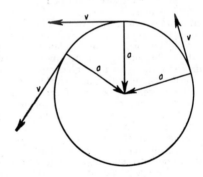

Fig. 4.

keep the body on its circular path; it is the *centripetal force.* Opposed to it is the radial "pull" of the body away from the center, the so-called *centrifugal force.* These two forces are counteracting; they are both expressed by the relation

$$F = m\,\frac{v^2}{r},$$ m being the mass of the revolving body.

By this and associated formulas, mechanical calculations are made of the forces and constructions necessary to keep circular moving parts in their proper orbits and to prevent their rupturing under tension. The power of the centrifugal force, pulling in space against the sun, is such that it has distorted the shape of the earth, producing a 13-mile bulge at the equator. It is likewise responsible for such phenomena as the blackout of aviators when they pull out of a power dive and the speed of the plane is so high that the centrifugal force greatly exceeds the force of gravity.

There is still another force not apparent in our daily lives but of importance in rotating systems not at rest relative to the earth. This is the *Coriolis force* (Gaspard Gustave de Coriolis, 1792–1843). Suppose, as in Fig. 5, a frame of reference, such as a disk or plate, is attached to the earth's surface (*S*) at a point *O* and revolves around that point. The Coriolis force will act out along the line *r* connecting the point of attachment *O* with any particle *A* moving on the rotating surface,

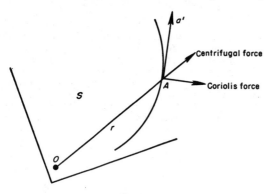

Fig. 5.

tending to make *A* fly off into space along this line. The force will be proportional to the square of the velocity of the rotating system and to the length of *r*. It is displayed in such situations as that of skaters on a revolving rink, and is responsible for the rather more important phenomenon of the trade winds.

Simple Harmonic Motion.—This important and frequently encountered type of motion has been described as uniform circular motion seen edgeways. It is vibratory, to and fro motion, wherein the body concerned goes through a repeating series of displacements, velocities, and accelerations, each completed in a regular period of time. As shown in Fig. 6, it may be regarded as the projection of uniform circular motion on a straight line (*AB*) in the plane of motion. As point *P,* for instance, moves around the circle counterclockwise, *P'* will move up and down the straight line in repeating motion between *d* and *j*. The *period* is the time required for a single vibration. *Displacement* is the distance of *P'* from its origin at any given time. Let *T* be the period; for the displacement *y* shown, and the period *T,* we will have

$$y = r \sin \theta = r \sin \omega t; \text{ and } T = \frac{2\pi}{\omega}.$$

In this type of motion, acceleration is always proportional to the displacement and opposite in direction. Harmonic motions occur widely in nature, as in all types of waves (see WAVES AND WAVE MOTION), released springs, and beams under suddenly applied loads; most importantly perhaps in the motion of pendulums. Galileo found long ago that the period of vibration of a pendulum depends upon its length and the acceleration of gravity at the place where it is located; also that within certain limits the period of any pendulum is the same regardless of the amplitude of its swing. These discoveries have resulted in the important present-day use of the pendulum in measuring the acceleration of gravity at different places on the earth's surface. See also HARMONIC ANALYSIS.

Work.—The term *work* (*δW*) is used in mechanics in a strictly defined sense much more limited than its popular connotation. It is a technical concept meaning the product of a force (*F*) times the displacement (*δs*) of the body or particle acted on, in the direction of the force; or *δW = F* cos *θ · δs,* where *θ* is the angle between the direction of *F* and of the displacement. If no motion takes place in the direction of the force (or of a component), then mechanically no work has been done. In mechanics, Atlas holding up the world for all eternity would have done no work. Thus, in mechanical parlance, although much force may be involved, no work is done in contacts between two bodies where there is no deformation of either and no resulting motion.

Similarly, no work is considered done in *rolling contact,* if no friction or sliding occurs. This seemingly strange concept becomes easier to accept when we reflect how much easier rolling is than sliding or dragging, and that machinery does indeed operate almost effortlessly, that is, without "work," on ball or roller bearings. Work, being force times displacement, is measured in units of these phenomena, generally either in foot-pounds or dyne centimeters (called "ergs").

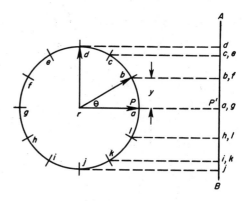

Fig. 6.

Method of Virtual Work.—So far the problems of mechanics have been discussed mainly in terms of one of the two principal methods used in their solution, the method of stable equilibrium or balancing of forces about a point. The considerations reviewed so far enable us to take account of an equally important alternative method of analysis. This involves the principle of *virtual work,* sometimes called the principle of *virtual displacements.* This method was first applied broadly by Jean Bernoulli in 1717, and was later developed by Lagrange as a foundation for a whole system of mechanical analysis. It consists in examination of the work done by forces in the infinitesimal displacement of a particle or system. Its general proposition is that a body is in equilibrium if the total work done by all the active forces in any infinitesimal displacement of the subject is zero; or

$$\delta W = \Sigma \left(F_x \, \delta x + F_y \, \delta y + F_z \, \delta z \right) = 0;$$

the *F*'s being the components of the active forces along the *x, y,* and *z* axes. The formula and method apply equally to the equilibrium of particles and, by modification, to particles or systems under constraint. The method is particularly useful in problems where only the equilibrium relationship of the external forces is sought and not the value of the internal forces or reactions. By proper selection of the force system, however, the reactive forces can be treated as active, and thus all reactions can also be determined by this method.

Energy.—The concept of *energy* is as important as any in the physical world, especially with the development of the postulates that mass and energy are interchangeable, and perhaps that only energy can be said to possess reality. Energy is defined as capacity to do work. It is classified as either *potential* or *kinetic*. "Potential" in this connection expresses the idea of "stored up," at rest but available. It is conceived that all bodies have this type of energy within them and that its quantity is measurable at any given time. Thus the work done in stretching a spring or in carrying a body to a height against the force of gravity is conceived of as stored up in the object as potential energy available for release. In the first case, the potential energy is equal to the work done in deformation, or $\frac{1}{2}Fd$, d being the increase in the length of the spring and F the final force applied in the stretching. The increase in the potential energy of a stone carried to the top of a cliff is equal to the product of its weight W (mg) by the height (h) to which it is carried. The general equation for both work and potential energy, which are equal in magnitude to each other, is Ml^2T^{-2}, the symbols denoting respectively mass, length (distance over which mass moves), and time (time during which mass moves). The kinds of potential energy just discussed are those of position. There are, of course, many other kinds, as the energy stored in coal, in dynamite, or in the chemistry of plants.

Potential energy when released becomes kinetic, the more familiar kind of energy observed in the released spring or in the rock as it crashes from the cliff. The general equation for kinetic energy (T) is one half of the mass of the body times the velocity squared; or, for motion of a particle in space and time, $\dot{T} = \dot{W}$, where $T = \frac{1}{2}mv^2 = \frac{1}{2}m(\dot{x}^2 + \dot{y}^2 + \dot{z}^2)$. Here W is work done, m is the mass, v is the velocity, and the x's, y's, and z's are the differentiated coordinates of the particle. For the kinetic energy of a system or body, summation of the energy of all

the component particles gives $T = \frac{1}{2}\sum_{i=1}^{n} m_i v_i^2$.

The last result is nothing but an affirmation of Newton's second law and leads directly to the key principle of the *conservation of energy*. Newton's law, symbolized simply for the motion of a particle, is $m\dfrac{dv}{dt} = F(x)$; v (velocity) being also $\dfrac{dx}{dt}$, then $m = \dfrac{d^2x}{dt^2} = F(x)$; and, by integration, $\frac{1}{2}mv^2 - \int_0^x F(x)dx = $ a constant.

Here $\frac{1}{2}mv^2$ is the kinetic, and $-\int_0^x F(x)dx$ the potential energy; so that the equation is a statement of the conservation of energy. This principle asserts as a universal rule that no energy can ever vanish nor can its total quantity be reduced; it may be transformed but never destroyed. For mechanics, it says that for any system the sum of its potential and kinetic energy stays constant, except for the "drain-off" effects of friction, which also accomplish no lessening of total energy, but only its transformation into heat. *Power* is the rate of doing work, or the rate at which energy is supplied. Its most commonly employed units

are, in English: horsepower, which denotes work at the rate of 550 foot-pounds per second; and joules per second (or watts).

Certain special considerations of *energy due to rotation* must be noted. Attempts to whirl a wheel by a handle at its axis will quickly convince us that a circular body with most of its weight in the rim is both harder to start and possessed of more momentum when started than one with a more equally distributed mass. The effect of the distribution of mass is expressed by the *moment of inertia,* a quantity denoted by I and defined for small particles as $I = mr^2$, where m is the mass of the particle and r its distance from the line or axis about which it is revolving.

Consider a body of any arbitrary shape rotating about a fixed axis and acted on by a force F at a distance R from the axis (Fig. 7). It can be shown that the moment of inertia of such a sys-

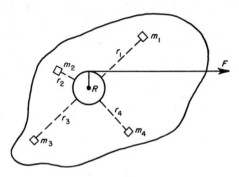

Fig. 7.

tem is the sum of the moments of inertia of all its particles of masses $m_1, m_2, \ldots m_n$, which are at perpendicular distances $r_1, r_2, \ldots r_n$, respectively, from the axis. Thus:

Moment of inertia $= I = m_1r_1^2 - m_2r_2^2 \ldots m_nr_n^2$

$$= \sum_{i=1}^{n} m_i r_i^2$$

In rotation each particle, possessing velocity, will have a kinetic energy of rotation equal to $\frac{1}{2}mv^2$, in terms of its mass and velocity. The speed of the various particles is not the same, however, so that the kinetic energy of the body can be found only by summing the products $\frac{1}{2}mv^2$ for all its particles. This sum is $\frac{1}{2}I\omega^2$ (ω equals angular velocity of body), which expresses the kinetic energy of the body in terms of its angular velocity and of its total moment of inertia. See also ENERGY

Friction and Machines.—*Friction* is the resistance of a surface to slipping or sliding on another surface with which it is in contact. Friction has physical value in that many of the motions made by man and his machines could not be accomplished without help from the resistance of friction. In mechanics, friction figures mainly as a robber of efficiency, turning applied energy into wasted heat. Its effect is conspicuous in machines. The typical advantage of a machine, reduced to its simplest terms, is shown in Fig. 8. Here the effect of the small force F is multiplied by the long lever arm OA so as to enable the force to raise the weight W to a higher position at W' with ease. A direct lift on W would have required many times the same force. If machines were ideal, all the force invested would be reflected in the work accomplished. No machine that would give this result has ever been produced. Friction is the reason.

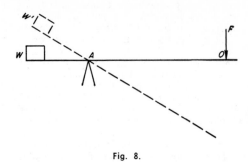

Fig. 8.

The force of friction is always tangential to the surfaces in contact; it does not depend upon the extent of those surfaces but upon their composition and condition. In Fig. 9, A and B are bodies in rough contact. R is the reaction of B on A. It resolves into the forces N, which is normal at the point of contact pressing the two surfaces together; and F, which is the force of

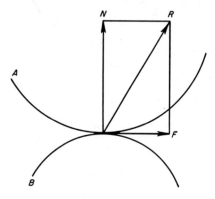

Fig. 9.

friction. If the contact were smooth, F would not exist. The *coefficient of friction*, written as μ, is equal to the tangent of the angle of friction. As soon as the angle between the normal N and the reaction R exceeds the angle of friction, slipping will occur. When this starts, the friction becomes kinetic, acting opposite to the direction of sliding and opposing it; and $\dfrac{F}{N} = \mu'$, the *coefficient of kinetic friction*. μ' is usually less than μ. A precaution of value is that when $\dfrac{F}{N} = \mu$, the system is at the point of slipping. See also FRICTION.

Generalized Coordinates.—The position of a particle or system is usually defined by its distance from each of a set of axial planes having fixed locations and relationships to each other. Of greater advantage and scope is the method of *generalized coordinates*. In this method, a set of variables is selected that will define the configuration of the given system (as, say, a rod lying on a table) but will not violate any constraints to motion that the system may have. Values are not assigned to these variables, or coordinates, in advance; it is evident that the variations in their values will determine any position that the system

may take. The number of the generalized coordinates expresses the number of *degrees of freedom* of the system. The coordinates of any particle in the system may be stated in terms of the generalized coordinates of the system, and its displacements in terms of increments in these coordinates.

Lagrange's Equations.—In connection with this principle, Lagrange developed his universal equations of motion. These may be summed up in his equation of motion for a system with n degrees of freedom:

$$\frac{d}{dt}\frac{\delta T}{\delta \dot{q}_r} - \frac{\delta T}{\delta q_r} = Q_r \quad (r = 1, 2 \ldots \ldots \ldots n).$$

In this, T is the kinetic energy expressed as a function of the q_r's, which are the generalized coordinates; Q_r represents the generalized forces, and is defined by the equation for the work δW done in a general displacement,

$$\delta w = \sum_{r=1}^{n} Q_r \delta q_r.$$

If the system is conservative, as are most systems considered in mechanics, that is, if the work done by the forces of the system in movement from one position to another is independent of the way that movement took place, the general equation of motion is then reduced to

$$Q_r = -\frac{\delta v}{\delta q_r} \quad (r = 1, 2 \ldots \ldots \ldots n).$$

Hamilton's Minimal Path.—Lagrangian equations do not tell us what path a system will take in moving from one configuration to another. But Hamilton, working from Lagrange's ideas, determined a function L of the variables of state (position and velocity) such that $\int_{t_1}^{t_2} L\, dt$ has a stationary value. From this he concluded that a particle or system moving according to Lagrange's equations will take a path along which this integral is a minimum. What this path will be is found through use of the Euler equations and the calculus of variations. This almost teleological conclusion that bodies move in space with a minimum quantity of motion had been foreshadowed by Maupertuis in his principle of least action, Pierre de Fermat (1601–1665) with his rule of least time, and others. This, the last significant development in Newtonian mechanics, was used by Albert Einstein (1879–1955) and others in developing the theories of the "newer physics." These found characteristics in nature that Newton knew nothing of, such as the variation of mass with velocity (see QUANTUM THEORY; RELATIVITY). These factors, however, have appreciable effect only in areas remote from ordinary human activities. For these activities, classical mechanics continues to be recognized as the adequate and valid description of the motions of matter in space.

See also KINEMATICS OF MACHINERY; PHYSICS—*Classical Physics* (Mechanics); STATICS.

Bibliography.—Mach, Ernst, *The Science of Mechanics* (La Salle, Ill., 1942); Margenau, Henry, *The Nature of Physical Reality* (New York 1950); Biezeno, Cornelis Benjamin, and Grammel, Richard, *Engineering Dynamics*, 4 vols. (Glasgow 1954–56); Den Hartog, Jacob Bieter, *Mechanical Vibrations*, 4th ed. (New York 1956); Hartman, James Busse, *Dynamics of Machinery* (New York 1956); Timoshenko, Stephen, and Young, Donovan,

Harold, *Engineering Mechanics,* 4th ed. (New York 1956); Synge, John Lighton, and Griffith, Byron Alexander, *Principles of Mechanics,* 3d ed. (New York 1959); Beer, F. P., and Johnston, E. R., *Mechanics for Engineers,* 2 vols., 2d ed. (New York 1962); Bullen, Keith E., *Introduction to the Theory of Mechanics,* 7th ed. (New York 1965); Leech, J. W., *Classical Mechanics,* 2d ed. (New York 1965); Zajac, Alfred, *Basic Principles and Laws of Mechanics* (Boston 1966); Fox, E. A., *Mechanics* (New York 1967).

WILLIAM H. DILLINGHAM.

MECHANIC'S LIEN, mê-kăn'ĭks lēn, in law, a kind of lien on real estate, created by constitution or statute, in favor of persons furnishing labor or materials for erecting buildings or making improvements. When it relates to materials, it is also sometimes called a materialman's lien. Like a mortgage, a mechanic's lien is an encumbrance on property, but unlike a mortgage, it is created by operation of law rather than by contract. Although not arising directly from a contract, a mechanic's lien exists only where a laborer or supplier either has an express or implied contract with the owner, or has the owner's authorization or consent, to make improvements on realty. This kind of lien is not recognized at common law or under general principles of equity jurisprudence. Statutes and constitutional provisions for mechanics' liens provide additional means for enforcing the payment of a debt, but create no new substantive rights.

A mechanic's lien ordinarily may attach only to privately owned property, including that of religious, educational, and charitable organizations, and not to public property. Most statutes provide for liens for materials furnished, but a few allow them only for services performed. In order for the lien to be established, the materials or labor in question must have gone into something which has attached to and become part of the real estate. Also, the work and materials must have been furnished for building purposes, as distinguished from general or unknown purposes. Buildings, structures, or improvements generally, or only specific kinds of them, may be subject to mechanics' liens, depending upon the governing statute. The lien will usually be allowed for fixtures (q.v.) and interior improvements, except trade fixtures. For example, heating, lighting, and water supply equipment, when installed with the intention of making them part of a building, will form the basis for a lien.

A mechanic's lien may be acquired by an individual, a partnership, or a corporation. The classes of persons entitled to a mechanic's lien are specifically enumerated in some statutes, while others simply provide benefits for "any person" performing labor or supplying materials. There is no requirement that laborers and materialmen make contracts directly with the owner; the right to a mechanic's lien extends to those working for and supplying materials to a contractor. Under some statutes, the right also extends to subcontractors and their employees and suppliers.

Some statutes require the filing or recording of contracts for alterations, improvements, and repairs in order for a mechanic's lien to attach. The purpose of filing is to give notice of the lien to subsequent purchasers. In order to be valid and enforceable, a mechanic's lien must be "perfected" by complying with certain statutory requirements. Notice of intent to claim a lien must be given to the owner in some cases. As a general rule, a mechanic's lien is measured by the amount due and unpaid for the work and materials furnished.

The right to a mechanic's lien may be waived by an express or implied agreement, or by an act such as taking some other security for the debt.

Consult "Mechanics' Liens," *Corpus Juris Secundum,* vol. 57 (Brooklyn 1948; supplement 1957).

RICHARD L. HIRSHBERG,
Attorney at Law.

MECHANICSBURG, mê-kăn'ĭks-bûrg, borough, Pennsylvania, in Cumberland County in the south central part of the state, 8 miles southwest of Harrisburg, at an altitude of 430 feet. It is on the Pennsylvania Railroad and near the Pennsylvania Turnpike. Situated in a farming area raising fruits, field crops, and hay, it has manufactures of clothing, automobile wheels, flavoring extracts, structural steel, and electrical supplies. One of the largest naval supply depots in the United States is located here.

The place was settled in 1790 and was called Drytown (because of the scarcity of water) until 1828, when it was incorporated and renamed, the new name alluding to the number of mechanics employed in its machine shops. Government is by council and manager. Pop. 8,123.

MECHANICSVILLE, Battle of, mê-kăn'ĭks-vĭl (also called the BATTLE OF BEAVER DAM CREEK), a battle of the American Civil War, fought near Mechanicsville, Va., on June 26, 1862. In April and May 1862, Gen. George B. McClellan, in command of the huge Army of the Potomac, had pushed his Peninsular campaign at a snail's pace from Yorktown, Va., to the environs of Richmond (see PENINSULA CAMPAIGN OF 1862). On May 31, Gen. Joseph E. Johnston, commanding the Confederate Army of Northern Virginia, had counterattacked, striking McClellan's left, which lay south of the Chickahominy River (see FAIR OAKS, BATTLES OF). Johnston, wounded during this bloody engagement, yielded the command to Robert E. Lee. McClellan's inability to estimate the size of his adversary's forces, together with his pathological caution, prevented him from taking advantage of his greatly superior numbers to push his campaign to a successful conclusion. His lack of action gave Thomas J. (Stonewall) Jackson time to finish driving the Federals from the Shenandoah Valley, and Lee took the opportunity to formulate a plan to defeat McClellan. After consultation with President Jefferson Davis, he called Jackson secretly from the valley immediately after the conclusion of his campaign there. When Jackson was on his way to join Lee, a Confederate deserter who defected to the Federal lines warned the Union high command. McClellan strengthened his defenses to meet what Lee expected would be a surprise attack.

McClellan's right wing, under Fitz-John Porter, lay on the north bank of the Chickahominy River, a sizable military obstacle. Porter's troops were entrenched along the east bank of a tributary, Beaver Dam Creek. The village of Mechanicsville lay to the west, across the creek, and from it the Mechanicsville Turnpike ran southwest into Richmond. The main body of the Army of the Potomac lay in front of Richmond, south of the Chickahominy. Porter guarded the supply routes from McClellan's base on the York River.

Lee's battle plan called for an envelopment of Porter's right. On June 22, Lee held a council with the generals to be involved in the operation— James Longstreet, Daniel H. Hill, Ambrose P.

Hill, and Jackson. To make the conference, Jackson rode 52 miles in 14 hours, leaving his army already well on its advance eastward from the valley. Because all members of the council were already familiar with the general outlines of the plan, Lee did not explain it in detail, leaving his subordinates to provide the proper implementation. On the eve of the battle, after Jackson was back with his command, a memorandum from Lee made some modifications. The final plan was for A. P. Hill (with D. H. Hill in reserve) to hold Porter in his position with a frontal attack while Jackson moved around the Union flank to strike at the Federal communications. Jackson's force was to spearhead the operation.

Lee set June 26 for the attack. In the early morning darkness, Longstreet and D. H. Hill moved from positions opposite McClellan's center to an area of concentration west of Mechanicsville, while A. P. Hill occupied a position nearer that town. In the forenoon, the Confederates pushed back some Union pickets. But Jackson did not appear at the appointed rendezvous at the hour called for in Lee's timetable. In fact, the Confederate commanders opposite Mechanicsville had no knowledge of his exact whereabouts.

At three in the afternoon, A. P. Hill grew impatient, fearing that there would not be enough daylight to conclude a battle successfully. Without knowing the position of Jackson's forces and without notifying Lee of his action, he moved to the attack; he seems to have expected Jackson to strike Porter's flank at any moment. Crossing Beaver Dam Creek, Hill assaulted the Federal entrenchments. Porter's men, suffering only minor casualties, threw back the Confederates with losses that for some units were catastrophic.

At five in the afternoon, Jackson reached the point designated in Lee's orders for junction with Hill. He understood that his force was to spearhead the attack, with Hill supporting his right. But Hill was gone, and Jackson had no information as to his movements. In an anguished quandary, Jackson, though he could hear sounds of a heavy engagement, decided to move no further and bivouacked for the night.

Lee's first effort to drive McClellan from the environs of Richmond failed for three reasons. Jackson was at least six hours late. Staff work, particularly in maintaining liaison among the several units of the complicated maneuver, was almost completely absent. (In the early years of the war, neither the Union nor the Confederate high command had an understanding of the organization and importance of staff work.) Finally, the operation failed because A. P. Hill took a responsibility that belonged to the commanding general. The evidence does not permit a completely satisfactory explanation of Jackson's failure to arrive on time, a failure that seems the more surprising when it is recalled that in the Shenandoah Valley, Jackson's soldiers had won the nickname "foot cavalry." Suffice it to say that Lee called on Jackson for a march that was long but possible. Though Jackson pressed the advance, a variety of delays impeded the progress of his army.

The action at Beaver Dam Creek had cost the Confederates over 1,500 killed and wounded out of an attacking force of some 10,000 men. About 5,000 Union troops were actively engaged, with casualties totaling less than 400. Lee had lost the battle of Mechanicsville, the first of the Seven Days' Battles (q.v.), but he did not give up the initiative. He struck McClellan the next day at Gaines' Mill (see GAINES' MILL, BATTLE OF).

Consult Freeman, Douglas Southall, *Lee's Lieutenants*, vol. 1 (New York 1942); Williams, Kenneth Powers, *Lincoln Finds a General*, vol. 1 (New York 1949).

RALPH H. GABRIEL,
Professor Emeritus of History, Yale University.

MECHANICVILLE, city, New York, in Saratoga County, at an altitude of 105 feet, on the Hudson River and the New York State Barge Canal system, 19 miles by rail north of Albany. It is served by the Boston and Maine and the Delaware and Hudson railroads, both of which have repair shops in the city. Mechanicville processes dairy products from the surrounding agricultural area, and manufactures pulp and paper products, knit goods, women's dresses, and bricks.

Settled before 1700, Mechanicville was incorporated as a village in 1859 and as a city in 1915. Government is of the commission type. Pop. 6,831.

MECHANISM, mĕk′a-nĭz′m, in philosophy, the theory that the universe and all its parts are like machines and can be described and explained mechanically. This involves (1) the deterministic view that every thing or event is necessitated; (2) that this occurs by efficient causes (causes which compel *a tergo*, "from behind"), rather than by final causes or purposes; (3) that it occurs in accordance with a few simple laws and (4) additively, so that the causal connections of wholes are resultants or functions deducible from the causal connections of their parts; and (5) that both wholes and parts are material or physical and hence extended, moving, and measurable in space.

Older mechanisms pictured the ultimate terms as indivisible solid particles. In the theories of ancient materialism and of René Descartes (1596–1650), who was a mechanist about everything but the human mind, these were supposed to vary infinitely, though only in shape and size. Later atomists postulated only a few standard varieties of particles, a different type for each chemical element or, more recently, still fewer varieties (electrons, protons, and the like) which make the chemical differences by their differences of aggregation. The first mechanisms conceived the particles as affecting one another by impact or push, and mechanists tried thus to explain even Newtonian gravitation, which ostensibly is attraction at a distance. Not very successful at this, mechanism adopted gravitation as the fundamental property of the world machine, and in this form got its supreme expression in the *Traité de Mécanique céleste* (1799–1825) of Pierre Simon de Laplace, who proved mathematically its adequacy to explain the origin and equilibrium of astronomical systems and argued that a superhuman intelligence could similarly calculate all the world's history, human as well as nonhuman.

Physics, however, by supplementing the idea of gravitation with that of magnetic and electrical fields, forced further revision of the mechanist's theories not only of the connections among the elemental parts but of the parts themselves, which are now less often thought of as hard lumps than as whorls, knots, or strains in the fields. The announcement of physicists that not strict determinism but a certain amount of chance seems to prevail among intra-atomic events apparently required a change from "Everything is determined mechanically" to "Everything is determined mechanically insofar as it is determined at all." The world is still a machine, but an electrical machine, and a somewhat loose-jointed one.

The ideal of strict mechanism remains to many minds the supreme type of simple systematic understanding. It has had considerable scientific confirmation in that most of chemistry has been reduced to (that is, explained in terms of) physics, much of biology and physiology reduced to chemistry, and a good deal of psychology reduced to biology and physiology.

It seems an intrinsic limitation of mechanism that since it explains things mainly or wholly by shapes, motions, and quantities, it is comparatively helpless about their qualities, particularly the indisputable perceptual qualities, such as seen colors or felt warmth. Its usual compromise is the argument that such qualities are epiphenomenal, that is, accompaniments and effects of characteristic mechanical processes, but having no effects of their own. The mechanist must accordingly add to his fundamental mechanical laws the many special laws correlating various mechanical configurations with various qualities.

Mechanism is opposed to any philosophy which declares that there are agencies fundamentally different from the physical and mechanical: to idealisms and dualisms, for example, which hold that the world is wholly or partly composed of and ruled by unique spiritual or mental entities; to vitalisms, which hold that there is an irreducible life principle; to finalisms or teleological philosophies, which hold that events happen for the sake of ends in a manner inexplicable by efficient causation; and to organicisms, which maintain that wholes are not exhausted in nor predictable from their parts. Related to the last are philosophies of "emergence," which hold that as certain sorts of complicated structures arise (living organisms, for instance), they exemplify new traits and laws not deducible from the old, though not contravening them either. Some philosophers of science would say that mechanism and emergence are relative to the state of science, since what cannot be mechanically reduced at one stage may be so at another. A metaphysical mechanist will not admit that a change of scientific concepts can affect the facts, but could concede that the facts may vindicate the mechanistic ideal only in a greater or less degree.

A familiar paradox about the doctrine is that while it explains life and mind on the analogy of automatic machines, automatic machines are just what we normally observe to be constructed for the purposes of life and mind. Mechanism about mundane things, therefore, has often been coupled, though it need not be, with deism in religion: God, in this view, is the Great Mechanical Engineer who made the world machine for His and our delectation.

See also DETERMINISM; MATERIALISM.

Bibliography.—Broad, Charlie Dunbar, "Mechanism and Its Alternatives," *The Mind and Its Place in Nature* (New York 1925); Pepper, Stephen C., "Mechanism," *World Hypotheses* (Berkeley, Calif., 1942); Nagel, Ernest, "The Meaning of Reduction in the Natural Sciences," in *Science and Civilization*, ed. by Robert C. Stauffer (Madison, Wis., 1949); reprinted in *Readings in the Philosophy of Science*, ed. by Philip P. Wiener (New York 1953). A slashing attack on mechanism by a philosophical biologist is Pierre Lecomte du Noüy's *Human Destiny* (New York 1947).

DONALD C. WILLIAMS,
Professor of Philosophy, Harvard University.

MECHELEN, měk′ĕ-lĕ[n] (Fr. MALINES; Eng. MECHLIN), town and commune, Belgium, in the Province of Antwerp, on the Dyle River, 14 miles north-northeast of Brussels and about the same distance south-southeast of Antwerp and northwest of Louvain. Mechelen has been the religious center of the country since 1560–1561, when Antoine Perrenot Cardinal de Granvelle was named primate of Belgium, a title which the archbishops of Mechelen have held ever since. The city was once noted for its lace manufacture and now produces chiefly furniture and textiles.

The Salian Franks occupied this territory in the early centuries of the Christian era, and Pepin the Short, the first Carolingian king and father of Charlemagne, conveyed the fief of Mechelen to a kinsman in 754. Charlemagne's grandson Charles II the Bald, king of the West Franks (r. 843–877) and Holy Roman emperor (875–877), gave it to the bishops of Liège. During the next few hundred years, these wealthy and powerful churchmen contributed much to the development of the lower town, on the right bank of the Dyle, and eventually, though less directly, to the growth of the "Free Town," on the left bank. Gradually Mechelen became involved in contests between the bishops and the Berthouts, lords of the Free Town, with the happy result that it was favored by both sides. From 1384 it was ruled by Philip the Bold and subsequent dukes of Burgundy. Margaret of Austria, who was born in Brussels in 1480 and was the widow of Philibert II, duke of Savoy, lived here when she became governor of the Low Countries in 1507. Before she died in 1530, she made Mechelen a brilliant social, artistic, and intellectual center. After her death, the town was caught up in the religious conflicts of the 16th century and was fought over many times by the French, Dutch, and English

A view of Mechelen, long the religious center of Belgium.

Monkmeyer

in the 17th and 18th centuries. The walls which surrounded the town and gave it a circular outline, like that of Louvain, were removed by the French in 1804 and have been replaced by boulevards. Like most cities in the Low Countries, Mechelen was bombarded and severely damaged during both world wars.

Radio Times Hulton Picture Library

The pulpit in the Cathedral of St. Rombaut at Mechelen.

In the center of the town is the beautiful Cathedral of St. Rombaut, begun about 1217 and added to during the next four centuries. Its 320-foot tower, which was begun in 1452 and was intended to reach a height of 570 feet, houses the famous Mechelen carillon of 49 bells, played by a master carillonneur. The cathedral contains Anthony van Dyck's famous painting, *The Crucifixion,* and the impressive mausoleum of Désiré Joseph Cardinal Mercier, the courageous Belgian primate of World War I, who lived in Mechelen. Other notable churches are the Grand Béguignage (mid-17th century); St. Catherine (mid-14th century); St. John (15th century), which contains *The Adoration of the Magi* by Peter Paul Rubens; and Notre Dame (begun in the late 14th century).

Interesting secular buildings include the Town Hall, a structure begun in the early 14th century to serve as a huge cloth market, and the Palais de Justice, built between 1507 and 1517, partly in Gothic and partly in French Renaissance style, following the dissimilar designs of two architects engaged by Margaret of Austria. There are also a number of very old Gothic houses which have withstood time and bombardment. Pop. (1952) commune 62,358.

MECKLENBURG, měk′lĕn-boŏrк, former state, Germany, situated in the lowlands of the northeast, on the coast of the Baltic Sea, be-

tween Schleswig-Holstein on the west, Lower Saxony (Niedersachsen) on the southwest, Brandenburg on the south, and East Pomerania (administered by Poland after 1945) on the east. After World War II, West Pomerania was included within the boundaries of Mecklenburg, increasing the total area from something over 6,000 square miles to 8,856 square miles. The enlarged state of Mecklenburg constituted the northernmost sector and about one fifth of the territory of the Soviet Zone of occupied Germany and the German Democratic Republic (East Germany) until 1952, when it was broken up into the districts of Rostock, Schwerin, and Neubrandenburg. Major cities in the area include Rostock (pop., 1955 est., 150,-000), a major port and oil-receiving center, the seat of a university, with shipyards and manufactures of agricultural machinery and tanks; Schwerin, an important dairying and transportation hub; Stralsund, a manufacturing city and seaport; Greifswald, site of a 500-year-old university; and Wismar, a fishing and manufacturing center.

The area is generally flat, though intersected by a few low ranges of hills, and is heavily forested. It is drained by the Peene, Uecl·er (Ücker), and Warnow rivers, all flowing into the Baltic Sea, and by the Elde River, a tributary of the Elbe. Lakes are plentiful, the larger ones including lakes Müritz, Schwerin, Kummerow, Plau, and Tollense. The climate is raw but not unhealthy, the temperature averaging about 46° F.; precipitation exceeds 20 inches during a normal year. Agriculture has prospered here for centuries. Fertile farm lands checker the entire region, decreasing only in the extreme south and along the wide expanses of sand and swamp which characterize the northern seacoast. Wheat, rye, corn, oats, barley, peas, beans, sugar beets, turnips, and

Eastfoto

A square in Rostock, an important port in Mecklenburg.

potatoes are staple crops, and livestock is raised. Baltic and North Sea fishing is also important, the fleets clustering near the major port cities and at the town of Sassnitz on Rügen Island. Though traditionally agrarian in its economy, Mecklenburg had several chemical plants and machine factories before World War II. After its separation from industrialized West Germany, efforts were made to build up heavy manufacturing, but a large sector of the labor force has continued to be engaged in the growing and processing of farm products.

History.—The Slavic Wends occupied the region, which then consisted almost entirely of dense forests, in the 6th century A.D. In the 12th century, it was colonized and partly Christianized by Henry the Lion, duke of Saxony, and the Wendish princes became nominal vassals of the Holy Roman Empire, in which they were granted ducal rank in 1348. Some medieval towns, notably Rostock and Wismar, were for a time relatively independent and prosperous as members of the Hanseatic League. The dukes adopted Protestantism in 1549, and the land was devastated during the Thirty Years' War (1618–1648), which left both peasants and townspeople in poverty for decades. Sweden, one of the participants in the war, retained control of parts of the German Baltic coast until well into the Napoleonic era.

In 1621 the duchy was divided into two parts, Mecklenburg-Schwerin and Mecklenburg-Güstrow; a redivision in 1701 created the duchies of Mecklenburg-Schwerin and Mecklenburg-Strelitz, which lasted until the end of World War I. Both were raised to grand duchies by the Congress of Vienna in 1815 and joined the German Empire in 1871, after supporting Prussia in its wars with Austria (1866) and France (1870–1871). The citizens sent elected representatives to the Reichstag during the days of the empire, but local government remained autocratic and nonrepresentative. The grand dukes were deposed in 1918, and the duchies became separate states of the republic. In 1934, after the Nazi coup, they were combined into a single state, which fell under the control of Soviet forces in 1945. Pop. (1956 est.) 2,156,100.

MECKLENBURG DECLARATION OF INDEPENDENCE, mĕk'lĕn-bûrg, in American history, a series of rebellious resolutions supposed to have been adopted on May 20, 1775, at Charlotte, Mecklenburg County, N.C., by a convention held at midnight and representing each militia company in the county. A report of the meeting and a text of the resolutions appeared in the Raleigh *Register* of April 30, 1819. This report was probably based on oral accounts by delegates who had attended the convention 44 years earlier. It was claimed that the original document and records relating to the meeting had been destroyed by fire in 1800.

Both in spirit and language, the Mecklenburg Declaration, as reconstructed in 1819, was a remarkable forerunner of the United States Declaration of Independence signed at Philadelphia in 1776. It described the citizenry as "a free and independent people," and declared that the colonies "are and of right ought to be a sovereign and self-governing association under the control of no other power but that of our God and the General Government of Congress." Similarities of phraseology between this document and the Declaration of Independence led many to doubt its authenticity, especially since one of the chief skeptics was Thomas Jefferson, the principal author of the more famous declaration. Jefferson disclaimed any knowledge of the Mecklenburg Declaration, and it was never established that the

North Carolinian signers of the Declaration of Independence of 1776 played a part in the composition of either document. By and large, however, the report of the Mecklenburg resolutions was accepted at face value. The anniversary of the supposed signing was proclaimed a legal holiday in North Carolina in 1831, and the date May 20, 1775, has remained upon the flag and seal of the state to the present day.

In 1838, Peter Force, a noted archivist (at that time also the mayor of Washington, D.C.), published the text of a series of "Resolves" adopted at Charlotte on May 31, 1775. He had apparently discovered these in a pre-Revolutionary issue of the New York *Journal.* The text which he reproduced was virtually substantiated during the 1840's when several copies of the May 31 resolutions were found, one even turning up in the British State Paper Office, having been sent to London in a letter of July 20, 1775, from colonial governor of Georgia. These so-called "Resolves of May 31," 20 in number, were signed by the same delegates who had claimed to be signatories of the declaration of May 20. They were aggressively anti-British and, in part, paralleled or duplicated the 1819 version of the document allegedly signed 11 days earlier. They did not in themselves, however, constitute a declaration of independence, nor did they contain the language which most closely resembled the national Declaration of Independence.

The authenticity of the Resolves of May 31 is no longer at issue, but a lively controversy has raged as to whether there had been two meetings and two sets of resolutions or only one convention and one set of resolutions, that of May 31. The consensus has favored the latter theory, though the "Declaration of Independence of May 20" has not been without its stanch defenders. In either case, the Resolves of May 31 give ample evidence that the intransigent, liberty-seeking spirit which was to sustain the American Revolution was widespread in North Carolina immediately after Lexington and Concord.

WILLIAM CUMMINGS,
Staff Editor, "The Encyclopedia Americana."

MECOPTERA, mē-kŏp'tēr-à, a rather small order of four-winged insects commonly known as scorpion flies. For the most part the wings are long and narrow, with many cross veins on the apical third or more. A few are wingless. The most important families are the Panorpidae and the Bittacidae. The Panorpidae are the true scorpion flies, being so named because the male genitalia are bulbous and shaped much like the sting of a scorpion. The antennae are moderately long and slender, ocelli are usually either absent or three in number, and the legs are long. The larvae are caterpillarlike and live in the soil under debris.

The bittacids are long and slender, with very long legs and resemble crane flies (Diptera). They are predaceous and are found in long grass and low foliage, on which they may hang suspended by their front legs and capture and hold prey with their hind legs. The Boreidae (snow scorpion flies) are wingless and are often found abundantly on snow.

CHARLES H. CURRAN.

MEDAL, mĕd"l, an emblem of metal, cast or struck, usually in the form of a coin but not circulated as money. It may be designed as a memento, as a token commemorating some event, as a prize or award of merit, as a recognition of heroic conduct or of victory in war, or for similar purposes. Among the earliest medals known are those awarded by the ancient Greeks to winners of athletic contests, and the custom of awarding medals in gold, silver, and bronze to winners of track and field events has continued to the present day. Medals in gold, silver, brass, or copper were cast as mementos of Roman emperors beginning with Augustus, the first of the imperial line (r. 27 B.C.–14 A.D.). Medals commemorating the reigns of kings of England date to William the Conqueror (r. 1066–1087). Such medals have portraits on the obverse; in some cases, the reverse is inscribed with dates of birth, coronation, death, and notable events of the reign. Similar medals honor French kings back to Louis XI (r. 1461–1483) and many Italian and German rulers. The papal series begins with Paul II (r. 1464–1471). In the United States, medals have been struck as mementos of the inauguration of every president since George Washington. In the early period, a die was made from these medals for presentation to Indian chiefs as a peace medal. On the reverse side was a design showing a tomahawk, a peace pipe, and crossed hands.

Medal making became a fine art during the Renaissance. In the 1400's and 1500's, such artists as Pisanello (Antonio Pisano), Filippo Lippi, Benvenuto Cellini, and Albrecht Dürer are notable for their medals. Cast medals predominated through the 15th century, but were superseded by die-struck medals in the 16th century. After the 18th century, France became the leading producer of artistic medals. The dies for early United States medals were made in France.

The earliest English military medal is believed to be that presented in 1480 to John Kendal, prior of the Knights of St. John of Jerusalem, for the relief of Rhodes. Queen Elizabeth I issued a medal commemorating the defeat of the Spanish Armada in 1588. The first medal with a ribbon was that for the English naval victory of the "Glorious First of June," 1794, against the French. Although the East India Company made a general distribution of medals for victories in India, and Horatio Nelson's prize agent passed out pewter medals for the battles of the Nile (1798) and Trafalgar (1805), the first official medal distributed to all ranks was that for Waterloo (1815).

The earliest military medal awarded in Britain's American colonies is said to be that given in 1756 by the city of Philadelphia to Col. (later Gen.) John Armstrong for an attack on the Indians at Kittanning, Pa. During the Revolutionary War, medals were awarded to American commanders winning important victories, and this custom continued through the quasi war with France (1798–1800), the Barbary wars (1801–1805, and 1815), the War of 1812, the Mexican War (1846–1848), and the Civil War. The Medal of Honor (or Congressional Medal of Honor, first authorized for 1861), campaign badges (first authorized in 1905), and subsequent decorations have superseded battle medals in the United States.

Among the medals awarded for merit, those issued by world's fairs have been notable. Many professional groups continue to recognize outstanding achievement by issuing medals.

See also DECORATIONS AND ORDERS; for the history of coins, see COINS.

DON RUSSELL.

MEDAL OF HONOR (often called the CONGRESSIONAL MEDAL OF HONOR). See DECORATIONS AND ORDERS—*United States.*

MEDALLION, mḗ-dăl'yŭn, originally a very large medal. Some Roman medallions in brass, gold, silver, and copper have been preserved from the early centuries of the Christian era and are much prized by coin collectors because of their scarcity. The term medallion was later adopted for use in the decorative arts to describe any part of an ornamental scheme which resembled a large medal or plaque, as, for example, an oval, round, or even rectangular design bearing a bust or portrait. In sculpture and architecture, a medallion is usually a full-length figure, a bust, a garland, or some geometrical design, executed in relief and enclosed in an oval frame. This motif was much favored by Renaissance architects for interior and exterior decoration.

The term is also applied to round or oval figures occurring either singly or in series in carpets and ornamental fabrics, and to certain lace patterns in garments. Oval or circular designs in illuminated manuscripts and printed books are likewise referred to as medallions, especially when they enclose portraits.

MEDAN, mȧ-dän', city, Indonesia, largest city on the island of Sumatra, and capital of North Sumatra Province (created in 1950). It is located on the Deli River, some 15 miles south of the outport of Belawan, where the river empties into the Strait of Malacca, and about 400 miles west-northwest of Singapore. Medan experienced tremendous growth during the 1940's and 1950's, due in great measure to development of the resources of the rich agricultural region in which it is situated. Tobacco, rubber, sisal, tea, palm oil, and coffee are produced; brick, tile, and some machinery are manufactured; and oilfields near the coast are being exploited. Medan has become a rail hub which links the major productive areas of northeastern Sumatra. There is an airport south of the city and a cable station at Belawan. There is also a radio station.

Medan was settled in the 1870's and was for many years a Dutch administrative center, the capital of the Sumatra East Coast government of the Netherlands East Indies. After 1945 it served for a time as the capital of the state of East Sumatra. Population (1961) 479,098.

MEDAWAR, med'ǝ-wär, **Peter Brian,** British biologist and medical scientist: b. Rio de Janeiro, Brazil, Feb. 28, 1915. He shared the 1960 Nobel Prize in physiology or medicine with Australian immunologist Frank Macfarlane Burnet for "their discovery of acquired immunological tolerance."

During World War II, Medawar turned his attention from a study of tissue growth to the medical problem of why skin grafts from a donor would not form a permanent graft on the body of a recipient. Experimenting with skin grafts on rabbits, Medawar found that an acquired immunological reaction caused a rabbit to reject the grafted "foreign" tissue. He discovered that the reaction was widespread and systemic, although it was not produced by antibodies, the agents usually responsible for an immunological reaction. Medawar then showed that the genetic relationship between donor and recipient determined how long a graft would last.

Influenced by Burnet's theories, Medawar and two students, R. E. Billingham and L. Brent, inoculated fetal mice with living cells from donor mice. They found that the recipient mice later proved tolerant of grafts from the same donor mice. This illustration of acquired immunological tolerance showed that organ transplants were possible and led to further study on ways to induce immunological tolerance in adult animals.

Medawar studied at Oxford and taught at Birmingham University and University College, London. In 1962 he became director of the National Institute for Medical Research in London.

MEDARY, Samuel, American political leader and editor: b. Montgomery County, Pa., Feb. 25, 1801; d. Columbus, Ohio, Nov. 7, 1864. He was brought up in Pennsylvania by Quaker parents, moved with them to Maryland in 1820, and in 1825 went to Batavia, Ohio, where he became active in the Democratic Party. Three years later, at Bethel, he cofounded the *Ohio Sun,* supporting Andrew Jackson for the presidency. Medary served in the Ohio legislature in 1834–1837 and for the next 10 years held the state post of superintendent of public printing. In the meantime he had purchased the *Western Hemisphere* of Columbus (1837), renaming it the *Ohio Statesman,* and as its editor for almost two decades, was first the spokesman and later the undisputed leader of the Democratic Party in the state. An aggressive advocate of national territorial expansion, he pressed for the annexation of Texas, and is sometimes credited (on little evidence) with originating the slogan "Fifty-four Forty or Fight!" during the Northwest Boundary Dispute of the mid-1840's. The adoption of the Ohio Constitution of 1851 was also largely due to his efforts.

Medary was governor of the Minnesota Territory (1857–1858) and of the Kansas Territory (1858–1860) during the latter part of the struggle between the proslavery and antislavery forces there. The Wyandotte Constitution, under which Kansas was admitted to the Union as a free state in 1861, was adopted (1859) during his administration, although he had previously favored the Lecompton Constitution, which was supported by the proslavery elements.

At Columbus in January 1861 he established the *Crisis,* a publication which he edited until his death, opposing the policies of the Lincoln administration as destructive of the Union and of the right of the individual states to enact their own law regarding slavery. His newspaper was banned in some parts of Ohio, its press was destroyed by a pro-Union mob in 1863, and he was widely denounced as a traitor, but he remained throughout the war an unyielding Peace Democrat, supporting the Ohio Copperhead leader Clement L. Vallandigham and campaigning in 1864 for the election of George B. McClellan as president. Many years later, a monument was erected in his honor at Columbus.

MEDEA, mē-dē'à, in classical mythology, an enchantress, daughter of Aëtes, king of Colchis in Asia, and niece of Circe, another sorceress. By her profound knowledge of the magical virtues of plants, she practiced powerful witchcraft and became the most famous magician of Greek mythology. Medea fell in love with Jason (q.v.) and helped him by her arts to acquire the Golden Fleece. She then fled with him on the *Argo,* murdering her brother to ensure their escape, and shared in the later adventures of the ship and its crew (see ARGONAUTS), arriving finally at Iolcus in Thessaly. There, according to one version of her story, she boiled Jason's father, Aeson in virtuous herbs, restoring his youth. She then persuaded the daughters of Pelias, Aeson's half brother and the usurper of his throne, to try the same process on Pelias, but gave them noxious herbs to use and thus induced his death. Another version has Medea demonstrating her powers of rejuvenation by cutting up an old ram, throwing the pieces into a pot of boiling water, uttering a charmed phrase, and then, by magic or trickery, producing from the pot a frisky young lamb. After this, she drugged Pelias and induced his daughters to dismember him, but withheld the magical incantation when the deed was done.

After 10 years of life with Medea, Jason deserted her to wed Creusa (sometimes called Glauce), daughter of Creon, king of Corinth. Medea presented to her rival, as a bridal gift, a poisoned gown which caused Creusa to die an agonized death. The sorceress then destroyed Creon and his palace by fire, murdered the two children that she had borne to Jason (some attribute the murder of Jason's children to the angered Corinthians), and escaped in a dragon-driven chariot. Ancient accounts next take Medea to various places and eventually return her to Colchis with a son, Medus, whom she had borne to Aegeus, king of Athens. At last she is represented as becoming immortal and marrying Achilles in the underworld.

The story of Medea, especially the Corinthian episode, has often provided a subject for ancient and modern tragedy. Aeschylus and Sophocles, among the Greeks, and Quintus Ennius and Ovid, among the Romans, took the theme for tragedies, but only fragments of these works exist. There are extant, however, the Greek *Medea* (q.v.) of Euripides and the Latin *Medea* of Lucius Annaeus Seneca. The story has also been dramatized in French by Pierre Corneille in *Médée* (1635) and in German by Franz Grillparzer in his trilogy *Das goldene Vliess* (published 1821). Luigi Cherubini used the myth for his Italian opera *Médée* (1797).

P. R. COLEMAN-NORTON,
Princeton University.

MEDEA, a tragedy by Euripides (q.v.), first performed in Athens in 431 B.C. Its theme is the sequel to the quest of the Golden Fleece by Jason and his Argonauts, an adventure which succeeded largely because Medea, the sorceress daughter of Aeëtes, king of Colchis, fell in love with Jason (see MEDEA). She helped him to steal the Fleece, deceived her father, murdered her brother, and fled to Greece with Jason, remaining his mistress, since legal marriage between Greeks and barbarians was impossible. The foregoing events are referred to in the play, as is Medea's contrivance of the death of Jason's usurping uncle, Pelias, king of Iolcus, by which she brought exile upon herself and her lover. They then went to Corinth, where the king, Creon, who had no sons, offered Jason the hand of his only daughter, Glauce. Jason, always practical, agreed to the marriage, thus becoming Creon's heir. The king, fearing Medea's wrath and her magical powers, ordered her exiled from Corinth, together with the two sons whom she had borne to Jason. At this point the action of the play begins.

Medea, her love for Jason turned to hatred, is prostrated by his perfidy, but even in her prostration begins to meditate on how best to avenge her wrongs. Creon comes to see that his sentence of banishment is carried out, but reluctantly grants her plea for a day's delay. Jason comes, seeking to justify his conduct and promising aid for her children. Aegeus, king of Athens, passes through Corinth. Medea appeals to him for sanctuary and

Gary Wagner

Judith Anderson (right) in the title role of *Medea*.

wins his promise of a haven in Athens. She then turns to her vengeance. In a second scene with Jason she feigns forgiveness, securing his pledge that their two sons shall not share her exile and his consent that they be allowed to bear her gifts to Jason's bride. The gifts are a magic robe and crown which, being donned, destroy the wearer with fire. Creon tries to help his daughter in her agony and shares her fate. Medea then kills her children and, in a final scene with Jason, denies to him even the dead bodies of his sons. She then escapes in a magic chariot drawn by winged serpents. Her vengeance is complete: Jason is left with no remnant of his former glory save the rotting wreck of his ship, the *Argo*, which, as she foretells, will collapse on him and kill him.

Gilbert Murray, author of one of the finest translations of the play, thus summarizes its central theme: "The *Medea*, in spite of its background of wonder and enchantment, is not a ro-mantic play but a tragedy of character and situation. It deals, so to speak, not with the romance itself, but with the end of the romance, a thing which is so terribly often the reverse of romantic." The fatal flaw in the romance of Jason and Medea reveals itself as the conflict between an adventurer who puts ambition and glory before everything else and a barbarian princess to whom passion is everything. Like Macbeth and Othello, Jason is destroyed by the weak spot in his own character. "The judgment pronounced on Jason," Murray writes, "comes not from any disinterested or peace-making God, but from his own victim transfigured into a devil."

Unlike *Macbeth* and *Othello*, however, the main interest throughout the play is directed to the instrument of the hero's destruction, in the person of Medea. Euripides endows her with as many human qualities as any character of such towering and vicious intemperance could exhibit without appearing altogether incongruous. In many of her scenes she is the universal type of outraged, proud woman betrayed by a lover. Nor does the playwright neglect to make the greatest dramatic capital out of the conflict in Medea's heart between her love for her children and her desire to inflict on Jason the ultimate in pain and degradation. Her vacillation between the two emotions, as she temporarily falters in her resolve to slaughter her sons, contributes to the terrible effect of the climax, in which hate is triumphant.

The play was first presented at a festival, with the works of other dramatists, in the year that marked the beginning of the Peloponnesian War. On that occasion, the Greeks awarded third prize to the *Medea*. Since classical times, however, critics have been nearly unanimous in ranking it with the two or three most dramatically effective of the 19 plays of Euripides that have come down to us. Some, indeed, have considered it his best work. Often staged in the modern theater, its central role is unusually demanding, but offers to the actress of sufficient intensity and discipline an opportunity for a truly bravura performance. A well-remembered production in the United States was that of 1947–1948, starring Judith Anderson and John Gielgud in an adaptation by Robinson Jeffers. Miss Anderson did it again on television in 1959.

MEDELLIN, mä-thê-yĕn', city, Colombia, capital of the Department of Antioquia, and an episcopal see, situated in a small valley more than 4,800 feet above sea level, near the Río Cauca, about 150 miles northwest of Bogotá. Founded in 1675, it soon became the leading community of the region, but remained virtually isolated and self-sufficient until late in the 19th century. Railroads and highways now provide adequate transportation facilities, and the city is well served by commercial airlines. Medellín ranks second in population among the cities of Colombia and is the country's chief industrial center. Favored by a healthy climate and by a vigorous and responsible city planning group, it has developed as a highly attractive residential area, with extensive boulevards and public parks, many modern buildings, and relatively little substandard housing. Sumptuous private estates look down on the city from the slopes of the valley, testifying to the economic wealth of the region.

Medellín benefited from the development of the gold and silver mines of Antioquia before World War I and later from the growth of the

C. Perry Weimer: House of Photography

The plaza in Medellín, the second largest city in Colombia, at an altitude of about 4,800 feet above sea level.

coffee plantations. Subsequently, steelworks, rolling mills, and sugar refineries, all of great capacity, were added. There are manufactures of pharmaceuticals, chemicals, electric appliances, foodstuffs, pottery, porcelain ware, cloth, candies, cigarettes, clocks, shoes, paper, and jewelry, and considerable trade in gold, silver, coffee, and sugar.

Medellín has a modern cathedral and several 17th century churches, a seminary, the government gold mint, a hospital, and many public buildings. It is the site of the University of Antioquia, Bolívar University, and several faculties of the University of Colombia. Pop. (1964) 772,887.

MEDFIELD, měd′fēld, town, Massachusetts, in Norfolk County, on the Charles River, at an elevation of 180 feet. Served by the New York, New Haven and Hartford Railroad, it is a residential suburb, 19 miles southwest of Boston. The public library houses historical relics. Medfield was settled in 1649 and incorporated in 1651. Pop. 6,021.

MEDFORD, měd′fẽrd, city, Massachusetts, in Middlesex County, at an altitude of 12 feet, on the navigable Mystic River, 5 miles northwest of Boston. It is served by the Boston and Maine Railroad and state and federal highways. A residential and industrial suburb of Boston, it manufactures machinery, waxes and polishes, chemicals, boxes and containers, furniture, truck bodies, wire fences, and toys, and engages in printing and publishing. It is the site of Tufts University, and of Jackson College for Women and the Fletcher School of Law and Diplomacy, both administered by Tufts. The Fletcher School, to whose operation Harvard University also contributes, trains students for government foreign service and for the management of international business and legal affairs.

In its earlier days, Medford was a center of manufacture of bricks and tiles, but it became most famous for its ships and its rum. A vessel was launched here as early as 1631, and shipbuilding prospered well into the 19th century, when Medford-built clipper ships engaged in the China trade and made fast voyages around Cape Horn to California. The last keel was laid in 1873. Medford rum was valued not only in New England but throughout the New World and in some parts of the Old, the last of the city's renowned distilleries ceasing operations in 1905.

Medford (first known as Meadford), one of the oldest communities in the state, was founded in 1630 and incorporated as a town in 1684. The Cradock House, a two-story fortresslike brick dwelling, with portholes, outside shutters, and walls 18 inches thick, was erected in 1634 and is still standing. The Royall House, rebuilt by Col. Isaac Royall in 1732 (restored in 1908), has attached slave quarters, the only such relic of slavery to be found in Massachusetts; the house was used as a headquarters by Gen. John Stark before the evacuation of Boston by the American forces in 1776. Outstanding examples of colonial architecture have been preserved from the pre-Revolutionary War period, when Medford was principally a town of merchants and a chief source of supplies to New Hampshire and Vermont. Paul Revere's famous ride took him through Medford, and a memorial tablet on the grounds of the public library lists the names of 59 of the town's citizens who fought as Minutemen at Lexington and Concord in 1775. The community was incorporated as a city in 1892 and adopted the city manager form of government in 1950. Pop. 64,971.

MEDFORD, city, Oregon, seat of Jackson County. It lies at an elevation of 1,382 feet in the Rogue River valley, 174 miles south of Eugene and 22 miles north of the California border, on federal and state highways. The city has an airport and is served by United, Pacific, and West Coast airlines. Freight service is provided by the Southern Pacific Railroad. Medford is situated in the center of a fruit-growing, dairying, farming, lumbering, and mining region. It is also a summer resort. The Rogue River National Forest is nearby, and the city is connected by highway with Crater Lake National Park, some 50 miles to the northeast. Medford was founded in 1883 and incorporated as a city two years later. Government is administered by a mayor and council. Pop. 24,425.

MEDIA, mē′dĭ-à, the ancient name of a region in what is now northwestern Iran, south of the Caspian Sea. It was bounded on the northwest by Armenia, on the west by Assyria and Babylonia, on the south by Susiana (Elam) and Persis, and on the east by Parthia. It consists largely of mountainous terrain around a plateau, on which is situated modern Teheran.

The archaeological history of this area has been pushed back into prehistoric times. Agriculture made its appearance on the shores of the Caspian as early as 10,000 B.C., according to radiocarbon dates. In the third and second millenniums B.C., the inhabitants of Media were prevailingly non-Semitic and non-Indo-European, but soon after the beginning of the Iron Age (12th century B.C.), the Indo-European Medes began to occupy the region, which was thenceforward named after them. Like their sister people, the Persians, the Medes belonged to the Indo-Aryan branch of the Indo-Europeans, being closely related in language and basic culture to the Vedic Indians, who invaded southwestern Asia and India from the north about the 17th century B.C. Medes and Persians both shared the Andronovo culture of southwestern Siberia in the Late Bronze Age, according to the discoveries of Soviet archaeologists working in this region since World War II. In any case, their invasion of northwestern Iran put an end to the Luristan culture, whose remarkable bronzes are found in nearly every important museum of Europe and America.

The name of the Medes and their country first appears in written sources about the middle of the 9th century B.C., when we find them mentioned in the Assyrian royal inscriptions as conquered foes. From then on, to the early 7th century B.C., the Median princes remained, in general, unwilling vassals of Assyria. The exact status of these princes toward the end of this period is defined in the longest treaty yet known from the ancient Orient. In 1955 the British found a huge clay tablet in the ruins of the Assyrian capital of Calah (Nimrud), in modern Iraq, which contained the entire treaty, dated in 672 B.C. At that time, the Median Empire had not yet been founded, and its first king (according to Herodotus, who dates him 700–674 B.C.) can at best have been a local chief not important enough to be mentioned in the Assyrian documents. His name, Deioces, was certainly not fictitious, since it was borne by another Median prince in the late 8th century B.C.

The Median Empire was thus probably created by the second king, Phraortes (c. 647–625 B.C.), whose accession coincided with the end of the

civil war between the Assyrian king Asshurbanapli (Ashurbanipal) and his brother, as a result of which Assyrian power was greatly weakened. His name reappears later among the dynastic names of the 6th century B.C. The next king, Cyaxares (q.v.), conquered Assyria in a series of onslaughts; Nineveh itself was destroyed by the Medes in 612. Before the end of his 40-year reign, Cyaxares seems to have been overlord of an empire which extended from the frontiers of Lydia, near modern Ankara, Turkey, to central Iran, if not even farther eastward. The kings of Persis, ancestors of the later kings of Persia, were also Median vassals.

Cyaxares was followed by Astyages (585–550 B.C.), the last independent king of Media, who was defeated by his son-in-law, Cyrus of Persia (Cyrus the Great), in a battle which saw the defection of the Median troops from their unpopular king. Cyrus set up a dual monarchy in which Medes and Persians had equal rights, at least in theory. The Medes endeavored to regain their independence during the civil wars and rebellions which followed the death (522 B.C.) of Cambyses, son of Cyrus, but in vain.

During the 300 years from the first appearance of the Medes in the Assyrian records to their conquest by the Persians, their civilization became strongly Assyrianized, as we know from many monuments and a number of inscriptions of Median chieftains. Assyrianizing monuments have been found at the Median capital, Ecbatana (now Hamadan, Iran), and a considerable quantity of art objects from a provincial capital at modern Ziwiye in western Media is scattered through various museums; it consists almost entirely of objects made in Assyria or by trained craftsmen in Media who imitated Assyrian originals.

According to later Zoroastrian tradition, the founder of the Parsi (Parsee) religion was a native of Media who lived in the 6th century B.C. This is not, however, the view of most modern students of the Avesta, who place Zoroaster's home further east, nor was it the view of ancient authorities, according to whom Zoroaster lived much earlier (perhaps about the 9th century B.C.).

Bibliography.—Cameron, George Glenn, *History of Early Iran* (Chicago 1936); Olmstead, Albert Ten Eyck, *History of the Persian Empire* (Chicago 1948); Wiseman, Donald John, *Chronicles of the Chaldaean Kings (626–556 B.C.)* (London 1956).

W. F. ALBRIGHT,
W. F. Spence Professor of Semitic Languages Emeritus, The Johns Hopkins University.

MEDIA, borough, Pennsylvania, seat of Delaware County, in the southeastern corner of the state, about 7 miles west of the city limits of Philadelphia, at an altitude of 210 feet. A pork-marketing center and residential suburb, it has several industrial establishments, including plastics manufacture, and is served by the Pennsylvania Railroad. It is associated in history with William Penn, having been settled in the 1680's by his followers, some of whom are buried here. It was incorporated in 1850. Government is by mayor and council. Pop. 5,803.

MEDIAL MORAINE. See MORAINE.

MEDIATION, mē-dĭ-ā′shŭn, in industrial relations, an offer or attempt by a neutral third party to give assistance to both of the interested parties in a labor-management or interunion negotiation, in order to facilitate agreement. The negotiating parties may accept the mediator's "good offices" without becoming obliged to follow his advice. The mediator may, in fact, be sparing with advice and concentrate on providing information, promoting discussion, probing for or developing areas of agreement, bringing to bear a moderating influence where personality conflicts are obscuring the real issues, citing formulas arrived at in other industries or in other localities, and otherwise helping the parties to find a mutually acceptable compromise.

Mediation occurs typically at an early stage in negotiations, with a view to forestalling serious or protracted disagreements and generally to promoting smooth industrial relations. It should not be confused with arbitration, which may be called for where serious disagreements have developed and normal collective-bargaining procedures have failed to resolve them. Acceptance of arbitration implies a commitment on the part of the contending parties to abide by the decision of the arbitrator, who acts as the adjudicator of the dispute. Thus arbitration is a wholly distinct function from mediation, though on many occasions the mediator in an unsuccessful series of negotiations has later been called upon to act as arbitrator. The term "conciliation" is more ambiguous; it may be used merely as a synonym for "collective bargaining" (whether or not a neutral third party is involved), or it may be a substitute for the term "mediation." In the latter sense, it often (though not always) implies mediation in its most positive form. A conciliator, for instance, may tender specific recommendations in the areas of greatest controversy.

Since unchecked industrial strife affects the general public, it was inevitable that national governments should eventually become active as third parties in labor disputes. Where mediation is concerned, democratic nations have hit upon a wide variety of approaches. In France, under an act of 1892, local justices were authorized to appoint labor-management committees, mediators, or both, at the request of either party to a dispute. The German Republic, at a low ebb in its industrial relations in 1923, established a permanent panel of "state conciliators" with the power to force arbitration whenever mediation and bargaining failed to produce agreement. New Zealand, in 1928, provided machinery for the selection of "conciliation committees," with workers and employers equally represented and a mediator functioning in the role of nonvoting chairman. An attempt to legislate industrial harmony was made in England as early as 1824, but the first reasonably effective law along this line was the Conciliation Act of 1896, which empowered the Board of Trade to investigate disputes and to appoint mediators. This measure was followed, in 1919, by the Industrial Courts Act, which established more permanent and well-defined machinery for both mediation and arbitration. The pattern that has emerged in the 20th century from the attempts of democracies to deal with this problem is the movement toward the establishment of standing boards of "career mediators," government-employed experts trained in the problems of labor and management and knowledgeable in the various techniques of industrial bargaining which prevail in their respective countries.

In the United States, mediation of major industrial disputes hardly existed in the 19th century or was the haphazard undertaking of some respected mutual friend of the contending parties.

In 1886 the governments of Massachusetts and New York, through legislation, set up public boards which successfully mediated enough disputes to inspire imitation by other states. Toward the turn of the century, the federal government began to attempt a mediatory role in certain industries, having on many previous occasions been called upon to act after long-simmering disputes had deteriorated into situations which endangered the public interest, private property, and even human life. The extension of governmental activity to include mediation, far from being motivated by a desire to enlarge the federal authority, was an attempt to avoid the necessity of such more dictatorial and unpopular measures as labor injunctions, forced arbitration, and the calling out of federal troops to enforce peace.

One of the earliest "permanent" federal mediation boards established by law in the United States (under the Erdman Act of 1898) consisted of only two members, the chairman of the Interstate Commerce Commission and his subordinate, the commissioner of the Bureau of Labor; they were empowered to mediate railroad labor disputes but not to initiate compulsory arbitration. The Newlands Act (1913) set up a four-member United States Board of Mediation which, during a period of about three years, helped to settle 46 of 61 railroad disputes without resort to arbitration. In 1917, to ensure the steady production of war goods, a Mediation Commission empowered to act in any of several industries was established on a temporary basis by President Woodrow Wilson. A Railroad Labor Board of nine members, not authorized to order arbitration proceedings, was set up in 1920. It was superseded in 1926 by a five-member United States Board of Mediation, and in 1934 by a three-man National Mediation Board.

By far the most important agency for mediation, however, began to evolve in 1913 with the creation of the Department of Labor, whose secretary was authorized to act as labor-management mediator and to appoint "commissioners of conciliation." This function of the department soon became the responsibility of a bureau known as the United States Conciliation Service. Increasingly active during the 1920's and 1930's, it was, in 1947, reconstituted as an independent agency with the title Federal Mediation and Conciliation Service (q.v.). In the late 1950's its large staff of specialists in labor relations was rendering help in as many as 15,000 separate cases annually.

See also ARBITRATION, INDUSTRIAL.

WILLIAM CUMMINGS,
Staff Editor, "The Encyclopedia Americana."

MEDIATION, in international affairs. See ARBITRATION, INTERNATIONAL.

MEDIATION SERVICE, Federal. See FEDERAL MEDIATION AND CONCILIATION SERVICE.

MEDICAGO, mĕd-ĭ-kā'gō, a genus of annual and perennial herbaceous legumes (family Leguminosae), whose 50 species are native mainly in the Mediterranean region, extending to central Europe and western Asia, and are often naturalized in other parts of the world. Several species are widely cultivated. Included in the genus are some of the world's most important forage crops, notably alfalfa (q.v.) or lucerne (*Medicago sativa*), black medic (*M. lupulina*), and bur clover (*M. hispida*). New strains of these and other species are continually being introduced to cultivation to increase the production of grazing animals. None of the species is used directly for human food. The leaves are composed of three toothed leaflets, borne pinnately. The small flowers are carried in slender, terminal spikelike racemes, those of the perennial species being mostly blue-violet or purple and those of the annuals mostly yellow. The fruits contain one to several seeds and are curved or variously coiled, sometimes spiny.

RICHARD M. STRAW.

MEDICAL DEPARTMENT, United States Army. See ARMY, DEPARTMENT OF THE.

MEDICAL DEPARTMENT, United States Navy. See NAVY, DEPARTMENT OF THE.

MEDICAL EDUCATION. All educational programs have four basic components—(1) students, (2) teachers, (3) curriculum content, and (4) the environment in which the educational process takes place. In the total structure of education medicine represents a special segment, and as such has its own particular needs in these basic areas.

Students.—The four basic components of an educational program are all interdependent, and the more closely each of them comes to approaching the ideal, the better qualified is the end product—in this instance, the physician. Nevertheless, there is agreement that if it were possible to define clearly the importance of each component out of context with the others, the students would be given first place. Because of this conviction considerable thought has been given to the selection of students for the study of medicine.

A general but not uniform characteristic of medical schools in the English-speaking world is their ability to exercise final authority in the admission of students. This privilege allows the faculty to utilize many factors other than previous academic achievement in the selection process. Under such circumstances, a committee of the medical faculty is given the responsibility of measuring each candidate in terms of proved scholastic achievement and also of making the more difficult assessment of intellectual potentiality. Through personal interviews, letters of recommendation from the candidate's previous teachers, and, in some instances, objective testing devices, the committee attempts to evaluate motivation, industry, aptitude, degree of emotional stability, character and personality, and evidence of good health. This system is utilized by medical schools in the United States, and although it is fully recognized that occasional errors of judgment are inevitable, the overall result is thought to be so good that it more than compensates for the errors.

Almost all prospective medical students in the United States take the medical college admissions test sponsored by the Association of American Medical Colleges. This test is designed to measure, in comparison with those of other students, the individual's ability to read, understand, and write at the professional school level; his quantitative ability; his understanding of modern society; and his knowledge of basic scientific concepts. Results of the test are available to medical school admission committees, which utilize them as one of many factors in deciding whether or not an applicant should be admitted to the study of medicine. Other objective testing methods are used to varying degrees by different schools. These often form part of a long-range experiment to help the schools design an admission procedure that will reduce errors of judgment to an absolute minimum.

United States medical schools require a minimum of three years of preparatory study, preferably in a college or university acceptable to the recognized regional accrediting agency. Nevertheless, three fourths of all students entering medical school in 1954 had completed four years of preparatory work.

In the belief that preparation for the study of medicine should provide an opportunity for a broad, balanced education with ample freedom to pursue individual interests, the Council on Medical Education and Hospitals of the American Medical Association has recommended (*Essentials of an Acceptable Medical School,* Chicago 1951) that required courses for premedical study include only physics, biology, and inorganic and organic chemistry. Since many medical schools specify additional course requirements and recommend others, prospective students should familiarize themselves with the requirements of the schools which they may wish to attend.

The existence of a selective admissions system is possible only when the number of students seeking admission is greater than the number of available positions in the first-year classes of medical schools. The excess of applicants over available positions in United States medical schools reached its peak in 1949, when only one third of the students who applied were accepted. Thereafter there was a gradual decline in the ratio, and in 1953 slightly more than half of all applicants were accepted.

By the mid-1950's the marked increase in the United States birth rate that began just before World War II was reflected in record high school enrollments, and it is expected that by 1960 medical schools will feel the impact of what has been aptly termed the tidal wave of students seeking advanced education in medicine as well as in other fields. In an effort to meet this anticipated increased number of applicants and to fulfill growing demands for medical service, several new medical schools are already in development, and many established schools are planning to expand their facilities in order to accommodate more students.

Information compiled in the 1954 *Report on Medical Education in the United States and Canada* (see *Bibliography*) by the Council on Medical Education and Hospitals indicates that since 1900 there had been an increase of 115 per cent in the number of graduates of approved medical schools, while during the same period the population of the United States approximately doubled. While the number of women graduates of medical schools gradually increased during this half century, the increase was only in proportion to the overall increase, so that the percentage of women graduating from medical school in the mid-1950's was not significantly greater than it had been 50 years before. This was true despite the fact that there remained only two medical schools in the United States that restricted admission to male students.

Not all students accepted for the study of medicine are able to complete their studies successfully. The adjustments which a young person undertaking medical studies must make are most pronounced during the first year in medical school, and it is not surprising that almost two thirds of all scholastic failures and withdrawals for personal reasons occur during this year. In 1955 approximately 5 per cent of the students enrolled in the first year were unable to continue their medical education. When the intellectual and emotional problems imposed on the new medical student are considered, however, this is a remarkably small attrition. In 1940 first-year attrition amounted to 10 per cent, and in 1935 it was 15 per cent. It does not seem unreasonable to assume that this improvement was due in large part to the more careful student selection process utilized in 1955 and to the rather widespread attention given to student counseling and guidance.

The cost of attending medical school is a matter of real concern to prospective students and their parents. Much information is available on this subject, but because of wide variations in costs from school to school and from student to student, data must be reduced to averages to have any significance. It has been found that the average student in the mid-1950's spent between $9,000 and $9,500 during four years of undergraduate medical study. A student who was unmarried and lived with his parents while attending a school with low tuition would spend significantly less than this amount, while one who attended a school away from home where tuition charges were high might spend considerably more.

Many scholarship and loan funds are available to needy and qualified medical students. Most such funds are administered by medical schools or their parent universities, but in some states financial assistance is available to residents of the respective states with the provision that the recipient agree to practice for a specified period in a rural area.

Teachers.—Institutions of higher education have two major functions: the communication of available knowledge (teaching) and the extension of the outer limits of knowledge (research). Teachers, as the second of the four basic components of an educational program, must be concerned with both of these functions. In medicine this concern is manifested by degrees of activity varying with the abilities and interests of the individual teacher and the time and facilities at his disposal in the institution in which he holds his appointment.

Although teaching activities in medicine tend increasingly to overlap, they have been divided traditionally into the two large areas of the basic medical sciences and the clinical sciences. The basic sciences are generally considered as those subjects—anatomy, biochemistry, physiology, pharmacology, microbiology, pathology (the last named falls in an intermediate pattern)—which relate concepts of biology, chemistry, mathematics, and physics to human biology. Clinical subjects—medicine, surgery, pediatrics, psychiatry, obstetrics—are those that focus the basic sciences into specific patterns of health and disease, including the measures that can be taken to maintain the former and to alleviate or cure the latter.

Teachers in the basic medical sciences in modern United States medical schools rarely engage in any professional activity outside of the responsibilities associated with their academic positions. Although they have advanced degrees (almost invariably at the doctoral level), in all but the subjects of pathology and pharmacology they are generally not medical school graduates. The full-time academic status and educational background of faculty members in the basic sciences are conducive to extensive research activity, and it would be unusual for a medical school to appoint an individual to such a position without some assurance of research accomplishment or potential.

One of the characteristics of medical schools in the United States is the low ratio of students to faculty: in the basic medical sciences there is one faculty member for every five students. This ratio lends itself to intensive, small-group, informal teaching in which the student-teacher relationship can be intimate and the student's role active.

The staffing pattern for clinical departments is much less uniform than that for the basic sciences. Most United States medical schools formerly depended for instruction in the clinical subjects almost entirely on competent practitioners with an interest in and talent for teaching. The tremendous expansion of the body of knowledge in medicine and the development of instruments and facilities for the utilization of that knowledge, however, induced medical schools to add physicians trained in the clinical areas and interested in teaching and research to their full-time staffs. Without the need for maintaining an outside private practice and its attendant physical and intellectual distractions, such clinicians are able to devote their entire energies to the supervision of teaching programs and to the development of more extensive research activities.

There remain only a few United States medical schools that continue to rely almost wholly on part-time and volunteer physicians for teaching the clinical subjects. At the other extreme, there are also only a few schools where all teaching in these subjects is now done by a full-time faculty. By far the commonest pattern is one in which there is a nucleus of full-time clinicians, particularly in the major clinical areas, who are responsible for the overall supervision of the teaching program and who can provide a needed continuity to it. The efforts of this nucleus are supplemented substantially by the devoted interest of competent practitioners, who usually receive as their only reward the satisfaction of having played a role in the passing on of knowledge to a new generation of physicians.

Curriculum Content.—The extraordinary progress that has taken place in medicine since 1900 perhaps can best be measured in its effect on life expectancy, which during this brief period of history has been extended by one third, representing an accomplishment greater than that achieved during the preceding 2,000 years. The resultant aging population has presented many social and economic problems that are not amenable to solution by principles that functioned adequately for a different type of population in 1900. Similarly, the medical needs of the population of the mid-1950's are significantly different, and physicians cannot be equipped to deal with them by means of an educational program designed for other purposes. For this reason, considerable thought and experimentation have been directed toward the design of a curriculum of medical education that would facilitate the education of physicians to meet contemporary requirements and to provide a basis for handling the changing needs of the future.

Because of the successful inroads made with regard to organic diseases, the first half of the 20th century has often been referred to as the golden age of medicine. Success in this area, combined with advancing knowledge in the disciplines concerned with human behavior and with a general awakening of social consciousness, gave medical educators an uneasy feeling that essential matters were not being properly focused for the students' attention. It was recognized that medicine had not performed satisfactorily when it cured a patient of a serious disease if he could not return to fruitful living because of problems related to his family, his work, and other sectors of the environment in which he lived. The recognition of the necessity of dealing with emotional problems and with all other aspects of the interactions between the patient with an organic disease and his total environment highlighted the concept of considering each patient as a total person. Under this concept the responsibility of the profession to the patient it serves is to render comprehensive medical care. The fundamental issues are clearly expressed in the following excerpt from the Commonwealth Fund's 1952 *Annual Report* (pp. 2-3, New York 1952):

Medical education . . . may now be in the second of three phases of adjustment. The first . . . has had scientific medicine as its objective and slogan, specialization as its dominant pattern, and the university medical center as its preferred instrument. The second, now unfolding, is a phase of transition in which the concept of comprehensive medicine is beginning to modify the definition of scientific medicine, in which there is some reaction against the extremes of specialization, and in which a few medical centers are beginning to re-examine their functions and achievements. . . . It is reasonable to hope that it will be followed by a third phase in which there will be some reconciliation between what has been called scientific medicine and what is now called comprehensive medicine . . . and some restructuring of both medical education and medical care to fit the needs of a more knowledgeable social order. . . . Scientific medicine should be medicine based upon the fullest and most exact knowledge of the patient that is available. . . . Scientific medicine has hitherto been weakest in relation to the patient's affective life and his social environment. The behavioral sciences are already helping the doctor to rely less on intuition and more on systematized knowledge as he approaches these facets of the patient. Not to make use of them so far as they are usable would seem to be unscientific.

An awareness of the desirability of placing added emphasis on teaching the behavioral sciences and the social and environmental factors in health and disease did not produce a ready means by which these objectives could be accomplished. The medical school curriculum was already so full as to cause concern, and there was general agreement that a greater number of subjects could not safely be added. The emergence of newly important areas as subjects that should be included serves to highlight the need for re-evaluation of the entire medical school curriculum.

An important step in this direction was the crystallization of the thoughts of many educators on the proper goals of undergraduate medical education. In "The Objectives of Undergraduate Medical Education" (*Journal of Medical Education*, vol. 28, p. 57, Chicago 1953), the following interdependent goals were suggested: the acquisition of fundamental professional knowledge, but not a complete, detailed knowledge of every medical and related discipline; the establishment of habits of careful judgment, with the student being given actual responsibility in real problems of health and disease; the attainment of the skills required to use this knowledge; and the development of basic intellectual attitudes and ethical principles.

Medical schools are under no compulsion to accept these objectives, but most of them have been carefully scrutinizing their curricula with essentially the same ultimate goals in view. The vital interest in teaching methods and content on the part of medical school faculties has been augmented by a series of teaching institutes sponsored by the Association of American Medical Colleges. The first two of these were held in 1951–1952 in conjunction with the American Psychiatric Association. Another such meeting, sponsored jointly by the Conference of Professors of Preventive Medicine and the Association of American Medical Colleges, was held in 1953. Two subsequent teaching institutes were held by 1955, and others were being contemplated.

That this concern with medical education is not limited to the United States is clearly indicated by the fact that the initial major project of the World Medical Association was the organization of the First World Conference on Medical Education, which was held in London in 1953. In Great Britain a similar and earlier anxiety regarding objectives and methods of attaining them led to the appointment of the Interdepartmental Committee on Medical Schools, whose published findings (see *Bibliography*) are generally known as the Goodenough report, from the name of the committee's chairman, Sir William M. Goodenough.

Each medical school has a separate and distinct nature that is determined by the characteristics of the community in which it exists, the personality traits and interests of its faculty and students, the facilities available, and many other intangible factors. This institutional personality finds expression in individual and usually differing approaches to and resolutions of problems. It was therefore neither expected nor desired that the ferment of the mid-1950's over the medical school curriculum would result in the development of any uniform design, but rather that there would be many types, each suitable to the institution concerned. There have, however, been evolving certain basic similarities.

All schools which have undertaken major curricular revisions have been cautious to retain the many components of proved value. It has been traditional of United States medical education in the 20th century that opportunities for intimate contact with patients be given to students according to their capabilities and under adequate supervision. The tendency is to enlarge these opportunities and to make them available as early as possible in the student's education. Laboratory experiments in the basic medical sciences as well as student responsibility for patients are evidences of the importance attached to the principle of active learning. This principle is being given even greater emphasis, and more care is devoted to the planning of laboratory work so that students may learn from each experiment basic concepts and not be overwhelmed with the technical details of the project.

Medical school departments are recognized as important features in the organization of a school, and a different type of structure undoubtedly would not encourage such productive work, especially in the fields of research and graduate education. Cooperative teaching efforts involving faculty from two or more departments often afford the student an opportunity to learn of the multiple parts of a biological process in a closely related and sequential manner so that the whole problem becomes clear to him. Teachers who participate in such exercises are more likely to be aware of the activities of other departments and to be enriched by the close working relationship with faculty members whose interests and areas of knowledge do not coincide with their own. When undertaken in the early years of medical study, such cooperative efforts involving faculty from the basic medical sciences and the clinical sciences present an opportunity for the student to appreciate the value of the basic sciences to his professional knowledge. When undertaken in the later years of medical study, they provide an ideal means of refreshing the student's (and the faculty's) knowledge of the basic sciences.

The high ratio of instructors to students lends itself to small-group teaching. All-class lectures are given less frequently, especially in the later years of medical study, and are replaced by small-group, informal seminars and conferences in which the student can play an active role. Nevertheless, although there is some feeling that more time has been allotted to all-class lectures than results would justify, it should not be assumed that there is any desire to discard such lectures completely.

Students now are often introduced to the behavioral sciences early in their medical school careers. Moreover, schools in increasing numbers are making environmental factors a reality to students through visits to patients in their own homes and places of work and through direct contact with the social agencies that can contribute to the patients' overall rehabilitation. There is a fairly general recognition that the acquisition of technical skills in the surgical areas is a part of graduate medical education; the undergraduate medical student is now expected to spend very little time in the operating room, and there remain only a few courses in animal surgery.

On the part of the faculty, there is developing an attitude that students should be considered as individuals participating in a graduate educational process. An inherent part of this attitude is the assumption that the student is a mature person capable of accepting a good deal of responsibility for his own professional development and education. It seems reasonable to predict that this attitude favors the student's "acquisition of enduring habits of work and thought and of enthusiasm for study so that the doctor may remain a student throughout his professional life," as Sir Henry Cohen stated in his paper *The Balanced Curriculum*, presented to the First World Conference on Medical Education.

The fundamental concept that the first two years of medical school should be devoted to the study of the basic medical sciences and the latter two years to the clinical sciences is unchanged. The important adjustment has been made in eliminating the exclusive element in this concept, so that the major but not the total emphasis in the first half of medical study is on the basic sciences and the major emphasis in the second half on the clinical sciences, with a goodly proportion of intermingling throughout all four years.

Since each medical school designs its curriculum to meet its own needs and objectives, there is considerable variation in detail from one school to another, but there is a general pattern that is applicable to most schools. The curriculum covers a four-year period, with the academic year consisting of 32 to 36 weeks. In the first year anatomy (including histology, embryology, and neuroanatomy), biochemistry, and physiology are the major subjects, to which the most time is allocated. The major subjects of the second year

are pathology, pharmacology, microbiology, physical diagnosis, and clinical laboratory diagnosis. The third year is ordinarily devoted to the inpatient clerkship, in which the student learns the application of the basic sciences and their clinical meaning through the study of hospitalized patients. Medicine and surgery are each usually given one quarter of the academic year, the other two quarters being divided among psychiatry, pediatrics, obstetrics and gynecology, and preventive medicine. The final year is commonly utilized for the study of the care of ambulant patients in the outpatient clinic and for the study of such specialties as otolaryngology, ophthalmology, orthopedics, and urology.

More detailed information on the curriculum and other major aspects of medical education can be found in the report of the Survey of Medical Education, *Medical Schools in the United States at Mid-Century*. This and the companion study on preprofessional education, *Preparation for Medical Education in the Liberal Arts College* (see *Bibliography*), are comprehensive studies that were undertaken because of the feeling, described above, of the need for re-evaluation of the total structure of medical education. The reports of these studies contain much information of great value to those interested in the education of physicians.

Environment.—The final basic component of a medical school is the environment that it provides for the educational process. The most important part of this component, the intellectual environment, defies description, for it is determined by the abilities and attitudes of the faculty and students and the parent university and community in general, but certain factual data with regard to the physical features that are of significance can be stated.

In 1955 there were 80 medical schools in complete operation in the United States, 1 in Puerto Rico, and 12 in Canada. Of these, 6 in the United States and 1 in Canada offered only the first two years of medical study, after which graduating students had to complete their studies in a four-year school, but 3 of the United States schools had completed plans and had facilities almost ready to expand into full four-year programs. An additional United States medical school was expected to graduate its first class in 1956. There were also 3 new medical schools in development, 1 of which enrolled its first students in September 1955; the 2 others were to open a year later.

The Council on Medical Education and Hospitals of the American Medical Association and the Association of American Medical Colleges serve as the accrediting agencies for United States medical schools. All schools in operation in 1955 were approved as offering opportunities for a sound education in medicine.

One or more medical schools were located in all but 11 of the states, and one of the developing schools was in a state that had not previously had a medical school. Of the 80 United States schools in complete operation, 36 were state owned, 3 were municipal institutions, and 41 were privately owned. All but 7 were integral parts of universities.

In the academic year 1953–1954, United States medical schools had over 28,000 medical students enrolled and almost 7,000 graduates. Both of these figures broke previous records, and with the completion of new schools and the expansion of existing ones it was anticipated that there would be a further increase of 10 to 15 per cent by 1960.

The schools vary in size from 2 which admit over 200 freshman each year to 5 which admit less than 50. The average entering class is somewhat greater than 90.

Enrollment in the entering class of 1953–1954 was restricted by 14 state-supported schools and 1 municipal school to residents of the state in which each school was located. In 8 other schools (all but 1 of which were state owned) out-of-state enrollments accounted for less than 10 per cent of the entering class. In 22 schools (all but 1 of which were privately owned) more than half of the entering students were out-of-state residents.

There is no United States medical school in which some instruction is not given to students other than those enrolled as undergraduate medical students. In fact, the number of other students who received part or all of their instruction from medical faculties in 1954–1955 was more than twice as great as the number of undergraduate medical students. These others were students of dentistry, pharmacy, and nursing, as well as interns, residents, and physicians taking postgraduate courses.

There is general agreement that formal education beyond that offered in the four years of medical school is necessary for all physicians before they begin any career in medicine. This view is in keeping with the concept embodied in the objectives of undergraduate medical education previously outlined, to the effect that the medical school should provide the foundation on which a career in medicine can be built. Although it is legally impossible to enter the practice of medicine without having successfully completed medical school studies, in almost half of the states of the United States there are not similar legal demands for additional training. Several medical schools formerly withheld the medical degree until the student had completed further training, but because it seemed educationally unsound to assume responsibility for training which the school could not adequately supervise, this requirement was discarded. Despite the absence of state or school requirements, however, students themselves have recognized the value of further training, as is evidenced by a study of the graduates of 1952. Not a single student in that class entered practice directly from medical school.

Most authorities are agreed that physicians should have at least two years of graduate education and training in a hospital before undertaking the practice of medicine. The first year of such hospital training is almost always in the form of an internship. Subsequent hospital training is entitled residency training, and the participants are known as residents.

Before the development of clinical clerkships graduates had had little previous opportunity for intimate contact with patients in the hospital or clinic. The internship was designed to provide the graduate's initial contact with patients, including some responsibility for their care. Since the clinical clerkship now largely fulfills the purpose for which the internship was created, the question has arisen as to the continued value of the internship. This question is complicated by the fact that most physicians now take further training as a resident in preparation for a career as a specialist or general practitioner. In addition, interns provide a hospital and its professional staff

with considerable service, so that there is a great deal of competition among hospitals in acquiring them. This competition is intensified by the presence of almost twice as many internship positions as there are graduates available to fill them.

Although there is no reason to believe that the question of the internship has been finally resolved, almost all graduates continue to accept such positions. An internship can be of great value to a young physician if it is designed as an educational experience graded toward the assumption of total responsibility for patient care. The most serious criticism of the internship system, and one which at times appears to be justified, is that the service benefits of the intern to the hospital assume precedence over the educational opportunities that are afforded him.

The Council on Medical Education and Hospitals early noted the need for establishing standards for hospitals offering internships, and in 1914 published the first of yearly lists of hospitals approved for intern training. The council also publishes *Essentials of an Approved Internship* (see *Bibliography*), which is designed to serve as a guide in setting up internship programs.

Three types of internship program are recognized—rotating, mixed, and straight. All are generally of 12 months' duration. A rotating internship is one which provides supervised practice in internal medicine, surgery, pediatrics, and obstetrics, and which includes experience in laboratory diagnosis and X-ray interpretation. It should provide not less than three consecutive months in both medicine and surgery and not less than two consecutive months in pediatrics and obstetrics. A mixed internship is one in which at least half of the total time is spent on one of the four major subjects, with additional experience in one or more of the others. A straight internship is one which provides experience in only one of the major services. Of the states that require an internship as a prerequisite to licensure examination, half specify that the internship be a rotating one.

With the growth of scientific and technical knowledge in medicine, the value of developing individuals with specialized knowledge and capabilities in specific areas of medicine became apparent. Initially such specialists came into being in the United States by taking advanced training under the supervision of recognized authorities in Europe. Later they themselves were in a position to impart their specialized knowledge to selected younger colleagues. This activity was gradually transferred to hospitals and led to the establishment of residency training programs. Eventually these physicians organized themselves according to areas of interest and established criteria for the purpose of certifying others with special training in the same field. These special groups became known as specialty boards, and such boards are now found in all specialized areas of medicine. The specialty boards are recognized by the Council on Medical Education and Hospitals, and standards acceptable to both the council and the specialty boards have been set up for residency training programs. The duration of such training after the internship has been completed varies from two to four years, depending on the specialty concerned.

There has also developed an awareness that physicians planning for careers in general practice, as well as those planning to specialize, could benefit from training beyond that available in the internship. Residency programs have therefore been established to provide this training.

Medicine by its very nature demands that those who profess to practice it must remain students for the rest of their professional lives. Physicians must not only keep abreast of significant new developments, but must also constantly review more static knowledge if they are to be in a position to render the best possible medical care to their patients. There are many ways in which physicians continue their education—by reading some of the hundreds of current medical journals and texts, by attending medical meetings, by enrolling in postgraduate courses, through consultations with colleagues, and through the utilization of such newer mediums of communication as closed-circuit television. This part of a physician's education determines to a large extent how well he continues to serve his patients. A broad survey of this entire field was completed in 1955 and published in a series of eight articles by Dr. Douglas D. Vollan in the *Journal of the American Medical Association* (see *Bibliography*).

Abraham Flexner, whose *Medical Education in the United States and Canada* (New York 1910) was a contribution of vast significance, stated in 1925: "From the earliest times, medicine has been a curious blend of superstition, empiricism and that kind of sagacious observation which is the stuff out of which ultimately science is made. Of these three strands—superstition, empiricism, and observation—medicine was constituted in the days of the priest-physicians of Egypt and Babylonia; of the same three strands it is still composed. . . ." The proportions of superstition and empiricism have been reduced substantially, and it is perhaps not unrealistic to hope that continued progress will leave them as barely detectable strands in a strong cable anchoring medicine both to science and to a sincere concern for patients as people.

Bibliography.—*Report of the Inter-Departmental Committee on Medical Schools* (London 1944); Hinsey, J. C., "Maintenance of a Continuing Supply of New Faculty Members," *Journal of the Association of American Medical Colleges*, vol. 25, pp. 379-395 (Chicago 1950); American Medical Association, Council on Medical Education and Hospitals, *Essentials of an Approved Internship* (Chicago 1952); id., *Essentials of Approved Residencies and Fellowships* (Chicago 1952); American Psychiatric Association, *Psychiatry and Medical Education* (Washington 1952); Berry, G. P., "Medical Education in Transition," *Journal of Medical Education*, vol. 28, p. 17 (Chicago 1953); Deitrick, John E., and Berson, Robert C., *Medical Schools in the United States at Mid-Century* (New York 1953); "Preventive Medicine in Medical Schools: Report of the Colorado Springs Conference, November 1952," *Journal of Medical Education*, vol. 28, p. 10 (Chicago 1953); Severinghaus, Aura E., Carman, Harry J., and Cadbury, William E., *Preparation for Medical Education in the Liberal Arts College* (New York 1953); American Medical Association, Council on Rural Health, *Medical Scholarship and Loan Funds* (Chicago 1954); Association of American Medical Colleges, *Admission Requirements, 1955* (Chicago 1954); Counts, S., and Stalnaker, J. M., "The Cost of Attending Medical School," *Journal of Medical Education*, vol. 29, p. 20 (Chicago 1954); "Directory of Approved Internships and Residencies," *Journal of the American Medical Association*, vol. 156, pp. 315-432 (Chicago 1954); *Proceedings of the First World Conference on Medical Education* (Oxford 1954); Turner, Edward L., Wiggins, Walter S., Vollan, Douglas D., and Tipner, Anne, "Report on Medical Education in the United States and Canada," *Journal of the American Medical Association*, vol. 154, p. 137 (Chicago 1954); Vollan, Douglas D., "Scope and Extent of Postgraduate Medical Education in the United States," "The Physician as a Lifelong Student," "The Objectives and Content of Postgraduate Medical Education," "Educational Methods in Postgraduate Teaching," "Time and Place Arrangements of Postgraduate Courses for Practicing Physicians," "Sponsorship and Administration of Postgraduate Medical Education," "Financing Postgraduate Medical Education," "The Future of Postgraduate Medical Education," *Journal of the American Medical Association*, vols. 157-58 (Chicago 1955).

WALTER S. WIGGINS, M.D.,
Associate Secretary, Council on Medical Education and Hospitals, American Medical Association.

MEDICAL JURISPRUDENCE (also known as FORENSIC MEDICINE or LEGAL MEDICINE) covers a wide field in which medicine comes into relation with law. It involves certification of the living and the dead, the study of violent and unnatural deaths, scientific criminal investigation, the duty of the medical examiner, procedure in courts of law, and considerations of medical ethics or proper standards of medical practice. One of its main subdivisions is the science of toxicology (q.v.).

The dead body is of paramount interest in any consideration of medical jurisprudence. Whenever a physician is called in a case in which a person is thought to be dead, he has three principal legal duties. These are (1) to be certain that the person is in fact dead; (2) to make adequate superficial examination so as to exclude medical grounds for suspicion that death was due to other than natural causes; and (3) to issue a death certificate if he is in a position to do so or, if not, to refer the case to the proper official (the medical examiner or coroner). The ordinary tests for death should be employed. Suspicion may be aroused if the body has been disposed of in some peculiar manner, or if it shows evidence of injury. In such cases a death certificate should be refused. Where strong suspicion of foul play exists, the body should not be moved until after the medical examiner arrives. A death certificate should be issued only by a qualified registered practitioner who is satisfied that the cause of death is a natural one and who is able to name it.

Many changes occur in the body after death. The most important are cadaveric spasm; the cooling of the body at the rate of about 2.5°F. for every hour for 6 hours, and an average loss of heat of 2°F. for the first 12 hours; lividity of the skin, which develops in less than an hour or two; *rigor mortis*, which may develop within 6 hours; and decomposition, which begins about 48 hours after death. Moreover, profound changes may be observed if the body has been immersed in water.

Identification of the dead is generally a police procedure and is concerned mainly with tracing missing persons. A file is maintained giving sex, age, height, weight, coloring of eyes and hair, distinguishing marks such as tattoos, and a record of fingerprints. In some cases it may be necessary to prove that the remains are human. Bloodstains on clothing, weapons, or automobiles or under the fingernails can usually be identified if of human origin.

Incised wounds are common in both suicidal and homicidal attacks. Suicidal wounds usually follow definite patterns, but in homicidal attacks cuts and stabs vary with the person inflicting the injury, and many stab wounds are so situated as to preclude self-infliction. Wounds made by firearms demand examination by experts in ballistics.

In cases of asphyxia the essential feature is a struggle to breathe against a respiratory impediment. In many cases two or three minutes elapse before a fatal termination results. Frequently, however, persons assaulted or strangled die in a few seconds from vagus nerve stimulation. Drowning may be suicidal, accidental, or homicidal. Some suspicious circumstance must be present to interpret a drowning as other than accidental.

Criminal abortion is the induced destruction and expulsion of the fetus from the mother by another person unlawfully. It is a felony, and if death results for the mother, the crime may be manslaughter. Infanticide is the slaying of a newborn infant before the birth has been reported; thereafter the crime is homicide. Rape is frequently the subject of legal prosecution, and the physician's testimony in court is most important in such cases.

The rights and obligations of physicians are fairly definite, though somewhat complex. The relationship in law between a physician and his patient is in the nature of an implied contract in which the physician is bound to treat the patient with reasonable skill, exercising due care and diligence and avoiding negligence. If he quits a case, he must give timely notice. He is not obliged to guarantee a cure. Malpractice is a term applied to the wrongful or improper practice of medicine resulting in injury to the patient. It may render a physician liable under both civil and criminal law. Certain information concerning a patient is sometimes privileged and cannot be revealed in court. A physician may be called into court to testify as an ordinary witness or as an expert witness. In the latter category he is expected to qualify by expert knowledge.

Consult Gonzales, Thomas A., and others, *Legal Medicine and Toxicology,* new ed. (New York 1940); Simpson, Cedric Keith, *Forensic Medicine,* 2d ed. (London 1952).

HAROLD WELLINGTON JONES, M.D.

MEDICAL LAKE, town, Washington, situated in Spokane County, at an altitude of 2,425 feet, on the Northern Pacific Railway, 15 miles southwest of Spokane. The town, which is built on the shores of a mile-long salt lake of the same name, was incorporated in 1889. Pop. (1960) 4,765.

MEDICAL LIBRARY ASSOCIATION.
See LIBRARIES—*11. Directory of Library Associations.*

MEDICAL MICROBIOLOGY. See
PLANTS AND PLANT SCIENCE—*13. Medical Microbiology.*

MEDICAL MISSION SISTERS. See
ORDERS, RELIGIOUS—*Roman Catholic Orders* (Orders of Women).

MEDICAL MYCOLOGY. See PLANTS
AND PLANT SCIENCE—*12. Medical Mycology.*

MEDICI, mâ'dĕ-chē (Fr. MÉDICIS), an Italian family prominent in the political and cultural history of Florence and Tuscany. The name first appears in Florentine records in the late 12th century. As wool merchants and later as bankers, the Medici gradually grew in wealth and power in the city. In 1378, at the time of the revolt of the *ciompi* (wool carders), Salvestro de' Medici (1331–1388) was serving as gonfalonier of justice. Except for the years 1494–1512 and 1527–1530, the family ruled Florence from 1434 until 1737, first while preserving nominal republican forms of government, then from 1531 as dukes of Florence, and finally, from 1569, as grand dukes

of Tuscany. The city and its environs were greatly embellished by the Medici; they built palaces and villas, churches and chapels, and their magnificent collections of paintings and sculpture formed the basis of the vast modern Uffizi and Pitti collections. The principal members of the family were the following:

GIOVANNI DE' MEDICI (also known as (GIOVANNI DI BICI DE' MEDICI), merchant and banker: b. 1360; d. Feb. 20, 1429. Through extensive trading and banking operations in Italy and other countries, he became very wealthy. Nevertheless, he continued the family tradition of supporting the lesser guilds against the ruling oligarchy. From 1421 until his death he was *de facto* ruler of Florence. Giovanni was the real founder of the Medici fortunes. He had two sons, Cosimo and Lorenzo, who were the respective progenitors of the elder and younger branches of the family.

ELDER BRANCH

COSIMO or COSMO DE' MEDICI (known as COSIMO THE ELDER; called posthumously PATER PATRIAE, Father of His Country): b. Florence, Sept. 27, 1389; d. Careggi, Aug. 1, 1464. The elder son of Giovanni de' Medici, he inherited a large fortune from his father, which he doubled through astute banking operations. The leading citizen of Florence, he was opposed by the Albizzi, who succeeded in having him banished from the city in 1433. In the following year, however, a new signory recalled him, and from then on he ruled the republic. He did not hold office himself, but controlled all political appointments. Cosimo used his wealth to encourage literature and the fine arts. He built villas and churches, founded the Medici Library and the Platonic Academy, and aided Greek scholars who had fled from Constantinople after its capture in 1453. Filippo Brunelleschi, Donatello, Lorenzo Ghiberti, and Fra Angelico were among the many artists who enjoyed his patronage.

PIERO DE' MEDICI (known as PIERO THE GOUTY; Ital. PIERO IL GOTTOSO): b. 1416; d. Dec. 2, 1469. The eldest son of Cosimo the Elder, he succeeded his father as *de facto* ruler of Florence in 1464. He was badly crippled by what is now recognized as arthritis, but was able to increase the family's wealth and to put down, in 1466, a conspiracy of the Pitti family. He married Lucrezia Tornabuoni, by whom he had two sons. His younger son, GIULIANO DE' MEDICI (1453–1478), ruled Florence together with his brother, Lorenzo, until his assassination by the Pazzi family. Giuliano's natural son, GIULIO DE' MEDICI (1478–1534), became Pope Clement VII (q.v.).

LORENZO DE' MEDICI (known as LORENZO THE MAGNIFICENT; Ital. LORENZO IL MAGNIFICO): b. Florence, Jan. 1, 1449; d. Careggi, April 8, 1492. With his younger brother, Giuliano, he succeeded his father, Piero, as ruler of Florence in 1469. In 1478 he narrowly escaped assassination by the Pazzi, who killed his brother in Florence Cathedral. When Giuliano's murderers were put to death, Pope Sixtus IV placed the city under an interdict. War broke out with the pope's supporters, who included Ferdinand I of Naples, with whom Lorenzo arranged a peace in 1480. In the same year the Florentine system of government was altered to provide for a permanent council of 70 members under complete Medici control. For the rest of his life, by means of astute diplomacy, Lorenzo was able to maintain peace in his domains. His rule was tyrannical and often capricious, but the city enjoyed great prosperity as well as enhanced prestige as a cultural center.

Lorenzo is considered the prototype of the Renaissance prince. He rivaled his grandfather in his patronage of arts and letters and was himself a poet, known for his lyrics, sonnets, and odes. Among the best known of his works are the lyric *Trionfo de Bacco e Arianna,* the *Selve d'amore,* the parodies *Il simposio o i beoni* and *Nencia da Barberino,* the short stories *Giacoppa* and *La Ginevra,* and the *Canzoni a ballo.* Scholars and writers, such as Politian and Luigi Pulci, flocked to his court, and great artists, among them Sandro Botticelli, Fra Filippo Lippi, Ghirlandajo, Andrea del Verrocchio, Antonio Pollaiuolo, Alessio Baldovinetti, the sculptors Benedetto da Maiano and Mino da Fiesole, and the young Michelangelo, worked in Florence. Some of their masterpieces went to enrich the Medici collections, and Lorenzo also added to the Medici Library.

Lorenzo was married to Clarice Orsini, by whom he had three sons. The second of them, GIOVANNI

Lorenzo de' Medici.

DE' MEDICI (1475–1521), became one of the most celebrated of the Renaissance popes, Leo X (q.v.).

GIULIANO DE' MEDICI, DUKE OF NEMOURS: b. 1479; d. Florence, March 17, 1516. The third son of Lorenzo the Magnificent, he went into exile with other members of his family in 1494 and did not return to Florence until 1512. Following his marriage with Philiberta of Savoy, niece of Francis I of France, he was invested by the king with the title of duke of Nemours. He was a patron of arts and letters, and his tomb in the Church of San Lorenzo, Florence, is a masterpiece of Michelangelo.

IPPOLITO DE' MEDICI: b. Urbino, 1511; d. Itri, Aug. 10, 1535. A natural son of the duke of Nemours, he was made joint ruler of Florence with his cousin Alessandro in 1523, under the regency of Silvio Cardinal Passerini. Expelled with Alessandro in 1527, he became a cardinal two years later. Ippolito was entrusted with a number of missions by his cousin Clement VII. He was a munificent patron of letters and en-

joyed the confidence of the Florentines, who sent him in 1535 to Emperor Charles V with their grievances about the tyranny and cruelty of Alessandro. He died on the way, however, probably a victim of poisoning.

PIERO DE' MEDICI: b. Feb. 15, 1471; d. Garigliano River, December 1503. The eldest son of Lorenzo the Magnificent, he was brought up at his father's court, where he was tutored by Politian. He lacked Lorenzo's capacity, however, and in 1494, two years after he succeeded his father, he surrendered four forts to the French invaders and was then driven from Florence by Girolamo Savonarola and his followers. Subsequently he entered the service of France, and he was drowned in the Garigliano River while escaping after the French defeat there on Dec. 28, 1503.

LORENZO DE' MEDICI, DUKE OF URBINO: b. Florence, Sept. 12, 1492; d. there, May 4, 1519. The son of Piero de' Medici, he became ruler of Florence in 1513 following the elevation of his uncle Giovanni to the papacy as Leo X. Three years later, Leo created him duke of Urbino. A weak and dissolute man, he died a year after his marriage (1518) to Madeleine de La Tour d'Auvergne. His tomb in the Church of San Lorenzo, Florence, designed by Michelangelo, is a companion piece to that of his uncle, the duke of Nemours. Lorenzo left an infant daughter, CATHERINE DE' MEDICI (CATHERINE DE MÉDICIS, 1519–1589, q.v.), who became queen of France; and a natural son, Alessandro.

ALESSANDRO DE' MEDICI, 1ST DUKE OF FLORENCE: b. Florence, 1519; d. there, Jan. 5, 1537. The natural son of the duke of Urbino, he was made joint ruler of Florence with his cousin Ippolito in 1523, under the regency of Silvio Cardinal Passerini. Both boys were expelled from the city in 1527. Three years later, however, Florence was captured by Emperor Charles V, who made Alessandro hereditary duke of Florence in 1531. In 1536 the duke married Charles' natural daughter, Margaret of Parma. Meanwhile, his debauchery and tyrannical rule had made him detested by the people of the city. In 1537 he was assassinated by his distant cousin Lorenzino de' Medici. Since he was the last male in direct descent of the elder branch of the family, succession to the dukedom passed to the younger branch, in the person of Cosimo I.

YOUNGER BRANCH

The younger branch of the family was descended from Giovanni de' Medici's younger son, LORENZO DE' MEDICI (known as LORENZO THE ELDER, 1395–1440), who devoted himself to banking. His son, PIER FRANCESCO DE' MEDICI (1430–1476), had two sons: LORENZO DE' MEDICI (known as LORENZO THE YOUNGER, 1463–1503), whose son, PIER FRANCESCO DE' MEDICI (1486–1525), was the father of Lorenzino; and GIOVANNI DE' MEDICI (1467–1498), who married Caterina Sforza, by whom he had a son, Giovanni delle Bande Nere.

LORENZO DE' MEDICI (known as LORENZINO): b. Florence, March 23, 1514; d. Venice, Feb. 26, 1548. The grandson of Lorenzo the Younger, he was the intimate companion of his distant cousin Alessandro de' Medici, 1st duke of Florence, but subsequently turned against him and, supposedly actuated by opposition to the duke's tyrannical rule and by the hope of restoring the Florentine republic, murdered him in 1537. He fled to Bologna and eventually to Venice, where, 10 years later, he was assassinated by agents of Cosimo I. Lorenzo is the hero of Alfred de Musset's play *Lorenzaccio*.

COSIMO I DE' MEDICI (known as COSIMO THE GREAT), grand duke of Tuscany: b. June 12, 1519; d. Castello, April 21, 1574. The son of Giovanni delle Bande Nere, he succeeded his distant cousin Alessandro de' Medici as duke of Florence in 1537. In the same year he crushed a revolt led by families exiled from the city during Alessandro's reign, and he executed most of his opponents. He increased the territory of the duchy to nearly twice its former size by such steps as the conquest of Siena (1555). In 1564 he associated his son Francesco with him as ruler of Florence. Five years later he received the title of grand duke of Tuscany from Pope Pius V (the title was confirmed by imperial patent to Francesco in 1575). Although Cosimo was tyrannical and cruel, he was an able ruler and patron of the arts.

FRANCESCO I, grand duke of Tuscany: b. Florence, March 25, 1541; d. Poggio a Caiano, Oct. 19, 1587. The eldest son of Cosimo I, he shared the administration of Florence with his father from 1564. He did not inherit Cosimo's capacity, however, and he was dominated by King Philip II of Spain and Emperor Maximilian II, his Habsburg relatives by marriage (his first wife was Joanna, sister of Maximilian). In 1574 he succeeded his father as grand duke, and in the following year his title was confirmed by imperial grant of his brother-in-law. Joanna died in 1578, and in the following year Francesco married his mistress, Bianca Capello (q.v.), who was proclaimed grand duchess. Soon thereafter the two died suddenly at their villa near Florence, possibly of poison given at the order of Francesco's brother Ferdinand I or intended by Bianca for Ferdinand himself. By his first wife, Francesco had a daughter, MARIA DE' MEDICI (MARIE DE MÉDICIS, 1573–1642, q.v.), who became queen of France. He was succeeded as grand duke by his brother FERDINAND I (q.v.).

COSIMO II DE' MEDICI, grand duke of Tuscany: b. May 12, 1590; d. Feb. 28, 1621. The elder son of Grand Duke Ferdinand I, he succeeded his father in 1609. In the preceding year he had married Maria Magdalena of Austria, sister of Emperor Ferdinand II, by whom he had seven children. Cosimo discontinued the Medici banking business. He was a patron of Galileo, whom he protected and honored with appointments as philosopher and mathematician extraordinary. He was succeeded by his eldest son, FERDINAND II (q.v.).

COSIMO III DE' MEDICI, grand duke of Tuscany: b. Aug. 14, 1642; d. Oct. 31, 1723. The elder son of Grand Duke Ferdinand II, he succeeded his father in 1670. The power of Tuscany had declined steadily under Ferdinand's rule, and the process was accelerated under Cosimo, who was weak and extravagant. He lived to be over 80, and during his last years, as it became apparent that his son and heir, Giovan Gastone, would be childless, the future of the grand duchy had already become an international question. Cosimo was married to his cousin, Marguerite Louise d'Orléans (d. 1721), daughter of Gaston, duc d'Orléans, and granddaughter of Maria de' Medici.

GIOVAN or GIAN GASTONE DE' MEDICI, grand duke of Tuscany: b. May 24, 1671; d. July 9, 1737. The younger son of Grand Duke Cosimo III, he succeeded his father in 1723. Weak and self-indulgent, he hastened the decline of Tuscany. Since

he had no children, the question of succession to the grand duchy occupied the powers even before his father's death. At first Don Carlos of Bourbon, the future King Charles III of Spain, was chosen, but in 1735, following the War of the Polish Succession, it was decided that the house of Lorraine (later Habsburg-Lorraine) should inherit Tuscany. Accordingly, Francis, duke of Lorraine (the future Emperor Francis I) became grand duke of Tuscany, and his successors continued to rule until 1859.

Pope Leo XI (Alessandro Ottaviano de' Medici, 1535–1605) was a member of a distant branch of the historic Florentine family. Pope Pius IV (Giovanni Angelo Medici, 1499–1565) belonged to a Milanese family of the same name.

See also FLORENCE—*History* (The Medici); ITALY—*History*.

Bibliography.—Young, George F., *The Medici* (New York 1933); Collison-Morley, Lacy, *The Early Medici* (New York 1936); Gutkind, Kurt Sigmar, *Cosimo de' Medici: Pater Patriae, 1389–1464* (London 1938); De Roover, Raymond Adrien, *The Medici Bank, Its Organization, Management, Operations, and Decline* (New York 1948); Schevill, Ferdinand, *The Medici* (New York 1949); Acton, Harold M. M., *The Last Medici* (New York 1958).

MEDICINE, History of. The history of medicine studies man's health and diseases throughout history and all human activities related to the goals of medicine. These goals are: to promote health, to prevent disease, to restore health, and to rehabilitate the patient.

The history of medicine, which is but one of the many facets of the story of civilization, covers the history of diseases, therapy, and prophylaxis; of medicine as an art, *technē*, or craft; of medical ideas; and of the social and economic conditions of mankind in relation to health through the centuries. Sources of study are any documents, works of art, instruments, and monuments containing a record of human activity bearing upon medicine. Of vital importance also is medical geography, which studies the course of medicine in space, just as history studies it in time; thus geography may be regarded as the anatomy of history, just as anatomy is the geography of medicine.

The history of medicine is discussed in this article under the following main headings:

1. Paleopathology, Primitive and Archaic Medicine	6. Medicine in the Renaissance (1453–1610)
2. Medicine in the Greek World (786–285 B.C.)	7. Medicine During the Baroque Period (1610–1700)
3. Medicine under the Roman Empire (285 B.C.–476 A.D.)	8. Medicine in the Age of Enlightenment (1700–1800)
4. Hindu, Chinese, Semitic, and Amerindian Medicine	9. Medicine in the 19th Century
5. Medicine in the Middle Ages (565–1453)	10. Medicine in the 20th Century

1. PALEOPATHOLOGY, PRIMITIVE AND ARCHAIC MEDICINE

Disease is a dynamic process that develops in time. Hence the first point to be considered is the antiquity of disease. Disease dates back before man: it was coincident with the first form of life on this planet. Microscopic and X-ray studies of prehistoric human fossils have revealed that osteitis, rachitism, and acromegaly already existed 25,000 years before the Christian era. Pleuritic and arteriosclerotic lesions have been found in the remains of Egyptian mummies. Disease in prehistoric man and animals took the same basic forms—metabolic and growth alterations, infections and tumors—as it does today.

Primitive Medicine.—Primitive medicine studies the diseases and healing methods of Neolithic man, who started civilization when he cut and polished stone. This medicine lasted from about 12,000 to 4,000 B.C., when the archaic cultures of Sumer, Egypt, India, and, later, China made their appearance. Sources of study are carved stones, folklore, myths and legends, psychoanalytic studies of the "magic thought" of primitive man, and primitive tribes still in existence today.

Minor diseases were treated with herbs, massage, poultices, and dieting. Major diseases and disabilities—smallpox, compound fractures, psychoses—were resolved by killing the patient, to prevent his becoming a burden, or else the aid of a healer was enlisted.

Besides the empirical healer, who employed rational physiotherapeutic and psychotherapeutic methods, there was also the medicine man or witch doctor, who was either noninspirational or inspirational. The latter, or shaman, usually a psychopath or schizophrenic, practiced exorcism and made prophecies, combining the functions of scientist, magician, priest, statesman, and bard.

The shaman's technique was based on the application of the principles of magic supported by the suggestive power of his spells. Though based solely on his emotional experiences, the shaman's magic was the forerunner of science, since it was man's first logical attempt to understand nature and to solve medical problems. Preventive magic regarded disease as a plus (entry of a foreign object or spirit into the body), or a minus (subtraction of the soul).

The medicine man had three main magic techniques: (1) *homeopathic,* based on the principle of similitude, such as the mutilation of an image of the enemy; (2) *contagious,* based on destruction of some part of the enemy's body, which, combined with homeopathic magic, made up *sympathetic* magic; and (3) *direct,* which called for special rituals. To prevent disease, defensive magic used *fetishes,* objects laden with magic powers; *amulets,* protective objects against black magic; and *talismans* or good-luck objects.

The shaman based his diagnoses on the concept that there was one disease only, which he identified with its cause, diagnosis and cure being one and the same; and his "case history" consisted of an inquiry into the existence of relevant magic fetishes, evil dreams, or broken taboos. Prognosis depended upon auguries and oracles. Treatment was based on the concept that disease was caused by the entry of a foreign body or spirit into the patient's body or by soul straying, and on the determination of its direct cause (magic, witchcraft, death dreams, or moral delinquency). Object intrusion was treated by magic, suction and object-extraction rituals, massage, steam baths, and vegetable drugs; spirit intrusion, by spells, exorcism, and bleeding.

Magic medicine, which lasted several thousand years and was based on the principle of doing no injury to the patient, took into account the psychic factor in each disease and endeavored to understand it, the therapy being expulsive in nature (bleeding, purging, diuresis, and catharsis).

Archaic Medicine.—The first great civilizations made their appearance in the sunny lands of Mesopotamia and Egypt some 4,000 years before Christ.

Mesopotamia.—Bounded by the two Biblical rivers, the Tigris and the Euphrates, Mesopotamia possessed a culture characteristic of a desert city situated on the route of the caravans. Cuneiform (pictographic) writing, consisting of marks made with a sharp reed on soft clay tablets, was invented in Mesopotamia. This writing was the most important event in the history of mankind until the invention of block printing.

Some 30,000 clay tablets, discovered in Mesopotamia and originating from the library of King Ashurbanipal (668–631 B.C.), reveal that dysentery and typhoid were rife there and that disease was regarded as a punishment inflicted by the gods against sinners. Magic was used by priest-physicians, who imparted their medical art secretly within the temple precincts and were aided by barbers in the lesser art of surgery. The basic method of diagnosis was hepatoscopy, or inspection of the liver of sacrificed animals. Astrology was practiced in an attempt to find some logic in the mechanics of the heavens. Materia medica included medicinal plants and mineral remedies, aided by physiotherapy and psychotherapy. One of the most important relics from this civilization is a block of black diorite on which is inscribed the Code of Hammurabi (c. 1690 B.C.), a part of which represents the first historical attempt to legislate the professional practice of medicine.

Egypt.—The gift of the Nile, Egypt, consisted of two riverside strips of fertile land bounded by rock, water, and sand. Here man created a civilization that used metals, wrote in hieroglyphics, and erected the pyramids. The seasonal overflow of the Nile compelled the Egyptians to create a feudal slave economy and a bureaucratic state, to help them maintain their periodically destroyed unity.

Egyptian medicine was magico-religious and empirico-rational, priests and sorcerers coexisting in harmony with physicians. Supplications and spells were used. Disease was considered to be possession by devils, and no progress took place in anatomy: despite the millions of corpses which were embalmed during the 31 dynasties that ruled over Egypt, nothing was learned about the human body.

Supplementary to the information gleaned from the examination of mummies, light has been shed on Egyptian medicine by the *Edwin Smith Surgical Papyrus* (17th century B.C., believed to be a copy of a much older work), a surgical treatise containing spells and incantations and details of various lesions and their physical and surgical treatment; by the *Ebers Papyrus,* later in date, which contains monographs on eye infections (common in a country scourged by sandstorms), and descriptions of skin, blood, and gynecological complaints; and by the Hearst and Berlin papyri.

Specialization was extreme, and besides court physicians there were priest-physicians and sorcerers. Being the least expensive, magico-religious medicine was the most popular, while rational medicine with its drugs and diets was reserved for the wealthy. Magical diagnosis was etiological—determination that the patient was possessed by the devil; rational diagnosis rested upon examination of symptoms. Anatomy was learned in kitchen and temple, where animals were slaughtered and sacrificed. Therapy depended on the use of animal, vegetable, and mineral materia medica. The geographical image of their land-irrigating canals inspired the Egyptian pathophysiology of "droughts" and "floods" traversing the blood "channels" in the human body. In Egypt appeared the first human medical figure known in history by his own name—Imhotep (fl. about 2980–2950 B.C.), prime minister, astrologer, architect of the Sakana pyramid, and physician, afterward deified and equated with Asclepius (Lat. Aesculapius) by the Greeks.

2. MEDICINE IN THE GREEK WORLD (786 B.C.– 285 B.C.)

To be a Greek in ancient Greece was to share a certain view of the universe peculiar to the Hellenic community. In a few hundred years Greece developed an "open sea" civilization, which retained its integrity through the centuries thanks to mythology and two epic poems, the *Iliad* and the *Odyssey,* and to the decennial Olympian games. Greece was a serfdom ruled by an aristocracy.

Greek medicine, as depicted in the *Iliad* and *Odyssey,* abounds with descriptions of wounds and traumas; the mortality rate after crude surgical treatment and the employment of medicinal herbs was as high as 78 per cent.

Influence of 6th Century B.C. Philosophers.—Hellenic medicine is an offshoot of the Greek philosophy of nature. The Greek philosophers of the 6th century B.C. were the first who sought to comprehend the universe rationally in terms of its fundamental elements: water (Thales of Miletus, 640?–546 B.C.), air (Anaximenes of Miletus, fl. 546 B.C.), and fire (Heraclitus of Ephesus, 536?–?475 B.C.). Democedes of Croton (fl. 525 B.C.), a traveling physician, and Empedocles of Agrigentum (493–443 B.C.) added the earth, and coordinated the concept of the four elements of the universe with that of the four humors of the human body, impairment of which was the source of all diseases. Empedocles accepted the blood and the heart as seats of the vital spark, or *pneuma,* and, with his notion of the antagonistic powers of love and hatred, was a precursor of Sigmund Freud. Pythagoras of Samos (fl. 530 B.C.) made the science of numbers the foundation of his philosophic system. His pupil, Alcmaeon of Croton (c. 500 B.C.), performed dissections on animals. Other Greek philosophers were Theophrastus, Parmenides of Elea, Diogenes of Apollonia, and Democritus of Abdera.

Cult of Asclepius.—Simultaneously with her naturalistic empirico-rational medicine, Greece cultivated a type of religious psychotherapy— the cult of Asclepius, which cropped up first in Thessaly and then spread southward to Asia Minor. The first gods of healing were Apollo, Artemis, and Athene, after which the healing art became apotheosized in the figure of a Thessalian prince called Asclepius (Lat. Aesculapius). Considered in mythology to be the son of Apollo, he was reputedly instructed in medicine by Chiron the Centaur; his staff with a coiled serpent was the origin of the caduceus, which became the symbol of medicine. The cult of Asclepius, based on psychotherapeutic miracles, was practiced by Asclepiads or priests in Epidaurus, Cos, Pergamum, and Tricea (modern Trikkala). The first altars to Asclepius stood in the open air and later developed into delightful temples in the midst of beautiful gardens. Sick pilgrims flocked in legions to the temples and, after purification through fasting and sacrifice at the feet of the gold and marble statues of the gods, dozed off into the incubatory temple trance, during which the priests administered drugs to them and made curative suggestions.

Hippocrates.—Greek empirico-rational medicine was represented by the school of Cnidus, concerned chiefly with diagnosis, and by that of Cos, which dealt mostly in *pronoia,* the act of telling the patient beforehand the course of his illness.

It was in the island of Cos that Hippocrates was born (c. 460?–?377 B.C.), some 1,200 years after Imhotep and 700 years before Galen. A new type of naturalist-physician, learned and kindly, Hippocrates regarded even "sacred" diseases, like epilepsy, as natural human afflictions. After much wandering as an itinerant Asclepiad through the sunny landscapes of the Hellenic world, Hippocrates died at Larissa. His fame lies in the Hippocratic Corpus or Collections, some 70 books first collated during the 3d century B.C. by Alexandrine scholars, the authorship of which cannot be conclusively established. Their content is naturalistic, concerned mainly with prognosis and with the patient rather than with the disease. Hippocrates asserted that there was not just one single disease but many, and he stressed the *vis medicatrix naturae,* the healing power of nature or *physis.*

Hippocrates separated medicine from philosophy (they were to be reunited later by Galen) and studied man as a whole. He adopted the theory of the four humors (blood, yellow bile, black bile, and phlegm), based perhaps on observation of the four layers formed by clotting blood; and of their properties (warm-wet, warm-dry, cold-dry, and cold-wet), any quantitative impairment of which could cause disease. The natural power of the *physis* during "crisis" expelled morbific matter from the human body by a process of "coction." Hippocratic therapy, sometimes expectant, sometimes stimulative of "coction," used few drugs, relying mostly on diet, ptisans, fresh air, massage, and hydrotherapy, and included the concept of *ponos* or suffering, identical with our modern concept of stress.

An itinerant craftsman, the Hippocratic physician was mainly concerned with making a fast accurate diagnosis and treating the disease by diet, herbs, and drugs, and occasionally by surgery. The Oath of Hippocrates introduced humanity and service into medicine, thereby leaving us a monument of ethics and morality.

Greek physicians (*periodeutas* or itinerant physicians, *iatros* or court physicians, *tekhnites* or artificers) learned their art through apprenticeship to experienced physicians who traveled from place to place and held their consultations in public squares. Disease to them was a natural process and a physical blemish. The patient was no longer considered a sinner; rather the sinner was considered a sick person who was physically incapacitated. Since disease was viewed as a disharmony in the *physis,* the physician became a *physiologos* capable of interpreting nature. He was particularly concerned with individual preventive medicine and hygiene, prescribing diet, gymnastics and physicomental hygiene.

Other Greek Schools.—Many streams of medical philosophy originated in the golden age of Greece, among them: the *Dogmatic* school (Thessalus of Cos, Draco, Diocles of Carystus), based on speculative thought; the *Empiric* Alexandrian school (Philinos of Cos, Archagathus of Peloponnesus, Herakleides of Tarentum), concerned with the study of diseases as groups of symptoms; the *Methodist* school (Themison of Laodicea); the *Encyclopedist* school (Aulus Cornelius Celsus); the *Pneumatic* school (Aretaeus of Cappadocia); the *Eclectic* school (Agathinus of Sparta); and the *Peripatetic* school (Plato, Zenon, Aristotle, Theophrastus).

To the last school belonged Socrates (470?–399 B.C.) and the Sophists, skilled in the use of the spoken word. Their philosophical heritage was gleaned by Plato (428/427–348/347 B.C.), a non-naturalist metaphysician, founder of the Academy. His concept of the unity of soul and body heralded psychosomatic medicine. He was also the first to use the word anesthesia. In his *Symposium,* a physician named Eryximachus describes medicine as "the art of learning the love affairs of the organs of the body."

To this school belonged also Zeno (335–263 B.C.), who lectured in his porch or *stoa* (hence the name Stoics), and Epicurus (342?–270 B.C.), who taught in his grove. Aristotle (384–322 B.C.), born when Plato was 43, later became tutor to Alexander the Great. His mind was a vast intellectual empire. He accepted the heart as the seat of the emotions and gave a teleological explanation of anatomy, asserting that knowledge comes through the senses and that while the true philosopher should begin his studies with medicine, the physician should end his with philosophy. His students included Theophrastus, Diocles of Carystus, Praxagoras of Cos, and Herophilus, who forged the link between Greek and Roman medicine.

Alexandrian School.—Hellenic learning jumped from Athens to Alexandria, the citadel built by Alexander the Great, when Ptolemy I Soter, the first of the dynasty of Greek rulers in Egypt, founded the Museum, or home for the Muses, with one of the most famous libraries in history, which attracted such men as Archimedes, Euclid, Strabo, and Eratosthenes. It was here that the first great clinical school, indeed the first university, in the world was founded, complete with laboratories and a publishing house, housing half a million works in papyrus scrolls. Alexandria's contribution to medicine was anatomical dissection, which opened the way to the concept that disease has its seat in the organs and not in the humors. In Alexandria were Herophilus of Chalcedon (335–280 B.C.), father of anatomy, and Erasistratus (c. 310–c. 250 B.C.), a surgeon who experimented in metabolism and discovered the tricuspid valve. Some of the followers of these two formed the Empiric school. Upon the death of Cleopatra, when Egypt became another province of Rome, the influence of the Alexandrian school began to decline.

Contributions of Greek Medicine.—The four great contributions of classical Greece to medical progress were: (1) the objective observation of disease as a natural occurrence, coupled with the maintenance of case records and the consideration of the *patient* rather than his disease as the chief object of study; (2) an ethical code of professional medical practice; (3) the concept of spontaneous healing by nature; and (4) the acceptance of the wise, modest, and humanitarian physician as a basic pillar of society.

3. MEDICINE UNDER THE ROMAN EMPIRE (285 B.C.–476 A.D.)

The Romans were magnificent soldiers and administrators, but they borrowed their medicine from the Greeks. Medicine was practiced first by priests of the Aesculapian cult, then by slaves, later by freed slaves, and finally by Greek physicians. Gaius Julius Caesar's edict of 46 B.C. improved the physician's social status by granting Roman citizenship to all freeborn Greek physicians practicing in Rome.

The first Greek physician known to have practiced in Rome was the freed slave and surgeon Archagathus (c. 220 B.C.), though the level of medicine was raised by Asclepiades of Bithynia (fl. mid-1st century B.C.), architect of a solidist system based on the notion of atoms interspersed with pores.

Counter to the classical or Hippocratic schools, other more "modern" schools flourished, such as the Methodist, the Pneumatic, and the Eclectic. Soranus of Ephesus (fl. early 2d century A.D.) wrote a treatise on midwifery and gynecology, and the sophisticated Celsus (fl. early 1st century A.D.), the Cicero of Roman medicine, wrote *De re medica,* a compilation of the medical learning of his time.

Disease was considered a physical deficiency and treated by drugs, physiotherapy, hydrotherapy, and surgery. Vivisection was performed on criminals, and comparative anatomy on apes. The leading figure in Roman medicine was Galen (129/130–199/200 A.D.), who left us an encyclopedia of medical lore never since equaled in size. An Eclectic, Galen revived the Hippocratic doctrines of the humors, the *pneuma,* and the *physis,* and studied anatomy in lesser animals. He proved that the arteries carried blood and asserted that the body was made of parts, not humors, and that it possessed natural spirits (born in the liver), vital spirits (born in the heart), and animal spirits (born in the brain). His concept of disease was anatomic, and thus essentially modern. For treatment he prescribed simples (galenicals), and promoted personal hygiene, sanitary engineering, and surgery.

The Romans aided the progress of collective hygiene and public health with their excellent water systems, baths, gymnasiums, municipal inspection of food, and sanitary engineering. The medical profession was granted legal status, and adequate legislation was passed on medical teaching, social service, and military and public health, all of which raised the social status of the physician.

4. HINDU, CHINESE, SEMITIC, AND AMERINDIAN MEDICINE

India.—Meanwhile, India was becoming a great nation in the East. In the 3d century B.C., Emperor Asoka (r. about 273–232/237 B.C.) created hospitals and academies. Medicine went through a Vedic period, during which epidemics were studied and surgery progressed, and a Brahmanic period, which saw the introduction of a physician's oath and the advent of the Hindu medical classics written by Charaka, Susruta, and Vaghbhatha (2d century A.D.), all based on the earlier Yajur-Veda (c. 700 B.C.), the crowning mystic document of archaic Hindu medicine. In the later writings, great stress was placed upon the organized teaching of medicine, drug compounding, obstetrics, and surgery, particularly rhinoplasty, since facial mutilation was a common form of punishment.

China.—China's culture, cradled in a nation always in peril of invasion, was influenced by Buddhist philosophies imported from India and by Confucianism in the north and Lao-Tzu's Taoism in the south. This civilization was far more advanced technologically than any Western civilization up to the Middle Ages, having developed the mariner's compass, gunpowder, silk, porcelain, and block printing centuries before they became known in Europe.

Chinese medicine, founded on Confucian principles, stepped from its initial period of magic to a cosmological period, and then to a period of botanical therapy, building up, all this while, a fantastic system of pathology, an ivory tower supported on theories devoid of reality. Diagnosis was based on examination of the tongue and the pulse, which was studied as though it were a musical instrument; 200 variations at 11 different points were described. Many drugs, such as ephedrine and camphor, were discovered in China. Acupuncture was practiced to reach the "channels" through which the blood and humors flowed, a procedure inspired by the irrigation canals used in the fields. Moxibustion, or subcutaneous application of combustible paper cones that were then ignited, and variolation were also practiced.

Semitic Medicine.—The Hebrew people of the land of Judah contributed to the creation of two great religions—Judaism and Christianity—as a means of purifying the soul, and to the establishment of public health as a means of fortifying the body. Just as the Homeric epics united the Greeks, so did the Bible unite the Jews. In its pages are recorded many diseases, from leprosy to epilepsy, as well as the earliest social prophylactic hygiene legislation.

Amerindian Medicine.—The Amerindian group of archaic cultures, Mayan, Aztec, and Incan, also followed the magical and empirical lines of primitive medicine.

5. MEDICINE IN THE MIDDLE AGES (565–1453)

The Middle Ages witnessed the propagation, assimilation, and synthesis of classical medicine; the intellectual labors of men like Roger Bacon (1214?–?1292), St. Albertus Magnus (1193?–1280), St. Thomas Aquinas (1225?–1274), and Arnaud de Villeneuve (Arnold of Villanova, 1235?–?1312); and the beginnings of the three great institutions upon which modern medicine is based—hospitals, universities, and public health.

During the 5th century the western half of the Roman Empire collapsed. The eastern part, under the protection of the great basileis, rulers of the Byzantine Empire, became the axis of the Christian world until the 15th century, when the Turks invaded Constantinople and established the Ottoman Empire. While the Mongols were invading Asia, Bedouin Arabs, urged on by the preachings of Mohammed, carved themselves a vast empire stretching from Spain to Cathay.

The Middle Ages were marked by the development of feudalism, a societal pyramid, with serfs constituting the broad base and great feudal lords at the apex. During this period the Crusades, the first and greatest collective adventure, took place, and the Mongol emperor, Kublai Khan, established contact with Europe through the voyage (1271–1295) of the Venetian Marco Polo.

Byzantine Medicine.—The first tributary through which medical lore traveled in the Middle Ages was Byzantine medicine, which, unable to develop in space, did so in time through the vast compilations of past medical learning gathered together by Oribasius (325–403), Aëtios (fl.

about 500), Alexander of Tralles (fl. mid-6th century), and Paul of Aegina (625–690). Christianity, deeming the sick person a potential saint, looked upon the heretic as a sick man, upon the priest as his best physician, the church as a hospital, and God as the Supreme Healer.

Arab Medicine.—The second medieval stream through which Hellenic medical wisdom traveled from the Eastern caliphate of Baghdad to the Western caliphate of Córdoba was Arabian medicine. Birthplace of Moorish medicine was Jundi Shapur, built on the Persian desert by the Byzantine Nestorius (d. about 451) upon his banishment from Constantinople for heresy. The Eastern caliphate was distinguished for its great physicians: al-Tabari (838–923), Rhazes (c. 865–925), Haly Abbas (930–994), and, above all, Avicenna (980–1037), humanist, bard, and author of the most popular work in the history of medicine, the *Canon Medicinae,* which reconciled Galen's teachings with Aristotle's and made Avicenna the dictator of medical learning. In the Western caliphate the leading physicians were the surgeon Abul Kasim (Albucasis, 936?–?1013), Avenzoar the clinician (1091?–1162), Averroës the philosopher (1126–1198), and the Jewish humanist Maimonides (1135–1204), author of *Guide for the Perplexed* and physician to the Sultan Saladin. In Toledo, Spain, where in the 12th century Christians, Jews, and Moors coexisted in harmony in a unique example of religious tolerance, the College of Translators carried on the great task of turning classical medical lore from Syrian and Arabic into Latin.

Arab contributions to medical progress were medical chemistry, the organization of pharmacy, and hospitals provided with music, fountains, and storytellers. The *Arabian Nights* provides an enlightening survey of the medical wisdom of Persia and Arabia.

Monastic Medicine.—The third medieval medical stream was monastic medicine, which was to give birth to the universities. Situated on the great pilgrimage roads, monasteries were a combination of temple, hospital, inn, and news center. Monte Cassino, a Benedictine monastery founded in the 6th century, was the cradle of religious medical instruction in Europe. Here the monk Constantine the African (Constantinus Africanus, 1020–1087) translated the Arabic versions of classical Greek works into Latin. For some 300 years (10th to 13th centuries), the medical school of Salerno flourished as the first lay center of medical teaching, where the title of "doctor" was granted. This great *civitas Hippocratica,* Hippocratic city, where various streams of culture merged, saw the birth of the great popular treatise on hygiene, *Regimen sanitatis Salernitanum,* probably written by Arnaud de Villaneuve, Catalan humanist, physician to popes and monarchs.

European Universities.—Next came the European universities, which epitomized medieval man's craving for learning. Universities flourished at Bologna, Montpellier, Paris, and later at Oxford and Cambridge, beginning originally as *universitates* or associations of students and associations of students and teachers. At Bologna the first *consilia,* or clinical case histories, were compiled and the first anatomical dissection performed. Many brilliant personalities added luster to these institutions. Bologna had among her students and teachers the surgeons Ugo Borgognoni of Lucca (d. 1252) and his son Theodoric (Teodorico, 1205–1298); William of Saliceto (1210?–1276/1277); Taddeo Alderotti (1223–1303); the astronomers Nicholas of Cusa (1401?–1464) and Nicolaus Copernicus (1473–1543), who was also a physician; and that master in dissection, Mondino de' Luzzi (1275–1326). Montpellier had Ramón Lull (1232/1235–?1315), the great Spanish mystic; Arnaud de Villeneuve; Henri de Mondeville (1260–1320), Bernard of Gordon (d. 1314); John of Gaddesden (1280–1361); and Guy de Chauliac (c. 1300–1368), the finest surgeon in the Middle Ages, whose book on surgery was the most famous in existence until the 16th century. The university in Paris, directed by the masters in contrast to Padua, which was run by the students, had that astounding humanist, Albertus Magnus, whose pupils numbered Roger Bacon, the English Franciscan who foretold X-rays, the airplane, and television; Thomas Aquinas; the physician Petrus Hispanus (1210?–1276), who became Pope John XXI; the surgeon Guido Lanfranchi (Lanfranco da Milan, d. about 1306); Jan Yperman (1275?–1330); and de Mondeville. Oxford shone with the genius of Michael Scot (c. 1175?–?1234), astrologer and physician; Bartholomaeus Anglicus (fl. 1230–1250), and *doctor mirabilis* Roger Bacon. Beautiful Padua had within her walls Pietro d'Abano (1250?–?1316), physician-philosopher who tutored Dante Alighieri (1265–1321); centuries later Andreas Vesalius and William Harvey attended Padua. Spain had universities at Córdoba, Salamanca, Barcelona, Valladolid, and Segovia. Latin was the language of science everywhere.

Medieval Man.—Living on the defensive, in constant fear of God, devils, famines, fires, and floods, men in the Middle Ages suffered "collective" diseases, such as the Black Death, smallpox, leprosy, and mental outbreaks, exemplified by the Flagellants and the Dancing Mania. Cities were cramped, and bathhouses were public, focuses of infection. On the other hand, the public market, center of daily life, was kept scrupulously clean, and foodstuffs were carefully inspected; a prophylactic epidemiology was established, based, as in the case of lepers, upon isolation of the diseased. Magic, astrology, amulets, relics, bezoars, and belief in the devil, gnomes, elves, fairies, incubi, and succubi continued to flourish. The chief method of diagnosis was uroscopy, and the canvases of the period depict the physician gazing at a phial filled with the golden fluid. Therapy consisted of cathartic diuretics, purges, bleeding, and sudorifics, supplemented by weird pharmaceuticals and opotherapy from the apothecaries' junkshops, including the panaceas theriaca and mithridate.

6. MEDICINE IN THE RENAISSANCE (1453–1610)

The Renaissance was not so much the beginning of the Modern Age as the end of the Middle Ages. Exploration overseas paralleled the exploration of the human body, both expressive of this period's craving for learning. The printing press facilitated human communication. It was an age of religious reforms and counterreforms and political experiments, while over the horizon the star of America was beginning to appear. Gunpowder put an end to feudalism and its castles. The mariner's compass gave new stimulus to seafaring. Most important were the revival of Greek culture, the new ideal of humanity, the exploration of the world, and the discovery of the beauty of the human form. The cosmography of land, sea, and sky moved forward at the helm of the explorers' ships; man's individuality stood out against the multicolored backdrop of the Renaissance; academies cropped up alongside the universities; and humanism blossomed with Petrarch, Giovanni Boccaccio, and Dante.

Great Humanists.—Among the great humanists of the Renaissance were Nicolaus Leonicenus (1428–1524); Geronimo (Girolamo) Cardano (1501–1576), physician, astrologer, and mathematician, who created "modern" psychiatry with his description of "moral insanity"; Thomas Linacre (1460?–1524), first president of the Royal College of Physicians in London; the Swiss Konrad von Gesner (1516–1565), physician and naturalist; Günther von Andernach (1487–1574) from Germany; Andrés de Laguna (1494?–1560), Luis de Mercado (1520–1606), and Francisco Valles (1524–1592) from Spain; and the great French humanist Jean Fernel (1497–1558), author of *Universa medicina*. Revolt against ancient dogma became manifest in such controversies as that posed by the Spanish martyr Michael Servetus (1511–1553), discoverer of pulmonary circulation, who strongly opposed the practice of giving sirupy medications for all ailments. Condemned by John Calvin for heresy, Servetus was burned alive on green wood at Geneva.

New Methods and Attitudes.—New instruments, such as optical lenses, the telescope, and the microscope, and new mercurial remedies and methods of necropsy exemplified the craving for novelty in the Renaissance. Clinical case histories progressed from the medieval *consilia* to the Renaissance *observationes*. New "individual" diseases appeared on the scene (in contrast to the "collective" diseases of the Middle Ages, typical of life under feudalism and the monastery), among them exanthematic typhus, diphtherial angina, and syphilis. Syphilis probably already existed in Europe, but it may have been aggravated by new virulent strains imported by Christopher Columbus' ships. The nature of syphilis and other epidemics was studied by Girolamo Fracastoro (1478–1553), physician and humanist, who gave the "love sickness" the poetic name of "syphilis" in his beautiful poem *Syphilis sive morbus Gallicus* (1530).

Paracelsus.—The three great rebels of the Renaissance were Paracelsus, Vesalius, and Ambroise Paré. Philippus Aureolus Paracelsus (Theophrastus Bombastus von Hohenheim, 1493?–1541) was born near Zurich. After a lifetime spent as an itinerant physician, he attacked the dogmatism of Galen and Avicenna and made a public bonfire of their works in Basel. He looked on diseases as actual entities and adopted the idea of an *archeus* or vital principle, which if weakened would cause disease. His therapy was based on the curative power of nature, and he believed that every disease had a remedy (*arcanum*) in the surrounding world. Paracelsus introduced many metals, minerals, tinctures, and essences, adopted a religious mythology teeming with sylphs, pygmies, nymphs, and salamanders, and was the precursor of medicinal chemistry.

Surgery: Paré.—Next to such Renaissance adventurers as the conquistador and the *condottiere,* there figured the surgeon, whose adventure lay in exploring the human frame which until then had been a terra incognita like the continent beyond the Atlantic. The importance of the barber in surgery increased, creating much conflict between the "long-robed" university surgeons and the "short-robed" barber-surgeons. Anatomical techniques improved, but fresh problems were posed by wounds caused by firearms. The course of surgery took a different turn with Ambroise Paré (1517?–1590), a barber-surgeon from Paris. On one occasion, having used up his stock of boiling sauce oil while treating the powder-infected wounds of war casualties, Paré successfully improvised a dressing of egg yolk blended with rose oil and turpentine. Plastic operations also improved with Gasparo Tagliacozzi of Bologna (1546–1599), and so did obstetrics, thanks to the higher esteem in which women were now held as a result of the works of Desiderius Erasmus (1469–1536), Juan Luis Vives (1492–1540), and Sir Thomas More (1478–1535). Ophthalmology also progressed, fostered by the more "visual" attitude toward life awakened by Leonardo da Vinci.

Opposition to Witch Hunting.—The quixotic crusade against witch hunting was started by the Swiss physician Johann Weyer (1515–1588). The existence of witches was then a universal belief, and more than 300,000 "witches" were burned in Europe by 1782. Witch hunting reached its peak when two inquisitors, Jacob Sprenger and Krämer, published the *Malleus maleficarum* (*Hammer of Evildoers,* c. 1487), a penal code for witches. Weyer, in his work *De praestigiis daemonum et incantationibus ac veneficiis (Concerning the Deceptions of Demons and Incantations and Poisons,* 1563), removed the stigma from witches by considering them mentally sick. Another worker in the field of mental illness was the brilliant Spaniard, Juan Luis Vives, tutor to royalty, voluntary exile at Bruges, and the father of modern psychology.

Anatomy: Leonardo da Vinci.—Leonardo da Vinci (1452–1519), one of the greatest geniuses in the history of human thought, performed many dissections, leaving some 1,500 anatomical sketches. In his 7,000 pages of notes, he left an anatomical ideal based upon the laws of nature, approaching science with the artist's eye and art with the scientist's mind. The multifaceted work on anatomy of this artist, physician, engineer, architect, and thinker heralded the work of Vesalius.

Vesalius.—Andreas Vesalius (1514–1564), a Belgian, became famous for his anatomical demonstrations in Padua. After publishing several anatomical works, he composed his own anatomy, with beautiful woodcuts made by Jan Stevenszoon van Calcar, a pupil of Titian, and sent it across the Alps on muleback to the printing house of Johannes Oporinus in Basel. This great work, *De humani corporis fabrica libri septem (Seven Books on the Structure of the Human Body),* published in June 1543, elicited such criticism that Vesalius went to Spain, where he served as court physician. He died on the island of Zante, having been shipwrecked there while returning from a pilgrimage to Jerusalem. Vesalius' fame rests not only on his anatomical knowledge but on his having developed a *new* anatomy, on his architectonic concept of the subject, on his having corrected some Galenic errors, on his having illustrated anatomy, and on his having regarded the human body as the fabric and statue of man. He was one of the mightiest figures in the history of medicine, his work being a prelude to modern science. Vesalius was Galenic in his physiology. His artistic representation of anatomy by means of skinned or fleshless men, posed against the Italian landscape, was a revolution in the art of teaching. His work was carried on by Gabriel Fallopius (Gabriello Fallopio, 1523–1562), the embryologist, who launched the concept of the "fibers," and by Hieronymus Fabricius ab Acquapendente (Geronimo or Girolamo Fabrizio, 1533–1619), who dissected the venous valves.

Renaissance physicians remained loyal to medieval tradition, accepting "catarrh" as the basis of pathology and expulsive therapy as the best cure. The social importance of physicians continued to increase, as shown in their elegant portraits bearing such signatures as Titian, Hans Holbein the Younger, and El Greco. Violent living fostered interest in the human body, its muscles and movements, since survival often depended on knowing the arts of killing and of self-protection.

7. MEDICINE DURING THE BAROQUE PERIOD (1610–1700)

In the 17th century mankind strove to adapt itself to a new order of things. Nations turned Protestant in religion, and republican in government, and the flight of a handful of Puritans on the *Mayflower* was to culminate in the democracy of the United States. Scientific academies prospered, and the first medical journal made its appearance in Paris in 1679. The concepts of nation, state, balance of power, and social classes were born. Baroque art stressed motion and emotion, which would exert its influence on the discovery of the motion of the blood. Nicolaus Copernicus' descriptive universe was replaced by the dynamic universe of Johannes Kepler, Galileo Galilei, and Sir Isaac Newton. René Descartes, Francis Bacon, and John Locke laid the rational and experimental foundations of philosophy. Physics strode forward under Christian Huygens and Blaise Pascal, and chemistry under Robert Boyle. Scientific quantitative mensuration began to replace empirical qualitative impressions. Descartes discussed the scientific value of doubt, the dichotomy between soma and psyche, and the mechanistic notion of the "human machine." Galileo originated the science of optics.

Progress in Anatomy.—Under the impact of Vesalius and Fabricius ab Aquapendente, anatomy made considerable advances. Outstanding were studies of the liver by Francis Glisson (1597–1677), of the pancreatic duct by Johann Georg Wirsung (1600–1643), of the parotid gland by Niels Stensen (1638–1686), and of the genitourinary glands by Thomas Bartholin (1616–1680) and William Cowper (1666–1709). Regnier de Graaf (1641–1673), Jan Swammerdam (1637–1680), and Fredrik Ruysch (1638–1731) injected colored substances into cadavers. Progress was made in anatomy by Raymond Vieussens (1641–1716), in otology by Antonio Maria Valsalva (1666–1723), and in ophthalmology by Anton van Leeuwenhoek (1632–1723) and Stensen. Vesalius' static *fabrica* was set in motion. Motion in space was replaced by *local* motion—blood vessels and secretory glands—the basis of modern physiology. The scepter of education passed from Padua to Leiden. Francesco Redi (1626?–1697/1698) introduced the idea of *contagium animatum* in opposition to the old Galenic etiology. The great anatomico-clinical monument of the period was the *Sepulchretum sive anatomica practica . . .* (1679), by Theophilus Bonet of Geneva, which contains more than 3,000 clinical case records.

Outstanding medical figure of the baroque period was William Harvey (1578–1657) of

MEDICINE, History of

Top: Bloodletting, an early form of medical therapy based on the supposed removal of "morbific humors," is illustrated in this 15th century drawing.

Center: The brutal treatment of the insane in 18th century England is portrayed in this scene from William Hogarth's series, *A Rake's Progress.*

Bottom: Street scene during the London plague of 1665. Corpses are placed in a cart while the town crier calls to the populace, "Bring out your dead."

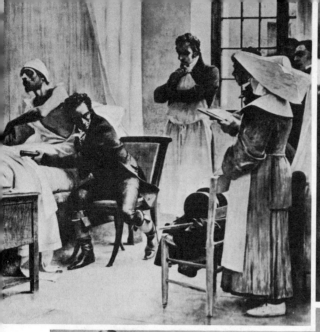

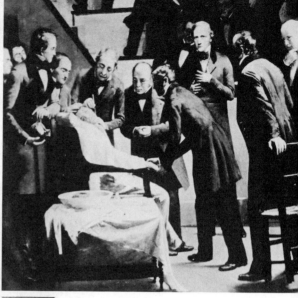

MEDICINE, History of

Top right: Painting records the first public use of ether as an anesthetic, in an operation at Massachusetts General Hospital, Oct. 16, 1846.

Top left: René Laënnec (1781–1826) demonstrates use of his stethoscope in the Hôpital Necker, Paris, in this painting by Théobald Chartran.

Center left: Carbolic acid spray as a surgical antiseptic, introduced by Joseph Lister, is shown in this early photograph (about 1870).

Bottom left: Dr. Charles McBurney, third from right, shown operating in New York City, made notable advances in treatment of appendicitis.

Bottom right: John Singer Sargent's "Four Doctors" of Johns Hopkins: left to right, W. H. Welch, pathology; W. S. Halsted, surgery; William Osler, medicine; and H. A. Kelly, gynecology.

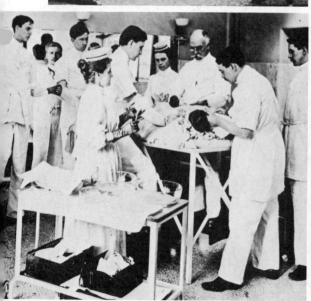

Folkestone, England, student at Cambridge and later at Padua, where he saw Fabricius ab Acquapendente dissecting the venous valves and listened to Galileo expounding the motion of the heavenly bodies. Returning to London at a time when Shakespeare's plays, resounding with words like "blood" and "heart," were at their height, and movement was the dominant factor in baroque art, Harvey experimentally demonstrated the circulation (motion) of the blood as reported in his Lumleian lecture (1616). His was a baroque physiology, *anatomia animata* in space, just as his embryology was *anatomia animata* in time. His theory, eventually fully accepted in Europe, was the basis of modern physiology.

Impetus of the Microscope.—After Harvey, the wish grew to discover the intrinsic texture of things invisible to the naked eye. Jean Fernel (1497–1558) and Fallopius had replaced the Galenic humoral physiology by their concept of the "fiber" as the basic unit of the body. The microscope, supposedly invented around 1590 by Zacharias Janssen, lensmaker of Middelburg, Netherlands, and rediscovered by Galileo, was put to practical use by Prince Federico Cesi (1585–1630) and Francesco Stelluti (1577–c. 1651), and employed by Marcello Malpighi (1628–1694), pioneer in microscopic anatomy, who described the capillary circulation. The Dutch merchant Leeuwenhoek built hundreds of microscopes and minutely studied plant and animal structures at Delft. It is significant that at the same time his neighbor, Jan Vermeer, the painter, was covering his canvases with minute details.

Jean Riolan (1577–1657) and Jean Pecquet (1622–1674) confirmed the lymphatic circulation first perceived by Gasparo Aselli (1581–1626). In showing that lymph circulates through special vessels and does not enter the liver, they demoted the liver from its importance under the Galenic system. With the discovery of the two principal fluids of the human body, blood and lymph, the dynamization of Vesalius' anatomy was completed.

Clinical Medicine.—In the baroque period, clinical medicine was illuminated by three sects: iatrophysicists, iatrochemists, and systematists.

Iatrophysicists.—The human body was regarded as a machine by the iatrophysicists, and pathology as a matter of "tensional state of the fibers" and density of the organic humors. Men like Kepler and Newton brought progress to the physiology of the senses. Other leading figures among them were Redi, who demolished the theory of spontaneous generation; Stensen; Giovanni Alfonso Borelli (1608–1679); Giorgio Baglivi (1669?–1707); and Sanctorius (Santorio Santorio, 1561–1636), originator of experimental mensuration in physiology, inventor of the clinical thermometer and pulse clock, and originator of the ideas that led to modern metabolism. Sanctorius lived for 30 years in a huge scale, weighing his "insensible perspiration" in states of action, rest, sadness, and sexual excitement.

Iatrochemists.—To the iatrochemists the body was a laboratory, and organic movement was the result of chemical ferments. Their leader was the Flemish mystic Jan Baptista van Helmont (1577?–1644), who located pathological processes in the diseased organs and considered water the substratum of the body, and the *archeus* the life-giving principle. His therapy of small doses of plant tinctures was a healthy reaction against the barbarous horse-doctoring of the age.

The finishing touch on his work was given by the rationalist Prussian Huguenot of French descent, Franciscus Sylvius (Franz de le Boë, 1614–1672). Next came Thomas Willis (1621–1675), who described the vascular ring at the base of the brain (circle of Willis) and internal secretions.

Systematists.—This sect was represented by Thomas Sydenham (1624–1689), who served as captain with the Cromwellian Roundheads, just as Harvey served with the king's men. Sydenham shut his textbooks and opened his eyes to the patients, and restored the Hippocratic concepts. His clinical case records are masterpieces. He used naturalistic remedies and described various morbid "species" as painstakingly as a botanist classifies his plants. He recommended clinical observation, treatment of the whole patient, and the study of diseases in particular instead of disease in general. This was the beginning of the diagnosis of one definite sickness in the patient. Sydenham divided diseases into the acute, biological, or animal (epidemiological), and the chronic, biographical, or human (psychosomatic).

Therapeutics.—New medicines were scanty in the baroque period, though from South America there did come cinchona and ipecacuanha. Surgery, which remained in the hands of barbers, made little progress, except perhaps in France and England, though Nicholas Tulp (1593–1674) and Ruysch in Holland and Fabricius of Hilden (1560–1634) in Germany were also distinguished.

Obstetrics and Surgery.—Obstetrics remained in the hands of midwives and unqualified surgeons, though a better method was devised for Caesarean sections, the forceps were introduced by Peter Chamberlen (1560–1631), and the first blood transfusion was performed. Clyster, bleeding, and purges were standbys for most physicians, whose pompous hats, black robes, scarlet heels, and louse-ridden periwigs elicited Molière's ridicule. Surgeons were assimilated into the medical profession and now wore long robes and mortarboards, while barber-surgeons gradually formed one guild.

The humanist and physician Sir Thomas Browne (1605–1682) tried to conciliate scientific skepticism and mystic faith in his excellent *Religio medici* (1642). Therapeutic "vampirism" or bleeding alternated with hot baths, and cupping reached its peak. Medicine was still practiced by charlatans, uroscopists, and tooth-pullers.

Beginnings of Medicine in the Americas.—Prior to the arrival of the Europeans, the Americas were populated by Indians, who followed an animistic religion and practiced shamanistic medicine. The conquistadores in the 16th century brought Spanish culture to the hemisphere. The first universities in the New World were founded in Mexico and Peru in 1551 and the first chair of medicine at the University of Mexico in 1580. The first medical book, *Opera medicinalis* by Francisco Bravo, was published in 1570, and the first degree of doctor in medicine in the Americas was granted in Peru in 1551.

Hygienic conditions among the first Puritan settlers in the English colonies in North America were abominable; nearly half of the *Mayflower* (1620) passengers died within three months after disembarking. Smallpox and typhus wrought havoc in the first colonies. There were no physicians and only a handful of surgeons, among them Thomas Wooton. Medicine was in the hands of clergymen. One, Deacon Samuel Fuller (1580–1633), functioned many years as a physician. Another cleric, Thomas Thacher (1620–1678), issued the first American medical publication, a broadside on smallpox (1677), and parson-physician Cotton Mather (1663–1728) promoted the first inoculations.

8. MEDICINE IN THE AGE OF ENLIGHTENMENT

The 18th century witnessed a Europe rent by political and religious struggles. Scientific life was centered in academies and universities, and scientific journals proliferated. Progress in the natural sciences (Marquis Pierre Simon de Laplace, Sir William Herschel) was remarkable. Physics adopted a rational mechanics with Leonhard Euler and James Watt, and a new force, electricity, began to revolutionize the world. Modern chemistry was born when Karl Wilhelm Scheele (1742–1786), Antoine Laurent Lavoisier (1743–1794), and Joseph Priestley (1733–1804), independently of each other, discovered oxygen, and Lavoisier discovered the analogy between combustion and hematosis. Biology marched forward with the work of Carolus Linnaeus (Carl von Linné, 1707–1778) and Comte Georges Louis Leclerc de Buffon (1707–1788).

Growth of Medical Schools.—A revolutionary change in clinical teaching was effected by Hermann Boerhaave (1668–1738), professor of clinical medicine and botany at Leiden, who taught medicine in a 12-bed hospital to more than half the physicians of Europe. Boerhaave wrote two slim clinical treatises, created a school that was the cradle of modern medical bedside teaching, and established the comparison of clinical diagnosis and case history with necropsy findings.

Three schools of medicine reaped the harvest of Leiden: the Old Vienna school, the Edinburgh school, and the English school.

The Old Vienna school was founded by Gerard van Swieten (1700–1772), who organized the medical faculty and set up clinics and libraries. His work was supplemented by the system of clinical observation and expectant therapy introduced by Anton de Haen (1704–1776). At about the same time in Vienna, Leopold Auenbrugger von Auenbrugg (1722–1809), physician and part-time musician, after watching his father testing wine levels by tapping the casks, began to diagnose chest ailments by tapping the chest and listening to the echoes. His discovery brought little reward in his lifetime, though recognition did come later in France thanks to René Théophile Hyacinthe Laënnec (1781–1826) and to Napoleon's physician, Jean Nicolas Corvisart des Marets (1755–1821), who originated modern surgical teaching in France and, despite his being rejected for the post of physician to the Necker Hospital because of his refusal to wear the required wig, became medical director of the Charité in Paris. Corvisart translated and popularized Auenbrugger's book, *Inventum novum ex percussione thoracis humani* . . . (1761; Fr. tr., 1808).

The English school was distinguished by the nosographers John Huxham (1692–1768), Richard Mead (1673–1754), John Fothergill (1712–1780), and William Pitcairn (1711–1791). This was the golden age of Scottish medicine at Edinburgh, where Alexander Monro (1697–1767) was succeeded by his son and grandson of the same name, and Francis Home (1719–1813), John and Charles Bell (1763–1820; 1774–1842), James Lind (1716–1794), William and John Hunter (1718–1783; 1728–1793), William Cullen (1710–1790),

and John Brown (1735–1788) were also among the professors. William Heberden (1710–1801) wrote a jewel of a description of angina pectoris, and William Withering (1741–1799) introduced digitalis in the treatment of dropsy.

Developments in Anatomy, Physiology, and Therapeutics.—Anatomy was based on the comparative study of morphology, proceeding from Fallopius' "texture" to Marie François Xavier Bichat's (1771–1802) "tissue," from animism to vitalism. The anatomists of the period include Giovanni Battista Morgagni (1682–1771), Antonio Scarpa (1747–1832), Jakob Benignus Winslow (1669–1760), William Cheselden (1688–1752), the Monros, and Antonio Gimbernat (1734–1816). The titan of physiology during the Enlightenment was the Swiss, Albrecht von Haller (1708–1777), who made his name in physiology. A great poet and an accomplished linguist, he wrote 2,000 scientific articles, 14,000 letters, and a mass of material on poetry, medicine, botany, philosophy, and religion. Despite his adherence to Catholicism, he corresponded with rakes like Giovanni Jacopo Casanova and atheists like Voltaire. Haller established irritability as the property of the muscles and sensitivity as the property of the nerves, and maintained that life was the specific property of living matter.

The physiology of respiration progressed under Robert Boyle (1627–1691), John Mayow (1645–1679) and particularly Lavoisier, a victim of the guillotine, who proved that the essential process of respiration is the combustion of hydrogen and carbon and the absorption of oxygen.

Pathological anatomy made progress thanks to Morgagni who at the age of 80 published his magnum opus (*De sedibus et causis morborum per anatomen indagatis,* 1761; Eng. tr., *The Seats and Causes of Diseases Investigated by Anatomy,* 1769), 5 books covering 70 personal letters, the only way of spreading knowledge since there were no medical journals. His great contribution was in proving that each disease had its seat in an organ. Morgagni was the first to classify diseases as anatomicopathological entities and to show the value of drawing a line between pathological and normal anatomy. Pathological anatomy became a dynamic process, since disease was a process in motion, in contrast to normal anatomy, which was static. Morgagni's gallery of the dead included maids and prostitutes, princesses, bishops, and bandits. He introduced the concept of disease as something located in the organs instead of floating through the vessels.

Abbé Lazzaro Spallanzani (1729–1799) studied the digestive processes in himself, swallowing little cloth bags and perforated tubes filled with food to prove that digestion was not a spontaneous putrefaction caused by germs in the organic solutions. His contemporary, Kaspar Friedrich Wolff (1733–1794), founder of modern embryology, revived the notion that organs become progressively differentiated and are not preformed. Ostracized by the scientific world, Wolff went to Russia at the invitation of Catherine the Great and there spent the last years of his life. Another clergyman, the Reverend Stephen Hales (1677–1761), studied blood pressure by introducing glass tubes into the veins and arteries of horses.

Rise of Specialization.—There now arose the age of specialization: cardiology, fostered by Antonio Giuseppe Testa (1756–1814); hematology, by Paul Gottfried Werlhof (1699–1767);

avitaminoses and pellagra, by Gaspar Casal (1679–1759); pediatrics, impelled by an increased interest in children stemming from the work of Jean Jacques Rousseau and Johann Heinrich Pestalozzi; and, toward the end of the century, psychiatry, stimulated by Joseph Daquin (1733–1815), Philippe Pinel (1745–1826), Johann Christian Reil (1759–1813), and others. Pinel, superintendent of the Salpêtrière, tried to turn diagnosis into an exact science based on an almost botanical classification of diseases, and made the earliest anatomicopathological classification of mental diseases. His chief distinction lies in having actively participated in the proclamation of the Declaration of the Rights of Man and the Citizen by the National Assembly (1789), and having introduced the rights established by the French Revolution at the Bicêtre Mental Hospital, thus liberating the mental patient from his chains.

Therapies continued on traditional lines: diet, bleeding, purges, and clysters, which were sometimes administered while the fashionable patient attended the theater, as Mme. de Maintenon and Ninon de Lenclos did. Phlebotomy became a true therapeutic "vampirism." Surgery progressed in France, where in 1731 the first Royal Academy of Surgery was chartered, separating the surgeons from the barbers. First director of this academy was Jean Louis Petit (1674–1750). His successor, Antoine Louis (1723–1792), collaborated with Joseph Ignace Guillotin (1738–1814) in perfecting the *louisine* or guillotine. Britain produced famous surgeons: William Cheselden, (1688–1752), Samuel Sharp (1700?–1778), Percivall Pott (1714–1788), Sir Charles and John Bell. The surgeon, by the stress laid by the Encyclopedists upon manual arts, became a technician.

A colossus in anatomy and surgery was the Scotsman John Hunter, apprentice to his brother William and a pupil of Cheselden. In his country house he kept hundreds of animals, from buffaloes to leopards, to study comparative anatomy. He reunited anatomy, medicine, and surgery upon a foundation of experimental and biological learning.

Obstetrics improved with the public introduction of the forceps (long a secret of the Chamberlen family) by Hugh Chamberlen in 1672, as did ophthalmology with the extraction of the crystalline lens by Jacques Daviel (1693–1762).

Curative Systems.—The most famous system in medicine was the animism of George Stahl (1660–1734), who opposed the materialism of vitalism. Stahl and a rival colleague at Halle, Prussia, Friedrich Hoffmann (1660–1742), accepted ether as the essential principle of life, transmitted by the nerves to the "fibers" and causing "atonies" or "hypertonies" if its nature was altered.

Vitalism.—Holding life to be a property of living matter, vitalism remained the prevalent system; it reached its full expression with Théophile de Bordeu (1722–1776), forerunner of endocrinology; Paul Joseph Barthez (1734–1806), Napoleon's physician, who established the ability of each organ to preserve the constancy of its properties; and Pinel. It was later revived by Bichat and Laënnec. In Scotland, the exponent of vitalism was William Cullen, whose neuropathology distinguished as the chief property of life the nervous "tone" of the solid parts, which if disturbed (spasm or atony) caused disease. He formulated the concept of "lesion of sensibility and movement, without inflammation of the organs" (today called organic neuroses).

Brunonian System.—Vitalism was opposed by another Scotsman, John Brown (1735–1788), student of Cullen, a parson and schoolmaster of dubious habits, who turned his attention to medicine. His own concept was that the fundamental quality of the living body lay in the excitability that mobilized organic energy, and that diseases were excesses or deficiencies (sthenias or asthenias) of such excitability and should be treated by the drastic *contraria contrariis* therapy. It has been said that the Brunonian system, which received the approval of the National Convention, destroyed more lives than the French Revolution and the Napoleonic Wars together, and Brown himself is believed to have succumbed to it when he took an overdose of laudanum. The system was modified in Germany by Reil, a pioneer of modern psychiatry, and by Christophe Wilhelm Hufeland (1762–1836), physician to Johann Wolfgang von Goethe.

Mesmerism.—Two other kinds of curative systems, based on the powers of suggestion, also flourished. Mesmerism was founded by the Viennese Franz Anton Mesmer (1734–1815), a friend of Wolfgang Amadeus Mozart. Mesmer claimed that the universe was full of a magnetic flux that could be mobilized by means of a magnet. (Subsequently his system veered toward clinical hypnotism as practiced by John Elliotson [1791–1868] and James Braid [1795?–1860].) In his "magnetic" chamber in Paris, assisted by soft music and by handsome young men, Mesmer, dressed in purple cloth, magnetic wand in hand, "treated" a great number of wealthy hysterical women.

Homeopathy.—Homeopathy was introduced by the German, Samuel Hahnemann (1755–1843), who, widowed at the age of 80, married a young society woman and moved from the provinces to Paris, where he practiced medicine for eight years more and became one of the best-known physicians in the French capital. Hahnemann's tenet was that the cause of acute diseases was an "impairment of the vital force." All diseases, he believed, were of a general nature, and he treated them with a mild form of another disease of a similar nature (*similia similibus curantur*).

Superstition and quackery also prospered, as proved by the success of the Venetian adventurers, Giacomo Casanova (1725–1798), Conte Alessandro di Cagliostro (1743–1795) with his elixir of life, the Comte de St. Germain, and the Scotsman James Graham (1745–1794) with his "Temple of Health" in London, where a high priestess was the future Lady Emma Hamilton. Graham's Temple was famous for its perfumed musical "celestial bed," which he claimed had electric currents that varied according to the vigor with which it was rocked by the persons ensconced therein.

Public Health.—The great figure in public health was Johann Peter Frank (1745–1821), physician to Czar Alexander I and self-appointed adviser to kings and emperors on how to protect their people's health. A reformer but not a revolutionary, he believed in a state "health police" to control the hygiene of the people at large. He laid down the laws of modern social hygiene, the application of which he entrusted to the all-powerful state and its sanitary police force.

The havoc wrought by epidemics was incalculable; during the 18th century more than 60 million people died from smallpox in Europe. Hygiene was practically nonexistent. Women's wigs were provided with small deposits of honey and vinegar in order to draw away the attentions of the lice, and kings like Louis XIV, as Mme. de Pompadour said, "stank like rotten meat." Reaction against such a state of affairs came from James Lind (1716–1794), originator of the hospital ship, and Lavoisier, who improved the jails and had several hospitals built in order to relieve the situation at the Hôtel Dieu in Paris, where six patients were lying in a bed and interns had to wear "nose bags" containing vinegar-soaked sponges because of the fetid odor in the wards. In 1796, William Tuke (1732–1822), a Quaker, founded the York Retreat for the insane. The physician became a social force, as evidenced by his scarlet satin clothes, powdered wig, silver-buckled shoes, gold-headed cane, and muff in portraits by Sir Joshua Reynolds, William Hogarth, and Thomas Rowlandson.

Discovery of Vaccination.—The great contribution of the 18th century was vaccination, discovered by the English physician Edward Jenner (1749–1823). While practicing in Berkeley, Jenner noticed that milkmaids contracted cowpox but never smallpox, which led him in 1796 to inoculate vaccine obtained from a milkmaid suffering from cowpox into a small boy, who, when later inoculated with smallpox, developed only a slight exanthema but not the disease. After a lengthy controversy, vaccination replaced Oriental variolation, brought to Europe from Constantinople by Lady Mary Wortley Montagu. Later, in 1803, the Spaniard Francisco Javier de Balmis introduced vaccination in Central America and in the East by taking 22 vaccinated children to Yucatán, the Philippines, and Macao and Canton in China.

Medicine in the American Colonies.—Life in the American colonies became stabilized during the 18th century. Medicine was learned through apprenticeship to a practicing physician, since few students were able to go to study in England, Scotland, or Holland. The physician was a surgeon from the very start. Some physicians became famous, for instance, William Shippen, Jr. (1736–1808), of Philadelphia, the first man to occupy a chair in medicine in the American colonies. The physician took home those patients requiring special attention. Homes for the helpless were established, and in 1751 the first hospital in Philadelphia, Pennsylvania Hospital, was founded on the initiative of Dr. Thomas Bond (1712–1784); it was followed 24 years later by the New York Hospital. In many of these projects a vital role was played by Benjamin Franklin (1706–1790), who practiced the ideals of the French Encyclopedists, applied electricity to paralysis, invented the lightning arrester and bifocal lenses, and collaborated in the foundation of the first hospital, the first school of medicine, and the first philosophical society in America, and made Philadelphia the cradle of American medicine.

Among the famous American physicians were Thomas Cadwalader (1708?–1799), who taught practical anatomy at Philadelphia; William Shippen, Jr., who lectured on obstetrics; and John Morgan (1735–1789), who founded the first medical college at the College of Philadelphia in 1765, and who delivered a commencement address that became the first book on medical education. In 1793 the population of Philadelphia was severely stricken by yellow fever, a plague which Benjamin Rush (1745–1813) treated with bleeding and purging. In 1797, in New York, three young physicians, Samuel L. Mitchill (1764–1831), Edward Miller (1760–1812), and Elihu H. Smith (1771–1798), founded the *Medical Repository,* the first medical review in the United States.

9. MEDICINE IN THE 19TH CENTURY

Nineteenth century medicine may be divided into two periods: that of the romantic revival and that of naturalistic positivism.

ROMANTIC REVIVAL (1800–1850)

The first half of the 19th century in Europe revolved round the military exploits of Napoleon I, which in France spurred the positivistic philosophy of Auguste Comte and in Germany the *Naturphilosophie* of Friedrich Wilhelm von Schelling and Georg Wilhelm Friedrich Hegel. The Industrial Revolution was on the way. Technical inventions multiplied, among them the steamboat (Robert Fulton, 1807), the locomotive (George Stephenson, 1814), the automobile with internal-combustion engine (Karl Benz, 1885), the telephone (Alexander Graham Bell, 1876), and radiotelegraphy (Guglielmo Marconi, 1895).

Histology and Anatomy.—Modern histology and topographical anatomy were founded at the beginning of this period by Bichat, who dissected 600 corpses during one winter session. For Bichat, disease had its seat not in organs generally but in one particular organ, organs being made up of "membranes" or tissues. He held that life was a "complex of functions which resisted death," consisting of vital force, reaction and resistance. Thus medical theory progressed from Galen's "single parts," Fallopius' "textures," Fabrizio ab Aquapendente's *ordimento,* the "fibers" of the baroque period, and Bordeu's mucous tissues, to the tissues as the basic unit in the living being.

The success of the microscope led to the development of the cell theory, which was conceived when the botanist Matthias Jakob Schleiden (1804–1881) showed that plants were composed of cells, and Theodor Schwann (1810–1882) applied this principle to animal organisms, their work being completed by Jacob Henle (1809–1885) and Robert Remak (1815–1865).

Physiology.—In France physiology took root in Bichat's vitalism, its greatest figures being François Magendie (1783–1855), René Antoine Ferchault de Réamur (1683–1757), Lazzaro Spallanzani (1729–1799), and Thomas Young (1773–1829). Progress was made in circulatory physiology (Bell; Marie Jean Pierre Flourens, 1794–1867; Robert Remak), respiratory physiology (Heinrich Gustav Magnus, 1802–1870), and the physiology of the senses (Johannes Evangelista Purkinje, 1787–1869; Thomas Young; Johannes Peter Müller, 1801–1858). Johann Kaspar Lavater's physiognomy and Franz Joseph Gall's and Johann Kaspar Spurzheim's phrenology enjoyed a brief vogue. The romantic speculations of natural philosophy were finally replaced by a genuine mensurational and practical examination of nature, or true natural science.

The leading figure of this period was Johannes Müller who, inspired by Goethe, dedicated himself to medicine. His encyclopedic work covered the nervous system, the sensory organs, the physiology of secretions, and embryology, for which he used the microscope, in contrast to Bichat's macroscopic anatomy.

New School of Vienna.—The New School of Vienna next sprang into existence, thanks to the greatest pathologist of the century, Baron

Karl von Rokitansky (1804–1878), who studied first the autopsy findings in some 100,000 dissections and then their clinical histories. He succeeded in separating clinical medicine from pathology, and regarded diseases as blood dyscrasias located in specific organs. At the same time, Joseph Skoda (1805–1881) laid the foundations of present-day physical diagnosis by devising a scientific terminology for the sounds heard in percussion and auscultation. Among their successors were Ferdinand von Hebra (1816–1880), who studied skin diseases; Joseph Hyrtl (1811–1894), the anatomist; and Ludwig Türck (1810–1868), the neurologist.

Advances in Specialized Fields.—Pediatrics, as a result in part of the interest in children aroused by Charles Dickens' novels, flourished under the leadership of Antoine Charles Ernst Barthez (1811–1891) and Charles Michel Billard (1800–1832). Neuropathology advanced with Domenico Cotugno (1736–1822), Johann Jacob Wepfer (1620–1695), and Moritz Heinrich Romberg (1795–1873); psychiatry with Johann Christian Friedrich Heinroth, (1773–1843), Jean Etienne Dominique Esquirol (1772–1840), François Emmanuel Fodéré (1764–1835), Jean Pierre Falret (1794–1870), and John Connolly (1794–1866); venereology with Philippe Ricord (1800–1889) and Abraham Colles (1773–1843); and dermatology with Jean Louis Alibert (1766–1837). In France and England, through Bichat, Laënnec, and Richard Bright (1789–1858), the general outlook became anatomicopathological, based on the spatial impairment of organ structures; in Germany, with Henle, it became pathophysiological and etiopathogenic. .

Surgery.—Surgery prospered in France, the armies of the Napoleons numbering many distinguished surgeons, including Baron Pierre François Percy (1754–1825); Baron Dominique Jean Larrey (1766–1842), who was present at Waterloo; Baron Guillaume Dupuytren (1777–1835); Charles Gabriel Pravaz (1791–1853), inventor of the hypodermic syringe; Josef François Malgaigne (1806–1865), Auguste Nélaton (1807–1873), and Jacques Mathieu Delpech (1777–1832). Leading surgeons in Great Britain were John Abernethy (1764–1831), Sir Astley Paston Cooper (1768–1841), the Bell brothers, and Colles; in Germany, Konrad Johann Martin Langenbeck (1776–1851) and Karl Ferdinand von Graefe (1787–1840); in Italy, Tommaso Rima (1775–1843); in the United States, Philip Syng Physick (1768–1837), J. Marion Sims (1813–1883), and Ephraim McDowell (1771–1830). Surgery was becoming more of an intellectual than a manual task, preservational instead of amputational, though the pleural and peritoneal cavities remained a mysterious inner sanctum. Plaster casts were now applied in the treatment of fractures, and improvements were made in vascular surgery. The greatest step forward was the discovery of surgical anesthesia.

Previously, Indian hemp, the soporific sponge, hypnotism, or laughing gas had been used for anesthesia. Crawford Williamson Long (1815–1878) and the dentist Horace Wells (1815–1848) had already used ether and nitrous oxide respectively. Surgical anesthesia began in 1846 when the dentist William Thomas Morton (1819–1868), coached in its use by Wells and physician-chemist Charles Thomas Jackson (1805–1880), anesthetized a patient for the surgeon John Collins Warren, Jr. Chloroform fumes were used in operations and deliveries by Dr. James Young Simpson (1811–1870) of Edinburgh.

Leading Figures in Medicine.—*France.*—Perhaps the most notable figure of this period was Corvisart's pupil René Laënnec (1781–1826), a Catholic realist, physician at the Necker Hospital in Paris. Faced with a young woman whose obesity made direct auscultation difficult and embarrassing, he had the inspiration to roll a quire of paper into a tube and apply it to her chest so as to listen to the "spoken tongue" of the diseased organs. This idea he got from having seen children in the street listening at one end of a hollow trunk to the noises made by a playmate at the other end. Thus the stethoscope came into being, and pathology, hitherto visual, now became auditory.

Other masters of the French school were: François Joseph Victor Broussais (1772–1838), who accepted phlegmasia or inflammation (gastroenteritis) as the source of all diseases and unleashed a period of therapeutic "vampirism" that increased the demand for leeches in France to more than 41 million a year; Larrey, surgeon to Napoleon and founder of modern military medicine; Guillaume Dupuytren, army anatomist; Pierre Bretonneau (1778–1862), celebrated for his description of typhoid fever; Pierre Charles Alexandre Louis (1787–1872), surgeon and inventor of modern medical statistics; Armand Trousseau (1801–1867), the great clinician (infantile tetanus); Jean Bouillaud (1796–1881), who found polyarthritis endocarditis as the source of all diseases; Jean Cruveilhier (1791–1874), who described phlebitis as the root of all pathology; and François Magendie (1783–1855), who taught Claude Bernard.

Great Britain.—Leading figures in Great Britain were Colles (fractures), John Cheyne (1777–1836, respiration), Robert Adams (1791–1875, heart block), Robert James Graves (1796–1853, exophthalmic goiter, feeding in febrile cases), Sir Dominic Corrigan (1802–1880, aortic insufficiency), William Stokes (1804–1878, respiration), and James Parkinson (1755–1824, paralysis agitans). The three colossi of Guy's Hospital were Richard Bright (nephritis), Thomas Addison (1793–1860, suprarenal melasma, syndrome of his name, the discovery of which was the commencement of modern endocrinology), and Thomas Hodgkin (1798–1866, syndrome of his name).

Germany.—Leading figures in Germany were Friedrich Wilhelm von Schelling (1775–1854), philosopher and physician *honoris causa,* who, following the Brunonian system, caused the death of Schlegel's daughter whom he was "treating"; the poet and medical theorist, Novalis (Baron Friedrich von Hardenberg, 1772–1801); Dietrich Georg Kieser (1779–1862), who regarded disease as a regression of the human being to an "animal and vegetable condition"; Christoph Wilhelm Hufeland (1762–1836); and Johann Lucas Schönlein (1793–1864).

Gynecology and Obstetrics.—Gynecology progressed with J. Marion Sims, James Y. Simpson, and Ephraim McDowell; obstetrics with the use of the forceps and the fight against puerperal fever (Oliver Wendell Holmes); ophthalmology advanced with ocular physiology, Goethe's theory of color vision, and the use of belladonna; and otology under the leadership of Jean Marie Gaspard Itard (1775–1838).

Therapeutics.—Empirical therapeutics prospered with the use of active vegetable principles and elements (morphine, veratrine, caffeine, strychnine, quinine, colchicine, atrophine, iodine, and bromide), while various empirical methods, such as the hydrotherapy of Vincenz Priessnitz (1799–1851) and the electrotherapy of Guillaume Benjamin Armand Duchenne (Duchenne de Boulogne, 1806–1875), coexisted with allopathy, homeopathy, isopathy, and therapeutic nihilism.

NATURALISTIC POSITIVISM (1850–1900)

In the second half of the 19th century medicine changed from European to national and vernacular. Progress in diagnosis was spectacular, reflecting man's sharpened curiosity about the universe and himself. Medical history, which in the Middle Ages had been made in the library just as today it is made in the laboratory, was in this period made mainly in the hospitals.

The discovery of nitrous oxide, chloroform, ether, and antiseptics (1870) made possible a finer, more delicate scientific surgery. Semeiological diagnosis was raised to the heights of artistic skill, and the etiological diagnosis of infections developed.

Fundamental developments in medicine during the century were the cellular concept of disease, which temporarily overthrew the humoral theory, later revived in endocrinology; the study of metabolism and nutrition, and the demonstration of the supremacy of the nervous system in governing the organism; the revival of the notion of unity between psyche and soma; the discovery of the microbial origin of infections; immunization, and the discovery of new drugs and instruments.

The human body was studied macroscopically in space (morphology, comparative anatomy, anthropology), microscopically (cytology, histopathology), and chronologically (genetics and embryology). Topographical and artistic anatomy, vital to the surgeon, progressed, and so did ethnology (Paul Broca, 1824–1880; Joseph Arthur de Gobineau, 1816–1882), and anthropometry.

Histology.—The genius of the German Rudolf Virchow (1821–1902) brought Hippocrates' humoral pathology to the intimate level of the cell and laid the foundations for the modern concept of disease. For Virchow, the cell was the fundamental element in the human body, each cell springing from another cell (*omnis cellula e cellula*). He regarded pathology as abnormal physiology and placed its seat in the cell instead of in the organ as Morgagni had, or in the tissue as had Bichat. Virchow asserted that the parts of the body formed a community of cellular units, a "republic of cells," its "classes" being the cells, its territory being the organs, the systems, and the organic apparatus; this "cellular democracy" was opposed to the ancient "absolutist empire" of blood humors.

Virchow's work oiled the wheels of histology, on which the first book published was by the Swiss Rudolf Albert von Kölliker (1817–1905). Disease was looked upon as a civil war between germs and leucocytes, the latter being the police force of the cell state. Histology received further impetus from Élie Metchnikoff (1845–1916) in Russia, Sir Almroth Edward Wright (1861–1947) in England, and the German Jacob Henle, the Vesalius of histology, a romantic revolutionary agitator who laid the foundations of *contagium animatum* and modern epidemiology when he identified the two forms of *contagium vivum* accepted in antiquity (*contagium* or contagious

matter originating in the patient; and *miasma,* contagious matter) with living organisms.

Progress in Specialized Fields.—Study of the human body in time resulted in its being thought of as a dynamic evolving form, the great exponents of comparative anatomy being Georges Cuvier (1769–1832), Sir Richard Owen (1804–1892), Thomas Henry Huxley (1825–1895), Karl Gegenbaur (1826–1903), and Edward Drinker Cope (1840–1897). Genetics strode on with Hugo De Vries (1848–1935, gene theory) and the Augustine abbot Gregor Johann Mendel (1822–1884), who, in studying peas, evolved the laws of heredity.

Embryology progressed after the nature of the egg and sperm and the dynamics of fertilization became known. This was all to be reinforced, at the beginning of the 20th century, by the revolutionary progress made by Alexis Carrel (1873–1944) and Hans Driesch (1867–1941) in the study of laboratory tissue cultures.

Modern physiology was born with Claude Bernard (1813–1878), who was born amid the sunny vineyards of the Saône Valley, served as an assistant apothecary, and later studied medicine in Paris. Influenced by Magendie's experimental and antivitalist views, Bernard first worked in a dismal cubbyhole in the Collège de France, then became a professor at the Sorbonne, taught his pupils how to "think physiologically," and left behind a notable school of followers (Paul Bert, 1833–1886; Arsène d'Arsonval, 1851–1940; Charles Édouard Brown-Séquard, 1817?–1894; Charles Richet, 1850–1935; Marcel Eugène Émile Gley, 1857–1930). He devised a method that started with observed reality and proceeded to its confirmation or rejection through analytical experiment, breaking it down into a series of component moments. Tracking down the metabolic fate of ingested foods, beginning with the sugars, he revealed in a series of brilliant experiments that the liver could secrete sugar starting with an intrinsic substance which he called glycogen (hepatic glycogenic function), and that the body secreted certain substances that passed into the blood. This became the basis of the concept of internal secretions. Bernard also established the following concepts: the *milieu intérieur,* or internal environment, and its stability as a "condition for a free and independent life"; the functional corelation of the organs; the specific correlation of the organs; the specific selectivity of toxic agents; the unity of physicochemical phenomena in the living being; and the principles of experimental physiological research. In his *Introduction à l'étude de la médicine expérimentale* (1865), a bible to scientists, he consolidated the philosophical positivism of his day and affirmed the need for teamwork with these words: *"L'Art c'est moi, la Science c'est nous."*

Other Advances.—In physiology remarkable advances were made in metabolism by Theodor Schwann (1810–1882), Baron Justus von Liebig (1803–1873), and Friedrich Wöhler (1800–1882); in internal secretions, in tropisms, in ferments and enzymes by Wilhelm Kühne (1837–1900) and Eduard Buchner (1860–1917); in perfusion, in thermodynamics, and in inscriptive recording (Ludwig's kymograph, Hutchinson's spirometer, Vierordt's sphygmograph, Einthoven's string galvanometer). Helmholtz' ophthalmoscope, Garcia's laryngoscope, thermoregulation, and physiological chemistry reflected other developments.

Clinical thermometry, now categorized as a

science, was founded by Karl August Wunderlich (1815–1877), who regarded fever as a reflection of nature's struggle against disease and taught how to read fever charts. Experimental public health was initiated by the Bavarian, Max von Pettenkofer (1818–1901), who championed fresh air, pure water, wholesome food, clean dwellings, and uncontaminated land as the best measures against disease. Against the contagionists Pettenkofer maintained that environmental conditions were the real causes of epidemics. To prove his contention, he drank, at the age of 74, a brew of cholera bacillus culture taken from a patient suffering from Asiatic cholera. He survived this heroic test and opened the way to modern public health practice.

The first half of the 19th century saw the death of the great French anatomists (Bichat, Corvisart, Pinel, and Laënnec). Leadership in this field then passed to England, under Bright, Addison, Sir James Paget (1814–1899), and Joseph Hodgson (1788–1869), and to America, under William Henry Welch (1850–1934), Simon Flexner (1863–1946), Harry Gideon Wells (1875–1943), and Theobald Smith (1859–1934).

Germ Theory of Disease.—The 19th century's greatest contribution to medical progress was the development of an etiopathogenic concept of disease. The "animate contagion" theory, whose heralds had been Fracastoro, Harvey, Father Athanasius Kircher (1602–1680), Francisco Enrico Acerbi (1785–1827), and Agostino Bassi (1773–1856), culminated in the work of Pasteur, Koch, and Behring, who established the germ theory of infection and laid the foundations of immunology.

Pasteur.—The founder of bacteriology was a Frenchman, Louis Pasteur (1822–1895), son of a tanner. He became a chemist, subsequently dean of the Faculté des Sciences at Lille and later director of scientific studies at the École Normale in Paris. Pasteur investigated lactic and butyric fermentations in alcohols, noting that they were caused by minute living organisms, which he differentiated into bacteria that required oxygen (aerobic) and bacteria that did not (anaerobic). Studying the "diseases" of wine, he verified that if contamination were prevented or the germs were destroyed by heat (pasteurization), the wine was preserved. Endeavoring to ascertain the origin of germs in damaged wine, milk, and beer, Pasteur proved that yeasts were the cause, not the consequence, of fermentation and that they came from the earth, air, and water. He thus identified microbes with the ancient and mysterious *contagium animatum*. Pasteur also discovered the cause of pébrine, the silkworm disease, and saved the French silk industry, just as he had saved the wine and dairy industries. His other achievements included protection of chickens and swine from cholera and splenic fever (anthrax) by means of inoculation with attenuated viruses or vaccines, and the development of an antihydrophobia vaccine. Seventy years before Sir Alexander Fleming, he investigated *Penicillium glaucum* and its effect on certain ferments, and proved that the products of bacteria, such as anthrax bacilli, could be destroyed by other bacteria, thus anticipating the antibiotics.

Koch and Behring.—Robert Koch (1843–1910), a German country doctor, discovered the causal germ of anthrax and its spores, this being the first time that a disease was specifically attributed to a germ. Koch unraveled the origin of splenic fever, identified the ancient *miasmata* and *contagium* with germs, fungi, bacteria, or spores, traced their natural history, and established the concept of microbic specificity for each infection. He also investigated wound infections, the methodology of disinfection, and the causal germ of tuberculosis.

Koch's work was supplemented by that of his pupil Emil von Behring (1854–1917), who discovered the toxins secreted by microbes and the organism's defense against them by antitoxins. His diphtheria antitoxin was the beginning of modern serotherapy and earned him the Nobel Prize in medicine (1901) which also was awarded to his teacher (1905).

Other Pioneers in Bacteriology.—The third founder of medical bacteriology was Edwin Klebs (1834–1913) who discovered the diphtheria bacillus (later isolated by Friedrich Löffler, 1852–1915), inoculated anthropoid apes with syphilis, and helped to establish the "empire" of the germ. There followed then a host of discoveries, among them phagocytosis by Metchnikoff; diphtheric toxin by Émile Roux (1853–1933); BCG antituberculosis vaccine by Albert Calmette (1863–1933); plague bacillus by Alexandre Émile John Yersin (1863–1943) and Shibasaburo Kitasato (1852–1931) working independently; the louse's role in petechial typhus by Charles Nicolle (1866–1936); diphtheria bacillus by Klebs and Löffler; antibodies and antigens by Jules Bordet (1870–1961); spirochete of syphilis by Fritz Schaudinn (1870–1934); bacteriology of septicemia by Georg Theodor August Gaffky (1850–1918); bacterial pleomorphism by Theobald Smith. Much successful work was done by David Bruce (1855–1930) and Sir Ronald Ross (1857–1932) on tropical diseases; Albert Neisser (1855–1916) and Augusto Ducrey (1860–1932) on gonorrhea; Flexner and Howard Taylor Ricketts (1871–1910) on Rocky Mountain spotted fever; W. H. Welch on *Staphylococcus albus*, and Jaime Ferran y Clua (1852–1929) on antialpha vaccine. All these achievements gave birth to the concept of biological therapy, based upon strengthening the two defenses of the organism, that is, the antibodies present in serum and the phagocytic action of leucocytes, and fostered the development of drugs that paralyzed or destroyed bacteria (bacteriostasis and bactericides).

Research on tropical diseases made headway with the expansion of the German and British empires into Africa and the Far East, and the causal germs of many tropical fevers, plagues, and dysenteries were discovered. Symbolic of this epic period was the Cuban Carlos Juan Finlay (1833–1915), the Latin American Pasteur, discoverer of the role of the mosquito in the transmission of yellow fever. Finlay's fame was universally acknowledged before he died, and he was crowned with many honors.

The therapeutic arsenal was enriched in the last quarter of the century with such drugs and methods as antipyrine, cocaine, chloral, bromides, sulfonal, antiseptics, X-rays, glandular extracts, immunobiology, and psychoanalysis.

Ehrlich.—Modern chemotherapy began with Paul Ehrlich (1854–1915), who was fascinated by the selectivity of dyes for certain organic tissues. In his institute at Frankfurt am Main, he plunged wholeheartedly into the search for substances with an intense chemical affinity for bacteria but little or none for cells. Modern chemotherapy began therefore as a chromotherapy or therapy by colors and became later a quest for "magic bullets" that would hit the germs and spare the cells. After 605 misfires, Ehrlich worked out an arsenical drug, 606 or Salvarsan, and for the first time an infection (syphilis) was specifically and successfully treated with a chemical compound. Later he developed the less toxic 914 or Neosalvarsan. While modern antibiotics have their roots in Galenic phytotherapy, Ehrlich's chemotherapy goes back to the heavy metals or non-Galenic medications employed by Paracelsus.

Internal Medicine.—Headway was made in internal medicine with the discovery of new physical and neurological signs, increased laboratory data, and the visualization of internal lesions through endoscopy, bronchoscopy, pyelography, biopsy, esophagoscopy, and X-rays. The "revolt" of cellular pathology and of the "democratic-republican" cell against the "aristocratic" mastery of the blood and nerves assisted the spatial, cellular localization of disease, and the concept of these lesions became more dynamic and general and less locational. Medicine became more pathophysiological and physicochemical in its substratum, with the subsequent development of the functional sign, of mensuration, and of the portrayal in charts, tables, and case histories of the course of disease, which was regarded as a measurable, historical, dynamic, and continuous process. The pathophysiological trend in medicine was successfully developed in France by Fernand Widal (1862–1929) and Henri Vaquez (1860–1936); in Germany by Friedrich Theodor von Frerichs (1819–1885), Moritz Traube (1818–1876), Adolf Kussmaul (1822–1902), Adolf von Strumpell (1853–1925), Moritz Heinrich Romberg (1795–1873), Georg Klemperer (1865–1946), and others; in England by Sir William Whitey Gull (1816–1890), Sir Samuel Wilks (1824–1911), Sir Thomas Barlow (1845–1945), and Thomas Clifford Allbutt (1836–1925), inventor of the pocket clinical thermometer; in Italy by Antonio Cardarelli (1832–1927) and Guido Baccelli (1832–1916); and in Spain by José de Letamendi (1828–1897) and Corral.

In pediatrics great progress was registered in pathophysiology, microbiology, congenital diseases, and prevention of ophthalmia. Neurology made headway with Duchenne, founder of the electrological treatment of nervous diseases; with Türck of Vienna in affections of the medullary fasciculi and location of the center of articulated speech; with Paul Broca (1824–1880), Carl Westphal (1833–1890), S. Weir Mitchell (1829–1914), and Nikolaus Friedreich (1825–1882) in hereditary ataxia; with John Hughlings Jackson (1835–1911) in Jacksonian epilepsy, nervous levels in neuropathology, and neurological ophthalmoscopy; and with Jean Martin Charcot (1825–1893), a brilliant speaker and teacher, whose work on hysteria was masterly from a "visual" standpoint though later it was largely replaced by the "auditory" approach of his pupil Sigmund Freud. Work in neurology was greatly supplemented at the beginning of the 20th century by Joseph Jules Dejerine (1849–1917), Pierre Marie (1853–1940), Joseph F. F. Babinski (1857–1932), Carl Wernicke (1848–1905), Sir William Richard Gowers (1845–1915), Charles Dana (1852–1935), Sir Victor Horsley (1857–1916), Sergei Sergeyevich Korsakov (1854–1900), Charles K. Mills (1845–1931), George Beard (1839–1883), George Huntington (1851–1916), William Alanson White (1870–1937), Smith Ely Jelliffe (1866–1945), G.

Lafora, and other noted neurologists.

Psychiatry.—The status of an independent science was acquired by psychiatry. Three German clinicians replaced the romantic mythology of the spirit by an anatomicopathological and clinical picture of the brain: Wilhelm Griesinger (1817–1868), Carl Westphal, and Theodore Hermann Meynert (1833–1892), who correlated the cell architecture of the brain with neuropsychiatric symptoms and nosological entities. The next step was the delimitation of clinical entities in psychiatry by Jean Pierre Falret (1794–1870) and Baron Richard von Krafft-Ebing (1840–1902) and the merger of somatological psychiatry, which considered mental infirmity as a manifestation of a somatic disease (Griesinger; Alois Alzheimer, 1864–1915; Franz Nissl, 1860–1919; Wernicke; Morel), with the descriptive, systematizing, clinical psychiatry of Falret and Emil Kraepelin (1856–1926). Kraepelin's work was the beginning of a scientific nosology in psychiatry, which it systematized and provided with a somatological and metabolic approach. This work was enhanced by the psychological studies of disease conducted by Pierre Janet (1859–1947) and Karl Jaspers (1883–   ); the psychotherapy of James Braid (1795?–1860), Ambroise Auguste Liébault (1823–1904), Josef Breuer (1842–1925), and Hippolyte Bernheim (1837–1919); and the social psychiatry of Benédict Augustin Morel (1809–1873), Jacques Joseph Moreau de Tours (1804–1884), Daniel Hack Tuke (1827–1895), and Dorothea Lynde Dix (1802–1887).

Freud.—In 1890, Sigmund Freud (1856–1939), a Viennese physician, began his overwhelming contributions to medical psychology by changing mental pathology from the visual to the auditory plane ("listening to" neuroses). His highly imaginative work was replete with clinical realism. His main contributions were the diagnostic and therapeutic assessment of human instincts, formulation of the concept of the various unconscious strata in the human mind, interrelationship between mental life and neurovegetative activity, historical integration of the event of the disease into the patient's biography, and the use of dialogue as a diagnostic aid and healing instrument.

Surgery.—Another stirring event in the history of medicine, antisepsis (elimination of infection in operations), occurred in 1867 with the publication by Joseph Lister (1827–1912) of a treatise on the antiseptic principles of operational surgery. Surgery passed through various stages: from the "heroic," to the antiseptic, to the aseptic (prevention of infection), to surgery of regions hitherto inaccessible, to prosthetic and reparational surgery, and lastly to plastic and "physiological" surgery.

The two chief obstacles in the path of surgery were overcome in the 19th century: pain, which demanded speedy operations; and infection, which had made surgery a heroic (extreme) resort. Lister's forerunners were Holmes and Semmelweis. Oliver Wendell Holmes (1809–1894), poet and physician, who studied in Boston and Paris, published in 1843 a paper in which he passionately propounded the view that puerperal fever, which killed thousands of women in childbirth, was contagious and was transmitted from patient to patient by physicians and nurses, and that delivery cases should not be attended by persons who had been in contact with puerperal fever cases or had been doing autopsies.

Semmelweis.—The same conclusion was reached by Ignaz Philipp Semmelweis (1818–1865), who after studying in Vienna and Pest (now a section of Budapest), joined the staff of a hospital in Vienna. He noticed a considerable discrepancy in the mortality rates in two different maternity wards, the one where midwives were trained having the greatest mortality. When a friend of his, accidentally pricked by a student during a necropsy, died of blood poisoning, he concluded that the fingers of the physicians and students attending confinement cases in the ill-starred ward were impregnated with "poisons" from victims of puerperal fever. Semmelweis promptly ordered all physicians and students to disinfect their hands in chlorine water, a measure that immediately reduced the mortality rate.

Lister.—Joseph Lister (1827–1912), son of a wine merchant, took his degree in London and practiced in Edinburgh, where he was professor of surgery. At that time it was still believed that contused injuries must suppurate, but Lister asked himself why simple fractures where the skin remained intact did not suppurate, and arrived at the conclusion that, in compound fractures, the air, which Pasteur had proved contained germs, contaminated the contused tissues. Hence, either the germs must be destroyed or the wound must be protected against them. Lister disinfected with carbolic acid both the air and the wounds, which he then occluded with a carbolic acid dressing. His method met with astonishing success and "Listerism" became generally accepted. Antisepsis was followed by asepsis, that is, chemical and physical methods of disinfection, chemical disinfection being reserved for the air and wounds and physical disinfection for instruments and wound dressings.

Other Leading Surgeons and Developments.—Among the great surgeons of this period were Charles Emanuel Sédillot (1804–1883), Joseph François Malgaigne (1806–1865), and Auguste Nélaton (1807–1873), in France; Bernhard von Langenbeck (1810–1887) and Theodor Billroth (1829–1894) in Germany; Paget and Sir Jonathan Hutchinson (1828–1913), Horseley, and Sir William Arbuthnot Lane (1856–1943) in Great Britain; Samuel David Gross (1805–1884), Henry Jacob Bigelow (1786–1879), Rudolph Matas (1860–1957), the Mayo brothers (William J., 1861–1939, and Charles H., 1865–1939), George Washington Crile (1864–1943), Harvey Cushing (1869–1937), and Alexis Carrel (1873–1944) in the United States; Emil Theodor Kocher (1841–1917) in Switzerland. Chloroform and ether anesthesia was replaced by local anesthesia (Carl Koller, 1857–1944) and by infiltration (Paul Reclus, 1847–1914), intraspinal (August Bier, 1861–1914; James L. Corning, 1855–1923; Matas; Co-Tui), endoneural (Crile, Cushing), sacral, venous, and arterial anesthesia (José Goyanes Capdevila, 1876–   ). Developments took place also in abdominal surgery (Billroth), thoracic and nerve surgery (Cushing), and endocrine surgery (Kocher, Jacques Louis Reverdin, 1842–1928). Exemplary surgeon of this period was Theodor Billroth, who operated on more than 8,000 patients in his Zurich clinic and investigated wound infections, correlating them with clinical temperatures. He published a memorable treatise on surgical pathology (*Allgemeine chirurgische Pathologie und Therapie*, 1863), and in Vienna spurred the progress of gastrointestinal surgery.

Headway was made in obstetrics and gynecology with the improvement of instruments and the vaginal approach in surgery (Sir Thomas Spencer Wells, 1818–1897; Ephraim McDowell, 1771–1830). Ophthalmology advanced with the invention of the ophthalmoscope in 1850 by Hermann von Helmholtz (1821–1894), and the practice of iridectomy (Albrecht von Graefe, 1828–1870); and otology progressed with the otoscope (Anton Friedrich von Tröltsch, 1829–1890), the otological speculum (Wilhelm Kramer, 1801–1876), and studies on the labyrinthine nystagmus (Robert Bárány, 1876–1936) and vertigo (Prosper Menière, 1799–1862). The laryngoscope was invented in 1855 by Manuel García and first used by Johann Nepomuk Czermak (1828–1873) and Türck. The bronchoscope was introduced by Chevalier Jackson, Sr. (1865–1958). Rhinology had its start with Czermak's rhinoscope. Surgical urology improved (Jean Casimir Félix Guyon, 1831–1920; Joaquin Albarrán, 1860–1912), as well as orthopedics and plastic surgery.

AMERICAN MEDICINE

In the second half of the 18th century, medical schools had been set up in the American colonies as medical departments in the universities. With the expansion of the United States westward in the 19th century, medical schools, without scientific tutelage, sprang up everywhere. Medical reform was initiated by the medical bodies of the universities and by the state governments as a result of national medical conventions held in 1846 and 1847 and the General Congress of Physicians, held in New York City in 1845, which laid down the requisites for grants of medical diplomas; and in 1847 the American Medical Association was born. Soon after, the state governments passed special legislation for medical schools, and Johns Hopkins University was opened in 1893, admitting only college graduates with a year's scientific training. The year 1908 saw the beginning of the great reform in medicine under Abraham Flexner.

Philadelphia was the leading center of medicine, followed closely by Boston, where Benjamin Waterhouse (1754–1846), a professor at Harvard University Medical School, introduced vaccination in 1800, using it on his son and later receiving the support of Thomas Jefferson. The third great medical center was New York, illuminated by Samuel Bard (1742–1821), George Washington's physician, and David Hosack (1769–1835). Pierre Louis in Paris trained many American physicians, including Alfred Stille (1813–1900), William Pepper (1810–1864), William W. Gerhard (1809–1872), Elisha Bartlett (1804–1855), Henry Ingersoll Bowditch (1808–1892), the public health pioneer, and the surgeon John Collins Warren (1778–1856). Surgery reflected the brilliance of Sims, Bigelow, Valentine Mott (1785–1865), and Gross, with the Midwest contributing the clinical studies of Austin Flint, Sr. (1812–1886), the work of Daniel Brainard (1812–1866) on surgery, and the work of Daniel Drake (1785–1852) on medical geography and medical education. Contributions by the United States to medicine in this period were the discovery of anesthesia, and the development of gynecologic surgery and gastric physiology.

Among the great pioneers in American medicine was John Morgan (1735–1789), who studied under William Hunter in London and Morgagni in Padua. He raised medicine to the rank of a university subject and organized the Philadelphia

School of Medicine, where years later the first medical diplomas were granted. He was the teacher of Benjamin Rush (1745?–1813), whom he preceded in the chair of practical and theoretic medicine. In his later years Rush was a revered figure in clinical medicine. A pioneer in occupational therapy in psychiatry, a great lecturer and abolitionist, a signer of the Declaration of Independence, he embodied the ideals of the Encyclopedists of the Enlightenment. Another famous physician was Ephraim McDowell in Kentucky, who, without anesthetics, performed the first resection of an ovarian cyst after carrying the patient on horseback on a journey lasting several winter days.

Another trail-breaking physician of the period was Daniel Drake of Kentucky, who studied under Rush, practiced in Cincinnati, and held the first chair in materia medica at Transylvania University, Lexington, Ky., the first medical school west of the Alleghenies. Realizing that the expansion westward required a medical geography and a larger education system, Drake traveled west and compiled a masterpiece on medical geography (*A Systematic Treatise . . . on the Principal Diseases of the Interior Valley of North America . . . ,* 2 vols., 1850–54). His contemporary, William Beaumont (1785–1853), learned medicine as apprentice to a physician, was licensed in Vermont, and served as army surgeon at Fort Mackinac, on Michilimackinac (Mackinac) Island, Mich., where over a period of nine years through 238 experiments, he studied a young Canadian trapper with a permanent gastric fistula caused by a blunderbuss shot.

Samuel Guthrie (1782–1848), an unlicensed physician and a pioneering chemist, discovered "sweet whisky" or chloroform in his rustic laboratory at Sacketts Harbor, N.Y., in 1831. Later it was used in obstetrics by the Scottish physician James Young Simpson. A great contribution was also made by the physician Samuel D. Gross (1805–1884), professor of pathology in Cincinnati, who published a valuable treatise of more than 1,000 pages on this subject (*Elements of Pathological Anatomy,* 1839).

Another great surgeon was J. Marion Sims (1813–1883), who studied in Philadelphia and settled in Montgomery, Ala., where he cured the dreaded vesicovaginal fistula—the first time this had been accomplished by surgical means.

A younger contemporary of Oliver Wendell Holmes, S. Weir Mitchell (1829–1914), poet, writer, and pupil of Claude Bernard, rendered numerous contributions to neurology. He initiated the rest cure and fattening diet in nervous diseases and wrote a series of "psychiatric" novels. A contemporary of his was John S. Billings (1838–1913), an army surgeon and medical director who participated in the Civil War and pioneered in building the largest medical library in America. Billings, with the assistance of Robert Fletcher (1823–1912) and the medical historian Fielding H. Garrison (1870–1935), founded the Surgeon General's Library (now the National Library of Medicine) in Washington, D.C., and started the library's monthly publication *Index Medicus.*

Towering above all was the Canadian, Sir William Osler (1849–1919), physician, researcher, humanist, philosopher, philanthropist, professor at McGill University in Montreal, Canada, and the universities of Pennsylvania, Johns Hopkins, and Oxford, and author of the most famous modern textbook on internal medicine (*Principles and Practice of Medicine,* 1891) and of a score of works on the blood platelets, multiple telangiectasis, erythema multiforme, and other subjects. Osler was the modern ideal of a kind, great physician and teacher.

10. MEDICINE IN THE 20TH CENTURY

The years of the 20th century include the atomic age, which began in 1945, and the space age, initiated in October 1957 with man's first attempt to conquer outer space.

Technical inventions and discoveries came fast in this century, among them the airplane (Wright brothers, 1903), radio (Lee De Forest, 1907), splitting of the atom (Ernest Rutherford, 1919), radar (A. Hoyt Taylor and Leo C. Young, 1922), television (John L. Baird, 1926). Progress in therapeutics had no parallel in the past. World population greatly increased, creating many social problems.

The natural sciences were propelled forward by Max Planck's quantum theory, which holds that the emission of light by radiant bodies is caused by indivisible explosions. Thus atoms were replaced by quanta or energy charges, and matter became discontinuous, like energy, and was reduced to a series of probability waves. This was followed by Albert Einstein's theory, which revolutionized the concepts of space and time just as the quantum theory upset our ideas on matter and energy. Matter now is considered a pocket in space and time, a flurry of electric charges, a probability wave rolling through the void of space. We accept atomic physics and speak of the space-time continuum, the discontinuity of matter, the identity of matter and energy, finite space, time relativity, a curved four-dimensional universe, and motion of matter by energy jumps.

Physics has become a basic principle in the technicalization of medicine, for medicine has switched from bacteriological and microchemical analysis to that of the atoms, and now studies bacteria and viruses under the electron microscope, as well as biochemical lesions, collagen diseases, and the hyaluronidase system. Modern diagnostic methods include electrophoresis and microspectrophotometry, the electrocardiogram in unison with electroencephalography and electromyography, and descendent pyelography in unison with intracardiac catheterization, ventriculography, stratigraphic radiography, or tomography.

Chemistry has become integrated with physics, with the progress in organic syntheses and the elucidation of chemical structures, catalytic actions and chain reactions, isotopy and nuclear chemistry. Biology has discovered intracellular entities such as viruses, genes, and microsomes, and is investigating whether viruses are living creatures, cell fragments, or microbial chemical seeds. Anatomy has been influenced by the notion that form is function. Modern methods of deep-freezing cadaver sections, anatomical cinematography, vascular injection, and the electron microscope have created a new physiological approach to anatomy. Physiology is now chiefly biochemical, studying hormonal functional interrelations, electrolytes, the neurovegetative system, and enzymes, with greater concentration on the adrenal-pituitary-hypothalamic system. Experimental psychology has prospered with Gestalt psychology (Wolfgang Köhler, 1887– ; Kurt Koffka, 1886–1941), phenomenological psychology (Karl Jaspers), and other psychologies. Outstanding figures, pupils of Freud, were Alfred Adler (1870–

1937, inferiority complexes) and Carl Gustav Jung, (1875–1961, collective unconscious, psychological types, and the "individuation" process). Anthropology has been spurred by the discovery of anthropoid fossil remains, and by research on blood groups and the Rh factor.

Outstanding is Hans Selye's (1907–) *stress* theory or concept of a syndrome of generic adaptation in response to nonspecific agents that produce cortico-adrenal hypertrophy, thymico-lymphatic involution, and intestinal ulceration. Cortico-adrenal hypertrophy, basic in this syndrome, is provoked by pituitary corticotropic hormones (ACTH) and somatotropic hormones (STH).

The physician's functions in modern society progress every day, from *healing* (helping the sick), to *knowing* (creating the picture man has of himself), to *preventing* disease, and to *rehabilitating* the patient. This has reduced mortality and increased life expectancy. Diseases "from without" (infection, intoxication, and traumatism) have diminished, while those "from within" (degeneration, stress, mental, incubatory, and circulatory diseases) have increased.

Medicine has become teamwork, and the physician requires the aid of countless technicians, and often examines his patients before they become ill (preventative medicine, q.v.). The bedside physician and the family doctor are being replaced by a physician who is at once scientist, educator, social worker, counselor, and statesman. Social health insurance and welfare schemes have increased, turning the relationship between physician and patient to a service under contract.

Outstanding contributions to medicine of the first half of the 20th century have occurred in vitamins, antibiotics and chemotherapeutics, endocrinology, surgery, psychiatry, and the "new" medical specialties.

Vitamins.—In 1900, Richard Willstätter (1872–1942) synthetized proline. In 1906, Sir Frederick Gowland Hopkins (1861–1947) demonstrated the existence of nutritional factors, and six years later he published the results of his research on the nutritional substances which that same year Casimir Funk (1884–1967) called "vitamins" (vital amines). The existence of deficiency diseases was then established. In 1913 research teams at the University of Wisconsin (Elmer V. McCollum, 1879–1967, and Harry Steenbock, 1886–1967) and at Yale (Thomas B. Osborne, 1859–1929 and Lafayette B. Mendel, 1872–1935) discovered vitamin A; in 1915 vitamin B was discovered, and in 1922 vitamin D. Later the antirachitic effect of ultraviolet light was shown to be produced by activation of a provitamin D. Other memorable events in this field were Mueller's discovery of methionine in 1922, the isolation of carotene in 1929, of the pure form of vitamin D₂ in 1932, of vitamin E in 1936, and of nicotinic acid in 1937; the discovery of pyridoxine or vitamin B₆ in 1938; and in 1948 the isolation of the active principle in liver, vitamin B₁₂. Nutritional science became enriched with the knowledge that the amino acids are the basic blocks with which the structure of protein molecules in the body is built. Noteworthy also are the use by George R. Minot (1885–1950) in 1926 of raw liver in pernicious anemia, and the new approach in the treatment of tropical diseases such as sprue and kwashiorkor.

Cancer.—Research in cancer is a combination of simultaneous activity in medical, biological, and physical fields, which may lead to early diagnosis and eradication of many of the malignancies such as skin and uterine cancer. Also being studied are the metabolism of cancerous cells and methods of arresting their growth by means of radioactive isotopes and nitrogenous mustards. Radioactive isotopes with a specific affinity for thyroid cancer, veritable "atomic-guided missiles," such as radioactive iodine, have been developed. We also have radioactive phosphorus, which slows down the development of leukemia, radioactive gold "seeds" for cancer of the tongue, and radioactive isotopes with "directional, built-in anticancer antennae" or antimetabolites.

Surgery.—Advances in surgery during the 20th century are astounding, stimulated by the two world wars and by modern locomotion and occupational accidents. Today the surgeon works as much with his brain as with his hands. Having no longer to fight against time, he tries to make his work "physiologically" perfect, reducing as much as possible psychological, nutritive, and surgical traumata in the patient. Pre- and postoperative preparation now has three objectives: to prevent infection, to eliminate pain, and to maintain a normal metabolism. Operations are based on a far more accurate diagnosis, depending as much on X-rays and laboratory tests as on clinical examination. Anesthetics are adapted to each type of operation. Antibiotics prevent infection; antihemorrhagic or anticoagulent agents prevent blood changes; and vitamins, fluids, amino acids, and mineral salts prevent dehydration and malnutrition. Physiotherapy promotes recovery and rehabilitation. New types of scalpels, sometimes smaller than a fingernail, are employed, and there are special lighting methods, electronic and radar devices for pinpointing organic processes, radioactive tracers, ultrasound, and fibrinolytic enzyme agents such as plasmin, which are true "chemical scalpels." There are heart-lung machines, artificial kidneys, and other artificial organs. Improvements in plastic, otological, and ocular surgery are notable, while those in cardiac surgery are spectacular. Surgery even contributed to neurology with the discovery by Wilder Graves Penfield (1891–) that electrical stimulation of the temporal lobes can expose zones in the cerebrum where stored memories, obliterated from the conscious mind, can be vividly revived under direct electrical stimulation.

New Instruments and Methods.—Among the new instruments and methods introduced in medicine and surgery are: Jackson's esophagoscope (1902); Einthoven's electrocardiograph (1903); Mackenzie's bullet detector (1915); Benedict's portable basal metabolism apparatus (1918); the arthroscope (1922); cholecystography by Evarts A. Graham and Warren R. Cole (1924); Busch's electron microscope (1926); Berger's electroencephalograph (1929); Schindler's gastroscope (1932); Starr's ballistocardiography (1939); E. C. Padgett's dermatome (1938); and O'Brien and McKinley's cyclone knife or microtome (1943).

Other spectacular achievements in surgery have been the first radical operation for treatment of uterine cancer by Ernst Wertheim (1900); Matas' endoaneurysm suture and Alexis Carrel's arterial end-to-end anastomosis (1902); Hugh H. Young's radical operation for prostatic cancer (1904); the frozen section method for surgical biopsies by Louis B. Wilson of the Mayo Clinic; Alfred Einhorn's spinal anesthesia with Novocain (1905); the abdominoperineal technique for operation of rectal cancer by William Ernest Miles of London (1907); continuous drip intravenous infusion by Matas (1911); the first valvotomy for relief of chronic constriction of the aorta by Theodore Tuffier (1914); resection of the pericardium in chronic adhesional pericarditis by Claude S. Beck (1924); the first total pneumonectomy for treatment of lung cancer by Evarts A. Graham (1933); leucotomy by Egas Moniz (1935); aorta resection (1944); and the transplant of kidneys and hearts in the 1960's.

Striking was the introduction in surgery of artificial hibernation, first employed by Simpson in 1905, revived in 1951 by Henri Marie Léon Laborit (1914–) and Pierre Huguenard, at first to potentiate anesthesia chemically in surgery, and later to produce a total neurovegetative block accompanied by induced hypothermy. For this purpose they used a "lytic cocktail" which had a neuroplegic effect, and which contained phenothiazine, promethazine, pyridosal, and neurovegetative hypnogenics and analgesic drugs, a concoction that "started the pituitary and adrenal endocrine couple off on a chemical holiday."

Remarkable has been the development of analgesics, whether narcotic, like morphine, or non-narcotic. For several years the salicylates were the model forms of non-narcotic analgesics. Later, a whole range of this type of drug was discovered, from aspirin to hydroxyphenylcinchonic acid, and from phenylbutazone to cortisone. Lately, more derivates and members of the morphine family have been developed, such as codeine, dihydromorphinone, and methylmorphine, as well as drugs having no direct relationship to morphine: meperidine, methadone, and alphaprodine.

Endocrinology.—A few of the events in endocrinology in the 20th century will suffice to give an idea of its vertiginous development: Joseph Babinski's and Alfred Fröhlich's report (1900 and 1901) on adiposogenital dystrophy; isolation of adrenalin from the adrenals by Jokichi Takamine (1901); discovery of intestinal "secretin" by Sir William Maddock Bayliss and Ernest Henry Starling (1902); preparation of a racemic adrenalin by Friedrich Stolz (1904) and Henry Drysdale Dakin (1905); isolation of pure thyroxin by Edward C. Kendall (1914); Starling's hormone theory, comparing them to "chemical messengers" in the blood (1905); isolation and employment of insulin by Sir Frederick G. Banting and Charles H. Best (1921); isolation of parathormone (parathyrin) by James B. Collip (1925); synthesis of thyroxin (1926); liver given in the treatment of anemia (1926); isolation of the gonadotrophic pituitary hormone by Selmar Aschheim and Bernhard Zondek; production of cortin; ovarian extracts containing sterone (1928); first extract of adrenal cortex (1929); research on pituitary basophilic adenoma (1932); isolation of progesterone (1934) and testosterone (1935), and of cortisone (1935) by Mason, Myers, and Kendall; discovery of the estrogenic action of stilbestrol (1938); isolation of adrenocorticotropic hormone (ACTH) by Choh Hao Li, Herman M. Evans, and Miriam E. Simpson, and by George Sayers, Abraham White, and Cyril Norman Hugh Long (1943); Kendall's E-compound or 17-hydroxy-11-dehydrocorticosterone (1945); prednisone and prednisolone (1954).

Antibiotics.—The discovery of antibiotics is perhaps the most revolutionary event in the history of medicine. The antibiotic age, which began in 1939–1940 with the work of René Dubos (1901–), Ernest B. Chain (1906–), and Sir Howard Walter Florey (1898–1968), and Selman Waksman (1888–), is the modern fruit of Pasteur's achievements in bacteriology, Lister's prophylactic chemotherapy against septic wounds, and Ehrlich's scientific chemotherapy. In 1922, Harold Raistrick (1890–) began the study of metabolic products which were secreted by molds and antimicrobial in their effect. Later, Dubos discovered thyrotricin and learned how to interfere with microbial metabolism.

Penicillin.—Penicillin was the result of an accident interpreted by genius. In 1928 Sir Alexander Fleming (1881–1955) noticed that some *Staphylococcus* cultures had been contaminated and destroyed by air-borne molds. From these fungal growths Fleming isolated a pure culture of *Penicillium notatum*, from which he extracted an active antimicrobial substance that he named penicillin. Some 12 years later, the Australian Sir Howard Walter Florey and his colleagues at Oxford University, Chain, Fletcher, Gardner, Heatley, and Jennings, working on Fleming's penicillin extract, improved its culture, extraction, and purification. The year 1941 saw the publication of clinical results with penicillin, which established the great bacteriostatic effect of penicillin and its low toxicity.

Other Discoveries.—The list of important discoveries in chemotherapy since 1900 is impressive: in 1908, P. Gelmo synthetized sulfanilamide; in 1910, Paul Ehrlich discovered Salvarsan; in 1917, Jay McLean isolated heparin, useful in thrombosis prevention; in 1921, Maurice C. Hall discovered that carbon tetrachloride eradicates *Ancylostoma* (hookworm); in 1935, Gerhard Domagk discovered the antimicrobial effects of Protonsil, a sulfanilamide derivate active against hemolytic streptococcus; in 1937, Merrit and Putnam discovered diphenylhydantoin, effective against erysipelas; in 1938, Sir Lionel Ernest Howard Whitby discovered sulfapyridine, effective against pneumonia; in 1940, Perrin H. Long introduced sulfathiazone in the United States, and Richard O. Robin found sulfadiazine effective in epidemic cerebrospinal meningitis; in 1941, H. R. Link and his coworkers isolated dicoumarin, a synthetic substitute for heparin; in 1943, Hoffman discovered LSD-25; in 1944 Waksman discovered streptomycin; in 1945, Balbina Johnson and her associates discovered bacitracin; in 1946, F. M. Berger and W. Bradley reported the efficacy of mephenesin as a muscular relaxant; in 1947, P. R. Burkholder discovered chloramphenicol; in 1948, Benjamin M. Duggar discovered chlortetracycline; in 1950, A. C. Finlay and a team of 10 others discovered oxytetracycline; B. J. Ludwig and E. C. Piech isolated meprobamate (1950), which was later developed by Berger; in 1952, J. M. Maguire and others isolated erythromycin, J. M. Mueller and others isolated reserpine, and C. R. Stephens and others discovered tetracycline; in 1954, B. A. Sobin and others discovered oleandomycin, R. Harned and E. Kropp discovered cycloserine, and isoniazid was introduced in the treatment of tuberculosis.

The Division of Antibiotics of the United States Department of Health, Education and Welfare tests and controls over 500,000 pounds of penicillin yearly. Similar control is exercised over another 2,000,000 pounds of the other antibiotics vital to public health. Exacting clinical studies have been directed by Dr. Chester S.

Keefer to determine the efficacy of penicillin and streptomycin. Antibiotics have greatly reduced postoperative infections, particularly in war casualties, have caused a decrease in the death rate from civilian accidents and traumatisms, and have diminished absenteeism in industry.

Antibiotics are changing medicine in its three facets: clinical, by compelling physicians to use new techniques and materials; research, by opening up new philosophical horizons on diseases, their prevention and treatment; and educational, by modifying the natural history of infections, their epidemiology and medical geography, and hence the university curriculum. Antibiotics are limiting the field of certain medical specialties. Urology and otorhinolaryngology, for instance, are beating a retreat before the antibiotic offensive, and even surgery has been forced to adopt a more conservative attitude.

Psychiatry.—One of the greatest medical tasks of the 20th century is to understand the nature of mental diseases. The new physiodynamic psychiatry has made three great contributions to our age: (1) it has integrated soma and psyche in clinical psychiatry and in the biochemical, endocrine, and metabolic approaches of psychiatric etiopathogenesis; (2) it has introduced the biographical factor, so vital in prognosis and in case histories; and (3) it has introduced biochemical and chemotherapeutic agents in psychiatric diagnosis and therapies. This last group includes the study of phenomena such as biochemical and endocrine changes in schizophrenia, hallucinogenics like mescaline and lysergic acid diethylamide (LSD) which create "pocket psychoses," adrenalin byproducts in the organism of schizophrenics, hormone balance, changes of the tricarboxylic cycle in cerebral metabolism, adrenal changes in psychosis, brain lipoproteins, hypothalamic and reticular formation functions, cerebral circulation, oxygen consumption, nerve tissues and their hormones, and the activities of the adrenal-hypothalamus-pituitary axis.

Eliminating such symptoms as agitation, hallucinations, and negativism, which make the mental patient "different" from other patients, restoring communication with the patient who is isolated as if on a walled island by his malady, and treating the mental patient like any other patient—are the great aims of modern psychiatry.

Psychoanalysis has made striking contributions to medicine by turning the spoken word into an exploratory and therapeutic instrument. It has also confirmed that instincts are qualitatively alike and that their alterations are quantitative. Furthermore, it has helped to individualize the study of mental disease.

Psychosomatic and psychobiographical medicine were developed by Georg Walther Groddeck (1866–1934), considered by some its father; by Lodolf von Krehl (1861–1937), who tried to integrate the natural sciences and those of the mind into a medical anthropology; and by Viktor von Weizsäcker (1886–1957) and Richard Siebeck (1883–) in Heidelberg, who developed medical "biography." This work was completed when the psychiatrist-philosopher Karl Jaspers classified diseases into "biological" and "biographical," and when Helen Flanders Dunbar (1902–1959), Stewart G. Wolf (1914–), made the psychobiological unity triumph over Cartesian dichotomy.

New Techniques.—Psychiatric therapy has advanced under the double aegis or organicistic conceptions of the etiology of mental diseases and the physiodynamic approach to their therapy. Presiding over psychiatric progress have been such investigators as Santiago Ramón y Cajal (1852–1934), Ivan Pavlov (1849–1936), and Sir Charles Scott Sherrington (1857–1952), and more recently Ugo Cerletti (1877–1963), Klaesi, Ladislas Joseph Meduna (1896–), Egas Moniz (1874–1956), Manfred Sakel (1900–1957), and Roy G. Hoskins (1880–1964). Therapeutic advances have been closely followed by neuropsychiatric advances, including the concepts of the central nervous system as a stimulus-conducting network subdivided into animal and vegetative branches, the neuron as a anatomico-functional unity, the hypothalamus, and the reticular formation.

Somatotherapies, born out of the new concepts on psychoses, are empirical methods of treating mental diseases by physiotherapy, chemotherapy, and psychosurgery. In 1933, Manfred J. Sakel of Vienna (later of New York) reported having treated psychoses by inducing a state of coma with insulin injections. The next year, Ladislas Joseph Meduna of Budapest (later of Chicago) reported having treated psychoses by producing convulsions with cardiazol injections. In 1935, Egas Moniz of Lisbon reported a successful leucotomy (lobotomy), thus creating a new specialty—psychosurgery. In 1938, Ugo Cerletti and Lucio Bini (1908–) of Rome announced their new electroshock treatment (ECT).

To the above must be added the achievements attained in endocrine and biochemical therapies by Hoskins, Finn Rudd, Max Reiss, Jacob Bernhard Jacobowsky (1893–), Ernest Danziger (1871–1930), the Sackler-van Ophuijsen-Creedmoor group, and others.

In their pioneering explorations of histamine, sex steroids, and thyroid substances as biochemotherapeutic agents, the Sackler-van Ophuijsen-Creedmoor group (New York) formulated a physiodynamic theory of the etiology and pathogenesis of the functional psychoses and demonstrated the relationships between endocrinology and psychiatry. This view permitted them to predict in 1949 that ACTH and cortisone would produce a psychosis when administered to certain patients, and enabled them to demonstrate a quantitative blood test to differentiate psychotic from nonpsychotic patients. It also led to the elucidation of sex differences in thyroid and thymus function.

New Drugs.—Perhaps the most revolutionary development in psychiatry today is the use of hallucinogenic and ataractic drugs. In 1943, A. Hoffman of Basel accidentally gave himself a "pocket" psychosis by ingesting some lysergic acid diethylamide (LSD). Also, mescaline and other drugs were studied. While this work was in progress, Rustom Jal Vakil, of King Edward VII Memorial Hospital, Bombay, India, had since 1940 been using in thousands of hypertension cases *Rauwolfia serpentina,* an ancient Indian root, and finally published (1949) his experiences with this drug, now called "reserpine," in the *British Heart Journal* (1949). Robert W. Wilkins (1906–), director of the Hypertension Clinic at Massachusetts Memorial Hospital, used *Rauwolfia* during 1950–1952 and reported on its sedative effect before the New England Cardiovascular Society (1952). The tranquilizing effect of *Rauwolfia* on mental patients was confirmed by Raymond Harris (1919–) of Albany Medical College in 1953.

Meanwhile, in France, research on antihistaminics had led to the discovery at the Rhône-Poulenc Laboratories of RP 4560, with which Mme. Courvoisier in 1951 cured experimentally induced anxiety in rats, and Laborit in 1952 cured anxiety in pregnant women. The same year Jean Paul Louis Delay (1907–) employed it successfully against mental disorders. This drug, chlorpromazine, reached the United States and Canada soon afterward, and Lehmann, Himwich, Ayd, Kinross-Wright, Winkelman, and others introduced it with success. All these drugs, which Howard Fabing and Cameron called ataraxics, belong to the family of the indoles, piperidines, amphetamines, and antihistamines. Their effect is to produce ataraxia, leaving the patient *ataraktos,* with peace of mind. They are among the most promising therapeutic drugs in psychiatry.

Scientific Research.—In the present century scientific research is a new tool for the exploration of the universe. In 1901 the Rockefeller Institute for Medical Research, where Simon Flexner (1863–1946) worked, was founded, fulfilling Francis Bacon's dream of a house of science. In 1902 the John McCormick Institute of Infectious Diseases, Chicago, and the Carnegie Institute of Washington were founded, and in 1913 the Henry Phipps Psychiatric Clinic of Baltimore. The greatest step forward in scientific research was the establishment of the great research laboratories: the Pasteur Institute, Paris; the Robert Koch Institute and the Paul Ehrlich Institute, Berlin; the Kitasato Institute for Infectious Diseases, Tokyo; Oswaldo Cruz Institute, Brazil; Lister Institute, London; and the Rockefeller Institute, New York.

Various fields of disease, the most important of which is cancer, have been investigated by American foundations, and the United States government has poured millions of dollars into a giant screening program for anticarcinogenic substances. Other problems under investigation have been maternal, fetal, and infantile mortality, arteriosclerosis and hypertension, cholesterol and fat metabolism, blood coagulation, hematic enzymes, and the dynamics of arterial tension. Rheumatism, alcoholism, and tuberculosis have been attacked with mass radiological examinations of entire populations and antibiotic treatment; whole populations have been treated in various parts of the world with penicillin in a mass attempt to eradicate yaws, syphilis, bejel, and similar infections; virus diseases, including the common cold and virus pneumonia, are under investigation as is cell permeability. The conquest of poliomyelitis with Jonas E. Salk's (1914–) vaccine has kindled the hope that other virus diseases may also be vanquished.

History of Medicine.—The history of medicine owes its progress to the dedicated efforts of the great medical historians of the century. Among these are: in German-speaking countries, J. H. Bass, Max Neuburger, Karl Sudhoff, Paul Diepgen, and Max Meyerhof; in France, C. A. E. Wickersheimer, Laignel-Lavastine, J. Vinchon, and P. Guiart; in Italy, David Giordano, Aldo Mieli, P. Capparoni, A. Castiglioni, L. Belloni, and A. Pazzini; in England, T. Clifford Allbutt, Charles Singer, W. Langdon-Brown, J. D. Rolleston, Sr., H. Rosseston, Douglas Guthrie (Edinburgh), and E. Ashworth Underwood; in Denmark, E. Gotfredsen; in Spain, E. García del Real, G. Marañón, and P. Laín Entralgo; in Portugal, L. de Pina and A. Silva Carvalho; in Rumania, V. Gomoiu; in Belgium, J. Tricot

Royer and Sondervorst; in Turkey, Suheyl Unver. Latin America has contributed: H. Valdizan, Juan Lastres, and C. Paz Soldán in Peru; A. Ruiz Moreno in Argentina; C. Martínez Durán in Guatemala; Díaz González in Venezuela; F. A. Flores and J. J. Izquierdo in Mexico; I. da Vasconcellos in Brazil; R. Pérez de los Reyes, H. Abascal, and C. Rodríguez Expósito in Cuba.

In the United States, from 1765 onward, the great physicians of the Philadelphia Medical School, Rush, Morgan, and Shippen, lectured regularly on the history of medicine. The first professor of medical history in the United States was Robley Dunglison (editor of the *American Medical Intelligencer,* now the *International Record of Medicine*), appointed in 1825 to the University of Virginia at the instance of Thomas Jefferson, then rector of the university. In 1876, John Shaw Billings was appointed lecturer in the history of medicine at Johns Hopkins University, and his work was completed by the Johns Hopkins Medical History Club and the "big four" of that hospital, Halsted, Welch, Kelly, and Osler. Great impetus was given to this subject by Fielding H. Garrison's *Introduction to the History of Medicine* (1913). Outstanding was the work of the beloved Paris-born Henry E. Sigerist (1891–1957), the greatest medical historian of all time, professor and director of the Institute of the History of Medicine, Johns Hopkins University. In his work he was ably assisted by John Rathbone Oliver, Owsei Temkin, Ludwig Edelstein, Erwin H. Ackernecht, Sanford V. Larkey, C. D. Leake, Genevieve Miller, and Edward E. Hume. Others came later: John F. Fulton, Arnold C. Klebs, E. C. Streeter, Richard Shryock, Ralph Major, G. W. C. Corner, Benjamin Spector, J. J. Walsh, E. R. Long, E. C. Kelly, David Riesman, Walther Riese, George Rosen, G. Arrington, Victor Robinson, I. Galdston, G. Zilboorg, Logan Clendening, George Urdang, A. A. Moll, Chauncy Leake, and George Sarton.

New Specialties.—New specialties are based on individual organs (as in cardiology), therapeutic methods (surgery), and environmental factors (tropical and industrial medicine). To this last category belong aeronautical and aerocosmic medicine.

Aeronautical medicine was initiated at the end of World War I for the purpose of helping in the conquest of outer space by relating medicine to astrophysics. Aerocosmic medicine studies man in flight through cosmic space in jet-propelled rockets and satellites. Military centers for aerocosmic medicine were first established in the United States in the late 1940's. Vehicles for flight in interplanetary space must be pressurized and air-conditioned and protected against cosmic rays and meteorites. Great technical problems must also be solved, such as acceleration, deceleration, spatial optics, decompression, and weightlessness, as well as reactions to thermic and mechanical interactions with the atmosphere when crossing the sound and heat barriers, psychological problems due to confinement within the rocket, the physiological day-and-night cycle, engine-generated gases, nutrition, excreta disposal, and human reactions to cosmic radiations, pressures, tensions, and temperatures.

Another new specialty is atomic medicine, which employs radioactivity to destroy diseased or necrosed human tissues. Among its devices are: the atomic pistol, which shoots radioactive gold "bullets" into cancerous tumors; injections of radioisotopes in solution; radioactive lamps to train radioactive cobalt rays on cancerous tissue only; radioactive iodine given orally in the form of "atomic cocktails," it being possible to measure with a Geiger counter the radioactive iodine absorbed; and direct exposure of the patient to radioactivity from a nuclear reactor.

Travel medicine was introduced at the First International Symposium on Health and Travel held in New York City in May 1955; discussions were devoted to principles of medicine, psychology, medical ecology, and medical geography to enable physicians to advise travelers of all ages, healthy or sick, on nutrition, clothing, psychological environmental adjustment, and strains and stresses encountered in journeys to strange places.

The progress achieved in medical geography, industrial and business medicine, military and naval medicine, and cybernetic medicine is rivaled only by that in international medicine due to two great organizations, the World Health Organization, which studies problems of world health and seeks to improve health standards, and the World Medical Association, a federation of medical associations.

Trends and Perspectives.—Medical research grows ever more distinguished for its advances in accuracy and speed of diagnosis. Auxiliary laboratory techniques have bridged the gap between clinical diagnosis and etiological diagnosis. Research is every day more a matter of teamwork.

Interest in geriatrics is increasing now that man's average life span has been extended by antibiotics and other life-prolonging drugs. The average span of social activity must also increase, for it is now considered that the retirement age of 65, normal in the past, is too early.

Correlation between psyche and soma is vitally important. Mind and body are now indissolubly welded together in the study of disease. Medicine is showing more interest in geosocial and financial conditions which may help to understand the sick more intimately, and is also intervening in world politics in an effort to prevent war, promote understanding between nations, solve economic problems due to food shortages or endemic plagues, and help mankind in its quest for well-being and happiness. Medicine is also being integrated with other sciences, especially physics, chemistry, engineering, and mathematics.

In the field of medical practice, medicine is concerned not with diagnosis, as in the past, but with healing, and in doing this quickly. Preventive medicine has been growing in importance, and prevention will in fact be the main objective of the medicine of the future. The great number of preventive techniques and medications available will make this objective all the easier to attain.

Medicine in its practical aspects has become universal, thanks to international medical organizations and to the fact that campaigns against epidemics know no frontiers. Medicine is becoming increasingly concerned with maintaining man's health. Health is now accepted as an active dynamic process involving, not the absence of disease, but the existence of a state of physical and mental well-being. Rehabilitation of the diseased is more than ever of vital importance, and this suggests the present status of medicine as a social science. The practice of medicine is based more and more on health centers and the socialization of medicine. Another sign of the times is woman's ever-increasing participation in medicine. In the field of medical education, medicine has adopted new audio-visual instruction methods based on radiotelephone, television, radar, and other devices. Although medical learning has been organized into increasingly specialized subjects, it is once more turning to medical humanism by studying the history of medicine as a facet of the history of civilization. Noteworthy is the increasing participation of the people in public health and their growing interest in medical problems, implying that the physician's role as a social counselor is increasing day by day. In particular we must not overlook the impact of medicine on 20th century art and culture, for this may be the beginning of the humanistic medical philosophy of the future.

Bibliography.—Garrison, Fielding H., *An Introduction to the History of Medicine*, 3d ed. (Philadelphia and London 1921); Osler, Sir William, *The Evolution of Modern Medicine* (New Haven 1921); Singer, Charles J., *The Evolution of Anatomy* (New York 1925); Sigerist, Henry E., *The Great Doctors*, tr. by Eden and Cedar Paul (New York 1933); paper reprint (New York 1958); Laignel-Lavastine, Maxime, *Histoire générale de la médecine*, 3 vols. (Paris 1936–1949); Robinson, Victor S., *The Story of Medicine* (New York 1931); rev. ed. (Philadelphia 1943); Guthrie, Douglas J., *A History of Medicine* (Philadelphia, London, and Toronto 1946); Castiglioni, Arturo, *A History of Medicine*, 2d ed., tr. by Edward B. Krumbhaar (New York 1947); Mettler, Cecilia C., *History of Medicine* (Philadelphia 1947); Sigerist, Henry E., *History of Medicine: Vol. 1, Primitive and Archaic Medicine* (New York 1951); Laín Entralgo, Pedro, *Historia de la medicina*, vol. 2 (Barcelona 1954); Major, Ralph H., *A History of Medicine*, 2 vols. (Springfield, Ill., 1954); Martí-Ibáñez, Félix, *Centaur: Essays on the History of Medical Ideas* (New York 1959); Martí-Ibáñez, Félix, ed., *Henry E. Sigerist on the History of Medicine* (New York 1960); Roemer, Milton I., ed., *Henry E. Sigerist on the Sociology of Medicine* (New York 1960).

FÉLIX MARTÍ-IBÁÑEZ, M.D., *Professor and Chairman of the Department of the History of Medicine, New York Medical College, Flower and Fifth Avenue Hospitals, New York City; Editor in Chief of "MD Medical Newsmagazine."*

MEDICINE DANCE, among American Indians, a dance conducted by the medicine men of the tribe for various purposes and in preparation for different events, such as warfare and the hunt. Both in the dance before a battle and in the conflict itself the medicine chief was the one man worthy of consideration. He would court the thick of the fight, if for no other reason than to show his immunity from danger.

The funeral dance of the Yaqui tribe of Mexico was a representative example of the medicine dance. The chief medicine man arranged the ceremony, which ensured the safe passage of the dead to the spirit world. The dancers, as many as 50, appeared in the center of the assembled tribal gatherings, naked except for loin cloths. Their bodies were painted in imitation of skeletons; over their heads they wore masks fringed with long horsehair, dyed in many hues, with eyelashes and eyebrows hanging over the rudely designed faces and beards reaching nearly to the waist. On their legs they fastened strings of rattles cut from rattlesnakes, and the sound of these was most gruesome to the spectators. Each dancer carried two knives, with which he gesticulated violently in imitation of the act of slaying imaginary enemies.

MEDICINE HAT, city, in the Province of Alberta, Canada, on the South Saskatchewan River, about 94 miles northeast of Lethbridge.

It is in a high, dry area (elevation 2,185 feet; precipitation variable but frequently below 12 inches) originally devoted to ranching and dry farming but now coming under gradual improvement by irrigation under a joint scheme of the Dominion and provincial governments. It is important also as a railway center, being a divisional point on the main line of the Canadian Pacific Railway where the Crow's Nest line branches off into southern Alberta and southeastern British Columbia. It was to the coming of the railway in 1883 that the town owed its birth. It is also on the Trans-Canada Highway and has a Trans-Canada airport with daily flights. The early discovery of one of the largest of known natural gas fields underlying the district, the product being almost pure methane, gave industry an immediate impetus. ("Medicine Hat has all hell for a basement" was a comment of Rudyard Kipling when present at the "blow-off" of a new well in 1902.) There are also large deposits of lignite in the vicinity. Flour and feed milling, grain elevators, foundries, lumber mills, and machine shops are located here.

The city handles the gas supply as well as its own water filtration and electric power and lighting systems. It has three business colleges, in addition to public and high schools and an academy. There are 22 churches, a hospital, a daily and weekly newspaper, a radio station, four banks, a chamber of commerce, and an industrial commissioner. The early population was recruited from Ontario, the Maritime provinces, and Great Britain, with a small infusion of Russo-Germans.

The curious place-name "Medicine Hat" is a translation of the Blackfoot Indian word "saamis" meaning the headdress of a medicine man. Various explanations of its application have been offered, several based on Indian legends, and one on the shape of a hill east of the town. A generally accepted one is that of a fight in which a Cree medicine man lost his professional headgear to a Blackfoot in the river. This and other local folklore, including the region of the Cypress Hills to the southeast —a rendezvous of the Cree and Blackfoot Plains Indians as well as of the Sioux under Sitting Bull after the defeat of Custer—have been collected in a brochure by F. W. Gershaw, a member of the Canadian Senate. Pop. 25,574.

Consult Wilfred Eggleson's *High Prairie*.

MEDICINE MAN, among the American Indians, South Sea Island tribes and other peoples, a man supposed to possess mysterious healing powers. Among most of them the medicine man occupies much the same position as that held in civilized communities by two of the learned professions—medical and clerical. The medicine man is both priest and physician, and is at once the repository of all that a tribe knows, fears and believes. In very low stages of human development, however, he is at best only a magician, dealing in terrors, possessed of occult powers, but laying claim to no special medical knowledge. Thus, among the aborigines of north Queensland, the tribal doctors do not attend the sick, an invalid being cared for by wife or mother. They are not ostentatious, a medicine man being distinguished by no insignia save a small bag for his talismans, death charms and other "credentials." Among the North American Indians medicine men are treated with great respect, and form a secret society with exclusive privileges and "exercise a terrible influence in degrading the people." It is curious to find that, as in Australia, the Indian medicine men are chiefly concerned to do positive harm. In cooperation with good and bad spirits, they bring about the deaths of men or dogs at a distance. Among the Ojibways they are a kind of broker in vengeance, and a coward or a hypocrite who wishes to be covertly avenged upon an enemy will bribe his tribal medicine man to employ the medical attendant of his victim. Then, if the victim dies, the instigators remain unsuspected, and the actual perpetrator of the crime probably goes scot free. Indian medicine men affect to suck out poison from a patient's body, or they cough up an arrow point or small, sharp piece of stone or bone which they suppose has been transferred from him to them by the evil spirit of another sorcerer. The medicine men of the Eskimos are even more extravagant in their pretensions. They profess themselves able to change into wood, stone or animal, or even to walk on the water, or to fly, but they make a condition, which is that "no one must see them."

MEDICINES. See CHEMICAL INDUSTRIES —*Pharmaceuticals;* DRUG TRADE.

MEDILL, mĕ-dĭl′, **Joseph**, American journalist: b. near St. John, New Brunswick, Canada, April 6, 1823; d. San Antonio, Tex., March 16, 1899. Having early removed to Massillon, Stark County, Ohio, he was admitted to the bar in 1846, practiced at New Philadelphia, and in 1849–1851 published at Coshocton the *Republican,* a Free-Soil paper. In 1852 he established at Cleveland the *Daily Forest City,* a Whig organ, which in 1853 was united with the *Free Democrat* and called the Cleveland *Leader.* In 1855 he sold his interest in the *Leader,* removed to Chicago, with two partners purchased the Chicago *Tribune,* advocated radical antislavery measures and supported Lincoln in 1860. He was a member of the Illinois constitutional convention of 1870; United States civil service commissioner in 1871 and in that year was elected mayor of Chicago. In 1874 he became editor in chief of the Chicago *Tribune,* in which position he remained until his death. It was largely due to his individual efforts that the city of Chicago was selected for the World's Fair of 1893.

MEDINA, mĕ-dē′nà, **Harold Raymond,** United States jurist: b. Brooklyn, N. Y., Feb. 16, 1888. Educated at Princeton University (A.B. 1909), he went on to Columbia Law School and gained his bachelor of laws in 1912. In the same year he was admitted to the New York bar and became associated until 1918 with the law firm of Davies, Auerbach and Cornell. From 1918 to 1947 he was senior member of the firm of Medina and Sherpick, and taught at Columbia as lecturer in law (1915–1917), associate in law (1917–1925), and as associate professor of law (1925–1947). As a practicing lawyer he was counsel for Herbert Singer, the only defendant acquitted during the trial of officials of the Bank of the United States (1931), and he successfully defended Anthony Cramer in the first treason case decided by the United States Supreme Court (1945). As both judge and lawyer he shared in effecting numerous reforms in court procedure.

In 1947 Medina was appointed by President Truman as judge on the United States District Court, Southern District of New York, and from January to October 1949 he presided over the nine-month trial of 11 Communists charged with and later convicted of conspiracy to teach and advocate the overthrow of the United States government by force and violence. In June 1951 the Supreme Court upheld the jury's conviction of the Communists as well as Medina's handling of the trial and the sentences he imposed. On June 11, 1951, he was appointed to succeed Judge Learned Hand (q.v.) on the U. S. Circuit Court of Appeals for the Second Circuit.

A prolific author and compiler in the field of law, Medina's works include: *Pleading and Practice Under New Civil Practice Act* (1922); *Cases on Federal Jurisdiction and Procedure* (1925); *Cases on New York Pleading and Practice* (1928); *Selected New York Practice Statutes* (1928); *Cases and Materials on Jurisdiction of Courts* (1931); *Medina's New York Civil Practice Manual* (1932); *Digest of New York Statute and Law* (1941); and *Summary of New York Pleading Practice and Evidence* (1941).

MEDINA, Sir **John Baptist,** Spanish portrait painter: b. Brussels, 1659; d. Edinburgh, Scotland, Oct. 5, 1710. The son of a Spanish officer who had married and settled in Brussels, then under Spanish rule, Medina studied painting in his native city under François Duchâtel. In his youth he married at Brussels Joanna Maria van Dael who bore him many children. Going to London in 1686 he established himself as a portrait painter, quickly gaining a reputation and many noble sitters. Two years later, one of his patrons, the munificent third earl of Leven (David Melville, 1660–1728), induced him to settle in Scotland; a subscription of £500 was collected to enable him to practice in Edinburgh. Accordingly he moved there with his large family. The antiquary George Vertue tells that he brought with him from his London studio "many postures for heads, the draperys painted—only to put the faces to them, cover'd them over with water-colours." By these mass production means he managed to paint a considerable number of paintings in a short time. He received so many commissions from the Scottish nobility that he was called "the Kneller of the North." He painted 20 portraits for the earl of Leven, including three of the earl himself. In Surgeons' Hall of Edinburgh's Royal College of Surgeons are several portraits of fellows of the college. The duke of Queensberry, as lord high commissioner of Scotland, knighted Medina in 1707, he being the last man in Scotland to receive that honor before the passage of the Act of Union the same year. He is also remembered for his drawings illustrating the Jonson edition of Milton's *Paradise Lost,* done during a visit to England in 1705. One of his sons, John (d. 1764), also practiced as a portrait painter, as did the latter's son John (1721–1796).

MEDINA, José Maria, Central American politician: b. Honduras, about 1815; d. Santa Rosa, Feb. 8, 1878. He was president of Honduras from 1862 to 1863, and was re-elected in 1864–1866 and in 1870. The war with Salvador in 1871 disturbed his successful administration and at the next election he was defeated by the

Liberal Party. Defeated again by Leiva in 1874 Medina raised an unsuccessfull revolt in 1875–1876 and in 1877 a second revolt was punished with death by court martial.

MEDINA, José Toribio, Chilean bibliographer, scholar and author: b. Santiago de Chile, Oct. 21, 1852; d. 1930. He received his education at the National Institute and the University of Santiago, being graduated in law at the latter institution in 1873. At the age of 22 he was appointed secretary of legation at Lima. In that city he made investigations in the archives and in 1878 after his return to Chile he published a history of Chilean literature. Already in 1874 he had published a metrical translation of Longfellow's *Evangeline.* In the War of the Pacific, Medina served in the army and at the close of the war was made judge in the provinces ceded by Peru. He was made secretary of legation at Madrid in 1884 and here also he delved into the Spanish archives dealing with the Spanish in America and especially the history of Chile. He returned to his native country after several years' residence in Europe. He went abroad again in 1902 and also visited the United States to make further historical studies. Medina's great work is the *Biblioteca hispanoamericana, 1493–1810,* 7 vols. (1898–1907), which contains notices of 10,000 works.

MEDINA, Vicente, Spanish poet: b. Archena, Murcia, 1866; d. 1936. Of humble origin, he earned wide fame after publication in 1898 of his *Aires murcianos* which profoundly influenced the character of regional poetry in Spain and Spanish America. He was not interested in mere depictions of the picturesque, or of physical and social aspects of an environment. He strove, rather, to capture the soul of the people through delineation of emotional conflicts and elemental human qualities.

MEDINA, mĕ-dē′nà (Arab. AL-MADINA), city, Arabia, 500 miles southeast of Palestine, 210 miles north of Mecca and about 120 miles from the Red Sea coast. It is reached from Damascus by an 820-mile railway journey. The city is celebrated for containing the tomb of Mohammed, whence it ranks second to Mecca as a pilgrimage resort of Islam. It is situated in the most fertile spot of all Hejaz, the streams of the vicinity tending to converge in this locality. An immense plain extends south from it; in every direction the view is bounded by hills and mountains. The town forms an oval, surrounded by a strong stone wall, 30 to 40 feet high, that dates from the 12th century, and is flanked with towers, while on a rock, at its northwest side, stands the castle. Of its four gates, the Bab-al-Salām, or Egyptian gate, is remarkable for its beauty. Medina has no large buildings except the great mosque, two smaller ones, a college and public baths. The houses are of stone, two stories high. Beyond the walls of the city, west and south, are suburbs consisting of low houses, yards, gardens and plantations. These suburbs have also their walls and gates. The mosque of the prophet stands at the east side of the city and resembles that at Mecca on a smaller scale. Its court is almost 500 feet in length, the dome is high and the three minarets picturesque. The tomb of the prophet, who died and was buried here in 632, is enclosed with a screen of iron filigree, at the south side of which the pilgrim goes through his devotions. The tombs of Fatima (Mohammed's daughter), abu-Bakr (first caliph, father of Mohammed's wife Aisha), and Omar I (the second caliph) are also here. The tombs of Mohammed and the others originally adjoined the mosque, which was rebuilt by Caliph Walid I (r. 705–715) to include them. The enlarged mosque was gutted by fire in 1256, shortly before the end of the Arab caliphate, and a virtually new building was erected after another fire in 1481.

The city was known as Yathrib until 622, when Mohammed fled here from Mecca (the Hegira) and made it his capital, calling it al-Madīnah (the city). It remained the seat of the Muslim caliphate after his death until 661, when the caliphs transferred their capital to Damascus. In 1517, Medina was acquired by the Turks, and it remained under their control until 1916, when the independent Arab kingdom of Hejaz (incorporated in Saudi Arabia in 1932) was formed. Pop. (1958 est.) 50,000.

MEDINA, mĕ-dī′nà, village, New York, in Orleans County, 30 miles northeast of Buffalo and 11 miles south of Lake Ontario. Located on the Barge Canal and the New York Central Railroad, at an altitude of 542 feet, in an agricultural area known for its high-grade dairy herds, it has fruit and vegetable canneries, furniture and textile factories, foundries, and machine shops. It was incorporated in 1832. Government is by mayor and council. Pop. 6,681.

MEDINA, city, Ohio, Medina County seat, 18 miles west of Akron. It is located at an altitude of 1,085 feet, in a diversified farm area (fruit, poultry, dairy products), and is served by the Baltimore & Ohio and the Akron Canton & Youngstown railroads and an airport. Its manufactured products include apiary supplies, aluminum castings, furnaces, toys, and candles. Platted in 1818, it was originally called Mecca. Government is administered by a mayor and council. Pop. 8,235.

MEDINA ANGARITA, mä-thē′nä äng-gä-rē′tä, **Isaías,** Venezuelan soldier and statesman: b. San Cristóbal, Táchira, Venezuela, July 6, 1897; d. Caracas, Sept. 15, 1953. Graduated from the Venezuelan Military Academy (1914), he was named army chief of staff and minister of war and navy by President Eleázar Lopez Contreras in 1936. In 1941 he succeeded the latter as president, instituting a program of moderate democratic reforms and pro-Allied foreign policy during World War II. He was overthrown in a coup by the left-of-center Acción Democrática in October 1945, and lived in exile in the United States until late in 1952.

MEDINA-SIDONIA, mä-thē′nä-sê-thō′nyä, 7TH DUKE OF (ALONSO PÉREZ DE GUZMÁN), Spanish admiral: b. Sept. 10, 1550; d. 1615. A descendant of the hero Alonso Pérez de Guzmán (q.v.) and a favorite of King Philip II, he was put in command of the Spanish Armada against England in 1588 (see ARMADA), despite his lack of naval experience and against his own wishes. The Armada suffered humiliating defeat, but Medina-Sidonia was retained as admiral. He was beaten again by the English at Cádiz (1596) and later by the Dutch off Gibraltar (1606).

MEDINA-SIDONIA, city, Spain, in Cádiz Province, Andalusia, about 20 miles east of Cádiz. Situated on a plateau in a wide plain where grain and livestock are raised, the city has flour mills, tanneries, and potteries. The ancient palace of the dukes of Medina-Sidonia (created 1445) and a Gothic cathedral are noteworthy buildings. Nearby are caves containing prehistoric paintings. Pop. (1950) 14,889.

MEDITATIONS OF MARCUS AURE-LIUS, The, mĕ-dĭ-tā′shŭnz, mär′kŭs ô-rē′lĭ-ŭs, the private memoranda of the Roman emperor Marcus Aurelius Antoninus (r. 161–180), who called these collected self-communings simply *To Himself* (*Ta eis heauton*). It is not known how this priceless monument was preserved. It is in Greek, out of devotion to the Greek Stoic philosophers, whose precepts had inspired the emperor. The work consists of notes couched in simple, straightforward style, compiled at such intervals as Marcus Aurelius could seize from his preoccupation with administrative and military matters to record his thoughts on the meaning of life and on how life should be lived.

The *Meditations* is not a book of confessions, but of careful examinations of conscience. It is the dramatic story of the soul of a man, taking counsel with himself, observing his own shortcomings, and exhorting himself, in the words of St. Paul, to think on "whatsoever things are true, . . . honest, . . . just, . . . pure, . . . lovely, . . . of good report" (Philippians 4:8). The work is prized as a document about one of antiquity's great philosophers, who resisted the temptation to write a reasoned treatise on ethics, preparing these notes with homely illustrations and apt quotations from philosophers, only for his own perusal when in a meditative mood. As a stimulus to thought and moral principles, it is "almost equal in ethical elevation to the Sermon on the Mount," according to John Stuart Mill, and has comforted and confirmed thousands of readers.

The *Meditations,* divided into 12 books by an early editor, is so much of a medley, except for the first book, that it is difficult to summarize satisfactorily each book's content. However, the emphasized themes appear to be these: book i, on lessons learned from persons who have influenced the author; book ii, on doing what we do; book iii, on obedience to God as evidence of true freedom; book iv, on the nonexistence of chance; book v, on life's real goods; book vi, on the supreme importance of the inner life; book vii, on suppressing impulse and on seeking self-content; book viii, on equanimity; book ix, on fate guiding the willing person; book x, on looking around, behind, and before oneself; book xi, on unselfishness; book xii, on departing life with satisfaction and without fear of death.

The *Meditations* has been translated into many modern tongues. Over 200 printings have been published in Great Britain alone since 1634, the date of its first appearance in English. The "authorized version"—so to speak—is George Long's translation, *The Thoughts of the Emperor Marcus Aurelius Antoninus* (London 1862), reprinted many times on into the 20th century, from which most English-reading persons know the words of Marcus Aurelius. The most convenient Greek text with English translation on opposite pages is by Charles R. Haines, *The Communings with Himself by Marcus Aurelius Antoninus, Emperor of Rome . . .* (London 1916). See also

MARCUS AURELIUS ANTONINUS—*Bibliography*.
P. R. COLEMAN-NORTON,
Princeton University.

MEDITATIONS POETIQUES, mā-dē-tȧ-syôn′ pô-ā-tēk′, the first book of poems by Alphonse de Lamartine, published March 11, 1820. In the *Méditations poétiques,* France was given not only another masterpiece but a warning of a coming literary revolution. Then only a salon celebrity, Lamartine had been working since 1816 on these poems, reciting them to friends in Paris. The slim volume of 24 poems, issued anonymously in an edition of 500, became an overnight sensation, partly because of the generous backing of a royalist press that approved the traditionalism and Catholicism of the author. However fresh the poems seemed to readers, they had been built on well-worn formulas. Much was in the *style noble,* and the themes were far from new; the verse bristled with sentimental Rousseauisms or clichés like the dying poet and the languorous heroine. To some critics it seemed another collection of odes and elegies that betrayed a cosmopolitan variety of influences, including Petrarch, Ossian, Edward Young's graveyard poetry, James Hervey's *Meditations and Contemplations,* and the vicomte de Parny. However, though basically classicist in composition and style, the poetry came from a man who found inspiration in his own experience and that of an uneasy generation still suffering from the *mal du siècle* that had followed the Napoleonic epic. Much of it sprang from Lamartine's tragic love affair with Mme. Julie Charles, who died of consumption in 1817, barely a year after he had met her.

Infused with melancholy and a pervading religiosity, the book was a moving and intense revelation of an individual's difficulties in adjusting to the frustrations of human existence. Unlike the merely virtuoso attempts of most poets of the preceding century, the fluid verse sounded resonantly musical. Women wept in reaction to its heavy charge of emotion. Appearing after the long drought of neoclassical versifying, the *Méditations* encouraged contemporary young poets to seek material within their own experience, to exploit the possibilities of the individual and the particular rather than dull generalities. Though Lamartine never belonged to any literary school, he inaugurated a literary revolution with the *Meditations* by indicating to the romanticists new directions that their poetic genius might take.

ALBERT J. GEORGE,
*Chairman, Department of Romance Languages,
Syracuse University.*

MEDITERRANEAN FRUIT FLY, mĕd-ĭ-tĕ-rā′nē-ȧn (*Ceratitis capitata*), a small black, brown, and yellow fly with pictured wings, belonging to the dipterous family Trupaneidae or Tephritidae. The males are readily recognized by the presence of a pair of bristles, strongly broadened at the apex, which are found on the front near the top of the head. The fly is a very general feeder and a most serious pest of fruits in tropical and subtropical regions of the Old World. It was discovered in a large area of the citrus belt in Florida early in 1929, and plans were immediately made for its extermination. Teams of entomologists scoured Florida to learn its distribution and the identity of its numerous food plants. Citrus and other fruits in the infested area were destroyed; wild citrus trees and other fruits in the area were eliminated. After a period of about three years, and at a cost of $6 million, the state was declared free of the "Medfly." A second outbreak occurred in 1956 but was quickly brought under control by airplane spraying of chlorinated hydrocarbon insecticides.

C. H. CURRAN.

MEDITERRANEAN SEA, a great inland sea of the Eastern Hemisphere, almost entirely enclosed by the continents of Europe, Asia, and Africa. It extends from longitude 5° 21′ W. to 36° 10′ E.—a distance of 2,320 miles. Its maximum breadth is 1,080 miles; its area, more than 1,140,000 square miles (including the Black Sea). The Strait of Gibraltar connects it with the Atlantic Ocean; the Dardanelles, the Sea of Marmora, and the Bosporus connect it with the Black Sea, which is a part of its natural basin; and the Suez Canal connects it with the Indian Ocean through the Red Sea. It is bounded on the north and northwest by Europe, on the south by Africa, and on the east by Asia. Its southern coast is comparatively level, with few good harbors, chief of which is the double harbor at Alexandria, Egypt. The northern coast is rugged and broken with long peninsulas, deep bays, gulfs, and numerous islands, and has many splendid harbors. The shore line of the Mediterranean is slightly more than 14,000 miles.

Hilty from Monkmeyer

One of the most famous islands in the Mediterranean Sea, Capri has beautiful scenery and a very pleasant climate.

Several names are given to the divisions of the Mediterranean, including the Levantine Sea in the east, the Aegean Sea, Ionian Sea, Adriatic, Tyrrhenian Sea (immediately west of Italy), and Balearic Sea. Its chief islands are the Balearics, Sardinia, Corsica, Sicily, Rhodes, Crete, Malta, and Cyprus. The Nile is the largest river emptying into it. Other principal rivers are the Ebro (Spain), the Rhone (France), and the Po (Italy).

Michael Short from Pix

Like most of the northern shores of the Mediterranean Sea, the coast of Corsica is rugged and irregular.

The Mediterranean has been called the world's most international sea, and its history records the endless struggle of many peoples for possession of its shores, which today are divided among almost 20 countries. It was the cradle of navigation, seaborne commerce, and international trade in the West, and from its peninsulas and islands came many pervasive and enduring elements in the civilization of the Western World—laws, art, literature, architecture, and the impulse for exploration.

The landlocked Mediterranean is practically tideless, although on parts of the African coast a rise of six feet sometimes occurs. In depth, the variation is great. The maximum is 14,401 feet in the eastern basin south of the Peloponnesus in Greece, and 12,216 feet in the western basin east of Sardinia. Its shallowest part is between the Sicilian coast and Cape Bon (Tunisia), where it is between 180 and 1,510 feet in depth. The surface temperature of the water is uniformly higher than that of the Atlantic, and the depth temperature is very much higher.

There is a strong current from the Black Sea, and because the evaporation in the Mediterranean is greater than in the Atlantic, a constant flow of surface water comes from the ocean. There is, however, a very deep and strong current which flows in the opposite direction, that is, from the sea to the ocean. This current is found at a depth of about 1,000 feet, and carries *out* a volume of water *less* than that brought *in* by the surface current from the ocean. Evaporation compensates for the difference. Due to great differences in temperature the vertical movement of the water is also marked, particularly in the eastern portion. In summer the prevailing winds are the Northeast Trades, while in winter the winds are mostly westerly.

More than 400 species of fish inhabit the Mediterranean, but not nearly so many useful kinds as are found in British and Scandinavian waters. The sea abounds in red coral, particularly on the coasts of the Balearic Islands, Sicily, Tunis, and Tripoli. The sponge, tunny, and sardine are important products of some of the coasts.

The present Mediterranean is but a small fragment of the sea which during the Jurassic and Cretaceous periods covered Syria, Palestine, and much of Egypt, Arabia, and Asia Minor, stretching eastward over what are now the Caucasus and Himalaya Mountains to the Pacific Ocean. In the early part of the Tertiary period, extensive portions of the bottom of this sea were lifted up and

became land. The movement was extremely slow.

So far as it has been explored, the floor of the Mediterranean shows more ruggedness than that of the Atlantic or Pacific oceans. Scientists are seeking through a series of cores taken from the bed of the sea to settle controversial problems concerning its history and that of the surrounding land. Long cores obtained from the floor off Algeria provide a record of volcanic activity through thousands of years, including great prehistoric eruptions of which we know nothing. The shores also abound in evidence of volcanic action, as in the still active volcanoes of Etna, Vesuvius, and Stromboli.

HAROLD F. BRANCH,
Archaeologist; author of "The Untrodden Way."

MEDIUM, in biology. See BACTERIA AND BACTERIOLOGY—*Laboratory Studies of Bacteria.*

MEDIUM, in spiritualism. See SPIRITUALISM.

MEDIUM, The, opera in two acts by Gian-Carlo Menotti (q.v.), with libretto by the composer, commissioned by the Alice M. Ditson Fund of Columbia University, where it was first sung (Brander Matthews Hall), May 8, 1946. The action occurs "in our time," in a parlor rigged up for "spiritualist" séances. According to the composer, *The Medium* "describes the tragedy of a woman caught between two worlds, a world of reality which she cannot wholly comprehend, and a supernatural world in which she cannot believe."

Monica, the daughter of the medium Baba ("Madame Flora"), is attracted by the mute boy Toby, her adopted brother; both are used by Baba in producing fake spirit messages and materializations. While Baba is heartlessly deceiving a bereaved couple with "messages" from their dead infant son, she feels a cold hand at her throat. Terrified, she tries to explain her deceptions to her victims, who wishfully refuse to believe her, insisting that the hand she felt was that of a spirit. Convinced that the mute boy has tried to kill her, Baba beats him and orders him from the house. She sinks into a drunken sleep. When Toby returns, seeking his beloved Monica, Baba revives, whereupon he conceals himself behind the curtains covering a cabinet. Seeing the curtains move, Baba seizes a revolver, shoots at them, and fatally wounds Toby, saying over and over "I've killed the ghost!" Heartbroken, Monica kneels beside Toby's body, looking searchingly into his eyes. Although Menotti is an intensely controversial figure, most critics unite in considering both the libretto and the score of *The Medium* his most considerable achievement.

HERBERT WEINSTOCK.

MEDJIDIEH, Order of. See DECORATIONS AND ORDERS—*Turkey.*

MEDLAR, měd'lẽr, the common name for a fruit tree, *Mespilus germanica,* of the rose family (Rosaceae), native from southern Europe to Persia and naturalized in central Europe and England. It is sometimes planted in the northeastern United States. The tree is 15 to 25 feet tall, often of twisted, twiggy growth, with oblong or elliptical leaves up to 5 inches long. The large, solitary white flowers appear in the spring. The small fruit is spherical, and differs from the pear in that the receptacle does not grow over the ovaries. When mature in the fall, the fruit is hard and bitter and is set aside until incipient decay softens and mellows it, when it may be eaten raw or made into preserves.

RICHARD M. STRAW.

MEDOC. See WINE.

MEDULLA OBLONGATA, mē-dŭl′à ŏb-lŏng-gā′tà, is the part of the brain stem which intervenes between the pons Varolii and the spinal cord. It is a very old part of the nervous system, judged from the standpoint of evolution. In it are located important centers that govern the activities of the heart, respiration, phonation, and to a considerable extent the functions of the gastrointestinal tract.

The medulla presents a truncated conical form, about one inch in length and two fifths to three fifths of an inch in thickness. It is round in outline caudally (toward the spinal cord) but flattens laterally as it approaches its junction with the pons Varolii. Its internal configuration, caudally, closely resembles that of the spinal cord, but from below upward greater and greater changes take place in its internal appearance, bringing about a gradual approximation of the internal structure of the medulla to that of the pons Varolii.

Four cerebral nerves make their exit from or entrance into the medulla. These are the 12th or hypoglossal, the 11th or spinal accessory, the 10th or vagus, and the 9th or glossopharyngeal nerves. The 8th or auditory nerve enters the brain stem at the pontomedullary sulcus, the line of demarcation ventrally and laterally between the pons and medulla; the 7th or facial nerve enters and leaves the brain stem at this point also. A considerable part of the first spinal nerve originates in the ventral gray matter within the lower portion of the medulla.

The anatomical structure of the medulla is exceedingly complicated. The chief pathway for volitional control over the muscles is provided by the pyramidal tracts, which enter the ventral portion of the medulla cephalically as the pyramids. As they descend, the pyramidal tracts in great part cross from one side to the other (the decussation of the pyramidal tracts), maintaining a lateral position in the spinal cord. Because of this decussation, lesions situated in the right side of the brain and upper brain stem cause a paralysis of the muscles of the left side of the body, and vice versa.

Immediately rostral and dorsal to the decussation of the pyramidal tracts, large masses of gray matter, connected with the central gray matter of the medulla, form in the dorsal white column to provide relay stations for the fibers of the medial and lateral spinomedullary tracts. The fibers arising from these cells proceed ventrally around and through the gray matter of the medulla and cross to the opposite side, forming the decussation of the medial (medullary) lemniscus (fillet), and proceed as the medial lemniscus upward to enter the thalamus of the side of the brain stem opposite to their origin. These masses of gray matter, which provide the relay in the spinal medullary tracts, consist of the nucleus gracilis medially and the nucleus cuneatus laterally. The fibers relayed in these nuclei conduct the discriminative (touch, position, movement, and posture) types of sensibility of the contralateral extremities and side of the body. The medial lemniscus is joined in the midbrain by the spinothalamic tracts (spinal lemniscus or fillet). These spinothalamic fibers have already crossed throughout almost the entire length of the spinal cord to the side opposite that of their entry, and conduct the affective (pain and temperature) types of sensibility. The crossing of the fibers of the medial (medullary) and spinal lemnisci provides the explanation for the fact that one side of the brain receives the great majority of impressions of all types from the opposite side of the face, body, and limbs.

The change in the appearance of the internal portion of the medulla is also materially modified by the appearance of new masses of gray matter constituting the lateral nucleus of the medulla and the medullary olives (inferior olivary nuclei, chief and accessory). These nuclei are closely associated with the cerebellum, both anatomically and functionally, but their exact significance is not clearly understood. See also BRAIN, ANATOMY OF.

Bibliography.—More detailed descriptions of the gross and microscopic appearance of the medulla oblongata can be obtained from Tilney, Frederick, and Riley, Henry Alsop, *The Form and Functions of the Central Nervous System* (New York 1938); Riley, Henry Alsop, *Atlas of the Basal Ganglia, Brain Stem and Spinal Cord* (Baltimore 1943); Mettler, Frederick Albert, *Neuroanatomy* (St. Louis 1948); and Ranson, Stephen Walter, *The Anatomy of the Nervous System* (Philadelphia 1953).

HENRY ALSOP RILEY, M.D.,
Professor Emeritus of Clinical Neurology, College of Physicians and Surgeons, Columbia University.

MEDUM, mē-dōōm′, town, Egypt, in Beni Suef Province, on the Nile River, about 20 miles northeast of Faiyûm. Medûm is the site of the pyramid of Snefru, first king of the 4th dynasty (r. 2614–2591 B.C.). Pop. (1947) 5,627.

MEDUSA. See GORGON.

MEDUSAE. See JELLYFISH.

MEDWALL, mĕd′wôl, **Henry,** English interlude writer: d. after 1500. Educated for the church at King's College, Cambridge, he became chaplain to John Cardinal Morton sometime after the latter was named archbishop of Canterbury in 1486. Of his two surviving works, the earlier is probably the interlude *Nature,* an allegory in the characteristic morality-play manner, distinguished for the realistic handling of its subject. More important is the interlude *Fulgens and Lucres,* the earliest truly secular play known in English and the first to have a love theme. It was first produced at Lambeth Palace, London, in 1497 at a banquet given by Archbishop Morton for the ambassadors from Spain and Flanders. The only known complete copy, printed by John Rastell between 1513 and 1519, is in the Huntington Library at Pasadena, Calif. The story is based on a dialogue printed by William Caxton in 1481, translated from the *De nobilitate controversia* (1428) of Buonascorso. It tells of Lucres, a Roman senator's daughter, whose hand is sought by two suitors, one rich and idle, the other poor but virtuous. The latter is finally successful. The play has a comic subplot in which the valets of the suitors are rivals for the affection of Lucres' maid.

MEDWAY, mĕd′wā, town, Massachusetts, in Norfolk County, on the Charles River, 22 miles southwest of Boston, at an altitude of 185 feet.

An industrial community served by the New York, New Haven and Hartford Railroad, its chief manufactured products are woolen textiles, shoes, and needles. Settled in 1657, it was set off from Medfield in 1713. Pop. 5,168.

MEDWAY RIVER, river, England, about 70 miles long, rising in the Ashdown Forest area of Sussex. It flows north into Kent, turns east at Tonbridge, passes Maidstone, and below Rochester forms a 12-mile estuary which joins the Thames estuary at Sheerness.

MEDWIN, mĕd'wĭn, **Thomas,** English author: b. Horsham, Sussex, England, March 20, 1788; d. there, Aug. 2, 1869. He was a cousin of Percy Bysshe Shelley, and a schoolfellow of Shelley's at Sion House, Brentford. After serving in the army for several years, Medwin resigned his commission and in the fall of 1821 went to Italy, where Shelley introduced him to Lord Byron at Pisa. Medwin kept notes of their talks, which he later published as *Journal of the Conversations of Lord Byron* (1824). The book, translated immediately into French and German, caused much controversy, some critics accusing Medwin of inaccuracy, others maintaining that Byron had falsified facts. Medwin's *Memoir of Percy Bysshe Shelley* (1833) was later expanded into *The Life of Percy Bysshe Shelley* (2 vols., 1847). He also translated the *Agamemnon* of Aeschylus into English verse (1832), and wrote *The Angler in Wales, or Days and Nights of Sportsmen* (2 vols., 1834) and the novel *Lady Singleton, or the World As It Is* (3 vols., 1843).

MEEHAN, mē'ăn, **Thomas,** American botanist: b. Potter's Bar, near London, England, March 21, 1826; d. Philadelphia, Pa., Nov. 19, 1901. Brought up on the Isle of Wight, where his father was an expert gardener, he began experiments in horticulture as a boy, producing a new race of fuchsia through hybridization, and publishing articles on his discoveries. In 1848 he emigrated to America, and a year later became superintendent of Bartram's Garden at Philadelphia, where he made a special study of trees which resulted in the publication of his first book, *The American Handbook of Ornamental Trees* (1853). He then opened his own nursery business in Philadelphia. Meehan edited the *Gardener's Monthly* (1859–1887), established *Meehan's Monthly* in 1891, and for many years was agricultural editor of *Forney's Weekly Press.* Elected to the Philadelphia Common Council in 1882, he furthered the formation of the City Parks Association and the establishment of many small parks throughout the city. His principal published work was *The Native Flowers and Ferns of the United States* (4 vols., 1878–80).

MEEKER, mē'kẽr, **Royal,** American economist: b. Silver Lake, Susquehanna County, Pa., Feb. 23, 1873; d. New Haven, Conn., Aug. 16, 1953. Educated at Iowa State College, Columbia University, and the University of Leipzig, Germany, he joined the faculty of Princeton University in 1905, and from 1908 to 1913 was assistant professor of political economy there. When Woodrow Wilson, who had been president of Princeton, entered the White House in 1913, Meeker was named United States commissioner of labor statistics, serving through both of Wilson's administrations. During this period he established the *Monthly Labor Review* published by the Bureau of Labor Statistics. In 1920–1923 he was chief of the scientific division of the League of Nations International Labor Office, founding the *International Labor Review* and other periodicals. He was connected with the Connecticut Department of Labor from 1932 until his retirement in 1946.

MEER, Jan van der, of Delft. See VERMEER, JAN.

MEER, mār, **Jan van der** (JAN VAN DER MEER VAN HAARLEM), Dutch painter: b. Haarlem, Netherlands, Oct. 22, 1628; d. there, buried Aug. 25, 1691. He is thought to have been a pupil of Rembrandt but, unlike the latter, was primarily a landscape painter. His canvases of the dunes and flatlands of Holland, done in the characteristic somber browns and greens of the period, have considerable warmth and charm.

JAN VAN DER MEER (1656–1705), called the Younger, his son and pupil, was also a painter and engraver, known for his landscapes with sheep. His work was influenced by contemporary styles in Italy, where he spent some years.

JAN VAN DER MEER (1630/1635–1688), another member of the family, was a historical and portrait painter of Utrecht.

MEERKAT. See SURICATE.

MEERSCHAUM, mẽr'shŭm (also called SEPIOLITE), a native hydrated magnesium silicate, white or cream in color. It is very light and, when dry, will float on water; hence the name, which means "sea foam." Although soft and easily carved, meerschaum is tough and durable and takes a good polish. It is used chiefly in pipe bowls. It is a weathering product of other magnesium minerals, such as magnesite and serpentine. Most of the meerschaum comes from the plains of Eskişehir (q.v.) in Turkey, where it has been mined for centuries. Here it occurs as nodules up to 8 or 10 inches in diameter in rock debris filling a valley. It is also found in Morocco, Greece, Spain, and in Utah, New Mexico, and California.

LEWIS S. RAMSDELL.

MEERUT, mā'rŭt, city, India, capital of Meerut District in the State of Uttar Pradesh. A comparatively high altitude makes the Meerut District (area 2,323 square miles) one of the healthiest areas in the plains of India. The rainfall is less than 30 inches a year, but the land, irrigated from the Ganges and Jumna rivers, is excellent for agriculture, the chief crops being wheat, millet, sugarcane, and cotton. The city, 37 miles northeast of Delhi, is a road and rail junction and trade center. Its chief industries are sugar, flour, and oilseed milling, steel smelting and refining, and manufacture of chemicals, carpets, hosiery, leather goods, pottery, soap, and vegetable oil.

Meerut dates back to the time of Asoka (r. about 274–237 B.C.). Not far from it once stood the ruins of Hastinapur, legendary capital of the Pandava warriors in the period of the *Mahābhārata* (possibly 800 B.C.). Meerut was taken by the Muslims in 1191. Timur (Tamerlane) captured it after sacking Delhi in 1398. After the death of Aurangzeb (1707), the country was overrun alternately by Sikh and Maratha invaders, and the city was the scene of attack and counterattack throughout most of the 18th century. About 1775 it was pacified after a fashion by Walter Reinhardt (a Walloon known as Sombre or Samru from his dark complexion), who came to India in the French service about 1750 and soon became the ringleader of a band of European deserters and sepoys. When he died in 1778, his widow, the Begum Samru, was recognized by the British as his successor. With the fall of Delhi in 1803, Meerut and much of the country round were ceded to the British. The rest came under British protection in 1805 and lapsed to the East India Company upon the begum's death in 1836. The outbreak of the so-called Indian (Sepoy) Mutiny began in Meerut on May 10, 1857. Pop. (1951) district 2,281,217; city 233,183.

RODERICK MARSHALL.

MEFISTOFELE, mä-fĕ-stō'fä-lä, an opera in four acts, a prologue, and an epilogue, by Arrigo Boïto, with libretto by the composer, after Johann Wolfgang von Goethe's *Faust.* It was first performed in Milan, Italy, on March 5, 1868. The cast includes: Marguerite (soprano); Helen of Troy (soprano); Martha (contralto); Pantalis (contralto); Faust (tenor); Wagner (tenor); Mefistofele (bass). The locale is Frankfurt, Germany, and Greece.

Prologue.—Mefistofele is sent to earth to tempt the overproud philosopher Faust.

Act I.—Faust and his student friend Wagner meet the disguised Mefistofele. In his study, Faust converses with the Evil One, who agrees to carry out all that Faust may ask in return for his soul—and then bears Faust away upon his cloak.

Act II.—While Faust strolls in the garden with Marguerite, Mefistofele pretends to woo her foolish mother, Martha. Later, on the heights of the Brocken, Faust and Mefistofele attend a Witches' Sabbath. The witches foretell Marguerite's pitiful fate and hand Mefistofele a crystal ball that he holds aloft, saying "Behold the earth!"

Act III.—Marguerite, about to be executed for the murder of her child, is out of her mind. When Faust tries to rescue her, Mefistofele insists that Faust now fulfill his part of their bargain. Marguerite dies as heavenly choirs chant peace and forgiveness.

Act IV.—Near a Grecian river, Faust and Mefistofele encounter Helen of Troy, with whom Faust falls passionately in love. She recounts the tragedy of Troy.

Epilogue.—Faust, repenting his misdeeds, rejects Mefistofele's offer to bear him anywhere in the universe upon his cloak. Reading in his Bible that repentant sinners can be redeemed, Faust prays for liberation from evil. He dies, whereupon Mefistofele vanishes. The heavenly choirs proclaim the triumph of good over evil.

Boïto, a musician of great erudition, but lacking in spontaneity, spent seven years meticulously revising *Mefistofele* after its unsuccessful Milan *première* (its success dates from Bologna, 1875). Especially familiar as excerpted from the revised *Mefistofele* are the magnificent *Prologue,* for bass, chorus, and orchestra; the tenor aria *Dai campi, dai prati;* the soprano aria *L'altra notte in fondo al mare;* and the soprano-tenor duet *Lontano, lontano.*

HERBERT WEINSTOCK.

MEGACLES, mĕg'à-klēz, Athenian politician: fl. mid-6th century B.C. He was the son of Alcmaeon and head of the family of the Alcmaeonidae. A moderate in politics, he at first opposed Pisistratus (q.v.), a democratic leader, but later aided him to gain power in Athens. When Pisistratus made himself tyrant in 560 B.C., Megacles helped to drive him from the city. After Pisistratus finally gained absolute control of the government (c. 543 B.C.), Megacles and the Alcmaeonidae fled from Athens and lived in exile.

MEGALITHIC MONUMENTS, mĕg-à-lĭth'ĭk mŏn'ŭ-mĕnts (from Gr. *megas,* large + *lithos,* stone). For centuries ordinary people and antiquaries in Europe have been intrigued by great prehistoric stone monuments like Stonehenge and Avebury (qq.v.) in Wiltshire, England; the alignments of Carnac in Brittany, France; and chambers or rooms such as New Grange in Ireland, Maes Howe in the Orkneys, and Bagneux in central France. The names at first given to these stone monuments—Giants' Graves, Le Palet de Roland, Arthur's Quoit, the Druidstones, or the Grotte des Fées—merely indicated ignorant speculation about their origin and purpose. In the early

Stonehenge, the most elaborate megalithic monument in England, is one of the best examples of the stone circle.

tombs of Japanese emperors up until the 7th century A.D. were built of megaliths, and megalithic monuments are still being constructed and used in Assam and Indonesia.

It was perhaps a natural development of 19th century diffusionist thought in archaeology and anthropology to assume that all megalithic monuments were connected, and there was for a while much talk of a megalithic "race" or "people" who spread all over the world from one center; Sir Grafton Elliot Smith and William James Perry identified that center as Egypt. Today we realize that there is no generic unity among all megalithic monuments and that techniques of megalithic construction originated in many parts of the world. What the builders of megaliths did have in common, however, was skill in transporting and erecting great stones, sometimes weighing from 50 to 100 tons.

Main Types.—Four main types of megalithic monuments are found in Europe: (1) the menhir or single standing stone; (2) the stone circle; (3) the alignment or stone row; and (4) the chamber or room. Menhirs vary in size from two to three feet up to the Grand Menhir Brisé of Locmariaquer in southern Brittany, now lying on the ground in three pieces, but originally standing 67 feet high. Brittany is the great country for menhirs; they are probably commemorative or cenotaphic in purpose. The British Isles is the great area for stone circles, which may be set up in the ground by themselves (for example, the Nine Maidens in Cornwall) or surrounded with a bank and ditch. These embanked stone circles are grouped with the remains of embanked wooden circles (woodhenges) and called henge monuments. The most famous henge monuments in England are Stonehenge and Avebury. Avebury is surrounded by a circular bank 4,450 feet in diameter; the original height from the top of the bank to the bottom of the ditch was 55 feet. Stone rows occur in southwest Britain, but the most famous area for them is the Carnac region of southern Brittany. Here the alignments of Kerlescan, Le Manio, and Ménec run for several miles and contain thousands of stones set in parallel rows leading to semicircles of stones. It seems likely that the stone circles and rows were some form of religious or secular assembly places.

Tombs.—The stone chambers, on the other hand, are tombs, probably of a family or neighborhood group used over a long period of time; sometimes as many as 200 to 300 skeletons are found in these collective communal vaults. The bodies were usually put in the tombs unburnt although cremation was also practiced. France has 6,000 of these tombs, Denmark 4,000, and the British Isles about 2,000. These figures, of course, refer only to surviving monuments; originally there were many more, and the megalith builders must have formed an important element in the peopling of early Europe. The chambers are built of large stones or orthostats set upright and roofed by capstones placed athwart the heads of the orthostats or by corbelled vaults made of small stones. They were probably for the most part enclosed in large long or round mounds of earth and stone; many of these still survive. The round barrow of New Grange is 270 feet in diameter, and the long barrow at West Kennet is 340 feet long by 75 feet broad. Elsewhere the covering mounds have disappeared, and the burial chambers are now freestanding.

Three main types of megalithic chamber tombs

The passage into Maes Howe, a huge chambered cairn in the Orkney Islands, which was probably built as a tomb.

19th century the word *megalith* was invented for these structures, and it was realized that megalithic monuments exist in many parts of the world as well as in Europe. They are found in North Africa, Abyssinia, Palestine, the Caucasus, the Deccan (India), Burma, and Indonesia. The

The alignments of stones in the Carnac area of Brittany extend for miles and contain thousands of megaliths.

are usually distinguished: (1) the single polygonal or rectangular chamber; (2) the Passage Grave, consisting of a passage leading into a circular polygonal or rectangular chamber; and (3) the Gallery Grave or long rectangular chamber (Fr. *allée couverte*). Sometimes the word *dolmen* is used for the first class, but this is a confusing usage as dolmen is the common word in France for all types of megalithic burial chamber. It is now generally thought that the megalithic burial chambers of Europe had a threefold origin: in south Russia; in Denmark, where graves of a nonmegalithic kind were translated into megalithic monuments; and in the West Mediterranean area, where rock-cut collective tombs were translated into surface megalithic structures in Malta, southern France, southern Iberia, and Sardinia. The builders of the West Mediterranean tombs were almost certainly colonists from the Aegean and brought with them the worship of an earth-mother goddess whose features they sometimes depicted on pots and idols buried with the dead, or on the walls of their tombs.

Illustration Research Service

Trethevy Quoit on Bodmin Moor, Cornwall, England.

The main period of the European megalithic monuments is from 2000 to 1500 B.C., but many were in use after that time. The great majority of the tombs have no metal in them and are therefore formally Neolithic, but the absence of metal from some tombs may be due to religious taboos.

Bibliography.—Fergusson, James, *Rude Stone Monuments in All Countries* (London 1872); Peet, Thomas Eric, *Rough Stone Monuments and Their Builders* (London and New York 1912); Forde, C. Daryll, "The Early Cultures of Atlantic Europe," *American Anthropologist*, vol. 32, pp. 14–100 (Menasha, Wis., 1930); Bailloud, G., and Boofzheim, P. Mieg de, *Les civilisations néolithiques de la France dans leur contexte européen* (Paris 1955); Daniel, Glyn E., *Lascaux and Carnac* (London 1955, New York 1957); Giot, P. R., *Menhirs et dolmens* (Chateaulin 1957); Daniel, Glyn E., *The Megalith Builders of Western Europe* (London 1958).

GLYN E. DANIEL,
Lecturer in Archaeology, Cambridge University.

MEGALOPOLIS, mĕg-à-lŏp'ô-lĭs, town, Greece, in Arcadia Nome, central Peloponnesus, 15 miles southwest of Tripolis. It is a trading point for tobacco, wheat, wine, potatoes, and other agricultural products.

Founded by Epaminondas the Theban, about 370 B.C. as the capital of the Arcadian League, a center of communications, and an outpost against Sparta, Megalopolis shifted its political affiliation to the Achaean League in 235–234 and in 222 was seized by the Spartans. Under the Roman domination of Greece, from 146 B.C. onward, it became an insignificant town. Ruins of the ancient city, one of the largest communities of the Peloponnesus, lie north of the present town. Population: (1961) 2,235.

MEGALOPTERA, mĕg-à-lŏp'tĕr-à, a small order of four-winged insects found in temperate and semitemperate regions. The adults are of medium to large size, and the wings have many cross veins. The larvae or naiads are aquatic and are found in sluggish to fast-flowing streams, where they prey upon the larvae of May flies, stone flies, and other stream inhabitants. The wings are held rooflike or flat over the body; the antennae are long, with many segments. The family Sialidae contains about 40 species, all of which are less than an inch in length. They are commonly known as sialids or alder flies and are seldom found far from their breeding places. The most famous of the Corydalidae are members of the genus *Corydalis,* the males of which have tapering, curved mandibles about half the length of the body. The common name is dobson fly. The larvae are commonly known as hellgrammites, crawlers, and toe-biters and· are highly prized as bait, especially for bass.

C. H. CURRAN.

MEGALOSAURUS. See DINOSAURS— *Order Saurischia* (Suborder Theropoda).

MEGANTIC, mĕ-găn'tĭc, town, Quebec, Canada, county town of Frontenac County. Situated at the north end of Lake Mégantic, about 10 miles from the Maine boundary, at an elevation of 1,300 feet, it is a popular summer and health resort. Pulp and lumber mills, with miscellaneous woodworking plants, are the main industries. Mégantic (officially *Lac-Mégantic*) is on the Canadian Pacific Railway and is the southern terminus of the Quebec Central line, about 150 miles south of the city of Quebec. It has an airport, and a main highway leads to Boston, Mass. It was incorporated as a town in 1907. Population: 6,958.

MEGAPHONE, mĕg'à-fōn, a hollow cone-shaped speaking instrument which magnifies the sound of the voice so that it can be heard at a considerable distance. The user, holding the megaphone like a horn, speaks into the smaller end, the instrument concentrating the sound waves and directing them wherever the speaker turns. Megaphones are usually made of light metal, plastic, or paperboard, and vary in size from less than a foot to more than two feet in length. The electrical megaphone used in some public address systems combines a microphone, amplifier, and cone loud-speaker.

MEGAPODE, mĕg'à-pōd, a bird of the family Megapodiidae, the members of which are also called brush turkeys or mound builders. There are about 10 species of megapodes, restricted to Australia, New Guinea, or the East Indies. They all resemble one another and are heavy, sluggish, fowllike birds with sturdy legs and toes equipped with long claws. The size of the biggest species is about two feet, and the predominant coloration combines shades of brown and gray, varied with white. Although the megapodes are not distinguished for their beauty, they are famous for their incubating habits, having devised an almost perfect incubator which relieves them of the necessity of building a conventional

New York Zoological Society Photo

A megapode or brush turkey (*Alectura lathami lathami*).

nest and of incubation duties. Sometimes this incubator utilizes the heat of the sun or of volcanic sands, but more often it uses heat generated by decomposing organic matter. The more typical method consists of building a large mound of mold or of soil mixed with organic debris, which the birds gather, and scratch together with their stout feet. On occasions this mound may reach a diameter of 40 feet and a height of 6 feet. A depression is dug in the mound at a well-calculated depth for optimum results, and the eggs are laid and buried. From time to time the adult aerates them if necessary by judicious scratching. At the end of about 40 days they hatch, and the young dig themselves out unaided. The young megapodes are precocious and fend for themselves the moment they leave the mound.

CHARLES VAURIE.

MEGARA, měg'à-rà, city, Greece, in Attica Nome, on the Isthmus of Corinth. It is 21 miles west of Athens on the railroad between Athens and Corinth and is a center for production of wine, olive oil, and flour.

During the 8th to 6th centuries B.C., Megara was a flourishing maritime city, the capital of ancient Megaris (q.v.), and grew wealthy from its woolen industry and its widespread trade. Of its many colonies established in Sicily and along the Black Sea, Byzantium (later Constantinople, now Istanbul) was the most celebrated. Megara's geographical situation between Athens and Corinth made the city-state the occasional victim of these more powerful neighbors from the 6th century B.C. onward. The climax came in the 5th century B.C., when Athens aided Megara against Corinth in 459 and then in 432 imposed an embargo (the so-called Megarian Decree) on Megara's trade with members of Athens' Delian League. This incident contributed to the outbreak of the Peloponnesian War (431–404), wherein

Megara suffered many invasions and much destruction. Though in the 4th century B.C. it regained some of its pristine prosperity, Megara declined in the 3d century B.C. and after the 2d century B.C. became a resort patronized by its Roman conquerors. Megara was the seat of the Megarian school of philosophy (see MEGARIAN SCHOOL) and in construction of aqueducts had no superior in the Greek world. Pop. (1951) 13,863.

Consult Highbarger, Ernest L., *The History and Civilization of Ancient Megara* (Baltimore 1927); Hanell, Krister, *Megarische Studien* (Lund 1934).

P. R. COLEMAN-NORTON,
Princeton University.

MEGARIAN SCHOOL, mē̆-gâr'ĭ-ăn, a sect of Greek philosophy, founded at Megara, Greece, by Euclid (450?–374 B.C.), a pupil of Socrates. It adapted the Socratic teaching on logic, and borrowed from Parmenides his concept of one absolute being and from Zeno of Elea his notion of the unreality of multiplicity and of motion, concluding that being includes all possibility and that virtue resides in the knowledge of being. The Megarics were characterized chiefly by their attention to eristic (the sophistic tendency for disputatious quibbling) and by their criticism of other philosophical schools. Like the other semi-Socratic schools, they probably had no corporate organization and disappeared by the end of the 4th century B.C.

P. R. COLEMAN-NORTON.

MEGARIS, měg'à-rĭs, a district of ancient Greece, between the Gulf of Corinth and the Saronic Gulf, on the Isthmus of Corinth. Its capital was Megara (q.v.).

MEGASTHENES, mē̆-găs'thē-nēz, Greek historian: fl. 300 B.C. In 302 B.C. he was sent by Seleucus I Nicator (see SELEUCIDS) as ambassador to the court of the Indian ruler Chandragupta (q.v.), where he remained until 291 B.C. Of his four-volume work *Indica,* describing Indian customs, religion, topography, flora, and fauna, only 34 fragments, chiefly in Strabo's *Geographica* and Arrian's *Indica,* remain.

Consult Jacoby, Felix, *Die Fragmente der griechischen Historiker,* vol. 3, part C, No. 715, pp. 604–39 (Leiden 1958).

MEGATHERIUM, měg-à-thē'rĭ-ŭm (from Gr. *megas,* great + *thērion,* beast), a giant extinct ground sloth. Over 20 feet long and as bulky as an elephant, this was the largest of the mammalian order Edentata. The long narrow head was small in comparison with the enormous body, the limbs and tail were massive but comparatively short. The skeletal structure indicates that *Megatherium* reared up on its hind legs and, supporting itself partly on its tail, used the large claws on the forepaws to strip the branches from trees. Its skull and tooth structure show that it lived on much the same food, chiefly leaves and twigs, as its living relatives the tree sloths. Its fossil remains have been found in the Pliocene and Pleistocene formations of North and South America. Richard Owen's classic monograph on the *Megatherium* appeared in the *Philosophical Transactions* of the Royal Society in 1851.

Consult Scott, William Berryman, *History of Land Mammals in the Western Hemisphere,* 2d ed. rev. (New York 1937); Colbert, Edwin Harris, *Evolution of the Vertebrates* (New York 1955).

GILES MACINTYRE.

MEGHNA RIVER, māg'nä, river, Pakistan, in East Bengal, formed by the branches of the Surma River. It is joined by the Padma (lower Ganges) southeast of Dacca after a course of about 130 miles, and flows into the Bay of Bengal, 90 miles to the south, forming the eastern mouth of the Ganges Delta. Navigation is dangerous because of the high tidal flood (bore), which rises to 20 feet in the spring.

MEGIDDO, mê-gĭd'ō, an ancient fortified hill town overlooking the Plain of Esdraelon in northern Palestine, about 15 miles southeast of Mount Carmel. From the earliest times it was of great strategic importance; one of the oldest roads in the world, the road from Egypt to Mesopotamia, crosses the ridge at this point. About 1468 B.C., Thutmose III of Egypt captured and looted the town. In the Song of Deborah it is mentioned (Judges 5:19) as the scene of the great battle fought during or soon after the Israelite invasion, about 1125 B.C.—though the city itself probably still lay in ruins. In the 10th century B.C., King Solomon fortified the place (I Kings 9:15) and stationed cavalry and chariots there; the University of Chicago expedition in 1928 uncovered the large stables of the fort. King Ahaziah died here about 840 B.C. (II Kings 9:27). Under Tiglath-pileser III (r. 745–727 B.C.) it became the capital of a province in the Assyrian Empire. In Roman times a legion was stationed here, giving its name Legio (el Lejjun) to the place. It has been held that the Armageddon of Revelation 16:16, where the kings from the East will assemble for the final earthly conflict, is the hill (*har* in Hebrew) of Megiddo; hence Gen. Edmund H. H. Allenby was called "Allenby of Armageddon" after his victory over the Turks in a battle near this site in 1918. But it is doubtful if the Greek word *Harmagedōn* will support this identification.

FREDERICK C. GRANT.

MEGRIM. See MIGRAINE.

MEGRUE, mĕ-grōō', **Roi Cooper,** American dramatist: b. New York, N.Y., June 12, 1883; d. there, Feb. 27, 1927. He graduated from Columbia University in 1903 and began writing for the stage while working in a playbroker's office. His first successful play was the melodrama *Under Cover,* which opened in Boston in 1913. The best of his subsequent plays included *It Pays to Advertise* (1914), on which Walter Hackett collaborated; *Abe and Mawruss* (1915), based on the *Potash and Perlmutter* stories of Montague Glass; *Under Sentence* (1916), with Irvin S. Cobb; and *Tea for Three* (1918), filmed in 1927.

MEHEMET ALI or **MEHMET ALI.** See MOHAMMED ALI.

MEHRING, mā'rĭng, **Franz,** German journalist, Socialist leader, and historian: b. Schlawe, Germany, Feb. 27, 1846; d. Berlin, Jan. 28, 1919. Educated at the University of Berlin, he distinguished himself in his earlier years as a democratic liberal journalist and in 1890 became affiliated with the Social Democratic Party. At the beginning of World War I he joined the left-wing antiwar "Spartacus" group (see SPARTACANS) formed by Karl Liebknecht and Rosa Luxemburg, collaborating with them on the programmatic "Junius" pamphlet (Eng. tr., *The Crisis in the German Social-Democracy,* 1918). In January 1918 he was elected to the Prussian Landtag as an Independent Social Democrat, continuing the fight against militarism and reaction in Germany until his death, two weeks after the assassination of Liebknecht and Luxemburg. Mehring's chief eminence was as a Marxist historian and biographer, notably for his *Geschichte der deutschen Sozialdemokratie* (2 vols., 1897–98; 12th ed., 4 vols., 1922) and *Karl Marx, Geschichte seines Lebens* (1918), as well as works on Gotthold Ephraim Lessing (1893) and Friedrich von Schiller (1905).

MEHUL, mā-ŭl', **Étienne (Nicolas)** French composer: b. Givet, Ardennes Department, France, June 22, 1763; d. Paris, Oct. 18, 1817. He showed great musical talent at an early age, and at 10 was organist of a convent in Givet. When he was 15, a wealthy patron enabled him to study in Paris, where the composer Christoph Gluck gave him advice and encouragement. *Euphrosine* (1790), the first of Méhul's works to be produced, was an immediate success, ushering in a new era in French *opéra comique.* During the next 17 years some two dozen of his operas were performed in Paris. *Joseph* (1807) is considered his masterpiece, and his overtures are regarded as the best of his instrumental works. He also wrote a number of cantatas and ballets. In 1795, Méhul became an inspector of the newly established Paris Conservatoire and the first musician elected to the Institut de France.

MEI LAN-FANG, mā' län'fäng', Chinese actor: b. Peking, China, Oct. 22, 1894; d. there, Aug. 8, 1961. Member of a well-known theatrical family, he became famous for his superb portrayal of female parts, highly stylized in accordance with the conventions of the classic Chinese theater and requiring skill in dancing and singing as well as in pantomime. Idolized in China, he was also acclaimed in Japan, England, Russia, and, in 1930, in the United States. He refused to perform for the Japanese during World War II, and in revenge the Japanese falsely reported his death in 1943. His popularity continued in China after the Chinese revolution, and he was highly honored by the Communist government although he refused to join the party until 1959.

MEIBOM, mī'bōm, **Heinrich,** German physician and anatomist: b. Lübeck, Germany, June 29, 1638; d. Helmstedt, March 26, 1700. He was professor of medicine at the University of Helmstedt from 1664 and also held the chair of history and poetry there from 1678. Meibom was the first to describe (1666) the ocular tarsal glands, also called Meibomian glands or Meibom's glands (see EYE—*Anatomy and Physiology:* Orbit).

MEIGGS, mĕgz, **Henry,** American railroad builder: b. Catskill, N.Y., July 7, 1811; d. Lima, Peru, Sept. 29, 1877. After operating a lumberyard in Williamsburg, N.Y., he went to San Francisco, Calif., in the gold rush of 1848 and made a fortune in the lumber trade. At the end of the boom, however, he had debts amounting to nearly a million dollars which he could not meet. In October 1854 he sailed secretly with his family for South America, working as a construction superintendent on the Santiago al Sur Railroad in Chile, and in 1861 secured a contract from the Chilean government to complete the railway from Valparaíso to Santiago which netted him a profit of more than a million dollars. Between 1868 and 1873 he contracted to build more than a thousand miles of railroad for the Peruvian government. His most ambitious undertaking was construction of the Callao, Lima & Oroya Railroad, one of the world's great engineering feats, which crosses the Andes in a series of viaducts and more than 60 tunnels, piercing Mount Meiggs (named for him) at over 15,000 feet. The construction of this line bankrupted both the Peruvian government and Meiggs. Before his death, however, he paid off most of his California debts and did much to beautify Lima with parks and boulevards.

MEIGHEN, mē′ĕn, **Arthur,** Canadian statesman: b. Anderson, Ontario, Canada, June 16, 1874; d. Toronto, Aug. 5, 1960. He graduated from the University of Toronto, studied law, and in 1902 was admitted to the Manitoba bar, practicing at Portage la Prairie. Elected to the Canadian House of Commons in 1908, he served almost continuously until 1926, becoming solicitor general for Canada in 1913 in the Conservative ministry of Sir Robert Laird Borden. In 1917 he became secretary of state and then minister of the interior, succeeding Borden as prime minister in July 1920, and also assuming the portfolio of external affairs. At the Prime Ministers' Conference of 1921, Meighen took the lead in opposing renewal of the Anglo-Japanese alliance in order to strengthen relations with the United States. He resigned upon defeat of the Conservatives in the December 1921 election, but was again prime minister from June to September 1926. In 1932 he entered the Senate, serving as minister without portfolio and Senate government leader (1932–1935) and retiring in 1942.

MEIGS, mĕgz, **Josiah,** American educator: b. Middletown, Conn., Aug. 21, 1757; d. Washington, D.C., Sept. 4, 1822. Brother of Return Jonathan Meigs (1740–1823, q.v.), he graduated from Yale College in 1778, was admitted to the bar (1783), and published the weekly New Haven *Gazette* from 1784 to 1788. After some years in Bermuda as an admiralty lawyer for American clients, he was named professor of mathematics and natural philosophy at Yale in 1794, resigning six years later because of his antipathy to the Federalist views of President Timothy Dwight. In 1801, when instruction began at the University of Georgia (chartered 1785), Meigs became president of the institution and its first really active executive; but eventually he quarreled with the trustees and resigned in 1810. Two years later President James Madison named him surveyor general of the United States, and he spent his remaining years in Washington, from 1814 as commissioner of the General Land Office.

CHARLES DELUCENA MEIGS (1792–1869), his son, studied medicine at the University of Pennsylvania and settled in Philadelphia, where he became a noted obstetrician and professor of obstetrics (1841–1861) at Jefferson Medical College.

JOHN FORSYTH MEIGS (1818–1882), son of the preceding, also became an eminent physician in Philadelphia, specializing in pediatrics. He was the author of *A Practical Treatise on the Diseases of Children* (1848), which remained a standard international classic for decades. The distinguished military engineer Montgomery Cunningham Meigs was his brother.

ARTHUR VINCENT MEIGS (1850–1912), son of John Forsyth and brother of William Montgomery Meigs, carried on the family medical tradition in Philadelphia, also as a pediatrician. He made important comparative studies of human and bovine milk, developed formulas for enriching cow's milk for human infant feeding, and devised the test for fat in milk known as Meigs's test. He was also the first to describe the capillaries in the heart muscle, called Meigs's capillaries.

MEIGS, mĕgz, **Return Jonathan,** American soldier and pioneer: b. Middletown, Conn., Dec. 17, 1740; d. at the Cherokee agency, Tenn., Jan. 28, 1823. After the Battle of Lexington, he marched a company of men to the aid of the American camp at Cambridge, Mass. He subsequently accompanied Benedict Arnold's expedition against Quebec and was taken prisoner. Following his release, he led a brilliant raid on the British at Sag Harbor, N.Y., in 1777. In 1779 he further distinguished himself under Anthony Wayne during the capture of Stony Point, N.Y. He retired from the army in 1781. As a surveyor for the Ohio Company, Meigs in 1788 led a group of pioneers to the mouth of Muskingum River where they founded a colony on the site of the future city of Marietta, Ohio. In 1801 he was appointed a Cherokee agent.

MEIGS, Return Jonathan, American public official, son of the preceding: b. Middletown, Conn., Nov. 17, 1764; d. Marietta, Ohio, March 29, 1824. He went to Marietta with his father in 1788 and became a prominent lawyer. In 1798 he was appointed a territorial judge and the following year he was elected to the territorial legislature. He was the first chief justice of Ohio (1803–1804) and a senator from Ohio (1807–1810). Meigs served as governor of that state from 1810 to 1814, during which period he was an active supporter of the War of 1812. He was postmaster general of the United States from 1814 to 1823.

MEIJI TENNO, mā′jê tĕn′nō, 122d emperor of Japan: b. Kyoto, Japan, Nov. 3, 1852; d. Tokyo, July 30, 1912. His given name was Mutsuhito, and he was the second son of Emperor Komei. He succeeded his father to the throne in January 1867 and was fully installed on Oct. 31, 1868, adopting the reign name of Meiji (enlightened rule). His reign was one of the most eventful in all Japanese history. During it the Japanese abandoned their long-established seclusion policy to enter the world community of nations, revolutionized their government, and began the program of modern social and industrial reform which precipitated them into a position of leadership in the Far East. By the time of Emperor Meiji's death, Japan was recognized as one of the great powers of the world.

After the opening of Japan to Western trade and influences in the middle of the 19th century, a group of radical young leaders pressed for political revolution, using the symbol of the emperor to create a modern centralized state. In January 1868 the emperor was "restored" as active head of state after nearly 1,000 years of rule by civil and military governors. During 1868 and 1869 the Tokugawa shogunate was destroyed and the new imperial government moved to Tokyo (the old city of Edo). On April 6, 1868, the new government issued in the name of Emperor Meiji the five-clause imperial oath, a statement of policy which laid the foundation for a modern government and looked to the adoption of domestic reforms under Western influence. In 1871 the autonomous provincial lords were replaced by a centralized provincial administration. During 1872–1873 the feudal system of land tenure was revised, and new systems of national education and military conscription were put into effect. Freedom of occupation and social mobility was granted, and the professional military (samurai) class was abolished. These reforms met their test in the armed uprisings of disgruntled samurai during 1874–1877, and the quelling of the Satsuma rebellion of 1877 demonstrated conclusively the stability of the new imperial government.

During the remainder of the Meiji period Japan met numerous critical problems. The need for a new form of government was worked out by 1889 when the Emperor Meiji granted a constitution, converting Japan into a constitutional monarchy with the position of the emperor assured as "sacred and inviolable." Japan's international status was assured with the revision by 1899 of the unequal treaties of 1858, the signing of the Anglo-Japanese Alliance of 1902, and the successful completion of wars against China (1894–1895) and Russia (1904–1905). The Japanese Empire by 1912 included the colonies of Formosa and Korea, and the Liaotung leased territory in Manchuria. Japan's rapid industrialization, spurred by aggressive foreign expansion, had already begun to affect social and economic conditions in Japan. After 1890 a vigorous party movement, which included socialist expression, enlivened Japanese politics. One of the major achievements of Emperor Meiji was the promulgation of the Rescript on Education, which set forth the ethical principles of a harmonious state based on traditional values.

The role of Emperor Meiji in the events of his reign was both direct and indirect. At the time of the Restoration the emperor was only 16 years old. His youthfulness made it possible for court members of the reform party, such as Sanjō Sanetomi and Iwakura Tomomi, to accomplish their ends through him. The young emperor provided the symbol under which political revolution was carried out. This same symbol became a powerful device for holding the country together after 1868. Eventually, as written into the constitution, the emperor became the keystone of the Japanese system of government. As Emperor Meiji came of age he took more active part in government. As a man he fulfilled admirably the image of the young nationalistic Japan pressing forward along many lines of reform. But he also maintained the importance of the traditional values of Japanese society. In political affairs the emperor delegated much to his chief advisors, such as Hirobumi Itō and Aritomo Yamagata. Yet he played a critical role as a moderating, unifying force between factions. In his personality the emperor was strong and forceful. Most frequently seen in public in military uniform, he acted the symbol of firm national leadership. While in favor of modern reform, he was most strongly influenced by the Confucian-based education provided by his tutor Motoda Eifu. He was married (1869) to Princess Haruko (1850–1914), of the Ichijō family.

Consult Sansom, Sir George Bailey, *The Western World and Japan* (New York 1950); Borton, Hugh, *Japan's Modern Century* (New York 1955); Beckmann, George M., *The Making of the Meiji Constitution* (Lawrence, Kans., 1957); Shively, D. H., "Motoda Eifu,"

Confucianism in Action, ed. by D. S. Nivison and A. P. Wright, pp. 302–333 (Stanford, Calif., 1959).

JOHN W. HALL
Griswold Professor of History, Yale University

MEIKLEJOHN, mik'əl-jon, **Alexander,** American educator: b. Rochdale, England, Feb. 3, 1872; d. Berkeley, Calif., Dec. 16, 1964. He went to the United States with his family when he was 8 years old. He graduated from Brown University in 1893. After taking his Ph.D. at Cornell (1897), he returned to Brown, where he taught philosophy, becoming dean of the college in 1901. In 1912 he was inaugurated as eighth president of Amherst College. An aggressive but constructive liberal, he was also a stimulating teacher and brought to Amherst promising young instructors and lecturers. He refused, however, to recognize his responsibility to the trustees or faculty and insisted on virtually autocratic authority. Forced to resign in 1923, in 1926 he was appointed head of the Experimental School at the University of Wisconsin. From 1933 to 1936 he was chairman of the School for Social Studies in San Francisco. In later years he lectured widely. In 1963, Meiklejohn was awarded the national Medal of Freedom by President Lyndon Johnson. His books include *The Liberal College* (1920), *The Experimental College* (1932), and *Free Speech and Its Relation to Self-Government* (1948).

MEILHAC, mĕ-yȧk', **Henri,** French playwright and librettist: b. Paris, France, Feb. 21, 1831; d. there, July 6, 1897. His first regular stage success was the play *Froufrou* (1869) written with Ludovic Halévy; his first remembered operetta libretto, that for Louis Pierre Deffès' *Le café du roi* (1861). With Halévy, he also wrote the texts of Jacques Offenbach's operettas *La belle Hélène, Barbe-Bleue, La vie parisienne, La grande-duchesse de Gérolstein, La Périchole,* and *Les brigands,* as well as for Georges Bizet's *Carmen* and Charles Lecocq's *Le petit duc.* Johann Strauss, Jr.'s *Die Fledermaus* is based on a Meilhac-Halévy vaudeville entitled *Le réveillon.* With Philippe Gille, Meilhac also wrote the libretto of Jules Massenet's *Manon.*

MEILLET, mĕ-yĕ', **Antoine,** French philologist and linguist: b. Moulins, France, Nov. 11, 1866; d. Châteaumeillant, Sept. 22, 1936. Educated at Vienna and Paris, he became professor at the École des Hautes Études (Paris) in 1891 and at the Collège de France in 1906. He was the most prominent figure of the French school of linguistics in the early 20th century, and his works continue to be of fundamental importance. In addition to numerous articles on all aspects of Indo-European and general linguistics, he wrote historical grammars of Common Slavic, Old Persian, Classical Armenian, and Greek and Latin. His two best-known works are the *Introduction a l'étude comparative des langues indo-européennes* (1903) and the *Dictionnaire étymologique de la langue latine* (with Alfred Ernout, 1932)

WILLIAM DIVER
Professor of Linguistics, Columbia University

MEIN KAMPF, mīn kämpf (MY STRUGGLE), the German National Socialist "bible," dictated by Adolf Hitler while he was imprisoned in the fortress of Landsberg am Lech, Bavaria, following the unsuccessful putsch of 1923, and dedicated to his followers killed in that attempt.

MEIOSIS, mī-ō′sĭs, a specialized kind of cell division that occurs in all sexually reproducing organisms. Meiosis is also known as *reduction division* because it results in the formation of germ cells that contain half the chromosome number normal for a species. In plants, the cells produced by meiosis become spores that divide a number of times with the reduced number of chromosomes; in animals, the cells produced by meiosis become gametes, either eggs or sperm. At fertilization, when cells from two parents fuse, the normal chromosome number is restored.

In meiosis, as in mitosis, each chromosome duplicates to form two daughter chromosomes, or chromatids. These chromatids then coil or condense during *prophase,* the first stage of cell division; become attached to spindle fibers at special sites on the chromosome known as centromeres, or kinetochores, during the next stage—*prometaphase;* line up on the spindle at *metaphase;* separate from each other at *anaphase;* and decondense to form daughter nuclei at *telophase.*

Meiosis differs from mitosis in four important ways. First, meiosis consists of two divisions, meiosis I and II, with only one duplication of chromosomes, resulting in four daughter cells, each with half the original number of chromosomes. Second, homologous, or similar, chromosomes undergo side-by-side pairing, or *synapsis.* Third, a recombination of parts occurs between the members of each pair of duplicated homologous chromosomes in a process known as *crossing-over.* Fourth, the splitting and separation of the centromere region of each duplicated chromosome is delayed until meiosis II.

Stages of Meiosis. After the chromosomes duplicate, meiosis I begins with an extended prophase, within which five successive stages are usually recognized: (1) *leptonema* in which the duplicated but unpaired chromosomes first begin to condense or coil and are visible as very thin threads; (2) *zygonema* during which homologous chromosomes pair side by side; (3) *pachynema* in which the chromosome pairs condense further to form shorter, thicker threads; (4) *diplonema* in which homologous chromosomes condense still further and begin to separate but remain held together by the presence of cross-over chromatids; (5) *diakinesis* during which the chromosomes condense and separate even more. Crossing-over, in which the breaking and rejoining of old chromatids leads to the formation of new composite chromatids, probably occurs during zygonema and pachynema stages.

At anaphase I the chromatids separate from each other except in the centromere region. The two chromatids of one chromosome move toward one end of the spindle, while the two chromatids of the homologous chromosome move toward the other end. The two daughter cells then enter a brief interphase, and then, without duplicating their chromosomes, enter meiosis II. During anaphase of meiosis II, the centromeres finally separate, and the daughter chromosomes, now single chromatids, move to opposite ends of the spindle. There, they decondense to form the nuclei of the four daughter cells.

PETER LUYKX
University of Miami, Coral Gables, Fla.

MEIR, me-ir′, **Golda** (1898–   ), first woman premier of Israel. She was born Golda Mabovitch in Kiev, Russia, on May 3, 1898. After moving to Milwaukee, Wis., with her family in 1906, she received her education at the Teacher's Seminary there. She became an active member of the Zionist Labor Party in Milwaukee and was a delegate to the World Jewish Congress.

In 1921 she emigrated to Palestine, where she changed her married name of Myerson to Meir. Active in the work of the Histadrut (Federation of Labor), she became a member of its executive committee. She was a leading figure in the movement to establish a Jewish state in Palestine, and as head of the political department of the Jewish Agency during 1946–1948, she conducted negotiations with the British high commissioner and with Haganah leaders.

When the state of Israel was established in 1948, Mrs. Meir was named to the parliament and soon afterward she became the first minister to the USSR. She then joined the Israeli cabinet, of which she was an influential member for 17 years, serving as minister of labor from 1949 to 1956 and as minister for foreign affairs from 1956 to 1966. She was named general secretary of the dominant Mapai (Israel Labor) party in 1966 and was selected to succeed the late Levi Eshkol as premier in March 1969.

MEISSEN PORCELAIN, a kind of ceramic ware made in Meissen, Germany, since the 18th century. It is the earliest variety of European porcelain, and one of the finest. Meissen ware is often called *Dresden china.* Prior to the invention of Meissen, European potters tried in vain to imitate the hard, white, translucent Chinese porcelain. Finally, by 1709, the alchemist J. F. Böttger, using local kaolin deposits, made a true porcelain with these qualities. In 1710, Augustus the Strong, Elector of Saxony, established a royal porcelain factory at Meissen, near Dresden, with Böttger in charge.

Meissen designs became increasingly complex. After 1720 the painter J. G. Heroldt introduced chinoiserie scenes and imitations of Oriental birds and flowers and, later, small landscapes and seascapes in panels on colored grounds. The sculptor J. J. Kändler, after 1731, modeled small porcelain figures from the theater and daily life and designed tableware with modeled decoration. By 1750 rococo styles predominated, and naturalistic *deutsche Blumen* (German flowers) replaced Oriental designs. Meissen porcelain, which inspired the products of the rival porcelain factories, deteriorated in the quality of its design after the 1760's. See also PORCELAIN.

MEISTERSINGER, mīs′tĕr-zĭng-ĕr (Eng. MASTERSINGERS), the name applied to German poet-musicians of the 15th and 16th centuries joined in the predominantly middle-class movement that superseded the more aristocratic *Minnesinger* (love singers) of the three preceding centuries. The *Meistersinger* were grouped in local guilds, some of which persisted into the 18th century (the one at Ulm was not discontinued until 1839). Best remembered of the real *Meistersinger*—largely because he is the central character of Richard Wagner's music drama *Die Meistersinger von Nürnberg*—is Hans Sachs (1494–1576).

The music of the *Meistersinger* was monophonic and was written out in plain-song notation. Its rhythm was relatively free, and its melodic line was often extravagantly decorated with coloratura. The melodies were commonly ternary—that is, in the three-section ABA pattern.

HERBERT WEINSTOCK.

MEISTERSINGER VON NÜRNBERG, Die, fôn nürn'bĕrҝ, a comic music drama by Richard Wagner (text by the composer), first performed at Munich, Germany, on June 21, 1868. The cast includes Eva Pogner (soprano), Magdalena (mezzo-soprano), Walther von Stolzing (tenor), David (tenor), Kunz Vogelgesang (tenor), Balthasar Zorn (tenor), Ulrich Eisslinger (tenor), Augustin Moser (tenor), Hans Sachs (bass), Sixtus Beckmesser (bass), Veit Pogner (bass), Konrad Nachtigall (bass), Fritz Kothner (bass), Hermann Ortel (bass), Hans Schwarz (bass), Hans Foltz (bass), A Night Watchman (bass), burghers of the guild, journeymen, apprentices, people of Nürnberg. The time is the 16th century.

Act I.—In St. Catharine's Church. Walther falls in love with Eva, whose father will give her as a bride to the mastersinger who wins the singing contest on St. John's Day. Walther persuades the mastersingers to let him take the test for admission to their guild. The malicious Beckmesser, also smitten with Eva, causes Walther to fail the test, but Hans Sachs has been much attracted by the young man's song.

Act II.—A street between Eva's home and Hans Sachs' workshop. Sachs learns that Eva returns Walther's love. Beckmesser serenades the disguised Magdalena, believing her to be Eva, who attempts to elope with Walther. After a street brawl, Sachs takes Walther into his workshop.

Act III.—A room in Sachs' house. Walther sings of a dream he has had during the night, and Sachs calls the result a mastersong, which he writes down, later permitting Beckmesser to take it away with him. Walther sings his prize song to Eva, and it is then formally baptized in a quintet (Sachs, Eva, Walther, Magdalena, David).

Scene 2.—A meadow, St. John's Day. During the singing contest, Beckmesser tries to sing the words of Walther's song to music of his own, thus arousing only ridicule. He then accuses Sachs of having composed the song, but the others believe Sachs' denial. When Walther sings his song, general enthusiasm results. The mastersingers wish to make him a member of their guild at once, but he refuses because of their earlier mistreatment of him, and is finally won over only by Hans Sachs. Walther then accepts. He and Eva, whose hand he has thus won, then crown Sachs with Walther's laurel wreath, and the opera ends amid general rejoicing.

HERBERT WEINSTOCK.

MEITNER, mīt'nĕr, **Lise,** Austrian physicist: b. Vienna, Austria, Nov. 7, 1878. She visited Berlin in 1907 to attend the lectures of Max Planck and stayed to join Otto Hahn at the Kaiser Wilhelm Institute. She and Hahn showed the existence of monoenergetic groups in beta-particle spectra in 1912 and discovered and named the element, protactinium, in 1917. Later she also studied and named the phenomenon of nuclear isomerism. In the 1930's Miss Meitner and Hahn investigated the products of the neutron bombardment of uranium, a study initiated by Enrico Fermi, and detected the new isomer U^{239}.

During the first years of Adolf Hitler's regime, Miss Meitner, though of Jewish extraction, was safe from harm because she was an Austrian national. After the Nazi absorption of Austria in 1938, however, she was forced to flee to Stockholm, Sweden. There, with Otto Robert Frisch, she published (January 1939) the suggestion that the uranium nucleus, on bombardment with neutrons, split in two (fission), and predicted the possibility of a chain reaction. This was quickly confirmed and proved to be the key discovery leading to the development of the atomic bomb and the nuclear reactor. She visited the United States after World War II, but later made Stockholm her permanent home.

ISAAC ASIMOV.

MEKNÈS, mĕk-nĕs' (Span. MEQUINEZ), city, Morocco, capital of Meknès Province, 33 miles west-southwest of Fez, at an altitude of 1,740 feet. Railways connect it with Rabat, Casablanca, Fez, and Tangier, and there is an airport. The city is the market center of a very rich agricultural region, which produces grain, grapes, olives, vegetables, and fruits. Industries include woolen milling, metalworking, distilling essential oils, processing of vegetables, fruit, palm fiber, and esparto, and, notably, weaving carpets. The principal attractions for tourists are the enormous market place, flanked by two gateways dating from the 17th–18th centuries, and the sultan's palace with grounds resembling Versailles.

Meknès was founded as an Almohade citadel in the 11th century and became prominent late in the 17th century, when Sultan Mulai Ismā'īl made it his capital and constructed his palace here. The city began to decline after 1728, when the capital of the sultanate was transferred to Fez. It was occupied by the French in 1911, when they established their protectorate over most of Morocco. Pop. (1960) 175,943.

MEKONG RIVER, mä-kông (Tibetan DzA CHU; Chin. LANTSANG; Thai MAE KHONG), river, Asia, one of the continent's great rivers, about 2,600 miles long. It rises in the Tibetan highlands of the Chinese Province of Tsinghai, flows southward through eastern Tibet and the western part of the Chinese Province of Yunnan, and is the boundary between Burma and Thailand (Siam) on the west and Laos on the east. Traversing Cambodia and South Vietnam, it empties through a wide delta into the South China Sea. Rapids in canyons prevent important navigation in its upper reaches, but the lower 340 miles permit passage of vessels of 15-foot draft. The Tonle Sap, a large lake in Cambodia, acts as the Mekong's natural flood reservoir. The delta is one of the world's largest rice-growing areas.

MELALEUCA, mĕl-à-lū'kà, a genus of shrubs and trees in the myrtle family (Myrtaceae) comprising over 100 species native in Australia and Tasmania, with one reaching the East Indies and Malaya. The name alludes to the black trunks and white branches of some species. Many have a showy bloom, similar to the closely related *Callistemon,* and are valuable drought-resistant ornamental plants. The small leaves, usually alternate and crowded, have oil glands, dotting the lower surfaces, that yield a fragrant odor when the leaves are crushed. The flowers are borne in globose heads or in subterminal spikes. They have small, five-parted calyces and corollas, and many long, conspicuous stamens gathered in five bundles, in shades of red, purple, yellow, or white. The fruits are hard, woody capsules which may persist on the branches for several years. The leaves of one species, *M. leucadendron,* yield cajuput oil, which has strong stimulant properties and is still somewhat used in the treatment of various skin diseases. The peoples of Malaysia use the oil as a general panacea, internally and externally, and the corky bark of the tree in the construction of shields.

R. M. STRAW.

MELAMPUS, mĕ-lăm'pŭs, in classical mythology, the earliest Greek prophet and physician, introducer of the worship of Dionysus into Greece. The most famous of the legends about him tells how his prophetic powers enabled him to escape from prison. Melampus attempted to aid his brother Bias, who wished to marry Pero but was required, as a condition of marriage, to regain cattle captured by Iphiclus from Tyro, Pero's grandmother. Caught and imprisoned, Melampus foretold from the speech of worms in the walls—he had acquired the ability to understand the language of all creatures—that the prison soon would collapse. Iphiclus was impressed, freed Melampus, and promised him the cattle, if Melampus could discover why Iphiclus was childless. Through conversation with a vulture, Melampus learned that Iphiclus' father Phylacus unknowingly had cast a charm of sterility on him. Melampus cured Iphiclus, received the cattle, and thus won Pero for Bias.

P. R. COLEMAN-NORTON.

MELANCHOLIA, mĕl-ăn-kō'lĭ-à, or **DEPRESSION,** dĕ-prĕsh'ŭn, a pathologic condition characterized by a sad, despondent mood, decrease of mental productivity, diminution of drive, and a general retardation or agitation. Besides these primary symptoms, there are often secondary symptoms, such as feelings of hopelessness, preoccupation with physiological functions of the body, pathologic feelings of guilt, nihilistic delusions, insomnia, loss of weight and appetite, decrease in sexual urge and in elimination—all of which are usually associated with severe depressive states. Pathophysiologically, this condition is characterized by reduced secretions, increased cerebral resistance to inhibiting drugs, and increased adrenal functioning.

Historically, the first description and definition of melancholia is found in the writings of Hippocrates (460?–?377 B.C.). He thought that it was caused by absorption of black bile into the system—hence the name, which literally means a condition produced by black bile. Throughout the Middle Ages and until the end of the 18th century, melancholia was considered to be produced by exclusively psychogenic factors such as love. At the end of the 18th and beginning of the 19th century, physiological notions of excitability and exhaustion of the nervous system began to be applied to the concept of melancholia. Emil Kraepelin in 1899 was the first to describe the manic-depressive psychosis, using the modern term "depression" as a substitute for melancholia. In 1904 Adolph Meyer proposed that "depression" be formally substituted for "melancholia." Modern psychiatry differentiates between *endogenous depression,* which is caused by physiological changes in the metabolism of the body, and *reactive depression* (sometimes called psychogenic depression), which is caused by unfavorable events not acceptable to the patient.

Depression can appear either as a reaction not associated with any other mental disturbance, or as part of a manic-depressive disease, or it may be concomitant with a schizophrenic or neurotic process. A distinction must be made between normal and pathologic depressive reactions. A normal reaction would be, for instance, mourning and grief for the loss of a beloved person, while the pathologic depressive reaction is not commensurate with its cause; it seems likely that the difference between the two reactions is mainly one of degree and of duration.

The classic and almost sovereign treatment of depressive states, convulsive therapy, was introduced in 1934 by L. J. Meduna. Subsequently, in the mid-1950's, a great number of stimulant drugs, most of them amino-oxidase inhibitors, were introduced in the treatment of depressive states. In milder cases they have proved quite useful and obviate the necessity of using convulsive treatment.

L. J. MEDUNA, M.D.,
Professor of Psychiatry, University of Illinois College of Medicine.

MELANCHTHON, mĕ-lăngk'thŭn (Hellenized name of PHILIPP SCHWARZERD), German reformer, theologian, and educator: b. Bretten, Germany, Feb. 16, 1497; d. Wittenberg, April 19, 1560. After the death of his father, his education was supervised by Johann Reuchlin (q.v.), his great-uncle. This famous humanist and Hebraic scholar guided his grandnephew through the Latin school at Pforzheim, and, in recognition of his achievements in the classics, named him "Melanchthon." Philipp received his B.A. from the University of Heidelberg in 1511 and his M.A. from the University of Tübingen in 1514. In 1518 he published *Institutiones grammaticae Graecae* (Rudiments of Greek Grammar), the first of his many textbooks for use in elementary grades and universities. His proficiency in Greek, Latin, and Hebrew and his extensive knowledge in the liberal arts won him the extravagant praise of Desiderius Erasmus of Rotterdam, foremost humanist scholar of the day.

Through Reuchlin, Melanchthon received a call to teach Greek at the University of Wittenberg, where he first met Martin Luther. Four days after his arrival he delivered (Aug. 29, 1518) a bold inaugural address, *De corrigendis adolescentiae studiis* (On Correcting the Studies of Youth), winning the acclaim of Luther, whose friend and collaborator he now became. Under Luther's influence, Melanchthon deepened his interest in theology and Scripture and fused his humanistic learning with evangelical faith. Even before coming to Wittenberg, Melanchthon's humanism was modified. His own inbred piety and wide readings in Wessel (Gansfort), William of Ockham, Aristotle, and the Bible had caused him to question the ultimacy of man's rational powers.

"Loci Communes."—The Leipzig debate (1519), in which Melanchthon skillfully assisted Luther, and the subsequent exchange of pamphlets with Johann Eck revealed Melanchthon as one of the most learned controversialists of the time. He sustained the arguments of Luther and clearly enunciated the principle of scriptural authority over against primacy of the pope. Melanchthon was never ordained, though he received the degree of bachelor of theology in 1519 and taught theology. His lectures on St. Paul's Epistle to the Romans, published in April 1521, became the first systematic statement of theology in Protestantism, the *Loci communes rerum theologicarum* (Commonplaces of Theology). The book was phenomenally successful. By 1525, 18 Latin editions had been printed, in addition to translations, and by 1560 more than 60 editions had appeared. Melanchthon's place as a leader and theologian of the Reformation was firmly established, but not without personal loss, for he suffered an irreparable break with his great-uncle Reuchlin, who remained a convinced Roman Catholic humanist.

On Nov. 25, 1520, Melanchthon married Katharina Krapp, daughter of the burgomaster of Wittenberg. Four children were born: Anna, 1522; Philip, 1525; George, 1527; and Magdalen, 1533. Magdalen married Kaspar Peucer, who was imprisoned for 12 years (from 1574) for promulgating Melanchthon's views after the reformer's death.

Educational Reforms.—Melanchthon was called the "Preceptor of Germany" for his work in founding preparatory schools and reorganizing the country's university systems. In 1528 he wrote a basic school plan, *Unterricht der Visitatoren* (Instructions for Visitors), to serve as a guide for inspectors of religious and educational conditions in Saxony. This plan was enacted into law, establishing the Protestant public school system. By 1555 more than 135 plans based on Melanchthon's model had appeared; at least 56 cities asked his aid in founding their schools. He helped to establish the universities of Marburg, Königsberg, and Jena and instituted basic reforms in Greifswald, Wittenberg, Cologne, Tübingen, Leipzig, Heidelberg, Rostock, and Frankfurt an der Oder. Melanchthon believed in learned piety, a cultivation of all the powers of man, with the fruits of religion as the goal. His views and activity revolutionized education in Germany.

Augsburg Confession.—Melanchthon was present at the Diet of Spires (Speyer) in 1529, when the German evangelicals protested a Roman Catholic resolution curbing their freedom of conscience and minority rights; from this came the term "Protestant." However, Melanchthon's spirit was conciliatory, and the divisions in Christendom caused him great anguish. The Augsburg Confession (1530), which he composed because Luther was under the emperor's ban, became the basic confession of Protestantism and influenced the making of all other Protestant creeds. It attempted to explain evangelical views without further alienating those who adhered to the papacy. But his spirit of compromise and hopefulness did not harmonize with the passions of the 16th century. Melanchthon's *Apology* (1531), a defense of the Augsburg Confession, ranks as one of the finest theological writings of the Reformation and is today a basic symbol in Lutheranism.

Melanchthon differed with Luther on the Lord's Supper, tending more to a concept of the spiritual presence of Christ in the bread and wine. He also rejected the tendency toward "determinism," which Luther seemed to express against Erasmus, and insisted that the will of man has a part in conversion; the Gospel and the Holy Spirit are primary, but the will of man must at least accept the gift of God, although it cannot merit divine favor. Luther raised no objection, but after Luther's death Melanchthon was bitterly attacked as a corrupter of genuine Lutheranism, a synergist, and a crypto-Calvinist.

Adiaphorist Controversy.—The controversy over adiaphora (nonessentials) cast a final spell of suspicion over Melanchthon that caused him to long to escape the rage of theologians. After Luther's death (1546) and the military defeat of the Protestants at Mühlberg (1547), an attempt was made to restore Catholicism throughout Germany. Melanchthon refused to yield on essential doctrines, but to preserve peace and keep Wittenberg as a Protestant symbol he compromised on nonessential doctrines and practices (the so-called Augsburg-Leipzig Interim, 1548). Melanchthon acted in accordance with his own and Luther's former views, but many opponents denounced him as a traitor.

Melanchthon stands next to Luther and John Calvin as a founder of Protestantism. More than any other reformer he sought to join the rationalistic side of the Renaissance and the evangelical faith of the Reformation.

Bibliography.—Melanchthon's basic writings are edited by Karl G. Bretschneider and Heinrich E. Bindseil, *Corpus reformatorum,* 28 vols. (Halle 1834–60). Additions are in Otto C. Clemen, *Supplementa Melanchthoniana,* vols. 1–2, 5–6 (Leipzig 1910–26). There is also a student's edition, *Melanchthons Werke* (Gütersloh 1951–   ).

Consult also Hartfelder, Karl, *Melanchthon als Praeceptor Germaniae* (Berlin 1889); Richard, James W., *Philip Melanchthon* (New York 1898); Ellinger, Georg, *Philipp Melanchthon* (Berlin 1902); Engelland, Hans, *Melanchthons Glauben und Handeln* (Munich 1931); Hill, Charles L., *Loci Communes of Philip Melanchthon* (Boston 1944); Manschreck, Clyde L., *Melanchthon: the Quiet Reformer* (New York 1958).

CLYDE L. MANSCHRECK, *Professor of Religion, Duke University.*

MELANESIA, měl-à-nē′zhà, a great zone of islands in the South Pacific Ocean named from the dark-skinned appearance of its inhabitants, called Melanesians. It comprises the huge island of New Guinea together with numerous archipelagoes to the north and east, including the Bismarcks, Solomons, New Hebrides, New Caledonia, and Fiji. It is one of three great regions into which tropical Oceania is divided, the others being Polynesia to the east and Micronesia to the north (see OCEANIA). Many of the islands immediately west of New Guinea, though classed as part of Malaysia, have population elements of the Melanesian type.

Politically, Melanesia is divided into seven territories under the control of four powers. The Netherlands holds Netherlands New Guinea, comprising the western half of that island and nearby groups, though its claim is disputed by Indonesia, which calls it West Irian. The southeast quarter of the island of New Guinea, with nearby islands, constitutes the Territory of Papua, an Australian possession; the northeast quarter is the Territory of New Guinea, a United Nations trust territory which also embraces the Bismarck Archipelago, the Admiralty Islands, and the northern Solomons (Bougainville, Buka); the two territories are jointly administered by Australia as the Territory of Papua and New Guinea. The United Kingdom has two jurisdictions, the British Solomon Islands Protectorate and Fiji. France holds New Caledonia and its small dependencies, while France and Great Britain jointly hold the New Hebrides Condominium.

Physical Features and Resources.—New Guinea forms part of what geologists call the Australian continental platform, while the islands north and east are tops of partially submerged mountain systems which traverse the floor of the Pacific Ocean. The surrounding seas call for skilled navigation because of the many coral reefs, currents, and channels. The climate near sea level is hot and humid. The region from New Hebrides westward is malarial, but New Caledonia and Fiji are free from malaria.

The natural vegetation, combining Asian- and Australian-type plants, consists mainly of tropical rain forests. There are also zones of coarse grasses and scrub, and mangrove swamps along the shores. Stands of pines occur on some islands and with other valuable timbers may be milled for export. New Guinea has extensive temperate grasslands in the high interior, and fresh-water sago swamps. The people variously stress in their diets such tropical roots and fruits as yams, taro, sweet potatoes, and bananas. Most soils are badly leached by heavy rains, but favorable soils occur on alluvial flats and in areas of continuing volcanism along the north New Guinea coast and eastward to the New Hebrides. Here commercial plantations are most frequent, growing coconuts and sometimes cacao, coffee, rubber, sugarcane, and tropical fruits.

The New Guinea area has various types of marsupial mammals such as survive in the Australian region. It also has a very rich bird life, including the cassowary and bird of paradise. Snakes, lizards, and crocodiles abound. Such fauna thin out in the islands to the east, where the main larger animals are rats and bats together with pigs, dogs, and chickens introduced by man. European settlers have added cattle, horses, and sometimes sheep. The principal indigenous flesh food is fish, with pig eaten particularly on ceremonial occasions. The seas yield trochus, pearl, and other commercially valuable shell.

Gold has been mined in Australian New Guinea since the 1880's and more recently in Fiji. The Dutch have an important petroleum field in the "Bird's Head" area of west New Guinea. In 1958, after long prospecting, a strike was also made in Australian Papua. New Caledonia contributes a considerable part of the world's nickel and chrome. Rock phosphate, iron, copper, and some other minerals have been worked on various islands. Yet little is known of the mineral resources in many parts of Melanesia, and only the most valuable of the known deposits have been mined.

The People.—Racial Types.

—Melanesians number about 3 million, broken into many little local groups differing more or less in language and custom. Most are of medium height, with frizzly hair and dark skin pigment, which results in their often being called an Oceanic Negroid (Negrolike) type. There is great variability from brown to almost blue-black and from tallness (the Fijians) to extreme shortness (the pygmy Negrito, or "little Negro," of west New Guinea).

The racial history of the region is very complex. Lowered ocean levels during the last glacial period, which was at its maximum about 30,000 years ago, made it possible for migrant bands of "early modern" men to cross narrowed sea channels from the Asiatic continental shelf to the Australian continental shelf. They evidently carried genetic strains which in subsequent breeding produced the rugged-faced Australian aborigine and the short to pygmy Negritoid (little, Negrolike) peoples of Tasmania and New Guinea. A prevalent racial type in west and south New Guinea and in inland parts of some of the other islands, with a large nose and other prominent features, may be derived from hybridizations of these early elements: it is often called

the Papuan type. (Papua is from a Malay word meaning "frizzly hair.") It contrasts with a prevalent, more Negroid type in the populations of north and east New Guinea and the coastal areas and small islands eastward to Fiji; generally broader faced with squat nose and thicker lips, it is often called the Melanesian type in a narrower sense. This seems to be a product of hybridizations of the earlier migrant elements, especially the Negritoid, with later peoples who came from the area of southeast Asia by canoe after the glacial decline. Until we know more about the complex racial history of the latter area, especially what are broadly called Proto-Malay (first Malay) elements which preceded the "flooding" of these western islands by Mongoloid genetic characters somewhat prior to the Christian era, our understanding of the Melanesian racial heritage must remain correspondingly uncertain.

Language.—The speech situation in Melanesia corresponds roughly to this racial distinction. Peoples of the Melanesian type usually speak languages of the great Malayo-Polynesian family, which was carried by overseas migrations from Madagascar (off Africa) to the easternmost Polynesian islands. Peoples of the Papuan type usually speak languages of evidently older derivation, differentiated (as are also the Australian aborigine languages) into many localized kinds of speech so unlike as to be quite unintelligible outside the immediate region. Some scholars profess to see a similar duality amid the many localized variations in social organization, religion, art, and other aspects of custom.

Way of Life.—Most Melanesians live in permanent villages dotted along the coasts and inland waterways, with adjacent gardens and fisheries. Houses are sometimes built on piles over the water. In forested country they usually scatter more sparsely in hamlets, perhaps shifting their houses as new gardens are cleared seasonally. Parts of the New Guinea highlands have large village settlements perched in defensible positions, with the sweet potato as the food staple. Much trading occurs in western Melanesia, in items such as shell, sago flour, salt, pots, and feathers. Among the tiny groups of inhabitants, surrounded by feuding, warlike neighbors, human relationships tend to be defined meticulously, so that family and kinship systems are complicated, and trading associations, secret societies, and other forms of intergroup organizations are marked by a kind of "international law" in miniature. The Papuan-type societies lean to patrilineal descent, while those of the Melanesian type vary in emphasizing matrilineal or patrilineal principles or both. Religion centers around beliefs in ancestral ghosts and animistic spirits, the practice of magic, fear of sorcery, and elaborate rituals, such as initiation ceremonies and secret-society gatherings. The often rich art traditions are closely associated with religious ideas, as in bodily decoration, sculpture such as masks and images, and lusty dance and "drama."

In west-central New Guinea there are still extensive forest and highland zones which have not been penetrated by the white man. Their populations are in the Stone Age, and warfare, sometimes with headhunting and cannibalism, makes their life precarious. As government patrols penetrate, however, such groups quickly settle down to peace, acquire trade goods, accept the more obviously effective Western medicines, cut trails and possibly roads, and supply laborers for mines and plantations. Most accessible Melanesian communities are Christianized, and many of their traditional customs have lapsed or become modified. Increasing numbers of the younger generation have a fair-to-good schooling; a few have university degrees. Since World War II the controlling authorities have emphasized training of Melanesian communities in district and local self-government, and selected young people are taught to be mechanics, radio operators, medical workers, and teachers. In Fiji, New Caledonia, and Australian New Guinea, Melanesian representatives sit with Europeans in the local legislatures.

Towns.—Each territory has a number of town settlements where European officials, traders, missionaries, and settlers have established themselves. Most are coastal ports, where harbors attracted vessels during the 19th century, but a few are inland mining towns. A few have grown into cities which have virtually all modern amenities. Such are Suva in Fiji (pop. 1956, 36,967) and Nouméa in New Caledonia (pop. 1957, 22,238). In Netherlands New Guinea the town centers include Hollandia (the capital), Merauke, Sorong, and Manokwari; in Australian New Guinea, Port Moresby (capital), Rabaul, Lae, Madang, and Wau; in the British Solomons, Honiara (capital) and Gizo; in the New Hebrides, Vila (capital) and Santo; in New Caledonia, Nouméa (capital), Bourail, La Foa, and Tiebaghi; in Fiji, Suva (capital), Lautoka, Levuka, and Vatukoula. Such centers have ethnically complex populations: local islanders, Europeans, part-islanders, Asians, and migrants from the outer island zones which they serve.

Communications.—Supplementing old trails and canoe routes, Europeans have brought the ship, the airplane, the radio telegraph, and to some extent roading. A shipping network connects the major ports with the larger world. Small motor and sailing vessels carry the inter-island and coastal traffic. Road systems rarely extend far beyond the ports because of the rugged terrain and heavy rains. Regular transoceanic air routes give quick access to the main urban centers. In the New Guinea area a busy air traffic by small planes provides connections with even remote government, mission, mining, and plantation centers.

History.—Malay traders have long penetrated western New Guinea to obtain bird-of-paradise plumes and other wanted goods. After Europeans had reached southeast Asia early in the 16th century, various Portuguese, Spanish, Dutch, English, and French voyagers passed through sections of Melanesia. In 1595 Álvaro de Mendaña de Neyra, a Spanish explorer, made an ill-fated attempt to found a colony in the Solomons. When the Dutch succeeded the Portuguese and Spaniards in control of the "Spice Islands" (Moluccas) in the 17th century, they acquired title to west New Guinea by virtue of a treaty with Malay rulers who counted it part of their domain. In 1828 the line was officially drawn across the middle of New Guinea as the eastern border of Netherlands sovereignty; but the Dutch did not begin to explore and pacify areas beyond a few coastal trading ports until the early 1900's.

The rest of Melanesia, too, was penetrated by Europeans considerably later than most of the other Pacific island areas. This was understandable in view of the hazards of navigating its waters, the warlike propensities of the people, and (in the western islands) the dreaded malaria. Missionaries largely pioneered the opening of Fiji in the 1830's and of New Caledonia about a decade later; the rest of Melanesia was little known until the 1870's. Venturesome traders then gradually penetrated the region, many selling guns and liquor, buying land, or recruiting (sometimes kidnaping) laborers for plantations in northern Australia and elsewhere. These activities, along with the introduction of new diseases, brought disruption and depopulation in their wake; the islanders often responded by killing settlers and missionaries. Warships of the great powers patrolled the coasts, and the worst abuses were prohibited by international agreements. Conversion of many groups to Christianity was initially accomplished by Polynesian teachers, especially from Tahiti and Samoa.

Modern political annexations started when France took New Caledonia in 1853, ostensibly to protect French missionaries. After much international rivalry in the Central Pacific, the United Kingdom raised its flag in Fiji in 1874. In 1884 Germany established a protectorate over the northeast coast of New Guinea and the Micronesian islands northward, where German nationals had developed commercial interests. The United Kingdom at the same time moved into Papua and in 1893 established its protectorate in the Solomons. A British and French naval commission supervised the New Hebrides for a decade prior to establishment of the joint condominium in 1906. In that year Great Britain transferred Papua to the newly formed Commonwealth of Australia.

In 1914 Australian forces occupied German New Guinea. In the peace settlement following World War I, the territory became a League of Nations mandate under Australian control; with the establishment of the United Nations after World War II, it was given the status of a trust territory. During the war, the Melanesian islands from the Solomons westward were scenes of bitter struggles between Japanese and Allied forces, so that Americans became familiar with names such as the Coral Sea, Guadalcanal, Rabaul, and Hollandia.

When, after World War II, the Republic of Indonesia was taking form, Dutch and Indonesian negotiators held the question of sovereignty over west New Guinea in abeyance. Since 1949 a bitter dispute has continued between the Dutch, who hold it as part of the Kingdom of the Netherlands, and the Indonesians, who claim it. Complicating the problem is the fact that Australia and New Zealand have declared themselves to be interested parties because of the strategic nature of the area in Pacific defense. The South Pacific Commission, a six-nation advisory and consultative body created in 1948, is advancing health, economic, and social development in all the Melanesian territories, as well as in Polynesia and Micronesia.

See PACIFIC OCEAN for map, and separate articles on individual islands.

Consult Keesing, Felix M., *The South Seas in the Modern World*, 2d ed. (New York 1945); Belshaw, Cyril S., *Island Administration in the South West Pacific* (London 1950); Oliver, Douglas L., *The Pacific Islands* (Cambridge, Mass., 1951); Elkin, Adolphus P., *Social Anthropology in Melanesia* (London 1953); *Pacific Islands Year Book* and *Pacific Islands Monthly* (Sydney).

FELIX M. KEESING,
Professor of Anthropology, Stanford University.

MELANIN. See COMPLEXION.—*Pigmentation.*

MELANORRHOEA. See VARNISH TREE.

MELANOSIS. See CHLOASMA.

MELANTERITE. See COPPERAS.

MELBA, měl'bà, DAME **Nellie** (stage name of HELEN PORTER MITCHELL), Australian operatic soprano: b. Richmond, near Melbourne, Australia, May 19, 1861; d. Sydney, Feb. 23, 1931. She had a good education in instrumental music but, because of her father's opposition, did not begin to study voice until after her marriage to Capt. Charles N. F. Armstrong in 1882. After a year of instruction by Mathilde Marchesi in Paris, she made her debut in Brussels (1887) as Gilda in *Rigoletto,* taking the name Melba for the city of Melbourne. An immediate popular and critical success, she rose rapidly to the height of fame as an international operatic star, appearing regularly at Covent Garden in London and (from 1893) at the Metropolitan Opera in New York City, with frequent tours of the Continent. She was made a Dame of the British Empire in 1918 and retired to Australia in 1926. Though not a great actress, she had a remarkably pure and flexible coloratura voice, which she managed with flawless and apparently effortless skill. She wrote an autobiography, *Melodies and Memories* (1925). Melba toast and peach Melba are named after the prima donna.

Consult Colson, Percy, *Melba* (London 1932).

MELBOURNE, měl'bẽrn, 2D VISCOUNT (WILLIAM LAMB), English statesman: b. ? London, England, March 15, 1779; d. Brocket Hall, near Hatfield, Hertfordshire, Nov. 24, 1848. He entered Trinity College, Cambridge, in 1796 and Lincoln's Inn in 1797. In 1804 he was called to the bar, and two years later he was elected to represent Leominster in the House of Commons. His marriage in 1805 to Lady Caroline Ponsonby, the eccentric daughter of the 3d earl of Bessborough, was an unhappy one. She became infatuated with Lord Byron in 1812, and in 1824 became mentally deranged, when she happened to meet the poet's funeral procession. Melbourne separated from her in 1825.

Because of his support of Catholic emancipation, Melbourne lost his seat in Parliament in 1812. He was re-elected in 1816, and from 1827 to 1828 served as chief secretary of Ireland, during the ministry of George Canning. After his father's death, he entered the House of Lords (1829). During the ministry of Lord Grey (1830–1834), he served as home secretary. Melbourne succeeded Grey as prime minister in July 1834, but was replaced in November by the Conservative, Sir Robert Peel. Melbourne's second ministry began in April 1835 and ended in May 1839. After a cabinet crisis over the Bedchamber Question (the queen wished to appoint her own lady attendants), Melbourne formed his third and last cabinet, and remained in power from May 1839 to August 1841. In 1842 he was struck by paralysis and thereafter took little part in politics.

Melbourne was a right wing Liberal (Whig) and not the moving spirit for the reforms which took place during his ministries. He was apathetic to the Reform Bill of 1832 and was opposed to parliamentary reform and the repeal of the corn laws. During his ministries, the most important legislation was the New Poor Law (1834), the Municipal Corporations Bill (1835), the Poor Law Bill (1838), and a bill (1840) which reformed the postal system and provided for a uniform penny postage. No action was taken on Canada, during Melbourne's third ministry, subsequent to the presentation of Lord Durham's famous *Report on the Affairs of British North America* (1839), and it was left to later governments to take up Durham's recommendations. In May 1839, Parliament also rejected the petition submitted by the Chartists, who called for sweeping parliamentary reforms. Melbourne was instrumental, after the death of William IV in 1837, in instructing the young Victoria in her responsibilities as a constitutional monarch. Public attention was focused on his private life from 1835 to 1836, when he was involved in a divorce suit (see NORTON, CAROLINE ELIZABETH).

Consult Cecil, Lord David, *Melbourne* (Indianapolis, Ind., 1954).

MELBOURNE, city, Australia, capital of the State of Victoria, situated on the Yarra River, two miles above its mouth on Hobson's Bay and on the north arm of Port Phillip Bay. Melbourne City, incorporated in 1842, was named after Lord Melbourne (William Lamb, 2d Viscount Melbourne), who was prime minister of England at the time of its founding. The city is governed by a lord mayor and city council.

The city and its very extensive suburbs occupy an undulating area of the Yarra Valley. The metropolitan area, which embraces 714 square miles, includes the suburbs of Carlton, Collingwood, Fitzroy, Brunswick, Coburg, South Melbourne, Richmond, Prahran, Kew, Hawthorn, Malvern, Camberwell, Caulfield, Brighton, Heidelberg, and Essendon. The business section of the city, approximately one square mile in area, is built on a grid plan, on the north bank of the Yarra. Streetcars form the chief means of transport within the city, and rail, streetcar, and bus services operate to the suburbs.

The Melbourne City Council controls nearly 8,000 acres. More than 1,000 acres of this area is taken up by parks and gardens, among them the Treasury Gardens, Flagstaff Gardens, Fitzroy Gardens, and the 102-acre Melbourne Botanic Gardens, which is beautifully landscaped and contains a fine collection of trees and plants. The cottage in which Capt. James Cook was born now stands in the Fitzroy Gardens. (As a tribute to the captain, who was the first to explore and chart Australia's eastern coast, the cottage was moved from England to Melbourne in 1934.)

Public buildings in the city include the state Parliament House, where the Legislative Council and Legislative Assembly meet; state administrative offices; law courts; the town hall; the natural history museum, with its excellent collection of Australian aboriginal artifacts—weapons, and domestic and ceremonial objects; the art gallery, with its important collection, containing many items bought under the bequest of Alfred Felton; and the public library, with its 750,000 books. Government House, residence of the state governor, stands immediately south of the Yarra. As the temporary seat of the Federal Parliament from 1901 to 1927, Melbourne was the administrative capital of Australia, and various offices, departments, and organizations of the federal government still maintain their headquarters in the city. The United States is represented by a consul general. Ecclesiastical buildings in Melbourne include St. Paul's (Anglican) Cathedral, St. Patrick's (Roman Catholic) Cathedral, Scots Church (Presbyterian), and Wesley Church (Methodist). Other notable places are the Stock Exchange, the Royal Mint, the Note and Stamp Printing Office, the Exhibition Building, and Her Majesty's Theatre.

The University of Melbourne (q.v.), located in Carlton, was founded in 1853. Other important schools in Melbourne are the Conservatorium of Music (established in 1910) and the Royal Melbourne Technical College (established in 1887). In addition to the coeducational public schools, there are many large private schools run by religious organizations. The city also is provided with facilities for almost every type of competitive sport and is particularly renowned for the Melbourne Cup (horse race) which has been run annually at Flemington since 1861. In 1956 the city was the site of the Olympic Games.

Melbourne is an important transportation center, a hub for rail, road, and air services, and for shipping. A board of harbor trust commissioners controls the port, which has 105 berths. In 1962 the volume of shipping exceeded 20 million tons gross; 1,830 overseas vessels (with a gross tonnage of 16,838,426) used the port. Imports from overseas totaled 4,640,741 tons and overseas exports totaled 1,400,614 tons. Principal imports were petroleum and its derivatives, vehicles, phosphate rock, paper, lumber, and iron and steel. Wool, flour, frozen meat, fruit, barley, and dairy produce were the chief exports. A total of 1,056 interstate vessels operated through Melbourne in 1962; principal imports were coal, iron and steel, raw sugar, lumber, and paper; exports comprised vehicles, machinery, oil and derivatives, and paper. More than a million passengers a year use Melbourne's airport at Essendon, and air freight handled exceeds 43 million pounds a year.

Road and air transportation companies are established in the city, as well as important firms engaged in commercial, financial, industrial, mining, or pastoral activities. Melbourne is also an important livestock market and a center for wool auctions. Engineering workshops are extensive and produce a wide range of items. Repair facilities are available for ships, locomotives, and aircraft. Manufacturing and processing industries have long been established; products include textiles and clothing, footwear, chemicals, paint, agricultural implements, electrical goods, machinery, cigarettes, and a wide range of processed foods. The automotive industry is well developed and growing; it has assembly plants for imported vehicles and also produces engines, accessories, and parts. Aircraft construction and research activities are centered in Melbourne; oil refineries have been established; and printing and packaging activities are highly developed. One evening and two morning newspapers are published; there are six commercial and two nationally operated radio stations and two commercial and one nationally operated television stations.

Melbourne owes its origin to settlers coming from Tasmania, beginning in 1835, notably John Batman and John Pascoe Fawkner. The town, named in 1837, was laid out by Robert Russell and Robert Hoddle. By 1841 Melbourne had a population of 5,000, and the next year it was proclaimed a city. Following the discovery of gold in the hinterland in 1851, Melbourne grew rapidly and for four decades was Australia's largest city. Its population was about 500,000 in 1901, when it became the temporary federal capital. According to the 1961 census, Melbourne City had a population of 76,483, and the metropolitan area of Melbourne had a total population of 1,907,366.

Consult Newnham, Wilfred H., *Melbourne, the Biography of a City* (Melbourne 1956).

R. M. YOUNGER.

MELBOURNE, měl'bẽrn, city, Florida, in Brevard County, at an altitude of 20 feet, on Indian River, 22 miles south of Cocoa. The city, which is served by the Florida East Coast Railway and by Eastern Airlines, is a shipping center for citrus fruits and vegetables. It is also a resort for sportsmen, hunters in search of small game, and anglers in pursuit of fresh- and salt-water fish. To the east, across Indian River, is Melbourne Beach, a bathing resort. Melbourne manufactures novelties and has a bottling works. The city, which has a daily newspaper founded in 1894, was first settled in 1878 and incorporated in 1888. Since 1926, it has been governed by a manager and five councilmen. Pop. 11,982.

MELBOURNE, University of. It was founded in 1853 and is located in Carlton, one of the suburbs of Melbourne, Australia. Trinity College, Ormond College, Queen's College, Newman College, and University Women's College are residential colleges affiliated with the university. The university has faculties of agriculture, architecture, arts, dental science, economics and commerce, education, engineering, law, medicine, music, science, and veterinary science. There were 11,451 students (63% of them full-time) and almost 900 faculty members in the 1961–1962 academic year. The university libraries contain nearly 300,000 volumes.

MELCHER, měl'chẽr, **Frederic G(ershom),** American publisher and editor: b. Malden, Mass., April 12, 1879; d. Montclair, N.J., March 9, 1963. From high school he went as a clerk with Lauriat and Company, Boston bookshop, where he became a popular salesman with a large personal following. From 1913 to 1918, he was manager of a bookstore in Indianapolis, Ind., the W. K. Stewart Company. Under his management the store thrived and built up a clientele of writers and artists, which included such prominent figures as Booth Tarkington, Vachel Lindsay, and James Whitcomb Riley. In 1918, Melcher moved to New York City and became coeditor of *Publishers' Weekly*. The following year, in collaboration with Franklin K. Mathiews, librarian of the Boy Scouts of America, he started Children's Book Week, which is now observed annually by libraries, schools, and booksellers throughout the country. In 1921, Melcher established the John Newbery Medal, awarded annually by the American Library Association for the most distinguished contribution to American literature for children. In 1937, he established the Caldecott Medal (named after the 19th century English artist and illustrator, Randolph Caldecott), which is awarded annually for the most distinguished American picture book for children. He was also influential in starting the quadrennial presentation, made by the American Booksellers Association, of 200 books for the library of the White House. Melcher was coeditor of *Publishers' Weekly* for 40 years, during which he supported every movement aimed to popularize book reading, and to him, in large measure, is due credit for the high quality of present-day children's books. See also LITERATURE FOR CHILDREN.

MELCHERS, měl′chěrz, **Gari** (in full JULIUS GARI), American painter: b. Detroit, Mich., Aug. 11, 1860; d. near Fredericksburg, Va., Nov. 30, 1932. In 1877, his father, who was a sculptor, sent him to study art at the Royal Academy, Düsseldorf, Germany, where Melchers worked under Eduard von Gebhardt. In 1881 Melchers entered the École des Beaux-Arts in Paris, and later, he studied with Gustave Boulanger and Jules Lefebvre. *The Letter,* his first picture accepted for an exhibition, was hung at the Salon of 1882. In 1884, after trips to Italy and the United States, he returned to Europe and worked both in Paris and in Egmond, The Netherlands.

Melchers was primarily a painter of genre, both religious and secular, and he excelled in scenes of Dutch peasant life. The motto, "Waar en Klaar" (True and Clear), inscribed over the door of his studio in Egmond, expressed his philosophy of art. *The Sermon,* hung at the Salon of 1886, established his fame, and at the International Exhibition of 1889, three of his works were on view. The rest of his life was filled with fame and fortune. Honors were heaped upon him, and his paintings were purchased for public buildings and famous art galleries. After 1914, he made his home in the United States.

Melchers' paintings are exhibited at the Musée du Luxembourg, Paris; the Metropolitan Museum of Art, New York City; the Art Institute, Chicago; the Carnegie Institute, Pittsburgh; the Pennsylvania Academy of Fine Arts, Philadelphia; the University of Michigan Library; the Detroit Public Library; the Detroit Institute of Arts; and at the State Capitol, Jefferson City, Mo. In Washington, D.C., his paintings are in the Library of Congress; the Freer Collection of the Smithsonian Institution; the Corcoran Gallery; and the Phillips Memorial Gallery.

MELCHERS, Henrik Melcher, Swedish musician: b. Stockholm, Sweden, May 30, 1882. He studied at the Stockholm Conservatory and in France at the Paris Conservatory. From 1925 to 1934, he taught harmony at the Stockholm Conservatory, and after 1934, counterpoint, composition and instrumentation. In 1932 he was elected a member of the Swedish Royal Academy of Music. His compositions, some of which show a French influence, include *Acht Zigeunerlieder* (*Eight Gypsy Songs,* 1910), with orchestra; *Swedish Rhapsody* (1914), an orchestral work; *Näcken* (*Seagod,* 1916), a symphonic piece; and *La Kermesse* (*Country Fair,* 1919).

MELCHERS, měl′kěrs, **Paulus,** German Roman Catholic prelate: b. Münster, Westphalia, Germany, Jan. 6, 1813; d. Rome, Italy, Dec. 14, 1895. He studied law at Bonn and theology at Munich, and in 1841 was ordained priest. In 1857 he was made bishop of Osnabrück and in 1866 appointed by Pope Pius IX as archbishop of Cologne. At the Vatican Council (1870), he was at first opposed to the proclamation of papal infallibility as dogma. Later he accepted it as dogma and excommunicated three professors who refused to declare themselves in agreement with it. During the Kulturkampf, his conspicuous activities brought him into collision with the government, and in 1874 he was fined and imprisoned for six months. In 1875, when he learned that he might be deported for refusing to resign his archbishopric, he fled the country and for the next nine years administered his diocese from the Netherlands. Because he was not free to return, he finally resigned in 1885. Pope Leo XIII then called him to Rome and created him cardinal (1885). During a serious illness in 1892, he joined the Jesuits.

MELCHIADES. See MILTIADES, SAINT.

MELCHIOR, měl′kǐ-ôr, a name given to one of the Magi who visited the infant Jesus. See WISE MEN FROM THE EAST, THE.

MELCHIOR, měl′kė-ôr, **Carl Joseph,** German banker: b. Hamburg, Germany, Oct. 13, 1871; d. there, Dec. 30, 1933. He was educated at Hamburg, Bonn, and Berlin. In 1902, he became a partner in the banking firm of M. M. Warburg and Company, and he remained with the firm throughout the rest of his life. Following World War I, he served as economic adviser to the German government at all the postwar political and reparations conferences. He was one of the six German delegates who negotiated the treaty at Versailles in 1919. From 1926 to 1930, he represented Germany on the finance committee of the League of Nations, and in 1930 was made committee chairman. He was appointed as a representative for Germany on the board of the Bank for International Settlements at Basel, Switzerland, in 1930, and in the same year was elected deputy chairman of the board, a position which he held until early in 1933, when the Nazi government removed him as German representative. Melchior also assisted in the preparation of an economic and social history of World War I, which was sponsored by the League of Nations and the Carnegie Endowment for International Peace.

MELCHIOR, měl′kyôr, **Lauritz Lebrecht Hommel,** operatic tenor: b. Copenhagen, Denmark, March 20, 1890. His career began early, when he sang as a boy soprano in an English church in Copenhagen. He made his operatic debut in 1913 in the baritone role of Silvio in Ruggiero Leoncavallo's *Pagliacci* at the Royal Opera House in Copenhagen. In 1918 he began singing tenor roles, and in 1924 made his debut at the Bayreuth Festival, where he soon established a reputation as an outstanding Wagnerian *Heldentenor* (heroic tenor). He made his debut at the Metropolitan Opera House, New York City, in 1926. His ability and stamina in the difficult and exhausting Wagnerian roles made him the leading Wagnerian tenor at the Metropolitan Opera. Within a decade he had sung the role of Tristan 100 times, and he very quickly established a record for having sung more performances of *Tristan, Siegfried,* and *Tannhäuser,* than any other singer, living or dead.

MELCHITES or **MELKITES,** měl′kǐts, a community of Christians who adhere to the

Byzantine rite, who use Arabic as their chief liturgical language, and who are subject first to the bishop of Rome (the pope) and secondly to the Melchite patriarch of Antioch (now Antakya, Turkey). The name is now usually applied only to Catholic. Uniats (see EASTERN RITE CHURCHES), although it has been and still is occasionally used to designate Orthodox Melchites, who broke with Rome following the schism of Photius (867) and of Michael Caerularius (1054).

The liturgy is ordinarily celebrated in Arabic, although, for special occasions, it is also celebrated entirely in Greek. Maximos IV Saigh, the present Melchite patriarch of Antioch (elected in 1947), who bears the personal title of "Patriarch of Antioch, Alexandria, Jerusalem, and all the East," is one of three Eastern rite Catholic partriarchs of Antioch. (The others are the Syrian and Maronite patriarchs.) There are also Orthodox patriarchs. The chief residence of the Melchite patriarch of Antioch is Damascus, Syria. He also resides during part of each year in Alexandria, Egypt, and in Jerusalem. Of the 375,000 Melchites, the majority in 1957 were located in Syria and Egypt; the rest were located in the Western Hemisphere and Australia. The United States in 1957 had 50,000, and Canada had about 1,000.

MELCHIZEDEK, mĕl-kĭz'ĕ-dĕk (in Douay Version MELCHISEDECH), the name of a pre-Aaronic and pre-Levitical priest-king mentioned in the Bible, Abraham, after returning from a battle with Chedorlaomer, king of Elam, was blessed by Melchizedek, king of Salem, and served bread and wine. Melchizedek received from Abraham a tenth of the spoils taken in the battle (Genesis 14:17–20). In the Epistle to the Hebrews, the author designates Christ as a high priest forever, after the order of Melchizedek (Hebrews 5:6–10). He explains Melchizedek's name as meaning "King of righteousness" and his title "King of Salem," as meaning "King of peace." According to the author of Hebrews, Melchizedek had no lineage and neither a beginning nor an end, but remained a priest continually (Hebrews 7:1–3).

MELCHTHAL, mĕlk'täl, **Arnold von** (also ARNOLD AN DER HALDEN), a legendary Swiss patriot of the late 13th and early 14th centuries. He was immortalized in Johann Christoph Friedrich Schiller's play, *Wilhelm Tell* (1804). Melchthal, who lived in what is now the Canton of Unterwalden, incurred the wrath of the Austrian governor and was compelled to flee to escape punishment, whereupon the governor seized Arnold's aged father and had his eyes put out. The son, enraged by this barbarity, with two friends, Walter Fürst of Uri and Werner Stauffacher of Schwyz, planned and successfully conducted a revolt against the Austrian oppressor. Near Brunnen, Switzerland is the Rütli (or Grütli), a meadow in which the three men are said to have sworn an oath uniting their respective cantons in a fight against the tyrannous rule of Austria. See also WILLIAM TELL.

MELCOMBE, BARON. See DODINGTON, GEORGE BUBB.

MELCOMBE-REGIS. See WEYMOUTH AND MELCOMBE-REGIS.

MELDOLLA, Andrea. See SCHIAVONE, ANDREA.

MELDOMETER. See MELTING POINT.

MELEAGER, mĕl-ê-ā'jẽr, Greek epigrammatist: b. probably Gadara, Palestine, c. 140 B.C.; d. about 70 B.C. Although he was a poet and a cynic philosopher, Meleager is remembered chiefly for his collection of about 130 epigrams. He was the first to bring together isolated epigrams for the sake of preserving them. He entitled his collection *Stephanos* (about 90 B.C.), meaning *Garland* or *Wreath,* and in the introduction likened each poet to a small flower. The poems, often erotic, are nearly all on the subject of love, and most of them are elegiac. The collection includes epigrams attributed to about 50 poets, from the most ancient lyric period of Greek poetry, down to Meleager's time. The use of the word "garland" for the title may have inspired "anthology," meaning "bouquet," which was first applied to a collection of poems in the Byzantine period.

Consult Wright, Frederick Adam, tr., "Meleager of Gadara," in *Poets of the Greek Anthology* (New York 1924).

MELEAGER, mĕl-ê-ā'jẽr, in Greek mythology, the hero of the Calydonian boar hunt. The earliest form of the story is found in the *Iliad.* When a monstrous boar devastated the land, Meleager (the son of Oeneus, king of Aetolia and of Althaea, the daughter of Thestius) gathered a band of heroes about him and, after a great struggle with considerable loss of life, slew the beast. The Aetolians and the Curetes then quarreled over the disposition of the boar's head and hide. During the quarrel, Meleager killed one of his maternal uncles. His mother, enraged by the death of her brother, cursed Meleager and prayed that the Erinyes might destroy him. The hero withdrew from the fight, but when the Curetes stormed the town, he entered the battle and put them to flight. According to Homer, Meleager never returned home, for the Erinyes had heard the curse of his mother and overtook him.

Later writers ascribe his death to Althaea, his mother, who shortly after Meleager's birth took possession of a fire brand which the Moirai said would continue to burn as long as he lived. Althaea had extinguished the brand and hidden it in a chest. When she heard that Meleager had killed her brothers, she burned the brand, and Meleager died. See also CALYDONIAN BOAR.

MELEDA. See MLJET.

MELEGNANO, mä-lâ-nyä'nô (formerly MARIGNANO), town, in northern Italy, in the province of Milano, about 10 miles southeast of Milan. The town is an agricultural center, but also manufactures a few products, such as textiles.

Two battles were fought in the vicinity. At the Battle of Marignano (still generally referred to by the former name of the town) on Sept. 13 and 14, 1515, the French fought under Francis I, together with the Venetians, and defeated the Duke of Milan and Swiss mercenaries. In the 19th century (June 8, 1859), the French gained a victory there over the Austrians. Pop. (1951) town 10,806; commune 11,170.

MELENDEZ VALDES, mȧl-lān'dȧth väl-dȧs', **Juan,** Spanish poet and politician: b. Ribera del Fresno, Spain, May 11, 1754; d. Montpellier, France, May 24, 1817. He wrote ballads while studying law at the University of Salamanca, where he became a protégé of the poet José Cadalso y Vázquez. In 1780, he was awarded a Spanish Academy prize for his pastoral poem, *Batilo*. A prize-winning comedy, *Las bodas de Camacho el rico* (*The Wedding of Camacho the Rich*), was ill received when produced on the stage, but his first volume of poems (1785) firmly established his literary reputation. He became a close friend of the statesman and author, Gaspar Melchor de Jovellanos, who secured his appointment as professor of the humanities at the University of Salamanca, a post he held from 1778 to 1789. Later Jovellanos appointed him to a succession of judicial posts. He was exiled from Madrid in 1797 at the fall of Jovellanos, and when Spanish government was restored following the Napoleonic invasion (1808–1813), he fled to France in 1813 because of his collaboration with the government of Joseph Bonaparte. Meléndez Valdés' many lyric poems, such as *El amor mariposa* (*Butterfly Love*), have been characterized as "agreeable anachronisms," even for his time, written in the florid and artificial manner of the 18th century, but with grace and music. His odes, such as *Oda a la Verdad* (*Ode to Truth*), reflect the artistic and philosophic sentiments of the era of Enlightenment.

MELETIUS or **MELITIUS,** mê-lē'shĭ-ŭs, Saint, bishop of Antioch in Syria: d. 381. He became bishop at Antioch in 360, at a time when the church there was torn with controversy between Arian and Nicene (orthodox) factions. A month after his consecration he was banished as a Nicene by the Arian emperor, Constantius II. He was recalled to his see by Emperor Julian the Apostate (r. 361–363), and twice again was banished. Finally reinstated in 378, he presided at the Council of Constantinople in 381, during the deliberations of which he died.

MELETIUS or **MELITIUS,** bishop of Lycopolis in Egypt: fl. 303–325 A.D. He refused to accept the terms laid down by Peter, bishop of Alexandria, for the return to the church of members who had renounced their faith during the persecutions of Diocletian (245–313). For this he was excommunicated by Peter, but after a period of banishment he returned to Egypt and founded a schismatic church. The Council of Nicaea in 325 permitted Meletian priests to function, subordinate to the bishop of Alexandria, and Meletius was allowed to retain the title of bishop, but without a see. Some Meletian schismatics appear to have survived, chiefly in Egypt, until the 8th century.

MELI, mȧ'lē, **Giovanni,** Sicilian poet and physician: b. Palermo, Sicily, March 6, 1740; d. there, Dec. 20, 1815. Writing in the Sicilian dialect, he gave literary expression to the Sicilian national character. From his pen came many odes, sonnets, and pastorals, the latter marked by a delicate feeling for nature. His early poem, the satirical *La fata galanti* (1762; *The Gallant Elf*), shows Virgilian influences. His many elegies, such as the collection entitled *La Buccolica* (1787; 5 elegies and 11 idylls), were fresh and spontaneous, while his mock heroic poem, *Don Chis-*ciotti i Sanciu Panza (1785–1787; *Don Quixote and Sancho Panza*), displayed a philosophic humanitarianism. Meli gave a prestige to the Sicilian dialect which was influential in the emergence of a Sicilian academy in Palermo.

Consult Di Giovanni, Alessio, *La vita e l'opera di Giovanni Meli* (Florence 1934).

MELIC GRASS, mĕl'ĭk, a common name for fairly tall grasses of the genus *Melica* (family Gramineae, tribe Festuceae) comprising about 60 species native to temperate and cool parts of the world, including 17 species in the United States. The culms are erect and simple; the leaves soft and flat; the panicles simple or compound, and narrow to widely spreading. The spikelets contain 2 to 6 florets, of which the terminal one or more may be sterile and reduced. The woody melic, *M. frutescens,* is a species with ranges in the southwestern deserts of the United States. It reaches a height of 6 feet and may be somewhat woody at the base. Some grasses of this genus have forage value.

Richard M. Straw.

MELIKOV. See Loris-Melikov, Count Mikhail Tariyelovich.

MELILLA, mȧ-lē'[l]yä, city, Spanish Africa, located on the north coast of Morocco about 165 miles east of Tangier and 30 miles west of the Algerian border. Occupied by Spain since 1497, it is administratively a part of the Province of Málaga in European Spain, and was not included in the cession of most of Spanish Morocco to the newly independent Kingdom of Morocco in 1956. Modern Melilla is built to the west and south of the old walled city, which lies on a peninsula in the Mediterranean. Melilla is an export center for iron and lead mined nearby, and an important fishing port. Its products include building materials, biscuits, and flour paste. The harbor possesses a dry dock.

In ancient times, the Phoenicians had a trading post, known as Rusaddir, on this site. The town was subsequently occupied by Carthaginians, Romans, Byzantines, and Berbers. In the 20th century it had a rapid Spanish population growth, and served as a base in the war against the Riffs (Berbers) under Abd-el-Krim (1921–1926). On July 17, 1936, a revolt of army officers in Melilla marked the beginning of the Spanish civil war. Pop. (1950) 81,182.

MELILOTUS, mĕl-ĭ-lō'tŭs, a genus of biennial and perennial herbs of the pea family (Leguminosae), comprising about 20 species native to central and southern Europe, western Asia, and northern Africa. Some of the species are cultivated widely as forage crops and have become naturalized as weeds. Especially common in the United States are the yellow (*Melilotus officinalis*) and white (*M. alba*) melilots or sweet clovers. These are tall branched plants with leaves of three, serrate to nearly entire leaflets, and with slender terminal spikelike clusters of small yellow or white flowers. The cut hay is very fragrant in drying due to the presence of a vanilla-scented substance, coumarin. Spoiled sweet clover hay is toxic to cattle because it contains a material, dicumarol, which prevents the clotting of blood and causes hemorrhage; as an anticoagulant it is medically important in the preventive treatment of thrombosis in the human circulatory system.

A preparation of melilot was formerly used as a neuralgia remedy but is probably of no value for this.

RICHARD M. STRAW.

MELIORISM, mēl′yŏ-rĭz′m, in philosophy, the doctrine that improvement of society through human effort is both possible and inevitable, and that, therefore, the world is gradually getting better and better because of such effort. Meliorism had a special appeal to the self-confident, expanding Western society of the 19th century. The name was probably first coined by the Victorian novelist, George Eliot (1819–1880), and the doctrines systematized by the English philosopher, James Sully, in his *Pessimism* (1877). In the 20th century the cataclysmic effects of two world wars left the doctrine with but few adherents.

MELISSA, mě-lĭs′å, a plant genus of mints. See BALM.

MELISSUS, mě-lĭs′ŭs, Greek philosopher: b. on the island of Samos in the Aegean Sea; fl. 5th century B.C. He commanded the Samian fleet against Athenian blockaders (442–440 B.C.), who finally conquered his native island. Melissus was a disciple of Parmenides and probably the last representative of the Eleatic School (q.v.). His fragmentary treatise, *On Nature or On Being,* teaches that being is eternal; is without beginning or end; is incorporeal; is simple because of its unity, which cannot be conceived from the combination of the traditional four elements of air, earth, fire, and water; and extends illimitably through space. Against the atomists he asserts that since void is nothing, void is unthinkable. With other Eleatics he finds that the foundations of all knowledge derived from experience are in themselves contradictory and that the reality of the actual world is inconceivable.

Bibliography.—Melissus' Greek fragments are collected by Hermann Diels, *Die Fragmente der Vorsokratiker,* 6th ed., vol. 1, pp. 268–276 (Berlin 1951), and are translated by Kathleen Freeman, *Ancilla to the Pre-Socratic Philosophers,* pp. 48–51 (Oxford 1948). She also discusses Melissus' philosophy in *The Pre-Socratic Philosophers,* 3d ed., pp. 164–171 (Oxford 1953).

P. R. COLEMAN-NORTON.

MELITA, mĕl′ĭ-tà, the ancient name of Malta, the island on which St. Paul was shipwrecked on his voyage as a prisoner to Rome about 58 A.D. Modern scholars have been able to trace his route (Acts 27:1–28:14). The prisoners were taken by ship from Caesarea in Palestine to Myra in Lycia, where they were transferred to a second ship bound for Italy. Because winter was at hand they sought shelter in a harbor on the south coast of Crete, but a violent wind blew the ship away from land, and fearing lest they be wrecked on the coast of North Africa, the sailors set their course westward. After two weeks of stormy passage they sighted land, and attempted to beach the ship. The ship was wrecked, but crew and passengers managed to reach shore on the island of Melita, where they found the crew of another Alexandrian ship wintering. In the spring this second ship carried the prisoners to Italy, with a pause at Syracuse in Sicily.

MELITOPOL, mĕl-ĭ-tô′p′l, city, USSR located in Zaporozhe Oblast in the southeastern steppe region of the Ukrainian SSR. The capital of the Melitopol district, it is situated on the west bank of the Molochnaya River about 25 miles north of the Sea of Azov, on the Kharkov-Sevastopol section of the Moscow-Crimea railway. During World War II the city was occupied by the German Army from the late summer of 1941 until the autumn of 1943, and suffered great war damage. By 1957, Melitopol had been completely rebuilt. The city, which had an annual fair in the 19th century, is the trade center for the surrounding agricultural area. It also has an engineering industry, producing diesel motors, compressors, flour mill equipment, and machine tools. Light industry for the processing of regional products include textiles, cotton cleaning, fruit canning, and meat packing. There is a teachers' college, a farm mechanization institute, and a fruit research station. Pop. (1959) 95,000.

ELLSWORTH RAYMOND.

MELKART or **MELKARTH,** mĕl′kärt, mĕl′kärth, god or *baal* of the city-state of Tyre in ancient Phoenicia. The name means Lord of the City. Melkart had a magnificent temple in Tyre which King Hiram, a contemporary of Solomon (986?–?933 B.C.), adorned with gold. He was the Baal whose worship was introduced into Samaria when Ahab married Jezebel, daughter of the king of Tyre, and against whom the prophet Elijah contended victoriously (I Kings 16:31–32; 18:1–46). He was the patron god of mariners and in time became the patron god of the Phoenician colonies in the western Mediterranean. Many of the heroic myths later associated with the Greek Hercules appear to have originated with Melkart. The symbolism of the two columns of gold and emerald in his Tyrian temple, representing the basic antagonism in the universe, came to be associated with the promontories of the Strait of Gibraltar, which the Greeks called the Pillars of Hercules. See also BAAL.

MELKITES. See MELCHITES.

MELL, mĕll, **Patrick Hues,** American educator and scientist: b. Penfield, Ga., May 24, 1850; d. Fredericksburg, Va., Oct. 12, 1918. Mell studied at the University of Georgia, receiving his A.B. degree in 1871 and Ph.D. in 1880. He was chemist for the Georgia Department of Agriculture from 1874 to 1877, then spent a year traveling through the mountains of Georgia, Alabama, and North Carolina collecting soil and mineral samples. From 1878 to 1902 he was professor of geology and botany at the State Agricultural and Mechanical College in Alabama (later the Alabama Polytechnic Institute); between 1884 and 1893 he was also head of the state weather service, and invented a system of weather signals used by the United States Weather Bureau. In addition, he served as botanist and meteorologist, and later director, of the Alabama Agricultural Experiment Station from 1888 to 1902, when he accepted the presidency of Clemson Agricultural College (later South Carolina Agricultural and Mechanical College), from which he retired in 1910.

Mell was a Southern pioneer in research climatology, hybridization of cotton, and mineralogy, but his greatest contribution was as an educator in the development of the agricultural and technical schools with which he was associated. In addition to a number of scientific publications, he wrote the *Life of Patrick Hues Mell* (1895), a biography of his father (1814–1888), a distinguished Baptist clergyman who was vice chancellor of the University of Georgia from 1860 to 1872.

MELLANBY, mĕl'lan-bĭ, Sɪʀ **Edward,** English medical educator and nutritionist: b. West Hartlepool, England, 1884; d. London, Jan. 30, 1955. After attending Cambridge University and serving as demonstrator in physiology (1909–1911) at St. Thomas' Hospital in London, Mellanby was appointed lecturer in physiology at the University of London in 1913, and shortly afterward was advanced to a professorship. In 1920 he became professor of pharmacology at Sheffield University, a post he held until 1933. He was a member of the Medical Research Council from 1931 to 1933, and its secretary from 1933 to 1949. In 1950 he helped found the Central Drugs Institute, a medical research center, at Lucknow, India.

Dr. Mellanby's research, especially in the field of nutrition, led to several important discoveries. He conducted a series of experiments (1915–1919) which demonstrated that rickets is caused by an absence in the diet of a sterol which, altered by exposure to ultraviolet light (irradiation), has some control over the rate of calcification. The irradiated sterol later became known as vitamin D. In 1948 he discovered that nitrogen trichloride (Agene), used at that time in bleaching nearly all the bread flour in the United States, was injurious to the nervous systems of small animals. His discovery led to the banning by the U.S. Food and Drug Administration in 1949 of this substance as a flour-bleaching agent.

Dr. Mellanby received honors from several governments and universities, and was knighted in 1937. He acted as chairman of the International Conference for the Standardization of Vitamins in 1931, 1934, and 1949. Besides writing numerous scientific articles, he was the author of *Nutrition and Diseases* (1934) and *A Story of Nutritional Research* (1950).

MELLON, mĕl'ŭn, **Andrew William,** American financier and public official: b. Pittsburgh, Pa., March 24, 1855; d. Southampton, N.Y., Aug. 26, 1937. His father, Thomas Mellon, was a lawyer and judge who became a successful banker in Pittsburgh. Early recognizing his son's financial ability—young Andrew had started a successful lumber business at the age of 17—he transferred to him in 1882 the ownership of the family bank, T. Mellon & Sons. In the next 35 years, the younger Mellon built up a great financial-industrial empire. Much of his success was due to his ability to foresee the growth potential of infant businesses, usually involving a process or patent of vital value to established industries, and, then financing them to robust maturity. Three such businesses were the electrolytic manufacture of aluminum, which Mellon built into the gigantic Aluminum Company of America; the manufacture of carborundum steel, which he similarly expanded into the Carborundum Company; and the industry based on Heinrich Koppers' invention of coke ovens which transformed into utilizable products industrial waste materials such as gas, sulphur, and coal tar. Mellon also helped found a construction company which built such major projects as the Panama Canal, and at one time he competed with John D. Rockefeller, Sr., in the Pennsylvania oil field. In 1889, with Henry Clay Frick, he organized the Union Trust Company of Pittsburgh, the major component of a financial complex which included the Union Savings Bank of Pittsburgh and the old family bank of T. Mellon &

Sons, now incorporated as the Mellon National Bank.

As a conservative Republican, Mellon was named secretary of the treasury by President Warren G. Harding in 1921, and served in that capacity under Harding and his Republican successors, Calvin Coolidge and Herbert Hoover, until 1932. Mellon's policies in the treasury fall into two categories, domestic and foreign. His domestic policies were based on reducing the government debt—largely inherited from World War I—and similarly lowering coporate and individual income taxes. All told, Mellon reduced the national debt from almost 26 billion dollars in 1921 to about 16 billion dollars in 1930, when the depression caused it to rise again. Taxes were reduced according to a plan which favored wealth on the theory that this stimulated business.

In foreign affairs, Mellon negotiated a series of agreements with European governments to pay off their World War I debts to the United States over a period of several decades. However, he failed to tie these agreements to a sound system of reparations payments by Germany to the debtor nations or, alternatively, to favor lowering United States tariffs to enable these countries to earn the money in trade to meet their debt repayments. Consequently, when the depression dried up normal sources of income, all these agreements were defaulted on except Finland's.

Mellon's popularity, which had been high in the prosperous 1920's, declined during the depression. In February 1932 he left the treasury to become ambassador to Great Britain, and in 1933, when a Democratic administration came into office, he returned to private life. In 1937, he gave his magnificent art collection to the nation together with $10 million for the erection of the National Gallery of Art in Washington, D.C. (See SMITHSONIAN INSTITUTION—*National Gallery of Art.*)

Consult Philip H. Love's favorable *Andrew W. Mellon* (Baltimore 1929), and Harvey O'Connor's critical *Mellon's Millions* (New York 1933).

MELLON INSTITUTE OF INDUSTRIAL RESEARCH, an endowed, nonprofit, corporate body founded in Pittsburgh, Pa., in 1913 by Andrew William Mellon (q.v.) and his brother Richard Beatty Mellon. In 1967, Mellon Institute merged with Carnegie Institute of Technology to form Carnegie-Mellon University (q.v.), of which the institute now forms a division.

According to the formally stated aims of the institute, it was established "for conducting comprehensive investigations on important problems in the fundamental and applied natural sciences, for training research workers and for providing technical information adaptable to professional, public and industrial advantage." The staff of the institute numbers over 500, and its annual research expenditures total about $7 million. Since 1913 it has published more than 60 books, several hundred bulletins, and thousands of research articles, and has obtained nearly 2,000 patents. Its periodical publications include the *Industrial Hygiene Digest,* the *Journal of the Air Pollution Control Association, APCA Abstracts,* and the *Mellon Institute News.*

Mellon Institute conducts research in a wide variety of fields including physics, chemistry, products and methods technology, and the conservation of health and resources. The institute initiated the large-scale study of air pollution and has contributed greatly to its control.

MELLONI, mäl-lō'nĕ, **Macedonio**, Italian physicist: b. Parma, Italy, April 11, 1798; d. Portici, Aug. 12, 1854. He studied in Parma and Paris, France, and from 1824 to 1831 taught physics at the university of Parma. After taking part in the abortive revolution of 1830 he went into exile in France, and for a time taught at the university of Montpellier. In 1839 he was allowed to return to Italy as director of the conservatory of arts and trades at Naples, on the promise that he would engage in no political activities. In 1847 he was appointed director of the observatory on Mount Vesuvius, but in 1849 was forced to resign under suspicion of having liberal sympathies, and retired to his villa in Portici near Naples.

Melloni's great research interest was in the field of radiant heat. He determined the properties of various substances in transmitting radiant heat, for which he introduced the term diathermancy (q.v.); he established the similarity of heat and light energy in many of their properties, and laid the foundation for the medical treatment known as diathermy. He studied radiant energy in the free atmosphere to determine the relative transmissive qualities of dry and humid air, and devised an electroscope for detecting small electric currents. He published numerous scientific papers in *Annales de chimie et physique* (*Annals of Chemistry and Physics*), and the first volume of a projected work on heat, *La thermocrose ou la coloration calorifique* (Naples 1850).

MELMOTH, Courtney. See PRATT, SAMUEL JACKSON.

MELODEON, AMERICAN ORGAN or **CABINET ORGAN,** mĕ-lō'dĕ-ŭn, a type of reed organ which was very popular in the United States in the late 19th century. It was invented by a workman in the French factory of Jacob Alexandre, who built harmoniums (see HARMONIUM). The melodeon resembled the harmonium in that it was diminutive in size and thus suitable for use in the home, and it employed metal reeds instead of pipes as in regular organs. It differed in applying the principle of suction—drawing the air inward through the reeds by suction bellows—rather than that of compression. The inventor, when his employer failed to appreciate the advantages of the suction principle, went to the United States, where the melodeon was developed by Jacob Estey of Brattleboro, Vt. and the firm of Mason and Hamlin in Boston, Mass. The melodeon had a pleasant flutelike tone which was further improved by "voicing" through curving the reeds.

In the late 19th and early 20th centuries the instrument was found in thousands of American homes as well as in small churches and meeting halls where pipe organs were not practical. It was eventually superseded by the piano and the electric organ.

MELODRAMA, mĕl'ô-drä-må (Gr. *melos,* song + *drama,* action), has two meanings. In its original sense it refers to a play or poem in which a musical background is provided for the spoken voice. Some of the Renaissance attempts to reconstitute Greek dramas presented an approximation of the speaking voice supported by chords. More recent examples of the use of melodrama in this sense are found in *Ariadne auf Naxos* and *Medea* (1775), by Georg Benda; in Richard Strauss' musical setting of *Enoch Arden* (1898) by Alfred, Lord Tennyson; and in *King David* (1921) by Arthur Honegger.

In its second and more frequent meaning, melodrama refers to a stage play which depends for its effect on strong, emotion-bound situations rather than character development. The origin of this usage can be traced to Jean Jacques Rousseau's *Pygmalion,* first performed in 1770, in which the spoken dialogue of the romantic play had a musical background. The melodramas popular in the 19th century, of which *East Lynne* is a classic example, were frequently without musical accompaniment, but for silent films in the early 20th century a pianist or organist normally provided appropriate music to heighten the effect of tense or emotional moments, and the later soap operas of radio and television introduced mood music at strategic points in the unfolding of the plot.

See also DRAMA.

MELODY, mĕl'ô-dĭ, in music, a succession of tones forming a separable unit and usually regarded as expressive. Melody is the most important of the three constitutive elements of almost all music, the other two being rhythm and harmony. More popularly, melody means an attractive tune or air.

Melody is unthinkable apart from rhythm. It is sometimes regarded as a pattern of changing pitch, and rhythm as a pattern of the time durations of successive tones. Although in much Western post-Renaissance music, melody may be regarded as tones heard in succession (or seen horizontally), and harmony as a succession of groups of tones heard simultaneously (or seen vertically), the two are not now wholly separable. Much ancient and medieval music consisted entirely of a single succession of tones. This *monophonic* music evolved into *contrapuntal* music in which two or more melodies are heard simultaneously. Both types are now heard impurely by most listeners, to whom, because of the development of the classic harmonic system, such successions of tones have come to imply, however subconsciously, supporting chordal progressions—that is, have become *homophonic*.

A melody is *diatonic* when most of its tones are native to a single key of the major or minor mode, and *chromatic* when a preponderance of its tones are not so native. It is *conjunct* when the intervals between the successive tones are mainly narrow; *disjunct* when these intervals are mainly wide.

Whether or not melody must imply tunefulness in the sense of in itself providing "sweetness" or pleasure, is a matter of dispute. What is certain is that the word music in any useful or widely accepted sense implies the presence of melody, melody that of rhythm and, to most modern listeners, that of harmony as well.

HERBERT WEINSTOCK.

MELOIDAE. See BLISTER BEETLES OR OIL BEETLES.

MELON, mĕl'ŭn, is the name popularly applied to the two most prominent members of the cucurbit family (Cucurbitaceae), the annual vining plant grown from seed for its various fruits. The two most familiar melons are the muskmelon (*Cucumis melo*) and watermelon (*Citrullus vulgaris*). The popular term cantaloupe is a misnomer since the botanical variety *Cucumis melo cantalupensis* is seldom found in the United States.

MUSKMELON

Varieties.—*Cucumis melo* has a number of botanical varieties, but the majority of the melons found on the American markets can be classified under the two botanical varieties *C. melo reticulatus* and *C. melo inodorus.*

Reticulatus includes most of the melons grown in the United States. The fruits are smaller than *inodorus,* with a ribbed and netted surface and a green undercolor which turns lighter and creamier with ripening. The relatively firm flesh is apricot colored and has a characteristic musky odor.

Inodorus includes the so-called winter melons which ripen later and keep better than *reticulatus.* Under this classification are the honeydew, honey ball, casaba, Crenshaw, and Persian melons. These melons are generally larger and smoother than the *reticulatus* group. They vary in appearance and flavor from the pale and globular Honeydew, with its light greenish flesh, to the dark green, finely netted Persian melon, with its bright orange flesh.

Other varieties of *Cucumis melo:*

Flexuosus has long, slender, sinuous fruits which vary from 1 to 3 inches in diameter, and from 18 to 36 inches in length, justifying the name snake or serpent melon. They are used either for preserves or as a curiosity.

Dudaim has small fruits usually about the size of an orange, with a brown, marbled surface. They are very fragrant and usually considered as ornamental.

Chito, the mango melon or lemon cucumber, is about the size of a lemon and is used for making mango preserves. The fruits are also known as orange melon and vegetable orange.

Cantalupensis takes its name from a village in Italy and is of a type found in Armenia. It has a hard rind and is scaly and warty in appearance.

History.—The species *Cucumis melo* may have been first cultivated in either southern Asia or Africa, and it is possible that different varieties came into cultivation independently in the two areas. Wild plants growing along the banks of the Niger River in West Africa were identified as *C. melo* by Sir Joseph Dalton Hooker, while cultivated varieties are found in a band extending from West Africa eastward through India. Hooker suggested that the domesticated *C. melo* might have evolved from *C. trigonus,* a wild species which has a distribution from Iran eastward across India into Malaya and northern Australia. The fruits of the wild varieties, and of many of the cultivated ones, are small—the size of a plum or lemon—and vary in flavor, color, and scent. Both wild and cultivated varieties are used in India for food or medicine.

Just where and when the sweet, large melons of modern times had their origin has not been determined. An area extending from northeastern Iran into Chinese Turkestan (Sinkiang) has long been famous for its melons; the Venetian traveler Marco Polo (1254–1324) wrote of Afghan Turkestan: "Here grow the best melons in the world. They are cut into round slices and dried in the sun. Thus dried they are sweeter than honey, and are exported to all countries." In this region melons form an important item of diet, and almost every village has developed its own strains or varieties. It is not known whether the large sweet melon evolved here or whether the area represents a secondary center of development.

The melon was apparently not known to the Romans until the imperial period. Since the Romans applied a general term for cucumber (*Cucumis sativus,* a related species) to what may have been a muskmelon, our first reasonably sure identification of the melon in ancient Rome is in the *Natural History* of Pliny (23–79 A.D.), where *melo-pepones* were described as having the golden color of the quince, and being noteworthy not only for their shape and odor but for the fact that, as soon as they were ripe, they detached themselves from the stalk. The muskmelon seems to have reached China somewhat later; the 8th century A.D., the date suggested by the Swiss botanist Alphonse de Candolle for its introduction into China, is frequently accepted for lack of additional evidence.

The cultivation of muskmelons in Spain was encouraged by the Moors, and with the Renaissance their use extended further into Europe. Melons were early introduced into the New World by Spanish explorers and conquerors. It is recorded that in 1494 companions of Columbus raised them, and muskmelons were reported in New Mexico as early as 1540. By the 19th century muskmelons were fairly widely raised in home gardens in the United States, but the fruit was seldom found in markets until about 1870, when improved transportation and storage facilities gave an impetus to commercial production. The muskmelon industry first began to assume importance around 1896 at Rocky Ford, Colo.; around 1905 the production center shifted to the Imperial Valley of California. By the 1950's the muskmelon had become one of the most important vegetable crops in the United States, with California, Arizona, and Texas leading in commercial production. Producing regions are also found in Michigan, Georgia, South Carolina, North Carolina, Indiana, Missouri, and Colorado.

Cultivation.—The melon is most successfully grown and develops the best flavor in a hot dry climate where the sunlight is intense and the growing season a long one. Furthermore, locations with high humidity mean an increase in the incidence of foliage diseases, which are often a serious deterrent to successful culture. Consequently, a large part of the crop is grown in an arid or semiarid region under irrigation.

It is possible to raise melons in areas having a short growing season if the seeds are started in greenhouses, hotbeds, or cold frames. In case the seeds are to be planted directly in field or garden, it is important to delay sowing until the frost hazard is completely eliminated. Plant protectors made of various kinds of paper are used in many parts of the United States to protect the plants against chilling following transplanting or early seeding in the fields.

Although melon plants react unfavorably to a strongly acid soil, a rather wide range of soil types may be utilized, provided the drainage is good. A sandy loam is considered ideal, particularly when early planting is a requisite feature, although in California clay loam is the principal soil used for melon production.

Diseases.—The muskmelon is subject to several diseases such as powdery mildew, anthracnose, fusarium wilt, and muskmelon mosaic. Control of fusarium wilt depends on crop rotation and the use of fusarium-resistant varieties, of which a number are available. Muskmelon mosaic is caused by a virus carried in the seed and transmitted to the plant by aphids. Use of virus-free seeds will protect young plants but will not ensure freedom from infection if the plants are grown near other sources of the disease.

Harvesting.—One of the major difficulties in the marketing of melons is the determination of the proper time of harvesting in terms of long distance shipping, for which the majority of the crop is intended. Immature harvesting often detracts from the flavor and quality of the marketed product.

WATERMELON

The widely cultivated watermelon, *Citrullus vulgaris,* includes among its varieties *C. vulgaris citroides,* the preserving melon or citron.

History.—The watermelon (*Citrullus vulgaris*) is found in the wild state in Africa, as far south as the Karroo Desert in South Africa, where it is one of the most important desert fruits, and it is widely cultivated in Africa. Since the wild form has not been found in Asia, although it is widely cultivated on that continent, Africa is generally accepted as the place of origin of the watermelon. Whether the fruit was known to the ancient Egyptians, as is sometimes claimed, is uncertain. Its cultivation in Asia does not seem to be of any great antiquity. Its first appearance in China was reported by a Chinese traveling in the 10th century A.D. among the Khitan people who then occupied north China. The Khitan were said to have obtained the watermelon from the Uigur, a Turkic tribe in the west, and in China the watermelon is known as "melon of the west." It may be inferred from this that the watermelon reached southern Asia at a somewhat earlier date. It is widely cultivated in India, Iran, Turkestan, southern Russia, and the region of the lower Danube River; throughout this area both the flesh and the parched seeds of the watermelon are very popular.

Although early French explorers found Indians growing watermelons in the Mississippi Valley, there are no extant records concerning the introduction of the watermelon into the New World from Europe. It is believed that *C. vulgaris* was brought to the New World directly from Africa, probably on early slave ships. Once established, it became a popular fruit in the United States.

Cultivation.—Like the muskmelon, the watermelon requires relatively high temperatures and a long growing season of not less than four frost-free months. It is, however, less affected by atmospheric humidity than is the muskmelon, and for this reason may be grown in a more varied climate. The states which lead in production are Florida, Texas, Georgia, California, and South Carolina. Other states in which watermelons are produced in quantity are Arizona, Arkansas, Indiana, Oklahoma, North Carolina, Mississippi, and Maryland. Actually, watermelons may be grown even in parts of Canada, provided varieties are selected which mature quickly in the shorter growing season. Such varieties are: Honey Cream, Dixie Cream, New Hampshire Midget, Rhode Island Red, and Klondyke and its various disease-resistant strains.

In regions with less than 120 frost-free days, the plants which are injured by even a light frost must be started indoors and transplanted to the field, a process which is practicable for only limited use. The use of plant protectors is essential where danger of frost is a hazard and where early marketability is important. Varieties suitable for the longer growing season in which most of the commercial crop is produced include the following: Dixie Queen, Florida Giant, Congo, Leesburg, Blacklee, Klondyke strains, Fairfax, and Charleston Gray. Strains of these varieties which are resistant to such destructive diseases as fusarium wilt and anthracnose are available.

Watermelon culture is quite similar to that of muskmelon, although the plants require more space and a somewhat longer growing season. Since the seeds will not germinate at temperatures of less than 70° F., planting must be delayed until the soil becomes warm. Well drained soils are essential, with the sandier types preferable. The watermelon is much more tolerant of acidity than is the muskmelon. In fact, a definitely acid soil with a pH of 5 (see SOIL), while not essential to production, nevertheless does not require lime application to reduce acidity. The watermelon is frequently grown in a general farm-crop rotation system with manure or soil-improving crops turned under to maintain organic matter.

Diseases.—The watermelon is attacked by the same insects and diseases as the muskmelon and cucumber, with the same controls applicable in each case. The most effective control measure continues to be the use, wherever possible, of disease-resistant strains or varieties.

Harvesting.—Determining the proper time of harvest presents a problem since the watermelon shows less evidence of maturity than any other common fruit or vegetable. Color and size provide no index, but with experience the picker may become reasonably adept at selecting ripe fruits.

Bibliography.—*Muskmelons,* Farmers' Bulletin No. 1468, U.S. Dept. of Agriculture (Washington 1951); *Watermelons,* Farmers' Bulletin No. 1394, U.S. Dept. of Agriculture (Washington 1951); Thompson, Homer C., and Kelly, William C., *Vegetable Crops,* 5th ed. (New York 1957); McCollum, J. P., and Ware, G. W., *Producing Vegetable Crops* (Danville, Ill., 1967).

FREEMAN S. HOWLETT,
Ohio State University.

MELOS, MILOS, or **MILO,** mē'lŏs (Gr. mē'lôs), island, Greece, most southwestern of the Cyclades in the Aegean Sea, about 70 miles east of the Peloponnesus. It is approximately 12 miles long and 6 miles wide, and is divided into two wings by a deep bay thrusting in from the northwest. Of volcanic origin, the rugged hills rise to a height of 2,465 feet at Prophet Elias. Grain, cotton, citrus fruits, olive oil, and wine are the chief products, and goats are raised. Sulphur, gypsum, and pumice are exported, as they have been since ancient times. Melos (formerly Plaka) is the principal town.

Melos was a center of the Aegean civilization in the 3d millennium B.C., and was a major source of the obsidian (volcanic glass) which was prized in the Mediterranean world for making tools before bronze came into general use. The island was colonized by Dorians from Laconia about 1,000 B.C. During the Peloponnesian War (431–404 B.C.) the island was ravaged by the Athenians, and never recovered its prosperity. The many archaeological treasures unearthed on Melos include the *Venus de Milo,* now in the Louvre. Pop. (1961) 4,910.

MELOZZO DA FORLÌ, mā-lôt'sō dä fōr-lē', Italian painter: b. Forlì, Italy, 1438; d. there, Nov. 8, 1494. Melozzo studied under the early master of the Umbrian school, Piero della Francesca, who taught him the principles of perspective. This became a consuming interest with the pupil, who was a pioneer in developing the use of foreshortening, which he used to create striking effects in decorating the cupolas with which contemporary Renaissance architects crowned their buildings. Melozzo painted mainly in Rome, where Pope Sixtus IV was his patron. Of his work, several sections of his frescoes for the now-destroyed Church of Santi Apostoli in Rome have survived. These include the *Ascension of Christ,* now in the Qurinal Palace, and a fragment of *Angels Making Music* in the Vatican gallery (Pinacoteca). Also in the Pinacoteca is his fresco, *Inauguration of the Vatican Library.*

MELPOMENE, mĕl-pŏm'ĕ-nē, one of the nine muses, the daughter of Zeus and Mnemosyne, the goddess of memory. Melpomene was the muse of tragedy. She is usually represented as a young woman wearing a mask of tragedy, with vine leaves circling her head.

MELROSE, mĕl'rōz, city, Massachusetts, located in Middlesex County, 7 miles north of Boston, at an altitude of 55 feet. It is served by the Boston and Maine Railroad. The surrounding area is largely industrial, but while Melrose manufactures some furniture, laboratory equipment, textile mill supplies, and chemicals, the city is primarily a residential suburb of Boston. Melrose was settled by the Puritan fathers in 1629; it became a municipality separate from Malden in 1650, was incorporated as a town in 1850, and became a city in 1899. The opera star, Geraldine Farrar, was born here. Melrose has a mayor and council government. Pop. 29,619.

MELROSE, village, Scotland, in Roxburghshire, on the south bank of the Tweed at the base of the Eildon Hills, about 20 miles from the English border. It is two miles east of Abbotsford, the home of Sir Walter Scott, and is the Kennaquhair of his novels, *The Abbot* and *The Monastery.* His *Lay of the Last Minstrel* gave Melrose's ruined abbey worldwide celebrity. The abbey, now a national monument, was founded by King David I of Scotland for the Cistercian Order in 1136. It was destroyed several times in the chronic border warfare. It is the burial place of the heart of Robert Bruce (d. 1329), and contains tombs of the redoubtable Douglas family. The ruins are an example of the late flamboyant Gothic style of architecture. Pop. (1961) 2,133.

MELROSE PARK, village, Illinois, in Cook County about 10 miles west of Chicago, at an altitude of 617 feet. It is served by the Chicago and North Western and the Indiana Belt Harbor railways. The town manufactures plastics, railroad car parts, and electrical equipment, but is mainly a residential community. It has a mayor-council form of government. Pop. 22,291.

MELTING POINT, the degree of temperature at which a solid material is transformed by heat into a liquid. Each material has its fixed melting point: ice melts at 0° Centigrade (32° Fahrenheit); aluminum at 660.2° C.; iron at 1539° C.; and tin at 231.9° C. In chemistry and metallurgy it is essential to know the melting point of the mineral or chemical compound being used in laboratory or factory. Because the melting point of any given substance is constant, knowledge of the melting point can be employed as a test of purity, for any deviation from the expected melting point is an indication that the substance is impure. It can also be employed in identifying a material. See also FUSION.

MELTON MOWBRAY, mĕl't'n mō'brā, urban district, England, in Leicestershire, 15 miles northeast of Leicester, on the right bank of the Wreak, at the junction of the Eye, 105 miles north by west of London. Melton Mowbray is famous for its pork pies and Stilton cheese. It owes its prosperity chiefly to being the seat of the Melton Hunt, which attracts the sporting world in great numbers during the winter months, extensive and luxurious hunting establishments being maintained here. Pop. (1961) 15,913.

MELTZER, mĕl'tsĕr, **Samuel James,** American physiologist: b. Kurland, Russia, March 22, 1851; d. Nov. 7, 1920. He received a general education at Königsberg, Prussia; studied philosophy and medicine at the University of Berlin 1875–1882 and removed to the United States in 1883, after which he practiced his profession in New York. From 1906 Dr. Meltzer was the head of the department of physiology and pharmacology at the Rockefeller Institute for Medical Research and consulting physician at Harlem Hospital. In 1917 he was commissioned major in the Medical Reserve Corps. Dr. Meltzer was a member of many medical and surgical societies. He published over 200 papers on biology, physiology, and aspects of scientific medicine.

MELUN, mē-lûn' (ancient MELODUNUM), town and commune, France, in Seine-et-Marne Department, on the Seine River, 26 miles southeast of Paris. The historic Forest of Fontainebleau is immediately to the south. Melun was a royal residence of the early Capetian kings, and the Romanesque Church of Notre Dame, on the island around which the town is built, dates from this period (11th century). Also of interest is the Church of St. Aspais (15th–16th century). The Château de Vaux-le-Vicomte, built (1656–1661) for Nicolas Fouquet, is nearby. The town has pharmaceutical and other industries. Pop. (1954) town 18,391; commune 20,219.

MELUSINA, mĕl-ü-sē'nȧ, or **MELUSINE,** in French myths, a beautiful nymph or fairy, who is represented as the daughter of Helmas, king of Albania, and the fairy Persine; and as having married Raymond, Count of Toulouse, who built the magnificent castle of Lusignan. According to the popular legend, Melusina was doomed to a periodical metamorphosis during which the lower part of her body assumed the form of a fish or serpent. On these occasions she exerted all her ingenuity to escape observation; but having been once accidentally seen by her husband in this condition, she swooned away, and soon afterward disappeared. Her form is said to be seen from time to time on the tower of Lusignan, clad in mourning and uttering deep lamentations. Her appearance was believed to indicate an impending calamity to the royal family.

MELVILLE or **MELVILL,** mĕl'vĭl, **Andrew,** Scottish reformer: b. Baldovie, near Montrose, Forfarshire, Scotland, Aug. 1, 1545; d. Sedan, France, 1622. He was educated at the grammar school of Montrose and St. Andrews University; studied two years (1564–1566) at the University of Paris; went to Poitiers to pursue his studies in the law; there became regent in the College of St. Marceon; and through the influence of Beza received an appointment to the chair of humanity in the academy of Geneva.

Returning to Scotland in 1574, he was at once appointed principal of the University of Glasgow, and in 1580 was made principal of St. Mary's College, St. Andrews. In 1582 he presented a petition to King James against the undue interference of the court in ecclesiastical affairs, for which he escaped imprisonment by going into England. Returning in 1585, he resumed his duties at St. Andrews, and was moderator of the General Assembly in 1587, 1589, 1594. In 1606 he was summoned to London by the king to confer on church matters, but because of his outspokenness he was committed to the Tower, and there remained until 1611. He was then released upon the solicitation of Henri de la Tour d'Auvergne (Duc de Bouillon), retired to France and became professor of Biblical theology in the University of Sedan.

MELVILLE, George Wallace, American naval officer and explorer: b. New York, Jan. 10, 1841; d. March 17, 1912. Educated at Brooklyn Polytechnic, he entered the navy as assistant engineer 1861, served through the war, and in 1879 accompanied George W. De Long's expedition on the *Jeannette* to discover the northeast passage. Of this party he was one of the few survivors; most of the others owed their lives to his indomitable courage and herculean strength—he carried a brother officer, weighing 175 pounds, upon his back, through ice and snow, at the same time superintending all movements of the crew and on occasion helping with the boat. He also commanded the subsequent search expeditions which recovered the *Jeannette's* records and De Long's body. In 1887 he was made chief of the bureau of steam engineering in the United States Navy, a post from which he retired in August 1903, having entirely reformed the service, put navy engineers on a professional rather than an artisan footing, introduced the triple screw on such successful ships as the *Columbia* and *Minneapolis,* saved the department a tremendous sum by his refusal to adopt a boiler which had proved unsatisfactory in the British Navy and designed 120 ships of over 700,000 horse power. Melville was made rear admiral in 1899, and retired in 1903. His book, *In the Lena Delta* (1885), describes his experiences in the *Jeannette* expedition.

MELVILLE, Herman, American author: b. New York, Aug. 1, 1819; d. there, Sept. 28, 1891. His grandfather, Major Thomas Melvill (original spelling of the name), was a member of the Boston Tea Party and prominent in civic affairs; in later life he became known as "the last of the cocked hats" and served Holmes as a model for "The Last Leaf." Gen. Peter Gansevoort, the maternal grandfather, successfully defended Ft. Stanwix during the American Revolution and was a leading citizen of Albany. Melville's father Allan conducted an importing business in New York which collapsed in 1830, after which the family moved to Albany, where the father died in 1832. Melville first attended the New York Male High School and later the Albany Academy, from which he withdrew after his father's death. He worked as a bank clerk, as a farm helper, and as assistant in his brother Gansevoort's fur factory, briefly attending the Albany Classical School. In 1837 he became a country schoolteacher at Pittsfield. He studied surveying and engineering at the Lansingburgh Academy

in the hope of securing employment on the Erie Canal. Unsuccessful in finding a vocation on land, he went to sea in 1839 as cabin boy aboard the *St. Lawrence,* a New York to Liverpool trading ship. This experience gave him the framework for his later novel, *Redburn* (1849). Upon his return he taught school briefly in Greenbush and Brunswick (N. Y.), then traveled west as far as Illinois. In 1841 he sailed as ordinary seaman on the *Acushnet,* a Fair Haven whaling ship. After 18 months he deserted at Nukuhiva in the Marquesas Islands and spent a month among the natives of the Typee [Taipi] Valley, escaping to Tahiti on an Australian whaling ship. After further whaling experience, he enlisted in the United States Navy at Honolulu and returned home aboard the frigate *United States,* landing in Boston in 1844.

His voyages furnished materials for his best published works. *Typee,* his first book, appeared in 1846 and was greeted with an acclaim which caused him to decide on authorship as his career. In 1847 he married Elizabeth Shaw, daughter of the chief justice of Massachusetts, after publication of his second South Seas romance, *Omoo* (1847). They made their home in New York, where Melville vainly tried to secure a government appointment. After publishing *Mardi* and *Redburn* in 1849, he made a short visit to England and the continent. *White-Jacket* appeared in 1850. For financial reasons he moved in that year to "Arrowhead," a farm in Pittsfield, where he completed his greatest novel, *Moby-Dick* (1851). This was followed a year later (1852) by *Pierre.* In 1856–1857 he made a voyage to the Holy Land and then spent three seasons lecturing on the South Seas, classical art, and travel. Meanwhile, *Israel Potter* (1855), *The Confidence-Man* (1857), and several essays and short stories had appeared. After a voyage to San Francisco in 1860, he moved permanently to New York in 1863. From 1866 to 1885 he served quietly as district inspector of customs in that city.

Having turned from prose to poetry, he published *Battle-Pieces and Aspects of the War* in 1866 and *Clarel,* a long narrative poem of the Holy Land, in 1876. Two more books of poetry, *John Marr and Other Sailors* (1888) and *Timoleon* (1891) appeared in his lifetime. At his death he left among his manuscripts a beautiful short novel, *Billy Budd,* which was first published in 1924. Relatively neglected in his own day after the spectacular initial success of *Typee* and *Omoo,* Melville was rediscovered after 1919 and is now generally regarded as one of the half dozen greatest American authors. See also MOBY-DICK; OMOO; TYPEE.

Bibliography.—Thorp, Willard, ed., *Herman Melville: Representative Selections* (New York 1938); Anderson, Charles Roberts, *Melville in the South Seas* (New York 1939); Matthiessen, F. O., *American Renaissance,* chapt. 9–12 (New York 1941); Arvin, Newton, *Herman Melville* (New York 1950); Gilman, William H., *Melville's Early Life and Redburn* (New York and London 1951); Howard, Leon, *Herman Melville: A Biography* (Berkeley and Los Angeles 1951).

TYRUS HILLWAY,
Associate Professor, Colorado State College of Education.

MELVILLE, town, Province of Saskatchewan, Canada, a divisional point on the Canadian National Railway system 280 miles northwest of Winnipeg on the main line and about 90 miles north of Regina on the Melville-Regina branch. It is in a high but productive agricultural area (elevation 1,810 feet), the leading local industries being a flour mill and creameries. There are four public and one separate school, a Lutheran college, a Roman Catholic hospital, three licensed grain elevators, and two banks. Pop. 5,690.

MELVILLE ISLAND, an island off the northwest coast of Northern Territory, Australia, at the entrance to Van Diemen Gulf, is 65 miles long and 40 miles wide; area about 2,400 square miles. It is hilly and densely wooded, especially with several species of eucalyptus. The earliest British settlement was made in 1824.

MELVILLE ISLAND, an island of Canada, in Franklin District, Northwest Territories, in the Arctic Ocean. It is the largest of the Parry Islands (q.v.). The island, 200 miles long and 30 to 130 miles wide, is generally hilly, with a few small ice-covered areas in the interior.

MELVILLE PENINSULA, North America, a northeastern projection of Franklin District in the Northwest Territories of Canada. Bounded on the north by Fury and Hecla Strait, on the east by Foxe Basin, and on the west by Committee Bay, it is about 250 miles long by 100 miles broad. Hilly in the north and center, it has many connected lakes in the south. On its south shore is Repulse Bay trading post.

MEMBRANE, *in anatomy and physiology,* a thin sheet-like tissue, more or less elastic, varying in structure and vital properties. Membranes absorb or secrete fluids, connect certain parts of the body, separate, envelop or form certain organs or act as partitions between two fluids or gases, permitting them to mingle. Mucous membranes line the canals, cavities and hollow organs which communicate externally by different apertures on the skin; for example, the digestive, respiratory and genito-urinary tracts. These membranes are soft and velvety and have on their free surface cells for absorption or motion and in their substance follicles which secrete mucus for lubricating and other purposes. Such secretions are saliva, gastric juice and pancreatic juice. Serous membranes, such as the peritoneum, pleura, the unicæ vaginales and pericardium, facilitate the motion of the organs they envelop (abdominal digestive organs, the lungs and heart) by reason of the serum they secrete, and also maintain the shape of these organs. Allied to the serous membranes are the synovial membranes lining movable joints. By reason of their smoothness and by aid of their lubricating serum the ends of bones move readily upon one another. Fibrous membranes (for example, periosteum, dura mater and perimysium), not moistened by any particular fluid, augment the solidity of organs they envelop, retain them in position, favor their motion and form canals and rings for the passage of different organs. The membranes which envelop the brain and are extended to cover the spinal cord are called meninges. (See MENINGITIS.) The membranes enclosing the fetus are called the placenta. Other special membranes are Descemet's membrane, which is the fourth layer of the cornea of the eye, and Bowman's membrane, which is the second.

MEMBRE, män-brā′, **Zenobius,** French missionary in America: b. Bapaume, France,

1645; d. Fort Saint Louis, Tex., 1687. He became a member of the Récollet Order; was sent as a missionary to Canada in 1675; accompanied La Salle in his western expedition; was with Tonti at Crèvecœur, where he helped bring about peace between the Iroquois and the Illinois; in 1682 went down the Mississippi with La Salle, and in the same year returned to France. For a time he was warden of a convent in his birthplace. But in 1684 he set out again with La Salle for the mouth of the Mississippi. He was left by La Salle at Fort Saint Louis and there massacred by the Indians. He wrote a description of his trip down the Mississippi, which was incorporated by his cousin, Christian le Clerq, into his *Etablissement de la Foi dans la Nouvelle France* (1691), and which was later unscrupulously copied by Hennepin (q.v.). This narrative has sometimes been attributed to La Salle.

MEMEL, mā′mĕl (Lithuanian KLAIPEDA; German MEMELGEBIET or MEMELLAND), territory, and its capital city, on the east coast of the Baltic Sea at the mouth of the Neman River, 70 miles northeast of Königsberg. The city was founded in 1252 by the Livonian order and later fortified by the Teutonic Knights. It was held at times by Sweden and Russia, but from the 17th century until World War I it was in Prussian possession, and Frederick William III of Prussia took refuge here during the Napoleonic Wars. The city was almost completely rebuilt after a disastrous fire in 1854. It has a large ice-free harbor, and exports great quantities of timber, flax and linseed, coal, manure, grain, and herring from Lithuania and Russia. Brandy, soap, and chemicals are produced, and there are also sawmills, iron foundries, breweries, and shipbuilding yards. Under the Treaty of Versailles, Memel was administered by France for the League of Nations, but Lithuania, claiming the city as its only good port, seized it on Jan. 15, 1923. It was surrendered to Germany on March 22, 1939, retaken by the Russian armies in 1944, and again made part of Lithuania under Soviet control in January 1945. The territory covers 1,026 square miles. Pop. (1961) city, 100,000.

MEMLING, mĕm′lĭng, or **MEMLINC, Hans,** Flemish painter: b. Mainz, about 1430; d. Bruges, 1495. He settled at Bruges 1478, of which town he was a prosperous citizen until his death. While all that is handed down of his biography is apocryphal, it is evident, from his works, that he was an imitator of Roger Van der Weyden, although he avoided the harshness and ungraceful drawing of that artist's style. He stood alone among the Flemish painters of his day in the religious tenderness of his pictures, their life-like expression, their exquisite coloring and modeling. His chief works are to be found in St. John's Hospital, Bruges, namely, the altarpiece, *Marriage of Saint Catherine* (1479); *Portrait of Maria Moreel as Sybilla Persica* (1480), and the 14 scenes illustrating the legend of Saint Ursula and the 11,000 Virgins of Cologne (1589). In the Academy of Bruges is a triptych of his in the central panel of which are Saints Christopher, Maurus and Aegidius, and on the wings, Burgomaster Moreel (who offered the picture) with his family. In the Royal Gallery at Turin is his *Seven Dolors of Mary*—a passion picture; in the Pinakothek at Munich a companion picture, *The Seven Joys of Mary*. Among Memling's works in the United States are the Portinari portraits in the Metropolitan Museum of Art, New York, and the *Madonna and Child with Angels* in the National Gallery, Washington.

Consult Friedlander, Max J., *From Van Eyck to Bruegel*, 2d ed. (New York 1965); Dumont, Georges-Henri, *Memling* (New York 1966).

MEMMI, Simone. See MARTINI, SIMONE.

MEMMINGEN, mĕm'ĭng-ĕn, city, Federal Republic of Germany, situated in Bavaria near the Iller River, 42 miles southwest of Augsburg. It has plants processing food and producing automobile bodies, machinery, wire, chemicals, textiles, paper, and furniture. The city is partly encircled by medieval walls, and it has two Gothic churches, a Renaissance town hall, and the Fugger House. Founded by the Welf family in the 11th century, Memmingen became a free imperial city in 1286. It passed to Bavaria in 1802. Pop. (1963) 29,801.

MEMMINGER, mĕm'ĭn-jĕr, **Christopher Gustavus,** American Confederate public official: b. Nayhingen, Württemberg, Germany, Jan. 9, 1803; d. Charleston, S.C., March 7, 1888. Taken to South Carolina in infancy, he was orphaned at the age of 4, and at 11 was adopted by Thomas Bennett, later governor of the state. Bennett sent him through South Carolina College, from which he was graduated in 1819, and gave him an opportunity to study law. Despite his attack on influential proponents of states' rights through his satire, *The Book of Nullification* (1830), Memminger was elected in 1836 to the legislature, where he sponsored notable banking laws. As commissioner of schools for Charleston from 1855, he helped to reorganize its school system. Although he was late in advocating secession, once convinced that this was the proper course he was active in the state secession convention and in the organization of the Confederate States of America. Appointed Confederate secretary of the treasury in 1861, he did not foresee a long war. His original fiscal program, based on taxation and bond issues, was altered to meet emergencies. He was never fully supported by the Confederate Congress and, blamed for the collapse of Confederate credit, he resigned in June 1864. In 1867 he resumed the practice of law. Reentering the state legislature in 1877, he resumed his leadership there, notably in the development of public schools for both whites and Negroes.

MEMNON, mĕm'nŏn, in Greek mythology, the son of Eos (Aurora) and Tithonus. A prince of Ethiopia, he was the nephew of Priam, for whom he fought at Troy. After he had killed Antilochus, he was himself killed by Achilles, but at his mother's plea was made immortal by Zeus. The Greeks gave his name to the Colossi of Memnon, two huge statues of Amenhotep III at Thebes, Egypt, one of which, the so-called vocal Memnon, emitted a musical note at sunrise (probably due to the action of sudden heat on the chilled, damp stone), said to be Memnon's greeting to his mother.

MEMORIAL DAY or DECORATION DAY, a holiday observed in most states of the United States on May 30, originally as an occasion for decorating the graves of soldiers killed in the Civil War, but since World War I as a day commemorating also those who died in later wars.

The custom of decorating soldiers' graves with flowers was observed locally after the Civil War, and on May 5, 1868, John A. Logan, then head of the Grand Army of the Republic, issued an order appointing May 30 of that year for "decorating the graves of comrades who died in defense of their country during the late rebellion." Memorial Day is observed in all states except Alabama, Georgia, and Mississippi, as well as in the District of Columbia, Puerto Rico, the Virgin Islands, the Canal Zone, and Guam. In Florida, May 30 is Memorial Day for the veterans of all wars, and in Virginia it is Confederate Memorial Day. In North Carolina and South Carolina only federal government offices are closed, and in Texas it is not a bank holiday. Besides Virginia, various Southern states observe Confederate Memorial Day as follows: April 26—Alabama, Florida, Georgia, and Mississippi; May 10—North Carolina and South Carolina; and June 3—Kentucky, Louisiana, and Tennessee.

MEMORIAL UNIVERSITY OF NEW-FOUNDLAND, the provincial university of Newfoundland, located in St. John's. It is Coeducational and is provincially supported and controlled. Founded in 1925, it was named Memorial University College in honor of Newfoundlanders who served in World War I. In 1949 it was given degree-granting authority and its present name by an act of the provincial legislature. Enrollment in the late 1960's totaled about 5,000.

The university offers undergraduate programs in arts and sciences, commerce, education, engineering, forestry, agriculture, and physical education; also premedical and predental programs. The graduate division offers degrees in many fields in the arts and sciences. The university conducts extension services and maintains an Institute of Social and Economic Research.

MEMORY, the mental processes of retaining and reviving former experiences. There is a common and fallacious belief that memory, like muscle, is subject to improvement through exercise. Memory, however, is a series of activities, not an entity. The term refers to the activities of learning, retaining, recalling, recognizing, and relearning. Each of these activities may be improved in efficiency, but memory, which is merely a convenient term to designate them, cannot be strengthened by a system of exercises.

In rote memory the original material is repeated verbatim, even though the meaning be neglected. It is possible to use mnemonic devices in order to facilitate the learning and the recall of meaningless items. Thus, a student of American history may use the mnemonic "St. Wapniacl" to learn and retain the offices in the cabinet of, say President Herbert Hoover, each letter standing for a title. *S* reminds the student of the secretary of state; *t*, treasury; *w*, war; and so on through *l*, labor. Memory-training courses, so called, are nothing but systems of mnemonic schemes for rote memorization. Logical memory involves the learning and the reproduction of the essential contents of experience. Whenever the factor of meaning is introduced into the learning process, efficiency is greatly improved. Mnemonic devices are, in fact, artificial schemes for establishing meaningful relationships among the items to be learned, retained, and revived. (See also MNEMONICS.)

Measures of intelligence usually contain test items dealing with rote and logical memory. Digits read at the rate of one a second are often used to measure immediate memory span. They are to be repeated in the order of presentation. A normal adult has little difficulty in repeating eight or nine unrelated digits. The logical-memory processes are tested by a more or less involved passage which is read by the examiner and summarized by the person tested. The score is determined by the number of essential ideas that are grasped. When the span is exceeded, a person becomes confused. Repeated study is then required to learn and retain the material for reproduction.

Interesting anecdotes describe the abilities of some persons to reproduce rote material. Samuel Taylor Coleridge related the tale of an ignorant servant girl who could repeat verbatim long passages of Hebrew. She had overheard her employer, a scholar, read aloud from rabbinical books, not a word of which she actually comprehended. It has been conjectured that some persons, like this girl, have unusually clear images. The young Wolfgang Amadeus Mozart, it is said, was able to remember a famous musical selection and to write the score he had heard once in the Sistine Chapel. This type of ability is said to depend on eidetic imagery. The German psychologist Erich Jaensch reported that two thirds of small children have clear, vivid (that is, eidetic) images.

Persons who blame themselves for having "a poor memory" usually find that they never had learned the material in the first place. In social gatherings names are seldom repeated after introductions. The guest may be self-conscious at the time, and later on it may be embarrassing to attempt to identify names and faces. A "memory expert" quickly makes an association between the name and the person while repeating the name. Hence retention and recall are facilitated.

In 1885, Hermann Ebbinghaus, a German experimental psychologist, reported on the results of a prolonged study of memorization processes. He devised a large number of nonsense syllables in order to have material devoid of association and equal in difficulty. He could repeat verbatim a list of 12 or 14 syllables after a single reading, but as he increased the number of syllables he required many additional readings to retain them. Unless he continued to review the task after a single correct reproduction, the rate of loss was high. Relatively the greatest loss occurred in the first hours after the rote learning had been concluded. Hence, after having mastered a list of items, the learner should review frequently right away. Occasional reviews later on may suffice to maintain the ability to reproduce the items.

Memorization of logical material is facilitated by the factors of interest, the uses to which it may be put in daily life, and the intent to recall it. Mere repetition is a poor way to memorize. The material has to be integrated into the experience of the learner if it is to be effectively used. Hence, whenever possible, recitations and discussions are helpful. They encourage what Ebbinghaus referred to as overlearning, or practice beyond the point of one reproduction. They may indicate relationships between the new material and that which has already been integrated into the past experiences of the learner.

Theoretically, all experiences affect the course of subsequent experiences. Thus, in a broad sense, nothing is ever completely forgotten if it made a vivid impression at the outset. Latin paradigms not studied since high school days may be quickly restored to their former efficiency by reviews in late adult life. Motor skills, like skating and swimming, may be more readily brought back by review in adult years because they were overlearned in childhood.

The processes of memory should not be considered as a metaphorical unwinding of a skein of yarn. The person does not "go back into the past," but utilizes past experiences in making responses to some present situation. A sequence of free associations may initiate a chain of reveries leading into a revival of experiences from early childhood. The person does not go back in a literal sense, but brings former experiences into relationships with contemporary images. Some "forgetting" may be due to the fact that former experiences were disquieting. Nevertheless, they may be remembered and indirectly assert themselves into contemporary experience, as through dreams, slips of the tongue, or spontaneous revivals touched off by chance factors.

Subjective factors often determine the content of a recall. Processes of imagination and those of memory are frequently confused. The processes of memory bear little resemblance to a photographic copy of an event, for they are influenced by all the complex psychological characteristics of the individual.

Consult Woodworth, Robert S., and Schlosberg, Harold, *Experimental Psychology*, rev. ed. (New York 1954); Wickens, Delos D., and Meyer, Donald R., *Psychology* (New York 1955).

PHILIP L. HARRIMAN,
Professor of Psychology, Bucknell University.

MEMPHIS, mĕm'fĭs, ancient city, Egypt, whose ruins lie near the apex of the Nile Delta, on the west bank of the river, 12 miles south of Cairo. Archaeologists have uncovered the remains of palaces; the temples of Ptah (chief god of the city), Ra, and Isis; the Serapeum, where the sacred bulls were buried; and two huge statues of Rameses II. Nearby are the pyramids of Saqqara and Giza.

According to tradition, Memphis was founded by Menes, the first king of Egypt, about 3110 B.C. It remained the capital of the kingdom until it was supplanted by Heracleopolis in the 9th dynasty (2154–c. 2100 B.C.). Even after Thebes became the capital in the 11th dynasty (2134–1999 B.C.), Memphis remained important as a religious and cultural center. In the 7th century B.C., it was taken by the Assyrians, and in 525 B.C. it fell to Cambyses, who made it the seat of a Persian satrapy. It was still a leading commercial center in the 4th century B.C., when it was visited by Alexander the Great, but with the rise of his city of Alexandria its importance declined. It was finally destroyed in the 7th century A.D., when its ruins were quarried by the Arabs for the building of al-Fustât, later known as Cairo.

MEMPHIS, city, Tennessee, seat of Shelby County, situated at an altitude of 275 feet, on the Mississippi River, 235 miles south of St. Louis. The largest city in the state, it is the most important commercial center and distributing point between St. Louis and New Orleans.

Communications.—Memphis has nine railroad systems operating 17 lines; they are the Southern; Illinois Central; Frisco Lines; Louisville & Nashville; Nashville, Chattanooga & St. Louis;

Missouri Pacific Lines; Rock Island; Gulf, Mobile and Ohio; and the Cotton Belt. Two railroad bridges span the Mississippi River at this point. One of these is a combined rail and highway bridge—the only toll-free bridge spanning the river between Saint Louis and New Orleans. Memphis is located on thirteen federal highways. Nine bus lines provide intercity highway transport between Memphis and other cities. Barge line transportation on the Mississippi reaches all river ports and provides an outlet for export trade through the port of New Orleans. The Federal Barge Line operates between Minnesota and the Gulf, while the Mississippi Valley Barge Line provides through service from Saint Louis and Cincinnati to Memphis and New Orleans. Service to the Pittsburgh area via the Ohio River is provided by the American Barge Line and the Union Barge Line.

Memphis has airport facilities sufficient to accommodate the largest flying ships under all weather conditions. There are 13 air lines. Service to the Atlantic and Pacific coasts and to the Great Lakes and Gulf areas is now provided in addition to service to the Florida Peninsula.

The city has six radio broadcasting stations.

Economic Resources and Development.— Memphis is located in the center of and serves the most rapidly developing agricultural section of the country. It is the commercial capital of the Mid-South area which embodies Southeast Missouri, Eastern Arkansas, Western Kentucky, and Tennessee, Northeast Alabama and the northern half of Mississippi. The center of cotton production is some 60 miles south of Memphis. This vast hinterland, some 200 by 300 miles in area, produces cotton, corn, rice, wheat, tobacco, soy beans, dairy products, fruits and vegetables. Considerable impetus has been given to livestock raising in recent years. Within this area are many natural resources from which are procured many diverse mineral products including coal, oil, natural gas, ball and kaolin clays, as well as stone and marble.

Memphis is the world's largest hardwood lumber market. Hundreds of square miles of hardwood forests lie in the Memphis area, and strict conservation practices assure the industry's supply.

By reason of its location on the Inland Waterways System, the cost of transportation on imports is very low. Memphis handles over 300,000 tons of steel annually. The city has over 700 plants engaged in manufacture, and is the center of a $2,500,000,000 annual market in wholesale and retail trade. Principal among these are automobiles, auto tires and tubes, auto bodies, furniture of many types, plywood and veneer, flooring, lumber, toys, mixed feeds, cosmetics, perfumes, toilet goods, food products, beverages, medicines, pharmaceuticals, batteries, piston rings, structural steel, automobile lifts, brick, roofing, asphalt products, meats, bakery products, bags, soap, mattresses, lubricants, tool handles, golf club shafts and heads, lard, paints, electric signs, ammunition, shuttleblocks, pulp for viscose rayon, cottonwood oil, railroad forgings, railroad brake shoes, sheet metal products, iron and steel castings and many other commodities. The city controls a trade area 71,326 square miles. Memphis has some of the strongest strictly wholesale firms in the country in dry goods, hardware, drugs, mill supplies, groceries, electrical products, and agricultural implements. Over 600 nationally-known manufacturers and wholesalers maintain their own warehouses or sales offices in Memphis. The city also has five large department stores and a mail-order house.

In addition to a branch of the Federal Reserve Bank, there are 6 banks and trust companies in the city. The total resources of these institutions (1949) was $492,672,439.

There are two daily newspapers, one daily and Sunday paper, and one weekly paper.

Public Improvements.—In recent years many improvements have been effected. These include great housing projects and the elimination of slum areas, the erection of Crump Stadium with a seating capacity of 25,000, Riverside Drive along the banks of the Mississippi, a public grain elevator, the elimination of grade crossings, etc. A new pumping station has doubled the city's water capacity. Buses have replaced the more cumbersome trolleys on a great part of the more important transit lines and new routes have been added. In 1939 Memphis completed negotiations for the purchase of the Memphis Power and Light Company, and immediately TVA power was brought to the entire city and power rates have been reduced an average of 37.9 per cent.

The new Memphis and Arkansas Bridge, a gigantic project, was opened to traffic in January 1950. It is a four-lane highway bridge.

A valuable addition to industrial Memphis will be the Tennessee Chute Project, on which construction was started in 1948. This $18,000,-000 project will provide a dam that will connect a large island in the river, just south of Memphis, to the mainland. This will give Memphis a deep, still-water harbor and 9,000 acres for industrial development on the new waterfront.

Port Facilities.—Memphis has a total of 7.88 miles of waterfront on the Mississippi and Wolf rivers. Memphis has municipally owned river terminals, including a package car terminal, carload terminal and river and rail grain elevators.

Civic Conditions.—The city is well laid out, and its further development is guided by a City Planning Commission. The wide, well-shaded and well-paved streets, the fine public and private buildings, the parks with numerous large trees, all make the city most attractive. Shelby County, in which Memphis is located, has 3,200 miles of paved and improved roads.

Memphis has 425 churches representing 28 denominations. Its superior educational advantages include the schools of pharmacy, dentistry and medicine of the University of Tennessee, Memphis State College, Southwestern University, the William R. Moore School of Technology, and the LeMoyne College for Negroes, University of Memphis Law School, Southern University College of Law, Southern College of Optometry, and Siena College. Its college preparatory schools include Christian Brothers College and St. Agnes Academy. Musical education is provided through the medium of the Memphis College of Music, the Memphis Conservatory of Music and numerous private studios. Memphis has 70 public schools including 11 senior high schools and nine junior high institutions. There are nine parochial schools, with an enrollment of 6,800. The public school enrollment is 46,947 pupils. Memphis has 10 public libraries, with a total of 264,864 volumes. Foremost of these are the Cossitt Library and the Goodwyn Institute Library, the latter being an endowed institution with an auditorium and lyceum lecture course.

Memphis is one of the foremost hospital centers of the South, having a total of 21 hospitals with 10,007 beds. Notable among these with Class A rating of the American Hospital Association, may be mentioned the Baptist Memorial, John Gaston Memorial Hospital, Methodist, St. Joseph's Crippled Adults and Crippled Children's hospitals. In addition to these, a United States Marine Hospital is located here as well as a United States Veterans' Hospital Facility No. 88. Memphis is provided with numerous clinics and private hospital institutions, and there are four sanitariums located just outside the city limits.

Local welfare institutions include the Anne Brinkley Home for Girls, the Mary Galloway Home for Aged Women, the Sunshine Home for Aged Men, the Tennessee Home for Incurables, and the Young Women's Christian Association and Young Men's Christian Association organizations. In addition, the city has three white orphanages and one colored orphanage.

The city has a municipal auditorium. The leading downtown clubs are the Catholic Club and the Rex Club. Other clubs are the University Club and the Nineteenth Century Club, the latter being a club for women. There are several country clubs, private and public golf courses operated by the Memphis Park Commission.

The city has been known as one of the cleanest cities in the United States for many years and has won national awards for its health and welfare work, and its noise-abatement campaigns.

Parks, Public Buildings, etc.—There are 41 improved parks with a total area of 1,421.58 acres. Two of the major parks are connected by a 12-mile boulevard or parkway encircling the city. The largest park is Riverside Park on the east side of the Mississippi River, just south of the city, containing 427 acres, much of which is left in its state of natural beauty. Next in point of size is Overton Park, one of the most beautiful parks of the South, located in the northeastern portion of the city and containing 355 acres. Within its boundaries are located the Memphis Zoological Garden, one of the finest in the nation, the Brooks Memorial Art Gallery, and the Open Air Theatre where some of the finest musical productions are performed each summer season. DeSoto Park is named for Hernando DeSoto, Spanish explorer. In this park near a great Indian mound, is a memorial, consisting of a ledge of rough granite with bronze tablets thereon, containing this inscription: "Near this spot Hernando De Soto discovered the Mississippi River in May 1541."

Russwood Park is the home of Memphis' Southern League baseball team, and E. H. Crump Stadium is the scene of outstanding college football games.

Recreational facilities are provided through 29 playgrounds, three swimming pools, seven community centers, 10 golf courses, 19 wading pools, 60 tennis courts, an athletic building for indoor sports, two stadiums and 12 baseball diamonds. The Park Commission has 100 persons on its recreational and playground staff. Of the 12 baseball diamonds, seven are equipped for night softball games, attracting approximately 300,000 per year.

Memphis has many fine buildings including the Custom House and Federal Building, the Shelby County Court House, the Criminal Courts Building and the Central Police Station, all of which are the finest examples of architecture. The city enjoys the distinction of having the largest ar-

tesian water system in the world, obtaining its city supply from an inexhaustible vein which runs as far as the Cumberland mountains in Tennessee. The waterworks are municipally owned and operated, with a capacity of 105,000,-000 gallons per day and with 906 miles of mains.

Modern sanitation methods obtain in its sewer system and $2,000,000 was expended in 1938 for improvements. Shelby County, in which Memphis is located, has one of the finest county hospitals in the United States which provides care for the indigent, sick and aged. Its Penal Farm is a modern institution in point of splendid facilities and methods employed. The Pink Palace Museum houses an attractive and extensive exhibit of mechanical arts. Memphis is the home of the Cotton Carnival, a week-long festival held each May, when the city honors "King Cotton" and his colorful court.

The Memphis Little Theatre presents a season of plays each winter, and the Memphis Auditorium books many famous persons from the theatrical world.

In writing of Memphis, one must not overlook Beale Street (or Avenue), where W. C. Handy wrote his immortal "Blues" songs. Modern Beale Street is now a far cry from the sinful street of the past—today it is a well-behaved, neon-lighted shopping district for Memphis' Negroes, but it is still a colorful and interesting street.

History.—The history of Memphis begins almost with the history of the United States. It was a landing and tenting place for the early explorers and missionaries. It was the home of the Chickasaw Indians, and the bluffs on which the city is located, 40 feet above high water and 80 feet above low water, have always been known as the Chickasaw Bluffs. Perhaps the first industry in America was established here in 1541 when DeSoto and his band of followers erected a shipyard for the construction of barges and piragues with which to cross the Mississippi River, then seven miles in width. In 1698 the French built forts on the site of what is now the city, and in 1794 the Spaniards erected forts at a time when Spain was claiming exclusive right to the lower Mississippi. Some of the foremost men in the United States owned lands in this vicinity and were interested in holding for their own country a right to free navigation on the Mississippi to the Gulf. Andrew Jackson, James Winchester and John Overton sent to Memphis in 1819 a small colony who established the first permanent settlement. In 1826 there were 500 persons in the settlement which was then incorporated as a town, and in 1849 a city charter was granted. The Union and Confederate forces tried to gain possession of the city at the beginning of the Civil War. On June 6, 1862 a Federal fleet under Commodore C. H. Davis conquered a Confederate fleet under Commodore J. E. Montgomery, thus placing Memphis in possession of the Union forces. General N. B. Forrest in command of Confederate forces entered the city in August 1864 and took several hundred prisoners. Memphis has always progressed commercially except during the Civil War, and when visited formerly by yellow fever epidemics. The great growth industrially has come within the last three decades. Its location has made the city a great railroad center; the surrounding forests made it a great industrial center; and the alluvial lands of the Saint Francis Basin, Yazoo Delta and the Valley of the Mississippi River will always make it a great commercial center. In 1855 yellow fever attacked the city, and again in 1867, 1873, 1878 and 1879. The epidemics of 1878 and 1879 so paralyzed the industries of the city that in 1879 Memphis was unable to liquidate the current indebtedness and the charter of the city was revoked. The former city was designated by the state legislature as "the taxing district of Shelby County." The control of the district was vested in a board of public works composed of five members, and a governing council composed of three commissioners. The council instituted the sewerage system, which practically eliminated the recurrence of yellow fever, improved civic conditions, liquidated the debts and in 1891 the place was reincorporated and again chartered as a city.

Population.—The growth of the city may be seen from the federal census reports. Pop. (1920) 162,351; (1930) 253,143; (1940) 292,942; (1960) 497,524. Only 1.5 per cent of Memphis' population is foreign born and 41.4 per cent is colored.

Consult Davis, J. D., *History of Memphis and the Old Times Papers* (Memphis 1873), most valuable for period prior to 1850; Williams, S. C., *Beginnings of West Tennessee, 1541–1841* (Johnson City 1930), objective; excellent background; Abernethy, T. P., *From Frontier to Plantation in Tennessee* (Chapel Hill 1932), best history, but ends in 1860; Hamer, P. M., *History of Tennessee,* 3 vols. (New York 1933), covers entire period; Capers, Jr., G. M., *The Biography of a River Town; Memphis: Its Heroic Age* (Chapel Hill 1939), excellent bibliography of primary and secondary sources, pages 269-279.

MEMPHIS (Tenn.), **Capture of.** At dusk June 5, 1862 the Union flotilla under command of Commodore C. H. Davis appeared near Memphis and anchored two miles above the city. The Confederate flotilla, Commodore J. E. Montgomery commanding, was lying at the Memphis levee. At daylight the Union fleet began to drop down toward the city, and the Confederates advanced to meet it. There were no troops protecting the city. The flotillas were composed of the following vessels:

Union	Guns	Confederate	Guns
Benton	16	Little Rebel	2
Louisville	13	Bragg	3
Carondelet	13	Beauregard	4
Cairo	13	Price	4
Saint Louis	13	Sumter	3
Queen of the West	ram	Lovell	4
Switzerland	ram	Thompson	4
Monarch	ram	Van Dorn	4
Lancaster	ram		
	68		28

Besides having more than twice the number of guns, the Union ordnance was much superior to that of the Confederates. The latter, however, made a desperate fight, which finally ended 10 miles below the city, with the result that the *Lovell, Beauregard* and *Thompson* were destroyed; and the *Little Rebel, Price, Sumter* and *Bragg* captured. The *Van Dorn* escaped. On the Union side only the *Queen of the West* was disabled.

Immediately after the fight the mayor, in reply to a summons to surrender, informed Commodore Davis that there were no troops with which to oppose him. The next morning detachments from troops under Col. C. N. Fitch, which accompanied the fleet, landed and took possession of the city.

General Grant arrived at Memphis June 23 and established the headquarters of the District of West Tennessee. He was recalled to Corinth July 15 and General Sherman was ordered to Memphis, reaching the city July 21. He restored the mayor and the city government, and made them responsible for civil order. He continued in command at Memphis until his forces left to joint General Grant in the final campaign for Vicksburg, having previously participated in the first move against that city.

The raid of Gen. N. B. Forrest, of Confederate cavalry fame, into Memphis occurred Aug. 21, 1864. The Union forces and commanding officers were completely surprised and barely escaped capture. Gen. C. C. Washburn, in command of the District of West Tennessee; Gen. R. P. Buckland of the District of Memphis, and Gen. S. A. Hurlbut were asleep in the city. General Forrest left the vicinity of Oxford August 18, with three brigades, making a forced march of nearly 100 miles. A strong detachment rode into the city at 4 o'clock in the morning, running over a regiment of 100-days men on picket, and capturing about 250 of them. This force divided into three and at once surrounded the quarters of the three officers named. Each, however, escaped.

MEMPHIS, city, Texas, in Hall County, altitude 2,067 feet, on the Fort Worth and Denver City Railroad, 85 miles southeast of Amarilla. Cotton processing is its principal industry. Pop. 3,332.

MEMPHREMAGOG, měm-frĕ-mä'gŏg, **Lake,** in the southern part of the province of Quebec, Canada, extending into Orleans County, in Vermont. It is about 30 miles long, north and south, and from one to four miles wide. It is irregular in shape, and along its shores are several striking indentations, in some places low and in some other parts high and rocky. The land on the west shore is mountainous, the altitude of the highest points being about 2,800 feet. The outlet is the Magog River, which flows into the St. Francis River. Along the shore are a number of villages, and in summer a steamer plies daily on the lake, connecting the chief towns and villages.

MENA, mä'nä, **Juan de,** Spanish poet: b. Cordova, Spain, about 1411; d. Torrelaguna, 1456. He was educated at Salamanca and at Rome and afterward was appointed secretary and court historian to John II, king of Castile. His allegorical poems, *Coplas de los Siete Pecados Mortales, Le Coronacion,* and *El Laberinto de Fortuna,* a poem founded on the *Divina Commedia* and published in the year 1496, all show the influence of Dante, for whom he held great respect and admiration. His collected works were published in 1528, entitled *Copilación de todas las obras de Juan de Mena.*

MENA, city, Arkansas, and Polk County seat; altitude 1,145 feet; 86 miles south of Fort Smith; on the Kansas City Southern Railroad. It is in a summer resort region of the Ouachita Mountains, is a shipping point for lumber, and the business center of a farm and dairy area raising truck crops, corn, peanuts, soybeans, berries and poultry. It has bottling works, flour mills, and manufactures of cream cheese, finished lumber, window sashes and doors, furniture, wooden handles, slate roofing, headings and staves. Pop. 4,368.

MENABREA, mä-nä-brâ′ä, COUNT **Luigi Federigo,** Italian soldier and statesman: b. Chambéry, in Savoy, Sept. 4, 1809; d. there, May 25, 1896. After completing a course in mathematics at the University of Turin and joining the engineers in the Sardinian army, he accepted the professorship of technical science at the military academy and at the University of Turin. Having been promoted to the rank of captain, he was used in the diplomatic corps for some time; was then elected deputy, serving both under the minister of war and the minister of the interior; and upon the outbreak of the war of Sardinia and France against Austria in 1859 he was appointed chief of the engineer corps. After Savoy was ceded to France, Menabrea was made a senator by Victor Emmanuel, and chief of the department of engineers, and as such planned the fortifications of Bologna, Piacenza and Pavia; in 1860 he was created a lieutenant-general, in that year laying siege to and after three months of fighting taking Gaeta. In 1861 he joined the Cabinet of Ricasoli as minister of marine; in 1862 he took over the portfolio of minister of public works. In 1866 he was Italian ambassador to the council which brought about the Treaty of Prague and ceded Venice to Italy. In 1867, when Rattazzi resigned, he formed a new ministry, himself becoming minister of foreign affairs. As premier he did much to place Italy in cordial relations with the outside world, and to settle internal dissensions, but his imprisonment of Garibaldi and the prevalent financial straits of the nation lost to him the confidence of the House of Deputies, and on Nov. 16, 1869 he resigned. In 1870 he became Italian ambassador at Vienna, was appointed to the same post at London in 1876 and in 1882 went to Paris, where he was stationed for 10 years.

The most important of his works are *Etudes sur la série de Lagrange* (1844–1847); *Le génie italien dans la campagne d'Ancone et de la Basse-Italie* (1866), and *République et Monarchie dans l'état actuel de la France* (1871).

MENAGE, mä-nàzh′, **Gilles,** French philologist and satirist: b. Angers, Aug. 15, 1613; d. Paris, July 23, 1692. After completing his early studies he became an advocate, practicing for some time at Paris, but, having conceived a profound disgust for that profession and all its adherents, he became an ecclesiastic, and for some time was a member of the household of the Cardinal de Retz, but subsequently took up his residence in the cloister of Notre Dame. A witty satire, entitled *Requéste des Dictionnaires,* published in 1638, and aimed at the *Dictionary* of the French Academy, prevented his becoming a member of that society.

His most important works are *Dictionnaire étymologique, ou Origines de la Langue Française* (1650–1694); *Origines de la Langue Italienne* (1669); *Miscellanea* (1652); *Poemata latina, gallica, graeca, et italica* (1656); *l'Anti-Baillet* (1690).

MENAGERIE, mê-năj′ẽr-ĭ, a collection of wild animals, exhibited in zoological gardens, in museums and by circus companies traveling from city to city. The term is now confined almost wholly to a collection exhibited in connection with a traveling circus, a permanent collection being styled a zoological park or "zoo." The menagerie of the typical circus is usually shown in a separate tent, so arranged that the public can make the round of the cages before taking their seats. The principal exhibits are usually elephants, a giraffe (when one is to be had), hippopotamus, rhinoceros, tapir, lions, tigers, bears, leopards (and others of the cat family), lynx, kangaroo, varieties of deer, monkeys, a few cages of snakes, and minor animals. See also CIRCUS; ZOOLOGICAL GARDENS.

MENAI STRAIT or **STRAITS,** měn′ī, the channel between Wales and Anglesey Island, is 14 miles long, and varies in width from 200 yards to ¾ mile. Menai Suspension Bridge and the celebrated Britannia Tubular Bridge connect Anglesey with the mainland. The tides and current are very strong at times, so that large vessels avoid the strait. See also BRIDGE—5.

MENAM, mä-näm′, **MEINAM, MAE NAM, ME NAM, CHAO PHRAYA,** or **CHAO PHYA,** a chief river of Thailand, rising in the Laos country, and flowing generally southward to enter the Gulf of Siam below Bangkok. Its length is about 750 miles, although strictly the name applies only to the 160-mile lower course which begins at the junction of the Ping and Nan rivers. It is navigable for small craft. It is subject to periodical overflows on which the crops of the rice fields along its banks are dependent.

MENANDER, the name of two Greek writers:

MENANDER, the comic dramatist: b. Athens, 343? B.C.; d. there, ?291 B.C. He was the pupil of Theophrastus, himself the pupil and successor of Aristotle as head of the Peripatetics, and author of *Characteres,* a somewhat more literary and popular enlargement of some ruling ideas of the Nicomachaean Ethics; he was by such a teacher well trained for his dramatic vocation. He was, moreover, a friend of Epicurus from early life, and may thus have been imbued with that bonhommie which rendered him so genial an interpreter of manners. He wrote a hundred comedies which are distinguished from those of Aristophanes by their refinement, their freedom from personal and political virulence, and their graceful, sometimes beautiful, delineation of feminine character. He was, however, outrivaled in popular favor by his contemporary Philemon, whose ribaldry was irresistible to the Athenian playgoers. Only some fragments of his works survive in the original, the most important of these relics having come to light in Egypt (1898). He was, however, closely imitated by Plautus and Terence, and in the *Bacchides, Stichus* and *Poenulus* of the former, and the *Andria, Eunuchus, Heautontimorumenos* and *Adelphi* of the latter we have very good representatives of the Greek dramatist's method and spirit. A fine antique statue of Menander is to be seen in the Vatican.

MENANDER, a rhetorician who flourished in the latter half of the 3d century B.C. He has left the rhetorical treatise *De Encomiis,* and from his analyses of the orations of Demosthenes, most of the scholia on that orator have been compiled.

Consult (on Menander the dramatist), Guizot, *Ménandre* (1855); Horkel, *Lebensweisheit des Komikers Menander* (1857); Smith, W., *A New Classical Dictionary* (1867).

MENARD, mě-närd', **Michel Branamour,** American pioneer: b. Laprairie, Lower Canada, Dec. 5, 1805; d. Galveston, Texas, Sept. 2, 1856. After working as a fur trader in Arkansas, where he lived among the Shawnee Indians, and in Texas, he began to acquire land and businesses in Texas. As a signatory of the Texas Declaration of Independence and later as a member of the Congress of Texas, he was influential in the formation of the state. Galveston was settled on a six-square mile tract of Menard's land by a company which he organized (1838), and Menard County, Texas, was named after him.

MENASHA, mě-năsh'à, city, Wisconsin, in Winnebago County, on the Fox River and Lake Winnebago, five miles south of Appleton. It is served by the "Soo" Line; Chicago and North Western; and Chicago, Milwaukee, St. Paul and Pacific railroads. The city's industries include printing and publishing and the manufacture of paper, and wood and paper products. Menasha is adjacent to Neenah and forms with it a continuous community. The twin cities were settled in the 1840's on land ceded to the United States government by the Menominee Indians. Of the two, Menasha became more industrial. Doty Island in the Fox River belongs partly to each city. The site of Jean Nicolet's landing in 1634 is marked on Menasha's side of the island. Pop. 14,647.

MENCIUS, měn'shǐ-ŭs (Latinized name of MENG-TSE or MÊNG-TZŬ), Chinese philosopher: b. Tsowhsien, in the ancient state of Lu (now Shantung Province), China, c. 372 B.C.; d. there, c. 289 B.C. Mencius, who bears the honorary title of the Second Sage, was one of the greatest of the early Confucians. During his lifetime, the governments of China were particularly oppressive, and Mencius for many years wandered about in search of a prince who would consent to govern in accordance with true and just principles. Failing to find such a ruler, he secluded himself and spent the rest of his life in perfecting his philosophy and in training his disciples. His works contain enlightened views of man and society. He believed in the basic goodness of man and had unbounded faith in the possibilities of progress under a good social and political system. He regarded all governments as coming from God, but at the same time, he believed in the responsibility of rulers to their people and of the nobility's right to depose or even put to death unworthy rulers. The people were for him the most important element in a nation, after them ranked the government, and last of all the monarch. The aim of a government, according to Mencius, should be the happiness and the education of the people, and any ruler who was content to leave his subjects in ignorance and misery deserved to be deposed. Mencius did not attain his revered position until the revival of Confucianism during the Sung dynasty, when the *Meng Tsu Shu* (*Book of Mencius*) became a part of the Four Books, which scholars committed to memory.

Consult *Mencius,* tr. by Leonard A. Lyall (London 1932); Richards, I. A., *Mencius on the Mind, Experiments in Multiple Definition* (New York 1932).

MENCKEN, měng'kěn, **H(enry) L(ouis),** American editor and satirist: b. Baltimore, Md., Sept. 12, 1880; d. there, Jan. 29, 1956. He received his formal education at the F. Knapp Institute and the Baltimore Polytechnic Institute. In 1899 he joined the Baltimore *Morning Herald* as a reporter. He became its editor in 1905, and in that year joined the Baltimore *Evening Sun,* for which he worked intermittently as editorial writer, columnist, and reporter until 1948. His first literary efforts were in the field of poetry and the short story, but, after discovering George Bernard Shaw and Friedrich Nietzsche, he abandoned creative writing for ideological warfare. Joining the magazine, *Smart Set,* in 1908, Mencken launched his campaign against prevailing values in American life and letters. In 1914 he and George Jean Nathan became coeditors of the magazine, and in 1924 they undertook the joint editorship of Alfred Knopf's new magazine of opinion, the *American Mercury,* which Mencken continued to edit until 1933.

Based on a union of scientific skepticism and Nietzschean ethics, Mencken's social criticism was directed primarily against the middle class, which he called the "booboisie." His antipathy for "Puritanism" and democracy led him to denounce the "genteel tradition" in American literature and to take up with ardor the cause of naturalism. With his mastery of the techniques of invective and shock, he became the apostle of ideological rebellion in the post-World War I years. His essays, particularly the *Prejudices* (six series, 1917–1927), which diagnosed with clinical precision the current social ills, acquired the status of scripture among young intellectuals. During the depression, however, he rapidly lost his following, and by 1930 his influence had become negligible. Perhaps his most important contribution to American literature was his championship of new writers, including Theodore Dreiser, James Branch Cabell, Sherwood Anderson, Sinclair Lewis, and Eugene O'Neill. And perhaps his most permanent work is the *American Language* (four revisions and two supplements, 1919–1948).

Among his many other writings are *George Bernard Shaw—His Plays* (1905); *Damn! A Book on Calumny* (1917); *In Defense of Women* (1917); *The American Credo* (with G. J. Nathan, 1920); *Treatise on Right and Wrong* (1934); and *Minority Report* (published posthumously, 1956). Mencken's autobiography is contained in three volumes, *Happy Days, 1880–1892* (1940); *Newspaper Days, 1899–1906* (1941); and *Heathen Days, 1890–1936* (1943).

MENDEL, měn'děl, **Gregor Johann,** Austrian botanist: b. Heinzendorf, near Odrau in Austrian Silesia (now Hynčice, near Odry in central Silesia, Czechoslovakia), July 22, 1822; d. Brünn, Austria (now Brno, Czechoslovakia), Jan. 6, 1884. Mendel is known today as the discoverer of the laws of inheritance named after him (see HEREDITY). His given name was Johann, but, according to custom, he assumed a new name, Gregor, when he entered the Augustinian Order. After completing his studies at a Gymnasium, he began his novitiate at the Abbey of St. Thomas in Brünn. He was ordained a priest in 1847, and since the Augustinians were obliged to supply a number of teachers for secondary schools, in 1851 he was sent to the University of Vienna for training in mathematics and the natural sciences.

Mendel studied in Vienna until 1853, and a year later he became a teacher of natural science and physics in the Realschule at Brünn, a position which he held for the next 14 years. During this period he engaged in the breeding experiments with peas and beans that led to his discovery of the fundamental laws of inheritance.

In 1868 Mendel was named abbot of his chapter, but the duties attending the new position soon forced him to give up his scientific studies. He did not engage directly in the current controversy between church and state, but he opposed what he regarded as discriminatory legislation and stubbornly defended his monastery against taxes levied exclusively on religious institutions. His gentle nature was embittered by these struggles, and he died, a lonely and saddened man, at the age of 61.

About 1856 Mendel began experiments in the monastery gardens. There he sowed varieties of garden peas and beans, and the hawkweeds, for purposes of cross fertilization and hybridization. The results of only a few of his experiments were published, and the two most important papers, "Experiments with Plant Hybrids" (1866) and "On Certain Hybrids of *Hieracium* Obtained by Artificial Fertilization" (1869), appeared in the rather obscure *Transactions* of the Brünn Natural History Society, where they remained unnoticed until long after his death. In 1900 the papers were discovered, Mendel's experiments were repeated, and their importance was realized and set forth, quite independently, by three leading botanists, Hugo De Vries in Holland, Karl Erich Correns in Germany, and by the Austrian, Erich Tschermak. The so-called "Mendelian Laws" (those relating to the uniformity of hybrids, to proportion and division, and above all, to the autonomy of characters) were formulated on the basis of data contained in the first paper. These laws have been fundamental in the flowering, since the turn of the century, of the science of genetics.

The choice of the pea, with the simple varietal characteristics of tall or short plants, and smooth or wrinkled seeds, was an extremely happy one. *Hieracium*, on the other hand, was most unsuitable for hybridization, since nothing was known in Mendel's day of its apogamy (ability to produce seeds without normal fertilization). It may have been the impossibility of verifying his earlier results with the hawkweeds that discouraged him from further experimentation. Mendel also occupied himself with experiments on the hybridization of bees, and with meteorological observations. See also GENETICS; MENDELISM.

Consult Iltis, Hugo, *Life of Mendel* (New York 1932); "Gregor Mendel and His Work," *Scientific Monthly*, vol. 56, pp. 414–423 (Washington, D.C.).

MENDELEYEV, myĕn-dyĭ-lyā'yĕf, **Dmitri Ivanovich**, Russian chemist: b. Tobolsk, Siberia, Feb. 7, 1834; d. St. Petersburg (now Leningrad), Feb. 2, 1907. He studied at the Pedagogical Institute in St. Petersburg, in 1863 became professor of chemistry at the St. Petersburg Institute of Technology, and in 1866 was appointed to a similar professorship at the University of St. Petersburg. Although he carried on significant research on gases and solutions, he is best known for his formulation of the periodic law (announced in 1869), which stated that the properties of elements are periodic functions of their atomic weights. The enunciation of the law was remarkable, because Mendeleyev was working with only 63 elements, all that were known at the time. He arranged these elements in the form of a table, in order of their increasing atomic weights, and discovered that the properties of the elements recurred at regular intervals. In his arrangement certain gaps occurred. Mendeleyev not only predicted that these gaps represented undiscovered elements, but in 1871, he actually described the properties of several elements which were discovered a few years later (gallium, 1875; scandium, 1879; germanium, 1886). His predictions were made, not only for the valence and general chemical activity, but he also gave precise numerical value for densities, melting points, and so forth. When the six inert gases were discovered at the end of the century, elements whose existence Mendeleyev could not have guessed at, as one more family of elements with similar properties, they fitted perfectly into his periodic table. During the 20th century, Mendeleyev's table has been rearranged, so that the elements are placed in order according to atomic number, rather than atomic weight, but since number and weight are almost identical, few changes have been made in Mendeleyev's original system.

From 1893, Mendeleyev served as director of the national bureau of weights and measures. He also acted as a consultant to the government on the development of the newly-founded petroleum industry. Among his various writings is his *Principles of Chemistry* (2 vols., 1868–1871; Eng. tr., 1905), which for many years was used as a standard textbook and was translated into various languages.

See also PERIODIC LAW.

Consult Posin, Daniel Q., *Mendeleyev; The Story of a Great Scientist* (New York 1948).

MENDELISM, mĕn'dĕl-ĭz'm, the basic principles of heredity discovered by Gregor Mendel through eight years of hybridizing varieties of the familiar garden pea. For purposes of hybridization, he selected, from specimens of the garden pea (*Pisum sativum*), plants which exhibited seven pairs of contrasting *characters*, for example, plants with tall or short stems, smooth or wrinkled seeds, varying colors of the seed-skins, inflated or constricted pods, and so forth. He preserved the seeds from his hybrids (the F_1 generation), planted them, observed in the crop (the F_2 generation) the characters selected for examination, then preserved the seeds of the new generation, planted them, and continued the experiment through several more generations. For each

RESULTS OF MENDEL'S EXPERIMENTS ON HEREDITY

Number of F_2 plants[1]	Structure	Property	Characters Dominant		Characters Recessive		Ratio
253	Seed	Form	5,474	smooth	1,850	wrinkled	2.96:1
258	Albumen	Color	6,022	yellow	2,001	green	3.01:1
929	Seed coats	Color	705	gray	224	white	3.15:1
1,181	Seed pods	Form	882	inflated	299	constricted	2.95:1
580	Unripe pods	Color	428	green	152	yellow	2.82:1
858	Flowers	Position	651	axial	207	terminal	3.14:1
1,064	Stem	Length	787	tall	277	dwarf	2.84:1
5,123 (total)			14,949 (total)		5,010 (total)		2.98:1 (mean ratio)

[1]*Pisum sativum*   Modified from "Principles of Genetics" (1950)

generation he counted both seeds and plants, thereby introducing statistical method into his studies (see Table).

The hybrid seeds from the crossing of tall and short plants, for example, produced an F_1 generation in which all plants were tall. When self-fertilized, the seeds of this F_1 generation produced an F_2 series in which, in one fourth of the plants, the character of shortness reappeared, unmodified by its passage through the F_1 generation. These dwarf plants, when self-fertilized, produced only dwarfs in succeeding generations. When the self-fertilized progeny of the remaining three fourths was further examined, it was seen that one fourth produced only tall plants which bred true in succeeding generations, while the remaining two fourths contained both the tall and the short character and continued to breed out the two pure and the hybrid lots in the same proportions, that is, 1:2:1. Thus the character of tallness was found to be *dominant* over shortness, and shortness, which was *recessive* in the F_1 generation, was found to be *segregated* in the F_2 generation, in which one fourth were pure tall, one half hybrid tall and short, and one fourth pure short. Tallness and shortness are therefore *unit characters* that remain distinct, however masked in the hybrids.

Subsequent studies have shown that dominance is not an essential feature of the Mendelian mode of inheritance, and that the hybrid form may be intermediate between contrasting parents. It is the orderly reappearance of characters in the succeeding generations, in the proportion of 3:1, that constitutes Mendel's "First Law."

The independent assortment of characters, when two or more factors (unit characters) are involved in the same experiment, constitutes Mendel's "Second Law" (the terms rule or principle are preferable to law). If two characters are present, the proportion becomes 9:3:3:1; if there are three, the figures are 27:9:9:9:3:3:3:1. The understanding and explanation of these modes of sorting out characters, or *factors,* required a generation of intensive study. See also HEREDITY; MENDEL, GREGOR JOHANN.

Consult Bateson, William, *Mendel's Principles of Heredity* (Cambridge, England, 1930); Sinnott, Edmund Ware, and others, *Principles of Genetics* (Chapel Hill, N.C., 1950).

KARL P. SCHMIDT.

MENDELSOHN, měn′děl-zōn, **Eric,** German-American architect: b. Allenstein, East Prussia, Germany (now Olsztyn, Poland), March 21, 1887; d. San Francisco, Calif., Sept. 15, 1953. He studied at the University of Munich (M.A., 1911), served during World War I with the corps of engineers in the German army, and in 1918 began architectural practice in Berlin. His Einstein Tower (1920–1921) at Potsdam, built as an observatory and astrophysical laboratory for experiments connected with Albert Einstein's theory of relativity, made Mendelsohn famous. In this structure, which appears carved or sculptured, can be seen the strong influence which the *Jugendstil* (*art nouveau* movement) and expressionism had on Mendelsohn. His later work, however, became more functional, as, for example, in the Schocken department store at Chemnitz. From 1933 to 1937 he practiced in England, and thereafter, until 1941, in Palestine, where some of his most creative work was done. He emigrated to the United States in 1941, and in 1945 settled in San Francisco. His work includes factories, power stations, department stores, houses, synagogues, laboratories, and hospital and university buildings.

Consult Whittick, Arnold, *Eric Mendelsohn,* 2d ed. (New York 1956).

MENDELSSOHN, Felix. See MENDELSSOHN-BARTHOLDY, JAKOB LUDWIG FELIX.

MENDELSSOHN, měn′děls-zōn, **Moses,** German Jewish philosopher: b. Dessau, Germany, Sept. 6, 1729; d. Berlin, Jan. 4, 1786. In his youth he received Jewish religious instruction and was particularly influenced by the writings of Maimonides. In 1743, at the age of 13, he went to Berlin, where despite poverty he was able to study languages, literature, mathematics, and philosophy. In 1754 he met Gotthold Ephraim Lessing, who was to remain his lifelong friend. Lessing later used Mendelssohn as the prototype for Nathan, the hero of his play, *Nathan der Weise* (*Nathan the Wise,* 1779). Mendelssohn's first work in German appeared in 1755, *Philosophische Gespräche* (*Philosophical Conversations*) and established his reputation in Germany as a philosopher of note. In 1763, he competed with various philosophers, among them Immanuel Kant, and with his *Abhandlung über die Evidenz in den metaphysischen Wissenschaften* won the prize of the Berlin Academy. In his *Phädon* (1767) he attempted to prove the immortality of the soul. His philosophy is most fully developed in *Jerusalem oder über religiöse Macht und Judentum* (1783; Eng. tr., *Jerusalem: A Treatise on Religious Power and Judaism,* 1852), in which he calls for religious tolerance and the separation of church and state. By the active role which he took, outside of Jewish communities, in the intellectual life of Europe, by his writings, and with his translations of the Pentateuch and the *Psalms* (1783), Mendelssohn gave a strong impetus to the Haskalah, the Jewish enlightenment movement. His work also had a strong effect in the 19th century of Reform Judaism. He was the grandfather of the composer, Felix Mendelssohn.

See also JEWISH HISTORY AND SOCIETY—11. *Haskalah* and 12. *Religious and Philosophical Movements* (Outstanding Jewish Philosophers).

MENDELSSOHN-BARTHOLDY, měn′-děls-zōn bär-tōl′dê, **Jakob Ludwig Felix,** German composer; b. Hamburg, Germany, Feb. 3, 1809; d. Leipzig, Nov. 4, 1847. Grandson of the philosopher Moses Mendelssohn (q.v.) and the first son and second of four children of Leah Salomon and Abraham Mendelssohn, a banker who appended to his surname that of his wife's Christianized brother when he himself adopted the Lutheran faith, the composer was free of financial problems throughout his life. His taste and talent for music became certain while he was a very young child. The boy and his gifted sister Fanny (later Fanny Hensel) took piano lessons from Marie Bigot in Paris in 1816; in Berlin, whither the family had moved in 1812, they studied literature with Carl Wilhelm Heyse, the father of the poet-novelist Paul Heyse; the piano with Ludwig Berger; the violin with Carl Wilhelm Henning; and harmony and composition with the director of the Singakademie, Karl Friedrich Zelter, a friend of Johann Wolfgang von Goethe. By 1820, Mendelssohn had made a public debut as a pianist (October 1818), had begun to compose extensively, and had been entered in the Singakademie.

Early Compositions.—During the next three years, he composed 12 string symphonies, three one-act operas, and a three-act opera entitled *Die beiden Neffen, oder Der Onkel aus Boston* (*Both Nephews, or the Uncle from Boston*). In 1821, and again in 1822, Mendelssohn visited Goethe, who was strongly impressed by the prodigy, whose name was rapidly becoming known throughout the German states. Before his 18th birthday, Mendelssohn had composed music that is still familiar today, including the *Rondo capriccioso* for piano and the overture to William Shakespeare's *A Midsummer Night's Dream* (composed as a piano duet in 1826, first played in orchestral form at Stettin in February 1827), had taken additional piano lessons from Ignaz Moscheles and, on extensive travels, had met many prominent musical figures of the day, including Maria Luigi Carlo Zenobio Salvatore Cherubini, Jacques Halévy, Christian Kalkbrenner, Giacomo Meyerbeer, Gioacchino Antonio Rossini, and Louis Spohr. His comic opera *Die Hochzeit des Camacho* (*Camacho's Wedding*) and the well-known Octet for Strings in E-Flat Major date from 1825. In 1826, Mendelssohn entered the University of Berlin, where he studied for three years. In 1828 he composed the overture *A Calm Sea and a Prosperous Voyage* after two poems by Goethe and began, with the enthusiastic support of his friend the actor-baritone Philipp Eduard Devrient, to prepare the Singakademie for the first performance of the *St. Matthew Passion* since Johann Sebastian Bach's death in 1750. That performance, on March 11, 1829 (it was repeated twice), importantly influenced the thereafter swiftly burgeoning reputation of Bach. In 1829, too, making his first appearance in London, Mendelssohn conducted his Symphony No. 1 in C Minor with the London Philharmonic Society, inaugurating his enduring popularity in England as pianist, composer, and conductor. He continued to compose swiftly and without apparent effort: pieces for piano solo and for varying chamber ensembles; songs; the *Reformation Symphony* No. 5 in D Major (1830–1832); and, during a visit to Italy during which he met Louis Hector Berlioz, the beginnings of both the *Scottish Symphony* No. 3 in A Minor-Major (completed 1842) and the *Italian Symphony* No. 4 in A Major-Minor (completed 1833).

Travels and Mature Works.—In Munich on Oct. 17, 1831, Mendelssohn was the soloist in the first performance of his Piano Concerto No. 1 in G Minor. Later that year and early in 1832 he visited Paris, meeting Frédéric François Chopin and Franz Liszt, and returned to England, where he composed the *Capriccio brillant* for piano and orchestra, the first book of *Songs without Words* for solo piano, and the *Hebrides* (*Fingal's Cave*) *Overture,* which he had first sketched out in 1830. In Berlin, in July 1832, he conducted the first performance of his choral setting of Goethe's *Die erste Walpurgisnacht* (revised 1843). Continuing to honor the many requests for his presence in London, Mendelssohn nevertheless conducted the Lower Rhine Festival at Düsseldorf in 1833, later that year settling temporarily in that city as general music director and there composing the overture *Das Märchen von der schönen Melusine,* after an opera libretto by Franz Grillparzer. In 1834 he composed the *Rondo brillant* for piano and orchestra and began the oratorio *St. Paul* (completed 1836).

In 1835, Mendelssohn left Düsseldorf for Leipzig, becoming conductor there of the Gewandhaus concerts and instituting his close friendship with Robert Schumann. *St. Paul* was a successful climax of the Lower Rhine Festival at Düsseldorf on May 22, 1836. In 1836, too, Mendelssohn became engaged to marry Cécile Charlotte Sophia Jeanrenaud, whose father had been pastor of the Walloon French Reformed Church at Frankfurt am Main; they were married on March 28, 1837, and their idyllically happy marriage produced three sons and two daughters.

In 1837, Mendelssohn met the English composer William (later Sir William) Sterndale Bennett, often regarded as his most devoted disciple. He also completed his Second Piano Concerto in D Minor, began to plan an oratorio dealing with the prophet Elijah, and conducted his *St. Paul* at the Birmingham (England) Festival. His eternally popular Violin Concerto in E Minor-Major was begun in 1838; the overture *Ruy Blas* after a play by Victor Hugo was composed in 1839. In 1841 he was appointed general music director at Berlin, but continued to live in Leipzig, and resigned the Berlin post in October 1844. During years crowded with travel and increasing honors, Mendelssohn poured out chamber music, unaccompanied choral pieces, piano works, songs, and church music. The cantata or choral symphony entitled *Lobgesang* (usually counted as Symphony No. 2) and the *Festgesang* were both composed in 1840, and the familiar *Variations sérieuses* for piano solo in 1841.

Mendelssohn completed the *Scottish Symphony* in January 1842 and conducted its first performance, at the Leipzig Gewandhaus, on March 3. When he repeated it in London on June 13, he was summoned to Buckingham Palace and showered with royal favors by Queen Victoria and Prince Albert. After his return to Germany, where he had been appointed *Kapellmeister* to Friedrich August II of Saxony, he resigned this new position to return to Leipzig and there, collaborating with Schumann and others, founded a conservatory of music. Meanwhile, Friedrich Wilhelm IV of Prussia had commissioned Mendelssohn to compose incidental music for Jean Baptiste Racine's *Athalie,* Sophocles' *Oedipus at Colonus,* and Shakespeare's *A Midsummer Night's Dream.* The last play was performed, with all of Mendelssohn's now-familiar music (including the Wedding March), at Potsdam on Oct. 14, 1843. In May and June 1844, Mendelssohn conducted five very successful Philharmonic concerts in London. In September he completed the Violin Concerto, which was heard for the first time at Leipzig on March 13, 1845. His health was deteriorating, and in December 1844 he retired from all official duties, settling at Frankfurt am Main. By September 1845 he had recuperated sufficiently to return to Leipzig as conductor at the Gewandhaus and professor of both piano and composition at the Conservatory of Music.

Final Years and Accomplishments.—In July 1846, Mendelssohn completed the oratorio *Elijah,* the first performance of which he conducted in England, at the Birmingham Festival, on August 26; he revised the oratorio completely after his return to Leipzig. His health was by this time alarming, but his habit of constant composition was not changed. After his tenth and final visit to England in April–May 1847, he began to compose an opera entitled *Lorelei* and another oratorio, *Christus,* neither of which was to be completed. The death of his beloved sister Fanny on May 14 caused Mendelssohn heartbroken grief and resulted in his complete physical collapse. During a summer visit to Switzerland in search of renewed health and vigor, he completed the last of his works, the String Quartet No. 6 in F Minor. Having returned to Leipzig in September, he died there on November 4, being three months less than 38 years of age. Among composers of the highest rank, only Wolfgang Amadeus Mozart and Franz Peter Schubert had shorter lives.

Reputation as Composer.—Mendelssohn's popularity and prestige, which were enormous in the German states, England, and Austria during his lifetime, continued to expand for decades after his death. In technique something of a classicist, he employed recognizably romantic musical ideas, and has thus come to be classified as an early romantic in music along with Karl Maria Friedrich Ernst von Weber, Robert Schumann, and Frédéric François Chopin. In recent decades his reputation has tended to recede somewhat, much of his music having come to seem naive and dusty to many 20th century listeners. Thus, though his Violin Concerto, *Scottish* and *Italian* symphonies, incidental music to *A Midsummer Night's Dream,* a few of the string quartets and other chamber pieces, and fewer of the piano pieces and songs are still much performed at professional concerts, the larger body of his music has either fallen into desuetude or been relegated to amateur performance. Mendelssohn's operas, most of his incidental music for plays (for Sophocles' *Antigone,* in addition to the plays mentioned above), his extensive church music, his oratorios and cantatas (except in England, where *St. Paul* and *Elijah* have faded only slightly), his unaccompanied choral works, his pieces for solo instruments and orchestra (the Violin Concerto excepted), much of his chamber music, most of his music for solo piano, his organ compositions, his vocal duets, and nearly all of his numerous solo songs (of which only his setting of Heinrich Heine's *Auf Flügeln des Gesanges* remains familiar) have suffered in both critical and popular esteem.

Some truth must be granted to the frequently repeated charge that Mendelssohn, a man of enormous charm without deeps, of a too-facile technique expended with too little effort, composed more music than his talent warranted. At evoking fairyland, in the swiftly rushing, sparkling sort of music represented by the *Rondo capriccioso,* the finest of the *Midsummer Night's Dream* pieces, the fast movements of the *Scottish* and *Italian* symphonies and the Violin Concerto, he has had no peer except Louis Hector Berlioz. But his attempts at seriousness, especially when tinged by a taste for philosophizing, tend to sound unctuous and insincere to modern listeners, particularly of the more sophisticated sort. However, his position among the great masters of musical creation, though not at or near the top, remains secure.

HERBERT WEINSTOCK

Bibliography.—Benedict, J., *A Sketch of the Life and Works of the Late Felix Mendelssohn-Bartholdy* (London 1850); Lampadius, Wilhelm Adolf, *Felix Mendelssohn-Bartholdy: ein Denkmal für seine Freunde* (Leipzig 1848), supplemented Eng. tr. by William Leonard Gage as *The Life of Felix Mendelssohn-Bartholdy* (Boston 1865); Reissmann, August, *Felix Mendelssohn-Bartholdy: sein Leben und seine Werke* (Berlin 1867); Hiller, Ferdinand, *Mendelssohn: Briefe und Erinnerugen* (Cologne 1874), Eng. tr. by M. E. von Glehn, *Mendelssohn: Letters and Recollections* (London 1874); Hensel, Sebastian, *Die Familie Mendelssohn,* 3 vols. (Berlin 1879), Eng. tr. by Carl Klingemann in 2 vols., *The Mendelssohn Family* (New York 1881); Rockstro, William Smyth, *Mendelssohn* (London 1884); Dahms, Walter, *Mendelssohn* (Berlin 1919); Kaufmann, Schima, *Mendelssohn, A Second Elijah* (New York 1934); Stratton, Stephen S., *Mendelssohn* (London 1901; rev. ed. 1934); Selden-Goth, Gisella, ed., *Letters* (New York 1945); Grove, Sir George, *Beethoven, Schubert, Mendelssohn* (London 1951), reprinting articles from the first four editions of *Grove's Dictionary of Music and Musicians* (London 1878–1940); Radcliffe, Philip, *Mendelssohn* (London 1954; New York 1963); Jacob, Heinrich E., *Felix Mendelssohn and His Times,* tr. by R. and C. Winston (Englewood Cliffs, N.J., 1963); Werner, Eric, *Mendelssohn,* tr. by D. Newlin (Glencoe, Ill., 1963).

MENDENHALL, mĕn′dĕn-hôl, **Thomas Corwin,** American physicist: b. near Hanoverton, Ohio, Oct. 4, 1841; d. Ravenna, March 22, 1924. Although he attended public schools and graduated from the Southwest Normal School at Lebanon, Ohio, in 1861, he was largely self-educated in mathematics and physics. He taught high school science with such success that he was elected in 1873 to the faculty of the Ohio Agricultural and Mechanical College (later Ohio State University). In 1878 he accepted a call to the chair of physics at the Imperial University, Tokyo, Japan, where he founded a laboratory and an observatory, and helped to organize a scientific society and a system of lectures. He returned to the Ohio State University in 1881, three years later accepted a position with the United States Signal Corps at Washington, and from 1886 to 1889 served as president of Rose Polytechnic Institute at Terre Haute, Ind. As superintendent of the United States Coast and Geodetic Survey (1889–1894), Mendenhall developed an improved instrument to measure the relative force of gravity with greater accuracy and planned a transcontinental series of gravity measurements. From 1894 he was president of Worcester Polytechnic Institute, until ill health forced him to retire in 1901. He received many scientific honors for his important contributions in the fields of electricity, gravity, seismology, and atmosphere electricity, and was the author of *A Century of Electricity* (1887).

MENDERES, mĕn-dĕ-rĕs′, **Adnan,** Turkish statesman: b. Aydin, Turkey, 1899; d. (executed) Imrali Island, Sept. 17, 1961. The son of a wealthy landowner, he was graduated from the American College at İzmir and took a law degree at the University of Ankara. He then returned to the family farm, where he introduced modern agricultural techniques. Entering politics, he won election to the National Assembly in 1930 and continued for some time in Kemal Atatürk's Republican People's Party. It was not until 1946, however, that he emerged as a political force in the country when, with Celâl Bayar and others, he organized the Democrat Party, the first genuine political opposition to the Republicans.

Following the Democrats' sweeping victory in the national elections of 1950, Menderes was named prime minister by President Bayar. The new regime continued the Atatürk reforms but introduced a system of free enterprise to supplant the state-controlled industries. In international affairs, Menderes aligned his country firmly with the West, bringing Turkey into such regional groupings as the North Atlantic Treaty Organization (1952), the Balkan Pact (1953), and the Baghdad Pact (1955). Soon after assuming office, Menderes embarked on a program of extending financial assistance to the peasants, encouraging private and foreign investment in the country, and organizing huge public developments. These measures—together with large-scale economic aid from the United States—combined to raise the Turkish standard of living to a new level, and the Democrat Party was continued in office by the election victories of 1954 and 1957.

With Menderes' free-spending policies, however, came severe monetary inflation. At the same time, he sought to stifle criticism of his regime with increasingly stringent curbs against the press and political opposition. By 1960 the government had extended its repression to include the judiciary and the universities, and the freedoms of speech and of assembly were curtailed. Resentment against these acts became widespread, culminating in a series of student demonstrations in April and May of that year which were met with harsh reprisals. Finally, on May 27, a military clique headed by Gen. Cemal Gürsel seized power and placed Menderes and scores of other government officials under arrest. Brought to trial on charges of corruption and unconstitutional acts, Menderes was condemned to death on Sept. 15, 1961, by a special court set up on Yassi Island, and two days later the former prime minister was hanged at the island prison of Imrali. Results of the general elections held one month after his death, however, indicated that Menderes still had a sizable following among the electorate.

MENDERES RIVER (also called Buyuk Menderes; anc. Maeander), river, Turkey, rising west of Afyonkarahisar and flowing west 250 miles to enter the Aegean south of Samos Island.

MENDERES RIVER (also called Kucuk Menderes; anc. Xanthus, q.v., or Scamander), river, Turkey, originating near Bayramic and flowing west 60 miles to empty into the Dardanelles, near the site of ancient Troy. A second Kucuk Menderes (anc. Caystrus or Cayster), rises in the Boz Mountains and flows 80 miles to the Gulf of Kusada.

MENDÈS, măn-děs′, **(Abraham) Catulle,** French writer: b. Bordeaux, France, May 22, 1841; d. St.-Germain, Feb. 8, 1909. A precocious poet, he was one of the initiators of the Parnassian school of poetry, founding the periodical *Revue fantaisiste* in 1861. With Louis Xavier de Ricard and other young poets, he contributed to the poetry anthology *Le Parnasse contemporain* (1866). From 1893 he was drama editor of the Paris *Journal*. Though regarded by most French critics as only a minor poet of the period, Mendès exhibited considerable versatility of form in his poetry, and was a prolific writer of romantic plays, erotic novels, and short stories. His works include the poetry volumes *Philomela* (1864), *Poésies* (1892); the novels *Le roi vierge* (1881), *Zo'har* (1886); the plays *La reine Fiammette* (1889), *Médée* (1898), *Le vierge d'Avila* (1905); and the literary histories *Légende du Parnasse contemporain* (1884), *Rapport sur le mouvement poétique de 1867 à 1900* (1902).

MENDES, měn′děs, **Frederic de Sola,** American Jewish rabbi: b. Montego Bay, Jamaica, British West Indies, July 8, 1850; d. New Rochelle, N.Y., Oct. 26, 1927. The son of a minister, he was educated in London and graduated (B.A. 1869) from London University. He also studied at the universities of Breslau and Jena (Ph.D. 1871), and received his rabbinic training at the Jewish Theological Seminary at Breslau (1870–1873). Becoming assistant minister of the Congregation Shaaray Tefila, New York City, in 1874, he took office as rabbi there four years later and was associated with that congregation (becoming rabbi emeritus in 1920) for over 53 years. An important scholar and influential conservative Jew of his day, he opposed radical reform Judaism, but gradually accepted his congregation's trend toward reform. Mendes founded and edited the *American Hebrew* magazine (1879–1885), and served as an editor of the *Jewish Encyclopedia*. His scholarly works include the translation, from the German of Meyer Kayserling, *The Life of Menasseh ben Israel* (1877), and the authorship of *Outlines of Jewish History* (1886).

MENDÈS-FRANCE, măn-děs-fräns′, **Pierre,** French economist and statesman: b. Paris, France, Jan. 11, 1907. A graduate of the École des Sciences Politiques, Université de Paris, and a doctor of law, he was at the age of 21 France's youngest advocate on admission to the bar. Mendès-France practiced law at Louviers and wrote several economic studies, including *L'Oeuvre financière du gouvernement Poincaré* (1928), which established his reputation as an authority on economics. Entering politics in 1932 as a Radical Socialist, he became the youngest deputy in the Chamber of Deputies, and was elected mayor of Louviers in 1934. He served briefly as undersecretary of state to the treasury in Léon Blum's Popular Front cabinet in 1938. Mobilized the following year, he won his aviation observer brevet in Syria, was arrested in North Africa after the German invasion of France, escaped from prison in 1942 to join Gen. Charles de Gaulle's Free French forces in London, and served with a French bombardment group. As commissioner of finances of the French Committee of National Liberation, he signed the Franco-British monetary accord of February 1944 and headed the French delegation to the Bretton Woods Monetary Conference in July. After the liberation of Paris, he became (Sept. 4, 1944) minister of national economy in the de Gaulle provisional government, but resigned the following year when his proposals for anti-inflationary economic measures were rejected. Refusing postwar offers of cabinet positions, he served on French technical missions and as a member (1947–1950) of the French delegation to the United Nations Economic and Social Council. At the request of President René Coty, he formed a cabinet on June 13, 1954, and was confirmed as premier five days later. As his own foreign minister, the new premier began direct negotiations with Red China's Premier Chou En-lai to establish a truce in Vietnam, which was accomplished on July 22. Mendès-France also succeeded in obtaining the National Assembly's approval of a substitute proposal for the European Defense Community after both Mendès-France and the Assembly had rejected the original provisions of the treaty. Despite these and other achievements, however, an adverse vote on his liberal North African policy lost him his office on Feb. 5, 1955, and he was succeeded by his former finance and foreign minister, Edgar Faure. As leader of the Radical Socialist Party, Mendès-France served from January to May 1956 in the cabinet of Premier Guy Mollet as minister of state without portfolio.

MENDIETA Y MONTEFUR, mân-dyä'tä ē mōn-tā-fōōr', **Carlos,** Cuban political leader: b. Vueltas, Cuba, Nov. 4, 1873; d. Havana, Sept. 27, 1960. He served in the forces of Antonio Maceo in the 1895 revolution against Spain. Although he was a sugar planter and physician, he spent most of his life, after Cuban independence was won, fighting for better government. He held numerous political offices and was representative to the National Legislature from 1901 to 1923. A leader in the unsuccessful revolt against Gerardo Machado, he was imprisoned and later exiled. He returned to Cuba in 1933 when the regime was overthrown, and in January 1934 he was named provisional president by Fulgencio Batista. He resigned in December 1935 after failing to establish a stable government.

MENDIP HILLS, měn'dĭp, a carboniferous limestone ridge, in Somerset, England. It extends some 25 miles northwest from Frome to Brean Down on the Bristol Channel, formerly extending to the uninhabited island of Steep Holme, 5 miles out at sea. The ridge has an average width of about 5 miles; its summit is an open plateau; and Black Down in the northwest is the highest point, 1,068 feet. Villages are scattered and their populations are small. The hills are noted for their numerous caves; those at Cheddar draw many visitors because of their fantastic stalactite formations, and Wookey Hole, another mecca for sightseers, is said to be the oldest known bone cavern in the country. Lead was worked in the hills in Roman times, and at Charterhouse-on-Mendip are the remains of a Roman amphitheater. Human and animal remains of prehistoric times have been found. Sheep and cattle graze on the hills and the village of Priddy has a popular sheep fair. The western edge of the ridge is a steep escarpment, at the foot of which are the cathedral city of Wells and the town of Cheddar, famous for its cheese.

Consult Gough, John W., *Mines of Mendip* (New York 1930); Balch, Herbert E., *Mendip-Cheddar: Its Gorge and Caves* (Wells, Eng., 1935).

H. GORDON STOKES.

MENDIVE, mān-dē'vä, **Rafael Maria de,** Cuban poet: b. Havana, Cuba, Oct. 24, 1821; d. there, Nov. 24, 1886. His first book of poems, *Passion-Flower* (1847), was widely popular. Exiled in 1869 because of his liberalism, he lived in New York City and the Bahamas until his return to his homeland. He is considered one of the outstanding Spanish-American poets.

MENDL, LADY. See DE WOLFE, ELSIE.

MENDOTA, měn-dō'tà, city, Illinois, in La Salle County, 83 miles west of Chicago. An agricultural and industrial community, Mendota is an important corn-canning center, and each August holds a popular Sweet Corn Festival. It has plants manufacturing farm and wood veneer machinery and a metal-fabricating plant. The *New Yorker* cartoonist, Helen E. Hokinson (1893–1949), was a native of Mendota and is buried here. The city, incorporated in 1863, has aldermanic government. Pop. 6,154.

MENDOTA HEIGHTS, village, Minnesota, in Dakota County, just south of St. Paul, at the confluence of the Mississippi and Minnesota rivers. It is a residential district on the site of the first permanent settlement in Minnesota. Founded as St. Peter's in 1834, it was renamed Mendota in 1837, and incorporated as Mendota Heights in 1956. The state's first stone house (1835), built by Minnesota's first governor, Henry H. Sibley, has been restored. Minneapolis-St. Paul International Airport and Mendota Bridge are nearby. Pop. 5,028.

MENDOTA LAKE. See FOUR LAKES.

MENDOZA, mân-dō'sä, **Antonio de,** Spanish colonial governor: b. near Granada, Spain, c. 1485; d. Lima, Peru, July 21, 1552. In 1535 Emperor Charles V, with whom he was in great personal favor, appointed him viceroy of New Spain (Mexico), being the first of 64 viceroys, with the longest administration and that which shows the best record in the history of that provincial government. He made many reforms, especially in relieving the oppressed natives; developed agriculture and mining; established the first Mexican mint; founded the first college; and introduced the first printing press.

In 1551 he became viceroy of Peru, where he caused to be prepared a code of laws that has been the basis of the colonial and, to a large extent, of the present legal system of the republic. It was under Mendoza's administration in Mexico that Francisco Vásquez de Coronado (q.v) undertook his famous exploring expedition.

MENDOZA, mân-dō'thä, **Diego Hurtado de,** Spanish author and statesman: b. Granada, Spain, c. 1503; d. Madrid, April 15, 1575. He was a great-grandson of the Marqués de Santillana, and was educated, as a younger son, for the church, but, after studying Arabic at Granada and the humanities at Salamanca, entered the army and in 1525 fought at Pavia. He acted as Charles V's ambassador to England in 1537, to Venice in 1539; was representative at the Council of Trent (1545), governor of Siena (1547), and imperial representative to the papal see in Rome (1549). With Philip II he quarreled and in 1564 was interned in Granada, only returning to court in 1574, soon before his death. To his stay in Italy was due his influence in making the Spanish lyric thoroughly Italianate; and from Italy he brought an unusual knowledge of the classics as well as a fine collection of Greek manuscripts. Mendoza also perfected the Spanish poetic epistle. The famous romance, *Lazarillo de Tormes* (q.v.), was long ascribed to him. But his greatest work is his history of the Moorish insurrection, *Guerra de Granada,* a model of historical impartiality on a theme for which knowledge of Arabic peculiarly fitted him, and painstakingly compiled over many years.

MENDOZA, Pedro de, Spanish soldier, explorer, and colonizer: b. Guadix, Granada, Spain, c. 1487; d. at sea, 1537. A favorite of Charles V, he fought in Italy, and in 1535 he led an expedition of 12 ships and 800 men from Spain to South America, largely at his own expense, sailing up the Río de la Plata and founding the first colony of Buenos Aires in 1536. His subsequent movements were unfortunate; Indian tribes and pestilence took toll of his men, three fourths of whom, including his brother Diego, were lost. Another brother, Gonzalo, came with reinforcements and rescued Mendoza from the ever-increasing hostile attacks and he managed to sail for home. But his health and reason were undermined, and he died on board ship.

MENDOZA, province, Argentina, on the frontier of Chile, of which until 1776 it was a part. The Andes Mountains on its border contain Aconcagua, the highest peak in the Western Hemisphere (22,835 ft.). A railroad crosses these mountains into Chile through the Uspallata Pass. The rivers Mendoza, Atuel, and Tunuyán supply hydroelectric power on their way to Desaguadero River on the eastern boundary, as well as plentiful irrigation for the agricultural products of fruit, grapes, olives, grain, and vegetables. Wine is a major industry, and the vineyards from vines brought from Spain in the 16th century are one of the major attractions for visitors. The province has many popular resorts with hot springs and swimming pools. There is some petroleum and other minerals, with petroleum refineries, cement works, and lumbering. See also ARGENTINA—*History.*

MENDOZA, city, Argentina, capital of Mendoza Province, at the foot of the Sierra de los Paramillos, 630 miles northwest of Buenos Aires, at an altitude of 2,575 feet, on the Transandine Railroad. On the west bank of the Canal Zanjón, in the center of the wine and fruit district, it is a beautiful city with wide streets, and irrigation ditches for its trees and parks, which are noted for their flowers. In 1861 an earthquake destroyed most of its buildings, but the city has been rebuilt with earthquake-proof houses. There is a large Italian population, and a vintage fiesta is held in April. Some manufacturing of cement, ceramics, and textiles is carried on. Pop. (1947) 92,243.

MENE, MENE, TEKEL, UPHARSIN, mē'nē, mē'nē, tĕk'ĕl, ū-fär'sĭn, Aramaic words traced on the wall at Belshazzar's feast, warning of his impending doom (Daniel 5:25). The Chaldaean wise men failed to interpret them so the queen advised the king to send for the prophet Daniel who deciphered them as: "God hath numbered thy kingdom, and finished it . . . ; Thou art weighed in the balances, and art found wanting; Thy kingdom is divided and given to the Medes and Persians." The king rewarded Daniel by proclaiming him third ruler of the kingdom but that night Belshazzar was slain and the kingdom taken by Darius. The exact meaning of the words and Daniel's interpretation continues to be a source of discussion among Biblical scholars.

Consult Hastings, James, ed., *Dictionary of the Bible* (New York 1942).

MENEDEMUS, mĕn-ĕ-dē'mŭs, Greek philosopher, founder of the Eretrian school of thought: b. Eretria 350? B.C.; died ?276 B.C. When sent on an expedition with the army into Megara, he became interested in the study of philosophy, and was a pupil of Plato's followers, including Stilpo and Phaedo of Ellis. He appears to have transferred the Elian school to Eretria, where he taught and wrote, but none of his actual writings have survived.

MENELAUS, mĕn-ĕ-lā'ŭs, in Greek legend, son of Atreus, king of Sparta, younger brother of Agamemnon, and husband of Helen of Troy. He appears in Homer's *Iliad* and *Odyssey,* and in Virgil's *Aeneid.* It was the kidnapping of his wife by Paris, who had been promised by Venus the most beautiful woman in the world, that caused the Trojan War (q.v.). He was one of the Greeks who concealed themselves in the wooden horse and conquered Troy, and he took Helen back to Sparta after a voyage of eight years. On his death he was taken to Elysium, and later was worshiped as a god.

MENELIK II, mĕn'ĕ-lĭk (Aby. NEGUS NEGUSTI, meaning King of Kings), emperor of Abyssinia (Ethiopia): b. Ankober, Ethiopia, Aug. 18, 1844; d. Addis Ababa, Dec. 22, 1913. Claiming descent from King Solomon and the queen of Sheba, Menelik was a son of Haeli Melicoth, king of Shoa. Failing to take his kingdom away from usurpers, he finally fell heir to it through marriage. After signing a treaty with Italy at Uccialli in 1889, he abrogated it in 1893 when he discovered the Italian version of the treaty gave Italy control of all foreign affairs. Obtaining no help from Queen Victoria, to whom he had appealed, he declared war against Italy and defeated the Italians at the Battle of Aduwa (Adowa) March 1896 and, as a result, the Treaty of Addis Ababa was signed in which Italy recognized the absolute independence of Abyssinia. The European countries recognized Menelik as emperor and concluded treaties with him. He cooperated with the British against Sudanese dervishes, attempted to open his country to Western civilization, but granted railway rights only when his sovereign rights were recognized. He was succeeded by his grandson Lij Yasu who was deposed in 1916 to be succeeded by Menelik's daughter, Zauditu, whose husband, Ras Taffari Makonnen, became negus in 1928, and after his wife's death, proclaimed himself Emperor Haile Selassie I (q.v.). See also ETHIOPIA.

MENENDEZ DE AVILES, mä-nän'däth thä ä-vē-lās', **Pedro,** Spanish mariner: b. Avilés, Asturias, Spain, 1519; d. Santander, Sept. 17, 1574. Menéndez had been captain general of the Spanish treasure fleets, but had fallen out of favor with the governing board and been imprisoned for a time. In 1565 he was commissioned by Philip II to equip an expedition to set up a colony in Florida. He founded St. Augustine in 1565 which was the first white settlement in Florida. In September of that year he attacked the French garrison at Fort Caroline, during the absence of part of the force which had set out to attack him but was storm-stayed and finally wrecked. Menendez slaughtered those remaining at the fort and also those saved from the shipwreck. He returned to Spain in 1567, visited America again in 1568 and 1570, sending a party of colonists to the Chesapeake and up the Rappahannock where they were massacred by the natives. He was recalled to Spain shortly before his death. See also FLORIDA—*History.*

MENENDEZ PIDAL, pē-thäl', **Ramón,** Spanish philologist: b. La Coruña, Spain, March 13, 1869. After completing his education at Madrid and Toulouse, Menéndez became professor of romance philology (1899–1939) in Madrid University, and in 1908–1911 published a critical study of *The Cid* (*Cantor de mio Cid*), in three volumes, which marked him as a distinguished scholar and critic. In 1913 he was made counselor of instruction in Spain, and he was visiting professor in American and South American universities (Johns. Hopkins 1909, Columbia 1938). An acknowledged authority on Spanish literature, especially epics and romance, he was also one of the great modern historians. Among his publications are *Origenes del Español* (1926) ; *La España del Cid* (1929; tr. into English by H. Sutherland, 1934) ; *Historia y Epopeya* (1934) ; *El Imperio Hispanico y los Cincos Reinos* (1950) ; *Spaniards in Their History,* tr. by Walter Starkie (1950) ; *Reliquias de la poesía épica española* (1951).

MENENDEZ Y PELAYO, ĕ pä-lä′yō, **Marcelino,** Spanish critic: b. Santander, Spain, Nov. 3, 1856; d. there, May 19, 1912. At the age of 22 Menéndez was professor of Spanish literature at the University of Madrid, where he had been a student, was elected to the Spanish Academy in 1881, and in 1899 became director of the Biblioteca Nacional (Spanish National Library). He served a term as senator in support of the conservative Catholic Party, was counselor of public instruction and chief of the board of archivists. The most important Spanish critic of his generation, he wrote *Historia de los Heterodoxes Españoles,* 3 vols. (1880–1882) ; *Historia de las I deas Estéticas en España* (1883–1891) ; *Estudios de critica filosófica* (1884–1908) ; *Antologia de Poetas Hispanoamericana* (1892) ; and *Origenes de la Novela* (1905–1910).

MENES, mē′nēz, or **MENA,** mē′nä (also Narmer), first king of the 1st dynasty of Egypt: fl. about 3100 B.C. The historian Herodotus relates that Menes founded Memphis, which he built on a piece of ground recovered from the Nile River by altering its course. Later archaeological finds confirmed that Menes united upper and lower Egypt in the Old Kingdom, which endured for over 1,000 years. He ruled as a god, introduced the beginnings of Egyptian civilization, and a code of gold values. His tomb was discovered at Negadr in 1897.

MENG-TSE or MENG-TZU. See Mencius.

MENGELBERG, mĕng′ĕl-bĕrк **(Josef) Willem,** Dutch musician: b. Utrecht, Netherlands, March 28, 1871; d. Chur, Switzerland, March 21, 1951. A Dutchman of German descent, Mengelberg studied in the Utrecht Music School, at Cologne Conservatory, and from 1891 to 1895 was municipal musical director at Lucerne. He was a guest conductor in many American and European orchestras, conducted frequently for the New York Philharmonic Orchestra between 1921 and 1930, and was most famous for conducting the Concertgebouw Orchestra in Amsterdam until 1945 where his rendering of Gustav Mahler and Tchaikovsky was widely acclaimed. He sometimes performed as a solo pianist. He was a National Socialist in his political sympathies and after World War II he was banned by the Netherlands Honor Council for collaborating, and went to live in Switzerland, where he died.

MENGER, mĕng′ĕr, **Karl,** Austrian economist: b. Neu-Sandez, Galicia, Austria, Feb. 23, 1840; d. Vienna, Feb. 26, 1921. One of a family of three brothers prominent in law, politics, and political economy, Karl Menger studied in Vienna and Prague, becoming professor of political economy at the University of Vienna from 1873 to 1903. In 1876 he was a tutor to Crown Prince

Rudolf. He gave up teaching for research in his subject, and became the founder of an Austrian school of national economy. He published several important works, among them *Grundsätze der Volkswirtschaftslehre (Foundations of Political Economy),* 1871, and his collected works in 4 volumes were published 1933–1936.

MENGS, mĕngs, **Anton Raphael,** German painter: b. Aussig, Bohemia, now Ustí, March 12, 1728; d. Rome, Italy, June 29, 1779. After studying with his father, who was a severe and critical master, Mengs worked for some years in Dresden and in Rome, where he carried out commissions for churches and villas. He worked in pastel and crayon, copied old masters successfully for clients, painted ceilings, frescoes, portraits, and altarpieces. Charles III of Spain employed him in Madrid, where he painted *The Apotheosis of Trajan* for the royal palace. In Rome again, he was commissioned by Pope Clement XIV to paint the ceiling of the Vatican Library. Believed by his contemporaries to be one of the great painters of Europe, his work marked the change from the baroque to a return to classicism. His work is to be found in museums in Vienna, Dresden, Madrid, Rome, and in Oxford colleges in England.

MENGTSZ or **MENG-TZU,** mĕng-dzŭ′, city, China, in southeast Yunnan Province on the Red River, 130 miles southeast of Kunming and 40 miles from the Tonkin border. It lies on a plateau at an altitude of 4,300 feet. The most important industry is tin mining from the nearby Kokiu mine which was first exported after the French Convention of 1887 had opened up trade with French Indochina. Pop. (1947 est.) 200,000.

MENHADEN, mĕn-hā′d′n, a species of fish (*Brevoortia tyrannus*) of the herring family Clupeidae, appearing in vast schools along the Atlantic Coast of America. Owing to the large number of local names applied to this species much confusion concerning its identity and distribution exists in the minds of fishermen and others. The Indian name "menhaden" is used chiefly in southern New England. North of Cape Cod the fish is called pogy, or occasionally hardhead; in New York and New Jersey, bunker or marshbunker; the fishermen of Delaware and Chesapeake bays know it as bay alewife, and in the latter region and southward also a bugfish or bughead; still farther south it becomes the fatback, and so on. From the other herrings the menhaden is readily distinguished by its very large head, large mouth, complex gill strainers, and crenulated scales. The body is deep, the fins small, the mouth toothless, and the color bluish and silvery, with one large and several small black spots.

Like some other pelagic and migratory fishes the menhaden is exceedingly irregular in its movements and variable in abundance and distribution from year to year, but its general range is from Nova Scotia to Brazil and oceanward, so far as observed, to the Gulf Stream. In spring it approaches the coasts and extends northward with the alewives and other species, probably for the purpose of spawning in brackish water, though little is actually known of its spawning habits. In winter Cape Hatteras marks the northern limit of its abundance. The menhaden swims in compact schools of large size, the movements of which at the surface, or sunken to a greater depth, are extremely irregular.

These irregularities are owing, no doubt, to corresponding variation in its food supply, which consists wholly of the minute organisms, both vegetable and animal (plankton), that are caught as the fish swims with open mouth, straining the water through its lips and gill-arches as it goes. Owing to its strong oily taste and extreme boniness its value as human food is very slight, but as furnishing food for other fishes, as bait, and for the manufacture of oil, fertilizer, soap, mixed feeds for livestock, and other products, it has a very great economic importance. Besides pound nets, many steamers are provided with purse seines and derricks, by means of which entire schools are taken at a haul and lifted on deck. The oil is extracted and the solid parts ground up for fertilizer at factories on shores. The product varies from year to year, but the total weight of fish taken runs into the hundreds of million pounds. The catch of fish and industries involved reached their highest level of importance in the latter part of the last century, then diminished, but now are an increasingly important industry.

The Fisheries reports of the Fish and Wildlife Service of the Department of the Interior show that in 1965 the menhaden catches ranked first in quantity and value in the Chesapeake, Middle and South Atlantic, and Gulf states, and formed a small but important proportion of the New England catch. See also FISHERIES.

C. W. COATES.

MENHIR, mĕn'hĭr (tall stone), a monolith, an upright rough stone tapering somewhat at the top, of various heights, found alone, in a circle, or in an avenue, usually on wild moors or hillsides, in Great Britain and in Brittany. The largest is at Locmariaquer, Brittany, and though fallen, stood at 62 feet. Menhirs were probably monuments on burial sites.

MENIERE'S SYNDROME, mā-nyâr' sĭn'-drōme, a disease of the middle ear, first described by the French physician, Émile Antoine Ménière, in 1861. A form of auditory vertigo, it is due to inflammation or hemorrhage caused by infectious diseases or even by a food allergy or arteriosclerosis. The symptoms are dizziness, nausea, a disturbance of equilibrium, and deafness, which usually persists. Treatment is by diet, especially salt elimination, and sometimes a slight operation to relieve pressure in the eustachian tubes, and some medication.

MENIN, mĕ-năN' (Flemish MEENEN), town, Belgium, in the Province of West Flanders, on the Lys River, and on the French border opposite Halluin, 7 miles southwest of Courtrai. It is a market center in a flax-growing region where linen is woven. It belonged to France at several periods in its history, and was occupied by the Germans in World War I in 1914, and again in 1918. As it was at an important crossing of the Lys, it was the scene of heavy fighting along the Menin road, where a terrific slaughter of Germans occurred which closed the road to Calais in the German advance. It was damaged again in World War II. Pop. (1961) 22,451.

MENINGITIS, inflammation of the membranes of the brain and spinal cord; inflammation of the dura alone is known as *pachymeningitis.* The acute pyogenic form of meningitis may be due to infection by the streptococcus, pneumococcus, micrococcus, or occasionally organisms other than the meningococcus which is responsible for the disease known as *epidemic cerebrospinal meningitis.* Occasionally a meningitis exists without bacterial origin (sterile meningitis), as when arising from the subarachnoid injection of gases, sera, and chemicals. In a great many cases a meningitis will develop as the result of trauma where the spine or head is injured. Tuberculous meningitis is due to the tubercle bacillus which lodges in the brain as a result of transference from some distant focus. This is not uncommon in tuberculous children and may be the end result of long continued bone tuberculosis. The term *leptomeningitis* as distinguished from *pachymeningitis* ordinarily refers to inflammation of the pia-arachnoid coverings of the brain and represents the pathology present in the different forms of meningitis described in this article.

No typical classification can be given for the varied and multiple causes of the disease, some of which have been referred to in the opening paragraph. Among exciting causes injury is most important. Compound fractures of the head and spine followed by infection are frequent. Old fractures, foreign bodies, and abscesses also are factors, and neighboring infections such as otitis media, and carbuncle of the face or lip may spread, by a retrograde process, to the meninges of the brain. Nasal sinus operations are sometimes followed by meningitis. Among diseases showing such a complication are pneumonia, whooping cough, and the acute exanthemata. Such organic diseases as chronic nephritis and heart disease may terminate in a meningitis. A classification of meningitis has been suggested which is of considerable practical value: (1) suppurative forms which includes the epidemic form (the most important), the pyogenic, and the influenzal form; (2) syphilitic meningitis; (3) tuberculous meningitis; (4) virus meningitis.

Meningococcus Meningitis.—This is also called epidemic cerebrospinal meningitis. The disease has been described by a host of writers over a period of many decades. The causal organism was determined in 1887 by Anton Weichselbaum (1845–1920) of Berlin. This was the *Diplococcus intracellularis meningitidis,* now called the *meningococcus.* Thomas Willis (1621–1675), of London, had described an epidemic in 1684 but it was not until 1805 that Gaspard Vieusseaux (1746–1814) gave the first accurate description of the disease as we now know it. There are four groups of meningococcus that can be demonstrated by agglutination tests. The infectious agent is commonly found in the nasopharynx of those ill with the disease and sometimes in the nasopharynx of healthy persons (carriers). Positive blood cultures of those ill with meningitis can often be demonstrated. It is conceded generally that the nose and throat passages are the ordinary ports of entry of the micrococcus. Most of the evidence now supports the belief that dissemination of the disease to other parts of the body is by way of the blood. A great majority of persons have a natural immunity to meningococcus infection although just why this is, is a matter of speculation.

Incidence of Meningitis.—Most of the epidemics have been reported from the United States. A serious outbreak was reported in 1806 in

Massachusetts. During the present century, one occurred in 1918 among troops just mobilized, and in the years 1915, 1916, and 1917 outbreaks were reported in England and Northern Europe during World War I. Epidemics among civil populations are spaced, apparently, about 12 years apart. In most of North America meningitis is endemic or sporadic. Even during epidemics it is a widely distributed and sometimes a localized disease, often being confined to small limited communities situated many miles apart. Most cases are seen in the late winter and spring months In children among civil populations the disease is more common than in adults. Under ordinary conditions the sexes fare about equally and the same is true of races. The mortality was once alarmingly high and constituted a terror to populations, but under modern methods of treatment this mortality has been greatly diminished.

Clinical Aspects.—According to the observations of medical authorities of great experience, no well defined clinical types exist. The disease may be manifested by 3 stages or phases: (1) an upper respiratory; (2) a general systemic; (3) a stage in which the infectious process is spread to the meninges. These stages have also been described as the *nasopharyngeal,* the stage of *septicemia,* and the stage of *meningococcus meningitis.* The incubation period is from 3 to 5 days, in exceptional cases 2 to 10 days. Meningitis is spread usually by carriers, often healthy persons, who harbor the bacteria in the nasal secretions (droplet infection). While the majority of persons possess immunity, others become infected and pass through the nasopharyngeal stage only, escaping the septicemic phase. In others the disease may progress to a generalized septicemia ending in a few days in recovery. In other cases, within a week or so, meningitis develops, with its evil consequences. Death may occur in the septicemic stage, the resulting toxemia being so severe that infection of the meninges has had insufficient time to develop. Generally, meningeal involvement can be detected within 48 hours and it is therefore of the utmost importance that a correct diagnosis be made and energetic and positive treatment be begun in the stage of sepsis, to prevent an impending meningitis which may render the case hopeless.

During this septic stage the patient is mentally clouded and dislikes being disturbed. Prostration may be so pronounced as to verge on coma. Various aches and pains are present in these severe and interval meningitis cases and the joints may become inflamed. The temperature is not usually extremely high (102° F. maximum) but this is not always a good omen. Hemorrhagic points or small spots in the skin are quite constant and are present mostly on the face, neck, and trunk. They are sometimes so abundant as to give the appearance of large purple blotches. Meningeal involvement may be slight or extensive and follows no set pattern. It is often masked by the gravity of the septicemia. In a large proportion of cases the disease progresses, within 10 days, to a point where the outcome will be apparent. Occasionally clinical recovery takes place over a period of two or three weeks when meningeal symptoms recur and the condition becomes chronic. In very severe fulminating cases death may occur within two days. Sometimes the eruption is mistaken, at first glance, for measles.

The so-called "ordinary" meningitis is the classic form in which meningeal involvement is the predominant feature and septicemia is of a minor nature. Here the onset is sudden but systemic reaction is moderate. The disease may develop in a period of a week. Headache and symptoms resembling those of influenza are present. Fever is likely to be much higher than in the fulminating infection. Vomiting may occur. The skin eruption is much less marked than that already described and shows pinkish patches becoming yellowish, hence the old term, *spotted fever.* Herpes of the lips is common. After some three days, meningeal irritation is evident in stiffness of the neck and spinal rigidity. In children this may be extreme, causing a backward curve of the spine (opisthotonos). During the height of the disease fever is high and respiration often irregular. The fever drops by lysis, after several weeks, rarely by crisis. Also in children a chronic recurrent meningitis may be observed. This was very common before the days of modern treatment but is now rare. If attacks recur they are less serious than the original.

Meningococcus meningitis presents some difficulties in diagnosis among children, in that the clinical signs are variable and indefinite in many cases. Retraction of the head is a valuable sign in young children. Lumbar puncture and evacuation and examination of the cerebrospinal fluid will usually confirm the diagnosis. The outlook for cases in which diagnosis is delayed unduly is more grave than where an early diagnosis is established, since prompt specific treatment is of the utmost importance. Some of the diseases that may be confused with meningococcus meningitis are suppurative leptomeningitis due to Pfeiffer's bacillus, in which, however, there is no skin eruption; tuberculous meningitis (in which the spinal fluid is clear); preparalytic poliomyelitis; alcoholism; uremia; diabetes.

The complications of meningitis are many. They may be divided into two groups: (1) those involving principally the central nervous system; (2) those in which complications are outside the meninges. In the first group are included affections of the eye, such as optic neuritis, which may result in partial or complete blindness, and those affecting the auditory nerve, ending often in total deafness. In the second group lung affections, especially pneumonia, are fairly common, and may result in death.

Treatment of Meningococcus Meningitis.—Prior to the use of serum therapy, treatment of meningitis was symptomatic and usually unsatisfactory. For more than a decade sulfathiazole and sulfadiazine have been used with astonishing success. Other sulfonamides have also been in use and in a series of about 2,500 cases treated by the many varieties, the mortality rate was reduced below 10 per cent. In general it will probably be found below that figure, perhaps as low as 5 or 6 per cent, for all cases and all ages. In special populations, like young adult males, it might run as low as 4 or 5 per cent. Penicillin has also been satisfactory in a limited number of cases (about 4 per cent mortality in some 48 cases treated in an epidemic in the United States Navy). Serum treatment is now seldom used. Isolation, bed rest, and careful nursing are important factors in lowering mortality.

Other Forms of Meningitis.—Pneumococcus and streptococcus meningitis may result from extracranial foci, such as pneumonia, empyema, and osteomyelitis, or by extension of a brain abscess. The symptoms vary little from the epidemic form except that they may be more severe. The spinal fluid shows a purulent fluid accompanied by the causal organism. The outlook is often unfavorable but if the primary focus can be located, chemotherapy may be helpful. In the pneumococcus infections penicillin and Aureomycin are especially effective. Influenza meningitis caused by *Hemophilus influenzae* (Pfeiffer's bacillus) is usually a disease of infants. Onset is sudden with vomiting and stiffness of the neck. Fever lasts two or three weeks. The causal agent can be recovered from the spinal fluid. Mortality is extremely high even with combined sulfonamide, streptomycin, and specific rabbit serum. Penicillin has not been notably effective. Acute syphilitic meningitis is seen occasionally. If antisyphilitic treatment is instituted clinical results are often good. Tuberculous meningitis is most often observed in very young children; the source of infection is from tuberculous foci in other parts of the body or from infected milk. The child almost always has a history of poor health for some time, is underweight, and exhibits headache, vomiting, and later convulsions or coma. Recovery is rare. No effective treatment is known. Antibiotics, especially streptomycin, have been used. See also BRAIN; ENCEPHALITIS LETHARGICA; IMMUNITY.

Consult Wilson, Graham S., and Miles, A. A., *Topley & Wilson's Principles of Bacteriology and Immunity,* 5th ed. (Baltimore 1964); Harrison, Tinsley R., and others, *Principles of Internal Medicine,* 5th ed. (New York 1966); Beeson, Paul B., and McDermott, Walsh, eds., *Textbook of Medicine,* 12th ed. (Philadelphia 1967).

HAROLD WELLINGTON JONES, M.D.

MENIPPUS, mê-nĭp'ŭs, Greek cynic philosopher: b. Gadara, Syria, fl. 1st half of the 2d century B.C. All his writings have been lost, and he is known entirely by what later writers say of him. Originally a slave, he bought his freedom and became a free Theban. In his dialogues, written in both verse and prose, he satirized his contemporaries, especially Epicureans and Stoics, with extreme sarcasm. Meleager (c. 140–c. 70 B.C.) includes some of Menippus' epigrams in his works; Marcus Terentius Varro (116–27 B.C.) wrote *Saturae Menippeae,* adapted from Menippus; and Lucian (2d century A.D.) introduces Menippus into his dialogues as "the most snarling of cynics." An anonymous French political lampoon of the late 16th century, *Satyre Ménippée,* perpetuates his name and reputation.

MENKEN, mĕng'kĕn, **Adah Bertha** (known as ADAH ISAACS MENKEN), American actress: b. near New Orleans, La., 1835; d. Paris, France, Aug. 10, 1868. The accounts of her parentage are conflicting, but she was undoubtedly the daughter of a Spanish Jew who died during her infancy. In 1856 she married Alexander Isaacs Menken, whose name she kept through her subsequent divorces and remarriages. She began her career as a dancer in New Orleans, and first appeared in the role of Mazeppa, based on the play by Byron, in a masculine part which was to make her famous, in Albany in 1861. She appeared in this part in San Francisco in 1863, delighting the Western writers, as she was to entrance the British in 1864, at Astley's in London. The greatest literary men and women of the day were her friends and she had the same success in Paris in *Les Pirates de la Savane.* In 1868 she published a book of verse *Infelicia,* dedicated to Charles Dickens. She was an unconventional figure on the staid Victorian scene. Allen T. Lesser has written a book about her, *Enchanting Rebel* (1947).

MENLO PARK, mĕn'lō, city, California, in San Mateo County, a residential community about 25 miles southeast of San Francisco. St. Patrick's Seminary (Roman Catholic, founded 1898), is situated here. The city was incorporated in 1874. Government is by city manager (adopted 1947). Pop. 26,957.

MENLO PARK, village, New Jersey, in Middlesex County, seven miles northeast of New Brunswick. In his laboratory here (1876–1887), commemorated by a tower, Thomas A. Edison invented the incandescent lamp and the phonograph.

MENNINGER, mĕn'ĭng-ēr, **Karl Augustus,** American psychiatrist: b. Topeka, Kans., July 22, 1893. After obtaining his medical degree at Harvard in 1917 and serving as assistant at the Boston Psychopathic Hospital, Menninger returned in 1919 to Topeka, where he and his father, Charles Frederick Menninger, established the Menninger Clinic for psychiatric research. In 1941, with his brother William, he founded the Menninger Foundation for psychiatric treatment, education, and research. During World War II he was adviser to the surgeon general of the United States Army, and was active in the development of the Winter Veterans' Administration Hospital at Topeka which became a center for psychiatric training. Menninger is clinical professor of psychiatry at the University of Kansas and consultant to a number of state and national organizations concerned with mental health. His publications include *The Human Mind* (1930; 3d rev. ed., 1945); *Man Against Himself* (1938); *Manual for Psychiatric Case Study* (1952); and *Theory of Psychoanalytic Technique* (1958). He edits the *Bulletin* of the Menninger Foundation and is on the editorial board of several psychiatric journals.

MENNO SIMONS, mĕn'ō sē'mŏns, Dutch religious reformer: b. Witmarsum, Friesland, 1496?; d. Wüstenfeld, Holstein, Jan. 31, 1561. He was ordained priest in the Roman Catholic Church and took pastoral work in the village of Pingium (1524), and from a study of the New Testament, undertaken (1530) to solve his doubts about transubstantiation, he was induced to become an evangelical preacher and finally left the church of his ordination. The martyrdom of Sicke Snyder at Leeuwarden for Anabaptism impelled him to consider the Scriptural grounds for infant baptism. He was finally converted to the cause of the Anabaptists (q.v.), but never sympathized with the excesses of Thomas Münzer and wrote a diatribe against John of Leyden (1535). In 1537, at the request of a number of Anabaptists of Groningen, he assumed the functions of an Anabaptist preacher and exercised, by his moderation, a most salutary influence on his fellow ministers. He now married, his change in faith having superseded his vow of celibacy, and began to travel as an evangelist not only in Friesland but throughout Holland and Germany as far as Livonia. Often suffering persecution he moved from place to place and finally settled in Wüstenfeld near Oldesloe, where he closed his ministry with the consciousness of having founded a large and flourishing sect. For its subsequent history, see MENNONITES.

Views of Menno Simons.—Menno preached a system of personal sanctity without the dogmatism or violent fanaticism of some of the Anabaptists. He was a man of pure moral and devotional enthusiasm, whose account of his own conversion reads like a passage from the *Confessions* of St. Augustine. He sums up the results of his labors as consisting in the conversion and recovery of the wicked. Yet he formulated a somewhat vague profession of faith. He believed in the divinity of Christ, who was born on earth *in* Mary, that is without taking upon him human flesh and blood. He rejected infant baptism, and baptized those only who made a personal profession of faith in Christ. He particularly emphasized the power of excommunication possessed by the Church, without which "the spiritual Kingdom of God on earth cannot," he said, "exist in purity and piety." He believed in the coming millenium (q.v.) ; he excluded civil magistrates from church membership on the ground that the church was a theocracy whose magistrates were the ministers. He declared that war and all taking and administering of oaths were unlawful, and regarded human science as useless, even pernicious to a Christian. These tenets, however, as modified by the explanations of Menno, differed little from those generally promulgated by the Reformed bodies of his day. His principal teaching was of a moral and practical character, encouraging all that was good and pure among his followers and sternly rebuking the guilty.

Menno's most important work was *Het Fundament der Cristelycke Leer* (1539; *The Foundations of Christian Doctrine*). A collection of his works, *Opera omnia theologica*, was published in Holland in 1681; a modern translation is the *Complete Writings,* translated from the Dutch by Leonard Verduin and edited by John C. Wenger, with a biography by Harold S. Bender (Scottdale, Pa., 1956).

MENNONITES, mĕn′ŏn-īts, a religious denomination found mostly in Europe and North and South America. The name comes from Menno Simons (1496?–1561, q.v.), a Dutch reformer whose field of activity was largely in North Germany in the neighborhood of Lübeck and Hamburg, although he traveled considerably in his church work, and was located for some time in Holland as well as in the Rhineland. The Mennonites of today are the descendants of the evangelical Anabaptists of the 16th century, the left wing of the Protestant Reformation.

Swiss Anabaptists.—The founder of the Anabaptists was Konrad Grebel (c. 1498–1526), who was originally a disciple of the Swiss reformer, Huldreich (Ulrich) Zwingli. Grebel gradually withdrew from Zwingli, beginning in 1523, and on Jan. 21, 1525, he formally launched the Anabaptist movement by baptizing a priest named Georg Blaurock, who had come to a like mind with Grebel. Blaurock in turn baptized a number of others. Grebel was a patrician of Zurich, Switzerland, and trained in the best universities of the day (Basel, Vienna, and Paris). Through the preaching of Zwingli, Grebel had come to an evangelical point of view, and through personal study of the Bible he had adopted such concepts as these :

(1) The church should be composed only of those who had repented of their sins and were walking in a newness of life. (Children were regarded as saved without formal church membership until they became mature enough to be converted.)

(2) Those persons who came to repentance and a faith commitment to Christ should be baptized on the confession of their faith. (The mode Grebel employed was affusion or pouring.)

(3) The church should be an absolutely free institution, having a voluntary membership; there should be no established religion.

(4) No force should be employed in matters of faith; people should be free to unite with the church, or to desist if they so chose. There should be no persecution of dissenters.

(5) Grebel understood the New Testament to teach that Christians can operate only on the basis of love. He felt that any institution which operated on the basis of force, including the sanction of taking human life, was outside the realm of the church, and could not be participated in by nonresistant followers of Christ; hence, he taught that Christians must abstain from the military, the constabulary, and even the magistracy.

(6) Grebel also taught, in obedience to the literal word of Christ, that Christians should not swear any sort of oath.

The Swiss authorities regarded the Anabaptist movement as a heresy of the worst sort, one that would dissolve the foundations of the established church (then Roman Catholic in name, but already non-Catholic in sentiment) as well as of the state itself. Severe persecution "unto the death" set in as early as 1525 and in time all but annihilated the Swiss Anabaptist movement except in the Canton of Bern where a small body of Anabaptists (*Täufer,* baptizers, as they were known) managed to survive.

Dutch Anabaptists.—Insofar as there was any connecting link between the Swiss Anabaptists and later Dutch Anabaptists it was in the person of an Independent, a former Lutheran named Melchior Hoffmann (1498–1543). He established small groups of secret followers, who were nicknamed Melchiorites, at various points in the Low Countries. Out of these Melchiorites arose a new movement, totally independent of the Swiss Anabaptists, led by two brothers, Obbe and Dirk Philips. These so-called Obbenites were established early in 1534. In January 1536, Menno Simons, a man who had become converted through a personal study of the Bible and of Martin Luther's writings, united with the Obbenites and soon became their outstanding leader. In contrast with Grebel, who died the year following his founding of Swiss Anabaptism, Menno lived for 25 years after uniting with the Dutch Anabaptists. He also wrote two dozen books and booklets which helped to spread his reformation ideas, and which greatly strengthened his Anabaptist congregations. He was a strong churchman, and helped mold his so-called "Mennist" followers into a unified denomination. He taught the same basic principles as Grebel (free church, baptism on confession of faith, nonresistance, rejection of the oath, the principle of freedom of conscience, and voluntarism in religion) and he insisted just as strenuously on high ethical standards of life and conduct.

Because of Menno. Simons' strong leadership and his influential writings, all Anabaptists ultimately came to be called Mennonites—the so-called Anabaptists of Münster, Germany, were annihilated within a few years of their founding —although until the 20th century the Swiss Mennonites called themselves *Taufgesinnten* (Baptists, literally, the Baptism-minded), and the Dutch used the equivalent term *Doopsgezinden.* The establishment in 1930 of the Mennonite World Conference, which meets every five years, has helped to popularize the use of the name Mennonites in all countries in which they are found.

American Mennonites.—The Mennonites

went to North America in five main waves:

(1) Several thousand Swiss Mennonites, wishing to escape the persecution and poverty of Europe, went to eastern Pennsylvania before the Revolutionary War. The first permanent settlement was made at Germantown, Pa., in 1683. Later Lancaster County became the stronghold of the group in the New World.

(2) After the Napoleonic era several more thousands from the Alsace, south Germany, and Switzerland located in western Pennsylvania, Ohio, Indiana, Illinois, Iowa, and Ontario, Canada, to escape the militarism of Europe.

(3) In the last three decades of the 19th century about 20,000 Mennonites, mostly of Dutch ancestry although including some Swiss groups also, migrated from Russia to the prairie states, North and South Dakota, Nebraska, Minnesota, Kansas, and Manitoba, Canada.

(4) After World War I about 20,000 more Mennonites, also mostly of Dutch ancestry, migrated from Europe to Canada and Paraguay, to escape the difficulties of life in the Soviet Union.

(5) Following World War II about 15,000 Mennonites from Russia and from the Danzig area of Poland located in Canada, Paraguay, and Brazil, to find full freedom of conscience.

World Membership.—In 1959 the baptized membership (young people are usually baptized in their teens) of the Mennonites was as follows: United States, 160,000; Canada, 53,000; Netherlands, 41,000; Soviet Union, 40,000 souls (number of baptized members unknown); Germany, 12,000; Mexico, 12,000; Paraguay, 7,000; France, 3,000; and Switzerland, 2,000. In addition, there were many thousands in such mission fields as India, Africa, and Java.

North American Congregations.—There are some twenty conferences of Mennonites in North America, although the Mennonites of Europe are no longer divided into different groups. These differing bodies in America are the consequence of different backgrounds in Europe, a reluctance to surrender trivial points of difference which mergers would require, and an excessive tendency to divide over the issue of how strict the discipline of the church should be. There are approximately 300,000 Mennonite souls in North America, of whom 225,000 are baptized; the remaining 75,000 (estimated) are children who have not yet been baptized. The age of baptism varies from about 12 to 18 in the several Mennonite groups.

Only five Mennonite bodies have more than 10,000 baptized members.

Mennonite Church.—The largest body is known simply as the Mennonite Church, although it is often written (Old) Mennonites to distinguish it from other groups. It has 78,000 members in North America and a scant 5,000 in foreign mission fields. This group employs *a cappella* music in divine worship, holds strictly to such historic doctrines as nonresistance (pacifism) and nonconformity to the world, requires its women members to wear during worship a small white prayer veiling similar to that in Whistler's *Portrait of the Artist's Mother,* baptizes converts by affusion, and formerly had a "love" (unsalaried) ministry exclusively. The group now maintains several colleges, a school of nursing, and a seminary to train its preachers. A minority of members wear a garb.

General Conference Mennonite Church.—The General Conference Mennonite Church, with 51,000 members, originated in 1860 in an effort to amalgamate all the Mennonite groups of North America. Many of the Mennonites who migrated to this continent from Russia united with the General Conference Mennonites. This group has no garb at all, they employ pianos and organs in their worship services, and theologically are quite similar to the larger Mennonite Church, although their discipline is milder.

Mennonite Brethren Church of North America.—The Mennonite Brethren Church began in Russian as a schismatic movement in 1860 under the influence of Baptist revivalism; this explains how they came to adopt immersion as their mode of baptism. They have no garb. Their strong emphasis on a conversion experience makes them somewhat resemble the early Wesleyan Methodists, although theologically they are solidly Mennonite. Slightly more than half of their 25,000 North American members live in Canada, and slightly less than half in the United States.

Old Order Amish Mennonite Church.—The most picturesque group is the Old Order Amish, who live in such centers as Lancaster County, Pa.; Holmes County, Ohio; and Elkhart County, Ind. The Amish are the followers of Jakob Amman, a Swiss Mennonite bishop who withdrew from the Mennonites in 1693 in the interest of a stricter discipline, including the "shunning" or social avoidance of those excommunicated from the church. The men wear beards, the women plain bonnets and shawls. Even the unbaptized children are tiny replicas of their parents, for they too wear the garb of the group. Worship services are held in private homes, and the language is a German (Palatine) dialect commonly known as Pennsylvania Dutch. The Amish number about 17,000.

Hutterian Brethren.—The fifth group does not employ the term Mennonite, although it also has Anabaptist origins (1528): the Hutterian Brethren or Hutterites, named for Jacob Hutter (d. 1536). In appearance the Hutterites are quite similar to the Amish. Their distinguishing emphasis is a Christian "community of goods." They live in colonies in which the group holds all property and real estate, and the members have no individual income. This attempt at a Christian communism of production and consumption has been a marked success economically. A majority of the 10,000 Hutterites live in Canada.

Other Bodies.—The next ten groups, listed in descending numerical order, have between 6,000 and 2,000 members each. They consist largely of small schismatic bodies who withdrew from the larger groups to practice a stricter discipline and to avoid the adoption of such newer forms of religious education as the Sunday school. This includes the Conservative Mennonite Conference; the Old Order (Wisler) Mennonites; the Church of God in Christ (Mennonite); the United Missionary Church (until 1947 the Mennonite Brethren in Christ); Sommerfelder Mennonites; Evangelical Mennonite Brethren; Beachy Amish Mennonites; Evangelical Mennonites (Conference of the Evangelical Mennonite Church); Old Colony Mennonites; and Evangelical Mennonites (in Canada), formerly named the Kleingemeinde. Of some eight other small groups having from 1,800 to 60 members, perhaps the most famous is that of the Reformed Mennonites, popularized by the novel, *Tillie, a Mennonite Maid,* by Helen R. Martin (New York 1904), a book of which Mennonites are very critical. All Mennonite groups have similar doctrinal beliefs, almost identical with those taught by the founding fathers in Europe.

Bibliography.—The best single source of information on the Mennonites is the *Mennonite Encyclopedia,* 4 vols.

(Scottdale, Pa., 1955–), ed. by Harold S. Bender and C. Henry Smith. Other good sources are: Bender, Harold S., *Two Centuries of American Mennonite Literature* (Goshen, Ind., 1929); Wenger, John C., *Glimpses of Mennonite History and Doctrine* (Scottsdale, Pa., 1949); Bender, Harold S., *Conrad Grebel* (Goshen, Ind., 1950); Horsch, John, *Mennonites in Europe*, 2d rev. ed. (Scottdale, Pa., 1950); Smith, C. Henry, *Story of the Mennonites*, 3d ed. (Newton, Kans., 1950); Braght, Thieleman J. van, *Martyr's Mirror*, tr. from the Dutch of 1660 by J. F. Sohm, rev. ed. (Scottdale, Pa., 1950); the *Mennonite Yearbook* (Scottdale, Pa., annually).

On Mennonite beliefs, consult Wenger, John C., *Separated unto God* (Scottdale, Pa., 1951); Hershberger, Guy F., *War, Peace, and Nonresistance*, 3d rev. ed. (Scottdale, Pa., 1953); Wenger, John C., *Introduction to Theology* (Scottdale, Pa., 1954); *Recovery of the Anabaptist Vision*, ed. by Guy F. Hershberger (Scottdale, Pa., 1957); and the *Mennonite Quarterly Review* (Goshen, Ind., 1927–).

JOHN C. WENGER,
Mennonite Bishop and Author.

MENOCAL, mä-nô-käl′, **Mario García,** Cuban engineer and political leader: b. Hanábana, Matanzas Province, Cuba, Dec. 16, 1866; d. Havana, Sept. 7, 1941. After studying engineering at Cornell University, Ithaca, N.Y., he returned to Cuba in 1891 as a railroad construction engineer. He took part in the Cuban War of Liberation (1895–1898), rising to the rank of major general. In 1908 he was an unsuccessful candidate for the presidency of the new republic. In 1913 he became president, and was re-elected for a second term (1917–1921) despite a liberal revolt in 1916 which was suppressed. In 1917 he brought Cuba into World War I as an ally of the United States. A conservative, Menocal encouraged foreign investment, and much of his period of office was marked by great prosperity, particularly in the sugar industry. His administration, at first efficient, was later charged by opponents as corrupt and extravagant, and a break in the world sugar market in 1920 led to serious financial difficulties in Cuba. Menocal supported Alfredo Zayas for the presidency in the 1920 elections. In 1924 he was defeated by Gen. Gerardo Machado y Morales, against whom he led an abortive revolt in 1931. Except for brief periods of imprisonment and exile Menocal remained active in Cuban politics as an opposition leader, but never again held public office. See also CUBA—*10. History* (Republic of Cuba).

MENOMINEE, mĕ-nŏm′ĭ-nê, city, Michigan, Menominee County seat, on Green Bay, Lake Michigan, at the mouth of the Menominee River, at an altitude of 595 feet. It is just opposite Marinette, Wis., with which it is connected by the Interstate Bridge, and is on a federal highway, about 150 miles north of Milwaukee, Wis. It is served by the Chicago and North Western, the Chicago, Milwaukee, St. Paul and Pacific, and (by car ferry across the lake to Frankfort) the Ann Arbor railway, and lake steamers. It is also served by the North Central Airlines. The $250,000 yacht basin and marina is a port of call for sailing and motor yachts, making the city a popular summer resort. The excellent harbor has ferry and steamship connections with other lake and foreign ports.

Menominee has important manufactures, including furniture, paper, wood products, fans, pumps, heavy machinery, electric goods, and chemicals. Other industries are sawmilling, meat packing, and fishing.

A trading post was established in 1799, and in 1832 the first steam sawmill was built. At the turn of the 20th century Menominee was the major port for the lumber industry of Michigan's Upper Peninsula, shipping more white pine than any other port in the world. The city was incorporated in 1883; it is governed by mayor and council. Pop. 11,289.

CATHERINE GRASSL.

MENOMINI or **MENOMINEE,** mê-nŏm′ĭ-nē (Ind., wild-rice men), a tribe of Amerindians of Algonquian linguistic stock, who lived in early times in upper Michigan around Michilimackinac (Mackinac) but were later found in Wisconsin along the Menominee River and Green Bay, ranging westward to the Mississippi River and southward to the Fox River. Their name was derived from their great use of wild rice as a staple food. Although many of their customs were quite similar to those of the neighboring Chippewa (q.v.), they seem to have a closer linguistic affinity with the Fox and Kickapoo tribes. Two important chieftains of the tribe were Oshkosh and Peshtigo.

The Menomini were living at the mouth of the Menominee River when first encountered by Jean Nicolet, the French explorer, about 1634. They were generally at peace with the white man, and after the signing of the treaty of 1854 they were settled on the Menomini Reservation in northeastern Wisconsin, where 3,029 lived in 1950.

Consult Hoffman, Walter J., "The Menominee Indians," *14th Annual Report*, Bureau of American Ethnology, 1892–1893, part 1 (Washington, D.C., 1896); Skinner, Alanson B., *Material Culture of the Menomini*, Indian Notes and Monographs, Miscellaneous No. 20 (Museum of the American Indian, Heye Foundation, New York 1921); Spindler, George D., *Sociocultural and Psychological Processes in Menomini Acculturation*, University of California Publications in Culture and Society, vol. 5 (Berkeley, Calif., 1955).

FREDERICK J. DOCKSTADER.

MENOMONIE, mê-nŏm′ô-nê, city, Wisconsin, Dunn County seat, on the Red Cedar River, 21 miles west of Eau Claire, at an altitude of 805 feet. It is on the Chicago, Milwaukee, St. Paul, and Pacific, and the Chicago, St. Paul, Minneapolis, and Omaha railroads, and state and federal highways. Formerly an important lumbering center, it processes and ships dairy products, flour, and stock feed. Other industries include the manufacture of aluminum ware, cigars, and bricks.

The city is the seat of Stout Institute, founded in 1893 as a vocational school, which became a state teachers' college in 1911. Menomonie was settled in the 1840's and received its charter in 1882; government is by a mayor and six councilmen. Pop. 8,624.

MENON, mê′nŏn, **V(engalil) K(rishnan) Krishna,** Indian statesman: b. Calicut, Kerala, India, May 3, 1897. He studied economics and law in Madras and in 1924 took up residence in England, where he continued his studies at the University of London. A militant advocate of Indian independence, he was the leading force in the reactivation of the India League, which he served as secretary from 1929 to 1947. In 1934 he was admitted to the English bar and, besides practicing law, was editor of the Twentieth Century Library and first editor of Pelican Books.

In 1947, when India became an independent state in the Commonwealth, Menon was named its first high commissioner in London, serving also (from 1949) as ambassador to Ireland. In 1952 he left these posts to become his country's spokesman at the United Nations, where his resolution on the repatriation of prisoners broke the deadlock in the Korean War. He entered the government of India in 1956 as minister without portfolio and a year later was named minister of defense. Throughout his career he has been a close collaborator and confidant of Prime Minister Jawaharlal Nehru and, like Nehru, an advocate of neutralism and of better understanding between the Communist and democratic camps.

MENOPAUSE, měn′ô-pôz, represents that period in a woman's life when menstruation no longer occurs. The changes which precede and follow the cessation of menstruation are a part of the climacteric. The physical changes of the climacteric period are somewhat similar to those of puberty. In puberty, when the ovaries first begin to function, the breasts enlarge, growth increases, menstruation is often irregular in time and amount, fatigue is noticeable, and changes in appetite occur. During the climacteric, when ovarian function decreases, these same symptoms may recur. However, the majority of well-adjusted women go through the climacteric period without any appreciable disturbance in physical and emotional well-being. About one woman in ten will have hot flashes associated with the menopause. These result from transient changes in the blood vessels which go to the body surfaces. Hot flashes followed by sweating are simply uncomfortable and disturb sleep at night. They may be untimely and soil clothing during the day. Hot flashes can be controlled by the judicious use of hormone medications. Menstruation may be regular and normal up to a certain date and stop abruptly. This is unusual. The most common manner in which the menopause occurs is by a gradual decrease in the amount of flow and by an occasional increase in the interval between periods. Excessive, frequent, and irregular bleeding during the climacteric are abnormal symptoms and should be brought to the attention of a physician.

While the menopause usually becomes manifest between the ages of 45 and 50 years, about one woman out of three will continue to menstruate normally after her 50th birthday. A natural menopause under 45 years of age is an uncommon occurrence. An induced menopause may be brought about by removal of the uterus. However, hysterectomy without removal of the ovaries does not cause a change of life. The ovaries are the feminizing organs. Although bleeding cannot occur after the uterus has been removed, the ovaries do continue to function and they contribute their hormonal influence to other body tissues.

Pregnancy is an uncommon but definite possibility during the climacteric and in the first year after the menopause.

JOHN PARKS, M.D.,
School of Medicine, George Washington University.

MENORCA, mä-nôr′kä, or **MINORCA,** mĭ-nôr′kà, island, Spain; second largest of the Balearic Islands, in the western Mediterranean, 25 miles northeast of Mallorca (Majorca) and 125 miles southeast of Barcelona. The island is about 30 miles long from northwest to southeast and approximately 10 miles wide, with a total area of about 264 square miles. The coastline is indented with many bays and rocky headlands,

particularly in the less fertile north, and fringed with islets. The southern coast, known as its Riviera, is more sheltered from the north winds and has a relatively calm, pleasant climate. The principal towns are Mahón on the southeastern coast, an important air and naval base with one of the finest harbors in the Mediterranean; and Ciudadela, a fishing port on the western tip with a 14th century cathedral and several fine churches and palaces. There is some agriculture on the southern plateau: potatoes, cereals, olives, grapes, hemp, and flax; and an abundance of citrus and other fruits. Cattle, sheep, and goats are raised, and bees are kept. Menorca has given its name to a breed of poultry (q.v.). Manufactures include shoes, cheese, metalware, textile, soap, wine, and sweets. A fine marble is quarried, as well as slate and lime. Deposits of iron, copper, and lead are little exploited because of the lack of fuel.

Menorca has many megaliths, called *talayotes:* stone tables, circles, and walls which date back to prehistoric times. Like other Mediterranean islands it was occupied in turn by Carthaginians, Romans, Vandals, and Moors. In the 13th century it was conquered by James I of Aragon; between 1535 and 1708 Mahón was held by a corsair; in 1709 Menorca was seized during the War of the Spanish Succession by the British, who held it until 1756 when the Spanish recovered it. The Treaty of Paris (1763) restored it to Great Britain, but Spain took it again in 1782. In 1798 it fell once again into the hands of the British, to be finally returned to Spain by the Treaty of Amiens in 1802. Menorca remained on the Loyalist side in the Spanish Civil War (1936–1939) until it surrendered to the Nationalists in February 1939. Pop. (1957 est.) 44,952.

HENRY HUMPHREY,
Staff Editor, "The Encyclopedia Americana."

MENOTTI, mä-nôt′tê, **Gian-Carlo,** Italian-American composer and librettist: b. Cadigliamo, Italy, July 7, 1911. He received his first music lessons from his mother, and wrote his first opera at the age of 11. After attending the Milan Conservatory he went to the United States in 1928 and studied with Rosario Scalero at the Curtis Institute of Music in Philadelphia, Pa. In 1933 he wrote the libretto and music for *Amelia Goes to the Ball,* an opera buffa, which was produced in 1937, first at the Philadelphia Academy of Music and later at the Metropolitan Opera House in New York City. *The Old Maid and the Thief,* an opera for radio commissioned by the National Broadcasting Company, was presented in 1939. *The Island God* received its première at the Metropolitan in 1942, and was followed by the composition of two ballets, *Sebastian* (1943) and *Errand into the Maze,* presented by Martha Graham in 1947. His melodramatic opera *The Medium* (q.v., 1946), won a popular success on Broadway, where it was accompanied by a satirical piece, *The Telephone* (q.v., 1947), and was later made into a motion picture. *The Consul* (1950), depicting the helplessness of stateless people in the hands of a totalitarian bureaucrat, was equally successful and won a Pulitzer Prize. The tender and imaginative *Amahl and the Night Visitors,* the story of a crippled boy who met the three kings bearing gifts to the Christ Child, was introduced on television in 1951 and repeated annually thereafter. *The Saint of Bleecker Street* (1954) won the New York Drama Critics

Circle Award as well as the Pulitzer Prize for Music. His *Maria Golovin* (1958), first presented at the World's Fair in Brussels, Belgium, was less favorably received.

Menotti has also composed a piano concerto, four pieces for string quartet, and other instrumental works, but he is best known as composer-librettist of operas. Mainly in the Italian tradition and musically eclectic, they are especially notable for having made opera acceptable to the general public under the guise of music dramas. During the summer of 1958 he organized the musical Festival of Two Worlds at Spoleto, Italy.

VENILA DRACHBAR.

MENPES, měm'pĭs, **Mortimer,** British painter and etcher: b. Adelaide, Australia, Feb. 22, 1859; d. England, April 1, 1938. He went to London at the age of 19 and studied for a while at South Kensington, but was largely self-taught. He spent three years in Brittany and traveled throughout Europe and Asia, as well as in Mexico and parts of Africa. After serving in South Africa as war artist for the periodical *Black and White* during the Boer War, he published *War Impressions* (1901), a collection of etchings, and the following year his *World Pictures* appeared. His sense of color and knowledge of draftsmanship enabled him to reproduce vividly the atmosphere of the localities he visited. He revived the art of printing in color from etched plates and personally supervised the reproductions of the *Menpes Series of Great Masters.* He claimed to have held more exhibitions than any of his contemporaries; well-known paintings included *The Bead Stringers, The Great Clock,* and *Traghetto.* Among his other publications were *Whistler as I Knew Him* (1904), *The People of India* (1910), and *Lord Kitchener* (1915).

MENSA, měn'sà, or **MONS MENSAE,** mŏnz měn'sē, in astronomy, the Table or Table Mountain, one of 14 southern constellations discovered by Nicolas Louis de Lacaille (q.v.) when he visited the Cape of Good Hope, South Africa, in 1751. It is named after Table Mountain in Cape Town, Union of South Africa. The constellation is an inconspicuous one near the South Pole, its brightest star being only of 5.3 magnitude.

MENSHEVIK, měn'shĕ-vĭk, a member of the conservative minority wing of the Russian Social-Democratic Labor Party. See BOLSHEVIK.

MENSHIKOV, myăn'y'-shĭ-kôf, PRINCE **Aleksandr Danilovich,** Russian soldier and statesman: b. Moscow, Russia, 1673; d. Berezov, Siberia, c. December 1729. The son of a court groom and, according to tradition, a street peddler in his youth, Menshikov became a soldier in the play regiments of Czarevich Peter before he assumed the throne as Peter I. Through François Lefort he became a friend of the czar, and after Lefort's death in 1699, his favorite. Menshikov accompanied Peter on his first trip to Europe, served with distinction in the Azov campaigns (1695–1696), was created a prince of the Holy Empire in 1706, and was made a field marshal after his victory in the Battle of Poltava (1709). He demonstrated great energy and ability in a number of important administrative positions, and worked closely with Peter in building the

city of St. Petersburg and developing Peter's far-reaching reform program. Menshikov was also notably corrupt, and was saved from disgrace for his embezzlements by the intervention of Empress Catherine, who had been his mistress before her marriage to Peter. On the death of Peter I, Menshikov was instrumental in placing the dowager empress on the throne as Catherine I, and during her brief reign (1725–1727) he was the actual ruler of Russia. On her death he made himself regent of the young Peter II, and had arranged a marriage between his daughter and the czar when members of the old nobility, angered by his arrogance, forced his imprisonment and exile (1727) to Siberia, where he died.

MENSHIKOV, PRINCE **Aleksandr Sergeyevich,** Russian soldier and statesman: b. Russia, Sept. 11, 1787; d. St. Petersburg, May 2, 1869. The great-grandson of Prince Aleksandr Danilovich Menshikov (q.v.), he served with Czar Alexander I against Napoleon I (1812–1815), rising to the rank of general. He was made governor general of Finland by Czar Nicholas I (1831), and head of the Russian navy (1836), which he reorganized on a more efficient basis. In 1853 he was sent as ambassador to the Sublime Porte at Constantinople on a mission to secure rights for the Orthodox Church and its members, a mission which ended in the outbreak of the Crimean War (q.v.). He was commander of the Russian forces in Crimea until his recall in early 1855 after the Russian defeat in the Battle of Inkerman.

MENSTRUATION, měn-strŏŏ-ā'shŭn (from Lat. *menstruus,* monthly), a physiologic process peculiar to human and higher anthropoid females, characterized by the passage of a non-clotting bloody fluid from the vagina. Each flowing episode is known as a menstrual period and usually lasts from three to five days; periods of less than three days or more than six days are exceptional and perhaps abnormal. The intervals between menstrual flow, which are called cycles, range from 21 to 42 days, although the great majority of women have cycles of from 25 to 32 days.

The initial menstrual period heralds the stage of life known as adolescence, which is normally established in the age range of 12 to 15 years, with occasional variations. The total amount of blood material passed in one period is not great. The menstrual periods continue to reappear in a cycle, of a duration, and in an amount peculiar to each individual. They may vary moderately without being considered unusual, but pronounced variations in the cycle, duration, or amount of flow should cause the individual to seek medical consultation. Despite lay opinion to the contrary, very few women are absolutely regular at a given date.

At the end of a menstruation the lining of the uterus, known as the endometrium, is very thin and broken. Within a few days it begins to proliferate and increase in thickness. By the time of ovulation, which is approximately 14 days before the next menstruation unless conception occurs, there is a moderate thickening of this lining. Following the escape of the egg from the ovary (ovulation) the endometrium prepares for the attachment of the fertilized egg. If conception fails the endometrium becomes slightly thicker and then undergoes a special process of engorgement and ultimately sheds (menstruation). Normally when conception occurs and the egg implants properly there is no menstruation until after delivery of the infant, although an occasional individual may have slight menstruallike bleeding in early pregnancy. Whether this is a normal process or a threatened miscarriage depends on circumstances.

The menstrual cycle is controlled principally by two glands of internal secretion: directly by the ovary and indirectly by the pituitary. Menstruation is a perfectly normal process for all women from adolescence until change of life or menopause (q.v.), and most women experience it without distress or inconvenience. Individuals may live their normal lives so far as activities of work, employment, care of household, and other routines are concerned. Normally the genital passage should be rested during the entire period of menstruation and until all evidence of the menstrual flow has vanished.

Disorders of Menstruation.—Among the disorders of menstruation is *amenorrhea* or the absence of menstrual periods, which may occur physiologically in association with pregnancy or menopause. Absences may also result from disease elsewhere in the body, such as a disturbance in the endocrinal glandular system, severe malnutrition, or injury to the ovary. The term *dysmenorrhea* means painful periods. Only infrequently does an individual have sufficient distress or annoyance to interfere with her routine activities. *Menorrhagia* implies excessive menstrual periods. It may be found in persons with tumors, polyps, cancer, certain blood complications, or a number of other conditions. *Polymenorrhea* indicates abnormally frequent periods. *Oligomenorrhea* refers to infrequent or scanty flow. *Metrorrhagia* means uterine bleeding unrelated to the menstrual cycle. All such abnormalities of menstruation should be investigated and treated by the family physician or a specialist. If the period is a little excessive, usually resting will give relief. Pain or distress in association with menstruation is observed in some individuals who work under tension; distress may also occur as a result of disease, especially of the tubes and ovaries. However most lower abdominal distress and backache experienced between menstrual periods and not increased during the periods are due to conditions outside the generative organs.

H. CLOSE HESSELTINE, M.D.,
Attending Obstetrician and Gynecologist, Chicago Lying-in Hospital.

MENSURAL MUSIC, měn'shŏŏr-ăl mū'zĭk (Lat. *musica mensurata*), is music in which the tones are of definite mathematically related durations. As long as music consisted largely of a single melody, as in plain song (q.v.) or Gregorian chant, the durations of its tones were indefinite, being determined in performance by the rhythms and accents of the words sung. Notation therefore long remained little more than a species of shorthand reminders to singers who already knew what they were expected to sing, and how it would be sung by their fellows and themselves. But when two and more distinct melodic lines began to be sung together, and perhaps more especially when two or more instruments began to play differing melodic lines simultaneously, the need for exact designation of the comparative durations of tones—that is, of notes representing tones to be played or sung—became imperative.

The need for exact designation of relative pitch similarly became acute at about the same time, for it was then that the system of vertical harmonic thought began to emerge in European music. The result of all this was the gradual evolution, evident as early as the 10th century, of the modern system of musical notation. This evolution, particularly rapid during the 13th and immediately succeeding centuries, was one prerequisite for the ensuing rich development of counterpoint, harmony, and modern rhythms.

HERBERT WEINSTOCK.

MENSURATION, měn-shŏŏ-rā'shŭn (Lat. *mensuratio,* from *metior,* to measure), the science of measuring, that branch of applied mathematics which deals with the finding of lengths of lines, areas of surfaces, and volumes of solids. The beginnings of the science undoubtedly go back to prehistoric times since even very primitive civilizations would find a need for crude measurements of length in the construction of buildings, of area for the division of land for cultivation, and of volume for the measuring out of foodstuffs.

Archaeologists have unearthed thousands of clay tablets at the sites of ancient Mesopotamian cities that date back as far as 2000 B.C. and which reveal a high level of computational ability. Many of the tablets deal with systems of weights and measures. From others we learn that the Sumerians and Babylonians of 2000 to 1600 B.C. were familiar with general rules for finding the area of a rectangle, the areas of at least special types of triangles, and the volume of a rectangular parallelepiped (box). Similarly, studies of papyri show roughly the same progress in Egypt at about the same dates. Not all of the methods used for mensuration by the Babylonians and the Egyptians were correct, however. Thus, for example, the Babylonians used the crude approximation to pi (ratio of the circumference of a circle to its diameter) of 3 whereas the actual value, to five decimal places, is 3.14159. Similarly, the Egyptians used an incorrect formula for finding the area of a general four-sided figure.

Measurement of Lengths.—All measurements of areas and volumes are ultimately based on measurements of lengths. Thus, for example, the area of a rectangle is the product of the length of the base and the length of the height. In order to measure a length one must, of course, have a unit of measurement such as the inch, centimeter, or mile. Many different units have been used in the past that are no longer in use, and we are still plagued by the existence of a large number of different and unrelated units for the measurement of lengths, areas, and volumes.

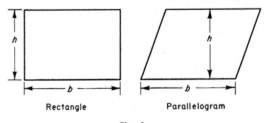

Rectangle　　　　　Parallelogram

Fig. 1.

(See WEIGHTS AND MEASURES for the different units and their relation to one another.) No matter what units are used one must be consistent throughout; for example, if one dimension of a plane figure is measured in inches so must the others be, and the area will then be measured in square inches. Similarly, if the dimensions of a solid are measured in centimeters, the volume will be measured in cubic centimeters.

The determination of a length is sometimes made directly by the use of a ruler, tape measure, or calipers, and sometimes indirectly by trigonometry. After the necessary lengths are determined (all measured in the same units) the areas and volumes of many plane figures and solids can be found by application of the proper formula.

Areas of Plane Figures.—The basic area is that of a *rectangle* where the area is given as the base times the height or, in symbols, $A = bh$.

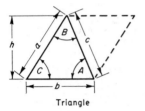 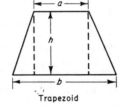

Triangle   Trapezoid

Fig. 2.

This is also the formula for the area of a *parallelogram* if we replace the concept of height by that of altitude as shown in Fig. 1. Since the *triangle* may be considered as half of a parallelogram (as shown by the dotted lines in Fig. 2), a formula for its area is $\frac{1}{2}bh$ where b is the base and h is the altitude.

In the case of the triangle, however, other formulas are frequently used such as

$$\tfrac{1}{2}ab \sin C, \ \tfrac{1}{2}bc \sin A, \ \tfrac{1}{2}ac \sin B$$

which involve trigonometry, and

$$\sqrt{s(s - a)(s - b)(s - c)} \text{ where}$$
$$s = \tfrac{1}{2}(a + b + c).$$

(Here a, b, and c are the three sides of the triangle and A, B, and C are the angles opposite the respective sides.)

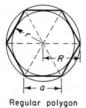

Regular polygon

Fig. 3.

By considering the *trapezoid* as two triangles plus a rectangle (as shown by the dotted lines in Fig. 2) it is easy to obtain the formula for its area,

$$\tfrac{1}{2}h(a + b),$$

where a and b are the parallel sides and h is the altitude. The *regular polygon,* in turn, may be considered as being made up of triangles. This is shown by the dotted lines in Fig. 3 where a is the length of a side, n the number of sides, r the radius of the inscribed circle, and R the

radius of the circumscribed circle. The area of the polygon is then given in terms of trigo-

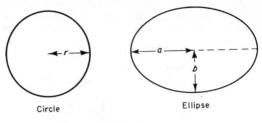

Circle   Ellipse

Fig. 4.

nometric functions as

$$\tfrac{1}{4}na^2 \cot \frac{180°}{n} = nr^2 \tan \frac{180°}{n} = \tfrac{1}{2}nR^2 \sin \frac{360°}{n}.$$

All of the areas discussed so far have been rather directly based on the primitive concept of the area of a rectangle—as can all areas whose boundaries are composed of straight line segments. The situation for areas with curved boundaries is quite different, however, and in general the determination of such areas requires the use of the calculus (q.v.). The two most commonly used areas with curved boundaries are the *circle* and the *ellipse* (Fig. 4). For both of these figures we may give the area in terms of the number pi (π) previously mentioned. Thus the area of a circle is πr^2 and the area of an ellipse is πab where r is the radius of the circle and a and b are the major and minor radii, respectively, of the ellipse. (It is usually sufficiently accurate to use π to two decimal places.) It is

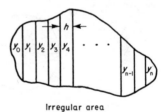

Irregular area

Fig. 5.

interesting to note, however, that while the circumference of a circle can be expressed simply as $2\pi r$, the circumference of an ellipse, as is shown in the calculus, can not be expressed in terms of algebraic or even trigonometric functions.

Even though it is not possible to find the areas of all plane figures by a direct algebraic or trigonometric formula, one can always make use of one of several approximation methods. For example, if the plane area is divided into n strips by equidistant parallel chords of lengths y_0, y_1, $y_2,\ldots,y_n$ as shown in Fig. 5, and if h is the common distance between them, the *trapezoidal* rule gives the approximate area as

$$h(\tfrac{1}{2}y_0 + y_1 + y_2 + y_3 + \ldots + y_{n-1} + \tfrac{1}{2}y_n).$$

A better approximation is given by *Simpson's* rule,

$$\tfrac{1}{3}h(y_0 + 4y_1 + 2y_2 + 4y_3$$
$$+ 2y_4 + \ldots + 4y_{n-1} + y_n),$$

where, here, n must be even.

Volumes and Surface Areas.—In our discussion of volumes and surface areas we will, for convenience, use the letter V for volume and the letter S for surface area. First, just as our basic area is that of the rectangle, so our basic volume

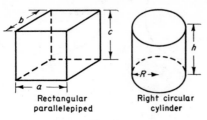

Rectangular parallelepiped   Right circular cylinder

Fig. 6.

is that of the *rectangular parallelepiped* with sides *a, b,* and *c* as shown in Fig. 6. For it we have

$$V = abc, \ S = 2(ab + ac + bc).$$

For the *right circular cylinder* of altitude h and radius R as shown in Fig. 6 we again use the number π and have

$$V = \pi R^2 h, \ S = 2\pi R h.$$

Similarly, for the right circular cone of altitude h and radius R as shown in Fig. 7 we have

$$V = \tfrac{1}{3}\pi R^2 h, \ S = \pi R \sqrt{R^2 + h^2};$$

and for the sphere of radius R shown in Fig. 7,

$$V = \tfrac{4}{3}\pi R^3, \ S = 4\pi R^2.$$

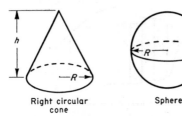

Right circular cone   Sphere

Fig. 7.

A *regular pyramid,* as shown in Fig. 8, resembles a circular cone except that its base is a regular polygon rather than a circle. Thus the area of its base can be found by the formulas discussed above under *Areas of Plane Figures* and we have

$$V = \tfrac{1}{3}(\text{area of base})h, \ S = \tfrac{1}{2}(\text{perimeter of base})s$$

where h is the altitude of the pyramid and s is its slant height.

Our final formula is that for the volume of the *frustrum* of a pyramid shown in Fig. 8. The ancient Egyptians apparently knew and used this rather complex formula (for the case when the base was a square) at a time when they were using incorrect formulas or had no formulas at all for the volumes of simpler solids. This formula is

$$V = \tfrac{1}{3}(A + A' + \sqrt{AA'})h$$

where A is the area of the lower base of the

frustrum, A' is the area of the upper base, and h is the altitude of the frustrum.

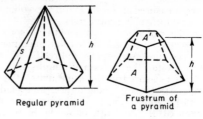

Regular pyramid   Frustrum of a pyramid

Fig. 8.

As is true in the case of plane areas, not all volumes or surface areas of even fairly simple solids can be found by the application of direct formulas. Recourse is then made to the calculus or to approximation formulas similar to those described above for plane areas.

Bibliography.—Hogben, Lancelot T., *Mathematics for the Million,* 3d ed. (New York 1951); Boyer, Lee E., *Introduction to Mathematics,* rev. ed. (New York 1955); Lopshits, A. M., *The Computation of Areas of Oriented Figures* (Boston 1963); Eves, Howard, *Introduction to the History of Mathematics,* rev. ed. (New York 1964); American Society of Tool and Manufacturing Engineers, *Handbook of Industrial Metrology* (New York 1967).

ROY DUBISCH,
Professor of Mathematics, Fresno State College.

MENTAL DEFICIENCY. See MENTAL RETARDATION.

MENTAL DISEASES. See PSYCHIATRY; PSYCHOLOGY OF THE ABNORMAL; PSYCHOPATHOLOGY; PSYCHOSIS.

MENTAL HEALTH, měn'tăl hělth, involves the development of a healthy attitude in the individual toward himself and toward the environment in which he lives so that he will achieve the maximum amount of self-fulfillment.

One of the clearest and most authoritative discussions of the concept of mental health is that of Marie Jahoda (see *Bibliography*). She states that it is not enough to say that mental health is the absence of mental disease. There is great variation from one culture to another as to what kinds of deviation from usual behavior may be considered "abnormal." Neither is it helpful to equate mental health with normality, because the term "normal" is equally undefinable. To say that mental health is a state of well-being is also unsatisfactory.

In her discussion of mental health, Dr. Jahoda finds it profitable to use six major categories of concepts. These are: (1) attitudes of an individual toward his own self; (2) the individual's style and degree of growth, development, or self-actualization; (3) integration of the personality; (4) autonomy, or the degree of independence from social influences; (5) the adequacy of the individual's perception of reality; and (6) environmental mastery.

Using this framework for ideas as to what constitutes mental health, it may be said that the mentally healthy person is confident and self-reliant, and has a realistic idea of the nature of his own capabilities. He has passed through the various stages of his own development, discarding forms of behavior and attitudes that have become unsuitable as he grows older, and has achieved a sense of purpose, balancing his own legitimate needs with an adequate concern for others. His personality is well integrated, indicating that he has achieved a satisfactory balance between the conscious and unconscious forces that motivate him. He is able to postpone temporary pleasures for some greater good at a later time. Some writers have also emphasized the need to achieve harmony between conscious and unconscious drives in order that the person may not be driven by unknown forces against his will.

Achievement of autonomy signifies that one's behavior is determined not so much by external events as by the inner organization of values, needs, beliefs, and desired goals. Thus it is postulated that a mentally healthy person is guided by his own sense of self-direction and not carried along by the opinions of others, regardless of their desirability. The mentally healthy person is able to see events in the world about him in terms of what they are really like, rather than in the nature of wish fulfillment. Such a person is able to put himself in the position occupied by other people, and thus to sense in a general way what they are thinking and feeling; this quality is called empathy or social sensitivity. And finally, environmental mastery suggests that the mentally healthy person has the ability to love, is adequate in his relation with others whether in work, play, or intimate relationships, and is able to meet the usual requirements of living in a community, to adapt himself to change, and to solve the ordinary problems that arise in everyday living. In simpler terms, environmental mastery suggests that the person with adequate mental health can endure a great deal of conflict, both internal and external, and that he acquires strength from mastering or overcoming obstacles as they arise.

The term "maturity" has essentially the same meaning as mental health but with the difference that allowance should be made for the age of the person under scrutiny. Actions that might be considered mature in a 10-year-old would very probably not be so interpreted in an individual 40 years of age.

Historical Background.—In 1900 Clifford W. Beers, a young man working in New York, developed a severe mental illness that caused him to attempt to end his life by jumping from a window. Subsequent examination at a general hospital revealed that he was severely depressed and suffering from delusions and hallucinations. After a trial period of about a month at home he did not improve and was admitted to a mental hospital. For the following three years he lived in a number of institutions designed to care for the mentally ill, but in all of them the treatment received seemed unbelievably inadequate and in many instances it was marked by excessive brutality. Upon his recovery in 1903 he began to work for greater awareness of the plight of those patients who were confined to mental hospitals, in order that they might receive humane treatment and the depth of understanding most conducive to recovery. His many letters to public officials, his visits to persons of wide influence, and finally the publication of his hospital experiences in the book, *A Mind That Found Itself* (1908), were key influences in the formation of the mental health movement, now one of the most significant forces of our time.

The Connecticut Society for Mental Hygiene was founded by Beers and 13 other public-spirited citizens in May 1908. Shortly thereafter, in 1909,

the National Committee for Mental Hygiene was organized. It engaged in a constantly increasing range of activities, designed not only to improve treatment of and attitudes toward those who have mental illness, but also to call attention to those factors in our social structure that tend to produce emotional disturbances. The latter effort has included work with schools and colleges, courts, probation officers, and religious organizations, as well as the establishment of various types of clinics, the training of mental health personnel, community education, and the development of research. A quarterly journal, *Mental Hygiene,* was established in 1917 and constitutes the most authoritative source in the United States for the dissemination of mental health concepts and descriptions of various approaches to the promotion of mental health. In 1950 two smaller organizations were merged with the National Committee of Mental Hygiene and the name was changed to the National Association for Mental Health.

Interest in mental health has led to organization along international as well as national and state lines. The first International Congress on Mental Hygiene was held in Washington in May 1930. Its proceedings, in two volumes of more than 1,600 pages, constitute a thorough résumé of the thinking about mental hygiene throughout the world at that time. Under the name of the International Congress on Mental Health similar conferences were held in Paris in 1947, in London in 1948, in Mexico City in 1951, and in Toronto in 1954. The World Federation for Mental Health was founded in 1948; it has many member associations from different countries. The United States association had 190 members in the late 1960's.

Nearly all the states in the United States have organizations working with the National Association for Mental Health, and many local associations in cities and towns are allied with the state groups. Although this rapid growth of a network of mental health agencies has at times resulted in much confusion and discussion of roles and functions, the net result has been to make many millions of persons aware of the necessity of improving mental health on a global scale, as well as on local and national levels.

Defining Needs and Goals.—The growth of so much interest in mental health has brought into sharp focus the need to define more accurately than has been heretofore possible the needs and goals of the movement as well as to clarify the concepts that are commonly employed. Accordingly in 1955 leaders in American medicine and psychiatry planned a comprehensive three-year study of these needs, goals, and concepts, the work itself being done by a group called the Joint Commission on Mental Illness and Health. It was sponsored by a number of organizations under the leadership of the American Medical Association and the American Psychiatric Association, and financed by an appropriation from the United States Congress through the National Institute of Mental Health of the United States Public Health Service. From the year 1956 this commission conducted studies and surveys of actual conditions pertaining to mental illness and health in the United States with the plan of producing a series of publications to serve as guides for future action as well as for the coordination of efforts in this field.

It is unfortunate, especially for those who need positive accomplishments to justify the expenditure of funds to promote mental health, that there are as yet few ways of estimating mental health in a community or nation. It cannot be said with certainty that the attempt to promote mental health results in a lessening of mental illness, yet most workers believe this to be true. The indexes of lack of mental health are numerous, and include crime rates, prevalence of suicide, alcoholism, drug addiction, divorce, juvenile delinquency, and prostitution. Most of these conditions have shown changes for the worse in recent years, at least so far as the United States is concerned.

As Adolf Meyer (1866–1950) pointed out many years ago, one may work toward mental health by making a list of all the things that are desirable and good in life and then give recommendations as to how to get them. This approach leads to excessive moralizing and helps but little in stimulating action. A more effective way is to make a survey of actual activities and conditions, pick out the points of difficulty, search for the causes and effects of the trouble, and devise ways of solving the problems that are discovered. Through research and experiments stemming from this latter method of approach a better understanding can be achieved, as well as an amelioration of the conditions which interfere with mental health.

Although studies by anthropologists throw much light on cultural conditions among different peoples and countries, there is no consensus as to which of many possible social systems may be regarded as best for the development of the healthy personality. Standards of mental health and psychopathology vary greatly from one culture or society to another. Behavior that is tolerated in one society may result in confinement to a mental hospital in another.

DEVELOPMENT OF MENTAL HEALTH IN CHILDREN

For the past two or three decades educators have paid increasing attention to the development of the "whole child," showing general agreement that a prime purpose of education is to aid children to grow into adults who are emotionally mature as well as capable of using their intellectual powers effectively. Critics of these newer trends often speak bitterly of the emphasis on "life adjustment" and urge a return to fundamentals of the school curriculum. Mental health workers do not favor pedagogical plans which decrease emphasis on subject matter, but instead they strive for enough attention to the child's personal needs to encourage the strongest possible motivation toward learning.

Among the studies that have contributed most to an understanding of children those of Erik H. Erikson (see *Bibliography*) stand out prominently. His formulation of the stages of development of the healthy personality is consistent with most theories of personality and is understandable to the layman. These stages include the development of a sense of trust, autonomy, initiative, duty and accomplishment, identity, intimacy, creativity (or parental sense), and integrity.

Sense of Trust.—This attitude is developed in the early months of life provided those who care for the child do so in such a way as to instill in him the expectation that when help is needed it will arrive somehow. If he is not loved or the meeting of his needs is habitually postponed to the point of acute discomfort the balance will be tipped in the direction of mistrust, setting the stage for various personality inadequacies later in life.

Sense of Autonomy.—The development of a mind and will of his own is especially prominent during the child's second and third years. In this period there is a delicate balance between fear and the attainment of confidence. The favorable outcome is self-control without loss of self-esteem. If this stage is not successfully worked through he may develop a lasting sense of doubt in others as well as in himself and a sense of shyness and shame.

Sense of Initiative.—By the age of four or five the child wants to find out what he can do on his own and imitates everyone. Aggression becomes more vigorous and conscience begins to develop. His fantasy is quite vivid. This is the time for a neat balance between permitting him some excesses of behavior, yet teaching him that there are certain limits beyond which he cannot go. Shame is a dangerous weapon at this or any other time. By avoiding excessive reprisals or punishments which cause constriction of the personality the proper sense of initiative can be developed and preserved.

These three stages are probably the most important for healthy personality development. If the individual passes through these successfully later difficulties seem to be more easily handled.

Sense of Duty and Accomplishment.—From the age of six up to the eleventh or twelfth year the child indulges in less fantasy and accomplishes a slower but steadier growth. If his early stages have been unhappy ones it is very easy for him to acquire a lasting sense of inferiority and inadequacy. Therefore encouragement and recognition for tasks done well are important. Success in this stage results in the development of a sense of industry or duty and accomplishment.

Sense of Identity.—Beginning with the onset of adolescence at about 12 years and extending into early adulthood comes a period of rapid change, confusion, contradictions, inconsistencies, and paradoxes. The gradual emancipation from parents with conflicting desires for dependence and independence, may bring about many differences of opinion between parents and child. It is the time in which the young boy or girl is trying to become sure of his own identity, to learn who and what he is, to develop goals and a sense of belonging to some coherent way of life in which his actions have meaning. He may find suitable models with whom he can indentify, he may become confused and suffer from a diffusion of goals and ideals, or he may react in a negative way, rejecting a responsible role in society—depending in a large measure on the supporting influence of his family, church, school, or community.

Sense of Intimacy.—The more a young person understands himself and feels sure of the affection and esteem of those close to him, the easier it is for him to develop relations of friendship, love, and inspiration with others. The capacity for forming such deep and satisfying relations with others, the sense of intimacy, may suffer in the presence of excessive pressures for efficiency. A sharing of inner resources with others requires much awareness of one's own personality characteristics and an acceptance of self.

Parental or Creative Sense.—This sense usually becomes most apparent when the young person begins to care for children of his own. The individual who develops it thinks of children as a trust of the community rather than extensions of his own personality. Concern for others takes reasonable preference over self-centered preoccupations. Without this sense an individual indulges himself, expects to be indulged, and goes through life acting in a childlike, immature way.

Sense of Integrity.—The final capstone to the healthy personality is the sense of integrity. A person with this quality exhibits the dominant ideals of his culture, is reasonable, and conveys sentiments of dignity and respect to those with whom he comes in contact. If children are to achieve this characteristic as they reach the stage of adults, it is necessary that a high proportion of the adults around them possess it to a considerable degree. Thus mental health and the acquisition of values consistent with a good society are inseparable.

During the whole period of childhood the slow steady pressure of parental attitudes is of vital importance, either for good or ill. A firm, friendly, consistent discipline, with parents holding themselves to the same high standards demanded of their children, is coming to be generally recognized as a priamry source of sound character structure.

APPLICATIONS OF MENTAL HEALTH PRINCIPLES

Since the goals of the mental health movement are so vast, new methods of sharing information have been sought between psychologists, psychiatrists, and social workers, and professional men and women in other fields in which human relations are very important.

Religious Counseling.—In recent years many signs of increasing collaboration between ministers or priests and mental health workers have appeared. For vast numbers of people their minister or priest is the only professional person with whom they have relatively easy personal contact. The problems brought to members of the clergy are often far removed from those about which they were instructed in their theological training. Therefore, many theological schools have introduced material into their curriculums designed to give their students greater skill in dealing with the infinite assortment of personal problems that will be brought to them in their church work. Such activity is commonly spoken of as pastoral counseling.

Grave difficulties face the clergyman who attempts to become an effective counselor. He may become so involved with the personal problems of his parishioners that he has insufficient time to pursue his theological studies or to prepare his sermons properly. He may come to view counseling as his primary task, then realize that at best he is an amateur psychologist and hence out of his field. A serious complication involving a person whom he has counseled may raise doubts in his mind as to his qualifications to do such work. To help throw additional light on how clergymen may make optimum use of modern knowledge of emotions, personality development, and relations between persons and groups, a number of special projects in religion and mental health have been organized at leading theological seminaries, notably Union Theological Seminary in New York, the theological schools of Loyola University in Chicago, Ill., and Yeshiva University in New York, and the Divinity School of Harvard University, Cambridge, Mass. From these and similar sources a flow of helpful literature on this vital subject may be expected.

Educational Programs.—Teachers in primary and secondary schools have become increasingly aware during the past two or three decades of how much the mental health of their pupils as well as their own emotional stability influences the processes of teaching and learning. Many national and international educational organizations have published valuable handbooks on the application of mental health principles in schools.

Interest in college mental health in the United States began early in the mental hygiene movement. Princeton University, University of Wisconsin, United States Military Academy, Washburn University of Topeka, Dartmouth and Vassar colleges, and Yale University were among the earliest institutions of higher learning to develop mental health programs. Such programs have gradually increased in number; they were in effect in many colleges in recent years, although many of them were limited in scope because of scarcity of funds and of suitably trained personnel.

A college mental health program consists of two main parts: the treatment of those students whose effectiveness is impaired by emotional conflicts, and the development of widespread awareness on the part of all members of the institution of the conditions in the community or in society which impair or promote mental health. When a college has an adequate program the experience of those who have worked with such colleges indicates that about 10 per cent of the students have emotional conflicts severe enough to warrant professional help in their management. The presenting condition in such illnesses may be approaching or actual academic failure, depression of mood, various anxiety states, physical symptoms (psychosomatic disorders), bizarre behavior, or even violence toward oneself or others.

As to the educational portion of a mental health program, constructive action may result from the study of student-faculty relations, counseling systems, effects of various teaching methods, causes of cheating, plagiarism, and disrespect for property, the effect of grading systems, and the administration of discipline. Social pressure resulting from membership in or rejection by campus organizations, attitudes of parents and alumni, emotional blocks to learning, and evidences of good or poor relations between individuals or groups in the college community also constitute legitimate objects of interest.

Uses in Industrial Management.—Application of mental health principles to the problems of industrial management have been stimulated by psychiatrists and psychologists who see the possibility of developing truly preventive measures against mental illness in business organizations, and by professors in business schools who have worked on meaures of improving human relations. The early interest and activities of psychiatrists in industry have been described by Alan A. McLean and Graham C. Taylor (see *Bibliography*). Such pioneers as Elton Mayo, Wallace B. Donham, and Fritz J. Roethlisberger have stimulated hundreds of studies on improvement of conditions of work within industrial institutions.

Any interference with good relations between individuals or groups in an organization may be expected to reduce efficiency and result in increased costs of whatever service or product the company offers. A psychiatrist or psychologist may profitably aid in preventing such interference by treating emotional illness through the resolution of conflicts, removing misunderstandings, conferring with appropriate persons about selection, promotion, and discharge procedures, and studying those factors which raise or lower the morale of employees and management. The improvement of safety by studying causes and prevention of accidents, the reduction of unnecessary absence from work, and the development of effective counseling of persons who are involved in quandaries are all essential duties of the industrial mental health worker.

Law Enforcement Problems.—One of the most effective channels for the promotion of mental health on a large scale is through the development of better methods of collaboration between representatives of the courts and other law enforcement agencies and psychiatrists, psychologists, and social workers. There are many difficulties in the way because of the difference in attitudes of most persons trained in legal procedures and those trained in dynamic psychology. Law and psychiatry have such different ways of defining behavior and accounting for its causes that communication between them is often only a series of misunderstandings. Yet awareness of the necessity for close cooperation is growing, and signs of success appear from time to time. In the Durham case in the District of Columbia in 1954 the principle was upheld that "an accused is not criminally responsible if his unlawful act was the product of mental disease or mental defect." Much disagreement persists on this point, many states still adhering to the much older "McNaghten's Rules," promulgated by Chief Justice Tindal of England in 1843, which declare that an accused is responsible so long as he knows (1) the nature and quality of his act and (2) that the act is "wrong."

To mental health workers who deal with persons in conflict with the law it is becoming increasingly apparent that hatred and forced deprivation of all privileges are not effective means of encouraging rehabilitation and the redevelopment of responsibilty. Yet many if not most of our social institutions for the control of human behavior seem to be based on the premise that publicly hurting the person who has done harm to others will be an effective deterrent to similar behavior in the future. Punishment is undoubtedly necessary if the web of morality that holds society together is to retain its strength, but the basic attitudes of those persons appointed by society to implement the necessary restraints on behavior are becoming increasingly important. The occasional harsh and sadistic behavior of some prison attendants toward their charges is only a personal application of the harsh and excessively primitive attitudes toward lawbreakers often expressed by leading citizens whose responsibilities are more remote. No psychiatrist or mental health specialist would wish to be represented as believing he knows the proper answers to the vast social problems presented by the criminal; he would only go on record as stating that these problems should be attacked with as much modern knowledge of human behavior as can be put to use.

Juvenile Delinquency.—The alarming increase of juvenile delinquency in the 1960's forced many communities into making studies to discover the causes of the delinquency and possible remedies. Antisocial behavior on the part of young boys and girls is not confined to any particular ethnic group, to crowded sections of cities, to families of low or high economic position, or to those who do not practice any religious observances. Instead it seems to reflect a failure on the part of the offending youngsters to make a satisfactory or positive identification with any person or group whose ideals are consistent with a smoothly functioning society. Thus it appears probable that at least some part of the problem of preventing boys and girls from identifying themselves with destructive forces in their community lies in giving them satisfying relations with their schoolmates and teachers; the remaining responsibility is shared by the family, the church, the courts, recreational agencies, and other groups which permit and encourage meaningful relations with people worthy of emulation. A crucial experience in the life of a boy or girl who has been apprehended in an antisocial act is the treatment he receives at that time from his friends and the agents of society. Firm but understanding and constructive efforts may divert a child to a useful career more easily at that point than at any other; punitive and senseless retaliation may confirm him in a course unacceptable to society. Hence the practice of good mental health principles is of the highest importance to all who deal with young offenders.

Fields for Social Action.—Most medical and civil authorities agree that mental health is our greatest health problem. Much information that would alleviate mental illness and promote mental health is already available if only it could be applied. Education to make use of what is available and research to further knowledge of better methods of mental health promotion are equally desirable, both to be carried on parallel to the treatment of those who suffer from mental illness or emotional disturbances.

In view of the magnitude of the tasks confronting any community that sets about improving the level of its mental health some limitation is necessary. A logical one is to work in areas of human relations that are productive of suffering and unhappiness. Some kinds of mental defect and mental illness may be prevented in part by such measures as better prenatal services, skillful delivery of infants, early treatment of infectious disease, and attention to nutritional and other growth factors in childhood. Sound principles of personality development should be taught universally, especially the vital role played in the child's development by continuous affection, nurture, and care. Other specific focuses for productive efforts include such activities as marriage counseling, pastoral counseling, court clinics, family agencies, sexual education, and discussion of the nuclear arms "race." Reduction of alcoholism, of gang warfare in cities, of absenteeism in industry, and of traffic accidents are other desirable goals for social action. Group opposition to health programs based on scientific advances, desegregation of the races in public schools, and the influence of mass communication media on emotional maturation are typical of controversial areas of interest.

The community or governmental unit which sets itself the task of alleviating mental illness and promoting mental health should first get a firm understanding of the problems involved, then attempt to select those institutions or groups which can be utilized most effectively in improving the lives of its citizens. Stated in very general terms, mental health can best be promoted through good family life, adequate schools, widespread recreational facilities, opportunities for spiritual training, and conditions for work that bring about a feeling of individual worth, accomplishment, and dignity.

From all these considerations it becomes obvious that a mental health program does not consist of piety or moralizing in a narrow sense. Instead, it is an attempt to improve relations between human beings in order to provide the greatest possible opportunity for self-fulfillment for all persons. Because this goal is so limitless efforts toward improvement are necessarily directed toward specific points of discord or suffering. Effective application of the basic principles of mental health calls for a deep and abiding respect for all human beings, regardless of their condition.

See also PSYCHOLOGY—*Mental Hygiene;* PSYCHOPATHOLOGY.

Bibliography

American Educational Research Association, *Mental and Physical Health* (Washington 1962).
Association for Supervision and Curriculum Development, *Learning and Mental Health in the School* (Washington 1966).
Ballak, Leopold, ed., *Handbook of Community Psychiatry and Community Mental Health* (New York 1963).
Biggs, John, Jr., *The Guilty Mind: Psychiatry and the Law of Homicide* (Baltimore 1967).
David, Henry P., *International Trends in Mental Health:* vol. 1, *Community and School* (New York 1966).
Deutsch, Albert, and Fishman, H., eds., *Encyclopedia of Mental Health,* 6 vols. (New York 1963).
Farnsworth, Dana L., *Mental Health in College and University* (Cambridge, Mass., 1957).
Jahoda, Marie, *Current Concepts of Positive Mental Health* (New York 1958).
Kornhauser, Arthur W., *The Mental Health of the Industrial Worker* (New York 1965).
Kotinsky, Ruth, and Witmer, Helen L., eds., *Community Programs for Mental Health* (Cambridge, Mass., 1955).
McLean, Alan A., and Taylor, Graham C., *Mental Health and the Business Community* (New York 1967).
Maier, Norman R. F., *Psychology in Industry,* 3d ed. (Boston 1965).
Mayo, Elton, *Human Problems of an Industrial Civilization* (New York 1960).
Michael, Donald N., *The Next Generation: The Prospects Ahead for the Youth of Today and Tomorrow* (New York 1965).
Ridenour, Nina, *Mental Health in the United States: A Fifty-Year History* (Cambridge, Mass., 1961).
Soddy, Kenneth, and Ahrenfeldt, Robert H., eds., *Mental Health and Contemporary Thought* (New York 1967).
Sutherland, Robert L., and Smith, B. K., eds., *Understanding Mental Health* (Princeton, N.J., 1965).
Torrance, Ellis Paul, *Mental Health and Constructive Behavior* (Belmont, Calif., 1965).
World Federation for Mental Health, *Population and Mental Health,* ed. by Henry P. David (New York 1964).

DANA L. FARNSWORTH, M.D.,
Director, University Health Services, Harvard University and Radcliffe College; Henry K. Oliver Professor of Hygiene, Harvard University; Physician, Massachusetts General Hospital.

MENTAL HOSPITAL. See HOSPITAL— *Care of the Mentally Ill.*

MENTAL ILLNESS. See PSYCHIATRY; PSYCHOPATHOLOGY; PSYCHOSIS.

MENTAL RETARDATES, Associations for Parents of. The organizational movement of parents with mentally retarded children to group together in associations for the purpose of being able better collectively to improve the welfare of their children began in the early 1930's. During the postwar period it expanded widely.

Among the reasons contributing to this growth are the following: (1) evidence that institutions operating under state appropriations are limited in what they can do for the children; (2) increasing awareness that the usual public school programs are unsuited for such children; (3) more general dissemination of knowledge of advances in techniques relating to mental retardation; (4) rise of questioning and challenge of the validity of the finality implicit in the words: "Nothing can be done for your child"; (5) desire of parents to learn what more can be done for these children and to pursue projects in their behalf; (6) strengthening conviction that the responsibility is social—that, just as funds are raised and appropriated for the benefit of the physically handicapped, so also should money be provided for building a fuller life for the mentally handicapped; and (7) realization that it is not enough spiritually just to care for one's own child.

The activities of these associations cover a wide range, being influenced by needs and reflecting available facilities. Some organizations, interested in improving state institutions, seek larger appropriations so that there will be adequate staffs and equipment, at the same time augmenting current funds by donations and doing many little things that bring pleasure to the children. Others devote their efforts to providing various services for children at home or in schools, such as clinics for diagnosis, therapy, and guidance; play and therapy groups; classes for children ineligible for enrollment in public schools; social clubs; sheltered workshops; vocational training centers; contacts for placement in industry; and educational classes for parents. Funds have been created to establish permanent homes or communities, and in several states, with the sponsorship of parent associations, bills have been enacted providing local aid for educating mentally retarded children.

The associations are nonprofit and, except in a few instances, membership is open to all interested persons. Members participate in the activities and regular meetings are held, often with speakers professional in the field of mental retardation. Through discussions thus afforded, parents come to accept the underlying problems as general and of broad community interest, detached from their emotional and subjective elements. Each association plans and pursues its projects, supplementing them in many cases by issuing news bulletins and pamphlets and fostering public education.

To further the common objectives of these groups the National Association of Parents and Friends of Mentally Retarded Children was formed in September 1950. Its purposes embraced all such children of all ages wherever they might be located. It served as a clearinghouse for information, fostered research and the training of personnel, acted as liaison with other bodies in this field, promoted legislation, and interpreted the movement to the general public. In 1953 the organization changed its name to the National Association for Retarded Children. By the late 1960's there were 100,000 individual members, with 50 state and 1,100 local groups. The association, with headquarters in New York City, has committees on international relations, education, vocational rehabilitation, governmental affairs, public health, early child care, recreation, parent guidance, and religious nurture.

WOODHULL HAY.

MENTAL RETARDATION is a limitation of intelligence due to lack of normal mental development rather than to mental disease or deterioration. It may be of any degree from dullness to profound idiocy. While the term covers many persons with a moderate handicap, it is most often applied to those with marked limitation of intelligence, whose mental capacity when adult will not be above that of an average child of 12. This group, also described as mentally deficient, subnormal, or feeble-minded, includes some 1 to 3 per cent of the general population. Mental deficiency is found in all classes of society and in all parts of the world. It has been known since the earliest times. Physical injury of the nervous system accounts for some cases; inherited factors, such as biochemical deficiencies, for others. Medical care consists chiefly of correcting remediable physical defects and improving general health. This does not change mental capacity but may improve the patient's ability to utilize his resources fully. Research encourages the hope that causes of retardation may be found, and some progress has been made toward prevention.

THE NATURE OF MENTAL RETARDATION

Mental deficiency or retardation must not be confused with mental illness. The mentally ill, psychotic, or insane person is one who has been normal but, due to known or unknown factors, has become mentally unbalanced. A mentally retarded individual is one in whom there is and always has been a lack of mental development.

The attitude of society toward the feeble-minded has progressed through the stages of abhorrence, rejection, and custody to sympathetic care. At present the emphasis is on suitable training and community supervision. The most highly developed program provides for the diversified needs of the group: (1) custody for those whose presence in the community would be inimical to its welfare; (2) specialized care for those whose needs cannot be met in the community; and (3) training for those who may, after the training period, take their places in the community with a minimum of supervision.

Primitive Attitude.—The mentally deficient members of early society were devoid of human rights and were left to fend for themselves. The Spartans disposed of them through abandonment, but Christianity preached tolerance toward all deviates, and similar attitudes of commiseration were a part of the teachings of other religions. The first recorded attempt to care for the feeble-minded was that offered by the bishop of Myra in the 4th century. That only custodial care—and not training—was offered may have been due to the fact that only the more pronounced and easily recognized cases of subnormality were identifiable.

During the Middle Ages the mentally deficient were confused with the insane, and the attitude toward them ranged from solicitude to persecution. It is likely that some care was given them in Flanders during the 13th century, but it was in France during the latter part of the 15th century and the early part of the 16th century that specialized care was organized by St. Vincent de Paul.

Scientific Approach.—The scientific care and training of the mentally deficient dates from the controversy which arose after the presentation by J. E. Marie Gaspard Itard (1774–1838) of the "Savage of Aveyron" before the Academy of Sciences in Paris in 1800. This 12-year-old boy, perhaps abandoned by his parents or lost in the woods at an early age, was the object of considerable scientific speculation as to the cause of his subnormal intelligence. Itard contended that he was untaught, and because of this was an idiot. But Philippe Pinel (1745–1826) held to the point of view that idiocy was congenital. Itard sought to substantiate his point of view and began a program of training. Although the boy was able to learn to some degree, Itard was finally forced to abandon the project of making him normal.

The clinical teaching program developed by Itard had in it many fine suggestions, and Itard's pupil, Édouard Seguin (1812–1880), devoted his life to the education of the feeble-minded. His system of sensory-motor training is described in detail in many of his writings. He came to America in 1850 and was an important influence in the establishment of the country's first institutions for the mentally deficient.

Early research laboratories, such as those established at Vineland, N. J., in 1906, and at Faribault, Minn., in 1910, under the direction of Henry H. Goddard and Fred Kuhlmann, respectively, contributed greatly to the understanding of the problem and to the development of training programs. The pioneer work of E. R. Johnstone and Joseph Beyers with the Committee on Provision, the publication of Goddard's *The Kallikak Family* (1912), and the introduction at Vineland, N. J., in 1909, of the original Binet-Simon tests for the measurement of intelligence are prominent milestones.

Understanding Mental Deficiency.—Specialists in a number of fields have made important contributions to the understanding of this group. The pediatrician, endocrinologist, pathologist, anthropologist, roentgenologist, psychiatrist, sociologist, educator, psychologist and others—each has made a significant contribution.

It early became apparent that mental deficiency could not be "cured" in the sense that a disease can be cured. Medical science is continuing to study the condition and some day a cure may be found, but at the present time the outlook for an early remedy is not hopeful.

The educator has discovered that the subnormal child can be trained within the limits of his ability, and many significant and highly worthwhile training programs have been developed. The sociologist has found that many can be helped to adjust to community life. The psychologist has established that he can be studied objectively, and his findings have been of considerable value to all other specialists concerned with the problems of mental deficiency.

Etiology.—The etiology or causative factors of mental deficiency are not thoroughly understood. In the individual case it is frequently extremely difficult to identify with certainty the specific cause or, perhaps, combination of causes.

During the past decade or two there has been a marked change in the overall concept of causation. Earlier research suggested that faulty heredity was a prominent factor in producing mental deficiency, but authorities rarely adhere to that point of view. While it is likely that it is still the most prominent single cause, the percentage of cases in which neuropathic ancestry is now considered to be the cause is very much lower than was previously thought to be true.

Upon thorough study of the antecedents and the growth and development of the individual child it is generally possible to determine whether the causative factors are endogenous or exogenous or, in other words, whether it is an hereditary or nonhereditary case, a primary or secondary case. Endogenous refers to gene variation, while exogenous refers to some modification of the organism.

Perhaps 50 per cent, or less, of the mentally retarded cases are endogenous in type, while the others are due to factors operating upon the organism prior to, during, or immediately following birth. Because of the difficulty of obtaining a truly representative sampling of the mentally deficient population, no estimate of the percentage of assigned causes is acceptable. Among the factors which have been found are: (1) injury *en utero*—injury during the birth process—and, infrequently, injury immediately following birth; (2) somatic variations due to little-understood changes in the functioning of the glands of internal secretion of the mother during the period of gestation; (3) diseases in early childhood accompanied by a high temperature. Other studies have pointed out that therapeutic X-ray treatment in the pelvic region of the pregnant mother —when such treatment is of a specified depth and frequency—will produce the microcephalic child; that incompatibility of the Rh factor in the blood of the mother may be found with a greater frequency in certain types of mental deficiency; and that an inordinate number of cases of mentally deficient children have a history of whooping cough at an early age.

Some of the hitherto rather well accepted causes—such as a fall in early childhood, alcoholism in the parents, fright, improper nourishment, and others of similar type—are no longer accepted with much credence.

Classification.—Mental deficiency is a symptom complex and is not a condition, the determination of which is dependent upon simple mental test results or the derivative of a mental test, the commonly used IQ (intelligence quotient). While the IQ may be helpful, as is the thermometer to a physician in diagnosing a disease, it fails when most critically needed. The skilled diagnostician relies upon a careful evaluation of such factors as birth conditions, genetic development, the results of formal and informal teaching, motor and verbal skills, and other evidences of maturation and responsiveness. In other words, the classification of mental deficiency is dependent upon exceedingly careful clinical studies.

The mentally deficient person is usually classified as to degree or grade. In the earliest days the profound mentally deficient, or feeble-minded, individual, as they were then called, was classified as the idiot; the next higher grade, as the imbecile; and the highest grade, as the feeble-minded. Goddard overcame this confusion by giving the name "moron" to the highest grade. Now there is a tendency to abandon the use, at least by some authorities, of these terms and to classify the mentally retarded into three main groups: the severely retarded (the idiot); the middle grade (imbecile); and the high grade (moron). These names are just as descriptive, and perhaps more so than the previously used designations, and the terms severely retarded, middle grade, and high grade do not carry with them unwarranted connotations.

The Severely Retarded.—The severely retarded mentally deficient person is generally the offspring of parents of healthy stock. The number of severely retarded individuals who come from poor stock—that is, the hereditary type—is relatively small. The condition is frequently recognizable at birth or at a very early age because of the unresponsiveness of the child to his surroundings, and readily recognized physical anomalies. At maturity the severely retarded mentally deficient individual is largely incapable of self-help, has little useful speech, is incapable of independent living, and is almost entirely dependent upon others for his comfort and welfare. This type of child at maturity rarely has a mental level in excess of three years and must be provided for throughout his entire life.

The Middle Grade.—The middle-grade child is not so easily detected at birth due to the fact that his retardation is less severe and is not particularly outstanding until perhaps the age of six months or a year. While this child can learn to take care of his bodily needs, be taught to perform many simple tasks, and move about quite freely in a limited environment, he is incapable, because of mental retardation, of managing his own affairs and, hence, is quite likely to become a social problem.

The High Grade.—The high-grade mentally deficient individual—and this group constitutes by far the largest number—is frequently unrecognized. He may be considered to be slow by his parents and teachers and "dumb" by his employer. The mental level concept is not of much help in classifying this grade. Indeed, clinicians adhere to the point of view that some individuals classifiable as normal may have a mental level as low as nine years and some high-grade mentally deficient individuals may have mental levels as high as 12 to 14 years. These individuals are very susceptible to training and, providing they have been in a situation and profited by a well-planned program, they may do much useful work. Because of their mental deficiency they always need some degree of external supervision. In many instances it is necessary to have this supplied by other persons, but it is possible to have it supplied by the situations in which they have been placed. Their scholastic potentials are not high, rarely exceeding the fifth grade; but in today's world there are a great many niches into which people may fit who are not able to read and calculate at high levels.

Clinical Varieties.—There are a number of clinical varieties, some of which are readily recognizable and occur with a frequency that is sufficient to cause mention to be made of them. The most frequently observed type is the Mongoloid type, miscalled because of the child's similarity in appearance to the child of the Mongolian race. Actually this type of mental deficiency appears throughout the entire world. It is reliably estimated that they appear two to three times in every 1,000 births. They are readily distinguishable by their slanting eyes, internal epicanthi, flat head, saddle-shaped nose, elongated and transverse-fissured tongue, short, stubby fingers, full and fissured lips, and general underdevelopment or hypoplasia. At maturity their mental level is generally between four and five years and rarely exceeds seven years. They have a sunny disposition and are playful and mischievous, although they can be outstandingly stubborn. They are the "aristocrats of the mentally deficient" because they appear in the better families. There is no agreement as to causal factors; but the discovery in 1958, by Dr. Jérôme Lejeune of the University of Paris and colleagues Drs. Marthe Gautier and Raymond Turpin, that mongols have an extra chromosome (a triple #21) opened new vistas. Biologists have since observed some 30 chromosomal anomalies associated with other diseases. In 1961 the French team also found that mongols have a tryptophan metabolism defect that may impair brain function. The findings stirred hope that a cure for mongolism may be found.

Cretinism is caused by severe thyroid imbalance that produces characteristic physiologic symptoms. Cretins are short in stature, being of the dwarf type and frequently also confused with the achondroplastic dwarf. The latter is a type of dwarfism frequently found in mental deficiency, characterized by a shortening of the long bones of the body. The torso is more or less normal, but the arms and legs are short due to a lack of a development of the chondrus, or the cartilage at the ends of the long bones.

The most frequent anomalies observed are the variations in cranial structure. Microcephaly, or small-headedness, is present in a large number of cases as is hydrocephaly, or large-headedness, due to excessive fluid in the brain cavity. Other conditions, such as dolichocephaly (long-headedness), appear frequently enough to be interesting but are not of importance.

Specialized Care and Training.—It is probably true that undue optimism will always prevail regarding the possibility of remedying mental deficiency. It is safe to say that there is no known training program or medical treatment which will so correct the defect in a mentally deficient individual that he will operate at normal levels of efficiency.

The mentally deficient require specialized care and training in the home, school, and community. The history of specialized care for the mentally deficient in the United States begins with the establishment in 1828 of the first experimental school, with an appropriation of $2,500 annually, in the Perkins Institute in Boston. This institution was incorporated in 1850 as the Massachusetts School for Idiotic and Feeble-Minded Youth, and in 1891 was renamed the Walter E. Fernald School and relocated at Waverly. New York State followed in the establishment of an institution in 1851, Ohio in 1857, Connecticut in 1858, Kentucky in 1860, and Illinois in 1865. The first private school for the care and training of the mentally deficient was established in 1852 at Media, Pa., and is now known as the Elwyn Training School and is located at Elwyn, Pa. Special classes in the public schools for the mentally retarded followed at a much later date— Providence in 1896, Chicago in 1898, New York in 1900, Philadelphia in 1901, and Los Angeles in 1902.

At the present time, although several states provide more than one residential institution for the specialized care of the mentally deficient of all ages, not all states make separate provisions for this type of individual. Special classes in the public schools are still inadequate, although more are being established from time to time. A great many of the states are recognizing the need for a differentiated attack upon the problem. This includes home training for the homebound, community classes, residential institution classes, and special classes in the public schools.

During World War II, authorities were astounded by two factors. One was the success attained by a great number of previously trained, high-grade mentally deficient boys in military service, and the degree of success attained by other mentally deficient boys and girls, young men, and young women in the war industries. Since that time there has been a marked reduction in the number of high-grade mentally deficient individuals on the waiting lists for the residential training schools. This is, no doubt, largely due to the fact that industry has found it possible to use these hands in simplified, routine operations.

While it is true that the mentally deficient contribute more than their share of social ills, it is not true to the extent once believed. They are the last to be hired and the first to be fired. They do appear more frequently on the relief rolls, and the estimated 1,500,000 in the United States cost the taxpayers a great deal of money. A careful estimate in 1947 placed this relief figure at more than $2,000,000,000.

It is not true, however, that most crimes are committed by the mentally deficient. In New Jersey a study was made in 1937 of 32,000 admissions to the penal, correctional, and juvenile training institutions extending over an 18-year period. In each of the reporting institutions well-trained psychologists saw each individual, making careful clinical studies. Out of the 32,000 admissions approximately 9 per cent were found to be mentally deficient. This is considerably lower than figures previously reported. It ranged from between 25 and 30 per cent in the juvenile delinquents to about 5 per cent in the male adult group.

A comparatively recent movement of some importance in the field has been the development of groups composed of the parents and friends of mentally retarded children who are interested in the development of additional and more adequate facilities and the better understanding of the problem. More than 100 such groups have come into being in the United States.

The single organization in the United States devoted exclusively to the problem of mental deficiency is the American Association on Mental Deficiency. This organization, founded in 1876, numbers among its membership only those who are working professionally in the field or primarily interested in mental deficiency. The association publishes the *American Journal of Mental Deficiency* and the *A.A.M.D. News*. The International Council for Exceptional Children, composed largely of educators, is interested in the retarded child as one of several groups of exceptional children. The National Association for Mental Health, primarily interested in the mentally ill, devotes some attention to mental deficiency. The National Association of Parents and Friends of the Mentally Retarded (see MENTAL RETARDATES, ASSOCIATIONS FOR PARENTS OF) is a lay organization in the field.

Bibliography.—Goddard, H. H., *The Kallikak Family* (New York 1912); Doll, E. A., *Clinical Studies in Feeble-Mindedness* (Boston 1917); Davies, S. P., *Social Control of the Mentally Deficient* (New York 1930); Itard, J. E. Marie Gaspard, *The Wild Boy of Aveyron*, tr. by George and Muriel Humphrey (New York 1932); Wallin, J.E.W., *Education of Mentally Handicapped Children* (New York 1955); Sarason, S.B., *Psychological Problems in Mental Deficiency*, 3d ed. (New York 1959); Benda, Clemens E., *Child with Mongolism* (New York 1960); Tredgold, A.F. and Soddy, K., *Textbook of Mental Deficiency*, 10th ed. (Baltimore 1964).

(L.N.Y.).

HOME CARE FOR THE RETARDED CHILD

Good home care is the greatest help for the retarded child. The first signs of retardation may be delayed teething, walking, and talking; lack of interest in the environment; and persistence of infantile habits. As soon as parents are aware that the child is not developing at the usual rate, advice should be sought from a specialist in this field or from a child-guidance clinic. A diagnosis indicating the degree of retardation is essential to good home management. Knowing the child's maximum possibilities, the parents should aim at helping him realize them and make the most of whatever ability he has. In daily training the chief consideration is to keep in mind the mental age of the child and manage him according to his capacity rather than according to his actual age. A subnormal child develops as other children do, but at a slower rate, so that when he reaches maturity and mental growth ceases he has not acquired average adult intelligence.

In general, all methods that benefit normal children will benefit the subnormal child if they are modified according to his ability to understand. Another general principle is that the family must be thought of as a whole, and a balanced family life maintained, without lavishing the means and time of the parents on the subnormal to the detriment of the normal. If the child requires so much attention that it is not possible to have a fairly normal home life, it may be desirable to seek institutional care.

Special measures will partly offset the special handicap. Retarded children sometimes have less than average resistance to disease, and precautions for maintaining health should be continuous. Even more important is the development of wholesome personality. In emotional stability retarded children vary as much as the normal. Some are very stable, others highly unstable. The backward child, however, is subject to emotional stresses not usually met by others. Ingenuity and patience may be needed to counter them. Security in the affection of parents, necessary for all children, is especially needed by the retarded, who suffer many rebuffs and disappointments outside the home.

Parents will do well to give constant evidence of affection and, while not indulging the child, give enough attention so that he has a feeling of personal recognition. To assure him the confidence and satisfaction that come from achievement, it is desirable to arrange chance for success through games and small tasks that are within his ability. Failures are to be avoided insofar as possible, and praise for accomplishment, however small, should be generous. The retarded child is often rejected by playmates of his own age, but he may play happily with younger children near his mental age. If he has brothers and sisters, they should be accustomed to including him in their pastimes, but not to a point where they feel him a burden or are denied the usual contacts with other children. Planned group play and simple outings are other devices for providing companionship and variety. Opportunities should be made for using all the faculties that are normal—for example, ability to sing.

When the child passes infancy, training toward self-help is begun. It is useless to attempt habit training until there is enough physiological development to enable the child to control functions, but it should begin as soon as practicable and continue until he can attend to personal needs. He can be encouraged to feed and help dress himself as soon as he has sufficient muscular coordination. Such training requires much patience, but it is very valuable to the child, besides relieving the mother of unnecessary work. Less important habits deserve consideration. Attention-getting devices, unpleasant mannerisms, or awkward gait and posture should be overcome if possible, since they mark the child as different from others. Indirect methods, such as imitation and suggestion, usually give better results than direct commands, which may make the child self-conscious.

Discipline should approximate that for normal children, but be adapted to the slower rate of learning. To be effective, discipline does not have to be severe, but it must be consistent. The subnormal child is somewhat more suggestible than the normal and has less sense of the consequences of his actions. Parents will therefore want to guard against undesirable friendships, especially as the child grows older and spends more time away from home. Reliable measures against making wrong associations are to provide companionship of the right kind, and to plan for plenty of occupation that holds the interest.

All but the most severely handicapped are capable of useful work. Mental defectives are found in a great variety of occupations but are best fitted for unskilled labor under supervision. In most cases, partial self-support is all that can be expected, but some are entirely self-supporting and even help relatives. The degree of deficiency roughly determines earning power, but other factors, such as stable personality and good work habits, influence employability. Preparation for the future begins in childhood. For those of very limited capacity, it is directed toward the maximum of self-help and usefulness, for those of higher intelligence to employability. The home program does not attempt to develop skills, but rather such habits and attitudes as courtesy, punctuality, self-confidence, feeling of responsibility, and ease in getting along with other people. Beginning with simple duties like dusting, washing vegetables, and feeding pets, the child shares in the activities of the home, at first with supervision, later without. If coordination is poor, work involving the large muscles is to be preferred. As he grows older, harder tasks, such as doing errands and making beds, are assigned. Proficiency compatible with increasing ability should be required. The child may be expected to do his share of repetitive jobs, like washing dishes, but he should not be made a household drudge. His activities should be varied and gradually broadened in scope, both inside and outside the home, and if there are any special aptitudes, they should be cultivated for possible economic value, but in any case for the satisfaction they give.

Often overlooked are the possibilities for usefulness of those too handicapped to be employable. By taking a large share of home duties, they sometimes free another member of the family for paid work, or add to the family income by acting as assistants. A measure of appreciation for such services goes far toward their contentment and happiness.

The care of a retarded child makes heavy demands on the family. Anxiety is often a chief part of the burden. Parents may find it a relief to give up specific objectives which may be unattainable, and set themselves a goal which it is possible to reach—namely, making the child as happy and as useful as his limitation permits.

(K.G.E.).

THE RETARDED PUPIL IN SCHOOL

In the schools of the United States there are many nonacademic pupils—those who, at the age of 15, will be unable to read at a sixth-grade level with interest and with profit. Such pupils should be considered in four categories: (1) the socially handicapped; (2) the socially maladjusted; (3) the clinical academic cases; and (4) the mentally deficient.

Socially Handicapped Pupils.—These are the children who are not working at normal grade level because of improper or insufficent instruction, physical defect, or poor home or neighborhood conditions. Such children are capable intellectually of doing normal or superior work. They are not doing such work because of external factors.

It is the business of the school with children in this category to see that, insofar as possible, every remediable physical or social handicap is removed or alleviated. Simultaneously the school must see, through proper guidance, that such pupils are started on an educational program that will aid them to realize their potentialities. The same program will not benefit all socially handicapped pupils. For those who have learned incorrectly a remedial program will be necessary. Those who have learned insufficiently will require a make-up program which will enable them to acquire the essential learning tools without being denied too much of the content appropriate for their social age. In both remedial and make-up programs, however, the teacher must face the fact that some content or cultural material must be eliminated in order to ensure the acquisition of the learning tools. Otherwise the pupil will be asked to do the impossible, and failure—emotional, social, physical, academic, or vocational—will result. For some socially handicapped pupils, therefore, a different developmental program must be provided. No socially handicapped pupil should be permitted to enter a remedial or make-up program unless it is reasonably certain that: (1) he will attain an actual sixth-grade proficiency by the end of his fifteenth year; or (2), being of college caliber, he will be given the sustained economic and emotional backing necessary to permit him to complete professional training. It is the business of the school to ensure sustained backing for pupils capable of utilizing it.

No one knows the incidence of the socially handicapped. Speaking from his experience in Delaware, George H. Henry wrote in *Harper's Magazine* (January 1946):

"By testing any graduating class of any high school in the country, the skeptic can see for himself what is an old story to teachers: that a third of the high school cannot read on a fifth-grade level or write a coherent paragraph reasonably free of errors. . . . The pupils who compose this lower one-third are not to be confused with the mentally backward (a far smaller group comprising only about five per cent of a school or less)."

The important thing to remember is that 90 per cent of the pupils in an average school are capable of achieving sixth-grade proficiency, not mere certification, before 16, provided that two steps are taken early enough: (1) their remediable handicaps are removed; and (2) they are placed on realistic, functioning educational programs.

Socially Maladjusted Pupils.—These children have an emotional disturbance which keeps them from doing the work of which they are capable intellectually. The disturbance may have come originally from defective environment, from

defective physique, or from defective mentality. In any case the deviation has resulted in a pattern or habit of action which these individuals cannot change without help.

The school has the same responsibilities toward the socially maladjusted as toward the socially handicapped: (1) to see that handicaps are removed or minimized; and (2) to make sure that the children have worthwhile school programs. But these responsibilities will entail different timing and methods than those employed for the socially handicapped.

For the socially maladjusted, whatever the primary cause or causes of the maladjustment, the emotional disturbance must be given precedence in treatment. And the treatment of this disturbance may, and probably will, so interfere with the school program that only a different developmental program can be expected to be of benefit to them either as children or as adults. This, of course, is equally true for a second reason. Although the fact is seldom or never mentioned in popular treatises, the general intellectual level of caught delinquents is exceptionally low: the lowest 10 per cent of the population intellectually furnishes about 50 per cent of the caught delinquents.

The different developmental program must be purposeful, however. Although relationship emphases will vary, the same educational goals or objectives that apply to all other children apply to the socially maladjusted. These children have the right to leave school capable of meeting adult responsibilities through contribution at the level of their potentialities.

About 1 out of 200 children is grossly maladjusted socially, and another 5 are in need of modified treatment. Both groups need the aid of clinical experts, but provision of functional school programs will help to arrest deterioration and prevent its onset. Schools, therefore, have three responsibilities with respect to the socially maladjusted: (1) to provide sufficient expert clinical service; (2) to provide different yet purposeful developmental school programs for the two groups of grossly maladjusted; and (3) to provide realistic school programs for all children as a preventive measure.

Clinical Academic Cases.—These are children who suffer from some specific defect in learning patterns, such as seeing words in reverse. Some experts feel that the basic cause is physiological; others, that it is emotional. Whatever the cause, a child should be turned over to an academic clinician as soon as such a handicap is discovered, since it is extremely important that the wrong pattern not be deepened. As with all nonacademic pupils, however, the real cause of the defect must be ascertained. A child may be learning ineffectively because of any one of a number of reasons: (1) a lack of concepts around which to build learning; (2) emotional blocking connected with learning; (3) emotional blocking not so connected, economic and cultural causes being especially important; (4) physical defect, particularly one due to dietary, glandular, visual, or auditory causes; (5) mental defect; (6) emotional defect; (7) poor or inadequate guidance; (8) incorrect curriculum; (9) insufficient teaching; (10) poor teaching; (11) poor learning; (12) clinical academic defect.

After the cause has been ascertained, a complete program should be outlined. Such a program would provide the following: (1) prognosis; (2) plans for amelioration or sublimation of the handicap, if possible; (3) educational plan; (4) guidance plan for child and family; (5) administrative plans to mesh subprograms and contributing personnel and to ensure that the program is carried out; (6) plans for continuous evaluation and replanning; and (7) plans for refitting the individual into society, where necessary or possible. The prognosis must be as honest as the diagnosis. A reading defect might require the services of an academic clinician, an ophthalmologist, a psychiatrist, a teacher of Braille, or a teacher of the retarded. And a reading deficiency might necessitate the initiation of a school program emphasizing long-time academic proficiency or vocational proficiency. Once started, however, an honest and intelligent program should be continued until some better program becomes apparent. Standards of promotion from one level to another within a school program, for instance, should be strict and honest. If a child cannot master a given curriculum, he should not have it. There is no education by osmosis, and there should be no planning by default.

At most there are very few true clinical academic cases. A somewhat larger number function in this way. For both groups, academic clinicians must be provided.

Mentally Deficient Pupils.—Technically, the terms "subnormal" or "inferior" are applicable to persons with below-average intelligence, and thus to about one fifth of the general population. The term "feeble-minded" has been pre-empted, though not technically, for use with individuals so defective intellectually that they will never be able to manage themselves or their affairs without a large amount of supervision. The terms "mentally deficient," "retarded," "mentally retarded," and "mentally handicapped," which can be used interchangeably, designate a smaller group than the subnormal or inferior, but, in common parlance, a larger group than the feeble-minded.

Of the one fifth of the general population that is below average in intelligence, the great majority can profit in reasonable degree from a modified regular school program, but some must be on a separate curriculum because their power of adjustment is limited. In other words, under fortunate circumstances the majority can profit from a modified regular program; under unfortunate circumstances they will need a different program. For those more grossly limited in power of adjustment—the mentally deficient—no degree of modification of the regular curriculum will provide profitable schooling. They cannot profit from a remedial or make-up program, either of which, ostensibly, would return them eventually to a regular program. The mentally deficient require a different developmental program.

Among the mentally deficient are the feeble-minded. These include the idiots, who cannot guard themselves against physical injury; the imbeciles, who are capable of a measure of self-help, ordinarily within an institution; and the low-grade morons, who often are capable of maintaining themselves in private competitive enterprise, provided they have constant supervision. Also included among the mentally deficient are many individuals who, under fortuitous circumstances, are capable of managing their affairs in adulthood without supervision, provided they have special education in childhood. These are the high-grade morons and certain borderline cases.

All inferiors are limited by constitutional defect. This limitation results, and is manifest, in a circumscribed power of adaptation to circumstances. For a given individual, inferior as well as normal and superior, happiness in a particular situation will result if the power of adaptation, internal and external, is equal to the demands of circumstance, internal and external. As a result, individuals reasonably similar in power may lead lives varying greatly in happiness or success. But no retardate is capable of getting enough from ordinary schooling to enable him to meet satisfactorily the demands of living. This is the distinguishing feature of mental deficiency.

Implications of Mental Deficiency.—Mental deficiency is actually a physical defect, but since it is not always apparent, it mistakenly is classified under a separate category. Moreover, since society for some reason has greater feelings of guilt about amentia than, for example, about dementia or blindness, persons with mental deficiency are accorded less consideration. We are sympathetic toward the blind child shown on the screen; we laugh at the comedian who imitates a moron. Many intelligent people who would be among the first to demand special service for the crippled, the blind, or the deaf would deny special service to the mentally deficient. Such people might put the idiot out of sight in an institution, but they would not give the more capable defective the special education that would enable him to keep out of an institution.

Mental deficiency has definite implications, many of which are unknown to the general public. A weak mind, for instance, is not accompanied ordinarily by a strong back. It is accompanied by a weak back, and physical defects are more than twice as frequent among the mentally deficient as among the normal. Moreover, the defective generally does not adjust easily to repetitive work, particularly on an assembly line. He works best in small groups where there is some change of operation and some personal contact with an overseer. Mental deficiency, especially among certain types, does not guarantee placidity. Not only does the lower intellectual group furnish a grossly undue proportion of caught delinquents, but the defective in the classroom is about five times as liable as the normal child to need specialized help with personal problems.

These characteristics have definite vocational implications. Only in the most unusual cases is the retardate able to maintain himself without supervision in semiskilled work; and studies, as distinguished from generalizations based on a few exceptional cases, repeatedly have shown that the retarded do best in unskilled work. Even here, however, they are competing with their more capable fellows, since about 20 per cent of the work in the United States falls at this level. Low-level jobs are terminal and not interim jobs for the mentally deficient, and yet such individuals often leave school without the necessary intensive preparation for the lowest-level jobs. By the very nature of mental deficiency, a boy so handicapped will not learn the required work casually. Thus, when the time of employment comes, the normal boy will get the job instead of the boy who is mentally deficient, not because the latter cannot do the work, but because he has not received the extra training that he needs in order to have equality of opportunity for employment. In order to obtain immediate employment and to retain it through his employable years, the mentally deficient must be better fitted for his work, in terms of particularized training, than his competitors who have average or better than average intelligence.

The basic characteristic of mental deficiency is limitation—in adaptive power, in associative power, in learning speed—and this limitation is so great that it extends to the learning and practicing of the simple operations which the average child picks up casually. Yet, upon leaving school, mentally deficient children must meet the competition of the more capable groups. Society does not give them any special consideration with respect to employment; in fact, ordinarily it discriminates against them. Therefore, the only protection of the mentally deficient against such a laissez-faire condition is special education.

A Valid Philosophy of Special Education. —Different philosophies have been utilized as a guide in the education of the retarded. Historically speaking, each may have been necessary at some stage in the development of a valid program, but some school systems still cling to a philosophy long discarded by more progressive systems.

An early philosophy, starting about 1900, could be termed the "relief" philosophy. Under this system, special education was established to relieve normal children in the regular grades, the emphasis being placed solely on their good. As a result of this negative attitude toward the mentally retarded, anything was possible or accepted in the special class. The children and some unfortunate teacher were thrown together in an out-of-the-way classroom, and the child's time was spent in meaningless nothingness.

A more enlightened but not more productive philosophy was that of "happiness," which also flourished in the early 1900's. Under this philosophy, special education was used to remove children from extremely unhappy classroom situations and to place them with their mental equals so that they would not suffer from the unfair competition of normal children. It was believed that, by giving the mentally deficient child command of the simplest academic tools, the most rudimentary manual skills, and the most generalized attitudes, he could be made into a reasonably self-sufficient, self-supporting citizen. This type of program failed because of the urbanization of society, the rise of cultural standards and educational levels, and the mechanization of industry. Experience showed that the mastery of simple academic skills, of generalized skills, and of generalized attitudes did not produce employable or contented individuals.

In the 1920's, with newer forms of education, many educators wishfully thought that the slow child was receiving an adequate education by performing certain manual parts of an activity, such as making dioramas or doing finger painting, while the more able child prepared reports and developed dramatic presentations. Time showed that such an emasculated program for the mentally deficient left them without any real facility in meeting adult responsibilities, slowed down the rate of progress for the more able, and degenerated eventually into that true form of segregation: remaining in the same room without worthwhile participation or emotional rapport.

In the 1930's, it was discovered that the retarded had some capabilities; and so the pendulum swung from "nothing" to "everything," and the emphasis was placed on a "return-to-the-grades" or "salvage" philosophy. Academic training was stressed out of all proportion to the children's needs or abilities. The kindest thing that can be said about the program which resulted was that it did not fool its victims.

Another philosophy, not more valid, was the "handwork" philosophy. In this the child was given something "real to do." He was urged to saw and hammer, plane and chisel; and somehow, some day, it was expected that he would take his place in the ranks of honest, skilled labor.

It is now recognized that no philosophy is valid for the education of the retarded that does not guide us toward providing an education beneficial to the retarded themselves. Such a philosophy must be based on a realistic view of the strengths and weaknesses of these children as well as on the place they eventually will occupy in society. It is believed that the retarded have a potential contribution to make to the world in which they live and that it is a primary function of special education to help the retarded to realize such potentialities.

As early as 1931 the Committee on Special Classes of the White House Conference on Child Health and Problems, in *Special Education: The Handicapped and the Gifted* (see *Bibliography*), stated:

"Serious consideration must be given to the curriculum best suited to the needs of subnormal [retarded] children. The aim is to develop the child's mental capacities and the control of his emotions to the point of adequate social adjustment and the curriculum must necessarily be determined in part by adult requisities. The first point to consider is what work these subnormal [retarded] will eventually be able to do."

In *A Guide to Curriculum Adjustment for Mentally Retarded Children* (see *Bibliography*), Dr. Elise H. Martens, senior specialist in the education of exceptional children in the United States Office of Education, said:

"Education for the mentally retarded is not different in its aim from education for any group of children. This aim is to teach the individual how to live better; to teach him to use all of his capacities; to teach him to become a useful member of the social group."

Dr. Charles Scott Berry wrote in *Education of Handicapped School Children in Michigan* (see *Bibliography*):

"There has been much time, money, and effort wasted in the education of subnormal [retarded] children through the failure to recognize clearly the proper aim of education in the case of this type of child. Since about 20% of the adult population are engaged in unskilled labor the folly of attempting to prepare children of the most inferior intelligence for skilled labor or for electrical work is self-evident. The aim of the teacher, after a thorough trial in the special class has demonstrated the impossibility of the pupils ever successfully doing regular grade work, should be to prepare him to become a law-abiding, self-supporting citizen in the simplest occupations."

Thus, conscientious educators have come to see that the retarded, if they are to realize their potentialities, must be given a different developmental program rather than a remedial or impractical adaptation of a normal program. Such education must give to each child a competency in (1) the technique of self-measurement; (2)

a knowledge of suitable job families and social requirements; (3) the technique of meshing abilities with vocational and social requirements; and (4) the desire for social contribution. The whole program for the mentally retarded must be built around the achievement of vocational and social competence, for here, if anywhere, the retarded will most nearly approach normalcy. This different developmental program is called occupational education.

Essentials of an Effective Program.—Occupational education seeks to give the retarded sufficient freedom to enable him to develop his capabilities for self-support and yet sufficient protection from the rigors of competition to keep him from being too hopelessly discouraged to utilize these capabilities. It provides a series of occupational-social skills leading toward a social maturity that includes occupational adjustment as a part of total adjustment. To accomplish this aim, the complete program includes the following:

(1) *Occupational information*—giving the pupil information concerning the work available to him (considering both youngster and community): how this work is done (job analyses); and what its importance is to the world.

(2) *Vocational guidance*—guiding the pupil to measure his own abilities against the requirements of the job in which he is interested; showing other jobs in the same work area.

(3) *Vocational training*—giving the pupil training in the manual skills found in the work area (25 per cent); training in the nonmanual skills necessary in the work area (25 per cent); training in the general habits, attitudes, and skills common to all good individuality, workmanship, and citizenship (50 per cent).

(4) *Vocational placement*—providing the individual with actual job placement.

(5) *Social placement*—adjusting the adult on the job and in the freedom of his first independence for as long a period as may be necessary.

In New York City the teacher is responsible for the first three of these phases, which he provides ordinarily in the classroom, using the eight following large cores of instruction:

Core	Chronological age
The home	7– 9
The neighborhood	10
The borough	11
The city	12
Study of job areas	13
Ways of choosing, getting, and holding a job	14
Ways of spending one's income wisely	15
The worker as a citizen and social being	16–17

Throughout these cores great emphasis is placed on the nonmanual or social skills. These are the skills, not of a manual or technical nature, that likewise are needed for living and working. Several recent studies show that from 60 to 80 per cent of workers lose their jobs for nonmanual reasons. Such skills include: personal health and appearance, manners, means of getting employment, means of keeping a job, means of adjusting to accidents and unemployment, ways to get along with the employer, ways to get along with fellow workers, budgets and banking, ways to travel in the city, suggestions for living at home or away from home, recreation, personal and group relationships, and citizenship.

The ordinary child learns many of these things in the process of living. For the re-

tarded, however, the mastery of these fields of knowledge and skill cannot be left to chance. This is true both because of the way the retarded learn and because service jobs, for which the majority of the retarded are best fitted, are more dependent for success upon general characteristics than upon the specific skills usually associated with vocational training. This training cannot be put off until the retarded is chronologically and socially mature enough to think of job seeking. Many of these skills must be consciously sought by teachers through careful grading and good teaching until they become in the children automatic responses to specific situations. In this regard the Committee on Special Classes of the White House Conference made two significant statements:

(1) "Subnormal [retarded] children obviously cannot acquire as much in quantity as the typical group and they also require more time for any given quantity than is the case with typical children.

(2) ". . . the lower the degree of potentiality the earlier should attention be centered on vocation. The subnormal [retarded] child can be put at productive work earlier than the child who needs more time for preliminary training but he should be prepared for his work as long as possible."

Few things are more certain than the fact of human variation. In one sense there is no such thing as an absolute standard of normalcy. People vary in stature, in color, in weight, in glandular balance, in visual acuity, in emotional balance, in mental ability. Some of these variations have a genetic basis or at least a prenatal basis; others arise largely from environmental circumstances. Most are conditioned by a complex interrelationship of prenatal and environmental factors. These differences account for much of the richness of life and also for many of its problems. The problem, therefore, for educators as well as for society as a whole, is to find a reasonably workable way to prevent the variation which is destructive in result without weakening the variation which is constructive. Obviously, no one knows with certainty how to do this. It is quite sure, however, that it must be attempted. In fact, it is being attempted, though far too seldom consciously and under an intelligent plan.

Like society in general, school people move with much more directness and with much more assurance where the object is concrete. Thus, the great majority of educators would attempt consciously to provide adequate school lunches to the undernourished or for the malnourished. They would provide showers, well-lighted rooms, recreational facilities, even competent vocational guidance and placement workers. There would be far less unanimity and assurance, however, in making realistic provision for the building of socially acceptable intellectual and emotional patterns. We not only know less of how such patterns are made; we are far less certain of the patterns we desire to make.

Throughout his life the individual is engaged in balancing (a continuing task) what he is (his tools, his spirituality, his thought processes, his emotional desires, his physical needs) against what he must do (his problems, human relationships, and physical surroundings) in order to achieve the greatest possible personal satisfaction at the level of his development (survival, physical enjoyment, gregariousness, aesthetics, logic, social contribution). More simply, every maturing individual is accommodating his changing body to his expanding responsibilities.

For at least 90 per cent of adolescents, achieving acceptable economic status implies achieving economic self-sufficiency. The young person without further training and experiences is expected to be able and willing (that is, emotionally able) to earn his own living in open competition with all others. It is easy of course to overestimate the importance of this fact, but the practice, among curriculum builders especially, is to underestimate it. Yet this and other adjustments or accommodations listed in this article are the required learnings of young people. Whatever the ostensible goals set up by educators, these are the learnings with which the school is expected to give great help. In other words, schools were established and are maintained to help young people achieve such competencies more easily. In a very real sense the nominal goals are merely the media by whose mastery school people have thought the required learnings could be achieved.

Almost all individuals fail sometimes; a few fail so repeatedly and so grossly that they must be considered as problems. Some of the problem children are not school problems in the ordinary use of the term. But before we can determine whether or not a child with a gross problem unmet is a school problem, we must decide what society reasonably can expect from a school. If a school is responsible only for giving pupils academic proficiency, then a school problem is only a child who is not making "normal" academic progress. If a school is responsible only for helping a child to make immediate adjustments, then even the child who acts "acceptably" only when nothing is demanded of him is not a school problem. If, however, a school is responsible for helping an individual to make a total adjustment, both while in school and throughout his life, then the school problem is the child who is not making reasonable progress along all the lines—spiritual, social, physical, emotional, vocational, and academic—which he presumably will need throughout his life.

Educators have recognized the desirability of modifying school programs to meet the needs of individual pupils. Too often, however, such modifications have been mere progressive "waterings down" of subject matter rather than an introduction of new content not technically academic in nature. The general order in which the school has placed its emphasis has been as follows: (1) academic proficiency; (2) occupational competency (largely the concern of vocational schools and commercial departments); (3) competency in social adjustment.

It is clear that for a great many pupils this order of emphasis cannot be justified, and that for at least 20 per cent of the pupils it must be reversed if education is to help such individuals appreciably. The three competencies naturally must be integrated, but the first objective must be to develop citizens capable of making total adjustments as readily and as satisfactorily as possible. This is necessary to ensure comparative maturity, both social and occupational, since almost every study which has been made of job holding and success reveals the need for personal qualities that will enable a person to make adjustments socially acceptable.

As a second objective, the schools must seek to develop economic and occupational competency of a type which will permit the young person to find a place where he can succeed in the world of work. This concern with the vocational objective does not mean that "occupational adjustment is the sole goal of the school program. Rather, what is meant is this: occupational adjustment is one of the inter-related, individual goals of the accepted program. . . . Education which does not seek occupational adjustment is incomplete." [1]

Academic competencies as such must take third place in school objectives for most pupils, especially when school goals are considered in terms of present day courses of study and curriculums. It is estimated that one child out of five of school age is not capable of benefiting at 16 years of age from a school program requiring mastery of academic skills beyond the sixth-grade level. With maturational promotion in effect in the elementary and junior high schools, it must be expected that senior high schools will have approximately this percentage of slow learners in their student bodies.

The retardation encountered will be the result of many factors, heredity being only one. Whatever the cause of the retardation, however, no practical change of teaching method will enable this group of pupils to master academic skills beyond the sixth-grade level. The adaptation of schooling to their needs and abilities involves far more than a meshing of educational guidance goals with existing grade levels and a slowing down of the rate of presentation. Instead, there is necessary a reconsideration of skills from many levels. A lower-level job from an economic standpoint may require the inclusion of certain skills from the standard eighth-grade level and the omission of others on the third-grade level. For example, certain jobs have certain vocabularies. A boy may be reading at the fourth-grade level; he may need to know 20 words at the eighth-grade level. He must be given these words irrespective of his reading level. In point are the words on social security and job applications. It should be stressed, however, that pupils are limited not only with respect to the degree of difficulty which they can master, but also with respect to the amount they can master even at the levels they can achieve. Thus, in order to get the time to teach —not merely to present—the words on a social security blank, it may be necessary to omit fractions with denominators above four, even though such fractions may be standard fifth-grade content and within the grasp of students capable of doing fifth-grade work. There must be long-term planning to ensure the teaching of first things first, both in the sense of order of presentation and in the sense of individual life needs. If it is a question of teaching a pupil to master fractions or to get along with his employer, the latter must be taught. If a pupil cannot be taught to get along with both the boys in his block and the boys halfway around the world, then the pupil must be taught to get along with the boys in his block.

The schools must be equally certain that the content is meaningful and challenging to the pupils. It would be absurd to use books of

[1] R. H. Hungerford and C. J. De Prospo, "Occupational Education and the Curriculum," *Occupational Education,* February 1946.

ninth-grade or even sixth-grade difficulty with a boy capable at the time of using only a fourth-grade book. It is equally absurd to use books with content, particularly social content, much below the pupil's needs and abilities. Thus, for a fourth-grade pupil of 15 years of age, a fourth-grade reader built around the interests of 11-year-old pupils may be almost as bad as a sixth-grade reader. The latter, the pupil is incapable of using mentally (for the time being); the former, the pupil is incapable of using for psychological backgrounds. Help can come from learning about the Eskimos only if such studies deal with the problems of the Eskimo father in bringing in enough blubber, making the man next door keep the dogs chained, and helping a son to realize that life is more than blubber or dogs. A real understanding of actual Eskimo life might be helpful, though probably not as helpful as content nearer home would be; generalizations about trivialities of Eskimo life cannot be justified.

It is the business of the school to give the individual, insofar as possible, all the experiences necessary for building the attitudes, skills, and habits he must use, at least in his beginning independence. Anything which does that is learning. Individualization of instruction is concerned quite as much with content as with technique. There is necessary a thorough reconsideration of the meaning of school goals. Even for the most retarded of the school group it is not necessary to omit or change any of the cardinal aims of education. It is necessary to reinterpret the meaning of applying goals to individual abilities and needs.

Occupational education is an inclusive program. It begins when the retardate enters the special class and does not cease until the need has ceased, however long that may be. It is an inclusive program also because it consciously attempts to prepare the child for many possible life situations. All encounter depressions, booms, war, and peace, and a complete education cannot leave an individual unprepared for any. This is true for all individuals; it is especially true for those who by very definition are unable to make quick and efficient adaptations to new situations.

Occupational education is not a technique of teaching. It is comparable to the social studies in that it provides a series of occupational-social skills leading toward social maturity. Because of its nature, however, it tends to become the interest core for all teaching in a special class. Occupational education is the content of instruction. As such it may be taught by any method, although it is believed that the activity or unit approach will produce the best results.

A continuing tendency in special education has been to try to lift the child above his capabilities. After viewing the total pattern of the individual in relation to this total life, occupational education teaches the possible skills basic to total adjustment. With this point of view, academic skills are relegated to their proper place, becoming only one part of the cores used for instruction.

All teaching presupposes the existence of goals based, at least suppositionally, upon an awareness of pupil needs (including real interests) and abilities. Occupational education consciously accepts responsibility for meeting pupil needs in the order of urgency. It does not limit pupil needs, but neither does it suppose that education occurs through osmosis. A boy does not become a worthwhile member of society by living in a town containing worthwhile members of society. A school has the responsibility of providing each pupil with the curriculum which will enable that pupil to function in school days and in adulthood in the most effective and happy way possible.

(L. N. Y.)   L. N. YEPSEN,
Director, Division of Classification and Education, Department of Institutions and Agencies, State of New Jersey.

(K. G. E.)   KATHARINE G. ECOB,
Consultant on Mental Hygiene, Veterans Administration; formerly with New York State Committee on Mental Hygiene.

(R. H. H.)   RICHARD H. HUNGERFORD,
Director, Bureau for Children with Retarded Mental Development, New York City Board of Education; Editor, "American Journal of Mental Deficiency."

Bibliography.—Berry, C. S., *Education of Handicapped School Children in Michigan*, Bulletin No. 11, Michigan Department of Public Instruction (Lansing, Mich., 1926); Whipple, H., D., *Making Citizens of the Mentally Limited* (Bloomington, Ill., 1927); Tredgold, A. F., *Mental Deficiency*, 5th ed. (New York 1929); Davies, S. P., *Social Control of the Mentally Deficient* (New York 1930); Berry, R. J. A., and Gordon, R. G., *The Mental Defective* (New York 1931); Scheidemann, N. V., *The Psychology of Exceptional Children* (Boston 1931); White House Conference on Child Health and Protection, Committee on Special Classes, *Special Education: The Handicapped and the Gifted* (New York 1931); Glueck, Eleanor, and Glueck, Sheldon, eds., *Preventing Crime: A Symposium* (New York 1936); Martens, E. H., *A Guide to Curriculum Adjustment for Mentally Retarded Children*, Bulletin No. 11, United States Office of Education (Washington 1936); id., *Occupational Experiences for Handicapped Adolescents in Day Schools*, Bulletin No. 30, United States Office of Education (Washington 1937); Educational Policies Commission, National Education Association, *Social Services and the Schools* (Washington 1939); *Meeting the Needs of the Mentally Retarded*, Bulletin No. 420, Pennsylvania Department of Public Instruction (Harrisburg, Pa., 1939); Garrison, K. C., *The Psychology of Exceptional Children* (New York 1940); Hungerford, R. H., "The Detroit Plan for the Occupational Education of the Mentally Retarded," *American Journal of Mental Deficiency*, pp. 102-08, July 1941; De Prospo, C. J., "Services of the Specialist in the Guidance and Placement of the Mentally Retarded," *American Journal of Mental Deficiency*, pp. 299-301, January 1944; Hungerford, R. H., "A Practical Program of Training and Service for the High Grade Defective and Borderline Group," *American Journal of Mental Deficiency*, pp. 414-16, April 1944; Hungerford R. H., and Rosenzweig, L. E., "The Mentally Retarded," *Journal of Exceptional Children*, pp. 210-13, May 1944; Raymond, C. S., "Retrospect and Prospect in Mental Deficiency," *American Journal of Mental Deficiency*, pp. 8-18, July 1944; Scharf, Louis, "Class Organization for the Use of Curricular Cores Based on Occupational Education," *Occupational Education*, pp. 49-60, December 1944; Femiani, Winifred, "The Mentally Retarded Go to High School," *High Points*, pp. 23-32, November 1945; Hungerford, R. H., and De Prospo, C. J., "Occupational Education and the Curriculum," *Occupational Education*, pp. 95-107, February 1946; Rosenzweig, L. E., and Hungerford, R. H., "The Place of the Retarded in a Day School," *Occupational Education*, pp. 1-9, October 1946; Wallin, J. E. W., *Children with Mental and Physical Handicaps* (New York 1949); Goldschmidt, W. R., *Man's Way* (New York 1959); Kanner, L., *History of the Care and Study of the Mentally Retarded* (Springfield, Ill., 1967).

MENTAL SPINE, in anatomy, the single or double tubercle on each side of the body of the mandible, for the attachment of the genioglossus and geniohyoid muscles.

MENTAL TESTS. Historical Background.—Modern psychology has been aptly characterized as an experimental science, and its preoccupation has been with the typical human being. There were trends, however, as early as the 1880's, that bore in the direction of emphasizing individual differences. One was the clinical study of abnormal personalities, and eventually some of the hospital psychiatrists turned to the psychologists and their laboratory instrumentation for many of their methods of examination.

Meanwhile, out of the laboratory experiment the mental test developed; for once experimentation had furnished a set of findings drawn up as laws about people in general, then the individual man could be examined and compared with man-in-general. When an experimental technique was used to determine a given person's particular ability or trait, it became not a psychological experiment, but a mental test. At first, the traits tested were mainly: reaction time; sensory keenness and sensory discrimination; memory abilities; motor accuracy, steadiness, and speed; imagination; word-association; and attention.

At the beginning of the 20th century attempts had been made at combining tests such as these and others to see which combinations might be fruitfully used. At Columbia University, J. McKeen Cattell was applying a battery consisting of a wide variety of laboratory-derived tests to the entering freshman and again to the graduating seniors, to see what changes due to age or to college environment might be brought to light.

Tests of General Intelligence.—Progress in the measuring of special aspects of psychological equipment became overshadowed by one achievement in particular. This was the successful combining and scaling of different tests to form a measuring rod for general intelligence. In 1905, 1908, and 1911, Alfred Binet (1857–1911) and Théodore Simon (1873–) devised a method, which would be more valid and more time-saving than were the teachers' judgments, for identifying those children in the schools of Paris that should have special attention. Their scale consisted essentially of series of problems and questions, to answer which demanded the exercise of "general intelligence." They were designed not as a test of the child's knowledge derived from school or home training, but as a test of his native capacity to acquire such knowledge. The child might be asked to follow out simple commands, to draw copies of complicated designs, to combine disarranged words into a sentence, to name some objects shown to him, or to tell what he would do in certain everyday situations described by the examiner. The tests were so graded that the easiest lay well within the range of the ability of the average 3-year-old, while the hardest taxed the ability of average adults. The scaling of these tests was done empirically, i.e., was based upon found results with Parisian children of all ages. For example, if, when tried, a given test was successfully passed by two-thirds to three-fourths of the 9-year-olds, but by a much smaller ratio of the 8-year-olds and a still smaller ratio of the 7-year-olds, it was then set up as a suitable test for "9-year-old intelligence." The tests accepted as best differentiating ability of the average 8-year-old were placed together, those for the average 9-year-old were placed together, and so on until for most age-years, a set of five tests was available; the whole series were finally combined into one scale, from age 3 to age 15 and to adult. By such a measuring rod it became possible to find out whether a given child tested was "at age," i.e., normal, or was retarded or superior.

The practical value of the Binet tests was not long in becoming recognized outside France. In America clinical psychologists were prompt in setting about the task of revising Binet's particular tests to the language and experience-background of the average American child, and of improving the scale and the procedures of administering and scoring. The scale most employed today is that constructed by Lewis M. Terman and Maud A. Merrill, which is the 1937 revision of the "Stanford-Binet" examination. They adopted from Wilhelm Stern the method of indicating the *relative* brightness of a child by his "intelligence quotient" or "IQ," found by dividing his "mental age" by his "chronological age." If a subject's IQ is around 100 per cent, then he has tested as somewhere near the average of children of his chronological age—he is of normal intelligence. If his IQ is 75, he has been found able to pass tests only of much younger ages than his and he is classed as mentally subnormal, or perhaps feebleminded.

Interest in intelligence testing has inspired a truly enormous amount of work. Most of this work has been based upon the use of tests as well accepted measures to determine what relationships may be found between intelligence and some other variable such as age, nationality, blood kinship, home status, occupation, and innumerable others. A few of the researches have been in the direction of critical inquiries into the nature of intelligence itself. Binet, and most others who have adopted his scale, have assumed that what the tests purport to measure is largely a native trait, intrinsic to the individual person. The point is reflected in the notion that the IQ of the same individual remains very closely the same throughout childhood. Thus, a boy at 5 years who tests 6 years in mental age, and so has an IQ of 6/5 or 120, will, when 15 years old, continue to have an IQ of 120, and will be mentally as bright as 18-year-olds. Obviously, this predictive function of the IQ has tremendous importance. There is a controversy, however, between those investigators who claim to have demonstrated that a child's IQ can be raised many points by furnishing him a stimulating environment and careful teaching in early years, and those who insist that such claims greatly exaggerate the possibilities.

Certain limitations in the Binet method of examining for intelligence have been recognized, and have led to the development of supplementary tests. (1) It cannot be as successfully employed with adults as with children. This arises from the fact that Binet originally standardized his tests only up to and through the age of 15 years; and the Stanford-Binet of 1937, though adding three more levels of brightness, still assumes 15 years as the "average adult" level. Then, too, the very content of many of the test items is unlikely to elicit the desired interest on the part of adults. Also many of the tests put a premium on the speed factor, whereas the slowing down in mental operations in later maturity has been found to be at no cost in accuracy. For the examining of adults on the other hand there are the *Wechsler-Bellevue Intelligence Scales* or the *Army Individual Test*. With these scales the final score of brightness is not calculated from mental age values of tests passed, but from the total number of points made on all tests, this total being then restated as a distance (in "standard deviations") above or below the average score made by adults of all ages. These have two advantages. The component tests fall into two general sorts: the verbal test and the performance test, which makes it possible to compare an examinee's facility in using words and symbols with his ability to manipulate objects and to perceive designs. Furthermore, the patterns of high and low scores on the respective component tests of the Bellevue scale vary characteristically with certain psychiatric groups (as the schizophrenic, the neurotic, the defective), so that not only brightness-level but clinical type of deviate can be recognized.

(2) The Binet type of test depends in part upon the examinee's ability to use language, oral and written; yet there are classes of people, whom it may be desirable to examine, who are illiterate or deaf, or who are unfamiliar with the English language. The oldest and best-known of the *performance* tests is the *form board* type, consisting of a baseboard bearing holes of varying shapes into which the examinee is instructed —by wordless hand motions if need be—to fit the appropriate blocks from among those supplied him. The *picture assembling* test is much like the popular jigsaw puzzle, with pictured objects or events which require some understanding and interpreting of them in order to completely assemble them. There is the *block design* test in which the examinee is shown a colored pattern and is instructed to copy this by putting together cubes with different colored faces and half-faces. Quite different is the *cube imitation* test: four cubes are set in a row before the subject, then the examiner taps them with a fifth cube in some standardized irregular order, and the subject is bidden to do likewise.

(3) The Binet method of intelligence measurement cannot be employed to test more than one individual at a time. This has led to the develop of *group* intelligence tests.

Group Tests.—The initial spurt of interest in group tests was occasioned by the recognition of their practical value, when the United States entered the First World War, in sorting out army recruits of varying levels of intelligence for promotion, discharge, special training, and other differential assignments. These men were drafted in such numbers that testing them individually proved unfeasible. In a group test the examinees are provided with printed booklets containing a variety of tests, each usually printed on a separate page and so arranged that it can not be seen in advance of or after the time during which work is to be done on it. The examiner uses a series of signals by which all examinees' starting and stopping of tests is controlled in concert. Each test is a series of questions or other items calling for penciled answers.

Just as in individual examining so in group examining there was seen to be a need for tests of nonlanguage or performance types. To meet this need there were developed printed problems that utilized designs rather than words. Since the First World War there has been a heavy output of group intelligence tests of both language and performance nature, including the *Army General Classification Test* employed in the Second World War.

Results of Intelligence Testing.—Just as the origin of intelligence tests lay in practical school demands, so their widest usefulness has been in connection with educational problems. For one thing, they have been quite widely employed to differentiate the children in school classes into the superior, average, and inferior sections; and over a wide area the differential treatment of the sectionized grades has obtained gratifying results. It should be pointed out that in dealing with the individual child, administrators recognize many factors other than native intelligence as contributing to his school success, such as health, home environment, and industry. Intelligence tests do not measure ability in all school subjects equally well; their results have been found to correlate better with grades made in composition, reading, and arithmetic, e.g., rather than with grades made in handwriting, handwork, drawing—or even spelling.

Group tests of the intelligence test type— though not so labeled—have been in well-nigh universal use in the induction of college freshmen, furnishing data for later reference in cases of disciplinary action or of counseling.

The greatest use of tests of intelligence, after educational and after military needs, is in vocational guidance. It is assumed that insofar as the different occupations and trades demand of people successfully pursuing them, different ranges of level of intelligence, then to learn the level of a given young man or woman is very material to guiding him successfully. This has been borne out in a very general way. However, success in a given occupation obviously depends upon so many other factors—interests, special aptitudes, personality makeup, and others —that the tests of general intelligence may be said to have more of an eliminative than a positive selective value.

Achievement Tests.—The impression made on psychologists and educators by the successes of the intelligence test movement led rapidly to the adoption of similar objective methods for measuring other abilities and traits. The impact upon school subject examinations was shown by the adoption of various test forms that freed their scoring from the influence of subjective impressions on the examiner's part. They included the answer of "true" or "false"; underscoring the correct answer out of alternatives; filling in a blank space with the correct word, or matching the relevant items in two arrays. These achievement tests are used to measure what level of facility or range of information the examinee has achieved in some particular area, as algebra, Italian, economics, or a nonacademic subject.

Aptitude Tests.—Another direction taken in the widening application of objective testing methods has been in the measuring of characteristics of a person that predict his ability to acquire, with training, some particular skill or knowledge. A celebrated battery of aptitude tests is that for *musical* talents devised by Carl E. Seashore. He has shown that "ability in music" really involves many components in a complex hierarchy, and for most of these he provided specific testing procedures. Phonograph disks are used to produce the sounds used in testing ability to discriminate differences in pitch, intensity, time interval, timbre, melody, and rhythm. The scores derived from these and other tests are then represented graphically as distances from a zero line, the resulting "profile" presenting a kind of picture of the examinee's various musical talents. Musical tests have been widely employed to direct attention to pupils who have unsuspected abilities calling for musical training, and they have also shown that in others musical training is an unwise investment. Other tests of music furnish vocabulary and question tests to measure musical knowledge.

Aptitude for *art* training has been tested in a variety of ways. One is by showing pairs of uncolored pictures or sets of four designs, the examinee to indicate his preference in each case, and then comparing these judgments with those previously obtained from art authorities. Many other art aptitudes, such as color preference, have been subjected to measurement.

Aptitude testing has shown much advancement in examining capacity for *mechanical* training. Some tests put a premium on the subject's ability to "get the hang" of a mechanical device, by asking him to assemble correctly into a working unit the separated parts of a bicycle bell, of a monkey wrench, of an electric light socket, or some such device. Other tests are directed at manual dexterities, as those involved in handling a complicated form board or stacking together some "wiggly" blocks. Then there are paper-and-pencil tasks, such as the kind that asks which pictured tool (screw driver, wrench) is used with each pictured object (a nut, a bit); or the kind that demands the quick putting of dots into small circles, or that involves counting how many blocks touch other blocks in a pictured pile of them.

Tests of other vocational aptitudes have been, and are being, developed. Tests of *clerical* aptitudes usually consist of operations not essentially different from those called for on the paper-and-pencil group intelligence tests; but they are directed to details that are especially relevant to the work of a business office, such as checking numbers or matching names.

The interest in vocational counseling, as well as the need which has been felt for sifting applicants for admission to the professional schools, have supported attempts to apply principles of aptitude measuring to the *learned professions*. The validation of these principles has been measured by comparing the scores of such applicants with the grades later made by the examinees in the professional school studies rather than with the degrees of success achieved still later in professional practice; and the value of these tests has been limited on the whole to selecting the persons who will do well in the professional fields in question.

In *medical aptitude* tests, the traits covered vary considerably; but taken together, they include tests of such things as knowledge of scientific facts, visual imagery, logical reasoning. Medical schools are using these tests to some extent for active selecting of candidates, but they are also maintaining a research attitude toward the question of their ultimate validity. There has not been as widespread acceptance of aptitude tests for admission to law schools as for admission to medical schools. For the study of engineering, aptitude tests have been devised ever since the end of the First World War; but there has not been persistent interest in comparing, validating, and standardizing the manifold available tests on a nationwide scale. Mathematical ability seems to be the most adequate single measure upon which ability to do the work of the engineering schools can be predicted, with facility in spatial thinking running second.

Interest Tests.—Success in an occupation certainly depends upon more than one's native ability developed by training; it depends upon his interests in many different directions. Consequently, aptitude tests frequently are supplemented by interest inventories. The examinee may be furnished elaborate lists of items concerning amusements, school subjects, people's peculiarities, personal possessions, and the like, and he is to indicate for each item whether he likes, dislikes, or is indifferent to it. The results are then studied to see whether or not the pattern of the examinee's likes-dislikes resembles that previously obtained from successful engineers, or life insurance salesmen, or other vocational groups. Where there is high correspondence, it is to be concluded that—capacity and training granted—there is evidence that the examinee would be happy in that occupation.

Personality Tests.—The great contemporary interest in problems of the total personality has led naturally to the development of approaches to the measuring of *personality*. But that word has many meanings; the approaches therefore are diverse.

The *questionnaire-inventory* method, developed during the First World War by Robert Sessions Woodworth (q.v.), has been adopted in myriad forms. Essentially this is not a test in which the subject actually faces a problem or situation, but a test which consists of a list of questions which the subject answers in the first person; e.g., "Are you easily moved to tears?" "Are you touchy on various subjects?" "Are you slow in making decisions?" In a form much in use, R. G. Bernreuter has picked 125 questions from many of the more successful inventories and recombined them. By applying different scoring keys which assign different weights to the various answers, the subject can be scored on six personality traits: neurotic tendency, self-sufficiency, introversion-extroversion, dominance-submission, self-confidence, and sociability. It can be seen readily that in the adoption of such self-questioning methods, whatever their internal consistency, their validation (the faithfulness with which they do measure what they purport to measure) must be a persistent problem.

Other scales in much use, especially by industrial concerns, assume certain "components" of the personality for which the tests may be scored: hysteroid, cycloid, schizoid, epileptoid, hypochondriacal, masculine-feminine, and others. Such terms come from the psychiatric hospital, and this use here recognizes that the deviations and eccentricities of mental illnesses are after all only exaggerations of variations to be found among the normal.

In clear contrast with the personality tests which limit the subject's responses to previously drawn-up alternatives and which consist of many discrete items, is the *projection* type of personality test. Therein the subject is free to react as he pleases—and this yields insight into his desires, phantasies, emotionality, dominant interests. The Swiss psychologist, Hermann Rorschach, seized upon the familiar ink-blot exercise as a way of revealing the profounder characteristics of a patient in his way of *seeing* or apprehending the blots. Standardized printed blots are presented one at a time to the individual for his oral responses. (In a form adapted to groups, the blots are thrown upon a screen and the examinees write out their responses.) Does the examinee see things as a whole, or does he emphasize the details? Is he influenced more by form, by movement sensations, or by coloring? Does he tend to see human beings, animals, plants, or landscapes? Are his responses individual with him, or much like those of other people? This may look like a piecemeal, item-by-item, analytic sort of approach, but it is far from that. All the tabulated details are arranged so that the skillful clinician can inspect them, not by adding and subtracting, but by apprehending them as a whole. It is not unlike the way one looks at a picture; and it should lead the clinician to a true picture of his examinee as a total personality—his expressiveness, interests, talents, temperament, and even his philosophy of life.

A newer projective technique, the "thematic apperception" test, employs a series of pictures, each depicting an ambiguous dramatic human event. The examinee is instructed to build up some fictional story illustrated by the picture, with preceding and subsequent events. In doing so he may be expected to read into the material some of his own personal problems and underlying strivings, the stories when taken together revealing a unifying thema.

Among the most important things in the organization of the personality are value attitudes. A method for determining the relative strengths of these consists of questions on specific problems or situations, the answers to which will reveal whether the examinee is influenced more by theoretic, economic, social, political, religious, or aesthetic considerations.

JOHN FREDERICK DASHIELL,
University of North Carolina.

Bibliography.—Yoakum, C. S., and Yerkes, R. M., *The Army Mental Tests* (New York 1920); Paterson, D. G., and others, *Minnesota Mechanical Ability Tests* (Minneapolis 1930); Fryer, Douglas, *The Measurement of Interests* others, *Minnesota Mechanical Ability Tests* (Minneapolis 1930); Fryer, Douglas, *The Measurement of Interests* (New York 1931); Symonds, Percival M., *Diagnosing Personality and Conduct* (New York 1931); Garrett, Henry E., and Schenck, M. R., *Psychological Tests, Methods, and Results* (New York 1933); Stanton, Hazel M., *Measurement of Musical Talent* (Iowa City 1935); Bingham, Walter Van Dyke, *Aptitudes and Aptitude Testing* (New York 1937); Terman, Lewis M., and Merrill, Maud A., *Measuring Intelligence* (Boston 1937); Greene, Edward B., *Measurements and Human Behavior* (New York 1941); Anastasi, Anne, *Psychological Testing*, 2d ed. (New York 1961); Thorndike, Robert L., and Hagen, E. P., *Measurement and Evaluation in Psychology and Education*, 2d ed. (New York 1961).

MENTHACEAE. See LABIATAE.

MENTHOL, měn'thŏl, $C_{10}H_{20}O$, an alicyclic or polymethylene compound, the most important member of the special class known as paramenthanols. It has the structure

$$
\begin{array}{c}
CH_3 \\
| \\
CH \\
H_2C \diagup \quad \diagdown CH_2 \\
| \qquad \qquad | \\
H_2C \qquad \qquad CHOH \\
\diagdown CH \diagup \\
| \\
CH \\
H_3C \diagup \quad \diagdown CH_3
\end{array}
$$

or 3-hydroxy-*p*-menthane. It is a white crystalline solid, melting at 42.5° C., and has a pungent and pleasant odor, imparting a cooling sensation to the mucous membranes of the nose and throat.

Menthol occurs in nature in oil of peppermint and other mint oils. The natural product is optically active and is levorotatory. Synthetic menthol, which may be made by adding hydrogen to a phenolic compound known as thymol, or 3-hydroxy-*p*-cymene, is a mixture of equal amounts of dextro and levorotatory menthanols. Menthol is employed in preparations for external use, primarily in ointments and sprays. It is a mild local anesthetic and also has anodyne and antispasmodic properties in treatment of irritations of the throat and nasal passages. It is also used in liqueurs, confectionery, perfumery, and cigarettes.

W. T. READ.

MENTON, män'tôn (Ital. MENTONE), town and commune, France, a leading winter and health resort of the French Riviera, on the Mediterranean in the Department of Alpes-Maritimes, about 13 miles northeast of Nice. It is charmingly situated on a promontory, with the new part of town at the base of the hill, atop which is the old quarter. The climate is mild and equable. There is considerable trade in fruit, flowers, and leaves used in the manufacture of perfumes, and olive oil. Founded in the 10th century, Menton belonged to the principality of Monaco from 1346 to 1848, and then was an independent republic until united with France in 1860. In the vicinity, on Italian territory, are the Grimaldi Caves, where the remains of prehistoric Cro-Magnon man were discovered. Pop. (1962) town 17,211; commune 20,069.

MENTOR, měn'tēr, in Greek mythology, the faithful friend of Odysseus, king of Ithaca, who entrusted to Mentor the care of his household during his absence in the Trojan War. Mentor was a guardian and tutor of Telemachus, Odysseus' son, whom the goddess Athena (assuming Mentor's form and acting as guide and prudent adviser), accompanied in the search for Odysseus after the war. In *Les aventures de Télémaque* (see TÉLÉMAQUE), the celebrated romance published in 1699 by François de Salignac de La Mothe-Fénelon, Mentor plays a conspicuous part, and his character of a sage counselor is more fully developed than in Homer's *Odyssey*, where Fénelon found much of his material. The word *mentor* is now used in the sense of a trustworthy adviser.

P. R. COLEMAN-NORTON.

MENTUHOTEP, měn'tōō-hō'těp, the last or family name of several kings of Egypt of the 11th Theban dynasty, which reunited the country and began the Middle Kingdom. The first, S'ANKHIBTAWI MENTUHOTEP I (2079–2062 B.C.), was unsuccessful in prosecuting the war with the northern kingdom of Heracleopolis. He left an extremely large but unfinished tomb. NEBHEPETRE MENTUHOTEP II (2061–2011 B.C.) had a long and glorious reign. In his 9th year he took Heracleopolis by storm and conquered the north. Later Egyptians honored him as the founder of the Middle Kingdom. With the end of civil strife, Nebhepetre embarked upon a period of vigorous campaigning to consolidate his borders and to reopen mines, quarries, and trade. Art flourished over the whole country, with a new naturalism and exquisite detail, as the local rulers who had gained considerable power during the years of breakdown and civil strife became hereditary nomarchs, maintaining their own provincial courts and constructing large, finely decorated tombs. Nebhepetre and his successors had the difficult task of exacting loyalty from these powerful nobles, and the measure of their ability was the success with which the nobles were dominated and their resources channeled toward the prosperity of the kingdom.

Artistically and architecturally Nebhepetre's greatest achievement was his tomb, which was built to the south of the resplendent later temple of Queen Hatshepsut at Deir el-Bahri and inspired its plan. His successor and eldest surviving son, S'ANKHKARE MENTUHOTEP III, reigned from 2010 to 1999 B.C. in peace and prosperity. He died with his tomb, half a mile south of his father's, unfinished. After some years about which we know little, NEBTAWIRE MENTUHOTEP IV ruled for about two years; the 11th dynasty ended in 1992 B.C. with his death. He is chiefly known for a series of inscriptions in the Hammamat quarries.

RICHARD A. PARKER,
Professor of Egyptology, Brown University.

MENUHIN, měn'ū-ĭn, **Yehudi,** American violinist: b. New York, N.Y., April 22, 1916. He moved to San Francisco with his parents in infancy and began violin lessons at the age of four, initially with Sigmund Anker and later with Louis Persinger. Menuhin made his first public appearance at seven with the San Francisco Orchestra (1924) and the following year played at the Manhattan Opera House in New York City. In 1926 he went to Europe to study with Georges Enesco and Adolf Busch, and on his return scored a triumph at Carnegie Hall (Nov. 25, 1927) with the New York Symphony Orchestra under Fritz Busch, playing Ludwig van Beethoven's Violin Concerto. For the next eight years he toured the United States and Europe with continued success and, after almost two years' retirement in California for further study, returned to the concert stage at the end of 1937.

During World War II, Menuhin gave over 500 concerts for the Allied armed forces, playing in the Pacific theater, Alaska, and Europe as well as the United States. Following the war, he played in the devastated countries of Europe, donating the greater part of his income from these tours to one humanitarian cause or another and raising several million dollars for the aid of the victims of Nazi persecution and refugees of all nations. He also toured Japan in 1951, India in 1952, Hungary in 1956, and Poland in 1957.

Menuhin has appeared from time to time in sonata recitals with his sister, Hephzibah Menuhin, a concert pianist. He has recorded many of the foremost works in violin literature, and from his scholarly researches has revived many forgotten classical compositions, including Robert Schumann's "lost" concerto, Felix Mendelssohn's juvenile concerto, Wolfgang Amadeus Mozart's juvenile *Adelaide* concerto, and the complete version of Niccolò Paganini's *Diabolic* concertos.

Consult Magidoff, Robert, *Yehudi Menuhin: the Story of the Man and the Musician* (New York 1955).

MENZEL, měn'tsěl, **Adolf (Friedrich Erdmann) von,** German painter, illustrator, and lithographer: b. Breslau, Germany (Pol. Wrocław), Dec. 8, 1815; d. Berlin, Feb. 9, 1905.

Having studied lithography with his father, he did a group of six lithographs at the age of 18, illustrating Johann Wolfgang von Goethe's *Künstlers Erdenwallen,* which immediately attracted attention. Four years later he had begun to draw historical scenes of Brandenburg and commenced painting in oils. Menzel's 400 woodblocks (1840) for Franz Kugler's *Geschichte Friedrichs des Grossen* were a turning point in the modern history of wood engraving in Germany. His 200 illustrations for the royal edition of the *Oeuvres de Frédéric le Grand* (1846–57) and 600 lithographs for *Die Armee Friedrichs des Grossen in ihrer Uniformierung* (3 vols., 1845–57) further demonstrated his originality, dramatic power, and historical accuracy. He became the painter-historian of the Hohenzollerns, *Krönung Wilhelms I in Königsberg* (1861–1865) and *Abreise Wilhelms I zur Armee 1870* (1871) being examples of his contemporary historical work. *Eisenwalzwerk* (1875), a painting of the interior of a rolling mill in Silesia, reveals Menzel's impressionistic treatment of the problem of light and shadow, in which he may have been influenced by his study of the English landscape painter John Constable. Other notable paintings are the *Ballsouper* (1878) and *Piazza d'Erbe in Verona* (1884).

MENZEL, Wolfgang, German author: b. Waldenburg, Germany (Pol. Wałbrzych), June 21, 1798; d. Stuttgart, April 23, 1873. He was editor (1825–1848) of the *Literaturblatt,* a supplement of the *Morgenblatt* in Stuttgart, and from 1852 to 1869 published an independent magazine of the same name. Often involved in controversy, he assailed with equal zeal the theological rationalists and political radicals; his attacks upon Johann Wolfgang von Goethe and other authors were matched for virulence by the criticisms upon Menzel himself by Heinrich Heine, Ludwig Börne, and other writers of the *Junges Deutschland* (q.v.) group. Menzel's writings include *Geschichte der Deutschen* (1824–25); *Die deutsche Literatur* (1828); *Furore* (1851), a historical novel of the Thirty Years' War; and *Die deutsche Dichtung* (1858–59).

MENZIES, men'zēz, **Sir Robert Gordon** (1894–   ), Australian prime minister, who in 16 successive years in office achieved domination of Australian politics to a degree never reached before. He was knighted in 1963 and retired in January 1966.

Menzies was born in Jeparit, Victoria, on Dec. 20, 1894. Educated at state schools and at Wesley College, Melbourne, he studied law at Melbourne University and began practice in 1918. He was elected to the Victorian parliament in 1928 and entered the federal House of Representatives six years later as a member of the newly formed United Australia Party (UAP). He was immediately named attorney general. In 1939 he became prime minister, but two years later he was forced to resign from the UAP leadership shortly before the Labor party gained power under John Curtin. Determined to reorganize non-Labor groups into a cohesive political force, Menzies was mainly responsible for the creation in 1944 of the Liberal party, and he became its leader.

With a policy aimed at removing restrictive controls maintained by Labor while retaining the expanded social welfare program, the Liberal-Country party coalition won the election of 1949, and Menzies again became prime minister. He came to office at a time of ferment over the issue of Communist influence in trade unions. He gave special attention to strengthening the powers of industrial tribunals as a means of improving industrial relations, but his attempt to outlaw the Communist party was blocked by the High Court. His administration won successive elections in 1951, 1954, 1955, 1958, 1961 and 1963.

Menzies held that Australia's prime responsibility was to build a stronger and more diversified economy and maintain a high standard of living, which in turn would attract new settlers and investment in industry; accordingly, an officially sponsored immigration program, rapid industrial growth, and accelerated development of resources became dominant features of his administration's domestic policy. Large-scale public works were undertaken, including major projects in water conservation, power generation, and transport.

Menzies became a senior figure at the annual conferences of Commonwealth prime ministers in London; also, he visited Washington each year for discussions. While nurturing traditional links with Britain, he worked zealously for firmer ties with the United States. His strong advocacy of regional defense arrangements for the western Pacific and southeast Asia area was rewarded in the ANZUS alliance (1951)—which he regarded as the key element in Australia's foreign policy and defense—and in SEATO (1955). See also PACIFIC COUNCIL; SOUTHEAST ASIA TREATY ORGANIZATION.

In the 1960's, Menzies supported Britain in defending Malaysia against Indonesian "confrontation" and backed the United States in its support of South Vietnam. His government sent Australian military units both to Malaysia and South Vietnam, and reintroduced military conscription in Australia in 1965.

Menzies' publications include *The Rule of Law During War* (1917); *The Forgotten People, and Other Studies in Democracy* (1943); and *Speech Is of Time* (1958).

R. M. YOUNGER
Author of "The Changing World: Australia"

MEPHISTOPHELES, mĕf-ĭ-stŏf'ĕ-lēz, a principal devil in medieval demonology, popularized in literature in Christopher Marlowe's *The Tragical History of Doctor Faustus* (c. 1588) and Johann Wolfgang von Goethe's *Faust* (1808, 1832). Various theories are held as to the etymology of the word; some scholars suppose it to be a Greek compound from the negative *mē, phōs* (light), and *philos* (loving), signifying "one who loves not light"; others surmise that it derives from Latin *mephitis* and Greek *philos,* meaning "loving the mephitic vapors of hell"; and still others believe it stems from the Hebrew *mephiz* (destroyer) and *tophel* (liar). In the Faust legend and its literary interpretations, Mephistopheles is the devil to whom Faust sells his soul in return for obedience to Faust's commands. He appears in Marlowe's drama as the literal embodiment of the medieval myth, a fallen angel, and thus possesses a melancholy dignity. In Goethe's version, he assumes the form of a real man of flesh and blood, a cynic who delights in selfish pleasure, the personification of the evil in man's nature. See also FAUST.

MERA, mā'rä, **Juan León,** Ecuadorian novelist and historian: b. Ambato, Ecuador, June 28, 1832; d. Atocha, near Ambato, Dec. 13, 1894. Conservative in outlook and a member of the Spanish Royal Academy, he wrote Ecuador's national hymn and was at various times provincial governor, deputy, and senator. His writings include legends, fables, biographical studies (especially a long one on Gabriel García Moreno), a *Historia de la Restauración en el Ecuador,* numerous short stories, and a novel, *Cumandá ó un drama entre salvajes* (1879). His fame today rests principally on *Cumandá,* one of the earliest literary approaches to the American Indian. In this novel, Mera leaned heavily on his models (René de Chateaubriand and James Fenimore Cooper), but there are, over and above the trite plot (the love of a white boy for a noble and courageous Indian girl who turns out to be his sister), moments of splendid beauty in which the landscape as well as the habits and customs of the Indians are faithfully depicted.

Consult Rolando, Carlos A., *Don Juan León Mera* (Guayaquil 1932); Toro Navas, Tarquino, *. . . Minarete* (Ambato 1938); Guevara, Dario C., *Juan León Mera o el hombre de cimas* (Quito 1944).

MERAMEC RIVER, mĕr'ȧ-măk, river, Missouri, rising in the Ozark Mountains east of Salem, in Dent County, and flowing 207 miles north, northeast, and southeast to enter the Mississippi at a point 20 miles south of St. Louis. The river provides excellent fishing, boating, and swimming facilities.

MERANO, mä-rä'nô, town and commune, Italy, in Bolzano Province, near the Austrian border, 15 miles northwest of Bolzano. It is a celebrated health and tourist resort situated on a sheltered south slope of the Tyrol Alps, and is noted for its mild and equable climate. The old town has a fine Gothic cathedral (1367), a museum, and a castle (15th century) which once was the seat of the counts of Tyrol. The new town has handsome villas and hotels. Merano is also an industrial center, producing furniture, pottery, jewelry, soap, insecticides, sausages, beer, and wine. It became the capitol of the Tyrol in the 12th century and received its city charter in 1305. It was long under Austrian rule, until ceded along with the south Tyrol to Italy in 1919. Population: (1961) town, 29,196.

MERCADANTE, mär-kä-dän'tä, **(Giuseppe) Saverio (Raffaele),** Italian composer: b. Altamura, Italy, bap. Sept. 17, 1795; d. Naples, Dec. 17, 1870. He studied composition under Nicola Antonio Zingarelli at the Collegio di San Sebastiano in Naples and produced his first opera, *L'apoteosi d'Ercole,* in that city in 1819. His next stage work, an *opera buffa, Elisa e Claudio* (Milan, 1821), won him an international reputation. For the next 12 years he traveled from city to city in Italy, Spain, Portugal, and Austria, composing several operas each year. In 1833 he settled in Novara as *maestro di cappella* of the cathedral, and here lost the sight of one eye, becoming totally blind in 1862. From 1840 he was director of the Naples Conservatory. In all, Mercadante wrote about 60 operas, of which *Il giuramento* (1837), *La vestale* (1840), and *Gli Orazi ed i Curiazi* (1846) may be singled out for mention. With the first of these he initiated a program of reform in operatic composition, intended to break away from traditional clichés and heighten the dramatic effect, and his work in this direction had an acknowledged influence on Giuseppe Verdi. He also wrote some 20 masses, a number of funeral symphonies, and considerable chamber music.

MERCANTILE LAW. See COMMERCIAL LAW.

MERCANTILISM, mûr′kăn-tĭl-ĭz′m, the name applied to a set of economic views prevailing in Europe from the 16th to 18th centuries. Adam Smith called it the "mercantile system," and the term "mercantilism" is derived from that.

It is misleading to regard mercantilism as a unified school of thought, however. Many scattered writers and pamphleteers from several European nations are classified as mercantilists. Their only common bond is found in their viewpoint, the viewpoint of the merchant.

The period in which mercantilism flourished witnessed the emergence of the national state from the feudal baronial system. Sovereign power was vested in a strong, central prince or ruler, who was identified with the nation. National power and prestige depended upon strength of arms, which could be obtained readily, and often only, by hiring professional soldiers. Thus the sovereign's war chest in the form of gold, silver, and other precious metals was crucial to the strength and greatness of the nation.

Policies.—The early mercantilist writers, often called bullionists, argued for the imposition of barriers to the export of bullion or precious metal in any form. In this way the national treasure would be preserved. This was in fact tried, but it did not help in adding to the nation's treasure because most European nations had few if any mines for the production of precious metals.

The solution hit upon was foreign trade. Gold and other treasure had become universally accepted means of settling debts, as commerce expanded and a money system replaced barter. If exports exceeded imports, the balance would have to be paid by the importing nation in specie (gold or other metallic money). This course of action would add to the nation's treasure. Thus an export balance came to be regarded as a "favorable balance of trade."

The mercantilists were themselves merchants and businessmen. Therefore, their analysis was translated directly into policy recommendations. They generally recommended bans on the export of specie, and severe restrictions on imports. Tariff barriers erected throughout Europe in the 17th and 18th centuries, and such undertakings as the English Navigation Acts, stand as testimony to the effectiveness of their writings.

A further extension of their policies lay in extreme encouragement of domestic industry. Industry that produced goods for export was encouraged because its products brought specie into the nation. Industry that produced goods otherwise imported was encouraged because it decreased the outward flow of specie. Import tariffs and quotas were imposed to protect the position of the former type of industry and the existence of the latter.

Colonial powers sought to add markets for their exports by expanding their overseas colonies. The prohibition of local manufacture in the American colonies of any goods that would compete with British industry was one factor leading to the American Revolution.

Weaknesses.—There were two major flaws in the mercantilists' position. First, many of them, particularly the bullionists, tended to confuse wealth with money or specie. They made the means an end in itself, and overlooked the fact that the satisfaction of human wants is the basic goal of all economic activity. Some even went so far as to condemn the use of land for agriculture, except for such export crops as tobacco, ignoring the fact that without food a nation cannot exist at all.

The second basic error in the mercantilists' position was that they regarded trade as a one-way phenomenon. In their view, the seller of goods for specie gained, while the buyer lost. Only with the publication of Adam Smith's dramatic treatment of specialization and trade (*Wealth of Nations,* 1776) were the mutual gains to be derived by both parties widely recognized. But despite generations of practical experience with the mutual gains from trade throughout the world, mercantilist thinking still persists in the policy recommendations of protectionists for import quotas and other trade restrictions.

Emperor Charles V in Spain, Oliver Cromwell in England, Jean Baptiste Colbert in France, and Frederick the Great in Prussia were all leading practitioners of mercantilism. The leading writer was Thomas Mun (1571–1641) in England.

See also ACTS OF TRADE; BALANCE OF TRADE; ECONOMICS—*The Nation and the Merchant.*

Consult Viner, Jacob, *Studies in the Theory of International Trade* (New York 1937); Heckscher, Eli F., *Mercantilism,* tr. by M. Shapiro, rev. ed., 2 vols. (New York 1956).

WILLIAM N. KINNARD, JR.,
Head, Business Department, The University of Connecticut.

MERCAPTANS, měr-kăp′tăns (also THIO-ALCOHOLS, or more correctly ALKANE THIOLS), compounds with the general formula R-SH, in which R stands for a simple or substituted carbon-hydrogen group. Mercaptans react to form metal derivatives. The word was derived from the Latin term *mercurium captans* (seizing mercury). The most noteworthy property of the lower members of the mercaptan series is an extremely disagreeable odor. Ethyl mercaptan, C_2H_5SH, is said to be capable of detection by smell when present only to the extent of two billionths of a milligram ($\frac{1}{200}$ of the amount of sodium detectable by the spectroscope). The odor decreases with increasing number of carbons in the molecule until mercaptans with nine carbon atoms have a relatively pleasant odor.

Mercaptans are quite reactive, forming metallic salts known as mercaptides, and are extensively employed in organic syntheses. They are most easily prepared by saturation of caustic soda solution with hydrogen sulphide and heating the product with a salt of an alkyl sulphuric acid.

In industry, mercaptans are flotation agents, and higher members are rubber plasticizers and also reagents in the manufacture of synthetic rubber. Mercaptans in motor fuels interfere with the action of the antiknock material, tetraethyl lead, and are removed in refinery operations by washing gasoline with a solution of a lead compound, sodium plumbite, or "doctor" solution.

W. T. READ

MERCATOR, mĕr-kā'tĕr, **Gerardus** (Latinized form of GERHARD KREMER, krā'mĕr), Flemish geographer: b. Rupelmonde, Flanders, March 5, 1512; d. Duisburg, Dec. 2, 1594. He studied at Louvain, and became a lecturer on geography and astronomy, making his instruments with his own hands. In 1544 he was arrested for heresy, being liberal in his views. He escaped, but 42 of those arrested with him were burnt alive. Recommended to Charles V, Mercator entered into the emperor's service, and executed for him a celestial globe of crystal, and a terrestrial globe of wood. In 1559 he retired to Duisburg and received the title of cosmographer to the Duke of Juliers. His last years were devoted to theological studies.

Mercator is known as the inventor of a method of projection called by his name, in which meridians and parallels of latitude cut each other at right angles, and are both represented by straight lines, which has the effect of enlarging the degrees of latitude as they recede from the equator. (See CHART—*Scales and Projections.*) The method is convenient in mapping small areas. His first maps on this projection were published in 1569; the principles were first explained by Edward Wright, in 1599, in his *Corrections of Errors in Navigation*, whence the discovery has sometimes been attributed to him. Mercator's *Tabulae Geographicae* (1578) is the best edition of the maps of Ptolemy. See MAP.

MERCATOR, Nicolaus. See KAUFMANN, NICOLAUS.

MERCED, city, California, seat of Merced County, 55 miles northwest of Fresno on U.S. Highway 99 and the Atchison, Topeka, and Santa Fe and the Southern Pacific railroads. Altitude 167 feet. Lying in the San Joaquin Valley, Merced is a trade and shipping center for an extensive agricultural region specializing in farming, dairying, fruitgrowing, and stock raising. Industries of the city include the manufacture of cement, fruit processing and packing, dairy products, and pottery.

The city has a library, sanitarium, county hospital, courthouse, national guard armory, three public parks and swimming pools. Nearby is the recreational center of Lake Yosemite, and Yosemite National Park lies 45 miles to the northeast. Founded in 1870, Merced received its first charter in 1889. It has a council-manager form of government. Pop. 20,068.

MERCEDES, mĕr-sā'dĕs, city, Texas, in Hidalgo County, 30 miles west-northwest of Brownsville on U.S. Highway 83 and the Missouri Pacific Railroad. Altitude 61 feet. Located in an agricultural region producing citrus fruits and vegetables, Mercedes is a center for packing, canning, processing, and shipping. The city's industrial production includes packed meat, cheese, clay products, oil and natural gas, and sheeet metal and machine shop products.

In 1949 a 1,840 mile pipe line to the New York region was begun. Founded in 1907, Mercedes was incorporated two years later. Its government is administered by a commission. Pop. 10,943.

MERCENARIES, mûr'sĕ-nĕr-ēz (also formerly called STIPENDIARIES, stī-pĕn'dĭ-ĕr-ēz), foreigners or others who received pay for their services as soldiers, especially as distinguished from government soldiers or those owing military service to the crown or nation.

Hired professional soldiers appear very early in the history of military organization. Foreign mercenaries were used in the armies of Alexander the Great and the Romans, and in England King Harold (1066) had a body of Danes in his army when he defeated the Norwegian king. These were the famous "housecarls" (from the Anglo-Saxon *hūscarl*) who were hired soldiers originally established in the kingdom by King Canute (1018–1035). William III had for some time a body of Dutch troops in his pay after he became king of England and throughout the 18th century Hessian and Hanoverian regiments were constantly in the pay of the British government for temporary purposes. Hessians fought for Great Britain in the Revolutionary War, and the landgrave of Hesse, who sold his troops at so much a head, received upward of $2,500,000 for Hessian soldiers lost in that struggle.

The most famous of all mercenaries were the Swiss soldiers, who were hired, sometimes by the cantons themselves, over all Europe, and formed many famous body guards. They were long employed by the French monarchs, and the Vatican at Rome still has its Swiss guards.

Other designations for mercenaries are *condottieri* (q.v.), who were Italian troops banded together and hired out to the city states in the Renaissance, and "soldiers of fortune," who pursue a military career for adventure and pleasure as well as for gain.

MERCER, mûr'sĕr, **Henry Chapman,** American archaeologist, antiquarian, and inventor: b. Doylestown, Pa., June 24, 1856; d. there, March 9, 1930. Graduating from Harvard in 1879, he was curator of American and prehistoric archaeology at the University of Pennsylvania from 1894 to 1897, and served as editor for anthropology in *American Naturalist* from 1893 to 1897. He made extensive investigations and studies in anthropology in America, discovering several unknown extinct species, and 1897 to 1917, made and presented to the Historical Society of Bucks County, Pa., an extensive collection of objects illustrating the Colonial and early history of the United States by means of the implements and handiwork of the pioneer settlers. In 1916 he built and presented to the society a fireproof museum for preserving the above collection.

Mercer established a pottery at Doylestown, Pa., in 1898, experimented upon and developed the processes of the Pennsylvania Germans for making and decorating pottery, inventing in 1899 a new method of manufacturing tiles for mural decoration and in 1902 a new process for making mosaics. His writings include *Lenape Stone* (1885); *Hill Caves of Yucatan* (1896); *Researches upon the Antiquity of Man in the Delaware Valley and Eastern United States* (1897); *Tools of the Nation Maker* (1897); *The Bible in Iron or the Pictured Stoves and Stoveplates of the Colonial United States* (1915); *Ancient Carpenter's Tools* (1925).

MERCER, Hugh, American general: b. Aberdeen, Scotland, about 1725; d. near Princeton, N. J., Jan. 12, 1777. Educated as a physician, he served as surgeon's assistant in the army of the Young Pretender at the battle of Culloden. Emigrating in 1747 to America, he settled in Pennsylvania, and resided there, in the practice of his profession, until 1755, when he volunteered in the expedition led by Braddock to Fort Duquesne. Later he moved to Virginia and at the outbreak of the Revolution joined the Continental army, and attained the rank of brigadier general. He subsequently accompanied Washington on his retreat through New Jersey, and rendered valuable assistance at the battle of Trenton. In the succeeding action at Princeton he was mortally wounded and died a week later. Mercer County, N. J., was named in his honor.

Consult Goolrick, J. T., *The Life of General Hugh Mercer* (New York 1906); *Dictionary of American Biography*, vol. 12 (New York 1933).

MERCER, John, English calico printer and chemist: b. Dean, near Blackburn, England, Feb. 21, .1791; d. Nov. 30, 1866. The son of a hand-loom weaver, he worked in weaving and cloth-printing shops from the age of nine, making his first experiments in dyeing cloth in 1807 and a few years later inventing several weaving designs. He was mainly self-educated and through his study of James Parkinson's *Chemical Pocket-Book* in 1814, he arrived at his first major discovery: a method of dyeing calico by the use of orange sulphide of antimony. As a chemist in the color shop of the Fort Bros. print works, he introduced into England a method of applying lead chromate as a cloth dye. He contributed a number of other improvements and inventions, and served as a partner in the firm from 1825 until its dissolution in 1848.

Mercer devoted the remainder of his life to his own chemical researches. In the field of theoretical chemistry, he suggested the first rational theory of catalytic action and his most far-reaching discovery was the process, called mercerizing (q.v.), of treating cotton cloth to improve its strength and adaptability for dyeing.

MERCER UNIVERSITY, Macon, Georgia, a coeducational Baptist institution opened at Penfield, Ga., as Mercer Institute on Jan. 14, 1833. Chief among the founders were the Rev. Jesse Mercer, early conceiver and patron for whom the school was named; Adiel Sherwood, D.D., who after coming to Georgia in 1818 established a theological school at his home near Eatonton; and Josiah Penfield, of Savannah, who at his death in 1827 bequeathed a fund for educating young ministers. Additional funds were provided by the Georgia Baptist Convention.

Conceived as a theological and classical school for ministerial students only, Mercer from its opening served a wider clientele; and in 1837 it obtained a charter giving it collegiate rank and changing the name to Mercer University. Thereafter it grew steadily.

During the administration of President Weaver (1918–1927), Mercer expanded rapidly. The campus was extended, new buildings were erected, the curriculum was revised, and nearly three-quarters of a million dollars were given to the institution by Georgia Baptists. Another period of physical growth and curriculum adjustment followed the inauguration of President Dowell. Mercer is now organized as a liberal arts college and school of law, with comprehensive curricula in the humanities, the social sciences, and the natural sciences.

In 1951 the working plant, covering about 65 acres, was valued at $3,191,613 and the endowment was $3,072,604. The plant, which includes three libraries, adequately meets the educational requirements of a student body numbering about 2,164 and dormitory and dining facilities are provided for both men and women students.

The teaching staff numbered 88 in 1960. Degrees conferred are B.A., B.S., LL.B., and M.A. Mercer is fully accredited by the various standardizing agencies, and the work done is accepted by the graduate schools of leading institutions in America and Europe.

MERCERIZING, mûr′sĕr-īz-ĭng, a process invented by John Mercer, of Lancaster, England, for treating cotton fiber or fabrics, first patented in 1851. The process consists of steeping the cloth in a solution of caustic alkali. The cloth shrinks about one-fourth and takes more brilliant colors in dyeing than unmercerized cotton goods. Cotton may be mercerized either in the yarn or in the cloth, and a variety of machines are made for this purpose. Some of these machines operating on the cloth employ a tension to obviate some after-shrinkage. This gives a greater yardage, but it reduces the gloss.

The name has sometimes been incorrectly extended to sizing of cloth to give it a better sheen. True mercerizing gives a luster to the cotton cloth, because the fibers are drawn closer and flattened, presenting a smooth surface that reflects the light. A variation in the caustic soda process is employed to give the modern crimped-of-crepe effects.

Consult Marsh, J. T., *Mercerizing* (New York 1941)

MERCERSBURG, mûr′sĕrz-bûrg, borough, Pennsylvania, in Franklin County, near the western rim of the Cumberland Valley at an altitude of 590 feet. It lies 17 miles west-southwest of Chambersburg and is served by the Pennsylvania Railroad. Situated in a productive agricultural region, it has considerable trade in dairy products and its local industries include a tannery, shirt factory, and lumber yard.

Mercersburg Academy, a well-known preparatory school for boys, had its origin here in 1836 with the founding of Marshall College. When Marshall College was moved to Lancaster, Pa., and combined with Franklin College in 1853, the Theological Seminary and preparatory department remained in Mercersburg. From this Mercersburg College developed and was superseded in 1893 by the Academy. Three miles from Mercersburg is Stony Batter, birthplace of James Buchanan, 15th president of the United States. Buchanan made his home in Mercersburg from 1796 to 1809.

The borough was first settled in 1730 by Scotch-Irish Presbyterians. In 1780 the town was laid out and named after Hugh Mercer, the Revolutionary War general. It was incorporated in 1831. Pop. 1,759.

MERCERSBURG THEOLOGY, a school of religious philosophy founded by Frederick Augustus Rauch (1806–1841) of the German Reformed Church in 1836, his work being taken up by John W. Nevin (q.v.) and Philip Schaff (q.v.). The name comes from the Mercersburg Theological Seminary of the German Reformed Church, whence the teaching of this system spread. The Mercersburg theology urged that the Church was not a voluntary society of believers but a historic and spiritual growth—an attitude showing markedly less hostility ·to the Roman Catholic

Church; that old confessions cannot express the modern faith in the Church; that the sacraments are more than symbols; that church worship should be orderly—hence the Liturgy (1858) and Order of Worship (1866); and that religious education is of prime importance.

MERCHANT ADVENTURERS, The Company of,

an association of English foreign traders with trading stations in Netherlands cities, also extending to Hamburg and other German ports, which enjoyed special privileges and exemptions similar to those of the Hanseatic League in London. Its earliest charter dates from 1407. It was a private company holding a monopoly of exporting certain manufactured articles, especially cloths, and its members were all subjects of the English crown, unlike the Staplers who included aliens as well as Englishmen and were limited to trading in unmanufactured products, particularly wool. Probably the nucleus of the Merchant Adventurers was formed of members of the Mercers' Company of London. New companies of Merchant Adventurers arose in the 16th and 17th centuries, especially during the reigns of Elizabeth and her immediate successors. These included the Muscovy, Levant, Guinea, Morocco, Eastland, Spanish, and East India companies. The Company of Merchant Adventurers trading to the Low Countries in the 18th century was called the Hamburg Company. From its inception in the early 15th century the company was in continuous rivalry with the Hansa, the German group that for centuries had monopolized the North Sea trade. This was intensified in 1545 when the Emperor Charles V cut off the Adventurers' trade with the Low Countries and the Hansa was thus able to obtain a monopoly of the English cloth export to Antwerp. In retaliation, the Hansa's London privileges were revoked in 1552; briefly restored, they were suspended in 1555. Queen Elizabeth in 1560 made peace with the Hansa; the terms excluded the Hansa from the Antwerp cloth trade and abolished their customs exemptions in London. Thus the Merchant Adventurers finally won their long trade war.

MERCHANT MARINE.

Down through the centuries two categories of vessels, merchant marines and navies, have carried on most of the world's seagoing activities. Those of the merchant marine known as merchantmen have been expected to make a profit for their owners by earning freight payments for carrying cargo; by earning passage money in transporting passengers; or by performing certain special functions, such as fishing or whaling. Navies, of course, have had the different mission of trying to maintain, by fighting if necessary, control of the sea lanes to enable the vessels of their own nations to move men and goods freely and safely and to keep the enemy from doing likewise. At times in the past the border line between the merchantman and the fighting ship was not always clearly drawn, but in modern times it has generally been quite distinct. A third category of maritime activity, rapidly increasing in recent years, has developed from the operation of yachts and other craft designed purely for pleasure.

A nation's merchant marine consists not only of ships but also of mariners and services. Allied with it have been numerous shore-based aspects, such as piers, pilotage, and other port functions;

Radio Times Hulton Picture Library

An unwilling victim is "shanghaied" by a press gang. In early days, the crews of vessels about to put to sea were often brought to their full complement by this method.

shipbuilding and repair yards; marine insurance, agents, brokers, ship chandlers, and other features. By and large, these have been fairly uniform among maritime nations, both in earlier times and today.

There is no need to discuss here the ships themselves, for they are treated fully elsewhere. (See SAILING VESSELS; SHIPS; STEAM VESSELS.) It is enough to say that merchantmen now fall into three major groups: passenger liners, dry cargo freighters, and tankers. Lesser types include barges, lighters, tugs, excursion boats, and ferries.

Merchant shipping activity began centuries ago in the days of the Phoenicians, the Egyptians, and other early traders in the Mediterranean. (See EXPLORATION AND DISCOVERY.) Gradually it spread to the other coasts of Europe. There were even international codes at very early dates, stipulating in detail how shipping should be conducted. The uniform, orderly development of merchant shipping, however, dates more or less from the period around 1600, at the time the Dutch, English, and French were taking in force to the high seas. The methods of doing things afloat and ashore would continue with relatively little change throughout the great age of sail down to the mid-19th century when the introduction of steam would bring in new features.

LIFE AND DUTIES OF THE MERCHANT MARINE

Shipboard Routine and Functions.—Aboard ship the duties and status of the officers and crew developed from several basic features which existed among ships of virtually all nations. Of these, the system of alternate four-hour watches was the most important. Except for the master and certain specialists, the crew was divided into a starboard and port watch, each headed by a mate. For four hours one watch would hold the deck with the mate in charge of navigation, one seaman steering the ship, another serving as lookout, and others cleaning up the deck. Every half hour the ship's bell would sound an additional stroke; when eight bells was reached the other watch would come on deck to take over. The watch from 4 P.M. to 8 P.M. was divided into two dogwatches, so that the actual hours on duty would change each day. In case of emergency, such as the necessity to shorten sail in a sudden squall, the cry of "All hands!" would interrupt

Helmsman of an oceangoing sailing ship of the 1880's.

the rest of the off-duty watch to rush everyone into action at once.

The most exacting part of a seaman's duties consisted of going aloft, out on a swaying yard-arm, to furl or let out the big, stiff canvas sails on a square-rigged brig, bark, or ship. The more experienced a seaman, the more effective he would be at such work, and the less likely to lose his footing and crash onto the deck or into the sea. For that reason there was a constant desire to get as many seasoned, able-bodied seamen as possible instead of green landsmen, ordinary seamen, or boys. Since the square-rigged naval vessels also needed such experienced mariners, it became part of national policy to encourage the merchant marine as a "nursery of seamen," so that there would be plenty in time of war when impressment would seize them for naval service. Queen Elizabeth I even used her position as head of the Church of England to make Wednesday as well as Friday a day when fish must be eaten; thus by doubling the demand for fish, the number of trained seamen had to be increased to meet that demand. One of the reasons for the American development of the schooner was that it could be operated by a smaller crew, since its fore-and-aft sails could be hoisted and lowered from the deck without having to send men aloft.

Those able-bodied and ordinary seamen, landsmen, and boys lived in the bow of the vessel in the forecastle, or "foc'sle" as it was usually abbreviated. Corresponding to the enlisted men of the navy they were sometimes known as foremast hands and would later be known officially as unlicensed personnel. The forecastles of those early days were dark, damp, and dreary; the men slept in tiers of bunks on the sides and ate at a table in between. With the "four-on-and-four-off" arrangement of watches, they never got more than four hours' sleep at a time, and even that could be interrupted, of course, by a call for "All hands!" See also separate article SEAMAN.

Between those foremast hands and the officers was a small group of specialists whom the crews sometimes called idlers because they did not stand regular watches. They corresponded somewhat to the chief petty officers in the navy and often lived in little separate cabins on deck. Chief among them was the boatswain, or "bosun," who had general immediate charge of deck operations. A carpenter was usually aboard to attend to repairs, while larger ships often had a sailmaker and sometimes a cooper for making casks. Much of

the morale of the crew depended upon the skill and efforts of the cook, for in the days before refrigeration the principal stand-bys were salt beef or salt pork, and ship's bread, which had more or less the consistency of dog biscuit. That monotonous diet, with its lack of vitamins, often led to scurvy until the English found that the use of lime juice (whence the name "limeys") helped to offset the condition. The Dutch in 1652 settled the Cape of Good Hope simply to be able to furnish the ships on the long run to the East Indies with fresh meat and vegetables.

The officers lived in cabins at the stern of the ship and exercised control there from the quarter-deck. It has been a cardinal and essential principle of ship operation, both mercantile and naval down through the years, that responsibility and authority be vested in one man, officially known as the "master" in the merchant marine and "commanding officer" in the navy, but commonly termed the "captain" in both services.

The master, both in early days and at present, has held his command at the pleasure of the owner or owners of the vessel. They appoint him and can also remove him unless, of course, he happens to be the sole owner of the vessel himself. In the days of sail the ownership of a vessel was often divided into 16ths or even 64ths among various individuals; one man would be appointed to handle the details as ship's husband, and he would normally have much to say about the selection and retention of the master. In much later days masters would have to pass government examinations before they could secure a license certifying their competence; but even then actual command still depended upon the will of the owner. The master did not have to stand watch, though he would usually take charge of the quarter-deck in leaving or entering port, or in very bad weather. The master has been eternally responsible, however, for whatever might happen to his vessel, even if an accident was the fault of a pilot or of a mate while he himself might be asleep below, or even if something went wrong in port while he was ashore. In compensation for that full responsibility, the master has also had full authority. Things can happen so fast at sea that there is often no time for consultation or discussion, and one man has to make split-second decisions. The laws of the maritime nations, moreover, have strongly upheld the authority of the master, even to the extent of punishing for mutiny any defiance of the decisions of the "old man." Those same laws, to be sure, have sought to protect the members of the crew from improper abuse of authority, but the courts have been apt to back up discipline aboard ship as a general principle.

Aside from the actual navigational matters, the captain has also been responsible for the formalities in clearing and entering the ship, and the rest of the inevitable paper work. In older days he was also likely to be responsible for many of the business transactions involved in selling a cargo and finding a return lading in its place; before the days of cable or radio the distant owner could not exercise continual control in such matters. Sometimes the master would be relieved of those business duties by a supercargo, a businessman directly representing the owners' interest, but that was not normal on ordinary voyages. Because of the captain's relationship to the business end of affairs his principal income was likely to come not from his small salary, but from primage, which meant 5 per cent or so of the vessel's freight earnings. A successful captain with good bargaining ability or with a command on a rich run could, before long, sometimes earn enough to become a shipowner or a merchant himself.

Associated with the master in the quarter-deck command were the mates, usually two until later days. Aside from getting experience for possible eventual command as masters themselves, they had important routine duties aboard ship. Each was in charge of a watch and for three four-hour periods each day had charge of the quarter-deck and the actual operation of the ship. In addition, the first, or chief, mate had particular responsibility for the proper stowing and unloading of the cargo, while the second mate, assisted by the boatswain, was expected to maintain the spars, rigging, and remainder of the ship in good condition.

One particular feature that distinguished the quarter-deck command from the foremast hands and the idlers was their knowledge of the mathematical mysteries of navigation. Originally, this consisted principally of "shooting the sun" with the quadrant or sextant to determine latitude. Not until the latter part of the 18th century did the use of the chronometer make it possible to find the longitude of the ship; until then that could be estimated only by dead reckoning. In view of possible death or disability of the master, it was important that at least the first mate should have a knowledge of navigation. It is probable that on many occasions disgruntled crews were prevented from overpowering their officers by the consideration that they could not find their way home without a knowledge of navigation.

The mates, it has been said, had a sort of "purgatory status." Their pay was usually small, not much more than that of the foremast hands. There were, however, certain compensations. They had authority; they were addressed as "Mister"; and they were in the line of command, with the possibility of being promoted to master. On some of the large Indiamen there might be three mates; on some passenger ships they would often be called "first officer," "second officer," and so on, because it sounded more impressive. In later days the mates, like the masters, would have to be licensed by the government.

Steam Personnel.—The first important change in that time-honored international shipboard hierarchy came from the gradual introduction of steam during the 19th century. Fewer men were required for the deck force than in

Seamen on the yardarms of a square-rigged sailing vessel.

square-riggers, but the principal innovation consisted of the engineer officers, who operated the machinery, and the husky "black gang" who served as coal passers and stokers.

Both in the merchant marines and in the navies the engineers were likely to be resented by the deck officers. The latter had been accustomed to matching their wits against the winds in order to move the ship as they desired. Now they simply signaled for "full speed ahead" or "stop," and a mechanical expert down in the engine room did the rest. The chief engineer and his assistants were, in the early days, often trained in the ironworks which made the engines and boilers, so that they would know what to do if things went wrong. Unlike the deck officers, whose experience did not particularly fit them for shore jobs, the engineers could often shift to industry or land transportation if they saw fit. The work of the "black gangs" in shoveling the coal from the bunkers and feeding it into the furnaces could be a grueling experience, especially in hot climates; it is said that in the Red Sea the stokehold temperatures sometimes rose as high as 140° F. The British gradually employed large numbers of Chinese, or lascars from India for such work. The gradual substitution of oil for coal after World War I removed the last really disagreeable service afloat. The burly coal passers and stokers were supplanted by a somewhat smaller number of oilers, firemen-water tenders, and wipers. The usual "watch below" consisted of one of each, under an assistant engineer.

The shift to steam also made a difference in the duties and size of the deck force. Instead of the good-sized group that had been needed for going aloft to shorten or let out sail, the usual deck watch on even a large steamship consisted of only three seamen—one to steer, another as lookout, and the third to stand by for odd jobs. Usually there would also be a couple of deck maintenance men who did not stand watch, but were kept busy with the incessant cleaning, scraping, painting, and similar duties. In addition to the deck and engine departments, every ship also had a steward's department, including cooks and messmen. On a cargo ship this was smaller than either of the others; on a passenger liner the steward's force was likely to be larger than both combined.

An impression of forecastle life on a 19th-century whaling ship, scrimshawed on a whale's tooth.

Cities Service Company

Captain and chief engineer converse aboard the Cities Service Company's 38,000-ton supertanker, S.S. W. *Alton Jones*, a ship which provides individual staterooms for all hands.

By the mid-1950's a 10,000-ton freighter required only a few more men than a 500- or 1,000-ton square-rigger of a century earlier. A typical cargo ship has a total complement of 47 men, of whom 12 are licensed officers. The 19 in the deck department include the master, 4 mates, a radio officer, a purser-pharmacist, a bosun (boatswain), 6 able-bodied seamen, 3 ordinary seamen, and 2 deck maintenance men. The 18 in the engine department consist of a chief engineer, 5 assistant engineers, 2 electricians, 3 oilers, 3 firemen-water tenders, 3 wipers, and an engine maintenance man. The 10 men of the steward's department include a chief steward, a chief cook, a cook and baker, an assistant cook, and 6 messmen-utility men.

The status of the shipmaster underwent several changes in the latter part of the 19th century. That dependence upon the engineers made ship handling a somewhat less exacting matter. Also important was the development of overseas communications. By 1875, at about the time that steamers were taking over much of the cargo carrying from sailing vessels, virtually all the major ports in the world, except in the mid-Pacific, were linked by ocean cables which could transmit messages almost instantaneously. This robbed the captains of their old importance as businessmen, for the owners could now keep constant track of distant markets. They could determine where and for how much a ship's cargo would be sold even before she arrived at her destination, and could likewise determine what her next move was to be. With their scope of action thus reduced, the captains generally lost their old primage percentage of freight earnings and were placed on a regular salaried basis. Some of the most pleasant and profitable masters' billets in later days were the commands of crack passenger liners where first-class passengers vied for the privilege of sitting at the captain's table.

While it is still possible to reach the position of officer "through the hawse hole," rising through the ranks from seaman or fireman, many officers of various nations are graduates of maritime schools. Originally, square-rigged "school ships" were the general rule and some still cling to that training. In the United States the schools are now ashore, though some of the training is aboard a steamship. In addition to the United States Merchant Marine Academy at Kings Point, on Long Island, New York, there are four state academies: Maine at Castine; Massachusetts at

Falmouth; New York at Fort Schuyler; and California at Vallejo.

Three less numerous categories of officers developed in the later days. Most passenger ships and some freighters carried pursers who looked out for the passengers and relieved the captain of much of his paper work. Passenger liners almost invariably carried a surgeon or ship's doctor, instead of depending upon what the captain or chief mate could do with his medicine chest. Finally the radio officer became a legal necessity as the 20th century progressed; freighters carried one, while passenger ships had to have three operators for continuous 24-hour service.

Maritime Unions.—Gradually steps were taken to improve the lot of the mariners, particularly in matters of safety, living conditions, and pay. One of the pioneers in this category was an English member of Parliament, Samuel Plimsoll, who was appalled at the unnecessary shipwrecks and loss of life at sea. During the last quarter of the 19th century he secured legislation to improve matters; his name is preserved in the "Plimsoll mark" which the government places on the side of a ship to show how deeply it may be safely loaded. In the United States the principal initiative came from an able and persistent Norwegian sailor, Andrew Furuseth, who called attention year after year to the dreary living and working conditions afloat and to the sorry situation ashore where crimps and boardinghouse keepers fleeced and exploited seamen. If a sailor left his ship before the end of the voyage, moreover, he was liable to arrest for desertion in many foreign ports. Furuseth's persistent efforts finally bore fruit in 1915 when Congress passed the Seamen's Act with the strong support of Senator Robert M. La Follette.

By the mid-1930's the American seamen's unions began to make great gains, and these improvements helped to make it constantly more expensive to operate vessels under the United States flag. The unions realized that regular scheduled steamship service is particularly vulnerable to interruption by strike, either by the seamen, by the longshoremen, or by both. After a series of costly strikes the National Maritime Union, the Seafarers' International Union, and the Sailors' Union of the Pacific began to secure much higher pay and various other concessions for the unlicensed personnel. For one thing, the centuries-old two-watch system at sea, with its "four-on-and-four-off" arrangement, gave way to three watches with a "four-on-and-eight-off" set-up. This meant that every ship had to have an extra mate and extra assistant engineer to head the third watch, as well as extra unlicensed deck and engine personnel. Generous concessions were also secured in the matter of overtime, which ran up the cost still further. Then came vacations, pensions, and other fringe benefits, so that by the late 1950's it was estimated that a seaman on an American-flag ship could earn about $7,000 a year if continually employed; most seamen did not work full time, and the average was around $4,500.[1] That was several times as much as aboard a foreign-flag ship. Although the Masters, Mates and Pilots, the Marine Engineers' Beneficial Association, and other officer unions also made substantial gains, the officers with their heavy responsibilities did not receive propor-

[1] United States Bureau of Labor Statistics, *Earnings and Employment of Seamen on U.S. Flag Ships* (Washington, November 1958).

tionally such extensive gains as the unlicensed personnel.

Along with the sharp increases in pay, the modern American seaman lives in quarters infinitely more comfortable than those of which Furuseth complained. In many of the later American ships there is privacy, with not more than two seamen to a room. There are well-equipped toilet facilities and comfortable lounges. The food, moreover, is a far cry from the old days of hardtack and "salt horse," thanks in part to refrigeration. For leisure hours there is usually a ship's library, while several reels of moving pictures are often put aboard for the voyage. On many foreign-flag ships there are fewer amenities of that sort.

The extent to which American-flag wages were drawing ahead of those under other flags is indicated in the following table for 1954. It shows the monthly basic pay (not including overtime and fringe benefit costs) for the principal licensed and unlicensed positions, except master, aboard a typical good-sized freighter.

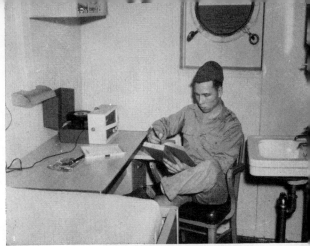

Sun Oil Company

Tankermen's cabins on the Sun Oil Company's S.S. *New Jersey Sun* are equipped with desks, wash basins, medicine cabinets, fluorescent lights, and bunks with innerspring mattresses.

COMPARISON OF MONTHLY BASIC PAY, 1954

	United States	British	Norwegian	Dutch
Deck Department				
Chief officer (mate)	$ 737	$ 173	$ 170	$ 155
2d officer (2d mate)	553	129	135	126
3d officer (3d mate)	510	108	115	94
Radio operator	501	142	131	72
Boatswain	400	91	110	82
Able-bodied seaman	314	78	96	71
Engine Department				
Chief engineer	1,030	218	193	222
2d (1st asst.) engineer	737	160	154	149
3d (2d asst.) engineer	554	130	136	116
Electrician	449	140	146	116
Fireman	314	79	97	72
Oiler	314	81	63	73
Wiper	294	78	63	60
Steward's Department				
Chief steward	390	125	114	101
Chief cook	361	102	117	96
Messman	242	75	61	40
Total crew	$30,341	$7,929	$7,239	$7,865

Source: House Merchant Marine and Fisheries Committee, *Hearings in Labor-Management Problems of the American Merchant Marine*, pp. 946–50 (Washington 1955).

The master's salary is not given in these official figures, but on American-flag ships in the 1950's it averaged around $1,200 a month or $14,400 a year. It will be noted that a mess attendant on an American-flag ship, a position requiring a minimum of skill and experience, received more base pay than the chief officer (and probably also the master), with all his training and responsibility, on a British, Norwegian, or Dutch ship. Between 1948 and 1954 the American pay scale had just about doubled, while the other three remained fairly stationary. It went still higher at the triennial renewals of union contracts in 1955 and 1958, with additional fringe benefits in particular.

DEVELOPMENT OF THE MERCHANT MARINE

Early Merchant Service.—In the great days of sail, between about 1600 and 1850, the services rendered by merchant shipping fall into three major groups: the long hauls on distant sea lanes, usually to other continents; the coastwise and other shorter trades; and fishing and whaling.

The long hauls naturally tended to employ the largest ships and to be the most profitable. In most cases they went to colonial outposts, and the colonizing nation was likely to reserve that lucrative traffic for its own vessels. The longest of those old regular sea routes ran from Europe around Africa to India, or even beyond to China, or what is now called Indonesia. It had originally been developed by the Portuguese and dated from 1497–1499 when Vasco da Gama, carrying out the exploration policy started in 1415 by Prince Henry the Navigator of Portugal, had rounded the Cape of Good Hope and proceeded to India where he secured a cargo of spices. For a century Portuguese vessels under royal control had made the annual voyage from Lisbon to Goa in India, returning with valuable ladings of spices and other oriental offerings.

Around 1600 the English and Dutch took over most of that trade under private companies chartered by their respective governments, with monopoly rights of trade and government in the eastern seas. Their stately East Indiamen, the aristocrats of the old merchant marines and usually the largest merchantmen afloat, made their lengthy voyages each year. The English East India Company's ships sailed from London to Bombay, Madras, or Calcutta in India, and later many went on to Canton in China for tea and silks; they often stopped at the island of St. Helena in the South Atlantic for provisions. The Dutch East India Company's vessels went from Amsterdam to Batavia (now Djakarta) in Java, stopping at Cape Town on the way. Because of the company monopolies, private English and Dutch traders could not send their vessels to those distant ports. Americans could visit there after they became independent in 1783, but private Englishmen could not trade with India until 1813, or with China until 1834. Because of the absence of competition, the Indiamen were apt to be operated in an expensive and not too efficient fashion. The commands of such vessels were eagerly sought because they paid far better than anything else in the merchant service. As time went on, the French, Danish, and other companies made similar voyages; John Paul Jones' famous *Bonhomme Richard* was a former French Indiaman. Beyond those regular main line routes to and from Europe the different nations carried on lucrative country trade with smaller vessels, often run by natives, all through the eastern seas. See also EAST INDIA COMPANIES.

The transatlantic routes were shorter than

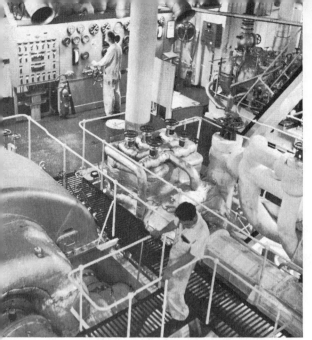

Cities Service Company

Engine room of a modern supertanker.

those long runs around Good Hope, but they were traveled by a much greater number of vessels. The earliest of the services to America consisted of the rigidly regulated "plate fleets" which the Spaniards sent each year to their colonies, a trade which began soon after 1500 and lasted until shortly after 1800. This was one of the first important examples of the convoy system, in which groups of cargo ships were shepherded across the seas by an escort of warships to protect them from attack by other navies or by buccaneers. Westward from Seville, or later Cádiz, in Spain, these fleets carried passengers and European cargo of various sorts. Part of the ships went to Panama and what is now Colombia, and the rest to Mexico. Then all joined at Havana for the return passage to Spain. The name "plate fleet" came from the very valuable cargoes of silver and gold which they brought home from the mines of Mexico and Peru. During most of those same years the Portuguese maintained less formal cargo service to and from their scattered ports along the coast of Brazil.

Around 1600, following the defeat of the Spanish Armada, the English, Dutch, and French began trading and colonizing activity in North America and the Caribbean area. With the development of sugar in the West Indies, a steady stream of valuable cargoes passed between England and her island possessions, particularly Jamaica, Barbados, and Antigua; between France and Martinique, Guadeloupe, and what is now Haiti; between the Netherlands and St. Eustatius, Curaçao, and other possessions; and even from Denmark and Sweden to their little Caribbean holdings. There was also a fair amount of traffic between France and her possessions in what is now Canada. That trade was overshadowed, however, by the steadily increasing traffic between England and her continental colonies, from New England down to Georgia on the stormy North Atlantic run which gradually became the most important of all sea lanes.

The most sinister of all the long hauls was the slave trade from the Guinea Coast and other

parts of Africa to the West Indian islands and to the mainland colonies of Portugal, Spain, and England, all the way from Brazil up to Chesapeake Bay. This was a trade in which the English ports of Bristol and Liverpool and the colonial port of Newport were particularly active. The slavers carried rum, colored cloth, trinkets, and other goods down to Africa and packed their holds with as many Negroes as they could carry. At times many of them died during the grim conditions of the "middle passage" to America. Those that survived were often exchanged for sugar, rum, or tobacco. England finally declared the slave trade illegal in 1807 and the United States in 1808, but, despite naval patrols on the pestilential coast, some of it continued to Cuba and Brazil well into the 19th century.

The Netherlands had the outstanding merchant marine of the period from 1600 to 1650, and even for a while beyond that. The Dutch performed wonders at sea, making Amsterdam the rich entrepôt of world trade where commodities from almost every port and region could be found. With a large and efficient merchant marine, well guarded by a powerful navy, the Dutch had a flourishing business not only with their own possessions in the East Indies, but also in carrying all sorts of commodities for everyone else. They had, moreover, a remarkable knack for opening up new business opportunities, introducing Negro slaves into Virginia, sugar into the West Indies, and coffee into Java in the East Indies from Mocha in Arabia.

After a half century of watching the Dutch outtrade them around the world, the English, in 1651, passed the first of their Navigation Acts (q.v.) designed to promote their own shipping. In particular they sought to reserve to themselves the lucrative long hauls to and from other continents, so they stipulated that all English trade with America, Africa, and Asia must be carried on in English ships with English crews. Between 1652 and 1674 the English and Dutch fought three closely contested naval wars. The Dutch fought bravely and well, but with their land frontier exposed to French invasion they eventually became so exhausted that the English won. By 1730 the British merchant marine was overtaking the Dutch and London was succeeding Amsterdam as the world's leading entrepôt. From that time on, the British merchant marine grew steadily in size.

One important aspect of that Navigation Act situation was that, until 1775, vessels built and manned in the American colonies counted legally as English ships with English crews. Because England lacked an adequate supply of ship timber and masts and had to import much of that material from the Baltic, vessels could be built about one third more cheaply in North America where oak and pine grew almost down to the water's edge, especially in New England. Consequently, the Yankees not only built vessels for the English, but also traded freely with the mother country and with other parts of the world. Up to the outbreak of the American Revolution about one third of all the vessels in British registry were American built.

In addition to those long routes from Europe around Good Hope or across the Atlantic there was a tremendous amount of maritime traffic, usually in smaller vessels, on shorter runs. Much of this was technically coasting trade between ports of a particular nation or colonial region.

Much, however, in Europe was with nearby ports of other countries. On the American seaboard, for instance, some of the coastwise voyages from New England to the South were long enough to carry a vessel from an English or Dutch port to the ports of several different countries on the Continent. In either case, smaller vessels, such as brigs, schooners, or sloops, were generally used in those short trades rather than the full-rigged, three-masted ships with their greater tonnage.

There was, however, one important technical difference between the coastwise trade and the other short runs. Almost every country reserved its coasting trade, like its colonial trade, to its own vessels. England did that in its Navigation Acts, and the United States, once it became free, did likewise in 1817. The Americans, in fact, would later extend the idea even to exclude foreign-flag vessels from the lengthy run around Cape Horn from east coast ports, such as New York, to west coast ports, such as San Francisco, as well as to outlying possessions, such as Hawaii.

Naturally such a monopoly was not possible where trade between two different countries was concerned. While the English Navigation Acts barred foreign vessels from the coasting trade and the long hauls from other continents, it stipulated that in the trade with the continent of Europe cargoes must come either in English ships or in ships of the producing country. In other words, wine from Bordeaux or Rochelle could come to London in English or French ships, but not in Dutch ones, which had previously carried on much of the service because of their efficiency and reasonable rates.

In England the principal coastwise service was in bringing coal, "sea coals" as they were called, from Newcastle down to London in collier brigs. That was a longer run than some of the short hauls to ports on the Continent. In America lively trading existed all along the coast, for it was much easier to exchange goods by sea than by land. There was also constant important trading on the relatively short hauls to the West Indies, carrying lumber and fish from New England, and flour from New York and Philadelphia southward, and bringing back sugar, molasses, and rum. Sometimes these Caribbean voyages fitted into longer triangular patterns involving other regions.

American shipping underwent some drastic changes during its "heroic age" between 1775 and 1815. At the close of the Revolution it no longer, of course, enjoyed the privileges of the British commercial system. American vessels could not trade with the British West Indies or be sold in Britain. On the other hand, they could now, for the first time, trade freely with the Mediterranean and Baltic, and also with India and other parts of the East. During the long Anglo-French wars, starting in 1793, neutral trading opportunities led to a highly profitable expansion of the American merchant marine.

Except on some of the major long trades many of the merchantmen of all nations were transients, counterparts of the later tramp ships. Instead of sticking to a particular route, they knocked around from port to port, wherever business offered. The *Mayflower,* for instance, in the years just before her celebrated voyage to Plymouth, appears to have been in and out of London occasionally—once on a voyage to Norway, once to Hamburg, and twice to Rochelle where she went once again after her return from

America. It is possible that she also engaged in the Greenland whale fishery during that period. As time went on, some ships tended to become regular traders, plying between two or more particular ports. They would carry the goods of the merchant or merchants who owned them, but would usually take other cargo as well in addition to passengers. Generally, however, there was no knowing just when they would sail; they might wait weeks for more cargo.

Line Service.—One of the important steps in merchant shipping development was the inauguration of still more regular service on particular routes, with vessels sailing on scheduled dates. This began in 1818 when the Black Ball Line of square-rigged packet ships commenced monthly sailings between New York and Liverpool, carrying passengers, mail, and the more valuable sort of cargo. This service of the American-flag "square-riggers on schedule" proved so valuable that several other lines quickly came into being, linking New York with London and Havre as well as Liverpool. Similar services ran southward along the coast to the cotton ports of Charleston, Savannah, Mobile, and New Orleans. Those regular sailings became known as "berth service," because a shipper could send his goods to a particular pier knowing that the line would

Engineers at the controls in the bridge of an oil tanker.

carry them on its next sailing.

That principle became even more highly developed with the advent of steamships on the longer runs. The best that sailing vessels could do was to sail on a particular date; their arrival depended upon how the winds happened to be blowing. The arrival of the British steamships *Sirius* and *Great Western* in New York from England in 1838 marked the beginning of permanent transatlantic service, for the pioneer run of the American steamship *Savannah* in 1819 had been mostly under sail and was not repeated.

The British government appreciated the value of the new steamship service in maintaining communication with its varied interests in distant parts of the world. The early marine engines used so much coal that there was not room for

The Merchant Marine Academy at Kings Point, Long Island.

sufficient cargo to meet expenses. That consideration led to the beginning of the policy of subsidies, or government aid to merchant shipping. Around 1840 the British granted mail subsidies on three major routes to companies which have ever since been outstanding: The Peninsular and Oriental to the East; the Royal Mail Steam Packet Company to the West Indies and later to South America; and the Cunard Line to North America—Halifax and Boston at first, later shifting to New York. During the next few years further subsidies were granted for line service to South Africa and numerous other regions.

Before long the United States followed suit as part of a remarkable decade (1845–1855) which came to be called the "glorious age" of its merchant marine. Several separate events combined to produce this period. Britain's abolition of its corn laws in 1846 opened a market for American grain, while its abolition of the Navigation Acts in 1849 admitted American ships to the China-London trade and to British registry. There was a tremendous influx of Irish and German immigrants. The acquisition of California, followed by the gold rush, led to the brilliant development of the California clippers—large, beautiful ships in which carrying capacity was sacrificed for speed. It also led to lines of subsidy steamships from New York and San Francisco to the Isthmus of Panama. The subsidy movement also produced the spectacular performance of the American-flag Collins liners to Liverpool, which established a better speed record than the Cunarders for a few years until they met with two major disasters. For a few years, in the mid-1850's, the American merchant marine almost equaled the British in size and excelled it in quality; the prestige of American shipbuilders and shipmasters was very high.

Then, even before the Confederate raiders damaged American-flag shipping in the Civil War, the decline began to set in. For a full half century following 1865, the American flag gradually disappeared from the distant sea routes to other continents. Whereas American-flag vessels had carried 90 per cent of the nation's commerce around 1800, they were carrying barely 9 per cent a century later.

One of the principal reasons for the American decline was the fact that Great Britain and some other European nations were much better able to build the new steamships with their iron and steam hulls than was the United States. It was a complete reversal of the old days up to 1830 when abundant ship timber and masts close

at hand had enabled the Americans to build more cheaply. Now the cost of construction in yards across the Atlantic was often a third less than in the United States.

During the 1870's steam made rapid advances at the expense of sail. The introduction of the compound engine enabled a ship to go much further on a ton of coal than had been possible in the earlier steamships. It now became practicable to carry heavy bulk cargo, such as wheat, sugar, or coal, by steamship. The opening of the Suez Canal in 1869 further accelerated the shift to steam because the baffling winds of the Red Sea made it very difficult for sailing vessels to use that valuable short cut to the East. Moderate sized steam freighters began to crowd the sailing vessels out of most of the important trades, except on such very long routes as those to Britain and the Continent, with wool or grain from Australia, grain from California, and nitrates from Chile.

While the red ensign of the British merchant marine continued to fly over more ships than any other flag, Germany made remarkable maritime progress during the 40 years before World War I. The Germans were able to build first-rate ships; they could operate them very efficiently and they found ample cargoes in their vigorous extension of world markets. The Scandinavian nations, particularly the Norwegians, developed

A merchant ship strikes a floating mine during World War I.

good-sized merchant marines consisting chiefly of freighters which carried tramp cargoes for others. The Dutch had a moderate-sized fleet of excellent ships which found rich business in trading with the Netherlands possessions in the East Indies, as well as on other long hauls. The Japanese, soon after throwing off their old isolation from the rest of the world, showed remarkable energy and skill in building and operating passenger liners and freighters. Various other countries had some merchant shipping; the French, like the Americans, clung to sail longer than most of the others. The Greeks were generally in the market for secondhand tonnage which could be purchased and operated cheaply.

The most conspicuous ships in these fleets were the crack passenger liners which raced across the North Atlantic to New York. In that field, which was apt to produce more glory than profit, the Cunard and White Star lines, under the British flag, received strenuous competition from the Germans with their Hamburg-American and North German Lloyd liners, while the French Line captured a fair amount of trade. More profitable, on the whole, were the medium-sized passenger-cargo ships, both in the North Atlantic service and on more distant runs. Some of these, especially on the routes from Argentina, Uruguay, Australia, and New Zealand, had refrigeration or "reefer" capacity for carrying fresh beef or mutton to Britain and the Continent.

The bulk of the world's cargoes, however, moved in the holds of the dry-cargo freighters which around 1900 averaged only about 4,000 to 5,000 gross tons and moved at only about 8 to 10 knots. Many of these, particularly in the Scandinavian merchant fleets, were tramps which plied no regular route but picked up cargoes wherever they were to be found, particularly in the seasonal movement of bulk commodities, such as sugar and wheat. As time went on, however, an increasing number of British, German, and some other freighters were organized into cargo lines which provided frequent, dependable scheduled berth service on most of the important sea routes. These lines, like some of the passenger services, were often organized into conferences on the various runs in order to keep rates uniform and avoid costly cutthroat competition.

Many such lines served American ports, connecting them with various regions beyond the seas, though not as adequately as Britain and Germany were served by their own lines to distant markets. Naturally those foreign lines seldom exerted themselves to develop American exports of commodities which their own factories could produce. Many distant cargoes, moreover, such as wool from Australia and South Africa, tea from Ceylon and India, and rubber from Malaya, reached the United States only after being carried hundreds of miles out of their way for transshipment at some British or German port.

The Americans, however, were not, as a whole, seriously concerned by their own lack of adequate shipping until the outbreak of World War I in 1914. Then, with the usual German services swept off the seas and the British sailings reduced, the Americans found themselves unable to meet the new demands of South America, Africa, and other distant regions for American exports, or to bring in manganese and other needed imports. With only a few seagoing coastal and intercoastal steamships available, the Americans resorted to sailing vessels which, for the last time in history, were able to render important service; dozens of big schooners and square-riggers were pressed into service on those long hauls. This lack of ships led Congress to pass the Shipping Act of Sept. 7, 1916, which set up the United States Shipping Board to handle the situation and also made provision for the acquisition of an American-flag merchant fleet under government auspices.

In the meantime the German submarine warfare was threatening the merchant fleets and overseas supplies of Britain and its allies. By the spring of 1917, when the United States entered the war, the submarines were taking a terrific toll and the situation looked desperate. The Shipping Board requisitioned all the nation's seagoing steamships for government operation and then launched a tremendous shipbuilding pro-

gram. Dozens of new shipyards were set up; the largest, at Hog Island below Philadelphia, Pa., had 50 shipways. The program was only just getting under way when the war ended in November 1918, but much of it was continued during the next three years. Altogether, 2,311 vessels were built. Most of these were steel dry-cargo freighters, but a few were passenger vessels or tankers, while 619 were less useful wooden or concrete ships.

This huge fleet suddenly placed the United States second only to Britain among the merchant marines of the world. It made possible a policy, which has been pursued ever since, of maintaining regular line service on a comprehensive network of essential trade routes, with government financial assistance wherever necessary. At the outset the Shipping Board directly operated a large number of such lines itself, but gradually the ships were sold at bargain rates at auction to private operators who agreed to maintain service on the particular routes. Congressional action in 1920 and 1928 made provision for certain financial assistance in the form of extra mail payments and construction loans.

Radio room of a modern merchant vessel.

By the mid-1930's it was obvious that these payments were not able to produce the desired results. The cost of operating American-flag ships was far more than in the foreign merchant marines. There was also the problem of "block obsolescence," for those Hog Islanders and other products of the 1917–1921 emergency program were all growing old together, approaching the 20-year limit which marked the normal life of a ship. The foreign merchant marines, moreover, were building new ships which were faster and more efficient than the American freighters.

Congress met that situation with the Merchant Marine Act of June 30, 1936, which established the principles of "operational differential" and "construction differential" subsidies on the essential trade routes. Instead of disguising these as payments for mail or naval purposes, Congress came out with an openly admitted subsidy policy, but at the same time took numerous precautions to be sure that effective, regular service with adequate ships would be maintained on the essential routes. The operational-differential subsidy was designed to make up the difference in cost between operating under the American or foreign flags. When, for instance, a freighter's cost of wages was some $30,000 a month under the American flag, as it was in 1954, and only about $7,500 under the flags of her British and Norwegian competitors, the government would pay the operator the $22,500 difference along with lesser differences in the cost of food, supplies, repairs, and insurance. This would enable the American shipowners to compete with the cheaper foreign operating costs. If, however, the American line made more than 10 per cent profit, the government would "recapture" half of the surplus up to the amount of the subsidy. Actually some of the lines thus returned their entire subsidy to the Maritime Commission or its successor, the United States Maritime Administration. See also COMMERCE, DEPARTMENT OF— *Functions.*

important were the so-called C-2 and C-3 freighters which were respectively 459 and 492 feet long, had 6,085 and 7,675 gross tons, and 8,794 and 12,500 dead-weight tons, with speeds of 15½ and 17 knots. It was planned to build 50 of these ships each year for 10 years to replace the old emergency fleets.

That program was barely getting under way when the submarine warfare of World War II called for another emergency program even more ambitious than that of the first war. It produced 5,777 ships totaling 56 million dead-weight tons. Of these 2,708 were large, slow Liberty ships, while 414 were Victory ships of similar size but more speed; 705 were tankers, 727 were minor types, and 682 were military types. But along with that emergency building, the Maritime Commission produced 541 of the C-2's, C-3's, and other types for its long-range program. This gave the United States an excellent nucleus of first-rate ships for its postwar fleet which became the largest in the world. Of the 71.0 million gross tons of world shipping in mid-1946 the

LINES HOLDING OPERATING-DIFFERENTIAL SUBSIDIES ON ESSENTIAL TRADE ROUTES, MID-1959

Route	From	To	Line
1	Atlantic	S. Amer., east coast	Moore-McCormack
2	Atlantic	S. Amer., west coast	Grace
3	Atlantic	Mexico, east coast	. . .
4	Atlantic	Caribbean	Grace; Moore-McCormack
5	N. Atlantic	United Kingdom; Rep. of Ireland	United States Lines
6	N. Atlantic	Scandinavia; Baltic	Moore-McCormack
7	N. Atlantic	German North Sea ports	United States Lines
8	N. Atlantic	Belgium; Netherlands	United States Lines; American Banner Line
9	N. Atlantic	Atlantic France; N. Spain	United States Lines
10	N. Atlantic	Mediterranean; Black Sea; etc.	Amer. Export; Amer. President
11	S. Atlantic	United Kingdom; N. Continent	United States Lines
12	Atlantic	Far East	United States Lines; Amer. President; Lykes
13	S. Atlantic; Gulf	Mediterranean; Black Sea; etc.	Lykes
14–1	Atlantic	West Africa	Farrell
14–2	Gulf	West Africa	Mississippi (Delta)
15A	Atlantic	South and East Africa	Farrell; Moore-McCormack
15B	Gulf	South and East Africa	Lykes
16	Atlantic; Gulf	Australasia	United States Lines
17	Atlantic; Pacific	Indonesia; Malaya	Amer. Mail; Amer. President; Lykes
18	Atlantic; Gulf	India; Persian Gulf; etc.	Amer. Export; Amer. President
19	Gulf	Caribbean	Lykes
20	Gulf	S. Amer., east coast	Mississippi (Delta)
21	Gulf	United Kingdom; N. Europe	Lykes; Bloomfield
22	Gulf	Far East	Lykes
23	Pacific	Caribbean	Grace; Moore-McCormack
24	Pacific	S. Amer., east coast	Moore-McCormack
25	Pacific	S. Amer., west coast; Cen. Amer.; Mexico	Grace
26A	Pacific	United Kingdom; Rep. of Ireland	. . .
26B	Pacific	Havre-Hamburg range	. . .
27	Pacific	Australasia	Oceanic
28	Pacific	Indonesia; Malaya; India; etc.	Amer. Mail; Amer. President
29	Pacific	Far East	Amer. Mail; Pacific Far East; Pacific Transport
31	Gulf	S. Amer., west coast	Gulf & South America
32	Great Lakes	Western Europe	Amer. Export
33	Great Lakes	Caribbean	Grace

While the operating-differential subsidy might be recaptured in boom periods, there were frequent lean years when it made the difference between profit and loss for a shipping line, and it became increasingly difficult to operate under the American flag without such aid.

The construction-differential subsidy was designed to offset the difference in building costs between American and foreign yards; it was designed particularly to keep American shipyards, with their higher costs, in operation. The government would pay up to half (later 55 per cent) of the cost of a vessel and would lend much of the rest to a line, to be repaid in installments. This arrangement was particularly timely, for the bulk of the ships in American lines needed replacement. The Maritime Commission designed several standard types which could be produced reasonably in considerable numbers. Particularly

United States had almost half at 35.3 gross tons while the United Kingdom totaled only 16.5, after which Norway trailed at 2.9. Many of the surplus American vessels were laid up at quiet anchorages in the Hudson River, the James River, the Columbia River, and elsewhere, just as they had been following World War I. During the Korean crisis in 1950–1952, more than 500 Liberty ships were brought out of reserve for active service. For complete figures see SHIPPING OF THE WORLD.

Passenger Traffic and Air Competition.— In one respect the American merchant marine was weaker than it had been before the war, and much weaker than the British. The number of passenger and passenger-cargo liners had fallen off sharply. This was a cause for some concern because the great British liners *Queen Mary* and *Queen Elizabeth,* the largest afloat, and the Amer-

MERCHANT MARINE

ican *America* (renamed *West Point*) had rendered invaluable service as troop transports during the war. Finally, in 1952, the new *United States* of the United States Lines restored the "blue riband" to America by proving herself the fastest liner in the world. Postwar travel was heavy, particularly to Europe in the summer and on cruises during the winter; the Cunard Line built one crack liner, the *Caronia,* especially for world cruises. Following the war, however, the passenger liners were receiving increasing competition from the overseas airlines which could render much faster service. Transpacific service and runs out through Asia to Australia had begun in the 1930's; transatlantic service had barely begun on the eve of World War II, but thereafter grew rapidly. By 1957 sea and air were almost identical—at about one million each in the number of passengers arriving from abroad at New York City, the western terminus for virtually all services. Of 53,676,000 dead-weight tons of new vessels under construction early in 1958[1], only 361,000 tons were passenger or passenger-cargo liners, as compared with 16,923,000 tons for dry-cargo freighters and 36,392,000 tons, more than 67 per cent, for tankers.

Tankers.—The preceding figures indicate graphically the constantly increasing importance of tankers in the merchant fleets of the world. In the early days of petroleum, kerosine, the principal product, was usually carried in sailing vessels as "case oil," with two 5-gallon cans in a wooden case. Bulk carriage, very much more economical, dated from 1886 with the construction of the first tanker, *Gluckauf,* with her hull divided into a dozen compartments. Such a vessel could be loaded and pumped out quickly without the delay and heavy expense that would become an increasing problem with dry-cargo vessels. The chief difficulty was the one-way traffic with no adequate return cargoes. "Dirty" tankers carried crude or heavy fuel oil; "clean" tankers carried gasoline and other refined products. Several important tanker routes developed, starting with the opening of the Gulf oilfields in Texas and vicinity. A major coastwise run brought the Gulf oil up past Cape Hatteras to northern ports, while transatlantic runs carried it to Europe. Later the Venezuelan oilfields served both regions. In the meantime, oil from the Middle East became increasingly important as part of the world supply. Some of it was transported in pipelines for considerable distance, but most of it moved by sea.

The tanker fleets grew constantly in size. At first most of them belonged to the large oil companies, but by the 1950's there was a tendency to charter privately owned tankers. The Norwegians went heavily into this business, as did a few wealthy Greeks, operating under various flags. It was found that big tankers were more economical to operate than small ones. During World War II the Maritime Commission, along with its Liberty ships, built many T-2 tankers which could carry around 130,000 barrels; by the late 1950's huge new ones were carrying almost three times that amount. In addition to tankers, a considerable number of huge ore ships have been built, both for ocean runs, such as iron ore from Venezuela, and for Great Lakes service. See also COMMERCE—*1. History;* TANKERS AND SUPERTANKERS.

Flags of Convenience.—In earlier days

[1] *American Merchant Marine Institute Bulletin* (New York, June 13, 1958).

Sun Oil Company

A tanker beats its way through a gale off Cape Hatteras.

the flag which a vessel flew was usually an indication of the country where she was owned, as was the hailing port painted on her stern. Gradually, differences in costs and other considerations began to lead shipowners to place their vessels under other flags while still retaining ownership. During the Civil War many northern vessels were transferred to British registry because of the Confederate raiders; later many American-owned vessels likewise flew Britain's red ensign for reasons of economy.

Since World War I, however, Panama and Liberia, which have virtually no regular shipping of their own, have gradually loaned the use of their flags until, by 1957, they ranked fourth and seventh respectively among the merchant fleets of the world. The first use of these so-called flags of convenience came during the early 1920's when two American-owned cruise ships were shifted to Panamanian registry so that they could serve liquor during the prohibition period. When the maritime unions began to secure drastic increases of pay for seamen on American-flag vessels, many other ships, including some of the big tanker fleets, likewise shifted to Panama. When it was found that such a shift meant substantial savings in taxation, in addition to freedom from wartime requisitioning, still more vessels followed suit. By 1939 the Panamanian merchant marine totaled 700,000 gross tons, or one twelfth the amount under the United States flag.

The postwar tanker boom suddenly boosted that total, but Panama was gradually outstripped by a rival which offered even more liberal terms. An American corporation which received a charter for the economic development of Liberia developed a system whereby, for a very modest fee, vessels could secure Liberian registry, even though most of them might never come within thousands of miles of Monrovia, its sole deepwater port.

By the end of 1956 the 6.5 million gross tons of the Liberian merchant fleet was exceeded only by the United States with 24.0, the United Kingdom with 23.3, and Norway with 7.7. Then, following the "legitimate" fleets of Japan, who was making a remarkable postwar recovery with 5.4 million gross tons, and France with 4.6, came Panama with 4.0. Honduras was also doing a modest business in such use of its flag. The use of these flags of convenience has been criticized severely by the regular maritime nations and also by the American maritime unions, whose costly wage scales have been among the major causes of the movement. Much of the new tanker tonnage, however, has been crowding into Liberian registry, particularly the ships with Greek or unsubsidized American owners.

In addition to these "flags of easy virtue," as they have been called, many new merchant marines have sprung up in the postwar period as manifestations of national pride. Israel and Ghana are examples of this new movement which has sent numerous flags to sea on missions previously performed by the ubiquitous merchant fleets of Britain, Norway, and the other traditional maritime powers.

Bibliography.—Thornton, R. H., *British Shipping* (New York 1939); Tyler, David B., *Steam Conquers the Atlantic* (New York 1939); Hutchins, John G. B., *The American Maritime Industries and Public Policy, 1789–1914* (Cambridge, Mass., 1941); Albion, Robert G., and Pope, J. B., *Sea Lanes in Wartime* (New York 1942); Marx, Daniel, Jr., *International Shipping Cartels* (Princeton 1953); Goldberg, Joseph P., *The Maritime Story; a Study in Labor-Management Relations* (Cambridge, Mass., 1958).

ROBERT G. ALBION,
Professor of History, Harvard University.

MERCHANT OF VENICE, The, a comedy by William Shakespeare, was entered in the Stationers Register on July 22, 1598, and published two years later as "The most excellent Historie of the *Merchant of Venice* With the extreame crueltie of *Shylocke* the Iewe towards the sayd Merchant, in cutting a iust pound of his flesh: and the obtayning of *Portia* by the choyse of three chests." Another quarto, falsely dated 1600, was not printed until 1619, and like the quartos of 1637 and 1652 it is a reprint without independent authority. The version in the First Folio of 1623 was also printed from the 1600 quarto but contains some alterations made in Jacobean times. The 1600 printing is therefore the substantive text; it was apparently based on the playwright's manuscript from which the promptbook had been prepared. The play was written earlier than 1598 and later than the trial of Dr. Roderigo Lopez, a Jewish physician, in 1594, which occasioned the revival of Christopher Marlowe's *The Jew of Malta* by the rival Admiral's Company in that year. It is probable that Shakespeare's was a competitive play for the Lord Chamberlain's Men. Various allusions make 1596 the most acceptable date for the play in its present form.

The stories which Shakespeare skillfully intertwined and adapted for *The Merchant of Venice* are old ones which exist in various forms. The bond and ring plots are combined in a 14th century *novella* by Ser Giovanni Fiorentino in a collection called *Il Pecorone,* published in 1558. The versions here are those closest to Shakespeare's play. The casket story the dramatist probably took from a medieval compilation, the *Gesta Romanorum,* which had been translated from Latin to English and published in 1577, and 1595. Elements of Shylock and the elopement of his daughter can be found in *The Jew of Malta,* 1589–1590. The matter of sources, however, is complex, and it is impossible to be dogmatic about what versions were actually used. It seems clear that Shakespeare, in addition to his combination of various tales, was responsible for motivating the entrance into the bond, cleaning up the casket story, introducing the law which condemned aliens for plotting against the life of a Venetian citizen, and developing the Jew into a realistic and credible character.

Three other characters are also rounded out: the melancholy idealist, Antonio, who embodies the Elizabethan cult of friendship; Bassanio, no mere fortune hunter but "best deserving of a fair lady," who chooses by substance, not appearance; and especially Portia, rich in personality as well as in estate. She has all the graces along with deep understanding and a sense of humor.

Changed attitudes are responsible for a frequent misunderstanding of Shylock. His importance is easily overstressed, but Shakespeare dropped him in the fourth act and devoted the last to clearing up the entanglements of the lovers. An Elizabethan would not have made a Jew a tragic hero in a comedy about a merchant of Venice and a series of wooings culminating in a happy ending. He is a dark and threatening cloud on the romantic horizon. Nor though he is the butt of gibes is he merely a comic figure expressing the anti-Semitism of a bygone age. Shakespeare presented his antagonist not only from the point of view of others but from his own, and Shylock's feelings are made understandable and at times sympathetic. It was Shakespeare who humanized him and wrote Portia's great speech of mercy and tolerance. The play is full of such poetic gems, sometimes utterly serious, in other places in delightful, musical banter. Thus it combines both ideas and reality with the otherworldliness of imaginative adventure.

The play was frequently acted in its own time and twice presented at court. Neglected in the Restoration, it was adapted and misinterpreted in the 18th century for performances in which Shylock was played by a comedian. The first great embodiment of the character was by Charles Macklin in 1741. He brought out his private calamities but stressed his cold malevolence. From this time on the play was popular, and productions included such stars as John Philip Kemble, John Henderson, and Edmund Kean, who made Shylock more sympathetic. The nineteenth century tended indeed to turn him into a symbol of a persecuted race, an interpretation which reached its culmination in the performance of Henry Irving in 1879. Ellen Terry was the Portia. The play has continued to fill theaters not only in Great Britain and the United States but all over the world. It has been one of the most frequently acted plays at the Memorial Theatre in Stratford, England, and was given in 1957 at the Festival Theatre in Stratford, Conn., with Morris Carnovsky as Shylock, and Katherine Hepburn as Portia.

Bibliography.—The most useful edition is by J. R. Brown, 7th rev. (Cambridge 1955); a convenient paperback is by G. L. Kittredge, notes ed. A. C. Sprague (Boston 1945). The *Variorum* ed. by H. H. Furness (Philadelphia 1888) contains early commentary but is out of print. For further discussion, see Stoll, E. E., *Shakespeare Studies* (New York 1927); Granville-Barker, H., *Prefaces to Shakespeare,* vol. 1 (Princeton 1946); and Parrott, T. M., *Shakespearean Comedy* (New York 1949).

ROBERT HAMILTON BALL,
Professor of English, Queens College of the City of New York.

MERCIER, mĕr-syä′, **Désiré Joseph,** Belgian cardinal: b. Braine l'Alleud, Belgium, Nov. 21, 1851; d. Brussels, Jan. 23, 1926. Educated at the Mechelen (Malines) Seminary, he attended the University of Louvain, was ordained priest in 1874, and appointed professor of philosophy at the seminary three years later. In 1882 Mercier was named to the newly created chair of Thomistic philosophy at Louvain University and thenceforward devoted himself to integrating the rapidly developing 19th century sciences with Catholic philosophy. Before his appointment he had studied under Jean Martin Charcot, the French neurologist to whom Sigmund Freud was indebted for some of his psychoanalytical theories. In 1894, as professor at the new Institut Supérieur de Philosophie in Louvain, Mercier became increasingly important in the Catholic intellectual world as a leader of the neo-Thomist movement. Named archbishop and primate of Belgium in 1906 and cardinal in 1907, he became *de facto* leader of his country in World War I when Belgium was overrun by the Germans and the king was at the front. Cardinal Mercier by his wise counsel to the Belgians and his courage in dealing with the invaders won worldwide popularity for himself and the Allied cause, particularly in America. After the war he was active in attempts to unite the Anglican and Roman Catholic faiths.

Simon, A., *Le Cardinal Mercier* (Brussels 1960).

MERCIER, Honoré, Canadian lawyer and politician: b. St. Athanase, Iberville County, Quebec, Canada, Oct. 15, 1840; d. Montreal, Oct. 30, 1894. Educated at Ste. Marie College in Montreal, he was editor of a Conservative newspaper (1862–1866) at St. Hyacinthe, where he also practiced law until 1882. He opposed the Canadian Confederation (1867) as inimical to the interests of French Canadians and in 1871 helped found the National Party. Mercier représented Rouville in the House of Commons (1872–1874) and from 1879 sat in the Quebec Assembly, serving briefly as solicitor general. Becoming Liberal leader of Quebec in 1883, his vigorous denunciation of the execution (1885) of Louis Riel (q.v.), leader of the Northwest Rebellion, helped defeat the Conservative Party and resulted in Mercier's election as premier of Quebec (1887–1891). He strengthened his position with French Canadians by putting through a bill compensating Jesuits for property confiscated by the crown, but he was dismissed from office in 1891 when it was alleged $100,000 authorized for railroad subsidization had been used for political purposes. Mercier was indicted on a criminal charge but acquitted.

MERCIER DE LA RIVIERE, rē-vyâr′, **Paul Pierre** (also LEMERCIER or LE MERCIER), French political scientist: b. 1720; d. Paris, France, ?1794. Councilor in the Parlement of Paris from 1747 to 1759 and intendant on the island of Martinique for five years thereafter, he became one of the leading theoreticians of the physiocrats (q.v.) after his return to Paris in 1764. In his major work, *L'ordre naturel et essentiel des sociétés politiques* (2 vols., 1767), Mercier de la Rivière developed the political side of physiocratic doctrine, advocating an enlightened "legal despotism" under an absolute monarch as the best form of government, and opposing representative government as anarchic. As a check on the monarch, Mercier relied on an independent magistracy with power to decide on the constitutionality of new laws.

MERCK, mĕrk, **Johann Heinrich,** German critic: b. Darmstadt, Germany, April 11, 1741; d. there, June 27, 1791. Educated at Giessen, Erlangen, and the Dresden Academy of Painting, he entered government service in Hesse-Darmstadt when he was 26, and from 1768 was paymaster of the army there. Merck's keen and caustic essays in the *Frankfurter Gelehrte Anzeigen,* Christoph Martin Wieland's *Merkur,* and Friedrich Nicolai's *Allgemeine Deutsche Bibliothek* made him one of the most respected and at the same time one of the most feared critics of his time. Among the first to recognize the genius of the youthful Johann Wolfgang von Goethe, he published Goethe's *Götz von Berlichingen* (1773) at his own expense; and although he often criticized the poet sharply in later years, they remained friends until Merck's death. Many of the characteristics of Mephistopheles in Goethe's *Faust* are believed to stem from Merck's wry personality. A series of tragedies in his personal life caused him finally to commit suicide.

MERCOEUR, mĕr-kûr′, DUC DE (PHILIPPE EMMANUEL DE LORRAINE), French soldier: b. Nomeny, France, Sept. 9, 1558; d. Nürnberg, Germany, Feb. 19, 1602. The son of Nicolas de Lorraine, who became duc de Mercoeur, he married Marie de Luxembourg, duchesse de Penthièvre, in 1575, the same year his sister married Henry III, king of France. Mercoeur was named governor of Brittany (1582) by his royal brother-in-law, but when Henry supported the Huguenots (1584) Mercoeur remained stanchly Catholic, and after the assassination of the 3d duc de Guise (1588) he assumed leadership of the Holy League in Brittany and sought to make his province independent. In campaigns against the Protestant Henry IV, successor to the murdered (1589) Henry III, he achieved some victories but submitted to the king at Angers (1598). Required to betroth his daughter to the king's natural son, the duc de Vendôme, who then became governor of Brittany, Mercoeur went to Hungary and served in the army of Emperor Rudolf II.

MERCURY, mûr′kṳ-rĭ, the English name for the Roman god Mercurius who, with winged hat and sandals, was messenger of the gods and divinity of the market place and of commerce. Mercurius was originally a Greek god, Hermes (q.v.).

MERCURY, the nearest planet to the sun and the smallest major planet in the solar system. It is a solid spherical body 3,100 miles in diameter and shines by reflected light from the sun. Mercury has no satellite. It revolves around the sun in an elliptical orbit in a *sidereal period* (reckoned from position of alignment with the sun and any given star to the same position again) of 88 days. The *synodical period* is 115.88 days. The average distance of Mercury from the sun is 36,000,000 miles compared with the earth's mean distance of 92,957,000 miles from the sun. Because of its relatively small orbit situated inside that of the earth, Mercury can never be seen in the sky more than 28° in angular separation (*elongation*) from the sun.

As Mercury in its orbital revolution moves to a maximum angular distance west of the sun in the sky, the planet rises just ahead of the sun in the early morning; in its position farthest east of the sun in the sky, Mercury sets just after the sun in the western twilight. Only in these two positions (near maximum western and eastern elongation, respectively) does Mercury appear as a conspicuous naked-eye object. Its average magnitude is then + 0.2. When Mercury is between the earth and the sun (in new phase or at *inferior conjunction*) only the side of the planet turned away from the earth is illuminated by the sun. When the planet is directly on the opposite side of the sun from the earth (in full phase or at *superior conjunction*) its fully lighted disc is turned toward the earth. In both of these cases, Mercury is directly in line with the sun and is lost in its glare.

Telescopically viewed, however, the maximum brightness actually occurs when the planet is at perihelion (its closest approach to the sun) and is near to, but not exactly at, superior conjunction and thus still fully illuminated. Its magnitude is then −1.8, or brighter than the star Sirius. With the unaided eye, the planet is best seen a few days before maximum eastern elongation (as an "evening star") in the spring, and shortly after maximum western elongation (as a "morning star") in autumn. The ancient Greeks believed that Mercury in these two positions represented two different planets; they named these Hermēs (Mercury) and Apollōn (Apollo) respectively.

In its motion around the sun, always inside the orbit of the earth, Mercury exhibits a recurring cycle of phases, passing from new to crescent to first quarter to gibbous to full phase and then through the cycle in reverse in a manner similar to that of the moon. Simultaneously, its distance from the earth varies from 48,000,000 miles at crescent phase (when its apparent diameter is 13" of arc) to 138,000,000 miles at full phase (when the apparent diameter is only 4½" of arc).

An earlier assumption of a common, synchronous rotation and revolution period of 88 days for Mercury has been refuted in recent years by Doppler radar-echo observations (see TELESCOPE —*Radio Telescopes*), combined with a reinterpretation of visual observations of the surface markings on Mercury. These mutually supporting results give a rotation period of 58.646 days (in a direct sense of rotation) with a probable error or ±0.01 day. The direction of the axis of rotation appears to be nearly perpendicular to the planet's orbital plane. Dynamic considerations point to the possibility of a resonance coupling between Mercury's rotation period and its revolution period, in a ratio of 2 to 3, as well as the likelihood of a small permanent rigidity for the planet. Radar observations indicate the planet's surface to be somewhat rougher than that of the moon.

Knowledge of the surface temperature of Mercury also has been enhanced in recent years by radio telescope data. While the temperature calculated to exist at the subsolar point—that is, the point on the surface directly below the sun—is above the melting point of lead, the thermal radiation from the fully sunlit disc of the planet turned toward earth at time of superior conjunction is not directly observable from earth, because of the intervening sun. The radio brightness temperatures at 2-centimeter wavelength, with

Mercury in phase angles between 40° and 130°, range from about 330° K to 210° K (+135° F to −81° F). These temperatures are representative of both the sunlit and dark portions of the planet, since the resolving power of a radio telescope cannot distinguish between portions of the disc.

Mercury's atmosphere is estimated from spectrographic measurements to be only about 0.0001% that of the earth's, and to have a carbon dioxide content of 0.3 to 7 grams per cubic centimeter.

The eccentricity or elliptical flattening of the planet's orbit is, next to that of Pluto, the greatest of any planet in the solar system. At perihelion Mercury is 28,600,000 miles from the sun and at aphelion it is 43,400,000 miles from the sun. From the relationships of Kepler's laws (q.v.), the planet moves with an orbital velocity of 35 miles per second at perihelion and only 23 miles per second at aphelion. As a result of this high orbital eccentricity and marked fluctuation in a consistently high orbital speed, Mercury is subject to a relativistic-mass variation in its orbit in addition to the gravitational perturbations induced by the other planets. The entire orbit actually spins very slowly around the sun in a fashion similar to that of a rotating wheel. In this motion there is a residual displacement of 42.56" per century in its line of apsides, a circumstance which has provided one of the few observational proofs for Einstein's general theory of relativity.

In its motion around the sun, Mercury may upon rare occasions pass directly between the earth and sun while being simultaneously at or near one of its orbital nodes, that is, crossing the plane of the earth's motion around the sun (the ecliptic). Mercury may then be seen telescopically as a small black dot crossing the disc of the sun from east to west, a phenomenon known as a *solar transit,* important for checking the lack of planetary atmosphere, the planet's predicted orbit, and perturbations therein. See also TRANSITS.

FERGUS J. WOOD,
Environmental Science Services Administration.

MERCURY, (also known as QUICKSILVER) the only metal which is liquid over a considerable range of temperature (from −38.85° C. to 356.9° C.). As a liquid it is approximately 13.6 times as heavy as water. It is the seventh in historical order of the metals known to the ancients, and played an important part in medieval alchemy.

Mercury has an atomic number of 80, and its accepted atomic weight is 200.61. Its symbol is Hg from the Latin *hydrargyrum,* liquid silver. There are six stable natural isotopes of mercury, totalling 99.9 per cent, with a range of abundance of 6.85 to 29.8 per cent, as well as radioactive isotopes, most of which are artificially produced. A sharp and narrow line in the spectrum of Mercury-198 is employed as a standard of length. In contact with glass under ordinary conditions, the high surface tension of mercury gives it a reversed meniscus, but Lyman James Briggs has shown that a practically flat surface characterizes the metal in a tube from which all gases have been removed.

Pure mercury is stable at ordinary temperatures in the presence of air, oxygen, carbon dioxide, and ammonia. Long heating at a moderate temperature in air causes the formation of red mercuric oxide, which decomposes at 500° C. into mercury and oxygen. These reactions were the basis of the experiments of Antoine Laurent Lavoisier in 1777 which led to his proof that oxygen is a component of the atmosphere. Sulphur and the halogens combine readily with mercury. It is relatively unreactive with dilute sulphuric and hydrochloric acid, but is attacked by nitric acid. Mercury has two electrons in its outermost shell and has a valence of both one and two. Ions of the element with the former valence are double and are represented as $(Hg_2)^{++}$, as indicated by X-ray studies and conductivity.

Mercury has been called the "metal of a thousand uses," but its annual world production rarely exceeds 10,000 tons, and is usually measured in terms of pounds. Occurring in nature mainly as mercuric sulphide, HgS, in the red mineral cinnabar (the precipitated sulphide is black), mercury from five mines accounts for about three quarters of all production: Almadén in Spain, a mine which has been worked for centuries, and one in Yugoslavia, Peru, Italy, and the United States. In this country, California and Nevada are the leading producers. United States production has fluctuated between 0.25 and 3.8 million pounds, and consumption averages around 4.0 million pounds. Two thirds of all mercury production is used for agriculture, electrical apparatus, electrolytic production of chlorine and caustic soda, and instruments. Mercury is handled and shipped in metal flasks, a single container holding 76 pounds as a standard weight. In the United States, ore runs from 5–12 per cent mercury content. The ore is ground and heated in retorts or furnaces, and collected in cast-iron condensers. Mercury vapor is a distinct health hazard in concentrations as low as 0.15 milligrams per cubic meter of air. It may be detected by the blackening of paper impregnated with a sulphide which passes over a photoelectric cell and actuates a warning alarm.

Metallic mercury is employed in large quantities in equipment in which there is relatively little loss, such as mercury boilers in a few power plants, in electrolytic cells, in electrical equipment, and in instruments. There is very little recovery of mercury from its compounds, and these represent the larger part of the annual market. The larger users of these compounds are the agricultural, pharmaceutical, and paint industries, and consumers of mercury catalysts. A minor use is in the manufacture of fulminates (q.v.) or detonators for explosives, the derivative being mercury fulminate.

Mercury compounds listed as commercial chemicals include: mercurous and mercuric chlorides and iodides, mercuric acetate, cyanide, oxide, naphthenate, nitrate, and sulphide. What is called mercurous oxide, a black solid, is a mixture of mercuric oxide and mercury. Mercuric oxide occurs in two forms, which are identical chemically, but in finely divided form the oxide is yellow, while coarser particles are red. Ammoniated mercury is a white material having the composition, $HgNH_2Cl$. Some organic mercury compounds are industrial fungicides, of which phenyl mercuric chloride is typical.

Mercury and mercury compounds are employed in electrical cells. A commercial dry battery is made up of mercury and zinc, their oxides, and potassium hydroxide. The Weston reference cell contains cadmium and mercury, their sulphates, and water. A calomel half-cell is made up of mercury and solid mercurous chloride in contact with a molar solution of potassium chloride. Compared with the standard hydrogen electrode, the voltage of the calomel electrode is 0.280 volts at $25°$ C. A standard reagent for the determination of ammonia is the Nessler solution, which contains a complex potassium mercuric iodide, whose color change is effected by small concentrations of ammonia.

Mercury compounds are of considerable importance in medicine. Calomel or mercurous chloride, Hg_2Cl_2 (whose name is derived from a Greek word meaning "beautiful black" because of the formation of a black mixture of mercury and ammonobasic mercuric chloride), was once a widely prescribed laxative. Medicinal mercury compounds are classified as antiseptics, diuretics, and fungicides. Mercuric chloride, or corrosive sublimate (q.v.), is very toxic and is dispensed in coffin-shaped tablets for disinfectant purposes. Ammoniated mercury and mercuric oleate, either alone or with finely divided mercury and mercuric oxide, are ingredients of ointments for external application. A common mild antiseptic is merbromin or Mercurochrome, a brominated fluorescein mercury derivative. Other antiseptics are derivatives of orthocresol and thiosalicylic acid. Mercurials have now been largely discarded in the treatment of venereal diseases, but mercury preparations are of increasing importance as diuretics. They are highly complex organic compounds, some being derivatives of dibasic acid amides, others containing aromatic rings, and still others being based on alkyl ureas. These mercurials are administered quite often along with theophylline, a purine related to caffeine. Such diuretics are said to be selectively concentrated in the kidney, where they inhibit kidney enzymes and spare these materials in other tissues. Resorption of water and sodium is also prevented.

W. T. READ,
Chemical Consultant.

MERCURY FULMINATE. See FULMINATES.

MERCURY ISLANDS, island group, New Zealand, off Coromandel Peninsula on the east coast of North Island, southeast of Great Barrier Island. The largest of the group are Great Mercury Island (about eight miles long) and Red Mercury Island. The name is derived from the fact that Capt. James Cook observed the transit of Mercury here in 1769.

MERCY, měr-sē', BARON **Franz von,** soldier of the Holy Roman Empire: b. Longwy, France, 1590; d. Nördlingen, Bavaria, Aug. 3, 1645. Born into a noble family of Lorraine, Mercy entered military service at an early age and fought almost throughout the Thirty Years' War (1618–1648) in armies of the Holy League. His valor in the first Battle of Breitenfeld (1631) won him the position of regimental commander in subsequent contests with Gustavus Adolphus in the Rhineland. Appointed general of the powerful Bavarian Army he was named field marshal when he defeated the French general Josias von Rantzau at the battle of Tuttlingen (1643). Thenceforward he met French armies under two great generals, the vicomte de Turenne and the duc d'Enghien (Louis II de Bourbon), in several inconclusive battles. He lost his life in a climactic battle of the long war, near Nördlingen.

MERCY, Sisters of, mûr'sĭ, a congregation of religious women in the Roman Catholic Church, with pontifical approval, founded in Dublin, Ireland, in 1831 by Mother Mary Catherine McAuley. The works of the sisters are education on the primary, secondary, and collegiate levels; the administration of hospitals, orphanages, and homes for working girls; and other spiritual and corporal works of mercy. The congregation spread rapidly and is now the second largest institute of religious women in the world, numbering thousands of sisters.

The first foundation of Sisters of Mercy in the United States was made at Pittsburgh, Pa., in 1843 by seven sisters from Carlow, Ireland. In 1959 there were close to 12,000 sisters in numerous mother houses scattered throughout the United States. Originally, the status of each mother house was that of an independent unit. In 1929, approximately one half of the membership in the United States amalgamated to form a single religious institute called the Sisters of Mercy of the Union. The remainder of the communities retained their autonomous organization. The religious habit worn by all Sisters of Mercy is of black wool, girded by a black leather cincture from which hangs a black rosary with the ebony Mercy cross. See also McAULEY, CATHERINE.

SISTER M. AQUINAS.

MERCYHURST COLLEGE, mûr'sĭ-hûrst, a college of liberal arts for women in Erie, Pa., founded by the Sisters of Mercy (q.v.) in 1926 as an outgrowth of St. Joseph's Academy (chartered 1871) and Normal Training School of Titusville, about 40 miles southeast of Erie. It is under the control of the Roman Catholic Church and confers the B.A. and B.S. degrees.

MEREDITH, mĕr'ĕ-dĭth, **Edwin Thomas,** American publisher and politician: b. Avoca, Iowa, Dec. 23, 1876; d. Des Moines, June 17, 1928. A farmer's son, educated in country schools and at Highland Park College (later Des Moines University), he assisted his grandfather in publishing the weekly *Farmer's Tribune* and was given the paper as a wedding present in 1896. Thereafter Meredith achieved great success with two magazines he founded: *Successful Farming* (1902), for Middle Western farmers, and *Better Homes and Gardens* (1924; originally, in 1922, *Fruit, Garden and Home*) a national publication. An unsuccessful Democratic candidate for senator (1941) and governor (1916), he was named secretary of agriculture (1920–1921) by President Woodrow Wilson.

MEREDITH, George, English poet and novelist: b. Hampshire (probably near Petersfield), England, Feb. 12, 1828; d. Box Hill, Surrey, May 18, 1909. His father, a tailor in Portsmouth, failed in business when Meredith was ten, and the boy became a ward in chancery. He spent two years in a Moravian school at Neuwied on the Rhine, and later was articled to a London solicitor, but did not complete his legal training. At twenty-one he married a daughter of Thomas Love Peacock (q.v.), the English writer, and they spent some years in poverty while Meredith tried to establish himself as an author. He published in 1851 a volume of poems in the style of Tennyson. This was followed by two short prose works, *The Shaving of Shagpat* (1856) and *Fa-*

rina (1857). Both were ingenious imitations of traditional types, the first being based on *The Arabian Nights* and the second on German folk tales; but both showed originality in their figurative language, fantastic humor, and symbolic implications. At this juncture his wife deserted him and their young son. Meredith withdrew from London to live in a cottage in the Surrey countryside.

His first novel, *The Ordeal of Richard Feverel* (1859), was a brilliant and complex psychological study of a boy whose father brings him up by a rigid system that excludes sex, with the result that Richard makes disastrous mistakes and suffers emotional torment. An idyllic love story is contrasted with the sophisticated standards of the upper class, and the prevailing mood is that of satiric comedy, though the outcome is tragic. The style ranges from witty epigram to lyrical imagery. As the book was banned as immoral, Meredith undertook a more conventional theme in his next novel, *Evan Harrington* (1861), a comedy which contained much transposed autobiography.

George Meredith

Brown Brothers

By this time he had become a reader for the publishing firm of Chapman & Hall, a position that brought him a regular income for the next 30 years. A second volume of poetry, in 1861, contained dramatic monologues of humble life and also *Modern Love,* a series of 16-line sonnets which subtly probe the conflicts of an incompatible marriage very like Meredith's own. His estranged wife died about this time, and he married again, happily, in 1864. Soon afterwards he settled at Box Hill, where he remained the rest of his life. *Emilia in England* (1864), later retitled *Sandra Belloni,* is a study of a musical genius, an impulsive, sincere girl set amid the shallow sentimentality and artificial conventions of society. A sequel, *Vittoria,* published three years later, showed Emilia becoming a great prima donna during the intrigues and battles of the Italian uprising of 1848. This was Meredith's nearest approach to a historical novel of panoramic scope, and was based on his experiences as a correspondent in the Austro-Italian war of 1866. Between these two novels he published *Rhoda Fleming,* a simpler and more tragic story of English rural life. His next novel, *The Adventures of Harry Richmond* (1871), was in a romantic vein, centering upon the fabulous figure of the hero's father, who claims royal parentage and almost succeeds in imposing his self-dramatization upon the world. This novel is less allusive in style than Meredith's others, and its picture of love and adventure in a German principality marks it as a forerunner of the romances of Stevenson.

In *Beauchamp's Career* (1876) Meredith undertook a more analytical study of political ideas, embodied in a visionary young man who sacrifices love and antagonizes his aristocratic relations in his campaign as a Radical candidate for Parliament. By this time Meredith had resigned himself to the fact that his novels were too subtle in scrutinizing motives and too oblique in style to be widely popular. His contempt for the sentimentality of much current fiction impelled him to develop a concept of his function which he expressed in an essay *On the Idea of Comedy and the Uses of the Comic Spirit* (1877), emphasizing the value of dispassionate yet tolerant comedy in establishing true standards of judgment. His theory was exemplified in *The Egoist* (1879), his most perfectly constructed novel; in it he exposes every facet of the egoism which he considered the dominant evil force in human relations. His next novel, *The Tragic Comedians* (1880), is less successful. It is an attempt to show the harmful effects of egoism in a political leader, but is hampered by staying too close to the career of a real person, the German Socialist Ferdinand Lassalle.

Somewhat the same handicap affected his next novel, *Diana of the Crossways* (1885), which was based on the life of the Hon. Mrs. Norton, an English writer who was the granddaughter of Richard Brinsley Sheridan. Nevertheless, this became his most popular book because its portrayal of a clever woman struggling against social prejudice appealed to the new feminist movement. About this time Meredith suddenly won appreciation in the United States, and in his own country also a few critics began to hail him as the greatest living novelist. His strongest wish, however, was for fame as a poet. In *Poems and Lyrics of the Joy of Earth* (1883), *Ballads and Poems of Tragic Life* (1887), and *A Reading of Earth* (1888) he developed a deeply philosophic theory of man's relationship with nature, based upon his own love of the winds and the woods, and accepting the modern evolutionary concept. In place of belief in an immortal soul he proclaimed obedience to the laws of nature and service to the welfare of the race as the bases for a happy life and a kind of survival after death. His concentrated symbolism made the poetry difficult for casual readers.

Meredith was now becoming afflicted with deafness and paralysis, and thereafter seldom left his country home, but a constant stream of visitors came to listen to his fascinating conversation. His last major novel, *One of Our Conquerors* (1890), contains perhaps his most penetrating psychology and most vigorous challenge to conventional moral values, but his idiosyncracies of manner are carried to such an extreme that it is his most difficult work to read. Two final novels, *Lord Ormont and his Aminta* (1894) and *The Amazing Marriage* (1895), are simpler and slighter works. One other book, *Celt and Saxon,* remained unfinished for many years and was published posthumously. He continued to write profound and often baffling poetry in his last decade.

See also DIANA OF THE CROSSWAYS; ORDEAL OF RICHARD FEVEREL, THE.

Bibliography.—The complete works are in the Memorial Edition, 29 vols. (New York 1909–1912). M. B.

Forman compiled an exhaustive *Bibliography of the Writings in Prose and Verse* (London 1922) and a guide to secondary material in *Meredithiana* (London 1924). The fullest biography is *The Ordeal of George Meredith,* by Lionel Stevenson (New York 1953). Other biographies, containing critical discussion, are by Siegfried Sassoon (London 1948) and Jack Lindsay (London 1955). Consult also René Galland, *George Meredith, les cinquante premières années* (Paris 1923). The themes and techniques of the novels are treated in Walter F. Wright's *Art and Substance in George Meredith* (Lincoln, Nebr., 1953). The only detailed study of the poetry is *The Poetry and Philosophy of George Meredith,* by George M. Trevelyan (London 1906).

LIONEL STEVENSON,
Professor of English, Duke University.

MEREDITH, James Howard, American human rights pioneer: b. Kosciusko, Miss., June 25, 1933. He grew up on the family farm and was educated in Kosciusko and St. Petersburg, Fla. Meredith served in the U.S. Air Force from 1951 to 1960. In 1960 he entered Jackson State College, but transferred to the University of Mississippi in 1962 with the assistance of a court order. Because he was black, his admission was at first resisted by most students and some professors and townspeople. His courage and determination won increasing respect, however, and he helped one of the South's most traditionalist universities make the transition from segregated to nonsegregated status. He graduated in 1963— the first Negro to do so. Meredith wrote *Three Years in Mississippi* (1966).

C. ERIC LINCOLN
Union Theological Seminary, New York

MEREDITH, Samuel, American statesman and financier: b. Philadelphia, Pa., 1741; d. Mount Pleasant Township, Feb. 10, 1817. Educated in private schools in Philadelphia and Chester, Pa., he entered his father's mercantile establishment and became active in colonial affairs, being a signer of the Philadelphia nonimportation resolutions in 1765. He was a deputy at the Provincial Convention in 1775 and during the revolution served as major, lieutenant colonel, and brigadier general of the Pennsylvania militia, distinguishing himself at the battles of Brandywine and Germantown in 1777. Thrice elected to the Pennsylvania Colonial Assembly (1778–1783), he served in the Congress of the Confederation from 1786 to 1788 and in the next year was named surveyor of the port of Philadelphia. In September 1789, at the invitation of George Washington, newly elected president, he became the first treasurer of the United States. He contributed to this office not only his ability for conservative financial management but more than $100,000 in cash, which the government was never able to repay. The owner of vast tracts of land, Meredith retired from office in 1801.

MEREDITH, William Morris, American lawyer and politician: b. Philadelphia, Pa., June 8, 1799; d. there, Aug. 17, 1873. Son of a well-to-do lawyer and banker, he graduated from the University of Pennsylvania at 13 and was admitted to the bar five years later. Active in state politics from the early 1820's, he became a leader of the Whig Party in Pennsylvania and was named secretary of the treasury by President Zachary Taylor when the latter took office in 1849. Meredith advocated a protective tariff and opposed the Compromise of 1850. He resigned on Taylor's death (1850). During the Civil War he was attorney general of Pennsylvania.

MERENDON, Sierra del, mā-rän-dôn', mountain range, Honduras, at the southern end of the western (Guatemalan) border. Mount Erapuca (8,200 feet) is at the junction of the Merendón with the Gallinero range to the north.

MERES, mērz, **Francis,** English clergyman and literary historian: b. Kirton-in-Holland, Lincolnshire, England, 1565; d. Wing, Rutlandshire, Jan. 29, 1647. Educated at Pembroke College, Cambridge, and later also at Oxford, he became rector of Wing in 1602 and continued there until his death. While living in London in 1598, he published the work which has perpetuated his memory, *Palladis Tamia, Wits Treasury,* a continuation of Nicholas Ling's *Politeuphuia: Wits Commonwealth* (1597). The most famous part of Meres' book is the essay "A Comparative Discourse of our English Poets with the Greek, Latin, and Italian Poets," in which he examines all the poets of England from Geoffrey Chaucer to his own contemporaries, including a unique list of William Shakespeare's works to date and a spurious but long-accepted description of the circumstances of Christopher Marlowe's death. Each English poet is compared with a counterpart in one of the other tongues. The book also contains chapters on "Philosophie," "Music," "Painting," and other essays on literature.

MEREZHKOVSKI, Russ. myĕ-ryĕsh-kôf'-skû-ĭ, Eng. mĕr-ĕsh-kôf'skĭ, **Dmitri Sergeyevich,** Russian writer: b. St. Petersburg (Leningrad), Russia, Aug. 2, 1865; d. Paris, France, Dec. 10, 1941. The son of a czarist official, he studied classical philology and philosophy at the University of St. Petersburg, and began to write poetry with a social content. In 1888 he went to the Crimea for his health and there met and married (1889) Zinaida Hippius who had just published the first of the poems which were to establish her as one of Russia's best-known writers at the turn of the century. Together they returned to St. Petersburg, and thenceforward in their writings and in social gatherings at their home they exerted great influence on the Russian intellectual world. Deeply religious and of a mystical nature, Merezhkovski sought a foundation for faith in the integration of the phenomenal and the transcendental, the flesh and the spirit, pagan Nature and Christian philosophy. His Religious-Philosophical Society (1900), advocating a neo-Christianity, was dissolved by the police, and he and his wife were forced to leave Russia (temporarily) when they supported the revolution of 1905. Antireligious Bolshevism proved even more distasteful and they settled in Paris in 1919. His best-known works are found in the trilogy *Khristos i Antikhrist* (1896–1905; Eng. tr., *Christ and the Antichrist,* 1938).

MERGANSER, mēr-găn'sēr, a diving duck of the genus *Mergus.* In its broad sense this genus consists of seven species, three of which inhabit North America. These are the common merganser or goosander (*M. merganser*), the red-breasted (*M. serrator*), and the hooded (*M. cucullatus*). The latter is considerably smaller than the other two and is often placed in a genus of its own (*Lophodytes*). It is, strictly speaking, the only purely American merganser as the other two species are also distributed widely in Eurasia. Mergansers may be distinguished by their narrow bills with serrated edges, which they use in catching live prey, usually fish, under water. In addition they may eat crawfish, frogs, or large water beetles and their larvae. Probably as the result of this diet, the merganser's flesh is rank and coarse and is not considered edible.

Donald S. Heintzelman from National Audubon Society

Hooded merganser (male).

Mergansers are often shot in the erroneous belief they destroy too many game or food fishes, but experts are now generally agreed their role is a beneficial one in reducing crowded fish populations and permitting the more rapid growth of survivors to "legal size." Mergansers chiefly inhabit fresh water: the hooded variety in well-timbered streams, swamps, or ponds; the common merganser frequents lakes or, occasionally, brackish inlets; while the red-breasted summers in fresh waters and winters at sea. Hooded and common varieties breed in cavities, preferably in stumps or hollow trees, but the red-breasted breeds on the ground under dense cover.

CHARLES VAURIE.

MERGENTHALER, mĕr'gĕn-tä-lĕr, **Ottmar,** American inventor: b. Hachtel, Germany, May 11, 1854; d. Baltimore, Md., Oct. 28, 1899. Upon completion of his apprenticeship to a watchmaker in Germany, he went to Washington, D.C. (1872), where he was employed for four years in the manufacture of scientific instruments. Moving to Baltimore in 1876 Mergenthaler was called in to remedy defects in a model of a newly devised writing machine and at the suggestion of its inventor, James O. Clephane, of Washington, built a full-scale machine which, however, was not satisfactory. In cooperation with Clephane, Mergenthaler eventually developed the first linotype machine (1884) which, in improved form, was first used commercially in 1886. He resigned his directorship in the company set up to manufacture the machines in 1888 but contributed more than 50 improvements to them before his death. See COMPOSING MACHINES—*Development* (The Linotype).

MERGER, mûr'jēr, in law, the combination of two or more business organizations into one, one firm surviving, the others losing their separate identities. Only the remaining firm retains its original name and charter, acquiring the assets of the others. This technique of business fusion differs from consolidation, which involves the formation of a completely new organization wherein all participating firms lose their original identities.

A merger may occur through the sale of assets, with payment either in cash or in stock of the purchasing company. The purchaser may choose instead to buy the other's stock, become a holding company, and then dissolve the subsidiary firm. Under statutory merger, the purchaser's stock is issued directly to the selling company's stockholders, the purchaser assumes the seller's assets and liabilities, and the selling firm is then dissolved.

The antitrust laws of the United States were originally ineffectual in dealing with mergers. The United States Steel case in 1920 was the first successful attack on close-knit combinations. Since World War II, antimerger enforcement in monopoly cases has increased greatly. See also CARTEL; COMBINATIONS AND MERGERS; MONOPOLY.

WILLIAM N. KINNARD, JR.

MERGUI ARCHIPELAGO, mûr-gwē', a chain of about 800 islands in the Andaman Sea, off the coast of Tenasserim in Burma, forming a part of the Lower Burma district of Mergui which has an area of 10,906 square miles. The islands are generally covered with jungle growth, and present many picturesque features, rising at some points to the height of 3,000 feet. The largest island is Tavoy, and others are King, Elphinstone, Ross, and St. Matthew islands. There is some mining of tin and tungsten on these islands and there are rubber plantations on several of the larger ones.

The chief town in the archipelago is Mergui, which is situated on a small island near the coast. This area is one of the wettest on the globe, rainfall exceeding 100 inches annually.

The inhabitants of the islands, mainly Selungs, give little attention to agriculture, obtaining their sustenance mainly by fishing, pearl gathering, and selling edible birds' nests. They are peaceful and industrious, but few in number. Pop. of Mergui town (1953) 33,697.

MERIDA, mā'rĕ-thä, **Carlos,** Mexican painter: b. Guatemala, Dec. 2, 1893. He studied in Paris (1910–1914) under Kees van Dongen and Anglada Camarasa, and returned to Guatemala where he began to explore the folklore themes of Central America. In 1919 he went to Mexico and held his first exhibition and in 1920 he joined a group of revolutionary Mexican painters under the leadership of David A. Siqueiros. With them he painted frescos in several government buildings, including in 1923 the children's library in the Ministry of Education Building, Mexico City.

A second trip to Paris (1927–1929) turned his interest to surrealism, and on his return to Mexico City, as professor of painting at the Escuela Centrale de Artes Plásticas, he propagated this form of art. He has exhibited in the United States and in Mexico and has written and illustrated *Tres motivos, huecograbado* (copperplate engravings, 1936); *Modern Mexican Artists* (1937); *Ten Interpretive Guides on Mexican Frescos* (1937); *Dances of Mexico* (10 color lithographs, 1938); *Carnival in Mexico* (1939); and *Mexican Costumes* (1941).

Mérida's painting has always been highly personal, emphasizing the abstract and symbolic aspect of the art. Out of his study of the Indian customs, dances, and art, he has evolved an expression that is truly poetic. Although he works in a variety of media, some of his finest painting has been done in watercolor. His handling of this medium is one of the most original and sensitive of the present century.

MERIDA, city, Mexico, capital of the State of Yucatán. It is situated on part of the great, low plain which comprises most of the state and is surrounded by henequen (sisal hemp) plantations. The climate is tropical. Numerous metal windmills in and around the city provide water from wells. The city was founded in 1542 by Francisco de Montejo the younger on the site of a Maya city called T'ho, and the early buildings were largely built of the stones from Maya temples and other native structures. The city has a strong Spanish tradition which is reflected in its architecture. The population, however, is largely Maya. The Montejo house, which dates from 1549, is located on the main plaza, as is the cathedral (1561–1598).

Mérida is the center of the Yucatán henequen industry, manufacturing rope, cordage, and coarse fabrics for sacking, and dyeing and weaving finer fabrics for small bags and hats. Cotton and leather goods are also made and there are numerous bottling works and breweries.

Some 75 miles to the east are the extensive and magnificent ruins of Chichén Itzá (q.v.), the sacred city of the Maya civilization during the New Empire. This place was settled by the Itzá people during the 6th century A.D. and reached its highest point 500 to 700 years later, to be completely abandoned about 1450. Even more elaborate in its architecture, although smaller in extent, is the Maya city of Uxmal (q.v.) whose ruins are about 55 miles south of Mérida. This was founded by the Xiu toward the end of the 10th century and abandoned about the same time as Chichén Itzá.

For many centuries Mérida was the most isolated of the larger Mexican cities since its only connection with the rest of the republic was by sea through Progreso, Yucatán's chief port, 23 miles distant by rail and highway to the north. With the coming of air transportation, this isolation was somewhat alleviated, for the Pan American Airways established a large airfield just outside the city. However, there was no land connection, except for a road and narrow gauge railroad that went only as far south as Campeche, until the road and railroad were linked with the rest of the republic in the 1950's. Other principal buildings in Mérida are those of the University of Yucatán and the Archaeological Museum. Pop. (1966) 100,394.

MERIDA, commune, Spain (Roman name AUGUSTA EMERITA), in the province of Badajoz, situated on the Guadiana River, 33 miles east-northeast of Badajoz. It is unique in Spain, and is in some points a rival of Rome itself because of the number and magnitude of its remains of Roman antiquity, built when it was the capital of the province of Lusitania. The Guadiana is here crossed by a Roman bridge of 64 arches (originally 81, but 17 were destroyed in 1812), with a length of 2,575 feet and a breadth of 26 feet. There is another Roman bridge over the Albarregas nearby, 450 feet long, 25 feet wide, and still quite perfect, in spite of the traffic of 18 centuries. Among other noteworthy Roman remains are an old fort (later a Moorish alcazar), aqueducts, a triumphal arch built by Trajan, and a colonnaded theater.

Mérida was founded in 23 B.C. by Augustus, and flourished in splendor under Roman and Moor until 1228, when it was taken from the Moors by Alfonso IX of Léon, after which it began to decline. Today it has undergone development and is an important stock-raising and agricultural center. Pop. (1950) 22,134.

MÉRIDA, town, Venezuela, capital of the State of Mérida, 30 miles south of Lake Maracaibo, at the foot of the Sierra Nevada de Mérida, at an altitude of 5,384 feet. Founded in 1558 by Spaniards, it is situated on the Venezuela-Columbia trans-Andean highway. It was almost totally destroyed by an earthquake in 1812, and again seriously damaged in 1894. Manufacturing consists of woolen and cotton goods, tobacco products, cordage, furniture, and vegetable oils. It is the seat of an archbishop, contains a fine cathedral, and is the site of Los Andes University, and a Jesuit college. The town is noted for its colonial traditions and architecture. Pop. (1961) 40,404.

MÉRIDA, Sierra Nevada de, (also Cordillera Mérida), a range of mountains in western Venezuela, an extension of the Andes, extending northeast from the Cordillera Oriental on the Colombian border between the Orinoco llanos and Maracaibo lowlands to Barquisimeto at the foot of the Caribbean coastal range. Its highest peak is La Columna (or Bolívar) at 16,411 feet. The trans-Andean highway travels the entire length of the range.

MERIDEN, mĕr'ĭ-d'n, city, Connecticut, in New Haven County, 17 miles northeast of New Haven. An industrial community, Meriden has a great variety of manufacturing, including silverware, ball-bearings, filters, lighting fixtures, jewelry, paper boxes, telephone and signaling equipment, hardware, and plastics.

The silver industry, responsible for Meriden's nickname, "The Silver City of the World," grew steadily from 1794, when Samuel Yale made and sold pewter buttons, through the time of Ashbil Griswold, who began the manufacture of britannia ware in 1808. In 1852, a group of small companies combined to form the Meriden Britannia Company. A few years later, this company bought the Rogers plant in Hartford where, in 1847, the Rogers brothers had discovered a successful method of plating other metals with silver by electrolysis. The Rogers brothers joined the company as managers. In 1898 the company's directors brought about the consolidation of several independent concerns to form the International Silver Company, largest manufacturers of silver and silverplate in the world.

Settled in 1661, and part of the Wallingford Plantation, Meriden was incorporated as a town in 1806. Part of the town obtained a city charter in 1867; town and city were consolidated in 1922. Meriden, whose name means "pleasant valley," is believed to have been named for an ancient market town in England. Inspired by the beauty of the surrounding countryside, and especially the Hanging Hills, Gerhart Hauptmann, who lived in Meriden in 1894, used this as the

background for his play *The Sunken Bell.*

Meriden has a mayor-council form of government, and an airport. It is the location of three state institutions: the Connecticut School for Boys, Undercliff Hospital, and the Wilcox Technical School. Hubbard Park, comprising approximately 1,000 acres of woodland and recreation areas, is topped by the famous landmark Castle Craig Tower. The city is the birthplace of the singer Rosa Ponselle. Pop. 51,850.

MARION E. COOK.

MERIDIAN, mĕ-rĭd'ĭ-ăn, city, Mississippi, seat of Lauderdale County, 96 miles east of Jackson, and serviced by an airport with facilities for jet airliners. It is an industrial, railroad, highway, and trade center. The region around the city comprises areas of forests and of fertile farmlands which produce cotton, commercial vegetables, and fruits. The principal sources of farm income are forestry, beef cattle, dairying, poultry, and hogs. In the city are stockyards, lumber mills, cotton gins, and creosoting plants. The Meridian factories produce hosiery, textiles, mattresses, shirts, and wallboard. The city is the site of the East Mississippi State Hospital, has a federal agricultural experiment station nearby, and is the location of a junior college. A United States Naval Auxiliary Air Station, a part of Naval Air Basic Training, is located 16 miles northeast.

Settled in 1831, Meridian developed rapidly after the advent of the railroad in 1854, and was incorporated in 1860. It became a supply depot and troop center during the Civil War, and was the temporary capital of Mississippi in 1863. Maj. Gen. William T. Sherman entered Meridian on Feb. 16, 1864, with 20,000 troops, after marching virtually unopposed from Vicksburg. His troops burned the arsenal, extensive storehouses, and cantonments, while over 10,000 men were employed in a systematic destruction of the railroads to and from the city, rendering Meridian useless as a rail center for the rest of the war. After the Civil War, Meridian was quickly rebuilt, again becoming a major rail center, and in the early part of the 20th century new industries began to be attracted there. In the early 1960's the city completed an extensive improvement program. Meridian has had a council-manager form of government since 1949. Pop. 49,374.

H.J. DEAR.

MERIDIAN, *in geography,* an imaginary half circle on the surface of the earth, perpendicular to the equator and passing through both geographic poles, which serves to define the longitude of any place (the angular distance of the place directly east or west of the prime meridian through Greenwich, England). The prime meridian, or 0° of longitude, is that meridian delineated by the central cross hair of the Airy transit instrument at the former site of the Royal Greenwich Observatory in Greenwich. The opposite half of a great circle extended from this cross hair through both geographic poles, and corresponding to longitude 180°, defines the position of the International Date Line (q.v.). Meridians also serve as the basis for the system of standard time zones, centered approximately 7½° on either side of standard time meridians, but possessing irregular boundaries. Standard time becomes successively one hour earlier for each 15° westward from the meridian of Greenwich, and one hour later for each 15° eastward from this same meridian. At the meridian of 180° longitude, an adjustment of one day is necessary.

In astronomy. The geographical meridian of any place projected onto the celestial sphere becomes the celestial meridian of that place. The celestial meridian passing through the north and south points of the horizon and through the zenith of any place is known as the local astronomical meridian. The sun crosses this meridian, or is said to transit or culminate, at local apparent noon. That portion of the local meridian between the two celestial poles which passes through the zenith of a place is known as the upper branch of the meridian; the remaining half of the same great circle extended is known as the lower branch.

See also ASTRONOMY; ASTRONOMY, PRACTICAL —*Meridian Astrometry*; LONGITUDE, TERRESTRIAL; TIME, INTERNATIONAL ZONES OF; TIME, MEASUREMENT AND DETERMINATION OF.

FERGUS J. WOOD.

MÉRIMÉE, mā-rē-mā′, **Prosper,** French man of letters: b. Paris, France, Sept. 28, 1803; d. Cannes, Sept. 23, 1870. After attending the Collège Henri IV, Mérimée studied law, but never practiced, preferring to enter the civil service. Following the revolution of July 1830 he was made secretary to the ministers of commerce and marine, and in 1831 he was appointed inspector of ancient monuments. In 1844 he was elected a member of the French Academy, and in 1853 he became a senator of France; in 1860 he was made a commander of the Legion of Honor. He began his literary career under the pseudonym "Joseph Lestrange" with two clever mystifications, *Le Théâtre de Clara Gazul* (1825), and *La Guzla* (1827), which he published as translations respectively of the plays of a Spanish actress and as Illyrian folk songs. These he followed with a historical novel, *Chronique du Règne de Charles IX* (1829). He also published several important works connected with his duties as inspector of ancient monuments, and he was the author of *Colomba* (1840), a very popular novel of the Corsican vendetta; *Carmen* (1847), a romance upon which the famous opera *Carmen* by Georges Bizet is founded; *Lettres à Une Inconnue* (1873), his most famous work, which throws an interesting light upon his enigmatical character; *Lettres à Une Autre Inconnue* (1875); *Lettres à Panizzi* (1881); and *Une Correspondance Inédite* (1896). The four works last named are Mérimée's most characteristic writings, revealing him as a loyal, devoted friend. They differ widely from his other works which, though often brilliant, are hard and unsympathetic, while these are tender and romantic.

A man of a melancholy, skeptical, and sensitive temper, and endowed with a powerful intellect, he was one of the greatest masters of imaginative prose in France in the 19th century.

See also CARMEN; COLOMBA.

MERINO, mẽ-rē′nō, a soft woolen or worsted fabric, introduced about 1826, and named from the wool of Merino sheep. The word is originally the title of an inspector of sheep pastures in Spain, and became attached to the short-wool Spanish sheep. The breed did not originate there, however, being imported from Africa by the Moors and bred by the Spanish. The wool was so highly regarded that Merino sheep have been exported for breeding all over the world, but especially to Australia. See also WOOL.

MERIONETHSHIRE, mĕr-ĭ-ŏn′ĕth-shĭr, county, Wales, bounded on the north by Caernarvon and Denbigh, on the east by Denbigh and Montgomery, on the southeast by Montgomery, on the south by the estuary of the Dyfi (Dovey), and on the west by Cardigan Bay. The area is 660 square miles. The surface is rugged and hilly; the highest peak is Cader Idris (2,927 feet). Rivers include the Dyfi, Dee, and Mawddach. Bala Lake, in the eastern part of the county, is the source of the Dee; it is the largest natural lake in Wales. Limestone and slate are quarried, and there are deposits of manganese ore. There is much pastureland, and the small, hardy Welsh ponies are raised. Dolgelly is the county town; it has replaced Harlech, the ancient capital of Gwynedd, and a center of resistance to the English. Pop. (1961) 39,007.

MERISTEMS. See PLANTS AND PLANT SCIENCE—2. *Anatomy* (Meristems).

MERIT, Order of, mĕr′ĭt, a British order designed as a special distinction for eminent persons without conferring a knighthood upon them. It was created by King Edward VII on June 26, 1902, and is awarded by the sovereign without ministerial advice. Alone among royal honors, the O.M. confers no precedence and no stated position at court functions; and no sum of money, no perquisite, accompanies it. The initials O.M., when written, are placed before any others except those denoting membership in the four great orders of chivalry; and the red and blue enamel cross of the order is not returned at the holder's death. Membership is limited in number to 24 living persons, with the addition of foreign honorary members. The Order of Merit is highly prized in Britain, and it is the only honor which, so far as is known, has never been declined. The first 12 members included, in addition to generals and admirals, Lord Rutherford, winner of the Nobel Prize for chemistry; Sir William Bragg, the physicist; Sir James Jeans, astronomer and physicist; and Sir James Frazer, anthropologist. Musicians, painters, and writers were among later recipients, the last category including T.S. Eliot. Florence Nightingale was the only woman ever to have held the order.

MERIVALE, mĕr′ĭ-vāl, **Charles,** English historian and ecclesiastic: b. London, England, March 8, 1808; d. Ely, Cambridgeshire, Dec. 27, 1893. He was the son of John Herman Merivale (1779–1844), a barrister, translator, and minor poet. After graduating from St. John's College, Cambridge University, in 1830, he studied theology and was ordained in the Church of England in 1833. He was rector of Lawford, Essex, from 1848 to 1869, and during this period was chaplain to the speaker of the House of Commons. In 1869 he declined the professorship of modern history at Cambridge but became dean of Ely, in which capacity he served until his death. His *History of the Romans Under the Empire* (7 vols., 1850–64), considered his greatest work, unduly glorified imperialism. *The Fall of the Roman Republics* (1853) was a popular epitome of a section of that work; and his *General History of Rome from the Foundation of the City to the Fall of Augustulus* (1875) was a summary of the whole. He also published histories of the conversion of the pagans. His *Autobiography and Letters,* edited by his daughter, appeared in 1899.

MERLE D'AUBIGNE, mĕrl'dō-bē-nyā', **Jean Henri,** Swiss ecclesiastical historian and Protestant preacher: b. Eaux Vives, now part of Geneva, Switzerland, Aug. 8, 1794; d. Geneva, Oct. 21, 1872. In 1819 he became pastor of the French Protestant church in Hamburg, Germany, and four years later was appointed court preacher in Brussels to William I of the Netherlands. After 1830, Merle d'Aubigné returned to Geneva, where he served until his death as professor of church history. He wrote several studies of the Reformation, but is best known for his two large-scale works. The *Histoire de la reformation du XVIe siècle* (5 vols., 1835–1853), was translated into most European languages. It was rendered into English as *History of the Reformation of the Sixteenth Century* (5 vols. in 1, 1854), and in many other editions, both of the whole and of its parts. The other major work, *Histoire de la reformation en Europe au temps de Calvin* (8 vols., 1863–1878), was translated into English as *History of the Reformation in Europe at the Time of Calvin* (8 vols., 1863–1878).

MERLIN, mûr'lĭn, a famous prophet and magician of the 5th century, closely associated with the Arthurian romances (q.v.). The stories of Merlin are confused by the presence of a second Merlin, an ancient bard and also a magician, who is believed to have lived about 570. To him an air of mystery and romance has been imparted by identifying him with the earlier and wholly legendary figure. Threads of history and fiction are woven together almost inextricably, and scholars have argued learnedly in defense of both a single and a double original for Merlin. Welsh tradition recognizes the two figures under the names Merlin Ambrosius (or Myrddin Emrys) and Merlin Silvester (or Myrddin Wyllt).

The 5th century legendary enchanter was said to have been born of a demon father (an incubus) and a Welsh princess. It was he, "the boy without a father," who explained to the king, Vortigern, why his tower would not stand, and told the symbolism of the two serpents discovered underneath the foundations. Many feats of divination were attributed to him. It was through his magic arts that Uther Pendragon became the father of Arthur, king of the Britons. The famous Round Table was established on Merlin's advice, and he helped Arthur select 50 of the knights who were to sit at it. Also, according to later stories which were popular, Merlin made a number of prophecies about the future of Britain. His role of sage and seer was such as to make his name synonymous with wisdom itself. Yet he was believed to have been enclosed forever in a bush in the wood, Brocéliande, the victim of a charm wrought by his mistress, Vivian, a charm which he himself had revealed to her.

The accounts of Merlin are to be traced to the *Historia Britonum,* an early 9th century work attributed to Nennius, but it was Geoffrey of Monmouth who first supplied the name Merlin, in his *Historia Regum Britanniae* (1137). Geoffrey is believed also to have composed a *Vita Merlini* in Latin verse. In the late 12th century, Robert de Boron wrote a trilogy of French poems, including an account of Merlin in which he followed Gregory. Sir Thomas Malory later borrowed from Boron's romance for his *Morte d'Arthur* (1470); and Edmund Spenser included Merlin the magician among his characters in *The Faerie Queene* (1589–1596).

The attractiveness of Merlin as a figure has not faded. The German poet, Karl Immermann, made his poetic drama *Merlin* (1832) an allegorical search into the mystery of life. Merlin also served Tennyson fo. *Merlin and Vivien* (1859), one of the *Idylls of the King*. In the 20th century the American poet Edwin Arlington Robinson sought to show in his *Merlin* (1917) that even the wisest men are deceived by passion, and unable to cope with problems of the modern world.

For bibliography see MORTE D'ARTHUR.

MERLIN, mĕr-lăn', COMTE **Philippe Antoine** (called MERLIN DE DOUAI), French jurist and politician: b. Arleux, near Douai, France, Oct. 30, 1754; d. Paris, Dec. 26, 1838. Admitted to the bar in 1775, he became a member of the States-General in 1789. During the period of the French Revolution and the Consulate (1789–1804) he was quite active in the government, serving as a member of the National Convention and the Committee of Public Safety. In 1794 he began a study of French civil and criminal law which resulted in many reforms, such as the abolition of branding and life imprisonment. He was minister of justice (1795–1799), and as *procureur-général* in the Court of Cassation (1801) he was largely responsible for fixing the interpretation of the Napoleonic Code. He was a councilor of state to Napoleon, who gave him the title of comte (1810). Exiled on the restoration of the monarchy (1815), he remained outside France until 1830.

MERMAID, mûr'mād, a mythical sea-dwelling creature of European folklore, resembling a woman but having a fishtail instead of legs. Mermaids are supposed to be able to lure imaginative, amorous men to destruction by enticing them into the depths of the sea; and, as a correlative, they are sometimes represented as securing their own destruction by quitting the sea, through marriage with a human husband. By this means they magically obtain temporarily a complete human form and soul, but always end in bringing disaster to one or both of the sacrilegious pair. Mermen are also occasionally heard of, but have a secondary role in the legendary lore of the sea.

The folkloric origins of the mermaid may go back to the semifish gods of ancient religions, such as the Philistine Dagon and the Chaldean Oannes. In medieval times, belief in the mermaid was widespread, and even in later centuries the creatures were sighted by sailors, including the Dutch explorer, Henry Hudson (d. 1611). It has been suggested by some that such marine animals as the dugong or the closely related manatee (qq.v.) may, at a distance, bear enough resemblance to a human female to have given vigor to the legend.

MERNEPTAH or **MERENPTAH.** See EGYPT—*Chronology.*

MERODACH. See BABYLONIA; NIMROD.

MERODACH-BALADAN, mē-rō'dăk-băl'a-dăn (Assyrian MARDUK-APAL-IDDINA, God has given a son), king of Babylon, fl. 721 B.C. A Chaldean prince, ruler of the state of Bīt Iakin in southern Babylonia, he took Babylon about 721 B.C. and was crowned king. With the support of the Elamites and other allies to the west he was able to resist his enemies the Assyrians for about 12 years. An example of his efforts to draw the Jews into his alliance against the Assyrians is the story of his sending a gift to King Hezekiah when the latter recovered from an illness (as told in Isaiah 39:1–8 and II Kings 20:12–19). Sargon of Assyria, the son of Shalmaneser, suppressed Merodach-baladan's allies, attacked Babylon in 710 B.C., and forced him to flee to the south. Sargon became king, but after his death (705 B.C.), Merodach-baladan regained the throne briefly. His policy of strengthening Chaldea eventually made it the most powerful state of the Neo-Babylonian Empire.

MEROE, měr′ô-ē, a ruin near Kabushia, was from 538 B.C. to 350 A.D. the capital of the Sudanese kingdom of Kush, which extended along the Nile from Aswan to Sennar on the Blue Nile. This kingdom was rich in cereals and herds. Surviving slag heaps show that Meroë itself was a smelting center, and it was the focus of land routes to the west, the Red Sea ports, and the interior of Africa. It was also a river port. There is evidence of contact with India. The earlier capital of Kush was Napata, near Kareima. From there King Piankhi marched on Egypt, which he and four successors ruled until displaced by the armies of Ashurbanipal (c. 665 B.C.). Egyptian influence on the Sudanese kingdom was strong: for centuries Kushite temples were built on the Egyptian plan and decorated with Egyptianizing reliefs and inscriptions in the Egyptian language. Members of the Kushite royal family were buried under pyramids and provided with Egyptian funerary texts. The copying of Egyptian forms decreased after the court moved to Meroë. It was briefly revived under Arqamani (Ergamenes, 225–200 B.C.), who may have been involved in an Upper Egyptian revolt during the reign of Ptolemy IV. In the reign of Augustus, the Kushites raided Philae, and the Roman general Gaius Petronius led a punitive expedition as far as Napata. From this time Qasr Ibrim (opposite Aniba) became the boundary between Kush and Roman Egypt. Meroë fell to Aksum (Axum), probably shortly before 350 A.D. The language of this kingdom used two scripts, both derived from Egypt. Although the alphabetic values of the signs are known and isolated words and phrases can be read, the relationship to other languages is not established; the grammar and vocabulary remain to be worked out.

Consult Arkell, A. J., *A History of the Sudan* (London 1955).

RICHARD A. PARKER.

MEROPE, měr′ô-pē, in classical mythology, the name of several women, of whom the most important are:

(1) Wife of Cresphontes, king of Messenia, and mother of Aepytus. Cresphontes was killed by Polyphontes, who usurped the throne and thereupon took Merope as his wife. Years later, Aepytus, in regaining his father's throne from Polyphontes, narrowly escaped death at the hands of Merope. The theme of Merope the widowed queen and mother has been used by Scipione Maffei, Voltaire, and many other European dramatists.

(2) One of the seven Pleiades, daughters of Atlas. In the Pleiades constellation, Merope is the least visible star because she is ashamed to have married a mortal (Sisyphus, king of Corinth), while her six sisters have mated with deities.

(3) Wife of Polybus, king of Corinth. Polybus and Merope were foster parents of Oedipus.

(4) Either the mother or the sister of Phaëthon.

(5) Daughter of Oenopion, king of Chios. She was beloved by Orion, the huntsman. Oenopion, disapproving of Orion's suit, made him drunk and then blinded him.

For seven more Meropes consult Roscher, Wilhelm Heinrich, *Ausführliches Lexikon der griechischen und römischen Mythologie,* vol. 2, part 2, cols. 2838–39 (Leipzig 1894–97).

P. R. COLEMAN-NORTON.

MEROPE, měr′ô-pě, an Italian tragedy in blank verse by the marchese (Francesco) Scipione di Maffei (1675–1755). Its first performance in Modena on Aug. 12, 1713, met with unprecedented and extraordinary success. Published the following year in Venice, there have since been more than 50 editions and imitations, and it has also been translated into many foreign languages. Still enjoying considerable fame in Italy, it is considered the best Italian tragedy before those of Vittorio Alfieri (q.v.). The predecessors of Maffei, including Giovanni Vincenzo Gravina (1664–1718), Pier Jacopo Martelli (1665–1727), Antonio Schinella Conti (1677–1749), and Saverio Bettinelli (1718–1808), had modeled their tragedies on either Greek or French authors, chiefly Jean Baptiste Racine (1639–1699) and Pierre Corneille (1606–1684). Thus, during a period of decadence in Italian literature, Maffei had no difficulty in introducing radical innovations in the Italian tragedy. He abolished the classical traditions of supernatural choruses, monotonous prologues, long monologues, and the nuncios, nurses, and oracles. At the same time, while retaining the French unities, especially with reference to time and place, Maffei concentrated his attention on simplicity of form and efficacy in performance.

The plot of the play is derived from Greek mythology as narrated in the 2d century B.C. by Apollodorus of Athens in his *Library,* Book II, chap. 8, sect. 5; and in the 2d century A.D. by Pausanias in his *Description of Greece,* Book IV, chap. 3, sects. 6–8. Polifonte has usurped the throne of Cresfonte, king of Messena. He has murdered Cresfonte, together with two of his children. Merope, Cresfonte's widow, anxious to protect her only surviving child, has the child kidnaped, entrusting him to the care of a friend, Polidoro. The son, raised away from Greece under the name of Egisto, attains manhood in ignorance of his royal lineage, and leaves his home to visit Greece. Traveling through Messena, Egisto is attacked by a robber whom he kills in self-defense. Arrested on a charge of homicide and theft of a precious gem, he is brought before Polifonte, who absolves him because circumstances lead him to believe that Egisto has killed Cresfonte's son. Merope, who had at first expressed sympathy for the young man, now also believes him to be the murderer of her own son, and she determines to avenge herself. While on the point of killing Egisto in his sleep, she discovers through Polidoro that he is her own son. When Egisto later learns the true story of his unhappy family, he kills Polifonte, who has planned to marry Merope in order to assure himself of the throne. The queen then announces to the tumultuous crowd that Egisto is her son, the legitimate heir to the throne, whereupon the populace acclaim him as their king.

The plot was used by Voltaire (1743), Alfieri (1782), and Matthew Arnold (1858). Nevertheless Maffei's *Merope* is superior in intensity of feeling and in dramatic treatment. The story was also utilized in several melodramas and operas.

Bibliography.—Maffei, Scipione, *Opuscoli e lettere . . . colla Merope, tragedia* (Milan 1844); *Studi maffeiani, raccolta per il primo centenario del Liceo Scipione Maffei* (Turin 1909); Copelli, Teresa, *Il teatro di Scipione Maffei* (Parma 1907); Maffei, Scipione, *Opere drammatiche e poesie varie, a cura di Antonio Avena* (Bari, Laterza, 1928).

HOWARD R. MARRARO,
Professor of Italian, Columbia University.

MEROPE, mā-rŏp′, one of the most highly esteemed of the 30 tragedies of Voltaire (q.v.), first performed in 1743 and generally considered to mark the climax of the author's career as a dramatist. The ancient Greek legend of the widowed queen Merope (q.v.) and her only surviving son, who thwarted the designs of the tyrant Polyphonte, had already been put on the French stage by Gabriel Gilbert, Jean de La Chapelle, Joseph de Lagrange-Chancel, and the baron de Longepierre (Hilaire-Bernard de Roqueleyne). Though Voltaire was well acquainted with their works, his principal source of inspiration for *Mérope* was Scipione Maffei's dramatic treatment of the same subject. Like Maffei, Voltaire sought to write a moving poetic drama, careful in construction and elevated in style, with maternal devotion rather than sexual love as its central interest. Gotthold Ephraim Lessing (1729–1781) was unjustified, however, in asserting that Voltaire did little more than copy the Italian *Merope*. In a letter of dedication to Maffei, Voltaire expressed his indebtedness to his predecessor but explained why he had felt obliged to rewrite the play according to his own standards. Moreover, in another letter under the pseudonym of M. de La Lindelle, Voltaire enumerated the sundry faults in Maffei's tragedy that were avoided in his own.

Working intermittently over a period of six years on this particular piece, Voltaire rightly held it to be "a Merope from my hand, a French tragedy where, without love, without the support of religion, a mother provides five full acts." Its rhymed Alexandrine verse and its acceptance of the unities marked it among contemporaries as in the great tradition of Jean Baptiste Racine (1639–1699). Adding to its popularity were certain dramatic effects, stemming in part from observation of the English stage, and various striking lines which served as vehicles for liberal ideas. *Mérope* was performed at the Comédie Française 340 times before being withdrawn from the repertory in 1869.

Consult *Oeuvres complètes de Voltaire,* ed. by Louis Moland, vol. 4 (Paris 1877); and Lancaster, Henry Carrington, *French Tragedy in the Time of Louis XV and Voltaire,* 2 vols. (Baltimore 1950).

OTIS E. FELLOWS,
Professor of French, Columbia University.

MEROSTOMATA, mĕr-ô-stō′mà-tà, a class of chelicerate arthropods, characterized as aquatic forms respiring by means of gills and with body divided into a protosome, bearing the che-

licerae and walking legs, and an opisthosome bearing the respiratory appendages that carry gill plates. The class is divided into the subclasses (or orders) Eurypterida or Gigantostraca, which somewhat resemble scorpions and are wholly extinct; and the Xiphosurida, represented by existing members known as horseshoe crabs. These are large creatures of bizarre appearance, having a crescentic shield covering the chelicerae and five pairs of walking legs, a smaller shield covering the flat flaps that bear the gill plates, and a long spike terminating the body. The sexes are separate. Breeding pairs come up on the beach, where the female deposits a mass of eggs in a hollowed place. These hatch in a state somewhat resembling the adult form, and the young molt at intervals.

Bibliography.—The best modern account of the Merostomata is found in the *Traité de zoologie,* ed. by Pierre P. Grassé, vol. 6 (Paris 1949), which includes a good bibliography.

LIBBIE H. HYMAN.

MEROVINGIANS, mĕr-ô-vĭn′jĭ-ănz, the first dynasty of Frankish kings, taking its name from its second king (or chieftain), Mérovée (Merowech, r. 448–458). Most Merovingian names have a number of variant spellings. The line originated as chieftains or kinglets of a tribe of the Salian group of Franks, who had settled in parts of modern Belgium and the Netherlands. First of the line was the obscure kinglet Clodion (r. 428–448), and he was followed by the half-legendary Mérovée, who may have aided the Roman general Flavius Aëtius in defeating the Huns under Attila (451). About 476, during the reign of Mérovée's son Childeric I (r. 458?–481), the Salians had expanded as far south as the Somme River. But it is with Clovis I (r. 481–511), the son of Childeric I, that the history of the Merovingians as a national dynasty really begins. Coming to power when he was 15 or so, Clovis married a Catholic princess, Clotilda of Burgundy, in 493, and was baptized himself, along with 3,000 Franks, on Christmas Day, 496. Before he died he had extended his authority, by conquest or assassination, so that he ruled additional Salian Franks, Ripuarian Franks, Alemanni, Visigoths, and others. His power stretched from beyond the Rhine River to the Pyrenees, thus roughly comprising a large part of modern France and territory to the east. From about 508, Paris was its capital.

At the death of Clovis, he divided the kingdom among his four sons, who increased the Merovingian possessions by adding Burgundy and Provence. Ultimately, through death and treachery, his son Clotaire (Lothaire) I became sole king in 558, but at Clotaire's death (561) the kingdom was again divided among his sons. Thus emerged the eastern kingdom of Austrasia (capital, Metz), the western kingdom of Neustria (capital, Soissons), and Burgundy, which was ruled in common with Neustria. Among the rulers of these petty kingdoms Chilperic I of Neustria (r. 561–584) was superior in ability but even more noted for his savagery. Under his son Clotaire II, infant ruler of Neustria from 584, the Frankish kingdoms were again united in 613. Clotaire's son, Dagobert I (r. 629?–?639), was the last strong Merovingian ruler, but even during his reign, the rebellious, power-seeking nobles forced him to make his son Sigebert III king of Austrasia. After Dagobert's death, the kingdoms were generally ruled separately by mayors of the palace, who were theoretically similar to prime ministers but actually held complete authority. Their nominal Merovingian superiors have been called the do-nothing kings (*les rois fainéants*), shadowy figures, many of whom acceded as children. Among these mayors was Pepin the Short, who in 751 deposed the last of the Merovingians, Childeric III. Pepin then became king of the Franks (r. 751–768), thus initiating the Carolingian dynasty. See FRANKS.

MERRIAM, mĕr'ĭ-ăm, **Charles Edward,** American political scientist and educator: b. Hopkinton, Iowa, Nov. 15, 1874; d. Rockville, Md., Jan. 8, 1953. Brother of John Campbell Merriam, paleontologist (1869–1945), he graduated at the State University of Iowa, studied political theory in Europe, and took his Ph.D. in 1900 at Columbia University. From 1900 he taught political science at the University of Chicago, becoming a professor in 1911 and chairman of the department from 1923 until his retirement in 1940. He was an unsuccessful candidate for Chicago mayor in 1911. From 1924 to 1927 he served as president of the Social Science Research Council, which he had helped to found. A member of the Hoover Commission on Recent Social Trends, in the 1930's he also served on various resource and planning boards under President Franklin Delano Roosevelt.

Merriam wrote extensively in his field, showing a marked tendency to relate political science to anthropology, psychology, sociology, and economics, rather than to law and history. Among his publications are *American Political Ideas . . . 1865–1917* (1920); *The American Party System* (1922); *The Role of Politics in Social Change* (1936); *The New Democracy and the New Despotism* (1939); and *Systematic Politics* (1945).

MERRICK, mĕr'ĭk, **Leonard,** English novelist and playwright: b. London, England, Feb. 21, 1864; d. there, Aug. 7, 1939. Born Leonard Miller, he was educated at Brighton College, employed for a time in South African diamond fields, and then went on the London stage, using the surname Merrick, which he later acquired by legal process. After two years as an actor, he began to write short stories and then novels, which had a modest or meager success although warmly received by his fellow craftsmen. He also wrote five plays, some in collaboration. Merrick's best-known novel was *Conrad in Quest of His Youth* (1903); others were *The Actor-Manager* (1898), *The Quaint Companions* (1903), and *The Position of Peggy* (1911). The above-named titles were reissued in 1918–1919 with introductions by J. M. Barrie, William Dean Howells, H. G. Wells, and Arthur Wing Pinero, respectively, as part of a special edition of Merrick's collected works made possible by his fellow authors.

MERRILL, mĕr'ĭl, **George Perkins,** American geologist: b. Auburn, Me., May 31, 1854; d. there, Aug. 15, 1929. He graduated from the University of Maine (B.S., 1879; Ph.D., 1889) and in 1881 accepted a position at the United States National Museum (Washington, D.C.). He worked there for the rest of his life, becoming head curator in 1897. Under his direction the museum's department of geology and paleontology built up one of the greatest collections in the world. From 1893 to 1915 he was also professor of geology at George Washington University. Through his pioneer research work on building stones, rock weathering, and meteorites, he made valuable contributions to science. His most important publications were *Stones for Building and Decoration* (1891); *A Treatise on Rocks, Rock-weathering and Soils* (1897); and *Non-metallic Minerals* (1904).

MERRILL, Stuart Fitzrandolph, American-French poet: b. Hempstead, N.Y., Aug. 1, 1863; d. Versailles, France, Dec. 1, 1915. Since in 1866 his father became attached to the United States legation in Paris, young Merrill was educated there, later attending Columbia Law School on his father's insistence. At the first opportunity he returned to France, and after 1892 remained there permanently. He had already published books of French verse, *Les gammes* (1887) and *Les fastes* (1891). A member of the symbolist group, including Stéphane Mallarmé and Paul Verlaine, he published also *Petits poèmes d'automne* (1895); *Une voix dans la foule* (1909); and others. His poems, said to be analogous in quality to the music of Claude Debussy, have received only fragmentary English translation.

Consult Henry, Marjorie Louise, *La contribution d'un américain au symbolisme français; Stuart Merrill* (Paris 1927).

MERRILL, city, Wisconsin, located at the confluence of the Wisconsin and Prairie rivers, 16 miles north of Wausau, at an elevation of 1,255 feet. It is the seat of Lincoln County. Served by the Chicago, Milwaukee, St. Paul, and Pacific Railroad, the city is a shipping center for a rich dairying and farming area. It is also the home of diversified small industries, producing paper, furniture, woolen goods, metal goods, shoes, and plastics. Nearby is Council Grounds State Forest, a 278-acre tract of timber.

Merrill's first settlement was a sawmill, built in 1847, and lumber and lumber milling were mainly responsible for the area's early growth, until the decline beginning about 1895. Originally Jenny Bull Falls and then Jenny, the name became Merrill in 1881. Government is by mayor and council. Pop. 9,451.

MERRIMAC, mĕr'ĭ-măk (originally MERRIMACK), United States Navy frigate, commissioned in 1856. Sunk by Union forces when the Norfolk Navy Yard was abandoned in 1861, she was raised by the Confederates, converted into an ironclad ram, and renamed the *Virginia*. See also MONITOR AND MERRIMACK.

MERRIMACK RIVER, mĕr'ĭ-măk, river, New Hampshire and Massachusetts, formed at Franklin, in south central New Hampshire, by the junction of the Pemigewasset and Winnepesaukee rivers, and flowing south into northeastern Massachusetts, where it turns to the northeast, flowing across the corner of Massachusetts to the Atlantic Ocean near Newburyport. The lower Merrimack is a broad estuary, shallow, but navigable by small boats as far as Haverhill, Mass. The river's course is marked by an abundance of rapids and waterfalls, producing a total drop of 269 feet along its length. During the 19th century, the water power thus so easily obtained was the cause of the development and prosperity of the entire region. Some of the country's cotton mills were erected on its banks, as well as woolen mills, carpet mills, and other manufactories. Besides Haverhill, other important towns on its banks in Massachusetts include Lawrence, Lowell, and Newburyport; in New Hampshire, Nashua, Manchester, Franklin, and Concord. The Merrimack has a length of 110 miles from the confluence of the Pemigewasset and Winnipesaukee rivers to its mouth; the drainage area of the river covers 5,000 square miles.

MERRIMAN, John Xavier, South African statesman: b. Street, Somersetshire, England, March 15, 1841; d. Aug. 2, 1926. He went to South Africa with his parents in 1849, and was educated at Rondebosch, near Capetown. In 1871 he was a diamond dealer in Kimberley, and during 1874–1875 he was a wine merchant in Capetown.

Meanwhile, in 1869 he had entered political life in Cape Colony, and he became commissioner of public works during 1881–1884 and treasurer general in 1890–1893. A close friend of Prime Minister Cecil Rhodes, he headed the Cape parliamentary committee which inquired into the Jameson raid of 1895. During 1898–1900 he was again treasurer general, and in 1908 he became prime minister of Cape Colony. As leader of the South African Party (formerly the Afrikaner Bond) he took a prominent part in formulating the constitution for a united South Africa. He vacated the Cape premiership when the Union of South Africa was constituted in 1910, and thereafter was a stanch supporter of the Union government which was headed by Gen. Louis Botha.

MERRIMAN, Mansfield, American civil engineer: b. Southington, Conn., 1848; d. June 7, 1925. He graduated at the Sheffield Scientific School, Yale University, in 1871, and during 1873–1875 he was a member of the United States Corps of Engineers. In 1875 he returned to Yale as instructor in civil engineering, and in 1878 he was appointed professor of civil engineering at Lehigh University; he vacated this chair in 1907 in order to devote his time to consultation, mainly in hydraulics. For five years he was associated with the geodetic survey of Pennsylvania, having charge of primary triangulation. He also conducted research in the fields of hydraulics, strength of materials, and pure mathematics. His works included *Elements of the Method of Least Squares* (1877); *The Mechanics of Materials* (1885); *Strength of Materials* (1897); *Elements of Sanitary Engineering* (1898); *Elements of Hydraulics* (1912).

MERRITT, Anna Lea, American artist: b. Philadelphia, Pa., Sept. 13, 1844; d. April 7, 1930. She studied in Dresden, Germany, under Heinrich Hoffman, and in England under Henry Merritt, whom she married in 1877. Thereafter most of her life was spent in London. She exhibited at the Royal Academy, and her *Love Locked Out* was the first work by a woman artist to be purchased by the Tate Gallery, London. Other examples of her paintings included *Piping Shepherd* (in the Pennsylvania Academy of Fine Arts, Philadelphia), *A Scene on the Grand Canal*, and *Venice*. Her portrait of James Russell Lowell hangs in the Memorial Hall, Harvard University. She also took up etching, executing a portrait of Sir Gilbert Scott and two portraits of Mary Wollstonecraft. In 1879 she published *Henry Merritt's Art Criticism and Romance;* she also wrote *A Hamlet in Old Hampshire* (1902) and *An Artist's Garden* (1908).

MERRITT, Wesley, American army officer: b. New York City, June 16, 1834; d. Washington, D.C., Dec. 3, 1910. He graduated at West Point in 1860, and served through the American Civil War. In 1863 he was promoted brigadier general of volunteers, and the next year he became brigadier general. From the close of the war he was chiefly on frontier duty down to 1879, and during 1882–1887 he served as superintendent of West Point. In 1887 he became a brigadier general in the United States Army, and in 1895 he was promoted major general. As commander in chief of United States forces in the Philippines in 1898, he cooperated with Admiral George Dewey in the capture of the city of Manila. He was retired in 1900.

MERRITT, William Hamilton, Canadian mining engineer: b. Saint Catherines, Ontario, 1855; d. Toronto, 1918. He was educated at Upper Canada College, the Royal Military School, and the Royal School of Mines, London. After his return to Canada he practiced in Toronto as a mining engineer, and subsequently he lectured in mining engineering at the Kingston School of Mines. In 1885 he took part in the operations to suppress the rebellion in Manitoba of Louis Riel, and during 1899–1902 he served with the Canadian forces in the South African War. He contributed papers to numerous learned societies, and published *Economic Minerals of Ontario* (1896) and *Field Testing for Gold and Silver* (1900).

MERRITTON, former town, Ontario, Canada, in Lincoln County on the Welland Ship Canal, now part of the city of St. Catherines. Just to the east of Merritton on June 24, 1813, the Battle of Beaver Dams was fought; 40 British soldiers and 200 Indians captured an American force of 650 men.

MERRY DEL VAL, mĕr'rĕ thĕl väl', **Rafael,** Roman Catholic prelate: b. London, England, Oct. 10, 1865; d. Rome, Italy, Feb. 26, 1930. His father was secretary to the Spanish legation in London. He accompanied his father to Rome when the latter was named Spanish ambassador to the Vatican, and in 1888 he was ordained in the priesthood. In 1892 he was appointed master of the robes and privy chamberlain to Leo XIII, and in 1897 he was papal delegate to Canada to investigate the question of separate Roman Catholic schools in Manitoba. He was consecrated titular archbishop of Nicaea in 1900, and in August 1903 he served as secretary of the conclave which elected Pope Pius X. In October of the latter year he succeeded Cardinal Mariano Rampolla as papal secretary of state, and he was created cardinal in November. From October 1914 until his death he was secretary of the congregation of the Holy Office. He wrote *The Truth of the Papal Claims* (1909).

MERRY WIVES OF WINDSOR, The, was Shakespeare's greatest prose play. It contains only about 15 per cent of verse lines, and in the spirit of its scenes it is equally subdued, save for a flash of the old fire in the fairy poetry at the close. John Dennis and Nicholas Rowe report a story, current at the opening of the 18th century and inherently plausible, to the effect that this play was written within two weeks to the special order of Queen Elizabeth, who desired to see Sir John Falstaff in love. The wish is worthy of the queen's taste, and the manner in which it was satisfied indicates that Shakespeare did not work spontaneously. In point of time the play belongs with the greatest comedies—with *Much Ado About Nothing, Twelfth Night,* and *As You Like It.* It was licensed for publication in January 1602 and most likely composed shortly before, for it is hard to believe that the Falstaff of this play can have been created while recollection of the great Falstaff of *Henry IV* (1597, 1598) was very fresh in the author's mind. There is a radical difference between the two characters. In the *Merry Wives* Falstaff loses most of his peculiar wit and all the graver, pathetic side of his character. He loses his charm, not only for the spectator but for his companions. There is a sense of positive disaster in seeing the invincibly lovable knight of *Henry IV* and *Henry V* betrayed by his own creatures, Nym and Pistol, just as there is in hearing the Titanic liar of the Gadshill episode ignominiously relating to Brook-Ford the whole sorry truth of his discomfiture. "I do begin to perceive that I am made an ass," he is forced to say in the final scene, and Shakespeare must have felt as keenly as his readers the pity of thus reducing Falstaff to the level of Dogberry and Bottom. The play is brisk and entertaining, and is constructed with masterly technique, but it deals wholly with the externals of character and with unlikely incidents. Its type-figures—Slender, Sir Hugh Evans, Dr. Caius, the Host—when compared with Mercutio, Sir Toby, or the old Falstaff, are like pygmies after giants. There is no reason to believe that *The Merry Wives of Windsor* was regarded with special favor by the Elizabethans. After the Restoration it seems to have become one of the most popular of Shakespeare's comedies, though Samuel Pepys registers emphatic dissent when noting in his diary that on Aug. 15, 1667, he saw *The Merry Wives of Windsor,* "which did not please me at all, in no part of it." Precisely a century after its first publication, in 1702, a revised version by Dennis was brought out with the title, *The Comical Gallant, or The Amours of Sir John Falstaff.* Since the rise of the romantic movement, it has been one of the least liked of Shakespeare's comedies.

TUCKER BROOKE.

MERSEN, Treaty of, effected Aug. 8, 870, at Mersen (Meerssen), Netherlands, between Charles the Bald of France and his half brother Louis of Germany by which Lotharingia or Lorraine, the kingdom of their nephew Lothair II (d. 869), was divided between the east and west Frankish realms—France and Germany. From this date the history of the two national divisions and of the European state system begins.

MERSEY, mûr′zĭ, river in northwest England formed by the junction of the rivers Goyt and Etherow in Derbyshire. It flows northwest and west between Cheshire and Lancashire into the Irish Sea through a large estuary that forms the harbor of Liverpool. From the right it re-

ceives the Tame, at Stockport, and the Irwell; and on the left its chief tributaries are the Bollin and the Weaver. At Eastham, on the estuary, is the entrance to the Manchester Ship Canal, 35½ miles in length, through which large ocean steamers have direct access to Manchester. Beneath the bed of the river, extending from Birkenhead to Liverpool, are a railway tunnel (opened in 1886) and a road tunnel (completed in 1930). The length of the Mersey, including the estuary, is 70 miles.

MERSHON, mĕr-shŏn′, **Ralph Davenport,** American electrical engineer and inventor: b. Zanesville, Ohio, July 14, 1868; d. Miami, Fla., Feb. 14, 1952. He graduated at Ohio State University in 1890, and the following year joined the staff of the Westinghouse Electric Company. Westinghouse transformers designed by him received an award at the Chicago Exposition in 1893. He retained his connection with the company, at Pittsburgh, Pa., and New York City until 1900, when he entered private practice as a consulting engineer. He designed and built several important high voltage transmission plants in Japan, South Africa, Canada, and various parts of the United States. His inventions included the six-phase rotary converter, a compounded rotary converter, a system of lightning protection for electrical apparatus, and a compensating voltmeter.

MERSIN, mĕr-sēn′, or **ICEL,** ê-chĕl′, seaport city, Turkey, seat of Içel vilayet, on the Mediterranean 40 miles west-southwest of Adana. Although the harbor is an open roadstead there is a considerable shipping trade. An American mission is located here. Pop. (1945) 33,148.

MERSON, mĕr-sôN′, **Luc Olivier** (also LUC OLIVIER-MERSON), French painter: b. Paris, May 21, 1846; d. Nov. 14, 1920. His first picture exhibited in the Salon was *Leucothea and Anaxandros* (1867). In 1869 he carried off the Grand Prix de Rome, the supreme ambition of art students, by his painting *The Soldier of Marathon.* He produced the same year *Apollo the Destroyer,* now in the Museum of Castres. In 1872 he painted *The Martyrdom of Saint Edmund of England* (Museum of Troyes). Thereafter he devoted his pencil to the portrayal of legendary and mythological scenes and incidents. His chief works in this class are *The Vision, a Legend of the 14th Century* (1873); *A Patriot Sacrifice* (1874); *Saint Michael* (1875); *Saint Francis and the Wolf of Agubbio* (1878); *Saint Isidore* (a triptych) (1879); *The Judgment of Paris witnessed by Eros* (1884); *Mankind and Fortune* (1892); *The Annunciation* (1903). He also frescoed with scenes from the life of Louis IX the walls of the Saint Louis gallery in the Palais de Justice at Paris.

MERTHYR TYDFIL, mûr′thĕr tĭd′vĭl, county borough, Wales, in Glamorganshire 24 miles by rail northwest of Cardiff. From an unimportant village in 1780, it became a prosperous center of iron and steel manufacturing owing to its situation near the valuable coal and mineral fields of South Wales. The industrial depression after World War I seriously affected the borough. Richard Trevithick's steam locomotive, the first to be tried on rails, successfully hauled a train of 10 tons of iron and 70 men on the Merthyr Tydfil-Pontypridd tramway in 1804. At the Dowlais iron works of Merthyr Tydfil, in 1856, Bessemer steel was first rolled into rails. The name of the borough is said to commemorate the martyrdom of Saint Tydfil, daughter of Brychan, who was put to death by the Saxons in the 5th century. Pop. (1961) 59,008.

MERTON, Walter de, English prelate: d. about Oct. 27, 1277. He served as chancellor of England during 1261–1263, and again in 1272–1274. In 1271 he was appointed justiciar, and from 1274 he was bishop of Rochester. He is best remembered as the founder of Merton College (q.v.).

MERTON COLLEGE. See OXFORD UNIVERSITY.

MERV, former name of the town of Mary, Turkmen Soviet Socialist Republic. See MARY.

MERWIN, Samuel, American author and editor: b. Evanston, Ill., Oct. 6, 1874; d. New York City, Oct. 17, 1936. He was educated at Northwestern University. In collaboration with Henry Kitchell Webster, a friend from his boyhood days, he later wrote fiction about railroad-building in the United States, attaining some success with *The Short Line War* (1899) and *Calumet K* (1901). He also published in 1901 a novel entitled *The Road to Frontenac,* and this was followed by others which included *His Little World* (1903) and *The Merry Anne* (1904). From 1905 to 1909 he was associate editor of *Success Magazine,* and he was editor for the next two years. During 1907 he visited China to study the trade in opium, an account of which he gave in the book *Drugging a Nation* (1908). His subsequent novels included *The Trufflers* (1916); *The Passionate Pilgrim* (1919); *The Moment of Beauty* (1924); *Lady Can Do* (1929); *Bad Penny* (1933). He was a nephew of Frances Elizabeth Willard (q.v.), whose views on woman suffrage he espoused.

MERYON, mā-ryôn', **Charles,** French etcher and engraver: b. Paris, Nov. 24, 1821; d. Charenton, Feb. 14, 1868. As a young man he served in the French Navy, which he was compelled to leave on account of ill health. Thereupon he turned to etching as a career, his chief works being picturesque spots in old Paris, many of which were subsequently destroyed. Between 1850 and 1854 he executed a series of 23 etchings known as *Eaux-fortes sur Paris,* by which he is best remembered. He met with little success, however, and lived in poverty until his mind failed and he was confined in a mental hospital, where he died.

MESA, mā'sȧ, city, Arizona, in Maricopa County 15 miles east of Phoenix; it is served by the Southern Pacific Railroad. Industrial activities are connected with the packing of vegetables and citrus fruits, and the ginning of cotton. The city was founded by Mormons in 1878. Government is by mayor and council. Pop. 33,772.

MESA, in geography, large, tabular, steep-sided blocks of land produced by the dissection of a plateau by the agency of rivers. The term is in common use in the great plateaus in the southwestern area of the United States. Smaller and less precipitous formations of the same type are frequently termed buttes.

MESA VERDE NATIONAL PARK, administered for the people of the United States by the National Park Service, a bureau of the Department of the Interior, is situated in southwestern Colorado. This area, comprising more than 51,000 acres, is a high tableland, rising abruptly from the floors of the Montezuma Valley on one side and the Mancos Valley on the other. Geologically it is the type locality of the Mesaverde formation of sandstones and shale that overlie the rocks of the Mancos formation, the whole exemplifying in striking scenic effects the forces of erosion which have worked upon the Rocky Mountain uplift. The surface of this mesa is broken by many canyons, the more rugged as they descend toward the Mancos. It is along these canyons, and in the great caverns of their sidewalls, with the overhanging rock serving as roofs, that the many hundreds of ancient villages of prehistoric Indians are found, to be visited yearly by an ever increasing number of tourists, and to be under constant study by those archaeologists whose patient research is slowly revealing the pattern of a fascinating phase of our pre-Columbian history.

Abandoned by the prehistoric people many centuries ago, and subject not only to the ravages of time but also to the unconscious vandalism of early plunderers, the cliff houses, pueblos, and pit houses are now given adequate federal protection. Visitors, though given every reasonable facility for enjoying the park, are required to observe the rules made necessary in pursuing the intent of the congressional organic act: the preservation of such park areas for the enjoyment and education of future generations. No cliff dwelling may be entered except in company of a park ranger. This rule does not apply to the ruins on the top of the mesa, which may be freely visited any time during the daylight hours by those who register at the park entrance or at the excellent Museum. For more than a thousand years sedentary Indians, unwarlike and mainly subsistent upon agriculture, lived in the Mesa Verde and surrounding regions. The discovery of the more important Mesa Verde pueblos was made in December 1888 by Richard Wetherell and Charles Mason, local cattlemen who were hunting stray stock on the mesa top. Later, Mason said "We had heard of Cliff Palace before we saw it. A Ute Indian named Acowitz had told us about it and we had always hoped to find it. The Utes were afraid of the ruins because of the spirits of the old people they believed to be there."

Beginning with a simple culture at about the opening of the Christian era, these people had reached by the end of the 13th century a high level that had even spread in some small degree to the wild tribes with whom they had contact. [The contact was not fortunate for the peaceable Pueblo people, as we shall see as we consider the four periods of progress that have been identified by the archaeologist.] Up to about the year 400 the outstanding craft of the Mesa Verde people was the weaving of baskets. They seem not to have had pottery, and their only missile weapon was the atlatl (throwing-stick). They lived in huts over shallow pits or in rough shelters on the floors of caves. Cooking, aside from roasting over coals, was done by means of putting hot stones in their well-made baskets. In the floors of their cave houses they stored some of the products of their meager fields on the mesa. The years from about 400 to 700 are known as the Modified Basket Maker period. Here we begin to encounter pottery of a plain gray type that supplanted baskets for such use as cooking and water carrying. The folk either invented for themselves the bow and arrow, or received it from the outside. Most important, they built houses. These were only head-high roofs over shallow pits, but they were homes for single families, in a total population that seems to have greatly increased. Weaving was practiced, and the farming had become more important. Toward the end of this period the roofed pits gave way to rectangular rooms with vertical walls, and these, grouped together, formed large villages. What is known as the Developmental Pueblo Period occupied the years from about 700 to 1000 A.D. The villages became more compact. The "pueblo" (giving it the Spanish word for village) was about to come to the full fruition of the Classic and final period in the culture of these people. It was a time of eager experiment. Many kinds of house walls were tried—adobe, adobe and poles, combination of stones and adobe —until they finally arrived at coursed masonry of superior artisanship. In the cluster of houses around open courts were pit houses for ceremonial purposes, now called kivas. The pottery was not only greatly improved, but each area had its own definite type. Cotton was woven. A strange innovation appeared, whereby a cradle made of wood was adopted, which had the effect of deforming the heads of the infants, flattening them on the back of the skull. At this point of the cultural development of the Mesa Verde people, and probably just about as their great period was beginning, this nonwarlike prosperous folk had become targets for nomadic bandits. The cliff dwellings that attract most attention from the modern visitor thus came into being. (See CLIFF DWELLERS.) Clearly these cave pueblos, or cliff houses, were a defensive step. Such impressive structures as Cliff Palace, Square Tower House, Spruce Tree House, and Long House were the product of this flowering period. A rigid social structure, with a highly ritualized religious ceremony had evolved from the first rude social behavior and beliefs. Now the pottery was not only more efficient, but the artist in the potter was achieving animal figures and geometrical designs, the finest ware having black figures upon light gray. There was a profusion of jewelry of turquoise and other colored stones. However, the end of the pueblo life was now in sight. What the invasion of hostile tribes could not do, the phenomenon of a radical climatic change did. Beginning about 1276 and continuing for 24 consecutive years there was insufficient moisture to grow crops. The springs failed and the rivers ceased to flow. One by one the villages were abandoned. The pueblo people simply shouldered what belongings they could carry and moved on, perhaps to the southward and eastward.

Consult Watson, Don, *Cliff Palace* (Ann Arbor 1940); Radin, Paul, *The Story of the American Indian* (New York 1944); National Park Service folder, Washington, revised and reprinted frequently.

FREEMAN TILDEN,
Author, "The National Parks."

MESCAL, měs-kăl′, a fiery liquor produced in Mexico from several species of agave. The most famous liquor, however, is made from the "hearts" of the species *Agave tequileana.* The city of Tequila, in the state of Jalisco, is the center of this particular industry. The Tequila agave resembles in the appearance of its stiff lancelike leaves the sisal hemp plant, though it sends out its leaves from a great bulb-like cellular mass which forms the heart of the plant. This heart, when denuded from its leaves and detached from the root, is cleft in two, and a dozen of these pieces make a fair load for a mule, for they must be transported from the fields where grown to the city, sometimes a journey of several miles. These hearts are roasted in pits, within the distillery enclosures, dug four or five feet deep and considerably wider. A hot fire is built of mesquite wood, and large stones distributed through the fuel. The "heads" are then heaped over the burning mass until a huge mound is formed, which is covered first with grass and then with earth, and the mass left several days to cook. When the mound is opened the raw product is found to have changed to a dull brown in color, and the juices to have been converted into sugar. White hot and steaming, the mass is taken to another pit, stone-paved, on the bottom of which revolves a heavy stone crusher, really an arrester operated by mule power. Here it is ground into pulp and the semiliquid mass carried in deep trays on the heads of Indians to the vats where it remains to ferment. Then it goes to the rude stills, and is run off as mescal.

The commercial mescal is a colorless liquor sometimes with a slight amber tint, though much of it is like alcohol. Some of the higher grades are given fancy names which serve as trademarks. It is far too strong a liquor to be drunk with impunity, though its fiery quality seems to suit the Mexican taste for hot things. Zotol is another liquor, made in the same way from the bulblike heart of a species of *Dasylirion*, which is said to be as strong as 95 per cent alcohol. These liquors should not be confounded with aguardiente, which is made from sugar cane. The Mexican name means burning water.

MESDAG, měs′däк, **Hendrik Willem,** Dutch marine painter: b. Groningen, Feb. 23, 1831; d. 1915. He was a banker, following in his father's footsteps, until his 36th year, when he devoted himself to art, studied under Alma-Tadema, who was a relative, and under Roelofs, and lived at The Hague, with a studio at Scheveningen. He took a foremost rank among modern painters of the sea, and conveyed the idea of water-masses and motions very felicitously. He presented his splendid collection of paintings and art objects to the nation. His pictures include *Fishing Boats at Scheveningen, Strand of Scheveningen, Morning on the Scheldt,* and *In Peril.*

MESENTERY, měs′ĕn-tĕr-ĭ, a double fold of the peritoneum which attaches the small intestine to the spinal column, but in such a manner as to permit great freedom of motion. The corresponding support of the large intestine is the mesocolon, with the mesorectum. The mesentery contains between its folds several blood-vessels, lacteals, lymphatics, nerves, and the ganglia called mesenteric glands, which are connected with the lymphatico-lacteal system.

It is about four inches wide, and extends nearly the whole length of the intestine. It is subject to several diseases, the most frequent of which is tubercular degeneration of some of its numerous glands. For this and other diseases of the mesentery, see PERITONITIS.

MESHA, mē'shà, king of Moab who ruled about 869–850 B.C. His deeds are described in the Old Testament (II Kings 3) and in the text of the Moabite Stone (q.v.), prepared in his capital at Dhiban (Dibon) to commemorate his country's independence from Israel. In spite of the harassment of his kingdom by the Israelites related in II Kings 3, he was able to accomplish the construction of a commercial road, a community water supply, and several fortified towns.

MESHCHERA, myĭsh-chě'rŭ, or **MESHCHORA**, watershed, USSR, in the central European part of the Russian SFSR, in Ryazan Oblast. The Oka River forms its southern boundary. The city of Kasimov is on its eastern edge, and Ryazan lies to the southwest. The Meshchera is an extensive swampy, forested area, with many lakes. Peat cutting is the chief industry, but lumbering and glass production are also carried on to some extent.

MESHED, mě-shěd' (Iranian MASHHAD, màsh-hàd'), city, Iran, situated at an altitude of 3,200 feet on the Kashaf River, 440 miles east-northeast of Teheran. It is the capital of the 9th Province (until 1938 called Khurasan) in northeastern Iran, and its proximity to the frontiers of the USSR and of Afghanistan has rendered it of considerable strategic importance. Connected with Teheran by railway, it is also a transportation and commercial center with many modern facilities, including a medical college, radio station, and airfield. Its fertile environs yield fruit, cotton, grain, and opium, and the chief industries of the city include the processing of cotton, wool, leather, and food, and the manufacture of carpets and leather goods.

Meshed is also important as the holy city of the Shi'ites who come to worship at its shrine, the 9th century tomb of the Imam Reza, the 8th Imam of the Shi'ites, for whom the city is named. The nearby Gauhar Shad Mosque was built in 1418 by the daughter-in-law of Tamerlane.

A successor of the ancient city of Tus which was destroyed by the Mongols in 1389 and whose ruins lie 15 miles to the northwest, Meshed grew up around the tomb of Imam Reza in the following century. It was many times invaded by marauding bands of Mongols, Turkomans, and Uzbeks, and in 1740 was remade the capital of Persia by Nadir Shah. During World War II, Soviet troops occupied the city until their general evacuation of the vicinity in 1946. Pop. (1956) 242,165.

MESILLA, mà-sē'yà, village, New Mexico, in Dona Ana County, a few miles southwest of Las Cruces, on the Rio Grande. With the surrounding territory, it was acquired by the United States through the Gadsden Purchase (1853). The region was captured by the Confederacy during the Civil War, and Mesilla was made its capital. The New Mexico College of Agriculture and Mechanic Arts is at nearby State College. The Organ Mountains lie to the east, and Mesilla Dam to the south. Pop. 1,264.

MESKO, měsh'kȯ, **Franc Ksaver**, Slovene poet and short story writer: b. Sv. Tomaž, near Maribor, Yugoslavia, Oct. 28, 1874. After studying for the ministry at Maribor (then Marburg, Germany) and Klagenfurt, Austria, Meško served a succession of Yugoslavian parishes before he settled near the village of Slovenjgradec in Slovenia. His first stories, like those of his compatriot, Ivan Cankar (1876–1918), introduced a new expression in Slovenian literature, characterized by profound psychological penetration, symbolism, and personal lyricism. His works include the novels *Hrast* (*The Oak,* 1896) and *Na poljani* (1907), and the short stories *Kam plovemo* (*Where are we going,* 1897); *Crtice* (*Sketches,* 1901–1902); *Ob tihih večerih* (*In the Silent Evening,* 1904); and *Mir Božji* (*The Peace of God,* 1906).

MESMER, měs'měr, Eng. měz'měr, **Franz** or **Friedrich Anton**, German physician after whom mesmerism was named: b. Iznang am Bodensee, near Rodolfzell, Baden, Germany, May 23, 1734; d. Meersburg, Baden, March 5, 1815. He was educated in medicine at the University of Vienna, where he presented his thesis on the supposedly magnetic influence of the stars on human beings. He began to practice curing diseases by the use of magnets, which he later discarded, believing that a magnetic fluid, which exerted a force he called animal magnetism, pervaded the universe and that he had a mysterious control over this force which enabled him to influence others. Although in Vienna he became a well-known patron of music—a friend of Christoph Willibald Gluck and of the young Mozart, whose opera *Bastien et Bastienne* was produced at his home, his theories became obnoxious to the Viennese medical profession, and in 1778 he went to Paris, where his curious methods (see HYPNOSIS) soon aroused considerable public attention and professional antagonism. In 1784 a committee of the Académie des Sciences, including such eminent men as Antoine Lavoisier, Dr. Joseph Guillotin, and Benjamin Franklin, reported on Mesmer's activities, acknowledging certain of his effects, but attributing them to causes other than so-called animal magnetism. Thus discredited, Mesmer left Paris and spent the remainder of his life in seclusion. His followers continued to practice those techniques which came to be called "mesmerism," but were for the most part regarded as charlatans.

Consult Purtscher, Nora (von Wydenbruck, *Doctor Mesmer; an Historical Study* (London 1947).

MESMERISM. See HYPNOSIS.

MESOHIPPUS. See HORSE—*Evolution of the Horse.*

MESOLITHIC. See ARCHAEOLOGY—*Old World.*

MESOMEDES, mě-sǒm'ě-dēs, a kithara player from Crete, who flourished in the early decades of the 2d century A.D. According to the Greek lexicographer Suidas, he was a freedman under the emperor Hadrian and wrote lyric poetry, including an encomium to Antoninus, Hadrian's favorite and successor. The extant corpus of Mesomedes' poetry includes two compositions in the *Anthologia graeca* and eight poems written in the Doric dialect, preserved in the Ottobonian Library in the Vatican. Also attributed to him are three hymns, *To the Muse, To the Sun,* and *To Nemesis,* which have survived with their original notation and are valued as authentic clues to the sound of ancient Greek music (q.v.). Although modern scholarship has upheld the attribution to Mesomedes of the latter two, the *Hymn to the Muse,* actually two separate pieces, has been dated about a century earlier.

MESON, mĕs'ŏn, mē'sŏn (also called MESOTRON, mĕs'ŏ-trŏn), originally a particle postulated by the Japanese physicist, Hideki Yukawa (1935), to account for the attractive forces in an atomic nucleus, and initially observed as a component of cosmic rays independently by J. C. Street and Edward C. Stevenson (1937) and by Seth Needermeyer and Carl David Anderson (1938). It has a mass intermediate between the electron and proton.

The observed cosmic ray μ mesons occur as positive and negative particles of unit electron charge and 215 electron masses. They have a spin of $\frac{1}{2}$ and therefore obey Fermi statistics and have only a very small nuclear interaction. They are radioactive and spontaneously decay in a vacuum to an electron and two neutral particles of small mass, presumably neutrinos with a mean lifetime of 2.1 microseconds. They are usually

of nucleons (protons or neutrons). See also COSMIC RADIATION; PARTICLE ACCELERATORS.

LYLE B. BORST,
Chairman, Department of Physics, New York University.

MESONERO Y ROMANOS, mā-sŏ-nā'rō ē rō-mä'nōs, **Ramon de,** Spanish journalist and essayist: b. Madrid, Spain, July 19, 1803; d. there, April 30, 1882. He first embarked upon a commercial career, but then turned to journalism and in 1836 founded a nonpolitical weekly, *Semanario pintoresco español,* which he continued to direct until 1842. An eminent representative of the 19th century *costumbrismo* (Spanish genre writing), he wrote *Panorama matritense* (1832–1835); *Tipos y caracteres* (1843–1862); and *Memorias de un setentón natural y vecino de Madrid* (1880).

MESONYCHIDAE, mĕs-ŏ-nĭk'ĭdē, a family of Creodonts which was highly specialized and prevailed on the North American continent during the Eocene period. They acquired a wolf-like form, with a very long, slender tail and a digitigrade gait indicating powers of speed beyond those of any other Creodont. Their heads, however, were disproportionately large and bear-like, indicating that they could not have been

Particle	Observed decay products	Mass m (Electron masses)	Lifetime (10^{-9} sec.)	Possible attribution
τ	3π	965.5 ± 0.7	~ 28	$\tau^{\pm} \rightarrow \pi^{+} + \pi^{-} + \pi^{\pm}$
ϑ°	2π	966 ± 10	0.10	$\vartheta^{\circ} \rightarrow \pi^{+} + \pi^{-}$
$\tau'(K_{\pi})$	$\pi(E < 57$ Mev$)$	975 ± 44	> 1	$\tau^{\pm} \rightarrow \pi^{\pm} + \pi^{\circ} + \pi^{\circ}$
$\chi(K_{\pi})$	π monoenergetic	955 ± 44	> 1	$\vartheta^{\pm} \rightarrow \pi^{\pm} + \pi^{\circ}$
$\varkappa(K_{\mu})$	μ continuous	1060 ± 35	~ 2	$\varkappa \rightarrow \mu + \nu + \gamma$ or $\rightarrow \mu + \nu + \nu$
K_{μ}	μ monoenergetic	914 ± 20	~ 28	$\varkappa_{\mu} \rightarrow \mu + \nu$

observed as the decay product of the heavier π meson.

The π mesons initially observed by Wilson M. Powell and others are now identified with the Yukawa particle. They are intimately associated with nuclear forces and have a strong nuclear interaction. They have integral spin and therefore obey Bose statistics. They are found with unit electron charge both positive and negative of mass 276 times the electron. They are radioactive and decay into a μ meson plus one neutrino with a mean lifetime of 0.025 microseconds. An uncharged π meson is found having a mass of 295 electron masses. It decays into two gamma rays with a lifetime of 10^{-14} seconds. The interaction cross section for π mesons on nucleons shows evidence of resonance structure and has a maximum value of 2.5 x 10^{-28} cm.^{2}.

Heavy Mesons.—Many heavier mesons have been observed or postulated. The accompanying table summarizes the characteristics of the more generally accepted varieties. Other less certain particles have been reported. Their relationships to each other and to the nucleus remain for future evaluation.

Hyperons.—Particles heavier than protons have been reported which decay into a proton (or neutron) and one or a number of mesons. They are presently considered to be excited states

rapid and aggressive in their habits; their teeth suggest that they lived principally on a vegetable diet. Their development into hyena-like creatures may be traced to nearly the close of the Eocene. The type genus of Mesonychidae was *Mesonyx.*

MESOPHYTE, mĕs'ŏ-fīt, a term used to designate any plant growing in a habitat that is neither too dry nor too wet. As a result mesophytes lack the many special adaptations characteristic of plants growing in extreme conditions. As the habitats range from very dry conditions to strictly aquatic ones, mesophytes are often difficult to differentiate from either xerophytes or hydrophytes but far outnumber them in most floras. Many deciduous trees and shrubs are mesophytes only during summer, as they become xerophytes after dropping their leaves.

THEODOR JUST,
Chicago Natural History Museum.

MESOPOTAMIA, mĕs-ŏ-pŏ-tā'mĭ-à; -tăm'-yà, a land that lies along and between the rivers Euphrates and Tigris in western Asia. It is bounded by the Anatolian plateau, the Iranian plateau, the Persian Gulf, and the Arabian and Syrian deserts. The name derives from Greek Μεσοποταμια, and means "land between the rivers." The Greeks, however, did not usually include Babylonia under that name.

Except for intermittent phases of single government, Mesopotamia consisted of a multitude of independent city-states prior to the 18th century B.C. Most of these were ruined in the wars of Hammurabi, king of Babylon. Two finally emerged: Assyria in Upper Mesopotamia and Babylonia in Lower Mesopotamia, each very different in character, but both sharing a common civilization.

Mesopotamia ceased to be politically independent after the Persians occupied Babylon in 539 B.C., but its cultural and economic importance was to remain considerable for some 1,800 years longer. During the last four of these centuries it steadily declined. The end came in 1258 A.D., when a Mongol invasion resulted in such destruction and loss of population that the irrigation system, upon which the welfare of the country depended, could no longer be repaired and maintained adequately.

Throughout almost the whole of the period from 539 B.C. to 1258 A.D. Mesopotamia and Persia formed a single political unit. The Persian Achaemenid dynasty was brought to an end by Alexander the Great in 331 B.C.; the Seleucids (Greeks) followed in 312 B.C., the Arsacids (Parthians) in 141 B.C., and the Sassanians (Persians) in 226 A.D. The Sassanians were overthrown by the Arabs in 637 A.D. and from then until 1258 both Mesopotamia and Persia formed part of the Caliphate. For most of this period of 1,800 years, the seat of government was in Mesopotamia, not Persia, the reason being that Mesopotamia surpassed Persia in population, wealth, culture, and communications. Except for the first and the last two centuries of this period the capital remained in the vicinity of ancient Babylon: first Seleucia, then Ctesiphon, and finally Baghdad.

The Mongol invasion of 1258 was followed by three centuries of anarchy, by the end of which Mesopotamia had sunk to an obscure and poverty-stricken province of the Turkish (Ottoman) empire. The scene of a hard-fought campaign between the Turks and the British in World War I, northwestern Mesopotamia was awarded to Syria after the war. From the remainder, a new state was formed, Iraq. For the geography of Mesopotamia see IRAQ; for political history, see ASSYRIA; CALIPHATE; IRAN; IRAQ.

In the field of modern knowledge Mesopotamia is important chiefly for the early civilization it nurtured, one of the two original sources of our Western civilization (the other being Egypt). So far as we know at present, civilization began when the hunters of western Asia (and adjacent Egypt) started turning to agriculture as their chief means of subsistence. Western Asia is mainly arid country and where the rainfall was scarce these early farmers tended to concentrate on the scanty rivers and streams. Of these, the Euphrates and Tigris are the only two of any considerable size. Over most of their course, only a short distance apart, they intersect the central part of Western Asia along the line where plain and mountain meet, and thus confer upon Mesopotamia, in addition to the advantage of an exceptionally rich agriculture, a position of high strategic and commercial importance. Who these early farmers were we do not know, though there is reason to believe they were neither Sumerians nor Semites. To the sphere of

primitive art they contributed elaborately decorated pottery, the so-called Hassuna, Samarra, and Tell Halaf ware in Upper Mesopotamia, superseded later by the coarser Al Ubaid ware, probably spreading from Lower Mesopotamia.

The Sumerian Period.—Many of the place names and names of deities in ancient Mesopotamia were neither Sumerian nor Semitic; and the same is probably true of a good number of the words for basic farming techniques and products. On the other hand most of the words for the institutions of city life are Sumerian, and many have later Semitic counterparts. It is possible therefore that the Sumerians were not the original settlers, but that it is they who are at least chiefly responsible for the transition to an urban economy. The date is very roughly 3500 B.C., rather earlier than later.

Although much still remains to be learned about this momentous development, it is reasonably probable that the chief factor in it was the need to construct and maintain a large and intricate system of canals in Lower Mesopotamia. This could hardly be achieved by the separate efforts of many small farming communities. It required cooperation and enforcement, for example, to allocate a limited supply of water. This in turn involved organization at least on a regional basis. These canals were needed for several purposes: to drain the marshes for their rich alluvial soil, to ensure a sufficient supply of water for irrigation, and to protect the country from devastating floods. The records show clearly that work on the canal system was to remain one of the dominant tasks of government, particularly in Lower Mesopotamia.

The outcome was a multitude of city-states. The supremacy among them, apparently a form of real hegemony, was held by various cities, by some more than once, as in the case of Uruk and Ur. It has been concluded that this possibly reflects an earlier loosely knit organization of regions, based upon a central sanctuary. This could best be termed an amphictyony; of such organizations the Greek amphictyony is the best known example, and early Israel may be another. The city of Nippur (q.v.), is the probable site of the central sanctuary, as it was the seat of the national deity, Enlil, and the chief religious center of Sumer as far back as the records go. The hegemony, so far as one can judge from the king list, went with control of this city, which, in historical times at least, was not an independent city-state.

That there may once have existed a Sumerian amphictyony is worth mentioning precisely because at the time of this writing it is merely an important possibility. In fact, much of what we can say about the earlier phases of Mesopotamian civilization belongs to this category of provisional conclusions, subject to further evidence and research. This state of our knowledge is due chiefly to the fact that writing was unknown at the beginning of urban civilization and for many centuries after it appeared, was confined chiefly to business documents. Gradually historical inscriptions and building inscriptions appear, but the large-scale use of writing for the purpose of recording Sumerian literature did not begin until after the end of the Sumerian period. In consequence there are serious gaps in our best source of information, contemporary texts, throughout the whole of the Sumerian period proper.

A Mesopotamian city-state seems to have been regarded as the private estate of the chief local deity. Thus, in Lower Mesopotamia, Nippur belonged to Enlil, originally god of the wind, Eridu belonged to Enki, god of sweet water, Lagash to Ningirsu (later Ninurta), god of war, Ur to Nanna, the moon-god. The sun-god, Utu, owned two cities in Lower Mesopotamia, Sippar and Larsa, whereas the goddess of love and war, Inanna, was mistress of Arba-Ila and Nineveh in Upper Mesopotamia, as well as being joint owner with the sky-god, An, of the city Uruk in Lower Mesopotamia.

The smaller cities were mostly seats of lesser deities, though if one of these smaller cities subsequently rose to power, the chief local deity would rise to correspondingly high status within the Mesopotamian pantheon. Notable instances are the rise of Marduk, god of Babylon, and the rise of Assur, god of the like-named city, the ancient capital of Assyria.

The god was the true king of the city-state. The mortal king was merely his chosen representative. As tenant-farmer administrating the god's domain, his duty was to provide for the needs of the gods (sacrifices), keep their houses (temples) in good repair, and rule the subjects of the god in the latter's name.

The more cities the king ruled, the more deities he represented. During those occasional intermittent phases when the city-states were united under single rule, as during part of the dynasty of Akkad (Accad), and part of the 3d dynasty of Ur, there was evident a tendency to deify the king himself. How far this extended beyond polite theory into the sphere of religious practice is not known. At any rate it never came to be the established view in Mesopotamia, as it had been from time immemorial in Egypt.

The priests assisted the king in his obligation to serve the gods, just as the lay officials of his government assisted him in his obligation to rule the subjects of the god. One of the priestly duties was to study the intricate ritual required in ministering to each deity exactly in the manner he desired. Another was the equally difficult problem of discovering the god's wishes and intentions, by means of omens, portents, and the like. Learning was chiefly confined to such sciences as these; only medicine and mathematics even approached the status of what we would term a science. The origin of Mesopotamian science is reflected in the fact that Enki, apart from being the god of learning, was also the god of magic.

A problem which greatly puzzled the ancients was that sometimes, in spite of all diligence and "science," the gods would visit totally unmerited disaster on state and individual. This problem is posed in myth and epic, particularly in the Babylonian story of the Flood. For floods were the most outstanding instance of divine irrationality, since they destroyed not only the wealth of the gods' servants but also the very estates of the gods themselves. Indeed, such weight did this problem possess that it was to break beyond the confines of literary motive, and in the so-called wisdom literature, closely akin to the Book of Job in the Old Testament, the problem of explaining unmerited misfortune carries Babylonian thought the nearest to philosophy it was ever to come.

The Semitic Period.—Already during the Sumerian period Semitic elements had been penetrating Sumer in appreciable numbers. Some of the kings who ruled about and before 2500 B.C. (for instance in Uruk and Mari) have Semitic names; and later, with the Semitic kings of the dynasty of Akkad, Semitic inscriptions as well as names appear. The Semitic language these people spoke was called Akkadian by their descendants. The name is connected with that of the city of Akkad founded by Sargon as the seat of a new dynasty. From the time of Sargon of Akkad the influence of the Semitic element in Sumer had been steadily increasing, and, as we approach the end of the Sumerian period, other Semites whom the Sumerians called Amurru begin to penetrate the country. A wall built to hold them out failed to stop the Amurru, and, when a few decades before or after 2000 B.C. the last Sumerian king was captured by Elamite invaders, the Sumerian element was finally absorbed into the Semitic.

Like the Akkadians before them, the Amurru adopted Sumerian religion and culture. Although the invaders were for the most part barbaric nomads, civilization continued without a break, the only major change being one of language. Sumerian ceased to be the language of everyday life and was relegated to the world of letters; it was kept alive to the very end of Mesopotamian civilization by the scribes, who even compiled elaborate dictionaries, the earliest known.

Sumerian was replaced, not by the West Semitic language of the Amurru, but by the language of their Semitic kinsmen, Akkadian. This rapidly rose to such prominence throughout the civilized world of the day that its use may be compared to that of French in 18th century Europe. For example, when an Egyptian Pharaoh corresponded with a Canaanite prince, the language used was neither Egyptian nor Canaanite, but Akkadian.

From the shocks it had suffered Mesopotamian civilization emerged as a synthesis of Sumerian and Semitic. But this was not achieved without a price. For the sphere of religion, art, and learning was to remain essentially Sumerian and so became divorced from the people. The latter, though ethnically mixed, became Semitic in speech, and thereby lost direct access to their cultural heritage. Moreover, fresh contributions were now impeded.

The result was that to a marked degree progress became confined to those fields where Sumerian influence was least. Semitic influence is most clearly perceptible outside the cultural sphere, as for instance in law and commerce. Already in the Code of Hammurabi, only some two centuries after the end of the Sumerian period, there are laws which have close parallels in the Old Testament, and which in outlook are far too primitive to be of Sumerian origin.

Whether the surprising achievements of Babylonian mathematics, such as rules to produce Pythagorean numbers, originated in the Sumerian or the Semitic period is not certain. On the other hand, the advances made in astronomy, which began in the Semitic period, reached their peak only under Greek rule. However, notwithstanding the importance of Greek contributions to astronomy, it is probable that in this field they took more from Babylonia than they gave.

It is in the field of literature that we most strongly feel the interplay of Sumerian and Semitic influence. Ancient Oriental literature is essentially religious in character, and, in consequence of the strong Sumerian influence in the field of religion, much in the Semitic literature of Mesopotamia is formal and artificial. But wherever the religious factor recedes to secondary importance, the literary genius of the Semites can be expected to break through. Good examples are the Epic of Creation as compared with the Epic of Gilgamesh. Both of these existed in Sumerian versions as well, but the major extant texts are Semitic in origin. The cumbersome Epic of Creation is steeped in religion. That is not the case in the Epic of Gilgamesh (q.v.), originally recorded on 12 tablets, of which the Old Babylonian Tablets II and III and the New Assyrian Tablet XI rank among the greatest and most important treasures in the early literature of mankind.

In religion, the synthesis took two main forms. The Semites either worshiped their own gods alongside the Sumerian gods, as for instance, Dagan or Adad (Hadad), who, in the city of Asshur, even shared a temple with the Sumerian god An, or else the Semitic gods were identified with Sumerian gods of like character by the simple means of adding a Semitic name to the existing Sumerian one. Of this latter process notable instances are Utu, identified with Shamash, and Inanna, identified with Ishtar.

In Mesopotamian architecture the most characteristic feature is the temple tower. Some of them hundreds of feet high, they consisted of superimposed platforms up to seven or eight in number, each smaller than the one below. At the top there was a small garden which probably contained the god's most private sanctuary. These towers go back to the Sumerian period but were to remain throughout characteristic landmarks of ancient Mesopotamia. How they originated is not yet certain; possibly as a place of refuge for the population (and the temple equipment) in times of flood. Together with the story of the flood, these towers are reflected in the Old Testament tradition, and later they figure in the accounts of Greek travelers, as for instance Herodotus.

With the arrival of the Greeks, Mesopotamian civilization had run its course. It was increasingly drawn into the orbit of Greek civilization until admiration for the foreign became so dominant that it led to imitation. See also ARCHAEOLOGY; ASSYRIA; ASSYRIOLOGY; BABYLONIA; CIVILIZATION.

M. ROWTON, *University of Chicago.*

Bibliography.—Harper, F. R., *The Code of Hammurabi* (Chicago 1904); Jastrow, M., *The Civilization of Assyria and Babylonia* (Philadelphia 1915); Meissner, B., . . . *Babylonien und Assyrien* (Heidelberg 1920–25); Delaporte, L., *Mesopotamia*, Eng. tr. (New York 1925); Driver, G. R., *The Assyrian Laws* (Oxford 1935); Lloyd, S., *Mesopotamia* (London 1936); Chiera, E., *They Wrote on Clay* (Chicago 1938); Christian, V., *Altertumskunde des Zweistromlandes*, Vol. 1 (Leipzig 1940); Dhorme, E. P., *Les Religions de Babylonie et d'Assyrie* (Paris 1945); Frankfort, H., *The Intellectual Adventure of Ancient Man* (Chicago 1946), in which see the important chapter on Mesopotamia by T. Jacobsen; Parrot, A., *Archéologie Mésopotamienne*, 2 vols. (Paris 1946–53); Heidel, A., *The Gilgamesh Epic*, 2d ed. (Chicago 1949); Parrot, A., *Ziggurats et tour de Babel* (Paris 1949); Contenau, G., *La Civilisation d'Assur et de Babylone* (Paris 1937); Heidel, A., *The Babylonian Genesis*, 2d ed. (Chicago 1951); Braidwood, R. J., *The Near East and the Foundations for Civilization* (Eugene, Ore. 1952); Driver, G. R., and Miles, J. C., *The Babylonian Laws* (Oxford 1952); Contenau, G., *Everyday Life in Babylon and Assyria* (New York 1954); Kramer, S. N., *The Sumerians* (Chicago 1963); Oppenheim, A. K., *Ancient Mesopotamia*, tr. by H. Harrison (New York 1965); Margueron, Jean-Claude, *Mesopotamia* (Cleveland 1965).

MESOZOIC ERA, in geology the large division of time following the Paleozoic Era and preceding the Cenozoic Era; some 130 million years commencing about 200 million years ago. The name, given by John Phillips in 1840, refers to the intermediate life. The era is of three periods, having the approximate durations in millions of years: Triassic, the oldest: 35; Jurassic: 40; and Cretaceous: 55.

Mesozoic North America.—The continent changed considerably during the era. In the beginning, the Atlantic region had coastal mountains formed in the preceding Appalachian Orogeny; these were eroded until they became a plain. In late Triassic, great fault-bounded depressed blocks formed from Nova Scotia to Georgia, receiving as much as six miles of sediment eroded from adjoining blocks raised as the basin sank. See NEWARK SERIES. Plains formed again during the Jurassic, to be covered by spreading seas in the Cretaceous. By the close of the era, the Atlantic Coast had much its present character, with moderate mountains west of shore-bordering sedimentary plains.

The early Mesozoic records along the Gulf of Mexico are not as accessible; but during Jurassic and Cretaceous it also had seas spreading over plains, eroded where late Paleozoic mountains had been formed. A seaway extended northwestward from central Mexico into southeastern Arizona, southern New Mexico, and extreme western Texas in Jurassic and Cretaceous time; this seaway was separated by a peninsula in Coahuila from the subsiding geosyncline along the Gulf.

The greatest changes were in the West. In early Triassic, the Pacific region continued to have widespread seas interrupted by volcanic and linear island ranges such as prevailed in the Paleozoic; toward the interior, seas interruptedly covered a subsiding belt from southern Nevada through eastern Idaho and the Canadian Rockies area, while stream plains covered the rather gradually sinking region to the east. In the middle of the era, in late Jurassic, the Nevadan Orogeny deformed a broad belt eastward from the British Columbia Coast ranges and the Sierra Nevada, while great volumes of lava invaded the cores of the mountains being formed. Later, marine waters were restricted to the immediate Pacific border and the interior. Sediment from the broad intervening highlands spread east into a broad geosyncline beneath the present Great Plains from the Mackenzie Valley to Texas. Later, in the Laramian Orogeny the ancestors of the present Rocky Mountains developed, much of the structure being gained at the very end of the era and early in the Cenozoic.

Mesozoic Life.—The plants developed profoundly during the Mesozoic era. Many plants like those now living, such as ferns and some conifers, were prevalent in the Triassic and Jurassic; but the true flowering plants, as well as the grasses, appeared in the Cretaceous. By late Mesozoic, forests and plains did not differ conspicuously in their flora from those of today.

Among invertebrates, changes are more apparent in some groups than in others. The ammonite ceaphalopods, flat-coiled chambered molluscs having strongly crenulated and fluted separating partitions, thrived from late Paleozoic through the Mesozoic, then disappeared quite suddenly; the last forms include some having irregular coiling. Among the foraminifera, the distinctive fusulinids did not survive the Paleozoic, and the orbitoids that became rock builders in the Tertiary had but a beginning in the Cretaceous. Modern types of corals replaced Paleozoic groups in the Triassic, and brachiopods, so abundant in the preceding era, became rather unimportant; these and other developments are not obvious to the layman.

The most spectacular Mesozoic organisms were among the vertebrates. Small, sprawling reptiles of the earliest Mesozoic developed into a great variety. Some, like *Tyrannosaurus* of the Cretaceous, stood erectly on two legs; enormous beasts like the Jurassic *Brontosaurus* carried tons of weight on four legs; some were armored, as the contemporary *Stegosaurus*, others horned as the late Cretaceous Triceratops. There were flying reptiles, pterodactyls, short-bodied swimming forms, like plesiosaurs, and fishlike ichthyosaurs; others were like the turtles, alligators, and snakes that have survived to the present. The first reptile-like bird, *Archaeopteryx* (q.v.), appeared in Jurassic times. Some primitive Triassic reptile is probably ancestral to the small, obscure mammals that lived in the Mesozoic, and became dominant when the dinosaurs suddenly disappeared at the close of the era. See also CRETACEOUS; JURASSIC; TRIASSIC.

MARSHALL KAY

MESQUITE, měs-kēt′, mě′skĕt, spiny shrubs or trees (*Prosopis*) of the family Mimosaceae, several species of which are common in the southwestern United States from Texas to California and southward to Mexico and tropical America. They have compound leaves divided into delicate leaflets, small greenish-white flowers borne in axillary spikes, and indehiscent pods—long and straight (*P. glandulosa, P. juliflora*) or coiled (*P. pupescens*)—which are used by the Indians for both food and fodder.

MESROP, měs′rŏp, **Saint** (sometimes MESROB; also called MAŠTOČ), Armenian bishop (390 A.D.), honored as the creator of the Armenian alphabet: b. Hasik, Province of Tarōn, Armenia, about 361; d. Valaršapat, Feb. 17, 441. A disciple of the Catholicos Nerses I, he served as secretary to the satrap of Persian Armenia, Khosrau (Chosroes), before taking Holy Orders and entering a monastery (382) in preparation for his ministry.

In 406 or 407 he organized and perfected a 36-letter Armenian alphabet, of which tradition has named him the inventor, although sacred texts in an Armenian script are suspected to have existed before his time. Thereafter he collaborated with the Catholicos, Sahak (Isaac), on an Armenian translation of the Bible, named *Mesropiana* or *Maštothsiana* after him, and also contributed to the formation of Armenian liturgy and ritual. On the death of Sahak in September 440, he succeeded to the latter's office, briefly and unofficially, however, as he died before he could be elected. His grave, near Etchmiadzin, is a place of pilgrimage and his feast is observed on Feb. 19 and November 25. A biography of him was written by his pupil Goriun (or Koriun).

MESSAGER, mě-sà-zhä′, **André Charles Prosper,** French composer and conductor: b. Montluçon, Allier, France, Dec. 30, 1853; d. Paris, Feb. 24, 1929. A student of Saint-Saëns, he won fame as a conductor at the Opéra Comi-

que in Paris (1898–1903; 1919–1920), Royal Opera in London (1901–1907), Paris Opéra (1908–1914), and Société des Concerts du Conservatoire (1908–1918). Of his numerous compositions, which include operas, ballets, and miscellaneous instrumental pieces, his comic operas were the most successful; among them, *La Basoche* (1890), *Les p'tites Michu* (1897), and *Véronique* (1898) were produced in London as well as Paris, and the last-named in America also.

MESSALA (or **MESSALLA**) **CORVINUS,** mě-sā′là (-săl′à) kôr-vī′nŭs, **Marcus Valerius,** Roman general, statesman, and patron of letters: b. 64 B.C.; d. 8 A.D. At Philippi (42 B.C.) he supported Brutus and Cassius, but after their defeat he allied himself with Antony until, disgusted with the latter's conduct, he joined Octavian. He distinguished himself at the Battle of Actium (31) and against the Aquitani (27). A well-known orator and historian, he was also noted for his high political principles and his patronage of literature, including the poet Tibullus and perhaps the author of the extant but anonymous *Panegyricus Messallae*.

MESSALINA, měs-à-lī′nà, **Valeria,** Roman empress noted for her profligacy: d. 48 A.D. The daughter of Marcus Valerius Messala Barbatus, she became the 3d wife of the emperor Claudius, after whose departure from Rome in 48, she was publicly married to her favorite paramour, Gaius Silius. She was betrayed to Claudius by her former lover, Narcissus, who had assisted her in many vicious acts, and was executed on Claudius' orders.

MESSENE, mě-sē′ně (modern Gr. MESSĒNĒ), town, Greece, in the nome of Messenia on the Pamisos River in southwest Peloponnesus, five miles west of Kalamata, with which it is connected by railroad. It is a market for the agricultural products of the environs, including olives, rice, cotton, figs, and wheat. Remains of its acropolis and other buildings have been preserved. Pop. (1940) 7,323.

MESSENIA, mě-sē′nĭ-à; modern Gr. mä-sě-nyē′ä, nome, Greece, in western Peloponnesus, bordered on the north by the nome of Elis, on the east by the Taygetus Mountains, and on the south and west by the Ionian Sea. The fertile central region, drained by the Pamisos River, yields citrus fruits, figs, wheat, olives, and cotton. Other industries include goat and hog raising, silk farming, and fishing. Its capital and chief industrial center is Kalamata. Within Messenia's boundaries are important traces of Mycenaean civilization, including beehive tombs, a walled town, and a huge palace, discovered near Pylos in 1939, which is thought to be the house of the Homeric Nestor.

A Doric settlement, Messenia is celebrated for her long struggle for independence from the Spartans, who subjugated her during the First Messenian War (8th century B.C.) and maintained their ascendency throughout the unsuccessful revolts of the Second (7th century B.C.) and Third (5th century B.C.) Messenian wars. After the latter, much of the population emigrated to Messina in Italy and to Naupaktus in Aetolia. In the next century, Messenia was restored to the Messenians by Epaminondas, the Theban general who gathered together the exiles from the various lands in which they were scattered. In 85 days they completed and fortified the town of Messene (369 B.C.), and maintained their independence until conquered by the Romans in 146 B.C.; in spite of conquest they preserved their customs and language. Pop. (1951) 227,871.

MESSERSCHMITT, mĕs'ẽr-shmĭt, **Wilhelm (Willy),** German pioneer aircraft designer and builder: b. Frankfort am Main, Germany, June 6, 1898. He designed his first airplane in 1916, organized his own aircraft manufacturing company in 1923, and merged it with the Bayerische Flugzeugwerke in 1938. His planes were remarkable for speed and four times broke world speed records; they were formidable German weapons in World War II. Messerschmitt became chairman of the German Institute for Research in Aviation at Brunswick in 1936, and in 1937 became a member of Adolf Hitler's War Council; he was fined as a war criminal after Germany's defeat.

MESSHED. See MESHED.

MESSIAH, mē-sī'à (or ANOINTED, Heb. MASHIAKH), the title (not the name) of the glorious king of Israel who is to reign in the age to come. In the Old Testament it is found only in Daniel 9:25 and following verses, where the Revised Standard Version reads "an anointed one." In the New Testament it is found only in John 1:41 and 4:25, where (in both cases) the word is explained as "Christ." But the idea of Messiahship, or Messianic vocation, or of the Messianic age is found repeatedly in both Testaments.

In ancient Israel, anointing with oil was a rite by which a king or high priest was set apart and consecrated for his office. By a transfer of meaning, the prophets also were described as anointed with the Spirit (as in Isaiah 61:1). So in the pseudepigraphic Psalms of Solomon, 17:32 and 18:5, 7, in the Apocalyptic literature, and in the Targums, the Messiah is the quasi-supernatural king whose coming is expected. This belief represented an age-old hope of national religious and political liberty and glory which goes back at least as far as the time of Isaiah, chapters 9 and 11, and Psalm 72, where the Messiah is specifically connected with the dynasty of King David (as also in Jeremiah 33:17, R.S.V., "David shall never lack a man to sit on the throne of the house of Israel").

This expectation is still an essential element in the great central prayer of the Jewish liturgy, the *Shemonch Esreh* or *Eighteen Benedictions.* Nevertheless, the Messianic hope was centered not so much in the coming of a person, the prince or king, as in the coming age of salvation, of righteousness and peace, of health, and of plenty, and so the belief took on other aspects. A vital religion necessarily expresses itself in a variety of forms and in a multiplicity of utopian dreams.

With the downfall of the Davidic monarchy, the final capture of Jerusalem by the Chaldaeans (in 587 B.C.), and the Babylonian Exile that followed this catastrophe, it became necessary to envision the restoration of the dynasty rather than its continuance and triumph. But even this was unacceptable to many, who looked for a pure theocracy or rule of a priestly hierarchy in which the prince would be a secondary figure. Still others thought of the Messianic era without reference to a personal ruler; that is, with no Mes-

siah; the promise, said some, had been fulfilled in Hezekiah.

Finally, under the influence of the long period of Persian domination (539–331 B.C.), various dualistic and transcendental emphases were introduced into Judaism, with the result that purely supernatural, angelic, heavenly beings took the place of earthly rulers (or stood above them and guided them), and were expected to control the final denouement of human history. Instead of the Messiah, the Book of Enoch, 46:3, pictures "the Son of Man who has righteousness," to whom the Last Judgment is to be committed—a divine being who was with God from the beginning and was "named before the Lord of Spirits before the signs [of the Zodiac] were hung up in heaven." Other figures expected at the end of the present world age are the Priest-King (Testament of Levi, chap. 18); "the anointed from Aaron and Israel" (Damascus Document 15:4 of the Dead Sea Scrolls); "a Prophet" (like Moses, Deuteronomy 18:15); or Moses, Elijah, or Jeremiah come back to earth; or even some purely angelic figure hitherto unknown.

These dramatis personae of the final judgment and inauguration of the age to come were not the traditional Messiah, but substitutes required by the conditions of the new era in which the Jews now lived. Political Messianism was highly dangerous under the Romans, as the false charges brought against Jesus of Nazareth clearly show. Thus the figure of the Messiah which meets us in the New Testament has many forms and analogues. The early Christians described Jesus as the Messiah (in Greek *Christos*), but the use of the term was soon given up and "Christ" became a proper name for Greek- and Latin-speaking Christians, which it has remained ever since. Among present-day Jews there are still some who look forward to the coming of a Messiah, but the concept has been largely reinterpreted.

FREDERICK C. GRANT,
Union Theological Seminary, New York City.

MESSIAH, an oratorio in three parts by George Frideric Handel, with text from the Bible arranged by Charles Jennens, Jr. (1700–1773). It was first performed at Dublin, Ireland, April 13, 1742, after a public rehearsal there on April 9. Within a few years *Messiah* became in England what it now remains throughout the English-speaking world, not only the most frequently performed oratorio, but also the most enduringly popular of extended musical compositions to English words. Called by Richard Alexander Streatfeild (*Handel,* 1909, p. 285) "the first instance in the history of music of an attempt to view the mighty drama of human redemption from an artistic standpoint." *Messiah* represents the final flowering of the baroque in music, standing parallel to such other masterworks of the time as the *B Minor Mass* and the *St. Matthew Passion* of Johann Sebastian Bach.

Handel began to compose *Messiah* on Aug. 22, 1741, when he was 56, and completed it in 23 days. The text, described by Jens Peter Larsen as "a representation of the fulfilment of Redemption through the Redeemer, Messiah," opens with a first part of 21 numbers devoted to the prophecy of God's intention to redeem mankind through the Messiah and then to the carrying out of His intention. Part two (23 numbers) recounts the accomplishment of redemption, mankind's rejection of God's intention, and the defeat of men in their attempt to oppose God's power. The final part (13 numbers) is a hymn of thanksgiving for the final overthrow of death.

Musically, the oratorio, accompanied by instrumental ensemble, is divided into purely orchestral passages; recitatives, both accompanied and *secco,* sometimes broadening out into ariosos; choruses; and solo songs and arias (for which Handel originally employed one soprano, one contralto, one tenor, two male altos, and two basses). Because Handel never published a definitive edition of *Messiah,* which he altered in detail during many performances, the establishment of a single unquestionable text is now impossible. Of the oratorio's 57 numbers, four may with equal reason be sung by either soprano or tenor; in five others, a choice between alternate versions must be made by editor or conductor. Among the numbers from *Messiah* which have atttained almost universal familiarity are the arias *He shall feed His flock* and *I know that my Redeemer liveth,* and the *Hallelujah* and *Amen* choruses.

For detailed information on all aspects of *Messiah,* consult Myers, Robert M., *Handel's Messiah: A Touchstone of Taste* (New York 1948); and Larsen, Jens Peter, *Handel's Messiah: Origins, Composition, Sources* (Copenhagen and New York 1957).

HERBERT WEINSTOCK,
Author of "Handel."

MESSIAH, The (Ger. DER MESSIAS), an epic poem by Friedrich Gottlieb Klopstock (q.v.), dealing with the life of Christ. Consisting of 19,458 lines, it is over three quarters as long as Homer's *Iliad,* but much shorter than some of the Italian epics. Klopstock conceived and in a large measure planned *Der Messias* during his middle teens while a student at the well-known classical school of Schulpforte, near Leipzig. After writing the first three cantos in prose, he recast them into unrhymed verse. When they first appeared in 1748 in the *Bremer Beiträge (Bremen Contributions),* a forward-looking periodical sponsored by a group of young writers, they created a sensation. Thereafter the completion of the 20-canto poem proceeded more and more desultorily, and it was not until 1773 that the last five cantos were published.

The historical importance of *Der Messias* can scarcely be exaggerated. By choosing dactylic hexameter, the meter of Homer and Virgil, Klopstock flouted the Francophiles led by Johann Christoph Gottsched and turned to the Anglophiles led by Johann Jakob Bodmer, whose translation of John Milton's *Paradise Lost* furnished the young poet with his cosmography. The first three cantos, being the effusions of youth, may still reward the imaginative reader, but the remaining ones are too carefully worked over. Pietism (q.v.) stifled the poet's inspiration, and his treatment of Christ's last week on earth and activity as triumphant Redeemer is not, despite the large and varied cast of characters, humanly interesting. Movement, the essential quality of narrative poetry, flags. Gotthold Ephraim Lessing's famous dictum, "The work is so full of feeling that the reader feels nothing at all," is only too apt. In short, Klopstock did not understand the conditions of epic, but even in his failure he created the poetic diction of Germany.

Consult Muncker, Franz, *Friedrich Gottlieb Klopstock* (Stuttgart 1900); Wöhlert, Hans, *Das Weltbild in Klopstocks Messias* (Halle 1915).

WALLACE BROCKWAY,
Consultant to the Bollingen Foundation.

Stephanie Dinkins

An annual event of the mid-August festivals in Messina, Sicily. Statues of the city's legendary founders, the giants Mata and Grifone, are pulled through the streets.

MESSINA, mĕ-sē'nà, city, Italy, capital of Messina Province, northeastern Sicily, a port on the Strait of Messina. By ferry across the strait, Messina is 5 miles west of Villa San Giovanni and 7 miles northwest of Reggio di Calabria, both on the tip of the Italian boot. A steppingstone to and from the peninsula of Italy, the city has one of the finest harbors in the world, protected by a sickle-shaped neck of land which led the Greeks to name the city Zancle (sickle). Messina exports the produce of the province's fertile fields: citrus fruits, olives, almonds, and carob beans; as well as the products of its own industries: macaroni and other *paste,* citrus extracts, wine, olive oil, soap, chemicals, cement, tobacco, and silk goods. There are also shipyards and foundries, and fishing is an important industry.

The University of Messina (q.v.) was founded in 1549. The 11th century cathedral has been twice restored, but most of the buildings in the city are modern. The region is subject to violent earthquakes, the most serious of which almost leveled Messina in 1908; the coastline dropped 26 inches and a 20-foot wave killed 30,000 of the inhabitants. Until the 19th century Messina's history had been one of continuous conquest and occupation. The city was founded about 724–730 B.C. by pirates from the Greek colony of Cumae in southern Italy. Anaxilas, tyrant of Rhegium (Reggio) across the strait, invited settlers there about 494 B.C. and named it Messana after Messene, his native city in Greece. Successively the Athenians took possession of the city (426 B.C.), the Carthaginians (396 B.C.), Dionysius I (about 392 B.C.), the Mamertines (288 B.C.), Hiero II (about 269 B.C.), Hannibal (264–241 B.C.), Pompey the Younger (43 B.C.), and Augustus (36 B.C.). In the Christian era, the Saracens took it in 843 A.D., the Normans in 1061, and Richard the Lion-Hearted sacked it in 1190. Beginning in the 13th century Spain and France contended for centuries for the control of Sicily, and it was not until 1860 that Garibaldi wrested Messina from the last Bourbon king, Francis II, and the city was incorporated in the new kingdom of Italy. Its last severe damage was in August 1943, when it was heavily bombed by the Allies before the Axis powers abandoned it to the Allies. Pop. of commune (1965) 263,254; of province (1961) 685,260. See also SICILY.

HENRY HUMPHREY,
Staff Editor, "The Encyclopedia Americana."

MESSINA, Strait of (ancient FRETUM SICULUM), a channel which separates northeastern Sicily from southwestern Italy and connects the Tyrrhenian and the Ionian seas. About 20 miles long from north to south, it broadens in width from about 2 miles in the north to about 10 miles in the south, and ranges in depth from 900 feet in the north to about 3,600 feet in the south. A strong current running with the tide makes its navigation somewhat difficult, but by no means as formidable as fabled by the ancients, to whom the rock of Scylla and the whirlpool of Charybdis seemed equally dangerous and almost unavoidable (see SCYLLA AND CHARYBDIS). The chief ports on the strait are Messina on Sicily, and Reggio di Calabria on the mainland.

MESSINA, University of, an institution of higher learning and general education in Messina, Italy, founded in 1548. Until 1641, when the Messina Senate assumed full control of the university, it was jointly administered by the senate and the Jesuits, the former supervising instruction in law, medicine, and the natural sciences, the latter having jurisdiction in mathematics, morality, philosophy, and theology. It was suppressed by the Spaniards in 1678, and reorganized by the Bourbons in 1838. When the earthquake of 1908 destroyed its buildings, it continued in temporary quarters until new buildings had been provided. It has departments of law and letters, medicine and surgery, philosophy, science, education, economics and commerce, veterinary medicine, and pharmacy. Affiliated with it are a botanical garden, institutes of biology and science, and an obstetrical school.

MESSMATES, Animal. See COMMENSALISM.

MESTA, měs'tȧ, Perle, American diplomat: b. Sturgis, Mich., c. 1890. The daughter of William B. Skirvin, who made a fortune in the Southwest in oil and real estate, and the widow of George Mesta, a Pittsburgh industrialist, she settled in Newport, R.I., in 1929 and was soon established as a society leader. She became active in politics in 1935 when she joined the National Woman's Party, serving as chairman of its public relations committee and later as a council member. At first a Republican, in 1941 she felt that the party had rejected Wendell Lewis Willkie's principles and so switched to the Democratic Party. Moving to Washington, D.C., the same year,

she became the foremost unofficial hostess in the capital, active in raising funds for the 1948 presidental election campaign and an enthusiastic supporter of President Harry S. Truman. In July 1949 she became minister to the Grand Duchy of Luxembourg, the third American woman to attain ministerial rank in the diplomatic service. She held this post until April 1953.

MESTA RIVER, (Gr. NÉSTOS; Turk. KARA SU), river, Greece. It rises in the Rhodope Mountains of southwestern Bulgaria, and flows south and southeast for about 150 miles to the Aegean Sea, forming a delta opposite the island of Thasos. The Greek port of Kavalla is on the western side of the delta. The river's lower course, known as the Nestos, forms the boundary between Thrace and Macedonia.

MESTROVIC, měsh'trò-vět-y'; Eng. -vĭch, **Ivan,** Croatian sculptor: b. Vrpolje, Croatia, Aug. 15, 1883; d. South Bend, Ind., Jan. 17, 1962. The son of a carpenter, he spent his boyhood in the Dalmatian village of Otavitze, working as a shepherd in the mountains. His father encouraged him in carving small figures in wood and stone, and when he was 15 apprenticed him for a year to a master mason in Split. From there, aided by friends who recognized his talent, he went to Vienna to study art. Poor and alone, he had trouble in finding a teacher, but finally obtained some teaching and at the end of a year was able to enter the Kunstakademie. There were one-man shows of his work at Belgrade (1904) and Zagreb (1905), and in 1907 he opened a studio in Paris, where he benefited from association with such sculptors as Auguste Rodin, Aristide Maillol, and Émile Bourdelle. From 1911 to 1914 Meštrović lived in Rome, making a special study of archaic Greek sculpture, then went to England, where his exhibitions won critical acclaim and brought him important commissions for portrait busts. During World War I he lived in Switzerland, returning to Yugoslavia in 1922 to become rector of the School of Fine Arts at Zagreb. The Brooklyn (New York) Museum held a large exhibition of his works in 1924 and acquired his *The Archangel Gabriel* (marble), and in 1947 he was given a one-man show at The Metropolitan Museum of Art. That year he became professor of fine arts at Syracuse University, going to Notre Dame University in the same capacity in 1955. He became a naturalized citizen of the United States in 1954. Represented in many of the world's leading museums, he became famous for the beauty and originality of his relief sculptures in wood and stone. Religion or legend inspired much of his work, and many of his pieces are heroic in style, notably his war memorials.

MESZAROS, mä'sä-rŏsh, Lázár, Hungarian soldier and patriot: b. Baja, Bacs-Bódrog County, Hungary, Feb. 20, 1796; d. Eywood, Herefordshire, England, Nov. 16, 1858. At first educated for the church, he later studied law at Pest, and in 1813 joined the Hungarian Army. Shortly afterward he entered the Austrian Army, took part in the campaigns of 1814–1815 against Napoleon, and later served in Italy as a colonel of hussars in forces commanded by Count Radetzky von Radetz. In 1848 he was chosen by Count Lajos Batthyány as minister of war in the first constitutional Hungarian cabinet. When Austria undertook to subjugate Hungary, Mészáros took command of the Hungarian forces in the north but on January 4 his army was routed at Kaschau (Košice). In April 1849, after the declaration of independence, he again took command of the Hungarian forces but was defeated at Szöreg and Temesvár in August and fled to Turkey. Subsequently he lived in England, France, the Island of Jersey, and in 1853 came to the United States.

META, mä'tä, an intendancy of central Colombia extending 32,903 square miles from Cordillera Oriental eastward between the Meta and Guaviare rivers. Undeveloped and sparsely populated, it has a tropical climate and but for the mountainous spurs of the Cordilleras at the east, consists of llanos (grasslands) suitable for cattle grazing. It produces balata gum, vanilla, timber, and coffee as well as subsistence crops. Its capital is Villavicencio. Pop. (1951) 67,492.

META, river, South America, which has its rise on the eastern slope of the Andes Mountains near Bogotá in Colombia. Formed by the junction of two small mountain streams which unite about 40 miles southeast of Bogotá, it then flows east-northeast into the Orinoco. Its course is 685 miles.

METABETCHOUAN, mĕt-ă-bĕt'chŏŏ-ăn, river, in south central Quebec, Canada, rising in the north part of the Laurentides Provincial Park and flowing 50 miles north into Lake St. John. A hydroelectric station is situated at its mouth.

METABOLISM, mĕ-tăb'ŏ-lĭz'm. In its broadest sense, the term metabolism is used to designate the sum total of chemical processes by which living organisms maintain themselves and carry out the activities characteristic of the living state. Many kinds of chemical events may be included within the framework of this definition—even the behavior of chemical compounds, such as sodium chloride and water, that merely pass through the body without undergoing any chemical change. However, metabolism is generally restricted to refer to the reactions concerned with the release or storage of energy within the organism. Metabolism involves two phases, anabolism and catabolism. Anabolism (q.v.) is used to describe processes that are synthetic or constructive in nature. Catabolism (katabolism) refers to processes by which complex molecules are broken down or simplified. In the organism, catabolism and anabolism go on simultaneously, though the relative intensity of the two processes may vary from time to time. During periods of active growth or during recovery from wasting disease, the balance is shifted in favor of anabolism; during starvation or fever, catabolism exceeds anabolism.

Source of Energy for Metabolism.—The energy used by organisms to support their vital activities is derived from food. The term food includes any substance taken in by the organism necessary for its survival and well-being. Inorganic compounds, vitamins, and other accessory substances are thus classified as foods, but in this account emphasis will be placed on foods which serve as sources of energy and as raw materials for growth. These energy-containing foods are carbohydrates, proteins, and fats.

Food is elaborated in nature through the photosynthetic activities of green plants. Photosynthesis (q.v.) is the basic metabolic process in the world of life, for, through it, organic compounds of high-energy content are synthesized from simple, inorganic precursors such as carbon dioxide and water. The process consists essentially of the chemical reduction of carbon dioxide by hydrogen atoms derived from water, with the production of sugar and oxygen. The sugar synthesized contains energy in potential or latent form. For photosynthesis to occur, an external source of energy is needed, and this is supplied by visible radiations from the sun. Photosynthesis is a complicated process, involving many reactions, not all of which require the presence of light, but the overall event may be summarized as

$$6CO_2 + 6H_2O \xrightarrow[\text{chlorophyll}]{\text{radiant energy}} C_6H_{12}O_6 + 6O_2.$$

The sugar molecules produced in photosynthesis may be converted into starch or other carbohydrates. They may also be partially broken down and then resynthesized into fat, or they may be partially broken down and combined with nitrogenous compounds to yield amino acids and proteins. By the various food chains that exist among plants and animals, the materials synthesized by green plants are passed on to herbivorous animals and then to carnivores. Thus, the ultimate source of all food energy in the world is photosynthesis. In passing from one organism to the next, the food may either be broken down to supply energy or used as raw material for growth.

Energy Content of Food.—The energy content of food is expressed in heat units, or *calories,* one calorie being the amount of energy required to raise the temperature of a kilogram of water from 15° to 16°C. In order to determine the amount of energy in food, an instrument known as a bomb calorimeter (see CALORIMETRY) is used. This is a device in which a measured amount of food can be burned completely, in the presence of oxygen, to its gaseous end-products, and the amount of heat energy liberated can be accurately measured. Average values for the energy obtained from one-gram samples of the primary foodstuffs are: carbohydrates, 4.1 calories; proteins, 5.7 calories; and fats, 9.3 calories. Within a given class of food, the energy content varies somewhat depending upon the chemical composition and the source of the food. Thus, among carbohydrates, glucose and starch yield, respectively, 3.75 and 4.2 calories per gram, and proteins and fats of animal origin on the whole have slightly higher caloric values than those from plant sources.

When carbohydrates or fats are burned in the animal body, the caloric yield per gram is the same as that obtained in the bomb calorimeter. This was first clearly demonstrated by Max Rubner, near the end of the last century, and proves that the *law of conservation of energy* applies to living systems as well as to nonliving systems. In the animal body, the energy yield from protein is only 4.1 calories per gram, whereas in the bomb calorimeter, the figure is 5.7. The discrepancy is due to the fact that combustion of protein in the calorimeter is complete, thus yielding the full quota of energy; in the body, protein is incompletely broken down, and some energy is still contained in the end-products—ammonia, urea, and uric acid. Certain microorganisms are able to oxidize these wastes of animal metabolism, and, thereby, to derive energy for their own life processes.

Mechanisms of Energy Release.—The vast majority of organisms, both plant and animal, derive energy by a process of cellular oxidation or respiration. In respiration, food molecules are burned in the presence of atmospheric oxygen into simpler compounds, such as carbon dioxide and water, and energy is released. The reactions involved in burning food to carbon dioxide and water in the body are not the same as when food is burned in a flame, but the amount of energy released in the two cases is equal. Cellular oxidation of food does not occur spontaneously, but it is brought about by the catalytic activity of specialized enzymes. For the organism, the most important end-result of cellular respiration is the release of energy and the channeling of the energy released into various vital activities.

Certain lower plants and animals live in the complete absence of oxygen or under conditions where the amount present is too low to be significant. These organisms, designated as *anaerobes,* derive their energy from the breakdown of food by processes, such as fermentation and putrefaction, in which free oxygen does not participate. In anaerobic metabolism, food substances do not break down completely, hence they release only a fraction of the total potential energy they contain. When glucose is broken down anaerobically into ethyl alcohol and carbon dioxide, the energy released is only about $\frac{1}{25}$ of that available from the complete oxidation of glucose to carbon dioxide and water.

Energy Transformations in the Organism.—The energy taken in by the organism as food may be converted into heat, or it may be used to perform work, or it may be stored in the form of intracellular and extracellular materials.

Heat.—Most of the energy released in organisms appears in the form of heat, for animals and plants are not capable of directing into useful activities all of the energy they liberate. In the living machine, no less than in man-made machines, heat production is an indication of inefficient utilization of released energy. In muscular activity, only a little more than one calorie for every five expended is available for doing work; the remaining four calories appear as heat. In other words, muscular activity is only a little more than 20 per cent efficient.

In "warm-blooded" animals, the heat released in metabolism is not completely wasted, for it is used to keep the body warm. Such animals generally produce much more heat than they require, but a constant body temperature can be maintained because of the operation of elaborate physiological mechanisms. In a few "cold-blooded" animals, heat production may also have significance. Thus, in winter time, the temperature of a cluster of bees in a hive may be many degrees higher than that of the environment.

Work.—Work performed by organisms may be mechanical or chemical. In animals, most of the work performed is mechanical and is represented by muscular contraction. In all organisms, a considerable amount of chemical work is performed in such processes as the synthesis of protoplasm to compensate for metabolic wear and tear and during growth. Work is also done in the synthesis and secretion of specific cell products, and in the maintenance of ionic or osmotic gradients between the inside of the cell or organism and its environment. In a number of organisms, the production of light or electricity represents work.

Storage.—Energy is stored in the body in potential form through the elaboration of new protoplasm, or of such cellular materials as starch, glycogen, or fat. Synthesis of new protoplasm represents growth, and this is an event of special prominence in the embryo and young organism. Some storage products are normally present at all times in the organism, and these are called upon as sources of energy during periods when food intake does not occur. The purpose of eating food is, then, to replenish the energy stores of the body. The amount of energy stored depends, obviously, upon the balance between energy intake in the form of food, and energy expenditure, as heat and work. Normally, in the mature organism, energy intake and expenditure equal each other and, in the long run, the weight of the individual remains constant. Too little or too much intake will lead to appropriate changes in the storage depots of the body. One of the unique characteristics of living organisms is the ability to consume their own tissues, as sources of energy, after storage materials have been largely exhausted.

Basal Metabolism.—The energy transformations described in the foregoing section may be summarized as follows:

Energy in food = Heat energy +

Work energy + Stored energy.

Only in animals has it proven possible to assess quantitatively the various components represented in the above equation and, for obvious reasons, most of the measurements have been made on man and other mammals. By placing an animal under conditions in which no external work is done, the total energy output of the animal will appear as heat, and, if food intake be prevented, the heat produced will be at the expense of stored reserves. Metabolism under such circumstances is described by the term *basal metabolism* or *basal metabolic rate* (BMR).

BMR can be measured either directly in terms of heat output, or indirectly through the gaseous exchange of the organism, since this exchange is proportional to the heat output. Direct measurement is made by means of an instrument of special design called a calorimeter (q.v.). This consists of a well-insulated chamber sufficiently large to accommodate the subject in a prone position. The heat given off by the subject is picked up by water which circulates through the chamber in a series of pipes, and the heat production can be determined by noting the rate of water flow and the difference in temperature between the incoming and outgoing streams. About one-quarter of the total energy liberated in the basal state is used to evaporate water that passes off in the expired air or from the surface of the body. This energy, representing latent heat of evaporation, cannot be measured by the calorimeter. However, it can be calculated after the total water evaporated by the subject has been absorbed and measured. Total heat production represents the sum of measured heat plus latent heat of evaporation.

Direct measurements of BMR are complicated not only by the elaborate and costly equipment required but also by the fact that measurements must usually be continued for a long period of time, so that it becomes difficult to maintain basal conditions. Accordingly, it is more common with human subjects to calculate energy output indirectly in terms of oxygen consumed and of the end-products of metabolism, carbon dioxide, and urea. The time required for such measurements may be as little as an hour, or less. Various methods are used for determining the gaseous exchange of animals and man. One of the simplest involves measuring the amount of oxygen withdrawn by the subject from a closed chamber containing air. Carbon dioxide produced is absorbed chemically and then weighed.

The heat liberated by an organism for a given volume of oxygen consumed depends upon the kind of foodstuff being burned. The caloric equivalent of a liter of oxygen in the combustion of carbohydrate is 5.047; for fat, it is 4.686, and for protein, 4.485. Thus, to calculate the calories of heat energy represented by a given volume of respired oxygen, it is necessary to know the kind and the relative proportions of the foodstuffs burned. Important in this connection is the *respiratory quotient* (RQ), i.e., the ratio of the volume of carbon dioxide produced to oxygen consumed, for this ratio depends upon the chemical composition of the foodstuff burned, and it can be used, therefore, to indicate its nature. For carbohydrate, the RQ is 1.0; for protein, 0.8, and for fat, 0.7. A value for the RQ intermediate between 1.0 and 0.7 denotes the combustion of a mixture of foodstuffs, and to determine the relative proportions of carbohydrates, proteins, and fats further calculations are necessary.

In practice, the amount of protein burned and the volume of oxygen and carbon dioxide concerned therewith are calculated from the nitrogen eliminated in the urine during the period of measurement. The number of calories from protein are then derived by multiplying the volume of oxygen consumed in the oxidation of protein by the calorific value 4.485.

The difference between the total respiratory exchange and that due to protein represents the metabolism of carbohydrate and fat. The value of the nonprotein RQ can be used to calculate (or, as is done in practice, to determine from standard tables) the calorific value of the oxygen consumed in the combustion of carbohydrate and fat. Thus, by adding the number of calories derived from protein to those from carbohydrate and fat, the total energy exchange can be obtained. When measurements of metabolism are carefully conducted, the results obtained by direct and indirect calorimetry agree to within a small fraction of 1 per cent.

When the greatest accuracy is not necessary, BMR is determined by assuming that the RQ is 0.82 and measuring only the oxygen consumed by the individual. This method is commonly used in clinical laboratories on human patients, and the BMR is then expressed as percentage deviation from standard average values. The BMR of an individual that deviates from the average by no more than plus or minus 10 per cent is regarded as normal.

Factors Affecting BMR.—The BMR of a normal adult human male ranges between 1,500 and 1,800 calories per day, but the absolute value may be affected by such factors, among others, as body size, sex, age, diet, and physiological condition of the individual. There is a direct proportionality between BMR and body size, that is, the larger the animal, the greater is the BMR. But BMR per kilogram of body weight decreases with increase in size of the animal. It is clear, therefore, that relatively more of a large animal's total bulk is metabolically inert than a smaller animal's.

One of the problems in metabolic studies today is to obtain a proper estimate of the metabolically active material in the body. At one time it was thought that heat production in animals was proportional to the total body surface. It is now clear, however, following the comparative studies of Francis Gano Benedict on the metabolism of animals ranging in size from the mouse to the elephant, that metabolism bears no simple relationship to body surface. Nevertheless, BMR standards are still often expressed in terms of calories per square meter of surface.

BMR varies with sex. The rate for the human female is approximately 10 per cent less than for the male, and the same difference can be demonstrated in a number of lower organisms as well.

In both males and females, BMR gradually falls with age. A five-year-old male child will have a basal heat production of 53 calories per hour per square meter of body surface. At 20 years of age, BMR will have fallen to 41 calories, and at 70 years of age, it will be approximately 35 calories. The high BMR of children explains, in part, their voracious appetites.

BMR is elevated during fever, and it is also influenced by the amount of secretion from the thyroid gland. When this secretion is high, the BMR may be 50 to 75 per cent greater than normal; during extreme hypothyroidism, BMR may be as low as 60 per cent of normal.

Total Metabolism.—Obviously, the BMR provides no information on the total energy expenditure of the organism. In general, for a moderately active individual, total metabolism is about twice the basal level. But total metabolism varies greatly, depending chiefly upon the physical activity of the individual, but also upon various physical and physiological factors, such as environmental temperature and humidity, emotional state, diet, etc. The importance of muscular activity in determining total metabolism is shown in the following table, abstracted from Abraham White and others.

Type of activity	Calories expended per hour
Sleeping	65
Awake, lying still (BMR)	77
Awake, sitting up	100
Standing relaxed	105
Light muscular exercise	170
Severe muscular exercise	450

By contrast with muscular activity, the energy demands of mental work are almost negligible. Benedict has shown that the energy requirement of an hour of intense brain work, represented by multiplying mentally numbers such as 67×83, can be met by an oyster cracker or one-half of a salted peanut. See also NUTRITION OF MAN; OBESITY.

Bibliography.—Prosser, C. L., and others, *Comparative Animal Physiology*, 2d ed. (Philadelphia 1961); Thannhauser, Siegfried, *Textbook of Metabolism and Metabolic Disorders*, 2 vols., 2d ed. (New York 1963-64); White, Abraham, and others, *Principles of Biochemistry*, 3d ed. (New York 1964); McMillan, A. J. S., *Introduction to Biochemistry*, vol. 1: *Metabolism of Carbohydrates, Proteins, and Fats* (New York 1966).

E. J. BOELL,
Osborn Zoological Laboratory, Yale University.

METACHROSIS, mĕt′à-krō′sĭs, the change of color brought about in the surface of certain animals either voluntarily or involuntarily to make them conform to their surroundings as explained in the article CHAMELEON.

The power possessed by these animals of adapting their color to their surroundings is of value in ensuring protection from enemies.

METAL FINISHING, mĕt″l fin′ĭsh-ĭng, a broad term that denotes the alteration of a metal surface to produce a new or different surface of special utility. The various processes include: (1) cleaning and pickling; (2) mechanical treatments (such as grinding, polishing, buffing, abrasive blasting, and tumbling); (3) chemical surface finishing; (4) metallic coating (by spraying, hot-dip, various forms of plating, or other methods); (5) conversion coating.

Cleaning and Pickling.—These are methods of removing organic and inorganic dirt, oxide, scale, or corrosion products from the metal as an essential step before applying finishing treatments. Precleaning is done by immersing the work in or spraying it with grease solvents; by immersing it in solvent vapors; or by agitating it in or spraying it with hot aqueous dispersions of solvents, or solutions of alkalis and surface active agents (surfactants). Steam cleaning is done mostly on large objects. Soaps are used largely to remove buffing dirt.

Final cleaning, important for finishing operations that produce coatings, is done chiefly by using various alkaline detergent mixtures as soak, spray, or electrolytic cleaners. In electrolytic cleaning, the work is made either the anode or cathode, or both. Heavy scale and oxide can be removed by shot-blasting or sandblasting; lighter scales by means of acids or deoxidizing compounds. Pickling (heavy oxide or scale removal with acids from steel) is done with either hot solutions of sulphuric acid (10 to 15 per cent by weight), temperature 150° to 180° F., or with strong hydrochloric acid solutions at room temperature.

Mechanical Treatments.—These vary with the quality of the finish desired. Grinding with bonded abrasive wheels containing aluminum oxide or silicon carbide removes gates and sprues and produces a coarse finish. Following grinding, polishing is done with flexible or semiflexible wheels or belts to which have been cemented aluminum oxide or silicon carbide abrasives. Buffing may then follow the polishing operation. In this operation canvas, leather, or felt wheels may be employed with a solid abrasive applied to the wheel by means of a buffing compound. Liquid abrasive materials are also sprayed onto wheels or belts. "Color buffing" is an operation used on plated coatings, or to produce a high luster on metals. A cloth or leather wheel is employed and the abrasive compound contains lime, rouge, or other soft polishing materials. In the abrasive blasting method of finishing metals, if coarse abrasives are used, they are impinged against the surface by means of air. This operation is usually done to remove heavy oxide or scale or to roughen and clean the surface. However, fine abrasives can be impinged against the surface by suspending them in water. The operation is called "vapor blasting."

Bulk work can be given finishes approximating polished or buffed surfaces by means of tumble or barrel burnishing. The objects may be tumbled with abrasives, such as aluminum oxide, tripoli, sand, or with media such as stone pebbles or metal slugs together with loose powdered abrasive.

Chemical Surface Finishing.—This includes processes that produce final finishes on metals by acid pickling, etching, chemical polishing, and electropolishing. Etching of copper surfaces is usually done with persulphates, chromate-containing compounds or salts of ferric iron. Chemical polishing, whereby a high luster is imparted to the surface, is done largely on zinc and aluminum. The objects to be polished are immersed in strong solutions of oxidizing acids, usually nitric acid with phosphoric acid. Electropolishing, whereby the object is made the anode in special electrolytes, is employed for finishing several metals, including aluminum, steel, copper alloys, zinc, iron, and stainless steel.

Metallic Coating Spraying.—Various metals may be sprayed upon surfaces by means of a special gun to which is fed metal wire or powder that is melted in the gun. Any metal available in the form of wire and fusible with oxyacetylene flame can be sprayed on almost any surface. Actually the two metals sprayed most widely are aluminum and zinc, although iron is also sprayed. Metal spraying is particularly suitable for large objects, such as storage tanks, bridges, and steel structures.

Hot-Dip Coatings.—Several metals can be successfully applied to other metals by melting one metal and dipping the article to be coated into the molten metal. The surface to be treated must be cleaned of grease or oxide, and fluxes are employed to remove any oxides that may form during processing. Metals most frequently applied by hot dipping are zinc (hot galvanizing), tin (hot tinning), lead, and aluminum. The purpose in all cases is to protect the metal coated.

Hot galvanizing is done by immersing the iron or steel in molten zinc. Similarly, hot tin coatings are applied by immersion to iron, steel, and copper. Pure lead coatings are not applied to iron or steel because molten lead does not alloy with iron. To bond the coatings, tin is usually used. (See GALVANIZING; TIN—*Tin Plate* and *Alloys.*) Aluminum alloys very readily with iron. However, the ever-present oxides on iron and aluminum mitigate against easy hot-dip coating of iron with aluminum. Commercial techniques are employed to keep the aluminum and the surface to be coated oxide free by means of hydrogen or inert gases.

Cementation or Diffusion Coatings.—Metals may be applied to other metals by packing a powdered metal around the subject to be coated and then heating the part in an inert atmosphere at a temperature where diffusion will occur. "Calorizing" is a trade name for the cementation of a metal surface by means of aluminum. It is used for preventing oxidation of iron at high temperatures which, for example, may be experienced in electric range heating elements. The articles to be treated are packed in a drum in a mixture of powdered aluminum, aluminum oxide, and flux. The drum is rotated slowly as it is heated in an inert or reducing atmosphere, usually of hydrogen, until a temperature from 850° to 950° C. has been obtained. Copper and brass may be coated at lower temperatures. Sherardizing is a process that produces zinc coatings on iron by diffusion. Chromium coatings can be applied to iron and steel surfaces by a technique similar to sherardizing. This process is called chromizing.

Peen Plating.—Peen plating is a process for coating one metal with another by mechanical means. It does not require heat. Small objects, such as nails, washers, and chains are particularly suitable for this technique. Zinc, brass, tin, and cadmium have been applied successfully. The objects to be coated are cleaned and are placed in a tumbling barrel with an impacting medium, a promoter solution to activate the metal, and the coating metal in the form of dust and water.

Gas Plating.—Gas plating is a thermal plating technique wherein the metal to be applied is present in the form of a gaseous compound, usually a carbonyl, and the metal is deposited from this gas by heating the object to be coated to a higher temperature, usually by induction, which breaks up the metal compound to its component gas and metal. Nickel is the metal most commonly deposited by this technique, although it is possible to plate out other metals, such as chromium and iron.

Vacuum Deposition.—The deposition of metals by vacuum vaporization is done on a large commercial scale on plastics; it is also used to apply metals to cast alloys such as zinc and lead. The article to be coated is first given a coat of clear lacquer or enamel which smooths the surface, filling holes and crevices. The metal to be deposited is vaporized in a tungsten loop in the vacuum chamber. The objects are rotated inside the chamber to permit coating of all of the surface. The metal most commonly employed for coating is aluminum, although gold, silver, and other metals capable of being vaporized can be deposited. The coatings formed are very thin and have poor abrasion resistance. Therefore, they are normally coated with a clear lacquer finish.

Chemical Reduction and "Electroless" Plating.—Silver, gold, and copper are applied to surfaces from aqueous solutions containing strong reducing agents. The technique is usually employed, however, for coating nonmetallic surfaces, such as glass (making of mirrors) and plastics. A reduction technique for applying metals, however, is being widely used for plating other metals, namely, "electroless" plating, that involves the reduction of nickel from one of its salts by means of sodium hypophosphite.

Chemical Displacement Coatings.—Deposition of a metal from aqueous solutions by chemical displacement is done with copper, tin, gold, and silver. The coatings produced are very thin, usually being less than $\frac{1}{100,000}$ inch.

Electroplating.—This is a widely used method for depositing coatings of numerous metals upon other metals or nonmetals by electrolytic means. (See ELECTROPLATING.)

Conversion Coating.—This is a method of metal finishing in which the surface treated is converted to a new compound, such as a phosphate, oxide, chromate, or sulphide, by chemical or electrolytic means.

Phosphate coatings are applied chiefly to iron and steel, zinc, and aluminum; oxide coatings to aluminum, copper, and steel; chromate coatings to zinc, cadmium, aluminum, copper, silver, and magnesium; and sulphide coatings to copper, copper alloys, and silver. The purposes of these coatings vary. Some are used chiefly as bases for painting or organic finishing, others to retard corrosion or for decorative purposes.

Consult Burns, Robert M., and Schuh, Arthur E., *Protective Coatings for Metals*, 2d ed. of work originally by Robert M. Burns and Walter W. Bradley (New York 1955); Metals and Plastics Publications, Inc., *Metal Finishing Guidebook—Directory* (Westwood, N.J., annually).

WALTER R. MEYER,
President, Enthone, Inc.

METALLOGRAPHY, mĕt′l-ŏg′ra-fĭ, the study of the structure of metals and the relation of this structure to the properties of the metal. Knowing the particular structure which is responsible for a specific property of a metal has led to a better understanding of these materials. It has provided engineers with the information necessary to specify metals for particular applications. For example, the average grain size is an engineering parameter now included in the commercial description of metals because metallographic observation revealed that the toughness of a metal (the energy required to cause fracture) is directly related to the average grain size of the crystals which make up the metal.

Important engineering properties of pure metals and alloys may be predicted from the study of their structure. Typical examples are corrosion resistance, impact strength, and machinability.

Specimen Preparation.—Techniques such as light microscopy, electron microscopy, and X-ray diffraction are used to study metallic structure. Whichever method is used, the first step is always careful preparation of the specimen. The surface to be studied must be polished to complete smoothness. A coarse grit is used to begin with, and is followed by successively finer and finer polishing papers. Next comes buffing on a rotating, cloth-covered polishing lap having very fine abrasives which are applied with a water solution. After the removal of every scratch and the attainment of a perfectly flat specimen, the sample is ready for etching.

Chemical etching with acids dissolves the boundaries between the grains and thereby delineates the crystal size of the metal. Phases of different composition or crystallographic orientation also will be attacked at different rates by an acid solution. Another technique for developing surface contrast is electroetching. In this method, the specimen is made anodic to a second metal, usually platinum, and the two are immersed in an electrolytic solution. Selective solution of the sample occurs as a function of composition and crystallography of the specimen constituents.

Heat tinting develops colors on the surface of a specimen which assist in identifying the

Fig. 1. Photomicrograph showing the design produced by the heat tinting of a titanium-iron-manganese alloy.

Elmats Ence

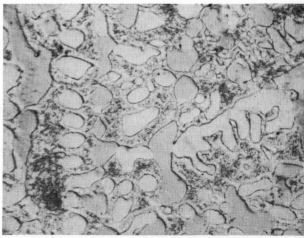

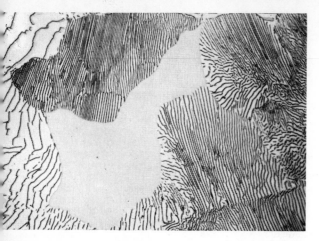

Fig. 2. Photomicrograph of an iron-carbon alloy.

various phases of the metal or alloy. A typical photomicrograph of a heat-tinted specimen taken at a magnification of 350 times is shown in Fig. 1. Three distinct colors are seen, each indicative of a phase of different composition in a titanium-iron-manganese alloy.

The tinting may be accomplished by exposing the sample to a predetermined oxidizing condition or, in some special cases, the specimen may be simply heated in air.

Examination of the Metal.—Once the metallic surface has been polished and etched, it is ready for examination either by light or electron optical methods. The choice of technique is dependent upon the desired observation magnification. Electron microscopy, because the lengths of the electron beam are much shorter than those of light, may be used for magnifications as high as 100,000 times. Light microscopes are generally limited to magnifications of 1,000 times.

Metallurgical microscopes, because they deal with opaque specimens, differ from biological ones in that light is reflected from the sample surface rather than transmitted through the material. This type of microscope is called a metallograph. A typical photomicrograph of steel produced by photographing the image on a metallograph is shown in Fig. 2.

The specimen is not usually examined directly in electron microscopy, but a replica is made of the surface with plastic or ceramic material. A high-velocity stream of electrons serves as the illumination, and magnetic coils act as lenses to control the flow of electrons and develop the magnification.

Although individual atoms have not as yet been seen by optical techniques, each new method of examining the structure of metals increases our understanding of crystals and helps us to predict the behavior of metals and alloys. See also METALLURGY; STEEL—4. *Steel Technology* (Heat Treatment).

Bibliography.—Williams, Richard S., and Homerburg, Victor O., *Principles of Metallography*, 5th ed. (New York 1948); Kehl, George L., *Principles of Metallographic Laboratory Practice*, 3d ed. (New York 1949); Shrager, Arthur M., *Elementary Metallurgy and Metallography* (New York 1949); Chalmers, Bruce, *Structure and Mechanical Properties of Metals* (New York 1951); Barrett, Charles S., *Structure of Metals*, 2d ed. (New York 1952); Rolfe, Robert T., *Dictionary of Metallography* (New York 1955); Greaves, Richard H., and

Wrighton, H., *Practical Microscopical Metallography*, 4th ed. (London 1957); Consultants Bureau, *Problems of Metallography and the Physics of Metals* (New York 1957).

SHELDON WEINIG,
President, Materials Research Corporation; Adjunct Professor, Cooper Union.

METALLOID, mĕt″l-oid, (1) in *chemistry,* an element, such as arsenic, antimony, and tellurium, which differs from metals in not being very electropositive and from nonmetals in not being very electronegative; and (2) in *metallurgy,* any of five elements—carbon, manganese, phosphorus, silicon, and sulphur—commonly present in iron and steel.

METALLURGY, mĕt″l-ûr-jĭ, mĕ-tăl′ẽr-jĭ, the science and art of extracting metals from their ores, of refining the metals, and of adapting them to use. In the broad sense, the field of metallurgy covers anything done to, for, or with metals, and their ores. One of the youngest sciences, metallurgy is nevertheless one of the oldest arts.

For the convenience of readers, this article is divided into the following sections:

1. Importance of Metallurgy   4. Extractive Metallurgy
2. History   5. Physical Metallurgy
3. Classifications   6. Bibliography

1. IMPORTANCE OF METALLURGY

It is almost impossible to think of any object used in everyday life that does not contain metal, or that does not require metal for its manufacture or production. Tools and machines, from typewriters to gasoline engines, are made chiefly of metals. All forms of transportation—automobiles, ships, aircraft, railroads—are moving masses of metal and metal components. Almost everything depends on metal, from the modern skyscraper to the production and distribution of electricity. With these facts in mind, it is not difficult to see that metallurgy influences every other industry—farming, transportation, manufacturing, construction, and power being among the major ones. As an industry and a wealth producer, metallurgy is second only to farming.

Although metallurgy does not include the fabrication and assembly of finished products, the metallurgist must be able to provide many different metals with great variations in properties to meet the demands of all the different articles made of metals. In many cases, the same metal or alloy must be adapted to meet different requirements and satisfy different purposes.

In its early days, metallurgy consisted largely of a collection of empirical facts. Trial and error determined the tools and methods used to perfect and carry out various processes. In modern times, scientific methods are used to evaluate, plan, produce, and perfect metallurgical processes. A constant challenge is posed by the ever-increasing demands for materials of greater strength, lightness, safety, reliability, electrical conductivity, electromagnetism and permanent magnetism, hardness, hardenability, cutting power, softness, cheapness, resistance to corrosion, resistance to radiation, and resistance to heat.

As a recognized branch of science and engineering, metallurgy has a great deal to offer as a vocation. The field encompasses so wide a scope, and involves so many industries and materials, that the work need never be routine. Then, too, the growth of the industry and the

Blister copper being poured from the converter in the foreground. The converting process is the last in the series of elimination processes which finally leave metallic copper. It is now about 99 percent pure and will be further refined electrolytically.

METALLURGY

METALLURGY

Top: By chemical analysis in the research laboratory, the content of crude ore and finished concentrates is determined.
Bottom: Steel specimen is heated in "muffle" furnace for study in developing its most useful properties.

constant demand for improved materials leads to employment stability equal to or better than any other engineering branch.

2. HISTORY

Since prehistoric times, wars have been fought over the wealth represented by mines and metallic deposits. Great conquests were spurred by desire to possess precious metals. As civilization advanced, the demand for precious metals increased, and with it there also grew a demand for industrial metals such as iron, steel, bronze, and lead. From all civilized countries, throughout the ages, pioneers have pushed from the centers of culture into new fields in quest of sources of metallic wealth. With the expansion of industry, there developed a demand for a very large and constantly growing supply of metals and alloys. Mineral resources, more than ever before, have become a great symbol and source of power.

The early history of metallurgy is colorful but incomplete. In the Old Testament there are over 80 references to iron alone. All early references to metals are associated with mythology, religion, and folklore. Chinese legend and tradition suggest that about 2800 B.C. the emperor Shên Nung discovered the process of smelting. It has also been said that the average Chinese of 500 B.C. was further advanced metallurgically than the average European of 1,500 years later.

An ancient clay tablet refers to the subject of ironmaking in a letter from the king of the Hittites to Rameses II (r. 1290–1223 B.C.) of Egypt. The early Romans developed a furnace for making iron, and in all probability brought the ironmaking art to Britain. The first recorded reference to steel in England was about 1267.

Samples of iron have been found that establish its early use. The oldest evidence of iron consists of the remains of some iron beads found in a predynastic (4000 B.C.) cemetery at Giza (Gizeh), near Cairo. The Great Pyramid of Khufu (Cheops, r. 2590–2568 B.C.), yielded a small iron sickle. By the time of Rameses II the use of iron was common in Egypt. Rings, spearheads, halberds, and tools of metal have been found in buildings of that period. The early forms of iron in use were probably meteoric iron, and all iron made by these primitive peoples was wrought iron.

Although more is known about the early history of iron, gold, because it is commonly found in a pure state in nature, was probably the first metal to be used. Copper was probably next, because it is frequently found in a relatively pure state and, being harder, could be fashioned into useful tools, rather than used just for ornament. Gold, silver, lead, mercury, copper, and the alloys brass and bronze, are also mentioned in the Bible.

The early users of metals were craftsmen. They evolved processes by which they could utilize some of the metals, but these were crude. They knew little or nothing about the actual chemical and physical changes they were producing. Starting in the middle of the 19th century, more and more attention was directed to developing the art of metal producing and metalworking, and gradually a science was evolved. New processes, employing the latest scientific developments came into being, economics began to assume importance, and the growth of civilization and industry began to make exacting demands.

The combining of iron and carbon to produce steel opened the way to a whole new technology, and today the steel industry is the backbone of our civilization. (See STEEL—5. Steel Production Throughout the World.)

In the nonferrous field, encompassing all metals other than iron and steel, strides of equal importance have been made. Industries were created to take advantage of the amazing properties of copper, lead, zinc, gold, and other metals that were known only casually in ancient times. Important metals such as aluminum, magnesium, and nickel came to the fore in the first half of the 20th century, and have been joined by such relative newcomers as titanium, zirconium, uranium, columbium, and tantalum. Research in metallurgy continues constantly, the findings of today providing working materials for tomorrow. The passage of a decade could render many common materials obsolete, while the passage of a century could establish a whole new technology.

3. CLASSIFICATIONS

The field of metallurgy can be divided into two basic divisions, differentiating between types of work performed. These divisions are extractive metallurgy, sometimes called chemical metallurgy, and physical metallurgy.

Extractive metallurgy deals with the liberation of metals by various chemical processes from the ores in which they are found. The extractive metallurgist is also charged with refining the metals to a purity that can be used in industry.

Physical metallurgy deals with the refined metals. This branch has a wide scope that ranges from a study of what the metals are and why they behave as they do, to production of a new or improved product through alloying or heat treating, and is concerned with the working and shaping of metals, by processes that change shape and size. Included in the broadest sense are machining, rolling, bending, and wire drawing, as well as casting and powder metallurgy.

Each of the two phases of metallurgy is usually subdivided into ferrous and nonferrous categories representing the metals themselves. Ferrous metallurgy is concerned with iron and steel and the alloys of iron and steel. Nonferrous metallurgy encompasses all metals and alloys with the exception of iron and steel and their alloys. The ferrous and nonferrous industries are separated, especially the basic metal producers. Ferrous producers make only iron and steel and their alloys, while nonferrous producers may make any number of different metals.

When a company covers all the activities from mining the ore and smelting to fabricating and finishing final products, it is known as an "integrated" company. Most of the large steel and nonferrous metal companies are integrated companies, embracing all phases of the industry from mining to finishing and selling the semifinished and final products made from the metals and their alloys. Steel foundries and iron foundries are examples of "nonintegrated" concerns, because they start with such raw materials as pig iron and scrap, and usually do not mine ore or smelt their own pig iron.

4. EXTRACTIVE METALLURGY

Of all the metals, only gold, occasionally copper, and to some extent silver, mercury, and bismuth can be found in the earth's crust in the metallic state. With but few exceptions, the metals occur as either sulphide or oxide minerals. The principal sulphide minerals are copper, lead, zinc, nickel, antimony, mercury, bismuth, molybdenum, and cadmium. Metals occurring as oxides are iron, tin, aluminum, chromium, tungsten, manganese, beryllium, zirconium, titanium, and uranium.

Ores can be very complex, and can contain more than one important metal, as well as a considerable amount of worthless material. Thus, to obtain a pure metal, it may be necessary to remove the gangue or worthless part of the ore, separate any of the metals that may remain, and purify the individual metals. The three basic chemical processes for separating metals from their ores are called *hydrometallurgy, pyrometallurgy,* and *electrometallurgy.*

Hydrometallurgy, which has assumed increased importance, utilizes a chemical solvent to leach (dissolve or separate) the metal from the ore, forming a solution from which the metal may then be obtained. For example, an aqueous solution of sodium or potassium cyanide might be used for some gold and silver ores, while an acid solution might be used for copper and zinc ores.

Pyrometallurgy is a process in which the chemical action is carried on by means of heat supplied by the burning of fuel, the operation usually taking place in a furnace. This is the oldest and most common method, and in many cases is the most economical. A sulphide ore is usually first roasted in air to form an oxide. The ore is then heated with a reducing agent such as coke or charcoal, which frees the metal. A flux is added to combine with the extraneous minerals or gangue and to form a slag, which separates from the liquid metal by gravity.

In *electrometallurgy,* the chemical action is carried on by means of electrical energy. This energy may be used directly, as in electrolysis of solutions or fused salt mixtures, or it may be used indirectly for its heating effect, as in electric furnaces. In many cases, hydrometallurgical or pyrometallurgical methods are used to free the metal, and electrolytic methods used for final purification.

As most ores mined today are low-grade ores —that is, they contain only a small percentage of valuable metals—a large bulk of material must be treated, which is a costly and time-consuming operation. Therefore methods are used to make a preliminary mechanical separation and remove as much of the worthless part as possible. This is called mineral beneficiation, or concentration.

Most metals are produced according to the following steps:

(1) Mining—removal of the ore from the earth's crust.

(2) Beneficiation or concentration—mechanical separation and removal of a large part of the worthless content of an ore to reduce the bulk of material to be treated in subsequent steps.

(3) Roasting (sulphide ores only)—removal of all or part of the sulphur.

(4) Smelting—fusion of the ore concentrate to obtain a crude metal or a matte.

(5) Refining—removal of all remaining impurities to leave a pure metal.

Beneficiation.—Beneficiation reduces the ore bulk and leaves a high-grade, concentrated product. This is accomplished by employing a variety of processes based on differences in certain mineral properties, such as specific gravity, magnetic properties, and chemical properties. Hand picking as a means of separating the valuable from the worthless contents is perhaps the oldest method of concentration, but is not practical for dealing with large quantities of ore.

The first step in beneficiation is to crush and grind the ore to separate the constituents. This is referred to as comminution. Several stages of crushing are necessary, and these are considered to be breaking and coarse crushing, intermediate and fine crushing, and grinding.

Once the ore is crushed to a suitable size, separation can be effected by classification, jigging, or bumping, all of which depend on the relative settling rates of different materials in a fluid medium; by flotation; or by magnetic separation.

In the classification method, using two different minerals of the same size and shape, the lighter can be made to rise in a rising current of water while the heavier sinks. Where the shape and weight are the same, the larger mineral having less specific gravity will sink more slowly in still water. Jigging and bumping methods also take advantage of differences in specific gravity. These processes depend on a mechanical agitation of the minerals and water to effect a gravity separation.

The most generally used concentration process is flotation. This process depends on causing the particles of one mineral to float in a liquid medium, usually water, leaving the other particles suspended in the liquid. Mineral particles with wettable surfaces do not float at the surface, while those particles whose surfaces have been made nonwettable are held at the water surface by surface tension forces. The surface properties of the minerals, on which the separation is based, are controlled by the use of various organic and inorganic chemicals. The large amount of water surface necessary is obtained by making a froth. The froth is obtained by blowing or beating air into the pulp of ore and water in flotation machines, and adding a small amount of frothing chemical to make the froth stable. This process has been advanced to a point where it has potential application for virtually all types of ores, both metallic and nonmetallic.

Magnetic separation is possible where it is desirable to separate magnetic materials from nonmagnetic materials. Different magnetic materials also can be separated from each other by utilizing different magnetic strengths.

Roasting.—Roasting is basically a heating of sulphide minerals in the presence of air to burn off all or part of the sulphur, converting the minerals to oxides either totally or in part.

Smelting.—Smelting involves the reduction of certain minerals in the ore or concentrate to the metallic state or a fused sulphide (matte). These ores or concentrates may be raw or roasted. In smelting ores of different metals, various fluxes are used to form a fusible and liquid slag with the nonvolatile and unreduced constituents accompanying the metal which is being recovered. In some cases silicon dioxide is added; in others, iron oxide or limestone. Occasionally soda salts, fluorspar, or other materials are required.

In some cases a crude metal is recovered as the result of reduction of oxides. This is true in the case of iron, lead, zinc, tin, and bismuth. Ferroalloys of manganese, tungsten, chromium, vanadium, and molybdenum are produced in the same way. Copper, nickel, and frequently antimony are first produced as fused sulphides (matte) and the metal is produced from this by a secondary operation.

Refining.—The metal obtained from smelting operations is usually not pure enough for use and must be further refined. One or more of the following methods may be utilized for refining: fire refining, electrolytic refining, chemical refining, distillation.

In fire refining, the crude metal is melted and subjected to oxidizing conditions either through application of air or the use of an oxidizing slag. This method is used only when the impurities can be oxidized and removed without serious loss of the metal being refined.

In electrolytic refining, the metal to be refined must be in a solution that will permit its deposition when a direct current is passed through the bath between two electrodes. Soluble impurities must be such that they are not deposited along with the pure metal, and it is preferred that impurities be insoluble.

In chemical refining, impurities are dissolved by chemical means. Acids or other chemicals can be used, but only when the action is limited to the impurities.

Distillation is used as a means of refining the volatile metals such as mercury, cadmium, and zinc. The metal to be refined is placed in a suitable retort and heated to the boiling point. The vapor must be collected in an appropriate condenser from which air is excluded. Where two or more volatile metals are present, fractional distillation must be practiced, and often several treatments are required before complete separation is obtained.

Recovery of Dust and Fume.—Roasting and smelting operations produce large quantities of dust and fume. Not only are these a nuisance and occasionally a hazard when emitted in populated areas or near vegetation, but the potential metal loss may be considerable. Therefore, means have to be provided for the recovery and collection of such material.

The first attempts to deal with the nuisance and recover the fume and dust were by means of brick chambers and zigzag flues, the flues extending in some cases for many thousands of feet. This proved moderately successful, but the finer particles refused to settle and escaped up the stack.

To collect the finer particles, woolen or cloth bags were employed. These were suspended from the roof of a building and the gas containing fume and dust was introduced through hoppers at the bottom. The gas traveled upward, depositing the solids on the inside of the bag; clean gas filtering through was drawn by a fan to the stack. Automatic bag filters were subsequently widely adopted. The bags are shaken automatically every few minutes, the dust collecting into the hoppers, from where it is removed by screw conveyors.

Certain types of gases, especially acid gases, are injurious to the bags, so the electrostatic method of dust precipitation is often used. The principle of electrical precipitation depends on the fact that a gas becomes charged when passed through a high-voltage field. As a result of the intense electrical field, the gas ions are carried from the discharging electrode to the collecting electrode. The suspended solids between the electrodes are caught up by the gas ions and become charged, and as a consequence are swept to the cathode, where they give up their charge and are deposited. Collected material is dislodged from the electrodes by an automatic rapping device and falls into bins.

Iron and Steel.—No event in the history of civilization equals in importance the development of the art of producing iron and steel. Iron was little used, however, until the invention of the blast furnace made large quantities of the metal available. The invention of large-scale refining methods such as the Bessemer and open hearth processes for producing steel followed. Today, the production of iron and steel is about 15 times that of all other metals combined.

Pig iron, the basic raw material from which all cast iron, wrought iron, and steel is made, is produced from iron ore in the blast furnace. Cast iron is obtained by purifying pig iron in a cupola or other furnace in which the composition of the iron can be varied. Wrought iron and steel are obtained by considerable furnace purification of the pig iron.

Pig iron is weak and brittle and cannot be used for structural purposes. It is usually poured into large ladles and taken while still molten to a cupola for making cast iron, or to the refining furnaces for making steel. If it cannot be used immediately, it is cast into blocks or pigs, which may be remelted later.

Cast iron is used in industry because of its low cost, good casting characteristics, high compressive strength, wear resistance, and good damping qualities. The principal types are: gray, white, malleable, ductile (nodular), and various alloy irons.

Steel can be manufactured in great quantity at small expense and with an almost infinite combination of desirable physical properties. Many parts formerly made of cast or wrought iron are now either cast or fabricated from steel.

The Blast Furnace.—The blast furnace produces pig iron by smelting or chemically reducing iron ore. It was invented in Germany during the early 14th century. Notable improvements have been made and the modern blast furnace reaches more than 100 feet in height and may produce 1,200 to 1,800 tons of pig iron per day. The charge is put in at the top. The molten iron and impurities are drawn off separately at the bottom as they accumulate. The hoppers at the top receive iron ore in the form of iron oxide, limestone, and coke. The limestone is a flux that helps reduce the iron oxide and unites with the ash of the coke and the impurities in the ore to form a slag, which melts near the bottom of the furnace. The coke also helps reduce the iron oxides, furnishes carbon to saturate the iron, and ultimately burns in the lower part of the furnace, supplying heat to melt the iron and slag. This slag floats on top of the molten iron, and is removed through the slag notch. A large volume of hot air is blown in at the bottom of the furnace to promote combustion of the coke and to help carry the gases upward. See also BLAST FURNACE; BLAST FURNACE PRACTICE, MODERN; IRON—4. *Pig Iron.*

Open-Hearth Process.—In 1856, Karl Wilhelm Siemens (1823–1883) patented the open-hearth furnace, which eventually became the largest producer of steel. The outstanding feature of this furnace is the intense heat obtainable by its regenerative process. The flame burns above a shallow vessel containing the charge of pig iron, steel scrap, iron ore, and flux. As the charge melts, the flux forms a slag which is raked off into slag pockets at the side of the furnace. Recarburizers and ferroalloys (high-alloy-content iron alloys) are added after refining to bring the steel to the desired composition, if the carbon, silicon, and manganese contents are lower than desired. This apparently wasteful procedure of eliminating the impurities and then adding them again in the desired amounts is, in reality, more efficient than trying to decrease them to just the right amounts. The proportions of pig iron, steel scrap, and iron ore added depend on various economic conditions as well as the grades of steel desired.

Bessemer Converter Process.—At about the same time that the open-hearth furnace was invented, Henry Bessemer (1813–1898) developed the refining process known by his name. This process requires no fuel. The heat is supplied by the oxidation of the impurities in the pig iron. Silicon and manganese occur in pig iron in sufficient quantities to increase the temperature of the molten iron when they are oxidized by even a blast of cold air. The Bessemer process takes advantage of this by blowing cold air in at the bottom of a pear-shaped vessel which has just been filled with molten pig iron from a blast furnace. As the air bubbles through the iron, silicon and manganese are oxidized to form a slag and the temperature gradually rises. Carbon is then oxidized and burns with a long flame from the mouth of the converter. After the carbon "blow," recarburizers and ferroalloys are added and the charge is dumped and cast into ingots. Because the process is rapid and simple, pig iron is sometimes refined in a Bessemer before being charged into the basic open hearth or the electric furnace (duplexing).

Electric Furnace Process.—The development of electric furnaces has been important to the steel industry because higher and more accurately controlled temperatures are obtainable, and because the charge may be exposed to an atmosphere that will not contaminate the metal. The high cost of electric power is one of the limiting factors and accounts for the fact that electric furnaces are used mainly for high-quality steel production, usually tool steels and alloy steels. The charge to the furnace can vary from almost all steel scrap to almost all pig iron or iron ore. Two types of furnaces are in general use for melting and smelting; the arc furnace and the induction furnace.

The electric furnace can produce steel of almost any desired purity and composition because various fluxes may be used and the operator can take samples from the melt from time to time, analyze them, and add whatever is needed to bring the steel to the desired composition. The operation is flexible and used even in small foundries, where small electric furnaces provide steel quickly and efficiently. The high temperatures obtainable permit easy melting of the higher alloy content steels.

See also FURNACE—4. *Electric Furnaces;* STEEL—3. *Manufacture* (Casting).

Reactive Metals.—A small number of metals, including titanium and zirconium, are so reactive that the general procedures outlined above cannot be used. These metals are reduced either directly from their ores or from an intermediate compound produced from the ore. High temperatures are needed and vacuum processes are used to prevent air contamination or to speed the reaction. Where intermediate compounds are the starting point, active reducing agents such as sodium or magnesium are used. Reduction is accomplished with or without fusion.

5. PHYSICAL METALLURGY

Physical metallurgy deals with the nature, structure, and physical properties of metals and alloys, as well as their application and adaptation. Included in this subject are working and fabricating, heat treating, joining, finishing, casting, and powder metallurgy. The science of metal physics is constantly growing, and research has resulted in remarkable improvements in metal products. In modern metallurgy, it is no longer satisfactory to compare metals and obtain only qualitative or comparative answers. Instead it is important to understand why a metal is like it is, what is known about it, how it will behave in service, and what modifications can be made. One of the ultimate aims is to have the science so exact that it will be possible to predict behavior—to take a new metal or alloy and be able, after examination, to say where and how it can best be used.

Fundamental studies of a metal are concerned with both the internal and external structure, and with determining and developing specific properties. Among the tools used are optical and electron microscopes for the study of metal and alloy structures, and X-rays for the study and determination of crystal structures. (See METALLOGRAPHY.) Part of the program is the development and carrying out of testing procedures to determine and study toughness, strength, hardness, corrosion resistance, behavior under stresses and strain, magnetic properties, elevated temperature properties, and nuclear properties.

As new technologies and industries develop, they tend to create metallurgical groups specializing in specific problems. Actually, of course, the metallurgy involved is the same—nuclear reactor metallurgy just concentrates more heavily on radiation properties of metals; jet engine metallurgy concentrates more on such matters as high temperature and high strength problems.

Working and Fabricating.—The working of metals and metal fabricating involve the use of mechanical forces and equipment to form shapes and sizes that are adaptable for specific uses. For example, a steel ingot, which is a casting made directly from a refining furnace, may be forged and rolled into sheet or bar. The sheet or bar forms may in turn be stamped, drawn, machined, or otherwise further altered. See FORGE, FORGING, AND FORGING MACHINES; METALWORKING; ROLLING MILLS; STEEL—3. *Manufacture.*

Heat Treating.—Heat treating is a combination of heating and cooling operations, timed and applied to a metal or alloy in the solid state in a way that will produce desired properties. In steels, hardness, softness, a combination of strength and ductility, and desired grain size can be obtained through heating to a previously determined temperature and then cooling at a rapid, moderate, or slow rate. Even in ancient times it was known that some steels could be hardened if they were heated to a bright red heat and then cooled rapidly, such as by plunging into water or oil.

In the heat treatment of steel, advantage is taken of the allotropic nature of steel, an alloy of iron and carbon. This means that iron exists in more than one crystal structure, and within the proper temperature ranges transforms from one structure to another. Carbon and certain other alloying elements influence the temperature and speed of transformation. See STEEL—4. *Steel Technology* (Heat Treatment).

Nonferrous metals do not have structures similar to steel, and the heat treatment is different. The hardening of nonferrous alloys depends on the precipitation of very small particles from solution. In many alloys the amount of an element which can be held in solid solution under slow cooling without being precipitated is greater at some elevated temperature than at room temperature. If such an alloy is cooled rapidly, the normal precipitation may be prevented, and there results a supersaturated solid solution at room temperature. In the supersaturated condition the metal is soft and may be worked to the desired shape. Then if this solid solution partially breaks down, at relatively low temperature, the precipitate may form in it in a manner which will cause the alloy to become progressively harder and stronger. This type of hardening and strengthening of an alloy is known as precipitation hardening. Maximum hardness is reached slowly at low temperature but is greater than when precipitation is carried out at higher temperatures.

Joining.—Many articles that are too big or too costly to be constructed in one piece can be made by joining several individually made parts. Joining may be done by fastening the pieces together by riveting or bolting, or by soldering, brazing, or welding. In processes in which the joining medium is melted, the strength of the joint depends upon adhesion or some slight alloying by diffusion. Soldering is an example of adhesion; in brazing, some of the filler-metal atoms diffuse into the solid base metal being joined. In welding the filler material, when present, and the parent metal are melted; after solidification the joint resembles the crystal structure of the casting. See BRAZING; SOLDER; WELDING.

Finishing.—Finishing consists of treating the surface of metal articles to give them better resistance to corrosion, wear, or fatigue, and a better appearance. See ELECTROPLATING; GALVANIZING; METAL FINISHING; STEEL—*4. Steel Technology* (Protective Coatings); TIN—*Tin Plate* and *Alloys* (Terneplate).

Casting.—Almost all of the refined metal produced is poured or cast into molds to form ingots. The ingots then are deformed mechanically into structural shapes of all kinds. Foundries produce the molten metals or alloys in open-hearth, electric arc or induction furnaces, or in gas- or oil-fired crucible furnaces. Before being poured into molds, molten metals must usually be degassed.

Molds into which metal is poured for solidification must withstand high temperatures without losing their strength or becoming soluble in the melt. For steel ingots, massive cast-iron molds are used, and ingots may weigh more than 300 tons. The thermal conductivity and heat capacity of the cast-iron molds are so high that the ingots solidify in them quickly, and the molds do not become excessively hot. This rapid cooling is not desirable for complex castings, and complicated molds are made of sand and a suitable binder. To form a cavity of the shape to be cast in the mold, the sand is packed around a pattern of wood or metal made to the dimensions of the casting desired. Feed heads or risers are provided to make up for shrinkage as the metal freezes, and sprues are located at proper places in the mold for introducing the molten metal. Hollow portions of a casting are formed with baked-sand cores secured inside the main cavity. After the casting has cooled sufficiently, the mold is broken away, cores are removed from the casting, and the excess metal forming the gates and risers is removed from the casting. Finishing operations include grit blasting to remove adhering sand and scale,

machining, and possibly heat treatment.

Precision casting is the term applied to the casting of fluid metals to form finished, close-tolerance products or parts. In modern practice, five techniques are used: (1) permanent mold castings; (2) plaster mold casting; (3) shell sand mold casting; (4) pressure die casting; (5) investment casting.

Permanent mold casting is done in iron or steel molds made in sections, so that the casting can be removed and the mold re-used. It is suitable for low melting point metals such as lead, aluminum, and magnesium.

Plaster mold casting is done in plaster of Paris molds made from a pattern, and usually destroyed to remove the casting.

In shell sand mold casting, the molds consist of shells made of a mixture of sand with resin, baked hard by heat from a precision-made cast-iron or aluminum alloy pattern of the shape to be cast.

Pressure die casting is a process in which intricate permanent steel molds are filled rapidly by injecting metal into them under high pressure. Alloys of low melting point are often die cast.

The investment casting process is the most flexible of these processes with respect to attainable intricacy, attainable precision, and variety of alloys which may be cast within the size limitations of the process. This process is the modern equivalent of the ancient lost wax process. The lost wax-investment method of casting to precise dimensions is said to have originated around 700 to 400 B.C. It has been used for statuary and jewelry and especially in dentistry. It has also been adapted to casting high melting point alloys that are unmachinable, notably blades for gas turbines. The process is especially suited for objects so irregular that a solid or even a rubber pattern could not be withdrawn from a sand or plaster mold.

As an example of the technique, the dentist inserts wax into the cavity of a tooth, and this wax pattern is then invested with a slurry of finely ground refractory which is allowed to set and then backed up by a suitable material. The pattern is the exact size and shape of the cavity. Before or during the baking of the investment, the wax pattern is melted out, leaving the investment ready to receive the metal. Casting may be done either centrifugally or by gravity. In centrifugal casting, the mold is spun rapidly during pouring of the molten metal, to ensure that the metal fills all areas.

Wax is not the only pattern material for this process. Certain plastics can be melted or volatilized out of the investment, and low-melting fusible alloys or even frozen mercury may be utilized. A peculiarity of frozen mercury is that two pieces of it weld together on merely being brought into contact. Many intricate shapes are cast from frozen mercury patterns.

See also ALLOYS—*Cast Steels, Cast Irons;* FOUNDRY PRACTICE; IRON—*3. Cast Iron;* STEEL—*3. Manufacture* (Casting).

Powder Metallurgy.—The powder metallurgy process dates back to 3000 B.C. when the Egyptians utilized something of its technique for making implements and weapons. Progress really did not start, however, until the classical experiments of William Hyde Wollaston (1766–1828) resulted in the production of solid platinum early in the 19th century. The process represents an important method of producing parts from powders of one or more metals, or of a combination of metals and nonmetals. It consists of preparing or obtaining the desired materials in powder form, mixing the powders together, compacting them at high pressures in dies of the desired shape, and then heating the pressed compact in a controlled atmosphere furnace at a temperature below the melting point of the major constitutent. The particles form into a strong unit by diffusion, and if the proper controls have been observed, the finished part requires little or no further working. High-precision parts may require a sizing operation, which is simply a repressing of the sintered compact in a sizing die. This is called coining.

Important advantages of the process are elimination of scrap, elimination of machining operations, adaptability to automatic mass production, good control of composition and structure, production of parts with controlled porosity, production of refractory metal parts that could not be prepared satisfactorily by any other method, and the ability to produce parts combining metals and nonmetals.

Important disadvantages are the high cost of dies, the lower physical properties usually obtained, high cost of raw materials, and limitation on the design of the part.

The process is especially suitable for the manufacture of high-production parts that would normally be machined from bar stock or castings by methods other than the automatic screw machine and multiple spindle operations. It is not generally competitive with sand, permanent mold, or die casting where little or no machining is required.

Among the refractory metals, tungsten, molybdenum, and tantalum are produced. Industrially important examples of parts produced by combinations of metal and nonmetal powders include the cemented carbides used as cutting tools, current collector brushes for electrical motors and generators, graphite bronze bearings, diamond drill core bits, metallic friction articles, and metal powder reinforced brake bands and clutch plates. Metal powder parts that cannot be made practically by other methods include self-lubricating porous bearings, metallic filters, laminated structures, radio and telephone cores. Powder metallurgy is also used to combine two or more metals without appreciable alloying to retain the individual characteristics of the metals, as in electrical contacts, welding electrodes, bimetallic products, and various types of jewelry.

Finishing of powder metallurgy parts, when necessary, follows the usual metal finishing operations. Prefinishing treatments may include pickling, degreasing, grit blasting, or electrolytic cleaning. Some metals may be made to form their own protective coatings by chemical or electrolytic action or by suitable heat treatment.

Furnaces, Refractories, and Fuels.—The furnaces used in extractive and physical metallurgy may be classified according to function or source of heat. A general functional classification would be: (1) furnaces used in extractive metallurgy—for roasting, smelting, and refining purposes; (2) furnaces used for melting—either for combining metals to form alloys or for obtaining metal for castings as in foundry work; (3) furnaces used for heat treatment, or for heating primary metal shapes like ingots and billets prior to hot-working operations. Using sources of heat as a criterion, furnaces can be classified as either fuel-fired furnaces or electric furnaces.

The parts of a furnace that are subjected to very high temperatures must be constructed of a material that will not melt, nor even soften extensively, at the temperature within the furnace; or else they must be cooled in some manner to maintain them at a lower temperature. Many furnaces are lined with refractories, which are materials of very high melting point, usually in the form of brick.

Refractory materials are considerably costlier than ordinary clay or brick, and are used only for furnace parts that are subjected to considerable heat. In most cases a furnace may be built of inexpensive brick, or steel plates, to give the necessary strength, and then the inside covered by a layer or layers of refractory brick. In some furnaces refractory clay may be rammed into certain parts, or loose refractory material may be thrown onto certain portions of the hearth. The commonly used refractories are the acid refractories—silica or fire clay; the basic refractories—magnesite, dolomite, alumina, zirconia; and the neutral refractories—chromite, graphite, silicon carbide.

The metallurgical industry consumes enormous quantities of combustible fuels. The selection of the best fuel for a particular process and efficient utilization of the fuel are matters of great technical and economic importance.

The leading metallurgical fuel in amount consumed is coal. Most of the coal is used as coke, since it is most suitable for the largest fuel-consuming furnace, the iron blast furnace. Oil is also of great importance for metallurgical purposes; and gas, both natural and manufactured, is also used in large and increasing amounts in metallurgical furnaces.

The chief combustible element in all fuels is carbon. In addition, most fuels contain a considerable amount of hydrogen, either as free hydrogen or combined as hydrocarbons. These are the only combustible elements of importance as heat producers.

See also BRICK—*Refractory Brick;* CHROMITE; REFRACTORIES.

6. BIBLIOGRAPHY

Dieter, George E., *Mechanical Metallurgy* (New York 1961); Guy, A. G., *Physical Metallurgy for Engineers* (Reading, Mass., 1962); Dennis, William H., *Metallurgy of the Ferrous Metals* (New York 1963); Parr, James G., *Man, Metals, and Modern Magic* (New York 1963); Smallman, R. E., *Modern Physical Metallurgy,* 2d ed. (Washington 1963); Avner, Sidney H., *An Introduction to Physical Metallurgy* (New York 1964); Heselwood, W. C., and others, *Instrumentation in the Metallurgical Industry* (New York 1964); Alexander, W. O., ed., *Metallurgical Achievements* (New York 1965); Rigers, Bruce A., *The Nature of Metals.* (Cambridge, Mass., 1965); Biringuccio, Vannoccio, Pirotechnia, tr. by Cyril S. Smith and Martha T. Gnudi (Cambridge, Mass., 1966); Cottrell, A. H., *Introduction to Metallurgy* (New York 1967); Gilchrist, J. D., *Extraction Metallurgy* (New York 1967); Simons, Eric N., *Guide to Uncommon Metals* (New York 1967).

ALVIN S. COHAN, *Metallurgical Engineer.*

METALS, mĕt"lz, chemical elements that have a metallic luster, and that in electrolysis carry a positive charge and are liberated at the cathode. Other characteristics of metals are high melting temperatures, low specific heat, good thermal and electrical conductivity, hardness, and the ability to be deformed permanently without fracture. The dividing line between metals and nonmetals is not a sharp one. However, more than 70 of the 102 known chemical elements are classed as metals; in addition, 10 are metals that are synthetically created by cyclotron and reactor bombardment of other elements, while the remaining elements are classed as nonmetals or inert gases.

In some applications, metals are used by themselves; usually they are in the form of alloys. An alloy is a union of two or more metals, or a metal and a nonmetal. Copper and tin, both metals, form the alloy bronze. Steel is an alloy of iron and carbon, a metal and a nonmetal. Pure gold is too soft for jewelry and coins and is generally alloyed with copper. Pure gold is 24 carat; 18 carat gold is generally used for jewelry, and contains 18 parts of gold or 75 per cent. Another alloying metal often used with gold is silver. Silver is used in alloy form to a large extent, particularly for coinage and silverware. In the United States sterling silver is usually 900 fine—it contains 900 parts per 1,000 of silver.

The following classification is a modern acceptance of the metal grouping in the periodic chart (see PERIODIC LAW):

CLASS Ia—*Light Metals:* lithium, sodium, potassium, rubidium, cesium, francium.

CLASS Ib—*Heavy Metals:* copper, silver, gold. These are typical metals and were known to the ancients. They exhibit the traditional qualities of metals.

CLASS IIa—*Light Metals:* beryllium, magnesium, calcium, strontium, barium, radium.

CLASS IIb—*Heavy Metals:* zinc, cadmium, mercury.

CLASS IIIa—*Heavy Metals:* scandium, yttrium, lanthanum, actinium; *Rare Earth Elements:* cerium, praseodymium, neodymium, prometheum, samarium, europium, gadolinium, terbium, dysprosium, holmium, erbium, thulium, ytterbium, lutecium.

CLASS IIIb—*Heavy Metals:* aluminum, gallium, indium, thallium.

CLASS IVa—*Heavy Metals:* titanium, zirconium, hafnium, thorium.

CLASS IVb—*Heavy Metals:* silicon, germanium, tin, lead.

CLASS Va—*Heavy Metals:* vanadium, columbium (or niobium), tantalum, protactinium.

CLASS Vb—*Heavy Metals:* arsenic, antimony, bismuth.

CLASS VIa—*Heavy Metals:* chromium, molybdenum, tungsten, uranium.

CLASS VIb—*Heavy Metals:* selenium, tellurium, polonium.

CLASS VII—*Heavy Metals:* manganese, technetium, rhenium.

CLASS VIII—*Heavy Metals:* iron, ruthenium, osmium, plutonium, cobalt, rhodium, iridium, nickel, palladium, platinum. This class contains the so-called platinum group of metals.

Elements heavier than uranium are all synthetic. These elements are neptunium (93), plutonium (94), americium (95), curium (96), berkelium (97), californium (98), einsteinium (99), fermium (100), mendelevium (101), and nobelium (102). All these have been discovered since 1940 as a result of atomic research.

Only 40 of the metal elements have commercial significance. These metals are: aluminum, antimony, arsenic, barium, beryllium, bismuth, cadmium, calcium, cerium, cobalt, columbium, copper, gold, iridium, iron, lead, lithium, magnesium, manganese, mercury, molybdenum, nickel, palladium, platinum, radium, rhenium, selenium, silicon, silver, sodium, tantalum, tellurium, thorium, tin, titanium, tungsten, uranium, vanadium, zinc, zirconium.

Metals and alloys are the most important of all structural materials. It would be difficult to name many items used in everyday life that do not contain metal in some form. Civilian and military aircraft, automotive equipment of all types, missiles, and rockets also depend upon metals.

Properties.—Depending upon the pressure to which it is subjected, and upon its temperature, a metal can exist as a solid, liquid, or gas. At room temperature and atmospheric pressure, only mercury is liquid, all others being solid.

The atoms of metals are arranged in geometric patterns or structures characteristic of the metal. These structures are described as space lattices, of which there are 14 types. Most of the common metals conform to one of three lattice types: body-centered cubic, face-centered cubic, and close-packed hexagonal.

SPACE LATTICES OF COMMON METALS AT ROOM TEMPERATURE

BODY-CENTERED CUBIC	FACE-CENTERED CUBIC	CLOSE-PACKED HEXAGONAL
Barium	Aluminum	Beryllium
Chromium	Calcium	Cadmium
Columbium	Copper	Cobalt
Iron	Gold	Magnesium
Molybdenum	Lead	Titanium
Tantalum	Nickel	Zinc
Uranium	Platinum	Zirconium
Vanadium	Silver	

An allotropic metal is one that exists in more than one lattice form. One space lattice will exist over a range of temperatures, and at a certain temperature changes to another lattice form. The different lattice forms are chemically identical, but have different physical properties. One of the best known allotropic metals is iron, which has a body-centered cubic lattice up to 910° C. Above 910° C., iron changes to a face-centered cubic structure, and at 1,400° C. it changes again to a body-centered cubic lattice type.

Metals and alloys are identified and classified by their chemical, physical, and mechanical properties. Some combination of all three properties will determine the choice of material for a specific use. Chemical properties include chemical and electrochemical reactivity (see ELECTROCHEMISTRY), corrodibility, oxidation at high temperature, and other characteristics. Physical properties include density, electrical and thermal conductivity, thermoelectric behavior, melting and boiling points, color, reflectivity, magnetic behavior, specific heat, heat of fusion, heat of vaporization, coefficient of thermal expansion, neutron absorption, thermionic emission, and penetrability of X-rays.

Mechanical properties are determined by conventional tests. Properties determined are hardness, tensile strength, bend test, impact strength, compression strength, fatigue strength, torsion, creep strength, and stress rupture. See STRENGTH OF MATERIALS; TESTING MACHINES.

One of the many important mechanical properties of a metal is its resistance to deformation. Strength, rigidity, hardness, resistance to wear, fatigue, and creep are all facets of resistance to deformation. A metal, to be useful, must not have so great a resistance to deformation that it becomes impossible to shape the metal by some practical method. Malleability and ductility refer to the ability of a metal to be worked without fracture. Malleability permits metal to be hammered or rolled into thin sheets or foil, ductility permits it to be drawn into wire. Toughness is a combination of ductility and strength. Elasticity is the property of a metal that permits it to return to its original shape after a certain amount of deformation.

One of the more useful properties of metals is corrosion resistance. Some metals, such as tantalum, titanium, platinum, and stainless steel, are so corrosion resistant as to resist attack by hot acids or corrosive gases; some metals, such as sodium, lithium, and potassium, have so low a corrosion resistance that the metal barely resists exposure to the atmosphere.

Gold, silver, platinum, bronze, brass, copper, aluminum, and stainless steel, in addition to their utility, are useful for their aesthetic value. They are used for jewelry, decoration, architecture, trim, and similar purposes. Baser metals can gain improved appearance and resistance to corrosion by coating with other metals, paint, enamel, or other substances. See CORROSION, ELECTROPLATING; METAL FINISHING.

High electrical conductivity, usually accompanied by high thermal conductivity, is another important metal feature. Silver, copper, and aluminum are the best conductors. Very few metals—iron, nickel, cobalt, germanium—are ferromagnetic—that is, have magnetic properties. However, many alloys have been developed with better magnetic properties than are possessed by any pure metals.

When heated, metals show a red, then yellow, and finally a clear, dazzling white color. The temperatures corresponding to these colors are approximately:

COLOR	DEGREES CENTIGRADE	DEGREES FAHRENHEIT
Visible color, black red	525	970
Dull red, low red	700	1,290
Red, incipient blood red	800	1,470
Cherry, bright red	900	1,650
Bright cherry	1,000	1,830
Dull orange	1,100	2,010
Bright orange	1,200	2,190
White	1,300	2,370
Bright white	1,400	2,550
Dazzling white	1,500	2,730

The most important metal is iron, which accounts for about 90 per cent of all metal used. Iron and steel form the ferrous metal group. Steel, the alloy of iron and carbon, is the basic material of construction in equipment for generating power and transmitting mechanical energy. The properties of steel are improved for specific applications by addition of other alloying elements in the form of ferroalloys. Important in this group of additions to steel are manganese, chromium, nickel, molybdenum, silicon, tungsten, and vanadium. Alloy steels make possible modern high-speed surface transportation—railroads, automobiles, and trucks. High-pressure and high-temperature equipment also depends on them.

Copper, aluminum, lead, zinc, magnesium and tin are among the principal nonferrous metals. Aluminum, magnesium, and titanium—all nonferrous metals—make up the light metal group and are responsible for most aircraft production.

Metals exist in the earth's crust in the following approximate amounts:

METAL	PER CENT OF EARTH'S CRUST (BY WEIGHT)	METAL	PER CENT OF EARTH'S CRUST (BY WEIGHT)
Silicon	28	Vanadium	0.015
Aluminum	8	Zinc	0.013
Iron	4.5	Nickel	0.008
Calcium	3.5	Copper	0.007
Sodium	2.5	Tungsten	0.006
Potassium	2.5	Lithium	0.006
Magnesium	2.2	Tin	0.004
Barium	0.8	Columbium	0.002
Titanium	0.46	Cobalt	0.002
Manganese	0.08	Lead	0.001
Zirconium	0.022	Molybdenum	0.001
Strontium	0.02		
Chromium	0.02		

All other metals exist in quantities less than 0.001 per cent (one thousandth of 1 per cent).

There is little relationship between the amount of a metal used, its price, and its availability in the earth's crust. Some metals may have their ore deposits scattered all over the globe, with few concentrated enough to permit economical mining. Some metals are difficult to separate in a pure state from their ores or compounds. In practice, metal prices vary widely, ranging from a fraction of a cent per pound for iron to hundreds of dollars per pound for such metals as gold, platinum, and rhodium.

Physical Constants.—Some physical constants of the metals are shown in the following table. The chemical symbol follows the name of the metal. The atomic number is the position in the periodic chart:

METAL AND SYMBOL	ATOMIC NUMBER	ATOMIC WEIGHT	MELTING POINT (DEGREES CENTIGRADE)	SPECIFIC GRAVITY (GRAMS PER CUBIC CENTIMETER)
Actinium (Ac)	89	228	1050	[1]
Aluminum (Al)	13	26.97	659.7	2.70
Americium (Am)	95	243	[1]	[1]
Antimony (Sb)	51	121.76	630.5	6.62
Arsenic (As)	33	74.91	814.0 [2]	5.73
Barium (Ba)	56	137.36	850	3.50
Berkelium (Bk)	97	249	[1]	[1]
Beryllium (Be)	4	9.02	1280	1.85
Bismuth (Bi)	83	209.00	271	9.80
Cadmium (Cd)	48	112.41	320.9	8.65
Calcium (Ca)	20	40.08	850	1.55
Californium (Cf)	98	249	[1]	[1]
Cerium (Ce)	58	140.13	804	6.73
Cesium (Cs)	55	132.91	28	1.90
Chromium (Cr)	24	52.01	1890	7.14
Cobalt (Co)	27	58.94	1495	8.90
Columbium (Cb) [3]	41	92.91	1950	8.57
Copper (Cu)	29	63.54	1083	8.94
Curium (Cm)	96	245	[1]	[1]
Dysporsium (Dy)	66	162.51	1485	8.56
Einsteinium (Es)	99	253	[1]	[1]
Erbium (Er)	68	167.27	1500	9.15
Europium (Eu)	63	152.0	826	5.24
Fermium (Fm)	100	255	[1]	[1]
Francium (Fr)	87	223	[1]	[1]
Gadolinium (Gd)	64	157.26	1350	7.86
Gallium (Ga)	31	69.72	29.8	5.91
Germanium (Ge)	32	72.60	958	5.36
Gold (Au)	79	197.0	1063.0	19.30
Hafnium (Hf)	72	178.50	1700	11.40
Holmium (Ho)	67	164.94	1490	8.799
Indium (In)	49	114.82	156.4	7.31
Iridium (Ir)	77	192.2	2454	22.42
Iron (Fe)	26	55.85	1535	7.87
Lanthanum (La)	57	138.92	920	6.19
Lead (Pb)	82	207.21	327.4	11.34
Lithium (Li)	3	6.940	186	0.53
Lutecium (Lu)	71	174.99	1650	9.849
Magnesium (Mg)	12	24.32	650	1.74
Manganese (Mn)	25	54.94	1260	7.44
Mendelevium (Mv)	101	256	[1]	[1]
Mercury (Hg)	80	200.61	−38.87	13.55
Molybdenum (Mo)	42	95.95	2625	10.20
Neodymium (Nd)	60	144.27	1024	7.05
Neptunium (Np)	93	237	[1]	[1]
Nickel (Ni)	28	58.71	1455	8.90
Nobelium (No)	102	[1]	[1]	[1]
Osmium (Os)	76	190.2	2700	22.50
Palladium (Pd)	46	106.4	1554	12.00
Platinum (Pt)	78	195.09	1773.5	21.45
Plutonium (Pu)	94	242	[1]	[1]
Polonium (Po)	84	210.0	600	[1]
Potassium (K)	19	39.10	63	0.86
Praseodymium (Pr)	59	140.92	940	6.78
Prometheum (Pm)	61	145	[1]	[1]
Protactinium (Pa)	91	231	3000	[1]
Radium (Ra)	88	226.05	960	5.00
Rhenium (Re)	75	186.22	3170	20.00
Rhodium (Rh)	45	102.91	1985	12.44
Rubidium (Rb)	37	85.48	39	1.53
Ruthenium (Ru)	44	101.1	2500	12.20
Samarium (Sm)	62	150.35	1052	7.49
Scandium (Sc)	21	44.96	1200	2.50
Selenium (Se)	34	78.96	220	4.81
Silicon (Si)	14	28.06	1420	2.42
Silver (Ag)	42	107.88	960.5	10.50
Sodium (Na)	11	22.991	97.7	0.97
Strontium (Sr)	38	87.63	770	2.60
Tantalum (Ta)	73	180.95	3027	16.60
Technetium (Tc)	43	99	2700	
Tellurium (Te)	52	127.61	450	6.24
Terbium (Tb)	65	158.93	1360	8.25
Thallium (Tl)	81	204.39	303	11.85

Thorium (Th)	90	232.05	1845	11.50
Thulium (Tm)	69	168.94	1550	9.318
Tin (Sn)	50	118.70	231.9	7.30
Titanium (Ti)	22	47.90	1820	4.50
Tungsten (W)	74	183.86	3370	19.30
Uranium (U)	92	238.07	1133	18.70
Vanadium (V)	23	50.95	1710	5.68
Ytterbium (Yb)	70	173.04	824	6.959
Yttrium (Y)	39	88.92	1552	4.472
Zinc (Zn)	30	65.38	419.5	7.14
Zirconium (Zr)	40	91.22	1900	6.40

[1] Not yet determined.   [2] Sublimes   [3] Also known as niobium (Nb).

See also METAL FINISHING; METALLOGRAPHY; METALLURGY; METALWORKING; IRON; STEEL; also separate articles on the individual metals.

Bibliography.—Aitchison, Leslie, *A History of Metals*, 2 vols (New York 1960); Hampel, C. A., ed., *Rare Metals Handbook*, 2d ed. (New York 1961); Parr, James G., *Man, Metals, and Modern Magic* (New York 1963); Chalmers, Bruce, *Principles of Solidification* (New York 1964); Rogers, Bruce A., *The Nature of Metals* (Cambridge, Mass., 1965); Datsko, Joseph, *Material Properties and Manufacturing Processes* (New York 1966).

ALVIN S. COHAN.

METALWORK, mĕt″l-wûrk, any work done in metals, but especially handiwork practiced as a decorative art, in which the design is executed in repoussé or relief. This may be accomplished either by carving or by hammering, as of thin sheet metal. The term includes jewelry and goldsmith's work; hence its materials are often precious metals, and its end personal adornment. But it is often applied to larger work, and especially to metal decoration in architecture. The Middle Ages were the great period of artistic metalwork, notably in connection with Gothic art. Even the more valuable metals were lavishly used in this epoch, as before in the Byzantine period, and since in the architecture of the Greek

A 12th century bronze relief depicting the Flight into Egypt, in the Church of St. Zeno in Verona, Italy.

Bildarchiv Foto Marburg

Church, especially in pre-Communist Russia. One of the foremost examples of Italian metalwork is the silver altar of the Chapel of St. James in the cathedral in Pistoia—the combined work of several artists over a period of more than a century. Also outstanding are the three great bronze doors in the baptistery of the cathedral at Florence, Italy, one by Andrea Pisano (1270?–1348) and the others by Lorenzo Ghiberti (1378–1455), each of the latter the work of more than a score of years. Benvenuto Cellini (1500–1571) was the greatest metalworker of the 16th century. Wrought ironwork dates back to ancient times; but it was between the 10th and the 18th centuries that it reached its most advanced forms in many European countries in the form of gates, grilles, and screens in ecclesiastical art, and in German locks and hinges of great beauty. The sepulchral brasses of German, French, and English churches should also be mentioned. See also BRONZE AND BRASS IN ART.

METALWORKING, mĕt″l-wŭr-kĭng, the act of processing metals from raw stock to achieve specified shape, size, and physical form. More specifically, the term usually is applied to various mechanical means of achieving this purpose, such as turning; milling, and broaching; planing, shaping, and slotting; gear cutting; pressworking; extrusion and drawing; and the use of torches and flames. These processes are described in this article. See also separate articles on BORING AND BORING MACHINES; DRILLS AND DRILLING; EXTRUSION; FORGE, FORGING, AND FORGING MACHINES; GRINDING; ROLLING MILLS; WELDING. In a broader sense, metalworking may include any method of changing the shape, size, and physical form of metals, from the art of jewelry making to such processes as casting, powder metallurgy, and heat treatment. See GOLDSMITHING; IRON; JEWELRY; METAL FINISHING; METALLURGY—*Physical Metallurgy* (Casting, Powder Metallurgy); and STEEL. For definitions of technical metalworking terms, see WORKSHOP TERMS.

Equipment.—Metalworking equipment in general is in a constant process of improvement. Cutting, processing, and handling speeds increase steadily; machines grow more powerful and stronger; vibration has been reduced; and coolants and lubricants are better applied to both workpieces and machines. New machines have been designed and constructed to accept new tool materials and new tooling ideas so that optimum advantage can be obtained from such progress.

With the acceleration in operating speeds made possible by new tools, methods, and machines, manual control has become increasingly impracticable. Automatic controls have been applied in increasing numbers to metalworking equipment. Results obtained with this automatic equipment far surpass any that could previously be achieved by manually controlled equipment and by comparatively skilled craftsmen and operators.

Not only has physical plant equipment been improved, but the methods by which this equipment is applied have altered rapidly since 1900. Work simplification, production efficiency, plant layout, operations research, planned programming, inventory control, cost accounting, data reduction, and equipment replacement methods have introduced scientific and mathematical thinking into metalworking. Inspection and statistical quality control procedures have kept step so that finished metal parts and products will accomplish the functions for which they have been designed.

Turning.—The backbone of any metalworking shop is the lathe. The lathe can be used, in addition to simple turning of diameters and facing of workpieces, for boring, forming, parting off, drilling, copying, reaming, tapping, and threading.[1] During the course of their machining, most parts are subjected to turning operations. Turning is usually an early operation in the production schedule to establish starting surfaces for subsequent secondary operations, such as grinding, milling, slotting, and gear cutting.

Basically, lathes are used to turn cylindrical or other solids of revolution by rotating raw stock or partially formed workpieces against a non-rotating tool and to face surfaces at right angles to the turning axis. Turning machines are made up of various combinations of components to satisfy more or less standard functions.

Self-contained motor drives are used in almost all turning machines. A rotating spindle can be revolved at speeds suitable to the diameter of the workpiece, the type of tools used, and the particu-

American Machinist

A large tracing lathe turns and faces a turbine housing. The light-colored, cone-shaped object at top is the model.

lar operation to be performed. Provision is made for holding the workpiece either between centers, in a collet or chuck, or on a faceplate. Turning machines include bedways on which the tailstock operates. The toolholder is also mounted in ways so that it can travel across the lathe bed to perform facing cuts.

Capacities of turning machines are given in terms of the maximum diameter of work that can be swung over the bedways and the maximum length of work that can be mounted between centers. Machines having collets or hollow chucks are rated by the maximum bar diameter that will

---

[1] The sketches that accompany this article illustrate the metalworking processes described. Each sketch shows fundamentals of the process and should be considered as surrounded by a rugged machine incorporating operating mechanisms that will produce the motions indicated. In every instance, a black arrow indicates a motion that is necessary to the operation; gray arrows indicate possible motions so that larger areas can be worked, or secondary motions resulting from work done on the part.

be accepted by the largest collet used.

The engine lathe is the general-purpose production turning machine. It can be used to machine a wide variety of work in small lots with a minimum investment in accessories and tooling. In addition to straight turning and facing, the engine lathe can be used for cutting tapers. A toolroom lathe is usually a small engine lathe that has been made accurately so that work done on it can be held to close tolerances. In a gap-bed lathe the bedways do not come up to the headstock, so that large-diameter workpieces can be faced.

The turret lathe is a higher-production machine, usually used on comparatively small workpieces. Its distinguishing feature is that the compound rest and tailstock are replaced by multiple-station toolholders. All the tools for a particular job can be mounted and preset in the turrets. A complete workpiece can be finished by indexing the various tools into cutting position in sequence. This considerably reduces cutting and handling time. Vertical turret lathes have heavy, unsymmetrical workpieces mounted on rotating tables. Horizontal turret lathes can take bar stock or individually chucked parts. Typical of the tools mounted in the turrets are single-point turning tools, drills, die heads for external threads, taps, boring tools, and powered milling cutters.

Automatic turning machines are profitable for long production runs where longer setup time and higher tool costs can be amortized. Frequently, one operator can run several automatic machines. Also, parts are more accurately duplicated because the human element is removed from the production cycle. Semiautomatic machines have automatic cutting cycles but workpieces are loaded manually. Fully automatic machines load the workpiece, perform all cutting operations, part the workpiece if it is produced from bar stock, and unload it. Further to increase production, multiple-spindle automatic machines are available. In these, several workpieces are mounted on individual spindles. At each spindle indexing station one or more tools operate on the workpiece. Thus, one part is completed at each index of the machine. Automatic screw machines are special automatics that use only bar stock. Swiss-type automatic screw machines were specially designed for use in making watch parts. Larger machines of the same type are also available. These machines are especially useful for making long, slender parts with high accuracy.

Duplicating lathes are used for reproducing shapes in production lots from solid masters or thin templates. A tracer follows the master and by means of air, hydraulic, or electrical control causes the single-point tool to form the workpiece to the correct shape.

Spinning lathes are used to form shapes of revolution from thin metal blanks without the removal of any material. A solid or segmented wooden block of the shape desired is rotated by the spindle. The blank is held between the block and a live center in the tailstock. As the flat blank is rotated, spinning tools form the metal to the shape of the block. Copper, brass, aluminum, and magnesium are the usual metals formed by spinning, although harder metals can be spun.

Milling.—Second only to turning in utility and frequency of use in the metalworking shop, milling is distinguished from every other metal cutting operation by the comma-shaped chip it produces. Milling is a roughing operation for a high rate of metal removal, but because of the shape of the chip, milling is an excellent finishing operation. Basically, milling is a chip-removing process in which a rotating cutter removes metal from workpieces mounted on a moving table. Milling is divided into *peripheral, face,* and *special.* Face milling is used to form accurate flat surfaces in one or more passes of the workpiece. Peripheral milling is used to cut slots or shapes into workpieces. Special machines and tools are used to sink dies (Kellering) and to cut threads, gears, and drill blanks.

Knee-and-column milling machines are used on short and medium production runs and in tool-room work. Vertical and horizontal machines of this type are used for face and peripheral milling respectively. Planer type milling machines are used for heavy work. They usually have both vertical and horizontal cutter heads. Some universal milling machines have spindles that can be rotated in a vertical plane so the cutter axis is vertical, horizontal, or at any angle in between.

With a horizontal spindle and peripheral cutting, it is obvious that the shape of the cutter teeth determines the shape of the cut. In gang milling, various shapes and sizes of cutters are used on a single horizontal arbor to form the desired shape with a single pass.

In peripheral milling, metal may be removed by up or down (climb) milling. Metal removal is accomplished in up milling by rotating the cutter against the direction of workpiece travel; in down milling the cutter rotation is in the direction of workpiece travel.

In certain instances, milling competes with broaching and grinding; in others, it competes with planing and shaping. It also competes with various thread-cutting processes.

Broaching.—Newest of the basic methods of cutting metals, broaching came into real prominence during World War II. With broaching, results can be achieved that would otherwise require the combination of several other machining processes. Savings in production time are large because finished work can be turned out as the result of a single pass and a single setup.

Broaching is a method of machining metals through use of a multiple-tooth tool that is pushed or pulled through a workpiece or that is moved along the surface of the workpiece. Variations of broaching machines use stationary tools and moving workpieces. Broaching is a generating process. The shape of the workpiece surface, the feed, the depth of cut, and the cutting speed depend primarily on tooth design, not on the machine, except for maximum limits such as length of stroke and power.

Teeth follow each other in a broach so there are no radial lines, which can be important when reciprocating parts must fit accurately. Each tooth removes approximately the same amount of material, except that the roughing teeth may remove greater amounts than finishing teeth. Large amounts of material can be removed by broaching, although in broach burnishing no material is removed. Since each tooth of the broach passes over the work only once per pass, broaches have exceptionally long lives.

Broach machines are available in both vertical and horizontal designs. Internal broaching is accomplished with either push- or pull-type machines. In order to speed up surface broaching cycles, because broaching cuts can be made in only one direction, workholders are usually indexed away from the tool so the workpieces can

American Machinist

The surfaces of metallic workpieces are faced by a horizontal milling machine equipped with carbide cutting teeth.

be unloaded and loaded while the ram is returning for another cutting stroke. To increase production further, dual-ram surface broaching machines are available. With these, as one ram is cutting and the other is returning to home position, a finished part can be unloaded and a blank loaded.

Internal broaching is an important process because holes of any cross section, regular, irregular, or tooth-shaped, for example, can be produced. The broach is started in a pilot hole and is then connected to the ram to be pulled through. Pushing of broaches is done only when the ratio of tool length to diameter is small.

A vertical broaching machine, with a tool of solid high-speed steel, at work on small steel parts.

American Machinist

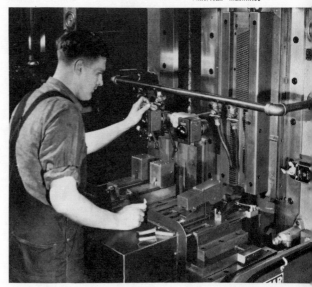

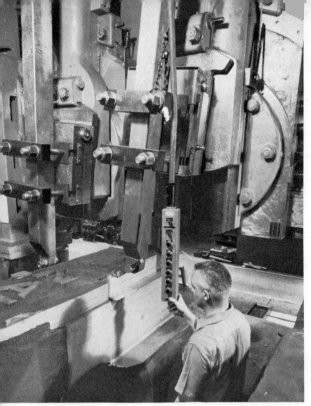

American Machinist

A double-head planer cuts part of a machine-tool frame. The worker can control the table motion and adjust tool-slide.

Planing, Shaping, and Slotting.—These three processes are quite similar but differ in significant details. In planing, the tool remains stationary while the workpiece, mounted on a table, passes underneath it; in shaping, the workpiece remains stationary while the tool passes over it; and in slotting, a shaper action is incorporated in a vertical machine. Planers and shapers are used

A rough-cut gear is fashioned automatically by a gear cutting machine. Tool depth can be adjusted for a finer cut.

American Machinist

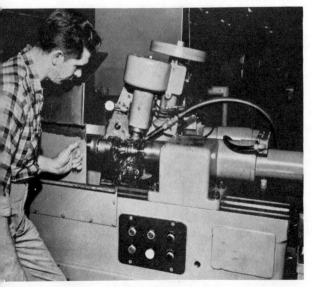

mainly for the machining of vertical, horizontal, or angular flat surfaces. They each use single-point tools that cut in only one direction, although some planers have been designed with duplicate tooling so they can cut on both strokes. With special tooling or procedures, planers and shapers can be used on curved surfaces.

Planers usually fall into two types. The first is a double housing design in which a housing supports each end of the cross rail. This type of planer usually has two cutting heads on the cross rail and one side-cutting head on each housing. The other type, the openside planer, has a column on one side of the machine only, and workpiece width is not restricted by column spacing. Through use of special linkages, cams, and hydraulic tracers, simple curves can be generated and parts duplicated by planing.

The shaper is a basic machine tool. It has a flexibility of setup to make it useful in toolrooms, die shops, and small-lot production plants. The shaper is also valuable because of its versatility in handling work that in many instances cannot be done on other machines. The most common type of shaper is the horizontal machine. It is used for producing surfaces and is also used for cutting slots. The actual slotting machine is in effect a shaper stood on its end.

Gear Cutting.—Production of gears requires special accessories and cutters for use with standard machine tools in low volume production or special machines for high volume production. Gear cutting is divided into three types: (1) *generating,* in which there is relative rolling between the cutter and gear blank and in which the tooth is formed; (2) *nongenerating,* in which cutters are formed in the shape of spaces between the desired teeth; and (3) *profiling* or tracing, in which templates are used to guide the cutting tool.

Modern high-production gear cutting demands the use of a generating process while other processes are used for small lots and experimental gears. As an example, a modern gear hobbing machine loads and unloads, adjusts the machine for pitch diameter controls, shifts the hob to distribute cutter wear, and sorts the finished gears without any operator attention.

To ensure correct operation, many gears are further finished after they are cut. Shaving, in which a minimum amount of metal is removed, can be used to achieve correct finish and required profile. Grinding, burnishing, and lapping are also used to finish gears. Gear rolling, in which the finished gear, especially a spline, is cold formed from solid stock, is applied in much the same manner as thread rolling.

Pressworking.—This includes work done on metals in presses ranging from simple embossing, coining, and blanking to deep draws, bends, and forging. The characteristics of the processes and the equipment used with each are almost automatically covered by their simplest names or definitions: piercing, perforating, slitting, trimming, shaving, bending, drawing, seaming, ironing, staking, and so forth. Flow of metal in the solid state, with or without heat, is common to all the press operations. Differences between operations and equipment lie principally in the severity of the metal flow.

A press is a heavy, strong piece of machinery designed to withstand the forces inherent in its use. A press comprises a frame, a punch platen, a die platen, a power source to raise the heavy

Right: A straightside mechanical press, one of several types used in industrial pressworking, stamps and draws dished parts of sheet metal.

American Machinist

METALWORKING

Below: A workpiece of hot, soft metal is forced through extruding dies by a hydraulically-operated machine. Molten glass is used as a lubricant.

American Machinist

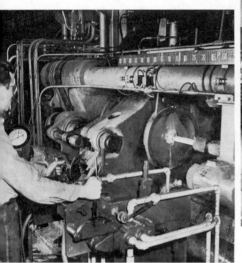

Below: An electric arc-welding machine joining metal plates. Filler metal is fed automatically from a reel.

American Machinist

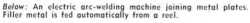

American Machinist

Above: Bar metal is cut into sections by a gas torch. The flame can be adjusted to cut cleanly to a desired depth.

METALWORKING

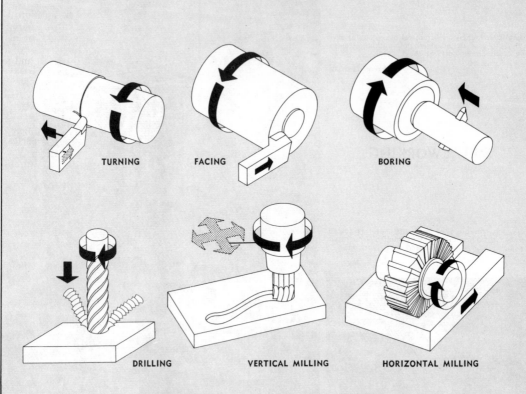

TURNING FACING BORING

DRILLING VERTICAL MILLING HORIZONTAL MILLING

The diagrams on this page illustrate the metalworking processes described in the text. Each diagram shows fundamentals of the process and should be considered as surrounded by a rugged machine incorporating operating mechanisms that will produce the motions indicated. In every instance, a black arrow indicates a motion that is necessary to the operation; shaded arrows indicate possible motions so that larger areas can be worked, or secondary motions resulting from work done on the part.

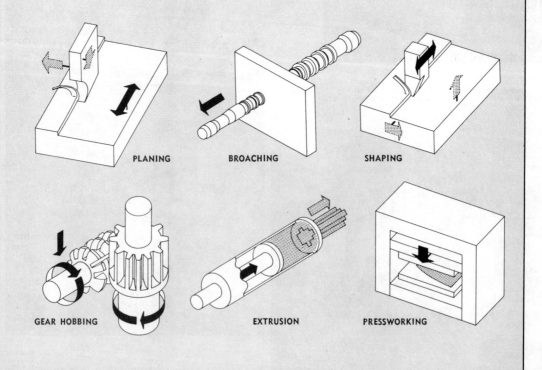

PLANING BROACHING SHAPING

GEAR HOBBING EXTRUSION PRESSWORKING

punch and/or to exert a squeeze on the metal, and controls to set the press cycle. The punch may be a cutting or forming member, and the die can be a flat plate or a forming member. Because of the elasticity of metals, punches and dies may not have the exact shape of the part to be made. If the metal will not be stressed beyond its elastic limit, allowance must be made for spring back. For more highly stressed metal, the forming action will cause permanent set without spring back.

Pressworking is done to impart size and shape to metal parts or to alter the physical and mechanical properties of the metal. Some presses are huge, high-production machines that can form the major portion of an airplane wing; others are manually operated for forming small, ornamental metal parts.

Extrusion and Drawing.—Extrusion is a process of squeezing hot metal through a die section so that it conforms to the cross section of the die. Rough gear forms, for example, can be extruded in long lengths and then sawed into individual gears. Sawing of such straight lines would normally be done by a mechanical hack saw or a circular saw, the latter probably having inserted carbide teeth. When it is necessary to saw contours, a band saw would be used.

Closely allied to the extrusion process is the wire-, rod , or tube-drawing process. Instead of being pushed through a die, the metal is pulled through. As with extrusion, regular or irregular internal holes can be produced by mandrels of the desired shape in the die section. To achieve the desired size, the metal is drawn through progressively smaller dies of ceramics, carbides, or diamonds.

Joining.—Since most products are made up of numerous components, the metalworking industry is vitally concerned with methods of joining parts. Nuts, bolts, and directly threaded members are widely used. Threading and tapping can be done on special equipment or on converted and specially tooled standard machine tools. In addition to the processes of riveting, welding, brazing, soldering, and mechanical joining, industrial adhesives have come into the metalworking industry. These synthetic materials have been widely used to join nonmetals to metallic parts and are also used to join metals to each other. Temperature limitations, which hampered rapid growth of such techniques, have been constantly expanded.

Torches and Flames.—These have many uses in metalworking. Parts can be cut quite accurately to shape with gas torches and various hardening processes use open flames. The change in metal structure introduced by heating and cooling cyles—that is heat treating—is important to metalworking. Metals can be processed in that condition which is easiest for cutting or forming and can then be heat-treated to achieve desired properties for use.

Bibliography.—Fraser, R. R., and Bedell, E. L., *General Metal: Principles, Procedures, and Projects*, 2d ed. (New York 1961); Ludwig, O. A., *Metalwork Technology and Practice*, 2d ed. (Bloomington, Ill., 1962); Robertson, J. G., *Metalwork* (London 1962); Begeman, Myron L., and Amstead, B. H., *Manufacturing Processes*, 5th ed. (New York 1963); Alexander, J. M., and others, *Recent Progress in Metal Working* (New York 1964); Crane, F. A. A., *Mechanical Working of Metals* (New York 1964); Lindberg, Roy A., *Processes and Materials of Manufacture* (Boston 1964); Rowe, G. W., *Introduction to the Principles of Metalworking* (New York 1965); Wilson, F. W., and Cox, R. W., eds., *Machining the Space-Age Metals* (Dearborn, Mich., 1965).

ROBERT A. WASON, III,
Associate Editor, "The Tool Engineer."

METAMERISM, mĕ-tăm′ẽr-ĭz′m, in zoology, the division of the body, from head to tail, into a succession of distinct segments, or metameres. Ideally each of the segments has identical or almost identical organs: a pair of appendages, a pair of excretory organs, a pair of gonads, and a ganglion of nerve cells. The boundaries of each segment are shown on the surface of the body as constrictions of the body wall.

The common earthworm serves as a good example of a metameric animal. The body is divided externally into a long series of segments and the segments contain almost identical muscles, excretory organs, ganglia and so forth. The head and tail segments are, of necessity, highly modified.

Metamerism has probably arisen on three separate occasions in evolution: in the ancestors of the tapeworms (Cestoda), of the annelid worms and Arthropoda, and of the Chordata (the vertebrates and their close relatives). There are several theories to account for the origin of segmentation. Probably the most reasonable idea is that animals with organs widely distributed throughout the body and using a snakelike locomotion evolved toward a segmented body plan because the division into segments favored their locomotion.

In the further evolution of segmented animals, the segments tend to lose their original uniformity so that the segmented divisions may be apparent only during embryonic development. Six metameres, for example, are fused together to form the insect head.

W. G. VAN DER KLOOT,
Associate Professor of Zoology, Cornell University.

METAMORPHIC ROCKS, mĕt′a-môr′fĭk rŏkz, in geology, those rocks produced by the alteration of igneous or sedimentary rocks through temperatures and pressures. Though they are generally considered to be a class of rocks to be compared with the sediments, formed by deposition from air or water at the earth's surface, or with the igneous rocks, formed by crystallization from molten substance, the distinctions are not absolute. A sediment becomes changed from the moment of its deposition; it is called metamorphic when the mineral constituents are appreciably changed in nature or structure. See also META-MORPHISM; ROCKS—*Metamorphic Rocks.*

MARSHALL KAY.

METAMORPHISM, mĕt′a-môr′fĭz′m, in geology, a term applied to the alteration of rocks. When rocks of sedimentary or igneous origin are so altered by changes in physical and chemical conditions that their crystalline structure or mineral orientation is appreciably changed, or the constituent minerals are reorganized with or without the addition of substance, the rocks are said to have undergone metamorphism. The term metamorphic rocks is generally restricted to those rocks produced through increases in pressures or temperatures or both, with increase in density; such changes have been called katamorphic, and the sequence of changes is progressive metamorphism. The rock thus produced becomes unstable as it is brought to lower temperatures and pressures such as are normal at the earth's surface, and tends to be altered to rock with minerals of lesser density; the changes have been called anamorphic, and the succession of changes is regressive or retrogressive metamorphism.

Increases in temperatures and pressures can cause recrystallization of the original mineral constituents into other minerals of the same composition, or recrystallization of the constituents into enlarged and reoriented form, as in the metamorphism of limestone to crystalline marble. Physical changes can cause interpenetration of original grains or crystals with loss of prosity, or the rock may be solidified by filling of interspaces by growth of added substance, as in the metamorphism of quartzite. In rocks of more complex composition and varied minerals, metamorphism can produce new minerals by the reconstitution of the substance in the original minerals, or by addition or subtraction of material. The growth and reorganization are greatly facilitated by the presence of water and other fluids. A normal argillite or shale will be progressively metamorphosed to phyllite and schist. Some minerals are stable under higher confining pressures, as under hydrostatic pressure; others retain stability under conditions of directed pressures or stress.

Metamorphism may have considerable areal extent. Progressive sequences of metamorphic grades can be recognized in rocks as they approach centers of higher temperature such as igneous intrusions; this is known as regional metamorphism, and the metamorphic rocks are said to lie in an aureole about the intrusion. Schists tend to change through chlorite schist, and through schists having biotite, garnet, staurolite, cyanite, andalusite, and sillimanite, minerals produced as successively higher temperatures were attained. As conditions of stress and rising temperature are commonly associated with deformation and depth, metamorphic rocks are prevalent in the past orogenic or mountain-making belts, particularly in the "roots" having great intrusions and sources of high temperatures. Many of the oldest rocks have been subjected to metamorphism, but conditions producing alteration have not been restricted to the oldest rocks. In addition to the products of regional metamorphism, there are local contact metamorphic rocks, such as those formed by the rise in temperature and escaping vapors at the contact of dikes and sills with their wall rocks.

Aside from marbles, formed of crystalline calcite by alteration of limestones, and quartzites, produced by the metamorphism of quartz sandstone, the common metamorphic rocks are characterized by foliation, the breaking along closely spaced partings. Argillaceous rocks under stress develop platy rock cleavage and are termed slate. Schists are composed of aggregates of minerals that break along the mineral cleavage, as in mica schist and hornblende schist. Gneiss is marked by minerals so arranged as to give a banded or layered appearance, either by the reorganization of minerals originally distributed in sedimentary layers, or spread in layers during rock flow as in some igneous rocks. Among the less common metamorphic rocks, serpentine is produced in the alteration of certain basic igneous rocks, and hornfels results when argillaceous rock is heated and altered at intrusive contacts. See also GEOLOGY—*Petrography and Petrology;* MARBLE; MINERALOGY; ROCKS—*Metamorphic Rocks;* SCHIST; SLATE.

Consult Harker, Alfred, *Metamorphism* (New York 1934); Turner, Francis J., and Verhoogen, Jean, *Igneous and Metamorphic Petrology* (New York 1951).

MARSHALL KAY,
Professor of Geology, Columbia University.

METAMORPHOSES, by Apuleius. See GOLDEN ASS, THE.

METAMORPHOSES, mĕt'à-môr'fô-sēz (TRANSFORMATIONS), a poem by Ovid (q.v.), published in Rome, 8 A.D., on the eve of the poet's exile. He later claimed to have destroyed his own copy, but the text was recovered from transcripts his friends had previously made.

The poem is in 15 books, in hexameter. For his material Ovid drew upon the stock of Greek and Roman legends of miraculous transformations, from the beginning of things, when Chaos was transformed into Cosmos, on down to his own day, when popular superstition identified as Julius Caesar the comet which had appeared after his death. (To Ovid, as to his modern readers, such tales were merely poetic fancies.) Among some 250 legends which he included, perhaps the most famous are those of Deucalion and Pyrrha, Daphne, Phaethon, Cadmus, Semele, Echo, Narcissus, Pyramus and Thisbe, Ino, Perseus and Andromeda, Niobe, Procne and Philomela, Medea, Theseus, Scylla, Daedalus and Icarus, Philemon and Baucis, Hercules, Orpheus, Adonis, and Thetis. In Ovid's handling, the transformations are little more than devices for rounding off each story and supplying an end link for the next. Though the poet himself tells most of the tales, he gives variety by such devices as having Orpheus tell one group, and the daughters of Minyas another.

Ovid closed the poem with a firm conviction that it had made his name immortal. He was right, not only for himself but for the stories he used. For nearly 2,000 years the *Metamorphoses* have been an inexhaustible source of material for poets, dramatists, and painters. Though many of the tales were also told by other Greek and Roman poets, it is Ovid's recensions of them that have been most often used in modern literatures.

DeLANCEY FERGUSON.

METAMORPHOSIS, mĕt'à-môr'fô-sĭs, the occurrence during a short period of postembryonic life of marked changes in the form of an animal. One familiar example of metamorphosis is the transformation of the tadpole into the frog, a second is the transformation of the caterpillar into the butterfly.

Metamorphosis is not confined to these two well-known examples; it has evolved independently in a number of evolutionary lines. One selective advantage of metamorphosis is that it allows the individual animal to exploit two dissimilar environments during its lifetime. The caterpillar, for example, usually lives by eating leaves and is well adapted for creeping about on its food plant. After metamorphosis the same animal has become a nectar-feeding butterfly, whose wings can carry it over long distances.

One of the best-studied examples of metamorphosis is the transformation of the tadpole into the frog. The tadpole is a strictly aquatic animal, with gills and a swimming tail. The tadpole has numerous small, horny teeth and a long, coiled intestine which equip it for eating and digesting plants and dead animals. The metamorphosis into the frog takes about 40 days, and during this period almost every organ is profoundly changed. The tail and gills are reabsorbed, legs appear and grow out, the eyes enlarge, the skeleton is altered, the teeth are lost and the mouth widens, and the intestine becomes short and broad. The outcome of these changes is the frog, an animal equipped for life as an amphibious feeder on living animals.

The onset of metamorphosis in the amphibia is triggered by the release of hormone from the tadpole's thyroid gland. A precocious metamorphosis can be elicited by putting a young tadpole into a solution containing thyroid hormone.

Many insects, such as the roach, gradually change in body form with each molt and these changes are called an incomplete metamorphosis.

But the true, or complete, metamorphosis of insects involves far more dramatic changes in form. The egg hatches out a larva, which is usually a crawling or burrowing, wormlike creature. The larva feeds and increases in size; its growth is punctuated by a series of molts. Within the larva there are already signs of the adult insect to come, for there are discrete pockets of cells—the imaginal discs—which will later form parts of the adult.

Toward the end of the last larval stage, the larva may spin a cocoon or bury itself in the ground. Then some of the larval tissues are completely broken down, while other larval tissues begin to be remodeled into adult organs. At the same time the imaginal discs begin to grow at a rapid rate, and start to form adult organs such as the wings and the compound eyes. The transition to the adult is interrupted by the molt of the larva into the pupa, which is a nonfeeding sessile stage intermediate between larva and adult. Within the pupa the development of the adult continues, and when the pupal skin is molted the adult, or imago, emerges.

During the larval life the development of the imaginal disc is held back by a hormone secreted by the corpora allata, a pair of small endocrine organs in the head. A premature metamorphosis may be obtained by surgically removing the corpora allata from a young larva.

Some of the parasitic insects have two distinct types of larvae and are therefore said to have a hypermetamorphosis. The first larva is an active crawler which sets out and burrows into the host. The next larval stage is an almost inert endoparasite. The remainder of the life history follows as described for complete metamorphosis.

In a number of the invertebrate phyla the egg develops into a motile larva which is quite unlike the parent. The second larva undergoes a metamorphosis into the adult forms. See also INSECTS—*Metamorphosis*.

W. G. VAN DER KLOOT,
Associate Professor of Zoology, Cornell University.

METAPHOR, mĕt'à-fēr, -fôr, in rhetoric, a figure of speech that, presupposing a similarity of two or more things, denotes one of them by terms properly or literally signifying the other, as if they were identical. The first two lines of Shakespeare's Sonnet 2 contain several words used metaphorically:

When forty winters shall besiege thy brow
And dig deep trenches in thy beauty's field . . .

Here, for example, the word "trenches" means wrinkles of age, and it suggests a similarity between wrinkles and ditches dug by besieging soldiers.

The similarity presupposed by a metaphor may be viewed simply as a common attribute of two or more things. "He is only a loud talker, an empty vessel" implies the disappointing difference between appearance and reality which one en-

counters in both an empty vessel and a talker who has nothing worthwhile to say. However, the presupposed similarity may also be viewed as a proportion of four or more terms. In "His biting words wounded me deeply" the implied proportion is "His words were to my sensibilities as teeth are to tender flesh."

Metaphors are used by speakers and writers, spontaneously or artfully, to make their meaning clear or forceful, to arouse emotion and inculcate attitudes, or to give pleasure. Many common expressions, originally metaphorical, have lost their figurative force and are used as if their meaning were purely literal, for example, "to sow dissension." See also SIMILE.

METAPHOSPHORIC ACID. See PHOSPHORIC ACID.

METAPHYSICAL POETS. See ENGLISH LITERATURE—*2. Renaissance Literature: 1500–1660* (The 17th Century: to 1660).

METAPHYSICS, mĕt'à-fĭz'ĭks, the division of philosophy which deals with first principles and the nature of reality. During its long development philosophy has gradually divided into four major areas of speculative thought. Each of the four is concerned with stating valid, intelligible opinions about problems of concern to all mankind. First, there is the field of ethics and morals. The purpose of this branch of philosophy is to expound the right standards for individual and group conduct. Ethics defines the *summum bonum,* or highest good; and it teaches man a proper sense of relative values. Second, there is aesthetics, which deals with standards whereby the beautiful and the ugly may be differentiated in works of art. Third, there is epistemology, or the theory of knowledge. This branch of philosophy seeks to answer the question, How can we be certain when we possess valid knowledge? The fourth branch, though not in order of its historical emergence, is metaphysics.

The term metaphysics has a broad and ambiguous connotation in the history of philosophy. Its importance relative to other divisions of philosophy has often been questioned. How to differentiate metaphysics from theology is a problem upon which much has been written. Aristotle, who may be called the Father of Metaphysics, seems to have regarded metaphysics and theology as similar inquiries. Both fields deal with knowledge about the nature of reality. Whereas theology has now come to denote the type of reasoning whereby faith is justified to human intelligence, metaphysics has acquired a broader scope. It is not confined to matters of fundamental truths about religion. Metaphysics, on the contrary, has a secular reference.

It is concerned with the manner in which we discriminate the real from what may be nothing but subjective or illusory experiences. For instance, the concert-goer listens to musical tones in various combinations. In the physics laboratory these tones are identified as sound waves of various types. The metaphysician is interested in determining whether the tones or the sound waves are the true reality. Through sensory experience and reflection man develops concepts about the world in which he lives. Various sciences, however, deal with the matter in entirely different ways. They are concerned with the molecular structures of what is present to sense, for example; and hence they describe reality in terms quite unlike those used to denote subjective impressions. The metaphysician seeks to reconcile this difference. Anyone who asks whether the world is actually what it appears to him to be, or whether his sensory impressions and reflections are distortions of reality, is a metaphysician. Furthermore, both layman and philosopher may wonder about the relative importance of material objects, of personality, of social living, and of religious convictions. This perplexity is another example of the type of speculative thought which is referred to as metaphysical.

Metaphysics is not necessarily an abstruse field of philosophy, interesting to none but the savant. It may be of immediate concern to everyone. For instance, the human being may be studied from the standpoint of histology, the science which describes the characteristics of tissues. Biochemists and physiologists add to the knowledge of human beings and their behavior and its organic substrate. Evolutionists and comparative anatomists furnish data of utmost importance for a valid knowledge of man. Is the human being an elaborate, complex mechanism evolved from lower forms of life? Does this reductive analysis so essential in the natural sciences present a valid understanding of the nature of human beings? These are metaphysical questions. They are familiarly known as the "nothing-but" and the "more-than" hypotheses about personality and its ultimate nature.[1] The metaphysician considers such problems in an objective, logical manner. He seeks to find answers that commend themselves to reason and that possess logical coherence with all other first principles about the nature of reality.

According to tradition, the term *metaphysics* was first used in connection with a complete edition of all the writings of Aristotle. Andronicus, a philosopher-teacher who lived on the Island of Rhodes, compiled Aristotle's essays on natural sciences, political theory, psychology, physics, and other subjects. Next to the volume dealing with physics, Andronicus (c.70 B.C.) placed a collection of essays on theology, first principles, the nature of reality, and cognate topics. He designated this volume "after physics" (Gr. *meta ta phusika*). The term alludes to nothing except the sequential position of the volume in a complete edition of Aristotle's essays. This point is of importance in an understanding of what is the legitimate field of metaphysics. Gradually, however, the term designated "after thoughts" of profound importance, not mere addenda. Not until the *Kritik der reinen Vernunft* was published by Kant in 1781 did the term begin to possess any precise denotation.

Misled by the connotations of *meta,* some writers have assumed that metaphysics deals with supranormal phenomena. Occult knowledge, abstruse opinions and concepts, and speculative thought about matters entirely remote from daily life are sometimes erroneously referred to as metaphysics. Neither by the etymology of the term nor by the writings of the early philosophers is this usage justified. Andronicus of Rhodes did not coin the term to denote those fields of knowledge which are beyond or above the techniques of reflective thinking. The early Greek philosophers, in fact, were certain that by the normal processes of reflection they could distinguish between the real and the apparent. The questions they raised in ancient times have repeatedly perplexed thoughtful men and women throughout the ages. These questions, not at all remote from the concerns of daily life, are of practical moment. The answers have a direct bearing upon human welfare.

To illustrate the scope of metaphysics, three major issues may be reviewed briefly. In each instance the metaphysicians have sought for intelligible answers through logical, coherent speculations. It is interesting to observe that no two metaphysicians have ever fully agreed about the valid solution of these issues. The divergence of opinions expounded by erudite philosophers throughout the centuries is one of the most challenging aspects of the history of thought. Comparisons of the great systems of metaphysics and a search for connective threads in the long history of philosophy make the study of interest to those students who have aptitude for speculative inquiry.

The Problem of the-One-and-the-Many.— The first illustrative problem is an intrusive, stimulating issue. Apparently, or actually, we live in a world which consists of a diversity of forms. Through our senses we detect a multiplicity of phenomena. Tones, noises, colors, odors, tastes, organic sensations of hunger—these are but a few of our varied and infinite experiences in everyday life. Is all human knowledge based upon, and basically limited to, sensory experience? That is a metaphysical question to which many philosophers have directed their inquiries.[2]

To go further, however, we may ponder upon a disparity between the world as we experience it and the world as it actually may exist. In the sciences, for instance, we strive to master the tenable reflections of empirical investigators. They describe reality in such terms as molecules, sound waves, gaseous particles, chemical elements, forces, and the like. Variables are isolated for experimental analysis. Knowledge seems to have a fragmented quality, each science dealing with a separate aspect of the world. The metaphysician asks whether this multiplicity and fragmentation indicates that reality consists of an infinite plurality of entities or whether for the convenience of scientific inquiry only a method of reductive analysis has been employed. Is there a basic, unifying reality behind the apparent multiplicity of phenomena and opinions? Is there a basic diversity in the world of nature and man?

Thales (c.600 B.C.) was the first to raise this issue in Occidental philosophy. He conjectured that all things arose from water, are basically composed of it, and eventually return to it. There is unity behind the apparent diversity. Reality is quite different from sensory experience, and mere appearance is deceptive and illusory. Pythagoras (c.530 B.C.) agreed that there is a basic oneness to reality and that the seeming multiplicity of phenomena is fallacious. He, however, found the essential unity in mathematical relationships. The basic realities are numbers, and all things are expressions of numerical relationships. Not so, taught Heraclitus (c.500 B.C.). Reality consists of diversities and of changes. There is no single unifying principle. Living things and inanimate objects alike are infinitely different and in eternal change.

The opinions of Thomas Hobbes (1588–1679)

---

[1] Cason, Helsey, "The Scientific Nature of Psychology," *Journal of Philosophy*, Vol. 31, p. 659 (1934).

[2] Precisely speaking, the question is an epistemological one, though past and current usages of "metaphysical" justify a wide connotation for the term.

illustrate the recurrence of this issue in the speculations of later philosophers. All knowledge, Hobbes believes, is dependent upon sensory experience. Through the processes of association it may become organized into coherent patterns, but these are merely chance occurrences effected by mechanical factors. Self-interest leads people to give up individual rights and prerogatives and submit to regulation by the state. Otherwise they would inevitably destroy one another. A pseudo-oneness—in the state imposed by the monarch—is a stern necessity, not a natural reality. Gottfried Wilhelm von Leibnitz (1632–1677) was a pluralist of quite a different persuasion. Reality, he wrote, consists of an infinite number of monads. They form a graduated series from the lowest to the highest. No two monads are alike. Baruch Spinoza (1632–1677), however, was impressed by the unity of reality. God is the sole reality. All else derives its substance from Him. Diversity is merely an illusion.

This illustrative problem directs attention to three aspects of metaphysics. First, and perhaps most intrusive, is the existence of a diversity of opinions. Even those metaphysicians who argued eloquently for the existence of an essential oneness must have been distressed by the fact that none but their most ardent and unreflective disciples completely agreed with them. Secondly, metaphysics deals with insistent problems, not with issues artificially created for the purpose of engaging in intellectual gymnastics. Whether ultimate reality is composed of a variety of entities, or whether there is an order and a unity in the world, is a very real and challenging issue. Thirdly, the issues of metaphysics are not the sole province of sophisticated philosophers. Everyone may at times assume the role of the metaphysician and think deeply about the nature and the meaning of the world. One may conjecture that there is unity (monism); a duality of mind and body, of matter and soul (dualism); or a plurality of entities (pluralism). The brilliant philosophers may employ erudite vocabularies filled with technical words, but their quest is basically the same as that of anyone who uses the familiar language of daily life.

The Materialistic-Idealistic Dilemma.—Another interesting metaphysical problem relates to the essential nature of reality. Does the world ultimately consist of matter and do the laws of mechanics suffice to account for everything? Democritus (c.400 B.C.) was convinced that basic reality consists of minute particles which he called atoms. Mechanical rearrangements of these atoms account for all events, even for thought. Purpose, relative values, and creative intelligence are illusory inferences. The natural sciences point the way to valid knowledge of reality. Indestructible, changeless, permanent elements lie at the basis of all reality. Atoms have material existence, so Democritus taught. They are small bits of matter, which might be thought of as the building stones of the universe. Atoms and the spaces between them compose the whole of reality, including the mind of man. The universe was created, and it is sustained, by the motions among atoms. All things may be accounted for in materialistic terms. Other views of reality, no matter how much they might satisfy the wish to believe, have no metaphysical justification, so Democritus maintained.

Plato (427–347 B.C.) took a position diametrically opposed to materialism. Both Democritus and Plato agreed that man's highest quest is for an intelligible, reasonable certainty about reality. They differed about the conclusions to which their metaphysical inquiries led them. Ideas, not material particles, are the ultimate realities which Plato discovered. Ideas are more than mere forms in the minds of thinkers, or even in the mind of God. They have a substantive form, and they constitute all that reality is. Ideas do not exist in a disordered, chaotic, evanescent fashion. On the contrary, they are the permanent realities in the universe, and they are organized into a coherent unity governed by intelligent purpose. Senses, therefore, give nothing but a crude, distorted view of what the nature of the universe actually is. Knowledge derived from sensation is inferior; that coming from reflection is a little better, though still imperfect; that coming from the apprehension of pre-existent ideas is the only genuine and valid wisdom. This wisdom negates the inferior knowledge leading to materialism. It inevitably leads the metaphysician to the point of view of idealism.

The foregoing brief account indicates three more characteristics of metaphysics. First, the history of philosophy may be studied as a centuries-old rivalry between the materialists and the idealists. The issue remains in contemporary metaphysics without a final solution. Secondly, it shows how many of the problems of metaphysics are closely related to cherished beliefs. It would be disquieting, to say the least, for a devoutly religious person to consider seriously the cogent arguments for a materialistic view of life. Equally disquieting would it be for a metaphysician to be denied an opportunity to speculate upon the materialism-idealism problem. No matter what his cherished hopes might be as to the final answer, he would weigh all phases of the problem and reach the conclusions warranted by logic. He might cite as Scriptural justification of his course of action that we must "prove all things and hold fast to that which is good." Thirdly, speculations about such an issue as this are even-tempered, objective, impartial, and coherent in metaphysics. Even when the issues bear upon personal, social, or religious values, the qualified metaphysician does not become emotional. In communicating his ultimate views, he takes the role of the expositor. To the theologian are often assigned those matters dealing with spiritual realities, the metaphysician preferring not to depart, or be tempted to depart, from his role as an impartial, objective reasoner.

The Problem of the Place of Metaphysics in Philosophy.—Paradoxically, a metaphysical debate has arisen over the issue of whether metaphysics has any real place in the broad field of philosophy. Too much zeal for speculative thinking, said the Sophists, unfits a man for the practical duties of life. Since philosophers have always dissented from one another in expounding their views about the ultimate nature of reality, metaphysics is a fruitless quest. It raises nothing but artificial problems and discovers no answers whatsoever. No problem can ever be solved once and for all. Consequently, so the Sophists believed, there are no absolutes or ultimates. Euthydemus, Callicles, and Thrasymachus—the radical young Sophists who appear in Plato's *Dialogues*—were derisive about the value of metaphysics.

David Hume (1711–1776) taught that all knowledge arises in sensory experience. We can never know anything except our impressions, and there is no way whatsoever of determining whether they are valid or not. The concept of cause-effect relationships is obviously a fallacious, untenable one. Impressions merely follow one another, and we are unjustified in attributing a causal relationship among them. Metaphysics, therefore, is a quest for knowledge that does not exist. It is fruitless, time-consuming, and trivial. We know nothing but our own past and present experiences or impressions. As for the future or for a reality lying behind them, we may conjecture in vain. The element of probability is so great that speculative thinking is a vain pursuit. Essentially, John Dewey (1859–1952) agrees that metaphysics is a useless, artificial branch of philosophy. An evolutionist, Dewey found no permanent, systematized ultimate reality. On the contrary, there are growth, change, impermanence, and development in the world. Therefore, speculation about origins, ends, purposes, and meanings are pointless. We should think of reality as something which is in the process of being made. According to Dewey, it should be pointed out, we may be able to guide the changes toward desirable, though ever-receding, outcomes. The means, however, will not be revealed by metaphysicians, so Dewey believed. Pragmatic justifications are our sole guide. With such views August Comte (1798–1857) had been in agreement long before. In fact, his six-volume work entitled *Cours de philosophie positive* (1830–1842) is, in a sense, a declaration of independence from metaphysics. In the United States one of the principal contemporary advocates of the view that philosophy should deal with issues far more important than metaphysical problems is Rudolf Carnap, of the University of California.

Lest these views be thought too modern and secular, let it be noted that Immanuel Kant (1724–1804) also reached the conclusion that metaphysics deals with non-existent problems. In mathematics and physics we may be able to arrive at a type of valid knowledge about ultimate reality. Such knowledge is universally true. The metaphysicians overlook the fact, so Kant held, that this knowledge pertains to nothing but the forms and the relationships of observed or hypothesized data. We are unable to transcend our experience. We can never know the thing-as-in-itself-it-really-is. They must exist, for otherwise we could not experience them. There is no basis for skepticism about the existence of objective realities. Neither is there any doubt about human inability to know what they actually are. Metaphysics, so Kant wrote in the second edition of his *Critique,* consists of nothing but fallacious opinions, confusions of perceptual reactions with reasoned thought, and incompatible views. The phenomenal world which metaphysicians vainly try to reconcile with the noumenal world is known through experience. Reality, however, can never be known for what it actually is. Concepts valid in the sensory-perceptual realm are completely unrelated to the transcendental principles of the mind. The real (noumenal) and the apparent (phenomenal) are forever irreconcilable.

This issue directs attention to a number of matters which are of concern to the metaphysicians. First, there is the problem of the impossibility or the certainty of valid knowledge about anything. In denying to metaphysics a place among the divisions of philosophy, Kant actually brought into focus a problem which others have considered at great length. Other philosophers have considered such a problem as that of differentiating the real from the illusory to be the very essence of metaphysics. Secondly, this issue shows how carefully the qualified philosopher defines his terms and strives to present coherent, tenable views. Some terms have what the semanticist would call "intensional meaning." In the graphic language of Hayakawa, the meaning "runs around in the head." Other terms have "extensional meaning." We may "point with the finger at what we designate." In metaphysics itself—man's most rigorous attempt to think clearly about first principles—even the greatest thinkers may shift from intensional to extensional terms. Thereby, they confuse the student, and disagree with one another. Thirdly, metaphysics cannot be dismissed as a major concern of speculative thinkers. Not even the eminent Immanuel Kant succeeded in removing metaphysics from philosophy. The intrusive and persisting issues which, by convention, have been assigned to metaphysics remain to this day as challenges for clear, reasoned thought. See also LOGIC; PHILOSOPHY.

Bibliography.—Marvin, W. T., *A First Book in Metaphysics* (New York 1912); Thilly, Frank, *History of Philosophy* (New York 1914); Gotshalk, D. W., *Metaphysics in Modern Times* (New York 1940); Emmet, D. M., *Nature of Metaphysical Thinking* (London 1945); Lazerowitz, M., *The Structure of Metaphysics* (New York 1955); Bochenski, I. M., *Contemporary European Philosophy* (Berkeley, Calif., 1956).

PHILIP L. HARRIMAN,
Bucknell University.

METAPONTUM, mĕ-tà-pŏn′tŭm, ancient city, Italy, located in what is now Puglia, between the mouths of the Basento and Bradano rivers, on the Gulf of Taranto. It was settled by Greeks in the 6th century B.C. The Greek philosopher Pythagoras taught here after being expelled from Crotona. Metapontum passed to the Romans after 275 B.C., but subsequently revolted to Hannibal of Carthage and was ruined.

METASEQUOIA GLYPTOSTRO-BOIDES, mĕ-tà-sĕ-kwoi′ȧ glĭp-tô-strô-boi′dēz, or **DAWN REDWOOD,** a tree native only to protected moist valleys in central China. It was first described in 1941 from Japanese and Korean fossils, but more widespread Northern Hemisphere fossils have since been identified. Living trees were found in China in 1945 and 1946, and were scientifically described in 1948—hence the species is actually a "living fossil." Classified in the family Taxodiaceae, with redwood and bald cypress, this conifer drops its needles in autumn. It is moderately hardy, reproduces by seeds and cuttings, and is now grown in cultivation.

METASOMATISM. See ROCKS.—*Metamorphic Rocks* (Classification).

METASTASIO, mä′tä-stä-zyȯ (originally PIETRO ANTONIO DOMENICO BONAVENTURA TRAPASSI), Italian poet and librettist: b. Rome, Italy, Jan. 3, 1698; d. Vienna, Austria, April 12, 1782. He was apprenticed to a goldsmith, but his precocious talent for poetry attracted the notice of the jurist and critic Gian Vicenzo Gravina, who adopted him, hellenized his name into Metastasio, and gave him a strict classical education. From Gravina he inherited a considerable estate in 1718, but it was soon spent, and he began the study of law under an attorney at Naples. Meanwhile he had taken minor clerical orders and brought out his first collection of verse, *Poesie di P. Metastasio* (1717), which included the *Giustino,* a tragedy composed when the author was only 14.

In Naples, Metastasio gained the patronage of Anna Francesca Pinelli di Sangro, for whom, on the occasion of her marriage to Antonio Pignatelli, marchese di Belmonte, in 1720, he composed an epithalamium, or wedding song. He soon gained other helpful friends, notably the prima donna Marianna Benti Bulgarelli, called La Romanina, who took him into her household, introduced him to the foremost composers and musicians of the day, made him study music and singing, and encouraged him to compose his first musical drama, or melodrama, *Didone abbandonata* (1723).

This and subsequent melodramas by Metastasio, set to music by celebrated composers, were received with acclaim. After 1730 he resided in Vienna as court poet to the Holy Roman emperor Charles VI and his daughter Maria Theresa. In Vienna, between 1730 and 1740, he composed his best melodramas, notably *Adriano in Siria* (1731), *Issipile* (1731), *Demetrio* (1732), *L'Olimpiade* (1733), *Demofoonte* (1733), *La Clemenza di Tito* (1734), *Achille in Sciro* (1736), *Temistocle* (1736), and *Zenobia* (1740).

His writings were celebrated for their ease and grace and for their suitability to the Italian vocal style that was predominant in 18th century musical drama and opera. After his death his works were neglected because the operatic style for which they were written gave way to a more orchestral manner originated and developed by German composers. Metastasio's works, including, in addition to his librettos, several critical works and much lyric verse, were edited in four volumes by Bruno Brunelli (Milan 1947–1954).

Consult Burney, Charles, *Life and Letters of Metastasio*, 3 vols. (London 1796); Russo, Luigi, . . . *Metastasio* (Bari 1921); Manganella, Renato (pseudonym Lucio d'Ambra), . . . *L'abate nei giardini di Vienna*. . . . (Bologna 1940).

METATARSUS. See Foot.

METATE, mȧ-tä′tä, a stone with a concave surface, used as a mortar for grinding grains or other substances by Indians of the southwestern United States and Latin America. See also Mortar.

METAURO, mȧ-tou′rō (ancient Metaurus), river, Italy, rising from headstreams in the Appenines, near Sansepolcro, and emptying into the Adriatic Sea near Fano. Its course, generally northeast, is 69 miles long. Near its banks, in 207 B.C., the Roman consuls Gaius Claudius Nero and Marcus Livius Salinator defeated and killed the Carthaginian general Hasdrubal.

METAXAS, mĕ-täk′sȧs, Gr. mĕ-tä-ksäs′, **Ioannis,** Greek army officer and dictator: b. Ithaca, Greece, April 12, 1871; d. Athens, Jan. 29, 1941. He received a military education in Greece and Germany, was assistant chief of staff in the Balkan War (1912–1913), and in 1915 became chief military adviser to King Constantine, with whom he shared pro-German sympathies in World War I. Constantine was exiled by a pro-Allied faction in Greece in 1917, and Metaxas was interned by French authorities (1917–1920). Subsequently he was a supporter of George II, pretender to the throne of Greece after the establishment of a republic in 1923–1924. George II was restored in 1935, and Metaxas was appointed to important cabinet posts, becoming war minister, foreign minister, and (in 1936) prime minister.

In August 1936, pleading civil unrest as his reason, he assumed dictatorial power and reorganized the still nominally monarchical government on Fascist lines.

Metaxas' continuing pro-German sympathies were reflected in his domestic and foreign policies, but when Italy attempted encroachments on Greek independence in October 1940, he led his country into war against Italy and Germany. A fortified line of defense, built in east Macedonia under his direction and named for him, was overrun by German troops in April 1941; and his regime, after surviving him for three months, was ended by the German occupation of Greece.

METAYER, mĕ-tā′yẽr, Fr. mȧ-tĕ-yā′, a name given in France to a tenant farmer who annually shares with his landlord the produce of his farm. *Metayage,* or share-cropping, is common in Europe and the southern United States. See also Cotton.—*Economic Problems* (Farm Tenancy).

METCALF, mĕt′kȧf, **Victor Howard,** American lawyer and statesman: b. Utica, N. Y., Oct. 10, 1853; d. Oakland, Cal., Feb. 20, 1936. He graduated from Yale in 1872 and from the Yale law school in 1876, and was an attorney in Utica between 1877 and 1879. He practiced in Oakland after 1879, and represented the third congressional district of California in Congress between 1899 and 1904. He was Secretary of Commerce and Labor (July 1904–December 1906) and Secretary of the Navy (December 1906–December 1908) in the cabinets of President Theodore Roosevelt.

METCALF, Willard Leroy, American landscape and figure painter: b. Lowell, Mass., July 1, 1853; d. New York, N. Y., March 9, 1925. He was an apprentice in the studio of George L. Brown, a Boston landscape artist, in 1876–1877, meanwhile studying at Lowell Institute, the Massachusetts Normal Art School, and the Boston Art Museum School. In 1881–1882 he visited the southwestern United States to collect specimens of birds and do exploration work for the Smithsonian Institution. Subsequently he was a pupil of Gustave Rodolphe Boulanger and Jules Joseph Lefebvre at the Académie Julien, Paris.

Metcalf was celebrated for his paintings of Vermont and New Hampshire landscapes. His style was realistic, and particularly suited to rendering delicate colors and textures. He was a member of Ten American Artists, the National Institute of Arts and Letters, and the American Society of Water Color Painters. His work is represented in numerous American art museums, including the Boston Museum of Fine Arts, the Chicago Art Institute, and the Corcoran Art Gallery, Washington, D.C.

METCALF, William, American metallurgist and steel manufacturer: b. Pittsburgh, Pa., Sept. 3, 1838; d. there, Dec. 5, 1909. He graduated from Rensselaer Polytechnic Institute in 1858 and subsequently became general superintendent of the Fort Pitt Foundry, Pittsburgh. Here he pioneered in the production of large castings and heavy machinery, supplying numerous big guns to the United States in the Civil War. Afterward he was managing director of the Crescent Steel Works; while serving in that capacity he specialized in the manufacture of fine crucible steels. After 1897 he was executive head of the Braeburn Steel Company. He was president of the

American Institute of Mining Engineers in 1881 and of the American Society of Civil Engineers in 1893. He published *Steel—A Manual for Steel-Users* (1896).

METCALFE, SIR **Charles Theophilus,** 1ST BARON, English Indian and colonial administrator: b. Calcutta, Jan. 30, 1785; d. Malshanger, near Basingstoke, Hampshire, England, Sept. 5, 1846. The son of a major in the Bengal Army and educated at Eton, the 15-year old boy sailed back to India in 1800, a writer in the East India Company's service. Four years later, he became political assistant to General Lake during the Mahratta war. Several increasingly important appointments followed. In 1822 he succeeded his brother in the baronetcy, and five years later obtained a seat on the supreme council. First governor of the new presidency of Agra, in 1835 he succeeded Lord Bentinck as provisional governor general of India. Resigning in 1838, he was appointed governor of Jamaica. Illness compelled his return to England in 1842, but the following year he went to Canada as governor general. A malignant disease compelled his retirement in 1845 when he was awarded a barony for distinguished service.

METCALFE, Samuel L., American physician and scientist: b. near Winchester, Va., 1798; d. 1856. In 1823 he was graduated in the medical department of Transylvania University; established a medical practice at New Albany, Ind., and visited England in 1831. Upon his return to his native country, he made a geological tour in Tennessee, North Carolina and Virginia. Later he settled in New York where he took up scientific work. He published *Narratives of Indian Warfare in the West* (1821); *A New Theory of Terrestrial Magnetism* (1833); *Caloric: Its Mechanical, Chemical and Vital Agencies in the Phenomena of Nature,* 2 vols., 1843 (2d ed., 1859).

METCHNIKOFF, Élie, Russian bacteriologist: b. Kharkov, Russia, May 15, 1845; d. Paris, France, July 15, 1916. Following his education at Kharkov, Metchnikoff studied at Giessen and Munich, and in 1870 he was appointed professor of zoology at Odessa. He held this post until 1882, when he resigned to devote himself to private researches into the anatomy of invertebrates. It was while working at lowly organized forms of life such as sponges that he first made the observations which constituted the basis of all his subsequent work. In 1888 he had attracted the notice of Louis Pasteur, the founder of the famous Pasteur Institute for the treatment of rabies, in Paris, and he was invited to become one of Pasteur's associates. In 1895 he succeeded as the director of the institute, a post which he held to the time of his death. In his study of longevity, Metchnikoff came to the belief that it should not be uncommon for persons to live to the age of 150 years. He found every indication that the human mechanism was calculated to last far longer than it actually does. His researches showed among other things that animals which had no large intestines lived to an advanced age, particularly birds, which preserve their youthful agility and spryness to the end of their long span. In the case of human beings, he found that even among those whose sufferings were terrible, there were few who wanted to be put out of their agony by death. They all wanted to live. If the

normal specific longevity were attained by human beings, he believed that old and not degenerate individuals would lose the instinct for life and acquire an instinct for death and that as they had fulfilled the normal cycle of life, they would accept death with the same relieved acquiescence as they now accept sleep. On his seventieth birthday, in 1915, Professor Metchnikoff received a present of a golden book, forming a unique record of the latest scientific researches, signed by men of science of the day. Although there was much controversy in the scientific world regarding his original ideas, he was fully recognized as one of the most eminent bacteriologists. In 1908 the Nobel Prize for medical research was divided between the late Dr. Paul Ehrlich, of Berlin, and Professor Metchnikoff. The $20,000 which he thus received he devoted entirely to the furtherance of his scientific researches. Personally he was not well off, and throughout his long life sacrificed all but the plainest living necessities to the cause of science. He was the author of a number of books including *Lectures on the Comparative Pathology of Inflammation* (London 1893); *Immunity in Infective Diseases* (New York 1905); *Etude sur la nature humaine; essai de philosophie optimiste* (1903). English translations of his lectures are *The New Hygiene* (Chicago 1907); *The Nature of Man* (New York 1910). He edited, with Sacquépée and others, *Médicaments microbiens* (1909). Consult *Annales de l'Institut Pasteur* (Paris), and Slosson, E. E., *Major Prophets of Today* (Boston 1914).

METELLA, Caecilia, daughter of Metellus Creticus and wife of Crassus the Younger. Her tomb on the Appian Way about 2 kilometers from Rome is one of the best-known surviving monuments of the Augustan age. It is a circular structure of 65-foot diameter on a square base. A frieze of garlands and bucranes circles the upper part. During the 13th century the tomb was incorporated in a fortress which three centuries later Pope Sixtus V (1521–1590) tore down to bring it again into full view.

METELLI, mĕ-tĕl′ĭ, a Roman family of the *gens Caecilia.* QUINTUS CAECILIUS METELLUS MACEDONICUS defeated the Achaeans, took Thebes and invaded Macedonia, and received a triumph 146 B.C. QUINTUS CAECILIUS METELLUS NUMIDICUS rendered himself illustrious by his successes against Jugurtha, the Numidian king. He took, in this expedition, the celebrated Marius (q.v.) as his lieutenant; was soon recalled to Rome, and accused of extortion and ill-management, but was acquitted of these charges. He celebrated a triumph at Rome 107 B.C. His son, QUINTUS CAECILIUS METELLUS received the surname of PIUS on account of the love which he displayed for his father when he besought the people to recall him from banishment in 99 B.C. In 83 B.C. he joined Sulla, with whom, three years later, he was united in the consulship. QUINTUS CAECILIUS METELLUS CRETICUS conquered Crete, and reduced it to a Roman province in 67 B.C. QUINTUS CAECILIUS METELLUS PIUS SCIPIO, the adopted son of Metellus Pius, in 52 B.C. was colleague in the consulship with Pompey, who had married his daughter Cornelia. Hence he exerted himself to the utmost to destroy the power of Caesar and strengthen that of his son-in-law. He commanded the center of Pompey's army at the Battle of Pharsalia, and thereafter fleeing to Africa was defeated by Caesar at Thapsus 46 B.C. He committed suicide.

METENIER, Oscar, French novelist and playwright: b. Sancoins, Cher, France, 1859; d. Saint Mandé, 1913. At the age of 24, Méténier became secretary to the police commissioner of Paris, a post he held for six years. In his novels and plays he made considerable use of the first-hand experience of underworld life gained during this period. Among his novels, which in general are quite daring, may be mentioned *La Chair* (1885); *Bohême bourgeoise* (1887); *Madame la Boule* (1889); *Barbe-Bleue* (1894). His plays include *En Famille* (1887); *La Casserole* (1889); and *Mademoiselle Fifi* (1896) adapted from de Maupassant's novel. In 1897, Méténier founded the Montmartre theater, Grand-Guignol, which soon became a theater specializing in sheer horror.

METEOR, mē'tē-ēr. The term is now restricted to cosmical bodies which enter the earth's atmosphere from without, but until a century or two ago it included other phenomena such as halos, auroras and rainbows. In some cases this makes it uncertain whether older writers were describing true meteoric bodies or their trains, or something purely ˙ atmospheric. The science of meteorology, which covers the phenomena of the earth's atmosphere, does not include the study of meteors, this latter being a branch of astronomy sometimes called meteoritics. As now used the term *meteor* denotes any type of body, coming from space, which makes its presence known by rapidly moving across the sky, its head generally starlike but sometimes with an apparent disk, and often leaving a luminous streak or train of light along its path. For descriptive purposes we have the terms *shooting star, fireball, bolide,* and *meteorite.* The first is a popular term denoting the average meteor; a fireball is a meteor at least as brilliant as the larger planets; a bolide is an exploding fireball; a meteorite is a fireball large enough to survive its fiery atmospheric journey and fall to the ground. All the other types are destroyed at considerable heights. The word *meteor* is used both in the general sense to cover all classes, and in the restricted sense to denote what used to be called a shooting star, that is, the fainter and far more numerous members of the family, such as may be seen on any night. The more recent term *meteoroid* covers all bodies mentioned before they enter our atmosphere.

It is difficult to separate the history of meteors and meteorites, so, while these latter are described in another article (see METEORITE), it is best to consider the development of ideas concerning their cosmical significance here. The fall of stones from the heavens is such an unexpected event, especially as it is usually accompanied by thunderous noises and often by smoke trains, that it must always have terrified primitive peoples, and later such events were doubtless recorded in official documents. Yet the oldest known record is that in the Book of Joshua, 10:11, where men fleeing from a battle are said to have been killed by "stones from heaven." We find that the Chinese, as early as 687 B.C., record the fall of meteorites and also describe fireballs and meteoric showers. Greek and Roman writers were less careful, some accounts being ambiguous. The oldest authentic one is of the large meteorite that fell in 467 B.C. at Aegospotami in Thrace. The oldest existing meteor-

ite, the exact date and place of fall of which are known, is the one that fell on Nov. 16, 1492, near Ensisheim, Alsace.

In the next three centuries, a good many meteorites fell in Europe, but the reaction against superstitions of the Middle Ages led the scientists of the day to such great skepticism that they refused to face facts, in some cases. Perhaps the most notorious instance refers to meteorites: in the 18th century the learned men of the day did not *believe* stones could fall from the skies, hence they affirmed they did not. Even the great French Académie des Sciences went on record denying that meteorites had an origin outside the atmosphere, despite accounts of falls by reliable witnesses, which were ridiculed, and the splendid pioneer work of Ernst F. F. Chladni about 1794. However, on April 26, 1803, a fall at L'Aigle in France, investigated by Jean B. Biot, finally convinced even the "philosophers," and the study of meteorites, as such, began. As for the more ordinary shooting stars, two German students, H. W. Brandes and J. F. Benzenberg, in 1798 carried out simultaneous observations from two stations some distance apart. Thus by the ordinary methods of triangulation, they were able to determine the approximate height at which meteors appeared and disappeared. Their average value for the points of disappearance was 98 kilometers. This proved they were far higher than clouds, but not at lunar or planetary distances. It should be mentioned that Sir Edmund Halley had calculated a fireball path in 1719, so the methods were well understood, but still scientists neglected meteors almost entirely, and we may truly say that meteoric astronomy was born on Nov. 13, 1833, when the great Leonid shower appeared over America.

The Leonids.—This shower is estimated to have furnished 200,000 meteors for a given station between midnight and dawn, numbers of them brilliant, and many leaving trains. The terror excited among the masses of the population was great, the superstitious fully expecting the end of the world was about to come. However, there were enough trained men who saw the phenomenon for several to detect that the meteors really had a radiant in the constellation Leo, that is, a point in the sky from which they seemed to shoot away as spokes from the hub of a wheel. It was quickly seen that this radiation was merely a perspective effect and that the meteors, before meeting the earth, were really moving in parallel paths. The position of the radiant fixes the direction in space from which the meteors come. As the radiant eventually was shown to be in the same position among the stars as seen from distant stations, this proved that the meteors came from space and did not originate in the atmosphere. From then on meteors have formed a definite branch of astronomy.

Professor Denison Olmsted of Yale University, New Haven, was the man who, at the time, made excellent observations on the Leonids and then concluded that what had occurred was due to the earth's encounter with a swarm of particles moving around the sun. John Locke, in America, in 1834 proved that the August meteors had a radiant in Perseus; and Lambert A. J. Quételet, of Belgium, in 1836 discovered from a study of older records that they appeared every August on about the same date. George Adolf Erman in 1839 developed a method for calculating the orbit of a meteor swarm; Sears C. Walker developed another in 1841; and it is stated that Palm H. L. Boguslawski had done so even earlier. Alexander C. Twining's work in 1862 pushed the knowledge of the Perseid orbit much further. But the truly great advances were made by Hubert A. Newton of Yale University and Giovanni V. Schiaparelli of Italy. The former in 1863 proved from a search of ancient annals that we had been meeting Leonid meteors in great showers at least back to 902 A.D., though the date then was October 12. He showed that this change of date was to be expected, as our calendar is based on the tropical year, whereas the meteors would follow the sidereal year. He gave a table showing there were great showers in the following years: 902, 931, 934, 1002, 1101, 1202, 1366, 1533, 1602, 1698, 1799, 1832, and 1833. From this he deduced a period for the stream of 33.25 years, and a shower was predicted for 1866 or 1867. (Since Newton's day, examination of Arabian, Chinese, Japanese, and Korean records have added showers in: 935, 967, 1035, 1037, 1237, 1238, 1465, 1466, 1532, and 1566.) This prediction was fulfilled by an excellent shower in 1866, another good one in 1867, and a fair one in 1868. None of these, however, was anything like as wonderful as that in 1833.

Before following the Leonids further, it must be stated that Schiaparelli was able to prove to his satisfaction that most meteors met the earth with nearly parabolic velocity, which is 42 kilometers per second. He further was the first to show that a meteor stream and a comet followed approximately the same orbit, this being done for the August Perseid meteors and Tuttle's comet, 1862 III. He embodied his researches into the first reference book on meteors (see *Bibliography*), which remained the standard work for over half a century and still should be read by all students of the subject.

Returning to the Leonids, there was general expectation of another grand shower in 1899, but, shortly before, two English astronomers, G. Johnstone Stoney and A. M. W. Downing, undertook the calculations of the perturbations which the meteors had undergone since 1866. We should pause to say that the Leonid orbit is an elongated ellipse, its aphelion point being near the orbit of Uranus. Meteors are scattered all around this orbit, which is really a cylinder several million miles in diameter, so that every November, when the earth passes through, we meet at least a few Leonids per hour. For a certain space, however, meteors are very much more concentrated, and this is roughly a tenth of the whole circumference. Hence it takes about three years for this denser part to pass, and we go through it either three or four times in succession. During these, greater showers occur. If we go, as in 1833, through the very densest part, wonderful showers are seen; if we miss the central mass and go through outlying regions of the stream, lesser displays are afforded. The calculations of Downing and Stoney showed that Jupiter and Saturn had so perturbed the densest part of the stream, as it passed near them, that it was probable it would wholly miss the earth in 1899. In 1898 the preliminary increase was indeed seen, and a good, if not spectacular, shower appeared, but the wretchedly poor display of both 1899 and 1900 more than vindicated the gloomy prediction. The 1901 Leonids, which had not been in position to be much influenced

by the planets, furnished a good display, but nothing comparable even to that of 1868. The main stream being thus "lost," it was impossible to compute exactly what should happen for the next return. Actually, on the night of Nov. 16-17, 1931 an excellent display occurred, comparable to that of 1901, but in no other year of the period did really great numbers of Leonids appear; hence again the earth had totally missed the densest part of the stream. The next return was expected between 1961 and 1967. On the morning of Nov. 17, 1966, a display of Leonid meteors rivaling that of 1833 was seen over the southwestern United States. However, it is not possible to assert what will happen in the future: perturbations may again shift the dense part of the stream into such a position that we will not pass through it. The Leonids follow the same orbit as the faint Tempel's comet, 1866 I.

Other Showers.—The Lyrid meteors of April were proved by Johann G. Galle in 1867 to follow the same orbit as Comet 1861 I, and the Andromedes (also called Andromedids or Bielids) and Biela's comet were proved to have the same orbit almost simultaneously by Edmund Weiss and Heinrich L. d'Arrest in 1867. Many other possible connections of meteor streams and comets were then explored, one—that of the Aquarid meteors of May and Halley's comet—being made probable though the observational data were very poor. In 1910 the final proof of this connection was given by Charles P. Olivier, based on new and adequate data. In 1916, meteors appearing in May and June, coming to a maximum on June 28, were proved independently by William F. Denning and Olivier to be connected with Pons-Winnecke's comet. In 1933 the splendid shower of Draconids, seen in Europe on October 9, was proved to follow the orbit of Giacobini-Zinner's comet. The possibility that this comet might furnish a meteor shower had been foretold some years before by Reverend Martin Davidson and by Denning. Lastly, the Taurid meteors of October, which do not give any "shower" in the popular sense, were proved to follow the orbit of Encke's comet by Fred L. Whipple. The other three annual showers, which furnish enough meteors to be worth noting here, the Quadrantids, Delta Aquarids, and Geminids, do not appear to have companion comets; the Orionids probably also are connected with Halley's comet. Some thousands of radiants of so-called minor streams have been published. At present, it is impossible to say what per cent represent real streams, though of course many do.

The Bielids furnished a grand shower on Nov. 27, 1872, a fine one in 1885, a good one in 1892, and an expiring effort in 1899. From then on few Bielids have been seen, either because the whole group has been so shifted that our earth misses them, or because the meteors have been dispersed so that the cross section of the stream is far larger and hence the meteors more sparsely scattered. As to Biela's comet itself, it divided into two in 1845, the twins were seen in 1852 at the next return, but never since (see COMET). Both the meteors and the comet were doubtless fragments of a much larger comet, and between them represent the last stages of its dispersal or destruction. The cases of the two meteor streams connected respectively with Pons-Winnecke's comet and with Giacobini-Zinner's comet illustrate very vividly how our earth may penetrate such streams on one or more occa-

METEOR

Above: A bolide—as a meteor of exceptional brightness is often called—crosses the camera field while the great spiral in Andromeda is being photographed.

Right: Meteorite found at Cape York, Greenland, weighing 36½ tons.

Below: New Quebec Crater, Quebec, from the air. The round crater is more than two miles across at the rim, and is of meteoritic origin. It was discovered in 1949.

Courtesy (1) and (2) The American Museum of Natural History; (3) National Geographic Society

METEOR

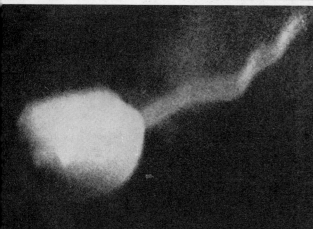

Above: Aerial view of the great Meteor Crater in Arizona, considered the largest known meteoritic crater until the discovery of the New Quebec Crater in Canada.

Left: The great fireball of March 24, 1933.

Below: The Willamette meteorite, found in the Willamette Valley near Oregon City, Oregon.

(Above and left) The American Museum of Natural History; (below) Hayden Planetarium of The American Museum of Natural History

sions and then planetary perturbations shift the meteor orbits so they no longer intersect ours. For example, the perihelion distance of the first comet in 1819 was 0.77 astronomical units, in 1915 was 0.97, and in 1939 was 1.10. Meantime the orbital inclination changed from $10°.7$ to $20°.1$. The result was that by 1916 the comet's orbit was literally pulled far enough from the sun to intersect ours and a fairly good display took place June 28. But the effects continued so that by the comet's next return in 1921, its orbit was wholly outside ours and a meeting with meteors moving therein impossible. As a consequence, since 1916 only outlying members of the stream have ever been seen—nothing which could be properly dignified as a "shower."

For the second comet, the period of which is 6.59 years, Denning on Oct. 10, 1926, identified a fair number of meteors as from a radiant which could be connected with the comet. Then on Oct. 9, 1933, a gorgeous shower appeared, observed in Europe, but it was over before darkness had come in America; in other words, it lasted only a few hours. Evidently in 1926 the earth penetrated the edge of the stream, in 1933 went through what was probably its center. This shower reappeared brilliantly in America on Oct. 9, 1946. The stream must be narrow. Both of the comets move with direct motion and belong to Jupiter's family. This means they are subject to great orbital changes. These latter have given us the chance to have meteor showers. In time to come we may hope that other streams may be switched into our path.

Frequencies.—The accompanying tables will indicate the average hourly and monthly number of meteors, and the average duration, date of maximum, and richness of the principal meteor streams. They are compiled from data secured through the American Meteor Society and other sources. They refer therefore mostly to middle northern latitudes, to clear nights without moonlight, and are for persons of good eyesight.

It will be noted that the second half of the year is much richer in meteors than the first, and that the same is true for the second half of the night. The first fact is due simply to the number and richness of the meteor streams intersected by the earth in the respective periods. The hourly duration comes as a result of the earth revolving in 24 hours, so the zone where it is 6 A.M. is on the exact front side with respect to its orbital motion; while the zone where it is 6 P.M. is exactly in the rear. The meteoric apex is the direction in which the earth is going at a given moment, defined by the tangent to the orbit. Our average orbital speed is 30 km/sec. (kilometers per second); that of meteors about 42 km/sec. It is easy to see then that we, in a unit

of time, meet many more than overtake us. Also the relative velocities of the two groups will be $42 + 30 : 42 - 30$ or $72 : 12$. When the earth's attraction is added to the heliocentric velocities of the meteors, this ratio becomes $73 : 16$. There is an important consequence when it is remembered that kinetic energy varies as the square of the velocity. Hence the ratio of the energy developed by a meteor coming from the apex at 6 A.M. to that of one of the same mass from the antiapex overtaking us at 6 P.M. is $73^2 : 16^2$ or about $20 : 1$. Therefore we might expect more meteors to survive their passage through our atmosphere in the evening than in the morning hours,

TABLE 2
HOURLY NUMBER OF METEORS FOR EACH MONTH

Month	Number of meteors per hour	Month	Number of meteors per hour
January	7	July	10
February	6	August	16
March	6	September	10
April	7	October	13
May	8	November	11
June	7	December	12

which is found to be statistically true. Also only larger bodies could survive during the morning hours.

Orbits.—The heliocentric orbits of all meteors are conic sections with the sun at the focus, but once the small body comes very near our earth, the attraction of the latter becomes dominant, and so, in our atmosphere, the meteor moves in a hyperbola with the earth's center as focus. The visible path being described usually in a second or less, and its length being only a few score miles, for the average meteor it is practically a straight line. By using observations from two or more stations, made simultaneously

TABLE 3

Name	Duration in days	Date of maximum	Hourly number of all meteors on this date
Quadrantids	4	Jan. 2	28
Lyrids	4	April 21	7
Eta Aquarids	8	May 4	7
Pons-Winnecke	?	June 28	?
Delta Aquarids	3	July 28	27
Perseids	25	Aug. 11	69
Draconids	1	Oct. 9	*
Orionids	14	Oct. 19	21
Leonids	7	Nov. 16	21
Andromedes	2	Nov. 20	?
Geminids	14	Dec. 12	23

* Brilliant shower in 1933 and in 1946.

on the same meteor, it is possible to compute the height at which it appeared and that at which it disappeared and the path length. If an accurate estimate of its duration is made, the velocity and, by well-known methods, its orbit in space can be computed. Even when, as is usual, the velocity is poorly determined, by assuming parabolic heliocentric velocity we derive an orbit which is nearly correct in several of the elements, especially the inclination and the perihelion distance.

The necessary observations for determining a meteor's path have mostly been made visually. During the past half century photography has begun to play a part, but even yet only the

TABLE 1
HOURLY NUMBER OF METEORS FOR WHOLE YEAR

Hour	Number of meteors per hour	Hour	Number of meteors per hour
6 P.M.	3.8	12	11.5
7	4.6	13*	13.1
8	5.6	14	14.4
9	6.8	15	15.0
10	8.2	16	14.8
11	9.8		

* 13 hours equals 1 A.M.

brighter meteors can be photographed. Visual observations consist in plotting the apparent path, as seen from each station, upon a star map. Knowing how far the stations are apart and their latitudes and longitudes, the base line can be established. The ends of the apparent path being measured with respect to the stars give the right ascensions and declinations of these points. Knowing the time, the altitudes and azimuths can then be computed. We now have, in principle, the case in trigonometry for solving a triangle when the base and adjacent angles are known. It is impossible to state how many meteors to date have had their height computed, but one would be safe in estimating the number to be several thousand—quite enough to give good average heights both for certain magnitude classes and special showers. Results based upon photographs are very much more accurate than visual, but as yet are fewer in number. This is because faint meteors do not impress themselves upon the plates and also the faster their angular velocity, the more difficult it becomes to photograph them. Short-focus lenses of large field of view and considerable aperture are best. With small fields of view, the chances for catching meteors decrease rapidly. At observatories where there are great collections of plates, notably Harvard University, Cambridge, Mass., and Sonneberg, Germany, statistical studies have been made. At Harvard, Willard D. Fisher, in 1927, examined 71,454 plates and found 213 trails. A later search at Harvard, covering 8,077 plates taken with two instruments in 1930–1935 inclusive, netted 59 meteors; 159 more meteor trails were found on other series there for these same six years. Cuno Hoffmeister reports that at Sonneberg (about 1937) on 10,729 plates 51 trails were detected.

By rotating a sector at high speed in front of a given lens, if a meteor is photographed, the path comes out as a line with a series of breaks thereon. If a photograph at another station is available, then the heights and length of path can be computed and, knowing the timing of the breaks, not only the meteor's average velocity can be found, but the velocity in each part of its path. Pioneer work along this line was done by William L. Elkin at Yale from 1891 to 1910, and more recent work at Harvard by F. L. Whipple. Interesting and important results, including proof of the slowing up of a meteor as it penetrates lower, have come from these programs, but observational difficulties have only recently permitted results on a large scale.

Spectra.—When it comes to meteor spectra, attempts made in the latter part of the 19th century with small visual spectroscopes need scarcely be mentioned in view of the relatively greater accuracy of photographs taken with objective prisms. The work of one man, Peter M. Millman, is so outstanding that it alone need be mentioned. He has, however, enlisted the aid of many observers, so that the actual plates come from various sources. In 44 spectra discussed before 1941, he finds two groups which he calls Y and Z. In the Y group of 33 spectra the two strong H and K lines of ionized calcium appear; these are absent in the 11 in Z group. Also 25 of Y are meteors belonging to the four most prolific annual showers, while 10 of Z are certainly sporadic. Iron is found in 37 spectra. Besides Fe, in order of number of cases are: Ca^+, Ca, Mn, Mg, Cr, Mg^+, Si^+, Si, Ni, Al, and Na.

This list of elements so far identified may be compared with those found in meteorites. It should be noted that all objective prism spectra are of very low dispersion and only prominent lines can be detected. As sporadic meteors form all of class Z, with one doubtful exception, it might well lead to belief in a considerable difference in structure between sporadic and the shower meteors, which latter seem to be debris of comets' nuclei. The term "sporadic meteor," as used here and elsewhere in this article, simply signifies that the meteor does not belong to one of the dozen or so best-known annual streams, or those known to be connected with some comet.

Mass.—The average meteor seems to be an extremely small body. To determine its size or mass, we remember that the equation for kinetic energy is $E = \frac{1}{2} m v^2$, where m is the mass and v the velocity of the moving body. Further it can be shown that no body can strike the earth with a smaller v than 11 km/sec., and it is nothing unusual for this figure to be as large as 70, 80, or even greater. It is then clear that v^2, expressed in the usual units, is a great quantity, and E may still be large, even when m is very small. By knowing how bright a meteor is, its path length, its duration, and how far it is from the observer, then a good estimate of the amount of light-energy it emits can be made. If all its E went into light, then our problem would be easier, but much goes into heat and probably also into other forms of energy. So assumptions are necessary. Accepting what seem the more probable, it is surprising to find that a meteor as bright as Jupiter may weigh only 4 grams, one as bright as Polaris 40 milligrams, and one just visible to the eye 1 milligram only. Fletcher G. Watson computes that daily the mass of meteors which strike us amounts to 1,000 kilograms, the meteors ranging from −10 to +30 magnitude. The latter are the smallest bodies which could move under gravitation and not be seriously affected by radiation pressure. He computes the true number of meteors, including those of +6 magnitude, or all visible to the eye, to be about 185,000,000 daily, while from +7 to +10 magnitude inclusive, or those visible in a small telescope, there would be 7 billion. These estimates are larger than most earlier ones, but are based upon more modern data.

Heights.—Meteors are mostly visible in that stratum of our atmosphere extending from 130 to 70 km. from the ground. Exceptional ones may begin higher and penetrate lower. It is obvious then that the average meteor one observes will be 70 to 200 kilometers distant. How can such minute bodies be seen so far? The answer is that they *are not*: it is the results of the energy they develop which we see. The small, solid body rushing through even the tenuous upper atmosphere continually strikes air molecules, heating them, and they in turn heat the surface. Those in front of the solid nucleus are greatly compressed so it is surrounded by an envelope of incandescent gas, much larger than the body itself. It must indeed be remembered that a lot of heating takes place and perhaps even some loss of mass occurs, before the body becomes visible. As it rushes into denser air, the surface is continually sloughed off, and the average meteor will be wholly consumed above the 70-km. level. However, the resulting debris, gas and dust, add to the earth's mass. The first stays in the atmosphere, the latter eventually settles. Traces can be found in polar snows and even deep-sea dredgings.

The geocentric velocity of a meteor seems to determine the height at which it first appears, the greater the velocity, the greater the beginning height. The Leonids, 70 km/sec., Perseids 56 km/sec., are cases in point. Results for 1932–1934 from work by the American Meteor Society (A.M.S.) give for Leonids $H_1 = 124$ km. (220 meteors) and $H_2 = 92$ km. (232 meteors). Results by Weiss on 49 Perseids give $H_1 = 115$ km. and $H_2 = 88$ km., respectively. A.M.S. results for sporadic meteors, observed on the same nights the Leonids appeared in 1932–1934, are $H_1 = 106$ km. (177 meteors), and $H_2 = 83$ km. (183 meteors). V. V. Fedynski for the period 1930–1933, using a new method, derived for 62 Leonids $H_1 = 128$ km., $H_2 = 92$ km. These agree excellently with the A.M.S. values as do those derived from the Yale photographic campaign by Elkin. Ernst Öpik, in his results of the Harvard-Cornell Meteor Expedition of 1931–1932, derives for what he calls "shower meteors" $H_1 = 103$ km., $H_2 = 85$ km., while for all meteors $H_1 = 95$ km., $H_2 = 82$ km. He preferred to use harmonic means which appear in all cases to make H_1 and H_2 smaller than arithmetic means. Large meteors or fireballs penetrate often to 30 km.

For photographic results by Whipple (1952) from two stations, shower and sporadic meteors combined, we find $H_1 = 98.6$ km. (144 meteors), $H_2 = 92.6$ km. (143 meteors); for Leonids only $H_1 = 108.6$ km. (6 meteors), $H_2 = 92.7$ km. (7 meteors); for Perseids $H_1 = 106.5$ km. (15 meteors), $H_2 = 84.0$ km. (14 meteors). In the past decade radio echo techniques have been extensively used for observation of meteors. The Canadian and English observers have been particularly successful. The latter, observing in daylight hours, have been able not only to detect the presence of meteors in our atmosphere, but have proved the existence of several prominent meteor streams. In addition to determining their hourly rate, their radiants were fixed with an accuracy comparable to that of most visual work. Later, in both countries mentioned, radio echoes have been further employed to determine the heights and velocities of individual meteors. In the few cases where comparison could be made with velocities secured by the photographic method agreement was good. The same remark can be made as to radiants. It is obvious that this new method has opened up an enormous field of research in meteoric astronomy as formerly, with dawn, all visual and photographic work had to cease, and in daytime only an occasional fireball could be seen. The basis of all this new method is that the meteor in its passage through our atmosphere leaves along its track a dense column of ionized matter, as well as producing the brilliant streak that we see. Radio echoes from these columns produce the phenomena which permit the results mentioned to be obtained. Work is also being done which may bring definite information about wind velocities at the heights where these ionized columns are produced.

Trains.—Most meteors leave an evanescent streak along their path which quickly disappears. The brighter ones often develop trains which last from one to many seconds. But exceptional meteors and fireballs occasionally leave trains which remain from a few minutes to even a couple of hours. Charles C. Trowbridge was the first to undertake serious researches upon long-enduring trains. His work appeared from 1906 to 1911.

In this he proved that the stratum in which night trains appeared was that from 72 to 105 km., mean value 87 km. As for the cause of luminosity, he assigned phosphorescense of the atmospheric gases following preceding ionization, and showed that duration and brightness of the trains agreed well with laboratory experiments. He showed that trains were cylindrical and that they rapidly expanded; also that their drift furnished the means of finding the direction of winds in the stratum where they occur. Velocities for drift up to 300 km/hr. were found, and it was further proved that thin layers, even when adjacent, had winds blowing in different directions and with different velocities. This means that the original train not only expands its diameter, but takes many forms, often fantastic in shape. In 1921, S. Kahlke, bringing the researches upon drifts partly up to date, showed that, for night trains over 80 km., a west wind was predominant over both America and Europe, but with a strong southern component for the former, a weak northern component for the latter. This he explains on the basis of the European observations being made in higher latitudes, on an average. For day trains, between 25 and 80 km. height, for Europe he found an east wind, but there were too few cases for much certainty.

In 1941 and 1947 Olivier published two far more extensive researches, based upon 1,493 meteor trains. The results for heights were divided into night, twilight, and day trains. Taking them in order: $H_1 = 104$ km. (5.3 meteors), $H_2 = 80$ km. (56 meteors); $H_1 = 71$ km. (26 meteors), $H_2 = 45$ km. (27 meteors); $H_1 = 45$ km. (9 meteors), $H_2 = 27$ km. (14 meteors). As to velocities, night trains gave 196 km. hour (75 cases), day and twilight trains 173 km. hour (16 cases). This indicates higher wind velocities, on an average, at greater heights. Motions in aurorae and noctilucent clouds give similar velocities. More recently the V-2 rockets and radar have both been successfully employed.

The trains left by bodies visible in daylight average, as said, much lower. These indeed must largely consist of dust and smoke, which show up by reflected sunlight. The night trains, on the contrary, cannot be so illuminated, and hence their light must be inherent. Twilight trains may be composite. The great fireball of March 24, 1933, over Oklahoma and New Mexico left a long-enduring train from 100 km. at the beginning to 25 km. height at its end. It also dropped stone meteorites. Explanation of how such a train, particularly the lower part, remained visible is more difficult. The upper part was in sunlight but at an altitude at which day trains do not usually extend. The sun had not risen for the lower, western end. Excellent photographs were secured of this train, as well as of a few others before or since.

Under the head of telescopic meteors may be included all which are fainter than $+6$ magnitude. Every observer at intervals must see a meteor shoot across the field of his telescope, but the number of serious studies of the little bodies have been few. With regard to shower meteors, observations have been made at the maxima of the Perseids and Bielids particularly. One interesting result by Adelbert Safarik in 1885 for the great shower of that year was that, in his telescope, he did not see many meteors fainter than $+9$ magnitude, and inferred that few smaller particles existed in the Bielid stream. Fletcher G.

Watson in 1936 concluded that "from a preliminary study of strong meteor showers we are led to expect relatively few telescopic shower members." Öpik concluded that most sporadic telescopic meteors had hyperbolic velocities and hence come from space beyond the solar system. J. Hoppe in 1935 considered that he was able to prove that the daily variation extended to telescopic meteors. In 1950, Olivier published results based upon 3,336 telescopic meteors found in the files of the American Meteor Society. One conclusion was that below magnitude +10 meteors do not grow more numerous by factors of from 2 to 4 per magnitude as has formerly been inferred by some.

Much of the best work has been done by amateurs securing results over long periods. Outstanding among such men was William F. Denning (1848–1931) whose work, over many decades, brought him deserved reputation. From about 1867 to 1872 there was an efficient association in Italy. The Meteor Section of the British Astronomical Association has been active for many decades, doing most excellent work. The American Meteor Society, founded in 1911, had up to 1955 made about 500,000 observations, perhaps one third of the meteors plotted and fully recorded, the rest mostly planned counts. In the USSR since 1920 there has been the greatest activity among both professionals and amateurs, and excellent work of every type is being done on meteors. In this connection I. S. Astapowitsch and V. V. Fedynski have been leaders. There is a flourishing society in Czechoslovakia. There is also a society in Japan doing good work. Individuals and groups in many European and other countries have functioned effectively.

Despite all that has been done, there is a vast field for future endeavor. This can be along two lines: devising new methods or instruments, or the attempt to use those we have in a more effective manner. Nearly all previous work has been done in Europe and North America; the Southern hemisphere has been relatively neglected. Statistical studies on such bodies as meteors should be made from many places on the earth, widely distributed, if we would have full information. Then there are problems which can best be attacked at fixed observatories. Primarily here would be wider application of photography and radar to meteors, both to secure more accurate paths and heights, but most of all to settle the vexing question of their velocities. So far, due to obvious selection, the velocities secured by photography must have been for slower moving bodies, or for the brighter ones. We need accurate velocities for the more average meteors. Not until these can be derived instrumentally can the question of where they originated be settled. If their heliocentric velocity is over 42 km/sec., then they are from outer space; if less, then in general they originated in the solar system. There has been great controversy on this point. Cuno Hoffmeister's important work, which appeared in 1924 and later, indicated that most meteors, omitting those belonging to the principal annual showers, had a strongly hyperbolic velocity. This was based on his interpretation of the daily variation. Also the majority of the 611 fireballs contained in the Von Niessl-Hoffmeister *Catalogue* (1925) give hyperbolic velocities. This latter result was strongly criticized by W. D. Fisher, and later by Charles C. Wylie, who believed that errors in the data are responsible for the high velocities

found. Yet the results of the Harvard-Cornell Expedition, both by the rocking-mirror method, which is a partly instrumental one, and by another approach to the problem, according to Öpik confirm the high velocities of sporadic meteors. But Watson (see *Bibliography*) indicates clearly that, as to the fireballs, he believes the large velocities erroneous. Whipple's work on the Taurid meteors, which Hoffmeister had worked out as an interstellar stream with high velocity, showed them to be connected with Encke's comet and really of low velocity. Whipple also finds among the numerous sporadic meteors observed photographically, in duplicate, at the Harvard stations practically none with a velocity greater than parabolic. Similar conclusions are arrived at by several observers employing the radar methods. Therefore, unless there is a serious effect due to selection, hyperbolic velocities must be comparatively few, and few meteors meet us coming from outside our solar system. Nevertheless, there it need for much more data before the question can be considered as finally settled.

The importance of meteor trains for studies of the upper atmosphere has already been explained. But determination of accurate heights and path lengths also give information as to the temperature, pressure, and possible composition of the stratosphere. We need more and better data. Studies of meteor rates help to determine the quantity of matter in space, and the density of meteor streams. In turn we are led to a better understanding of the composition and course of dissolution of comets.

Origin.—At present, all theories of evolution in the astronomical sense are in a state of flux, or, it would be better to state that no one has general acceptance among scientists. Such being the case, it is impossible to be certain as to where or how meteors originated. We may say that shower meteors are debris of comet nuclei. But are these tiny bodies indeed the building block of evolution or its debris? If such small bodies could form out in space from molecules or atoms of gas, the former would be a very comfortable hypothesis. Though recently theories along this line have been advanced by several able scientists, there remain many unexplained difficulties. Therefore, to the writer the debris hypothesis at present seems the more logical. In this, meteors are debris of evolutionary processes by which large bodies are born into the embryonic stage. From here on some attain full growth, others are destroyed before, or perhaps after, reaching it. For every large fragment, say of asteroid size, there would be innumerable small ones, down to the dimensions of dust. These tiny particles, scattered in vast numbers through space, give us our meteors; those a little larger, and hence far less numerous, our meteorites. In historic times we have not met a body of the next order of size, that of a small asteroid, but our earth is itself of moderate area, space is vast, and human history short. There is not the least reason to doubt such bodies do exist. We should hasten to add that some meteorites, the orbits of which have been calculated, originated in the solar system: we know of asteroids of short period which come inside our orbit. It being the writer's opinion that the same processes, which formed them here, formed similar bodies in distant systems, the only question we need ask further is how the sporadic debris escaped into space. The answer would be rather technical but should follow the same type of explanation as how a comet can attain hyperbolic velocity, which we occasionally find has occurred. Studies of space absorption and the masses of spiral nebulae also lead independently to belief that innumerable particles of meteoric size and larger exist beyond the confines of the solar system. While a complete account of why they are there cannot as yet be given with any certainty, we have good reasons for believing that they are there.

See also GRAPHICAL ANALYSIS; METEORITE.

Bibliography.—Schiaparelli, Giovanni V., *Le stelle cadenti* (1873); Hawkins, Gerald S., *The Physics and Astronomy of Meteors, Comets, and Meteorites* (New York 1964); Page, Thornton, and Page, Lou Williams, eds., *Neighbors of the Earth* (New York 1965).

CHARLES P. OLIVIER,
Former Director, Flower and Cook Astronomical Observatories, University of Pennsylvania.

METEOR CRATER, in Arizona, is the best known and most studied of all such formations. That it was formed by the impact of an enormous meteorite or group of meteorites was first definitely proved by Daniel Moreau Barringer. The crater is roughly circular, average diameter 4,150 feet, depth 570 feet. Its bottom is filled with debris to a further depth of 600 feet. It is surrounded by a wall from 130 to 160 feet high, composed of large boulders and other material which were ejected when the crater was formed. The rim's present mass is probably 300 million tons. Great numbers of meteorites, large and small, were found scattered within a radius of five miles out from the crater. The whole area is formed of parallel strata: the top Kaibab limestone, then Coconino sandstone, lastly Supai red limestone. Inside the crater, the edges of the strata show uplifting and in the southwest quadrant a very definite arching as though bodily pushed into a curve by an intruding body from below. There is no volcanic activity in the immediate vicinity and indeed such a theory of its origin is now wholly discredited.

Beginning with 1903 mining operations were begun by Barringer, and since his death in 1929 continued by his sons. As the original mass must have been some millions of tons to make such a crater, and as analysis of the surrounding meteorites indicate a high monetary value per ton, the aim has been to locate and recover the main mass. The difficulties were extremely great due to shattering of the surrounding strata to fully half a mile outward. Borings in the crater itself were very disappointing, but later a shaft sunk in the southwest rim encountered material at 1,376 feet which the drill could not penetrate. Later, tests were made with the magnetometer, electric resistivity method, and the Worden Gravitometer all indicating that a large mass still remained buried. However, theoretical studies by a number of able men led to the conclusion that the original mass was converted into vapor by the enormous force of contact. Therefore only further mining operations can give a definite answer to its survival and size.

CHARLES P. OLIVIER,
Former Director, Flower and Cook Observatories, University of Pennsylvania.

METEORITE, mē′tē-ēr-īt, a solid mass which enters the earth's atmosphere from outside and survives its fiery passage to fall upon the earth's surface. The difference between a meteorite and a meteor, or shooting star, is that the latter is small enough to be totally destroyed in the atmosphere (see also METEOR). Before its encounter with the earth, a meteorite travels in an orbit which is a conic section, our sun being at one focus. As the meteorite closely approaches the earth, the earth's attraction adds to the body's heliocentric velocity; hence it can be proved that the minimum velocity with which an outside body can strike the earth's atmosphere is 11 km./sec. (kilometers per second), while the maximum has reached perhaps eight times this value. The minimum velocity is the velocity a body would attain falling from infinity to the earth under the gravitation of the earth only. This would be the case when a body overtakes the earth at 6 P.M., both moving in the same direction. The maximum velocity would occur when a body met the earth head on at 6 A.M.

Just before collision with the atmosphere, the temperature of the meteoritic body would be that of a small airless planet at one astronomical unit from the sun, or about $4°$ C. As the meteorite enters our atmosphere, even in the tenuous upper regions, the body is heated by collision with air molecules, the friction or heating becoming greater as it penetrates lower. Meantime a large gas cap forms in front, the gases therein being tremendously compressed and carried along with it. The surface becomes greatly heated, and in fact melts and sloughs off. Eventually the resistance, due to increased air density, not only slows but virtually stops the body at a height of some 20 to 30 km. from the earth.

Having lost much or all of its cosmical velocity, the body continues to drop from this height principally as the result of the earth's gravitational attraction. The loss of cosmical velocity explains why no meteorite actually seen to fall has ever penetrated deeply into the ground. The greatest penetrations known are only a few meters, while small meteorites are found lying on the surface. One even fell upon lake ice a few inches thick without breaking it.

As the time of passage through the air amounts to only a few seconds, heat has no chance to penetrate from the surface into the interior by conduction. The heating and melting are therefore superficial. Although the outer crust of meteorites is doubtless warm when they first fall, accounts of their being extremely hot, or setting fire to vegetation, seem certainly exaggerated. If they fall at night, they are usually visible at a height of 120 km. (75 miles) or more down to 20 or 30 km.; below this, it is doubtful if many are seen. Some have the brilliancy of the full moon and may become even brighter when they burst or flare up. Such bursting is doubtless due to tremendous air pressure on their front surfaces, plus sudden surface expansions. A meteorite acts like a typical fireball while visible in its atmospheric path. The rapid passage through the air, which is violently disturbed, often produces sounds like rolling thunder, artillery fire, or even explosions. These are sometimes violent enough to shake houses. If the body falls during daylight, it is usually detected at lower heights and, by contrast against the sunlit sky, will not be so brilliant. A meteorite "fall" is often accompanied by clouds of smoke and dust, which debris at times remains visible for long intervals after the body itself has fallen. Some meteorites "explode" into many fragments; others fall in a single mass (or at least only one body is found). In the first case, fragments may be dispersed over an area of as much as several square miles.

When a meteorite is found, its surface to the depth of about one millimeter has a black, fused crust, composed of the material most recently melted which was not brushed off by the air during passage. Iron-type meteorites (called "iron") usually have pitted surfaces, the smaller depressions looking not unlike deep thumbmarks. When a meteorite has lain on or in the ground for a long time, larger cavities are formed by the removal of the less refractory materials through erosion and weathering. Stone meteorites, unless promptly found, are likely to be permanently lost. This is because they look not unlike ordinary rocks and disintegrate rather rapidly. Irons, on the contrary, may survive for centuries and still be recognizable. Curiously, however, only one meteorite has been found embedded in ancient strata. This was discovered in the Pliocene gravels of the Klondike.

Origin.—There currently are two possible hypotheses as to the formation of meteorites: (1) they come from small masses of gas and dust which somehow condense out in space; (2) they are debris of larger bodies which have disintegrated. While certain eminent men have leaned to the former theory, no one has been able to show how the extremely complex meteoritic structure could evolve under such conditions. Unless this point can be explained, the second theory would seem much more probable. Here we are at liberty to think of an exploded planet, asteroid, or (possibly) star, and of the disintegrated nuclei of comets. There seem to be no grounds for believing that meteorites could be fragments of our earth.

Determination of the age of meteorites is important to the question of their origin. Helium and lead are products of radioactive elements, and the rate of radioactive decay which produces them is known. Hence the total amount of helium accumulated in the meteorite at any period, divided by the rate of production of helium by radioactive decay, gives the age of the meteorite. The method is more applicable to irons than to stones, it being assumed that gases can escape from the latter and not from the former, once solidification of the minerals has taken place. Pioneer work by Fritz Paneth, William D. Urry, and W. Koeck on 23 irons indicated their meteorite ages as being from 10^8 (100 million) years for the "youngest" to 2.8×10^9 (2.8 billion) years for the "oldest." If these ages are correct, none seems older than the earth. Measurements on the Pultusk stones (see section on *Important Meteorites*) gave 5×10^8 years, but this estimate is probably much too low, as the stones are at least semiporous. The results depend on the assumption that there has been no leakage of internal gases; but in millions of years, meteorites moving in what is a practically perfect vacuum and heated on each approach to our sun (or any other star) may well lose some of their gas. More recent researches on stony meteorites give much greater ages. Various methods involving radioactive decay were used. For the "youngest" meteorites the ages averaged 2.4 billion years (four determinations); for the "oldest," 4.4 billion years. Many single meteorites were used in each determination, so that their total number was several dozen.

Some meteorites at least have such low velocities that we know they belong to the solar system and originated therein. Some of their orbits resemble those of short-period comets. For others, observations (which are always very uncertain as to duration) give hyperbolic orbits. If these orbits are, in fact, hyperbolic, then these meteorites came from other parts of space.

Composition.—Meteorites are roughly called either irons or stones, but the more accurate classification is as follows: (1) irons or siderites, consisting mostly of nickeliferous iron; (2) stony-irons or siderolites, in which iron and stony matter are mixed in large amounts; (3) stones or aerolites, consisting mostly of stony matter. There are two subdivisions of the latter class: (a) stones poor in iron, generally without round chondrules, and (b) chondrites, with some bronzite, olivine, and nickel-iron, and many rounded chondrules. No new elements have been detected in meteorites by either chemical or spectroscopic analysis. This may indicate that the same elements exist everywhere in space. Yet combinations of minerals are found in meteorites which do not occur on earth. This is part of the evidence that these bodies were formed elsewhere and came to us fully developed.

Meteorites, even of the same class, differ considerably in composition. On an average, however, when we compare stone meteorites with the earth's crust, we find over five times the percentage of iron and only about three fourths that of oxygen and silicon. Other well-known elements common to both earth and meteorites have quite different percentages.

The stones, in general, belong to a very basic class of rocks, low in silicic acid but high in iron and magnesium. They have the characteristics of igneous rather than sedimentary rocks. They are very complex in structure and much fragmented. Many show intrusions of other minerals which must have occurred after their original consolidation.

The irons consist essentially of alloys of iron, nickel, and cobalt, with which are commonly associated a phosphide, schreibersite, and a sulphide, troilite. In this type have been found small quantities of the noble metals, including gold, iridium, and platinum. When the surface of an iron meteorite which usually contains from 7 to 15 per cent of nickel is polished and then treated with acid, it shows characteristic patterns of intersecting bands, known as Widmanstätten figures. These are due to the inequality of the acid's action upon thick or thin plates (layers) of the various constituents, which are largely kamacite and taenite. The latter is richer in nickel than the former, and the bands narrower. The bands are edges of plates arranged parallel to the faces of an octahedron, the form assumed in crystallization. Such meteorites must have formed under conditions of high temperature and great pressure, and must once have been in a liquid state and cooled slowly. They did not form in the presence of free oxygen. Reports of the finding of bacteria in meteorites are believed to be incorrect.

History.—The Old Testament Book of Joshua records the death of men in battle by the fall of "stones from heaven." In modern times, we have no authentic accounts of deaths from meteorites, but at least 25 have damaged buildings, and one person is known to have been struck. However, there have been numerous narrow escapes from injury or death. There is reason to believe that the (original) image of Diana at Ephesus, which "fell down from Jupiter," must have been a meteorite (see STONE WORSHIP). Several Greek and Roman writers describe the fall of other stones from heaven, which were thereafter held in veneration. The Chinese record a fall in 644 B.C. The sacred black stone built into the Kaaba (q.v.) at Mecca, which is still extant, is believed to be a meteorite. Despite the skepticism of 18th century scientists, a few meteorites which fell in Europe before 1800 were preserved. The German physicist Ernst F. F. Chladni in 1794 seems to have been the first eminent man to give scientific reasons for believing that certain metallic masses could not have been formed on the earth. In 1803, the researches of Jean B. Biot first convinced his colleagues that witnesses' accounts of the fall at L'Aigle, France, were true and that the stones came from space.

Distribution and Recovery.—Taking the United States as an example, the distribution of meteorites is most surprising. The southern Appalachian region seems much favored, as are Texas, New Mexico, and Arizona; but few have been found in the four very populous states of Illinois, Massachusetts, New York, and Pennsylvania. Due largely to the work of Harvey H. Nininger, many have been found in Colorado and Kansas. No doubt, thorough surveys in other states would turn up numerous meteorites, but no good explanation has been given for the curious distribution so far shown. Obviously, regions of small rainfall are most favorable for meteorite survival and eventual discovery, since weathering and erosion are at a minimum. Only a few of the total falls of meteorites have been recovered. The earth is about three fourths covered by water, and virtually all meteorites that fall on water are lost. There are also vast, uninhabited polar, desert, and jungle regions. Even when small masses fall in thickly settled areas, unless the exact place of fall is known and at once examined, the chances for finding the meteorite are poor. It would be a very liberal estimate to say that one out of every hundred is recovered. Hence the number of recorded meteorite falls represents a misleading statistic.

Important Meteorites.—The largest meteorite discovered, if we omit the highly controversial Adrar or Chinguetti mass, is that still lying near Grootfontein, South-West Africa, called the Hoba West Meteorite, an iron whose present weight is estimated at 60 metric tons.[1] The iron shale around this meteorite weighs an additional 20 tons. The date of discovery, sometimes given as 1920, is uncertain, but the body has surely been lying there for centuries. The Adrar mass, discovered in 1916 by a French officer in the region of that name in the Sahara, was said to be immensely large. However, numerous later attempts to locate it all have failed. The largest American meteorite (33.1 tons) is the Ahnighito, or "The Tent," brought from Greenland by Admiral Robert E. Peary in 1897. This and the Willamette from Oregon (14.2 tons) are both irons and are in the Hayden Planetarium in New York City. Mexico possesses four very large irons: Bacubirito (24.5 tons), Chupaderos I (14.1 tons), Morito (10.1 tons), and Chupaderos II (6.8 tons). Another very large iron is Moosi (12 tons) in Tanzania, East Africa. However, no record survives of the fall of any of the meteorites mentioned above.

Turning to stone meteorites, we find a different result. This is in part because irons will last

[1] The metric ton, 2,205 pounds or 1,000 kilograms, is used throughout this section.

for thousands of years, if large, and still be recognizable, while stones decay. The largest known single stony mass fell Feb. 18, 1948, in Norton County, Kans. Its weight was 1,073 kilograms (2,360 pounds). The larger mass which fell at Paragould, Ark., on Feb. 17, 1930, weighed 338 kilograms (744 pounds). The aggregate weight of other fragments from this fall was 73 kilograms (161 pounds). The next in size, Knyahinya, Czechoslovakia, weighed 293 kilograms (645 pounds). Two very large ones which were broken into fragments either in the atmosphere or on impact fell at Long Island, Kans. (total weight of fragments 564 kilograms or 1,241 pounds), and Bjurböle, Finland (330 kilograms or 726 pounds). All of these were seen to fall. The fall at Pultusk, Poland, on Jan. 30, 1868, seems to break all records. About 100,-000 fragments were picked up, the largest weighing 9 kilograms (20 pounds), the smallest perhaps 1 gram. Of these about 200 kilograms (440 pounds) have been preserved. The Estherville, Iowa, fall of May 10, 1879, also furnished thousands of fragments (total weight 338 kilograms or 744 pounds). At Holbrook, Ariz., on July 19, 1912, some 15,000 stones fell (total 219 kilograms or 482 pounds). At present, many more falls are composed of stony than of iron meteorites, the proportion being about 9 to 1. Most of the irons seen to fall have consisted of a single mass; the stony falls may consist of from one to many thousands of bodies.

Meteor Craters.—By far the most important effects produced upon the earth's surface by the fall of outside bodies are the so-called meteor craters. Several have been discovered, and doubtless there are many others. They were probably caused, at least in some cases, by the impact of not one mass but of a rather compact group of meteorites, perhaps the nucleus of a small comet. The best known is Meteor Crater (q.v.), near Winslow, Ariz. It is about 4,150 feet in diameter and about 570 feet deep, with a rim that is from 130 to 160 feet above the surrounding plain. Its bottom is filled to an extra depth of 600 feet by pulverized rock. Thousands of meteorites, weighing in the aggregate 10 to 20 tons, have been picked up in the vicinity.

There is a group of 13 craters at Henbury, Australia, the largest being 660 by 360 feet, the smallest only 30 feet wide. Iron meteorites have been excavated from some of the smaller craters.

The larger Odessa Crater in Texas is 530 feet in diameter and less than 18 feet deep, and has a very low rim. There is a companion 80-foot crater. Many small meteorite fragments have been found there.

The so-called Siberian Craters, formed on June 30, 1908, are also famous, although no real crater survives. The still visible results were caused by a group of meteorites which crossed Siberia from south to north, falling at a spot in longitude 101° 57' E., latitude 60° 55' N. It was not until 1927 that an expedition under L. A. Kulik found the place, so that observers were interviewed and data collected long after the event. Around the slightly depressed area, out to a radial distance of 30 to 50 kilometers, the forests had been seared and flattened, the trees lying with their tops away from the center. No meteorites are known to have been recovered. The principal damage had been done by a blast of superheated air, carried along by the solid fragments, where air and fragments struck the ground. The fall occurred in an uninhabited swampy area. Had it occurred in a great city, the city would have been largely destroyed.

More recently, several great craters, all believed to be meteoric in origin, have been located. Wolf Crater, in northwestern Australia, is about a half mile in diameter and 100 feet deep. New Quebec Crater (q.v., formerly called Chubb Crater) in northern Quebec, Canada, is the largest known. It is 2½ miles in diameter, and part of its rim, composed of fragmented granite, is 550 feet high. The interior is filled by a lake whose level considerably exceeds that of others nearby. In the East Pamir highlands of the USSR two companion craters exist, the larger being 260 feet in diameter and 50 feet deep, and the smaller 52 feet in diameter. In this case there is a legend about a "fiery star" which fell there two or three centuries ago. On Feb. 12, 1947, a swarm of iron meteorites fell in southeastern Siberia. At least 106 craters, the largest 90 feet in diameter, were formed. A considerable weight of iron meteorites was recovered, and it is estimated that perhaps 1,000 tons formed the original mass. Several other "craters" have been suspected of being formed by impact, but cannot yet be so classified with absolute certainty.

Bibliography.—Mason, Brian, Meteorites (New York 1962); Moore, C. B., ed., Researches on Meteorites (New York 1962); Kuiper, Gerard P., and Middlehurst, B. M., The Moon, Meteorites and Comets (Chicago 1963); Hawkins, G. S., The Physics and Astronomy of Meteors, Comets, and Meteorites (New York 1964); Heide, Fritz, Meteorites (Chicago 1964); Krinov, E. L., Giant Meteorites (New York 1966); United Nations Educational, Scientific, and Cultural Organization, Directory of Meteorite Collisions and Meteorite Research (New York 1967).

CHARLES P. OLIVIER,
Former Director, Flower and Cook Astronomical Observatories, University of Pennsylvania.

METEOROLOGICAL STATIONS, mē-tē-ŏr-ô-lŏj'ĭ-kăl.

A meteorological station, or, as it is sometimes called, a meteorological observing station, is defined internationally as a station approved by a meteorological service for the purpose of making meteorological observations and reports. The person who makes the observations or reports at a meteorological station is called a meteorological observer, or weather observer. (See also METEOROLOGY.)

International coordination and the setting of international standards, procedures, and practices for the operation of meteorological stations are a part of the responsibilities of the World Meteorological Organization (WMO), created in 1950 as a special agency of the United Nations. The first such world body was the International Meteorological Organization, established in 1878. At present, tens of thousands of meteorological stations are scattered over the face of the earth, both on land and sea. The resulting observations are exchanged internationally to an extent which surpasses even the exchange of letters between the postal services of the world.

Of the many ways of classifying meteorological stations, two in particular are important: the first is to classify them according to the type of observations taken. The second is to classify them according to their primary physical characteristics.

Stations by Type of Observations.—The types of stations are listed in ascending order of complexity, each (except the last) being capable of performing the routines of those types which precede them: rainfall, climatological, synoptic, pilot balloon, rawin, radiosonde, rawinsonde, and special observation stations.

Rainfall Stations.—These measure the amount of precipitation on a daily, monthly, and annual basis. A rainfall station normally is located in an exposed place convenient to a voluntary rainfall observer where a rain gauge is used to catch and measure the amount of rain as it falls. In winter a snow stick may be used to measure the depth of freshly fallen snow. The rainfall observer records the amount of precipitation that has fallen each day, and normally submits monthly reports to the national meteorological service. Because of the importance of rainfall for agriculture and hydroelectric power development, to mention only two of many vital uses, and because of the complexity of rainfall patterns, there is almost no limit to the number of rainfall stations that are required in any agricultural area or on any catchment area for water storage.

Climatological Stations.—In addition to the rain gauge, climatological stations are normally equipped with accurately calibrated maximum and minimum thermometers. The observer, who in most instances serves voluntarily, takes readings of the rain gauge and the maximum and minimum thermometers each morning at the same time, seven days a week, 365 days a year, and enters these readings together with general notes on the weather, on a monthly summary sheet, which is forwarded to the national meteorological service. The observations taken at these stations are valuable in developing building codes, establishing heating requirements in buildings, designing drainage installations for built-up areas, planning flood control, and performing many other activities vital to healthy community life.

Synoptic Stations.—Next in ascending order of complexity are the synoptic stations. At such stations weather observations are taken simultaneously throughout the world at times fixed by international agreement. For many years the internationally agreed times for the taking of primary synoptic weather observations have been 0000, 0600, 1200, and 1800 Greenwich Mean Time (GMT). The reports from these stations contain the values of a wide variety of weather elements, and are exchanged by high-speed modern telecommunications among neighboring countries. In fact, in any main center in North America or Europe, weather observations are assembled from a network of synoptic stations over the whole of the Northern Hemisphere within a matter of one or two hours of the time the observations were actually taken.

At the synoptic stations, in addition to measuring the rainfall and the maximum and minimum temperatures, the observer records wind speed and direction, visibility, present and past weather, atmospheric pressure and the nature and rate of change of that pressure, temperature, and dew point, and a complete classification of the clouds in the sky by type, amount, height of base, and direction of motion. All of these elements are measured and recorded each day by instrumental and visual means. The observer codes the results in a series of five-figure groups for rapid communication. These weather observations are exchanged free of charge throughout the world. They are also mailed monthly to the national climatological center. Many of the synoptic stations take four additional observations at intermediate three-hourly periods (0300, 0900, 1500,

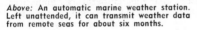

Above: An automatic marine weather station. Left unattended, it can transmit weather data from remote seas for about six months.

Right: The S.S. *Anton Dohrn,* a combination hospital ship and weather station, belongs to the government of West Germany.

Upper right: The *Anton Dohrn* meteorologist checks the temperature of the North Atlantic, an important indicator of forthcoming changes in weather.

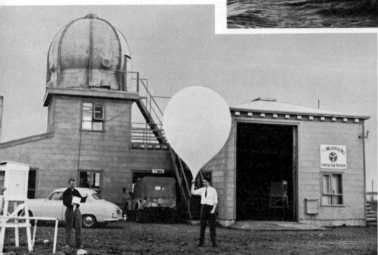

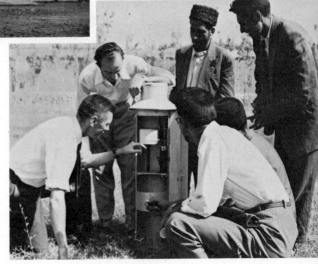

METEOROLOGICAL STATIONS

Above: A radiosonde station at Keflavik, Iceland. Supported jointly by the countries which use its services, the station provides weather information vital to safe air travel in the North Atlantic.

Center right: A mobile station of the U.S. Weather Bureau, making special observations to aid in the prevention of forest fires.

Right: An instructor, sent to Afghanistan by the World Meteorological Organization to train local personnel for a national weather service, explains a rainfall gauge to a student group.

(Top left, right, and center) Birnback; (center left) United Nations; (others) World Meteorological Service.

and 2100 GMT). A smaller number of specialized stations, located so as to guard the national and international air routes of the world, take observations every hour.

Pilot Balloon Stations.—Before the development of radar, the only way by which the meteorological observer could, on a routine basis, determine the direction and speed of winds aloft was to release hydrogen-filled rubber balloons some three feet in diameter, adjusted to rise at a fixed rate of ascent, and to follow these balloons through a theodolite. By knowing the rate of ascent and reading the azimuth and elevation angles from the theodolite at fixed intervals, the observer obtained the wind speed and direction by trigonometry. Between the two world wars, with the rapid growth of aviation, a knowledge of the upper winds became extremely important, and large numbers of these pilot balloon stations were set up, particularly in the Northern Hemisphere.

The limitation of following a hydrogen-filled balloon visually is that once the balloon enters a cloud, no further information is obtained. Moreover, the balloons cannot be flown successfully in precipitation because rain or snow affects their rate of ascent. It is therefore essentially a fair-weather method of observing, and the role of such stations is gradually being assumed by rawin stations. Nevertheless, they have the advantage of being simple and inexpensive and will therefore continue in operation for many years.

FPG

Midget radio transmitters attached to balloons can report weather conditions at heights up to 100,000 feet.

Rawin Stations.—With the development of radar and radio direction finding, it became possible to obtain the speed and direction of winds aloft by releasing hydrogen-filled balloons to which were attached radar targets, responders, or small airborne transmitters, and tracking the ascent with radar or radio direction-finding equipment. "Rawin," the code name of stations equipped to do this work, is a contraction of "radio-wind." The big advantage of this technique is that data can be obtained to heights as great as 100,000 feet, regardless of whether there is cloud or precipitation. These stations are gradually replacing the pilot balloon stations, but their chief drawbacks are the expense of operation and the complexity of the ground equipment. The hydrogen-filled balloons to carry radar reflectors or transmitters aloft are large (six feet in diameter when inflated at sea level) and are difficult to handle. Special balloon-filling sheds are required, and in high winds the act of releasing the balloons requires the efforts of two men.

Radiosonde Stations.—After World War I, in the service of aviation, special meteorological aircraft made daily ascents with a variety of instruments to measure the temperature, humidity, and pressure and to observe the cloud layers between the surface and around 20,000 feet. These pioneers in upper air meteorological observation played a very important part in the development of the science of meteorology. They worked often at considerable personal risk, as oxygen apparatus, blind-flying equipment, and the variety of navigation aids now taken as commonplace were not then available.

The demand for observations at greater and greater heights, and the desire to have these observations regardless of whether conditions were fit for the flight of aircraft, led to the development of the radiosonde, which is an airborne measuring and radio-telemetering instrument. It is sent aloft on a free hydrogen-filled balloon and measures and transmits the ambient pressure, temperature, and humidity at frequent intervals. The radiosonde was brought into quantity production shortly before the outbreak of World War II; since then hundreds of these stations have been set up in the Western Hemisphere alone. The airborne equipment is expendable; therefore, the cost of operating a radiosonde station is considerable. Observations are taken at internationally agreed times throughout the world (0000 and 1200 GMT) each day, and the results are exchanged by radio and telegraph among all the countries of the world.

Similar observations can be taken by dropping the instruments from high-flying aircraft specially equipped for receiving the signals. The rate of descent of the equipment is kept down to about 1,000 feet per minute by a parachute. The equipment is known as a dropsonde.

Rawinsonde Stations.—Some of the most complex of all meteorological observations are taken at rawinsonde stations. As the name implies, the equipment combines the functions of rawin and radiosonde stations, and incorporates all the latest techniques of radar or radio direction finding with radio telemetering and automatic computing.

Special Observation Stations.—A number of special meteorological stations have also been developed to take observations in what is called physical meteorology. These include stations for the routine chemical analysis of the atmosphere, and for measurements of the ozone content of the air, atmospheric electricity, solar radiation, and others. Such stations are destined to play increasingly important roles in the advancement of meteorology and its practical applications.

METEOROLOGICAL STATIONS

Stations by Physical Characteristics.—
In this classification, stations may be listed in the following five groups: land, ship, ocean weather, aircraft, and automatic meteorological stations.

Land Stations.—By far the largest number of meteorological stations are located on land and are staffed with trained meteorological observers. These land stations vary in complexity of equipment all the way from the simplest kind of rain gauge to large and expensive rawinsonde installations, complete with their own electric generating plants, radio transmitters, radar domes, and quarters for married personnel.

Ship Stations.—Similar information from the ocean areas is obtained from the largest single voluntary scientific effort in the world today. Practically all ocean-going merchant ships are equipped to take synoptic meteorological observations, and part of the training of a ship's officer includes the knowledge necessary to take and record such data. Observations on board ship are taken by the ship's officer without additional remuneration. The responsibility is normally discharged by the officer of the watch. The resulting weather message is transmitted as quickly as possible to the nearest shore station. These observations from the oceans enable the national meteorological services to provide forecasts and storm warnings, which are, in return, broadcast to all ships. The observations from ships also contribute very materially to the provision of meteorological service to the continents.

Ocean Weather Stations.—There are areas in the oceans, outside normal shipping lanes, from which reports from merchant ships are seldom, if ever, received. Moreover, while merchant ships can and do discharge the duties of synoptic stations, they are not equipped for the radiosonde and rawinsonde observations on which international aviation depends. For these reasons networks of ocean weather stations have been established in the Atlantic and Pacific. An ocean weather station is a fixed geographical position in the ocean continuously attended by a ship equipped to take rawinsonde and synoptic observations and, as ancillary benefits, to provide communication, navigation, and search and rescue services. To ensure that the station is always manned, two or three ships are required per station. These ships rotate, each doing a tour of duty of three to four weeks on the station and then being relieved by the next ship.

This international effort is carried on in the Atlantic Ocean under the terms of an international agreement in which all countries operating aircraft over the ocean participate. The countries with major aeronautical interests, such as the United States, the United Kingdom, Canada, France, the Netherlands, Norway, and Sweden, operate ships manning nine ocean weather stations, while countries with smaller aeronautical interest pay cash contributions. In the Pacific Ocean, under a bilateral agreement between Canada and the United States, Canada maintains one station and the United States two.

Aircraft Stations.—By agreement under the International Civil Aviation Organization, all aircraft flying the intercontinental civil air routes of the world are required to take, each hour, observations of the weather encountered on the flight, and to pass them promptly to the control station. These reports are then passed on to the adjacent forecast office and, in turn, to all other

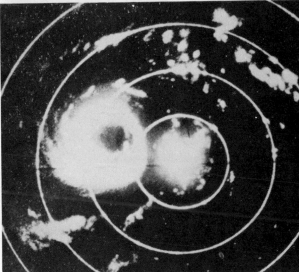

Top: Crew members photograph a hurricane from a patrol plane window, a part of the Hurricane Research Project. *Bottom:* Clearly visible on the radarscope, the hurricane shows its characteristic counterclockwise motion.

interested forecast offices in the world. They are a valuable supplement to the weather ship observations over the oceans and help to fill the gaps in the polar and other remote areas of the continents traversed by the air routes.

However, these civil aircraft fly specific routes, the ships follow defined shipping lanes, and there are not enough ocean weather ships to fill all the gaps in the network of reporting stations. A few countries, principally the United Kingdom and the United States, operate aircraft specially equipped with meteorological instruments on regular reconnaissance flights to help fill these gaps. The aircraft take frequent weather observations and occasional dropsonde descents, and transmit all information to the control stations. Weather reconnaissance aircraft have been successfully used in locating and following hurricanes and typhoons, and have contributed greatly to our scientific knowledge of these destructive tropical storms.

Automatic Meteorological Stations.—A meteorological station is referred to as automatic when it is capable of taking meteorological ob-

Meteorological Branch, Department of Transport, Toronto

At climatological stations an observer takes readings of maximum and minimum thermometers and a rain gauge every day at the same time. Most observers serve voluntarily.

servations, coding the results, and transmitting the reports, all without the presence of a meteorological observer. Strictly speaking, a radiosonde instrument is a type of automatic meteorological station, but because of its highly specialized role it is not classed as such. The term "automatic meteorological station" or "automatic weather station" is reserved for land-, ice-, or sea-based installations capable of operating unattended over substantial periods of time. These station fall into two main divisions: (1) those taking regular observations in remote areas, such as deserts, polar ice, or rugged mountains; and (2) those taking frequent observations in settled areas. Secondary airports are in the latter category. Automatic stations are desirable where the presence of staffs of trained observers is either impractical or economically unjustifiable. Installations in remote, isolated areas demand the ultimate in reliability and ruggedness, and must be completely self-contained. Frequently, however, only a relatively small selection of the meteorological variables need to be measured. On the other hand, installations in settled areas are usually required to measure as many as possible of the variables included in an aviation weather report. They can be inspected and adjusted at frequent intervals by a service man, and can rely on local municipal power supply and telegraph lines for transmission purposes. They can, therefore, be much more sophisticated.

A number of countries are developing automatic stations for operation in remote areas. One of the most successful is the Alekseyev-Beacon,

developed by Y. K. Alekseyev of the USSR Arctic Institute in Leningrad, for use on the floating ice of the Arctic Ocean. Two such devices were put into operation in 1956. The station is flown in and set up on an ice floe, and can operate for one year unattended. It weighs about 450 pounds and has a clock, radio transmitter, and batteries hermetically sealed in a balloon which is suspended in the water below the ice, thus ensuring that it will be kept at a constant temperature above freezing. The instruments are mounted on a duraluminum mast, and the station transmits temperature, pressure, and wind speed and direction twice daily. The position of the station as it drifts with the ice is determined by radio direction finding from two shore stations, and can be worked up to a distance of 1,000 miles.

The meteorological service of France has developed, and has in use, a number of automatic weather stations in the Sahara Desert. This type of station transmits pressure, temperature, humidity, wind speed and direction, and rainfall, either by radio (with a range of up to 800 miles) or by land line. The values of the readings are sent out in standard Morse code and therefore may be received by any station equipped with an ordinary wireless-telegraph receiver set. The electric current is provided by a battery of accumulators charged by a wind generator. Two independent radio transmitters provide day and night frequencies, while a mechanical translater is set in motion every three hours by a time-control unit to send the full meteorological report.

Developments in the United States have been focused on equipment suitable for operation in settled areas, principally at smaller airports, and capable of transmitting directly to the national weather teleprinter system in the North American hourly aviation code. A number of such stations are in operation, reporting cloud height, visibility, temperature, dew point, wind direction, wind speed, altimeter setting, and precipitation. The meteorological instruments in the automatic station are all of well-proved standard design, but great ingenuity has been used to quantize the readings and convert them to digital signals capable of operating a standard weather teletype. Readings are made very frequently and are stored electronically for transmission either at fixed times or on demand. Research on how to incorporate automatic observing of the remaining elements that make up a complete weather observation is continuing.

Work has also been going on in the development of buoy-mounted automatic weather stations. These were used in elementary form in the Pacific theater in World War II by United States forces. More advanced models have been used by the United States Navy in hurricane research, and may also be applied in conjunction with general research on the limnology and hydrology of the Great Lakes.

Meteorological Networks.—The aggregate of meteorological stations over an area or region is called a network, as, for instance, a network of rainfall stations, a network of climatological stations, or a network of synoptic stations. It is part of the responsibility of the World Meteorological Organization to publish a list of these networks, giving the names and geographical locations of land stations, and the names and call signs of ship stations. In addition, each land station which takes synoptic, rawin, radiosonde, or rawinsonde observations is assigned a five-

figure international index number by which it is
recognized by meteorologists throughout the world.
The list of index numbers is also published by the
WMO and is made available to all countries, as
is information on the actual observational routine
of each station.

The question of how close one meteorological
station should be to another in order to obtain
an adequate sampling of the physical characteristics of the atmosphere is an extremely complex
problem, and has been the subject of a continuing study by an international panel of experts
of the WMO, set up in 1951. Certain factors are
obvious. For example, the variations in rainfall
from place to place are so large that rainfall
stations in populated parts of the world must
be separated by distances measured in not more
than tens of miles. On the other hand, since the
rate of change in the atmosphere at high levels
is generally less than that near the surface of the
earth, rawinsonde stations can be spaced several
hundred miles apart and still present a reasonably
adequate network. Heavily traveled air routes
of the world and other special areas, however,
may require a network of greater density. Broadly
speaking, a denser network is required in the
temperate than in the tropical latitudes.

The polar regions present a special challenge
because of the high cost of maintaining observing stations in these latitudes. Iceland and Greenland have stations financed internationally by the
North Atlantic countries. Canada maintains an
Arctic network supplemented by five stations
jointly operated with the United States. The
USSR has a network of stations in northern
Russia and Siberia, besides its temporary stations
on the floating polar ice.

During 1957–1958, in support of the International Geophysical Year (q.v.), there was established for the first time an adequate network of
meteorological observing stations in Antarctica
(58 including the sub-Antarctic area). These
observations initiated valuable research and development, and it was hoped that at least some
of the stations could be maintained on a continuing basis after the end of the IGY.

National networks of meteorological stations
vary considerably from country to country: To
some extent they are an index of a country's
economic development. The underdeveloped countries are noticeably deficient in networks and,
consequently, in the meteorological advice required in planning agriculture and other activities.

P. D. McTaggart-Cowan,
*Director, Meteorological Branch, Department of
Transport, Toronto, Canada.*

METEOROLOGY, mē-tē-ēr-ŏl′ō-gĭ, the
science of the atmosphere, involving the application of the principles of physics and mathematics
to phenomena in the air around and above the
earth. Meteorology has many branches: atmospheric electricity; weather forecasting; atmospheric turbulence; weather control; atmospheric
pollution; analysis of weather maps; the physics
of clouds and precipitation; meteorological instrumentation and methods of observation; climatology, which is the science of the average weather
conditions; micrometeorology, the study of atmospheric phenomena that are observed in small
areas; and hydrometeorology, the study of the
water cycle. (This cycle traces the disposition of
moisture from the initial evaporation of ocean

World Meteorological Organization

In Antarctica, penguins gather about an automatic weather station. Installed by Australian meteorologists, it
operates unattended, making regular observations of meteorological variables and transmitting the results.

water into the air through its subsequent condensation to form clouds, its precipitation from
these clouds as rain or snow, and its eventual
runoff by way of streams and rivers back to the
sea.)

Significance of Atmospheric Science.—We
live in the "ocean of air" and are constantly
affected by its temperature, humidity, motion,
clouds, and precipitation. These direct, immediate
influences are too obvious to need elaboration.
Indirect, long-range effects of the atmosphere
on mankind have increased as civilization has
grown. Man constantly seeks ways of rendering
himself independent of the weather through such
various artifices as furnaces and air conditioners,
drought-resistant varieties of grain, radar navigation in fog, instrument-landing systems for
aircraft, and so on. But these methods of obtaining independence have not kept pace with the
increasing dependence of civilization on weather.
To cite a few examples: the launching of a
rocket is critically dependent on atmospheric
turbulence; industrial, automobile exhaust-fume,
and other waste products are beginning to pollute
the atmosphere faster than it can cleanse itself;
jet aircraft have small fuel reserves and cannot
risk a flight to a terminal where weather conditions may delay the landing; and the use of water
may soon exceed the supply naturally provided by
precipitation. See also Drought.

History of Meteorology.—The growth of
meteorology as a science has been chronologically
the outcome of: (1) the invention of accurate
instruments for observing the weather; (2) the
collection of data over the world for long periods;
(3) improved methods of communication for the
purpose of weather forecasting and (4) in recent
years, the development of high-speed computers
for processing and analyzing weather data.

It is likely that measurements of rainfall with crude rain gages were made by agrarian tribes in prehistoric times, and it is known that such measurements were made in India as early as the 4th century B.C. The next instrument to come into use was the wind vane. Experience with observations of clouds, wind direction, and rainfall must have produced some fairly good amateur weather forecasters in ancient times, though the value of the experience gained was doubtless reduced by superstitious belief in capricious gods.

The invention of the thermometer about 1593 by Galileo Galilei (1564–1642) and the barometer in 1643 by Evangelista Torricelli (1608–1647) opened the way for the development of accurate weather observations. Beginning as early as the 15th century, a number of instruments for measuring humidity were constructed, including one by Leonardo da Vinci (1452–1519), but the most commonly used instrument, the hair hygrometer, was invented by Horace Bénédict de Saussure (1740–1799) in 1783. Seven years later Reinhard Woltmann (1757–1837) developed the first really practical anemometer designed to measure wind speed. Thus, by 1790 the basic instruments had been invented: the rain gage, thermometer, barometer, hygrometer, wind vane, and anemometer.

Many individuals, Thomas Jefferson among them, kept weather diaries in which notes were made on the daily weather. These diaries are an important source of information about the climate of the 18th and 19th centuries. Organized systems of collecting weather data developed slowly in the 19th century. In 1820 Heinrich Wilhelm Brandes (1777–1834) constructed the first weather map by collecting observations made in Europe on March 6, 1783. But lack of rapid communications prevented the use of observations for weather forecasting. The invention of the telegraph in 1848 solved this problem, and can, in a sense, be regarded as the single event which marked the beginning of modern meteorology. Shortly thereafter, telegraphic weather services were organized in the United States and many other countries. The daily succession of weather maps made possible by the telegraph stimulated scientific investigation of weather processes. By 1900 charts had been constructed showing the prevailing wind systems of the lower atmosphere and the major storm tracks. It was known that rising air cools by expansion until the water vapor condenses into clouds and precipitation. Some meteorologists had suggested that storms form at the boundary between cold and warm air masses. But almost the only way a meteorologist could earn a living was by routine observation and forecasting of the weather. Basic research in atmospheric science was practically nonexistent.

During World War I, Vilhelm Bjerknes (1862–1951) and his collaborators in Norway proposed a model of weather processes that is still the standard. They distinguished between different types of air masses, particularly polar and tropical; they showed that there is often a sharp boundary between air masses which they called a "front," obviously by analogy with the front on a battlefield; and they designed a model of the typical atmospheric low pressure systems of middle latitudes which shows how the air masses interact and the fronts move and develop during the life history of such an atmospheric "low." Between the two world wars, details of this model were worked out and applied in weather analysis and forecasting.

An important development was the beginning of regular observations of pressure, temperature, and humidity in the upper air. At first, kites were used for this purpose, then airplanes, and finally the radiosonde came into common use in the 1930's. Upper winds have been observed regularly by means of balloons since World War I, but the radiosonde made it possible to construct maps of upper air conditions that were comparable to the surface weather map.

Until World War II, atmospheric science had very little support and was overshadowed by the practical operation of weather forecasting. During this war, the recognized importance of meteorology in military operations provided a tremendous boost to the science, especially in the United States where thousands of meteorologists were trained in the universities and the government began to spend millions of dollars on meteorological research. World War II marked the beginning of a productive era for meteorology. Radar, intended as a means of detecting enemy aircraft, turned out to be an excellent means of observing clouds and precipitation far beyond the limits of the naked eye. Rockets, intended for destructive purposes, provide valuable information about conditions in the very high atmosphere. Earth satellites, placed into orbit by rockets, are being used as a kind of superobserver of the weather. The satellites Tiros I and II (April 1, Nov. 23, 1960) have transmitted thousands of pictures of cloud systems from average heights of 450 miles (I) and 400 miles (II) providing a broad view of weather systems never before possible. Incoming radiation from the sun and outgoing radiation from the earth can be observed from satellites. Finally, electronic computors, developed during and since the war, help to solve the two most difficult problems of atmospheric science: the rapid analysis and forecasting of weather by mathematical methods, and the solution of equations that explain the nature of atmospheric processes. See also SATELLITE, ARTIFICIAL; SPACE RESEARCH; UPPER ATMOSPHERE, SOUNDING METHODS OF THE.

The Scale of Atmospheric Processes.—A fundamental consideration of atmospheric science is the size of the phenomenon that is being examined. Just as a coarse fish net will catch only big fish, so an observational network with widely spaced stations will reveal only the larger atmospheric phenomena. A tornado, which is small and short lived, is not very likely to be detected in the usual network of weather stations. Some of the important processes of the atmosphere, such as convergence and rotation, have quite different values according to the scale on which they are measured. To understand such processes, one must keep in mind that the air motion, temperature, pressure, and other properties are controlled not only by very large pressure systems hundreds of miles in diameter, but also by smaller transient systems, and even by local effects due to hills, valleys, and other topographic features of small size.

In the following sections, the explanation of atmospheric phenomena will start with the smallest scale, sometimes called the microscale; and will proceed to the next largest, the mesoscale; then to the "synoptic" scale; and finally to the macroscale. Micrometeorology is concerned with phenomena such as thunderstorms up to a few miles in diameter and with a life of minutes or an hour or two; mesometeorology, with phenomena whose scale is a few miles to a hundred miles and whose life span is a few hours; synoptic meteorology, with the familiar highs and lows and fronts of the daily weather map; and macrometeorology, with the planetary pressure systems that persist for a whole season.

CLOUDS

Types of Clouds.—A cloud is composed of minute particles of water or ice, or of both. The three basic cloud forms are stratus, a flat cloud; cumulus, a puffy cloud; and cirrus, a feathery cloud. By combining these basic forms with each other and with alto, meaning high, and nimbus, meaning rain cloud, the names of the ten genera of clouds are obtained.

In fair weather the genus cumulus is often seen. Sometimes the white puffy cumulus grows vertically into a towering cumulonimbus, the thunderstorm cloud. Stratus is a low, gray cloud layer. In a typical sequence of clouds preceding a period of rain, one sees first the genus cirrus high in the sky. Some cirrocumulus, a thin white layer with small ripples, may also be seen, but it is rare. The feathery cirrus clouds increase and gradually merge into a thin overcast of cirrostratus, in which a halo may be seen around the sun or moon. The cirrostratus thickens and lowers, becoming altostratus. As the thickening continues, the altostratus becomes dark and shapeless and begins to precipitate rain or snow. The cloud is then called nimbostratus. The altostratus may be preceded or accompanied by altocumulus and stratocumulus, layers of rounded masses of cloud. The altocumulus is higher in the sky, so the cloud masses appear smaller than in stratocumulus. See also CLOUDS.

Observation of Clouds.—Weather observers make regular observations of the types of clouds that are present over their station. For each type, a record is made of the amount of sky covered, the direction of motion, and the altitude. The altitude of a cloud layer above the ground may be determined in several ways. An experienced observer can estimate the altitude rather accurately. At airfields, pilots ascending or descending through a cloud base fix the height by referring to their altimeter and report the height to the observer. A balloon with a known rate of ascent may be released from the ground. The time elapsed until the balloon disappears into the cloud, multiplied by the rate of ascent, gives the altitude. At night a light beam is projected upward against a cloud, and the height of the spot on the cloud base is found by triangulation. The *ceilometer* projects a pulsed beam of light which can be distinguished from daylight by means of a photocell, so that it can be used both day and night. With a suitable recording device the ceilometer gives a continuous automatic record of cloud height.

The ceiling is the height above ground of the lowest layer of cloud that covers at least half the sky. Safe minimum ceilings for landing or take-off have been established at airports for various types of aircraft and instrument-landing systems.

Cloud Structure.—The water droplets in a cloud are tiny spheres with diameters ranging from 1 to 80 ten-thousandths of an inch. The average droplet is about 20 ten-thousandths of an inch in diameter. It falls, relative to the surrounding air, at a speed of about 15 feet per minute. There are from 400 to 4,000 droplets in one cubic inch of cloud. Even so, the liquid water in

a cloud constitutes only one or two millionths of its total volume.

The cloud droplets grow by condensation of water vapor from the air on hygroscopic nuclei, tiny particles a few millionths of an inch in diameter. These particles are composed principally of salt from sea spray and sulfurous and nitrous acids from combustion. They have a special affinity for water, so that condensation takes place on them even when the humidity is less than 100 per cent.

A cloud may also contain ice crystals, which can be created either by deposition of water vapor in the form of ice on certain types of nuclei, or by freezing of a supercooled water droplet. There are many shapes of ice crystals in clouds —hexagonal plates; needles; hollow prisms; and dendrites, which are branching hexagonal flakes of an infinite variety of patterns.

Photometeors.—When light from the sun or moon passes through a cloud or falling precipitation certain optical phenomena known as photometeors may be seen. A halo is a white ring around the sun or moon caused by refraction of light in the ice crystals of cirrostratus clouds. Since these clouds often precede a period of precipitation, the halo is a popular, though not reliable, sign of bad weather to come. The principal halo has an angular radius of 22°. Sometimes it appears faintly reddish on the inside and violet on the outside. Associated with the halo are a number of phenomena that are rarely seen: a pillar of light above and below the sun or moon; the circumzenithal arc, a small bright arc of a circle centered at the zenith, the point of sky directly overhead; sun dogs, bright spots on the halo at the same altitude as the sun; and others. The corona is a colored ring of small diameter centered on the sun or moon, caused by diffraction of light by liquid cloud droplets. *Irisation* refers to colors, usually green and pink, appearing on clouds, not in rings but often in parallel bands. The rainbow is caused by refraction and reflection of light in raindrops. It always appears in a direction opposite the sun from the observer and, contrary to ancient tradition, may signify either passing bad weather when it is seen in the east or approaching storm conditions when seen in the west (in the normal course of frontal weather movements). The primary rainbow has an angular radius of 41°, with violet color on the inside through the visible spectrum to red on the outside. See also ANTHELION; CORONA; HALO; PARASELENE; PARHELION; RAINBOW.

PRECIPITATION

The Mechanisms of Precipitation.—Cloud particles are so small that they are either supported by rising air currents or, if they fall from the cloud, are evaporated before reaching the ground. Cloud particles may grow large enough to fall to the earth's surface as precipitation either by coalescence of droplets or by the colloidal instability due to coexistence of water droplets and ice particles.

Coalescence simply means that some droplets grow by collision with other droplets. When they collide, two droplets may bounce off each other or may coalesce into one droplet, depending upon factors such as surface tension, electrical charge, and relative velocity. The larger droplet formed by coalescence falls faster and overtakes small droplets, some of which it collects. As the process continues a few of the original tiny droplets become raindrops and fall from the cloud.

The coexistence of water droplets and ice particles is possible because the tiny droplets do not readily freeze and may remain liquid at temperatures well below freezing. At these temperatures the saturation vapor pressure over ice is less than over liquid water. Therefore, there is a tendency for vapor to be deposited in the form of ice on the ice particles, while the droplets evaporate. The transfer of water by evaporation from the droplets and deposition in solid form on the ice particles causes the latter to grow to a size where they can fall freely.

Attempts to stimulate precipitation by artificial methods are based on the theory that natural mechanisms of precipitation are inefficient. Injection of particles of silver iodide and other chemicals, dry ice, or sprays of water droplets into a cloud is supposed to enhance one or the other of the two principal mechanisms. There is some slight evidence that precipitation can be stimulated artificially; but a great amount of research needs to be done before man can control precipitation to any significant extent.

Precipitation Forms.—Drizzle is precipitation in the form of small drops less than two hundredths of an inch in diameter. It falls from low stratus clouds and often is accompanied by fog and poor visibility. Raindrops are larger than drizzle drops. Freezing drizzle or rain occur when the drops are supercooled, so that they freeze on contact with the ground or with objects such as buildings and trees. The deposit of ice so formed is called glaze. If freezing rain continues for very long, an ice storm results; the accumulated weight of ice causes limbs to break off trees and telephone and power lines to fall.

Sleet consists of frozen raindrops; it is made up of transparent or translucent pellets of ice, with diameters less than two tenths of an inch, which bounce when they hit hard surfaces. Hail takes the form of balls of ice from two tenths of an inch to two inches or more in diameter. It falls in thunderstorms, where the upward air currents are strong enough to sustain ice pellets while they grow to the size of hailstones.

Snow is composed of hexagonal ice crystals, often displaying elaborate branching from the six sides of the crystal. A snow crystal may be as large as one third of an inch in diameter. In a typical fall of snow the snow crystals become interlocked, forming larger aggregates called snowflakes. Snow pellets are white, opaque grains of ice, up to two tenths inch in diameter; they are crisp and may bounce from a hard surface. Snow grains are very small, white, opaque grains of ice, flat, with diameter less than four one-hundredths of an inch. Ice prisms are tiny crystals in the shape of needles, columns, or plates that seem almost suspended in the air. A blizzard is a very cold, strong wind filled with drifting or falling snow. (See also BLIZZARD; PRECIPITATION; SNOW AND SNOW CRYSTALS.)

Dew is produced by condensation of water vapor from the air on relatively cool objects at the ground. It does not "fall." Hoarfrost is a white deposit of ice in the form of scales, needles, or feathers on the ground during a night when the temperature is below freezing. (See also DEW; FROST.)

In a shower the intensity of precipitation changes rapidly. A shower is usually associated with swelling cumulus or cumulonimbus clouds. Rain, snow, hail, and snow pellets may fall in showers. A light snow shower is sometimes called a snow flurry.

Measurement of Precipitation.—The amount of precipitation falling in a certain time interval is measured in a rain gauge, the oldest and simplest of all meteorological instruments. The rain gauge is a cylinder which catches the precipitation falling into the open top. In the gauge used in the United States, the precipitation is funneled into a smaller cylinder, exaggerating the true depth by a factor of 10 so it can be more accurately determined with a measuring stick. If the precipitation is snow or some other solid form, it is melted and the depth of melted water is measured. The weighing gauge records the weight of accumulated water on a chart which is labeled in terms of equivalent depth.

When snow is on the ground, regular measurements of its depth are made at weather stations. One inch of snow is roughly equivalent to one-tenth inch of rain, but this ratio varies considerably according to whether the snow is closely packed or loose. Since snow tends to drift, the average of several depth measurements around the observing station is taken as the representative depth.

Weather Radar.—A weather radar set broadcasts an intermittent signal in a narrow beam at a wavelength of a few centimeters. The signal is reflected from raindrops and snowflakes that are in clouds or falling from clouds. The distance is determined by the time required for a reflected pulse to return to the radar set at the speed of light. The distribution of precipitation-bearing clouds can be displayed either on a plan-position-indicator, which gives a horizontal view, or on a range-height-indicator, which gives a vertical cross section. The radar can be thought of as an extension of human vision into wavelengths beyond the infrared and over distances many times the normal range of vision. Simply as a mapping device the weather radar is extremely useful; it can also be used to estimate the amount of rain water in a cloud, the drop sizes, and the turbulent motions of the cloud. See also RADAR—*Airborne Radar*.

Distribution of Precipitation.—Precipitation is one of the most irregular of the meteorological elements. Rain gauges just a few miles apart may show quite different readings, especially in showery weather. Even during a period of weeks or months, the total precipitation may vary significantly between nearby areas. Only over a period of years does this small-scale variability begin to smooth out. In a general sense, the amount of precipitation is greatest in the tropics and equatorial regions and decreases toward the poles. It is heavier on the windward side of mountains than on the leeward side, and heavier in coastal regions than in the interior of continents. Warm ocean currents favor precipitation while cold currents suppress it. (See also HYDROLOGY; RAINFALL.)

The greatest amount of precipitation observed in a one-year period was 1,041 inches at Cherrapunji, India, between August 1860, and July 1861. At the other end of the time scale, the greatest one-minute rainfall observed was 0.69 inch at Jefferson, Iowa, on July 10, 1955.

TEMPERATURE

Temperature Scales and Measurement.—Temperature is a measure of the heat content of

METEOROLOGY

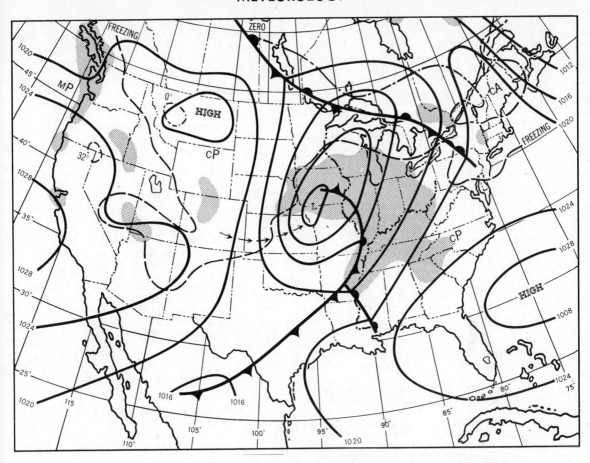

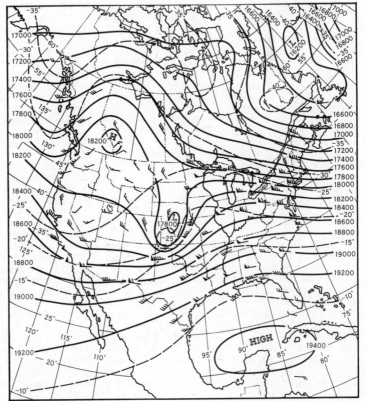

Above: Example of a daily weather map for 1 A.M., Eastern Standard Time, compiled from observations taken at approximately 200 selected stations.

Right: Example of a 500-millibar constant pressure chart based on radiosonde observations begun between 6 P.M. and 7 P.M. and collected by 10:30 P.M., Eastern Standard Time.

Based on material supplied by the Weather Bureau, U.S. Department of Commerce a substance. When two substances are in contact with each other, heat flows from the one at higher temperature to the one at lower temperature. In meteorology three scales of temperature are used. On the Fahrenheit scale the freezing point of water is at 32° F. and the boiling point at 212° F. On the centigrade scale, now officially known as the Celsius scale, water freezes at 0° C. and boils at 100° C. Thus, one degree on the Celsius scale is equivalent to one and eight-tenths degree on the Fahrenheit scale. The absolute temperature is simply the Celsius temperature plus 273 degrees. (See also Absolute Temperature; Celsius; Thermometer.)

The thermometer most used to measure air temperature is a glass tube with a thin hollow bore and a bulb at one end. It contains mercury or alcohol; in very cold climates alcohol must be used because mercury freezes at −38° F. As the temperature rises, the mercury or alcohol expands and rises in the thin bore of the tube. A scale on the tube shows the temperature according to the height of the liquid.

A maximum thermometer has a constriction between the bulb and the tube which prevents the mercury from returning to the bulb when the temperature falls. Thus, its reading is the highest temperature since the thermometer was last set. It is set to the current temperature by spinning the thermometer so that centrifugal force pushes the excess mercury through the constriction into the bulb.

A minimum thermometer contains alcohol and includes a small glass index in the bore. Surface tension at the end of the alcohol column pulls the index back as the temperature falls, and the index remains at the lowest temperature. The minimum thermometer is reset by tipping it until the force of gravity returns the index to the top of the alcohol column.

Recording thermometers, or thermographs, are usually of the bimetal type. Two bars of different metals, such as Invar and brass, are welded together. The two metals expand at different rates as the temperature rises, so the welded bar is forced to bend. The bending is magnified by levers and the temperature indication is recorded on a chart by a pen at the end of the lever system. (See also Thermograph.)

Thermometers must be exposed properly or they will not show the true air temperature. They must be shielded to keep the rays of the sun from striking them and to keep the thermometer from losing heat by radiation at night. A thermometer exposed in sunshine reads well above the air temperature.

The temperature of the sea surface is an important meteorological quantity because the exchange of heat between the sea and atmosphere affects weather processes. Sea temperature is regularly observed and reported by ships. Ground temperature is also of some importance but is not regularly measured or reported.

A combined quantity known as "degree days" is computed by subtracting the mean temperature of a day from 65° F. For example, on a day when the mean temperature is 50° F., the corresponding value is 15 degree days. If the mean temperature is 65° F. or greater, the number of degree days is zero. The consumption of heating fuel is closely related to this quantity. The efficiency of a heating plant can be estimated from the amount of fuel burned for each degree-day unit.

Temperature Variation in the Lower Atmosphere.—In the lower part of the atmosphere, called the troposphere, temperature generally decreases upward. The rate of decrease is called the *lapse rate;* its average value in the troposphere is about 3.6° F. per 1,000 feet. Sometimes the temperature increases upward in certain layers; such an increase is called an *inversion.*

When a mass of air rises or sinks, it is expanded or compressed, respectively, because atmospheric pressure decreases upward. When it expands the air cools and when it is compressed it warms. Since the exchange of heat between such a mass of air and the surrounding air is quite slow, the processes of expansion and compression may be considered *adiabatic*—that is, without exchange of heat. The adiabatic lapse rate is the rate at which rising air cools by expansion; its value for dry air is 5.4° F. per 1,000 feet. The average lapse rate, 3.6° F. per 1,000 feet, is less than this; hence, rising air is likely to be cooler and heavier than the surrounding air, so that it tends to fall back to its original level. The atmosphere is then said to be in stable equilibrium. If the lapse rate is greater than 5.4° F., rising air is warmer and lighter than the surrounding air and tends to keep on rising; this condition is called unstable equilibrium. The adiabatic lapse rate is less than 5.4° F. per 1,000 feet if the air contains saturated water vapor; thus, the state of equilibrium depends upon whether the air is "saturated" or not.

HUMIDITY

Definitions and Measurement of Humidity.—Humidity is the amount of water vapor in the air. The specific humidity is the mass of water vapor in a unit mass of air. It ranges from nearly zero in very dry air up to a maximum of about 40 grams of water vapor in 1 kilogram of air, a proportion of 4 per cent. One of the paradoxes of meteorology is the fact that this small proportion of water vapor is responsible for most of the weather: fog, clouds, and precipitation. It is also responsible for much of the heat exchange in the atmosphere. About 600 calories of heat are required to evaporate 1 gram of water. The vapor carries this latent heat locked up within it and releases it when the vapor condenses into liquid water.

The vapor pressure is the partial pressure exerted by the water vapor; that is to say, it is the pressure that would be exerted even if no air were mixed with the vapor. For any given temperature, there is a maximum vapor pressure called the saturation vapor pressure. If the vapor pressure exceeds the maximum, some condensation takes place and reduces the pressure to the maximum value for that temperature. The common expression, "saturated air," is inaccurate because the water vapor is saturated, not the air. The saturation vapor pressure is determined by temperature and has nothing to do with the capacity of air to contain vapor.

Relative humidity is the ratio of the actual vapor pressure to the saturation vapor pressure. When the relative humidity is 100 per cent, the water vapor is saturated. The relative humidity is sometimes slightly greater than 100 per cent; the vapor is then supersaturated and condensation may be expected. Relative humidity can be measured directly by the hair hygrometer. Strands of hair elongate when the humidity increases and contract when it decreases. The elongation and contraction are magnified by levers which move a pointer across a scale, or, in the hygrograph, move a pen up and down on a chart on a clock-driven drum.

The hair hygrometer is not very accurate and has to be calibrated from time to time. In weather stations humidity is measured by means of the psychrometer, which consists of two thermometers mounted so they can be whirled together through the air or ventilated by a fan. One thermometer has a piece of moistened cloth covering its bulb. Its reading is called the wet-bulb temperature, and the reading of the other thermometer is the dry-bulb temperature, which is the actual temperature of the air. Evaporation of water from the cloth on the bulb of the wet-bulb thermometer absorbs heat and cools the air passing the bulb. The wet-bulb temperature is, therefore, always lower than the actual air temperature, except in saturated conditions when it is the same. Tables are used to find the humidity of the air from the dry- and wet-bulb readings.

If air is cooled sufficiently it reaches the dew-point temperature where the vapor begins to condense. This is the temperature for which the existing vapor pressure is the saturation vapor pressure. The dew point can be measured directly by cooling a bright metal surface until a film of moisture is deposited on it. The temperature of the metal surface is then the dew-point temperature. See also DROSOMETER; HYGROMETRY.

Effects of Humidity.—The wet-bulb temperature is the lowest temperature to which air can be cooled by evaporating water into it. For this reason it is a significant temperature for human comfort in hot weather, because the body cannot be cooled effectively by evaporation of perspiration if the wet-bulb temperature is high. A formula combining the dry- and wet-bulb temperatures gives an index which is related both to human comfort in hot weather and to loads on air conditioners.

Humidity is important for human activities in many ways besides comfort. In certain manufacturing processes the humidity must be carefully controlled. Forest rangers keep a close watch on the humidity, as dry air greatly increases the danger of forest fires. Low humidity also increases the danger of fires in buildings. In winter, when heating results in very low humidity inside a building, a fire may easily start and spread with great rapidity. Furthermore, a study of the relation between atmospheric humidity and fire frequency in New York City in summer has shown that there are nearly twice as many fires when the humidity is below 50 per cent as when it is above 90 per cent.

VISIBILITY

Obstructions to Vision.—The ability of a person to see an object at a distance depends on several factors: the person's eyesight, the amount of illumination, the contrast in brightness between the object and the background, and the scattering and absorption of light in the atmosphere between the object and the observer. The latter factor is determined by various meteorological obstructions to vision. These are the hydrometeors, which are liquid and frozen particles such as rain and snow, and the lithometeors, which are particles of smoke, dust, or sand.

Many of the hydrometeors have been defined in the section *Precipitation.* Nonprecipitating hydrometeors are fog, mist, and blowing snow.

Fog is a cloud on the ground. There are four ways in which fog may form. A mass of air moving over a cold surface may be cooled below its original dew-point temperature; this is the main cause of the dense fogs at sea off the coast of Newfoundland. Secondly, air may be cooled at night by radiational loss of heat until fog forms; ground fogs form in this manner. Thirdly, rain falling through cold air evaporates until the vapor in the air becomes saturated. Finally, air moving up a slope may be cooled by expansion until fog forms. Mist is a suspension of microscopic water droplets or wet hygroscopic particles which does not reduce the visibility as much as fog. Ice fog is composed of minute ice crystals. Blowing snow is snow raised from the ground by the wind.

Among the lithometeors are haze, a suspension in the air of extremely small, dry particles; smoke, a suspension of small particles produced by combustion; blowing dust and blowing sand, lifted by the wind from the ground; and dust storm and sandstorm, resulting from the action of a strong, turbulent wind on the earth's surface. See also FOG.

Atmospheric Pollution.—A growing problem of modern civilization is the pollution of the atmosphere by many kinds of gases and particles that are harmful to human beings, crops, and structures. These substances are produced by combustion in factories, incinerators, home furnaces, and automobile motors; and by the explosion of atom and hydrogen bombs. They are removed from the atmosphere by the gradual settling out of particles and the "scavenging" effect of precipitation. However, they are not always removed fast enough. When the atmosphere is stable and stagnant, the pollution may steadily increase. Thousands of deaths in London within a few days have been ascribed to pulmonary complications caused by polluted air. See also SMOKE ABATEMENT.

WIND

Measurement of Wind.—Wind is the motion of air. Its speed may be expressed in miles per hour, meters per second, or knots. One knot is a speed of one nautical mile per hour or 1.15 statute miles per hour. Wind direction is the direction from which the wind is blowing. It may be expressed in compass points, so that, for example, a wind blowing from west toward east is called a west wind. It may also be given in degrees, from 0° for a north wind clockwise around to 90° for an east wind, 180° for a south wind, and 270° for a west wind.

Wind speed and direction may be estimated by observing the effects of the wind on trees, flags, smoke plumes from chimneys, vegetation, or on the sea surface. Wind is measured by a wind vane, which points into the wind direction, and an anemometer, which shows the speed. A common type of anemometer is the cup anemometer, consisting of three or four cups mounted on arms about a vertical axis so that the wind forces the cups to rotate about the axis. The speed of rotation is a measure of the wind speed. Another common type has a propeller mounted on a vane. The vane keeps the propeller facing the wind, thus giving the direction, and the speed of rotation of the propeller gives the wind speed. (See also ANEMOMETER; WIND VANE.)

Winds above the earth's surface are observed principally with balloons which travel with the wind and are tracked by various methods. The motion of a pilot balloon is observed through a theodolite, a telescope whose orientation is indicated by scales for vertical and horizontal angles. The height of the pilot balloon is known at any given time because it rises at a known rate. Hence, by use of trigonometry, its horizontal positions at successive times can be determined and its speed calculated. A more accurate method makes use of a balloon to which a suitable target is attached. The target is tracked by a radar instrument. In a third method, a radio direction finding device tracks a small radio transmitter attached to a balloon. Winds at very high levels in the atmosphere are estimated from observations of the motion of meteor trails.

Local Winds.—The sea breeze is experienced along coasts when air over the land is warmer than air over the sea. This condition is most common in the afternoon and in spring. The relatively cool, dense air over the sea spreads inland under the warm air, bringing a drop in temperature of several degrees.

Mountain and valley winds are caused by unequal cooling or heating of air along the slopes. At night the air near the surface of a slope cools more than air at the same level away from the slope. It is therefore heavier and flows down the slope, accumulates in valleys, and flows down the valleys toward the plains. In daytime, air near the surface of a slope is heated excessively. It rises and is replaced by air blowing up the slopes.

The foehn, known as the chinook in the Rocky Mountains, is a warm, dry wind coming down from the mountains toward the plains. It is driven by the prevailing winds blowing across the mountain ranges. The air of the foehn has become dry by precipitating part of its moisture in the mountains, and it has been heated by compression as it moves to lower levels where the air pressure is greater.

The mistral is a famous wind along the southern coast of France. Cold air from central Europe, moving southward, funnels into the Rhone Valley and speeds up. It reaches the coast as a strong, cold wind, unpleasant, sometimes with enough force to cause damage. The mistral is an example of drainage winds that are accelerated when forced to blow through narrow passes. See also WINDS—*Local Winds* (Glossary of Winds).

Turbulence.—The motion of the atmosphere is not smooth. Wind speed and direction fluctuate over a wide range of frequencies. These fluctuations, called turbulence, are one of the most difficult problems of meteorology. Turbulence mixes the atmosphere more effectively than does the motion of molecules. The transfer of heat, momentum, and moisture by turbulence is something like one million times more effective than molecular conduction, friction, and diffusion. Such transfers of properties must be taken into account in explaining and forecasting the weather. Turbulent fluctuations of the wind are caused by irregularities of the surface, unequal heating, and instability of the atmosphere, but they are not related to these factors by simple laws. Therefore, the effects of turbulence cannot be predicted exactly.

LOCAL STORMS

The Thunderstorm.—When the atmosphere is unstable and sufficient moisture is present, the vertical currents in cumulus clouds climb higher and higher, building cumulonimbus clouds whose tops may reach an altitude of six to eight miles. Within the cumulonimbus the cloud droplets and particles of ice grow by condensation of vapor and by coalescence and fall out of the cloud. Successive layers of water freeze on some of the ice particles so that they grow into hailstones. Powerful electrical charges are created. The difference in electrical potential between the cloud and the ground, and between different parts of the cloud, results in strokes of lightning. The rapid heating and expansion of air along the path of a lightning stroke causes the noise of thunder. Inside the cloud a mass of cold air rushes downward and outward, producing the strong, gusty, cold wind at the forward edge of the thunderstorm.

The cumulonimbus cloud of a thunderstorm is not always visible from the ground, as it may be obscured by a low layer of altostratus or nimbostratus. When it is visible, a patient observer, concentrating on the protuberances of the cloud, can see that it is in constant agitation, parts of the cloud growing swiftly while other parts are collapsing. This "boiling" of the cloud is most vividly shown by time-lapse motion pictures, by means of which the motions are speeded up about 30 times on the screen. The energy of one thunderstorm is equivalent to several atom bombs.

The precipitation in a thunderstorm is showery, alternating between downpours of large drops and light rainfall in smaller drops. Sometimes the upward air currents in the cloud are suddenly cut off. Then raindrops which were supported by the currents fall out in a torrent known as a cloudburst. This can be very damaging to crops and can result in a flash flood, which overflows stream beds so quickly that people in its path do not have time to escape. Hail is a fairly common form of precipitation from thunderstorms. It breaks the glass of greenhouses and flattens growing crops. Thunderstorms in winter may precipitate snow instead of rain.

Thunder originates as a sharp sound and is heard as such when lightning strikes nearby. At greater distances the sound becomes more prolonged and rumbling, because of reflections and variations in the paths followed by the sound toward the listener. Sound travels at about one-fifth of a mile per second, while light travels 186,000 miles per second. Hence, the distance to a lightning stroke can be estimated by counting the seconds between the time when the stroke is seen and the time when the first sound of thunder is heard. If the number of seconds is divided by five, the quotient is the distance in miles. Lightning may ruin electrical equipment and start fires. Thunder seems more frightening but does no harm in itself; in fact, the thunder one hears is from lightning that has already done its damage. Lightning seeks out objects that rise above the surrounding terrain. For this reason, it is better not to stand in open spaces or near isolated trees during a thunderstorm. (See also LIGHTNING.)

Lightning radiates a complex electromagnetic signal that causes static in a radio. Detection of certain frequencies of this signal by a method known as *sferics* permits thunderstorms to be located at distances of hundreds of miles. (See also STATIC.) Two widely separated receiving stations, with directional antennas, find the bearing of the thunderstorm where the signal originates. Lines drawn on a map from each station toward the direction of the signal intersect at its source.

Saint Elmo's fire (q.v.) is a luminous electrical discharge from elevated objects such as lightning rods, ship masts, and the wing tips of aircraft in flight.

The wind squall that heralds the arrival of a thunderstorm often is strong enough to damage or destroy trees and buildings and capsize small boats. On the arrival of the squall, the air temperature drops abruptly and the pressure rises sharply. The relief from the heat of a summer afternoon is usually only temporary; after the storm passes the temperature rises and the air is quite humid from evaporation of the rain.

Thunderstorms are caused by instability of the vertical forces in the atmosphere. Heating of air near the surface is the most common cause of this instability. Hence, the frequency of thunderstorms is generally greatest when and where surface heating by sunshine is greatest. With respect to time, they are most frequent in the afternoon and in summer. With respect to place, they are most frequent in tropical regions and over continents, because sunshine heats land surfaces more rapidly than water surfaces. In some areas near the equator, thunderstorms occur on more than half the days of the year.

The Tornado.—Sometimes a severe thunderstorm spawns the most violent storm of all, the tornado. Air rushing inward and upward in a thunderstorm may, in suitable conditions, start spinning about a vertical axis. Simultaneously, the pressure falls at the center of spin. The closer the air gets to the center the faster it spins and the lower is its pressure. Near the center of a tornado the pressure may be 900 millibars, only about 90 per cent of normal, and the whirling winds may blow with speeds in excess of 300 miles per hour.

The tornado is a small storm, about 300 yards in diameter, but extremely destructive. It has two destructive forces: its winds and its explosive force. The winds are strong enough to destroy trees and houses, roll automobiles over and over, move freight cars, and carry a person or any object as large and heavy as a person for several hundred yards. The explosive force on buildings results from the sudden decrease of air pressure when the center of a tornado strikes. The pressure of the air inside the building against the walls and roof is not compensated by an equal pressure on the outside, and the building explodes.

Besides being relatively small storms, tornadoes have a short life, averaging only about a half hour. Their mean speed of travel along their path is about 30 miles per hour and the average length of the path is only a few miles. Despite their small size and brief life, tornadoes accomplish considerable damage in the United States, where as many as a thousand may occur in one year.

PRESSURE

Measurement of Pressure.—Pressure is a force divided by the area upon which it acts. A fundamental unit of pressure is a dyne per square centimeter. One dyne is the force required to accelerate a mass of one gram to a speed of one centimeter per second in a period of one second. The millibar is 1,000 dynes per square centimeter and is the unit of pressure most frequently used in meteorology.

The mercurial barometer is a glass tube containing mercury, closed at the upper end and opening into a reservoir of mercury at the bottom. Atmospheric pressure, exerted on the open reservoir, supports the mercury at a certain height in the glass tube. This height is another commonly used measure of pressure. It may be expressed as inches of mercury or millimeters of mercury. One inch of mercury at standard temperature and gravity is equivalent to 33.86 millibars.

The aneroid barometer is an evacuated metal chamber that responds to the variations of atmospheric pressure on its surface. The responses are magnified by levers and the pressure is read on a scale. The aneroid barograph has a rotating drum on which the pressure is recorded with a pen. The pressure altimeter is an aneroid barometer calibrated in terms of heights corresponding to various pressures. It is used in aircraft to determine altitude. See also BAROMETER.

Pressure Variations.—Because of its weight, the atmosphere is compressed down toward the earth's surface. The amount of compression at a particular level, and hence the pressure there, is proportional to the mass of air lying above that level. Therefore, the pressure is greatest at sea level, where its average value is 1,013.2 millibars or 29.92 inches of mercury. At an altitude of 18,000 feet or 3.4 miles the pressure is half the sea level value. The decrease of pressure upward in the atmosphere is of fundamental importance in weather processes; because, when a mass of air rises, the pressure on it decreases and the mass expands and cools, just as air released from a tire cools by expansion. The cooling of the rising mass eventually brings its temperature down to the point where the water vapor is saturated and begins to condense into clouds. Cooling of rising air and warming of descending air are expressed in terms of the adiabatic lapse rate, discussed above in the section on *Temperature*.

Air pressure at a fixed point changes with time for two reasons: the regular daily tidal oscillation of the atmosphere, and the passage of moving pressure systems of various types. The diurnal oscillation gives a maximum of pressure at 10 A.M. and 10 P.M. local time and a minimum at 4 A.M. and 4 P.M. The range is greatest at the equator, where it is 2.6 millibars, and least at the poles, where it is practically zero. Meteorologists have not yet determined to what extent this oscillation is a true tide induced by the gravitational attraction of the sun and magnified by a natural resonance of the atmosphere, or to what extent it is induced by the daily heating of the atmosphere by the sun.

Moving pressure systems of all sizes, from the tornado to atmospheric highs hundreds of miles in diameter, cause irregular local variations. These are generally greater than the regular diurnal oscillation, ranging up to a rise of 50 millibars or more in a strong high and a drop of 100 millibars or more in tornadoes and hurricanes.

The variation of pressure in the horizontal direction is usually no more than one ten-thousandth as great as the decrease in the vertical. Only in a tornado does the horizontal variation equal or exceed the vertical variation. At sea level the pressure drops about 1 millibar for each 10 meters of altitude, or about 1 inch of mercury for each 1,000 feet. The rate of decrease is proportional to the air density; hence, at higher altitudes, where the density is less, pressure decreases less rapidly with altitude. See also

Hypsometry—*Barometric Methods.*

Pressure and Wind.—The atmosphere is nearly in hydrostatic equilibrium. This means that the decrease of pressure upward is just sufficient to balance the force of gravity downward. When the balance is not exact, upward or downward currents of air are created.

Wind is caused by horizontal variations of pressure. For example, if the pressure decreases from west toward east, there is a force pushing the masses of air toward east. This is called the pressure-gradient force. In local winds, such as sea breezes and mountain winds, the air moves mostly from higher toward lower pressure. But on a larger scale, such as the scale represented by a weather map, the deflecting force of the earth's rotation becomes effective; and the wind tends to blow parallel to isobars, or lines of equal pressure.

This deflecting force is known as the Coriolis force after the French mathematician who first described it. It can be demonstrated with a phonograph turntable. If one draws a piece of chalk straight across a spinning record, then stops the record, one can see that the chalk mark is curved. Similarly, air moving across the face of the earth tends to follow a straight path in space while the earth spins beneath it. To an earthbound observer, it appears that the air is deflected to the right in the Northern Hemisphere and to the left in the Southern Hemisphere.

Meteorologists have invented an idealized type of wind called the geostrophic wind. The geostrophic wind blows parallel to isobars, with the pressure-gradient force and the Coriolis force acting at right angles to the wind direction and canceling each other. In the Northern Hemisphere the pressure-gradient force acts to the left of the wind and the Coriolis force to the right; in the Southern Hemisphere the forces are reversed. Above the earth's surface the winds of the free atmosphere are often close to geostrophic. Deviations from geostrophic wind are caused by friction, especially near the earth's surface, where the wind blows at an angle toward lower pressure; by centrifugal force due to curvature of the path followed by the air; and by changing pressure gradients to which the air motion cannot respond immediately. See also Winds—*The Gradient Wind.*

THE WEATHER MAP

Collection and Dissemination of Observations.—The weather elements described in the preceding sections are observed regularly at thousands of weather stations all over the world. At some stations, especially at airports, observations are made every hour and more frequently when the weather is changing rapidly. The standard observations for the surface weather map are made four times a day, at midnight, 6:00 A.M., noon, and 6:00 P.M., Greenwich time. The observations of upper winds are made four times a day; and the observations of pressure, temperature, and humidity aloft are made twice a day. The network of weather observing stations is supplemented at intervening points by cooperative observers who, serving without pay, record each day's maximum and minimum temperature and precipitation.

Weather observations are collected efficiently and swiftly by telephone, telegraph, teletype, and radio. Observations for a certain area are collected at one point in that area and then relayed by teletype and radio to other areas. Weather data for the whole United States are available by teletype at any point in the country within two hours after the observations have been made. The observations are transmitted in codes which permit a great amount of information to be expressed in a few symbols. It is this well-organized system of collection and dissemination that makes weather forecasting possible.

The Surface Weather Map.—The most important chart used by forecasters is the surface weather map. On this chart are plotted for each station the amount of cloudiness, the types of clouds and height of the lowest cloud, wind direction and speed, temperature, dew point, visibility, present weather, pressure reduced to sea level, pressure change in the past three hours, weather of the past six hours, and amount of precipitation. The weather analyst can see at a glance the state of the weather at one time over the region covered by the map; hence, the chart is called the synoptic chart. By extension of this idea, meteorologists, when referring to observations, sometimes use the term "synoptic" in the sense of "simultaneous."

The data in the raw, plotted form represent point values of elements which actually vary continuously between points. Hence, to make the surface weather map useful, it must be analyzed with lines showing a picture of the weather that is continuous across the map. Such lines might be drawn for each element plotted; but this procedure is not practical, partly because too many lines would be required and partly because some elements, such as visibility, are so variable that their distribution is not adequately shown in an ordinary synoptic network. It is common practice to draw isobars, or lines of equal pressure, in order to delineate the pressure systems. (See also Isobar.) Fronts, the boundaries between masses of air of different properties, are also drawn. In addition, areas where precipitation is occurring may be shaded; types of air masses may be indicated by symbols; and isallobars, lines of equal pressure change, may be drawn for the three-hour changes.

The necessity of using pressure observations reduced to sea level leads to difficulties in the isobaric analysis of weather maps containing mountainous regions. Sea-level pressures are a necessity because the vertical variation of pressure is so much greater than the horizontal variation. If pressure were not reduced to a fixed level, isobars would represent the altitudes of observing stations more than they would the horizontal pressure variations. But in order to reduce pressure to sea level one must assume a fictitious column of air between sea level and the altitude of the station. The temperature assumed for the fictitious air column at high stations significantly affects the pressure computed for sea level. Hence, in mountainous regions the reduced pressure is sometimes meaningless.

The Constant Pressure Chart.—Observations above the earth's surface are obtained primarily by means of balloons and balloon-borne instruments, and to a lesser extent from aircraft. Special observations of the very high atmosphere are made with rockets. The radiosonde is a small instrument carried aloft by a balloon. It contains an aneroid barometer, a resistance thermometer, a hygrometer, and a radio transmitter. Readings of the instruments are automatically sent by the radio to a ground receiver. The altitude corresponding to a given pressure is computed by means of the hydrostatic equation, which expresses the balance between the weight of air and the force due to the decrease of pressure upward. (See also UPPER ATMOSPHERE, SOUNDING METHODS OF THE—*Development of the Radiosonde.*)

Upper air observations are customarily analyzed for selected pressure levels. On these constant pressure charts are plotted for each station the altitude at which the particular pressure was observed, the temperature, dew point, and wind. The charts are analyzed with contours, lines of equal altitude. Contours on a constant pressure surface correspond to isobars on a constant height surface. This method of analysis has been adopted because many of the fundamental equations of meteorology are simpler when applied to surfaces of constant pressure. The idealized wind called geostrophic wind blows parallel to contours and its speed is greater where the contours are closer together. In addition to contours, other lines drawn on constant pressure charts include fronts; isotherms, or lines of equal temperature; and isotachs, or lines of equal wind speed.

The observations obtained by a radiosonde may also be plotted on a special type of thermodynamic chart. The primary coordinates of the thermodynamic chart are pressure and temperature. The plotted sounding forms a zigzag line joining the observed pairs of values of temperature and pressure. Analysis of individual soundings gives the meteorologist much information about the vertical structure of the atmosphere, the nature of temperature inversions, and the stability. See also GRAPHICAL ANALYSIS—*Weather Forecasting from Single-Station Analysis.*

Pressure Systems.—Isobars on the surface map and contours on the constant pressure chart form characteristic patterns known as pressure systems. An area in which the isobars or contours form closed lines about a point with minimum pressure or height is called a low; if they form closed lines about a point of maximum pressure or height the area is called a high. A line along which the pressure or altitude is relatively low is a trough line; and a line along which the value is relatively high is a ridge line. Where a trough line crosses a ridge line the area is known as a col.

Generally speaking, upward air currents, clouds, and precipitation are found in a low and in the vicinity of a trough line; while downward currents and clear skies are found in a high and near a ridge line. However, these relationships are not dependable and should not be used as the sole basis for predicting the weather. The barometer alone may be better than nothing at all; but labels such as "cloudy," "stormy," or "clearing" on the barometer should not be taken very literally.

Air Masses.—An air mass is a large body of air, several hundred miles across, which has certain characteristic properties. An ideal air mass is homogeneous in the horizontal; but a real air mass exhibits some variation of temperature, humidity, and other properties, particularly after it has moved away from the region where the properties were acquired from the underlying surface. This region, the source region, is a part of the earth's surface with uniform properties over a large area. For example, central Canada in winter is covered with snow; if a mass of air stagnates there for several days it becomes cold

and dry, with a strong temperature inversion in the lowest layer. It is then called a polar continental air mass, with the symbol cP. As another example, a body of air that remains over a tropical ocean for several days becomes warm and moist. This is a tropical maritime air mass, with symbol mT. Other common air masses are the moist, cool polar maritime (mP) formed over the oceans in high latitudes, and the hot, dry tropical continental (cT) formed over subtropical deserts. Arctic air, with symbol A, is a very cold air mass that forms in Arctic regions in winter. Equatorial air, E, is quite warm and moist up to high levels.

When an air mass moves away from its source region its properties are progressively modified and it becomes less and less homogeneous. The United States is a region of transition, where polar and Arctic air masses from the north meet tropical air masses from the south.

Fronts.—The boundary zone between two different air masses is sometimes diffuse ·and sometimes sharp. When it is sharp it is called a frontal surface; the line of intersection between a frontal surface and a horizontal surface is called a front. The boundary between polar and tropical air is the polar front. If a diffuse boundary zone between two air masses becomes sharper, *frontogenesis* is said to have occurred.

The ideal front is a perfect discontinuity of temperature, that is, a thin line with warm air on one side and cold air on the other. Mixing processes in the atmosphere prevent such a perfect discontinuity from forming; a real front is a zone of transition from 30 miles up to perhaps 100 miles in width. Nevertheless, in weather analysis the fronts are drawn as thin lines and are regarded, in some respects, as nearly ideal discontinuities.

A frontal surface is neither vertical nor horizontal. It slopes upward over the cold air mass, which lies in the shape of a wedge beneath the lighter, warm air mass. The slope of a frontal surface is described mathematically in terms of its rate of rise with horizontal distance; for example, a slope of one in a hundred, or 1:100, means that the surface rises 1 mile in a distance of 100 miles. Frontal slopes vary between the approximate limits of 1:50 and 1:250.

A cold front is one along which the cold air is advancing against the warm air and displacing it; while along a warm front the cold air is retreating and the warm air is replacing it. If the cold air mass is neither advancing nor retreating, the front is called a stationary front. Usually along a front there is conflict between the two air masses, each of which is trying to displace the other. Hence the air masses converge toward the front and, having no other place to go, must rise along the frontal surface. It is this convergence and lifting of air, with resulting adiabatic cooling, that causes cloudiness and precipitation along frontal surfaces.

A front lies in a trough of low pressure. At an ideal front, the isobars or contours would make a sharp angle pointing toward higher pressure. They are drawn this way on weather charts even though fronts are not ideal. The geostrophic relation between wind and isobars, according to which the wind is parallel to the isobars, requires that the wind shift direction when a front passes a station. In the Northern Hemisphere the wind veers, or changes direction clockwise, when a front passes. For example, the wind may shift from southwest to northwest. In the Southern Hemisphere a frontal passage causes the wind to back, or shift counterclockwise, such as from northwest to southwest.

Although a front is fundamentally a discontinuity of temperature, it is also, in most cases, a zone of transition for other weather elements, particularly the dew-point temperature and to some extent visibility, cloudiness, and precipitation, because these elements are likely to be different in the two contrasting air masses.

The Extratropical Cyclone.—In the area of a low, around a point of minimum pressure, the winds circulate counterclockwise in the Northern Hemisphere and clockwise in the Southern Hemisphere. Such a pressure system and its circulating winds is called a cyclone. Cyclones are large weather systems some hundreds of miles across; they should not be confused with tornadoes, which are sometimes known colloquially, but incorrectly, as "cyclones." Two kinds of cyclone are distinguished according to their region of origin and their characteristics: the extratropical cyclone and the tropical cyclone. The tropical cyclone is more symmetrical, the isobars being nearly circular, and it forms solely in a tropical maritime air mass. It contains no fronts until it moves to higher latitudes, where it may draw in a polar air mass which lies in juxtaposition with the tropical air.

Most extratropical cyclones form along a front. The polar front theory of cyclones is another of the ideal models used in weather analysis to represent a rather complex phenomenon in a reasonably simple manner. According to the polar front theory, *cyclogenesis,* or the creation of a new cyclone, begins when a small wavelike disturbance appears on a front. At the peak of the wave the pressure begins to fall. If the wavelength is within certain limits, the wave grows in amplitude and the pressure continues to fall. At this stage the cyclone is called a young wave cyclone. It is moving generally from west toward east. On its forward side, warm air is displacing cold air, so this front is a warm front. To its rear, the cold air is moving forward and the front here is a cold front. Between the cold front and warm front is a pie-shaped area of warm air called the warm sector. The pressure is lowest at the peak of the warm sector where the front changes from a cold to a warm front.

Extending 200 or 300 miles ahead of the surface warm front is a system of clouds. At the extreme forward edge the clouds are cirrus. As one approaches the warm front the cirrus clouds merge into an overcast of cirrostratus, then lower and thicken, becoming altostratus and altocumulus. Nearer the warm front one finds the low, thick, shapeless nimbostratus from which steady rain or snow is falling. In the warm sector the weather conditions depend on the stability of the tropical air mass. If it is stable, as is usually the situation in western Europe, there are stratus clouds precipitating drizzle. If it is unstable, as in midwestern United States, one finds cumulus clouds and scattered showers. Warm sectors in the United States frequently contain a squall line, a line of showers and thunderstorms ahead of the cold front and roughly parallel to it. At the cold front the weather is showery and clears quickly when the cold front passes.

During the first day or two of its existence, the cyclone deepens, which means that the pressure falls, and simultaneously the cold front begins to overtake the warm front at the peak of the warm sector. This process is called *occlusion,* and the front formed where the cold front overtakes the warm front is an occluded front. The occluded front lengthens as the process of occlusion extends farther from the center, and the warm sector is progressively wiped out. In actual fact the warm air does not disappear but is lifted above the earth's surface. During occlusion, the center of low pressure remains at the tip of the occluded front, corresponding to the original peak of the warm sector. When occlusion is complete, the cyclone is deepest and strongest, and from that time on it is likely to fill and die.

The development of a wave cyclone in the Southern Hemisphere is a mirror image of that in the Northern Hemisphere, reflected at the equator. Thus, if one holds a weather map for the Northern Hemisphere upside down and views it in a mirror, he sees the wind circulation, the frontal pattern, and the relative positions of the warm and cold air masses as they would appear on a weather map for the Southern Hemisphere.

The Tropical Cyclone and the Hurricane.—In its source region, tropical maritime air is uniformly warm and moist up to about 4,000 feet above the surface of the tropical oceans. At that average level a temperature inversion is found. Above the inversion the air mass is warm and dry. The inversion is a stabilizing influence, acting as a "lid" on upward currents in the moist lower layer, so that cumulus clouds are unable to grow vertically.

Occasionally a low pressure trough, opening toward the equatorial region, forms in the tropical air. Within the trough, convergence of air lifts the temperature inversion and weakens or destroys it. Then the cumulus are able to grow into cumulonimbus clouds. Hence, in these troughs, called easterly waves, showers and thunderstorms may be observed. If the thunderstorms become concentrated in an area of the easterly wave, the pressure falls and a cyclonic circulation develops. This is a tropical cyclone.

Tropical cyclones are regions of squally, thundery weather with diameter of 100 to several hundred miles. They are fairly symmetrical, the isobars tending to form concentric circles about the lowest pressure, with uniformly warm, humid air. They are carried along by the trade winds from east toward west, then toward north and northeast around the vast subtropical high pressure system. Their path in the Southern Hemisphere is a mirror image—from east toward west, then toward south and southeast. It is sometimes exceedingly difficult to detect a tropical cyclone in its early stages, because it may form in an area where there are no island stations or ships to observe it. When there is some evidence pointing to an incipient tropical cyclone, meteorologists watch the area closely and make the most of any observations they may chance to receive. As a cyclone approaches the mainland of the United States, "hurricane hunters" fly out in specially equipped airplanes for a thorough weather reconnaissance of the area.

When the winds of a tropical cyclone reach 75 miles per hour, the storm is called a hurricane; in the western North Pacific it is called a typhoon. Tornadoes and hurricanes are similar storms except for size. If a tornado could be spread out laterally from its diameter of about 300 yards to 300 miles or more, it would make a good substitute for a hurricane. Like a tornado, a hurricane is a vortex of winds circling cyclonically about a center where the pressure may be 100 millibars below normal. The winds are strongest on the edge of the inner core, called the calm eye. Inside the eye, the winds are light and the sky may be partly clear. Outside the eye, the sky is overcast and heavy rain accompanies the strong winds.

Hurricanes are most frequent in summer and fall. They occur in all tropical oceans except the South Atlantic. Their strength is greatest while they remain over the ocean; it is likely to be dissipated rapidly when they move over land because of friction with the land surface and because the supply of water vapor from the warm ocean surface is cut off. The energy of a hurricane is derived mostly from the latent heat of condensation of water vapor. This energy is tremendous. In a well-developed hurricane the kinetic energy of the winds at any moment is of the order of 200 billion kilowatt-hours. At the rate of one cent per kilowatt-hour, this amount of energy would be worth two billion dollars if it could be harnessed and used. Unfortunately, a hurricane's energy is concentrated on destruction which, in extreme cases, may amount to the loss of several hundred million dollars in property and hundreds of lives. See also HURRICANE.

The Anticyclone.—The opposite of the cyclone is the anticyclone, an area of high pressure hundreds of miles in diameter with winds circulating clockwise in the Northern Hemisphere and counterclockwise in the Southern Hemisphere. There are two kinds of anticyclone, the cold and the warm. In the cold anticyclone the high pressure is caused by the extra weight of cold, dense air. It does not extend very high in the atmosphere, generally not more than two miles. It is associated with cold air masses such as polar continental air and moves with the cold mass.

The warm anticyclone, sometimes called the "dynamic" anticyclone, extends to higher levels than the cold anticyclone. It is more lethargic, tending to remain in one area for a considerable time. Thus, it acts as a "block" for moving cyclones, which are forced to go around its periphery. It may dominate the weather of an area for days or weeks, giving clear skies and in summer very hot weather.

In both types of anticyclone, the air of the lower atmosphere is subsiding, or sinking. The subsiding air is compressed as it is subjected to the greater pressure near the earth's surface. Compression warms the air, and since there is no supply of water vapor to moisten the air, the increased temperature leads to decreased relative humidity and evaporation of clouds. The air does not subside all the way to the earth's surface. The limit of its descent is marked by a subsidence inversion. This inversion stabilizes the atmosphere, so that cumulus clouds in the lowest layer do not grow upward. Pollution originating from combustion at the surface is trapped below the inversion, making the sky hazy; and, when there is not enough wind to carry the pollution away, the concentration may become harmful to life. See also ANTICYCLONE.

WEATHER FORECASTING

The Nature of the Problem of Forecasting.—Weather forecasting is only one of many important branches of meteorology, but most of the financial support for the study of the atmosphere is supplied by government agencies primarily for the purpose of forecasting.

The stated accuracy of weather forecasts depends upon the method used to verify them. If sufficient tolerance is permitted, it may be said that the accuracy is high. For example, if a forecast of temperature is counted correct when it is within five degrees of the observed temperature, then nearly all forecasts of temperature will verify. If the tolerance is lowered to one degree, a good many forecasts will not verify. Evaluation of forecast accuracy must be related to the way in which the forecasts are used. No system of verification is satisfactory for all purposes.

The weather is an exceedingly complex phenomenon. A disturbance so small that it cannot be detected in the synoptic network may grow into a cyclone within a day. While it grows, the disturbance interacts with other pressure systems, changing their characteristics. Although these processes are governed by known physical laws, the problem of prediction is complicated by mathematical complexity of the laws and lack of sufficient observations to show the exact state of the atmosphere at a given moment.

Weather phenomena can be recognized over a tremendous range of scale, as explained in the introductory paragraphs of this article. When forecasting nighttime minimum temperatures for a fruitgrowing district, the forecaster must keep in mind the effect of cold air drainage into small valleys as well as the effect of large-scale pressure systems. A forecast of thundershowers for New York City means that rain will occur in some parts of the city but not necessarily in all parts. The forecaster does not know who will get wet.

General Methods of Forecasting.—Because of the complexity of the problem, weather forecasting has been based largely on empirical methods. Two of these methods constitute the greater part of the science of forecasting. The analog method utilizes the past behavior of the atmosphere as a model of its future behavior. If today's weather map resembles, in its essential parts, a situation that has occurred before, one may expect that today's weather will develop in the same way as its analog did in the past. This method by itself is inadequate, because no two weather maps are alike in all essential details. Each map is a new challenge; prediction may be guided by other similar maps but cannot be based entirely upon them.

The other empirical method is extrapolation of trends. The observed motion of a cyclone over the past day or two can be extended forward to give a prediction of its future position. Its rate of deepening can be extrapolated to give its future pressure. The growth and motion of a precipitation system, as observed on the last few weather maps, suggest the intensity and location that may be expected later. This is a powerful method of forecasting, but not sufficient in itself. Trends change from time to time, for a deepening cyclone cannot deepen forever and a precipitation area cannot grow indefinitely.

These two empirical methods are apt to yield predictions that are contradictory or physically impossible. The forecaster must call on his knowledge of the physical processes and his experience to adjust the predictions. The skill of a forecaster is most apparent at this point, where forecasting becomes something of an art. When he has arrived at his final prediction, the forecaster constructs prognostic charts showing the expected pattern of the future weather. He then interprets the charts in terms of forecasts describing the expected weather in various areas of the region for which he is responsible. These forecasts are transmitted by teletype to other weather stations, newspapers, and radio and television stations for dissemination to the public. The prognostic charts and the current weather charts prepared in the National Weather Analysis Center in Washington, D.C., are sent over a weather facsimile network for the information of meteorologists throughout the area of the United States.

Numerical Weather Prediction.—High-speed electronic computers have opened the way to weather prediction by mathematical methods in place of the empirical methods of the past. These computers have both the capacity for storing information and the speed that are necessary for useful solutions of the equations of meteorology. Without such computers a numerical calculation of a weather forecast would take so much time that the predicted weather would come and go long before the calculation could be completed.

The basic principle of the method of numerical weather prediction can be illustrated by a very simple example. A particle of air at rest in a pressure field is accelerated from higher to lower pressure by a force proportional to the pressure gradient. The acceleration can be calculated and multiplied by a small time interval to give the velocity attained by the air a short time later. This process of iteration is repeated, and the velocity and position of the particle are determined as a function of time. But, after the air particle starts moving, it is subjected to another force at right angles to its path, the Coriolis force, which is proportional to the velocity of the air. So in each short time interval, the acceleration due to the Coriolis force is computed, and the resulting velocity component at right angles to the original path is determined. The particle of air, responding to both the pressure-gradient force and the Coriolis force, follows a curved path until it is moving approximately parallel to the isobars.

In this kind of computation one must keep at a minimum the errors introduced by the assumption that gradients, forces, and accelerations are constant over short distances and during each time interval of the iteration. The errors can be reduced by shortening the space and time intervals but this in turn increases the total time required for the computation. The errors not only may lead to an erroneous forecast but also may render the computation unstable so that the calculated quantities increase beyond reason, or in the terminology used, the computation "blows up." Meteorologists are seeking the best ways to write the equations to produce accurate and detailed predictions.

The electronic computers are capable of taking coded weather reports directly from the teletype, decoding them, correcting certain errors, analyzing the present weather situation, calculating the forecasted weather, and presenting the forecast in the form of a printed prognostic chart. The computers can be programmed to perform any logical computation or decision, and their usefulness is limited only by man's ability to give them the correct instructions to work with in solving the problems at hand.

See also COMPUTERS—*3. Continuous Computers.*

THE VERTICAL STRUCTURE OF THE ATMOSPHERE

Composition of the Atmosphere.—Pure, dry air is a mixture of 78 per cent nitrogen, 21 per cent oxygen, and 1 per cent argon, by volume. There are traces of carbon dioxide, ozone, neon, krypton, helium, hydrogen, xenon, nitrous oxide, and methane. The proportions of the principal constituents are essentially the same up to at least 40 miles above the earth's surface. At higher levels the oxygen molecules begin to dissociate into oxygen atoms, and all the constituents of air are partly ionized by ultraviolet rays from the sun.

Of the rare gases, ozone is perhaps the most important because of its absorption of solar radiation. The maximum concentration of ozone is found near 14 miles. Although the total amount of ozone in the atmosphere would form a layer only about one tenth of an inch thick at a temperature of 0° C. and sea-level pressure, ozone is quite effective in absorbing the very short waves of sunshine, thus protecting man from these harmful rays.

Water vapor is a variable constituent of moist air, its proportion ranging from near zero in a very dry air mass up to about 6 per cent by volume, or 4 per cent by weight, in a hot, moist air mass. Water vapor is important because it is the only atmospheric constituent that condenses into liquid form or freezes at the temperatures that occur in the atmosphere. Both water vapor and carbon dioxide are effective in absorbing radiation in the longer wavelengths of the infra-red region of the spectrum. Such radiation originates at the earth's surface, at clouds, and even in clear air.

Other variable constituents are the gases and particles originating from combustion; particles of dust, sand, and salt carried aloft by the wind; volcanic dust; water droplets and ice crystals in clouds and precipitation; and radioactive material from the explosion of atom and hydrogen bombs.

The Layers of the Atmosphere.—In the lowest layer of the atmosphere, called the troposphere, the air temperature normally decreases upward with an average lapse rate of 3.6° F. per 1,000 feet. At an altitude of about 5 miles at the poles and 10 miles near the equator, this lapse rate ceases and the temperature becomes nearly constant with increasing altitude up to about 20 miles. The layer of constant temperature is the stratosphere, and the boundary zone between the stratosphere and troposphere is the tropopause.

Above the tropopause various names have been given to layers with characteristic properties. The names have not been standardized and some of the layers overlap. The ozonosphere is the layer of maximum ozone content; it lies in the upper part of the stratosphere. Above the stratosphere is a warm layer caused by absorption of short-wave solar radiation by ozone. This warm layer lies above the ozonosphere because the absorption of short waves by ozone is nearly complete before the sun's rays penetrate to the layer of maximum ozone. The warm layer, which extends to 40 miles, has been called both the chemosphere and the mesosphere. (See also ATMOSPHERE—*Divisions of the Atmosphere.*)

The ionosphere, extending from 40 miles to 300 miles, is the layer in which the atmospheric gases are partly ionized by the ultraviolet rays from the sun. The aurora, the brilliant display sometimes called the "northern lights," is caused by charged particles from the sun striking the ionosphere. The ionosphere can be divided into separate layers according to the nature of the ionization. These layers, such as the E layer and the F₂ layer, reflect radio waves and make possible long-distance communication by radio. Beyond the ionosphere the atmosphere gradually becomes more and more attenuated, with no definite upper limit. (See also AURORA BOREALIS; IONOSPHERICS.)

The average altitude of the tropopause is 7 miles, at a pressure of 230 millibars, a temperature of −70° F., and with a density three tenths of the density of air at sea level. In the mesosphere the temperature rises to about the same as the average temperature at sea level, then drops to about −100° F. at the mesopause, where the ionosphere begins. The pressure at the mesopause is only three one-hundredths of a millibar. In the ionosphere the temperature increases upward. At the upper limit of the ionosphere, 300 miles, the temperature is estimated to be 1600° F. and the pressure is only one three-hundred-billionth of the sea level pressure.

A million or more meteors enter the atmosphere every day at speeds of many miles per second. Most meteors are tiny specks of matter. Friction with the atmosphere heats them to incandescence and vaporizes them at altitudes of 30 to 90 miles. We observe them as "shooting stars." Very rarely a meteor is large enough to survive its passage through the atmosphere and reach the earth's surface. See also METEOR; METEORITE.

THE GENERAL CIRCULATION

The Atmospheric Heat Balance.—The *solar constant* is a measure of insolation, the radiant energy received from the sun at the outer limit of the earth's atmosphere. It is approximately 1.94 gram-calories per minute on one square centimeter of a surface at right angles to the sun's rays at the earth's mean (average) distance from the sun. A calorie is the amount of heat required to raise the temperature of one gram of water one degree Celsius. Because of the curvature of the earth and because only half of its surface is illuminated at one time, the average amount of insolation received at right angles to the earth's outer atmospheric surface is one half calorie per square centimeter per minute. This energy is concentrated in the short wavelength end of the electromagnetic spectrum, with maximum intensity in the range of visible light. Reflection back to space by clouds and by the earth's ground surface amounts to about 40 per cent of the incoming energy; this ratio of reflected to incoming energy is called the *albedo*. The remaining 60 per cent, an average of three tenths of a calorie per square centimeter per minute, is transformed into heat energy which drives the winds and maintains the warmth of the atmosphere and earth's surface, and is eventually radiated back to space in the invisible infrared wavelengths.

Over a period of a year or longer, the energy loss by infrared radiation from the earth and atmosphere is almost exactly equal to the energy gain from insolation. Thus, a heat balance is maintained. Theories have been advanced to explain changes of climate by changes in energy received from the sun; but these theories cannot be confirmed because the observed variations of the solar constant are approximately within the limits of the errors of observation.

The Planetary Winds.—Insolation is strongest in equatorial regions, where the sun's rays are perpendicular to the earth's surface, and least at the poles. This unequal heating provides the energy for the large-scale circulation of the atmosphere. The general circulation is divided into three major wind belts: the trade winds, which blow from the northeast in the Northern Hemisphere and from the southeast in the Southern Hemisphere; the prevailing westerlies of middle latitudes; and the polar easterlies of high latitudes. Between the trade winds of the two hemispheres lies the doldrums, a region of calms also known as the intertropical convergence zone. Between the trade winds and the prevailing westerlies are the horse latitudes, another region of calms at about 30° latitude. Between the prevailing westerlies and the polar easterlies is the polar front. Tropical cyclones form in the intertropical convergence zone and extratropical cyclones form along the polar front.

At increasing heights the separate wind systems gradually merge into one system of westerlies circulating about the poles, except that easterly winds persist to high levels over the tropics in summer. Near the level of the tropopause is found the jet stream, a narrow band of very fast westerlies. In the Northern Hemisphere in winter, the average position of the jet stream is 8 miles above the surface at latitude 27° N.; in summer it is 7 miles above the surface at 42° N. Winds of the jet stream average 75 miles per hour in winter and 35 miles per hour in summer; speeds greater than 200 miles per hour have been observed. In the stratosphere the west winds diminish with increasing height and eventually become easterlies at very high levels.

Associated with these planetary winds are vertical currents which are the primary factor in determining the average cloudiness and precipitation of a latitude belt. In the doldrums the warm, moist trade winds from the two hemispheres converge and rise, producing clouds and heavy precipitation. In the horse latitudes the air subsides, warms by compression, and spreads out. Deserts are found in this zone. In the polar front zone, cyclones, clouds, and precipitation result from the convergence of the polar easterlies against the relatively warm and moist westerlies, which are forced to rise over the sloping polar frontal surface. (See also CLIMATE— *Winds at Middle Latitudes*.)

A large-scale deviation from the planetary wind system is the monsoon of Asia. In summer the air is heated strongly over the continent of Asia. A vast low pressure area covers most of the continent. Air from the Pacific and Indian oceans converges into the low, rises, and precipitates heavy rainfall. In winter the Asiatic low is replaced by a high, with winds diverging outward from the continent to the oceans. Monsoons over other continents are much weaker than the Asiatic monsoon, and are generally not detectable.

The Semipermanent Pressure Systems.— Because of the relationship between wind and pressure, the planetary winds are related to large highs and lows. These pressure systems are called "semipermanent" because their position and intensity change little from day to day. The doldrums belt is one of low pressure, the so-called equatorial low. The horse latitudes form a belt of high pressure, broken up into large subtropical anticyclones. In the low pressure belt coinciding with the polar front zone are found semipermanent cyclones, particularly the Icelandic low and the Aleutian low of the Northern Hemisphere. In the polar regions is the polar high.

Weather Control.—Control of the weather by man would have an incalculable economic value and a profound effect on our way of life. Intensive studies of possible ways of controlling the weather have been carried on since World War II. It seems that the possibilities are greatest for phenomena of small scale and least for those of large scale, because the energy of atmospheric processes exceeds the energy sources controlled by man except for phenomena of the size of a thunderstorm. In order to circumvent this problem of energy, ways are being sought to tip the balance in a delicately balanced situation by means of a relatively small amount of energy. Artificial rain making (see RAIN MAKING) employs this approach, on the theory that some clouds will produce rain only if stimulated by injections of dry ice, silver iodide, or other substances into them.

There is, at the present time, little hope of changing the climate of a large region. Deserts, which are caused by subsidence of air in the subtropical anticyclones, cannot be converted into fertile regions by increasing the rainfall unless the circulation in the large anticyclones can be changed. But we can gain some comfort from our ignorance about the mechanics of the general circulation; when we understand the mechanics better we may find ways of influencing the circulation. See also METEOROLOGICAL STATIONS; WEATHER BUREAU.

Bibliography.—Malone, T. F., ed., *Compendium of Meteorology* (Boston 1951); Middleton, W. E. K., and Spilhaus, A. F., *Meteorological Instruments*, 3d rev. ed. (Toronto 1953); Taylor, G. F., *Elementary Meteorology* (New York 1954); Riehl, Herbert, *Tropical Meteorology* (New York 1954); Trewartha, Glenn T., *Introduction to Weather and Climate* (New York 1954); Saucier, W. J., *Principles of Meteorological Analysis* (Chicago 1955); World Meteorological Organization, *International Cloud Atlas—Abridged Atlas* (Geneva 1956); Spar, Jerome, *The Way of the Weather* (Mankato, Minn., 1957); Petterssen, Sverre, *Introduction to Meteorology*, 2d ed. (New York 1958); Byers, H. R., *General Meteorology*, 3d ed. (New York 1959); also *Bulletin* and *Journal of Meteorology* published by the American Meteorological Society (Boston); *Weatherwise* published by the American Meteorological Society (Boston); *Weather* and *Quarterly Journal of the Royal Meteorological Society* published by the Royal Meteorological Society (London); *Tellus* published by the Swedish Geophysical Society (Stockholm); *Monthly Weather Review* and *Daily Weather Map* published by the U.S. Weather Bureau (Washington).

JAMES E. MILLER,
Professor of Meteorology, New York University.

METEOROLOGY, Marine, differs from that of land areas chiefly from the fact that the rays of the sun penetrate more deeply into the ocean substance than into the land and that the diffusion of this heat through the water body is practically uniform. The ocean thus becomes a vast storage reservoir of heat which is but slowly returned to the atmosphere. The effect upon the ocean climate is to render it more equable. See also CLIMATE; METEOROLOGY; OCEANOGRAPHY; WEATHER BUREAU.

METER, mē′tĕr, a mechanical device or instrument for automatically measuring, indicating, and recording the quantity measured.

Gas Meter.—This is an automatic instrument which measures the volume of gas flowing through a pipeline. There are two types: (1) the *wet meter,* in which a drum submerged in liquid is rotated by the entering gas; indicators geared to the axis of the drum indicate the amount of gas flowing through the instrument; (2) the *dry* meter, in which the gas entering the instrument displaces a piston, the extent of the displacement being shown on a dial.

Water Meter.—This mechanical device measures and automatically records the quantity of water flowing through a pipe. There are three types: (1) *positive,* which measures the actual volume of water; (2) *inferential,* which measures the velocity of the flowing water; and (3) *proportional,* which measures a fractional part of the full flow. See also CURRENT METER; WATER METER.

Electric Meters.—These instruments are designed to measure either electrical current or energy, or its potential, resistance, inductance, or capacitance. There are three general types of electric meters: (1) the *electrolytic* meter; (2) the *clock* meter; and (3) the *motor* meter. The latter is most generally used. For other types of meters see under AMPEREMETER; ELECTRICAL MEASUREMENTS; ELECTRICAL TERMS; ELECTROMETER; GALVANOMETER.

METHANE, mĕth′ān, CH_4, is the first member of the aliphatic or paraffin series of hydrocarbons of the type formula C_nH_{2n+2}. It is a very stable and abundant substance, being the principal component of natural gas. The methane content of natural gas varies between 50 and 98 per cent, but is commonly nearer the higher value. A typical gas will contain around 85 per cent methane, up to 9 per cent ethane, 3 per cent propane, the remainder being higher hydrocarbons and nitrogen. This sample before distribution contained some low-boiling liquids which were removed and blended with petroleum distillates. Since methane is a product of the decomposition of vegetable matter, it is often called marsh gas. Pockets of methane are often found in coal deposits, and as firedamp are a source of danger and the cause of numerous mine disasters. Methane is also evolved in certain sewage disposal processes and may be used as a source of heat and power.

In the carbonization of coal for the production of industrial and metallurgical coke a gas is formed which contains methane to the extent of 30 to 40 per cent. Carburetted water gas, made up mainly of carbon monoxide and hydrogen, owes its added heat value to 10 to 15 per cent methane, which results from the thermal decomposition of enriching oil. Since methane is practically always a product of the pyrolysis of hydrocarbons, petroleum refinery gases are rich in methane.

Pure methane may be prepared in the laboratory by heating dry sodium acetate with a mixture of caustic soda and quicklime, and by decomposing either methyl magnesium iodide or aluminum carbide with water. Both carbon monoxide and carbon may be reduced, by hydrogen at high temperature, to methane. Compressed methane is available in commercial cylinders, but the bulk of this gas is utilized as it is produced without being separated from the substances that accompany it.

Methane is comparatively unreactive toward such reagents as nitric acid and sulphuric acid, but can be converted into a series of substitution products ranging from methyl chloride, to carbon tetrachloride. However these substances are more commonly prepared by other methods so that mixtures of the four possible compounds are avoided. Methane is a common source of hydrogen, being acted on by steam in the presence of a catalyst, the accompanying carbon dioxide being scrubbed out from the hydrogen. A method of making so-called "synthesis gas" for the production of liquid hydrocarbons from natural gas involves the partial combustion of methane with commercial oxygen to carbon monoxide and hydrogen. Subsequent reactions carried out at high temperature in the presence of a catalyst result in higher molecular weight hydrocarbons and oxygenated derivatives. Methane and ammonia may be made to react to form hydrogen cyanide, a starting substance in the plastics industry. Acetylene may be made from methane either by thermal methods or by a low voltage electrical discharge, but neither method is in commercial operation. Methane and other hydrocarbons in natural gas are the source of various types of industrial carbon, the most important being "gas black" for the rubber industry.

The boiling point of methane is —161.7°C., hence it is rarely liquefied except when necessary to remove helium from the natural gas of the Southwestern states. Methane has no color nor odor and its density is approximately 0.56 that of air. Its heat of combustion is 1113 British thermal units (gross), the gas being measured at 60°F. and 30 inches barometric pressure. Methane forms explosive mixtures with air in proportions which range from 5.8 to 13.3 per cent.

W. T. READ,
Chemical Adviser, General Staff, Department of the Army; Former Dean, School of Chemistry, Rutgers University.

METHOD OF LEAST SQUARES. See LEAST SQUARES, METHOD OF.

METHODISM is a general name describing the practical religious movement of personal experience and social responsibility set in motion in the 18th century by the experience, preaching, hymn writing, and organizing genius of two British Anglican priests, John Wesley (1703–1791) and Charles Wesley his brother (1707–1788) (qq.v.).

The thirteen and one-quarter million Methodists in the world, two thirds of whom are in the United States, are loosely bound together in the Ecumenical Methodist Council, conferences of which met in London (1881), Washington (1891), London (1901), Toronto (1911), London (1921), Atlanta (1931), and Springfield (1947).

HISTORY

Oxford Beginnings.—At first strictly Anglican and rubrical, the movement began at Oxford University in November 1729 when John Wesley, returning from service under his father, Samuel Wesley (1662–1735), as a curate in Lincolnshire, joined a group of Christ Church students who were taking weekly communion with his brother Charles. At the time John was 26, Charles 22. The group, never exceeding 30, was bound together by personal influence and mutually agreed upon habits and usages including the common study of the Greek Testament, regular fasting, the observance of stated hours for private devotion, the visitation of the sick, the poor, and prisoners, and instruction of neglected children.

The name *Methodists* was one of a number of derisive epithets used to describe the group. Because it continued to be an accurate description, Methodism was finally accepted as the official name of the movement. A doggerel current at the time expresses the significance of the name like this:

> By rule they eat, by rule they drink,
> Do all things else by rule but think,
> Method alone must guide them all,
> Whence Methodists themselves they call.

The Aldersgate Experience.—While between 1733 and 1735 the first Oxford Methodism was becoming more patristic, John Wesley fell under the influence of William Law's devotional ideas most clearly expressed in his *Serious Call to a Devout and Holy Life* (1728). Wesley's spiritual experience was further advanced during his unsuccessful service as a missionary of the Society for the Propagation of the Gospel to the Indians in Georgia (Feb. 6, 1736, to Dec. 2, 1737) by his industrious translation of 33 hymns from the German into English and by daily contact with the Moravians in their joyful faith, their earnest prayer, and in their conviction of the merits of the religious method of justification through faith. In Georgia the young priest sang in his own translation Dessler's words: "Into Thy gracious hands I fall and with the arms of faith embrace: O King of Glory, hear my call! O raise me, heal me by Thy grace!" Returning to London, Wesley suffered from disappointment over his spiritual ineffectiveness in the new world, disaffection resulting from a love affair, and spiritual unrest kindled by his contact with the Moravians. Influenced especially by the Moravian Peter Böhler to alter his belief that religion was only an intellectual and moral habit, that is, a methodical union of intellectual belief, voluntary self-submission, and punctilious performance of the routines of the Church and the general duties of life without concern for the intervention of the supernatural and divine in life, Wesley wrote on March 5, 1738: "By Peter Böhler in the hands of a great God I was fully convinced of the want of that faith whereby we are saved." The text "if any man be in Christ, he is a new creature" increasingly expressed the object of Wesley's quest to be born again.

On May 24, 1738, at the end of a day of earnest spiritual seeking, Wesley, dressed in the habit of an Anglican priest, sat down in a prayer meeting being held in a secluded room on Aldersgate Street, London. He listened to a layman reading aloud Luther's *Preface to the Epistles to the Romans*. Of the ensuing experience, Wesley says: "While he (Luther) was describing the change which God works in the heart through faith in Christ, I felt my heart strangely warmed. I felt I did trust in Christ, Christ alone, for salvation; and an assurance was given me that He had taken away my sins, even mine, and saved me from the law of sin and death." This experience of the "heart strangely warmed" became a motivating religious experience characteristic of Methodism. Among Methodists this *day* of the *Aldersgate Experience*, May 24, 1738, and the *hour* of "quarter to nine" identify a vivid, dated conversion. William E. H. Lecky in his *History of England in the Eighteenth Century* (1882) calls the experience on Aldersgate Street an *"epoch in English history."*

The Evangelical Mission.—Following the Aldersgate Experience and after a visit to the Moravian center at Herrnhut on the continent, Wesley, feeling now the assurance of salvation through Christ, began his life mission. During the 53 strenuous years which followed he preached some 40,000 sermons and traveled a quarter of a million miles, mostly on horseback, keeping a detailed journal which literally is a guidebook of the British Isles.

The Wesley who emerged from Aldersgate and Herrnhut preached a gospel of a "new birth" by which men became "new creatures." This new birth depended neither on churchly form, creed, priestly prerogative, sacramental grace, or influence; it was the free gift of God's grace to repentant men. Wesley came to have one dominating objective: by preaching and personal influence to raise up a body of converted men who themselves would become witnesses to truth by which he had been saved. Under this inspiration he preached a persuasive gospel; as a consumate organizer he formed living witnesses into classes and societies. *Preaching power in the pulpit and private and personal influence in the class room became the two characteristic forms of Methodist activity. The power-link between the pulpit and the class meeting was the doctrine and experience of conversion.*

A word needs to be said about John Wesley's effective method of preaching. He spoke in short, economical phrases, using his eyes in such a way that each person in the congregation felt himself alone pierced and knew that the words were meant especially for him. Three of Wesley's simple observations about Christian method may help to explain his practical and direct program for Christian living.

1. "Read and meditate upon the 13th chapter of the 1st *Epistle to the Corinthians.*"

2. "If we see God in all things, and do all for Him, then all things are easy."

3. *"Do all the good you can, by all the means you can, in all the ways you can, in all the places you can, at all the times you can, to all the people you can, as long as ever you can."*

Evolution of a Church.—The unsectarian evangelical efforts of John and Charles Wesley and their associates were in reality the activity of another sect in process of formation as a church. When established churches closed their doors to him and clergy took offense at his doctrines, Wesley in 1739 took recourse, as his Oxford friend, George Whitefield (1714–1770), was already doing, to preaching in the open fields to immense crowds and in an old arsenal in Moorfields called "The Foundery" which he transformed into a "meeting house." From this point the history of the evolution of Methodism as a church may be summarized in 10 steps:

The *first step* in the evolution of the church was the formation of religious societies through which the Wesleys exercised their spiritual influence. These societies were in part imitated from the Moravians and in part were the continuation of societies related to the Church of England, being successors of those groups which sprang up in the last years of the Stuarts to compensate for the decay of Puritanism within the Anglican Church.

The *second step* was taken in 1739 when Wesley, to avoid an antinomian quietism growing among the Moravians in England, formally separated from the Moravians to establish a society of his own at the Foundery as mentioned above. This became the first society under the direct control of Wesley and the beginning of the Wesleyan Methodist Society.

The *third step* was taken in 1740 because the clergy excluded the Wesleys from their pulpits and repelled them and their converts from the Lord's Supper. The brothers therefore took the decisive step of administering the sacrament to their societies themselves in their own meeting rooms, both at Bristol and at Kingswood. The only link which now connected the administration of the sacrament to these societies with the Church of England was that the preachers who served the Lord's Supper were among its priests.

The *fourth step* was taken in 1741 when Wesley called out lay preachers to itinerate under his direction. To the societies founded and sustained with the aid of these preachers, who were absolutely under Wesley's personal control, the two brothers in their extensive journeys administered the sacraments as they were able. Despite Wesley's injunctions that his societies should generally keep to their parish churches, the societies wanted to have their own full Sunday services and to have the sacraments administered by their own preachers. The development of these preachers into ministers and of the societies into fully organized churches was the natural result of Wesley's designation of spiritual agents to carry on the work that was continually opening up before him.

The *fifth step* was taken in 1742 with the division of the societies into classes with leaders appointed as lay spiritual helpers and subpastors, and as stewards to take and give account of moneys received and expended.

The *sixth step* was by the Wesley Brothers in 1743, who published the *Rules of the United Societies* which have continued unaltered as the rules of Wesleyan Methodism. The Society was described as a "company of men having the form, and seeking the power of godliness, united in order to pray together, to receive the word of exhortation, and to watch over one another in love, that they may help each other to work out their salvation." The condition of membership in the societies was stated as a "desire to flee from the wrath to come and to be saved from their sins." The minimum customary contribution was a penny a week to "help the poor"; later the contributions were paid more generally toward "the support of the gospel."

The *seventh step* was taken in 1744 when Wesley held his first annual conference composed of preachers whom he personally selected. These early conferences were chiefly useful for the settlement of points of doctrine and discipline and for the examination and accreditation of fellow laborers. The aging of the brothers and the authority of the evolving church so far existing only as a personal authority of the two brothers exercised either directly or by their official delegates, moreover, led Wesley in 1784 to provide for the perpetuation of his work by a deed poll enacted by Parliament which vested in trustees for the use of "the people called Methodists" under the jurisdiction of the conference as to the appointment of ministers and preachers all the preaching places and trust property of the connection. The legal conference was defined as 100 itinerant preachers named by Wesley with power given to this "legal hundred" to fill vacancies in their own numbers, to admit and expel preachers, and to station them from year to year. Indeed, no preacher was allowed to remain more than three years in one station. By the constitution of this conference Wesley consolidated his movement into a distinct religious organization with legally corporate character and large property holdings.

The *eighth step* was taken when Wesley began to ordain ministers. This step gave the societies a yet more definite character as a separate church, yet Wesley protested that his societies were not a church. They were only a "society," the "United Society," the society of the "People Called Methodists," the "Methodist Society." In fact Wesley held the members of his society to be members of the Church of England, except for professed Dissenters whom he defined in a letter to Charles as those "who for conscience sake refused to join in the services of the church or partake of the sacraments administered therein." He interpreted the "Church of England" to mean "all the believers in England, except Papists and Dissenters, who have the word of God and the sacraments administered among them."

By 1746 Wesley abandoned his ecclesiastical high-churchmanship and revolutionized his views on ecclesiastical organization by reading Lord Chancellor King's account of the primitive church. From this time on he consistently maintained that the "uninterrupted succession was a fable which no man ever did or could prove." Indeed he was convinced by Lord King's book that the office of bishop was originally one and the same with that of presbyter. From this position he drew the practical inference that he himself was a "Scriptural Episcopos" and that he had as much right as any primitive or missionary bishop to ordain ministers as his representatives and helpers to administer the sacraments. Despite this belief he held this right in abeyance for three fifths of a century until at length he was constrained to exercise it. In doing so he in effect led the way toward making his society a distinct and independent church.

The *ninth step* was taken in 1784 when the independence of the American colonies made necessary the organization of a separate Methodism for America. Wesley declared that the colonial Methodists should be "totally disintangled from both the state and the English hierarchy." By giving formal ordination and letters to Thomas Coke, former curate of South Petherton and presbyter of the Church of England, Wesley commissioned Coke to preside over the "Flock in America" as presbyter and superintendent. Coke in turn associated himself with Francis Asbury (1745–1816), a preacher in the Wesleyan Conference in London. Asbury had come to America in 1771 as a volunteer missionary to the 400 Methodists in America. Against Wesley's order issued immediately before the outbreak of the Revolutionary War, Asbury alone refused to return to England.

The *tenth step* was taken at the Christmas Conference convened in Balitmore, Maryland, on Dec. 24, 1784. Sixty preachers met with Coke, approved an organizational plan submitted by Wesley, accepted his liturgy and hymnal, adopted the Articles of Religion with the addition of a clause recognizing the civil government and with the inclusion of a prayer for the rulers of the United States. The conference elected Coke and Asbury to the episcopal office. Asbury, with the approval of the Conference, was ordained by Coke. Thus Episcopal Methodism began in America with bishops considered only as chief administrative officers among the presbyters whom they superintended.

At the time of John Wesley's death in 1791 Methodism in Great Britain, the Isle of Man, and the Channel Islands numbered 19 circuits, 227 preachers, and 57,562 members; in Ireland 29 circuits, 67 preachers, and 14,006 members; in the West Indies and British America 19 preachers and 5,300 members; and in the United States 43,265 members.

DIVISION AND REUNION

In America.—Methodism as a church became divided as a result of two wars and the philosophy of political independence which affected church organization. The American Revolution precipitated the first major cleavage along nationalistic lines. In the year that the battles at Lexington and Concord were fought, all the Methodist preachers except Asbury and Thomas Rankin left America. Indeed during the war a Methodist was classified as a Tory until he proved himself otherwise. Wesley, to make the position of the Methodists more difficult, declared: "We Methodists are no republicans and never intend to be." Following the Treaty of 1783, however, Wesley released the Methodists from their British connections and urged them "to stand fast in that liberty wherewith God has so strangely made them free." Methodism in the new union separated from British Methodism on nationalistic lines.

The first important division within the new Church in the United States led to the organization of the *Methodist Protestant Church*. The Methodist Protestant group insisted on the right of a layman to vote on any question in any church meeting and the administration of the church without bishops. "Having no traditional prejudices in favor of a divine right monarchy or a divine right hierarchy," they said, they took for their model "the church without a bishop and the state without a king." By insistence upon these two principles the Methodist Protestants sought to bring church government, as they said, into harmony with the Republic and to make it conform to the principles of the "Kingdom of God." The Methodist Protestants, being unable to work out their reform within the Methodist Episcopal Church, assembled 114 delegates at Baltimore on Nov. 2, 1830, to separate and found the Methodist Protestant Church.

The second important division in America occurred in 1844 when the *Methodist Episcopal Church, South,* separated from the Methodist Episcopal Church. On the northern side the division was considered to have resulted from the slavery issue; on the southern side it was considered merely to be a constitutional issue over the powers of the episcopacy. After years of discussion, negotiation, and litigation, the Cape May Commission, established in 1876 by joint membership and action of the Methodist Episcopal Church and the Methodist Episcopal Church, South, reached terms of amity according to which each body recognized the other as a legitimate branch of Methodism and laid the basis for a peace which moved steadily toward reunion. The Methodist Episcopal Church, the Methodist Episcopal Church, South, and the Methodist Protestant Church, by a Declaration of Union issued at Kansas City, Missouri, on May 10, 1939, came together again as a united church with more than eight million members under the name of *The Methodist Church*. In a ceremony in Dallas, Texas, on April 23, 1968, the Methodist Church and the Evangelical United Brethren Church merged to form the *United Methodist Church*. The union of the two churches makes the United Methodist Church the second largest Protestant church in the United States. The Evangelical United Brethren Church had similar doctrines and organization, but had originated among German immigrants in Pennsylvania.

The Methodist Church in America also was organized along color lines. The *African Methodist Episcopal Zion Church* (1,100,000 members) was organized in 1796 out of the old John Street Methodist Church in New York. The *African Methodist Episcopal Church* (1,116,301) was originated in Philadelphia in 1816 and extended throughout the South after the Civil War. The Colored Methodist Episcopal Church was organized with the approval of the General Conference of the Methodist Episcopal Church, South, in 1870 to bring its colored membership, at the request of the colored members, into a separate ecclesiastical body. In 1956 the name of the church was changed to the *Christian Methodist Episcopal Church* (466,718). After the 1939 unification all Negro membership was organized in the Central Jurisdiction, an administrative unit which included all Negro Conferences. The Central Jurisdiction was abolished by the 1968 merger.

The *Yearbook of American Churches* for 1968 records 19 independent varieties of Methodism in the United States with a membership of nearly 2,500,000. The largest among these churches are the Congregational Methodist Church (1852), Evangelical Methodist Church (1946), Free Methodist Church of North America (1860), Reformed Methodist Union Episcopal Church (1885), Reformed Zion Union Apostolic Church (1869), Union American Methodist Episcopal Church (1850), and the Wesleyan Methodist Church of America (1843).

In Great Britain.—Division in Great Britain began in 1797 when Alexander Kilham, expelled from the Wesleyan Conference for his violent zeal directed toward abolishing the distinction between ministers and laymen, founded the *New Connection*. Other divisions resulted in the organization of *Primitive Methodist, Bible Christians, Protestant Methodists,* the *Wesleyan Methodist Association,* and the *Wesleyan Reformers*. In 1857 the Protestant Methodists, the Wesleyan Methodist Association, and the Wesleyan Reformers formed a union as the *United Methodist Free Churches*. In 1907 these were incorporated with the Methodist New Connection and the Bible Christians as the *United Methodist Church*. In 1932 the Wesleyan Methodists, the Primitive Methodists, and the United Methodists merged into one church as the *United Conference of Methodist Churches*. One special separation deserves mention. In the 1860's William Booth withdrew from the ministry of the New Connection to organize the *Salvation Army* as an international quasi-military religious organization to bring religion and social service to the masses, finding opposition to his specialized ministry not to his liking in the Church in which he had been ordained.

In Canada.—The history of Methodist expansion in Canada parallels the opening and settlement of the Dominion itself. Spread oftener by laymen than by preachers, Methodism was introduced into Newfoundland by Laurence Coughlan in 1765. Yorkshire Methodists settling in Nova Scotia in response to a call for British colonists, United Empire Loyalists in New Brunswick, soldiers of General Wolfe's army in Quebec, the Heck family migration to Ontario, missionaries to upper Canada and the Indians, encouragement from the Hudson's Bay Company, and saddle bag itinerants pressing westward to the Pacific all contributed to the spread of Methodism across the new continent.

On June 10, 1925, *The Methodist Church,* formed in 1884 by the merger of four Methodist branches (The Methodist Church in Canada, the Methodist Episcopal Church in Canada, the Primitive Methodist Church in Canada, and the Bible Christian Church) united with the Congregational Churches of Canada, the Presbyterian Church in Canada, and the Local Union Churches in Western Canada to form *The United Church of Canada*. The Methodist Church was the only one of the three denominations entering the union to bring into the United Church all its local churches. Negotiations looking toward this union, begun in 1899, were completed by the enactment of necessary legislation by the Parliament of Canada in 1924 and by the legislatures of the various provinces from 1924 to 1926. In 1930 the Wesleyan Methodist Church of Bermuda joined with the United Church of Canada as a Presbytery of the Maritime Conference. The United Church is carrying on negotiations looking toward organic union with the British and African Methodist Episcopal Churches (colored) whereby the two bodies may merge with the United Church of Canada.

Congregational in polity, the basic organization of the United Church is much like that of The Methodist Church in the United States except that it has no bishops and no elected or appointed ecclesiastical hierarchy.

In 1968 a merger of the Evangelical United Brethren Church and the United Church of Canada, retaining the *United Church of Canada* as its name. The combined membership is 1,074,203 with eleven conferences, 5,390 preaching places, approximately 3,500 ministers, and 4,605 church schools. Overseas missions are carried on in West Africa, Central India, Japan, Korea, and Trinidad.

The basic literature of the United Church consists of the *Hymnary* (1930) containing the great hymns of the ecumenical church drawn largely from the Presbyterian, Congregational, Methodist, Anglican, and Moravian churches; the *Book of Common Prayer;* the *Statement of Faith;* the *Catechism;* and the *Manual* which contains the doctrinal standards, constitution, and laws for the government of the church. The official church paper is *The United Church Observer* (1939) the product of a merger of several smaller publications. The general officers of the United Church of Canada are located in Toronto, Ontario.

Among the Germans.—The practical nature of Methodism was nowhere more obvious than in the mission of the Methodist Episcopal Church to the Germans. Concerned with effective ministry to the German immigrants swarming into the United States in the 19th century, Bishop

Joshua Soule on Aug. 19, 1835, in concluding the Ohio Annual Conference appointed Wilhelm Nast as "German Missionary." A seminary classmate of David Friedrich Strauss, Nast came to the United States to settle at West Point as librarian of the United States Military Academy. Hearing a sermon of Wilbur Fisk in the West Point Chapel, Nast came under the influence of the Methodists, finding "grace abundant to his needs." Nast began his preaching as a German missionary in Cincinnati, holding class meetings in the home of James Gamble, an Irish soap maker. Itinerating in areas settled by German immigrants, Nast established Methodist societies and organized his advances into German-language speaking conferences. By 1915 the German work in the United States was organized into ten annual conferences extending from ocean to ocean and from Canada to Mexico. The German work was carried on in 761 churches with 644 preachers caring for 60,270 members. Including the Methodists in Germany and German-speaking sections of Europe, the German Methodist movement grew to about 120,000 members and 1,200 preachers.

Episcopal Methodism was carried from the United States to Germany by Ludwig Sigmund Jacoby, a Jew converted in Cincinnati under the preaching of Nast. Jacoby married Amalie Therese Nuelsen, a devout Catholic converted in Cincinnati under the preaching of Peter Schmucker. Pastor and Frau Jacoby arrived in Bremen on Nov. 10, 1849. Working against prejudice and the legal status of the established church, the Methodists gained a permanent footing and developed on the continent in organic relationship with the Methodist Episcopal Church in the United States. In 1874 the Bethany Society with motherhouse in Frankfurt am Main began a deaconess work which was to become a major contribution to the Methodist Church.

The strains of World War I together with the assimilation of the Germans in language and custom led to the integration of the German Methodism into the English-speaking church. Liquidation of German Methodism was begun by an enabling act passed by the 1924 General Conference and completed with the disbanding of the East German Conference in 1943.

The principal journal of German Methodism was *Der Christliche Apologete*, established by Nast as editor in 1839, edited by him until 1892, until 1918 by his son Albert, and until 1936 by a Swiss scholar, August J. Bucher. *Der Christliche Apologete* celebrated its centennial in 1939 and then discontinued publication.

The statesman of German Methodism was Bishop John L. Nuelsen, elected to the episcopacy in 1908 and assigned to administer continental Methodism in 1912. "Our battle," said Bishop Nuelsen, "is against sin, the flesh, the devil, and his works."

The work in Germany continues under the Germany Central Conference with episcopal headquarters at Frankfurt am Main where the German Methodist Theological Seminary is located and under the Provisional Central Conference of Central and Southern Europe with episcopal headquarters in Geneva, Switzerland.

The traditions of German Methodists were bound together into the history of the Methodist Church by the heroic efforts of John A. Diekmann, who became president of Bethesda Institutions in Cincinnati in 1922.

The Methodists also developed strength among the Scandinavians, Chinese, Japanese, Italians, and Latin Americans in the United States. The Northern European Central Conference, administered from Stockholm, continues as a substantial overseas area of Methodist work.

PROTESTANT COOPERATION

The Methodists in the United States constitute the largest constituent body of the Federal Council of the Churches of Christ in America, a general Protestant federation organized at Philadelphia in 1908. The Methodists have also played a leading role in the organization of the World Council of Churches, established by constitution promulgated at Amsterdam, Holland, in 1948. The Methodist layman, John R. Mott, became the first honorary president of the Assembly and Bishop G. Bromley Oxnam, of the New York Area of the Methodist Church, president of the Federal Council of the Churches of Christ in America from 1944 to 1946, became one of the six World Council presidents.

DOCTRINE

Methodist theology expresses an eclectic evangelical Arminianism. Wesley explained his conception of doctrine in 53 sermons known as the four volume edition of 1787-1788 and in his *Explanatory Notes Upon the New Testament* (1755). To a generation which believed in heaven and hell as objective entities in the other world, to Englishmen advised by Calvinists that God had predestined every man, some to hell and some to heaven for eternity, Wesley offered the comforting assurance that any man seeking to be saved from his sins and desiring to live the Christian life could by an act of faith find God's grace abundant to his needs and could be born again. The sovereignty of God, according to the Methodist preaching, was so exercised as to be compatible with the freedom of man, divine grace originating, maintaining, and perfecting man as God's free gift. The sequence of Methodist spiritual psychology runs from original sin through repentance, justification by faith, the witness of the spirit defined as the consciousness of the divine favor through the atonement of Jesus Christ, and Christian perfection.

Methodists recognize the two sacraments as ordained by Christ to be baptism and the Supper of the Lord. To Methodists a sacrament is a certain sign of grace and of God's good will toward man by which God works invisibly in man to quicken, strengthen, and confirm man's faith in God. Baptism is both the mark of difference which distinguishes a Christian from others and a sign of regeneration and new birth. The Supper of the Lord is a sign of love that Christians ought to have among themselves one to another and a symbol of man's redemption by Christ's death. The visible Church of Christ to the Methodists is a congregation of faithful men in which the "pure word of God" is preached and the sacraments duly administered according to "Christ's ordinance." The local church is a society of persons who have professed the faith and have joined together in the fellowship of a Christian congregation in order to pray together, to receive the word of exhortation, and to watch over one another in love, that they may help each other to work out their salvation. Any confusion in the theological position of Methodism is explained by its pragmatic concern for practical rather than ecclesiastical detail.

POLITY

The organization of Methodism is divided into two general forms by British and American Methodism.

British Methodism.—During his life Wesley acted between conferences as patriarch and visitor with summary and supreme jurisdiction. By a letter produced after his death he begged the members of the Legal Hundred to assume no advantage over other preachers in any respect. Instead of appointing bishops, therefore, the preachers divided the country into districts with operating committees within these districts. Presently chairmen were elected for the whole conference each year.

American Methodism.—In the United States the organization of The Methodist Church is episcopal, with bishops serving as superintending presbyters rather than as prelatical or diocesan officers. The bishops, elected by jurisdictional conferences oversee the spiritual and temporal affairs of the church, preside in the General Jurisdictional, Central, and Annual conferences, annually appoint preachers, district superintendents, deaconesses, and connectional officers, and execute the policies and programs established by the General, Jurisdictional, and Annual conferences. The bishops are organized in three groups: a College of Bishops composed of all the bishops assigned to or elected by a Jurisdictional or Central conference; a Council of Bishops composed of all the bishops of all the jurisdictions and central conferences; and a Conference of Methodist Bishops composed of all the bishops elected by the General, Jurisdictional, and Central conferences, and bishops of affiliated autonomous Methodist Churches meeting each quadrennium immediately prior to the General Conference or on call of the Council of Bishops.

Bishops for purposes of residential and presidential supervision are assigned to convenient geographical areas by a jurisdictional conference upon the recommendation of a Committee on Episcopacy composed of ministerial and lay delegates.

Jurisdictions.—The United States is divided into six jurisdictions, namely the Northeastern, Southeastern, Central (Negro), North Central, South Central, and Western.

Conferences.—For effective action, the work of the Methodist Church is organized in a pattern of conferences. The quadrennial "General Conference" exercises supreme legislative and policymaking power for the entire church over all active connectional matters. The "Quadrennial Jurisdictional Conference" meets after the adjournment of the General Conference, elects bishops, and plans details for carrying out the program of the General Conference within the jurisdiction. Delegates to both the General and the Jurisdictional conferences, are elected by the Annual Conference. The *Annual Conference* is the *basic body in the church.* It is composed of all traveling preachers and lay members elected by each pastoral charge. District Conferences are informal administrative units of the Annual Conference corresponding to the geographical districts presided over by an administrative officer known as a district superintendent appointed by the bishop presiding over the Annual Conference. The "Quarterly Conference," presided over by the district superintendent, is the governing body of the pastoral charge. Central Conferences are administrative units for the work of the church outside the United States to promote evangelistic,

educational, missionary, and benevolent interests and institutions. These bodies elect their own bishops.

Recognizing the need for national leadership, the Methodist Church provides for Affiliated Autonomous Churches defined as self-governing churches in whose establishment The Methodist Church has assisted and with which it is cooperating through its Board of Missions and Church Extension.

Administrative Agencies.—Among the administrative agencies of the United Methodist Church are the Council of World Service and Finance; Board of Christian Social Concerns, composed of the Division of Alcohol Problems and General Welfare, Division of Human Relations and Economic Affairs, and the Division of Peace and World Order; General Board of Education including the Division of Higher Education, Division of the Local Church, and the Editorial Division; Board of Evangelism; Board of Hospitals and Homes; Board of Lay Activities; Board of Missions, composed of the National, World and Woman's Divisions, Joint Commission on Education and Cultivation, and the Joint Committee on Missionary Personnel; Board of Publication; Commission on Chaplains; Commission on Ecumenical Affairs; Commission on Public Relations and Methodist Information; Commission on Camp Activities (military); Commission on Interjurisdictional Relations; Commission on Promotion and Cultivation; Commission on Worship; Committee for Overseas Relief.

The 1968 Annual Conference of the United Methodist Church voted to set up a 4-year program to meet the problems of the urban crisis and to create a youth corps for service in depressed areas. The conference established a $20 million fund to finance the program, which is the largest amount ever given by an American Church for such purposes.

STATISTICS

In 1968 the United Methodist Church, the major Methodist Church in the United States, had a membership of 11,035,313. Other pertinent statistics are: 42,144 churches; 33,004 ordained ministers; 7,110,708 persons enrolled in church schools; 1,609 missionaries overseas; local and district property valued at $5,090,815,990. Other institutions include 14 seminaries, 8 universities, 124 colleges and secondary schools, 78 hospitals, and 217 children's homes and homes for the aged.

LITERATURE

The basic literature of the Methodist Church includes the *Discipline of the Methodist Church,* published quadrennially; *The Methodist Hymnal; The Christian Advocate,* weekly journal; and extensive periodical and instructional literature published by the administrative agencies of the church. The publishing interests of the church are organized in the Methodist Publishing House (founded in 1789 as the Methodist Book Concern), the profits of which are annually distributed through the annual conferences as pensions to retired preachers.

PAUL F. DOUGLASS
President, The American University

Bibliography

Bucke, E. S., and others, eds., *A History of American Methodism,* 3 vols. (New York 1949–1957).
Crozier, D., ed. *Methodist Fact Book* (Evanston 1964).
Douglass, P. F., *The Story of German Methodism* (New York 1939).

Goodloe, Robert W., and others, *The Story of Methodism* (Nashville 1967).

Harmon, Nolan B., *Understanding the Methodist Church* (Nashville 1955).

Moore, J. M., *Methodism in Belief and Action* (New York 1946).

Muelder, W. G., *Methodism and Society in the 20th Century* (Nashville 1966).

Sweet, W. W. *Methodism in American History* (New York 1933).

Sweet, W. W., *The Methodists: A Collection of Source Material* (Chicago 1946).

Warner, W. J., *The Wesleyan Movement in the Industrial Revolution* (London 1930).

METHODIST PUBLISHING HOUSE,

The, a company established in 1789 in Philadelphia as The Methodist Book Concern. It has branches in 14 cities and publishes thousands of books and pamphlets each year.

METHODIST YOUTH FELLOWSHIP,

The. When the three Methodist bodies united in 1939, it was necessary to unify the youth work in the three churches. This union was completed in 1941 when the Methodist Youth Fellowship was launched. The name was chosen by a vote of the young people throughout the church. The details of organization were largely planned by youth groups, although the responsibilities for promoting the program lie with the Youth Department of the Board of Education of the Methodist Church. The Methodist Youth Fellowship includes all of the young people connected with the church school between the ages of 12 and 23 years, inclusive. This includes those attending the Sunday morning sessions of the church school, Sunday evening meetings such as Epworth League (q.v.), Christian Endeavor, and University of Life, or other youth groups within the church.

The national organization is known as the National Conference of the Methodist Youth Fellowship. Its membership is composed of presidents of annual conference youth organizations, the presidents of state or regional student organizations, representatives from the staff of the agencies working with youth in church, and selected young people designated by the conference.

The Methodist Youth Fellowship is organized in each annual conference of the Methodist Church and provision is made for district and subdistrict organization where desired. In the local church, the Methodist Youth Fellowship is divided into three departments: (1) intermediate (ages 12, 13, and 14); (2) senior (ages 15, 16, and 17); and (3) young people (ages 18 to 23). Intermediates do not participate in the program beyond the local church. Provision is made for two types of youth organization. Plan I provides for a unified plan with one set of officers serving for all functions within a given age range. Plan II provides for separate organization for morning and evening sessions or as many divisions as seem advisable for the local church.

The activities of the organization on each age level (conference, district, subdistrict, and local church) are carried on through four commissions: Commission on Worship and Evangelism; Commission on World Friendship; Commission on Community Service; and Commission on Recreation and Leisure. The National Conference of the Methodist Youth Fellowship is responsible for specific projects in the youth field and has its own secretary who is a co-operating member of the Youth Department and the Department of Student Work in the Board of Education of the Methodist Church.

METHODIUS, mē-thō′dĭ-ŭs, **Saint.** See CYRIL AND METHODIUS, SAINTS.

METHOW, mĕt′hou, river, in the north central part of the State of Washington. Rising in the Chelan National Forest, it flows southeasterly and merges with the Columbia River just east of the town of Pateros. The Methow drains the larger part of the western half of Okanogan County. The narrow valley to which the river gives its name has no large towns, and is given over principally to farms, orchards, and pasture lands. It is especially well known for its apple orchards.

METHUEN, mĕth′ū-ĭn, 3D BARON (PAUL SANFORD METHUEN), English general: b. Corsham Court, Wiltshire, England, Sept. 1, 1845; d. there, Oct. 30, 1932. He is descended from John Methuen who effected the treaty, named after him, between England and Portugal in 1703. He studied at Eton; entered the Scots Fusilier Guards in 1864; saw special service on the Gold Coast in 1873; received a medal for bravery in the Ashanti War in 1874; became attaché in Berlin (1878), assistant quartermaster general Home District (1881), and quartermaster general in the Egyptian War (1882). He was in command of the Home District from 1892 to 1897; and commanded a division in the unsuccessful attempt at the beginning of the South African War to relieve Kimberley. At Magersfontein (1899) he was defeated. With Lord Roberts he marched on Pretoria in May 1901. In March 1902 he was captured between Vryburg and Lichtenburg, but immediately released. His ill success in South Africa was attributed to the difficult circumstances, and he was placed over the Eastern Command after the Boer War. In 1907 he was commander in chief in South Africa, in 1909 governor of Natal, was created fieldmarshal in 1911; in 1915–1919 governor of Malta; and after 1920 governor of the Tower.

METHUEN, town, Massachusetts, in Essex County; altitude 105 feet; on the Spicket River; 28 miles northwest of Boston, on the Boston and Maine Railroad. Its industrial products are yarn, shoddy, worsted cloth, shoes, wooden heels, brooms and weaving equipment. The Nevins Memorial Hall and Library, and Methuen Memorial Music Hall are notable buildings.

First settlement of the site was made about 1642; it was included within the limits of Haverhill until 1725, when it was incorporated as a separate municipality. In 1917 it was chartered as a city, but in 1921 it returned to representative town meeting government. It was named for Sir Paul Methuen, pre-Revolutionary official. Pop. 28,114.

METHUEN TREATY, a commercial treaty between Great Britain and Portugal, signed in 1703 and annulled in 1835, dealing with the tariff on wines and wool, negotiated by John Methuen, the British ambassador.

METHUSELAH, mē-thū′zē-là ("a man with a dart"?), Hebrew patriarch. The name appears in old manuscripts also as Mathusala and Mathusale. It has been variously translated as "Man of God," "Man of the Javelin," "Man of Sin," "Man of Selah." Because Selah was a title of the god Sin, these other derivations are possible. He is remarkable as the oldest man mentioned in the Bible, his age being stated in Genesis 5:27 as 969 years. According to Hebrew chronology and to that of the Samaritan version (which, however, reduces his age to 720 years), he died in the year of the Flood; but the Septuagint calculation makes him die six years earlier. Few will be found who believe that a man ever attained such an age. The most rational conclusion is that the original writer had in mind a period different from the year of 365 days.

METHYL, mĕth'il. The simplest and most common organic radical is known as methyl and has the formula CH_3. It will be readily seen that this corresponds to one molecule of methane, CH_4, from which one atom of hydrogen has been removed, and it would not be expected to be a stable substance. As will be pointed out later in the discussion of free radicals, it has only momentary and fugitive existence in organic reactions.

The term radical, while still in common use in the chemistry of carbon compounds, is not employed to any extent in discussing the chemistry of other elements. The term originally applied to any group of atoms present in a number of similar compounds which conferred certain specific chemical properties on all of them. Inorganic radicals were such groups as sulphate (SO_4), nitrate (NO_3), and ammonium (NH_4). With the development of the modern theory of ionization it was recognized that these groups existed, when compounds containing them were dissolved in liquids of high dielectric properties. Such radicals are known to possess electrical charges due to an excess or deficiency of one or more electrons, and are regarded as negative or positive ions.

Ionization is a much less common phenomenon in carbon chemistry, but in spite of the fact that only comparatively few organic radicals can exist longer than a fraction of a second, the idea of setting apart such groups and learning more about their influence in an entire organic molecule is still very useful and generally employed.

The hydrocarbon radicals are generally regarded as hydrocarbons from which an atom of hydrogen has been removed. Their names indicate their origin as: methyl, CH_3 from methane, CH_4; butyl, C_4H_9, from butane, C_4H_{10}. An exception is phenyl, C_6H_5, which bears a similar relation to benzene, C_6H_6. The name, however, is derived from phenol, C_6H_5OH.

As an example of the effect of different radicals on the properties of the same parent substance, the alkyl resorcinols may be cited. The resorcinols, in which R stands for any alkyl radical of the formula C_nH_{2n+1}, may be represented as $RC_6H_3(OH)_2$. Beginning with methyl and using those radicals with a single straight carbon chain, the antiseptic properties gradually increase with each additional carbon until the radical is hexyl, C_6H_{11}. Further increase in the length of chain is marked by a steady decrease in physiological activity.

For instructional purposes organic chemists very commonly think of many carbon compounds as being derived by the replacement of one or more hydrogen atoms by another atom or group of atoms. It is, of course, well known that relatively few carbon compounds are actually made in this way in spite of the recent rise in the use of petroleum hydrocarbons as chemical raw materials. Using the idea of hydrocarbons as a point of origin, a few substances may be considered as typical. The methyl group from methane is present in all of these substances: methyl chloride, CH_3Cl; methyl alcohol, CH_3OH; methyl cyanide, CH_3CN; methylamine, CH_3NH_2; and dimethyl ether, CH_3OCH_3.

In the middle of the past century, it was believed that the free methyl radical was produced when an iodine atom was removed from methyl iodide, CH_3I, by zinc. It was only when methods of determining molecular weights were developed that it was shown that the supposed methyl was in reality CH_3CH_3 or C_2H_6, ethane. So for many years the idea that free radicals were formed in chemical reactions and subsequently combined was an abstraction. In 1897 Prof. Moses Gomberg of the University of Michigan, in preparing hexaphenylethane, $(C_6H_5)_3C—C(C_6H_5)_3$, found that a free radical, triphenylmethyl, $(C_6H_5)_3C$, was formed when the saturated hydrocarbon was put into solution. Since that time a considerable number of free radicals have been made in which several ring structures in each molecule are involved.

A still more important development in the study of the mechanism of organic reactions has been in the field of unstable free radicals that are simpler than the stable free radicals heavily loaded with ring structures. Such studies deal with a series of relatively simple steps involving both free radicals and free atoms. Only the most fundamental concepts are given here.

As early as 1925 Prof. Hugh S. Taylor of Princeton suggested that free radicals might be involved in chain reactions such as the mercury photosensitized hydrogenation of ethylene. Active free radicals and atoms may be produced by heat, by the use of sensitizers, by photochemical effects, and by electrical methods. A common method of detecting and estimating free atoms and radicals is by their reactions with metallic mirrors previously deposited in glass tubes. The products of such reactions can be isolated as metallic alkyls. Other methods include the use of isotopes, paramagnetism, exchange reactions, and such physical determinations as rate of diffusion, heats of reactions, and optical effects. A typical thermal reaction involving a free radical is:

$$CH_3 + I \rightarrow CH_3I$$

METHYL ALCOHOL. See ALCOHOL and METHYL.

METHYLATED SPIRIT, is ethyl or grain alcohol to which has been added several per cent of methanol, methyl alcohol. While most methanol is now made synthetically, the product of destructive distillation of wood, or the common wood alcohol of commerce, it is preferred as a denaturant, being equally as toxic and possessing an unmistakable and unpleasant odor due to various impurities. The term methylated spirit is not now in common use, various grades of commercial alcohol being known as specially denatured and completely denatured and containing a number of different denaturants depending on industrial uses.

METIS. See ZEUS.

METOL. See NEGATIVES, DEVELOPMENT AND TREATMENT OF.

METONIC CYCLE. See CALENDAR.— *Lunisolar Cycles.*

METRIC SYSTEM, the decimal system of weights and measures based upon the meter and the gram as represented by standards preserved at the International Bureau of Weights and Measures, Sèvres, France. The primary standard of length is a bar of platinum alloyed with 10 per cent of iridium. The bar has an X-shaped cross section, with a plane surface along the bottom of the groove formed by two branches of the X. The basic unit, the meter, is defined as the distance between two lines engraved across that surface near the ends of the bar, when the bar is at the temperature of melting ice (0° Centigrade or Celsius). The basic unit of mass is the gram, but the primary standard has a mass of 1,000 grams, or one kilogram. The standard is a simple cylinder made of the same platinum-iridium alloy as the meter bar. Its height and its diameter are about 3.9 centimeters, or a little more than 1.5 inches.

Larger and smaller units are derived from the basic ones in decimal steps, and their names are formed by adding the following prefixes to the basic names:

mega-	= 1,000,000	deci-	= 0.1
kilo-	= 1,000	centi-	= 0.01
hecto-	= 100	milli-	= 0.001
deca-	= 10	micro-	= 0.000001

History.—The development of the metric system began in efforts of the revolutionary government in France in 1789 to devise a simple system to supplant the diverse units then in use in various parts of that country. The French scientists, however, hoped to establish a system suitable for all times and all peoples. They therefore proposed to base the system upon permanent natural standards. The meter was to be the ten-millionth part of a meridional quadrant of the earth; the gram was to be the mass of one cubic centimeter of water at the temperature at which water is most dense. This general plan was approved by the National Assembly of France in 1791, but the surveys and other measurements necessary to fix the size of the units were not completed until 1798. A standard meter bar and a standard kilogram, both made of platinum, were then accepted by a conference including delegates from ten countries, and in 1799 these standards were legally adopted as the basis for all measurements in France. Since they were deposited in the Archives of the republic, they became known as the "meter and kilogram of the Archives." Because of inevitable errors of measurement these standards did not have exactly the values intended, and it was soon realized that certainty and continuity of values were more important than adherence to the original plan of using natural standards. Consequently standards made later were derived from the standards of the Archives and not from the size of the earth and the density of water. However, the liter, the basic unit of capacity, was still defined as the volume filled by one kilogram of water at the temperature of maximum density. Later measurements showed that the liter thus defined is equal to 1.000028 cubic decimeters, instead of exactly one cubic decimeter or 1,000 cubic centimeters as

it was intended to be. This difference is of no importance in ordinary measurements, but makes it necessary for chemists to distinguish between milliliters and cubic centimeters.

The use of familiar weights and measures is so ingrained in the lives of people that a radical change meets strong objections. So in spite of the simplicity of the decimal metric system, diverse local units remained in use in France for many years. Finally, a law enacted July 4, 1837, forbade the use of any units other than those of the metric system after Jan. 1, 1840.

The advantages of the metric system were so great that its use gradually spread to many countries besides France. Several countries, including Great Britain and the United States, passed laws permitting the use of the metric system although they did not adopt it as supplanting the older customary units in commerce and industry. For example, the Congress of the United States on July 28, 1866, enacted a law providing that "it shall be lawful throughout the United States of America to employ the weights and measures of the metric system; and no contract or dealing, or pleading in any court, shall be deemed invalid or liable to objection because the weights and measures expressed or referred to therein are weights and measures of the metric system."

The growing use of the system led to demands for more copies of the metric standards and for an international organization to assure their uniformity. Conferences convened by the French government in 1870, 1872, and 1875 resulted in the signing, May 20, 1875, of a treaty, the Convention of the Meter, under which a permanent organization was eventually created. Eighteen countries soon ratified the treaty: Argentina, Austria, Belgium, Brazil, Denmark, France, Germany, Hungary, Italy, Norway, Peru, Portugal, Russia, Spain, Sweden, Switzerland, Turkey, and the United States. Countries which joined in the organization later included Australia, Bulgaria, Canada, Chile, Czechoslovakia, the Dominican Republic, Finland, Great Britain, Ireland, Japan, Mexico, Netherlands, Poland, Rumania, Siam, Uruguay, and Yugoslavia; so that in 1954 there were 35 member countries.

Regulation of Standards.—For the purpose of maintaining the standards and using or adapting them as necessary to meet current needs the treaty set up a three-step organization. The top authority is a General Conference on Weights and Measures, which is convened at intervals of 6 years and includes delegates from all member countries. Under the General Conference there is a permanent International Committee on Weights and Measures having 18 members, each of whom must be from a different country. This committee meets at 2-year intervals. It makes recommendations on problems referred to it by the General Conference, and supervises the operations of the International Bureau of Weights and Measures, which is the third part of the organization.

The International Bureau is located at Sèvres, a suburb of Paris, on a plot of ground dedicated by the government of France as international territory. The bureau is the principal working unit of the organization. It not only cares for the primary or prototype standards, but periodically compares the primary standards of the various member countries, which are sent back to it for this purpose; calibrates other standards; and carries on research to improve standards and methods of measurement. The bureau also serves as a permanent secretariat for the business of the General Conference and the International Committee. The International Bureau is housed in a historical structure known as the Pavillon de Breteuil which is situated on the edge of the Parc de Saint-Cloud, close to the road from Paris to Versailles, on the south side of the Seine and near the Manufacture Nationale de Porcelaine de Sèvres. It was in very poor condition at the time it was assigned to the International Committee in 1875. In 1930 the Rockefeller Foundation provided funds for repair and extension of the laboratories.

The treaty of 1875 set up an organization to provide permanent international standards, but many years of work were required to obtain suitable materials and to prepare meter bars and kilograms from them. To assure the permanence of the standards, the committee in charge of the work had already decided to use a platinum-iridium alloy instead of pure platinum, but alloys which had been made in 1874 were found to contain some impurities. When a satisfactory alloy was finally obtained, 31 meter bars and 40 kilograms were made from it. These were carefully compared in 1888 with the meter and the kilogram of the Archives by the International Bureau. The ones which had length and mass closest to those of the Archive standards were selected as international prototypes and deposited with a few of the other copies in a vault at the International Bureau eight meters underground. They are removed only on rare occasions to meet some special need, such as the most important comparisons of other standards.

The first General Conference under the treaty of 1875 was held in September 1889. It distributed by lot to the various member countries the meter bars and kilograms which had been calibrated along with the international prototypes, each standard being accompanied by a certificate stating how much it differed from the prototype. The United States was allotted meters No. 21 and No. 27, and kilograms No. 4 and No. 20. Meter No. 27 and kilogram No. 20 were received and formally accepted by President Benjamin Harrison in Washington on Jan. 2, 1890. They have since that time been considered as the basic standards of the United States. These, and the other two standards, which were delivered in July 1890, were deposited in the Office of Weights and Measures, then a part of the United States Coast and Geodetic Survey, in the Treasury Department. On April 5, 1893, the superintendent of weights and measures, with the approval of the secretary of the treasury, announced that thereafter the customary units, the yard and the pound, would be derived from the meter and the kilogram in accordance with the act of Congress of July 28, 1866.

When the National Bureau of Standards was established, July 1, 1901, the standards were transferred to it. From time to time the national standard meters and kilograms belonging to the various countries have been sent back to the International Bureau at Sèvres for comparison with the international standards. These comparisons have shown no change in the relative values of the standards greater than the uncertainty of the measurements or weighings, except for the standards of one or two countries which showed evidence of careless use.

Secondary Units.—In the derivation of sec-ondary units various combinations of basic metric units have been used. The centimeter-gram-second (cgs.) system is most commonly used in scientific work. In that system the unit of force, the dyne, is the force required to give a mass of one gram a unit acceleration, that is, to change its velocity by one centimeter per second in one second. The erg, the cgs. unit of work or energy, is the amount of work done when a force of one dyne acts for a distance of one centimeter.

The units of the cgs. system are small, and in practical engineering work a system called mks., based upon the meter, the kilogram, and the second, is more convenient. The mks. unit of force is the force which will give to a mass of one kilogram an acceleration of one meter per second per second. It is called the newton, and is equal to 100,000 dynes. A force of one newton acting for a distance of one meter does the mks. unit of work, the joule, which equals 10,000,000 ergs. The power required to do one joule of work in a second is one watt; electrical devices are commonly rated in watts or kilowatts. The other common electrical units, such as ohm, volt, and ampere, are part of the mks. system.

Proposed New Standards.—Although the metric standards made of platinum-iridium have served their purpose very well, many scientists have believed that the system should eventually be based upon natural standards of even greater permanence, and possibly of greater precision. In particular, wavelengths of light have long been considered as possible substitutes for the metal bar as the ultimate reference standard of length. However, the waves given off by natural materials which seemed most suitable for this purpose have always been found to be really mixtures of waves of slightly different length. This complexity of the waves is caused by the presence in each material of various "isotopes" which have atoms differing in weight although so similar in structure that they can not be separated by ordinary chemical procedures. Research on atomic structure has made it possible to produce materials each containing only a single isotope and giving waves more suitable for precise standards of length. In 1953 an Advisory Committee of the International Committee on Weights and Measures, including members from 11 countries, recommended that some wavelength produced by a single-isotope material be adopted to supersede the meter bar. The committee did not recommend a specific material because isotopes of mercury, of krypton, and of cadmium were proposed by different countries. The proposed action would not change the magnitude of the meter but would simply define it as a specified member of wave-lengths.

Standards in English-Speaking Countries.—The metric system is used exclusively in all continental European countries; it is the legal system in all of Latin America and in several Asiatic countries, although older units often remain in use. China, India, and Indonesia have planned to introduce it gradually to replace their numerous local units. In brief, practically the whole world, excepting the English-speaking countries, uses or plans to use the metric system; and even in English-speaking countries that system is used in nearly all work in science.

While the customary United States units are defined by reference to the metric standards, British units are derived quite independently from "imperial" standards adopted by act of Parliament. These standards are older than the international meter and kilogram and not so well designed. They have apparently changed slightly. The British pound is smaller than that of the United States by about one part in 5 million; the British yard, foot, and inch are smaller by four parts in a million. The United States inch equals 2.540005 centimeters, the British inch 2.539996 centimeters. To remedy this discrepancy the adoption of the exact value 2.54 centimeters in both countries has been proposed. Canada, by act of Parliament, took this step on May 28, 1951, declaring its yard to be 0.9144 meter. British units of capacity differ markedly from those in use in the United States, as is shown in the table of metric equivalents following.

METRIC UNITS, ABBREVIATIONS OF NAMES, AND EQUIVALENTS IN AMERICAN AND BRITISH UNITS

Length—

10 millimeters (mm.)	= 1 centimeter (cm.)	
100 centimeters	= 1 meter (m.)	
1,000 meters	= 1 kilometer (km.)	
1 centimeter	= 0.3937 inch	
1 meter	= 3.2808 feet	
1 meter	= 1.0936 yards	
1 kilometer	= 0.6214 mile	

Area—

10,000 square meters (m²)	= 1 hectare (ha.)
1 hectare	= 2.471 acres

Capacity—

1,000 milliliters (ml.)	= 1 liter (l.)
100 liters	= 1 hectoliter (hl.)
1 milliliter	= 0.0610 cubic inch

In the United States

1 milliliter	= 0.2705 fluid dram
1 milliliter	= 0.0338 fluid ounce
1 liter	= 1.0567 liquid quarts
1 liter	= 0.9081 dry quart
1 liter	= 0.2642 gallon
1 hectoliter	= 2.8378 bushels

In Great Britain

1 milliliter	= 0.2816 fluid dram
1 milliliter	= 0.0352 fluid ounce
1 liter	= 0.8799 quart
1 liter	= 0.2200 gallon
1 hectoliter	= 2.7497 bushels

Mass or Weight—

1,000 milligrams (mg.)	= 1 gram (g.)
1,000 grams	= 1 kilogram (kg.)
1,000 kilograms	= 1 metric ton (t.)
1 gram	= 15.4324 grains
1 gram	= 0.0353 avoirdupois ounce
1 gram	= 0.0322 troy ounce
1 kilogram	= 2.2046 avoirdupois pounds
1 metric ton	= 1.1023 tons (of 2,000 lb.)
1 metric ton	= 0.9842 ton (of 2,240 lb.)

Bibliography.—Fischer, Louis A., *History of the Standard Weights and Measures of the United States,* Miscellaneous Publication 64, U.S. Bureau of Standards (Washington 1925); Guillaume, Charles Édouard, *La création du Bureau International des Poids et Mesures et son oeuvre* (Paris 1927); U.S. Bureau of Standards, *International Metric System of Weights and Measures,* Miscellaneous Publication 135 (Washington 1932); id., *Units of Weights and Measures (United States Customary and Metric); Definitions and Tables of Equivalents,* Miscellaneous Publication 121 (Washington 1936); Briggs, Lyman J., "The National Standards of Measurement," *Reviews of Modern Physics,* 11:111-120, April 1939; Darwin, Sir Charles, and others, "A Discussion on Units and Standards," *Proceedings,* Royal Society (London), Series A, July 9, 1946; Moreau, Henri, "Le système métrique et le Bureau International des Poids et Mesures," *La Nature,* pp. 353-358, December 1948; id., "The Genesis of the Metric System and the Work of the International Bureau of Weights and Measures," tr. from the French by R. E. Oesper, *Journal of Chemical Education,* 30: 3-20, January 1953.

E. C. CRITTENDEN,

Member, International Committee on Weights and Measures.

METROLOGY. See WEIGHTS AND MEASURES.

METRONOME, mĕ′trô-nōm (from Gr. *metron,* a measure, and *nomos,* a law), a mechanical device for indicating, by beats or ticks, the exact tempo of a musical composition. In 1816, Johann Mälzel constructed a clockwork instrument having a pendulum mounted on a pivot between two weights or bobs, at either end, with a graduated slide, on which the upper bob could be moved up or down, for adjusting the number of beats to be sounded per minute. The double pendulum had been invented previously by a mechanist named Dietrich Nikolaus Winkel who declined to cede his rights to Mälzel. Mälzel thereupon appropriated the principle and applied it to the graduated slide he had himself invented. Although an appointed commission in Holland decided the resulting dispute in Winkel's favor, the decision came too late to benefit him, and Mälzel has come to be regarded as the inventor of the metronome. It became a standard instrument, and composers or publishers of music often indicate the tempo of a piece by specifying the number of beats, corresponding to a note of given value, such as a half, quarter, or eighth note, that should occur per minute according to the metronome. Such tempo indications are preceded by the initials M. M. (for Mälzel's Metronome). In 1938 an electric metronome was placed on the market, operated by a synchronous electric current, without a pendulum.

METROPOLIS, mê-trŏp′ô-lĭs, city, Illinois, located in Massac County, of which it is the county seat, 28 miles northeast of Cairo, on the Ohio River. It is an agricultural marketing center, with light manufacturing plants producing underwear, gloves, and furniture. The city has a Carnegie library, a hospital, and a courthouse. Nearby, in 1757, Fort Massac was built by the French. The fort was destroyed by the Cherokee Indians and its site was subsequently occupied by the British (1765–1778). The fort was rebuilt by Anthony ("Mad Anthony") Wayne in 1794. A neighboring settlement became the city of Massac; between it and the fort was Metropolis City, which in 1843 became a county seat. The two cities were merged under the present name in 1892. In 1908 the site of the fort was designated as a state park. It was here that George Rogers Clark (q.v.) crossed the Ohio on his way into the Northwest Territory. Pop. 7,339.

METROPOLITAN, mĕt-rô-pŏl′ĭ-tăn, in ecclesiastical usage, a name for an archbishop, whose see is commonly the chief place or metropolis of an ecclesiastical province. In the Orthodox Eastern churches, a metropolitan ranks above a bishop and below a patriarch. In the Roman Catholic Church an archbishop may bear the title of metropolitan even though he does not have a metropolis as a see.

METROPOLITAN MUSEUM OF ART, The, New York, N. Y., the largest art museum in the United States, founded in 1870. Its collections cover a period of 5,000 years and represent all the great cultures of the world. The present building is in Central Park, fronting Fifth Avenue at 82d Street. The original galleries were opened in 1880, but various wings were subsequently added, notably the Pierpont Morgan Wing (opened 1917) and the American Wing (opened 1924). Special collections include the Benjamin Altman Collection (notable for Dutch paintings,

Renaissance decorative arts, and Oriental rugs and ceramics) ; the Theodore M. Davis Collection (notable for Italian paintings, Egyptian antiquities and European and Oriental decorative arts) ; the Michael Friedsam Collection (notable for early French and Netherlandish paintings and European and Oriental decorative arts) ; the H. O. Havemeyer Collection (notable for 19th century French paintings, Oriental paintings and decorative arts and prints) ; the George Blumenthal Collection (notable for paintings and decorative arts of the Middle Ages and the Renaissance) ; the Jules S. Bache Collection, which includes masterpieces of all the European schools of painting.

The collection of prints consists of woodcuts, engravings, etchings and lithographs dating from 1450 to the present.

The Egyptian Wing presents a vivid chronological picture of a highly-developed civilization. Outstanding in the display is a mastabeh tomb erected about 4,400 years ago for a Memphite dignitary named Pery-neb, rebuilt in its original form. The arts of Greece and Rome are well represented. Notable are a Greek statue, the best preserved of the early Attic Kouroi, and a bronze statuette of a horse from the 5th century B.C.

The collection of ancient art of Mesopotamia, Persia, Palestine, and Syria was augmented through substantial purchases made in 1947 and is represented by sculpture, metalwork, and pottery. Notable examples of ancient Assyrian art are a colossal winged bull and winged lion and a number of reliefs, the gifts of John D. Rockefeller, Jr., and of J. Pierpont Morgan.

The collections of Near Eastern art from Egypt, Turkey, Syria, Iraq, Iran, and India are highlighted by outstanding Oriental carpets, Arabic glass, Islamic pottery and metalwork inlaid with gold and silver. A number of Syrian mosque lamps and other pieces of enameled glass of the 13th and 14th centuries are among the rarest and most precious objects.

The collection of Far Eastern art is notable for a fine selection of Chinese sculpture, which includes superb pieces ranging in date from the late Chou dynasty (about 1050–249 B.C.) to the Ch'ing (1644–1912). Other oustanding phases of the collections are the early Chinese potteries, the later decorated porcelains, the early bronzes and the extensive group of paintings.

The collections of medieval art in the Metropolitan Museum together with those at The Cloisters form the most important assemblage of medieval art in America. Collecting toward the turn of the century by the late J. Pierpont Morgan and subsequent gifts to the Museum by his son, J. P. Morgan, brought to the Museum world-famous groups of Early Christian, Byzantine, Romanesque and Gothic objects.

The decorative arts of the Renaissance include numerous outstanding objects from the well-known Morgan, Altman, Havemeyer, Friedsam, Blumenthal, and Wentworth collections. Notable are the intarsia room from the Ducal Palace at Gubbio, the sculpture, the majolica and the goldsmith's work including the famed Cellini cup in the Altman Collection. French decorative arts of the 17th and 18th centuries are well represented as are the decorative arts of England from Elizabethan times through the 18th century.

The collection of musical instruments of all nations with some 4,400 objects, is the most comprehensive assemblage of this kind in the world. It includes prehistoric instruments as well as those of Europe, Asia, Africa, Oceanica and America. Reconstruction work, still in progress, has brought many instruments back into playing condition.

The collections of Arms and Armor—consisting of armor, weapons, horse equipment and other war gear from both Europe and the Orient and dating mainly from 1400–1800—ranks with European national collections in scope and quality. Signed works by the best-known artist-armorers of Augsburg, Nürnberg, and Milan and over 450 pieces with historical associations are included.

The American Wing is devoted to American decorative arts from the 17th through the first quarter of the 19th century. In rooms, most of them reconstructed with original woodwork, there have been assembled furniture, metalwork, ceramics, glass, prints and paintings to present the characteristic background of our ancestors.

The collection of the Costume Institute (formerly the Museum of Costume Art, at 18 East 50th Street) includes some 10,000 items of costume and accessories ranging from the 17th to the 20th centuries and a library of reference materials—periodicals, costume histories, old costume plates, patterns, sketches of Paris openings, etc.

Study-storages of costume, millinery, shoes and other accessories; specially-equipped designer workrooms where designers may work in privacy, a classroom and library facilities are available to Costume Institute members. Changing special exhibitions of historic and regional costumes are open to the public.

METROPOLITAN OPERA, one of the leading operatic organizations in the world, presenting opera and music drama at the Metropolitan Opera House (popularly called the "Met") in New York City. Since 1932 its official title has been the Metropolitan Opera Association, Inc. This title includes singers, instrumentalists, and other artists and technicians who participate directly in its productions, but these persons as a group are referred to informally as the Metropolitan Opera Company.

Beginning in 1883, a succession of organizations, under various types of management, functioned in the Metropolitan Opera House at Broadway and 39th Street until that building was sold and the company moved into a new Metropolitan Opera House in 1966. The new building is part of the Lincoln Center for the Performing Arts at Broadway and 63rd Street.

HISTORY

Early Years.—The Metropolitan Opera-House Company, Ltd., opened its auditorium, built at a cost of about $1,732,000, on Oct. 22, 1883. The architect, Josiah Cleaveland Cady, had not previously designed a theater and is reported to have boasted that he "had never entered a playhouse." The interior of the auditorium was luxuriously furnished, but the plain, homely, yellow-brick facade was unsightly, and the inadequate stage equipment quickly became a handicap to the producers. Henry E. Abbey, although appointed manager by a board of directors, ran the first season as a private venture and incurred a personal deficit estimated at from $300,000 to $600,000.

The initial performance was of Gounod's *Faust,* with Christine Nilsson, Sofia Scalchi, Italo Campanini, Giuseppe del Puente, and Franco Novara as the leading singers, and Auguste Vianesi as conductor. On the second night of the season, October 24, Marcella Sembrich, later to become one of the company's leading singers, sang the title role in Donizetti's *Lucia di Lammermoor.* All of the operas that season, including Wagner's *Lohengrin,* were sung in either French or Italian.

The stockholders directly sponsored the second season, under the leadership of the German-born conductor Leopold Damrosch. As director of the New York Symphony, he was able to use that orchestra for the operas he conducted, all of which were sung in German. Damrosch died before the season ended, and his son Walter replaced him. For the following season and those through 1890–1891, the company was headed by Edmund C. Stanton as executive director, Anton Seidl as first conductor, and Walter Damrosch as second conductor. The policy of presenting opera in German was continued, and first American performances were given of Wagner's *Die Meistersinger, Tristan und Isolde,* and the *Ring* cycle. Major new artists in this German period were Amalia Materna, Marianne Brandt, Lilli Lehmann, Max Alvary, Emil Fischer, Albert Niemann, and Anton Schott.

For the 1891–1892 season, a triumvirate was in charge—Abbey (the first manager), Edward Schoeffel (a silent partner), and Maurice Grau (a Bohemian-born opera impresario). On Aug. 27, 1892, a fire destroyed much of the backstage area of the building, with the result that the following season was cancelled. Through reorganization, the controlling group then became the Metropolitan Opera and Real Estate Company, formed to represent the interests of certain boxholders. The new company became the owner of the opera house and leased the building to each successive producing agency, which paid no rent but gave the stockholders the use of the parterre boxes for all subscription performances. The company continued as owner of the house until its dissolution in 1940, when the Metropolitan Opera Association raised $1,057,000 through public subscription and obtained possession of the building.

The first lessors were Abbey, Schoeffel, and Grau, who reopened the house on Nov. 27, 1893, with a performance of *Faust.* The cast included Emma Eames, Jean Lassalle, and the brothers Jean and Édouard de Reszke. During the next decade, known as the Metropolitan's "golden age of song," these singers appeared, along with other such distinguished artists as Lillian Nordica, Pol Plançon, Emma Calvé, Nellie Melba, Ernestine Schumann-Heink, Antonio Scotti, Louise Homer, and Milka Ternina. During this period all operas were sung in their original language.

The three-man directorate was dissolved in 1896, and the company was inactive for one season until Grau took charge alone in 1898. When he retired because of ill health in 1903, the Conried Metropolitan Opera Company was formed on a stockholding basis. The new organization had 12 directors headed by Heinrich Conried, an Austrian who had managed an illustrious German repertory at the Irving Place Theatre in New York City.

During the Conried regime, which lasted until 1908, Wagner's *Parsifal* had its first stage performance outside of Bayreuth on Dec. 24, 1903. Other notable events were the Metropolitan debut of Enrico Caruso (Nov. 23, 1903), marking the beginning of one of the most successful careers there, and a single performance of Richard Strauss' *Salome* (Jan. 22, 1907), which had to be dropped because of public indignation at its subject matter. Newcomers to the company included Olive Fremstad, Geraldine Farrar, and Feodor Chaliapin.

Gatti-Casazza's Management.—Conried resigned on Feb. 11, 1908, and the producing organization then became known as the Metropolitan Opera Company, with a joint management. Giulio Gatti-Casazza, who had been general director of La Scala in Milan, was appointed general manager, and Andreas Dippel, a leading tenor, became administrative manager. Gatti-Casazza brought Arturo Toscanini with him from La Scala as chief conductor, and Gustav Mahler was engaged as chief conductor of the German repertory. The double management proved unsatisfactory, and after two years Dippel resigned in order to assume management of the Philadelphia–Chicago Opera Company. Gatti-Casazza continued as manager until 1935.

In 1910 the Metropolitan bought out its big rival, Oscar Hammerstein's opera company, for $1.2 million. Mahler left the Metropolitan in 1910, and Toscanini left in 1915. Caruso's death in 1921 and Farrar's retirement in 1922 deprived the company of two of its major box-office attractions. However, many noted artists joined during Gatti-Casazza's tenure: Emmy Destinn, Frances Alda, Leo Slezak, Clarence Whitehill, Luisa Tetrazzini, Maria Jeritza, Amelita Galli-Curci, Elisabeth Rethberg, Rosa Ponselle, Lucrezia Bori, Frieda Hempel, Giovanni Martinelli, Beniamino Gigli, Lawrence Tibbett, Ezio Pinza, Edward Johnson, Claudia Muzio, Lotte Lehmann, and Lauritz Melchior. In Gatti-Casazza's final season, Kirsten Flagstad made her debut (Feb. 2, 1935), and her performances of Wagnerian roles, together with Melchior's, stimulated public interest in Wagner.

The economic depression that began in 1929 made itself felt at the Metropolitan. The 1929–1930 season ended with the company's first deficit in 20 years, and the accumulated profits of $1.1 million were quickly eaten up. A 10% cut in salary was accepted by most of the personnel. Otto H. Kahn, who had been a member of the board of directors since 1903 and the influential chairman of the majority stockholders' committee since 1924, resigned as both chairman and president of the company on Oct. 26, 1931. With Kahn's departure, much of the wealthy patronage on which the Metropolitan had largely depended for its maintenance was withdrawn, and the organization turned to the public for support. A fund-raising campaign had brought in $150,000 by the spring of 1932. That year the company was reorganized as the Metropolitan Opera Association, Inc., on a membership instead of a stockholding basis.

The following season was cut from 24 to 16 weeks, and a further cut in salary was accepted by most of the artists and technicians. In 1933 another appeal for funds had to be made, and a "Save the Metropolitan" campaign for $300,000 was waged by a subsidiary group formed to enlist public support.

A factor that proved invaluable to the Metropolitan in its campaign for funds was the series of Saturday afternoon broadcasts, which began in the 1932–1933 season, following the success of an initial broadcast of Humperdinck's *Hänsel und Gretel* on Dec. 31, 1931. Public interest was also

The Metropolitan Opera moved into new quarters for the start of its 1966 season. The new Metropolitan Opera House is part of the Lincoln Center for Performing Arts on New York City's upper West Side. The old opera house, in midtown Manhattan, was demolished.

Louis Mélançon

stimulated by the Metropolitan Opera Guild, an independent membership organization founded in 1935 by Mrs. August Belmont. The Guild published *Opera News* for its members and arranged special matinees for school children at nominal ticket prices. During this period the company was helped financially by gifts from the Juilliard Foundation and the Carnegie Corporation.

Edward Johnson's Management.—Herbert Witherspoon, who had previously sung bass roles at the Metropolitan and had later been director of the Chicago Opera, was appointed to succeed Gatti-Casazza in 1935. Edward Johnson, a leading tenor with the company since 1922, was also appointed as assistant general manager to direct a series of supplementary spring sessions. When Witherspoon died of a heart attack on May 10, 1935, Johnson succeeded him as general manager.

By the end of World War II, the Metropolitan's finances had become stabilized, sometimes at the expense of artistic purposes, since little money was spent on new productions. But attendance had grown to near capacity, and profits were realized from spring tours to principal American cities.

During Johnson's regime, which lasted until 1950, the company ventured into English versions of foreign works, and more American-born singers were engaged, among them Helen Traubel, Risë Stevens, Eleanor Steber, Leonard Warren, Charles Kullman, Jan Peerce, Richard Tucker, Roberta Peters, and Jerome Hines. Singers from other countries included Bidu Sayão, Marjorie Lawrence, Zinka Milanov, Licia Albanese, Jussi Bjoerling, John Brownlee, and Salvatore Baccaloni. Prominent conductors included Sir Thomas Beecham, George Szell, Bruno Walter, Fritz Busch, Fritz Stiedry, and Fritz Reiner.

Rudolf Bing's Management.—In 1950, Johnson was succeeded as general manager by Rudolf Bing. A Viennese impresario, Bing had directed the opera festivals at Glyndebourne, England, and was the first director of the Edinburgh Festival.

In 1951, $750,000 was raised by public subscription. In 1952, Mrs. Belmont was instrumental in the formation of the National Council of the Metropolitan Opera, a nationwide group whose members contributed large sums of money annually. The council helped finance new productions

and supervised annual auditions for new singers. Also in 1952 the public contributed $1.5 million, mostly used to renovate the opera house.

On Jan. 7, 1955, Bing presented Marian Anderson as Ulrica in Verdi's *Un Ballo in Maschera,* marking the first performance by a Negro of a leading role at the Metropolitan. Among the other singers engaged by Bing were Joan Sutherland, Renata Tebaldi, Maria Callas, Victoria de los Angeles, Birgit Nilsson, Montserrat Caballé, Guilietta Simionato, Eileen Farrell, Leontyne Price, Mirella Freni, Elisabeth Schwarzkopf, Franco Corelli, Tito Gobbi, and Carlo Bergonzi. Bing also engaged outstanding stage directors and designers from both the United States and Europe to enliven old productions and to stage new ones; conductors under his management included Dimitri Mitropoulos, Eugene Ormandy, Leopold Stokowski, Georg Solti, Leonard Bernstein, and Thomas Schippers.

The New "Met."—On April 16, 1966, the Metropolitan marked its last appearance in the original opera house with a gala concert, before moving to its new home at Lincoln Center. Designed by Wallace K. Harrison, the new Metropolitan Opera, with a seating capacity of 3,800 (compared to 3,625 for the former house), was erected at a cost of $45,700,000. Money for the project came from private, corporate, and foundation sources; the only public gifts were from foreign governments. The acoustics of the new house were superior to those of the old one, and the backstage facilities were lavishly comprehensive. Murals by Marc Chagall adorned the lobby.

On Sept. 16, 1966, the new house opened with the premiere of an American opera especially commissioned for the occasion—Samuel Barber's *Antony and Cleopatra.* The cast was headed by Leontyne Price, Rosalind Elias, Jess Thomas, Justino Diaz, and Ezio Flagello. Thomas Schippers was the conductor.

The cost of moving to the new house and of paying for elaborate new productions left the Metropolitan in a bleak financial position. However, despite this difficulty, the Metropolitan expanded its activities, and by the 1968–1969 season it was operating on a year-round basis, with a 31-week season in New York, an annual spring tour, and various summer projects, such as free concert performances of opera in the New York City parks.

RAYMOND S. ERICSON
Music Editor, "The New York Times."

Further Reading: Eaton, Quaintance, *Opera Caravan, Adventures of the Metropolitan on Tour, 1883–1956* (New York 1957); Kolodin, Irving, *The Metropolitan Opera, 1883–1966* (New York 1967); Seltsam, William Henry, ed., *Metropolitan Opera Annals* (New York 1947) and supplements.

METTERNICH, met′ər-niκH, **Clemens Wenzel Nepomuk Lothar,** PRINCE, Austrian statesman: b. Coblenz, May 15, 1773; d. Vienna, June 11, 1859. He was educated at Strasbourg; when only 17 represented the Westphalian princes at the coronation of Leopold II; settled in Vienna in 1794; and asured himself a place in diplomacy by marrying the granddaughter of the Austrian chancellor, Count Wanzel von Kaunitz, in 1795. This marriage not only gave him entry to the best society, but brought wealth, and at the Congress of Rastatt he represented the Westphalian collegium, where he served his apprenticeship in politics. In 1801 he was sent to Dresden by Austria; two years later to Berlin; there a part of his mission was to cultivate the friendship of the French ambassador. He did this so well that that official induced Napoleon to suggest to Austria that Metternich would be a most acceptable representative at the Tuileries; and so in 1806 he was sent to Paris, where he ingratiated himself with Caroline Murat, sister to Napoleon, and with Prince Charles Maurice de Talleyrand. On the outbreak of the war between France and Austria, Metternich was put to much personal inconvenience by Napoleon, who forcibly detained him for some time. Thereafter he entered eagerly into the anti-Napoleonic league; assisted in the formation of the Quadruple Alliance; and as Germany proved successful, took no part in the national sentiment which arose, but directed himself solely to the aggrandizement of Austria, hence doing his best to preserve the French boundaries as they had been and to render Austria the only gainer among the powers by the reapportionment of Europe. He is credited with having planned and brought about the marriage of Napoleon and Marie Louise. In the years that followed he carried things his own way in Austria, planned the Holy Alliance and was extremely reactionary in his internal and foreign policies. In the difficult times of Napoleon's supremacy and his fall Metternich guided Austrian policies with a masterly hand. As a diplomatist he was the equal of any of his time. In 1814 he visited England and formed the Quadruple Alliance. He was the master spirit at the Congress of Vienna and for 15 years thereafter was the leading statesman of Europe. The Revolution of 1830 in France showed the ill-success of his program; and the risings of 1848 and the insurrection in Vienna itself made it necessary for the Emperor Ferdinand to demand his resignation. He kept some power even then, his counsel being frequently sought.

Bibliography.—Malleson, G. B., *Life of Prince Metternich* (New York 1888); Sandeman, J. A. C., *Metternich, Life and Career* (New York 1911); Buckland, C., *Metternich and the British Government 1809–13* (London 1932); Auernheimer, R., *Prince Metternich, Statesman and Lover* (Toronto 1940); Cecil, A., *Metternich 1773–1859: a Study of the Period and Personality* (London 1943); Kraehe, Enno E., *Metternich's German Policy,* 2 vols.: vol. 1, *Contest with Napoleon, 1799–1814* (Princeton 1963); Haas, Arthur G., *Metternich: Reorganization and Nationality, 1813–1818* (Knoxville, Tenn., 1964).

METUCHEN, mĕ-tŭch′ĕn, borough and residential suburb, New Jersey, in Middlesex County, five miles west-northwest of Perth Amboy; altitude 100 feet. It is served by the Pennsylvania Railroad. Manufactures include insulation materials, metal products, and chemicals. Pop. 14,041.

METZ, mĕts, city, France, capital of Moselle Department, on the junction of the Moselle and Seille rivers, 178 miles east-northeast of Paris. Formerly it was an important fortress and center of control of a group of forts. Its manufactures include woolens, cottons, hosiery, hats, muslin, glue, and leather, as well as machine-tools, elevators, agricultural equipment, household articles. It has also printing and brewing establishments.

History.—Metz was anciently known as Divodurum; later the Romans gave it the name Mediomatrica; under the Gallo-Romans (1st and 2d century) it was called Mettis, of which Metz is a contraction. The Romans built military roads through the territory, and a fine aqueduct, of which traces remain. It was sacked by Attila in the 5th century, and, after the retirement of the Huns, the Franks occupied Metz and made it the capital of Austrasia. In 870 it was included in East Francia, and developed under German influence. Its prosperity increased, and in the 13th century, as a free imperial city, it attained the zenith of its prosperity. It was taken by the French in 1552, and Charles IV issued there, in that same year, the Golden Bull. The Peace of Westphalia (1648) confirmed the rights of the French to own Metz, together with the rest of Alsace-Lorraine.

The peaceful existence of this territory came to an end in 1870 with the outbreak of the Franco-Prussian War, when several battles were fought under the walls of Metz and in its neighborhood. The town capitulated after a two-months siege on Oct. 28 with 180,000 officers and men under the command of Marshal Achille Bazaine. It was included in the cession of territory to Germany at the peace of 1871.

After World War I the Peace of Versailles (1919) restored Metz to France. But during World War II it was for more than four years once more under German occupation. It was liberated on Nov. 19, 1944 by the American Third Army.

Metz has a handsome cathedral of late Gothic design, and several other ancient churches and monuments, among them the Palais de Justice. On its wall a bas-relief commemorates the treaties of commerce and of mutual defense between America and France negotiated by Benjamin Franklin in 1778. A monument to Lafayette by the American sculptor Paul Weyland Bartlett, commemorating American participation in liberating Metz during World War I, was destroyed by the Germans in World War II. Pop. (1962) 101,496.

MEUNIER, mŭ-nyā′, **Constantin,** Belgian artist: b. Brussels, Belgium, April 12, 1831; d. there, April 4, 1905. An historical and genre painter, he first studied sculpture at the Brussels Academy and with C. A. Fraikin, then painting as a pupil of F. J. Navez. He turned from religious and historical subjects to vividly realistic depictions of life in the colliery district amid whose unlovely surroundings he long made his home. His *Martyrdom of St. Stephen* in the Ghent Museum is quite in the spirit of Ribera and shocks the mind by its brutal literalness. *The Peasants' Rebellion* is an example of his energy and force as a realist in modern life. His statue *The Lost Son* is in the Berlin National Gallery.

MEURICE, mû-rēs', **François Paul,** French dramatist: b. Paris, France, 1820; d. there, Dec. 11, 1905. He was educated at the Collége Charlemagne and entered upon a literary career. He worked for a time in collaboration with Jean Dumas, with whom he made a translation of Hamlet, and was entrusted by Victor Hugo, his brother-in-law, with the publication of his complete works (46 vols., 1880–1885). He published *Benvenuto Cellini* (1852); *Fanfan la Tulipe* (1858); *Cadio* (1868); *Le Songe de l'Amour* (1889).

MEURSIUS, mûr'sĕ-ŭs, **Johannes** (Latin form of JAN DE MEURS), Dutch scholar and historian: b. Lovsduinen, Feb. 9, 1579; d. Sept. 20, 1639. Besides *Glossarium Graeco-Barbarum* (1614); and *Athenae Batavae* (1625); for his edition of Greek authors he wrote numerous introductory essays which J. F. Gronovius reprinted in *Thesaurus Antiquitatum Graecarum*. His complete works were edited by Lami, 12 vols. (Florence 1741–1763).

MEUSE (Flem. *Maes*; Du. *Maas*), a river which rises in northeastern France in the department of Haute-Marne and flows in a generally northerly course through France, Belgium and Holland into the North Sea where it forms a common delta with the Rhine. Its source is on the plateau of Langres, about six miles west-northwest of Bourbonne-les-Bains. Above Neufchâteau (Vosges) it runs underground for a distance of over three miles. In the neighborhood of Maastricht it forms a 31-mile sector of the boundary between Belgium and Holland. Its principal affluents are the Chiers, Semois, Lesse, Sambre, Ourthe and Roer. Parts of its course in Belgium and Holland have been canalized. The principal French cities on the Meuse are Verdun, Sedan, Mézières and Givet; Belgian cities are Dinant, Namur, Huy, and Liége; Dutch cities are Maastricht, Roermond, Venlo, Dordrecht, and Rotterdam. During World War I the upper valley of the Meuse was the scene of the most sanguinary battles, including the Battle of Verdun.

MEUSE, a northeastern department of France having an area of 2,410 square miles. The capital is Bar-le-Duc. Meuse is bounded on the north by Belgium and the department of Ardennes; east by Meurthe-et-Moselle; south by Vosges and Haute-Marne; and west by Marne and Ardennes. When France was departmentalized during the Revolution, the Meuse was constituted from a portion of Lorraine, that is, from parts of the Three Bishoprics, the Barrois and Clermontais, and derived its name from the River Meuse (q.v.) which flows centrally through it from south to north-northwest. Approximately half the department is contained in the Meuse basin. The northeastern part comprises the valley of the Orne, a tributary of the Moselle, and the Chiers. In the western part the Aisne with its tributary the Aire take their rise, the mingled

waters flowing west to join the Seine. Here too is the Ornain, affluent of the Saulx, their waters debouching into the Marne. Main waterways are the canal connecting the Marne and Rhine and the Eastern Canal, which parallels the Meuse, the two having a length of 145 miles.

A rolling fertile terrain, with a rather large forested area (about one quarter), the department has no mountains. Its highest elevation, in the southwest on the line of the watershed dividing the Seine and Meuse basins, rises to only 1,388 feet. The main crops are wheat, oats, rye, barley, and potatoes. Viticulture is a minor activity. Industrial activities include lumbering, quarrying, paper milling, cheese manufactures, glass works, distilleries and flour mills. At Ligny-en-Barrois scientific instruments are manufactured. The department is divided into four arrondisements: Bar-le-Duc, Commercy, Verdun, and St. Mihiel; and these are divided into 28 cantons and 586 communes. Pop. (1962) 215,985.

MEXCALA, mäs-kä'lä, or **RIO DE LAS BALSAS,** rē'ô ~~thä~~ läz väl'säs, river, Mexico, in the southern part, which has its rise in the mountains southeast of the City of Mexico, and flows generally south and west for 426 miles to the Pacific. It is on the boundary line between the states of Michoacán and Guerrero. The port of Zacatula is at its mouth. It is a swift-flowing stream, with numerous low cascades and rapids.

MEXIA, mĕ-hā'à, city, Texas, in Limestone County; altitude 534 feet; 29 miles southeast of Corsicana; on the Southern Pacific, and Burlington-Rock Island railroads. In 1920 there was an oil boom here, but now the oil industries are second to agriculture in contribution to the city's prosperity, and cottonseed oil, textiles, and machinery are the principal products of its industry. It has the commission form of government. Pop. 6,121.

MEXICALI, mĕ-hĕ-kä'lĕ, town, Mexico, capital of Northern Territory, Lower California, near Calexico, Calif.; agricultural center in the Imperial Valley area. Pop. (1960) 172,554.

MEXICAN ARCHAEOLOGY. See MEXICO—3. *Racial Composition, Population Trends and Health.*

MEXICAN BOLL WEEVIL. See BOLL WEEVIL.

MEXICAN HAIRLESS DOG, a small terrier-like dog, of uncertain origin, without hair except a tuft on the crown of the head, another on the tail and a few scattering wisps on the body; the skin is grayish black, wrinkled and dry. Clavigero describes a large hairless dog found among the Mexicans by the Spanish conquerors, whose puppies were esteemed as an edible delicacy; and others are recorded as having occurred in ancient Peru and on various of the West Indian islands.

MEXICAN JUMPING BEAN. See JUMPING BEANS.

MEXICAN LITERATURE. See MEXICO—19. *Literature.*

MEXICAN ONYX, a stained and banded

variety of calcite or aragonite. It is not true onyx.

MEXICAN RUBBER TREE. See Castilla Elastica.

MEXICAN SUBREGION, a faunal district of the Neotropical region embracing the low hot coast region of Mexico.

MEXICAN WAR. The annexation of Texas in 1845 laid the foundation for the war with Mexico. Although Texas had been for many years practically free, and had been recognized by the United States, England, France and other countries, yet Mexico still refused to acknowledge its independence. When therefore the United States proposed to admit Texas into the Union, Mexico gave warning that the annexation would be equivalent to a declaration of war, and March 6, 1845 protested, and soon afterward withdrew her minister and severed diplomatic relations. Her acts, however, scarcely justified her threats, as at that time at least little or no preparation was made for war. It has, therefore, been claimed that had the American government used a conciliatory policy, peace might have been preserved and friendly relations re-established.

At the moment, however, the Mexican people and authorities were in a rather belligerent attitude, due in part to pride, and in part to an expectation that the United States would soon be involved in a war with Great Britain over the Oregon boundary, in which case Mexico would have a powerful ally to aid her. Did President Polk at this point seek to strengthen this hope in the minds of the Mexicans, intending at the proper moment to make a compromise and peace with England, as was done, and thus leave Mexico at the mercy of the United States? Perhaps history can never answer the question, but events at least seemed to march in harmony with the thought. For Mexico soon found herself in the dilemma that she must either sell California to the United States, receiving in return a goodly sum of money to appease her pride, or engage in a war to sustain her honor and territorial integrity. Mexico bravely, but perhaps not wisely, chose the latter alternative, not fully realizing the inequality of the contestants, nor the depth of the humiliation to which she would be subjected. Doubtless President Polk preferred to acquire California without war; but its acquisition was to be the principal measure of his administration. Hence if war was the only means to secure it, war it must be; at least enough to get possession of the desired territory.

Causes of the War.—The immediate occasion of the war was the dispute in regard to the western boundary of Texas. Proclaiming her independence in 1836 Texas asserted that her western boundary was the Rio Grande to its source, thence due north to the 42d degree of north latitude. The following year the United States recognized her independence, and in December 1845, by a joint resolution, admitted her into the Union as a state, providing that boundary disputes were to be settled by the United States. President Polk accepted the boundary line claimed by Texas, and Jan. 13, 1846 ordered Gen. Zachary Taylor to march to the eastern bank of the Rio Grande as the western boundary of the United States. Mexico insisted that the Nueces River—100 miles eastward—was the true western boundary of Texas, and therefore that General Taylor was now on Mexican soil. On April 25, 1846, the first blood was shed in a conflict between a band of Mexican troops that had crossed to the eastern side of the Rio Grande and a company of American soldiers. The news of this action was immediately communicated by General Taylor to President Polk, who sent his now noted message to Congress, asserting that war was begun by the act of Mexico on United States soil. Congress accepted, after a stormy debate in the Senate, the President's statement, and war was recognized as existing.

Other causes than the two already noted were also at work, and help to make a decision in regard to the justness of the war still more difficult. Mexico for many years had been in a chronic state of revolution. The natural result followed. American citizens in Mexico sustained property losses and doubtless were frequently unjustly arrested and even imprisoned. Claims arising from these causes had been in part settled under a convention of 1840; but many of them were still pending. Some were just; more, either unjust or extravagant in amount. President Polk united these unsettled claims with the boundary question, and demanded that Mexico receive an envoy extraordinary with power to settle both—on its face an eminently fair proposition. On the other hand, Mexico professed to be ready to receive an ambassador to settle the boundary dispute, but declined to receive John Slidell as United States minister, when he was commissioned to settle all disputes, insisting that the two questions were distinct in kind and origin and should not be united. President Polk in his message asserted that this action of Mexico was in violation of her promise to receive a minister, and hence justified his administration in its measures, and forced him to take possession of the disputed territory.

The need of more slave territory was perhaps another factor in causing the war. At least many from the South took an aggressive position on all questions in dispute between the two countries and thus made a peaceable settlement more difficult. Both the economic and the political reasons for more territory began to be felt by 1846—the one to have new soil over which to spread the land-exhausting system of slavery; and the other to have new territory out of which to carve new slave states that the equilibrium between slave and free states might be maintained. Some other forces tending to arouse the war and aggressive spirit may be noted. The cry of "manifest destiny" played a part. Many, especially in the West, felt that the Pacific Ocean was the natural western boundary of the United States. They also demanded the "Golden Gate" that commerce might be opened up with the Orient. The two great parties—the Whigs and the Democrats—divided quite sharply on the question; in fact so completely that the war became almost a party, instead of a national, issue. The Democrats, as a rule, supported the administration and its claim that the war was just. The Whigs, on the contrary, asserted that it was a most unholy and unrighteous war, and characterized it as Polk's war. Abraham Lincoln, entering Congress in 1847, became a severe critic of the policy pursued, while Thomas Corwin of Ohio went so far as to use this language: "If I were a Mexican I would tell you, 'Have you not room in your own country to bury your dead men? If you come into mine we will greet you with bloody hands, and welcome you to hospitable graves.'"

President Polk summarized his reasons for recommending that Congress recognize war as existing as follows: "The grievous wrongs perpetrated by Mexico upon our citizens throughout a long period of years remain unredressed; and solemn treaties . . . have been disregarded. . . . Our commerce with Mexico has been almost annihilated." He then adds: "As war exists, and . . . exists by the act of Mexico herself, we are called upon, by every consideration of duty and patriotism, to vindicate, with decision the honor, the rights, and the interests of our country."

The Campaigns.—The war with Mexico was accepted as a fact by Congress, May 13, 1846. There were four principal fields of action in its prosecution. (1) Along the Rio Grande, under the command of Gen. Zachary Taylor; (2) in California, where Capt. John Charles Frémont and Commodore Robert Field Stockton were in command; (3) in New Mexico, with Colonel Stephen Watts Kearny leading the United States forces; and (4) from Veracruz to Mexico City, under the command of Gen. Winfield Scott, the commander in chief of the United States armies. Everywhere success attended the arms of the United States. Perhaps it was the first war in history, lasting two years, in which no defeat was sustained by one party, and no victory won by the other.

General Taylor defeated the Mexican troops at Palo Alto, May 8, 1846; at Resaca de la Palma the following day, and captured Matamoros on the 18th. He remained near that city for some weeks to recruit his army and prepare to advance into the interior. On September 24 he entered Monterrey, after a siege of four days, and a gallant resistance by the Mexicans. Taylor's most famous victory, however, was won Feb. 22–23, 1847, at Buena Vista. General Scott gave orders, which fell into the hands of Antonio López de Santa Anna, the Mexican general, for General Taylor to send some nine regiments to aid Scott in his proposed attack on Veracruz. Santa Anna immediately marched his whole command against Taylor, expecting to crush him in this weakened condition. It was 20,000 men against about 5,000. But the skill of Taylor, the persistence of his army, the organization and equipment of the United States troops, won a great victory. Taylor became the hero of the hour, and Buena Vista made him an irresistible presidential candidate.

Frémont's course in California has been a subject of keen controversy. As leader of an exploring expedition he was already in northern California, and early in 1846 was recalled to the Sacramento Valley. California was the goal of the political policy of Polk's administration. The means to secure its acquisition were uncertain. It might be gained by war; or by filling the territory with settlers from the United States, who in course of time might bring it into the Union as Texas had already been annexed; or it might be effected by securing the goodwill of the native Californians who were already jealous of Mexican rule. The latter policy seems to have been the one adopted by the administration. The United States consul at Monterey,

California, Thomas Oliver Larkin, was developing this policy with a good prospect of success, it is claimed, when Frémont appeared on the scene. He seems to have developed a fourth policy, namely, the establishment of an independent government under the control of settlers from the United States in the Sacramento Valley. This movement resulted in the so-called Bear Flag Republic, and virtual civil war between the native Californians and the newer settlers. At this moment the Mexican War began and the Bear Flag was replaced by the Stars and Stripes. It has been claimed by some California historians that Frémont's course, had not the Mexican War come at the moment it did, might have lost California to the United States. The native Californians, alienated as they were by his course, might have put themselves under an English protectorate in revenge for the treatment accorded them. Be this as it may, by the end of 1846 all California was conquered and held by United States troops, and Frémont was regarded as the hero who had won the "Golden Gate" by his energy and decision.

Santa Fé was captured by Colonel Kearny, Aug. 18, 1846, and New Mexico secured with almost no loss of life. By the end of the year, therefore, all the territory that the administration desired was in the possession of its armies, but Mexico was still unconquered.

Scott had been chafing in Washington during the summer and fall of 1846 while Taylor was winning his brilliant victories. He asked to go to the front to assume chief command, but the administration retained him at the capital under the plea of needing his advice. As it happened this Democratic war was officered by Whig generals. Scott had already been a candidate for the Whig nomination for the presidency. The charge was now made that Scott was kept from command for fear that success might make him a more formidable candidate in 1848. Finally, when he was sent to the front in January 1847, the cry was raised that the purpose was to dim the luster of Taylor's victories, or at least to divide the popular support between the two generals in such a way as to destroy the political prospects of both.

General Scott invested Veracruz in March 1847, and by the 27th had captured the fortress of San Juan de Ulúa, which had been thought to be almost impregnable, and was ready to enter the city. On April 8 he started into the interior, and on the 18th captured Cerro Gordo; the 19th, Jalapa; and the 22d, Perote. On May 15 he entered the important city of Puebla. Remaining here for some weeks he again advanced, in August, toward the capital, and on the 10th came in sight of the city. Two important victories were won August 20—at Contreras and at Churubusco. He captured Molino del Rey, September 8, and the victory of Chapultepec, September 12–13, gave him Mexico City itself, which he entered on September 14 with an army of only 6,000 men.

The war was practically over, but the victory was so complete that it began to be a question whether there was any government left with sufficient power to negotiate a treaty of peace. An agitation began with friends both in and out of Congress, as well as in the cabinet, looking to the annexation of the whole of Mexico. John C. Calhoun on the one hand, Daniel Webster and a majority of the Whigs on the other, joined hands to defeat this plan. President Polk was finally forced to make the ultimate decision. Nicholas Trist was sent in March 1847 to Mexico to make a treaty of peace. Failing, he was ordered in the fall to return to Washington; but disobeying instructions he remained in Mexico, and on Feb. 2, 1848, concluded a treaty of peace in harmony with his original instructions. The administration was in a quandary. To ratify meant to condone the disobedience of Trist. To reject meant a prolongation of the war, and time to perfect the intrigue for the annexation of "All Mexico." President Polk, after some hesitation, decided to send the treaty to the Senate for its consideration. Received February 23, it was ratified, after some amendments, March 10, by a vote of 38 to 14. On May 30, ratifications were exchanged and the war was at an end.

The Mexicans had fought bravely, even stubbornly and at times skillfully, yet in every contest, even when the odds were greatly in their favor, without a single victory. In part superior leadership and training won for the soldiers of the northern republic; in part their cooler and more persistent character; but in the main it was not bravery, nor generalship, nor even character that won. It was science and education applied in the equipment of the armies, the guns of the soldiers, the cannon, and the powder in the arsenals which made the one so much more effective than the other that the most daring bravery was no counterpoise.

The Treaty of Peace.—The treaty of Guadalupe Hidalgo gave to the administration of President Polk the territory that his diary informs us he intended to acquire, California and New Mexico. Mexico in return for the loss of its fairest northern provinces was paid $15,000,-000, and released from all claims of all kinds held by citizens of the United States against her, estimated at $3,250,000, which the United States assumed. Boundary lines were drawn, and provision made in regard to other questions at issue between the two countries.

Results.—Usually successfully waged wars redound to the credit of the party in power. In this case, however, the Democratic Party, the author and supporter of the war, was defeated by the Whig Party, the party of opposition and criticism, in the presidential election of 1848. The Whigs made use of the popularity of a successful general (Taylor) to defeat the party that had made his glory possible. Evidently the people were ready to accept the fruits of the war, but also ready to punish the party they believed had wrought in a wrong manner.

A large number of young officers, destined to renown in later years, proved their worth in this war. Ulysses S. Grant and William T. Sherman, Robert E. Lee, "Stonewall" Jackson, and Jefferson Davis, in the great Civil War, foreshadowed, in this Mexican struggle, the greatness that was to be theirs in the "days that tried men's souls" from 1861 to 1865.

The acquisition of some 522,568 square miles of territory—about one sixth of the modern continental United States—was the most important immediate as well as remote result. It was important in the issues that its acquisition precipitated. Should it be slave or free territory? Who should determine its institutions? Out of this question grew the larger one, who had the right to control the institutions of the territories

in general? To settle the first question David Wilmot, a Democrat of Pennsylvania, proposed the celebrated Wilmot Proviso which would exclude slavery forever from all territory acquired from Mexico. Four long years of intense and bitter debate followed. This question and a series of others were settled temporarily in the Compromise of 1850. The second question was answered by the phrase "nonintervention," which meant, or soon came to mean, one thing to Douglas and the Northern Democrats, and another to Davis and the South. Three main theories were evolved or defended in answer to the third query: (1) that Congress had the right to control the institutions of the territories and could make them slave or free at its will; (2) the Dickinson-Cass-Douglas doctrine of popular or "squatter" sovereignty—the doctrine that the people of a territory themselves, while yet in a territorial status, determined their own institutions; (3) the radical Southern view that slaves were property, and, as property, might be taken into any territory—the common public domain of the states—with no constitutional power anywhere to hinder or prevent.

The new territory was important secondly in its industrial and political effect on the nation. The United States now had an outlook on the Pacific Ocean comparable to that on the Atlantic. China, Japan and the Orient were brought within the circle of its influence. Conditions favorable to further expansion were prepared. In addition to the great effect on commerce thus prefigured, that on wealth and industry was not less. The gold, silver, copper, and other mineral wealth of the Rocky Mountain region was turned into the pockets of the people of the United States. This vast addition of territory and wealth tended also to emphasize national pride and ambition; to arouse a still more intense belief in "manifest destiny"; to develop a more optimistic tone, and perhaps also to produce a more materialistic spirit.

HOWARD W. CALDWELL,
University of Nebraska.

Bibliography.—Ripley, H. S., *The War with Mexico,* 2 vols. (New York 1849); Grant, Ulysses S., *Personal Memoirs,* 2 vols. (New York 1885–86); Rives, G. L., *The United States and Mexico, 1821–1848,* 2 vols. (New York 1913); DeVoto, Bernard, *The Year of Decision: 1846* (Boston 1943); Bill, Alfred H., *Rehearsal for Conflict, the War with Mexico* (New York 1947); Henry, Robert S., *The Story of the Mexican War* (New York 1950); Singletary, Otis, *The Mexican War* (Chicago 1960); Brooks, Nathan C., *A Complete History of the Mexican War* (Glorieta, N.Mex., 1965); Price, Glenn W., *Origins of the War with Mexico* (Philadelphia 1967).

MEXICO, měk′sĭ-kō, Span. mě′hě-kô (officially LOS ESTADOS UNIDOS MEXICANOS; The Mexican United States), republic, is bounded to the north by the United States of America, and to the south and southeast by Guatemala and British Honduras. Within the country, the name México is chiefly reserved for the capital, known to the English-speaking world as Mexico City; the nation as a whole being generally referred to simply as *la república* (the republic).

The most important features of geographical relief are the lofty Central Plateau bordered by two mountain ranges and these ranges themselves, the Sierra Madre Oriental on the east and the Sierra Madre Occidental on the west.

Although Mexico is usually considered as being in North America, it is perhaps more accurate from the point of view of physical geogra-

phy to include in North America only that portion
between the southern border of the United States
and the Sierra Volcánica Transversal (see section *The Land*); assigning the territory south
of this sierra to Central America. The national
territory is divided into almost equal parts by the
Tropic of Cancer, or latitude 23°27'N., which
transverses it.

The name and the national emblem of Mexico
are derived from the Aztecs who, according to
tradition, departed from Aztlan (thought to be
in the northwestern part of the republic) in 820
A.D., and after a peregrination of many centuries
arrived at what is today the Valley of Mexico.
It is believed that they chose this site on the
banks of what was then the principal lake, in
response to a prophecy which instructed them
to settle where they saw an eagle holding a serpent in its claws. The name Mexico was derived from the word Mexitli—another name for
the Aztec god of war, Huitzilopochtli—to which
was added the suffix *co,* signifying "place."

Coat of arms.

The eagle seen by the Aztecs was conserved
as a symbol through the years, and when independence was achieved in 1821 it was adopted as
the national emblem, which it is today. The
flag, consisting of three wide vertical stripes,
green at the hoist, white in the center, and red
at the fly, with the emblem—the eagle standing
on a cactus devouring a serpent—in the center,
dates from 1821 when the Plan of Iguala (see
section *Mexico from 1810 to 1910*) was approved.
A minor change in design was made by an act of
April 14, 1823. The words of the national hymn
whose first line is *Mexicanos, al grito de guerra*
were written by Francisco Gonzáles Bocanegra;
and its music, by Jaimě Nunó.

Spanish is the official language. The metric
system is in use and the monetary unit is the
peso, consisting of 100 centavos.

For the convenience of the reader, the historical, political, economic, and social development
of Mexico is discussed in the following articles,
written by eminent Mexican authorities.

1. THE LAND. Mexico lies south of the
United States, and north and west of Guatemala
and British Honduras. It is otherwise limited
by the Pacific Ocean on the west and by extensions of the Atlantic Ocean—the Gulf of Mexico
and Caribbean Sea—on the east. The total length
of the coastlines is 6,212 miles. The northernmost point of Mexico is at the confluence of the
Gila and Colorado rivers, at latitude 32°41'N.
Its southernmost point is the mouth of the
Suchiate River at latitude 14°30'N.

The border with the United States was established, following the annexation of Texas by
the United States in 1845 and the war with that
country in 1846–1848, by the Treaty of Guadalupe Hidalgo, Feb. 2, 1848. This treaty was later
modified by the Gadsden Purchase, also known
as the Treaty of Mesilla, Dec. 30, 1853, by which
the United States annexed other territories of
the Mexican states of Sonora and Chihuahua.
The frontier with Guatemala was determined by
two treaties, of Sept. 27, 1882, and May 19, 1894.
The frontier with British Honduras was established by treaty with Great Britain, July 8, 1893.

The calculations of the Dirección de Geografía y Meteorología place the area of Mexico
at 760,579 square miles, excluding the continental
shelf, which was declared incorporated into the
national territory by President Manuel Ávila
Camacho, Oct. 30, 1945; the decree being ratified
by the legislature in a special session, Jan. 16,
1946. The area of the continental shelf claimed
by Mexico is 154,633 square miles.

PHYSIOGRAPHY

Mexico is divided into nine physiographic
provinces, as follows:

Northwestern Mexico.—(1) *Peninsula of
Lower California.*—This is the continuation of a
series of anticlines extending along the western
part of the North American continent and comprising the Alaska Range, the Coast Mountains
of British Columbia, the Cascade Range, the
Sierra Nevada, and the Sierra de Baja (Lower)
California. The anticlines of the Sierra de Baja
California produced extensive lava flows during
the Upper Tertiary period, but the region seems
to have remained quiet throughout the Quaternary.

(2) *Gulf of California and Adjacent Lowlands.*—These are the continuation of the depressions, the basin, and range complex found
throughout the western part of North America;
including the basins of the Yukon, Fraser and
Columbia rivers, and the Great Basin of the

western United States. Faulting has been extensive in the Gulf of California. In adjacent plains of the states of Sonora, Sinaloa, and Nayarit are found elongated volcanic edifices of the Tertiary period.

North and Central Mexico and Yucatán Peninsula.—(3) *Sierra Madre Occidental and Sierra Madre Oriental.*—The former, which follows the western coast at some distance inland, is the most important manifestation of relief in Mexico, as well as of the entire continent; being in other places known as the Rocky Mountains. No evidence has been found of volcanic activity during the Quaternary period in the Sierra Madre Occidental, except in the southern part. The foldings of this range take on an east-west orientation, cross the Central Plateau and continue in the Sierra Madre Oriental, which follows the eastern coast at a distance from the Gulf of Mexico. The latter range began to take form during the Upper Middle Cretaceous, as the result of foldings which continued during the Tertiary. Its great elevation is interrupted only here and there from Monterrey to the Isthmus of Tehuantepec. Volcanism was active in the central part of the Sierra Madre Oriental during Quaternary times; elsewhere the range has been quiet.

(4) *Mexican Central Plateau.*—This plateau, lying between the Sierra Madre Occidental and the Sierra Madre Oriental, is the continuation of the Great Plains of the western United States and Canada. It was formed mostly by marine sedimentations during the Cretaceous period, then emerged from the sea during an uplift which continued during Tertiary and Quaternary times. The plateau is crossed by folds of the Sierra Madre Occidental and the Sierra Madre Oriental systems, and by a transverse range beginning in the State of Durango and continuing across the states of Zacatecas, Guanajuato, Querétaro, and Hidalgo to the borders of Puebla. This last is characterized by numerous volcanic edifices, products of the Oligocene and Miocene periods. To the south of this range once again are found isolated plateaus, such as El Bajío (the high valley of the Central Plateau which includes most of Guanajuato and parts of Querétaro, Michoacán, Jalisco, and Aguascalientes) and the so-called valleys of Toluca, Mexico, Tlaxcala, Puebla, and Tehuacán, all of which are limited in the south by the Sierra Volcánica Transversal. Only in this last zone of the Central Plateau do earthquakes still occur.

(5) *Gulf Coastal Plain and Yucatán Peninsula.*—This division is a continuation of the coastal plain which begins east of the Appalachian Mountains and continues into Florida and along the Gulf coast of the United States. It embraces the Mexican states of Tamaulipas, Veracruz, and Tabasco, and the Yucatán Peninsula; then the plain submerges into the Yucatán Channel, later to reappear in Cuba. The uplifting of this coastal plain in Mexico began toward the end of the Cretaceous period and has continued, despite numerous recessions, through the Tertiary and Quaternary. The relief of the region drops precipitously down from the highlands on the west, tapering off into a plain of very slight inclination. Except for some regions of the central and southern parts of Veracruz, which are seismic zones due to their proximity to the tectonic region of southern Mexico, the coastal plain is free of earthquakes in the present era.

(6) *Sierra Volcánica Transversal.*—The Transverse Volcanic Range rises south of the Central Plateau and north of the Balsas Depression. Its historical geology is very similar to that of the neighboring physiographic divisions, with interruptions from time to time by effusions of lava, which have formed a series of lofty volcanic edifices along the 19th meridian from coast to coast. It is a region of tectonic as well as of volcanic earthquakes. The Sierra Volcánica Transversal includes the famous Popocatepetl, Citlaltepetl (Pico de Orizaba), and Colima, old but still active volcanoes, as well as the newer Jorullo and Paricutín.

Southern Mexico.—(7) *Balsas Depression.*—The depression of the Balsas River in the states of Michoacán and Guerrero, with the depressions of the rivers Atoyac (in Puebla), and Nochistlán, Verde, and Tehuantepec (the last three in Oaxaca), is part of a geosyncline which also includes the Gulf of California and the other great depressions of the continent associated with it. This region underwent the same uplifts of the Upper Cretaceous and Tertiary periods as its southern neighbor, the Sierra Madre del Sur. The foldings which formed the depression itself began during the Oligocene and continued into the Quaternary. It is also a region of frequent tectonic earthquakes.

(8) *Sierra Madre del Sur.*—This sierra, which crosses the states of Colima, Michoacán, Guerrero, and Oaxaca, is the continuation of the Sierra de Baja California and the other mountain ranges linked with it. This region experienced an uplift beginning in the Upper Cretaceous period. During the Cenozoic, the uplifting continued, accompanied by the foldings which created the mountainous relief. The present tectonic character of the Sierra Madre del Sur is reflected by frequent earthquakes.

(9) *Isthmus Region and Chiapas.*—The three physiographic divisions described immediately above end at the Isthmus of Tehuantepec, where their physiographic elements taper off to a low altitude and are scarcely distinguishable one from another. Farther east, however, in the State of Chiapas the three phenomena once again appear more pronouncedly, clearly dividing the region into three zones. The mountainous region of the Sierra Septentrional de Chiapas, in the north of that state, is a prolongation of the Sierra Madre Oriental, being prolonged even farther into Guatemala, British Honduras, Cuba, Haiti, the Dominican Republic, and Puerto Rico. The central depression of Chiapas is a continuation of the Balsas Depression and the associated depressions of the states of Oaxaca and Guerrero. This series of depressions continues through Guatemala and British Honduras into the Caribbean, where it is known as the Bartlett Deep. The Sierra Madre de Chiapas, in the west, is a prolongation of the Sierra Madre del Sur which continues across Guatemala and Honduras, later reappearing in Jamaica and Haiti. In this physiographic division, volcanic activity is at present concentrated in the south.

Volcanoes.—Volcanism in Mexico was at its maximum activity during Tertiary times, especially during the Oligocene period, although it has continued to the present. Volcanic activity is concentrated mainly along the 19th meridian of latitude, in the range formed by various volcanic edifices, called the Sierra Volcánica Transversal. The most important volcanoes of this range, with their approximate heights, are: Colima Volcano (12,984 feet) and the Nevado de Colima (14,108 feet), in western Jalisco; El Quinceo (9,016 feet) and Tancitaro (11,148 feet), in Michoacán; the Nevado de Toluca (14,944 feet), in Mexico State; Cempoala (14,036 feet), in Morelos; Popocatepetl (17,705 feet) and Ixtaccihuatl (17,671 feet), both within sight of Mexico City; Malinche (14,623 feet), between Tlaxcala and Puebla; and Citlaltepetl, or Pico de Orizaba (18,843 feet), the highest point in the republic; and Cofre de Perote (13,475 feet), in Veracruz.

In the Revillagigedo Islands, lying along the 19th parallel in the Pacific, are found Monte Evermann, on Socorro Island, and Monte Gallegos and Monte Tent on Clarión Island. Smaller Mexican volcanoes include: Ceboruco (7,100 feet) and Sanganguey, in Nayarit; Tequila, in Jalisco; Calmini, Virgenes, and Loreto in the Sierra de Baja California; Chacahua, Ometepec, and Pochutla in the Sierra Madre del Sur; the volcanoes of the Tres Marías Islands off the coast of Nayarit; and San Bartolomé, Zontehuitz, San Cristóbal, Hueytepec, and Chicón, in Chiapas. The youngest volcanoes of Mexico are Jorullo (4,331 feet; erupted first in 1759) and Paricutín (in 1943), both in Michoacán.

Rivers and Lakes.—The principal rivers of Mexico, with their alternate names and approximate total lengths, are given in the following paragraphs.

Rivers which drain into the Gulf of California are: the Colorado, most of whose course is in the United States; the Concepción (or Magdalena, 200 miles long); Sonora (250 miles); Yaqui (420 miles); Mayo (220 miles); Fuerte (175 miles—350 miles with its affluent the Verde); Sinaloa (200 miles); and Culiacán (175 miles).

Those entering the Pacific are, in central Mexico, the San Pedro (250 miles—upper course called the Mezquital) and Santiago (600 miles—upper course, above Lake Chapala, called the Lerma). In the south are the Balsas (450 miles —upper course called the Atoyac in Puebla and the Mexcala in Guerrero) and its affluent the Tepalcatepec (150 miles), the Verde (200 miles—upper course called the Atoyac), Tehuantepec (150 miles), and Suchiate (100 miles) on the Guatemala border.

The most important river draining into the Gulf of Mexico in the north is the Rio Grande (or Bravo), most of whose course separates Mexico from the United States. Its chief tributaries from the Mexican side are the Conchos (300 miles) and the Salado (210 miles—upper course called the Sabinas). The San Fernando (170 miles) and Soto la Marina (160 miles) are also in the north. In the central region are the Pánuco (100 miles), which is formed by the junction of the Moctezuma (175 miles) and the Santa María (200 miles)—the lower course of the Pánuco is also called the Tamuin—as well as the Tuxpan (or Tuxpam, 100 miles), Tecolutla (257 miles), and Nautla (162 miles). In the south are the Papaloapan (or Papaloápam, 75 miles—195 miles with its headstream, the Tuxtepec), Coatzacoalcos (175 miles), Grijalva (400 miles—middle course also called Chiapa), and Usumacinta (600 miles—upper course called the Chixoy). The Grijalva and Usumacinta are connected near the coast. The Hondo (150 miles) drains into the Caribbean Sea after forming the border between Quintana Roo and British Honduras.

The Papaloapan is the most important river of Mexico, occupying seventh rank among the rivers of the world in volume of water discharged; the rate at times reaching 8,000 cubic meters per second at Tlacotalpan, where its force is greatest. The Lerma-Santiago River is also of great importance. The Lerma rises in the mountains near Toluca and drains into Lake Chapala, the largest (417 square miles) and one of the most beautiful lakes in Mexico. By way of the Santiago River, Lake Chapala drains into the Pacific, as noted above.

In the interior there are many rivers which do not drain into the ocean but into lakes which have no outlet. In the northwest of the Central Plateau, the Casas Grandes (250 miles long) drains into Lake Guzmán (56 square miles in area); the Santa María (200 miles) into Lake Santa María (30 square miles); and the Carmen (150 miles) into Lake Patos. These three rivers and lakes are in Chihuahua. In the west of the plateau, the Cadena (94 miles) drains into Lake Palomas, Chihuahua. The areas of lakes Patos and Palomas are variable, due to irrigation operations. Also in the west, the Nazas (180 miles) formerly drained into Lake Mayrán, in Coahuila; and the Aguanaval (250 miles), into Lake Viesca, also in Coahuila. These two rivers were dammed, however, and have water only in the rainy season. In Michoacán, lakes Pátzcuaro (100 square miles) and Cuitzeo (160 square miles) have no outlet to the sea; nor has Lake Sayula (79 square miles) in Jalisco.

The Moctezuma River, an affluent of the Pánuco as mentioned above, now drains the ancient lacustrian basins of the Valley of Mexico, where of five lakes, Texcoco, Zumpango, Xaltocán, Chalco, and Xochimilco, the last named is the only survivor, although only Chalco is absolutely dry in all seasons.

Islands.—Mexico possesses numerous islands off both coasts, many of which are uninhabited. The principal islands in the Gulf of Mexico and Caribbean Sea, all of which are populated, are Carmen, on which is the port of Carmen, Campeche; and Cozumel and Mujeres islands off Quintana Roo. Mujeres is notable for being the first Mexican land discovered, by Francisco Fernández de Córdoba on March 1, 1517.

In the Pacific the only populated islands are Cedros (Northern Lower California), which has a plant for packing sea food; Margarita (Southern Lower California), a naval base; and Tiburón, home of the Seri Indians, in the Gulf of California off the coast of Sonora.

Nevertheless, it is in the Pacific that Mexico has her most interesting islands, among them Socorro and Clarión in the Revillagigedos, 300 to 500 miles from the nearest point on the continent.

Guadalupe Island is one of the most interesting islands in the world. Located 180 miles west of northern Lower California, it rises sharply from the abyssal depths of the ocean to an altitude of 4,498 feet. Guadalupe is the home of the only surviving elephant seals (or sea elephants; *Macrorhinus angustirostris*).

Climate and Vegetation.—In general, altitude and rainfall are more important than latitude in determining climate. According to the classification of Wladmir Köppen, the following types of climate are found in Mexico:

(1) Tropical humid climate with rains throughout the year (type Af), in northeastern Chiapas, the southwestern tip of Campeche, southeastern Veracruz, and Tabasco except along the coast. Here the vegetation is tropical rain forest, characterized by angiospermous trees, both monocotyledons and dicotyledons, to which cling lianas or vines and epiphytes or parasitic plants. Among the trees of greatest economic importance are red cedar, mahogany, lignum vitae, quebracho, ceiba, brazilwood, logwood, and sapodilla, as well as tropical fruit trees.

(2) Tropical humid climate with intense monsoon rains in summer (Am), along the Atlantic slopes of the Sierra Madre Oriental, across the State of Veracruz, along the north of the Sierra Septentrional de Chiapas, and in the south of Campeche and Quintana Roo.

The natural vegetation is tropical forest, which is composed of the same class of trees as the tropical rain forest, but without lianas and epiphytes. Thus it is less dense than the rain forest. Among its most important species, in addition to those noted as belonging to the tropical rain forest, are avocados, custard apples, magnolias, guavas, and cacao trees.

The tropical forests of Quintana Roo, Campeche, and Chiapas constitute the primary forest region of the country. Their trees, which are hardwood, are used in furniture making and other industries. The sapodilla should be mentioned for the importance of its latex as a raw material that yields chicle. Mexico is one of the world's leading exporters of chicle, of which some 2,642,-000 pounds were produced by the country in the year 1964.

These forests are subjected to an immoderate exploitation, but their exuberant growth facilitates natural reforestation.

(3) Tropical humid climate, with rainfall in summer (Aw), in the coastal plain of Veracruz, the north of the Yucatán Peninsula, the Pacific coastal plain from central Sinaloa to Chiapas, part of the Balsas Depression, and the central depression of Chiapas. Vegetation is of the tropical savannah-type grassland, consisting chiefly of herbaceous plants, among which may be mentioned amaranth, jicama, gourds, pineapples, and bananas.

(4) Dry climates, steppe (BS) and desert (BW), are found in the northern stretches of the Central Plateau, in the plains of Sonora and Sinaloa, the Peninsula of Lower California, in a strip all along the western side of the Sierra Madre Oriental, and in the extreme northwest of Yucatán. In all these regions the steppe climate surrounds the desert.

There is also a type of steppe vegetation on the plateaus that extend from San Luis Potosí through eastern Puebla as far as the central plateaus of Oaxaca, as well as in the lowest part of the Balsas Depression and in other depressions, such as that of Lake Cuitzeo.

The steppe vegetation is grass and drought-resistant plants, whereas the desert has only drought-resistant plants or naked sands and rocks. Among the most important types of drought-resistant plants are cacti, agave, yucca, mesquite, candelilla, and guayule.

(5) Temperate humid climate with rains in winter (Cs) is characteristic of the northwest region of the Peninsula of Lower California. The vegetation here is either grassland or prairie (see classification 8).

(6) Temperate humid climate with rains throughout the year (Cf) occurs in the upper reaches of the sierras, and is characterized by coniferous forests.

These forests are formed chiefly of gymnospermous conifers, of which the most important are pines, oyamel (*Abies religiosa*), *abeto*, the common juniper, and the ahuehuete (*Taxodium mucronatum*). These softwood trees are found in the San Pedro Mártir and Juárez sierras in northern Lower California, in the Sierra Madre Occidental, the Sierra Madre Oriental, the Sierra Volcánica Transversal, in the highest regions of the Sierra Madre del Sur, and in the Sierra Madre de Chiapas. Being found the length of the country and being located near centers of population, they are exploited on a national scale. They supply wood for building and furniture, as well as wood pulp and resins used by medicine and industry, such as pitch and turpentine. The coniferous forests have been subjected to an immoderate exploitation, but are protected to a certain extent by their location in the mountains. The exploitation of pine represents about three quarters of the forest production of the country.

(7) Temperate humid climate with scant rainfall in all seasons (Cx') is found only in northern Tamaulipas and in some mountainous areas of Nuevo León and Coahuila. Steppe vegetation prevails (see classification 4).

(8) Temperate humid climate with rainfall in summer (Cw) occurs on the western slope of the Sierra Madre Occidental, in the southern valleys of the Central Plateau, in the Sierra Madre del Sur, the Sierra Madre de Chiapas, and in the northern mountainous region of the latter state. Vegetation is prairie grassland. The vegetation of the temperate humid prairies is formed chiefly of grasses, among the most important of which are epazote (*Chenopodium ambrosioides*), zacaton (*Epicampes macroura*), and otate (*Gradua amplexifolia*).

(9) Polar climate due to altitude (EB) is found in the higher elevations of some mountains. This classification has two subtypes: (ET) tundra vegetation, consisting of lichens and bunch grasses, is found on the Nevado de Colima, Nevado de Toluca, Cofre de Perote, and Malinche, as well as at corresponding elevations on the still higher volcanoes; the climate of perpetual ice (EF) occurs in the most elevated regions of Citlaltepetl, Popocatepetl, and Ixtaccihuatl.

Mixed Forest of Temperate Regions.—This type of forest is characterized by dicotyledonous angiosperms and gymnospermous conifers; thus, besides the conifers, there are live oaks, oaks, willows, and ash and walnut trees, among others. The mixed forests are found on the western slope of the Sierra Madre Occidental, southern slope of the Sierra Volcánica Transversal, northern slope of the Sierra Septentrional de Chiapas, and the eastern slopes of the northern and southern parts of the Sierra Madre de Chiapas.

The mixed forests, like the forests of softwood conifers (classification 6, above), are thus found the length of the country, and are exploited on a national scale. Since many of the mixed forests extend into the southern valleys of the Central Plateau, however, they have suffered a more severe exploitation than have the coniferous forests. Live oaks, oaks, and walnut trees are used chiefly in furniture making; pines, for building, furniture, and to obtain resins.

Fauna.—The animals belong to the two great

zoogeographical regions of the American continent, the Nearctic and the Neotropical, since the boundary between the two is in Mexico. This boundary crosses the Gulf and Pacific coastal plains roughly at the Tropic of Cancer, but altitude then forces it southward along the Sierra Madre Oriental in the east and the Sierra Madre Occidental in the west until it reaches the Sierre Volcánica Transversal, where it crosses the interior of the country in an east-west direction. North of this boundary the fauna is almost exclusively Nearctic (of the Rocky Mountain subregion); south of it the fauna is neotropical.

Among Nearctic mammals are the wild sheep, pronghorn, and several species of deer and bear; among Nearctic mammals with Neotropical components are the tapir, puma, jaguar, and various deer. Neotropical mammals include marsupials, such as the opossum, and those of the American type, such as the armadillo and monkeys.

Bibliography.—Köppen, Wladimir, *Grundriss der Klimakunde* (Berlin 1931); Schuchert, Charles, *Historical Geology of the Antillean-Caribbean Region* (New York 1935); Sánchez, Pedro C., *Estudio orogénico de la República Mexicana* (Tacubaya, D. F., Mexico, 1936); id., *Estudio hidrológico de la República Mexicana* (Mexico City 1938); Vivó, Jorge A., and Gómez, José C., *Climatología de México* (Mexico City 1946); Yarza, Luz Esperanza, *Los volcanes de México* (Mexico City 1946); O'Gorman, Edmundo, *Historia de las divisiones territoriales de México* (Mexico City 1948); Vivó, Jorge A., *Geografía de México* (Mexico City 1949); Krutch, Joseph Wood, *The Forgotten Peninsula: A Naturalist in Baja California* (New York 1961); Ewing, Russell C., ed., *Six Faces of Mexico* (Tucson, Ariz., 1966); Simpson, Lesley Byrd, *Many Mexicos*, rev. ed. (Berkeley, Calif., 1966).

CARLOS R. BERZUNZA,
Colonel, Mexican Army; Professor of Geography, Universidad Nacional de México, Escuela Superior de Guerra, and Mexico City College.

2. POLITICAL DIVISIONS AND POPULATION.

The initial political division, of Mexico, similar to the present division, was incorporated in the federal Constitution of Oct. 4, 1824, which divided the federation into 19 states and 4 territories, and adopted the federal popular representative form of government. The states included Texas; the territories, Upper California and New Mexico (Santa Fe). These two territories, as well as Texas—whose declaration of independence in 1836 was not recognized by Mexico—and parts of the states of Coahuila, Chihuahua, and Sonora, were ceded to the United States in the treaties of Guadalupe Hidalgo in 1848 and Mesilla (Gadsden Purchase) in 1853. The territorial extension of Mexico before these treaties was approximately 1,544,400 square miles; hence it is now less than half what it was during the colonial period and the first years of independence.

Under the Constitution of 1857 the republic was reorganized into 24 states and 1 territory. The constitution promulgated Feb. 5, 1917 recognized 28 states, 3 territories, and the Federal District, which corresponds to the District of Columbia in the United States. The admission of the Territory of Northern Lower California as a state on Jan. 16, 1952, however, changed the organization of Mexico to 29 states, 2 territories (Southern Lower California and Quintana Roo), and the Federal District, which are tabulated on the accompanying table, with their respective areas, capitals, and populations according to 1967 official estimates. States and territories are divided into *municipios* (municipalities) of which there are several thousand. The Federal Dis-

State or territory	Square miles	Total population[1]	Capital city	Populations of capitals[2]
North—				
Chihuahua	94,831	1,678,000	Chihuahua	221,500
Coahuila	58,068	1,162,000	Saltillo	126,300
Durango	47,691	919,000	Durango	137,900
Nuevo León	25,137	1,535,000	Monterrey	900,600
San Luis Potosí	24,417	1,355,000	San Luis Potosí	181,700
Tamaulipas	30,734	1,379,000	Ciudad Victoria	50,000
Zacatecas	28,124	1,931,000	Zacatecas	40,000
North Pacific—				
Lower California, North	27,655	896,000	Mexicali	350,200
Lower California, South (Terr.)	27,978	100,000	La Paz	21,000
Nayarit	10,547	532,000	Tepic	40,000
Sinaloa	22,582	1,106,000	Culiácan	125,600
Sonora	70,483	1,136,000	Hermosillo	167,700
Central—				
Aguascalientes	2,499	302,000	Aguascalientes	157,000
Federal District	573	6,815,000	Mexico City	3,353,000
Guanajuato	11,805	2,193,000	Guanajuato	38,000
Hidalgo	8,058	1,218,000	Pachuca	96,000
Jalisco	31,152	3,139,000	Guadalajara	1,183,000
Mexico	8,268	2,576,000	Toluca	87,000
Michoacán	23,202	2,329,000	Morelia	140,100
Morelos	1,917	546,000	Cuernavaca	40,000
Puebla	13,125	2,438,000	Puebla	360,600
Querétaro	4,432	444,000	Querétaro	81,000
Tlaxcala	1,555	431,000	Tlaxcala	8,000
Gulf of Mexico—				
Campeche	19,664	224,000	Campeche	50,000
Quintana Roo (Terr.)	19,630	72,000	Chetumal	12,000
Tabasco	9,783	644,000	Villahermosa	55,440
Veracruz	27,759	3,409,000	Jalapa	165,000
Yucatán	14,867	775,000	Mérida	193,800
South Pacific—				
Chiapas	28,731	1,470,000	Tuxtla Gutiérrez	45,000
Colima	2,010	221,000	Colima	45,000
Guerrero	24,887	1,524,000	Chilpancingo	20,000
Oaxaca	36,374	2,072,000	Oaxaca	75,000
Total	758,358[3]	45,671,000		

[1] Government estimates, 1967; about half the population was classified formally as rural, though closer to 60 per cent lived under essentially rural conditions in 1966. Net population increase per year is 3.5 per cent, one of world's highest rates. [2] Conservative estimates, 1967. [3] Does not include uninhabited islands (2,224 square miles) or continental shelf (154,633 square miles).

trict includes Mexico City, the national capital, and 12 surrounding villages.

Population.—In its 1960 census, Mexico had a population of 34,923,129. This was an increase of 36 per cent over the 1950 figure of 25,791,017. The rate of increase has been most noticeable in the states of North Lower California, Zacatecas, Nuevo León, Sonora, Chihuahua, and Morelos, and in the Federal District and the territory of Quintana Roo.

The crude birth rate in 1965 was 44.2 per 1,000 inhabitants, and the crude death rate was 9.5 per 1,000. The death rate, which was 26.1 per 1,000 in 1921, has been going down steadily, but the birth rate is one of the highest in the world. As a result the net population increase per year reached 1,500,000 persons during the 1960's. For the economic effects of this rapid growth see section 6. *Economic, Industrial, Agricultural, and Financial Factors* (Population).

Chief Cities.—In the late 1960's about half of the population was formally considered to be urban—that is, living in places with more than 2,500 inhabitants. However, rural conditions prevailed for some 60 per cent of the total population. Government estimates for 1967 show that 23 cities had populations of over 100,000 each. (There were only four such cities in 1940.)

Aside from Mexico City and the state capitals, the most populous were Ciudad Juárez (448,400), Tijuana (339,700), León (306,700), Torreón (227,600), Veracruz (185,900), Matamoros (151,-600), Tampico (147,700), and Nuevo Laredo (129,400).

Five of the 23 largest cities in Mexico are on or near the United States border.

Editorial Staff,
"The Encyclopedia Americana."

3. RACIAL COMPOSITION, POPULATION TRENDS, AND HEALTH.

Mexico ranks among the most populous of those Latin American countries with a mixed racial origin. Mestizo (mixed) elements make up the preponderant part of the population, but a large part of this population is Indian.

Indians.—The criteria which have served to characterize the Indians as such are very diverse, since the problem of defining what is Indian is not easily solved. Alfonso Caso, in "Definición del indio y de lo indio" (see *Bibliography*), says:

An Indian is one who feels that he belongs to an Indian community; an Indian community is one in which non-European physical elements predominate, which speaks an Indian language by preference, which possesses a large proportion of Indian elements in its material and spiritual culture, and which, finally, has a social sense of being an isolated community among the communities which surround it, which makes it distinguish itself both from white and mestizo groups.

The foregoing definition, of a practical nature (above all for the end of applying social and economic measures), is very far from what might be expected as a biological definition. Nevertheless, the statistician is more interested in knowing whether a population group lives in accordance with the characteristics of Indian culture than whether that group possesses the physical and psychic traits corresponding to a given race. Furthermore, after the many contacts which have taken place in the past, not only in the Mexican population but over the entire globe, it is useless to continue insisting on pure races.

For many years the linguistic criterion was the only one considered valid for purposes of the census. This was criticized by anthropologists like Manuel Gamio, and beginning with 1940 later censuses took into account not only language but the presence of other cultural traits, which bring students of these statistics closer to reality! Theoretically, perhaps, it might be thought that biological data would be the only sure data for classification, but this is invalidated by racial mixture. Therefore, although as was stated above, Caso's concept seems to clash with the scientific rigor of physical anthropology, it is the only one valid for the social ends aimed at.

Within the same Indian group, classified as such because of language, can be found the physical variations which are precisely those which make classifications difficult. A typical example, among many others, is provided by the Trique Indians of the Mixtec area, in the State of Oaxaca; those living in the mountains differ completely from those along the coast as regards physical characteristics, and even psychic ones, and yet they are grouped together because they speak the same language.

The classification of the Indian population from the point of view of physical anthropology has been only slightly satisfactory because it has not always been possible to collect a sufficient amount of data, evaluated statistically. Nevertheless, the available statistical material does permit an overall picture adequate for forming a criterion with respect to that mosaic of native races and languages which constitutes the modern Mexican people. There is a series of coincident facts which are easily perceived, without going into details. The Indian tribes of high physical stature are found in the northwest of Mexico, and as one goes southeast they become smaller in stature. In general, this seems also to hold true for head shapes (cephalic index), since the most brachycephalous (short-headed) groups are found in the southeast, and the most dolichocephalous (longheaded) groups in the northwest. There are, however, clear exceptions to this.

Pre-Hispanic Population.—It has been noted that the Indian part of the population forms a large demographic nucleus. Since the present-day Mexican has developed from Indian roots, what is known of the Indians' origin, distribution, and principal differentiating characteristics must now be treated.

It is agreed among most anthropologists that the first inhabitants of Mexico, as of the Americas in general, were predominantly of Asiatic origin. An eclectic theory of the populating of the Americas admits both the arrival of migrations by way of the Bering Strait and sporadic influences from Polynesia. The precise date of arrival has not been agreed upon, but dates ranging from 10,000 to 40,000 years ago have been suggested. The 1952 discovery at Santa Isabel Ixtapan, in Mexico state, of the skeleton of a mammoth of the Pleistocene period along with projectile points and scrapers indicates the area was already populated by hunters then. In 1967, near Puebla, similar tools were unearthed that may be more than 35,000 years old.

It is interesting to note that a high percentage of the modern Indian population is medium-headed (mesocephalic) or brachycephalous, and that the places where the bones of dolichocephalous Indians have been found are sites which have been long uninhabited, as, for example, those of the Pericu Indians of the southernmost part of the Peninsula of Lower California. The present-day Indians with tendencies toward long-headedness are likewise found in marginal areas. This has been interpreted as indicating that longheads formed the first migratory waves and were displaced by shortheaded peoples and forced into less favorable regions. Much has been said of such migratory waves and there is much difference of opinion among the various authors.

In general, the hunting, fishing, and gathering groups of pre-Hispanic Mexico occupied the north, where environmental conditions are less favorable for the evolution of more complex cultures. On the other hand, the areas which anthropologists have named Meso-America (central and southern Mexico, British Honduras, Guatemala, western Honduras, and El Salvador) saw the flourishing of a whole series of peoples whose cultural manifestations have surprised modern man.

The question of what influence the environmental conditions may have had on the physical aspect and method of reacting of the diverse inhabitants of the Mexican territory has not been investigated, perhaps because of the complications which would arise, but it is easy to deduce that the people who reached the Central Plateau from the north did so in large measure under the pressure of the scarcity of means for supporting life. Nomadic tribes, with an economy based on hunting and gathering, suffered great privations in the mountains and deserts of the north. The climate in this region is very extreme, and such living conditions were surely a sufficient stimulus for them to venture southward. Once in less inclement territory, with abundant food and better possibilities for supporting life, they must have changed from a widespread nomadic existence to one close to a sedentary mode.

Later, when agriculture had satisfied their basic needs, they could begin to create all that series of cultural accomplishments whose remains we admire. It is clear that the same impulse which guided the first inhabitants of the plateau stimulated subsequent waves and was the origin of conquests and reconquests by the many peoples of whom archaeologists and historians speak. This was the panorama through which passed Chichimecs of different origin, Toltecs, Mayas, Mixtecs, Zapotecs, Tarascans, Aztecs, and others. These constant clashes always brought as a consequence more or less permanent contacts which resulted in group mixture, with a natural interchange of customs, language, myths, techniques, and what interests us here, biological mixture. Mixture certainly caused many of the variations we observe, but it is also certain that the environment acted on them, leaving more or less permanent characteristics.

There was much less movement from south to north. In the majority of cases it consisted of readjustments, or of changes sought by centers of population already established, whose commerce and highly evolved population required slaves and artisans. It is natural that good living conditions should permit an increase of population, either through a high birth rate or by the immigration of subjugated groups.

Centers of Concentration.—Upon their arrival, the Spaniards found an extensive territory, very unevenly populated. In some areas there was a large concentration of population—responsible chroniclers are of the opinion that the great Tenochtitlan (on the site of Mexico City) had no less than 60,000 houses, which is to say about 300,000 inhabitants, and in addition a series of widespread tributary towns.

The metropolis was the seat of the dominant group, the Aztecs, whose hegemony extended southward to modern Central America. In the northwest its power did not extend as far, reaching only to the borders of Michoacán. Beyond this point there are only records of a multitude of seminomadic or completely nomadic tribes, of whose customs and languages we have information, but whose numbers it is difficult to calculate.

The major concentration of population at the time of the Spanish conquest was thus located in the plateau. Perhaps in earlier times the coast and the tropical plains had had the greatest population, since the ruins in the Maya zone bespeak very large concentrations in those regions. Only the presence of hundreds of thousands of workers can explain the building of huge edifices which were already in ruins upon the arrival of Europeans in Mexico.

Teotihuacán, with its enormous pyramids and its area of some 11 square miles with abundant remains of dwellings, must have been another great center of population, but its inhabitants were dispersed long before the conquest, perhaps by the push of tribes which were barbarian but full of combative vigor. The same fate overtook other large centers of population such as Monte Albán, Tula (Tollan), and Xochicalco.

Of all these, the only ones remaining upon the arrival of Hernán Cortés (Hernando Cortez) were the urban centers of the Valley of Mexico, seats of the great chiefs who with Montezuma (Moctezuma) formed the triple alliance of the cities of Tlacopan, Texcoco (or Tetzcoco), and Tenochtitlan, with Tlatelolco only recently dominated. We have sufficient information on the Aztecs to substantiate their flourishing civilization. That their population was constantly increasing is proven by the need of the Aztecs for expansion, notwithstanding the fact that war and other calamities must have reduced their numbers very frequently.

Outside the Aztec Empire perhaps the major center of population was Tlaxcala, for which a population of about 500,000 has been calculated for that period. The Tarascans in Michoacán formed another nucleus of demographic importance.

Precise data are lacking with respect to the total population on the eve of the conquest. Each of the investigators, like their informants, makes personal appraisals that do not resist analysis. According to the historian Gonzalo Aquirre Beltrán, the one that is perhaps closest to reality is Angel Rosenblat, who after a careful analysis estimates that 4.5 million Indians were living in the territory that now forms Mexico in 1519, the year the Spaniards reached Tenochtitlan.

Conquest and Colony.—In 1570 the Indian population diminished to 3,366,860, and in 1646, according to Aguirre Beltrán, it dropped to only 1,269,607. This tremendous decline has been variously explained. In Tenochtitlan alone, the war which decimated more than one third of the population was a tremendous depopulating factor at the beginning of the conquest. Not only did the conquest cause death directly, but it

MEXICO

Total Population, 45,671,000

STATES and TERRITORIES

Aguascalientes, 243,363 ....H 6
Baja California, 520,165 ....B 1
Baja California Sur (terr.), 81,594 ....C 3
Campeche, 168,219 ....O 7
Chiapas, 1,210,870 ....N 8
Chihuahua, 1,226,793 ....F 2
Coahuila, 907,734 ....H 3
Colima, 164,450 ....G 7
Distrito Federal, 4,870,876..........L 1
Durango, 760,836 ....G 4
Guanajuato, 1,735,490 ....J 6
Guerrero, 1,186,716 ....J 8
Hidalgo, 994,598 ....K 6
Jalisco, 2,443,261 ....H 6
México, 1,897,851 ....K 7
Michoacán, 1,851,876 ....H 7
Morelos, 387,264 ....K 7
Nayarit, 389,929 ....G 6
Nuevo León, 1,078,848 ....K 4
Oaxaca, 1,727,266 ....L 8
Puebla, 1,973,837 ....L 7
Querétaro, 355,045 ....J 6
Quintana Roo (terr.), 50,169 .....P 7
San Luis Potosí, 1,048,297 ....J 5
Sinaloa, 838,404 ....F 4
Sonora, 783,378 ....D 2
Tabasco, 496,340 ....N 7
Tamaulipas, 1,024,182 ....K 4
Tlaxcala, 346,699 ....N 1
Veracruz, 2,727,899 ....L 7
Yucatán, 614,049 ....P 6
Zacatecas, 817,831 ....H 5

CITIES and TOWNS

Acámbaro, 26,187 ....J 7
Acaponeta, 8,462 ....G 5
Acapulco de Juárez, 49,149..........J 8
Acatlán, 7,268 ....K 7
Acatzingo, 6,672 ....N 2
Acayucan, 12,831 ....M 8
Actlzayanca, 1,392 ....N 1
Actopan, 1,242 ....Q 1
Agua Caliente ....A 1
Agualeguas, 2,426 ....J 3
Agua Prieta, 15,339 ....E 1
Aguascalientes, 152,293 ....H 6
Aguililla, 4,036 ....H 7
Ahuacatlán, 4,982 ....G 6
Ahualulco, 8,292 ....G 6
Ajuchitlán, 3,170 ....J 7
Alamo, 6,438 ....L 6
Alamos, 3,602 ....E 3
Aldama, Chihuahua, 5,294 ....G 2
Aldama, Tamaulipas, 2,067 ....L 5
Aljojuca, 2,642 ....O 1
Allende, Coahuila, 9,418 ....J 2
Allende, Nuevo León, 6,497 ....J 4
Almoloya, 3,387 ....K 1
Altamira, 2,620 ....K 5
Altar, 1,116 ....D 1
Altotonga, 5,584 ....P 1
Alvarado, 12,548 ....M 7
Amatlán, 3,041 ....P 2
Amealco, 2,201 ....K 6
Ameca, 17,588 ....H 6
Amecameca, 12,291 ....L 1
Amozoc de Mota, 7,019 ....N 2
Angostura, 1,372 ....E 4
Antiguo Morelos, 912 ....K 5
Apan, 8,640 ....M 1
Apatzingán, 19,568 ....J 7
Apizaco, 15,705 ....N 1
Aquiles Serdán, 4,357 ....G 2
Aramberri, 1,311 ....J 5
Arandas, 17,071 ....H 6
Arizpe, 1,410 ....D 1
Atlixco, 30,650 ....M 2
Atotonilco, 14,430 ....H 6
Autlán de Navarro, 17,017 ....G 7
Ayutla, 2,658 ....K 8
Azcapotzalco, 63,857 ....L 1
Azoyú, 2,545 ....K 8
Bacadéhuachi, 1,406 ....D 2
Bacalar, 619 ....P 7
Bacanora, 772 ....E 2
Bacerac, 1,016 ....E 1
Bacubirito, 420 ....F 4
Bácum, 1,508 ....D 3
Badiraguato, 666 ....F 4
Balancán, 2,554 ....O 8
Balleza, 870 ....F 3
Bamoa, 1,934 ....E 4
Batopilas, 502 ....F 3
Batuc, 1,267 ....E 2
Baviácora, 1,317 ....E 2
Bavispe, 925 ....E 1
Boca del Río, 2,660 ....Q 1
Bolonchén de Rejón, 1,540 ....P 7
Buenaventura, 2,780 ....F 2
Burgos, 541 ....K 4
Caborca, 9,338 ....C 1
Cadereyta, Nuevo León, 8,042.....K 4
Cadereyta, Querétaro, 1,635 ....K 6
Calera, 5,504 ....H 5
Calkiní, 5,611 ....O 6
Calpulalpam, 6,551 ....M 1
Calvillo, 5,735 ....H 6
Camargo, 7,902 ....K 3
Campeche, 43,874 ....O 7
Cananea, 19,683 ....D 1
Canatlán, 5,077 ....G 4
Candela, 2,240 ....J 3
Cárdenas, S. Luis Potosí, 12,461 ....K 6
Cárdenas, Tabasco, 4,583 ....N 8
Carmen, 21,164 ....N 7
Casas Grandes, 1,102 ....F 1
Catemaco, 8,702 ....M 7
Cedral, 4,221 ....J 5
Celaya, 58,851 ....J 6
Celestún, 840 ....O 6
Cerralvo, 4,057 ....J 3
Cerritos, 9,989 ....K 5
Chalchihuites, 3,951 ....G 5
Chalco de Díaz, 7,595 ....M 1
Champotón, 4,694 ....O 7
Chapulco, 1,520 ....O 2
Charcas, 9,105 ....J 5
Chetumal, 12,855 ....Q 7
Chiapa, 6,960 ....N 8
Chiautempan, 11,296 ....N 1
Chichiquila, 1,159 ....O 1
Chicoloapan, 3,672 ....M 1
Chietla, 4,651 ....M 2
Chignahuapan, 3,081 ....N 1
Chignautla, 1,937 ....N 1
Chihuahua, 209,650 ....G 2
Chilapa, 7,368 ....K 8
Chilpancingo, 18,022 ....K 8
China, 2,494 ....K 4
Choix, 1,923 ....E 3
Cholula, 12,833 ....M 1
Ciudad Acuña, 20,048 ....J 2
Ciudad Altamirano, 6,014 ....J 7
Ciudad Camargo, 18,951 ....G 3
Ciudad de las Casas, 23,343..........O 8
Ciudad del Maíz, 4,767 ....K 5
Ciudad García, 15,016 ....H 5
Ciudad Guzmán, 30,941 ....H 7
Ciudad Juárez, 415,580 ....F 1
Ciudad Madero, 53,628 ....L 5
Ciudad Mante, 22,919 ....K 5
Ciudad Mendoza, 16,051 ....O 2
Ciudad Obregón, 67,956 ....E 3
Ciudad Serdán, 9,942 ....O 2
Ciudad Victoria, 50,797 ....K 5
Coalcomán, 7,695 ....H 7
Coatepec, 18,022 ....P 1
Coatzacoalcos, 37,300 ....M 7
Cocorit, 3,819 ....E 3
Cocula, 10,119 ....G 6
Coixtlahuaca, 1,600 ....L 8
Colima, 43,518 ....H 7
Colón, 2,716 ....K 6
Colotlán, 6,337 ....H 5
Comalcalco, 7,745 ....N 7
Comitán, 15,409 ....O 8
Comondú, 540 ....D 3
Compostela, 7,658 ....G 6
Concepción del Oro, 8,452 ....J 4
Concordia, 4,099 ....G 5
Córdoba, 47,448 ....P 2
Cosalá, 1,692 ....F 4
Cosamaloapan, 16,944 ....M 7
Cosautlán, 1,659 ....P 1
Coscomatepec de Bravo, 5,187....P 2
Cosío, 1,350 ....H 5
Cosoleacaque, 5,665 ....M 7
Cotija, 8,059 ....H 7
Coyame, 791 ....G 2
Coyoacán, 54,866 ....L 1
Coyotepec, 5,967 ....L 1
Coyuca, 3,124 ....J 7
Coyutla, 3,880 ....L 6
Cozumel, 2,085 ....Q 6
Cruillas, 415 ....K 4
Cuatro Ciénegas de Carranza, 3,931 ....H 3
Cuautitlán, 8,378 ....L 1
Cuautla, 12,427 ....L 2
Cuencamé, 2,982 ....H 4
Cuernavaca, 37,144 ....L 2
Cuicatlán, 1,978 ....L 8
Cuitlahuac, 3,634 ....P 2
Culiacán, 118,842 ....F 4
Cumpas, 2,314 ....D 2
Cuna de la Independencia Nacional, 12,311 ....J 6
Cunduacán, 1,792 ....N 7
Cusihuiriáchic, 378 ....F 2
Cuyoaco, 993 ....O 1
Doctor Arroyo, 3,085 ....K 5
Durango, 131,232 ....G 4
Dzitbalché, 3,666 ....P 6
Ebano, 5,564 ....K 5
Ejutla, 5,194 ....L 8
El Dorado, 6,423 ....F 4
El Fuerte, 5,331 ....E 3
El Oro, Durango, 4,224 ....G 4
El Oro, México, 3,507 ....K 7
El Plan ....M 8
El Salto, 6,947 ....G 5
Empalme, 18,964 ....D 2
Encarnación, 8,710 ....H 6
Ensenada, 42,561 ....A 1
Escuinapa, 9,920 ....G 5
Escuintla, 3,468 ....N 9
Españita, 989 ....M 1
Espita, 5,161 ....Q 6
Etchojoa, 4,075 ....E 3
Fresnillo, 35,582 ....H 5
Frontera, 8,375 ....N 7
Fronteras, 548 ....E 1
Galeana, Chihuahua, 744 ....F 1
Galeana, Nuevo León, 3,127 ....J 4
García de la Cadena, 1,754 ....H 6
General Bravo, 1,718 ....K 4
General Cepeda, 3,832 ....J 4
Gómez Palacio, 61,174 ....G 4
González, 3,270 ....K 5
Granados, 1,124 ....E 2
Guadalajara, 1,105,930 ....H 6
Guadalupe, Chihuahua, 1,864..........F 3
Guadalupe, S. L. Potosí, 904 ....J 5
Guadalupe, Zacatecas, 7,888 ....H 5
Guanacevi, 1,148 ....G 4
Guanajuato, 28,212 ....J 6
Guasave, 17,510 ....E 4
Guaymas, 34,865 ....D 3
Guazapares, 430 ....E 3
Güemes, 664 ....K 5
Guerrero, Chihuahua, 2,719 ....F 2
Guerrero, Tamaulipas, 3,409 ....K 3
Guzmán, 72 ....F 1
Halachó, 4,543 ....O 6
Hecelchakán, 3,879 ....O 6
Hermosillo, 154,987 ....D 2
Heroica Nogales, 37,657 ....D 1
Hidalgo, Durango, 707 ....G 3
Hidalgo, Tamaulipas, 3,394 ....K 4
Hopelchén, 3,006 ....P 7
Huajuapan, 8,531 ....L 8
Huamantla, 10,154 ....N 1
Huaquechula, 1,929 ....M 2
Huatabampo, 10,228 ....D 3
Huatlatlauca, 1,274 ....N 2
Huatusco de Chicuellar, 8,680....P 2
Hauchinango, 12,317 ....L 6
Huautla, 6,862 ....L 7
Huehuetlán, 2,924 ....M 2
Huejotzingo, 7,390 ....M 1
Huejutla, 3,849 ....K 6
Huetamo, 6,191 ....J 7
Hueyotlipan, 1,520 ....M 1
Huimanguillo, 4,537 ....N 8
Huitzuco, 6,354 ....K 7
Huixtla, 12,327 ....N 9
Hunucmá, 6,616 ....O 6
Ignacio de la Llave, 2,629 ....Q 2
Iguala de la Independencia, 26,845 ....K 7
Imuris, 1,003 ....D 1
Indé, 1,278 ....G 4
Irapuato, 83,768 ....J 6
Isla Mujeres, 557 ....Q 6
Iturbide, 752 ....P 7
Ixcatlán, 2,820 ....L 8
Ixmiquilpan, 1,752 ....K 6
Ixtapalapa, 25,517 ....L 1
Ixtenco, 5,655 ....N 1
Ixtepec, 12,087 ....M 8
Ixtla, 6,769 ....L 2
Ixtlán, 8,330 ....G 6
Izamal, 8,633 ....P 6
Izúcar de Matamoros, 16,556 ....M 2
Jala, 3,803 ....G 6
Jalacingo, 2,831 ....P 1
Jalapa, Tabasco, 1,286 ....N 8
Jalapa, Veracruz, 66,269 ....P 1
Jalpa, 6,213 ....H 6
Jalpa de Méndez, 5,133 ....N 7
Jalpan, 1,008 ....K 6
Jáltipan de Morelos, 8,588 ....M 8
Jamiltepec, 2,028 ....K 8
Jantetelco, 1,351 ....L 2
Jaumave, 1,884 ....K 5
Jico, 6,965 ....P 1
Jilotepec, 2,689 ....K 7
Jiménez, 14,904 ....G 3
Jojutla, 11,555 ....L 2
Jonacatepec, 3,250 ....M 2
Jonuta, 1,482 ....N 7
Juan Aldama, 7,742 ....H 4
Juárez, 1,152 ....J 3
Juchipila, 3,459 ....H 6
Juchique de Ferrer, 983 ....Q 1
Juchitán, 19,797 ....M 8
Juquila, 1,822 ....L 8
Juxtlahuaca, 2,618 ....K 8
La Babia, 28 ....H 2
La Barca, 16,273 ....H 6
La Concordia, 1,879 ....N 9
La Cruz, Chihuahua, 1,049 ....G 3
La Cruz, Sinaloa, 2,740 ....F 5
La Dura, 376 ....E 2
Lagos, 23,636 ....J 6
La Junta, 3,234 ....F 2
Lampazos, 2,699 ....J 3
La Paz, 24,253 ....D 5
La Piedad, 24,337 ....H 6
La Purísima, 598 ....D 3
Las Cruces, 713 ....F 2
Las Vigas, 4,762 ....P 1
La Trinitaria, 2,370 ....N 9
La Yesca, 508 ....G 6
León, 290,634 ....J 6
Lerdo, 17,682 ....H 4
Lerma, 1,719 ....L 1
Libres, 2,443 ....O 1
Linares, 13,592 ....K 4
Llera, 1,653 ....K 5
Los Mochis, 38,307 ....E 4
Los Reyes de Salgado, 9,796 ....H 7
Loxicha, 761 ....L 9
Madera, 7,314 ....F 2
Magdalena, 9,445 ....D 1
Malpaís, 2,533 ....O 1
Mamantel, 89 ....O 7
Manuel Benavides, 801 ....H 2
Manzanillo, 19,950 ....G 7
Mapastepec, 4,664 ....N 9
Mapimí, 2,998 ....G 4
Maravasco, 2,967 ....H 4
Mascota, 5,267 ....G 6
Matamoros, Coahuila, 13,770 ....H 4
Matamoros, Tamaulipas, 141,341 ....L 4
Matehuala, 19,927 ....J 5
Matías Romero, 10,187 ....M 8
Maxcanú, 5,139 ....O 6
Mazapil, 1,777 ....J 4
Mazatán, 644 ....E 2
Mazatlán, 75,751 ....F 5
Medellín, 583 ....Q 2
Melchor Ocampo, 647 ....H 4
Meoqui, 10,287 ....G 2
Mérida, 200,394 ....P 6
Mexicali, 317,041 ....B 1
Mexico City (México) (capital), 3,287,334 ....L 1
Mezquital, 837 ....G 5
Mier, 4,120 ....K 3
Miguel Azua, 7,173 ....H 4
Minatitlán, 35,350 ....M 8
Mineral del Monte, 10,061 ....K 6
Miquihuana, 1,777 ....K 5
Misantla, 9,201 ....P 1
Mocorito, 4,223 ....F 4
Moctezuma, S. L. Potosí, 1,333 ....J 5
Moctezuma, Sonora, 2,148 ....E 2
Monclova, 43,077 ....J 3
Montemorelos, 11,641 ....K 4
Monterrey, 849,677 ....J 4
Morelia, 133,764 ....J 7
Morelos, Coahuila, 3,096 ....J 2
Morelos, Puebla, 2,709 ....O 2
Moroleón, 17,954 ....J 6
Motul, 10,351 ....P 6
Mulatos, 496 ....E 2
Mulegé, 846 ....C 3
Muna, 4,443 ....P 6
Múzquiz, 12,971 ....J 3
Nacozari, 2,745 ....E 1
Nadadores, 1,890 ....J 3
Naolinco de Victoria, 3,658 ....P 1
Naucalpan, 10,365 ....L 1
Nautla, 1,432 ....L 6
Nava, 3,118 ....J 2
Navojoa, 30,560 ....E 3
Navolato, 9,188 ....E 4
Nazas, 2,738 ....G 4
Nieves, 3,147 ....H 5
Nochistlán, Oaxaca, 3,172 ....L 8
Nochistlán, Zacatecas, 7,293 ....H 6
Nogales, 11,219 ....P 2
Nombre de Dios, 3,159 ....G 5
Nonoava, 1,582 ....F 3
Nopalucan, 2,783 ....O 1
Nueva Rosita, 34,302 ....J 2
Nuevo Laredo, 123,449 ....J 3
Nuevo Morelos, 580 ....K 5
Nuri, 808 ....E 3
Oaxaca, 72,370 ....L 8
Ocampo, Chihuahua, 375 ....E 2
Ocampo, Coahuila, 1,298 ....H 3
Ocampo, Tamaulipas, 3,348 ....K 5
Ocotepec, 953 ....O 1
Ocotlán, Jalisco, 25,416 ....H 6

Total pop.—1967 off. est.; capital & cities (over 100,000)—1966 off. est.; other pops—1960 final census.

MEXICO

States Indicated by Numbers

1 Tlaxcala   6 Querétaro
2 Morelos   7 Guanajuato
3 Distrito Federal   8 Aguascalientes
4 México   9 Nayarit
5 Hidalgo   10 Colima

MEXICO
CONIC PROJECTION
SCALE OF MILES
0   100   200
SCALE OF KILOMETRES
0   100   200   300

National Capitals .... ☆   State Capitals .... ⊙
International Boundaries ....   State Boundaries ....
Railroads ....

Copyright by C.S. HAMMOND & Co., N.

dispersed many groups which, not being able to adapt themselves to new conditions of life, thus perished. In addition, contacts with sick Europeans and Negroes, helped by the exhaustion due to fatigue and inadequate nourishment, let loose truly catastrophic epidemics, such as those of smallpox in 1520, measles in 1529, and typhus in 1545, which took millions of lives. Gilberto Loyo cites the fact that some 2 million Indians died of matlazahuatl (Mexican typhus or tabardillo) between 1573 and 1577. The inhuman exploitation to which the Indians were subjected, the change in their way of life, their removal to different zones, and so forth, were other factors which explain the decrease in population suffered in the first periods of the conquest. The European and Negro populations may be considered still insignificant, but mestizos and *Criollos* (native-born whites) began to multiply rapidly.

The paternalistic laws for the protection of the Indians, in spite of their remaining dead letters in large part, gave rise to a situation of social as well as demographic importance. In an attempt to free the Indians from the exhausting labor to which they were subjected in the mines and in the cultivation of sugar cane, and so forth, permission was obtained in 1501 to bring Negro slaves to the Spanish colonies. In Mexico most of these were settled in the hot lands of Veracruz and Guerrero; still others were taken to the mines in Zacatecas.

Aguirre Beltrán gives the population figures in the accompanying table (the terms Euro-, Afro-, and Indo- indicate mixtures in which European, African, or Indian characteristics predominated in the mestizos).

since they had on their side all the privileges of its racial and economic condition, felt neglected before the hierarchical superiority of the Spaniards, to whom the crown entrusted the official duties.

This accumulation of circumstances unfavorable to the harmony and progress of colonial society was the leaven which, after receiving an incentive from the ideas of revolutionary France, brought on the struggle for independence.

The nucleus of white Spaniards was never numerous—only 7,904 individuals in 1793, from which it may be inferred that only a few thousand men had control of the political, judicial, military, and ecclesiastical functions, and like positions. The decline of the Indian population had finally ceased about this time and a slight increase had begun. The mestizos and mulattos were also increasing in numbers. In a total population of 3,799,561 in 1793, it is calculated that 61.1 per cent were Indians and 38.6 per cent were mestizos and mulattos; of the remainder, 0.2 per cent were Spaniards and *Criollos* and 0.1 per cent were Negroes.

Later Population Trends.—The struggle for independence (1810–1821), like all wars, brought about a series of upheavals, as well as a slight decrease in population. Soon, however, there occurred a readjustment favorable to population gains.

In conclusion it may be said that the present population of Mexico is predominantly mestizo, and that a large proportion, 20 to 25 per cent of the total population, has Indian cultural characteristics. The Indian population has been growing, although from the linguistic point of view

Year	Spaniards and *Criollos*	Negroes	Indians	Euro-mestizos	Afro-mestizos	Indo-mestizos	Total
1570	6,644	20,569	3,366,860	11,067	2,437	2,435	3,410,012
1646	13,780	35,089	1,269,607	168,568	116,529	109,042	1,712,615

Social Structure.—The Negroes, with the Indians, formed the lowest stratum of colonial society, and their conditions of misery were the motive for the constant unrest manifested through mutinies and rebellions. From the mixtures among them arose the so-called castes. The word "caste," eminently biological, was given a derogatory meaning in the colonial period, comprising not so much the physical characteristics of the individuals as their social extraction, without forgetting their racial mixture. The attempt to define precisely the last degree of difference between such mixtures, as the various combinations passed through generation after generation, gave rise to terms which were ridiculously elaborate and often artificial.

The mestizos, who in the beginning had been well regarded—to the extent that some were admitted into the Spanish nobility—were relegated to a secondary status as they grew in numbers. They were considered quarrelsome individuals, and they, for their part, feeling themselves humiliated by the whites, showed their resentment in violent form. On the other hand, the mestizos looked down on the Indians for having been conquered, thus showing themselves to be what they were, unadapted beings who participated in the social environment only with difficulty.

The native-born whites, or *Criollos,* comprising a class which could have been the elite,

the great majority are interested in learning Spanish in addition to their mother language and in adopting various elements of Western culture. Since the Revolution of 1910 various programs have been undertaken to provide them with lands and with economic and cultural media, to achieve the homogenization of the population.

Indian Health and Diet.—Various circumstances have influenced the disappearance of innumerable Indian groups, above all in northern Mexico, but in those places occupied by individuals who had reached a sufficiently advanced state of cultural evolution, the Indian was able to resist all that man and nature brought against him. In addition, the conquerors and the other white rulers who followed them through time, knew that land without someone to work it lacks value —from an economic point of view, the Indians were one with the land, a most valuable factor which had to be conserved. Hacienda owners bought their land making sure that with it went a sufficient number of laborers to exploit it.

Thousands of these laborers, principally members of the rural population, have continued to live in very precarious hygienic conditions. Water-borne diseases cause very serious disorders among them, weakening them physically. It is certain, however, that little by little they have become naturally immunized against the diseases brought by Europeans and Africans. There were no returns of the great epidemics like those of the 16th century mentioned above. Nevertheless there still remain wide areas in which malaria, tuberculosis, and parasitic diseases continue to reduce their numbers. Some maladies have thrived specifically among the Indians, such as onchocerciasis, which occurs in an extensive zone of Chiapas, and pinta in Guerrero, Morelos, Michoacán, and other states.

It has been said that the Indian diet is inadequate and poor in nutrition, and that their feeble resistance to disease results from this. Such an assertion is in general false, since besides the fact that the Indian is not especially susceptible to disease, various other causes may have unfavorable effects on his resistance. The Indian diet may not include a series of foods which are considered basic in the diet of Western civilization, such as milk, eggs, and meat, but the nutritive content of such products is supplied by other foods containing the necessary factors. The basic Indian diet is composed of corn (maize), beans, and chili peppers, and in the highlands, pulque, a drink extracted from agave plants. This diet is supplemented with a series of vegetable and animal products which vary according to the region. Even in extremely poor regions, such as the Mezquital Valley inhabited by Otomí Indians, where the basic foods are corn, chilies, and pulque, the Indians have found additional foods, such as insects, larvae (including the grubs found on maguey plants, and caterpillars), and other animal products, which with beans, mesquite, and fresh vegetables complement their diet so that sicknesses due to nutritional deficiencies are not encountered among them.

Bibliography.—Loyo, Gilberto, *La política demográfica de México* (Mexico City 1935); Comas, Juan, *La antropología física en México y Centroamérica*, publication No. 68 of the Instituto Panamericano de Geografía e Historia (Mexico City 1943); Martínez del Río, Pablo, *Los orígenes americanos* (Mexico City 1943); Fuente, Julio de la, "Sobre nutrición y enfermedades de indios," *América Indígena*, vol. 5, No. 3 (Mexico City 1945); Aguirre Beltrán, Gonzalo, *La población negra de México* (Mexico City 1946); Instituto Nacional Indigenista, "Densidad cana," *Memorias*, vol. 1, no. 1 (Mexico City 1950); City 1946); Instituto Nacional Indigenista, "Densidad de la población de habla indígena en la República Mexicana" *Memorias*, vol. 1, no. 1 (Mexico City 1950); Lewis, Oscar, *Five Families: Mexican Case Studies in the Culture of Poverty* (New York 1959).

EUSEBIO DÁVALOS HURTADO,
Secretary, Escuela Nacional de Antropología e Historia; Director, Museo Nacional de Antropología, Mexico City.

NATIONAL HEALTH

The death rates of a population are one of the best expressions of its state of health, since it is to be expected that a decline in death rate indicates a reasonable adaptation of sanitation and technical control to factors of climate and social conditions.

Mortality Rates.—The Mexican death rate has been going down steadily since 1930, when it was 26.6 per thousand inhabitants, although the most rapid drop has been since World War II. The average death rate during the years 1941–1945 was 21.5 per thousand inhabitants; during the five-year period 1946–1950 it was 17.4; but by 1965 it had dropped to 9.5, which compared favorably with that of many of the most advanced countries of the world. In one respect, however, the Mexican record was still extremely high: an infant mortality rate in 1965 of 60.7 per 1,000 live births.

At the beginning of the 1950's, the death rates were highest in the Central Region,[1] a fact that would indicate that the most densely populated area and cultural center of Mexico presented a greater sanitary problem than other regions in the notably hazardous tropics. Only two states of the Central Region, Jalisco and Michoacán (16.4 and 16.9), presented rates slightly below the national average, and three of them, Mexico, Puebla, and Tlaxcala (23.2, 23.5, and 24.3) had the highest mortality rates in the country. With the exception of Northern Lower California (17.5) in the North Pacific Region, and Colima and Oaxaca (17.9 and 21.7) in the South Pacific Region, the death rates in the states of the other four regions were lower than the national average for the period 1946–1950.

Infant Mortality Rates.—Infant mortality plays an important role in the high general death rate. Although it too has been declining, it is still very high; 29.4 per cent of the total number of deaths during 1950 were due to deaths of children under the age of one year. The average infant death rate for 1946–1950 showed that one out of every ten children born alive died before it reached the age of one year. Again, it was in the Central Region that by far the highest infant mortality rates occurred. The Federal District (134.4) and the states of Mexico (145.5) and Tlaxcala (146.8) included in this region had the highest rates in the whole country in 1946–1950.

Causes of Death.—In the period 1941–1950, the principal causes of death were diarrhea and enteritis, pneumonia, and malaria.

The decline in the number of deaths caused by diarrhea and enteritis, as well as by dysentery, typhoid and paratyphoid fever, can only be attributed to better general sanitary conditions, such as improved water supply and drainage, greater hygiene in the food supply, and to education and other factors.

The high number of deaths caused by pneumonia was due principally to inadequate housing conditions and clothing. In spite of the hope offered by the use of sulfa drugs and antibiotics, mortality declined only slightly and tended to remain more or less the same.

The high death rate from malaria was due, on the one hand, to special environmental conditions, and on the other, to the lack of adequate communications, the poverty, and the low standard of hygienic education characteristics of the *tierra caliente* (hot country) where malaria is endemic, that is, the southern part of Mexico and along the Pacific and Gulf coasts.

A serious problem was presented by the considerable isolation of the majority of Mexico's rural population and a shortage of physicians who were willing to sacrifice comfort and to live among people often opposed to their services because of their nonscientific conception of the causes of disease. According to the census of 1940, only 8.7 per cent of physicians were practicing in rural areas, which contained 57.4 per cent of the total population. In order to solve this problem, the federal government in 1936 organized a bureau now known as the Dirección General de Servicios Médicos Rurales Cooperativos, and every medical student is obliged to practice his profession in some rural area during five

[1] For a listing of the states comprising these regions, see *Political Divisions and Population.*

Eric Schwab, from WHO

From a Mexican village, a World Health Organization team sets out on horseback for the mountains, where it will fight malaria with insecticide sprays.

months immediately before receiving his degree. The government has established a number of official agencies to care for the poor in urban areas, and since 1943 has enforced a program of social insurance, which includes medical attention, in several of the largest cities in Mexico.

Consult Whetten, Nathan L., *Rural Mexico* (Chicago 1948); Secretaría de Salubridad y Asistencia, *Memoria, 1943–45* (Mexico City 1951).

JOHANNA FAULHABER,
Physical Anthropologist, Museo Nacional de Antropología.
Revised by the Editors of "The Encyclopedia Americana."

4. THE INDIAN GROUPS. These groups still form an important part of Mexico's population. The area of present-day distribution of Indian groups which, to a greater or lesser degree, maintain their ethnic characteristics and group consciousness, coincides generally with the areas inhabited by sedentary peoples in pre-Hispanic times. These are central and southern Mexico and a strip in the northwest along the Pacific coast and the Gulf of California (in Sinaloa and Sonora) and the Sierra Madre Occidental. It was there that "the settled Indian was fitted into the colonial and modern economic scheme, in fact this was built upon him" (Alfred L. Kroeber, *Cultural and Natural Areas of Native North America,* University of California Press, 1939). There is a rough correlation between the pre-Hispanic density of population and cultural development, and the strength of Indian groups today.

The Indian groups may be defined on the basis of the following characteristics: (1) they are composed of individuals who are predominantly Indian from the physical point of view; (2) they possess group consciousness (they consider themselves Indian), and are considered Indians by outsiders; (3) with but few exceptions, they speak Indian languages; (4) in differing degrees they maintain in their cultures a larger proportion of pre-Hispanic or preindustrial elements than the proportion of these elements in the national (or modern Mexican) culture. The persistence of pre-Hispanic and preindustrial elements of culture is especially evident in technology and economy.

As regards point 1, there is some degree of *mestizaje* (white and Negro admixture) in most Indian groups. Nevertheless, in Mexico, cultural differences are vastly more important in the characterization of Indian groups than racial differences. The Indian who abandons his Indian mother tongue and becomes assimilated to modern Mexican culture becomes a Mexican, and is socially accepted as one. In some areas, such as the Isthmus of Tehuantepec and the Mixtec area, the use of group names (*tehuano, mixteco*) to designate specific ethnic groups is being lost. The tendency is to use these terms as regional names, regardless of racial and cultural origins.

With regard to point 4, several centuries of colonial rule and, more recently, the impact of Western industrial civilization have modified the Indian cultures to a varying extent. It is impossible to generalize about the degree of assimilation of Indian groups to modern Mexican culture.

Socially, the Indian groups form rural communities which are generally subordinate to the semiurban or urban Ladino groups; the latter consisting of individuals who speak Spanish and participate in modern Mexican culture. Racially, the Ladinos are very mixed, with a considerable proportion of white admixture. However, the distinction is cultural rather than racial, and there are possibilities of passage from Indian to Ladino, through cultural and social changes. In some areas, the relationship between Indian groups and Ladinos comes close to being a caste system—for example, in Chiapas. In other areas this relationship is rather that of a class system. This seems to depend on the different economic development of the various regions. Some Indian groups, such as the Maya in the Quintana Roo forests, the Lacandon in the Chiapas jungle, the Huichol in the mountains of Nayarit, the Tarahumara (or Tarahumare) in the mountains of western Chihuahua, live in isolation, without maintaining relationship with Ladinos.

Linguistic Divisions.—The only general criterion which permits a statistical evaluation of the importance of the Indian groups in modern Mexico is the linguistic one. According to the 1940 census there were 1,237,018 individuals more than five years old who spoke only Indian languages (monolinguals), and 1,253,891 individuals more than five years of age who were bilinguals or plurilinguals, speaking Spanish as well as one or more native languages. The total number (2,490,909) of monolinguals and bilinguals more than five years old represented 15 per cent of the total population in that age category. The corresponding figures from the 1960 census showed 1,104,955 monolinguals and 1,925,299 bilinguals, or a total of 3,030,254, a relative reduction in view of the fact that the total population of Mexico increased some 77 per cent during the 20-year period.

Taking the Indian population by groups, the most important is made up of the people who speak Nahuatl, the language of the Aztecs (355,295 monolinguals; 360,071 bilinguals; total: 715,366), and live in the states of Puebla, Veracruz, Hidalgo, Morelos, Guerrero, and in the Federal District. All the figures refer to the population more than five years of age, in 1940. There follow, in order of importance: Maya (131,836 monolinguals; 114,011 bilinguals; total 245,847), in Yucatán, Campeche, and Quintana Roo (see also the article MAYA); Mixtec (111,391; 124,994; total 236,385), in Oaxaca and the adjacent zone of Guerrero; Zapotec (111,660; 104,661; total 216,321), in Oaxaca; Otomí (94,693; 87,404; total 182,097), in Hidalgo and the State of Mexico; Totonac (58,561; 59,242; total 117,803), in Veracruz and Puebla; Mazatec (45,254; 55,743; total 100,997), in Oaxaca and Puebla.

Among the groups smaller than 100,000 we find the Tzotzil (75,207, total of monolinguals and bilinguals) in Chiapas; Mazahua (68,855) in the State of Mexico; Tzeltal (66,861) in Chiapas; Mixe (51,261) in Oaxaca; Huastec, or Huaxtec (46,631) in Veracruz and San Luis Potosí; Chinantec (37,577) in Oaxaca; Tarascan (34,880) in Michoacán; Chol (34,624) in Chiapas; Tlapanec (27,698) in Guerrero; Tarahumara (26,007) in Chihuahua; Chatino (16,794) in Oaxaca; Zoque (15,732) in Chiapas and Oaxaca; Amuzgo, or Amishgo (13,219) in Guerrero and Oaxaca; Mayo (12,831) in Sonora and Sinaloa; Tojolabal (11,653) in Chiapas; Cuicatec (10,005) in Oaxaca. There also exist many groups of less than 10,000 individuals.

Bibliography.—Redfield, Robert, *Tepoztlán, a Mexican Village* (Chicago 1930); Redfield, Robert, and Villa Rojas, Alfonso, *Chan Kom, a Maya Village* (Washington 1934); Bennett, Wendell C., and Zingg, Robert M., *The Tarahumara, an Indian Tribe of Northern Mexico* (Chicago 1935); Parsons, Elsie, *Mitla, Town of the Souls* (Chicago 1936); Redfield, Robert, *The Folk Culture of Yucatan* (Chicago 1941); Beals, Ralph L., *The Contemporary Culture of the Cáhita Indians* (Washington 1945); Villa Rojas, Alfonso, *The Maya of East Central Quintana Roo* (Washington 1945); Beals, R. L., *Cheran: A Sierra Tarascan Village* (Washington 1946); Foster, George M., *Empire's Children: the People of Tzintzuntzan* (Washington 1948); Pozas, Ricardo, *Juan Pérez Jolote: biografía de un Tzotzil* (Mexico City 1948); de la Fuente, Julio, *Yalalag: una villa Zapoteca serrana* (Mexico City 1949); Instituto Indigenista Nacional, *Población de habla indígena de la República Mexicana* (Mexico City 1950); Lewis, Oscar, *Life in a Mexican Village: Tepoztlán Restudied* (Champaign, Ill., 1951); Kelly, Isabel, and Palerm, Angel, *The Tajín Totonac: Part 1, History, Subsistence, Shelter, and Technology* (Washington 1952); Stoppleman, Joseph W. F., *People of Mexico* (New York 1966).

PEDRO ARMILLAS,
*Instituto Nacional de Antropología e Historia,
Mexico City.*

5. THE WAY OF LIFE. Modern Mexican life presents a complex of striking contrasts: Parisian fashions alongside Aztec mantles; Coca-Cola and the thousand-year-old nectar of the gods, pulque; the baseball field and the bull ring; and most significant, minds molded in ancient ritualistic patterns mastering 20th-century machine tools. As in the Far East, the new has met with the old, the European with the native. A clash was inevitable, and the results—economic, political, and social—are only now taking definitive form.

Food and Drink.—In Aztec times the basic diet consisted of corn (maize), beans, and chili. Corn was prepared in an infinite variety of ways, the most popular being the *tortilla*, a thin, flat, unleavened bread. Tamales (corn dough steamed in corn husks) and the less well-known *pozole* (corn soup) were common fare. The ancient Mexicans supplemented their diet with turkeys, boars, rabbits, fowl, and a great variety of fruits, herbs, and insects. All these foods have retained their importance and still may be said to constitute the main diet of the Indian population. Cattle, wheat, and certain fruits such as oranges, apples, and grapes were perhaps the most significant European contributions.

Following the Spanish tradition, the main meals are the *desayuno* (breakfast), the *comida* (a large meal of several courses served about two o'clock in the afternoon), and the *merienda* (a very light supper at eight or nine in the evening). In the large cities this customary eating pattern has changed somewhat during this century. Many of the middle class now favor a lunch at midday, as in the United States, and a heavier *cena* (supper) in the evening.

The most popular drink of the Indians is pulque, the fermented juice of the maguey, a cactus plant. Its alcoholic content is slight. More potent than pulque are tequila and mezcal, also derived from the maguey. The excellent beers of the European type brewed at Monterrey, Nuevo León, in the north, and at Orizaba, Veracruz, near the east coast, are extremely popular throughout the republic and have replaced pulque to a considerable extent.

Dress.—In pre-Hispanic times among the majority of the Indian population, dress was extremely simple. Men usually wore a loincloth, sandals, and a cotton mantle (the Aztec *tilma*) draped and tied over the right shoulder. A long cotton blouse and a skirt held to the waist by a sash constituted the general female attire. The Spanish manner of dressing changed male clothing habits radically: the natives of most rural districts are now to be seen wearing white cotton trousers, a shirt, and inevitably, a straw hat. Except in the warmest areas, they will usually be seen wearing or carrying a serape (or *sarape*), a woolen blanket whose design and colors vary from region to region. This is perhaps the only Aztec remnant in male attire, and stems from both the ancient cotton *tilma* and the Spanish capote, or cape. The women of some Indian groups may still be seen dressed in the ancient, pre-Hispanic blouse and skirt. Statistics reveal that approximately one half of the population has not adopted shoes of the European type.

In the cities the average well-to-do or middle-class Mexican wears very much the same clothing as is worn in the United States or Europe. A certain amount of formality, not so often seen in the United States, is noticeable among the men; materials are darker as a rule, tailoring is conservative, and sports clothes are not as commonly accepted. Hats are seldom worn by women, and on those rare occasions when head covering is in order, the *rebozo* (shawl), the veil, and the Spanish mantilla are the most common forms of headgear among all social classes. A revival of interest in folk costumes has taken place since about 1940. The decorative *rebozo,* as an article of high fashion, has come into its own. *Huaraches,* the attractive native sandals, have become increasingly popular for resort wear among the Mexicans.

Sports.—The traditional spectacle and main source of hero worship in Mexican life, bullfighting, has continued to maintain its popular appeal. Nevertheless, some *toreo* impresarios and enthusiasts lament the fact that the new generation is turning more and more to football (which in the United States would be called soccer), basketball, and baseball as recreational outlets. The decades after 1920 witnessed an ever-increasing interest in these athletic "imports." Contrary to the general trend in the United States, the emphasis in Mexican sports is primarily on the amateur and the spontaneous. In the larger cities a Sunday morning finds thousands engaging personally in ball games; even the most primitive native villages generally can boast an open-air field, equipped at least for basketball.

A growing rivalry, sportswise, between the various colleges has created a demand for better playing fields and more adequate spectator accommodations. The Olympic Stadium of the Universidad Nacional easily seats 100,000 persons. Radical in design, this great elliptical bowl is the sports center of the capital's ultramodern University City, which was dedicated in 1952.

On the professional level, *frontón* (or *jai-alai*), a court game of Basque origin, maintains an almost fanatical following. Betting is an integral part of the game and fortunes can be made—or lost—nightly at the Frontón México in Mexico City.

Fiestas.—The great Christian festivals are still celebrated with considerable liturgical pomp, attracting enormous crowds of the devout to churches and shrines. Household celebrations of these same feasts are often occasions for informal gatherings. One of the foremost among these great holy days is *Los Santos Reyes* ("The Holy Kings," that is Epiphany, or the feast of

the Wise Men). On this day, January 6, children receive their gifts from the Three Kings of the East; the Santa Claus tradition is unknown except among the city sophisticates. *Semana Mayor* (Holy Week) inspires a truly popular outburst of religious fervor. A number of Indian communities have become famous for their Passion plays and public processions on Friday of this week.

The most significant Aztec religious festival, the feast of the offerings to the spirits of the dead, oddly enough coincided with the remembrance of the faithful departed in the Catholic calendar (November 2). Many pagan practices persist to this time: special household altars are prepared and covered with curious ceremonial breads (*pan de muerto*), meat dishes, *tortillas,* cigarettes, toys, and other articles to placate the dead.

December 12 finds hundreds of thousands of Mexicans, particularly the Indians, converging on Mexico City and thronging the great basilica of the Virgin of Guadalupe, patroness of the republic, which is north of the city.

The nine days preceding Christmas represent the happiest and most carefree of the religious year. *Posadas* (literally "inns"), representing the journey of Mary and Joseph to Bethlehem and their search for an inn, are enacted nightly in many homes. In more recent years these celebrations have taken on a more frivolous tone, and cocktails and dancing have come to be expected.

Regional Differences.—These, as they are found today, are direct or indirect results of the colonial policies followed by the conquerors during the three centuries of Spanish hegemony.

In the southern part of Mexico the European colonizers encountered flourishing centers of native culture, such as the Aztec, Maya, and Zapotec confederations. Sedentary in nature, these ethnic groups tilled the land, consolidated their political positions, and had reached a high point of refinement in the arts and sciences. While many of their political, social, and religious institutions suffered an almost total eclipse with the conquest, the basic patterns of folk culture persisted and came to constitute an integral component of the Hispanic-Mexican civilization. With these groups the Spanish crown accepted and even encouraged intermarriage, which resulted in the emergence of the mestizo (mixed) population.

On the other hand, in the northern desert stretches the Spanish settlers found only barbarous, nomadic tribes. Agricultural stability was virtually unknown, and life was devoted to hunting, fishing, foraging, and intertribal warfare. In a word, the culture pattern of this region was strikingly similar to that prevailing among the Indians in United States territory. As often happens with such marginal and submarginal groups, contact with the European resulted either in the annihilation or cultural ineffectiveness of the native. At the present time, tribes such as the Tarahumara of Chihuahua and the Yaqui of Sonora roam the plains and mountain ranges exactly as they have in centuries past; the Indian reservation is an institution unknown to the Mexican people. These fiercely independent tribes take little part in civic activity, and numerically constitute an almost negligible part of the modern population.

European stock, therefore, has remained relatively pure in northern Mexico. This in turn has facilitated the assimilation of ideas, customs, and attitudes from the United States. Such has not been the case in certain southern states, such as Oaxaca, Puebla, Guerrero, Tlaxcala, and Chiapas.

While inhabitants of both regions possess a deep-rooted consciousness of national spirit, the southern mestizos and Indians tend to regard the *norteños* (northerners) as more frank, thrifty, businesslike, and self-assertive, though too "Americanized" in their language, manners, and general way of life. Mexicans of the north, particularly in Sonora, Chihuahua, Coahuila, and Nuevo León, find it difficult to accept their southern neighbors' Indian ceremoniousness, passivity, and general fatalistic attitude. Mexico City is a case in itself, with an atmosphere all its own. Here, Indian currents and those from Europe and the United States have found a meeting place, contributing to the formation of a complex, cosmopolitan way of life.

Bibliography.—Spratling, William, *Little Mexico* (New York 1932); Vásquez Santa Ana, Higinio, *Fiestas y costumbres mexicanas* (Mexico City 1940); Vivó, Jorge A., ed., *México prehispánico* (Mexico City 1946); Toor, Frances, *A Treasury of Mexican Folkways* (New York 1947); Whetten, Nathan L., *Rural Mexico* (Chicago 1948); Mosk, Sanford A., *Industrial Revolution in Mexico* (Berkeley, Calif., 1954); Lewis, Oscar, *Pedro Martínez* (New York 1964); Hayner, Norman S., *New Patterns in Old Mexico* (New Haven, Conn., 1966).

FERNANDO HORCASITAS,
Professor of History, Mexico City College.

6. ECONOMIC, INDUSTRIAL, AGRICULTURAL, AND FINANCIAL FACTORS.

The economic situation of Mexico offers a picture which reflects her level of natural and human resources and her system of economic institutions, both public and private. Mexico is a product of her geography, her demographic structure and movements, and her history, pre-Hispanic, colonial, and independent. Remodeled by her revolution, fought from 1913 to 1925, she is engaged in an economic development which asserts her national independence and adds greatly to her wealth and income measured above all in the general welfare of her citizens—displaying, moreover, an authentic determination to strive with the rest of the world for pacific ends.

Territory.—Frank Tannenbaum has said that "Mexico is a beautiful place in which to live, but a tough place in which to make a living" (*Mexico; the Struggle for Peace and Bread*, Knopf, New York 1950).

Mexico's geography is violent and diversified. In a space equivalent to a little more than one fifth that of the United States including Alaska, her physical geography imposes severe obstacles to the settlement and the efforts of her inhabitants, and to the easy circulation and consumption of the fruits of their labor. Since most of her territory contains rugged mountains, vast deserts, and jungle lands, which can be only sparsely inhabited, there are only limited areas where the temperature and climate, the precipitation and the soil's fertility constitute an environment that is favorable to the full development of an economic culture. Mexico lacks the advantages of great navigable rivers, wide and safe ports, as well as facilities for the laying of the paths of ground communication by means of which her natural resources might attain a maximum value.

But when everything is considered this same varied geography opens up an infinite number of possibilities to the persevering efforts of the Mexicans. On the diverse climatic levels, from the *tierra caliente* (hot land) of the coastal lowlands or subtropical zones to the alpine passes, grow the most varied botanical and zoological species of economic value to man. The geological structure encloses mineral deposits which attracted the greed of conquerors eager for gold and silver, offered modest reserves of iron and coal in the preliminary stages of Mexico's modern industrialization since the beginning of this century, and later added petroleum and industrial and strategic minerals whose exploitation has meant a vital contribution to the economy. Adding to all this a respectable hydroelectric potential, Mexico has sufficient effective assets for waging the battle for economic progress, without the limitations of countries like Cuba, Venezuela, Bolivia, or El Salvador, whose economy is based on one or a limited number of products, or of those other countries to which nature has denied the bases of adaptation to the changing requirements of a modern economy. Her geographic location is to be envied: the wide northern frontier places Mexico right next to the strongest and most prosperous economic power in the world; her coasts look out upon the two great oceans of present-day civilization; and the Isthmus of Tehuantepec links Mexico to a Latin America which considers her the leading partner in the community of Spanish-speaking peoples.

Despite impressive advances since about 1925, the beginning of peaceful and constructive revolution, Mexico has realized barely a minimum part of her economic potential. Perhaps some of her resources have been overestimated through a misunderstood patriotism; also, over broad regions of her territory there exist forms of primitive human life which act as a factor retarding progress, the elimination of which will be slow and difficult. But the deficient knowledge and superficial exploitation of her resources may soon be replaced by a serious inventory and a deep exploration of the Mexican potential, providing gratifying surprises to coming generations, and assuring their full employment to meet the increasing demands of progress. It is generally believed, not solely among Mexicans but especially among foreigners, that Mexico is paving the way to a better utilization of her resources, and that there remain many plus-values to be gained. To climb step by step to more and more elevated levels of this mastery is the ultimate goal and the surest pledge for the future well-being of the Mexicans.

Population.—The total population growth of Mexico is quite considerable, and the rate keeps increasing. The census of population reflect this enormous development: 1930, 16.6 million inhabitants; 1940, 19.7 million; 1950, 25.8 million; 1960, 35 million; 1967 estimate, 45.7 million. During the 1930's the average yearly increase was 310,000 inhabitants; during the 1940's about 610,000; during the 1950's about 920,000.

This very substantial increase in population possesses a significant economic importance: year after year the demographic increase spells greater pressure upon available resources. But this situation is further aggravated, first, because the economically active population does not grow at the same rate as the total (active population in relation to the total: 31 per cent in 1930; 30 per cent in 1940; 29.5 per cent in 1950; 31 per cent in 1960); and second, because

the agricultural population has continued to increase in absolute terms (between 1930, when it
amounted to 3.6 million, and 1960 when it had
more than doubled). At the same time its percentage level in the economically active population of the country has been decreasing. In 1930
it accounted for 70.6 per cent; in 1940, 65.4 per
cent; in 1950, 58.0 per cent; and in 1960, 54.2
per cent.

Transportation.—For the normal economic
development of a growing nation, a well-planned,
efficient system of transportation is almost unanimously considered as indispensable. The reader
is referred to the section in this series on *Transportation and Communications* for this information.

NATURAL RESOURCES

Minerals.—*Precious Metals.*—The proverbial
wealth of Mexico in minerals for more than
three and a half centuries was based on the
circumstance that the precious metals were, according to the ideas of mercantilism, the most
conspicuous indication of the wealth of nations
and the economic potentiality of states; and that
Mexico stood out as the leading producer of
argentiferous metal. The entire world accumulation of silver barely totaled 50 million kilograms (a kilogram equals 32.2 ounces troy) until
the exploitation of the Mexican mines in the
Guanajuato region began in 1555. Since then
over 200 million kilograms of silver have been
extracted from the Mexican subsoil, the peak
of production taking place in the five-year period
1926–1930, with more than 3 million kilograms
per year. Despite declining figures (2.6 million

kilograms in 1942; 1.29 million in 1964) Mexico
still leads in world production, with 16 per cent
in 1965, although today it is closely followed by
the United States, a country which exercises the
decisive influence over this precious metal by
virtue of being the primary purchaser of the
product and the principal investor in Mexican
silver mining. The decline in silver is not due so
much to the exhaustion or scarcity of reserves
as to the impact of phenomena manifested since
the period following World War I, among them
the discard or decline of metallic monetary standards, the oscillations of United States silver policies, and the disturbing effects of political
changes after 1946 in countries of the Orient and
southern Asia, such as China and India, which
in the past fed the demand for silver by their
high propensity for hoarding.

In comparison with this extremely valuable
Mexican silver production, the exploitation of
gold-bearing lode deposits results in quantitatively modest returns. While the productive
capacity at the end of the 18th century was, on
a yearly average, 1,610 kilograms, with an approximate value of one million pesos of that era,
and although the production for 1965 (6,712
kilograms, valued at almost 95 million pesos)
represented quite an increase, the income from
Mexican gold production occupied rather a low
place in the country's mineral production in 1965,
while the income from silver in the same year
amounted to almost 650 million pesos. Base
metals are even more important today.

Other Minerals.—In the course of the years
other minerals required for the industrial uses
of our manufacturing epoch have replaced the

MEXICO

MINERAL RESOURCES

precious metals in their importance to Mexico.

The table below shows Mexican mineral production, other than petroleum and natural gas, for 1965. Besides ranking first in world production of silver, Mexico is among the four leading producers of sulfur, lead, and zinc. In terms of the value of production, the leading Mexican minerals were, in 1965: zinc, lead, silver, copper, sulfur, iron, fluorspar, manganese, mercury, and coal, each with a production value of more than 100 million pesos (1 peso = U.S. $0.08). While Mexico remains a leading mineral-producing nation, the value of its agricultural production is greater than that of its minerals, and rapid industrialization is changing the former status of Mexico as mainly a supplier of raw materials, such as ores.

MINERAL PRODUCTION IN 1965

Mineral	Metric Tons	Value in Pesos
Antimony	4,461	58,034,000
Arsenic	10,127	13,722,000
Barites	368,685	59,126,000
Bismuth	465	42,079,000
Cadmium	775	56,735,000
Coal	2,005,662	136,385,000
Copper	55,248	535,077,000
Fluorspar	726,716	206,859,000
Gold	6.4	88,242,000
Graphite	40,413	26,482,000
Iron	1,526,107	389,157,000
Lead	166,780	734,099,000
Manganese	83,574	138,733,000
Mercury	662	137,711,000
Molybdenum	81	2,074,000
Selenium	8.2	1,020,000
Silver	1,153	599,071,000
Sulfur	1,585	460,937,000
Tin, refined	466	22,745,000
Tungsten	110	3,818,000
Zinc	233	961,774,000

Over the years, the development of Mexico's mineral resources involved large investments by private U.S. concerns—the best customers for most of the minerals. However, by a law passed in 1961, foreign investors were to own no more than 49 per cent of any such company, but this law has yet to be fully enforced.

Since 1959, uranium ore of various kinds has been discovered in Chihuahua, Durango, Querétaro, and Sonora. The mineral found at Moctezuma, Sonora, has been named, accordingly, moctezumite. These uranium-ore deposits may prove valuable as interest continues to grow in nuclear power plants for civilian use. More and more utility companies are building reactors. Nuclear power is also beginning to be used for desalination plants; and nuclear engineering tools are being devised, especially for blasting.

Coal and Iron.—Three nonreplaceable raw materials of the Mexican subsoil present problems of a different character: coal, iron, and petroleum. Coal and iron are the mainstays of industrialization thus far. But in Mexico, until recent years, they lay either hidden or unexploited. In the 1940's the total production of pit coal, extracted almost entirely in Chihuahua, barely exceeded a yearly average of 1 million metric tons (0.05 per cent of world production at the time). A lack of progress in the exploitation of known deposits is revealed by the fact that the average monthly extraction in 1937 was 103,500 tons, a figure not attained in any month in 1950.

There is no doubt today that Mexico's coal resources are large. They include high-grade coking coal at Sabinas in Coahuila. Modern treatment processes have been introduced at the same time that geologic-mineral explorations have been

extended. There are excellent deposits in Oaxaca and Chiapas as well as in Coahuila. In 1965 the total output of coal amounted to 2 million metric tons.

Mexico was once thought to be poor in iron ore. It seemed that the only promising deposit of good quality (60 per cent iron) was that in the Cerro de Mercado of Durango, which contributed to the siderurgical prosperity of Monterrey from the beginning of the century. The reserves there were estimated at no more than 50 million tons. Yet, as in the case of coal, it is now known that Mexico has large undeveloped reserves. Among the most promising fields is Peña Colorada in the state of Colima. In 1964 Mexico produced 1.4 million tons of high-grade (60 per cent iron) ore. In 1965 its mills produced 1.15 million tons of pig iron and 2.4 million tons of steel ingots.

The foregoing is in very encouraging contrast to previous figures: in 1940, just over 70,000 tons of iron ore; in 1945, 175,000; and in 1950, 285,000. Only 130,000 tons of iron and steel were produced in 1940. Then output increased to 300,000 tons in 1947 and continued to rise thereafter. During this period, however, total Mexican production was heavily dependent on imports of iron, scrap, and steel. In exploiting its resources, Mexico has had the difficult problem of transportation to overcome because the sites are often in very rough country. Exploration and road building both continue.

Mining Policies.—For a good many years the main problem of Mexican mining was the clash of interests between foreign investors and the Mexican economy. Foreign investments in Mexican mining amounted to 626 million pesos in 1940 and 892 million in 1948. Including the nationalized production of petroleum and natural gas, this economic sector gave employment to only 1.8 per cent of the economically active population, the same in 1940 as in 1950. Thus there was the paradox that the mining labor force presented the highest index of productivity among all activities, a deceptive look that faded when set beside the relatively high capitalization in mining.

A concrete fact is the high fiscal income issuing from the mining enterprises. In 1951 they paid 800 million pesos in taxes to the government, an amount comprising 20 per cent of the federal income; the value of production of mining enterprises being only 5.84 per cent of the gross national product in that year. The mining entrepreneurs complain that the government has abandoned them, as evidenced by such a heavy tax burden and by the fact that the greater part of government incentives is concentrated in the field of manufacturing enterprises. In the opinion of the miners, the extractive industry languishes for want of a strong stimulus—without reaching the high productive figures of 1926–1929—and thus the bases for the success of the industrial programs are reduced and narrowed.

The government, however, justifies these high tax charges by the fact that minerals constitute an exhaustible reserve whose earnings for the most part go to foreigners, aggravating the problem of deficits in the balance of payments—an injury even more revealing when one considers that it is necessary to import the finished products of Mexican mineral raw materials in order to satisfy the needs of ultimate consumption and, above all, of equipment for manufacturing plants in Mexico.

Without a doubt, Mexican mining enterprises

have not passed beyond the most elemental levels in the field of transformation industry (preparation of concentrates), due to which circumstance mining products account for a high percentage of the load carried by Mexican railroads, a factor deeply disconcerting to the country's very poor system of transportation.

The only viable solution in this field would consist in leveling the taxes imposed on mining until they were fixed at a rate similar to other incomes derived from capital. In exchange for this, the enterprises should undertake to compromise so as to reinvest a sizable portion of their profits in installations of high transformation, capable of producing a part of the articles needed for national consumption, thus saving production costs, tariffs, and costs of insurance and transportation, all of which are at present ultimately shifted onto the Mexican consumer.

Petroleum.—In dealing with the Mexican petroleum problem, the temper of the nation and the will of its leaders are fully revealed. The *chapopote* of the natives before the conquest, the *stercor diabolus* (devil's dung) of the missionary friars, petroleum has been the best exponent of Mexican history in the 20th century. In 1900 and 1901 Englishmen and United States citizens began drillings in the Isthmus of Tehuantepec and in La Huasteca (Lower Pánuco River region), respectively. In the rich zone called Faja de Oro, in Veracruz, a concession of the British company El Águila, the well Potrero del Llano No. 4 gushed forth in 1910, and its production in a few years reached the incredible figure of 157.1 million barrels (1920), to which were added healthy contributions from the fields of the Huasteca Petroleum Company and the Poza Rica zone in Coatzintla, Veracruz.

At the beginning of the 1920's (maximum production, 1921: 193.4 million barrels) Mexico was second in world production, although considerably below the United States. But the appearance of strong, successful competitors in the world market, particularly Venezuela, brought Mexican production to a low of 32.8 million barrels in 1932, in the midst of a world depression. As a defense against unilateral decisions of the petroleum companies, in an attempt to guard this valuable asset of national patrimony by removing it as much as possible from the fluctuations of the world market, and in order to satisfy the requirements of Mexican transportation and of industry, President Lázaro Cárdenas decreed the nationalization of petroleum on March 18, 1939, relying upon the legal basis of the Mining Ordinances (Ordenanzas de Minería) promulgated by Philip II in 1559 and Article 27 of the Constitution of 1917, and upon the assent of all sectors of opinion of the Mexican people. The Mexican professor Jesús Silva Herzog and the Committee on Interstate and Foreign Commerce of the United States House of Representatives have each described with considerable erudition (see *Bibliography*), and each from a different point of view, this transcendental event, viewed by foreign investors and governments as one of the worst attempts against the institution of property and human rights. Since that time the ability of the Mexican people to attempt a technological exploit reserved until then for the oligopolies of the great industrial powers has stood trial. (See also the following subsection on economic policy.)

The report of the director of Petróleos Mexicanos (which exploits the nationalized petroleum resources), published March 18, 1952, summed up the strides made in these terms (comparing the years 1946 and 1951 except as noted): the crude petroleum reserves increased from 1,058 million barrels to 1,424 million; adding the equivalents of reserves of natural gas and distilled products, the hydrocarbon reserves of the nation rose to 1,796 million barrels. Annual production increased from 49 million barrels to 79 million. The number of wells drilled in 1951 was 268, as compared with 64 (1947). Refining plants at Azcapotzalco, Federal District; Salamanca, Guanajuato; Reynosa, Árbol Grande, and Ciudad Madero, Tamaulipas; and Mata Redonda, Minatitlán, and Bella Vista, Veracruz, went from a production of 42 million barrels (1945) to 57 million (1951); distributed products rose from 34 million barrels to 50.6 million. Exports were raised from 9.7 million barrels to 22 million. Revenues of Petróleos Mexicanos rose from 570 million pesos to 1,839 million ($66 million and $213 million, respectively). The sum invested in explorations rose from 28 million pesos ($3.3 million) to 177 million pesos ($20.4 million). Taxes paid to the Mexican government increased from 191 million pesos ($22 million) to 505 million ($58 million).

During the 1960's a number of new oil areas were announced but the most intensive exploitation was that of the Poza Rica field (discovered in 1938) and nearby Excolín and Mecatepec. Proved reserves of chief fields in 1962 amounted to almost 3 billion barrels of oil and more than 350 million cubic meters of natural gas. In 1965, Mexico produced around 118 million barrels of oil and 14 billion cubic meters of gas. In fact, Mexico was exceeded only by the United States, the USSR, and Canada in the production of natural gas; but Mexico's rank in oil production had slipped back to 12th place. Mexico was forced to export crude oil and fuel oil, for which prices were comparatively low, and to import the higher-priced kerosene and gasoline.

ELECTRIC ENERGY

Perhaps one of the most eloquent indices of the economic development of Mexico is that expressed in the increase registered by the generation and consumption of electricity, for residential purposes as well as for those associated with the production of goods and services, in the private sector and in the public. In 1933 the total generation of electricity was 1,529 million kilowatt-hours, of which 204 million were generated privately by industry and 23 million were imported, with a total consumption of 1,351 million kilowatt-hours. The corresponding figures for 1950 were a total of 4,423 million kilowatt-hours generated (1949.5 million hydroelectric; 2474.0 million thermic), 874 million generated privately, 125 million imported, and a total consumption of 4,187 million kilowatt-hours. The total billing recorded by the Dirección General de Electricidad was for 208 million pesos in 1949, and 383 million in 1950.

Since then, demand has steadily increased, particularly as the result of industrialization. To meet the demand, Mexico has been stepping up the development of its waterpower sites. Among them are the $100-million Infiernillo installation on the Balsas River and the $330-million Malpaso project in Tabasco. There were almost 3,000 generating plants by 1965, which had a capacity of about 6 million kilowatts. In 1966 some 18,500 million kilowatt hours were generated.

In addition to the companies that initiated the country's electrification in the early years of the present century, led by the powerful Compañía

Mexicana de Luz y Fuerza Motriz, the government also has been seriously concerned with the problem of creating, through juridical regulations and direct promotions, the bases for this service, so fundamental and indispensable to the fostering and growth of Mexican industries and services. The Comisión Federal de Electricidad (Federal Electricity Commission) was instituted on Aug. 14, 1937, and is governed by the statute of Jan. 14, 1949. Its objective is to "organize and direct a national system of generation, transmission, and distribution of electric energy, on a nonprofit basis, with the aim of getting the greatest possible returns at a minimum cost for the benefit of the general interest." Its most important creation is what is now called the Sistema Hidroeléctrico Miguel Alemán, which was actually begun in 1937 during the administration of Lázaro Cárdenas, and was completed in the late 1950's. This comprises seven hydroelectric plants with a total capacity of about 404,000 kilowatts.

The most pressing problems of the immediate future consist in raising the capacity of generation to such an extent that lack of electricity will not curb the country's economic development, and then achieving the standardization of frequencies and voltages. During the years 1948–1950 more than 670 million pesos were invested by the Comisión Federal de Electricidad, the Compañia Mexicana de Luz y Fuerza Motriz, and the Nueva Compañía Eléctrica de Chapala. The major portion of investments were made by the Comisión Federal, which utilized more than 300 million pesos in international credits; the Compañía Mexicana obtained a credit of $25 million in 1949 from the International Bank of Reconstruction and Development, guaranteed by the Mexican government; the Eléctrica de Chapala in turn received a credit of $3.5 million which it invested almost entirely between 1948 and 1950. Forty-two per cent of the investments were made through internal financing and the remainder originated in international organizations.

FISHING

Of the five large fishing areas into which the country is divided, and which produced a total of 187,884 metric tons in 1965, the most important were Zone 1, comprising North and South Lower California, Sonora, Sinaloa, and Nayarit (1949 production, 100,000 tons; valued at 40 million pesos), and Zone 2, comprising Tamaulipas and Veracruz (1949 production, 13,000 tons; valued at 19 million pesos). The two main species caught were tuna fish (50,000 tons, in 1948; value 116 million pesos) and shrimp (18,000 tons in 1949; value 42 million pesos).

Those employed totally or partially in this extractive industry number some 20,000 persons, although the number of fishermen organized in cooperatives does not exceed 9,000. The local character of much of the fishing—mainly in marshy waters along the coast—the inadequate operating equipment (most of the boats are less than three-ton), and the limitation of the internal market (consumption in large internal urban centers continues to decrease), are decisive factors in the low production and reduced income obtained by the fishing community.

On Oct. 25, 1945, Mexico reaffirmed her sovereignty over her continental shelf, presupposing an extension of her jurisdiction much farther than the nine-mile limit to jurisdictional waters in effect since 1935. A recognition of this declaration, especially by the United States and Cuba, would avoid numerous conflicts brought on by discussions over limits and invasion of these areas by the fishing operations of foreigners.

Bibliography.—Gordon, Wendell C., *The Expropriation of Foreign-owned Property in Mexico* (Washington 1941); Silva Herzog, Jesús, *El petróleo en México* (Mexico City 1942); *Conferencia de mesa redonda, campaña electoral del Presidente Miguel Alemán* (Mexico City 1946); Othón de Mendizábal, Miguel, *Obras completas*, 6 vols. (Mexico City 1946); Secretaría de Gobernación, *Seis años de actividad nacional* (Mexico City 1946); González Reyna, Jenaro, *Riqueza minera y yacimientos mineros de México* (Mexico City 1947); Committee on Interstate and Foreign Commerce, U.S. House of Representatives, *Fuel Investigation—Mexican Petroleum*, Report No. 2470 (Washington 1949); Noyola Vázquez, J. F., *Desequilibrio fundamental y fomento económico en México* (Mexico City 1949); Tannenbaum, Frank, *Mexico; the Struggle for Peace and Bread* (New York 1950); Carrillo Flores, Antonio, *El desarrollo económico de México* (Mexico City 1951); *Directorio del gobierno federal* (Mexico City 1950, 1951); Navarrete Jr., Alfredo, *Estabilidad de cambios, el ciclo y el desarrollo económico* (Mexico City 1951); Escuela de Economía, *El desarrollo económico de México* (Mexico City 1952); Iturriaga, José, *La estructura social y cultural de México* (Mexico City 1952); Zea, Leopoldo, *Conciencia y posibilidad del mexicano* (Mexico City 1952); Vernon, Raymond, *The Dilemma of Mexico's Development* (Cambridge, Mass., 1963); Bennett, Robert L., *The Financial Sector and Economic Development; the Mexican Case* (Baltimore, Md., 1965); Bernstein, Marvin D., *The Mexican Mining Industry, 1890–1950* (Yellow Springs, Ohio, 1966); Pérez López, Enrique, and others, *Mexico's Recent Economic Growth* (Austin, Texas 1967).

AGRICULTURE

Land Reform.—Since the birth of the movement for independence in 1810 the greater mass of Mexicans have felt, in a silent, vague manner, the desire for access to possession of land. Neither the disentailment (*desamortización*) law nor the Reform Laws, of the 19th century, succeeded in fully destroying the colonial structure of land tenancy, and the reforms of Porfirio Díaz strengthened the hacienda system based on large estates and the servile condition of rural laborers, instead of establishing the foundation for a thorough agrarian reform. In 1910 it was estimated that two per cent of the population owned over 80 per cent of the land, and that 80 to 90 per cent of the rural population was landless.

The revolution of Francisco Madero (1910–1911) confined itself to overthrowing the juridical and political apparatus of the Porfirian regime. It was the armed uprising (1911) of Emiliano Zapata in Morelos, and his demand that the lands be restored to the people, that communicated to the entire country the galvanic emotion of a profound agrarian revolution. The first official reaction was the promulgation of the law of Jan. 6, 1915, issued by Venustiano Carranza in Veracruz, whose principles were embodied in Article 27 of the Constitution of 1917. This article recognized the social function of private property; the right of towns, villages, and communities to be endowed with land and water; the setting of a maximum to the properties of each economic entity, whether individual or collective; the special protection of small property; and the eminent dominion of the nation over the soil and subsoil.

There was great faith in the thaumaturgical powers of the legal text, in the idea that a mere change in ownership or dominion would solve the problem and satisfy those who were so eager for land. But distributions without adequate title, brought about in an anarchical manner, could not serve as a firm base for the reform; nor could the peons on former estates or in villages change overnight into people with the mentality of nonwage earners, into technicians capable of valuing the lands assigned to them to their own advantage and that of the country; nor did their education permit them to submit to the rigors of a collectivist discipline, and neither they nor the country possessed the credits and equipment necessary for carrying the technological revolution into the fields. A brilliant Ley de Crédito Agrícola (Agricultural Credit Law) composed by learned jurists, which clearly stated problems and solutions, did not go beyond being an item in the files; nor did the Banco Nacional de Crédito Agrícola y Ganadero (National Agricultural and Livestock Credit Bank), established March 8, 1926, have better luck, except in some few districts where there happened to be self-denying, energetic men as directors.

President Cárdenas gave the widespread spirit of the agrarian reform a legal vigor and condition of fact by the Código Agrario (Agrarian Code) of 1934, extensive distributions of land, and the institution of the Banco Nacional de Crédito Ejidal in 1934, which gave each large rural sector its own credit organization. His period in power (1934–1940) represents the peak in the distribution of large estates.

LAND DISTRIBUTION

	Hectares (= 2.471 acres)	Persons Benefited
1915–1921	453,000	86,000
1922–1933	7,000,000	700,000
1934–1940	18,000,000	1,250,000
1941–1950	7,800,000	1,415,000
1951–1967	20,747,000	1,380,000
Total	54,000,000	3,624,000

In this way the *ejido* system was established. An *ejido* is land held in common by a single village; the word may also refer to the farm community itself. On some *ejidos* each family has its own parcel of land to cultivate. Such parcels are limited to 10 hectares or less and may include forest land, pasture, and even desert as well as arable land. The family head does not own the parcel so, by law, he cannot rent, sell, or use it as collateral for a loan. He can, however, pass it on to his heir—to only one son, though he may have several sons. On the other kind of *ejido,* commercial crops are farmed collectively. This is the pattern of the Laguna cotton district and of the henequen (sisal) plantations of Yucatán.

Farms may be owned outright but are limited by law to no more than 100 hectares of irrigated land or 200 hectares of nonirrigated land. The limits of an individual farm are set according to the type of soil and the use to which it is put. Like the *ejidos* the privately owned farms may include several kinds of land.

By the late 1960's well over half of the farm population was settled in *ejidos,* which included some 25 per cent of Mexico's total land area. The *ejidos* also accounted for about half the total crop lands and over half the irrigated land.

Yet in spite of this long great effort, serious agricultural problems persisted, and thousands of campesinos remained landless. The population had continued to multiply at one of the highest rates in the world, and there was little good land left to distribute. Irrigation could not be used much further; water levels in some irrigated tracts were already sinking.

In the production of food crops, Mexico had very nearly caught up with its ballooning population. Some aspects of the farm problem showed more clearly in the production of commercial crops. By 1968 the situation had become critical in the henequen-growing state of Yucatán. The fiber plant has been the main crop of Yucatán's economy since henequen became commercially valuable in the 19th century; and for a long time the state had a world monopoly on henequen production. In recent years, however, Brazil, Haiti, and various African countries have been offering stiff competition. Synthetic fibers have offered another kind of competition. One result has been overproduction. This led to a fall of 40 per cent in the world market price of henequen between 1964 and 1968.

The inroads on the earnings of the farmers—most of them Indians—of the henequen collectives of Yucatán were so severe that thousands could not eke out the barest living. The fiber plant has been grown on almost a third of the state's land and has involved about half of its population of around 700,000. To keep these people going the Agrarian Bank, the national government's chief financial agency, has been subsidizing the industry to the tune of $10 to $12 million a year. Most of the henequen fiber produced had been exported to the United States. Because of its policy of selling its stockpiles of the fiber, it shared in the blame for depressing prices.

In 1968, Cordemex, a company owned by the national government of Mexico, began operating several plants for processing the fiber into finished products: carpets, cloth, rope, bags. Initially these plants employed 1,500 workers at wages considerably higher than the income of the henequen farmers.

The Lerma Plan, launched in 1966, with a $150 million loan from the Inter-American Development Bank, aimed to raise the living conditions and the productivity of some 8 million persons living in the poor rural sections of western Mexico.

Irrigation.—By the 1960's some 4.25 million hectares had been added to Mexico's potentially productive land. Among the major projects, combining power, flood control, or both with irrigation, were El Palmito Dam, on the Nazas River; Don Martín Dam, on the Salado River; La Angostura Dam, on the Yaqui River; Falcon Dam (a joint Mexican-United States project), on the Rio Grande; several regional projects, on the Papaloapan and Tepalcatepec rivers, and in the states of Sonora, Campeche, and Sinaloa. The $330 million Malpaso project in Tabasco, on the Grijalva River, is bringing a great change in the living conditions of the communities there.

Crops.—The very wide zone of traditional agriculture offers few possibilities for technological reform. The predominant crop is corn, mostly consumed by the families of the cultivators themselves, with little remaining for the market. In this type of cultivation there is no crop rotation, merely an insertion of beans to complete the wretched rural diet. On the other hand, the lands under "new agriculture" open up a field that is propitious for the cultivation of plants like cotton, sugar beets, or oilseeds, whose product is destined almost exclusively for the market, at the most profitable revenue levels. Such crops serve as raw materials for industry, or are intended for export.

Corn.—This grain, grown almost everywhere in Mexico, constitutes one of the gravest problems of the country's agricultural economy.

Major advances were achieved thanks to genetic studies made in experimental agricultural camps under the Instituto de Investigaciones Agrícolas and the Oficina de Estudios Especiales (Rockefeller Foundation) of the Secretaría de Agricultura y Ganadería (Department of Agriculture and Livestock). Despite these efforts, however, this grain has frequently been imported, in some years in volumes as considerable as 109,000 tons (1926), 117,500 (1933), or 162,800 (1944).

According to investigations by the engineer Ernesto Reza Rivera, the average annual corn production in the five-year period 1930–1934 was 1.8 million metric tons and the average rural price per ton was 56 pesos; while in 1945–1949 the average annual production was 2.6 million tons and the

in the 20 years from 1930 to 1949, in answer to pressure exerted by the demand of sections of the population which are entering more generous diet zones. Comparing the five-year periods 1930–1934 and 1945–1949: the average annual production registered only a slight advance (391,000 metric tons to 418,000 metric tons); the average rural price per ton rose (103.60 pesos to 417.20 pesos), though not to the same degree as the price of corn.

The sizable deficit registered by this cereal in relation to consumption needs, and the displacement of the interests of farmers toward other more profitable cultivations (like cotton and oilseeds) are shown in the heavy wheat imports that were required: 122,000 tons in 1940; 447,000 tons in 1948. An interesting fact to be underscored is

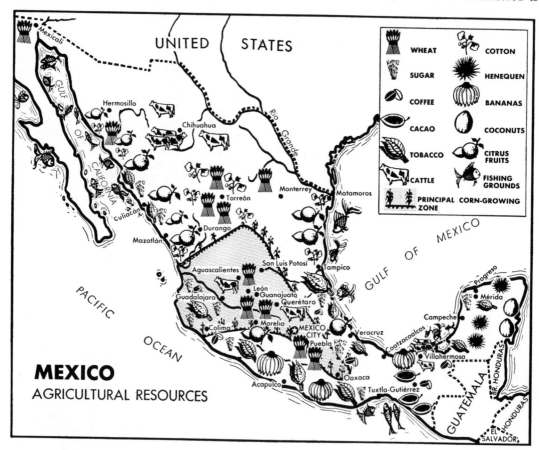

MEXICO
AGRICULTURAL RESOURCES

price was 385.50 pesos per ton. This tremendous price increase is expressive of an inflationary tendency, made acute by devaluations and other causes, phenomena which are also reflected in the production values, which increased almost tenfold from 1930–1934 to 1945–1949.

In 1965, Mexico produced about 8.7 million metric tons of corn, accounting for some 6 per cent of the total world production of the grain. In most years, Mexico is now self-sufficient in corn—which is produced primarily for domestic consumption and ordinarily does not enter into the nation's foreign trade. Though corn remains one of the two staples of the Mexican diet (the other is beans), consumption of wheat in place of corn is rising.

Wheat.—Special attention is merited by the case of wheat, whose consumption almost doubled

that wheat production, which amounted to about 500,000 metric tons at mid-century, increased to 2,088,000 tons by 1965.

Cotton.—The cultivation of cotton has shown a vigorous increase, especially since 1946, due to full use of the soils of the Laguna district in Coahuila, and also areas of Chihuahua, Northern Lower California, Durango, and Tamaulipas. The cultivations are achieved entirely under a system of irrigation. Although the returns are far from those of the traditional cultivators of cotton in other countries, the yields have not only permitted Mexico to become almost entirely independent in regard to raw materials for domestic industry, but also provide a sizable surplus which, along with the higher prices in the world market and other favorable circumstances, furnished a great incentive for the expansion of the cotton plantations.

A motive for concern, however, is the fact that relief of international tension, together with agronomical advances in other productive areas of the world and a partial stagnation in the Mexican textile industry, can create serious fluctuations in foreign demand and disturb the development of the Mexican cotton economy. The United States absorbed nine tenths of the cotton exports in 1950, at a value of 761 million pesos.

Beginning around 1950, cotton became Mexico's leading export; and for most years since then Mexico has been the world's fifth leading producer of cotton (after the United States, the Soviet Union, Communist China, and India). For the years 1955–1959 Mexico's yearly average of cotton production amounted to about 440,000 metric tons, which represented a considerable advance over the 1950 production figure of 260,000 metric tons. The 1966 figure was 519,000 metric tons, about 5 per cent of total world production. The latest figures reflected in part the much larger acreage devoted to cotton.

Henequen.—Within the Mexican agricultural economy, henequen—a hard fiber resembling sisal, but coming from the *Agave fourcroydes*—represents a monoculture in a region especially endowed with very suitable soil conditions, the Yucatán Peninsula. Until 1915 Mexican henequen production regulated the world export market for this fiber. Competition from new productive areas, the Philippines and Indonesia, the social repercussions of the revolution and the agrarian reform, as also the relative technological stagnation of the Mexican henequen centers—which, at first, gave their traditional technique and even their mechanical inventions to those countries interested in this crop —resulted in a decline in production, still further increased by the substitution of other products similar to henequen. Between 1930–1934 and 1945–1949 the average annual yield declined from 1,146 to 798 kilograms per hectare; production remained stationary, at a little more than 100,000 metric tons annually between 1930 and 1952. In 1964 some 160,200 metric tons of fiber were produced but the value was faltering.

Coffee, Vanilla, Chick-peas.—Other export crops, such as coffee, vanilla, and chick-peas, have experienced serious reversals since 1948, without asserting themselves as products of fundamental permanence in the agricultural economy of Mexico.

Coffee, produced mainly in Veracruz, Chiapas, and Oaxaca (70,837 metric tons in 1952), maintained the same values, almost without modification, between 1930 and 1949, but the yield declined. However, since 1953 coffee has been Mexico's second most important export crop. The 1965 output amounted to 180,000 metric tons.

Vanilla encounters difficulties in competition from synthetic products, and although production has been increasing since 1935 (179 tons in 1952), at values that likewise have increased (9.2 million pesos in 1950), it does not show signs of establishing itself securely as a promising crop for the future. Vanilla is produced chiefly in Veracruz.

The chick-pea (*garbanzo*) harvests, mainly from Sinaloa, Guanajuato, Jalisco, and Michoacán, traditionally went to Spain, almost the sole purchaser. The decline of this market resulted in an accumulation of stock from several harvests, with the exchange operation (1951) with Spain relieving the situation only in a passing manner. Production in 1952 was some 83,000 metric tons.

Livestock.—The extensive grazing and cattle-raising regions in the north of the country, despite the absence of a steady supply of water, managed to acquire the importance predicted by the early leaders of the struggle for independence. However, the internal market, because of poor communications with the large consumer centers in central Mexico, failed to provide sufficient stimulus. Thus, cattle-raising (14.4 million head in 1948; value, 2,872 million pesos) was oriented primarily toward exportation "on the hoof" to the United States, but the *aftosa* fever epidemic (hoof and mouth disease), which affected many states of the republic after 1947, meant the total suspension of such commerce until 1951. In this situation only the meat-packing industry managed to benefit when heavy demands from European countries in the first years after World War II resulted in an atmosphere of prosperity for such enterprises. Production in 1950 was 14.8 million head. Fifteen years later, in 1965, there were 33.1 million head. Cattle continue to be exported even though Mexico's own supply of meat is sometimes short.

In recent years, in order to augment domestic supplies of meat, the national government has been encouraging farmers to keep goat herds and more pigs and sheep. Some 3.84 million hides of all kinds were produced in 1964; and 532,576 tons of meat in 1965.

Agriculture in General.—In 1966, agriculture accounted for 17 per cent of Mexico's gross national product and 46 per cent of the value of her exports, and employed 49 per cent of the country's total labor force. But productivity per capita remained low, and many rural families, with a high birth rate, were still living in primitive conditions. In some of the poorest areas, *ejido* farmers were breaking or evading the law to increase their desperately meager incomes. Renting their *ejido* parcels illegally, they sought work elsewhere as farm hands.

Yet the outlook for Mexican agriculture was by no means completely somber. All over the country in recent years, *acción communal* (self-help) groups have been forming in the villages. By their own efforts they have been building new schools, new roads, waterworks. They are the end results of the work of the National Indigenous Institute, founded in 1950 by the government to bring the Indians (a very large part of the population) into the mainstream of Mexican life. From the institute's regional centers, villages are urged and guided into various projects and shown that if they help themselves the government will help them.

In October 1967, President Gustavo Díaz Ordaz handed out land titles for over one million hectares, in the state of Chihuahua, to 9,600 *campesinos*. It was the largest single distribution of land ever made in Mexico and was probably the last that could be made on such a scale. Few authorities would dispute the probability that the land-distribution program would peter out within a few years.

Bibliography.—*Conferencia de mesa redonda, campaña electoral del Presidente Miguel Alemán* (Mexico City 1946); Secretaría de Gobernación, *Seis años de actividad nacional* (Mexico City 1946); Noyola Vázquez, Juan Francisco, *Desequilibrio fundamental y fomento económico en México* (Mexico City 1949); Carrillo Flores, Antonio, *Practices, Methods and Problems Involved in the Domestic Financing of Economic Development in Mexico* (United Nations, New York, 1950); Tannenbaum, Frank, *Mexico; the Struggle for Peace and Bread* (New York 1950); Carrillo Flores, Antonio, *El desarrollo económico de México* (Mexico City 1951); *Directorio del gobierno federal* (Mexico City 1950, 1951); Navarrete Jr., Alfredo, *Estabilidad de cambios, el ciclo y el desarrollo económico* (Mexico City 1951); Escuela de Economía, *El desarrollo económico de México* (Mexico City 1952).

INDUSTRY

Process of Industrialization. Mexico's desire to become industrialized dates back to the beginning of its independent life (1821). Certain patriotic and learned statesmen, such as Lucas Alamán (1792–1853), were concerned with offering government help—in a modest but well-meant gesture of federal aid—so that the country might benefit immediately from the technical advances of the Industrial Revolution which started in England and certain regions of the Old World. In the field of the entrepreneur, Esteban de Antuñano founded La Constancia Mexicana in Puebla in 1837. This was the first modern textile company in Mexico, as measured by the standards of the time. In the public field the Banco de Avío and the Dirección Industrial were established in 1831; the former to finance the importation of machinery and raw materials for private concerns, the latter to implement the new economic policy. Their great interest lies in the fact that they reflect a youthful but decided sense of planning, inspired by the necessity of furthering, in accordance with Mexican aspirations, an industrial development whose integration was hindered by demographic, politico-economic, fiscal, and educational problems.

These farsighted men, acting in difficult times and with poor resources, believed that industrialization must not grow as an isolated vine, but must surround itself with other developments; it must not mean the wealth of a few fortunate entrepreneurs but must bring about a general welfare. This inspiration was renewed a century later, after the Revolution of 1910. On its correct application, without forgetting any useful factor, depends the successful future of Mexico.

The Liberal epoch, strongly evident in the Constitution of 1857, although fortunate in many other aspects, was not as successful in its attempt to accomplish the industrial development of Mexico as was the previous period. The greatest accomplishment was in the epoch—politically a dictatorship—in which Gen. Porfirio Díaz ruled (1876–1911). The present industrial development of Mexico dates from the last 20 years of the 19th century. It is reminiscent, particularly in the emphasis on transportation, of the growth of Germany in the time of Georg Friedrich List (1789–1846), although on a smaller scale.

This earlier concern for industrialization was interrupted by the widespread revolutionary activity between 1910 and 1925. During this period, the peaceful atmosphere and the right institutional organization for a definite progress in the production field were lacking.

The brilliant and well-aimed administration of Gen. Plutarco Elías Calles (1924–1928) provided the bases of organization for subsequent steps up to the present. The administration of Gen. Lázaro Cárdenas (1934–1940) emphasized agrarian reform, attempted to incorporate the great Indian masses into the cultural work of the country, converted the labor class into the forgers of Mexico's future, and strongly affirmed Mexican economic sovereignty in regard to the nationalization problem, as evidenced in the petroleum industry and railroads. His aim in industrialization was directed toward processing the soil's products to the greatest possible extent in their place of origin, in order to avoid the disadvantages emerging from a concentration of manufacturing in urban centers.

With less emphasis on the agrarian revolution, although still endeavoring to create a farmer with sufficient purchasing power, Gen. Manuel Ávila Camacho's regime (1940–1946) underscored the necessity of industrialization for the economic progress of Mexico—in addition to his cooperation in the war effort of the democratic powers in World War II. The early 1940's were a period of weak investments by industrialists, both nationals and foreigners. Some economists attributed this partial withdrawal to fear that new and important industrial promotions would be in danger of a future nationalization program by the government. In the opinion of others, however, much capital available for investment had been liberated as a result of the agrarian reform, and awaited only the advent of the proper occasion for new industrial undertakings. That opportunity came during the administration of President Ávila Camacho. The outbreak and spread of World War II deprived Mexico of imported necessities and encouraged investors to establish light industries, to expand those that could provide basic products, and to improve necessary public services. The government, by offering investors valuable incentives, also contributed to this development. Among the encouragements offered, the Ley de Industrias de Transformación (Transformation Industries Law) of April 21, 1941 (amended Dec. 31, 1945) may be mentioned as an example. This provided for important tax exemptions for new and necessary industries with respect to machinery, equipment, and importation of raw materials, and it also eliminated the fiscal encumbrance of the first schedule of the income tax for maximum periods of from 5 to 10 years.

The Oficina de Investigaciones Industriales of the Banco de México, which supervised the implementation of the above-mentioned law, obtained complete information on nearly 900 industries benefited by this plan, and provided the government with very useful criteria for a future program of industrial protection. Of course some of the industries that arose as a result of the incentives offered by the law disappeared when World War II ended and foreign competition re-entered Mexico and the international market. The majority, however, subsisted and even improved; this being, together with the presence of older companies and those that were modernized, the reason for the obvious industrial progress of Mexico during the presidential term of Miguel Alemán (1946–1952).

Evidence of the progress achieved is found in the fact that government pump-priming is no longer necessary to industrial investment. An effort is being made, thanks to acquired experience, to channel new investments into fields where gaps are still to be found, preferring a localization that will fit national industrialization into an integrated plan. At the same time, an attempt is being made to promote companies producing basic materials used by secondary industries, in order to reduce the economy's dependence on foreign economies, whose cyclical oscillations disturb Mexico's development. This does not mean, however, that Mexico expects to attain an impossible self-sufficiency; the object is to push the available means, now increasing in number, to the purchase of capital goods, so necessary in sustaining the rhythm of industrialization.

Debate Over Basic Policy.—There has been a great controversy, international in scope, in regard to this subject. As far as the Mexicans are concerned, industrialization is justified for many reasons, among them the following: the fact that it concerns a country which has a diversified economy; the necessity of absorbing—especially in the secondary industries—important numbers of the excessive farm population; and the convenience of giving foreign companies an opportunity to make sizable profits, while at the same time preventing the continuous drain of natural resources resulting from the exportation of exhaustible raw materials. Foreign writers, for their part, have generally tried to show the advantages of an international division of labor, making of Mexico a nation limited essentially to providing the superindustrialized countries with raw materials. Those countries furnishing capital feared that Mexico, with its limited financial resources and with its exportations of raw materials as the almost exclusive source of its wealth, would not be able ultimately to sustain its industrialization rhythm without falling into painful and repeated devaluations. The fact is that despite an almost permanent deficit in its balance of payments, Mexico is reaching higher and higher levels of development and is directing its policies toward the safeguarding and improvement of the positions gained.

The persistent attempts of authors in the United States to analyze the problem is to be highly appreciated—with regard to industrialization, especially the efforts of Sanford Alexander Mosk (see *Bibliography*) and Frank Tannenbaum, who, in *Mexico, the Struggle for Peace and Bread* (1950), adopted the view of industrialization held by the Cárdenas administration (1934–1940), mentioned above. Their recommendations emphasize the necessity of attaining a more considerate and proportionate development of the human and material resources actually available. If in some cases a return to the "philosophy of small things" is suggested, this advice does not mean a return to rural and backward forms, but reflects a desire to rescue the unmistakable human qualities of the Mexican from the destructive forces of urban crowds arising from the rapid progress of industrialization.

The fundamental aim of the industrialization program is the creation of a large national market for industrial products on the basis of a healthy stability, even an increase, in the farmer's income. Thus a fruitful industrialization, pleasing to Mexican patriotism and constantly attempting to raise the people's income, is advancing by firm steps. Mexico has sufficiently demonstrated its capacity to produce more and more of the goods which satisfy its economic needs; the government aims at developing an equal ability to raise the general purchasing power of the masses of its population, so that all its inhabitants may reach a higher and more satisfactory standard of living.

Production.—Industrial production has registered an amazing development: its total value increased from 2,113 million pesos in 1939, to 9,514 million in 1946, and to 16,794 million in 1950, according to data quoted by Ramón Beteta, then secretary of the Treasury. These data to a large extent reflect the effects of monetary devaluation. But taking the total volume of production in manufacturing in 1939 as a base equal to 100, the percentage for 1946 was 174.6 and for 1950, 228.2. If industrial production is considered as a whole, including manufacturing, mining, petroleum, and electric energy, the flow of industrial goods increased during the 1960's at about 8 per cent a year.

In the following paragraphs is a summary of data of some of the heavy and light industries most characteristic of the modern industrial development of Mexico. These are only small samples of the industrial development which has reached all manufacturing branches. By the 1960's they included industries that required a large amount of financing, costly technological equipment, or both, which not so many years before had been out of Mexico's reach. Through its national credit agency, the Nacional Financiera, the Mexican Government is the major stimulus. The agency both provides funds and directs development. Toward the end of the 1960's, at least two thirds of the capital that is supplied for industrial development was Mexican.

The automotive industry well illustrates what has been happening. At one time all cars and trucks were imported from the United States. Then car assembly was launched in Mexico, but the parts still had to be imported. In 1962 about 95 per cent of the Mexican market, at that time estimated at 85,000 cars and trucks a year, was dominated by the three major United States automotive concerns, General Motors, Ford, and Chrysler. That year the Mexican Government initiated a four-year campaign to "Mexicanize" the auto industry. Prices were frozen (to shut out expensive models) and quotas were opened to almost all the auto-producing countries. At first the Mexican market was flooded with European and Japanese cars, mainly compacts; but price ceilings and other measures reduced the makes to nine—the most popular and best suited to Mexico —by the end of 1963. However, the most influential act was that of September 1964 by which at least 60 per cent (by value) of any car sold in Mexico must be manufactured there. The result has been heavy investment by leading U.S. and German firms in the building of plants in Mexico.

Iron and Steel.—The only company producing pig iron at the beginning of the present century was the Compañía Fundidora, of Monterrey, whose first furnace started production in 1903 with a volume of somewhat less than 22,000 metric tons a year. (All tons in the following are metric.) In 1950 it had two furnaces, with a daily theoretical capacity of 800 tons, and the annual production amounted to a total of 119,000 tons of pig iron and 139,000 tons of steel. La Consolidada, founded in 1912 (with branches in Piedras Negras, Coahuila; Mexico City; and Tlalnepantla, State of Mexico), had open-hearth furnaces with a yearly theoretical production of 100,000 tons of ingots in 1950, producing mainly from scrap from northern Mexico and the southern United States. A third large enterprise, Altos Hornos de México, rose in answer to the limitation of supplies caused by World War II. It was financed by the Nacional Financiera, a government institution, and was established at Monclova, Coahuila, in 1942. It was limited initially to the production of steel and tin plate.

The volume of production of the iron and steel smelting plants in Mexico was 164,000 tons in 1943 and 300,000 in 1950, with respective values of 73.5 million and 415 million pesos. This, in 1950, represented a little over 9 per cent of the total value of the country's manufacturing production. Scrap importation, almost exclusively from the United States, was 119,000 tons in 1950. The importation of iron (pig iron) and steel (ingots and bars) totaled 30,000 tons, with a value of 22 million pesos, in 1950. As reserves of iron ore and coal are being exploited, Mexico is becoming more self-sufficient in iron and steel.

Cement.—This has acquired a central significance among construction materials. As late as 1900, cement had to be imported from the United States and Germany. The first factory was established in Mexico in 1903; in 1950 there were 12 plants in operation, with a production of 1,480,000 metric tons valued at 148 million pesos (in 1939, 537,464 tons and a value of 22 million pesos). With a yearly rate of growth of 11 per cent of its volume of production, this industry is one of the most forceful in the country and one of the main supports of its development. Importation is practically nil (3,000 tons in 1950). In spite of local progress, this industry is faced with the problems of balancing the supply with an increasing demand, giving a correct location to new plants, organizing transportation and distribution, and taking advantage of favorable conditions for the exportation of its products.

Rayon.—The first governmental attempts to stimulate the building of a rayon factory appeared in 1935. In 1942, thanks to financing by the Nacional Financiera, La Celanese was established in Ocotlán, Jalisco, starting production in 1947 with 2,000 metric tons. In 1950 it produced 5,000 tons, with a value of 81.5 million pesos. This initial step was followed by the founding of a plant in Zacapu, Michoacán, with a production (1950) of 3,000 tons a year. At the same time, imports, which amounted to 3,240 tons in 1946 (the entire rayon consumption of the country) and to 1,435 tons in 1950, have been reduced. The main problem is the dependence of this industry on its raw material, cellulose, which must be imported. The production of cellulose in Mexico is one of the important goals to be pursued in the coming decades of the economic development of the country.

Fertilizers.—Among the chemical industries, a group which attained the most impressive progress after 1940, those manufacturing fertilizers are truly essential to Mexico because of their significance to agricultural progress. In order to satisfy the food demands of a constantly increasing population, the scarce arable lands (around 8 million hectares in 1950) must be given the nitrogen they lack due both to the natural physical condition of the soil and to the effects of an irrational agricultural exploitation during many centuries. The magnitude of the problem is apparent in the fact that in 1947 the entire country consumed only 21,000 tons of fertilizers. In 1944, Guanos y Fertilizantes de México (financed by the Nacional Financiera) started its productive activities, although on a small scale, with its three plants, in Guadalajara, San Luis Potosí city, and the Federal District. A plant at Cuautitlán, State of Mexico, was founded in 1951, with a yearly production of 66,200 metric tons of ammonium sulphate, utilizing gas from the Poza Rica oilfields in Veracruz as raw material. This plant also was financed by the Nacional Financiera. The production of the Cuautitlán plant, one of the most perfect of its kind, is subject to such a large demand that plans for further expansion in fertilizer production, limited only by the difficulties in acquiring equipment, and, as in other cases, the scarce transportation facilities for the products, are more than justified.

Cotton Textiles.—Among the so-called light industries, the textile branch deserves special mention. Cotton is particularly significant because of its century-old tradition and its great importance in modern times, as well as because of the large number of workers employed and the pressing need of increasing production—especially of low cost fabrics, since several million inhabitants in the rural districts lack the most indispensable clothing and cannot satisfy that vital necessity due to their limited purchasing power. In 1945 the cotton tex-

tile factories manufactured products with a value of 676 million pesos; in 1950, 1,162 million. In the latter year, the raw material consumed had a value of 359 million pesos. The cotton textile industry employs 48,000 looms and 1,000,000 spindles. In 1950, of the 180 plants of this branch, only 10 were completely modern, 15 were modernized, 46 were established after 1925, and 109 before that date. Many managers, with their amortized plants and with difficulties in matters of credit, besides the numerous labor conflicts, are not in favor of the modernization of their equipment, as stimulated by the government. The workers, for their part, regard this technological progress with suspicion, believing, perhaps with good reason, that it will result in the unemployment of some 25,000 workers.

Until 1939, production greatly exceeded demand, and the managers, compelled by labor legislation and the impossibility of reducing working hours and wages, overstocked their warehouses and suffered losses which meant bankruptcy for some of them. World War II, with all the misery it brought to humanity, provided an advantageous and unexpected outlet for this industry. Stocks were easily disposed of, and all the productive capacity, including that of machines which might very well be considered museum pieces, was raised above theoretical output in order to satisfy the necessities of not only the Mexican population, deprived of imports, but also the demand of other countries whose markets were normally supplied by the great industrial countries then at war.

In this, as in other cases of eventual benefits brought about by the war, profits were not directed toward the most productive and beneficial uses for the country: the consumption of luxuries by those already profiting was increased; while those interested in modernizing found their efforts to acquire machinery and equipment obstructed by slow deliveries. A drift of huge profits toward investment in real estate took place, which forced prices upward. In the postwar period, after a severe decrease in exports of cotton fabrics due to the fact that foreign markets recovered their former providers, this branch of the textile industry went through a crisis which only the few modernized plants were in a condition to meet. To end this situation permanently, internal consumption must be increased with low-cost fabrics for the large masses of the population so poorly dressed and with such small incomes. The government is attending to this problem, which affects both the industry and the standard of living of numerous consumers, with a plan to increase the production of cheap fabrics, which was drastically curtailed by private manufacturers after 1940.

Shoes.—In regard to the great problem of the purchasing power of low-income classes, the shoe industry is somewhat similar to that of cotton fabrics. According to the 1940 census, of a total of 18,900,000 inhabitants questioned only 49 per cent wore shoes, 23 per cent wore *huaraches* (a sandal of popular use) and 28 per cent went barefoot. In 1950, production for this manufacturing sector was 67 million pesos, representing only 1.47 per cent of the total value of Mexican industrial production. For the more than 150 factories, some with completely modern equipment, there are nearly 1,000 workshops, most of them domestic, using in many cases rented machinery. To this we must add a large number of unregistered workshops, which contribute about

MEXICO

Above: Lake Chapala, with an area of 417 square miles, is the largest lake in Mexico.

Right: A holiday scene in the "floating gardens" of Xochimilco, a popular resort near Mexico City.

Below: Hotel section along the beach at Mazatlán, a tourist center and largest port on Mexico's Pacific coast.

(Top and right) Otto Done; (bottom) Max Tatch, from Shostal

MEXICO

Above left: The Palace of Fine Arts in Mexico City houses exhibition galleries as well as a theater.

Above: Condominio Building on Central Plaza in Monterrey, with pool and fountain in foreground.

Left: La Parroquia, the 16th century cathedral of Cuernavaca, in Early Franciscan style.

Below: University of Mexico School of Engineering, with mural (right) by David Alfaro Siqueiros.

25 per cent to the total production. The output in general is low and consequently the workers' wages are also very meager. Not so retail prices, however, which are high because of the intervention of many distributors who carry their profits to the limit of consumers' purchasing power. The 10 million pairs of shoes produced in 1950 supplied only 33 per cent of the potential demand. Nevertheless, due to the fact that Mexico can supply the larger part of the raw materials needed by this industry, and because of the high qualifications of certain sectors of the manual labor force, and other favorable circumstances, this industry foresees a prosperous future.

General Prospects.—In the early 1950's it was assumed that Mexico had the necessary bases for a considerable volume of industrialization and that it could continue to industrialize at the rate of the decade 1940–1950. However, besides financial difficulties, several other problems were recognized, among them: the need to steer new undertakings, with government participation, toward the achievement of wide local benefits and higher revenue and away from harmful political interference; and the persistently high percentage of agricultural workers. More than 15 years later the problem of rural poverty was still far from being solved. In other respects, Mexico had made giant strides toward both industrialization and a balanced economy. During the 1950's industrial production increased at an average annual rate of 8 per cent, and by 1960 a diversified industrial complex was well established, with an output of both consumer and production goods.

Between 1950 and 1961 the gross national product leaped by 240 per cent. In absolute figures it climbed to $19.4 billion in 1965. That same year the national income amounted to $17.5 billion, which averages out to an income per capita of $412 (14 per cent higher than that of 1963). This was aside from the effects of the profit-sharing law passed in 1964, by which an employee receives, on the average, about two extra weeks pay as his share of company earnings. While there had been some inflation, production far outdistanced the cost of living, as a few 1965 economic indexes show: industrial production (1958 = 100), 168; agricultural production (1956–57 = 100), 181; and cost of living (1958 = 100), 118. By January 1966, Mexico had maintained an overall economic growth rate of between 8 and 12 per cent a year for more than 12 years. It had the most stable economy in all Latin America, and Latin America's only hard currency. Parallel with these advances, tourism has been making an ever greater contribution to national income. In 1966, gross earnings from tourism amounted to $319.8 million.

Bibliography.—*Conferencia des mesa redonda, campaña electoral del Presidente Miguel Alemán* (Mexico City 1946); Secretaría de Gobernación, *Seis años de actividad nacional* (Mexico City 1946); Noyola Vázquez, Juan Francisco, *Desequilibrio fundamental y fomento económico en México* (Mexico City 1949); Mosk, Sanford A., *Industrial Revolution in Mexico* (Berkeley, Calif., 1950); Tannenbaum, Frank, *Mexico; the Struggle for Peace and Bread* (New York 1950); Escuela de Economía, *El desarrollo económico de Mexico* (Mexico City 1952); Mosk, Sanford A., *The Industrial Revolution in Mexico* (Berkeley, Calif., 1954); Vernon, Raymond, *The Dilemma of Mexico's Development* (Cambridge, Mass., 1963); Ewing, Russell C., ed., *Six Faces of Mexico* (Tucson, Ariz., 1966).

FINANCIAL FACTORS

Profound changes have taken place in Mexico's economic and social life since 1925. On March 18 of that year the promulgation of the income tax law (effective in 1926) began the reform of the Mexican fiscal system and the establishment of the public revenue on a sound basis. The rehabilitation of the public credit was initiated in the same year, together with concern for a balanced budget, and during the next year (1926) the bases of agricultural credit were outlined, a most important factor in the attainment of the agrarian reform.

Financial Institutions.—*Banks.*—On Aug. 25, 1925, and on the basis of Article 28 of the Constitution of 1917, the Banco de México was founded. During its early life, the Banco de México went through an initial stage of participating, as did other private institutions, in the activities of a commercial bank, except for its unique privilege of coining, stabilizing the rate of exchange, and regulating interest rates. It was only when the Ley Monetaria (Monetary Law) of July 25, 1931 was passed, and other reforms, substantially ended on April 12, 1932, took effect, that this central institute started functioning as a bank of banks: establishing a rediscount system and regulating the amount of reserves to be held by private banks in the Banco de México as a guarantee for customers' deposits; aiming at the rationalization of credit; regulating the circulation of money; and defending the purchasing power of the peso in Mexico and abroad.

This banking reform was soon followed by the creation of a series of public banks to satisfy the specific needs of the economic development of Mexico: for agricultural credits, the Banco Nacional de Crédito Agrícola (1926)—now the Banco Nacional de Crédito Agrícola y Ganadero —and, later, the Banco Nacional de Crédito Ejidal (1935); for public works, the Banco Nacional Hipotecario y de Obras Públicas (1933); for industrial development, the Nacional Financiera (1934); for foreign commerce, the Banco Nacional de Comercio Exterior (1937); for the film industry, the Banco Nacional Cinematográfico (1941); for the development of cooperatives, the Banco Nacional de Fomento Cooperativo (1941); for small business, the Banco Nacional del Pequeño Comercio (1942); and, of lesser importance, for credits to members of the armed forces, the Banco Nacional del Ejército y la Armada (1947).

The Banco de México was an efficient collaborator with the government in the financing of public works, and made use of all its resources to check the inflation process as World War II accelerated the course of economic recovery from the depression of the 1930's, with the bank's cooperation. This central institute reduced to a minimum the speculations which were particularly active in raw materials and foodstuffs, and which were aggravated by "hot" or "refugee" money flying from countries at war. It handled with good judgment the eventual excess in the balance of payments during the war years, and channeled the effects of the deferred demand for capital goods, so necessary to a continuation of the country's industrialization.

Beyond the classical functions of the central bank's policies—the regulation of interest rates and open-market operations—the Banco de México realized that monetary maneuvers are only part of economic policies and therefore united its efforts to those of the government in the task of strengthening and increasing the economic power of the nation. For this purpose, the bank established a qualitative control on the total volume of private banking credit, by raising reserve requirements and by establishing so-called *topes de cartera* (portfolio maximums). The object was to channel the credit activities of private banking houses, limiting those for commercial purposes and, at the same time, expanding those of a productive character, particularly in agriculture, industry, and basic utilities. As late as 1949 the composition of the portfolios of deposit banks, in the aggregate, was as follows: commercial credits, 48.3 per cent; industrial, 38.8 per cent; agricultural, 8.6 per cent; livestock credits, 3.9 per cent; mining, 0.4 per cent. On September 30 of that year all new deposits entrusted to banks in the future were neutralized; however, the disposal of 70 per cent of them for loans having a proved productive character was authorized. Later, the capacity of commercial banks to extend credit was curtailed, limiting it to ten times the capital, plus the reserves of the institution concerned.

Mexican banking institutions (Banco de México, national specialized institutions, and private institutions together) had total resources as follows: in 1945, 8,285.3 million pesos; 1946, 8,520 million; 1947, 8,981.5 million; 1948, 10,677.5 million; 1949, 12,385.3 million; and 1950, 15,660.4 million. Converted into dollars according to exchange rates in the respective years, the resources of the Mexican banking system were reduced from $1,700 million in 1945 to $1,400 million in 1949, surpassing the first figure only in 1950, when the resources amounted to $1,810 million. The Banco de México had resources in 1945 of a value of 3,416 million pesos; declining in 1946 to 3,231.1 million and remaining at 3,271.2 million in 1947; but starting a rising curve in the following years: 1948, 3,813.1 million; 1949, 4,400.8 million; 1950, 5,620.7 million; and 1951, 5934.0 million. The second group (other national institutions) registered a constant increase—the most important in the entire system—in the course of those seven years (1945, 1,103.2 million pesos; 1951, 4,247.3 million). The same is true of the private institutions (1945, 3,765.5 million pesos; 1950, 6,796.8 million). In 1949 this last group led in resources, with 42 per cent of the total; followed by the Banco de México, with 35 per cent; leaving 23 per cent for other national institutions. The institutions of the system as a whole had on hand gold, silver, and foreign exchange with a value of 1,588.6 million pesos in 1949, and 2,725.4 million in 1951.

In 1949 a significant decrease was apparent in the net balances credited to Mexican banking houses by enterprises and individuals in the country; however, the system's balance in foreign money showed a very substantial increase. According to the report of the Banco de México for 1951 (published in 1952), the commercial banks, during that year, had raised the credit operations of 1950 by 24.1 per cent. During the same year (1951) the aggregate composition of the portfolios of commercial banks was as follows: 38 per cent, operations with industry; 19 per cent, agricultural credits; 36 per cent, commercial credits; 2 per cent, transportation credits; 5 per cent, consumer credits. These figures indicate an increase in the importance given to productive operations, and the favorable effect of the selective control measures of the Banco de México. However, a marked narrowness is apparent in the liquid assets of private enterprises; in 1952 private banks were softening the restrictive measures of the Mexican monetary authorities.

It is interesting to point out that the Banco de México, aside from its normal monetary and banking activities, plays a fundamentally important part in the economic development of Mexico. Other Latin American countries (Chile and Venezuela particularly) have limited their central banks to traditional activities, centralizing their objectives in regard to economic development—without any coordinating activities with the incentive programs of the government executive power —in special institutions, the *corporaciones de fomento* (development corporations). In Mexico, the central bank has taken over many of those functions, and has prevailed over the specialized public banking houses as a whole, which are organized in a system of autonomous institutions. The close connections for development purposes that the Banco de México has with the federal departments of the Treasury (Hacienda) and National Economy (Economía Nacional) must be emphasized, as also the activities of some of its own departments, in particular the Oficina de Investigaciones Industriales (Bureau of Industrial Investigations), its economic planning section. The bank also has very close relations with the Nacional Financiera in the field of industrial development.

Nacional Financiera.—The Nacional Financiera commenced its activities in June 1934. During its first stage (until 1940) it grew at a slow rate, but accumulated valuable experience. In 1937 it began turning its attention toward the stock market and issued its first bonds. In the following years it felt the blows of the unstable exchange situation, the nationalization of the petroleum industry (1938) and the beginning of World War II (1939). In 1940, legislation was passed, naming as the objectives of the Nacional Financiera:

The vigilance and regulation of the security market, the stimulation of capital investments to create and expand productive enterprises and public utilities, and the representation, as fiduciary and agent, of the federal government and the municipal and state entities in regard to the issue and placement of stock.

In its second stage (1940–1947) important events took place. In 1941 the first participating certificates (*certificados de participación*) were issued to strengthen the position of government bonds and to begin the absorption of monetary excess in a period in which the flow of circulation was increasing constantly. These certificates, which allow their owners to participate in the enterprises financed by the Nacional Financiera, are in increasing demand by private persons because of high profit and redemption practically at sight.

The first industrial promotions were also begun in 1941—Cementos Guadalajara (cement) and Compañía Industrial de Atenquique (paper)—and the first credit ($30 million) was obtained from the Export-Import Bank in the United States. In 1942 the Altos Hornos de México (steel and plate) was established in Monclova, Coahuila, and in 1943 Guanos y Fertilizantes de México (fertilizers) and the Carbonífera Unida de Palau (coal mining) were instituted, among other incorporated promotions. At the beginning of the postwar period (second half of 1945) the Nacional Financiera devoted more than 72 million pesos to the Ferrocarriles Nacionales (railroads) and 68 million to Petróleos Mexicanos (petroleum). Between 1946 and 1947 five important sugar mills were established, in order to liquidate the national deficit in the supply of that article. Also in 1946, the Comisión Nacional de Valores (National Securities Commission) was created to control the floating of capital stock and bond issues of new or enlarged corporations, and construction of Ayotla Textil (textiles), Industria Eléctrica de México (electrical equipment and household appliances) and other companies was started.

The third stage began in 1947 with the amendment of the law of 1940, raising the Nacional Financiera's capital from 20 million pesos to 100 million, turning it into an agent with power to negotiate long- and short-term credits from foreign, international, and private institutions, and establishing the bases of development which future promotions must follow. In 1947 Química Mexicana (chemicals), Viscosa Mexicana (rayon textiles), and other no less important companies were formed, and Sosa Texcoco (soda), Cementos Portland del Bajío (cement), Empacadora de Tampico (canning), and Vidriera Guadalupana (glass) started production. The International Bank for Reconstruction and Development in 1949 granted a credit of $34.1 million to develop electrification and $17.9 million to restore the railroads. In 1950 the study of a railroad plant was started and negotiations were begun with an Italian company for the assembly and manufacture of trucks in Mexico. In 1951 new promotions were companies for: coke and derivatives at Monclova, Coahuila; railroad car construction in Hidalgo; diesel trucks in Hidalgo; and two cellulose plants in Michoacán.

The issue of participating certificates was so successful that between 1941 and 1949 their total amount rose to 324 million pesos, and in 1950 it reached 713 million (in January 1952, 1,216 million). On Dec. 31, 1950 a new amendment was added to the legislation of 1940, and Export-Import Bank credits of $293.6 million were extended, of which $133 million had been already disposed of at the time; on Dec. 31, 1951 the authorized total was $382.6 million, of which $194.8 million had been disposed of. Between 1946 and 1950 the Nacional Financiera's total investment in industrial financing increased from 374 to 1,147 million pesos.

Public Finance.—In Mexico, as in the rest of the Latin American countries, the government has had a deep influence on economic development since 1940. In order to foster this progress, the Mexican government absorbed, through taxes, 11.4 per cent of the gross national product in 1939, 8.4 per cent in 1947, and 10.3 per cent in 1950 according to the economist Víctor Urquidi. Its effect is reflected more strongly in capitalization than in consumption: public entities, during the period 1946–1949, devoted from 31 per cent to 38 per cent of their expenses to the net formation of capital, either directly or as credits, guarantees, and other contributions. This represents from 29 per cent to 36 per cent of the net total capitalization of the country.

The net expenses of all forms of government were 753 million pesos in 1939, 2,352 million in 1946, and 5,834 million in 1951. In this last year, 4,158 million pesos were spent by the federal government; 330 million by the Federal District; 600 million by the states and territories; and 170 million by the *municipios* (municipalities)—the balance may be attributed to the expenses of various autonomous bodies. Investment expenses in 1951 amounted to 1,617.5 million pesos.

The budget results have been as follows—

deficits or surpluses indicated by (+) or (—) —1936, +6.7 million pesos; 1946, —65 million; 1947, —401.2 million; 1948, —392.5 million; 1949, —49.1 million; 1950, —342.1 million; 1951, —558.5 million.

The main sources of revenue of the federal government have been: the income tax (which amounted to 7.5 per cent of the net receipts in 1939 and more than 20 per cent on an average from 1943 to 1951—25.7 per cent in the latter year); taxes on foreign trade, which have lost much of their importance as compared with other periods (34.5 per cent in 1939, 30 per cent in 1951); taxes on natural resources (44 million pesos or 7.6 per cent in 1939, and 287 million or 7.2 per cent in 1951); and taxes on industry and transportation (22.8 per cent in 1939, 6.1 per cent in 1951). Taxation on sales, excluding the sale of food and other essential products, however, became heavier—a tax on commercial incomes, instituted in 1948 to replace the stamp tax, furnishes the federal government with 1.8 per cent of ,net sales, and the states with 1.2 per cent. In 1948 an extra rate of 15 per cent ad valorem was established on exports to absorb 50 per cent of the exchange profits produced by the devaluation of the peso.

In 1940 an amendment to the income tax was introduced, placing an additional burden on excess profits in order to stimulate reinvestment of surpluses. In the first year (1940) this tax yielded 43.7 million pesos; in 1950, 60 million. The burden of the Mexican taxpayer is relatively light in comparison with that of people of other countries—even more so if the government's participation in economic development works is considered.

According to data compiled by the Secretaría de Bienes Nacionales (Department of National Property), which controls government purchases and payments to contractors, the finished projects which were supervised by that executive agency amounted, cumulatively, for the period from Jan. 1, 1947 to March 31, 1952, to 1,603.4 million pesos. Of this amount, 1,052.7 million pesos represented productive works of direct benefit (294.2 million in agriculture, and 758.5 million in communications), and 550.6 million represented projects for social welfare (of these 492.3 million for urban services, and 58.3 million for educational and assistance purposes). Commitments represented a total of 3,076.1 million pesos for projects, leaving therefore a balance of works in process valued at 1,472.7 million pesos.

The internal public debt was quoted on Dec. 31, 1950 as amounting to 2,079.5 million pesos, in circulation, with 1,284.9 million payable interest—a total, therefore, of 3,364.4 million pesos. The external public debt on the same date amounted to 230.6 million pesos, 15 million having been redeemed up to 1950. The balance due, therefore, amounts to 215.6 million pesos. The credit terms expire on Jan. 1, 1963 for guaranteed debts and the rest in 1968.

Of the total internal public debt in 1950, approximately 1,619 million pesos were held by the Banco de México, 180 million by the Nacional Financiera, and 279 million by other investors.

National Income.—Following the example given after 1940 by the more progressive countries (among them the Netherlands, Sweden, and the United States), Mexico has been concerned with studying the size and composition of its gross national product. It is evident that these large-scale (macroeconomic) data, although approximate, can give a summarized idea of the progress achieved year after year, permit rough comparisons with other nations, and offer the bases, even though they be provisional, which indicate the trends of future economic progress. The four usual components of these types of studies—consumers', business enterprises', governmental, and foreign accounts—provide a pattern of the economic structure defined in broad outlines at the end of each fiscal period, even though such a picture may have a static character. If to this are added studies which bring one in contact with the income-expense relations (input-output, sources and allocations), and if, lastly, the net national income is found, Mexico will have achieved a great advance in statistical methods as compared with previous eras.

The national income at factor cost, according to the more reliable provisional figures, rose from 5,737 million pesos in 1939 to 15,551 million in 1944, 37,816 million in 1950, and 140 billion in 1965. For the same years, the gross national product at market prices (in which figure depreciation is included, subsidies are deducted, and indirect taxes are added) amounted respectively to 6,744 million, 17,317 million, 43,299 million, and 155 billion. (Similar improvements were shown in most other categories discussed in this section.)

The account of consumers (considered as final distributors) shows, in salaries and nominal wages, on the income side, 1,792 million pesos in 1939, 3,719 million in 1944, and 7,491 million in 1949; and for the savings record, on the side of disposable income, the meager sums of 6.9 million, 175 million, and —186 million.

The consolidated account of the gross product of business enterprises shows, among other important entries, nominal distributed profits with a value of 1,067 million pesos in 1939, 5,007 million in 1944, and 8,454 million in 1949; and undistributed profits of 376 million, 508 million, and 3,116 million.

The federal government's gross investment was as follows: 247.7 million pesos (1939); 713.7 million (1944); 3,007.5 million (1951). Allocations to the four main categories of expenses were—agriculture and natural resources: 39.7 million pesos (1939); 124.8 million (1944); 595.9 million (1951); communications and transportation: 143.2 million (1939); 387.5 million (1944); 1,172.9 million (1951); electrical works and fuel: 27.0 million (1939); 60.4 million (1944); 687.9 million (1951); social and municipal works: 25.7 million (1939); 92.0 million (1944); 430.2 million (1951).

In the foreign account, in current transactions, the commercial balance in 1950 showed a deficit of $63.5 million (exports $533.8 million; imports $597.3 million); and in 1951 this deficit was raised to $353.1 million (exports $569.8 million; imports $922.9 million). The tourists' account, an important item in the "invisible" account, showed a net income of $162.5 million in 1950, and $175.1 million in 1951. Personal payments from abroad, particularly those received by workers in the United States, amounted to nearly $20 million in 1950, and $30 million in 1951.

In regard to the saving and investment account it is sufficient to state that the gross national savings (which balance with the gross national investments) amounted to 649 million pesos in 1939, 1,730 million in 1944, and 5,937 million in 1950.

Contributions of the main economic sectors to the national income in 1950 were, in nominal figures: wholesale and retail commerce, 30.9 per cent; agriculture, 14.1 per cent; manufacturing, 18.3 per cent; rents and interest, 6.0 per cent; private services, 7.4 per cent; government services, 5.1 per cent; mining and petroleum, 4.5 per cent; and transportation and communications, 4.3 per cent.

Taking the Mexican nation as a whole, and even making the elementary adjustments that have been made, the preceding data imply that the balance is satisfactory in regard to the past, and the general tendency for the future is clear and encouraging. But an impressive problem is immediately apparent if one is not influenced by the blurred per capita values. Carefully grouping the available data under a new light, the income derived from labor, in percentage of the gross national product, was 30.5 per cent in 1939, 23.7 per cent in 1944, and 23.8 per cent in 1950. On the other hand, the income (profits) derived from capital was 26.2 per cent in 1939, 37.6 per cent in 1944, and 41.4 per cent in 1950. In other words, in contrast with superdeveloped countries where labor participation in the gross national product increased at a fast rate after 1930, in Mexico the tendencies are moving in the opposite direction. If attention is turned to one of the first theses of the present examination—the swift demographic growth of Mexico's population—one finds, clearly defined, a task which cannot be delayed and an ultimate goal for future administrations of the country: to invert the terms of the problem, arbitrating solutions by which economic development may be attained without as costly a sacrifice by the lower economic classes of the population. To reach this objective, without at the same time decreasing the investors' legitimate profits—but on the contrary, raising them, not because of the increased consumption but as a result of its extension to vast potential zones—is undoubtedly the worthiest project for accomplishment by the Mexican government, with the help of all of the country's productive factors.

Bibliography.—Pani, Alberto J., *La reforma hacendaria y la revolución* (Mexico City 1926); Ortiz Mena, Raúl, *La moneda mexicana; análisis histórico de sus fluctuaciones* (Mexico City 1942); *Conferencia de mesa redonda, campaña electoral del Presidente Miguel Alemán* (Mexico City 1946); Secretaría de Gobernación, *Seis años de actividad nacional* (Mexico City 1946); Noyola Vázquez, Juan Francisco, *Desequilibrio fundamental y fomento económico en México* (Mexico City 1949); Carrillo Flores, Antonio, *Practices, Methods and Problems Involved in the Domestic Financing of Economic Development in Mexico* (United Nations, New York, 1950); Tannenbaum, Frank, *Mexico; the Struggle for Peace and Bread* (New York 1950); Carrillo Flores, Antonio, *El desarrollo económico de México* (Mexico City 1951); *Directorio del gobierno federal* (Mexico City 1950, 1951); Navarrete Jr., Alfredo, *Estabilidad de cambios, el ciclo y el desarrollo económico* (Mexico City 1951); Pani, Alberto J., *Los orígenes de la política crediticia en México* (Mexico City 1951); Salas Villagómez, Manuel, *La deuda pública en México* (Mexico City 1951); Escuela de Economía, *El desarrollo económico de México* (Mexico City 1952); Bennett, Robert L., *The Financial Sector and Economic Development; the Mexican Case* (Baltimore, Md., 1965); Brothers, Dwight S., *Mexican Financial Development* (Austin, Texas, 1965).

FOREIGN TRADE

Since the end of World War I Mexico's trade relations, and its trends, have reflected the importance of the United States as the primary world creditor. That country's capacity of production introduced very important changes in the volume and composition of Mexican foreign trade. In 1935-1939 Europe furnished Mexico with only a third of Mexican imports, Germany and the United Kingdom being the main exporters; Mexico obtained six tenths of its imports from the United States, which in turn purchased two thirds of Mexican exports during the same period. Europe received only one fourth of Mexican exports.

After 1940, during World War II, the United States became the only important market for Mexican imports and exports, although Mexican products were in demand in other countries in Latin America, and even in South Africa and southern Asia. In the peak year, 1943, imports from and exports to the United States were 88.5 per cent and 87 per cent, respectively, of the Mexican total.

The year 1948 began a return to more normal relations. The highly developed nations recovered their traditional markets, but on the other hand Mexico intensified the importation of capital goods, durable goods, and raw materials, so necessary for the industrialization programs. These included equipment for manufactures and assembly plants, railroad equipment, cellulose and nylon. Mexican imports from Latin America fell to prewar levels (2.5 per cent); even lower in 1952 (0.9 per cent), when Canada furnished 2.5 per cent of Mexican imports. Europe advanced to 13 per cent of Mexican imports, at the expense of the United States, imports from which were reduced to some 80 per cent.

In 1965, the United States remained Mexico's principal market for exports (63 per cent) and its chief supplier of imports (66 per cent). Mexico was the best U.S. customer in Latin America. Japan, the Latin American republics, and Western Europe took most of the remainder of Mexico's exports.

Editorial Staff
"The Encyclopedia Americana"

MODERN ECONOMIC POLICY

The Mexican social revolution began Nov. 20, 1910, with the uprising in Chihuahua. The armed struggle lasted seven years. It accounted for thousands of lives, and destroyed, mainly in the rural areas, part of the riches that had been accumulated during the 30 peaceful years of the rule of President Porfirio Díaz. Nevertheless, everything considered, the bitter fighting opened the way for the profound changes that were carried out in the economic structure of the country, as well as in its political organization and legal institutions.

The foundations of modern Mexican political economy were laid during the years 1925 and 1926, when Plutarco Elías Calles was president; this is the same policy that has been continued into 1953 and which will, most likely, go on in the near future. It has been improved with the years. No doubt the continuity of purpose for nearly 30 years and the desire of each new government to improve on the achievements of its predecessors have played a very important part in the economic advance of the nation. This would explain the progress achieved in the economy and the confidence which is noticeable in wide sectors of the population.

Legal Bases.—The new constitution, promulgated Feb. 5, 1917, contains Articles 27 and 123, which were aimed at satisfying popular demand for reform in the social and economic fields. Both articles have since had boundless repercussions on the economic development of Mexico.

Article 27 sets forth the following principles:

The rights of ownership of the land and water comprised within the boundaries of the national territory belong primarily to the nation, which has had and has the right of transferring their control to private individuals, thus giving rise to private property.

Expropriations can be carried out only for reasons of public utility and through indemnity.

The nation shall always have the right to impose on private property regulations in the public interest, as well as the right to control the exploitation of any natural elements that can be so exploited, in order to distribute public wealth on an equable basis and to care for its conservation. To this end, whatever regulations are deemed necessary will be issued for the fragmentation of *latifundia* [large estates]; for the development of private property; for the creation of new agricultural centers enjoying the tenure of indispensable land and water; for the encouragement of agriculture and to avoid the destruction of natural elements and whatever damage property may suffer to the detriment of society. Villages, ranches, and communities lacking land and water supply, or not having a sufficient amount for the needs of the community, shall have a right to being endowed with them, taking them from neighboring properties, but always respecting small holdings.

The article later continues:

The acquisition of the private property necessary to achieve the ends stated, shall be considered [as having been made on the basis] of public utility.

Regarding ownership of the subsoil, the following paragraph from Article 27 states:

The nation shall have direct control of all minerals or matter found in seams, layers, concentrations, or veins forming deposits the nature of which may be different from that of the components of the soil, such as minerals from which metals and metalloids used in industry are extracted, veins of precious stones, salt mines and also salt ponds formed directly by sea water, the products derived from the breaking up of rocks, when their exploitation makes underground working necessary, phosphates that can be used as fertilizers, solid mineral fuels, petroleum, and all carbohydrates in liquid or gaseous form.

Article 123 concerns labor laws. Among other provisions, it sets forth the following, which are the most important:

1. An eight-hour working day.

2. Children under 12 years are forbidden to work.

3. A weekly day of rest.

4. Protection to women about to become mothers, who must cease to do work requiring considerable physical effort three months before childbirth, and will also enjoy one full month's compulsory rest after childbirth; receiving their full pay and keeping their job, with every right that they shall have acquired as stated in their contract.

5. The minimum wage shall be sufficient to provide for the normal needs of the worker's life, education, and legitimate pleasures of the man considered the head of the family.

6. The employer is required to provide schools for the worker's children when the industrial premises are situated at a considerable distance from any populated area.

7. Employers are held to be responsible in certain cases of occupational accidents and sickness.

8. The right is granted for both employers and employees to organize to defend their interests; the former are granted the right to close their plants, the latter the right to strike.

Application.—These two constitutional articles have had a far-reaching influence on Mexico's economic policy since 1917. The agrarian reform has been steadily changing the old system of land exploitation through large holdings, found in the haciendas that had been in existence since colonial times. Article 27 has been the basis on which the breaking up of these large estates has been carried out, thus giving rise to the communal landholdings of the Indian villages and also to small private property. In altering the organization of private property in rural areas, it has also been found necessary to carry out certain changes in the agricultural and cattle-raising policy of the whole nation, as will be described below.

Article 27 has also had a certain influence on mining laws and on government policy concerning petroleum. The mining companies, mostly British- or United States-controlled, had never raised any international problems for the Mexican government; on the other hand, the oil companies had always been the cause of disagreements, sometimes far-reaching, between Mexico and the other two countries. Of the capital invested in oil in Mexico at the time of expropriation, United States firms held approximately 38 per cent, British firms 60 per cent, and Mexican firms 2 per cent. The expropriation of the holdings of these firms in March 1938 was based on Article 27.

Article 123 was regulated by rules set forth in the Ley del Trabajo (Labor Law) of 1929. This law and the before-mentioned article together regulate economic and social relations between workers and employers.

Land Reform.—There was no clearly defined economic policy in the years from 1917 to 1924, under presidents Venustiano Carranza, Adolfo de la Huerta, and Álvaro Obregón. The only sign of an economic policy was the distribution of land to the villages. The peace had not yet been consolidated; those were years of reconstruction, of discussion of new plans aiming at transforming the country's organization.

The distribution of land could not be put off, since there was a general and urgent demand from the agricultural masses; without it, no lasting peace would have been possible, in spite of every Mexican's anxiety to be done with fighting. According to the census of 1910 there were in Mexico only 840 hacienda-owners, who—it was estimated—owned among them three fourths of the national territory; while, according to the same census, there were over 3 million agricultural workers without land. It thus became imperative to start distribution right away, without waiting to draw up a well-thought-out technical plan. The crying need of land had been the main cause of the revolution.

From early in 1916 until Dec. 31, 1924, 3,292,-332 acres of land were distributed among various agricultural communities, with benefits accruing to 178,829 families. But it must be pointed out that they were given land which in many cases was of poor quality, without machinery, without fertilizers, and without facilities for obtaining credit. Naturally enough, the results were not very satisfactory; indeed, in some cases they were completely negative.

Credit.—In the years 1925 to 1926, it was clearly seen that the agricultural problem could not be satisfactorily solved if the government were content with merely giving land to the people, who were applying for it in ever-increasing numbers. It was at the same time necessary to grant them credit at long, medium, and short terms; long-term credit, in order to enable them to build irrigation ditches, storehouses for produce, and the like; medium-term, so that they would be able to buy agricultural machinery, such as plows, tractors, and trucks; and short-term, to make it possible for them to buy seeds and to live before the harvest. For these purposes the Banco Nacional de Crédito Agrícola (National Agricultural Credit Bank) was

founded March 1, 1926; followed shortly after by the founding of small credit institutions, called *bancos agrícolas ejidales,* to provide credit for communal village lands (*ejidos*). By 1935 these small banks had been closed. They had failed, partly because they operated with very small capital. But the Banco Nacional de Crédito Ejidal was founded in their stead in the same year, 1935, and became one of the two great credit organizations which work with capital supplied by the federal government. The Banco Nacional de Crédito Agrícola had, up to Dec. 31, 1950, granted credit to a value of 1,247 million pesos, of which it had recovered 936 million. Its capital was then 213 million. As for the Banco Nacional de Crédito Ejidal, it had on the same date a capital of 250 million pesos, had loaned 1,637 million, and the recovery amounted to 1,314 million. The federal government constantly supplies the banks with new funds.

More recently some private banking institutions have also provided funds on credit for agriculture, mostly in small amounts; among them the Banco Nacional de México, founded in 1884.

But in spite of governmental policy, it has been impossible to meet in full the demand of the nation's agriculture for credit. There are still many unsatisfied needs, which can only be attended to very slowly.

Irrigation.—The year 1926 also saw the beginning of extensive irrigation work aimed at reclaiming new lands for agricultural uses. This program has progressed uninterruptedly and continues on an increasing scale, as can be seen from the work started at the end of 1947 on the Papaloápan (Papaloápam) River in Veracruz and the Tepalcatepec in Michoacán. When the Papaloápan project is finished, Mexico will have one of the largest irrigation systems in the world.

Education.—It was also in 1926 that the first agricultural schools were organized. Their purpose was to teach agricultural workers and their children new methods of cultivation. There were 15 agricultural schools in the country in 1952, apart from the Escuela Nacional de Agricultura (National School of Agriculture) at Chapingo, State of Mexico, where a seven-year course is given, leading to the degree of agricultural engineer. The other 15 have less comprehensive plans of study, for a total of 5,000 students, who are to play an important role in the modernization of Mexican rural areas.

Minerals.—It can be said that the government has given almost complete freedom to mining firms, apart from its intervention through a system of taxation and its subsidies to cooperatives that continue to exploit impoverished properties, in order to keep such sources of employment operating as far as possible.

But the case of petroleum is entirely different. After 1917 the Mexican government had many serious, sometimes extremely serious, difficulties with the oil companies. About the middle of 1937 after a week-long strike which seriously affected the country's economy, the oil workers submitted to the companies certain demands which the latter refused to meet, arguing that their resources did not make such concessions possible. The workers demanded larger salaries and the improvement of social services, such as medical attention, hospitalization, indemnity in case of occupational accidents, and more holidays with pay. The workers' demands meant an increase in expenditure of 90 million pesos and the companies were ready to meet them to an extent of only 13.5 million. Thus the conflict was not easy to solve.

The usual procedure in dealing with such conflicts is for the labor authorities to appoint three experts who draw up a report on the financial situation of the company or companies, as well as recommendations expressing their opinion as to the most suitable way to end the dispute. Experts were, therefore, appointed. They drew up their report and recommendations within the appointed time, stating that the oil companies could well afford to increase their expenses by 26.5 million pesos without any undue strain. The labor authorities, after hearing the objections that employers as well as employees raised to the experts' report, gave their final decision, which was in agreement with the recommendations of the experts. The companies did not agree and appealed to the Supreme Court. The court confirmed the decision of the labor authorities. The companies, however, refused to accept the decision of the Supreme Court and took a rebellious attitude. It was then, on March 18, 1938 that the government decreed their expropriation.

The first years of Petróleos Mexicanos—this was the name of the official firm which took over the companies' properties—were difficult, years spent in organizing; but as of 1953 it could be said that the Mexican oil industry was firmly established and was progressing from day to day. A new oil pipeline was built from Poza Rica to Salamanca, where a new refinery was completed in 1951, with an output of 30,000 barrels daily; hundreds of new wells have been drilled and new fields discovered. Oil production, which under the foreign companies totaled 119 million barrels in the three years 1934 to 1936, increased to 215 million barrels from 1949 to 1951 inclusive. The output of crude oil in 1965 was approximately 117 million barrels. Eventually the foreign companies were compensated for the expropriations; the last foreign concession being bought by the government in 1950. The oil industry is controlled by Pemex (Petróleos Mexicanos).

Transportation.—The building of motor roads was started during Gen. Plutarco Elías Calles' term of office (1924–1928); and has continued uninterruptedly. The road-building policy has tried to fulfill two aims: to join production centers with consumers, and to favor the tourist trade.

Much less has been done to develop the railways. Efforts are being made to modernize them and to put them in a position to meet the growing demand for transport efficiently, but this requires the investment of considerable sums of money. See also the section *Transportation and Communications*.

Industrialization.—A policy favoring the establishment of new industry was initiated in 1939–1940, during the last two years of President Lázaro Cárdenas' term of office. Facilities were given by granting exemption from the payment of taxes for a few years and also loans on a long-term basis. The Nacional Financiera (see below) was important in this financing. Industrialization gained a new impetus during World War II, and an even greater one after 1946. During the war there was a great lack of certain goods, sometimes indispensable ones, which had previously been easily imported from foreign countries, especially the United States. This influenced Mexicans to push on with the creation of new industries and to strengthen those already in existence.

However, Mexican statesmen, as well as economists, know full well that their country will never be able to equal the United States in industrial potentialities. But they also know that Mexico has a very good chance of becoming industrially powerful; among other reasons because it has iron, coal, oil, ample possibilities of enlarging its electric resources, and a good number of other raw materials. Moreover, economists as well as statesmen realize that industrialization will help to raise the standard of living of an important sector of the community.

Tariffs.—Mexico has always been a protectionist country, sometimes more and sometimes less, according to the circumstances. After 1940 economic policy concerning foreign trade was based openly on protection for new industries and on the opening up of new sources of employment, as in the case of automobile assembly plants. The customs duty payable on unassembled cars is very low, while that on assembled motor cars is extremely high. There is an organization, the Comisión de Aranceles (Tariff Commission), whose job it is to study and recommend to the Treasury Department (Secretaría de Hacienda y Crédito Público) any necessary changes in import and export tariffs. This commission is made up of representatives from several federal departments, and from the Confederation of Chambers of Commerce and Industry. Certain tariffs are raised on occasion, following Treasury requirements. This, of course, does not happen often.

Financial Institutions.—The Banco de México, being the central bank, is mainly concerned with loans to other banks, the issue of paper currency, the control of currency circulation and foreign exchange, and is the financial agent of the federal government. The Banco de México was founded by law on Aug. 25, 1925 and opened for business on September 1 of that year.

Besides the Banco de México, and the Banco Nacional de Crédito Agrícola and the Banco Nacional de Crédito Ejidal (described above), there are other banking institutions most of whose stock is owned by the federal government. Among these, the Nacional Financiera, the Banco Hipotecario Urbano y de Obras Públicas, and the Banco Nacional de Comercio Exterior deserve mention.

The Nacional Financiera has become very important since about 1939, mainly because of its intervention in financing new industries. It owns the greater part of the stock in many of them. Its policy consists in contributing whatever capital it may be necessary to add to private investments to facilitate the creation of new industry that will play a useful part in the economic progress of the nation. As soon as these industrial concerns are fully developed, however, the Nacional Financiera tries to get rid of its stock by sale to private investors. Sometimes this institution issues bonds to bearer to be placed among various investors. These bonds return an annual interest of six or seven per cent, as for instance, *certificados de participación* (participation certificates) and *bonos de caminos* (highway bonds). It also buys on the stock exchange.

The Banco Nacional Hipotecario Urbano y de Obras Públicas (National Urban and Public Works Hypothecary Bank) is concerned mainly with loans to states and *municipios* (municipalities) for the construction of sewage facilities and waterworks. The Banco Nacional de Comercio Exterior (National Foreign Trade Bank) controls, among other things, certain business operations carried out between Mexico and foreign countries.

There are, besides, a number of private credit institutions that help in the economic development of the country and sometimes make considerable profits. Most of them are banks doing only deposit and discount operations, and they issue loans usually on a short-term basis. They have grown considerably in number since 1940; both because banking has turned out to be very lucrative in Mexico, and because of the facilities granted by the Ley General de Instituciones de Crédito (General Law for Banking Institutions), in 1937 and thereafter, and the stimulating policy of the Treasury Department. Banking policy has consisted in authorizing the formation of new banking concerns, always in accordance with the law and wisely defined to avoid duplication. It is the job of an official institution, the Comisión Nacional Bancaria (National Banking Commission), to keep a constant watch over all banking concerns and so to secure the public interest.

Taxation and Expenditures.—In the 1920's the federal government depended on mining and petroleum taxation for a considerable part of its revenue. Such taxation has steadily been losing importance since 1942. The income tax, which became effective for the first time in Mexico in 1926, now accounts for most of such income and grows constantly. A comparison of the years 1940 and 1951 shows that the income of the federal treasury, reckoned in dollars, increased fivefold; the increase of production and the development of business, as well as an improved budgeting technique accounting for the increment.

A fact of singular importance, which reveals a certain aspect of the government's economic policy, can be observed in its expenditure. The War Department headed the list of public expenditure in 1925, while in 1950, for instance, communications came first, followed by capital investments; education came third; waterworks fourth; followed by national defense in fifth place.

The most serious problem of Mexico as regards contemporary economic policy is the achievement of a better distribution of the national income, since the mass of the people has in no way enjoyed the undeniable overall increase of such income.

Bibliography.—Tannenbaum, Frank, *The Mexican Agrarian Revolution* (Washington 1929); Simpson, Eyler N., *The Ejido* (Chapel Hill, N.C., 1937); Millan, Verna Carleton, *Mexico Reborn* (Boston 1939); Whetten, Nathan L., *Rural Mexico* (Chicago 1948); Mosk, Sanford A., *Industrial Revolution in Mexico* (Berkeley, Calif., 1949); Lavin, José Domingo, *Petróleo* (Mexico City 1950); Tannenbaum, Frank, *Mexico; the Struggle for Peace and Bread* (New York 1950); Vernon, Raymond, *Public Policy and Private Enterprise in Mexico* (Cambridge, Mass., 1964); Wilkie, J. W., *The Mexican Revolution: Federal Expenditure and Social Change Since 1910* (Berkeley, Calif., 1967).

JESÚS SILVA HERZOG,
Universidad Nacional de México.
Revised by the Editors.

7. LABOR MOVEMENT.

The lack of an industrial movement during the 19th century retarded the growth of labor unions in Mexico during that period. Few labor groups were formed, the most important being the Gran Círculo de Obreros (Grand Circle of Workers), founded in 1876.

Labor activity increased up to 1884, when it was effectively suppressed by Porfirio Díaz.

From 1865 to 1877 there was a period of labor unrest with many strikes.

In 1906 the Círculo de Obreros Libres (Circle of Free Workers) was founded, and a series of strikes was organized by this group among textile workers to obtain an eight-hour day and minimum wage levels, but these strikes were broken in the same year.

During the years 1907 to 1911 new organizations made their appearance in Mexico City. The most important of these was the linotypist union, Unión Linotipográfica de la República Mexicana. The Casa del Obrero Mundial (World Worker's House), founded in Mexico City in 1912, was the first labor organization to receive government backing. It was supported by President Venustiano Carranza's government, and during the revolution organized the so-called red battalions which fought on the side of that government.

CROM.—In 1918 dissident elements of the Casa del Obrero Mundial founded the Confederación Regional Obrera Mexicana (Regional Confederation of Mexican Workers) and affiliated themselves with the Amsterdam Syndicalist Federation. The leader of this group was Luis Morones, who later served under President Plutarco Elías Calles as minister of commerce, industry and labor. Morones, called "Czar of Labor" by the American writer Lesley Byrd Simpson, and his followers were the founders of Mexican labor *liderismo,* an absolute domination of union and members by the leaders; strikes often being called or stopped according to their personal interests. Morones and the CROM's central governing committee, the Grupo Acción, attained the peak of their power during the Calles administration.

The CROM had an initial membership of 7,000 members. By 1927 it counted 2,500,000 members in its ranks. During the years 1924 to 1926 it was affiliated with 76 national organizations, 106 unions located in the Federal District, and with about 1,000 syndicalist groups and 1,500 peasant unions scattered throughout Mexico. Without a doubt, the CROM was the most important labor body in Mexican history. In 1936 it became a member of the London World Syndicalist Federation.

CTM.—The speed with which the CROM grew was matched by the rapidity with which it disintegrated, a decline due to its submissiveness to the government and loss of zeal. The groups that broke off met in a unification congress in 1936, which resulted in the organization known as the Confederación de Trabajadores Mexicanos (Confederation of Mexican Workers). The CTM had a starting membership of 20,000 workers. By 1940 its membership had increased to well over a million. This powerful labor group has as its motto, "Toward a Classless Society," and had as its leader the Soviet sympathizer Vicente Lombardo Toledano, who in 1936 also became the leader of a new international labor group, the Confederación de Trabajadores de la América Latina (Latin American Workers' Confederation).

The CTM suffered a severe drop in membership in 1942, which was in great part due to the communistic policies followed by its leaders. The loss of membership, however, continued even after 1949, when it broke with the Communist elements with which it was infiltrated.

Newer Unions.—Vicente Lombardo Toledano, who was ousted as leader of the CTM in 1949, organized a new labor body, known as the

MEXICO

View of canal from bridge, Xochimilco.

View of stairs of Temple of Quetzalcoatl,
San Juan, Teotihuacán.

The Cathedral of Mexico City is the finest and largest in Mexico.

MEXICO

Ewing Galloway

The Castle—ruins of Chichen-Itza, Yucatan.

Silberstein from Monkmeyer

Modern Mexican school in suburb of Mexico City.

Mexican Government Railway System

Pyramid of the Sun, near Mexico City.

Fritz Henle from Monkmeyer

Paseo de la Reforma, Mexico City.

Ewing Galloway

The observatory at the Chichen-Itza ruins.

Silberstein from Monkmeyer

Front of the Cardiac Institute in Mexico City.

Unión General de Obreros y Campesinos de México (General Workers and Peasants Union of Mexico) in the same year.

Luis Morones organized the Proletaria Nacional (National Proletariat) in 1952, which was closely linked with the *Peronista* movement emanating from Argentina and represented by the Comisión para la Unidad Obrera de Ibero América (Commission for Ibero-American Labor Unity). Three minor unions fused to form the Proletaria Nacional: the Confederación Nacional Proletaria (National Proletarian Confederation) of anarchist-syndicalist tendencies; the Confederación Nacional de Trabajo (National Labor Confederation) of communistic tendencies; and the Confederación de Obreros y Campesinos de México (Confederation of Workers and Peasants of Mexico). Prior to the merging of these three groups there were in Mexico approximately 15 national and central unions, without any link among themselves. By 1950 there were 165 federations, 20 worker syndical confederations, an employers syndical confederation, and over 8,200 local unions of all types, with more than half a million workers.

Legislation.—The Congress of Queretaro incorporated "liberty of professional association" in the Constitution of 1917. In 1929 Congress passed the Ley del Trabajo (Labor Law), establishing the Special Minimum Wage Commission, conciliation and arbitration boards, and other labor bodies. Unions were declared "public corporations subject to industrial law" by the Supreme Court in 1938.

Strikes.—The report of the National Workers Confederation Committee of the CTM, published in Mexico City in April 1938, gives the strike statistics in the following table:

Year	Strikes	Year	Strikes
1920	173	1928	7
1921	310	1929	14
1922	197	1930	15
1923	146	1931	21
1924	136	1932	56
1925	51	1933	13
1926	23	1934	202
1927	16	1935	642
		1936	659

No information is available on the numbers of strikers participating. As will be seen, the number of strikes gradually declined after 1921, the year in which the revolution may be said to have been consolidated by President Alvaro Obregón, until the effects of the great economic depression were felt in Mexico during the administration of Lázaro Cárdenas. No information is available for the years 1937–1940.

The *Compendio estadístico* (1951) of the Dirección General de Estadística gives the information in the following table.

Year	Strikes	Strikers	Year	Strikes	Strikers
1941	142	12,892	1944	887	165,744
1942	98	13,643	1945	220	48,055
1943	766	81,557	1946	207	10,202

The labor conciliation boards settled 87,327 labor-management conflicts in 1941–1946.

Consult Chávez Orozco, Luis, *Historia económica y social de México* (Mexico City 1938); *Memoria de los grupos socialistas de México* (Mérida 1950); López Apa-ricio, Alfonso, *El movimiento obrero en México* (Mexico City 1952).

NARCISO MOLINS FÁBREGA,
Ethnologist, Escuela Nacional de Antropología.

8. TRANSPORTATION AND COMMUNICATIONS. Mexican transportation reflects the difficult conditions under which the system was constructed. From 600 kilometers (1 km. equals .62 statute mile) of railways in 1875, the total increased to 23,672 kilometers of standard-gauge track in 1965. By the same year, roads totaled 58,278 kilometers, 51,461 of these hard-surfaced. With 8 national airlines, 32 main airports, and over 1,000 other airports, practically the whole country had air service. Veracruz and Tampico were the chief of 49 ocean ports. In 1965 there were 24 steamships and 1,759 motorboats of at least 5 tons each. The oil fleet consisted of 19 tankers and 196 other vessels.

The initial planning of land transport routes conformed to no strong national or logical criteria. During the Díaz regime (1877–1911) communication lines were developed to facilitate export of raw materials via ports and borders, and to supply the national capital with imported articles. This was reflected in the predominance of foreign investment in railroads, in correlation with investments in mining and agriculture. Not until 1907 was the Ferrocarriles Nacionales de México created, with the government as majority participant. The nationalization of railways occurred in 1937 under President Cárdenas in hope of alleviating the shortage of rail facilities (11.9 km. of track per 1,000 sq. km. of area). The expansion of railway facilities has been handicapped by deficit conditions, by deterioration of fixed equipment and rolling stock, by high wage budgets for a multitude of low-wage workers, and the heavy expense of renting numerous passenger and freight cars from the United States.

During the administrations (1940–1952) of presidents Manuel Ávila Camacho and Miguel Alemán appropriations for the Secretaría de Comunicaciones y Obras Públicas (Department of Communications and Public Works) consistently exceeded those for any other department. Trunkline communications have been improved and augmented, and new feeder lines have been incorporated into Mexican economic and cultural life many areas hitherto isolated.

Motor vehicles numbered 1,244,717 in 1965; about half of these were passenger cars, the rest trucks, motorcycles, and buses. Of the 827,739 telephones, all but about 5,000 were operated by public companies, and 83.8 per cent of the total were automatic.

Besides a modern postal system, in 1965 Mexico had 460 radio-broadcasting stations and 8.3 million radio sets; and 31 television stations and 1.1 million television sets. More than 200 daily newspapers were being published, with a combined circulation of 4,428,000.

Editorial Staff, "The Encyclopedia Americana"

Air Transport.—Between 1930 and 1949 the total number of kilometers flown by commercial aviation increased nearly tenfold (from 4 million to 37.8 million km.). The number of passengers carried in 1930 was 21,000; in 1951 the corresponding figure was 1,128,385. In 1950 there were 38 airports and 165 smaller landing fields in Mexico; by 1952, public investment in airport construction and repair amounted to 94 million pesos. From 1940–1948 private companies invested 132 million pesos. New airports completed in 1951 included those at Campeche and León, and one of the most beautiful and efficient airports in Mexico, that of Guadalajara. The 29 domestic and 6 international airlines serve virtually every town and city of importance. Air cargo includes agricultural produce, industrial goods, sea foods, even jungle products, such as chicle. There are three schools of civil aeronautics; one, the Cinco de Mayo in Puebla, is a dependency of the Secretaría de Comunicaciones y Obras Públicas.

Railroads.—Twenty-one railroad companies operating some 1,449 miles of track were registered in 1948 with the Secretaría de Comunicaciones y Obras Públicas; the balance of about 22,300 km. being government-operated. In 1940 work began on the Ferrocarril del Sureste (Southeastern Railroad), which crosses innumerable rivers and marshlands and connects the Peninsula of Yucatán with the national network; this was completed in 1950. On the opposite side of the country the costly Ferrocarril Sonora–Baja California, which crosses the desert called Desierto de Altar and links Lower California with the rest of the country, was also completed. In July 1950, construction was begun on the Durango-Mazatlán line; the importance of this project is evident in the expectation that it will benefit 30 per cent of Mexico's population. Over 11 miles of tunnels and more than 1,000 meters of bridging will be required on this line. A line from Mexico City to Tuxpan, Veracruz, was under construction in 1952, while a new modern passenger terminal and a new freight terminal were being completed in Mexico City. A rational plan of laying heavier tracks was adopted after 1946 to facilitate higher speeds and the carrying of heavier loads; diesel units have been acquired, and a plant to manufacture railway cars is being promoted.

Highways.—The creation, in 1925, of the Comisión Nacional de Caminos provided the first positive impulse, reinforced later by the administrative efforts of the Department of Communications and Public Works, which undertook an ambitious plan of highway construction in cooperation with various state governments; under President Alemán annual appropriations for this purpose averaged 300 million pesos. From 1925 to 1940, the yearly average of construction was about 664 km. (total: 9,968 km.) and this average rose to 1,333 km. per year between 1941 and 1949. Approximately 22,000 km. were constructed up to 1949; 57 per cent were paved, 33 per cent "improved," and 10 per cent were dirt roads. During the 25 years, 2,135 million pesos were expended, of which nine tenths came from the federal government.

By 1951 main trunk routes were undertaken to tap the vast regions of Yucatán and Lower California. Construction of the Carretera Internacional del Noroeste (Northwest International Highway) from Guadalajara, Jalisco, to Nogales, Sonora (1,069 miles), was pushed intensively. At Mazatlán, this highway will connect with the Matamoros, Tamaulipas-Mazatlán, Sinaloa highway.

The year 1952 saw the completion of the 728-mile coast-to-coast road from Tampico, Tamaulipas, to Barra de Natividad, Jalisco, except for the paving of 170 miles of the section Barra de Natividad-Acatlán. Construction was in progress on the Transisthmus highway from Coatzacoalcos, Veracruz, to Salina Cruz, Oaxaca. The

Mexico City-Cuernavaca superhighway, inaugurated in 1952, is a 22-meter boulevard; each of the double lanes is 7.5 meters wide. Entrance boulevards 30 to 40 meters wide had been completed for the Mexico City-Acapulco and the Guadalajara-Chapala highways.

Other completed roads include the 1,327-mile Mexico City-Ciudad Juárez route, the 760-mile Mexico City-Nuevo Laredo route, and the Carretera Cristóbal Colón (846 miles) which links the capital with Ciudad Cuauhtémoc, Chiapas, on the Guatemala border. The opening of the latter constituted a milestone in Mexican highway development, for it completed Mexico's part of the Pan American Highway and made it possible to travel on good roads from Fairbanks, Alaska, to Guatemala.

Local Roads.—The federal government's extensive program of building local roads, designed to bring a majority of the small towns and agricultural areas within range of first-class trunk highways, began with creation of a new bureau within the Department of Communications and Public Works to develop this type of road. Automobile assembling firms and tire manufacturers offered to pay an additional tax of 10 per cent, and thus financed these roads in part. A presidential decree of Oct. 12, 1949 inaugurated a plan of dividing the cost of local roads equally between the federal government, state governments, and private enterprise. Construction allocations and priorities depend upon the anticipated volume and type of traffic. Some of these roads are constructed with an absolute minimum of investment, but are designed to facilitate improvement as traffic may require. In 1952, 273 miles of such roads had been completed, and 1,324 additional miles were under construction. Some of these are gravel roads four meters wide, others are asphalt roads up to nine meters wide.

Telecommunications.—Telegraph services have been modernized by radio relay stations, multiplex transmission and printing, and other devices for simultaneous transmission of several messages on the same line. The telegraph system functions in liaison with urban and long-distance telephone systems. No state capital or city of importance lacks long-distance telephone service. There are about 214 radio broadcasting stations, and four television stations in 1952.

Pipelines.—In 1950 the daily transport capacity of oil pipelines was 817,000 barrels of crude petroleum and other products. Between 1938 and 1950, five gas pipelines totaling 447 km. in length and with a daily carrying capacity of 410 million cubic feet were constructed. Another pipeline from Monterrey to Torreón (340 km.; daily capacity, 100 million cu. ft.) was under construction in 1952.

Harbors.—There are ten harbors on the Pacific coast and twelve on the Gulf of Mexico. Of the former, Guaymas; Yavaros, Sonora; Mazatlán; Manzanillo; and Acapulco are natural harbors; on the east coast there is but one natural harbor: Ciudad del Carmen. The only breakwaters are at Veracruz, Tampico, Coatzacoalcos, and Salina Cruz.

The decreasing relative importance of sea and rail transport on the one hand and the increasing importance of air and highway transport on the other carries implications for Mexico's efforts to modernize and extend both fixed and mobile equipment. Coordination and integration of these systems depend on the skill with which government agencies estimate the services that each factor can render most effectively in relation to the needs of the national economy.

CARLOS R. BERZUNZA,
Colonel, Mexican Army; Professor of Geography, Universidad Nacional de México, Escuela Superior de Guerra, and Mexico City College.

MANUEL SÁNCHEZ SARTO,
Professor of Economics, Universidad Nacional de México; Head, Department of Economics, Mexico City College; Economic Adviser, Banco de México.

9. THE PRESS. The stormy history of Mexico during most of the 19th century is reflected in its journalism; political journalism was the order of the day, as were colorful names.

The first newspaper of consequence to be printed in Mexico was a *Gaceta de México* (*Mexico Gazette*), founded in 1805 by Juan Villaurrutia, a court judge, and suspended in the same year. However, a great number of pamphlets, leaflets, and journals were published soon after, under the freedom of the press briefly granted by the Spanish Constitution of 1812. Among the many publications circulating in Mexico at the time, the most outstanding were *El Pensador Mexicano* (*The Mexican Thinker*) published by Fernández de Lizardi and *El Juguetillo* (*The Plaything*) published by Carlos María Bustamante; both in Mexico City. In the same year, however, Viceroy Francisco Javier Venegas, under the pretext that the newspapers were abusing the liberty of the press granted under the constitution, suspended these and fourteen other publications. This resulted in a flood of illegal pamphlets and leaflets, which were distributed throughout Mexico.

The burning issue of the times was the independence of Mexico from Spain. Among the publications favoring independence in 1811–1812 were *El Despertador Mexicano* (*The Mexican Awakener*), published at Guadalajara as a result of Miguel Hidalgo's entry into that city; *El Ilustrador Mexicano* (*The Mexican Illustrator*), published at Zitácuaro by Andrés Quintana Roo; *El Despertador Michoacano* (*The Michoacano Awakener*), at Valladolid (now Morelia); *El Correo Americano del Sur* (*The South American Courier*) at Oaxaca, and *El Mexicano Independiente* (*The Mexican Independent*) published by José María Morelos at Iguala. The Spaniards countered by publishing the newspapers *El Fenix* (*The Phoenix*), *El Ateneo* (*The Athenaeum*), and *El Español* (*The Spaniard*); all at Mexico City, 1811–1812.

After the Independence.—After Agustín de Iturbide's army had entered Mexico City in 1821, Carlos María Bustamante published the *Avispa de Chilpancingo* (*Chilpancingo Wasp*), with other minor publications making their appearance. When Iturbide had proclaimed himself emperor the *Gaceta de México* mentioned above became the *Gaceta Imperial*. Iturbide suspended those newspapers which directed attacks against his government and it was not until his downfall in 1823 that newspaper publishing gained new force. In 1824 the Freemasons belonging to the Scottish rite, and conservative in policy, founded *El Águila Mexicana* (*The Mexican Eagle*), while those of the York rite, liberal in policy, founded *El Observador* (*The Observer*) in the same year, together with the *Correo de la Federación* (*Federation Courier*), and in 1825, the *Amigo del Pueblo* (*Friend of the People*). The advanced Liberals had founded the *Estrella Polar* (*Polar Star*) and *El Fantasma* (*The Phantom*) in 1824. The journals of this period were shortlived and were mostly political publications.

Santa Anna Period.—Although Antonio López de Santa Anna was as much opposed to the freedom of the press as his predecessors had been, a great many publications made their appearance under his government. In 1841 *El Siglo XIX* (*The 19th Century*), a most influential Liberal newspaper, made its appearance in Mexico City. Eleven other publications of a political or professional nature were also published during this period. The *El Monitor Constitucional* (*The Constitutional Monitor*), a publication of great influence and longevity, was first published in 1842. Its name was changed in 1844 to *El Monitor Republicano* (*The Republican Monitor*).

During the occupation by United States troops (1847–1848) two newspapers favoring them were published in the State of Veracruz. These were *El Boletín de Veracruz* (*The Veracruz Bulletin*) and the Xalapa (Jalapa) *Estrella Americana* (*American Star*). Opposed to the occupation were the Mexico City *El Eco del Comercio* (*The Echo of Commerce*) and *La Patria* (*The Nation*). After the occupation was ended, Santa Anna published *La Palanca* (*The Lever*), opposed to President Mariano Arista; and another newspaper, *El Universal* (*The Universal*), favoring a monarchy with a European ruler, made its entrance onto the journalistic stage. This newspaper was destroyed by an enraged mob on Aug. 13, 1855. *El Monitor Republicano,* which had ceased publication, now reappeared, and following Santa Anna's fall from power (1855) the *Heraldo Liberal* (*Liberal Herald*) was born. The struggle between the Liberal republican press and the Conservative press now reached its highest peak.

French Occupation, Maximilian's Empire, and Reform Period.—The cleavage between the Liberal and Conservative parties was greatly accentuated during this period and was reflected in the press. The following publications favoring the monarchy were published during Maximilian's reign (1864–1867): *La Monarquía* (*The Monarchy*); *L'Estafette* (*The Courier,* published in French); *La Patria,* no relation to that mentioned above; *La Sociedad* (*The Society*); *El Cronista* (*The Chronicler*); *El Espíritu del Pueblo* (*The Spirit of the People*); *El Franco-Mexicano* (*The Franco-Mexican*); *La Constitución Social* (*The Social Constitution*); *La Raza de México* (*The Mexican Race*); and others. Opposed to the monarchy were: *La Orquesta* (*The Orchestra*); *El Hijo del Ahuizote* (*The Son of the Ahuizote*); *La Sombra* (*The Shadow*); *La Cucaracha* (*The Cockroach*); *El Espejuelo del Diablo* (*The Devil's Mirror*); *El Clamor Progresista* (*The Progressive Clamor*); *El Año Nuevo* (*The New Year*); *La Voz del Pueblo* (*The Voice of the People*); and *El Payaso* (*The Clown*). Marshal Achille Bazaine, commander of the French forces, prohibited opposition journals from publishing in 1863; however, *El Payaso* and *El Hijo del Ahuizote* reappeared and continued in business up to the regime of Porfirio Díaz.

The administration (1867–1872) of President Benito Juárez was notable in that complete freedom of the press existed. A great number of periodicals were published during this period. His government was the subject of bitter attacks by the pro-Catholic press, namely *La Voz de México* (*The Voice of Mexico*) and *La Idea Católica* (*The Catholic Idea*), but in spite of this opposition they were permitted to continue functioning without interference from the government.

Porfirio Díaz Dictatorship.—The stability of the Díaz government (1876–1911) resulted in the creation of sound journals and journalistic principles. Many papers were opposed to the government, but there were also many which defended it. In 1896, Rafael Reyes Espindola (1860–1922) founded *El Imparcial* (*The Impartial*), the first Mexican daily to have a well-trained editorial and reportorial staff and the latest in printing presses. In 1906, with the growth of opposition to Díaz, *El Imparcial,* pro-Díaz, *El Popular,* slightly leftist, and *El País* (*The Country*), Catholic and pro-Díaz, vied for the public's favor.

Contemporary Journalism.—The end of the Porfirio Díaz dictatorship in 1911 marks the rise of modern Mexican journalism. Between the years 1910 and 1917 the most outstanding newspapers were: *El Antireeleccionista* (*The Anti-Reelectionist*), the most important of those defending the Constitutionalist revolution; *El Imparcial; El Debate* (*The Debate*), pro-Díaz; *El Nuevo México* (*The New Mexico*), anti-Díaz; *La Nueva Era* (*The New Era*), pro-Díaz; *El Mañana* (*Tomorrow*), anti-Madero; *La Tribuna* (*The Tribune*); and the anti-Díaz *El Mexicano* (*The Mexican*), *El Pueblo* (*The People*), and *El Universal.*

Excelsior was founded in 1917, as was *El Universal,* which papers were inspired by United States journalistic methods and editorial policies.

The approximate circulations of important Mexico City newspapers in 1953 were: *La Prensa* (*The Press*, tabloid) 119,300; *Excelsior,* 91,367; *El Universal,* 83,751; *Novedades* (*News*), 80,000; *Ultimas Noticias* (*Latest News;* noon and afternoon daily published by the *Excelsior*), 79,940; *El Universal Gráfico* (pictorial tabloid published by *El Universal*), 25,307; *El Nacional* (*The National,* government journal), 25,000; *El Popular* (official organ of the labor organization Confederación de Trabajadores Mexicanos), 12,000; and the sports daily *Esto* (*This*), 10,000. There is an English-language daily, *The News* (circulation 10,000), and an English section in the *Excelsior.* The *Journal Française du Mexique* (3,000), is the only French daily of consequence.

There are countless weekly magazines published in Mexico City, of which the most important are: *Todo* (*All*), approximate circulation in 1953, 30,000; *Revista de Revistas* (*Review of Reviews*), 25,000; *Hoy* (*Today*), 20,000; *Mañana* (*Tomorrow*), 20,000; and *Tiempo* (*Time*), 20,000, which in format closely resembles the *Time* magazine of the United States. A great variety of bullfighting periodicals, such as *Redondel* (30,000) and *Claridades* (21,500), are published weekly, with another group of periodicals dedicated to all the sports practiced in Mexico. In the provinces a great number of publications are published daily or weekly, rivaling in number those published in Mexico City. Of these the largest daily papers are *El Norte* of Monterrey, *Diario de Yucatán* of Mérida, and *El Informador* of Guadalajara. The García

Valseca newspaper chain publishes seventeen out-of-town newspapers.

Statistical Data.—The number of readers per copy in 1950 was 21.7, which places Mexico considerably below the United States and Great Britain. However, among the Spanish-speaking countries, Mexico occupies first place in readers per copy. In 1936 (the last year for which figures are available) the number of readers per daily was 23.1 per copy; weekly publications, 28.4 per copy; and monthlies, 24.8 per copy.

The total number of publications in Mexico in May 1952 was 1,515, of which 136 were dailies; 321 weeklies; 651 monthlies; others, 407. They may be divided by subject matter as follows: 841 general information (including 32 whose appearance was so irregular that they are not included in the foregoing); 208 religious; 184 technical scientific; 69 cultural; 44 literary; 43 political; 38 for children; 34 sports; 24 labor; and 62 miscellaneous. These figures show the progress that has been made in Mexico, and the evolutionary step taken from political journalism to informative journalism, a phenomenon which reflects the stability and coming of age of a country.

Bibliography.—Chávez Orozco, Luis, *Historia económica y social de México* (Mexico City 1938); Sierra, Justo, *Evolución política del pueblo mexicano* (Mexico City 1940); Palavicini, Félix, *México, historia de su evolución constructiva* (Mexico City 1945); Henestrosa, Andrés, and Fernández de Castro, José A., *Periodismo y periodistas de Hispano América* (Mexico City 1947).

NARCISO MOLINS FÁBREGA,
Journalist; Ethnologist, Escuela Nacional de Antropología.

10. GOVERNMENT. Government is the organism for the administration and realization of the aims of the state. In the case of the Aztecs, their government, as it was encountered by the Spaniards, had undergone considerable evolution since the first tribe settled on the site of Mexico City, then an island in Lake Texcoco (or Tetzcoco). In the first third of the 16th century the supreme political, judicial, administrative, and military authority was vested in the *tlacatecuhtli,* or *hueytlatoani,* who was elected by a council of four electors from the nobility. After the election of the first *hueytlatoani,* named Acamapichtli, however, this office was always bestowed upon his descendants. It thus appears that the Aztecs were governed by a single dynasty, the last of whom was Montezuma II.

To describe the colonial government would be to repeat the history of the viceroyalty (see the section *Spanish Conquest and Colony*).

During the Spanish domination Mexico was ruled by laws emanating from the Spanish crown. After its initial declaration of independence in 1810, New Spain was granted some concessions in the Spanish Constitution of 1812, which went into effect Sept. 28, 1812, but was suspended on December 5 following, and due to events in Spain was not again put into effect until 1820, only a year before Mexico achieved its independence.

Meanwhile, the Constitution of Apatzingán, abolishing slavery, had been promulgated by the Mexican insurgents on Oct. 22, 1814. Although it was never put into effect, this constitution is historically interesting, since it clearly states the concepts of the liberator, José María Morelos y Pavón, and his inner circle of followers, who established the organization of the country on a self-governing basis. It provided for universal suffrage, a congress which was to appoint a three-man executive, and a supreme court.

The independence of Mexico was achieved in 1821. Nevertheless, the new government was dominated by the landed gentry and the clergy for many years until the thorough-going reforms of the Constitution of 1857 were achieved.

On Feb. 24, 1821, the Plan of Iguala, considered the first Mexican constitution, was signed by Vicente Guerrero and Agustín de Iturbide, and the country was organized as a constitutional monarchy. After the overthrow of Iturbide's short-lived empire, a constitutional act of Jan. 31, 1824 reflecting various Anglo-American influences of the 18th century, was decreed and went into effect on October 4 of the same year, establishing a federal republic.

A movement toward a more centralized government took place on April 22, 1833, when a statement of basic principles was issued. These were the basis of the so-called Siete Leyes Constitucionales (Seven Constitutional Laws) of Dec. 29, 1836. This code was quite explicit with regard to individual rights, although it did not recognize freedom of religion, and organized a centralized republic, changing the states into departments. The Siete Leyes were later rejected by Antonio López de Santa Anna in his decree of June 12, 1843 (the so-called Bases Orgánicas), by which he virtually re-established the centralist organization of 1821. The federalist Constitution of 1824 was re-established, Aug. 22, 1846, to promote unity during the war with the United States.

The Plan of Ayutla, which led to the overthrow of Santa Anna in 1855, was proclaimed on March 10, 1854, and later modified at Acapulco. This federalist constitution contained a declaration of the rights of man and certain advanced ideas.

The Reform, or Constitution of 1857 (promulgated February 5), re-established the Constitution of 1824, but contained the germ of a truly liberal law creating the right of judicial protection (see *Legislation and Jurisprudence*).

In the Revolution of 1910, a violent uprising finally terminated the dictatorship of Gen. Porfirio Díaz, under which a wealthy minority oppressed the miserably poor masses. Venustiano Carranza convoked a constituent congress in Querétaro, which approved a new political constitution on Jan. 31, 1917. It was promulgated Feb. 5, 1917.

Constitution of 1917.—The Mexican government was established in the following forms:

(1) *Constitutional*, because it is governed by the Constitution of 1917, which is the fundamental charter and basis of its politico-administrative organization. This constitution establishes the other characteristics of the government.

(2) *Republican*, since the national sovereignty rests with the people, from whom are derived all public powers; they having at all times the right to reform or modify the form of their government.

(3) *Representative*, because the people, by means of organisms created by the constitution, exercise their control over the government.

(4) *Democratic*, for these powers are exercised by each and every Mexican citizen.

(5) *Federal*, for the nation is composed of states, internally free and sovereign political entities joined together by a federal pact, or constitution, which determines the relationship and powers of the federal and local governments.

(6) *Presidential*, because the president freely appoints his aides and cabinet ministers, and because of the independence which the latter enjoy in relation to the legislative chambers.

The government is exercised by federal and local authorities. The federal government is divided for its functions into legislative, executive, and judicial branches.

Legislative Branch.—This is divided into two houses. The Cámara de Diputados (House of Representatives) is composed of national constituent representatives (*diputados*), directly elected for three years, one for each 150,000 inhabitants or fraction over 75,000. Each representative has an elected alternate who takes his place in case of absence or death. In no case may there be less than two representatives for each state, nor less than one per territory. The election of July 6, 1952 named 160 representatives. The other house, the Cámara de Senadores (Senate), is composed of two members (*senadores*) from each state and two from the Federal District, also directly elected and replaced in their totality every six years. An alternate is also elected for each senator. Territories are not represented in the Senate.

Together the two houses compose the Congress of the Union. Their resolutions are called laws, if issued by the Congress, or decrees, if issued by the president when invested by the Congress with extraordinary powers. Their ordinary period of sessions is from September 1 to December 31, at the latest. During their recess there is a permanent congressional commission composed of 29 members (15 representatives and 14 senators).

Executive Branch.—The executive power is vested in a single individual, the president, who is selected by direct election for a term of six years beginning on December 1, and is not eligible for re-election. He must be Mexican by birth, the son of Mexicans by birth, at least 35 years old, and may not be a clergyman, nor have been in active military service for at least six months before election.

There is no vice president. If a vacancy occurs during the first three years of a presidential term, new elections are held; if it occurs during the last three years, Congress may elect a successor for the remainder of the term.

The Ley de Secretarías y Departamentos de Estado enumerates and distributes the administrative matters entrusted to each branch of the executive power. This law came into effect on Dec. 7, 1946; it was reformed on May 1, 1947. The following are the cabinet posts:

(1) Secretaries (heads of the *secretarías*) of: Gobernación (Interior); Relaciones Exteriores (Foreign Relations); Hacienda y Crédito Público (Treasury); Defensa Nacional (National Defense); Marina Nacional (Navy); Agricultura y Ganadería (Agriculture and Livestock); Comunicaciones y Obras Públicas (Communications and Public Works); Economía Nacional (National Economy); Educación Pública (Public Education); Salubridad y Asistencia (Health and Welfare); Trabajo y Previsión Social (Labor and Social Welfare); Recursos Hidráulicos (Hydraulic Resources); and Bienes Nacionales e Inspección Administrativa (National Properties and Administrative Inspection).

(2) Department chiefs (heads of the following *departamentos*): Agrario (Agrarian); Distrito Federal (Federal District); and Industria Militar (Military Industry).

(3) Presidential cabinet assistants: attorney general of the republic; district attorney of the Federal District and territories; and the governors of the territories.

Judicial Branch.—The judicial power is vested in the Supreme Court of the Nation, circuit courts, district courts, and the federal public minister, who is appointed by and subordinate to the attorney general of the republic. See also the section *Legislation and Jurisprudence*.

State and Territorial Governments.—The basic unit of state government is the free *municipio* (municipality) administered by its municipal council (*ayuntamiento*). The president of the *municipio* and the members of the *ayuntamiento* are directly elected by popular vote. There is no intermediate authority between the *municipios* and the state governments, consisting of a governor and a Cámara de Diputados, both directly elected by popular vote. The governors' terms are limited to six years by federal law, and neither they, nor the members of the legislatures, nor the officials of the *municipios* may be immediately re-elected, without an intervening term. The state officials are appointed by the governors.

The *municipio* is also the basis of government in the territories. Governors of territories are named by the president of the republic, and they name the other officials. There are no territorial legislatures.

CARLOS R. BERZUNZA,
Colonel, Mexican Army; Professor of Geography, Universidad Nacional de México, Escuela Superior de Guerra, and Mexico City College.

11. POLITICAL PARTIES.

11. POLITICAL PARTIES. The political struggles of Mexico after independence was achieved in 1821 took place between two ill-defined groups loosely labeled Conservatives and Liberals. The Conservatives were the party of the professional soldiers, the church, and the large landowners—in other words, the group which had inherited the economic and political power of the colonial period. The Liberals were the party of the middle class, the merchants, the nascent industrialists, and toward the end of the century, the industrial workers. The peasant group was largely controlled by the church and therefore cannot be considered as belonging to the Liberal group.

With minor interruptions, the Conservatives ruled the country from independence until the overthrow of Antonio López de Santa Anna by the Liberals in 1855. The Liberals then embarked on a program of reform which culminated in the Reform Laws (Leyes de la Reforma) of 1859–1860, decreed by Benito Juárez, which destroyed the economic power of the church by breaking up its extensive land holdings. The Conservatives, furthermore, were compromised in the unsuccessful scheme of Napoleon III to set Maximilian on the throne of Mexico. The long dictatorship (1884–1911) of Porfirio Díaz was thus born under the auspices of a Liberal victory.

The 20th Century.—Peace reigned throughout Mexico under Díaz. This was a period of material progress, railway construction, and industrial growth, but it weighed heavily on the peasants and workers. The political, military, and peasant rebellions, which appeared during the period, continued through the Revolution of 1910 up to the revolt of Gen. Saturnino Cedillo in 1938 during the presidency of Lázaro Cárdenas.

The Díaz period saw the emergence of new political parties, based on opposition to or support of the regime. San Luis Potosí was the birthplace (in 1901) of the anti-Díaz Club Liberal (Liberal Club), while in Mexico City the Asociación Liberal Reformista (Liberal Reformist Association) made its appearance. In 1908 both the pro-Díaz Club Reeleccionista (Re-electionist Club) and the group known as the *Científicos* ("Scientists") were formed, with definite despotic tendencies; in the same year the Partido Liberal de la Oposición (Liberal Opposition Party) emerged, and supported Francisco Madero against Díaz in the elections of 1910. Although Díaz was declared elected, the Partido Constitucional Progresista (Constitutional Progressive Party), also opposed to the re-election of Díaz, which would have meant a continuation of the dictatorship, carried Madero to power, with the aid of revolts by Pascual Orozco and Francisco Villa in the north in 1910, and by Emiliano Zapata in the south in 1911. Both rebellions, however, were peasant uprisings and did not accept revolutionary guidance from the cities.

Party labels had little meaning in the chaotic period which followed. Madero was assassinated by Victoriano Huerta, who assumed the presidency, 1913–1914. Venustiano Carranza drove Huerta from office, his regime lasting until 1920 when he was overthrown, and elections were held. Gen. Alvaro Obregón was elected president with the support of the Partido Laborista Mexicano (Mexican Labor Party), founded by the labor leader Luis Morones. It is interesting to note that the Partido Comunista de México (Communist Party of Mexico) was founded in 1922

In 1924 Plutarco Elías Calles was elected president. In 1929 he founded the Partido Nacional Revolucionario (or PNR; National Revolutionary Party) as the official government party. The PNR has continued in existence, under various names, up to the present period. This political organization is a conglomeration of individual adherents, groups of varying political interests, and labor unions—all interested in maintaining the party in power. The army, which until 1914 had been a support of the conservatives, has become the supporter of constitutional rights and guardian of the conquests of the revolution.

During President Calles' term the Ley de Cultos was passed. This law was a definite blow at the church, and gave rise to the *Cristero* (Christist) revolt which began in 1927 and lasted up to President Portes Gil's regime in 1929. Gen. Lázaro Cárdenas, who gained wide popularity with the peasants and received the political support of the labor union Confederación de Trabajadores Mexicanos, in 1938 changed the name of the PNR to Partido de la Revolución Mexicana (PRM; Party of the Mexican Revolution), which launched as its candidate for the presidency in 1940 Gen. Manuel Ávila Camacho, who defeated Gen. Juan Andreu Almazan. General Almazan's Partido Revolucionario de Unificación Nacional (National Revolutionary Unification Party) was backed by groups similar to those which comprised the PRM.

President Avila Camacho in 1946 changed the name of the official party to Partido Revolucionario Institucional (PRI; Revolutionary Institutional Party) which presented Miguel Alemán as its candidate for the presidency in the elections of that year. Alemán, the first civilian president after a long series of revolutionary generals, defeated Ezequiel Padilla by a vote announced as 1,800,829 to 431,487. Padilla was supported by the Partido Democrático Mexicano (Mexican Democratic Party), which was formed by dissident right-wing elements of the PRI.

The Revolutionary Institutional Party has continued to dominate Mexican politics. In the 1952 elections, Adolfo Ruiz Cortines, the PRI candidate, won a sweeping victory over the candidates of the opposition parties. The 1958 elections likewise resulted in a landslide victory for the PRI candidate, Adolfo López Mateos. In 1964 the party's candidate, Gustavo Díaz Ordaz, won about 90 percent of the popular vote. The PRI also captured about 90 percent of the seats in the lower chamber of the legislature. The chief opposition parties are the Partido Acción Nacional (PAN), a conservative pro-Catholic party founded in 1939; the Partido Popular Socialista (PPS), a Marxist group founded in 1948; the Partido Nacionalista de Mexico, a nationalist and pro-Catholic party founded in 1946; and the Partido Auténtico de la Revolución Mexicana (PARM).

Consult Sierra, Justo, *Evolución política del pueblo mexicano* (Mexico City 1940); also the declarations of various parties—Partido Nacional Revolucionario, *Constitución* (Mexico City 1934); Partido de la Revolución Mexicana, *Declaración de principios, programa y estatutos* (Mexico City 1938); Partido de Acción Nacional, *Declaración de principios* (Mexico City 1940); Partido Popular, *Razón histórica, principios, programa y estatutos* (Mexico City 1948); Partido Revolucionario Institucional, *Declaración de principios, programa y estatutos* (Mexico City 1950).

NARCISO MOLINS FÁBREGA,
Journalist; Ethnologist, Escuela Nacional de Antropología.

12. LEGISLATION AND JURISPRU-
DENCE. Although Mexico had every intention of modifying its constitutional law upon achieving its independence in 1821, a large part of Spanish law, which had been in force during the colonial period, was in fact preserved for many years. It had been variously codified and was used throughout the Spanish Empire and in the laws of the Indies, applicable to New Spain (Mexico) and other colonies. Therefore, Mexico belongs by legal tradition to the system of civil law, not of common law.

CONSTITUTIONAL AND ADMINISTRATIVE LAW

The first documents of Mexican public law were three documents of 1821, the Plan of Iguala (February 24), signed by Agustín de Iturbide and Vicente Guerrero, the Convention (or Treaty) of Córdoba (August 24) signed by Iturbide and Viceroy Juan O'Donojú, but not ratified by Spain, and the Act of Independence (September 28) signed by the governing junta, which tended to organize the new state as a monarchy; and, after the fall of the ephemeral empire of Iturbide, the liberator of Mexico, the Constitution of 1824. The constitution, which had been inspired mainly by the United States model and showed some influence of the Spanish Constitution of 1812, founded a democratic, representative, federal republic. This gave rise to a long-standing conflict between monarchists and centralists, those who favored a unitarian, not federal, government, on one side, and republicans and federalists on the other.

Following the trends of this struggle, the Siete Leyes Constitucionales (Seven Constitutional Laws) of 1836 and the Bases Orgánicas (Organic Bases) of 1843, both of which were constitutional changes, marked a return to republican centralization, and the decision of the Junta de Notables (Assembly of Notables) of 1863, a return to monarchic centralization under Maximilian of Austria. On the other hand the Acta de Reformas (Reform Act, amendments to the Constitution of 1824) drawn up in 1847, and the Constitution of 1857 insisted on a federal republic. This prevailed in the end, after the execution of the Emperor Maximilian in 1867.

Constitution of 1917.—The Revolution of 1910, which put an end to the regime of Gen. Porfirio Díaz, led to the proclamation of the Constitution of 1917. This turned out to be a revision of the one of 1857, and curbed the latter's excessive individualism, having very definite social tendencies, especially as regards certain public rights (such as freedom of commerce), the right to own land, and industrial relations. This constitution, which is still in force, although it has undergone various reforms, upheld a republican government which is democratic, representative, and federal, with a threefold division of power (executive, judicial, and legislative), and a presidential system. The federal authority has no power other than that granted by the constitution, since all other power is understood to be the prerogative of the member states of the federation. Nevertheless, it sets forth the principles to be observed by the various state constitutions in the organization of their governments, which must be democratic, representative, with a division of power, and have as the basis of political and administrative division the free *municipio* (municipality).

The constitution includes a chapter declaring fundamental public rights (limitations to the activities of public power), in which are named various individual guarantees. It is of a rigid type: the approval of two thirds of the members of both houses of the federal Congress, as well as of a majority of the legislative councils of the states of the union, is needed for any change in its provisions.

Legislature and Executive.—The Congress of the Union, made up of two chambers (Representatives and Senators), whose members are elected by popular vote, is vested with the legislative power. Apart from having the powers usually vested in a federal legislative body, it may also legislate on such matters as education, commerce, labor, mining, and on everything concerned with the territories and the Federal District, which is the residence of federal power and includes Mexico City. The president of the republic, who is elected by direct universal suffrage, is the head of the executive administration; he appoints and discharges the members of his cabinet, and he alone can issue directives for the enactment of and compliance with the law. (See also the section *Government*.)

Judiciary.—The federal judicial power is vested in the district judges (*jueces de distrito*), circuit courts (*tribunales de circuito*), and the Suprema Corte de Justicia de la Nación (Supreme Court). Their principal function is to watch over adherence to the constitution through the traditional *juicio de amparo* (judgment of protection), the most valuable and useful creation of Mexican law, the object of which is to repeal, on the petition of the interested party and only in so far as concerns the individual in his particular case, the ruling of any authority, executive, legislative, or judicial, state or federal, which may be against the constitution because of a violation of fundamental public rights guaranteed by the constitution, or because a federal ruling encroaches on the prerogatives of the states, or a state ruling encroaches on federal prerogatives. Any precedents set in five rulings of the Supreme Court in five similar cases are considered binding on the courts of the whole republic, except for the Supreme Court itself, which may alter later decisions, explaining whatever reasons it may have for such action.

Social Provisions.—Constitutional provisions relating to real property, trade, and industrial relations have been the source of numerous laws supplementing the principles of the constitution, such as the Ley sobre Monopolios (Monopoly Law) of 1931, Ley Federal del Trabajo (Federal Labor Law) of 1933, Código Agrario (Agrarian Code) of 1934, Ley del Seguro Social (Social Security Law) of 1943, and Ley de Facultades del Ejecutivo en Materia Económica (Law of the Powers of the Executive in Economic Matters) of 1950. The inclusion of these provisions in the constitution is explained by the desire of the constituent power that came from the revolution to make them prevail over changes of government.

Private property is guaranteed, and may be expropriated only by reason of public utility and with indemnity. But the state may impose on property such limits and regulations as are compatible with the public interest, and it may control the exploitation of those natural resources (such as minerals) susceptible of appropriation, in order to achieve a fair distribution of public wealth and its conservation. To this end, and in order to solve the agrarian problem, the state may order large estates to be broken up, may foster the development of small agrarian properties, and may create new centers of agricultural population. Agrarian legislation is directed mainly to restoring to villages the communal water and land of which they were deprived in the past, and to providing them for communities that do not already possess them, taking them from neighboring property, but without harming the small units already in existence. Such land is subject to special provisions which aim at full private property. Apart from this, the nation is the sole owner of all mineral deposits and, except for petroleum, may grant the rights of exploitation to private persons. Petroleum is exploited exclusively by a state enterprise, Petróleos Mexicanos, an autonomous organization commonly known as Pemex.

As regards commerce, monopolies are forbidden, as well as exclusive control of essential goods, anything that may interfere with free competition in manufacturing or commerce, any action aimed at raising prices, and generally anything intended to give exclusive or undue advantage to one or several persons, to the detriment of the general public or of a particular social class. In the exercise of this principle the law allows the setting of ceiling prices for goods considered as essential, compulsory sales, and even in some cases the control of sources of production. At the same time, official organizations have been set up to compete in inland and international trade. These enjoy special privileges and franchises not granted private tradesmen.

As regards labor, workers are protected with respect to working hours, place of work, minimum wages, holidays, and unjustified dismissal, and are provided with social security against sickness of the worker or his family, invalidism, unemployment, old age, and with death benefits. These are brought about through individual, collective, or industrial contracts, which may never be lower than the minimum advantages which the law grants labor. Minors and women workers are also protected, and the right to strike or stop work for causes specified by law is granted. There are special tribunals to try labor conflicts, and their decisions are binding. See also the section *Economic, Industrial, Agricultural, and Financial Factors* (Modern Economic Policy).

CIVIL LAW

Until 1870 Mexican civil law was essentially the same as Spanish civil law, which was in force when independence was declared (1821). The Código Civil para el Distrito y Territorios Federales (Civil Code for the Federal District and Territories) was published in 1370, and this was soon replaced by another in 1884, which was in turn replaced by that in force, which dates back to 1932. The states have always adopted for their own use, with slight variations, the Civil Code for the Federal District. This code belongs to the group known as the Napoleonic codes, although it has been influenced by Spanish and Argentine civil legislation, and by the Swiss Code of Obligation. It controls family relations, succession, property, possessions, *derechos reales* (such as mortgages and easements), obligations, and contracts. Together with the recognition of the right to private property and the autonomy of will in contracts, a marked tendency toward the protection of social interests can be observed, get-

ting away from the individualism of the code of 1884.

Commercial Codes.—Spanish law concerning trading matters was also accepted in its greater part until the Código de Comercio (Code of Commerce), applicable throughout the republic, was written in 1884. A new Code of Commerce was published in 1889. Both were along the lines of codes of the Latin countries of Europe, that is to say, Spain, France, Italy, and Portugal. The Code of 1889, however, is now valid only in certain fields, such as general trading operations, maritime commerce, and mercantile lawsuits, since, while awaiting the issuance of a new code, several laws have been passed which replace some of its chapters. The most important of these laws are the laws on: Títulos y Operaciones de Crédito (Securities and Credit Transactions) of 1932; Sociedades Mercantiles (Corporations) of 1934; Contrato de Seguro (Insurance Contracts) of 1935; Instituciones de Seguro (Insurance Concerns) of 1935; two measures relating to national financial institutions, Nacional Financiera (1940) and Banco de México (1941); Instituciones de Crédito y Organizaciones Auxiliares (Banking Institutions and Auxiliary Organizations) of 1941; Quiebras y Suspensión de Pagos (Bankruptcy and Suspension of Payments) of 1943; (and Instituciones de Fianzas (Bonding Companies) of 1950. It cannot be said that this new mercantile legislation follows a definite school, but Italian influence is predominant.

Penal Codes.—Excepting occasional decrees mainly of a political character, Spanish penal law continued to be applied in Mexico until the first Código Penal para el Distrito y Territorios Federales (Penal Code for the Federal District and Territories) was published in 1871. It followed the theories of the classical school and, as regards procedure, adhered to the fundamental rights of the defendant, clearly set out in the declaration of rights of the Constitution of 1857. This code remained in force until 1929, when it was replaced by the Código Penal and the Código de Procedimientos Penales (Code of Penal Procedure), which followed the most modern theories of the time. As these were found difficult to execute in the Mexican environment, they were in turn abrogated and replaced in 1931 by codes having the same names. The codes of 1931, also based on new ideas concerning penal matters, but of an eclectic nature, are more practical and have survived with practically no change. The states have largely adopted the penal legislation of the Federal District.

Summing up, it can be said that Mexico enjoys legislation that is modern in every branch, but is relatively unsettled because of the special political, social, and economic conditions of a country which is in the process of development and which has not yet worked out a system that may be called fully its own, fitting its particular idiosyncrasy.

Bibliography.—Macedo, Miguel S., *Datos para el estudio del nuevo código civil del Distrito Federal* (Mexico City 1884); Pallares, Jacinto, *Curso completo del derecho mexicano* (Mexico City 1901); Rabasa, Emilio, *La constitución y la dictadura* (Mexico City 1912); id., *El juicio constitucional* (Mexico City 1919); Macedo, Miguel S., *Apuntes para la historia del derecho penal mexicano* (Mexico City 1931); García Téllez, Ignacio, *Motivos, colaboración y concordancias del nuevo código civil mexicano* (Mexico City 1932); Ceniceros, J. A., and Garrido, J. L., *La ley penal mexicana* (Mexico City 1934); Wheless, Joseph, ed. and tr., *Compendium of the Laws of Mexico* (St. Louis 1938); Borja Soriano, Manuel, *Teoría general* *de las obligaciones,* 2 vols. (Mexico City 1939); Fernández del Castillo, Germán, *La propiedad y la expropiación en el derecho mexicano actual* (Mexico City 1939); Tena, Felipe de J., *Derecho mercantil mexicano,* 2 vols. (Mexico City 1938–39); Gómiz, José, and Muñoz, Luis, *Elemento de derecho civil mexicano* (Mexico City 1942); Escuela Libre de Derecho, *Evolución del derecho mexicano; 1912–1942,* 2 vols. (Mexico City 1943); Esquivel Obregón, Toribio, *Apuntes para la historia del derecho en México,* 3 vols. (Mexico City 1937–43); Fraga, Gabino, *Derecho administrativo* (Mexico City 1948); De la Cueva, Mario, *Derecho del trabajo* (Mexico City 1949); Schoenrich, Otto, tr., *Civil Code for the Federal District and Territories of Mexico, and the Mexican Laws on Alien Landownership* (New York 1950).

DAVID CASARES NICOLÍN,
Professor of the General Theory of the State, Escuela Libre de Derecho, Mexico City.

13. NATIONAL DEFENSE.

The armed forces of Mexico, as well as the whole country, have undergone a radical evolution, in accordance with advances throughout the world after World War II. The Secretaría de la Defensa Nacional (Department of National Defense) and the Secretaría de la Marina Nacional (Department of the Navy) were created on Dec. 1, 1940. These agencies had previously been joined together, under the title of the Secretaría de Guerra y Marina (Department of War and Navy).

Navy.—The Department of the Navy includes not only the fleet but also the merchant marine, and the bureaus of Obras Marítimas (Maritime Works), Dragado (Dredging), and Faros (Lighthouses) which previously belonged to the Secretaría de Comunicaciones y Obras Públicas (Department of Communications and Public Works), as well as the Departamento de Pesca (Bureau of Fishing), which had formed part of the autonomous Departamento de Caza y Pesca (Department of Hunting and Fishing). Thus, everything relating to the sea has been brought under the control of one department of the government.

The navy constructs its own lighthouses. On July 24, 1951, the port works of Mazatlán were completed, permitting the entry of ships drawing 24 feet of water. A dry dock functions at Salina Cruz, Oaxaca, for ships of 20,000 tons displacement, and another for 10,000-ton ships is in service at San Juan de Ulúa, in the port of Veracruz.

There are eight naval zone headquarters. On the Gulf of Mexico are the First, at Tampico; Third, at Veracruz; Fifth, at Carmen; and Seventh, at Mujeres Island. On the Pacific are the Second, at Margarita Island; Fourth, at Guaymas; Sixth, at Manzanillo; and Eighth, at Acapulco.

The naval academy, Heróica Escuela Naval Militar, formerly in the city of Veracruz, is at Antón Lizardo, Veracruz, in buildings completed in 1952. These are also the site of the Naval War College. The instruction imparted at the naval academy is considered among the best in the world in its field. There are also a naval aviation school at Veracruz and a school for sailors at Mazatlán. For the merchant marine, the Fernando Siliceo Nautical School at Veracruz is provided by the Department of the Navy.

The naval units are: 4 frigates, 3 gunboat-transports, 1 transport, 21 coast patrol craft, 4 auxiliary coast patrol craft, and 2 auxiliary ships. There is one marine battalion, and marine detachments, in each naval zone. The navy has about 8,000 men.

Army.—The army and its air force have achieved a notable progress in the years since 1940. The army takes considerable pride in its origins during the Revolution of 1910. By modern standards, its training and discipline place it among the best in Latin America. New officers for the army are procured from the graduates of the military academy, Heróico Colegio Militar, at Popotla, Federal District. There are also the following service schools: engineer, medical, signal, cavalry, noncommissioned officers, male nurses, nurses, and the Escuela Superior de Guerra (War College) in Mexico City; the latter being the highest level of studies in the army.

The regular army units are: 1 infantry division, 1 mechanized brigade, 1 mechanized cavalry regiment, 1 mixed brigade of presidential guards, 51 infantry battalions, 20 cavalry regiments, 2 artillery regiments, 3 independent artillery companies, 1 coast artillery battery, 2 battalions of combat engineers, 1 radar observation company, 1 signal battalion, and 1 quartermaster battalion. The corps of engineers is divided territorially into 8 engineer districts. The army and air force number about 60,000 men, exclusive of those called to the colors under the national military training program.

There is a central military hospital, modern in every respect, and an isolation hospital, both located in the capital, and six other military hospitals distributed throughout the republic. Mexican military surgeons enjoy great professional prestige.

Air Force.—This arm is part of the army, but has its own tradition—not only because the 201st Fighter Squadron fought on the Pacific front in World War II with the forces of the United States and other Allied nations, but also because Mexican pilots were the first to drop aerial bombs on warships, in 1913 during the revolution. It is composed of: 4 groups, 1 training group, 10 separate squadrons, and 1 battalion of paratroopers. Schools operated are the military flying school at Guadalajara; and the meteorology school, aviation mechanics school, and the parachutist school company at Mexico City.

National Military Service.—On Aug. 20, 1940 universal military training was commenced, obligating all 18-year-old youths to receive one year of basic training in the army. The draftees are organized under reserve officers into 43 infantry divisions, each of 3 regiments, plus 8 nondivisional regiments, all distributed according to population throughout the nation.

Military Territorial Divisions.—By a presidential decree of Feb. 20, 1952, the national territory was reorganized and divided into nine military regions (later one more was added), each commanded by a lieutenant general. Thus the 32 military zones, previously the base of territorial division, were subordinated to the respective regional headquarters, located as follows: the First, at Mexico City; Second, at Veracruz; Third, at Mérida, Yucatán; Fourth, at Ixtepec, Oaxaca; Fifth, at Guadalajara; Sixth, at Tijuana, Lower California; Seventh, at Hermosillo, Sonora; Eighth, at Torreón, Coahuila; Ninth, at Monterrey; and Tenth, at Irapuato, Guanajuato.

Military Industry.—On May 1, 1947 the Law of Secretariats and Departments of State was revised, creating the Departamento de la Industria Militar. This cabinet department is charged with the operation of the munitions and arms factories which supply the national armed forces.

CARLOS R. BERZUNZA,
Colonel, Mexican Army; Professor of Geography, Universidad Nacional de México, Escuela Superior de Guerra, and Mexico City College.

14. EDUCATION. Pre-Hispanic.

When the Spaniards led by Hernán Cortés conquered Mexico, they encountered among the natives a fairly well-organized system of education. The education of the Maya and Aztec populations may serve as typical examples, although they are not the only Indian educational systems that might be mentioned.

Mayan education, which like science, was entrusted to their priests, was the medium through which religion and scientific learning were transferred to new generations. It is known that these learned men achieved a notable exactitude in astronomy and mathematics, and that their literary, architectural, and artistic achievements in general were of a high order. None of this could have been accomplished without an organized and efficient educational system.

Among the Aztecs, infant education was under the care of the parents, who were charged with responsibility for the physical development of their children, in conformance with a plan which indicated even the quantity of food that should be given to children and the exercises and tasks that gradually were to be entrusted to them.

The education of the Aztec people was imparted in three types of schools: the *calmecac,* the *telpochcalli,* and the *cuicalco*. The *calmecac,* joined to the great temple of the Aztec capital, Tenochtitlan, was a school for the children of both sexes of noble families, priests, military chiefs, and merchants. The education given in the *calmecac* was oriented toward the formation of public officials of the state, the priesthood, and the upper hierarchies of the army. The youths studied there from the time they were 15 until they became 22. Young girls studied in accordance with their own program appropriate to the social function of their sex, and remained in the *calmecac* completely separated from the males and under the care of instructors. The studies in the *calmecac* embraced astronomy, cosmogony, reading of the calendars, arithmetic, singing, dancing, civil and penal procedures, and military instruction.

The *telpochcalli* was an academy of the popular type; there being one in each section of the city of Tenochtitlan. At the age of 15, the sons of farmers and artisans entered these schools, remaining in them until they were 22. The teaching was oriented toward the formation of good soldiers and army officers. It consisted, fundamentally, in a gradual series of severe physical exercises to keep the students healthy and to make them strong. Knowledge of use of arms and training for combat were also taught; the latter included practice in real battles under the direction of an experienced chieftain. The excellence acquired in these practices was rewarded by distinctions which gave the young man the right to use insignia and to hold military rank. These aided the man ultimately in his entry into the army.

The *cuicalco* was a kind of general school where all the other young people of both sexes were concentrated to learn songs, dances, and religious rites under the direction of priests and matrons.

In general, Aztec education exalted the warlike virtues, respect for parents and hierarchical superiors, the cultivation of a rigid morality, the formation of religious feeling, and love of country.

Colonial.—Once the Indian peoples had been subjugated, the conquerors showed an inexorable determination to destroy the cultural institutions of the conquered. This determination is explained as a means of preventing a political and social resurgence of the conquered peoples and as a method of imposing the Catholic religion, whose propagation had been the moral justification of the conquest. As the Mexican education was intimately connected with the old religion and as it was directed toward the formation of a haughty and aggressive spirit, it was logically the target of the intolerance of the dominators.

The various religious orders that were coming to the colony founded schools in the various cities and monopolized education during the entire colonial epoch.

The new education, established in the country during the three centuries in which it was called Nueva España (New Spain), had well-distinguished characteristics. The first objectives, as far as the education of the people in general was concerned, were those of instructing them for conversion to Catholicism and imposing on them feelings of subjection toward the new social hierarchy and of resignation with respect to their destiny.

Experiments in Indian Education.—In 1536 Fray Juan de Zumárraga (1468–1548), later to become the first bishop of Mexico, with the aid of the first viceroy, Antonio de Mendoza, founded the Imperial Colegio de Santa Cruz de Tlatelolco, just north of Mexico City, dedicated exclusively to the education of Indian children. In the beginning, this school imparted elementary and advanced studies; later it was limited merely to advanced education, and it finally became an elementary school.

The children were taught in their own language, Nahuatl, and their instruction was directed by such eminent men as Fray Bernardino de Sahagún (1499?–1590). The school proposed that the Indians instructed in it be converted into missionaries of the Catholic faith and given the responsibility of going out to convert their own peoples.

Santa Cruz de Tlatelolco had such amazing success that notable Indians imbued with the humanistic spirit left its lecture halls to become teachers of the Spaniards themselves, and eventually they opened their own way to positions as mayors and governors in the colony.

But while progressive and generous spirits existed in the colony, there were many intolerant and distrustful persons in leading posts. The latter became alarmed at the success of Santa Cruz de Tlatelolco and began a decided policy of hostility against the school, until in 1595 they were successful in reducing it to an elementary institution. Its brief existence was nevertheless sufficient to demonstrate graphically the great possibilities of the native population.

In 1540, Vasco de Quiroga (1470–1565), first bishop of Michoacán, founded the Colegio de San Nicolás Obispo, in Pátzcuaro, dedicated to the Indians. In this school also, the teachers spoke to the children in the language of their fathers, Tarascan, because, as Bishop Quiroga said, this was the only bridge over which he could reach the brain and the heart of the Indians. The teaching of subjects was organized around practical activities. The children practiced agriculture for certain hours; in others, the apprenticeship of crafts. These crafts were those which the great educator felt would best take advantage of the native artisan tradition then extant, the available raw materials, the new experiences that his European culture had brought, and the great artistic aptitudes of his students.

The experiment of Vasco de Quiroga had such a powerful effect and left such a deep impression that, after four centuries, his deeds still live in the minds of his people. Nor have they forgotten the artistic crafts he taught; even today their work attracts the admiration of both Mexicans and foreigners.

University of Mexico.—In 1539, Fray Bartolomé de las Casas assumed the initiative for the creation of a university in Mexico City and took the plan to Emperor Charles V, who in 1551, ordered the foundation of the Real y Pontificia Universidad de México (Royal and Pontifical University of Mexico), granting it the same privileges that were enjoyed by the University of Salamanca, Spain, and a subsidy for its maintenance. It opened its doors in 1553, and the pope confirmed the foundation and privileges in 1555. Thus was born the greatest institution of higher learning in the country, now called, in full, the Universidad Nacional Autónoma de México (National Autonomous University of Mexico). The National University and the University of San Marcos in Lima, Peru, are thus the oldest universities in the Americas.

The 19th Century.—With the consummation of independence in 1821, and for many years thereafter, education underwent practically no alteration, but eventually criticism against a system of education that was monopolized by the clergy and that retained medieval methods of teaching brought on a vigorous change. José María Luis Mora (1794–1850) and Valentín Gómez Farías (1781–1858) were among the ideologists of the new movement.

Gómez Farías became president of the republic in 1833 and immediately initiated an educational reform. A commission, whose duty it was to study the condition in which the centers of education were maintained, in order to propose reforms, found that the University of Mexico was a "useless, unreformable, and pernicious institution."

Until the Liberal triumph in 1865, education was a field in which incidents in the conflict between Liberals and Conservatives were well reflected. The latter were the partisans of a regime of privilege and intolerance in behalf of the Catholic Church and of a social order similar to that of the colony. The Liberals, on the other hand, aspired to a regime of religous tolerance, to the separation of church and state, and to a democratic political organization within a federal system.

While schools supported by the church declined, the Lancasterian Company, which operated through private initiative and with a government subsidy, handled the most important field of study, primary education. The success of the Lancasterian schools, organized in conformity with the ideas of the English educator Joseph Lancaster (for which see LANCASTERIAN SCHOOLS), dominated this field from 1822 to 1890.

In 1865 the Liberals, led by Benito Juárez, triumphed definitively and initiated the reorganization of education. The University of Mexico, which had been closed three times (1833, 1857, and 1861) and reestablished each time, was finally closed in 1865, since it was considered a center of the reactionary mentality; its doors remaining shut until 1910.

Higher education was established in separate professional schools, with the Escuela Nacional Preparatoria (National Preparatory School) as a common basis. The latter school, founded in 1867, taught teaching methods and prepared persons for entry into the professional schools. Its organization, the work of Dr. Gabino Barreda (1818–1881), was founded on the positivistic philosophy of Auguste Comte. It gave special preference to the teaching of the sciences and eliminated all religious or dogmatic teaching; scientific, positive, and demonstrable truth being considered valid against all types of speculative science. The plan of studies followed the order of the Comtian law of the historical appearance of the sciences: mathematics, astronomy, physics, chemistry, biology, and sociology.

To end the influence of the clergy through the educational activities of the priests, normal schools were founded, and the professional teacher, with a specialized preparation, then appeared. From that time, normal schools prepared lay teachers with Liberal views and ideas. Those who directed this movement with notable competence were: Enrique C. Rébsamen (1857–1904), of Swiss origin; Enrique Laubscher, who in 1883 founded the first kindergarten in Mexico; and Carlos A. Carrillo (1855–1903). The educational method in vogue, called the intuitive method, consisted in putting the child in direct contact with things and nature instead of telling him about them. Justo Sierra (1848–1912), undersecretary of justice and public instruction under the regime of Gen. Porfirio Díaz, was the representative of the government in educational matters.

New Education.—By 1920 the revolution which had put an end to the Díaz dictatorship had consolidated its triumph, and in 1921 the Secretaría de Educación Pública y Bellas Artes (Department of Public Education and Fine Arts) was created. It was charged with the development of educational programs and served as an organ of the federal government.

The situation that the new regime immediately encountered may be summed up: (1) a great amount of popular ignorance, with an illiteracy rate of 66 per cent; and (2) a standardized pedagogic organization imported from urban Europe, without adaptation to the necessities and characteristics of Mexico, where a large group of the population is rural.

Government-sponsored education and the educational methods adopted were a reaction against this state of affairs. The government increased, in proportions without precedent, its budgets for education—in 1921 it was four times larger than in 1920 (when it was 2,218,165 pesos); in 1922 it was 13 times larger, and in 1923 it became 15 times larger than in the initial year.

Illiteracy.—To instruct the illiterate adult population, anti-illiteracy (*desanalfabetización*) campaigns were organized and night schools were created. As a result of these efforts, the proportion of adult illiteracy has been steadily reduced—from 70 per cent in 1910, to 66 per cent in 1921; to 59 per cent in 1930; to 47.8 per cent in 1940, and to 35 per cent in 1960.

Rural Schools.—Special schools were created for the rural population, beginning with 85 in 1922. The rural school was defined in 1926 as a school in which it was proposed: (1) to better the conditions of life in the community by teaching better methods of work; (2) to teach less within classrooms and more outside in the community; and (3) to teach a practical program, the knowledge to be learned to be selected according to the necessities of communal life and to be acquired in the course of managed activities to satisfy rural needs. It is not merely a rudimentary education, but a special kind of education for country people, and includes all grades from the lowest to the highest. The aim was to create a secondary educational system, and later to add a higher education. The rural schools were very successful and grew rapidly from practically nothing. In 1949 there were already 18,840 spread throughout the country.

To prepare a teaching personnel adequate for the rural schools, regional normal schools were founded; however, these were unable to produce teachers in proportion to the number of schools that were being created, and many persons without previous preparation had to be accepted. To prepare the latter group, the Instituto Federal de Capacitación was created in 1945. Their needs are being met by means of a combination of courses by mail, and short, intensive periods of study in classes.

Cultural Missions.—The *misiones culturales* were created in 1923 with a view to reducing the differences in conditions of life between city and country. Various specialists, such as agronomists, hygienists, social workers, technicians, and others, under the direction of a normal school teacher, went to the more distant and undeveloped places, which they themselves chose. There they developed programs for the improvement of economic and social life in the community, working with the citizens. The latter, upon cooperating in the program for their own betterment, learned superior methods of work and life, whose value is lasting.

Indian Education.—Indian education is focused in a special manner, since at an early date the conviction was reached that the imposition of the Spanish language on the Indian population, which speaks a variety of tongues, is not an adequate way to educate the Indian, because it produces resistances, and stumbles upon other difficulties that neutralize the effort. On the other hand, it is much easier to impart useful, scientific, and technical knowledge in the mother tongue, achieving an immediate educational influence, while at the same time opening an accessible and interesting way to learn Spanish, and a sure way of integrating the rural Indian peoples into the national community. Complementing this educational program, periodicals are published in the native languages at experimental centers. These publications have had spectacular results.

Toward a Mexican Pedagogy.—In 1925, the Departamento de Psicopedagogía e Higiene (Department of Pedagogic Psychology and Hygiene) was created, which in 1939 was transformed into the Instituto Nacional de Psicopedagogía (National Institute of Pedagogic Psychology). The institute's mission is that of organizing scientific investigations into Mexican social and scholastic methods.

It is proposed eventually to build up a pedagogy that answers to reality and is not merely an exotic importation. In the same spirit, the Instituto de Perfeccionamiento de Maestros de Ensenanza Secundaria (Teacher's Institute of Secondary Instruction), transformed later into the Escuela Normal Superior (Superior Normal School), was founded in 1937 for graduate teachers to improve their work.

Higher Education.—The disputes between radicals and conservatives that made the life of the university so unfortunate in the 19th century were resolved in 1929 by giving legal autonomy to the National University and a substantial subsidy from the government for its maintenance. The course of studies in the humanities and in the formation of the liberal professions of the traditional type has been left to the university. Under these conditions it prospers, and has also been converted into the leader of the network of other universities established in the principal cities of the country.

On the other hand, the aspiration toward a higher education that would place the more advanced scientific knowledge and technique at the service of the industrial development of the country, noted before in the Liberal ideologies of the 19th century, was made a reality with the establishment (1936) of the Instituto Politécnico Nacional (National Polytechnic Institute) in Mexico City during the administration of President Cárdenas. Built upon the same basis as the national institute, but with adaptations to local necessities and resources, local technological institutes exist in various states and others are being set up. Among the most noted of these educational centers are those at Monterrey and Guadalajara.

The education of technicians in the field of agriculture and cattle raising relies upon various agricultural schools of the middle grades, in whose courses more than 5,000 students are enrolled, and upon three schools of the upper levels. The latter are the Escuela Nacional de Agricultura, located in Chapingo, State of Mexico, and the agricultural schools of Narro, Coahuila, and Ciudad Juárez, Chihuahua. The first named dates from 1854; all the others are the work of the educational reforms which grew out of the revolution.

Educational Policies.—The development of the contemporary educational work which has been described does not follow a constant rhythm, either in intensity or in technical organizational efficiency. The economic vicissitudes of the government and the greater or lesser progressivism and interest of the political leaders in office have made the intensity and the effectiveness of the educational endeavor variable. The impulse given to education by presidents Obregón (1920–1924), Calles (1924–1928), and Cárdenas (1934–1940) should be mentioned, since during their administrations education received a generous attention, expressed in the large portions of the general government budgets designated for its use.

The first secretary of public education in the constructive era of the revolution was José Vasconcelos, from 1921–1924, but the credit for orienting and constructing the new Mexican education along definite lines goes to the group of professional teachers who constituted the staff of the Secretaría de Educación Pública during the more fruitful years. Distinguished teachers gathered around Professor Lauro Aguirre (1883–1928), who edited the magazine *Educación.* Among these was Professor Moisés Sáenz (1888–1941), who was undersecretary of public education (1925–1930), in the administration of General Calles, which, in fact, implied responsibility for the technical direction of the programs. Lauro Aguirre was placed in charge of the preparation of new teachers in the reform of normal-school education, and Alfredo Uruchurtu (1884–1940) became the chief administrator of this program. José María Bonilla (1872–   ) and later Rafaél Ramírez (1885–   ) were in charge of organizing rural education. José Guadalupe Nájera (1889–   ) assumed the office of chief of the cultural missions. Other posts of similar importance were occupied by professors Manuel Barranco (1881–1945), José Arturo Pichardo (1863–1933), and Leopoldo Kiel (1876–1943). This is the team which, from the technical-pedagogical point of view, effected the most skillful, transcendental, and ample work of education in the history of Mexico.

In more recent years, with the start (1940) of the administration of President Ávila Camacho, the vigorous rhythm characteristic of the early years has yielded to a slow decline, as a consequence of the practical exclusion of professional teachers from the direction of educational endeavors. Their successors have not had a clear and deep vision of the meaning of the new educational institutions; thus they did not continue the development of those institutions with the same enthusiasm and ability. Their lack of deep concern for education is shown by the following data.

The financing of education took 6.78 per cent of the general expenses of the federal government in 1950. For this same work, 13.35 per cent of the general budget was applied in 1937, while in 1923 it was 15 per cent. This has necessarily affected the quality and the amplitude of the service. In 1950, for example, the proportion of the population of primary school age being adequately instructed was reduced to 44.6 per cent; contrasting with 54.7 per cent in 1938 and 71.8 per cent in 1939.

The decline proved to be transitory, however, and the progress of education picked up speed in the 1960's. More than 26 per cent of the 1967 national budget was allotted to education.

Bibliography.—Sáenz, Moisés, and Priestley, Herbert I., *Some Mexican Problems* (Chicago 1926); Secretaría de Educación Pública, *La educación pública en México a través de los informes presidenciales* (Mexico City 1926); Sáenz, Moisés, "Newer Aspects of Education in Mexico," *Bulletin of the Pan American Union*, September 1929; Alegría, Paula, *La educación en México antes y después de la conquista* (Mexico City 1936); Sánchez, George Isidore, *Mexico: a Revolution by Education* (New York 1936); Booth, George C., *Mexico's School-made Society* (Stanford, Calif., 1941); Bonilla, Guillermo, *Report on the Cultural Missions of Mexico* (Washington 1945); González Blacaller, C., *Bosquejo histórico de la educación en México* (Mexico City 1951); Ruiz, Ramón E., *Mexico: The Challenge of Poverty and Illiteracy* (San Marino, Calif., 1963).

ISMAEL RODRÍGUEZ ARAGÓN,
Former Director, Escuela Nacional de Maestros and Escuela Normal Superior.

15. CHURCH AND STATE.

Relations between church and state in Mexico have passed through a multitude of vicissitudes which have oscillated between complete harmony and open war. To understand the situation of those relations in modern times it is necessary to know the historic antecedents. For the purposes of this article, therefore, the study has been divided into six historical periods.

Indian Basis.—The tyrannical and primitive political forms which the Spaniards encountered in that part of the New World which today is the Mexican Republic were of a theocratic and warlike type, with diverse shadings among the different peoples. All of them were idolatrous, but particularly so were the most powerful, the Aztecs, who dominated the Central Plateau, and who practiced a barbaric worship based on human sacrifice and even cannibalism, in which the number of victims came to 100,000 annually. Although they had priests and warriors as different social castes, a real institutional distinction between political method and religious organization did not exist.

Discovery and Conquest.—The Catholic monarchs, Ferdinand and Isabella, and afterwards Charles V and Philip II, as also their successors, took an apostolic view of the discoveries and conquests that, beginning with Christopher Columbus, they made in the New World. Thus, with respect to the conquest, they considered the propagation of the Christian faith in the newly discovered lands as their primary duty.

Hernán Cortés and the other conquerors were nearly always accompanied by missionaries. They not only required of the Indians submission to the king of Spain; they also destroyed temples and idols in order to uproot the sanguinary religion of the Indians and asked them to adopt the Catholic faith. In other words, the Spanish state patronized the conversion of the Indians. It also prescribed wise laws for the incorporation of these Indians into Christian civilization. In spite of this, however, the conquerors and the delegates of the Spanish government committed many real abuses; at the same time, the cause of the natives was continually defended by the missionaries, such as Fray Toribio de Benavente (known as Motolinia), and by bishops like Juan de Zumárraga and Vasco de Quiroga.

In the work of evangelization undertaken in America, the Spanish crown received special privileges from the church, which allowed it to intervene in ecclesiastical discipline. Among these were the concession of tithes, the royal Indian patronage (*patronato real*), and the tribunal of the Inquisition. The tithes—or rather the proportion of the gross products of the fields and herds—that the inhabitants paid to the church for the support of its personnel, its worship, and its pious works were granted to Spain by Pope Alexander VI in 1501. In return the church imposed on the government the obligation of defraying these expenses. The rulers accepted the concession, but retained only two ninths of the collection, leaving the balance to the church.

The Bull *Universalis Ecclesiae* issued by Pope Julian II in 1508, and the wide interpretation that the Spanish monarchs gave to it, allowed them, among other things, the right to present candidates to fill the bishoprics and ecclesiastical offices, to issue royal licenses before churches, monasteries, and hospitals could be built, and to issue governmental permits before the bulls and other papal documents could be published and obeyed in the Indies. Numerous unjustified acts were committed by the kings and their officials in the government of the church in New Spain (Mexico) under the pretext of this royal patronage.

For its share, the government endeavored to prevent people who did not profess the Catholic faith from going to New Spain, with the end of maintaining the unity of the faith. Within this policy Philip II, by royal decree in 1569, established the Holy Office of the Inquisition in

New Spain, with the object of preserving the religious unity of the area, isolating heretics, and punishing their errors with the rigor demanded by the laws of the crown. Many have exaggerated the cruelty of the procedures and the penalties of the Inquisition, which in reality were ordinary for that period. From the solemn foundation of the tribunal until its suppression in 1820, only 36 persons were delivered by that tribunal to the secular arm for capital punishment by burning; this in 11 *autos de fé* from 1574 to 1715. After the latter year no death sentences were imposed.

Colony.—French influence and the organization of Freemasonry drove the Spanish government, in the last third of the 18th century and the beginning of the 19th, to a cooling of religious ardor and to a growing intervention in church affairs, which culminated in the Spanish Constitution of 1812 and in subsequent policy, all of which was reflected clearly in New Spain until that colony gained its independence in 1821. One of the most evident earlier manifestations of this change in religious policy was the dissolution and expulsion of the Jesuits from the Spanish dominions in 1767, during the reign of Charles III, and the occupation by government officials of the property belonging to that order, which was one of the most prosperous and active and was dedicated principally to teaching. Mention should also be made of government obstruction, in Spain and in the colony, to the extension of teaching and welfare work, which until then had been completely in the hands of the church and the religious orders. Some of the latter had to withdraw from New Spain or were deprived of their buildings by the government on the pretext of benefiting the national economy, and were fenced in with obstacles that impeded the discharge of their responsibilities.

Independence.—The people of New Spain and their leaders had remained eminently Catholic. It was very natural, therefore, that the Catholic religion should be the only one permitted and protected by the laws—in the constitutional project elaborated at Apatzingán under the direction of the insurgent José María Morelos in 1814 during the struggle for independence; in the Plan of Iguala, which served as a basis for the effective realization of independence in 1821, and was drawn up principally by Agustín de Iturbide; and even in the republican Constitution of 1824, written after the fall of Iturbide, who had been proclaimed emperor in the interim. The first independent governments sought to preserve privileges, such as the royal patronage which the kings of Spain had enjoyed in matters pertaining to religion, but were not successful.

The attack on the privileges of the Catholic Church was initiated—at first secretly, then in public form—principally because of the influence of Freemasonry established in Mexico. In 1833 the vice president of the republic, Valentín Gómez Farías, acting as president by permission of President Antonio López de Santa Anna, issued a series of expanding decrees to oppress the Catholic Church and to deprive it of its privileges. Among other measures, it dissolved the Royal and Pontifical University of Mexico (founded 1551) in the capital, secularized learning, and above all sought to interfere directly in parish affairs. A general clamor and various armed uprisings obliged President Santa Anna to intervene (1834) and to abandon some of these arrangements. Nevertheless, Gómez Farías, without success, had planned to nationalize the property of the church and to convert the priests into functionaries paid by the government.

Constitution of 1857 and Reform Laws.—There was a short period of harmony on the religious question until, triumphant in the Revolution of Ayutla (1854–1855), the ultraradical Liberals came to power. Under the presidency (1855–1857) of Ignacio Comonfort, plain civil war existed between the Conservatives, friends of the church, and the Liberals, their enemies. In 1855 Benito Juárez, as minister of justice and ecclesiastical matters, put forth a law which disentailed property held in *manos muertas* (mortmain), which obliged corporations, especially religious corporations, to sell their properties. A little later, in 1859, nationalization of all the property belonging to religious corporations was decreed. This, made under the pretext that the church, enormously rich, had abused its power by intrigues in politics, had as its only object the crushing of the church; as a result many politicians and foreigners became rich, buying up many of its lands at low prices. A great number of churches, schools, and hospitals were converted by the government to other uses.

Meanwhile, the Liberal Party in power had promulgated the Constitution of 1857. This established liberty for all religions and freedom of education, to stimulate the rivalry with Catholicism, deprived the priests of civil rights, disregarded the religious orders and gave the federal government the right to intervene in matters of religious procedure and in relations between the clergy and the people. With the civil war newly started again, the government led by Benito Juárez set forth the laws called the Reform Laws (1859–1860), which included the law nationalizing the property of the clergy and carried to an extreme the reprisals against the Catholic Church. After the downfall of the imperial adventure of Maximilian of Austria, whose regime (1861–1867) did not basically alter the religious situation, even though it tempered it notably, the Liberal Party remained definitively the victor, and in 1874 had the Reform Laws included in the constitution.

A long period of peace came in 1876, under the rule of Gen. Porfirio Díaz, the "strong man" who remained in power until 1911, when he was overthrown by the revolution led by Francisco Madero. During the regime of Díaz the laws against the church were maintained with vigor, but the church enjoyed, *de facto,* sufficient liberty, although certain policies of oppression were carried out, such as disregard of the legal status of ecclesiastical corporations, and prohibitions of public religious ceremonies outside the churches and of the use of special dress by priests and religious officials.

Constitution of 1917 and Its Application.—The Revolution of 1910 was not antireligious in origin, but it became so in a series of movements which culminated in the Constitution of 1917. The new constitution carried to the extreme the attacks on the church contained in the previous Constitution of 1857. Nevertheless, its provisions were not forcibly applied until 1926, the year in which President Plutarco Elías Calles let loose a true persecution against every kind of religious manifestation, commencing with limiting the number of priests to a ridiculously small figure, prohibiting foreign priests from performing the sacred offices in Mexico, as well as preventing all religious rites and religious instruction in private schools and even in homes; all under the threat of severe penalties, since all infractions of the laws on religious matters were considered criminal.

The clergy chose to suspend all ceremonies. A popular rebellion (the so-called *Cristero* movement) opposed the law for three years, but did not overthrow the government; because the latter was aided by foreign governments, the *Cristeros* could not obtain arms. Finally, in 1929, President Emilio Portes Gil reached an understanding with the church. Although the persecuting laws were not repealed, they were not applied in large part, or were executed with tolerance.

The church was again attacked in 1934 at the beginning of the administration of President Lázaro Cárdenas, principally in the matter of instruction. The Marxist tendency of the government led it to impose socialistic and antireligious education, and even to amend the constitution in that year.

From 1937, however, the *de facto* situation of the church and of religious matters in general has much improved. Relative liberty is enjoyed, since the antireligious laws that are in effect are in large part not applied, and the legislation relating to Marxist education was abolished in 1942–1946. As of 1952, benevolent, although unofficial, relations exist between church and state. From the constitutional and legal point of view, everyone may profess the religion of his choice in Mexico, but the public religious ceremonies must be held within precincts of the churches, in accordance with regulations that are dictated by and are under the vigilance of the authorities. Ecclesiastical corporations lack legal capacity and are not able to acquire property either directly or indirectly. All buildings dedicated to worship or religious education have been converted into national property. The priests do not have political rights, nor can they dedicate themselves to teaching or charity work. Both public and private religious education in the schools is prohibited.

Bibliography.—Alamán, Lucas, *Historia de México desde los primeros movimientos que prepararon la independencia en el año de 1808 hasta la época presente* (Mexico City 1849–52); Kelley, Francis C., *Blood-drenched Altars* (Milwaukee 1935); Planchet, Regis, *El robo de los bienes de la iglesia ruina de los pueblos* (Mexico City 1939); Cuevas, Mariano, *Historia civil de México* (Mexico City 1940); Bravo Ugarte, José, *Historia de México* 3 vols. (Mexico City 1941–44); Cuevas, Mariano, *Historia de la iglesia en México*, 5 vols. (Mexico City 1946–47); Alamán, Lucas, *Disertaciones sobre la historia de la República Mexicana desde la época de la conquista hasta la independencia*, 3 vols. (Mexico City 1944–49); Pereyra, Carlos, *México falsificado* (Mexico City 1949); Schlarman, Joseph H., *Mexico: a Land of Volcanoes; from Cortés to Alemán* (Milwaukee 1950); García Gutiérrez, Jesús, *Apuntes para la historia del regio patronato indiano hasta 1857* (Mexico City 1951).

DAVID CASARES NICOLÍN,
Professor of the General Theory of the State, Escuela Libre de Derecho, Mexico City.

16. PRE-HISPANIC ART. Mural Painting.

—The great epoch of Indian mural painting, as far as both quantity and quality of output are concerned, coincides with the period which archaeologists label "Classic" (300 A.D. to 900 A.D.). At Teotihuacán, the great metropolis of central Mexico, a large number of murals have been discovered already, and it seems likely that more will come to light in the future. It is possible to distinguish an early style of painting at this site. This is found in a building which may be dated at 200 A.D. Its mural decoration is based on interlocking geometric designs with some symbolic religious motifs. The most recent style (dated roughly from 400 to 800 A.D.) is naturalistic, but not realistic. The content of the paintings is religious: they represent gods, priests, and sacred animals. Plants are also represented and some paintings even contain suggestions of landscapes. One of the most outstanding scenes represents the paradise of the water gods. Its liveliness of composition contrasts with the usual hieratic rigidity of Teotihuacán art.

The style of these paintings is characterized as follows: areas of flat colors delimited by contour lines; absence of modeling; no attempts to suggest space through the use of perspective or by other means. The technique used is partly fresco, partly tempera, on a base of calcium carbonate mixed with finely ground quartz sand. All the colors analyzed are mineral colors. Red was probably produced with hematite; yellow and orange with limonite and goethite; black possibly with magnesite; green with malachite or azurite. Reds were painted directly on the wet surface of the wall; greens were never painted in this fashion, but were applied as tempera over the white surface formed by the dry base. The application of transparent green on this white base results in a particularly brilliant green.

The murals of the big tombs of Monte Albán near Oaxaca (tombs Nos. 103, 104, and 105) belong to the same period. These paintings represent gods and goddesses, or priests dressed in cult ornaments. Here, as in Teotihuacán, the style is hieratic, but lines are drawn with greater freedom. The color scheme includes yellow, red, green, blue, white, gray, and black.

In 1946, ruins belonging to the Classic Maya civilization were discovered at Bonampak, in the Chiapas jungle. Among its buildings is one containing three rooms painted with different scenes. One of these shows richly dressed chiefs; servants dressing other men, perhaps chief priests, in ceremonial costumes; and musicians and dancers. Another gives an impressive picture of a battle and of victorious chiefs, surrounded by their guard, confronting a group of prisoners. The third painting represents another group of chiefs, musicians, and a big dance. Particularly significant is the fact that each of the paintings shows differences in rhythm, composition, and color scheme, according to its special content. The battle scene is characterized by the violent rhythm of broken lines and by somber colors. The scenes in which groups of chiefs appear show a composition of horizontal and vertical lines in equilibrium, and brilliant colors. The dancing scene shows an agitated rhythm of massed colors and undulating lines, which suggest movement. The technique employed in these paintings is also partly fresco, partly tempera. The color scheme includes yellow ocher, Indian red, orange red, burnt sienna, emerald green, dark green, turquoise blue, dark blue, white, and black. The Bonampak paintings are assigned to the 8th century A.D.

To a period after 1000 A.D. belong the paintings of mythological subjects which cover the altars of Tizatlán near Tlaxcala. The figures of gods are painted in the same style as the codices and the polychrome pottery of the Mixtec region of Oaxaca and the Valley of Puebla. This style, therefore, has received the name Mixtec-Puebla. Murals, painted in Mixtec-Puebla style, have also been found at Mitla, near Oaxaca. They represent mythological scenes, painted in red on a white background. An extension of this style toward the north has been found on the altar of Tamuin, in San Luis Potosí, near Valles. This painting, similarly red on white, shows a procession of gods and other figures.

In Yucatán, the murals of the Temple of the

Jaguars and the Temple of the Warriors at Chichén Itzá belong to the period of Toltec influence, from 1000 to 1200 A.D. They depict scenes from the conquest of the country by the Itzá. These pictures definitely show an attempt to depict the landscape realistically, and to convey an impression of spaciousness.

Mural paintings are also found in a number of buildings in the Maya ruins of Tulum, in Quintana Roo. They represent mythological scenes. The Tulum buildings are dated after 1000 A.D.

Another mural, which belongs to the last centuries before the Spanish conquest, decorates one of the rooms in the temples of Malinalco, in the State of Mexico, 25 miles south-southeast of Toluca. It represents a procession of warriors, armed with lances and shields.

Painted Books.—The miniatures contained in the painted books form an important aspect of Indian art; comparable on the one hand to the great art of mural painting, and on the other to some types of decorated pottery. Some of the miniatures show exquisite composition, drawing, movement, and coloring. They were painted on deerskin or on bark paper, dressed with white chalk. They deal with the calendar, ritual, mythology, and history. None of the picture books which have been preserved seem to go back further than 1000 A.D. Nevertheless, remains of similar books, consisting of heaps of alternate layers of thin chalk and powdered paint, have been found in tombs that are several centuries older.

The few pre-Hispanic codices which have survived the ravages of time and men are classified stylistically as follows:

(1) Aztec: The most important of these, from the artistic point of view, are the sections of the *Codex Borbonicus* which deal with the divining calendar and with the ritual of the months.

(2) Historical Mixtec: This group comprises a number of codices, which contain genealogies of Mixtec lords, and depict their acts of prowess.

(3) *Codex Borgia* group: This consists of codices which deal with the calendar, astronomy, divining, and mythology. The codices of groups 2 and 3 are firmly drawn and vividly colored, and differ only slightly in style. According to the art expert Salvador Toscano, this slight difference may be due to their different content.

(4) Maya: These are characterized by freedom of drawing, sensitiveness of line, and by the elegant sophistication of Maya art.

Decorated Pottery and Lacquer Work.—The pre-Hispanic potters did not know the potter's wheel. They usually shaped and modeled pots by hand, but they were also acquainted with the use of molds. A large number of techniques were used to decorate pottery. Due to limitations of space, only three types of decorated pottery will be discussed here: the painted pottery of Tlaxcala, Puebla, and the Mixtec region, produced after 1000 A.D.; the ritual champlevé-decorated pottery of Teotihuacán, produced between about 300 and about 700 A.D.; and stucco-decorated pottery, which is related to lacquer work.

The Mixtec-Puebla style employed in painting polychrome ware is identical with the style used in painting murals and codices in the same regions. The ware is decorated with figures of gods and animals, and with symbolic or simply decorative motifs painted in purple, orange, yellow, blue-gray, white, black, and other colors, and burnished to a high gloss.

The ritual vases of Teotihuacán were often first painted solid deep brown or brownish red, then polished and fired. After firing, the background was scraped away with some sharp instrument, leaving the figures outlined in silhouette and slightly raised above the scraped surface. Details within the silhouettes were shown by incising. The dark colors and brilliant finish of the unscraped portions contrast sharply with the mat background, showing the natural color of the clay or painted with cinnabar. Though not painting, the technique produces the effects of painting in two colors. The figures of gods, priests, religious symbols, and the like used to decorate this Teotihuacán champlevé pottery are the same as those painted in the great murals of the site.

Stucco decoration was applied after the vessels were fired. Two different techniques were in use. The first, called *paint-cloisonné*, was used mainly in western Mexico. A thick coat of paint was first applied over the entire surface of the vessel. This base was scraped to form depressions, and these were filled with the different pigments to be used in the composition. The areas of paint thus imbedded in the base were separated by narrow ridges, in which the base showed through, and which outlined the motifs. In the second technique, successive layers of paint were applied over the vessel. Parts of each layer were cut away to show the portions of the lower layers intended to form the design. Available evidence indicates that this second technique is older than the other. It was used in central and southern Mexico and in Guatemala. It seems certain that some organic adhesive or solvent was used, in both cases, to fix the colors.

These two pre-Hispanic stucco techniques employed to decorate pottery are similar to the lacquer techniques still used in Michoacán and Guerrero to decorate gourds or wood. In Michoacán, the *paint-cloisonné* technique is used, with a varnish made from an insect (*Coccus axin*). In Olinalá, Guerrero, the technique of successive layers is employed, with oil from the lime-leaved sage (*Salvia hispanica*) as the solvent medium. Furthermore, Gordon Ekholm found remains of gourd vessels with *paint-cloisonné* decoration in his excavations in Sinaloa. It cannot be doubted that much lacquer work was done on gourds and wood, but that the perishable nature of the material has made preservation very rare.

Monumental Sculpture.—The majority of pre-Hispanic sculptures were conceived either in terms of compact blocks, or pictorially in two dimensions only. The representation of mass in the three-dimensional terms proper to sculpture is rare in Indian art. The development of a true sense of space in sculpture was inhibited, in some cases, by technical inability to liberate form from the stone. In such cases, the sculptor surrendered to the material. In others, the lack of a true sense of space is due to either conscious aesthetic considerations which conceive form as a closed-in unitary whole, or to functional reasons. A large part of pre-Hispanic stone sculpture was conceived as an integral part of architecture. Therefore flat or low-relief carvings are more frequent than sculpture in the round. However, the same flat conception is found in minor sculpture in baked clay or precious stones; though modeled in the round, these figurines were intended to be seen only from one side.

The so-called *danzantes* (dancers) belonging to the earliest period of Monte Albán are either figures incised on slabs or flat reliefs. In these, the figures were made to stand out slightly by carving out the background, though no modeling of any kind was attempted. They represent unusually animated human figures, and are attributed to the beginning of the Christian era or a little before.

The oldest stone sculpture in central Mexico is that of Teotihuacán, dating from about 200 to 500 A.D. Teotihuacán sculpture is wholly conceived in architectural terms; its forms are massive cubes with a minimum of modeling. The reliefs of the Temple of the Plumed Serpent at Xochicalco, Morelos, show greater freedom of form, combined with a more sensual and whimsical style. They are attributed to the 9th century A.D.

The main works of sculpture in the ruins of Tollan (modern Tula), the Toltec capital, are flat reliefs on the fronts of the great pyramid and on the pillars of the portico of the temple. Even the colossal warriors which also supported the portico, though carved in the round, were sculpted following the techniques employed in flat relief. The Toltec period dates are from about 900 to about 1200 A.D.

Only during the last centuries before the Spanish conquest did monumental sculpture reach its zenith in central Mexico, both in quantity and quality. There exist remarkably realistic, austere, and expressive works of this period. Some achieved great economy of form, such as the head of the eagle knight, in the Museo Nacional de Antropología in Mexico City. Others are noteworthy for the sense of movement achieved within a compact block and for their plastic modeling, such as the figure of Quetzalcoatl in the Musée de l'Homme in Paris; or the great Coatlicue, the earth goddess, in the Museo Nacional de Antropología, in which the abundance of detail and the sophistication of execution do not detract from the grandeur of the whole.

There are few examples of the sculpture of the Huastec area of northern Veracruz and of the adjacent zones of San Luis Potosí and Hidalgo. From the Totonac region, north central Veracruz, the reliefs of the site of El Tajín, carved between 600 and 900 A.D., are noteworthy. Sculptured stone yokes, the so-called palmate stones ("palmas"), and flat stone representations of heads or complete figures in profile are also called Totonac, especially when they bear characteristic scroll designs. However, the area of distribution of these objects is much wider than the historic Totonac area.

The Olmec area of southern Veracruz and western Tabasco is famous for its colossal heads, for monolithic altars carved with figures in high relief and for other sculptures from Tres Zapotes, San Lorenzo, and La Venta. Another masterwork of Olmec statuary, and one of the best pieces of ancient Mexican art, is the figure called *The Wrestler*. It represents a man dressed in a loincloth, seated on the ground, apparently stretching his shoulder and arm muscles. The statue is truly three-dimensional in conception and was executed with great mastery of form and movement. It was found in Minatitlán, Veracruz, and belongs to a private collector in Mexico City. The dating of Olmec sculptures remains controversial; nevertheless, there are grounds for dating them between 300 and 600 A.D.

In the part of the Maya area now in Mexico, Palenque, Chiapas, is outstanding for the quality of its stucco reliefs and stone carvings. The stucco decoration is executed in deeply carved relief, with an extraordinary plasticity of forms. The stone carvings are flat relief or slightly modeled low relief. They were painted, and are thus classifiable more as painting than as sculpture. The carvings of the altars of the Temple of the Cross (dated 642 A.D.), the Temple of the Sun, and the Temple of the Foliated Cross (dated 692 A.D.) are well known. During excavations made in 1952 a similar carving was found in a secret chamber in the Temple of the Inscriptions. This stone covered a monolithic sarcophagus in which a great personage was buried. Palenque art is characterized by its naturalistic style, the grace and refinement in the representation of human form and movement, and its decorative splendor. The carvings show an extraordinary sensitiveness of line. Paradoxically, the carvers of Palenque were not sculptors, but excellent draftsmen who, like Hans Holbein the Younger, and Jean Auguste Dominique Ingres, used line to produce the illusion of mass. Many carvings in flat relief or low relief cover the steles, lintels, jambs, and panels of other ruins in the Maya zone of Chiapas, Tabasco, and the Peninsula of Yucatán. These belong to the middle Classic or late Classic periods (about 500 to 900 A.D.). Later, Toltec influence reached Yucatán. This is exemplified by the carvings and sculptures of Chichén Itzá (about 987 to about 1204 A.D.).

The sculpture of Michoacán is known from a few examples only. They tend to be cubic in shape and are schematically and roughly worked.

Ceramic Sculpture.—Sculpture in Mexico begins with the hand-modeled figurines of baked clay belonging to the Archaic period, which lasted to about the time of Christ. The oldest ones seem to be expressions of a fertility cult, involving the symbolic use of female figurines. Many Archaic figurines are conventional in type and seem to have been produced according to standard formulas which did not permit much leeway for the expression of creative impulses. Nevertheless, in others the creative will of the artist is clearly visible, even within the established conventions. The tradition of sculptured clay figurines of religious character lasted in central Mexico up to the Spanish conquest. After the peak period of Teotihuacán, however, they were cast from molds, resulting in a series of conventional types of little artistic value.

In Oaxaca, clay sculpture consists mainly of funerary urns, with different styles corresponding to successive periods. The most abundant of these are of the epoch Monte Albán III (400 to 700 A.D.). These funeral urns of Monte Albán III are heavily structured and covered with ornamentation which had ritual meaning.

In the Maya area, the older figurines of Jaina Island, off the Campeche coast, are small masterworks of realistic art. They are hand-modeled and represent warriors, priests, ballplayers, and women. They are dated at about 600 A.D. The Jaina figurines of a later period (roughly from 700 to 1000 A.D.) are mold-made and conventional in style; nearly all represent women and animals.

In western Mexico (Colima, Jalisco, and Nayarit) baked clay statuary achieved extraordinary development and artistic importance. These western ceramic sculptures are characterized by great economy of form. They portray psychological states with jovial irony. Although intended as funerary art, they faithfully reproduce scenes from everyday life. They may have been inspired by religious ideas, according to which life in the mansion of the dead was thought to be a continuation of life on earth.

Masks.—Masks of stone, wood, baked clay, and bone form an important aspect of pre-Hispanic art. They were used in magic, and for religious and funerary purposes. During religious ceremonies, the priests covered their faces with masks representing the faces of the gods. In the representations of the gods, their faces are also often seen covered with masks. In funeral ceremonies, the dead body was completely wrapped in cloth, and a mask was placed on top of the bundle. The face of the personage buried in the secret chamber of the Temple of the Inscriptions, mentioned above under *Monumental Sculpture,* was covered with a mask composed of hundreds of jade tesserae pasted on a coat of stucco. The eyes of the mask were made of shell, with obsidian irises.

The use of masks is attested since Archaic times. Aesthetically, the stone masks of the Teotihuacán culture deserve special mention. They show great simplification of the features of the human face, but within a basically naturalistic conception. The absence of individuality is striking, especially since they were probably used to represent the faces of the dead in funeral ceremonies. The art expert Paul Westheim has said that they were not realistic representations, but plastic representations of a concept. There are also Teotihuacán masks of baked clay, painted in many colors, which form the basic element of great incense burners. These are made in the same style as the stone masks. Equally outstanding are the miniature masks carved in Olmec style from semiprecious stones such as jade or jadeite, real masterworks of lapidary art.

A few wooden masks have been preserved. These are covered with mosaics of turquoise, jadeite, shell, mother-of-pearl, and lignite. The British Museum in London and the Prehistoric and Ethnographic Museum in Rome have the best examples. Some are also found in the Museum of the American Indian in New York. There also exist masks made from the frontal portions of the human skull, which are covered with mosaic. The British Museum owns the best specimen.

Lapidary Work and Mosaic. — The pre-Hispanic craftsmen worked jade, jadeite, turquoise, obsidian, rock crystal, and other hard minerals. The most beautiful works of Indian lapidary art are little figures, little masks, and anthropomorphic votive hatchets of Olmec style, worked in jade or jadeite. The most famous work in rock crystal is the human skull in the British Museum. Jadeite, obsidian, rock crystal, and alabaster were also used to make vases. Examples are the jadeite jug in the shape of the water god in the Museo Nacional de Antropología in Mexico City; the obsidian vase in the shape of a monkey in the same museum; the alabaster vase also shaped like a monkey in the Bliss Collection, National Gallery of Art, Washington; and the rock crystal cup from Tomb 7 at Monte Albán, now in the museum at Oaxaca. Ear plugs, breast pendants, and other jewelry were also made from these materials. Turquoise was used in mosaic, together with jade, coral, shell, and other materials. The small mosaic pieces were generally glued on a wood or leather base, occasionally on bone or stone.

A number of the most outstanding mosaic works are mentioned above under *Masks.* To these should be added: the wooden helmet in the British Museum; the handles of the sacrificial knives in the British Museum and in the Prehistoric and Ethnographic Museum in Rome; the wooden vases in the British Museum and at Copenhagen; the discs in the Museum of the American Indian, New York, and those found at Chichén Itzá; and the two-headed serpent in the British Museum.

Wood and Bone Carving and Shell Engraving. — Due to the perishable nature of the material, few wooden carvings have been preserved. Enough are known, however, to give an idea of the remarkable craftsmanship of the pre-Hispanic wood carvers. A number of slit drums (*teponaztlis*) and skin-covered drums (*huehuetls*) have been preserved. These are decorated with mythological scenes. Also preserved are a number of finely carved ceremonial spear throwers. The most remarkable bone objects are the spatulate objects found in Tomb 7 at Monte Albán; they are decorated in Mixtec-Puebla style with calendrical inscriptions and mythological figures. In the Huastec area (the northern part of what is now the State of Veracruz), engraving was used to decorate shell gorgets.

Weaving and Featherwork. — The art of pre-Hispanic weavers is known only from descriptions by ancient authors, and from representations of textiles in painting and sculpture. The chronicles tell us about the types of fabrics produced, and the patterns used are clearly shown in the artistic representations. Cotton was used to make high-quality textiles; agave fiber to make coarse fabrics only. Pre-Hispanic featherwork won high praise from the chroniclers. The lack of feather ornaments in representations of art older than 300 A.D. seems to indicate that this craft developed only after this date. Feather ornaments were in great fashion during the Classic period. At the time of the Spanish conquest, feathers were used for headdresses, fans, and cloaks, and feather mosaic was used to decorate shields. Only a few pre-Hispanic examples of this delicate craft have been preserved. The most beautiful of these are the great quetzal feather headdress of Montezuma II, and a shield, decorated with the figure of a fabled animal, the *ahuitzotl;* both are in the Kaiserliche Schatzkammer in Vienna.

Metalwork. — The tradition of metalwork was of relatively recent development; it does not seem to antedate 900 A.D. The pre-Hispanic metalworkers used gold, silver, copper, and some tin and lead. They alloyed copper with gold, copper with tin, and copper with lead. The technical processes known were: hammering, casting, welding, gilding, plating, and inlaying. Castings were made using the cire-perdue (lost-wax) process, in which the mold is shaped around a wax model of the object to be cast. They employed the *mise-en-couleur* process to gild objects. This produced a gilded surface on copper-gold alloy of low precious-metal content. The surface copper was dissolved by treating it with acids (probably plant juices) and subjecting it to heat. Pieces which are part gold, part silver were produced by welding. Abundant use of filigree characterized the style of Mexican metalwork.

The first rank in technique and artistry was held by the metalworkers of the Mixtec region. The jewels found in Tomb 7 at Monte Albán and presently in the museum at Oaxaca (rings, necklaces, breast pendants, and so forth) are good examples of their excellent work. Copper and silver were both worked in Michoacán, but the artistic quality of this work is low. In Yucatán, during the Toltec period, the local artists used the technique of *repoussé* to represent animated scenes of the conquest of the Maya by the Itzá on discs of imported gold. These scenes have great artistic value.

Consult Burland, Cottie A., *Art and Life in Ancient Mexico* (Oxford, Eng., 1948); Emmerich, Andre, *Art Before Columbus; the Art of Ancient Mexico* (New York 1963); Edwards, Emily, *Painted Walls in Mexico* (Austin, Texas, 1966).

PEDRO ARMILLAS,
Instituto Nacional de Antropología e Historia,
Mexico City.

17. COLONIAL AND MODERN ART.

Indian painting had very little influence on colonial painting. There were great differences between the two: while the former drew inspiration from Indian mythology and found expression in hieroglyphs and symbols, the latter was devoted predominantly to the Roman Catholic religion and, in common with all European art, favored the use of natural forms.

Mexican colonial art, which could more accurately be described as the art of New Spain, can be divided into four periods: primitive, comprising approximately the 50 years following the conquest of Mexico in 1521; renaissance, a reflection of European Renaissance seen through Spain, lasting a short 25 or 30 years; baroque, developed during the 17th and a great part of the 18th century; and lastly, the period of the neoclassic academicians, during the last years of the 18th century and up to the beginning of the struggle for independence in 1810.

Painting.—*Primitive Period.*—Although pre-Hispanic painting had no direct influence on the art of New Spain, paintings by Indian artists are found in the years following the conquest; however, they used the forms of European art brought over by the Spaniards.

The first school of painting was founded in the capital of New Spain about 1525, only a few years after the conquest, by the Franciscan friar Pedro de Gante; Indian painters like Cuauhtli, Xochitótotl, Xóchmitl, Marcos Cipac and others studied there. Very few of their works have been preserved, but we still have a portrait of Fray Domingo de Betanzos on wood, and the image called the *Virgin of Guadalupe,* probably painted by Cipac shortly before the middle of the 16th century.

The first mural paintings were done about the same time in the cloisters of monasteries, following the fresco technique. The names of the artists are unknown, but it can be safely assumed that in many cases they were Indians, directed by the friars, who found inspiration in European paintings and engravings. The subjects are sometimes simply Italian ornamental themes (so-called grotesque). The most important, however, are usually representations of religious subjects and images of Christ and the saints; although in an exceptional case (at Atotonilco, Hidalgo) the Renaissance influence was so strong as to prompt the reproduction of two great figures, those of Plato and Aristotle, in Renaissance costume. Good examples of this type of work are found in the monasteries of Huejotzingo, Puebla; Acolman, Mexico State; Actopan, Hidalgo; Epazoyucan, Hidalgo; and many others.

Renaissance.—It is perhaps not very accurate to call renaissance painters those who flourished in the last 30 years of the 16th century, but it would be difficult to find another name suitable for them; indeed, their painting is the same as that of the Spanish Renaissance, with its twofold Flemish and Italian influence.

Andrés de Concha, Juan de Arrúe (1565–c.1637), and Simón Pereyns were painters of this period. Pereyns, the most important, was Flemish, and his works belong to the Flemish Renaissance style. He was born before 1550, came to Mexico in 1566, and probably died at the end of the century. His work may still be seen at Huejotzingo; in *La Virgen del Perdón (Virgin of Forgiveness)*, a good painting in the style of the 16th-century Flemish Madonnas, in the Cathedral of Mexico City; and in many other paintings.

The period which followed can be described as one of transition between renaissance and baroque. The outstanding painter was Baltasar de Echave y Orio, also called Echave el Viejo (the Elder; c.1548–after 1612). He was of Basque origin and came to Mexico at an early age in 1573. Echave's painting was done at the end of the 16th century and in the first quarter of the 17th. He borrowed from both Italians and Flemish, but the two influences never blended adequately. Echave used rich and intense colors. Some of his work is preserved in the Palacio de Bellas Artes in Mexico City. His son, Baltasar de Echave Ibía (1583–1640), has been called "the blue Echave" by Manuel Toussaint because of his marked preference for this color. Several religious paintings of his have been preserved, as well as the portrait of an unknown lady.

Of the same time were Sebastián López de Arteaga (1610–1656), a good portrait painter, and Alonso López de Herrera (d. about 1654), called "the Divine," who achieved great fame. The latter was talented and possessed a remarkable knowledge of his craft. He followed the Italian school; critics have pointed out the influence of Titian. Luis Juárez (fl. 1610–1630), a weaker but very prolific contemporary painter, had leanings towards mysticism. His paintings show certain traits which class him clearly within the baroque tendencies which began at that time.

Baroque.—Mexican baroque architecture is varied and rich, but baroque painting is not. The contrast is all the more remarkable because there is no doubt that baroque painting in New Spain came directly, almost exclusively, from Spanish painting, which reached its highest peak in the 17th century with such masters as Diego Velázquez, Francisco de Zurbarán, and Bartolomé Esteban Murillo. Evidently the distance was too great, and as a consequence painting in Mexico falls well below the Spanish level. The work of Mexican baroque painters was commonplace, a very weak reflection of the Spanish originals, whose excellence made them unattainable.

Baltasar de Echave y Rioja (1632–1682), grandson of Echave el Viejo, was one of the first completely baroque painters. He achieved dramatic effects through the movement which he put in the various elements of his paintings.

Among other painters of the time may be mentioned Juan Correa (c.1649–1738), Cristóbal de Villalpando (c.1649–c.1714), and the brothers Juan Rodríguez Juárez (1675–1728) and Nicolás Rodríguez Juárez (1667–1734), all of whom favored religious subjects, and make good use of color and light effects, with hardly discernible differences. Their painting, in true baroque fashion, is complicated and sumptuous, and they show a marked preference for a purely decorative and spectacular treatment.

The Mexican baroque entered a new phase in the 18th century, when the already few possibilities of expression were further reduced. Inspiration was still found in Spanish painting, which was also in a decadent state, after its great 17th century. In Spain, the disciples of Murillo had turned his softness of color into a nauseous surfeit of tender pinks and blues. Such an evil example produced in Mexico an art of set formulas which prescribed rose-colored flesh, except in the case of ascetics, who were to be depicted as of yellowish complexion; carelessness in the treatment of robes; pitch-colored backgrounds, the better to show soft colors in the first planes; and several such defective methods, monotonously repeated. Two names should be mentioned in such a panorama, Ibarra and Cabrera. José de Ibarra (1688–1756) possessed good technique, but his use of color followed the trends outlined above. His self-portrait is among his best works. The reputation of Miguel Cabrera (1695–1768) as a good painter has come down almost to our times; the only explanation for this is to be found in a general decadence of taste, since his work was, to begin with, inconsistent—probably owing mainly to the great number of pictures he painted—and then, although his drawing was good, his composition was generally bad. All this apart from his sharing in the generally defective coloring of the aftermath of a great period.

Academicians.—The Royal Academy of San Carlos was opened in 1781 for the purpose of giving instruction in fine arts. It marked the end of a very decadent baroque, and its being replaced by neoclassicism. Two of the important painters that came out of this school before the end of the colonial era are José Luis Rodríguez Alconedo (1749–1815) and Rafael Ximeno y Planes. The former was an excellent silversmith and painter, but his output was small. His self-portrait in pastels is his best work. This is now in the Academia de Bellas Artes at Puebla.

Rafael Ximeno y Planes (1761–1825) was born in Spain, studied in Mexico and Rome, and came back to Mexico in 1795 to direct the academy. He painted many excellent portraits, such as that of the sculptor and architect Manuel Tolsá. He used oil for much of his work and tempera in some murals, like those in the cupola of the cathedral of Mexico City and the chapel of the old Mining College; there Manuel Toussaint found a clear influence of Giovanni Battista Tiepolo.

Sculpture.—*Primitive Period.*—The process is similar to that observed in painting: to begin with, Indians worked on European figures, and managed to leave in them a strong expression of their own sensitivity. The results were primitive and ingenuous pieces of sculpture, now revealing a certain childishness, now a certain ruggedness bordering at times on the monstrous.

There are some crucifixes left from those early times, which are carved in soft wood (patol), and are copies of Spanish originals. Some work was also done in papier-mâché.

We may also consider as sculpture the reliefs executed on the walls of monasteries and churches. These are mostly images of saints, symbols, or even purely ornamental shapes. There are good examples of this type of work in the monasteries of Calpan, Puebla; Tepoztlán, Morelos; Tlalmanalco, Mexico State; Yuriria, Guanajuato; and others. Like the frescoes done at the time, these reliefs seem to have been modeled on copper engravings or woodcuts of various origin.

Renaissance and Baroque.—Again there is a strong parallel with painting. The best of Spain's sculpture was done by Alonso Cano, Pedro de Mena, Juan Martínez Montañes, and others; in Mexico, sculptors filled church exteriors with carved stone figures, and the inside with numerous polychrome or *estofado* wooden sculptures. *Estofado* sculptures are wooden images covered with stucco or plaster, on which gold leaf is applied. Lines are drawn on this with a burin and colors are sometimes applied on top.

Architecture and sculpture blended in wonderful, frequently gigantic reredos which were usually made in three tiers with a finishing motif at the top, a central panel and from two to four panels on each side. They contain oil paintings and sculptures inside niches. Each part was usually executed in a different architectural style. The sculpting work, done by different persons, covered every bit of available space—thousands of columns, friezes, cornices, brackets, all of it carved in wood and lined with gold leaf; here indeed is the glitter and light and shadow play typical of baroque fancy.

The first reredos were in the richly ornamented plateresque style, following the Renaissance influence; among these are the ones at Xochimilco near Mexico City, and, better still, at Huejotzingo, Puebla, executed by Simón Pereyns. But the great period of reredos came later, in the 17th century, when the full influence of the baroque was felt. In all of them we find twisted columns, fewer paintings, and a greater number of sculpted figures; they are full of garlands, angels, symbols, all of them admirably carved and in great profusion. The Churrigueresque type in the 18th century gave sculptors and wood carvers their boldest conceptions, the result being such masterpieces as the reredos of Tepotzotlán, Mexico State; Querétaro; and Salamanca, Guanajuato.

Academicians.—In delivering the *coup de grâce* to baroque art, the Academy of San Carlos put a stop to the development of reredos; but, perhaps as a compensation, it was then that statuary received full attention, just because then each statue began to be considered as an end in itself, not as part of a great mass of a reredos, where each statuette, engulfed in the great mass of decor, lost its identity.

Puebla and Querétaro were the two centers of sculpture in the last years of the viceroys. The names Cora and Villegas became famous in Puebla as those of two families that gave several well-known sculptors; the outstanding ones in Querétaro were Mariano Arce and Mariano Perusquía. A great architect of Celaya, Guanajuato, Francisco Eduardo Tresguerras (1759–1833) also executed a number of sculptures.

The best sculptor of the academic movement in Mexico was Manuel Tolsá (1757–1816), also an architect, whose equestrian statue of the Spanish king Charles IV, in bronze, is preserved in Mexico City as one of its most beautiful and appreciated monuments.

Minor Arts.—Native precursors are of importance in some of the minor arts, such as silverwork and feather mosaic. The decadence of the last dates from early times and it is now almost lost. Otherwise the native element took refuge in popular arts like ceramics, the Michoacán and Guerrero *jícaras* (wooden bowls), and few others. In the majority of cases, however, the European arts became predominant, and even materials and tools were imported.

As was to be expected, the development followed closely the growth of the colonial regime. The increase in population and wealth, the growth of the cities—above all the capital city—the luxury and pomp of the wealthy classes, the baroque leaning to ostentatiousness and flamboyance, all these favored the development of industrial art in the 17th and 18th centuries. Since such arts vary according to regional and personal characteristics, it is possible to come to know them only through very specialized studies. It is sufficient here to say that they were carefully fostered in New Spain. Jewelry, ornaments, and religious objects of the highest class were made of precious metals, and many Mexican towns still show with pride their iron and bronze grillwork, locks, ancient arms, and other objects. As for woodwork, fine carved furniture and inlaid work in ivory, tortoise shell, bone, and silver were made. Among luxury goods, fine work was done in dyed or gilded leather cordovan and *guadameci* (embossed leather), as well as in weaving and embroidery. Ceramics were also prominent, ranging from that which originated in the pre-Hispanic past to that inherited through Spain from the Arabs, such as the Talavera style of glazed tiles developed at Puebla. The Museo Nacional de Historia and the Museo de Arte Religioso in Mexico City, the Museo José Luis Bello in Puebla and other regional museums, as well as many private collections, have abundant examples of such crafts.

19TH CENTURY ART

Because of the troubled beginnings of independent Mexico, artistic activities were at a very low ebb. The plastic arts lived on the remains of colonial art, creating nothing new. It was not until 1839 that steps were taken to reorganize the Academy of San Carlos. Two Spanish masters, the painter Pelegrín Clavé and the sculptor Manuel Vilar, were engaged to effect a reform in the plan of studies, and arrived shortly after.

Apart from his work as a teacher and director, Pelegrín Clavé (1810–1880) also painted a number of pictures which were well liked. He arrived in Mexico in 1846 to assume the directorship of the Academy of San Carlos, and his influence was instrumental in bringing about a change, indispensable at the time. He did not limit his work to religious paintings, but drew inspiration also from history and fiction. In his portraits he strove for likeness to the model, using gay, brilliantly colored silks and velvets which replaced the monotonous dark shades that obtained in colonial times. In so doing he followed the style whose principal exponent in Europe was then Jean Auguste Dominique Ingres.

The most promising of Clavé's students, Santiago Rebull (1829–1902), Felipe Gutiérrez (1824–1904), and José Salomé Pina (1830–1909), were sent to continue their studies in Rome, and their work was admired in several exhibitions given in Mexico between 1850 and 1865. Ramón Sagredo (1834–1872) and Juan Cordero (1824–1884) are of the same school, though they belong to a later period; also, toward the end of the century, Luis Monroy and Félix Parra (1845–1910). All of them painted portraits, and historical and religious paintings. Their asset was a thorough knowledge of their craft; their handicaps those of the academic movement: limitation, lack of vitality, artificiality, and conventionalism.

It was also a Spanish master, Manuel Vilar, who, coming to Mexico with Clavé in 1846, gave a new impulse to sculpture. His stay in Mexico was shorter than that of Clavé, but during it he endeavoured to teach correct academic sculpture. His most proficient students were Miguel Noreña and Gabriel Guerra (1847–1893), who made several praiseworthy pieces. They worked together on the monument to Cuauhtemoc which is now in the Paseo de la Reforma in Mexico City; Noreña made the hero's statue, and Guerra the four high reliefs adorning the base. The five pieces are in bronze.

Landscape painting in Mexico was begun in the second half of the 18th century, when the Academy of San Carlos arranged for the Italian landscape painter Eugenio Landesio to come to Mexico to teach his specialty; this he did for some 20 years. His most outstanding student was José María Velasco (1840–1912), whose works are mostly landscapes. Velasco always kept to a high standard of achievement and some of his paintings are of the very highest quality; of these are two large canvases of the Valley of Mexico, which are in the Museo de Artes Plásticas.

In 1903 the Catalan painter Antonio Fabrés was appointed to direct the academy. Under him Mexican painting continued along the decadent way it had again fallen into, by following the mistaken road of "photographic" realism, with certain leanings toward the French manner. Two artists are perhaps worth mentioning: Leandro Izaguirre (1867–1941) and Julio Ruelas (1871–1907). The second was an extremely capable but warped draughtsman.

Jesús F. Contreras (1866–1902) should be mentioned among the sculptors of the time. In spite of the loss of an arm, he executed a number of statues for the capital and other cities of Mexico.

Meanwhile, some Mexican artists who were studying in Europe and others who had stayed in their own country were venting their dissatisfaction with the state of the arts. These fostered the awakening of the movement which was to bring far-reaching changes not long after. But very few people then realized that the most important artistic effort was being made in a small printing workshop that was publishing stories, prayers, plays for marionettes, and *corridos* (popular narrative songs) in leaflets and sheets that were sold for two or three centavos. Woodcuts and copper prints had been made in New Spain since the 16th century. The first lithograph press was founded in 1826, shortly after independence had been won, and that type of work was assiduously cultivated during the 19th century.

Manuel Manilla (1830–c.1890) and José Guadalupe Posada (1851–1913) were doing their work for the publisher Antonio Vanegas Arroyo in Mexico City, illustrating with their engravings that genuinely popular literature. Posada's engravings, though showing the influence of Francisco José de Goya and Honoré Daumier, have such a strong Mexican character and such extraordinary strength and emotivity that they are, without a doubt, the best product of Mexican art in the 19th century. They not only announce the following period; they link up with it.

MODERN ART

The last European art movement whose influence was felt in Mexico was the impressionist—very strong in Europe and fully a 19th-century movement; very weak in Mexico and felt rather late. Among Mexican artists, it was best known to Alfredo Ramos Martínez (1875–1946) and Dr.

Atl (1877–   ), both of whom had lived for many years in Italy and France. They imparted their knowledge to young Mexican painters in 1910, and the result was, not an impressionist movement in Mexico, but rather the desire to seek some reform, something new and different.

Joaquín Clausel (1885–1936), a young landscape painter of great sensitivity, was the best exponent of impressionism in Mexico. Another young painter, Saturnino Herrán (1887–1918), used impressionist trends blended with a national feeling for subject and color, suggesting the discovery of a type of art of his own; unfortunately, he died before he could bring it to fruition.

Meanwhile the revolution had broken out, and during the most active years, 1914–1916, the political struggle and the battlefield demanded everybody's full attention. Some artists were abroad; others, like Dr. Atl and José Clemente Orozco, had embraced the revolutionary cause and were waging their own war, using their art as a weapon through political newspapers. Such an upheaval as the revolution brought about had of necessity to result in something new; it would have been impossible to return to the old ideas and forms of expression.

When peace came in 1921, a cultured and intelligent man, José Vasconcelos (1882–   ), was appointed minister of public education. Vasconcelos sought above all to create, and in this endeavor he saw fit to offer new opportunities to artists, making available to them public buildings which they could brighten with their artistic imagination.

Diego Rivera had been living in Europe from the first years of the century, having gone there after being awarded a scholarship by the academy, but he had returned to Mexico at the time of Vasconcelos' accession to the ministry. Together with Xavier Guerrero (1896–   ), Alva de la Canal, Jean Charlot (1898–   ), David Alfaro Siqueiros, Orozco, and others, he formed the Syndicate of Painters and Sculptors, and prepared to decorate the old and new buildings that the government was making available. They decided to do fresco or encaustic paintings on walls, to make them easily accessible to the common man and to prevent their being shut up in halls, like the oils and watercolors of old. In sculpture, they abandoned bronze and plaster casting, preferring to carve stone in the footsteps of pre-Hispanic sculptors. Thus was born that interesting phenomenon, perhaps the aspect of modern Mexico best known to the non-Spanish-speaking world, its postrevolutionary art.

Each artist followed his own path, all of them different. Some disappeared; others went on, growing in stature. The original group was followed by another, and a third group of artists began its career toward the middle of the 20th century. It is, therefore, inconvenient to follow the process as a whole; to avoid confusion it is best to refer individually to each of the artists that deserve to be mentioned within the strict limits of this short study.

Rivera.—Diego Rivera was born at Guanajuato in 1886. He studied at the academy in Mexico City and went to Europe in 1906, remaining there until 1921, except for a short visit to Mexico at the time the revolution was beginning. He worked in Mexico after 1921, except for visits to the USSR and the United States, where he did some paintings in the cities of San Francisco, Detroit, and New York. He tried

various styles and used several techniques in his early days (realism, impressionism, and cubism; oil, tempera, and collage), but his important work began in 1922, and must be studied in two great sections: murals and easel paintings.

Rivera painted his first mural in 1922 in the Anfiteatro Bolívar of the Escuela Nacional Preparatoria in Mexico City, using encaustic paint. It has a vast theme of Man, Nature, and Life. The composition is excellent, but in the subject's treatment one can detect strong Italian and Byzantine influences. A short time later he decorated the ground floor of the Secretaría de Educación Pública (Public Education Department) also in the capital. It is here that social themes and subjects based on the Mexican Revolution of 1910 make their first appearance. In 1927 Rivera painted murals on the walls and vaulting of the former chapel (now the Escuela Nacional de Agricultura) at Chapingo, northeast of Mexico City. The subjects were land and the agrarian reform; the composition as well as the use of design and color are excellent. It can be said without hesitation that the Chapingo frescoes are Rivera's masterpiece, which he has been unable to surpass. After 1929, he devoted his frescoes in the Palacio de Cortés in Cuernavaca and the Palacio Nacional in Mexico City to subjects taken from the history of Mexico and the coming socialist revolution. He repainted, in the Palacio de Bellas Artes in Mexico City, the fresco that he had started—and had been forbidden to finish—for Rockefeller Center, New York. More recently, he has been engaged almost exclusively in trying to make a grand apology for Mexican cultures before the coming of the Spaniards. Through political ideology, he has fallen into practicing the art of propaganda.

His easel paintings, nearly always oil on canvas, show more varied qualities. He has painted popular Mexican types, portrayed with great dignity and devoid of picturesqueness; some landscapes; some life studies; and many portraits. They are in museums and private collections, mainly in Mexico and the United States.

Orozco.—José Clemente Orozco was born at Zapotlán, Jalisco, in 1883, and studied at the academy in Mexico City, where he died in 1949. He made cartoons and illustrations for some of the revolutionary papers, and later held an exhibition of paintings and other small works. Like Rivera and several other Mexican painters, he took to mural painting in 1922 and after that date his important work was in his frescoes, though he also did a great number of works in oil and tempera, as well as drawings and lithographs. His most important murals are found in the following places: Escuela Nacional Preparatoria (1922 and 1926), the Supreme Court building (1940), and the Hospital de Jesús (1942), all in Mexico City; in the United States at Pomona College, California, and Dartmouth College, New Hampshire; the library at Jiquilpan, Michoacán; and the university, Palacio de Gobierno (Government Building), and Hospicio Cabañas (Cabañas Foundling Home) in Guadalajara. The three last were painted in or about 1938 and they are, on the whole, the best. Of special note is the fresco on the cupola of the old chapel of the Hospicio Cabañas. There is, besides, an impressive array of Orozco's oils, drawings, and other easel work, all of a very high quality.

Orozco cultivated a very personal style, which

is in some ways slightly reminiscent of expressionism, but the peculiar characteristics he imparted to it give it a character of his own. It is above all virile, austere, sometimes fierce; there is in it none of the voluptuousness often found in Diego Rivera's work, but on the other hand, it usually has much more strength and movement; it is dynamic in its subjects and treatment, and it moves the observer—just as Diego Rivera's style is static. Some critics have insisted that Orozco is the best Mexican painter of the 20th century. This is difficult to judge, however, when most of the other painters are still living and it cannot be said how or what they will paint in the future. Nevertheless, it can be definitely stated that Orozco was an inspired artist and a great master of the craft of fresco painting.

Siqueiros.—David Alfaro Siqueiros, born at Chihuahua in 1898, has lived a very full life as a Mexican revolutionary, a union leader, and a soldier in the Spanish Civil War, always fighting vehemently for the extreme left. He was one of the pioneers of modern Mexican painting. He has painted in North and South America, and his restless spirit has impelled him to try new materials and methods—undoubtedly in an attempt to modernize art, but it is difficult to see that the results achieved have justified such innovations. He has done murals and easel work, and his political passion has often carried him beyond the realm of art. There is no doubt that he is a good painter; but, so far, only a few portraits and human figures can be said to have lasting qualities.

The painters mentioned, and others who have followed them, are driven mainly by an all-pervading social consciousness: they accuse, they protest, they fight. This is certainly a most important aspect in much of modern Mexican painting, and it is an aspect which the outside observer and the foreign critic, Europeans especially, do not seem to comprehend—perhaps because they are steeped in a pure art tradition which is not part of the Mexican way of life.

Other Painters.—Painters whom we can call independent have worked alongside those who express social or political themes. Among them should be mentioned Francisco Goitia (1884–   ), who gave pictorial expression to the misery and grief of the poor; in the austerity of his *Tata Jesucristo* he has achieved one of the most dramatic paintings of modern art. Goitia is also a landscape painter. Doctor Atl (pseudonym of Gerardo Murillo; 1877–   ) is a prolific painter of strong and concise landscapes, using varied techniques. Manuel Rodríguez Lozano (1896–   ) has, with great intelligence and self-control, followed his own path in paintings of a strong poetic feeling allied to fine drawing and a sensitively quiet use of color. Rufino Tamayo (1899–   ) is undoubtedly one of the best Mexican painters, but the style he has cultivated since about 1940 has placed him nearer the modern international school and farther from Mexican painting.

There is a later group of painters which has been named the second generation of modern Mexican painting. Of these, the following have done outstanding work: Carlos Orozco Romero (1898–   ); Julio Castellanos (1905–1947), whose death before he could be said to have reached maturity cut short a highly promising career; Federico Cantú (1908–   ); Agustín

Lazo (1900–   ); and Jesús Guerrero Galván (1910–   ).

In the last group, or third generation, are included those painters who are still young, but whose work is sufficient to reveal their talent. Among them should be mentioned Raúl Anguiano (1915–   ), Juan Soriano (1920–   ), and Ricardo Martínez de Hoyos (1918–   ). It is hardly fitting even to try to judge these painters, who are now in their prime and who, because of their age, are still susceptible to change.

Sculpture.—By contrast, modern sculpture, though starting at the same time as modern painting, in 1922, is still very far from achieving the development and fruition that accrued to painting. The experiment of the Escuela de Talla Directa (School of Direct Carving) was very interesting because of the return the school advocated to the straightforward, austere technique that had produced so many masterpieces in pre-Hispanic Mexico. But the results did not come up to expectations, nor was the experiment long continued. Some giant-size statues have been carved —the best example is the statue of José María Morelos on the island of Janitzio in Lake Pátzcuaro—but results have been bad in every case: witness the Pípila Monument in Guanajuato, among others. Mexican sculptors have followed various tendencies, from realism to abstractionism, and they have sometimes created work which is praiseworthy, but never really meaningful or talented. The phenomenon has a parallel in many other places; it seems that our times are not propitious to sculpture. The best known Mexican sculptors are: Ignacio Asúnsolo (1890–   ), Luis Albarrán, Carlos Bracho (1899–   ), Manuel Centurión (1865–1948), Federico Canessi, Germán Cueto (1893–   ), Mardonio Magaña (1866–1947), Luis Ortiz Monasterio (1906–   ), Juan Olaguíbel (1897–   ), Guillermo Toussaint, Guillermo Ruiz, and Francisco Zúñiga.

Engraving.—This art, which became so important in prerevolutionary days with José Guadalupe Posada, has continued in its various forms: wood, copper, etchings, and lithographs. It can be said that, like painting, Mexican engraving now holds an important place. The principal places where engraving is carried out are in Mexico City: the Taller de Gráfica Popular (Popular Printing Workshop); the Escuela de Artes del Libro (School of Book Arts); and the two schools dedicated to plastic art, that of the National University and the one supported by the Secretaría de Educación Pública (Public Education Department). Some of the best engravers are: Francisco Díaz de León (1897–   ), Leopoldo Méndez (1903–   ), Carlos Alvarado Lang (1905–   ), Alfredo Zalce (1908–   ), Abelardo Ávila (1909–   ), José Julio (1912–   ), Mariano Paredes (1912–   ), and Julio Prieto (1912–   ).

Photography.—Photography has also made a place for itself among the arts. In the first part of the 20th century two photographers did notable work: Lupercio and Guillermo Kahlo (d. 1941). Three great foreign photographers resided in the country between 1920 and 1930, Edward Weston, Tina Modotti, and Serge M. Eisenstein. Their influence stimulated Mexican photography and raised its standards. The most distinguished photographers of recent times have been: Emilio Amero, Manuel Alvarez Bravo and Lola Alvarez Bravo, A. Jiménez, and Luis Márquez.

FOLK ART

The art critic Justino Fernández, in *El arte moderno en México* (Mexico City 1937), has made the following statement which is still valid:

The general characteristics which can be found in this popular Mexican activity are: a great artistic feeling, especially in so far as decoration is concerned; a high degree of vitality, as can be observed from the number of objects produced and attention to detail; a concern with method to such a degree that it looks like routine; and extraordinary fantasy. It can therefore be said that Mexico holds the third place, after China and Japan, as a producer of folk art.

The only possible classification of folk art, since it follows no school and shows no particular period of development, is according to objects and sometimes to its sources of inspiration. In the following the objects are referred to according to their importance.

Folk painting is found mainly in religious subjects, in small paintings on sheet metal or cloth called *retablos* (another meaning of the word—in English, *retable*—which is used to describe the ornamental pieces of architecture or sculpture covering walls at the back of altars in many churches), showing figures or scenes with great ingenuousness and sometimes with a certain graceful, almost childish clumsiness. A lot of nonreligious painting was done in the decoration of *pulquerías* (taverns where pulque, a popular drink made from the fermented sap of the maguey, is sold). This custom, however, has been almost completely lost.

Folk art finds magnificent expression in weaving. Fabrics are woven in many different ways and for many uses: tablecloths, serapes (woolen blankets to be worn), *rebozos* (scarves of cotton or silk), garments, and ornamental pieces. The techniques are nearly always of Spanish origin, and so are the designs, though in certain regions (Oaxaca, Chiapas, and Michoacán) native influence can be clearly seen in embroidery or colored fabrics. Weaving can be best classified according to regions, since costumes and their ornaments serve best to differentiate popular regional characteristics.

Lacquered goods—vessels, boxes, toys; sometimes furniture and other objects—are also of great interest. The principal centers of production are Olinalá in Guerrero, and Pátzcuaro and Uruapan in Michoacán. The process followed in Olinalá is as follows: scenes and ornaments are painted in color on a black base; or else one single color is applied, on which certain parts are scraped to suggest lacework. In Pátzcuaro it is usual to paint in several colors, nearly always on a black base. The practice of this art had almost disappeared, but it was revived and has become almost as important as it once was in the 18th and 19th centuries. In Uruapan, colors are rubbed into the wood, using black as the background, and the whole is covered with a damp-resisting lacquer.

Leather and iron are worked following the tradition of Spanish arts and crafts. There are slight variations due to the influence of national characteristics. The working of gold and silver, which became so important in vice-regal times, has disappeared in many parts. Gold is being worked following the traditional manner in Oaxaca; and silver in Taxco, Guerrero.

Furniture with regional characteristics, following popular designs and motifs, was being built as late as the 19th century. These designs have been widely used by mechanized industry, and for that reason have changed and lost value.

A great variety of pots have always been made of clay and glass. These continue to be made; as well as toys and other useful and ornamental objects of the same materials. Glass blowing is carried out with great success at Guadalajara and Mexico City. Pottery exists practically everywhere, but as is the case with weaving, takes on distinctive characteristics according to the region. Such peculiarities tend to disappear nowadays, owing to facilities for interchange—whenever a certain type of pot or decoration becomes fashionable, it is immediately imitated by potters whose production ought to have completely different characteristics.

The manufacture of cheap toys has reached into practically the whole country, and offers a very wide variety. Many materials are used—fired clay, wood, wire, rags, paper, cardboard, tin, wax, and even chewing gum—and they are turned out in every kind of animal shape, dolls, and all sorts of objects, most often painted over with strong, contrasting colors.

The human form, apart from being used in clay, rag, wooden, or cardboard puppets, is also borrowed for the manufacture of masks, which may represent comical, awe-inspiring, or grotesque faces, or skulls; sometimes also animal heads. The masks are often children's toys, but in some cases are intended to cover the faces of dancers or actors taking part in dances or religious plays acted during specific celebrations.

The human form is also represented in the so-called Judases, which are small or large cardboard or papier-mâché figures (some being six or more feet tall) to which firecrackers are attached. The "Judases" are burnt publicly on the Saturday of Holy Week.

Piñatas (clay pots covered with colored paper in the shape of animals, ships, stars, and the like) and the crèches or Nativity scenes, with their clay and wax figures made up to represent Biblical scenes or scenes of regional customs, are all expressions of popular art which take place around Advent and Christmas.

Candies are often made or decorated in ways which allow them to be classed as popular art. Perhaps the most remarkable are the small figures made of sugar paste, like *alfeñique* (boiled sugar candy of different colors) and other candies in the shape of animals and objects. Most often they are made to represent skeletons, skulls, and the like, and are made, bought, and eaten around All Souls' Day (November 2), when the so-called pan de muerto (bread of the dead) is also eaten in various regional varieties.

All the folk arts are very poor in the northern states and greatly varied in the central and southern ones. They have also tended to disappear, due to several reasons. Sometimes it is because of the mechanization of industry; sometimes because easier means of communication have tended to standardize the formerly different production of each region; sometimes because the growing market for such goods has made manufacturers anxious to please the taste of the majority of buyers, often foreign tourists who prefer picturesqueness and mistaken Mexicanized motifs to genuine decoration, which is usually more austere.

The ornamental motifs in these arts and crafts are usually flowers, birds, and scenes and objects taken from nature, stylized according to the taste peculiar to the region or the artist.

MEXICO

F. Henle from Monkmeyer
Bill Sprattling's outside silver workshop at Taxco.

Mexican Government Railway System
A Pueblan potter at work.

Monkmeyer
Interior of Bill Sprattling's silver workshop.

MEXICO

Mexican tiled kitchen.

Mexican Government Railway System

Homes of peasants and gardens in the shadow of the mountains. Mt. Ixtachihuatl off in the distance.

Sometimes they are geometrical shapes of ancient origin. In certain cases short legends are written —"Souvenir Of . . ." or proper names, and so forth. Very seldom is the human figure used, but a very usual subject is death, represented by various symbols or allegories: skulls, skeletons, bones, coffins, funeral processions, tombs, and the like, used in the manufacture of masks, puppets, toys, bread, and candy. The reasons for this— atavism, reminiscence of forgotten cults, the character of the people, their interpretation of life, everything that may have originated and may justify the preference shown for death in folk art—may be studied, perhaps, only through ethnological and historical research. It is sufficient for the present study to record the facts as related to art.

Bibliography.—Atl, Dr., *Las artes populares de México,* 2 vols. (Mexico City 1922); Romero de Terreros, Manuel, *Las artes industriales en la Nueva España* (Mexico City 1923); Brenner, Anita, *Idols Behind Altars* (New York 1929); Museum of Modern Art, *Frescoes,* Diego Rivera's works (New York 1933); Universidad Nacional de México, *Anales del Instituto de Investigaciones Estéticas* (Mexico City 1933—); Wolfe, Bertram D., *Diego Rivera: His Life and Times* (New York 1939); Museum of Modern Art, *Twenty Centuries of Mexican Art* (New York 1940); Fernández, Justino, *José Clemente Orozco; forma e idea* (Mexico City 1942); id., *Prometeo; ensayo sobre pintura contemporánea* (Mexico City 1945); Orozco, José Clemente, *Autobiografía* (Mexico City 1945); Toussaint, Manuel, *Arte colonial en México* (Mexico City 1948); Wilder, Elizabeth Weismann, *Mexico in Sculpture, 1521–1821* (Cambridge, Mass., 1950); *Diego Rivera; 50 años de su labor artística* (Mexico City 1951); *Siqueiros, por la via de una pintura neorrealista . . . ,* text in Spanish, English, and French, with 215 reproductions (Mexico City 1951); Cranfill, Thomas M., *The Muse in Mexico* (Austin, Texas, 1959); Charlot, Jean, *The Mexican Mural Renaissance, 1920–1925* (New Haven, Conn., 1963); Edwards, Emily, *Painted Walls in Mexico* (Austin, Texas, 1966).

JOSÉ ROJAS GARCIDUEÑAS,
Professor of Literature, Universidad Nacional de México; Researcher, Instituto de Investigaciones Estéticas.

18. ARCHITECTURE. Pre-Hispanic Architecture.

—In discussing pre-Hispanic architecture in Mexico one cannot limit one's field of interest to the present-day boundaries of the Mexican Republic, and hope to understand all the architectural manifestations of that period. This is due to the fact that the culture out of which it arose extended far to the south, while limited narrowly in its extension toward the north. Reference here will therefore be made only to the geographical and cultural area which archaeologists call Meso-America, that is, central and southern Mexico, British Honduras, Guatemala, western Honduras, and El Salvador.

There has been remarkably little excavation, considering the great number of monuments left by pre-Hispanic cultures. Thus only the first phase of architectural investigation has been completed: that of describing and classifying the known material in basic ways. The systematic study of techniques and of the development of forms, as well as the evaluation of styles and aesthetics, awaits the future.

Archaic Culture in Central Mexico.—The first architectural development with which we are acquainted in Meso-America belongs to the level of cultural development characterized by farming and pottery. Its technology, religious ideas, and patterns of urban association are characteristic of a very wide geographical area.

Cuicuilco.—The one well-preserved monument which belongs to this culture and which has been studied sufficiently is found in the Valley of Mexico, south of Mexico City, and is called the Pyramid of Cuicuilco. Shortly after its construction, apparently, the monument was covered over by a layer of basaltic lava, averaging eight meters in thickness. (One meter equals 3.28 feet.) This accounts for its relatively good state of preservation. The monument was excavated by Byron Cummings of the University of Arizona in 1922.

Despite the fact that the building is called a pyramid, it really consists of four superimposed truncated cones. These decrease in size. The first has a diameter of 135 meters, the last a diameter of 70 meters. The layout is oriented almost exactly along a north-south axis, with one end formed by a ramp and stairway leading up to the entrance. This solid construction serves as a platform for an upper construction of wood of which only traces remain. The body of the pyramid is filled with a mixture of clay and rocks, while the outside was faced with stones. Part of this facing is preserved in the upper portions.

The radioactivity of organic remains, analyzed by means of carbon isotope 14 (radiocarbon method) has yielded 600 B.C. as a possible date for the site.

Classic Cultures in Central Mexico.— *Teotihuacán*—The most important material remains of the new cultural horizon in the Valley of Mexico, a horizon which to some degree extended throughout Meso-America, and which is characterized basically by the formation of great urban centers, is the archaeological city called Teotihuacán. It is situated in a small valley, about 25 miles northeast of Mexico City, to the east of the Valley of Mexico and subsidiary to it. The development of the city may be dated very roughly between the 1st century A.D. and the 8th or 9th centuries A.D. Its beginnings tie into the Archaic culture; its terminal phase links up with the Toltec horizon by way of developments at Azcapotzalco, where its culture was carried on. While Teotihuacán has been studied intermittently since the middle of the 19th century, its methodical study by Manuel Gamio, Ignacio Marquina, Sigvald Linné, Pedro Armillas, and others has been under way only since 1922.

The city plan is laid out around a basic north-south axis formed by the Avenue of the Dead (*Miccaotli*), 55 meters wide, which compensates for the unevenness of the terrain by means of ascending tiers. The Avenue of the Dead is about 2,500 meters long, with indefinite limits toward the southern end. The main religious and secular monuments are situated close to the axis and perpendicular to it. Other streets also run parallel or perpendicular to the main axis.

The initial plan determined by these axes was followed rigidly throughout the city's growth. Lines not in harmony with it were avoided. Curved lines are completely absent. Axes also relate the complexes of ceremonial buildings to each other, but these relations do not serve to tie the whole into one aesthetic unit. On the contrary, each building group forms a closed-in unit with scant ties to the other groups.

The main axis, the Avenue of the Dead, is cut off at the extreme northern end by the building called the Pyramid of the Moon. In front of this building the big avenue widens into a rectangular plaza, 150 meters long along the front of the pyramid, and 120 meters wide. West of this axis rise the groups called the Temple of Agriculture and the Group of the Columns; east of it the Pyramid of the Sun and the buildings which surround it. To the south lies the so-called Group of Superimposed Buildings, and, just before the avenue crosses the San Juan River, the one watercourse which traverses the city, is the Viking Fund Group. On the other side of the river, and virtually in line with the prolongation of the axis of the Pyramid of the Sun, lies the complex of the Temple of Quetzalcoatl, also called the Ciudadela (Fortress).

Due both to their location and dimensions, the most important of the buildings mentioned are the Pyramid of the Sun, the Pyramid of the Moon, and the Temple of Quetzalcoatl. The typical plan of these buildings erected for religious purposes consists of a base formed by the superimposed terraces which supported a small temple. None of the small temples have been preserved. The entire complex is surrounded by a platform on three or four sides. The Pyramid of the Sun, 64.46 meters high, with a square base 225 meters on each side, wholly dominates its surrounding platform. This relation has been inverted in the case of the Temple of Quetzalcoatl. The platform, with sides 400 meters long, is vastly larger than the pyramid, which measures only 40 meters at the base.

It has been possible to recognize three distinct periods in the development of these buildings. They are evident primarily in the evolution of the surfaces of the terraces which rise in layers to form the platforms. During the earliest period, the surface is a simple slope. The last step is represented by the architectural form called the "Teotihuacán panel." This consists of a rectangular compartment, outlined by a flat molding, which juts out over a sloping platform one third the size of the whole terrace layer. The inside may or may not be decorated with paintings as well as with sculptured forms. On the Temple of Quetzalcoatl, for example, the heads of two different types of serpents, evidently symbols of water deities, are arranged in strict order within a geometric design.

The system of construction employed in nearly all the buildings at Teotihuacán is very similar. Basically, it consists in heaping up earth, rocks, and adobe, together with retaining walls made of lava, into solid inner bodies for the pyramidal platforms. The retaining walls sometimes form a framework throughout the building. The panels with moldings that jut out are made of whole stone slabs which hold up the weight of the panel, and are faced with ordinary stones and lime stucco. Only the Temple of Quetzalcoatl has facings entirely of cut stones, which protrude into the body of the building.

The layout of buildings used as homes has received less study. It is possible, however, to distinguish buildings near the great temples, which seem to have been used by the priestly class. They show a quite systematic distribution of rooms, with porticos in front, around sunken courts intended for religious purposes. These courts were common to a number of housing units. The habitation area seems to have been very large, so that the large religious buildings formed only the center of an urban aggregate of great proportions.

Later buildings were generally superimposed on earlier ones, following either the vertical or the longitudinal axes of these buildings. The later buildings thus often hid the earlier ones wholly or in part. This custom was followed not only in the case of the great temples but also in the case of human habitations. It constitutes a characteristic common to all Meso-America.

Teotihuacán architecture is important not only in terms of itself, but also because it made its influence felt in such widely different areas as the states of Sinaloa and Tamaulipas in the north of Mexico and the highlands of the Republic of Guatemala to the south.

Cholula.—In pre-Hispanic times this city, now eight miles west of Puebla, was the most important religious and urban center in the Valley of Puebla. Few remains exist, since the colonial city was built over the ruins of the pre-Hispanic city. The most important monument, the main pyramid, was excavated systematically after 1931. As a result, five different architectural periods are known. Each period is characterized by a pyramidal structure of different size, each of which incorporated the pyramid of the preceding epoch.

The phases which stand out most clearly are I, II and IV. One must remember that I is the oldest and that at the time of the conquest the Spaniards found the pyramid unused and in ruins, during the last phase (V).

The structure belonging to phase I resembles in shape the Pyramid of the Sun at Teotihuacán, although its dimensions are obviously smaller. It measures 113 meters by 107 and is typically oriented toward the west, with a deviation of 17°. Five stepped terraces of structured pyramidal shape lead up to the topmost platform, which lies 17 or 18 meters above the surrounding terrain. Each stepped terrace is thus roughly 2.5 meters high.

The most outstanding characteristic of this structure is perhaps the special decoration of the panels which were later added to the slopes. These include polychrome paintings of greatly enlarged insect heads. In style and technique, they seem to be contemporary with the two earliest periods at Teotihuacán.

During phase II the building was completely covered over and its dimensions greatly enlarged. A side of its square base came to measure 190 meters. Its height of 34 meters was distributed among nine terraces, each shaped like a truncated pyramid, but each subdivided into 12 steps 0.30 meters high. The whole edifice thus came to represent a platform with stairways running up each one of its four sides. This continuity, which so strongly emphasized horizontal lines, is interrupted at only four points on each side where open-air drains from the platform above project vertically.

This monument is unique in Mexico, due both to the originality of its conception and to the maximum of emphasis on horizontal lines in its construction. No other building is known in which the same arrangement has been employed.

The works belonging to phase IV, the last phase of importance, cover the preceding ones and lend the edifice its present character. They are sadly ruined on the outside, but seem to have comprised two enormous terraces with sloping surfaces, separated by a wide passage on three sides, while on the fourth side one surface led into another and formed a single slope.

The dimensions of this pyramid are the largest found in any monument built in Mexico. It has a square base with sides 400 meters long and a height of 62 meters, nearly the height of the Pyramid of the Sun.

Transition Period in Central Mexico.—
Xochicalco.—The ruins of Xochicalco are located
17 miles southwest of the city of Cuernavaca in
the Valley of Morelos. From the cultural and
architectural point of view, they seem to represent
a point of transition between the Classic cultures
and the Toltec period, both in terms of time, and
in terms of their geographical location as a link
between the cultures of the south and the Valley
of Mexico.

In contrast to Teotihuacán and Cholula, the
ruins are situated on the lateral spur of a
mountain, the natural shape of which has been
modified by five stepped terraces which tend to
organize the terrain into horizontal levels and a
surrounding area. The general layout of the terraced area follows a north-south axis 1,200 meters
long and an east-west axis 700 meters long.

The top platform is reached by means of two
walks formed by staircases which begin in the
south and west. It measures roughly 300 meters
by 200 meters, and supports the chief buildings
of the city. The most important of these buildings in terms of location, state of preservation,
and architectural style is located where the general axes of the city cross. It consists of one
body, the profile of which is formed by a slope
that covers two thirds of its total height, and of
an unbroken floor which juts out over the slope
and rises on a beveled cornice. The temple which
rose on this platform seems to have had a similar
silhouette, though only the part belonging to the
slope has been preserved. The outside of the
whole construction is finished with reliefs of cut
and worked stone. These represent the undulating figure of a plumed serpent, which shelters
seated human figures and the symbol of the new
fire in its curves. A number of authors have
called attention to the stylistic similarity of the
human figures to Maya representations. Remains
of polychrome stucco, which once completely covered architecture and sculpture, are found in different parts of the whole monument.

There are other monuments adjoining the terraces, which form true esplanades. The most
interesting of these is the ball court, which in
layout and front elevations shows similarities to
the ball courts of Copán and Piedras Negras in
the Maya area, and to the ball court of the Toltec
city of Tollan (Tula).

In contrast to the metropolis of Teotihuacán,
Xochicalco seen as a whole gives the impression
that the planner, in striving to attain the shapes
of stepped pyramids, has attempted to erect one
gigantic pyramid. Its body is formed by the
natural prominence of the hill of Xochicalco; its
stepped tiers are defined by the surrounding terraces.

Toltec Period in Central Mexico.—The
fall of Teotihuacán as a cultural center marks a
profound break in the development of architecture
on the plateau, though it does not imply a complete abandonment of the architectural forms and
arrangements produced during the city's period.

Pottery shows a cultural continuation of the
Teotihuacán period; in architecture this is represented by decorative elements which appear at
Tollan and which were developed during the preceding period. Among the latter elements may
be mentioned the special type of panel employed
at Tollan (this represents the last step in the evolution of the panel of Teotihuacán and is described
below); the merlons of battlements in the shape
of a transversal section of a snail; the represen-

tations of Tlaloc, god of the rain; the general arrangement of the pyramidal platforms in religious
structures; and the layout of courts surrounded
by rooms in structures used as homes.

Tollan.—The city of Tollan, the modern Tula,
located in the Valley of Tula in Hidalgo, was the
center of the new cultural horizon. Excavations
were carried on there sporadically after 1873, but
systematic excavations were made only from 1940
to 1945. As a result a number of buildings of
artistic and archaeological value are known, and
proof has been obtained that this city was the
capital of the Toltec Empire mentioned in the
Indian chronicles before the Spanish conquest.

The building which gives the clearest idea of
Toltec architecture is Temple B or Temple of
Tlahuizcalpantecuhtli, which forms part of the
northern side of the main plaza of the city. It
consists of five superimposed terraces decorated
with unusually shaped panels, which are divided
into three horizontal strips. The lowest forms a
slope roughly one third of the total height; the
top one consists of a continuous frieze delimited
by two smooth moldings with alternating figures
of jaguars and coyotes. In the middle strip,
panels which stand out alternate with sunken
ones. These show eagles devouring human
hearts, and a figure which combines human features with those of bird and serpent. A stairway
on the southern side facing the plaza ascends to
an upper platform where there are remains of
columns in the form of anthropomorphic "atlases," eight of which held up the flat roof of a
temple. The entrance to the temple was divided
into three spaces by columns in the shape of serpents. The tail of each serpent formed a kind of
capital, while the head formed the base. Three
corridors of pillars, with square sections and decorated with the images of warriors, stood in front
of this temple and connected it with the plaza.

All the decorative elements mentioned are repeated with remarkable exactness on the buildings at Chichén Itzá in northern Yucatán which
belong to the period of Toltec influence. This
supports the supposition that Temple B is older
than the Toltec emigration to the south and Yucatán, which took place during the reign of Ce Acatl
Topiltzin Quetzalcoatl, in the katun 2 Ahau
(987–1007 A.D.), according to the Maya chronicles.

There are a number of other buildings, apart
from the one just described. Among these are
Mound A, remarkable for its size, but little
known, and two ball courts, one on the western
end of the main plaza, and the other north of
Temple B. These ball courts are of undoubted
importance within the general plan of the city
and exhibit close similarities to the one at Xochicalco.

Other known buildings are the ones surrounding Temple B and the so-called Palace of Cielito
which show the development of porticos around
courts, with a layout similar to the buildings of
Teotihuacán, but with greater use of isolated
supports and more control over them.

Generally it may be said that Tollan lacks the
monumental conception evident at Teotihuacán
and Xochicalco. The principle of axes of a city
has been lost, while the general orientation of
buildings along a 17° deviation has been preserved. Religious architecture still dominates,
but secular architecture has certainly gained in
impulse and has come to use more differentiated
elements, such as the pillar and the atlas-type

column. These are used to further a tendency toward relating architecture to the needs of interior structure and decoration, stripping it of the wholly external character typical of Teotihuacán.

The decorative sculpture on the buildings lends them an air of greater luxury and ostentation, retreating from the tendency of the preceding period towards the schematic and geometric. Yet the abundance of new decorative elements gives rise to the impression that there existed a creative tendency to produce new forms, without the refinement and control over aesthetic and technical expressions needed to carry these motifs to a high level of maturity.

Post-Toltec Period in Central Mexico.— *Tenayuca.*—In this small present-day village, eight miles north-northwest of Mexico City, and once of great importance as the center of Chichimec power after the eclipse of Toltec rule, there are some remains which have been well studied in excavations carried on by the Instituto Nacional de Antropología e Historia.

A series of successively superimposed architectural structures belong to an equivalent number of periods. From the earliest period to the latest, the layout used is always the same. It is characterized by three or four stepped terraces with more or less sloping surfaces, which support an upper platform with twin temples. These can be reached by way of a staircase divided in the middle by a double ramp.

Mention may be made of a type of low wall formed by closely spaced serpents which coil back upon themselves and surround the pyramid on the three sides of lesser importance.

The decorative and architectural poverty of these monuments and the repetition of the same arrangements seem to indicate a standstill in the evolution of styles during the three centuries preceding the Spanish conquest.

The known remains of the great temple of the old Aztec city of Tenochtitlán in Mexico City and of the temple there in the barrio (quarter) of Tlaltelolco resemble the Tenayuca pyramid in style.

Valley of Oaxaca.— *Monte Albán.*—This ancient city, six miles west of the modern city of Oaxaca, is primarily interesting for its overall plan in which the highest portion of a hill rising 400 meters above the valley has been used for its buildings. The main center includes a rectangular plaza surrounded by buildings on its two larger sides and delimited on the two shorter sides by two great platforms. The main axis of the plaza is marked by four low structures which stand in line. The principle of organization in terms of parallel or perpendicular axes is absent in this arrangement, which is characterized, however, by a series of relations set up by visual perspective which have determined the position and dimension of each monument.

The central part represents a great center of monumental buildings. The spurs of the mountain have been absorbed by means of stepped terraces, containing a large number of tombs. The whole complex is thus one great necropolis. Four periods of architectural development are recognizable in the form and system of construction of the tombs; these periods are also evident in the development of ceramics. The city flourished during the Classical period in central Mexico, and was abandoned about the end of the 8th century A.D., though it was used later as a burial ground.

The slopes of the stepped terraces of the main buildings are decorated with a special type of panel, called *escapulario,* used principally on ramps. It consists of alternating lower vertical elements and horizontal top ornaments of varying height.

Mitla.—This city, 26 miles southeast of Oaxaca, flourished during the Toltec period in central Mexico, after the decline of Monte Albán. The monuments of Mitla were known throughout the colonial period. They are preserved in part due to their stone construction which is, technically speaking, perhaps the best in Meso-America.

The city consists of five groups of buildings, clearly the same in layout. Each is made up of three extended constructions on top of platforms which surround a plaza on three sides, leaving the fourth open. These buildings bear decorations unique in Meso-American architecture. The decorations consist of three strips of panels similar to those found at Monte Albán, with square compartments containing Greek frets of great variety, which were produced by a type of stone mosaic. These buildings are also outstanding from the architectural point of view due to the use of great stone lintels on the doorways, and due to the division of halls by monolithic columns which held up the roof. The lintels are up to seven meters long and 1.20 meters wide.

Gulf Coast.— *El Tajín.*—This city, which flourished near modern Papantla in northern Veracruz during the Classical period in central Mexico, is not sufficiently known; but special mention should be made of its best preserved building, the so-called Pyramid of the Niches. The pyramid consists of six stepped terraces. Square niches, formed by laying flagstones vertically and horizontally, are crowned by a wide cornice. The effect of lights and shadows in the niches gives the onlooker an impression of great height and the total effect is very picturesque. The number of niches appears to equal the number of days in the solar year and there has been much speculation about their use. The general silhouette of the building has a slope of close to 45°.

Maya Area.— Maya architecture represents the most differentiated type of architecture within the entire cultural complex of Meso-America. Its stylistic development leads almost without interruptions from the beginnings of the 4th century A.D. to the middle of the 15th century. In terms of modern political geography, the monuments of Maya culture are scattered through Guatemala, particularly in Petén Department; British Honduras; the west of the Republic of Honduras; and the southeast of the Mexican Republic, which includes the Peninsula of Yucatán and the states of Chiapas and Tabasco. For methodological considerations, however, archaeologists divide the Maya area into the regions used below.

Petén Region.—According to the opinion of Sylvanus Griswold Morley (1883–1946), which is generally accepted, the first Maya cities to develop were Uaxactún and Tikal.

At Uaxactún, 37 miles north-northeast of the modern city of Flores, probably the oldest monument is the substructure E-VIII, excavated by the Carnegie Institution of Washington. It consists of a low stepped base with four stairs and ramps decorated with grotesque faces. The whole monument is covered over with a thick layer of stucco. Its construction is dated at earlier than the Maya date 8.14.0.0.0. (317 A.D.), due to its association with Chicanel-type pottery. The construction above this base was of wood only.

One of the characteristic elements of Maya architecture, the corbeled arch, is found for the first time in Group A-V, dated a little later than 328 A.D. From this date on, it is used with variations in forms and materials throughout Maya architecture.

The prototype of the temple in the shape of a pyramid reaches its greatest development in the Maya city of Tikal, 27 miles northeast of Flores. There, five great structures were built, with the highest 70 meters high. The latter, Temple IV, consists of a stepped base of nine terraces and an upper construction of three chambers parallel to the façade, and walls up to seven meters thick, which support a cresting, 14 meters high, in the rear portion.

Copán and Quiriguá.—Due to the custom of setting up dated memorial steles observed in all the Maya cities, we know that Copán, 35 miles west of Santa Rosa in western Honduras, thrived from 450 A.D. to 800.

The architectural monuments show a more perfect type of construction, involving the use of cut stone and less use of stucco. Decorative sculpture made great use of human and animal forms, as well as of plant themes, and is found concentrated around doors and along the façades around archways.

The most important monuments are Temple 22, Temple 11, and the Stair of the Hieroglyphics. The first of these rises on a base formed by a single terrace and consists of two halls parallel to the façade, and two others perpendicular to the ends of the first two. The entrance leading from the outside into the first hall is formed by the mouth of a grotesque face; the communicating door between the first and the second hall is ornamented with human figures in high relief, which surround the door on all sides. A high step of the stairs is similarly decorated.

The Stairway of the Hieroglyphics begins at the east end of the main plaza. The fronts of its 63 steps are decorated with more than 2,500 hieroglyphics, and at every section sculptured figures rise from the center of the ramp.

The layout and the orientation of the buildings at Copán show some points of contact between this city and the cities of central Mexico. The Maya city of Quiriguá, in Izabal Department, eastern Guatemala, has little importance from the architectural point of view; its few buildings are patterned on those found at Copán.

Usumacinta River Drainage, Tabasco, and Chiapas.—Three of the most important cities of the Maya area are located in this region: Yaxchilán, Piedras Negras, and Palenque. Their general plan has been adapted to mountainous terrain; their urban pattern does not follow a clearly defined plan. The pattern consists of unequal terraces and steps, which tend to organize the terrain, and which create groups around plazas and courts.

Piedras Negras, in Petén Department, Guatemala, 90 miles west-northwest of Flores, is at one and the same time the most ruined of these cities and the richest of the three in the sculptured decoration of its steles, lintels, and thrones.

Yaxchilán, in Chiapas, possesses well-preserved buildings such as Structure 33. These consist of only one hall, which runs parallel to the main front, and transversal buttresses which

support a large cresting formed by two wedged and leaning walls and which come together at the center of the building. The lintels of all of the buildings are stone and most of them are sculptured.

The Temple of the Sun at Palenque, State of Chiapas, Mexico, is its most representative structure. It is constructed of flat stones or flagstones and is thickly decorated with stucco. It has a double hall, and in the rear a small sanctuary with a corbeled arch which covers a panel sculptured in low relief. This panel shows human figures flanking a representation of the sun and four columns of hieroglyphics around the edges.

Southern and Northern Campeche.—These two regions are usually called Río Bec and Chenes respectively. They seem to represent an intermediate step between the architecture of the Petén region and the architecture of northern Yucatán.

The decorative forms of both groups are very similar. They make great use of the grotesque face. In the first of these zones there are simulated temples which do not contain any interior rooms whatsoever.

The most important cities of the first group are Río Bec and Xpuhil; of the second, Hochob, Tabasqueño, and Dzibilnocac.

Puuc in Yucatán.—In the north of the Peninsula of Yucatán there exist small complexes of cities and building groups which are notable for exact and careful stonework, for special types of decoration, among which geometric elements predominate, and for their stress of the horizontal lines in the buildings. It is possible that these buildings are coeval with Toltec influence, which is clearly evident from 1000 A.D. on, and which possibly began before that date.

The most important city for its size in puuc (Maya renaissance) style is Uxmal, 40 miles south of Mérida. Its general layout does not obey a strictly preconceived plan, but is clearer than that of most Maya cities.

The most important buildings extend horizontally and consist of corridors of rooms, raised on low platforms. Yet some also show considerable development into pyramidal structures, such as the chief pyramid, called the House of the Wizard, and also the structure called the House of the Old Woman.

Buildings with many rooms are almost always grouped in rectangular fashion: four buildings, the sides of which do not touch, around a court. To this type belong the so-called Nunnery Quadrangle, the House of the Doves, the Cemetery, and some others that are less well preserved.

The most outstanding building of puuc style is called the Governor's House. It is constructed on top of a platform with sides 150 meters long, and directly on a base seven meters high. The building proper consists of twin corridors of rooms with a front of 98 meters. The façade is divided into component parts. The middle one is the biggest. It consists of a flat area formed by the walls and a much-decorated higher area which belongs to the arches. Along this decorated higher surface geometric motifs, grotesque faces, and lattice work alternate along diagonal lines.

Remains of a ball court excavated by the Carnegie Institution's archaeologist, S. G. Morley, have also been preserved.

Toltec Influence in Yucatán.—The similarities between Toltec and Maya architecture became known when systematic excavations were begun in 1940 in the Toltec city of Tollan (now Tula). According to Indian chronicles, corroborated by archaeology, this cultural current originated in central Mexico in the beginning of the second millennium A.D., although it seems certain that less profound contacts existed before.

The following architectural and urban elements are characteristic of this influence: layout of the entire city according to one plan, and more or less exact relationship of the axes of different buildings to each other; columns in the shape of plumed serpents; slopes at the base of walls; creation of great roofed-in spaces with corridors of pillars and columns; atlas-type figures; and use of merlons.

The buildings most representative of this influence are the Temple of Kukulkán (or El Castillo), the Temple of the Warriors, and the ball court at Chichén Itzá, 72 miles east-southeast of Mérida. The first two buildings have substructures which belong to an earlier period, but which also reveal Toltec influence.

In the same city there are other buildings which certainly belong to a previous period. These show more Maya style in their architecture, with grotesque faces as decoration, as is evident in the group of the Nunnery. These Maya elements continue in the buildings of the period of Toltec influence, together with the system of construction based on the corbeled arch.

Toltec influence is also visible in the much ruined cities of Mayapán, 24 miles south-southeast of Mérida, and Tulum, on the coast of Quintana Roo.

COLONIAL ARCHITECTURE

The architectural development of the colony shows various phases which are related in part to local conditions, both political and social, and in part to the development of styles in Europe. The first phase comprises the years from 1521 to 1550, a period which corresponds to the conquest of New Spain (Mexico). In the second half of the 16th century and at the beginning of the 17th century, Renaissance influences are felt; just as in the following years and during all of the 18th century the baroque style is developed to its ultimate consequences. The last 30 years of the colonial period reflect in Mexico the neoclassical tendencies current in Europe.

From 1521 to 1550.—Immediately after the conquest of the Aztec capital, Tenochtitlan, on the site of Mexico City, feverish activity was displayed to furnish the conquerors with churches and dwellings. In building the churches, the basilica type was adopted, as in the original cathedral of Mexico City. Another characteristic type was the so-called open chapel, which could accommodate the immense congregations of newly converted Indians, and which has certain analogies with the architecture of the natives. An example of this type of chapel open to the sky is that attached to the Monastery of Tlalmanalco, State of Mexico, which is arcaded; the arcades being profusely ornamented with sculptured archivolts in the plateresque style. Other examples are the churches at Actopan, Hidalgo; Yautepec, Morelos; and the Royal Chapel at Cholula, Puebla.

From 1550 to 1630.—During this period the building of great "fortress monasteries" belonging to the Franciscan, Augustinian, and Dominican orders was carried out. These edifices, springing up all over the country, served as active centers for the Christianization of the natives.

The general disposition of the monasteries is almost always the same. A thick-walled masonry church with a single nave, and rib vaulting supporting an arched stone roof was prevalent. Its exterior was generally undecorated except for the area around the entrance, above which there might be a small rose window. To the right of the church the monastery proper is found, together with one or two large patios around which are placed various dependencies. These constructions are surrounded by a great uncovered courtyard or atrium, which is enclosed by chapels and a battlemented wall.

It is easy to perceive in these monasteries the Romanesque, Gothic, and plateresque influences. The outstanding examples of this architectural type are found in the monasteries at Huejotzingo and Tepeaca, in Puebla; Acolman, Mexico State; Actopan, Hidalgo; and Atlatlahucan, Morelos.

In this same period the construction of great cathedrals, such as those of Mexico City and Puebla, was undertaken. These two edifices were not completed until the middle of the 17th century, however, and are predominantly neoclassical, although they incorporate many styles inside and out.

Baroque.—The monastic orders followed the expanding frontier of Hispanic civilization and were replaced in the rapidly growing cities by the secular clergy. The baroque style, which makes its appearance in Mexico after the first 25 years of the 17th century, coincides with the most flourishing economic period in New Spain and, due to its characteristics of form, it developed as the most suitable manner of expressing the amalgamated feelings of Spaniard and native. As a result the baroque style crystallized in Mexico into a group of works which, because of their number and quality, form the most genuine artistic manifestation of the colonial period, and at the same time constitute the most differentiated style when compared with the art of the mother country, Spain.

Within the baroque period, which maintained its output for more than 150 years, a line of evolution can be traced, which, starting from the forms of the Renaissance, began to develop a new style guided by the premises of expression and movement at all costs, until it reached the ultimate consequences of these principles.

The development of baroque style in Mexico is usually divided into two phases, the first of which is known as baroque proper and the second as Churrigueresque. Certain examples which show the proportions and regularities of the Renaissance combined with baroque principles are the churches of Jesús María, completed in 1621, and of San Lorenzo, completed in 1650, both in Mexico City. Toward the end of the century there appeared the ornamentation of the body of the columns, and finally the twisted or spiral column which forms the most typical element of this first phase. Church portals were heavily ornamented with carvings and a profusion of sculptured figures placed in niches. The interiors were also exuberantly decorated. Brightly painted, carved stucco covered walls and sections of ceilings with innumerable heads, figures, and varieties of decorative motifs. The baroque style was also adapted to large residences and colleges. Besides certain buildings erected in the capital, mention should be made of other groups having definite local traits, such as the churches of the valleys of Oaxaca and Puebla, among which the churches of Santo Domingo in Oaxaca, San Francisco Acatepec and the Chapel of the Rosary in Puebla are outstanding.

Churrigueresque.—The second phase, typified by the almost exclusive use of the reversed pyramid as an ornamental support in façades and altars, appears for the first time in the Altar of the Kings of the cathedral of Mexico City. This altar, begun in 1718, is the work of Jerónimo de Balbos.

A great number of churches in Mexico City were built in the new fashion, which carried the baroque to its limits in fantasy and inventiveness and created even more elaborate church façades, and *retablos* (decorative altar pieces) of richly carved, gilded wood as a background to an array of small polychromed statues. Among such churches are the Sagrario Metropolitano and the Church of La Santísima Trinidad (both the work of Lorenzo Rodríguez), the Balvanera Chapel in the Church of San Francisco, the Church of La Santa Veracruz, and the Church of La Enseñanza. Churrigueresque extended itself to all corners of the colony and formed local focuses, the most important of which rose among the cities of the central regions. The finest examples of this style are the churches of Santa Rosa and Santa Clara in Querétaro, La Valenciana in Guanajuato, San Agustín in Salamanca, and the Del Carmen Church in San Luis Potosí, among others that might be mentioned.

In the final manifestations of baroque style the concept of architectural elements was lost; ornamental moldings, and animal, vegetable, and anthropomorphous leitmotifs being substituted for it. (See also the section *Colonial and Modern Art.*)

Neoclassicalism.—During the last quarter of the 18th century, in partial juxtaposition to baroque, there appeared the neoclassical style, imported directly from Spain with the arrival in Mexico of architects such as Manuel Tolsá, Antonio González Velázquez, Jerónimo Gil, and others. Tolsá, an architect and sculptor, and a native of Valencia, completed the cathedral of Mexico City and built the Real Seminario de Minería there. Of native architects, mention should be made of Ignacio Costera, Francisco Eduardo Tresguerras, designer of the Church of Nuestra Señora del Carmen in Celaya and the Palacio Real in Guanajuato, and José Manzo who worked mainly in Puebla. The neoclassical style did not terminate with the end of the colonial era, but lasted until the middle of the 19th century.

Domestic Urban Architecture.—This architecture, which showed far less variation than that of churches and public buildings, generally arranged rooms around a paved patio which was enclosed on four sides and contained the family garden, the rooms opening directly onto the patio. Most public buildings, of one or two stories, also incorporated the patio in their design. The houses, built of stone, stuccoed brick, or adobe, were usually severely plain outside. There were some notable exceptions to this, however, such as the Casa de Alfeñique ("Sugar-paste House"), built in Puebla in 1790, whose walls are faced with unglazed red and glazed blue tiles and a lavish white stucco trim, the latter giving the mansion its nickname.

MODERN ARCHITECTURE

To understand fully the development of modern architecture in Mexico, it is necessary to bear in mind its immediate antecedents in Europe, where its first manifestations occurred. These first manifestations appeared in Mexico in the middle of the 19th century, although they did not crystallize into a true artistic style until much later.

The 19th and Early 20th Centuries.—Whether one turns to the Europe of this period, or to Spanish America—in this case particularly to Mexico, where remarkable works of architecture were produced during the colonial period—a deep fracture becomes evident in a Western artistic tradition, which for an uninterrupted period of 5,000 years had produced an architecture in stone. The new architect, allowing himself to be carried away by a completely subjective taste, and utterly disdaining the deepest roots of style, turned to the latest artistic novelties exhumed by archaeologists and historians to find a repertory of anachronous forms which he applied with scientific coldness to the ornamentation of his façades. Thus an architecture was developed that copied the Gothic cathedral in building its churches, Greek temples in its banking buildings, and which even reproduced architectural forms alien to Western culture, such as Arabian patios and Mayan temples.

In this process of copying the forms of other arts, toward the end of the 19th century architecture reached a new phase characterized by the copying of nature itself; executing this copy not as a means of expression, but rather as a finality in itself. This is the artistic mode known as *art nouveau* (new art). The noble art of architecture, which fundamentally had expressed itself through the severe forms of geometry, now found itself transformed into an art of naturalistic ornamentation.

The situation in which architecture found itself was typified in Mexico by the arrival of two architects, Lorenzo de la Hidalga, a Spaniard who arrived in 1838, and Xavier Caballari, an Italian who reached Mexico in 1856. It must be noted that the period immediately following Mexican independence (1821) had marked a critical moment for the Academy of Architecture, which for a time was forced to close its doors and only regained impetus through the efforts of Javier Echeverría and José Bernardo Couto, chairmen of its Board of Trustees. It was they who decided to avail the academy of the services of de la Hidalga and Caballari.

Within the eclectic tendencies referred to above were executed the baldachin of the cathedral of Mexico City, which replaced the original one in Churrigueresque style, the Teatro Nacional (National Theater) inaugurated in 1844, and the dome of the Sanctuary of Santa Teresa. All three of these structures in the capital were the work of de la Hidalga and may be characterized as the last germination of that neoclassicism which took hold in Mexico in the final years of its colonial period.

The Italian Caballari is important not so much for his personal output as because of the impulse he brought to the Academy of Architecture, modifying its curricula by fusing architectural and engineering studies into a single course.

The second half of the 19th century was dominated by influences emanating from France, whence radiated the prevalent fashions and taste, not only in architecture but in other fields of life as well. The principal Mexican architects of the period were trained in the École des Beaux-Arts in Paris, bringing its teachings back to the academy in Mexico.

The architect Emilio Dondé (d. 1905) designed luxurious mansions and built the Church of San Felipe de Jesús in Mexico City in a style somewhat similar to Romanesque-Byzantine. Antonio Rivas Mercado, counted among the finest architects of his time, erected the Independence Monument in the Paseo de la Reforma in the capital. This not only ranks among the noblest architectural works of its period, but also served to introduce technical innovations, such as the use of supporting piles driven to great depths. These were introduced to offset the sponginess of the subsoil.

At the dawn of the 20th century another work of colossal dimensions was begun in Mexico City, the Palacio de Bellas Artes (Palace of Fine Arts). This was entrusted to the Italian architect Adamo Boari, who applied to it the forms of *art nouveau,* giving Mexico what is possibly the finest example of that architectural style in all the world; certainly the most finished. Boari's general layout is clear and well-ordered, and fineness of design and good proportions are notable in the details.

Other buildings of less importance were constructed in the capital in the most varied styles: the Edificio de Correos (Post Office Building), also by Boari, in Gothic; the pavilion of the Alameda de Santa María, in Spanish Moorish; and the Secretaría de Gobernación (Department of the Interior) in the style of the Renaissance.

In all these constructions, as in their counterparts in Europe, two new structural materials are made use of—steel and concrete. Nevertheless, the use of these did not yield, at the time, any apparent changes in the conception of architectural forms.

Contemporary Architecture.—Having examined the architectural production of the second half of the 19th century and the beginning of the 20th, one is able to investigate the architecture usually called modern or contemporary. A very brief reference to the aesthetic ideas which preceded it and which served to form the intellectual atmosphere in which it began will first be made.

The purely objective consideration of an artistic work is a tendency, based on certain of Immanuel Kant's philosophical considerations, which gained great momentum during the last third of the 19th century. In its historical application to the field of architecture it was championed by the German art theorist Konrad Fiedler, who saw the specific values of architecture as exclusively formal and spatial, the spatial ones deriving from the formal. Fiedler likewise maintained in his writings the basic predicate that the prime factor in architecture is "functionalism," considered as the need of covering an enclosed space. Similar ideas and even more radical ones were upheld by the eminent German architect Gottfried Semper, who proclaimed the technogenetic roots of architectural art.

Modern architecture rose out of the activity generated by these ideas, in the first decade of this century, some 15 years prior to its appearance in Mexico. It is necessary to refer to these ideas because of their widespread influence in contemporary Mexican architecture.

The first productions of modern architecture in Mexico were produced in the first interval of social stability following the Revolution of 1910. The head of the new architectural movement was a young architect, José Villagrán García, who attained the professorship of architectural theory in the National University in Mexico City and formed a small but integrated group with Mauricio R. Campos, Enrique del Moral, Juan O'Gorman, Juan Legarreta, and others, who soon became the stalwarts of the new architecture. This group contended against the Academy of Fine Arts, which they regarded as simply a follower of architectures of the past. According to the new ideals, architecture was to be eminently "functional" and was to solve the needs of man considered as a whole, in all his psychic and physical complexity.

Faithful to these ideas and in collaboration with his students, Villagrán García in 1925 brought to completion the laboratories of the Instituto de Higiene (Institute of Hygiene) in Popotla, a suburb of Mexico City, this being the first accomplishment of the new architecture in the republic.

The various blendings of ideas and a greater radicalism in their creative thought, together with the influence of the Swiss architect Le Corbusier, which was immediately felt by the pioneering group, moved O'Gorman and Legarreta toward a solution of the problems created by what were called "popular" dwellings of the masses. Together they began the construction of groups of "popular" homes and schools between the years 1931 and 1934. This architectural tendency, combined with ideas of a social and political nature, led to the creation of the so-called advanced school of construction by O'Gorman and the engineer José A. Cuevas in 1932.

Nevertheless, this appearance of modern architecture did not in the least suppress the great profusion of works representative of opposite ideas, among which mention should be made of the conceptions determined by the influence of the Paris Salon of Decorative Arts, and also of the various attempts to originate a "national" architecture. Among the first group mentioned one finds the works of Juan Segura, such as the Ermita Building in Tacubaya, a suburb of Mexico City, the open-air theater in Colonia Hipódromo, a residential section of the capital, and some of the works of Carlos Obregón Santacilia (1898–   ), such as the interior of the Bank of Mexico, also in Mexico City. In all these works may be noted the geometric stylizations of classical forms intermixed with surviving elements of *art nouveau.*

The attempts to form a "national" architecture have been of much greater importance, owing to the number of works those attempts have produced. The system followed in each case has always been to take forms or conceptions belonging to past periods of Mexican history and to adapt them to present needs and problems. In this fashion, the architect Amabilis brought to his constructions decorative elements of Mayan architecture from the Yucatán Peninsula. Obregón Santacilia adapted the typical dwellings of the 19th century, called *viviendas,* furnishing them with ventilation, illumination, hygienic conditions, and other modern improvements. In the reconstruction (1930–1934) of the Palacio de Bellas Artes, carried out by Federico

Mariscal (1881–   ), discreet use was made of pre-Hispanic themes, as in other constructions of the same architect.

In addition to these attempts, carried out by trained architects within the limits of discretion and archaeological knowledge, there have been other very numerous productions of private architecture and sometimes even of public buildings, executed generally by engineers and contractors devoid of professional skill. These productions, which have given a special countenance to certain entire residential sections of Mexico City, can be classified within the generic and derogatory denomination of Californian-colonial. In these productions one finds elements grotesquely copied from colonial architecture, profusely decorated with fireplaces, coats of arms, rustic touches, and the like. The most deplorable technical and structural qualities are combined with a taste that can only be described as ridiculous and anachronous.

Leaving aside those tendencies, which may be called heterodox, and once more taking up the new movement, it should be said that the most important fruits of modern Mexican architecture appeared during the decade of 1940–1950, brought into being in the large edifices built along the important avenues of Mexico City and in the great collective projects sponsored by various government agencies.

The first of the great privately owned buildings in the capital was that of the La Nacional Insurance Company, its design and constructions deftly carried out by the architect Manuel Ortiz Monasterio and the engineer Calderón. This type of building, similar in general outline to the skyscraper of the United States, has been also used in the constructions of the brothers Francisco (1894–   ) and Luis (1908–   ) Martínez Negrete who erected the San Antonio Building and the Seguros de México Building. Other great buildings have sprung up along the famous Paseo de la Reforma, giving this boulevard the definite quality of a commercial avenue. Among these the following should be mentioned: the building at Number 1 Reforma, designed by the brothers Martínez Negrete; the La Fragua Building by Mario Pani (1911–   ); and the vast central building of the Instituto del Seguro Social (Social Security Institute) by Obregón Santacilia.

Among the great groups of buildings designed for government agencies is the Hospital City in the capital, which is part of the general plan for the construction of hospitals in all parts of Mexico sponsored by Gustavo Baz while he was secretary of public health and social assistance, and which has been only partially completed. The design and construction of public schools throughout Mexico is also worthy of mention. This work is being carried out by the Committee for the Construction of Schools and by the Buildings Division of the Department of Public Instruction, under the direction of the architects José Luis Cuevas and Pedro Ramírez Vásquez.

Special mention should be made of the University City in the capital, begun in 1950 and dedicated in 1952. This work, of great transcendency from an architectural point of view, is the fruitful result of the collaboration of the best Mexican architects, headed by Enrique del Moral and Mario Pani, who are the directors of the project.

The formal characteristics of modern architecture in Mexico are very similar to the corresponding ones in Europe and the United States: elementary combination of geometrical volumes, a marked tendency towards a horizontal line, and an almost absolute exclusion of the curved line. When the latter is used, it is expressed mainly in the form of parabolas and ellipses.

Special attention is paid to the function which is to be fulfilled by the building, rationalist logic is applied to the use of materials and technique, and there is a growing interest in expressing a definite aesthetic idea. Any element that tends to obscure the expression of form is eliminated. Interior and exterior space is fused, not limited. All these are significant traits of modern Mexican architecture. Particular mention should be made of the importance granted by the Mexican architect to the use of colors as an element of ornamentation which underscores and gives added clarity to architectural form.

RICARDO ROBINA,
Architect.

19. LITERATURE. Mexican literature, like every other aspect of what we understand as Mexican culture, is not of a wholly indigenous nature. The roots of Mexico are found both in the native pre-Hispanic culture and in the Spanish culture. These two aspects have blended in varying proportions to form present-day Mexico.

Pre-Hispanic Period.—The most important pre-Hispanic peoples—the Maya, Tarascans, Otomís, Mixtecs, Zapotecs, and Nahuas; mainly the Aztecs among the last—all created important literary works, which undoubtedly were numerous. Unfortunately, these were almost completely lost when European civilization was superimposed on Indian cultures, for the native literatures were all oral and their creators had not yet perfected literary texts. Their hieroglyphs could express only concrete facts or symbols of concepts—thus all codices were records of history, taxes, or mythology—and they were useless to communicate that beauty of expression which is indispensable in literature.

Very few works were saved from the upheaval caused by the conquest, to be later transcribed into European writing; some books were, however, saved in this way, such as the Maya *Popol Vuh* and a few epic and lyric poems, mainly Otomí and Nahua, all of them relating to a period immediately before the conquest and all anonymous, with the exception of a few songs attributed to Nezahualcoyotl. Many modern scholars, however, doubt that this 15th-century king of Texcoco was the real author of these poems. In any case, these few monuments of a lost literature have exerted no direct influence in the awakening of what must now be considered as Mexican literature.

The true roots of the literature of Mexico are to be found in Spanish literature, in which at the time of the conquest (1521) one could already find outstanding examples of every literary genre, and which was soon to embark on its golden century, so amazingly rich.

The 16th Century.—The first type of work—not strictly literary—produced in New Spain (Mexico) was the chronicle. The best examples are found among the chronicles of the conquest, such as the *Cartas de relación* of Hernán Cortés and the *Historia de la conquista* (published 1632) of Bernal Díaz del Castillo, and among the religious chronicles—in those of the friars Toribio

Motolinia, and Jerónimo de Mendieta, whose *Historia eclesiástica indiana* (published 1870) is an account of the conversion of the Indian peoples to Christianity, and in the remarkable research work of Friar Bernardino de Sahagún, who wrote the *Historia general de las cosas de Nueva España* (first published 1829–1830).

Another primitive genre was the drama used for the evangelization of the Indians, which consisted of adaptions in the native tongues of the religious drama of medieval Europe. Its very purpose made it a short-lived phenomenon, to which many references are found but of which very few works are left.

A dramatic movement equivalent to that called *prelopista* (before Lope de Vega, 1562–1635) in Spanish literature soon made itself felt in the towns of New Spain where Spaniards lived, mainly in the capital. The year 1574 saw the performance, in honor of Pedro Moya de Contreras on his investiture as archbishop of Mexico, of the allegorical work *Desposorio espiritual del pastor Pedro y la iglesia mexicana* by the presbyter Juan Pérez Ramírez, the first writer born in Mexico (1543–?) and perhaps the first in the whole of the American continent. A short time later the *Tragedia del triunfo de los santos* was played. The author of this verse play with a medieval theme is unknown, but he was probably a Jesuit, and he shows a marked Renaissance influence. The most important writer of this time was Hernán González de Eslava (1534–1600?), of whom we have 16 *Coloquios espirituales y sacramentales*, religious and allegorical plays similar to the medieval mystery plays. They are uneven works, but the fact that some of them deal with local Mexican themes is of special interest.

Epic and lyric poetry were also cultivated from very early times. Francisco de Terrazas (c.1525–1600) was a good poet following in the steps of the school of Seville. Also important were Pedro de Trejo (c.1534–c.1600) and Fernando de Córdova y Bocanegra (1565–1589); but the outstanding writer of the period was Bernardo de Balbuena (c.1567–1627), who wrote three long poetic works: *La grandeza mexicana,* a eulogy of Mexico (1604); *El siglo de oro* (1608), a pastoral novel in imitation of Jacopo Sannazaro; and *Bernardo* (1624). The last, dealing with the semilegendary hero Bernardo del Carpio, is one of the best epic poems of its time.

Besides literary works in the Spanish language there were writings in the native tongues, decreasing in number as the years advanced; also works in Latin, of which the most important in the 16th century are some *Dialogues* (1554), descriptions of social and intellectual life by Francisco Cervantes de Salazar (c.1514–1575), a distinguished professor of the Royal University of Mexico (founded in 1551). Other prominent, though not so literary, writers are found among historians, jurists, physicians, mathematicians, and above all theologians, among whom the most important is the Augustinian friar Alonso de la Veracruz (1504–1584).

Baroque.—The great baroque period, the richest and most fruitful in New Spain, begins at the end of the 16th century and continues to the second half of the 18th. The literary genres already initiated were continued and developed in accordance with the basic characteristics of the Spanish baroque—superabundance, flamboyance, and dynamism.

After Balbuena, epic poems tend to disappear and none of them are really important; but the name of Arias de Villalobos, whose poem *Canto intitulado Mercurio* (1623) concerns the arrival of one of the viceroys, should be mentioned in passing.

Of special note is the case of Carlos de Sigüenza y Góngora (1645–1700), a remarkable author who wrote successfully in such varied fields as narrative (*Aventuras de Alonso Ramírez,* 1690); lyric poetry, of which he left many examples; history; geography; mathematics; and astronomy, with his bombastic explanation of a comet. But his most important work is a chronicle and compilation which he made on the occasion of two poetic competitions, and which he entitled *Triunfo parthénico* (1683).

The first important name in the baroque theater is that of Juan Ruiz de Alarcón y Mendoza. He was born about 1576 and studied in the Royal University of Mexico. He then went to Spain, where his dramas were played with those of Lope de Vega, Tirso de Molina, and other authors of the Spanish golden century. He was appointed to the Consejo de Indias (Council of the Indies) in 1626 and died in Madrid in 1639. Some of the most important among his plays are *Los favores del mundo, La verdad sospechosa, Los pechos privilegiados,* and *El examen de maridos.* Ruiz de Alarcón belonged to Lope de Vega's dramatic cycle in the Spanish theater, but had certain personal values, paying particular attention to form and the psychology of his characters. His influence was felt directly in the French classical theater, and he is surely, as Alfonso Reyes states, the foremost Mexican writer of international renown.

The remaining playwrights of the baroque period were much less important, but Eusebio Vela (1688–1737), a mixture of author, producer, and actor, should be mentioned. He did a great deal of work in Mexico and it is known that he wrote some 14 plays, of which only three remain. The influence of the Spanish dramatist Pedro Calderón de la Barca toward the end of the period is incontestable.

Lyric poetry was written profusely during the baroque period; a competition held about 1680 brought forth over 500 poems. Among poets of note were Luis de Sandoval y Zapata, Alonso Ramírez de Vargas, and Matías de Bocanegra (1612–1668). Sandoval and Ramírez were more Gongoristic in their metaphors; Bocanegra's style was sweeter, but less coloristic. His claim to fame is based on his *Canción a la vista de un desengaño* (c.1650), a sort of precursor of neoclassicism which breaks away from the two great baroque tendencies holding absolute sway over the literary production of the times, the pompous *culteranismo* and the deliberately ambiguous metaphors and puns of conceptism. Nor must one omit Friar Miguel de Guevara (c.1585–c.1646), who is credited with the sonnet *No me mueve mi Dios para quererte,* one of the best in the Spanish language.

But before all these must be placed the name of Juana Inés de la Cruz, born near Mexico City in 1648 (or perhaps, according to older documentation, in 1651). Precocious and intelligent, she was for a time at the viceroy's court; but later entered the Convent of San Jerónimo, where she died in 1695. She was a woman of great talent and very wide culture, the author of religious works, a musical treatise now lost, some religious and some secular plays, like *Los empeños de una casa* and *El divino Narciso*, and a great number of poems, many of them first rate, especially *Primer sueño*. This poem, nearly 1,000 lines in length, deals with a broad and universal subject in a continuous succession of extremely lyrical baroque metaphors, and is a poetic interpretation of a dream—in the human body, in nature, in the cosmos—followed by the awakening and the return to life and to conscious being. Within the baroque style is a forerunner of modern literature based on the experiences of the subconscious. Such extensive writings place their author not only in the first rank in her time but among the best writers in the Spanish language.

Literary production shows a very definite decadence in every branch in the first half of the 18th century, reaching extremes of exaggeration, confusion, senselessness, and bad taste. The baroque had exhausted its possibilities; new trends were in the making. One of the effects was a drifting of intellectual interest mainly to the sciences, as far removed as possible from the exclusively literary activity of the previous period.

The most remarkable product of this new trend in New Spain was the writings of the group of Jesuits exiled from Spain and her colonies in 1767 by order of the king. They published their work in Italy, and although circumstances forced them to write in Italian or in Latin, as a group they caused the first awakening of the consciousness of Mexico, now fully distinguished from its Spanish origin. The most important were Francisco Xavier (or Javier) Clavijero, author of a comprehensive history of pre-Hispanic Mexico, *Storia antica del Messico* (Cesena 1780–1781); Rafael Landívar, author of *Rusticatio Mexicana* (Bologna 1782), in which he described the beauty of the Mexican countryside and customs; the historians Francisco Xavier Alegre and Andrés Cavo; and the aesthetician José Márquez.

Neoclassicism.—In ousting the baroque, neoclassicism gave rise to a type of formally correct lyric poetry, but showed a marked preference for minor themes and a certain weakening sweetness. Examples of this type of writing are found in the work of Father José Manuel Sartorio (1746–1828) and Friar Manuel Navarrete (1768–1809).

During the struggle for independence (1810–1821), as was to be expected, writers concentrated on the political conflict, and it is this trend that the scanty production of the times followed. The most important name was that of José Joaquín Fernández de Lizardi (1776–1827) who wrote many political works under the pseudonym El Pensador Mexicano (The Mexican Thinker). His novels *El Periquillo Sarniento, La Quijotita y su prima,* and *Don Catrín de la Fachenda,* in which he criticizes the customs of the times, are far more important to us nowadays. These were the first novels to be written in Spanish America. The picaresque *El Periquillo Sarniento* (1816) was translated into English by Katherine Anne Porter, as *The Itching Parrot,* in 1941.

The 19th Century.—Men of letters of the first few years of independent Mexico fall into two groups: neoclassicists and romanticists. Of note among the former were: Manuel Sánchez de Tagle (1782–1860), José María Heredia (1803–1839), Manuel Carpio (1791–1860), José Joaquín Pesado (1801–1861), and the playwright Manuel

Eduardo de Gorostiza (1789–1851), who is best remembered for his plays *Contigo pan y cebolla, Indulgencia para todos,* and *Don Dieguito.*

Romanticism came to Mexico shortly after the country's independence, as a French influence. Young writers took to it with devoted zeal. Of these were José Ignacio Rodríguez Galván (1812–1842), a prolific but inaccurate poet, author of two romantic dramas, *El privado del virrey* and *Muñoz, visitador de México;* and Fernando Calderón (1809–1845), also a poet, and author of the plays *Herman, o la vuelta del cruzado* and *Ana Bolena,* among others, as well as a play in which he criticizes the customs of the times, *A ninguna de las tres.* Among the early romantic novelists were Florencio María del Castillo (1828–1863), Juan Díaz Covarrubias (1837–1859), and Justo Sierra O'Reilly (1814–1861). The last leaned toward the historical novel, as did Eligio Ancona (1830–1893), and Vicente Riva Palacio (1832–1896). Manuel Payno (1870–1894) preferred the novel of adventure.

About the middle of the century there was an almost uninterrupted 20 years of wars and civil wars (1847–1867)—including the invasion from the United States, which wrested from the nation half its territory, the Liberal reform movement, which succeeded in breaking the power of the Roman Catholic Church, and the French invasion and the country's struggle against Maximilian's empire. All these factors encouraged the development of new literary forms: oratory, political essays, and history. Prominent in these fields were Francisco Zarco (1829–1869), Ignacio Ramírez (1818–1879), Clemente de Jesús Munguía (1810–1868), and others. José María Luis Mora (1794–1850), Lucas Alamán (1792–1853) and Manuel Orozco y Berra (1818–1881) dealt with political history.

When peace came, a second and last romantic flowering took place, with the poets Manuel Acuña (1849–1873), Manuel M. Flores (1840–1885), Agustín F. Cuenca (1850–1884); the playwright José Peón Contreras (1843–1907); and the novelist Pedro Castera (1838–1906).

The trend of the last genre was toward the novel of manners, with such authors as Guillermo Prieto (1818–1897) and José T. de Cuéllar (1830–1894); but it soon drifted toward realism, whose first adherent was Luis G. Inclán (1846–1875), followed by Ignacio Altamirano (1834–1893), Rafael Delgado (1853–1914), José López Portillo y Rojas (1850–1923), and Federico Gamboa (1864–1939). The novel of the turn of the century was inspired by the French and Spanish realistic novel, but by its very nature—because of its method, which was based on the observation of surrounding reality, in taking note and making use of it—it gave rise to novels which differed more and more consciously from their European models and which took on more of the country, the people, and the color of Mexico; in other words, the true Mexican novel was being created.

Poetry, which has always been a most important literary activity in Mexico, as well as in the whole of Spanish America, also experienced a considerable change, influenced by French Parnassianism and symbolism, in those years of transition between romanticism and modernism.

Histories of Spanish American literature also mention the premodernistic poets of the transition period; first place always being given to Manuel Gutiérrez Nájera (1859–1895), who was also an extremely fine and nimble prose writer.

The triumph of modernism dates from about 1890, and the movement lasted for more than 20 years. The poets of modernism were Efrén Rebolledo (1877–1929), erotic and curt; José Juan Tablada (1871–1945), who made use of Japanese exoticism, and became a brilliant newspaperman; and Amado Nervo (1870–1919), who started from modernism and went on to achieve a more personal style. The latter achieved international renown in the Spanish-speaking world and great honors were bestowed on him at his death.

Though modernism was predominant, there were also other types of poets. Manuel José Othón (1858–1906) was classical by education and style. He was perhaps the poet who wrote best about the Mexican landscape. Salvador Díaz Mirón (1853–1928) sought perfection in form, and left a relatively small but magnificent production. Luis G. Urbina (1868–1934), always faithful to romanticism, was also a good critic and a fine prose writer.

The names of a few humanists must be added, men of profound classical culture, translators of the Greek and Latin classics and themselves careful writers in their own tongue, though often writing in Latin. Among these are Ignacio Montes de Oca y Obregón (1890–1921), Joaquín Arcadio Pagaza (1839–1919), Federico Escobedo (1874–1949), Francisco de P. Herrasti (1879–1940), the brothers Gabriel (1905–1949) and Alfonso (1909–   ) Méndez Plancarte, and Octaviano Valdés (1901–   ).

The 20th Century.—The Mexican Revolution of 1910 brought about a profound and all-embracing political and social upheaval. Mexican literature could not escape its impact, though its effect was felt late.

Novels.—The realistic novel mentioned above welcomed the warm echo of the revolution and a new branch sprang forth. This has been called by some "the novel of the revolution"; but the name is inexact, for much of the production did not, properly speaking, consist of novels, but rather of tales or anecdotes, sometimes memoirs, and short stories were abundantly written.

The general opinion is that the novel of the revolution began with *Los de abajo* (1916) of Mariano Azuela (1873–1952), author of some short biographies and a long series of novels, the best of which are *Malayerba, Sin amor,* and *La luciérnaga.* His best known work, *Los de abajo,* translated by Enrique Munguía as *The Underdogs* (1929), is no doubt a good novel, mainly because of its background and its characters. The structure leaves much to be desired, but this is a common occurrence in this author and, indeed, in most of the Mexican fiction writers of the present century. Generally speaking, Martín Luis Guzmán (1887–   ) is a better writer. Novelist, essayist, newspaperman, and politician, he is the author of a book of tales, *El águila y la serpiente* (1928), without doubt the best of its kind that has been written about the Mexican Revolution. This work was translated by Harriet de Onís as *The Eagle and the Serpent* (1930). There are other, not so successful, writers of this type of novel, such as José Rubén Romero (1890–1952), Rafael Muñoz (1899–   ), and others.

Some authors, like Ermilo Abreu Gómez (1895–   ), Francisco Monterde (1894–   ), and Julio Jiménez Rueda (1896–   ), followed a trend which started in the third decade of the century and which sought inspiration in the times of the viceroys; hence it was called *colonialismo.* The authors mentioned have written excellent short stories, novels, dramas, and works of criticism; but realizing the mistake of finding inspiration exclusively in dead forms, they made a timely departure from their original aims. Artemio de Valle-Arizpe (1888–   ) alone has kept up the error.

The appraisal of Mexican social problems and the revision of certain historical opinions in favor of the Indian, as against the Spanish, roots of Mexican culture—so-called *indigenismo*—inspired many of the more recent short story and novel writers, most of whom are enjoying the fullness of their creative powers. Among these should be mentioned: Andrés Henestrosa (1908–   ), José Mancisidor (1894–   ), Mauricio Magdaleno (1906–   ), José Revueltas (1914–   ), Alberto Quiroz (1909–   ), Efrén Hernández (1903–   ), and Agustín Yáñez (1904–   ).

Poetry.—This art, meanwhile, had been following varied paths. Shortly before the outbreak of the revolution, the more sensitive writers foresaw the exhaustion of modernism and the need for a poetic revival. Beginning in 1909, this revival was led by Enrique González Martínez (1871–1952), physician and diplomat, who throughout his long life created works of such importance as to place him in the lead in Mexican literature. Also very important is Ramón López Velarde (1881–1921). His contribution was to make a place in poetry for provincial and familiar things, in a language full of tender sensitivity and unexpected imagery.

A group of young writers conceived the idea, imperfectly understood by most people, of strengthening the bonds, at that time not very solid, between the literature of Mexico and that of other countries. They published a literary review, *Contemporáneos* (1928–1931), from which the group of its contributors was named. Their writings were usually accessible only to an intellectual minority, but usually kept to very high standards of achievement. They wrote a great deal of poetry, some prose fiction, and some drama. Of this group were Jaime Torres Bodet (1902–   ), Xavier Villaurrutia (1903–1950), the brothers José (1901–   ) and Celestino Gorostiza (1904–   ), Gilberto Owen (1905–1952), Jorge Cuesta (1903–1942), and Bernardo Ortiz de Montellano (1899–1949), among others.

Lyric poetry has always been favored by women writers in Mexico. The number of women poets has grown and their standards have improved considerably in modern times. Important work has been done since about 1930 by Concha Urquiza, Margarita Michelena, and Guadalupe Amor.

Drama.—The first of the literary genres to be cultivated in Mexico, from the days immediately following the conquest in the 16th century, entered a period of decadence after the baroque era. The decline continued during the following two centuries, and with ever-quickening tempo after independence. After the turn of the century, psychological drama replaced moral plays in the European theater; the romantic theater was followed by realism, under the strong influence of the Scandinavians through the Théâtre Libre of André Antoine in Paris. Whatever drama was written in those days in Mexico has only an historical interest for us. The only name worth mentioning is that of Marcelino Dávalos (1871–1923), a facile poet and author of several well-constructed plays; but their subjects were romantic and their characters distorted by an excessively realistic point of view.

Before the revolution every theater was kept busy showing various kinds of the Spanish type of operetta called zarzuelas. The revolution, however, caused a very specific change and innovation, the Mexican review, in which criticism and politics carried the day. Unfortunately, it never reached a really artistic or literary level.

Tentative efforts made after 1920 later turned into an open and decided attempt at creating a Mexican theater movement, which would blaze a trail for the artistic expression of the country. José Joaquín Gamboa (1878–1931) and Víctor Manuel Díez Barroso (1890–1936) are the outstanding writers of those years. Taken together, their works clearly reflect the evolution of the theater, similar to that of Europe, from the naturalistic drama to the drama subsequent to the influence of Henrik Ibsen. But it is perhaps more important to point out the struggle toward the achievement of a national drama movement, which was being conducted both by individuals and by experimental groups like the Comedia Mexicana, the Teatro de Ulises, and the Teatro de Orientación. These struggled on, partially encouraged by insufficient and sporadic government grants. It has been only comparatively recently, really since 1946, that the government has seriously undertaken to encourage authors and actors working exclusively in Mexican media. It is fitting to mention among contemporary authors Xavier Villaurrutia (1903–1950), and above all Rodolfo Usigli (1905–   ), author of first-rate plays like *Otra primavera, Media tono,* and *El gesticulador.* Usigli's best qualities are in the precision and psychological vigor of his characters, in the construction of his plays, and in the powerful social and political criticism which they contain.

Essays.—Very few essays have been written by Mexican authors. They are first found with the introduction of modernism, mixed and confused with newspaper articles and critical reviews. This form later gained new importance with the impulse given to it by the group that was called Ateneo de la Juventud (Athenaeum of Youth), later renamed Ateneo de México, toward 1910. It was a splendid group of people, highly productive under the guidance of the eminent Santo Dominican intellectual Pedro Henríquez Ureña. Of this group were the essayists, and also philosophers, Antonio Caso (1883–1946), José Vasconcelos (1882–   ), Julio Torri (1889–   ), and Alfonso Reyes (1889–1959). Essay writing was also taken up later by Xavier Villaurrutia, Andrés Iduarte (1905–   ), Octavio Paz (1914–   ), and various others; but above them all stands Alfonso Reyes, a native of Monterrey, who apart from being a diplomat for 30 years, has successfully written short stories and dramas, and has done extensive research and literary criticism. His works are legion. A few of the most important are: *Cuestiones estéticas* (1911); *Visión de Anáhuac* (1917); *Huellas* (poetry, 1922); *Ifigenia cruel* (poetry, 1924); *Capítulos de literatura española* (1939); *La crítica en la edad ateniense* (1941); *La experiencia literaria* (1942); *El deslinde* (1944); and his version of the *Iliad* (1952). Alfonso Reyes is, without a doubt, the most important, of greater

literary knowledge, and the most devoted and most careful writer that Mexico has ever produced. See also LATIN AMERICA—*10. Literature.*

Bibliography.—Menéndez Pelayo, Marcelino, *Historia de la poesia hispanoamericana* (Madrid 1911); Coester, Alfred, *The Literary History of Spanish America* (New York 1928); Jiménez Rueda, Julio, *Historia de la literatura mexicana,* 4th ed. (Mexico City 1946); Hespelt, E. H., ed., *An Outline History of Spanish American Literature* (New York 1947); Reyes, Alfonso, *Letras de Nueva España* (Mexico City 1948); Martínez, José Luis, *Literatura mexicana del siglo XX* (Mexico City 1950); Cranfill, Thomas M. *The Muse in Mexico* (Austin, Texas, 1959); Brushwood, John, *Mexico in Its Novel* (Austin 1967).

JOSÉ ROJAS GARCIDUEÑAS, *Professor of Literature, Universidad Nacional de México; Researcher, Instituto de Investigaciones Estéticas.*

20. MUSIC. Pre-Hispanic.—Of the music of prehistoric Mexico, only instruments (clay whistles), found under the lava that forms the Pedregal de San Ángel on the southern outskirts of the capital, have been preserved.

In the 4th to 10th centuries the Maya culture flourished in southern Mexico, Guatemala, and western Honduras. The large monuments of the region—temples, palaces, and pyramids—as well as their reliefs and statues, are proofs of the refinement attained by Maya culture. After a short period of decadence this culture sprang up again on the Yucatán Peninsula in the 10th century.

In reality very little is known concerning the customs of the Mayas. With regard to music, we know that they had a singer and a principal director in charge of the instruments that accompanied the dances with which they celebrated their religious festivals. These instruments, which are well known through the frescoes discovered in 1946 at Bonampak, Chiapas, were: conchs used as horns, of raucous sound; large trumpets, probably of wood; turtle shells struck with the horns of deer; wooden oboes; whistles and flutes of cane and deer bones; drums; and the *tunkul,* which the Aztecs called the *teponaztli.* Conchs and the *tunkul* served particularly to call the people to the temples.

The *tunkul,* or two-tone slit drum, made from the trunk or limb of a hardwood tree such as the sapodilla, is an instrument without equal in the ancient world. It consists of a wooden cylinder placed on its side, generally from two to three feet long and about a foot in diameter, which has been hollowed out through the base. The latter is left open, except for a "pillow" at each end to support the instrument. In the center of the upper part are two small tongues produced by two parallel longitudinal slits connected by another, in the form of an H. These tongues are struck with rubber-tipped sticks and produce the two tones, the musical interval varying with such factors as the length and mass of each tongue.

Music and dance played a very important role in Maya worship and in that of the Mixtecs and Zapotecs of Oaxaca and the Tarascans of Michoacán.

The Texcocans, who in the reign of Nezahualcoyotl (15th century) were the most civilized of the peoples in the Nahua confederation, had schools and fraternities similar to academies for the cultivation of poetry and music.

The musical life of the Aztecs has come to us in more detail. The wealthy class had its own group of singers, and generally composers also. The great lords and the temples had for their exclusive service chanters, or composers of songs. In a like manner, the king had his musicians, perhaps poets also, who extolled in their songs the warlike deeds of the king, his lineage, and his great wealth.

In each of the 18 months of the Aztec year there was at least one important celebration, for each of which the dances, songs, and the dress were distinct. In the large festivals, in which there were up to 8,000 dancers, the first two or three circles of people were formed by the older lords and priests; the others, after leaving a space for the jesters who rambled about performing as buffoons, were formed by the youths. The Aztecs, however, danced as much in private festivals as in public ceremonies.

Dance and song were carefully taught not only in the *calmecac,* where the sons of the nobles were educated, but also in the great temple, where the young girls of the noblest houses lived, and in the *telpochcalli,* where the plebeian youths were educated.

The sounding of the alarm in the city of Tenochtitlan was given with the terrible *huehuetl* of the great temple. This was a "drum" about three feet high and 1.5 feet in diameter, made of a hollowed tree trunk, over the top of which was stretched a deer or jaguar skin, while the bottom was supported by feet. It was beaten with the hands, fingers, or sticks as various usages required.

The instrument of warfare, to communicate orders, was the conch, of frightful sound. The signal for combat was communicated by *teponaztlis* which the chiefs carried at their sides, that of the supreme chief being made of gold.

Colonial.—Together with the rest of the culture of the Indians, their music fell victim to the implacable persecution of the friars. To the peremptory prohibitions placed on the music and dances of the Indians, one must add, as the cause of the absolute extermination of Indian music, the early opening of schools of religious music in the churches and convents. In fact, scarcely had the final capture of Tenochtitlan (now Mexico City) taken place, when Fray Pedro de Gante in 1524 founded the first music school, at Texcoco, to teach the Indians the musical essentials for the religious services, and the making of instruments. This school was moved to Mexico City in 1527, and in a short time there was scarcely a church or convent without a music school, or a town without Indian singers. Their teachers found great talent for music and declared that "they advance in months what in Spain the Spaniards do in two years."

Thus, in the hands of the conquerors, ended the great Indian music—the music that had been composed for the Indian lords and that which had accompanied the temple ceremonies. Only rural and pastoral music remained, defended by the jungle or the rugged mountains. Its pure remains are now to be found principally among the Seri Indians of Tiburón Island, Sonora; the Yaqui of southern Sonora; the Tarahumara of Chihuahua; the Huichol of Nayarit; the Cora of Jalisco; the Lacandon of Chiapas; and the Maya of the Yucatán Peninsula.

Very little of the dazzling sparkle of the Renaissance came to New Spain. Musical life in the colony remained as if in a state of sleep. In the theaters, there were only frivolous little songs and immodest little dances, done by assembled companies of castoffs from Spain. The devout, however, had the occasion to hear in their vespers, their matins, their tierces, and solemn masses something of what the great mystic composers of Europe produced.

Four colonial composers are worthy of note because of the high quality of their works. José de Lienas, whose style shows that he lived in the second half of the 16th century, was an able polyphonic composer. Hernando (or Fernando) Franco reached Mexico City in 1575 and died in 1585. He was choirmaster of the cathedral and his compositions consist of religious works in the best style of the Roman school. Antonio de Salazar is known to have been choirmaster in the cathedral between 1685 and 1715. His works are religious: motets, masses, hymns, and a great number of *villancicos.* José María Aldana, who died in 1810, was a violinist in the cathedral and the composer of numerous religious works, including a *Te Deum* and a Mass in D Major.

The people showed an extraordinary musical activity. *Jarabes, sones,* and *huapangos* of a thousand suggestive names are touched upon in the reports of the epoch—and the archives of the Inquisition. Everywhere they were spoken of as diabolical inventions; on all sides there arose a clamor which called these popular songs shameful, indecent, and sinful.

The folk music of Mexico is the result of three currents: the Indian, the European, and that of the Negroes brought as slaves by the conquerors. The *corrido,* a narrative ballad which derives from the Spanish *romance,* and the *canción* are two song types found all over Mexico. The most characteristic dance forms, generally accompanied by singing, are: the *son,* found almost everywhere; the *chilena* of Guerrero; the *jarana* of the Yucatán Peninsula; the *huapango* of the Gulf coast, principally in Veracruz and Tamaulipas; and the *jarabe,* of which the most popular types are those of Jalisco and Michoacán and the *jarabe largo* of Veracruz. *Jarabes* are suites of *sones* danced by couples without embracing. The three types differ from one another in the *sones* which make them up and in the steps by which they are danced.

The 19th Century.—The musical geography of the country was defined during this century. The *jarabe* divided into the Jalisco and Michoacán types; the *canción* of the Bajío and that of the Central Plateau established a style full of Italian influence; African influence fastened itself along the Gulf coast; and the Viennese waltz found shelter among the islanders of Lake Pátzcuaro in Michoacán.

The 19th century, with the independence of Mexico (1821), also brought the first effective importation to the musical life of the country. For the first time, musicians of merit arrived and Mexico heard Italian music sung by large opera companies.

Three main impulses initiated the musical movement in the country: the founding in Mexico City of the Sociedad Filarmónica by Mariano Elizaga in 1825, and of the Gran Sociedad Filarmónica by José Antonio Gómez in 1839, and the establishment of the Sociedad Filarmónica Mexicana by Agustín Caballero in 1866. From these three were born the Conservatorio Nacional (founded 1877), symphonic and solo concerts, and choral organizations and concerts.

Ricardo Castro (1864–1907) and Julio Ituarte (1845–1905) composed fantasies dealing with Mexican themes. Castro's principal works are a piano concerto and the operas *La Leyenda de Rudel* and *Atzimba*. Aniceto Ortega (1823–1875) composed the opera *Guatimotzin* (another name for Cuauhtemoc, the last Aztec emperor), which was presented in 1871 and had an extraordinary success. Two other composers, Felipe Villanueva (1862–1893) and Juventino Rosas (1868–1894), succeeded in gaining universal renown with two waltzes: Villanueva with the *Vals Poético;* Rosas with *Sobre las Olas*. Villanueva was also the composer of the opera *Keofar,* presented in 1893.

The first artist to make the name of Mexico known to the European continent was Angela Peralta (1854–1883), a soprano with a prodigious voice and great talent that aroused tremendous enthusiasm during a tour of the principal cities of Italy and France.

At the end of the 19th century, Carlos J. Meneses (1863–1929) started the symphonic movement in Mexico, formed a true symphonic orchestra, and made known the most important works of that class of music.

Modern.—Music in the 20th century follows the paths of nationalism, timidly aimed at by Castro and Ituarte. The latest European currents are represented: the German by the violinist and composer Julián Carrillo (1875–   ), author of numerous treatises and of the theory of Sound 13, based on the subdivision of the semitone; and the French by Gustavo E. Campa (1863–1934). The latter's most important work is the opera *El Rey Poeta,* based on the life of Nezahualcoyotl, the 15th century poet-king of Texcoco.

During the Revolution of 1910 the great composer and pianist Manuel M. Ponce (1882–1948) brought the music of the people into aristocratic salons with his stylizations of Mexican folk songs. After the revolution had ended, the interest of Mexican musicians and musicographers was oriented toward folk music, led by Ponce. The latter, José Rolón (1883–1945), Candelario Huizar (1888–   ), the pianist and composer Silvestre Revueltas (1899–1940), and Carlos Chávez (1899–   ) began to produce works which used the essentials of Indian or mestizo music, according to the personal inclinations of each composer, and thus a national style continued to form. Rolón is particularly known for his heroic poem *Cuauhtemoc* (1929), the symphonic suite *Zapotlán* (1941), and a concerto for piano and orchestra (1942); Huizar, for several symphonies, and the symphonic poems *Imágenes* (1929), *Pueblerinas* (1931), and *Surco* (1935); Revueltas, one of Mexico's most gifted composers, for the orchestral works *Cuauhnahuac* (1933), *Janitzio* (1933), and *Sensemayá* (for orchestra and chorus; 1938), and music for the film *Redes* (1935); Chávez, for his ballets *El Fuego Nuevo* (1921); *Los Cuatro Soles* (1926), and *H.P.* (for "Horsepower," 1926–1927), and the symphonies *Sinfonía de Antígona* (1933) and *Sinfonía India* (1936).

The principal works of Luis Sandi (1905–   ) are *Norte* and *Theme and Variations* for orchestra; *El Venado* for Mexican orchestra, performed in New York in 1940 under the title of *Yaqui Music;* the opera *Carlota,* presented in 1948; the ballet *Bonampak,* presented in 1951; as well as a string quartet, and *Troyanas* for chorus and small orchestra. With the exceptions of the last two compositions and *Carlota,* the nationalistic style predominates in Sandi's works.

The profound difference between the 20th century and previous periods is that while there were Mexican composers before the 20th century, they produced Italian, French, and German music; now Mexican musicians produce music which is increasingly Mexican in character.

During the second quarter of the century there was realized a transformation that tended to modernize the musical language of the composers and the taste of the public. Carlos Chávez, first as director (1928–1934) of the Conservatorio Nacional, and later as director of the Orquesta Sinfónica de México, besides being a notable composer, was the soul of this movement.

Among the Mexican artists most famous in Mexico are: the singers Fanny Anitúa, José Mojica, Irma González, Oralia Domínguez, and Carlos Puig; and the pianists Angélica Morales and Miguel García Mora.

Mexico has eight orchestras: the National, the University, the Mexico City, and the Chamber Orchestra of Mexico, all in the capital, and the orchestras of Jalapa, Mérida, Guadalajara, and Guanajuato; as well as five choruses: the Madrigalistas, the Conservatory Chorus, the Boys Chorus of the Conservatory, the Boys Chorus of Morelia, and the Male Chorus of the Escuela Nocturna de Música; and also the National Opera Company.

The most distinguished composers of the middle of the 20th century, in addition to those previously mentioned are: Daniel Ayala Pérez (1908–   ), Miguel Bernal Jiménez (1910–   ), Salvador Contreras (1912–   ), Blas Galindo (1910–   ), and Pablo Moncayo (1912–   ), who may be catalogued as belonging to the nationalistic school; Eduardo Hernández Moncada (1899–   ), Rodolfo Halffter (1900–   ), Jesús Bal y Gay (1905–   ), Luis Herrera de la Fuente (1916–   ), and Carlos Jiménez Mabarak (1916–   ), who follow more or less advanced modern currents; and José Francisco Vázquez (1893–   ), whose style may be called postromantic, as may that of Miguel Bernal Jiménez.

Bibliography.—Lumholtz, Karl, *Unknown Mexico* (New York 1902); García Cubas, Antonio, *El libro de mis recuerdos* (Mexico City 1904); López de Gomara, Francisco, *Hispania Victrix* (Madrid 1925); Campos, Rubén M., *El folklore y la música mexicana* (Mexico City 1928); Saldívar, Gabriel, *Historia de la música en México* (Mexico City 1934); Mendoza, Vicente T., *Romance y corrido* (Mexico City 1939); Copland, Aaron, *Our New Music* (New York 1941); Mayer Serra, Otto, *Panorama de la música mexicana* (Mexico City 1941); *Enciclopedia de la música* (Mexico City 1944); Salazar, Adolfo, *La música moderna* (Buenos Aires 1944); *México y la cultura* (Mexico City 1946); Stevenson, Robert, *Music in Mexico; a Historical Survey* (New York 1952); Simmons, M. E., *The Mexican Corrido as a Source for Interpretive Study of Modern Mexico* (New York 1957).

Useful material may also be found in the *Anales* (*Annals*) of the Instituto de Investigaciones Estéticas and the *Anuario* (*Annual*) of the Sociedad Folklórica de México.

LUIS SANDI,
Composer; Director, Madrigalistas Chorus; Chief, School Music Section, Instituto Nacional de Bellas Artes; Director General, Juventudes Musicales de México.

21. MOTION PICTURES. The first Mexican cinematographic activities were of a documentary nature. Photographers of the turn of the century, such as Salvador Toscano (1872–1947), have left us a wealth of documentary films on the Porfirio Díaz regime and the Mexican Revolution of 1910. *El Grito de Dolores* (1910), based on the stirring appeal to revolt from Spain made by Father Miguel Hidalgo in 1810, was the first motion picture to be filmed in Mexico. Natives of the region were employed to represent the patriots and Spanish soldiers. During the actual filming they became so imbued with their roles that near bloodshed occurred.

In the year 1916, one of the bloodiest of the revolution, the first filming company, México Lux, was founded. Sporadic and ill-directed efforts to create other filming companies had met with little success and it was not until World War I cut off the supply of European films that the Mexican film industry began to produce on a fairly healthy basis. Various other companies were founded during the war years, the most prominent being Azteca Films owned by Germán Camus, Productora Quetzal owned by Jorge Stahl, and Bandera Films. The films which received the widest acclaim and popularity abroad were *Santa* (1917), a melodrama taken from Federico Gamboa's Mexican novel; *Tabaré* (1917), an Indian story; and *El Automóvil Gris* (1919), a cops-and-robbers thriller.

With the war over, Hollywood production created a crisis in the infant motion picture industry of Mexico. This crisis was further aggravated by the introduction of the "talkies." However, this proved to be a blessing in disguise, since the Mexican movie-going public began to insist on films with dialogue spoken in their own language.

During the 1930's a vast source of potential customers was opened up among rural and village inhabitants. Many well-known cinema personalities embarked on their film careers at this time. The director Emilio Fernández (1909–   ); Gabriel Figueroa (1907–   ), cameraman of world-wide fame; the brothers Andrés (1900–   ), Fernando (1900–   ), Domingo (1901–   ), and Julián (1910–   ) Soler, actors; Jorge Negrete (1911–   ), Mexican singing cowboy; Andrea Palma, actress; Arturo de Córdova (1908–   ), actor; and Mario Moreno (1911–   ), known as Cantinflas, mimic and comic, imitator of the likable Mexican "low-lifer" and idol of the Mexican movie-going public, all got their start in the film industry during the 1930's.

Many Spanish-speaking actors in Hollywood were lured south of the border by the nascent Mexican filming industry. Such well-known artists as Virginia Fabregas (1880–   ) and José Mojica (1895–   ), the singer who later gave up fame and fortune to join the Franciscan Order, became leading figures in Mexican films. The greatest film presentation of this period was the cowboy musical *Allá en el Rancho Grande* (1936), the vehicle that carried Tito Guizar to success and popularity as a matinee idol. Artistically, *La Noche de los Mayas,* portraying an Indian legend, produced in 1939, was perhaps the best film of this era.

Since the Mexican film industry caters primarily to a national market, a great many of its films draw on historical or folklore themes. Mexican producers seem to have mastered this type of medium. Such fine films as *María Candelaria* (1943), dealing with the clash of urban and rural cultures in a village near Mexico City, with Dolores del Río in the stellar role, and *Río Escondido* (1947), which portrayed the repercussions arising from the introduction of a school in a Mexican village and had the lovely María Félix (1914–   ) as the feature star, are proofs of the excellence and high artistic quality of their productions. On universal themes, they have produced works which have received world acclaim, such as *Doña Bárbara* (1943), starring María Félix. This was based on the Venezuelan novel by Rómulo Gallegos.

With minor setbacks, the Mexican film industry has continued to expand. In 1952 Mexico occupied first place among the Spanish-speaking countries as a producer of films, followed by Argentina and Spain. Excluding the USSR, Mexico ranked fourth in world ratings as a producer of motion pictures.

FILM PRODUCTION

Year	Films Produced	Reviewed	Average Filming Cost (pesos)
1931	2	0	40,000
1932	8	4	45,000
1933	18	12	50,000
1934	25	25	55,000
1935	21	26	58,000
1936	22	18	75,000
1937	36	32	81,000
1938	50	43	128,000
1939	37	37	135,000
1940	27	32	75,000
1941	46	28	156,000
1942	49	47	278,000
1943	67	57	350,000
1944	78	63	580,000
1945	79	63	648,000
1946	74	79	579,000
1947	54	60	450,000
1948	82	72	400,000
1949	109	101	450,000
1950	125	104	480,000
1951	102	112	540,000
1952	94	99	600,000

The origin of films exhibited in Mexico is shown in the following table:

Country of Origin	1949	1950	1951	1952
United States	250	228	243	274
Mexico	101	104	112	99
France	20	23	18	22
Great Britain	17	7	3	19
Spain	20	13	16	15
Italy	6	13	10	10
Argentina	8	4	6	3

An insignificant number of Portuguese, Chilean, Russian, and Japanese films were also exhibited during these years.

The Banco Nacional Cinematográfico, a public bank founded in 1941 to assist in developing the Mexican film industry by furnishing 50 per cent of the capital, which financed 30 per cent of the films produced in 1946, classified film production as the fourth major industry in the country in the latter year. By 1951 it had declined to seventh place in importance. In 1951 there were approximately 26,000 people working in the film business, with a total investment of 618 million pesos. Approximately 50 studios are owned by Churubusco, Azteca, Clasa, San Angel Inn, and Tepeyac studios, all of which are located near Mexico City. Tepeyac boasts the largest studio in the world.

There were 130 motion picture theaters in Mexico City and 2,021 others scattered throughout the country in 1952. Mexico City theaters during the fiscal year 1950–1951 grossed 14,065,434.85 pesos and paid 2,165,013 pesos in taxes to the government.

According to data furnished by the *Anuario Estadístico,* in 1934, 70.1 per cent of all spectators attended the cinema, 22.5 per cent attended the legitimate theater, 2.4 per cent attended sports events, and 1.7 per cent attended bullfights and cockfights. In 1947 cinema attendance had increased to 92.4 per cent, while theater attendance dropped to 1.7 per cent, with sports attendance and attendance at bullfighting and cockfighting events remaining unchanged.

In world competition, Mexican films have consistently placed in the high rankings. In 1946 at the Cannes Film Festival the photographer Gabriel Figueroa won acclaim with *María Candelaria;* in 1947 at Brussels he again triumphed with *Enamorada* (1946), a drama of the revolution. In the same year he was awarded the International Prize at Venice for *La Perla* (1945), a drama dealing with fishermen; Pedro Armendáriz (1912–) and María Elena Márquez were given trophies for their acting in this film. Figueroa also won a prize at Locarno for *La Perla* in 1947. In the next year at Madrid Figueroa won the photography prize for *Río Escondido,* while Emilio Fernández won acclaim for his direction. Figueroa and Fernández duplicated this feat at Prague in 1948. In 1950 at Madrid the first prize went to *El Dolor de los Hijos* (1950), a melodrama. Once again Figueroa's photography won a prize, for the rural drama *Pueblerina* (1948). At Venice in 1950 Figueroa gained further laurels for *La Malquerida* (1949), based on the drama by the Spaniard Jacinto Benavente. In the next year at Cannes the Mexican-Spanish director Luis Buñuel won acclaim for *Los Olvidados* (1950), exhibited in the United States as *The Young and the Damned,* a film dealing with Mexican adolescents. In 1953 at Cannes a special prize was awarded to Emilio Fernández for *La Red,* a drama of the Pacific coast of Mexico, involving two men and a woman and the resulting play of passions.

Following an old Hollywood custom, the Academia de Artes y Ciencias Cinematográficas (founded in 1948) presents an "Ariel," which is similar to the Hollywood "Oscar," to the best director, the best photographer, and to the best actors of the year.

Bibliography.—Palavacini, Félix, *México, historia de su evolución constructiva* (Mexico City 1945); Departamento Financiero de la Nacional Financiera, *La estructura social de México* (Mexico City 1951); *Mañana,* May 12, 1951.

NARCISO MOLINS-FÁBREGA,
Journalist; Ethnologist, Escuela Nacional de Antropología.

22. SCIENCE AND SCIENTIFIC INSTITUTIONS. Astronomy.

—There are several centers devoted to astronomy (astrophysics in particular) and related fields, such as the Tonanzintla Astrophysical Observatory, established in 1942, in the State of Puebla, where a group of workers is concentrating on the investigation of novae, spectrography of stars, and so forth, and the Observatorio Astronómico Nacional (National Astronomical Observatory), founded in 1878, in Tacubaya, near Mexico City, which for many years has been in charge of the Mexican portion of the chart of the sky. Smaller observatories at state universities and colleges carry on descriptive astronomical work. An astronomical society (Sociedad Astronómica de México) has existed in Mexico City since 1902. It maintains a small observatory for amateur study.

Geography and Geodesy.—Geodetic and geographic work is under the care of a federal government agency, the Dirección General de Geografía, Meteorología e Hidrografía, also located in Tacubaya, Federal District. Unfortunately, lack of sufficient appropriations has somewhat hampered its work, and the old charts to the scales of 1:100,000 and 1:500,000 were never finished, or contain a considerable number of blanks where modern facilities for geographic work could be employed, or more study should be done. However, very useful topographic charts for most of the states have been published, as well as other charts for different purposes. The army has a cartographic office, in charge of the new 1:100,000 map of Mexico, using air navigation charts and other data, of which 26 sheets had appeared by the beginning of 1953. The state government of Jalisco also maintains a geographic institute at Guadalajara.

The Sociedad Mexicana de Geografía y Estadística (Mexican Society of Geography and Statistics), established in 1833, and its branches in most states, have large collections of maps of all kinds, as well as much other data useful to geographers, meteorologists, and cartographers. A bulletin of a specialized nature has been published by the society at more or less regular intervals since 1839.

Geology.—The geological sciences have been taken over from the old Instituto de Geología in Mexico City (founded in 1891 and now a division of the Universidad Nacional de México) by several organizations, official and semiofficial. Large collections of rocks and fossils are kept for research at the institute, and there is a large library and other facilities for study. Its publications reach a large number, covering all fields of geology. Structural and historical geological studies are carried out on a large scale by the government petroleum agency, Petróleos Mexicanos, geohydrological work is done by the Secretaría de Recursos Hidráulicos, a department of the federal government, and mining geological investigations are conducted by the Instituto Nacional para el Estudio de los Recursos Minerales (National Institute for the Study of Mineral Resources) established in Mexico City in 1944; all of these extend their studies to the whole country. The Bank of Mexico, through its Geological Department, has concentrated on coal and iron resources. All these agencies occasionally publish the results of their work. There is also the Sociedad Geológica Mexicana (Mexican Geological Society), in the capital, founded in 1904, and the Asociación Mexicana de Geólogos Petroleros (Mexican Association of Petroleum Geologists), organized in 1949, both with publications in the form of bulletins and maps.

Meteorology.—A new center for meteorological studies in the Gulf of Mexico was established in the port of Veracruz in 1950, in connection with the Servicio Meteorológico Mexicano (Mexican Meteorological Service), at Tacubaya, founded in 1877 by President Porfirio Díaz. Some states, like Jalisco and Yucatán, also have local networks of meteorological stations for weather forecasting. In Mexico City a meteorological chart is published daily, with forecasts for the next 24 hours in the whole country, and also a meteorological bulletin once a month, with summaries of national, state, and regional observations. The Sociedad Mexicana de Geografía y Estadística, mentioned under *Geography and Geodesy,* is also active in this field.

Physics and Chemistry.—These are the least developed branches of scientific research in Mexico, although many theoretical mathematical studies by Mexican workers on several aspects of both sciences have received international recognition. There is a Sociedad Mexicana de Física (Mexican Physics Society), founded in 1951, in the capital, with a bimonthly bulletin, and the Universidad Nacional maintains an institute in each of the corresponding fields. A small laboratory for nuclear research was established on the university campus in Mexico City in 1951. The new technological institutes in different states will undoubtedly contribute to the development of new studies. As regards chemistry in particular, except for practical problems of an industrial nature, very little work of an original character has been done. Technical education and organizations are entirely professional.

Biology.—This is the best-represented field of scientific study, both in the pure and in the applied aspects. A long tradition of interest in plants and animals, coming down from pre-Hispanic days, has brought about a continuity in their investigation which other scientific studies have not enjoyed in the past. This interest in living beings includes native human populations, which offer a rich array of physical and cultural traits of great attraction to research (see section on *Anthropology*). The Sociedad Mexicana de Historia Natural (Mexican Natural History Society), in the capital, founded in 1868, embraces all fields of biological studies and publishes a well-known review. The Mexican societies of Hydrobiology (Hidrobiología) and Entomology (Entomología) organized in Mexico City in 1950 may also be mentioned among scientific organizations in this field.

Botany.—Botanical investigation of a systematic nature is done at the Herbario Nacional (National Herbarium), founded in 1788 and since 1929 a department of the Instituto de Biología of the Universidad Nacional, and at the Instituto Botánico (Botanical Institute) established in 1948 at Tuxtla Gutiérrez, Chiapas. Agricultural botany is studied in the Mexico City office of the Rockefeller Foundation, and at several less important agencies, like the Instituto Técnico Agrícola (Technological Agricultural Institute) of the sisal growers association, founded in 1934 at Mérida, Yucatán. There is also a Department of Agronomy at the Instituto Tecnólogico y de Estudios Superiores in Monterrey. Obviously cereals receive more attention in most states than other crops, but here and there small laboratories carry on research on special problems, such as pest control in citrus plants, and the like.

Forest products are most important in northern and southern Mexico, and the lumber industry maintains an interest in the study of areas in Durango and Chihuahua, in northern Mexico, as well as in the tropical rain forests in Campeche, Yucatán, and Quintana Roo, in southern Mexico. Some enterprising firms have started a scientific survey of possibilities, in the charge of properly trained staffs. There are several learned societies whose members are interested, as professionals or amateurs, in forest plants problems, and most of these organizations publish bulletins, special papers, and semitechnical information.

There are some 50 national parks in different regions of the country, largely so declared on the basis of an idealistic acceptance of the necessity of conserving natural resources rather than on a scientific understanding of the realities of Mexico. Studies of some of these national parks, like the Izta-Popo National Park, close to Mexico City, where some of the most famous volcanoes of the country are located, have been published.

Zoology.—Zoological studies are conducted in the capital at the Universidad Nacional's Instituto de Biología (founded in 1929) which has a natural history museum, at the Escuela Nacional de Ciencias Biológicas (National School of Biological Sciences), founded in 1936 and now a division of the Instituto Politécnico Nacional, and at other institutions of lesser academic standing. There are also museums of natural history in some state capitals, like Tuxtla Gutiérrez, Guanajuato, and Guadalajara, and most colleges and universities maintain

collections of local interest. Applied zoology is developing swiftly in fisheries, cattle raising, and other aspects. There is an Instituto de Pesquería del Pacífico (Institute of Pacific Fisheries), founded in 1947 at Guaymas, Sonora, a Comisión Federal para el Fomento de la Piscicultura Rural (Federal Commission for the Development of Rural Pisciculture), founded in 1949 in Mexico City, and various zootechnic laboratories in the states. For the Sociedad Mexicana de Historia Natural see the section on *Biology*.

Physiology and Medicine.—There are research laboratories in several professional schools and hospitals, such as the Instituto Nacional de Cardiología (National Cardiological Institute), founded in 1946, the Instituto de Salubridad y Enfermedades Tropicales (Health and Tropical Diseases Institute), founded in 1939, and the Instituto de Higiene (Institute of Hygiene), founded in 1904. The first two are in Mexico City; the last near by at Popotla. Most hospitals maintain laboratories for special studies, and there is a great number of medical publications of all kinds, as well as societies and other groups for pure and applied research.

The Academia Nacional de Medicina de México, founded in 1864, represents the highest institution of its kind in the republic, and is housed in the old building of the medical college of the Universidad Nacional. As soon as new buildings for this school are finished, the old quarters will be turned over to medical societies in Mexico City for the establishment of a medical museum and appropriate libraries of professional character.

Anthropology.—Anthropology is centered in the Escuela Nacional de Antropología e Historia (National School of Anthropology and History), founded in 1937, in the Museo Nacional de Antropología (National Museum of Anthropology) in Mexico City, and in other agencies in that city and the state capitals. Some state governments like those of Michoacán, Veracruz, and Yucatán, maintain anthropological departments. There is a Sociedad Mexicana de Antropología, founded in 1937, in the capital, which publishes an annual review, as well as other societies for special studies. The Instituto Indigenista Interamericano (Inter-American Indian Institute), organized in 1940 in Mexico City and supported by the governments of the American republics, has several publications. The Instituto Panamericano de Geografía e Historia, founded in 1929 at Tacubaya, Federal District, also publishes a well-known annual bulletin in the field of anthropological bibliography. Lastly, there is an Instituto Nacional Indigenista (National Indian Institute), established in Mexico City in 1948, for ethnographical investigation.

MANUEL MALDONADO-KOERDELL,
Professor of Paleontology, Instituto Politécnico Nacional and Escuela Nacional de Antropología e Historia; Paleontologist, Gerencia de Exploración, Petróleos Mexicanos.

23. PHILOSOPHY. Colonial Mexico.—

The cultures existing in Mexico before its conquest (1521) by the Spaniards possessed cosmic myths and moral ideas which may be considered as elements of a philosophy in the sense of *Welt-* and *Lebensanschauung* (outlooks on the universe and life), although founded neither upon scientific nor indeed upon rational bases as a philosophy in the strict sense. A philosophy in this sense was introduced into Mexico by the Spaniards, and was stimulated mainly through the foundation of the university, Real y Pontificia Universidad (now the Universidad Nacional) de México, in 1551, and other centers of culture similar to those in Spain whose activities were partially devoted to the teaching of philosophy and to the development of scholasticism. The Spanish Augustinian monk Fray Alonso de la Veracruz (1504–1584) may be considered the father of this discipline in Mexico. He was the first professor of philosophy in the university and the author of didactic works, one of which, the *Recognitio Summularum* (1554), was the first philosophical treatise printed in the Americas.

During its first decades the colony was influenced by intellectual movements, more or less related to a philosophy in the strict sense, such as Renaissance humanism, utopianism, and Erasmism. These movements inspired works of beneficent colonization such as that performed by Bishop Vasco de Quiroga (1470–1565) in Michoacán. During these same years the colony was engaged in juridical issues and in various philosophically slanted polemics which followed in the wake of the conquest, mainly through the intervention of Fray Bartolomé de las Casas (1474–1566), the most celebrated of these polemists. However, when these influences and polemics had died out or at least had tempered themselves, the history of philosophy in Mexico until the second half of the 18th century was confined almost exclusively to the formulation of scholastic thought, although the problems, methods, and doctrines of modern science and philosophy were active in the minds of certain exceptional personalities, among them Carlos de Sigüenza y Góngora (1645–1700), who wrote on a wide variety of subjects, and the poetess Juana Inés de la Cruz (1651–1695).

At the beginning of the second half of the 18th century, a group of young Jesuits, cognizant of European philosophy and science, initiated a reform which affected mainly the teaching of natural philosophy as performed by their order. This was the introduction in their teaching of experimental and exact modern science (so-called experimental philosophy). The Jesuits Francisco Javier Clavigero (or Clavijero; 1731–1787), Francisco Javier Alegre (1729–1788), and Diego José Abad (1727–1779) were the best-known members of this group, due to the works they published in Italy (although these were not of a philosophical nature) after the expulsion of the Jesuit Order from the dominions of the Spanish crown in 1767. This expulsion, however, did not check the success of the reform, because of the zealous activity of a brilliant group of men, of whom the principal ones were disciples of the Jesuits.

With the sanction given by the university to the *Elementa recentioris philosophiae* (1774) of Juan Benito Díaz de Gamarra, a priest of the Order of the Oratory, modern philosophy and science in Mexico achieved a significant victory under the banner of an eclecticism similar to that of Europe in the 17th and 18th centuries. This eclecticism had been diffused in Spain and her colonies as a doctrine extremely well suited to the introduction of modern science and philosophy. Father José Antonio de Alzate (1729–1799), in whose honor the present Mexican Academy of Sciences was named, and others, criticized and satirized traditional scholasticism, cultivated the exact, natural, and human sciences, particularly in their relation to Mexico, and championed the cause of the scientific disciplines, principally in the practical field.

In the fulfillment of their task, the members of this group utilized cultural newspapers, among which the most renowned was Alzate's own *Gazeta de Literatura*. The scientific expeditions of Spaniards and other men of different nationalities, including that of the illustrious Alexander von Humboldt (1769–1859), stimulated their work. The foundation of new cultural centers, among which that of the Real Seminario de Minería (Royal School of Mines), in 1792, deserves mention, helped them in their activities. Thus they created a new intellectual environment in which philosophy in the full and applied sense of the 18th century had the leading part. The intellectual career of Miguel Hidalgo before his *Grito de Dolores* (1810), which launched the movement against Spain, offers convincing evidence that this philosophical movement was a decisive forerunner of Mexican independence.

Independent Mexico.—During the struggle for the consolidation of a country which had declared its independence, the philosophical tradition born of the colonial period suffered intermittent crises. The frequent closing of the academic halls of the university gave eloquent testimony to its precarious defense against the political philosophy of liberalism, the most important of the new philosophies of this period, whose main exponent was the ideologist José María Luis Mora (1794–1850). The university was definitively closed in 1865, and the triumph of the Liberals under Benito Juárez established the doctrine of positivism as the official philosophy of the country under the direction of the physician Gabino Barreda (1818–1881), founder of the Escuela Nacional Preparatoria (National Preparatory School) in 1867. This institution was responsible for the education or at least the philosophical orientation of the Mexican leaders, some of whom were members of the group known as the *científicos* ("scientists"), who preached economic progress and guided the public life of their nation during the successive regimes of Gen. Porfirio Díaz until the Revolution of 1910. During the latter year the outstanding *científico,* Justo Sierra (1848–1912), realizing that a reconciliation of the national culture and the new foreign ideological orientations was imperative, succeeded in re-establishing the university and in restoring within its walls a measure of freedom in the teaching of philosophy.

Likewise in 1910 constructive efforts to the same worthy cause were contributed by the group known as the Ateneo de la Juventud, among whose illustrious members were José Vasconcelos (1882–   ) and Antonio Caso (1883–1946), the two great masters of philosophy of modern Mexico, and also Alfonso Reyes (1889–1959). The latter was one of the most eminent of Latin American intellectuals. His ideological essays make excursions into the domain of philosophy; his *El deslinde* (1944) completely masters the realm of philosophy of literature. Caso presents in the most personal of his philosophical works, *La existencia como economía, desinterés y caridad* (3d ed. 1943), a veritable Christian existentialism, although before that term became popular. Vasconcelos has developed in his voluminous *Metafísica* (1929), *Ética* (1931), *Estética* (1935), and his later equally extensive *Lógica Orgánica* (1945), a system which fuses various philosophical influences from Plotinus to Henri Bergson into a very personal neospiritualism culminating in mystical aestheticism.

Samuel Ramos (1897–   ), in his *El perfil del hombre y la cultura en México* (1934), emerges as the main forerunner of the most interesting movement in the recent development of philosophical thought in Mexico, one which tends to elaborate a philosophy of the Mexican and his culture. This movement was initiated in 1945 by the Grupo Filosófico Hyperión led by Leopoldo Zea (1912–   ).

In the modern intellectual life of Mexico the principal directions of contemporary philosophy are well represented, chiefly: neo-Thomism, by Oswaldo Robles (1905–   ); neo-Kantianism, by Francisco Larroyo (1908–   ) and Guillermo Hector Rodríguez (1910–   ); the philosophy of values, by Eduardo García Máynez (1908–   ), active also in the field of juridical logic, and José Romano Muñoz (1890–   ); also phenomenology, existentialism, and historicism by some of those already named, as well as other Mexicans, and by a group of Spaniards in exile in Mexico since 1938. These latter are working principally in the exposition and critical interpretation of the last-mentioned philosophical trends and in the history of ideas in Spain and Mexico.

Bibliography.—Ramos, Samuel, *Historia de la filosofía en México* (Mexico City 1943); Zea, Leopoldo, *El positivismo en México* (Mexico City 1943); id., *Apogeo y decadencia del positivismo en México* (Mexico City 1944); Navarro, Bernabé, *La introducción de la filosofía moderna en México* (Mexico City 1948); Gallegos Rocafull, J. M., *El pensamiento mexicano en los siglos XVI y XVII* (Mexico City 1951); Gaos, José, *En torno a la filosofía mexicana*, 2 vols. (Mexico City 1952–53).

JOSÉ GAOS,
Professor of Philosophy, Universidad Nacional de México.

24. PREHISTORY AND PRE-HISPANIC HISTORY.

Setting.—Mexico is a land of strong geographical contrasts, a fact which greatly influenced the development of native civilizations. The arid lands of the north, to the east of the Sierra Madre Occidental, offered few incentives for the establishment of farmers before the introduction of European technology. This zone was occupied in pre-Hispanic times by nomadic food gatherers, with a very scattered population and a simple culture. This also applies to Lower California. The alluvial plains of the northwest, along the coast of the Pacific Ocean and the Gulf of California, irrigated by the rivers flowing from the Sierra Madre Occidental, and the well-watered mountains themselves, are exceptions to this. These northwestern regions were occupied, at the time of the conquest, by farming peoples who formed a link between the civilized peoples to the south and the cultivators of the southwestern United States.

To the south of a line drawn roughly from the mouth of the Pánuco River, on the coast of the Gulf of Mexico in northern Veracruz, to the mouth of the Santiago River, in Nayarit on the Pacific coast, the Indians took advantage of environmental conditions more favorable to agriculture, and developed complex sedentary cultures. Within the area south of this line, including central and southern Mexico, Guatemala, British Honduras, and the western parts of Honduras and El Salvador, there are extremes of environment, ranging from tropical rain-forest lowlands, through semiarid savanna country and fertile semitropical and temperate intermountain valleys, to cool uplands. These strong contrasts of relief within small areas result in the proximity of very diverse life zones, which, being complementary from the viewpoint of natural resources, have stimulated trade and conquests. These interregional relationships contributed to the development of basically similar cultures all over this territory—notwithstanding differences in patterns of regional specialization—constituting the culture area named Meso-America by ethnologists. Some of the most advanced American Indian cultures, having reached the stage of urban civilization, flourished here.

Sources of Information.—A consistent picture of cultural development covering at most 3,000 years and ending with the Spanish conquest can be traced for only a few areas of central and southern Mexico. It is based mainly on the historical reconstruction made possible through interpretations of findings in archaeological excavations. Only for the last centuries of this period do we have information based on reliable native historical sources.

These Indian sources could be classified in three groups, as follows:

(1) Native history preserved in the original form of folded books of picture writing. Due to the pictorial character of Indian writing these books were only summaries, consisting mainly of personal names, place names, and dates, with indications of the birth, marriage, and death of the personages, conquests, and so forth. The details were filled in by an oral tradition transmitted in the form of epics. Some of these epic poems have been preserved transcribed in the histories of group 2. Only a few of these books have survived the accidents of conquests, systematic destruction by overzealous friars and priests, or the ravages of time. On the basis of a group of picture-writing books known to have been made in the northern Oaxaca-southern Puebla region, Alfonso Caso was able to compile a list of Mixtec royal genealogies, going back to 692 A.D. according to his assertion. A preliminary account of this discovery was published in Caso's "El mapa de Teozacoalco," *Cuadernos Americanos* (Mexico City, September–October 1949).

(2) Histories written down (from formal oral tradition, or as transcriptions and interpretations of picture writing) after the Spanish conquest, in the Indian languages with the Latin script, or in Spanish. Quite a few of these refer to central Mexico, but the information they provide does not go back beyond the Toltec period (c.900 A.D.–c.1200). To this group belongs the *Relación de Michoacán,* which includes data for only the last two centuries before the Spanish conquest, and also the several *Books of Chilam Balam* of Yucatán. These books include historical data going back to the 5th century A.D., but only from the 10th century onward can we derive a consistent historical picture.

(3) Interesting historical information is found scattered in the answers to inquiries made by Spanish officials in the first decades of the colonial regime (particularly in the *Relaciones Geográficas,* 1579–1582), in petitions of the Indians to the Spanish authorities, and in other sources. These are valuable in that they reflect personal memories and what the people remembered as being historically important. They represent the limited local version of events, which can be compared with official history. Of course, the data provided by sources of this type cover only the last decades before the Spanish conquest.

The deciphered inscriptions of the so-called Long Count system of the ancient Maya give us a chronological framework for the greatest part of the first millennium of our era. However, it must be noted that the correspondence between

Maya Long Count dates and our calendar has not been securely established. Several different correlations of the Long Count with the Gregorian calendar have been suggested. J. Eric S. Thompson's correlation is accepted by a majority of specialists. According to it, the Long Count inscriptions cover the period from about 300 A.D. to 900 A.D. The dates given in this article, when referring to this period, are based on that correlation. Evidence from trade relations and stylistic evidence permit the transfer of dates from the Maya area to central Mexico, where no such chronological framework exists.

The method of dating through the radioactivity of organic remains by carbon isotope 14 has been applied to Meso-American materials, but since this method is in the experimental stage, the dates produced cannot be considered as absolutely reliable. Certainly, some of the dates for central Mexico conflict with other sources of evidence.

Ancient Hunters and Plant Gatherers.— The oldest evidences of human occupation in Mexico have been found in the upper layers of a geological formation named Becerra, dating from the very end of Pleistocene times. Mammoths, American horses, and other extinct animals constituted the Becerra fauna.

In the second half of the 19th century, the French Commission Scientifique du Mexique discovered stone implements in geological formations bearing remains of fossil elephants and bisons in the region of Juchipila, Jalisco; in the State of Guanajuato; and near Tacubaya, in the Federal District. In 1946, a small waste flake of obsidian, showing apparent use by man, was found lying below the head of an imperial mammoth (*Archidiskodon imperator*) in a Becerra bed, near Tepexpan, State of Mexico. In 1947, at the same locality and in the same geological layer, was found the skeleton of a man 55 to 65 years old, but there is some controversy about the possibility of this skeleton of so-called Tepexpan man —who would have lived some 10,000 years ago— being an intrusive burial of later date. Finally, in March 1952 another *Archidiskodon* skeleton, also lying in a Becerra stratum, was excavated at Santa Isabel Ixtapan, near Tepexpan. A flint projectile point was found amid the ribs and five other flint and obsidian tools around the skeleton. The projectile point belongs to the type named Scottsbluff, also found associated with the remains of extinct fauna in the high plains region of the United States. Other cultural remains dated at Becerra times are: a fossil llama bone carved in the form of an animal head, found in 1870 near Tequixquiac, and several obsidian, chalcedony, and bone artifacts found by Helmut de Terra after 1946 at Tequixquiac, El Risco, and San Francisco Mazapan. All these localities are in the Valley of Mexico, not far from Tepexpan.

Geologists date the end of the Becerra epoch at about 10,000 years ago. The radiocarbon method yielded dates ranging from earlier than 16,000 to about 4,000 years ago for materials (wood, peat, stems, and roots of aquatic plants) found in the upper Becerra formation. The last date is much later than expected and too recent to be accepted without question. However, the dating of Scottsbluff points in the high plains in the postglacial period from 8,000 to 4,000 years ago may support a date later than 10,000 years ago for the findings at Santa Isabel Ixtapan. Other findings of human skeletal remains

or stone artifacts, supposedly very ancient, have been made at different times and in different regions, but for one reason or another full evidence is lacking concerning the antiquity claimed.

For central Mexico, at present, there is a gap in our knowledge of several thousand years between the age of the hunters of mammoths and the earliest known cultures of sedentary farmers from which a continuous sequence of cultural development can be traced up to the time of the Spanish conquest. This gap may be filled by the culture represented by a great number of artifacts, predominantly made of basalt, including grinding stones, found at several places and grouped under the term "Chalco industry." It has been claimed that they represent a culture based on the gathering of wild plants rather than on hunting. Helmut de Terra, the discoverer, dated them from 10,000 to 4,000 years ago, but most of these artifacts were found on the surface, giving no basis for safe geological dating. Furthermore, the association of all these artifacts in a simple tradition of stoneworking is highly questionable. However, the surveys made in northwestern Mexico show that there was a southern extension (in Sonora and perhaps also in Chihuahua) of the prehistoric plant-gathering Cochise culture of the southwestern United States

Archaic Farmers.— Remains representing the beginnings of agriculture and sedentary life have not yet been found in Mexico. The oldest known cultures of sedentary farmers—called by archaeologists "Archaic," "Formative," or "Middle" cultures—were already very complex. Undoubtedly they were the products of a long tradition of sedentary life and the development of crafts whose antecedents are still to be found.

Not a single complete excavation of an Archaic site has been made; however, the findings made in testing trenches and pits permit one to draw a sketchy picture of life in those times. In what follows, the Archaic cultures in the Valley of Mexico, which are the best known, will mainly be referred to.

Thick fertile alluvial soils, a temperate climate, fish in the lakes and wild fowl living along their marshy shores, and game on the wooded slopes of the surrounding mountains, made the valley very favorable to settlement. Subsistence was based upon cultivation of corn (maize). Beans and squash were probably cultivated, and the products of the agave and prickly pear were probably used. Hunting and fishing were secondary economic activities. The importance of hunting for the first part of this period is attested by the abundance of deer bones found in the middens; later, game became scarcer. Remains of cotton textiles have also been found. The Valley of Mexico is too high for the cultivation of cotton and thus its use surely indicates commercial relations with the neighboring semitropical regions of Morelos, Guerrero, or the southern part of Puebla. These relations are also proved by the distribution of pottery types and terra-cotta figurines. Also, shells from both coasts (from the Pacific in the early period, from the Gulf of Mexico later) which were used for ornaments, and jade and other fine stones from outside the valley reveal extended commercial relations. Tools were made of stone and bone. The basic technological patterns already well established in the Archaic period lasted—with few additions or modifications—until the introduction of European techniques. Forms, techniques, and motifs of decoration in Archaic pottery are quite elaborate.

Permanent settlements inhabited over long periods of time are indicated by thick deposits of refuse. Little evidence of house types has been found; however, it seems that the walls were of wattle, daubed with mud, a type of wall still in general use in rural Mexico. It is assumed that they were covered by thatched roofs. Only for the last part of the Archaic period do we have evidence of stone building.

Nothing is known about political organization and very little about social structure. Some social differentiation can be inferred from the evidence supplied by burials. Such differentiation does not, however, seem to have attained the complexity of clear-cut class distinctions. The religious ideas of these Archaic farmers manifest themselves characteristically in a fertility cult. This seems indicated by abundant finds of female figurines of baked clay. Such a cult in all probability furnished the basis for the worship of the mother of the gods, the earth goddess, so important in late pre-Hispanic times. Two-headed figurines and above all bipartite masks—expressive of the concepts of life and death—seem to contain the germ of an idea most important in later times, the principle of duality. Conspicuously lacking are formalized representations of gods and symbols associated with a priestly cult, which achieved great development later, in the period of the Classic civilizations.

Radiocarbon dates for charcoal found in early Archaic middens would place the beginnings of this period not later than 1500 B.C. These fall several centuries earlier than the dates accepted by archaeologists before 1950. If we accept the radiocarbon dates, we are faced with a period of about 1,000 years without significant cultural development and with only very minor changes in pottery styles, evidencing a remarkably conservative culture. While this is possible, other considerations lead one to ask for further confirmation of these dates, before accepting them as definitive.

During the last few centuries before the Christian era the homogeneous peasant communities of earlier times were giving rise to more differentiated societies in most of Meso-America. Everywhere in central and southern Mexico, as well as in the highlands and on the Pacific coast of Guatemala, some villages were growing into towns at this time. In the Valley of Mexico, Tlatilco, an extensive site northwest of Mexico City, may well represent an example of this transition. Adequate information on the excavations of this site have not yet been published. Nevertheless, a careful analysis of the evidence found in its great cemetery, excavated in the 1940's, throws light on the changes in social structure corresponding to the development from the homogeneous village culture to the more differentiated and sophisticated town culture. Even before 500 B.C. (according to radiocarbon dating) some towns had enough economic power and control of human resources to build groups of large artificial mounds for religious purposes. Thus, at Cuicuilco, near Tlalpan in the south of the valley, several truncated conical platforms—the largest measuring 390 feet in diameter at the base and 75 feet in height—were raised as bases for altars. This largest mound has a solid mud nucleus and a stone-faced exterior. A large pyramidal mound at Yaxuná, in Yucatán, also belongs to this stage.

Other significant new features appearing at this time are calendar and hieroglyphic writing, the earliest examples of which are found in the carved stones with calendric inscriptions uncovered under buildings of later age in the ruins of Monte Albán, near Oaxaca.

Classic Civilizations.—What archaeologists call "Classic" in Meso-America is the period from about the time of Christ, or shortly afterward, to about 900 A.D., when brilliant civilizations flourished and fell. These civilizations had no metal tools, or, for that matter, metallurgy of any kind. Only from about 750 A.D. were some metal ornaments of a gold-copper alloy traded into southern Meso-America (Honduras, El Salvador, and Guatemala) from Panama or Costa Rica.

Systems of overland transportation were poorly developed. Meso-America lacked large animals which might have been domesticated for use as pack animals, such as the Peruvian llama, or for pulling and riding. The wheel was known, but used only for toys. The prevalence of mountainous terrain may then, as now, have inhibited its use in transportation. Goods were transported overland by human carriers. The rivers of Meso-America do not constitute good waterways. Only the lake areas of the Valley of Mexico and of Michoacán (as well as Lake Atitlán in Guatemala) offered facilities for inland water transportation by canoes. This fact accounts for the importance of these areas in pre-Hispanic history. It would seem that maritime transportation along the coast was important only around the Peninsula of Yucatán. However, the productivity of agriculture was developed to the point of being able to support a dense population, part of which was concentrated around large religious centers or in true urban communities. Surplus produce allowed these communities to divert tremendous amounts of energy to the glory of the gods, to the service of their earthly representatives, and to honor the dead.

In central Mexico, the largest city that flourished during this period was Teotihuacán, whose ruins are now about 25 miles northeast of Mexico City. About 300 A.D., the urbanized area of this site covered more than 500 acres; by 700 A.D. it had expanded to cover more than 1,750 acres. We do not know how far the suburbs extended. The nucleus of the city is made up of large temples, of which the most dominant is the great pyramid (the so-called Pyramid of the Sun) which stands 64.46 meters (about 212 feet) high. The temple with the largest ground plan is the square enclosure dedicated to Quetzalcoatl, the Feathered Serpent (a symbol of the water gods), which measures 440 yards on each side. Inside this enclosure there is a pyramid which served as the base for the temple proper, a great ceremonial plaza, and the living quarters of the priests. The great Avenue of the Dead, which forms the axis of the city, and the streets were paved with mortar; there was a complete system of underground drainage. In the residential sections, buildings were densely clustered. The large number of rooms found in the relatively few houses that have been excavated, and their decoration, which often included elaborate murals, indicate that these were the dwellings of an upper class. A cluster of more than 200 rooms and courts, grouped in units of different sizes, excavated in 1935 by Sigvald Linné on the eastern periphery of the site, suggests private houses, possibly for a middle class of merchants. We have no information about the dwellings of the lower class.

Monte Albán, located on top of a hill, was the metropolis of the central valleys of Oaxaca. Many temples and a great number of well-built tombs, built under the floors of dwellings, have been discovered there. Cobá, in Quintana Roo, was the center of a system of causeways radiating to outlying sites. The longest causeway extends 62 miles west, to Yaxuná. Other important centers of this period were El Tajín, in the coastal plain of northern Veracruz, and Palenque, in Chiapas, one of the westernmost sites of the Maya area. It seems that the flourishing epoch of the Olmec culture of southern Veracruz and western Tabasco should be placed in this period.

The monumental architecture of the Classic period implies a well-organized control of the labor force. Hieroglyphic writing, developments in mathematics such as the use of zero and the positional concept in the writing of numbers, astronomy, and the calendar, mark the achievements of intellectual culture.

Trade was very extensive. It is attested mainly for manufactured luxury items. We also have evidence for trade of either prime materials, such as obsidian, fine-quality flint, or other stones used in the production of tools, or of the finished tools themselves. A fine type of pottery, probably produced in southern Puebla, was traded as far as Teotihuacán in the Valley of Mexico, to Colima in the west, and to Copán in Honduras. Food must have been an important trade item, considering the great urban population, which could not have been self-sufficient. The supporting area of the largest centers, such as Teotihuacán and Monte Albán, must have been very large.

The importance of temples and the development of religious art (see the section *Pre-Hispanic Art*) seems to indicate that religion was the main integrating force of society. The main deities were the water gods, the gods of vegetation and corn, the god of fire, and in the southern regions (Oaxaca and the Maya area) a bat god. Noteworthy by its absence is the cult of the gods of war.

Most of the settlements are located in open ground, with obvious disregard for defense, and lacking—so far as is known—any artificial protective works. The ruins of Monte Albán are an exception to this, in that they are located on top of an easily defensible hill rising 1,300 feet above the surrounding valley. Nevertheless, the excavations have failed to produce any indication whatever that the site was selected with defensive purposes in mind or that it was at any time used as a fortress.

Transition Period.—This location of the sites and absence of defensive works and the absence of representations of warriors in art at the peak of the Classic period seem to indicate that external relations were predominantly pacific. Later, warfare acquired greater importance. Warriors and battle scenes became prominent in art. According to present evidence the earliest examples of such representations occur in the Usumacinta River drainage (western Maya area) and are dated about 630 A.D. Central Mexican tradition tells us of the conquest of Cholollan (modern Cholula, near Puebla)—formerly a center of the Teotihuacán culture—by the Olmec-Xicalanca people, about the end of the 8th century. Approximately at the same time, Teotihuacán was violently destroyed and never rebuilt. Monte Albán was abandoned, its buildings fell into ruin, and the site was subsequently used only as a burial ground. Farther south, one after another the Mayan centers of civilization in the previous centuries were also deserted. The causes of this general crisis are not yet known, but the consequences were unquestionably a change from societies patterned on a seemingly theocratic basis to more secular-militaristic ones. The settlement pattern changed accordingly. After the 9th or 10th centuries many cities and towns established in open country were protected by stone walls, or by palisades and moats. In addition, many settlements with large, permanent populations were located on hilltops and were, in most cases, solidly fortified as well.

It seems that the ruins of Xochicalco, in Morelos, correspond to the epoch of transition between this period and the following one, or about the 9th to 10th centuries. The site is composed of three parts: the acropolis, on a steep hill, a ceremonial and residential section—seemingly for the upper class—surrounded by ramparts and moats; the citadel on top of a neighboring, higher hill; and a suburban area on flat ground, protected by these hills and by deep ravines.

Toltec Period (c.900 A.D.–c.1200 A.D.)— About the beginning of the 10th century a conqueror called Ce Tecpatl Mixcoatl entered the Valley of Mexico. He was the chief of a barbarian people arriving from the northwest (possibly from Zacatecas, Jalisco, or the Lerma River basin). Mixcoatl established his capital at Culhuacán in the Valley of Mexico, and extended his conquests in the south to the neighboring Valley of Morelos and northern Guerrero. Soon, these invaders absorbed the civilization of central Mexico. Such a process of acculturation was repeated later, after the fall of Tollan, by the Aztecs and other Chichimec groups. Mixcoatl's son, Ce Acatl Topiltzin, is the most important figure in Toltec history. He was the founder of Tollan (now Tula, Hidalgo), where he established the capital of his empire. The name Toltec is derived from the name of this city. Internal disturbances put an end to the rule of Ce Acatl and he was forced into exile. A new dynasty began at Tollan, with Matlacxochitl as the first king. Famine, epidemics, and war mark the history of this period, until Tollan was destroyed and Huemac, its last king, was killed or hanged himself in a cave on the Hill of Chapultepec. A dispersion of the Toltec lords took place. They took refuge in their possessions to the south and the southeast. At that time the Chichimecs took over most of the former Toltec territories in central Mexico; however, Toltec tradition was kept alive at Culhuacán. (See also TOLTECS.)

In Yucatán, local tradition records the arrival of foreign invaders toward the end of the 10th century. Their legendary leader was named Kukulcán. This title is the literal translation in Maya of the Nahua word Quetzalcoatl (Feathered Serpent), the title of Ce Acatl Topiltzin. There is no doubt of the connection between these events and the history of Tollan. Excavations at Tula (Tollan) and at Chichén Itzá, in Yucatán, have demonstrated close cultural connections between the two sites. But there are reasons to believe that this leader was not the same Ce Acatl referred to previously. The title Quetzalcoatl or Kukulcán seems to have been applied to different men at different times.

Toltec invaders also reached the highlands of

Guatemala. They conquered the local populations belonging to the highland branch of the Maya and established dynasties which lasted until the Spanish conquest.

It would seem that during the Toltec period the valleys of Puebla and Tlaxcala, and parts of the valleys of Mexico and Morelos, were under the domination of the Olmec-Xicalanca people, mentioned above as conquerors of Cholollan about the end of the 8th century. It is believed that they were people of Chocho-Popoloca and Mixtec origin, related to or identical with the Nonoalca, one of the ethnic components of the Toltecs. In Oaxaca, Mitla, a site famous for the beautiful stone relief mosaic on the walls of the palaces, flourished during this period, after the decline of Monte Albán.

It was during the Toltec period that metallurgy became widespread in Meso-America. However, metal was used mostly for ornaments. For the epoch prior to 900 A.D., there is at present no evidence of metal in Meso-America besides that brought into the southern areas through trade with Panama, previously mentioned; however, metallurgical techniques could be older than this date in the archaeologically little-known area of western Mexico. In this area, copper (or bronze) metallurgy was well developed in later times, and cast copper bells, apparently from western Mexico, were traded as far north as southern Arizona at about 1000 A.D.

From About 1200 A.D. to the Spanish Conquest.

—In central Mexico, a troubled period followed the fall of Tollan. Previous plagues and wars had resulted in serious depopulation, and the outcome of political disintegration created a chaotic situation. At that time, different peoples —collectively designated by the Indian historical sources as Chichimecs—invaded the Valley of Mexico and the neighboring regions. Among them were the Aztecs. The term "Chichimec" requires clarification. It was used to designate peoples of very different cultural types and ethnic origins, including: (1) the northern food-gathering nomads; (2) farming peoples from the north, culturally simpler than the civilized peoples of central and southern Mexico; and (3) the descendants of civilized colonists established in the northwest in former times, returning to central Mexico after the fall of Tollan. Indian history emphasizes the importance of the role played by peoples of the first type during the period of the invasions, and by their descendants in the history of the following centuries. Some modern scholars overstress this point, and the author believes that critical analysis of the historical sources will prove that most of the invaders, and certainly those who were to provide the politically dominant element of later centuries, belonged to the second and third types. As a result of the movement of peoples, northern territories previously occupied by sedentary farmers were abandoned to nomadic food gatherers. The frontier of civilization thus receded somewhat in the direction of the south.

The 13th century is an obscure period during which the newcomers established new dynasties in the Valley of Mexico and conquered the dominions of the Olmec-Xicalanca people and their allies in the southern part of the valley and in Morelos, Puebla, and Tlaxcala. Cholollan (Cholula) fell to the Chichimecs about 1292 (the traditional date, 1168, has been corrected by more recent studies in pre-Hispanic chronology), and the Olmec-Xicalanca were expelled toward the northeast and southeast.

City-States in the Valley of Mexico.—Out of this confusion emerged, at the end of the 13th century and the beginning of the 14th, several city-states in mutual competition for hegemony. There was an Otomí kingdom, with its capital at Xaltocan in the north of the Valley of Mexico, whose territories extended beyond, as far north as Oxitipan on the border of the Huastec region —the Huastecs (or Huaxtecs) being an isolated Maya tribe living in northern Veracruz. It lasted until 1395, when the Tepanecs conquered Xaltocan.

The other major powers in the valley were, at first, Culhuacán—where the last vestige of Toltec tradition and legitimacy was kept alive—and a new Chichimec kingdom, founded by the invaders, whose capital was originally established at Tenayocan (in the Valley of Mexico northwest of Mexico City) and was later moved to Tetzcoco (or Texcoco). Culhuacán was decisively defeated in 1347, and an 80-year period of Tepanec supremacy followed, with Azcapotzalco as the capital and Coatlichan, Amaquemecan (now Amecameca), Huexotzinco (now Huejotzingo), and Cuauhnahuac (now Cuernavaca) as allies; Tetzcoco being relegated to a subordinated position. The Tepanecs had arrived in the Valley of Mexico from the neighboring Valley of Toluca. Ethnically they belonged to the group Otomí-Matlatzinca-Mazahua. The core of their dominions was the regions in the northwestern section of the Valley of Mexico and north and west of it, occupied by the Otomí and related peoples. At its peak, just before its fall, the Tepanec Empire expanded to the east and south, incorporating— through conquests and political alliances—territories occupied by Nahua peoples, and covered over 15,000 square miles of central Mexico—from Itzmiquilpan (now Ixmiquilpan) in the north to Tlachco (today's Taxco) in the south, and possibly to the Balsas River in the south, and from Tollocan (modern Toluca) and Ixtlahuacan in the west to Tollantzinco (modern Tulancingo, in Hidalgo) and Huexotzinco in the east. Besides the intensively cultivated and densely populated Valley of Mexico and other plateau territories, the Tepanecs thus dominated the semitropical lands of Morelos and northern Guerrero, which supplied the plateau with cotton, not cultivated in higher altitudes, native paper, jade, copper, and feathers.

To curb the danger of rebellion of the vassal lords, Tezozomoc, only king of Azcapotzalco during the period of Tepanec supremacy, imposed several of his sons as kings of different vassal city-states, murdering the kings of local dynasties when necessary. However, at Tezozomoc's death (1427), a rebellion broke out under the leadership of Itzcoatl, king of Tenochtitlan (see AZTECS) and Nezahualcoyotl, legitimate heir to the kingdom of Tetzcoco. This rebellion had the characteristics of a civil war in that public opinion within each city-state was divided. Bitter internal fighting and political murders were the result. The success of the rebellion was favored by dynastic troubles, because Tezozomoc's son and successor, Maxtla, not being the first born, was not the legitimate heir and was considered a usurper. The rebellion had the help of the Tlaxcalans who, as eastern neighbors of the Tepanec Empire, were probably fearful of its expansion. The war began with the storming of Azcapotzalco (1428) and ended in 1431 when the rebels took Coyoacán, Maxtla's own fief, and lib-

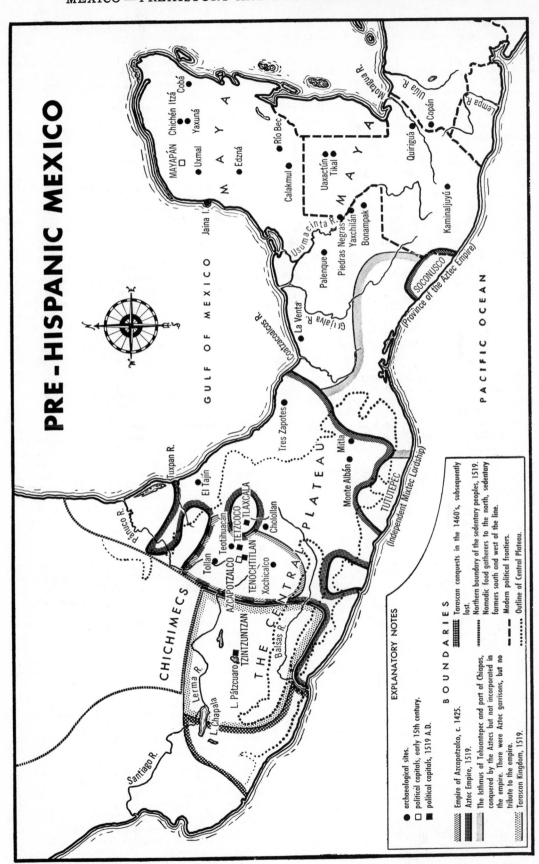

PRE-HISPANIC MEXICO

GULF OF MEXICO

PACIFIC OCEAN

MAYA

Cobá
Chichén Itzá
Yaxuná
MAYAPÁN
Uxmal
Edzná
Río Bec
Calakmul
Uaxactún
Tikal
Quiriguá
Copán
Kaminaljuyú
Jaina I.
Palenque
Piedras Negras
Yaxchilán
Bonampak
La Venta
SOCONUSCO
(Province of the Aztec Empire)

Usumacinta R.
Grijalva R.
Coatzacoalcos R.
Motagua R.
Ulúa R.
Lempa R.

Tres Zapotes
Mitla
Monte Albán
TUTUTEPEC
(Independent Mixtec Lordship)

Tuxpan R.
El Tajín
Teotihuacán
TETZCOCO
TLAXCALA
Cholollan
Tollan
AZCAPOTZALCO
TENOCHTITLAN
Xochicalco
THE CENTRAL PLATEAU

Pánuco R.
Balsas R.
Lerma R.
L. Pátzcuaro
TZINTZUNTZAN
L. Chapala
Santiago R.

CHICHIMECS

EXPLANATORY NOTES

- ● archaeological sites.
- □ political capitals, early 15th century.
- ■ political capitals, 1519 A.D.

Empire of Azcapotzalco, c. 1425.

Aztec Empire, 1519.

The Isthmus of Tehuantepec and part of Chiapas, conquered by the Aztecs but not incorporated in the empire. There were Aztec garrisons, but no tribute to the empire.

Tarascan Kingdom, 1519.

BOUNDARIES

Tarascan conquests in the 1460's, subsequently lost.

Northern boundary of the sedentary peoples, 1519. Nomadic food gatherers to the north, sedentary farmers south and west of the line.

Modern political frontiers.

Outline of Central Plateau.

erated Tetzcoco. As a result of the war, and to fill the political vacuum left by the destruction of the Tepanec Empire, a triple alliance was established, including the two victorious powers (Tenochtitlan and Tetzcoco) and Tlacopan, as a minor member representing the vanquished. Despite frictions between the three confederate powers this confederacy proved successful in maintaining the political stability of the valley until the coming of the Spaniards, and in uniting forces for external conquests.

Between 1431 and 1440, Nezahualcoyotl extended the power of Tetzcoco toward the northeast, to Tziuhcoac on the border of the Huastec area.

Aztec Expansion.—Itzcoatl, for his part, extended the conquests of the Aztecs toward the south, through Morelos and northern Guerrero to the Balsas River. From the rule of Montezuma I (Moteczuma Ilhuicamina; r. 1440–1468) on, the Aztecs of Tenochtitlan gained hegemony over the confederacy and subordinated the foreign policy of their allies to their own ends. Montezuma I extended his conquests up to the Gulf coast in central Veracruz. Axayacatl (r. 1469–1481) completed the encirclement of Tlaxcala and conquered the Matlatzinca territories of the Valley of Toluca in the 1470's, though he failed in his effort to invade Michoacán. Ahuitzotl (r. 1486–1502) was a great conqueror. He conquered a part of the Huastec area to the northeast. To the south, he reached the coast of Guerrero and established bases in Oaxaca which facilitated the conquests of his successor. He crossed the Isthmus of Tehuantepec, conquered the Soconusco (the Chiapas coast) and established garrisons in the Chiapas highlands up the modern Guatemalan border. Montezuma II (Moteczuma Xocoyotzin; r. 1502–1520) overcame the Mixtecs and Zapotecs of Oaxaca, with the exception of the powerful Mixtec lordship of Tututepec on the Pacific coast, which maintained its independence until the coming of the Spaniards.

Thus in less than nine decades the Aztecs and their allies built an empire which comprised about 75,000 square miles and between 5 and 6 million people. These conquests did not aim at the acquisition of land for colonization, but rather to incorporate the political and military resources of the conquered peoples into the empire, to open trade routes, to dominate markets, and to obtain tribute. The tribute books of the empire give us information about its extent, the organization of its provinces, and the heavy tribute which they had to pay. Two copies of these tribute books have been preserved. One, the *Matrícula de Tributos* in the Museo Nacional de México, was probably painted for Hernán Cortés; the other, *Codex Mendoza* in the Bodleian Library, Oxford, was painted for the first Spanish viceroy, Antonio de Mendoza.

Due to environmental and cultural factors, the Aztecs did not attempt to expand northward into Chichimec territory. Geographical conditions discouraged colonization, and it was impossible to extract tribute from the nomad hunters. Their conquests to the east and to the south were made in territory occupied by civilized groups, politically fragmented into rather small principalities. Whenever they encountered other centralized states, they met with failure.

Tlaxcalans.—For the reason just mentioned, the Tlaxcalans (or Tlaxcaltecs) to the east of the Valley of Mexico, with about 200,000 people

occupying a territory of about 1,600 square miles, were successful in rebuffing the Aztec attacks. This was true in spite of the fact that over a period of about 60 years, until 1519, the Tlaxcalans were completely surrounded by provinces of the Aztec Empire, and thus subjected to a severe economic blockade and constant military pressure. Systems of fortification encircled the territory of Tlaxcala on both sides of the frontier.

Tarascans.—To the west, after the conquest of the Valley of Toluca by the Aztec king Axayacatl in the 1470's, the only enemy left was the Tarascan kingdom of Michoacán. Axayacatl's attempt to invade Tarascan territory met with a crushing defeat at Taximaroa (now Ciudad Hidalgo, Michoacán). From then on, the two states were involved in constant warfare, and systems of forts and garrisons were maintained along the disputed frontier.

At the time of the Spanish conquest, the Tarascan kingdom comprised about 25,000 square miles and a population estimated at 1,000,000. The core of the kingdom was the region of Lake Pátzcuaro and the sierra to the west of the lake. The Tarascans showed strong social and political cohesion and the same expansionist tendencies as the Aztecs, although they were less urbanized than the inhabitants of the Valley of Mexico. The integration of the Tarascan state began about 1370, under the rule of Tariacuri, who conquered northwestern Michoacán and adjacent Jalisco, as well as the middle Balsas River basin to the south. When he died the kingdom divided into three parts. Pátzcuaro, Tzintzuntzan, and Coyuca (now Coyuca de Catalán, Guerrero) were the capitals of these splinter states. King Tzitzic Pandacuare reunited the three principalities, extended his conquests toward the southwest, and reached the Pacific coast in the 1460's. He was responsible for the defeat of Axayacatl's attempted invasion at Taximaroa. Subsequently, the Tarascans lost their dominions on the Pacific coast, but proved successful against the Aztecs. In the early 1500's they threw back another attempted invasion at Indaparapeo, and exerted aggressive pressure on the southern part of the Tarascan-Aztec frontier. On the northern frontier, Tarascan activities remained limited to forays against the Chichimecs in El Bajío (chiefly the modern states of Guanajuato and Querétaro) in order to protect their border, without attempting a permanent conquest of the region.

For the history of the Maya see the separate article MAYA.

Bibliography.—Spinden, Herbert J., *Ancient Civilizations of Mexico and Central America* (New York 1928); Thompson, John Eric, *Mexico Before Cortez* (New York 1933); Linné, Sigvald, *Archaeological Researches at Teotihuacan, Mexico* (New York 1934); Vaillant, George C., *Aztecs of Mexico* (Garden City, N. Y., 1941); Linné, Sigvald, *Mexican Highland Cultures*, tr. by M. Leijer (Stockholm 1942); Barlow, Robert H., *The Extent of the Empire of the Culhua Mexica* (Berkeley, Calif., 1949).

PEDRO ARMILLAS,
Instituto Nacional de Antropología e Historia, Mexico City.

25. SPANISH CONQUEST AND COLONY.

The Spanish conquest of Mexico at first represented a cultural clash but eventually there developed an amalgamation of cultures. On the one hand was the Spanish culture, with a strong medieval tinge; on the other, the Indian, in central Mexico dominated and made homogeneous by the Aztecs. The conquerors had varied backgrounds, but most of those coming to the new world were concerned with the dual purpose of propagating the Catholic faith and of raising themselves in the social scale. They were men of strong ambition.

The conquest started from Cuba. In 1517 the expedition of Francisco Hernández (or Fernández) de Córdoba reached Yucatán, where it was defeated in the bay called Mala Pelea (literally, bad fight), and explored the coast of Campeche. In 1518 a second expedition, under Juan de Grijalva, left Cuba and explored the coast as far north as San Juan de Ulúa, off the modern city of Veracruz.

The results obtained encouraged other adventurers who, headed by Hernán Cortés (1485–1547), took part in another expedition ordered by the Cuban governor, Diego Velázquez. Although chosen by the governor, Cortés had to balk several attempts by the former to replace him, and on Feb. 18, 1519, set sail without authorization. The stages of the voyage were: Cozumel Island, off Yucatán; the Grijalva River, Tabasco; the Isla de Sacrificios and San Juan de Ulúa; and a final landing near the site of modern Veracruz.

The Aztec emperor, Montezuma II (more correctly Moctezuma), frightened by omens and the legend of Quetzalcoatl, which prophesied a return of that god from the east, did everything short of violence to prevent Cortés from advancing inland. Cortés, however, noting the dissensions and fears within the country, proceeded to convert his expedition into an occupation.

The municipality of Veracruz was founded April 27, and communications with Velázquez were broken off. Cortés then arranged to have the municipal authorities of the new town select him captain general, and a ship was sent to Spain to secure the royal ratification. The other ships were burned and, on August 14, Cortés led his expedition inland toward the Aztec capital of Tenochtitlan, on an island in Lake Texcoco on the site of modern Mexico City, leaving a small garrison at Veracruz. During the advance, an alliance was made with the Tlaxcalans, perennial enemies of the Aztecs, who after testing the power of the Spaniards in two battles became their allies and gave a fundamental assistance to the conquest.

In October, Cortés reached Cholula, where, confronted with attempted treachery, he and his men killed many hundreds of the inhabitants. Montezuma's hopes of stopping the expedition were frustrated and he succumbed to fatalistic despair. The Spaniards reached Tenochtitlan on Nov. 8, 1519. Hoping through the emperor to control his subjects, Cortés seized Montezuma soon after, but it was clear that the Aztecs would not long submit.

When the city's population was at its most antagonistic to the Spaniards, Pánfilo de Narváez, sent by Governor Velázquez, arrived in Mexico to arrest Cortés. Leaving Pedro de Alvarado (1495?–1541) in command of Tenochtitlan, Cortés returned with a small force to Cempoala, where he surprised and captured Narváez and enlisted his men in his own force. In Tenochtitlan, meanwhile, in the mistaken belief that a gathering of Aztecs for a religious ceremonial was a prelude to an attack on the Spaniards, Alvarado had massacred a large number of Indians. Cortés returned to find the Spaniards besieged. Montezuma tried to pacify his people but was stoned and killed.

On the night of June 30–July 1, 1520, the Spaniards and Tlaxcalans, carrying away much of its wealth, fought their way out of the city over the causeways which connected it to Tlacopan on the mainland, with the loss of many men. Those taken prisoner were sacrificed. Cortés wept over his losses on what is remembered as la noche triste (the dismal night), and the Spaniards retreated to Tlaxcala.

Montezuma's brother, Cuitlahuac, defender of Tenochtitlan, became emperor. He renewed his alliances with the Indian lords, but the populace was weakened by epidemics, in one of which Cuitlahuac died. He was succeeded by the last of the emperors, Cuauhtemoc.

Cortés made several expeditions to prepare the taking of Tenochtitlan; the first from Segura de la Frontera (now Tepeaca, Puebla), the second from Texcoco, the last from south of Tenochtitlan. Having done this preparatory work, the next year, with forces enlarged by groups recently arrived from Cuba, he again attacked the Aztec capital. The siege began on May 26, 1521, lasting until August 13, and destroying the city. Cuauhtemoc was captured, and later taken as a hostage by Cortés on his expedition to Honduras in the course of which he was executed (1525).

Once Tenochtitlan had been taken, Spanish expansion spread in several directions—to the north with the expedition (1522) of Cortés to the Pánuco River; to the west with the expedition (1522–1524) of Cristóbal de Olid into Colima and Jalisco; and to the northwest with the expedition (1535) of Cortés to Lower California. The areas of modern Guatemala and El Salvador were conquered by Pedro de Alvarado in 1524–1526. Olid led an expedition into Honduras (1524), where he came in conflict with Spaniards advancing from the south. Having overcome these, he renounced his allegiance to Cortés, but was defeated by Francisco de las Casas and killed. Cortés himself then undertook an arduous expedition to Honduras, 1524–1526. Numerous expeditions were made against the Maya in Yucatan, but they were not conquered until the campaigns of Francisco de Montejo the Younger in 1540–1546.

COLONY

The conquest did not end with the epic period; part of the Central Plateau and the northern part of the country remained to be settled. The dynamics of the movements which occupied these regions grew out of the characteristics of the colonizing groups. Because the traditions of inheritance within the Spanish family, based on primogeniture as well as custom, offered little hope for the younger sons, these tended to become adventurers. Land grants given by the crown covered a vast territory, sparsely populated. Those unable to obtain grants moved on still farther to unclaimed land.

Social and Economic Organization.—The Spanish colonizer tended to superimpose, both physically and socially, his community on the native ones. He subordinated the Indian population to his own juridical and economic institutions, placing it at the bottom of the seigniorial organization, topped by himself. Since the colonizer had come to America in search of social betterment, which in 15th and 16th century Europe was based on the seigniorial system, labor was performed by the lower strata, with the upper classes supervising or performing military duties.

These upper classes also included the missionaries and governmental officers, generally from Spain.

When the territory had been conquered, it was organized in conformity with contracts made between the king and the conquerors. Booty obtained directly from war, such as Indian slaves, pearls, gold, and feathers, must be differentiated from the lasting privileges, such as the marquisates, *encomiendas,* and *repartimientos* granted by the king. Holders of such privileges had the double duty of exploiting the Indians and of giving them a tie with the colony. They were charged with assimilating the Indians into the new social and economic order, besides converting them to the faith.

Indian Labor and the Problem of Conscience. —Labor for agriculture, mining, industry, and construction in the colony was always supplied principally by the Indians, although Negro slaves and mestizos (persons of mixed Spanish and Indian blood) were also used. Much of the profuse labor legislation was designed to protect these laborers against abuse.

Indian enslavement was one of the important results of the conquest, and was considered its logical consequence; but while the Spaniards applied the Roman concept, under which a slave was equivalent to a "thing," slavery among the Indians consisted of various grades of liberty, only seldom (in the case of slaves sold in the markets) descending to the Roman concept. The abuses of the conquerors and these differences in concepts of slavery led to protests being sent to the king by ecclesiastical groups, government officials, and soldiers. The missionary and historian Fray Bartolomé de las Casas (1474–1566) should be remembered among the distinguished leaders in this struggle for Indian freedom.

The Spanish crown was exposed to pressures from conflicting sides. On the one hand it was sympathetic to the spiritual and religious viewpoint; on the other, it saw the material value of slavery as an economic factor. The crown hesitated until Nov. 20, 1542, when the Leyes Nuevas (New Laws) established freedom as a principle and forbade the acceptance of slaves sold by Indians. Even "just" wars were no longer to be considered legal sources of slaves and the slavery of women and children was forbidden. The institution endured as a punishment for those who resisted the colonial system. The Indian remained as a serf, tied by the obligations of paying tribute and providing personal service. The comparative liberty of the Indian, however, furthered the slavery of the Negroes, who were brought to New Spain by foreign traders to supply the need for labor.

Up to 1549, the principal device for utilizing Indian labor was the *encomienda.* This was a royal concession granting a Spaniard (usually one of the conquerors) part of the tribute in goods and labor that was due the king from a particular group of Indians, in return for which the *encomendero* was obligated to protect his Indians, supervise their education and religious indoctrination, and provide vocational training. Indians rendered personal services to the *encomendero* for no more than 20 days consecutively, with a month elapsing between each period of service. All women, and children under 12, were exempt from personal service.

First introduced into the Antilles, with disastrous consequences to the Indian population, the *encomienda* as organized by Cortés in New Spain was designed to avoid the worst abuses of the Antilles. In any case, some means of utilizing Indian labor was necessary if the colony were to be maintained, and for their part, the conquered Indians needed protectors who had a personal interest in their welfare.

Nevertheless, the extension of the *encomienda* system in New Spain was opposed by the crown both in the name of humanity and because, with its feudal implications, it challenged the growing concept of centralized absolute power. On June 20, 1523, Charles V issued the Cédula de Valladolid, designed to bring the *encomiendas* to an abrupt end, but enforcement was impossible in the face of furious colonial opposition and the order was nullified.

A similar attempt was made in the Leyes Nuevas of Nov. 20, 1542, which forbade the granting of new *encomiendas,* canceled those that were held without legal title and those held by viceroys, governors, royal officials, prelates, monasteries, and hospitals. *Encomiendas* were no longer to be passed on by inheritance; on the death of the *encomendero,* his *encomienda* was to revert to the crown. The intent was the complete abolition of the system in a generation, but again the royal commands were not enforced. With the *Cédulas de Malinas* of Oct. 20, 1545, Charles retreated from his position, but did insist on abolishing personal services to the *encomendero.*

After 1573, the privileges of an *encomendero* were reduced to the right to collect a tribute from his Indians. He was still obligated to protect and instruct them, but no longer had seigniorial power over them. The *encomiendas* that remained were extinguished during the 18th century.

As the *encomienda* system was whittled away, it was replaced by a forced *repartimiento.* Under this ancient Spanish method of recruiting labor, the Indians were forced to work at agriculture, mining, and construction, but their services were on a temporary basis, under contract, and the employer to whom they were consigned had to pay wages.

Government.—At first, the government was subordinate to the Audiencia of Santo Domingo. But this changed when Spanish dominion extended throughout the continent and the home government began to centralize. Cortés organized the colony on Oct. 30, 1520, naming it Nueva España (New Spain), and in 1522 was named governor and captain general. Its center was erected on the site of modern Mexico City and it included all of modern Mexico, somewhat later the captaincy general of Guatemala, and after the discovery of the western shores of the modern United States it extended northward as far as Alaska.

Royal treasury officials took over the government during Cortés' expedition to Hibueras (Honduras), which began on Oct. 12, 1524. During his absence a conflict broke out between his followers and more newly arrived officials. This subsided upon his return in 1526, but late in the next year he returned to Spain to defend himself before the king.

The first *audiencia,* a supreme court with executive functions, was sent from Spain and assumed the conduct of public affairs from December 1528 to the end of 1530, a period noted in the history of Mexico for its destructiveness. These first *oidores* (members of the *audiencia*) were its president, Beltrán Nuño de Guzmán, and Alonso Parada, Francisco Maldonado, Juan

Ortíz de Matienzo, and Diego Delgadillo. Parada and Maldonado died shortly after reaching Mexico. Guzmán, Matienzo, and Delgadillo remained, and made themselves wealthy by despoiling Cortés, his captains, and his soldiers, and by exploiting the Indians without restraint. They appropriated 100,000 Indians in *encomienda* and levied such heavy tributes on them that, besides storing up great wealth for themselves, the exploiters had enough grain and clothing left over to sell to the public.

Cortés returned to New Spain in 1530, no longer as governor, but only captain general and marquis of the Valley of Oaxaca, and the next year saw the arrival of the second *audiencia* to replace the first. More carefully selected than their predecessors, its *oidores* were Sebastián Ramírez de Fuenleal, bishop of Santo Domingo, Juan Salmerón, Francisco Ceynos, the celebrated Vasco de Quiroga, and Alonso Maldonado. All worked in cooperation with the first bishop of Mexico, Juan de Zumárraga (1468–1548), who had opposed the excesses of the first *audiencia*. Aside from their regular duties, they conducted trials of *residencia* to hear charges against the first *audiencia*, and took a census of Cortés' approximately 23,000 vassals, as well as making a general inquiry into the complicated activities of the conqueror of Mexico. The *oidores* were in the position of defenders of the crown's interests against the ambitions of Cortés, but on the whole they performed this duty without resorting to the violence that had marked the actions of their predecessors. In 1540, after a long conflict with the first viceroy, Cortés left New Spain, never to return.

Viceroyalty.—The first viceroy of New Spain, Antonio de Mendoza, was appointed in 1529 and held office from November 1535 to October 1550.

Although the viceroys seldom held office for more than six years, the frequent turnover was offset by the strictness of the system, which provided for a trial of *residencia* at the end of each viceroy's term. A new viceroy followed the *relación* (report) of his predecessor and heard the opinion of the *oidores*. He presided over the *audiencia*, and his functions were those of governor, superintendent of the royal treasury, and vice patron of the church.

The *audiencia* was an important juridical institution. Its decisions in relatively important cases were final; in cases of great importance an appeal could be made to the Council of the Indies in Spain. Its president, or all its members, substituted when the viceroy was absent, to maintain the administrative functions.

Lower levels of government were administered by provincial governors, and by *corregidores* and *alcaldes mayores*, officials with similar functions, who represented the royal authority in smaller districts. Special *corregidores* were appointed to govern the Indian towns. In addition there were the autonomous *municipios* (municipalities) governed by their own councils (*ayuntamientos*).

The personalities of the viceroys are important because they were the direct representatives of the king, in whose person was centered all government power, legislative, judicial, and administrative. Since the king was recognized as God's representative, the government's right to rule was considered both natural and divine.

Antonio de Mendoza made an auspicious beginning and set an impressive example for his successors. He worked closely with the second *audiencia*, and on the whole his government was marked by justice and order, establishing an important tradition of orderly administration in New Spain. Mendoza also waged several difficult Indian wars, notably the one called the Mixton War (1541) in Jalisco, and in 1540 sent a futile expedition under Francisco Vázquez Coronado in search of the legendary Seven Cities of Cíbola.

His successor, Luis de Velasco, in office October 1550–July 1564, was outstanding in promoting the spread of Spanish civilization northward, and his protection of Indian rights earned him the title "Father of the Indians."

Another noteworthy viceroy was Fray Payo Enríquez de Rivera, in office 1673–1680. Although his administration was routine and unexciting, it was just and progressive. Significant material gains were made and the viceroy was well loved.

Royal Control.—The viceroy was the king's personal representative in New Spain. Generally, the king governed his colonies through the Council of the Indies (Consejo de Indias), but at times he sent direct royal orders. Organized by Charles V in 1524 to advise him on matters concerning the Indies, the council came to exercise supreme legislative, executive, and judicial power over the colonies until the creation of the Universal Secretariat of the Indies in 1714 reduced it to the functions of a supreme court. While the Spanish Constitution of Cádiz was in force (1812–1814, 1820–1824), the council disappeared, but it was re-established for ten years, 1824 to 1834.

The Casa de Contratación (House of Trade) was another institution fundamental to the administration of the colony. Founded in 1503, little by little it assumed the management of all commerce in the Indies, as well as immigration, exploration, and legal problems involving merchants and shippers. Situated in Seville, the only port in Spain legally authorized to handle shipping to and from the Indies, the Casa had absolute control over all legitimate colonial commerce. The ports of entry in New Spain were Veracruz on the Gulf and Acapulco on the Pacific. The result of this monopoly was harmful to the Spanish Empire, since large-scale smuggling by both Spaniards and foreigners flourished, and a consequent contempt for law and authority was fostered. The Casa de Contratación was transferred to Cádiz in 1717.

The exploration activities of the Casa de Contratación were also of great importance. Its navigation school was directed by Amerigo Vespucci (1451–1512), who was assisted and succeeded by other world-renowned seamen. The merchant tribunals known as *consulados*, which were established in Spanish America and later throughout the world, developed out of the Casa de Contratación.

Mining.—This industry was fundamental to the prosperity of New Spain, as well as old Spain. It was the output of American mines that made Spain the first power of the Western World. All mines and subsoil rights belonged to the crown, but were rented to those who discovered them, the crown obtaining a fifth (the royal *quinto*) of the output. Failure to work the mine was grounds for expropriation.

Mineowners were a favored class, enjoying numerous political and social privileges. All the prime materials for mining were tax-free. Mercury, essential for the extraction of silver by the patio process, was allotted in proportion to ore production. To expedite their affairs, the mine-owners formed the Cuerpo de la Minería de la Nueva España on May 4, 1774. The organization conducted a court, a bank (Banco de Avío), and in 1792 established a college of mining (Real Seminario de Minería de México) to train technicians. A mining code, the Ordenanzas de Minería, was formulated May 22, 1783, while José de Gálvez was minister of the Indies, under the wise direction of Joaquín Velázquez de León.

Of the 500 mines in New Spain, the richest was La Valenciana in Guanajuato, which at its peak in 1800 produced some 3 million pounds troy of silver. Total production of the mines of New Spain from 1537 to 1821 was 2,151,581,961 pesos, with the peso during that period roughly equivalent to a dollar.

Church.—One of the major objectives of the Spanish crown in undertaking the conquest of the Americas was the conversion of the natives to Catholicism. In addition, the clergy, particularly the great religious orders, was the main source of education in the colonies, both secular and spiritual education being dependent on the development of religious institutions.

In order to coordinate ecclesiastical administration and relations between church and state, problems closely intertwined in colonial development, the Spanish rulers Ferdinand and Isabella obtained the right to control the relations between the papacy and the church in America. This important concession, known as the *patronato real* (royal patronage), was granted by the Vatican in several bulls between 1493 and 1508. Later, sweeping concessions allowed royal intervention in parish policies, church doctrine, administration of the sacrament, choral services in the cathedrals, rules of religious orders, church elections, and in general in all matters except those referring to faith and general discipline. In spite of this unusual distribution of authority, relations between church and state were usually amicable during the colonial period.

The first Catholic diocese was established at Tlaxcala in 1527, upon the arrival of its bishop, Julian Garcés, a Dominican. Subsequently, ten more were established. These dioceses, working through their parishes, which nearly always had a hospital and a school, were centers of education, public welfare, and social life. At the end of the 16th century, there were 474 parishes, and by 1810 there were 1,070.

The main task of the ordinary clergy was the establishment of the regular church in New Spain, while members of the various religious orders busied themselves with the conversion of the Indians. A good many of the methods used by religious missionaries originated in New Spain and were, little by little, adopted by the lay clergy.

Franciscans.—This order was the first to reach New Spain. Three Franciscan friars of Flemish origin arrived at Veracruz on Aug. 13, 1523: Juan de Tecto (Dekkers), Juan de Aora (Van Den Auwera), and the noted educator, Pedro de Gante (that is "of Ghent"). They quickly applied themselves to learning the Indian languages, and another famous group, known as "the Twelve," reached Veracruz on May 13, 1524, entrusted with a mission from Pope Adrian VI. They were Martín de Valencia, their leader; Martín de Jesús (or de la Coruña), who later led the missionaries who with Cortés attempted

to colonize Lower California in 1535–1536; Francisco de Soto, Francisco Jiménez, Juan de Ribas, Juan Suárez, Antonio de Ciudad Rodrigo, Toribio de Benavente (known as Motolinia), who was known for his charity and poverty, later a historian and one of the founders of Puebla; García de Cisneros, and Luis de Fuensalida, accompanied by two lay brothers, Andrés de Córdoba and Juan de Palos.

In New Spain the order was organized in five "provinces": Santo Evangelio in the capital (founded 1535), San José of Yucatán (1539), San Pedro y San Pablo of Michoacán (1565), Santiago of Jalisco (1606), and San Francisco of Zacatecas (1606). Until they became provinces, the *custodias* of Yucatán, Michoacán, Jalisco, and Zacatecas were subordinate to the Province of Santo Evangelio. Similarly dependent were the *custodias* of Peru, Nicaragua, Guatemala, and Florida. The Franciscans carried Christianity to almost all of the country and provided missionaries of high qualities. Besides contributing such noted men as Juan de Zumárraga, first bishop of Mexico, and the saintly Marcos Ramirez de Prado, bishop of Michoacán from 1640 to 1666, they wrote many of the basic works on history and the Indian languages.

Dominicans.—The first Dominicans to reach New Spain were twelve that arrived in company with a royal official, Luis Ponce de León, July 2, 1526. Five died the first year, and four returned to Spain. Gradually, they renewed and increased their forces and established four provinces: Santiago of Mexico (1532), San Vicente of Chiapas and Guatemala (1551), San Hipólito of Oaxaca (1595), and the Province of Puebla (1656). In a famous controversy over the nature of the Indians—were they rational human beings with souls to be saved, or a nonhuman species?—the Dominicans were furiously involved under the leadership of Bartolomé de las Casas in defense of Indian rationality. Although it converted Indians on a mass basis, the order later entertained doubts concerning the religious capacity of the Indian population.

Through the University of Mexico and the Inquisition, the Dominicans displayed their characteristic orthodoxy and mastery of doctrine. Prominent leaders of the order were Las Casas, Bishop Garcés, and Antonio Alcalde, who became bishop of Yucatán in 1767, and in 1771 bishop of Guadalajara, where he founded the university and charitable institutions.

Augustinians.—The first Augustinians landed at San Juan de Ulúa on May 22, 1533. Two provinces were established: El Santo Nombre de Jesús of Mexico (1587) and San Nicolás de Tolentino of Michoacán (1602). The special role of the Augustinians was the organization and direction of Indian communities. They did valuable missionary work and were distinguished as teachers in the University of Mexico.

Jesuits.—The Jesuit Province of Mexico was founded by 17 men who reached Mexico on Sept. 28, 1572. The province lasted 195 years, a brief life compared to those of the other orders. The important influence of the Jesuits was exerted through the colleges of San Pedro y San Pablo (1573) and San Gregorio Magno (1586) in the capital, and through a network of colleges and residences in the center of the country, which were dedicated to raising the cultural, moral, and religious level of the ruling class, both the Spanish-born *Peninsulares* and colonials of pure Spanish blood (*Criollos*). A group of missions in the northwest sought to save Indian souls while improving their material welfare. Intellectually, the Jesuits contributed to the knowledge of linguistics and other sciences. In 1767 they were expelled by Charles III from all Spanish territory and the order was suppressed by Pope Clement XIV in 1773.

Other Orders.—The Alcantarines (1580) erected the Custodia of San Diego de Alcalá, making it a province in 1599; the Carmelites established themselves in 1585; the Mercedarians, in 1589; and the Benedictines, in 1602.

The Mexican Order of St. Philip installed its first oratory in 1702. Besides these, there were other masculine orders as well as orders for women, such as the Conceptionists (1540), the Dominican nuns (1580), the Poor Clares (1570), and the Capuchin nuns (1704), the Brigittines (1743), and the Company of Mary (1754).

Education.—The clergy was the chief source of education in New Spain. It must be remembered that in the 16th century education was for the upper class. Therefore, in the towns the priests generally taught religion only—since it was felt that the Indian population had no need of other knowledge—but, at times, European trades were taught to Indians in the parishes. Vasco de Quiroga, who was bishop of Michoacán from 1538 to 1565, put into practice an important educational experiment when, inspired by Thomas More's *Utopia,* he organized Michoacán into units, the inhabitants of each unit being instructed in a different trade.

When monastic schools developed, they showed a tendency to turn into universities, but the University of Mexico itself was founded by royal decree in 1551 and opened its doors in 1553. The others that appeared were colleges, with university standing, organized according to medieval ideas.

A great many institutions appeared independently of the university in the 17th century, and were the vehicles for the absorption of the Enlightenment and rationalism, philosophic theories which later inspired the groups that prepared the independence of Mexico.

Press.—The introduction of the printing press in 1535 was a cultural factor of importance. The oldest book known to have been printed by Juan Pablos, owner of the second press brought to New Spain, describes itself as "Short and most complete Christian doctrine in the Mexican and Castilian language, which contains the things most necessary to our holy Catholic Faith, for the profit of the indigenous Indians and the salvation of their souls." This book was published in 1539.

Among the first printers of note (with the dates they were active) were Pedro Balli (1574–1608), Pedro Ocharte (1562–1592), Antonio Espinosa (1558–1576), Diego López Dávalos (1601–1611), and the Calderóns: Bernardo; his wife, Paula Benavides; his son, Antonio Calderón; his father-in-law, Juan de Ribera; and his granddaughter, María de la Rivera Calderón Benavides. Of all those of the viceregal period, the Calderón imprint survived longest (1631–1768). Printing houses were numerous in the 18th century.

In Puebla, the press was first used in 1640; in Oaxaca, in 1720; in Guadalajara, in 1793; and in Veracruz, in 1794. One of the Mexican printing presses, that of Father Juan José Eguiara (d. 1763), had Greek and Hebrew types. A total of some 12,000 works was published in the colonial era.

Newspapers, published as broadsides by the viceroyalty, appeared as early as the 16th century. The first *Gaceta de México* (founded 1667), of irregular publication, was followed by the *Mercurio de México.* The second *Gaceta de México* (1784–1809) was directed by Manuel Valadés. It was replaced in 1810 by the *Gaceta del Gobierno de México.*

Bourbon Era.—The entrance of the Bourbons into Spain (1700), in the person of Philip V, grandson of the French king Louis XIV, greatly changed Spanish thought. Centralism in the French style was emphasized, and rights of autonomy and liberties that might diminish the royal power were rejected. Difficulties with the Jesuits increased until finally, in 1767, they were expelled. The concept of wealth changed, new values being placed on the potentialities of production. Work was honored, science was applied, and social legislation was drafted.

Viceroys.—The first viceroy of the Bourbon kings, Fernando de Alencastre Noroña y Silva, duke of Linares and marquis of Valdefuentes, was in office from 1711 to 1716. First of the great viceroys of the new epoch, his work in collaboration with the tribunal of the *acordada,* which devoted itself to making the highways safe, ended an epidemic of highway robbery that had been a grave problem of the viceroyalty. In the capital he constructed the aqueduct of the Arcos de Belén. He also established cities in the north, and made an excellent study of ecclesiastical and state officials, a frank appraisal of faults, virtues, and procedures, which facilitated the work of later viceroys.

Juan de Acuña, marquis of Casa Fuerte (1722–1734), was called "the Great Governor." He ordered a survey of fortifications in the interior provinces of the north, which extended over four years. In the capital, he constructed the treasury and customhouse buildings.

Antonio María Bucareli y Ursúa (1771–1779) was conspicuous for his personal integrity and administrative ability. As an example of the former, he submitted his luggage to the customs inspection in Mexico City and courteously refused the gift traditionally offered by the city to new viceroys. As an administrator, he succeeded in balancing the budget. Impressed by the fall of Havana to the British in 1762, he organized the defense of New Spain, completing the fortress of San Carlos de Perote near Jalapa, building a fort at Acapulco, and reinforcing the defenses of San Juan de Ulúa at Veracruz. He reorganized the army and collected a gift of 1,299,000 pesos from private individuals to build warships. He established new charitable institutions, started primary schools, and accelerated the teaching of Spanish to the Indians.

Juan Vicente de Güemes Pacheco y Padilla, second Count of Revillagigedo (1789–1794), was an effective administrator who governed with intelligence and strength. He initiated the lighting and paving of the streets of Mexico City.

Transition.—The ideological change introduced by the Bourbons reached the colony in the middle of the 18th century, beginning with the arrival of such capable viceroys as Bucareli and Revillagigedo, who showed genuine concern for the welfare of the colony. In 1786, the French concept of colonial structure brought the subdivision of New Spain into 12 *intendencias,* headed by officers responsible only to the crown, which strengthened Spanish control over the colony in the face of foreign threats. Despite the abolition of *encomiendas* and *repartimientos,* and the *corregidores* of the Indian towns, many of whom had become miniature despots, social and administrative reforms reached the colony too late to satisfy it.

A spirit of restlessness already prevailed. Viceroy Miguel de la Grúa Talamanca y Branciforte, marquis of Branciforte, who had succeeded Revillagigedo, opposed without success the entrance of the ideology of the French Revolution, and, paradoxically, through exiles from his regime who went to the United States, he prepared the way for the introduction of that country's constitutional ideas into the colony.

Disintegration.—Definite political disintegration arrived in 1808, with the Napoleonic invasion of Spain. As a result of the imprisonment of Charles IV and his son, Ferdinand VII, which raised the problem of sovereignty, the Spaniards in rebellion against the French created municipal juntas (councils) dedicated to the restoration of Ferdinand to the throne. A similar movement took place in Mexico City, where the *ayuntamiento* decreed that in the absence of the king Viceroy José de Iturrigaray was to rule without superior orders.

Taking the opposite view, the members of the *audiencia* (all Spaniards) declared that they represented the will of the populace. Iturrigaray was replaced by Viceroy Pedro de Garibay, and the *audiencia* put itself forward as the representative of the people.

From this issue evolved the first independence movement. Beginning with opposition to French orders and a determination to hold the throne for Ferdinand, it reached a climax with the declaration of absolute independence by the priest Miguel Hidalgo in the town of Dolores, Guanajuato, Sept. 16, 1810.

Bibliography.—Díaz del Castillo, Bernal, *The Discovery and Conquest of Mexico, 1517–1521,* tr. by A. P. Maudslay (New York 1928); Cortés, Hernán, *Five Letters, 1519–1526,* tr. by Bayard Morris (New York 1929); Simpson, Lesley Byrd, *The Encomienda in New Spain* (Berkeley, Calif., 1929); Arciniegas, Germán, *Este pueblo de América* (Mexico City 1945); Simpson, Lesley Byrd, *Many Mexicos,* rev. ed. (New York 1946); Bravo Ugarte, José, *Historia de México* (Mexico City 1947); Tannenbaum, Frank, *Mexico; the Struggle for Peace and Bread* (New York 1950).

Carlos Bosch García,
Secretary, Comisión de Historia, Instituto Panamericano de Geografía e Historia.

26. MEXICO FROM 1810 TO 1910.

It was in an atmosphere propitious to rebellion that news of the Napoleonic invasion of Spain and the abdications of Charles IV and his son, Ferdinand VII, reached Mexico in 1808. Joseph Bonaparte sat on the Spanish throne, but the Spanish colonies in America refused to recognize him.

In Mexico, the *Criollos,* native-born persons of Spanish ancestry, asserted that sovereignty had devolved on the people, while the *Peninsulares,* persons born in Spain, who feared a movement for independence, supported the juntas (councils) which governed the parts of Spain not occupied by the French. The viceroy, José de Iturrigaray, who for reasons of personal ambition favored the *Criollos,* was seized by a group of wealthy *Peninsulares* on the night of Sept. 15-16, 1808, and replaced by a provisional viceroy, Pedro de

Garibay. Nevertheless, the lack of legitimate authorities and the ideological restlessness of the times continued to encourage a revolt.

Garibay was replaced by Archbishop Francisco Javier de Lizana later in the same year, and on Sept. 14, 1810, only two days before the movement for independence was launched by the *Grito de Dolores,* Francisco Javier Venegas, a viceroy sent by the regency formed by the juntas in Spain, took office in Mexico.

Declaration of Independence.—At Querétaro, a modest group of *Criollo* and mestizo intellectuals and military men was preparing a conspiracy. Among them, Miguel Hidalgo (1753–1811), parish priest of Dolores and father of Mexican independence, represented revolutionary thought; Ignacio Allende (1779–1811), captain of the Queen's Regiment, the military. Their attempts to convert others came to the attention of the government and orders were issued for their arrest. Warned in time, by a bold stroke at dawn on Sept. 16, 1810, in the town of Dolores (now Dolores Hidalgo, Guanajuato), Hidalgo proclaimed the independence in the so-called *Grito de* (Cry of) *Dolores.* With the title of general, and leading an improvised army of his Indian parishioners, which grew in size as it advanced, he began a campaign of liberation. The revolt quickly became an uprising of the oppressed masses, dreadful because of the passions it unleashed, and as a consequence the wealthy *Criollos* were driven to support the government. Hidalgo captured Celaya, next the rich city of Guanajuato, and then Valladolid (now Morelia), where he proclaimed the abolition of slavery. The cities of Zacatecas, San Luis Potosí, Guadalajara, and Saltillo were taken by other groups of insurgents.

Hidalgo then continued toward the capital. Nevertheless, after a victory of his ill-organized army, which then numbered about 80,000 men, over some 7,000 Spanish troops at Monte de las Cruces between the valleys of Toluca and Mexico, Oct. 30, 1810, he turned back to Valladolid and finally established his government at Guadalajara. His soldiers now began to leave him.

Felix Calleja, the cleverest and most illustrious of the royal officers, recaptured Guanajuato from Allende, and when the latter joined Hidalgo at Guadalajara, he decisively defeated the insurgent army at the bridge of Calderón on the banks of the Lerma River, Jan. 17, 1811. Hidalgo and Allende escaped toward the north, trying to reach the border of the United States, but were captured at Acatita de Baján, Coahuila, on March 21. Hidalgo was tried and shot at Chihuahua, July 30, 1811.

Morelos.—The first destructive impetus of the insurrection was followed by a desire to justify it. The priest José María Morelos (1765–1815), who continued the movement begun by Hidalgo, is known both for his political and his military activities. Morelos had raised an army of some 9,000 men in what is now the State of Guerrero. Among his able subordinates were Mariano Matamoros (1770?–1814) and Vicente Guerrero (1783–1831). As chief of the insurgent forces, Morelos carried the war into the modern states of Guerrero, Oaxaca, and Morelos, while other insurgents fought in the Central Plateau and other areas.

Calleja was occupied in putting down the insurrection in the north and Michoacán, but early in 1812 he turned south. Morelos resisted him at the memorable siege of Cuautla, in the modern State of Morelos, March 5-May 2, 1812; then fought his way out. When Calleja returned to the capital, Morelos reoccupied Cuautla and undertook a campaign in east central Mexico, taking Orizaba and other towns west of Veracruz. The meeting of a national congress at Chilpancingo in 1813, which issued a declaration of independence and published the Constitution of Apatzingán, Oct. 22, 1814, was made possible by his zeal and decision.

In February 1813, however, Venegas returned to Spain, and Calleja replaced him as viceroy. The exhaustion of the country now turned more and more people in favor of the government. Morelos was defeated in attempting to capture Valladolid, mainly through the efforts of a royalist officer, Agustín de Iturbide, and again defeated at Puruarán, where Matamoros was captured and later shot. Oaxaca, Cuautla, and Chilpancingo fell to the royalists, and Morelos, heart of the rebellion, was himself captured following a defeat at Tezmalaca, Guerrero, while conducting the national congress to Tehuacán. He was tried and shot at San Cristóbal Ecatepec, near the capital, on Dec. 22, 1815.

With the death of Morelos, the few remaining rebellious groups, led by Guerrero, were restricted to the mountains of the south and Guanajuato.

In 1816 Calleja was replaced as viceroy by Juan de Apodaca, who granted pardons from the Spanish crown to all who would submit, and the new viceroy almost managed to pacify the country. In 1817, only the Spaniard Francisco Javier Mina (1789–1817), a true example of the militant liberal, who had come from Spain to fight for the insurgents in Guanajuato, menaced the peace of the viceroyalty, from April until October, when he too was captured and shot.

Iturbide.—In 1820, at Cádiz, Spain, Gen. Rafael del Riego rebelled against the absolutist regime of Ferdinand VII, and the king was forced to swear to abide by the liberal Constitution of 1812 in order to retain his throne. This political change in the mother country had important repercussions in Mexico. The *Peninsulares* feared the liberal reforms, while the Mexican insurgents saw the possibility of finally reaching an agreement with Spain.

Agustín de Iturbide, former royalist commander in the Bajío region, who in 1820 was appointed to end Vicente Guerrero's rebellion in the south, saw an opportunity of conciliating the dissimilar interests of Mexico's political parties, now tired of the armed struggle. He succeeded in gaining the confidence of Guerrero, the support of the clergy—who feared that the Spanish liberal government would disentail the church properties held in mortmain—and acceptance by the *Criollos*. Iturbide adopted the Plan of Iguala, Feb. 24, 1821, which was agreed to by Guerrero. This was a program of reforms or political changes, also called the Three Guaranties: the independence of Mexico; the union of *Peninsulares* and Americans; and one religion, Catholicism. By the summer of 1821 nearly all Mexico had rallied to the plan.

On July 30, a liberal viceroy, Juan O'Donojú, arrived at Veracruz to succeed Apodaca. Iturbide was fortunate in being able to place his army between the new viceroy and the capital, and obtained his acquiescence to the Plan of Iguala in the Convention of Córdoba, Aug. 24, 1821. Thus after an active military and propaganda campaign, Iturbide's triumphant army entered the capital of the new country on Sept. 27, 1821.

The Captaincy General of Guatemala, comprising Chiapas and the five modern nations between Mexico and Panama, had also declared its independence in 1821 and in the next year was incorporated in Iturbide's empire. Many difficulties were found in annexation, however, and following Iturbide's abdication all but Chiapas separated from Mexico in 1823.

Struggle for Shaping the State.—During the next 36 years the Mexicans were resolutely to seek institutions to change the former colonial political body. Carried away by the promises of political liberalism and the ideals of freedom and equality, in a struggle against reality, they were to experience many disappointments before arriving at the Constitution of 1857.

Which form of government was to inaugurate Mexico's life as an independent nation? Iturbide, backed by the royalists and clergy, favored a constitutional monarchy, since it was believed that the political habits of the country were more in accordance with a monarchy than a republic. The people welcomed the consummation of independence with great enthusiasm, but soon realized that their difficulties were not over and that the situation of their country was difficult and full of danger. The heavy loss in lives and property occasioned by the separation from Spain was forgotten for the moment, but soon poverty, disorder, and unrest again brought the governing groups into conflict.

Spain refused to recognize the Convention of Córdoba, and free trade, the substitute for Spanish commercial policies so anxiously awaited, and in which so much hope had been placed, could not be regularized. An exhausted exchequer and an undisciplined, hungry populace complicated the administrative task.

In hope of bringing order to the nation, the army proclaimed Iturbide emperor on May 18, 1822. Congress was dissolved, and the farce of setting up an imperial court increased the national expenses. Almost immediately, those favoring a popular representative government rose in rebellion; in December, Gen. Antonio López de Santa Anna proclaimed the republic in Veracruz and was joined by many of Mexico's former leaders in the war against Spain, including Guerrero. Iturbide could not curb the new revolution. He abdicated, March 19, 1823, and left for exile. A congressional decree outlawed him if he should return to the country, and when, hoping to regain his prestige and ascendency, he landed at Soto La Marina the next year, this decree was used to condemn him. He was shot at Padilla on July 19, 1824.

Once the monarchy had been discarded, the struggle continued over the question of whether Mexico was to be a federal or a centralized republic. It was believed that federation was a magic formula to bring happiness to the people, but few serious attempts at decentralization were actually carried out. The federal Constitution of Jan. 31, 1824 was the result of temporizations by the liberals, the army, and the clergy. It was in force until 1836, after which there followed in quick succession various experiments in centralized and federal forms of government (see also the section *Government*).

The political parties defined their views under the names of Liberals, who were generally federalists and in favor of reducing the power of the church; and Conservatives, who were generally centralists, sometimes royalists, and were supported by the great landowners. Freemasons were active politically, those of the Scottish rite enlisting in the Conservative Party; those of the York rite, in the Liberal. Neither party, however, was able to unify the country's opinion and support behind it. In this situation appeared the military *caudillos*, who supported this or that regime according to their preferences.

The first president was a veteran of the struggle for independence, Guadalupe Victoria, who was in office from 1824 to 1829, when following a revolt, Vicente Guerrero was installed. Within a few months Guerrero was overthrown by his vice president, Anastasio Bustamante (1829), and in 1832 the latter was put out of office by Santa Anna, the most prominent of the *caudillos*, who in 1829 at Tampico had received the surrender of King Ferdinand's last attempt to reconquer Mexico.

Santa Anna left the powers of his office to his vice president, Valentín Gómez Farías, under whom took place the so-called Reform of 1833, which separated church and state and provided for secular education. The next year, however, Santa Anna assumed power on behalf of the Conservatives, and the reform was largely nullified. A new constitution (the so-called Seven Constitutional Laws), centralizing the government, was promulgated on Dec. 29, 1836. This, and the activities of settlers from the United States in Texas led to the secession of that province in the same year. Santa Anna was unable to put down the rebellion and retired to his estate in Veracruz.

After a short interim, Bustamante again became president (1837–1841). In 1838 a French fleet attacked and occupied the port of Veracruz with the object of collecting indemnities claimed by its nationals. Santa Anna, who participated in the defense, regained some of his former popularity and was able to make himself president again in 1841–1842. On June 12, 1843 a highly centralized constitution (the so-called Bases Orgánicas) was adopted, and Santa Anna was president under it in 1844. He was overthrown and was succeeded by José Joaquín Herrera (1844–1845). The latter was replaced in 1846 by Mariano Paredes, under whom war began with the United States.

During this chaotic period agriculture was neglected, mining could not be made to prosper, and the incipient industrialization could not be protected. The greater part of the governmental receipts went to the army, which had to be paid to prevent insurrections. The treasury was bolstered by internal and foreign loans which tied up the customs revenues, and the urgent financial needs of succeeding governments made dishonest transactions very easy. This difficult situation was exploited by a group of foreign traders and speculators. Some measure of Mexico's difficulties may be seen in the fact that the country had some 30 changes of chief executives between 1824 and 1848.

The war with the United States in 1846–1848, a conflict which had been maturing since the early years of the century, caught the country in complete prostration. The military campaign showed the Mexicans how disorganized and weak they were. By the Treaty of Guadalupe Hidalgo, Feb. 2, 1848, Mexico was forced to cede half her territory to the United States. (See also

Mexican War; and the section *Relations with the United States*.)

Decisive Decade (1857–1867).—The federalist Constitution of 1824 had been restored following the fall of Paredes in 1846, in an effort to unify the people during the war. After Santa Anna, who had returned to fight, had left the country in 1848, José Joaquín Herrera again became president (1848–1851) and was succeeded, peacefully for the first time in Mexico's history, by Mariano Arista (1851–1853). The latter, however, was driven from office by the Conservatives, who then restored Santa Anna as dictator. But the political problem was now reaching a climax.

In 1855 Santa Anna was overthrown for the last time by a group under the leadership of Juan Álvarez, once a lieutenant of Morelos, and Ignacio Comonfort, with the Plan of Ayutla, March 10, 1854, which called for a federal constitution. The accumulated demands for an end to privilege and oligarchical groups mark the succeeding period as one of social revolution.

While Álvarez was acting president, August to December 1855, his minister of justice, Benito Juárez, abolished the privileges of the army and clergy by means of the Ley (Law) Juárez. Álvarez was then succeeded by Comonfort, whose secretary of the treasury, Miguel Lerdo de Tejada, set forth the Ley Lerdo of 1856, disentailing properties in order to put the holdings of religious communities into circulation. These laws were to be the basis for the economic and political regeneration of the country.

Meanwhile a constituent congress had drafted a new constitution, which was promulgated on Feb. 5, 1857. The principles it proclaimed were considered too bold and too advanced by some, and it was also prejudicial to an important social group, encountering the open opposition of the Conservatives. President Comonfort himself soon turned against the constitution and a Conservative coup was executed in the capital by Gen. Félix Zuloaga. Comonfort's defection began the so-called War of the Reform (1858–1861).

The duty of defending the Liberal institutions fell upon Benito Juárez (1806–1872), as president of the Supreme Court of Justice. His government was pursued by the Conservatives, led by Zuloaga and Gen. Miguel Miramón, until it was established at Veracruz, where Juárez promulgated the Leyes de Reforma (Reform Laws), 1859–1860, as an extreme means of achieving the economic and social policy of the Liberals. These laws included the nationalization of property owned by the church, the establishment of civil marriage, the secularization of cemeteries, the abolition of monastic orders, the separation of church and state, and the establishment of freedom of worship. While Veracruz proved impregnable against Miramón, Santos Degollado and Jesús González Ortega led the Liberal Army to success. After the latter's victory over Miramón in the Battle of Calpulálpam, Dec. 22, 1860, the Liberal troops again occupied the capital, and Juárez was elected president in March 1861.

After this three-year war, the task of reorganizing the country was difficult. Some Conservative groups were still fighting in various regions, and traffic through the country was insecure due to gangs of highway bandits. The expenses of the war and the destruction of national wealth had exhausted the treasury, and

Juárez found it necessary to suspend payment on the public debt (Decree of July 17, 1861).

Encouraged by Mexican Conservatives, France and Spain joined England in a triple alliance (Treaty of London, Oct. 31, 1861) under the pretext of demanding payment of the debt. Napoleon III, however, planned to intervene directly in Mexico, since he could then aid the Confederacy in the Civil War being fought in the United States, and could, furthermore, establish a European prince on the throne of Mexico. When the foreign troops arrived at Veracruz (December 1861 to January 1862), Juárez sent delegates to discuss their differences within the limits of honor. The Spanish and English representatives, Juan Prim and Sir Charles Wyke, recognized Mexico's rights and re-embarked their troops. Only the French failed to come to an agreement and revealed their true intentions by invading the country. The clerical and Conservative group joined them. The French marched toward the capital, but were defeated at Puebla, May 5, 1862, in a famous battle which greatly surprised the foreign countries and covered Mexican arms with glory. As Napoleon III was now compelled to send re-enforcements to conquer the country, his help to the Confederacy was delayed, thus benefiting the Union cause. The re-enforced French soldiers under generals Élie Frédéric Forey and Achille Bazaine defeated the Mexicans, and entered the capital in June 1863. Juárez' government was pursued northward, through San Luis Potosí, Saltillo, and Monterrey, finally reaching Paso del Norte (now Ciudad Juárez).

The so-called Junta de Notables (Assembly of Notables) made up of rich Mexican Conservatives, in agreement with Napoleon III, then offered Archduke Maximilian of Austria a throne in Mexico, assuring him that all Mexicans wanted him for their monarch. This prince renounced his rights in Europe and made burdensome concessions to Napoleon in exchange for his support. He and his wife Carlota still believed that they had been summoned by all Mexico, but were disillusioned by their cold reception in June 1864.

At first, Maximilian had the support of the Conservatives, but as he wished to follow a policy of adjustment and moderation and did not revoke the Reform Laws, he lost their backing and that of the clergy. Nor could the country's rebelliousness be brought to an end; where least expected, groups of patriots would appear.

The enterprise thus became long and expensive for the French. All their hopes for gaining important commercial advantages failed. Following the Union victory in the United States (1865), the Monroe Doctrine was invoked, and Napoleon III abandoned his Mexican adventure in 1866. To keep their throne, Maximilian and Carlota appealed to the courts of Europe, and even tried to come to an agreement with Juárez. The latter obtained the help of the United States and little by little his generals defeated the imperial forces. Maximilian surrendered at Querétaro, May 14, 1867, and on June 19 was shot, to the amazement of Europe.

Republic Restored.—On July 15, 1867, Benito Juárez announced to the nation that the enemy had been defeated, and declared that "among individuals as among nations the respect for the rights of others is peace." Again Juárez was faced with a postwar problem, which meant the liquidation of rebel groups, the enactment of the Constitution of 1857 and the Reform Laws, and the start of a "progressive revolution" that would inaugurate a new era in Mexico.

In the elections of 1867, Juárez defeated one of his generals, Porfirio Díaz (1830–1915), and in those of 1871 he again triumphed over Díaz and Sebastián Lerdo de Tejada (1825–1889). Díaz, dissatisfied with the returns of the election, rebelled with the Plan of La Noria (1871), condemning the re-election of the president. Juárez' prestige proved greater than the armed revolt, but a short time later Juárez died (July 18, 1872). He was succeeded by Sebastián Lerdo de Tejada, president of the Supreme Court of Justice, a man of great talent and a distinguished Liberal, who had followed Juárez during the French intervention. At first, Lerdo's government was very popular. He incorporated the Reform Laws in the constitution and halted railroad construction for fear of United States imperialism. But his intellectual rectitude prevented him from following a policy of conciliation and his somewhat haughty manner made enemies of his former sympathizers. When he announced that he would seek re-election, Díaz revolted, with the Plan of Tuxtepec (1876), again condemning the re-election of the president. After the Battle of Tecoac, in which Gen. Manuel González destroyed Lerdo's forces, Díaz triumphantly entered the capital on Dec. 23, 1876.

Porfirian Era.—Porfirio Díaz promised order and peace. He was a good administrator, a famous officer, and a lover of progress. Upon being elected to the presidency, he inaugurated a long regime that was to change the aspect of the country. Following his first presidential term he entrusted the post to Gen. Manuel González (1880–1884); afterward, he had the constitution reformed so as to re-elect himself indefinitely. In 1904 the office of vice president was created, for which Díaz chose Ramón Corral.

The dictatorship of Díaz welcomed foreign investment, encouraged railroad construction, and entered into commercial treaties; in general, under the direction of Finance Minister José Limantour, it ended the colonial economic regime. It expedited laws for colonization and land surveys, but without effectively benefiting immigration or the protection of agriculture. In mining, the principles of concession and the denunciation of unworked properties were kept. Petroleum, however, was now granted as the property of the owner of the land, a principle which was to have far-reaching consequences in post-Porfirian Mexico. Industry prospered, principally with English capital, and material improvements, such as the construction of harbors, canals, and buildings, were of great importance.

Education was carried forward in secular institutions through application of the Law of Public Instruction of 1867, which was based on the doctrines of French positivism. Toward the end of the Díaz regime ambitious cultural works were undertaken, existing facilities, such as the National Library and the National Museum, were improved, and numerous writers and poets contributed to the Europeanization of Porfirian culture.

The material progress of the country was evident, but the dictatorship nullified political progress, and the creation of a new wealthy class postponed the solution of the social problem. The work of progress did not reach the immense Indian population, living in poverty and debt peonage in the fields. Great numbers of the communal lands (*ejidos*) owned by Indian villages had been alienated, and the ownership of land had been concentrated in fewer and fewer hands.

General Díaz and his ministers grew old in power, opposition increased, and the disorder that the dictator's death might bring was feared. A vice president more popular than Corral was wanted. This was one of the themes of a notable book of the time, *La sucesión presidencial en 1910* (1908), written by a member of a wealthy family of Coahuila, Francisco Madero (1873–1913). Madero, representing the popular restlessness, ran for election in 1910, but Díaz reelected himself, again naming Ramón Corral as vice president. On Nov. 20, 1910, Madero revolted, inaugurating the overthrow of the regime.

Bibliography.—*México a través de los siglos*, vol. 4 (Mexico City and Barcelona, n.d.); Bancroft, Hubert H., *History of Mexico*, 6 vols. (San Francisco 1883–88); Priestley, Herbert I., *The Mexican Nation* (New York 1923); Gruening, Ernest, *Mexico and Its Heritage* (New York 1931); Teja Zabre, Alfonso, *Breve historia de México* (Mexico City 1934); Parkes, Henry B., *History of Mexico* (Boston 1938); Zavala, Silvio, "México contemporáneo," *Historia de América*, vol. 11 (Buenos Aires 1941); Simpson, Lesley B., *Many Mexicos*, rev. ed. (New York 1946); Sierra, Justo, *Evolución política del pueblo Mexicano* (Mexico City 1950).

María del Carmen Velázquez,
Professor of History, Universidad Nacional de México.

27. MODERN MEXICO.

Outbreak of the Revolution.—Francisco Madero pointed out his reasons for beginning the armed movement against the Díaz regime in his Plan of San Luis Potosí (dated Oct. 5, 1910): an intolerable tyranny in exchange for a shameful peace imposed by force, which had favored only a few; a complete contempt of the country's constitution; a mercenary justice; a congress at the dictator's orders; everything arranged so that Díaz could maintain himself in power. This political retrogression had produced a deep ill feeling in the country, intensified in 1910 with the naming of Ramón Corral to the vice presidency. On the social side, there was the problem of the land and the peons.

Madero's party adopted the slogan, "Sufragio Efectivo, No Reelección" (Effective Suffrage, No Re-election). Their leader declared that he had entered the political struggle honestly and would have been elected president but for electoral frauds. In so doing he put himself at the head of all the Mexicans who wanted to protest with guns in their hands against the illegality of the elections and the violation of the national will.

The revolution thus began spread rapidly. In Santa Clara, Puebla, Aquiles Serdán proclaimed the revolt in November 1910, but was killed almost immediately. At about the same time Pascual Orozco proclaimed it in Ciudad Guerrero, Chihuahua. The revolt in the north was joined by Francisco Villa. In March 1911 Emiliano Zapata rose in rebellion in Morelos, demanding land and better living conditions for the peons.

The Federal Army, commanded by Díaz' generals, could not contain the uprisings. On May 21, 1911 an armistice was signed between the Federal forces and the revolutionaries. Díaz sent a delegate to sign an agreement with the rebels, then renounced the presidency, May 25.

The secretary of foreign affairs, Francisco León de la Barra, was named provisional president. In special elections, in October 1911, Francisco Madero was elected president and was sworn into office on November 6.

Madero had been elected with the strictest legality—but there were other questions besides that of democratic suffrage. The new president came to terms with the moneyed classes and other influential groups of the Porfirian regime, and thus the social, economic, and religious questions were left unsolved, and the revolutionary groups remained in arms.

The Zapata revolutionaries in Morelos, dissatisfied because Madero had not carried further the revolution begun with such success, protested energetically in the Plan of Ayala of Nov. 25, 1911. Their slogan was "Tierra y Libertad" (Land and Liberty), and it proposed the complete destruction of the Porfirian system and an agrarian reform. Pascual Orozco rebelled against Madero in March 1912, but was driven out of Mexico by Gen. Victoriano Huerta. Bernardo Reyes attempted to revolt in Nuevo León, and Félix Díaz, a nephew of the former dictator, rose in Veracruz, but these also were put down.

The delicate international situation was another of Madero's problems. The United States remained vigilant, watching events, especially along the border, but its ambassador, Henry Lane Wilson, favored active military intervention against Madero's government. In April 1912, Wilson entered a claim for damages for injury to lives and properties of American citizens resulting from the revolutionary fighting, and he did everything in his power to cause the intervention of his country in the internal affairs of Mexico.

On Feb. 9, 1913, Félix Díaz and General Reyes, who had been imprisoned in the capital, were freed by troops who had rebelled against Madero. Reyes was killed, but Díaz and the rebels took refuge in the Ciudadela (Citadel). There followed ten days of uncertainty, intrigue, and fighting in the city, known as the "Tragic Ten Days." Madero's commander, Huerta, taking advantage of the bloody fighting, arrested the president and Vice President José María Pino Suárez on February 18, obtained their resignations, and on February 22 had them shot while they were being transported from the National Palace to the penitentiary. The usurper Victoriano Huerta, supported by Ambassador Wilson and the reactionary Porfirian group, then took over the presidency. His government was recognized by Great Britain and several other countries, but not by the United States.

Carranza.—Huerta's treason angered the governor of Coahuila, Venustiano Carranza, who was to be the organizer of the revolution, as well as Zapata, Villa, and other revolutionaries. Supported by numerous military leaders, Carranza launched the Plan of Guadalupe of March 26, 1913, disowning the government of Huerta. The latter lost Wilson's backing when the ambassador resigned his post following the election of President Wilson in the United States.

On April 9, 1914, some United States sailors landed in Tampico in search of provisions. They were arrested by Mexican soldiers and later released upon proving their nationality. This incident provoked an exchange of notes between Mexico and the United States. Huerta adopted a provocative attitude, the result of which was that the new government of the United States broke off relations with his government and in February lifted the arms embargo to authorize the sending of munitions to the usurper's enemies. Later, it ordered United States marines to land in Veracruz (April 21, 1914). This intervention and invasion caused an energetic patriotic reaction in Mexico.

Meanwhile other revolutionary groups had joined Carranza, declaring him chief of the Constitutionalist Army. In March 1914 they attacked the city of Torreón, and their capture of Zacatecas in June was the decisive blow against Huerta's forces. From there, Gen. Alvaro Obregón of the Constitutionalist Army advanced to Teoloyucan, near Mexico City, where the rest of the Federal Army surrendered. Huerta abandoned the capital on July 15, 1914, and went into exile. When Carranza entered Mexico City in August, he had to face the difficulties with the United States. Since these had concerned the usurping government, he demanded that the United States forces leave Veracruz, and the port was evacuated in November 1914.

Villa, who enjoyed great popularity in the north, and Zapata, who was fighting for his ideals in the south, had been unwilling to recognize Carranza's leadership, since it seemed to them that he was interested only in the political part of the revolution, rather than its social and economic causes. The partisans of Villa and Carranza thereupon decided to call a convention to agree on a plan of future reforms. The convention met briefly in Mexico City, and later at Aguascalientes, a neutral city, in October 1914, but Villa, distrustful of Carranza, then disowned his authority and marched on Mexico City.

Carranza was obliged to leave the capital for Veracruz; nevertheless, this port city was a more favorable location, since it was beyond reach of his enemies, and the customs duties provided funds. In Veracruz, Carranza began to organize the revolutionary government, and initiated the agrarian reform with the law of Jan. 6, 1915. Meanwhile, his generals were fighting the partisans of Villa and Zapata. These groups attempted to establish a national government in the capital, and discussed social and agrarian reform at sessions of the Supreme Revolutionary Convention. They were driven from Mexico City in January 1915, however, and Alvaro Obregón decisively defeated Villa in the Battle of Celaya in March, forcing him to retreat to the north. The Supreme Revolutionary Convention, subjected to the hazards of war, finally took refuge in Morelos, where it was dissolved when Carranza's troops marched in. Zapata continued his resistance until he was killed in 1919.

The United States recognized the government of Carranza in October 1915. Frustrated in his ambitions, and unable to obtain arms from the United States on account of this recognition, Villa had a group of United States citizens shot in January 1916 and on March 9 attacked the town of Columbus, New Mexico. The United States then sent Gen. John Pershing on a punitive expedition. Carranza ordered the defense of Mexican territory, thus creating a very difficult situation. Nor would he enter into any agreement as long as United States troops remained in Mexico. When, in February 1917, the troops finally left the country, the two governments had not reached an agreement, and Pershing's troops had not been able to capture Villa.

In order to restore constitutional methods in Mexico, Carranza called elections, in September 1916, for a constituent congress, thus fulfilling promises made in the Plan of Guadalupe and providing for the incorporation of revolutionary legislation in the Constitution of 1857. This congress met in the city of Querétaro from Dec. 1, 1916 to Jan. 31, 1917, and formulated a new constitution, which was promulgated on Feb. 5, 1917. Once the triumph of the Constitutionalist forces had been consolidated, Carranza called special elections for president, representatives (*diputados*), and senators; being himself elected president of the republic.

The Constitution of 1917 established a representative, democratic, federal republic. Some of its articles represent very advanced social tendencies, as well as the outlines for a national utilization of the national wealth. Articles 5, 27, 123, and 130 are especially important because of the reforms they envisaged and because of their consequences in national and international politics.

Article 5 established the principle that no one may be forced to render personal services without just compensation and without his full consent. Article 130 undertakes the difficult problem of relations between the state and the church, and grants the federal authorities the right to oversee religious worship and the relations between the church and the people. Article 27 is the basis of the agrarian reform and of regulations for the exploitation of the subsoil. Article 123 refers to labor and social planning, and establishes the basis for labor contracts. (Details of Articles 27 and 123 are given in the section *Economic, Agricultural, Industrial, and Financial Factors—Modern Economic Policy*).

The history of Mexico after 1917 may be viewed as an effort to carry out the principles and lines of policy laid down by this constitution. The effort has not always been constant and sustained. Often violated by personal ambition, foreign pressure, or the avarice of various social groups, it has nevertheless triumphed over other social and political policies which have been proposed for the country.

One of Carranza's measures was his decree of Feb. 19, 1918, declaring Mexican petroleum to be an inalienable national resource and beginning a long struggle to bring petroleum under Mexican control.

Post-Revolutionary Governments. — Carranza attempted to impose Ignacio Bonillas as his successor in the elections of 1920, but Alvaro Obregón, a leader of Carranza's partisans, used the old procedure of seizing power by armed force. He rose with the Plan of Agua Prieta (April 23, 1920) in defense of popular suffrage, and was joined by others of the military, notably generals Plutarco Elías Calles and Adolfo de la Huerta. Carranza, fleeing from the capital, was murdered at Tlaxcalantongo, Puebla, May 21, 1920. De la Huerta then became provisional president, and the remnants of other anti-Carranza forces abandoned the struggle. On July 27, 1920, Villa, who had maintained a futile opposition in the north, surrendered to the new government. The few followers of Zapata who had remained in arms in Morelos also came to terms.

Obregón was elected president on September 5, and took office on Dec. 1, 1920.

Obregón.—Prosperity increased under Obregón, and labor unions flourished, particularly the Confederación Regional de Obreros Mexicanos, which had been organized' in 1918. Obregón's administration also marks the beginning of modern Mexican education, in the hands of José Vasconcelos, secretary of public education from 1921 to 1924. Elementary education was increased, and literacy campaigns and school-building programs were undertaken. During 1923, Obregón antagonized the clergy when he expelled the apostolic delegate for transgressing the laws. Catholics openly objected to this measure, but the real conflict was delayed until the administration of Calles, to whom Obregón left the presidency at the end of his term in 1924, but not without having overcome a revolt by de la Huerta in 1923–1924.

Calles.—Under the new administration prosperity continued, and the labor movement attracted increasing numbers of workers. The fiscal system was put on a sound basis in 1925, when nonproductive taxes were abolished and government income was increased by the levy of an income tax. The Banco de México was also founded in that year. Due to programs of material improvement, dating from Calles' administration and thereafter, means of transportation and communication have brought towns and villages which had been isolated for centuries into contact with the rest of the country; and schools, public buildings, and hospitals have changed the colonial or Porfirian appearance of many cities.

In 1925–1926 the Congress passed laws enforcing the provisions of the Constitution of 1917 in regard to foreign-owned land and Mexican mineral resources. This led to a diplomatic conflict with the United States, which alleged that the laws were confiscatory. The dispute was settled in 1927, but the Mexican government did not retreat from its stand on any of the basic questions.

In February 1927 the church publicly repudiated the Constitution of 1917. Calles faced the ensuing conflict by putting the anticlerical measures of 1917 into effect. Ecclesiastical property was nationalized and foreign priests and the archbishop were expelled, together with other prelates. In October the so-called *Cristeros* rose in arms to fight for *Cristo Rey* (Christ the King). The revolt was centered in Jalisco and Guanajuato; there, and in other states there were bloody persecutions and reprisals.

At the end of Calles' term, the constitutional provision against re-election was set aside, and Obregón ran again. He was re-elected, but before taking office was assassinated, July 17, 1928, by the Catholic fanatic León Toral. A lawyer, Emilio Portes Gil, was elected by Congress as provisional president.

Portes Gil, Ortiz Rubio, and Rodríguez.—Relations between the government and the church became more conciliatory in 1929. In March of that year Calles founded the party successively called Partido Nacional Revolucionario, Partido de la Revolución Mexicana, and Partido Revolucionario Institucional, Mexico's dominant political party, to which all presidents after Portes Gil belonged. Its first nominee, Pascual Ortiz Rubio, defeated José Vasconcelos in special elections held in 1929.

After the new president had taken office,

Mexico entered the worst of the world depression. The economic situation and a conflict within his administration, in which he was opposed by Calles, led to the president's resignation on Sept. 3, 1932. Gen. Abelardo Rodríguez was elected by Congress to fill out the remainder of the term.

Cárdenas.—In 1934 Lázaro Cárdenas was elected to a six-year term, in accordance with a constitutional reform of April 29, 1933. Social legislation, agrarian reform, and economic development received a new impetus from Cárdenas, who represented the more liberal wing of the official party. The president came into conflict with Calles in 1935, and in the next year Calles was deported.

An important pillar of the Cárdenas regime was the Confederación de Trabajadores Mexicanos, a new labor organization founded in 1936 in opposition to the older Confederación Regional Obrera Mexicana and led by Vicente L. Toledano. The circle of the official party was widened in 1938 to include workers and peasants, in order to give them a share in the political and economic direction of the country.

In 1936, when Cárdenas decided to reform Article 3 of the constitution, dealing with education, the religious situation again became critical; but relations between church and state thereafter were improved, due less to changes in legislation than to a conciliatory attitude on the part of the government. (See also section *15. Church and State* in this article.)

A major objective of the Cárdenas administration was agrarian reform. To this end the distribution of lands, which had been somewhat in abeyance, was increased, and various institutions through which farmers could obtain credit were established.

In 1938 the government completed the long-standing effort to bring Mexican petroleum resources under national control by expropriating foreign-owned oil companies. (See also section *6. Economic, Industrial, Agricultural, and Financial Factors* in this article.) This important move aroused great popular enthusiasm in Mexico and led to a diplomatic controversy with Great Britain and the United States, which was finally settled after an agreement for indemnifying the owners had been reached in 1944.

Ávila Camacho.—In the elections of 1940, Gen. Manuel Ávila Camacho was victorious over Gen. Juan Andreu Almazán. The new administration was notable for an increasing rate of industrialization and the entrance into Mexico of large amounts of refugee capital from Europe during World War II. The government severed diplomatic relations with Japan on Dec. 8, 1941, a day after the attack on Pearl Harbor, and with Germany and Italy on December 11. War against all three Axis powers was declared on May 28, 1942. Mexico became a member of the United Nations on Nov. 7, 1947.

Alemán and Ruiz Cortines.—In 1946, Camacho was succeeded by Miguel Alemán, the first civilian to be elected president since 1911. During his presidency, industrialization increased rapidly. He was succeeded in 1952 by another civilian, Adolfo Ruiz Cortines. Ruiz Cortines continued his predecessor's policy of concentration on industrial growth. Mexico became increasingly prosperous, in part because his economic policy encouraged substantial capital investments by United States businessmen.

López Mateos and Díaz Ordaz.—In 1958, Adolfo López Mateos, former secretary of labor, was elected to the presidency. He continued the policy of encouraging industrialization. Mexico's industrial growth rate became one of the highest in the world. He instituted a sweeping land-reform program and irrigation projects to encourage the growth of agriculture. He was succeeded in 1964 by Gustavo Díaz Ordaz, former minister of the interior.

Bibliography.—Cabrera, Luis, *Obras políticas* (Mexico City 1921); Meléndez, José T., *Historia de la revolución mexicana* (Mexico City 1936); Cline, Howard F., *United States and Mexico* (Cambridge, Mass., 1953); Simpson, Lesley B., *Many Mexicos*, 3d ed. rev. (Berkeley, Calif., 1959); Brandenburg, Frank, *The Making of Modern Mexico* (New York 1964); Cosío Villages, Daniel, *American Extremes* (Austin, Texas, 1964); Hundley, Norris, *Dividing the Waters* (Berkeley, Calif., 1966); Ross, Stanley, ed., *Is the Mexican Revolution Dead?* (New York 1966).

María del Carmen Velázquez,
Professor of History, Universidad Nacional de México.

28. RELATIONS WITH THE UNITED STATES. Early Relations and Border Problems.

—The independence of Latin America early in the 19th century forced England and the United States into a new field of rivalry. The English, who had traded illegally with the Spanish colonies, signed treaties of friendship, commerce, and navigation with them after their declarations of independence. For its part, the United States felt the threat of European influence to its interests in the Western Hemisphere.

During its colonial past, New Spain (Mexico) had had border friction with its northern neighbor. This was intensified by the vague borders of the Louisiana Territory, sold by the French to the United States in 1803, after being acquired from Spain. The Spanish authorities considered the Mississippi River as the limit of the territory, while the United States insisted on the Rio Grande. The discussion lasted several years, and was ended by the Adams-Onís Treaty of Feb. 22, 1819, under the terms of which Spanish claims in Florida were exchanged with the United States for its claims to the territory lying between the Rio Grande and the Sabine River. This treaty established the boundary line as follows: from the Gulf of Mexico at the mouth of the Sabine River, north along the west bank of the Sabine to latitude 32°N.; due north from this point to the Red River; west along the Red to longitude 100°W.; north along this meridian to the Arkansas River; west along the southern bank of the Arkansas to its source; due north from this point to latitude 42°N.; and west along this line to the Pacific.

The Treaty of 1819, however, had been arranged between the United States and Spain, not with Mexico, which in 1821 became independent. Thus, the new republic inherited the problem. Mexico also inherited the problems of colonizing its frontier territories and of conducting trade with the United States. This trade went between Santa Fe, then in northern Mexico, and the area centering around St. Louis, and was complicated by numberless smuggling and hunting expeditions which violated the border in both directions.

A further troublesome inheritance was the threat of United States expansion westward and southward, one reason for which was the plantation economy of the southern United States, with its dependence on slave labor and large expanses of agricultural territory. Southern desire to extend its way of life into new territories, to counterbalance the extension of nonslave territory in the North, influenced United States policy along its borders with Mexico, and naturally aroused Mexican suspicion and resistance. United States insistence on the need for new land in the southwest seemed all the less reasonable to Mexico because of the still huge undeveloped areas in the western United States.

England, shrewdly realizing that it was in a position to develop commercial relations with Mexico without becoming involved in political or territorial disagreements, improved its position in proportion as Mexican-United States relations deteriorated. The most significant reflection of United States concern over the position it felt England was attaining was contained in the declaration of the Monroe Doctrine of Dec. 2, 1823, calling a halt to European expansion in the Western Hemisphere. Although directed chiefly against Spain and Russia, the doctrine was also an effort by the United States to accomplish in the field of politics what it could not at the time accomplish in the field of trade. Pending the time when it could compete with the trade of Europe, particularly that of England, the United States wished to keep the Latin American market as open as possible. Attainment of the necessary commercial vigor and a sufficiently expanding economy to develop this market fully did not come until after the Civil War.

Indian tribes, frontiersmen, and traders moved back and forth across the border, and such American colonizers as Stephen Austin settled in Texas (in 1821) on Mexican territory. Mexico made efforts to define her frontiers in conformity with the Adams-Onís Treaty of 1819, but the United States refused to acknowledge that the treaty was valid with Mexico unless further border modifications were made.

In the time of Iturbide's empire (1822–1823), immediately after independence, Mexico attempted to win full *de jure* recognition of her government by the United States. Iturbide sent Manuel Zozaya, with full diplomatic powers, as first Mexican minister to Washington. Since in spite of this, between 1822 and 1825 no treaty was ratified between Mexico and the United States, and in light of the expansionism of the latter country, the original Mexican good feeling turned against her northern neighbor. "In time," wrote Zozaya of the United States. "they will be our sworn enemies, and foreseeing this we should treat them as such from the present day." Zozaya's viewpoint shaped the Mexican attitude.

Under the Constitution of 1824, Mexico became a federal republic. Joel Roberts Poinsett was sent as the first American minister in 1825. Poinsett seemed to have real qualifications for the position, but most of his recommendations were rejected by Mexico. He proposed construction of a new road between Santa Fe and St. Louis to make possible the passage of wagon trains, a treaty which would recognize the borders of the Treaty of 1819, and a "most favored nation" tariff agreement between the two nations. Yielding to Mexican opposition to these plans, however, he accepted the Mexican terms and in January 1826 signed a treaty of friendship, trade, and navigation, by which Mexico was recognized by the United States, but which bypassed a settlement of the frontier question.

The situation remained static until the end of Poinsett's mission in 1829, despite his government's insistence on frontier changes, because the Mexican government recalled Zozaya's warning and it seemed that any change in the position of the border would set a dangerous precedent. As a result, the United States refused to ratify the Treaty of 1819 on borders and Mexico did not ratify Poinsett's treaty of friendship, trade, and navigation.

Poinsett's efforts to exert political influence in Mexico in order to obtain the privileges desired by the United States, since the volume of trade with his country was not sufficient to impose its conditions, were sharply criticized by the Mexicans and led to disputes between Poinsett and the British minister, Henry George Ward. When Poinsett assisted in the formation of a lodge of York Rite Freemasons, which promptly became a Mexican political party (the *Yorkinos*), he aroused so much enmity that he was forced to leave the country. After his departure, bad feeling was further aggravated, at times because of lack of tact on the part of succeeding ministers, who insisted on border changes, and by violations of the Mexican border and abuses of Mexican custom officials.

Texas Question and Mexican War.—Above all, bad feeling was created by the part played by the United States in Texan independence, the basis of which was the effort of the Southern states to expand slave territory. The constant and often violent changes of government in Mexico did not help matters, and the anarchy which frequently prevailed encouraged American diplomatic representatives to seek settlement of the frontier question by influencing Mexican government officials. Anthony Butler, who was United States minister from October 1829 to January 1836, for example, tried to obtain the cession of Texas by strategically distributing 100,000 pesos among government officials. Butler suggested extending the southwestern border of the United States all the way to the Pacific, arguing that this was necessary so that a fishing industry could be established in the vicinity of San Francisco and transcontinental communications facilitated.

When Texas, defying the Mexican government, proclaimed its independence in 1836, Mexico tried to reconquer it. The campaign of reconquest was led by Gen. Antonio López Santa Anna, who won the Battle of the Alamo (March 6, 1836) but lost the decisive Battle of San Jacinto (April 21, 1836).

With the independence of Texas, which claimed the Rio Grande as its southern boundary, established by force but not legally recognized by Mexico, Mexican-United States relations were placed under an increased strain. The United States recognized Texas as a new nation in 1837, and other nations followed its lead in granting recognition. Mexico nevertheless continued to insist on its sovereignty over Texas and considered as unfriendly any intervention between itself and its rebellious state.

The problem came to a head in November 1844 after a heated discussion in Mexico City between José María Bocanegra and Manuel Crescencio Rejón for Mexico, and Benjamin Edwards Green and Wilson Shannon for the United States. Rejón analyzed the policies of the United States and charged that its preconceived objective had been to obtain Texas. In January 1845 he said

that annexation of Texas by the United States would be considered as a declaration of war against Mexico. Despite this serious position, Mexico was unable to mobilize because of the anarchy and confusion reigning at the time.

The Texas question, as it involved Mexico and the United States, was approaching a climax. Diplomatic relations were broken off in January 1846 and Mexico stopped payment on claims that, despite the work of two arbitration conventions (1839 and 1843), were still pending.

When war came in May 1846, the United States based its declaration of war on the claim that Mexico had begun hostilities by invading United States territory (that is, territory north of the Rio Grande previously claimed by Texas), and "shedding American blood." Mexico, however, denied any invasion and based its stand on the question of Texas. The war is still a matter of great controversy, but at the time many persons in the United States felt it unjustified, and two later presidents, Lincoln and Grant, publicly deplored the action of their country.

Because of internal weakness, Mexico was not able to oppose the United States armies effectively, but spectacular battles were fought (see MEXICAN WAR).

Final peace, sealed by the Treaty of Guadalupe Hidalgo (Feb. 2, 1848), was signed on behalf of the United States by Nicholas Philip Trist, who disregarded his instructions to accept terms regarded by some in the United States as too lenient. Through the treaty, however, Mexico lost half of her territory, including New Mexico, Arizona, all of Upper California, and parts of what are now other states. This treaty established a new boundary line as follows: from the Gulf of Mexico three leagues from land opposite the mouth of the Rio Grande, following the middle of that river to the southern boundary of New Mexico; thence west along that boundary to its western end; north along the western boundary of New Mexico to the first branch of the Gila River; west along the middle of that branch and the middle of the Gila to its junction with the Colorado; thence west along the division between Upper and Lower California to the Pacific Ocean.

Gadsden Purchase.—The peace treaty of 1848 did not solve the problems between the two countries, and the actual position of the southern boundary of New Mexico remained in dispute until the Gadsden Purchase. The southwest border of the United States still was not drawn far enough south to satisfy the promoters of a coast-to-coast railroad, who feared having their trains run too close to the border. Indians from the United States continued to attack Mexican territory and the responsibility of checking them, accepted by the United States in Article 11 of the Treaty of Guadalupe Hidalgo, proved so heavy that that government tried to revoke the clause. Projects for building a canal or railroad across the Isthmus of Tehuantepec were also pending, and were further complicated by concessions made by the Mexican government to individuals, who in turn passed them on to British subjects.

Still desiring more territory, the United States took advantage of the Mexican government's chronic need for money to negotiate the Gadsden Purchase (Treaty of Mesilla) of Dec. 30, 1853, by which Article 11 of the previous treaty was abrogated, the border moved to its present position (for which see UNITED STATES—*Area and*

Boundaries), and the building of the Southern Pacific Railroad was made possible.

Relations with the United States After 1853.

—A few years later, the United States fought its Civil War, emerging from the struggle in 1865 with an economic, political, and social structure based on an industrial system which had been ripening in the North and which demanded foreign markets and new fields for investment of capital. Confirmation of industrialism as the national pattern was quickly reflected in United States foreign policy.

During the Civil War, the French invasion of Mexico had installed Maximilian as emperor (1864–1867), in defiance of the Monroe Doctrine. The end of the Civil War, and Mexican resistance led by Benito Juárez, ended the French experiment and Maximilian's life. The re-established Mexican republic received United States support.

During the prolonged presidency (1876–1880 and 1884–1911) of Porfirio Díaz, development of United States industrialization fitted in with material betterment in Mexico, and United States as well as European capital flowed into the country. Through investments, and indirect political influence designed to protect its investors, the United States gained considerable control over the Mexican economy during the Porfirian era. But the material progress made under Díaz was not matched by proportionate social progress, and eventually this pressure produced the Revolution of 1910 and the overthrow of the regime.

The United States began to become aware of the social and economic problems that foreign investment brought to Mexico, and modified its policies so that, despite such incidents during the revolution as the bombardment and occupation of Veracruz by United States Marines in 1914 and Francisco Villa's raid on Columbus, N. M., in 1916, relations were improved.

After the revolution, the most important in Mexico's history, nationalism increased, some foreign properties were expropriated, and foreign investments in major industries were limited.

Then came the era of the Good Neighbor policy, inaugurated in 1933, with hope for understanding based on something more than merely material concerns, and even the acceptance by the United States of the principle that Mexico was entitled to limit economic penetration by foreign capital. (See section *Economic, Industrial, Agricultural, and Financial Factors.*)

Efforts toward mutual understanding seem to have smoothed out the major causes of friction, and *rapprochement* has been strengthened by intellectual movements which began in various universities, and extended through private scientific institutions which have financed exchange students, researchers, and teachers, who contribute to the cause by studying each other's country.

Bibliography.—Rippy, James Fred, *The United States and Mexico* (New York 1931); Callahan, James Morton, *American Foreign Policy in Mexican Relations* (New York 1932); Bosch García, Carlos, *Problemas Diplomáticos del México Independiente* (Mexico City 1947).

CARLOS BOSCH GARCÍA,
Secretary, Comisión de Historia, Instituto Panamericano de Geografía e Historia.

Note: The foregoing 28 articles on Mexico were prepared under the joint direction of the editors of THE ENCYCLOPEDIA AMERICANA and Dr. Pedro Armillas of the Instituto Nacional de Antropología e Historia, Mexico City.

MEXICO, mĕk'sĭ-kō (Span. mě'hĕ-kō), state of the Republic of Mexico. Located in the south central section, it is the central portion of a plateau rising 8,000 feet above sea level. Running from northwest to southeast through the center of the state is a range of well-wooded mountains which separate the Valley of Mexico from a second plateau area in which is located the state capital, Toluca.

The state is one of the richest in the republic. Agriculture and mining are equally well developed and there is an increasing amount of industry. Cereals, sugar, the maguey cactus, fruit, dairy products, and livestock are the main products of agriculture, while silver, gold, copper and lead are mined in quantity. Manufactures are concentrated mainly in the area immediately north of the Federal District, an expansion of industries from Mexico City. Cotton and woolen goods, fibers, paper, flour, glass, pottery and bricks, wines and spirits, and metal products are produced. The area of the state is 8,286 square miles; pop. (1960) 1,897,851, of which 61.3 per cent was rural.

MEXICO, city, Missouri, seat of Audrain County, is located on Salt River, 25 miles northeast of Columbia, on the Wabash, the Gulf, Mobile and Ohio and the Burlington Route railroads. It is in a farming area raising grains and soybeans, and is noted as a mule market and horse breeding center. There are large deposits of fine fire clay in the county, and the city's manufactured products include fire brick, stove linings, flour, shoes, and soybean products. Missouri Military Academy is here. The city was settled in 1833, incorporated in 1862, and has a council-manager form of government. Pop. 12,889.

MEXICO, Federal District of (Span. DISTRITO FEDERAL), area, Republic of Mexico, which is set aside for the exclusive use of the federal government, so that government will not be hampered by state interference. In this it is like the District of Columbia in the United States. The Federal District was created in 1824. The State of Mexico, of which it was formerly a part, bounds it on the east, north, and west; on the south it is bounded by Morelos.

It is the southeastern portion of the Valley of Mexico, and contains Mexico City, the national capital, which is also the capital of the Federal District. The district is smaller than any of the Mexican states or territories, but has a greater population. In 1950 only 5.43 per cent of the population was rural. The most important manufactures are concentrated in Mexico City and its suburbs. Area 573 square miles; pop. (1960) 4,870,876. See also MEXICO CITY.

MEXICO, Gulf of, an arm of the Atlantic Ocean, bounded on the north by the United States and on the south and west by Mexico. It is oval in form; its greatest length is, from east to west, about 1,000 miles; from north to south, about 800 miles; area about 716,000 square miles. It has a continuous coastline of about 3,000 miles. Its maximum depth (Sigsbee Deep) is about 12,425 feet, and the average depth is about 4,700 feet. The outlet of the gulf is on the east, between the peninsulas of Yucatán and Florida, a distance of about 475 miles. In this outlet is the island of Cuba, which is separated from Florida by the Straits of Florida, 110 miles wide, and from Yucatán by the Yucatán Channel, 120 miles wide.

The Yucatán Channel opens into the Caribbean Sea, and the Straits of Florida into the Atlantic.

The temperature of the gulf is from eight degrees to nine degrees higher than in the Atlantic in the same latitude. The temperature at the point of greatest depth is 39.5° F. The range of the tides is small: from about two and a half feet at the neap tides to about four feet in the spring. The chief current is a branch of the Equatorial Current, which enters the Gulf of Mexico through the Yucatán Channel. It exits through the Straits of Florida and joins the Antilles Current to form the Florida Current, which is the beginning of the Gulf Stream system. Prevailing winds from the north blow from September to March, and from the south from March to September. Severe gales occur in the winter, and hurricanes may be encountered in late summer or early autumn.

The northern part of the gulf, from Mexico to Florida, is really a coastal plain averaging from 40 to 100 miles wide. The basin off the Mexican coast sinks rapidly to the submarine plain, and reaches its maximum depth a short distance from shore. The Gulf of Campeche is the largest indentation.

The chief ports are Havana, Cuba; Veracruz and Tampico, Mexico; and Galveston, Houston, Port Arthur, Beaumont, New Orleans, Mobile, and Tampa, in the United States.

MEXICO CITY is the capital of Mexico. It is also the capital of the Federal District, an area of 573 square miles set aside for the exclusive use of the federal government. The city is located in central Mexico, on a small plain near the south end of the large central plateau of the Sierra Madre. It is about 200 miles west of Veracruz, on the Gulf of Mexico, and 190 miles northeast of the Pacific port of Acapulco. The city lies at an altitude of 7,349 feet, on the former bed of Lake Texcoco, and is dominated by the snowcapped volcanoes of Popocatepetl and Iztaccihuatl.

Mexico City was founded by the Aztecs in 1321 as their capital. Called Tenochtitlán by the Aztecs, it is the oldest continuously inhabited capital in North America. Its recent rapid growth has made it one of the world's largest cities. Its population, about 500,000 in 1900, had reached an estimated 3,353,000 by 1967, with another 2,100,000 in its suburbs. Thus it is one of the Western Hemisphere's largest cities.

Mexico City is situated in a beautiful high valley with fertile soil, an abundance of water, and a springlike climate. Its natural beauty, together with the ruins and remains of earlier civilizations, makes it one of the most attractive tourist centers in the world. The city bears witness to several cultures. Its history includes the prehistoric and Aztec eras, the centuries of Spanish colonial rule, and the brief period of French influence in the 19th century, when Napoleon III chose Maximilian of Austria to rule as emperor of Mexico. Modern Mexico City is a rapidly expanding industrial center with striking modern architecture.

Geography.—The valley in which Mexico City is situated has no natural outlet. Until the Canal de Desaugue was completed in 1900, the summer rainy season caused the valley's numerous streams to overflow, at times creating disastrous floods. The 30-mile canal was cut through the mountains to join the Pánuco River flowing to the Gulf of Mexico. A serious disadvantage, which has even brought suggestions of transferring the city to another location, is the unstable, spongy, silt deposit on which the foundations of the buildings must rest. The canal, though a great engineering feat, unfortunately accelerated the sinking of certain areas of the capital. Examples of sinking are seen in the ancient Palace of Mines, built in colonial days, and the modern white Palace of Fine Arts adjoining Alameda Park and erected in 1910 by President Porfirio Díaz to celebrate the centennial of Mexico's independence. Such buildings noticeably sink annually, and engineers are at a loss to find means of stabilizing them.

The city is also hampered by being constructed on a great geological fault, stretching from Acapulco to Veracruz, which causes earthquakes. Though severe tremors are not common, one occurred on July 28, 1957, causing an estimated property damage of $25,600,000 largely in the neighborhood of the Paseo de la Reforma, where many of the new skyscrapers are located. While most of the old buildings escaped serious injury, almost 100 modern buildings were ordered temporarily closed. However, the 44-story Latin American Tower, highest in Latin America, did not even suffer the breaking of a windowpane. The tower's "floating island" foundation was planned by architect Frank Lloyd Wright, and is similar to the foundation of Wright's Imperial Hotel in Tokyo, Japan.

As the city has expanded and water has continued to be drawn from the former lake bed, an unusual system has developed, the Caracol (which means "snail"). A spiraling canal, it sucks up excess water, which then evaporates. It has helped to firm the spongy foundation, though at the cost of lowering the water table. The city's water supplies must be brought from deep in the mountains.

Federal District.—Mexico City is situated in a Federal District similar to the District of Columbia in the United States. The district was established in 1824 so that the federal government would not be hampered by state interference. It was originally part of the state of Mexico, which now borders it on three sides. The population of the Federal District has expanded much more rapidly than that of the country as a whole. By 1960 it numbered 4,870,876, nine times larger than in 1900.

The governor of the district is appointed by the president. Residents have a certain amount of self-government through elected local *ayuntamientos,* or town councils. These work in consultation with the Superior Governing Council of the Federal Council, composed of the governor of the Federal District, the president of the Superior Board of Health, and the director general of public works.

Landmarks and Monuments.—From the great Square of Zócalo at the center of the city, a business street, Madero Avenue, leads west into El Paseo de la Reforma, one of the world's most beautiful thoroughfares. This wide, tree-shaded, flower-bedecked boulevard, three miles long, is interrupted at intervals by *glorietas* (circles) adorned with monuments, and leads to the great wrought-iron gates of Chapultepec Park. In these three miles lie six centuries of history—Aztec, Spanish, Mestizo (Spanish-Indian), United States (1847–1848, during the Mexican War), French (Empire), and modern Mexican.

Surrounding the Zócalo are the great public buildings—the National Palace, the Municipal Palace, the cathedral, and the Arcade of Tradesmen. All these were built shortly after the Spanish Conquest, under Hernán Cortés in the 16th century, on the ground occupied as the governmental and religious center of the Aztec capital Tenochtitlán. Here the wily Cortés tricked Emperor Montezuma (Moctezuma) II into entertaining him, while he examined the military and religious defenses of what the Spaniards described as the "city of palaces" and also, because of its many canals, as the "Venice of the New World." Mexican and foreign archaeologists have combed almost every foot of the ground for examples of Aztec, Toltec, and even more primitive civilizations. Relics, such as the famous Aztec calendar, fill the National Museum.

The National Palace occupies the site of Cortés' own house on the east side of the plaza. Begun in 1692, but much altered subsequently, the present building houses the executive offices of the Mexican president, the National Treasury, the Defense Ministry, the National Archives, and the National Museum. Above the central portal of the palace hangs the Liberty Bell rung by Miguel Hidalgo y Costilla (q.v.) in 1810 to rally the people to the struggle for freedom from Spain. Every year at 11 o'clock on the night of September 15, crowds surge into the plaza to hear the president ring the bell and repeat the celebrated *Grito de Delores* from the balcony.

What was probably the first church on the North American continent was erected in 1525 on the north side of the Zócalo above the ruins of the great temple dedicated to the Aztec god of war. The cathedral, now occupying the site, was begun in 1573; the main structure was finished in 1667 and the towers in 1791. During the two centuries of its building, the plans were changed several times, which accounts for the lack of a feeling of architectural unity in the interior (387 feet long, 177 feet wide, 179 feet high). It is said to be the largest church in the New World. Here were crowned the two Mexican emperors, Augustín de Iturbide (1822) and the Austrian Archduke Maximilian (1864).

Since the days of Cortés, the west side of the Zócalo has been allocated to arcades sheltering a variety of shops. The south side is occupied by the Palacio Municipal (City Hall). Other old buildings in the Zócalo section are the School of Medicine, the National Preparatory School, the Ministry of Education, the Hospital de Jesus Nazareno. The School of Medicine was begun in 1732 as headquarters for the Holy Office of the Inquisition, and the cells of victims may still be seen there. A cornerstone of a nearby edifice indicates the home of the first printing press in America established in the year 1539.

The National Preparatory School was formerly the Jesuit College of San Ildefonso; on the walls and stairways are murals by Diego Rivera and other famous modernists. What may be the longest series of murals painted by a single artist (Rivera) are those depicting Mexico's social revolution. They completely occupy the walls of the first, second, and third floors of the blocklong Ministry of Education. Beginning with pictures of the cruelties inflicted on the Indians by the early Spanish landlords, they continue with striking pictures of rural schools, and with the artist's concept of the exploitation of Mexico by northern capitalists.

Madero Avenue leads by way of the Palace of Tiles (now occupied by a restaurant) to the white marble Palace of Fine Arts, which historically marks the break between the old Díaz regime and the modern social revolution which began in ·1910. Planned by Díaz as an architectural and social reproduction of the Opera in Paris, it was changed, following his expulsion, into a popular center for music, painting, lectures, and public receptions. To such affairs special welcome seems to be extended to the general public, especially to members of labor unions and teachers in public schools, who crowd performances of grand opera, art exhibitions, and government-sponsored entertainments.

Just west of the Palace of Fine Arts is the Alameda, a downtown park some three blocks long; and three blocks farther along from the Alameda is the statue of Charles IV of Spain, popularly known as *El Caball'to* (the little horse), marking the beginning of El Paseo de la Reforma which was planned by Maximilian and Carlota to echo the grandeur of Paris' Champs-Élysées. After the execution of the emperor by the forces of Benito Pablo Juárez in 1867 and the mad Carlota's return to Europe, the boulevard was somewhat neglected; but in recent years luxury hotels, government buildings, foreign embassies (including that of the United States), modern apartments, private palaces, and completely new pavements have restored its grandeur.

In tree-shaded Chapultepec Park is the rocky hill which was the first point in the Valley of Mexico taken and fortified by the invading Aztecs. On this hill Montezuma II had his summer palace, and at the same site, in 1783, Chapultepec Castle was begun. During the early 1860's Maximilian and Carlota rebuilt and redecorated the castle for their residence. Afterward it became the residence of President Díaz, and later a public museum. The Inter-American Conference on Problems of War and Peace was held in the castle in 1945, and here was signed the Act of Chapultepec, which committed the nations of the Americas to the united defense of the Western Hemisphere.

During the Mexican War (q.v.), the National Military School at the rear of the hill was the scene of the last defense of the city by the cadets of the school, before General Winfield Scott's forces entered the city on Sept. 14, 1847. The spot where the cadets fell became a patriot shrine. A century later, Harry S. Truman, as president of the United States, stood on the same spot and returned the captured flags.

Mexico City's numerous suburban additions display various types of architecture and illustrate the Mexican characteristic of boldness. One suburb is built on lava where grow colorful plants and flowers as well as native trees. Old towns, like San Angelo and Coyoacán (where royalty first settled), now a part of the city, still contain old homes lovingly preserved by descendants of the conquistadors or by newer foreign settlers. Their gardens emphasize the ancient Indian love of flowers, transmitted through the Spaniards to the Mexicans to become a national passion.

Other points of interest farther from the city proper, but easily reached, are numerous. Xochimilco, the "floating gardens," 15 miles from the center of the city, is a favorite Sunday and holiday excursion point. Visitors hire small flower-bedecked boats and are propelled along the canals, while vendors in other boats offer flowers, food, music, and souvenirs. Xochimilco, "land sown with flowers," was constructed near Mexico City long before the Spanish Conquest and is often described as Mexico's Venice. In a lake the Aztecs constructed a settlement on rafts covered with earth and planted gardens on them; later, when the waters of the lake receded, the plants took root on the lake bottom and held fast.

About 28 miles northeast of the capital stand the remains of the pre-Aztec city now known as San Juan Teotihuacán, covering in all eight square miles. At the center of this city rises the Pyramid of the Sun, nearly 220 feet high. Nearby are

Marilu Pease from Monkmeyer

Murals in stone adorn Mexico City's Ministry of Communications and Public Works.

the smaller, but similar, Pyramid of the Moon and many other examples of pre-Aztec civilization.

Social and Industrial Development.—The visitor to Mexico City will miss the significance of much of its modern development, unless he appreciates the profound social revolution which began in 1910 and continued for the next 25 years. The work of modern muralists, such as Diego Rivera, is only one evidence of the fundamental changes made by the revolution in the land system, organized labor, socialized education, and separation of state and church. Though halted for a time by Mexico's entry into World War II, these reforms have continued to be important to an understanding of Mexican architecture, education, politics, search for freedom, and efforts to create a good life for all the people.

Education.—The revolutionary spirit is especially demonstrated in the new home of the National University. Founded in 1551, the institution was long dominated by the Roman Catholic Church. During long periods of the 19th century it was closed by Liberal governments unable to introduce lay scientific courses. Radical intellectuals controlled the institution during the revolution of 1910 and made it the instrument of a new national school system emphasizing a social centered education. In 1929, following one of the worst of the student strikes, the university was made autonomous, that is, responsible for its own life. A daring plan was soon approved to collect the many overcrowded schools of law, medicine, engineering, and others scattered over the city and to move them to an immense campus on an ancient lava bed formerly regarded as waste land. This large suburban site was planned to accommodate 25,000 students. After representatives of the university had visited many of the world's great universities, a plan was adopted to build a complete university including a central rectory and library, lecture halls, laboratories, faculty residences, sports fields, and a stadium seating 125,000 people. The stadium, a tremendous swimming pool nearby, and facilities built in other parts of the city were the setting for the 1968 Olympic Games.

Industry.—Mexico City is not only the cultural and political center of the nation, but also the heart of its economic and industrial life. The industries of the city and surrounding areas include textile milling, flour milling, brewing, and manufacture of rubber goods, cement, steel, and construction materials. Of increasing importance is the making of cigarettes, soap, leather, shoes, electrical supplies, and furniture; the number of chain stores is increasing. To avoid high import duties on finished products, assembly plants for iron and steel products, such as automobiles, have been created.

Transportation.—The city is the most important transportation center in the republic and is connected with all the chief Mexican seaports and interior cities by railway, highway, and airlines. The Pan American Highway runs to Laredo, Texas, on the north and to Guatemala and Panama on the south. Excellent air service is available to all points in the United States and Europe. Such good transportation has helped to make the city a center for international conventions and organizations.

History.—Mexico City traditionally was founded in 1176 by the Aztecs, who called it Tenochtitlán and made it their capital about 1321. The Spaniards under Hernán Cortés captured it in 1519, were expelled from it in 1520, and rewon it in 1521. They razed the old city and built a new city, which became the metropolis of New Spain and was governed by the Spaniards until 1821, when it fell to Mexican revolutionists, led by Gen. Agustín de Iturbide. United States forces, commanded by Gen. Winfield Scott, occupied Mexico City in 1847 during the Mexican War. The French occupied it from 1863 until the Mexicans, under Gen. Benito Pablo Juárez, ousted them in 1867. During the revolution begun in 1910, it was occupied briefly from 1914 to 1915 by Gens. Francisco (Pancho) Villa and Emiliano Zapata.

SAMUEL GUY INMAN.